I0844682

VOLUME 2

L ~ Z

The Outline Bible Five Translation

PRACTICAL WORD STUDIES IN THE NEW TESTAMENT

Five Translations

- King James Version
- New King James Version
- New International Version
- New American Standard
- New Living Translation

VOLUME 2

L ~ Z

The Outline Bible Five Translation

PRACTICAL WORD STUDIES IN THE NEW TESTAMENT

Leadership Ministries Worldwide
PO Box 21310
Chattanooga, TN 37424-0310

Publisher & Distributor

DEDICATED:

To all the men and women of the world
who preach and teach the Gospel of our
Lord Jesus Christ
and
To the Mercy and Grace of God.

- Demonstrated to us in Christ Jesus our Lord.

   "In whom we have redemption through His blood, the
   forgiveness of sins, according to the riches of His grace."   (Eph. 1:7)

- Out of the mercy and grace of God His Word has flowed.
   Let every person know that God will have mercy upon him,
   forgiving and using him to fulfill His glorious plan of salvation.

   "For God so loved the world, that he gave his only begotten Son,
   that whosoever believeth in him should not perish, but have everlasting life. For God sent not his Son into the world to condemn the
   world; but that the world through him might be saved."   (Jn 3:16-17)

   "For this is good and acceptable in the sight of God our Saviour; who
   will have all men to be saved, and to come unto the knowledge of the
   truth."   (I Tim. 2:3-4)

The Preacher's Outline and Study Bible®
is written for God's people to use
in their study and teaching of God's Holy Word.

OUR VISION, PASSION & PURPOSE:

- To share the Word of God with the world.
- To help the believer, both minister and layman alike, in his understanding, preaching, and teaching of God's Word.
- To do everything we possibly can to lead men, women, boys, and girls to give their hearts and lives to Jesus Christ and to secure the eternal life which He offers.
- To do all we can to minister to the needy of the world.
- To give Jesus Christ His proper place, the place which the Word gives Him. Therefore — No work of Leadership Ministries Worldwide will ever be personalized.

TABLE OF CONTENTS

HOW TO USE...
THE PRACTICAL WORD STUDY

When you look up an English word, this simple, easy-to-use word study chart will give you the following information:

(#1) The English Word

(#2) How Five Different Translations Use the Same Word

(#3) The Preacher's Outline & Sermon Bible® Reference where you can secure additional information

(#4) The Greek Word, English Transliteration, Pronunciation, and Grammatical Parsing

(#5) The Reference Number for the Root Word from the Three Major Concordances

(#6) The Verse Written Out for Five Major Translations with the Key Word(s) in Bold Type

(#7) The Actual Greek Text (Textus Receptus [GNS] and UBS4-NA27 [GNT]) with the Key Word(s) in Bold)

(#8) The Greek Meaning of the Word Defined with Simple, Easy-to-Understand Terms

(#9) The Practical Application For Study, Preaching, And Teaching

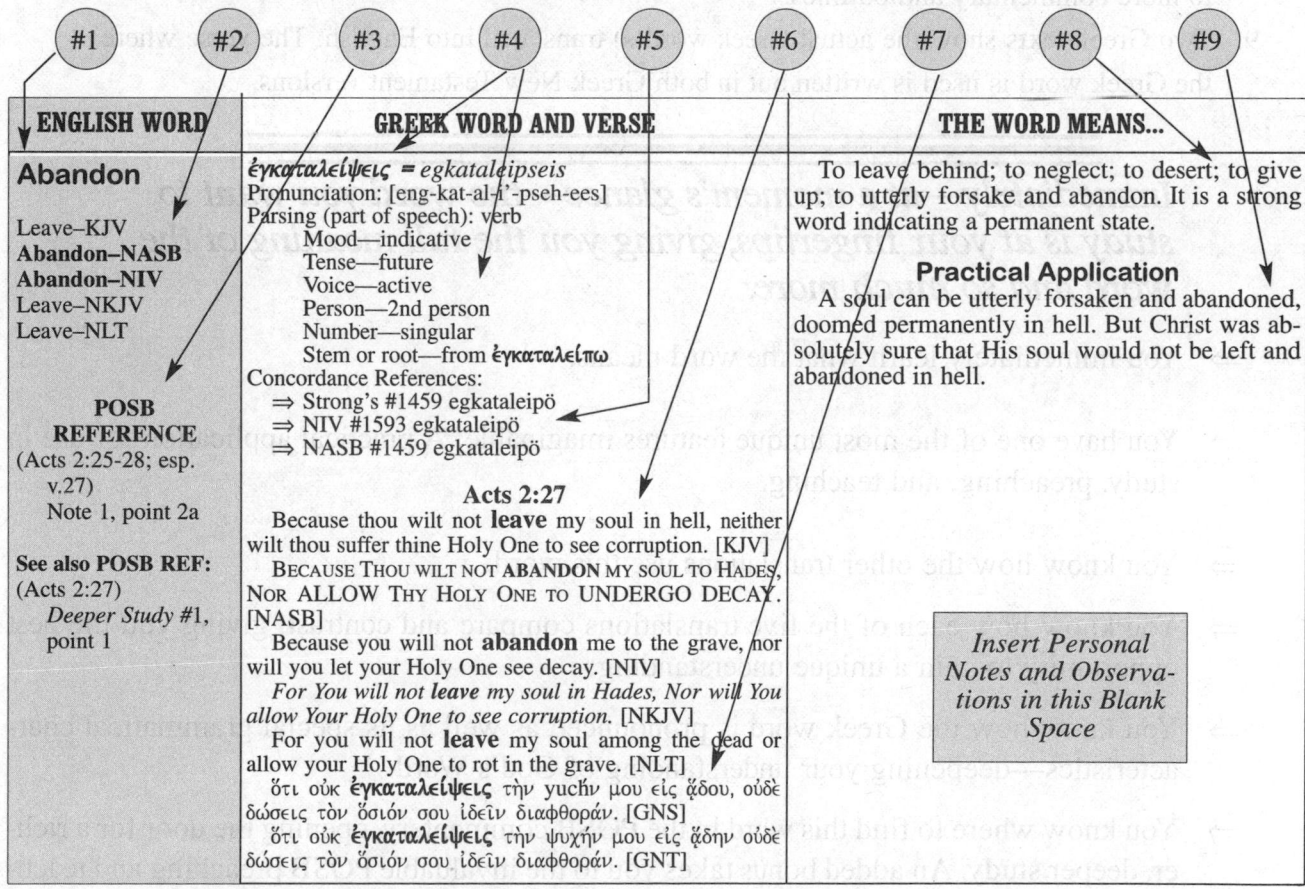

| #1 | #2 | #3 | #4 | #5 | #6 | #7 | #8 | #9 |

ENGLISH WORD	GREEK WORD AND VERSE	THE WORD MEANS...

Abandon
 	
Leave–KJV
Abandon–NASB
Abandon–NIV
Leave–NKJV
Leave–NLT
 	
**POSB
REFERENCE**
(Acts 2:25-28; esp.
v.27)
Note 1, point 2a
 	
See also POSB REF:
(Acts 2:27)
Deeper Study #1,
point 1
	ἐγκαταλείψεις = *egkataleipseis*
	Pronunciation: [eng-kat-al-i'-pseh-ees]
	Parsing (part of speech): verb
	  Mood—indicative
	  Tense—future
	  Voice—active
	  Person—2nd person
	  Number—singular
	  Stem or root—from ἐγκαταλείπω
	Concordance References:
	  ⇒ Strong's #1459 egkataleipö
	  ⇒ NIV #1593 egkataleipö
	  ⇒ NASB #1459 egkataleipö
	
	Acts 2:27
	Because thou wilt not **leave** my soul in hell, neither wilt thou suffer thine Holy One to see corruption. [KJV]
	BECAUSE THOU WILT NOT **ABANDON** MY SOUL TO HADES, NOR ALLOW THY HOLY ONE TO UNDERGO DECAY. [NASB]
	Because you will not **abandon** me to the grave, nor will you let your Holy One see decay. [NIV]
	*For You will not **leave** my soul in Hades, Nor will You allow Your Holy One to see corruption.* [NKJV]
	For you will not **leave** my soul among the dead or allow your Holy One to rot in the grave. [NLT]
	ὅτι οὐκ **ἐγκαταλείψεις** τὴν ψυχήν μου εἰς ᾅδου, οὐδὲ δώσεις τὸν ὅσιόν σου ἰδεῖν διαφθοράν. [GNS]
	ὅτι οὐκ **ἐγκαταλείψεις** τὴν ψυχήν μου εἰς ᾅδην οὐδὲ δώσεις τὸν ὅσιόν σου ἰδεῖν διαφθοράν. [GNT]
		To leave behind; to neglect; to desert; to give up; to utterly forsake and abandon. It is a strong word indicating a permanent state.
		
		Practical Application
		A soul can be utterly forsaken and abandoned, doomed permanently in hell. But Christ was absolutely sure that His soul would not be left and abandoned in hell.
		
		Insert Personal Notes and Observations in this Blank Space

Read on for more ...
...SPECIAL FEATURES

SPECIAL FEATURES OF...
THE PRACTICAL WORD STUDY

1. The Full Meaning of Each Word is given.
2. Five Major Translations are given to show just how the English word is used.
3. Practical Application is given for each word.
4. The Greek Word is given and phonetically pronounced. No more embarrassing stumbles from the pulpit or lectern trying to pronounce the Greek word.
5. Full and easy-to-understand parsing is given using simple, meaningful terms.
6. Concordance numbers from all three of the major concordances are given for each word: the concordance numbers from Strong's, the NIV, and the NASB. This allows for a quick, more exhaustive search for a particular word.
7. Each Scripture verse is written out in full, providing clear understanding with the key word in bold type.
8. **The Preacher's Outline & Sermon Bible** Reference is given for quick and easy access to more commentary and outlines.
9. Two Greek texts show the actual Greek word(s) translated into English. The verse where the Greek word is used is written out in both Greek New Testament versions.

Immediately—at a moment's glance—the word you want to study is at your fingertips, giving you the full meaning of the word and so much more:

⇒ You immediately learn what the word means.

⇒ You have one of the most unique features imaginable: A practical application for use in study, preaching, and teaching.

⇒ You know how the other translations use this word.

⇒ You know how each of the five translations compare and contrast, giving you the best opportunity to gain a unique understanding.

⇒ You know how the Greek word is pronounced as well as its special grammatical characteristics—deepening your understanding of God's Word.

⇒ You know where to find this word in the POSB commentary, opening the door for a richer, deeper study. An added bonus takes you to the invaluable POSB preaching and teaching outlines, giving you additional preparation for your message or lesson.

⇒ You know where to find the word from your favorite concordance.

A BRIEF HISTORICAL OVERVIEW OF THE TRANSLATIONS

One of the great benefits of the *Practical Word Studies In The New Testament (PWS)* is the use of five popular English translations. The reader will quickly discover the value of being able to compare the translations with one another. Below is a quick overview of the five translations. (Note: they are listed in chronological order.)

1. KING JAMES VERSION—KJV (or the AUTHORIZED VERSION—AV)

⇒ **DATE**: The KJV (both Old and New Testaments) was published in 1611.

⇒ **PURPOSE**: "That a translation be made of the whole Bible, as constant as can be to the original Hebrew and Greek; and this to be set out and printed, without any marginal notes, and only to be used in all Churches of England in time of divine service"—from *History of the English Bible* by F. F. Bruce; New York: Oxford University Press, 1978, third edition, p.96.

⇒ **HISTORY**: The idea for a new translation came out of the Hamton Court Conference in January 1604. At the forefront was Dr. John Reynolds (or Rainolds), the President of Corpus Christi College in Oxford England. The momentum for a translation that would replace the Geneva Bible was halting at first. However, with the blessing and strong leadership of King James I of England, the translation by 47 translators soon began. The KJV was translated from the earliest known Greek and Hebrew texts.

Note carefully King James' very own words on why he desired a new Bible translation:

"I profess...I could never yet see a Bible well translated in English; but I think that, of all, that of Geneva is the worst. I wish some special pains were taken for a uniform translation, which should be done by the best-learned men in both Universities, then reviewed by the Bishops, presented to the Privy Council, lastly ratified by Royal authority, to be read in the whole Church, and none other." —Bruce, p.96-97.

⇒ **FEATURES OF THE KJV**: Since its inception in 1611, it remains the best-selling Bible in the world. The KJV is noted for its poetic beauty, for its majestic literary splendor using "The King's English."

2. NEW AMERICAN STANDARD BIBLE—NASB

⇒ **DATE**: The NASB (both Old and New Testaments) was published in 1971.

⇒ **PURPOSE**: "The Editorial Board had a twofold purpose in making this translation: to adhere as closely as possible to the original languages of the Holy Scriptures, and to make the translation in a fluent and readable style according to current English usage."

The fourfold aim of the Lockman Foundation as printed in each copy of the NASB is as follows:

1. These publications shall be true to the original Hebrew and Greek.
2. They shall be grammatically correct.
3. They shall be understandable to the masses.
4. They shall give the Lord Jesus Christ His proper place, the place which the Word gives Him; therefore, no work will ever be personalized.

⇒ **HISTORY**: "The King James Version, a landmark in the history of English Bible translation, is a revision of the Bishops' Bible of 1568. The KJV became the basis for the English Revised Version appearing in 1881 (New Testament) and 1885 (Old Testament). The American counterpart of this last work was published in 1901 as the American Standard Version. The ASV, a product of both British and American scholarship, has been highly regarded for its scholarship, and accuracy.

Recognizing the values of the American Standard Version, The Lockman Foundation felt an urgency to preserve these and other lasting values of the ASV, by incorporating recent discoveries of Hebrew and Greek textual sources and by rendering it into more current English. Therefore, in 1959 a new translation project was launched, based on the time-honored principles of translation of the ASV and KJV. **The result is the *New American Standard Bible®*.** Under the sponsorship of The Lockman Foundation of La Habra, California, a dedicated team of scholars worked for more than ten years to produce the *New American Standard Bible*."—from The Lockman Foundation web site.

⇒ **FEATURES OF THE NEW AMERICAN STANDARD BIBLE**: This translation is noted as the most accurate, word for word, translation available. The NASB translation attempts to bridge the beauty of the King's English with a language that can be understood by the contemporary reader. "The *NASB®* is excellent for Bible study because it aims at a precise translation of the original Hebrew, Aramaic, and Greek. As such, it renders, where practical, the original order of words and phrases. In passages where this literalness produces unacceptable English, the translators used modern English idioms and indicated the literal renderings in marginal notes. In New Testament Greek, questions are worded in a way that shows whether the expected answer is yes or no. The *NASB®* translation is faithful to this treatment. In places where the English language would describe past action with a past-tense verb, the Greek uses the present tense for special vividness. The *NASB®* indicates such cases with an asterisk (or star) before the past-tense verb. Among the other distinctives are the *NASB*'s clear indicating of all phrases that quote or allude to the Old Testament; it includes quotation marks for dialogue and quoted material and capitalizes personal pronouns and words referring to Deity; and supplied words are in italic type."—from The Lockman Foundation web site.

3. NEW INTERNATIONAL VERSION—NIV

⇒ **DATE**: The NIV New Testament was published in 1973. The NIV Old Testament was published in 1979.

⇒ **PURPOSE**: "From the beginning of the project, the Committee on Bible Translation held to certain goals for the New International Version: that it would be an accurate translation and one that would have clarity and literary quality and so prove suitable for public and private reading, teaching, preaching, memorizing and liturgical use. The Committee also sought to preserve some measure of continuity with the long tradition of translating the Scriptures into English."—from the Preface of the NIV Study Bible, Zondervan, 1985.

⇒ **HISTORY**: "The New International Version is a completely new translation of the Holy Bible made by over a hundred scholars working directly from the best available Hebrew, Aramaic and Greek texts. It had its beginning in 1965 when, after several years of exploratory study by committees from the Christian Reformed Church and the National Association of Evangelicals, a group of scholars met at Palos Heights, Illinois, and concurred in the need for a new translation of the Bible in contemporary English. This group, though not made up of official church representatives, was transdenominational. Its conclusion was endorsed by a large number of leaders from many denominations who met in Chicago in 1966.

"Responsibility for the new version was delegated by the Palos Heights group to a self-governing body of fifteen, the Committee on Bible Translation, composed for the most part of biblical scholars from colleges, universities and seminaries. In 1967 the New York Bible Society (now the International Bible Society) generously undertook the financial sponsorship of the project—a sponsorship that made it possible to enlist the help of many distinguished scholars. The fact that participants from the United States, Great Britain, Canada, Australia and New Zealand worked together give the project its international scope. That they were from many denominations—including Anglican, Assemblies of God, Baptist, Brethren, Christian Reformed, Church of Christ, Evangelical Free, Lutheran, Mennonite, Methodist, Nazarene, Presbyterian, Wesleyan and other churches—helped to safeguard the translation from sectarian bias."—from the Preface of the NIV Study Bible, Zondervan, 1985.

⇒ **FEATURES OF THE NEW INTERNATIONAL VERSION**: This translation is a popular modern-language Bible. It attempts to find the balance between two translation methods: the literal method and the dynamic translation method. Many Bible scholars credit the NIV for both its accuracy and its readability.

4. NEW KING JAMES VERSION—NKJV

⇒ **DATE**: The New King James Version NT was published in 1979. The New King James Version OT was published in 1982.

⇒ **PURPOSE**: "In the Preface to the 1611 edition, the translators of the Authorized Version, known popularly as the King James Bible, state that it was not their purpose 'to make a new translation…but to make a good one better.' Indebted to the earlier work of William Tyndale and others, they saw their best contribution to consist in revising and enhancing the excellence of the English versions which had sprung from the Reformation of the sixteenth century. In harmony with the purpose of the King James scholars, the translators and editors of the present work [NKJV] have not pursued a goal of innovation. They have perceived the Holy Bible, New King James Version, as a continuation of the labors of the earlier translators, thus unlocking for today's readers the spiritual treasures found especially in the Authorized Version of the Holy Scriptures." —from the preface, The New Open Bible Study Edition, Thomas Nelson, 1990, p.12.

⇒ **HISTORY**: "The versions of 1881, 1901, and 1952 had used a New Testament Greek text that differed considerably from the traditional text and from the great majority of biblical manuscripts. There was growing concern among large segments of the Christian community that there was insufficient reason for many of these differences.

"In 1975 Thomas Nelson Publishers, successor to the British firm that had first published the English Revised Version (1885), the American Standard Version (1901), and the Revised Standard Version (1952), determined to evaluate interest in a possible new revision. Such a revision would retain the traditional text while taking into account of variant readings in footnotes.

"Because any revision of the Scriptures must meet the needs of public worship, Christian education and personal reading and study, leading clergymen and lay Christians were invited to meetings in Chicago, Illinois, and Nashville, Tennessee, in 1975, and in London, England, in 1976 to discuss the need for revision. Almost one hundred church leaders from a broad spectrum of Christian churches gave strong endorsement to a new revision.

"Biblical scholars representing a broad cross section of evangelical Christendom were selected to work on this major project. They came from Canada, England, Scotland, New Zealand, Australia, the Netherlands, and Taiwan, as well as from the United States, so that the New King James Version would reflect internationally accepted English use.

"Each translator worked privately and recommended changes in the King James text. In the translator's work he used the *Biblia Hebraica Stuttgartensia* (for the Old Testament) or the Scrivener Greek Text (for the New Testament) and a copy of the 1611 King James Version as revised in 1769 (the edition in general use today). His work was then submitted to the executive editor for the Old or New Testament. An elaborate concordance and word studies of the English, Greek, and Hebrew were prepared especially for this revision by the executive editors and their associates. In addition, using the original texts, the King James Bible, and other guidelines, the executive editor for the Old or New Testament carefully reviewed each scholar's work. Where necessary, they made recommendations for further changes or, in some cases, for restoration of the King James reading....Throughout the entire editing process, the work was regularly reviewed by the clergy and lay advisors who served on the British and North American Overview Committees. The final exhaustive review process was carried out by a separate Executive Review Committee for each Testament over a period of four years...The review process was completed in July 1981, at St. Andrews University in northeast Scotland, not far from King James' residence, historic Stirling Castle."—from the forward, The New Open Bible Study Edition, Thomas Nelson, 1990, p.10-11.

⇒ **FEATURES OF THE NEW KING JAMES VERSION**: The NKJV is noted as the translation that retains the elegant style of the KJV while "modernizing" the language. The NKJV is a word for word translation, replacing archaic words with contemporary ones.

5.   NEW LIVING TRANSLATION—NLT

⇒ **DATE**: The New Living Translation was published in 1996.

⇒ **PURPOSE**: "The goal of any Bible translation is to convey the meaning of the ancient Hebrew and Greek texts as accurately as possible to the modern reader. The New Living Translation is based on the most recent scholarship in the theory of translation. The challenge for the translators was to create a text that would make the same impact in the life of modern readers that the original text had for the original readers. In the New Living translation, this is accomplished by translating entire thoughts (rather than just words) into natural, everyday English. The end result is a translation that is easy to read and understand and that accurately communicates the meaning of the original text."—from A Note To Readers, The New Living Translation, Tyndale, 1996.

⇒ **HISTORY**: "With 40 million copies in print, *The Living Bible* has been meeting a great need in people's hearts for more than thirty years. But even good things can be improved, so ninety evangelical scholars from various theological backgrounds and denominations were commissioned in 1989 to begin revising *The Living Bible*. The end result of this seven year process in the *Holy Bible*, New Living Translation—a general-purpose translation that is accurate, easy to read, and excellent for study."—from A Note To Readers, The New Living Translation, Tyndale, 1996.

⇒ **FEATURES OF THE NEW LIVING TRANSLATION**: The NLT is a meaning-for-meaning translation. "The goal of any Bible translation is to convey the **meaning** of the ancient Hebrew and Greek texts as accurately as possible to the modern reader. The New Living Translation is based on the most recent scholarship in the theory of translation. The challenge for the translators was to create a text that would make the same **impact** in the life of modern readers that the original text had for the original readers. In the New Living Translation, this is accomplished by translating **entire thoughts** (rather than just words) into natural, everyday English. The end result is a translation that is easy to read and understand and that accurately communicates the meaning of the original text."—from Tyndale's web site.

A BRIEF HISTORICAL OVERVIEW OF THE GREEK NEW TESTAMENT

Throughout history, God has preserved the integrity of the Bible as it has been passed down from generation to generation. Because of God's love for man and His wisdom and power, we can trust the authority of the Bible. It is important to know how we got the Bible and why we can trust its authority for our lives. There are three principle sources for the New Testament text that give us our English Bibles:

1. There are the Greek manuscripts (some 4,000 to 5,000 in number).
   a. The earliest form of these Greek manuscripts is called "papyri." This paper scroll was made from the Egyptian papyrus plant that grew on the banks of the Nile River.
   b. From the fourth to tenth century, the manuscripts were written on parchment from animal skins. Of the many manuscripts, four stand out for their authority:
      1) *The Sinaitic Codex* was written in the fourth century and contains the entire New Testament. Discovered in a monastery on Mt. Sinai by Constantin Tischendorf, it was brought to Russia in 1859. In 1933 it was purchased by the British government from the Soviets. This important manuscript is on display at the British Museum in London England.
      2) *The Vatican Codex* was also written in the fourth century. It contains the complete New Testament except for the Pastoral epistles, a portion of Hebrews, and the book of Revelation. It is on display in the Library of the Vatican in Rome Italy.
      3) The *Alexandrian Codex* was written in the fifth century. It contains the complete New Testament except for most of the Gospel of Matthew and portions of John and 2 Corinthians. This manuscript contains almost all of the Greek Old Testament. A gift to King James I, it is on display at the British Museum.
      4) The *Ephraem Codex* was written in the fifth century. It contains the New Testament but in fragmentary form. This manuscript is on display in the National Library of Paris France.
2. There are different versions that had a significant impact on the New Testament text, the most important being Jerome's Latin Vulgate (382 A.D.)
3. There are the quotations of the New Testament from the writings of the early church fathers; men like Ambrose, Athanasius, Augustine, Clement of Alexandria, Irenaeus, Jerome, and Origen. The majority of their writings are in Greek and Latin.

IMPORTANT DATES AND EVENTS IN THE
HISTORY OF THE NEW TESTAMENT

NAME OF MANUSCRIPT OR TRANSLATION	DATE	AUTHOR/EDITOR	HISTORICAL FACTS/REMARKS
The Original Autographs	Most of the New Testament books were written before the destruction of the Temple in Jerusalem by Rome in A.D.70	The New Testament writers	The original autographs are perfect, without error. The whole Bible is God's inerrant, infallible revelation to man, and is to be the only supreme authority in all matters of faith and conduct.
The Earliest Greek Manuscripts	Written in the second and third centuries	Early Church fathers	⇒ The earliest Greek manuscripts were written on papyrus.
The Codex Manuscripts	Dated as early as the fourth century	Scribes, monks	⇒ The Codex Manuscripts are the basis for most modern editions of the Greek New Testament.
The Majority Text (from the Byzantine family of Greek Manuscripts)	Dated in the 15th century	Scribes, monks	⇒ The Majority Text became the basis of all English translations of the New Testament until the nineteenth century.
The Gutenberg Bible	Dated in the fifteenth century (1456)	Johann Gutenberg	⇒ The Latin Vulgate edition of the Bible was the first Bible to be printed from a printing press. 47 known copies still exist.
The Complutensian Polygot	Dated in the sixteenth century (1522)	Cardinal Ximenes of Spain	⇒ The Complutensian Polygot was the first printed Greek New Testament from a printing press.

NAME OF MANUSCRIPT OR TRANSLATION	DATE	AUTHOR/EDITOR	HISTORICAL FACTS/REMARKS
The Textus Receptus	Dated in the sixteenth century (1516)	Desiderius Erasmus	⇒ The Textus Receptus (TR) is based primarily on the manuscripts from the Byzantine text family. ⇒ The TR influenced biblical studies and theology for centuries. ⇒ The TR was the first published Greek New Testament made available for sale.
The Revision of the Textus Receptus	Dated in the sixteenth century (1550-1551)	Robert (Estienne) or Stephanus	⇒ This popular edition of the TR became the standard until the late nineteenth century. ⇒ It was Stephanus who inserted verse divisions.
The Revision of the Textus Receptus	Dated in the sixteenth century (1565-1604)	Theodore Beza	⇒ Beza published nine editions of the TR. ⇒ Beza popularized the form of Erasmus and Stephanus.
The King James Version	Dated in the seventeenth century (1611)	47 translators	⇒ The KJV is based upon the Textus Receptus.
Bengel's Greek New Testament	Dated in the eighteenth century (1734)	Johann Bengel	⇒ Bengel followed the Textus Receptus, but also offered comments and corrections in the text in the margin.
Westcott and Hort's Greek New Testament	Dated in the nineteenth century (1881-1882)	Brooke Foss Westcott and Fenton John Anthony Hort	⇒ Westcott and Hort's Greek text became known as a "critical text." They departed from the Textus Receptus and worked from other Greek manuscripts. ⇒ Their work become the forerunner for modern Greek New Testament translations; i.e. The Greek New Testament UBS4, the fourth edition of the United Bible Society's standard New Testament text in the original Greek language.
The Greek New Testament (GNT UBS4 - NA27)	First copyright was in 1966. Later revisions were completed in 1968 and 1975	Edited by Kurt Aland, Matthew Black, Carlo M. Martini, Bruce M. Metzger, and Allen Wikgren, in cooperation with the Institute for New Testament Textual Research, Munster/Westphalia, Fourth Edition (with exactly the same text as the Nestle - Aland 27th Edition of the Greek New Testament)	⇒ Most modern translations are based upon this Greek text.

ABBREVIATIONS

BIBLE ABBREVIATIONS

KJV	=	King James Version
NASB	=	New American Standard Bible
NIV	=	New International Version
NKJV	=	New King James Version
NLT	=	New Living Translation
GNS	=	The F. H. A. Scrivener 1881 - Theodore Beza 1598 Textus Receptus Greek New Testament, ASCII edition
GNT	=	The Greek New Testament (UBS4 - NA27)
RV	=	Revised Version

BIBLE RESOURCES ABBREVIATIONS

POSB	=	The Preacher's Outline & Sermon Bible®
PWS	=	Practical Word Studies in the New Testament

NEW TESTAMENT ABBREVIATIONS

Mt.	=	Matthew
Mk.	=	Mark
Lk.	=	Luke
Jn.	=	John
Acts	=	Acts
Ro.	=	Romans
1 Cor.	=	1 Corinthians
2 Cor.	=	2 Corinthians
Gal.	=	Galatians
Eph.	=	Ephesians
Ph.	=	Philippians
Col.	=	Colossians
1 Th.	=	1 Thessalonians
2 Th.	=	2 Thessalonians
1 Tim.	=	1 Timothy
2 Tim.	=	2 Timothy
Tit.	=	Titus
Phile.	=	Philemon
Heb.	=	Hebrews
Jas.	=	James
1 Pt.	=	1 Peter
2 Pt.	=	2 Peter
1 Jn.	=	1 John
2 Jn.	=	2 John
3 Jn.	=	3 John
Jude	=	Jude
Rev.	=	Revelation

MISCELLANEOUS ABBREVIATIONS

&	=	And
Arg.	=	Argument
Bckgrd.	=	Background
Bc.	=	Because
Circ.	=	Circumstance
Concl.	=	Conclusion
Cp.	=	Compare
Ct.	=	Contrast
Dif.	=	Different
e.g.	=	For example
Et.	=	Eternal
f.	=	Following
Govt.	=	Government
Id.	=	Identity or Identification
Illust.	=	Illustration
K.	=	Kingdom, K. of God, K. of Heaven, etc.
No.	=	Number
N.T.	=	New Testament
O.T.	=	Old Testament
Pt.	=	Point
Quest.	=	Question
Rel.	=	Religion
Resp.	=	Responsibility
Rev.	=	Revelation
Rgt.	=	Righteousness
Thru	=	Through
V.	=	Verse
Vs.	=	Verses
Vs.	=	Versus

ENGLISH WORD	GREEK WORD AND VERSE	THE WORD MEANS...

#2278
Labor–
Labour
 	
Labour–KJV
Labor–NASB
Labor–NIV
Labor–NKJV
Work hard–NLT
 	
POSB
REFERENCE
(1 Tim.4:10)
Note 6
	κοπιῶμεν = kopiōmen
	Pronunciation: [kop-ee-o'-mehn]
	Parsing (part of speech): verb
	    Mood—indicative
	    Tense—present
	    Voice—active
	    Person—1st person
	    Number—plural
	    Stem or root—from κοπιάω
	Concordance References:
	  ⇒ Strong's #2872 kopiaō
	  ⇒ NIV #3159 kopiaō
	  ⇒ NASB #2872 kopiaō
	
	1 Tim. 4:10
	For therefore we both **labour** and suffer reproach, because we trust in the living God, who is the Saviour of all men, specially of those that believe. [KJV]
	For it is for this we **labor** and strive, because we have fixed our hope on the living God, who is the Savior of all men, especially of believers. [NASB]
	(And for this we **labor** and strive), that we have put our hope in the living God, who is the Savior of all men, and especially of those who believe. [NIV]
	For to this *end* we both **labor** and suffer reproach, because we trust in the living God, who is *the* Savior of all men, especially of those who believe. [NKJV]
	We **work hard** and suffer much in order that people will believe the truth, for our hope is in the living God, who is the Savior of all people, and particularly of those who believe. [NLT]
	εἰς τοῦτο γὰρ **κοπιῶμεν** καὶ ὀνειδιζόμεθα, ὅτι ἠλπίκαμεν ἐπὶ Θεῷ ζῶντι, ὅς ἐστι σωτὴρ πάντων ἀνθρώπων, μάλιστα πιστῶν. [GNS]
	εἰς τοῦτο γὰρ **κοπιῶμεν** καὶ ἀγωνιζόμεθα, ὅτι ἠλπίκαμεν ἐπὶ θεῷ ζῶντι, ὅς ἐστιν σωτὴρ πάντων ἀνθρώπων μάλιστα πιστῶν. [GNT]
		To labor; to work; to work hard. It means arduous labor, strenuous work.
		
		Practical Application
		The good minister labors and labors, works and works to the point of fatigue and exhaustion; to the point that he can go no further. He exerts every ounce of energy and effort in his body for the sake of God and Christ. And note: he is even willing to suffer reproach for Christ. He continues to minister even when men ridicule, revile, mock, curse, and persecute him. Why?
		  ⇒ Because God is the living God. The minister's work and message are based upon the truth; what he is doing is truth. It is all for the living God.
		  ⇒ Because Jesus Christ is the Savior of all men. All men can be saved, actually delivered from the grip of sin, death, and condemnation.
		
		Therefore the good minister must labor, no matter the reproach. He must share the glorious news: man can now be reconciled to God and live forever.

#2279
Labor–Labour
 	
Labour–KJV
Toil–NASB
Labor–NIV
Labor–NKJV
Nothing you do–NLT
 	
POSB
REFERENCE
(1 Cor.15:58)
Note 6, point 3
	κόπος = kopos
	Pronunciation: [kop'-os]
	Parsing (part of speech): noun
	    Case—nominative
	    Gender—masculine
	    Number—singular
	    Stem or root—from κόπος, ου
	Concordance References:
	  ⇒ Strong's #2873 kopos
	  ⇒ NIV #3160 kopos
	  ⇒ NASB #2873 kopos
	
	1 Cor. 15:58
	Therefore, my beloved brethren, be ye stedfast, unmovable, always abounding in the work of the Lord, forasmuch as ye know that your **labour** is not in vain in the Lord. [KJV]
	Therefore, my beloved brethren, be steadfast, immovable, always abounding in the work of the Lord, knowing that your **toil** is not *in* vain in the Lord. [NASB]
	Therefore, my dear brothers, stand firm. Let nothing move you. Always give yourselves fully to the work of the Lord, because you know that your **labor** in the Lord is not in vain. [NIV]
	Therefore, my beloved brethren, be steadfast, immovable, always abounding in the work of the Lord, knowing that your **labor** is not in vain in the Lord. [NKJV]
	So, my dear brothers and sisters, be strong and steady, always enthusiastic about the Lord's work, for you know that **nothing you do** for the Lord is ever useless. [NLT]
	ὥστε, ἀδελφοί μου ἀγαπητοί, ἑδραῖοι γίνεσθε, ἀμετάκίνητοι, περισσεύοντες ἐν τῷ ἔργῳ τοῦ Κυρίου πάντοτε, εἰδότες ὅτι ὁ **κόπος** ὑμῶν οὐκ ἔστι κενὸς ἐν Κυρίῳ. [GNS]
	Ὥστε, ἀδελφοί μου ἀγαπητοί, ἑδραῖοι γίνεσθε, ἀμετάκίνητοι, περισσεύοντες ἐν τῷ ἔργῳ τοῦ κυρίου πάντοτε, εἰδότες ὅτι ὁ **κόπος** ὑμῶν οὐκ ἔστιν κενὸς ἐν κυρίῳ. [GNT]
		To labor; to toil; to suffer hardship. The word always means never cease, never stop, never slacken up, never quit, never retire; toiling and working to the point of exhaustion and fatigue, to the point of collapse.
		
		Practical Application
		The believer is to abound in the work of the Lord. The believer's labor will not be in vain, that is, left empty and unrewarded. The believer who...
		  • is steadfast,
		  • is unmoveable,
		  • is always abounding and laboring in the work of the Lord,
		  • will be rewarded: resurrected and given a new body.

ENGLISH WORD	GREEK WORD AND VERSE	THE WORD MEANS...

#2280
Labor–Labour
 	
Labour–KJV
Labor–NASB
Labor–NIV
Labor–NKJV
Work–NLT
 	
POSB
REFERENCE
(Col.1:29)
Note 5, point 1
	κοπιῶ = *kopiö*
	Pronunciation: [kop-ee-o']
	Parsing (part of speech): verb
	  Mood—indicative
	  Tense—present
	  Voice—active
	  Person—1st person
	  Number—singular
	  Stem or root—from κοπιάω
	Concordance References:
	⇒ Strong's #2872 kopiaö
	⇒ NIV #3159 kopiaö
	⇒ NASB #2872 kopiaö
	
	Col. 1:29
	Whereunto I also **labour**, striving according to his working, which worketh in me mightily. [KJV]
	And for this purpose also I **labor**, striving according to His power, which mightily works within me. [NASB]
	To this end I **labor**, struggling with all his energy, which so powerfully works in me. [NIV]
	To this *end* I also **labor**, striving according to His working which works in me mightily. [NKJV]
	I **work** very hard at this, as I depend on Christ's mighty power that works within me. [NLT]
	εἰς ὃ καὶ **κοπιῶ**, ἀγωνιζόμενος κατὰ τὴν ἐνέργειαν αὐτοῦ, τὴν ἐνεργουμένην ἐν ἐμοὶ ἐν δυνάμει. [GNS]
	εἰς ὃ καὶ **κοπιῶ** ἀγωνιζόμενος κατὰ τὴν ἐνέργειαν αὐτοῦ τὴν ἐνεργουμένην ἐν ἐμοὶ ἐν δυνάμει. [GNT]
		To labor; to work; to work hard; to toil and to struggle in labor and work to the point of exhaustion, fatigue, and pain.
		
		Practical Application
		It is the picture of an athlete struggling, agonizing, and pushing himself well beyond his capacity in order to achieve his objective. This is the call of God to the minister: to labor and work just as diligently as Paul and as the most dedicated athlete.

#2281
Labor
 	
Labour–KJV
Toil–NASB
Hard work–NIV
Labor–NKJV
Hard work–NLT
 	
POSB
REFERENCE
(Rev.2:2-3; esp. v.2)
Note 3, point 1
	κόπον = *kopon*
	Pronunciation: [kop'-on]
	Parsing (part of speech): noun
	  Case—accusative
	  Gender—masculine
	  Number—singular
	  Stem or root—from κόπος, ου
	Concordance References:
	⇒ Strong's #2873 kopos
	⇒ NIV #3160 kopos
	⇒ NASB #2873 kopos
	
	Rev. 2:2
	I know thy works, and thy **labour**, and thy patience, and how thou canst not bear them which are evil: and thou hast tried them which say they are apostles, and are not, and hast found them liars: [KJV]
	'I know your deeds and your **toil** and perseverance, and that you cannot endure evil men, and you put to the test those who call themselves apostles, and they are not, and you found them to be false; [NASB]
	I know your deeds, your **hard work** and your perseverance. I know that you cannot tolerate wicked men, that you have tested those who claim to be apostles but are not, and have found them false. [NIV]
	I know your works, your **labor**, your patience, and that you cannot bear those who are evil. And you have tested those who say they are apostles and are not, and have found them liars; [NKJV]
	"I know all the things you do. I have seen your **hard work** and your patient endurance. I know you don't tolerate evil people. You have examined the claims of those who say they are apostles but are not. You have discovered they are liars. [NLT]
	Οἶδα τὰ ἔργα σου, καὶ τὸν **κόπον** σου, καὶ τὴν ὑπομονήν σου, καὶ ὅτι οὐ δύνῃ βαστάσαι κακούς, καὶ ἐπειράσω τοὺς φάσκοντας εἶναι ἀποστόλους καὶ οὐκ εἰσί, καὶ εὗρες αὐτοὺς ψευδεῖς, [GNS]
	Οἶδα τὰ ἔργα σου καὶ τὸν **κόπον** καὶ τὴν ὑπομονήν σου καὶ ὅτι οὐ δύνῃ βαστάσαι κακούς καὶ ἐπείρασας τοὺς λέγοντας ἑαυτοὺς ἀποστόλους καὶ οὐκ εἰσίν καὶ εὗρες αὐτοὺς ψευδεῖς, [GNT]
		Hard work; to labor; to toil; to labor to the point of weariness, sweat, and exhaustion; to work and labor to the limit of one's ability.
		
		Practical Application
		The church *worked* and labored for Christ. The church was a working church, a laboring church, a church committed to serve Christ and to serve Him to the fullest.

ENGLISH WORD	GREEK WORD AND VERSE	THE WORD MEANS...

#2282
Labored–
Laboured
 	
Laboured–KJV
Labored–NASB
Worked–NIV
Labored–NKJV
Worked–NLT
 	
POSB
REFERENCE
(1 Cor.15:8-10; esp. v.10)
Note 5, point 3
	ἐκοπίασα = ekopiasa
	Pronunciation: [eh-kop-ee'-ah-sah]
	Parsing (part of speech): verb
	    Mood—indicative
	    Tense—aorist
	    Voice—active
	    Person—1st person
	    Number—singular
	    Stem or root—from κοπιάω
	Concordance References:
	⇒ Strong's #2872 kopiaö
	⇒ NIV #3159 kopiaö
	⇒ NASB #2872 kopiaö
	
	1 Cor. 15:10
	But by the grace of God I am what I am: and his grace *which was bestowed* upon me was not in vain; but I **laboured** more abundantly than they all: yet not I, but the grace of God which was with me. [KJV]
	But by the grace of God I am what I am, and His grace toward me did not prove vain; but I **labored** even more than all of them, yet not I, but the grace of God with me. [NASB]
	But by the grace of God I am what I am, and his grace to me was not without effect. No, I **worked** harder than all of them—yet not I, but the grace of God that was with me. [NIV]
	But by the grace of God I am what I am, and His grace toward me was not in vain; but I **labored** more abundantly than they all, yet not I, but the grace of God *which was* with me. [NKJV]
	But whatever I am now, it is all because God poured out his special favor on me and not without results. For I have **worked** harder than all the other apostles, yet it was not I but God who was working through me by his grace. [NLT]
	χάριτι δὲ Θεοῦ εἰμι ὅ εἰμι, καὶ ἡ χάρις αὐτοῦ ἡ εἰς ἐμὲ οὐ κενὴ ἐγενήθη, ἀλλὰ περισσότερον αὐτῶν πάντων **ἐκοπίασα**, οὐκ ἐγὼ δὲ ἀλλ ἡ χάρις τοῦ Θεοῦ ἡ σὺν ἐμοί. [GNS]
	χάριτι δὲ Θεοῦ εἰμι ὅ εἰμι, καὶ ἡ χάρις αὐτοῦ ἡ εἰς ἐμὲ οὐ κενὴ ἐγενήθη, ἀλλὰ περισσότερον αὐτῶν πάντων **ἐκοπίασα**, οὐκ ἐγὼ δὲ ἀλλὰ ἡ χάρις τοῦ Θεοῦ [ἡ] σὺν ἐμοί. [GNT]
		To labor; to work; to work hard; to labor to the point of being weary and exhausted; to become tired because of hard work.
		
		Practical Application
		Because God had done so much for him, Paul labored ever so diligently for God. Note his statement: he labored more than all the others that served Christ. Why? Because he owed it to Christ: he had sinned so terribly against the Lord. Note that he even gives the credit for his labor to the grace of God.

#2283
Laboreth
 	
Laboureth–KJV
Hard-working–NASB
Hardworking–NIV
Hard-working–NKJV
Hardworking–NLT
 	
POSB
REFERENCE
(2 Tim. 2:6)
NoteNote 5
	κοπιῶντα = kopiönta
	Pronunciation: [kop-ee-own'-tah]
	Parsing (part of speech): verb
	    Mood—participle
	    Tense—present
	    Voice—active
	    Gender—masculine
	    Number—singular
	    Stem or root—from κοπιάω
	Concordance References:
	⇒ Strong's #2872 kopiaö
	⇒ NIV #3159 kopiaö
	⇒ NASB #2872 kopiaö
	
	2 Tim. 2:6
	The husbandman that **laboureth** must be first partaker of the fruits. [KJV]
	The **hard-working** farmer ought to be the first to receive his share of the crops. [NASB]
	The **hardworking** farmer should be the first to receive a share of the crops. [NIV]
	The **hard-working** farmer must be first to partake of the crops. [NKJV]
	Hardworking farmers are the first to enjoy the fruit of their labor. [NLT]
	τὸν **κοπιῶντα** γεωργὸν δεῖ πρῶτον τῶν καρπῶν μεταλαμβάνειν. [GNS]
	τὸν **κοπιῶντα** γεωργὸν δεῖ πρῶτον τῶν καρπῶν μεταλαμβάνειν. [GNT]
		Hardworking; to labor; to work hard; to become very weary and tired. It means labor that is diligent, laborious, exhausting.
		
		Practical Application
		It is the picture of a farmer who toils to the point of becoming weary, so tired that he cannot put one foot in front of the other.
		Note a most significant point: it is the diligent farmer who arduously labors—who labors to the point of exhaustion—that shall will be the *first* to partake of the fruit. The slothful farmer…
		• is the last to receive the reward of his harvest and fruit.
		• never bears a full harvest and never receives the reward of a full harvest.
		The reason is that the slothful farmer either plants less seed or plants later than he should. And he never weeds or harvests the fields like he should. Note the point: it is the diligent farmer who shall will be the first to be rewarded. He shall will be the first to partake of the fruit of the harvest.
		The point is true of the Christian believer as well. The diligent believer shall will be rewarded first by God; that is, he shall will be given a greater reward by God.

ENGLISH WORD	GREEK WORD AND VERSE	THE WORD MEANS...

#2284
Labors–
Labours
 	
Labours–KJV
Labors–NASB
Hard work–NIV
Labors–NKJV
Worked to exhaus-
tion–NLT
 	
POSB
REFERENCE
(2 Cor.6:5)
Note 4
	κόποις = *kopois*
	Pronunciation: [kop'-oys]
	Parsing (part of speech): noun
	  Case—dative
	  Gender—masculine
	  Number—plural
	  Stem or root—from κόπος, ου
	Concordance References:
	  ⇒ Strong's #2873 kopos
	  ⇒ NIV #3160 kopos
	  ⇒ NASB #2873 kopos
	
	2 Cor. 6:5
	In stripes, in imprisonments, in tumults, in **labours**, in watchings, in fastings; [KJV]
	In beatings, in imprisonments, in tumults, in **labors**, in sleeplessness, in hunger, [NASB]
	In beatings, imprisonments and riots; in **hard work**, sleepless nights and hunger; [NIV]
	In stripes, in imprisonments, in tumults, in **labors**, in sleeplessness, in fastings; [NKJV]
	We have been beaten, been put in jail, faced angry mobs, **worked to exhaustion**, endured sleepless nights, and gone without food. [NLT]
	ἐν πληγαῖς, ἐν φυλακαῖς, ἐν ἀκαταστασίαις, ἐν κόποις, ἐν ἀγρυπνίαις, ἐν νηστείαις, [GNS]
	ἐν πληγαῖς, ἐν φυλακαῖς, ἐν ἀκαταστασίαις, ἐν κόποις, ἐν ἀγρυπνίαις, ἐν νηστείαις, [GNT]
		Hard work, labors, toils, efforts; laborious-laborous work to the point of exhaustion.
		
		Practical Application
		As we study the life of Paul, one striking characteristic about Paul's ministry becomes clear: he never stopped preaching, teaching, or ministering —not until he just had to have rest. He was not lazy, lethargic, slothful, or complacent. He got up in the mornings and put his hand to the plow: working, praying, studying, ministering, and witnessing—just as God had called him.

#2285
Labour
 	
Labour–KJV
Ambition–NASB
Make it goal–NIV
Make it aim–NKJV
Aim is–NLT
 	
POSB
REFERENCE
(2 Cor.5:9-10; esp.
v.9)
Note 4
	φιλοτιμούμεθα = *philotimoumetha*
	Pronunciation: [fil-ot-im-oo'-meh-tha]
	Parsing (part of speech): verb
	  Mood—indicative
	  Tense—present
	  Voice—middle or passive deponent
	  Person—1st person
	  Number—plural
	  Stem or root—from φιλοτιμέομαι
	Concordance References:
	  ⇒ Strong's #5389 philotimeomai
	  ⇒ NIV #5818 philotimeomai
	  ⇒ NASB #5389 philotimeomai
	
	2 Cor. 5:9
	Wherefore we **labour**, that, whether present or absent, we may be accepted of him. [KJV]
	Therefore also we have as our **ambition**, whether at home or absent, to be pleasing to Him. [NASB]
	So we **make it** our **goal** to please him, whether we are at home in the body or away from it. [NIV]
	Therefore we **make it** our **aim**, whether present or absent, to be well pleasing to Him. [NKJV]
	So our **aim is** to please him always, whether we are here in this body or away from this body. [NLT]
	διὸ καὶ φιλοτιμούμεθα, εἴτε ἐνδημοῦντες, εἴτε ἐκδημοῦντες, εὐάρεστοι αὐτῷ εἶναι. [GNS]
	διὸ καὶ φιλοτιμούμεθα, εἴτε ἐνδημοῦντες εἴτε ἐκδημοῦντες, εὐάρεστοι αὐτῷ εἶναι. [GNT]
		To make a goal; to constantly aim; to be constantly ambitious; to strive earnestly.
		
		Practical Application
		Judgment stirs in us the longing to please God and to receive our heavenly home. Judgment stirs "laborslabours" (*philotimoumetha*) in order to please God in life. The word means The word means that Paul says that he is to be judged; therefore, he works his fingers to the bone. Why? That he may please (*euarestoi*) God.

#2286
Labour
 	
Labour–KJV
Diligent–NASB
Make every effort–
NIV
Diligent–NKJV
Do our best–NLT
 	
POSB
REFERENCE
(Heb.4:11-13; esp. v.11)
Note 5, point 1
	σπουδάσωμεν = *spoudasömen*
	Pronunciation: [spoo-dah'-so-mehn]
	Parsing (part of speech): verb
	  Mood—subjunctive
	  Tense—aorist
	  Voice—active
	  Person—1st person
	  Number—plural
	  Stem or root—from σπουδάζω
	Concordance References:
	  ⇒ Strong's #4704 spoudazo
	  ⇒ NIV #5079 spoudazö
	  ⇒ NASB #4704 spoudazo
		To make every effort, labor; to be diligent, do one's best, work hard, endeavor, to give all diligence, be zealous, eagerly strive, exert one's self, and make haste.
		To make every effort; to labor; to be diligent; to do your best; to work hard; to endeavor, give all diligence, be zealous, strive eagerly, exert one's self, and make haste.
		
		Practical Application
		A person must labor to enter God's rest or else he will fall into unbelief. There is no place for sleepiness or laziness, complacency or lethargy. Unless a person labors with all diligence, he will fall just as Israel fell. And

ENGLISH WORD	GREEK WORD AND VERSE	THE WORD MEANS...
	Hebrews 4:11 Let us **labour** therefore to enter into that rest, lest any man fall after the same example of unbelief. [KJV] Let us therefore be **diligent** to enter that rest, lest anyone fall through *following* the same example of disobedience. [NASB] Let us, therefore, **make every effort** to enter that rest, so that no one will fall by following their example of disobedience. [NIV] Let us therefore be **diligent** to enter that rest, lest anyone fall according to the same example of disobedience. [NKJV] Let us **do our best** to enter that place of rest. For anyone who disobeys God, as the people of Israel did, will fall. [NLT] σπουδάσωμεν οὖν εἰσελθεῖν εἰς ἐκείνην τὴν κατάπαυσιν, ἵνα μὴ ἐν τῷ αὐτῷ τις ὑποδείγματι πέσῃ τῆς ἀπειθείας. [GNS] σπουδάσωμεν οὖν εἰσελθεῖν εἰς ἐκείνην τὴν κατάπαυσιν, ἵνα μὴ ἐν τῷ αὐτῷ τις ὑποδείγματι πέσῃ τῆς ἀπειθείας. [GNT]	remember Israel's experience: the people would labor for awhile and then fall back for awhile; labor again and then fall back again. Israel lived an up-and-down life, and the nation was not allowed to enter God's rest. There is no place for inconsistency, no place for living an up-and-down life—not in God's rest. Diligence—laboring every day—is an absolute essential. We must labor or else fall from God's rest as Israel fell.

#2287
Labour
 	
Labour–KJV
Toil–NASB
Hard work–NIV
Labor–NKJV
Hard work–NLT
 	
**POSB
REFERENCE**
(Rev.2:2-3; esp. v.2)
Note 3, point 1
	κόπον = kopon
	Pronunciation: [kop'-on]
	Parsing (part of speech): noun
	  Case—accusative
	  Gender—masculine
	  Number—singular
	  Stem or root—from κόπος, ου
	Concordance References:
	⇒ Strong's #2873 kopos
	⇒ NIV #3160 kopos
	⇒ NASB #2873 kopos
	
	Rev. 2:2
	I know thy works, and thy **labour**, and thy patience, and how thou canst not bear them which are evil: and thou hast tried them which say they are apostles, and are not, and hast found them liars: [KJV]
	'I know your deeds and your **toil** and perseverance, and that you cannot endure evil men, and you put to the test those who call themselves apostles, and they are not, and you found them *to be* false; [NASB]
	I know your deeds, your **hard work** and your perseverance. I know that you cannot tolerate wicked men, that you have tested those who claim to be apostles but are not, and have found them false. [NIV]
	I know your works, your **labor**, your patience, and that you cannot bear those who are evil. And you have tested those who say they are apostles and are not, and have found them liars; [NKJV]
	"I know all the things you do. I have seen your **hard work** and your patient endurance. I know you don't tolerate evil people. You have examined the claims of those who say they are apostles but are not. You have discovered they are liars. [NLT]
	Οἶδα τὰ ἔργα σου, καὶ τὸν **κόπον** σου, καὶ τὴν ὑπομονήν σου, καὶ ὅτι οὐ δύνῃ βαστάσαι κακούς, καὶ ἐπειράσω τοὺς φάσκοντας εἶναι ἀποστόλους καὶ οὐκ εἰσί, καὶ εὗρες αὐτοὺς ψευδεῖς, [GNS]
	Οἶδα τὰ ἔργα σου καὶ τὸν **κόπον** καὶ τὴν ὑπομονήν σου καὶ ὅτι οὐ δύνῃ βαστάσαι κακούς καὶ ἐπείρασας τοὺς λέγοντας ἑαυτοὺς ἀποστόλους καὶ οὐκ εἰσίν καὶ εὗρες αὐτοὺς ψευδεῖς, [GNT]
		Hard work; to labor; to toil; to labor to the point of weariness, sweat, and exhaustion; to work and labor to the limit of one's ability.
		
		Practical Application
		The church *worked and labored* for Christ. The church was a working church, a laboring church, a church committed to serve Christ and to serve Him to the fullest.

#2288
Lacked
 	
Lacked–KJV
Needy–NASB
Needy–NIV
Lacked–NKJV
Poverty–NLT
	ἐνδεής == endeēs
	Pronunciation: [en-deh-ace']
	Parsing (part of speech): pronominal adjective
	  Case—nominative
	  Gender—masculine
	  Number—singular
	  Stem or root—from ἐνδεής, ές
	Concordance References:
	⇒ Strong's #1729 endees
		Needy; the poor; the person who lacks; the poor; and lives in poverty.
		
		Practical Application
		The idea is that no family, no man, no woman, no child was neglected. No one was left without the necessities of life; no one had to face a day without the food, clothing, or shelter that he needed to take care of himself or of

ENGLISH WORD	GREEK WORD AND VERSE	THE WORD MEANS...
POSB REFERENCE (Acts 4:34-37; esp. v.34) Note 3, point 1	⇒ NIV #1890 endeës ⇒ NASB #1729 endees **Acts 4:34** Neither was there any among them that **lacked**: for as many as were possessors of lands or houses sold them, and brought the prices of the things that were sold, [KJV] For there was not a **needy** person among them, for all who were owners of land or houses would sell them and bring the proceeds of the sales, [NASB] There were no **needy** persons among them. For from time to time those who owned lands or houses sold them, brought the money from the sales [NIV] Nor was there anyone among them who **lacked**; for all who were possessors of lands or houses sold them, and brought the proceeds of the things that were sold, [NKJV] There was no **poverty** among them, because people who owned land or houses sold them [NLT] οὐδὲ γὰρ **ἐνδεής** τις ὑπῆρχεν ἐν αὐτοῖς· ὅσοι γὰρ κτήτορες χωρίων ἡ οἰκιῶν ὑπῆρχον, πωλοῦντες ἔφερον τὰς τιμὰς τῶν πιπρασκομένων, [GNS] οὐδὲ γὰρ **ἐνδεής** τις ἦν ἐν αὐτοῖς· ὅσοι γὰρ κτήτορες χωρίων ἡ οἰκιῶν ὑπῆρχον, πωλοῦντες ἔφερον τὰς τιμὰς τῶν πιπρασκομένων [GNT][GNT]	his dear family. All of God's dear children people were taken care of.

#2289
Lacking
 	
Slothful–KJV
Lagging behind–NASB
Lacking–NIV
Lagging–NKJV
Lazy–NLT
 	
POSB REFERENCE (Romans 12:11) Note 2, point 1
	ὀκνηροί = *oknëroi*
	Pronunciation: [ok-nay-roy']
	Parsing (part of speech): adjective
	    Case—nominative
	    Gender—masculine
	    Number—plural
	    Stem or root—from **ὀκνηρός**, ά, όν
	Concordance References:
	⇒ Strong's #3636 oknëros
	⇒ NIV #3891 oknëros
	⇒ NASB #3636 oknëros
	
	Romans 12:11
	Not **slothful** in business; fervent in spirit; serving the Lord; [KJV]
	Not **lagging behind** in diligence, fervent in spirit, serving the Lord; [NASB]
	Never be **lacking** in zeal, but keep your spiritual fervor, serving the Lord. [NIV]
	Not **lagging** in diligence, fervent in spirit, serving the Lord; [NKJV]
	Never be **lazy** in your work, but serve the Lord enthusiastically. [NLT]
	ᾗ σπουδῇ μὴ **ὀκνηροί**· τῷ πνεύματι ζέοντες· τῷ Κυρίῳ δουλεύοντες· [GNS]
	τῇ σπουδῇ μὴ **ὀκνηροί**, τῷ πνεύματι ζέοντες, τῷ κυρίῳ δουλεύοντες [GNT]
		To be lazy, slow moving, sluggish, lethargic, complacent, hesitating, delaying, slothful, lagging behind.
		
		Practical Application
		The believer is to serve the Lord. The charge is twofold. Do not lack in zeal; do not be lacking in diligence. The exhortation is clear: the believer must...
		• not be lazy or slow moving in zeal.
		• not be sluggish or lethargic in diligence.
		• not be hesitating or delaying in earnestness.
		• not be lagging behind.
		
		The believer just cannot approach life in a lackadaisical, easy-going, slow-moving fashion. The world is reeling in pain, with millions starving and suffering due to man's selfishness and sin, hoarding, disease, war, death—and the list could go on and on. The believer must not give in to sluggishness and complacency. He must serve the Lord with all diligence and zeal and earnestness. He must be enthusiastic in his service.

#2290
Lagging Behind– Lagging
 	
Slothful–KJV
Lagging behind– NASB
Lacking–NIV
Lagging–NKJV
Lazy–NLT
 	
POSB REFERENCE (Romans 12:11) Note 2, point 1
	ὀκνηροί = *oknëroi*
	Pronunciation: [ok-nay-roy']
	Parsing (part of speech): adjective
	    Case—nominative
	    Gender—masculine
	    Number—plural
	    Stem or root—from **ὀκνηρός**, ά, όν
	Concordance References:
	⇒ Strong's #3636 oknëros
	⇒ NIV #3891 oknëros
	⇒ NASB #3636 oknëros
	
	Romans 12:11
	Not **slothful** in business; fervent in spirit; serving the Lord; [KJV]
	Not **lagging behind** in diligence, fervent in spirit, serving the Lord; [NASB]
	Never be **lacking** in zeal, but keep your spiritual fer-
		To be lazy, slow moving, sluggish, lethargic, complacent, hesitating, delaying, lagging behind.
		
		Practical Application
		The believer is to serve the Lord. The charge is twofold: do not lag behind in diligence; do not be slothful in business. The exhortation is clear: the believer must...
		• not be lazy or slow moving in zeal.
		• not be sluggish or lethargic in diligence.
		• not be hesitating or delaying in earnestness.
		• not be lagging behind.
		
		(See **Lacking** for more practical application)

ENGLISH WORD	GREEK WORD AND VERSE	THE WORD MEANS...
	vor, serving the Lord. [NIV] Not **lagging** in diligence, fervent in spirit, serving the Lord; [NKJV] Never be **lazy** in your work, but serve the Lord enthusiastically. [NLT] τῇ σπουδῇ μὴ **ὀκνηροί**· τῷ πνεύματι ζέοντες· τῷ Κυρίῳ δουλεύοντες· [GNS] τῇ σπουδῇ μὴ **ὀκνηροί**, τῷ πνεύματι ζέοντες, τῷ κυρίῳ δουλεύοντες, [GNT]	

#2291
Laid Upon
 	
Laid upon–KJV
Under compulsion–NASB
Compelled–NIV
Laid upon–NKJV
Compelled–NLT
 	
POSB REFERENCE
(1 Cor.9:16)
Note 1
	ἀνάγκη ἐπίκειται = *anagkē epikeitai*
	Pronunciation: [an-ang-kay' ep-ik'-eh-ee-tah-ee]
	Parsing *anagkē* (part of speech): noun
	   Case—nominative
	   Gender—feminine
	   Number—singular
	   Stem or root—from *ἀνάγκη*, ης
	Parsing *epikeitai* (part of speech): verb
	   Mood—indicative
	   Tense—present
	   Voice—middle or passive deponent
	   Person—3rd person
	   Number—singular
	   Stem or root—from *ἐπίκειμαι*
	Concordance References:
	⇒ Strong's #318+1945 anagkē epikeimai
	⇒ NIV #340+2130 anagkē epikeimai [compelled]
	⇒ NASB #318+1945 anagkē epikeimai
	
	1 Cor. 9:16
	For though I preach the gospel, I have nothing to glory of: for necessity is **laid upon** me; yea, woe is unto me, if I preach not the gospel! [KJV]
	
	For if I preach the gospel, I have nothing to boast of, for I am **under compulsion**; for woe is me if I do not preach the gospel. [NASB]
	
	Yet when I preach the gospel, I cannot boast, for I am **compelled** to preach. Woe to me if I do not preach the gospel! [NIV]
	
	For if I preach the gospel, I have nothing to boast of, for necessity is **laid upon** me; yes, woe is me if I do not preach the gospel! [NKJV]
	
	For preaching the Good News is not something I can boast about. I am **compelled** by God to do it. How terrible for me if I didn't do it! [NLT]
	
	ἐὰν γὰρ εὐαγγελίζωμαι, οὐκ ἔστι μοι καύχημα· **ἀνάγκη** γάρ μοι **ἐπίκειται**· οὐαὶ δέ μοί ἐστιν, ἐὰν μὴ εὐαγγελίζωμαι. [GNS]
	
	ἐὰν γὰρ εὐαγγελίζωμαι, οὐκ ἔστιν μοι καύχημα· **ἀνάγκη** γάρ μοι **ἐπίκειται**· οὐαὶ γάρ μοί ἐστιν ἐὰν μὴ εὐαγγελίσωμαι. [GNT]
		To be pressed, compelled, constrained, required; to be duty bound, gripped with a sense of duty; to preach the gospel. It means to be urged, under force, under compulsion, imposed upon.
		
		Practical Application
		God had called Paul to preach the gospel; therefore, it was his charge, his work, his business, his call in life. He could not do otherwise: he was compelled to preach. His preaching was not a matter of choice; he had not chosen to be a preacher. His preaching was a matter of duty. If he did not preach, he would be disobeying God and would be missing the very purpose for his life upon earth.

#2292
Lamb
 	
Lamb–KJV
Lamb–NASB
Lamb–NIV
Lamb–NKJV
Lamb–NLT
 	
POSB REFERENCE
(Rev.5:6-7; esp. v.6)
Note 2, point 2
	ἀρνίον = *arnion*
	Pronunciation: [ar-nee'-ahn]
	Parsing (part of speech): noun
	   Case—nominative
	   Gender—neuter
	   Number—singular
	   Stem or root—from *ἀρνίον*, ου
	Concordance References:
	⇒ Strong's #721 arnion
	⇒ NIV #768 arnion
	⇒ NASB #721 arnion
	
	Rev. 5:6
	And I beheld, and, lo, in the midst of the throne and of the four beasts, and in the midst of the elders, stood a **Lamb** as it had been slain, having seven horns and seven eyes, which are the seven Spirits of God sent forth into all the earth. [KJV]
	
	And I saw between the throne (with the four living creatures) and the elders a **Lamb** standing, as if slain, having seven horns and seven eyes, which are the seven
		Lamb, sheep.
		
		Practical Application
		Note this: A.T. Robertson, the Greek scholar, points out that the word for *lamb* throughout the New Testament is *ho amnos*. But throughout Revelation, John uses another word *arnion*, and he uses the word twenty-nine times for the crucified Christ. The difference is this: the word chosen by John stresses the slaughter, suffering, pain, agony, and humiliation of Christ. And *all the suffering* is still seen in heaven. As Robertson says: "The Lamb is now alive, but...with the marks of the sacrifice" (*Word Pictures in the New Testament*, Vol.6, p.334).
		
		The point is this: Jesus Christ is the perfect sacrifice for our sins. He lived a sinless life when He was upon earth; He was the Ideal and Perfect Man. Therefore, whatever Jesus Christ did as the Perfect and Ideal Man, it could stand for and

ENGLISH WORD	GREEK WORD AND VERSE	THE WORD MEANS...

Spirits of God, sent out into all the earth. [NASB]

Then I saw a **Lamb**, looking as if it had been slain, standing in the center of the throne, encircled by the four living creatures and the elders. He had seven horns and seven eyes, which are the seven spirits of God sent out into all the earth. [NIV]

And I looked, and behold, in the midst of the throne and of the four living creatures, and in the midst of the elders, stood a **Lamb** as though it had been slain, having seven horns and seven eyes, which are the seven Spirits of God sent out into all the earth. [NKJV]

I looked and I saw a **Lamb** that had been killed but was now standing between the throne and the four living beings and among the twenty-four elders. He had seven horns and seven eyes, which are the seven spirits of God that are sent out into every part of the earth. [NLT]

καὶ εἶδον, καὶ ἰδού, ἐν μέσῳ τοῦ θρόνου καὶ τῶν τεσσάρων ζῴων καὶ ἐν μέσῳ τῶν πρεσβυτέρων, **ἀρνίον** ἑστηκὸς ὡς ἐσφαγμένον, ἔχον κέρατα ἑπτὰ καὶ ὀφθαλμοὺς ἑπτά, οἵ εἰσι τὰ ἑπτὰ τοῦ Θεοῦ πνεύματα τὰ ἀπεσταλμένα εἰς πᾶσαν τὴν γῆν. [GNS]

Καὶ εἶδον ἐν μέσῳ τοῦ θρόνου καὶ τῶν τεσσάρων ζῴων καὶ ἐν μέσῳ τῶν πρεσβυτέρων **ἀρνίον** ἑστηκὸς ὡς ἐσφαγμένον ἔχων κέρατα ἑπτὰ καὶ ὀφθαλμοὺς ἑπτὰ οἵ εἰσιν τὰ [ἑπτὰ] πνεύματα τοῦ θεοῦ ἀπεσταλμένοι εἰς πᾶσαν τὴν γῆν. [GNT]

cover us. When He died for our sins, He died as the Ideal and Perfect sacrifice. His sacrifice for our sins was perfectly acceptable to God. His sacrifice for sin stands for and covers us.

#2293
Lambs

Lambs–KJV
Lambs–NASB
Lambs–NIV
Lambs–NKJV
Lambs–NLT

**POSB
REFERENCE**
(Jn.21:16; esp. v.15)
Note 3, point 2

ἀρνία = arnia
Pronunciation: [ar-nee'-ah]
Parsing (part of speech): noun
    Case—accusative
    Gender—neuter
    Number—plural
    Stem or root—from **ἀρνίον**, ου
Concordance References:
  ⇒ Strong's #721 arnion
  ⇒ NIV #768 arnion
  ⇒ NASB #721 arnion

John 21:15
So when they had dined, Jesus saith to Simon Peter, Simon, *son* of Jonas, lovest thou me more than these? He saith unto him, Yea, Lord; thou knowest that I love thee. He saith unto him, Feed my **lambs**. [KJV]

So when they had finished breakfast, Jesus said to Simon Peter, "Simon, *son* of John, do you love Me more than these?" He said to Him, "Yes, Lord; You know that I love You." He said to him, "Tend My **lambs**." [NASB]

When they had finished eating, Jesus said to Simon Peter, "Simon son of John, do you truly love me more than these?""Yes, Lord," he said, "you know that I love you."Jesus said, "Feed my **lambs**." [NIV]

So when they had eaten breakfast, Jesus said to Simon Peter, "Simon, *son* of Jonah, do you love Me more than these?" He said to Him, "Yes, Lord; You know that I love You." He said to him, "Feed My **lambs**." [NKJV]

After breakfast Jesus said to Simon Peter, "Simon son of John, do you love me more than these?""Yes, Lord," Peter replied, "you know I love you.""Then feed my **lambs**," Jesus told him. [NLT]

Ὅτε οὖν ἠρίστησαν, λέγει τῷ Σίμωνι Πέτρῳ ὁ Ἰησοῦς, Σίμων Ἰωνᾶ, ἀγαπᾷς με πλέον τούτων; λέγει αὐτῷ, Ναί Κύριε· σὺ οἶδας ὅτι φιλῶ σε. λέγει αὐτῷ, Βόσκε τὰ **ἀρνία** μου. [GNS]

Ὅτε οὖν ἠρίστησαν λέγει τῷ Σίμωνι Πέτρῳ ὁ Ἰησοῦς, Σίμων Ἰωάννου, ἀγαπᾷς με πλέον τούτων; λέγει αὐτῷ, Ναί, κύριε, σὺ οἶδας ὅτι φιλῶ σε. λέγει αὐτῷ, Βόσκε τὰ **ἀρνία** μου. [GNT]

Lambs in a figurative sense applied to certain people.

Practical Application
Who are these "lambs?" The lambs are children, young converts, the handicapped or believers who need special attention. Scripture identifies the lambs and sheep as the flock of God, that is, as the church of God. Both the lambs and sheep are to be fed on the Word of God and fed in the same way.

ENGLISH WORD	GREEK WORD AND VERSE	THE WORD MEANS...

#2294
Lament
 	
Be afflicted–KJV
Be miserable–NASB
Grieve–NIV
Lament–NKJV
Deep grief–NLT
 	
POSB
REFERENCE
(Jas 4:9)
Note 3
	ταλαιπωρήσατε = talaipõrēsate
	Pronunciation: [tal-ahee-po-ray'-sah-teh]
	Parsing (part of speech): verb
	    Mood—imperative
	    Tense—aorist
	    Voice—active
	    Person—2nd person
	    Number—plural
	    Stem or root—from ταλαιπωρέω
	Concordance References:
	  ⇒ Strong's #5003 talaipõreõ
	  ⇒ NIV #5415 talaipõreõ
	  ⇒ NASB #5003 talaipõreõ
	
	James 4:9
	Be afflicted, and mourn, and weep: let your laughter be turned to mourning, and your joy to heaviness. [KJV]
	Be miserable and mourn and weep; let your laughter be turned into mourning, and your joy to gloom. [NASB]
	Grieve, mourn and wail. Change your laughter to mourning and your joy to gloom. [NIV]
	Lament and mourn and weep! Let your laughter be turned to mourning and your joy to gloom. [NKJV]
	Let there be tears for the wrong things you have done. Let there be sorrow and **deep grief**. Let there be sadness instead of laughter, and gloom instead of joy. [NLT]
	ταλαιπωρήσατε καὶ πενθήσατε καὶ κλαύσατε· ὁ γέλως ὑμῶν εἰς πένθος μετατραπήτω, καὶ ἡ χαρὰ εἰς κατήφειαν.[GNS]
	ταλαιπωρήσατε καὶ πενθήσατε καὶ κλαύσατε. ὁ γέλως ὑμῶν εἰς πένθος μετατραπήτω καὶ ἡ χαρὰ εἰς κατήφειαν. [GNT]
		To lament; to grieve; to be afflicted; to be miserable; to be distressed; to suffer deep grief; to endure toils (A.T. Robertson. *Word Pictures in the New Testament*, Vol. 6, p.53); to discipline and to voluntarily abstain (William Barclay. *The Letters of James and Peter*, p.127).
		
		Practical Application
		How can we overcome temptation? Endure. Be deeply and mournfully concerned. Note how descriptive this verse is:
		
		Lament and mourn and weep! Let your laughter be turned to mourning and your joy to gloom. (James 4:9). [NKJV]
		
		The picture is this: when temptation strikes us, it is not time...
		  • to be laughing
		  • to be joking around
		  • to be lighthearted
		  • to be complacent
		  • to be at ease
		  • to be jolly
		  • to be teasing
		  • to be unconcerned
		  • to be uncomfortable
		  • to be lying around
		Temptation is affliction; therefore, it is time to be disciplined and to control the comforts and joys of life. Temptation is a time for rigorous warfare—for battle and the discipline and endurance of battle.

#2295
Lamented–
Lamenting
 	
Lamented–KJV
Lamenting–NASB
Wailed for–NIV
Lamented–NKJV
Grief-stricken–NLT
 	
POSB
REFERENCE
(Lk.23:27)
Note 2
	ἐθρήνουν = ethrēnoun
	Pronunciation: [eh-thray-noon]
	Parsing (part of speech): verb
	    Mood—indicative
	    Tense—imperfect
	    Voice—active
	    Person—3rd person
	    Number—plural
	    Stem or root—from θρηνέω
	Concordance References:
	  ⇒ Strong's #2354 thrēneõ
	  ⇒ NIV #2577 thrēneõ
	  ⇒ NASB #2354 thrēneõ
	
	Luke 23:27
	And there followed him a great company of people, and of women, which also bewailed and **lamented** him. [KJV]
	And there were following Him a great multitude of the people, and of women who were mourning and **lamenting** Him. [NASB]
	A large number of people followed him, including women who mourned and **wailed for** him. [NIV]
	And a great multitude of the people followed Him, and women who also mourned and **lamented** Him. [NKJV]
	Great crowds trailed along behind, including many **grief-stricken** women. [NLT]
	Ἠκολούθει δὲ αὐτῷ πολὺ πλῆθος τοῦ λαοῦ, καὶ γυναικῶν αἳ καὶ ἐκόπτοντο καὶ ἐθρήνουν αὐτόν. [GNS]
	Ἠκολούθει δὲ αὐτῷ πολὺ πλῆθος τοῦ λαοῦ καὶ γυναικῶν αἳ ἐκόπτοντο καὶ ἐθρήνουν αὐτόν. [GNT]
		To be grief-stricken; to lament; to wail; to cry out loud; to mourn; to groan; to weep for; to sing out a dirge.
		
		Practical Application
		In this Scripture, the women were crying out, unable to hold back the pain cutting their hearts. Some of the people, of course, had been followers of Jesus for a long time and were feeling the depth of their Lord's sufferings. Other onlookers, as in any crowd witnessing severe suffering, felt only a natural tenderness and lament over one suffering so much.

ENGLISH WORD	GREEK WORD AND VERSE	THE WORD MEANS...

#2296
Large
 	
Great–KJV
Great–NASB
Large–NIV
Great–NKJV
Large–NLT
 	
POSB
REFERENCE
(Mk.4:1-2; esp. v.1)
Note 1
	πλεῖστος = *pleistos*
	Pronunciation: [plees-tos]
	Parsing (part of speech): adjective
	    Type—superlative
	    Case—nominative
	    Gender—masculine
	    Number—singular
	    Stem or root—from πολύς, πολλή, πολύ
	Concordance References:
	⇒ Strong's #4183 polus
	⇒ NIV #4498 polus
	⇒ NASB #4183 polus
	
	Mark 4:1
	    And he began again to teach by the sea side: and there was gathered unto him a **great** multitude, so that he entered into a ship, and sat in the sea; and the whole multitude was by the sea on the land. [KJV]
	    And He began to teach again by the sea. And such a very **great** multitude gathered to Him that He got into a boat in the sea and sat down; and the whole multitude was by the sea on the land. [NASB]
	    Again Jesus began to teach by the lake. The crowd that gathered around him was so **large** that he got into a boat and sat in it out on the lake, while all the people were along the shore at the water's edge. [NIV]
	    And again He began to teach by the sea. And a **great** multitude was gathered to Him, so that He got into a boat and sat *in it* on the sea; and the whole multitude was on the land facing the sea. [NKJV]
	    Once again Jesus began teaching by the lakeshore. There was such a **large** crowd along the shore that he got into a boat and sat down and spoke from there. [NLT]
	    Καὶ πάλιν ἤρξατο διδάσκειν παρὰ τὴν θάλασσαν, καὶ συνήχθη πρὸς αὐτὸν ὄχλος **πολύς**, ὥστε αὐτὸν ἐμβάντα εἰς τὸ πλοῖον καθῆσθαι ἐν τῇ θαλάσσῃ, καὶ πᾶς ὁ ὄχλος πρὸς τὴν θάλασσαν ἐπὶ τῆς γῆς ἦν. [GNS]
	    Καὶ πάλιν ἤρξατο διδάσκειν παρὰ τὴν θάλασσαν· καὶ συνάγεται πρὸς αὐτὸν ὄχλος **πλεῖστος**, ὥστε αὐτὸν εἰς πλοῖον ἐμβάντα καθῆσθαι ἐν τῇ θαλάσσῃ, καὶ πᾶς ὁ ὄχλος πρὸς τὴν θάλασσαν ἐπὶ τῆς γῆς ἦσαν. [GNT]
		Large, numerous, many, abundant, very great; a great deal of, a large number of, plenty of.
		
		Practical Application
		    The multitude was so large that they overflowed the seashore, and they pressed in upon Jesus so much that He was forced into a boat.

#2297
Large Millstone
 	
Millstone–KJV
Millstone–NASB
Millstone–NIV
Millstone–NKJV
Large millstone–NLT
 	
POSB
REFERENCE
(Lk.17:2)
Deeper Study #1
	λίθος μυλικός = *lithos mulikos*
	Pronunciation: [li-thos mul-i-kos]
	Parsing *lithos* (part of speech): noun
	    Case—nominative
	    Gender—masculine
	    Number—plural
	    Stem or root—from λίθος, ου
	Parsing *mulikos* (part of speech): adjective
	    Case—nominative
	    Gender—masculine
	    Number—singular
	    Stem or root—from μυλικός, ή, όν
	Concordance References:
	⇒ Strong's #3458 mulos+3684 onikos
	⇒ NIV #3345 lithos+3683 mulikos [millstone]
	⇒ NASB #3037 lithos+3457a mulikos
	
	Luke 17:2
	    It were better for him that a **millstone** were hanged about his neck, and he cast into the sea, than that he should offend one of these little ones. [KJV]
	    "It would be better for him if a **millstone** were hung around his neck and he were thrown into the sea, than that he should cause one of these little ones to stumble. [NASB]
	    It would be better for him to be thrown into the sea with a **millstone** tied around his neck than for him to cause one of these little ones to sin. [NIV]
	    It would be better for him if a **millstone** were hung around his neck, and he were thrown into the sea, than that
		The huge millstone, the one that the oxen or donkey pulled around to grind the grain. It was not the small hand millstone used by the women to grind a little grain at a time.
		
		Practical Application
		    Note: the very fact that Jesus referred to the huge millstone shows how great this sin is. The person would be held to the bottom of the sea by the most awful and terrible weight. The sin of leading others astray is the most awful sin that can be committed. Jesus is stressing that its condemnation will be awful and terrible.

ENGLISH WORD	GREEK WORD AND VERSE	THE WORD MEANS...
	he should offend one of these little ones. [NKJV] It would be better to be thrown into the sea with a **large millstone** tied around the neck than to face the punishment in store for harming one of these little ones. [NLT] λυσιτελεῖ αὐτῷ εἰ **μύλος ὀνικὸς** περίκειται περὶ τὸν τράχηλον αὐτοῦ, καὶ ἔρριπται εἰς τὴν θάλασσαν, η ἵνα σκανδαλίση ἕνα τῶν μικρῶν τούτων. [GNS] λυσιτελεῖ αὐτῷ εἰ **λίθος μυλικὸς** περίκειται περὶ τὸν τράχηλον αὐτοῦ καὶ ἔρριπται εἰς τὴν θάλασσαν η ἵνα σκανδαλίση τῶν μικρῶν τούτων ἕνα. [GNT]	

#2298
Lasciviousness
 	
Lasciviousness–KJV
Sensuality–NASB
Lewdness–NIV
Lewdness–NKJV
Eagerness for lustful pleasure–NLT
 	
POSB REFERENCE
(Mk.7:22)
Deeper Study #11
 	
See also POSB REF:
(2 Cor.12:19-21; esp. v.21)
Note 3, point 2
(Gal.5:19-21; esp. v.19)
Note 2
(1 Pt.4:3)
Note 3, point 1
	ἀσέλγεια = *aselgeia*
	Pronunciation: [as-elg'-i-ah]
	Parsing (part of speech): noun
	    Case—nominative
	    Gender—feminine
	    Number—singular
	    Stem or root—from ἀσέλγεια, ας
	Concordance References:
	  ⇒ Strong's #766 aselgeia
	  ⇒ NIV #816 aselgeia
	  ⇒ NASB #766 aselgeia
	
	Mark 7:22
	Thefts, covetousness, wickedness, deceit, **lasciviousness**, an evil eye, blasphemy, pride, foolishness: [KJV]
	Deeds of coveting *and* wickedness, *as well as* deceit, **sensuality**, envy, slander, pride *and* foolishness. [NASB]
	Greed, malice, deceit, **lewdness**, envy, slander, arrogance and folly. [NIV]
	Thefts, covetousness, wickedness, deceit, **lewdness**, an evil eye, blasphemy, pride, foolishness. [NKJV]
	Adultery, greed, wickedness, deceit, **eagerness for lustful pleasure**, envy, slander, pride, and foolishness. [NLT]
	πλεονεξίαι, πονηρίαι, δόλος, **ἀσέλγεια**, ὀφθαλμὸς πονηρός, βλασφημία, ὑπερηφανία, ἀφροσύνη· [GNS]
	μοιχεῖαι, πλεονεξίαι, πονηρίαι, δόλος, **ἀσέλγεια**, ὀφθαλμὸς πονηρός, βλασφημία, ὑπερηφανία, ἀφροσύνη· [GNT]
		Debauchery; lasciviousness; lewdness; eagerness for lustful pleasure; sensuality and indecency; shamelessness; uncontrolled, undisciplined, and unrestrained lust and passion.
		
		Practical Application
		A chief characteristic of the behavior is open and shameless indecency. It means unrestrained evil thoughts and behavior. It is giving in to brutish and lustful desires, a readiness for any pleasure. It is a person who knows no restraint, an individual who has sinned so much that he no longer cares what people say or think. It is something far more distasteful than just doing wrong. The person who misbehaves usually tries to hide his wrong, but a lascivious man does not care who knows about his exploits or shame. He wants; therefore, he seeks to take and gratify. Decency and opinion do not matter. When he initially began to sin, he did as all people do: he misbehaved in secret. But eventually, the sin got the best of him—to the point that he no longer cared who saw or knew. He became the subject of a master—the master of habit, of the thing itself. People become the slaves of such things as unbridled lust, wantonness, licentiousness, outrageousness, shamelessness, insolence (Mark 7:22), wanton manners, filthy words, indecent body movements, immoral handling of males and females (Romans 13:13), carnality, gluttony, and sexual immorality (1 Peter 4:3; 2 Peter 2:2, 18). (Cp. 2 Cor. 12:21; Galatians 5:19; Ephes. 4:19; 2 Peter 2:7.)

#2299
Lasciviousness
 	
Lasciviousness–KJV
Licentiousness–NASB
License for immorality–NIV
Lewdness–NKJV
Immoral lives–NLT
 	
POSB REFERENCE
(Jude 1:4)
Note 5
	ἀσέλγειαν = *aselgeian*
	Pronunciation: [as-elg'-i-ahn]
	Parsing (part of speech): noun
	    Case—accusative
	    Gender—feminine
	    Number—singular
	    Stem or root—from ἀσέλγεια, ας
	Concordance References:
	  ⇒ Strong's #766 aselgeia
	  ⇒ NIV #816 aselgeia
	  ⇒ NASB #766 aselgeia
	
	Jude 1:4
	For there are certain men crept in unawares, who were before of old ordained to this condemnation, ungodly men, turning the grace of our God into **lasciviousness**, and denying the only Lord God, and our Lord Jesus Christ. [KJV]
	For certain persons have crept in unnoticed, those who were long beforehand marked out for this condemnation, ungodly persons who turn the grace of our God into **licentiousness** and deny our only Master and Lord, Jesus Christ. [NASB]
	For certain men whose condemnation was written
		License for immorality; lasciviousness; licentiousness; immoral living; lustful desires; sensuality; shamelessness.
		
		Practical Application
		No matter what the false teaching is, it will enslave. The false teacher who denies Christ and God's Word removes the supreme authority over man's life. Therefore, man is basically free to live in selfishness and greed, desire and lust. He is left to seek as much pleasure and as many possessions as he desires upon earth. But in the end, man discovers something. The more he gets, the more he wants. It may be comfort, money, sex, position, or authority; it does not matter. Man's nature is such that he wants more and more. Man must be restrained by an authority above himself, that is, by God and by God's Word. If he is not, then he becomes enslaved to his passions and to the corruption of the world. This is one of the terrible fallacies of all false teachings. They all enslave man to this world: not a single false teaching can usher a man through the door of

ENGLISH WORD	GREEK WORD AND VERSE	THE WORD MEANS...
	about long ago have secretly slipped in among you. They are godless men, who change the grace of our God into a **license for immorality** and deny Jesus Christ our only Sovereign and Lord. [NIV]	death into eternal life. Only Jesus Christ can do that. Note the clear truth: whatever overcomes a man, that very thing enslaves him.
	For certain men have crept in unnoticed, who long ago were marked out for this condemnation, ungodly men, who turn the grace of our God into **lewdness** and deny the only Lord God and our Lord Jesus Christ. [NKJV]	⇒ If a false teacher overcomes a man, then the man is enslaved to that teaching. ⇒ If the world overcomes a man, then the man is enslaved by the world.
	I say this because some godless people have wormed their way in among you, saying that God's forgiveness allows us to live **immoral lives**. The fate of such people was determined long ago, for they have turned against our only Master and Lord, Jesus Christ. [NLT]	
	παρεισέδυσαν γὰρ τινες ἄνθρωποι, οἱ πάλαι προγεγραμμένοι εἰς τοῦτο τὸ κρίμα, ἀσεβεῖς, τὴν τοῦ Θεοῦ ἡμῶν χάριν μετατιθέντες εἰς **ἀσέλγειαν**, καὶ τὸν μόνον δεσπότην Θεόν, καὶ Κύριον ἡμῶν Ἰησοῦν Χριστὸν ἀρνούμενοι. [GNS]	
	παρεισέδυσαν γὰρ τινες ἄνθρωποι, οἱ πάλαι προγεγραμμένοι εἰς τοῦτο τὸ κρίμα, ἀσεβεῖς, τὴν τοῦ θεοῦ ἡμῶν χάριτα μετατιθέντες εἰς **ἀσέλγειαν** καὶ τὸν μόνον δεσπότην καὶ κύριον ἡμῶν Ἰησοῦν Χριστὸν ἀρνούμενοι. [GNT]	

#2300
Last Hour
 	
Last time–KJV
Last hour–NASB
Last hour–NIV
Last hour–NKJV
Last hour–NLT
 	
**POSB
REFERENCE**
(1 Jn.2:18)
Note 1, point 1
	ἐσχάτη ὥρα = *eschatē hōra*
	Pronunciation: [es'-khat-ay ho'-rah]
	Parsing *eschatē* (part of speech): adjective
	    Case—nominative
	    Gender—feminine
	    Number—singular
	    Stem or root—from ἔσχατος, η, ον
	Parsing *hōra* (part of speech): noun
	    Case—nominative
	    Gender—feminine
	    Number—singular
	    Stem or root—from ὥρα, ας
	Concordance References:
	⇒ Strong's #2078 eschatos + 5610 hōra
	⇒ NIV #2274 eschatos [last] + 6052 hōra [hour]
	⇒ NASB #2078 eschatos + 5610 hōra
	
	1 John 2:18
	Little children, it is the **last time**: and as ye have heard that antichrist shall come, even now are there many antichrists; whereby we know that it is the last time. [KJV]
	Children, it is the **last hour**; and just as you heard that antichrist is coming, even now many antichrists have arisen; from this we know that it is the last hour. [NASB]
	Dear children, this is the **last hour**; and as you have heard that the antichrist is coming, even now many antichrists have come. This is how we know it is the last hour. [NIV]
	Dear children, this is the **last hour**; and as you have heard that the antichrist is coming, even now many antichrists have come. This is how we know it is the last hour. [NKJV]
	Dear children, the **last hour** is here. You have heard that the Antichrist is coming, and already many such antichrists have appeared. From this we know that the end of the world has come. [NLT]
	Παιδία, **ἐσχάτη ὥρα** ἐστί, καὶ καθὼς ἠκούσατε ὅτι ὁ ἀντίχριστος ἔρχεται, καὶ νῦν ἀντίχριστοι πολλοὶ γεγόνασιν· ὅθεν γινώσκομεν ὅτι ἐσχάτη ὥρα ἐστίν. [GNS]
	Παιδία, **ἐσχάτη ὥρα** ἐστίν, καὶ καθὼς ἠκούσατε ὅτι ἀντίχριστος ἔρχεται, καὶ νῦν ἀντίχριστοι πολλοὶ γεγόνασιν, ὅθεν γινώσκομεν ὅτι ἐσχάτη ὥρα ἐστίν. [GNT]
		The last hour; the last time; the final hour; the last moment.
		
		Practical Application
		Believers must know that it is the last hour, that the midnight hour is about to strike for the end of the world. Note the term "the last hour" (*eschatē hōra*). It means the midnight hour when the world is to end (see POSB note, Last Days—2 Peter 3:3 for discussion).

ENGLISH WORD	GREEK WORD AND VERSE	THE WORD MEANS...

#2301
Last Time
 	
Last time–KJV
Last hour–NASB
Last hour–NIV
Last hour–NKJV
Last hour–NLT
 	
POSB
REFERENCE
(1 Jn.2:18)
Note 1, point 1
	ἐσχάτη ὥρα = *eschatē hōra*
	Pronunciation: [es'-khat-ay ho'-rah]
	Parsing *eschatē* (part of speech): adjective
	    Case—nominative
	    Gender—feminine
	    Number—singular
	    Stem or root—from ἔσχατος, η, ον
	Parsing *hōra* (part of speech): noun
	    Case—nominative
	    Gender—feminine
	    Number—singular
	    Stem or root—from ὥρα, ας
	Concordance References:
	⇒ Strong's #2078 eschatos + 5610 hōra
	⇒ NIV #2274 eschatos [last] + 6052 hōra [hour]
	⇒ NASB #2078 eschatos + 5610 hōra
	
	1 John 2:18
	  Little children, it is the **last time**: and as ye have heard that antichrist shall come, even now are there many antichrists; whereby we know that it is the last time. [KJV]
	  Children, it is the **last hour**; and just as you heard that antichrist is coming, even now many antichrists have arisen; from this we know that it is the last hour. [NASB]
	  Dear children, this is the **last hour**; and as you have heard that the antichrist is coming, even now many antichrists have come. This is how we know it is the last hour. [NIV]
	  Little children, it is the **last hour**; and as you have heard that the Antichrist is coming, even now many antichrists have come, by which we know that it is the last hour. [NKJV]
	  Dear children, the **last hour** is here. You have heard that the Antichrist is coming, and already many such antichrists have appeared. From this we know that the end of the world has come. [NLT]
	  Παιδία, ἐσχάτη ὥρα ἐστί, καὶ καθὼς ἠκούσατε ὅτι ὁ ἀντίχριστος ἔρχεται, καὶ νῦν ἀντίχριστοι πολλοὶ γεγόνασιν· ὅθεν γινώσκομεν ὅτι ἐσχάτη ὥρα ἐστίν. [GNS]
	  Παιδία, ἐσχάτη ὥρα ἐστίν, καὶ καθὼς ἠκούσατε ὅτι ἀντίχριστος ἔρχεται, καὶ νῦν ἀντίχριστοι πολλοὶ γεγόνασιν, ὅθεν γινώσκομεν ὅτι ἐσχάτη ὥρα ἐστίν. [GNT]
		The last hour; the last time; the final hour; the last moment.
		
		### Practical Application
		  Believers must know that it is the last time, that the midnight hour is about to strike for the end of the world. Note the term "the last time" (*eschatē hōra*). It really means *the last hour*, the midnight hour when the world is to end (see POSB note, Last Days—2 Peter 3:3 for discussion).

#2302
Last Times
 	
Latter times–KJV
Later times–NASB
Later times–NIV
Latter times–NKJV
Last times–NLT
 	
POSB
REFERENCE
(1 Tim.4:1)
Note 1
	ὑστέροις καιροῖς = *husterois kairois*
	Pronunciation: [hoos'-tehr-oys kai'-roys]
	Parsing *husterois* (part of speech): adjective
	    Type—comparative
	    Case—dative
	    Gender—masculine
	    Number—plural
	    Stem or root—from ὕστερος, α, ον
	Parsing *kairois* (part of speech): noun
	    Case—dative
	    Gender—masculine
	    Number—plural
	    Stem or root—from καιρός, οῦ
	Concordance References:
	⇒ Strong's #5305 husteros + 2540 kairos
	⇒ NIV #5731 husteros [later] + 2789 kairos [times]
	⇒ NASB #5305 husteros + 2540 kairos
	
	1 Tim. 4:1
	  Now the Spirit speaketh expressly, that in the **latter times** some shall depart from the faith, giving heed to seducing spirits, and doctrines of devils; [KJV]
	  But the Spirit explicitly says that in **later times** some will fall away from the faith, paying attention to deceitful spirits and doctrines of demons, [NASB]
		Later times; latter times; last times; final times. It means a little later on, not far out in the future.
		
		### Practical Application
		  False teachers will arise in the last days of history. That is, false teachers were to arise within the church almost immediately and continue on through our day and on to the end of time. The point is well made: the church and the genuine believer have to be constantly on guard against false teaching. The terrible danger of false teaching always confronts the church and believer. And note: this is a revelation of the Spirit of God Himself. It is not the idea of some preacher seeking recognition because of his novel idea. It is the warning of God's Spirit.

ENGLISH WORD	GREEK WORD AND VERSE	THE WORD MEANS...
	The Spirit clearly says that in **later times** some will abandon the faith and follow deceiving spirits and things taught by demons. [NIV] Now the Spirit expressly says that in **latter times** some will depart from the faith, giving heed to deceiving spirits and doctrines of demons, [NKJV] Now the Holy Spirit tells us clearly that in the **last times** some will turn away from what we believe; they will follow lying spirits and teachings that come from demons. [NLT] Τὸ δὲ Πνεῦμα ῥητῶς λέγει, ὅτι ἐν **ὑστέροις καιροῖς** ἀποστήσονταί τινες τῆς πίστεως, προσέχοντες πνεύμασι πλάνοις καὶ διδασκαλίαις δαιμονίων, [GNS] Τὸ δὲ πνεῦμα ῥητῶς λέγει ὅτι ἐν **ὑστέροις καιροῖς** ἀποστήσονταί τινες τῆς πίστεως προσέχοντες πνεύμασιν πλάνοις καὶ διδασκαλίαις δαιμονίων, [GNT]	

#2303
 Later Times— Latter Times
 	
 Latter times–KJV
 Later times–NASB
 Later times–NIV
 Latter times–NKJV
 Last times--NLT
 	
 POSB REFERENCE
 (1 Tim.4:1)
 Note 1
	ὑστέροις καιροῖς = husterois kairois
	 Pronunciation: [hoos'-tehr-oys kai'-roys]
	 Parsing husterois (part of speech): adjective
	      Type—comparative
	      Case—dative
	      Gender—masculine
	      Number—plural
	      Stem or root—from ὕστερος, α, ον
	 Parsing kairois (part of speech): noun
	      Case—dative
	      Gender—masculine
	      Number—plural
	      Stem or root—from καιρός, οῦ
	 Concordance References:
	 ⇒ Strong's #5305 husteros + 2540 kairos
	 ⇒ NIV #5731 husteros [later] + 2789 kairos [times]
	 ⇒ NASB #5305 husteros + 2540 kairos
	
	 1 Tim. 4:1
	 Now the Spirit speaketh expressly, that in the **latter times** some shall depart from the faith, giving heed to seducing spirits, and doctrines of devils; [KJV]
	
	 But the Spirit explicitly says that in **later times** some will fall away from the faith, paying attention to deceitful spirits and doctrines of demons, [NASB]
	
	 The Spirit clearly says that in **later times** some will abandon the faith and follow deceiving spirits and things taught by demons. [NIV]
	
	 Now the Spirit expressly says that in **latter times** some will depart from the faith, giving heed to deceiving spirits and doctrines of demons, [NKJV]
	
	 Now the Holy Spirit tells us clearly that in the **last times** some will turn away from what we believe; they will follow lying spirits and teachings that come from demons. [NLT]
	
	 Τὸ δὲ Πνεῦμα ῥητῶς λέγει, ὅτι ἐν **ὑστέροις καιροῖς** ἀποστήσονταί τινες τῆς πίστεως, προσέχοντες πνεύμασι πλάνοις καὶ διδασκαλίαις δαιμονίων, [GNS]
	
	 Τὸ δὲ πνεῦμα ῥητῶς λέγει ὅτι ἐν **ὑστέροις καιροῖς** ἀποστήσονταί τινες τῆς πίστεως προσέχοντες πνεύμασιν πλάνοις καὶ διδασκαλίαις δαιμονίων, [GNT]
		Later times; latter times; last times; final times. It means a little later on, not far out in the future.
		
		 Practical Application
		 False teachers will arise in the later days of history. That is, false teachers were to arise within the church almost immediately and continue on through our day and on to the end of time. (See **Last Times** for more practical application).

#2304
 Laugh
 	
 Laugh–KJV
 Laugh–NASB
 Laugh–NIV
 Laugh–NKJV
 Laugh–NLT
 	
 POSB REFERENCE
 (Lk.6:20-23; esp. v.21)
 Note 1, point 3c
	γελάσετε = gelasete
	 Pronunciation: [ghel-ah'-seh-teh]
	 Parsing (part of speech): verb
	      Case—indicative
	      Tense—future
	      Voice—active
	      Person—2nd person
	      Number—plural
	      Stem or root—from γελάω
	 Concordance References:
	 ⇒ Strong's #1070 gelaō
	 ⇒ NIV #1151 gelaō
	 ⇒ NASB #1070 gelaō
		Loud laughter that arises from a deep-seated joy and comfort.
		
		 Practical Application
		 The laughter comes from two things.
		 1. It comes from seeing the end of sin and shame, sorrow and suffering, tragedy and trauma.
		 2. It comes from being comforted.

ENGLISH WORD	GREEK WORD AND VERSE	THE WORD MEANS...
	Luke 6:21	
	Blessed *are ye* that hunger now: for ye shall be filled. Blessed *are ye* that weep now: for ye shall **laugh**. [KJV]	
	"Blessed *are* you who hunger now, for you shall be satisfied. Blessed *are* you who weep now, for you shall **laugh**. [NASB]	
	Blessed are you who hunger now, for you will be satisfied. Blessed are you who weep now, for you will **laugh**. [NIV]	
	Blessed *are you* who hunger now,For you shall b filled.Blessed *are you* who weep now,For you shall **laugh**. [NKJV]	
	God blesses you who are hungry now, for you will be satisfied. God blesses you who weep now, for the time will come when you will **laugh** with joy. [NLT]	
	μακάριοι οἱ πεινῶντες νῦν, ὅτι χορτασθήσεσθε. μακάριοι οἱ κλαίοντες νῦν· ὅτι **γελάσετε**. [GNS]	
	μακάριοι οἱ πεινῶντες νῦν, ὅτι χορτασθήσεσθε. μακάριοι οἱ κλαίοντες νῦν, ὅτι **γελάσετε**. [GNT]	

#2305
Law–
Law of Moses
 	
Law–KJV
Law–NASB
Law–NIV
Law–NKJV
Law of Moses–NLT
 	
POSB
REFERENCE
(Mt.5:17-18; esp. v.17)
Note 1
Deeper Study #2
	νόμον = nomon
	Pronunciation: [nom'-on]
	Parsing (part of speech): noun
	    Case—accusative
	    Gender—masculine
	    Number—singular
	    Stem or root—from *νόμος, ου*
	Concordance References:
	⇒ Strong's #3551 nomos
	⇒ NIV #3795 nomos
	⇒ NASB #3551 nomos
	
	Matthew 5:17
	Think not that I am come to destroy the **law**, or the prophets: I am not come to destroy, but to fulfil. [KJV]
	"Do not think that I came to abolish the **Law** or the Prophets; I did not come to abolish, but to fulfill. [NASB]
	"Do not think that I have come to abolish the **Law** or the Prophets; I have not come to abolish them but to fulfill them. [NIV]
	"Do not think that I came to destroy the **Law** or the Prophets. I did not come to destroy but to fulfill. [NKJV]
	"Don't misunderstand why I have come. I did not come to abolish the **law of Moses** or the writings of the prophets. No, I came to fulfill them. [NLT]
	Μὴ νομίσητε ὅτι ἦλθον καταλῦσαι τὸν **νόμον** η τοὺς προφήτας· οὐκ ἦλθον καταλῦσαι ἀλλὰ πληρῶσαι. [GNS]
	Μὴ νομίσητε ὅτι ἦλθον καταλῦσαι τὸν **νόμον** η τοὺς προφήτας· οὐκ ἦλθον καταλῦσαι ἀλλὰ πληρῶσαι. [GNT]
		The law; the law of Moses; the four different writings of the Jews.
		
		Practical Application
		1. It referred to the Ten Commandments.
		2. It referred to the first five books of the Bible, that is the Pentateuch.
		3. It referred to the law and the prophets, that is, all the Scripture of the Old Testament.
		4. It referred to the oral or the Scribal Law.
		
		God's law, given in the Old Testament, was not enough for the Jews. They reasoned that if the law were really God's Word, then it must include—have embodied within it—every conceivable rule and regulation for conduct. Therefore, they took the great principles of the law and reduced them to thousands upon thousands of rules and regulations. These rules and regulations became the oral or Scribal Law.
		There were two groups who gave their lives to the teaching and keeping of the law.
		1. The Scribes: they were the writers and teachers of the law (See POSB *Deeper Study #1*—Lk.6:2).
		2. The Pharisees: they were the strict followers of the law (See POSB *Deeper Study #3*—Acts 23:8).

#2306
Lawlessness
 	
Iniquity–KJV
Lawlessness–NASB
Wickedness–NIV
Lawlessness–NKJV
Sin will be rampant–NLT
 	
POSB
REFERENCE
(Mt.24:12)
Deeper Study #6
 	
See also POSB REF:
(Mt.7:23)
Note 3, point 2
(2 Cor.6:14-16; esp. v.14)
Note 2
	ἀνομίαν = anomian
	Pronunciation: [an-om-ee'-ahn]
	Parsing (part of speech): noun
	    Case—accusative
	    Gender—feminine
	    Number—singular
	    Stem or root—from *ἀνομία, ας*
	Concordance References:
	⇒ Strong's #458 anomia
	⇒ NIV #490 anomia
	⇒ NASB #458 anomia
	
	Matthew 24:12
	And because **iniquity** shall abound, the love of many shall wax cold. [KJV]
	"And because **lawlessness** is increased, most people's love will grow cold. [NASB]
	Because of the increase of **wickedness**, the love of most will grow cold, [NIV]
	And because **lawlessness** will abound, the love of many will grow cold. [NKJV]
	Sin will be rampant everywhere, and the love of
		Lawlessness, wickedness, iniquity, unrighteousness; sin that is rampant; a gross transgression of the law; unauthorized acts or conduct; evil-doing.
		
		Practical Application
		Unbelievers do not obey God. They live and do as they wish, not as God says. Rejecting God and what He says they go about doing their own thing. They rebel against God and His commandments, living lawless and unrighteous lives. What is lawlessness? It is taking license...
		• with the law and righteousness
		• with morality and discipline
		
		It is neglect of or opposition to the law of God; it is substituting the will of self in the place of God's will (1 John 3:4). It is looking to self or to the world instead of looking to God. It is following the course of self and the desires of self

ENGLISH WORD	GREEK WORD AND VERSE	THE WORD MEANS...
	many will grow cold. [NLT] καὶ διὰ τὸ πληθυνθῆναι τὴν **ἀνομίαν** ψυγήσεται ἡ ἀγάπη τῶν πολλῶν· [GNS] καὶ διὰ τὸ πληθυνθῆναι τὴν **ἀνομίαν** ψυγήσεται ἡ ἀγάπη τῶν πολλῶν. [GNT]	instead of following the course of God. (See POSB *Deeper Study #1*—Matthew 7:23 for discussion).

#2307
Lawyer
 	
Lawyer–KJV
Lawyer–NASB
Expert in the law–NIV
Lawyer–NKJV
Expert in religious
law–NLT
 	
**POSB
REFERENCE**
(Mt.22:35)
Deeper Study #1
	νομικός = *nomikos*
	Pronunciation: [nom-ik-os']
	Parsing (part of speech): pronominal adjective
	    Case—nominative
	    Gender—masculine
	    Number—singular
	    Stem or root—from **νομικός, ή, όν**
	Concordance References:
	  ⇒ Strong's #3544 nomikos
	  ⇒ NIV #3788 nomikos
	  ⇒ NASB #3544 nomikos
	
	Matthew 22:35
	Then one of them, *which was* a **lawyer**, asked *him a question,* tempting him, and saying, [KJV]
	And one of them, a **lawyer**, asked Him *a question,* testing Him, [NASB]
	One of them, an **expert in the law**, tested him with this question: [NIV]
	Then one of them, a **lawyer**, asked *Him a question,* testing Him, and saying, [NKJV]
	One of them, an **expert in religious law**, tried to trap him with this question: [NLT]
	καὶ ἐπηρώτησεν εἷς ἐξ αὐτῶν **νομικὸς** πειράζων αὐτόν, [GNS]
	καὶ ἐπηρώτησεν εἷς ἐξ αὐτῶν [**νομικὸς**] πειράζων αὐτόν, [GNT]
		An expert in the law; an expert in religious law; a lawyer; a profession of laymen who studied, taught, interpreted, and dealt with the practical questions of Jewish law.
		
		Practical Application
		They were a special group within the profession commonly called Scribes (cp. Mark 12:28). They functioned both in the court and synagogues (cp. Luke 7:30; Luke 10:25; Luke 11:45, 46, 52; Luke 14:3; Titus 3:13). They apparently dealt with the study and interpretation of the law.

#2308
Lay Aside
 	
Lay aside–KJV
Lay aside–NASB
Throw off–NIV
Lay aside–NKJV
Strip off–NLT
 	
**POSB
REFERENCE**
(Heb.12:1)
Note 2, point 1
	ἀποθέμενοι = *apothemenoi*
	Pronunciation: [ap-oth-eh'-mehn-oy]
	Parsing (part of speech): verb
	    Mood—participle
	    Tense—aorist
	    Voice—middle
	    Case—nominative
	    Gender—masculine
	    Person—1st person
	    Number—plural
	    Stem or root—from **ἀποτίθημι**
	Concordance References:
	  ⇒ Strong's #659 apotithēmi
	  ⇒ NIV #700 apotithēmi
	  ⇒ NASB #659 apotithēmi
	
	Hebrews 12:1
	Wherefore seeing we also are compassed about with so great a cloud of witnesses, let us **lay aside** every weight, and the sin which doth so easily beset us, and let us run with patience the race that is set before us, [KJV]
	Therefore, since we have so great a cloud of witnesses surrounding us, let us also **lay aside** every encumbrance, and the sin which so easily entangles us, and let us run with endurance the race that is set before us, [NASB]
	Therefore, since we are surrounded by such a great cloud of witnesses, let us **throw off** everything that hinders and the sin that so easily entangles, and let us run with perseverance the race marked out for us. [NIV]
	Therefore we also, since we are surrounded by so great a cloud of witnesses, let us **lay aside** every weight, and the sin which so easily ensnares *us,* and let us run with endurance the race that is set before us, [NKJV]
	Therefore, since we are surrounded by such a huge crowd of witnesses to the life of faith, let us **strip off** every weight that slows us down, especially the sin that so easily hinders our progress. And let us run with endurance the race that God has set before us. [NLT]
	Τοιγαροῦν καὶ ἡμεῖς τοσοῦτον ἔχοντες περικείμενον
		To throw off; to lay aside; to strip off; to get rid of; to put off; to remove as in taking off clothes.
		
		Practical Application
		We must lay aside every weight and lay aside the sin that so easily traps us. Anything that does not build us up and make us stronger is excess weight that slows us down. The Christian runner must do exactly what the Olympic runner does: strain to remove all excess weight. He must do nothing—absolutely nothing—that hinders or hampers him from running at full speed. He must strip off all unnecessary weight.

PRACTICAL WORD STUDIES
in the NEW TESTAMENT

ENGLISH WORD	GREEK WORD AND VERSE	THE WORD MEANS...
	ἡμῖν νέφος μαρτύρων, ὄγκον **ἀποθέμενοι** πάντα καὶ τὴν εὐπερίστατον ἁμαρτίαν, δι' ὑπομονῆς τρέχωμεν τὸν προκείμενον ἡμῖν ἀγῶνα, [GNS] Τοιγαροῦν καὶ ἡμεῖς τοσοῦτον ἔχοντες περικείμενον ἡμῖν νέφος μαρτύρων, ὄγκον **ἀποθέμενοι** πάντα καὶ τὴν εὐπερίστατον ἁμαρτίαν, δι' ὑπομονῆς τρέχωμεν τὸν προκείμενον ἡμῖν ἀγῶνα [GNT]	

#2309
Lay Down
 	
Slumbered–KJV
Drowsy–NASB
Drowsy–NIV
Slumbered–NKJV
Lay Down–NLT
 	
POSB REFERENCE
(Mt.25:5)
Deeper Study #3
	ἐνύσταξαν = *enustaxan*
	Pronunciation: [eh-noos-tadz'-an]
	Parsing (part of speech): verb
	    Mood—indicative
	    Tense—aorist
	    Voice—active
	    Person—3rd person
	    Number—plural
	    Stem or root—from νυστάζω
	Concordance References:
	  ⇒ Strong's #3573 nustazō
	  ⇒ NIV #3818 nustazō
	  ⇒ NASB #3573 nustazō
	
	Matthew 25:5
	While the bridegroom tarried, they all **slumbered** and slept. [KJV]
	"Now while the bridegroom was delaying, they all got **drowsy** and *began* to sleep. [NASB]
	The bridegroom was a long time in coming, and they all became **drowsy** and fell asleep. [NIV]
	But while the bridegroom was delayed, they all **slumbered** and slept. [NKJV]
	When the bridegroom was delayed, they all **lay down** and slept. [NLT]
	χρονίζοντος δὲ τοῦ νυμφίου **ἐνύσταξαν** πᾶσαι καὶ ἐκάθευδον. [GNS]
	χρονίζοντος δὲ τοῦ νυμφίου **ἐνύσταξαν** πᾶσαι καὶ ἐκάθευδον. [GNT]
		To grow drowsy; to slumber; to lay down to sleep; to nod; to nap; to drift off to sleep.
		
		Practical Application
		Note that the bridesmaids allowed themselves to lie down, then lying down led to sleep. We must guard against lying down, against cooling off. Lying down will lead to a cooling of fervor. A little loss of fervor may not seem too serious; but the first step, as small as it may seem, leads to heavy eyelids.

#2310
Laying Aside
 	
Laying aside–KJV
Putting aside–NASB
Rid...of–NIV
Laying aside–NKJV
Get rid of–NLT
 	
POSB REFERENCE
(1 Pt.2:1)
Note 1
	Ἀποθέμενοι = *Apothemenoi*
	Pronunciation: [ap-oth-eh'-mehn-oy]
	Parsing (part of speech): verb
	    Mood—participle (imperative sense)
	    Tense—aorist
	    Voice—middle
	    Case—nominative
	    Gender—masculine
	    Person—2nd person
	    Number—plural
	    Stem or root—from ἀποτίθημι
	Concordance References:
	  ⇒ Strong's #659 apotithēmi
	  ⇒ NIV #700 apotithēmi
	  ⇒ NASB #659 apotithēmi
	
	1 Peter 2:1
	Wherefore **laying aside** all malice, and all guile, and hypocrisies, and envies, and all evil speakings, [KJV]
	Therefore, **putting aside** all malice and all guile and hypocrisy and envy and all slander, [NASB]
	Therefore, **rid** yourselves **of** all malice and all deceit, hypocrisy, envy, and slander of every kind. [NIV]
	Therefore, **laying aside** all malice, all deceit, hypocrisy, envy, and all evil speaking, [NKJV]
	So **get rid of** all malicious behavior and deceit. Don't just pretend to be good! Be done with hypocrisy and jealousy and backstabbing. [NLT]
	Ἀποθέμενοι οὖν πᾶσαν κακίαν καὶ πάντα δόλον καὶ ὑποκρίσεις καὶ φθόνους καὶ πάσας καταλαλιάς, [GNS]
	Ἀποθέμενοι οὖν πᾶσαν κακίαν καὶ πάντα δόλον καὶ ὑποκρίσεις καὶ φθόνους καὶ πάσας καταλαλιάς, [GNT]
		To get rid of; to lay aside; to put aside.
		
		Practical Application
		The Greek word for "laying aside" (*apothemenoi*) means to put off one's clothing; to cleanse oneself of those things that defile. Both meanings are applicable in this verse (A.T. Robertson. *Word Pictures in the New Testament*, Vol.6, p.94). There are some things that defile the believer. He is to take these things and strip them off just as he would strip off his clothes; he is to cleanse himself from all that defiles him. Five things in particular are mentioned, and note: all five have to do with what has just been said in the former passage. We are to love one another fervently with a pure heart. The very things that we are to strip off are the things that dirty and soil our love. They have to do with how we treat one another, with our behavior toward our Christian brothers and sisters.

1225

ENGLISH WORD	GREEK WORD AND VERSE	THE WORD MEANS...

#2311
Lazy
 	
Slothful–KJV
Lagging behind–
NASB
Lacking–NIV
Lagging–NKJV
Lazy–NLT
 	
POSB
REFERENCE
(Romans 12:11)
Note 2, point 1
	ὀκνηροί = oknëroi
	Pronunciation: [ok-nay-roy']
	Parsing (part of speech): adjective
	    Case—nominative
	    Gender—masculine
	    Number—plural
	    Stem or root—from ὀκνηρός, ά, όν
	Concordance References:
	  ⇒ Strong's #3636 oknëros
	  ⇒ NIV #3891 oknëros
	  ⇒ NASB #3636 oknëros
	
	Romans 12:11
	Not **slothful** in business; fervent in spirit; serving the Lord; [KJV]
	Not **lagging behind** in diligence, fervent in spirit, serving the Lord; [NASB]
	Never be **lacking** in zeal, but keep your spiritual fervor, serving the Lord. [NIV]
	Not **lagging** in diligence, fervent in spirit, serving the Lord; [NKJV]
	Never be **lazy** in your work, but serve the Lord enthusiastically. [NLT]
	τῇ σπουδῇ μὴ ὀκνηροί· τῷ πνεύματι ζέοντες· τῷ Κυρίῳ δουλεύοντες· [GNS]
	τῇ σπουδῇ μὴ ὀκνηροί, τῷ πνεύματι ζέοντες, τῷ κυρίῳ δουλεύοντες, [GNT]
		To be lazy, slow moving, sluggish, lethargic, complacent, hesitating, delaying, lagging behind.
		
		Practical Application
		The believer is to serve the Lord. The charge is twofold. Do not be lazy in your work; do not be slothful in business; do not be lagging in zeal. The word "lazy" (*oknëroi*) means to be lazy, slow moving, sluggish, lethargic, complacent, hesitating, delaying. The word "work" (*spoude*) means business, diligence, zeal, earnestness. The exhortation is clear: the believer must...
		• not be lazy or slow moving in zeal.
		• not be sluggish or lethargic in diligence.
		• not be hesitating or delaying in earnestness.
		• not be lagging behind.
		
		The believer just cannot approach life in a lackadaisical, easy-going, slow-moving fashion. The world is reeling in pain, with millions starving and suffering due to man's selfishness and sin, hoarding, disease, war, death—and the list could go on and on. The believer must not give in to sluggishness and complacency. He must serve the Lord with all diligence and zeal and earnestness. He must be enthusiastic in his service.

#2312
Lead Astray
 	
Seduce–KJV
Deceive–NASB
Lead astray–NIV
Deceive–NKJV
Lead astray–NLT
 	
POSB
REFERENCE
(1 Jn.2:26)
Note 3
	πλανώντων = planöntön
	Pronunciation: [plan-on'-ton']
	Parsing (part of speech): verb
	    Mood—participle
	    Tense—present
	    Voice—active
	    Case—genitive
	    Gender—masculine
	    Number—plural
	    Stem or root—from πλανάω
	Concordance References:
	  ⇒ Strong's #4105 planaö
	  ⇒ NIV #4414 planaö
	  ⇒ NASB #4105 planaö
	
	1 John 2:26
	These *things* have I written unto you concerning them that **seduce** you. [KJV]
	These things I have written to you concerning those who are trying to **deceive** you. [NASB]
	I am writing these things to you about those who are trying to **lead** you **astray**. [NIV]
	These things I have written to you concerning those who *try to* **deceive** you. [NKJV]
	I have written these things to you because you need to be aware of those who want to **lead** you **astray**. [NLT]
	ταῦτα ἔγραψα ὑμῖν περὶ τῶν πλανώντων ὑμᾶς. [GNS]
	Ταῦτα ἔγραψα ὑμῖν περὶ τῶν πλανώντων ὑμᾶς. [GNT]
		To lead astray; to seduce; to deceive; to be mistaken.
		
		Practical Application
		A false teacher is one who attempts to lead us away from Jesus Christ, from the glorious truth that He is the Son of God who came to earth to die for our sins. The false teacher deceives people; that is, he teaches that man can become acceptable to God by some other way than Jesus Christ. He teaches that there are other ways to God, other approaches, other religions, other truths. He seduces and leads people astray; he deceives people into following some other teaching. Note this: the tense is continuous action in the Greek. That is, false teachers are continually teaching false doctrine. They are always teaching a false doctrine and always trying to seduce people.
		Believers must be on constant guard against false teaching. So much is at stake: the very promise of God. We will abandon the faith if we listen to the deception and go astray. We must continue to follow Christ; we must let the gospel abide and take up a permanent residence in our lives.

#2313
Leadership–
Leadership
Ability
 	
Ruleth–KJV
Leads–NASB
Leadership–NIV
Leads–NKJV
	προϊστάμενος = proistamenos
	Pronunciation: [proy-stah-mehn-os]
	Parsing (part of speech): verb
	    Mood—participle
	    Tense—present
	    Voice—middle
	    Case—nominative
	    Gender—masculine
	    Number—singular
	    Stem or root—from προϊστημι
		Be a leader; have authority over; manage; care for; give help; engage in.
		
		Practical Application
		There is the gift of leadership (*proistamenos*). This means the ability of ruling, leadership, authority, administration, government. Note that this person is to lead with diligence (*spoude*), that is, with haste, zeal, desire, and concentrated attention.

ENGLISH WORD	GREEK WORD AND VERSE	THE WORD MEANS...
Leadership ability–NLT **POSB REFERENCE** (Rom.12:6-8, esp. v.8) Note 2, point 6	Concordance References: ⇒ Strong's #4291 proistēmi ⇒ NIV #4613 proistēmi ⇒ NASB #4291 proistēmi **Romans 12:8** Or he that exhorteth, on exhortation: he that giveth, *let him do it* with simplicity; he that **ruleth**, with diligence; he that sheweth mercy, with cheerfulness. [KJV] Or he who exhorts, in his exhortation; he who gives, with liberality; he who **leads**, with diligence; he who shows mercy, with cheerfulness. [NASB] If it is encouraging, let him encourage; if it is contributing to the needs of others, let him give generously; if it is **leadership**, let him govern diligently; if it is showing mercy, let him do it cheerfully. [NIV] He who exhorts, in exhortation; he who gives, with liberality; he who **leads**, with diligence; he who shows mercy, with cheerfulness. [NKJV] If your gift is to encourage others, do it! If you have money, share it generously. If God has given you **leadership ability**, take the responsibility seriously. And if you have a gift for showing kindness to others, do it gladly. [NLT] εἴτε ὁ παρακαλῶν, ἐν τῇ παρακλήσει· ὁ μεταδιδοὺς ἐν ἁπλότητι, ὁ **προϊστάμενος**, ἐν σπουδῇ· ὁ ἐλεῶν ἐν ἱλαρότητι. [GNS] εἴτε ὁ παρακαλῶν ἐν τῇ παρακλήσει· ὁ μεταδιδοὺς ἐν ἁπλότητι, ὁ **προϊστάμενος** ἐν σπουδῇ, ὁ ἐλεῶν ἐν ἱλαρότητι. [GNT]	

#2314
Leads
 	
Ruleth–KJV
Leads–NASB
Leadership–NIV
Leads–NKJV
Leadership ability–NLT
 	
POSB REFERENCE
(Rom.12:6-8, esp. v.8)
Note 2, point 6
	προϊστάμενος = *proistamenos*
	Pronunciation: [proy-stah-mehn-os]
	Parsing (part of speech): verb
	  Mood—participle
	  Tense—present
	  Voice—middle
	  Case—nominative
	  Gender—masculine
	  Number—singular
	  Stem or root—from προϊστημι
	Concordance References:
	⇒ Strong's #4291 proistēmi
	⇒ NIV #4613 proistēmi
	⇒ NASB #4291 proistēmi
	
	Romans 12:8
	Or he that exhorteth, on exhortation: he that giveth, *let him do it* with simplicity; he that **ruleth**, with diligence; he that sheweth mercy, with cheerfulness. [KJV]
	Or he who exhorts, in his exhortation; he who gives, with liberality; he who **leads**, with diligence; he who shows mercy, with cheerfulness. [NASB]
	If it is encouraging, let him encourage; if it is contributing to the needs of others, let him give generously; if it is **leadership**, let him govern diligently; if it is showing mercy, let him do it cheerfully. [NIV]
	He who exhorts, in exhortation; he who gives, with liberality; he who **leads**, with diligence; he who shows mercy, with cheerfulness. [NKJV]
	If your gift is to encourage others, do it! If you have money, share it generously. If God has given you **leadership ability**, take the responsibility seriously. And if you have a gift for showing kindness to others, do it gladly. [NLT]
	εἴτε ὁ παρακαλῶν, ἐν τῇ παρακλήσει· ὁ μεταδιδοὺς ἐν ἁπλότητι, ὁ **προϊστάμενος**, ἐν σπουδῇ· ὁ ἐλεῶν ἐν ἱλαρότητι. [GNS]
	εἴτε ὁ παρακαλῶν ἐν τῇ παρακλήσει· ὁ μεταδιδοὺς ἐν ἁπλότητι, ὁ **προϊστάμενος** ἐν σπουδῇ, ὁ ἐλεῶν ἐν ἱλαρότητι. [GNT]
		Be a leader; have authority over; manage; care for; give help; engage in.
		
		Practical Application
		There is the gift of leading (*proistamenos*). This means the ability of ruling, leadership, authority, administration, government. Note that this person is to lead with diligence (*spoude*), that is leadership with haste, zeal, desire, and concentrated attention.

ENGLISH WORD	GREEK WORD AND VERSE	THE WORD MEANS...
#2315 **Learned Man** Eloquent man–KJV Eloquent man–NASB **Learned man–NIV** Eloquent man–NKJV Eloquent speaker–NLT **POSB REFERENCE** (Acts 18:24) Note 2	ἀνὴρ λόγιος = *anër logios* Pronunciation: [an'-ayr log'-ee-os] Parsing *anër* (part of speech): noun 　　Case—nominative 　　Gender—masculine 　　Number—singular 　　Stem or root—from ἀνήρ, ἀνδρός Parsing *logios* (part of speech): adjective 　　Case—nominative 　　Gender—masculine 　　Number—singular 　　Stem or root—from λόγιος, α, ον Concordance References: ⇒　Strong's #435 anër + 3052 logios ⇒　NIV #467 anër [man] + 3360 logios [learned] ⇒　NASB #435 anër + 3052 logios **Acts 18:24** And a certain Jew named Apollos, born at Alexandria, an **eloquent man**, *and* mighty in the scriptures, came to Ephesus. [KJV] 　Now a certain Jew named Apollos, an Alexandrian by birth, an **eloquent man**, came to Ephesus; and he was mighty in the Scriptures. [NASB] 　Meanwhile a Jew named Apollos, a native of Alexandria, came to Ephesus. He was a **learned man**, with a thorough knowledge of the Scriptures. [NIV] 　Now a certain Jew named Apollos, born at Alexandria, an **eloquent man** *and* mighty in the Scriptures, came to Ephesus. [NKJV] 　Meanwhile, a Jew named Apollos, an **eloquent speaker** who knew the Scriptures well, had just arrived in Ephesus from Alexandria in Egypt. [NLT] 　Ἰουδαῖος δέ τις Ἀπολλῶς ὀνόματι, Ἀλεξανδρεὺς τῷ γένει, **ἀνὴρ λόγιος**, κατήντησεν εἰς Ἔφεσον, δυνατὸς ὢν ἐν ταῖς γραφαῖς· [GNS] 　Ἰουδαῖος δέ τις Ἀπολλῶς ὀνόματι, Ἀλεξανδρεὺς τῷ γένει, **ἀνὴρ λόγιος**, κατήντησεν εἰς Ἔφεσον, δυνατὸς ὢν ἐν ταῖς γραφαῖς. [GNT]	Learned man; eloquent man or speaker. **Practical Application** 　The term "learned man" or "eloquent man" can mean either learned or eloquent. In this case it probably means both. But note the point: it was the Scriptures that Apollos... • learned so well. • spoke forth so eloquently or forcefully.
#2316 **Learning** **Learning–KJV** Instruction–NASB Teach–NIV **Learning–NKJV** Teach–NLT **POSB REFERENCE** (Rom.15:4) Note 2, point 1	διδασκαλίαν = *didaskalian* Pronunciation: [did-ahs-kal-ee'-ahn] Parsing (part of speech): noun 　　Case—accusative 　　Gender—feminine 　　Number—singular 　　Stem or root—from διδασκαλία, ας Concordance References: ⇒　Strong's #1319 didaskalia ⇒　NIV #1436 didaskalia ⇒　NASB #1319 didaskalia **Romans 15:4** For whatsoever things were written aforetime were written for our **learning**, that we through patience and comfort of the scriptures might have hope. [KJV] 　For whatever was written in earlier times was written for our **instruction**, that through perseverance and the encouragement of the Scriptures we might have hope. [NASB] 　For everything that was written in the past was written to **teach** us, so that through endurance and the encouragement of the Scriptures we might have hope. [NIV] 　For whatever things were written before were written for our **learning**, that we through the patience and comfort of the Scriptures might have hope. [NKJV] 　Such things were written in the Scriptures long ago to **teach** us. They give us hope and encouragement as we wait patiently for God's promises. [NLT] 　ὅσα γὰρ προεγράφη, εἰς τὴν ἡμετέραν **διδασκαλίαν** προεγράφη, ἵνα διὰ τῆς ὑπομονῆς καὶ τῆς παρακλήσεως τῶν γραφῶν τὴν ἐλπίδα ἔχωμεν. [GNS]	What is taught; teaching; doctrine; act of teaching; instruction. **Practical Application** 　In a strong church, everyone studies the Scripture. This is a great verse on the purpose of the Holy Scriptures. In very simple terms, it tells us why God gave us the Bible. 　The Scriptures were written for our... • learning (*didaskalian*), • instruction, • direction, • guidance.

ENGLISH WORD	GREEK WORD AND VERSE	THE WORD MEANS...
	ὅσα γὰρ προεγράφη, εἰς τὴν ἡμετέραν **διδασκαλίαν** ἐγράφη, ἵνα διὰ τῆς ὑπομονῆς καὶ διὰ τῆς παρακλήσεως τῶν γραφῶν τὴν ἐλπίδα ἔχωμεν. [GNT]	

#2317
Leave
 	
Leave–KJV
Abandon–NASB
Abandon–NIV
Leave–NKJV
Leave–NLT
 	
POSB REFERENCE
(Acts 2:25-28; esp. v.27)
Note 1, point 2a
 	
See also POSB REF:
(Acts 2:27)
Deeper Study #1, point 1
	ἐγκαταλείψεις = egkataleipseis
	Pronunciation: [eng-kat-al-i'-pseh-ees]
	Parsing (part of speech): verb
	    Mood—indicative
	    Tense—future
	    Voice—active
	    Person—2nd person
	    Number—singular
	    Stem or root—from ἐγκαταλείπω
	Concordance References:
	⇒ Strong's #1459 egkataleipō
	⇒ NIV #1593 egkataleipō
	⇒ NASB #1459 egkataleipō
	
	Acts 2:27
	Because thou wilt not **leave** my soul in hell, neither wilt thou suffer thine Holy One to see corruption. [KJV]
	BECAUSE THOU WILT NOT **ABANDON** MY SOUL TO HADES, NOR ALLOW THY HOLY ONE TO UNDERGO DECAY. [NASB]
	Because you will not **abandon** me to the grave, nor will you let your Holy One see decay. [NIV]
	*For You will not **leave** my soul in Hades, Nor will You allow Your Holy One to see corruption. [NKJV]*
	For you will not **leave** my soul among the dead or allow your Holy One to rot in the grave. [NLT]
	ὅτι οὐκ **ἐγκαταλείψεις** τὴν ψυχήν μου εἰς ἅδου, οὐδὲ δώσεις τὸν ὅσιόν σου ἰδεῖν διαφθοράν. [GNS]
	ὅτι οὐκ **ἐγκαταλείψεις** τὴν ψυχήν μου εἰς ἅδην οὐδὲ δώσεις τὸν ὅσιόν σου ἰδεῖν διαφθοράν. [GNT]
		To leave behind; to neglect; to desert; to give up; to utterly forsake and abandon. It is a strong word indicating a permanent state.
		
		Practical Application
		A soul can be utterly forsaken and abandoned, doomed permanently in hell. But Christ was absolutely sure that His soul would not be left and abandoned in hell.

#2318
Led
 	
Led–KJV
Led–NASB
Led–NIV
Led–NKJV
Led–NLT
 	
POSB REFERENCE
(Rom.8:14)
Note 7
	ἄγονται = agontai
	Pronunciation: [ag'-on-tah-ee]
	Parsing (part of speech): verb
	    Mood—indicative
	    Tense—present
	    Voice—passive
	    Person—3rd person
	    Number—plural
	    Stem or root—from ἄγω
	Concordance References:
	⇒ Strong's #33 agō
	⇒ NIV #72 agō
	⇒ NASB #33 agō
	
	Romans 8:14
	For as many as are **led** by the Spirit of God, they are the sons of God. [KJV]
	For all who are being **led** by the Spirit of God, these are sons of God. [NASB]
	Because those who are **led** by the Spirit of God are sons of God. [NIV]
	For as many as are **led** by the Spirit of God, these are sons of God. [NKJV]
	For all who are **led** by the Spirit of God are children of God. [NLT]
	ὅσοι γὰρ Πνεύματι Θεοῦ **ἄγονται**, οὗτοι εἰσιν υἱοὶ Θεοῦ. [GNS]
	ὅσοι γὰρ πνεύματι θεοῦ **ἄγονται**, οὗτοι υἱοὶ θεοῦ εἰσιν. [GNT]
		To lead; to bring; to go.
		
		Practical Application
		The Spirit leads the believer. There are several ideas in the Greek word "lead" or "led" (*agontai*). There is the idea of carrying and bearing along. The Spirit leads the believer and carries him through the trials of this life. He bears the believer up, carrying him over the corruptions of this world.
		There is the idea of leading and guiding along. The Spirit leads and guides the believer along the way of righteousness and truth. He guides the believer by moving in advance and going ahead of him. He blazes the path, making sure the believer knows where to walk (cp. John 16:13; cp. Galatians 5:18; 2 Peter 1:21).
		There is the idea of directing on a course and of bringing along to an end. The Spirit directs the believer where to go and how to get there, and He actually brings the believer to his destined end. The Spirit actually becomes involved in the life of the believer, directing him to live righteously and conforming him to the image of Christ. He actually brings the believer to his destined end, that is, to heaven, to live eternally in the presence of God Himself.
		This is one of the great powers of the Holy Spirit, the power to lead the believer and to become involved in his life.

#2319
Left
 	
Went forth–KJV
Went forth–NASB
	ἐξῆλθεν = exēlthen
	Pronunciation: [ex-ayl'-thehn]
	Parsing (part of speech): verb
	    Mood—indicative
	    Tense—aorist
	    Voice—active
		To leave; to go forth; to cross over; to go; to set out.
		
		Practical Application
		The idea being conveyed is purpose. Jesus

ENGLISH WORD	GREEK WORD AND VERSE	THE WORD MEANS...
Left–NIV Went out–NKJV Crossed–NLT **POSB REFERENCE** (Jn.18:1-3; esp. v.1) Note 1	Person—3rd person Number—singular Stem or root—from ἐξέρχομαι Concordance References: ⇒ Strong's #1831 exerchomai ⇒ NIV #2002 exerchomai ⇒ NASB #1831 exerchomai **John 18:1** When Jesus had spoken these words, he **went forth** with his disciples over the brook Cedron, where was a garden, into the which he entered, and his disciples. [KJV] When Jesus had spoken these words, He **went forth** with His disciples over the ravine of the Kidron, where there was a garden, into which He Himself entered, and His disciples. [NASB] When he had finished praying, Jesus **left** with his disciples and crossed the Kidron Valley. On the other side there was an olive grove, and he and his disciples went into it. [NIV] When Jesus had spoken these words, He **went out** with His disciples over the Brook Kidron, where there was a garden, which He and His disciples entered. [NKJV] After saying these things, Jesus **crossed** the Kidron Valley with his disciples and entered a grove of olive trees. [NLT] Ταῦτα εἰπὼν ὁ Ἰησοῦς **ἐξῆλθε** σὺν τοῖς μαθηταῖς αὐτοῦ πέραν τοῦ χειμάρρου τοῦ Κεδρὼν, ὅπου ἦν κῆπος, εἰς ὃν εἰσῆλθεν αὐτὸς καὶ οἱ μαθηταὶ αὐτοῦ. [GNS] Ταῦτα εἰπὼν Ἰησοῦς **ἐξῆλθεν** σὺν τοῖς μαθηταῖς αὐτοῦ πέραν τοῦ χειμάρρου τοῦ Κεδρὼν ὅπου ἦν κῆπος, εἰς ὃν εἰσῆλθεν αὐτὸς καὶ οἱ μαθηταὶ αὐτοῦ. [GNT]	was going forth deliberately, for a specific purpose, knowing exactly what He was doing. Jesus "left" to prepare Himself spiritually. He was facing *the hour* to which God had called Him, the hour of His death. (See POSB note, Hour—John 2:3-5; POSB *Deeper Study #1*—John 12:23-24). He knew that God's will was for Him to die for the sins of the world. He knew the awful separation from God that sin causes; therefore, He knew that He was to be cut off from God's presence, that God would have to forsake and turn His back upon Him because of sin. He was feeling the awful pressure of God's coming judgment upon sin which was to be exercised upon Him. In the flesh, He wanted to flee; He wanted another way to be chosen to save man (Matthew 26:39, 42, 44). Yet He... • was *committed* to God. • was totally *devoted* to His Father. • *must* do God's will. But to do God's will, He had to have God's help. He had to pray and seek God's face. In some special way He desperately needed God to meet His need. It was for this reason that He headed for the garden. He was seeking to be alone with His Father, to have His Father strengthen Him for the terrible ordeal and judgment of the cross.
#2320 **Left All Alone** Desolate–KJV Left alone–NASB **Left all alone–NIV** Left alone–NKJV Truly alone–NLT **POSB REFERENCE** (1 Tim.5:4-8; esp. v.5) Note 2, point 2	μεμονωμένη = memonömenë Pronunciation: [meh-mon-o'-meh-nay] Parsing (part of speech): verb Mood—participle Tense—perfect Voice—passive Case—nominative Gender—feminine Number—singular Stem or root—from μονόομαι Concordance References: ⇒ Strong's #3443 monoö ⇒ NIV #3670 monoö ⇒ NASB #3443 monoö **1 Tim. 5:5** Now she that is a widow indeed, and **desolate**, trusteth in God, and continueth in supplications and prayers night and day. [KJV] Now she who is a widow indeed, and who has been **left alone** has fixed her hope on God, and continues in entreaties and prayers night and day. [NASB] The widow who is really in need and **left all alone** puts her hope in God and continues night and day to pray and to ask God for help. [NIV] Now she who is really a widow, and **left alone**, trusts in God and continues in supplications and prayers night and day. [NKJV] But a woman who is a true widow, one who is **truly alone** in this world, has placed her hope in God. Night and day she asks God for help and spends much time in prayer. [NLT] ἡ δὲ ὄντως χήρα καὶ **μεμονωμένη** ἤλπικεν ἐπὶ Θεὸν, καὶ προσμένει ταῖς δεήσεσι καὶ ταῖς προσευχαῖς νυκτὸς καὶ ἡμέρας. [GNS] ἡ δὲ ὄντως χήρα καὶ **μεμονωμένη** ἤλπικεν ἐπὶ θεὸν καὶ προσμένει ταῖς δεήσεσιν καὶ ταῖς προσευχαῖς νυκτὸς καὶ ἡμέρας, [GNT]	To be left all alone; to be desolate; to be truly alone. **Practical Application** Widowed parents who are true Christians are to live above reproach. Who are "widows who are really in need," the persons who are to be cared for by the church? The person who is "left all alone" (*memonömenë*): left completely alone without husband, children, or close kin.

ENGLISH WORD	GREEK WORD AND VERSE	THE WORD MEANS...
#2321 **Left Alone** Desolate–KJV **Left alone–NASB** Left all alone–NIV **Left alone–NKJV** Truly alone–NLT **POSB** **REFERENCE** (1 Tim.5:4-8; esp. v.5) Note 2, point 2	μεμονωμένη = *memonōmenē* Pronunciation: [meh-mon-o'-meh-nay] Parsing (part of speech): verb 　Mood—participle 　Tense—perfect 　Voice—passive 　Case—nominative 　Gender—feminine 　Number—singular 　Stem or root—from μονόομαι Concordance References: ⇒　Strong's #3443 monoö ⇒　NIV #3670 monoö ⇒　NASB #3443 monoö **1 Tim. 5:5** Now she that is a widow indeed, and **desolate**, trusteth in God, and continueth in supplications and prayers night and day. [KJV] Now she who is a widow indeed, and who has been **left alone** has fixed her hope on God, and continues in entreaties and prayers night and day. [NASB] The widow who is really in need and **left all alone** puts her hope in God and continues night and day to pray and to ask God for help. [NIV] Now she who is really a widow, and **left alone**, trusts in God and continues in supplications and prayers night and day. [NKJV] But a woman who is a true widow, one who is **truly alone** in this world, has placed her hope in God. Night and day she asks God for help and spends much time in prayer. [NLT] ἡ δὲ ὄντως χήρα καὶ **μεμονωμένη** ἤλπικεν ἐπὶ Θεὸν, καὶ προσμένει ταῖς δεήσεσι καὶ ταῖς προσευχαῖς νυκτὸς καὶ ἡμέρας. [GNS] ἡ δὲ ὄντως χήρα καὶ **μεμονωμένη** ἤλπικεν ἐπὶ θεὸν καὶ προσμένει ταῖς δεήσεσιν καὶ ταῖς προσευχαῖς νυκτὸς καὶ ἡμέρας, [GNT]	To be left all alone; to be desolate; to be truly alone. ### Practical Application Widowed parents who are true Christians are to live above reproach. Who are "widows indeed," the persons who are to be cared for by the church? The person who is "left alone" (*memonōmenē*): left completely alone without husband, children, or close kin.
#2322 **Left His Case** Committed–KJV Entrusting–NASB Entrusted–NIV Committed–NKJV **Left his case–NLT** **POSB** **REFERENCE** (1 Pt.2:21-24; esp. v.23) Note 2, point 3c	παρεδίδου = *paredidou* Pronunciation: [par-ed-id'-oo] Parsing (part of speech): verb 　Mood—indicative 　Tense—imperfect 　Voice—active 　Person—3rd person 　Number—singular 　Stem or root—from παραδίδωμι Concordance References: ⇒　Strong's #3860 paradidömi ⇒　NIV #4140 paradidömi ⇒　NASB #3860 paradidömi **1 Peter 2:23** Who, when he was reviled, reviled not again; when he suffered, he threatened not; but **committed** *himself* to him that judgeth righteously: [KJV] And while being reviled, He did not revile in return; while suffering, He uttered no threats, but kept **entrusting** *Himself* to Him who judges righteously; [NASB] When they hurled their insults at him, he did not retaliate; when he suffered, he made no threats. Instead, he **entrusted** himself to him who judges justly. [NIV] Who, when He was reviled, did not revile in return; when He suffered, He did not threaten, but **committed** *Himself* to Him who judges righteously; [NKJV] He did not retaliate when he was insulted. When he suffered, he did not threaten to get even. He **left his case** in the hands of God, who always judges fairly. [NLT] ὃς λοιδορούμενος οὐκ ἀντελοιδόρει, πάσχων οὐκ ἠπείλει, **παρεδίδου** δὲ τῷ κρίνοντι δικαίως· [GNS] ὃς λοιδορούμενος οὐκ ἀντελοιδόρει, πάσχων οὐκ ἠπείλει, **παρεδίδου** δὲ τῷ κρίνοντι δικαίως· [GNT]	Entrusted, committed, handed over; to deliver into the hands of. ### Practical Application Jesus Christ handed over His life to God; He delivered His life into the hands and keeping of God. Again, He did not have to suffer death, for He had the power to stop it all. But He had come to save men; therefore, he willingly suffered, committing His death and cause into the hands of God. He knew that God would raise Him up to prove His claim to be the Son of God, the Savior of the world.

ENGLISH WORD	GREEK WORD AND VERSE	THE WORD MEANS...
#2323 **Leper** **Leper–KJV** **Leper–NASB** Man with leprosy– NIV **Leper–NKJV** Man with leprosy– NLT **POSB** **REFERENCE** (Mk.1:40) Note 1	*λεπρός = lepros* Pronunciation: [lep-ros'] Parsing (part of speech): pronominal adjective 　　Case—nominative 　　Gender—masculine 　　Number—singular 　　Stem or root—from λεπρός, οῦ Concordance References: ⇒　Strong's #3015 lepros ⇒　NIV #3320 lepros ⇒　NASB #3015 lepros **Mark 1:40** And there came a **leper** to him, beseeching him, and kneeling down to him, and saying unto him, If thou wilt, thou canst make me clean. [KJV] And a **leper** came to Him, beseeching Him and falling on his knees before Him, and saying to Him, "If You are willing, You can make me clean." [NASB] A **man with leprosy** came to him and begged him on his knees, "If you are willing, you can make me clean." [NIV] Now a **leper** came to Him, imploring Him, kneeling down to Him and saying to Him, "If You are willing, You can make me clean." [NKJV] A **man with leprosy** came and knelt in front of Jesus, begging to be healed. "If you want to, you can make me well again," he said. [NLT] Καὶ ἔρχεται πρὸς αὐτὸν **λεπρὸς** παρακαλῶν αὐτόν, καὶ γονυπετῶν αὐτόν, καὶ λέγων αὐτῷ, ὅτι Ἐὰν θέλῃς, δύνασαί με καθαρίσαι. [GNS] Καὶ ἔρχεται πρὸς αὐτὸν **λεπρὸς** παρακαλῶν αὐτόν [καὶ γονυπετῶν] καὶ λέγων αὐτῷ ὅτι Ἐὰν θέλῃς δύνασαί με καθαρίσαι. [GNT]	A person with the skin disease of leprosy. **Practical Application** It is a gross destruction of the skin that had no natural cure or treatment during Bible times. Symtoms are... • a loss of feeling in a patch of skin • damage to the nervous system • potential paralysis • loss of extremities Leprosy was the most feared disease of the ancient world. The man with leprosy was considered the most unclean, revolting, and hideous person imaginable. Leprosy itself was thought to be the result of terrible sin and actually became the most dramatic type of sin in the minds of people. There was no known cure for leprosy; only God was considered powerful enough to cure the disease. Therefore, in cleansing the leper, Jesus was demonstrating His Messiahship. He was demonstrating that He had the power to cleanse the most unclean, no matter how terrible their uncleanness. 1.　The man with leprosy was considered utterly unclean—physically and spiritually. He could not approach within six feet of any person, including family members. "The person with such an infectious disease must wear torn clothes, let his hair be unkempt, cover the lower part of his face and cry out, 'Unclean! Unclean!'" (Leviticus 13:45). 2.　He was judged as dead—the living dead. He had to wear a black garment so he could be recognized as from among the dead. 3.　He was banished as an outcast, totally ostracized from society—considered without hope of going to heaven. "As long as he has the infection he remains unclean. He must live alone; he must live outside the camp." (Lev.13:46). He could not live within the walls of any city; his dwelling had to be outside the city gates. 4.　He was thought to be polluted, incurable by any human means whatsoever. Leprosy could be cured by God and His power alone. (Note how Christ proves His Messiahship and deity by healing the man with leprosy.) 　　Imagine the anguish and heartbreak of the leper being completely cut off from family and friends and society. Imagine the emotional and mental pain. There are other recorded instances of men with leprosy being healed (cp. Matthew 10:8; Matthew 11:5; Mark 1:40; Luke 7:22; Luke 17:12; and perhaps Matthew 26:6; cp. Mark 14:3).
#2324 **Leprosy, Man** **With** Leper–KJV Leper–NASB **Man with leprosy–** **NIV** Leper–NKJV **Man with leprosy–** **NLT**	*λεπρός = lepros* Pronunciation: [lep-ros'] Parsing (part of speech): pronominal adjective 　　Case—nominative 　　Gender—masculine 　　Number—singular 　　Stem or root—from λεπρός, οῦ Concordance References: ⇒　Strong's #3015 lepros ⇒　NIV #3320 lepros ⇒　NASB #3015 lepros	A person with the skin disease of leprosy. **Practical Application** It is a gross destruction of the skin that had no natural cure or treatment during Bible times. Symtoms are... • a loss of feeling in a patch of skin • damage to the nervous system • potential paralysis • loss of extremities Leprosy was the most feared disease of the

ENGLISH WORD	GREEK WORD AND VERSE	THE WORD MEANS...
POSB REFERENCE (Mk.1:40) Note 1	**Mark 1:40** And there came a **leper** to him, beseeching him, and kneeling down to him, and saying unto him, If thou wilt, thou canst make me clean. [KJV] And a **leper** came to Him, beseeching Him and falling on his knees before Him, and saying to Him, "If You are willing, You can make me clean." [NASB] A **man with leprosy** came to him and begged him on his knees, "If you are willing, you can make me clean." [NIV] Now a **leper** came to Him, imploring Him, kneeling down to Him and saying to Him, "If You are willing, You can make me clean." [NKJV] A **man with leprosy** came and knelt in front of Jesus, begging to be healed. "If you want to, you can make me well again," he said. [NLT] Καὶ ἔρχεται πρὸς αὐτὸν **λεπρὸς** παρακαλῶν αὐτὸν, καὶ γονυπετῶν αὐτὸν, καὶ λέγων αὐτῷ, ὅτι Ἐὰν θέλῃς, δύνασαί με καθαρίσαι. [GNS] Καὶ ἔρχεται πρὸς αὐτὸν **λεπρὸς** παρακαλῶν αὐτὸν [καὶ γονυπετῶν] καὶ λέγων αὐτῷ ὅτι Ἐὰν θέλῃς δύνασαί με καθαρίσαι. [GNT]	ancient world. The man with leprosy was considered the most unclean, revolting, and hideous person imaginable. Leprosy itself was thought to be the result of terrible sin and actually became the most dramatic type of sin in the minds of people. There was no known cure for leprosy; only God was considered powerful enough to cure the disease. Therefore, in cleansing the leper, Jesus was demonstrating His Messiahship. He was demonstrating that He had the power to cleanse the most unclean, no matter how terrible their uncleanness. 1. The man with leprosy was considered utterly unclean—physically and spiritually. He could not approach within six feet of any person, including family members. "The person with such an infectious disease must wear torn clothes, let his hair be unkempt, cover the lower part of his face and cry out, 'Unclean! Unclean!'" (Lev.13:45). 2. He was judged as dead—the living dead. He had to wear a black garment so he could be recognized as from among the dead. 3. He was banished as an outcast, totally ostracized from society—considered without hope of going to heaven. "As long as he has the infection he remains unclean. He must live alone; he must live outside the camp." (Lev.13:46). He could not live within the walls of any city; his dwelling had to be outside the city gates. 4. He was thought to be polluted, incurable by any human means whatsoever. Leprosy could be cured by God and His power alone. (Note how Christ proves His Messiahship and deity by healing the man with leprosy.) Imagine the anguish and heartbreak of the leper being completely cut off from family and friends and society. Imagine the emotional and mental pain. There are other recorded instances of men with leprosy being healed (cp. Matthew 10:8; Matthew 11:5; Mark 1:40; Luke 7:22; Luke 17:12; and perhaps Matthew 26:6; cp. Mark 14:3).
#2325 **Let** Yield–KJV Presenting–NASB Offer–NIV Present–NKJV **Let–NLT** **POSB REFERENCE** (Rom.6:13) *Deeper Study #2*	παριστάνετε = *paristanete* Pronunciation: [par-is'-tahn-eh-teh] Parsing (part of speech): verb 　Mood—imperative 　Tense—present 　Voice—active 　Person—2nd person 　Number—plural 　Stem or root—from παρίστημι and παριστάνω Concordance References: ⇒ Strong's #3936 paristēmi ⇒ NIV #4225 paristēmi ⇒ NASB #3936 paristēmi **Romans 6:13** Neither **yield** ye your members *as* instruments of unrighteousness unto sin: but yield yourselves unto God, as those that are alive from the dead, and your members *as* instruments of righteousness unto God. [KJV] And do not go on **presenting** the members of your body to sin *as* instruments of unrighteousness; but present yourselves to God as those alive from the dead, and your members *as* instruments of righteousness to God. [NASB]	To present; to bring into one's presence; to show; to yield; to dedicate; to provide; to send; to prove. It means to offer; to put at the disposal of; to give; to grant; to turn over to. **Practical Application** The believer must not let the members of his body sin. The believer is not to yield the members of his body to be instruments or tools of unrighteousness. If he takes a member of his body and uses it as an instrument or tool of unrighteousness, he sins. The members of a person's body refer to all the parts of the body: the eyes, ears, mouth, tongue, hands, feet, mind, or any of the covered and dressed parts. No believer is to offer or give any part of his body over to unrighteousness. To do so is to sin. The tense is present action, so the believer is to be constantly on guard against allowing any member of his body to be yielded to sin. Note: the word "let" has the idea of struggling. It is a struggle to fight

ENGLISH WORD	GREEK WORD AND VERSE	THE WORD MEANS...
	Do not **offer** the parts of your body to sin, as instruments of wickedness, but rather offer yourselves to God, as those who have been brought from death to life; and offer the parts of your body to him as instruments of righteousness. [NIV] And do not **present** your members *as* instruments of unrighteousness to sin, but present yourselves to God as being alive from the dead, and your members *as* instruments of righteousness to God. [NKJV] Do not **let** any part of your body become a tool of wickedness, to be used for sinning. Instead, give yourselves completely to God since you have been given new life. And use your whole body as a tool to do what is right for the glory of God. [NLT] μηδὲ **παριστάνετε** τὰ μέλη ὑμῶν ὅπλα ἀδικίας τῇ ἁμαρτίᾳ· ἀλλὰ παραστήσατε ἑαυτοὺς τῷ Θεῷ ὡς ἐκ νεκρῶν ζῶντας, καὶ τὰ μέλη ὑμῶν ὅπλα δικαιοσύνης τῷ Θεῷ. [GNS] μηδὲ **παριστάνετε** τὰ μέλη ὑμῶν ὅπλα ἀδικίας τῇ ἁμαρτίᾳ, ἀλλὰ παραστήσατε ἑαυτοὺς τῷ θεῷ ὡσεὶ ἐκ νεκρῶν ζῶντας καὶ τὰ μέλη ὑμῶν ὅπλα δικαιοσύνης τῷ θεῷ. [GNT]	against sin and to control and protect the members of our bodies.
#2326 **Let These [Sayings] Sink Down Into Your Ears** Let these [sayings] sink down into your ears–KJV Let these [words] sink into your ears–NASB Listen carefully–NIV Let these [words] sink down into your ears–NKJV Listen to me–NLT **POSB REFERENCE** (Lk.9:44-45; esp. v.44) Note 4, point 1	**Θέσθε ὑμεῖς εἰς τὰ ὦτα ὑμῶν** = *Thesthe humeis eis ta öta humön* Pronunciation: [thes-theh hu-meh-ees ice tah o-tah hu-mown] Parsing *Thesthe* (part of speech): verb 　　Mood—imperative 　　Tense—aorist 　　Voice—middle 　　Person—2nd person 　　Number—plural 　　Stem or root—from τίθημι Parsing *öta* (part of speech): noun 　　Case—accusative 　　Gender—neuter 　　Number—plural 　　Stem or root—from οὖς, ὠτός Concordance References: ⇒　Strong's #1519 eis + 3588 ho +3775 ous + 4771 su + 4771 su + 5087 tithemi ⇒　NIV # 1650+3836+4044+5148+5148+5502 eis ho ous su su tithëmi [Listen carefully] ⇒　NASB #1519 eis + 3588 ho +3775 ous + 4771 su + 4771 su + 5087 tithemi **Luke 9:44** **Let these sayings sink down into your ears**: for the Son of man shall be delivered into the hands of men. [KJV] "**Let these words sink into your ears**; for the Son of Man is going to be delivered into the hands of men." [NASB] "**Listen carefully** to what I am about to tell you: The Son of Man is going to be betrayed into the hands of men." [NIV] "**Let these words sink down into your ears**, for the Son of Man is about to be betrayed into the hands of men." [NKJV] "**Listen to me** and remember what I say. The Son of Man is going to be betrayed." [NLT] **Θέσθε ὑμεῖς εἰς τὰ ὦτα ὑμῶν** τοὺς λόγους τούτους· ὁ γὰρ υἱὸς τοῦ ἀνθρώπου μέλλει παραδίδοσθαι εἰς χεῖρας ἀνθρώπων. [GNS] **Θέσθε ὑμεῖς εἰς τὰ ὦτα ὑμῶν** τοὺς λόγους τούτους· ὁ γὰρ υἱὸς τοῦ ἀνθρώπου μέλλει παραδίδοσθαι εἰς χεῖρας ἀνθρώπων. [GNT]	Put these sayings into your ears. Give special attention to them. **Practical Application** Apparently, the disciples began to think about the earthly reign of Jesus. The power of God demonstrated that Jesus had the power to conquer the earth and subject all men to Himself. Their hopes were stirred. But note what Jesus did. He rebuked their thoughts of a physical and material Messiah. He again had to show them that God's Messiah had to die in order to save the world.

ENGLISH WORD	GREEK WORD AND VERSE	THE WORD MEANS...

#2327
 	
Let These [Words] Sink (Down) Into Your Ears
 	
Let these [sayings] sink down into your ears–KJV
Let these [words] sink into your ears–NASB
Listen carefully–NIV
Let these [words] sink down into your ears–NKJV
Listen to me–NLT
 	
POSB REFERENCE
(Lk.9:44-45; esp. v.44)
Note 4, point 1
	Θέσθε ὑμεῖς εἰς τὰ ὦτα ὑμῶν = *Thesthe humeis eis ta öta humön*
	Pronunciation: [thes-theh hu-meh-ees ice tah o-tah hu-mown]
	Parsing *Thesthe* (part of speech): verb
	    Mood—imperative
	    Tense—aorist
	    Voice—middle
	    Person—2nd person
	    Number—plural
	    Stem or root—from τίθημι
	Parsing *öta* (part of speech): noun
	    Case—accusative
	    Gender—neuter
	    Number—plural
	    Stem or root—from οὖς, ὠτός
	Concordance References:
	    ⇒ Strong's #1519 eis + 3588 ho +3775 ous + 4771 su + 4771 su + 5087 tithemi
	    ⇒ NIV # 1650+3836+4044+5148+5148+5502 eis ho ous su su tithëmi [Listen carefully]
	    ⇒ NASB #1519 eis + 3588 ho +3775 ous + 4771 su + 4771 su + 5087 tithemi
	
	Luke 9:44
	Let these sayings sink down into your ears: for the Son of man shall be delivered into the hands of men. [KJV]
	"**Let these words sink into your ears**; for the Son of Man is going to be delivered into the hands of men." [NASB]
	"**Listen carefully** to what I am about to tell you: The Son of Man is going to be betrayed into the hands of men." [NIV]
	"**Let these words sink down into your ears**, for the Son of Man is about to be betrayed into the hands of men." [NKJV]
	"**Listen to me** and remember what I say. The Son of Man is going to be betrayed." [NLT]
	Θέσθε ὑμεῖς εἰς τὰ ὦτα ὑμῶν τοὺς λόγους τούτους· ὁ γὰρ υἱὸς τοῦ ἀνθρώπου μέλλει παραδίδοσθαι εἰς χεῖρας ἀνθρώπων. [GNS]
	Θέσθε ὑμεῖς εἰς τὰ ὦτα ὑμῶν τοὺς λόγους τούτους· ὁ γὰρ υἱὸς τοῦ ἀνθρώπου μέλλει παραδίδοσθαι εἰς χεῖρας ἀνθρώπων. [GNT]
		Put these sayings into your ears. Give special attention to them.
		
		Practical Application
		Apparently, the disciples began to think about the earthly reign of Jesus. The power of God demonstrated that Jesus had the power to conquer the earth and subject all men to Himself. Their hopes were stirred.
		(See **Let These Sayings Sink Down Into Your Ears** for more practical application.)

#2328
 	
Let Your Mind Dwell On
 	
Think on–KJV
Let your mind dwell on–NASB
Think about–NIV
Meditate on–NKJV
Think about–NLT
 	
POSB REFERENCE
(Philip.4:8-9; esp. v.8)
Note 2
	λογίζεσθε = *logizesthe*
	Pronunciation: [log-id'-zehs-theh]
	Parsing (part of speech): verb
	    Mood—imperative
	    Tense—present
	    Voice—middle or passive deponent
	    Person—2nd person
	    Number—plural
	    Stem or root—from λογίζομαι
	Concordance References:
	    ⇒ Strong's #3049 logizomai
	    ⇒ NIV #3357 logizomai
	    ⇒ NASB #3049 logizomai
	
	Philip. 4:8
	Finally, brethren, whatsoever things are true, whatsoever things *are* honest, whatsoever things *are* just, whatsoever things *are* pure, whatsoever things *are* lovely, whatsoever things *are* of good report; if *there be* any virtue, and if *there be* any praise, **think on** these things. [KJV]
	Finally, brethren, whatever is true, whatever is honorable, whatever is right, whatever is pure, whatever is lovely, whatever is of good repute, if there is any excellence and if anything worthy of praise, **let your mind dwell on** these things. [NASB]
		To think about; to think on; to let one's mind dwell on; to calculate; to evaluate; to consider, reflect, reason, and ponder.
		
		Practical Application
		The idea is that of focusing our thoughts until they shape our behavior. The truth is:
		    ⇒ what we think is what we become.
		    ⇒ where we have kept our minds is where we are.
		    ⇒ our thoughts shape our behavior.
		    ⇒ what we do is what we think.
		
		William Barclay says,
		...it is a law of life that, if a man thinks of something often enough and long enough, he will come to the stage when he cannot stop thinking about it. His thoughts will be quite literally in a groove out of which he cannot jerk them (The Letters to the Philippians, Colossians, and Thessalonians, p.97).
		
		A person who centers his thoughts upon the world and its things will live for the world and its things: money, wealth, lands, property, hous-

ENGLISH WORD	GREEK WORD AND VERSE	THE WORD MEANS...
	Finally, brothers, whatever is true, whatever is noble, whatever is right, whatever is pure, whatever is lovely, whatever is admirable—if anything is excellent or praiseworthy—**think about** such things. [NIV] Finally, brethren, whatever things are true, whatever things *are* noble, whatever things *are* just, whatever things *are* pure, whatever things *are* lovely, whatever things *are* of good report, if *there is* any virtue and if *there is* anything praiseworthy—**meditate on** these things. [NKJV] And now, dear brothers and sisters, let me say one more thing as I close this letter. Fix your thoughts on what is true and honorable and right. Think about things that are pure and lovely and admirable. **Think about** things that are excellent and worthy of praise. [NLT] Τὸ λοιπόν, ἀδελφοί, ὅσα ἐστὶν ἀληθῆ, ὅσα σεμνά, ὅσα δίκαια, ὅσα ἁγνά, ὅσα προσφιλῆ, ὅσα εὔφημα, εἴ τις ἀρετὴ καὶ εἴ τις ἔπαινος, ταῦτα **λογίζεσθε**· [GNS] Τὸ λοιπόν, ἀδελφοί, ὅσα ἐστὶν ἀληθῆ, ὅσα σεμνά, ὅσα δίκαια, ὅσα ἁγνά, ὅσα προσφιλῆ, ὅσα εὔφημα, εἴ τις ἀρετὴ καὶ εἴ τις ἔπαινος, ταῦτα **λογίζεσθε**· [GNT]	es, possessions, position, power, recognition, honor, social standing, fame, and a host of other worldly pursuits. Very simply stated, a person who centers his thoughts... • upon the flesh and its lusts will live to satisfy the flesh through such things as pride, self, greed, pleasure, and sex. • upon the eyes and their lust will live to satisfy the eyes and their lust through such things as the immoral, pornographic filth flaunted in magazines, films, books, and television; the exposing of the human body; dressing to attract attention; looking a second time. • upon the pride of life will live to satisfy such things as the desire for recognition, honor, position, and authority. A mind set upon the world and the flesh is what leads to anxiety and worry, emptiness and restlessness (Phil. 4:6-7). A worldly mind never knows peace—not true peace, not the peace of God. God will never allow a worldly mind to have peace, for it is the restlessness of the human soul that He uses to reach men for salvation. The point is this: when a person accepts Jesus Christ, his mind is renewed by the Spirit of God.

#2329
Lewdness
 	
Lasciviousness–KJV
Sensuality–NASB
Lewdness–NIV
Lewdness–NKJV
Eagerness for lustful pleasure–NLT
 	
POSB REFERENCE
(Mk.7:22)
Deeper Study #11
 	
See also POSB REF:
(2 Cor.12:19-21; esp. v.21)
Note 3, point 2
(Gal.5:19-21; esp. v.19)
Note 2
(1 Pt.4:3)
Note 3, point 1
	ἀσέλγεια = aselgeia
	Pronunciation: [as-elg'-i-a]
	Parsing (part of speech): noun
	    Case—nominative
	    Gender—feminine
	    Number—singular
	    Stem or root—from ἀσέλγεια, ας
	Concordance References:
	  ⇒ Strong's #766 aselgeia
	  ⇒ NIV #816 aselgeia
	  ⇒ NASB #766 aselgeia
	
	Mark 7:22
	Thefts, covetousness, wickedness, deceit, **lasciviousness**, an evil eye, blasphemy, pride, foolishness: [KJV]
	Deeds of coveting *and* wickedness, *as well as* deceit, **sensuality**, envy, slander, pride *and* foolishness. [NASB]
	Greed, malice, deceit, **lewdness**, envy, slander, arrogance and folly. [NIV]
	Thefts, covetousness, wickedness, deceit, **lewdness**, an evil eye, blasphemy, pride, foolishness. [NKJV]
	Adultery, greed, wickedness, deceit, **eagerness for lustful pleasure**, envy, slander, pride, and foolishness. [NLT]
	πλεονεξίαι, πονηρίαι, δόλος, **ἀσέλγεια**, ὀφθαλμὸς πονηρός, βλασφημία, ὑπερηφανία, ἀφροσύνη· [GNS]
	μοιχεῖαι, πλεονεξίαι, πονηρίαι, δόλος, **ἀσέλγεια**, ὀφθαλμὸς πονηρός, βλασφημία, ὑπερηφανία, ἀφροσύνη· [GNT]
		Debauchery; lasciviousness; lewdness; eagerness for lustful pleasure; sensuality and indecency; shamelessness; uncontrolled, undisciplined, and unrestrained lust and passion.
		
		Practical Application
		A chief characteristic of the behavior is open and shameless indecency. It means unrestrained evil thoughts and behavior. It is giving in to brutish and lustful desires, a readiness for any pleasure. It is a person who knows no restraint, an individual who has sinned so much that he no longer cares what people say or think. It is something far more distasteful than just doing wrong. The person who misbehaves usually tries to hide his wrong, but a lewd man does not care who knows about his exploits or shame. He wants; therefore, he seeks to take and gratify. Decency and opinion do not matter. When he initially began to sin, he did as all people do: he misbehaved in secret. But eventually, the sin got the best of him—to the point that he no longer cared who saw or knew. He became the subject of a master—the master of habit, of the thing itself. People become the slaves of such things as unbridled lust, wantonness, licentiousness, outrageousness, shamelessness, insolence (Mark 7:22), wanton manners, filthy words, indecent body movements, immoral handling of males and females (Romans 13:13), carnality, gluttony, and sexual immorality (1 Peter 4:3; 2 Peter 2:2, 18). (Cp. 2 Cor. 12:21; Galatians 5:19; Ephes. 4:19; 2 Peter 2:7.)

#2330
Lewdness
 	
Chambering–KJV
Sexual promiscuity–NASB
	κοίταις = koitais
	Pronunciation: [koy'-tays]
	Parsing (part of speech): noun
	    Case—dative
	    Gender—feminine
	    Number—plural
	    Stem or root—from κοίτη, ης
		Sexual immorality; sexual promiscuity; sexual impurity; adultery, lewdness, fornication (pre-marital sex).
		
		Practical Application
		The charge is straightforward. The believer is not to participate...

ENGLISH WORD	GREEK WORD AND VERSE	THE WORD MEANS...
Sexual immorality–NIV **Lewdness–NKJV** Adultery–NLT **POSB REFERENCE** (Rom.13:13) Note 4, point 3	Concordance References: ⇒ Strong's #2845 koitë ⇒ NIV #3130 koitë ⇒ NASB #2845 koitë **Romans 13:13** Let us walk honestly, as in the day; not in rioting and drunkenness, not in **chambering** and wantonness, not in strife and envying. [KJV] Let us behave properly as in the day, not in carousing and drunkenness, not in **sexual promiscuity** and sensuality, not in strife and jealousy. [NASB] Let us behave decently, as in the daytime, not in orgies and drunkenness, not in **sexual immorality** and debauchery, not in dissension and jealousy. [NIV] Let us walk properly, as in the day, not in revelry and drunkenness, not in **lewdness** and lust, not in strife and envy. [NKJV] We should be decent and true in everything we do, so that everyone can approve of our behavior. Don't participate in wild parties and getting drunk, or in **adultery** and immoral living, or in fighting and jealousy. [NLT] ὡς ἐν ἡμέρᾳ, εὐσχημόνως περιπατήσωμεν, μὴ κώμοις καὶ μέθαις, μη **κοίταις** καὶ ἀσελγείαις, μὴ ἔριδι καὶ Ζήλῳ. [GNS] ὡς ἐν ἡμέρᾳ εὐσχημόνως περιπατήσωμεν, μὴ κώμοις καὶ μέθαις, μὴ **κοίταις** καὶ ἀσελγείαις, μὴ ἔριδι καὶ ζήλῳ, [GNT]	• in wild parties • in getting drunk • in adultery • in immoral living • in jealousy

#2331
Lewdness
 	
Lasciviousness–KJV
Sensuality–NASB
Debauchery–NIV
Lewdness–NKJV
Immorality–NLT
 	
POSB REFERENCE
(1 Pt.4:3)
Note 3, point 1
	ἀσελγείαις = *aselgeiais*
	Pronunciation: [as-elg'-i-ah-is]
	Parsing (part of speech): noun
	   Case—dative
	   Gender—feminine
	   Number—plural
	   Stem or root—from ἀσέλγεια, ας
	Concordance References:
	⇒ Strong's #766 aselgeia
	⇒ NIV #816 aselgeia
	⇒ NASB #766 aselgeia
	
	1 Peter 4:3
	For the time past of our life may suffice us to have wrought the will of the Gentiles, when we walked in **lasciviousness**, lusts, excess of wine, revellings, banquetings, and abominable idolatries: [KJV]
	For the time already past is sufficient for you to have carried out the desire of the Gentiles, having pursued a course of **sensuality**, lusts, drunkenness, carousals, drinking parties and abominable idolatries. [NASB]
	For you have spent enough time in the past doing what pagans choose to do—living in **debauchery**, lust, drunkenness, orgies, carousing and detestable idolatry. [NIV]
	For we *have spent* enough of our past lifetime in doing the will of the Gentiles—when we walked in **lewdness**, lusts, drunkenness, revelries, drinking parties, and abominable idolatries. [NKJV]
	You have had enough in the past of the evil things that godless people enjoy—their **immorality** and lust, their feasting and drunkenness and wild parties, and their terrible worship of idols. [NLT]
	ἀρκετὸς γὰρ ἡμῖν ὁ παρεληλυθὼς χρόνος τὸ βίου τὸ θέλημα τῶν ἐθνῶν κατεργάσασθαι, πεπορευμένους ἐν **ἀσελγείαις**, ἐπιθυμίαις, οἰνοφλυγίαις, κώμοις, πότοις, καὶ ἀθεμίτοις εἰδωλολατρείαις· [GNS]
	ἀρκετὸς γὰρ ὁ παρεληλυθὼς χρόνος τὸ βούλημα τῶν ἐθνῶν κατειργάσθαι πεπορευμένους ἐν **ἀσελγείαις**, ἐπιθυμίαις, οἰνοφλυγίαις, κώμοις, πότοις καὶ ἀθεμίτοις εἰδωλολατρίαις. [GNT]
		Debauchery, lasciviousness, sensuality, immorality, vice, filthiness, indecency, shamelessness, license, lustful desire; without restraint; lewdness.
		
		Practical Application
		A chief characteristic of the behavior is open and shameless indecency. It means unrestrained evil thoughts and behavior. It is giving in to brutish and lustful desires, a readiness for any pleasure. It is a man who knows no restraint, a man who has sinned so much that he no longer cares what people say or think. It is something far more distasteful than just doing wrong. The man who misbehaves usually tries to hide his wrong, but a sensual man does not care who knows about his exploits or shame. He wants; therefore he seeks to take and gratify. Decency and opinion do not matter. Initially when he began to sin, he did as all men do: he misbehaved in secret. But eventually, the sin got the best of him—to the point that he no longer cared who saw or knew. He became the subject of a master—the master of habit, of the thing itself.

ENGLISH WORD	GREEK WORD AND VERSE	THE WORD MEANS...
#2332 **Lewdness** Lasciviousness–KJV Licentiousness–NASB License for immorality–NIV **Lewdness–NKJV** Immoral lives–NLT **POSB REFERENCE** (Jude 1:4) Note 5	*ἀσέλγειαν* = *aselgeian* Pronunciation: [as-elg'-i-ahn] Parsing (part of speech): noun 　Case—accusative 　Gender—feminine 　Number—singular 　Stem or root—from *ἀσέλγεια*, ας Concordance References: 　⇒ Strong's #766 aselgeia 　⇒ NIV #816 aselgeia 　⇒ NASB #766 aselgeia **Jude 1:4** For there are certain men crept in unawares, who were before of old ordained to this condemnation, ungodly men, turning the grace of our God into **lasciviousness**, and denying the only Lord God, and our Lord Jesus Christ. [KJV] For certain persons have crept in unnoticed, those who were long beforehand marked out for this condemnation, ungodly persons who turn the grace of our God into **licentiousness** and deny our only Master and Lord, Jesus Christ. [NASB] For certain men whose condemnation was written about long ago have secretly slipped in among you. They are godless men, who change the grace of our God into a **license for immorality** and deny Jesus Christ our only Sovereign and Lord. [NIV] For certain men have crept in unnoticed, who long ago were marked out for this condemnation, ungodly men, who turn the grace of our God into **lewdness** and deny the only Lord God and our Lord Jesus Christ. [NKJV] I say this because some godless people have wormed their way in among you, saying that God's forgiveness allows us to live **immoral lives**. The fate of such people was determined long ago, for they have turned against our only Master and Lord, Jesus Christ. [NLT] παρεισέδυσαν γάρ τινες ἄνθρωποι, οἱ πάλαι προγεγραμμένοι εἰς τοῦτο τὸ κρίμα, ἀσεβεῖς, τὴν τοῦ Θεοῦ ἡμῶν χάριν μετατιθέντες εἰς **ἀσέλγειαν**, καὶ τὸν μόνον δεσπότην Θεόν, καὶ Κύριον ἡμῶν Ἰησοῦν Χριστὸν ἀρνούμενοι. [GNS] παρεισέδυσαν γάρ τινες ἄνθρωποι, οἱ πάλαι προγεγραμμένοι εἰς τοῦτο τὸ κρίμα, ἀσεβεῖς, τὴν τοῦ θεοῦ ἡμῶν χάριτα μετατιθέντες εἰς **ἀσέλγειαν** καὶ τὸν μόνον δεσπότην καὶ κύριον ἡμῶν Ἰησοῦν Χριστὸν ἀρνούμενοι. [GNT]	License for immorality; lasciviousness; licentiousness; immoral living; lustful desires; sensuality; shamelessness. **Practical Application** No matter what the false teaching is, it will enslave. The false teacher who denies Christ and God's Word removes the supreme authority over man's life. Therefore, man is pretty much free to live in selfishness and greed, desire and lust. He is pretty much left to seek as much pleasure and as many possessions as he desires upon earth. But in the end, man discovers something. The more he gets, the more he wants. It may be comfort, money, sex, position, or authority; it does not matter. Man's nature is such that he wants more and more. Man must be restrained by an authority above himself, that is, by God and by God's Word. If he is not, then he becomes enslaved to his passions and to the corruption of the world. This is one of the terrible fallacies of all false teachings. They all enslave man to this world: not a single false teaching can usher a man through the door of death into eternal life. Only Jesus Christ can do that. Note the clear truth: whatever overcomes a man, that very thing enslaves him. 　⇒ If a false teacher overcomes a man, then the man is enslaved to that teaching. 　⇒ If the world overcomes a man, then the man is enslaved by the world.
#2333 **Liberality** **Liberality–KJV** **Liberality–NASB** Generosity–NIV **Liberality–NKJV** Generosity–NLT **POSB REFERENCE** (2 Cor.8:1-5; esp. v.2) Note 1, point 1	*ἁπλότητος* = *haplotētos* Pronunciation: [hap-lot'-ay-tos] Parsing (part of speech): noun 　Case—genitive 　Gender—feminine 　Number—singular 　Stem or root—from *ἁπλότης*, ητος Concordance References: 　⇒ Strong's #572 haplotēs 　⇒ NIV #605 haplotes 　⇒ NASB #572 haplotēs **2 Cor. 8:2** How that in a great trial of affliction the abundance of their joy and their deep poverty abounded unto the riches of their **liberality**. [KJV] That in a great ordeal of affliction their abundance of joy and their deep poverty overflowed in the wealth of their **liberality**. [NASB] Out of the most severe trial, their overflowing joy and their extreme poverty welled up in rich **generosity**. [NIV] That in a great trial of affliction the abundance of their joy and their deep poverty abounded in the riches of their	Generosity; liberality; singleness of mind; sincerely; with an open and free heart. **Practical Application** The churches of Macedonia determined to give, to open their hearts and give all they could. The point is this: they knew the Lord—really knew Him—and they were committed to living for the Lord. Therefore, when someone needed help, they were ready to help. They gave liberally. They gave with great generosity.

ENGLISH WORD	GREEK WORD AND VERSE	THE WORD MEANS...
	liberality. [NKJV] Though they have been going through much trouble and hard times, their wonderful joy and deep poverty have overflowed in rich **generosity**. [NLT] ὅτι ἐν πολλῇ δοκιμῇ θλίψεως ἡ περισσεία τῆς χαρᾶς αὐτῶν καὶ ἡ κατὰ βάθους πτωχεία αὐτῶν ἐπερίσσευσεν εἰς τὸ πλοῦτον τῆς **ἁπλότητος** αὐτῶν. [GNS] ὅτι ἐν πολλῇ δοκιμῇ θλίψεως ἡ περισσεία τῆς χαρᾶς αὐτῶν καὶ ἡ κατὰ βάθους πτωχεία αὐτῶν ἐπερίσσευσεν εἰς τὸ πλοῦτος τῆς **ἁπλότητος** αὐτῶν· [GNT]	

#2334
Liberality
 	
Simplicity–KJV
Liberality–NASB
Generously–NIV
Liberality–NKJV
Generously–NLT
 	
POSB REFERENCE
(Rom.12:6-8; esp. v.8)
Note 2, point 5
	ἐν ἁπλότητι = en haplotëti
	Pronunciation: [en hap-lot'-ay-tee]
	Parsing *haplotëti* (part of speech): noun
	    Case—dative
	    Gender—feminine
	    Number—from ἁπλότης, ητος
	Concordance References:
	⇒ Strong's #572 + 1722 haplotës en
	⇒ NIV #605 + 1877 haplotës en [generously]
	⇒ NASB #572 + 1722 haplotës en
	
	Romans 12:8
	Or he that exhorteth, on exhortation: he that giveth, *let him do it* with **simplicity**; he that ruleth, with diligence; he that sheweth mercy, with cheerfulness. [KJV]
	
	Or he who exhorts, in his exhortation; he who gives, with **liberality**; he who leads, with diligence; he who shows mercy, with cheerfulness. [NASB]
	
	If it is encouraging, let him encourage; if it is contributing to the needs of others, let him give **generously**; if it is leadership, let him govern diligently; if it is showing mercy, let him do it cheerfully. [NIV]
	
	He who exhorts, in exhortation; he who gives, with **liberality**; he who leads, with diligence; he who shows mercy, with cheerfulness. [NKJV]
	
	If your gift is to encourage others, do it! If you have money, share it **generously**. If God has given you leadership ability, take the responsibility seriously. And if you have a gift for showing kindness to others, do it gladly. [NLT]
	
	εἴτε ὁ παρακαλῶν, ἐν τῇ παρακλήσει· ὁ μεταδιδοὺς **ἐν ἁπλότητι**, ὁ προϊστάμενος, ἐν σπουδῇ· ὁ ἐλεῶν ἐν ἱλαρότητι. [GNS]
	
	εἴτε ὁ παρακαλῶν ἐν τῇ παρακλήσει· ὁ μεταδιδοὺς **ἐν ἁπλότητι**, ὁ προϊστάμενος ἐν σπουδῇ, ὁ ἐλεῶν ἐν ἱλαρότητι. [GNT]
		Generosity; simplicity; sincerity; singlehearted devotion
		
		Practical Application
		The word has several ideas. It means...
		• to give with sincerity and in simplicity.
		• to give with singleness of heart and without show.
		• to give liberally and generously.
		The point is this: God gives some persons the special gift to make money in order to have plenty to help others and to spread the gospel around the world. These persons...
		• must give generously. God gave them the gift of making money in order to have enough to fulfill the will of God for the world. Therefore, they must give liberally.
		• must not hoard and bank and misuse their gift of wealth.
		• must not give grudgingly and complaining about having to give.
		• must not give to attract attention or to heap honor upon themselves.
		• must not give to boost their own egos and pride.

#2335
License For Immorality
 	
Lasciviousness–KJV
Licentiousness–NASB
License for immorality–NIV
Lewdness–NKJV
Immoral lives–NLT
 	
POSB REFERENCE
(Jude 1:4)
Note 5
	ἀσέλγειαν = aselgeian
	Pronunciation: [as-elg'-i-ahn]
	Parsing (part of speech): noun
	    Case—accusative
	    Gender—feminine
	    Number—singular
	    Stem or root—from ἀσέλγεια, ας
	Concordance References:
	⇒ Strong's #766 aselgeia
	⇒ NIV #816 aselgeia
	⇒ NASB #766 aselgeia
	
	Jude 1:4
	For there are certain men crept in unawares, who were before of old ordained to this condemnation, ungodly men, turning the grace of our God into **lasciviousness**, and denying the only Lord God, and our Lord Jesus Christ. [KJV]
	
	For certain persons have crept in unnoticed, those who were long beforehand marked out for this condemnation, ungodly persons who turn the grace of our God into **licentiousness** and deny our only Master and Lord, Jesus Christ. [NASB]
	
	For certain men whose condemnation was written about long ago have secretly slipped in among you. They
		License for immorality; lasciviousness; licentiousness; immoral living; lustful desires; sensuality; shamelessness.
		
		Practical Application
		No matter what the false teaching is, it will enslave. The false teacher who denies Christ and God's Word removes the supreme authority over man's life. Therefore, man is basically free to live in selfishness and greed, desire and lust. He is left to seek as much pleasure and as many possessions as he desires upon earth. But in the end, man discovers something. The more he gets, the more he wants. It may be comfort, money, sex, position, or authority; it does not matter. Man's nature is such that he wants more and more. Man must be restrained by an authority above himself, that is, by God and by God's Word. If he is not, then he becomes enslaved to his passions and to the corruption of the world. This is one of the terrible fallacies of all false teachings. They all enslave man to this world: not a single false teaching can usher a man through the door of

ENGLISH WORD	GREEK WORD AND VERSE	THE WORD MEANS...
	are godless men, who change the grace of our God into a **license for immorality** and deny Jesus Christ our only Sovereign and Lord. [NIV] For certain men have crept in unnoticed, who long ago were marked out for this condemnation, ungodly men, who turn the grace of our God into **lewdness** and deny the only Lord God and our Lord Jesus Christ. [NKJV] I say this because some godless people have wormed their way in among you, saying that God's forgiveness allows us to live **immoral lives**. The fate of such people was determined long ago, for they have turned against our only Master and Lord, Jesus Christ. [NLT] παρεισέδυσαν γάρ τινες ἄνθρωποι, οἱ πάλαι προγεγραμμένοι εἰς τοῦτο τὸ κρίμα, ἀσεβεῖς, τὴν τοῦ Θεοῦ ἡμῶν χάριν μετατιθέντες εἰς **ἀσέλγειαν**, καὶ τὸν μόνον δεσπότην Θεόν, καὶ Κύριον ἡμῶν Ἰησοῦν Χριστὸν ἀρνούμενοι. [GNS] παρεισέδυσαν γάρ τινες ἄνθρωποι, οἱ πάλαι προγεγραμμένοι εἰς τοῦτο τὸ κρίμα, ἀσεβεῖς, τὴν τοῦ θεοῦ ἡμῶν χάριτα μετατιθέντες εἰς **ἀσέλγειαν** καὶ τὸν μόνον δεσπότην καὶ κύριον ἡμῶν Ἰησοῦν Χριστὸν ἀρνούμενοι. [GNT]	death into eternal life. Only Jesus Christ can do that. Note the clear truth: whatever overcomes a man, that very thing enslaves him. ⇒ If a false teacher overcomes a man, then the man is enslaved to that teaching. ⇒ If the world overcomes a man, then the man is enslaved by the world.

#2336
Licentious-
ness
 	
Lasciviousness–KJV
Licentiousness–NASB
License for immoral-
ity–NIV
Lewdness–NKJV
Immoral lives–NLT
 	
POSB
REFERENCE
(Jude 1:4)
Note 5
	ἀσέλγειαν = aselgeian
	Pronunciation: [as-elg'-i-ahn]
	Parsing (part of speech): noun
	   Case—accusative
	   Gender—feminine
	   Number—singular
	   Stem or root—from *ἀσέλγεια, ας*
	Concordance References:
	⇒ Strong's #766 aselgeia
	⇒ NIV #816 aselgeia
	⇒ NASB #766 aselgeia
	
	Jude 1:4
	For there are certain men crept in unawares, who were before of old ordained to this condemnation, ungodly men, turning the grace of our God into **lasciviousness**, and denying the only Lord God, and our Lord Jesus Christ. [KJV]
	
	For certain persons have crept in unnoticed, those who were long beforehand marked out for this condemnation, ungodly persons who turn the grace of our God into **licentiousness** and deny our only Master and Lord, Jesus Christ. [NASB]
	
	For certain men whose condemnation was written about long ago have secretly slipped in among you. They are godless men, who change the grace of our God into a **license for immorality** and deny Jesus Christ our only Sovereign and Lord. [NIV]
	
	For certain men have crept in unnoticed, who long ago were marked out for this condemnation, ungodly men, who turn the grace of our God into **lewdness** and deny the only Lord God and our Lord Jesus Christ. [NKJV]
	
	I say this because some godless people have wormed their way in among you, saying that God's forgiveness allows us to live **immoral lives**. The fate of such people was determined long ago, for they have turned against our only Master and Lord, Jesus Christ. [NLT]
	
	παρεισέδυσαν γάρ τινες ἄνθρωποι, οἱ πάλαι προγεγραμμένοι εἰς τοῦτο τὸ κρίμα, ἀσεβεῖς, τὴν τοῦ Θεοῦ ἡμῶν χάριν μετατιθέντες εἰς **ἀσέλγειαν**, καὶ τὸν μόνον δεσπότην Θεόν, καὶ Κύριον ἡμῶν Ἰησοῦν Χριστὸν ἀρνούμενοι. [GNS]
	
	παρεισέδυσαν γάρ τινες ἄνθρωποι, οἱ πάλαι προγεγραμμένοι εἰς τοῦτο τὸ κρίμα, ἀσεβεῖς, τὴν τοῦ θεοῦ ἡμῶν χάριτα μετατιθέντες εἰς **ἀσέλγειαν** καὶ τὸν μόνον δεσπότην καὶ κύριον ἡμῶν Ἰησοῦν Χριστὸν ἀρνούμενοι. [GNT]
		License for immorality; lasciviousness; licentiousness; immoral living; lustful desires; sensuality; shamelessness.
		
		Practical Application
		No matter what the false teaching is, it will enslave. The false teacher who denies Christ and God's Word removes the supreme authority over man's life. Therefore, man is basically free to live in selfishness and greed, desire and lust. He is left to seek as much pleasure and as many possessions as he desires upon earth. But in the end, man discovers something. The more he gets, the more he wants. It may be comfort, money, sex, position, or authority; it does not matter. Man's nature is such that he wants more and more. Man must be restrained by an authority above himself, that is, by God and by God's Word. If he is not, then he becomes enslaved to his passions and to the corruption of the world. This is one of the terrible fallacies of all false teachings. They all enslave man to this world: not a single false teaching can usher a man through the door of death into eternal life. Only Jesus Christ can do that. Note the clear truth: whatever overcomes a man, that very thing enslaves him.
		⇒ If a false teacher overcomes a man, then the man is enslaved to that teaching.
		⇒ If the world overcomes a man, then the man is enslaved by the world.

ENGLISH WORD	GREEK WORD AND VERSE	THE WORD MEANS...

#2337
Lie
 	
Lie–KJV
Lie–NASB
Lie–NIV
Lie–NKJV
Lie–NLT
 	
POSB REFERENCE
(Col.3:8-11; esp. v.9)
Note 2, point 1f
	ψεύδεσθε = *pseudesthe*
	Pronunciation: [psyoo'-dehs-theh]
	Parsing (part of speech): verb
	  Mood—imperative
	  Tense—present
	  Voice—middle or passive deponent
	  Person—2nd person
	  Number—plural
	  Stem or root—from ψεύδομαι
	Concordance References:
	⇒ Strong's #5574 pseudomai
	⇒ NIV #6017 pseudomai
	⇒ NASB #5574 pseudomai
	
	Col. 3:9
	Lie not one to another, seeing that ye have put off the old man with his deeds; [KJV]
	Do not **lie** to one another, since you laid aside the old self with its *evil* practices, [NASB]
	Do not **lie** to each other, since you have taken off your old self with its practices [NIV]
	Do not **lie** to one another, since you have put off the old man with his deeds, [NKJV]
	Don't **lie** to each other, for you have stripped off your old evil nature and all its wicked deeds. [NLT]
	μὴ **ψεύδεσθε** εἰς ἀλλήλους, ἀπεκδυσάμενοι τὸν παλαιὸν ἄνθρωπον σὺν ταῖς πράξεσιν αὐτοῦ, [GNS]
	μὴ **ψεύδεσθε** εἰς ἀλλήλους, ἀπεκδυσάμενοι τὸν παλαιὸν ἄνθρωπον σὺν ταῖς πράξεσιν αὐτου [GNT]
		To lie; to live a lie; to be false. The word lying means that which is false. It is untruthfulness, deception, misrepresentation, exaggeration.
		
		Practical Application
		A lie does at least three things.
		1. Lying misrepresents the truth. It camouflages and hides the truth. The person lied to does not know the truth; therefore, he has to act or live upon a lie. If the lie is serious, it can be very damaging.
		2. Lying deceives a person. It leads a person astray. A person deceives...
		• to get what he wants.
		• to seduce someone.
		• to cover up or hide something.
		• to cause harm or hurt.
		  The point to see is that lying is a deception, and deception eventually causes misunderstanding, disappointment, bewilderment, helplessness, and emotional upheaval.
		3. Lying builds a wrong relationship, a relationship built upon sinking sand. Two people cannot possibly be friends or live together if the relationship is based upon lies.

#2338
Lies
 	
Guile–KJV
Guile–NASB
Deceitful–NIV
Deceit–NKJV
Lies–NLT
 	
POSB REFERENCE
(1 Pt.3:10)
Note 1
	δόλον = *dolon*
	Pronunciation: [dol'-on]
	Parsing (part of speech): noun
	  Case—accusative
	  Gender—masculine
	  Number—singular
	  Stem or root—from δόλος, ου
	Concordance References:
	⇒ Strong's #1388 dolos
	⇒ NIV #1515 dolos
	⇒ NASB #1388 dolos
	
	1 Peter 3:10
	For he that will love life, and see good days, let him refrain his tongue from evil, and his lips that they speak no **guile**: [KJV]
	For, "LET HIM WHO MEANS TO LOVE LIFE AND SEE GOOD DAYS REFRAIN HIS TONGUE FROM EVIL AND HIS LIPS FROM SPEAKING **GUILE**. [NASB]
	For, "Whoever would love life and see good days must keep his tongue from evil and his lips from **deceitful** speech. [NIV]
	For"He who would love life,And see good days, Let him refrain his tongue from evil, And his lips from speaking **deceit**. [NKJV]
	For the Scriptures say, "If you want a happy life and good days, keep your tongue from speaking evil, and keep your lips from telling **lies**. [NLT]
	Ὁ γὰρ θέλων ζωὴν ἀγαπᾶν, καὶ ἰδεῖν ἡμέρας ἀγαθάς, παυσάτω τὴν γλῶσσαν αὐτοῦ ἀπὸ κακοῦ, καὶ χείλη αὐτοῦ τοῦ μὴ λαλῆσαι **δόλον**· [GNS]
	ὁ γὰρ θέλων ζωὴν ἀγαπᾶν καὶ ἰδεῖν ἡμέρας ἀγαθὰς παυσάτω τὴν γλῶσσαν ἀπὸ κακοῦ καὶ χείλη τοῦ μὴ λαλῆσαι **δόλον**, [GNT]
		Deceitful, guile, lies, trickery, treachery.
		
		Practical Application
		A lying tongue is...
		• a false tongue
		• a cheating tongue
		• a treacherous tongue
		• a deceptive tongue
		• a deceitful tongue
		• a mistreating tongue
		• a beguiling tongue
		• a flattering tongue
		We deceive and smooth talk others in order to get what we are after or to protect ourselves. But note what Scripture says: the very first step to loving and enjoying life is to keep our tongues from deceiving and beguiling others. Lying leads to sin and sin destroys. Just think about the lying tongues that have...
		• destroyed marriages
		• damaged friendships
		• caused injuries
		• prevented promotions
		• disturbed children
		• ruined reputations
		• aroused fights
		• maimed bodies
		• caused wars
		If we wish to love and enjoy life, we must stop our tongues from speaking evil and from deceiving others. We must control and discipline our tongues.

#2339
Life
 	
Life–KJV
Life–NASB
Life–NIV
Life–NKJV
	ψυχὴν = *psuchēn*
	Pronunciation: [psoo-khayn']
	Parsing (part of speech): noun
	  Case—accusative
	  Gender—feminine
	  Number—singular
	  Stem or root—from ψυχή, ῆς
	Concordance References:
		Life, soul, mind, heart. It means the inner life; the natural, animal life; the earthly life that quickly passes away; the fading, aging, decaying, corruptible life of the earth.
		
		Practical Application
		The warning to the materialist is clear. No

ENGLISH WORD	GREEK WORD AND VERSE	THE WORD MEANS...
Life–NLT **POSB** **REFERENCE** (Lk.9:24) Note 2	⇒ Strong's #5590 psuchë ⇒ NIV #6034 psuchë ⇒ NASB #5590 psuchë **Luke 9:24** For whosoever will save his **life** shall lose it: but whosoever will lose his **life** for my sake, the same shall save it. [KJV] "For whoever wishes to save his **life** shall lose it, but whoever loses his **life** for My sake, he is the one who will save it. [NASB] For whoever wants to save his **life** will lose it, but whoever loses his **life** for me will save it. [NIV] For whoever desires to save his **life** will lose it, but whoever loses his **life** for My sake will save it. [NKJV] If you try to keep your **life** for yourself, you will lose it. But if you give up your **life** for me, you will find true **life**. [NLT] ὃς γὰρ ἂν θέλῃ τὴν **ψυχὴν** αὐτοῦ σῶσαι, ἀπολέσει αὐτήν· ὃς δ' ἂν ἀπολέσῃ τὴν ψυχὴν αὐτοῦ ἕνεκεν ἐμοῦ, οὗτος σώσει αὐτήν. [GNS] ὃς γὰρ ἂν θέλῃ τὴν **ψυχὴν** αὐτοῦ σῶσαι ἀπολέσει αὐτήν· ὃς δ' ἂν ἀπολέσῃ τὴν ψυχὴν αὐτοῦ ἕνεκεν ἐμοῦ οὗτος σώσει αὐτήν. [GNT]	man can gain the whole world, but what if he could? All the pleasure and wealth and power and fame are nothing compared with his soul. There are four primary reasons why the soul is far superior to the things of this earth. 1. Everything fades and passes away. A person possesses something only for a short time. 2. Everything cannot be used all at once. Everything sits and remains unused most of the time. ⇒ Clothes sit. ⇒ A car sits. ⇒ Power goes unused. ⇒ Popularity and fame quickly pass and are forgotten. 3. The human soul is eternal. The soul never dies and never ceases to exist. It will live forever either with God or apart from God. 4. The human soul is of more value than the whole world.

#2340
Life
 	
Stature–KJV
Life's span–NASB
Life–NIV
Stature–NKJV
Life–NLT
 	
POSB
REFERENCE
(Lk.12:22-28; esp.
v.25)
Note 1, point 3
 	
See also POSB REF:
(Mt.6:27)
Note 4
	ἡλικίαν = hëlikian
	Pronunciation: [hay-lik-ee'-ahn]
	Parsing (part of speech): noun
	   Case—accusative
	   Gender—feminine
	   Number—singular
	   Stem or root—from ἡλικία, ας
	Concordance References:
	⇒ Strong's #2244 hëlikia
	⇒ NIV #2461 hëlikia
	⇒ NASB #2244 hëlikia
	
	Luke 12:25
	And which of you with taking thought can add to his **stature** one cubit? [KJV]
	"And which of you by being anxious can add a *single* cubit to his **life's span**? [NASB]
	Who of you by worrying can add a single hour to his **life**? [NIV]
	And which of you by worrying can add one cubit to his **stature**? [NKJV]
	Can all your worries add a single moment to your **life**? Of course not! [NLT]
	τίς δὲ ἐξ ὑμῶν μεριμνῶν δύναται προσθεῖναι ἐπὶ τὴν **ἡλικίαν** αὐτοῦ πῆχυν ἕνα; [GNS]
	τίς δὲ ἐξ ὑμῶν μεριμνῶν δύναται ἐπὶ τὴν **ἡλικίαν** αὐτοῦ προσθεῖναι πῆχυν; [GNT]
		Height, quality, life, or stature gained by growth; but sometimes it also means age or life span.
		
		Practical Application
		The point is striking: worry is senseless—just as senseless as trying to add to one's height or lengthen a minute to one's life span (when it is time for one to pass on). All statures and all bodies are not normal and perfectly formed. The world is corruptible and imperfect (see POSB note—Matthew 6:19-20). But there is a glorious hope in God—a hope that acknowledges that God does love and care and has promised a new heavens and earth that will be perfect. In that perfect heavens and earth all bodies will be normal and perfectly formed. God will "wipe away all tears" (Rev. 21:4; cp. Rev. 21:1-7).

#2341
Life
 	
Life–KJV
Life–NASB
Life–NIV
Life–NKJV
Life–NLT
 	
POSB
REFERENCE
(Jn.10:10)
Deeper Study #1
 	
See also POSB REF:
(1 Jn.5:11)
Deeper Study #1
	ζωὴν = zöën
	Pronunciation: [dzo-ayn']
	Parsing (part of speech): noun
	   Case—accusative
	   Gender—feminine
	   Number—singular
	   Stem or root—from ζωή, ῆς
	Concordance References:
	⇒ Strong's #2222 zoe
	⇒ NIV #2437 zoe
	⇒ NASB #2222 zoe
	
	John 10:10
	The thief cometh not, but for to steal, and to kill, and to destroy: I am come that they might have **life**, and that they might have *it* more abundantly. [KJV]
	"The thief comes only to steal, and kill, and destroy; I came that they might have **life**, and might have *it* abundantly. [NASB]
	The thief comes only to steal and kill and destroy; I
		Life; life as opposed to death and dying.
		
		Practical Application
		The word "life" (*zöën*) and the verb "to live" or "to have life" (*zen*) have a depth of meaning. (See POSB *Deeper Study #2*—John 1:4; POSB *Deeper Study #1*—John 17:2-3.)
		1. Life is the energy, the force, the power of being.
		2. Life is the opposite of perishing. It is deliverance from condemnation and death. It is the stopping or cessation of deterioration, decay, and corruption (John 3:16; John 5:24, 29; John 10:28).
		3. Life is eternal (*aionios*). It is forever. It is the very life of God Himself (John 17:3). However, eternal life does not refer just to duration. Living forever would be a curse for

ENGLISH WORD	GREEK WORD AND VERSE	THE WORD MEANS...
	have come that they may have **life**, and have it to the full. [NIV] The thief does not come except to steal, and to kill, and to destroy. I have come that they may have **life**, and that they may have *it* more abundantly. [NKJV] The thief's purpose is to steal and kill and destroy. My purpose is to give **life** in all its fullness. [NLT] ὁ κλέπτης οὐκ ἔρχεται εἰ μὴ ἵνα κλέψῃ καὶ θύσῃ καὶ ἀπολέσῃ· ἐγὼ ἦλθον ἵνα **ζωὴν** ἔχωσι καὶ περισσὸν ἔχωσιν. [GNS] ὁ κλέπτης οὐκ ἔρχεται εἰ μὴ ἵνα κλέψῃ καὶ θύσῃ καὶ ἀπολέσῃ· ἐγὼ ἦλθον ἵνα **ζωὴν** ἔχωσιν καὶ περισσὸν ἔχωσιν. [GNT]	some persons. The idea of eternal life is also quality, a certain kind of life, a life that consistently knows love, joy, peace, power, and responsibility (John 10:10). 4. Life is satisfaction (John 6:35). 5. Life is security and enjoyment (John 10:10). 6. Life is found only in God. God is the source and author of life, and it is God who has appointed Jesus Christ to bring life to man. Jesus Christ gives the very life of God Himself (John 5:26; John 6:27, 40; John 10:28; John 17:23). 7. Life has now been revealed. It has been unveiled and is clearly seen in Jesus Christ. Jesus Christ shows man what life is (John 1:4-5; John 5:26; 1 John 1:2). 8. Life only comes to a man by believing in Jesus Christ. A man outside Jesus Christ only exists. He merely has the existence of an animal. Real life is found only in God. This is to be expected and it is logically true, for God is the Creator of life. As the Creator of life, He alone knows what life really is and what it is supposed to be (John 3:36; John 5:24; John 6:47). This is the reason He sent His Son, the Lord Jesus Christ, into the world: to show men what life is. When a person looks at Jesus Christ, he sees exactly what life is, exactly what it involves (cp. Galatians 5:22-23): Life lived in Jesus Christ is... • love • joy • peace • patience • kindness • goodness • faithfulness • gentleness • and self-control

#2342
# Life's Span 	
 	
Stature–KJV
Life's span–NASB
Life–NIV
Stature–NKJV
Life–NLT
 	
POSB REFERENCE
(Lk.12:22-28; esp. v.25)
Note 1, point 3
 	
See also POSB REF:
(Mt.6:27)
Note 4
	ἡλικίαν = *hēlikian*
	Pronunciation: [hay-lik-ee'-ahn]
	Parsing (part of speech): noun
	    Case—accusative
	    Gender—feminine
	    Number—singular
	    Stem or root—from ἡλικία, ας
	Concordance References:
	  ⇒ Strong's #2244 hēlikia
	  ⇒ NIV #2461 hēlikia
	  ⇒ NASB #2244 hēlikia
	
	## Luke 12:25
	And which of you with taking thought can add to his **stature** one cubit? [KJV]
	
	"And which of you by being anxious can add a *single* cubit to his **life's span**? [NASB]
	
	Who of you by worrying can add a single hour to his **life**? [NIV]
	
	And which of you by worrying can add one cubit to his **stature**? [NKJV]
	
	Can all your worries add a single moment to your **life**? Of course not! [NLT]
	
	τίς δὲ ἐξ ὑμῶν μεριμνῶν δύναται προσθεῖναι ἐπὶ τὴν **ἡλικίαν** αὐτοῦ πῆχυν ἕνα; [GNS]
	
	τίς δὲ ἐξ ὑμῶν μεριμνῶν δύναται ἐπὶ τὴν **ἡλικίαν** αὐτοῦ προσθεῖναι πῆχυν; [GNT]
		Height, quality, stature, life, or status gained by growth; but sometimes it also means age or life's span.
		
		## Practical Application
		The point is striking: worry is senseless—just as senseless as trying to add to one's height or lengthen a minute to one's life span (when it is time for one to pass on). All statures and all bodies are not normal and perfectly formed. The world is corruptible and imperfect (see POSB note—Matthew 6:19-20). But there is a glorious hope in God—a hope that acknowledges that God does love and care and has promised a new heavens and earth that will be perfect. In that perfect heavens and earth, all bodies will be normal and perfectly formed. God will "wipe away all tears" (Rev. 21:4; cp. Rev. 21:1-7).

ENGLISH WORD	GREEK WORD AND VERSE	THE WORD MEANS...

#2343
Life Cannot Be Spoken Against
 	
Blameless–KJV
Above reproach–NASB
Above reproach–NIV
Blameless–NKJV
Life cannot be spoken against–NLT
 	
POSB REFERENCE
(1 Tim.3:2-3; esp. v.2)
Note 2, point 1
	ἀνεπίλημπτον = *anepilēmpton*
	Pronunciation: [an-ep-il'-amp-ton]
	Parsing (part of speech): adjective
	    Case—accusative
	    Gender—masculine
	    Number—singular
	    Stem or root—from ἀνεπίλημπτος, ον
	Concordance References:
	  ⇒ Strong's #423 anepilēmptos
	  ⇒ NIV #455 anepilēmptos
	  ⇒ NASB #423 anepilēmptos
	
	1 Tim. 3:2
	A bishop then must be **blameless**, the husband of one wife, vigilant, sober, of good behaviour, given to hospitality, apt to teach; [KJV]
	An overseer, then, must be **above reproach**, the husband of one wife, temperate, prudent, respectable, hospitable, able to teach, [NASB]
	Now the overseer must be **above reproach**, the husband of but one wife, temperate, self-controlled, respectable, hospitable, able to teach, [NIV]
	A bishop then must be **blameless**, the husband of one wife, temperate, sober-minded, of good behavior, hospitable, able to teach; [NKJV]
	For an elder must be a man whose **life cannot be spoken against**. He must be faithful to his wife. He must exhibit self-control, live wisely, and have a good reputation. He must enjoy having guests in his home and must be able to teach. [NLT]
	δεῖ οὖν τὸν ἐπίσκοπον **ἀνεπίλημπτον** εἶναι, μιᾶς γυναικὸς ἄνδρα, νηφάλιον, σώφρονα, κόσμιον, φιλόξενον, διδακτικόν· [GNS]
	δεῖ οὖν τὸν ἐπίσκοπον **ἀνεπίλημπτον** εἶναι, μιᾶς γυναικὸς ἄνδρα, νηφάλιον σώφρονα κόσμιον φιλόξενον διδακτικόν, [GNT]
		To be without fault; to be without rebuke; to be above reproach; to live an innocent life; to have a life that cannot be spoken against; to be without blemish, spot, or defect.
		
		Practical Application
		The minister or overseer of God must be qualified; he must meet some personal qualifications; he must be a person of great Christian character. The minister or overseer must have a "life (that) cannot be spoken against" (*anepilēmpton*): blameless; not open to attack; not able to be criticized by the enemy at all (*The Pulpit Commentary*, Vol.21, p.50). He must be completely above reproach.

#2344
Light
 	
Light–KJV
Light–NASB
Light–NIV
Light–NKJV
Light–NLT
 	
POSB REFERENCE
(Jn.12:36)
Deeper Study #5
	φωτός = *phōtos*
	Pronunciation: [fo-tos]
	Parsing (part of speech): noun
	    Case—genitive
	    Gender—neuter
	    Number—singular
	    Stem or root—from φῶς, φωτός
	Concordance References:
	  ⇒ Strong's #5457 phōs
	  ⇒ NIV #5890 phōs
	  ⇒ NASB #5457 phōs
	
	John 12:36
	While ye have light, believe in the light, that ye may be the children of **light**. These things spake Jesus, and departed, and did hide himself from them. [KJV]
	"While you have the light, believe in the light, in order that you may become sons of **light**." These things Jesus spoke, and He departed and hid Himself from them. [NASB]
	Put your trust in the light while you have it, so that you may become sons of **light**." When he had finished speaking, Jesus left and hid himself from them. [NIV]
	While you have the light, believe in the light, that you may become sons of **light**." These things Jesus spoke, and departed, and was hidden from them. [NKJV]
	Believe in the light while there is still time; then you will become children of the **light**." After saying these things, Jesus went away and was hidden from them. [NLT]
	ἕως τὸ φῶς ἔχετε, πιστεύετε εἰς τὸ φῶς, ἵνα υἱοὶ **φωτός** γένησθε. Ταῦτα ἐλάλησεν ὁ Ἰησοῦς, καὶ ἀπελθὼν ἐκρύβη ἀπ' αὐτῶν. [GNS]
	ὡς τὸ φῶς ἔχετε, πιστεύετε εἰς τὸ φῶς, ἵνα υἱοὶ **φωτός** γένησθε. Ταῦτα ἐλάλησεν Ἰησοῦς, καὶ ἀπελθὼν ἐκρύβη ἀπ' αὐτῶν. [GNT]
		Light; light that illuminates a person's darkened soul.
		
		Practical Application
		Light is one of the great words of Scripture. (See POSB *Deeper Study* #1—John 8:12.)
		1. God is light and in Him is no darkness at all (1 John 1:5).
		2. Jesus Christ is the Light of the world—the very embodiment of the heavenly light (John 8:12; John 9:5).
		3. The light of the knowledge of God is seen in the face of Jesus Christ (2 Cor. 4:6).
		4. Jesus Christ "lights every man" who comes into the world (John 1:9).
		5. Believers are said to become "children of light" through belief in the Light, Jesus Christ Himself (John 12:36).
		6. Believers have been transferred from the dominion of darkness into the Kingdom of Christ, the inheritance of light (Col. 1:13).
		7. Before they come to Christ, believers are not only in darkness but are an embodiment of darkness. But when they come to Christ, believers are placed in the Light and become an embodiment of the Light itself (Ephes. 5:8).
		8. Believers are the light of the world (Matthew 5:14-16).
		9. Believers are to set their light on a lampstand—to make their light conspicuous (Matthew 5:15).
		10. Evildoers shun the light (John 3:20f).
		11. The creation of light is a picture of the expulsion of spiritual darkness (Genesis 1:2f).

ENGLISH WORD	GREEK WORD AND VERSE	THE WORD MEANS...

#2345
Like Passions
 	
Like passions–KJV
Same nature–NASB
Human like–NIV
Same nature–NKJV
Human beings like–NLT
 	
POSB REFERENCE
(Acts 14:14-18; esp. v.15)
Note 3, point 1
	ὁμοιοπαθεῖς = homoiopatheis
	Pronunciation: [hom-oy-op-ath-ice']
	Parsing (part of speech): adjective
	    Case—nominative
	    Gender—masculine
	    Number—plural
	    Stem or root—from ὁμοιοπαθής, ές
	Concordance References:
	⇒ Strong's #3663 homoiopathēs
	⇒ NIV #3926 homoiopathēs
	⇒ NASB #3663 homoiopathēs
	
	Acts 14:15
	And saying, Sirs, why do ye these things? We also are men of **like passions** with you, and preach unto you that ye should turn from these vanities unto the living God, which made heaven, and earth, and the sea, and all things that are therein: [KJV]
	
	and saying, "Men, why are you doing these things? We are also men of the **same nature** as you, and preach the gospel to you in order that you should turn from these vain things to a living God, WHO MADE THE HEAVEN AND THE EARTH AND THE SEA, AND ALL THAT IS IN THEM. [NASB]
	
	"Men, why are you doing this? We too are only men, **human like** you. We are bringing you good news, telling you to turn from these worthless things to the living God, who made heaven and earth and sea and everything in them. [NIV]
	
	And saying, "Men, why are you doing these things? We also are men with the **same nature** as you, and preach to you that you should turn from these useless things to the living God, who made the heaven, the earth, the sea, and all things that are in them, [NKJV]
	
	"Friends, why are you doing this? We are merely **human beings like** yourselves! We have come to bring you the Good News that you should turn from these worthless things to the living God, who made heaven and earth, the sea, and everything in them. [NLT]
	
	καὶ λέγοντες, Ἄνδρες, τί ταῦτα ποιεῖτε; καὶ ἡμεῖς ὁμοιοπαθεῖς ἐσμεν ὑμῖν ἄνθρωποι, εὐαγγελιζόμενοι ὑμᾶς ἀπὸ τούτων τῶν ματαίων ἐπιστρέφειν ἐπὶ τὸν Θεὸν ζῶντα, ὃς ἐποίησε τὸν οὐρανὸν καὶ τὴν γῆν καὶ τὴν θάλασσαν, καὶ πάντα τὰ ἐν αὐτοῖς· [GNS]
	
	καὶ λέγοντες, Ἄνδρες, τί ταῦτα ποιεῖτε; καὶ ἡμεῖς ὁμοιοπαθεῖς ἐσμεν ὑμῖν ἄνθρωποι εὐαγγελιζόμενοι ὑμᾶς ἀπὸ τούτων τῶν ματαίων ἐπιστρέφειν ἐπὶ θεὸν ζῶντα, ὃς ἐποίησεν τὸν οὐρανὸν καὶ τὴν γῆν καὶ τὴν θάλασσαν καὶ πάντα τὰ ἐν αὐτοῖς· [GNT]
		Like, passions, same; to be like in every way. It means the same nature.
		
		Practical Application
		It means that all men have the same...
		• heart (Psalm 33:15)
		• feelings
		• infirmities
		• temptations (1 Cor. 10-13)
		• sufferings
		• aging and dying bodies (Hebrews 9:27)

#2346
Like Precious
 	
Like precious–KJV
Same kind–NASB
As precious as–NIV
Like precious–NKJV
Same precious–NLT
 	
POSB REFERENCE
(2 Pt.1:1)
Note 2
	ἰσότιμον = isotimon
	Pronunciation: [ee-sot'-ee-mon]
	Parsing (part of speech): adjective
	    Case—accusative
	    Gender—feminine
	    Number—singular
	    Stem or root—from ἰσότιμος, ον
	Concordance References:
	⇒ Strong's #2472 isotimos
	⇒ NIV #2700 isotimos
	⇒ NASB #2472 isotimos
	
	2 Peter 1:1
	Simon Peter, a servant and an apostle of Jesus Christ, to them that have obtained **like precious** faith with us through the righteousness of God and our Saviour Jesus Christ: [KJV]
	
	Simon Peter, a bond-servant and apostle of Jesus Christ, to those who have received a faith of the **same kind** as ours, by the righteousness of our God and Savior, Jesus Christ: [NASB]
	
	Simon Peter, a servant and apostle of Jesus Christ, To
		As precious as; equally valuable; of the same kind.
		
		Practical Application
		Note this: the faith of Jesus Christ is the same *precious faith* that is given to all believers. The Greek word that Peter uses for "precious" (*isotimon*) is an unusual word. This is the only time it is used in the New Testament. It is really a double word. The *isos* means *equal*, and *time* means *honor* (A.T. Robertson. *Word Pictures in the New Testament*, Vol.6, p.147). Therefore, by *precious faith* is meant *like faith*, a faith that is like everyone else's faith. This is a most wonderful thing. It means that we are all given the very same faith; we are all equal in value and honor and privilege before God. God does not discriminate; He does not have favorites. God loves us all equally, and He values and honors us all as much as He did Peter, James, John and Paul.

ENGLISH WORD	GREEK WORD AND VERSE	THE WORD MEANS...
	those who through the righteousness of our God and Savior Jesus Christ have received a faith **as precious as** ours: [NIV] Simon Peter, a bondservant and apostle of Jesus Christ, To those who have obtained **like precious** faith with us by the righteousness of our God and Savior Jesus Christ: [NKJV] This letter is from Simon Peter, a slave and apostle of Jesus Christ. I am writing to all of you who share the **same precious** faith we have, faith given to us by Jesus Christ, our God and Savior, who makes us right with God. [NLT] Σίμων Πέτρος, δοῦλος καὶ ἀπόστολος Ἰησοῦ Χριστοῦ, τοῖς **ἰσότιμον** ἡμῖν λαχοῦσι πίστιν ἐν δικαιοσύνῃ τοῦ Θεοῦ ἡμῶν καὶ σωτῆρος ἡμῶν Ἰησοῦ Χριστοῦ· [GNS] Συμεὼν Πέτρος δοῦλος καὶ ἀπόστολος Ἰησοῦ Χριστοῦ τοῖς **ἰσότιμον** ἡμῖν λαχοῦσιν πίστιν ἐν δικαιοσύνῃ τοῦ θεοῦ ἡμῶν καὶ σωτῆρος Ἰησοῦ Χριστοῦ, [GNT]	

#2347
Like The Rest
 	
Course–KJV
Course–NASB
Ways–NIV
Course–NKJV
Like the rest–NLT
 	
POSB
REFERENCE
(Eph.2:1-2; esp. v.2)
Note 2
	αἰῶνα = *aiöna*
	Pronunciation: [ahee-ohn'-ah]
	Parsing (part of speech): noun
	    Case—accusative
	    Gender—masculine
	    Number—singular
	    Stem or root—from **αἰών**, ῶνος
	Concordance References:
	⇒ Strong's #165 aiön
	⇒ NIV #172 aiön
	⇒ NASB #165 aiön
	
	Ephes. 2:2
	Wherein in time past ye walked according to the **course** of this world, according to the prince of the power of the air, the spirit that now worketh in the children of disobedience: [KJV]
	
	In which you formerly walked according to the **course** of this world, according to the prince of the power of the air, of the spirit that is now working in the sons of disobedience. [NASB]
	
	In which you used to live when you followed the **ways** of this world and of the ruler of the kingdom of the air, the spirit who is now at work in those who are disobedient. [NIV]
	
	In which you once walked according to the **course** of this world, according to the prince of the power of the air, the spirit who now works in the sons of disobedience, [NKJV]
	
	You used to live just **like the rest** of the world, full of sin, obeying Satan, the mighty prince of the power of the air. He is the spirit at work in the hearts of those who refuse to obey God. [NLT]
	
	ἐν αἷς ποτε περιεπατήσατε κατὰ τὸν **αἰῶνα** τοῦ κόσμου τούτου, κατὰ τὸν ἄρχοντα τῆς ἐξουσίας τοῦ ἀέρος, τοῦ πνεύματος τοῦ νῦν ἐνεργοῦντος ἐν τοῖς υἱοῖς τῆς ἀπειθείας· [GNS]
	
	ἐν αἷς ποτε περιεπατήσατε κατὰ τὸν **αἰῶνα** τοῦ κόσμου τούτου, κατὰ τὸν ἄρχοντα τῆς ἐξουσίας τοῦ ἀέρος, τοῦ πνεύματος τοῦ νῦν ἐνεργοῦντος ἐν τοῖς υἱοῖς τῆς ἀπειθείας· [GNT]
		Ways, course, world order, age, universe.
		
		Practical Application
		The sinner "lives just like the rest of the world." This simply means he follows the world in its...
		
		• opinions
		• life
		• speculations
		• pleasures
		• selfishness
		• purposes
		• technology
		• possessions
		• positions
		• popularity
		• honor
		• religion
		• values
		• science
		• standards

#2348
Like-Minded
 	
One mind–KJV
Like-minded–NASB
One mind–NIV
One mind–NKJV
Harmony–NLT
	τὸ αὐτὸ φρονεῖτε = *to auto phroneite*
	Pronunciation: [to ow-to' fron-eh'-ee-teh]
	Parsing *phroneite* (part of speech): verb
	    Mood—imperative
	    Tense—present
	    Voice—active
	    Person—2nd person
	    Number—plural
	    Stem or root—from **φρονέω**
	Concordance References:
	⇒ Strong's #846+3588 autos ho + 5426 phroneö
	⇒ NIV #899+3836 autos ho [one] + 5858 phroneö
		One mind; to be like-minded; to be in harmony; to be of one mind in faith, belief, purpose, mission, and ministry.
		
		Practical Application
		Note that God is the Author, the Giver of love and peace. The believer must therefore accept the challenge to be of one mind with other believers and live accordingly.

ENGLISH WORD	GREEK WORD AND VERSE	THE WORD MEANS...
POSB REFERENCE (2 Cor.13:11-13; esp. v.11) Note 3, point 3	[mind] ⇒ NASB #846+3588 autos ho + 5426 phroneö **2 Cor. 13:11** Finally, brethren, farewell. Be perfect, be of good comfort, be of **one mind**, live in peace; and the God of love and peace shall be with you. [KJV] Finally, brethren, rejoice, be made complete, be comforted, be **like-minded**, live in peace; and the God of love and peace shall be with you. [NASB] Finally, brothers, good-by. Aim for perfection, listen to my appeal, be of **one mind**, live in peace. And the God of love and peace will be with you. [NIV] Finally, brethren, farewell. Become complete. Be of good comfort, be of **one mind**, live in peace; and the God of love and peace will be with you. [NKJV] Dear brothers and sisters, I close my letter with these last words: Rejoice. Change your ways. Encourage each other. Live in **harmony** and peace. Then the God of love and peace will be with you. [NLT] Λοιπόν, ἀδελφοί, χαίρετε· καταρτίζεσθε, παρακαλεῖσθε, **τὸ αὐτὸ φρονεῖτε**, εἰρηνεύετε· καὶ ὁ Θεὸς τῆς ἀγάπης καὶ εἰρήνης ἔσται μεθ' ὑμῶν. [GNS] Λοιπόν, ἀδελφοί, χαίρετε, καταρτίζεσθε, παρακαλεῖσθε, **τὸ αὐτὸ φρονεῖτε**, εἰρηνεύετε, καὶ ὁ θεὸς τῆς ἀγάπης καὶ εἰρήνης ἔσται μεθ' ὑμῶν. [GNT]	

#2349
Listen Carefully
 	
Let these [sayings] sink down into your ears–KJV
Let these [words] sink into your ears–NASB
Listen carefully–NIV
Let these [words] sink down into your ears–NKJV
Listen to me–NLT
 	
POSB REFERENCE (Lk.9:44-45; esp. v.44) Note 4, point 1
	Θέσθε ὑμεῖς εἰς τὰ ὦτα ὑμῶν = *Thesthe humeis eis ta öta humön*
	Pronunciation: [thes-theh hu-meh-ees ice tah o-tah hu-mown]
	Parsing *Thesthe* (part of speech): verb
	    Mood—imperative
	    Tense—aorist
	    Voice—middle
	    Person—2nd person
	    Number—plural
	    Stem or root—from τίθημι
	Parsing *öta* (part of speech): noun
	    Case—accusative
	    Gender—neuter
	    Number—plural
	    Stem or root—from οὖς, ὠτός
	Concordance References:
	⇒ Strong's #1519 eis + 3588 ho +3775 ous + 4771 su + 4771 su + 5087 tithemi
	⇒ NIV # 1650+3836+4044+5148+5148+5502 cis ho ous su su tithēmi [Listen carefully]
	⇒ NASB #1519 eis + 3588 ho +3775 ous + 4771 su + 4771 su + 5087 tithemi
	
	Luke 9:44
	Let these sayings sink down into your ears: for the Son of man shall be delivered into the hands of men. [KJV]
	"**Let these words sink into your ears**; for the Son of Man is going to be delivered into the hands of men." [NASB]
	"**Listen carefully** to what I am about to tell you: The Son of Man is going to be betrayed into the hands of men." [NIV]
	"**Let these words sink down into your ears**, for the Son of Man is about to be betrayed into the hands of men." [NKJV]
	"**Listen to me** and remember what I say. The Son of Man is going to be betrayed." [NLT]
	Θέσθε ὑμεῖς εἰς τὰ ὦτα ὑμῶν τοὺς λόγους τούτους· ὁ γὰρ υἱὸς τοῦ ἀνθρώπου μέλλει παραδίδοσθαι εἰς χεῖρας ἀνθρώπων. [GNS]
	Θέσθε ὑμεῖς εἰς τὰ ὦτα ὑμῶν τοὺς λόγους τούτους· ὁ γὰρ υἱὸς τοῦ ἀνθρώπου μέλλει παραδίδοσθαι εἰς χεῖρας ἀνθρώπων. [GNT]
		Put these sayings into your ears. Give special attention to them.
		
		Practical Application
		Apparently, the disciples began to think about the earthly reign of Jesus. The power of God demonstrated that Jesus had the power to conquer the earth and subject all men to Himself. Their hopes were stirred.
		But note what Jesus did. He rebuked their thoughts of a physical and material Messiah. He again had to show them that God's Messiah had to die in order to save the world.

ENGLISH WORD	GREEK WORD AND VERSE	THE WORD MEANS...

#2350
Listen To
 	
Heed–KJV
Pay...attention to–NASB
Pay...attention...to–NIV
Heed–NKJV
Listen...to–NLT
 	
POSB REFERENCE
(Heb.2:1)
Note 1
	προσέχειν = *prosechein*
	Pronunciation: [pros-ekh'-een]
	Parsing (part of speech): verb
	    Mood—infinitive
	    Tense—present
	    Voice—active
	    Stem or root—from προσέχω
	Concordance References:
	⇒ Strong's #4337 prosechō
	⇒ NIV #4668 prosechō
	⇒ NASB #4337 prosechō
	
	Hebrews 2:1
	Therefore we ought to give the more earnest **heed** to the things which we have heard, lest at any time we should let *them* slip. [KJV]
	For this reason we must **pay** much closer **attention to** what we have heard, lest we drift away *from it.* [NASB]
	We must **pay** more careful **attention**, therefore, **to** what we have heard, so that we do not drift away. [NIV]
	Therefore we must give the more earnest **heed** to the things we have heard, lest we drift away. [NKJV]
	So we must **listen** very carefully **to** the truth we have heard, or we may drift away from it. [NLT]
	Διὰ τοῦτο δεῖ περισσοτέρως ἡμᾶς **προσέχειν** τοῖς ἀκουσθεῖσι, μή ποτε παραρρυῶμεν. [GNS]
	Διὰ τοῦτο δεῖ περισσοτέρως **προσέχειν** ἡμᾶς τοῖς ἀκουσθεῖσιν, μήποτε παραρυῶμεν. [GNT]
		To pay attention to; to heed; to listen to; to listen very carefully; to be careful; to be on guard; to consider carefully; to keep watch over.
		
		Practical Application
		Note how intense the warning is: we must *listen to* the gospel. We must *listen very carefully to* the gospel. We are to pay the utmost attention to the gospel of salvation:
		⇒ to listen more closely than ever before.
		⇒ to pay more attention than ever before.

#2351
Listen To Appeal
 	
Be of good comfort–KJV
Be comforted–NASB
Listen to appeal–NIV
Be of good comfort–NKJV
Encourage each other–NLT
 	
POSB REFERENCE
(2 Cor.13:11-13; esp. v.11)
Note 3
	παρακαλεῖσθε = *parakaleisthe*
	Pronunciation: [par-ak-al-eehs'-the]
	Parsing (part of speech): verb
	    Mood—imperative
	    Tense—present
	    Voice—passive
	    Person—2nd person
	    Number—plural
	    Stem or root—from παρακαλέω
	Concordance References:
	⇒ Strong's #3870 parakaleō
	⇒ NIV #4151 parakaleō
	⇒ NASB #3870 parakaleō
	
	2 Cor. 13:11
	Finally, brethren, farewell. Be perfect, **be of good comfort**, be of one mind, live in peace; and the God of love and peace shall be with you. [KJV]
	Finally, brethren, rejoice, be made complete, **be comforted**, be like-minded, live in peace; and the God of love and peace shall be with you. [NASB]
	Finally, brothers, good-by. Aim for perfection, **listen to** my **appeal**, be of one mind, live in peace. And the God of love and peace will be with you. [NIV]
	Finally, brethren, farewell. Become complete. **Be of good comfort**, be of one mind, live in peace; and the God of love and peace will be with you. [NKJV]
	Dear brothers and sisters, I close my letter with these last words: Rejoice. Change your ways. **Encourage each other**. Live in harmony and peace. Then the God of love and peace will be with you. [NLT]
	Λοιπόν, ἀδελφοί, χαίρετε· καταρτίζεσθε, **παρακαλεῖσθε**, τὸ αὐτὸ φρονεῖτε, εἰρηνεύετε· καὶ ὁ Θεὸς τῆς ἀγάπης καὶ εἰρήνης ἔσται μεθ' ὑμῶν. [GNS]
	Λοιπόν, ἀδελφοί, χαίρετε, καταρτίζεσθε, **παρακαλεῖσθε**, τὸ αὐτὸ φρονεῖτε, εἰρηνεύετε· καὶ ὁ Θεὸς τῆς ἀγάπης καὶ εἰρήνης ἔσται μεθ' ὑμῶν. [GNT]
		To be comforted; to encourage each other; to cheer up; to be assured, consoled. The word could also mean "be exhorted"; that is, listen and heed what I have said.
		
		Practical Application
		If the believers of the church would do these four things...
		• aim for perfection
		• listen to Paul's appeal
		• be of one mind
		• live in peace
		
		...then the God of love and peace would be with them. Note that God is the Author, the Giver of love and peace. Therefore, if a man wishes to know true love and true peace, he must accept the challenge to live accordingly.

#2352 **Listen To Me** Let these [sayings] sink down into	Θέσθε ὑμεῖς εἰς τὰ ὦτα ὑμῶν = *Thesthe humeis eis ta ōta humōn* Pronunciation: [thes-theh hu-meh-ees ice tah o-tah hu-mown] Parsing *Thesthe* (part of speech): verb Mood—imperative	Put these sayings into your ears; give special attention to them; listen to me; listen carefully. **Practical Application** Apparently, the disciples began to think about

ENGLISH WORD	GREEK WORD AND VERSE	THE WORD MEANS...

your ears–KJV
Let these [words] sink into your ears–NASB
Listen carefully–NIV
Let these [words] sink down into your ears–NKJV
Listen to me–NLT
 	
POSB REFERENCE
(Lk.9:44-45; esp. v.44)
Note 4, point 1
	Tense—aorist
	Voice—middle
	Person—2nd person
	Number—plural
	Stem or root—from τίθημι
	Parsing *ōta* (part of speech): noun
	    Case—accusative
	    Gender—neuter
	    Number—plural
	    Stem or root—from οὖς, ὠτός
	Concordance References:
	⇒ Strong's #1519 eis + 3588 ho +3775 ous + 4771 su + 4771 su + 5087 tithemi
	⇒ NIV # 1650+3836+4044+5148+5148+5502 eis ho ous su su tithëmi [Listen carefully]
	⇒ NASB #1519 eis + 3588 ho +3775 ous + 4771 su + 4771 su + 5087 tithemi
	
	Luke 9:44
	Let these sayings sink down into your ears: for the Son of man shall be delivered into the hands of men. [KJV]
	"**Let these words sink into your ears**; for the Son of Man is going to be delivered into the hands of men." [NASB]
	"**Listen carefully** to what I am about to tell you: The Son of Man is going to be betrayed into the hands of men." [NIV]
	"**Let these words sink down into your ears**, for the Son of Man is about to be betrayed into the hands of men." [NKJV]
	"**Listen to me** and remember what I say. The Son of Man is going to be betrayed." [NLT]
	Θέσθε ὑμεῖς εἰς τὰ ὦτα ὑμῶν τοὺς λόγους τούτους· ὁ γὰρ υἱὸς τοῦ ἀνθρώπου μέλλει παραδίδοσθαι εἰς χεῖρας ἀνθρώπων. [GNS]
	Θέσθε ὑμεῖς εἰς τὰ ὦτα ὑμῶν τοὺς λόγους τούτους· ὁ γὰρ υἱὸς τοῦ ἀνθρώπου μέλλει παραδίδοσθαι εἰς χεῖρας ἀνθρώπων. [GNT]
		the earthly reign of Jesus. The power of God demonstrated that Jesus had the power to conquer the earth and subject all men to Himself. Their hopes were stirred.
		    But note what Jesus did. He rebuked their thoughts of a physical and material Messiah. He again had to show them that God's Messiah had to die in order to save the world.

#2353
Listened–Listening
 	
Heard–KJV
Listening–NASB
Listening–NIV
Heard–NKJV
Listened–NLT
 	
POSB REFERENCE
(Acts 16:14)
Note 4
	ἤκουεν = *ëkouen*
	Pronunciation: [ey-koo'-ehn]
	Parsing (part of speech): verb
	    Mood—indicative
	    Tense—imperfect
	    Voice—active
	    Person—3rd person
	    Number—singular
	    Stem or root—from ἀκούω
	Concordance References:
	⇒ Strong's #191 akouö
	⇒ NIV #201 akouö
	⇒ NASB #191 akouö
	
	Acts 16:14
	And a certain woman named Lydia, a seller of purple, of the city of Thyatira, which worshipped God, **heard** *us*: whose heart the Lord opened, that she attended unto the things which were spoken of Paul. [KJV]
	And a certain woman named Lydia, from the city of Thyatira, a seller of purple fabrics, a worshiper of God, was **listening**; and the Lord opened her heart to respond to the things spoken by Paul. [NASB]
	One of those **listening** was a woman named Lydia, a dealer in purple cloth from the city of Thyatira, who was a worshiper of God. The Lord opened her heart to respond to Paul's message. [NIV]
	Now a certain woman named Lydia **heard** *us*. She was a seller of purple from the city of Thyatira, who worshiped God. The Lord opened her heart to heed the things spoken by Paul. [NKJV]
	One of them was Lydia from Thyatira, a merchant of expensive purple cloth. She was a worshiper of God. As
		Listening, listen, heard; to receive news of; to understand.
		
		Practical Application
		    The word "listening" (*ëkouen*) means she really perked up and paid attention. She listened and kept on listening, giving utmost attention to the gospel.

ENGLISH WORD	GREEK WORD AND VERSE	THE WORD MEANS...
	she **listened** to us, the Lord opened her heart, and she accepted what Paul was saying. [NLT] καί τις γυνὴ ὀνόματι Λυδία, πορφυρόπωλις, πόλεως Θυατείρων σεβομένη τὸν Θεόν, **ἤκουεν**· ἧς ὁ Κύριος διήνοιξε τὴν καρδίαν, προσέχειν τοῖς λαλουμένοις ὑπὸ τοῦ Παύλου. [GNS] καί τις γυνὴ ὀνόματι Λυδία, πορφυρόπωλις πόλεως Θυατείρων σεβομένη τὸν θεόν, **ἤκουεν**, ἧς ὁ κύριος διήνοιξεν τὴν καρδίαν προσέχειν τοῖς λαλουμένοις ὑπὸ τοῦ Παύλου. [GNT]	

#2354
 	
Listened Intently
 	
Gave heed–KJV
Giving attention–NASB
Paid close attention–NIV
Heeded–NKJV
Listened intently– NLT
 	
POSB REFERENCE
(Acts 8:6)
Note 2, point 2
	προσεῖχον = *proseichon*
	Pronunciation: [pros-eekh'-on]
	Parsing (part of speech): verb
	    Mood—indicative
	    Tense—imperfect
	    Voice—active
	    Person—3rd person
	    Number—plural
	    Stem or root—from προσέχω
	Concordance References:
	  ⇒ Strong's #4337 prosechö
	  ⇒ NIV #4668 prosechö
	  ⇒ NASB #4337 prosechö
	
	Acts 8:6
	And the people with one accord **gave heed** unto those things which Philip spake, hearing and seeing the miracles which he did. [KJV]
	And the multitudes with one accord were **giving attention** to what was said by Philip, as they heard and saw the signs which he was performing. [NASB]
	When the crowds heard Philip and saw the miraculous signs he did, they all **paid close attention** to what he said. [NIV]
	And the multitudes with one accord **heeded** the things spoken by Philip, hearing and seeing the miracles which he did. [NKJV]
	Crowds **listened intently** to what he had to say because of the miracles he did. [NLT]
	προσεῖχον τέ οἱ ὄχλοι τοῖς λεγομένοις ὑπὸ τοῦ Φιλίππου ὁμοθυμαδόν, ἐν τῷ ἀκούειν αὐτοὺς καὶ βλέπειν τὰ σημεῖα ἃ ἐποίει. [GNS]
	προσεῖχον δὲ οἱ ὄχλοι τοῖς λεγομένοις ὑπὸ τοῦ Φιλίππου ὁμοθυμαδὸν ἐν τῷ ἀκούειν αὐτοὺς καὶ βλέπειν τὰ σημεῖα ἃ ἐποίει· [GNT]
		To pay close attention; to give attention; to listen intently; to respond to; to keep watch over.
		
		Practical Application
		The believer must "listen intently;" must keep his mind and heart upon the message.

#2355
 	
Listening
 	
Hearing–KJV
Listening–NASB
Listening–NIV
Listening–NKJV
Discussing–NLT
 	
POSB REFERENCE
(Lk.2:46-47; esp. v.46)
Note 3, point 2a
	ἀκούοντα = *akouonta*
	Pronunciation: [ah-koo'-on-tah]
	Parsing (part of speech): verb
	    Mood—participle
	    Tense—present
	    Voice—active
	    Case—accusative
	    Gender—masculine
	    Number—singular
	    Stem or root—from ἀκούω
	Concordance References:
	  ⇒ Strong's #191 akouö
	  ⇒ NIV #201 akouö
	  ⇒ NASB #191 akouö
	
	Luke 2:46
	And it came to pass, that after three days they found him in the temple, sitting in the midst of the doctors, both **hearing** them, and asking them questions. [KJV]
	And it came about that after three days they found Him in the temple, sitting in the midst of the teachers, both **listening** to them, and asking them questions. [NASB]
	After three days they found him in the temple courts, sitting among the teachers, **listening** to them and asking them questions. [NIV]
	Now so it was *that* after three days they found Him in
		To listen to; to hear; to attend; to hearken; to perceive; to receive news of; to give heed to.
		
		Practical Application
		In this Scripture, Jesus was "listening" to what the teachers said. He listened closely, attentively, with rapt attention.

ENGLISH WORD	GREEK WORD AND VERSE	THE WORD MEANS...
	the temple, sitting in the midst of the teachers, both **listening** to them and asking them questions. [NKJV] Three days later they finally discovered him. He was in the Temple, sitting among the religious teachers, **discussing** deep questions with them. [NLT] καὶ ἐγένετο, μεθ' ἡμέρας τρεῖς εὗρον αὐτὸν ἐν τῷ ἱερῷ, καθεζόμενον ἐν μέσῳ τῶν διδασκάλων, καὶ **ἀκούοντα** αὐτῶν, καὶ ἐπερωτῶντα αὐτούς. [GNS] καὶ ἐγένετο μετὰ ἡμέρας τρεῖς εὗρον αὐτὸν ἐν τῷ ἱερῷ καθεζόμενον ἐν μέσῳ τῶν διδασκάλων καὶ **ἀκούοντα** αὐτῶν καὶ ἐπερωτῶντα αὐτούς· [GNT]	

#2356
Live
 	
Walk–KJV
Walk–NASB
Live–NIV
Walk–NKJV
Live–NLT
 	
POSB
REFERENCE
(Romans 6:3-5, esp. v.4)
Note 2, point 2b
	περιπατήσωμεν = *peripatēsōmen*
	Pronunciation: [per-ee-pat-ay'-so-mehn]
	Parsing (part of speech): verb
	  Mood—subjunctive
	  Tense—aorist
	  Voice—active
	  Person—1st person
	  Number—plural
	  Stem or root—from περιπατέω
	Concordance References:
	⇒ Strong's #4043 peripateō
	⇒ NIV #4344 peripateō
	⇒ NASB #4043 peripateō
	
	Romans 6:4
	Therefore we are buried with him by baptism into death: that like as Christ was raised up from the dead by the glory of the Father, even so we also should **walk** in newness of life. [KJV]
	
	Therefore we have been buried with Him through baptism into death, in order that as Christ was raised from the dead through the glory of the Father, so we too might **walk** in newness of life. [NASB]
	
	We were therefore buried with him through baptism into death in order that, just as Christ was raised from the dead through the glory of the Father, we too may **live** a new life. [NIV]
	
	Therefore we were buried with Him through baptism into death, that just as Christ was raised from the dead by the glory of the Father, even so we also should **walk** in newness of life. [NKJV]
	
	For we died and were buried with Christ by baptism. And just as Christ was raised from the dead by the glorious power of the Father, now we also may **live** new lives. [NLT]
	
	συνετάφημεν οὖν αὐτῷ διὰ τοῦ βαπτίσματος εἰς τὸν θάνατον· ἵνα ὥσπερ ἠγέρθη Χριστὸς ἐκ νεκρῶν διὰ τῆς δόξης τοῦ πατρός, οὕτως καὶ ἡμεῖς ἐν καινότητι ζωῆς **περιπατήσωμεν**. [GNS]
	
	συνετάφημεν οὖν αὐτῷ διὰ τοῦ βαπτίσματος εἰς τὸν θάνατον, ἵνα ὥσπερ ἠγέρθη Χριστὸς ἐκ νεκρῶν διὰ τῆς δόξης τοῦ πατρός, οὕτως καὶ ἡμεῖς ἐν καινότητι ζωῆς **περιπατήσωμεν**. [GNT]
		To walk; to go or move about; to live; to conduct oneself.
		
		Practical Application
		God's purpose for raising us up with Christ is dynamic and meaningful. It involves living in a whole new life. The word "live" (*peripatēsōmen*) means to walk about, to walk step by step, to control and order our behavior, to constantly and habitually live "a new life."
		
		Think about it for a moment. When Christ died, he laid aside His old life and left it behind Him. Therefore, when He arose, He took on a totally new life, a changed life, a resurrected life. It is His new life, His changed and resurrected life, that is given to us. In the Bible the word "new" often carries the idea of purity, righteousness, holiness, godliness. The believer...
		
		• receives a "newbirth" (1Peter1:23; 1 Peter 2:2).
		• receives a "new heart" (Ezekiel 11:19; Ezekiel 18:31).
		• becomes a "new creation" (2 Cor. 5:17; Galatians 6:15).
		• becomes a "new self" (Ephes. 4:24; Col. 3:10).
		
		God's very purpose for placing us in the resurrected life of Jesus Christ is that we might live in Christ, live soberly, righteously and godly in this present world. The true believer puts off the old man of sin and puts on the new man of righteousness and godliness. He lives a pure, clean, and holy life.

#2357
Live
 	
Rest–KJV
Abide–NASB
Live–NIV
Rest–NKJV
Rests–NLT
 	
POSB
REFERENCE
(Acts 2:25-28; esp. v.26)
Note 1, point 1c
	κατασκηνώσει = *kataskēnōsei*
	Pronunciation: [ka-tah-skay-no-seh-ee]
	Parsing (part of speech): verb
	  Mood—indicative
	  Tense—future
	  Voice—active
	  Person—3rd person
	  Number—singular
	  Stem or root—from κατασκηνόω
	Concordance References:
	⇒ Strong's #2681 kataskēnoō
	⇒ NIV #2942 kataskēnoō
	⇒ NASB #2681 kataskēnoō
	
	Acts 2:26
	Therefore did my heart rejoice, and my tongue was glad; moreover also my flesh shall **rest** in hope: [KJV]
		To live; to rest; to abide; to nest; to dwell.
		
		Practical Application
		The word "live" means to tabernacle or pitch a tent. Jesus' flesh rested, tabernacled, pitched its tent, encamped and made its abode upon hope—the hope of conquering death, of being resurrected. Hope of living forever was the basis and foundation of Jesus' life, that for which He lived. He focused His whole life upon the hope of the cross and of the glorious resurrection from the dead (cp. Paul's testimony—Phil. 3:7-16, esp. Phil. 3:11).

ENGLISH WORD	GREEK WORD AND VERSE	THE WORD MEANS...
	'THEREFORE MY HEART WAS GLAD AND MY TONGUE EXULTED; MOREOVER MY FLESH ALSO WILL **ABIDE** IN HOPE; [NASB] Therefore my heart is glad and my tongue rejoices; my body also will **live** in hope, [NIV] *Therefore my eart rejoiced, and my tongue was glad; Moreover my flesh also will **rest** in hope.* [NKJV] No wonder my heart is filled with joy, and my mouth shouts his praises! My body **rests** in hope. [NLT] Διὰ τοῦτο εὐφράνθη ἡ καρδία μου, καὶ ἠγαλλιάσατο ἡ γλῶσσά μου· ἔτι δὲ καὶ ἡ σάρξ μου **κατασκηνώσει** ἐπ' ἐλπίδι· [GNS] διὰ τοῦτο ηὐφράνθη ἡ καρδία μου καὶ ἠγαλλιάσατο ἡ γλῶσσά μου, ἔτι δὲ καὶ ἡ σάρξ μου **κατασκηνώσει** ἐπ' ἐλπίδι, [GNT]	

#2358
Live
 	
Conversation–KJV
Conduct–NASB
Conduct–NIV
Conduct–NKJV
Live–NLT
 	
POSB
REFERENCE
(Philip.1:27)
Note 1
	πολιτεύεσθε = *politeuesthe*
	Pronunciation: [pol-it-yoo'-ehs-theh]
	Parsing (part of speech): verb
	    Mood—imperative
	    Tense—present
	    Voice—middle or passive deponent
	    Person—2nd person
	    Number—plural
	    Stem or root—from πολιτεύομαι
	Concordance References:
	  ⇒ Strong's #4176 politeuomai
	  ⇒ NIV #4488 politeuomai
	  ⇒ NASB #4176 politeuomai
	
	Philip. 1:27
	Only let your **conversation** be as it becometh the gospel of Christ: that whether I come and see you, or else be absent, I may hear of your affairs, that ye stand fast in one spirit, with one mind striving together for the faith of the gospel; [KJV]
	
	Only **conduct** yourselves in a manner worthy of the gospel of Christ; so that whether I come and see you or remain absent, I may hear of you that you are standing firm in one spirit, with one mind striving together for the faith of the gospel; [NASB]
	
	Whatever happens, **conduct** yourselves in a manner worthy of the gospel of Christ. Then, whether I come and see you or only hear about you in my absence, I will know that you stand firm in one spirit, contending as one man for the faith of the gospel [NIV]
	
	Only let your **conduct** be worthy of the gospel of Christ, so that whether I come and see you or am absent, I may hear of your affairs, that you stand fast in one spirit, with one mind striving together for the faith of the gospel, [NKJV]
	
	But whatever happens to me, you must **live** in a manner worthy of the Good News about Christ, as citizens of heaven. Then, whether I come and see you again or only hear about you, I will know that you are standing side by side, fighting together for the Good News. [NLT]
	
	μόνον ἀξίως τοῦ εὐαγγελίου τοῦ Χριστοῦ **πολιτεύεσθε**, ἵνα εἴτε ἐλθὼν καὶ ἰδὼν ὑμᾶς, εἴτε ἀπὼν, ἀκούσω τὰ περὶ ὑμῶν, ὅτι στήκετε ἐν ἑνὶ πνεύματι, μιᾷ ψυχῇ συναθλοῦντες τῇ πίστει τοῦ εὐαγγελίου, [GNS]
	
	Μόνον ἀξίως τοῦ εὐαγγελίου τοῦ Χριστοῦ **πολιτεύεσθε**, ἵνα εἴτε ἐλθὼν καὶ ἰδὼν ὑμᾶς εἴτε ἀπὼν ἀκούσω τὰ περὶ ὑμῶν, ὅτι στήκετε ἐν ἑνὶ πνεύματι, μιᾷ ψυχῇ συναθλοῦντες τῇ πίστει τοῦ εὐαγγελίου [GNT]
		Behavior; conduct; to live one's life.
		
		### Practical Application
		A.T. Robertson points out that this word is used only twice in the New Testament (Acts 23:1; Phil. 1:27) (*Word Pictures in the New Testament*, Vol.4, p.441). Usually, when the New Testament refers to behavior or conduct, it uses a word meaning how a person should walk about day by day (*peripatein*). But Paul switches the word in writing to the Philippians. Why? The reason is significant. Philippi was a proud Roman colony. In fact, it was famous as a miniature Rome. A city became a Roman colony by one of two ways. At first, Rome founded colonies throughout the outer reaches of the Empire to keep the peace and to guard against invasions from barbaric hordes. Veteran soldiers, ready for retirement, were usually granted citizenship if they would go out to settle these colonies. Later on, however, a city was granted the distinctive title of a Roman Colony for loyalty and service to the Empire. The distinctive thing about these colonies was their fanatic loyalty to Rome. The citizens kept all their Roman ties: the Roman language, titles, customs, affairs, and dress. They refused to allow any infiltration of local influence whatsoever. They totally rejected the influence of the world around them. They were Roman colonists within an alien environment.
		
		This is the reason Paul uses the word *politeuesthe*. It means conduct and behavior; but more accurately, it means the conduct and behavior of *citizenship*, of a person who is the citizen of a great nation. The Philippian church knew exactly what Paul was saying: they were citizens of heaven. Therefore, they must...
		
		• keep their close ties with heaven.
		• speak the clean and pure language of heaven.
		• bear the title of heaven, Christian, and do so proudly.
		• bear witness to the customs of heaven.
		• carry on the affairs of heaven.
		• dress as a citizen of heaven.
		• allow no infiltration of worldly influence whatsoever.
		• live and conduct themselves as a heavenly colony within a polluted and dying environment.

ENGLISH WORD	GREEK WORD AND VERSE	THE WORD MEANS...

#2359
Live
 	
Walk–KJV
Walk–NASB
Walk–NIV
Walk–NKJV
Live–NLT
 	
POSB
REFERENCE
(1 Jn.2:6)
Note 4
	περιπατεῖν = *peripatein*
	Pronunciation: [per-ee-pat-een]
	Parsing (part of speech): verb
	    Mood—infinitive
	    Tense—present
	    Voice—active
	    Stem or root—from περιπατέω
	Concordance References:
	  ⇒ Strong's #4043 peripateö
	  ⇒ NIV #4344 peripateö
	  ⇒ NASB #4043 peripateö
	
	1 John 2:6
	He that saith he abideth in him ought himself also so to **walk**, even as he walked. [KJV]
	The one who says he abides in Him ought himself to **walk** in the same manner as He walked. [NASB]
	Whoever claims to live in him must **walk** as Jesus did. [NIV]
	He who says he abides in Him ought himself also to **walk** just as He walked. [NKJV]
	Those who say they **live** in God should live their lives as Christ did. [NLT]
	ὁ λέγων ἐν αὐτῷ μένειν ὀφείλει, καθὼς ἐκεῖνος περιεπάτησε, καὶ αὐτὸς οὕτω **περιπατεῖν**. [GNS]
	ὁ λέγων ἐν αὐτῷ μένειν ὀφείλει καθὼς ἐκεῖνος περιεπάτησεν καὶ αὐτὸς [οὕτως] **περιπατεῖν**. [GNT]
		To walk; to live; to act; to behave. The word "live" (*peripatein*) is continuous action. It means to keep on living; to continuously live.
		
		Practical Application
		If a person says that he abides in Christ, he must be a responsible person. He should live as Jesus Christ lived. In fact, the word s*hould* means debt, constraint, obligation. The person who professes Jesus Christ, who claims that he knows God, is obligated to live as Jesus Christ lived. He is in debt to live as Christ lived. How did Christ walk upon earth? He lived...
		• believing and trusting God.
		• worshipping and praying to God.
		• fellowshipping and communing with God.
		• giving and sacrificing all He was and had to God.
		• seeking and following after God.
		• teaching and telling others about God.
		• loving and caring for others just as God said to do.
		• obeying and keeping all of God's commandments.
		This is the responsible man, the man who lives what he professes. If he professes to know God, he lives even as the Lord Jesus Christ lived upon earth. He believes and trusts God; he worships and prays to God, and he does all the other things that Christ did. He walks in the footsteps of Christ, doing exactly what Christ did. This is the person who knows God.

#2360
Live A Life
 	
Walk–KJV
Walk–NASB
Live a life–NIV
Walk–NKJV
Way you live–NLT
 	
POSB
REFERENCE
(Col.1:10)
Note 2
	περιπατῆσαι = *peripatēsai*
	Pronunciation: [per-ee-pat-ays'-ah-ee]
	Parsing (part of speech): verb
	    Mood—infinitive
	    Tense—aorist
	    Voice—active
	    Stem or root—from περιπατέω
	Concordance References:
	  ⇒ Strong's #4043 peripateö
	  ⇒ NIV #4344 peripateö
	  ⇒ NASB #4043 peripateö
	
	Col. 1:10
	That ye might **walk** worthy of the Lord unto all pleasing, being fruitful in every good work, and increasing in the knowledge of God; [KJV]
	So that you may **walk** in a manner worthy of the Lord, to please *Him* in all respects, bearing fruit in every good work and increasing in the knowledge of God; [NASB]
	And we pray this in order that you may **live a life** worthy of the Lord and may please him in every way: bearing fruit in every good work, growing in the knowledge of God, [NIV]
	That you may **walk** worthy of the Lord, fully pleasing *Him,* being fruitful in every good work and increasing in the knowledge of God; [NKJV]
	Then the **way you live** will always honor and please the Lord,' and you will continually do good, kind things for others. All the while, you will learn to know God better and better. [NLT]
	περιπατῆσαι ὑμᾶς ἀξίως τοῦ Κυρίου εἰς πᾶσαν ἀρεσκείαν, ἐν παντὶ ἔργῳ ἀγαθῷ καρποφοροῦντες καὶ αὐξανόμενοι εἰς τὴν ἐπιγνώσιν τοῦ Θεοῦ· [GNS]
	περιπατῆσαι ἀξίως τοῦ κυρίου εἰς πᾶσαν ἀρεσκείαν, ἐν παντὶ ἔργῳ ἀγαθῷ καρποφοροῦντες καὶ αὐξανόμενοι τῇ ἐπιγνώσει τοῦ θεοῦ, [GNT]
		To live a life; to walk; to conduct oneself; how a person's lives his life
		
		Practical Application
		Knowing the will of God is of no value until we have committed our lives to do it.
		  ⇒ The phrase "live a life" (*peripatesai*) means that we *set* our lives—our behavior and conduct—after Christ.
		  ⇒ The word "worthy" (*axios*) means to have the weight of or to weigh as much as something else (Kenneth Wuest, *Ephesians and Colossians,* Vol.1, p.176).
		
		This means an amazing thing: our life is to weigh as much as the life of Christ. Our conduct is to conform to the will of God as much as the conduct of Christ. We are to live a life just as worthy as the life of Christ. The will of God is to control our behavior as much as it did the behavior of Christ.

ENGLISH WORD	GREEK WORD AND VERSE	THE WORD MEANS...

#2361
 	
 Live A Life
 	
 Shew–KJV
 Show–NASB
 Show–NIV
 Show–NKJV
 Live a Life–NLT
 	
 POSB REFERENCE
 (Jas 3:13)
 Note 1
	δειξάτω = *deixatö*
	 Pronunciation: [di-zah-tow']
	 Parsing (part of speech): verb
	     Mood—imperative
	     Tense—aorist
	     Voice—active
	     Person—3rd person
	     Number—singular
	     Stem or root—from δείκνυμι
	 Concordance References:
	 ⇒ Strong's #1166 deiknumi
	 ⇒ NIV #1259 deiknumi
	 ⇒ NASB #1166 deiknumi
	
	 James 3:13
	 Who *is* a wise man and endued with knowledge among you? let him **show** out of a good conversation his works with meekness of wisdom. [KJV]
	 Who among you is wise and understanding? Let him **show** by his good behavior his deeds in the gentleness of wisdom. [NASB]
	 Who is wise and understanding among you? Let him **show** it by his good life, by deeds done in the humility that comes from wisdom. [NIV]
	 Who *is* wise and understanding among you? Let him **show** by good conduct *that* his works *are done* in the meekness of wisdom. [NKJV]
	 If you are wise and understand God's ways, **live a life** of steady goodness so that only good deeds will pour forth. And if you don't brag about the good you do, then you will be truly wise! [NLT]
	 Τίς σοφὸς καὶ ἐπιστήμων ἐν ὑμῖν; **δειξάτω** ἐκ τῆς καλῆς ἀναστροφῆς τὰ ἔργα αὐτοῦ ἐν πραΰτητι σοφίας. [GNS]
	 Τίς σοφὸς καὶ ἐπιστήμων ἐν ὑμῖν; **δειξάτω** ἐκ τῆς καλῆς avnastrofῆς τὰ ἔργα αὐτοῦ ἐν πραΰτητι σοφίας. [GNT]
		To show; to live a life; to prove; to reveal; to bring about.
		
		 Practical Application
		 Note the words "live a life" (*deixatö*). It is one word in the Greek, and it is emphatic, strongly emphasized. This means that the wise teacher will strongly show forth these traits. These two traits will be clearly seen in the wise teacher's life: those who are "wise and understanding."

#2362
 	
 Live For Themselves
 	
 Contentious–KJV
 Selfishly ambitious– NASB
 Self-seeking–NIV
 Self-seeking–NKJV
 Live for themselves– NLT
 	
 POSB REFERENCE
 (Romans 2:8)
 Deeper Study #4
	ἐριθείας = *eritheias*
	 Pronunciation: [er-ith-i'-ahs]
	 Parsing (part of speech): noun
	     Case—genitive
	     Gender—feminine
	     Number—singular
	     Stem or root—from ἐριθεία, ας
	 Concordance References:
	 ⇒ Strong's #1537 ek + 2052 eritheia
	 ⇒ NIV #2249 eritheia
	 ⇒ NASB #2052 eritheia
	
	 Romans 2:8
	 But unto them that are **contentious**, and do not obey the truth, but obey unrighteousness, indignation and wrath, [KJV]
	 but to those who are **selfishly ambitious** and do not obey the truth, but obey unrighteousness, wrath and indignation. [NASB]
	 But for those who are **self-seeking** and who reject the truth and follow evil, there will be wrath and anger. [NIV]
	 But to those who are **self-seeking** and do not obey the truth, but obey unrighteousness—indignation and wrath, [NKJV]
	 But he will pour out his anger and wrath on those who **live for themselves**, who refuse to obey the truth and practice evil deeds. [NLT]
	 τοῖς δὲ ἐξ **ἐριθείας**, καὶ ἀπειθοῦσι μὲν τῇ ἀληθείᾳ πειθομένοις δὲ τῇ ἀδικίᾳ, θυμὸς καὶ ὀργὴ, [GNS]
	 τοῖς δὲ ἐξ **ἐριθείας** καὶ ἀπειθοῦσι τῇ ἀληθείᾳ πειθομένοις δὲ τῇ ἀδικίᾳ ὀργὴ καὶ θυμός. [GNT]
		To strive; to struggle; to fight; to quarrel; to wrangle; to argue; to debate; to be divisive, factious, contentious, argumentative, and belligerent; to live for self; selfish rivalry; selfish ambition.
		
		 Practical Application
		 The evil-doer does not like what God says; therefore, he strives against it. He wrangles and wrestles, struggles and fights against God. He refuses to buckle under and surrender to God's will. When dealing with God, the evil-doer lives for himself.

ENGLISH WORD	GREEK WORD AND VERSE	THE WORD MEANS...

#2363
Live In
 	
Dwell in–KJV
Dwell within–NASB
Dwell in–NIV
Dwell in–NKJV
Live in–NLT
 	
POSB
REFERENCE
(Col.3:16)
Note 2, point 1
	ἐνοικείτω ἐν = enoikeitō en
	Pronunciation: [en-oy-keh'-o en]
	Parsing (part of speech): verb
	  Mood—imperative
	  Tense—present
	  Voice—active
	  Person—3rd person
	  Number—singular
	  Stem or root—from ἐνοικέω
	Concordance References:
	⇒ Strong's #1722+1774 en enoikeō
	⇒ NIV #1877+1940 en enoikeō [dwell in]
	⇒ NASB #1722+1774 en enoikeō
	
	Col. 3:16
	Let the word of Christ **dwell in** you richly in all wisdom; teaching and admonishing one another in psalms and hymns and spiritual songs, singing with grace in your hearts to the Lord. [KJV]
	Let the word of Christ richly **dwell within** you, with all wisdom teaching and admonishing one another with psalms and hymns and spiritual songs, singing with thankfulness in your hearts to God. [NASB]
	Let the word of Christ **dwell in** you richly as you teach and admonish one another with all wisdom, and as you sing psalms, hymns and spiritual songs with gratitude in your hearts to God. [NIV]
	Let the word of Christ **dwell in** you richly in all wisdom, teaching and admonishing one another in psalms and hymns and spiritual songs, singing with grace in your hearts to the Lord. [NKJV]
	Let the words of Christ, in all their richness, **live in** your hearts and make you wise. Use his words to teach and counsel each other. Sing psalms and hymns and spiritual songs to God with thankful hearts. [NLT]
	ὁ λόγος τοῦ Χριστοῦ **ἐνοικείτω ἐν** ὑμῖν πλουσίως, ἐν πάσῃ σοφίᾳ· διδάσκοντες καὶ νουθετοῦντες ἑαυτοὺς ψαλμοῖς, καὶ ὕμνοις, καὶ ᾠδαῖς πνευματικαῖς, ἐν χάριτι ᾄδοντες ἐν τῇ καρδίᾳ ὑμῶν τῷ Κυρίῳ. [GNS]
	ὁ λόγος τοῦ Χριστοῦ **ἐνοικείτω ἐν** ὑμῖν πλουσίως, ἐν πάσῃ σοφίᾳ διδάσκοντες καὶ νουθετοῦντες ἑαυτούς, ψαλμοῖς ὕμνοις ᾠδαῖς πνευματικαῖς ἐν [τῇ] χάριτι ᾄδοντες ἐν ταῖς καρδίαις ὑμῶν τῷ θεῷ. [GNT]
		To dwell in; to live in; to be at home or to make a home; to abide or dwell within.
		
		Practical Application
		The choice is up to the believer: the Word of Christ does not naturally live within the believer's heart. The believer must make room within his heart for the Word of Christ. He must let the Word of Christ enter his heart and make a home within his life. He must let the Word of Christ live and abide in his heart. The believer must clean out all the old furnishings of his life and let the Word of Christ settle down as the permanent resident within his heart.

#2364
Live In
Harmony
With
 	
One mind–KJV
Harmonious–NASB
Live in harmony
with–NIV
One mind–NKJV
One mind–NLT
 	
POSB
REFERENCE
(1 Pt.3:8)
Note 1
	ὁμόφρονες = homophrones
	Pronunciation: [hom-of'-ron-ehs]
	Parsing (part of speech): adjective
	  Case—nominative
	  Gender—masculine
	  Number—plural
	  Stem or root—from ὁμόφρων, ον
	Concordance References:
	⇒ Strong's #3675 homophrōn
	⇒ NIV #3939 homophrōn
	⇒ NASB #3675 homophrōn
	
	1 Peter 3:8
	Finally, *be ye* all of **one mind**, having compassion one of another, love as brethren, *be* pitiful, *be* courteous: [KJV]
	To sum up, let all be **harmonious**, sympathetic, brotherly, kindhearted, and humble in spirit; [NASB]
	Finally, all of you, **live in harmony with** one another; be sympathetic, love as brothers, be compassionate and humble. [NIV]
	Finally, all *of you be* of **one mind**, having compassion for one another; love as brothers, *be* tenderhearted, *be* courteous; [NKJV]
	Finally, all of you should be of **one mind**, full of sympathy toward each other, loving one another with tender
		To live in harmony; to be of one mind; to be harmonious; to be like-minded; to be of the same mind.
		
		Practical Application
		Believers must live in harmony (*homophrones*). Believers must keep their minds on the same things. They must focus their minds upon Jesus Christ and His mission.

ENGLISH WORD	GREEK WORD AND VERSE	THE WORD MEANS...

#2369
Live Wisely
 	
Sober minded–KJV
Sensible–NASB
Self-controlled–NIV
Sober-minded–NKJV
Live wisely–NLT
 	
**POSB
REFERENCE**
(Tit.2:6)
Note 5
	σωφρονεῖν = *sōphronein*
	Pronunciation: [so-fron-een]
	Parsing (part of speech): verb
	  Mood—infinitive
	  Tense—present
	  Voice—active
	  Stem or root—from σωφρονέω
	Concordance References:
	  ⇒ Strong's #4993 sōphroneō
	  ⇒ NIV #5404 sōphroneō
	  ⇒ NASB #4993 sōphroneō
	
	Titus 2:6
	Young men likewise exhort to be **sober minded**. [KJV]
	  Likewise urge the young men to be **sensible**; [NASB]
	  Similarly, encourage the young men to be **self-controlled**. [NIV]
	  Likewise exhort the young men to be **sober-minded**, [NKJV]
	  In the same way, encourage the young men to **live wisely** in all they do. [NLT]
	  Τοὺς νεωτέρους ὡσαύτως παρακάλει **σωφρονεῖν**· [GNS]
	  τοὺς νεωτέρους ὡσαύτως παρακάλει **σωφρονεῖν** [GNT]
		To be self controlled; to be sober minded; to have sober judgment; to be clear minded; to be sensible; to live wisely; to be serious; to be temperate, controlled, disciplined, restrained; curbing emotions, passions, and desires.
		
		Practical Application
		What does it mean to "live wisely?" It means to have a mind that is sound, sensible, and focused upon pure and clean thoughts and meaningful things. It means to control one's mind and life and to keep them focused upon the purpose, meaning, and significance of life. It means to control everything in life. This is critical for young men.

#2370
Live With
 	
Communion–KJV
Fellowship–NASB
Fellowship–NIV
Communion–NKJV
Live with–NLT
 	
**POSB
REFERENCE**
(2 Cor.6:14-16; esp.
v.14)
Note 2, point 2
	κοινωνία = *koinōnia*
	Pronunciation: [koy-nohn-ee'-ah]
	Parsing (part of speech): noun
	  Case—nominative
	  Gender—feminine
	  Number—singular
	  Stem or root—from κοινωνία, ας
	Concordance References:
	  ⇒ Strong's #2842 koinōnia
	  ⇒ NIV #3126 koinōnia
	  ⇒ NASB #2842 koinōnia
	
	2 Cor. 6:14
	Be ye not unequally yoked together with unbelievers: for what fellowship hath righteousness with unrighteousness? and what **communion** hath light with darkness? [KJV]
	  Do not be bound together with unbelievers; for what partnership have righteousness and lawlessness, or what **fellowship** has light with darkness? [NASB]
	  Do not be yoked together with unbelievers. For what do righteousness and wickedness have in common? Or what **fellowship** can light have with darkness? [NIV]
	  Do not be unequally yoked together with unbelievers. For what fellowship has righteousness with lawlessness? And what **communion** has light with darkness? [NKJV]
	  Don't team up with those who are unbelievers. How can goodness be a partner with wickedness? How can light **live with** darkness? [NLT]
	  Μὴ γίνεσθε ἑτεροζυγοῦντες ἀπίστοις· τίς γὰρ μετοχὴ δικαιοσύνῃ καὶ ἀνομίᾳ; τίς δὲ **κοινωνία** φωτὶ πρὸς σκότος; [GNS]
	  Μὴ γίνεσθε ἑτεροζυγοῦντες ἀπίστοις· τίς γὰρ μετοχὴ δικαιοσύνῃ καὶ ἀνομίᾳ, ἢ τίς **κοινωνία** φωτὶ πρὸς σκότος; [GNT]
		Fellowship; communion; to live with; to share; to be in union, in partnership, in a bound fellowship; to be closely bound together; to have a close, mutual relationship.
		
		Practical Application
		It means to be so closely bound together that there is open and mutual sharing: what one has belongs to the other. The point is clear: there is no such fellowship or union between light and darkness. On the contrary, light and darkness are mutually exclusive, of different natures entirely. They cannot coexist.

#2371
Live With
 	
Dwell with–KJV
Live with–NASB
Live with–NIV
Dwell with–NKJV
Give honor–NLT
	συνοικοῦντες = *sunoikountes*
	Pronunciation: [soon-oy-koon-tehs]
	Parsing (part of speech): verb
	  Mood—participle (imperative sense)
	  Tense—present
	  Voice—active
	  Case—nominative
	  Gender—masculine
	  Person—2nd person
	  Number—plural
		To live with; to dwell with; to remain with; to reside with; to dwell together; to give honor.
		
		Practical Application
		Alan Stibbs points out that it is a word that is often used in the Greek for sexual intercourse. It is similar to the Hebrew verb *to know* which means that a man and woman *know* each other sexually (cp. Genesis 4:1; Matthew 1:25). (*The*

ENGLISH WORD	GREEK WORD AND VERSE	THE WORD MEANS...
POSB REFERENCE (1 Pt.3:7) Note 1	Stem or root—from συνοικέω Concordance References: ⇒ Strong's #4924 sunoikeō ⇒ NIV #5324 sunoikeō ⇒ NASB #4924 sunoikeō **1 Peter 3:7** Likewise, ye husbands, **dwell with** *them* according to knowledge, giving honour unto the wife, as unto the weaker vessel, and as being heirs together of the grace of life; that your prayers be not hindered. [KJV] You husbands likewise, **live with** *your wives* in an understanding way, as with a weaker vessel, since she is a woman; and grant her honor as a fellow heir of the grace of life, so that your prayers may not be hindered. [NASB] Husbands, in the same way be considerate as you **live with** your wives, and treat them with respect as the weaker partner and as heirs with you of the gracious gift of life, so that nothing will hinder your prayers. [NIV] Husbands, likewise, **dwell with** *them* with understanding, giving honor to the wife, as to the weaker vessel, and as *being* heirs together of the grace of life, that your rayers may not be hindered. [NKJV] In the same way, you husbands must **give honor** to your wives. Treat her with understanding as you live together. She may be weaker than you are, but she is your equal partner in God's gift of new life. If you don't treat her as you should, your prayers will not be heard. [NLT] Οἱ ἄνδρες ὁμοίως, **συνοικοῦντες** κατὰ γνῶσιν, ὡς ἀσθενεστέρῳ σκεύει τῷ γυναικείῳ ἀπονέμοντες τιμήν, ὡς καὶ συγκληρονόμοι χάριτος ζωῆς, εἰς τὸ μὴ ἐκκόπτεσθαι τὰς προσευχὰς ὑμῶν. [GNS] Οἱ ἄνδρες ὁμοίως, **συνοικοῦντες** κατὰ γνῶσιν ὡς ἀσθενεστέρῳ σκεύει τῷ γυναικείῳ, ἀπονέμοντες τιμήν ὡς καὶ συγκληρονόμοις χάριτος ζωῆς εἰς τὸ μὴ ἐγκόπτεσθαι τὰς προσευχὰς ὑμῶν. [GNT]	*First Epistle General of Peter.* "The Tyndale New Testament Commentaries," p.127). The point is this: the husband is to *live with his wife* and with no one else. He is not to *know* anyone else; he is not to have sexual intercourse with any other woman. The husband has a wife and he is to live with her in purity, righteousness, and holiness, and not as an adulterer. Note one other fact as well: to live with his wife means that he is not to be gone all of the time. He stays at home and lives with her: he is a close and supportive companion. He is not out and away from the home all of the time pursuing his own interests and hobbies. A good husband dwells at home; he is close to his wife and he is supportive of her in all of life. In fact, the term *live with* actually means to live together. The husband and wife are a team; they are as one body, one body that lives and dwells and moves together. This is not to do away with individuality. But individuality never has been and never will be the problem within a marriage of normal people. The problem with normal people will always be denying self and sacrificially giving oneself to one's spouse. *Husbands* must always remember this: they are to live with—to live and move and have their being with—their wives.

#2372
Lives
 	
Dwelleth–KJV
Dwell–NASB
Lives–NIV
Dwells–NKJV
Lives–NLT
 	
POSB REFERENCE (Col.2:9-10; esp. v.9) Note 2, point 1
	κατοικεῖ = *katoikei*
	Pronunciation: [kat-oy-keh'-ee]
	Parsing (part of speech): verb
	    Mood—indicative
	    Tense—present
	    Voice—active
	    Person—3rd person
	    Number—singular
	    Stem or root—from **κατοικέω**
	Concordance References:
	⇒ Strong's #2730 katoikeō
	⇒ NIV #2997 katoikeō
	⇒ NASB #2730 katoikeō
	
	Col. 2:9
	For in him **dwelleth** all the fulness of the Godhead bodily. [KJV]
	For in Him all the fulness of Deity **dwells** in bodily form, [NASB]
	For in Christ all the fullness of the Deity **lives** in bodily form, [NIV]
	For in Him **dwells** all the fullness of the Godhead bodily; [NKJV]
	For in Christ the fullness of God **lives** in a human body, [NLT]
	ὅτι ἐν αὐτῷ **κατοικεῖ** πᾶν τὸ πλήρωμα τῆς θεότητος σωματικῶς, [GNS]
	ὅτι ἐν αὐτῷ **κατοικεῖ** πᾶν τὸ πλήρωμα τῆς θεότητος σωματικῶς, [GNT]
		Lives, dwells; to live in. The word *"lives"* (*katoikei*) means to be at home; to stay at home; to be permanently settled and present.
		
		Practical Application
		This tells us...
		• that the fullness of God has always dwelt in Christ, even before He came to earth (John 1:1, 18; John 17:5, 24; Phil. 2:6).
		• that the fullness of God dwelt in Christ when Christ was walking upon earth in a human body (John 1:14, 18; 1 John 1:1-3).
		• that the fullness of God was not just a temporary gift to Christ.
		
		What does all this mean to us in practical day-to-day living? It means two wonderful things.
		1. First, God is not far off in outer space someplace. God is not unconcerned with the world. God has not just created the world and wound it up, to leave it on its own to fly throughout space with man's making out the best he can. God is interested and concerned with the world—so much so that He has come to earth to show how vitally concerned He is.
		2. God is love, not evil. Only a God of evil would leave man in the dark where he would have to grope and grasp and stumble about in order to find God. A God of love would reveal Himself and show man...
		• the way to God.
		• the truth of God, man, and his world.
		• the life that man is to live (John 14:6).

ENGLISH WORD	GREEK WORD AND VERSE	THE WORD MEANS...

#2373
Lives
 	
Conversation–KJV
Character–NASB
Lives–NIV
Conduct–NKJV
Not translated–NLT
 	
POSB
REFERENCE
(Heb.13:5-6; esp. v.5)
Note 5
	τρόπος = tropos
	Pronunciation: [trop'-os]
	Parsing (part of speech): noun
	  Case—nominative
	  Gender—masculine
	  Number—singular
	  Stem or root—from τρόπος, ου
	Concordance References:
	  ⇒ Strong's #5158 tropos
	  ⇒ NIV #5573 tropos
	  ⇒ NASB #5158 tropos
	
	Hebrews 13:5
	Let your **conversation** *be* without covetousness; *and* be content with such things as ye have: for he hath said, I will never leave thee, nor forsake thee. [KJV]
	  Let your **character** be free from the love of money, being content with what you have; for He Himself has said, "I will never desert you, nor will I ever forsake you," [NASB]
	  Keep your **lives** free from the love of money and be content with what you have, because God has said, "Never will I leave you; never will I forsake you." [NIV]
	  Let your **conduct** *be* without covetousness; *be* content with such things as you have. For He Himself has said, *"I will never leave you nor forsake you."* [NKJV]
	  Stay away from the love of money; be satisfied with what you have. For God has said, "I will never fail you. I will never forsake you." [NLT]—Not Translated
	  ἀφιλάργυρος ὁ **τρόπος**, ἀρκούμενοι τοῖς παροῦσιν· αὐτὸς γὰρ εἴρηκεν, Οὐ μή σε ἀνῶ, οὐδ' οὐ μήσε ἐγκαταλίπω. [GNS]
	  Ἀφιλάργυρος ὁ **τρόπος**, ἀρκούμενοι τοῖς παροῦσιν. αὐτὸς γὰρ εἴρηκεν, Οὐ μή σε ἀνῶ οὐδ' οὐ μή σε ἐγκαταλίπω, [GNT]
		Character, conversation, lives, ways, conduct. Thomas Hewitt points out that the Greek word for "lives" (*tropos*) means *manner of life*, or *the way of thought and life* (*The Epistle to the Hebrews.* "Tyndale New Testament Commentaries," p.206).
		
		Practical Application
		  The believer's life, yes, his very thoughts are to be free from covetousness, the love of money. His thoughts are to be focused upon Christ and the glorious hope of eternity, not upon this passing world and its possessions. The believer is to have no secret lust for the things of this world.

#2374
Lives–Living
 	
Dwell–KJV
Dwells–NASB
Lives–NIV
Dwells–NKJV
Living–NLT
 	
POSB
REFERENCE
(Romans 8:9)
Note 4, point 1
	οἰκεῖ = oikei
	Pronunciation: [oy-keh'-ee]
	Parsing (part of speech): verb
	  Mood—indicative
	  Tense—present
	  Voice—active
	  Person—3rd person
	  Number—singular
	  Stem or root—from οἰκέω
	Concordance References:
	  ⇒ Strong's #3611 oikeö
	  ⇒ NIV #3861 oikeö
	  ⇒ NASB #3611 oikeö
	
	Romans 8:9
	  But ye are not in the flesh, but in the Spirit, if so be that the Spirit of God **dwell** in you. Now if any man have not the Spirit of Christ, he is none of his. [KJV]
	  However, you are not in the flesh but in the Spirit, if indeed the Spirit of God **dwells** in you. But if anyone does not have the Spirit of Christ, he does not belong to Him. [NASB]
	  You, however, are controlled not by the sinful nature but by the Spirit, if the Spirit of God **lives** in you. And if anyone does not have the Spirit of Christ, he does not belong to Christ. [NIV]
	  But you are not in the flesh but in the Spirit, if indeed the Spirit of God **dwells** in you. Now if anyone does not have the Spirit of Christ, he is not His. [NKJV]
	  But you are not controlled by your sinful nature. You are controlled by the Spirit if you have the Spirit of God **living** in you. (And remember that those who do not have the Spirit of Christ living in them are not Christians at all.) [NLT]
	  ὑμεῖς δὲ οὐκ ἐστὲ ἐν σαρκὶ, ἀλλὰ ἐν πνεύματι, εἴπερ Πνεῦμα Θεοῦ **οἰκεῖ** ἐν ὑμῖν. εἰ δέ τις Πνεῦμα Χριστοῦ οὐκ ἔχει, οὗτος οὐκ ἔστιν αὐτοῦ. [GNS]
	  ὑμεῖς δὲ οὐκ ἐστὲ ἐν σαρκὶ ἀλλὰ ἐν πνεύματι, εἴπερ πνεῦμα θεοῦ **οἰκεῖ** ἐν ὑμῖν. εἰ δέ τις πνεῦμα Χριστοῦ οὐκ ἔχει, οὗτος οὐκ ἔστιν αὐτοῦ. [GNT]
		Lives, dwells; lives in (1 Tim.6:16).
		
		Practical Application
		  The Spirit lives within the believer, putting the Spirit of Christ within him.
		  The power of the Spirit is seen in the word "lives" or "living" (*oikei*). The word "lives" is the picture of a home (*oikei*). The Holy Spirit lives within the believer: He makes His home, takes up residence, and lives within the believer just as we live in our homes.

ENGLISH WORD	GREEK WORD AND VERSE	THE WORD MEANS...
#2375 **Living** Quick–KJV **Living–NASB** **Living–NIV** **Living–NKJV** **Living–NLT** **POSB** **REFERENCE** (Heb.4:11-13; esp. v.12) Note 5, point 2a	Ζῶν = Zön Pronunciation: [zone] Parsing (part of speech): verb 　Mood—participle 　Tense—present 　Voice—active 　Case—nominative 　Gender—masculine 　Number—singular 　Stem or root—from ζάω Concordance References: ⇒　Strong's #2198 zaö ⇒　NIV #2409 zaö ⇒　NASB #2198 zaö **Hebrews 4:12** 　For the word of God *is* **quick**, and powerful, and sharper than any twoedged sword, piercing even to the dividing asunder of soul and spirit, and of the joints and marrow, and *is* a discerner of the thoughts and intents of the heart. [KJV] 　For the word of God is **living** and active and sharper than any two-edged sword, and piercing as far as the division of soul and spirit, of both joints and marrow, and able to judge the thoughts and intentions of the heart. [NASB] 　For the word of God is **living** and active. Sharper than any double-edged sword, it penetrates even to dividing soul and spirit, joints and marrow; it judges the thoughts and attitudes of the heart. [NIV] 　For the word of God *is* **living** and powerful, and sharper than any two-edged sword, piercing even to the division of soul and spirit, and of joints and marrow, and is a discerner of the thoughts and intents of the heart. [NKJV] 　For the word of God is full of **living** power. It is sharper than the sharpest knife, cutting deep into our innermost thoughts and desires. It exposes us for what we really are. [NLT] 　**ζῶν** γὰρ ὁ λόγος τοῦ Θεοῦ, καὶ ἐνεργὴς, καὶ τομώτερος ὑπὲρ πᾶσαν μάχαιραν δίστομον, καὶ διϊκνούμενος· ἄχρι μερισμοῦ ψυχῆς τὲ καὶ πνεύματος, ἁρμῶν τε καὶ μυελῶν, καὶ κριτικὸς ἐνθυμήσεων καὶ ἐννοιῶν καρδίας. [GNS] 　**Ζῶν** γὰρ ὁ λόγος τοῦ θεοῦ καὶ ἐνεργὴς καὶ τομώτερος ὑπὲρ πᾶσαν μάχαιραν δίστομον καὶ διϊκνούμενος ἄχρι μερισμοῦ ψυχῆς καὶ πνεύματος, ἁρμῶν τε καὶ μυελῶν, καὶ κριτικὸς ἐνθυμήσεων καὶ ἐννοιῶν καρδίας· [GNT]	Living, quick, alive; coming to life; bringing to life. **Practical Application** 　The Word of God is "living" (*Zön*). It is alive and living. The idea is that the Word of God is always alive and active; it is always working and quickening its message to the human heart. Therefore, God's word of promise is not a dead and meaningless word of promise; it is living and full of life to the heart of the believer.
#2376 **Living As You** **Should** Order–KJV Good discipline– 　NASB Orderly–NIV Good order–NKJV **Living as you** **should–NLT** **POSB** **REFERENCE** (Col.2:5) Note 4	τάξιν = taxin Pronunciation: [tax'-in] Parsing (part of speech): noun 　Case—accusative 　Gender—feminine 　Number—singular 　Stem or root—from τάξις, εως Concordance References: ⇒　Strong's #5010 taxis ⇒　NIV #5423 taxis ⇒　NASB #5010 taxis **Col. 2:5** 　For though I be absent in the flesh, yet am I with you in the spirit, joying and beholding your **order**, and the stedfastness of your faith in Christ. [KJV] 　For even though I am absent in body, nevertheless I am with you in spirit, rejoicing to see your **good discipline** and the stability of your faith in Christ. [NASB] 　For though I am absent from you in body, I am present with you in spirit and delight to see how **orderly** you are and how firm your faith in Christ is. [NIV] 　For though I am absent in the flesh, yet I am with you in spirit, rejoicing to see your ***good* order** and the stead-	Orderly, good discipline, living as you should. The word "order" [living as you should] (*taxin*) means to maintain military discipline, array, and arrangement; to hold a solid front (The Amplified New Testament); to hold the military line unbroken and intact (A.T. Robertson, *Word Pictures in the New Testament*, Vol.4, p.489). **Practical Application** 　Note that the believers of the Colossian church were being attacked by false teaching even as Paul was writing to them. But they were responding like a victorious army. They were maintaining their discipline and holding their order and standing fast. Note also the importance of the minister's encouragement: Paul says that he was with them *in spirit*, joying and watching them gain the victory over the false teachers.

ENGLISH WORD	GREEK WORD AND VERSE	THE WORD MEANS...
	fastness of your faith in Christ. [NKJV] For though I am far away from you, my heart is with you. And I am very happy because you are **living as you should** and because of your strong faith in Christ. [NLT] εἰ γὰρ καὶ τῇ σαρκὶ ἄπειμι, ἀλλὰ τῷ πνεύματι σὺν ὑμῖν εἰμι, χαίρων καὶ βλέπων ὑμῶν τὴν **τάξιν**, καὶ τὸ στερέωμα τῆς εἰς Χριστὸν πίστεως ὑμῶν. [GNS] εἰ γὰρ καὶ τῇ σαρκὶ ἄπειμι, ἀλλὰ τῷ πνεύματι σὺν ὑμῖν εἰμι, χαίρων καὶ βλέπων ὑμῶν τὴν **τάξιν** καὶ τὸ στερέωμα τῆς εἰς Χριστὸν πίστεως ὑμῶν. [GNT]	

#2377
Living Bread
 	
Living bread–KJV
Living bread–NASB
Living bread–NIV
Living bread–NKJV
Living bread–NLT
 	
POSB
REFERENCE
(Jn.6:47-51; esp. v.51)
Note 3, point 3a
	ὁ ἄρτος ὁ ζῶν = *ho artos ho zōn*
	Pronunciation: [ho ar-tos ho zown]
	Parsing *artos* (part of speech): noun
	  Case—nominative
	  Gender—masculine
	  Number—singular
	  Stem or root—from ἄρτος, ου
	Parsing *zōn* (part of speech): verb
	  Mood—participle
	  Tense—present
	  Voice—active
	  Case—nominative
	  Gender—masculine
	  Person—1st person
	  Number—singular
	  Stem or root—from ζάω
	Concordance References:
	  ⇒ Strong's #2198 zao + 740 artos
	  ⇒ NIV #2409 zaö [living] + 788 artos [bread]
	  ⇒ NASB #2198 zao + 740 artos
	
	John 6:51
	I am the **living bread** which came down from heaven: if any man eat of this bread, he shall live for ever: and the bread that I will give is my flesh, which I will give for the life of the world. [KJV]
	
	"I am the **living bread** that came down out of heaven; if anyone eats of this bread, he shall live forever; and the bread also which I shall give for the life of the world is My flesh." [NASB]
	
	I am the **living bread** that came down from heaven. If anyone eats of this bread, he will live forever. This bread is my flesh, which I will give for the life of the world." [NIV]
	
	I am the **living bread** which came down from heaven. If anyone eats of this bread, he will live forever; and the bread that I shall give is My flesh, which I shall give for the life of the world." [NKJV]
	
	I am the **living bread** that came down out of heaven. Anyone who eats this bread will live forever; this bread is my flesh, offered so the world may live." [NLT]
	
	ἐγώ εἰμι ὁ ἄρτος ὁ ζῶν, ὁ ἐκ τοῦ οὐρανοῦ καταβάς· ἐάν τις φάγῃ ἐκ τούτου τοῦ ἄρτου, ζήσεται εἰς τὸν αἰῶνα. καὶ ὁ ἄρτος δὲ ὃν ἐγὼ δώσω, ἡ σάρξ μού ἐστιν, ἣν ἐγὼ δώσω ὑπὲρ τῆς τοῦ κόσμου ζωῆς. [GNS]
	
	ἐγώ εἰμι ὁ ἄρτος ὁ ζῶν ὁ ἐκ τοῦ οὐρανοῦ καταβάς· ἐάν τις φάγῃ ἐκ τούτου τοῦ ἄρτου ζήσει εἰς τὸν αἰῶνα, καὶ ὁ ἄρτος δὲ ὃν ἐγὼ δώσω ἡ σάρξ μού ἐστιν ὑπὲρ τῆς τοῦ κόσμου ζωῆς. [GNT]
		Living Bread, food.
		
		Practical Application
		The Bread is living; it is a life (John 1:4; John 5:26). The words are literally, "the Bread, the Living." (Cp. John 6:35, 41, 48.) The purpose of bread is to give life. (See POSB *Deeper Study* #2—John 1:4; POSB *Deeper Study* #1—John 10:10; POSB *Deeper Study* #1—John 17:2-3.) Bread gives life by...
		1. nourishing and sustaining.
		2. satisfying.
		3. energizing.
		4. creating desire (the need) for more (See POSB note—Luke 4:3-4. Cp. Neh. 9:15).
		5. being partaken on a regular basis.
		
		Christ (and the Word of God) gives life to the believer by doing the same five things as bread.

#2378
Lofty Words And Brilliant Ideas
 	
Excellency of speech or of wisdom–KJV
Superiority of speech or of wisdom– NASB
	ὑπεροχὴν λόγου η σοφίας = *huperochēn logou ē sophias*
	Pronunciation: [hoop-er-okh-ayn' log'-oo ay sof-ee'-ahs]
	Parsing *huperochēn* (part of speech): noun
	  Case—accusative
	  Gender—feminine
	  Number—singular
	  Stem or root—from ὑπεροχή, ῆς
	Parsing *logou* (part of speech): noun
	  Case—genitive
	  Gender—masculine
	  Number—singular
		Eloquent words; superior, elevated, preeminent words; words that rise above.
		
		Practical Application
		Remember Paul is speaking about words, not so much about himself, although the behavior of a person could be involved. Paul did not try to sound more superior, more elevated, and more eloquent in his preaching than did others. He was not concerned in the least with his preaching's rising above and being more preeminent

ENGLISH WORD	GREEK WORD AND VERSE	THE WORD MEANS...

Eloquence or superior wisdom–NIV
Excellence of speech or of wisdom–NKJV
Lofty words and brilliant ideas–NLT
 	
POSB REFERENCE
(1 Cor.2:1)
Note 1, point 1
	Stem or root—from **λόγος**, ου
	Parsing *sophias* (part of speech): noun
	    Case—genitive
	    Gender—feminine
	    Number—singular
	    Stem or root—from **σοφία**, ας
	Concordance References:
	⇒ Strong's #3056 logos + 2228 ë + 4678+5247 sophia huperochë
	⇒ NIV #3364 logos [eloquence] + 2445 ë [or] + 5053+5667 sophia huperochë [superior wisdom]
	⇒ NASB #3056 logos + 2228 ë + 4678+5247 sophia huperochë
	
	1 Cor. 2:1
	And I, brethren, when I came to you, came not with **excellency of speech or of wisdom**, declaring unto you the testimony of God. [KJV]
	And when I came to you, brethren, I did not come with **superiority of speech or of wisdom**, proclaiming to you the testimony of God. [NASB]
	When I came to you, brothers, I did not come with **eloquence or superior wisdom** as I proclaimed to you the testimony about God. [NIV]
	And I, brethren, when I came to you, did not come with **excellence of speech or of wisdom** declaring to you the testimony of God. [NKJV]
	Dear brothers and sisters, when I first came to you I didn't use **lofty words and brilliant ideas** to tell you God's message. [NLT]
	Κἀγὼ ἐλθὼν πρὸς ὑμᾶς, ἀδελφοί, ἦλθον οὐ καθ' **ὑπεροχὴν λόγου η σοφίας** καταγγέλλων ὑμῖν τὸ μυστήριον τοῦ Θεοῦ. [GNS]
	Κἀγὼ ἐλθὼν πρὸς ὑμᾶς, ἀδελφοί, ἦλθον οὐ καθ' **ὑπεροχὴν λόγου η σοφίας** καταγγέλλων ὑμῖν τὸ μυστήριον τοῦ θεοῦ. [GNT]
		and recognized than the preaching of others. Paul did not seek to impress the Corinthians with superior wisdom or brilliant ideas.

#2379
Long For
 	
Desire–KJV
Long for–NASB
Crave–NIV
Desire–NKJV
Crave–NLT
 	
POSB REFERENCE
(1 Pt.2:2-3; esp. v.2)
Note 2
	ἐπιποθήσατε = *epipothësate*
	Pronunciation: [ep-ee-poth-ay'-sah-teh]
	Parsing (part of speech): verb
	    Mood—imperative
	    Tense—aorist
	    Voice—active
	    Person—2nd person
	    Number—plural
	    Stem or root—from **ἐπιποθέω**
	Concordance References:
	⇒ Strong's #1971 epipotheö
	⇒ NIV #2160 epipotheö
	⇒ NASB #1971 epipotheö
	
	1 Peter 2:2
	As newborn babes, **desire** the sincere milk of the word, that ye may grow thereby: [KJV]
	Like newborn babes, **long for** the pure milk of the word, that by it you may grow in respect to salvation, [NASB]
	Like newborn babies, **crave** pure spiritual milk, so that by it you may grow up in your salvation, [NIV]
	As newborn babes, **desire** the pure milk of the word, that you may grow thereby, [NKJV]
	You must **crave** pure spiritual milk so that you can grow into the fullness of your salvation. Cry out for this nourishment as a baby cries for milk, [NLT]
	ὡς ἀρτιγέννητα βρέφη, τὸ λογικὸν ἄδολον γάλα **ἐπιποθήσατε**, ἵνα ἐν αὐτῷ αὐξηθῆτε, [GNS]
	ὡς ἀρτιγέννητα βρέφη τὸ λογικὸν ἄδολον γάλα **ἐπιποθήσατε**, ἵνα ἐν αὐτῷ αὐξηθῆτε εἰς σωτηρίαν, [GNT]
		To crave; to desire; to long for; to yearn for. It means to crave, yearn, and long for the Word of God.
		
		Practical Application
		The believer is to long for one thing—the milk of God's Word. The charge is an imperative, a command: "You desire, crave, and yearn for the pure spiritual milk of the Word. And the craving and yearning are to be constant." The phrase "long for" (*epipothësate*) is a strong one, very strong. It paints the picture of being an absolute essential, of hungering and thirsting after the Word. If a believer is to grow, it is absolutely essential that he hunger and thirst after the milk of the Word.

ENGLISH WORD	GREEK WORD AND VERSE	THE WORD MEANS...

#2380
Longer, No–Longer, For You Can No
 	
No longer–KJV
For you can no longer–NASB
Because [you] cannot–NIV
For you can no longer–NKJV
You are going to be dismissed–NLT
 	
POSB REFERENCE
(Lk.16:1-7; esp. v.2)
Note 1, point 2a
	οὐ γὰρ δύνῃ = *ou gar dunë*
	Pronunciation: [oo gar doo-nay]
	Parsing *dunë* (part of speech): verb
	    Mood—indicative
	    Tense—present
	    Voice—middle or passive dep
	    Person—2nd person
	    Number—singular
	    Stem or root—from δύναμαι
	Concordance References:
	⇒ Strong's #1063 gar + dunamai 1410 + 3756 ou
	⇒ NIV #1142 gar [because] + 1538 dunamai + 4024 ou [cannot]
	⇒ NASB #1063 gar + dunamai 1410 + 3756 ou
	
	Luke 16:2
	And he called him, and said unto him, How is it that I hear this of thee? give an account of thy stewardship; for thou mayest be **no longer** steward. [KJV]
	"And he called him and said to him, 'What is this I hear about you? Give an account of your stewardship, **for you can no longer** be steward.' [NASB]
	So he called him in and asked him, 'What is this I hear about you? Give an account of your management, **because you cannot** be manager any longer.' [NIV]
	So he called him and said to him, 'What is this I hear about you? Give an account of your stewardship, **for you can no longer** be steward.' [NKJV]
	So his employer called him in and said, 'What's this I hear about your stealing from me? Get your report in order, because **you are going to be dismissed**.' [NLT]
	καὶ φωνήσας αὐτὸν, εἶπεν αὐτῷ, Τί τοῦτο ἀκούω περὶ σοῦ; ἀπόδος τὸν λόγον τῆς οἰκονομίας σου· **οὐ γὰρ δύνῃση** ἔτι οἰκονομεῖν. [GNS]
	καὶ φωνήσας αὐτὸν εἶπεν αὐτῷ, Τί τοῦτο ἀκούω περὶ σοῦ; ἀπόδος τὸν λόγον τῆς οἰκονομίας σου, **οὐ γὰρ δύνῃ** ἔτι οἰκονομεῖν. [GNT]
		Because you cannot; for you can no longer; you are going to be dismissed; not capable of; cannot do; not able to do.
		
		Practical Application
		In this Scripture, the manager is required to give an account of his actions, to prepare a final accounting. Two facts are important in this point.
		1. The Lord hears that the steward has been misusing His "possessions" (cp. Lk.16:1). Note: the Lord had only heard about the embezzlement. The full evidence against the steward was not yet fully known. The Lord gave the steward a chance to prove his trust and faithfulness. The accounting did not mean that the steward would be dismissed from the Lord's estate (heaven, Kingdom of God), only that he must prove his trust and faithfulness. Of course, if the steward had not been faithful in looking after the Lord's goods, then he would be dismissed: "because you can no longer (*ou gar dunë*) be my steward."
		2. The final accounting is at death (Hebrews 9:27). If the steward is found to have been untrustworthy, he will be dismissed and discharged from the Lord's estate (kingdom, heaven, eternal life. See POSB *Deeper Study* #3—Matthew 19:23-24.)

#2381
Longing
 	
Desire–KJV
Desire–NASB
Desire–NIV
Desire–NKJV
Longing–NLT
 	
POSB REFERENCE
(Rom.10:1-3; esp. v.1)
Note 1
	εὐδοκία = *eudokia*
	Pronunciation: [yoo-dok-ee'-ah]
	Parsing (part of speech): noun
	    Case—nominative
	    Gender—feminine
	    Number—singular
	    Stem or root—from εὐδοκία, ας
	Concordance References:
	⇒ Strong's #2107 eudokia
	⇒ NIV #2306 eudokia
	⇒ NASB #2107 eudokia
	
	Romans 10:1
	Brethren, my heart's **desire** and prayer to God for Israel is, that they might be saved. [KJV]
	Brethren, my heart's **desire** and my prayer to God for them is for *their* salvation. [NASB]
	Brothers, my heart's **desire** and prayer to God for the Israelites is that they may be saved. [NIV]
	Brethren, my heart's **desire** and prayer to God for Israel is that they may be saved. [NKJV]
	Dear brothers and sisters, the **longing** of my heart and my prayer to God is that the Jewish people might be saved. [NLT]
	Ἀδελφοί, ἡ μὲν **εὐδοκία** τῆς ἐμῆς καρδίας καὶ ἡ δέησις πρὸς τὸν Θεὸν ὑπὲρ τοῦ Ἰσραήλ ἐστιν εἰς σωτηρίαν. [GNS]
	Ἀδελφοί, ἡ μὲν **εὐδοκία** τῆς ἐμῆς καρδίας καὶ ἡ δέησις πρὸς τὸν θεὸν ὑπὲρ αὐτῶν εἰς σωτηρίαν. [GNT]
		Goodwill, pleasure, favor; desire, purpose, choice. The word "longing" (*eudokia*) means desiring, willing, yearning, craving.
		
		Practical Application
		Paul had a burning desire for Israel's salvation. He loved his people and loved them deeply. He craved and yearned to see the salvation of his people. If he saw their salvation, his desire would be fulfilled.
		Note that Paul prayed for Israel's salvation. They could be saved; their rejection of Christ was not hopeless. The door of salvation is open to all men, the Jew as well as the Gentile.

#2382
Longsuffering
	μακροθυμία = *makrothumia*
	Pronunciation: [mak-roth-oo-mee'-ah]
	Parsing (part of speech): noun
	    Case—nominative
	    Gender—feminine
		Patience, longsuffering; bearing and suffering a long time; perseverance; being constant, steadfast, and enduring.

ENGLISH WORD	GREEK WORD AND VERSE	THE WORD MEANS...
Longsuffering–KJV Patience–NASB Patience–NIV **Longsuffering–NKJV** Patience–NLT **POSB REFERENCE** (Gal.5:22-23; esp. v.22) Note 1 **See also POSB Ref:** (2 Cor. 6:6-7; esp. v.6) Note 5	Number—singular Stem or root—from **μακροθυμία**, ας Concordance References: ⇒ Strong's #3115 makrothumia ⇒ NIV #3429 makrothumia ⇒ NASB #3115 makrothumia **Galatians 5:22** But the fruit of the Spirit is love, joy, peace, **longsuffering**, gentleness, goodness, faith, [KJV] But the fruit of the Spirit is love, joy, peace, **patience**, kindness, goodness, faithfulness, [NASB] But the fruit of the Spirit is love, joy, peace, **patience**, kindness, goodness, faithfulness, [NIV] But the fruit of the Spirit is love, joy, peace, **longsuffering**, kindness, goodness, faithfulness, [NKJV] But when the Holy Spirit controls our lives, he will produce this kind of fruit in us: love, joy, peace, **patience**, kindness, goodness, faithfulness, [NLT] ὁ δὲ καρπὸς τοῦ Πνεύματός ἐστιν ἀγάπη, χαρά, εἰρήνη, **μακροθυμία**, χρηστότης, ἀγαθωσύνη, πίστις, [GNS] Ὁ δὲ καρπὸς τοῦ πνεύματός ἐστιν ἀγάπη χαρά εἰρήνη, **μακροθυμία**, χρηστότης ἀγαθωσύνη, πίστις, [GNT]	**Practical Application** God's Spirit gives the believer a patience that never gives in; that is never broken no matter what attacks it. ⇒ Pressure and hard work may fall upon us, but the Spirit of God helps us be patient under it all. ⇒ Disease or accident or old age may afflict us, but the Spirit of God helps us to be patient under it. ⇒ Discouragement and disappointment may attack us, but the Spirit of God helps us to be patient under it. ⇒ People may do us wrong, abuse, slander, and injure us; but the Spirit of God helps us to be patient under it all. Two significant things need to be noted about patience. 1. Patience never strikes back. Common sense tells us that a person who is attacked by others could strike back and retaliate. *But* the Christian believer is given the power of patience—the power to be patient with the situation or person for a long, long time. 2. Patience is one of the great traits of God. As pointed out in this verse, it is a fruit of God's very own Spirit, a fruit that is to be in the life of the believer.
#2383 **Longsuffering** **Longsuffering–KJV** Patient–NASB Patient–NIV **Longsuffering–NKJV** Patient–NLT **POSB REFERENCE** (2 Pt.3:9) Note 2	**μακροθυμεῖ** = *makrothumei* Pronunciation: [mak-roth-oo-meh' ee] Parsing (part of speech): verb Mood—indicative Tense—present Voice—active Person—3rd person Number—singular Stem or root—from **μακροθυμέω** Concordance References: ⇒ Strong's #3114 makrothumeö ⇒ NIV #3428 makrothumeö ⇒ NASB #3114 makrothumeö **2 Peter 3:9** The Lord is not slack concerning his promise, as some men count slackness; but is **longsuffering** to us-ward, not willing that any should perish, but that all should come to repentance. [KJV] The Lord is not slow about His promise, as some count slowness, but is **patient** toward you, not wishing for any to perish but for all to come to repentance. [NASB] The Lord is not slow in keeping his promise, as some understand slowness. He is **patient** with you, not wanting anyone to perish, but everyone to come to repentance. [NIV] The Lord is not slack concerning *His* promise, as some count slackness, but is **longsuffering** toward us, not willing that any should perish but that all should come to repentance. [NKJV] The Lord isn't really being slow about his promise to return, as some people think. No, he is being **patient** for your sake. He does not want anyone to perish, so he is giving more time for everyone to repent. [NLT] οὐ βραδύνει ὁ Κύριος τῆς ἐπαγγελίας, ὥς τινες βραδύτητα ἡγοῦνται· ἀλλὰ **μακροθυμεῖ** εἰς ἡμᾶς, μὴ βουλόμενός τινας ἀπολέσθαι ἀλλὰ πάντας εἰς μετάνοιαν χωρῆσαι. [GNS] οὐ βραδύνει κύριος τῆς ἐπαγγελίας, ὥς τινες βραδύτητα ἡγοῦνται, ἀλλὰ **μακροθυμεῖ** εἰς ὑμᾶς, μὴ βουλόμενός τινας ἀπολέσθαι ἀλλὰ πάντας εἰς μετάνοιαν χωρῆσαι. [GNT]	To be patient; to be longsuffering; to wait patiently. **Practical Application** God is longsuffering (*makrothumei*). The word means... • that God is patient with us. • that God bears and suffers a long time with us. • that God perseveres and is constant in suffering with us. • that God is steadfast and enduring in being patient with us. Very simply, God is slow to give in and to judge and condemn us. God loves and cares for us despite our sin and rebellion, cursing and rejection. This is the very reason He sent Christ to save us. He loves and cares for us; therefore, He is suffering a long time with us.

ENGLISH WORD	GREEK WORD AND VERSE	THE WORD MEANS...

#2384
Look
 	
Look–KJV
Look–NASB
Fix...eyes...on–NIV
Look–NKJV
Look–NLT
 	
**POSB
REFERENCE**
(2 Cor.4:17-18; esp.
v.18)
Note 8, point 2
	σκοπούντων = *skopountōn*
	Pronunciation: [skop-oon'-tone]
	Parsing (part of speech): verb
	  Mood—participle
	  Tense—present
	  Voice—active
	  Case—genitive
	  Gender—masculine
	  Person—1st person
	  Number—plural
	  Stem or root—from σκοπέω
	Concordance References:
	  ⇒ Strong's #4648 skopeō
	  ⇒ NIV #5023 skopeō
	  ⇒ NASB #4648 skopeō
	
	2 Cor. 4:18
	While we **look** not at the things which are seen, but at the things which are not seen: for the things which are seen *are* temporal; but the things which are not seen *are* eternal. [KJV]
	While we **look** not at the things which are seen, but at the things which are not seen; for the things which are seen are temporal, but the things which are not seen are eternal. [NASB]
	So we **fix** our **eyes** not **on** what is seen, but on what is unseen. For what is seen is temporary, but what is unseen is eternal. [NIV]
	While we do not **look** at the things which are seen, but at the things which are not seen. For the things which are seen *are* temporary, but the things which are not seen *are* eternal. [NKJV]
	So we don't **look** at the troubles we can see right now; rather, we look forward to what we have not yet seen. For the troubles we see will soon be over, but the joys to come will last forever. [NLT]
	μὴ **σκοπούντων** ἡμῶν τὰ βλεπόμενα, ἀλλὰ τὰ μὴ βλεπόμενα· τὰ γὰρ βλεπόμενα πρόσκαιρα· τὰ δὲ μὴ βλεπόμενα αἰώνια. [GNS]
	μὴ **σκοπούντων** ἡμῶν τὰ βλεπόμενα ἀλλὰ τὰ μὴ βλεπόμενα· τὰ γὰρ βλεπόμενα πρόσκαιρα, τὰ δὲ μὴ βλεπόμενα αἰώνια. [GNT]
		To look to; to fix eyes on; to watch; to focus one's eyes and attention on a set goal or end; to look on with undistracted focus.
		
		Practical Application
		The goal, of course, is spending eternity with God in the new heavens and earth. The minister does not look at the things which are seen (the physical and corruptible), but at things which are not seen (the spiritual and incorruptible).
		The reason is strikingly clear: the things which are seen are temporal (brief, temporary, fading, passing, fleeting, transient) but the things which are not seen are eternal (lasting, endless, forever, permanent, immortal, glorious).

#2385
Look
 	
Look–KJV
Eagerly wait–NASB
Eagerly await–NIV
Eagerly wait–NKJV
Eagerly waiting–NLT
 	
**POSB
REFERENCE**
(Philip.3:20-21; esp.
v.20)
Note 3, point 2
	ἀπεκδεχόμεθα = *apekdechometha*
	Pronunciation: [ap-ek-dekh'-om-ethh-ah]
	Parsing (part of speech): verb
	  Mood—indicative
	  Tense—present
	  Voice—middle or passive deponent
	  Person—1st person
	  Number—plural
	  Stem or root—from ἀπεκδέχομαι
	Concordance References:
	  ⇒ Strong's #553 apekdechomai
	  ⇒ NIV #587 apekdechomai
	  ⇒ NASB #553 apekdechomai
	
	Philip. 3:20
	For our conversation is in heaven; from whence also we **look** for the Saviour, the Lord Jesus Christ: [KJV]
	For our citizenship is in heaven, from which also we **eagerly wait** for a Savior, the Lord Jesus Christ; [NASB]
	But our citizenship is in heaven. And we **eagerly await** a Savior from there, the Lord Jesus Christ, [NIV]
	For our citizenship is in heaven, from which we also **eagerly wait** for the Savior, the Lord Jesus Christ, [NKJV]
	But we are citizens of heaven, where the Lord Jesus Christ lives. And we are **eagerly waiting** for him to return as our Savior. [NLT]
	ἡμῶν γὰρ τὸ πολίτευμα ἐν οὐρανοῖς ὑπάρχει, ἐξ οὗ
		To eagerly await; to look; to await expectantly. It means to yearn, to eagerly look and wait for the coming of the Lord Jesus to take His dear people to heaven.
		
		Practical Application
		The believer's life is to be focused upon the return of Christ. He is to be looking for the Lord's return—constantly looking—looking every day of his life.
		Kenneth Wuest points out that the Greek words "eagerly await" or "look" (*apekdechometha*) is made up of three words put together. There is...
		• the word "receive" which speaks of welcoming as the welcoming of a guest. It also has the idea of preparation for the guest.
		• the word "off" which speaks of withdrawing one's attention from other objects.
		• the word "out" which has the idea of waiting for, of stretching out the neck and waiting out or for the return of Christ. (*Philippians,* Vol.1, p.102.)

ENGLISH WORD	GREEK WORD AND VERSE	THE WORD MEANS...
	καὶ Σωτῆρα **ἀπεκδεχόμεθα**, Κύριον Ἰησοῦν Χριστόν· [GNS] ἡμῶν γὰρ τὸ πολίτευμα ἐν οὐρανοῖς ὑπάρχει, ἐξ οὗ καὶ σωτῆρα **ἀπεκδεχόμεθα** κύριον Ἰησοῦν Χριστόν, [GNT]	
#2386 **Look After** Looking diligently–KJV See to it–NASB See to it–NIV Looking carefully–NKJV **Look after–NLT** **POSB REFERENCE** (Heb.12:15-17; esp. v.15) Note 2	*ἐπισκοποῦντες* = *episkopountes* Pronunciation: [ep-ee-skop-oon'-tehs] Parsing (part of speech): verb 　Mood—participle (imperative sense) 　Tense—present 　Voice—active 　Case—nominative 　Gender—masculine 　Person—2nd person 　Number—plural 　Stem or root—from ἐπισκοπέω Concordance References: 　⇒ Strong's #1983 episkopeō 　⇒ NIV #2174 episkopeō 　⇒ NASB #1983 episkopeō **Hebrews 12:15** **Looking diligently** lest any man fail of the grace of God; lest any root of bitterness springing up trouble *you,* and thereby many be defiled; [KJV] **See to it** that no one comes short of the grace of God; that no root of bitterness springing up causes trouble, and by it many be defiled; [NASB] **See to it** that no one misses the grace of God and that no bitter root grows up to cause trouble and defile many. [NIV] **Looking carefully** lest anyone fall short of the grace of God; lest any root of bitterness springing up cause trouble, and by this many become defiled; [NKJV] **Look after** each other so that none of you will miss out on the special favor of God. Watch out that no bitter root of unbelief rises up among you, for whenever it springs up, many are corrupted by its poison. [NLT] **ἐπισκοποῦντες** μή τις ὑστερῶν ἀπὸ τῆς χάριτος τοῦ Θεοῦ· μή τις ῥίζα πικρίας ἄνω φύουσα ἐνοχλῇ, καὶ διὰ ταύτης μιανθῶσι πολλοί· [GNS] **ἐπισκοποῦντες** μή τις ὑστερῶν ἀπὸ τῆς χάριτος τοῦ θεοῦ, μή τις ῥίζα πικρίας ἄνω φύουσα ἐνοχλῇ καὶ δι' αὐτῆς μιανθῶσιν πολλοί, [GNT]	See to it; to look diligently; to look after; to be on the watch; to look carefully; to take the oversight of; to serve as overseer. **Practical Application** There are dangers that threaten the faith of believers. Therefore, believers must look after themselves and after others. It is of utmost importance, of a critical nature, for there are dangers. Therefore, be on the lookout and search diligently lest one fall into one of these dangers and fail to lay hold of the grace [salvation] of God.
#2387 **Look At** To see–KJV **Look at–NASB** **Look at–NIV** To see–NKJV To see–NLT **POSB REFERENCE** (Mt.28:1) Note 2, point 2a	*θεωρῆσαι* = *theōrēsai* Pronunciation: [theh-o-rayeh'-sah-ee] Parsing (part of speech): verb 　Mood—infinitive 　Tense—aorist 　Voice—active 　Stem or root—from θεωρέω Concordance References: 　⇒ Strong's #2334 theōreō 　⇒ NIV #2555 theōreō 　⇒ NASB #2334 theōreō **Matthew 28:1** In the end of the sabbath, as it began to dawn toward the first *day* of the week, came Mary Magdalene and the other Mary **to see** the sepulchre. [KJV] Now after the Sabbath, as it began to dawn toward the first *day* of the week, Mary Magdalene and the other Mary came to **look at** the grave. [NASB] After the Sabbath, at dawn on the first day of the week, Mary Magdalene and the other Mary went to **look at** the tomb. [NIV] Now after the Sabbath, as the first *day* of the week began to dawn, Mary Magdalene and the other Mary came **to see** the tomb. [NKJV] Early on Sunday morning, as the new day was dawning, Mary Magdalene and the other Mary went out **to see**	To look at; to see; to contemplate; to gaze; to observe in order to grasp; to perceive. **Practical Application** We can learn from the example of the two women who came to the empty tomb: They came to be close to their Lord, the One who meant so much to them, to mourn over Him, to think through all that had happened. This is an important point, for it perhaps explains why the women were more prepared to believe the miracle of the resurrection.

ENGLISH WORD	GREEK WORD AND VERSE	THE WORD MEANS...
	the tomb. [NLT] 'Οψὲ δὲ σαββάτων, τῇ ἐπιφωσκούσῃ εἰς μίαν σαββάτων, ἦλθε Μαρία ἡ Μαγδαληνὴ καὶ ἡ ἄλλη Μαρία **θεωρῆσαι** τὸν τάφον. [GNS] 'Οψὲ δὲ σαββάτων, τῇ ἐπιφωσκούσῃ εἰς μίαν σαββάτων ἦλθεν Μαριὰμ ἡ Μαγδαληνὴ καὶ ἡ ἄλλη Μαρία **θεωρῆσαι** τὸν τάφον. [GNT]	

#2388
Look At
 	
Look upon–KJV
Look at–NASB
Look at–NIV
Look on–NKJV
Look at–NLT
 	
POSB
REFERENCE
(Lk.9:37-40; esp. v.38)
Note 1, point 1
	ἐπιβλέψαι ἐπὶ = epiblepsai epi
	Pronunciation: [ep-ee-ble'-psah-ee ep-ee]
	Parsing *epiblepsai* (part of speech): verb
	    Mood—infinitive
	    Tense—aorist
	    Voice—active
	    Stem or root—from **ἐπιβλέπω**
	Concordance References:
	⇒ Strong's #1909 epi + 1914 epiblepo
	⇒ NIV #2093 epi + 2098 epiblepö [look at]
	⇒ NASB #1909 epi + 1914 epiblepo
	
	Luke 9:38
	And, behold, a man of the company cried out, saying, Master, I beseech thee, **look upon** my son: for he is mine only child. [KJV]
	And behold, a man from the multitude shouted out, saying, "Teacher, I beg You to **look at** my son, for he is my only *boy,* [NASB]
	A man in the crowd called out, "Teacher, I beg you to **look at** my son, for he is my only child. [NIV]
	Suddenly a man from the multitude cried out, saying, "Teacher, I implore You, **look on** my son, for he is my only child. [NKJV]
	A man in the crowd called out to him, "Teacher, **look at** my boy, who is my only son. [NLT]
	καὶ ἰδοὺ, ἀνὴρ ἀπὸ τοῦ ὄχλου ἀνεβόησε, λέγων, Διδάσκαλε, δέομαί σου, **ἐπιβλέψον ἐπὶ** τὸν υἱόν μου, ὅτι μονογενής ἐστι μοί· [GNS]
	καὶ ἰδοὺ ἀνὴρ ἀπὸ τοῦ ὄχλου ἐβόησεν λέγων, Διδάσκαλε, δέομαί σου **ἐπιβλέψαι ἐπὶ** τὸν υἱόν μου, ὅτι μονογενής μοί ἐστιν, [GNT]
		To look at; to look upon; to look on; to show special attention to.
		
		Practical Application
		The word for "look at" is a medical term. It means to carefully examine the patient, to look at with pity.

#2389
Look Down On
 	
Despise–KJV
Regard with contempt–NASB
Look down on–NIV
Despise–NKJV
Look down on–NLT
 	
POSB
REFERENCE
(Romans 14:3-4, esp. v.3)
Note 2
	ἐξουθενείτω = exoutheneitö
	Pronunciation: [ex-oo-then-ee'-tow]
	Parsing (part of speech): verb
	    Mood—imperative
	    Tense—present
	    Voice—active
	    Person—3rd person
	    Number—singular
	    Stem or root—from **ἐξουθενέω**
	Concordance References:
	⇒ Strong's #1848 exoutheneö
	⇒ NIV #2024 exoutheneö
	⇒ NASB #1848 exoutheneö
	
	Romans 14:3
	Let not him that eateth **despise** him that eateth not; and let not him which eateth not judge him that eateth: for God hath received him. [KJV]
	Let not him who eats **regard with contempt** him who does not eat, and let not him who does not eat judge him who eats, for God has accepted him. [NASB]
	The man who eats everything must not **look down on** him who does not, and the man who does not eat everything must not condemn the man who does, for God has accepted him. [NIV]
	Let not him who eats **despise** him who does not eat, and let not him who does not eat judge him who eats; for God has received him. [NKJV]
	Those who think it is all right to eat anything must not **look down on** those who won't. And those who won't eat certain foods must not condemn those who do, for God has accepted them. [NLT]
		To look down on; to despise; to refuse to accept; to regard with contempt; to hold in contempt; to reject; to treat as meaningless and utterly wrong.
		
		Practical Application
		Three reasons are given for not looking down on and judging one another, three reasons that stand as a warning to believers.
		1. God Himself has received the strong believer. The believer who walks in the liberty of Christ and does not live a strict life has been accepted by God, no matter what the more legalistic believer may think. There may be some man-made religious rules which he does not observe, but he has trusted Christ, and he obeys the Word of God. Therefore, he is not to be criticized and judged, but he is to be accepted into the fellowship of the more legalistic believer.
		2. No one has the *right* to judge the Lord's servant. Note: both believers belong to the Lord; both are the servants of the Lord. Therefore, the Lord alone has the right to judge them. Believers do not have the *right to play God* by judging each other. They have no right to condemn and pass judgment upon one another's behavior and works, for they do not belong to one another. They each belong to Christ; therefore, He alone determines

ENGLISH WORD	GREEK WORD AND VERSE	THE WORD MEANS...
	ὁ ἐσθίων τὸν μὴ ἐσθίοντα μὴ **ἐξουθενείτω**, καὶ ὁ μὴ ἐσθίων τὸν ἐσθίοντα μὴ κρινέτω· ὁ Θεὸς γὰρ αὐτὸν προσελάβετο. [GNS] ὁ δὲ ἐσθίων τὸν μὴ ἐσθίοντα μὴ **ἐξουθενείτω**, ὁ δὲ μὴ ἐσθίων τὸν ἐσθίοντα μὴ κρινέτω, ὁ θεὸς γὰρ αὐτὸν προσελάβετο. [GNT]	whether or not they stand or fall and are accepted or rejected. 3. God *will make* the believer stand. There is no question about the matter: the believer will stand, for God is able to make him stand (Rom.14:4).
#2390 **Look For** Seek–KJV **Look for–NASB** **Look for–NIV** Seek–NKJV Find–NLT **POSB REFERENCE** (Acts 11:25-26; esp. v.25) Note 3	ἀναζητῆσαι = *anazēteō* Pronunciation: [an-ad-zay-teh'-sah-ee] Parsing (part of speech): verb 　　Mood—infinitive 　　Tense—aorist 　　Voice—active 　　Stem or root—from ἀναζητέω Concordance References: ⇒　Strong's #327 anazēteō ⇒　NIV #349 anazēteō ⇒　NASB #327 anazēteō **Acts 11:25** Then departed Barnabas to Tarsus, for to **seek** Saul: [KJV] 　　And he left for Tarsus to **look for** Saul; [NASB] 　　Then Barnabas went to Tarsus to **look for** Saul, [NIV] 　　Then Barnabas departed for Tarsus to **seek** Saul. [NKJV] 　　Then Barnabas went on to Tarsus to **find** Saul. [NLT] ἐξῆλθε δὲ εἰς Ταρσὸν ὁ Βαρνάβας **ἀναζητῆσαι** Σαῦλον, [GNS] ἐξῆλθεν δὲ εἰς Ταρσὸν **ἀναζητῆσαι** Σαῦλον, [GNT]	To look for; to seek; to find; to search after. It means to search for, to search back and forth, up and down; to make a thorough search. **Practical Application** 　　The church sought additional staff—to have an adequate teaching staff. Barnabas is the one who is the focus of attention in this point, but the church was bound to have sensed the need for additional staff and given its approval. The point is this: the need was sensed, and the decision was made to seek for help. The only question was who should be secured. A unique person was needed, a person who not only had a Jewish background, but who knew the Greek language and culture and could relate to both Gentile and Jew alike. The person also needed to be fearless and bold in his witness for Christ because of the godless, immoral society of Antioch. 　　Barnabas knew such a man: Saul of Tarsus. So he set out to find him. Paul had been busy throughout Syria and Cilicia preaching Christ (Galatians 1:21). Apparently, Barnabas had difficulty finding him. But note: he knew God's will, so he did not give up the search. He kept searching until he found God's choice. What a dynamic lesson for all churches in seeking help and in building a church staff!
#2391 **Look Forward To** Looking for–KJV Looking for–NASB **Look forward to– NIV** Looking for–NKJV **Look forward to– NLT** **POSB REFERENCE** (2 Pt.3:12) Note 2, point 1	προσδοκῶντας = *prosdokōntas* Pronunciation: [pros-dok-own'-tahs] Parsing (part of speech): verb 　　Mood—participle 　　Tense—present 　　Voice—active 　　Case—accusative 　　Gender—masculine 　　Person—2nd person 　　Number—plural 　　Stem or root—from προσδοκάω Concordance References: ⇒　Strong's #4328 prosdokaō ⇒　NIV #4659 prosdokaō ⇒　NASB #4328 prosdokaō **2 Peter 3:12** **Looking for** and hasting unto the coming of the day of God, wherein the heavens being on fire shall be dissolved, and the elements shall melt with fervent heat? [KJV] 　　**Looking for** and hastening the coming of the day of God, on account of which the heavens will be destroyed by burning, and the elements will melt with intense heat! [NASB] 　　As you **look forward to** the day of God and speed its coming. That day will bring about the destruction of the heavens by fire, and the elements will melt in the heat. [NIV] 　　**Looking for** and hastening the coming of the day of God, because of which the heavens will be dissolved, being on fire, and the elements will melt with fervent heat? [NKJV] 　　You should **look forward** to that day and hurry it	To look forward to; to look for; to expect. The word means to wait; to wait patiently but expectantly; to eagerly anticipate and long for the day of God; to be in expectation (W.E. Vine. *Expository Dictionary of New Testament Words*). **Practical Application** 　　Believers must look forward to and seek to bring the day of God about. The day of God refers to the day when God will dissolve and destroy the heavens and earth, the day when God "will bring about the destruction of the heavens by fire, and the elements will melt in the heat." (2 Peter 3:12) (See POSB note—2 Peter 3:10 for discussion). What is to be the attitude of the believer toward the *day of God*? The believer is to "look forward to" (*prosdokōntas*) the day of God.

ENGLISH WORD	GREEK WORD AND VERSE	THE WORD MEANS...
	along—the day when God will set the heavens on fire and the elements will melt away in the flames. [NLT] προσδοκῶντας καὶ σπεύδοντας τὴν παρουσίαν τῆς τοῦ Θεοῦ ἡμέρας, δι' ἣν οὐρανοὶ πυρούμενοι λυθήσονται, καὶ στοιχεῖα καυσούμενα τήκεται; [GNS] προσδοκῶντας καὶ σπεύδοντας τὴν παρουσίαν τῆς τοῦ θεοῦ ἡμέρας δι' ἣν οὐρανοὶ πυρούμενοι λυθήσονται καὶ στοιχεῖα καυσούμενα τήκεται. [GNT]	

#2392
 	
 Look On
 	
 Look upon–KJV
 Look at–NASB
 Look at–NIV
 Look on–NKJV
 Look at–NLT
 	
 POSB REFERENCE
 (Lk.9:37-40; esp. v.38)
 Note 1, point 1
	ἐπιβλέψαι ἐπὶ = epiblepsai epi
	 Pronunciation: [ep-ee-ble'-psah-ee ep-ee]
	 Parsing epiblepsai (part of speech): verb
	     Mood—infinitive
	     Tense—aorist
	     Voice—active
	     Stem or root—from ἐπιβλέπω
	 Concordance References:
	   ⇒ Strong's #1909 epi + 1914 epiblepo
	   ⇒ NIV #2093 epi + 2098 epiblepö [look at]
	   ⇒ NASB #1909 epi + 1914 epiblepo
	
	 Luke 9:38
	 And, behold, a man of the company cried out, saying, Master, I beseech thee, **look upon** my son: for he is mine only child. [KJV]
	 And behold, a man from the multitude shouted out, saying, "Teacher, I beg You to **look at** my son, for he is my only *boy,* [NASB]
	 A man in the crowd called out, "Teacher, I beg you to **look at** my son, for he is my only child. [NIV]
	 Suddenly a man from the multitude cried out, saying, "Teacher, I implore You, **look on** my son, for he is my only child. [NKJV]
	 A man in the crowd called out to him, "Teacher, **look at** my boy, who is my only son. [NLT]
	 καὶ ἰδού, ἀνὴρ ἀπὸ τοῦ ὄχλου ἀνεβόησε, λέγων, Διδάσκαλε, δέομαί σου, **ἐπιβλέψον ἐπὶ** τὸν υἱόν μου, ὅτι μονογενής ἐστι μοί· [GNS]
	 καὶ ἰδοὺ ἀνὴρ ἀπὸ τοῦ ὄχλου ἐβόησεν λέγων, Διδάσκαλε, δέομαί σου **ἐπιβλέψαι ἐπὶ** τὸν υἱόν μου, ὅτι μονογενής μοί ἐστιν, [GNT]
		To look at; to look upon, to look on; to pay special attention to.
		
		 Practical Application
		 The word for "look on" is a medical term. It means to carefully examine the patient, to look upon with pity.

#2393
 	
 Look On
 	
 Behold–KJV
 Take note–NASB
 Consider–NIV
 Look on–NKJV
 Hear–NLT
 	
 POSB REFERENCE
 (Acts 4:29-30; esp. v.29)
 Note 4, point 1b
	ἔπιδε ἐπὶ = epide epi
	 Pronunciation: [ep-i'-deh ep-ee]
	 Parsing epide (part of speech): verb
	     Mood—imperative
	     Tense—aorist
	     Voice—active
	     Person—2nd person
	     Number—singular
	     Stem or root—from ἐπεῖδον
	 Parsing epi (part of speech): preposition
	     Case—accusative
	     Stem or root—from ἐπι
	 Concordance References:
	   ⇒ Strong's #1896 + 1909 epeidon epi
	   ⇒ NIV #2078 + 2093 epeidon epi
	   ⇒ NASB #1896 + 1909 epeidon epi
	
	 Acts 4:29
	 And now, Lord, **behold** their threatenings: and grant unto thy servants, that with all boldness they may speak thy word, [KJV]
	 "And now, Lord, **take note** of their threats, and grant that Thy bond-servants may speak Thy word with all confidence, [NASB]
	 Now, Lord, **consider** their threats and enable your servants to speak your word with great boldness. [NIV]
	 Now, Lord, **look on** their threats, and grant to Your servants that with all boldness they may speak Your word, [NKJV]
	 And now, O Lord, **hear** their threats, and give your servants great boldness in their preaching. [NLT]
		To consider; to behold; to take note; to hear; to look upon.
		
		 Practical Application
		 The church was asking God to concentrate and focus upon the persecution; to deal with it and to overrule the enemy; to give whatever was necessary to endure through it all.

ENGLISH WORD	GREEK WORD AND VERSE	THE WORD MEANS...
	καὶ τὰ νῦν, Κύριε, **ἔπιδε ἐπὶ** τὰς ἀπειλὰς αὐτῶν, καὶ δὸς τοῖς δούλοις σου μετὰ παρρησίας πάσης λαλεῖν τὸν λόγον σου, [GNS] καὶ τὰ νῦν, Κύριε, **ἔπιδε ἐπὶ** τὰς ἀπειλὰς αὐτῶν καὶ δὸς τοῖς δούλοις σου μετὰ παρρησίας πάσης λαλεῖν τὸν λόγον σου, [GNT]	

#2394
Look Over
 	
See–KJV
Look over–NASB
See–NIV
See–NKJV
Meet–NLT
 	
POSB REFERENCE
(Mt.22:11-14; esp. v.11)
Note 4, point 1
	θεάσασθαι = *theasasthai*
	Pronunciation: [theh-ahs'-ahs-thigh]
	Parsing (part of speech): verb
	  Mood—infinitive
	  Tense—aorist
	  Voice—middle deponent
	  Stem or root—from θεάομαι
	Concordance References:
	⇒ Strong's #2300 theaomai
	⇒ NIV #2517 theaomai
	⇒ NASB #2300 theaomai
	
	Matthew 22:11
	And when the king came in to **see** the guests, he saw there a man which had not on a wedding garment: [KJV]
	"But when the king came in to **look over** the dinner guests, he saw there a man not dressed in wedding clothes, [NASB]
	"But when the king came in to **see** the guests, he noticed a man there who was not wearing wedding clothes. [NIV]
	But when the king came in to **see** the guests, he saw a man there who did not have on a wedding garment. [NKJV]
	But when the king came in to **meet** the guests, he noticed a man who wasn't wearing the proper clothes for a wedding. [NLT]
	εἰσελθὼν δὲ ὁ βασιλεὺς **θεάσασθαι** τοὺς ἀνακειμένους εἶδεν ἐκεῖ ἄνθρωπον οὐκ ἐνδεδυμένον ἔνδυμα γάμου· [GNS]
	εἰσελθὼν δὲ ὁ βασιλεὺς **θεάσασθαι** τοὺς ἀνακειμένους εἶδεν ἐκεῖ ἄνθρωπον οὐκ ἐνδεδυμένον ἔνδυμα γάμου, [GNT]
		To see; to look at; to view attentively; to observe; to carefully look over; to closely look upon and contemplate and inspect; to visit.
		
		Practical Application
		The stress is upon the person who is looking over the situation. He beholds and inspects. The idea is that God entered the banqueting feast *for the purpose* of looking over and inspecting the guests. He wanted to make sure everyone and everything was in order for His Son's great celebration. Not anyone can be allowed to detract from His Son by being improperly dressed or clothed. (See POSB note—Romans 13:14 and POSB *Deeper Study* #2—Righteousness, Romans 13:14; POSB note—2 Cor. 5:21. See POSB *Deeper Study* #2, Justification—Romans 4:22; POSB note—Romans 5:1.)

#2395
Look Upon
 	
Look upon–KJV
Look at–NASB
Look at–NIV
Look on–NKJV
Look at–NLT
 	
POSB REFERENCE
(Lk.9:37-40; esp. v.38)
Note 1, point 1
	ἐπιβλέψαι ἐπὶ = *epiblepsai epi*
	Pronunciation: [ep-ee-ble'-psah-ee ep-ee]
	Parsing *epiblepsai* (part of speech): verb
	  Mood—infinitive
	  Tense—aorist
	  Voice—active
	  Stem or root—from ἐπιβλέπω
	Concordance References:
	⇒ Strong's #1909 epi + 1914 epiblepo
	⇒ NIV #2093 epi + 2098 epiblepō [look at]
	⇒ NASB #1909 epi + 1914 epiblepo
	
	Luke 9:38
	And, behold, a man of the company cried out, saying, Master, I beseech thee, **look upon** my son: for he is mine only child. [KJV]
	And behold, a man from the multitude shouted out, saying, "Teacher, I beg You to **look at** my son, for he is my only *boy,* [NASB]
	A man in the crowd called out, "Teacher, I beg you to **look at** my son, for he is my only child. [NIV]
	Suddenly a man from the multitude cried out, saying, "Teacher, I implore You, **look on** my son, for he is my only child. [NKJV]
	A man in the crowd called out to him, "Teacher, **look at** my boy, who is my only son. [NLT]
	καὶ ἰδού, ἀνὴρ ἀπὸ τοῦ ὄχλου ἀνεβόησε, λέγων, Διδάσκαλε, δέομαί σου, **ἐπιβλέψον ἐπὶ** τὸν υἱόν μου, ὅτι μονογενής ἐστι μοί· [GNS]
	καὶ ἰδοὺ ἀνὴρ ἀπὸ τοῦ ὄχλου ἐβόησεν λέγων, Διδάσκαλε, δέομαί σου **ἐπιβλέψαι ἐπὶ** τὸν υἱόν μου, ὅτι μονογενής μοί ἐστιν, [GNT]
		To look at; to look upon; to look on; to show special attention to.
		
		Practical Application
		The word for "look upon" is a medical term. It means to carefully examine the patient, to look upon with pity.

ENGLISH WORD	GREEK WORD AND VERSE	THE WORD MEANS...

#2396
Looked At
 	
Beheld–KJV
Looked at–NASB
Looked at–NIV
Looked at–NKJV
Looking intently–NLT
 	
POSB REFERENCE
(Jn.1:42)
Note 6, point 1
	ἐμβλέψας = emblepsas
	Pronunciation: [em-blehps'-ahs]
	Parsing (part of speech): verb
	  Mood—participle
	  Tense—aorist
	  Voice—active
	  Case—nominative
	  Gender—masculine
	  Number—singular
	  Stem or root—from ἐμβλέπω
	Concordance References:
	⇒ Strong's #1689 emblepō
	⇒ NIV #1838 emblepō
	⇒ NASB #1689 emblepō
	
	John 1:42
	And he brought him to Jesus. And when Jesus **beheld** him, he said, Thou art Simon the son of Jona: thou shalt be called Cephas, which is by interpretation, A stone. [KJV]
	He brought him to Jesus. Jesus **looked at** him, and said, "You are Simon the son of John; you shall be called Cephas" (which is translated Peter). [NASB]
	And he brought him to Jesus. Jesus **looked at** him and said, "You are Simon son of John. You will be called Cephas" (which, when translated, is Peter). [NIV]
	And he brought him to Jesus. Now when Jesus **looked at** him, He said, "You are Simon the son of Jonah. You shall be called Cephas" (which is translated, A Stone). [NKJV]
	Then Andrew brought Simon to meet Jesus. **Looking intently** at Simon, Jesus said, "You are Simon, the son of John—but you will be called Cephas" (which means Peter). [NLT]
	καὶ ἤγαγεν αὐτὸν πρὸς τὸν Ἰησοῦν. ἐμβλέψας δὲ αὐτῷ ὁ Ἰησοῦς εἶπε, Σὺ εἶ Σίμων ὁ υἱὸς Ἰωνᾶ· σὺ κληθήση Κηφᾶς, -- ὃ ἑρμηνεύεται Πέτρος. -- [GNS]
	ἤγαγεν αὐτὸν πρὸς τὸν Ἰησοῦν. ἐμβλέψας αὐτῷ ὁ Ἰησοῦς εἶπεν, Σὺ εἶ Σίμων ὁ υἱὸς Ἰωάννου, σὺ κληθήση Κηφᾶς ὃ ἑρμηνεύεται Πέτρος. [GNT]
		To look at; to behold; to look intently; to look upon with an intense, earnest look; to concentrate; to stare and gaze upon; to look directly at; to look straight at; to look closely at.
		
		Practical Application
		Jesus looked into the innermost being of Peter. Note two significant facts.
		1. Jesus "looks at" a person: studies and knows him intimately. This is both a comfort and a warning, depending upon a person's response.
		2. Jesus sees the potential within a person and longs to change that person to make him everything he can become.

#2397
Looked At–
Looked Upon
 	
Looked upon–KJV
Beheld–NASB
Looked at–NIV
Looked upon–NKJV
Saw–NLT
 	
POSB REFERENCE
(1 Jn.1:1)
Note 2, point 3
	ἐθεασάμεθα = etheasametha
	Pronunciation: [eh-theh-ah'-sahm-eth-ah]
	Parsing (part of speech): verb
	  Mood—indicative
	  Tense—aorist
	  Voice—middle deponent
	  Person—1st person
	  Number—plural
	  Stem or root—from θεάομαι
	Concordance References:
	⇒ Strong's #2300 theaomai
	⇒ NIV #2517 theaomai
	⇒ NASB #2300 theaomai
	
	1 John 1:1
	That which was from the beginning, which we have heard, which we have seen with our eyes, which we have **looked upon**, and our hands have handled, of the Word of life; [KJV]
	What was from the beginning, what we have heard, what we have seen with our eyes, what we **beheld** and our hands handled, concerning the Word of Life— [NASB]
	That which was from the beginning, which we have heard, which we have seen with our eyes, which we have **looked at** and our hands have touched—this we proclaim concerning the Word of life. [NIV]
	That which was from the beginning, which we have heard, which we have seen with our eyes, which we have **looked upon**, and our hands have handled, concerning the Word of life— [NKJV]
		To look at; to look upon; to behold; to observe; to notice; to see; to gaze and look upon for a long time in order to study and understand and grasp.
		
		Practical Application
		It means to look intensely and earnestly; it means to grasp the meaning and significance of a person. John is testifying that he and the other apostles and believers looked and gazed upon Jesus Christ in order...
		• to study and understand Him.
		• to seek and grasp the meaning and significance of His person.
		
		A person will never see and understand who Christ is by just glancing at Him. If a person wants to know Christ, he has to look intensely and seriously; he has to seek to understand if Christ really is who John and other believers claim He is.

ENGLISH WORD	GREEK WORD AND VERSE	THE WORD MEANS...
	The one who existed from the beginning is the one we have heard and seen. We **saw** him with our own eyes and touched him with our own hands. He is Jesus Christ, the Word of life. [NLT] Ὃ ἦν ἀπ' ἀρχῆς, ὃ ἀκηκόαμεν, ὃ ἑωράκαμεν τοῖς ὀφθαλμοῖς ἡμῶν, ὃ **ἐθεασάμεθα**, καὶ αἱ χεῖρες ἡμῶν ἐψηλάφησαν, περὶ τοῦ λόγου τῆς ζωῆς [GNS] Ὃ ἦν ἀπ' ἀρχῆς, ὃ ἀκηκόαμεν, ὃ ἑωράκαμεν τοῖς ὀφθαλμοῖς ἡμῶν, ὃ **ἐθεασάμεθα** καὶ αἱ χεῖρες ἡμῶν ἐψηλάφησαν περὶ τοῦ λόγου τῆς ζωῆς [GNT]	

#2398
Looked Down On
 	
Despised–KJV
Viewed others with contempt–NASB
Looked down on– NIV
Despised–NKJV
Scorned–NLT
 	
POSB REFERENCE
(Lk.18:9)
Note 1, point 3
	ἐξουθενοῦντας = *exouthenountas*
	Pronunciation: [ex-oo-then-oon'-tas]
	Parsing (part of speech): verb
	    Mood—participle
	    Tense—present
	    Voice—active
	    Case—accusative
	    Gender—masculine
	    Number—plural
	    Stem or root—from ἐξουθενέω
	Concordance References:
	⇒ Strong's #1848 exoutheneö
	⇒ NIV #2024 exoutheneö
	⇒ NASB #1848 exoutheneö
	
	Luke 18:9
	And he spake this parable unto certain which trusted in themselves that they were righteous, and **despised** others: [KJV]
	And He also told this parable to certain ones who trusted in themselves that they were righteous, and **viewed others with contempt:** [NASB]
	To some who were confident of their own righteousness and **looked down on** everybody else, Jesus told this parable: [NIV]
	Also He spoke this parable to some who trusted in themselves that they were righteous, and **despised** others: [NKJV]
	Then Jesus told this story to some who had great self-confidence and **scorned** everyone else: [NLT]
	Εἶπε δὲ καὶ πρός τινας τοὺς πεποιθότας ἐφ' ἑαυτοῖς ὅτι εἰσὶ δίκαιοι, καὶ **ἐξουθενοῦντας** τοὺς λοιπούς, τὴν παραβολὴν ταύτην· [GNS]
	Εἶπεν δὲ καὶ πρός τινας τοὺς πεποιθότας ἐφ' ἑαυτοῖς ὅτι εἰσὶν δίκαιοι καὶ **ἐξουθενοῦντας** τοὺς λοιποὺς τὴν παραβολὴν ταύτην· [GNT]
		To despise; to view others with contempt; to look down on; to scorn; to set at naught; to count as nothing, as unimportant and insignificant; to refuse to accept; to reject.
		
		Practical Application
		Such persons feel and act as though they are above and better, more important and significant, than others. They shy away from, ignore and neglect, pass by and downgrade, criticize and talk about...
		• the poor
		• the unfortunate
		• the poorly dressed
		• the homeless
		• the downcast
		• the derelict
		• the undernourished

#2399
Looked On
 	
Looked on–KJV
Fixing his gaze upon– NASB
Stared at–NIV
Observed–NKJV
Stared at–NLT
 	
POSB REFERENCE
(Acts 10:1-8; esp. v.4)
Note 1, point 3c
	ἀτενίσας = *atenisas*
	Pronunciation: [ah-ten-i'-sahs]
	Parsing (part of speech): verb
	    Mood—participle
	    Tense—aorist
	    Voice—active
	    Case—nominative
	    Gender—masculine
	    Number—singular
	    Stem or root—from ἀτενίζω
	Concordance References:
	⇒ Strong's #816 atenizö
	⇒ NIV #867 atenizö
	⇒ NASB #816 atenizö
	
	Acts 10:4
	And when he **looked on** him, he was afraid, and said, What is it, Lord? And he said unto him, Thy prayers and thine alms are come up for a memorial before God. [KJV]
	And **fixing his gaze upon** him and being much alarmed, he said, "What is it, Lord?" And he said to him, "Your prayers and alms have ascended as a memorial before God. [NASB]
	Cornelius **stared at** him in fear. "What is it, Lord?" he asked. The angel answered, "Your prayers and gifts to
		To stare at; to look on; to fix one's gaze upon; to look straight at.
		
		Practical Application
		Cornelius "looked on," that is, fastened his eyes, gazed, focused his attention; he was startled, frightened.

ENGLISH WORD	GREEK WORD AND VERSE	THE WORD MEANS...
	the poor have come up as a memorial offering before God. [NIV] And when he **observed** him, he was afraid, and said, "What is it, lord?" So he said to him, "Your prayers and your alms have come up for a memorial before God. [NKJV] Cornelius **stared at** him in terror. "What is it, sir?" he asked the angel. And the angel replied, "Your prayers and gifts to the poor have not gone unnoticed by God! [NLT] ὁ δὲ **ἀτενίσας** αὐτῷ καὶ ἔμφοβος γενόμενος εἶπε, Τί ἐστι, Κύριε; εἶπε δὲ αὐτῷ, Αἱ προσευχαί σου καὶ αἱ τε ἐλεημοσύναι σου ἀνέβησαν εἰς μνημόσυνον ἐνώπιον τοῦ Θεοῦ. [GNS] ὁ δὲ **ἀτενίσας** αὐτῷ καὶ ἔμφοβος γενόμενος εἶπεν, Τί ἐστιν, κύριε; εἶπεν δὲ αὐτῷ, Αἱ προσευχαί σου καὶ αἱ ἐλεημοσύναι σου ἀνέβησαν εἰς μνημόσυνον ἔμπροσθεν τοῦ θεοῦ. [GNT]	

#2400
Looked Steadfastly, While They
 	
While they looked steadfastly–KJV
Were gazing intently–NASB
Were looking intently up–NIV
While they looked steadfastly–NKJV
Were straining their eyes–NLT
 	
POSB REFERENCE
(Acts 1:9; esp. v.10)
Note 4
	ἀτενίζοντες ἦσαν = atenizontes ësan
	Pronunciation: [at-en-id'-zon-tes ay-san]
	Parsing *atenizontes* (part of speech): verb
	  Mood—participle
	  Tense—present
	  Voice—active
	  Case—nominative
	  Gender—masculine
	  Number—plural
	  Stem or root—from ἀτενίζω
	Concordance References:
	⇒ Strong's #1510 eimi + 816 atenizō
	⇒ NIV #1639 eimi [were] + 867 atenizō [looking intently up]
	⇒ NASB #1510 eimi + 816 atenizō
	
	Acts 1:10
	And **while they looked stedfastly** toward heaven as he went up, behold, two men stood by them in white apparel; [KJV]
	And as they **were gazing intently** into the sky while He was departing, behold, two men in white clothing stood beside them; [NASB]
	They **were looking intently up** into the sky as he was going, when suddenly two men dressed in white stood beside them. [NIV]
	And **while they looked steadfastly** toward heaven as He went up, behold, two men stood by them in white apparel, [NKJV]
	As they **were straining their eyes** to see him, two white-robed men suddenly stood there among them. [NLT]
	καὶ ὡς ἀτενίζοντες ἦσαν εἰς τὸν οὐρανὸν πορευομένου αὐτοῦ, καὶ ἰδοὺ ἄνδρες δύο παρειστήκεισαν αὐτοῖς ἐν ἐσθῆτι λευκῇ, [GNS]
	καὶ ὡς ἀτενίζοντες ἦσαν εἰς τὸν οὐρανὸν πορευομένου αὐτοῦ, καὶ ἰδοὺ ἄνδρες δύο παρειστήκεισαν αὐτοῖς ἐν ἐσθήσεσι λευκαῖς, [GNT]
		To look intently; to look steadfastly; to gaze intently; to fix one's eyes on; to stare; to look directly at.
		
		Practical Application
		The Lord ascended somewhat slowly in a dramatic, spectacular fashion. Why depart in this way? For the sake of the disciples. There are several significant reasons why they needed such a dramatic departure. (See POSB note, Jesus Christ, Exaltation—Acts 2:33-36 for more discussion.)
		1. Christ needed to dramatize and enforce His final departure.
		2. Christ needed to dramatize and enforce His claim upon the disciples.
		3. Christ needed to dramatize and enforce His return to earth, that it would take place exactly as He said. (See POSB note—Acts 1:10-11 for discussion.)
		4. Christ needed to dramatize and enforce that the disciples were not to be standing around "looking intently up into the sky." They were to get to the business at hand. They were to return to the upper room and...
		• "wait" and pray for the presence and power of the Holy Spirit.
		• move out witnessing to a world lost and reeling in desperate need.
		(See POSB note—Acts 1:9-10 for a detailed discussion of this topic.)

#2401
Looking
 	
Considering–KJV
Looking–NASB
Watch–NIV
Considering–NKJV
Be careful–NLT
 	
POSB REFERENCE
(Gal.6:1)
Note 3
	σκοπῶν = skopōn
	Pronunciation: [skop-own]
	Parsing (part of speech): verb
	  Mood—participle (imperative sense)
	  Tense—present
	  Voice—active
	  Case—nominative
	  Gender—masculine
	  Person—2nd person
	  Number—singular
	  Stem or root—from σκοπέω
	Concordance References:
	⇒ Strong's #4648 skopeō
	⇒ NIV #5023 skopeō
	⇒ NASB #4648 skopeō
		To watch; to carefully consider; to look to oneself; to keep one's attention on; to fix eyes on; to take note of; to think about oneself and to give attention to oneself. It means to keep an attentive eye on oneself.
		
		Practical Application
		If we really watch and consider the matter, then we will reach out in love and gentleness to help our fallen brothers. We have to help them, for we are all ever so subject to being caught in a sin.

ENGLISH WORD	GREEK WORD AND VERSE	THE WORD MEANS...
	### Galatians 6:1 Brethren, if a man be overtaken in a fault, ye which are spiritual, restore such an one in the spirit of meekness; **considering** thyself, lest thou also be tempted. [KJV] Brethren, even if a man is caught in any trespass, you who are spiritual, restore such a one in a spirit of gentleness; *each one* **looking** to yourself, lest you too be tempted. [NASB] Brothers, if someone is caught in a sin, you who are spiritual should restore him gently. But **watch** yourself, or you also may be tempted. [NIV] Brethren, if a man is overtaken in any trespass, you who *are* spiritual restore such a one in a spirit of gentleness, **considering** yourself lest you also be tempted. [NKJV] Dear brothers and sisters, if another Christian is overcome by some sin, you who are godly should gently and humbly help that person back onto the right path. And **be careful** not to fall into the same temptation yourself. [NLT] Ἀδελφοί, ἐὰν καὶ προληφθῇ ἄνθρωπος ἔν τινι παραπτώματι, ὑμεῖς οἱ πνευματικοὶ καταρτίζετε τὸν τοιοῦτον ἐν πνεύματι πραότητος, **σκοπῶν** σεαυτόν, μὴ καὶ σὺ πειρασθῇς. [GNS] Ἀδελφοί, ἐὰν καὶ προλημφθῇ ἄνθρωπος ἔν τινι παραπτώματι, ὑμεῖς οἱ πνευματικοὶ καταρτίζετε τὸν τοιοῦτον ἐν πνεύματι πραΰτητος, **σκοπῶν** σεαυτόν μὴ καὶ σὺ πειρασθῇς. [GNT]	

#2402
## Looking 	
 	
Looking–KJV
Fixing eyes–NASB
Fix eyes–NIV
Looking–NKJV
Keeping eyes–NLT
 	
POSB REFERENCE
(Heb.12:2)
Note 3
	ἀφορῶντες = *aphorōntes*
	Pronunciation: [af-or-own'-tehs]
	Parsing (part of speech): verb
	    Mood—participle
	    Tense—present
	    Voice—active
	    Case—nominative
	    Gender—masculine
	    Person—1st person
	    Number—plural
	    Stem or root—from ἀφοράω
	Concordance References:
	  ⇒ Strong's #872 aphoraō
	  ⇒ NIV #927 aphoraō
	  ⇒ NASB #872 aphoraō
	
	### Hebrews 12:2
	Looking unto Jesus the author and finisher of *our* faith; who for the joy that was set before him endured the cross, despising the shame, and is set down at the right hand of the throne of God. [KJV]
	
	Fixing our **eyes** on Jesus, the author and perfecter of faith, who for the joy set before Him endured the cross, despising the shame, and has sat down at the right hand of the throne of God. [NASB]
	
	Let us **fix** our **eyes** on Jesus, the author and perfecter of our faith, who for the joy set before him endured the cross, scorning its shame, and sat down at the right hand of the throne of God. [NIV]
	
	Looking unto Jesus, the author and finisher of *our* faith, who for the joy that was set before Him endured the cross, despising the shame, and has sat down at the right hand of the throne of God. [NKJV]
	
	We do this by **keeping** our **eyes** on Jesus, on whom our faith depends from start to finish. He was willing to die a shameful death on the cross because of the joy he knew would be his afterward. Now he is seated in the place of highest honor beside God's throne in heaven. [NLT]
	
	ἀφορῶντες εἰς τὸν τῆς πίστεως ἀρχηγὸν καὶ τελειωτὴν Ἰησοῦν, ὃς ἀντὶ τῆς προκειμένης αὐτῷ χαρᾶς, ὑπέμεινεν σταυρόν, αἰσχύνης καταφρονήσας, ἐν δεξιᾷ τε
		To fix one's eyes on; to keep one's eyes on; to look. The word "looking" (*aphorōntes*) means to fix your eyes upon Jesus. It also means to fix your mind upon Him (Kenneth Wuest. *Hebrews*, Vol. 2, p.214).
		
		### Practical Application
		We may and should look at the example of other believers, but we should always be *looking to Jesus*. The Christian runner is to focus his eyes and mind upon Jesus Christ. Why? Because Jesus Christ Himself ran the race of faith when He was upon earth, and He shows us exactly how to run it.

ENGLISH WORD	GREEK WORD AND VERSE	THE WORD MEANS...
	τοῦ θρόνου τοῦ Θεοῦ εκάθισεν. [GNS] ἀφορῶντες εἰς τὸν τῆς πίστεως ἀρχηγὸν καὶ τελειωτὴν Ἰησοῦν, ὃς ἀντὶ τῆς προκειμένης αὐτῷ χαρᾶς ὑπέμεινεν σταυρὸν αἰσχύνης καταφρονήσας ἐν δεξιᾷ τε τοῦ θρόνου τοῦ Θεοῦ κεκάθικεν. [GNT]	

#2403
 Looking Carefully
 	
 Looking diligently– KJV
 See to it–NASB
 See to it–NIV
 Looking carefully– NKJV
 Look after–NLT
 	
 POSB REFERENCE
 (Heb.12:15-17; esp. v.15)
 Note 2
	ἐπισκοποῦντες = *episkopountes*
	 Pronunciation: [ep-ee-skop-oon'-tehs]
	 Parsing (part of speech): verb
	     Mood—participle (imperative sense)
	     Tense—present
	     Voice—active
	     Case—nominative
	     Gender—masculine
	     Person—2nd person
	     Number—plural
	     Stem or root—from ἐπισκοπέω
	 Concordance References:
	 ⇒ Strong's #1983 episkopeö
	 ⇒ NIV #2174 episkopeö
	 ⇒ NASB #1983 episkopeö
	
	 Hebrews 12:15
	 Looking diligently lest any man fail of the grace of God; lest any root of bitterness springing up trouble *you,* and thereby many be defiled; [KJV]
	 See to it that no one comes short of the grace of God; that no root of bitterness springing up causes trouble, and by it many be defiled; [NASB]
	 See to it that no one misses the grace of God and that no bitter root grows up to cause trouble and defile many. [NIV]
	 Looking carefully lest anyone fall short of the grace of God; lest any root of bitterness springing up cause trouble, and by this many become defiled; [NKJV]
	 Look after each other so that none of you will miss out on the special favor of God. Watch out that no bitter root of unbelief rises up among you, for whenever it springs up, many are corrupted by its poison. [NLT]
	 ἐπισκοποῦντες μή τις ὑστερῶν ἀπὸ τῆς χάριτος τοῦ Θεοῦ· μή τις ῥίζα πικρίας ἄνω φύουσα ἐνοχλῇ, καὶ διὰ ταύτης μιανθῶσι πολλοί· [GNS]
	 ἐπισκοποῦντες μή τις ὑστερῶν ἀπὸ τῆς χάριτος τοῦ Θεοῦ, μή τις ῥίζα πικρίας ἄνω φύουσα ἐνοχλῇ καὶ δι' αὐτῆς μιανθῶσιν πολλοί, [GNT]
		See to it; to look diligently; to look after; to be on the watch; to look carefully; to take the oversight of; to serve as overseer.
		
		 Practical Application
		 There are dangers that threaten the faith of believers. Therefore, believers must look diligently after themselves and after others. It is of utmost importance, of a critical nature. Therefore, be on the lookout and search diligently lest one fall into one of these dangers and fail to lay hold of the grace fo God [salvation].

#2404
 Looking Diligently
 	
 Looking diligently– KJV
 See to it–NASB
 See to it–NIV
 Looking carefully– NKJV
 Look after–NLT
 	
 POSB REFERENCE
 (Heb.12:15-17; esp. v.15)
 Note 2
	ἐπισκοποῦντες = *episkopountes*
	 Pronunciation: [ep-ee-skop-oon'-tehs]
	 Parsing (part of speech): verb
	     Mood—participle (imperative sense)
	     Tense—present
	     Voice—active
	     Case—nominative
	     Gender—masculine
	     Person—2nd person
	     Number—plural
	     Stem or root—from ἐπισκοπέω
	 Concordance References:
	 ⇒ Strong's #1983 episkopeö
	 ⇒ NIV #2174 episkopeö
	 ⇒ NASB #1983 episkopeö
	
	 Hebrews 12:15
	 Looking diligently lest any man fail of the grace of God; lest any root of bitterness springing up trouble *you,* and thereby many be defiled; [KJV]
	 See to it that no one comes short of the grace of God; that no root of bitterness springing up causes trouble, and by it many be defiled; [NASB]
	 See to it that no one misses the grace of God and that no bitter root grows up to cause trouble and defile many. [NIV]
		See to it; to look diligently; to look after; to be on the watch; to look carefully; to take the oversight of; to serve as overseer.
		
		 Practical Application
		 There are some great dangers that threaten the faith of believers. Therefore, believers must look diligently after themselves and after others. It is of utmost importance, of a critical nature. Therefore, be on the lookout and search diligently lest one fall into one of these dangers.

ENGLISH WORD	GREEK WORD AND VERSE	THE WORD MEANS...
	Looking carefully lest anyone fall short of the grace of God; lest any root of bitterness springing up cause trouble, and by this many become defiled; [NKJV] **Look after** each other so that none of you will miss out on the special favor of God. Watch out that no bitter root of unbelief rises up among you, for whenever it springs up, many are corrupted by its poison. [NLT] ἐπισκοποῦντες μή τις ὑστερῶν ἀπὸ τῆς χάριτος τοῦ Θεοῦ· μή τις ῥίζα πικρίας ἄνω φύουσα ἐνοχλῇ, καὶ διὰ ταύτης μιανθῶσι πολλοί· [GNS] ἐπισκοποῦντες μή τις ὑστερῶν ἀπὸ τῆς χάριτος τοῦ θεοῦ, μή τις ῥίζα πικρίας ἄνω φύουσα ἐνοχλῇ καὶ δι' αὐτῆς μιανθῶσιν πολλοί, [GNT]	

#2405
Looking For
 	
Looking for–KJV
Looking for–NASB
Look forward to–NIV
Looking for–NKJV
Look forward to–NLT
 	
**POSB
REFERENCE**
(2 Pt.3:12)
Note 2, point 1
	προσδοκῶντας = *prosdoköntas*
	Pronunciation: [pros-dok-own'-tahs]
	Parsing (part of speech): verb
	    Mood—participle
	    Tense—present
	    Voice—active
	    Case—accusative
	    Gender—masculine
	    Person—2nd person
	    Number—plural
	    Stem or root—from προσδοκάω
	Concordance References:
	  ⇒ Strong's #4328 prosdokaö
	  ⇒ NIV #4659 prosdokaö
	  ⇒ NASB #4328 prosdokaö
	
	2 Peter 3:12
	Looking for and hasting unto the coming of the day of God, wherein the heavens being on fire shall be dissolved, and the elements shall melt with fervent heat? [KJV]
	
	Looking for and hastening the coming of the day of God, on account of which the heavens will be destroyed by burning, and the elements will melt with intense heat! [NASB]
	
	As you **look forward to** the day of God and speed its coming. That day will bring about the destruction of the heavens by fire, and the elements will melt in the heat. [NIV]
	
	Looking for and hastening the coming of the day of God, because of which the heavens will be dissolved, being on fire, and the elements will melt with fervent heat? [NKJV]
	
	You should **look forward to** that day and hurry it along—the day when God will set the heavens on fire and the elements will melt away in the flames. [NLT]
	
	προσδοκῶντας καὶ σπεύδοντας τὴν παρουσίαν τῆς τοῦ Θεοῦ ἡμέρας, δι' ἣν οὐρανοὶ πυρούμενοι λυθήσονται, καὶ στοιχεῖα καυσούμενα τήκεται; [GNS]
	
	προσδοκῶντας καὶ σπεύδοντας τὴν παρουσίαν τῆς τοῦ θεοῦ ἡμέρας δι' ἣν οὐρανοὶ πυρούμενοι λυθήσονται καὶ στοιχεῖα καυσούμενα τήκεται. [GNT]
		To look forward to; to look for; to expect. The word means to wait; to wait patiently but expectantly; to eagerly anticipate and long for the day of God; to be in expectation (W.E. Vine. *Expository Dictionary of New Testament Words*).
		
		### Practical Application
		Believers must look for and seek to bring the day of God about. The day of God refers to the day when God will dissolve and destroy the heavens and earth, the day when the universe "shall be set aflame by fire and shall be dissolved, and the elements shall melt with fervent heat" [KJV] (2 Peter 3:12; see POSB note—2 Peter 3:10 for discussion). What is to be the attitude of the believer toward the *day of God*? The believer is to be "looking for" (*prosdoköntas*) the day of God.

#2406
**Looking
  Intently**
 	
Beheld–KJV
Looked at–NASB
Looked at–NIV
Looked at–NKJV
**Looking intently–
NLT**
 	
**POSB
REFERENCE**
(Jn.1:42)
	ἐμβλέψας == *emblepsas*
	Pronunciation: [em-blehps'-ahs]
	Parsing (part of speech): verb
	    Mood—participle
	    Tense—aorist
	    Voice—active
	    Case—nominative
	    Gender—masculine
	    Number—singular
	    Stem or root—from ἐμβλέπω
	Concordance References:
	  Strong's #1689 emblepö
	  NIV #1838 emblepö
	  NASB #1689 emblepö
	
	John 1:42
	And he brought him to Jesus. And when Jesus **beheld**
		To look at; to behold; to look intently; to look upon with an intense, earnest look; to concentrate; to stare and gaze upon; to look directly at; to look straightstratight at; to look closely at.
		
		### Practical Application
		Jesus looked into the innermost being of Peter. Note two significant facts.
		1. Jesus "looks at" a person: studies and knows him intimately. This is both a comfort and a warning, depending upon a person's response.
		2. Jesus sees the potential within a person and

ENGLISH WORD	GREEK WORD AND VERSE	THE WORD MEANS...
Note 6, point 1	him, he said, Thou art Simon the son of Jona: thou shalt be called Cephas, which is by interpretation, A stone. [KJV] He brought him to Jesus. Jesus **looked at** him, and said, "You are Simon the son of John; you shall be called Cephas" (which is translated Peter). [NASB] And he brought him to Jesus. Jesus **looked at** him and said, "You are Simon son of John. You will be called Cephas" (which, when translated, is Peter). [NIV] And he brought him to Jesus. Now when Jesus **looked at** him, He said, "You are Simon the son of Jonah. You shall be called Cephas" (which is translated, A Stone). [NKJV] Then Andrew brought Simon to meet Jesus. **Looking intently** at Simon, Jesus said, "You are Simon, the son of John—but you will be called Cephas" (which means Peter). [NLT] καὶ ἤγαγεν αὐτὸν πρὸς τὸν Ἰησοῦν. **ἐμβλέψας** δὲ αὐτῷ ὁ Ἰησοῦς εἶπε, Σὺ εἶ Σίμων ὁ υἱὸς Ἰωνᾶ· σὺ κληθήσῃ Κηφᾶς, -- ὃ ἑρμηνεύεται Πέτρος. -- [GNS] ἤγαγεν αὐτὸν πρὸς τὸν Ἰησοῦν. **ἐμβλέψας** αὐτῷ ὁ Ἰησοῦς εἶπεν, Σὺ εἶ Σίμων ὁ υἱὸς Ἰωάννου, σὺ κληθήσῃ Κηφᾶς ὃ ἑρμηνεύεται Πέτρος. [GNT]	longs to change that person to make him everything he can become.
#2407 **Looking Intently Up, Were** While they looked stedfastly–KJV Were gazing intently–NASB **Were looking intently up–NIV** While they looked stcadfastly–NKJV Were straining their eyes–NLT **POSB REFERENCE** (Acts 1:9-10; esp. v.10) Note 4	**ἀτενίζοντες ἦσαν** = atenizontes ēsan Pronunciation: [at-en-id'-zon-tes ay-san] Parsing *atenizontes* (part of speech): verb 　Mood—participle 　Tense—present 　Voice—active 　Case—nominative 　Gender—masculine 　Number—plural 　Stem or root—from ἀτενίζω Concordance References: ⟹　Strong's #1510 eimi + 816 atenizō ⟹　NIV #1639 eimi [were] + 867 atenizō [looking intently up] ⟹　NASB #1510 eimi + 816 atenizō ## Acts 1:10 And **while they looked stedfastly** toward heaven as he went up, behold, two men stood by them in white apparel; [KJV] And as they **were gazing intently** into the sky while He was departing, behold, two men in white clothing stood beside them; [NASB] They **were looking intently up** into the sky as he was going, when suddenly two men dressed in white stood beside them. [NIV] And **while they looked steadfastly** toward heaven as He went up, behold, two men stood by them in white apparel, [NKJV] As they **were straining their eyes** to see him, two white-robed men suddenly stood there among them. [NLT] καὶ ὡς **ἀτενίζοντες ἦσαν** εἰς τὸν οὐρανὸν πορευομένου αὐτοῦ, καὶ ἰδοὺ ἄνδρες δύο παρειστήκεισαν αὐτοῖς ἐν ἐσθῆτι λευκῇ, [GNS] καὶ ὡς **ἀτενίζοντες ἦσαν** εἰς τὸν οὐρανὸν πορευομένου αὐτοῦ, καὶ ἰδοὺ ἄνδρες δύο παρειστήκεισαν αὐτοῖς ἐν ἐσθήσεσι λευκαῖς, [GNT]	Were looking intently up; while they looked steadfastly; were gazing intently; were straining their eyes; to fix one's eyes on; to stare; to look directly at. ### Practical Application The Lord ascended somewhat slowly in a dramatic, spectacular fashion. Why depart in this way? For the sake of the disciples. There are several significant reasons why they needed such a dramatic departure. (See POSB note, Jesus Christ, Exaltation—Acts 2:33-36 for more discussion.) 1. Christ needed to dramatize and enforce His final departure. 2. Christ needed to dramatize and enforce His claim upon the disciples. 3. Christ needed to dramatize and enforce His return to earth, that it would take place exactly as He said. (See POSB note—Acts 1:10-11 for discussion.) 4. Christ needed to dramatize and enforce that the disciples were not to be standing around "looking intently up into the sky." They were to get to the business at hand. They were to return to the upper room and... • "wait" and pray for the presence and power of the Holy Spirit. • move out witnessing to a world lost and reeling in desperate need. (See POSB note—Acts 1:9-10 for a detailed discussion of this topic.)
#2408 **Looking On** Beheld–KJV **Looking on–NASB** Before...eyes–NIV Watched–NKJV Watching–NLT	**βλεπόντων** = blepontōn Pronunciation: [blep'-own-tone] Parsing (part of speech): verb 　Mood—participle 　Tense—present 　Voice—active 　Case—genitive 　Gender—masculine 　Number—plural 　Stem or root—from βλέπω	To see; to behold; to look upon; to watch. ### Practical Application Jesus Christ began to slowly arise from the earth, ascending ever upward toward the sky above. The disciples were shocked and spellbound, gazing at the spectacular sight. They were beholding one of the most dramatic and phenomenal events ever experienced:

ENGLISH WORD	GREEK WORD AND VERSE	THE WORD MEANS...
POSB REFERENCE (Acts 1:9) Note 4	Concordance References: ⇒ Strong's #991 blepö ⇒ NIV #1063 blepö ⇒ NASB #991 blepö ### Acts 1:9 And when he had spoken these things, while they **beheld**, he was taken up; and a cloud received him out of their sight. [KJV] And after He had said these things, He was lifted up while they were **looking on**, and a cloud received Him out of their sight. [NASB] After he said this, he was taken up **before** their very **eyes**, and a cloud hid him from their sight. [NIV] Now when He had spoken these things, while they **watched**, He was taken up, and a cloud received Him out of their sight. [NKJV] It was not long after he said this that he was taken up into the sky while they were **watching**, and he disappeared into a cloud. [NLT] καὶ ταῦτα εἰπών, **βλεπόντων** αὐτῶν ἐπήρθη, καὶ νεφέλη ὑπέλαβεν αὐτὸν ἀπὸ τῶν ὀφθαλμῶν αὐτῶν. [GNS] καὶ ταῦτα εἰπὼν **βλεπόντων** αὐτῶν ἐπήρθη, καὶ νεφέλη ὑπέλαβεν αὐτὸν ἀπὸ τῶν ὀφθαλμῶν αὐτῶν. [GNT]	⇒ the Ascension of the Lord Jesus Christ. ⇒ the return of God's Son into heaven, into the spiritual world and dimension of being.

#2409
Loose
 	
Loose–KJV
Loose–NASB
Loose–NIV
Loose–NKJV
Allow–NLT
 	
POSB REFERENCE
(Mt.18:17-18; esp. v.18)
Note 2, point 2
	λύσητε = lusëte
	Pronunciation: [loo'-say-teh]
	Parsing (part of speech): verb
	  Mood—subjunctive
	  Tense—aorist
	  Voice—active
	  Person—2nd person
	  Number— plural
	  Stem or root—from λύω
	Concordance References:
	⇒ Strong's #3089 luö
	⇒ NIV #3395 luö
	⇒ NASB #3089 luö
	
	### Matthew 18:18
	Verily I say unto you, Whatsoever ye shall bind on earth shall be bound in heaven: and whatsoever ye shall **loose** on earth shall be loosed in heaven. [KJV]
	"Truly I say to you, whatever you shall bind on earth shall be bound in heaven; and whatever you **loose** on earth shall be loosed in heaven. [NASB]
	"I tell you the truth, whatever you bind on earth will be bound in heaven, and whatever you **loose** on earth will be loosed in heaven. [NIV]
	Assuredly, I say to you, whatever you bind on earth will be bound in heaven, and whatever you **loose** on earth will be loosed in heaven. [NKJV]
	I tell you this: Whatever you prohibit on earth is prohibited in heaven, and whatever you **allow** on earth is allowed in heaven. [NLT]
	Ἀμὴν λέγω ὑμῖν, ὅσα ἐὰν δήσητε ἐπὶ τῆς γῆς, ἔσται δεδεμένα ἐν τῷ οὐρανῷ· καὶ ὅσα ἐὰν **λύσητε** ἐπὶ τῆς γῆς, ἔσται λελυμένα ἐν τῷ οὐρανῷ. [GNS]
	Ἀμὴν λέγω ὑμῖν· ὅσα ἐὰν δήσητε ἐπὶ τῆς γῆς ἔσται δεδεμένα ἐν οὐρανῷ, καὶ ὅσα ἐὰν **λύσητε** ἐπὶ τῆς γῆς ἔσται λελυμένα ἐν οὐρανῷ. [GNT]
		To unbind, to loosen what has been bound or tied. To loose a person means to set him free from spiritual bondage.
		
		### Practical Application
		Why is it so important to free offending believers from the clutches of sin? There are several passages of Scripture that issue a severe warning and speak of the sinful behavior of believers...
		• sinful behavior that causes loss of all reward by fire—a loss so great one is stripped as much as a burned-out building. It is the loss of all except the bare salvation of oneself (1 Cor. 3:11-15, esp. 1 Cor. 3:15).
		• sinful behavior that destroys the flesh so that the Spirit may be saved (1 Cor. 5:5).
		• sinful behavior that can cause a person to become a castaway (1 Cor. 9:27).
		• sinful behavior that causes death for a believer (1 Cor. 11:29-30, esp. 1 John 5:30; 1 John 5:16).
		• sinful behavior that merits no escape (Hebrews 2:1-3; Hebrews 12:25f).
		• sinful behavior that prohibits a person from ever repenting again (Hebrews 6:4f).
		• sinful behavior that causes a person to miss God's rest (Hebrews 4:1f).
		• sinful behavior that prohibits any future sacrifice for sins and merits terrible punishment (Hebrews 10:26f).
		• sinful behavior that entangles a person in the pollutions of the world after he has come to the knowledge of the Lord Jesus Christ (2 Peter 2:20).
		• sinful behavior that leads to death (1 John 5:16).

ENGLISH WORD	GREEK WORD AND VERSE	THE WORD MEANS...

#2410
Lord
 	
Lord, the–KJV
Lord, the–NASB
Lord, the–NIV
Lord, the–NKJV
Lord, the–NLT
 	
POSB
REFERENCE
(Mt.21:2-5; esp. v.3)
Note 2, point 1a
 	
See also POSB REF:
(Lk.19:29-35; esp. v.31)
Note 2, point 2
(Acts 2:36)
Deeper Study #2
	Ὁ κύριος = *o kurios*
	Pronunciation: [ho koo'-ree-os]
	Parsing *kurios* (part of speech): noun
	    Case—nominative
	    Gender—masculine
	    Number—singular
	    Stem or root—from κύριος, ου
	Concordance References:
	  ⇒ Strong's #2962 kurios
	  ⇒ NIV #3836 ho [the] + 3261 kurios [Lord]
	  ⇒ NASB #2962 kurios
	
	Matthew 21:3
	And if any *man* say ought unto you, ye shall say, **The Lord** hath need of them; and straightway he will send them. [KJV]
	"And if anyone says something to you, you shall say, '**The Lord** has need of them,' and immediately he will send them." [NASB]
	If anyone says anything to you, tell him that **the Lord** needs them, and he will send them right away." [NIV]
	And if anyone says anything to you, you shall say, '**The Lord** has need of them,' and immediately he will send them." [NKJV]
	If anyone asks what you are doing, just say, '**The Lord** needs them,' and he will immediately send them." [NLT]
	καὶ ἐάν τις ὑμῖν εἴπῃ τι, ἐρεῖτε ὅτι **ὁ Κύριος** αὐτῶν χρείαν ἔχει· εὐθέως δὲ ἀποστελεῖ αὐτούς. [GNS]
	καὶ ἐάν τις ὑμῖν εἴπῃ τι, ἐρεῖτε ὅτι **Ὁ κύριος** αὐτῶν χρείαν ἔχει· εὐθὺς δὲ ἀποστελεῖ αὐτούς. [GNT]
		Lord, master, owner, mentor, supreme authority.
		
		Practical Application
		Used apart from Christ, the word "Lord" was a title of respect (i.e. "Master" or "Sir"). In reference to the resurrected and exalted Christ, it means:
		⇒ "Jesus our Lord" (2 Peter 1:2).
		⇒ "My Lord and my God" (John 20:28).
		⇒ "Both Lord and Christ" (Acts 2:36).
		⇒ "The Lord of all" (Acts 10:36).
		⇒ "The Lord of glory" (1 Cor. 2:8; James 2:1).
		⇒ "The Lord of lords" (Rev. 17:14).
		⇒ "The Lord our God" (Rev. 19:1).
		⇒ "The Lord God [Theos, Jehovah]" (1 Peter 3:15; cp. Isaiah 8:13).
		⇒ "The Lord your God" (Matthew 4:7; Luke 4:12).
		⇒ "The Lord [Jehovah]" (1 Peter 2:3; cp. Psalm 34:8; Mark 1:2-3; cp. Isaiah 40:3; Malachi 3:1).
		⇒ "Lord Jesus" (Acts 7:59; Acts 8:16; Acts 9:29; 2 Cor. 1:14; 2 Thes. 1:7; Hebrews 13:20; Rev. 22:20).
		⇒ "Christ the Lord" (Luke 2:11).
		⇒ "The Son of Man is Lord" (Mark 2:28).
		⇒ "The Lord of David" (Mark 12:35-37).
		⇒ "The [Lord] owner of the house" (Mark 13:35).

#2411
Lord
 	
Lord–KJV
Rabboni–NASB
Rabbi–NIV
Rabboni–NKJV
Teacher–NLT
 	
POSB
REFERENCE
(Mk.10:51-52; esp. v.51)
Note 6, point 4
	Ῥαββουνι = *Rabboni*
	Pronunciation: [hrab-bon-ee']
	Parsing (part of speech): noun
	    Case—vocative
	    Gender—masculine
	    Number—singular
	    Stem or root—from ῥαββουνί
	Concordance References:
	  ⇒ Strong's #4462 rhabboni or *rhabbouni*
	  ⇒ NIV #4808 hrabbouni
	  ⇒ NASB #4462 hrabbouni
	
	Mark 10:51
	And Jesus answered and said unto him, What wilt thou that I should do unto thee? The blind man said unto him, **Lord**, that I might receive my sight. [KJV]
	And answering him, Jesus said, "What do you want Me to do for you?" And the blind man said to Him, "**Rabboni**, *I want* to regain my sight!" [NASB]
	"What do you want me to do for you?" Jesus asked him. The blind man said, "**Rabbi**, I want to see." [NIV]
	So Jesus answered and said to him, "What do you want Me to do for you?" The blind man said to Him, "**Rabboni**, that I may receive my sight." [NKJV]
	"What do you want me to do for you?" Jesus asked. "**Teacher**," the blind man said, "I want to see!" [NLT]
	καὶ ἀποκριθεὶς λέγει αὐτῷ ὁ Ἰησοῦς, Τί θέλεις ποιήσω σοι; Ὁ δὲ τυφλὸς εἶπεν αὐτῷ, **Ῥαββουνι**, ἵνα ἀναβλέψω. [GNS]
	καὶ ἀποκριθεὶς αὐτῷ ὁ Ἰησοῦς εἶπεν, Τί σοι θέλεις ποιήσω; ὁ δὲ τυφλὸς εἶπεν αὐτῷ, **Ῥαββουνι**, ἵνα ἀναβλέψω. [GNT]
		Rabbi, Lord, Rabboni, Teacher, Master.
		
		Practical Application
		It is a title of reverent respect. Note the possessive "my." The heart of Bartimaeus reached out to Jesus, desiring to belong to Him.

ENGLISH WORD	GREEK WORD AND VERSE	THE WORD MEANS...
#2412 **Lord** Lord–KJV Lord–NASB Sir–NIV Lord–NKJV Sir–NLT **POSB** **REFERENCE** (Jn.6:34-35; esp. v.34) Note 4, point 1 **See also POSB REF:** (Jn.4:48-49; esp. v.49) Note 2, point 2	*Κύριε = Kurie* Pronunciation: [koo'-ree] Parsing (part of speech): noun 　Case—vocative 　Gender—masculine 　Number—singular 　Stem or root—from **κύριος**, ου Concordance References: ⇒　Strong's #2962 kurios ⇒　NIV #3261 kurios ⇒　NASB #2962 kurios **John 6:34** Then said they unto him, **Lord**, evermore give us this bread. [KJV] They said therefore to Him, "**Lord**, evermore give us this bread." [NASB] "**Sir**," they said, "from now on give us this bread." [NIV] Then they said to Him, "**Lord**, give us this bread always." [NKJV] "**Sir**," they said, "give us that bread every day of our lives." [NLT] εἶπον οὖν πρὸς αὐτόν, **Κύριε**, πάντοτε δὸς ἡμῖν τὸν ἄρτον τοῦτον. [GNS] Εἶπον οὖν πρὸς αὐτόν, **Κύριε**, πάντοτε δὸς ἡμῖν τὸν ἄρτον τοῦτον. [GNT]	Sir, Lord, Master, Owner, Mister. **Practical Application** In this Scripture, it means an address of respect. The people requested the Bread of God. The people called Jesus "Lord" (*Kurie*), but how much they understood of His deity is not known. Apparently, it was just an address of respect. However, the point is clear in the Bible. When a person asks for the Bread of God, he must call Jesus "Lord" and be ready to submit to Him as Lord, serving Jesus day by day (cp. Luke 9:23; Romans 10:13).
#2413 **Lord** Lord–KJV Lord–NASB Lord–NIV Lord–NKJV Lord–NLT **POSB** **REFERENCE** (1 Cor.12:3) Note 4	*Κύριος = Kurios* Pronunciation: [koo'-ree-os] Parsing (part of speech): noun 　Case—nominative 　Gender—masculine 　Number—singular 　Stem or root—from **κύριος**, ου Concordance References: ⇒　Strong's #2962 kurios ⇒　NIV #3261 kurios ⇒　NASB #2962 kurios **1 Cor. 12:3** Wherefore I give you to understand, that no man speaking by the Spirit of God calleth Jesus accursed: and *that* no man can say that Jesus is the **Lord**, but by the Holy Ghost. [KJV] Therefore I make known to you, that no one speaking by the Spirit of God says, "Jesus is accursed"; and no one can say, "Jesus is **Lord**," except by the Holy Spirit. [NASB] Therefore I tell you that no one who is speaking by the Spirit of God says, "Jesus be cursed," and no one can say, "Jesus is **Lord**," except by the Holy Spirit. [NIV] Therefore I make known to you that no one speaking by the Spirit of God calls Jesus accursed, and no one can say that Jesus is **Lord** except by the Holy Spirit. [NKJV] So I want you to know how to discern what is truly from God: No one speaking by the Spirit of God can curse Jesus, and no one is able to say, "Jesus is **Lord**," except by the Holy Spirit. [NLT] διὸ γνωρίζω ὑμῖν, ὅτι οὐδεὶς ἐν Πνεύματι Θεοῦ λαλῶν λέγει, ἀνάθεμα Ἰησοῦν, καὶ οὐδεὶς δύναται εἰπεῖν, **Κύριον** Ἰησοῦν, εἰ μὴ ἐν Πνεύματι Ἁγίῳ. [GNS] διὸ γνωρίζω ὑμῖν ὅτι οὐδεὶς ἐν πνεύματι θεοῦ λαλῶν λέγει, Ἀνάθεμα Ἰησοῦς, καὶ οὐδεὶς δύναται εἰπεῖν, **Κύριος** Ἰησοῦς, εἰ μὴ ἐν πνεύματι ἁγίῳ. [GNT]	Lord (of God and Christ), Master; His Majesty. **Practical Application** It refers to God Himself, that is, Jehovah, Yahweh, the One who is proclaimed throughout Scripture to be the Sovereign LORD of the Universe. To call Jesus "Lord" is to acknowledge His deity, that He is God Himself. The point is this: no man can please God by calling Jesus Lord apart from the Holy Spirit. Any person can speak the words that "Jesus is Lord," but for a person to please God, he must *acknowledge* within his heart and life that Jesus is Lord. The word *acknowledge* is the key: it means to surrender one's heart to Jesus *as the Lord of one's life*. And no person is going to do this, not really, unless he is moved upon by the Spirit of God. However, when a person is moved upon by the Spirit to say that Jesus is Lord, the person surrenders all he is and has to serve Jesus. To summarize very simply, saying that Jesus is Lord does not mean to merely mouth the words; it means to be stirred within the heart by the Spirit of God to *confess* that one's life belongs to Jesus *as Lord*. It means to give everything that a person is and has to Christ, acknowledging Him to be the Sovereign Majesty of the universe, the very Son of God Himself.

ENGLISH WORD	GREEK WORD AND VERSE	THE WORD MEANS...

#2414
Lord

Lord–KJV
Lord–NASB
Sovereign Lord–NIV
Lord–NKJV
Sovereign Lord–NLT

**POSB
REFERENCE**
(Acts 4:24)
Deeper Study #1

See also POSB REF:
(Rev.6:10)
Note 3

Δέσποτα = *Despota*
Pronunciation: [des-pot'-ah]
Parsing (part of speech): noun
  Case—vocative
  Gender—masculine
  Number—plural
  Stem or root—from δεσπότης, ου
Concordance References:
⇒ Strong's #1203 despotes
⇒ NIV #1305 despotēs
⇒ NASB #1203 despotes

Acts 4:24

And when they heard that, they lifted up their voice to God with one accord, and said, **Lord**, thou *art* God, which hast made heaven, and earth, and the sea, and all that in them is: [KJV]

And when they heard *this,* they lifted their voices to God with one accord and said, "O **Lord**, it is Thou who DIDST MAKE THE HEAVEN AND THE EARTH AND THE SEA, AND ALL THAT IS IN THEM, [NASB]

When they heard this, they raised their voices together in prayer to God. "**Sovereign Lord**," they said, "you made the heaven and the earth and the sea, and everything in them. [NIV]

So when they heard that, they raised their voice to God with one accord and said: "**Lord**, You *are* God, who made heaven and earth and the sea, and all that is in them, [NKJV]

Then all the believers were united as they lifted their voices in prayer: "O **Sovereign Lord**, Creator of heaven and earth, the sea, and everything in them—[NLT]

οἱ δὲ ἀκούσαντες ὁμοθυμαδὸν ἦραν φωνὴν πρὸς τὸν Θεὸν, καὶ εἶπον, **Δέσποτα**, σὺ ὁ Θεὸς ὁ ποιήσας τὸν οὐρανὸν καὶ τὴν γῆν καὶ τὴν θάλασσαν καὶ πάντα τὰ ἐν αὐτοῖς· [GNS]

οἱ δὲ ἀκούσαντες ὁμοθυμαδὸν ἦραν φωνὴν πρὸς τὸν θεὸν καὶ εἶπαν, **Δέσποτα**, σὺ ὁ ποιήσας τὸν οὐρανὸν καὶ τὴν γῆν καὶ τὴν θάλασσαν καὶ πάντα τὰ ἐν αὐτοῖς, [GNT]

Sovereign Lord, Sovereign Master, Sovereign Ruler.

Practical Application

It is the word used by slaves in referring to their master, slaves who are totally subjected to the lord and master of their domain. God is being addressed as "Lord," the Sovereign Majesty, the Creator, Ruler, and Lord of the universe and of all life. He alone is God and Sovereign Lord. No one else is—no person, no being, no ruling power, visible or invisible, physical or spiritual (cp. Romans 8:38-39; Col. 1:16).

#2415
Lord

Lord–KJV
Lord–NASB
Lord–NIV
Lord–NKJV
Lord–NLT

**POSB
REFERENCE**
(Philip.2:11)
Deeper Study #1

See also POSB REF:
(Jas 1:1)
Note 1

κύριος = *kurios*
Pronunciation: [koo'-ree-os]
Parsing (part of speech): noun
  Case—nominative
  Gender—masculine
  Number—singular
  Stem or root—from κύριος, ου
Concordance References:
⇒ Strong's #2962 kurios
⇒ NIV #3261 kurios
⇒ NASB #2962 kurios

Philip. 2:11

And *that* every tongue should confess that Jesus Christ *is* **Lord**, to the glory of God the Father. [KJV]

And that every tongue should confess that Jesus Christ is **Lord**, to the glory of God the Father. [NASB]

And every tongue confess that Jesus Christ is **Lord**, to the glory of God the Father. [NIV]

And *that* every tongue should confess that Jesus Christ *is* **Lord**, to the glory of God the Father. [NKJV]

And every tongue will confess that Jesus Christ is **Lord**, to the glory of God the Father. [NLT]

καὶ πᾶσα γλῶσσα ἐξομολογήσηται ὅτι **Κύριος**, Ἰησοῦς Χριστὸς, εἰς δόξαν Θεοῦ πατρός. [GNS]

καὶ πᾶσα γλῶσσα ἐξομολογήσηται ὅτι **κύριος** Ἰησοῦς Χριστὸς εἰς δόξαν θεοῦ πατρός. [GNT]

Lord, Master, Owner, Sir.

Practical Application

Jesus was called "Lord" from the very first of His ministry (Matthew 8:2) and He accepted the title. He even called Himself "Lord" (Matthew 7:21). The word had been a title of respect throughout history. During the Roman empire, it became the official title of Roman emperors. It was also a title given to the gods. The Hebrew title Adonai is translated "Lord" (Genesis 15:2), so is Jehovah (Matthew 1:20-22; Matthew 2:15; Matthew 3:3; Matthew 4:7, 10; Matthew 11:25; Matthew 21:9; Mark 12:29-30; Luke 1:68; Luke 2:9). Both titles, Adonai and Jehovah, are translated "Lord" in Matthew 22:44. Jesus Himself called God the Father, "Lord" (Matthew 4:7, 10). But the title is more often given to Jesus. There is no question but that Jesus was recognized as Lord, being identical with the Old Testament Jehovah and Adonai (Matthew 3:3; Matthew 12:8; Matthew 21:9; Matthew 22:43-45; Luke 1:43; John 14:8-10; John 20:28; Acts 9:5). When Jesus is called Lord, it means that He is Master and Owner, the King of kings and Lord of lords, the only true God. He is Jehovah, Adonai, God Himself.

ENGLISH WORD	GREEK WORD AND VERSE	THE WORD MEANS...
#2416 **Lose Heart** Faint–KJV Faint–NASB **Lose heart–NIV** Discouraged–NKJV Discouraged–NLT **POSB** **REFERENCE** (Heb.12:5-7, esp. v.5) Note 1, point 2	ἐκλύου = *ekluou* Pronunciation: [ek-loo'-oo] Parsing (part of speech): verb 　Mood—imperative 　Tense—present 　Voice—passive 　Person—2nd person 　Number—singular 　Stem or root—from ἐκλύομαι Concordance References: ⇒　Strong's #1590 ekluö ⇒　NIV #1725 ekluö ⇒　NASB #1590 ekluö **Hebrews 12:5** And ye have forgotten the exhortation which speaketh unto you as unto children, My son, despise not thou the chastening of the Lord, nor **faint** when thou art rebuked of him: [KJV] And you have forgotten the exhortation which is addressed to you as sons, "MY SON, DO NOT REGARD LIGHTLY THE DISCIPLINE OF THE LORD, NOR **FAINT** WHEN YOU ARE REPROVED BY HIM; [NASB] And you have forgotten that word of encouragement that addresses you as sons: "My son, do not make light of the Lord's discipline, and do not **lose heart** when he rebukes you, [NIV] And you have forgotten the exhortation which speaks to you as to sons: *"My son, do no despise the chastening of the LORD, Nor be **discouraged** when you are rebuked by Him;* [NKJV] And have you entirely forgotten the encouraging words God spoke to you, his children? He said, "My child, don't ignore it when the Lord disciplines you, and don't be **discouraged** when he corrects you. [NLT] καὶ ἐκλέλησθε τῆς παρακλήσεως, ἥτις ὑμῖν ὡς υἱοῖς διαλέγεται, Υἱέ μου, μὴ ὀλιγώρει παιδείας Κυρίου, μηδὲ **ἐκλύου**, ὑπ' αὐτοῦ ἐλεγχόμενος· [GNS] καὶ ἐκλέλησθε τῆς παρακλήσεως, ἥτις ὑμῖν ὡς υἱοῖς διαλέγεται, Υἱέ μου, μὴ ὀλιγώρει παιδείας κυρίου μηδὲ **ἐκλύου** ὑπ' αὐτοῦ ἐλεγχόμενος· [GNT]	To lose heart; to be faint; to be discouraged; to give up; to give out; to lose heart; to collapse; to buckle under; to lose courage; to weaken. **Practical Application** 　The trials and sufferings of this world can become extremely heavy and painful—sometimes almost too much to bear. The rebuking hand of God that convicts us to repent and to correct our behavior becomes almost unbearable. 　In either case, we are not to lose heart or give up. We are to turn totally to God in trust and dependence, asking for His help and strength. We have the glorious assurance that He will deliver us victoriously through all. He will make us stronger and make us a much greater witness for Him. God will save us and live within our hearts and lives—save us both now and eternally—save us even through death itself so that we may live with Him forever and ever in the new heavens and earth (1 Peter 3:10-13; Rev. 21:1f).
#2417 **Lose Heart,** **Not (To)** Not to faint–KJV **Not to lose heart–** **NASB** Not give up–NIV **Not lose heart–NKJV** Never give up–NLT **POSB** **REFERENCE** (Lk.18:1) Note 1, point 4	μὴ ἐγκακεῖν = *më egkakein* Pronunciation: [may ek-kak-eh'-een] Parsing *egkakein* (part of speech): verb 　Mood—infinitive 　Tense—present 　Voice—active 　Stem or root—from ἐγκακέω Concordance References: ⇒　Strong's #3361 me +1573 egkakeo ⇒　NIV #3590 më [not] + 1591 egkakeö [give up] ⇒　NASB #3361 me +1573 egkakeo **Luke 18:1** And he spake a parable unto them *to this end,* that men ought always to pray, and **not to faint**; [KJV] Now He was telling them a parable to show that at all times they ought to pray and **not to lose heart**, [NASB] Then Jesus told his disciples a parable to show them that they should always pray and **not give up**. [NIV] Then He spoke a parable to them, that men always ought to pray and **not lose heart**, [NKJV] One day Jesus told his disciples a story to illustrate their need for constant prayer and to show them that they must **never give up**. [NLT] Ἔλεγε δὲ καὶ παραβολὴν αὐτοῖς πρὸς τὸ δεῖν πάντοτε προσεύχεσθαι, καὶ **μὴ ἐκκακεῖν**, [GNS] Ἔλεγεν δὲ παραβολὴν αὐτοῖς πρὸς τὸ δεῖν πάντοτε προσεύχεσθαι αὐτοὺς καὶ **μὴ ἐγκακεῖν**, [GNT]	Not to lose heart; not to faint; not to tire of; not to become discouraged; not to turn coward, or give up, or give in to evil. **Practical Application** 　There is need for perseverance in prayer, for praying over a long period of time and not giving in and becoming discouraged. God's people are to pray and keep on praying until Christ returns, no matter how long He may be delayed.

ENGLISH WORD	GREEK WORD AND VERSE	THE WORD MEANS...

#2418
Lose None–
Lose Nothing–
Lose Even One,
Not
 	
Lose nothing–KJV
Lose nothing–NASB
Lose none–NIV
Lose nothing–NKJV
Not lose even one–
NLT
 	
POSB
REFERENCE
(Jn.6:39)
Note 4, point 2
	μὴ ἀπολέσω = mē apolesö
	Pronunciation: [may ap-ol'-leh-sow]
	Parsing apolesö (part of speech): verb
	  Mood—indicative OR subjunctive
	  Tense—future OR aorist
	  Voice—active
	  Person—1st person
	  Number—singular
	  Stem or root—from ἀπόλλυμι
	Concordance References:
	  ⇒ Strong's #3361 me + 622 apollumi
	  ⇒ NIV #3590 mē [none] + 660 apollumi [lose]
	  ⇒ NASB #3361 me + 622 apollumi
	
	John 6:39
	And this is the Father's will which hath sent me, that of all which he hath given me I should **lose nothing**, but should raise it up again at the last day. [KJV]
	"And this is the will of Him who sent Me, that of all that He has given Me I **lose nothing**, but raise it up on the last day. [NASB]
	And this is the will of him who sent me, that I shall **lose none** of all that he has given me, but raise them up at the last day. [NIV]
	This is the will of the Father who sent Me, that of all He has given Me I should **lose nothing**, but should raise it up at the last day. [NKJV]
	And this is the will of God, that I should **not lose even one** of all those he has given me, but that I should raise them to eternal life at the last day. [NLT]
	τοῦτο δέ ἐστι τὸ θέλημα τοῦ πέμψαντός με πατρός, ἵνα πᾶν ὃ δέδωκέ μοι, **μὴ ἀπολέσω** ἐξ αὐτοῦ, ἀλλὰ ἀναστήσω αὐτὸ ἐν τῇ ἐσχάτῃ ἡμέρᾳ. [GNS]
	τοῦτο δέ ἐστιν τὸ θέλημα τοῦ πέμψαντός με, ἵνα πᾶν ὃ δέδωκέν μοι **μὴ ἀπολέσω** ἐξ αὐτοῦ, ἀλλὰ ἀναστήσω αὐτὸ [ἐν] τῇ ἐσχάτῃ ἡμέρᾳ. [GNT]
		That He will not lose anything, not even a fragment, not any part of what God has given to Him. No person, not a single one, will be lost; not to possess.
		
		Practical Application
		It was true while He was on earth: He lost none (John 17:12). It will also be true of every believer throughout history.

#2419
Loss
 	
Diminishing–KJV
Failure–NASB
Loss–NIV
Failure–NKJV
Turned down–NLT
 	
POSB
REFERENCE
(Romans 11:11-12,
esp. v.12)
Note 1, point 3
	ἥττημα = hëttëma
	Pronunciation: [hayt'-tay-mah]
	Parsing (part of speech): noun
	  Case—nominative
	  Gender—neuter
	  Number—singular
	  Stem or root—from ἥττημα, τος
	Concordance References:
	  ⇒ Strong's #2275 hëttëma
	  ⇒ NIV #2488 hëttëma
	  ⇒ NASB #2275 hëttëma
	
	Romans 11:12
	Now if the fall of them be the riches of the world, and the **diminishing** of them the riches of the Gentiles; how much more their fulness? [KJV]
	Now if their transgression be riches for the world and their **failure** be riches for the Gentiles, how much more will their fulfillment be! [NASB]
	But if their transgression means riches for the world, and their **loss** means riches for the Gentiles, how much greater riches will their fullness bring! [NIV]
	Now if their fall is riches for the world, and their **failure** riches for the Gentiles, how much more their fullness! [NKJV]
	Now if the Gentiles were enriched because the Jews **turned down** God's offer of salvation, think how much greater a blessing the world will share when the Jews finally accept it. [NLT]
	εἰ δὲ τὸ παράπτωμα αὐτῶν πλοῦτος κόσμου, καὶ τὸ **ἥττημα** αὐτῶν πλοῦτος ἐθνῶν, πόσῳ μᾶλλον τὸ πλήρωμα αὐτῶν; [GNS]
	εἰ δὲ τὸ παράπτωμα αὐτῶν πλοῦτος κόσμου καὶ τὸ **ἥττημα** αὐτῶν πλοῦτος ἐθνῶν, πόσῳ μᾶλλον τὸ πλήρωμα αὐτῶν. [GNT]
		Defeat; failure; diminishing loss; turning down.
		
		Practical Application
		God assures the glorious restoration of Israel and a rich period for the whole earth. Note the sharp contrast...
		  • between "full" and "riches."
		  • between "loss" and "riches."
		
		The word "loss" (hëttëma) means diminishing, defeat, injury. It means that Israel became impoverished spiritually. Israel was spiritually injured and defeated; the Jewish people lost the blessings of salvation. Now...
		  • if the spiritual fall of Israel led to the riches of salvation being carried to the world...
		  • if the spiritual loss of Israel led to the riches of salvation being carried to the Gentiles...
		
		...how much more will the fullness (the restoration of Israel) bring the blessings of God to earth?

ENGLISH WORD	GREEK WORD AND VERSE	THE WORD MEANS...
#2420 **Lost** Cast away–KJV Forfeits–NASB Forfeit–NIV **Lost–NKJV** Forfeit–NLT **POSB REFERENCE** (Lk.9:25) *Deeper Study #2*	ζημιωθείς = zēmiötheis Pronunciation: [dzay-mee-o'-thace] Parsing (part of speech): verb 　Mood—participle 　Tense—aorist 　Voice—passive 　Case—nominative 　Gender—masculine 　Number—singular 　Stem or root—from ζημιόω Concordance References: 　⇒ Strong's #2210 zēmioö 　⇒ NIV #2423 zēmioö 　⇒ NASB #2210 zēmioö **Luke 9:25** 　For what is a man advantaged, if he gain the whole world, and lose himself, or be **cast away**? [KJV] 　"For what is a man profited if he gains the whole world, and loses or **forfeits** himself? [NASB] 　What good is it for a man to gain the whole world, and yet lose or **forfeit** his very self? [NIV] 　For what profit is it to a man if he gains the whole world, and is himself destroyed or **lost**? [NKJV] 　And how do you benefit if you gain the whole world but lose or **forfeit** your own soul in the process? [NLT] 　τί γὰρ ὠφελεῖται ἄνθρωπος, κερδήσας τὸν κόσμον ὅλον, ἑαυτὸν δὲ ἀπολέσας, η **ζημιωθείς**; [GNS] 　τί γὰρ ὠφελεῖται ἄνθρωπος κερδήσας τὸν κόσμον ὅλον ἑαυτὸν δὲ ἀπολέσας η **ζημιωθείς**; [GNT]	To forfeit; to cast away; to harm; to suffer the loss of; to lose what is of greatest value; to be punished by forfeiting and losing. **Practical Application** 　Note that this is a stated fact, an inevitable and sure result. The person who seeks to please himself is doomed to "be destroyed or lost." He tried to find himself here on earth, but he never did. He lost himself. He lost the greatest things in all the world: certainty, assurance, confidence, and satisfaction of knowing that he is eternally secure and destined to live and serve God forever.
#2421 **Lost** **Lost–KJV** **Lost–NASB** **Lost–NIV** **Lost–NKJV** **Lost–NLT** **POSB REFERENCE** (Lk.15:4) *Deeper Study #1*	ἀπολωλός = apolölos Pronunciation: [ap-ol'-o-los] Parsing (part of speech): verb 　Mood—participle 　Tense—perfect 　Voice—active 　Case—accusative 　Gender—neuter 　Number—singular 　Stem or root—from ἀπόλλυμι Concordance References: 　⇒ Strong's #622 apollumi 　⇒ NIV #660 apollumi 　⇒ NASB #622 apollumi **Luke 15:4** 　What man of you, having an hundred sheep, if he lose one of them, doth not leave the ninety and nine in the wilderness, and go after that which is **lost**, until he find it? [KJV] 　"What man among you, if he has a hundred sheep and has lost one of them, does not leave the ninety-nine in the open pasture, and go after the one which is **lost**, until he finds it? [NASB] 　"Suppose one of you has a hundred sheep and loses one of them. Does he not leave the ninety-nine in the open country and go after the **lost** sheep until he finds it? [NIV] 　"What man of you, having a hundred sheep, if he loses one of them, does not leave the ninety-nine in the wilderness, and go after the one which is **lost** until he finds it? [NKJV] 　"If you had one hundred sheep, and one of them strayed away and was lost in the wilderness, wouldn't you leave the ninety-nine others to go and search for the **lost** one until you found it? [NLT] 　Τίς ἄνθρωπος ἐξ ὑμῶν ἔχων ἑκατὸν πρόβατα, καὶ ἀπολέσας ἕν ἐξ αὐτῶν, οὐ καταλείπει τὰ ἐννενήκονταεννέα ἐν τῇ ἐρήμῳ, καὶ πορεύεται ἐπὶ τὸ **ἀπολωλός**, ἕως εὕρῃ αὐτό. [GNS] 　Τίς ἄνθρωπος ἐξ ὑμῶν ἔχων ἑκατὸν πρόβατα καὶ ἀπολέσας ἐξ αὐτῶν ἓν οὐ καταλείπει τὰ ἐνενήκοντα ἐννέα ἐν τῇ ἐρήμῳ καὶ πορεύεται ἐπὶ τὸ **ἀπολωλὸς** ἕως εὕρῃ αὐτό; [GNT]	To be lost; to be on a road to destruction; to perish; to destroy; to lose; to lose eternal life; to be spiritually destitute; to be cut off; to vanish; to be wasted. **Practical Application** 　The sheep was lost because of self. A sheep loses itself in one of five ways. 1. The sheep is attracted by something out "in the wilderness," away from the flock of the Shepherd. What the sheep sees is more attractive and appealing. It tempts and seduces him, and he lusts after it (cp. 1 John 2:16). 2. The sheep is aimless, not paying attention to what is going on. It aimlessly wanders off, and while it is getting lost, the sheep does not know it is losing its way. The sheep is already lost when it discovers it is lost. 3. The sheep refuses to heed the warnings of the shepherd and the example of the other sheep (cp. 1 John 2:16). 4. The sheep is not attached enough to the shepherd or to the other sheep. He does not have the bond or union he should have. Therefore, he stays off by himself, eating and resting and working alone until eventually he wanders off without anyone knowing it, including himself (Hebrews 10:25). 5. The sheep does not trust the shepherd. It does not think the shepherd will take care and see that there is satisfying food. It goes astray in search of greener pasture and more satisfying food (see POSB note—Matthew 18:14 for the help of others needed by the shepherd to care for the sheep).

ENGLISH WORD	GREEK WORD AND VERSE	THE WORD MEANS...

#2422
Lost
 	
Lost–KJV
Perishing–NASB
Perishing–NIV
Perishing–NKJV
Perishing–NLT
 	
POSB
REFERENCE
(2 Cor.4:3-4; esp. v.3)
Note 3
	ἀπολλυμένοις = apollumenois
	Pronunciation: [ap-ol'-loo-mehn-oys]
	Parsing (part of speech): verb
	  Mood—participle
	  Tense—present
	  Voice—middle or passive
	  Case—dative
	  Gender—masculine
	  Number—plural
	  Stem or root—from ἀπόλλυμι
	Concordance References:
	  ⇒ Strong's #622 apollumi
	  ⇒ NIV #660 apollumi
	  ⇒ NASB #622 apollumi
	
	2 Cor. 4:3
	But if our gospel be hid, it is hid to them that are **lost**: [KJV]
	And even if our gospel is veiled, it is veiled to those who are **perishing**, [NASB]
	And even if our gospel is veiled, it is veiled to those who are **perishing**. [NIV]
	But even if our gospel is veiled, it is veiled to those who are **perishing**, [NKJV]
	If the Good News we preach is veiled from anyone, it is a sign that they are **perishing**. [NLT]
	εἰ δὲ καὶ ἔστι κεκαλυμμένον τὸ εὐαγγέλιον ἡμῶν, ἐν τοῖς **ἀπολλυμένοις** ἐστὶ κεκαλυμμένον· [GNS]
	εἰ δὲ καὶ ἔστιν κεκαλυμμένον τὸ εὐαγγέλιον ἡμῶν, ἐν τοῖς **ἀπολλυμένοις** ἐστὶν κεκαλυμμένον, [GNT]
		Perishing; to be lost; to be in the process of being destroyed or ruined, corrupted and put to death; to be wasted; to be executed.
		
		Practical Application
		The gospel is "hid" to men because they are "lost" (*apollumenois*). Men are on the road to being lost, to perishing. They have turned away from God and are traveling in the opposite direction along the road that leads to perdition.

#2423
Lost All Sensitivity
 	
Past feeling–KJV
Having become callous–NASB
Lost all sensitivity–NIV
Past feeling–NKJV
Don't care anymore about right and wrong–NLT
 	
POSB
REFERENCE
(Eph.4:17-19; esp. v.19)
Note 1, point 4
	ἀπηλγηκότες = apëlgëkotes
	Pronunciation: [ap-ayl'-gay'-ko-tehs]
	Parsing (part of speech): verb
	  Mood—participle
	  Tense—perfect
	  Voice—active
	  Case—nominative
	  Gender—masculine
	  Number—plural
	  Stem or root—from ἀπαλγέω
	Concordance References:
	  ⇒ Strong's #524 apalgeō
	  ⇒ NIV #556 apalgeō
	  ⇒ NASB #524 apalgeō
	
	Ephes. 4:19
	Who being **past feeling** have given themselves over unto lasciviousness, to work all uncleanness with greediness. [KJV]
	And they, **having become callous**, have given themselves over to sensuality, for the practice of every kind of impurity with greediness. [NASB]
	Having **lost all sensitivity**, they have given themselves over to sensuality so as to indulge in every kind of impurity, with a continual lust for more. [NIV]
	Who, being **past feeling**, have given themselves over to lewdness, to work all uncleanness with greediness. [NKJV]
	They **don't care anymore about right and wrong**, and they have given themselves over to immoral ways. Their lives are filled with all kinds of impurity and greed. [NLT]
	ἵτινες **ἀπηλγηκότες** ἑαυτοὺς παρέδωκαν τῇ ἀσελγείᾳ, εἰς ἐργασίαν ἀκαθαρσίας πάσης ἐν πλεονεξίᾳ. [GNS]
	οἵτινες **ἀπηλγηκότες** ἑαυτοὺς παρέδωκαν τῇ ἀσελγείᾳ εἰς ἐργασίαν ἀκαθαρσίας πάσης ἐν πλεονεξίᾳ. [GNT]
		To lose all sensitivity; to be past feeling; to become callous; not to care anymore about right and wrong; to become insensible, hardened.
		
		Practical Application
		Unbelievers reach a point where they lose all sensitivity for God and His standard of morality. The more a person walks without God, the more callous a person becomes to God. The more a person walks in sin, the more callous his conscience becomes to righteousness. Sin becomes more and more acceptable. The person's conscience no longer bothers him. He reaches a point of *losing all sensitivity*. The believer is not to return to sin. He is not to walk as other men walk—in sin, becoming callous and insensitive to God.

ENGLISH WORD	GREEK WORD AND VERSE	THE WORD MEANS...

#2424
Loud Voice
 	
Cried–KJV
Cried out–NASB
A loud voice–NIV
Cried out–NKJV
Shouted–NLT
 	
**POSB
REFERENCE**
(Jn.7:37-39; esp. v.37)
Note 2
	ἔκραξεν = *ekraxen*
	Pronunciation: [eh-krahd'-zehn]
	Parsing (part of speech): verb
	   Mood—indicative
	   Tense—aorist
	   Voice—active
	   Person—3rd person
	   Number—singular
	   Stem or root—from κράζω
	Concordance References:
	  ⇒ Strong's #2896 krazö
	  ⇒ NIV #3189 krazö
	  ⇒ NASB #2896 krazö
	
	John 7:37
	In the last day, that great *day* of the feast, Jesus stood and **cried**, saying, If any man thirst, let him come unto me, and drink. [KJV]
	Now on the last day, the great *day* of the feast, Jesus stood and **cried out**, saying, "If any man is thirsty, let him come to Me and drink. [NASB]
	On the last and greatest day of the Feast, Jesus stood and said in **a loud voice**, "If anyone is thirsty, let him come to me and drink. [NIV]
	On the last day, that great *day* of the feast, Jesus stood and **cried out**, saying, "If anyone thirsts, let him come to Me and drink. [NKJV]
	On the last day, the climax of the festival, Jesus stood and **shouted** to the crowds, "If you are thirsty, come to me! [NLT]
	Ἐν δὲ τῇ ἐσχάτῃ ἡμέρᾳ τῇ μεγάλῃ τῆς ἑορτῆς εἱστήκει ὁ Ἰησοῦς, καὶ **ἔκραζε**, λέγων, Ἐάν τις διψᾷ ἐρχέσθω πρός με, καὶ πινέτω. [GNS]
	Ἐν δὲ τῇ ἐσχάτῃ ἡμέρᾳ τῇ μεγάλῃ τῆς ἑορτῆς εἱστήκει ὁ Ἰησοῦς καὶ **ἔκραξεν** λέγων, Ἐάν τις διψᾷ ἐρχέσθω πρός με καὶ πινέτω. [GNT]
		To cry or call out with a loud voice; to shout in order to be heard; to exclaim; to scream; to shriek; to yell.
		
		Practical Application
		It was on "the last day, that great day of the feast," the day when the people marched in the processional seven times that Jesus made His phenomenal claim. Some imagine Jesus' shouting His claim just as the people finished saying, "grant us success" (Psalm 118:25).
		Imagine the scene: Jesus did two unusual things. He "stood" (a teacher always sat in that day), and He said in "a loud voice" (*ekraxen*), shouting loudly. Both actions would startle and shock the people to attention. Picture thousands of voices praying to God for the fruitful rains in the coming season, reciting: "grant us success." Then all of a sudden, piercing the air, comes the thundering cry:
		
		If anyone is thirsty, let him come to me and drink. Whoever believes in me, as the Scripture has said, streams of living water will flow from within him. (John 7:37-38) [NIV]
		
		Jesus made three phenomenal claims.
		1. Jesus Christ is the source of life: He is the One who can quench the real thirst of man's being, who can meet the desperate need of man for prosperity, the real fruit and bounty of life.
		2. Jesus Christ is the source of abundant life. Rivers of *living water* can flow out from a person. An abundance of life can be experienced (see POSB *Deeper Study #1*—John 1:4; POSB *Deeper Study #1*—John 10:10).
		3. Jesus Christ is the source of the Holy Spirit. Streams of living water refer to the Holy Spirit. This is a crucial verse, for it is the only place "living waters" is defined. When Jesus spoke of giving "living water," He meant He would give the Holy Spirit to a person. The presence of the Holy Spirit, of course, meant the experience of abundant and eternal life. Note: it is only the believer in Christ who receives the Holy Spirit. Belief in Him is essential. Christ is the Giver of the Spirit. (See POSB note—John 4:13-14 for more discussion.)

#2425
Loud Voice
 	
Loud voice–KJV
Loud voice–NASB
Called out–NIV
Loud voice–NKJV
Loud voice, called to him in a–NLT
 	
**POSB
REFERENCE**
(Acts 14:8-13; esp. v.10)
Note 2, point 1e
	εἶπεν μεγάλῃ φωνῇ = *eipen megalë phönë*
	Pronunciation: [ep'-ee meg'ah-lay fo-nay']
	Parsing *eipen* (part of speech): verb
	   Mood—indicative
	   Tense—aorist
	   Voice—active
	   Person—3rd person
	   Number—singular
	   Stem or root—from εἶπον αορ οφ λέγω
	Parsing *megalë* (part of speech): adjective
	   Case—dative
	   Gender—feminine
	   Number—singular
	   Stem or root—from μέγας
	Parsing *phönë* (part of speech): noun
	   Case—dative
	   Gender—feminine
	   Number—singular
		To call out; to call out with a loud voice, a loud cry, at the top of voice; to give a shout.
		
		Practical Application
		Paul did not reach out for the man; he did not touch the man at all. He simply spoke to the man. The power was of Christ and the faith was within the man. The man had to exercise his faith, believe in and really trust in the Lord Jesus, to be healed just as he did to be saved.

ENGLISH WORD	GREEK WORD AND VERSE	THE WORD MEANS...
	Stem or root—from φωνη Concordance References: ⇒ Strong's #4483+3173+5456 legö megas phönë ⇒ NIV #3306+3489+5889 legö megas phönë [called out] ⇒ NASB #4483+3173+5456 legö megas phönë **Acts 14:10** Said with a **loud voice**, Stand upright on thy feet. And he leaped and walked. [KJV] Said with a **loud voice**, "Stand upright on your feet." And he leaped up and *began* to walk. [NASB] And **called out**, "Stand up on your feet!" At that, the man jumped up and began to walk. [NIV] Said with a **loud voice**, "Stand up straight on your feet!" And he leaped and walked. [NKJV] So Paul **called to him in a loud voice**, "Stand up!" And the man jumped to his feet and started walking. [NLT] εἶπε μεγάλῃ τῇ **φωνῇ**, Ἀνάστηθι ἐπὶ τοὺς πόδας σου ὀρθός. καὶ ἥλλετο καὶ περιεπάτει. [GNS] εἶπεν μεγάλῃ **φωνῇ**, Ἀνάστηθι ἐπὶ τοὺς πόδας σου ὀρθός. καὶ ἥλατο καὶ περιεπάτει. [GNT]	

#2426
Love
 	
Love–KJV
Love–NASB
Love–NIV
Love–NKJV
Love–NLT
 	
POSB REFERENCE
(Mt.5:44)
Deeper Study #1
	ἀγαπᾶτε = agapate
	Pronunciation: [ag-ap-ah'-teh]
	Parsing (part of speech): verb
	  Mood—imperative
	  Tense—present
	  Voice—active
	  Person—2nd person
	  Number—plural
	  Stem or root—from ἀγαπάω
	Concordance References:
	⇒ Strong's #25 agapao
	⇒ NIV #26 agapao
	⇒ NASB #25 agapao
	
	Matthew 5:44
	But I say unto you, **Love** your enemies, bless them that curse you, do good to them that hate you, and pray for them which despitefully use you, and persecute you; [KJV]
	"But I say to you, **love** your enemies, and pray for those who persecute you [NASB]
	But I tell you: **Love** your enemies and pray for those who persecute you, [NIV]
	But I say to you, **love** your enemies, bless those who curse you, do good to those who hate you, and pray for those who spitefully use you and persecute you, [NKJV]
	But I say, **love** your enemies! Pray for those who persecute you! [NLT]
	ἐγὼ δὲ λέγω ὑμῖν, **ἀγαπᾶτε** τοὺς ἐχθροὺς ὑμῶν, εὐλογεῖτε τοὺς καταρωμένους ὑμᾶς, καλῶς ποιεῖτε τοὺς μισοῦντας ὑμᾶς, καὶ προσεύχεσθε ὑπὲρ τῶν ἐπηρεαζόντων ὑμᾶς, καὶ διωκόντων ὑμᾶς· [GNS]
	ἐγὼ δὲ λέγω ὑμῖν, **ἀγαπᾶτε** τοὺς ἐχθροὺς ὑμῶν καὶ προσεύχεσθε ὑπὲρ τῶν διωκόντων ὑμᾶς, [GNT]
		The most supreme love, the love of God.
		
		Practical Application
		The Greeks interpreted love in four ways, and used four different words to describe which kind of love was meant:
		1. There was "*eros*" love. This is love that arises from passion, infatuation, and sexual attraction. It is the love (passion) of a man for a woman. The word is never used in the New Testament.
		2. There was "*storge*" love. This is love that arises from affection, a natural born affection, the affection of family love. It is the love and natural affection between parent and child. The word is never used in the New Testament [apart from two compounds—"*astorgos*" (Ro.1:31; 2 Ti.3:3) and "*philostorgos*" (Ro.12:10)].
		3. There was "*phileo*" or "*philadelphia*" love. This is love that arises from affection also, but from a different kind. It is a deep, intense, and warm affection. It is an affection that fills a person's heart with warmth and tenderness, with a sense of preciousness and a deep consciousness of loving and of being loved. It is the love of deep affection and feelings toward those who are very near and very dear to one's heart (see POSB notes—Jn.21:15-17).
		4. There was "*agape*" love. This is a sacrificial love that does well and wishes well—no matter the circumstance. It is a love that disciplines and corrects harmful indulgence and misbehavior, no matter the cost to self. It is a love that demonstrates kindness, benevolence, and esteem even in the midst of stormy situations. It is the love of the mind, reason, and choice. Simply stated, agape love is a sacrificial love, that is, a love that cares, gives, and works for another person's good—no matter how the person may respond or treat one (see POSB notes—Jn.21:15-17).

ENGLISH WORD	GREEK WORD AND VERSE	THE WORD MEANS...

#2427
Love
 	
Charity–KJV
Love–NASB
Love–NIV
Love–NKJV
Love–NLT
 	
POSB
REFERENCE
(1 Cor.13:1-13; esp. v.1)
Deeper Study #1
 	
See also POSB REF:
(Rom.5:6-11; esp. v.8)
Introduction
(Col.3:14)
Note 9
(I Tim.1:5-6: esp. v.5)
Note 3
(2 Pet.1:5-7; esp.v.7)
Note 1, point 7
(2 Jn.1:5)
Deeper Study #1
	ἀγάπην = *agapēn*
	Pronunciation: [ag-ah'-payn]
	Parsing (part of speech): noun
	  Case—accusative
	  Gender—feminine
	  Number—singular
	  Stem or root—from ἀγάπη, ης
	Concordance References:
	⇒ Strong's #26 agapē
	⇒ NIV #27 agapē
	⇒ NASB #26 agapē
	
	1 Cor. 13:1
	Though I speak with the tongues of men and of angels, and have not **charity**, I am become *as* sounding brass, or a tinkling cymbal. [KJV]
	If I speak with the tongues of men and of angels, but do not have **love**, I have become a noisy gong or a clanging cymbal. [NASB]
	If I speak in the tongues of men and of angels, but have not **love**, I am only a resounding gong or a clanging cymbal. [NIV]
	Though I speak with the tongues of men and of angels, but have not **love**, I have become sounding brass or a clanging cymbal. [NKJV]
	If I could speak in any language in heaven or on earth but didn't **love** others, I would only be making meaningless noise like a loud gong or a clanging cymbal. [NLT]
	Ἐὰν ταῖς γλώσσαις τῶν ἀνθρώπων λαλῶ καὶ τῶν ἀγγέλων, **ἀγάπην** δὲ μὴ ἔχω, γέγονα χαλκὸς ἠχῶν ἢ κύμβαλον ἀλαλάζον. [GNS]
	Ἐὰν ταῖς γλώσσαις τῶν ἀνθρώπων λαλῶ καὶ τῶν ἀγγέλων, **ἀγάπην** δὲ μὴ ἔχω, γέγονα χαλκὸς ἠχῶν ἢ κύμβαλον ἀλαλάζον. [GNT]
		Love, the "God-kind" of love; Christian love; the highest level of concern and interest.
		
		Practical Application
		The meaning of *agape love* is more clearly seen by contrasting it with the various kinds of love. There are essentially four kinds of love. Whereas the English language has only the word *love* to describe all the affectionate experiences of men, the Greek language had a different word to describe each kind of love.
		1. There is *passionate love* or *eros love*. This is the physical love between sexes; the patriotic love of a person for his nation; the ambition of a person for power, wealth, or fame. Briefly stated, *eros love* is the base love of a man that arises from his own inner passion. Sometimes *eros love* is focused upon good and other times it is focused upon bad. It should be noted that *eros love* is never used in the New Testament.
		2. There is *affectionate love* or *storge love*. This is the kind of love that exists between parent and child and between loyal citizens and a trustworthy ruler. *Storge love* is also not used in the New Testament.
		3. There is an *endearing love*, the love that cherishes. This is *phileo love*, the love of a husband and wife for each other, of a brother for a brother, of a friend for the dearest of friends. It is the love that cherishes, that holds someone or something ever so dear to one's heart.
		4. There is *selfless and sacrificial love* or *agape love*. Agape love is the love of the mind, of the reason, of the will. It is the love that goes so far...
		  • that it loves a person even if he does not deserve to be loved.
		  • that it actually loves the person who is utterly unworthy of being loved.
		  Note: For more discussion concerning love, see POSB note, pt. 4, *Love*—John 21:15-17 and POSB *Deeper Study* #1, pt.4, *Love*—1 Cor.13:1-13.

#2428
Love
 	
Love–KJV
Love–NASB
Love–NIV
Love–NKJV
Love–NLT
 	
POSB
REFERENCE
(Gal.5:22-23; esp. v.22)
Note 1
	ἀγάπη = *agapē*
	Pronunciation: [ag-ah'-pay]
	Parsing (part of speech): noun
	  Case—nominative
	  Gender—feminine
	  Number—singular
	  Stem or root—from ἀγάπη, ης
	Concordance References:
	⇒ Strong's #26 agapē
	⇒ NIV #27 agapē
	⇒ NASB #26 agapē
	
	Galatians 5:22
	But the fruit of the Spirit is **love**, joy, peace, longsuffering, gentleness, goodness, faith, [KJV]
	But the fruit of the Spirit is **love**, joy, peace, patience, kindness, goodness, faithfulness, [NASB]
	But the fruit of the Spirit is **love**, joy, peace, patience, kindness, goodness, faithfulness, [NIV]
	But the fruit of the Spirit is **love**, joy, peace, longsuffering, kindness, goodness, faithfulness, [NKJV]
	But when the Holy Spirit controls our lives, he will produce this kind of fruit in us: **love**, joy, peace, patience, kindness, goodness, faithfulness, [NLT]
		Love; the highest form of Christian love and concern.
		
		Practical Application
		Agapē love is the love of the mind, of the reason, of the will. It is the love that goes so far...
		  • that it loves regardless of feelings—whether a person feels like loving or not.
		  • that it loves a person even if the person does not deserve to be loved.
		  • that it actually loves the person who is utterly unworthy of being loved.
		Note four significant points about agape love.
		1. Selfless or agape love is the love of God, the very love possessed by God Himself. It is the love demonstrated in the cross of Christ.
		2. Selfless or agape love is a gift of God. It can be experienced only if a person knows God *personally*—only if a person has received the love of God, that is, Christ Jesus, into his heart and life. Agape love has to be shed abroad (poured out, flooded, spread about) by the Spirit of God within the heart of a person.

ENGLISH WORD	GREEK WORD AND VERSE	THE WORD MEANS...
	ὁ δὲ καρπὸς τοῦ Πνεύματός ἐστιν **ἀγάπη**, χαρά, εἰρήνη, μακροθυμία, χρηστότης, ἀγαθωσύνη, πίστις, [GNS] Ὁ δὲ καρπὸς τοῦ πνεύματός ἐστιν **ἀγάπη** χαρά εἰρήνη, μακροθυμία, χρηστότης ἀγαθωσύνη, πίστις [GNT]	3. Selfless or agape love is the greatest thing in all of life according to the Lord Jesus Christ. 4. Selfless or agape love is the greatest possession and gift in human life according to the Scripture (1 Cor. 13:1-13).

#2429
Love
 	
Love–KJV
Love–NASB
Love–NIV
Love–NKJV
Love–NLT
 	
POSB REFERENCE
(Eph.5:25-33; esp. v.25)
Note 2, point 1
 	
See also POSB REF:
(Col.3:19)
Note 2
	ἀγαπᾶτε = *agapate*
	Pronunciation: [ag-ap-ah'-teh]
	Parsing (part of speech): verb
	   Mood—imperative
	   Tense—present
	   Voice—active
	   Person—2nd person
	   Number—plural
	   Stem or root—from **ἀγαπάω**
	Concordance References:
	  ⇒ Strong's #25 agapaō
	  ⇒ NIV #26 agapaō
	  ⇒ NASB #25 agapaō
	
	Ephes. 5:25
	Husbands, **love** your wives, even as Christ also loved the church, and gave himself for it; [KJV]
	Husbands, **love** your wives, just as Christ also loved the church and gave Himself up for her; [NASB]
	Husbands, **love** your wives, just as Christ loved the church and gave himself up for her [NIV]
	Husbands, **love** your wives, just as Christ also loved the church and gave Himself for her, [NKJV]
	And you husbands must **love** your wives with the same love Christ showed the church. He gave up his life for her [NLT]
	οἱ ἄνδρες, **ἀγαπᾶτε** τὰς γυναῖκας ἑαυτῶν, καθὼς καὶ ὁ Χριστὸς ἠγάπησε τὴν ἐκκλησίαν, καὶ ἑαυτὸν παρέδωκεν ὑπὲρ αὐτῆς· [GNS]
	Οἱ ἄνδρες, **ἀγαπᾶτε** τὰς γυναῖκας, καθὼς καὶ ὁ Χριστὸς ἠγάπησεν τὴν ἐκκλησίαν καὶ ἑαυτὸν παρέδωκεν ὑπὲρ αὐτῆς, [GNT]
		Love; the highest form of Christian love and concern.
		
		Practical Application
		The love which the husband is to have for his wife is the very love of God Himself (*agapë* love). *Agapë* love is a selfless and unselfish love, a giving and sacrificial love. It is the love of the mind and will as well as of the heart. It is not only a love of affection and feelings; it is a love of the *will and commitment*. It is a love that wills and commits itself to love a person. It is the love that works for the highest good of the person loved...
		• that loves even if the person *does not deserve to be loved*.
		• that loves even if the person is *utterly unworthy of being loved*.
		Just imagine! What would happen in most marriages if the husband so loved his wife, loved her...
		• with a selfless and unselfish love.
		• with a giving and sacrificial love.
		• with a love of the will as well as of the heart.
		• with a love of commitment as well as of *affection*.
		One thing that would happen in most marriages would be this: the wife would melt in the husband's arms and willingly accept his authority as the head of the family.
		Note that the standard of the husband's love is the love of Christ for the church. The love of Christ for the church can be described in one simple statement: Christ *gave Himself* for the church. Christ loved the church so much that He gave Himself—*sacrificed Himself totally*—gave all He was and had for it. This is the love the husband is to have for his wife.

#2430
Love
 	
Love–KJV
Love–NASB
Love–NIV
Love–NKJV
Love–NLT
 	
POSB REFERENCE
(Rev.3:18-20; esp. v.19)
Note 5, point 2
 	
See also POSB REF:
(Jn.21:15)
Note 2
	φιλῶ = *philō*
	Pronunciation: [fil-o']
	Parsing (part of speech): verb
	   Mood—subjunctive
	   Tense—present
	   Voice—active
	   Person—1st person
	   Number—singular
	   Stem or root—from **φιλέω**
	Concordance References:
	  ⇒ Strong's #5368 phileō
	  ⇒ NIV #5797 phileō
	  ⇒ NASB #5368 phileō
	
	Rev. 3:19
	As many as I **love**, I rebuke and chasten: be zealous therefore, and repent. [KJV]
	'Those whom I **love**, I reprove and discipline; be zealous therefore, and repent. [NASB]
	Those whom I **love** I rebuke and discipline. So be earnest, and repent. [NIV]
	As many as I **love**, I rebuke and chasten. Therefore be zealous and repent. [NKJV]
		To love. It means a dear love, a tender, fatherly love. Phileo love is the love of tender affection, of warm and deep feelings within the heart. It is the deep and precious love of those near and dear to one's heart. It is brotherly love, a love between family members, a love that would die for its brother.
		
		Practical Application
		Christ counsels them to be zealous and to repent. Note what Christ says: He loves them. They are lukewarm and indifferent to Him, only half-committed to Him, but He still loves them. This is the reason He rebukes and chastens the lukewarm and half-committed person. It is not out of anger that Christ tells people they are doing wrong, sinning, coming short, and are doomed. He tells them out of love. They must know they are doing wrong in order to correct their behavior. They must know that judgment lies ahead so that they will do whatever is need-

ENGLISH WORD	GREEK WORD AND VERSE	THE WORD MEANS...
	I am the one who corrects and disciplines everyone I **love**. Be diligent and turn from your indifference. [NLT] ἐγὼ ὅσους ἐὰν **φιλῶ**, ἐλέγχω καὶ παιδεύω. ζήλωσον οὖν καὶ μετανόησον. [GNS] ἐγὼ ὅσους ἐὰν **φιλῶ** ἐλέγχω καὶ παιδεύω· ζήλευε οὖν καὶ μετανόησον. [GNT]	ed to save themselves. The Lord's rebuke and chastening hand is for one purpose only: that they might see the love of Christ—see their wrong, correct their behavior, and change their lives. He wants people to possess the fullness of life and the hope of eternal life.

#2431
Love
 	
Love–KJV
Love–NASB
Love–NIV
Love–NKJV
Love–NLT
 	
**POSB
REFERENCE**
(Tit.3:4-5; esp. v.4)
Note 1, point 2
	φιλανθρωπία = *philanthrōpia*
	Pronunciation: [fil-anh'-thro-pi-ah]
	Parsing (part of speech): noun
	    Case—nominative
	    Gender—feminine
	    Number—singular
	    Stem or root—from **φιλανθρωπία**, ας
	Concordance References:
	  ⇒ Strong's #5363 philanthrōpia
	  ⇒ NIV #5792 philanthrōpia
	  ⇒ NASB #5363 philanthrōpia
	
	Titus 3:4
	But after that the kindness and **love** of God our Saviour toward man appeared, [KJV]
	But when the kindness of God our Savior and *His* **love** for mankind appeared, [NASB]
	But when the kindness and **love** of God our Savior appeared, [NIV]
	But when the kindness and the **love** of God our Savior toward man appeared, [NKJV]
	But then God our Savior showed us his kindness and **love**. [NLT]
	ὅτε δὲ ἡ χρηστότης καὶ ἡ **φιλανθρωπία** ἐπεφάνη τοῦ σωτῆρος ἡμῶν Θεοῦ, [GNS]
	ὅτε δὲ ἡ χρηστότης καὶ ἡ **φιλανθρωπία** ἐπεφάνη τοῦ σωτῆρος ἡμῶν θεοῦ, [GNT]
		Love, kindness.
		
		Practical Application
		Salvation comes from God's "love" (*philanthrōpia*). This means that God's love reached out toward man; that God has a deep-seated affection for man and that He has showered His affection upon man by saving him. The word has the idea of compassion in it. God loves man so much that His affection and compassion are stirred to save men. God loves us so much that He must act to handle the sin and death problems for man and provide an escape from condemnation.

#2432
Love–Loved
 	
Love–KJV
Love–NASB
Love–NIV
Love–NKJV
Loved–NLT
 	
**POSB
REFERENCE**
(Eph.2:4-5; esp. v.4)
Note 1, point 1b
	ἀγάπην ἠγάπησεν = *agapēn ēgapēsen*
	Pronunciation: [ag-ah'-payn eyg-ap-ay'-sehn]
	Parsing (part of speech): noun
	    Case—accusative
	    Gender—feminine
	    Number—singular
	    Stem or root—from **ἀγάπη**, ης
	Parsing (part of speech): verb
	    Mood—indicative
	    Tense—aorist
	    Voice—active
	    Person—3rd person
	    Number—singular
	    Stem or root—from **ἀγαπάω**
	Concordance References:
	  ⇒ Strong's #25+26 agapaō agapē
	  ⇒ NIV #26+27 agapaō agapē
	  ⇒ NASB #25+26 agapaō agapē
	
	Ephes. 2:4
	But God, who is rich in mercy, for his great **love** wherewith he loved us, [KJV]
	But God, being rich in mercy, because of His great **love** with which He loved us, [NASB]
	But because of his great **love** for us, God, who is rich in mercy, [NIV]
	But God, who is rich in mercy, because of His great **love** with which He loved us, [NKJV]
	But God is so rich in mercy, and he **loved** us so very much, [NLT]
	ὁ δὲ Θεὸς, πλούσιος ων ἐν ἐλέει, διὰ τὴν πολλὴν **ἀγάπην** αὐτοῦ ἦν **ἠγάπησεν** ἡμᾶς, [GNS]
	ὁ δὲ θεὸς πλούσιος ων ἐν ἐλέει, διὰ τὴν πολλὴν **ἀγάπην** αὐτοῦ ἦν **ἠγάπησεν** ἡμᾶς, [GNT]
		Love; to prove one's love.
		
		Practical Application
		God is love; He is full of love (*agapē*): a selfless and sacrificial love; a love of the mind, of the reason, of the will as well as of the heart and affections. It is the love that goes so far...
		• that it loves a person even if he does not deserve to be loved.
		• that it loves the person who is utterly unworthy of being loved.
		• that it is compelled to sacrifice itself for its enemies (Romans 5:8, 10).

ENGLISH WORD	GREEK WORD AND VERSE	THE WORD MEANS...

#2433
Love All That Is Good
 	
Lover of good men–KJV
Loving what is good–NASB
Loves what is good–NIV
Lover of what is good– NKJV
Love all that is good–NLT
 	
POSB REFERENCE
(Tit.1:7-8; esp. v.8)
Note 3, point 2b
	φιλάγαθον = philagathon
	Pronunciation: [fil-ag'-ath-on]
	Parsing (part of speech): adjective
	    Case—accusative
	    Gender—masculine
	    Number—singular
	    Stem or root—from φιλάγαθος, ον
	Concordance References:
	  ⇒ Strong's #5358 philagathos
	  ⇒ NIV #5787 philagathos
	  ⇒ NASB #5358 philagathos
	
	Titus 1:8
	But a lover of hospitality, a **lover of good men**, sober, just, holy, temperate; [KJV]
	But hospitable, **loving what is good**, sensible, just, devout, self-controlled, [NASB]
	Rather he must be hospitable, one who **loves what is good**, who is self-controlled, upright, holy and disciplined. [NIV]
	But hospitable, a **lover of what is good**, sober-minded, just, holy, self-controlled, [NKJV]
	He must enjoy having guests in his home and must **love all that is good**. He must live wisely and be fair. He must live a devout and disciplined life. [NLT]
	ἀλλὰ φιλόξενον, **φιλάγαθον**, σώφρονα, δίκαιον, ὅσιον, ἐγκρατῆ, [GNS]
	ἀλλὰ φιλόξενον **φιλάγαθον** σώφρονα δίκαιον ὅσιον ἐγκρατῆ, [GNT]
		Loves what is good; loving what is good; love all that is good. The Greek means a lover of good things as well as of good people.
		
		Practical Application
		The minister or steward of God must love all that is good (*philagathon*). The minister of God loves good no matter where he finds it, in people or things. He loves the poor and the homeless, the weak and the suffering, as well as the wealthy and healthy. And the minister loves to do good things for everyone, no matter who they are.

#2434
Love As Brothers– Love As Brethren
 	
Love as brethren–KJV
Brotherly–NASB
Love as brothers–NIV
Love as brothers–NKJV
Loving one another–NLT
 	
POSB REFERENCE
(1 Pt.3:8)
Note 3
	φιλάδελφοι = philadelphoi
	Pronunciation: [fil-ad'-el-foy]
	Parsing (part of speech): adjective
	    Case—nominative
	    Gender—masculine
	    Number—plural
	    Stem or root—from φιλάδελφος, ον
	Concordance References:
	  ⇒ Strong's #5361 philadelphos
	  ⇒ NIV #5790 philadelphos
	  ⇒ NASB #5361 philadelphos
	
	1 Peter 3:8
	Finally, *be ye* all of one mind, having compassion one of another, **love as brethren**, *be* pitiful, *be* courteous: [KJV]
	To sum up, let all be harmonious, sympathetic, **brotherly**, kindhearted, and humble in spirit; [NASB]
	Finally, all of you, live in harmony with one another; be sympathetic, **love as brothers**, be compassionate and humble. [NIV]
	Finally, all *of you be* of one mind, having compassion for one another; **love as brothers**, *be* tenderhearted, *be* courteous; [NKJV]
	Finally, all of you should be of one mind, full of sympathy toward each other, **loving one another** with tender hearts and humble minds. [NLT]
	Τὸ δὲ τέλος, πάντες ὁμόφρονες, συμπαθεῖς, **φιλάδελφοι**, εὔσπλαγχνοι, φιλόφρονες· [GNS]
	Τὸ δὲ τέλος πάντες ὁμόφρονες, συμπαθεῖς, **φιλάδελφοι**, εὔσπλαγχνοι, ταπεινόφρονες, [GNT]
		To love as brothers; to be brotherly; to love one another; to love another believer.
		
		Practical Application
		There is no greater force than love. If two people truly love each other, they will do anything for the other. There is no greater bond on earth than true love. This is especially true of the love between believers. Why? Is there a difference between the love that believers have for one another and the love that neighbors have for one another? Scripture says yes, emphatically yes. Believers are to have a different kind of love than neighbors have for one another. The love that believers are to have for one another is what the Greek calls *philadelphia* love, a very special kind of love.

#2435
Love Each Other With True Christian Love
 	
Brotherly love–KJV
Love of the brethren–NASB
	φιλαδελφία = philadelphia
	Pronunciation: [fil-ad-el-fee'-ahs]
	Parsing (part of speech): noun
	    Case—genitive
	    Gender—feminine
	    Number—singular
	    Stem or root—from φιλαδελφία, ας
	Concordance References:
	  ⇒ Strong's #5360 philadelphia
	  ⇒ NIV #5789 philadelphia
	  ⇒ NASB #5360 philadelphia
		Brotherly love; love of the brothers shown among God's people; loving one another as brothers; brotherly kindness.
		
		Practical Application
		Note that the love existing among believers is a special kind of love. It is "to love each other with true Christian love" (*philadelphia*), a very special love that exists between brothers and sisters within a loving family, brothers and sisters

ENGLISH WORD	GREEK WORD AND VERSE	THE WORD MEANS...
Loving each other as brothers–NIV Brotherly love–NKJV **Love each other with true Christian love–NLT** **POSB REFERENCE** (Heb.13:1) Note 1, point 1	**Hebrews 13:1** Let **brotherly love** continue. [KJV] Let **love of the brethren** continue. [NASB] Keep on **loving each other as brothers**. [NIV] Let **brotherly love** continue. [NKJV] Continue to **love each other with true Christian love**. [NLT] Ἡ **φιλαδελφία** μενέτω. [GNS] Ἡ **φιλαδελφία** μενέτω. [GNT]	who truly cherish one another. It is the kind of love... • that binds each other together as a family, as a brotherly clan. • that binds each other in an unbreakable union. • that holds each other ever so deeply within the heart. • that knows deep affection for each other. • that nourishes and nurtures each other. • that shows concern and looks after the welfare of each other. • that joins hands with each other in a common purpose under one father (Leon Morris. *The Epistles of Paul to the Thessalonians*. "Tyndale New Testament Commentary," p.80).

#2436
Love For Brothers
 	
Love of the brethen–KJV
Love of the brethen–NASB
Love for brothers–NIV
Love of the brethren–NKJV
Love for each other–NLT
 	
**POSB
REFERENCE**
(1 Pt.1:22-25; esp. v.22)
Introduction
	φιλαδελφίαν = philadelphian
	Pronunciation: [fil-ad-el-fee'-ahn]
	Parsing (part of speech): noun
	   Case—accusative
	   Gender—feminine
	   Number—singular
	   Stem or root—from *φιλαδελφία, ας*
	Concordance References:
	⇒ Strong's #5360 philadelphia
	⇒ NIV #5789 philadelphia
	⇒ NASB #5360 philadelphia
	
	1 Peter 1:22
	Seeing ye have purified your souls in obeying the truth through the Spirit unto unfeigned **love of the brethren**, *see that ye* love one another with a pure heart fervently: [KJV]
	Since you have in obedience to the truth purified your souls for a sincere **love of the brethren**, fervently love one another from the heart, [NASB]
	Now that you have purified yourselves by obeying the truth so that you have sincere **love for** your **brothers**, love one another deeply, from the heart. [NIV]
	Since you have purified your souls in obeying the truth through the Spirit in sincere **love of the brethren**, love one another fervently with a pure heart, [NKJV]
	Now you can have sincere **love for each other** as brothers and sisters because you were cleansed from your sins when you accepted the truth of the Good News. So see to it that you really do love each other intensely with all your hearts. [NLT]
	τὰς ψυχὰς ὑμῶν ἡγνικότες ἐν τῇ ὑπακοῇ τῆς ἀληθείας διὰ Πνεύματος εἰς **φιλαδελφίαν** ἀνυπόκριτον, ἐκ καθαρᾶς καρδίας ἀλλήλους ἀγαπήσατε ἐκτενῶς· [GNS]
	τὰς ψυχὰς ὑμῶν ἡγνικότες ἐν τῇ ὑπακοῇ τῆς ἀληθείας εἰς **φιλαδελφίαν** ἀνυπόκριτον, ἐκ [καθαρᾶς] καρδίας ἀλλήλους ἀγαπήσατε ἐκτενῶς [GNT]
		Love for brothers; love of the brethren; love for others; brotherly kindness.
		
		Practical Application
		There is no greater force than love. If two people truly love each other, they will do anything for the other. There is no greater bond on earth than true love. This is especially true of the love between believers. Why? Is there a difference between the love that believers have for one another and the love that neighbors have for one another? Scripture says yes, emphatically yes. Believers are to have a different kind of love than neighbors have for one another. The love that believers are to have for one another is what the Greek calls *philadelphian* love, a very special kind of love. The word is "scarcely found except in Christian writings" (B.C. Coffin. *First Peter*. "The Pulpit Commentary," Vol.22, p.11.) *Philadelphian love* means *brotherly love*, the very special love that exists between the brothers and sisters within a loving family, brothers and sisters who truly cherish each other. It is the kind of love...
		• that binds one another together as a family, as a brotherly clan.
		• that binds one another in an unbreakable union.
		• that holds one another ever so deeply within the heart.
		• that knows deep affection for one another.
		• that nourishes and nurtures one another.
		• that shows concern and looks after the welfare of one another.
		
		The importance of believers loving one another with a *philadelphian love* cannot be over stressed.

#2437
Love For Each Other
 	
Love of the brethen–KJV
Love of the brethen–NASB
	φιλαδελφίαν = philadelphian
	Pronunciation: [fil-ad-el-fee'-ahn]
	Parsing (part of speech): noun
	   Case—accusative
	   Gender—feminine
	   Number—singular
	   Stem or root—from *φιλαδελφία, ας*
	Concordance References:
	⇒ Strong's #5360 philadelphia
		Love for brothers; love for others; brotherly kindness.
		
		Practical Application
		There is no greater force than love. If two people truly love each other, they will do anything for the other. There is no greater bond on earth than true love. This is especially true of the love between believers. Why? Is there a differ-

ENGLISH WORD	GREEK WORD AND VERSE	THE WORD MEANS...
Love for brothers–NIV Love of the brethren–NKJV **Love for each other–NLT** **POSB REFERENCE** (1 Pt.1:22-25; esp. v.22) Introduction	⇒ NIV #5789 philadelphia ⇒ NASB #5360 philadelphia **1 Peter 1:22** Seeing ye have purified your souls in obeying the truth through the Spirit unto unfeigned **love of the brethren**, *see that ye* love one another with a pure heart fervently: [KJV] Since you have in obedience to the truth purified your souls for a sincere **love of the brethren**, fervently love one another from the heart, [NASB] Now that you have purified yourselves by obeying the truth so that you have sincere **love for** your **brothers**, love one another deeply, from the heart. [NIV] Since you have purified your souls in obeying the truth through the Spirit in sincere **love of the brethren**, love one another fervently with a pure heart, [NKJV] Now you can have sincere **love for each other** as brothers and sisters because you were cleansed from your sins when you accepted the truth of the Good News. So see to it that you really do love each other intensely with all your hearts. [NLT] τὰς ψυχὰς ὑμῶν ἡγνικότες ἐν τῇ ὑπακοῇ τῆς ἀληθείας διὰ Πνεύματος εἰς **φιλαδελφίαν** ἀνυπόκριτον, ἐκ καθαρᾶς καρδίας ἀλλήλους ἀγαπήσατε ἐκτενῶς· [GNS] Τὰς ψυχὰς ὑμῶν ἡγνικότες ἐν τῇ ὑπακοῇ τῆς ἀληθείας εἰς **φιλαδελφίαν** ἀνυπόκριτον, ἐκ [καθαρᾶς] καρδίας ἀλλήλους ἀγαπήσατε ἐκτενῶς [GNT]	ence between the love that believers have for one another and the love that neighbors have for one another? Scripture says yes, emphatically yes. Believers are to have a different kind of love than neighbors have for one another. The love that believers are to have for one another is what the Greek calls *philadelphian* love, a very special kind of love. (See **Love For Brothers,** for additional discussion.)
#2438 **Love For Other Christians** Brotherly kindness–KJV Brotherly kindness–NASB Brotherly kindness–NIV Brotherly kindness–NKJV **Love for other Christians–NLT** **POSB REFERENCE** (2 Pt.1:5-7; esp. v.7) Note 1, point 6	**φιλαδελφίαν** = *philadelphian* Pronunciation: [fil-ad-el-fee'-ahn] Parsing (part of speech): noun 　　Case—accusative 　　Gender—feminine 　　Number—singular 　　Stem or root—from **φιλαδελφία**, ας Concordance References: ⇒ Strong's #5360 philadelphia ⇒ NIV #5789 philadelphia ⇒ NASB #5360 philadelphia **2 Peter 1:7** And to godliness **brotherly kindness**; and to brotherly kindness charity. [KJV] And in *your* godliness, **brotherly kindness**, and in *your* brotherly kindness, love. [NASB] And to godliness, **brotherly kindness**; and to brotherly kindness, love. [NIV] To godliness **brotherly kindness**, and to brotherly kindness love. [NKJV] Godliness leads to **love for other Christians**, and finally you will grow to have genuine love for everyone. [NLT] ἐν δὲ τῇ εὐσεβείᾳ τὴν **φιλαδελφίαν**, ἐν δὲ τῇ φιλαδελφίᾳ τὴν ἀγάπην. [GNS] ἐν δὲ τῇ εὐσεβείᾳ τὴν **φιλαδελφίαν**, ἐν δὲ τῇ φιλαδελφίᾳ τὴν ἀγάπην. [GNT]	Brotherly kindness; love for other Christians; loving each other as brothers; the very special love that exists between brothers and sisters within a loving family; brothers and sisters who truly cherish one another. **Practical Application** It is the kind of love... • that binds one another together as a family, as a brotherly clan. • that binds one another in an unbreakable union. • that holds one another ever so dearly within the heart. • that knows deep affection for one another. • that nourishes and nurtures one another. • that shows concern for and looks after the welfare of one another. • that joins hands with one another in a common purpose *under one father* (Leon Morris. *The Epistles of Paul to the Thessalonians.* "Tyndale New Testament Commentary," p.80). How can people possibly love one another like this when they are not true blood brothers and sisters? Here is how. The Greek word "brother" (*adelphos*) means *from the same womb*. The word used for love is "phileo" which means deep-seated affection and care, deep and warm feelings within the heart. It is the kind of love that holds a person near and dear to one's heart. Now note: the two Greek words are combined together by the writer to convey what he means by brotherly love or *love for other Christians.* ⇒ People who have *brotherly love* have come from the same womb, that is, from the same source. They have been *born again* by the Spirit of God through faith in the Lord Jesus Christ. When they receive this new birth, God

ENGLISH WORD	GREEK WORD AND VERSE	THE WORD MEANS...
		gives them a new spirit—a spirit that melts and binds their hearts and lives in love for all the family of God. Believers may not even know one another. They may even be from different parts of the world, but there is a *brotherly love* between them because they have been given a new birth and a new spirit of love by God. They are brothers and sisters in the family of God—the family of those who truly believe in God's Son, the Lord Jesus Christ—the family who has received a new spirit that binds them together in brotherly love. This new spirit, of course, comes from the Holy Spirit of God Himself. (See POSB *Deeper Study* #3, Fellowship—Acts 2:42 for more discussion.)

#2439
Love Of The Brethen
 	
Love of the brethen– KJV
Love of the brethen– NASB
Love for brothers–NIV
Love of the brethren– NKJV
Love for each other– NLT
 	
POSB REFERENCE
(1 Pt.1:22-25; esp. v.22)
Introduction
	φιλαδελφίαν = *philadelphian*
	Pronunciation: [fil-ad-el-fee'-ahn]
	Parsing (part of speech): noun
	  Case—accusative
	  Gender—feminine
	  Number—singular
	  Stem or root—from φιλαδελφία, ας
	Concordance References:
	⇒ Strong's #5360 philadelphia
	⇒ NIV #5789 philadelphia
	⇒ NASB #5360 philadelphia
	
	1 Peter 1:22
	Seeing ye have purified your souls in obeying the truth through the Spirit unto unfeigned **love of the brethren,** *see that ye* love one another with a pure heart fervently: [KJV]
	Since you have in obedience to the truth purified your souls for a sincere **love of the brethren**, fervently love one another from the heart, [NASB]
	Now that you have purified yourselves by obeying the truth so that you have sincere **love for** your **brothers**, love one another deeply, from the heart. [NIV]
	Since you have purified your souls in obeying the truth through the Spirit in sincere **love of the brethren**, love one another fervently with a pure heart, [NKJV]
	Now you can have sincere **love for each other** as brothers and sisters because you were cleansed from your sins when you accepted the truth of the Good News. So see to it that you really do love each other intensely with all your hearts. [NLT]
	τὰς ψυχὰς ὑμῶν ἡγνικότες ἐν τῇ ὑπακοῇ τῆς ἀληθείας διὰ Πνεύματος εἰς **φιλαδελφίαν** ἀνυπόκριτον, ἐκ καθαρᾶς καρδίας ἀλλήλους ἀγαπήσατε ἐκτενῶς· [GNS]
	Τὰς ψυχὰς ὑμῶν ἡγνικότες ἐν τῇ ὑπακοῇ τῆς ἀληθείας εἰς **φιλαδελφίαν** ἀνυπόκριτον, ἐκ [καθαρᾶς] καρδίας ἀλλήλους ἀγαπήσατε ἐκτενῶς [GNT]
		Love for brothers; love of the brethren; love for others.
		
		Practical Application
		There is no greater force than love. If two people truly love each other, they will do anything for the other. There is no greater bond on earth than true love. This is especially true of the love between believers. Why? Is there a difference between the love that believers have for one another and the love that neighbors have for one another? Scripture says yes, emphatically yes. Believers are to have a different kind of love than neighbors have for one another. The love that believers are to have for one another is what the Greek calls *philadelphian* love, a very special kind of love. (See **Love For Brothers,** for additional discussion.)

#2440
Love Of The Brethren
 	
Brotherly love–KJV
Love of the brethren– NASB
Loving each other as brothers–NIV
Brotherly love–NKJV
Love each other with true Christian love–NLT
	φιλαδελφία = *philadelphia*
	Pronunciation: [fil-ad-el-fee'-ahs]
	Parsing (part of speech): noun
	  Case—genitive
	  Gender—feminine
	  Number—singular
	  Stem or root—from φιλαδελφία, ας
	Concordance References:
	⇒ Strong's #5360 philadelphia
	⇒ NIV #5789 philadelphia
	⇒ NASB #5360 philadelphia
	
	Hebrews 13:1
	Let **brotherly love** continue. [KJV]
	Let **love of the brethren** continue. [NASB]
	Keep on **loving each other as brothers**. [NIV]
	Let **brotherly love** continue. [NKJV]
	Continue to **love each other with true Christian**
		Brotherly love; love of the brothers shown among God's people; loving one another as brothers.
		
		Practical Application
		Note that the love existing among believers is a special kind of love. It is "love of brethren" [brothers] (*philadelphia*), the very special love that exists between brothers and sisters within a loving family, brothers and sisters who truly cherish one another. It is the kind of love...
		• that binds each other together as a family, as a brotherly clan.
		• that binds each other in an unbreakable union.
		• that holds each other ever so deeply within

ENGLISH WORD	GREEK WORD AND VERSE	THE WORD MEANS...
POSB REFERENCE (Heb.13:1) Note 1, point 1	love. [NLT] Ἡ φιλαδελφία μενέτω. [GNS] Ἡ φιλαδελφία μενέτω. [GNT]	the heart. • that knows deep affection for each other. • that nourishes and nurtures each other. • that shows concern and looks after the welfare of each other. • that joins hands with each other in a common purpose *under one father* (Leon Morris. *The Epistles of Paul to the Thessalonians.* "Tyndale New Testament Commentary," p.80). How can people possibly love one another like this when they are not true blood brothers and sisters? Here is how. The Greek word "brother" (*adelphos*) means *from the same womb.* The word used for "love" is *phileo* which means deep-seated affection and care, deep and warm feelings within the heart. It is the kind of love that holds a person near and dear to one's heart. Now note: the two Greek words are combined together by the writer to convey what he means by *love of the brethren.* ⇒ People who have brotherly love have come from the same womb, that is, from the same source. They have been *born again* by the Spirit of God through faith in the Lord Jesus Christ. And when they receive this new birth, God gives them a new spirit—a spirit that melts and binds their hearts and lives in love for all the family of God. Believers may not even know each other. They may even be from different parts of the world, but there is a *brotherly love* between them because they have been given a new birth and a new spirit of love by God. They are brothers and sisters in the family of God—the family of those who truly believe in God's Son, the Lord Jesus Christ—the family who have received a new spirit that binds them together in brotherly love.

#2441
Love Only Themselves
 	
 Lovers of their own selves–KJV
 Lovers of themselves–NIV
 Lovers of self–NASB
 Lovers of themselves–NKJV
 Love only themselves–NLT
 	
 POSB REFERENCE (2 Tim. 3:2-4; esp. v.2) Note 2, point 1
	φίλαυτοι = *philautoi*
	 Pronunciation: [fil'-ow-toy]
	 Parsing (part of speech): adjective
	    Case—nominative
	    Gender—masculine
	    Number—plural
	    Stem or root—from φίλαυτος, ον
	 Concordance References:
	⇒ Strong's #5367 philautos
	⇒ NIV #5796 philautos
	⇒ NASB #5367 philautos
	
	 2 Tim. 3:2
	 For men shall be **lovers of their own selves,** covetous, boasters, proud, blasphemers, disobedient to parents, unthankful, unholy, [KJV]
	 For men will be **lovers of self,** lovers of money, boastful, arrogant, revilers, disobedient to parents, ungrateful, unholy, [NASB]
	 People will be **lovers of themselves,** lovers of money, boastful, proud, abusive, disobedient to their parents, ungrateful, unholy, [NIV]
	 For men will be **lovers of themselves,** lovers of money, boasters, proud, blasphemers, disobedient to parents, unthankful, unholy, [NKJV]
	 For people will **love only themselves** and their money. They will be boastful and proud, scoffing at God, disobedient to their parents, and ungrateful. They will consider nothing sacred. [NLT]
		Lovers of themselves; lovers of their own selves; lovers of self; lovers of only themselves; to be self-centered, selfish.
		
		 Practical Application
		 The first mark of the last days will be a godless world. Why will the last days be perilous? Because the world will be godless. Note how the terrible marks of the last days sound very much like a picture of today.
		 People will *love only themselves* (*philautoi*): this does not mean the normal and natural love of life and of oneself that we should all have. It means selfishness and self-centeredness...
		• to focus upon oneself and one's own pleasure and flesh instead of upon God and other people.
		• to put oneself before others: wife, husband, parent, child, friend, neighbor, God.
		• to put one's own will before God's will.
		• to seek one's own desires without considering others.
		• to go after what one wants even if it is unwise and hurts others.
		• to feel that everyone and everything should revolve around oneself.
		• to focus upon one's own pleasure and flesh

ENGLISH WORD	GREEK WORD AND VERSE	THE WORD MEANS...
	ἔσονται γὰρ οἱ ἄνθρωποι **φίλαυτοι**, φιλάργυροι, ἀλαζόνες, ὑπερήφανοι, βλάσφημοι, γονεῦσιν ἀπειθεῖς, ἀχάριστοι, ἀνόσιοι, [GNS] ἔσονται γὰρ οἱ ἄνθρωποι **φίλαυτοι** φιλάργυροι ἀλαζόνες ὑπερήφανοι βλάσφημοι, γονεῦσιν ἀπειθεῖς, ἀχάριστοι ἀνόσιοι [GNT]	and ignore the crying needs of the desperate and dying. Self love sets one up like a god and feels that nothing matters as much as the pleasure of oneself. In the last days people will love themselves more than they love anyone else. Selfishness will be one of the terrible marks of the last days.

#2442
 Love Their Husbands
 	
 Love their husbands– KJV
 Love their husbands– NASB
 Love their husbands– NIV
 Love their husbands– NKJV
 Love their husbands– NLT
 	
 POSB REFERENCE
 (Tit.2:4-5; esp. v.4)
 Note 4, point 2
	φιλάνδρους = *philandrous*
	 Pronunciation: [fil’-an-droos]
	 Parsing (part of speech): adjective
	    Case—accusative
	    Gender—feminine
	    Number—plural
	    Stem or root—from **φίλανδρος**
	 Concordance References:
	   ⇒ Strong’s #5362 philandros
	   ⇒ NIV #5791 philandros
	   ⇒ NASB #5362 philandros
	
	 Titus 2:4
	 That they may teach the young women to be sober, to **love their husbands**, to love their children, [KJV]
	 That they may encourage the young women to **love their husbands**, to love their children, [NASB]
	 Then they can train the younger women to **love their husbands** and children, [NIV]
	 That they admonish the young women to **love their husbands**, to love their children, [NKJV]
	 These older women must train the younger women to **love their husbands** and their children, [NLT]
	 ἵνα σωφρονίζωσι τὰς νέας, **φιλάνδρους** εἶναι, φιλοτέκνους, [GNS]
	 ἵνα σωφρονίζωσιν τὰς νέας **φιλάνδρους** εἶναι, φιλοτέκνους [GNT]
		To love one’s husband.
		
		 Practical Application
		 Young women are to love their husbands. Note: this particular command is to *young women* which means that the marriages are young marriages. The only way young married couples can become united and bound together and have the kind of life they desire is by loving each other. Therefore, young wives must love their husbands...
		 • with a selfless and unselfish love.
		 • with a giving and sacrificial love.
		 • with a quiet and peaceable love.
		 • with a love of the will as well as of the heart.
		 • with a love of commitment as well as of affection.
		
		 The word used here for love (*philandrous*) actually stresses affection, care, tenderness, warmth, and feelings. The young wives are to have *affection* for their husband.

#2443
 Love Their Money
 	
 Covetous–KJV
 Lovers of money– NASB
 Lovers of money–NIV
 Lovers of themselves–NKJV
 Love their money– NLT
 	
 POSB REFERENCE
 (2 Tim. 3:2-4; esp. v.2)
 Note 2, point 2
	φιλάργυροι = *philarguroi*
	 Pronunciation: [fil-ar’-goo-roy]
	 Parsing (part of speech): adjective
	    Case—nominative
	    Gender—masculine
	    Number—plural
	    Stem or root—from **φιλάργυρος**, ον
	 Concordance References:
	   ⇒ Strong’s #5366 philarguros
	   ⇒ NIV #5795 philarguros
	   ⇒ NASB #5366 philarguros
	
	 2 Tim. 3:2
	 For men shall be lovers of their own selves, **covetous**, boasters, proud, blasphemers, disobedient to parents, unthankful, unholy, [KJV]
	 For men will be lovers of self, **lovers of money**, boastful, arrogant, revilers, disobedient to parents, ungrateful, unholy, [NASB]
	 People will be lovers of themselves, **lovers of money**, boastful, proud, abusive, disobedient to their parents, ungrateful, unholy, [NIV]
	 For men will be **lovers of themselves**, lovers of money, boasters, proud, blasphemers, disobedient to parents, unthankful, unholy, [NKJV]
	 For people will **love** only themselves and **their money**. They will be boastful and proud, scoffing at God, disobedient to their parents, and ungrateful. They will consider nothing sacred. [NLT]
	 ἔσονται γὰρ οἱ ἄνθρωποι φίλαυτοι, **φιλάργυροι**, ἀλαζόνες, ὑπερήφανοι, βλάσφημοι, γονεῦσιν ἀπειθεῖς, ἀχάριστοι, ἀνόσιοι, [GNS]
	 ἔσονται γὰρ οἱ ἄνθρωποι φίλαυτοι **φιλάργυροι** ἀλαζόνες ὑπερήφανοι βλάσφημοι, γονεῦσιν ἀπειθεῖς, ἀχάριστοι ἀνόσιοι [GNT]
		To be lovers of money or possessions; to be fond of money or possessions; to be covetous.
		
		 Practical Application
		 The word means lovers of money and possessions. People will want more and more and bigger and bigger and better and better, and they will seldom be satisfied with what they have. In the last days people will focus upon...
		 • money, banking more and more.
		 • houses in the best neighborhoods, on the seashore, in the mountains, and by the rivers.
		 • furnishings and property.
		 • possessions—such as clothes, jewelry, antiques, art, and vehicles.
		 • travel, seeing more and more sights.
		 • property, stocks and bonds—owning more and more.
		 • power—controlling more and more.
		
		 Men will love money, what it buys and allows them to do, and they will covet more and more of it in order to buy things. Their eyes and hearts will be focused upon money instead of God. They will indulge and hoard instead of meeting the desperate needs of the poor and lost of the world.

ENGLISH WORD	GREEK WORD AND VERSE	THE WORD MEANS...

#2444
Love, Truly–
Love–
Lovest
 	
Lovest–KJV
Love–NASB
Truly Love–NIV
Love–NKJV
Love–NLT
 	
POSB
REFERENCE
(Jn.21:15)
Note 2
	ἀγαπᾷς = *agapas*
	Pronunciation: [ag-ap-ahs']
	Parsing (part of speech): verb
	    Mood—indicative
	    Tense—present
	    Voice—active
	    Person—2nd person
	    Number—singular
	    Stem or root—from ἀγαπάω
	Concordance References:
	⇒ Strong's #25 agapao
	⇒ NIV #26 agapao
	⇒ NASB #25 agapao
	
	John 21:15
	So when they had dined, Jesus saith to Simon Peter, Simon, *son* of Jonas, **lovest** thou me more than these? He saith unto him, Yea, Lord; thou knowest that I love thee. He saith unto him, Feed my lambs. [KJV]
	So when they had finished breakfast, Jesus said to Simon Peter, "Simon, *son* of John, do you **love** Me more than these?" He said to Him, "Yes, Lord; You know that I love You." He said to him, "Tend My lambs." [NASB]
	When they had finished eating, Jesus said to Simon Peter, "Simon son of John, do you **truly love** me more than these?" "Yes, Lord," he said, "you know that I love you."Jesus said, "Feed my lambs." [NIV]
	So when they had eaten breakfast, Jesus said to Simon Peter, "Simon, *son* of Jonah, do you **love** Me more than these?" He said to Him, "Yes, Lord; You know that I love You." He said to him, "Feed My lambs." [NKJV]
	After breakfast Jesus said to Simon Peter, "Simon son of John, do you **love** me more than these?" "Yes, Lord," Peter replied, "you know I love you." "Then feed my lambs," Jesus told him. [NLT]
	Ὅτε οὖν ἠρίστησαν, λέγει τῷ Σίμωνι Πέτρῳ ὁ Ἰησοῦς, Σίμων Ἰωνᾶ, **ἀγαπᾷς** με πλέον τούτων; λέγει αὐτῷ, Ναί Κύριε· σὺ οἶδας ὅτι φιλῶ σε. λέγει αὐτῷ, Βόσκε τὰ ἀρνία μου. [GNS]
	Ὅτε οὖν ἠρίστησαν λέγει τῷ Σίμωνι Πέτρῳ ὁ Ἰησοῦς, Σίμων Ἰωάννου, **ἀγαπᾷς** με πλέον τούτων; λέγει αὐτῷ, Ναί, κύριε, σὺ οἶδας ὅτι φιλῶ σε. λέγει αὐτῷ, Βόσκε τὰ ἀρνία μου. [GNT]
		To love, truly love.
		
		Practical Application
		In Christ, God was showing the world a new kind of love—agape love. Agape love is a love so new that a new meaning had to be given to the Greek word "agape." Agape became the love that was willing to give and die even for an enemy. The early Christian leaders recognized this new dimension of love, so they lifted the meaning of agape love up to God's love for the world. Agape love is the highest level of love possible; it is the love of God: "For God so loved the world that he gave his one and only Son, that whoever believes in him shall not perish but have eternal life" (John 3:16).
		Agape love is the love of the mind, of the reason, and of the will. It is a love that is born of choice; one simply chooses to love regardless of feelings. A person may insult, injure, or humiliate; but agape love chooses to seek only the highest good for that person. It is sacrificial love, a love that is willing to die even for its enemies.

#2445
Lovely
 	
Lovely–KJV
Lovely–NASB
Lovely–NIV
Lovely–NKJV
Lovely–NLT
 	
POSB
REFERENCE
(Philip.4:8-9; esp. v.8)
Note 2, point 1e
	προσφιλῆ = *prosphilë*
	Pronunciation: [pros-fee-lay']
	Parsing (part of speech): adjective
	    Case—nominative
	    Gender—neuter
	    Number—plural
	    Stem or root—from προσφιλής, ές
	Concordance References:
	⇒ Strong's #4375 prosphilës
	⇒ NIV #4713 prosphilës
	⇒ NASB #4375 prosphilës
	
	Philip. 4:8
	Finally, brethren, whatsoever things are true, whatsoever things *are* honest, whatsoever things *are* just, whatsoever things *are* pure, whatsoever things *are* **lovely**, whatsoever things *are* of good report; if *there be* any virtue, and if *there be* any praise, think on these things. [KJV]
	Finally, brethren, whatever is true, whatever is honorable, whatever is right, whatever is pure, whatever is **lovely**, whatever is of good repute, if there is any excellence and if anything worthy of praise, let your mind dwell on these things. [NASB]
	Finally, brothers, whatever is true, whatever is noble, whatever is right, whatever is pure, whatever is **lovely**, whatever is admirable—if anything is excellent or praiseworthy—think about such things. [NIV]
		Lovely, pleasing, winsome, kind, gracious; things that excite love and kindness.
		
		Practical Application
		The believer's thoughts are not to be thoughts of unkindness and meanness, grumbling and murmuring, criticism and reaction. The believer's thoughts are to be focused upon things that are lovely—that build up people, not tear them down.

ENGLISH WORD	GREEK WORD AND VERSE	THE WORD MEANS...
	Finally, brethren, whatever things are true, whatever things *are* noble, whatever things *are* just, whatever things *are* pure, whatever things *are* **lovely**, whatever things *are* of good report, if *there is* any virtue and if *there is* anything praiseworthy—meditate on these things. [NKJV] And now, dear brothers and sisters, let me say one more thing as I close this letter. Fix your thoughts on what is true and honorable and right. Think about things that are pure and **lovely** and admirable. Think about things that are excellent and worthy of praise. [NLT] Τὸ λοιπόν, ἀδελφοί, ὅσα ἐστὶν ἀληθῆ, ὅσα σεμνά, ὅσα δίκαια, ὅσα ἁγνά, ὅσα **προσφιλῆ**, ὅσα εὔφημα, εἴ τις ἀρετὴ καὶ εἴ τις ἔπαινος, ταῦτα λογίζεσθε· [GNS] Τὸ λοιπόν, ἀδελφοί, ὅσα ἐστὶν ἀληθῆ, ὅσα σεμνά, ὅσα δίκαια, ὅσα ἁγνά, ὅσα **προσφιλῆ**, ὅσα εὔφημα, εἴ τις ἀρετὴ καὶ εἴ τις ἔπαινος, ταῦτα λογίζεσθε· [GNT]	
#2446 **Lover Of Good Men** **Lover of good men– KJV** Loving what is good– NASB Loves what is good– NIV Lover of what is good– NKJV Love all that is good– NLT **POSB REFERENCE** (Tit.1:7-8; esp. v.8) Note 3, point 2b	φιλάγαθον = *philagathon* Pronunciation: [fil-ag'-ath-on] Parsing (part of speech): adjective 　　Case—accusative 　　Gender—masculine 　　Number—singular 　　Stem or root—from φιλάγαθος, ον Concordance References: ⇒　Strong's #5358 philagathos ⇒　NIV #5787 philagathos ⇒　NASB #5358 philagathos **Titus 1:8** But a lover of hospitality, a **lover of good men**, sober, just, holy, temperate; [KJV] But hospitable, **loving what is good**, sensible, just, devout, self-controlled, [NASB] Rather he must be hospitable, one who **loves what is good**, who is self-controlled, upright, holy and disciplined. [NIV] But hospitable, a **lover of what is good**, sober-minded, just, holy, self-controlled, [NKJV] He must enjoy having guests in his home and must **love all that is good**. He must live wisely and be fair. He must live a devout and disciplined life. [NLT] ἀλλὰ φιλόξενον, **φιλάγαθον**, σώφρονα, δίκαιον, ὅσιον, ἐγκρατῆ, [GNS] ἀλλὰ φιλόξενον **φιλάγαθον** σώφρονα δίκαιον ὅσιον ἐγκρατῆ, [GNT]	Loving what is good; loving all that is good. The Greek means a lover of good things as well as of good people. **Practical Application** The minister or steward of God must be a lover of good men (*philagathon*). The minister of God loves good no matter where he finds it, in people or things. He loves the poor and the homeless, the weak and the suffering, as well as the wealthy and healthy. And the minister loves to do good things for everyone, no matter who they are.
#2447 **Lover Of What Is Good** Lover of good men– KJV Loving what is good– NASB Loves what is good– NIV **Lover of what is good– NKJV** Love all that is good– NLT **POSB REFERENCE** (Tit.1:7-8; esp. v.8) Note 3, point 2b	φιλάγαθον = *philagathon* Pronunciation: [fil-ag'-ath-on] Parsing (part of speech): adjective 　　Case—accusative 　　Gender—masculine 　　Number—singular 　　Stem or root—from φιλάγαθος, ον Concordance References: ⇒　Strong's #5358 philagathos ⇒　NIV #5787 philagathos ⇒　NASB #5358 philagathos **Titus 1:8** But a lover of hospitality, a **lover of good men**, sober, just, holy, temperate; [KJV] But hospitable, **loving what is good**, sensible, just, devout, self-controlled, [NASB] Rather he must be hospitable, one who **loves what is good**, who is self-controlled, upright, holy and disciplined. [NIV] But hospitable, a **lover of what is good**, sober-minded, just, holy, self-controlled, [NKJV] He must enjoy having guests in his home and must **love all that is good**. He must live wisely and be fair. He must live a devout and disciplined life. [NLT] ἀλλὰ φιλόξενον, **φιλάγαθον**, σώφρονα, δίκαιον, ὅσιον, ἐγκρατῆ, [GNS] ἀλλὰ φιλόξενον **φιλάγαθον** σώφρονα δίκαιον ὅσιον ἐγκρατῆ, [GNT]	Loving what is good; loving all that is good. The Greek means a lover of good things as well as of good people. **Practical Application** The minister or steward of God must be a lover of what is good (*philagathon*). The minister of God loves good no matter where he finds it, in people or things. He loves the poor and the homeless, the weak and the suffering, as well as the wealthy and healthy. And the minister loves to do good things for everyone, no matter who they are.

ENGLISH WORD	GREEK WORD AND VERSE	THE WORD MEANS...

#2448
Lovers Of Money
 	
Covetous–KJV
Lovers of money–NASB
Lovers of money–NIV
Lovers of money–NKJV
Love their money–NLT
 	
POSB REFERENCE
(2 Tim. 3:2-4; esp. v.2)
Note 2, point 2
	φιλάργυροι = *philarguroi*
	Pronunciation: [fil-ar'-goo-roy]
	Parsing (part of speech): adjective
	    Case—nominative
	    Gender—masculine
	    Number—plural
	    Stem or root—from φιλάργυρος, ον
	Concordance References:
	⇒ Strong's #5366 philarguros
	⇒ NIV #5795 philarguros
	⇒ NASB #5366 philarguros
	
	2 Tim. 3:2
	For men shall be lovers of their own selves, **covetous**, boasters, proud, blasphemers, disobedient to parents, unthankful, unholy, [KJV]
	For men will be lovers of self, **lovers of money**, boastful, arrogant, revilers, disobedient to parents, ungrateful, unholy, [NASB]
	People will be lovers of themselves, **lovers of money**, boastful, proud, abusive, disobedient to their parents, ungrateful, unholy, [NIV]
	For men will be lovers of themselves, **lovers of money**, boasters, proud, blasphemers, disobedient to parents, unthankful, unholy, [NKJV]
	For people will **love** only themselves and **their money**. They will be boastful and proud, scoffing at God, disobedient to their parents, and ungrateful. They will consider nothing sacred. [NLT]
	ἔσονται γὰρ οἱ ἄνθρωποι φίλαυτοι, **φιλάργυροι**, ἀλαζόνες, ὑπερήφανοι, βλάσφημοι, γονεῦσιν ἀπειθεῖς, ἀχάριστοι, ἀνόσιοι, [GNS]
	ἔσονται γὰρ οἱ ἄνθρωποι φίλαυτοι **φιλάργυροι** ἀλαζόνες ὑπερήφανοι βλάσφημοι, γονεῦσιν ἀπειθεῖς, ἀχάριστοι ἀνόσιοι [GNT]
		To be lovers of money; to be fond of money or possessions; to be covetous.
		
		Practical Application
		The word means lovers of money and possessions. People will want more and more and bigger and bigger and better and better, and they will seldom be satisfied with what they have. In the last days people will focus upon...
		• money, banking more and more.
		• houses in the best neighborhoods, on the seashore, in the mountains, and by the rivers.
		• furnishings and property.
		• possessions—such as clothes, jewelry, antiques, art, and vehicles.
		• travel, seeing more and more sights.
		• property, stocks and bonds—owning more and more.
		• power—controlling more and more.
		
		Men will love money, what it buys and allows them to do, and they will covet more and more of it in order to buy things. Their eyes and hearts will be focused upon money instead of God. They will indulge and hoard instead of meeting the desperate needs of the poor and lost of the world.

#2449
Lovers Of Self
 	
Lovers of their own selves–KJV
Lovers of self–NASB
Lovers of themselves–NIV
Lovers of themselves–NKJV
Love only themselves–NLT
 	
POSB REFERENCE
(2 Tim. 3:2-4; esp. v.2)
Note 2, point 1
	φίλαυτοι = *philautoi*
	Pronunciation: [fil'-ow-toy]
	Parsing (part of speech): adjective
	    Case—nominative
	    Gender—masculine
	    Number—plural
	    Stem or root—from φίλαυτος, ον
	Concordance References:
	⇒ Strong's #5367 philautos
	⇒ NIV #5796 philautos
	⇒ NASB #5367 philautos
	
	2 Tim. 3:2
	For men shall be **lovers of their own selves**, covetous, boasters, proud, blasphemers, disobedient to parents, unthankful, unholy, [KJV]
	For men will be **lovers of self**, lovers of money, boastful, arrogant, revilers, disobedient to parents, ungrateful, unholy, [NASB]
	People will be **lovers of themselves**, lovers of money, boastful, proud, abusive, disobedient to their parents, ungrateful, unholy, [NIV]
	For men will be **lovers of themselves**, lovers of money, boasters, proud, blasphemers, disobedient to parents, unthankful, unholy, [NKJV]
	For people will **love only themselves** and their money. They will be boastful and proud, scoffing at God, disobedient to their parents, and ungrateful. They will consider nothing sacred. [NLT]
	ἔσονται γὰρ οἱ ἄνθρωποι **φίλαυτοι**, φιλάργυροι, ἀλαζόνες, ὑπερήφανοι, βλάσφημοι, γονεῦσιν ἀπειθεῖς, ἀχάριστοι, ἀνόσιοι, [GNS]
	ἔσονται γὰρ οἱ ἄνθρωποι **φίλαυτοι** φιλάργυροι ἀλαζόνες ὑπερήφανοι βλάσφημοι, γονεῦσιν ἀπειθεῖς, ἀχάριστοι ἀνόσιοι [GNT]
		Lovers of themselves; lovers of their own selves; lovers of self; lovers of only themselves; to be self-centered; selfish.
		
		Practical Application
		The first mark of the last days will be a godless world. Why will the last days be perilous? Because the world will be godless. Note how the terrible marks of the last days sound very much like a picture of today.
		People will be *lovers of self* (*philautoi*): this does not mean the normal and natural love of life and of oneself that we should all have. It means selfishness and self-centeredness. It means selfishness and self-centeredness. (See **Love Only Themselves**, for additional discussion.)

ENGLISH WORD	GREEK WORD AND VERSE	THE WORD MEANS...

#2450
 	
Lovers Of Their Own Selves
 	
Lovers of their own selves–KJV
Lovers of self–NASB
Lovers of themselves–NIV
Lovers of themselves–NKJV
Love only themselves–NLT
 	
POSB REFERENCE
(2 Tim. 3:2-4; esp. v.2)
Note 2, point 1
	φίλαυτοι = *philautoi*
	Pronunciation: [fil'-ow-toy]
	Parsing (part of speech): adjective
	    Case—nominative
	    Gender—masculine
	    Number—plural
	    Stem or root—from φίλαυτος, ον
	Concordance References:
	  ⇒ Strong's #5367 philautos
	  ⇒ NIV #5796 philautos
	  ⇒ NASB #5367 philautos
	
	2 Tim. 3:2
	For men shall be **lovers of their own selves**, covetous, boasters, proud, blasphemers, disobedient to parents, unthankful, unholy, [KJV]
	For men will be **lovers of self**, lovers of money, boastful, arrogant, revilers, disobedient to parents, ungrateful, unholy, [NASB]
	People will be **lovers of themselves**, lovers of money, boastful, proud, abusive, disobedient to their parents, ungrateful, unholy, [NIV]
	For men will be **lovers of themselves**, lovers of money, boasters, proud, blasphemers, disobedient to parents, unthankful, unholy, [NKJV]
	For people will **love only themselves** and their money. They will be boastful and proud, scoffing at God, disobedient to their parents, and ungrateful. They will consider nothing sacred. [NLT]
	ἔσονται γὰρ οἱ ἄνθρωποι φίλαυτοι, φιλάργυροι, ἀλαζόνες, ὑπερήφανοι, βλάσφημοι, γονεῦσιν ἀπειθεῖς, ἀχάριστοι, ἀνόσιοι, [GNS]
	ἔσονται γὰρ οἱ ἄνθρωποι φίλαυτοι φιλάργυροι ἀλαζόνες ὑπερήφανοι βλάσφημοι, γονεῦσιν ἀπειθεῖς, ἀχάριστοι ἀνόσιοι [GNT]
		Lovers of themselves; lovers of their own selves; lovers of self; lovers of only themselves; to be self-centered; selfish.
		
		Practical Application
		The first mark of the last days will be a godless world. Why will the last days be perilous? Because the world will be godless. Note how the terrible marks of the last days sound very much like a picture of today.
		People will be *lovers of their own selves* (*philautoi*): this does not mean the normal and natural love of life and of oneself that we should all have. It means selfishness and self-centeredness. (See **Love Only Themselves,** for additional discussion.)

#2451
 	
Lovers Of Themselves
 	
Lovers of their own selves–KJV
Lovers of self–NASB
Lovers of themselves–NIV
Lovers of themselves–NKJV
Love only themselves–NLT
 	
POSB REFERENCE
(2 Tim. 3:2-4; esp. v.2)
Note 2, point 1
	φίλαυτοι = *philautoi*
	Pronunciation: [fil'-ow-toy]
	Parsing (part of speech): adjective
	    Case—nominative
	    Gender—masculine
	    Number—plural
	    Stem or root—from φίλαυτος, ον
	Concordance References:
	  ⇒ Strong's #5367 philautos
	  ⇒ NIV #5796 philautos
	  ⇒ NASB #5367 philautos
	
	2 Tim. 3:2
	For men shall be **lovers of their own selves**, covetous, boasters, proud, blasphemers, disobedient to parents, unthankful, unholy, [KJV]
	For men will be **lovers of self**, lovers of money, boastful, arrogant, revilers, disobedient to parents, ungrateful, unholy, [NASB]
	People will be **lovers of themselves**, lovers of money, boastful, proud, abusive, disobedient to their parents, ungrateful, unholy, [NIV]
	For men will be **lovers of themselves**, lovers of money, boasters, proud, blasphemers, disobedient to parents, unthankful, unholy, [NKJV]
	For people will **love only themselves** and their money. They will be boastful and proud, scoffing at God, disobedient to their parents, and ungrateful. They will consider nothing sacred. [NLT]
	ἔσονται γὰρ οἱ ἄνθρωποι φίλαυτοι, φιλάργυροι, ἀλαζόνες, ὑπερήφανοι, βλάσφημοι, γονεῦσιν ἀπειθεῖς, ἀχάριστοι, ἀνόσιοι, [GNS]
	ἔσονται γὰρ οἱ ἄνθρωποι φίλαυτοι φιλάργυροι ἀλαζόνες ὑπερήφανοι βλάσφημοι, γονεῦσιν ἀπειθεῖς, ἀχάριστοι ἀνόσιοι [GNT]
		Lovers of themselves; lovers of their own selves; lovers of self; lovers of only themselves; to be self-centered; selfish.
		
		Practical Application
		The first mark of the last days will be a godless world. Why will the last days be perilous? Because the world will be godless. Note how the terrible marks of the last days sound very much like a picture of today.
		People will be *lovers of themselves* (*philautoi*): this does not mean the normal and natural love of life and of oneself that we should all have. It means selfishness and self-centeredness. (See **Love Only Themselves,** for additional discussion.)

ENGLISH WORD	GREEK WORD AND VERSE	THE WORD MEANS...

#2452
 Loves To Do Evil
 	
 Lusteth–KJV
 Sets its desire against– NASB
 Desires contrary to– NIV
 Lusts–NKJV
 Loves to do evil–NLT
 	
 POSB REFERENCE
 (Gal.5:16-18; esp. v.17)
 Note 1
	ἐπιθυμεῖ κατά = *epithumei kata*
	 Pronunciation: [ep-ee-thoo-mee' kat-ah']
	 Parsing *epithumei* (part of speech): verb
	     Mood—indicative
	     Tense—present
	     Voice—active
	     Person—3rd person
	     Number—singular
	     Stem or root—from ἐπιθυμέω
	 Parsing *kata* (part of speech): preposition
	     Case—genitive
	     Stem or root—from κατά
	 Concordance References:
	 ⇒ Strong's #1937 epithumeō + 2596 kata
	 ⇒ NIV #2121 epithumeō [desires] + 2848 kata [contrary to]
	 ⇒ NASB #1937 epithumeō + 2596 kata
	
	 ### Galatians 5:17
	 For the flesh **lusteth** against the Spirit, and the Spirit against the flesh: and these are contrary the one to the other: so that ye cannot do the things that ye would. [KJV]
	 For the flesh **sets its desire against** the Spirit, and the Spirit against the flesh; for these are in opposition to one another, so that you may not do the things that you please. [NASB]
	 For the sinful nature **desires** what is **contrary to** the Spirit, and the Spirit what is contrary to the sinful nature. They are in conflict with each other, so that you do not do what you want. [NIV]
	 For the flesh **lusts** against the Spirit, and the Spirit against the flesh; and these are contrary to one another, so that you do not do the things that you wish. [NKJV]
	 The old sinful nature **loves to do evil**, which is just opposite from what the Holy Spirit wants. And the Spirit gives us desires that are opposite from what the sinful nature desires. These two forces are constantly fighting each other, and your choices are never free from this conflict. [NLT]
	 ἡ γὰρ σὰρξ **ἐπιθυμεῖ κατὰ** τοῦ Πνεύματος, τὸ δὲ Πνεῦμα κατὰ τῆς σαρκός· ταῦτα δὲ ἀντίκειται ἀλλήλοις, ἵνα μὴ ἃ ἐὰν θέλητε, ταῦτα ποιῆτε. [GNS]
	 ἡ γὰρ σὰρξ **ἐπιθυμεῖ κατὰ** τοῦ πνεύματος, τὸ δὲ πνεῦμα κατὰ τῆς σαρκός, ταῦτα γὰρ ἀλλήλοις ἀντίκειται, ἵνα μὴ ἃ ἐὰν θέλητε ταῦτα ποιῆτε. [GNT]
		A yearning passion for; a love to do evil; to long for; to desire; to lust for.
		
		 ### Practical Application
		 The flesh fights for dominance. It loves to do evil against the Spirit, struggles and fights to control the man. The picture is that of a tug of war (A.T. Robertson. *Word Pictures in the New Testament*, Vol.4, p.311). The flesh stands contrary to the Spirit—toe to toe, face to face—and it seeks to control man.
		 Every person has experienced the flesh's...
		 • yearning
		 • pulling
		 • desiring
		 • wanting
		 • grasping
		 • craving
		 • hungering
		 • thirsting
		 • longing
		 • taking
		
		 Every person knows what it is to have his sinful nature lusting after something, to have it yearning and yearning to lay hold of something. The sinful nature is very strong and difficult to control. This is the first reason why a believer's only hope to control the sinful nature is the Spirit of God.

#2453
 Loves What Is Good– Loving What Is Good
 	
 Lover of good men– KJV
 Loving what is good– NASB
 Loves what is good– NIV
 Lover of what is good– NKJV
 Love all that is good– NLT
 	
 POSB REFERENCE
 (Tit.1:7-8; esp. v.8)
 Note 3, point 2b
	φιλάγαθον = *philagathon*
	 Pronunciation: [fil-ag'-ath-on]
	 Parsing (part of speech): adjective
	     Case—accusative
	     Gender—masculine
	     Number—singular
	     Stem or root—from φιλάγαθος, ον
	 Concordance References:
	 ⇒ Strong's #5358 philagathos
	 ⇒ NIV #5787 philagathos
	 ⇒ NASB #5358 philagathos
	
	 ### Titus 1:8
	 But a lover of hospitality, a **lover of good men**, sober, just, holy, temperate; [KJV]
	 But hospitable, **loving what is good**, sensible, just, devout, self-controlled, [NASB]
	 Rather he must be hospitable, one who **loves what is good**, who is self-controlled, upright, holy and disciplined. [NIV]
	 But hospitable, a **lover of what is good**, sober-minded, just, holy, self-controlled, [NKJV]
	 He must enjoy having guests in his home and must **love all that is good**. He must live wisely and be fair. He must live a devout and disciplined life. [NLT]
	 ἀλλὰ φιλόξενον, **φιλάγαθον**, σώφρονα, δίκαιον, ὅσιον, ἐγκρατῆ, [GNS]
	 ἀλλὰ φιλόξενον **φιλάγαθον** σώφρονα δίκαιον ὅσιον ἐγκρατῆ, [GNT]
		Loves what is good, loving what is good, love all that is good. The Greek means a lover of good things as well as of good people.
		
		 ### Practical Application
		 The minister or steward of God must love what is good (*philagathon*). The minister of God loves good no matter where he finds it, in people or things. He loves the poor and the homeless, the weak and the suffering, as well as the wealthy and healthy. And the minister loves to do good things for everyone, no matter who they are.

ENGLISH WORD	GREEK WORD AND VERSE	THE WORD MEANS...

#2454
 	
Loving Each Other As Brothers
 	
Brotherly love–KJV
Love of the brethren–NASB
Loving each other as brothers–NIV
Brotherly love–NKJV
Love each other with true Christian love–NLT
 	
POSB REFERENCE
(Heb.13:1)
Note 1, point 1
	φιλαδελφία = *philadelphia*
	Pronunciation: [fil-ad-el-fee'-ahs]
	Parsing (part of speech): noun
	    Case—genitive
	    Gender—feminine
	    Number—singular
	    Stem or root—from φιλαδελφία, ας
	Concordance References:
	  ⇒ Strong's #5360 philadelphia
	  ⇒ NIV #5789 philadelphia
	  ⇒ NASB #5360 philadelphia
	
	Hebrews 13:1
	Let **brotherly love** continue. [KJV]
	Let **love of the brethren** continue. [NASB]
	Keep on **loving each other as brothers**. [NIV]
	Let **brotherly love** continue. [NKJV]
	Continue to **love each other with true Christian love**. [NLT]
	Ἡ φιλαδελφία μενέτω. [GNS]
	Ἡ φιλαδελφία μενέτω. [GNT]
		Brotherly love; love of the brothers shown among God's people; loving one another as brothers.
		
		Practical Application
		Note that the love existing among believers is a special kind of love. It is a "love" (*philadelphia*)—a very special love—that exists between brothers and sisters within a loving family, brothers and sisters who truly cherish one another. It is the kind of love...
		• that binds each other together as a family, as a brotherly clan.
		• that binds each other in an unbreakable union.
		• that holds each other ever so deeply within the heart.
		• that knows deep affection for each other.
		• that nourishes and nurtures each other.
		• that shows concern and looks after the welfare of each other.
		• that joins hands with each other in a common purpose *under one father* (Leon Morris. *The Epistles of Paul to the Thessalonians.* "Tyndale New Testament Commentary," p.80).

#2455
 	
Loving One Another
 	
Love as brethren–KJV
Brotherly–NASB
Love as brothers–NIV
Love as brothers–NKJV
Loving one another–NLT
 	
POSB REFERENCE
(1 Pt.3:8)
Note 3
	φιλάδελφοι = *philadelphoi*
	Pronunciation: [fil-ad'-el-foy]
	Parsing (part of speech): adjective
	    Case—nominative
	    Gender—masculine
	    Number—plural
	    Stem or root—from φιλάδελφος, ον
	Concordance References:
	  ⇒ Strong's #5361 philadelphos
	  ⇒ NIV #5790 philadelphos
	  ⇒ NASB #5361 philadelphos
	
	1 Peter 3:8
	Finally, *be ye* all of one mind, having compassion one of another, **love as brethren**, *be* pitiful, *be* courteous: [KJV]
	To sum up, let all be harmonious, sympathetic, **brotherly**, kindhearted, and humble in spirit; [NASB]
	Finally, all of you, live in harmony with one another; be sympathetic, **love as brothers**, be compassionate and humble. [NIV]
	Finally, all *of you be* of one mind, having compassion for one another; **love as brothers**, *be* tenderhearted, *be* courteous; [NKJV]
	Finally, all of you should be of one mind, full of sympathy toward each other, **loving one another** with tender hearts and humble minds. [NLT]
	Τὸ δὲ τέλος, πάντες ὁμόφρονες, συμπαθεῖς, φιλάδελφοι, εὔσπλαγχνοι, φιλόφρονες· [GNS]
	Τὸ δὲ τέλος πάντες ὁμόφρονες, συμπαθεῖς, φιλάδελφοι, εὔσπλαγχνοι, ταπεινόφρονες, [GNT]
		To love as brothers; to be brotherly; to love one another; to love another believer.
		
		Practical Application
		There is no greater force than love. If two people truly love each other, they will do anything for the other. There is no greater bond on earth than true love. This is especially true of the love between believers. Why? Is there a difference between the love that believers have for one another and the love that neighbors have for one another? Scripture says yes, emphatically yes. Believers are to have a different kind of love than neighbors have for one another. The love that believers are to have for one another is what the Greek calls *philadelphia* love, a very special kind of love.

#2456
 	
Lovingly
 	
Cherisheth–KJV
Cherishes–NASB
Cares for–NIV
Cherishes–NKJV
Lovingly–NLT
	θάλπει = *thalpei*
	Pronunciation: [thal'-peh-ee]
	Parsing (part of speech): verb
	    Mood—indicative
	    Tense—present
	    Voice—active
	    Person—3rd person
	    Number—singular
	    Stem or root—from θάλπω
	Concordance References:
	  ⇒ Strong's #2282 thalpo
		To care for; to cherish; to lovingly care for; to take care of.
		
		Practical Application
		The word "lovingly" (*thalpei*) means to hold ever so dear within the heart; to treat with warmth, tenderness, care, affection, and appreciation.

ENGLISH WORD	GREEK WORD AND VERSE	THE WORD MEANS...
POSB REFERENCE (Eph.5:25-33; esp. v.29) Note 2, point 2a	⇒ NIV #2499 thalpö ⇒ NASB #2282 thalpö **Ephes. 5:29** For no man ever yet hated his own flesh; but nourisheth and **cherisheth** it, even as the Lord the church: [KJV] For no one ever hated his own flesh, but nourishes and **cherishes** it, just as Christ also *does* the church, [NASB] After all, no one ever hated his own body, but he feeds and **cares for** it, just as Christ does the church—[NIV] For no one ever hated his own flesh, but nourishes and **cherishes** it, just as the Lord *does* the church. [NKJV] No one hates his own body but **lovingly** cares for it, just as Christ cares for his body, which is the church. [NLT] οὐδεὶς γάρ ποτε τὴν ἑαυτοῦ σάρκα ἐμίσησεν, ἀλλ ἐκτρέφει καὶ **θάλπει** αὐτήν, καθὼς καὶ ὁ Κύριος τὴν ἐκκλησίαν· [GNS] οὐδεὶς γάρ ποτε τὴν ἑαυτοῦ σάρκα ἐμίσησεν ἀλλὰ ἐκτρέφει καὶ **θάλπει** αὐτήν, καθὼς καὶ ὁ Χριστὸς τὴν ἐκκλησίαν, [GNT]	

#2457
Lowliness Of Mind
 	
Lowliness of mind– KJV
Humility of mind– NASB
Humility–NIV
Lowliness of mind– NKJV
Humble–NLT
 	
POSB REFERENCE (Philip.2:3) Deeper Study #1
 	
See also POSB REF: (1 Pt.5:5) Note 2
	ταπεινοφροσύνη = *tapeinophrosunē*
	Pronunciation: [tap-i-nof-ros-oo'-nay]
	Parsing (part of speech): noun
	    Case—dative
	    Gender—feminine
	    Number—singular
	    Stem or root—from ταπεινοφροσύνη, ης
	Concordance References:
	⇒ Strong's #5012 tapeinophrosunē
	⇒ NIV #5425 tapeinophrosunē
	⇒ NASB #5012 tapeinophrosunē
	
	Philip. 2:3
	Let nothing *be done* through strife or vainglory; but in **lowliness of mind** let each esteem other better than themselves. [KJV]
	Do nothing from selfishness or empty conceit, but with **humility of mind** let each of you regard one another as more important than himself; [NASB]
	Do nothing out of selfish ambition or vain conceit, but in **humility** consider others better than yourselves. [NIV]
	Let nothing *be done* through selfish ambition or conceit, but in **lowliness of mind** let each esteem others better than himself. [NKJV]
	Don't be selfish; don't live to make a good impression on others. Be **humble**, thinking of others as better than yourself. [NLT]
	μηδὲν κατ' ἐριθείαν η κενοδοξίαν, ἀλλὰ τῇ **ταπεινοφροσύνῃ** ἀλλήλους ἡγούμενοι ὑπερέχοντας ἑαυτῶν· [GNS]
	μηδὲν κατ' ἐριθείαν μηδὲ κατὰ κενοδοξίαν ἀλλὰ τῇ **ταπεινοφροσύνῃ** ἀλλήλους ἡγούμενοι ὑπερέχοντας ἑαυτῶν, [GNT]
		Humility, lowliness of mind; *to offer* oneself as lowly and submissive; to walk in a spirit of lowliness; *to present* oneself as lowly and low-lying in mind; to be of low degree and low rank; not to be high-minded, proud, haughty, arrogant, or assertive.
		
		Practical Application
		Note: a humble person may have a high position, power, wealth, fame, and much more; but he carries himself in a spirit of lowliness and submission. He denies himself for the sake of Christ and in order to help others.
		Men have always looked upon humility as a vice. A lowly man is often looked upon as a coward, a cringing, despicable, slavish type of person. Men fear humility. They feel humility is a sign of weakness and will make them the object of contempt and abuse and cause them to be shunned and overlooked.
		Because of this, men ignore and shun the teaching of Christ on humility. This is tragic:
		⇒ for a humble spirit is necessary for salvation (Matthew 18:3-4).
		⇒ for God's idea of humility is not weakness and cowardice.
		God makes people strong, the strongest they can possibly be. By humility God does not mean what men mean. God infuses a new and strong spirit within a person and causes that person to conquer all throughout life. He just does not want the person walking around in pride. He wants the person to do what the definition says: *to offer* himself in a spirit of submissiveness and lowliness; not to act high-minded, proud, haughty, arrogant, or assertive.

#2458
Lowly
 	
Base–KJV
Meek–NASB
Timid–NIV
Lowly–NKJV
Timid–NLT
	ταπεινός = *tapeinos*
	Pronunciation: [tap-i-nos']
	Parsing (part of speech): adjective
	    Case—nominative
	    Gender—masculine
	    Number—singular
	    Stem or root—from ταπεινός, ή, όν
	Concordance References:
	⇒ Strong's #5011 tapeinos
		Timid, meek, base, humble, lowly, gentle.
		
		Practical Application
		Some were saying that Paul was a coward. This is what is meant by the word "lowly" (*tapeinos*). They were saying that Paul was bold in his instructions; that is, he rebuked the church when he was writing to them, but he was a coward when it came to speaking face to face with them.

ENGLISH WORD	GREEK WORD AND VERSE	THE WORD MEANS...
POSB REFERENCE (2 Cor.10:1-2; esp. v.1) Note 1	⇒ NIV #5424 tapeinos ⇒ NASB #5011 tapeinos **2 Cor. 10:1** Now I Paul myself beseech you by the meekness and gentleness of Christ, who in presence am **base** among you, but being absent am bold toward you: [KJV] Now I, Paul, myself urge you by the meekness and gentleness of Christ— I who am **meek** when face to face with you, but bold toward you when absent! [NASB] By the meekness and gentleness of Christ, I appeal to you—I, Paul, who am "**timid**" when face to face with you, but "bold" when away! [NIV] Now I, Paul, myself am pleading with you by the meekness and gentleness of Christ—who in presence am **lowly** among you, but being absent am bold toward you. [NKJV] Now I, Paul, plead with you. I plead with the gentleness and kindness that Christ himself would use, even though some of you say I am bold in my letters but **timid** in person. [NLT] Αὐτὸς δὲ ἐγὼ Παῦλος παρακαλῶ ὑμᾶς διὰ τῆς πραότητος καὶ ἐπιεικείας τοῦ Χριστοῦ, ὃς κατὰ πρόσωπον μὲν **ταπεινὸς** ἐν ὑμῖν, ἀπὼν δὲ θαρρῶ εἰς ὑμᾶς· [GNS] Αὐτὸς δὲ ἐγὼ Παῦλος παρακαλῶ ὑμᾶς διὰ τῆς πραΰτητος καὶ ἐπιεικείας τοῦ Χριστοῦ, ὃς κατὰ πρόσωπον μὲν **ταπεινὸς** ἐν ὑμῖν, ἀπὼν δὲ θαρρῶ εἰς ὑμᾶς· [GNT]	
#2459 **Lure** Enticed–KJV Enticed–NASB Enticed–NIV Enticed–NKJV **Lure–NLT** **POSB REFERENCE** (Jas 1:14-16; esp. v.14) Note 2, point 1	δελεαζόμενος = *deleazomenos* Pronunciation: [del-eh-ad'-zo-mehn-os] Parsing (part of speech): verb 　Mood—participle 　Tense—present 　Voice—passive 　Case—nominative 　Gender—masculine 　Number—singular 　Stem or root—from δελεάζω Concordance References: ⇒ Strong's #1185 deleazö ⇒ NIV #1284 deleazö ⇒ NASB #1185 deleazö **James 1:14** But every man is tempted, when he is drawn away of his own lust, and **enticed**. [KJV] But each one is tempted when he is carried away and **enticed** by his own lust. [NASB] But each one is tempted when, by his own evil desire, he is dragged away and **enticed**. [NIV] But each one is tempted when he is drawn away by his own desires and **enticed**. [NKJV] Temptation comes from the **lure** of our own evil desires. [NLT] ἕκαστος δὲ πειράζεται, ὑπὸ τῆς ἰδίας ἐπιθυμίας ἐξελκόμενος καὶ **δελεαζόμενος**. [GNS] ἕκαστος δὲ πειράζεται ὑπὸ τῆς ἰδίας ἐπιθυμίας ἐξελκόμενος καὶ **δελεαζόμενος**· [GNT]	To entice, lure, trap, catch, seduce. It means to lure and bait just as a person lures and baits a fish. **Practical Application** Every man—there are no exceptions—has temptation that comes from the lure of his own evil desires. The picture is this: man has good desires, natural and normal desires. Therefore, when he begins to think about or look at something, he very naturally desires it. His desire is normal behavior. The problem arises when the thing is forbidden or is harmful. If he looks at and thinks about the forbidden or harmful thing, he begins to lust and is enticed or lured to go after it. This is the very beginning stage of temptation. Man focuses his desire upon the forbidden or harmful thing. He begins to pay attention to what he should not look at; he begins to think about the things of the flesh and of the world. Thereby, he is tempted by the lure of his own evil desires.
#2460 **Lust** Wantonness–KJV Sensuality–NASB Debauchery–NIV **Lust–NKJV** Immoral living–NLT	ἀσελγείαις = *aselgeiais* Pronunciation: [as-elg'-i-ah-is] Parsing (part of speech): noun 　Case—dative 　Gender—feminine 　Number—plural 　Stem or root—from ἀσέλγεια, ας Concordance References: ⇒ Strong's #766 aselgeia ⇒ NIV #816 aselgeia ⇒ NASB #766 aselgeia	Debauchery; sensuality; lust; running wild; licentiousness; wantonness; homosexuality; lasciviousness; living a wild, partying, and immoral life. **Practical Application** It is excess lust, unbridled lust that consumes one's thoughts and behavior through... • looks and dress • films and pictures • dances and parties • suggestions and gestures

ENGLISH WORD	GREEK WORD AND VERSE	THE WORD MEANS...
POSB REFERENCE (Rom.13:13) Note 4, point 4	**Romans 13:13** Let us walk honestly, as in the day; not in rioting and drunkenness, not in chambering and **wantonness**, not in strife and envying. [KJV] Let us behave properly as in the day, not in carousing and drunkenness, not in sexual promiscuity and **sensuality**, not in strife and jealousy. [NASB] Let us behave decently, as in the daytime, not in orgies and drunkenness, not in sexual immorality and **debauchery**, not in dissension and jealousy. [NIV] Let us walk properly, as in the day, not in revelry and drunkenness, not in lewdness and **lust**, not in strife and envy. [NKJV] We should be decent and true in everything we do, so that everyone can approve of our behavior. Don't participate in wild parties and getting drunk, or in adultery and **immoral living**, or in fighting and jealousy. [NLT] ὡς ἐν ἡμέρᾳ, εὐσχημόνως περιπατήσωμεν, μὴ κώμοις καὶ μέθαις, μὴ κοίταις καὶ **ἀσελγείαις**, μὴ ἔριδι καὶ ζήλῳ. [GNS] ὡς ἐν ἡμέρᾳ εὐσχημόνως περιπατήσωμεν, μὴ κώμοις καὶ μέθαις, μὴ κοίταις καὶ **ἀσελγείαις**, μὴ ἔριδι καὶ ζήλῳ, [GNT]	• books and pamphlets • songs and music • talk and jokes • touch and behavior • sensuality, indecency, vice
#2461 Lust Inordinate affection– KJV Passion–NASB **Lust–NIV** Passion–NKJV **Lust–NLT** **POSB REFERENCE** (Col.3:5-7; esp. v.5) Note 1, point 1c	**πάθος** = *pathos* Pronunciation: [path'-os] Parsing (part of speech): noun Case—accusative Gender—neuter Number—singular Stem or root—from **πάθος**, ους Concordance References: ⇒ Strong's #3806 pathos ⇒ NIV #4079 pathos ⇒ NASB #3806 pathos **Col. 3:5** Mortify therefore your members which are upon the earth; fornication, uncleanness, **inordinate affection**, evil concupiscence, and covetousness, which is idolatry: [KJV] Therefore consider the members of your earthly body as dead to immorality, impurity, **passion**, evil desire, and greed, which amounts to idolatry. [NASB] Put to death, therefore, whatever belongs to your earthly nature: sexual immorality, impurity, **lust**, evil desires and greed, which is idolatry. [NIV] Therefore put to death your members which are on the earth: fornication, uncleanness, **passion**, evil desire, and covetousness, which is idolatry. [NKJV] So put to death the sinful, earthly things lurking within you. Have nothing to do with sexual sin, impurity, **lust**, and shameful desires. Don't be greedy for the good things of this life, for that is idolatry. [NLT] Νεκρώσατε οὖν τὰ μέλη ὑμῶν τὰ ἐπὶ τῆς γῆς, πορνείαν, ἀκαθαρσίαν, **πάθος**, ἐπιθυμίαν κακήν, καὶ τὴν πλεονεξίαν, ἥτις ἐστὶν εἰδωλολατρεία, [GNS] Νεκρώσατε οὖν τὰ μέλη τὰ ἐπὶ τῆς γῆς, πορνείαν ἀκαθαρσίαν **πάθος** ἐπιθυμίαν κακήν, καὶ τὴν πλεονεξίαν, ἥτις ἐστὶν εἰδωλολατρία, [GNT]	Lust; inordinate affection; lustful passion; craving; strong desire; intense arousal; a driving lust. **Practical Application** It is, of course, a desire and craving for the wrong things such as the second and third helping of food, alcohol, drugs, nudity, pornography, suggestive and filthy literature, illicit affairs, extra-marital sex and a host of other lusts.
#2462 Lust **Lust–KJV** **Lust–NASB** Evil desire–NIV Desires–NKJV Evil desires–NLT	**ἐπιθυμίας** = *epithumias* Pronunciation: [ep-ee-thoo-mee'-ahs] Parsing (part of speech): noun Case—genitive Gender—feminine Number—singular Stem or root—from **ἐπιθυμία**, ας Concordance References: ⇒ Strong's #1939 epithumia ⇒ NIV #2123 epithumia ⇒ NASB #1939 epithumia	Evil desire, lust, passion, longing. It means to crave either good or evil. There are good desires and bad desires. **Practical Application** Every man—there are no exceptions—is tempted when he is drawn away by his own lusts and enticed. The picture is this: man has good desires, natural and normal desires. Therefore, when he begins to think about or look at something, he very naturally desires it. His desire is normal

ENGLISH WORD	GREEK WORD AND VERSE	THE WORD MEANS...
POSB REFERENCE (Jas.1:14-16; esp. v.14) Note 2	**James 1:14** But every man is tempted, when he is drawn away of his own **lust**, and enticed. [KJV] But each one is tempted when he is carried away and enticed by his own **lust**. [NASB] But each one is tempted when, by his own **evil desire**, he is dragged away and enticed. [NIV] But each one is tempted when he is drawn away by his own **desires** and enticed. [NKJV] Temptation comes from the lure of our own **evil desires**. [NLT] ἔκαστος δὲ πειράζεται, ὑπὸ τῆς ἰδίας **ἐπιθυμίας** ἐξελκόμενος καὶ δελεαζόμενος. [GNS] ἔκαστος δὲ πειράζεται ὑπὸ τῆς ἰδίας **ἐπιθυμίας** ἐξελκόμενος καὶ δελεαζόμενος [GNT]	behavior. The problem arises when the thing is forbidden or is harmful. If he looks at and thinks about the forbidden or harmful thing, he begins to lust and is enticed or lured to go after it. This is the very beginning stage of temptation. Man focuses his desire upon the forbidden or harmful thing. He begins to pay attention to what he should not look at; he begins to think about the things of the flesh and of the world. Thereby he is tempted and drawn away by his own lusts and enticements.
#2463 Lust–Lusts Lusts–KJV Lusts–NASB Lust–NIV Lusts–NKJV Lust–NLT **POSB REFERENCE** (1 Pt.4:3) Note 3	**ἐπιθυμίαις** = *epithumiais* Pronunciation: [ep-ee-thoo-mee'-ah-ees] Parsing (part of speech): noun Case—dative Gender—feminine Number—plural Stem or root—from ἐπιθυμία, ας Concordance References: ⇒ Strong's #1939 epithumia ⇒ NIV #2123 epithumia ⇒ NASB #1939 epithumia **1 Peter 4:3** For the time past of *our* life may suffice us to have wrought the will of the Gentiles, when we walked in lasciviousness, **lusts**, excess of wine, revellings, banquetings, and abominable idolatries: [KJV] For the time already past is sufficient *for you* to have carried out the desire of the Gentiles, having pursued a course of sensuality, **lusts**, drunkenness, carousals, drinking parties and abominable idolatries. [NASB] For you have spent enough time in the past doing what pagans choose to do—living in debauchery, **lust**, drunkenness, orgies, carousing and detestable idolatry. [NIV] For we *have spent* enough of our past lifetime in doing the will of the Gentiles—when we walked in lewdness, **lusts**, drunkenness, revelries, drinking parties, and abominable idolatries. [NKJV] You have had enough in the past of the evil things that godless people enjoy—their immorality and **lust**, their feasting and drunkenness and wild parties, and their terrible worship of idols. [NLT] ἀρκετὸς γὰρ ἡμῖν ὁ παρεληλυθὼς χρόνος τὸ βίου τὸ θέλημα τῶν ἐθνῶν κατεργάσασθαι, πεπορευμένους ἐν ἀσελγείαις, **ἐπιθυμίαις**, οἰνοφλυγίαις, κώμοις, πότοις, καὶ ἀθεμίτοις εἰδωλολατρείαις· [GNS] ἀρκετὸς γὰρ ὁ παρεληλυθὼς χρόνος τὸ βούλημα τῶν ἐθνῶν κατειργάσθαι πεπορευμένους ἐν ἀσελγείαις, **ἐπιθυμίαις**, οἰνοφλυγίαις, κώμοις, πότοις καὶ ἀθεμίτοις εἰδωλολατρίαις. [GNT]	Lust, desire. It means strong desire or craving and passion; it means that the pull of sin is sometimes very, very strong. **Practical Application** All men know what it is to lust after things, after more and more, and never to be satisfied even after the things are secured. (See POSB note—1 Peter 1:14; POSB note—1 Peter 2:11 for more discussion.)
#2464 Lust For More Greediness–KJV Greediness–NASB Lust for more–NIV Greediness–NKJV Greed–NLT **POSB REFERENCE** (Eph.4:17-19; esp. v.19) Note 1, point 7	**πλεονεξία** = *pleonexia* Pronunciation: [pleh-on-ex-ee'-ah] Parsing (part of speech): noun Case—dative Gender—feminine Number—singular Stem or root—from πλεονεξία, ας Concordance References: ⇒ Strong's #4124 pleonexia ⇒ NIV #4432 pleonexia ⇒ NASB #4124 pleonexia **Ephes. 4:19** Who being past feeling have given themselves over unto lasciviousness, to work all uncleanness with **greediness**. [KJV] And they, having become callous, have given them-	To lust for more; to be greedy. It means avarice, coveting, craving, grasping, desiring to have more and more; hoarding all one can get and still craving more. **Practical Application** It is being enslaved and held in bondage by the things of this earth: for example, food, drink, and a host of fleshly sins and self-centered behavior. Believers are not to walk in such a life. They are not to walk as other men walk.

ENGLISH WORD	GREEK WORD AND VERSE	THE WORD MEANS...
	selves over to sensuality, for the practice of every kind of impurity with **greediness**. [NASB] Having lost all sensitivity, they have given themselves over to sensuality so as to indulge in every kind of impurity, with a continual **lust for more**. [NIV] Who, being past feeling, have given themselves over to lewdness, to work all uncleanness with **greediness**. [NKJV] They don't care anymore about right and wrong, and they have given themselves over to immoral ways. Their lives are filled with all kinds of impurity and **greed**. [NLT] οἵτινες ἀπηλγηκότες ἑαυτοὺς παρέδωκαν τῇ ἀσελγείᾳ, εἰς ἐργασίαν ἀκαθαρσίας πάσης ἐν **πλεονεξίᾳ**. [GNS] οἵτινες ἀπηλγηκότες ἑαυτοὺς παρέδωκαν τῇ ἀσελγείᾳ εἰς ἐργασίαν ἀκαθαρσίας πάσης ἐν **πλεονεξίᾳ**. [GNT]	

#2465
Lusteth–Lusts
 	
Lusteth–KJV
Sets its desire against–NASB
Desires contrary to–NIV
Lusts–NKJV
Loves to do evil–NLT
 	
**POSB
REFERENCE**
(Gal.5:16-18; esp. v.17)
Note 1
	ἐπιθυμεῖ κατὰ = epithumei kata
	Pronunciation: [ep-ee-thoo-mee' kat-ah']
	Parsing epithumei (part of speech): verb
	   Mood—indicative
	   Tense—present
	   Voice—active
	   Person—3rd person
	   Number—singular
	   Stem or root—from ἐπιθυμέω
	Parsing kata (part of speech): preposition
	   Case—genitive
	   Stem or root—from κατά
	Concordance References:
	⇒ Strong's #1937 epithumeö + 2596 kata
	⇒ NIV #2121 epithumeö [desires] + 2848 kata [contrary to]
	⇒ NASB #1937 epithumeö + 2596 kata
	
	Galatians 5:17
	For the flesh **lusteth** against the Spirit, and the Spirit against the flesh: and these are contrary the one to the other: so that ye cannot do the things that ye would. [KJV]
	For the flesh **sets its desire against** the Spirit, and the Spirit against the flesh; for these are in opposition to one another, so that you may not do the things that you please. [NASB]
	For the sinful nature **desires** what is **contrary to** the Spirit, and the Spirit what is contrary to the sinful nature. They are in conflict with each other, so that you do not do what you want. [NIV]
	For the flesh lusts against the Spirit, and the Spirit against the flesh; and these are **contrary to** one another, so that you do not do the things that you wish. [NKJV]
	The old sinful nature **loves to do evil**, which is just opposite from what the Holy Spirit wants. And the Spirit gives us desires that are opposite from what the sinful nature desires. These two forces are constantly fighting each other, and your choices are never free from this conflict. [NLT]
	ἡ γὰρ σὰρξ **ἐπιθυμεῖ κατὰ** τοῦ Πνεύματος, τὸ δὲ Πνεῦμα κατὰ τῆς σαρκός· ταῦτα δὲ ἀντίκειται ἀλλήλοις, ἵνα μὴ ἃ ἐὰν θέλητε, ταῦτα ποιῆτε. [GNS]
	ἡ γὰρ σὰρξ **ἐπιθυμεῖ κατὰ** τοῦ πνεύματος, τὸ δὲ πνεῦμα κατὰ τῆς σαρκός, ταῦτα γὰρ ἀλλήλοις ἀντίκειται, ἵνα μὴ ἃ ἐὰν θέλητε ταῦτα ποιῆτε. [GNT]
		A yearning passion for; a love to do evil; to long for; to desire; to lust for; to covet.
		
		Practical Application
		The flesh fights for dominance. It lusts against the Spirit, struggles and fights to control the man. The picture is that of a tug of war (A.T. Robertson. *Word Pictures in the New Testament*, Vol.4, p.311). The flesh stands contrary to the Spirit—toe to toe, face to face—and it seeks to control man.
		Every person has experienced the flesh's...
		• yearning
		• pulling
		• desiring
		• wanting
		• grasping
		• grabbing
		• craving
		• hungering
		• thirsting
		• longing
		• taking
		
		Every person knows what it is to have his sinful nature lusting after something, to have it yearning and yearning to lay hold of the thing. The sinful nature is very strong and difficult to control. This is the first reason why a believer's only hope to control the sinful nature is the Spirit of God.

#2466
Lusts
 	
Lusts–KJV
Desires–NASB
Desire–NIV
Desires–NKJV
Evil things–NLT
	ἐπιθυμίας = epithumias
	Pronunciation: [ep-ee-thoo-mee'-ahs]
	Parsing (part of speech): noun
	   Case—accusative
	   Gender—feminine
	   Number—plural
	   Stem or root—from ἐπιθυμία, ας
	Concordance References:
	⇒ Strong's #1939 epithumia
	⇒ NIV #2123 epithumia
	⇒ NASB #1939 epithumia
		Desire; lust; loving to do evil things; a strong desire; a yearning passion for; an all-consuming craving.
		
		Practical Application
		The word is used in a good sense three different times in Scripture (Luke 22:15; Phil. 1:23; 1 Thes. 2:17). A person is to turn his strong desires toward righteousness and godliness; however, a person has to struggle to turn away from the

ENGLISH WORD	GREEK WORD AND VERSE	THE WORD MEANS...
POSB REFERENCE (Jn.8:44) *Deeper Study #1*	**John 8:44** Ye are of your father the devil, and the **lusts** of *your* father ye will do. He was a murderer from the beginning, and abode not in the truth, because there is no truth in him. When he speaketh a lie, he speaketh of his own: for he is a liar, and the father of it. [KJV] "You are of *your* father the devil, and you want to do the **desires** of your father. He was a murderer from the beginning, and does not stand in the truth, because there is no truth in him. Whenever he speaks a lie, he speaks from his own *nature;* for he is a liar, and the father of lies. [NASB] You belong to your father, the devil, and you want to carry out your father's **desire**. He was a murderer from the beginning, not holding to the truth, for there is no truth in him. When he lies, he speaks his native language, for he is a liar and the father of lies. [NIV] You are of *your* father the devil, and the **desires** of your father you want to do. He was a murderer from the beginning, and *does not* stand in the truth, because there is no truth in him. When he speaks a lie, he speaks from his own *resources,* for he is a liar and the father of it. [NKJV] For you are the children of your father the Devil, and you love to do the **evil things** he does. He was a murderer from the beginning and has always hated the truth. There is no truth in him. When he lies, it is consistent with his character; for he is a liar and the father of lies. [NLT] ὑμεῖς ἐκ πατρὸς τοῦ διαβόλου ἐστὲ, καὶ τὰς **ἐπιθυμίας** τοῦ πατρὸς ὑμῶν θέλετε ποιεῖν. ἐκεῖνος ἀνθρωποκτόνος ἦν ἀπ' ἀρχῆς, καὶ ἐν τῇ ἀληθείᾳ οὐκ ἔστηκεν, ὅτι οὐκ ἔστιν ἀλήθεια ἐν αὐτῷ. ὅταν λαλῇ τὸ ψεῦδος, ἐκ τῶν ἰδίων λαλεῖ· ὅτι ψεύστης ἐστὶ καὶ ὁ πατὴρ αὐτοῦ. [GNS] ὑμεῖς ἐκ τοῦ πατρὸς τοῦ διαβόλου ἐστὲ καὶ τὰς **ἐπιθυμίας** τοῦ πατρὸς ὑμῶν θέλετε ποιεῖν. ἐκεῖνος ἀνθρωποκτόνος ἦν ἀπ' ἀρχῆς καὶ ἐν τῇ ἀληθείᾳ οὐκ ἔστηκεν, ὅτι οὐκ ἔστιν ἀλήθεια ἐν αὐτῷ. ὅταν λαλῇ τὸ ψεῦδος, ἐκ τῶν ἰδίων λαλεῖ, ὅτι ψεύστης ἐστὶν καὶ ὁ πατὴρ αὐτοῦ. [GNT]	desire to please himself. A person's natural tendency is the desire or lust to satisfy self before others, in particular when survival and comfort are at stake. 1. The very nature of a person is lust, the lust of the flesh and of the mind (Ephes. 2:2-3). Sinful and evil lust show that people are by nature... • the children of wrath. • the children of disobedience. • the children of the spirit who is the prince and power of the air, that is, the devil. 2. The very nature of a person and of the world is lust, a tendency both to be and to get. What a person discovers is that his cravings are never satisfied; they have to be controlled. There is something within a person's innermost being that craves for more and more; but as more and more is taken, the lust does not diminish, it grows. It craves for still more and more. A person's cravings are never satisfied; his only answer is to control them by the power of Christ (see POSB note, Lust—James 4:2 for a discussion of the Spirit of God's control. Cp. Galatians 5:22-23.)
#2467 **Lusts** **Lusts–KJV** **Lusts–NASB** Sinful desires–NIV **Lusts–NKJV** Desired–NLT **POSB REFERENCE** (Romans 1:24-25; esp. v.24) Note 2, point 1	**ἐπιθυμίαις** = epithumiais Pronunciation: [ep-ee-thoo-mee'-ah-ees] Parsing (part of speech): noun Case—dative Gender—feminine Number—plural Stem or root—from ἐπιθυμία, ας Concordance References: ⇒ Strong's #1939 epithumia ⇒ NIV #2123 epithumia ⇒ NASB #1939 epithumia **Romans 1:24** Wherefore God also gave them up to uncleanness through the **lusts** of their own hearts, to dishonour their own bodies between themselves: [KJV] Therefore God gave them over in the **lusts** of their hearts to impurity, that their bodies might be dishonored among them. [NASB] Therefore God gave them over in the **sinful desires** of their hearts to sexual impurity for the degrading of their bodies with one another. [NIV] Therefore God also gave them up to uncleanness, in the **lusts** of their hearts, to dishonor their bodies among themselves, [NKJV] So God let them go ahead and do whatever shameful things their hearts **desired**. As a result, they did vile and degrading things with each other's bodies. [NLT] Διὸ καὶ παρέδωκεν αὐτοὺς ὁ Θεὸς ἐν ταῖς **ἐπιθυμίαις** τῶν καρδιῶν αὐτῶν εἰς ἀκαθαρσίαν τοῦ ἀτιμάζεσθαι τὰ	Desire, longing; lust, passion; covetousness; sinful desires. ### Practical Application Their hearts are filled with shameful...desires or "lusts" (*epithumiais*), that is, passionate cravings and urges. They long after things that displease God and that dishonor their bodies. God cares deeply about the human body, and he judges any person who abuses the body. (See POSB outline—Matthew 6:11 and POSB *Deeper Study #6*—Matthew 6:11; POSB note—1 Cor. 3:16; POSB note—1 Cor. 3:17; POSB *Deeper Study #1*—1 Cor. 6:18; POSB note—1 Cor. 6:19; POSB note—1 Cor. 6:20; cp. 1 Thes. 4:3-5 for more discussion.) In the Greek the lusts or desires are said to be "in [*en*] their own hearts." [KJV] Sin takes place in the heart before it takes place by act.

ENGLISH WORD	GREEK WORD AND VERSE	THE WORD MEANS...
	σώματα αὐτῶν ἐν αὐτοῖς· [GNS] Διὸ παρέδωκεν αὐτοὺς ὁ θεὸς ἐν ταῖς ἐπιθυμίαις τῶν καρδιῶν αὐτῶν εἰς ἀκαθαρσίαν τοῦ ἀτιμάζεσθαι τὰ σώματα αὐτῶν ἐν αὐτοῖς· [GNT]	

#2468
Lusts
 	
Lusts–KJV
Lusts–NASB
Evil desires–NIV
Lusts–NKJV
Lust–NLT
 	
**POSB
REFERENCE**
(2 Tim. 2:22)
Note 1
 	
See also POSB REF:
(Rom.6:12)
Note 2, point 2
(Rom.1:24-25; esp.
v.24)
Note 2, point 1
	ἐπιθυμίας = epithumias
	Pronunciation: [ep-ee-thoo-mee'-ahs]
	Parsing (part of speech): noun
	    Case—accusative
	    Gender—feminine
	    Number—plural
	    Stem or root—from *ἐπιθυμία, ας*
	Concordance References:
	  ⇒ Strong's #1939 epithumia
	  ⇒ NIV #2123 epithumia
	  ⇒ NASB #1939 epithumia
	
	2 Tim. 2:22
	Flee also youthful **lusts**: but follow righteousness, faith, charity, peace, with them that call on the Lord out of a pure heart. [KJV]
	Now flee from youthful **lusts**, and pursue righteousness, faith, love *and* peace, with those who call on the Lord from a pure heart. [NASB]
	Flee the **evil desires** of youth, and pursue righteousness, faith, love and peace, along with those who call on the Lord out of a pure heart. [NIV]
	Flee also youthful **lusts**; but pursue righteousness, faith, love, peace with those who call on the Lord out of a pure heart. [NKJV]
	Run from anything that stimulates youthful **lust**. Follow anything that makes you want to do right. Pursue faith and love and peace, and enjoy the companionship of those who call on the Lord with pure hearts. [NLT]
	τὰς δὲ νεωτερικὰς **ἐπιθυμίας** φεῦγε· δίωκε δὲ δικαιοσύνην, πίστιν, ἀγάπην, εἰρήνην μετὰ τῶν ἐπικαλουμένων τὸν Κύριον ἐκ καθαρᾶς καρδίας. [GNS]
	τὰς δὲ νεωτερικὰς **ἐπιθυμίας** φεῦγε, δίωκε δὲ δικαιοσύνην πίστιν ἀγάπην εἰρήνην μετὰ τῶν ἐπικαλουμένων τὸν κύριον ἐκ καθαρᾶς καρδίας. [GNT]
		Evil desires, lusts. It means passionate desires and cravings. It can mean either good or bad desires, and its meaning is always to be determined by the context (Wuest).
		
		Practical Application
		The point is this: passionate desire and craving is normal and natural. God made us to desire and crave. It is when we use our passions to hurt and damage that they become evil. What are the *lusts* of youth?
		⇒ *The desires of the eye*: youths desire to have and possess. To have and possess are normal desires, but the normal desire can lead to the lust for possessions and people.
		⇒ *The desires of the flesh*: youths desire the companionship of the opposite sex. Attraction is normal and leads to marriage and the carrying on of the human race. However, the normal desire can lead to illicit sex and immorality.
		⇒ *The desire for acceptance*: youths want friends. They want to fit in with their peers. They want approval, and they want to be recognized. This is normal, but it can lead to compromise—the compromise of one's values and morality and of the truth. It can also lead to rebellion against authority.
		⇒ *The desire to achieve*: youths desire to be successful, to find their place in the world. However, this can lead to seeking authority and power over people and to the manipulation and using of people for one's own ends.
		⇒ *The desire for recognition*: youths desire to be the *top gun*, the star, the best looking, the smartest, the most popular. They constantly picture themselves as winning the game in the last seconds, winning the beauty pageant, winning the contest, being the one most recognized; and a host of other daydreams. This can lead to either pride and arrogance or to a sense of inferiority and low self-image. It can lead either to the hurting of the less gifted or to the downing of oneself.
		⇒ *The desire to act and to act now*: youths, bursting with energy and idealism, want to see things done now. This can lead to impatience and to the mistreatment of people: bypassing and disregarding the peace and security of other people.
		⇒ *The desire to be original and creative*: youths want to have the new and fresh idea, the better thought, and the better way for doing things. This can lead to a critical and argumentative spirit. It can also lead to cheating in order to be recognized. It can lead to the restating and rewording of things and ideas and claiming that they are creative ideas.
		
		The charge to youth is direct and forceful: flee youthful lusts.

ENGLISH WORD	GREEK WORD AND VERSE	THE WORD MEANS...

#2469
Lusts
 	
Lusts–KJV
Desires–NASB
Desires–NIV
Desires–NKJV
Desires–NLT
 	
POSB
REFERENCE
(2 Tim. 4:3-4; esp. v.3)
Note 3, point 2
	ἐπιθυμίας = epithumias
	Pronunciation: [ep-ee-thoo-mee'-ahs]
	Parsing (part of speech): noun
	    Case—accusative
	    Gender—feminine
	    Number—plural
	    Stem or root—ἐπιθυμία, ας
	Concordance References:
	  ⇒ Strong's #1939 epithumia
	  ⇒ NIV #2123 epithumia
	  ⇒ NASB #1939 epithumia
	
	2 Tim. 4:3
	For the time will come when they will not endure sound doctrine; but after their own **lusts** shall they heap to themselves teachers, having itching ears; [KJV]
	For the time will come when they will not endure sound doctrine; but *wanting* to have their ears tickled, they will accumulate for themselves teachers in accordance to their own **desires**; [NASB]
	For the time will come when men will not put up with sound doctrine. Instead, to suit their own **desires**, they will gather around them a great number of teachers to say what their itching ears want to hear. [NIV]
	For the time will come when they will not endure sound doctrine, but according to their own **desires**, *because* they have itching ears, they will heap up for themselves teachers; [NKJV]
	For a time is coming when people will no longer listen to right teaching. They will follow their own **desires** and will look for teachers who will tell them whatever they want to hear. [NLT]
	ἔσται γὰρ καιρὸς ὅτε τῆς ὑγιαινούσης διδασκαλίας οὐκ ἀνέξονται, ἀλλὰ κατὰ τὰς **ἐπιθυμίας** τὰς ἰδίας ἑαυτοῖς ἐπισωρεύσουσι διδασκάλους, κινηθόμενοι τὴν ἀκοήν· [GNS]
	ἔσται γὰρ καιρὸς ὅτε τῆς ὑγιαινούσης διδασκαλίας οὐκ ἀνέξονται ἀλλὰ κατὰ τὰς ἰδίας **ἐπιθυμίας** ἑαυτοῖς ἐπισωρεύσουσιν διδασκάλους κινηθόμενοι τὴν ἀκοήν [GNT]
		Desire; lust; loving to do evil things; a strong desire; a yearning passion for; an all-consuming craving.
		
		Practical Application
		People will want teachers who will allow them to live like they desire. The Greek actually says that people will be *dominated* "by their own lusts or desires" (*epithumias*). They will be living lives of lusts, cravings, and gratifications—lives that seek the gratification of the flesh through...
		• sex and immorality
		• recognition and honor
		• power and authority
		• status and position
		• money and possessions
		• image and approval
		• discipline and control
		• religion and personal righteousness
		• good works and benevolence
		Such lusts and cravings will so dominate people's lives that they will seek ministers and teachers who will tickle their ears with the message of personal development and self-image.

#2470
Lusts
 	
Lusts–KJV
Pleasures–NASB
Desires–NIV
Desires for pleasure–
NKJV
Desires–NLT
 	
POSB
REFERENCE
(Jas.4:1)
Note 1
	ἡδονῶν = hēdonōn
	Pronunciation: [hay-don-own']
	Parsing (part of speech): noun
	    Case—genitive
	    Gender—feminine
	    Number—plural
	    Stem or root—from ἡδονή, ῆς
	Concordance References:
	  ⇒ Strong's #2237 hēdonē
	  ⇒ NIV #2454 hēdonē
	  ⇒ NASB #2237 hēdonē
	
	James 4:1
	From whence *come* wars and fightings among you? *come they* not hence, *even* of your **lusts** that war in your members? [KJV]
	What is the source of quarrels and conflicts among you? Is not the source your **pleasures** that wage war in your members? [NASB]
	What causes fights and quarrels among you? Don't they come from your **desires** that battle within you? [NIV]
	Where do wars and fights *come* from among you? Do *they* not *come* from your **desires for** pleasure that war in your members? [NKJV]
	What is causing the quarrels and fights among you? Isn't it the whole army of evil **desires** at war within you? [NLT]
	Πόθεν πόλεμοι καὶ μάχαι ἐν ὑμῖν; οὐκ ἐντεῦθεν, ἐκ τῶν **ἡδονῶν** ὑμῶν τῶν στρατευομένων ἐν τοῖς μέλεσιν ὑμῶν; [GNS]
		Desires, lusts, pleasures, passions. It means to crave pleasure; to crave gratification.
		
		Practical Application
		This Scripture says that lust for pleasure and gratification war within our bodies. The picture is that of constant warfare, of our bodies craving, yearning, pulling, urging, desiring, and grasping after whatever will gratify our pleasure. We want and want, desire and desire, and the battle of wanting and desiring rages on and on within our bodies. Our bodies are a battlefield of wants and desires. Every person knows what it is to experience this warfare, to have his flesh yearning and yearning after something. Lust is strong and difficult to control. In fact, few people control it completely. A few people may control their lust in what are called the gross and visible sins such as vengeance and murder, but they gratify their lust in acceptable things such as over-eating and selfishness, in buying and hoarding more than what is needed, and in looking when they should not look.
		The point is this: man is a walking civil war; lust after lust wages war within him, seeking gratification and pleasure. Man senses desire after desire, wanting to lift the restraint and to cut loose to enjoy the pleasure of the lust. It may be the lust for...

ENGLISH WORD	GREEK WORD AND VERSE	THE WORD MEANS...
	Πόθεν πόλεμοι καὶ πόθεν μάχαι ἐν ὑμῖν; οὐκ ἐντεῦθεν, ἐκ τῶν **ἡδονῶν** ὑμῶν τῶν στρατευομένων ἐν τοῖς μέλεσιν ὑμῶν; [GNT]	• food and more food • drink and more drink • drugs and more drugs • sex and more sex • possessions and more possessions • money and more money • property and more property • land and more land • recognition and more recognition • popularity and more popularity • authority and more authority • vengeance and more vengeance As stated, lust after lust wars within our members seeking its pleasure and gratification. Man is a civil war of lust and desire, of pleasure and gratification raging within his body and its members.

#2471
Lusts
 	
Lusts–KJV
Lusts–NASB
Passions–NIV
Lusts–NKJV
Desires–NLT
 	
POSB
REFERENCE
(Tit.3:3)
Note 2
 	
See also POSB REF:
(Tit.2:12)
Note 2, point 2d
	ἐπιθυμίας = *epithumias*
	Pronunciation: [ep-ee-thoo-mee'-ahs]
	Parsing (part of speech): noun
	   Case—accusative
	   Gender—feminine
	   Number—plural
	   Stem or root—from **ἐπιθυμία**, ας
	Concordance References:
	  ⇒ Strong's #1939 epithumia
	  ⇒ NIV #2123 epithumia
	  ⇒ NASB #1939 epithumia
	
	Titus 3:3
	For we ourselves also were sometimes foolish, disobedient, deceived, serving divers **lusts** and pleasures, living in malice and envy, hateful, *and* hating one another. [KJV]
	For we also once were foolish ourselves, disobedient, deceived, enslaved to various **lusts** and pleasures, spending our life in malice and envy, hateful, hating one another. [NASB]
	At one time we too were foolish, disobedient, deceived and enslaved by all kinds of **passions** and pleasures. We lived in malice and envy, being hated and hating one another. [NIV]
	For we ourselves were also once foolish, disobedient, deceived, serving various **lusts** and pleasures, living in malice and envy, hateful and hating one another. [NKJV]
	Once we, too, were foolish and disobedient. We were misled by others and became slaves to many wicked **desires** and evil pleasures. Our lives were full of evil and envy. We hated others, and they hated us. [NLT]
	ἦμεν γάρ ποτε καὶ ἡμεῖς ἀνόητοι, ἀπειθεῖς, πλανώμενοι, δουλεύοντες **ἐπιθυμίαις** καὶ ἡδοναῖς ποικίλαις, ἐν κακίᾳ καὶ φθόνῳ διάγοντες, στυγητοί, μισοῦντες ἀλλήλους. [GNS]
	Ἦμεν γάρ ποτε καὶ ἡμεῖς ἀνόητοι, ἀπειθεῖς, πλανώμενοι, δουλεύοντες **ἐπιθυμίαις** καὶ ἡδοναῖς ποικίλαις, ἐν κακίᾳ καὶ φθόνῳ διάγοντες, στυγητοί, μισοῦντες ἀλλήλους. [GNT]
		Passions, lusts, desires, pleasures. It means desire, lust, loving to do evil things, a strong desire, a yearning passion for, an all-consuming craving. The word (*epithumias*) means passionate cravings, desires, and urges.
		
		Practical Application
		Man is enslaved by the things of the world, things that damage his body—that make him greedy and selfish—that destroy his spirit and doom him to destruction.
		But thanks be to God our Savior. He has saved us and delivered us from the enslavements of this world, the enslavements of lust and pleasure that destroy our bodies and souls. The wonderful news is that any person can be delivered from the destructive lusts and pleasures of this world. How? Through our Lord Jesus Christ. If a person will turn away from the destructive passions, lusts and pleasures and turn to Christ, God will deliver him. God will give him the power to conquer the lusts and enslavements of this world.

#2472
Luxury, In
 	
Sumptuously–KJV
In splendor–NASB
In luxury–NIV
Sumptuously–NKJV
In luxury–NLT
 	
POSB
REFERENCE
(Lk.16:19-21; esp.
	λαμπρῶς = *lampros*
	Pronunciation: [lamp-rows]
	Parsing (part of speech): adjective
	   Type—adverb
	   Stem or root—from **λαμπρῶς**
	Concordance References:
	  ⇒ Strong's #2983 lambano
	  ⇒ NIV #3289 lampros
	  ⇒ NASB #2988 lampros
	
	Luke 16:19
	There was a certain rich man, which was clothed in purple and fine linen, and fared **sumptuously** every day: [KJV]
		To live in luxury; to live in splendor. The word means that the rich man was flamboyant, displaying his wealth in materialistic ways.
		
		Practical Application
		His sin was *self-indulgence, comfort, ease, luxury, extravagant living.* He sought the things and pleasures of this world. He was complacent, hoarding and allowing money to lie around making more and more for himself and his estate while needs lay all around him—right at his gate. He neglected and ignored others, most significantly, Lazarus. The needs of a degenerate

ENGLISH WORD	GREEK WORD AND VERSE	THE WORD MEANS...
v.19) *Deeper Study* #1 point 1	"Now there was a certain rich man, and he habitually dressed in purple and fine linen, gaily living **in splendor** every day. [NASB] "There was a rich man who was dressed in purple and fine linen and lived **in luxury** every day. [NIV] "There was a certain rich man who was clothed in purple and fine linen and fared **sumptuously** every day. [NKJV] Jesus said, "There was a certain rich man who was splendidly clothed and who lived each day **in luxury**. [NLT] "Ἄνθρωπος δέ τις ἦν πλούσιος, καὶ ἐνεδιδύσκετο πορφύραν καὶ βύσσον, εὐφραινόμενος καθ᾽ ἡμέραν **λαμπρῶς**. [GNS] "Ἄνθρωπος δέ τις ἦν πλούσιος, καὶ ἐνεδιδύσκετο πορφύραν καὶ βύσσον εὐφραινόμενος καθ᾽ ἡμέραν **λαμπρῶς**. [GNT]	world concerned him little, if at all. He wanted what others in the world had, plenty for themselves and more. The world acknowledged and honored those who had plenty, and he wanted such recognition and honor for himself. He wanted what others had and he wanted to keep up with them.

#2473
Lying
 	
Lying–KJV
Falsehood–NASB
Falsehood–NIV
Lying–NKJV
Falsehood–NLT
 	
POSB
REFERENCE
(Eph.4:25)
Note 1
	ψεῦδος = *pseudos*
	Pronunciation: [psyoo'-dos]
	Parsing (part of speech): noun
	  Case—accusative
	  Gender—neuter
	  Number—singular
	  Stem or root—from ψεῦδος, ους
	Concordance References:
	⇒ Strong's #5579 pseudos
	⇒ NIV #6022 pseudos
	⇒ NASB #5579 pseudos
	
	Ephes. 4:25
	Wherefore putting away **lying**, speak every man truth with his neighbour: for we are members one of another. [KJV]
	Therefore, laying aside **falsehood**, SPEAK TRUTH, EACH ONE *of you,* WITH HIS NEIGHBOR, for we are members of one another. [NASB]
	Therefore each of you must put off **falsehood** and speak truthfully to his neighbor, for we are all members of one body. [NIV]
	Therefore, putting away **lying**, *"Let each one of you speak truth with his neighbor,"* for we are members of one another. [NKJV]
	So put away all **falsehood** and "tell your neighbor the truth" because we belong to each other. [NLT]
	Διὸ ἀποθέμενοι τὸ **ψεῦδος** λαλεῖτε ἀλήθειαν ἕκαστος μετὰ τοῦ πλησίον αὐτοῦ· ὅτι ἐσμὲν ἀλλήλων μέλη. [GNS]
	Διὸ ἀποθέμενοι τὸ **ψεῦδος** λαλεῖτε ἀλήθειαν ἕκαστος μετὰ τοῦ πλησίον αὐτοῦ, ὅτι ἐσμὲν ἀλλήλων μέλη. [GNT]
		Falsehood, deceit, lying, counterfeit, distortion, fabrication. It is untruthfulness, deception, misrepresentation, exaggeration.
		
		Practical Application
		A lie does at least three things.
		1. Lying misrepresents the truth. It camouflages and hides the truth. The person lied to does not know the truth; therefore, he has to act or live upon a lie. If the lie is serious, it can be very damaging:
		⇒ A lie about a business deal can cost money and cause terrible loss.
		⇒ A lie about the salvation of the gospel can cost a person the hope of eternal life.
		⇒ A lie about loving someone can stir emotions that lead to destruction.
		2. Lying deceives a person. It leads a person astray. A person deceives...
		• to get what he wants.
		• to seduce someone.
		• to cover up or hide something.
		• to cause harm or hurt.
		The point to see is that lying is a deception, and deception eventually causes misunderstanding, disappointment, bewilderment, helplessness, and emotional upheaval.
		3. Lying builds a wrong relationship, a relationship built upon sinking sand. Two people cannot possibly be friends or live together if the relationship is based upon lies. Lying destroys...
		• confidence
		• assurance
		• security
		• love
		• trust
		• hope

ENGLISH WORD	GREEK WORD AND VERSE	THE WORD MEANS...

#2474
Made
 	
Made–KJV
Made–NASB
Made–NIV
Coming–NKJV
Appeared–NLT
 	
POSB
REFERENCE
(Philip.2:7)
Note 3, point 2
	γενόμενος = *genomenos*
	Pronunciation: [ghin'-om-eh-nos]
	Parsing (part of speech): verb
	    Mood—participle
	    Tense—aorist
	    Voice—middle deponent
	    Case—nominative
	    Gender—masculine
	    Number—singular
	    Stem or root—from *γίνομαι*
	Concordance References:
	⇒ Strong's #1096 ginomai
	⇒ NIV #1181 ginomai
	⇒ NASB #1096 ginomai
	
	Philip. 2:7
	But made himself of no reputation, and took upon him the form of a servant, and was **made** in the likeness of men: [KJV]
	But emptied Himself, taking the form of a bond-servant, and being **made** in the likeness of men. [NASB]
	But made himself nothing, taking the very nature of a servant, being **made** in human likeness. [NIV]
	But made Himself of no reputation, taking the form of a bondservant, *and* **coming** in the likeness of men. [NKJV]
	He made himself nothing; he took the humble position of a slave and **appeared** in human form. [NLT]
	ἀλλ ἑαυτὸν ἐκένωσε, μορφὴν δούλου λαβών, ἐν ὁμοιώματι ἀνθρώπων **γενόμενος·** καὶ σχήματι εὑρεθεὶς ὡς ἄνθρωπος, [GNS]
	ἀλλὰ ἑαυτὸν ἐκένωσεν μορφὴν δούλου λαβών, ἐν ὁμοιώματι ἀνθρώπων **γενόμενος·** καὶ σχήματι εὑρεθεὶς ὡς ἄνθρωπος [GNT]
		To be made; to become; to appear. It means a definite entrance into time.
		
		Practical Application
		It is not a permanent state. Jesus became a man, but it was not to be a permanent state. It was only for a time, a particular period. In the fullness of time, He made a definite entrance into the world as a man.
		Note that Jesus Christ did not come to earth as a prince or some great leader upon earth. He did not come to receive the homage and service of men. He came as the humblest of men, as a servant to serve men. "He was brought up meanly, probably working with his supposed father at his trade. His whole life was a life of humiliation, meanness, poverty, and disgrace; he had nowhere to lay his head, lived upon alms, was a man of sorrows and acquainted with grief, did not appear with external pomp or any marks of distinction from other men. This was the humiliation of his life" (*Matthew Henry's Commentary*, Vol.6, p.732f).

#2475
Made Alive Together With
 	
Quickened together with–KJV
Made alive together with–NASB
Made alive with–NIV
Made alive together with–NKJV
Made alive with–NLT
 	
POSB
REFERENCE
(Col.2:13)
Note 1, point 2b
	συνεζωοποίησεν σὺν = *sunezöopoiësen sun*
	Pronunciation: [soon-dzo-op-oy-ay'-sehn soon]
	Parsing *sunezöopoiësen* (part of speech): verb
	    Mood—indicative
	    Tense—aorist
	    Voice—active
	    Person—3rd person
	    Number—singular
	    Stem or root— from *συζωοποιέω*
	Parsing *sun* (part of speech): preposition
	    Case—dative
	    Stem or root—from *σύν*
	Concordance References:
	⇒ Strong's #4806+4862 suzöopoieö sun
	⇒ NIV #5188+5250 suzöopoieö sun [made alive with]
	⇒ NASB #4806+4862 suzöopoieö sun
	
	Col. 2:13
	And you, being dead in your sins and the uncircumcision of your flesh, hath he **quickened together with** him, having forgiven you all trespasses; [KJV]
	And when you were dead in your transgressions and the uncircumcision of your flesh, He **made** you **alive together with** Him, having forgiven us all our transgressions, [NASB]
	When you were dead in your sins and in the uncircumcision of your sinful nature, God **made** you **alive with** Christ. He forgave us all our sins, [NIV]
	And you, being dead in your trespasses and the uncircumcision of your flesh, He has **made alive together with** Him, having forgiven you all trespasses, [NKJV]
	You were dead because of your sins and because your sinful nature was not yet cut away. Then God **made** you **alive with** Christ. He forgave all our sins. [NLT]
	καὶ ὑμᾶς νεκροὺς ὄντας ἐν τοῖς παραπτώμασι καὶ τῇ ἀκροβυστίᾳ τῆς σαρκὸς ὑμῶν, **συνεζωοποίησε σὺν**
		Made alive with; quickened; to make alive; to bring to life.
		
		Practical Application
		God makes the believer alive with Christ. The believer is brought to life *from the dead*. How?
		⇒ By being "together with Christ."
		
		What does this mean, to be "together with Christ"? Simply this: when we trust Christ—really trust Him—God takes our trust and identifies us with Him. God places us *together with Christ*. This means a most wonderful thing: it means that we were with Christ in His death and resurrection.
		Therefore, when Christ died for our sins, we died with Him. God identifies us with Him, therefore, we never have to die for our sins. The penalty for our sins has already been paid; Christ paid for them. Christ bore the guilt, judgment, condemnation, and punishment for our sins. Consequently, we are *forgiven all our sins* (Gal.2:20; 1 Pet.2:24).

ENGLISH WORD	GREEK WORD AND VERSE	THE WORD MEANS...
	αὐτῷ, χαρισάμενος ὑμῖν πάντα τὰ παραπτώματα, [GNS] καὶ ὑμᾶς νεκροὺς ὄντας [ἐν] τοῖς παραπτώμασιν καὶ τῇ ἀκροβυστίᾳ τῆς σαρκὸς ὑμῶν, **συνεζωοποίησεν** ὑμᾶς **σὺν** αὐτῷ, χαρισάμενος ἡμῖν πάντα τὰ παραπτώματα. [GNT]	
#2476 **Made Alive Together With** Quickened together with–KJV **Made alive together with–NASB** **Made alive with–NIV** **Made us alive together with–NKJV** Gave us life–NLT **POSB REFERENCE** (Eph.2:4-5; esp. v.5) Note 1, point 2b	**συνεζωοποίησεν** = sunezöopoiësen Pronunciation: [soon-ehd-zo-op-oy-ee'-sehn] Parsing (part of speech): verb Mood—indicative Tense—aorist Voice—active Person—3rd person Number—singular Stem or root— from **συζωοποιέω** Concordance References: ⇒ Strong's #4806 suzöopoieö ⇒ NIV #5188 suzöopoieö ⇒ NASB #4806 suzöopoieö **Ephes. 2:5** Even when we were dead in sins, hath **quickened** us **together with** Christ, (by grace ye are saved;) [KJV] Even when we were dead in our transgressions, **made us alive together with** Christ (by grace you have been saved), [NASB] **Made** us **alive with** Christ even when we were dead in transgressions—it is by grace you have been saved. [NIV] Even when we were dead in trespasses, **made** us **alive together with** Christ (by grace you have been saved), [NKJV] That even while we were dead because of our sins, he **gave us life** when he raised Christ from the dead. (It is only by God's special favor that you have been saved!) [NLT] καὶ ὄντας ἡμᾶς νεκροὺς τοῖς παραπτώμασι **συνεζωοποίησε** τῷ Χριστῷ· -- χάριτί ἐστε σεσῳσμένοι· -- [GNS] καὶ ὄντας ἡμᾶς νεκροὺς τοῖς παραπτώμασιν **συνεζωοποίησεν** τῷ Χριστῷ, χάριτί ἐστε σεσῳσμένοι [GNT]	To make alive; to quicken; to give life. **Practical Application** We were dead in trespasses and sins, but God has made us alive. Why has God made us alive? Because of His very nature. God does not have a nature like most men picture: distant, disinterested, unconcerned, vengeful, and fearful.
#2477 **Made Complete** Perfection–KJV **Made complete–NASB** Perfection–NIV **Made complete–NKJV** Restoration to maturity–NLT **POSB REFERENCE** (2 Cor.13:7-10; esp. v.9) Note 2	**κατάρτισιν** = katartisin Pronunciation: [kat-ar'-tis-in] Parsing (part of speech): noun Case—accusative Gender—feminine Number—singular Stem or root—from **κατάρτισις**, εως Concordance References: ⇒ Strong's #2676 katartisis ⇒ NIV #2937 katartisis ⇒ NASB #2676 katartisis **2 Cor. 13:9** For we are glad, when we are weak, and ye are strong: and this also we wish, even your **perfection**. [KJV] For we rejoice when we ourselves are weak but you are strong; this we also pray for, that you be **made complete**. [NASB] We are glad whenever we are weak but you are strong; and our prayer is for your **perfection**. [NIV] For we are glad when we are weak and you are strong. And this also we pray, that you may be **made complete**. [NKJV] We are glad to be weak, if you are really strong. What we pray for is your **restoration to maturity**. [NLT] χαίρομεν γὰρ ὅταν ἡμεῖς ἀσθενῶμεν, ὑμεῖς δὲ δυνατοὶ ἦτε· τοῦτο δὲ καὶ εὐχόμεθα, τὴν ὑμῶν **κατάρτισιν**. [GNS] χαίρομεν γὰρ ὅταν ἡμεῖς ἀσθενῶμεν, ὑμεῖς δὲ δυνατοὶ ἦτε· τοῦτο καὶ εὐχόμεθα, τὴν ὑμῶν **κατάρτισιν**. [GNT]	Perfection; excellence; made whole; made complete, restoring to maturity; to repair what is broken and to restore it to a more perfect condition. **Practical Application** Paul was glad when the believers were strong in the Lord and he was able to appear weak, that is, when he did not have to be exercising authority and discipline. At such times, the believers and the church were growing toward perfection. What the Corinthian church needed was to become strong and perfected, that is, repaired and restored, to have its fellowship cleansed of critics and false teachers.

ENGLISH WORD	GREEK WORD AND VERSE	THE WORD MEANS...

#2478
Made Complete
 	
Made perfect–KJV
Perfected–NASB
Made complete–NIV
Made perfect–NKJV
Made complete–NLT
 	
POSB REFERENCE
(Jas. 2:21-24; esp. v.22)
Note 5
	ἐτελειώθη = eteleiöthë
	Pronunciation: [eh-tel-i-o'-thay]
	Parsing (part of speech): verb
	  Mood—indicative
	  Tense—aorist
	  Voice—passive
	  Person—3rd person
	  Number—singular
	  Stem or root—from τελειόω
	Concordance References:
	⇒ Strong's #5048 teleioö
	⇒ NIV #5457 teleioö
	⇒ NASB #5048 teleioö
	
	James 2:22
	Seest thou how faith wrought with his works, and by works was faith **made perfect**? [KJV]
	You see that faith was working with his works, and as a result of the works, faith was **perfected**; [NASB]
	You see that his faith and his actions were working together, and his faith was **made complete** by what he did. [NIV]
	Do you see that faith was working together with his works, and by works faith was **made perfect**? [NKJV]
	You see, he was trusting God so much that he was willing to do whatever God told him to do. His faith was **made complete** by what he did—by his actions. [NLT]
	βλέπεις ὅτι ἡ πίστις συνήργει τοῖς ἔργοις αὐτοῦ, καὶ ἐκ τῶν ἔργων ἡ πίστις ἐτελειώθη; [GNS]
	βλέπεις ὅτι ἡ πίστις συνήργει τοῖς ἔργοις αὐτοῦ καὶ ἐκ τῶν ἔργων ἡ πίστις ἐτελειώθη, [GNT]
		Made complete; made perfect; perfected; to completely finish; carried to the end.
		
		Practical Application
		By his works Abraham's faith was made complete (eteleiöthë), that is, finished, completed, carried to the end. Abraham's faith was proven, shown to be a complete faith. A true and living faith works: it completes and finishes its course. If a faith does not work or act or complete or finish its course, it is a dead faith—an incomplete, unfinished, and unproven faith.

#2479
Made Light Of
 	
Made light of–KJV
Paid no attention–NASB
Paid no attention–NIV
Made light of–NKJV
Ignored them–NLT
 	
POSB REFERENCE
(Mt.22:3-7; esp. v.5)
Note 2, point 3
	ἀμελήσαντες = amelësuntes
	Pronunciation: [am-el-ay'-sahn-tehs]
	Parsing (part of speech): verb
	  Mood—participle
	  Tense—aorist
	  Voice—active
	  Case—nominative
	  Gender—masculine
	  Number—plural
	  Stem or root—from ἀμελέω
	Concordance References:
	⇒ Strong's #272 ameleö
	⇒ NIV #288 ameleö
	⇒ NASB #272 ameleö
	
	Matthew 22:5
	But they **made light of it**, and went their ways, one to his farm, another to his merchandise: [KJV]
	"But they **paid no attention** and went their way, one to his own farm, another to his business, [NASB]
	"But they **paid no attention** and went off—one to his field, another to his business. [NIV]
	But they **made light of** it and went their ways, one to his own farm, another to his business. [NKJV]
	But the guests he had invited **ignored them** and went about their business, one to his farm, another to his store. [NLT]
	οἱ δὲ ἀμελήσαντες ἀπῆλθον, ὁ μὲν εἰς τὸν ἴδιον ἀγρόν, ὁ δὲ εἰς τὴν ἐμπορίαν αὐτοῦ· [GNS]
	οἱ δὲ ἀμελήσαντες ἀπῆλθον, ὃς μὲν εἰς τὸν ἴδιον ἀγρόν, ὃς δὲ ἐπὶ τὴν ἐμπορίαν αὐτοῦ· [GNT]
		To pay no attention; to make light of; to turn away; to neglect; to ignore; to care little if any; to be careless; to disregard.
		
		Practical Application
		In the Greek this is an aorist participle: the subjects of the King were making light of the King's gracious invitation to attend His Son's wedding banquet.
		They were definite in their decision not to attend the Great Wedding Banquet or Marriage Feast. They were careless and negligent about it. They were too busy to be concerned with the King's invitation, too busy with the world, making a living and getting more and more for pleasure and comfort (cp. James 4:13).

#2480
Made New
 	
Renewed–KJV
Renewed–NASB
Made new–NIV
Renewed–NKJV
Spiritual renewal–NLT
	ἀνανεοῦσθαι = ananeousthai
	Pronunciation: [an-an-eh-oos-tha-ee]
	Parsing (part of speech): verb
	  Mood—infinitive
	  Tense—present
	  Voice—passive
	  Stem or root—from ἀνανεόω
	Concordance References:
	⇒ Strong's #365 ananeoomai
		Renewed; made new, readjusted, changed, turned around, and regenerated. It is spiritual renewal.
		
		Practical Application
		The mind of man has been affected by sin. It desperately needs to be made new. The mind is far from perfect. It is *basically worldly*, that is...

ENGLISH WORD	GREEK WORD AND VERSE	THE WORD MEANS...
POSB REFERENCE (Eph.4:23) *Deeper Study #2*	⇒ NIV #391 ananeoomai ⇒ NASB #365 ananeoomai **Ephes. 4:23** And be **renewed** in the spirit of your mind; [KJV] And that you be **renewed** in the spirit of your mind, [NASB] To be **made new** in the attitude of your minds; [NIV] And be **renewed** in the spirit of your mind, [NKJV] Instead, there must be a **spiritual renewal** of your thoughts and attitudes. [NLT] ἀνανεοῦσθαι δὲ τῷ πνεύματι τοῦ νοὸς ὑμῶν, [GNS] ἀνανεοῦσθαι δὲ τῷ πνεύματι τοῦ νοὸς ὑμῶν [GNT]	• selfish • self-centered • self-seeking • centered on this world • centered on the flesh • centered on this life

#2481
 Made Nothing
 	
 Made...no reputation– KJV
 	
 Emptied–NASB
 	
 Made...nothing–NIV
 	
 Made...no reputation– NKJV
 	
 Made nothing–NLT
 	
 POSB REFERENCE (Philip.2:7) Note 3, point 1
	ἐκένωσεν = ekenōsen
	 Pronunciation: [eh-ken-o'-sehn]
	 Parsing (part of speech): verb
	     Mood—indicative
	     Tense—aorist
	     Voice—active
	     Person—3rd person
	     Number—singular
	     Stem or root—from κενόω
	 Concordance References:
	 ⇒ Strong's #2758 kenoö
	 ⇒ NIV #3033 kenoö
	 ⇒ NASB #2758 kenoö
	
	 Philip. 2:7
	 But made himself of no **reputation**, and took upon him the form of a servant, and was made in the likeness of men: [KJV]
	 But **emptied** Himself, taking the form of a bond-servant, and being made in the likeness of men. [NASB]
	 But **made** himself **nothing**, taking the very nature of a servant, being made in human likeness. [NIV]
	 But made Himself of no **reputation**, taking the form of a bondservant, *and* coming in the likeness of men. [NKJV]
	 He **made** himself **nothing**; he took the humble position of a slave and appeared in human form. [NLT]
	 ἀλλ᾽ ἑαυτὸν ἐκένωσε, μορφὴν δούλου λαβών, ἐν ὁμοιώματι ἀνθρώπων γενόμενος· καὶ σχήματι εὑρεθεὶς ὡς ἄνθρωπος, [GNS]
	 ἀλλὰ ἑαυτὸν ἐκένωσεν μορφὴν δούλου λαβών, ἐν ὁμοιώματι ἀνθρώπων γενόμενος· καὶ σχήματι εὑρεθεὶς ὡς ἄνθρωπος [GNT]
		Made [himself] nothing; to have no reputation; to empty oneself; to be completely empty.
		
		 Practical Application
		 Jesus Christ made Himself of no reputation; that is, He *made Himself nothing*. It is the picture of pouring water out of a glass until it is empty or of dumping something until it is all removed (William Barclay. *The Letters to the Philippians, Colossians, and Thessalonians*, p.44). The very picture of being completely empty stirs a feeling of just how far Christ went in humbling Himself for us. What was it that was poured or emptied out of Jesus Christ when He left heaven and came to earth? (This is what theologians call the *kenosis theory*.) Note that this passage does not say. It only says that Christ *made Himself nothing*. Other Scriptures, however, give some indication. (See POSB note, pt.4—Mark 13:32 for more discussion.)
		 1. Christ did not lay aside His deity when He came to earth. He could not cease to be who He was: God. No person can ever cease to be who he is. A person may take on different traits and behave differently; a person may change his behavior and looks, but he is the same person in being, nature, and essence. Jesus Christ is God; therefore, He is always God—He always possesses the nature of God (See POSB notes—John 1:1-2 for more discussion).
		 2. Christ laid aside some of His rights as God:
		 ⇒ He laid aside His right *to experience only the glory* and majesty, honor and worship of heaven. In coming to earth as a man, He was to experience anything but glory and majesty, honor and worship. Men would treat Him far differently than they would a heavenly being.
		 ⇒ He laid aside His right *to appear only in heaven* and to appear only as the Sovereign God of heaven. In coming to earth as a man, He was, of course, to appear as a man on earth.

#2482
 Made Of A Woman
 	
 Made of a woman– KJV
 	
 Born of a woman– NASB
 	
 Born of a woman–NIV
	γενόμενον ἐκ γυναικός = genomenon ek gunaikos
	 Pronunciation: [ghin'-om-eh-non ek goo-nee-kos]
	 Parsing *genomenon* (part of speech): verb
	     Mood—participle
	     Tense—aorist
	     Voice—middle deponent
	     Case—accusative
	     Gender—masculine
	     Number—singular
	     Stem or root—from γίνομαι
	 Parsing *ek* (part of speech): preposition
	     Case—genitive
		Born of a woman; made of a woman.
		
		 Practical Application
		 Christ came into the world just as all men do, through a woman. But note the most glorious truth: He was "sent" by God. Jesus Christ was "His Son," the Son of God. God spoke the Word and the woman conceived miraculously. The Virgin Birth did take place: God's very own Son has been sent into the world *as a man* to save people. (See POSB *Deeper Study #3*, Jesus

ENGLISH WORD	GREEK WORD AND VERSE	THE WORD MEANS...

Born of a woman–NKJV
 	
Born of a woman–NLT
 	
POSB REFERENCE
(Gal.4:4-7; esp. v.4)
Note 2
	Stem or root—from ἐκ
	Parsing *gunaikos* (part of speech): noun
	   Case—genitive
	   Gender—feminine
	   Number—singular
	   Stem or root—from γυνή, αικός
	Concordance References:
	⇒ Strong's #1096 ginomai + 1537 ek + 1135 gunë
	⇒ NIV #1181 ginomai [born] + 1666 ek [of] + 1222 gunë [woman]
	⇒ NASB #1096 ginomai + 1537 ek + 1135 gunë
	
	Galatians 4:4
	But when the fulness of the time was come, God sent forth his Son, **made of a woman**, made under the law, [KJV]
	But when the fulness of the time came, God sent forth His Son, **born of a woman**, born under the Law, [NASB]
	But when the time had fully come, God sent his Son, **born of a woman**, born under law, [NIV]
	But when the fullness of the time had come, God sent forth His Son, **born of a woman**, born under the law, [NKJV]
	But when the right time came, God sent his Son, **born of a woman**, subject to the law. [NLT]
	ὅτε δὲ ἦλθε τὸ πλήρωμα τοῦ χρόνου, ἐξαπέστειλεν ὁ Θεὸς τὸν υἱὸν αὐτοῦ, **γενόμενον ἐκ γυναικός**, γενόμενον ὑπὸ νόμον, [GNS]
	ὅτε δὲ ἦλθεν τὸ πλήρωμα τοῦ χρόνου, ἐξαπέστειλεν ὁ θεὸς τὸν υἱὸν αὐτοῦ, **γενόμενον ἐκ γυναικός**, γενόμενον ὑπὸ νόμον, [GNT]
		Christ, Birth—Matthew 1:16; POSB *Deeper Study* #8—Matthew 1:23; POSB note—Luke 1:27 and POSB *Deeper Study* #1—Luke 1:27; POSB note—Luke 1:34-35. Especially see Luke 1:27.)

#2483
Made Perfect
 	
Consecrated–KJV
Made perfect–NASB
Made perfect–NIV
Perfected–NKJV
Made perfect–NLT
 	
POSB REFERENCE
(Heb.7:28)
Note 4
	τετελειωμένον = *teteleiömenon*
	Pronunciation: [teh-tel-i-o'-mehn-on]
	Parsing (part of speech): verb
	   Mood—participle
	   Tense—perfect
	   Voice—passive
	   Case—accusative
	   Gender—masculine
	   Number—singular
	   Stem or root—from τελειόω
	Concordance References:
	⇒ Strong's #5048 teleioō
	⇒ NIV #5457 teleioō
	⇒ NASB #5048 teleioō
	
	Hebrews 7:28
	For the law maketh men high priests which have infirmity; but the word of the oath, which was since the law, maketh the Son, who is **consecrated** for evermore. [KJV]
	For the Law appoints men as high priests who are weak, but the word of the oath, which came after the Law, appoints a Son, **made perfect** forever. [NASB]
	For the law appoints as high priests men who are weak; but the oath, which came after the law, appointed the Son, who has been **made perfect** forever. [NIV]
	For the law appoints as high priests men who have weakness, but the word of the oath, which came after the law, *appoints* the Son who has been **perfected** forever. [NKJV]
	Those who were high priests under the law of Moses were limited by human weakness. But after the law was given, God appointed his Son with an oath, and his Son has been **made perfect** forever. [NLT]
	ὁ νόμος γὰρ ἀνθρώπους καθίστησιν ἀρχιερεῖς, ἔχοντας ἀσθένειαν· ὁ λόγος δὲ τῆς ὁρκωμοσίας τῆς μετὰ τὸν νόμον, υἱὸν εἰς τὸν αἰῶνα **τετελειωμένον**. [GNS]
	ὁ νόμος γὰρ ἀνθρώπους ἀθίστησιν ἀρχιερεῖς ἔχοντας ἀσθένειαν, ὁ λόγος δὲ τῆς ὁρκωμοσίας τῆς μετὰ τὸν νόμον υἱὸν εἰς τὸν αἰῶνα **τετελειωμένον**. [GNT]
		Perfected, consecrated; made perfect, complete.
		
		Practical Application
		Jesus Christ is the High Priest with a perfect appointment. Men—mere men—are appointed to be priests by the law. The law can appoint no one else but men with infirmities and weaknesses—men who are imperfect, frail, sinful, and dying. But the glorious message of this passage offers eternal hope for man. Why? Because God has given us two wonderful things: God has given His Word, His precious promise that He will give us a perfect and eternal High Priest to save us, and God has sworn that He will fulfill His Word. God has assured us with a double surety. Jesus Christ, the Son of God, is consecrated forever more. The phrase "made perfect" (*teteleiömenon*) means perfected. Jesus Christ is the perfected and eternal High Priest promised and sworn by God to save man. What greater salvation and surety could we ask than to have God send His own Son to perfect us and to give us eternal life and the glorious privilege of living forever with Him—the glorious privilege of ruling and reigning with Him throughout all of eternity.

ENGLISH WORD	GREEK WORD AND VERSE	THE WORD MEANS...

#2484
Made Perfect
 	
Made perfect–KJV
Perfected–NASB
Made complete–NIV
Made perfect–NKJV
Made complete–NLT
 	
POSB
REFERENCE
(Jas. 2:21-24; esp. v.22)
Note 5
	ἐτελειώθη = eteleiöthë
	Pronunciation: [eh-tel-i-o'-thay]
	Parsing (part of speech): verb
	  Mood—indicative
	  Tense—aorist
	  Voice—passive
	  Person—3rd person
	  Number—singular
	  Stem or root—from τελειόω
	Concordance References:
	⇒ Strong's #5048 teleioö
	⇒ NIV #5457 teleioö
	⇒ NASB #5048 teleioö
	
	James 2:22
	Seest thou how faith wrought with his works, and by works was faith **made perfect**? [KJV]
	You see that faith was working with his works, and as a result of the works, faith was **perfected**; [NASB]
	You see that his faith and his actions were working together, and his faith was **made complete** by what he did. [NIV]
	Do you see that faith was working together with his works, and by works faith was **made perfect**? [NKJV]
	You see, he was trusting God so much that he was willing to do whatever God told him to do. His faith was **made complete** by what he did—by his actions. [NLT]
	βλέπεις ὅτι ἡ πίστις συνήργει τοῖς ἔργοις αὐτοῦ, καὶ ἐκ τῶν ἔργων ἡ πίστις **ἐτελειώθη**; [GNS]
	βλέπεις ὅτι ἡ πίστις συνήργει τοῖς ἔργοις αὐτοῦ καὶ ἐκ τῶν ἔργων ἡ πίστις **ἐτελειώθη**, [GNT]
		To be made complete; to be made perfect; to be perfected; to completely finish; to be carried to an end.
		
		Practical Application
		By his works Abraham's faith was made perfect (*eteleiöthë*), that is, finished, completed, carried to the end. Abraham's faith was proven, shown to be a complete faith. A true and living faith works: it completes and finishes its course. If a faith does not work or act or complete or finish its course, it is a dead faith—an incomplete, unfinished, and unproven faith.

#2485
Made Right In God's Sight
 	
Justified–KJV
Justified–NASB
Justified–NIV
Justified–NKJV
Made right in God's sight–NLT
 	
POSB
REFERENCE
(Romans 5:1)
Note 1, point 3
 	
See also POSB REF:
(Gal.2:15-16; esp. v.16)
Deeper Study #1
	Δικαιωθέντες = Dikaiöthentes
	Pronunciation: [dik-ah-ee'-o-then-tehs]
	Parsing (part of speech): verb
	  Mood—participle
	  Tense—aorist
	  Voice—passive
	  Case—nominative
	  Gender—masculine
	  Person—1st person
	  Number—plural
	  Stem or root—from δικαιόω
	Concordance References:
	⇒ Strong's #1344 dikaioö
	⇒ NIV #1467 dikaioö
	⇒ NASB #1344 dikaioö
	
	Romans 5:1
	Therefore being **justified** by faith, we have peace with God through our Lord Jesus Christ: [KJV]
	Therefore having been **justified** by faith, we have peace with God through our Lord Jesus Christ, [NASB]
	Therefore, since we have been **justified** through faith, we have peace with God through our Lord Jesus Christ, [NIV]
	Therefore, having been **justified** by faith, we have peace with God through our Lord Jesus Christ, [NKJV]
	Therefore, since we have been **made right in God's sight** by faith, we have peace with God because of what Jesus Christ our Lord has done for us. [NLT]
	Δικαιωθέντες οὖν ἐκ πίστεως εἰρήνην ἔχομεν πρὸς τὸν Θεὸν διὰ τοῦ Κυρίου ἡμῶν Ἰησοῦ Χριστοῦ, [GNS]
	Δικαιωθέντες οὖν ἐκ πίστεως εἰρήνην ἔχομεν πρὸς τὸν θεὸν διὰ τοῦ κυρίου ἡμῶν Ἰησοῦ Χριστοῦ [GNT]
		To count righteous; to put into a right relationship (with God); to show or prove to be right. It means to reckon, to credit, to account, to judge, to treat, to look upon as righteous. It does not mean to make a man righteous. All Greek verbs which end in "oun" mean not to make someone something, but merely to count; to judge; to treat someone as something.
		
		Practical Application
		There are three major points to note about justification.
		1. Why justification is necessary:
		  a. Justification is necessary because of the sin and alienation of man. Man has rebelled against God and taken his life into his own hands.
		    Man has become sinful and ungodly, an enemy of God, pushing God out of his life and wanting little if anything to do with God. Man has separated and alienated himself from God.
		  b. Justification is necessary because of the anger and wrath of God. "God is angry with the wicked every day" (Psalm 7:11). Sin has aroused God's anger and wrath. God is angry over man's...
		    • rebellion
		    • sin
		    • hostility
		    • ungodliness
		    • unrighteousness
		    • desertion
		2. Why God justifies a man: God justifies a man because of His Son Jesus Christ. When a man believes in Jesus Christ, God takes that man's faith and counts it as righteousness. The man is not righteous, but God considers and cred-

ENGLISH WORD	GREEK WORD AND VERSE	THE WORD MEANS...
		its the man's faith as righteousness. Why is God willing to do this? a. God is willing to justify man because He loves man that much. God loves man so much that He sent His Son into the world and sacrificed Him in order to justify man (John 3:16; Romans 5:8). b. God is willing to justify man because of what His Son Jesus Christ has done for man. ⇒ Jesus Christ has secured the ideal righteousness for man. ⇒ Jesus Christ came into the world to die for man. ⇒ Jesus Christ came into the world to arise from the dead and thereby to conquer death for man. Now, as stated above, when a man believes in Jesus Christ—really believes—God takes that man's belief and... • counts it as the righteousness (perfection) of Christ. The man is counted as righteous in Christ. • counts it as the death of Christ. The man is counted as having already died in Christ, as having already paid the penalty for sin in the death of Christ. • counts it as the resurrection of Christ. The man is counted as already having been resurrected in Christ. Very simply, God loves His Son Jesus Christ so much that He honors any man who honors His Son by believing in Him. He honors the man by taking the man's faith and counting (crediting) it as righteousness and by giving him the glorious privilege of living with Christ forever in the presence of God. 3. How God justifies a man: the words "made right in God's sight" (*Dikaiōthentes*) is a legal term taken from the courts. It pictures man on trial before God. Man is seen as having committed the most heinous of crimes; he has rebelled against God and broken his relationship with God. How can he restore that relationship? Within human courts if a man is acquitted, he is declared innocent, but this is not true within the Divine Court. When a man appears before God, he is anything but innocent; he is utterly guilty and condemned accordingly. But when a man sincerely trusts Christ, then God takes that man's faith and counts it as righteousness. By such, God counts the man—judges him, treats him—as if he were innocent. The man is not made innocent; he is guilty. He knows it and God knows it, but God treats him as innocent. "God justifies the ungodly"—an incredible mercy, a wondrous grace. (See POSB notes—Romans 4:1-3; POSB *Deeper Study* #1—Romans 4:1-25; POSB *Deeper Study* #2—Romans 4:22.) How do we know this? How can we know for sure that God is like this? Because Jesus Christ said so. He said that God loves us. We are sinners, yes; but Christ said that we are very, very dear to God. (Note: for a detailed discussion of this topic see POSB note 1, point 3—Romans 5:1).

ENGLISH WORD	GREEK WORD AND VERSE	THE WORD MEANS...

#2486
Made Right In God's Sight
 	
Righteousness–KJV
Righteousness–NASB
Righteousness–NIV
Righteousness–NKJV
Made right in God's sight–NLT
 	
POSB REFERENCE
(Heb.11:7)
Note 2, point 3
	δικαιοσύνης = *dikaiosunës*
	Pronunciation: [dik-ah-ee-os-soo'-nays]
	Parsing (part of speech): noun
	  Case—genitive
	  Gender—feminine
	  Number—singular
	  Stem or root—from δικαιοσύνη, ης
	Concordance References:
	⇒ Strong's #1343 dikaiosunē
	⇒ NIV #1466 dikaiosunē
	⇒ NASB #1343 dikaiosunē
	
	Hebrews 11:7
	By faith Noah, being warned of God of things not seen as yet, moved with fear, prepared an ark to the saving of his house; by the which he condemned the world, and became heir of the **righteousness** which is by faith. [KJV]
	By faith Noah, being warned by God about things not yet seen, in reverence prepared an ark for the salvation of his household, by which he condemned the world, and became an heir of the **righteousness** which is according to faith. [NASB]
	By faith Noah, when warned about things not yet seen, in holy fear built an ark to save his family. By his faith he condemned the world and became heir of the **righteousness** that comes by faith. [NIV]
	By faith Noah, being divinely warned of things not yet seen, moved with godly fear, prepared an ark for the saving of his household, by which he condemned the world and became heir of the **righteousness** which is according to faith. [NKJV]
	It was by faith that Noah built an ark to save his family from the flood. He obeyed God, who warned him about something that had never happened before. By his faith he condemned the rest of the world and was **made right in God's sight**. [NLT]
	Πίστει χρηματισθεὶς Νῶε περὶ τῶν μηδέπω βλεπομένων, εὐλαβηθεὶς, κατεσκεύασε κιβωτὸν εἰς σωτηρίαν τοῦ οἴκου αὐτοῦ· δι' ἧς κατέκρινε τὸν κόσμον, καὶ τῆς κατὰ πίστιν **δικαιοσύνης** ἐγένετο κληρονόμος. [GNS]
	Πίστει χρηματισθεὶς Νῶε περὶ τῶν μηδέπω βλεπομένων, εὐλαβηθεὶς κατεσκεύασεν κιβωτὸν εἰς σωτηρίαν τοῦ οἴκου αὐτοῦ δι' ἧς κατέκρινεν τὸν κόσμον, καὶ τῆς κατὰ πίστιν **δικαιοσύνης** ἐγένετο κληρονόμος. [GNT]
		Righteousness; to be made right in God's sight.
		
		Practical Application
		Noah was made right in God's sight (*dikaiosunës*). Noah believed God and God counted his faith as righteousness. He "became heir of the righteousness *which is by faith.*" As Matthew Henry says, Noah had faith in the *promised Seed*, the Savior whom God was someday going to send to earth (*Matthew Henry's Commentary*, Vol. 6, p.941). There is nothing else upon earth that can cause God to count a man righteous but faith—faith in the *promised Seed*, the Savior of the world, even the Lord Jesus Christ.

#2487
Made Well
 	
Made whole–KJV
Cured–NASB
Healed–NIV
Made...well–NKJV
Healed–NLT
 	
POSB REFERENCE
(Mt.14:36)
Note 6
	διεσώθησαν = *diesöthësan*
	Pronunciation: [dee-so'-thay-sahn]
	Parsing (part of speech): verb
	  Mood—indicative
	  Tense—aorist
	  Voice—passive
	  Person—3rd person
	  Number—plural
	  Stem or root—from διασῴζω
	Concordance References:
	⇒ Strong's #1295 diasözö
	⇒ NIV #1407 diasözö
	⇒ NASB #1295 diasözö
	
	Matthew 14:36
	And besought him that they might only touch the hem of his garment: and as many as touched were **made** perfectly **whole**. [KJV]
	And they began to entreat Him that they might just touch the fringe of His cloak; and as many as touched it were **cured**. [NASB]
	And begged him to let the sick just touch the edge of his cloak, and all who touched him were **healed**. [NIV]
	And begged Him that they might only touch the hem of His garment. And as many as touched *it* were **made**
		To be healed or cured through and through; to be made whole through and through; to be rescued.
		
		Practical Application
		A complete restoration takes place within the person. The person is completely cured, spiritually and inwardly, as well as physically and outwardly.

ENGLISH WORD	GREEK WORD AND VERSE	THE WORD MEANS...
	perfectly **well**. [NKJV] The sick begged him to let them touch even the fringe of his robe, and all who touched it were **healed**. [NLT] καὶ παρεκάλουν αὐτόν, ἵνα μόνον ἅψωνται τοῦ κρασπέδου τοῦ ἱματίου αὐτοῦ· καὶ ὅσοι ἥψαντο **διεσώθησαν**. [GNS] καὶ παρεκάλουν αὐτὸν ἵνα μόνον ἅψωνται τοῦ κρασπέδου τοῦ ἱματίου αὐτοῦ· καὶ ὅσοι ἥψαντο **διεσώθησαν**. [GNT]	
#2488 **Made Well** Made...whole–KJV **Made...well–NASB** **Made...well–NIV** **Made...well–NKJV** **Made...well–NLT** **POSB** **REFERENCE** (Lk.17:15-19; esp. v.19) Note 3, point 5	*σέσωκέν* = sesöken Pronunciation: [seh-so-ken'] Parsing (part of speech): verb 　Mood—indicative 　Tense—perfect 　Voice—active 　Person—3rd person 　Number—singular 　Stem or root—from σώζω Concordance References: ⇒ Strong's #4982 sözö ⇒ NIV #5392 sözö ⇒ NASB #4982 sözö **Luke 17:19** And he said unto him, Arise, go thy way: thy faith hath **made** thee **whole**. [KJV] And He said to him, "Rise, and go your way; your faith has **made** you **well**." [NASB] Then he said to him, "Rise and go; your faith has **made** you **well**." [NIV] And He said to him, "Arise, go your way. Your faith has **made** you **well**." [NKJV] And Jesus said to the man, "Stand up and go. Your faith has **made** you **well**." [NLT] καὶ εἶπεν αὐτῷ, Ἀναστὰς πορεύου· ἡ πίστις σου **σέσωκέ** σε. [GNS] καὶ εἶπεν αὐτῷ, Ἀναστὰς πορεύου· ἡ πίστις σου **σέσωκέν** σε. [GNT]	To be made well; to be made whole; to be saved; to be delivered; to be cured; to be rescued; to be preserved; to be made better. **Practical Application** The verb "made well" is literally "has saved you." The man was clearly whole in body. This could be easily seen, but one could not see the spiritual and inward cleansing. Jesus was telling the man that his sins were forgiven; He was giving the man the assurance of salvation.
#2489 **Made Whole** Made whole–KJV Cured–NASB Healed–NIV Made well–NKJV Healed–NLT **POSB** **REFERENCE** (Mt.14:36) Note 6	*διεσώθησαν* = diesöthësan Pronunciation: [dee-so'-thay-sahn] Parsing (part of speech): verb 　Mood—indicative 　Tense—aorist 　Voice—passive 　Person—3rd person 　Number—plural 　Stem or root—from διασώζω Concordance References: ⇒ Strong's #1295 diasözö ⇒ NIV #1407 diasözö ⇒ NASB #1295 diasözö **Matthew 14:36** And besought him that they might only touch the hem of his garment: and as many as touched were **made** perfectly **whole**. [KJV] And they began to entreat Him that they might just touch the fringe of His cloak; and as many as touched it were **cured**. [NASB] And begged him to let the sick just touch the edge of his cloak, and all who touched him were **healed**. [NIV] And begged Him that they might only touch the hem of His garment. And as many as touched *it* were **made** perfectly **well**. [NKJV] The sick begged him to let them touch even the fringe of his robe, and all who touched it were **healed**. [NLT] καὶ παρεκάλουν αὐτόν, ἵνα μόνον ἅψωνται τοῦ κρασπέδου τοῦ ἱματίου αὐτοῦ· καὶ ὅσοι ἥψαντο **διεσώθησαν**. [GNS] καὶ παρεκάλουν αὐτὸν ἵνα μόνον ἅψωνται τοῦ κρασπέδου τοῦ ἱματίου αὐτοῦ· καὶ ὅσοι ἥψαντο **διεσώθησαν**. [GNT]	To be healed or cured through and through; to be made whole through and through; to rescue. **Practical Application** A complete restoration takes place within the person. The person is completely cured, spiritually and inwardly, as well as physically and outwardly.

ENGLISH WORD	GREEK WORD AND VERSE	THE WORD MEANS...

#2490
Made Whole
 	
Made...whole–KJV
Made...well–NASB
Made...well–NIV
Made...well–NKJV
Made...well–NLT
 	
**POSB
REFERENCE**
(Lk.17:15-19; esp.
v.19)
Note 3, point 5
	σέσωκέν = sesöken
	Pronunciation: [seh-so-ken']
	Parsing (part of speech): verb
	    Mood—indicative
	    Tense—perfect
	    Voice—active
	    Person—3rd person
	    Number—singular
	    Stem or root—from σῴζω
	Concordance References:
	  ⇒ Strong's #4982 sözö
	  ⇒ NIV #5392 sözö
	  ⇒ NASB #4982 sözö
	
	Luke 17:19
	And he said unto him, Arise, go thy way: thy faith hath **made** thee **whole**. [KJV]
	And He said to him, "Rise, and go your way; your faith has **made** you **well**." [NASB]
	Then he said to him, "Rise and go; your faith has **made** you **well**." [NIV]
	And He said to him, "Arise, go your way. Your faith has **made** you **well**." [NKJV]
	And Jesus said to the man, "Stand up and go. Your faith has **made** you **well**." [NLT]
	καὶ εἶπεν αὐτῷ, Ἀναστὰς πορεύου· ἡ πίστις σου **σέσωκέ** σε. [GNS]
	καὶ εἶπεν αὐτῷ, Ἀναστὰς πορεύου· ἡ πίστις σου **σέσωκέν** σε. [GNT]
		To be made well; to be made whole; to be saved; to be delivered; to be cured; to be rescued; to be preserved; to be made better.
		
		Practical Application
		The verb "made whole" is literally "has saved you." The man was clearly whole in body. This could be easily seen, but one could not see the spiritual and inward cleansing. Jesus was telling the man that his sins were forgiven; He was giving the man the assurance of salvation.

#2491
Madness, Filled With
 	
Filled with madness–KJV
Filled with rage–NASB
Furious–NIV
Filled with rage–NKJV
Wild with rage–NLT
 	
**POSB
REFERENCE**
(Lk.6:6-11; esp. v.11)
Note 3, point 5
	ἐπλήσθησαν ἀνοίας = eplësthësan anoias
	Pronunciation: [eh-playce'-thay-san' an-oy-ahs]
	Parsing *eplësthësan* (part of speech): verb
	    Mood—indicative
	    Tense—aorist
	    Voice—passive
	    Person—3rd person
	    Number—plural
	    Stem or root—from πίμπλημι
	Parsing *anoias* (part of speech): noun
	    Case—genitive
	    Gender—feminine
	    Number—singular
	    Stem or root—from ἄνοια, ας
	Concordance References:
	  ⇒ Strong's #454+4130 anoia pletho
	  ⇒ NIV #486+4398 anoia pimplëmi [furious]
	  ⇒ NASB #454+4130 anoia pletho
	
	Luke 6:11
	And they were **filled with madness**; and communed one with another what they might do to Jesus. [KJV]
	But they themselves were **filled with rage**, and discussed together what they might do to Jesus. [NASB]
	But they were **furious** and began to discuss with one another what they might do to Jesus. [NIV]
	But they were **filled with rage**, and discussed with one another what they might do to Jesus. [NKJV]
	At this, the enemies of Jesus were **wild with rage** and began to discuss what to do with him. [NLT]
	αὐτοὶ δὲ **ἐπλήσθησαν ἀνοίας**· καὶ διελάλουν πρὸς ἀλλήλους, τί ἂν ποιήσειαν τῷ Ἰησοῦ. [GNS]
	αὐτοὶ δὲ **ἐπλήσθησαν ἀνοίας** καὶ διελάλουν πρὸς ἀλλήλους τί ἂν ποιήσαιεν τῷ Ἰησοῦ. [GNT]
		To be furious; to be filled with wild, insane rage; to be controlled by foolishness, stupidity.
		
		Practical Application
		Jesus had confronted the religionists with the truth. They had been shown unmistakably what true religion is. They were now faced with the dilemma: they had to either accept true religion, Jesus and His teaching, or else oppose Him. They chose to oppose Him, but they needed political help, so they went out to form an alliance with the Herodians (see POSB *Deeper Study* #2—Matthew 22:16). Note a significant fact: despite enormous philosophical differences, there was no difference between the religious and political leaders in behavior (the Pharisees and the Herodians). Position, power, and security had corrupted their hearts and minds. They both plotted to destroy a person (Jesus) who opposed them.

#2492
Magic Arts
 	
Sorceries–KJV
Sorceries–NASB
Magic arts–NIV
Sorceries–NKJV
	φαρμάκων = pharmakön
	Pronunciation: [far-mak-own']
	Parsing (part of speech): noun
	    Case—genitive
	    Gender—neuter
	    Number—plural
	    Stem or root—from φάρμακον, ου
		Magic arts, sorceries, witchcraft.
		
		Practical Application
		Note that the Greek word (*pharmakön*) is close to the spelling of the English word *pharmacy*, that is, a place that handles drugs. Magic arts include all kinds of witchcraft, the use of

ENGLISH WORD	GREEK WORD AND VERSE	THE WORD MEANS...
Witchcraft–NLT **POSB REFERENCE** (Rev.9:20-21; esp.v.21) Note 4, point 2c	Concordance References: ⇒ Strong's #5331 pharmakon ⇒ NIV #5760 pharmakon ⇒ NASB #5331 pharmakon **Rev. 9:21** Neither repented they of their murders, nor of their **sorceries**, nor of their fornication, nor of their thefts. [KJV] And they did not repent of their murders nor of their **sorceries** nor of their immorality nor of their thefts. [NASB] Nor did they repent of their murders, their **magic arts**, their sexual immorality or their thefts. [NIV] And they did not repent of their murders or their **sorceries** or their sexual immorality or their thefts. [NKJV] And they did not repent of their murders or their **witchcraft** or their immorality or their thefts. [NLT] καὶ οὐ μετενόησαν ἐκ τῶν φόνων αὐτῶν, οὔτε ἐκ τῶν **φαρμακειῶν** αὐτῶν, οὔτε ἐκ τῆς πορνείας αὐτῶν, οὔτε ἐκ τῶν κλεμμάτων αὐτῶν. [GNS] καὶ οὐ μετενόησαν ἐκ τῶν φόνων αὐτῶν οὔτε ἐκ τῶν **φαρμάκων** αὐτῶν οὔτε ἐκ τῆς πορνείας αὐτῶν οὔτε ἐκ τῶν κλεμμάτων αὐτῶν. [GNT]	drugs or of evil spirits to gain control over the lives of others or over one's own life. In the present context, it would include all forms of magic arts including astrology, palm reading, seances, fortune telling, crystals, and other forms of witchcraft.

#2493
**Magnifies–
Magnify**
 	
Magnify–KJV
Exalts–NASB
Glorifies–NIV
Magnifies–NKJV
Praise–NLT
 	
**POSB
REFERENCE**
(Lk.1:46)
Note 1, point 2
	Μεγαλύνει = Megalunei
	Pronunciation: [meg-al-oo'-neh-ee]
	Parsing (part of speech): verb
	    Mood—indicative
	    Tense—present
	    Voice—active
	    Person—3rd person
	    Number—singular
	    Stem or root—from μεγαλύνω
	Concordance References:
	⇒ Strong's #3170 megalunö
	⇒ NIV #3486 megalunö
	⇒ NASB #3170 megalunö
	
	Luke 1:46
	And Mary said, My soul doth **magnify** the Lord, [KJV]
	And Mary said: "My soul **exalts** the Lord, [NASB]
	And Mary said: "My soul **glorifies** the Lord [NIV]
	And Mary said: "My soul **magnifies** the Lord, [NKJV]
	Mary responded, "Oh, how I **praise** the Lord. [NLT]
	Καὶ εἶπε Μαριάμ, [GNS]—**Luke 1:46**
	Μεγαλύνει ἡ ψυχή μου τὸν Κύριον, καὶ ἠγαλλίασε τὸ πνεῦμά μου ἐπὶ τῷ Θεῷ τῷ σωτῆρί μου, [GNS]—**Luke 1:47**
	Καὶ εἶπεν Μαριάμ, [GNT]—**Luke 1:46**
	Μεγαλύνει ἡ ψυχή μου τὸν κύριον, καὶ ἠγαλλίασεν τὸ πνεῦμά μου ἐπὶ τῷ θεῷ τῷ σωτῆρί μου, [GNT]—**Luke 1:47**
	NOTE: This greek word (**Μεγαλύνει**) in verse 47 is translated in verse 46 in English Bibles.
		To exalt; to magnify; to highly regard; to glorify; to praise; to declare the greatness of.
		
		Practical Application
		The idea is habitual; that is, it was the habit of Mary's soul to magnify or glorify the Lord.

#2494
Magnify God
 	
Magnify God–KJV
Exalting God–NASB
Praising God–NIV
Magnify God–NKJV
Praising God–NLT
 	
**POSB
REFERENCE**
(Acts 10:46)
Note 2
	μεγαλυνόντων τὸν θεόν = *megalunontön ton theon*
	Pronunciation: [meh-gah-loon-on-toan ton they-on]
	Parsing *megalunontön* (part of speech): verb
	    Mood—participle
	    Tense—present
	    Voice—active
	    Case—genitive
	    Gender—masculine
	    Number—plural
	    Stem or root—from μεγαλύνω
	Concordance References:
	⇒ Strong's #3170 megalunö + 3588 ho + 2316 theos
	⇒ NIV #3486 megalunö + 3836 ho + 2536 theos
	⇒ NASB #3170 megalunö + 3588 ho + 2316 theos
		To praise God; to magnify God; to exalt God.
		
		Practical Application
		Note: the speaking in tongues led the Gentile believers into a glorious and joyful praise of God. They *magnified God* (*megalunontön ton theon*). They were caught up in an ecstatic praise of the Lord. The "speaking with tongues" seems to be the sign that the Holy Spirit had fallen upon the Gentiles. Both Peter and the Jewish believers needed a sign, a sign that would leave no doubt that the Gentiles were saved. Speaking in tongues, that is, breaking out in an ecstatic praise of God, was such a sign. It was the sign that

ENGLISH WORD	GREEK WORD AND VERSE	THE WORD MEANS...
	Acts 10:46 For they heard them speak with tongues, and **magnify God**. Then answered Peter, [KJV] For they were hearing them speaking with tongues and **exalting God**. Then Peter answered, [NASB] For they heard them speaking in tongues and **praising God**.Then Peter said, [NIV] For they heard them speak with tongues and **magnify God**. Then Peter answered, [NKJV] And there could be no doubt about it, for they heard them speaking in tongues and **praising God**.Then Peter asked, [NLT] ἤκουον γὰρ αὐτῶν λαλούντων γλώσσαις, καὶ **μεγαλυνόντων τὸν Θεόν**. τότε ἀπεκρίθη ὁ Πέτρος, [GNS] ἤκουον γὰρ αὐτῶν λαλούντων γλώσσαις καὶ **μεγαλυνόντων τὸν θεόν**. τότε ἀπεκρίθη Πέτρος, [GNT]	would leave no doubt whatsoever. Note: it is this that utterly shocked the Jewish believers who were with Peter; for the Gentiles were, as Peter says, receiving "the Holy Spirit *as well as we*" (Acts 10:47. See POSB *Deeper Study #1*—Acts 2:1-4. Also see POSB *Deeper Study #4*, Tongues—Acts 2:4 for more discussion.)

#2495
Maidservant
 	
Handmaid–KJV
Bondslave–NASB
Servant–NIV
Maidservant–NKJV
Servant–NLT
 	
POSB REFERENCE
(Lk.1:38)
Note 8
	δούλη = *doulë*
	Pronunciation: [doo'-lay]
	Parsing (part of speech): noun
	    Case—nominative
	    Gender—feminine
	    Number—singular
	    Stem or root—from δούλη, ης
	Concordance References:
	⇒ Strong's #1399 doulë
	⇒ NIV #1527 doulë
	⇒ NASB #1399 doulë
	
	Luke 1:38
	And Mary said, Behold the **handmaid** of the Lord; be it unto me according to thy word. And the angel departed from her. [KJV]
	And Mary said, "Behold, the **bondslave** of the Lord; be it done to me according to your word." And the angel departed from her. [NASB]
	"I am the Lord's **servant**," Mary answered. "May it be to me as you have said." Then the angel left her. [NIV]
	Then Mary said, "Behold the **maidservant** of the Lord! Let it be to me according to your word." And the angel departed from her. [NKJV]
	Mary responded, "I am the Lord's **servant**, and I am willing to accept whatever he wants. May everything you have said come true." And then the angel left. [NLT]
	εἶπε δὲ Μαριάμ, Ἰδοὺ ἡ **δούλη** Κυρίου· γένοιτό μοι κατὰ τὸ ῥῆμά σου. καὶ ἀπῆλθεν ἀπ' αὐτῆς ὁ ἄγγελος. [GNS]
	εἶπεν δὲ Μαριάμ, Ἰδοὺ ἡ **δούλη** κυρίου· γένοιτό μοι κατὰ τὸ ῥῆμά σου. καὶ ἀπῆλθεν ἀπ' αὐτῆς ὁ ἄγγελος. [GNT]
		Slave girl; a handmaid; a female servant; a maid servant; a bondslave.
		
		Practical Application
		Mary was saying that she was a bondslave, willing to sell herself out completely to God. She would possess herself no longer but would give herself completely to God.

#2496
Maintain
 	
Maintain–KJV
Engage–NASB
Devote–NIV
Maintain–NKJV
Do–NLT
 	
POSB REFERENCE
(Tit.3:8)
Note 1
	προΐστασθαι = *proistasthai*
	Pronunciation: [pro-is'-tahs-tha-ee]
	Parsing (part of speech): verb
	    Mood—infinitive
	    Tense—present
	    Voice—middle
	    Stem or root—from προΐστημι
	Concordance References:
	⇒ Strong's #4291 proistēmi
	⇒ NIV #4613 proistēmi
	⇒ NASB #4291b proistēmi
	
	Titus 3:8
	This is a faithful saying, and these things I will that thou affirm constantly, that they which have believed in God might be careful to **maintain** good works. These things are good and profitable unto men. [KJV]
	This is a trustworthy statement; and concerning these things I want you to speak confidently, so that those who have believed God may be careful to **engage** in good deeds. These things are good and profitable for men. [NASB]
		To devote; to maintain; to engage; to do; to manage; to care for; to set before; to give attention to; to be forward and eager and diligent in doing good works.
		
		Practical Application
		Believers must do good works and keep on doing them. It means...
		• to keep on doing good works.
		• to sustain good works.
		• to persevere in doing good works.
		• to carry on good works.
		
		It even has the idea of sustaining good works against all odds regardless of circumstances and difficulties. It means to persevere in good works even in the midst of opposition or danger.

ENGLISH WORD	GREEK WORD AND VERSE	THE WORD MEANS...
	This is a trustworthy saying. And I want you to stress these things, so that those who have trusted in God may be careful to **devote** themselves to doing what is good. These things are excellent and profitable for everyone. [NIV] This is a faithful saying, and these things I want you to affirm constantly, that those who have believed in God should be careful to **maintain** good works. These things are good and profitable to men. [NKJV] These things I have told you are all true. I want you to insist on them so that everyone who trusts in God will be careful to **do** good deeds all the time. These things are good and beneficial for everyone. [NLT] πιστὸς ὁ λόγος, καὶ περὶ τούτων βούλομαί σε διαβεβαιοῦσθαι, ἵνα φροντίζωσι καλῶν ἔργων **προΐστασθαι** οἱ πεπιστευκότες τῷ Θεῷ. ταῦτά ἐστι τὰ καλὰ καὶ ὠφέλιμα τοῖς ἀνθρώποις· [GNS] Πιστὸς ὁ λόγος· καὶ περὶ τούτων βούλομαί σε διαβεβαιοῦσθαι, ἵνα φροντίζωσιν καλῶν ἔργων **προΐστασθαι** οἱ πεπιστευκότες θεῷ· ταῦτά ἐστιν καλὰ καὶ ὠφέλιμα τοῖς ἀνθρώποις. [GNT]	

#2497
Majestic Splendor
 	
Majesty–KJV
Majesty–NASB
Majesty–NIV
Majesty–NKJV
Majestic splendor–NLT
 	
POSB REFERENCE
(2 Pt.1:16-18; esp. v.16)
Note 2
	μεγαλειότητος = *megaleiotētos*
	Pronunciation: [meg-al-i-ot'-ay-tos]
	Parsing (part of speech): noun
	    Case—genitive
	    Gender—feminine
	    Number—singular
	    Stem or root—from μεγαλειότης, ητος
	Concordance References:
	  ⇒ Strong's #3168 megaleiotēs
	  ⇒ NIV #3484 megaleiotēs
	  ⇒ NASB #3168 megaleiotēs
	
	2 Peter 1:16
	For we have not followed cunningly devised fables, when we made known unto you the power and coming of our Lord Jesus Christ, but were eyewitnesses of his **majesty**. [KJV]
	
	For we did not follow cleverly devised tales when we made known to you the power and coming of our Lord Jesus Christ, but we were eyewitnesses of His **majesty**. [NASB]
	
	We did not follow cleverly invented stories when we told you about the power and coming of our Lord Jesus Christ, but we were eyewitnesses of his **majesty**. [NIV]
	
	For we did not follow cunningly devised fables when we made known to you the power and coming of our Lord Jesus Christ, but were eyewitnesses of His **majesty**. [NKJV]
	
	For we were not making up clever stories when we told you about the power of our Lord Jesus Christ and his coming again. We have seen his **majestic splendor** with our own eyes. [NLT]
	
	οὐ γὰρ σεσοφισμένοις μύθοις ἐξακολουθήσαντες ἐγνωρίσαμεν ὑμῖν τὴν τοῦ Κυρίου ἡμῶν Ἰησοῦ Χριστοῦ δύναμιν καὶ παρουσίαν, ἀλλ' ἐπόπται γενηθέντες τῆς ἐκείνου **μεγαλειότητος**. [GNS]
	
	Οὐ γὰρ σεσοφισμένοις μύθοις ἐξακολουθήσαντες ἐγνωρίσαμεν ὑμῖν τὴν τοῦ κυρίου ἡμῶν Ἰησοῦ Χριστοῦ δύναμιν καὶ παρουσίαν ἀλλ' ἐπόπται γενηθέντες τῆς ἐκείνου **μεγαλειότητος**. [GNT]
		Majesty, majestic splendor, greatness. The words "majestic splendor" (*megaleiotētos*) means the majesty of God, the *divine nature* of God (Michael Green. *The Second Epistle of Peter and The Epistle of Jude.* "The Tyndale New Testament Commentaries," p.83). It means that the *majesty and glory* of God filled and surrounded Christ when He walked upon earth.
		
		Practical Application
		The early disciples and believers knew that Jesus Christ was the Savior of men because they saw the majesty and glory of God in His life and works. Jesus Christ went to great pains to reveal the majesty and glory of God; He proved time and again that He was the Son of God.

#2498
Majesty
 	
Mighty power–KJV
Greatness–NASB
Greatness–NIV
Majesty–NKJV
	μεγαλειότητι = *megaleiotēti*
	Pronunciation: [meg-al-i-ot'-ay-tee]
	Parsing (part of speech): noun
	    Case—dative
	    Gender—feminine
	    Number—singular
	    Stem or root—from μεγαλειότης, ητος
	Concordance References:
	  ⇒ Strong's #3168 megaleiotēs
		Majesty, greatness, glory, mighty power; a display of God's glory and power.
		
		Practical Application
		They marvelled at "the majesty of God." Note that Jesus brought honor to God, not to Himself.

ENGLISH WORD	GREEK WORD AND VERSE	THE WORD MEANS...
Display of [God's] power–NLT **POSB REFERENCE** (Lk.9:42-43; esp. v.43) Note 3, point 2	⇒ NIV #3484 megaleiotēs ⇒ NASB #3168 megaleiotēs ### Luke 9:43 And they were all amazed at the **mighty power** of God. But while they wondered every one at all things which Jesus did, he said unto his disciples, [KJV] And they were all amazed at the **greatness** of God. But while everyone was marveling at all that He was doing, He said to His disciples, [NASB] And they were all amazed at the **greatness** of God. While everyone was marveling at all that Jesus did, he said to his disciples, [NIV] And they were all amazed at the **majesty** of God. But while everyone marveled at all the things which Jesus did, He said to His disciples, [NKJV] Awe gripped the people as they saw this **display of God's power**. While everyone was marveling over all the wonderful things he was doing, Jesus said to his disciples, [NLT] ἐξεπλήσσοντο δὲ πάντες ἐπὶ τῇ **μεγαλειότητι** τοῦ Θεοῦ. Πάντων δὲ θαυμαζόντων ἐπὶ πᾶσιν οἷς ἐποίεν ὁ Ἰησοῦς, εἶπε πρὸς τοὺς μαθητὰς αὐτοῦ, [GNS] ἐξεπλήσσοντο δὲ πάντες ἐπὶ τῇ **μεγαλειότητι** τοῦ θεοῦ. Πάντων δὲ θαυμαζόντων ἐπὶ πᾶσιν οἷς ἐποίει εἶπεν πρὸς τοὺς μαθητὰς αὐτοῦ, [GNT]	

#2499
Majesty
 	
Majesty–KJV
Majesty–NASB
Majesty–NIV
Majesty–NKJV
Majestic splendor–NLT
 	
POSB REFERENCE
(2 Pt.1:16-18; esp. v.16)
Note 2
	μεγαλειότητος = *megaleiotētos*
	Pronunciation: [meg-al-i-ot'-ay-tos]
	Parsing (part of speech): noun
	  Case—genitive
	  Gender—feminine
	  Number—singular
	  Stem or root—from μεγαλειότης, ητος
	Concordance References:
	⇒ Strong's #3168 megaleiotēs
	⇒ NIV #3484 megaleiotēs
	⇒ NASB #3168 megaleiotēs
	
	### 2 Peter 1:16
	For we have not followed cunningly devised fables, when we made known unto you the power and coming of our Lord Jesus Christ, but were eyewitnesses of his **majesty**. [KJV]
	For we did not follow cleverly devised tales when we made known to you the power and coming of our Lord Jesus Christ, but we were eyewitnesses of His **majesty**. [NASB]
	We did not follow cleverly invented stories when we told you about the power and coming of our Lord Jesus Christ, but we were eyewitnesses of his **majesty**. [NIV]
	For we did not follow cunningly devised fables when we made known to you the power and coming of our Lord Jesus Christ, but were eyewitnesses of His **majesty**. [NKJV]
	For we were not making up clever stories when we told you about the power of our Lord Jesus Christ and his coming again. We have seen his **majestic splendor** with our own eyes. [NLT]
	οὐ γὰρ σεσοφισμένοις μύθοις ἐξακολουθήσαντες ἐγνωρίσαμεν ὑμῖν τὴν τοῦ Κυρίου ἡμῶν Ἰησοῦ Χριστοῦ δύναμιν καὶ παρουσίαν, ἀλλ' ἐπόπται γενηθέντες τῆς ἐκείνου **μεγαλειότητος**. [GNS]
	Οὐ γὰρ σεσοφισμένοις μύθοις ἐξακολουθήσαντες ἐγνωρίσαμεν ὑμῖν τὴν τοῦ κυρίου ἡμῶν Ἰησοῦ Χριστοῦ δύναμιν καὶ παρουσίαν ἀλλ' ἐπόπται γενηθέντες τῆς ἐκείνου **μεγαλειότητος**. [GNT]
		Majesty, majestic splendor, greatness. The word "majesty" (*megaleiotētos*) means the majesty of God, the *divine nature* of God (Michael Green. *The Second Epistle of Peter and The Epistle of Jude.* "The Tyndale New Testament Commentaries," p.83). It means that the *majesty and glory* of God filled and surrounded Christ when He walked upon earth.
		
		### Practical Application
		The early disciples and believers knew that Jesus Christ was the Savior of men because they saw the majesty and glory of God in His life and works. Jesus Christ went to great pains to reveal the majesty and glory of God; He proved time and again that He was the Son of God.

#2500 **Make Allowance**	ἀνεχόμενοι = *anechomenoi* Pronunciation: [an-ekh'-om-ehn-oy] Parsing (part of speech): verb Mood—participle (imperative sense)	To bear with; to be patient with; to make allowance for; forbearance; to hold back; to put up with; to refrain; to endure; to control.

ENGLISH WORD	GREEK WORD AND VERSE	THE WORD MEANS...

Forbearing–KJV
Bearing with–NASB
Bear with–NIV
Bearing with–NKJV
Make allowance–NLT

**POSB
REFERENCE**
(Col.3:13)
Note 7

Tense—present
Voice—middle
Case—nominative
Gender—masculine
Person—2nd person
Number—plural
Stem or root—from ἀνέχομαι
Concordance References:
⇒ Strong's #430 anechomai
⇒ NIV #462 anechomai
⇒ NASB #430 anechomai

Col. 3:13

Forbearing one another, and forgiving one another, if any man have a quarrel against any: even as Christ forgave you, so also do ye. [KJV]

Bearing with one another, and forgiving each other, whoever has a complaint against anyone; just as the Lord forgave you, so also should you. [NASB]

Bear with each other and forgive whatever grievances you may have against one another. Forgive as the Lord forgave you. [NIV]

Bearing with one another, and forgiving one another, if anyone has a complaint against another; even as Christ forgave you, so you also must do. [NKJV]

You must **make allowance** for each other's faults and forgive the person who offends you. Remember, the Lord forgave you, so you must forgive others. [NLT]

ἀνεχόμενοι ἀλλήλων, καὶ χαριζόμενοι ἑαυτοῖς ἐάν τις πρός τινα ἔχῃ μομφήν· καθὼς καὶ ὁ Χριστὸς ἐχαρίσατο ὑμῖν, οὕτω καὶ ὑμεῖς· [GNS]

ἀνεχόμενοι ἀλλήλων καὶ χαριζόμενοι ἑαυτοῖς ἐάν τις πρός τινα ἔχῃ μομφήν· καθὼς καὶ ὁ κύριος ἐχαρίσατο ὑμῖν, οὕτως καὶ ὑμεῖς· [GNT]

Practical Application

People have to put up with a great deal of things when dealing with us. There is a reason for this: every one of us is guilty of...
• some weakness
• some unattractive behavior
• some wrong behavior
• some mistreatment
• some neglect
• some failure
• some bad habit
• some irritating behavior

There are some things about us that just turn some people off. None of us escapes this fact. In addition, everyone of us does things that irritate some people. Again, there is no escaping the fact. Every person has flaws and weaknesses that are readily apparent to anyone who looks at him carefully.

But note: this is not what Scripture says to do. Scripture says that the believer is to put on the clothing of forbearance. The believer is to forbear the flaws of others. He is to put up with and bear with the weaknesses of other believers.

#2501
Make Atonement For

Make reconciliation for–KJV

Make propitiation for–NASB

Make atonement for–NIV

Make propitiation for–NKJV

Offer a sacrifice–NLT

**POSB
REFERENCE**
(Heb.2:17-18; esp. v.17)
Note 2, point 3

ἱλάσκεσθαι = hilaskesthai
Pronunciation: [hil-as'-keh-thah-ee]
Parsing (part of speech): verb
    Mood—infinitive
    Tense—present
    Voice—middle deponent
    Case—accusative
    Stem or root—from ἱλάσκομαι
Concordance References:
⇒ Strong's #2433 hilaskomai
⇒ NIV #2661 hilaskomai
⇒ NASB #2433 hilaskomai

Hebrews 2:17

Wherefore in all things it behoved him to be made like unto his brethren, that he might be a merciful and faithful high priest in things pertaining to God, to **make reconciliation for** the sins of the people. [KJV]

Therefore, He had to be made like His brethren in all things, that He might become a merciful and faithful high priest in things pertaining to God, to **make propitiation for** the sins of the people. [NASB]

For this reason he had to be made like his brothers in every way, in order that he might become a merciful and faithful high priest in service to God, and that he might **make atonement for** the sins of the people. [NIV]

Therefore, in all things He had to be made like *His* brethren, that He might be a merciful and faithful High Priest in things *pertaining* to God, to **make propitiation for** the sins of the people. [NKJV]

Therefore, it was necessary for Jesus to be in every respect like us, his brothers and sisters, so that he could be our merciful and faithful High Priest before God. He then could **offer a sacrifice** that would take away the sins of the people. [NLT]

ὅθεν ὤφειλε κατὰ πάντα τοῖς ἀδελφοῖς ὁμοιωθῆναι, ἵνα ἐλεήμων· γένηται καὶ πιστὸς ἀρχιερεὺς τὰ πρὸς τὸν

To make atonement for; to make reconciliation for; to make propitiation for; to offer a sacrifice. It means to sacrifice or to make a covering, satisfaction, payment, or appeasement for sin.

Practical Application

Jesus Christ became the High Priest so that He could make atonement for the sins of the people.

It was, of course, the task of the High Priest to offer up the animal sacrifice for the sins of the people. This is the picture being painted of Christ. But note one distinct difference: Jesus Christ Himself is the atonement for man's sin. It was not His teachings, power, example, or life that made Christ the atonement. It was His blood: His sacrifice, His death, His sufferings, His cross that caused God to accept Jesus as the atonement. It is the blood of Christ that God accepts as...
• the *sacrifice* for our sins.
• the *covering* for our sins.
• the *satisfaction* for our sins.
• the *payment* for the penalty of our sins.
• the *appeasement* of His wrath against sin.

When Christ died for man...
• the righteousness of God was satisfied.
• the perfection of God was satisfied.
• the justice of God was satisfied.

Jesus Christ became the *atonement*—the covering and satisfaction for the sins of man. He became the High Priest in order to make atonement for our sins.

ENGLISH WORD	GREEK WORD AND VERSE	THE WORD MEANS...
	θεόν, εἰς τὸ **ἱλάσκεσθαι** τὰς ἁμαρτίας τοῦ λαοῦ. [GNS] ὅθεν ὤφειλεν κατὰ πάντα τοῖς ἀδελφοῖς ὁμοιωθῆναι, ἵνα ἐλεήμων γένηται καὶ πιστὸς ἀρχιερεὺς τὰ πρὸς τὸν θεόν εἰς τὸ **ἱλάσκεσθαι** τὰς ἁμαρτίας τοῦ λαοῦ. [GNT]	

#2502
Make Disciples
 	
Teach–KJV
Make disciples–
NASB
Make disciples–NIV
Make disciples–
NKJV
Make disciples–NLT
 	
POSB
REFERENCE
(Mt.28:19-20; esp.
v.19)
Note 3, point 1
	μαθητεύσατε = *mathëteusate*
	Pronunciation: [math-ayt-yoo'-sa-tay]
	Parsing (part of speech): verb
	   Mood—imperative
	   Tense—aorist
	   Voice—active
	   Person—2nd person
	   Number—plural
	   Stem or root—from **μαθητεύω**
	Concordance References:
	  ⇒ Strong's #3100 mathëteuö
	  ⇒ NIV #3411 mathëteuö
	  ⇒ NASB #3100 mathëteuö
	
	Matthew 28:19
	Go ye therefore, and **teach** all nations, baptizing them in the name of the Father, and of the Son, and of the Holy Ghost: [KJV]
	"Go therefore and **make disciples** of all the nations, baptizing them in the name of the Father and the Son and the Holy Spirit, [NASB]
	Therefore go and **make disciples** of all nations, baptizing them in the name of the Father and of the Son and of the Holy Spirit, [NIV]
	Go therefore and **make disciples** of all the nations, baptizing them in the name of the Father and of the Son and of the Holy Spirit, [NKJV]
	Therefore, go and **make disciples** of all the nations, baptizing them in the name of the Father and the Son and the Holy Spirit. [NLT]
	πορευθέντες οὖν **μαθητεύσατε** πάντα τὰ ἔθνη, βαπτίζοντες αὐτοὺς εἰς τὸ ὄνομα τοῦ Πατρὸς καὶ τοῦ Υἱοῦ καὶ τοῦ Ἁγίου Πνεύματος· [GNS]
	πορευθέντες οὖν **μαθητεύσατε** πάντα τὰ ἔθνη, βαπτίζοντες αὐτοὺς εἰς τὸ ὄνομα τοῦ πατρὸς καὶ τοῦ υἱοῦ καὶ τοῦ ἁγίου πνεύματος, [GNT]
		To make disciples; to teach; to attach ourselves to those persons who will follow our Lord until they can, in turn, make disciples.
		
		Practical Application
		Our Lord was not only telling us "to go and evangelize," He was telling us *how* to go and *how* to evangelize. He was not only giving His ultimate *objective* and overriding purpose, He was giving *the method* to use in evangelizing the world.
		Think about the word "make disciples" (*mathëteusate*). What does our Lord mean by "make disciples"? Does it not mean that we are to do what He did: make disciples and do things with them as He did. Is He not telling us to do exactly as He did?
		What *did* He do? Christ "came to seek and save that which was lost" (Luke 19:10). He sought the lost, those who were willing to commit their lives to Him. And when He found such a person, He saved that person. When Christ found a person who was willing to commit his life, Christ attached Himself to that person. Christ began to mold and make that person into His image. The word *attach* is the key word. It is probably the word that best describes discipleship. Christ made disciples of men by attaching Himself to them; and through that personal attachment, they were able to observe His life and conversation; and in seeing and hearing, they began to absorb and assimilate His very character and behavior. They began to follow Him and to serve Him more closely. In simple terms this is what our Lord did. This is the way He made disciples. This was His mission and His method, His obsession: to attach Himself to willing believers.

#2503
Make Every
Effort
 	
Strive–KJV
Strive–NASB
Make every effort–
NIV
Strive–NKJV
Work hard–NLT
 	
POSB
REFERENCE
(Lk.13:24)
Note 2, point 2
	Ἀγωνίζεσθε = *Agönizesthe*
	Pronunciation: [ag-o-nid'-zehs-theh]
	Parsing (part of speech): verb
	   Mood—imperative
	   Tense—present
	   Voice—middle or passive deponent
	   Person—2nd person
	   Number—plural
	   Stem or root—from **ἀγωνίζομαι**
	Concordance References:
	  ⇒ Strong's #75 agonizomai
	  ⇒ NIV #76 agönizomai
	  ⇒ NASB #75 agonizomai
	
	Luke 13:24
	Strive to enter in at the strait gate: for many, I say unto you, will seek to enter in, and shall not be able. [KJV]
	"**Strive** to enter by the narrow door; for many, I tell you, will seek to enter and will not be able. [NASB]
	"**Make every effort** to enter through the narrow door, because many, I tell you, will try to enter and will not be able to. [NIV]
	"**Strive** to enter through the narrow gate, for many, I say to you, will seek to enter and will not be able. [NKJV]
	"The door to heaven is narrow. **Work hard** to get in,
		To make every effort; to compete; to agonize, strive, struggle, contend, work hard, exert to the fullest, labor fervently.
		
		Practical Application
		A person has to "make every effort" to be saved. Wholehearted dedication and effort are required. But note a critical point: the idea is not that a person works for his salvation, but that he diligently seeks God. He casts himself totally upon the belief that God is, that God actually exists (cp. Hebrews 11:6). It is the spirit, the attitude, the heart that sets itself upon God, refusing to be diverted or to be committed to anything else. It is the total commitment of one's life to God for salvation.

ENGLISH WORD	GREEK WORD AND VERSE	THE WORD MEANS...
	because many will try to enter, [NLT] 'Αγωνίζεσθε εἰσελθεῖν διὰ τῆς στενῆς πύλης· ὅτι πολλοί, λέγω ὑμῖν, ζητήσουσιν εἰσελθεῖν, καὶ οὐκ ἰσχύσουσιν. [GNS] 'Αγωνίζεσθε εἰσελθεῖν διὰ τῆς στενῆς θύρας, ὅτι πολλοί, λέγω ὑμῖν, ζητήσουσιν εἰσελθεῖν καὶ οὐκ ἰσχύσουσιν. [GNT]	

#2504
Make Every Effort
 	
Endeavouring–KJV
Being diligent–NASB
Make every effort–NIV
Endeavoring–NKJV
Always keep yourselves–NLT
 	
POSB REFERENCE
(Eph.4:3)
Note 2
	σπουδάζοντες = *spoudazontes*
	Pronunciation: [spoo-dad'-zon-tes]
	Parsing (part of speech): verb
	    Mood—participle (imperative sense)
	    Tense—present
	    Voice—active
	    Case—nominative
	    Gender—masculine
	    Person—2nd person
	    Number—plural
	    Stem or root—from σπουδάζω
	Concordance References:
	⇒ Strong's #4704 spoudazō
	⇒ NIV #5079 spoudazō
	⇒ NASB #4704 spoudazō
	
	Ephes. 4:3
	Endeavouring to keep the unity of the Spirit in the bond of peace. [KJV]
	Being diligent to preserve the unity of the Spirit in the bond of peace. [NASB]
	Make every effort to keep the unity of the Spirit through the bond of peace. [NIV]
	Endeavoring to keep the unity of the Spirit in the bond of peace. [NKJV]
	Always keep yourselves united in the Holy Spirit, and bind yourselves together with peace. [NLT]
	σπουδάζοντες τηρεῖν τὴν ἑνότητα τοῦ Πνεύματος ἐν τῷ συνδέσμῳ τῆς εἰρήνης. [GNS]
	σπουδάζοντες τηρεῖν τὴν ἑνότητα τοῦ πνεύματος ἐν τῷ συνδέσμῳ τῆς εἰρήνης· [GNT]
		To make every effort; to work hard; to be eager; to do one's best, being diligent, to work at, taking care and doing one's very best, and to make haste to do it.
		
		Practical Application
		The only way to walk worthy of God's great calling is to work at keeping the peace and unity which God has given us. Nothing cuts the heart of God like divisiveness between His people, divisiveness which tears apart His church. The very thing God is doing is creating a new body of people to live together in the love and unity of His Son. He is going to create a new heavens and earth in which there will be no other spirit. Therefore, He expects us to live in the love and unity of His Spirit now.

#2505
Make Every Effort
 	
Be diligent–KJV
Be diligent–NASB
Make every effort–NIV
Be diligent–NKJV
Make every effort–NLT
 	
POSB REFERENCE
(2 Pt.3:14)
Note 4
	σπουδάσατε = *spoudasate*
	Pronunciation: [spoo-das-teh]
	Parsing (part of speech): verb
	    Mood—imperative
	    Tense—aorist
	    Voice—active
	    Person—2nd person
	    Number—plural
	    Stem or root—from σπουδάζω
	Concordance References:
	⇒ Strong's #4704 spoudazō
	⇒ NIV #5079 spoudazō
	⇒ NASB #4704 spoudazō
	
	2 Peter 3:14
	Wherefore, beloved, seeing that ye look for such things, **be diligent** that ye may be found of him in peace, without spot, and blameless. [KJV]
	Therefore, beloved, since you look for these things, **be diligent** to be found by Him in peace, spotless and blameless, [NASB]
	So then, dear friends, since you are looking forward to this, **make every effort** to be found spotless, blameless and at peace with him. [NIV]
	Therefore, beloved, looking forward to these things, **be diligent** to be found by Him in peace, without spot and blameless; [NKJV]
	And so, dear friends, while you are waiting for these things to happen, **make every effort** to live a pure and blameless life. And be at peace with God. [NLT]
	Διό, ἀγαπητοί, ταῦτα προσδοκῶντες, **σπουδάσατε** ἄσπιλοι καὶ ἀμώμητοι αὐτῷ εὑρεθῆναι ἐν εἰρήνῃ. [GNS]
	Διό, ἀγαπητοί, ταῦτα προσδοκῶντες **σπουδάσατε** ἄσπιλοι καὶ ἀμώμητοι αὐτῷ εὑρεθῆναι ἐν εἰρήνῃ [GNT]
		To make every effort; to be diligent; to do one's very best; to work hard; to be eager; to strive earnestly; to be zealous in seeking after.
		
		Practical Application
		Believers must make every effort for the coming of Christ. The believer is to be diligent, that is, eager, earnest and zealous, in preparing himself for the return of the Lord. Why? So that the Lord will find him prepared.

ENGLISH WORD	GREEK WORD AND VERSE	THE WORD MEANS...

#2506
Make Every Effort
 	
Labour–KJV
Diligent–NASB
Make every effort–NIV
Diligent–NKJV
Do our best–NLT
 	
POSB REFERENCE
(Heb.4:11-13; esp. v.11)
Note 5, point 1
	σπουδάσωμεν = *spoudasömen*
	Pronunciation: [spoo-dah'-so-mehn]
	Parsing (part of speech): verb
	    Mood—subjunctive
	    Tense—aorist
	    Voice—active
	    Person—1st person
	    Number—plural
	    Stem or root—from σπουδάζω
	Concordance References:
	⇒ Strong's #4704 spoudazö
	⇒ NIV #5079 spoudazö
	⇒ NASB #4704 spoudazö
	
	Hebrews 4:11
	Let us **labour** therefore to enter into that rest, lest any man fall after the same example of unbelief. [KJV]
	Let us therefore be **diligent** to enter that rest, lest anyone fall through following the same example of disobedience. [NASB]
	Let us, therefore, **make every effort** to enter that rest, so that no one will fall by following their example of disobedience. [NIV]
	Let us therefore be **diligent** to enter that rest, lest anyone fall according to the same example of disobedience. [NKJV]
	Let us **do our best** to enter that place of rest. For anyone who disobeys God, as the people of Israel did, will fall. [NLT]
	σπουδάσωμεν οὖν εἰσελθεῖν εἰς ἐκείνην τὴν κατάπαυσιν, ἵνα μὴ ἐν τῷ αὐτῷ τις ὑποδείγματι πέσῃ τῆς ἀπειθείας. [GNS]
	σπουδάσωμεν οὖν εἰσελθεῖν εἰς ἐκείνην τὴν κατάπαυσιν, ἵνα μὴ ἐν τῷ αὐτῷ τις ὑποδείγματι πέσῃ τῆς ἀπειθείας. [GNT]
		To make every effort, labor; to be diligent, do one's best, work hard, endeavor, to give all diligence, be zealous, eagerly strive, exert one's self, and make haste.
		
		Practical Application
		A person must make every effort to enter God's rest or else he will fall into unbelief. There is no place for sleepiness or laziness, complacency or lethargy. Unless a person makes every effort, he will fall just as Israel fell. And remember Israel's experience: the people would labor for a while and then fall back for awhile; labor again and then fall back again. Israel lived an up-and-down life, and the nation was not allowed to enter God's rest. There is no place for inconsistency, no place for living an up-and-down life—not in God's rest. Diligence—laboring every day—is an absolute essential. We must make every effort or else fall from God's rest as Israel fell.

#2507
Make It Aim—Make It Goal
 	
Labour–KJV
Ambition–NASB
Make it...goal–NIV
Make it...aim–NKJV
Aim is–NLT
 	
POSB REFERENCE
(2 Cor.5:9-10; esp. v.9)
Note 4
	φιλοτιμούμεθα = *philotimoumetha*
	Pronunciation: [fil-ot-im-oo'-meh-tha]
	Parsing (part of speech): verb
	    Mood—indicative
	    Tense—present
	    Voice—middle or passive deponent
	    Person—1st person
	    Number—plural
	    Stem or root—from φιλοτιμέομαι
	Concordance References:
	⇒ Strong's #5389 philotimeomai
	⇒ NIV #5818 philotimeomai
	⇒ NASB #5389 philotimeomai
	
	2 Cor. 5:9
	Wherefore we **labour**, that, whether present or absent, we may be accepted of him. [KJV]
	Therefore also we have as our **ambition**, whether at home or absent, to be pleasing to Him. [NASB]
	So we **make it** our **goal** to please him, whether we are at home in the body or away from it. [NIV]
	Therefore we **make it** our **aim**, whether present or absent, to be well pleasing to Him. [NKJV]
	So our **aim is** to please him always, whether we are here in this body or away from this body. [NLT]
	διὸ καὶ φιλοτιμούμεθα, εἴτε ἐνδημοῦντες, εἴτε ἐκδημοῦντες, εὐάρεστοι αὐτῷ εἶναι. [GNS]
	διὸ καὶ φιλοτιμούμεθα, εἴτε ἐνδημοῦντες εἴτε ἐκδημοῦντες, εὐάρεστοι αὐτῷ εἶναι. [GNT]
		To make a goal; to constantly aim, to be constantly ambitious, to strive earnestly.
		
		Practical Application
		Judgment stirs the longing to please God and to receive our heavenly home. Judgment stirs us to make it our goal (*philotimoumetha*) in life to please God. Paul says that he is to be judged; therefore, he works his fingers to the bone. Why? That he may please (*euarestoi*) God.

#2508
Make Known
 	
Declare–KJV
Make known–NASB
Remind–NIV
	Γνωρίζω = *Gnörizö*
	Pronunciation: [gno-rid'-zo]
	Parsing (part of speech): verb
	    Mood—indicative
	    Tense—present
	    Voice—active
	    Person—1st person
		To remind; to declare; to tell; to present; to make known.
		
		Practical Application
		Paul is not reminding the Corinthians of the gospel, he is...

ENGLISH WORD	GREEK WORD AND VERSE	THE WORD MEANS...
Declare–NKJV Remind–NLT **POSB** **REFERENCE** (1 Cor.15:1-2; esp. v.1) Note 1	Number—singular Stem or root—from γνωρίζω Concordance References: ⇒ Strong's #1107 gnörizö ⇒ NIV #1192 gnörizö ⇒ NASB #1107 gnörizö **1 Cor. 15:1** Moreover, brethren, I **declare** unto you the gospel which I preached unto you, which also ye have received, and wherein ye stand; [KJV] Now I **make known** to you, brethren, the gospel which I preached to you, which also you received, in which also you stand, [NASB] Now, brothers, I want to **remind** you of the gospel I preached to you, which you received and on which you have taken your stand. [NIV] Moreover, brethren, I **declare** to you the gospel which I preached to you, which also you received and in which you stand, [NKJV] Now let me **remind** you, dear brothers and sisters, of the Good News I preached to you before. You welcomed it then and still do now, for your faith is built on this wonderful message. [NLT] Γνωρίζω δὲ ὑμῖν, ἀδελφοί, τὸ εὐαγγέλιον ὃ εὐηγγελισάμην ὑμῖν, ὃ καὶ παρελάβετε, ἐν ᾧ καὶ ἑστήκατε, [GNS] Γνωρίζω δὲ ὑμῖν, ἀδελφοί, τὸ εὐαγγέλιον ὃ εὐηγγελισάμην ὑμῖν, ὃ καὶ παρελάβετε, ἐν ᾧ καὶ ἑστήκατε, [GNT]	• declaring it as though they had never heard it. • proclaiming it as though they had never sat before it. • making it known as though they had never known it.

#2509
Make Known
 	
Certify–KJV
Know–NASB
Know–NIV
Make known–NKJV
Solemnly assure–NLT
 	
POSB
REFERENCE
(Gal.1:11-12; esp.
v.11)
Note 2
	Γνωρίζω = Gnörizö
	Pronunciation: [gno-rid'-zo]
	Parsing (part of speech): verb
	    Mood—indicative
	    Tense—present
	    Voice—active
	    Person—1st person
	    Number—singular
	    Stem or root—from γνωρίζω
	Concordance References:
	⇒ Strong's #1107 gnörizö
	⇒ NIV #1192 gnörizö
	⇒ NASB #1107 gnörizö
	
	Galatians 1:11
	But I **certify** you, brethren, that the gospel which was preached of me is not after man. [KJV]
	For I would have you **know**, brethren, that the gospel which was preached by me is not according to man. [NASB]
	I want you to **know**, brothers, that the gospel I preached is not something that man made up. [NIV]
	But I **make known** to you, brethren, that the gospel which was preached by me is not according to man. [NKJV]
	Dear brothers and sisters, I **solemnly assure** you that the Good News of salvation which I preach is not based on mere human reasoning or logic. [NLT]
	Γνωρίζω δὲ ὑμῖν, ἀδελφοί, τὸ εὐαγγέλιον τὸ εὐαγγελισθὲν ὑπ' ἐμοῦ, ὅτι οὐκ ἔστι κατὰ ἄνθρωπον. [GNS]
	Γνωρίζω γὰρ ὑμῖν, ἀδελφοί, τὸ εὐαγγέλιον τὸ εὐαγγελισθὲν ὑπ' ἐμοῦ ὅτι οὐκ ἔστιν κατὰ ἄνθρωπον· [GNT]
		To certify; to make known; to solemnly assure.
		
		Practical Application
		The minister proclaimed the gospel. Some critics of Paul were saying that he was not a true apostle of the Lord Jesus because he had not been a follower of the Lord when the Lord was upon the earth. Therefore, what he was teaching was a man-made gospel taught by mistaken and misguided men.
		Note that the phrase "make known" (*Gnörizö*) is a solemn phrase, a strong declaration that what follows is of crucial importance and needs to be heard.

#2510
Make Mistakes
 	
Offend–KJV
Stumble in–NASB
Stumble in–NIV
Stumble in–NKJV
	πταίομεν = ptaiomen
	Pronunciation: [ptah'-ee-o-mehn]
	Parsing (part of speech): verb
	    Mood—indicative
	    Tense—present
	    Voice—active
	    Person—1st person
	    Number—plural
	    Stem or root—from πταίω
		To stumble in; to offend; to make mistakes; to go wrong, astray.
		
		Practical Application
		The tongue stumbles and sins often, stumbles in word after word. Note: "we all make mistakes" (stumble, fall, sin). This includes teachers

ENGLISH WORD	GREEK WORD AND VERSE	THE WORD MEANS...
Make...mistakes–NLT **POSB REFERENCE** (Jas. 3:2) Note 2	Concordance References: ⇒ Strong's #4417 ptaiö ⇒ NIV #4760 ptaiö ⇒ NASB #4417 ptaiö **James 3:2** For in many things we offend all. If any man **offend** not in word, the same is a perfect man, and able also to bridle the whole body. [KJV] For we all **stumble in** many ways. If anyone does not stumble in what he says, he is a perfect man, able to bridle the whole body as well. [NASB] We all **stumble in** many ways. If anyone is never at fault in what he says, he is a perfect man, able to keep his whole body in check. [NIV] For we all **stumble in** many things. If anyone does not stumble in word, he *is* a perfect man, able also to bridle the whole body. [NKJV] We all **make** many **mistakes**, but those who control their tongues can also control themselves in every other way. [NLT] πολλὰ γὰρ **πταίομεν** ἅπαντες. εἴ τις ἐν λόγῳ οὐ πταίει, οὗτος τέλειος ἀνήρ, δυνατὸς χαλιναγωγῆσαι καὶ ὅλον τὸ σῶμα. [GNS] πολλὰ γὰρ **πταίομεν** ἅπαντες. εἴ τις ἐν λόγῳ οὐ πταίει, οὗτος τέλειος ἀνήρ δυνατὸς χαλιναγωγῆσαι καὶ ὅλον τὸ σῶμα. [GNT]	as well as other believers. No believer—no matter how great a teacher he is or who he is—is free from stumbling and falling. In fact, note what the verse says: "In many things" we all stumble. We do not just occasionally fall and sin; we are always coming up short before God. And this includes all teachers or preachers as well as all other believers. What is the proof of this? When some believers live such pure and righteous lives and walk so faithfully among us, how can Scripture say that they are always offending and stumbling? Look at the tongue; the tongue shows us.
#2511 **Make Propitiation For** Make reconciliation for–KJV **Make propitiation for–NASB** Make atonement for–NIV **Make propitiation for–NKJV** Offer a sacrifice–NLT **POSB REFERENCE** (Heb.2:17-18; esp. v.17) Note 2, point 3	ἱλάσκεσθαι = hilaskesthai Pronunciation: [hil-as'-keh-thah-ee] Parsing (part of speech): verb Mood—infinitive Tense—present Voice—middle deponent Case—accusative Stem or root—from ἱλάσκομαι Concordance References: ⇒ Strong's #2433 hilaskomai ⇒ NIV #2661 hilaskomai ⇒ NASB #2433 hilaskomai **Hebrews 2:17** Wherefore in all things it behoved him to be made like unto his brethren, that he might be a merciful and faithful high priest in things pertaining to God, to **make reconciliation for** the sins of the people. [KJV] Therefore, He had to be made like His brethren in all things, that He might become a merciful and faithful high priest in things pertaining to God, to **make propitiation for** the sins of the people. [NASB] For this reason he had to be made like his brothers in every way, in order that he might become a merciful and faithful high priest in service to God, and that he might **make atonement for** the sins of the people. [NIV] Therefore, in all things He had to be made like *His* brethren, that He might be a merciful and faithful High Priest in things *pertaining* to God, to **make propitiation for** the sins of the people. [NKJV] Therefore, it was necessary for Jesus to be in every respect like us, his brothers and sisters, so that he could be our merciful and faithful High Priest before God. He then could **offer a sacrifice** that would take away the sins of the people. [NLT] ὅθεν ὤφειλε κατὰ πάντα τοῖς ἀδελφοῖς ὁμοιωθῆναι, ἵνα ἐλεήμων· γένηται καὶ πιστὸς ἀρχιερεὺς τὰ πρὸς τὸν Θεόν, εἰς τὸ **ἱλάσκεσθαι** τὰς ἁμαρτίας τοῦ λαοῦ. [GNS] ὅθεν ὤφειλεν κατὰ πάντα τοῖς ἀδελφοῖς ὁμοιωθῆναι, ἵνα ἐλεήμων γένηται καὶ πιστὸς ἀρχιερεὺς τὰ πρὸς τὸν θεόν εἰς τὸ **ἱλάσκεσθαι** τὰς ἁμαρτίας τοῦ λαοῦ. [GNT]	To make atonement for; to make reconciliation for; to make propitiation for; to offer a sacrifice. It means to sacrifice or to make a covering, satisfaction, payment, or appeasement for sin. **Practical Application** Jesus Christ became the High Priest so that He could make propitiation for the sins of the people. It was, of course, the task of the High Priest to offer up the animal sacrifice for the sins of the people. This is the picture being painted of Christ. But note one distinct difference: Jesus Christ Himself is the propitiation for man's sin. It was not His teachings, power, example, or life that made Christ the propitiation. It was His blood: His sacrifice, His death, His sufferings, His cross that caused God to accept Jesus as the propitiation. It is the blood of Christ that God accepts as... • the *sacrifice* for our sins. • the *covering* for our sins. • the *satisfaction* for our sins. • the *payment* for the penalty of our sins. • the *appeasement* of His wrath against sin. When Christ died for man... • the righteousness of God was satisfied. • the perfection of God was satisfied. • the justice of God was satisfied. Jesus Christ became the *propitiation*—the covering and satisfaction for the sins of man. He became the High Priest in order to make propitiation for our sins.

ENGLISH WORD	GREEK WORD AND VERSE	THE WORD MEANS...

#2512

Make Reconciliation For

Make reconciliation for–KJV

Make propitiation for–NASB

Make atonement for–NIV

Make propitiation for–NKJV

Offer a sacrifice–NLT

**POSB
REFERENCE**
(Heb.2:17-18; esp.
v.17)
Note 2, point 3

ἱλάσκεσθαι = hilaskesthai

Pronunciation: [hil-as'-keh-thah-ee]

Parsing (part of speech): verb

   Mood—infinitive

   Tense—present

   Voice—middle deponent

   Case—accusative

   Stem or root—from ἱλάσκομαι

Concordance References:

  ⇒ Strong's #2433 hilaskomai

  ⇒ NIV #2661 hilaskomai

  ⇒ NASB #2433 hilaskomai

Hebrews 2:17

Wherefore in all things it behoved him to be made like unto his brethren, that he might be a merciful and faithful high priest in things pertaining to God, to **make reconciliation for** the sins of the people. [KJV]

Therefore, He had to be made like His brethren in all things, that He might become a merciful and faithful high priest in things pertaining to God, to **make propitiation for** the sins of the people. [NASB]

For this reason he had to be made like his brothers in every way, in order that he might become a merciful and faithful high priest in service to God, and that he might **make atonement for** the sins of the people. [NIV]

Therefore, in all things He had to be made like *His* brethren, that He might be a merciful and faithful High Priest in things *pertaining* to God, to **make propitiation for** the sins of the people. [NKJV]

Therefore, it was necessary for Jesus to be in every respect like us, his brothers and sisters, so that he could be our merciful and faithful High Priest before God. He then could **offer a sacrifice** that would take away the sins of the people. [NLT]

ὅθεν ὤφειλε κατὰ πάντα τοῖς ἀδελφοῖς ὁμοιωθῆναι, ἵνα ἐλεήμων γένηται καὶ πιστὸς ἀρχιερεὺς τὰ πρὸς τὸν Θεόν, εἰς τὸ **ἱλάσκεσθαι** τὰς ἁμαρτίας τοῦ λαοῦ. [GNS]

ὅθεν ὤφειλεν κατὰ πάντα τοῖς ἀδελφοῖς ὁμοιωθῆναι, ἵνα ἐλεήμων γένηται καὶ πιστὸς ἀρχιερεὺς τὰ πρὸς τὸν θεόν εἰς τὸ **ἱλάσκεσθαι** τὰς ἁμαρτίας τοῦ λαοῦ. [GNT]

To make atonement for; to make reconciliation for; to make propitiation for; to offer a sacrifice. It means to sacrifice or to make a covering, satisfaction, payment, or appeasement for sin.

Practical Application

Jesus Christ became the High Priest so that He could make reconciliation for the sins of the people.

It was, of course, the task of the High Priest to offer up the animal sacrifice for the sins of the people. This is the picture being painted of Christ. But note one distinct difference: Jesus Christ Himself is the propitiation for man's sin. It was not His teachings, power, example, or life that made Christ the propitiation. It was His blood: His sacrifice, His death, His sufferings, His cross that caused God to accept Jesus as the propitiation. It is the blood of Christ that God accepts as...

- the *sacrifice* for our sins.
- the *covering* for our sins.
- the *satisfaction* for our sins.
- the *payment* for the penalty of our sins.
- the *appeasement* of His wrath against sin.

When Christ died for man...

- the righteousness of God was satisfied.
- the perfection of God was satisfied.
- the justice of God was satisfied.

Jesus Christ became the *propitiation*—the covering and satisfaction for the sins of man. He became the High Priest in order to make propitiation for our sins.

#2513

Make Strong

Established–KJV

Established–NASB

Make...strong–NIV

Established–NKJV

Grow strong–NLT

**POSB
REFERENCE**
(Romans 1:10-13; esp.
v.11)
Note 4, point 1,
thought 1

στηριχθῆναι = sterichthēnai

Pronunciation: [stay-rix'-thay-nah-ee]

Parsing (part of speech): verb

   Mood—infinitive

   Tense—aorist

   Voice—passive

   Case—accusative

   Stem or root—from στηρίζω

Concordance References:

  ⇒ Strong's #4741 stērizō

  ⇒ NIV #5114 stērizō

  ⇒ NASB #4741 stērizō

Romans 1:11

For I long to see you, that I may impart unto you some spiritual gift, to the end ye may be **established**; [KJV]

For I long to see you in order that I may impart some spiritual gift to you, that you may be **established**; [NASB]

I long to see you so that I may impart to you some spiritual gift to **make** you **strong**—[NIV]

For I long to see you, that I may impart to you some spiritual gift, so that you may be **established**— [NKJV]

For I long to visit you so I can share a spiritual blessing with you that will help you **grow strong** in the Lord. [NLT]

ἐπιποθῶ γὰρ ἰδεῖν ὑμᾶς, ἵνα τι μεταδῶ χάρισμα ὑμῖν πνευματικὸν εἰς τὸ **στηριχθῆναι** ὑμᾶς, [GNS]

ἐπιποθῶ γὰρ ἰδεῖν ὑμᾶς, ἵνα τι μεταδῶ χάρισμα ὑμῖν πνευματικὸν εἰς τὸ **στηριχθῆναι** ὑμᾶς, [GNT]

To make firm; to make strong; to establish; to fix; to make fast; to strengthen; to set.

Practical Application

Paul wished to *impart some spiritual gift* to the believers. Why? So that they might be more deeply established in the faith. The term spiritual gift (*charisma*) means a gift of grace. The term often refers to specific gifts given by the Holy Spirit (Romans 12:6-8), but here it means *the truths* of the grace of God, of His spiritual blessings to man revealed in Christ Jesus our Lord. Very simply, Paul longed to share the truths of the gospel with the believers at Rome. God's spiritual blessings were overflowing in his heart, and he was aching to share the gift of God's blessings.

ENGLISH WORD	GREEK WORD AND VERSE	THE WORD MEANS...
	body than for your whole body to be thrown into hell. [NIV] If your right eye **causes** you to **sin**, pluck it out and cast *it* from you; for it is more profitable for you that one of your members perish, than for your whole body to be cast into hell. [NKJV] So if your eye—even if it is your good eye—**causes** you to **lust**, gouge it out and throw it away. It is better for you to lose one part of your body than for your whole body to be thrown into hell. [NLT] εἰ δὲ ὁ ὀφθαλμός σου ὁ δεξιὸς **σκανδαλίζει** σε, ἔξελε αὐτὸν καὶ βάλε ἀπὸ σοῦ· συμφέρει γάρ σοι ἵνα ἀπόληται ἓν τῶν μελῶν σου, καὶ μὴ ὅλον τὸ σῶμά σου βληθῇ εἰς γέενναν. [GNS] εἰ δὲ ὁ ὀφθαλμός σου ὁ δεξιὸς **σκανδαλίζει** σε, ἔξελε αὐτὸν καὶ βάλε ἀπὸ σοῦ· συμφέρει γάρ σοι ἵνα ἀπόληται ἓν τῶν μελῶν σου καὶ μὴ ὅλον τὸ σῶμά σου βληθῇ εἰς γέενναν. [GNT]	

#2518
**Male
   Prostitutes**
 	
Effeminate–KJV
Effeminate–NASB
Male prostitutes–NIV
Homosexuals–NKJV
**Male prostitutes–
   NLT**
 	
**POSB
REFERENCE**
(1 Cor.6:9)
Note 2, point 4
	μαλακοί = *malakoi*
	Pronunciation: [mal-ak-oy-ee']
	Parsing (part of speech): pronominal adjective
	   Case—nominative
	   Gender—masculine
	   Number—plural
	   Stem or root—from μαλακός, ή, όν
	Concordance References:
	   ⇒ Strong's #3120 malakos
	   ⇒ NIV #3434 malakos
	   ⇒ NASB #3120 malakos
	
	1 Cor. 6:9
	Know ye not that the unrighteous shall not inherit the kingdom of God? Be not deceived: neither fornicators, nor idolaters, nor adulterers, nor **effeminate**, nor abusers of themselves with mankind, [KJV]
	
	Or do you not know that the unrighteous shall not inherit the kingdom of God? Do not be deceived; neither fornicators, nor idolaters, nor adulterers, nor **effeminate**, nor homosexuals, [NASB]
	
	Do you not know that the wicked will not inherit the kingdom of God? Do not be deceived: Neither the sexually immoral nor idolaters nor adulterers nor **male prostitutes** nor homosexual offenders [NIV]
	
	Do you not know that the unrighteous will not inherit the kingdom of God? Do not be deceived. Neither fornicators, nor idolaters, nor adulterers, nor **homosexuals**, nor sodomites, [NKJV]
	
	Don't you know that those who do wrong will have no share in the Kingdom of God? Don't fool yourselves. Those who indulge in sexual sin, who are idol worshipers, adulterers, **male prostitutes**, homosexuals, [NLT]
	
	η οὐκ οἴδατε ὅτι ἄδικοι βασιλείαν Θεοῦ οὐ κληρονομήσουσι; μὴ πλανᾶσθε· οὔτε πόρνοι, οὔτε εἰδωλολάτραι, οὔτε μοιχοὶ, οὔτε **μαλακοὶ**, οὔτε ἀρσενοκοῖται, [GNS]
	
	η οὐκ οἴδατε ὅτι ἄδικοι θεοῦ βασιλείαν οὐ κληρονομήσουσιν; μὴ πλανᾶσθε· οὔτε πόρνοι οὔτε εἰδωλολάτραι οὔτε μοιχοὶ οὔτε **μαλακοὶ** οὔτε ἀρσενοκοῖται [GNT]
		Male prostitutes; effeminate; a homosexual pervert; gay.
		
		Practical Application
		The sin of homosexuality takes place in the heart. Men and women *burn within*, crave the sin before they commit the act. It is their burning, their lusting, their craving that sets them aflame to pursue the shameful act. Their heart burns after other men and women, not after God. Therefore, they stand condemned, and God is forced to judge them. They "will not inherit the kingdom of God. Do not be deceived."

#2519
Malice
 	
Wickedness–KJV
Wickedness–NASB
Malice–NIV
Wickedness–NKJV
Wickedness–NLT
	πονηρίαι = *poneriai*
	Pronunciation: [pon-ay-ree'-ah-ee]
	Parsing (part of speech): noun
	   Case—nominative
	   Gender—feminine
	   Number—plural
	   Stem or root—from πονηρία, ας
	Concordance References:
	   ⇒ Strong's #4189 ponēría
	   ⇒ NIV #4504 ponēría
	   ⇒ NASB #4189 ponēría
		To be depraved; to be malicious; to be wicked; to be actively evil; to do mischief; to trouble others and cause harm; to be malicious; to be dangerous and destructive.
		
		Practical Application
		It is malice, hatred, and ill will. It is an active malice, a desire within the heart to do harm and to corrupt people. It is actually pursuing others in order to seduce them or to harm them.

ENGLISH WORD	GREEK WORD AND VERSE	THE WORD MEANS...
POSB REFERENCE (Mk.7:22) *Deeper Study #9*	**Mark 7:22** Thefts, covetousness, **wickedness**, deceit, lasciviousness, an evil eye, blasphemy, pride, foolishness: [KJV] Deeds of coveting and **wickedness**, as well as deceit, sensuality, envy, slander, pride and foolishness. [NASB]	
See also POSB REF: (Lk.11:39-41; esp. v.39) Note 2, point 1	Greed, **malice**, deceit, lewdness, envy, slander, arrogance and folly. [NIV] Thefts, covetousness, **wickedness**, deceit, lewdness, an evil eye, blasphemy, pride, foolishness. [NKJV] Adultery, greed, **wickedness**, deceit, eagerness for lustful pleasure, envy, slander, pride, and foolishness. [NLT] πλεονεξίαι, **πονηρίαι**, δόλος, ἀσέλγεια, ὀφθαλμὸς πονηρός, βλασφημία, ὑπερηφανία, ἀφροσύνη· [GNS] μοιχεῖαι, πλεονεξίαι, **πονηρίαι**, δόλος, ἀσέλγεια, ὀφθαλμὸς πονηρός, βλασφημία, ὑπερηφανία, ἀφροσύνη· [GNT]	
#2520 **Malice** **Malice–KJV** **Malice–NASB** **Malice–NIV** **Malice–NKJV** Wickedness–NLT **POSB REFERENCE** (1 Cor.5:8) Note 3 See also POSB REF: (Eph.4:7-10; esp. v.10) Note 1 (Col.3:8-11; esp. v.8) Note 2, point 1c (1 Pt.2:1) Note 1, point 1	*κακίας* = *kakias* Pronunciation: [kak-ee'-ahs] Parsing (part of speech): noun ⎯Case—genitive ⎯Gender—feminine ⎯Number—singular ⎯Stem or root—from **κακία**, ας Concordance References: ⇒ Strong's #2549 kakia ⇒ NIV #2798 kakia ⇒ NASB #2549 kakia **1 Cor. 5:8** Therefore let us keep the feast, not with old leaven, neither with the leaven of **malice** and wickedness; but with the unleavened bread of sincerity and truth. [KJV] Let us therefore celebrate the feast, not with old leaven, nor with the leaven of **malice** and wickedness, but with the unleavened bread of sincerity and truth. [NASB] Therefore let us keep the Festival, not with the old yeast, the yeast of **malice** and wickedness, but with bread without yeast, the bread of sincerity and truth. [NIV] Therefore let us keep the feast, not with old leaven, nor with the leaven of **malice** and wickedness, but with the unleavened *bread* of sincerity and truth. [NKJV] So let us celebrate the festival, not by eating the old bread of **wickedness** and evil, but by eating the new bread of purity and truth. [NLT] ὥστε ἑορτάζωμεν, μὴ ἐν ζύμῃ παλαιᾷ, μηδὲ ἐν ζύμῃ **κακίας** καὶ πονηρίας, ἀλλ' ἐν ἀζύμοις εἰλικρινείας καὶ ἀληθείας. [GNS] ὥστε ἑορτάζωμεν μὴ ἐν ζύμῃ παλαιᾷ μηδὲ ἐν ζύμῃ **κακίας** καὶ πονηρίας ἀλλ' ἐν ἀζύμοις εἰλικρινείας καὶ ἀληθείας. [GNT]	Malice, wickedness, hateful feelings, evil. **Practical Application** The word "malice" (*kakias*) indicates that some in the church were apparently opposing the shameful man's presence in the church (1 Cor.5:6). But those who supported the man stood their ground, and malice set in between the two groups. The word means two things. 1. In a general sense, it means wickedness, all kinds and forms of evil. It is a word that strikes at all the vices of men. 2. In a narrow sense, it means malice, deep-seated feelings against a person; hatred that lasts on and on; intense and long-lasting bitterness against a person. It means ill will, actually wishing that something bad would happen to a person. It means to be vicious, spiteful, and to hold a grudge. It means that a person has turned his heart over to evil: ⇒ He no longer has any good feelings toward the other person—none whatsoever. ⇒ He could care less if something bad happened to the person. The charge is strong: believers are to strip off malice—all of their evil and wickedness and all of their ill feelings against others. Believers are to be pure and clean, and they are to live pure and clean lives before their brothers and sisters in the Lord.
#2521 **Malice** Malignity–KJV **Malice–NASB** **Malice–NIV** Evil-mindedness– NKJV Malicious behavior– NLT **POSB REFERENCE** (Romans 1:29) *Deeper Study #10*	*κακοηθείας* = *kakoëtheias* Pronunciation: [kak-o-ay'-thee-ahs] Parsing (part of speech): noun ⎯Case—genitive ⎯Gender—feminine ⎯Number—singular ⎯Stem or root—from **κακοήθεια**, ας Concordance References: ⇒ Strong's #2550 kakoëtheia ⇒ NIV #2799 kakoëtheia ⇒ NASB #2550 kakoëtheia **Romans 1:29** Being filled with all unrighteousness, fornication, wickedness, covetousness, maliciousness; full of envy, murder, debate, deceit, **malignity**; whisperers, [KJV] Being filled with all unrighteousness, wickedness, greed, evil; full of envy, murder, strife, deceit, **malice**; they are gossips, [NASB] They have become filled with every kind of wicked-	Malignity, malice, meanness; evil disposition; evil in nature; evil done for the sake of evil. **Practical Application** It is a spirit full of evil and malice and injury, a character that is as evil as it can be. It is a person who always looks for the worst in other people and always passes on the worst about them. It is the person who so often ruins other people both in reputation and body and in mind and spirit. It is a person so full of evil that he is always ruining others either by word or violence.

ENGLISH WORD	GREEK WORD AND VERSE	THE WORD MEANS...
	ness, evil, greed and depravity. They are full of envy, murder, strife, deceit and **malice**. They are gossips, [NIV] Being filled with all unrighteousness, sexual immorality, wickedness, covetousness, maliciousness; full of envy, murder, strife, deceit, **evil-mindedness**; *they are* whisperers, [NKJV] Their lives became full of every kind of wickedness, sin, greed, hate, envy, murder, fighting, deception, **malicious behavior**, and gossip. [NLT] πεπληρωμένους πάση ἀδικία πορνεία, πονηρία πλεονεξία κακία· μεστοὺς φθόνου, φόνου, ἔριδος, δόλου, **κακοηθείας**· [GNS] πεπληρωμένους πάση ἀδικία πονηρία πλεονεξία κακία, μεστοὺς φθόνου φόνου ἔριδος δόλου **κακοηθείας**, ψιθυριστάς [GNT]	

#2522
Malice
 	
Malice–KJV
Malice–NASB
Malice–NIV
Malice–NKJV
Evil–NLT
 	
POSB
REFERENCE
(Tit.3:3)
Deeper Study #4
	κακία = *kakia*
	Pronunciation: [kak-ee'-ah]
	Parsing (part of speech): noun
	    Case—dative
	    Gender—feminine
	    Number—singular
	    Stem or root—from κακία, ας
	Concordance References:
	    ⇒ Strong's #2549 kakia
	    ⇒ NIV #2798 kakia
	    ⇒ NASB #2549 kakia
	
	Titus 3:3
	For we ourselves also were sometimes foolish, disobedient, deceived, serving divers lusts and pleasures, living in **malice** and envy, hateful, and hating one another. [KJV]
	
	For we also once were foolish ourselves, disobedient, deceived, enslaved to various lusts and pleasures, spending our life in **malice** and envy, hateful, hating one another. [NASB]
	
	At one time we too were foolish, disobedient, deceived and enslaved by all kinds of passions and pleasures. We lived in **malice** and envy, being hated and hating one another. [NIV]
	
	For we ourselves were also once foolish, disobedient, deceived, serving various lusts and pleasures, living in **malice** and envy, hateful and hating one another. [NKJV]
	
	Once we, too, were foolish and disobedient. We were misled by others and became slaves to many wicked desires and evil pleasures. Our lives were full of **evil** and envy. We hated others, and they hated us. [NLT]
	
	ἦμεν γάρ ποτε καὶ ἡμεῖς ἀνόητοι, ἀπειθεῖς, πλανώμενοι, δουλεύοντες ἐπιθυμίαις καὶ ἡδοναῖς ποικίλαις, ἐν **κακία** καὶ φθόνω διάγοντες, στυγητοί, μισοῦντες ἀλλήλους. [GNS]
	
	Ἦμεν γάρ ποτε καὶ ἡμεῖς ἀνόητοι, ἀπειθεῖς, πλανώμενοι, δουλεύοντες ἐπιθυμίαις καὶ ἡδοναῖς ποικίλαις, ἐν **κακία** καὶ φθόνω διάγοντες, στυγητοί, μισοῦντες ἀλλήλους. [GNT]
		Malice, evil, wickedness, depravity. The word means evil disposition or evil in nature. It is a spirit full of evil and malice and injury, a character that is as evil as it can be. It is a person who always looks for the worst in other people and always passes on the worst about them. It is the person who so often ruins other people by word or violence and ruins them both in reputation and body and in mind and spirit.
		
		Practical Application
		There are some people who would never actively strike or harm a person, yet they have experienced feelings against another person. The feelings arose from some argument or difference within the family, with a neighbor, or at work, school, or play. And the feelings were strong, so strong that the person could care less if something bad happened to the other person. And most people have even had feelings...
		• that wished something bad upon others.
		• that downgraded and tore down others.
		
		Tragically, these feelings even occur within families. People hold malice within their hearts; they are unconcerned about something bad happening to others. But thanks be to God our Savior, who has provided forgiveness for this terrible sin—both forgiveness and deliverance. And He will forgive and deliver any person who turns away from his malice and bitterness against others and turns to Him.

#2523
Malicious Behavior
 	
Malignity–KJV
Malice–NASB
Malice–NIV
Evil-mindedness–NKJV
Malicious behavior–NLT
 	
POSB
REFERENCE
	κακοηθείας = *kakoëtheias*
	Pronunciation: [kak-o-ay'-thee-ahs]
	Parsing (part of speech): noun
	    Case—genitive
	    Gender—feminine
	    Number—singular
	    Stem or root—from κακοήθεια, ας
	Concordance References:
	    ⇒ Strong's #2550 kakoëtheia
	    ⇒ NIV #2799 kakoëtheia
	    ⇒ NASB #2550 kakoëtheia
	
	Romans 1:29
	Being filled with all unrighteousness, fornication, wickedness, covetousness, maliciousness; full of envy, murder, debate, deceit, **malignity**; whisperers, [KJV]
		Malignity, malice, meanness; evil disposition; evil in nature; evil done for the sake of evil.
		
		Practical Application
		It is a spirit full of evil and malice and injury, a character that is as evil as it can be. It is a person who always looks for the worst in other people and always passes on the worst about them. It is the person who so often ruins other people both in reputation and body and in mind and spirit. It is a person so full of evil that he is always ruining others either by word or violence.

ENGLISH WORD	GREEK WORD AND VERSE	THE WORD MEANS...
(Romans 1:29) *Deeper Study* #10	Being filled with all unrighteousness, wickedness, greed, evil; full of envy, murder, strife, deceit, **malice**; they are gossips, [NASB] They have become filled with every kind of wickedness, evil, greed and depravity. They are full of envy, murder, strife, deceit and **malice**. They are gossips, [NIV] Being filled with all unrighteousness, sexual immorality, wickedness, covetousness, maliciousness; full of envy, murder, strife, deceit, **evil-mindedness**; *they are* whisperers, [NKJV] Their lives became full of every kind of wickedness, sin, greed, hate, envy, murder, fighting, deception, **malicious behavior**, and gossip. [NLT] πεπληρωμένους πάσῃ ἀδικίᾳ πορνείᾳ, πονηρίᾳ πλεονεξίᾳ κακίᾳ· μεστοὺς φθόνου, φόνου, ἔριδος, δόλου, **κακοηθείας**·[GNS] πεπληρωμένους πάσῃ ἀδικίᾳ πονηρίᾳ πλεονεξίᾳ κακίᾳ, μεστοὺς φθόνου φόνου ἔριδος δόλου **κακοηθείας**, ψιθυριστάς [GNT]	

#2524
Malicious Gossips
 	
False accusers–KJV
Malicious gossips–NASB
Slanderers–NIV
Slanderers–NKJV
Speaking evil of others–NLT
 	
POSB REFERENCE
(Tit.2:3)
Note 3, point 2
 	
See also POSB REF:
(2 Tim. 3:2-4; esp. v.3)
Note 2, point 11
	διαβόλους = *diabolous*
	Pronunciation: [dee-ab'-ol-oos]
	Parsing (part of speech): adjective
	   Case—accusative
	   Gender—feminine
	   Number—plural
	   Stem or root—from διάβολος, ου
	Concordance References:
	⇒ Strong's #1228 diabolos
	⇒ NIV #1333 diabolos
	⇒ NASB #1228 diabolos
	
	Titus 2:3
	The aged women likewise, that they be in behaviour as becometh holiness, not **false accusers**, not given to much wine, teachers of good things; [KJV]
	Older women likewise are to be reverent in their behavior, not **malicious gossips**, nor enslaved to much wine, teaching what is good, [NASB]
	Likewise, teach the older women to be reverent in the way they live, not to be **slanderers** or addicted to much wine, but to teach what is good. [NIV]
	The older women likewise, that they be reverent in behavior, not **slanderers**, not given to much wine, teachers of good things— [NKJV]
	Similarly, teach the older women to live in a way that is appropriate for someone serving the Lord. They must not go around **speaking evil of others** and must not be heavy drinkers. Instead, they should teach others what is good. [NLT]
	Πρεσβύτιδας ὡσαύτως ἐν καταστήματι ἱεροπρεπεῖς, μὴ **διαβόλους**, μὴ οἴνῳ πολλῷ δεδουλωμένας, καλοδιδασκάλους, [GNS]
	πρεσβύτιδας ὡσαύτως ἐν καταστήματι ἱεροπρεπεῖς, μὴ **διαβόλους** μηδὲ οἴνῳ πολλῷ δεδουλωμένας, καλοδιδασκάλους, [GNT]
		Slanderers, false accusers, malicious gossips, speaking evil of others, talebearers, gossipers, a person who goes about talking about others, stirring up mischief and disturbance.
		
		Practical Application
		This is so terrible a sin that the devil himself is called a "slanderer," a "malicious gossip" (*diabolous*).

#2525
Maliciousness
 	
Maliciousness–KJV
Evil–NASB
Depravity–NIV
Maliciousness–NKJV
Hate–NLT
 	
POSB REFERENCE
(Rom.1:29)
Deeper Study #5
	κακία = *kakia*
	Pronunciation: [kak-ee'-ah]
	Parsing (part of speech): noun
	   Case—dative
	   Gender—feminine
	   Number—singular
	   Stem or root—from κακία, ας
	Concordance References:
	⇒ Strong's #2549 kakia
	⇒ NIV #2798 kakia
	⇒ NASB #2549 kakia
	
	Romans 1:29
	Being filled with all unrighteousness, fornication, wickedness, covetousness, **maliciousness**; full of envy, murder, debate, deceit, malignity; whisperers, [KJV]
		Evil; wickedness; hateful feelings; malice; viciousness; ill will; spite; a grudge; worry (Mt. 6:34).
		
		Practical Application
		Maliciousness (*kakia*) means that a man has turned his heart completely over to evil.
		⇒ He no longer has any good within—none whatsoever.
		⇒ He is full of viciousness and malice.
		⇒ He is actively pursuing evil with a vengeance.

ENGLISH WORD	GREEK WORD AND VERSE	THE WORD MEANS...
	Being filled with all unrighteousness, wickedness, greed, **evil**; full of envy, murder, strife, deceit, malice; they are gossips, [NASB] They have become filled with every kind of wickedness, evil, greed and **depravity**. They are full of envy, murder, strife, deceit and malice. They are gossips, [NIV] Being filled with all unrighteousness, sexual immorality, wickedness, covetousness, **maliciousness**; full of envy, murder, strife, deceit, evil-mindedness; *they are* whisperers, [NKJV] Their lives became full of every kind of wickedness, sin, greed, **hate**, envy, murder, fighting, deception, malicious behavior, and gossip. [NLT] πεπληρωμένους πάσῃ ἀδικίᾳ πορνείᾳ, πονηρίᾳ πλεονεξίᾳ **κακίᾳ·** μεστοὺς φθόνου, φόνου, ἔριδος, δόλου, κακοηθείας· [GNS] πεπληρωμένους πάσῃ ἀδικίᾳ πονηρίᾳ πλεονεξίᾳ **κακίᾳ**, μεστοὺς φθόνου φόνου ἔριδος δόλου κακοηθείας, ψιθυριστάς [GNT]	

#2526
Malignity
 	
Malignity–KJV
Malice–NASB
Malice–NIV
Evil-mindedness–NKJV
Malicious behavior–NLT
 	
POSB
REFERENCE
(Romans 1:29)
Deeper Study #10
	κακοηθείας = *kakoëtheias*
	Pronunciation: [kak-o-ay'-thee-ahs]
	Parsing (part of speech): noun
	    Case—genitive
	    Gender—feminine
	    Number—singular
	    Stem or root—from **κακοήθεια**, ας
	Concordance References:
	⇒ Strong's #2550 kakoëtheia
	⇒ NIV #2799 kakoëtheia
	⇒ NASB #2550 kakoëtheia
	
	Romans 1:29
	Being filled with all unrighteousness, fornication, wickedness, covetousness, maliciousness; full of envy, murder, debate, deceit, **malignity**; whisperers, [KJV]
	
	Being filled with all unrighteousness, wickedness, greed, evil; full of envy, murder, strife, deceit, **malice**; they are gossips, [NASB]
	
	They have become filled with every kind of wickedness, evil, greed and depravity. They are full of envy, murder, strife, deceit and **malice**. They are gossips, [NIV]
	
	Being filled with all unrighteousness, sexual immorality, wickedness, covetousness, maliciousness; full of envy, murder, strife, deceit, **evil-mindedness**; *they are* whisperers, [NKJV]
	
	Their lives became full of every kind of wickedness, sin, greed, hate, envy, murder, fighting, deception, **malicious behavior**, and gossip. [NLT]
	
	πεπληρωμένους πάσῃ ἀδικίᾳ πορνείᾳ, πονηρίᾳ πλεονεξίᾳ κακίᾳ· μεστοὺς φθόνου, φόνου, ἔριδος, δόλου, **κακοηθείας·** [GNS]
	
	πεπληρωμένους πάσῃ ἀδικίᾳ πονηρίᾳ πλεονεξίᾳ κακίᾳ, μεστοὺς φθόνου φόνου ἔριδος δόλου **κακοηθείας**, ψιθυριστάς [GNT]
		Malignity, malice, meanness; evil disposition; evil in nature; evil done for the sake of evil.
		
		Practical Application
		It is a spirit full of evil and malice and injury, a character that is as evil as he can be. It is a person who always looks for the worst in other people and always passes on the worst about them. It is the person who so often ruins other people both in reputation and body and in mind and spirit. It is a person so full of evil that he is always ruining others either by word or violence.

#2527
Mammon
 	
Mammon–KJV
Mammon–NASB
Money–NIV
Mammon–NKJV
Money–NLT
 	
POSB
REFERENCE
(Mt.6:24)
Note 3
	μαμωνᾷ = *mamōna*
	Pronunciation: [mam-mo-nah']
	Parsing (part of speech): noun
	    Case—dative
	    Gender—masculine
	    Number—singular
	    Stem or root—from μαμωνᾶς, ᾶ
	Concordance References:
	⇒ Strong's #3126 mamōnas
	⇒ NIV #3440 mamōnas
	⇒ NASB #3126 mamōnas
	
	Matthew 6:24
	No man can serve two masters: for either he will hate the one, and love the other; or else he will hold to the one, and despise the other. Ye cannot serve God and **mammon**. [KJV]
		Money, wealth or any material thing that has value to a person. This means property, possessions, money, stocks, bonds, precious metals or jewels.
		
		Practical Application
		The word mammon or money is neutral, but as the Scripture states, mammon or money acquires a negative connotation when it becomes more important than a relationship with God.
		
		The secret to contentment is not money. This is shocking, for the rich cling to and hoard their money, and the rest of mankind is forever seeking to get more and more money. But God is clear about the matter: money and wealth do not

ENGLISH WORD	GREEK WORD AND VERSE	THE WORD MEANS...

"No one can serve two masters; for either he will hate the one and love the other, or he will hold to one and despise the other. You cannot serve God and **mammon**. [NASB]

"No one can serve two masters. Either he will hate the one and love the other, or he will be devoted to the one and despise the other. You cannot serve both God and **Money**. [NIV]

"No one can serve two masters; for either he will hate the one and love the other, or else he will be loyal to the one and despise the other. You cannot serve God and **mammon**. [NKJV]

"No one can serve two masters. For you will hate one and love the other, or be devoted to one and despise the other. You cannot serve both God and **money**. [NLT]

οὐδεὶς δύναται δυσὶ κυρίοις δουλεύειν· ἢ γὰρ τὸν ἕνα μισήσει, καὶ τὸν ἕτερον ἀγαπήσει· ἢ ἑνὸς ἀνθέξεται, καὶ τοῦ ἑτέρου καταφρονήσει· οὐ δύνασθε Θεῷ δουλεύειν καὶ **μαμμωνᾷ**. [GNS]

Οὐδεὶς δύναται δυσὶ κυρίοις δουλεύειν· ἢ γὰρ τὸν ἕνα μισήσει καὶ τὸν ἕτερον ἀγαπήσει, ἢ ἑνὸς ἀνθέξεται καὶ τοῦ ἑτέρου καταφρονήσει. οὐ δύνασθε θεῷ δουλεύειν καὶ **μαμμωνᾷ**. [GNT]

bring contentment. There are four reasons why this is true.
1. Money tempts and enslaves.
2. Money can cause many foolish and hurtful lusts.
3. Money drowns men in destruction and perdition. Wealth can be "a personal monster, which plunges its victims into an ocean of complete destruction" (Donald Guthrie. *The Pastoral Epistles.* "Tyndale New Testament Commentaries," p.113). The idea is this: the person who falls into the foolish and hurtful lusts of this world will be utterly destroyed and ruined, both in body and soul. And the destruction and ruin will be for eternity (A.T. Robertson. *Word Pictures in the New Testament*, Vol.4, p.593).
4. Money—that is, the love of money—is the root of all evil. Note the three reasons why:
⇒ The love of money causes people to covet, and covetousness is idolatry.
⇒ The love of money causes people to wander away from the faith. It causes people to go after the lusts of this world.
⇒ The love of money causes people to pierce themselves through with many sorrows. The things, possessions, and lusts of this world do not satisfy nor fulfill a person's heart and life. Money cannot bring contentment to a person. The love of money only consumes and eats a person with grief (A.T. Robertson. *Word Pictures in the New Testament*, Vol.4, p.594). It pierces the heart with a void—the void of emptiness and worry, anxiety, and insecurity. Money cannot buy love, health, and deliverance from death. Money cannot buy God; it cannot buy assurance, not the assurance and confidence of living forever.

#2528

Man Without The Spirit

Natural man–KJV
Natural man–NASB
Man without the Spirit–NIV
Natural man–NKJV
People who aren't Christians–NLT

POSB REFERENCE
(1 Cor.2:14)
Note 1

ψυχικὸς = *psuchikos*
Pronunciation: [psoo-khee-kos']
Parsing (part of speech): adjective
    Case—nominative
    Gender—masculine
    Number—singular
    Stem or root—from ψυχικός, ή, όν
Concordance References:
⇒ Strong's #5591 psuchikos
⇒ NIV #6035 psuchikos
⇒ NASB #5591 psuchikos

1 Cor. 2:14

But the **natural man** receiveth not the things of the Spirit of God: for they are foolishness unto him: neither can he know them, because they are spiritually discerned. [KJV]

But a **natural man** does not accept the things of the Spirit of God; for they are foolishness to him, and he cannot understand them, because they are spiritually appraised. [NASB]

The **man without the Spirit** does not accept the things that come from the Spirit of God, for they are foolishness to him, and he cannot understand them, because they are spiritually discerned. [NIV]

But the **natural man** does not receive the things of the Spirit of God, for they are foolishness to him; nor can he know *them,* because they are spiritually discerned. [NKJV]

Man without the Spirit; unspiritual; a natural man; a man who has physical life or who is living.

Practical Application

The root word is soul (*psuche*), which simply means the life of a man, the consciousness, the breath, the energy, the being of a man. The soul is the animal life of a man. Men and animals are breathing and conscious beings. They are living souls. This is clearly pointed out in the creation of animal life. When God was creating the world and He had finished the creation of vegetation, He said:

"Let the water teem with living creatures [hephesh, Hebrew], and let birds fly above the earth across the expanse of the sky." (Genesis 1:20) [NIV]

What God was saying is that the life He was then creating was different from the vegetation He had just created. The things that were now being created were "living souls (*hephesh*)," things that breathe and possess consciousness—things that have "souls," life, and consciousness within their bodies.

PRACTICAL WORD STUDIES
in the NEW TESTAMENT

ENGLISH WORD	GREEK WORD AND VERSE	THE WORD MEANS...
	But **people who aren't Christians** can't understand these truths from God's Spirit. It all sounds foolish to them because only those who have the Spirit can understand what the Spirit means. [NLT] ψυχικὸς δὲ ἄνθρωπος οὐ δέχεται τὰ τοῦ Πνεύματος τοῦ Θεοῦ· μωρία γὰρ αὐτῷ ἐστι, καὶ οὐ δύναται γνῶναι, ὅτι πνευματικῶς ἀνακρίνεται [GNS] ψυχικὸς δὲ ἄνθρωπος οὐ δέχεται τὰ τοῦ πνεύματος τοῦ θεοῦ, μωρία γὰρ αὐτῷ ἐστιν, καὶ οὐ δύναται γνῶναι, ὅτι πνευματικῶς ἀνακρίνεται. [GNT]	The point is this: the natural man is a living soul, an animal soul; he is a man who is living on this earth, just as an animal. However, that is all he is doing. He is living in the flesh only. He has gotten no further than the flesh, no further than his animal life. He has never progressed to the level of the spiritual.
#2529 **Manifest** **Manifest–KJV** Disclose–NASB Show–NIV **Manifest–NKJV** Reveal–NLT **POSB REFERENCE** (Jn.14:21) *Deeper Study* #3	ἐμφανίσω = emphanisö Pronunciation: [em-fahn-ee'-so] Parsing (part of speech): verb 　Mood—indicative 　Tense—future 　Voice—active 　Person—1st person 　Number—singular 　Stem or root—from ἐμφανίζω Concordance References: ⇒　Strong's #1718 emphanizo ⇒　NIV #1872 emphanizo ⇒　NASB #1718 emphanizo **John 14:21** He that hath my commandments, and keepeth them, he it is that loveth me: and he that loveth me shall be loved of my Father, and I will love him, and will **manifest** myself to him. [KJV] "He who has My commandments and keeps them, he it is who loves Me; and he who loves Me shall be loved by My Father, and I will love him, and will **disclose** Myself to him." [NASB] Whoever has my commands and obeys them, he is the one who loves me. He who loves me will be loved by my Father, and I too will love him and **show** myself to him." [NIV] He who has My commandments and keeps them, it is he who loves Me. And he who loves Me will be loved by My Father, and I will love him and **manifest** Myself to him." [NKJV] Those who obey my commandments are the ones who love me. And because they love me, my Father will love them, and I will love them. And I will **reveal** myself to each one of them." [NLT] ὁ ἔχων τὰς ἐντολάς μου καὶ τηρῶν αὐτάς, ἐκεῖνός ἐστιν ὁ ἀγαπῶν με· ὁ δὲ ἀγαπῶν με, ἀγαπηθήσεται ὑπὸ τοῦ πατρός μου· καὶ ἐγὼ ἀγαπήσω αὐτὸν, καὶ ἐμφανίσω αὐτῷ ἐμαυτόν." [GNS] ὁ ἔχων τὰς ἐντολάς μου καὶ τηρῶν αὐτὰς ἐκεῖνός ἐστιν ὁ ἀγαπῶν με· ὁ δὲ ἀγαπῶν με ἀγαπηθήσεται ὑπὸ τοῦ πατρός μου, κἀγὼ ἀγαπήσω αὐτὸν καὶ ἐμφανίσω αὐτῷ ἐμαυτόν. [GNT]	To show; to manifest; to disclose; to reveal; to appear; to make known. **Practical Application** When manifest (*emphanisö*) is used in the sense of an unveiling or revelation, it suggests that a new thing has come to light, that something never known by man before is made known. Some mystery has now been revealed. It is something that cannot be discovered by man's reason or wisdom. It is a mystery that is hidden from man and beyond his grasp. Here in John 14:21-22, it means that Jesus' presence is revealed (brought to light), illuminated, manifested, quickened in the life of the believer. It means that He manifests Himself to His disciples in a very special way. He discloses His person, His nature, His goodness. He illuminates Himself within their hearts and lives. He gives a very special consciousness within their souls. (See POSB note—John 14:21-22; POSB *Deeper Study* #1—Acts 2:1-4.)
#2530 **Mansions** **Mansions–KJV** Dwelling places–NASB Rooms–NIV **Mansions–NKJV** Rooms–NLT **POSB REFERENCE** (Jn.14:2) Note 2, point 3	μοναί = monai Pronunciation: [mon-ah-ee'] Parsing (part of speech): noun 　Case—nominative 　Gender—feminine 　Number—plural 　Stem or root—from μονή, ῆς Concordance References: ⇒　Strong's #3438 mone ⇒　NIV #3665 mone ⇒　NASB #3438 mone **John 14:2** In my Father's house are many **mansions**: if it were not so, I would have told you. I go to prepare a place for you. [KJV] "In My Father's house are many **dwelling places**; if	Rooms, mansions, dwelling places, abiding places. It means places, residences, dwellings, areas, spaces for living, homes. **Practical Application** What a glorious hope! How much clearer could Jesus be: *a place* for every one of us—a place for every believer to dwell and live. Just as we have dwellings and homes here on earth, so Jesus promises us dwellings and homes (rooms) in heaven. And note: there is no shortage. There are *"many mansions."* (In the other gospels, Jesus talks a great deal about believers inheriting huge areas or places, even whole realms and kingdoms, which probably mean the heavenly bodies

ENGLISH WORD	GREEK WORD AND VERSE	THE WORD MEANS...

it were not so, I would have told you; for I go to prepare a place for you. [NASB]

In my Father's house are many **rooms**; if it were not so, I would have told you. I am going there to prepare a place for you. [NIV]

In My Father's house are many **mansions**; if *it were* not *so*, I would have told you. I go to prepare a place for you. [NKJV]

There are many **rooms** in my Father's home, and I am going to prepare a place for you. If this were not so, I would tell you plainly. [NLT]

ἐν τῇ οἰκίᾳ τοῦ πατρός μου **μοναὶ** πολλαί εἰσιν· εἰ δὲ μή, εἶπον αν ὑμῖν; πορεύομαι ἐτοιμάσαι τόπον ὑμῖν. [GNS]

ἐν τῇ οἰκίᾳ τοῦ πατρός μου **μοναὶ** πολλαί εἰσιν· εἰ δὲ μή, εἶπον αν ὑμῖν ὅτι πορεύομαι ἐτοιμάσαι τόπον ὑμῖν; [GNT]

all throughout the universe that will be recreated in the new heavens and earth; 2 Peter 3:10-13; Rev. 21:1. See POSB note—Matthew 19:28; POSB note—Matthew 24:45-47; POSB note—Matthew 25:20-23.)

Note how Jesus stressed the truth and reality of "God's house" and its "mansions": "If it were not so, I would have told you." Jesus did not lie. He told only the truth. Note something else: one thing is essential to inherit these rooms—belief in Christ (John 14:1).

#2531
Many Days

Many days–KJV
Many days–NASB
Many days–NIV
Many days–NKJV
After a while–NLT

POSB REFERENCE
(Acts 9:23)
Deeper Study #1

ἡμέραι ἰκαναι = *hēmerai hikanai*
Pronunciation: [hay-mer'-ah-ee hik-an-ah-ee']
Parsing *hēmerai* (part of speech): noun
    Case—nominative
    Gender—feminine
    Number—plural
    Stem or root—from ἡμέρα
Parsing *hikanai* (part of speech): adjective
    Case—nominative
    Gender—feminine
    Number—plural
    Stem or root—from ἰκανός
Concordance References:
⇒ Strong's #2425 hikanos + 2250 hēmera
⇒ NIV #2653 hikanos [many] + 2465 hēmera [days]
⇒ NASB #2425 hikanos + 2250 hēmera

Acts 9:23
And after that **many days** were fulfilled, the Jews took counsel to kill him: [KJV]

And when **many days** had elapsed, the Jews plotted together to do away with him, [NASB]

After **many days** had gone by, the Jews conspired to kill him, [NIV]

Now after **many days** were past, the Jews plotted to kill him. [NKJV]

After a while the Jewish leaders decided to kill him. [NLT]

Ὡς δὲ ἐπληροῦντο **ἡμέραι ἰκαναί**, συνεβουλεύσαντο οἱ Ἰουδαῖοι ἀνελεῖν αὐτόν· [GNS]

Ὡς δὲ ἐπληροῦντο **ἡμέραι ἰκαναί**, συνεβουλεύσαντο οἱ Ἰουδαῖοι ἀνελεῖν αὐτόν· [GNT]

Many days; after a while.

Practical Application
This is a term indicating a short time (Acts 9:19).

#2532
Many Times

At sundry times–KJV
In many portions–NASB
At many times–NIV
At various times–NKJV
Many times–NLT

POSB REFERENCE
(Heb.1:1-2; esp. v.1)
Note 1, point 1

Πολυμερῶς = *Polumerōs*
Pronunciation: [pol-oo-mer'-oce]
Parsing (part of speech): adverb adjective
    Stem or root—from πολυμερῶς
Concordance References:
⇒ Strong's #4181 polumerōs
⇒ NIV #4495 polumerōs
⇒ NASB #4181 polumerōs

Hebrews 1:1
God, who **at sundry times** and in divers manners spake in time past unto the fathers by the prophets, [KJV]

God, after He spoke long ago to the fathers in the prophets **in many portions** and in many ways, [NASB]

In the past God spoke to our forefathers through the prophets **at many times** and in various ways, [NIV]

God, who **at various times** and in various ways spoke in time past to the fathers by the prophets, [NKJV]

Long ago God spoke **many times** and in many ways to our ancestors through the prophets. [NLT]

Πολυμερῶς καὶ πολυτρόπως πάλαι ὁ Θεὸς λαλήσας

At many times; that is, in many portions; in many parts; in many separate revelations; at many different times; little by little.

Practical Application
God's Word is found in the prophets. In ancient times God spoke to man by His prophets, that is, by persons whom He had chosen to proclaim His Word to the world. Who are these persons? They are the men and women of the Old Testament Scriptures. But note a significant fact: God spoke through the prophets...

- in "many times"
- in many ways

What does this mean? No man could possibly receive and understand or explain the whole revelation of God. God and the truth of God are too big for any one man. Therefore, God had to

ENGLISH WORD	GREEK WORD AND VERSE	THE WORD MEANS...
	at the gracious words which were falling from His lips; and they were saying, "Is this not Joseph's son?" [NASB] All spoke well of him and were **amazed** at the gracious words that came from his lips. "Isn't this Joseph's son?" they asked. [NIV] So all bore witness to Him, and **marveled** at the gracious words which proceeded out of His mouth. And they said, "Is this not Joseph's son?" [NKJV] All who were there spoke well of him and were **amazed** by the gracious words that fell from his lips. "How can this be?" they asked. "Isn't this Joseph's son?" [NLT] καὶ πάντες ἐμαρτύρουν αὐτῷ, καὶ **ἐθαύμαζον** ἐπὶ τοῖς λόγοις τῆς χάριτος, τοῖς ἐκπορευομένοις ἐκ τοῦ στόματος αὐτοῦ, καὶ ἔλεγον, Οὐχ οὗτος ἐστιν οἱ υἱός Ἰωσήφ; [GNS] Καὶ πάντες ἐμαρτύρουν αὐτῷ καὶ **ἐθαύμαζον** ἐπὶ τοῖς λόγοις τῆς χάριτος τοῖς ἐκπορευομένοις ἐκ τοῦ στόματος αὐτοῦ καὶ ἔλεγον, Οὐχὶ υἱός ἐστιν Ἰωσήφ οὗτος; [GNT]	

#2537
Marveled–
Marvelled
 	
Marvelled–KJV
Marveled–NASB
Surprised–NIV
Marveled–NKJV
Astonished–NLT
 	
POSB
REFERENCE
(Jn.4:27)
Note 3
	ἐθαύμαζον = ethaumazon
	Pronunciation: [eh-thou-mah'-sahn]
	Parsing (part of speech): verb
	    Mood—indicative
	    Tense—imperfect
	    Voice—active
	    Person—3rd person
	    Number—plural
	    Stem or root—from θαυμάζω
	Concordance References:
	  ⇒ Strong's #2296 thaumazo
	  ⇒ NIV #2513 thaumazö
	  ⇒ NASB #2296 thaumazo
	
	John 4:27
	And upon this came his disciples, and **marvelled** that he talked with the woman: yet no man said, What seekest thou? or, Why talkest thou with her? [KJV]
	
	And at this point His disciples came, and they **marveled** that He had been speaking with a woman; yet no one said, "What do You seek?" or, "Why do You speak with her?" [NASB]
	
	Just then his disciples returned and were **surprised** to find him talking with a woman. But no one asked, "What do you want?" or "Why are you talking with her?" [NIV]
	
	And at this point His disciples came, and they **marveled** that He talked with a woman; yet no one said, "What do You seek?" or, "Why are You talking with her?" [NKJV]
	
	Just then his disciples arrived. They were **astonished** to find him talking to a woman, but none of them asked him why he was doing it or what they had been discussing. [NLT]
	
	Καὶ ἐπὶ τούτῳ ἦλθον οἱ μαθηταὶ αὐτοῦ, καὶ **ἐθαύμαζον** ὅτι μετὰ γυναικὸς ἐλάλει· οὐδεὶς μέντοι εἶπε, Τί ζητεῖς; ἤ, Τί λαλεῖς μετ' αὐτῆς; [GNS]
	
	Καὶ ἐπὶ τούτῳ ἦλθαν οἱ μαθηταὶ αὐτοῦ καὶ **ἐθαύμαζον** ὅτι μετὰ γυναικὸς ἐλάλει· οὐδεὶς μέντοι εἶπεν, Τί ζητεῖς ἤ Τί λαλεῖς μετ' αὐτῆς; [GNT]
		To be astonished, amazed, bewildered; to be surprised; to marvel; to wonder.
		
		Practical Application
		Just as Jesus made His phenomenal claims (See John 4:13-26), the disciples arrived. They marvelled because He was talking with the woman. There were two reasons for their reaction.
		1. She was a woman. The Rabbis of that day would not be *alone* or *talk* with women in public. They feared what people might think and say. Very honestly, there is some merit to this idea. A person, especially a leader, must guard himself and his thoughts around the opposite sex. Of course, one can carry the practice too far. Wisdom and self-control are both needed.
		2. She was a Samaritan, a person considered despicable, below their social standing, unfit to be seen with in public. Note how Christ tore down the barriers of both problems, and how the disciples controlled their tongue from questioning and gossiping.

#2538
Masquerade
 	
Transformed–KJV
Disguise–NASB
Masquerade–NIV
Transform–NKJV
Pretending–NLT
	μετασχηματίζονται = metaschēmatizontai
	Pronunciation: [met-askh-ay-mat-id'-zon-tah-ee]
	Parsing (part of speech): verb
	    Mood—indicative
	    Tense—present
	    Voice—middle
	    Person—3rd person
	    Number—plural
	    Stem or root—from μετασχηματίζω
	Concordance References:
	  ⇒ Strong's #3345 metaschēmatizō
	  ⇒ NIV #3571 metaschēmatizō
	  ⇒ NASB #3345 metaschēmatizō
		To masquerade; to disguise; to pretend; to transform; to fashion; to change one's outward appearance.
		
		Practical Application
		They pose as "gentlemen of the cloth," but they are nothing but cloth (A.T. Robertson. *Word Pictures in the New Testament*, Vol. 4, p.259). They are false ministers.

ENGLISH WORD	GREEK WORD AND VERSE	THE WORD MEANS...
POSB REFERENCE (2 Cor.11:13-15; esp. v.15) Note 6	**2 Cor. 11:15** Therefore it is no great thing if his ministers also be **transformed** as the ministers of righteousness; whose end shall be according to their works. [KJV] Therefore it is not surprising if his servants also **disguise** themselves as servants of righteousness; whose end shall be according to their deeds. [NASB] It is not surprising, then, if his servants **masquerade** as servants of righteousness. Their end will be what their actions deserve. [NIV] Therefore *it is* no great thing if his ministers also **transform** themselves into ministers of righteousness, whose end will be according to their works. [NKJV] So it is no wonder his servants can also do it by **pretending** to be godly ministers. In the end they will get every bit of punishment their wicked deeds deserve. [NLT] οὐ μέγα οὖν εἰ καὶ οἱ διάκονοι αὐτοῦ μετασχηματίζονται ὡς διάκονοι δικαιοσύνης, ὧν τὸ τέλος ἔσται κατὰ τὰ ἔργα αὐτῶν. [GNS] οὐ μέγα οὖν εἰ καὶ οἱ διάκονοι αὐτοῦ μετασχηματίζονται ὡς διάκονοι δικαιοσύνης· ὧν τὸ τέλος ἔσται κατὰ τὰ ἔργα αὐτῶν. [GNT]	

#2539
 Master
 	
 Master–KJV
 Master–NASB
 Master–NIV
 Master–NKJV
 Master–NLT
 	
 POSB REFERENCE (Lk.17:12-14; esp. v.13) Note 2, point 3a
	ἐπιστάτα = *epistata*
	 Pronunciation: [ep-is-tat'-ah]
	 Parsing (part of speech): noun
	     Case—vocative
	     Gender—masculine
	     Number—singular
	     Stem or root—from ἐπιστάτης, ου
	 Concordance References:
	   ⇒ Strong's #1988 epistatēs
	   ⇒ NIV #2181 epistatēs
	   ⇒ NASB #1988 epistatēs
	
	 Luke 17:13
	 And they lifted up their voices, and said, Jesus, **Master**, have mercy on us. [KJV]
	 And they raised their voices, saying, "Jesus, **Master**, have mercy on us!" [NASB]
	 And called out in a loud voice, "Jesus, **Master**, have pity on us!" [NIV]
	 And they lifted up *their* voices and said, "Jesus, **Master**, have mercy on us!" [NKJV]
	 Crying out, "Jesus, **Master**, have mercy on us!" [NLT]
	 καὶ αὐτοὶ ἦραν φωνὴν, λέγοντες, Ἰησοῦ ἐπιστάτα, ἐλέησον ἡμᾶς. [GNS]
	 καὶ αὐτοὶ ἦραν φωνὴν λέγοντες, Ἰησοῦ ἐπιστάτα, ἐλέησον ἡμᾶς. [GNT]
		The Master, The Chief, the Commander, the Overseer, the One who has the power to meet needs.
		
		 Practical Application
		 They called Jesus "Master." The Greek word for "Master" is not *Rabbi*, the Teacher; but it is *epistata*, which means the Chief, the Commander, the Overseer, the One who has the power to meet needs. Note: the need is not for instruction (*Rabbi*), but for healing; and by healing, they meant both the cleansing of their physical bodies and the spiritual sin which had caused their disease. The Jews always connected leprosy with sin, so this is definitely what they meant. They recognized Jesus to be the Master who could cleanse both the body and spirit, who could give them both healing and forgiveness of sins.

#2540
 Master
 	
 Master–KJV
 Teacher–NASB
 Teacher–NIV
 Teacher–NKJV
 Teacher–NLT
 	
 POSB REFERENCE (Jn.11:28) *Deeper Study #1*
	Ὁ διδάσκαλος = *ho didaskalos*
	 Pronunciation: [ho did-as'-kal-os]
	 Parsing *didaskalos* (part of speech): noun
	     Case—nominative
	     Gender—masculine
	     Number—singular
	     Stem or root—from διδάσκαλος, ου
	 Concordance References:
	   ⇒ Strong's #1320 didaskalos
	   ⇒ NIV #1437 didaskalos
	   ⇒ NASB #1320 didaskalos
	
	 John 11:28
	 And when she had so said, she went her way, and called Mary her sister secretly, saying, **The Master** is come, and calleth for thee. [KJV]
	 And when she had said this, she went away, and called Mary her sister, saying secretly, "**The Teacher** is here, and is calling for you." [NASB]
		The Teacher, Master, Rabbi.
		
		 Practical Application
		 The definite article "the" (*ho*) is important. Jesus is not just another teacher like all other teachers. He is *the* Teacher, the teaching Master. This means at least two things.
		 1. Jesus is the Supreme Teacher, the very best teacher who has ever lived. He is known for being the greatest of teachers. No one compares or even comes close to comparing with Him. He stands alone as *the Teacher*.
		 2. Jesus is the Master, the Lord, the Teacher of all men. In calling Jesus *the* Teacher, there is the idea of His Lordship and deity. Note that He claims deity Himself: "Ye call me 'Teacher' and 'Lord' and rightly so, for that is what I am" (John 13:13). His being *the*

ENGLISH WORD	GREEK WORD AND VERSE	THE WORD MEANS...
	And after she had said this, she went back and called her sister Mary aside. "The Teacher is here," she said, "and is asking for you." [NIV] And when she had said these things, she went her way and secretly called Mary her sister, saying, "The Teacher has come and is calling for you." [NKJV] Then she left him and returned to Mary. She called Mary aside from the mourners and told her, "The Teacher is here and wants to see you." [NLT] καὶ ταῦτο εἰποῦσα ἀπῆλθε, καὶ ἐφώνησε Μαρία τὴν ἀδελφὴν αὐτῆς λάθρα, εἰποῦσα, Ὁ διδάσκαλος πάρεστι καὶ φωνεῖ σε. [GNS] Καὶ τοῦτο εἰποῦσα ἀπῆλθεν καὶ ἐφώνησεν Μαριὰμ τὴν ἀδελφὴν αὐτῆς λάθρα εἰποῦσα, Ὁ διδάσκαλος πάρεστιν καὶ φωνεῖ σε. [GNT]	*Teacher* is tied closely with His being *the Lord*. In fact, logic alone would tell us that *the Lord* would be *the greatest Teacher* among all men.

#2541
Master
 	
Master–KJV
Teacher–NASB
Teacher–NIV
Teacher–NKJV
Teacher–NLT
 	
POSB REFERENCE
(Mt.8:19)
Deeper Study #2
 	
See also POSB REF:
(1 Tim.2:3-7; esp. v.7)
Note 3, point 5
	Διδάσκαλε = *Didaskale*
	Pronunciation: [did-as'-kal-eh]
	Parsing (part of speech): noun
	  Case—vocative
	  Gender—masculine
	  Number—singular
	  Stem or root—from διδάσκαλος, ου
	Concordance References:
	⇒ Strong's #1320 didaskalos
	⇒ NIV #1437 didaskalos
	⇒ NASB #1320 didaskalos
	
	Matthew 8:19
	And a certain scribe came, and said unto him, **Master**, I will follow thee whithersoever thou goest. [KJV]
	
	"And a certain scribe came and said to Him, "**Teacher**, I will follow You wherever You go." [NASB]
	
	"Then a teacher of the law came to him and said, "**Teacher**, I will follow you wherever you go. [NIV]
	
	Then a certain scribe came and said to Him, "**Teacher**, I will follow You wherever You go." [NKJV]
	
	Then one of the teachers of religious law said to him, "**Teacher**, I will follow you no matter where you go!" [NLT]
	
	καὶ προσελθὼν εἷς γραμματεὺς εἶπεν αὐτῷ, Διδάσκαλε, ἀκολουθήσω σοι ὅπου ἐὰν ἀπέρχῃ. [GNS]
	
	καὶ προσελθὼν εἷς γραμματεὺς εἶπεν αὐτῷ, Διδάσκαλε, ἀκολουθήσω σοι ὅπου ἐὰν ἀπέρχῃ. [GNT]
		Teacher, Master, Rabbi in both the Greek and Hebrew.
		
		Practical Application
		To call someone a "master" or "teacher" was to confer a title of great respect upon that person. This person was considered to be an expert in Old Testament Law.

#2542
Master Builder
 	
Masterbuilder–KJV
Master builder– NASB
Expert builder–NIV
Master builder– NKJV
Expert builder–NLT
 	
POSB REFERENCE
(1 Cor.3:10)
Note 1
	ἀρχιτέκτων = *architektōn*
	Pronunciation: [ar-khee-tek'-tone]
	Parsing (part of speech): noun
	  Case—nominative
	  Gender—masculine
	  Number—singular
	  Stem or root—from ἀρχιτέκτων, ονος
	Concordance References:
	⇒ Strong's #753 architektōn
	⇒ NIV #802 architektōn
	⇒ NASB #753 architektōn
	
	1 Cor. 3:10
	According to the grace of God which is given unto me, as a wise **masterbuilder**, I have laid the foundation, and another buildeth thereon. But let every man take heed how he buildeth thereupon. [KJV]
	
	According to the grace of God which was given to me, as a wise **master builder** I laid a foundation, and another is building upon it. But let each man be careful how he builds upon it. [NASB]
	
	By the grace God has given me, I laid a foundation as an **expert builder**, and someone else is building on it. But each one should be careful how he builds. [NIV]
	
	According to the grace of God which was given to me, as a wise **master builder** I have laid the foundation, and another builds on it. But let each one take heed how he
		Expert builder, masterbuilder. It means the superintendent or architect of the building project.
		
		Practical Application
		Paul says that he was the one who planned the church at Corinth. He was the one who laid the foundation, who began and superintended the founding of the church.

ENGLISH WORD	GREEK WORD AND VERSE	THE WORD MEANS...
	builds on it. [NKJV] Because of God's special favor to me, I have laid the foundation like an **expert builder**. Now others are building on it. But whoever is building on this foundation must be very careful. [NLT] Κατὰ τὴν χάριν τοῦ Θεοῦ τὴν δοθεῖσάν μοι, ὡς σοφὸς **ἀρχιτέκτων** θεμέλιον τέθεικα, ἄλλος δὲ ἐποικοδομεῖ. ἕκαστος δὲ βλεπέτω πῶς ἐποικοδομεῖ. [GNS] Κατὰ τὴν χάριν τοῦ θεοῦ τὴν δοθεῖσάν μοι ὡς σοφὸς **ἀρχιτέκτων** θεμέλιον ἔθηκα, ἄλλος δὲ ἐποικοδομεῖ. ἕκαστος δὲ βλεπέτω πῶς ἐποικοδομεῖ. [GNT]	

#2543
Masterpiece
 	
Workmanship–KJV
Workmanship–NASB
Workmanship–NIV
Workmanship–NKJV
Masterpiece–NLT
 	
POSB REFERENCE
(Eph.2:10)
Note 2
	ποίημα = *poiëma*
	Pronunciation: [poy'-ee-mah]
	Parsing (part of speech): noun
	    Case—nominative
	    Gender—neuter
	    Number—singular
	    Stem or root—from ποίημα, τος
	Concordance References:
	⇒ Strong's #4161 poiëma
	⇒ NIV #4473 poiëma
	⇒ NASB #4161 poiëma
	
	### Ephes. 2:10
	For we are his **workmanship**, created in Christ Jesus unto good works, which God hath before ordained that we should walk in them. [KJV]
	
	For we are His **workmanship**, created in Christ Jesus for good works, which God prepared beforehand, that we should walk in them. [NASB]
	
	For we are God's **workmanship**, created in Christ Jesus to do good works, which God prepared in advance for us to do. [NIV]
	
	For we are His **workmanship**, created in Christ Jesus for good works, which God prepared beforehand that we should walk in them. [NKJV]
	
	For we are God's **masterpiece**. He has created us anew in Christ Jesus, so that we can do the good things he planned for us long ago. [NLT]
	
	αὐτοῦ γάρ ἐσμεν **ποίημα**, κτισθέντες ἐν Χριστῷ Ἰησοῦ ἐπὶ ἔργοις ἀγαθοῖς, οἷς προητοίμασεν ὁ Θεὸς, ἵνα ἐν αὐτοῖς περιπατήσωμεν. [GNS]
	
	αὐτοῦ γάρ ἐσμεν **ποίημα**, κτισθέντες ἐν Χριστῷ Ἰησοῦ ἐπὶ ἔργοις ἀγαθοῖς οἷς προητοίμασεν ὁ θεὸς, ἵνα ἐν αὐτοῖς περιπατήσωμεν. [GNT]
		Workmanship, masterpiece; that which is created or made.
		
		### Practical Application
		1. We are God's masterpiece, created in Christ Jesus. The believer experiences two creations, both a natural birth and a spiritual birth. The spiritual birth is the point of this verse. When a man believes in Jesus Christ, God *creates him in Christ*. What does this mean?
		⇒ It means that God *quickens the spirit* of the believer, making his spirit alive. Whereas the believer's spirit was dead to God, God creates it anew and makes it alive to God.
		⇒ It means that God causes the believer to be *born again spiritually*.
		⇒ It means that God actually places His *divine nature* into the heart of the believer.
		⇒ It means that God actually makes a *new creature* of the believer.
		⇒ It means that God actually creates a *new man* out of the believer.
		⇒ It means that God *renews the believer* by the Holy Spirit.
		2. We are created to do good things. God saves man *for good things* not by good things. F.F. Bruce points out that the believer is God's "masterpiece" (*poiema*), God's work of art (*The Epistle to the Ephesians*, p.52). God fashions man and creates a masterpiece. God's masterpiece is always a work of art. The believer does not create the beauty, the art that shows in the canvas of his life. The believer just shows that he is God's masterpiece by the life he lives and displays. Works are an evidence of salvation. Those who walk in trespasses and sins (Ephes. 2:1-2) show that they are not God's workmanship, no matter what profession they make. God's people give ample evidence of the *power of a new life* which operates in them.
		
		Note that God has *ordained* us to walk in good things. Doing good things is not an option for the believer; it is the very nature of the believer. If a man has been created in Christ—if God has truly worked in him—the man does good works. His very nature dictates it. He cannot do otherwise. He is not perfect, and he fails; but he keeps coming back to God and falling upon his knees, believing and asking forgiveness, and getting back up and going forth once again to do all the good he can. As stated, it is his nature. He is a new creation to do good things. Therefore, he does them. Just like a tree, he bears the fruit of his nature.

ENGLISH WORD	GREEK WORD AND VERSE	THE WORD MEANS...

#2544
Masters
 	
Masters–KJV
Teachers–NASB
Teachers–NIV
Teachers–NKJV
Teachers–NLT
 	
POSB
REFERENCE
(Jas. 3:1-12; esp v.1)
Note 1
	διδάσκαλοι = didaskaloi
	Pronunciation: [did-as'-kal-oy]
	Parsing (part of speech): noun
	   Case—nominative
	   Gender—masculine
	   Number—plural
	   Stem or root—from διδάσκαλος, ου
	Concordance References:
	⇒ Strong's #1320 didaskalos
	⇒ NIV #1437 didaskalos
	⇒ NASB #1320 didaskalos
	
	James 3:1
	My brethren, be not many **masters**, knowing that we shall receive the greater condemnation. [KJV]
	Let not many of you become **teachers**, my brethren, knowing that as such we shall incur a stricter judgment. [NASB]
	Not many of you should presume to be **teachers**, my brothers, because you know that we who teach will be judged more strictly. [NIV]
	My brethren, let not many of you become **teachers**, knowing that we shall receive a stricter judgment. [NKJV]
	Dear brothers and sisters, not many of you should become **teachers** in the church, for we who teach will be judged by God with greater strictness. [NLT]
	Μὴ πολλοὶ **διδάσκαλοι** γίνεσθε, ἀδελφοί μου, εἰδότες ὅτι μεῖζον κρίμα ληψόμεθα. [GNS]
	Μὴ πολλοὶ **διδάσκαλοι** γίνεσθε, ἀδελφοί μου, εἰδότες ὅτι μεῖζον κρίμα λημψόμεθα. [GNT]
		Teachers, masters, rabbis.
		
		Practical Application
		Temptations and trials are common to all, but especially to teachers. Masters or teachers are pointed out as being especially subject...
		• to the sins of the tongue (James 3:1-12, esp. James 3:1).
		• to misunderstanding true wisdom (James 3:13-18, esp. James 3:13).
		Teachers are being specially addressed. Note James 3:1 where the word master (*didaskaloi*) is actually used, and James 3:2 where James, who is a teacher, says *we* are all guilty of sin, especially the sin of the tongue. Note also James 3:13-18 where the wise man (teacher) of who is within the church is addressed.
		What is the first temptation common to us all, but especially to teachers? That of misusing the tongue.

#2545
Matter
 	
Matter–KJV
Forest–NASB
Forest–NIV
Forest–NKJV
Forest–NLT
 	
POSB
REFERENCE
(Jas 3:5-6; esp. v.5)
Note 4
	ὕλην = hulën
	Pronunciation: [hoo-layn']
	Parsing (part of speech): noun
	   Case—accusative
	   Gender—feminine
	   Number—singular
	   Stem or root—from ὕλη, ης
	Concordance References:
	⇒ Strong's #5208 hulë
	⇒ NIV #5627 hulë
	⇒ NASB #5208 hulë
	
	James 3:5
	Even so the tongue is a little member, and boasteth great things. Behold, how great a **matter** a little fire kindleth! [KJV]
	So also the tongue is a small part of the body, and yet it boasts of great things. Behold, how great a **forest** is set aflame by such a small fire! [NASB]
	Likewise the tongue is a small part of the body, but it makes great boasts. Consider what a great **forest** is set on fire by a small spark. [NIV]
	Even so the tongue is a little member and boasts great things. See how great a **forest** a little fire kindles! [NKJV]
	So also, the tongue is a small thing, but what enormous damage it can do. A tiny spark can set a great **forest** on fire. [NLT]
	οὕτω καὶ ἡ γλῶσσα μικρὸν μέλος ἐστί, καὶ μεγάλαυχεῖ. ἰδού, ὀλίγον πῦρ ἡλίκην **ὕλην** ἀνάπτει. [GNS]
	οὕτως καὶ ἡ γλῶσσα μικρὸν μέλος ἐστὶν καὶ μεγάλα αὐχεῖ. Ἰδοὺ ἡλίκον πῦρ ἡλίκην **ὕλην** ἀνάπτει· [GNT]
		Forest, wood, matter. The word "matter" (*hulën*) means wood or forest, hence the matter or raw material of a thing (Marvin Vincent. *Word Studies in the New Testament*, Vol. 1, p.747f). Therefore, it means that a great forest is set on fire by only a little spark of fire.
		
		Practical Application
		So it is with the tongue. The tongue is a fire that can set a whole forest of lives and relationships on fire, consuming and destroying all that lies in its path. It is a world of iniquity; it can cause what seems to be a world of sin and destruction when it is set ablaze. Just think about the great and terrible damage that has been done by the fire of words, rumors, talebearing, and remarks that are sharp or cutting. Think about the...
		• marriages destroyed
		• children disturbed
		• friendships damaged
		• reputations ruined
		• wars fought
		• fights aroused
		• injuries caused
		• bodies maimed
		• promotions denied
		
		The list could go on and on, but the point is well made. The tongue can be a little fire that sets ablaze and consumes a whole forest of people and relationships.

#2546
Mature
 	
Perfect–KJV
Perfect–NASB
	τέλειοι = teleioi
	Pronunciation: [tel'-i-oy]
	Parsing (part of speech): adjective
	   Case—nominative
	   Gender—masculine
	   Number—plural
		Mature, perfect, fully developed; full grown, complete, whole.
		
		Practical Application
		A person becomes more mature (*teleioi*). The

ENGLISH WORD	GREEK WORD AND VERSE	THE WORD MEANS...
Mature–NIV Perfect–NKJV Fully developed–NLT **POSB REFERENCE** (Jas. 1:4) Note 3 **See also POSB REF:** (1 Cor.2:6) Note 1	Stem or root—from τέλειος, α, ον Concordance References: ⇒ Strong's #5046 teleios ⇒ NIV #5455 teleios ⇒ NASB #5046 teleios **James 1:4** But let patience have her perfect work, that ye may be **perfect** and entire, wanting nothing. [KJV] And let endurance have its perfect result, that you may be **perfect** and complete, lacking in nothing. [NASB] Perseverance must finish its work so that you may be **mature** and complete, not lacking anything. [NIV] But let patience have *its* perfect work, that you may be **perfect** and complete, lacking nothing. [NKJV] So let it grow, for when your endurance is **fully developed**, you will be strong in character and ready for anything. [NLT] ἡ δὲ ὑπομονὴ ἔργον τέλειον ἐχέτω, ἵνα ἦτε **τέλειοι** καὶ ὁλόκληροι, ἐν μηδενὶ λειπόμενοι. [GNS] ἡ δὲ ὑπομονὴ ἔργον τέλειον ἐχέτω, ἵνα ἦτε **τέλειοι** καὶ ὁλόκληροι ἐν μηδενὶ λειπόμενοι. [GNT]	word does not mean mature in the sense of becoming a mature person. The word means *perfection of purpose*. It has to do with an end, an aim, a goal, a purpose. It means fit, mature, fully grown at a particular stage of growth. For example, a fully grown child is a perfect child; he has reached his childhood and achieved the purpose of childhood. It does not mean perfection of character, that is, being without sin. It is fitness, maturity for task and purpose. It is full development, maturity of godliness. (See POSB note—Ephes. 4:12-13; cp. Phil. 3:12; 1 John 1:8, 10.) When a person stands against trials and temptations and conquers them... • he perfects the purpose God intended. That is, he becomes a stronger and more pure person—a person who is a little more like Jesus. • he perfects his task and purpose for being on earth a little bit more. God has a twofold purpose for every believer: to become more and more like Jesus and to do a specific task or job while on earth. When the believer perseveres against and conquers trials or temptations, he perfects both purposes a little bit more. He becomes more like Jesus, and he finishes his task a little more.

#2547
May Come To
 	
Access–KJV
Access–NASB
Access–NIV
Access–NKJV
May come to–NLT
 	
**POSB
REFERENCE**
(Eph.2:18)
Note 5
 	
See also POSB REF:
(Romans 5:2)
Note 3, point 2
	προσαγωγὴν = prosagōgēn
	Pronunciation: [pros-ag-ogue-ayn']
	Parsing (part of speech): noun
	  Case—accusative
	  Gender—feminine
	  Number—singular
	  Stem or root—from προσαγωγή, ῆς
	Concordance References:
	⇒ Strong's #4318 prosagōgē
	⇒ NIV #4643 prosagōgē
	⇒ NASB #4318 prosagōgē
	
	Ephes. 2:18
	For through him we both have **access** by one Spirit unto the Father. [KJV]
	For through Him we both have our **access** in one Spirit to the Father. [NASB]
	For through him we both have **access** to the Father by one Spirit. [NIV]
	For through Him we both have **access** by one Spirit to the Father. [NKJV]
	Now all of us, both Jews and Gentiles, **may come to** the Father through the same Holy Spirit because of what Christ has done for us. [NLT]
	ὅτι δι' αὐτοῦ ἔχομεν τὴν **προσαγωγὴν** οἱ ἀμφότεροι ἐν ἑνὶ Πνεύματι πρὸς τὸν πατέρα. [GNS]
	ὅτι δι' αὐτοῦ ἔχομεν τὴν **προσαγωγὴν** οἱ ἀμφότεροι ἐν ἑνὶ πνεύματι πρὸς τὸν πατέρα. [GNT]
		Access; to bring to; to move to; to introduce; to present.
		
		Practical Application
		The thought is that of being in a royal court and being presented and introduced to the King of kings. Jesus Christ is the One who throws open the door into God's presence. He is the One who presents us to God, the Sovereign Majesty of the universe.
		Note that it is the Holy Spirit who escorts us into God's presence. The idea is that of daily access—hour by hour, moment by moment. The Holy Spirit keeps us in the presence of God.
		⇒ The Holy Spirit is the Divine Nature of God within us that gives us permanent access into God's presence. (John 3:5; Romans 8:11; 2 Peter 1:4).
		⇒ The Holy Spirit is the One who works in us to stir us to move more and more into God's presence (Romans 8:14; Galatians 4:6-7).
		⇒ The Holy Spirit is the constant companion with us, teaching us to live in God's presence (John 14:26; 1 Cor. 2:12-13).
		⇒ The Holy Spirit is the One within us who bears witness that we are children of God and should approach God continually (Romans 8:15-16; Galatians 4:4-6).

#2548
May It Never Be
 	
God forbid–KJV
**May it never be–
NASB**
Not at all–NIV
Certainly not–NKJV
Of course not–NLT
	μὴ γένοιτο = mē genoito
	Pronunciation: [may ghin'-oy-tow]
	Parsing *genoito* (part of speech): verb
	  Mood—optative
	  Tense—aorist
	  Voice—middle dep
	  Person—3rd person
	  Number—singular
	  Stem or root—from γίνομαι
	Concordance References:
	⇒ Strong's #1096 + 3361 ginomai mē
		God forbid; not at all; may it never be.
		
		Practical Application
		The question is, "If you say some Jews do not believe and are condemned, doesn't that void God's promises and make God a liar?" Or to say it another way, "What if some disbelieve and reject God's Word, will their unbelief cause God to void His Word and promises? God promised the Jews a special place and special privileges

ENGLISH WORD	GREEK WORD AND VERSE	THE WORD MEANS...

POSB REFERENCE
(Romans 3:5-8; esp. v.4)
Note 3, point 1

See also POSB REF:
(Romans 11:1)
Note 1

⇒ NIV #1181 + 3590 ginomai mē [Not at all]
⇒ NASB #1096+ 3361 ginomai mē

Romans 3:4

God forbid: yea, let God be true, but every man a liar; as it is written, That thou mightest be justified in thy sayings, and mightest overcome when thou art judged. [KJV]

May it never be! Rather, let God be found true, though every man be found a liar, as it is written, "That Thou mightest be justified in Thy words, And mightest prevail when Thou ART JUDGED." [NASB]

Not at all! Let God be true, and every man a liar. As it is written: "So that you may be proved right when you speak and prevail when you judge." [NIV]

Certainly not! Indeed, let God be true but every man a liar. As it is written: *"That You may be justified in Your words, And may overcome when You are judged."* [NKJV]

Of course not! Though everyone else in the world is a liar, God is true. As the Scriptures say, "He will be proved right in what he says, and he will win his case in court." [NLT]

μὴ γένοιτο· γινέσθω δὲ ὁ Θεὸς ἀληθής, πᾶς δὲ ἄνθρωπος ψεύστης, καθὼς γέγραπται, Ὅπως ἂν δικαιωθῇς ἐν τοῖς λόγοις σου, καὶ νικήσεις ἐν τῷ κρίνεσθαί σε. [GNS]

μὴ γένοιτο· γινέσθω δὲ ὁ θεὸς ἀληθής, πᾶς δὲ ἄνθρωπος ψεύστης, καθὼς γέγραπται, Ὅπως ἂν δικαιωθῇς ἐν τοῖς λόγοις σου καὶ νικήσεις ἐν τῷ κρίνεσθαί σε. [GNT]

through Abraham and his seed (see POSB *Deeper Study #1*—John 4:22). If some Jews do not believe God's promises and God condemns them, isn't He breaking His promise to Abraham and his seed? Isn't He voiding His Word and Covenant and making Himself a liar? God's Word could not be based on heart religion and on moral character alone. There has to be something else, something outward—a rite (circumcision, baptism, church membership)—that shows we are religious (Jews). If we go through the rite or ritual, then God is bound to accept us. He has so promised to accept us. He is not going to break His Word."

The application of this question concerns every religionist. The thinking religionist poses the same objection and question: "If you say some religionists do not believe and are condemned, doesn't that void God's Word and make God a liar? God's Word promises the religious person special privileges and the hope of eternal life. His Word tells us to believe Christ and to possess His Word, be baptized and join the fellowship of the church. If we do that and God still condemns us, is He not voiding His Word and becoming a liar?"

⇒ God forbid.
⇒ God will be faithful. His Word and promise of salvation will stand even if *every* man lies about believing and lies about giving his heart to serve Jesus.
⇒ God will prove His Word: He will be justified and proven faithful in what He has said. He will still save *any person* who gives his heart to Jesus and obeys Jesus.
⇒ In fact, God will overcome; He will prove His Word another way. He will judge all who make a false profession and who judge Him and His Word, who accuse Him of being unfaithful and voiding His Word. David himself said that God would judge the unfaithful or disobedient man (Psalm 51:4). David had sinned greatly, not keeping the commandments of God, so God judged David and charged him with sin. David did the right thing: he confessed his sin and repented and began to live righteously. But David did something else: he declared that God's charge and judgment against him were *just*, that God was perfectly justified. And God was, for God is always just, and He is always justified in what He says and does.

#2549
Meaningless

Frustrate–KJV
Nullify–NASB
Set aside–NIV
Set aside–NKJV
Meaningless–NLT

POSB REFERENCE
(Gal.2:19-21; esp. v.21)
Note 5

ἀθετῶ = *athetō*
Pronunciation: [ath-eh-to]
Parsing (part of speech): verb
    Mood—indicative
    Tense—present
    Voice—active
    Person—1st person
    Number—singular
    Stem or root—from ἀθετέω
Concordance References:
⇒ Strong's #114 athetō
⇒ NIV #119 athetō
⇒ NASB #114 athetō

Galatians 2:21
I do not **frustrate** the grace of God: for if righteous-

To set aside, void, invalidate, ignore, make ineffective, and nullify; to frustrate; to reject; to refuse; to be meaningless.

Practical Application
If a man sees the grace of God as meaningless (*athetō*) and seeks righteousness by the law, then Christ died in vain. The person who preaches that a man can be good enough—that he can work enough and keep enough law—to become righteous and acceptable to God...

• voids and does away with the love and grace of God.
• makes the death of Christ empty and meaningless.

ENGLISH WORD	GREEK WORD AND VERSE	THE WORD MEANS...
	ness come by the law, then Christ is dead in vain. [KJV] "I do not **nullify** the grace of God; for if righteousness comes through the Law, then Christ died needlessly." [NASB] I do not **set aside** the grace of God, for if righteousness could be gained through the law, Christ died for nothing!" [NIV] I do not **set aside** the grace of God; for if righteousness *comes* through the law, then Christ died in vain." [NKJV] I am not one of those who treats the grace of God as **meaningless**. For if we could be saved by keeping the law, then there was no need for Christ to die. [NLT] οὐκ **ἀθετῶ** τὴν χάριν τοῦ Θεοῦ· εἰ γὰρ διὰ νόμου δικαιοσύνη, ἄρα Χριστὸς δωρεὰν ἀπέθανεν. [GNS] οὐκ **ἀθετῶ** τὴν χάριν τοῦ θεοῦ· εἰ γὰρ διὰ νόμου δικαιοσύνη, ἄρα Χριστὸς δωρεὰν ἀπέθανεν. [GNT]	The only way a man can live for God is by trusting the grace and love of God, that is, by trusting the death of Jesus Christ for His righteousness.

#2550
Meaningless Repetitions
 	
Vain repetitions–KJV
Meaningless repetitions–NASB
Babbling–NIV
Vain repetitions–NKJV
Babble–NLT
 	
POSB REFERENCE
(Mt.6:7)
Deeper Study #1
	βατταλογήσητε = *battologesete*
	Pronunciation: [bat-tol-og-ay say-teh]
	Parsing (part of speech): verb
	   Mood—subjunctive or imperative
	   Tense—aorist
	   Voice—active
	   Person—2nd person
	   Number—plural
	   Stem or root—from βατταλογέω
	Concordance References:
	⇒ Strong's #945 battalogeö
	⇒ NIV #1006 battalogeö
	⇒ NASB #945 battalogeö
	
	Matthew 6:7
	But when ye pray, use not **vain repetitions**, as the heathen do: for they think that they shall be heard for their much speaking. [KJV]
	
	"And when you are praying, do not use **meaningless repetition**, as the Gentiles do, for they suppose that they will be heard for their many words. [NASB]
	
	And when you pray, do not keep on **babbling** like pagans, for they think they will be heard because of their many words. [NIV]
	
	And when you pray, do not use **vain repetitions** as the heathen do. For they think that they will be heard for their many words. [NKJV]
	
	"When you pray, don't **babble** on and on as people of other religions do. They think their prayers are answered only by repeating their words again and again. [NLT]
	
	Προσευχόμενοι δὲ μὴ **βατταλογήσητε**, ὥσπερ οἱ ἐθνικοί· δοκοῦσι γὰρ ὅτι ἐν τῇ πολυλογίᾳ αὐτῶν εἰσακουσθήσονται. [GNS]
	
	Προσευχόμενοι δὲ μὴ **βατταλογήσητε** ὥσπερ οἱ ἐθνικοί, δοκοῦσιν γὰρ ὅτι ἐν τῇ πολυλογίᾳ αὐτῶν εἰσακουσθήσονται. [GNT]
		To babble; to use many phrases; to speak idle or vain words; to speak meaningless words.
		
		Practical Application
		The phrase "meaningless repetitions" (*battologesete*) means at least two things.
		1. It means saying the same words over and over again without putting one's heart and thought into what is being said.
		2. It means using certain religious words or phrases (sometimes over and over again) and thinking God hears because one is using such religious talk.

#2551
Means
 	
Discerned–KJV
Appraised–NASB
Discerned–NIV
Discerned–NKJV
Means–NLT
 	
POSB REFERENCE
(1 Cor.2:14)
Note 1, point 3
	ἀνακρίνεται = *anakrinetai*
	Pronunciation: [an-ak-ree'-neh-tah-ee]
	Parsing (part of speech): verb
	   Mood—indicative
	   Tense—present
	   Voice—passive
	   Person—3rd person
	   Number—singular
	   Stem or root—from ἀνακρίνω
	Concordance References:
	⇒ Strong's #350 anakrinō
	⇒ NIV #373 anakrinō
	⇒ NASB #350 anakrinō
	
	1 Cor. 2:14
	But the natural man receiveth not the things of the Spirit of God: for they are foolishness unto him: neither can he know them, because they are spiritually **discerned**. [KJV]
		Discerned, investigated, judged, scrutinized, examined, appraised, estimated.
		
		Practical Application
		Spiritual things have to be discerned by a living spirit, not by a natural man—a man without the Spirit—not by a man who is primarily living by his animal nature. Spiritual things can be discerned only by a spirit that is living. Spiritual things can be...
		• investigated only by a living spirit.
		• judged only by a living spirit.
		• examined only by a living spirit.
		• estimated and valued only by a living spirit.

ENGLISH WORD	GREEK WORD AND VERSE	THE WORD MEANS...
	But a natural man does not accept the things of the Spirit of God; for they are foolishness to him, and he cannot understand them, because they are spiritually **appraised**. [NASB] The man without the Spirit does not accept the things that come from the Spirit of God, for they are foolishness to him, and he cannot understand them, because they are spiritually **discerned**. [NIV] But the natural man does not receive the things of the Spirit of God, for they are foolishness to him; nor can he know *them*, because they are spiritually **discerned**. [NKJV] But people who aren't Christians can't understand these truths from God's Spirit. It all sounds foolish to them because only those who have the Spirit can understand what the Spirit **means**. [NLT] ψυχικὸς δὲ ἄνθρωπος οὐ δέχεται τὰ τοῦ Πνεύματος τοῦ Θεοῦ· μωρία γὰρ αὐτῷ ἐστι, καὶ οὐ δύναται γνῶναι, ὅτι πνευματικῶς **ἀνακρίνεται**· [GNS] ψυχικὸς δὲ ἄνθρωπος οὐ δέχεται τὰ τοῦ πνεύματος τοῦ θεοῦ, μωρία γὰρ αὐτῷ ἐστιν, καὶ οὐ δύναται γνῶναι, ὅτι πνευματικῶς **ἀνακρίνεται**· [GNT]	

#2552
Mediator
 	
Mediator–KJV
Mediator–NASB
Mediator–NIV
Mediator–NKJV
The one who guarantees–NLT
 	
**POSB
EFERENCE**
(Heb.8:6)
Note 1
	μεσίτης = *mesitēs*
	Pronunciation: [mes-ee'-tace]
	Parsing (part of speech): noun
	  Case—nominative
	  Gender—masculine
	  Number—singular
	  Stem or root—from μεσίτης, ου
	Concordance References:
	  ⇒ Strong's #3316 mesitēs
	  ⇒ NIV #3542 mesitēs
	  ⇒ NASB #3316 mesitēs
	
	Hebrews 8:6
	But now hath he obtained a more excellent ministry, by how much also he is the **mediator** of a better covenant, which was established upon better promises. [KJV]
	
	But now He has obtained a more excellent ministry, by as much as He is also the **mediator** of a better covenant, which has been enacted on better promises. [NASB]
	
	But the ministry Jesus has received is as superior to theirs as the covenant of which he is **mediator** is superior to the old one, and it is founded on better promises. [NIV]
	
	But now He has obtained a more excellent ministry, inasmuch as He is also **Mediator** of a better covenant, which was established on better promises. [NKJV]
	
	But our High Priest has been given a ministry that is far superior to the ministry of those who serve under the old laws, for he is **the one who guarantees** for us a better covenant with God, based on better promises. [NLT]
	
	νυνὶ δὲ διαφορωτέρας τέτειχε λειτουργίας, ὅσῳ καὶ κρείττονός ἐστι διαθήκης **μεσίτης**, ἥτις ἐπὶ κρείττοσιν ἐπαγγελίαις νενομοθέτηται. [GNS]
	
	νυν[ὶ] δὲ διαφορωτέρας τέτυχεν λειτουργίας, ὅσῳ καὶ κρείττονός ἐστιν διαθήκης **μεσίτης**, ἥτις ἐπὶ κρείττοσιν ἐπαγγελίαις νενομοθέτηται. [GNT]
		Mediator; one who guarantees; intermediary, broker. It means someone who stands between two parties and brings them together. The mediator is a negotiator, a middle person, an arbitrator, a go-between.
		
		Practical Application
		    This is Jesus Christ, but there is one distinct and unique difference between Jesus Christ and human mediators. Jesus Christ is the *Perfect Mediator*. He is the Mediator chosen by God Himself to stand between God and man. Jesus Christ was chosen to be the Mediator because He is perfect. He presents the terms of the covenant perfectly. He does not lie, deceive, twist, change, add to, take away from, or misrepresent the terms of God's covenant. He spells out and proclaims the truth of the terms clearly and perfectly.

#2553
Meditate On
 	
Think on–KJV
Let your mind dwell on–NASB
Think about–NIV
Meditate on–NKJV
	λογίζεσθε = *logizesthe*
	Pronunciation: [log-id'-zehs-theh]
	Parsing (part of speech): verb
	  Mood—imperative
	  Tense—present
	  Voice—middle or passive deponent
	  Person—2nd person
	  Number—plural
	  Stem or root—from λογίζομαι
		To think about; to think on; to let one's mind dwell on; to calculate; to evaluate; to consider, reflect, reason, and ponder.
		
		Practical Application
		    The idea is that of focusing our thoughts until they shape our behavior. The truth is:
		  ⇒ what we think is what we become.
		  ⇒ where we keep our minds is where we are.

ENGLISH WORD	GREEK WORD AND VERSE	THE WORD MEANS...
Think about–NLT **POSB REFERENCE** (Philip.4:8-9; esp. v.8) Note 2	Concordance References: ⇒ Strong's #3049 logizomai ⇒ NIV #3357 logizomai ⇒ NASB #3049 logizomai **Philip. 4:8** Finally, brethren, whatsoever things are true, whatsoever things *are* honest, whatsoever things *are* just, whatsoever things *are* pure, whatsoever things *are* lovely, whatsoever things *are* of good report; if *there be* any virtue, and if *there be* any praise, **think on** these things. [KJV] Finally, brethren, whatever is true, whatever is honorable, whatever is right, whatever is pure, whatever is lovely, whatever is of good repute, if there is any excellence and if anything worthy of praise, **let your mind dwell on** these things. [NASB] Finally, brothers, whatever is true, whatever is noble, whatever is right, whatever is pure, whatever is lovely, whatever is admirable—if anything is excellent or praiseworthy—**think about** such things. [NIV] Finally, brethren, whatever things are true, whatever things *are* noble, whatever things *are* just, whatever things *are* pure, whatever things *are* lovely, whatever things *are* of good report, if *there is* any virtue and if *there is* anything praiseworthy—**meditate on** these things. [NKJV] And now, dear brothers and sisters, let me say one more thing as I close this letter. Fix your thoughts on what is true and honorable and right. Think about things that are pure and lovely and admirable. **Think about** things that are excellent and worthy of praise. [NLT] Τὸ λοιπόν, ἀδελφοί, ὅσα ἐστὶν ἀληθῆ, ὅσα σεμνά, ὅσα δίκαια, ὅσα ἁγνά, ὅσα προσφιλῆ, ὅσα εὔφημα, εἴ τις ἀρετὴ καὶ εἴ τις ἔπαινος, ταῦτα **λογίζεσθε**· [GNS] Τὸ λοιπόν, ἀδελφοί, ὅσα ἐστὶν ἀληθῆ, ὅσα σεμνά, ὅσα δίκαια, ὅσα ἁγνά, ὅσα προσφιλῆ, ὅσα εὔφημα, εἴ τις ἀρετὴ καὶ εἴ τις ἔπαινος, ταῦτα **λογίζεσθε**· [GNT]	⇒ our thoughts shape our behavior. ⇒ what we do is what we think. William Barclay says, *"...it is a law of life that, if a man thinks of something often enough and long enough, he will come to the stage when he cannot stop thinking about it. His thoughts will be quite literally in a groove out of which he cannot jerk them"* (The Letters to the Philippians, Colossians, and Thessalonians, p.97). A person who centers his thoughts upon the world and its things will live for the world and its things: money, wealth, lands, property, houses, possessions, position, power, recognition, honor, social standing, fame, and a host of other worldly pursuits. Very simply stated, a person who centers his thoughts... • upon the flesh and its lusts will live to satisfy the flesh through such things as pride, self, greed, pleasure, and sex. • upon the eyes and their lust will live to satisfy the eyes and their lust through such things as the immoral, pornographic filth flaunted in magazines, films, books, and television; the exposing of the human body; dressing to attract attention; looking a second time. • upon the pride of life will live to satisfy such things as the desire for recognition, honor, position, and authority. A mind set upon the world and the flesh is what leads to anxiety and worry, emptiness and restlessness (Phil. 4:6-7). A worldly mind never knows peace—not true peace, not the peace of God. God will never allow a worldly mind to have peace, for it is the restlessness of the human soul that He uses to reach men for salvation. The point is this: when a person accepts Jesus Christ, his mind is renewed by the Spirit of God.

#2554
Meek
 	
Meek–KJV
Gentle–NASB
Meek–NIV
Meek–NKJV
Gentle and lowly–NLT
 	
POSB REFERENCE
(Mt.5:5)
Note 4
	πραεῖς = *praeis*
	Pronunciation: [prah-ees']
	Parsing (part of speech): pronominal adjective
	    Case—nominative
	    Gender—masculine
	    Number—plural
	    Stem or root—from πραΰς, πραεῖα, πραΰ
	Concordance References:
	⇒ Strong's #4239 prau`s
	⇒ NIV #4558 praus
	⇒ NASB #4239b praus
	
	Matthew 5:5
	Blessed are the **meek**: for they shall inherit the earth. [KJV]
	"Blessed are the **gentle**, for they shall inherit the earth. [NASB]
	Blessed are the **meek**, for they will inherit the earth. [NIV]
	Blessed *are* the **meek**, For they shall inherit the earth. [NKJV]
	God blesses those who are **gentle and lowly**, for the whole earth will belong to them. [NLT]
	Μακάριοι οἱ **πραεῖς**, ὅτι αὐτοὶ κληρονομήσουσι τὴν γῆν. [GNS]
	μακάριοι οἱ **πραεῖς**, ὅτι αὐτοὶ κληρονομήσουσιν τὴν γῆν. [GNT]
		To be meek or gentle; to have a strong, but tender and humble, life.
		
		### Practical Application
		It is a strong yet teachable spirit. It is not being weak, bowing or spineless. It is a man who is strong, very strong, yet he is humble and tender. It is a man with all the emotions and ability to take and conquer, but he is able to control himself. It is discipline—a man disciplined because he is God-controlled. The opposite of meekness is arrogance or pride. In too many persons, there is an air of sufficiency and superiority. A meek person knows that he has needs and does not have all the answers.

ENGLISH WORD	GREEK WORD AND VERSE	THE WORD MEANS...

#2555
Meek
 	
Base–KJV
Meek–NASB
Timid–NIV
Lowly–NKJV
Timid–NLT
 	
**POSB
REFERENCE**
(2 Cor.10:1-2; esp.
v.1)
Note 1
	ταπεινός = tapeinos
	Pronunciation: [tap-i-nos']
	Parsing (part of speech): adjective
	    Case—nominative
	    Gender—masculine
	    Number—singular
	    Stem or root—from ταπεινός, ή, όν
	Concordance References:
	  ⇒ Strong's #5011 tapeinos
	  ⇒ NIV #5424 tapeinos
	  ⇒ NASB #5011 tapeinos
	
	2 Cor. 10:1
	Now I Paul myself beseech you by the meekness and gentleness of Christ, who in presence am **base** among you, but being absent am bold toward you: {KJV}
	Now I, Paul, myself urge you by the meekness and gentleness of Christ— I who am **meek** when face to face with you, but bold toward you when absent! [NASB]
	By the meekness and gentleness of Christ, I appeal to you—I, Paul, who am "**timid**" when face to face with you, but "bold" when away! [NIV]
	Now I, Paul, myself am pleading with you by the meekness and gentleness of Christ—who in presence *am* **lowly** among you, but being absent am bold toward you. [NKJV]
	Now I, Paul, plead with you. I plead with the gentleness and kindness that Christ himself would use, even though some of you say I am bold in my letters but **timid** in person. [NLT]
	Αὐτὸς δὲ ἐγὼ Παῦλος παρακαλῶ ὑμᾶς διὰ τῆς πραότητος καὶ ἐπιεικείας τοῦ Χριστοῦ, ὃς κατὰ πρόσωπον μὲν **ταπεινὸς** ἐν ὑμῖν, ἀπὼν δὲ θαρρῶ εἰς ὑμᾶς· [GNS]
	Αὐτὸς δὲ ἐγὼ Παῦλος παρακαλῶ ὑμᾶς διὰ τῆς πραΰτητος καὶ ἐπιεικείας τοῦ Χριστοῦ, ὃς κατὰ πρόσωπον μὲν **ταπεινὸς** ἐν ὑμῖν, ἀπὼν δὲ θαρρῶ εἰς ὑμᾶς· [GNT]
		Timid, meek, base, humble, lowly, gentle.
		
		Practical Application
		Some were saying that Paul was a coward. This is what is meant by the word "meek" (*tapeinos*). They were saying that Paul was bold in his instructions; that is, he rebuked the church when he was writing to them, but he was a coward when it came to speaking face to face with them.

#2556
Meekness
 	
Meekness–KJV
Gentleness–NASB
Gentleness–NIV
Gentleness–NKJV
Gentleness–NLT
 	
**POSB
REFERENCE**
(Gal.5:22-23; esp.
v.23)
Note 1, point 8
 	
See also POSB REF:
(Jas.3:13)
Note 1, point 2
	πραΰτης = prautēs
	Pronunciation: [prah-ot'-ace]
	Parsing (part of speech): noun
	    Case—nominative
	    Gender—feminine
	    Number—singular
	    Stem or root—from πραΰτης, ητος
	Concordance References:
	  ⇒ Strong's #4240 prautēs
	  ⇒ NIV #4559 prautēs
	  ⇒ NASB #4240 prautēs
	
	Galatians 5:23
	Meekness, temperance: against such there is no law. [KJV]
	Gentleness, self-control; against such things there is no law. [NASB]
	Gentleness and self-control. Against such things there is no law. [NIV]
	Gentleness, self-control. Against such there is no law. [NKJV]
	Gentleness, and self-control. Here there is no conflict with the law. [NLT]
	πραΰτης, ἐγκράτεια· κατὰ τῶν τοιούτων οὐκ ἔστι νόμος. [GNS]
	πραΰτης ἐγκράτεια· κατὰ τῶν τοιούτων οὐκ ἔστιν νόμος. [GNT]
		Gentleness, meekness. It means to be gentle, tender, humble, mild, considerate, but strongly so.
		
		Practical Application
		Meekness has the strength to control and discipline, and it does so at the right time.
		1. Meekness has *a humble state of mind*. But this does not mean the person is weak, cowardly, and bowing. The gentle person simply loves people and loves peace; therefore, he walks humbly among men regardless of their status and circumstance in life. Associating with the poor and lowly of this earth does not bother the gentle person. He desires to be a friend to all and to help all as much as possible.
		2. Meekness has *a strong state of mind*. It looks at situations and wants justice and right to be done. It is not a weak mind that ignores and neglects evil and wrong doing, abuse and suffering.
		  ⇒ If someone is suffering, gentleness steps in to do what it can to help.
		  ⇒ If evil is being done, gentleness does what it can to stop and correct it.
		  ⇒ If evil is running rampant and indulging itself, gentleness actually strikes out in anger. However, note a crucial point: the anger is always at the right time and against the right thing.

ENGLISH WORD	GREEK WORD AND VERSE	THE WORD MEANS...
		3. Meekness has *strong self-control*. The gentle person controls his spirit and mind. He controls the lusts of his sinful nature. He does not give way to ill-temper, retaliation, passion, indulgence, or license. The gentle person dies to himself, to what his sinful nature (his flesh) would like to do, and he does the right thing—exactly what God wants done.

#2557
Meekness
 	
Meekness–KJV
Gentleness–NASB
Gentleness–NIV
Gentleness–NKJV
Gentleness–NLT
 	
**POSB
REFERENCE**
(1 Tim.6:11)
Note 2, point 6
	πραϋπαθίαν = praupathian
	Pronunciation: [prauh-pah'-thee-ahn]
	Parsing (part of speech): noun
	    Case—accusative
	    Gender—feminine
	    Number—singular
	    Stem or root—from πραϋπάθεια, ας
	Concordance References:
	  ⇒ Strong's #4236 praupathia
	  ⇒ NIV #4557 praupathia
	  ⇒ NASB #4236 praupathia
	
	1 Tim. 6:11
	But thou, O man of God, flee these things; and follow after righteousness, godliness, faith, love, patience, **meekness**. [KJV]
	But flee from these things, you man of God; and pursue righteousness, godliness, faith, love, perseverance and **gentleness**. [NASB]
	But you, man of God, flee from all this, and pursue righteousness, godliness, faith, love, endurance and **gentleness**. [NIV]
	But you, O man of God, flee these things and pursue righteousness, godliness, faith, love, patience, **gentleness**. [NKJV]
	But you, Timothy, belong to God; so run from all these evil things, and follow what is right and good. Pursue a godly life, along with faith, love, perseverance, and **gentleness**. [NLT]
	Σὺ δέ ὦ ἄνθρωπε τοῦ Θεοῦ, ταῦτα φεῦγε· δίωκε δὲ δικαιοσύνην, εὐσέβειαν, πίστιν, ἀγάπην, ὑπομονήν, **πραόπατητα**· [GNS]
	Σὺ δέ, ὦ ἄνθρωπε θεοῦ, ταῦτα φεῦγε· δίωκε δὲ δικαιοσύνην εὐσέβειαν πίστιν, ἀγάπην ὑπομονήν **πραϋπαθίαν**. [GNT]
		Gentleness, meekness, humility. Meekness means to be gentle, tender, humble, mild, considerate, but strongly so.
		
		Practical Application
		Meekness has the strength to control and discipline, and it does so at the right time.
		1. Meekness has *a humble state of mind*. But this does not mean the person is weak, cowardly, and bowing. The meek person simply loves people and loves peace; therefore, he walks humbly among men regardless of their status and circumstance in life. Associating with the poor and lowly of this earth does not bother the meek person. He desires to be a friend to all and to help all as much as possible.
		2. Meekness has *a strong state of mind*. It looks at situations and wants justice and right to be done. It is not a weak mind that ignores and neglects evil and wrong-doing, abuse and suffering.
		⇒ If someone is suffering, meekness steps in to do what it can to help.
		⇒ If evil is being done, meekness does what it can to stop and correct it.
		⇒ If evil is running rampant and indulging itself, meekness actually strikes out in anger. However, note a crucial point: the anger is always at the right time and against the right thing.
		3. Meekness has *strong self-control*. The meek person controls his spirit and mind. He controls the lusts of his flesh. He does not give way to ill-temper, retaliation, passion, indulgence, or license. The meek person dies to himself, to what his flesh would like to do, and he does the right thing—exactly what God wants done.

#2558
Meekness
 	
Meekness–KJV
Gentleness–NASB
Humility–NIV
Meekness–NKJV
Don't brag–NLT
 	
**POSB
REFERENCE**
(Jas. 3:13)
Note 1, point 2
 	
See also POSB REF:
(Tit.3:2)
Note 6
	πραΰτητι = prautēti
	Pronunciation: [prah-oo'-tay-tee]
	Parsing (part of speech): noun
	    Case—dative
	    Gender—feminine
	    Number—singular
	    Stem or root—from πραΰτης, ητος
	Concordance References:
	  ⇒ Strong's #4240 prautēs
	  ⇒ NIV #4559 prautēs
	  ⇒ NASB #4240 prautēs
	
	James 3:13
	Who is a wise man and endued with knowledge among you? let him show out of a good conversation his works with **meekness** of wisdom. [KJV]
	Who among you is wise and understanding? Let him show by his good behavior his deeds in the **gentleness** of wisdom. [NASB]
	Who is wise and understanding among you? Let him show it by his good life, by deeds done in the **humility**
		Humility, meekness, gentleness; to be gentle, tender, humble, mild, considerate, but strongly so.
		
		Practical Application
		Meekness has the strength to control and discipline; and it does so at the right time.
		1. Meekness has *a humble state of mind*. But this does not mean the teacher is weak, cowardly, and bowing. The meek teacher simply loves people and loves peace; therefore, he walks humbly among men regardless of their status and circumstance in life. Associating with the poor and lowly of this earth does not bother the meek teacher. He desires to be a friend to all and to help all as much as possible.
		2. Meekness has *a strong state of mind*. It looks at situations and wants justice and right to be done. It is not a weak mind that ignores and

ENGLISH WORD	GREEK WORD AND VERSE	THE WORD MEANS...
	that comes from wisdom. [NIV] Who is wise and understanding among you? Let him show by good conduct that his works are done in the **meekness** of wisdom. [NKJV] If you are wise and understand God's ways, live a life of steady goodness so that only good deeds will pour forth. And if you **don't brag** about the good you do, then you will be truly wise! [NLT] Τίς σοφὸς καὶ ἐπιστήμων ἐν ὑμῖν; δειξάτω ἐκ τῆς καλῆς ἀναστροφῆς τὰ ἔργα αὐτοῦ ἐν **πραΰτητι** σοφίας. [GNS] Τίς σοφὸς καὶ ἐπιστήμων ἐν ὑμῖν; δειξάτω ἐκ τῆς καλῆς ἀναστροφῆς τὰ ἔργα αὐτοῦ ἐν **πραΰτητι** σοφίας. [GNT]	neglects evil and wrongdoing, abuse and suffering. ⇒ If someone is suffering, humility steps in to do what it can to help. ⇒ If evil is being done, humility does what it can to stop and correct it. ⇒ If evil is running rampant and indulging itself, humility actually strikes out in anger. However, note a crucial point: the anger is always at the right time and against the right thing. 3. Meekness has *strong self-control*. The humble teacher controls his spirit and mind. He controls the lusts of his flesh. He does not give way to ill-temper, retaliation, passion, indulgence, or license. The meek teacher dies to himself, to what his flesh would like to do, and he does the right thing—exactly what God wants done. In summary, the meek man walks in a humble, tender, but strong state of mind; denies himself, giving utmost consideration to others. He shows a control and righteous anger against injustice and evil. A humble man forgets and lives for others because of what Christ has done for him.

#2559
Meet
 	
See–KJV
Look over–NASB
See–NIV
See–NKJV
Meet–NLT
 	
POSB
REFERENCE
(Mt.22:11-14; esp. v.11)
Note 4, point 1
	θεάσασθαι = *theasasthai*
	Pronunciation: [theh-ahs'-ahs-thigh]
	Parsing (part of speech): verb
	    Mood—infinitive
	    Tense—aorist
	    Voice—middle deponent
	    Stem or root—from θεάομαι
	Concordance References:
	  ⇒ Strong's #2300 theaomai
	  ⇒ NIV #2517 theaomai
	  ⇒ NASB #2300 theaomai
	
	Matthew 22:11
	And when the king came in to **see** the guests, he saw there a man which had not on a wedding garment: [KJV]
	
	"But when the king came in to **look over** the dinner guests, he saw there a man not dressed in wedding clothes, [NASB]
	
	"But when the king came in to **see** the guests, he noticed a man there who was not wearing wedding clothes. [NIV]
	
	But when the king came in to **see** the guests, he saw a man there who did not have on a wedding garment. [NKJV]
	
	But when the king came in to **meet** the guests, he noticed a man who wasn't wearing the proper clothes for a wedding. [NLT]
	
	εἰσελθὼν δὲ ὁ βασιλεὺς **θεάσασθαι** τοὺς ἀνακειμένους εἶδεν ἐκεῖ ἄνθρωπον οὐκ ἐνδεδυμένον ἔνδυμα γάμου· [GNS]
	
	εἰσελθὼν δὲ ὁ βασιλεὺς **θεάσασθαι** τοὺς ἀνακειμένους εἶδεν ἐκεῖ ἄνθρωπον οὐκ ἐνδεδυμένον ἔνδυμα γάμου, [GNT]
		To see; to look at; to view attentively; to observe; to carefully look over; to closely look upon and contemplate and inspect; to visit.
		
		Practical Application
		The stress is upon the person who is looking over the situation. He beholds and inspects. The idea is that God entered the banqueting feast *for the purpose* of looking over and inspecting the guests. He wanted to make sure everyone and everything was in order for His Son's great celebration. Not anyone can be allowed to detract from His Son by being improperly dressed or clothed. (See POSB note—Romans 13:14 and POSB *Deeper Study* #2—Righteousness, Romans 13:14; POSB note—2 Cor. 5:21. See POSB *Deeper Study* #2, Justification—Romans 4:22; POSB note—Romans 5:1.)

#2560
Memorial, As–
Memorial, For
 	
For...memorial–KJV
As...memorial–NASB
As...memorial offering–NIV
For...memorial–
	εἰς μνημόσυνον = *eis mnëmosunon*
	Pronunciation: [ice mnay-mos'-oo-non]
	Parsing *mnëmosunon* (part of speech): noun
	    Case—accusative
	    Gender—neuter
	    Number—singular
	    Stem or root—from μνημόσυνον, ου
	Concordance References:
	  ⇒ Strong's #1519 eis + 3422 mnëmosunon
	  ⇒ NIV #1650 eis [as] + 3649 mnëmosunon [memorial offering]
	  ⇒ NASB #1519 eis + 3422 mnëmosunon
		A memorial offering; a memorial.
		
		Practical Application
		The word means that the sincerity of Cornelius' heart caught God's eye. Cornelius was seeking God, desiring to please God, to know God and to do God's will. Therefore, God could not miss him. He had to make sure that Cornelius heard the message of salvation.

ENGLISH WORD	GREEK WORD AND VERSE	THE WORD MEANS...
NKJV Have not gone unnoticed–NLT **POSB** **REFERENCE** (Acts 10:1-6; esp. v.4) *Deeper Study #1*	**Acts 10:4** And when he looked on him, he was afraid, and said, What is it, Lord? And he said unto him, Thy prayers and thine alms are come up **for** a **memorial** before God. [KJV] And fixing his gaze upon him and being much alarmed, he said, "What is it, Lord?" And he said to him, "Your prayers and alms have ascended **as** a **memorial** before God. [NASB] Cornelius stared at him in fear. "What is it, Lord?" he asked. The angel answered, "Your prayers and gifts to the poor have come up **as** a **memorial offering** before God. [NIV] And when he observed him, he was afraid, and said, "What is it, lord?" So he said to him, "Your prayers and your alms have come up for a **memorial** before God. [NKJV] Cornelius stared at him in terror. "What is it, sir?" he asked the angel. And the angel replied, "Your prayers and gifts to the poor **have not gone unnoticed** by God! [NLT] ὁ δὲ ἀτενίσας αὐτῷ καὶ ἔμφοβος γενόμενος εἶπε, Τί ἐστι, Κύριε; εἶπε δὲ αὐτῷ, Αἱ προσευχαί σου καὶ αἱ τε ἐλεημοσύναι σου ἀνέβησαν **εἰς μνημόσυνον** ἐνώπιον τοῦ Θεοῦ. [GNS] ὁ δὲ ἀτενίσας αὐτῷ καὶ ἔμφοβος γενόμενος εἶπεν, Τί ἐστιν, κύριε; εἶπεν δὲ αὐτῷ, Αἱ προσευχαί σου καὶ αἱ ἐλεημοσύναι σου ἀνέβησαν **εἰς μνημόσυνον** ἔμπροσθεν τοῦ θεοῦ. [GNT]	
#2561 **Memorial** **Offering** For...memorial–KJV As...memorial–NASB **As...memorial offering– NIV** For...memorial–NKJV Have not gone unnoticed–NLT **POSB** **REFERENCE** (Acts 10:1-6; esp. v.4) *Deeper Study #1*	**εἰς μνημόσυνον** = *eis mnēmosunon* Pronunciation: [ice mnay-mos'-oo-non] Parsing *mnēmosunon* (part of speech): noun 　　Case—accusative 　　Gender—neuter 　　Number—singular 　　Stem or root—from μνημόσυνον, ου Concordance References: ⇒　Strong's #1519 eis + 3422 mnēmosunon ⇒　NIV #1650 eis [as] + 3649 mnēmosunon [memorial offering] ⇒　NASB #1519 eis + 3422 mnēmosunon **Acts 10:4** And when he looked on him, he was afraid, and said, What is it, Lord? And he said unto him, Thy prayers and thine alms are come up **for** a **memorial** before God. [KJV] And fixing his gaze upon him and being much alarmed, he said, "What is it, Lord?" And he said to him, "Your prayers and alms have ascended **as** a **memorial** before God. [NASB] Cornelius stared at him in fear. "What is it, Lord?" he asked.The angel answered, "Your prayers and gifts to the poor have come up **as** a **memorial offering** before God. [NIV] And when he observed him, he was afraid, and said, "What is it, lord?" So he said to him, "Your prayers and your alms have come up for a **memorial** before God. [NKJV] Cornelius stared at him in terror. "What is it, sir?" he asked.And the angel replied, "Your prayers and gifts to the poor **have not gone unnoticed** by God! [NLT] ὁ δὲ ἀτενίσας αὐτῷ καὶ ἔμφοβος γενόμενος εἶπε, Τί ἐστι, Κύριε; εἶπε δὲ αὐτῷ, Αἱ προσευχαί σου καὶ αἱ τε ἐλεημοσύναι σου ἀνέβησαν **εἰς μνημόσυνον** ἐνώπιον τοῦ Θεοῦ. [GNS]	A memorial offering; a memorial. **Practical Application** The word means that the sincerity of Cornelius' heart caught God's eye. Cornelius was seeking God, desiring to please God, to know God and to do God's will. Therefore, God could not miss him. He had to make sure that Cornelius heard the message of salvation.

ENGLISH WORD	GREEK WORD AND VERSE	THE WORD MEANS...
	ὁ δὲ ἀτενίσας αὐτῷ καὶ ἔμφοβος γενόμενος εἶπεν, Τί ἐστιν, κύριε; εἶπεν δὲ αὐτῷ, Αἱ προσευχαί σου καὶ αἱ ἐλεημοσύναι σου ἀνέβησαν **εἰς μνημόσυνον** ἔμπροσθεν τοῦ θεοῦ. [GNT]	
#2562 **Men Of Flesh** Carnal–KJV **Men of flesh–NASB** Worldly–NIV Carnal–NKJV Belonged to this world–NLT **POSB REFERENCE** (1 Cor.3:1-4; esp. v.1) *Deeper Study #1*	σαρκίνοις = *sarkinois* Pronunciation: [sar-kee'-noys] Parsing (part of speech): pronominal adjective 　Case—dative 　Gender—masculine 　Number—plural 　Stem or root—from σάρκινος, η, ον Concordance References: ⇒　Strong's #4560 sarkinos ⇒　NIV #4921 sarkinos ⇒　NASB #4560 sarkinos **1 Cor. 3:1** And I, brethren, could not speak unto you as unto spiritual, but as unto **carnal**, even as unto babes in Christ. [KJV] And I, brethren, could not speak to you as to spiritual men, but as to **men of flesh**, as to babes in Christ. [NASB] Brothers, I could not address you as spiritual but as **worldly**—mere infants in Christ. [NIV] And I, brethren, could not speak to you as to spiritual *people* but as to **carnal**, as to babes in Christ. [NKJV] Dear brothers and sisters, when I was with you I couldn't talk to you as I would to mature Christians. I had to talk as though you **belonged to this world** or as though you were infants in the Christian life. [NLT] Καὶ ἐγώ, ἀδελφοί, οὐκ ἠδυνήθην λαλῆσαι ὑμῖν ὡς πνευματικοῖς, ἀλλ' ὡς **σαρκίνοις**, ὡς νηπίοις ἐν Χριστῷ. [GNS] Κἀγώ, ἀδελφοί, οὐκ ἠδυνήθην λαλῆσαι ὑμῖν ὡς πνευματικοῖς ἀλλ' ὡς **σαρκίνοις**, ὡς νηπίοις ἐν Χριστῷ. [GNT]	Worldly, carnal, fleshly, unspiritual, belonging to this world. **Practical Application** The ending "*inois*" (*sarkinois*) means "to be made of." Paul is saying that the Corinthians were human beings, made of flesh. Their problem was that they were living as though they were nothing but flesh. They were still living at the human level of life. They had never gotten beyond the affairs and material things of this life. They acted as though this world was all there was.
#2563 **Mention** Declare–KJV Instruction–NASB Directives–NIV Instructions–NKJV **Mention–NLT** **POSB REFERENCE** (1 Cor.11:17) Note 1	παραγγέλλων = *paraggellon* Pronunciation: [par-ang-gel'-lone] Parsing (part of speech): verb 　Mood—participle 　Tense—present 　Voice—active 　Case—nominative 　Gender—masculine 　Person—1st person 　Number—singular 　Stem or root—from παραγγέλλω Concordance References: ⇒　Strong's #3853 paraggellö ⇒　NIV #4133 paraggellö ⇒　NASB #3853 paraggellö **1 Cor. 11:17** Now in this that I **declare** unto you I praise you not, that ye come together not for the better, but for the worse. [KJV] But in giving this **instruction**, I do not praise you, because you come together not for the better but for the worse. [NASB] In the following **directives** I have no praise for you, for your meetings do more harm than good. [NIV] Now in giving these **instructions** I do not praise *you*, since you come together not for the better but for the worse. [NKJV] But now when I **mention** this next issue, I cannot praise you. For it sounds as if more harm than good is done when you meet together. [NLT] Τοῦτο δὲ **παραγγέλλων** οὐκ ἐπαινῶ, ὅτι οὐκ εἰς τὸ κρεῖττον ἀλλ εἰς τὸ ἧττον συνέρχεσθε. [GNS] Τοῦτο δὲ **παραγγέλλων** οὐκ ἐπαινῶ ὅτι οὐκ εἰς τὸ κρεῖσσον ἀλλὰ εἰς τὸ ἧσσον συνέρχεσθε. [GNT]	To command; to give strict orders; to give instructions; to charge. **Practical Application** Note how forceful Paul is: "When I mention (*paraggellon*) this next issue, I cannot praise you." His forcefulness stresses the awesome importance of the Lord's Supper and the absolute necessity to celebrate it as it should be celebrated.

ENGLISH WORD	GREEK WORD AND VERSE	THE WORD MEANS...

#2564
Merchant Of Expensive Purple Cloth
 	
Seller of purple–KJV
Seller of purple fabrics–NASB
Dealer in purple cloth–NIV
Seller of purple–NKJV
Merchant of expensive purple cloth–NLT
 	
POSB REFERENCE
(Acts 16:14)
Note 2
	πορφυρόπωλις = *porphuropölis*
	Pronunciation: [por-foo-rop'-o-lis]
	Parsing (part of speech): noun
	    Case—nominative
	    Gender—feminine
	    Number—singular
	    Stem or root—from πορφυρόπωλις, ιδος
	Concordance References:
	    ⇒ Strong's #4211 porphuropölis
	    ⇒ NIV #4527 porphuropölis
	    ⇒ NASB #4211 porphuropölis
	
	### Acts 16:14
	And a certain woman named Lydia, a **seller of purple**, of the city of Thyatira, which worshipped God, heard us: whose heart the Lord opened, that she attended unto the things which were spoken of Paul. [KJV]
	And a certain woman named Lydia, from the city of Thyatira, a **seller of purple fabrics**, a worshiper of God, was listening; and the Lord opened her heart to respond to the things spoken by Paul. [NASB]
	One of those listening was a woman named Lydia, a **dealer in purple cloth** from the city of Thyatira, who was a worshiper of God. The Lord opened her heart to respond to Paul's message. [NIV]
	Now a certain woman named Lydia heard *us*. She was a **seller of purple** from the city of Thyatira, who worshiped God. The Lord opened her heart to heed the things spoken by Paul. [NKJV]
	One of them was Lydia from Thyatira, a **merchant of expensive purple cloth**. She was a worshiper of God. As she listened to us, the Lord opened her heart, and she accepted what Paul was saying. [NLT]
	καί τις γυνὴ ὀνόματι Λυδία, **πορφυρόπωλις**, πόλεως Θυατείρων σεβομένη τὸν Θεόν, ἤκουεν· ἧς ὁ Κύριος διήνοιξε τὴν καρδίαν, προσέχειν τοῖς λαλουμένοις ὑπὸ τοῦ Παύλου. [GNS]
	καί τις γυνὴ ὀνόματι Λυδία, **πορφυρόπωλις** πόλεως Θυατείρων σεβομένη τὸν Θεόν, ἤκουεν, ἧς ὁ κύριος διήνοιξεν τὴν καρδίαν προσέχειν τοῖς λαλουμένοις ὑπὸ τοῦ Παύλου. [GNT]
		Dealer in purple cloth; seller of purple; seller of purple fabrics; merchant of expensive purple cloth.
		
		### Practical Application
		Purple fabrics were in great demand in the Roman world. Purple was used on the toga or outer garments by the royalty of Rome. Therefore, as in every society, the lower classes desired what the upper class had. Royal purple always has been and still is a common term.

#2565
Mercies
 	
Mercies–KJV
Mercies–NASB
Compassion–NIV
Mercies–NKJV
Every mercy–NLT
 	
POSB REFERENCE
(2 Cor.1:3)
Note 1
	οἰκτιρμῶν = *oiktirmön*
	Pronunciation: [oyk-tir-mon']
	Parsing (part of speech): noun
	    Case—genitive
	    Gender—masculine
	    Number—plural
	    Stem or root—from οἰκτιρμός, οῦ
	Concordance References:
	    ⇒ Strong's #3628 oiktirmos
	    ⇒ NIV #3880 oiktirmos
	    ⇒ NASB #3628 oiktirmos
	
	### 2 Cor. 1:3
	Blessed be God, even the Father of our Lord Jesus Christ, the Father of **mercies**, and the God of all comfort; [KJV]
	Blessed be the God and Father of our Lord Jesus Christ, the Father of **mercies** and God of all comfort; [NASB]
	Praise be to the God and Father of our Lord Jesus Christ, the Father of **compassion** and the God of all comfort, [NIV]
	Blessed be the God and Father of our Lord Jesus Christ, the Father of **mercies** and God of all comfort, [NKJV]
	All praise to the God and Father of our Lord Jesus Christ. He is the source of **every mercy** and the God who comforts us. [NLT]
	Εὐλογητὸς ὁ Θεὸς καὶ πατὴρ τοῦ Κυρίου ἡμῶν Ἰησοῦ Χριστοῦ, ὁ πατὴρ τῶν **οἰκτιρμῶν** καὶ Θεὸς πάσης
		Compassion, pity, and mercy. It means looking upon people in need and having compassion and mercy upon them.
		
		### Practical Application
		⇒ Note that God is not the God of mercy but the Father of mercy. His very nature and behavior toward us is that of a Father, not of a God. He is our Father, a Father who is merciful and compassionate and who showers His mercies and compassions upon us.
		⇒ Note that the word "mercies" [see parsing] is plural. God does not show mercy just once, nor just here and there. God showers His compassion upon us continuously (cp. Romans 12:1; Phil. 2:1; Col. 3:12; Hebrews 10:28).

ENGLISH WORD	GREEK WORD AND VERSE	THE WORD MEANS...
	παρακλήσεως, [GNS] Εὐλογητὸς ὁ θεὸς καὶ πατὴρ τοῦ κυρίου ἡμῶν Ἰησοῦ Χριστοῦ, ὁ πατὴρ τῶν **οἰκτιρμῶν** καὶ θεὸς πάσης παρακλήσεως, [GNT]	
#2566 **Mercies** **Mercies–KJV** Compassion–NASB Compassion–NIV **Mercies–NKJV** Mercy–NLT **POSB** **REFERENCE** (Col.3:12) Note 2	**οἰκτιρμοῦ** = *oiktirmou* Pronunciation: [oyk-tir-mon'] Parsing (part of speech): noun 　　Case—genitive 　　Gender—masculine 　　Number—singular 　　Stem or root—from **οἰκτιρμός**, οῦ Concordance References: 　⇒　Strong's #3628 oiktirmos 　⇒　NIV #3880 oiktirmos 　⇒　NASB #3628 oiktirmos **Col. 3:12** Put on therefore, as the elect of God, holy and beloved, bowels of **mercies**, kindness, humbleness of mind, meekness, longsuffering; [KJV] And so, as those who have been chosen of God, holy and beloved, put on a heart of **compassion**, kindness, humility, gentleness and patience; [NASB] Therefore, as God's chosen people, holy and dearly loved, clothe yourselves with **compassion**, kindness, humility, gentleness and patience. [NIV] Therefore, as *the* elect of God, holy and beloved, put on tender **mercies**, kindness, humility, meekness, long-suffering; [NKJV] Since God chose you to be the holy people whom he loves, you must clothe yourselves with tenderhearted **mercy**, kindness, humility, gentleness, and patience. [NLT] Ἐνδύσασθε οὖν, ὡς ἐκλεκτοὶ τοῦ Θεοῦ, ἅγιοι καὶ ἠγαπημένοι, σπλάγχνα **οἰκτιρμῶν**, χρηστότητα, ταπεινοφροσύνην, πραότητα, μακροθυμίαν· [GNS] Ἐνδύσασθε οὖν, ὡς ἐκλεκτοὶ τοῦ θεοῦ, ἅγιοι καὶ ἠγαπημένοι, σπλάγχνα **οἰκτιρμοῦ** χρηστότητα ταπεινοφροσύνην πραΰτητα μακροθυμίαν, [GNT]	Compassion, mercy, pity, tenderheartedness. **Practical Application** God has had so much mercy upon us, the one thing we should do is to show mercy to others. Compassion and pity should flood our hearts for the... • lost • wayward • lonely • homeless • hungry • aged • hurting • diseased • poor • empty • unclothed • orphaned Of course, the list could go on and on. The point is that the believer no longer has the right to overlook the needy of the world. He is now a new man. A part of the clothing of the new man is the garment of compassion; the believer is to be clothed with compassion. He is to have mercy and reach out to meet the needs of the world—reach out with all he is and has, holding back nothing so long as a single need exists.
#2567 **Merciful** **Merciful–KJV** **Merciful–NASB** **Merciful–NIV** **Merciful–NKJV** **Merciful–NLT** **POSB** **REFERENCE** (Mt.5:7) Note 6	**ἐλεήμονες** = *eleëmones* Pronunciation: [el-eh-ay'-mon-es] Parsing (part of speech): pronominal adjective 　　Case—nominative 　　Gender—masculine 　　Number—plural 　　Stem or root—from **ἐλεήμων**, ον Concordance References: 　⇒　Strong's #1655 eleëmön 　⇒　NIV #1798 eleëmön 　⇒　NASB #1655 eleëmön **Matthew 5:7** Blessed are the **merciful**: for they shall obtain mercy. [KJV] "Blessed are the **merciful**, for they shall receive mercy. [NASB] Blessed are the **merciful**, for they will be shown mercy. [NIV] Blessed *are* the **merciful**,Fo they shall obtain mercy. [NKJV] God blesses those who are **merciful**, for they will be shown mercy. [NLT] Μακάριοι οἱ **ἐλεήμονες**· ὅτι αὐτοὶ ἐλεηθήσονται. [GNS] μακάριοι οἱ **ἐλεήμονες**, ὅτι αὐτοὶ ἐλεηθήσονται. [GNT]	To show kindness, compassion, benevolence, and forgiveness; to be merciful. **Practical Application** In this Scripture it means to have a forgiving spirit and a compassionate heart. It is showing mercy and being benevolent. It is forgiving those who are wrong, yet it is much more. It is empathy; it is getting right inside the person and feeling right along with him. It is a deliberate effort, an act of the will to understand the person and to meet his need by forgiving and showing mercy. It is the opposite of being hard, unforgiving, and unfeeling. God forgives only those who forgive others. A person receives mercy only if he is merciful (cp. Mt.6:12; Jas.2:13).
#2568 **Merciful**	**ἱλάσθητί** = *hilasthëti* Pronunciation: [hil-as'-thay-tee] Parsing (part of speech): verb 　　Mood—imperative 　　Tense—aorist	Propitiated; to have mercy on; to be merciful; to make atonement for.

ENGLISH WORD	GREEK WORD AND VERSE	THE WORD MEANS...
Merciful–KJV **Merciful–NASB** Mercy on–NIV **Merciful–NKJV** **Merciful–NLT** **POSB REFERENCE** (Lk.18:13) Note 4, point 3b	Voice—passive Person—2nd person Number—singular Stem or root—from ἱλάσκομαι Concordance References: ⇒ Strong's #2433 hilaskomai ⇒ NIV #2661 hilaskomai ⇒ NASB #2433 hilaskomai **Luke 18:13** And the publican, standing afar off, would not lift up so much as his eyes unto heaven, but smote upon his breast, saying, God be **merciful** to me a sinner. [KJV] "But the tax-gatherer, standing some distance away, was even unwilling to lift up his eyes to heaven, but was beating his breast, saying, 'God, be **merciful** to me, the sinner!' [NASB] "But the tax collector stood at a distance. He would not even look up to heaven, but beat his breast and said, 'God, have **mercy on** me, a sinner.' [NIV] And the tax collector, standing afar off, would not so much as raise *his* eyes to heaven, but beat his breast, saying, 'God, be **merciful** to me a sinner!' [NKJV] "But the tax collector stood at a distance and dared not even lift his eyes to heaven as he prayed. Instead, he beat his chest in sorrow, saying, 'O God, be **merciful** to me, for I am a sinner.' [NLT] καὶ ὁ δὲ τελώνης μακρόθεν ἑστὼς οὐκ ἤθελεν οὐδὲ τοὺς ὀφθαλμοὺς εἰς τὸν οὐρανόν ἐπᾶραι, ἀλλ' ἔτυπτεν τὸ στῆθος αὐτοῦ, λέγων, Ὁ Θεός, ἱλάσθητί μοι τῷ ἁμαρτωλῷ. [GNS] ὁ δὲ τελώνης μακρόθεν ἑστὼς οὐκ ἤθελεν οὐδὲ τοὺς ὀφθαλμοὺς ἐπᾶραι εἰς τὸν οὐρανόν, ἀλλ' ἔτυπτεν τὸ στῆθος αὐτοῦ λέγων, Ὁ θεός, ἱλάσθητί μοι τῷ ἁμαρτωλῷ. [GNT]	**Practical Application** The sinner cried for mercy. There are two things to note. 1. He called himself "the sinner" (*to hamarto-lo*). This is critical: he did not feel he was just "a sinner" like everyone else, which would mean he was also as good as everyone else. But he felt he was "the sinner," the one who had hurt and shamed God more than anyone else, the one who was more undeserving than anyone else. There was nothing good within him, nothing to commend him to God, nothing to make him acceptable to God. 2. He cried for mercy. The word "merciful" (*hilasthëti*) is really the word for "propitiated." He prayed for God to remove His anger and judgment from him. He deserved God's anger and judgment, but he begged God to turn His anger and judgment away. He felt he would die from the pressure within his chest unless God forgave him and gave him peace and assurance of forgiveness. He wanted to be reconciled to God; he wanted God to remove His judgment from him and to accept him. Now note: he knew the only way he could ever be accepted by God was for God to have mercy upon him and to forgive his sins. He had no good thing about him, no righteousness to offer God. If he were going to be saved by God, God had to accept him simply because he came to God in all the desperation and sincerity of his heart and begged God for mercy. God alone was his hope, and mercy alone was all he could plead.
#2569 **Mercy** **Mercy–KJV** **Mercy–NASB** **Mercy–NIV** **Mercy–NKJV** **Mercy–NLT** **POSB REFERENCE** (Eph.2:4-5; esp. v.4) Note 1, point 1a **See also POSB REF:** (1 Tim.1:2) *Deeper Study* 2 (1 Pt.1:3) Note 1, point 1 (Jas. 3:7-18; esp. v.17) Note 3 (Tit.3:4-5; esp. v.5) Note 1	ἐλέει = *eleei* Pronunciation: [el'-eh-ee] Parsing (part of speech): noun Case—dative Gender—neuter Number—singular Stem or root—from ἔλεος, ους Concordance References: ⇒ Strong's #1656 eleos ⇒ NIV #1799 eleos ⇒ NASB #1656 eleos **Ephes. 2:4** But God, who is rich in **mercy**, for his great love wherewith he loved us, [KJV] But God, being rich in **mercy**, because of His great love with which He loved us, [NASB] But because of his great love for us, God, who is rich in **mercy**, [NIV] But God, who is rich in **mercy**, because of His great love with which He loved us, [NKJV] But God is so rich in **mercy**, and he loved us so very much, [NLT] ὁ δὲ Θεὸς, πλούσιος ων ἐν ἐλέει, διὰ τὴν πολλὴν ἀγάπην αὐτοῦ ἣν ἠγάπησεν ἡμᾶς, [GNS] ὁ δὲ θεὸς πλούσιος ωνσ ἐν ἐλέει, διὰ τὴν πολλὴν ἀγάπην αὐτοῦ ἣν ἠγάπησεν ἡμᾶς, [GNT]	Feelings of mercy, compassion, pity, affection, kindness. **Practical Application** Two things are essential in order to have mercy: seeing a need and being able to meet that need. God sees our need and feels for us (Ephes. 2:1-3). Therefore, He acts; He has mercy upon us. • God withholds His judgment. • God provides a way for us to be saved. Mercy arises from a heart of love: God has mercy upon us because He loves us. His mercy has been demonstrated in two great ways: • God has withheld His judgment from us—withheld it even when we deserve it. • God has provided a way for us to be saved through the Lord Jesus Christ. When Jesus Christ died, He died for our sins. He took our sins upon Himself and bore the judgment of sin for us. Therefore, if we trust Christ as our Savior, God *does not count* sin against us. Instead, He *counts the righteousness* of Christ for us. We become acceptable to God through the righteousness of Christ. The great mercy of God is... • that He allowed Christ, His very own Son, to die for us. He actually allowed His own Son to bear the punishment of our sins for us. • that he loves us so much that He will forgive our sins if we will only trust Christ.

ENGLISH WORD	GREEK WORD AND VERSE	THE WORD MEANS...
		The point is this: it is absolutely necessary for both the minister and the disciple to know and possess the mercy of God and of Christ. A person who has not experienced the mercy of God does not know God. Of all people, the minister and disciple of Christ must know the mercy of God.

#2570
Mercy
 	
Mercies–KJV
Compassion–NASB
Compassion–NIV
Mercies–NKJV
Mercy–NLT
 	
POSB
REFERENCE
(Col.3:12)
Note 2
	οἰκτιρμοῦ = oiktirmou
	Pronunciation: [oyk-tir-mon']
	Parsing (part of speech): noun
	    Case—genitive
	    Gender—masculine
	    Number—singular
	    Stem or root—from οἰκτιρμός, οῦ
	Concordance References:
	  ⇒ Strong's #3628 oiktirmos
	  ⇒ NIV #3880 oiktirmos
	  ⇒ NASB #3628 oiktirmos
	
	Col. 3:12
	Put on therefore, as the elect of God, holy and beloved, bowels of **mercies**, kindness, humbleness of mind, meekness, longsuffering; [KJV]
	And so, as those who have been chosen of God, holy and beloved, put on a heart of **compassion**, kindness, humility, gentleness and patience; [NASB]
	Therefore, as God's chosen people, holy and dearly loved, clothe yourselves with **compassion**, kindness, humility, gentleness and patience. [NIV]
	Therefore, as *the* elect of God, holy and beloved, put on tender **mercies**, kindness, humility, meekness, long-suffering; [NKJV]
	Since God chose you to be the holy people whom he loves, you must clothe yourselves with tenderhearted **mercy**, kindness, humility, gentleness, and patience. [NLT]
	Ἐνδύσασθε οὖν, ὡς ἐκλεκτοὶ τοῦ Θεοῦ, ἅγιοι καὶ ἠγαπημένοι, σπλάγχνα **οἰκτιρμῶν**, χρηστότητα, ταπεινοφροσύνην, πρᾳότητα, μακροθυμίαν· [GNS]
	Ἐνδύσασθε οὖν, ὡς ἐκλεκτοὶ τοῦ θεοῦ, ἅγιοι καὶ ἠγαπημένοι, σπλάγχνα **οἰκτιρμοῦ** χρηστότητα ταπεινοφροσύνην πραΰτητα μακροθυμίαν, [GNT]
		Compassion, mercy, pity, tenderheartedness.
		
		Practical Application
		God has had so much mercy upon us, that the one thing we should do is to show mercy to others. Compassion and pity should flood our hearts for the...
		  • lost
		  • wayward
		  • lonely
		  • homeless
		  • hungry
		  • aged
		  • hurting
		  • diseased
		  • poor
		  • empty
		  • unclothed
		  • orphaned
		
		Of course, the list could go on and on. The point is that the believer no longer has the right to overlook the needy of the world. He is now a new man. A part of the clothing of the new man is the garment of compassion; the believer is to be clothed with compassion. He is to have mercy and reach out to meet the needs of the world—reach out with all he is and has, holding back nothing so long as a single need exists.

#2571
Mercy, Every
 	
Mercies–KJV
Mercies–NASB
Compassion–NIV
Mercies–NKJV
Every mercy–NLT
 	
POSB
REFERENCE
(2 Cor.1:3)
Note 1
	οἰκτιρμῶν = oiktirmōn
	Pronunciation: [oyk-tir-mon']
	Parsing (part of speech): noun
	    Case—genitive
	    Gender—masculine
	    Number—plural
	    Stem or root—from οἰκτιρμός, οῦ
	Concordance References:
	  ⇒ Strong's #3628 oiktirmos
	  ⇒ NIV #3880 oiktirmos
	  ⇒ NASB #3628 oiktirmos
	
	2 Cor. 1:3
	Blessed be God, even the Father of our Lord Jesus Christ, the Father of **mercies**, and the God of all comfort; [KJV]
	Blessed be the God and Father of our Lord Jesus Christ, the Father of **mercies** and God of all comfort; [NASB]
	Praise be to the God and Father of our Lord Jesus Christ, the Father of **compassion** and the God of all comfort, [NIV]
	Blessed *be* the God and Father of our Lord Jesus Christ, the Father of **mercies** and God of all comfort, [NKJV]
	All praise to the God and Father of our Lord Jesus Christ. He is the source of **every mercy** and the God who comforts us. [NLT]
	Εὐλογητὸς ὁ Θεὸς καὶ πατὴρ τοῦ Κυρίου ἡμῶν Ἰησοῦ Χριστοῦ, ὁ πατὴρ τῶν **οἰκτιρμῶν** καὶ Θεὸς πάσης
		Compassion, pity, and mercy. It means looking upon people in need and having compassion and mercy upon them.
		
		Practical Application
		⇒ Note that God is not the God of mercies but the Father of mercies. His very nature and behavior toward us is that of a Father, not of a God. He is our Father, a Father who is merciful and compassionate and who showers His mercies and compassions upon us.
		⇒ Note that the phrase "every mercy" [see parsing] is plural. God does not show mercy just once, nor just here and there. God showers His compassion upon us continuously (cp. Romans 12:1; Phil. 2:1; Col. 3:12; Hebrews 10:28).

ENGLISH WORD	GREEK WORD AND VERSE	THE WORD MEANS...
	παρακλήσεως, [GNS] Εὐλογητὸς ὁ θεὸς καὶ πατὴρ τοῦ κυρίου ἡμῶν Ἰησοῦ Χριστοῦ, ὁ πατὴρ τῶν **οἰκτιρμῶν** καὶ θεὸς πάσης παρακλήσεως, [GNT]	

#2572
Mercy On
 	
Merciful–KJV
Merciful–NASB
Mercy on–NIV
Merciful–NKJV
Merciful–NLT
 	
POSB REFERENCE
(Lk.18:13)
Note 4, point 3b
	ἰλάσθητί = *hilasthëti*
	Pronunciation: [hil-as'-thay-tee]
	Parsing (part of speech): verb
	    Mood—imperative
	    Tense—aorist
	    Voice—passive
	    Person—2nd person
	    Number—singular
	    Stem or root—from ἰλάσκομαι
	Concordance References:
	    ⇒ Strong's #2433 hilaskomai
	    ⇒ NIV #2661 hilaskomai
	    ⇒ NASB #2433 hilaskomai
	
	Luke 18:13
	And the publican, standing afar off, would not lift up so much as his eyes unto heaven, but smote upon his breast, saying, God be **merciful** to me a sinner. [KJV]
	    "But the tax-gatherer, standing some distance away, was even unwilling to lift up his eyes to heaven, but was beating his breast, saying, 'God, be **merciful** to me, the sinner!' [NASB]
	    "But the tax collector stood at a distance. He would not even look up to heaven, but beat his breast and said, 'God, have **mercy on** me, a sinner.' [NIV]
	    And the tax collector, standing afar off, would not so much as raise *his* eyes to heaven, but beat his breast, saying, 'God, be **merciful** to me a sinner!' [NKJV]
	    "But the tax collector stood at a distance and dared not even lift his eyes to heaven as he prayed. Instead, he beat his chest in sorrow, saying, 'O God, be **merciful** to me, for I am a sinner.' [NLT]
	    καὶ ὁ δὲ τελώνης μακρόθεν ἑστὼς οὐκ ἤθελεν οὐδὲ τοὺς ὀφθαλμοὺς εἰς τὸν οὐρανὸν ἐπᾶραι, ἀλλ' ἔτυπτεν τὸ στῆθος αὐτοῦ, λέγων, Ὁ Θεός, **ἰλάσθητί** μοι τῷ ἁμαρτωλῷ. [GNS]
	    ὁ δὲ τελώνης μακρόθεν ἑστὼς οὐκ ἤθελεν οὐδὲ τοὺς ὀφθαλμοὺς ἐπᾶραι εἰς τὸν οὐρανόν, ἀλλ' ἔτυπτεν τὸ στῆθος αὐτοῦ λέγων, Ὁ θεός, **ἰλάσθητί** μοι τῷ ἁμαρτωλῷ. [GNT]
		Propitiated, to have mercy on; to be merciful; to make atonement for.
		
		Practical Application
		    The sinner cried for mercy. There are two things to note.
		1. He called himself "the sinner" (*to hamartolo*). This is critical: he did not feel he was just "a sinner" like everyone else, which would mean he was also as good as everyone else. But he felt he was "the sinner," the one who had hurt and shamed God more than anyone else, the one who was more undeserving than anyone else. There was nothing good within him, nothing to commend him to God, nothing to make him acceptable to God.
		2. He cried for mercy. The word "mercy" (*hilastheti*) is really the word for "propitiated." He prayed for God to remove His anger and judgment from him. He deserved God's anger and judgment, but he begged God to turn His anger and judgment away. He felt he would die from the pressure within his chest unless God forgave him and gave him peace and assurance of forgiveness. He wanted to be reconciled to God; he wanted God to remove His judgment from him and to accept him.
		    Now note: he knew the only way he could ever be accepted by God was for God to have mercy upon him and to forgive his sins. He had no good thing about him, no righteousness to offer God. If he were going to be saved by God, God had to accept him simply because he came to God in all the desperation and sincerity of his heart and begged God for mercy. God alone was his hope, and mercy alone was all he could plead.

#2573
Mere Talkers
 	
Vain talkers–KJV
Empty talkers–NASB
Mere talkers–NIV
Idle talkers–NKJV
Useless talk–NLT
 	
POSB REFERENCE
(Tit.1:10-12; esp. v.10)
Note 1, point 2
	ματαιολόγοι = *mataiologoi*
	Pronunciation: [mat-ah-yol-og'-oy]
	Parsing (part of speech): pronominal adjective
	    Case—nominative
	    Gender—masculine
	    Number—plural
	    Stem or root—from ματαιολόγος, ου
	Concordance References:
	    ⇒ Strong's #3151 mataiologos
	    ⇒ NIV #3468 mataiologos
	    ⇒ NASB #3151 mataiologos
	
	Titus 1:10
	For there are many unruly and **vain talkers** and deceivers, specially they of the circumcision: [KJV]
	    For there are many rebellious men, **empty talkers** and deceivers, especially those of the circumcision, [NASB]
	    For there are many rebellious people, **mere talkers** and deceivers, especially those of the circumcision group. [NIV]
	    For there are many insubordinate, both **idle talkers** and deceivers, especially those of the circumcision, [NKJV]
	    For there are many who rebel against right teaching; they engage in **useless talk** and deceive people. This is especially true of those who insist on circumcision for sal-
		Mere talkers; vain talkers; empty talkers; useless talk.
		
		Practical Application
		    They were saying and teaching things that amounted to nothing and were worthless. Their teaching helped no one—not permanently and not eternally. Their teaching was not able to overcome sin and death—not able to bring true forgiveness of sin and eternal life to a person.

ENGLISH WORD	GREEK WORD AND VERSE	THE WORD MEANS...
	vation. [NLT] Εἰσὶ γὰρ πολλοὶ καὶ ἀνυπότακτοι, **ματαιολόγοι** καὶ φρεναπάται, μάλιστα οἱ ἐκ τῆς περιτομῆς, [GNS] Εἰσὶν γὰρ πολλοὶ [καὶ] ἀνυπότακτοι, **ματαιολόγοι** καὶ φρεναπάται, μάλιστα οἱ ἐκ τῆς περιτομῆς, [GNT]	

#2574
Message
 	
Testimony–KJV
Testimony–NASB
Testimony–NIV
Testimony–NKJV
Message–NLT
 	
POSB
REFERENCE
(1 Cor.2:1)
Note 1, point 3
	μυστήριον = *mustērion*
	Pronunciation: [mus-tay'-ree-on]
	Parsing (part of speech): noun
	    Case—accusative
	    Gender—neuter
	    Number—singular
	    Stem or root—from μυστήριον, ου
	Concordance References:
	⇒ Strong's #3142 mustērion
	⇒ NIV #3457 mustērion
	⇒ NASB #3142 mustērion
	
	1 Cor. 2:1
	And I, brethren, when I came to you, came not with excellency of speech or of wisdom, declaring unto you the **testimony** of God. [KJV]
	And when I came to you, brethren, I did not come with superiority of speech or of wisdom, proclaiming to you the **testimony** of God. [NASB]
	When I came to you, brothers, I did not come with eloquence or superior wisdom as I proclaimed to you the **testimony** about God. [NIV]
	And I, brethren, when I came to you, did not come with excellence of speech or of wisdom declaring to you the **testimony** of God. [NKJV]
	Dear brothers and sisters, when I first came to you I didn't use lofty words and brilliant ideas to tell you God's **message**. [NLT]
	Κἀγὼ ἐλθὼν πρὸς ὑμᾶς, ἀδελφοί, ἦλθον οὐ καθ' ὑπεροχὴν λόγου η σοφίας καταγγέλλων ὑμῖν τὸ **μυστήριον** τοῦ Θεοῦ. [GNS]
	Κἀγὼ ἐλθὼν πρὸς ὑμᾶς, ἀδελφοί, ἦλθον οὐ καθ' ὑπεροχὴν λόγου η σοφίας καταγγέλλων ὑμῖν τὸ **μυστήριον** τοῦ θεοῦ. [GNT]
		The testimony, the witness, the message or revelation of God.
		
		Practical Application
		The glorious message or revelation of God is Jesus Christ and Him crucified (1 Cor. 2:2). Preaching is not delivering eloquent speeches nor sound advice on...
		• self-development
		• self-image
		• positive thinking
		• philosophy
		• religion and its rituals
		• education
		• science
		• new and novel ideas
		• history
		
		All of these have their place, and what truth lies within each needs to be taught; but they are not the subjects that are to be preached by God's ministers to a lost world that is reeling under the weight of lonely, empty, starving, and suffering masses of people. The genuine preacher of God is to preach the testimony (marturion, mystery, revelation) of God.

#2575
Message
 	
Testifying–KJV
Testifying–NASB
Declared–NIV
Testifying–NKJV
Message–NLT
 	
POSB
REFERENCE
(Acts 20:20-21; esp. v.21)
Note 3, point 3
	διαμαρτυρόμενος = *diamarturomenos*
	Pronunciation: [dee-am-ar-too'-rom-ehn-os]
	Parsing (part of speech): verb
	    Mood—participle
	    Tense—present
	    Voice—middle or passive deponent
	    Case—nominative
	    Gender—masculine
	    Person—1st person
	    Number—singular
	    Stem or root—from διαμαρτύρομαι
	Concordance References:
	⇒ Strong's #1263 diamarturomai
	⇒ NIV #1371 diamarturomai
	⇒ NASB #1263 diamarturomai
	
	Acts 20:21
	Testifying both to the Jews, and also to the Greeks, repentance toward God, and faith toward our Lord Jesus Christ. [KJV]
	Solemnly **testifying** to both Jews and Greeks of repentance toward God and faith in our Lord Jesus Christ. [NASB]
	I have **declared** to both Jews and Greeks that they must turn to God in repentance and have faith in our Lord Jesus. [NIV]
	Testifying to Jews, and also to Greeks, repentance toward God and faith toward our Lord Jesus Christ. [NKJV]
	I have had one **message** for Jews and Gentiles alike—the necessity of turning from sin and turning to God, and of faith in our Lord Jesus. [NLT]
		To declare; to testify; to warn; to give a strong, sobering message.
		
		Practical Application
		Paul taught powerfully, as a man under oath. This is seen in the word "message" (*diamarturomenos*). He proclaimed the truth as a man of truth. He spoke with authority, as one who had the right of God Himself to testify.

ENGLISH WORD	GREEK WORD AND VERSE	THE WORD MEANS...
	διαμαρτυρόμενος Ἰουδαίοις τε καὶ Ἕλλησι τὴν εἰς Θεὸν μετάνοιαν καὶ τὴν πίστιν τὴν εἰς τὸν Κύριον ἡμῶν Ἰησοῦν Χριστόν. [GNS] διαμαρτυρόμενος Ἰουδαίοις τε καὶ Ἕλλησιν τὴν εἰς Θεὸν μετάνοιαν καὶ πίστιν εἰς τὸν κύριον ἡμῶν Ἰησοῦν. [GNT]	

#2576
Message Of Knowledge
 	
Word of knowledge–KJV
 	
Word of knowledge–NASB
 	
Message of knowledge–NIV
 	
Word of knowledge–NKJV
 	
Gift of special knowledge–NLT
 	
POSB REFERENCE
(1 Cor.12:8-10; esp. v.8)
Note 3, point 2
	λόγος γνώσεως = logos gnōseōs
	Pronunciation: [logos gno'-seh-os]
	Parsing gnōseōs (part of speech): noun
	    Case—genitive
	    Gender—feminine
	    Number—singular
	    Stem or root—from γνῶσις, εως
	Concordance References:
	⇒ Strong's #3056 logos + 1108 gnōsis
	⇒ NIV #3364 logos [message of] + 1194 gnōsis [knowledge]
	⇒ NASB #3056 logos + 1108 gnōsis
	
	1 Cor. 12:8
	For to one is given by the Spirit the word of wisdom; to another the **word of knowledge** by the same Spirit; [KJV]
	For to one is given the word of wisdom through the Spirit, and to another the **word of knowledge** according to the same Spirit; [NASB]
	To one there is given through the Spirit the message of wisdom, to another the **message of knowledge** by means of the same Spirit, [NIV]
	For to one is given the word of wisdom through the Spirit, to another the **word of knowledge** through the same Spirit, [NKJV]
	To one person the Spirit gives the ability to give wise advice; to another he gives the **gift of special knowledge**. [NLT]
	ᾧ μὲν γὰρ διὰ τοῦ Πνεύματος δίδοται λόγος σοφίας, ἄλλῳ δὲ **λόγος γνώσεως**, κατὰ τὸ αὐτὸ Πνεῦμα· [GNS]
	ᾧ μὲν γὰρ διὰ τοῦ πνεύματος δίδοται λόγος σοφίας, ἄλλῳ δὲ **λόγος γνώσεως** κατὰ τὸ αὐτὸ πνεῦμα, [GNT]
		Message, word of knowledge; a gift of practical knowledge.
		
		Practical Application
		This is practical knowledge. It is knowing what to do in the day-to-day situations that arise. It is knowing how to apply the wisdom that one has to daily living. It is being able to make practical application of truth to life. It does no good to know truth unless a person knows how to use the truth.
		The *message of knowledge* is the gift to share with others how they should live; the ability to apply truth to their lives in day-to-day living; the ability to make practical application of truth to life.

#2577
Message Of Wisdom
 	
Word of wisdom–KJV
Word of wisdom–NASB
 	
Message of wisdom–NIV
 	
Word of wisdom–NKJV
Ability to give wise advice–NLT
 	
POSB REFERENCE
(1 Cor.12:8-10; esp. v.8)
Note 3, point 1
	σοφίας λόγος = sophias logos
	Pronunciation: [sof-ee'-ahs log'-os]
	Parsing sophias (part of speech): noun
	    Case—genitive
	    Gender—feminine
	    Number—singular
	    Stem or root—from σοφία, ας
	Concordance References:
	⇒ Strong's #3056 logos + 4678 sophia
	⇒ NIV #3364 logos [message of] + 5053 sophia [wisdom]
	⇒ NASB #3056 logos + 4678 sophia
	
	1 Cor. 12:8
	For to one is given by the Spirit the **word of wisdom**; to another the word of knowledge by the same Spirit; [KJV]
	For to one is given the **word of wisdom** through the Spirit, and to another the word of knowledge according to the same Spirit; [NASB]
	To one there is given through the Spirit the **message of wisdom**, to another the message of knowledge by means of the same Spirit, [NIV]
	For to one is given the **word of wisdom** through the Spirit, to another the word of knowledge through the same Spirit, [NKJV]
	To one person the Spirit gives the **ability to give wise advice**; to another he gives the gift of special knowledge. [NLT]
	ᾧ μὲν γὰρ διὰ τοῦ Πνεύματος δίδοται λόγος **σοφίας**, ἄλλῳ δὲ **λόγος** γνώσεως, κατὰ τὸ αὐτὸ Πνεῦμα· [GNS]
	ᾧ μὲν γὰρ διὰ τοῦ πνεύματος δίδοται λόγος **σοφίας**, ἄλλῳ δὲ **λόγος** γνώσεως κατὰ τὸ αὐτὸ πνεῦμα, [GNT]
		Message or word of wisdom; the ability to give wise advice; insight, intelligence, knowledge, the wisdom of God.
		
		Practical Application
		The wisdom of God is the truth which God has now revealed to man; it is the whole system of truth revealed by God—the truth about God and man and the world. Therefore, the message of wisdom is the gift to share the wisdom and truth of God with men—to share the truth in simple and understandable language.

ENGLISH WORD	GREEK WORD AND VERSE	THE WORD MEANS...

#2580
Messiah
 	
Christ–KJV
Christ–NASB
Christ–NIV
Christ–NKJV
Messiah–NLT
 	
**POSB
REFERENCE**
(Mk.1:1)
Deeper Study #2
 	
See also POSB REF:
(Jn.1:20)
Deeper Study #2
(Mt.22:41-42; esp.
v.42)
Note 2, point 1
(Mk.12:35)
Note 2, point 1
	Χριστοῦ = *Christou*
	Pronunciation: [khris-too']
	Parsing (part of speech): noun
	    Case—genitive
	    Gender—masculine
	    Number—singular
	    Stem or root—from Χριστός, οῦ
	Concordance References:
	  ⇒ Strong's #5547 Christos
	  ⇒ NIV #5986 Christos
	  ⇒ NASB #5547 Christos
	
	Mark 1:1
	The beginning of the gospel of Jesus **Christ**, the Son of God; [KJV]
	The beginning of the gospel of Jesus **Christ**, the Son of God. [NASB]
	The beginning of the gospel about Jesus **Christ**, the Son of God. [NIV]
	The beginning of the gospel of Jesus **Christ**, the Son of God. [NKJV]
	Here begins the Good News about Jesus the **Messiah**, the Son of God. [NLT]
	Ἀρχη τοῦ εὐαγγελίου Ἰησοῦ **Χριστου** υἱοῦ Θεοῦ. [GNS]
	Ἀρχὴ τοῦ εὐαγγελίου Ἰησοῦ **Χριστου** [υἱοῦ θεοῦ]. [GNT]
		The Christ; the Messiah; the Anointed One.
		
		Practical Application
		The words "Christ" and "Messiah" (*Christou*) are the same word. *Messiah* is the Hebrew word and *Christ* is the Greek word. Both words refer to the same person and mean the same thing: the *Anointed One*. The Messiah is the *Anointed One of God*. Matthew says Jesus "is called Christ" (Matthew 1:16); that is, He is recognized as the *Anointed One of God*, the Messiah Himself.
		In the day of Jesus Christ, people feverishly panted for the coming of the long-promised Messiah. The weight of life was harsh, hard, and impoverished. Under the Romans the people felt that God could not wait much longer to fulfill His promise. Such longings for deliverance left the people gullible. Many arose who claimed to be the Messiah and led the gullible followers into rebellion against the Roman State. The insurrectionist Barabbas, who was set free in the place of Jesus at Jesus' trial, is an example (Mark 15:6f). (See POSB notes—Matthew 1:1; POSB *Deeper Study #2*—Matthew 3:11; POSB notes—Matthew 11:1-6; POSB note—Matthew 11:2-3; POSB *Deeper Study #1*—Matthew 11:5; POSB *Deeper Study #2*—Matthew 11:6; POSB note—Luke 7:21-23.)
		The Messiah was thought to be several things. (See POSB note, Davidic Prophecies—Luke 3:24-31.)
		1. Nationally, He was to be the leader from David's line who would free the Jewish state as an independent nation and lead it to be the greatest nation the world had ever known.
		2. Militarily, He was to be a great military leader who would lead Jewish armies victoriously over all the world.
		3. Religiously, He was to be a supernatural figure straight from God who would bring righteousness over all the earth.
		4. Personally, He was to be the One who would bring peace to the whole world.
		Jesus Christ accepted the title of Messiah on three different occasions (Matthew 16:17; Mark 14:61; John 4:26). The name "Jesus" shows Him to be man. The name "Messiah" shows Him to be God's Anointed One, God's very own Son. *Messiah* is Jesus' official title. It identifies Him officially as *Prophet* (Deut. 18:15-19), *Priest* (Psalm 110:4), and *King* (2 Samuel 7:12-13). These three officials were always anointed with oil, a symbol of the Holy Spirit who was to perfectly anoint the Christ, the Messiah (Matthew 3:16; Mark 1:10-11; Luke 3:21-22; John 1:32-33). (See POSB note—Luke 3:32-38 for more discussion, verses and fulfillment.)

#2581
Met Together
 	
Were together–KJV
Were together–NASB
Were together–NIV
Were together–NKJV
Met together–NLT
	ἦσαν ἐπὶ τὸ αὐτὸ = *ësan epi to auto*
	Pronunciation: [ay-san eh-pee to aw-to]
	Parsing *ësan* (part of speech): verb
	    Mood—indicative
	    Tense—imperfect
	    Voice—active
	    Person—3rd person
	    Number—plural
	    Stem or root—from εἰμί
		Were together; met together.
		
		Practical Application
		This means they were together in the same place because they were of the same call, mind, and purpose. It does not mean just being in the same location and place. They would not have been together unless they had been of the same spirit and purpose. This is critical to God's call.

ENGLISH WORD	GREEK WORD AND VERSE	THE WORD MEANS...
POSB REFERENCE (Acts 2:44-45; esp. v.44) Note 4, point 2	Parsing *epi* (part of speech): preposition Case—accusative Stem or root—from ἐπί Parsing *auto* (part of speech): pronominal adjective Case—accusative Gender—neuter Number—singular Stem or root—αὐτός, ή, ὁ Concordance References: ⇒ Strong's #1510 eimi + 846 + 1909 + 3588 autos epi ho ⇒ NIV #1639 eimi [were] + 899+ 2093+ 3836 autos epi ho [together] ⇒ NASB #1510 eimi + 846 + 1909 + 3588 autos epi ho **Acts 2:44** And all that believed **were together**, and had all things common; [KJV] And all those who had believed **were together**, and had all things in common; [NASB] All the believers **were together** and had everything in common. [NIV] Now all who believed **were together**, and had all things in common, [NKJV] And all the believers **met together** constantly and shared everything they had. [NLT] πάντες δὲ οἱ πιστεύοντες **ἦσαν ἐπὶ τὸ αὐτὸ** καὶ εἶχον ἄπαντα κοινά, [GNS] πάντες δὲ οἱ πιστεύοντες **ἦσαν ἐπὶ τὸ αὐτὸ** καὶ εἶχον ἄπαντα κοινά [GNT]	
#2582 **Met Together Continually** Continued with one accord–KJV Continually devoting themselves to–NASB Joined...constantly–NIV **Met together continually–NLT** **POSB REFERENCE** (Acts 1:12-15; esp. v.14) Note 1, point 4	**ἦσαν προσκαρτεροῦντες** = ësan proskarterountes Pronunciation: [ay-sahn pros-kar-ter-oon'-tes] Parsing *proskarterountes* (part of speech): verb Mood—participle Tense—present Voice—active Case—nominative Gender—masculine Number—plural Stem or root—from προσκαρτερέω Concordance References: ⇒ Strong's #1510 eimi + 4342 proskartereö ⇒ NIV #1639 eimi + 4674 proskartereö ⇒ NASB #1510 eimi + 4342 proskartereö **Acts 1:14** These all **continued with one accord** in prayer and supplication, with the women, and Mary the mother of Jesus, and with his brethren. [KJV] These all with one mind were **continually devoting themselves to** prayer, along with the women, and Mary the mother of Jesus, and with His brothers. [NASB] They all **joined** together **constantly** in prayer, along with the women and Mary the mother of Jesus, and with his brothers. [NIV] These all **continued with one accord** in prayer and supplication, with the women and Mary the mother of Jesus, and with His brothers. [NKJV] They all **met together continually** for prayer, along with Mary the mother of Jesus, several other women, and the brothers of Jesus. [NLT] οὗτοι πάντες **ἦσαν προσκαρτεροῦντες** ὁμοθυμαδὸν τῇ προσευχῇ καὶ τῇ δεήσει, σὺν γυναιξὶ καὶ Μαριά τῇ μητρὶ τοῦ Ἰησοῦ, καὶ σὺν τοῖς ἀδελφοῖς αὐτοῦ. [GNS] οὗτοι πάντες **ἦσαν προσκαρτεροῦντες** ὁμοθυμαδὸν τῇ προσευχῇ σὺν γυναιξὶν καὶ Μαριὰμ τῇ μητρὶ τοῦ Ἰησοῦ καὶ τοῖς ἀδελφοῖς αὐτοῦ. [GNT]	Joined constantly; to continue with one accord; continually devoting themselves; met together continually; to be in regular attendance. **Practical Application** The word is strong. They continued, persevered, endured, persisted, stuck to praying.
#2583 **Might–Mighty**	ἰσχύος = ischuos Pronunciation: [is-khoo-os'] Parsing (part of speech): noun Case—genitive	Strength, might, power, force, ability. It means the Lord's ability to use His strength and force wisely, that is, in perfection.

ENGLISH WORD	GREEK WORD AND VERSE	THE WORD MEANS...
Might–KJV **Might–NASB** **Mighty–NIV** **Might–NKJV** **Mighty–NLT** **POSB REFERENCE** (Eph.6:10-11; esp. v.10) Note 1, point 1	Gender—feminine Number—singular Stem or root—from ἰσχύς, ύος Concordance References: ⇒ Strong's #2479 ischus ⇒ NIV #2709 ischus ⇒ NASB #2479 ischus **Ephes. 6:10** Finally, my brethren, be strong in the Lord, and in the power of his **might**. [KJV] Finally, be strong in the Lord, and in the strength of His **might**. [NASB] Finally, be strong in the Lord and in his **mighty** power. [NIV] Finally, my brethren, be strong in the Lord and in the power of His **might**. [NKJV] A final word: Be strong with the Lord's **mighty** power. [NLT] Τὸ λοιπόν, ἀδελφοί μου, ἐνδυναμοῦσθε ἐν Κυρίῳ, καὶ ἐν τῷ κράτει τῆς **ἰσχύος** αὐτοῦ. [GNS] Τοῦ λοιποῦ, ἐνδυναμοῦσθε ἐν κυρίῳ καὶ ἐν τῷ κράτει τῆς **ἰσχύος** αὐτοῦ. [GNT]	**Practical Application** The believer is to be strong in the sovereign unlimited power of the Lord—in the power of His might—in His ability to use His power exactly as it should be used. (See POSB outline—Ephes. 1:19-23 and POSB notes—Ephes. 1:19-23 for more discussion on the power of God.) But note the significant point: the believer's strength is not human, fleshly strength; it is not the strength of anything within this world. The believer's strength is found *in the Lord*—in a living, dynamic relationship with Him. The Lord is the source of the believer's strength. There is no other source that can give man the strength to overcome this world with all its trials and temptations and death.

#2584
Mightily
 	
Mightily–KJV
Powerfully–NASB
Vigorously–NIV
Vigorously–NKJV
Powerful–NLT
 	
**POSB
REFERENCE**
(Acts 18:27-28; esp.
v.28)
Note 8, point 2a
	εὐτόνως = *eutonös*
	Pronunciation: [yoo-ton'-oce]
	Parsing (part of speech): adjective
	  Type— adverb
	  Stem or root—from εὐτόνως
	Concordance References:
	⇒ Strong's #2159 eutonös
	⇒ NIV #2364 eutonös
	⇒ NASB #2159 eutonös
	
	Acts 18:28
	For he **mightily** convinced the Jews, and that publickly, shewing by the scriptures that Jesus was Christ. [KJV]
	For he **powerfully** refuted the Jews in public, demonstrating by the Scriptures that Jesus was the Christ. [NASB]
	For he **vigorously** refuted the Jews in public debate, proving from the Scriptures that Jesus was the Christ. [NIV]
	For he **vigorously** refuted the Jews publicly, showing from the Scriptures that Jesus is the Christ. [NKJV]
	He refuted all the Jews with **powerful** arguments in public debate. Using the Scriptures, he explained to them, "The Messiah you are looking for is Jesus." [NLT]
	εὐτόνως γὰρ τοῖς Ἰουδαίοις διακατηλέγχετο δημοσίᾳ ἐπιδεικνὺς διὰ τῶν γραφῶν εἶναι τὸν Χριστόν, Ἰησοῦν. [GNS]
	εὐτόνως γὰρ τοῖς Ἰουδαίοις διακατηλέγχετο δημοσίᾳ ἐπιδεικνὺς διὰ τῶν γραφῶν εἶναι τὸν Χριστὸν Ἰησοῦν. [GNT]
		Vigorously, mightily, powerfully.
		
		Practical Application
		The word "mightily" (*eutonös*) means that Apollos used the Scriptures with power, straining earnestly to prove that Jesus is the Christ, the true Messiah.

#2585
Mighty Deeds
 	
Mighty deeds–KJV
Miracles–NASB
Miracles–NIV
Mighty deeds–NKJV
Miracles–NLT
 	
**POSB
REFERENCE**
(2 Cor.12:11-12; esp.
v.12)
Note 1
	δυνάμεσιν = *dunamesin*
	Pronunciation: [doo'-nam-eh-sin]
	Parsing (part of speech): noun
	  Case—dative
	  Gender—feminine
	  Number—plural
	  Stem or root—from δύναμις, εως
	Concordance References:
	⇒ Strong's #1411 dunamis
	⇒ NIV #1539 dunamis
	⇒ NASB #1411 dunamis
	
	2 Cor. 12:12
	Truly the signs of an apostle were wrought among you in all patience, in signs, and wonders, and **mighty deeds**. [KJV]
	The signs of a true apostle were performed among you
		Miracles, mighty deeds; an act of supernatural power; great works; powerful deeds.
		
		Practical Application
		Every minister should ask himself:
		⇒ Could I *defend* my ministry if it became necessary to defend it?
		⇒ Is my ministry *proven* by the signs of the ministry?
		⇒ Is the presence and power of God *upon* my life and work?
		⇒ Is my commitment to the ministry *equal to the commitment* of faithful ministers?

ENGLISH WORD	GREEK WORD AND VERSE	THE WORD MEANS...
	with all perseverance, by signs and wonders and **miracles**. [NASB] The things that mark an apostle—signs, wonders and **miracles**—were done among you with great perseverance. [NIV] Truly the signs of an apostle were accomplished among you with all perseverance, in signs and wonders and **mighty deeds**. [NKJV] When I was with you, I certainly gave you every proof that I am truly an apostle, sent to you by God himself. For I patiently did many signs and wonders and **miracles** among you. [NLT] τὰ μὲν σημεῖα τοῦ ἀποστόλου κατειργάσθη ἐν ὑμῖν ἐν πάσῃ ὑπομονῇ, ἐν σημείοις καὶ τέρασι καὶ **δυνάμεσι**. [GNS] τὰ μὲν σημεῖα τοῦ ἀποστόλου κατειργάσθη ἐν ὑμῖν ἐν πάσῃ ὑπομονῇ, σημείοις τε καὶ τέρασιν καὶ **δυνάμεσιν**. [GNT]	
#2586 **Mighty Power** **Mighty power**–KJV Greatness–NASB Greatness–NIV Majesty–NKJV Display of [God's] power–NLT **POSB REFERENCE** (Lk.9:42-43; esp. v.43) Note 3, point 2	**μεγαλειότητι** = *megaleiotēti* Pronunciation: [meg-al-i-ot'-ay-tee] Parsing (part of speech): noun 　Case—dative 　Gender—feminine 　Number—singular 　Stem or root—from μεγαλειότης, ητος Concordance References: ⇒　Strong's #3168 megaleiotēs ⇒　NIV #3484 megaleiotēs ⇒　NASB #3168 megaleiotēs **Luke 9:43** And they were all amazed at the **mighty power** of God. But while they wondered every one at all things which Jesus did, he said unto his disciples, [KJV] And they were all amazed at the **greatness** of God. But while everyone was marveling at all that He was doing, He said to His disciples, [NASB] And they were all amazed at the **greatness** of God.While everyone was marveling at all that Jesus did, he said to his disciples, [NIV] And they were all amazed at the **majesty** of God. But while everyone marveled at all the things which Jesus did, He said to His disciples, [NKJV] Awe gripped the people as they saw this **display of God's power**. While everyone was marveling over all the wonderful things he was doing, Jesus said to his disciples, [NLT] ἐξεπλήσσοντο δὲ πάντες ἐπὶ τῇ **μεγαλειότητι** τοῦ Θεοῦ. Πάντων δὲ θαυμαζόντων ἐπὶ πᾶσιν οἷς ἐποίει ὁ Ἰησοῦς, εἶπε πρὸς τοὺς μαθητὰς αὐτοῦ, [GNS] ἐξεπλήσσοντο δὲ πάντες ἐπὶ τῇ **μεγαλειότητι** τοῦ θεοῦ. Πάντων δὲ θαυμαζόντων ἐπὶ πᾶσιν οἷς ἐποίει εἶπεν πρὸς τοὺς μαθητὰς αὐτοῦ, [GNT]	Majesty, greatness, glory, mighty power; a display of God's glory and power. **Practical Application** They marvelled at "mighty power." Note that Jesus brought honor to God, not to Himself.
#2587 **Mighty Powers Who Rule This World** Rulers of world–KJV World forces–NASB Powers of...world–NIV Rulers of...age-NKJV **Mighty powers...who rule this world–NLT**	**κοσμοκράτορας** = *kosmokratoras* Pronunciation: [kos-mok-rat'-ore-ahs] Parsing (part of speech): noun 　Case—accusative 　Gender—masculine 　Number—plural 　Stem or root—from κοσμοκράτωρ, ορος Concordance References: ⇒　Strong's #2888 kosmokratōr ⇒　NIV #3179 kosmokratōr ⇒　NASB #2888 kosmokratōr **Ephes. 6:12** For we wrestle not against flesh and blood, but against principalities, against powers, against the **rulers** of the darkness **of** this **world**, against spiritual wickedness in high places. [KJV] For our struggle is not against flesh and blood, but	Powers of the world; rulers of the world; world forces; the mighty powers who rule this world. **Practical Application** Who is this? It refers to Satan and his demons. The forces of evil are the rulers of darkness, the rulers who blind the minds of men lest they believe the glorious gospel of eternal salvation. F.F. Bruce words it well: Satan and his demonic forces *"rank among the highest angel-princes in the hierarchy of the heavenly places, yet all of them owe their existence to Christ, through whom they were created [Col. 1:16], and who is accordingly*

ENGLISH WORD	GREEK WORD AND VERSE	THE WORD MEANS...
	ἔρχομαι. [GNS] καλέσας δὲ δέκα δούλους ἑαυτοῦ ἔδωκεν αὐτοῖς δέκα μνᾶς καὶ εἶπεν πρὸς αὐτούς, Πραγματεύσασθε ἐν ᾧ ἔρχόμαι. [GNT]	
#2591 **Mind.** Mind–KJV Mind–NASB Mind–NIV Mind–NKJV Mind–NLT **POSB REFERENCE** (Mk.12:30) Note 2, point 2	*διανοίας* = *dianoia* Pronunciation: [dee-an'-oy-ah] Parsing (part of speech): noun 　Case—genitive 　Gender—feminine 　Number—singular 　Stem or root—from διάνοια, ας Concordance References: ⇒ Strong's #1271 dianoia ⇒ NIV #1379 dianoia ⇒ NASB #1271 dianoia **Mark 12:30** And thou shalt love the Lord thy God with all thy heart, and with all thy soul, and with all thy **mind**, and with all thy strength: this is the first commandment. [KJV] And you shall love the Lord your God with all your heart, and with all your soul, and with all your **mind**, and with all your STRENGTH.' [NASB] Love the Lord your God with all your heart and with all your soul and with all your **mind** and with all your strength.' [NIV] *And you shall love the LORD your God with all your heart, with all your soul, with all your **mind**, and with all your strength.'* This *is* the first commandment. [NKJV] And you must love the Lord your God with all your heart, all your soul, all your **mind**, and all your strength.' [NLT] καὶ ἀγαπήσεις Κύριον τὸν Θεόν σου ἐξ ὅλης τῆς καρδίας σου, καὶ ἐξ ὅλης τῆς ψυχῆς σου, καὶ ἐξ ὅλης τῆς **διανοίας** σου, καὶ ἐξ ὅλης τῆς ἰσχύος σου. αὕτη πρώτη ἐντολή. [GNS] καὶ ἀγαπήσεις κύριον τὸν θεόν σου ἐξ ὅλης τῆς καρδίας σου καὶ ἐξ ὅλης τῆς ψυχῆς σου καὶ ἐξ ὅλης τῆς **διανοίας** σου καὶ ἐξ ὅλης τῆς ἰσχύος σου. [GNT]	Mind, thoughts, reasoning; the seat of reasoning, understanding, intention, purpose and attitude. **Practical Application** God has given intellectual powers to man. Man thinks, reasons, and understands. Christ says that our minds and thoughts are to be centered upon God. We are to love God "with all our mind."
#2592 **Mind** Mind–KJV Mind–NASB Thinking–NIV Mind–NKJV Not translated–NLT **POSB REFERENCE** (Eph.4:17-19; esp. v.17) Note 1, point 1	*νοός* = *noos* Pronunciation: [noose] Parsing (part of speech): noun 　Case—genitive 　Gender—masculine 　Number—singular 　Stem or root—from νοῦς, νοός, νοΐ, νοῦν Concordance References: ⇒ Strong's #3563 nous ⇒ NIV #3808 nous ⇒ NASB #3563 nous **Ephes. 4:17** This I say therefore, and testify in the Lord, that ye henceforth walk not as other Gentiles walk, in the vanity of their **mind**, [KJV] This I say therefore, and affirm together with the Lord, that you walk no longer just as the Gentiles also walk, in the futility of their **mind**, [NASB] So I tell you this, and insist on it in the Lord, that you must no longer live as the Gentiles do, in the futility of their **thinking**. [NIV] This I say, therefore, and testify in the Lord, that you should no longer walk as the rest of the Gentiles walk, in the futility of their **mind**, [NKJV] With the Lord's authority let me say this: Live no longer as the ungodly do, for they are hopelessly confused. [NLT]—NOT TRANSLATED Τοῦτο οὖν λέγω καὶ μαρτύρομαι ἐν Κυρίῳ, μηκέτι ὑμᾶς περιπατεῖν καθὼς καὶ τὰ λοιπὰ ἔθνη περιπατεῖ, ἐν ματαιότητι τοῦ **νοὸς** αὐτῶν, [GNS] Τοῦτο οὖν λέγω καὶ μαρτύρομαι ἐν κυρίῳ, μηκέτι ὑμᾶς περιπατεῖν, καθὼς καὶ τὰ ἔθνη περιπατεῖ ἐν ματαιότητι τοῦ **νοὸς** αὐτῶν, [GNT]	Thinking, mind, discernment, purpose, thought. The mind (*noos*) includes the ability to will and to do the truth as well as know the truth; it includes morality as well as reasoning and understanding. **Practical Application** When men push God out of their minds, their minds are void and empty of God and of His truth and morality. *God is not in their thoughts.* Their minds are ready to be filled with some other god or supremacy, that is, with the things of the world: ⇒ worldly pleasures ⇒ worldly possessions ⇒ worldly power ⇒ worldly position ⇒ worldly religions ⇒ worldly ideas ⇒ worldly honor ⇒ worldly gods

ENGLISH WORD	GREEK WORD AND VERSE	THE WORD MEANS...

#2593
Mind Controlled By The Spirit
 	
Spiritually minded–KJV
Mind set on the Spirit–NASB
Mind controlled by the Spirit–NIV
Spiritually minded–NKJV
Holy Spirit controls your mind–NLT
 	
POSB REFERENCE
(Romans 8:5-8, esp. v.6)
Note 3, point 2
	τὸ φρόνημα τοῦ πνεύματος = *to phronēma tou pneumatos*
	Pronunciation: [to fron'-ay-mah too pnyoo'-mah-tos]
	Parsing *phronēma* (part of speech): noun
	  Case—nominative
	  Gender—neuter
	  Number—singular
	  Stem or root—from φρόνημα, τος
	Parsing *pneumatos* (part of speech): noun
	  Case—genitive
	  Gender—neuter
	  Number—singular
	  Stem or root—from πνεῦμα, τος
	Concordance References:
	⇒ Strong's #3588 ho + 5427 phronēma + 3588 ho + 4151 pneuma
	⇒ NIV #3836 ho [the] + 5859 phronēma [mind] + 3836 ho [the] + 4460 pneuma [Spirit]
	⇒ NASB #3588 ho + 5427 phronēma + 3588 ho + 4151 pneuma
	
	Romans 8:6
	For to be carnally minded is death; but **to be spiritually minded** is life and peace. [KJV]
	For the mind set on the flesh is death, but **the mind set on the Spirit** is life and peace, [NASB]
	The mind of sinful man is death, but **the mind controlled by the Spirit** is life and peace; [NIV]
	For to be carnally minded *is* death, but to be **spiritually minded** *is* life and peace. [NKJV]
	If your sinful nature controls your mind, there is death. But if **the Holy Spirit controls your mind**, there is life and peace. [NLT]
	τὸ γὰρ φρόνημα τῆς σαρκὸς θάνατος· τὸ δὲ **φρόνημα τοῦ πνεύματος** ζωὴ καὶ εἰρήνη· [GNS]
	τὸ γὰρ φρόνημα τῆς σαρκὸς θάνατος, τὸ δὲ **φρόνημα τοῦ πνεύματος** ζωὴ καὶ εἰρήνη· [GNT]
		The self, mind, inner life, disposition controlled by the Holy Spirit; the mind set on the Spirit; to be spiritually minded.
		
		Practical Application
		The words "mind controlled by the Spirit" (*to phronēma tou pneumatos*) mean to be possessed by the Spirit or to be dominated by the Spirit. It means that the man who walks after the Spirit minds "the things of the Spirit" day by day. And note: it is the Spirit of God who draws the believer's mind to focus upon spiritual things. The Spirit of God lives within the believer. He is there to work within the believer, both to will and to do God's pleasure. He is there to keep the mind and thoughts of the believer focused upon spiritual things.

#2594
Mind Of Sinful Man
 	
Carnally minded–KJV
Mind set on the flesh–NASB
Mind of sinful man–NIV
To be carnally minded–NKJV
Sinful nature controls your mind–NLT
 	
POSB REFERENCE
(Rom.8:5-8; esp. v.6)
Note 3, point 1
	τὸ φρόνημα τῆς σαρκὸς = *to phronēma tēs sarkos*
	Pronunciation: [to fron'-ay-mah tace sar-kos]
	Parsing *phronēma* (part of speech): noun
	  Case—nominative
	  Gender—neuter
	  Number—singular
	  Stem or root—from φρόνημα, τος
	Parsing *sarkos* (part of speech): noun
	  Case—genitive
	  Gender—feminine
	  Number—singular
	  Stem or root—from σάρξ
	Concordance References:
	⇒ Strong's #3588 ho + 5427 phronēma + 3588 ho + 4561 sarx
	⇒ NIV #3836 ho [The] + 5859 phronēma [mind] + 3836 ho [Not in English] + 4922 sarx [sinful man]
	⇒ NASB #3588 ho + 5427 phronēma + 3588 ho + 4561 sarx
	
	Romans 8:6
	For **to be carnally minded** is death; but to be spiritually minded is life and peace. [KJV]
	For **the mind set on the flesh** is death, but the mind set on the Spirit is life and peace, [NASB]
	The mind of sinful man is death, but the mind controlled by the Spirit is life and peace; [NIV]
	For **to be carnally minded** is death, but to be spiritually minded is life and peace. [NKJV]
	If your **sinful nature controls your mind**, there is death. But if the Holy Spirit controls your mind, there is life and peace. [NLT]
	τὸ γὰρ **φρόνημα τῆς σαρκὸς** θάνατος· τὸ δὲ φρόνημα τοῦ πνεύματος ζωὴ καὶ εἰρήνη· [GNS]
	τὸ. γὰρ **φρόνημα τῆς σαρκὸς** θάνατος, τὸ δὲ φρόνημα τοῦ πνεύματος ζωὴ καὶ εἰρήνη· [GNT]
		To have a worldly, carnal, fleshly, mind and thoughts; to be controlled by your own sinful desires; to be unspiritual.
		
		Practical Application
		This is one of the most important passages in all of Scripture, for it discusses the human mind:
		
		For he is the kind of man who is always thinking about the cost...(Proverbs 23:7) [NIV]
		
		Where a man keeps his mind and what he thinks about determine who he is and what he does. If a man keeps his mind and thoughts in the gutter, he becomes part of the filth in the gutter. If he keeps his mind upon the *good*, he becomes good. If he focuses upon achievement and success, he achieves and succeeds. If his mind is filled with religious thoughts, he becomes religious. If his thoughts are focused upon God and righteousness, he becomes godly and righteous. A man becomes and does what he thinks. It is the law of the mind.

ENGLISH WORD	GREEK WORD AND VERSE	THE WORD MEANS...

#2595
 	
Mind On, Set–
Minds On, Set
 	
Set affection on–KJV
Set mind on–NASB
Set minds on–NIV
Set mind on–NKJV
Thoughts–NLT
 	
POSB
REFERENCE
(Col.3:1-4; esp. v.2)
Note 2
	φρονεῖτε = *phroneite*
	Pronunciation: [fron-eh'-ee-teh]
	Parsing (part of speech): verb
	   Mood—imperative
	   Tense—present
	   Voice—active
	   Person—2nd person
	   Number—plural
	   Stem or root—from φρονέω
	Concordance References:
	  ⇒ Strong's #5426 phroneö
	  ⇒ NIV #5858 phroneö
	  ⇒ NASB #5426 phroneö
	
	Col. 3:2
	  Set your **affection on** things above, not on things on the earth. [KJV]
	  Set your **mind on** the things above, not on the things that are on earth. [NASB]
	  Set your **minds on** things above, not on earthly things. [NIV]
	  Set your **mind on** things above, not on things on the earth. [NKJV]
	  Let heaven fill your **thoughts**. Do not think only about things down here on earth. [NLT]
	  τὰ ἄνω φρονεῖτε, μὴ τὰ ἐπὶ τῆς γῆς. [GNS]
	  τὰ ἄνω φρονεῖτε, μὴ τὰ ἐπὶ τῆς γῆς. [GNT]
		To set one's mind on; to set one's thoughts on; to have one's mind controlled. It means mind; to set and focus one's mind constantly upon heavenly things, not upon earthly things.
		
		Practical Application
		  Very simply, the things of Christ and of heaven are to consume the believer's life and mind. But for the believer to keep his mind upon the things of Christ he must know what those things are. Therefore, the question naturally arises: What are the things of Christ and the things of heaven which are to consume our thoughts?
		  The resurrection of Christ tells us what the things of Christ and of heaven are. It is His resurrection that allows us to be "*risen with Christ*." Remember: we actually take part and participate in the resurrection of Christ. This is a *positional relationship* to God. As stated in the former note, when we accept Christ, God places us in Christ positionally. He begins to see us *in* Christ, *already seated in the heavenlies and perfected forever* (cp. Ephes. 2:4-7). It is because of this glorious position which God has given us that we should seek the things of Christ and of heaven.

#2596
 	
Mind Set On
The Flesh
 	
Carnally minded–KJV
Mind set on the
flesh–NASB
Mind of sinful man–
  NIV
Carnally minded–
  NKJV
Sinful nature controls
  your mind–NLT
 	
POSB
REFERENCE
(Rom.8:5-8; esp. v.6)
Note 3, point 1
	τὸ φρόνημα τῆς σαρκὸς = *to phronema tës sarkos*
	Pronunciation: [to fron'-ay-mah tace sar-kos]
	Parsing *phronëma* (part of speech): noun
	   Case—nominative
	   Gender—neuter
	   Number—singular
	   Stem or root—from φρόνημα, τος
	Parsing *sarkos* (part of speech): noun
	   Case—genitive
	   Gender—feminine
	   Number—singular
	   Stem or root—from σάρξ
	Concordance References:
	  ⇒ Strong's #3588 ho + 5427 phronëma + 3588 ho + 4561 sarx
	  ⇒ NIV #3836 ho [The] + 5859 phronëma [mind] + 3836 ho [Not in English] + 4922 sarx [sinful man]
	  ⇒ NASB #3588 ho + 5427 phronëma + 3588 ho + 4561 sarx
	
	Romans 8:6
	  For **to be carnally minded** is death; but to be spiritually minded is life and peace. [KJV]
	  For **the mind set on the flesh** is death, but the mind set on the Spirit is life and peace, [NASB]
	  The mind of sinful man is death, but the mind controlled by the Spirit is life and peace; [NIV]
	  For to be **carnally minded** *is* death, but to be spiritually minded *is* life and peace. [NKJV]
	  If your **sinful nature controls your mind**, there is death. But if the Holy Spirit controls your mind, there is life and peace. [NLT]
	  τὸ γὰρ φρόνημα τῆς σαρκὸς θάνατος· τὸ δὲ φρόνημα τοῦ πνεύματος ζωὴ καὶ εἰρήνη· [GNS]
	  τὸ γὰρ φρόνημα τῆς σαρκὸς θάνατος, τὸ δὲ φρόνημα τοῦ πνεύματος ζωὴ καὶ εἰρήνη· [GNT]
		To have a worldly, carnal, fleshly, mind and thoughts; to be controlled by your own sinful desires; to be unspiritual.
		
		Practical Application
		  This is one of the most important passages in all of Scripture, for it discusses the human mind:
		
		  As he [a man] thinks within himself, so he is (Proverbs 23:7). [NASB]
		
		  Where a man keeps his mind and what he thinks about determine who he is and what he does. If a man keeps his mind and thoughts in the gutter, he becomes part of the filth in the gutter. If he keeps his mind upon the *good*, he becomes good. If he focuses upon achievement and success, he achieves and succeeds. If his mind is filled with religious thoughts, he becomes religious. If his thoughts are focused upon God and righteousness, he becomes godly and righteous. A man becomes and does what he thinks. It is the law of the mind.

#2597
 	
Mind Set On
The Spirit
 	
Spiritually minded–
  KJV
	τὸ φρόνημα τοῦ πνεύματος = *to phronëma tou pneumatos*
	Pronunciation: [to fron'-ay-mah too pnyoo'-mah-tos]
	Parsing *phronëma* (part of speech): noun
	   Case—nominative
	   Gender—neuter
	   Number—singular
		Mind controlled by the Spirit; spiritually minded.
		
		Practical Application
		  The words "mind set on the Spirit" (*to phronëma tou pneumatos*) mean to be possessed

ENGLISH WORD	GREEK WORD AND VERSE	THE WORD MEANS...
Mind set on the Spirit–NASB Mind controlled by the Spirit–NIV Spiritually minded–NKJV Holy Spirit controls your mind–NLT **POSB REFERENCE** (Romans 8:5-8, esp. v.6) Note 3, point 2	Stem or root—from φρόνημα, τος Parsing *pneumatos* (part of speech): noun Case—genitive Gender—neuter Number—singular Stem or root—from πνεῦμα, τος Concordance References: ⇒ Strong's #3588 ho + 5427 phronëma + 3588 ho + 4151 pneuma ⇒ NIV #3836 ho [the] + 5859 phronëma [mind] + 3836 ho [the] + 4460 pneuma [Spirit] ⇒ NASB #3588 ho + 5427 phronëma + 3588 ho + 4151 pneuma **Romans 8:6** For to be carnally minded is death; but to be **spiritually minded** is life and peace. [KJV] For the mind set on the flesh is death, but **the mind set on the Spirit** is life and peace, [NASB] The mind of sinful man is death, but **the mind controlled by the Spirit** is life and peace; [NIV] For to be carnally minded *is* death, but to be **spiritually minded** *is* life and peace. [NKJV] If your sinful nature controls your mind, there is death. But if **the Holy Spirit controls your mind**, there is life and peace. [NLT] τὸ γὰρ φρόνημα τῆς σαρκὸς θάνατος· **τὸ** δὲ **φρόνημα τοῦ πνεύματος** ζωὴ καὶ εἰρήνη· [GNS] τὸ γὰρ φρόνημα τῆς σαρκὸς θάνατος, **τὸ** δὲ **φρόνημα τοῦ πνεύματος** ζωὴ καὶ εἰρήνη· [GNT]	by the Spirit or to be controlled and dominated by the Spirit. It means that the man who walks after the Spirit minds "the things of the Spirit" day by day. And note: it is the Spirit of God who draws the believer's mind to focus upon spiritual things. The Spirit of God lives within the believer. He is there to work within the believer, both to will and to do God's pleasure; He is there to keep the mind and thoughts of the believer focused upon spiritual things.
#2598 Minister Minister–KJV Minister–NASB Minister–NIV Minister–NKJV Special messenger– NLT **POSB REFERENCE** (Rom.15:16) Note 3	λειτουργὸν = *leitourgon* Pronunciation: [li-toorg-own'] Parsing (part of speech): noun Case—accusative Gender—masculine Number—singular Stem or root—from λειτουργός, οῦ Concordance References: ⇒ Strong's #3011 leitourgos ⇒ NIV #3313 leitourgos ⇒ NASB #3011 leitourgos **Romans 15:16** That I should be the **minister** of Jesus Christ to the Gentiles, ministering the gospel of God, that the offering up of the Gentiles might be acceptable, being sanctified by the Holy Ghost. [KJV] To be a **minister** of Christ Jesus to the Gentiles, ministering as a priest the gospel of God, that my offering of the Gentiles might become acceptable, sanctified by the Holy Spirit. [NASB] To be a **minister** of Christ Jesus to the Gentiles with the priestly duty of proclaiming the gospel of God, so that the Gentiles might become an offering acceptable to God, sanctified by the Holy Spirit. [NIV] That I might be a **minister** of Jesus Christ to the Gentiles, ministering the gospel of God, that the offering of the Gentiles might be acceptable, sanctified by the Holy Spirit. [NKJV] A **special messenger** from Christ Jesus to you Gentiles. I bring you the Good News and offer you up as a fragrant sacrifice to God so that you might be pure and pleasing to him by the Holy Spirit. [NLT] εἰς τὸ εἶναί με **λειτουργὸν** Ἰησοῦ Χριστοῦ εἰς τὰ ἔθνη, ἱερουργοῦντα τὸ εὐαγγέλιον τοῦ Θεοῦ, ἵνα γένηται ἡ προσφορὰ τῶν ἐθνῶν εὐπρόσδεκτος, ἡγιασμένη ἐν Πνεύματι Ἁγίῳ. [GNS] εἰς τὸ εἶναί με **λειτουργὸν** Χριστοῦ Ἰησοῦ εἰς τὰ ἔθνη, ἱερουργοῦντα τὸ εὐαγγέλιον τοῦ Θεοῦ, ἵνα γένηται ἡ προσφορὰ τῶν ἐθνῶν εὐπρόσδεκτος, ἡγιασμένη ἐν πνεύματι ἁγίῳ. [GNT]	Servant, minister, special messenger. **Practical Application** The minister of God is called to minister the gospel of God. When Paul called himself a minister (*leitourgon*), the Greek word was often used to refer to the priests of the Old Testament. This is a beautiful passage describing the nature of the Christian ministry. The Christian ministry is seen as a priestly ministry. However, we must always remember that the ministry is not an office to make atonement for sin, nor to offer a propitiatory sacrifice to God. It is a ministry of preaching the gospel under the influence of the Holy Spirit. The purpose of the ministry is this: to bring men to the point where they will offer themselves as living sacrifices, holy, acceptable to God (cp. Romans 12:1-2). A minister's only priesthood is the preaching of the gospel, and his only offering is the offering of redeemed and sanctified men to God. He is not a mediator between God and men; he does not offer propitiatory sacrifices. He is only an instrument which God uses to share the gospel of salvation with men. He is a priest only in the sense that he serves the gospel of God to men and brings men to God through the gospel of God. Note what the "offering" was that God wanted Paul to make: the offering of the Gentiles, of human lives. God wanted Paul to bring people to Him. This is the task of ministers: to offer the lives of men, women, boys, and girls to God.

ENGLISH WORD	GREEK WORD AND VERSE	THE WORD MEANS...
#2599 **Minister** **Minister–KJV** Helper–NASB Helper–NIV Assistant–NKJV Assistant–NLT **POSB REFERENCE** (Acts 13:5-6; esp. v.5) Note 2, point 2	ὑπηρέτην = *hupéretēn* Pronunciation: [hoop-ay-ret'-ayn] Parsing (part of speech): noun 　　Case—accusative 　　Gender—masculine 　　Number—singular 　　Stem or root—from ὑπηρέτης, ου Concordance References: 　⇒ Strong's #5257 hupéretēs 　⇒ NIV #5677 hupéretēs 　⇒ NASB #5257 hupéretēs **Acts 13:5** And when they were at Salamis, they preached the word of God in the synagogues of the Jews: and they had also John to their **minister**. [KJV] And when they reached Salamis, they began to proclaim the word of God in the synagogues of the Jews; and they also had John as their **helper**. [NASB] When they arrived at Salamis, they proclaimed the word of God in the Jewish synagogues. John was with them as their **helper**. [NIV] And when they arrived in Salamis, they preached the word of God in the synagogues of the Jews. They also had John as *their* **assistant**. [NKJV] There, in the town of Salamis, they went to the Jewish synagogues and preached the word of God. (John Mark went with them as their **assistant**.) [NLT] καὶ γενόμενοι ἐν Σαλαμῖνι, κατήγγελλον τὸν λόγον τοῦ Θεοῦ ἐν ταῖς συναγωγαῖς τῶν Ἰουδαίων· εἶχον δὲ καὶ Ἰωάννην ὑπηρέτην. [GNS] καὶ γενόμενοι ἐν Σαλαμῖνι κατήγγελλον τὸν λόγον τοῦ θεοῦ ἐν ταῖς συναγωγαῖς τῶν Ἰουδαίων. εἶχον δὲ καὶ Ἰωάννην ὑπηρέτην. [GNT]	Helper, minister, assistant, attendant, servant. **Practical Application** Mark was ministering under Barnabas and Paul, being discipled by them—helping, serving, ministering right with them, learning all he could. Apparently he was somewhat younger.
#2600 **Minister– Ministered** **Ministered–KJV** Minister–NASB Take care–NIV Ministered–NKJV Help–NLT **POSB REFERENCE** (Philip.2:25) Note 1, point 5	λειτουργὸν = *leitourgon* Pronunciation: [li-toorg-on'] Parsing (part of speech): noun 　　Case—accusative 　　Gender—masculine 　　Number—singular 　　Stem or root—from λειτουργός, οῦ Concordance References: 　⇒ Strong's #3011 leitourgos 　⇒ NIV #3313 leitourgos 　⇒ NASB #3011 leitourgos **Philip. 2:25** Yet I supposed it necessary to send to you Epaphroditus, my brother, and companion in labour, and fellow soldier, but your messenger, and he that **ministered** to my wants. [KJV] But I thought it necessary to send to you Epaphroditus, my brother and fellow worker and fellow soldier, who is also your messenger and **minister** to my need; [NASB] But I think it is necessary to send back to you Epaphroditus, my brother, fellow worker and fellow soldier, who is also your messenger, whom you sent to **take care** of my needs. [NIV] Yet I considered it necessary to send to you Epaphroditus, my brother, fellow worker, and fellow soldier, but your messenger and the one who **ministered** to my need; [NKJV] Meanwhile, I thought I should send Epaphroditus back to you. He is a true brother, a faithful worker, and a courageous soldier. And he was your messenger to **help** me in my need. [NLT] ἀναγκαῖον δὲ ἡγησάμην Ἐπαφρόδιτον τὸν ἀδελφὸν καὶ συνεργὸν καὶ συστρατιώτην μου, ὑμῶν δὲ ἀπόστολον, καὶ **λειτουργὸν** τῆς χρείας μου, πέμψαι πρὸς ὑμᾶς· [GNS]	To take care; to minister; to help; to be a servant. **Practical Application** Epaphroditus was a very special minister (*leitourgon*). William Barclay points out that this word would have great meaning to the Greek minds of the Philippian church. The word (*leitourgon*) was a great word and was used only of great men. The title was bestowed only upon great benefactors, men who loved their city, culture, arts, or sports so much that they gave huge sums of money to support these functions. The person was looked upon as a great servant or minister given over to his cause. (*The Letters to the Phillipians, Colossians, and Thessalonians,* p.61.) Paul is here bestowing the great title of minister (*leitourgon*) upon Epaphroditus. Epaphroditus was an extraordinary minister of God who ministered to Paul's needs. He was not a quitter! He was not a coward!

ENGLISH WORD	GREEK WORD AND VERSE	THE WORD MEANS...
	Ἀναγκαῖον δὲ ἡγησάμην Ἐπαφρόδιτον τὸν ἀδελφὸν καὶ συνεργὸν καὶ συστρατιώτην μου, ὑμῶν δὲ ἀπόστολον καὶ **λειτουργὸν** τῆς χρείας μου, πέμψαι πρὸς ὑμᾶς, [GNT]	

#2601
Ministers
 	
Ministers–KJV
Servants–NASB
Servants–NIV
Ministers–NKJV
Servants–NLT
 	
POSB
REFERENCE
(1 Cor.3:5)
Note 1
	διάκονοι = *diakonoi*
	Pronunciation: [dee-ak'-on-oy]
	Parsing (part of speech): noun
	    Case—nominative
	    Gender—masculine
	    Number—plural
	    Stem or root—from διάκονος, ου
	Concordance References:
	  ⇒ Strong's #1249 diakonos
	  ⇒ NIV #1356 diakonos
	  ⇒ NASB #1249 diakonos
	
	1 Cor. 3:5
	Who then is Paul, and who is Apollos, but **ministers** by whom ye believed, even as the Lord gave to every man? [KJV]
	What then is Apollos? And what is Paul? **Servants** through whom you believed, even as the Lord gave opportunity to each one. [NASB]
	What, after all, is Apollos? And what is Paul? Only **servants**, through whom you came to believe—as the Lord has assigned to each his task. [NIV]
	Who then is Paul, and who *is* Apollos, but **ministers** through whom you believed, as the Lord gave to each one? [NKJV]
	Who is Apollos, and who is Paul, that we should be the cause of such quarrels? Why, we're only **servants**. Through us God caused you to believe. Each of us did the work the Lord gave us. [NLT]
	τίς οὖν ἐστι Παῦλος; τίς δὲ Ἀπολλώς; ἀλλ η **διάκονοι** δι᾽ ὧν ἐπιστεύσατε, καὶ ἑκάστῳ ὡς ὁ Κύριος ἔδωκεν, [GNS]
	τί οὖν ἐστιν Ἀπολλῶς; τί δέ ἐστιν Παῦλος; **διάκονοι** δι᾽ ὧν ἐπιστεύσατε, καὶ ἑκάστῳ ὡς ὁ κύριος ἔδωκεν. [GNT]
		A servant, an attendant, a helper, or a waiter on tables.
		
		Practical Application
		The stress is upon the lowly status of the service. Ministers; yes, even all believers, are not *lords* over God's flock and church; they are the lowly servants. They are the servants of God and the servants of God's people.

#2602
Ministers
 	
Ministers–KJV
Servants–NASB
Servants–NIV
Servants–NKJV
Servants–NLT
 	
POSB
REFERENCE
(1 Cor.4:1-2; esp. v.1)
Note 1
	ὑπηρέτας = *hupēretas*
	Pronunciation: [hoop-ay-ret'-ahs]
	Parsing (part of speech): noun
	    Case—accusative
	    Gender—masculine
	    Number—plural
	    Stem or root—from ὑπηρέτης, ου
	Concordance References:
	  ⇒ Strong's #5257 hupēretēs
	  ⇒ NIV #5677 hupēretēs
	  ⇒ NASB #5257 hupēretēs
	
	1 Cor. 4:1
	Let a man so account of us, as of the **ministers** of Christ, and stewards of the mysteries of God. [KJV]
	Let a man regard us in this manner, as **servants** of Christ, and stewards of the mysteries of God. [NASB]
	So then, men ought to regard us as **servants** of Christ and as those entrusted with the secret things of God. [NIV]
	Let a man so consider us, as **servants** of Christ and stewards of the mysteries of God. [NKJV]
	So look at Apollos and me as mere **servants** of Christ who have been put in charge of explaining God's secrets. [NLT]
	Οὕτως ἡμᾶς λογιζέσθω ἄνθρωπος ὡς **ὑπηρέτας** Χριστοῦ καὶ οἰκονόμους μυστηρίων Θεοῦ. [GNS]
	Οὕτως ἡμᾶς λογιζέσθω ἄνθρωπος ὡς **ὑπηρέτας** Χριστοῦ καὶ οἰκονόμους μυστηρίων θεοῦ. [GNT]
		Servants, attendants, helper, an under-rower.
		
		Practical Application
		It refers to the slaves who sat in the belly of the large ships and pulled at the great oars to carry the boat through the sea. Christ is the Master of the ship and each believer is *one of the slaves of Christ*. Note: he is only one of many under-rowing servants. Remember also that slaves in the belly of the ship were bound by chains. They were allowed to do nothing but serve the master of the ship. The believer is a bound slave of Christ: he exists only to row for the Master. He does not and cannot serve anyone else.

#2603 **Ministry**	διακονίαν = *diakonian* Pronunciation: [dee-ak-on-ee'-ahn] Parsing (part of speech): noun Case—accusative	Service; ministry, contribution, help, support, mission; perhaps office of deacon or authority (Ro.12.7).

ENGLISH WORD	GREEK WORD AND VERSE	THE WORD MEANS...
Ministry–KJV Service–NASB Serving–NIV **Ministry–NKJV** Serving–NLT **POSB REFERENCE** (Rom.12:6-8; esp. v.7) Note 2, point 2	Gender—feminine Number—singular Stem or root—from διακονία, ας Concordance References: ⇒ Strong's #1248 diakonia ⇒ NIV #1355 diakonia ⇒ NASB #1248 diakonia **Romans 12:7** Or **ministry**, let us wait on our ministering: or he that teacheth, on teaching; [KJV] If **service**, in his serving; or he who teaches, in his teaching; [NASB] If it is **serving**, let him serve; if it is teaching, let him teach; [NIV] Or **ministry**, *let us use it* in *our* ministering; he who teaches, in teaching; [NKJV] If your gift is that of **serving** others, serve them well. If you are a teacher, do a good job of teaching. [NLT] εἴτε **διακονίαν**, ἐν τῇ διακονίᾳ· εἴτε ὁ διδάσκων, ἐν τῇ διδασκαλίᾳ· [GNS] εἴτε **διακονίαν** ἐν τῇ διακονίᾳ, εἴτε ὁ διδάσκων ἐν τῇ διδασκαλίᾳ, [GNT]	**Practical Application** The word is often used of a servant or of a person who serves and ministers to others in the most practical ways. Therefore, the meaning would be the very special ability to serve, minister, aid, help and assist others—to assist them in such a way that they are built up and truly helped. It is the most practical of gifts. Most of us know a few people who are always willing and who are unusually gifted to help others when help is needed. All of us can help, and all of us can develop our willingness and ability to help, but there are some believers who are unusually gifted with the very special gift of ministry.
#2604 Miracles Mighty deeds–KJV **Miracles–NASB** **Miracles–NIV** Mighty deeds–NKJV **Miracles–NLT** **POSB REFERENCE** (2 Cor.12:11-12; esp. v.12) Note 1	δυνάμεσιν = *dunamesin* Pronunciation: [doo'-nam-eh-sin] Parsing (part of speech): noun Case—dative Gender—feminine Number—plural Stem or root—from δύναμις, εως Concordance References: ⇒ Strong's #1411 dunamis ⇒ NIV #1539 dunamis ⇒ NASB #1411 dunamis **2 Cor. 12:12** Truly the signs of an apostle were wrought among you in all patience, in signs, and wonders, and **mighty deeds**. [KJV] The signs of a true apostle were performed among you with all perseverance, by signs and wonders and **miracles**. [NASB] The things that mark an apostle—signs, wonders and **miracles**—were done among you with great perseverance. [NIV] Truly the signs of an apostle were accomplished among you with all perseverance, in signs and wonders and **mighty deeds**. [NKJV] When I was with you, I certainly gave you every proof that I am truly an apostle, sent to you by God himself. For I patiently did many signs and wonders and **miracles** among you. [NLT] τὰ μὲν σημεῖα τοῦ ἀποστόλου κατειργάσθη ἐν ὑμῖν ἐν πάσῃ ὑπομονῇ, ἐν σημείοις καὶ τέρασι καὶ **δυνάμεσι**. [GNS] τὰ μὲν σημεῖα τοῦ ἀποστόλου κατειργάσθη ἐν ὑμῖν ἐν πάσῃ ὑπομονῇ, σημείοις τε καὶ τέρασιν καὶ **δυνάμεσιν**. [GNT]	Miracles, mighty deeds; an act of supernatural power; great works; powerful deeds. **Practical Application** Every minister should ask himself: ⇒ Could I *defend* my ministry if it became necessary to defend it? ⇒ Is my ministry *proven* by the signs of the ministry? ⇒ Is the presence and power of God *upon* my life and work? ⇒ Is my commitment to the ministry *equal to the commitment* of faithful ministers?
#2605 Miraculous Signs– Miracles **Miracles–KJV** Signs–NASB **Miraculous signs– NIV** Signs–NKJV **Miraculous signs– NLT**	σημεῖα = *sēmeia* Pronunciation: [say-mi'-ah] Parsing (part of speech): noun Case—accusative Gender—neuter Number—plural Stem or root—from σημεῖον, ου Concordance References: ⇒ Strong's #4592 sēmeion ⇒ NIV #4956 sēmeion ⇒ NASB #4592 sēmeion	Miraculous signs; miracles; supernatural; extraordinary. **Practical Application** In this Scripture, it means a sign that characterizes the person of Christ, the nature and character of Christ. There are four words used in the Bible for miracles or signs. These words are used to describe the works of God and they show why people believed in Jesus. 1. *Teras* means the spectacular, staggering, amazing, dazzling signs. Many believed in

ENGLISH WORD	GREEK WORD AND VERSE	THE WORD MEANS...

POSB REFERENCE
(Jn.2:23)
Note 1, point 2

See also POSB REF:
(Jn.2:23)
Deeper Study #1

John 2:23

Now when he was in Jerusalem at the passover, in the feast day, many believed in his name, when they saw the **miracles** which he did. [KJV]

Now when He was in Jerusalem at the Passover, during the feast, many believed in His name, beholding His **signs** which He was doing. [NASB]

Now while he was in Jerusalem at the Passover Feast, many people saw the **miraculous signs** he was doing and believed in his name. [NIV]

Now when He was in Jerusalem at the Passover, during the feast, many believed in His name when they saw the **signs** which He did. [NKJV]

Because of the **miraculous signs** he did in Jerusalem at the Passover celebration, many people were convinced that he was indeed the Messiah. [NLT]

Ὡς δὲ ἦν ἐν Ἱεροσολύμοις ἐν τῷ πάσχα ἐν τῇ ἑορτῇ, πολλοὶ ἐπίστευσαν εἰς τὸ ὄνομα αὐτοῦ, θεωροῦντες αὐτοῦ τὰ **σημεῖα** ἃ ἐποίει. [GNS]

Ὡς δὲ ἦν ἐν τοῖς Ἱεροσολύμοις ἐν τῷ πάσχα ἐν τῇ ἑορτῇ, πολλοὶ ἐπίστευσαν εἰς τὸ ὄνομα αὐτοῦ θεωροῦντες αὐτοῦ τὰ **σημεῖα** ἃ ἐποίει· [GNT]

Jesus because of the spectacular signs He performed. However, such belief made a person only a spectator, not a participant in His life. The word *teras* also means the sensational; that is, it appeals to the sensations of men. Many believed and followed Jesus because it made them feel good and comfortable and secure. Such belief is weak and often fails. This word is never used by itself to initiate faith in the Lord Jesus. If a person is to have genuine faith in the Lord Jesus, he must have some basis other than the spectacular sign (*teras*).

2. *Dunamis* means power—unusual, extraordinary power; effective, explosive power. There were those who were attracted to Jesus because of the unusual power (*dunamis*) they witnessed. They believed because of the power. Such is a legitimate belief and leads to salvation for everyone who believes.

3. *Ergon* means distinctive works, deeds, and miracles. Such works come from God (John 14:10) and bear witness to Christ. They point men to Christ (John 5:36; John 10:25). Some men look at the very special works of Christ and believe because of the works (*ergon*).

4. *Semeion* (*sēmeia*) means a sign that characterizes the person, his nature and character. A few throughout Jesus' ministry did believe because they saw in the miracles exactly who He was, the very Son of God. However, the word "semeion" is also used of those who believed the signs, but did not have the highest or right kind of faith. Their faith was not a faith that committed itself (see POSB *Deeper Study* #2—John 2:24).

#2606
Mischief

Mischief–KJV
Fraud–NASB
Trickery–NIV
Fraud–NKJV
Trickery–NLT

POSB REFERENCE
(Acts 13:8-11; esp. v.10)
Note 4, point 3

ῥᾳδιουργίας = *hradiourgias*
Pronunciation: [hrad-ee-oorg-ee'-ahs]
Parsing (part of speech): noun
  Case—genitive
  Gender—feminine
  Number—singular
  Stem or root—from ῥᾳδιουργία, ας
Concordance References:
⇒ Strong's #4468 hradiourgia
⇒ NIV #4816 hradiourgia
⇒ NASB #4468 hradiourgia

Acts 13:10

And said, O full of all subtilty and all **mischief**, thou child of the devil, thou enemy of all righteousness, wilt thou not cease to pervert the right ways of the Lord? [KJV]

And said, "You who are full of all deceit and **fraud**, you son of the devil, you enemy of all righteousness, will you not cease to make crooked the straight ways of the Lord? [NASB]

"You are a child of the devil and an enemy of everything that is right! You are full of all kinds of deceit and **trickery**. Will you never stop perverting the right ways of the Lord? [NIV]

And said, "O full of all deceit and all **fraud**, *you* son of the devil, *you* enemy of all righteousness, will you not cease perverting the straight ways of the Lord? [NKJV]

"You son of the Devil, full of every sort of **trickery** and villainy, enemy of all that is good, will you never stop perverting the true ways of the Lord? [NLT]

εἶπεν, Ὦ πλήρης παντὸς δόλου καὶ πάσης ῥᾳδιουργίας, υἱὲ διαβόλου, ἐχθρὲ πάσης δικαιοσύνης, οὐ

Trickery, mischief, fraud, unscrupulousness. It means to be full of all wickedness, fraud, villainy, and sleight of hand; moving about with ease and working against good; doing all kinds and forms of evil.

Practical Application

The judgment is from the Holy Spirit, not from Paul. What Paul did was not of himself: not of his emotions, not of personal resentment. The judgment came from the Holy Spirit. God had tolerated enough of the man's sin, hostility, and destruction. His sins were great. There was...

• the sin of all deceit (*pantos dolou*): full of all craftiness, guile, trickery, deceit, treachery, seeking to bait and catch, to enslave in error and untruth.

• the sin of all fraud (*pases rhaidiourgias*).

• the sin of being a son of the devil: being possessed and controlled by the devil; doing and working the will and works of the devil (cp. John 8:44; 1 John 3:10).

• the enemy of all righteousness: opposing all that is right and honest and just; all that is pure and moral and clean.

• the one who "makes crooked the straight ways of the Lord": distorting, twisting, adding to and taking away from the character of God and His Word, the holy Scriptures. (Paul is quoting Hosea 14:9. Cp. Isaiah 40:4; Isaiah 42:16; Luke 3:5.)

ENGLISH WORD	GREEK WORD AND VERSE	THE WORD MEANS...
	ἐκκλησίας. [GNS] Κατ' ἐκεῖνον δὲ τὸν καιρὸν ἐπέβαλεν Ἡρῴδης ὁ βασιλεὺς τὰς χεῖρας **κακῶσαί** τινας τῶν ἀπὸ τῆς ἐκκλησίας. [GNT]	

#2611
Mistreated
 	
Spitefully entreated–KJV
Mistreated–NASB
Insult–NIV
Insulted–NKJV
Treated shamefully–NLT
 	
POSB REFERENCE
(Lk.18:32-33; esp. v.32)
Note 2, point 1b
	ὑβρισθήσεται = hubristhēsetai
	Pronunciation: [hoo-bris'-thay-seh-tah-ee]
	Parsing (part of speech): verb
	  Mood—indicative
	  Tense—future
	  Voice—passive
	  Person—3rd person
	  Number—singular
	  Stem or root—from ὑβρίζω
	Concordance References:
	⇒ Strong's #5195 hubrizō
	⇒ NIV #5614 hubrizō
	⇒ NASB #5195 hubrizō
	
	Luke 18:32
	For he shall be delivered unto the Gentiles, and shall be mocked, and **spitefully entreated**, and spitted on: [KJV]
	"For He will be delivered to the Gentiles, and will be mocked and **mistreated** and spit upon, [NASB]
	He will be handed over to the Gentiles. They will mock him, **insult** him, spit on him, flog him and kill him. [NIV]
	For He will be delivered to the Gentiles and will be mocked and **insulted** and spit upon. [NKJV]
	He will be handed over to the Romans to be mocked, **treated shamefully**, and spit upon. [NLT]
	παραδοθήσεται γὰρ τοῖς ἔθνεσι, καὶ ἐμπαιχθήσεται, καὶ **ὑβρισθήσεται**, καὶ ἐμπτυσθήσεται, [GNS]
	παραδοθήσεται γὰρ τοῖς ἔθνεσιν καὶ ἐμπαιχθήσεται καὶ **ὑβρισθήσεται** καὶ ἐμπτυσθήσεται [GNT]
		To insult; to reproach; to treat with insolence and contempt; to be outraged; to mistreat; to treat disgracefully; to treat shamefully and despitefully.
		
		Practical Application
		Jesus was to be delivered to the Gentiles, and the Jews were going to be the ones to deliver Him into Gentile hands. This fact was to symbolize both the religionists and the world— both were going to reject God's Son and put Him to death. Neither could accept Him and His message of total self-denial.

#2612
Mocked
 	
Mocked–KJV
Mocked–NASB
Mocked–NIV
Mocked–NKJV
Ignore God–NLT
 	
POSB REFERENCE
(Gal.6:7-9; esp. v.7)
Note 2, point 1
	μυκτηρίζεται = muktērizetai
	Pronunciation: [mook-tay-rid'-zeh-tah-ee]
	Parsing (part of speech): verb
	  Mood—indicative
	  Tense—present
	  Voice—passive
	  Person—3rd person
	  Number—singular
	  Stem or root—from μυκτηρίζω
	Concordance References:
	⇒ Strong's #3456 muktērizō
	⇒ NIV #3682 muktērizō
	⇒ NASB #3456 muktērizō
	
	Galatians 6:7
	Be not deceived; God is not **mocked**: for whatsoever a man soweth, that shall he also reap. [KJV]
	Do not be deceived, God is not **mocked**; for whatever a man sows, this he will also reap. [NASB]
	Do not be deceived: God cannot be **mocked**. A man reaps what he sows. [NIV]
	Do not be deceived, God is not **mocked**; for whatever a man sows, that he will also reap. [NKJV]
	Don't be misled. Remember that you can't **ignore God** and get away with it. You will always reap what you sow! [NLT]
	Μὴ πλανᾶσθε, Θεὸς οὐ **μυκτηρίζεται**· ὃ γὰρ ἐὰν σπείρῃ ἄνθρωπος τοῦτο καὶ θερίσει. [GNS]
	Μὴ πλανᾶσθε, θεὸς οὐ **μυκτηρίζεται**. ὃ γὰρ ἐὰν σπείρῃ ἄνθρωπος, τοῦτο καὶ θερίσει· [GNT]
		To mock; to make a fool of; to ignore God; to turn one's nose up at God.
		
		Practical Application
		By rejecting God's minister, the teacher whom God had sent to them, the Galatians were rejecting God. They were not only mocking and turning their noses up at the teacher of God, but they were mocking God. However, Scripture declares in no uncertain terms: "God cannot be mocked. a man reaps what he sows." If a man sows a life...
		• that is not present when the teacher teaches,
		• that is not attentive and learning what the teacher teaches,
		• that does not bear testimony to what the teacher teaches,
		• that does not participate with the teacher in his ministry,
		• that does not encourage others to learn from the teacher,
		...if a man sows this rejection, this turning up of the nose, he rejects and turns his nose up at God. And if he rejects God, he will be rejected by God. Whatever a man sows toward his teacher, he reaps. He will bear the judgment of his behavior toward God's teacher.

#2613
Mockers
 	
Despisers–KJV
Scoffers–NASB
	καταφρονηταί = kataphronētai
	Pronunciation: [kat-af-ron-ay-tah-ee]
	Parsing (part of speech): noun
	  Case—vocative
	  Gender—masculine
	  Number—plural
	  Stem or root—from καταφρονητής, οῦ
		Scoffers; scorners; mockers; cynics; mimics. It means to look down upon; think lightly of; act against.
		
		Practical Application
		The Savior brings judgment upon men. Since

ENGLISH WORD	GREEK WORD AND VERSE	THE WORD MEANS...
Scoffers–NIV Despisers–NKJV **Mockers–NLT** **POSB REFERENCE** (Acts 13:23-41; esp. v.41) Note 3, point 7	Concordance References: ⇒ Strong's #2707 kataphronētēs ⇒ NIV #2970 kataphronētēs ⇒ NASB #2707 kataphronētēs **Acts 13:41** Behold, ye **despisers**, and wonder, and perish: for I work a work in your days, a work which ye shall in no wise believe, though a man declare it unto you. [KJV] 'Behold, you **scoffers**, and marvel, and perish; For I am accomplishing a work in your days, A work which you will never believe, though someone should describe it to you.'" [NASB] "'Look, you **scoffers**, wonder and perish, for I am going to do something in your days that you would never believe, even if someone told you.'" [NIV] "Behold, you **despisers**, Marvel and perish! For I work a work in your days, A work which you will by no means believe, Though oe were to declare it to you.'" [NKJV] 'Look you **mockers**, be amazed and die! For I am doing something in your own day, something you wouldn't believe even if someone told you about it.'" [NLT] Ἴδετε, οἱ **καταφρονηταί**, καὶ θαυμάσατε καὶ ἀφανίσθητε· ὅτι ἔργον ἐγὼ ἐργάζομαι ἐν ταῖς ἡμέραις ὑμῶν, ἔργον ᾧ οὐ μὴ πιστεύσητε ἐάν τις ἐκδιηγῆται ὑμῖν. [GNS] Ἴδετε, οἱ **καταφρονηταί**, καὶ θαυμάσατε καὶ ἀφανίσθητε, ὅτι ἔργον ἐργάζομαι ἐγὼ ἐν ταῖς ἡμέραις ὑμῶν, ἔργον ὃ οὐ μὴ πιστεύσητε ἐάν τις ἐκδιηγῆται ὑμῖν. [GNT]	He has come, men must beware lest what the prophet declared come upon them (Habakkuk 1:5). ⇒ They can be "mockers" (*kataphronētai*). ⇒ They can wonder and perish. The idea is that a man can perish wondering if Jesus is truly the Savior and if the Word preached is true (Acts 13:38-39). (See POSB *Deeper Study #2*, Perish—John 3:16.)

**#2614
Moment**
 	
Cubit–KJV
Cubit–NASB
Hour–NIV
Cubit–NKJV
Moment–NLT
 	
**POSB
REFERENCE**
(Mt.6:27)
Note 4
	πῆχυν = *pēchun*
	Pronunciation: [pay'-khoon]
	Parsing (part of speech): noun
	    Case—accusative
	    Gender—masculine
	    Number—singular
	    Stem or root—from πῆχυς, εως
	Concordance References:
	⇒ Strong's #4083 pēchus
	⇒ NIV #4388 pēchus
	⇒ NASB #4083 pēchus
	
	Matthew 6:27
	Which of you by taking thought can add one **cubit** unto his stature? [KJV]
	"And which of you by being anxious can add a single **cubit** to his life's span? [NASB]
	Who of you by worrying can add a single **hour** to his life? [NIV]
	Which of you by worrying can add one **cubit** to his stature? [NKJV]
	Can all your worries add a single **moment** to your life? Of course not. [NLT]
	τίς δὲ ἐξ ὑμῶν μεριμνῶν δύναται προσθεῖναι ἐπὶ τὴν ἡλικίαν αὐτοῦ **πῆχυν** ἕνα; [GNS]
	τίς δὲ ἐξ ὑμῶν μεριμνῶν δύναται προσθεῖναι ἐπὶ τὴν ἡλικίαν αὐτοῦ **πῆχυν** ἕνα; [GNT]
		An hour, a moment, a cubit.
		
		Practical Application
		In this Scripture, the word speaks of a time, a moment, in a person's life that is past and can never be added to.

**#2615
Moment**
 	
Cubit–KJV
Cubit–NASB
Hour–NIV
Cubit–NKJV
Moment–NLT
	πῆχυν = *pēchun*
	Pronunciation: [pay'-khoon]
	Parsing (part of speech): noun
	    Case—accusative
	    Gender—masculine
	    Number—singular
	    Stem or root—from πῆχυς, εως
	Concordance References:
	⇒ Strong's #4083 pēchus
	⇒ NIV #4388 pēchus
	⇒ NASB #4083 pēchus
		Cubit, hour, moment. The word "moment" literally means measure of space, or distance (approximately 18 inches); but it can also mean a measure of time or age (John 9:21). It is an age, a time of life.
		
		Practical Application
		In this context, the word speaks of a time that is past. So the verse can read either "who can add one cubit to his stature" or "a single hour or moment to his life span."

ENGLISH WORD	GREEK WORD AND VERSE	THE WORD MEANS...
POSB REFERENCE (Lk.12:22-28; esp. v.25) Note 1, point 3	**Luke 12:25** And which of you with taking thought can add to his stature one **cubit**? [KJV] "And which of you by being anxious can add a *single* **cubit** to his life's span? [NASB] Who of you by worrying can add a single **hour** to his life? [NIV] And which of you by worrying can add one **cubit** to his stature? [NKJV] Can all your worries add a single **moment** to your life? Of course not! [NLT] τίς δὲ ἐξ ὑμῶν μεριμνῶν δύναται προσθεῖναι ἐπὶ τὴν ἡλικίαν αὐτοῦ **πῆχυν** ἕνα; [GNS] τίς δὲ ἐξ ὑμῶν μεριμνῶν δύναται ἐπὶ τὴν ἡλικίαν αὐτοῦ προσθεῖναι **πῆχυν**; [GNT]	
#2616 **Moment** Moment–KJV Moment–NASB Flash–NIV Moment–NKJV Moment–NLT **POSB REFERENCE** (1 Cor.15:51-52; esp. v.52) Note 2, point 2	ἀτόμῳ = *atomö* Pronunciation: [at'-om-o] Parsing (part of speech): pronominal adjective Case—dative Gender—neuter Number—singular Stem or root—from ἄτομος, ον Concordance References: ⇒ Strong's #823 atomos ⇒ NIV #875 atomos ⇒ NASB #823 atomos **1 Cor. 15:52** In a **moment**, in the twinkling of an eye, at the last trump: for the trumpet shall sound, and the dead shall be raised incorruptible, and we shall be changed. [KJV] In a **moment**, in the twinkling of an eye, at the last trumpet; for the trumpet will sound, and the dead will be raised imperishable, and we shall be changed. [NASB] In a **flash**, in the twinkling of an eye, at the last trumpet. For the trumpet will sound, the dead will be raised imperishable, and we will be changed. [NIV] In a **moment**, in the twinkling of an eye, at the last trumpet. For the trumpet will sound, and the dead will be raised incorruptible, and we shall be changed. [NKJV] It will happen in a **moment**, in the blinking of an eye, when the last trumpet is blown. For when the trumpet sounds, the Christians who have died will be raised with transformed bodies. And then we who are living will be transformed so that we will never die. [NLT] ἐν **ἀτόμῳ**, ἐν ῥιπῇ ὀφθαλμοῦ, ἐν τῇ ἐσχάτῃ σάλπιγγι· σαλπίσει γάρ, καὶ οἱ νεκροὶ ἐγερθήσονται ἄφθαρτοι, καὶ ἡμεῖς ἀλλαγησόμεθα. [GNS] ἐν **ἀτόμῳ**, ἐν ῥιπῇ ὀφθαλμοῦ, ἐν τῇ ἐσχάτῃ σάλπιγγι· σαλπίσει γάρ καὶ οἱ νεκροὶ ἐγερθήσονται ἄφθαρτοι καὶ ἡμεῖς ἀλλαγησόμεθα. [GNT]	In a flash; in a moment; indivisible, that which cannot be cut. **Practical Application** The resurrection will be a quick, sudden change. It (*atomö*) is the word from which we get the English word *atom*. The idea is that the resurrection will take place so quickly... • that one could not divide the time into two moments. • that one could not blink an eye.
#2617 **Money** Mammon–KJV Mammon–NASB Money–NIV Mammon–NKJV Money–NLT **POSB REFERENCE** (Mt.6:24) Note 3	μαμωνᾷ = *mamöna* Pronunciation: [mam-mo-nah'] Parsing (part of speech): noun Case—dative Gender—masculine Number—singular Stem or root—from μαμωνᾶς, ᾶ Concordance References: ⇒ Strong's #3126 mamönas ⇒ NIV #3440 mamönas ⇒ NASB #3126 mamönas **Matthew 6:24** No man can serve two masters: for either he will hate the one, and love the other; or else he will hold to the one, and despise the other. Ye cannot serve God and **mammon**. [KJV] "No one can serve two masters; for either he will hate the one and love the other, or he will hold to one and despise the other. You cannot serve God and **mammon**.	Money, wealth or any material thing that has value to a person. This means property, possessions, money, stocks, bonds, precious metals or jewels. **Practical Application** The word money is neutral, but as the Scripture states, money acquires a negative connotation when it becomes more important than a relationship with God. The secret to contentment is not money. This is shocking, for the rich cling to and hoard their money, and the rest of mankind is forever seeking to get more and more money. But God is clear about the matter: money and wealth do not bring contentment. There are four reasons why this is true. 1. Money tempts and enslaves.

ENGLISH WORD	GREEK WORD AND VERSE	THE WORD MEANS...
	[NASB] "No one can serve two masters. Either he will hate the one and love the other, or he will be devoted to the one and despise the other. You cannot serve both God and **Money**. [NIV] "No one can serve two masters; for either he will hate the one and love the other, or else he will be loyal to the one and despise the other. You cannot serve God and **mammon**. [NKJV] "No one can serve two masters. For you will hate one and love the other, or be devoted to one and despise the other. You cannot serve both God and **money**. [NLT] οὐδεὶς δύναται δυσὶ κυρίοις δουλεύειν· ἢ γὰρ τὸν ἕνα μισήσει, καὶ τὸν ἕτερον ἀγαπήσει· ἢ ἑνὸς ἀνθέξεται, καὶ τοῦ ἑτέρου καταφρονήσει· οὐ δύνασθε Θεῷ δουλεύειν καὶ **μαμμωνᾷ**. [GNS] Οὐδεὶς δύναται δυσὶ κυρίοις δουλεύειν· ἢ γὰρ τὸν ἕνα μισήσει καὶ τὸν ἕτερον ἀγαπήσει, ἢ ἑνὸς ἀνθέξεται καὶ τοῦ ἑτέρου καταφρονήσει. οὐ δύνασθε θεῷ δουλεύειν καὶ **μαμμωνᾷ**. [GNT]	2. Money can cause many foolish and hurtful lusts. 3. Money drowns men in destruction and perdition. Wealth can be "a personal monster, which plunges its victims into an ocean of complete destruction" (Donald Guthrie. *The Pastoral Epistles.* "Tyndale New Testament Commentaries," p.113). The idea is this: the person who falls into the foolish and hurtful lusts of this world will be utterly destroyed and ruined, both in body and soul. And the destruction and ruin will be for eternity (A.T. Robertson. *Word Pictures in the New Testament*, Vol.4, p.593). 4. Money—that is, the love of money—is the root of all evil. Note the three reasons why: ⇒ The love of money causes people to covet, and covetousness is idolatry. ⇒ The love of money causes people to wander away from the faith. It causes people to go after the lusts of this world. ⇒ The love of money causes people to pierce themselves through with many sorrows. The things, possessions, and lusts of this world do not satisfy nor fulfill a person's heart and life. Money cannot bring contentment to a person. The love of money only consumes and eats a person with grief (A.T. Robertson. *Word Pictures in the New Testament*, Vol.4, p.594). It pierces the heart with a void—the void of emptiness and worry, anxiety, and insecurity. Money cannot buy love, health, and deliverance from death. Money cannot buy God; it cannot buy assurance, not the assurance and confidence of living forever.

#2618
Money Bag
 	
Purse–KJV
Purse–NASB
Purse-NIV
Money bag–NKJV
Not translated–NLT
 	
**POSB
REFERENCE**
(Lk.10:4)
Note 4, point 1
	βαλλάντιον = *ballantion*
	Pronunciation: [bal-an'-tee-on]
	Parsing (part of speech): noun
	   Case—accusative
	   Gender—neuter
	   Number—singular
	   Stem or root—from βαλλάντιον, ου
	Concordance References:
	  ⇒ Strong's #905 balantion
	  ⇒ NIV #964 ballantion
	  ⇒ NASB #905 balantion
	
	Luke 10:4
	Carry neither **purse**, nor scrip, nor shoes: and salute no man by the way. [KJV]
	"Carry no **purse**, no bag, no shoes; and greet no one on the way. [NASB]
	Do not take a **purse** or bag or sandals; and do not greet anyone on the road. [NIV]
	Carry neither **money bag**, knapsack, nor sandals; and greet no one along the road. [NKJV]
	Don't take along any money, or a traveler's bag, or even an extra pair of sandals. And don't stop to greet anyone on the road. [NLT] NOT TRANSLATED
	μὴ βαστάζετε **βαλλάντιον**, μὴ πήραν, μὴ ὑποδήματα· καὶ μηδένα κατὰ τὴν ὁδὸν ἀσπάσησθε. [GNS]
	μὴ βαστάζετε **βαλλάντιον**, μὴ πήραν, μὴ ὑποδήματα, καὶ μηδένα κατὰ τὴν ὁδὸν ἀσπάσησθε. [GNT]
		Purse, money bag, money pouch.
		
		Practical Application
		What did a money pouch have to do with a believer's life? In this Scripture, they were not to carry a money-bag, purse, ballantion or a traveller's bag (*pera*) or two pair of sandals. They were to trust God for provisions, not worrying about money for food, housing, or clothing (Matthew 6:24-34). Worrying about such things would be cumbersome, taking away precious time that should be spent in ministering. Also, they were preaching a message of faith and trust in God. They needed to live what they were preaching and become a living picture of the dependency that God wants from every man.

#2619 **Moral Excellence**	ἀρετήν = *aretēn* Pronunciation: [ar-et-ayn'] Parsing (part of speech): noun Case—accusative	Goodness, virtue; moral excellence and goodness of character; moral strength and moral courage.

ENGLISH WORD	GREEK WORD AND VERSE	THE WORD MEANS...
Virtue–KJV **Moral excellence–NASB** Goodness–NIV Virtue–NKJV **Moral excellence–NLT** **POSB REFERENCE** (2 Pt.1:5-7; esp. v.5) Note 1, point 1	Gender—feminine Number—singular Stem or root—from ἀρετή, ῆς Concordance References: ⇒ Strong's #703 aretë ⇒ NIV #746 aretë ⇒ NASB #703 aretë **2 Peter 1:5** And beside this, giving all diligence, add to your faith **virtue**; and to virtue knowledge; [KJV] Now for this very reason also, applying all diligence, in your faith supply **moral excellence**, and in your moral excellence, knowledge; [NASB] For this very reason, make every effort to add to your faith **goodness**; and to goodness, knowledge; [NIV] But also for this very reason, giving all diligence, add to your faith **virtue**, to virtue knowledge, [NKJV] So make every effort to apply the benefits of these promises to your life. Then your faith will produce a life of **moral excellence**. A life of moral excellence leads to knowing God better. [NLT] καὶ αὐτὸ τοῦτο δὲ σπουδὴν πᾶσαν παρεισενέγκαντες, ἐπιχορηγήσατε ἐν τῇ πίστει ὑμῶν τὴν **ἀρετήν**, ἐν δὲ τῇ ἀρετῇ τὴν γνῶσιν, [GNS] καὶ αὐτὸ τοῦτο δὲ σπουδὴν πᾶσαν παρεισενέγκαντες ἐπιχορηγήσατε ἐν τῇ πίστει ὑμῶν τὴν **ἀρετήν**, ἐν δὲ τῇ ἀρετῇ τὴν γνῶσιν, [GNT]	**Practical Application** It means manliness; being an excellent person in life, a real man or a real woman in life; living life just like one should, in the most excellent way. It means always choosing the excellent way.
#2620 **Moral Filth** Filthiness–KJV Filthiness–NASB **Moral filth–NIV** Filthiness–NKJV Filth–NLT **POSB REFERENCE** (Jas. 1:19-21; esp. v.21) Note 1, point 3	ῥυπαρίαν = hruparian Pronunciation: [hroo-par-ee'-ahn] Parsing (part of speech): noun Case—accusative Gender—feminine Number—singular Stem or root—from ῥυπαρία, ας Concordance References: ⇒ Strong's #4507 hruparia ⇒ NIV #4864 hruparia ⇒ NASB #4507 hruparia **James 1:21** Wherefore lay apart all **filthiness** and superfluity of naughtiness, and receive with meekness the engrafted word, which is able to save your souls. [KJV] Therefore putting aside all **filthiness** and all that remains of wickedness, in humility receive the word implanted, which is able to save your souls. [NASB] Therefore, get rid of all **moral filth** and the evil that is so prevalent and humbly accept the word planted in you, which can save you. [NIV] Therefore lay aside all **filthiness** and overflow of wickedness, and receive with meekness the implanted word, which is able to save your souls. [NKJV] So get rid of all the **filth** and evil in your lives, and humbly accept the message God has planted in your hearts, for it is strong enough to save your souls. [NLT] διὸ ἀποθέμενοι πᾶσαν **ῥυπαρίαν** καὶ περισσείαν κακίας, ἐν πραΰτητι δέξασθε τὸν ἔμφυτον λόγον, τὸν δυνάμενον σῶσαι τὰς ψυχὰς ὑμῶν. [GNS] διὸ ἀποθέμενοι πᾶσαν **ῥυπαρίαν** καὶ περισσείαν κακίας ἐν πραΰτητι, δέξασθε τὸν ἔμφυτον λόγον τὸν δυνάμενον σῶσαι τὰς ψυχὰς ὑμῶν. [GNT]	Moral filth, filthiness, impurity. **Practical Application** The picture is that of *taking off* a dirty garment and putting it aside. A person must put off every dirty thing and lay it off to the side away from himself. If he enjoys the dirt and filth, then his mind is going to be on it. His mind will not be clear, not enough to hear the Word of God. William Barclay makes the point that the Greek word for "filthiness" [moral filth] (*hruparian*) is taken from the Greek word *rupos*. The word is sometimes used to refer to *wax in the ear* (*The Letters of James and Peter*, p.66). The picture is descriptive: a person with wax in the ear cannot hear the Word of God, not clearly. Therefore, he must take the wax out of his ear and put it away or else he will be deaf to the Word of God.
#2621 **More And More At Home** Dwell–KJV Dwell–NASB Dwell–NIV	κατοικῆσαι = katoikēsai Pronunciation: [kat-oy-kay'-sah-ee] Parsing (part of speech): verb Mood—infinitive Tense—aorist Voice—active Stem or root—from κατοικέω Concordance References: ⇒ Strong's #2730 katoikeō	To dwell; to live in; to inhabit; to be more and more at home. It means a permanent, not a temporary, dwelling. It means to take up permanent residence; to live in a home; to enter, settle down, and be at home. **Practical Application** When a person believes in Jesus Christ for the

ENGLISH WORD	GREEK WORD AND VERSE	THE WORD MEANS...
Dwell–NKJV **More and more at home–NLT** **POSB REFERENCE** (Eph.3:17) Note 3 **See also POSB REF:** (Col.1:19) Note 5	⇒ NIV #2997 katoikeō ⇒ NASB #2730 katoikeō **Ephes. 3:17** That Christ may **dwell** in your hearts by faith; that ye, being rooted and grounded in love, [KJV] So that Christ may **dwell** in your hearts through faith; and that you, being rooted and grounded in love, [NASB] So that Christ may **dwell** in your hearts through faith. And I pray that you, being rooted and established in love, [NIV] That Christ may **dwell** in your hearts through faith; that you, being rooted and grounded in love, [NKJV] And I pray that Christ will be **more and more at home** in your hearts as you trust in him. May your roots go down deep into the soil of God's marvelous love. [NLT] κατοικῆσαι τὸν Χριστὸν διὰ τῆς πίστεως ἐν ταῖς καρδίαις ὑμῶν· ἐν ἀγάπῃ ἐρριζωμένοι καὶ τεθεμελιωμένοι [GNS] κατοικῆσαι τὸν Χριστὸν διὰ τῆς πίστεως ἐν ταῖς καρδίαις ὑμῶν, ἐν ἀγάπῃ ἐρριζωμένοι καὶ τεθεμελιωμένοι, [GNT]	first time, Christ enters his life. Therefore, the believer is not praying for Christ to enter the hearts and lives of believers; Christ is already in their hearts and lives. What then does this request mean? Just what the verse says: ⇒ that Christ would be at home and live in a permanent sense within the believer. ⇒ that the believer would be aware and conscious of Christ within his heart—always aware and conscious that Christ has taken up residence within him. ⇒ that the believer would let Christ control and guide his life—permanently and constantly—because Christ is at home in his heart. It is the presence of Christ within that motivates the believer to follow Christ. The more the believer is aware and conscious of Christ within him, the more he will *walk and live* in Christ.

#2622
 	
Morning, Early In The–Morning, In The
 	
In the morning–KJV
In the morning–NASB
Early in the morning–NIV
In the morning–NKJV
In the morning–NLT
 	
POSB REFERENCE
(Mt.21:18)
Deeper Study #1
	Πρωΐ = *proi*
	Pronunciation: [pro-ee']
	Parsing (part of speech): adjective
	    Type—adverb
	    Stem or root—from πρωΐ
	Concordance References:
	⇒ Strong's #4404 prōi
	⇒ NIV #4745 prōi
	⇒ NASB #4404 prōi
	
	Matthew 21:18
	Now **in the morning** as he returned into the city, he hungered. [KJV]
	Now **in the morning**, when He returned to the city, He became hungry. [NASB]
	Early in the morning, as he was on his way back to the city, he was hungry. [NIV]
	Now **in the morning**, as He returned to the city, He was hungry. [NKJV]
	In the morning, as Jesus was returning to Jerusalem, he was hungry, [NLT]
	Πρωΐας δὲ ἐπανάγων εἰς τὴν πόλιν, ἐπείνασε· [GNS]
	Πρωΐ δὲ ἐπανάγων εἰς τὴν πόλιν ἐπείνασεν. [GNT]
		Early morning, very early, the fourth or last watch of the previous night (Mark 1:35).
		
		Practical Application
		Jesus began the events of Tuesday so early it was in the wee hours of the morning, or according to Jewish time, in the last hours of the previous day.

#2623
 	
Mortify
 	
Mortify–KJV
Putting to death–NASB
Put to death–NIV
Put to death–NKJV
Turn from–NLT
 	
POSB REFERENCE
(Romans 8:12-13, esp. v.13)
Note 6, point 2c
	θανατοῦτε = *thanatoute*
	Pronunciation: [than-at-oo'-teh]
	Parsing (part of speech): verb
	    Mood—indicative
	    Tense—present
	    Voice—active
	    Person—2nd person
	    Number—plural
	    Stem or root—from θανατόω
	Concordance References:
	⇒ Strong's #2289 thanatoō
	⇒ NIV #2506 thanatoō
	⇒ NASB #2289 thanatoō
	
	Romans 8:13
	For if ye live after the flesh, ye shall die: but if ye through the Spirit do **mortify** the deeds of the body, ye shall live. [KJV]
	For if you are living according to the flesh, you must die; but if by the Spirit you are **putting to death** the deeds of the body, you will live. [NASB]
	For if you live according to the sinful nature, you will die; but if by the Spirit you **put to death** the misdeeds of the body, you will live, [NIV]
	For if you live according to the flesh you will die; but
		To put to death; to mortify; to turn from. The idea is that of denying, subjecting, subduing, deadening, destroying the strength of.
		
		Practical Application
		The power to mortify the evil deeds of the body comes "through the Spirit." However, note this: we deny the evil deeds, and then the Spirit gives the strength to deaden and to subdue their strength. We are involved just as the Spirit is involved. He cannot destroy the strength of sin unless we exercise our will and work to destroy it ourselves, and we cannot will and work at it apart from Him. Both the Spirit and ourselves have to be involved, each doing his part if we wish the evil deeds of the body to be put to death. To repeat the point above: we exercise our will to deny the evil deeds, and then the Spirit immediately steps in to deaden the pull and strength of the evil deed. If we do not want the evil deeds of our body destroyed, if we want to continue living in the sins of the flesh, if we want nothing to do with the Spirit—then the

ENGLISH WORD	GREEK WORD AND VERSE	THE WORD MEANS...
	if by the Spirit you **put to death** the deeds of the body, you will live. [NKJV] For if you keep on following it, you will perish. But if through the power of the Holy Spirit you **turn from** it and its evil deeds, you will live. [NLT] εἰ γὰρ κατὰ σάρκα ζῆτε, μέλλετε ἀποθνῄσκειν· εἰ δὲ πνεύματι τὰς πράξεις τοῦ σώματος **θανατοῦτε**, ζήσεσθε. [GNS] εἰ γὰρ κατὰ σάρκα ζῆτε, μέλλετε ἀποθνῄσκειν· εἰ δὲ πνεύματι τὰς πράξεις τοῦ σώματος **θανατοῦτε**, ζήσεσθε. [GNT]	Spirit can do nothing for us. God loves us too much to force us; He will not override our choices. But if we honestly will to follow the Spirit and honestly desire to destroy the evil deeds of our body, the Spirit will step in and give the power to do so. He will break the power of sin: He will deaden and subdue the strength of it.

#2624
Most Excellent
 	
Most excellent–KJV
Most excellent–NASB
Most excellent–NIV
Most excellent–NKJV
Not translated–NLT
 	
POSB REFERENCE
(Lk.1:3)
Note 3, point 4a
	κράτιστε = *kratiste*
	Pronunciation: [krat'-is-teh]
	Parsing (part of speech): adjective
	    Type—superlative
	    Case—vocative
	    Gender—masculine
	    Number—singular
	    Stem or root—from κράτιστος, η, ον
	Concordance References:
	⇒ Strong's #2903 kratistos
	⇒ NIV #3196 kratistos
	⇒ NASB #2903 kratistos
	
	Luke 1:3
	It seemed good to me also, having had perfect understanding of all things from the very first, to write unto thee in order, **most excellent** Theophilus, [KJV]
	it seemed fitting for me as well, having investigated everything carefully from the beginning, to write it out for you in consecutive order, **most excellent** Theophilus; [NASB]
	Therefore, since I myself have carefully investigated everything from the beginning, it seemed good also to me to write an orderly account for you, **most excellent** Theophilus, [NIV]
	It seemed good to me also, having had perfect understanding of all things from the very first, to write to you an orderly account, **most excellent** Theophilus, [NKJV]
	Having carefully investigated all of these accounts from the beginning, I have decided to write a careful summary for you, [NLT]—NOT TRANSLATED
	ἔδοξε κἀμοὶ παρηκολουθηκότι ἄνωθεν πᾶσιν ἀκριβῶς, καθεξῆς σοι γράψαι, **κράτιστε** Θεόφιλε, [GNS]
	ἔδοξε κἀμοὶ παρηκολουθηκότι ἄνωθεν πᾶσιν ἀκριβῶς καθεξῆς σοι γράψαι, **κράτιστε** Θεόφιλε, [GNT]
		Most excellent, most noble.
		
		Practical Application
		It is a title of rank and honor given to those in authority. The same title is used of Felix and Festus (Acts 23:26; Acts 24:3; Acts 26:25).

#2625
Most Surely Believed
 	
Most surely believed–KJV
Accomplished–NASB
Fulfilled–NIV
Fulfilled–NKJV
Took place–NLT
 	
POSB REFERENCE
(Lk.1:1)
Note 1, point 2
 	
See also POSB REF:
(Lk.21:24)
Note 5, point 1
	πεπληροφορημένων = *peplërophorëmenön*
	Pronunciation: [pe-play-rof-or-ee-men-own]
	Parsing (part of speech): verb
	    Mood—participle
	    Tense—perfect
	    Voice—passive
	    Case—genitive
	    Gender—neuter
	    Number—plural
	    Stem or root—from πληροφορέω
	Concordance References:
	⇒ Strong's #4135 plerophoreo
	⇒ NIV #4442 plërophoreö
	⇒ NASB #4135 plerophoreo
	
	Luke 1:1
	Forasmuch as many have taken in hand to set forth in order a declaration of those things which are **most surely believed** among us, [KJV]
	Inasmuch as many have undertaken to compile an account of the things **accomplished** among us, [NASB]
	Many have undertaken to draw up an account of the things that have been **fulfilled** among us, [NIV]
	Inasmuch as many have taken in hand to set in order a narrative of those things which have been **fulfilled**
		To fill; to fill up; to make full; to come to an end; to bring to completion; to finish. It means things that were fulfilled, that were accomplished, that were actually performed, or that had run their full course (cp. 2 Tim. 4:5).
		
		Practical Application
		Luke is saying that the *things of Christ* were not only believed, but they were also accomplished or fulfilled among the believers of that day. The *things* (events, matters) of Christ actually took place; they were purposeful; they were destined to be accomplished and fulfilled.
		The point is this: the things of Christ are a record of historical events, things that actually happened and that actually fulfilled the purpose of God. Therefore, the things are "most surely believed among us [believers]." What are the things accomplished and believed? Both the things of the New Testament and of the Old Testament. The whole Bible is a record of "those things."

ENGLISH WORD	GREEK WORD AND VERSE	THE WORD MEANS...
	among us, [NKJV] Most honorable Theophilus:Many people have written accounts about the events that **took place** among us. [NLT] Ἐπειδήπερ πολλοὶ ἐπεχείρησαν ἀνατάξασθαι διήγησιν περὶ τῶν **πεπληροφορημένων** ἐν ἡμῖν πραγμάτων, [GNS] Ἐπειδήπερ πολλοὶ ἐπεχείρησαν ἀνατάξασθαι διήγησιν περὶ τῶν **πεπληροφορημένων** ἐν ἡμῖν πραγμάτων, [GNT]	

#2626
Motions Of Sins, The
 	
Motions of sins, the–KJV
Sinful passions, the–NASB
Sinful passions, the–NIV
Sinful passions, the–NKJV
Sinful desires–NLT
 	
POSB REFERENCE
(Rom.7:5)
Note 3, point 1b
	τὰ παθήματα τῶν ἁμαρτιῶν = *ta pathēmata tōn hamartiōn*
	Pronunciation: [tah pah-thay-mah-tah tone ha-mar-tee-own]
	Parsing *pathēmata* (part of speech): noun
	  Case—nominative
	  Gender—neuter
	  Number—plural
	  Stem or root—from πάθημα, τος
	Parsing *hamartiōn* (part of speech): noun
	  Case—genitive
	  Gender—feminine
	  Number—plural
	  Stem or root—from ἁμαρτία, ας
	Concordance References:
	⇒ Strong's #3588 ho + 3804 pathēma + 3588 ho + 266 hamartia
	⇒ NIV #3836 ho [Not in English] + 4077 pathēma [passions] + 3836 ho [the] + 281 hamartia [sinful]
	⇒ NASB #3588 ho + 3804 pathēma + 3588 ho + 266 hamartia
	
	Romans 7:5
	For when we were in the flesh, **the motions of sins**, which were by the law, did work in our members to bring forth fruit unto death. [KJV]
	For while we were in the flesh, **the sinful passions**, which were aroused by the Law, were at work in the members of our body to bear fruit for death. [NASB]
	For when we were controlled by the sinful nature, **the sinful passions** aroused by the law were at work in our bodies, so that we bore fruit for death. [NIV]
	For when we were in the flesh, **the sinful passions** which were aroused by the law were at work in our members to bear fruit to death. [NKJV]
	When we were controlled by our old nature, **sinful desires** were at work within us, and the law aroused these evil desires that produced sinful deeds, resulting in death. [NLT]
	ὅτε γὰρ ἦμεν ἐν τῇ σαρκί, **τὰ παθήματα τῶν ἁμαρτιῶν** τὰ διὰ τοῦ νόμου ἐνηργεῖτο ἐν τοῖς μέλεσιν ἡμῶν εἰς τὸ καρποφορῆσαι τῷ θανάτῳ, [GNS]
	ὅτε γὰρ ἦμεν ἐν τῇ σαρκί, **τὰ παθήματα τῶν ἁμαρτιῶν** τὰ διὰ τοῦ νόμου ἐνηργεῖτο ἐν τοῖς μέλεσιν ἡμῶν, εἰς τὸ καρποφορῆσαι τῷ θανάτῳ· [GNT]
		Sinful passions; motions of sins; sinful desires.
		
		Practical Application
		It is alive and active in that it arouses sinful passions or "the motions of sins" (*ta pathēmata tōn hamartiōn*). The law not only points out sin, it actually arouses feelings and stirs the emotions to do the forbidden.

#2627
Mourn
 	
Mourn–KJV
Mourn–NASB
Mourn–NIV
Mourn–NKJV
Mourn–NLT
 	
POSB REFERENCE
(Mt.5:4)
Note 3
	πενθοῦντες = *penthountes*
	Pronunciation: [pen-thoon-tes]
	Parsing (part of speech): verb
	  Mood—participle
	  Tense—present
	  Voice—active
	  Case—nominative
	  Gender—masculine
	  Number—plural
	  Stem or root—from πενθέω
	Concordance References:
	⇒ Strong's #3996 pentheō
	⇒ NIV #4291 pentheō
	⇒ NASB #3996 pentheō
		To mourn; to have a broken heart; to experience sorrow.
		
		Practical Application
		The Greek is the strongest word possible for mourning. It is like the deep mourning and wailing that occurs over the death of a loved one. It is sorrow—a desperate, helpless sorrow. In this Scripture it is a sorrow for sin, a broken heart over evil and suffering. It is a brokenness of self that comes from seeing Christ on the cross and realizing that our sins put Him there (cp. Jas.4:9).

ENGLISH WORD	GREEK WORD AND VERSE	THE WORD MEANS...
	Matthew 5:4 Blessed are they that **mourn**: for they shall be comforted. [KJV] "Blessed are those who **mourn**, for they shall be comforted. [NASB] Blessed are those who **mourn**, for they will be comforted. [NIV] Blessed *are* those who **mourn**, for they shall be comforted. [NKJV] God blesses those who **mourn**, for they will be comforted. [NLT] Μακάριοι οἱ **πενθοῦντες**· ὅτι αὐτοὶ παρακληθήσονται. [GNS] μακάριοι οἱ **πενθοῦντες**, ὅτι αὐτοὶ παρακληθήσονται. [GNT]	

#2628
Mourned–Mourning
 	
Mourned–KJV
Mourned–NASB
Filled with grief–NIV
Mourned–NKJV
Mourning–NLT
 	
POSB REFERENCE
(1 Cor.5:2)
Note 2
	ἐπενθήσατε = epenthēsate
	Pronunciation: [eh-pen-thay'-sah-teh]
	Parsing (part of speech): verb
	   Mood—indicative
	   Tense—aorist
	   Voice—active
	   Person—2nd person
	   Number—plural
	   Stem or root—from πενθέω
	Concordance References:
	⇒ Strong's #3996 pentheō
	⇒ NIV #4291 pentheō
	⇒ NASB #3996 pentheō
	
	1 Cor. 5:2
	And ye are puffed up, and have not rather **mourned**, that he that hath done this deed might be taken away from among you. [KJV]
	And you have become arrogant, and have not **mourned** instead, in order that the one who had done this deed might be removed from your midst. [NASB]
	And you are proud! Shouldn't you rather have been **filled with grief** and have put out of your fellowship the man who did this? [NIV]
	And you are puffed up, and have not rather **mourned**, that he who has done this deed might be taken away from among you. [NKJV]
	And you are so proud of yourselves! Why aren't you **mourning** in sorrow and shame? And why haven't you removed this man from your fellowship? [NLT]
	καὶ ὑμεῖς πεφυσιωμένοι ἐστέ, καὶ οὐχὶ μᾶλλον **ἐπενθήσατε**, ἵνα ἐξαρθῇ ἐκ μέσου ὑμῶν ὁ τὸ ἔργον τοῦτο ποιήσας. [GNS]
	καὶ ὑμεῖς πεφυσιωμένοι ἐστέ καὶ οὐχὶ μᾶλλον **ἐπενθήσατε**, ἵνα ἀρθῇ ἐκ μέσου ὑμῶν ὁ τὸ ἔργον τοῦτο πράξας; [GNT]
		To be filled with grief; to mourn; to grieve over; to experience sorrow.
		
		Practical Application
		The word "mourned" (*epenthēsate*) is the word used for grieving and mourning over the dead. The people in this Scripture should have been so grieved that they were driven to prayer. Their need was not to be glorying in their so-called spirituality and strength as a church; their need was to mourn over the sin in their midst, begging God to help them restore the fallen brother or to remove him and the sin from their fellowship through love and correction.

#2629
Mourned–Mourning
 	
Bewailed–KJV
Mourning–NASB
Mourned–NIV
Mourned–NKJV
Grief-stricken–NLT
 	
POSB REFERENCE
(Lk.23:27)
Note 2
	ἐκόπτοντο = ekoptonto
	Pronunciation: [eh-kop'-tawn-tow]
	Parsing (part of speech): verb
	   Mood—indicative
	   Tense—imperfect
	   Voice—middle
	   Person—3rd person
	   Number—plural
	   Stem or root—from κόπτω
	Concordance References:
	⇒ Strong's #2875 koptō
	⇒ NIV #3164 koptō
	⇒ NASB #2875 koptō
	
	Luke 23:27
	And there followed him a great company of people, and of women, which also **bewailed** and lamented him. [KJV]
	And there were following Him a great multitude of the people, and of women who were **mourning** and lament-
		To mourn; to be grief stricken; to lament; to wail; to cut, strike, smite, beat.
		
		Practical Application
		They were cut to the core of their hearts, actually feeling pain for Jesus. A natural response to the Lord's sufferings is not enough. A person must understand why Christ suffered and must feel a godly sorrow over Christ's having to bear the sins of the world (see POSB *Deeper Study* #1—2 Cor. 7:10).

ENGLISH WORD	GREEK WORD AND VERSE	THE WORD MEANS...

	ing Him. [NASB]
	    A large number of people followed him, including women who **mourned** and wailed for him. [NIV]
	    And a great multitude of the people followed Him, and women who also **mourned** and lamented Him. [NKJV]
	    Great crowds trailed along behind, including many **grief-stricken** women. [NLT]
	    Ἠκολούθει δὲ αὐτῷ πολὺ πλῆθος τοῦ λαοῦ, καὶ γυναικῶν αἳ καὶ **ἐκόπτοντο** καὶ ἐθρήνουν αὐτόν. [GNS]
	    Ἠκολούθει δὲ αὐτῷ πολὺ πλῆθος τοῦ λαοῦ καὶ γυναικῶν αἳ **ἐκόπτοντο** καὶ ἐθρήνουν αὐτόν. [GNT]	

#2630
Moved
 	
Moved–KJV
Stirred–NASB
Stirred–NIV
Moved–NKJV
Stirred–NLT
 	
**POSB
REFERENCE**
(Mt.21:10-11; esp. v.10)
Note 5
	ἐσείσθη = *eseisthē*
	Pronunciation: [eh-sees'-thay]
	Parsing (part of speech): verb
	    Mood—indicative
	    Tense—aorist
	    Voice—passive
	    Person—3rd person
	    Number—singular
	    Stem or root—from σείω
	Concordance References:
	⇒ Strong's #4579 seiö
	⇒ NIV #4940 seiö
	⇒ NASB #4579 seiö
	
	Matthew 21:10
	    And when he was come into Jerusalem, all the city was **moved**, saying, Who is this? [KJV]
	    And when He had entered Jerusalem, all the city was **stirred**, saying, "Who is this?" [NASB]
	    When Jesus entered Jerusalem, the whole city was **stirred** and asked, "Who is this?" [NIV]
	    And when He had come into Jerusalem, all the city was **moved**, saying, "Who is this?" [NKJV]
	    The entire city of Jerusalem was **stirred** as he entered. "Who is this?" they asked. [NLT]
	    καὶ εἰσελθόντος αὐτοῦ εἰς Ἱεροσόλυμα **ἐσείσθη** πᾶσα ἡ πόλις λέγουσα, Τίς ἐστιν οὗτος; [GNS]
	    καὶ εἰσελθόντος αὐτοῦ εἰς Ἱεροσόλυμα **ἐσείσθη** πᾶσα ἡ πόλις λέγουσα, Τίς ἐστιν οὗτος; [GNT]
		To stir up; to be shaken to the core, to the foundations. This word implies that nothing is spared—everything that can be shaken will be shaken.
		
		Practical Application
		    When Jesus Christ makes His presence known, every fabric of society is affected. Note what happened when He entered Jerusalem:
		⇒ The Romans sensed that a popular uprising might be in the making.
		⇒ The Herodians, who were the Jewish ruling party, feared they would be overthrown and lose their power.
		⇒ The Pharisees were stirred to new depths of envy and malice.
		⇒ The common people were convinced that their day of liberation had finally arrived in Jesus of Nazareth.

#2631
Moved
 	
Groaned–KJV
Deeply moved–NASB
Deeply moved–NIV
Groaned–NKJV
Moved–NLT
 	
**POSB
REFERENCE**
(Jn.11:33-36; esp. v.33)
Note 5, point 1
	ἐνεβριμήσατο = *enebrimēsato*
	Pronunciation: [en-eh-brim-ay'-sah-tow]
	Parsing (part of speech): verb
	    Mood—indicative
	    Tense—aorist
	    Voice—middle deponent
	    Person—3rd person
	    Number—singular
	    Stem or root—from ἐμβριμάομαι
	Concordance References:
	⇒ Strong's #1690 embrimaomai
	⇒ NIV #1839 embrimaomai
	⇒ NASB #1690 embrimaomai
	
	John 11:33
	    When Jesus therefore saw her weeping, and the Jews also weeping which came with her, he **groaned** in the spirit, and was troubled, [KJV]
	    When Jesus therefore saw her weeping, and the Jews who came with her, also weeping, He was **deeply moved** in spirit, and was troubled, [NASB]
	    When Jesus saw her weeping, and the Jews who had come along with her also weeping, he was **deeply moved** in spirit and troubled. [NIV]
	    Therefore, when Jesus saw her weeping, and the Jews who came with her weeping, He **groaned** in the spirit and was troubled. [NKJV]
	    When Jesus saw her weeping and saw the other people wailing with her, he was **moved** with indignation and was deeply troubled. [NLT]
	    Ἰησοῦς οὖν ὡς εἶδεν αὐτὴν κλαίουσαν, καὶ τοὺς
		To be deeply moved; to groan in the spirit; to be agitated by grief and sorrow.
		
		Practical Application
		    Jesus is moved in understanding and feeling and compassion for all who are hurting and suffering. In this Scripture, we see Jesus gripped with intense emotion. He was deeply moved...
		• by Mary, who was so broken in sorrow.
		• by Martha, who was gripped by pain and hurt.
		• by those who were really feeling the death of Lazarus and the sorrow of the family.
		• by the terrible tragedy of death and the pain it causes.
		• by the terrible price He was soon to pay conquering death. (This was certainly glimpsed by Jesus in such a scene as He was now experiencing.)

ENGLISH WORD	GREEK WORD AND VERSE	THE WORD MEANS...
	συνελθόντας αὐτῇ Ἰουδαίους κλαίοντας, **ἐνεβριμήσατο** τῷ πνεύματι, καὶ ἐτάραξεν ἑαυτόν, [GNS] Ἰησοῦς οὖν ὡς εἶδεν αὐτὴν κλαίουσαν καὶ τοὺς συνελθόντας αὐτῇ Ἰουδαίους κλαίοντας, **ἐνεβριμήσατο** τῷ πνεύματι καὶ ἐτάραξεν ἑαυτόν· [GNT]	

#2632
Murder
 	
Murder–KJV
Murder–NASB
Murder–NIV
Murder–NKJV
Murder–NLT
 	
POSB
REFERENCE
(Romans 1:29)
Deeper Study #7
 	
See also POSB REF:
(Mk.7:21)
Deeper Study #6
	φόνου = *phonou*
	Pronunciation: [fo'-noo]
	Parsing (part of speech): noun
	    Case—genitive
	    Gender—masculine
	    Number—singular
	    Stem or root—from φόνος, ου
	Concordance References:
	  ⇒ Strong's #5408 phonos
	  ⇒ NIV #5840 phonos
	  ⇒ NASB #5408 phonos
	
	Romans 1:29
	Being filled with all unrighteousness, fornication, wickedness, covetousness, maliciousness; full of envy, **murder**, debate, deceit, malignity; whisperers, [KJV]
	Being filled with all unrighteousness, wickedness, greed, evil; full of envy, **murder**, strife, deceit, malice; they are gossips, [NASB]
	They have become filled with every kind of wickedness, evil, greed and depravity. They are full of envy, **murder**, strife, deceit and malice. They are gossips, [NIV]
	Being filled with all unrighteousness, sexual immorality, wickedness, covetousness, maliciousness; full of envy, **murder**, strife, deceit, evil-mindedness; *they are* whisperers, [NKJV]
	Their lives became full of every kind of wickedness, sin, greed, hate, envy, **murder**, fighting, deception, malicious behavior, and gossip. [NLT]
	πεπληρωμένους πάσῃ ἀδικίᾳ πορνείᾳ, πονηρίᾳ πλεονεξίᾳ κακίᾳ· μεστοὺς φθόνου, **φόνου**, ἔριδος, δόλου, κακοηθείας· [GNS]
	πεπληρωμένους πάσῃ ἀδικίᾳ πονηρίᾳ πλεονεξίᾳ κακίᾳ, μεστοὺς φθόνου **φόνου** ἔριδος δόλου κακοηθείας, ψιθυριστάς [GNT]
		To kill, to take the life of another.
		
		Practical Application
		Murder is a sin against the sixth commandment. Jesus Christ taught that this commandment means far more than just prohibiting the killing of people. He enlarged the meaning to include both the anger that is aroused within the heart and the lawless motives that drive a person to kill others (cp. Mt.5:21-22).

#2633
Murders
 	
Murders–KJV
Not translated–NASB
Not translated–NIV
Murders–NKJV
Not translated–NLT
 	
POSB
REFERENCE
(Gal.5:19-21; esp.
v.21)
Note 2
	φόνοι = *phonoi*
	Pronunciation: [fon'-oy]
	Parsing (part of speech): noun
	    Case—genitive
	    Gender—masculine
	    Number—plural
	    Stem or root—from **fevnw**
	Concordance References:
	  ⇒ Strong's #5408 phonos
	  ⇒ NIV #Not Translated
	  ⇒ NASB #Not Translated
	
	Galatians 5:21
	Envyings, **murders**, drunkenness, revellings, and such like: of the which I tell you before, as I have also told you in time past, that they which do such things shall not inherit the kingdom of God. [KJV]
	Envying, drunkenness, carousing, and things like these, of which I forewarn you just as I have forewarned you that those who practice such things shall not inherit the kingdom of God. [NASB]—Not Translated
	And envy; drunkenness, orgies, and the like. I warn you, as I did before, that those who live like this will not inherit the kingdom of God. [NIV]—Not Translated
	Envy, **murders**, drunkenness, revelries, and the like; of which I tell you beforehand, just as I also told *you* in time past, that those who practice such things will not inherit the kingdom of God. [NKJV]
	Envy, drunkenness, wild parties, and other kinds of sin. Let me tell you again, as I have before, that anyone
		To murder; to kill, to take the life of another person.
		
		Practical Application
		Murder is a sin against the sixth commandment.

ENGLISH WORD	GREEK WORD AND VERSE	THE WORD MEANS...
	living that sort of life will not inherit the Kingdom of God. [NLT]—Not Translated φθόνοι, **φόνοι**, μέθαι, κῶμοι, καὶ τὰ ὅμοια τούτοις· ἃ προλέγω ὑμῖν, καθὼς καὶ προεῖπον, ὅτι οἱ τὰ τοιαῦτα πράσσοντες βασιλείαν Θεοῦ οὐ κληρονομήσουσιν. [GNS] φθόνοι, μέθαι, κῶμοι καὶ τὰ ὅμοια τούτοις, ἃ προλέγω ὑμῖν καθὼς προεῖπον ὅτι οἱ τὰ τοιαῦτα πράσσοντες βασιλείαν θεοῦ οὐ κληρονομήσουσιν. [GNT]	
#2634 **Murmur–Murmured** **Murmured–KJV** Grumbling–NASB Grumble–NIV Complained–NKJV **Murmur–NLT** **POSB REFERENCE** (Jn.6:41-43; esp. v.41) Note 1	Ἐγόγγυζον = Egogguzon Pronunciation: [eh-gong-good'-zon] Parsing (part of speech): verb 　Mood—indicative 　Tense—imperfect 　Voice—active 　Person—3rd person 　Number—plural 　Stem or root—from γογγύζω Concordance References: ⇒　Strong's #1111 gogguzö ⇒　NIV #1197 gogguzö ⇒　NASB #1111 gogguzo **John 6:41** The Jews then **murmured** at him, because he said, I am the bread which came down from heaven. [KJV] 　The Jews therefore were **grumbling** about Him, because He said, "I am the bread that came down out of heaven." [NASB] 　At this the Jews began to **grumble** about him because he said, "I am the bread that came down from heaven." [NIV] 　The Jews then **complained** about Him, because He said, "I am the bread which came down from heaven." [NKJV] 　Then the people began to **murmur** in disagreement because he had said, "I am the bread from heaven." [NLT] 　Ἐγόγγυζον οὖν οἱ Ἰουδαῖοι περὶ αὐτοῦ, ὅτι εἶπεν, Ἐγώ εἰμι ὁ ἄρτος ὁ καταβὰς ἐκ τοῦ οὐρανοῦ. [GNS] 　Ἐγόγγυζον οὖν οἱ Ἰουδαῖοι περὶ αὐτοῦ ὅτι εἶπεν, Ἐγώ εἰμι ὁ ἄρτος ὁ καταβὰς ἐκ τοῦ οὐρανοῦ, [GNT]	To grumble; to murmur against; to mutter; to whisper undertones; to grouse; to complain. **Practical Application** The Jews murmured against Him. The word refers to the grumbling, the buzzing, the discontent that arises from a crowd that is upset and confused; that is, misunderstanding, rejecting, and opposing a speaker.
#2635 **Murmured Against** **Murmured against–KJV** Scolding–NASB Rebuked harshly–NIV Criticized sharply–NKJV Scolded harshly–NLT **POSB REFERENCE** (Mk.14:4-5; esp. v.5) Note 2	ἐνεβριμῶντο = eneboimonto Pronunciation: [en-eh-brim-own'-tow] Parsing (part of speech): verb 　Mood—indicative 　Tense—imperfect 　Voice—middle or passive deponent 　Person—3rd person 　Number—plural 　Stem or root—from ἐμβριμάομαι Concordance References: ⇒　Strong's #1690 embrimaomai ⇒　NIV #1839 embrimaomai ⇒　NASB #1690 embrimaomai **Mark 14:5** For it might have been sold for more than three hundred pence, and have been given to the poor. And they **murmured against** her. [KJV] 　"For this perfume might have been sold for over three hundred denarii, and the money given to the poor." And they were **scolding** her. [NASB] 　It could have been sold for more than a year's wages and the money given to the poor." And they **rebuked** her **harshly**. [NIV] 　For it might have been sold for more than three hundred denarii and given to the poor." And they **criticized** her **sharply**. [NKJV] 　"She could have sold it for a small fortune and given the money to the poor!" And they **scolded** her **harshly**. [NLT] 　ἠδύνατο γὰρ τοῦτο πραθῆναι ἐπάνω τριακοσίων	To growl, rebuke, murmur against, scold; to speak harshly against. **Practical Application** In this Scripture, what disturbed the disciples was not the fact that Mary anointed Jesus. Anointing Him was easy enough to understand since it was a common custom of the day. What disturbed them was the gift she gave. The gift... • seemed too valuable and priceless. • seemed unnecessary and thoughtless. • seemed misplaced and wasted. • seemed too costly and sacrificial. • seemed to be a foolish and senseless act.

ENGLISH WORD	GREEK WORD AND VERSE	THE WORD MEANS...
	δηναρίων, καὶ δοθῆναι τοῖς πτωχοῖς. καὶ **ἐνεβριμῶντο** αὐτῇ. [GNS] ἠδύνατο γὰρ τοῦτο τὸ μύρον πραθῆναι ἐπάνω δηναρίων τριακοσίων καὶ δοθῆναι τοῖς πτωχοῖς· καὶ **ἐνεβριμῶντο** αὐτῇ. [GNT]	

#2636
Murmurings
 	
Murmurings–KJV
Grumbling–NASB
Complaining–NIV
Complaining–NKJV
Complaining–NLT
 	
POSB
REFERENCE
(Philip.2:14)
Note 3
	γογγυσμῶν = *goggusmōn*
	Pronunciation: [gong-goos-mown']
	Parsing (part of speech): noun
	    Case—genitive
	    Gender—masculine
	    Number—plural
	    Stem or root—from γογγυσμός, οῦ
	Concordance References:
	  ⇒ Strong's #1112 goggusmos
	  ⇒ NIV #1198 goggusmos
	  ⇒ NASB #1112 goggusmos
	
	Philip. 2:14
	Do all things without **murmurings** and disputings: [KJV]
	Do all things without **grumbling** or disputing; [NASB]
	Do everything without **complaining** or arguing, [NIV]
	Do all things without **complaining** and disputing, [NKJV]
	In everything you do, stay away from **complaining** and arguing, [NLT]
	πάντα ποιεῖτε χωρὶς **γογγυσμῶν** καὶ διαλογισμῶν, [GNS]
	πάντα ποιεῖτε χωρὶς **γογγυσμῶν** καὶ διαλογισμῶν, [GNT]
		Complaining, murmuring, grumbling, whispering, quarreling.
		
		Practical Application
		Note: it means the quiet, soft, behind-the-back undertone of complaining and murmurings. It is the kind of criticism, dissatisfaction, fault-finding and gossip that goes on within small groups or cliques.
		The results of murmurings are far worse than people ever think. This is the primary reason God forbids murmurings in no uncertain terms. Murmuring...
		• hurts
		• damages
		• divides
		• tears down
		• downs a person
		• says "look at me"
		• elevates selfish opinion
		• opposes God's will
		• hinders progress
		• stymies growth
		• misleads people
		• is self-centered
		• pushes people away from Christ and the church

#2637
Must
 	
Must–KJV
Must–NASB
Must–NIV
Must–NKJV
Had to–NLT
 	
POSB
REFERENCE
(Mt.16:21-23; esp.
v.21)
Note 1
 	
See also POSB REF:
(Lk.9:21-22; esp. v.22)
Note 4, point 2
(Lk.13:31-33 esp.
v.33)
Note 2, point 2
(Lk.24:44-49 esp.
v.44)
Note 2, point 2
(Jn.3:4-8; esp. v.7)
Note 3, point 4
(Jn.4:1-9; esp. v.4)
Note 1, point 1
(Jn.9:4)
Note 2, point 3a
(Jn.10:14-16; esp.
v.16)
Note 2, point 4c
	δεῖ = *dei*
	Pronunciation: [die]
	Parsing (part of speech): verb
	    Mood—indicative
	    Tense—present
	    Voice—active
	    Person—3rd person
	    Number—singular
	    Stem or root—from δεῖ
	Concordance References:
	  ⇒ Strong's #1163 dei
	  ⇒ NIV #1256 dei
	  ⇒ NASB #1163 dei
	
	Matthew 16:21
	From that time forth began Jesus to shew unto his disciples, how that he **must** go unto Jerusalem, and suffer many things of the elders and chief priests and scribes, and be killed, and be raised again the third day. [KJV]
	From that time Jesus Christ began to show His disciples that He **must** go to Jerusalem, and suffer many things from the elders and chief priests and scribes, and be killed, and be raised up on the third day. [NASB]
	From that time on Jesus began to explain to his disciples that he **must** go to Jerusalem and suffer many things at the hands of the elders, chief priests and teachers of the law, and that he must be killed and on the third day be raised to life. [NIV]
	From that time Jesus began to show to His disciples that He **must** go to Jerusalem, and suffer many things from the elders and chief priests and scribes, and be killed, and be raised the third day. [NKJV]
	From then on Jesus began to tell his disciples plainly that he **had to** go to Jerusalem, and he told them what would happen to him there. He would suffer at the hands of the leaders and the leading priests and the teachers of religious law. He would be killed, and he would be raised
		Must go; to be compelled; to consider no other options; ought; should; had to go, an absolute necessity, an imperative, a compulsion, destiny.
		
		Practical Application
		The words "must [*dei*] go" are strong: a constraint, an imperative, a necessity was laid upon Christ. He had no choice. His death and resurrection had been planned and willed by God through all eternity. The prophets had predicted it: He must fulfill the will of God, for God had ordained His death (cp. Matthew 26:54; Luke 24:26, 46).
		The entire life and ministry of Jesus Christ was governed by what He "must" do. The same must be true for the believer also. We must...
		• be born again (John 3:7).
		• become less as He becomes greater (John 3:30).
		• worship God in spirit and in truth (John 4:24).
		• do the work of God who sent Christ (John 6:28).
		• follow Christ if we are going to serve Him (John 12:26).
		• love one another (John 13:34).
		• remain in the vine—connected to Christ—if we are to bear fruit (John 15:4).

ENGLISH WORD	GREEK WORD AND VERSE	THE WORD MEANS...
	on the third day. [NLT] Ἀπὸ τότε ἤρξατο ὁ Ἰησοῦς δεικνύειν τοῖς μαθηταῖς αὐτοῦ ὅτι **δεῖ** αὐτὸν ἀπελθεῖν εἰς Ἱεροσόλυμα, καὶ πολλὰ παθεῖν ἀπὸ τῶν πρεσβυτέρων καὶ ἀρχιερέων καὶ γραμματέων, καὶ ἀποκτανθῆναι, καὶ τῇ τρίτῃ ἡμέρᾳ ἐγερθῆναι. [GNS] Ἀπὸ τότε ἤρξατο ὁ Ἰησοῦς δεικνύειν τοῖς μαθηταῖς αὐτοῦ ὅτι **δεῖ** αὐτὸν εἰς Ἱεροσόλυμα ἀπελθεῖν καὶ πολλὰ παθεῖν ἀπὸ τῶν πρεσβυτέρων καὶ ἀρχιερέων καὶ γραμματέων καὶ ἀποκτανθῆναι καὶ τῇ τρίτῃ ἡμέρᾳ ἐγερθῆναι. [GNT]	
#2638 **Must** Ought–KJV Ought–NASB Should–NIV Ought–NKJV **Must–NLT** **POSB** **REFERENCE** (Lk.18:1) Note 1, point 2	**δεῖν** = *dein* Pronunciation: [dine] Parsing (part of speech): verb 　Mood—infinitive 　Tense—present 　Voice—active 　Case—accusative 　Stem or root—from δεῖ Concordance References: 　⇒ Strong's #1163 dei 　⇒ NIV #1256 dei 　⇒ NASB #1163 dei **Luke 18:1** And he spake a parable unto them to this end, that men **ought** always to pray, and not to faint; [KJV] Now He was telling them a parable to show that at all times they **ought** to pray and not to lose heart, [NASB] Then Jesus told his disciples a parable to show them that they **should** always pray and not give up. [NIV] Then He spoke a parable to them, that men always **ought** to pray and not lose heart, [NKJV] One day Jesus told his disciples a story to illustrate their need for constant prayer and to show them that they **must** never give up. [NLT] Ἔλεγε δὲ καὶ παραβολὴν αὐτοῖς πρὸς τὸ **δεῖν** πάντοτε προσεύχεσθαι, καὶ μὴ ἐκκακεῖν, [GNS] Ἔλεγεν δὲ παραβολὴν αὐτοῖς πρὸς τὸ **δεῖν** πάντοτε προσεύχεσθαι αὐτοὺς καὶ μὴ ἐγκακεῖν, [GNT]	Must, should, ought. It means a strong sense of duty and responsibility. **Practical Application** The words "must never give up" have the idea of necessity. It is absolutely necessary that men persevere in prayer.
#2639 **Must Believe** **Must believe–KJV** **Must believe–NASB** **Must believe–NIV** **Must believe–NKJV** **Must believe–NLT** **POSB** **REFERENCE** (Heb.11:6) Note 5, point 2a	**πιστεῦσαι δεῖ** = *pisteusai dei* Pronunciation: [pist-yoo'-sah-ee die] Parsing *pisteusai* (part of speech): verb 　Mood—infinitive 　Tense—aorist 　Voice—active 　Stem or root—from πιστεύω Parsing *dei* (part of speech): verb 　Mood—indicative 　Tense—present 　Voice—active 　Person—3rd person 　Number—singular 　Stem or root—from δεῖ Concordance References: 　⇒ Strong's #4100 pisteuō + 1163 dei 　⇒ NIV #4409 pisteuō [believe] + 1256 dei [must] 　⇒ NASB #4100 pisteuō + 1163 dei **Hebrews 11:6** But without faith it is impossible to please him: for he that cometh to God **must believe** that he is, and that he is a rewarder of them that diligently seek him. [KJV] And without faith it is impossible to please Him, for he who comes to God **must believe** that He is, and that He is a rewarder of those who seek Him. [NASB] And without faith it is impossible to please God, because anyone who comes to him **must believe** that he exists and that he rewards those who earnestly seek him. [NIV] But without faith *it is* impossible to please *Him,* for he	To believe in; must believe in; must have confidence in; must have faith in. **Practical Application** The person who comes to God must believe two things. 1. He *must believe* in God—that God is—that God exists. The words "must believe" (*pisteusai dei*) mean necessary and essential, absolutely necessary and essential. A.T. Robertson says it is a "moral necessity to have faith....The very Existence of God is a matter of intelligent faith...so that men are left without excuse (Romans 1:19f)" (*Word Pictures in the New Testament*, Vol. 5, p.420f). 　⇒ A person must look at the world (heaven and earth) and at himself—at the existence, design, order, and end of all things—and believe in God. 　⇒ A person must look at the Word of God, the Holy Bible, and believe in God. 　⇒ A person must look at Jesus Christ, the very Son of God, who reveals God to man, and believe in God. 2. He *must believe* that God rewards those who diligently seek Him. Note the word "diligently" (*ekzetousin*). It means to *seek out God*; to diligently seek to find Him and to follow

ENGLISH WORD	GREEK WORD AND VERSE	THE WORD MEANS...
	who comes to God **must believe** that He is, and *that* He is a rewarder of those who diligently seek Him. [NKJV] So, you see, it is impossible to please God without faith. Anyone who wants to come to him **must believe** that there is a God and that he rewards those who sincerely seek him. [NLT] χωρὶς δὲ πίστεως ἀδύνατον εὐαρεστῆσαι· **πιστεῦσαι** γὰρ **δεῖ** τὸν προσερχόμενον τῷ Θεῷ, ὅτι ἔστι, καὶ τοῖς ἐκζητοῦσιν αὐτὸν μισθαποδότης γίνεται. [GNS] χωρὶς δὲ πίστεως ἀδύνατον εὐαρεστῆσαι· **πιστεῦσαι** γὰρ **δεῖ** τὸν προσερχόμενον τῷ θεῷ ὅτι ἔστιν καὶ τοῖς ἐκζητοῦσιν αὐτὸν μισθαποδότης γίνεται. [GNT]	Him. God does not reward the sleepy-eyed, complacent, non-thinker, half-interested, worldly-minded, pleasure seeker. God rewards those who diligently seek to know and follow Him. The idea is that we must be in earnest and persevere and endure to the end. What is the reward to those who diligently seek God? It is the same reward given to Abel and Enoch: righteousness and God's care in this life and deliverance from death unto eternal life.

#2640
Must Love Me More
 	
Hate not–KJV
Not hate–NASB
Not hate–NIV
Not hate–NKJV
Must love me more–NLT
 	
POSB REFERENCE
(Lk.14:26)
Note 2
	οὐ μισεῖ = *ou misei*
	Pronunciation: [oo mis-eh'-ee]
	Parsing *ou* (part of speech): particle
	    Type—negative
	    Stem or root—from οὐ
	Parsing *misei* (part of speech): verb
	    Mood—indicative
	    Tense—present
	    Voice—active
	    Person—3rd person
	    Number—singular
	    Stem or root—from μισέω
	Concordance References:
	  ⇒ Strong's #3756 ou + 3404 miseo
	  ⇒ NIV #4024 ou [not] + 3631 miseö [hate]
	  ⇒ NASB #3756 ou + 3404 miseo
	
	### Luke 14:26
	If any man come to me, and **hate not** his father, and mother, and wife, and children, and brethren, and sisters, yea, and his own life also, he cannot be my disciple. [KJV]
	
	"If anyone comes to Me, and does **not hate** his own father and mother and wife and children and brothers and sisters, yes, and even his own life, he cannot be My disciple. [NASB]
	
	"If anyone comes to me and does **not hate** his father and mother, his wife and children, his brothers and sisters—yes, even his own life—he cannot be my disciple. [NIV]
	
	"If anyone comes to Me and does **not hate** his father and mother, wife and children, brothers and sisters, yes, and his own life also, he cannot be My disciple. [NKJV]
	
	"If you want to be my follower you **must love me more** than your own father and mother, wife and children, brothers and sisters—yes, more than your own life. Otherwise, you cannot be my disciple. [NLT]
	
	Εἴ τις ἔρχεται πρός με, καὶ **οὐ μισεῖ** τὸν πατέρα ἑαυτοῦ, καὶ τὴν μητέρα, καὶ τὴν γυναῖκα, καὶ τὰ τέκνα, καὶ τοὺς ἀδελφοὺς, καὶ τὰς ἀδελφάς, ἔτι τε καὶ τὴν ἑαυτοῦ ψυχὴν, οὐ δύναται μου μαθητής εἶναί. [GNS]
	
	Εἴ τις ἔρχεται πρός με καὶ **οὐ μισεῖ** τὸν πατέρα ἑαυτοῦ καὶ τὴν μητέρα καὶ τὴν γυναῖκα καὶ τὰ τέκνα καὶ τοὺς ἀδελφοὺς καὶ τὰς ἀδελφάς ἔτι τε καὶ τὴν ψυχὴν ἑαυτοῦ, οὐ δύναται εἶναί μου μαθητής. [GNT]
		Not showing preference, disregard; not hate; not detest.
		
		### Practical Application
		The words "must love me more" are strong. Christ was not saying that one's family and one's self were to be literally hated. The true believer is to love even his enemies (Luke 6:27). What then did Christ mean? Very simply...
		
		• Christ is to be first in a person's life: before family, even before self.
		
		• Christ is to be put before family: even if one's family opposes his decision to follow Christ.
		
		• Christ is to be put first: before the companionship and comfort and pleasure of family and home.
		
		• All—even family and self—are to be put behind Christ and His mission. All must be denied and put behind a person's love and devotion to Christ and His cause.

#2641
Mutually Encouraged
 	
Comforted together–KJV
 	
Encouraged together–NASB
 	
Mutually encouraged–NIV
 	
Encouraged together–NKJV
	συμπαρακληθῆναι = *sumparaklēthēnai*
	Pronunciation: [soom-par-ak-leh'-thay-nah-ee]
	Parsing (part of speech): verb
	    Mood—infinitive
	    Tense—aorist
	    Voice—passive
	    Case—accusative
	    Stem or root—from συμπαρακαλέομαι
	Concordance References:
	  ⇒ Strong's #4837 sumparakaleö
	  ⇒ NIV #5220 sumparakaleö
	  ⇒ NASB #4837 sumparakaleö
		To be encouraged together; to be mutually encouraged; to be strengthened and consoled together.
		
		### Practical Application
		Paul wished to be mutually encouraged with other believers. Paul expected to be taught and strengthened by the believers as well as to teach and to strengthen them. There was to be a mutual sharing among all. Paul expected all believers to be actively sharing the gospel. He even expected them to share with him so that he might grow and be more firmly rooted in the faith.

ENGLISH WORD	GREEK WORD AND VERSE	THE WORD MEANS...
Encouraged by yours–NLT **POSB REFERENCE** (Romans 1:10-13; esp. v.12) Note 4, point 2	**Romans 1:12** That is, that I may be **comforted together** with you by the mutual faith both of you and me. [KJV] That is, that I may be **encouraged together** with you while among you, each of us by the other's faith, both yours and mine. [NASB] That is, that you and I may be **mutually encouraged** by each other's faith. [NIV] That is, that I may be **encouraged together** with you by the mutual faith both of you and me. [NKJV] I'm eager to encourage you in your faith, but I also want to be **encouraged by yours**. In this way, each of us will be a blessing to the other. [NLT] τοῦτο δέ ἐστι, **συμπαρακληθῆναι** ἐν ὑμῖν διὰ τῆς ἐν ἀλλήλοις πίστεως ὑμῶν τε καὶ ἐμοῦ. [GNS] τοῦτο δέ ἐστιν **συμπαρακληθῆναι** ἐν ὑμῖν διὰ τῆς ἐν ἀλλήλοις πίστεως ὑμῶν τε καὶ ἐμοῦ. [GNT]	

#2642
Mystery
 	
Mystery–KJV
Mystery–NASB
Secret–NIV
Mystery–NKJV
Secret–NLT
 	
POSB REFERENCE
(1 Cor.2:7)
Deeper Study #1
	ἐν μυστηρίῳ = *en mustēriō*
	Pronunciation: [en moos-tay'-ree-o]
	Parsing (part of speech): noun
	    Case—dative
	    Gender—neuter
	    Number—singular
	    Stem or root—from μυστήριον, ου
	Concordance References:
	⇒ Strong's #1722+3466 en mustërion
	⇒ NIV #1877+3696 en mustërion [secret]
	⇒ NASB #1722+3466 en mustërion
	
	1 Cor. 2:7
	But we speak the wisdom of God in a **mystery**, even the hidden wisdom, which God ordained before the world unto our glory: [KJV]
	But we speak God's wisdom in a **mystery**, the hidden wisdom, which God predestined before the ages to our glory; [NASB]
	No, we speak of God's **secret** wisdom, a wisdom that has been hidden and that God destined for our glory before time began. [NIV]
	But we speak the wisdom of God in a **mystery**, the hidden *wisdom* which God ordained before the ages for our glory, [NKJV]
	No, the wisdom we speak of is the **secret** wisdom of God, which was hidden in former times, though he made it for our benefit before the world began. [NLT]
	ἀλλὰ λαλοῦμεν σοφίαν Θεοῦ **ἐν μυστηρίῳ**, τὴν ἀποκεκρυμμένην, ἣν προώρισεν ὁ Θεὸς πρὸ τῶν αἰώνων εἰς δόξαν ἡμῶν· [GNS]
	ἀλλὰ λαλοῦμεν θεοῦ σοφίαν **ἐν μυστηρίῳ**, τὴν ἀποκεκρυμμένην, ἣν προώρισεν ὁ θεὸς πρὸ τῶν αἰώνων εἰς δόξαν ἡμῶν· [GNT]
		A secret; a mystery; a fact or truth that man is unable to discover by himself; a fact or truth that has to be revealed to man.
		
		Practical Application
		It is a fact or truth that had been hidden and kept secret by God until it was time for it to be revealed. It does not mean something hard to understand or something strange and mysterious as a magical trick. It does not mean that there is something mysterious about God. It means some fact or truth...
		• that is known only by God.
		• that God reveals to man because He loves man and man desperately needs to know the truth.
		There are several important mysteries or secrets revealed in the Bible.
		1. The mystery of the gospel, that is, God's wisdom which is Christ crucified (1 Cor. 1:23-24; 1 Cor. 2:7; Ephes. 6:19).
		2. The mysteries of the Kingdom of heaven (See POSB note—Matthew 13:10-11; cp. Matthew 13:1-52).
		3. The mystery of Israel's blindness and restoration (Romans 11:25-27).
		4. The mystery of the believers' resurrection, which will enable them to live an incorruptible life with God (1 Cor. 15:51-52; 1 Thes. 4:13-18).
		5. The mystery of God's will: that He is to gather together and unify all things in Christ—unify them in a spirit of peace and harmony—all things, both visible and invisible (Ephes. 1:9-10).
		6. The mystery of the church and of God's universal love: that both Jew and Gentile are included in the church (Ephes. 3:4-6; cp. 1 Cor. 2:7-12; Romans 16:25).
		7. The mystery of the church: that the church is the bride and body of Christ (Ephes. 5:30-32; cp. Ephes. 5:22-33).
		8. The mystery of the indwelling Christ, of "Christ in you, the hope of glory" (Col. 1:26-27; Galatians 2:20).
		9. The mystery of godliness or of Christ; of God's coming to earth in human flesh in the person of Jesus Christ (Col. 2:2, 9; 1 Tim. 3:16; Col. 4:3; 2 Cor. 5:19).
		10. The mystery of iniquity and of sin in the world and of man's disobedience to God

ENGLISH WORD	GREEK WORD AND VERSE	THE WORD MEANS...
		(2 Thes. 2:7; Ephes. 2:2). 11. The mystery of the seven stars or local churches and pastors (Rev. 1:20). 12. The mystery of Babylon in the end time (Rev. 17:5, 7).

#2643
Mystery
 	
Mystery–KJV
Mystery–NASB
Mystery–NIV
Mystery–NKJV
Secret–NLT
 	
POSB
REFERENCE
(Romans 16:25-26; esp. v.25)
Note 3, point 1
 	
See also POSB REF:
(Rom.11:25-26; esp. v.25)
Note 1, point 1
(Eph.3:3-5; esp. v.4)
Note 2
	μυστηρίου = *mustëriou*
	Pronunciation: [moos-tay'-ree-oo]
	Parsing (part of speech): noun
	   Case—genitive
	   Gender—neuter
	   Number—singular
	   Stem or root—from μυστήριον, ου
	Concordance References:
	⇒ Strong's #3466 mustërion
	⇒ NIV #3696 mustërion
	⇒ NASB #3466 mustërion
	
	Romans 16:25
	Now to him that is of power to stablish you according to my gospel, and the preaching of Jesus Christ, according to the revelation of the **mystery**, which was kept secret since the world began, [KJV]
	Now to Him who is able to establish you according to my gospel and the preaching of Jesus Christ, according to the revelation of the **mystery** which has been kept secret for long ages past, [NASB]
	Now to him who is able to establish you by my gospel and the proclamation of Jesus Christ, according to the revelation of the **mystery** hidden for long ages past, [NIV]
	Now to Him who is able to establish you according to my gospel and the preaching of Jesus Christ, according to the revelation of the **mystery** kept secret since the world began [NKJV]
	God is able to make you strong, just as the Good News says. It is the message about Jesus Christ and his plan for you Gentiles, a plan kept **secret** from the beginning of time. [NLT]
	Τῷ δὲ δυναμένῳ ὑμᾶς στηρίξαι κατὰ τὸ εὐαγγέλιόν μου καὶ τὸ κήρυγμα Ἰησοῦ Χριστοῦ, κατὰ ἀποκάλυψιν **μυστηρίου** χρόνοις αἰωνίοις σεσιγημένου [GNS]
	[Τῷ δὲ δυναμένῳ ὑμᾶς στηρίξαι κατὰ τὸ εὐαγγέλιόν μου καὶ τὸ κήρυγμα Ἰησοῦ Χριστοῦ, κατὰ ἀποκάλυψιν **μυστηρίου** χρόνοις αἰωνίοις σεσιγημένου, [GNT]
		Secret, mystery, deep truth (of something formerly unknown but now revealed).
		
		Practical Application
		The mystery of the gospel had been a secret since the world began. The word "mystery" (*mustëriou*) does not mean something obscure and difficult to understand nor something that has to be searched out and solved by men. It simply means...
		• some truth that was not previously known.
		• some truth that could not be discovered by human reason.
		• some truth that had to be revealed by God if it were ever to be known.
		
		The gospel could never have been known by man. It is not a creation of man's mind, of his rationalizations, concepts, thoughts, and ideas as to how man is to become reconciled to God. Man could never and can never figure out how to become acceptable to God. No man in this physical world could ever penetrate the spiritual world, no matter what some have claimed.

#2644
Myths
 	
Fables–KJV
Myths–NASB
Myths–NIV
Fables–NKJV
Myths–NLT
 	
POSB
REFERENCE
(1 Tim.1:4)
Note 2, point 1
	μύθοις = *muthois*
	Pronunciation: [moo'-thoys]
	Parsing (part of speech): noun
	   Case—dative
	   Gender—masculine
	   Number—plural
	   Stem or root—from μῦθος, ου
	Concordance References:
	⇒ Strong's #3454 muthos
	⇒ NIV #3680 muthos
	⇒ NASB #3454 muthos
	
	1 Tim. 1:4
	Neither give heed to **fables** and endless genealogies, which minister questions, rather than godly edifying which is in faith: so do. [KJV]
	Nor to pay attention to **myths** and endless genealogies, which give rise to mere speculation rather than furthering the administration of God which is by faith. [NASB]
	Nor to devote themselves to **myths** and endless genealogies. These promote controversies rather than God's work—which is by faith. [NIV]
	Nor give heed to **fables** and endless genealogies, which cause disputes rather than godly edification which is in faith. [NKJV]
	Don't let people waste time in endless speculation
		Myths, fables, stories. The word "myths" (*muthois*) refers to *all forms* of false and fictional teaching or doctrine.
		
		Practical Application
		It means the *false ideas* and speculations of men about God and Christ and the teachings of God's Word. The doctrines of men are only speculations, fables, narratives, stories, fictions, and falsehoods (A.T. Robertson. *Word Pictures in the New Testament*, Vol.4, p.561).

ENGLISH WORD	GREEK WORD AND VERSE	THE WORD MEANS...

	over **myths** and spiritual pedigrees. For these things only cause arguments; they don't help people live a life of faith in God. [NLT]
	    μηδὲ προσέχειν **μύθοις** καὶ γενεαλογίαις ἀπεράντοις, αἵτινες ζητήσεις παρέχουσι μᾶλλον ἢ οἰκοδομίαν Θεοῦ τὴν ἐν πίστει-. [GNS]
	    μηδὲ προσέχειν **μύθοις** καὶ γενεαλογίαις ἀπεράντοις, αἵτινες ἐκζητήσεις παρέχουσιν μᾶλλον ἢ οἰκονομίαν θεοῦ τὴν ἐν πίστει. [GNT]	

ENGLISH WORD	GREEK WORD AND VERSE	THE WORD MEANS...

interest in your welfare. [NIV]

For I have no one like-minded, who will **sincerely** care for your state. [NKJV]

I have no one else like Timothy, who **genuinely** cares about your welfare. [NLT]

οὐδένα γὰρ ἔχω ἰσόψυχον, ὅστις **γνησίως** τὰ περὶ ὑμῶν μεριμνήσει, [GNS]

οὐδένα γὰρ ἔχω ἰσόψυχον, ὅστις **γνησίως** τὰ περὶ ὑμῶν μεριμνήσει· [GNT]

deep and genuine, a true concern.

#2651
Nature

Nature–KJV
Instinctively–NASB
Nature–NIV
Nature–NKJV
Instinctively–NLT

**POSB
REFERENCE**
(Romans 2:11-15; esp.
v.14)
Note 4, point 3a

φύσει = *phusei*
Pronunciation: [foo'-see]
Parsing (part of speech): noun
　　Case—dative
　　Gender—feminine
　　Number—singular
　　Stem or root—from φύσις, εως
Concordance References:
⇒　Strong's #5449 phusis
⇒　NIV #5882 phusis
⇒　NASB #5449 phusis

Romans 2:14

For when the Gentiles, which have not the law, do by **nature** the things contained in the law, these, having not the law, are a law unto themselves: [KJV]

For when Gentiles who do not have the Law do **instinctively** the things of the Law, these, not having the law, are a law to themselves, [NASB]

(Indeed, when Gentiles, who do not have the law, do by **nature** things required by the law, they are a law for themselves, even though they do not have the law, [NIV]

For when Gentiles, who do not have the law, by **nature** do the things in the law, these, although not having the law, are a law to themselves, [NKJV]

Even when Gentiles, who do not have God's written law, **instinctively** follow what the law says, they show that in their hearts they know right from wrong. [NLT]

ὅταν γὰρ ἔθνη τὰ μὴ νόμον ἔχοντα **φύσει** τὰ τοῦ νόμου ποιῇ, οὗτοι νόμον μὴ ἔχοντες, ἑαυτοῖς εἰσι νόμος· [GNS]

ὅταν γὰρ ἔθνη τὰ μὴ νόμον ἔχοντα **φύσει** τὰ τοῦ νόμου ποιῶσιν, οὗτοι νόμον μὴ ἔχοντες ἑαυτοῖς εἰσιν νόμος· [GNT]

Nature, natural condition; instinct.

Practical Application
The heathen have a threefold witness, a witness that is strong enough to lead them to God.
1. Men have their nature—the nature of man that speaks loudly and clearly—that points toward God. Note exactly what the verse says.
　⇒ Men may not have the law (the Scriptures)...
　⇒ But they can do the law by nature.
　⇒ They can become "a law unto themselves."

There is that within man, within his nature (*phusei*), that can stir him to do the law. Man has within him an instinctive knowledge of right and wrong. His very nature gives him the opportunity to do what is right.
　　Something else is meant here as well. Man can look at nature (creation) and see that he is part of it. He can instinctively see by nature the great eternal power and deity of God. (See POSB note—Romans 1:20 for a list of the things nature reveals about God.)
2. Men have their consciences that bear witness to what is right and wrong. When they do right, they sense approval; when they do wrong, they sense reproach. Man's conscience gives him the opportunity to live righteously and to do good.
3. Men have their thoughts, their reasoning ability which can approve or disapprove, excuse or accuse them and others. Men's thoughts bear witness to how they should and should not live, whether their behavior is excused (acceptable) or accused (condemned).

#2652
Nature

Form–KJV
Form–NASB
Nature–NIV
Form–NKJV
Not translated–NLT

**POSB
REFERENCE**
(Philip.2:6)
Note 2, point 2

μορφῇ = *morphë*
Pronunciation: [mor-fay']
Parsing (part of speech): noun
　　Case—dative
　　Gender—feminine
　　Number—singular
　　Stem or root—from μορφή, ῆς
Concordance References:
⇒　Strong's #3444 morphë
⇒　NIV #3671 morphë
⇒　NASB #3444 morphë

Philip. 2:6

Who, being in the **form** of God, thought it not robbery to be equal with God: [KJV]

Who, although He existed in the **form** of God, did not regard equality with God a thing to be grasped, [NASB]

Who, being in very **nature** God, did not consider equality with God something to be grasped, [NIV]

Who, being in the **form** of God, did not consider it robbery to be equal to God, [NKJV]

Nature, form, appearance, model. It means the permanent, constant being of a person. It is the very essence of a person, that part of him that never changes. It is the unchangeable being.

Practical Application
Jesus Christ is *in the nature of God*. William Barclay points out that there is another Greek word translated "form" (*schema*). In contrast, it means the fleeting, outward form of a person that is always changing. For example, a man is always changing (*schema*) in looks because of age and fashion. But his manhood (*morphë*) never changes. (*The Letters to the Philippians, Colossians, and Thessalonians*, p.44.)
　　This means a most glorious thing. Jesus is of the very essence and being and image of God. He is the divine, unchangeable God Himself. He dwells in the very perfection and essence of God; He possesses the very attributes of God Himself.

ENGLISH WORD	GREEK WORD AND VERSE	THE WORD MEANS...
	Though he was God, he did not demand and cling to his rights as God. [NLT]—NOT TRANSLATED ὃς ἐν **μορφῇ** Θεοῦ ὑπάρχων, οὐχ ἁρπαγμὸν ἡγήσατο τὸ εἶναι ἴσα Θεῷ, [GNS] ὃς ἐν **μορφῇ** θεοῦ ὑπάρχων οὐχ ἁρπαγμὸν ἡγήσατο τὸ εἶναι ἴσα θεῷ, [GNT]	*Who being the brightness of his glory, and the express image of his person, and upholding all things by the word of his power, when he had by himself purged our sins, sat down on the right hand of the Majesty on high (Hebrews 1:3).* *Who is the image of the invisible God, the firstborn of every creature (Col. 1:15).*

#2653
Nature
 	
Person–KJV
Nature–NASB
Being–NIV
Person–NKJV
God–NLT
 	
POSB
REFERENCE
(Heb.1:3)
Note 5
	ὑποστάσεως = *hupostaseōs*
	Pronunciation: [hoop-os'-tas-eh-os]
	Parsing (part of speech): noun
	    Case—genitive
	    Gender—feminine
	    Number—singular
	    Stem or root—from ὑπόστασις, εως
	Concordance References:
	  ⇒ Strong's #5287 hupostasis
	  ⇒ NIV #5712 hupostasis
	  ⇒ NASB #5287 hupostasis
	
	Hebrews 1:3
	Who being the brightness of his glory, and the express image of his **person**, and upholding all things by the word of his power, when he had by himself purged our sins, sat down on the right hand of the Majesty on high; [KJV]
	
	And He is the radiance of His glory and the exact representation of His **nature**, and upholds all things by the word of His power. When He had made purification of sins, He sat down at the right hand of the Majesty on high; [NASB]
	
	The Son is the radiance of God's glory and the exact representation of his **being**, sustaining all things by his powerful word. After he had provided purification for sins, he sat down at the right hand of the Majesty in heaven. [NIV]
	
	Who being the brightness of His glory and the express image of His **person**, and upholding all things by the word of His power, when He had by Himself purged our sins, sat down at the right hand of the Majesty on high, [NKJV]
	
	The Son reflects God's own glory, and everything about him represents **God** exactly. He sustains the universe by the mighty power of his command. After he died to cleanse us from the stain of sin, he sat down in the place of honor at the right hand of the majestic God of heaven. [NLT]
	
	ὃς ὢν ἀπαύγασμα τῆς δόξης, καὶ χαρακτὴρ τῆς **ὑποστάσεως** αὐτοῦ, φέρων τε τὰ πάντα τῷ ῥήματι τῆς δυνάμεως αὐτοῦ, δι' ἑαυτοῦ καθαρισμὸν ποιησάμενος τῶν ἁμαρτιῶν ἡμῶν, ἐκάθισεν ἐν δεξιᾷ τῆς μεγαλωσύνης ἐν ὑψηλοῖς, [GNS]
	
	ὃς ὢν ἀπαύγασμα τῆς δόξης καὶ χαρακτὴρ τῆς **ὑποστάσεως** αὐτοῦ, φέρων τε τὰ πάντα τῷ ῥήματι τῆς δυνάμεως αὐτοῦ, καθαρισμὸν τῶν ἁμαρτιῶν ποιησάμενος ἐκάθισεν ἐν δεξιᾷ τῆς μεγαλωσύνης ἐν ὑψηλοῖς, [GNT]
		Being, person, nature, substance.
		
		### Practical Application
		Jesus Christ is the very substance, the very Being, Person, and Embodiment of God.

#2654
Necessities
 	
Necessities–KJV
Hardships–NASB
Hardships–NIV
Needs–NKJV
Hardships–NLT
 	
POSB
REFERENCE
(2 Cor.6:4-5; esp. v.4)
Note 3
	ἀνάγκαις = *anagkais*
	Pronunciation: [an-ang-kah-ees]
	Parsing (part of speech): noun
	    Case—dative
	    Gender—feminine
	    Number—plural
	    Stem or root—from ἀνάγκη, ης
	Concordance References:
	  ⇒ Strong's #318 anagkē
	  ⇒ NIV #340 anagkē
	  ⇒ NASB #318 anagkē
		Hardships; inescapable hardships, difficulties; the privation, distress, trouble, and pain suffered in life.
		
		### Practical Application
		William Barclay points out that the word literally means "the necessities of life" (*The Letters to the Corinthians*, p.238). A minister or servant is called upon to face the necessities of life: he has to eat and drink, clothe and shelter himself and his family; and he has to face the sorrows and struggles and pains of life, includ-

ENGLISH WORD	GREEK WORD AND VERSE	THE WORD MEANS...
	2 Cor. 6:4 But in all things approving ourselves as the ministers of God, in much patience, in afflictions, in **necessities**, in distresses, [KJV] But in everything commending ourselves as servants of God, in much endurance, in afflictions, in **hardships**, in distresses, [NASB] Rather, as servants of God we commend ourselves in every way: in great endurance; in troubles, **hardships** and distresses; [NIV] But in all things we commend ourselves as ministers of God: in much patience, in tribulations, in **needs**, in distresses, [NKJV] In everything we do we try to show that we are true ministers of God. We patiently endure troubles and **hardships** and calamities of every kind. [NLT] ἀλλ' ἐν παντὶ συνίσταντες ἑαυτοὺς ὡς Θεοῦ διάκονοι, ἐν ὑπομονῇ πολλῇ, ἐν θλίψεσιν, ἐν **ἀνάγκαις**, ἐν στενοχωρίαις, [GNS] ἀλλ' ἐν παντὶ συνίσταντες ἑαυτοὺς ὡς θεοῦ διάκονοι, ἐν ὑπομονῇ πολλῇ, ἐν θλίψεσιν, ἐν **ἀνάγκαις**, ἐν στενοχωρίαις, [GNT]	ing death itself—sometimes beyond what the average citizen has to face. Only one thing can carry the minister or servant through the necessities and experiences of life: endurance. He must steadfastly endure for the sake of the Lord Jesus Christ and His ministry.

#2655
Needs
 	
Necessities–KJV
Hardships–NASB
Hardships–NIV
Needs–NKJV
Hardships–NLT
 	
POSB REFERENCE
(2 Cor.6:4-5; esp. v.4)
Note 3
	ἀνάγκαις = *anagkais*
	Pronunciation: [an-ang-kah-ees]
	Parsing (part of speech): noun
	    Case—dative
	    Gender—feminine
	    Number—plural
	    Stem or root—from **ἀνάγκη**, ης
	Concordance References:
	⇒ Strong's #318 anagkē
	⇒ NIV #340 anagkē
	⇒ NASB #318 anagkē
	
	2 Cor. 6:4
	But in all things approving ourselves as the ministers of God, in much patience, in afflictions, in **necessities**, in distresses, [KJV]
	But in everything commending ourselves as servants of God, in much endurance, in afflictions, in **hardships**, in distresses, [NASB]
	Rather, as servants of God we commend ourselves in every way: in great endurance; in troubles, **hardships** and distresses; [NIV]
	But in all things we commend ourselves as ministers of God: in much patience, in tribulations, in **needs**, in distresses, [NKJV]
	In everything we do we try to show that we are true ministers of God. We patiently endure troubles and **hardships** and calamities of every kind. [NLT]
	ἀλλ' ἐν παντὶ συνίσταντες ἑαυτοὺς ὡς Θεοῦ διάκονοι, ἐν ὑπομονῇ πολλῇ, ἐν θλίψεσιν, ἐν **ἀνάγκαις**, ἐν στενοχωρίαις, [GNS]
	ἀλλ' ἐν παντὶ συνίσταντες ἑαυτοὺς ὡς θεοῦ διάκονοι, ἐν ὑπομονῇ πολλῇ, ἐν θλίψεσιν, ἐν **ἀνάγκαις**, ἐν στενοχωρίαις, [GNT]
		Hardships; inescapable hardships, difficulties; the privation, distress, trouble, and pain suffered in life.
		
		Practical Application
		William Barclay points out that the word literally means "the necessities of life" (*The Letters to the Corinthians*, p.238). A minister or servant is called upon to face the necessities of life: he has to eat and drink, clothe and shelter himself and his family; and he has to face the sorrows and struggles and pains of life, including death itself—sometimes beyond what the average citizen has to face. Only one thing can carry the minister or servant through the necessities and experiences of life: endurance. He must steadfastly endure for the sake of the Lord Jesus Christ and His ministry.

#2656
Needy
 	
Lacked–KJV
Needy–NASB
Needy-NIV
Lacked–NKJV
Poverty–NLT
 	
POSB REFERENCE
(Acts 4:34-37; esp. v.34)
Note 3, point 1
	ἐνδεής = *endeēs*
	Pronunciation: [en-deh-ace']
	Parsing (part of speech): pronominal adjective
	    Case—nominative
	    Gender—masculine
	    Number—singular
	    Stem or root—from **ἐνδεής**, ές
	Concordance References:
	⇒ Strong's #1729 endees
	⇒ NIV #1890 endeēs
	⇒ NASB #1729 endees
	
	Acts 4:34
	Neither was there any among them that **lacked**: for as many as were possessors of lands or houses sold them, and brought the prices of the things that were sold, [KJV]
		Needy; the poor; the person who lacks and lives in poverty.
		
		Practical Application
		The idea is that no family, no man, no woman, no child was neglected. No one was left without the necessities of life; no one had to face a day without the food, clothing, or shelter that he needed to take care of himself or of his dear family. All of God's dear people were taken care of.

ENGLISH WORD	GREEK WORD AND VERSE	THE WORD MEANS...
	For there was not a **needy** person among them, for all who were owners of land or houses would sell them and bring the proceeds of the sales, [NASB] There were no **needy** persons among them. For from time to time those who owned lands or houses sold them, brought the money from the sales [NIV] Nor was there anyone among them who **lacked**; for all who were possessors of lands or houses sold them; and brought the proceeds of the things that were sold, [NKJV] There was no **poverty** among them, because people who owned land or houses sold them [NLT] οὐδὲ γὰρ **ἐνδεής** τις ὑπῆρχεν ἐν αὐτοῖς· ὅσοι γὰρ κτήτορες χωρίων η οἰκιῶν ὑπῆρχον, πωλοῦντες ἔφερον τὰς τιμὰς τῶν πιπρασκομένων, [GNS] οὐδὲ γὰρ **ἐνδεής** τις ἦν ἐν αὐτοῖς· ὅσοι γὰρ κτήτορες χωρίων η οἰκιῶν ὑπῆρχον, πωλοῦντες ἔφερον τὰς τιμὰς τῶν πιπρασκομένων [GNT]	

#2657
Never Give Up
 	
Faint not–KJV
Not lose heart–NASB
Not lose heart–NIV
Not lose heart–NKJV
Never give up–NLT
 	
POSB REFERENCE
(2 Cor.4:1)
Note 1
	οὐκ ἐγκακοῦμεν = ouk egkakoumen
	Pronunciation: [ook ek-kak-oo'-mehn]
	Parsing *egkakoumen* (part of speech): verb
	    Mood—indicative
	    Tense—present
	    Voice—active
	    Person—1st person
	    Number—plural
	    Stem or root—from ἐγκακέω
	Concordance References:
	  ⇒ Strong's #3756 ou + 1573 egkakeö
	  ⇒ NIV #4024 ou [not] +1591 egkakeö [lose heart]
	  ⇒ NASB #3756 ou + 1573 egkakeö
	
	2 Cor. 4:1
	Therefore seeing we have this ministry, as we have received mercy, we **faint not**; [KJV]
	
	Therefore, since we have this ministry, as we received mercy, we do **not lose heart**, [NASB]
	
	Therefore, since through God's mercy we have this ministry, we do **not lose heart**. [NIV]
	
	Therefore, since we have this ministry, as we have received mercy, we do **not lose heart**. [NKJV]
	
	And so, since God in his mercy has given us this wonderful ministry, we **never give up**. [NLT]
	
	Διὰ τοῦτο ἔχοντες τὴν διακονίαν ταύτην, καθὼς ἠλεήθημεν, **οὐκ ἐκκακοῦμεν**· [GNS]
	
	Διὰ τοῦτο, ἔχοντες τὴν διακονίαν ταύτην καθὼς ἠλεήθημεν, **οὐκ ἐγκακοῦμεν** [GNT]
		Not to lose heart; not to tire of; not to faint; not to become weary; never give up; not become discouraged, spiritless, fainthearted, despondent, or discouraged.
		
		Practical Application
		The ministry demands constancy, demands that one never give up. Paul did not quit or give up for any reason, not even because of persecution or weariness and exhaustion.

#2658
Never Gives Up
 	
Beareth–KJV
Bears–NASB
Protects–NIV
Bears–NKJV
Never gives up–NLT
 	
POSB REFERENCE
(1 Cor.13:4-7; esp. v.7)
Note 2, point 12
	στέγει = stegei
	Pronunciation: [steg'-ee]
	Parsing (part of speech): verb
	    Mood—indicative
	    Tense—present
	    Voice—active
	    Person—3rd person
	    Number—singular
	    Stem or root—from στέγω
	Concordance References:
	  ⇒ Strong's #4722 stegö
	  ⇒ NIV #5095 stegö
	  ⇒ NASB #4722 stegö
	
	1 Cor. 13:7
	Beareth all things, believeth all things, hopeth all things, endureth all things. [KJV]
	
	Bears all things, believes all things, hopes all things, endures all things. [NASB]
	
	It always **protects**, always trusts, always hopes, always perseveres. [NIV]
	
	Bears all things, believes all things, hopes all things, endures all things. [NKJV]
	
	Love **never gives up**, never loses faith, is always hopeful, and endures through every circumstance. [NLT]
		To protect; to bear; to never give up; to endure; to put up with; to stand.
		
		Practical Application
		It means both to cover all things and to bear up under all things. Love does both: it stands up under the weight and onslaught of all things, and it covers up the faults of others. It has no pleasure in exposing the wrong and weaknesses of others. Love bears up under any neglect, abuse, ridicule—anything that is thrown against it.

ENGLISH WORD	GREEK WORD AND VERSE	THE WORD MEANS...
	πάντα **στέγει**, πάντα πιστεύει, πάντα ἐλπίζει, πάντα ὑπομένει. [GNS] πάντα **στέγει**, πάντα πιστεύει, πάντα ἐλπίζει, πάντα ὑπομένει. [GNT]	

#2659
Never Had God's Written Law
 	
Without law–KJV
Without the law–NASB
Apart from the law–NIV
Without law–NKJV
Never had God's written law–NLT
 	
POSB REFERENCE
(Romans 2:11-15; esp. v.12)
Note 4, point 1a
	ἀνόμως = *anomōs*
	Pronunciation: [an-om'-oce]
	Parsing (part of speech): adjective adverb
	    Stem or root—from **ἀνόμως**
	Concordance References:
	  ⇒ Strong's #460 anomōs
	  ⇒ NIV #492 anomōs
	  ⇒ NASB #460 anomōs
	
	Romans 2:12
	For as many as have sinned **without law** shall also perish without law: and as many as have sinned in the law shall be judged by the law; [KJV]
	For all who have sinned **without the Law** will also perish without the Law; and all who have sinned under the Law will be judged by the Law; [NASB]
	All who sin **apart from the law** will also perish apart from the law, and all who sin under the law will be judged by the law. [NIV]
	For as many as have sinned **without law** will also perish without law, and as many as have sinned in the law will be judged by the law [NKJV]
	God will punish the Gentiles when they sin, even though they **never had God's written law**. And he will punish the Jews when they sin, for they do have the law. [NLT]
	ὅσοι γὰρ **ἀνόμως** ἥμαρτον, ἀνόμως καὶ ἀπολοῦνται· καὶ ὅσοι ἐν νόμῳ ἥμαρτον, διὰ νόμου κριθήσονται· [GNS]
	ὅσοι γὰρ **ἀνόμως** ἥμαρτον, ἀνόμως καὶ ἀπολοῦνται, καὶ ὅσοι ἐν νόμῳ ἥμαρτον, διὰ νόμου κριθήσονται [GNT]
		Apart from the law; to be without the law; to never have God's written law.
		
		Practical Application
		The man who sins without "God's written law" (*anomos*) will also perish apart from the law. The word for "law" is a general word. It refers to the law of God in both the Scriptures and nature. Therefore, the man who does not have the law of Scripture does have the law of nature to guide him. If he sins against the law of nature, he will still be judged and perish. He had the opportunity to know through nature itself.

#2660
New Life
 	
Regeneration–KJV
Regeneration–NASB
Rebirth–NIV
Regeneration–NKJV
New Life–NLT
 	
POSB REFERENCE
(Tit.3:5)
Note 2, point 1
 	
See also POSB REF:
(Mt.19:28)
Note 2
	παλιγγενεσίας = *paliggenesias*
	Pronunciation: [pal-ing-ghen-es-ee'-ahs]
	Parsing (part of speech): noun
	    Case—genitive
	    Gender—feminine
	    Number—singular
	    Stem or root—from **παλιγγενεσία**, ας
	Concordance References:
	  ⇒ Strong's #3824 paliggenesia
	  ⇒ NIV #4098 paliggenesia
	  ⇒ NASB #3824 paliggenesia
	
	Titus 3:5
	Not by works of righteousness which we have done, but according to his mercy he saved us, by the washing of **regeneration**, and renewing of the Holy Ghost; [KJV]
	He saved us, not on the basis of deeds which we have done in righteousness, but according to His mercy, by the washing of **regeneration** and renewing by the Holy Spirit, [NASB]
	He saved us, not because of righteous things we had done, but because of his mercy. He saved us through the washing of **rebirth** and renewal by the Holy Spirit, [NIV]
	Not by works of righteousness which we have done, but according to His mercy He saved us, through the washing of **regeneration** and renewing of the Holy Spirit, [NKJV]
	He saved us, not because of the good things we did, but because of his mercy. He washed away our sins and gave us a **new life** through the Holy Spirit. [NLT]
	οὐκ ἐξ ἔργων τῶν ἐν δικαιοσύνῃ ὧν ἐποιήσαμεν ἡμεῖς, ἀλλὰ κατὰ τὸν αὐτοῦ ἔλεον ἔσωσεν ἡμᾶς, διὰ λουτροῦ **παλιγγενεσίας** καὶ ἀνακαινώσεως Πνεύματος
		Rebirth, regeneration, new life, renewal. It means to be regenerated or given new life; to be given a new birth; to be renewed or revived; to be spiritually reborn or converted.
		
		Practical Application
		Salvation is a spiritual rebirth; it is a person being *born again* by the Spirit of God.

ENGLISH WORD	GREEK WORD AND VERSE	THE WORD MEANS...

Ἁγίου, [GNS]

οὐκ ἐξ ἔργων τῶν ἐν δικαιοσύνῃ ἃ ἐποιήσαμεν ἡμεῖς ἀλλὰ κατὰ τὸ αὐτοῦ ἔλεος ἔσωσεν ἡμᾶς διὰ λουτροῦ **παλιγγενεσίας** καὶ ἀνακαινώσεως πνεύματος ἁγίου, [GNT]

#2661
New Man

New man–KJV
New self–NASB
New self–NIV
New man–NKJV
New nature–NLT

**POSB
REFERENCE**
(Eph.4:24)
Deeper Study #3

καινὸν ἄνθρωπον = *kainon anthrōpon*
Pronunciation: [kahee-non' anth'-ro-pon]
Parsing *kainon* (part of speech): adjective
    Case—accusative
    Gender—masculine
    Number—singular
    Stem or root—from **καινός**, ή, όν
Parsing *anthrōpon* (part of speech): noun
    Case—accusative
    Gender—masculine
    Number—singular
    Stem or root—from **ἄνθρωπος**, ου
Concordance References:
⇒ Strong's #2537 kainos + 444 anthrōpos
⇒ NIV #2785 kainos [new] + 476 anthrōpos [self]
⇒ NASB #2537 kainos + 444 anthrōpos

Ephes. 4:24

And that ye put on the **new man**, which after God is created in righteousness and true holiness. [KJV]

And put on the **new self**, which in the likeness of God has been created in righteousness and holiness of the truth. [NASB]

And to put on the **new self**, created to be like God in true righteousness and holiness. [NIV]

And that you put on the **new man** which was created according to God, in true righteousness and holiness. [NKJV]

You must display a **new nature** because you are a new person, created in God's likeness—righteous, holy, and true. [NLT]

καὶ ἐνδύσασθαι τὸν **καινὸν ἄνθρωπον**, τὸν κατὰ Θεὸν κτισθέντα ἐν δικαιοσύνῃ καὶ ὁσιότητι τῆς ἀληθείας. [GNS]

καὶ ἐνδύσασθαι τὸν **καινὸν ἄνθρωπον** τὸν κατὰ θεὸν κτισθέντα ἐν δικαιοσύνῃ καὶ ὁσιότητι τῆς ἀληθείας. [GNT]

New man, new self, new nature.

Practical Application

It is a man *regenerated, renewed, born again* who has become spiritually minded. It is a new man created by Christ; he has been given a holy nature and an incorruptible life. It is opposed to the *old man* with a corrupt nature. It is a man who is...

• in fellowship with God.
• obedient to God's will.
• devoted to God's service.

There are two Greek words translated by the English word *new*. There is the word *neos* which refers to something new that has just been made, but there are already many others existing just like it. There is the word kainos which refers to something new, something just made, and there is nothing like it in existence. *Kainos* is the word used here. Jesus Christ makes a *new man* entirely—a creation unlike any other creation existing. The Gentile believer is not made into a Jew; neither is a Jewish believer made into a Gentile. Each, through the Lord Jesus Christ, is made into *a new kind of person—a new man in God*. Every person *can begin life all over again*; every person can have a new beginning, a new life by coming to Jesus Christ.

How is this possible? By the power of God. When a person believes in God's Son, the Lord Jesus Christ—really believes and entrusts his life into the hands of Jesus Christ—God creates the spirit of the person in righteousness and true holiness. God takes the faith of the person and *credits it as the righteousness of Jesus Christ*. God actually credits the person's faith *as the perfect righteousness and holiness of Jesus Christ*. Therefore, the person stands before God in the righteousness and holiness of Jesus Christ. But note: this is not all that God does. He does more marvelous things for the believer—all having to do with creating the believer into a new person.

1. God quickens the spirit of the believer and makes his spirit alive. Whereas the believer's spirit was dead to God, God creates it and makes it alive to God.
2. God causes the believer to be born again spiritually.
3. God actually places His divine nature into the heart of the believer.
4. God actually creates a new man out of the believer.
5. God renews the believer by the Holy Spirit.

#2662
New Nature

New man–KJV
New self–NASB
New self–NIV
New man–NKJV
New nature–NLT

καινὸν ἄνθρωπον = *kainon anthrōpon*
Pronunciation: [kahee-non' anth'-ro-pon]
Parsing *kainon* (part of speech): adjective
    Case—accusative
    Gender—masculine
    Number—singular
    Stem or root—from **καινός**, ή, όν
Parsing *anthrōpon* (part of speech): noun

New man, new self, new nature.

Practical Application

It is a man *regenerated, renewed, born again* who has become spiritually minded. It is a new man created by Christ; he has been given a holy nature and an incorruptible life. It is opposed to

ENGLISH WORD	GREEK WORD AND VERSE	THE WORD MEANS...
POSB REFERENCE (Eph.4:24) *Deeper Study* #3	Case—accusative Gender—masculine Number—singular Stem or root—from ἄνθρωπος, ου Concordance References: ⇒ Strong's #2537 kainos + 444 anthröpos ⇒ NIV #2785 kainos [new] + 476 anthröpos [self] ⇒ NASB #2537 kainos + 444 anthröpos **Ephes. 4:24** And that ye put on the **new man**, which after God is created in righteousness and true holiness. [KJV] And put on the **new self**, which in the likeness of God has been created in righteousness and holiness of the truth. [NASB] And to put on the **new self**, created to be like God in true righteousness and holiness. [NIV] And that you put on the **new man** which was created according to God, in true righteousness and holiness. [NKJV] You must display a **new nature** because you are a new person, created in God's likeness—righteous, holy, and true. [NLT] καὶ ἐνδύσασθαι τὸν **καινὸν ἄνθρωπον**, τὸν κατὰ Θεὸν κτισθέντα ἐν δικαιοσύνῃ καὶ ὁσιότητι τῆς ἀληθείας. [GNS] καὶ ἐνδύσασθαι τὸν **καινὸν ἄνθρωπον** τὸν κατὰ θεὸν κτισθέντα ἐν δικαιοσύνῃ καὶ ὁσιότητι τῆς ἀληθείας. [GNT]	the *old man* with a corrupt nature. It is a man who is... • in fellowship with God. • obedient to God's will. • devoted to God's service. (See **New Man** for more discussion).

#2663
New Self
 	
New man–KJV
New self–NASB
New self–NIV
New man–NKJV
New nature–NLT
 	
POSB REFERENCE (Eph.4:24) *Deeper Study* #3
	καινὸν ἄνθρωπον = kainon anthröpon
	Pronunciation: [kahee-non' anth'-ro-pon]
	Parsing *kainon* (part of speech): adjective
	  Case—accusative
	  Gender—masculine
	  Number—singular
	  Stem or root—from καινός, ή, όν
	Parsing *anthröpon* (part of speech): noun
	  Case—accusative
	  Gender—masculine
	  Number—singular
	  Stem or root—from ἄνθρωπος, ου
	Concordance References:
	⇒ Strong's #2537 kainos + 444 anthröpos
	⇒ NIV #2785 kainos [new] + 476 anthröpos [self]
	⇒ NASB #2537 kainos + 444 anthröpos
	
	Ephes. 4:24
	And that ye put on the **new man**, which after God is created in righteousness and true holiness. [KJV]
	And put on the **new self**, which in the likeness of God has been created in righteousness and holiness of the truth. [NASB]
	And to put on the **new self**, created to be like God in true righteousness and holiness. [NIV]
	And that you put on the **new man** which was created according to God, in true righteousness and holiness. [NKJV]
	You must display a **new nature** because you are a new person, created in God's likeness—righteous, holy, and true. [NLT]
	καὶ ἐνδύσασθαι τὸν **καινὸν ἄνθρωπον**, τὸν κατὰ Θεὸν κτισθέντα ἐν δικαιοσύνῃ καὶ ὁσιότητι τῆς ἀληθείας. [GNS]
	καὶ ἐνδύσασθαι τὸν **καινὸν ἄνθρωπον** τὸν κατὰ θεὸν κτισθέντα ἐν δικαιοσύνῃ καὶ ὁσιότητι τῆς ἀληθείας. [GNT]
		New man, new self, new nature.
		
		Practical Application
		It is a man *regenerated, renewed, born again* who has become spiritually minded. It is a new man created by Christ; he has been given a holy nature and an incorruptible life. It is opposed to the *old man* with a corrupt nature. It is a man who is...
		• in fellowship with God.
		• obedient to God's will.
		• devoted to God's service.
		(See **New Man** for more discussion).

#2664
No Condemnation
	Οὐδὲν κατάκριμα = Ouden katakrima
	Pronunciation: [oo-dehn' kat-ak'-ree-mah]
	Parsing *katakrima* (part of speech): noun
	  Case—nominative
	  Gender—neuter
		No condemnation, blame, censure, denunciation, or reproach.
		
		Practical Application
		"No condemnation" (*Ouden katakrima*)

ENGLISH WORD	GREEK WORD AND VERSE	THE WORD MEANS...
No condemnation–KJV No condemnation–NASB No condemnation–NIV No condemnation–NKJV No condemnation–NLT **POSB REFERENCE** (Rom.8:1) Note 1, point 1	Number—singular Stem or root—from **κατάκριμα**, τος Concordance References: ⇒ Strong's #3762 oudeis + 2631 katakrima ⇒ NIV #4029 oudeis [no] + 2890 katakrima [condemnation] ⇒ NASB #3762 oudeis + 2631 katakrima **Romans 8:1** There is therefore now **no condemnation** to them which are in Christ Jesus, who walk not after the flesh, but after the Spirit. [KJV] There is therefore now **no condemnation** for those who are in Christ Jesus. [NASB] Therefore, there is now **no condemnation** for those who are in Christ Jesus, [NIV] *There is* therefore now **no condemnation** to those who are in Christ Jesus, who do not walk according to the flesh, but according to the Spirit. [NKJV] So now there is **no condemnation** for those who belong to Christ Jesus. [NLT] Οὐδὲν ἄρα νῦν **κατάκριμα** τοῖς ἐν Χριστῷ Ἰησοῦ, μὴ κατὰ σάρχα περιπατοῦσιν, ἀλλὰ κατὰ πνεῦμα. [GNS] Οὐδὲν ἄρα νῦν **κατάκριμα** τοῖς ἐν Χριστῷ Ἰησοῦ· [GNT]	means that the believer is not doomed and damned, but is freed from the penalty and condemnation of sin; he is not judged as a sinner, but is delivered from the condemnation of death and hell; he is not judged to be unrighteous, but is counted to be righteous. Very simply stated, the person who is in Christ is safe and secure from condemnation now and forever. He will not be judged as a sinner; he will not face condemnation. He is beyond condemnation; he will never be condemned for sin; he will never be separated from the love of God which is in Christ Jesus our Lord (cp. John 3:16; Romans 8:33-39). (But remember: the believer is to be judged for his faithfulness to Christ. He will be judged for how responsible he is—for how well he uses his "spiritual gifts" for Christ—for how diligently he serves Christ in the work of God. The judgment of the believer will take place at the great judgment seat of Christ.)

#2665
No Different From What Others Experience
 	
Common to man–KJV
 	
Common to man–NASB
 	
Common to man–NIV
 	
Common to man–NKJV
 	
No different from what others experience–NLT
 	
POSB REFERENCE
(1 Cor.10:11-13; esp. v.13)
Note 3, point 3
	ἀνθρώπινος = *anthrōpinos*
	Pronunciation: [anth-ro'-pee-nos]
	Parsing (part of speech): adjective
	    Case—nominative
	    Gender—masculine
	    Number—singular
	    Stem or root—from *ἀνθρώπινος*, η, ον
	Concordance References:
	⇒ Strong's #442 anthrōpinos
	⇒ NIV #474 anthrōpinos
	⇒ NASB #442 anthrōpinos
	
	1 Cor. 10:13
	There hath no temptation taken you but such as is **common to man**: but God is faithful, who will not suffer you to be tempted above that ye are able; but will with the temptation also make a way to escape, that ye may be able to bear it. [KJV]
	No temptation has overtaken you but such as is **common to man**; and God is faithful, who will not allow you to be tempted beyond what you are able, but with the temptation will provide the way of escape also, that you may be able to endure it. [NASB]
	No temptation has seized you except what is **common to man**. And God is faithful; he will not let you be tempted beyond what you can bear. But when you are tempted, he will also provide a way out so that you can stand up under it. [NIV]
	No temptation has overtaken you except such as is **common to man**; but God is faithful, who will not allow you to be tempted beyond what you are able, but with the temptation will also make the way of escape, that you may be able to bear it. [NKJV]
	But remember that the temptations that come into your life are **no different from what others experience**. And God is faithful. He will keep the temptation from becoming so strong that you can't stand up against it. When you are tempted, he will show you a way out so that you will not give in to it. [NLT]
	πειρασμὸς ὑμᾶς οὐκ εἴληφεν εἰ μὴ **ἀνθρώπινος**· πιστὸς δὲ ὁ Θεός, ὃς οὐκ ἐάσει ὑμᾶς πειρασθῆναι ὑπὲρ ὃ δύνασθε, ἀλλὰ ποιήσει σὺν τῷ πειρασμῷ καὶ τὴν ἔκβασιν, τοῦ δύνασθαι ὑμᾶς ὑπενεγκεῖν. [GNS]
	πειρασμὸς ὑμᾶς οὐκ εἴληφεν εἰ μὴ **ἀνθρώπινος**· πιστὸς δὲ ὁ θεός, ὃς οὐκ ἐάσει ὑμᾶς πειρασθῆναι ὑπὲρ ὃ δύνασθε ἀλλὰ ποιήσει σὺν τῷ πειρασμῷ καὶ τὴν ἔκβασιν τοῦ δύνασθαι ὑπενεγκεῖν. [GNT]
		Common to man; a universal human characteristic; a human temptation that falls to the lot of man.
		
		Practical Application
		This is an amazing promise. Think about it. No temptation...
		
		• is superhuman.
		• is unique.
		• is beyond man's capacity to handle.
		• is terrifying in any sense of the word.
		
		Every single temptation that attacks the believer is *no different from what others experience*. *All men* face the same temptation. This means a wonderful thing: some men have already overcome it. Yes, many fell, caved in to the temptation, but some demonstrated the will and energy to overcome it.

ENGLISH WORD	GREEK WORD AND VERSE	THE WORD MEANS...
#2666 **No Hesitation** Nothing doubting–KJV Without misgivings–NASB **No hesitation–NIV** Doubting nothing–NKJV Not to worry about–NLT **POSB REFERENCE** (Acts 11:4-15; esp. v.12) Note 2, point 3	μηδὲν διακρίναντα = *mēden diakrinanta* Pronunciation: [may-dehn' dee-ak-ree'-nahn-tah] Parsing *diakrinanta* (part of speech): verb 　Mood—participle 　Tense—aorist 　Voice—active 　Case—accusative 　Gender—masculine 　Person—1st person 　Number—singular 　Stem or root—from διακρίνω Concordance References: ⇒　Strong's #3367 mēdeis + 1252 diakrinō ⇒　NIV #3594 mēdeis [no] + 1359 diakrinō [hesitation] ⇒　NASB #3367 mēdeis + 1252 diakrinō **Acts 11:12** And the spirit bade me go with them, **nothing doubting**. Moreover these six brethren accompanied me, and we entered into the man's house: [KJV] "And the Spirit told me to go with them **without misgivings**. And these six brethren also went with me, and we entered the man's house. [NASB] The Spirit told me to have **no hesitation** about going with them. These six brothers also went with me, and we entered the man's house. [NIV] Then the Spirit told me to go with them, **doubting nothing**. Moreover these six brethren accompanied me, and we entered the man's house. [NKJV] The Holy Spirit told me to go with them and **not to worry about** their being Gentiles. These six brothers here accompanied me, and we soon arrived at the home of the man who had sent for us. [NLT] εἶπε δὲ μοι τὸ Πνεῦμά συνελθεῖν αὐτοῖς, **μηδὲν διακρινόμενον**. ἦλθον δὲ σὺν ἐμοὶ καὶ οἱ ἓξ ἀδελφοὶ οὗτοι, καὶ εἰσήλθομεν εἰς τὸν οἶκον τοῦ ἀνδρός· [GNS] εἶπεν δὲ τὸ πνεῦμά μοι συνελθεῖν αὐτοῖς **μηδὲν διακρίναντα**. ἦλθον δὲ σὺν ἐμοὶ καὶ οἱ ἓξ ἀδελφοὶ οὗτοι καὶ εἰσήλθομεν εἰς τὸν οἶκον τοῦ ἀνδρός. [GNT]	Not to hesitate; not to have misgivings; not to worry about; not to doubt. **Practical Application** It means that they were to make no distinction. God tells Peter in no uncertain terms, "Go with them [the Gentiles] making no distinctions." The same command is given to all believers of all generations. Believers are not to make distinctions, not to discriminate in proclaiming the gospel. What an indictment against so many! How many *withdraw* from the poor? How many do not reach out to people of other races and social classes?
#2667 **No Interest In What Is Good** Despisers of those that are good–KJV Haters of good–NASB Not lovers of good–NIV Despisers of good–NKJV **No interest in what is good–NLT** **POSB REFERENCE** (2 Tim. 3:2-4; esp. v.3) Note 1, point 14	ἀφιλάγαθοι = *aphilagathoi* Pronunciation: [af-il-ag'-ath-oy] Parsing (part of speech): adjective 　Case—nominative 　Gender—masculine 　Number—plural 　Stem or root—from ἀφιλάγαθος, ον Concordance References: ⇒　Strong's #865 aphilagathos ⇒　NIV #920 aphilagathos ⇒　NASB #865 aphilagathos **2 Tim. 3:3** Without natural affection, trucebreakers, false accusers, incontinent, fierce, **despisers of those that are good**, [KJV] Unloving, irreconcilable, malicious gossips, without self-control, brutal, **haters of good**, [NASB] Without love, unforgiving, slanderous, without self-control, brutal, **not lovers of** the **good**, [NIV] Unloving, unforgiving, slanderers, without self-control, brutal, **despisers of good**, [NKJV] They will be unloving and unforgiving; they will slander others and have no self-control; they will be cruel and have **no interest in what is good**. [NLT] ἄστοργοι, ἄσπονδοι, διάβολοι, ἀκρατεῖς, ἀνήμεροι, **ἀφιλάγαθοι**, [GNS] ἄστοργοι ἄσπονδοι διάβολοι ἀκρατεῖς ἀνήμεροι **ἀφιλάγαθοι** [GNT]	Not lovers of good, despisers of those who are good, haters of good, no interest in what is good, an enemy to goodness. **Practical Application** People will *have no interest in what is good* (*aphilagathoi*): this refers to people despising both good people and good things. In the last days people will be embarrassed... • to speak up for what is right. • to take a stand for what is good. • to be known as a good person. • to be a friend to good people. People will want to fulfill their desires and to satisfy their flesh; they will want to party, indulge, look, feel, taste, experience, possess, take, and fit in and be acceptable with the crowd. They will let morality and justice go, rejecting whatever restraint they feel. They will actually despise righteousness and want nothing to do with anyone who speaks up for what is right.

ENGLISH WORD	GREEK WORD AND VERSE	THE WORD MEANS...

#2668
No Partiality
 	
Without partiality–KJV
Unwavering–NASB
Impartial–NIV
Without partiality–NKJV
No partiality–NLT
 	
POSB REFERENCE
(Jas 3:17-18; esp. v.17)
Note 3, point 2g
	ἀδιάκριτος = *adiakritos*
	Pronunciation: [ad-ee-ak-'ree-tos]
	Parsing (part of speech): adjective
	  Case—nominative
	  Gender—feminine
	  Number—singular
	  Stem or root—from ἀδιάκριτος, ον
	Concordance References:
	  ⇒ Strong's #87 adiakritos
	  ⇒ NIV #88 adiakritos
	  ⇒ NASB #87 adiakritos
	
	James 3:17
	But the wisdom that is from above is first pure, then peaceable, gentle, and easy to be intreated, full of mercy and good fruits, **without partiality**, and without hypocrisy. [KJV]
	But the wisdom from above is first pure, then peaceable, gentle, reasonable, full of mercy and good fruits, **unwavering**, without hypocrisy. [NASB]
	But the wisdom that comes from heaven is first of all pure; then peace-loving, considerate, submissive, full of mercy and good fruit, **impartial** and sincere. [NIV]
	But the wisdom that is from above is first pure, then peaceable, gentle, willing to yield, full of mercy and good fruits, **without partiality** and without hypocrisy. [NKJV]
	But the wisdom that comes from heaven is first of all pure. It is also peace loving, gentle at all times, and willing to yield to others. It is full of mercy and good deeds. It shows **no partiality** and is always sincere. [NLT]
	ἡ δὲ ἄνωθεν σοφία πρῶτον μὲν ἁγνή ἐστιν, ἔπειτα εἰρηνική, ἐπιεικής, εὐπειθής, μεστὴ ἐλέους καὶ καρπῶν ἀγαθῶν, **ἀδιάκριτος** καὶ ἀνυπόκριτος. [GNS]
	ἡ δὲ ἄνωθεν σοφία πρῶτον μὲν ἁγνή ἐστιν, ἔπειτα εἰρηνική, ἐπιεικής, εὐπειθής, μεστὴ ἐλέους καὶ καρπῶν ἀγαθῶν, **ἀδιάκριτος**, ἀνυπόκριτος. [GNT]
		Impartial, without partiality, unwavering, no partiality, no favoritism.
		
		Practical Application
		True wisdom shows no partiality (*adiakritos*). This word in the Greek actually means two things.
		1. The wise teacher is impartial; he shows no partiality or favoritism to anyone.
		2. The wise teacher is undivided in his convictions and judgments. He knows the truth, exactly what God's Word says, and he will not entertain false ideas or teachings. He is totally committed and undivided in following and teaching God's Word.

#2669
No Reply
 	
Speechless–KJV
Speechless–NASB
Speechless–NIV
Speechless–NKJV
No Reply–NLT
 	
POSB REFERENCE
(Mt.22:11-14; esp. v.12)
Note 4, point 1c
	ἐφιμώθη = *ephimōthē*
	Pronunciation: [eh-fee-mo'-thay]
	Parsing (part of speech): verb
	  Mood—indicative
	  Tense—aorist
	  Voice—passive
	  Person—3rd person
	  Number—singular
	  Stem or root—from φιμόω
	Concordance References:
	  ⇒ Strong's #5392 phimoö
	  ⇒ NIV #5821 phimoö
	  ⇒ NASB #5392 phimoö
	
	Matthew 22:12
	And he saith unto him, Friend, how camest thou in hither not having a wedding garment? And he was **speechless**. [KJV]
	And he said to him, 'Friend, how did you come in here without wedding clothes?' And he was **speechless**. [NASB]
	'Friend,' he asked, 'how did you get in here without wedding clothes?' The man was **speechless**. [NIV]
	So he said to him, 'Friend, how did you come in here without a wedding garment?' And he was **speechless**. [NKJV]
	'Friend,' he asked, 'how is it that you are here without wedding clothes?' And the man had **no reply**. [NLT]
	καὶ λέγει αὐτῷ, Ἑταῖρε, πῶς εἰσῆλθες ὧδε μὴ ἔχων ἔνδυμα γάμου; ὁ δὲ **ἐφιμώθη**. [GNS]
	καὶ λέγει αὐτῷ, Ἑταῖρε, πῶς εἰσῆλθες ὧδε μὴ ἔχων ἔνδυμα γάμου; ὁ δὲ **ἐφιμώθη**. [GNT]
		Muzzled, muted, speechless, silenced, tongue-tied, closed-mouthed; not able to reply.
		
		Practical Application
		The man had no reply (*ephimōthē*). He had no excuse. He stood guilty of disrespect and dishonor for wearing the wrong wedding clothes, a garment that was not right for a kingly occasion. The wedding clothes were unclean.

ENGLISH WORD	GREEK WORD AND VERSE	THE WORD MEANS...

Noble–NIV
Good–NKJV
Honorable–NLT
 	
**POSB
REFERENCE**
(1 Tim.3:1)
Note 1
	Stem or root—from καλός, ή, όν
	Concordance References:
	  ⇒ Strong's #2570 kalos
	  ⇒ NIV #2819 kalos
	  ⇒ NASB #2570 kalos
	
	1 Tim. 3:1
	This is a true saying, If a man desire the office of a bishop, he desireth a **good** work. [KJV]
	It is a trustworthy statement: if any man aspires to the office of overseer, it is a **fine** work he desires to do. [NASB]
	Here is a trustworthy saying: If anyone sets his heart on being an overseer, he desires a **noble** task. [NIV]
	This *is* a faithful saying: If a man desires the position of a bishop, he desires a **good** work. [NKJV]
	It is a true saying that if someone wants to be an elder, he desires an **honorable** responsibility. [NLT]
	Πιστὸς ὁ λόγος· Εἴ τις ἐπισκοπῆς ὀρέγεται, **καλοῦ** ἔργου ἐπιθυμεῖ· [GNS]
	πιστὸς ὁ λόγος. Εἴ τις ἐπισκοπῆς ὀρέγεται, **καλοῦ** ἔργου ἐπιθυμεῖ. [GNT]
		task." Note that the position of the ministry is not what is stressed, but the work of the ministry. The emphasis is not the esteem and honor of the profession. The emphasis is upon the work of the ministry. It is the work that is honorable, excellent, beneficial, and productive. The work of the ministry is a "noble task."

#2675
Nobleman
 	
Nobleman–KJV
Royal official–NASB
Royal official–NIV
Nobleman–NKJV
Government official–
  NLT
 	
**POSB
REFERENCE**
(Jn.4:46-47; esp. v.46)
Note 1
	βασιλικός = *basilikos*
	Pronunciation: [bas-il-ee-kos']
	Parsing (part of speech): pronominal adjective
	    Case—nominative
	    Gender—masculine
	    Number—singular
	    Stem or root—from βασιλικός, ή, όν
	Concordance References:
	  ⇒ Strong's #937 basilikos
	  ⇒ NIV #997 basilikos
	  ⇒ NASB #937 basilikos
	
	John 4:46
	So Jesus came again into Cana of Galilee, where he made the water wine. And there was a certain **nobleman**, whose son was sick at Capernaum. [KJV]
	He came therefore again to Cana of Galilee where He had made the water wine. And there was a certain **royal official**, whose son was sick at Capernaum. [NASB]
	Once more he visited Cana in Galilee, where he had turned the water into wine. And there was a certain **royal official** whose son lay sick at Capernaum. [NIV]
	So Jesus came again to Cana of Galilee where He had made the water wine. And there was a certain **nobleman** whose son was sick at Capernaum. [NKJV]
	In the course of his journey through Galilee, he arrived at the town of Cana, where he had turned the water into wine. There was a **government official** in the city of Capernaum whose son was very sick. [NLT]
	Ἦλθεν οὖν ὁ Ἰησοῦς πάλιν εἰς τὴν Κανὰ τῆς Γαλιλαίας, ὅπου ἐποίησε τὸ ὕδωρ οἶνον. καὶ ἦν τις **βασιλικὸς**. οὗ ὁ υἱὸς ἠσθένει ἐν Καπερναούμ· [GNS]
	Ἦλθεν οὖν πάλιν εἰς τὴν Κανὰ τῆς Γαλιλαίας, ὅπου ἐποίησεν τὸ ὕδωρ οἶνον. καὶ ἦν τις **βασιλικὸς** οὗ ὁ υἱὸς ἠσθένει ἐν Καφαρναούμ. [GNT]
		A royal official; a nobleman; a government official; a secular leader. This man was an official of the King's royal court.
		
		Practical Application
		Needs confront every human being. Eventually the severe needs arising from accident, illness, disease, suffering, and death strike everyone. No one is exempt. One may be an official in government or even the King himself—it does not matter. The day eventually comes when every person needs help. The severe disasters of life are beyond any person's control.

#2676
Noised Abroad
 	
Noised abroad–KJV
Sound
  occurred–NASB
Heard...sound–NIV
Sound
  occurred–NKJV
Heard...sound–NLT
	γενομένης φωνῆς = *genomenēs phōnēs*
	Pronunciation: [ghin'-om-eh-nace fo-nays']
	Parsing *genomenēs* (part of speech): verb
	    Mood—participle
	    Tense—aorist
	    Voice—middle deponent
	    Case—genitive
	    Gender—feminine
	    Number—singular
	    Stem or root—from γίνομαι
	Parsing *phōnēs* (part of speech): noun
	    Case—genitive
	    Gender—feminine
		To hear a sound, noise, roar.
		
		Practical Application
		The Greek says, "When this sound was heard." It was apparently the sound of the thunderous blast caused by God that brought the people rushing to the scene.

ENGLISH WORD	GREEK WORD AND VERSE	THE WORD MEANS...
POSB REFERENCE (Acts 2:5-11; esp. v.6) Note 5, point 2	Number—singular Stem or root—from φωνή, ῆς Concordance References: ⇒ Strong's #1096 ginomai + 5456 phönë ⇒ NIV #1181 ginomai [heard] + 5889 phönë [sound] ⇒ NASB ##1096 ginomai + 5456 phönë ### Acts 2:6 Now when this was **noised abroad**, the multitude came together, and were confounded, because that every man heard them speak in his own language. [KJV] And when this **sound occurred**, the multitude came together, and were bewildered, because they were each one hearing them speak in his own language. [NASB] When they **heard** this **sound**, a crowd came together in bewilderment, because each one heard them speaking in his own language. [NIV] And when this **sound occurred**, the multitude came together, and were confused, because everyone heard them speak in his own language. [NKJV] When they **heard** this **sound**, they came running to see what it was all about, and they were bewildered to hear their own languages being spoken by the believers. [NLT] γενομένης δὲ τῆς **φωνῆς** ταύτης, συνῆλθε τὸ πλῆθος, καὶ συνεχύθη, ὅτι ἤκουον εἷς ἕκαστος τῇ ἰδίᾳ διαλέκτῳ λαλούντων αὐτῶν. [GNS] γενομένης δὲ τῆς **φωνῆς** ταύτης συνῆλθεν τὸ πλῆθος καὶ συνεχύθη, ὅτι ἤκουον εἷς ἕκαστος τῇ ἰδίᾳ διαλέκτῳ λαλούντων αὐτῶν. [GNT]	
#2677 **No Effect, Of– None Effect** **Of none effect–KJV** Invalidating–NASB Nullify–NIV **Of no effect–NKJV** Break–NLT **POSB REFERENCE** (Mk.7:13) *Deeper Study* #2	ἀκυροῦντες = *akurountes* Pronunciation: [ak-oo-roon'-tehs] Parsing (part of speech): verb Mood—participle Tense—present Voice—active Case—nominative Gender—masculine Person—2nd person Number—plural Stem or root—from ἀκυρόω Concordance References: ⇒ Strong's #208 akuroö ⇒ NIV #218 akuroö ⇒ NASB #208 akuroö ### Mark 7:13 Making the word of God **of none effect** through your tradition, which ye have delivered: and many such like things do ye. [KJV] Thus **invalidating** the word of God by your tradition which you have handed down; and you do many things such as that." [NASB] Thus you **nullify** the word of God by your tradition that you have handed down. And you do many things like that." [NIV] Making the word of God **of no effect** through your tradition which you have handed down. And many such things you do." [NKJV] As such, you **break** the law of God in order to protect your own tradition. And this is only one example. There are many, many others." [NLT] **ἀκυροῦντες** τὸν λόγον τοῦ Θεοῦ τῇ παραδόσει ὑμῶν ᾗ παρεδώκατε· καὶ παρόμοια τοιαῦτα πολλὰ ποιεῖτε. [GNS] **ἀκυροῦντες** τὸν λόγον τοῦ θεοῦ τῇ παραδόσει ὑμῶν ᾗ παρεδώκατε· καὶ παρόμοια τοιαῦτα πολλὰ ποιεῖτε. [GNT]	To nullify; to be of no effect; to make void, ineffective; to annul; to cancel; to disregard; to deprive of authority and power; to invalidate. ### Practical Application In this Scripture, Christ is rebuking anyone who places human traditions on an equal or higher authority than the Word of God. Jesus charged the religionists with setting aside God's Word for tradition. Religious traditions may be described as institutional or personal. 1. Institutional traditions are such things as rituals, rules, regulations, schedules, forms, services, procedures, organizations—anything that gives order and security to the persons involved. 2. Personal traditions are such things as church attendance, prayers, habits, ceremonies, objects which a person uses (somewhat superstitiously) to keep himself religiously secure. Jesus was attacking the fact that so many religionists put their traditions first while neglecting and ignoring God's Word (see POSB notes—Matthew 12:1-8; POSB note—Matthew 12:10 and POSB *Deeper Study* #1—Matthew 12:10).

ENGLISH WORD	GREEK WORD AND VERSE	THE WORD MEANS...

#2678
Nonsense, As,
Like
 	
Idle tales–KJV
As nonsense–NASB
Like nonsense–NIV
Idle tales–NKJV
Like nonsense–NLT
 	
POSB
REFERENCE
(Lk.24:9-11; esp. v.11)
Note 6
	ὡσεὶ λῆρος = *hösei lëros*
	Pronunciation: [ho-seh-ee lay-ros]
	Parsing *hösei* (part of speech): conjunction
	    Type—subordinating
	    Stem or root—from ὡσεὶ
	Parsing *lëros* (part of speech): noun
	    Case—nominative
	    Gender—masculine
	    Number—singular
	    Stem or root—from λῆρος, ου
	Concordance References:
	⇒ Strong's #5616 hösei + 3026 lëros
	⇒ NIV #6059 hösei [like] + 3333 lëros [nonsense]
	⇒ NASB #5616 hösei + 3026 lëros
	
	### Luke 24:11
	But they did not believe the women, because their words seemed to them **like nonsense**. [NIV]
	And their words seemed to them as **idle tales**, and they believed them not. [KJV]
	And these words appeared to them **as nonsense**, and they would not believe them. [NASB]
	And their words seemed to them like **idle tales**, and they did not believe them. [NKJV]
	but the story sounded **like nonsense**, so they didn't believe it. [NLT]
	καὶ ἐφάνησαν ἐνώπιον αὐτῶν **ὡσεὶ λῆρος** τὰ ῥήματα αὐτῶν, καὶ ἠπίστουν αὐταῖς. [GNS]
	καὶ ἐφάνησαν ἐνώπιον αὐτῶν **ὡσεὶ λῆρος** τὰ ῥήματα ταῦτα, καὶ ἠπίστουν αὐταῖς. [GNT]
		Ridiculous talk, idle tales, wild imagination, empty talk; like or as nonsense.
		
		### Practical Application
		After the resurrection of Christ, there was the immediate unbelief of the disciples. The women rushed to the disciples to share the glorious news. But the news "seemed to them like nonsense" (*hösei lëros*). "They did not believe." The Greek word is disbelieved (*epistoun*) and is in the imperfect active tense which means they "kept on disbelieving," kept on putting no trust or confidence in what the women were claiming. They were gripped with a skeptical, unbelieving spirit.

#2679
Not Accus-
tomed To
 	
Unskillful–KJV
Not accustomed to–
NASB
Not acquainted with–NIV
Unskilled–NKJV
Doesn't know much–NLT
 	
POSB
REFERENCE
(Heb.5:13)
Note 3
	ἄπειρος = *apeiros*
	Pronunciation: [ap'-i-ros]
	Parsing (part of speech): adjective
	    Case—nominative
	    Gender—masculine
	    Number—singular
	    Stem or root—from ἄπειρος, ον
	Concordance References:
	⇒ Strong's #552 apeiros
	⇒ NIV #586 apeiros
	⇒ NASB #552 apeiros
	
	### Hebrews 5:13
	For every one that useth milk is **unskillful** in the word of righteousness: for he is a babe. [KJV]
	For everyone who partakes only of milk is **not accustomed to** the word of righteousness, for he is a babe. [NASB]
	Anyone who lives on milk, being still an infant, is **not acquainted with** the teaching about righteousness. [NIV]
	For everyone who partakes *only* of milk *is* **unskilled** in the word of righteousness, for he is a babe. [NKJV]
	And a person who is living on milk isn't very far along in the Christian life and **doesn't know much** about doing what is right. [NLT]
	πᾶς γὰρ ὁ μετέχων γάλακτος **ἄπειρος** λόγου δικαιοσύνης· νήπιος γάρ ἐστι. [GNS]
	πᾶς γὰρ ὁ μετέχων γάλακτος **ἄπειρος** λόγου δικαιοσύνης, νήπιος γάρ ἐστιν· [GNT]
		Not acquainted with; unskillful; not accustomed to; does not know much; inexperienced in.
		
		### Practical Application
		A person becomes immature because of being unskilled in the Word. The Hebrew believers remained unskillful in the Word of righteousness. They professed Christ and His righteousness, but they had never grasped or experienced Him—not fully—not in a mature sense. Note the verse: although this person is a church member, "he is still an infant."

#2680
Not Acquainted
With
 	
Unskillful–KJV
Not accustomed to–NASB
Not acquainted with–
NIV
	ἄπειρος = *apeiros*
	Pronunciation: [ap'-i-ros]
	Parsing (part of speech): adjective
	    Case—nominative
	    Gender—masculine
	    Number—singular
	    Stem or root—from ἄπειρος, ον
	Concordance References:
	⇒ Strong's #552 apeiros
	⇒ NIV #586 apeiros
	⇒ NASB #552 apeiros
		Not acquainted with; unskillful; not accustomed to; does not know much; inexperienced in.
		
		### Practical Application
		A person becomes immature because he is not acquainted with the Word. The Hebrew believers remained unskillful in the Word of righteousness. They professed Christ and His righteousness, but they had never grasped or

ENGLISH WORD	GREEK WORD AND VERSE	THE WORD MEANS...
Unskilled–NKJV Doesn't know much–NLT **POSB REFERENCE** (Heb.5:13) Note 3	**Hebrews 5:13** For every one that useth milk is **unskillful** in the word of righteousness: for he is a babe. [KJV] For everyone who partakes only of milk is **not accustomed to** the word of righteousness, for he is a babe. [NASB] Anyone who lives on milk, being still an infant, is **not acquainted with** the teaching about righteousness. [NIV] For everyone who partakes *only* of milk *is* **unskilled** in the word of righteousness, for he is a babe. [NKJV] And a person who is living on milk isn't very far along in the Christian life and **doesn't know much** about doing what is right. [NLT] πᾶς γὰρ ὁ μετέχων γάλακτος **ἄπειρος** λόγου δικαιοσύνης· νήπιος γάρ ἐστι. [GNS] πᾶς γὰρ ὁ μετέχων γάλακτος **ἄπειρος** λόγου δικαιοσύνης, νήπιος γάρ ἐστιν· [GNT]	experienced Him—not fully—not in a mature sense. Note the verse: although this person is a church member, "he is a babe."

#2681
Not Any Thing
 	
Not any thing–KJV
Nothing–NASB
Nothing–NIV
Nothing–NKJV
Nothing–NLT
 	
**POSB
REFERENCE**
(Jn.1:3)
Note 2, point 4b
	οὐδὲ ἕν = *oude hen*
	Pronunciation: [oo-day hen]
	Parsing *oude* (part of speech): adjective
	    Type—adverb
	    Stem or root—from οὐδέ
	Parsing *hen* (part of speech): pronominal adjective
	    Type—cardinal
	    Case—nominative
	    Gender—neuter
	    Number—singular
	    Stem or root—from εἷς, μία, ἕν
	Concordance References:
	  ⇒ Strong's #1520 heis + 3761 oude
	  ⇒ NIV #1651 heis + 4028 oude [nothing]
	  ⇒ NASB #1520 heis + 3761 oude
	
	John 1:3
	All things were made by him; and without him was **not any thing** made that was made. [KJV]
	All things came into being by Him, and apart from Him **nothing** came into being that has come into being. [NASB]
	Through him all things were made; without him **nothing** was made that has been made. [NIV]
	All things were made through Him, and without Him **nothing** was made that was made. [NKJV]
	He created everything there is. **Nothing** exists that he didn't make. [NLT]
	πάντα δι' αὐτοῦ ἐγένετο, καὶ χωρὶς αὐτοῦ ἐγένετο **οὐδὲ ἕν**, ὃ γέγονεν. [GNS]
	πάντα δι' αὐτοῦ ἐγένετο, καὶ χωρὶς αὐτοῦ ἐγένετο **οὐδὲ ἕν**. ὃ γέγονεν [GNT]
		Not even one thing, not a single thing, not even a detail was made apart from Him.
		
		Practical Application
		Note a critical point for mankind. The world is God's; He made it, every element of it, one by one. This means several things.
		1. God is not off in some distant place far removed from the world, unconcerned and disinterested in what happens to the world. God cares about the world. He cares deeply, even about the most minute detail and smallest person. He cares about everything and every person in the world.
		2. The problems of the world are not due to God and His attitude. The problems of the world are due to sin, to the attitude and evil of man's heart.
		3. The answer to the world's problems is not man and his technical skill. The answer is Christ: for men to turn to Christ, surrendering and giving their lives to know Christ in the most personal and intimate way possible. Then, and only then, can men set their lives and world in order as God intends.

#2682
Not At All
 	
God forbid–KJV
May it never be–NASB
Not at all–NIV
Certainly not–NKJV
Of course not–NLT
 	
**POSB
REFERENCE**
(Romans 3:5-8; esp. v.4)
Note 3, point 1
 	
See also POSB REF:
(Romans 11:1)
Note 1
	μὴ γένοιτο = *më genoito*
	Pronunciation: [may ghin'-oy-tow]
	Parsing *genoito* (part of speech): verb
	    Mood—optative
	    Tense—aorist
	    Voice—middle deponent
	    Person—3rd person
	    Number—singular
	    Stem or root—from γίνομαι
	Concordance References:
	  ⇒ Strong's #1096 + 3361 ginomai më
	  ⇒ NIV #1181 + 3590 ginomai më [Not at all]
	  ⇒ NASB #1096+ 3361 ginomai më
	
	Romans 3:4
	God forbid: yea, let God be true, but every man a liar; as it is written, That thou mightest be justified in thy sayings, and mightest overcome when thou art judged. [KJV]
	May it never be! Rather, let God be found true, though every man be found a liar, as it is written, "That
		God forbid; not at all; may it never be; certainly not; of course not.
		
		Practical Application
		The question is, "If you say some Jews do not believe and are condemned, doesn't that void God's promises and make God a liar?" Or to say it another way, "What if some disbelieve and reject God's Word, will their unbelief cause God to void His Word and promises? God promised the Jews a special place and special privileges through Abraham and his seed (see POSB Deeper Study #1—John 4:22). If some Jews do not believe God's promises and God condemns them, isn't He breaking His promise to Abraham and his seed? Isn't He voiding His Word and Covenant and making Himself a liar? God's Word could not be based on heart religion and on

ENGLISH WORD	GREEK WORD AND VERSE	THE WORD MEANS...
	Thou mightest be justified in Thy words, And mightest prevail when Thou ART JUDGED." [NASB] **Not at all**! Let God be true, and every man a liar. As it is written: "So that you may be proved right when you speak and prevail when you judge." [NIV] **Certainly not**! Indeed, let God be true but every man a liar. As it is written: *"That You may be justified in Your words, And may overcome when You are judged."* [NKJV] **Of course not**! Though everyone else in the world is a liar, God is true. As the Scriptures say, "He will be proved right in what he says, and he will win his case in court." [NLT] μὴ γένοιτο· γινέσθω δὲ ὁ Θεὸς ἀληθής, πᾶς δὲ ἄνθρωπος ψεύστης, καθὼς γέγραπται, "Ὅπως ἂν δικαιωθῇς ἐν τοῖς λόγοις σου, καὶ νικήσεις ἐν τῷ κρίνεσθαί σε. [GNS] μὴ γένοιτο· γινέσθω δὲ ὁ Θεὸς ἀληθής, πᾶς δὲ ἄνθρωπος ψεύστης, καθὼς γέγραπται, "Ὅπως ἂν δικαιωθῇς ἐν τοῖς λόγοις σου καὶ νικήσεις ἐν τῷ κρίνεσθαί σε. [GNT]	moral character alone. There has to be something else, something outward—a rite (circumcision, baptism, church membership)—that shows we are religious (Jews). If we go through the rite or ritual, then God is bound to accept us. He has so promised to accept us. He is not going to break His Word." The application of this question concerns every religionist. The thinking religionist poses the same objection and question: "If you say some religionists do not believe and are condemned, doesn't that void God's Word and make God a liar? God's Word promises the religious person special privileges and the hope of eternal life. His Word tells us to believe Christ and to possess His Word, be baptized and join the fellowship of the church. If we do that and God still condemns us, is He not voiding His Word and becoming a liar?" ⇒ God forbid. ⇒ God will be faithful. His Word and promise of salvation will stand even if *every* man lies in his believing and lies about giving his heart to serve Jesus. ⇒ God will prove His Word: He will be justified and proven faithful in what He has said. He will still save *any person* who gives his heart to Jesus and obeys Jesus. ⇒ In fact, God will overcome; He will prove His Word another way. He will judge all who make a false profession and who judge Him and His Word, who accuse Him of being unfaithful and voiding His Word. David himself said that God would judge the unfaithful or disobedient man (Psalm 51:4). David had sinned greatly, not keeping the commandments of God, so God judged David and charged him with sin. David did the right thing: he confessed his sin and repented and began to live righteously. But David did something else: he declared that God's charge and judgment against him were *just*, that God was perfectly justified. And God was, for God is always just, and He is always justified in what He says and does.

#2683
Not Double-Tongued
 	
Not doubletongued–KJV
Not double tongued–NASB
Sincere–NIV
Not double-tongued–NKJV
Integrity–NLT
 	
POSB REFERENCE
(1 Tim.3:8)
Note 1, point 2
	μὴ διλόγους = mē dilogous
	Pronunciation: [may dil'-og-oos]
	Parsing *dilogous* (part of speech): adjective
	    Case—accusative
	    Gender—masculine
	    Number—plural
	    Stem or root—from δίλογος, ον
	Concordance References:
	⇒ Strong's #1351+3361 dilogos mē
	⇒ NIV #1474+3590 dilogos mē [sincere]
	⇒ NASB #1351+3361 dilogos mē
	
	1 Tim. 3:8
	Likewise must the deacons be grave, **not double-tongued**, not given to much wine, not greedy of filthy lucre; [KJV]
	Deacons likewise must be men of dignity, **not double-tongued**, or addicted to much wine or fond of sordid gain, [NASB]
	Deacons, likewise, are to be men worthy of respect, **sincere**, not indulging in much wine, and not pursuing dishonest gain. [NIV]
	Likewise deacons *must be* reverent, **not double-**
		To be sincere; to have integrity. It means a person is not to be double-tongued, two-faced, or insincere.
		
		## Practical Application
		
		Deacons must not be doubletongued (*dilogous*): bearing tales, gossiping, saying "one thing to one person and something different to another [person]" (Donald Guthrie. *The Pastoral Epistles*. "Tyndale New Testament Commentaries, p.84); saying one thing to a person's face and something else behind his back. No more descriptive word could be chosen than "double-tongued."
		
		The quality of *not being double-tongued* is important. As a deacon ministers through visitation (going from house to house), he is often tempted to gossip or say one thing to one person and something else to another person. He is also tempted to evade or smooth talk issues. Therefore, he must be a man of integrity, a man

ENGLISH WORD	GREEK WORD AND VERSE	THE WORD MEANS...
	tongued, not given to much wine, not greedy for money, [NKJV] In the same way, deacons must be people who are respected and have **integrity**. They must not be heavy drinkers and must not be greedy for money. [NLT] διακόνους ὡσαύτως σεμνούς, **μὴ διλόγους**, μὴ οἴνῳ πολλῷ προσέχοντας, μὴ αἰσχροκερδεῖς, [GNS] Διακόνους ὡσαύτως σεμνούς, **μὴ διλόγους**, μὴ οἴνῳ πολλῷ προσέχοντας, μὴ αἰσχροκερδεῖς, [GNT]	who speaks the straight truth—a man who is as honest as the day is long.

#2684
Not Hate
 	
Hate not–KJV
Not hate–NASB
Not hate–NIV
Not hate–NKJV
Must love me more–NLT
 	
POSB
REFERENCE
(Lk.14:26)
Note 2
	οὐ μισεῖ = *ou misei*
	Pronunciation: [oo mis-eh´-ee]
	Parsing *ou* (part of speech): particle
	    Type—negative
	    Stem or root—from οὐ
	Parsing *misei* (part of speech): verb
	    Mood—indicative
	    Tense—present
	    Voice—active
	    Person—3rd person
	    Number—singular
	    Stem or root—from μισέω
	Concordance References:
	⇒ Strong's #3756 ou + 3404 miseo
	⇒ NIV #4024 ou [not] + 3631 miseö [hate]
	⇒ NASB #3756 ou + 3404 miseo
	
	Luke 14:26
	If any man come to me, and **hate not** his father, and mother, and wife, and children, and brethren, and sisters, yea, and his own life also, he cannot be my disciple. [KJV]
	
	"If anyone comes to Me, and does **not hate** his own father and mother and wife and children and brothers and sisters, yes, and even his own life, he cannot be My disciple. [NASB]
	
	"If anyone comes to me and does **not hate** his father and mother, his wife and children, his brothers and sisters—yes, even his own life—he cannot be my disciple. [NIV]
	
	"If anyone comes to Me and does **not hate** his father and mother, wife and children, brothers and sisters, yes, and his own life also, he cannot be My disciple. [NKJV]
	
	"If you want to be my follower you **must love me more** than your own father and mother, wife and children, brothers and sisters—yes, more than your own life. Otherwise, you cannot be my disciple. [NLT]
	
	Εἴ τις ἔρχεται πρός με, καὶ **οὐ μισεῖ** τὸν πατέρα ἑαυτοῦ, καὶ τὴν μητέρα, καὶ τὴν γυναῖκα, καὶ τὰ τέκνα, καὶ τοὺς ἀδελφοὺς, καὶ τὰς ἀδελφάς, ἔτι τε καὶ τὴν ἑαυτοῦ ψυχὴν, οὐ δύναταί μου μαθητής εἶναί. [GNS]
	
	Εἴ τις ἔρχεται πρός με καὶ **οὐ μισεῖ** τὸν πατέρα ἑαυτοῦ καὶ τὴν μητέρα καὶ τὴν γυναῖκα καὶ τὰ τέκνα καὶ τοὺς ἀδελφοὺς καὶ τὰς ἀδελφάς ἔτι τε καὶ τὴν ψυχὴν ἑαυτοῦ, οὐ δύναται εἶναί μου μαθητής. [GNT]
		Not showing preference, disregard, not hate; not detest.
		
		Practical Application
		The words "not hate" are strong. Christ was not saying that one's family and one's self were to be literally hated. The true believer is to love even his enemies (Luke 6:27). What then did Christ mean? Very simply...
		
		• Christ is to be first in a person's life: before family, even before self.
		
		• Christ is to be put before family: even if one's family opposes his decision to follow Christ.
		
		• Christ is to be put first: before the companionship and comfort and pleasure of family and home.
		
		• All—even family and self—are to be put behind Christ and His mission. All must be denied and put behind a person's love and devotion to Christ and His cause.

#2685
Not Have In Mind
 	
Savourest not–KJV
Not setting your mind–NASB
Not have in mind–NIV
Not mindful–NKJV
Seeing things merely from a human point of view–NLT
	οὐ φρονεῖς = *ou phroneis*
	Pronunciation: [oo fron-eh´-ees]
	Parsing *phroneis* (part of speech): verb
	    Mood—indicative
	    Tense—present
	    Voice—active
	    Person—2nd person
	    Number—singular
	    Stem or root—from φρονέω
	Concordance References:
	⇒ Strong's #3756 ou + #5426 phroneö
	⇒ NIV #4024 ou [not] + 5858 phroneö [have in mind]
	⇒ NASB #3756 ou + #5426 phroneö
	
	Mark 8:33
	But when he had turned about and looked on his disciples, he rebuked Peter, saying, Get thee behind me, Satan:
		To think; to mind; to have a certain mindset; to see things merely from a human point of view.
		
		Practical Application
		It is a word that is governed by human choice, an act of a person's will. Peter did not have his mind, his thinking, in line with God's mind and thoughts. His tastes were different from God's tastes. Peter's thoughts and tastes were worldly and self-pleasing, not spiritual and pleasing to God. He was using human reasoning, not God's reasoning. The thought that God's Son had to die and shed His blood for the sins of the world was disgraceful to Peter. In his mind such a concept was unfit for God.

ENGLISH WORD	GREEK WORD AND VERSE	THE WORD MEANS...
POSB REFERENCE (Mk.8:32-33; esp. v.33) Note 2, point 3 **See also POSB REF:** (Mt.16:21-23; esp. v.23) Note 1, point 4	for thou **savourest not** the things that be of God, but the things that be of men. [KJV] But turning around and seeing His disciples, He rebuked Peter, and said, "Get behind Me, Satan; for you are **not setting your mind** on God's interests, but man's." [NASB] But when Jesus turned and looked at his disciples, he rebuked Peter. "Get behind me, Satan!" he said. "You do **not have in mind** the things of God, but the things of men." [NIV] But when He had turned around and looked at His disciples, He rebuked Peter, saying, "Get behind Me, Satan! For you are **not mindful** of the things of God, but the things of men." [NKJV] Jesus turned and looked at his disciples and then said to Peter very sternly, "Get away from me, Satan! You are **seeing things merely from a human point of view**, not from God's." [NLT] ὁ δὲ ἐπιστραφείς, καὶ ἰδὼν τοὺς μαθητὰς αὐτοῦ ἐπετίμησε τῷ Πέτρῳ, λέγει, Ὕπαγε ὀπίσω μου, Σατανᾶ· ὅτι **οὐ φρονεῖς** τὰ τοῦ Θεοῦ, ἀλλὰ τὰ τῶν ἀνθρώπων. [GNS] ὁ δὲ ἐπιστραφείς καὶ ἰδὼν τοὺς μαθητὰς αὐτοῦ ἐπετίμησεν Πέτρῳ καὶ λέγει, Ὕπαγε ὀπίσω μου, σατανᾶ, ὅτι **οὐ φρονεῖς** τὰ τοῦ θεοῦ ἀλλὰ τὰ τῶν ἀνθρώπων. [GNT]	
#2686 **Not Have To** Ought not–KJV Not necessary–NASB **Not...have to–NIV** Ought not–NKJV Clearly predicted–NLT **POSB REFERENCE** (Lk.24:15-27; esp. v.26) Note 2, point 3b	οὐχὶ ἔδει = ouchi edei Pronunciation: [oo-chee eh-dee] Parsing *edei* (part of speech): verb 　　Mood—indicative 　　Tense—imperfect 　　Voice—active 　　Person—3rd person 　　Number—singular 　　Stem or root—from δεῖ Concordance References: ⇒　Strong's #3780 ouchi + 1163 dei ⇒　NIV #4049 ouchi [not] + 1256 dei [have to] ⇒　NASB #3780 ouchi + 1163 dei **Luke 24:26** **Ought not** Christ to have suffered these things, and to enter into his glory? [KJV] "Was it **not necessary** for the Christ to suffer these things and to enter into His glory?" [NASB] Did **not** the Christ **have to** suffer these things and then enter his glory?" [NIV] **Ought not** the Christ to have suffered these things and to enter into His glory?" [NKJV] Wasn't it **clearly predicted** by the prophets that the Messiah would have to suffer all these things before entering his time of glory?" [NLT] οὐχὶ ταῦτα **ἔδει** παθεῖν τὸν Χριστὸν καὶ εἰσελθεῖν εἰς τὴν δόξαν αὐτοῦ; [GNS] οὐχὶ ταῦτα **ἔδει** παθεῖν τὸν Χριστὸν καὶ εἰσελθεῖν εἰς τὴν δόξαν αὐτοῦ; [GNT]	Not have to, ought not, not necessary, clearly predicted. **Practical Application** It means that the death of Christ was an absolute necessity. The words "not have to" are strong. They mean there was a constraint, an imperative, a necessity laid upon the Messiah to die and arise. He had no choice. His death and resurrection had been planned and willed by God through all eternity.
#2687 **Not Lose Heart** Faint not–KJV **Not lose heart–NASB** **Not lose heart–NIV** **Not lose heart–NKJV** Never give up–NLT **POSB REFERENCE** (2 Cor.4:1) Note 1	οὐκ ἐγκακοῦμεν = ouk egkakoumen Pronunciation: [ook ek-kak-oo'-mehn] Parsing *egkakoumen* (part of speech): verb 　　Mood—indicative 　　Tense—present 　　Voice—active 　　Person—1st person 　　Number—plural 　　Stem or root—from ἐγκακέω Concordance References: ⇒　Strong's #3756 ou + 1573 egkakeō ⇒　NIV #4024 ou [not] +1591 egkakeō [lose heart] ⇒　NASB #3756 ou + 1573 egkakeō	Not to lose heart; not to tire of; not to faint; not to become weary; never give up; not become discouraged, spiritless, fainthearted, despondent, or discouraged. **Practical Application** The ministry demands constancy, demands that one never faint. Paul did not quit or give up for any reason, not even because of persecution or weariness and exhaustion.

ENGLISH WORD	GREEK WORD AND VERSE	THE WORD MEANS...
	2 Cor. 4:1 Therefore seeing we have this ministry, as we have received mercy, we **faint not**; [KJV] Therefore, since we have this ministry, as we received mercy, we do **not lose heart**, [NASB] Therefore, since through God's mercy we have this ministry, we do **not lose heart**. [NIV] Therefore, since we have this ministry, as we have received mercy, we do **not lose heart**. [NKJV] And so, since God in his mercy has given us this wonderful ministry, we **never give up**. [NLT] Διὰ τοῦτο ἔχοντες τὴν διακονίαν ταύτην, καθὼς ἠλεήθημεν, οὐκ **ἐκκακοῦμεν**· [GNS] Διὰ τοῦτο, ἔχοντες τὴν διακονίαν ταύτην καθὼς ἠλεήθημεν, οὐκ **ἐγκακοῦμεν** [GNT]	

#2688
Not Lovers Of Good
 	
Despisers of those that are good–KJV
Haters of good–NASB
Not lovers of...good–NIV
Despisers of good–NKJV
No interest in what is good–NLT
 	
POSB REFERENCE
(2 Tim. 3:2-4; esp. v.3)
Note 1, point 14
	ἀφιλάγαθοι = aphilagathoi
	Pronunciation: [af-il-ag'-ath-oy]
	Parsing (part of speech): adjective
	  Case—nominative
	  Gender—masculine
	  Number—plural
	  Stem or root—from ἀφιλάγαθος, ον
	Concordance References:
	⇒ Strong's #865 aphilagathos
	⇒ NIV #920 aphilagathos
	⇒ NASB #865 aphilagathos
	
	2 Tim. 3:3
	Without natural affection, trucebreakers, false accusers, incontinent, fierce, **despisers of those that are good**, [KJV]
	Unloving, irreconcilable, malicious gossips, without self-control, brutal, **haters of good**, [NASB]
	Without love, unforgiving, slanderous, without self-control, brutal, **not lovers of** the good, [NIV]
	Unloving, unforgiving, slanderers, without self-control, brutal, **despisers of good**, [NKJV]
	They will be unloving and unforgiving; they will slander others and have no self-control; they will be cruel and have **no interest in what is good**. [NLT]
	ἄστοργοι, ἄσπονδοι, διάβολοι, ἀκρατεῖς, ἀνήμεροι, **ἀφιλάγαθοι**, [GNS]
	ἄστοργοι ἄσπονδοι διάβολοι ἀκρατεῖς ἀνήμεροι **ἀφιλάγαθοι** [GNT]
		Not lovers of good, despisers of those who are good, haters of good, no interest in what is good, an enemy to goodness.
		
		Practical Application
		People will not be *lovers of good (aphilagathoi)*: this refers to people despising both good people and good things. In the last days, people will be embarrassed...
		• to speak up for what is right.
		• to take a stand for what is good.
		• to be known as a good person.
		• to be a friend to good people.
		
		People will want to fulfill their desires and to satisfy their flesh; they will want to party, indulge, look, feel, taste, experience, possess, take, and fit in and be acceptable with the crowd. They will let morality and justice go, rejecting whatever restraint they feel. They will actually despise righteousness and want nothing to do with anyone who speaks up for what is right.

#2689
Not Make Light Of
 	
Despise not–KJV
Not regard lightly–NASB
Not make light of–NIV
Do not despise–NKJV
Don't ignore it–NLT
 	
POSB REFERENCE
(Heb.12:5-7; esp. v.5)
Note 1, point 1
	μὴ ὀλιγώρει = mē oligōrei
	Pronunciation: [may ol-ig-o-reh'-ee]
	Parsing *oligōrei* (part of speech): verb
	  Mood—imperative
	  Tense—present
	  Voice—active
	  Person—2nd person
	  Number—singular
	  Stem or root—from ὀλιγωρέω
	Concordance References:
	⇒ Strong's #3361 mē + 3643 oligōreō
	⇒ NIV #3590 mē [not] + 3902 oligōreō [make light of]
	⇒ NASB #3361 mē + 3643 oligōreō
	
	Hebrews 12:5
	And ye have forgotten the exhortation which speaketh unto you as unto children, My son, **despise not** thou the chastening of the Lord, nor faint when thou art rebuked of him: [KJV]
	And you have forgotten the exhortation which is addressed to you as sons, "My son, do **not regard lightly** the discipline of the Lord, Nor FAINT WHEN YOU ARE REPROVED BY Him; [NASB]
	And you have forgotten that word of encouragement that addresses you as sons: "My son, do **not make light of** the Lord's discipline, and do not lose heart when he
		Not to make light of; not to regard lightly; not to despise; not to ignore; not to think lightly of; not to scorn; not to make little of, treat lightly.
		
		Practical Application
		When we are being taught, disciplined, or corrected, there is always the danger of...
		• despising it
		• scorning it
		• making light of it
		• treating it too lightly
		
		Too often, we pay little attention to the discipline and correction of God: to the tug and pull of the Spirit of God, to the little consequences and sufferings of our hearts, to the little things that happen to us. As a result, we continue right on in our little irresponsible behaviors and sins. The little flaws and sins get bigger and bigger until finally the roof caves in and the consequences involve so much destruction and suffering that we can no longer ignore them.
		Why do we suffer so much in this life? Because of our irresponsibilities and sins—because we do not heed the discipline and cor-

ENGLISH WORD	GREEK WORD AND VERSE	THE WORD MEANS...
	rebukes you, [NIV] And you have forgotten the exhortation which speaks to you as to sons: "My son, **do not despise** the chastening of the Lord, Nor be discouraged when you are rebuked by Him; [NKJV] And have you entirely forgotten the encouraging words God spoke to you, his children? He said, "My child, **don't ignore it** when the Lord disciplines you, and don't be discouraged when he corrects you. [NLT] καὶ ἐκλέλησθε τῆς παρακλήσεως, ἥτις ὑμῖν ὡς υἱοῖς διαλέγεται, Υἱέ μου, **μὴ ὀλιγώρει** παιδείας Κυρίου, μηδὲ ἐκλύου, ὑπ' αὐτοῦ ἐλεγχόμενος· [GNS] καὶ ἐκλέλησθε τῆς παρακλήσεως, ἥτις ὑμῖν ὡς υἱοῖς διαλέγεται, Υἱέ μου, **μὴ ὀλιγώρει** παιδείας κυρίου μηδὲ ἐκλύου ὑπ' αὐτοῦ ἐλεγχόμενος· [GNT]	rection of God when we first begin to act irresponsibly. If we heeded the discipline of God, then we could correct our small misbehavior and no big sin would happen. This would mean that much of the great sufferings in the world would never happen. The point is this: we are not to make light of the discipline of God—not to scorn it nor take and treat it lightly. We are to heed it. As we do, life will be much easier, and we will be stronger and much more triumphant and victorious.

#2690
Not Malicious Gossips
 	
Not slanderers–KJV
Not malicious gossips–NASB
Not malicious talkers–NIV
Not slanderers–NKJV
Not speak evil–NLT
 	
POSB REFERENCE
(1 Tim.3:11-12; esp. v.11)
Note 3, point 1b
	μὴ διαβόλους = *mē diabolous*
	Pronunciation: [may dee-ab'-ol-oos]
	Parsing *diabolous* (part of speech): adjective
	    Case—accusative
	    Gender—feminine
	    Number—plural
	    Stem or root—from διάβολος, ου
	Concordance References:
	⇒ Strong's #3361 mē + 1228 diabolos
	⇒ NIV #3590 mē [not] + 1333 diabolos [malicious talkers]
	⇒ NASB #3361 mē + 1228 diabolos
	
	1 Tim. 3:11
	Even so must their wives be grave, **not slanderers**, sober, faithful in all things. [KJV]
	Women must likewise be dignified, **not malicious gossips**, but temperate, faithful in all things. [NASB]
	In the same way, their wives are to be women worthy of respect, **not malicious talkers** but temperate and trustworthy in everything. [NIV]
	Likewise *their* wives *must be* reverent, **not slanderers**, temperate, faithful in all things. [NKJV]
	In the same way, their wives must be respected and must **not speak evil** of others. They must exercise self-control and be faithful in everything they do. [NLT]
	γυναῖκας ὡσαύτως σεμνάς, **μὴ διαβόλους**, νηφαλίους, πιστὰς ἐν πᾶσι. [GNS]
	γυναῖκας ὡσαύτως σεμνάς, **μὴ διαβόλους**, νηφαλίους, πιστὰς ἐν πᾶσιν. [GNT]
		Not malicious talkers, slanderers, malicious gossips; not to speak evil.
		
		Practical Application
		The wife of a deacon must not be a "malicious gossip" (*mē diabolous*): a talebearer, gossiper; a person who goes about talking about others, stirring up mischief and disturbance.

#2691
Not Malicious Talkers
 	
Not slanderers–KJV
Not malicious gossips–NASB
Not malicious talkers–NIV
Not slanderers–NKJV
Not speak evil–NLT
 	
POSB REFERENCE
(1 Tim.3:11-12; esp. v.11)
Note 3, point 1b
	μὴ διαβόλους = *mē diabolous*
	Pronunciation: [may dee-ab'-ol-oos]
	Parsing *diabolous* (part of speech): adjective
	    Case—accusative
	    Gender—feminine
	    Number—plural
	    Stem or root—from διάβολος, ου
	Concordance References:
	⇒ Strong's #3361 mē + 1228 diabolos
	⇒ NIV #3590 mē [not] + 1333 diabolos [malicious talkers]
	⇒ NASB #3361 mē + 1228 diabolos
	
	1 Tim. 3:11
	Even so must their wives be grave, **not slanderers**, sober, faithful in all things. [KJV]
	Women must likewise be dignified, **not malicious gossips**, but temperate, faithful in all things. [NASB]
	In the same way, their wives are to be women worthy of respect, **not malicious talkers** but temperate and trustworthy in everything. [NIV]
	Likewise *their* wives *must be* reverent, **not slanderers**, temperate, faithful in all things. [NKJV]
	In the same way, their wives must be respected and must **not speak evil** of others. They must exercise self-control and be faithful in everything they do. [NLT]
		Not malicious talkers, slanderers, malicious gossips; not to speak evil.
		
		Practical Application
		The wife of a deacon must not be a "malicious talker" (*mē diabolous*): a talebearer, gossiper; a person who goes about talking about others, stirring up mischief and disturbance.

ENGLISH WORD	GREEK WORD AND VERSE	THE WORD MEANS...
	γυναῖκας ὡσαύτως σεμνάς, **μὴ διαβόλους**, νηφαλίους, πιστὰς ἐν πᾶσι. [GNS] γυναῖκας ὡσαύτως σεμνάς, **μὴ διαβόλους**, νηφαλίους, πιστὰς ἐν πᾶσιν. [GNT]	

#2692
Not Mindful
 	
Savourest not–KJV
Not setting your mind–NASB
Not have in mind–NIV
Not mindful–NKJV
Seeing things merely from a human point of view–NLT
 	
POSB REFERENCE
(Mk.8:32-33; esp. v.33)
Note 2, point 3
 	
See also POSB REF:
(Mt.16:21-23; esp. v.23)
Note 1, point 4
	οὐ φρονεῖς = ou phroneis
	Pronunciation: [oo fron-eh'-ees]
	Parsing *phroneis* (part of speech): verb
	    Mood—indicative
	    Tense—present
	    Voice—active
	    Person—2nd person
	    Number—singular
	    Stem or root—from **φρονέω**
	Concordance References:
	⇒ Strong's #3756 ou + #5426 phroneö
	⇒ NIV #4024 ou [not] + 5858 phroneö [have in mind]
	⇒ NASB #3756 ou + #5426 phroneö
	
	Mark 8:33
	But when he had turned about and looked on his disciples, he rebuked Peter, saying, Get thee behind me, Satan: for thou **savourest not** the things that be of God, but the things that be of men. [KJV]
	But turning around and seeing His disciples, He rebuked Peter, and said, "Get behind Me, Satan; for you are **not setting your mind** on God's interests, but man's." [NASB]
	But when Jesus turned and looked at his disciples, he rebuked Peter. "Get behind me, Satan!" he said. "You do **not have in mind** the things of God, but the things of men." [NIV]
	But when He had turned around and looked at His disciples, He rebuked Peter, saying, "Get behind Me, Satan! For you are **not mindful** of the things of God, but the things of men." [NKJV]
	Jesus turned and looked at his disciples and then said to Peter very sternly, "Get away from me, Satan! You are **seeing things merely from a human point of view**, not from God's." [NLT]
	ὁ δὲ ἐπιστραφείς, καὶ ἰδὼν τοὺς μαθητὰς αὐτοῦ ἐπετίμησε τῷ Πέτρῳ, λέγει, Ὕπαγε ὀπίσω μου, Σατανᾶ· ὅτι **οὐ φρονεῖς** τὰ τοῦ Θεοῦ, ἀλλὰ τὰ τῶν ἀνθρώπων. [GNS]
	ὁ δὲ ἐπιστραφείς καὶ ἰδὼν τοὺς μαθητὰς αὐτοῦ ἐπετίμησεν Πέτρῳ καὶ λέγει, Ὕπαγε ὀπίσω μου, σατανᾶ, ὅτι **οὐ φρονεῖς** τὰ τοῦ θεοῦ ἀλλὰ τὰ τῶν ἀνθρώπων. [GNT]
		To think; to mind; to have a certain mindset; to see things merely from a human point of view.
		
		Practical Application
		It is a word that is governed by human choice, an act of a person's will. Peter did not have his mind, his thinking, in line with God's mind and thoughts. His tastes were different from God's tastes. Peter's thoughts and tastes were worldly and self-pleasing, not spiritual and pleasing to God. He was using human reasoning, not God's reasoning. The thought that God's Son had to die and shed His blood for the sins of the world was disgraceful to Peter. In his mind such a concept was unfit for God.

#2693
Not Necessary
 	
Ought not–KJV
Not necessary–NASB
Not have to–NIV
Ought not–NKJV
Clearly predicted–NLT
 	
POSB REFERENCE
(Lk.24:15-27; esp. v.26)
Note 2, point 3b
	οὐχὶ ἔδει = ouchi edei
	Pronunciation: [oo-chee eh-dee]
	Parsing *edei* (part of speech): verb
	    Mood—indicative
	    Tense—imperfect
	    Voice—active
	    Person—3rd person
	    Number—singular
	    Stem or root—from **δεῖ**
	Concordance References:
	⇒ Strong's #3780 ouchi + 1163 dei
	⇒ NIV #4049 ouchi [not] + 1256 dei [have to]
	⇒ NASB #3780 ouchi + 1163 dei
	
	Luke 24:26
	Ought not Christ to have suffered these things, and to enter into his glory? [KJV]
	"Was it **not necessary** for the Christ to suffer these things and to enter into His glory?" [NASB]
	Did **not** the Christ **have to** suffer these things and then enter his glory? [NIV]
	Ought not the Christ to have suffered these things and to enter into His glory?" [NKJV]
		Not have to, ought not, not necessary, clearly predicted; must not; should not.
		
		Practical Application
		It means that the death of Christ was an absolute necessity. The words "not necessary" are strong. They mean there was a constraint, an imperative, a necessity laid upon the Messiah to die and arise. He had no choice. His death and resurrection had been planned and willed by God through all eternity.

ENGLISH WORD	GREEK WORD AND VERSE	THE WORD MEANS...
	Wasn't it **clearly predicted** by the prophets that the Messiah would have to suffer all these things before entering his time of glory?" [NLT] οὐχὶ ταῦτα ἔδει παθεῖν τὸν Χριστὸν καὶ εἰσελθεῖν εἰς τὴν δόξαν αὐτοῦ; [GNS] οὐχὶ ταῦτα ἔδει παθεῖν τὸν Χριστὸν καὶ εἰσελθεῖν εἰς τὴν δόξαν αὐτοῦ; [GNT]	
#2694 **Not New Christian** Not...novice–KJV Not...new convert–NASB Not...recent convert–NIV Not...novice–NKJV **Not...new Christian–NLT** **POSB REFERENCE** (1 Tim.3:6) Note 4	μὴ νεόφυτον = me neophuton Pronunciation: [may neh-of'-oo-ton] Parsing *neophuton* (part of speech): adjective 　Case—accusative 　Gender—masculine 　Number—singular 　Stem or root—from νεόφυτος, ον Concordance References: ⇒ Strong's #3361 me + 3504 neophutos ⇒ NIV #3590 me [not] + 3745 neophutos [recent convert] ⇒ NASB #3361 me + 3504 neophutos **1 Tim. 3:6** **Not** a **novice**, lest being lifted up with pride he fall into the condemnation of the devil. [KJV] And **not** a **new convert**, lest he become conceited and fall into the condemnation incurred by the devil. [NASB] He must **not** be a **recent convert**, or he may become conceited and fall under the same judgment as the devil. [NIV] **Not** a **novice**, lest being puffed up with pride he fall into the *same* condemnation as the devil. [NKJV] An elder must **not** be a **new Christian**, because he might be proud of being chosen so soon, and the Devil will use that pride to make him fall. [NLT] μὴ νεόφυτον, ἵνα μὴ τυφωθεὶς εἰς κρίμα ἐμπέσῃ τοῦ διαβόλου. [GNS] μὴ νεόφυτον, ἵνα μὴ τυφωθεὶς εἰς κρίμα ἐμπέσῃ τοῦ διαβόλου. [GNT]	Not a recent convert, novice, new Christian. **Practical Application** 　The minister or elder of God must be spiritually qualified. He must not be a new Christian (*me neophuton*), that is, a new convert or a new church member. He must have been a convert or church member for a long time... • long enough to have become rooted and grounded in the Lord and His Word. • long enough to have become spiritually mature. • long enough to have proven his testimony for Christ. • long enough to be well known and respected by other believers. • long enough to be able to minister to others and to teach them to minister. 　Note why a new Christian must not be given a position of leadership in the church: because he may become prideful and "the Devil will use that pride to make him fall." Satan was expelled from heaven because of pride. It was pride that caused his fall and brought condemnation upon him. When a person is given a significant responsibility before he has become rooted and grounded in the faith, he is most likely going to fall and be condemned just as Satan fell and was condemned. We must always remember what Matthew Henry points out: "Pride...is a sin that turned angels into devils" (*Matthew Henry's Commentary*, Vol.6, p.815). We must guard against pride. We must guard against putting a person in a position of leadership that will tempt him to feel more important than he is.
#2695 **Not New Convert** Not...novice–KJV **Not...new convert–NASB** Not...recent convert–NIV Not...novice–NKJV Not...new Christian–NLT **POSB REFERENCE** (1 Tim.3:6) Note 4	μὴ νεόφυτον = me neophuton Pronunciation: [may neh-of'-oo-ton] Parsing *neophuton* (part of speech): adjective 　Case—accusative 　Gender—masculine 　Number—singular 　Stem or root—from νεόφυτος, ον Concordance References: ⇒ Strong's #3361 me + 3504 neophutos ⇒ NIV #3590 me [not] + 3745 neophutos [recent convert] ⇒ NASB #3361 me + 3504 neophutos **1 Tim. 3:6** **Not** a **novice**, lest being lifted up with pride he fall into the condemnation of the devil. [KJV] And **not** a **new convert**, lest he become conceited and fall into the condemnation incurred by the devil. [NASB] He must **not** be a **recent convert**, or he may become conceited and fall under the same judgment as the devil. [NIV] **Not** a **novice**, lest being puffed up with pride he fall into the *same* condemnation as the devil. [NKJV] An elder must **not** be a **new Christian**, because he might be proud of being chosen so soon, and the Devil	Not a recent convert, novice, new Christian. **Practical Application** 　The minister or elder of God must be spiritually qualified. He must not be a new convert (*me neophuton*), that is, a novice or a new church member. He must have been a convert or church member for a long time... • long enough to have become rooted and grounded in the Lord and His Word. • long enough to have become spiritually mature. • long enough to have proven his testimony for Christ. • long enough to be well known and respected by other believers. • long enough to be able to minister to others and to teach them to minister. 　Note why a new convert must not be given a position of leadership in the church: because he may become conceited and "fall into the condemnation incurred by the devil." Satan was expelled from heaven because of pride. It was pride that caused his fall and brought condemnation upon him. When a person is given a signif-

ENGLISH WORD	GREEK WORD AND VERSE	THE WORD MEANS...
	will use that pride to make him fall. [NLT] μὴ **νεόφυτον**, ἵνα μὴ τυφωθεὶς εἰς κρίμα ἐμπέσῃ τοῦ διαβόλου. [GNS] μὴ **νεόφυτον**, ἵνα μὴ τυφωθεὶς εἰς κρίμα ἐμπέσῃ τοῦ διαβόλου. [GNT]	icant responsibility before he has become rooted and grounded in the faith, he is most likely going to fall and be condemned just as Satan fell and was condemned. We must always remember what Matthew Henry points out: "Pride...is a sin that turned angels into devils" (*Matthew Henry's Commentary*, Vol.6, p.815). We must guard against pride. We must guard against putting a person in a position of leadership that will tempt him to feel more important than he is.
#2696 **Not Novice** **Not...novice–KJV** Not...new convert–NASB Not...recent convert–NIV **Not...novice–NKJV** Not...new Christian–NLT **POSB REFERENCE** (1 Tim.3:6) Note 4	μὴ **νεόφυτον** = *më neophuton* Pronunciation: [may neh-of'-oo-ton] Parsing *neophuton* (part of speech): adjective 　　Case—accusative 　　Gender—masculine 　　Number—singular 　　Stem or root—from νεόφυτος, ον Concordance References: ⇒　Strong's #3361 më + 3504 neophutos ⇒　NIV #3590 më [not] + 3745 neophutos [recent convert] ⇒　NASB #3361 më + 3504 neophutos **1 Tim. 3:6** **Not** a **novice**, lest being lifted up with pride he fall into the condemnation of the devil. [KJV] And **not** a **new convert**, lest he become conceited and fall into the condemnation incurred by the devil. [NASB] He must **not** be a **recent convert**, or he may become conceited and fall under the same judgment as the devil. [NIV] **Not** a **novice**, lest being puffed up with pride he fall into the *same* condemnation as the devil. [NKJV] An elder must **not** be a **new Christian**, because he might be proud of being chosen so soon, and the Devil will use that pride to make him fall. [NLT] μὴ **νεόφυτον**, ἵνα μὴ τυφωθεὶς εἰς κρίμα ἐμπέσῃ τοῦ διαβόλου. [GNS] μὴ **νεόφυτον**, ἵνα μὴ τυφωθεὶς εἰς κρίμα ἐμπέσῃ τοῦ διαβόλου. [GNT]	Not a recent convert, novice, new Christian. **Practical Application** The minister or bishop of God must be spiritually qualified. He must not be a novice (*më neophuton*), that is, a new convert or a new church member. He must have been a convert or church member for a long time... • long enough to have become rooted and grounded in the Lord and His Word. • long enough to have become spiritually mature. • long enough to have proven his testimony for Christ. • long enough to be well known and respected by other believers. • long enough to be able to minister to others and to teach them to minister. Note why a novice must not be given a position of leadership in the church: lest he may become prideful and "fall into the condemnation of the devil." Satan was expelled from heaven because of pride. It was pride that caused his fall and brought condemnation upon him. When a person is given a significant responsibility before he has become rooted and grounded in the faith, he is most likely going to fall and be condemned just as Satan fell and was condemned. We must always remember what Matthew Henry points out: "Pride...is a sin that turned angels into devils" (*Matthew Henry's Commentary*, Vol.6, p.815). We must guard against pride. We must guard against putting a person in a position of leadership that will tempt him to feel more important than he is.
#2697 **Not Pugnacious** No striker–KJV **Not...pugnacious–NASB** Not violent–NIV Not violent–NKJV Not...violent–NLT **POSB REFERENCE** (1 Tim.3:2-3; esp. v.3) Note 2, point 9	μὴ **πλήκτην** = *më plëktën* Pronunciation: [may playke'-tayn] Parsing (part of speech): noun 　　Case—accusative 　　Gender—masculine 　　Number—singular 　　Stem or root—from πλήκτης, ου Concordance References: ⇒　Strong's #3361 më + 4131 plëktës ⇒　NIV #3590 më [not] + 4438 plëktës [violent] ⇒　NASB #3361 më + 4131 plëktës **1 Tim. 3:3** Not given to wine, **no striker**, not greedy of filthy lucre; but patient, not a brawler, not covetous; [KJV] **Not** addicted to wine or **pugnacious**, but gentle, uncontentious, free from the love of money. [NASB] Not given to drunkenness, **not violent** but gentle, not quarrelsome, not a lover of money. [NIV] Not given to wine, **not violent**, not greedy for money, but gentle, not quarrelsome, not covetous; [NKJV] He must **not** be a heavy drinker or be **violent**. He must be gentle, peace loving, and not one who loves	Not violent; no striker; not pugnacious, not quicktempered. **Practical Application** The minister or elder must not be a "pugnacious" (*më plëktën*): not combative or violent, not contentious or quarrelsome, not a person who strikes out and contends with another person. The minister must not be a person who strikes other people or who becomes easily upset, irritated, or aggravated with others. He uses neither hand nor tongue against anyone. On the contrary, he is kind, gentle, and longsuffering with others.

ENGLISH WORD	GREEK WORD AND VERSE	THE WORD MEANS...
	money. [NLT] μὴ πάροινον, **μὴ πλήκτην**, μὴ αἰσχροκερδῆ, ἀλλ᾽ ἐπιεικῆ, ἄμαχον, ἀφιλάργυρον· [GNS] μὴ πάροινον **μὴ πλήκτην**, ἀλλὰ ἐπιεικῆ ἄμαχον ἀφιλάργυρον, [GNT]	
#2698 **Not Receive** Receiveth not–KJV Not accept–NASB Not accept–NIV **Not receive–NKJV** Can't understand–NLT **POSB** **REFERENCE** (1 Cor.2:14) Note 1, point 1	οὐ δέχεται = *ou dechetai* Pronunciation: [oo dekh'-eh-tah-ee] Parsing *dechetai* (part of speech): verb 　　Mood—indicative 　　Tense—present 　　Voice—middle or passive deponent 　　Person—3rd person 　　Number—singular 　　Stem or root—from δέχομαι Concordance References: ⇒　Strong's #3756 ou + 1209 dechomai ⇒　NIV #4024 ou [not] + 1312 dechomai [accept] ⇒　NASB #3756 ou + 1209 dechomai **1 Cor. 2:14** 　　But the natural man **receiveth not** the things of the Spirit of God: for they are foolishness unto him: neither can he know them, because they are spiritually discerned. [KJV] 　　But a natural man does **not accept** the things of the Spirit of God; for they are foolishness to him, and he cannot understand them, because they are spiritually appraised. [NASB] 　　The man without the Spirit does **not accept** the things that come from the Spirit of God, for they are foolishness to him, and he cannot understand them, because they are spiritually discerned. [NIV] 　　But the natural man does **not receive** the things of the Spirit of God, for they are foolishness to him; nor can he know them, because they are spiritually discerned. [NKJV] 　　But people who aren't Christians **can't understand** these truths from God's Spirit. It all sounds foolish to them because only those who have the Spirit can understand what the Spirit means. [NLT] ψυχικὸς δὲ ἄνθρωπος **οὐ δέχεται** τὰ τοῦ Πνεύματος τοῦ Θεοῦ· μωρία γὰρ αὐτῷ ἐστι, καὶ οὐ δύναται γνῶναι, ὅτι πνευματικῶς ἀνακρίνεται· [GNS] ψυχικὸς δὲ ἄνθρωπος **οὐ δέχεται** τὰ τοῦ πνεύματος τοῦ θεοῦ, μωρία γὰρ αὐτῷ ἐστιν, καὶ οὐ δύναται γνῶναι, ὅτι πνευματικῶς ἀνακρίνεται [GNT]	Not receive; not accept; not take; not welcome; not bear with; to refuse and regret; not obtain. **Practical Application** 　　The man without the Spirit is the natural man. He does not accept the things that come from the Spirit of God. The phrase "not receive" (*dechetai*) means that spiritual things are not welcomed as a guest, are not accepted. It means to refuse and reject. Spiritual things are of little, if any, concern to the natural man. His mind is primarily upon this world, upon... • bigger and better things • acquiring more and more • desires and feelings • wants and cravings • position and wealth • attention and recognition • ambition and promotion • socials and parties • play and recreation • comfort and ease • drinking and eating • dress and appearance 　　The natural man's life and mind are spent focusing upon the natural, upon this world and not upon the spiritual; therefore, in God's eyes he is classified as the natural man. His heart welcomes only the world; it is closed to God. God is not welcomed into his life. Therefore, he does not accept the things that come from the Spirit of God.
#2699 **Not Recent Convert** Not...novice–KJV Not...new convert–NASB **Not...recent convert–NIV** Not...novice–NKJV Not...new Christian–NLT **POSB** **REFERENCE** (1 Tim.3:6) Note 4	μὴ νεόφυτον = *më neophuton* Pronunciation: [may neh-of'-oo-ton] Parsing *neophuton* (part of speech): adjective 　　Case—accusative 　　Gender—masculine 　　Number—singular 　　Stem or root—from νεόφυτος, ον Concordance References: ⇒　Strong's #3361 më + 3504 neophutos ⇒　NIV #3590 më [not] + 3745 neophutos [recent convert] ⇒　NASB #3361 më + 3504 neophutos **1 Tim. 3:6** 　　**Not** a **novice**, lest being lifted up with pride he fall into the condemnation of the devil. [KJV] 　　And **not** a **new convert**, lest he become conceited and fall into the condemnation incurred by the devil. [NASB] 　　He must **not** be a **recent convert**, or he may become conceited and fall under the same judgment as the devil. [NIV] 　　**Not** a **novice**, lest being puffed up with pride he fall into the *same* condemnation as the devil. [NKJV] 　　An elder must **not** be a **new Christian**, because he	Not a recent convert, novice, new Christian. **Practical Application** 　　The minister or overseer of God must be spiritually qualified. He must not be a recent convert (*më neophuton*), that is, a novice or a new church member. He must have been a convert or church member for a long time... • long enough to have become rooted and grounded in the Lord and His Word. • long enough to have become spiritually mature. • long enough to have proven his testimony for Christ. • long enough to be well known and respected by other believers. • long enough to be able to minister to others and to teach them to minister. 　　Note why a recent convert must not be given a position of leadership in the church: lest he become conceited and "fall under the same judgment as the devil." Satan was expelled from heaven because of pride. It was pride that caused

ENGLISH WORD	GREEK WORD AND VERSE	THE WORD MEANS...
	might be proud of being chosen so soon, and the Devil will use that pride to make him fall. [NLT] μὴ νεόφυτον, ἵνα μὴ τυφωθεὶς εἰς κρίμα ἐμπέσῃ τοῦ διαβόλου. [GNS] μὴ νεόφυτον, ἵνα μὴ τυφωθεὶς εἰς κρίμα ἐμπέσῃ τοῦ διαβόλου. [GNT]	his fall and brought condemnation upon him. When a person is given a great responsibility before he has become rooted and grounded in the faith, he is most likely going to fall and be condemned just as Satan fell and was condemned. We must always remember what Matthew Henry points out: "Pride...is a sin that turned angels into devils" (*Matthew Henry's Commentary*, Vol.6, p.815). We must guard against pride. We must guard against putting a person in a position of leadership that will tempt him to feel more important than he is.
#2700 **Not Regard Lightly** Despise not–KJV **Not regard lightly–NASB** Not make light of–NIV Do not despise–NKJV Don't ignore it–NLT **POSB REFERENCE** (Heb.12:5-7; esp. v.5) Note 1, point 1	μὴ ὀλιγώρει = mē oligōrei Pronunciation: [may ol-ig-o-reh'-ee] Parsing *oligōrei* (part of speech): verb 　　Mood—imperative 　　Tense—present 　　Voice—active 　　Person—2nd person 　　Number—singular 　　Stem or root—from ὀλιγωρέω Concordance References: ⇒ Strong's #3361 mē + 3643 oligōreō ⇒ NIV #3590 mē [not] + 3902 oligōreō [make light of] ⇒ NASB #3361 mē + 3643 oligōreō **Hebrews 12:5** And ye have forgotten the exhortation which speaketh unto you as unto children, My son, **despise not** thou the chastening of the Lord, nor faint when thou art rebuked of him: [KJV] And you have forgotten the exhortation which is addressed to you as sons, "My son, do **not regard lightly** the discipline of the Lord, Nor FAINT WHEN YOU ARE REPROVED By Him; [NASB] And you have forgotten that word of encouragement that addresses you as sons: "My son, do **not make light of** the Lord's discipline, and do not lose heart when he rebukes you, [NIV] And you have forgotten the exhortation which speaks to you as to sons: "My son, **do not despise** the chastening of the Lord, Nor be discouraged when you are rebuked by Him; [NKJV] And have you entirely forgotten the encouraging words God spoke to you, his children? He said, "My child, **don't ignore it** when the Lord disciplines you, and don't be discouraged when he corrects you. [NLT] καὶ ἐκλέλησθε τῆς παρακλήσεως, ἥτις ὑμῖν ὡς υἱοῖς διαλέγεται, Υἱέ μου, μὴ ὀλιγώρει παιδείας Κυρίου, μηδὲ ἐκλύου, ὑπ' αὐτοῦ ἐλεγχόμενος· [GNS] καὶ ἐκλέλησθε τῆς παρακλήσεως, ἥτις ὑμῖν ὡς υἱοῖς διαλέγεται, Υἱέ μου, μὴ ὀλιγώρει παιδείας κυρίου μηδὲ ἐκλύου ὑπ' αὐτοῦ ἐλεγχόμενος· [GNT]	Not to make light of; not to regard lightly; not to despise; not to ignore; not to think lightly of; not to scorn; not to make little of, treat lightly. **Practical Application** When we are being taught, disciplined, or corrected, there is always the danger of... 　• despising it. 　• scorning it. 　• making light of it. 　• treating it too lightly. Too often, we pay little attention to the discipline and correction of God: to the tug and pull of the Spirit of God, to the little consequences and sufferings of our hearts, to the little things that happen to us. As a result, we continue right on in our little irresponsible behaviors and sins. The little flaws and sins get bigger and bigger until finally the roof caves in and the consequences involve so much destruction and suffering that we can no longer ignore them. 　Why do we suffer so much in this life? Because of our irresponsibilities and sins—because we do not heed the discipline and correction of God when we first begin to act irresponsibly. If we heeded the discipline of God, then we could correct our small misbehavior and no big sin would happen. This would mean that much of the great sufferings in the world would never happen. 　The point is this: we are not to regard lightly the discipline of God—not to scorn it nor take and treat it lightly. We are to heed it. As we do, life will be much easier, and we will be stronger and much more triumphant and victorious.
#2701 **Not Return** Came not as yet–KJV Came no more–NASB **Not return–NIV** Came no more–NKJV Didn't return–NLT **POSB REFERENCE** (2 Cor.1:23-2:4; esp. v.23) Note 1, 2	οὐκέτι ἦλθον = ouketi ēlthon Pronunciation: [oo-keh-tee ale'-thon] Parsing *ēlthon* (part of speech): verb 　　Mood—indicative 　　Tense—aorist 　　Voice—active 　　Person—1st person 　　Number—singular 　　Stem or root—from ἔρχομαι Concordance References: ⇒ Strong's #3765 ouketi + 2064 erchomai ⇒ NIV #4033 ouketi [not] + 2262 erchomai [return] ⇒ NASB #3765 ouketi + 2064 erchomai	Did not return; did not make his way back; did not go back. **Practical Application** The statement, "I did not return," can be equally translated, "I came no more to Corinth." This, too, points toward Paul's having made a quick visit to Corinth after writing his first letter, a visit that resulted in the people's rejecting him and breaking his heart (see POSB Introduction, Special Features, pt. 3—1 Corinthians for more discussion).

ENGLISH WORD	GREEK WORD AND VERSE	THE WORD MEANS...
POSB REFERENCE (1 Tim.3:11-12; esp. v.11) Note 3, point 1b	Women must likewise be dignified, **not malicious gossips**, but temperate, faithful in all things. [NASB] In the same way, their wives are to be women worthy of respect, **not malicious talkers** but temperate and trustworthy in everything. [NIV] Likewise their wives *must be* reverent, **not slanderers**, temperate, faithful in all things. [NKJV] In the same way, their wives must be respected and must **not speak evil** of others. They must exercise self-control and be faithful in everything they do. [NLT] γυναῖκας ὡσαύτως σεμνάς, **μὴ διαβόλους**, νηφαλίους, πιστὰς ἐν πᾶσι. [GNS] γυναῖκας ὡσαύτως σεμνάς, **μὴ διαβόλους**, νηφαλίους, πιστὰς ἐν πᾶσιν. [GNT]	

#2706
 Not To Delay
 	
 Not delay–KJV
 Do not delay–NASB
 At once–NIV
 Not to delay–NKJV
 Come as soon as possible–NLT
 	
 POSB REFERENCE (Acts 9:36-39; esp. v.38) Note 2, point 3c
	Μὴ ὀκνήσῃς = *Mē oknēsēs*
	 Pronunciation: [may hok-nay'-says]
	 Parsing *oknēsēs* (part of speech): verb
	     Mood—subjunctive or imperative
	     Tense—aorist
	     Voice—active
	     Person—2nd person
	     Number—singular
	     Stem or root—from ὀκνέω
	 Concordance References:
	 ⇒ Strong's #3361 + 3635 mē okneō
	 ⇒ NIV #3590 + 3890 mē okneō [at once]
	 ⇒ NASB #3361 + 3635 mē okneō
	
	 ### Acts 9:38
	 And forasmuch as Lydda was nigh to Joppa, and the disciples had heard that Peter was there, they sent unto him two men, desiring him that he would **not delay** to come to them. [KJV]
	
	 And since Lydda was near Joppa, the disciples, having heard that Peter was there, sent two men to him, entreating him, "**Do not delay** to come to us." [NASB]
	
	 Lydda was near Joppa; so when the disciples heard that Peter was in Lydda, they sent two men to him and urged him, "Please come **at once!**" [NIV]
	
	 And since Lydda was near Joppa, and the disciples had heard that Peter was there, they sent two men to him, imploring him **not to delay** in coming to them. [NKJV]
	
	 But they had heard that Peter was nearby at Lydda, so they sent two men to beg him, "Please **come as soon as possible!**" [NLT]
	
	 ἐγγὺς δὲ οὔσης Λύδδης τῇ Ἰόππῃ, οἱ μαθηταὶ ἀκούσαντες ὅτι Πέτρος ἐστὶν ἐν αὐτῇ, ἀπέστειλαν δύο ἄνδρας πρὸς αὐτὸν παρακαλοῦντες **μὴ ὀκνῆσαι** διελθεῖν ἕως αὐτῶν. [GNS]
	
	 ἐγγὺς δὲ οὔσης Λύδδας τῇ Ἰόππῃ οἱ μαθηταὶ ἀκούσαντες ὅτι Πέτρος ἐστὶν ἐν αὐτῇ ἀπέστειλαν δύο ἄνδρας πρὸς αὐτὸν παρακαλοῦντες, **Μὴ ὀκνήσῃς** διελθεῖν ἕως ἡμῶν. [GNT]
		At once; without delay; to come as soon as possible.
		
		 ### Practical Application
		 It means not to hesitate, not to be reluctant, but to act and act now, quickly, without questioning.

#2707
 Not To Worry About
 	
 Nothing doubting–KJV
 Without misgivings–NASB
 No hesitation–NIV
 Doubting nothing–NKJV
 Not to worry about–NLT
	μηδὲν διακρίναντα = *mēden diakrinanta*
	 Pronunciation: [may-dehn' dee-ak-ree'-nahn-tah]
	 Parsing *diakrinanta* (part of speech): verb
	     Mood—participle
	     Tense—aorist
	     Voice—active
	     Case—accusative
	     Gender—masculine
	     Person—1st person
	     Number—singular
	     Stem or root—from διακρίνω
	 Concordance References:
	 ⇒ Strong's #3367 mēdeis + 1252 diakrinō
	 ⇒ NIV #3594 mēdeis [no] + 1359 diakrinō [hesitation]
	 ⇒ NASB #3367 mēdeis + 1252 diakrinō
		Not to hesitate; not to have misgivings; not to worry about; not to doubt.
		
		 ### Practical Application
		 It means that they were to make no distinction. God tells Peter in no uncertain terms, "Go with them [the Gentiles] making no distinctions."
		
		 The same command is given to all believers of all generations. Believers are not to make distinctions, not to discriminate in proclaiming the gospel. What an indictment against so many! How many *withdraw* from the poor? How many do not reach out to people of other races and social classes?

ENGLISH WORD	GREEK WORD AND VERSE	THE WORD MEANS...
POSB REFERENCE (Acts 11:4-15; esp. v.12) Note 2, point 3	**Acts 11:12** And the spirit bade me go with them, **nothing doubting**. Moreover these six brethren accompanied me, and we entered into the man's house: [KJV] "And the Spirit told me to go with them **without misgivings**. And these six brethren also went with me, and we entered the man's house. [NASB] The Spirit told me to have **no hesitation** about going with them. These six brothers also went with me, and we entered the man's house. [NIV] Then the Spirit told me to go with them, **doubting nothing**. Moreover these six brethren accompanied me, and we entered into the man's house. [NKJV] The Holy Spirit told me to go with them and **not to worry about** their being Gentiles. These six brothers here accompanied me, and we soon arrived at the home of the man who had sent for us. [NLT] εἶπε δὲ μοι τὸ Πνεῦμά συνελθεῖν αὐτοῖς, **μηδὲν διακρινόμενον**. ἦλθον δὲ σὺν ἐμοὶ καὶ οἱ ἓξ ἀδελφοὶ οὗτοι, καὶ εἰσήλθομεν εἰς τὸν οἶκον τοῦ ἀνδρός· [GNS] εἶπεν δὲ τὸ πνεῦμά μοι συνελθεῖν αὐτοῖς **μηδὲν διακρίναντα**. ἦλθον δὲ σὺν ἐμοὶ καὶ οἱ ἓξ ἀδελφοὶ οὗτοι καὶ εἰσήλθομεν εἰς τὸν οἶκον τοῦ ἀνδρός. [GNT]	
#2708 **Not Violent** No striker–KJV Not...pugnacious– NASB **Not violent–NIV** **Not violent–NKJV** **Not...violent–NLT** **POSB REFERENCE** (1 Tim.3:2-3; esp. v.3) Note 2, point 9	**μὴ πλήκτην** = *më plëktën* Pronunciation: [may playke'-tayn] Parsing (part of speech): noun Case—accusative Gender—masculine Number—singular Stem or root—from πλήκτης, ου Concordance References: ⇒ Strong's #3361 më + 4131 plëktës ⇒ NIV #3590 më [not] + 4438 plëktës [violent] ⇒ NASB #3361 më + 4131 plëktës **1 Tim. 3:3** Not given to wine, **no striker**, not greedy of filthy lucre; but patient, not a brawler, not covetous; [KJV] **Not** addicted to wine or **pugnacious**, but gentle, uncontentious, free from the love of money. [NASB] Not given to drunkenness, **not violent** but gentle, not quarrelsome, not a lover of money. [NIV] Not given to wine, **not violent**, not greedy for money, but gentle, not quarrelsome, not covetous; [NKJV] He must **not** be a heavy drinker or be **violent**. He must be gentle, peace loving, and not one who loves money. [NLT] μὴ πάροινον, **μὴ πλήκτην**, μὴ αἰσχροκερδῆ, ἀλλ ἐπιεικῆ, ἄμαχον, ἀφιλάργυρον· [GNS] μὴ πάροινον **μὴ πλήκτην**, ἀλλὰ ἐπιεικῆ ἄμαχον ἀφιλάργυρον, [GNT]	Not violent; no striker; not pugnacious, not quicktempered. ## Practical Application The minister or bishop must not be a "violent" (*më plëktën*) person: not combative, not contentious or quarrelsome, not a person who strikes out and contends with another person. The minister must not be a person who strikes other people or who becomes easily upset, irritated, or aggravated with others. He uses neither hand nor tongue against anyone. On the contrary, he is kind, gentle, and longsuffering with others.
#2709 **Note** Mark–KJV Keep your eye on– NASB Watch out for–NIV **Note–NKJV** Watch out for–NLT **POSB REFERENCE** (Rom.16:17-18; esp. v.17) Note 1, point 1c	**σκοπεῖν** = *skopein* Pronunciation: [skop-een'] Parsing (part of speech): verb Mood—infinitive Tense—present Voice—active Stem or root—from σκοπέω Concordance References: ⇒ Strong's #4648 skopeö ⇒ NIV #5023 skopeö ⇒ NASB #4648 skopeö **Romans 16:17** Now I beseech you, brethren, **mark** them which cause divisions and offences contrary to the doctrine which ye have learned; and avoid them. [KJV] Now I urge you, brethren, **keep your eye on** those who cause dissensions and hindrances contrary to the teaching which you learned, and turn away from them. [NASB]	To mark; to note; to keep one's eye on; to look at; to observe; to focus upon; to contemplate; to scrutinize; to pay attention to; to watch out (for); to be careful. ## Practical Application "Note" (*skopein*) the divisive person. It is the divisive person himself who is to be avoided and turned away from, not just his sin. We are not to have anything to do with a divisive person... • for we give the appearance of approving of what he is doing. • for we run the risk of being influenced by and stumbling over what he says and does.

ENGLISH WORD	GREEK WORD AND VERSE	THE WORD MEANS...
POSB REFERENCE (1 Cor.15:58) Note 6, point 3	**1 Cor. 15:58** Therefore, my beloved brethren, be ye stedfast, unmovable, always abounding in the work of the Lord, forasmuch as ye know that your **labour** is not in vain in the Lord. [KJV] Therefore, my beloved brethren, be steadfast, immovable, always abounding in the work of the Lord, knowing that your **toil** is not in vain in the Lord. [NASB] Therefore, my dear brothers, stand firm. Let nothing move you. Always give yourselves fully to the work of the Lord, because you know that your **labor** in the Lord is not in vain. [NIV] Therefore, my beloved brethren, be steadfast, immovable, always abounding in the work of the Lord, knowing that your **labor** is not in vain in the Lord. [NKJV] So, my dear brothers and sisters, be strong and steady, always enthusiastic about the Lord's work, for you know that **nothing you do** for the Lord is ever useless. [NLT] ὥστε, ἀδελφοί μου ἀγαπητοί, ἑδραῖοι γίνεσθε, ἀμετακίνητοι, περισσεύοντες ἐν τῷ ἔργῳ τοῦ Κυρίου πάντοτε, εἰδότες ὅτι ὁ **κόπος** ὑμῶν οὐκ ἔστι κενὸς ἐν Κυρίῳ. [GNS] Ὥστε, ἀδελφοί μου ἀγαπητοί, ἑδραῖοι γίνεσθε, ἀμετακίνητοι, περισσεύοντες ἐν τῷ ἔργῳ τοῦ κυρίου πάντοτε, εἰδότες ὅτι ὁ **κόπος** ὑμῶν οὐκ ἔστιν κενὸς ἐν κυρίῳ. [GNT]	• is always enthusiastic about the Lord's work, • will be rewarded: resurrected and given a new body.
#2714 Nought **Nought–KJV** Contempt–NASB Ridiculed–NIV Contempt–NKJV Ridiculing–NLT **POSB REFERENCE** (Lk.23:8-11; esp. v.11) Note 3, point 4	ἐξουθενήσας = exouthenēsas Pronunciation: [ex-oo-then-eh'-sas] Parsing (part of speech): verb Mood—participle Tense—aorist Voice—active Case—nominative Gender—masculine Number—singular Stem or root—from ἐξουθενέω Concordance References: ⇒ Strong's #1848 exoutheneō ⇒ NIV #2024 exoutheneō ⇒ NASB #1848 exoutheneō **Luke 23:11** And Herod with his men of war set him at **nought**, and mocked him, and arrayed him in a gorgeous robe, and sent him again to Pilate. [KJV] And Herod with his soldiers, after treating Him with **contempt** and mocking Him, dressed Him in a gorgeous robe and sent Him back to Pilate. [NASB] Then Herod and his soldiers **ridiculed** and mocked him. Dressing him in an elegant robe, they sent him back to Pilate. [NIV] Then Herod, with his men of war, treated Him with **contempt** and mocked *Him,* arrayed Him in a gorgeous robe, and sent Him back to Pilate. [NKJV] Now Herod and his soldiers began mocking and **ridiculing** Jesus. Then they put a royal robe on him and sent him back to Pilate. [NLT] **ἐξουθενήσας** δὲ αὐτὸν ὁ Ἡρῴδης σὺν τοῖς στρατεύμασιν αὐτοῦ, καὶ ἐμπαίξας, περιβαλὼν αὐτὸν ἐσθῆτα λαμπράν, ἀνέπεμψεν αὐτὸν τῷ Πιλάτῳ. [GNS] **ἐξουθενήσας** δὲ αὐτὸν [καὶ] ὁ Ἡρῴδης σὺν τοῖς στρατεύμασιν αὐτοῦ καὶ ἐμπαίξας περιβαλὼν ἐσθῆτα λαμπρὰν ἀνέπεμψεν αὐτὸν τῷ Πιλάτῳ. [GNT]	To ridicule; to count as nothing; to make nothing of; to despise; to look down upon; to reject; to think something is unimportant; to count as zero—therefore, to treat with utter contempt. **Practical Application** Note the contrast in the verse. Herod sat there as King with "his men of war" surrounding him, and Jesus stood there beaten and battered in torn, ragged clothes. Herod, judging by appearance, counted the Man who claimed to be the Son of God as nothing. This Man and His claim did not matter, not to Herod.
#2715 Nourishes– Nourisheth **Nourisheth–KJV** **Nourishes–NASB** Feeds–NIV	ἐκτρέφει = ektrephei Pronunciation: [ek-tref'-eh-ee] Parsing (part of speech): verb Mood—indicative Tense—present Voice—active Person—3rd person Number—singular Stem or root—from ἐκτρέφω	To feed; to clothe; to nurture; to look after until she is mature in the marriage and then to continue nourishing her as long as she lives. **Practical Application** The love which the husband is to have for his wife is the very same love he has for his own body. This is a startling statement. Note again

ENGLISH WORD	GREEK WORD AND VERSE	THE WORD MEANS...
Nourishes–NKJV Cares–NLT **POSB REFERENCE** (Eph.5:25-33; esp. v.29) Note 2, point 2	Concordance References: ⇒ Strong's #1625 ektrephö ⇒ NIV #1763 ektrephö ⇒ NASB #1625 ektrephö **Ephes. 5:29** For no man ever yet hated his own flesh; but **nourisheth** and cherisheth it, even as the Lord the church: [KJV] For no one ever hated his own flesh, but **nourishes** and cherishes it, just as Christ also does the church, [NASB] After all, no one ever hated his own body, but he **feeds** and cares for it, just as Christ does the church—[NIV] For no one ever hated his own flesh, but **nourishes** and cherishes it, just as the Lord *does* the church. [NKJV] No one hates his own body but lovingly **cares** for it, just as Christ cares for his body, which is the church. [NLT] οὐδεὶς γάρ ποτε τὴν ἑαυτοῦ σάρκα ἐμίσησεν, ἀλλ **ἐκτρέφει** καὶ θάλπει αὐτήν, καθὼς καὶ ὁ Κύριος τὴν ἐκκλησίαν· [GNS] οὐδεὶς γάρ ποτε τὴν ἑαυτοῦ σάρκα ἐμίσησεν ἀλλὰ **ἐκτρέφει** καὶ θάλπει αὐτήν, καθὼς καὶ ὁ Χριστὸς τὴν ἐκκλησίαν, [GNT]	what it says: the husband is to love his wife just as much as he loves *his own body*. This means that he is to care for his wife as he does his own body. What a difference would exist in marriage if the husband just *cares for* his wife as he does his own body. Think through the meaning of the two words for just a moment and imagine the difference that could exist.
#2716 **Nullify** Of none effect–KJV Invalidating–NASB **Nullify–NIV** Of no effect–NKJV Break–NLT **POSB REFERENCE** (Mk.7:13) *Deeper Study #2*	ἀκυροῦντες = *akurountes* Pronunciation: [ak-oo-roon'-tehs] Parsing (part of speech): verb 　Mood—participle 　Tense—present 　Voice—active 　Case—nominative 　Gender—masculine 　Person—2nd person 　Number—plural 　Stem or root—from ἀκυρόω Concordance References: ⇒ Strong's #208 akuroö ⇒ NIV #218 akuroö ⇒ NASB #208 akuroöt **Mark 7:13** Making the word of God **of none effect** through your tradition, which ye have delivered: and many such like things do ye. [KJV] Thus **invalidating** the word of God by your tradition which you have handed down; and you do many things such as that." [NASB] Thus you **nullify** the word of God by your tradition that you have handed down. And you do many things like that." [NIV] Making the word of God **of no effect** through your tradition which you have handed down. And many such things you do." [NKJV] As such, you **break** the law of God in order to protect your own tradition. And this is only one example. There are many, many others." [NLT] **ἀκυροῦντες** τὸν λόγον τοῦ Θεοῦ τῇ παραδόσει ὑμῶν ᾖ παρεδώκατε· καὶ παρόμοια τοιαῦτα πολλὰ ποιεῖτε. [GNS] **ἀκυροῦντες** τὸν λόγον τοῦ θεοῦ τῇ παραδόσει ὑμῶν ᾖ παρεδώκατε· καὶ παρόμοια τοιαῦτα πολλὰ ποιεῖτε. [GNT]	To nullify; to be of no effect; to set aside; to make void, ineffective; to annul; to cancel; to disregard; to deprive of authority and power; to invalidate. **Practical Application** In this Scripture, Christ is rebuking anyone who places human traditions on an equal or higher authority than the Word of God. Jesus charged the religionists with setting aside God's Word for tradition. Religious traditions may be described as institutional or personal. 1. Institutional traditions are such things as rituals, rules, regulations, schedules, forms, services, procedures, organizations—anything that gives order and security to the persons involved. 2. Personal traditions are such things as church attendance, prayers, habits, ceremonies, objects which a person uses (somewhat superstitiously) to keep himself religiously secure. Jesus was attacking the fact that so many religionists put their traditions first while neglecting and ignoring God's Word. (See POSB notes—Matthew 12:1-8; POSB note—Matthew 12:10 and POSB *Deeper Study #1*—Matthew 12:10).
#2717 **Nullify** Frustrate–KJV **Nullify–NASB** Set aside–NIV Set aside–NKJV Meaningless–NLT	ἀθετῶ = *athetö* Pronunciation: [ath-eh-to] Parsing (part of speech): verb 　Mood—indicative 　Tense—present 　Voice—active 　Person—1st person 　Number—singular	To set aside, void, invalidate, ignore, make ineffective, and nullify; to frustrate; to be meaningless. **Practical Application** If a man sets aside the grace of God and seeks righteousness by the law, then Christ died in

ENGLISH WORD	GREEK WORD AND VERSE	THE WORD MEANS...
POSB REFERENCE (Gal.2:19-21; esp. v.21) Note 5	Stem or root—from ἀθετέω Concordance References: ⇒ Strong's #114 atheteö ⇒ NIV #119 atheteö ⇒ NASB #114 atheteö **Galatians 2:21** I do not **frustrate** the grace of God: for if righteousness come by the law, then Christ is dead in vain. [KJV] "I do not **nullify** the grace of God; for if righteousness comes through the Law, then Christ died needlessly." [NASB] I do not **set aside** the grace of God, for if righteousness could be gained through the law, Christ died for nothing!" [NIV] I do not **set aside** the grace of God; for if righteousness *comes* through the law, then Christ died in vain." [NKJV] I am not one of those who treats the grace of God as **meaningless**. For if we could be saved by keeping the law, then there was no need for Christ to die. [NLT] οὐκ **ἀθετῶ** τὴν χάριν τοῦ Θεοῦ· εἰ γὰρ διὰ νόμου δικαιοσύνη, ἄρα Χριστὸς δωρεὰν ἀπέθανεν. [GNS] οὐκ **ἀθετῶ** τὴν χάριν τοῦ Θεοῦ· εἰ γὰρ διὰ νόμου δικαιοσύνη, ἄρα Χριστὸς δωρεὰν ἀπέθανεν. [GNT]	vain. The person who preaches that a man can be good enough—that he can work enough and keep enough law—to become righteous and acceptable to God... • voids and does away with the love and grace of God. • makes the death of Christ empty and meaningless. The only way a man can live for God is by trusting the grace and love of God, that is, by trusting the death of Jesus Christ for His righteousness.

#2718
Nurture
 	
Nurture–KJV
Discipline–NASB
Training–NIV
Training–NKJV
Discipline–NLT
 	
POSB REFERENCE (Eph.6:4) Note 2, point 2
	παιδεία = *paideia*
	Pronunciation: [pahee-di'-ah]
	Parsing (part of speech): noun
	  Case—dative
	  Gender—feminine
	  Number—singular
	  Stem or root—from παιδεία, ας
	Concordance References:
	⇒ Strong's #3809 paideia
	⇒ NIV #4082 paideia
	⇒ NASB #3809 paideia
	
	Ephes. 6:4
	And, ye fathers, provoke not your children to wrath: but bring them up in the **nurture** and admonition of the Lord. [KJV]
	And, fathers, do not provoke your children to anger; but bring them up in the **discipline** and instruction of the Lord. [NASB]
	Fathers, do not exasperate your children; instead, bring them up in the **training** and instruction of the Lord. [NIV]
	And you, fathers, do not provoke your children to wrath, but bring them up in the **training** and admonition of the Lord. [NKJV]
	And now a word to you fathers. Don't make your children angry by the way you treat them. Rather, bring them up with the **discipline** and instruction approved by the Lord. [NLT]
	καὶ οἱ πατέρες, μὴ παροργίζετε τὰ τέκνα ὑμῶν, ἀλλ᾽ ἐκτρέφετε αὐτὰ ἐν **παιδείᾳ** καὶ νουθεσίᾳ Κυρίου. [GNS]
	Καὶ οἱ πατέρες, μὴ παροργίζετε τὰ τέκνα ὑμῶν ἀλλὰ ἐκτρέφετε αὐτὰ ἐν **παιδείᾳ** καὶ νουθεσίᾳ κυρίου. [GNT]
		To train; to nurture; to discipline. The word "nurture" (*paideia*) means "the whole training and education of children which [involves]...the cultivation of mind and morals...commands and admonitions...reproof and punishment...correcting mistakes and curbing the passions...the increase of virtue" (Thayers Greek - English Lexicon).
		
		Practical Application
		A parent is to bring up a child in the ways of the Lord, in the nurture and admonition of the Lord.

ENGLISH WORD	GREEK WORD AND VERSE	THE WORD MEANS...

#2719
Oath, Bound With An–
Oath, Bound Under An
 	
Bound...under a curse–KJV
Bound...under an oath–NASB
Bound...with an oath–NIV
Bound...under an oath–NKJV
Bound...with an oath–NLT
 	
POSB REFERENCE
(Acts 23:12-15; esp. v.12)
Note 1, point 1
	ἀνεθεμάτισαν = anethematisan
	Pronunciation: [an-eth-ehm-aht-i'-sahn]
	Parsing (part of speech): verb
	  Mood—indicative
	  Tense—aorist
	  Voice—active
	  Person—3rd person
	  Number—plural
	  Stem or root—from ἀναθεματίζω
	Concordance References:
	⇒ Strong's #332 anathematizö
	⇒ NIV #354 anathematizö
	⇒ NASB #332 anathematizö
	
	Acts 23:12
	And when it was day, certain of the Jews banded together, and **bound** themselves **under a curse**, saying that they would neither eat nor drink till they had killed Paul. [KJV]
	And when it was day, the Jews formed a conspiracy and **bound** themselves **under an oath**, saying that they would neither eat nor drink until they had killed Paul. [NASB]
	The next morning the Jews formed a conspiracy and **bound** themselves **with an oath** not to eat or drink until they had killed Paul. [NIV]
	And when it was day, some of the Jews banded together and **bound** themselves **under an oath**, saying that they would neither eat nor drink till they had killed Paul. [NKJV]
	The next morning a group of Jews got together and **bound** themselves **with an oath** to neither eat nor drink until they had killed Paul. [NLT]
	Γενομένης δὲ ἡμέρας, ποιήσαντες τινες τῶν Ἰουδαίων συστροφὴν, **ἀνεθεμάτισαν** ἑαυτούς, λέγοντες μήτε φαγεῖν μήτε πίειν ἕως οὗ ἀποκτείνωσι τὸν Παῦλον. [GNS]
	Γενομένης δὲ ἡμέρας ποιήσαντες συστροφὴν οἱ Ἰουδαῖοι **ἀνεθεμάτισαν** ἑαυτοὺς λέγοντες μήτε φαγεῖν μήτε πίειν ἕως οὗ ἀποκτείνωσιν τὸν Παῦλον. [GNT]
		To be bound with an oath; to be bound under a curse; to bind by a solemn vow.
		
		Practical Application
		The oath was what may be called a religious oath. It was an *anathema*; that is, they devoted themselves to God; they would not eat or drink until they had killed Paul. They actually thought they would be pleasing God by getting rid of Paul.

#2720
Obey
 	
Keep–KJV
Keep–NASB
Obey–NIV
Keep–NKJV
Obey–NLT
 	
POSB REFERENCE
(Jn.14:15)
Note 1, point 1
	τηρήσετε = tërësete
	Pronunciation: [tay-ray'-seh-teh]
	Parsing (part of speech): verb
	  Mood—indicative
	  Tense—future
	  Voice—active
	  Person—2nd person
	  Number—plural
	  Stem or root—from τηρέω
	Concordance References:
	⇒ Strong's #5083 tereo
	⇒ NIV #5498 tereo
	⇒ NASB #5083 tereo
	
	John 14:15
	If ye love me, **keep** my commandments. [KJV]
	"If you love Me, you will **keep** My commandments. [NASB]
	"If you love me, you will **obey** what I command. [NIV]
	"If you love Me, **keep** My commandments. [NKJV]
	"If you love me, **obey** my commandments. [NLT]
	Ἐὰν ἀγαπᾶτέ με, τὰς ἐντολὰς τὰς ἐμὰς **τηρήσατε**. [GNS]
	Ἐὰν ἀγαπᾶτέ με, τὰς ἐντολὰς τὰς ἐμὰς **τηρήσετε**· [GNT]
		To obey; to keep in focus with the eyes; to observe; to give uncompromised attention to; to guard; to fulfill a responsibility; to pay attention to.
		
		Practical Application
		In this Scripture, the meaning of this word is better understood in the context of confessed love for Christ.
		Obedience is not optional for believers. Jesus stated a simple fact that must be clearly understood: "If you love me, you will obey (*tërësete*) what I command." This is the correct translation. Jesus is not giving an *optional commandment*, "If you love me, [then, optional] obey what I command." He is saying that the man who truly loves Him *will* obey His commandments. To the believer, there is no option. He loves Jesus; therefore, he obeys His commandments. In this the believer is not claiming perfection, but he is claiming to love Jesus and to believe with all his heart that Jesus is the Son of God. Therefore, he diligently seeks Jesus, and he seeks to please Him in all that he does (cp. Hebrews 11:6).

#2721
Obey
	πράσσῃς = prassës
	Pronunciation: [pras'-sayce]
	Parsing (part of speech): verb
	  Mood—subjunctive
	  Tense—present
		Do, practice, keep, observe, obey, perform, play.
		
		Practical Application
		The religionist believes that a ritual is the way

ENGLISH WORD	GREEK WORD AND VERSE	THE WORD MEANS...
Keep–KJV Practice–NASB Observe–NIV Keep–NKJV **Obey–NLT** **POSB REFERENCE** (Romans 2:25-27; esp. v.25) Note 3	Voice—active Person—2nd person Number—singular Stem or root—from πράσσω Concordance References: ⇒ Strong's #4238 prassö ⇒ NIV #4556 prassö ⇒ NASB #4238 prassö **Romans 2:25** For circumcision verily profiteth, if thou **keep** the law: but if thou be a breaker of the law, thy circumcision is made uncircumcision. [KJV] For indeed circumcision is of value, if you **practice** the Law; but if you are a transgressor of the Law, your circumcision has become uncircumcision. [NASB] Circumcision has value if you **observe** the law, but if you break the law, you have become as though you had not been circumcised. [NIV] For circumcision is indeed profitable if you **keep** the law; but if you are a breaker of the law, your circumcision has become uncircumcision. [NKJV] The Jewish ceremony of circumcision is worth something only if you **obey** God's law. But if you don't obey God's law, you are no better off than an uncircumcised Gentile. [NLT] περιτομὴ μὲν γὰρ ὠφελεῖ, ἐὰν νόμον **πράσσῃς**· ἐὰν δὲ παραβάτης νόμου ᾖς, ἡ περιτομή σου ἀκροβυστία γέγονεν. [GNS] περιτομὴ μὲν γὰρ ὠφελεῖ ἐὰν νόμον **πράσσῃς**· ἐὰν δὲ παραβάτης νόμου ᾖς, ἡ περιτομή σου ἀκροβυστία γέγονεν. [GNT]	to secure God's praise or approval (for example, circumcision, baptism, and church membership). Just take the word circumcision and substitute whatever ritual a church says is essential for salvation and the meaning of the passage becomes clear. For example, take the ritual of church membership. "Church membership profits a man if he keeps the law: but if he breaks the law, his church membership is made or counted as unchurch membership." If a religionist does not obey (*prassës*) God's law and Word, then his ritual does not count. The man becomes... • unbaptized • unchurched • uncircumcised • unwhatever The point is obedience, not ritual. A person is acceptable to God because he lives for God and obeys Him, not because he has undergone some ritual.
#2722 Obey Obey–KJV Obey–NASB Obey–NIV Obey–NKJV Obey–NLT **POSB REFERENCE** (Eph.6:1-3; esp. v.1) Note 1 See also POSB REF: (Col.3:20) Note 3	ὑπακούετε = hupakouete Pronunciation: [hoop-ak-oo'-eh-teh] Parsing (part of speech): verb Mood—imperative Tense—present Voice—active Person—2nd person Number—plural Stem or root—from ὑπακούω Concordance References: ⇒ Strong's #5219 hupakouö ⇒ NIV #5634 hupakouö ⇒ NASB #5219 hupakouö **Ephes. 6:1** Children, **obey** your parents in the Lord: for this is right. [KJV] Children, **obey** your parents in the Lord, for this is right. [NASB] Children, **obey** your parents in the Lord, for this is right. [NIV] Children, **obey** your parents in the Lord, for this is right. [NKJV] Children, **obey** your parents because you belong to the Lord, for this is the right thing to do. [NLT] Τὰ τέκνα, **ὑπακούετε** τοῖς γονεῦσιν ὑμῶν ἐν Κυρίῳ· τοῦτο γάρ ἐστι δίκαιον. [GNS] Τὰ τέκνα, **ὑπακούετε** τοῖς γονεῦσιν ὑμῶν [ἐν κυρίῳ]· τοῦτο γάρ ἐστιν δίκαιον. [GNT]	To obey; to submit to; to comply with; to hearken; to heed; to adhere to; to respond to; to follow the directions or guidance of some instruction. **Practical Application** Children are to obey their parents. When a parent guides and directs a child, the child is to obey the parent. But what about the problems that are so repulsively evident in society: the problems of parental abuse—the problems of physical abuse, sexual abuse, and mental abuse? Is a child to obey a parent when the parent is so devilishly wrong? No! A thousand times no! This is not what Scripture is talking about. (See POSB note, Children—Ephes. 6:1-3 for discussion of child abuse.) Scripture is talking about the normal day-to-day instructions and guidance which parents give to children. Children are to obey their parents *in all instructions*. What happens when older children have different opinions? They feel like they should be able... • to have something • to do something • to go someplace • to come in late Differences always arise, and yet God says that the child is to obey *in all* things. Does this mean the parent is always right? No. It means that the child has a unique opportunity to learn discipline, control, and order.

ENGLISH WORD	GREEK WORD AND VERSE	THE WORD MEANS...

#2723
Obey, Did Not
 	
Believed not–KJV
Disobedient–NASB
Disobeyed–NIV
Did not obey–NKJV
Disobeyed–NLT
 	
**POSB
REFERENCE**
(Heb.3:13-19; esp.
v.18)
Note 3, point 7
	ἀπειθήσασιν = apeithēsasin
	Pronunciation: [ap-i-thay'-sah-sin]
	Parsing (part of speech): verb
	  Mood—participle
	  Tense—aorist
	  Voice—active
	  Case—dative
	  Gender—masculine
	  Number—plural
	  Stem or root—from ἀπειθέω
	Concordance References:
	⇒ Strong's #544 apeitheō
	⇒ NIV #578 apeitheō
	⇒ NASB #544 apeitheō
	
	Hebrews 3:18
	And to whom sware he that they should not enter into his rest, but to them that **believed not**? [KJV]
	And to whom did He swear that they should not enter His rest, but to those who were **disobedient**? [NASB]
	And to whom did God swear that they would never enter his rest if not to those who **disobeyed**? [NIV]
	And to whom did He swear that they would not enter His rest, but to those who **did not obey**? [NKJV]
	And to whom was God speaking when he vowed that they would never enter his place of rest? He was speaking to those who **disobeyed** him. [NLT]
	ισι δὲ ὤμοσε μὴ εἰσελεύσεσθαι εἰς τὴν κατάπαυσιν αὐτοῦ, εἰ μὴ τοῖς **ἀπειθήσασι**; [GNS]
	τίσιν δὲ ὤμοσεν μὴ εἰσελεύσεσθαι εἰς τὴν κατάπαυσιν αὐτοῦ εἰ μὴ τοῖς **ἀπειθήσασιν**; [GNT]
		To disobey; to fail to believe; to be disobedient; to refuse to be persuaded; to refuse to believe; to withhold belief.
		
		Practical Application
		It is a person who just refuses to be persuaded despite the evidence that Jesus Christ is truly the Savior of the world; the kind of person who chooses to continue living for the world and self despite the fact of coming judgment. The unbeliever will not be allowed to enter God's promised land of heaven nor God's eternal rest.

#2724
Obeyed
 	
Fear–KJV
Reverence–NASB
Holy fear–NIV
Godly fear–NKJV
Obeyed–NLT
 	
**POSB
REFERENCE**
(Heb.11:7)
Note 1, point 1
	εὐλαβηθείς = eulabētheis
	Pronunciation: [yoo-lab-ay'-theh-ees]
	Parsing (part of speech): verb
	  Mood—participle
	  Tense—aorist
	  Voice—passive deponent
	  Case—nominative
	  Gender—masculine
	  Number—singular
	  Stem or root—from εὐλαβέομαι
	Concordance References:
	⇒ Strong's #2125 eulabeomai
	⇒ NIV #2326 eulabeomai
	⇒ NASB #2125 eulabeomai
	
	Hebrews 11:7
	By faith Noah, being warned of God of things not seen as yet, moved with **fear**, prepared an ark to the saving of his house; by the which he condemned the world, and became heir of the righteousness which is by faith. [KJV]
	By faith Noah, being warned by God about things not yet seen, in **reverence** prepared an ark for the salvation of his household, by which he condemned the world, and became an heir of the righteousness which is according to faith. [NASB]
	By faith Noah, when warned about things not yet seen, in **holy fear** built an ark to save his family. By his faith he condemned the world and became heir of the righteousness that comes by faith. [NIV]
	By faith Noah, being divinely warned of things not yet seen, moved with **godly fear**, prepared an ark for the saving of his household, by which he condemned the world and became heir of the righteousness which is according to faith. [NKJV]
	It was by faith that Noah built an ark to save his family from the flood. He **obeyed** God, who warned him about something that had never happened before. By his faith he condemned the rest of the world and was made right in God's sight. [NLT]
	πίστει χρηματισθεὶς Νῶε περὶ τῶν μηδέπω
		Fear, holy fear; to reverence; to obey; to be moved with fear. The word "obeyed" (eulabētheis) means with godly fear (A.T. Robertson. *Word Pictures in the New Testament*, Vol. 5, p.421). It has the idea of...
		• reverence.
		• standing in awe of God and His warning.
		• taking heed lest one fall under God's judgment.
		• diligently taking God at His Word.
		• immediately acting upon what God says.
		
		Practical Application
		There was a time in world history when the earth had become so wicked that it was filled with corruption and violence. It was so corrupt that every imagination of man's heart was corrupt and evil. Man had reached the point of no return; he would never repent and return to God. God was left with no choice: the earth had to be destroyed. But there was one man on earth who was godly—Noah. Noah worshipped and honored God in his life. Therefore, God warned Noah of the coming judgment upon the earth.
		⇒ God told Noah to prepare an ark and the ark would save him, his family, and two of every animal.
		⇒ God also told Noah to warn the world of coming judgment.
		Noah believed God's warning of coming judgment, and he began to build the ark with a godly fear and reverence, knowing that what God said would come true. God's judgment would fall upon the earth; Noah believed it and knew it by faith.

ENGLISH WORD	GREEK WORD AND VERSE	THE WORD MEANS...
	βλεπομένων, **εὐλαβηθεὶς**, κατεσκεύασε κιβωτὸν εἰς σωτηρίαν τοῦ οἴκου αὐτοῦ· δι' ἧς κατέκρινε τὸν κόσμον, καὶ τῆς κατὰ πίστιν δικαιοσύνης ἐγένετο κληρονόμος. [GNS] Πίστει χρηματισθεὶς Νῶε περὶ τῶν μηδέπω βλεπομένων, **εὐλαβηθεὶς** κατεσκεύασεν κιβωτὸν εἰς σωτηρίαν τοῦ οἴκου αὐτοῦ δι' ἧς κατέκρινεν τὸν κόσμον, καὶ τῆς κατὰ πίστιν δικαιοσύνης ἐγένετο κληρονόμος. [GNT]	
#2725 **Obey–Obeys** Keepeth–KJV Keeps–NASB **Obeys–NIV** Keeps–NKJV **Obey–NLT** **POSB REFERENCE** (1 Jn.2:5) Note 3	τηρῇ = *tërë* Pronunciation: [tay-ray] Parsing (part of speech): verb Mood—subjunctive Tense—present Voice—active Person—3rd person Number—singular Stem or root—from τηρέω Concordance References: ⇒ Strong's #5083 tëreö ⇒ NIV #5498 tëreö ⇒ NASB #5083 tëreö **1 John 2:5** But whoso **keepeth** his word, in him verily is the love of God perfected: hereby know we that we are in him. [KJV] But whoever **keeps** His word, in him the love of God has truly been perfected. By this we know that we are in Him: [NASB] But if anyone **obeys** his word, God's love is truly made complete in him. This is how we know we are in him: [NIV] But whoever **keeps** His word, truly the love of God is perfected in him. By this we know that we are in Him. [NKJV] But those who **obey** God's word really do love him. That is the way to know whether or not we live in him. [NLT] ὃς δ' ἂν **τηρῇ** αὐτοῦ τὸν λόγον, ἀληθῶς ἐν τούτῳ ἡ ἀγάπη τοῦ Θεοῦ τετελείωται. ἐν τούτῳ γινώσκομεν ὅτι ἐν αὐτῷ ἐσμεν· [GNS] ὃς δ' ἂν **τηρῇ** αὐτοῦ τὸν λόγον, ἀληθῶς ἐν τούτῳ ἡ ἀγάπη τοῦ θεοῦ τετελείωται, ἐν τούτῳ γινώσκομεν ὅτι ἐν αὐτῷ ἐσμεν. [GNT]	To obey; to keep; to hold; to take to heart; to pay attention to. **Practical Application** The word "obeys" (*tërë*) is continuous action. It means to continue on and not to stop. It means day-by-day obedience. If we obey God's Word day-by-day, then we learn more and more about God; we learn to love Him more and more. His love becomes perfected, completed, and fulfilled in us.
#2726 **Objects Of Worship** Devotions–KJV **Objects of...worship–NASB** **Objects of worship–NIV** **Objects of...worship–NKJV** Altars–NLT **POSB REFERENCE** (Acts 17:23) Note 3, point 1	τὰ σεβάσματα = *ta sebasmata* Pronunciation: [tah seb'-as-mah-tah] Parsing *sebasmata* (part of speech): noun Case—accusative Gender—neuter Number—plural Stem or root—from σέβασμα, τος Concordance References: ⇒ Strong's #3588 ho + 4574 sebasma ⇒ NIV #3836 ho + 4934 sebasma ⇒ NASB #3588 ho + 4574 sebasma **Acts 17:23** For as I passed by, and beheld your **devotions**, I found an altar with this inscription, TO THE UNKNOWN GOD. Whom therefore ye ignorantly worship, him declare I unto you. [KJV] "For while I was passing through and examining the **objects of** your **worship**, I also found an altar with this inscription, 'TO AN UNKNOWN GOD.' What therefore you worship in ignorance, this I proclaim to you. [NASB] For as I walked around and looked carefully at your **objects of worship**, I even found an altar with this inscription: TO AN UNKNOWN GOD. Now what you worship as something unknown I am going to proclaim to you. [NIV]	Objects of worship; altars; places of devotion and worship. **Practical Application** It means the objects of worship such as idols, altars, images.

ENGLISH WORD	GREEK WORD AND VERSE	THE WORD MEANS...
	For as I was passing through and considering the **objects of** your **worship**, I even found an altar with this inscription: TO THE UNKNOWN GOD. Therefore, the One whom you worship without knowing, Him I proclaim to you: [NKJV] For as I was walking along I saw your many **altars**. And one of them had this inscription on it—'To an Unknown God.' You have been worshiping him without knowing who he is, and now I wish to tell you about him. [NLT] διερχόμενος γὰρ καὶ ἀναθεωρῶν **τὰ σεβάσματα** ὑμῶν, εὗρον καὶ βωμὸν ἐν ᾧ ἐπεγέγραπτο, Ἀγνώστῳ Θεῷ. ὃν οὖν ἀγνοοῦντες εὐσεβεῖτε, τοῦτον ἐγὼ καταγγέλλω ὑμῖν. [GNS] διερχόμενος γὰρ καὶ ἀναθεωρῶν **τὰ σεβάσματα** ὑμῶν, εὗρον καὶ βωμὸν ἐν ᾧ ἐπεγέγραπτο, Ἀγνώστῳ Θεῷ. ὃ οὖν ἀγνοοῦντες εὐσεβεῖτε, τοῦτο ἐγὼ καταγγέλλω ὑμῖν. [GNT]	
#2727 **Obligated–** **Obligation,** **Under** Debtor–KJV **Under obligation–** **NASB** **Obligated–NIV** Debtor–NKJV Great sense of obliga- tion–NLT **POSB** **REFERENCE** (Rom.1:14-15; esp. v.14) Note 5, point 1 **See also POSB REF:** (Rom.8:12-13; esp. v.12) Note 6, point 1	**ὀφειλέτης** = *opheiletēs* Pronunciation: [of-i-let'-ace] Parsing (part of speech): noun 　Case—nominative 　Gender—masculine 　Number—singular 　Stem or root—from ὀφειλέτης, ου Concordance References: ⇒ Strong's #3781 opheiletēs ⇒ NIV #4050 opheiletēs ⇒ NASB #3781 opheiletēs **Romans 1:14** I am **debtor** both to the Greeks, and to the Barbarians; both to the wise, and to the unwise. [KJV] I am **under obligation** both to Greeks and to barbarians, both to the wise and to the foolish. [NASB] I am **obligated** both to Greeks and non-Greeks, both to the wise and the foolish. [NIV] I am a **debtor** both to Greeks and to barbarians, both to wise and to unwise. [NKJV] For I have a **great sense of obligation** to people in our culture and to people in other cultures, to the educated and uneducated alike. [NLT] Ἕλλησί τε καὶ βαρβάροις, σοφοῖς τε καὶ ἀνοήτοις **ὀφειλέτης** εἰμί· [GNS] Ἕλλησίν τε καὶ βαρβάροις, σοφοῖς τε καὶ ἀνοήτοις **ὀφειλέτης** εἰμί, [GNT]	To be obligated; to be in debt; to owe; to be bound by duty; to have a great sense of obligation or debt. **Practical Application** The Greek is impossible to translate into English, for two ideas are being expressed by Paul. He was "under obligation"... ● because Christ had done so much for him (saved him). ● because Christ had called him to preach (given him a task to do). The obligation was deeply felt by Paul. The idea is that it was intense, unwavering, unrelentless, powerful. The sense of obligation just would not let Paul go. He was compelled to preach the gospel; therefore, he could do nothing else. He was obligated and duty-bound to preach it. He actually felt that he owed the gospel to the world; therefore, if he kept quiet, it would be worse than knowing the cure for the most terrible disease of history but refusing to share it.
#2728 **Obscene** **Stories** Filthiness–KJV Filthiness–NASB Obscenity–NIV Filthiness–NKJV **Obscene stories–NLT** **POSB** **REFERENCE** (Eph.5:4) Note 4, point 1	**αἰσχρότης** = *aischrotēs* Pronunciation: [ah-hee-skhrot'-ace] Parsing (part of speech): noun 　Case—nominative 　Gender—feminine 　Number—singular 　Stem or root—from αἰσχρότης, ητος Concordance References: ⇒ Strong's #151 aischrotēs ⇒ NIV #157 aischrotēs ⇒ NASB #151 aischrotēs **Ephes. 5:4** Neither **filthiness**, nor foolish talking, nor jesting, which are not convenient: but rather giving of thanks. [KJV] And there must be no **filthiness** and silly talk, or coarse jesting, which are not fitting, but rather giving of thanks. [NASB] Nor should there be **obscenity**, foolish talk or coarse joking, which are out of place, but rather thanksgiving. [NIV] Neither **filthiness**, nor foolish talking, nor coarse jesting, which are not fitting, but rather giving of thanks. [NKJV]	Obscenity, filthiness; to tell obscene stories; to display indecent behavior. **Practical Application** The believer is never, not once, to be engaged in "obscene stories" (*aischrotēs*): using the mouth in obscene, shameful, foul, polluted, base, immoral conduct and conversation. What an indictment of our day—a day of sodomy and perversion. And note: the word refers to both conduct and speech. How polluted and foul mouthed so many have become—so much so that society could easily be known as a second Sodom and Gomorrah.

ENGLISH WORD	GREEK WORD AND VERSE	THE WORD MEANS...
	the poor have come up as a memorial offering before God. [NIV] And when he **observed** him, he was afraid, and said, "What is it, lord?" So he said to him, "Your prayers and your alms have come up for a memorial before God. [NKJV] Cornelius **stared at** him in terror. "What is it, sir?" he asked the angel.And the angel replied, "Your prayers and gifts to the poor have not gone unnoticed by God! [NLT] ὁ δὲ **ἀτενίσας** αὐτῷ καὶ ἔμφοβος γενόμενος εἶπε, Τί ἐστι, Κύριε; εἶπε δὲ αὐτῷ, Αἱ προσευχαί σου καὶ αἱ τε ἐλεημοσύναι σου ἀνέβησαν εἰς μνημόσυνον ἐνώπιον τοῦ Θεοῦ. [GNS] ὁ δὲ **ἀτενίσας** αὐτῷ καὶ ἔμφοβος γενόμενος εἶπεν, Τί ἐστιν, κύριε; εἶπεν δὲ αὐτῷ, Αἱ προσευχαί σου καὶ αἱ ἐλεημοσύναι σου ἀνέβησαν εἰς μνημόσυνον ἔμπροσθεν τοῦ Θεοῦ. [GNT]	
#2733 **Observing** Beheld–KJV **Observing–NASB** Watched–NIV Saw–NKJV Watched–NLT **POSB REFERENCE** (Mk.12:41-42; esp. v.41) Note 1	ἐθεώρει = etheōrei Pronunciation: [eh-theh-o-reh'-ee] Parsing (part of speech): verb 　Mood—indicative 　Tense—imperfect 　Voice—active 　Person—3rd person 　Number—singular 　Stem or root—from θεωρέω Concordance References: ⇒　Strong's #2334 theōreō ⇒　NIV #2555 theōreō ⇒　NASB #2334 theōreō **Mark 12:41** And Jesus sat over against the treasury, and **beheld** how the people cast money into the treasury: and many that were rich cast in much. [KJV] And He sat down opposite the treasury, and began **observing** how the multitude were putting money into the treasury; and many rich people were putting in large sums. [NASB] Jesus sat down opposite the place where the offerings were put and **watched** the crowd putting their money into the temple treasury. Many rich people threw in large amounts. [NIV] Now Jesus sat opposite the treasury and **saw** how the people put money into the treasury. And many who were rich put in much. [NKJV] Jesus went over to the collection box in the Temple and sat and **watched** as the crowds dropped in their money. Many rich people put in large amounts. [NLT] Καὶ καθίσας ὁ Ἰησοῦς κατέναντι τοῦ γαζοφυλακίου, **ἐθεώρει** πῶς ὁ ὄχλος βάλλει χαλκὸν εἰς τὸ γαζοφυλάκιον· καὶ πολλοὶ πλούσιοι ἔβαλλον πολλά. [GNS] Καὶ καθίσας κατέναντι τοῦ γαζοφυλακίου **ἐθεώρει** πῶς ὁ ὄχλος βάλλει χαλκὸν εἰς τὸ γαζοφυλάκιον. καὶ πολλοὶ πλούσιοι ἔβαλλον πολλά· [GNT]	To observe, watch, behold, look at, notice; to see; to carefully observe; to look on; to gaze upon; to perceive. **Practical Application** Christ was deliberately observing, discerning the motives of the people as they made their offerings. Christ knows the motives—the sacrifices made or the "tips" offered—behind every gift given to Him. There is a great difference between giving what one can spare and giving sacrificially, actually giving up something in order to give. Sacrificial giving costs something. Sacrificial giving is giving when it hurts, when a person has nothing left, nothing to spare. The difference needs to be stressed, for God expects sacrificial giving. If the world is ever to be reached for Christ and its desperate needs met then every believer must give sacrificially.
#2734 **Obstacle** Occasion to fall–KJV **Obstacle–NASB** **Obstacle–NIV** Cause to fall–NKJV **Obstacle–NLT** **POSB REFERENCE** (Rom.14:13-15; esp. v.13) Note 6	σκάνδαλον = skandalon Pronunciation: [skan'-dal-on] Parsing (part of speech): noun 　Case—accusative 　Gender—neuter 　Number—singular 　Stem or root—from σκάνδαλον, ου Concordance References: ⇒　Strong's #4625 skandalon ⇒　NIV #4998 skandalon ⇒　NASB #4625 skandalon **Romans 14:13** Let us not therefore judge one another any more: but judge this rather, that no man put a stumblingblock or an	To trap; to snare; to do something that causes a person to stumble and fall; that which causes sin or gives occasion for sin; that which causes stumbling or trouble; obstacle; occasion to fall; stumbling block. **Practical Application** It has reference in particular to leading or causing someone to sin. The exhortation is strong: believers are not to be criticizing and judging each other; they are to be judging themselves. Every single believer is to be constantly looking at his own life making sure... • that he is not putting a stumbling block in

ENGLISH WORD	GREEK WORD AND VERSE	THE WORD MEANS...
	occasion to fall in his brother's way. [KJV] Therefore let us not judge one another anymore, but rather determine this— not to put an **obstacle** or a stumbling block in a brother's way. [NASB] Therefore let us stop passing judgment on one another. Instead, make up your mind not to put any stumbling block or **obstacle** in your brother's way. [NIV] Therefore let us not judge one another anymore, but rather resolve this, not to put a stumbling block or a **cause to fall** in *our* brother's way. [NKJV] So don't condemn each other anymore. Decide instead to live in such a way that you will not put an **obstacle** in another Christian's path. [NLT] Μηκέτι οὖν ἀλλήλους κρίνωμεν· ἀλλὰ τοῦτο κρίνατε μᾶλλον, τὸ μὴ τιθέναι πρόσκομμα τῷ ἀδελφῷ η **σκάνδαλον**. [GNS] Μηκέτι οὖν ἀλλήλους κρίνωμεν· ἀλλὰ τοῦτο κρίνατε μᾶλλον, τὸ μὴ τιθέναι πρόσκομμα τῷ ἀδελφῷ η **σκάνδαλον**. [GNT]	his brother's path to God, not even a single obstacle or hindrance of any kind. • that he is not doing a single thing that will cause his brother to stumble or fall into sin. If a believer is constantly looking at his own life and guarding against becoming a stumbling block, he does not have time to judge and talk about his brother.

#2735
Obstacles
 	
Offences–KJV
Hindrances–NASB
Obstacles–NIV
Offenses–NKJV
Upset people's
    faith–NLT
 	
POSB
REFERENCE
(Rom.16:17-18; esp.
    v.17)
    Note 1, point 1
	σκάνδαλα = *skandala*
	Pronunciation: [skan'-dal-ah]
	Parsing (part of speech): noun
	    Case—accusative
	    Gender—neuter
	    Number—plural
	    Stem or root—from **σκάνδαλον**, ου
	Concordance References:
	⇒ Strong's #4625 skandalon
	⇒ NIV #4998 skandalon
	⇒ NASB #4625 skandalon
	
	Romans 16:17
	Now I beseech you, brethren, mark them which cause divisions and **offences** contrary to the doctrine which ye have learned; and avoid them. [KJV]
	
	Now I urge you, brethren, keep your eye on those who cause dissensions and **hindrances** contrary to the teaching which you learned, and turn away from them. [NASB]
	
	I urge you, brothers, to watch out for those who cause divisions and put **obstacles** in your way that are contrary to the teaching you have learned. Keep away from them. [NIV]
	
	Now I urge you, brethren, note those who cause divisions and **offenses**, contrary to the doctrine which you learned, and avoid them. [NKJV]
	
	And now I make one more appeal, my dear brothers and sisters. Watch out for people who cause divisions and **upset people's faith** by teaching things that are contrary to what you have been taught. Stay away from them. [NLT]
	
	Παρακαλῶ δὲ ὑμᾶς, ἀδελφοί, σκοπεῖν τοὺς τὰς διχοστασίας καὶ τὰ **σκάνδαλα**, παρὰ τὴν διδαχὴν ἣν ὑμεῖς ἐμάθετε, ποιοῦντας· καὶ ἐκκλίνατε ἀπ' αὐτῶν. [GNS]
	
	Παρακαλῶ δὲ ὑμᾶς, ἀδελφοί, σκοπεῖν τοὺς τὰς διχοστασίας καὶ τὰ **σκάνδαλα** παρὰ τὴν διδαχὴν ἣν ὑμεῖς ἐμάθετε ποιοῦντας, καὶ ἐκκλίνετε ἀπ' αὐτῶν· [GNT]
		That which causes sin or gives occasion for sin; that which causes stumbling or trouble, obstacle. The word "obstacles" (*skandala*) means laying a stumbling block in someone's way or causing someone to fall.
		
		Practical Application
		The most effective way for Satan to get a foothold into a strong church is to quietly and insidiously move a divisive person into some teaching or leadership position where he can influence immature believers. Paul knew this, so he left the warning until the end of his letter. It is a warning that must be heeded by a strong church if it is to keep its witness for the Lord.

#2736
Obstinate
 	
Hardened–KJV
Hardened–NASB
Obstinate–NIV
Hardened–NKJV
Rejected–NLT
	ἐσκληρύνοντο = *esklërunonto*
	Pronunciation: [es-sklay-roo'-non-tow]
	Parsing (part of speech): verb
	    Mood—indicative
	    Tense—imperfect
	    Voice—passive
	    Person—3rd person
	    Number—plural
	    Stem or root—from **σκληρύνω**
	Concordance References:
	⇒ Strong's #4645 sklërunö
	⇒ NIV #5020 sklërunö
	⇒ NASB #4645 sklërunö
		To be obstinate, to be hardened, to be rejected; to be stubborn. It means to be as hard as a stone; to be unfeeling and difficult, standing in opposition.
		
		Practical Application
		Many were obstinate and did not believe, being disobedient to the call of God to salvation.

ENGLISH WORD	GREEK WORD AND VERSE	THE WORD MEANS...
POSB REFERENCE (Acts 19:2-9; esp. v.9) Note 2, point 2d	**Acts 19:9** But when divers were **hardened**, and believed not, but spake evil of that way before the multitude, he departed from them, and separated the disciples, disputing daily in the school of one Tyrannus. [KJV] But when some were becoming **hardened** and disobedient, speaking evil of the Way before the multitude, he withdrew from them and took away the disciples, reasoning daily in the school of Tyrannus. [NASB] But some of them became **obstinate**; they refused to believe and publicly maligned the Way. So Paul left them. He took the disciples with him and had discussions daily in the lecture hall of Tyrannus. [NIV] But when some were **hardened** and did not believe, but spoke evil of the Way before the multitude, he departed from them and withdrew the disciples, reasoning daily in the school of Tyrannus. [NKJV] But some **rejected** his message and publicly spoke against the Way, so Paul left the synagogue and took the believers with him. Then he began preaching daily at the lecture hall of Tyrannus. [NLT] ὡς δέ τινες **ἐσκληρύνοντο** καὶ ἠπείθουν, κακολογοῦντες τὴν ὁδὸν ἐνώπιον τοῦ πλήθους, ἀποστὰς ἀπ' αὐτῶν ἀφώρισε τοὺς μαθητάς, καθ' ἡμέραν διαλεγόμενος ἐν τῇ σχολῇ τυράννου τινός. [GNS] ὡς δέ τινες **ἐσκληρύνοντο** καὶ ἠπείθουν κακολογοῦντες τὴν ὁδὸν ἐνώπιον τοῦ πλήθους, ἀποστὰς ἀπ' αὐτῶν ἀφώρισεν τοὺς μαθητὰς καθ' ἡμέραν διαλεγόμενος ἐν τῇ σχολῇ Τυράννου. [GNT]	
#2737 **Obtained** **Obtained–KJV** Received–NASB Received–NIV **Obtained–NKJV** Share–NLT **POSB REFERENCE** (2 Pt.1:1) Note 2, point 2	λαχοῦσιν = *lachousin* Pronunciation: [la-khoo'-sin] Parsing (part of speech): verb Mood—participle Tense—aorist Voice—active Case—dative Gender—masculine Person—2nd person Number—plural Stem or root—from λαγχάνω Concordance References: ⇒ Strong's #2975 lagchanö ⇒ NIV #3275 lagchanö ⇒ NASB #2975 lagchanö **2 Peter 1:1** Simon Peter, a servant and an apostle of Jesus Christ, to them that have **obtained** like precious faith with us through the righteousness of God and our Saviour Jesus Christ: [KJV] Simon Peter, a bond-servant and apostle of Jesus Christ, to those who have **received** a faith of the same kind as ours, by the righteousness of our God and Savior, Jesus Christ: [NASB] Simon Peter, a servant and apostle of Jesus Christ, To those who through the righteousness of our God and Savior Jesus Christ have **received** a faith as precious as ours: [NIV] Simon Peter, a bondservant and apostle of Jesus Christ, To those who have **obtained** like precious faith with us by the righteousness of our God and Savior Jesus Christ: [NKJV] This letter is from Simon Peter, a slave and apostle of Jesus Christ. I am writing to all of you who **share** the same precious faith we have, faith given to us by Jesus Christ, our God and Savior, who makes us right with God. [NLT] Σίμων Πέτρος, δοῦλος καὶ ἀπόστολος Ἰησοῦ Χριστοῦ, τοῖς ἰσότιμον ἡμῖν **λαχοῦσι** πίστιν ἐν δικαιοσύνῃ τοῦ Θεοῦ ἡμῶν καὶ σωτῆρος ἡμῶν Ἰησοῦ Χριστοῦ· [GNS] Συμεὼν Πέτρος δοῦλος καὶ ἀπόστολος Ἰησοῦ Χριστοῦ τοῖς ἰσότιμον ἡμῖν **λαχοῦσιν** πίστιν ἐν δικαιοσύνῃ τοῦ θεοῦ ἡμῶν καὶ σωτῆρος Ἰησοῦ Χριστοῦ, [GNT]	Received, obtained, shared. It means to secure by lot; to receive by allotment; to be given a share or a portion. **Practical Application** The faith of Jesus Christ is obtained, not earned. No person deserves the precious faith of Jesus Christ. No person can work and earn it. It is a gift of God, a free gift that is given to every person who believes in Jesus Christ.

ENGLISH WORD	GREEK WORD AND VERSE	THE WORD MEANS...

#2738
Obtained Our Introduction
 	
Access–KJV
Obtained our intro-duction–NASB
Access–NIV
Access–NKJV
Brought us into this place–NLT
 	
POSB REFERENCE
(Romans 5:2)
Note 3, point 2
	προσαγωγὴν = prosagōgēn
	Pronunciation: [pros-ag-ogue-ayn']
	Parsing (part of speech): noun
	    Case—accusative
	    Gender—feminine
	    Number—singular
	    Stem or root—from προσαγωγή, ῆς
	Concordance References:
	⇒ Strong's #4318 prosagōgē
	⇒ NIV #4643 prosagōgē
	⇒ NASB #4318 prosagōgē
	
	Romans 5:2
	By whom also we have **access** by faith into this grace wherein we stand, and rejoice in hope of the glory of God. [KJV]
	Through whom also we have **obtained our intro-duction** by faith into this grace in which we stand; and we exult in hope of the glory of God. [NASB]
	Through whom we have gained **access** by faith into this grace in which we now stand. And we rejoice in the hope of the glory of God. [NIV]
	Through whom also we have **access** by faith into this grace in which we stand, and rejoice in hope of the glory of God. [NKJV]
	Because of our faith, Christ has **brought us into this place** of highest privilege where we now stand, and we confidently and joyfully look forward to sharing God's glory. [NLT]
	δι' οὗ καὶ τὴν **προσαγωγὴν** ἐσχήκαμεν τῇ πίστει εἰς τὴν χάριν ταύτην ἐν ᾗ ἐστήκαμεν, καὶ καυχώμεθα ἐπ' ἐλπίδι τῆς δόξης τοῦ Θεοῦ" [GNS]
	δι' οὗ καὶ τὴν **προσαγωγὴν** ἐσχήκαμεν [τῇ πίστει] εἰς τὴν χάριν ταύτην ἐν ᾗ ἐστήκαμεν καὶ καυχώμεθα ἐπ' ἐλπίδι τῆς δόξης τοῦ θεοῦ. [GNT]
		Access, to bring to, to move to, to introduce, to present. It is the freedom or right to enter.
		
		Practical Application
		Note it is through Christ that we have obtained our introduction into this grace. The thought is that of being in a royal court and being presented and introduced to the King of kings. Jesus Christ is the One who throws open the door into God's presence. He is the One who presents us to God, the Sovereign Majesty of the universe.

#2739
Occasion To Fall
 	
Occasion to fall–KJV
Obstacle–NASB
Obstacle–NIV
Cause to fall–NKJV
Obstacle–NLT
 	
POSB REFERENCE
(Rom.14:13-15; esp. v.13)
Note 6
	σκάνδαλον = skandalon
	Pronunciation: [skan'-dal-on]
	Parsing (part of speech): noun
	    Case—accusative
	    Gender—neuter
	    Number—singular
	    Stem or root—from σκάνδαλον, ου
	Concordance References:
	⇒ Strong's #4625 skandalon
	⇒ NIV #4998 skandalon
	⇒ NASB #4625 skandalon
	
	Romans 14:13
	Let us not therefore judge one another any more: but judge this rather, that no man put a stumblingblock or an **occasion to fall** in his brother's way. [KJV]
	Therefore let us not judge one another anymore, but rather determine this— not to put an **obstacle** or a stumbling block in a brother's way. [NASB]
	Therefore let us stop passing judgment on one anoth-er. Instead, make up your mind not to put any stumbling block or **obstacle** in your brother's way. [NIV]
	Therefore let us not judge one another anymore, but rather resolve this, not to put a stumbling block or a **cause to fall** in *our* brother's way. [NKJV]
	So don't condemn each other anymore. Decide instead to live in such a way that you will not put an **obstacle** in another Christian's path. [NLT]
	Μηκέτι οὖν ἀλλήλους κρίνωμεν· ἀλλὰ τοῦτο κρίνατε μᾶλλον, τὸ μὴ τιθέναι πρόσκομμα τῷ ἀδελφῷ η **σκάνδαλον**. [GNS]
	Μηκέτι οὖν ἀλλήλους κρίνωμεν· ἀλλὰ τοῦτο κρίνατε μᾶλλον, τὸ μὴ τιθέναι πρόσκομμα τῷ ἀδελφῷ η **σκάνδαλον**. [GNT]
		That which causes sin or gives occasion for sin; that which causes stumbling or trouble; obstacle. The words "occasion to fall" (*skan-dalon*) mean to trap to snare; to do something that causes a person to stumble and fall.
		
		Practical Application
		It has reference in particular to leading or causing someone to sin. The exhortation is strong: believers are not to be criticizing and judging each other; they are to be judging them-selves. Every single believer is to be constantly looking at his own life making sure...
		• that he is not putting a stumbling block in his brother's path to God, not even a single obstacle or hindrance of any kind.
		• that he is not doing a single thing that will cause his brother to stumble or fall into sin.
		• If a believer is constantly looking at his own life and guarding against becoming a stumbling block, he does not have time to judge and talk about his brother.

ENGLISH WORD	GREEK WORD AND VERSE	THE WORD MEANS...

#2740
Occupy
 	
Occupy–KJV
Do business–NASB
Put...to work–NIV
Do business–NKJV
Invest–NLT
 	
POSB
REFERENCE
(Lk.19:13)
Note 3, point 2
Deeper Study #2
	Πραγματεύσασθε = *Pragmateusasthe*
	Pronunciation: [prag-mat-yoo'-sahs-theh]
	Parsing (part of speech): verb
	  Mood—imperative
	  Tense—aorist
	  Voice—middle deponent
	  Person—2nd person
	  Number—plural
	  Stem or root—from πραγματεύομαι
	Concordance References:
	  ⇒ Strong's #4231 pragmateuomai
	  ⇒ NIV #4549 pragmateuomai
	  ⇒ NASB #4231 pragmateuomai
	
	Luke 19:13
	And he called his ten servants, and delivered them ten pounds, and said unto them, **Occupy** till I come. [KJV]
	"And he called ten of his slaves, and gave them ten minas, and said to them, '**Do business** with this until I come back.' [NASB]
	So he called ten of his servants and gave them ten minas. '**Put** this money **to work**,' he said, 'until I come back.' [NIV]
	So he called ten of his servants, delivered to them ten minas, and said to them, '**Do business** till I come.' [NKJV]
	Before he left, he called together ten servants and gave them ten pounds of silver to **invest** for him while he was gone. [NLT]
	καλέσας δὲ δέκα δούλους ἑαυτοῦ, ἔδωκεν αὐτοῖς δέκα μνᾶς, καὶ εἶπε πρὸς αὐτούς, **Πραγματεύσασθε** ἕως ἔρχομαι. [GNS]
	καλέσας δὲ δέκα δούλους ἑαυτοῦ ἔδωκεν αὐτοῖς δέκα μνᾶς καὶ εἶπεν πρὸς αὐτούς, **Πραγματεύσασθε** ἐν ᾧ ἔρχομαι. [GNT]
		To invest; to do business; to put to work; to trade; to occupy.
		
		Practical Application
		The word "occupy" is a word of diligent action. It is from the root word meaning to walk, to set in motion; and to continue in motion. The servant is to labor diligently, never letting up but using all the Lord has given him to look after. This is the only time the word is used in the New Testament (cp. Isaiah 35:3; Hebrews 12:28; Hebrews 12:12).

#2741
Of Course Not
 	
God forbid–KJV
May it never be–
  NASB
Not at all–NIV
Certainly not–NKJV
Of course not–NLT
 	
POSB
REFERENCE
(Romans 3:5-8; esp.
v.4)
Note 3, point 1
 	
See also POSB REF:
(Romans 11:1)
Note 1
	μὴ γένοιτο = *më genoito*
	Pronunciation: [may ghin'-oy-tow]
	Parsing *genoito* (part of speech): verb
	  Mood—optative
	  Tense—aorist
	  Voice—middle deponent
	  Person—3rd person
	  Number—singular
	  Stem or root—from γίνομαι
	Concordance References:
	  ⇒ Strong's #1096 + 3361 ginomai më
	  ⇒ NIV #1181 + 3590 ginomai më [Not at all]
	  ⇒ NASB #1096+ 3361 ginomai më
	
	Romans 3:4
	God forbid: yea, let God be true, but every man a liar; as it is written, That thou mightest be justified in thy sayings, and mightest overcome when thou art judged. [KJV]
	May it never be! Rather, let God be found true, though every man be found a liar, as it is written, "THAT THOU MIGHTEST BE JUSTIFIED IN THY WORDS, AND MIGHTEST PREVAIL WHEN THOU ART JUDGED." [NASB]
	Not at all! Let God be true, and every man a liar. As it is written: "So that you may be proved right when you speak and prevail when you judge." [NIV]
	Certainly not! Indeed, let God be true but every man a liar. As it is written: *That You may be justified in Your words, And may overcome when You are judged.* [NKJV]
	Of course not! Though everyone else in the world is a liar, God is true. As the Scriptures say, "He will be proved right in what he says, and he will win his case in court." [NLT]
	μὴ γένοιτο· γινέσθω δὲ ὁ Θεὸς ἀληθής, πᾶς δὲ ἄνθρωπος ψεύστης, καθὼς γέγραπται, Ὅπως ἂν δικαιωθῇς ἐν τοῖς λόγοις σου, καὶ νικήσεις ἐν τῷ κρίνεσθαί σε. [GNS]
		God forbid; not at all; may it never be; certainly not; of course not.
		
		Practical Application
		The question is, "If you say some Jews do not believe and are condemned, doesn't that void God's promises and make God a liar?" Or to say it another way, "What if some disbelieve and reject God's Word, will their unbelief cause God to void His Word and promises? God promised the Jews a special place and special privileges through Abraham and his seed (see POSB *Deeper Study #1*—John 4:22). If some Jews do not believe God's promises and God condemns them, isn't He breaking His promise to Abraham and his seed? Isn't He voiding His Word and Covenant and making Himself a liar? God's Word could not be based on heart religion and on moral character alone. There has to be something else, something outward—a rite (circumcision, baptism, church membership)—that shows we are religious (Jews). If we go through the rite or ritual, then God is bound to accept us. He has promised to so accept us. He is not going to break His Word."
		The application of this question concerns every religionist. The thinking religionist poses the same objection and question: "If you say some religionists do not believe and are condemned, doesn't that void God's Word and make God a liar? God's Word promises the religious person special privileges and the hope of eternal life. His Word tells us to believe Christ and to possess His Word, to be baptized and join the

ENGLISH WORD	GREEK WORD AND VERSE	THE WORD MEANS...
	μὴ γένοιτο· γινέσθω δὲ ὁ θεὸς ἀληθής, πᾶς δὲ ἄνθρωπος ψεύστης, καθὼς γέγραπται, Ὅπως ἂν δικαιωθῇς ἐν τοῖς λόγοις σου καὶ νικήσεις ἐν τῷ κρίνεσθαί σε. [GNT]	fellowship of the church. If we do that and God still condemns us, is He not voiding His Word and becoming a liar?"
		⇒ God forbid.
		⇒ God will be faithful. His Word and promise of salvation will stand even if *every* man lies about believing and lies about giving his heart to serve Jesus.
		⇒ God will prove His Word: He will be justified and proven faithful in what He has said. He will still save *any person* who obediently gives his heart to Jesus.
		⇒ In fact, God will overcome; He will prove His Word another way. He will judge all who make a false profession and who judge Him and His Word, who accuse Him of being unfaithful and voiding His Word. David himself said that God would judge the unfaithful or disobedient man (Psalm 51:4). David had sinned greatly, not keeping the commandments of God, so God judged David and charged him with sin. David did the right thing: he confessed his sin and repented and began to live righteously. But David did something else: he declared that God's charge and judgment against him were *just*, that God was perfectly justified. And God was, for God is always just, and He is always justified in what He says and does.

#2742
 	
Of God
 	
Of God–KJV
Of God–NASB
Of God–NIV
Of God–NKJV
Of God–NLT
 	
POSB REFERENCE
(Jn.1:29)
Note 1, point 3
	τοῦ θεοῦ = *tou theou*
	Pronunciation: [too they-oo]
	Parsing *tou* (part of speech): determiner
	    Type—definite article
	    Case—genitive
	    Gender—masculine
	    Number—singular
	    Stem or root—from ὁ, ἡ, τό pl. οἱ, αἱ, τά
	Parsing *theou* (part of speech): noun
	    Case—genitive
	    Gender—masculine
	    Number—singular
	    Stem or root—from θεός, οῦ
	Concordance References:
	  ⇒ Strong's #3588 ho + 2316 theos
	  ⇒ NIV #3836 ho [of] + 2536 theos [God]
	  ⇒ NASB #3588 ho + 2316 theos
	
	John 1:29
	The next day John seeth Jesus coming unto him, and saith, Behold the Lamb **of God**, which taketh away the sin of the world. [KJV]
	The next day he saw Jesus coming to him, and said, "Behold, the Lamb **of God** who takes away the sin of the world! [NASB]
	The next day John saw Jesus coming toward him and said, "Look, the Lamb **of God**, who takes away the sin of the world! [NIV]
	The next day John saw Jesus coming toward him, and said, "Behold! The Lamb **of God** who takes away the sin of the world! [NKJV]
	The next day John saw Jesus coming toward him and said, "Look! There is the Lamb **of God** who takes away the sin of the world! [NLT]
	Τῇ ἐπαύριον βλέπει ὁ Ἰωάννης τὸν Ἰησοῦν ἐρχόμενον πρὸς αὐτόν, καὶ λέγει, Ἴδε ὁ ἀμνὸς **τοῦ θεοῦ**, ὁ αἴρων τὴν ἁμαρτίαν τοῦ κόσμου. [GNS
	Τῇ ἐπαύριον βλέπει τὸν Ἰησοῦν ἐρχόμενον πρὸς αὐτόν καὶ λέγει, Ἴδε ὁ ἀμνὸς τοῦ θεοῦ ὁ αἴρων τὴν ἁμαρτίαν τοῦ κόσμου. [GNT]
		Of, from, about, regarding, concerning, out from God.
		
		Practical Application
		The "Lamb of God" is not of men, but of God. The idea is that the Lamb belonged to God; that is, God gave, supplied, and provided the Lamb for sacrifice. (Cp. Genesis 22:8 where God provided the lamb for Abraham as a substitute for Isaac.) This glorious truth speaks volumes on...
		• the unbelievable love of God for man (John 3:16; Romans 5:1).
		• the great sacrifice and humiliation Christ underwent for man (Phil. 2:6-8; 1 Peter 2:24).
		• the forgiveness of sins and salvation which came from God's grace and not from man's resources and works (Ephes. 2:8-9; Titus 2:4-7).
		• the deity of Christ, His being *of God* (see POSB Master Subject Index, Jesus Christ, Deity).

ENGLISH WORD	GREEK WORD AND VERSE	THE WORD MEANS...
#2743 **Of Him** **Of him–KJV** By His doing–NASB Because of him–NIV **Of Him–NKJV** God alone made it possible–NLT **POSB** **REFERENCE** (1 Cor.1:30-31; esp. v.30) Note 4	ἐξ αὐτοῦ = ex autou Pronunciation: [ex ow-too'] Parsing autou (part of speech): noun Type—pronoun Case—genitive Gender—masculine Person—3rd person Number—singular Stem or root—from αὐτός, ή, ό Concordance References: ⇒ Strong's #1537 ek + 846 autos ⇒ NIV #1666 ek [because of] + 899 autos [him] ⇒ NASB #1537 ek + 846 autos **1 Cor. 1:30** But **of him** are ye in Christ Jesus, who of God is made unto us wisdom, and righteousness, and sanctification, and redemption: [KJV] But **by His doing** you are in Christ Jesus, who became to us wisdom from God, and righteousness and sanctification, and redemption, [NASB] It is **because of him** that you are in Christ Jesus, who has become for us wisdom from God—that is, our righteousness, holiness and redemption. [NIV] But **of Him** you are in Christ Jesus, who became for us wisdom from God—and righteousness and sanctification and redemption—[NKJV] **God alone made it possible** for you to be in Christ Jesus. For our benefit God made Christ to be wisdom itself. He is the one who made us acceptable to God. He made us pure and holy, and he gave himself to purchase our freedom. [NLT] ἐξ αὐτοῦ δὲ ὑμεῖς ἐστε ἐν Χριστῷ Ἰησοῦ, ὃς ἐγενήθη ἡμῖν σοφία ἀπὸ Θεοῦ, δικαιοσύνη τε καὶ ἁγιασμὸς, καὶ ἀπολύτρωσις, [GNS] ἐξ αὐτοῦ δὲ ὑμεῖς ἐστε ἐν Χριστῷ Ἰησοῦ, ὃς ἐγενήθη σοφία ἡμῖν ἀπὸ θεοῦ, δικαιοσύνη τε καὶ ἁγιασμὸς καὶ ἀπολύτρωσις, [GNT]	Because of (God); out of God; out of His nature (of love and salvation); by God's doing. **Practical Application** God chooses the believer to be in Christ (see POSB *Deeper Study* #1, Position in Christ–Romans 8:1 for discussion). The stress is that it is God who saves a person; the person does not save himself, no matter how capable he is nor how much good he may do. How is God able to save people? By Christ. God presented Christ to the world as the wisdom and righteousness of God.
#2744 **Of No Effect–** **Of None Effect** **Of none effect–KJV** Invalidating–NASB Nullify–NIV **Of no effect–NKJV** Break–NLT **POSB** **REFERENCE** (Mk.7:13) *Deeper Study* #2	ἀκυροῦντες = akurountes Pronunciation: [ak-oo-roon'-tehs] Parsing (part of speech): verb Mood—participle Tense—present Voice—active Case—nominative Gender—masculine Person—2nd person Number—plural Stem or root—from ἀκυρόω Concordance References: ⇒ Strong's #208 akuroö ⇒ NIV #218 akuroö ⇒ NASB #208 akuroö **Mark 7:13** Making the word of God **of none effect** through your tradition, which ye have delivered: and many such like things do ye. [KJV] Thus **invalidating** the word of God by your tradition which you have handed down; and you do many things such as that." [NASB] Thus you **nullify** the word of God by your tradition that you have handed down. And you do many things like that." [NIV] Making the word of God **of no effect** through your tradition which you have handed down. And many such things you do." [NKJV] As such, you **break** the law of God in order to protect your own tradition. And this is only one example. There are many, many others." [NLT] ἀκυροῦντες τὸν λόγον τοῦ Θεοῦ τῇ παραδόσει ὑμῶν ᾗ παρεδώκατε· καὶ παρόμοια τοιαῦτα πολλὰ ποιεῖτε. [GNS] ἀκυροῦντες τὸν λόγον τοῦ θεοῦ τῇ παραδόσει ὑμῶν ᾗ παρεδώκατε· καὶ παρόμοια τοιαῦτα πολλὰ ποιεῖτε. [GNT]	To nullify; to be of no effect; to make void, ineffective; to annul; to cancel; to disregard; to deprive of authority and power; to invalidate. **Practical Application** In this Scripture, Christ is rebuking anyone who places human traditions on an equal or higher authority than the Word of God. Jesus charged the religionists with setting aside God's Word for tradition. Religious traditions may be described as institutional or personal. 1. Institutional traditions are such things as rituals, rules, regulations, schedules, forms, services, procedures, organizations—anything that gives order and security to the persons involved. 2. Personal traditions are such things as church attendance, prayers, habits, ceremonies, objects which a person uses (somewhat superstitiously) to keep himself religiously secure. Jesus was attacking the fact that so many religionists put their traditions first while neglecting and ignoring God's Word. (See POSB notes—Matthew 12:1-8; POSB note—Matthew 12:10 and POSB *Deeper Study* #1—Matthew 12:10).

ENGLISH WORD	GREEK WORD AND VERSE	THE WORD MEANS...

#2745
Of Sin
 	
Under sin–KJV
Under sin–NASB
Of sin–NIV
Under sin–NKJV
Of sin–NLT
 	
**POSB
REFERENCE**
(Gal.3:22)
Note 5
	ὑπὸ ἁμαρτίαν = *hupo hamartian*
	Pronunciation: [hoop-o' ham-ar-tee'-ahn]
	Parsing *hupo* (part of speech): preposition
	    Case—accusative
	    Stem or root—from ὑπό
	Parsing *hamartian* (part of speech): noun
	    Case—accusative
	    Gender—feminine
	    Number—singular
	    Stem or root—from ἁμαρτία, ας
	Concordance References:
	  ⇒ Strong's #5259 hupo + 266 hamartia
	  ⇒ NIV #5679 hupo [of] + 281 hamartia [sin]
	  ⇒ NASB #5259 hupo + 266 hamartia
	
	Galatians 3:22
	But the scripture hath concluded all **under sin**, that the promise by faith of Jesus Christ might be given to them that believe. [KJV]
	But the Scripture has shut up all men **under sin**, that the promise by faith in Jesus Christ might be given to those who believe. [NASB]
	But the Scripture declares that the whole world is a prisoner **of sin**, so that what was promised, being given through faith in Jesus Christ, might be given to those who believe. [NIV]
	But the Scripture has confined all **under sin**, that the promise by faith in Jesus Christ might be given to those who believe. [NKJV]
	But the Scriptures have declared that we are all prisoners **of sin**, so the only way to receive God's promise is to believe in Jesus Christ. [NLT]
	ἀλλὰ συνέκλεισεν ἡ γραφὴ τὰ πάντα ὑπὸ ἁμαρτίαν, ἵνα ἡ ἐπαγγελία ἐκ πίστεως Ἰησοῦ Χριστοῦ δοθῇ τοῖς πιστεύουσι. [GNS]
	ἀλλὰ συνέκλεισεν ἡ γραφὴ τὰ πάντα ὑπὸ ἁμαρτίαν, ἵνα ἡ ἐπαγγελία ἐκ πίστεως Ἰησοῦ Χριστοῦ δοθῇ τοῖς πιστεύουσιν. [GNT]
		Of sin, under sin; to be shut up as a prisoner in the hopeless depths or solitary confinement of a dungeon.
		
		Practical Application
		    How do we know that the law does not justify or make a person acceptable to God? Because the law imprisons all men under sin.

#2746
**Offence–
Offense**
 	
Offence–KJV
Offense–NASB
Stumbling block–NIV
Offense–NKJV
Hindered from finding
the Lord–NLT
 	
**POSB
REFERENCE**
(2 Cor.6:3)
Note 1
	προσκοπήν = *proskopēn*
	Pronunciation: [pros-kop-ayn']
	Parsing (part of speech): noun
	    Case—accusative
	    Gender—feminine
	    Number—singular
	    Stem or root—from προσκοπή, ῆς
	Concordance References:
	  ⇒ Strong's #4349 proskopē
	  ⇒ NIV #4683 proskopē
	  ⇒ NASB #4349 proskopē
	
	2 Cor. 6:3
	Giving no **offence** in any thing, that the ministry be not blamed: [KJV]
	Giving no cause for **offense** in anything, in order that the ministry be not discredited, [NASB]
	We put no **stumbling block** in anyone's path, so that our ministry will not be discredited. [NIV]
	We give no **offense** in anything, that our ministry may not be blamed. [NKJV]
	We try to live in such a way that no one will be **hindered from finding the Lord** by the way we act, and so no one can find fault with our ministry. [NLT]
	μηδεμίαν ἐν μηδενὶ διδόντες **προσκοπήν**, ἵνα μὴ μωμηθῇ ἡ διακονία· [GNS]
	μηδεμίαν ἐν μηδενὶ διδόντες **προσκοπήν**, ἵνα μὴ μωμηθῇ ἡ διακονία, [GNT]
		Stumbling block; to give cause for offense; to stumble; to strike against; to hinder someone from finding the Lord.
		
		Practical Application
		    Paul wanted his life and ministry to be so consistent that he would never give any reason for anyone to reject or to turn sour on the Lord Jesus Christ. Paul was careful; he guarded his behavior and conduct lest he cause a person to stumble and fall and reject the gospel of Christ. Note the reason: he did not want to be a poor reflection upon the ministry. Paul knew the nature of man, that people looked for excuses to reject Christ and to avoid His church. He knew that some people were always searching for juicy gossip to use against the followers of Christ and especially against the ministers of the gospel. He also knew that God had called him to the ministry of His Son, the Lord Jesus Christ, and that no higher call could be issued. Therefore, Paul sought to bring only honor to the ministry and to the name of the Lord Jesus Christ.

ENGLISH WORD	GREEK WORD AND VERSE	THE WORD MEANS...

#2747
Offence–
Offense
 	
Offence–KJV
Blameless–NASB
Blameless–NIV
Offense–NKJV
Blameless–NLT
 	
POSB
REFERENCE
(Philip.1:9-10; esp.
v.10)
Note 7, point 3
	ἀπρόσκοποι = *aproskopoi*
	Pronunciation: [ap-ros'-kop-oy]
	Parsing (part of speech): adjective
	    Case—nominative
	    Gender—masculine
	    Number—plural
	    Stem or root—from ἀπρόσκοπος, ον
	Concordance References:
	  ⇒ Strong's #677 aproskopos
	  ⇒ NIV #718 aproskopos
	  ⇒ NASB #677 aproskopos
	
	Philip. 1:10
	That ye may approve things that are excellent; that ye may be sincere and without **offence** till the day of Christ; [KJV]
	So that you may approve the things that are excellent, in order to be sincere and **blameless** until the day of Christ; [NASB]
	So that you may be able to discern what is best and may be pure and **blameless** until the day of Christ, [NIV]
	That you may approve the things that are excellent, that you may be sincere and **offense** till the day of Christ, [NKJV]
	For I want you to understand what really matters, so that you may live pure and **blameless** lives until Christ returns. [NLT]
	εἰς τὸ δοκιμάζειν ὑμᾶς τὰ διαφέροντα, ἵνα ἦτε εἰλικρινεῖς καὶ **ἀπρόσκοποι** εἰς ἡμέραν Χριστοῦ, [GNS]
	εἰς τὸ δοκιμάζειν ὑμᾶς τὰ διαφέροντα, ἵνα ἦτε εἰλικρινεῖς καὶ **ἀπρόσκοποι** εἰς ἡμέραν Χριστοῦ, [GNT]
		Blameless; without offense; clear; faultless; inoffensive.
		
		Practical Application
		A growing love is needed to keep us blameless, from causing others to stumble. We must always guard against being blameless (*aproskopoi*) or a stumbling block to others. Note: we must be willing to choose the best and the excellent for the sake of others. We may be able to control, but others may not be able to control...
		• drinking
		• television
		• social functions
		• the latest fashion and dress
		• dancing
		• movies
		• eating
		• makeup
		
		The list could go on and on with almost everything we do. We must control everything we do, not slipping over into the questionable—sometimes not even doing the acceptable and good. We must choose the best. Discern what is best. Why?
		⇒ To keep from causing a brother to stumble.
		⇒ To offer up to the Lord the very best we can. This point should *break our hearts*. Just think how often we have chosen to do less than the best for our Lord. We have offered up to Him behavior, words, thoughts, deeds, works that were second best—and we knew it! How His heart must have been cut—especially when He went to the ultimate limit in loving and giving Himself for us.

#2748
Offences–
Offenses
 	
Offences–KJV
Hindrances–NASB
Obstacles–NIV
Offenses–NKJV
Upset people's faith–
NLT
 	
POSB
REFERENCE
(Rom.16:17-18; esp.
v.17)
Note 1, point 1
	σκάνδαλα = *skandala*
	Pronunciation: [skan'-dal-ah]
	Parsing (part of speech): noun
	    Case—accusative
	    Gender—neuter
	    Number—plural
	    Stem or root—from σκάνδαλον, ου
	Concordance References:
	  ⇒ Strong's #4625 skandalon
	  ⇒ NIV #4998 skandalon
	  ⇒ NASB #4625 skandalon
	
	Romans 16:17
	Now I beseech you, brethren, mark them which cause divisions and **offences** contrary to the doctrine which ye have learned; and avoid them. [KJV]
	Now I urge you, brethren, keep your eye on those who cause dissensions and **hindrances** contrary to the teaching which you learned, and turn away from them. [NASB]
	I urge you, brothers, to watch out for those who cause divisions and put **obstacles** in your way that are contrary to the teaching you have learned. Keep away from them. [NIV]
	Now I urge you, brethren, note those who cause divisions and **offenses**, contrary to the doctrine which you learned, and avoid them. [NKJV]
	And now I make one more appeal, my dear brothers and sisters. Watch out for people who cause divisions and **upset people's faith** by teaching things that are contrary to what you have been taught. Stay away from them. [NLT]
		Hindrances; that which causes sin or gives occasion for sin; that which causes stumbling or trouble; obstacles. The word "offenses" (*skandala*) means laying a stumbling block in someone's way or causing someone to fall.
		
		Practical Application
		The most effective way for Satan to get a foothold into a strong church is to quietly and insidiously move a divisive person into some teaching or leadership position where he can influence immature believers. Paul knew this, so he left the warning until the end of his letter. It is a warning that must be heeded by a strong church if it is to keep its witness for the Lord.

ENGLISH WORD	GREEK WORD AND VERSE	THE WORD MEANS...
	Παρακαλῶ δὲ ὑμᾶς, ἀδελφοί, σκοπεῖν τοὺς τὰς διχοστασίας καὶ τὰ **σκάνδαλα**, παρὰ τὴν διδαχὴν ἣν ὑμεῖς ἐμάθετε, ποιοῦντας· καὶ ἐκκλίνατε ἀπ᾽ αὐτῶν. [GNS] Παρακαλῶ δὲ ὑμᾶς, ἀδελφοί, σκοπεῖν τοὺς τὰς διχοστασίας καὶ τὰ **σκάνδαλα** παρὰ τὴν διδαχὴν ἣν ὑμεῖς ἐμάθετε ποιοῦντας, καὶ ἐκκλίνετε ἀπ᾽ αὐτῶν· [GNT]	

#2749
Offend
 	
Offend–KJV
Makes you stumble–NASB
Causes...sin–NIV
Causes...sin–NKJV
Causes...lust–NLT
 	
POSB REFERENCE
(Mt.5:29)
Note 4
	σκανδαλίζει = *skandalizei*
	Pronunciation: [skan-dal-idz-eh-ee]
	Parsing (part of speech): verb
	  Mood—indicative
	  Tense—present
	  Voice—active
	  Person—3rd person
	  Number—singular
	  Stem or root—from **σκανδαλίζω**
	Concordance References:
	⇒ Strong's #4624 skandalizö
	⇒ NIV #4997 skandalizö
	⇒ NASB #4624 skandalizö
	
	Matthew 5:29
	And if thy right eye **offend** thee, pluck it out, and cast it from thee: for it is profitable for thee that one of thy members should perish, and not that thy whole body should be cast into hell. [KJV]
	"And if your right eye **makes you stumble**, tear it out, and throw it from you; for it is better for you that one of the parts of your body perish, than for your whole body to be thrown into hell. [NASB]
	If your right eye **causes** you to **sin**, gouge it out and throw it away. It is better for you to lose one part of your body than for your whole body to be thrown into hell. [NIV]
	If your right eye **causes** you to **sin**, pluck it out and cast it from you; for it is more profitable for you that one of your members perish, than for your whole body to be cast into hell. [NKJV]
	So if your eye—even if it is your good eye—**causes** you to **lust**, gouge it out and throw it away. It is better for you to lose one part of your body than for your whole body to be thrown into hell. [NLT]
	εἰ δὲ ὁ ὀφθαλμός σου ὁ δεξιὸς **σκανδαλίζει** σε, ἔξελε αὐτὸν καὶ βάλε ἀπὸ σοῦ· συμφέρει γάρ σοι ἵνα ἀπόληται ἓν τῶν μελῶν σου, καὶ μὴ ὅλον τὸ σῶμά σου βληθῇ εἰς γέενναν. [GNS]
	εἰ δὲ ὁ ὀφθαλμός σου ὁ δεξιὸς **σκανδαλίζει** σε, ἔξελε αὐτὸν καὶ βάλε ἀπὸ σοῦ· συμφέρει γάρ σοι ἵνα ἀπόληται ἓν τῶν μελῶν σου καὶ μὴ ὅλον τὸ σῶμά σου βληθῇ εἰς γέενναν. [GNT]
		To stumble; to fall away; to sin; to succumb to lust; to offend; to be baited; to be lured; to be tripped up; to cause someone to sin or fall into sin.
		
		Practical Application
		In this particular Scripture, the eyes and hands are said to be stumbling blocks.

#2750
Offend
 	
Offend–KJV
Causes...to stumble–NASB
Causes...to sin–NIV
Causes...to stumble–NKJV
Causes...to lose faith–NLT
 	
POSB REFERENCE
(Mk.9:42)
Note 1
	σκανδαλίσῃ = *skandalisë*
	Pronunciation: [skan-dal-i'-see]
	Parsing (part of speech): verb
	  Mood—subjunctive
	  Tense—aorist
	  Voice—active
	  Person—3rd person
	  Number—singular
	  Stem or root—from **σκανδαλίζω**
	Concordance References:
	⇒ Strong's #4624 skandalizö
	⇒ NIV #4997 skandalizö
	⇒ NASB #4624 skandalizö
	
	Mark 9:42
	And whosoever shall **offend** one of *these* little ones that believe in me, it is better for him that a millstone were hanged about his neck, and he were cast into the sea. [KJV]
	"And whoever **causes** one of these little ones who
		To cause a person to sin or stumble; to offend or cause a person to lose faith.
		
		Practical Application
		Christ seemed to be saying, "The most terrible sin of all is leading another person to sin. There is no sin any worse than leading another person astray. It is the worst conceivable sin." There are several ways we cause others to sin.
		1. By leading them into sin and teaching them to sin. "Oh, come on, no one will know. It's not going to hurt you."
		
		2. By example, things that we do. Example is not a direct vocal suggestion. We are not necessarily aware that "the child" sees or is observing us; nevertheless, he sees and learns from what we do. He thinks to himself: "If

ENGLISH WORD	GREEK WORD AND VERSE	THE WORD MEANS...

	believe **to stumble**, it would be better for him if, with a heavy millstone hung around his neck, he had been cast into the sea. [NASB]
	
	   "And if anyone **causes** one of these little ones who believe in me **to sin**, it would be better for him to be thrown into the sea with a large millstone tied around his neck. [NIV]
	
	   "But whoever **causes** one of these little ones who believe in Me **to stumble**, it would be better for him if a millstone were hung around his neck, and he were thrown into the sea. [NKJV]
	
	   "But if anyone **causes** one of these little ones who trusts in me **to lose faith**, it would be better for that person to be thrown into the sea with a large millstone tied around the neck. [NLT]
	
	   καὶ ὃς ἂν **σκανδαλίσῃ** ἕνα τῶν μικρῶν τούτων τῶν πιστευόντων εἰς ἐμέ, καλόν ἐστι αὐτῷ μᾶλλον, εἰ περίκειται λίθος μύλικὸς περὶ τὸν τράχηλον αὐτοῦ, καὶ βέβληται εἰς τὴν θάλασσαν. [GNS]
	
	   Καὶ ὃς ἂν **σκανδαλίσῃ** ἕνα τῶν μικρῶν τούτων τῶν πιστευόντων [εἰς ἐμέ], καλόν ἐστιν αὐτῷ μᾶλλον εἰ περίκειται μύλος ὀνικο [GNT]
		it's all right for him, then it is bound to be all right for me."
		
		3. By overlooking or passing over wrong; by giving soft names to it; by considering some sins to be merely minor sins. "Oh, that's all right. There's not that much to it. It isn't going to hurt anyone. Don't pay any attention to it. Just forget it."
		
		4. By ridiculing or poking fun at, or by joking and sneering at a person's attempt to do right. "Oh, don't be a fuddy-duddy, a square; you're acting like a fanatic. You and your religion."
		
		5. By looking at, touching, and tasting some things that are socially acceptable but that are sinful to God. They are harmful, habit forming, and physically stimulating when they should not be. "Wow, look at that." "Taste that." "What a turn on!"
		
		6. By persecuting and threatening "a child" or a believer. The threat can range all the way from loss of promotion, job, friendship, or acceptance, to imprisonment and death.

#2751
Offend
 	
Offend–KJV
Stumble in–NASB
Stumble in–NIV
Stumble in–NKJV
Make...mistakes–NLT
 	
**POSB
REFERENCE**
(Jas.3:2)
Note 2
	πταίομεν = ptaiomen
	Pronunciation: [ptah'-ee-o-mehn]
	Parsing (part of speech): verb
	   Mood—indicative
	   Tense—present
	   Voice—active
	   Person—1st person
	   Number—plural
	   Stem or root—from πταίω
	Concordance References:
	  ⇒ Strong's #4417 ptaiö
	  ⇒ NIV #4760 ptaiö
	  ⇒ NASB #4417 ptaiö
	
	James 3:2
	   For in many things we offend all. If any man **offend** not in word, the same is a perfect man, and able also to bridle the whole body. [KJV]
	
	   For we all **stumble in** many ways. If anyone does not stumble in what he says, he is a perfect man, able to bridle the whole body as well. [NASB]
	
	   We all **stumble in** many ways. If anyone is never at fault in what he says, he is a perfect man, able to keep his whole body in check. [NIV]
	
	   For we all **stumble in** many things. If anyone does not stumble in word, he *is* a perfect man, able also to bridle the whole body. [NKJV]
	
	   We all **make** many **mistakes**, but those who control their tongues can also control themselves in every other way. [NLT]
	
	   πολλὰ γὰρ **πταίομεν** ἅπαντες. εἴ τις ἐν λόγῳ οὐ πταίει, οὗτος τέλειος ἀνήρ, δυνατὸς χαλιναγωγῆσαι καὶ ὅλον τὸ σῶμα. [GNS]
	
	   πολλὰ γὰρ **πταίομεν** ἅπαντες. εἴ τις ἐν λόγῳ οὐ πταίει, οὗτος τέλειος ἀνήρ δυνατὸς χαλιναγωγῆσαι καὶ ὅλον τὸ σῶμα. [GNT]
		To stumble in; to offend; to make mistakes; to go wrong, astray.
		
		Practical Application
		   The tongue stumbles and sins often, stumbles in word after word. Note: "we all offend" (stumble, fall, sin). This includes teachers as well as other believers. No believer—no matter how great a teacher he is or who he is—is free from stumbling and falling. In fact, note what the verse says: "In many things" we all stumble. We do not just occasionally fall and sin; we are always coming up short before God. And this includes all teachers or preachers as well as all other believers. What is the proof of this? When some believers live such pure and righteous lives and walk so faithfully among us, how can Scripture say that they are always offending and stumbling? Look at the tongue; the tongue shows us.

#2752
**Offend–
Offense**
 	
Offend–KJV
Offense–NASB
	σκανδαλίσωμεν = skandalisömen
	Pronunciation: [skan-dal-li'-sow-mehn]
	Parsing (part of speech): verb
	   Mood—subjunctive
	   Tense—aorist
	   Voice—active
	   Person—1st person
		To give offense; to offend; to insult.
		
		Practical Application
		   When used as a verb the word "offend" (*skandalizo*) means to put a snare or stumbling block in someone's way; to cause someone to trip or fall. When used as a noun the word

ENGLISH WORD	GREEK WORD AND VERSE	THE WORD MEANS...
Offend–NIV **Offend–NKJV** **Offend–NLT** **POSB REFERENCE** (Mt.17:27) Note 4	Number—plural Stem or root—from σκανδαλίζω Concordance References: ⇒ Strong's #4624 skandalizō ⇒ NIV #4997 skandalizō ⇒ NASB #4624 skandalizō **Matthew 17:27** Notwithstanding, lest we should **offend** them, go thou to the sea, and cast an hook, and take up the fish that first cometh up; and when thou hast opened his mouth, thou shalt find a piece of money: that take, and give unto them for me and thee. [KJV] "But, lest we give them **offense**, go to the sea, and throw in a hook, and take the first fish that comes up; and when you open its mouth, you will find a stater. Take that and give it to them for you and Me." [NASB] "But so that we may not **offend** them, go to the lake and throw out your line. Take the first fish you catch; open its mouth and you will find a four-drachma coin. Take it and give it to them for my tax and yours." [NIV] Nevertheless, lest we **offend** them, go to the sea, cast in a hook, and take the fish that comes up first. And when you have opened its mouth, you will find a piece of money; take that and give it to them for Me and you." [NKJV] However, we don't want to **offend** them, so go down to the lake and throw in a line. Open the mouth of the first fish you catch, and you will find a coin. Take the coin and pay the tax for both of us." [NLT] ἵνα δὲ μὴ **σκανδαλίσωμεν** αὐτούς, πορευθεὶς εἰς θάλασσαν βάλε ἄγκιστρον, καὶ τὸν ἀναβάντα πρῶτον ἰχθὺν ἆρον, καὶ ἀνοίξας τὸ στόμα αὐτοῦ εὑρήσεις στατῆρα· ἐκεῖνον λαβὼν δὸς αὐτοῖς ἀντὶ ἐμοῦ καὶ σοῦ. [GNS] ἵνα δὲ μὴ **σκανδαλίσωμεν** αὐτούς, πορευθεὶς εἰς θάλασσαν βάλε ἄγκιστρον καὶ τὸν ἀναβάντα πρῶτον ἰχθὺν ἆρον, καὶ ἀνοίξας τὸ στόμα αὐτοῦ εὑρήσεις στατῆρα· ἐκεῖνον λαβὼν δὸς αὐτοῖς ἀντὶ ἐμοῦ καὶ σοῦ. [GNT]	"offend" (*skandalon*) means something that causes someone to stumble, trip, fall, or slip back. It is anything that arouses prejudice within others; anything that is a roadblock or a hindrance to others; anything that causes others to fall by the wayside. It is important to note that the stumbling block is sometimes good, and those who stumble are the ones in the wrong. For example, Christ is said to be a "rock that makes them fall of offense" (Romans 9:33) and His cross is said to "offend some"; that is, it is a stumbling block to some (Galatians 5:11).

#2753
Offended
 	
Offended–KJV
Fall away–NASB
Fall away–NIV
Stumble–NKJV
Desert–NLT
 	
POSB REFERENCE
(Mt.26:31)
Deeper Study #1
 	
See also POSB REF:
(Mk.14:27)
Note 1, point 1
	σκανδαλισθήσεσθε = *skandalisthēsesthe*
	Pronunciation: [skan-dal-is'-thay-sehs-theh]
	Parsing (part of speech): verb
	  Mood—indicative
	  Tense—future
	  Voice—passive
	  Person—2nd person
	  Number—plural
	  Stem or root—from σκανδαλίζω
	Concordance References:
	⇒ Strong's #4624 skandalizō
	⇒ NIV #4997 skandalizō
	⇒ NASB #4624 skandalizō
	
	Matthew 26:31
	Then saith Jesus unto them, All ye shall be **offended** because of me this night: for it is written, I will smite the shepherd, and the sheep of the flock shall be scattered abroad. [KJV]
	Then Jesus said to them, "You will all **fall away** because of Me this night, for it is written, 'I WILL STRIKE DOWN THE SHEPHERD, AND THE SHEEP OF THE FLOCK SHALL BE SCATTERED.' [NASB]
	Then Jesus told them, "This very night you will all **fall away** on account of me, for it is written:' 'I will strike the shepherd, and the sheep of the flock will be scattered.' [NIV]
	Then Jesus said to them, "All of you will be made to **stumble** because of Me this night, for it is written: 'I will strike the Shepherd, And the sheep of the flock will be scattered.' [NKJV]
		To stumble; to cause to stumble; to be led into sin; to be offended; to fall (because of Christ). (See POSB *Deeper Study #1*—Matthew 26:31).
		
		Practical Application
		When facing Christ, men stumble over three things. (For a thorough discussion see POSB *Deeper Study #9*—Matthew 21:44 and POSB *Deeper Study #10*—Matthew 21:44 cp. POSB note—Luke 20:17-18.)
		1. Men stumble over who Christ is (John 6:54-58, 60, 66).
		2. Men stumble over the cross of Christ (1 Cor. 1:21-23, esp. 1 Cor. 1:23).
		3. Men stumble over the cross God calls them to bear (see POSB note—Luke 9:23 and POSB *Deeper Study #1*—Luke 9:23).

ENGLISH WORD	GREEK WORD AND VERSE	THE WORD MEANS...
	"Tonight all of you will **desert** me," Jesus told them. "For the Scriptures say, 'God will strike the Shepherd, and the sheep of the flock will be scattered.' [NLT] Τότε λέγει αὐτοῖς ὁ Ἰησοῦς, Πάντες ὑμεῖς **σκανδαλισθήσεσθε** ἐν ἐμοὶ ἐν τῇ νυκτὶ ταύτῃ, γέγραπται γάρ, Πατάξω τὸν ποιμένα, καὶ διασκορπισθήσεται τὰ πρόβατα τῆς ποίμνης· [GNS] Τότε λέγει αὐτοῖς ὁ Ἰησοῦς, Πάντες ὑμεῖς **σκανδαλισθήσεσθε** ἐν ἐμοὶ ἐν τῇ νυκτὶ ταύτῃ, γέγραπται γάρ, Πατάξω τὸν ποιμένα, καὶ διασκορπισθήσονται τὰ πρόβατα τῆς ποίμνης. [GNT]	

#2754
Offended
 	
Offended–KJV
Stumbling–NASB
Go astray–NIV
Stumble–NKJV
Fall away–NLT
 	
POSB REFERENCE
(Jn.16:1)
Note 1
	σκανδαλισθῆτε = skandalisthēte
	Pronunciation: [skan-dal-is'-thay-teh]
	Parsing (part of speech): verb
	    Mood—subjunctive
	    Tense—aorist
	    Voice—passive
	    Person—2nd person
	    Number—plural
	    Stem or root—from **σκανδαλίζω**
	Concordance References:
	  ⇒ Strong's #4624 skandalizo
	  ⇒ NIV #4997 skandalizo
	  ⇒ NASB #4624 skandalizo
	
	John 16:1
	These things have I spoken unto you, that ye should not be **offended**. [KJV]
	"These things I have spoken to you, that you may be kept from **stumbling**. [NASB]
	"All this I have told you so that you will not **go astray**. [NIV]
	"These things I have spoken to you, that you should not be made to **stumble**. [NKJV]
	"I have told you these things so that you won't **fall away**. [NLT]
	Ταῦτα λελάληκα ὑμῖν, ἵνα μὴ **σκανδαλισθῆτε**· [GNS]
	Ταῦτα λελάληκα ὑμῖν ἵνα μὴ **σκανδαλισθῆτε**. [GNT]
		To go astray; to fall away; to cause to stumble or sin; to be offended; to stumble and to trip.
		
		Practical Application
		Jesus warned the believer that religionists would persecute His followers. Jesus warned the believer because He wants to prevent the believer from slipping away. The believer can stumble and fall over persecution. Persecution can...
		• cause a believer to question his beliefs.
		• cause a believer to weaken and return to the way of false religion.
		• silence a believer and his witness.
		• cause a believer to deny Jesus.

#2755
Offer
 	
Yield–KJV
Presenting–NASB
Offer–NIV
Present–NKJV
Let–NLT
 	
POSB REFERENCE
(Rom.6:13)
Deeper Study #2
	παριστάνετε = paristanete
	Pronunciation: [par-is'-tahn-eh-teh]
	Parsing (part of speech): verb
	    Mood—imperative
	    Tense—present
	    Voice—active
	    Person—2nd person
	    Number—plural
	    Stem or root—from **παρίστημι** and παριστάνω
	Concordance References:
	  ⇒ Strong's #3936 paristēmi
	  ⇒ NIV #4225 paristēmi
	  ⇒ NASB #3936 paristēmi
	
	Romans 6:13
	Neither **yield** ye your members as instruments of unrighteousness unto sin: but yield yourselves unto God, as those that are alive from the dead, and your members as instruments of righteousness unto God. [KJV]
	And do not go on **presenting** the members of your body to sin as instruments of unrighteousness; but present yourselves to God as those alive from the dead, and your members as instruments of righteousness to God. [NASB]
	Do not **offer** the parts of your body to sin, as instruments of wickedness, but rather offer yourselves to God, as those who have been brought from death to life; and offer the parts of your body to him as instruments of righteousness. [NIV]
	And do not **present** your members as instruments of unrighteousness to sin, but present yourselves to God as being alive from the dead, and your members as instruments of righteousness to God. [NKJV]
		To present; to bring into one's presence; to show; to yield; to dedicate; to provide; to send; to prove. It means to offer; to put at the disposal of; to give; to grant; to turn over to.
		
		Practical Application
		The believer must not offer the parts of his body to sin. The believer is not to offer the parts of his body to be instruments or tools of wickedness. If he takes a part of his body and uses it as an instrument or tool of wickedness, he sins. The parts of a person's body refer to all the parts of the body: the eyes, ears, mouth, tongue, hands, feet, mind, or any of the covered and dressed parts. No believer is to offer or give any part of his body over to wickedness. To do so is to sin. The tense is present action, so the believer is to be constantly on guard against allowing any part of his body to be offered to sin. Note: the word "offer" has the idea of struggling. It is a struggle to fight against sin and to control and protect the parts of our bodies.

ENGLISH WORD	GREEK WORD AND VERSE	THE WORD MEANS...
	Do not **let** any part of your body become a tool of wickedness, to be used for sinning. Instead, give yourselves completely to God since you have been given new life. And use your whole body as a tool to do what is right for the glory of God. [NLT] μηδὲ **παριστάνετε** τὰ μέλη ὑμῶν ὅπλα ἀδικίας τῇ ἁμαρτίᾳ· ἀλλὰ παραστήσατε ἑαυτοὺς τῷ Θεῷ ὡς ἐκ νεκρῶν ζῶντας, καὶ τὰ μέλη ὑμῶν ὅπλα δικαιοσύνης τῷ Θεῷ. [GNS] μηδὲ **παριστάνετε** τὰ μέλη ὑμῶν ὅπλα ἀδικίας τῇ ἁμαρτίᾳ, ἀλλὰ παραστήσατε ἑαυτοὺς τῷ θεῷ ὡσεὶ ἐκ νεκρῶν ζῶντας καὶ τὰ μέλη ὑμῶν ὅπλα δικαιοσύνης τῷ θεῷ. [GNT]	
#2756 **Offer A Sacrifice** Make reconciliation for–KJV Make propitiation for–NASB Make atonement for–NIV Make propitiation for–NKJV **Offer a sacrifice–NLT** **POSB REFERENCE** (Heb.2:17-18; esp. v.17) Note 2, point 3	ἱλάσκεσθαι = *hilaskesthai* Pronunciation: [hil-as'-keh-thah-ee] Parsing (part of speech): verb 　　Mood—infinitive 　　Tense—present 　　Voice—middle deponent 　　Case—accusative 　　Stem or root—from ἱλάσκομαι Concordance References: ⇒　Strong's #2433 hilaskomai ⇒　NIV #2661 hilaskomai ⇒　NASB #2433 hilaskomai **Hebrews 2:17** Wherefore in all things it behoved him to be made like unto his brethren, that he might be a merciful and faithful high priest in things pertaining to God, to **make reconciliation for** the sins of the people. [KJV] Therefore, He had to be made like His brethren in all things, that He might become a merciful and faithful high priest in things pertaining to God, to **make propitiation for** the sins of the people. [NASB] For this reason he had to be made like his brothers in every way, in order that he might become a merciful and faithful high priest in service to God, and that he might **make atonement for** the sins of the people. [NIV] Therefore, in all things He had to be made like *His* brethren, that He might be a merciful and faithful High Priest in things *pertaining* to God, to **make propitiation for** the sins of the people. [NKJV] Therefore, it was necessary for Jesus to be in every respect like us, his brothers and sisters, so that he could be our merciful and faithful High Priest before God. He then could **offer a sacrifice** that would take away the sins of the people. [NLT] ὅθεν ὤφειλε κατὰ πάντα τοῖς ἀδελφοῖς ὁμοιωθῆναι, ἵνα ἐλεήμων· γένηται καὶ πιστὸς ἀρχιερεὺς τὰ πρὸς τὸν Θεόν, εἰς τὸ **ἱλάσκεσθαι** τὰς ἁμαρτίας τοῦ λαοῦ. [GNS] ὅθεν ὤφειλεν κατὰ πάντα τοῖς ἀδελφοῖς ὁμοιωθῆναι, ἵνα ἐλεήμων γένηται καὶ πιστὸς ἀρχιερεὺς τὰ πρὸς τὸν θεόν εἰς τὸ **ἱλάσκεσθαι** τὰς ἁμαρτίας τοῦ λαοῦ. [GNT]	To make atonement for; to make reconciliation for; to make propitiation for; to offer a sacrifice. It means to sacrifice or to make a covering, satisfaction, payment, or appeasement for sin. **Practical Application** Jesus Christ became the High Priest so that He could make propitiation for the sins of the people. It was, of course, the task of the High Priest to offer up the animal sacrifice for the sins of the people. This is the picture being painted of Christ. But note one distinct difference: Jesus Christ Himself is the propitiation for man's sin. It was not His teachings, power, example, or life that made Christ the propitiation. It was His blood: His sacrifice, His death, His sufferings, His cross that caused God to accept Jesus as the propitiation. It is the blood of Christ that God accepts as... • the *sacrifice* for our sins. • the *covering* for our sins. • the *satisfaction* for our sins. • the *payment* for the penalty of our sins. • the *appeasement* of His wrath against sin. When Christ died for man... • the righteousness of God was satisfied. • the perfection of God was satisfied. • the justice of God was satisfied. Jesus Christ became the *propitiation*—the covering and satisfaction for the sins of man. He became the High Priest in order to make propitiation for our sins.
#2757 **Offered** Gave it–KJV Gave it–NASB **Offered–NIV** Gave it–NKJV Gave it–NLT **POSB REFERENCE** (Mk.14:23-24; esp. v.23) Note 2, point 3	ἔδωκεν = *edoken* Pronunciation: [eh-dow'-kehn] Parsing (part of speech): verb 　　Mood—indicative 　　Tense—aorist 　　Voice—active 　　Person—3rd person 　　Number—singular 　　Stem or root—from δίδωμι Concordance References: ⇒　Strong's #1325 didōmi ⇒　NIV #1443 didōmi ⇒　NASB #1325 didōmi **Mark 14:23** And he took the cup, and when he had given thanks, he **gave it** to them: and they all drank of it. [KJV]	To offer; to give to; to present. **Practical Application** Christ offered the cup once for all. Note the word "offered" or "gave it" (*edoken*) is in the Greek aorist tense. He died once and only once (Romans 6:10), and man partakes of His death once and only once (Romans 6:6).

ENGLISH WORD	GREEK WORD AND VERSE	THE WORD MEANS...
POSB REFERENCE (Gal.2:7-10; esp. v.7) Note 5	**Galatians 2:7** But **contrariwise**, when they saw that the gospel of the uncircumcision was committed unto me, as the gospel of the circumcision was unto Peter; [KJV] But **on** the **contrary**, seeing that I had been entrusted with the gospel to the uncircumcised, just as Peter had been to the circumcised [NASB] **On** the **contrary**, they saw that I had been entrusted with the task of preaching the gospel to the Gentiles, just as Peter had been to the Jews. [NIV] But **on** the **contrary**, when they saw that the gospel for the uncircumcised had been committed to me, as *the gospel* for the circumcised *was* to Peter [NKJV] They saw that God had given me the responsibility of preaching the Good News to the Gentiles, just as he had given Peter the responsibility of preaching to the Jews. [NLT]—Not Translated ἀλλὰ **τοὐναντίον**, ἰδόντες ὅτι πεπίστευμαι τὸ εὐαγγέλιον τῆς ἀκροβυστίας, καθὼς Πέτρος τῆς περιτομῆς, [GNS] ἀλλὰ **τοὐναντίον** ἰδόντες ὅτι πεπίστευμαι τὸ εὐαγγέλιον τῆς ἀκροβυστίας καθὼς Πέτρος τῆς περιτομῆς, [GNT]	oned the truth that God gives to every man a particular task.
#2766 **On Every Side** On every side–KJV In every way–NASB On every side–NIV On every side–NKJV On every side–NLT **POSB REFERENCE** (2 Cor.4:7-9; esp. v.8) Note 2, point 1	ἐν παντί = *en panti* Pronunciation: [en pahn-tee] Parsing *panti* (part of speech): pronominal adjective Case—dative Gender—neuter Number—singular Stem or root—from πᾶς, πᾶσα, πᾶν Concordance References: ⇒ Strong's #1722 en + 3956 pas ⇒ NIV #1877 en [on] + 4246 pas [every side] ⇒ NASB #1722 en + 3956 pas **2 Cor. 4:8** We are troubled **on every side**, yet not distressed; we are perplexed, but not in despair; [KJV] We are afflicted **in every way**, but not crushed; perplexed, but not despairing; [NASB] We are hard pressed **on every side**, but not crushed; perplexed, but not in despair; [NIV] *We are* hard pressed **on every side**, yet not crushed; *we are* perplexed, but not in despair; [NKJV] We are pressed **on every side** by troubles, but we are not crushed and broken. We are perplexed, but we don't give up and quit. [NLT] ἐν **παντὶ** θλιβόμενοι, ἀλλ' οὐ στενοχωρούμενοι· ἀπορούμενοι ἀλλ' οὐκ ἐξαπορούμενοι· [GNS] ἐν **παντὶ** θλιβόμενοι ἀλλ' οὐ στενοχωρούμενοι, ἀπορούμενοι ἀλλ' οὐκ ἐξαπορούμενοι, [GNT]	On every side; everywhere; in every imaginable way and place and occasion. **Practical Application** The minister experiences all kinds of trouble and pressure. He sometimes feels as though he is pressured and troubled beyond what he can bear. It is as though a heavy weight is pressing in upon him and about to crush him. But then God steps in to save him from being distressed and crushed. The presence and power of God sustain His dear minister.
#2767 **On Guard** Beware–KJV On...guard–NASB On...guard–NIV Beware–NKJV Beware–NLT **POSB REFERENCE** (Rom.12:15-19; esp. v.15) Note 2, point 1	φυλάσσεσθε = *phulassesthe* Pronunciation: [foo-las'-say-the] Parsing (part of speech): verb Mood—imperative Tense—present Voice—middle Person—2nd person Number—plural Stem or root—from φυλάσσω Concordance References: ⇒ Strong's #5442 phulassō ⇒ NIV #5875 phulassō ⇒ NASB #5442 phulassō **Luke 12:15** And he said unto them, Take heed, and **beware** of covetousness: for a man's life consisteth not in the abundance of the things which he possesseth. [KJV] And He said to them, "Beware, and be **on** your **guard** against every form of greed; for not even when one has an	To be on guard; to beware; to guard oneself; to keep safe; to defend; to protect oneself from some dangerous enemy. **Practical Application** What is the purpose of such a strong warning? Why should a person seek protection from coveteousness and greed? Because it is a craving, a desire for more and more. It is greediness, a dissatisfaction with what is enough. It includes the cravings for both material things and fleshly indulgence. It is desiring what belongs to others; snatching at something that belongs to others; a love of having, a cry of give me, give me (cp. 2 Peter 2:14). ⇒ It is a lust so deep within a man that he finds his happiness in things instead of in God.

ENGLISH WORD	GREEK WORD AND VERSE	THE WORD MEANS...
	abundance does his life consist of his possessions." [NASB] Then he said to them, "Watch out! Be **on** your **guard** against all kinds of greed; a man's life does not consist in the abundance of his possessions." [NIV] And He said to them, "Take heed and **beware** of covetousness, for one's life does not consist in the abundance of the things he possesses." [NKJV] Then he said, "**Beware**! Don't be greedy for what you don't have. Real life is not measured by how much we own." [NLT] εἶπε δὲ πρὸς αὐτούς, Ὁρᾶτε καὶ **φυλάσσεσθε** ἀπὸ πάσης πλεονεξίας· ὅτι οὐκ ἐν τῷ περισσεύειν τινὶ ἡ ζωὴ αὐτοῦ ἐστιν ἐκ τῶν ὑπαρχόντων αὐτοῦ. [GNS] εἶπεν δὲ πρὸς αὐτούς, Ὁρᾶτε καὶ **φυλάσσεσθε** ἀπὸ πάσης πλεονεξίας, ὅτι οὐκ ἐν τῷ περισσεύειν τινὶ ἡ ζωὴ αὐτοῦ ἐστιν ἐκ τῶν ὑπαρχόντων αὐτῷ. [GNT]	⇒ It is a covetousness so deep that it desires the power that things bring more than the things themselves. ⇒ It is an intense appetite for gain; a passion for the pleasure that things can bring. It goes beyond the pleasure of possessing things for their own sakes.
#2768 **On Guard** Take heed–KJV **On guard–NASB** Careful–NIV Take heed–NKJV Watch out–NLT **POSB REFERENCE** (Lk.21:34-35; esp. v.34) Note 1	Προσέχετε = prosechete Pronunciation: [pros-ekh'-eh-teh] Parsing (part of speech): verb 　Mood—imperative 　Tense—present 　Voice—active 　Person—2nd person 　Number—plural 　Stem or root—from προσέχω Concordance References: ⇒ Strong's #4337 prosechō ⇒ NIV #4668 prosechō ⇒ NASB #4337 prosechō **Luke 21:34** And **take heed** to yourselves, lest at any time your hearts be overcharged with surfeiting, and drunkenness, and cares of this life, and so that day come upon you unawares. [KJV] "Be **on guard**, that your hearts may not be weighted down with dissipation and drunkenness and the worries of life, and that day come on you suddenly like a trap; [NASB] "Be **careful**, or your hearts will be weighed down with dissipation, drunkenness and the anxieties of life, and that day will close on you unexpectedly like a trap. [NIV] "But **take heed** to yourselves, lest your hearts be weighed down with carousing, drunkenness, and cares of this life, and that Day come on you unexpectedly. [NKJV] "**Watch out**! Don't let me find you living in careless ease and drunkenness, and filled with the worries of this life. Don't let that day catch you unaware, [NLT] Προσέχετε δὲ ἑαυτοῖς, μήποτε βαρυνθῶσιν ὑμῶν αἱ καρδίαι ἐν κραιπάλῃ καὶ μέθῃ καὶ μερίμναις βιωτικαῖς, καὶ αἰφνίδιος ἐφ' ὑμᾶς ἐπιστῇ ἡ ἡμέρα ἐκείνη· [GNS] Προσέχετε δὲ ἑαυτοῖς μήποτε βαρηθῶσιν ὑμῶν αἱ καρδίαι ἐν κραιπάλῃ καὶ μέθῃ καὶ μερίμναις βιωτικαῖς καὶ ἐπιστῇ ἐφ' ὑμᾶς αἰφνίδιος ἡ ἡμέρα ἐκείνη [GNT]	To give attention; to focus one's mind; to watch out; to guard; to beware; to take care; to be on guard; to pay close attention to; to carefully consider. **Practical Application** The end time and the day of the Lord's return demands taking care. Note this important fact: the believer is to be careful; that is, to guard his life. How? By not engaging in worldliness. His heart is not to be weighed down (barethosin): heavy, weighed down, burdened, overloaded, filled up, indulged.
#2769 **On Guard** Watch–KJV On...alert–NASB **On...guard–NIV** Watch–NKJV **On guard–NLT** **POSB REFERENCE** (1 Cor.16:13-14; esp. v.13) Note 4	Γρηγορεῖτε = Grēgoreite Pronunciation: [gray-gor-ee'-teh] Parsing (part of speech): verb 　Mood—imperative 　Tense—present 　Voice—active 　Person—2nd person 　Number—plural 　Stem or root—from γρηγορέω Concordance References: ⇒ Strong's #1127 grēgoreō ⇒ NIV #1213 grēgoreō ⇒ NASB #1127 grēgoreō	To be on guard; to be on alert; to watch; to be awake, alert, alive, and constantly on guard; never to be sleepy-eyed or sluggish; never to let one's guard down. **Practical Application** There are five charges in this exhortation, and all five are in the present tense; that is, this is the way believers are to live. These things are to be continually done. 1. "Be on guard" (Grēgoreite): to be awake, alert, and constantly on guard; never to be sleepy-eyed or sluggish; never to let one's guard down.

ENGLISH WORD	GREEK WORD AND VERSE	THE WORD MEANS...
	1 Cor. 16:13 **Watch** ye, stand fast in the faith, quit you like men, be strong. [KJV] Be **on** the **alert**, stand firm in the faith, act like men, be strong. [NASB] Be **on** your **guard**; stand firm in the faith; be men of courage; be strong. [NIV] **Watch**, stand fast in the faith, be brave, be strong. [NKJV] Be **on guard**. Stand true to what you believe. Be courageous. Be strong. [NLT] Γρηγορεῖτε, στήκετε ἐν τῇ πίστει, ἀνδρίζεσθε, κραταιοῦσθε. [GNS] Γρηγορεῖτε, στήκετε ἐν τῇ πίστει, ἀνδρίζεσθε, κραταιοῦσθε. [GNT]	2. "Stand firm in the faith": do not listen or give heed to false teachers and false doctrine; do not question the word and truth of Christ. Stand against those who mishandle and abuse the Word of God. 3. "Be men of courage" means either to be courageous as real men or to quit living like immature men. It means to live as courageous men of God. 4. "Be strong": to grow in strength; to be men of real strength; to stand against the world and its enticements. 5. Do everything in love (v.17): The believer is to live "in" love and to do everything "in" love. Remember the love chapter, 1 Cor. 13. The greatest answer to the division and other problems within the church is love. Love must prevail in the hearts and behavior of believers and their church.

#2770
Once
 	
Once–KJV
Once–NASB
Once–NIV
Once–NKJV
Once–NLT
 	
**POSB
REFERENCE**
(Heb.9:27-28; esp. v.27)
Note 3, point 1
	ἅπαξ = *hapax*
	Pronunciation: [hap'-ax]
	Parsing (part of speech): adjective
	    Type—adverb
	    Stem or root—from ἅπαξ
	Concordance References:
	  ⇒ Strong's #530 hapax
	  ⇒ NIV #562 hapax
	  ⇒ NASB #530 hapax
	
	Hebrews 9:27
	And as it is appointed unto men **once** to die, but after this the judgment: [KJV]
	And inasmuch as it is appointed for men to die **once** and after this comes judgment, [NASB]
	Just as man is destined to die **once**, and after that to face judgment, [NIV]
	And as it is appointed for men to die **once**, but after this the judgment, [NKJV]
	And just as it is destined that each person dies only **once** and after that comes judgment, [NLT]
	καὶ καθ' ὅσον ἀπόκειται τοῖς ἀνθρώποις ἅπαξ ἀποθανεῖν, μετὰ δὲ τοῦτο κρίσις· [GNS]
	καὶ καθ' ὅσον ἀπόκειται τοῖς ἀνθρώποις ἅπαξ ἀποθανεῖν, μετὰ δὲ τοῦτο κρίσις, [GNT]
		Once, on one occasion, one time, just this once, this time.
		
		Practical Application
		Man dies and he dies once—only once. There is no second chance. This is the emphasis of "once" (*hapax*). Man has only one chance to be forgiven, saved, and redeemed—only one chance to become acceptable to God and receive the inheritance of the promise, that is, eternal life. Man dies, and when he dies, his opportunity is over. Jesus Christ died in this world and in the time frame of this life. He did not die in some other world nor in the time frame of some other world. He died upon earth *as* a Man *for* men. Therefore, there will never again be a chance to be covered by His sacrifice other than in this world and in this life. Men die and they die only once, never again to live upon the earth.

#2771
Once And Forever
 	
Uttermost–KJV
Forever–NASB
Completely–NIV
Uttermost–NKJV
Once and forever–NLT
 	
**POSB
REFERENCE**
(Heb.7:25)
Note 1, point 3
	εἰς τὸ παντελές = *eis to panteles*
	Pronunciation: [ice to pan-tel-ehs]
	Parsing *panteles* (part of speech): pronominal adjective
	    Case—accusative
	    Gender—neuter
	    Number—singular
	    Stem or root—from παντελής, ές
	Concordance References:
	  ⇒ Strong's #1519+3588+3838 eis ho panteles
	  ⇒ NIV #1650+3836+4117 eis ho panteles [completely]
	  ⇒ NASB #1519+3588+3838 eis ho panteles
	
	Hebrews 7:25
	Wherefore he is able also to save them to the **uttermost** that come unto God by him, seeing he ever liveth to make intercession for them. [KJV]
	Hence, also, He is able to save **forever** those who draw near to God through Him, since He always lives to make intercession for them. [NASB]
	Therefore he is able to save **completely** those who come to God through him, because he always lives to intercede for them. [NIV]
	Therefore He is also able to save to the **uttermost** those who come to God through Him, since He always lives to make intercession for them. [NKJV]
		Completely; to the uttermost; forever, once and forever.
		
		Practical Application
		Jesus Christ is able to save all persons once and forever. What does it mean to be saved completely, once and forever (*panteles*)? It means to be saved "completely, perfectly, finally and for all time and eternity" (Amplified New Testament). It means that Jesus Christ presents us to God as perfect. He presents us in His righteousness as perfected forever. Therefore in Christ—because He makes intercession for us and because He stands before God as the perfect and eternal sacrifice for our sins—we become acceptable to God. But it means much more. In outline form, when Jesus Christ saves us once and forever, it means...
		• that He saves us from sin, death and condemnation (John 5:24; Romans 8:34).
		• that He saves us to live with God eternally (John 3:16; Romans 8:39).
		• that He saves us to be the citizens of the new heaven and earth (2 Peter 3:10-13;

ENGLISH WORD	GREEK WORD AND VERSE	THE WORD MEANS...
	Therefore he is able, **once and forever**, to save everyone who comes to God through him. He lives forever to plead with God on their behalf. [NLT] ὅθεν καὶ σώζειν **εἰς τὸ παντελὲς** δύναται τοὺς προσερχομένους δι' αὐτοῦ τῷ θεῷ, πάντοτε ζῶν εἰς τὸ ἐντυγχάνειν ὑπὲρ αὐτῶν. [GNS] ὅθεν καὶ σώζειν **εἰς τὸ παντελὲς** δύναται τοὺς προσ' ερχομένους δι' αὐτοῦ τῷ θεῷ, πάντοτε ζῶν εἰς τὸ ἐντυγχάνειν ὑπὲρ αὐτῶν. [GNT]	Rev. 21:1f). • that He saves us to rule and reign over the universe right along with Him throughout all of eternity (Luke 12:42-44; Luke 22:28-29; 1 Cor. 6:2-3).
#2772 **One Abnor-mally Born** One born out of due time–KJV One untimely born–NASB **One abnormally born–NIV** One born out of due time–NKJV I had been born at the wrong time–NLT **POSB REFERENCE** (1 Cor.15:8-10; esp. v.8) Note 5	τῷ ἐκτρώματι = tō ektrōmati Pronunciation: [tow ek'-tro-mah-tee] Parsing *ektrōmati* (part of speech): noun Case—dative Gender—neuter Number—singular Stem or root—from ἔκτρωμα, τος Concordance References: ⇒ Strong's #3588 ho + 1626 ektrōma ⇒ NIV #3836 ho [one] +1765 ektrōma [abnormally born] ⇒ NASB #3588 ho + 1626 ektrōma **1 Cor. 15:8** And last of all he was seen of me also, as of **one born out of due time**. [KJV] And last of all, as it were to **one untimely born**, He appeared to me also. [NASB] And last of all he appeared to me also, as to **one abnormally born**. [NIV] Then last of all He was seen by me also, as by **one born out of due time**. [NKJV] Last of all, I saw him, too, long after the others, as though **I had been born at the wrong time**. [NLT] ἔσχατον δὲ πάντων ὡσπερεὶ **τῷ ἐκτρώματι** ὤφθη κἀμοί. [GNS] ἔσχατον δὲ πάντων ὡσπερεὶ **τῷ ἐκτρώματι** ὤφθη κἀμοί. [GNT]	A miscarriage, an abortion, an unnatural birth, a child born out of time; born at the wrong time. **Practical Application** Paul is simply saying that he did not follow the Lord when the Lord walked upon the earth, but he saw and began to follow the Lord after He had left the earth, after His ascension into heaven. Paul is, of course, referring to his experience on the Damascus road (Acts 9:1f), and perhaps to the visions granted him (2 Cor. 12:1f).
#2773 **One Accord** One accord–KJV One mind–NASB Together–NIV One accord–NKJV Together–NLT **POSB REFERENCE** (Acts 1:14) *Deeper Study #1*	ὁμοθυμαδόν = homothumadon Pronunciation: [hom-oth-oo-mad-on'] Parsing (part of speech): adjective adverb Stem or root—from ὁμοθυμαδόν Concordance References: ⇒ Strong's #3661 homothumadon ⇒ NIV #3924 homothumadon ⇒ NASB #3661 homothumadon **Acts 1:14** These all continued with **one accord** in prayer and supplication, with the women, and Mary the mother of Jesus, and with his brethren. [KJV] These all with **one mind** were continually devoting themselves to prayer, along with the women, and Mary the mother of Jesus, and with His brothers. [NASB] They all joined **together** constantly in prayer, along with the women and Mary the mother of Jesus, and with his brothers. [NIV] These all continued with **one accord** in prayer and supplication, with the women and Mary the mother of Jesus, and with His brothers. [NKJV] They all met **together** continually for prayer, along with Mary the mother of Jesus, several other women, and the brothers of Jesus. [NLT] οὗτοι πάντες ἦσαν προσκαρτεροῦντες **ὁμοθυμαδὸν** τῇ προσευχῇ καὶ τῇ δεήσει, σὺν γυναιξὶ καὶ Μαριά τῇ μητρὶ τοῦ Ἰησοῦ, καὶ σὺν τοῖς ἀδελφοῖς αὐτοῦ. [GNS] οὗτοι πάντες ἦσαν προσκαρτεροῦντες **ὁμοθυμαδὸν** τῇ προσευχῇ σὺν γυναιξὶν καὶ Μαριὰμ τῇ μητρὶ τοῦ Ἰησοῦ καὶ τοῖς ἀδελφοῖς αὐτοῦ. [GNT]	Together, one mind, one accord; the same mind or spirit; oneness of mind and heart. It means to be one in spirit and purpose. *Homos* means same and *thumos* means spirit or mind. **Practical Application** The believers, all 120 of them in the upper room, were of the same spirit, of the same mind. The idea is they were after the same thing, the baptism of the Holy Spirit. They were focusing and concentrating their thoughts and energies upon seeking God for the promise of His Spirit. The word is used only eleven times in Scripture, ten of those times are found in Acts, one is found in Romans. ⇒ Together in prayer (Acts 1:14; Acts 4:24). ⇒ Together in one place (Acts 2:1). ⇒ Together in daily worship and the Lord's supper (Acts 2:46; Acts 5:12). ⇒ Together in obedience (Acts 8:6). ⇒ Together in a business meeting (Acts 15:25). ⇒ Togetherness is needed to glorify God (Romans 15:6).

ENGLISH WORD	GREEK WORD AND VERSE	THE WORD MEANS...

#2774
One Born Out Of Due Time
 	
One born out of due time–KJV
One untimely born–NASB
One abnormally born–NIV
One born out of due time–NKJV
I had been born at the wrong time–NLT
 	
POSB REFERENCE
(1 Cor.15:8-10; esp. v.8)
Note 5
	τῷ ἐκτρώματι = tō ektrōmati
	Pronunciation: [tow ek'-tro-mah-tee]
	Parsing ektrōmati (part of speech): noun
	   Case—dative
	   Gender—neuter
	   Number—singular
	   Stem or root—from ἔκτρωμα, τος
	Concordance References:
	⇒ Strong's #3588 ho + 1626 ektrōma
	⇒ NIV #3836 ho [one] +1765 ektrōma [abnormally born]
	⇒ NASB #3588 ho + 1626 ektrōma
	
	1 Cor. 15:8
	And last of all he was seen of me also, as of **one born out of due time**. [KJV]
	And last of all, as it were to **one untimely born**, He appeared to me also. [NASB]
	And last of all he appeared to me also, as to **one abnormally born**. [NIV]
	Then last of all He was seen by me also, as by **one born out of due time**. [NKJV]
	Last of all, I saw him, too, long after the others, as though **I had been born at the wrong time**. [NLT]
	ἔσχατον δὲ πάντων ὡσπερεὶ **τῷ ἐκτρώματι** ὤφθη κἀμοί. [GNS]
	ἔσχατον δὲ πάντων ὡσπερεὶ **τῷ ἐκτρώματι** ὤφθη κἀμοί. [GNT]
		A miscarriage, an abortion, an unnatural birth, a child born out of time; born at the wrong time.
		
		Practical Application
		Paul is simply saying that he did not follow the Lord when the Lord walked upon the earth, but he saw and began to follow the Lord after He had left the earth, after His ascension into heaven. Paul is, of course, referring to his experience on the Damascus road (Acts 9:1f), and perhaps to the visions granted him (2 Cor. 12:1f).

#2775
One Mind
 	
One mind–KJV
Like-minded–NASB
One mind–NIV
One mind–NKJV
Harmony–NLT
 	
POSB REFERENCE
(2 Cor.13:11-13; esp. v.11)
Note 3
	τὸ αὐτὸ φρονεῖτε = to auto phroneite
	Pronunciation: [to ow-to' fron-eh'-ee-teh]
	Parsing phroneite (part of speech): verb
	   Mood—imperative
	   Tense—present
	   Voice—active
	   Person—2nd person
	   Number—plural
	   Stem or root—from φρονέω
	Concordance References:
	⇒ Strong's #846+3588 autos ho + 5426 phroneō
	⇒ NIV #899+3836 autos ho [one] + 5858 phroneō [mind]
	⇒ NASB #846+3588 autos ho + 5426 phroneō
	
	2 Cor. 13:11
	Finally, brethren, farewell. Be perfect, be of good comfort, be of **one mind**, live in peace; and the God of love and peace shall be with you. [KJV]
	Finally, brethren, rejoice, be made complete, be comforted, be **like-minded**, live in peace; and the God of love and peace shall be with you. [NASB]
	Finally, brothers, good-by. Aim for perfection, listen to my appeal, be of **one mind**, live in peace. And the God of love and peace will be with you. [NIV]
	Finally, brethren, farewell. Become complete. Be of good comfort, be of **one mind**, live in peace; and the God of love and peace will be with you. [NKJV]
	Dear brothers and sisters, I close my letter with these last words: Rejoice. Change your ways. Encourage each other. Live in **harmony** and peace. Then the God of love and peace will be with you. [NLT]
	Λοιπόν, ἀδελφοί, χαίρετε· καταρτίζεσθε, παρακαλεῖσθε, **τὸ αὐτὸ φρονεῖτε**, εἰρηνεύετε· καὶ ὁ Θεὸς τῆς ἀγάπης καὶ εἰρήνης ἔσται μεθ' ὑμῶν. [GNS]
	Λοιπόν, ἀδελφοί, χαίρετε, καταρτίζεσθε, παρακαλεῖσθε, **τὸ αὐτὸ φρονεῖτε**, εἰρηνεύετε, καὶ ὁ θεὸς τῆς ἀγάπης καὶ εἰρήνης ἔσται μεθ' ὑμῶν. [GNT]
		One mind; to be like-minded; to be in harmony; to be of one mind in faith, belief, purpose, mission, and ministry.
		
		Practical Application
		Note that God is the Author, the Giver of love and peace. The believer must therefore accept the challenge to be of one mind with other believers and live accordingly.

ENGLISH WORD	GREEK WORD AND VERSE	THE WORD MEANS...

#2776
One Mind
 	
One accord–KJV
One mind–NASB
Together–NIV
One accord–NKJV
Together–NLT
 	
POSB
REFERENCE
(Acts 1:14)
Deeper Study #1
	ὁμοθυμαδόν = *homothumadon*
	Pronunciation: [hom-oth-oo-mad-on']
	Parsing (part of speech): adjective adverb
	   Stem or root—from ὁμοθυμαδόν
	Concordance References:
	  ⇒ Strong's #3661 homothumadon
	  ⇒ NIV #3924 homothumadon
	  ⇒ NASB #3661 homothumadon
	
	Acts 1:14
	These all continued with **one accord** in prayer and supplication, with the women, and Mary the mother of Jesus, and with his brethren. [KJV]
	These all with **one mind** were continually devoting themselves to prayer, along with the women, and Mary the mother of Jesus, and with His brothers. [NASB]
	They all joined **together** constantly in prayer, along with the women and Mary the mother of Jesus, and with his brothers. [NIV]
	These all continued with **one accord** in prayer and supplication, with the women and Mary the mother of Jesus, and with His brothers. [NKJV]
	They all met **together** continually for prayer, along with Mary the mother of Jesus, several other women, and the brothers of Jesus. [NLT]
	οὗτοι πάντες ἦσαν προσκαρτεροῦντες ὁμοθυμαδόν τῇ προσευχῇ καὶ τῇ δεήσει, σὺν γυναιξὶ καὶ Μαριά τῇ μητρὶ τοῦ Ἰησοῦ, καὶ σὺν τοῖς ἀδελφοῖς αὐτοῦ. [GNS]
	οὗτοι πάντες ἦσαν προσκαρτεροῦντες ὁμοθυμαδόν τῇ προσευχῇ σὺν γυναιξὶν καὶ Μαριὰμ τῇ μητρὶ τοῦ Ἰησοῦ καὶ τοῖς ἀδελφοῖς αὐτοῦ. [GNT]
		Together, one mind, one accord; the same mind or spirit; oneness of mind and heart. It means to be one in spirit and purpose. *Homos* means same and *thumos* means spirit or mind.
		
		Practical Application
		The believers, all 120 of them in the upper room, were of the same spirit, of the same mind. The idea is they were after the same thing, the baptism of the Holy Spirit. They were focusing and concentrating their thoughts and energies upon seeking God for the promise of His Spirit.
		The word is used only eleven times in Scripture, ten of those times are found in Acts, one is found in Romans.
		  ⇒ Together in prayer (Acts 1:14; Acts 4:24).
		  ⇒ Together in one place (Acts 2:1).
		  ⇒ Together in daily worship and the Lord's supper (Acts 2:46; Acts 5:12).
		  ⇒ Together in obedience (Acts 8:6).
		  ⇒ Together in a business meeting (Acts 15:25).
		  ⇒ Togetherness is needed to glorify God (Romans 15:6).

#2777
One Mind
 	
One mind–KJV
Like-minded–NASB
One mind–NIV
One mind–NKJV
Harmony–NLT
 	
POSB
REFERENCE
(2 Cor.13:11-13; esp. v.11)
Note 3
	τὸ αὐτὸ φρονεῖτε = *to auto phroneite*
	Pronunciation: [to ow-to' fron-eh'-ee-teh]
	Parsing *phroneite* (part of speech): verb
	   Mood—imperative
	   Tense—present
	   Voice—active
	   Person—2nd person
	   Number—plural
	   Stem or root—from φρονέω
	Concordance References:
	  ⇒ Strong's #846+3588 autos ho + 5426 phroneō
	  ⇒ NIV #899+3836 autos ho [one] + 5858 phroneō [mind]
	  ⇒ NASB #846+3588 autos ho + 5426 phroneō
	
	2 Cor. 13:11
	Finally, brethren, farewell. Be perfect, be of good comfort, be of **one mind**, live in peace; and the God of love and peace shall be with you. [KJV]
	Finally, brethren, rejoice, be made complete, be comforted, be **like-minded**, live in peace; and the God of love and peace shall be with you. [NASB]
	Finally, brothers, good-by. Aim for perfection, listen to my appeal, be of **one mind**, live in peace. And the God of love and peace will be with you. [NIV]
	Finally, brethren, farewell. Become complete. Be of good comfort, be of **one mind**, live in peace; and the God of love and peace will be with you. [NKJV]
	Dear brothers and sisters, I close my letter with these last words: Rejoice. Change your ways. Encourage each other. Live in **harmony** and peace. Then the God of love and peace will be with you. [NLT]
	Λοιπόν, ἀδελφοί, χαίρετε· καταρτίζεσθε, παρακαλεῖσθε, τὸ αὐτὸ φρονεῖτε, εἰρηνεύετε· καὶ ὁ Θεὸς τῆς ἀγάπης καὶ εἰρήνης ἔσται μεθ' ὑμῶν. [GNS]
	Λοιπόν, ἀδελφοί, χαίρετε, καταρτίζεσθε, παρακαλεῖσθε, τὸ αὐτὸ φρονεῖτε, εἰρηνεύετε, καὶ ὁ Θεὸς τῆς ἀγάπης καὶ εἰρήνης ἔσται μεθ' ὑμῶν. [GNT]
		One mind; to be like-minded; to be in harmony; to be of one mind in faith, belief, purpose, mission, and ministry.
		
		Practical Application
		Note that God is the Author, the Giver of love and peace. The believer must therefore accept the challenge to live in harmony with other believers and live accordingly.

ENGLISH WORD	GREEK WORD AND VERSE	THE WORD MEANS...
Opposing ideas–NIV **Contradictions–NKJV** **Oppose–NLT** **POSB REFERENCE** (1 Tim.6:20-21; esp. v.20) Note 2, point 2b	⇒ NIV #509 antithesis ⇒ NASB #477 antithesis ### 1 Tim. 6:20 O Timothy, keep that which is committed to thy trust, avoiding profane and vain babblings, and **oppositions** of science falsely so called: [KJV] O Timothy, guard what has been entrusted to you, avoiding worldly and empty chatter and the **opposing arguments** of what is falsely called "knowledge"— [NASB] Timothy, guard what has been entrusted to your care. Turn away from godless chatter and the **opposing ideas** of what is falsely called knowledge, [NIV] O Timothy! Guard what was committed to your trust, avoiding the profane *and* idle babblings and **contradictions** of what is falsely called knowledge— [NKJV] Timothy, guard what God has entrusted to you. Avoid godless, foolish discussions with those who **oppose** you with their so-called knowledge. [NLT] Ὦ Τιμόθεε, τὴν παρακαταθήκην φύλαξον, ἐκτρεπόμενος τὰς βεβήλους κενοφωνίας καὶ **ἀντιθέσεις** τῆς ψευδωνύμου γνώσεως· [GNS] Ὦ Τιμόθεε, τὴν παραθήκην φύλαξον ἐκτρεπόμενος τὰς βεβήλους κενοφωνίας καὶ **ἀντιθέσεις** τῆς ψευδωνύμου γνώσεως, [GNT]	contrary to God's glorious revelation in Christ and in the Word of God. The minister of God—in fact, any person—is a fool to stand against truth and fact, whether of God or of true science.

#2787
 	
## Opposition Arose 	
 	
Arose–KJV
Rose up–NASB
Opposition arose–NIV
Arose–NKJV
Started–NLT
 	
**POSB
REFERENCE**
(Acts 6:9-10; esp. v.9)
Note 2, point 2
	ἀνέστησαν = anestēsan
	Pronunciation: [an-is'-tay-san]
	Parsing (part of speech): verb
	    Mood—indicative
	    Tense—aorist
	    Voice—active
	    Person—3rd person
	    Number—plural
	    Stem or root—from ἀνίστημι
	Concordance References:
	⇒ Strong's #450 anistemi
	⇒ NIV #482 anistēmi
	⇒ NASB #450 anistemi
	
	### Acts 6:9
	Then there **arose** certain of the synagogue, which is called the synagogue of the Libertines, and Cyrenians, and Alexandrians, and of them of Cilicia and of Asia, disputing with Stephen. [KJV]
	But some men from what was called the Synagogue of the Freedmen, including both Cyrenians and Alexandrians, and some from Cilicia and Asia, **rose up** and argued with Stephen. [NASB]
	Opposition arose, however, from members of the Synagogue of the Freedmen (as it was called)—Jews of Cyrene and Alexandria as well as the provinces of Cilicia and Asia. These men began to argue with Stephen, [NIV]
	Then there **arose** some from what is called the Synagogue of the Freedmen (Cyrenians, Alexandrians, and those from Cilicia and Asia), disputing with Stephen. [NKJV]
	But one day some men from the Synagogue of Freed Slaves, as it was called, **started** to debate with him. They were Jews from Cyrene, Alexandria, Cilicia, and the province of Asia. [NLT]
	ἀνέστησαν δέ τινες τῶν ἐκ τῆς συναγωγῆς τῆς λεγομένης Λιβερτίνων, καὶ Κυρηναίων, καὶ Ἀλεξανδρέων, καὶ τῶν ἀπὸ Κιλικίας καὶ Ἀσίας, συζητοῦντες τῷ Στεφάνῳ. [GNS]
	ἀνέστησαν δέ τινες τῶν ἐκ τῆς συναγωγῆς τῆς λεγομένης Λιβερτίνων καὶ Κυρηναίων καὶ Ἀλεξανδρέων καὶ τῶν ἀπὸ Κιλικίας καὶ Ἀσίας συζητοῦντες τῷ Στεφάνῳ, [GNT]
		Opposition arose; stood up.
		
		### Practical Application
		Five synagogues in particular stood up against Stephen. They opposed what he was preaching. There was a strong reason for the opposition of the Grecian Jews. They and their forefathers had been forcibly deported out of their homeland and scattered across the world by the Romans. While living in the foreign lands of the world, they had remained faithful to their Jewish religion. The message of Jesus Christ was a threat to them and their religion.

ENGLISH WORD	GREEK WORD AND VERSE	THE WORD MEANS...

#2788
Oppositions

Oppositions–KJV
Opposing arguments–NASB
Opposing ideas–NIV
Contradictions–NKJV
Oppose–NLT

**POSB
REFERENCE**
(1 Tim.6:20-21; esp.
v.20)
Note 2, point 2b

ἀντιθέσεις = antitheseis
Pronunciation: [an-tith'-es-is]
Parsing (part of speech): noun
    Case—accusative
    Gender—feminine
    Number—plural
    Stem or root—from ἀντίθεσις, εως
Concordance References:
⇒   Strong's #477 antithesis
⇒   NIV #509 antithesis
⇒   NASB #477 antithesis

1 Tim. 6:20

O Timothy, keep that which is committed to thy trust, avoiding profane and vain babblings, and **oppositions** of science falsely so called: [KJV]

O Timothy, guard what has been entrusted to you, avoiding worldly and empty chatter and the **opposing arguments** of what is falsely called "knowledge"— [NASB]

Timothy, guard what has been entrusted to your care. Turn away from godless chatter and the **opposing ideas** of what is falsely called knowledge, [NIV]

O Timothy! Guard what was committed to your trust, avoiding the profane *and* idle babblings and **contradictions** of what is falsely called knowledge— [NKJV]

Timothy, guard what God has entrusted to you. Avoid godless, foolish discussions with those who **oppose** you with their so-called knowledge. [NLT]

Ὦ Τιμόθεε, τὴν παρακαταθήκην φύλαξον, ἐκτρεπόμενος τὰς βεβήλους κενοφωνίας καὶ **ἀντιθέσεις** τῆς ψευδωνύμου γνώσεως· [GNS]

Ὦ Τιμόθεε, τὴν παραθήκην φύλαξον ἐκτρεπόμενος τὰς βεβήλους κενοφωνίας καὶ **ἀντιθέσεις** τῆς ψευδωνύμου γνώσεως, [GNT]

Opposing ideas, oppositions, opposing arguments, contradiction; to oppose. It means antithesis, that is, to stand against some thesis, truth, or fact.

Practical Application
What is being condemned is the false knowledge of men, the things that men teach that are contrary to God's glorious revelation in Christ and in the Word of God. The minister of God—in fact, any person—is a fool to stand against truth and fact, whether of God or of true science.

#2789
Ordained

Ordained–KJV
Appointed–NASB
Appointed–NIV
Appointed–NKJV
Selected–NLT

**POSB
REFERENCE**
(Mk.3:14)
Deeper Study #1

ἐποίησεν = epoiesen
Pronunciation: [eh-poy-eh'-sen]
Parsing (part of speech): verb
    Mood—indicative
    Tense—aorist
    Voice—active
    Person—3rd person
    Number—singular
    Stem or root—from ποιέω
Concordance References:
⇒   Strong's #4160 poieö
⇒   NIV #4472 poieö
⇒   NASB #4160 poieö

Mark 3:14

And he **ordained** twelve, that they should be with him, and that he might send them forth to preach, [KJV]

And He **appointed** twelve, that they might be with Him, and that He might send them out to preach, [NASB]

He **appointed** twelve—designating them apostles—that they might be with him and that he might send them out to preach [NIV]

Then He **appointed** twelve, that they might be with Him and that He might send them out to preach, [NKJV]

Then he **selected** twelve of them to be his regular companions, calling them apostles. He sent them out to preach, [NLT]

καὶ **ἐποίησε** δώδεκα, ἵνα ὦσι μετ' αὐτοῦ, καὶ ἵνα ἀποστέλλῃ αὐτοὺς κηρύσσειν, [GNS]

καὶ **ἐποίησεν** δώδεκα [οὓς καὶ ἀποστόλους ὠνόμασεν] ἵνα ὦσιν μετ' αὐτοῦ καὶ ἵνα ἀποστέλλῃ αὐτοὺς κηρύσσειν [GNT]

To be ordained, chosen, designated, commissioned, picked, elected, selected, or appointed.

Practical Application
The word is taken from the Greek root word *poieö* which means to do, to make, to appoint with credential. The word is often used to refer to a persons being appointed to some high position or office. The picture is that of Jesus Christ, the future King of the universe, taking twelve men and appointing them to be His. He appointed (ordained) them to the *office* of being His ministers and representatives on earth.

ENGLISH WORD	GREEK WORD AND VERSE	THE WORD MEANS...
Teachings–NIV Traditions–NKJV Christian teaching– NLT **POSB REFERENCE** (1 Cor.11:2) Note 1 **See also POSB REF:** (2 Thes.2:15) Note 4	Number—plural Stem or root—from παράδοσις, εως Concordance References: ⇒ Strong's #3862 paradosis ⇒ NIV #4142 paradosis ⇒ NASB #3862 paradosis **1 Cor. 11:2** Now I praise you, brethren, that ye remember me in all things, and keep the **ordinances**, as I delivered them to you. [KJV] Now I praise you because you remember me in everything, and hold firmly to the **traditions**, just as I delivered them to you. [NASB] I praise you for remembering me in everything and for holding to the **teachings**, just as I passed them on to you. [NIV] Now I praise you, brethren, that you remember me in all things and keep the **traditions** just as I delivered *them* to you. [NKJV] I am so glad, dear friends, that you always keep me in your thoughts and you are following the **Christian teaching** I passed on to you. [NLT] Ἐπαινῶ δὲ ὑμᾶς, ἀδελφοί, ὅτι πάντα μου μέμνησθε καὶ καθὼς παρέδωκα ὑμῖν τὰς **παραδόσεις** κατέχετε. [GNS] Ἐπαινῶ δὲ ὑμᾶς ὅτι πάντα μου μέμνησθε καί, καθὼς παρέδωκα ὑμῖν, τὰς **παραδόσεις** κατέχετε. [GNT]	**Practical Application** This is important to see, for this passage is dealing... • with traditions. • with unwritten laws of behavior. • with customs. • with local practice. • with preferences of a particular people or body. • with long-established patterns of a people or group. Leon Morris quotes J.B. Lightfoot: "The prominent idea of *paradoseis* [tradition]...is that of an authority external to the teacher himself." Leon Morris himself says: *This is another way of putting the truth...that the gospel is not of human origin, and the preacher is not at liberty to substitute his own thoughts for that which he has received (The Epistles of Paul to the Thessalonians. "Tyndale New Testament Commentaries," p.138).*
#2795 **Orgies** Revellings–KJV Carousing–NASB **Orgies–NIV** Revelries–NKJV Wild parties–NLT **POSB REFERENCE** (Gal.5:19-21; esp. v.21) Note 2 **See also POSB REF:** (Rom.13:13) Note 4, point 1	κῶμοι = kōmoi Pronunciation: [ko'-moy] Parsing (part of speech): noun Case—nominative Gender—masculine Number—plural Stem or root—from κῶμος, ου Concordance References: ⇒ Strong's #2970 kōmos ⇒ NIV #3269 kōmos ⇒ NASB #2970 kōmos **Galatians 5:21** Envyings, murders, drunkenness, **revellings**, and such like: of the which I tell you before, as I have also told you in time past, that they which do such things shall not inherit the kingdom of God. [KJV] Envying, drunkenness, **carousing**, and things like these, of which I forewarn you just as I have forewarned you that those who practice such things shall not inherit the kingdom of God. [NASB] And envy; drunkenness, **orgies**, and the like. I warn you, as I did before, that those who live like this will not inherit the kingdom of God. [NIV] Envy, murders, drunkenness, **revelries**, and the like; of which I tell you beforehand, just as I also told *you* in time past, that those who practice such things will not inherit the kingdom of God. [NKJV] Envy, drunkenness, **wild parties**, and other kinds of sin. Let me tell you again, as I have before, that anyone living that sort of life will not inherit the Kingdom of God. [NLT] φθόνοι, φόνοι, μέθαι, **κῶμοι**, καὶ τὰ ὅμοια τούτοις· ἃ προλέγω ὑμῖν, καθὼς καὶ προεῖπον, ὅτι οἱ τὰ τοιαῦτα πράσσοντες βασιλείαν Θεοῦ οὐ κληρονομήσουσιν. [GNS] φθόνοι, μέθαι, **κῶμοι** καὶ τὰ ὅμοια τούτοις, ἃ προλέγω ὑμῖν καθὼς προεῖπον ὅτι οἱ τὰ τοιαῦτα πράσσοντες βασιλείαν θεοῦ οὐ κληρονομήσουσιν. [GNT]	Orgies, rioting, carousing, wild parties. It means reveling, carousing, partying, feasting, intemperance, debauchery, unrestrained revelry and indulgence, giving license to basic urges. **Practical Application** This word graphically describes a life of uncontrolled license, indulgence, and pleasure; taking part in wild parties or in drinking parties; lying around indulging in feeding the lusts of the flesh.
#2796 **Orgies** Revellings–KJV Carousals–NASB	κῶμοις = kōmois Pronunciation: [ko'-moys] Parsing (part of speech): noun Case—dative Gender—masculine Number—plural	Orgies, revellings, carousals; feasting, uncontrolled license, indulgence, and pleasure; taking part in wild parties or in drinking parties or in orgies; lying around indulging in feeding the lusts of the flesh, the desires of the sinful nature.

ENGLISH WORD	GREEK WORD AND VERSE	THE WORD MEANS...
Orgies–NIV Revelries–NKJV Feasting–NLT **POSB REFERENCE** (1 Pt.4:3) Note 3, point 4	Stem or root—from κῶμος, ου Concordance References: ⇒ Strong's #2970 kömos ⇒ NIV #3269 kömos ⇒ NASB #2970 kömos **1 Peter 4:3** For the time past of our life may suffice us to have wrought the will of the Gentiles, when we walked in lasciviousness, lusts, excess of wine, **revellings**, banquetings, and abominable idolatries: [KJV] For the time already past is sufficient for you to have carried out the desire of the Gentiles, having pursued a course of sensuality, lusts, drunkenness, **carousals**, drinking parties and abominable idolatries. [NASB] For you have spent enough time in the past doing what pagans choose to do—living in debauchery, lust, drunkenness, **orgies**, carousing and detestable idolatry. [NIV] For we *have spent* enough of our past lifetime in doing the will of the Gentiles—when we walked in lewdness, lusts, drunkenness, **revelries**, drinking parties, and abominable idolatries. [NKJV] You have had enough in the past of the evil things that godless people enjoy—their immorality and lust, their **feasting** and drunkenness and wild parties, and their terrible worship of idols. [NLT] ἀρκετὸς γὰρ ἡμῖν ὁ παρεληλυθὼς χρόνος τὸ βίου τὸ θέλημα τῶν ἐθνῶν κατεργάσασθαι, πεπορευμένους ἐν ἀσελγείαις, ἐπιθυμίαις, οἰνοφλυγίαις, **κώμοις**, πότοις, καὶ ἀθεμίτοις εἰδωλολατρείαις· [GNS] ἀρκετὸς γὰρ ὁ παρεληλυθὼς χρόνος τὸ βούλημα τῶν ἐθνῶν κατειργάσθαι πεπορευμένους ἐν ἀσελγείαις, ἐπιθυμίαις, οἰνοφλυγίαις, **κώμοις**, πότοις καὶ ἀθεμίτοις εἰδωλολατρίαις. [GNT]	**Practical Application** It is a graphic picture of a life that is out of control, a life that has cast off reason and pursued a course of carousals.
#2797 **Orphans** Comfortless–KJV **Orphans–NASB** **Orphans–NIV** **Orphans–NKJV** **Orphans–NLT** **POSB REFERENCE** (Jn.14:18-20; esp. v.18) Note 4, point 1	ὀρφανούς = orphanous Pronunciation: [or-fan-oos'] Parsing (part of speech): pronominal adjective 　Case—accusative 　Gender—masculine 　Number—plural 　Stem or root—from ὀρφανός, ή, όν Concordance References: ⇒ Strong's #3737 orphanos ⇒ NIV #4003 orphanos ⇒ NASB #3737 orphanos **John 14:18** I will not leave you **comfortless**: I will come to you. [KJV] "I will not leave you as **orphans**; I will come to you. [NASB] I will not leave you as **orphans**; I will come to you. [NIV] I will not leave you **orphans**; I will come to you. [NKJV] No, I will not abandon you as **orphans**—I will come to you. [NLT] οὐκ ἀφήσω ὑμᾶς **ὀρφανούς**· ἔρχομαι πρὸς ὑμᾶς. [GNS] Οὐκ ἀφήσω ὑμᾶς **ὀρφανούς**, ἔρχομαι πρὸς ὑμᾶς. [GNT]	Orphans; comfortless; to be without care of parents; to be alone; to be helpless; to be friendless. **Practical Application** Jesus would not leave them to struggle through the trials of life alone. Jesus' presence with His followers began with His resurrection and with the coming of the Holy Spirit. Jesus was saying that He would come to the believer in the person of the Holy Spirit.
#2798 **Other Way– Other Way, Some** **Some other way–KJV** **Some other way– NASB**	ἀλλαχόθεν = allachothen Pronunciation: [al-lach-oth'-ehn] Parsing (part of speech): adjective 　Type—adverb 　Stem or root—from ἀλλαχόθεν Concordance References: ⇒ Strong's #237 allachothen ⇒ NIV #249 allachothen ⇒ NASB #237a allachothen	To come from elsewhere; to come from some other way; to sneak over. **Practical Application** Some shepherds climb into the sheepfold *from* "some other way" (allachothen). The word from is important. It indicates origin. The false shepherd comes from and originates from...

ENGLISH WORD	GREEK WORD AND VERSE	THE WORD MEANS...

| | unfruitful. [NASB]

Our people must learn to devote themselves to doing what is good, in order that they may provide for daily necessities and not live unproductive lives. [NIV]

And let **our** *people* also learn to maintain good works, to *meet* urgent needs, that they may not be unfruitful. [NKJV]

For **our people** should not have unproductive lives. They must learn to do good by helping others who have urgent needs. [NLT]

μανθανέτωσαν δὲ καὶ **οἱ ἡμέτεροι** καλῶν ἔργων προΐστασθαι εἰς τὰς ἀναγκαίας χρείας, ἵνα μὴ ὦσιν ἄκαρποι. [GNS]

μανθανέτωσαν δὲ καὶ **οἱ ἡμέτεροι** καλῶν ἔργων προΐστασθαι εἰς τὰς ἀναγκαίας χρείας, ἵνα μὴ ὦσιν ἄκαρποι. [GNT] | to do good with their money. They are to help those in need, ministering to help meet the needs of the world. And they are to support men such as Zenas and Apollos, both layman and minister, who have given their lives and time to serve Christ. They are to financially support the spread of the gospel around the world. |

| **#2803**
Ours

Ours–KJV
Our people–NASB
Our people–NIV
Our people–NKJV
Our people–NLT

POSB REFERENCE
(Tit.3:14)
Note 6 | οἱ ἡμέτεροι = *hoi hēmeteroi*
Pronunciation: [oy hay-met'-er-oy]
Parsing *hēmeteroi* (part of speech): pronominal adjective
    Case—nominative
    Gender—masculine
    Person—1st person
    Number—plural
    Stem or root—from ἡμέτερος, α, ον
Concordance References:
  ⇒ Strong's #3588 ho + 2251 hēmeteros
  ⇒ NIV #3836 ho + 2466 hēmeteros [Our people]
  ⇒ NASB #3588 ho + 2251 hēmeteros

Titus 3:14
And let **ours** also learn to maintain good works for necessary uses, that they be not unfruitful. [KJV]

And let **our people** also learn to engage in good deeds to meet pressing needs, that they may not be unfruitful. [NASB]

Our people must learn to devote themselves to doing what is good, in order that they may provide for daily necessities and not live unproductive lives. [NIV]

And let **our** *people* also learn to maintain good works, to *meet* urgent needs, that they may not be unfruitful. [NKJV]

For **our people** should not have unproductive lives. They must learn to do good by helping others who have urgent needs. [NLT]

μανθανέτωσαν δὲ καὶ **οἱ ἡμέτεροι** καλῶν ἔργων προΐστασθαι εἰς τὰς ἀναγκαίας χρείας, ἵνα μὴ ὦσιν ἄκαρποι. [GNS]

μανθανέτωσαν δὲ καὶ **οἱ ἡμέτεροι** καλῶν ἔργων προΐστασθαι εἰς τὰς ἀναγκαίας χρείας, ἵνα μὴ ὦσιν ἄκαρποι. [GNT] | Our people, ours.

Practical Application
Note that Paul calls the believers of Crete "ours" (*hoi hēmeteroi*), an endearing term. The Amplified Bible says:

And let our [own people really] learn to apply themselves to good deeds—to honest labor and honorable employment—so that they may be able to meet necessary demands whenever the occasion may require and not be living idle and uncultivated and unfruitful lives.

The point is that believers are to work and labor in order to make money, and then they are to do good with their money. They are to help those in need, ministering to help meet the needs of the world. And they are to support men such as Zenas and Apollos, both layman and minister, who have given their lives and time to serve Christ. They are to financially support the spread of the gospel around the world. |

| **#2804**
Out Of

From–KJV
Out of–NASB
From–NIV
From–NKJV
From–NLT

POSB REFERENCE
(Jn.6:33)
Note 3, point 1a

See also POSB REF:
(Jn.3:13)
Note 6, point 1 | ἐκ = *ek*
Pronunciation: [ek]
Parsing (part of speech): preposition
    Case—genitive
    Stem or root—from ἐκ
Concordance References:
  ⇒ Strong's #1537 ek
  ⇒ NIV #1666 ek
  ⇒ NASB #1537 ek

John 6:33
For the bread of God is he which cometh down **from** heaven, and giveth life unto the world. [KJV]

"For the bread of God is that which comes down **out of** heaven, and gives life to the world." [NASB]

For the bread of God is he who comes down **from** heaven and gives life to the world." [NIV]

For the bread of God is He who comes down **from** heaven and gives life to the world." [NKJV]

The true bread of God is the one who comes down **from** heaven and gives life to the world." [NLT] | From, out of.

Practical Application
Jesus came out of (*ek*) the spiritual world into the physical world, out of the heavenly dimension of being into the earthly dimension of being. Jesus came out of...
• the incorruptible world into the corruptible world.
• the glorious world into the dishonorable world.
• the powerful world into the weak world.
• the spiritual world into the natural world. (Cp. 1 Cor. 15:42-44).

He came down from (out of) heaven. No man can ascend up into heaven; no man can penetrate the spiritual world. Flesh is flesh, that is, born of the earth; therefore, it is earthly (1 Cor. 15:47). |

ENGLISH WORD	GREEK WORD AND VERSE	THE WORD MEANS...
	ὁ γὰρ ἄρτος τοῦ Θεοῦ ἐστιν ὁ καταβαίνων ἐκ τοῦ οὐρανοῦ, καὶ ζωὴν διδοὺς τῷ κόσμῳ. [GNS] ὁ γὰρ ἄρτος τοῦ θεοῦ ἐστιν ὁ καταβαίνων ἐκ τοῦ οὐρανοῦ καὶ ζωὴν διδοὺς τῷ κόσμῳ. [GNT]	However, Jesus Christ was different from all other men. His origin was out of heaven, out of the spiritual world and dimension of being. (See POSB *Deeper Study* #1—John 3:31; POSB note—John 1:18; POSB *Deeper Study* #1—John 14:6, POSB *Deeper Study* #2—John 14:6, POSB *Deeper Study* #3—John 14:6 for discussion.)

#2805
 Out Of...Mind
 	
 Beside ourselves–KJV
 Beside ourselves– NASB
 Out of...mind–NIV
 Beside ourselves– NKJV
 Crazy–NLT
 	
 POSB REFERENCE
 (2 Cor.5:13)
 Note 3
	ἐξέστημεν = *exestēmen*
	 Pronunciation: [ex-is'-tay-mehn]
	 Parsing (part of speech): verb
	    Mood—indicative
	    Tense—aorist
	    Voice—active
	    Person—1st person
	    Number—plural
	    Stem or root—from ἐξίστημι and ἐξιστάνω
	 Concordance References:
	 ⇒ Strong's #1839 existēmi
	 ⇒ NIV #2014 existēmi
	 ⇒ NASB #1839 existēmi
	
	 2 Cor. 5:13
	 For whether we be **beside ourselves**, it is to God: or whether we be sober, it is for your cause. [KJV]
	 For if we are **beside ourselves**, it is for God; if we are of sound mind, it is for you. [NASB]
	 If we are **out of** our **mind**, it is for the sake of God; if we are in our right mind, it is for you. [NIV]
	 For if we are **beside ourselves**, *it is* for God; or if we are of sound mind, *it is* for you. [NKJV]
	 If it seems that we are **crazy**, it is to bring glory to God. And if we are in our right minds, it is for your benefit. [NLT]
	 εἴτε γὰρ ἐξέστημεν, Θεῷ· εἴτε σωφρονοῦμεν, ὑμῖν. [GNS]
	 εἴτε γὰρ ἐξέστημεν, θεῷ· εἴτε σωφρονοῦμεν, ὑμῖν. [GNT]
		To be crazy; to be beside oneself; to be out of one's mind; to be insane.
		
		 Practical Application
		 One of the charges against Paul was that he was out of his mind (*exestemen*), that he was mad, insane. It means to act in the extreme, abnormally, unlike what others act. Paul was charged with being a "fool" for Christ. Note that he accepts the charge as true.

#2806
 Outbursts Of Anger
 	
 Wraths–KJV
 Angry tempers–NASB
 Outbursts of anger– NIV
 Outbursts of wrath– NKJV
 Outbursts of anger– NLT
 	
 POSB REFERENCE
 (2 Cor.12:19-21; esp. v.20)
 Note 3, point 2
	θυμοί = *thumoi*
	 Pronunciation: [thoo-moy']
	 Parsing (part of speech): noun
	    Case—nominative
	    Gender—masculine
	    Number—plural
	    Stem or root—from θυμός, ου
	 Concordance References:
	 ⇒ Strong's #2372 thumos
	 ⇒ NIV #2596 thumos
	 ⇒ NASB #2372 thumos
	
	 2 Cor. 12:20
	 For I fear, lest, when I come, I shall not find you such as I would, and that I shall be found unto you such as ye would not: lest there be debates, envyings, **wraths**, strifes, backbitings, whisperings, swellings, tumults: [KJV]
	 For I am afraid that perhaps when I come I may find you to be not what I wish and may be found by you to be not what you wish; that perhaps there may be strife, jealousy, **angry tempers**, disputes, slanders, gossip, arrogance, disturbances; [NASB]
	 For I am afraid that when I come I may not find you as I want you to be, and you may not find me as you want me to be. I fear that there may be quarreling, jealousy, **outbursts of anger**, factions, slander, gossip, arrogance and disorder. [NIV]
	 For I fear lest, when I come, I shall not find you such as I wish, and *that* I shall be found by you such as you do not wish; lest *there be* contentions, jealousies, **outbursts of wrath**, selfish ambitions, backbitings, whisperings, conceits, tumults; [NKJV]
	 For I am afraid that when I come to visit you I won't
		Outbursts of anger; angry tempers; wrath; fiery anger; intense fits of anger.
		
		 Practical Application
		 Paul was stricken with fear, fear lest the church fail to be what it should be and reject him and his ministry. Paul feared that the church would fail to deal with the carnal critics and continue putting up with their evil attacks against him. He lists eight evils, including outbursts of anger (*thumoi*), that were and still are characteristic of divisive critics in the church.

ENGLISH WORD	GREEK WORD AND VERSE	THE WORD MEANS...
	like what I find, and then you won't like my response. I am afraid that I will find quarreling, jealousy, **outbursts of anger**, selfishness, backstabbing, gossip, conceit, and disorderly behavior. [NLT] φοβοῦμαι γὰρ μή πως ἐλθὼν οὐχ οἵους θέλω εὕρω ὑμᾶς, κἀγὼ εὑρεθῶ ὑμῖν οἷον οὐ θέλετε· μή πως ἔρις, ζῆλοι, **θυμοί**, ἐριθεῖαι, καταλαλιαί, ψιθυρισμοί, φυσιώσεις, ἀκαταστασίαι· [GNS] φοβοῦμαι γὰρ μή πως ἐλθὼν οὐχ οἵους θέλω εὕρω ὑμᾶς κἀγὼ εὑρεθῶ ὑμῖν οἷον οὐ θέλετε· μή πως ἔρις, ζῆλος, **θυμοί**, ἐριθεῖαι, καταλαλιαί, ψιθυρισμοί, φυσιώσεις, ἀκαταστασίαι· [GNT]	

#2807
Outbursts Of Anger
 	
Wrath–KJV
Outbursts of anger– NASB
Fits of rage–NIV
Outbursts of wrath– NKJV
Outbursts of anger– NLT
 	
POSB REFERENCE
(Gal.5:19-21; esp. v.20)
Note 2
	θυμοί = *thumoi*
	Pronunciation: [thoo-moy']
	Parsing (part of speech): noun
	  Case—nominative
	  Gender—masculine
	  Number—plural
	  Stem or root—from θυμός, ου
	Concordance References:
	  ⇒ Strong's #2372 thumos
	  ⇒ NIV #2596 thumos
	  ⇒ NASB #2372 thumos
	
	Galatians 5:20
	Idolatry, witchcraft, hatred, variance, emulations, **wrath**, strife, seditions, heresies, [KJV]
	Idolatry, sorcery, enmities, strife, jealousy, **outbursts of anger**, disputes, dissensions, factions, [NASB]
	Idolatry and witchcraft; hatred, discord, jealousy, **fits of rage**, selfish ambition, dissensions, factions [NIV]
	Idolatry, sorcery, hatred, contentions, jealousies, **outbursts of wrath**, selfish ambitions, dissensions, heresies, [NKJV]
	Idolatry, participation in demonic activities, hostility, quarreling, jealousy, **outbursts of anger**, selfish ambition, divisions, the feeling that everyone is wrong except those in your own little group, [NLT]
	εἰδωλολατρία, φαρμακεία, ἔχθραι, ἔρεις, ζῆλοι, **θυμοί**, ἐριθεῖαι, διχοστασίαι, αἱρέσεις, [GNS]
	εἰδωλολατρία, φαρμακεία, ἔχθραι, ἔρις, ζῆλος, **θυμοί**, ἐριθεῖαι, διχοστασίαι, αἱρέσεις, [GNT]
		Fits of rage; outbursts of anger; wrath; an intense feeling of indignation.
		
		Practical Application
		It is a violent, explosive temper; quick-tempered explosive reactions that arise from stirred and boiling emotions. But it is anger which fades away just as quickly as it arose. It is not anger that lasts.

#2808
Outbursts Of Wrath
 	
Wraths–KJV
Angry tempers–NASB
Outbursts of anger– NIV
Outbursts of wrath– NKJV
Outbursts of anger– NLT
 	
POSB REFERENCE
(2 Cor.12:19-21; esp. v.20)
Note 3, point 2
	θυμοί = *thumoi*
	Pronunciation: [thoo-moy']
	Parsing (part of speech): noun
	  Case—nominative
	  Gender—masculine
	  Number—plural
	  Stem or root—from θυμός, ου
	Concordance References:
	  ⇒ Strong's #2372 thumos
	  ⇒ NIV #2596 thumos
	  ⇒ NASB #2372 thumos
	
	2 Cor. 12:20
	For I fear, lest, when I come, I shall not find you such as I would, and that I shall be found unto you such as ye would not: lest there be debates, envyings, **wraths**, strifes, backbitings, whisperings, swellings, tumults: [KJV]
	For I am afraid that perhaps when I come I may find you to be not what I wish and may be found by you to be not what you wish; that perhaps there may be strife, jealousy, **angry tempers**, disputes, slanders, gossip, arrogance, disturbances; [NASB]
	For I am afraid that when I come I may not find you as I want you to be, and you may not find me as you want me to be. I fear that there may be quarreling, jealousy, **outbursts of anger**, factions, slander, gossip, arrogance and disorder. [NIV]
	For I fear lest, when I come, I shall not find you such
		Outbursts of anger; angry tempers; wrath; fiery anger; intense fits of anger.
		
		Practical Application
		Paul was stricken with fear, fear lest the church fail to be what it should be and reject him and his ministry. Paul feared that the church would fail to deal with the carnal critics and continue putting up with their evil attacks against him. He lists eight evils, including outbursts of wrath (*thumoi*), that were and still are characteristic of divisive critics in the church.

ENGLISH WORD	GREEK WORD AND VERSE	THE WORD MEANS...
	as I wish, and *that* I shall be found by you such as you do not wish; lest *there be* contentions, jealousies, **outbursts of wrath**, selfish ambitions, backbitings, whisperings, conceits, tumults; [NKJV] For I am afraid that when I come to visit you I won't like what I find, and then you won't like my response. I am afraid that I will find quarreling, jealousy, **outbursts of anger**, selfishness, backstabbing, gossip, conceit, and disorderly behavior. [NLT] φοβοῦμαι γὰρ μή πως ἐλθὼν οὐχ οἵους θέλω εὕρω ὑμᾶς, κἀγὼ εὑρεθῶ ὑμῖν οἷον οὐ θέλετε· μή πως ἔρις, ζῆλοι, **θυμοί**, ἐριθεῖαι, καταλαλιαί, ψιθυρισμοί, φυσιώσεις, ἀκαταστασίαι· [GNS] φοβοῦμαι γὰρ μή πως ἐλθὼν οὐχ οἵους θέλω εὕρω ὑμᾶς κἀγὼ εὑρεθῶ ὑμῖν οἷον οὐ θέλετε· μή πως ἔρις, ζῆλος, **θυμοί**, ἐριθεῖαι, καταλαλιαί, ψιθυρισμοί, φυσιώσεις, ἀκαταστασίαι· [GNT]	

#2809
 	
Outbursts Of Wrath
 	
Wrath–KJV
Outbursts of anger–NASB
Fits of rage–NIV
Outbursts of wrath– NKJV
Outbursts of anger– NLT
 	
POSB REFERENCE
(Gal.5:19-21; esp. v.20)
Note 2
	θυμοί = *thumoi*
	Pronunciation: [thoo-moy']
	Parsing (part of speech): noun
	   Case—nominative
	   Gender—masculine
	   Number—plural
	   Stem or root—from θυμός, ου
	Concordance References:
	  ⇒ Strong's #2372 thumos
	  ⇒ NIV #2596 thumos
	  ⇒ NASB #2372 thumos
	
	Galatians 5:20
	Idolatry, witchcraft, hatred, variance, emulations, **wrath**, strife, seditions, heresies, [KJV]
	Idolatry, sorcery, enmities, strife, jealousy, **outbursts of anger**, disputes, dissensions, factions, [NASB]
	Idolatry and witchcraft; hatred, discord, jealousy, **fits of rage**, selfish ambition, dissensions, factions [NIV]
	Idolatry, sorcery, hatred, contentions, jealousies, **outbursts of wrath**, selfish ambitions, dissensions, heresies, [NKJV]
	Idolatry, participation in demonic activities, hostility, quarreling, jealousy, **outbursts of anger**, selfish ambition, divisions, the feeling that everyone is wrong except those in your own little group, [NLT]
	
	εἰδωλολατρία, φαρμακεία, ἔχθραι, ἔρεις, ζῆλοι, **θυμοί**, ἐριθεῖαι, διχοστασίαι, αἱρέσεις, [GNS]
	
	εἰδωλολατρία, φαρμακεία, ἔχθραι, ἔρις, ζῆλος, **θυμοί**, ἐριθεῖαι, διχοστασίαι, αἱρέσεις, [GNT]
		Fits of rage; outbursts of anger; fury; wrath; an intense feeling of indignation.
		
		Practical Application
		It is a violent, explosive temper; quick-tempered explosive reactions that arise from stirred and boiling emotions. But it is anger which fades away just as quickly as it arose. It is not anger that lasts.

#2810
 	
Overbearing
 	
Selfwilled–KJV
Self-willed–NASB
Overbearing–NIV
Self-willed–NKJV
Arrogant–NLT
 	
POSB REFERENCE
(Tit1:7-8; esp. v.7)
Note 3, point 1a
	αὐθάδη = *authadë*
	Pronunciation: [ow-thad'-ay]
	Parsing (part of speech): adjective
	   Case—accusative
	   Gender—masculine
	   Number—singular
	   Stem or root—from αὐθάδης, ες
	Concordance References:
	  ⇒ Strong's #829 authadës
	  ⇒ NIV #881 authades
	  ⇒ NASB #829 authadës
	
	Titus 1:7
	For a bishop must be blameless, as the steward of God; not **selfwilled**, not soon angry, not given to wine, no striker, not given to filthy lucre; [KJV]
	For the overseer must be above reproach as God's steward, not **self-willed**, not quick-tempered, not addicted to wine, not pugnacious, not fond of sordid gain, [NASB]
	Since an overseer is entrusted with God's work, he must be blameless—not **overbearing**, not quick-tempered, not given to drunkenness, not violent, not pursuing dishonest gain. [NIV]
		Overbearing, self-willed, self-pleasing, arrogant, haughty, and self-centered.
		
		Practical Application
		It is a person who thinks too highly of himself, who looks at his own things and ignores or neglects the things of others. It is a person who is harsh to others; who criticizes, grumbles, and condemns others; who downs others and elevates himself in his own mind.

ENGLISH WORD	GREEK WORD AND VERSE	THE WORD MEANS...
	For a bishop must be blameless, as a steward of God, not **self-willed**, not quick-tempered, not given to wine, not violent, not greedy for money, [NKJV] An elder must live a blameless life because he is God's minister. He must not be **arrogant** or quick-tempered; he must not be a heavy drinker, violent, or greedy for money. [NLT] εἰ γὰρ τὸν ἐπίσκοπον ἀνέγκλητον εἶναι, ὡς Θεοῦ οἰκονόμον· μὴ **αὐθάδη**, μὴ ὀργίλον, μὴ πάροινον, μὴ πλήκτην, μὴ αἰσχροκερδῆ, [GNS] δεῖ γὰρ τὸν ἐπίσκοπον ἀνέγκλητον εἶναι ὡς θεοῦ οἰκονόμον, μὴ **αὐθάδη**, μὴ ὀργίλον, μὴ πάροινον, μὴ πλήκτην, μὴ αἰσχροκερδῆ, [GNT]	

#2811
## Overcharged 	
 	
Overcharged–KJV
Weighted
  down–NASB
Weighed down–NIV
Weighed down–NKJV
Filled with–NLT
 	
**POSB
REFERENCE**
(Lk.21:34-35, esp.
v.34)
Note 1
	βαρηθῶσιν = *barëthösin*
	Pronunciation: [ba-ray'-tho-sin]
	Parsing (part of speech): verb
	  Mood—subjunctive
	  Tense—aorist
	  Voice—passive
	  Person—3rd person
	  Number—plural
	  Stem or root—from βαρέω
	Concordance References:
	⇒ Strong's #925 baruno or #916 bareö
	⇒ NIV #976 bareö
	⇒ NASB #916 bareö
	
	### Luke 21:34
	And take heed to yourselves, lest at any time your hearts be **overcharged** with surfeiting, and drunkenness, and cares of this life, and so that day come upon you unawares. [KJV]
	
	"Be on guard, that your hearts may not be **weighted down** with dissipation and drunkenness and the worries of life, and that day come on you suddenly like a trap; [NASB]
	
	"Be careful, or your hearts will be **weighed down** with dissipation, drunkenness and the anxieties of life, and that day will close on you unexpectedly like a trap. [NIV]
	
	"But take heed to yourselves, lest your hearts be **weighed down** with carousing, drunkenness, and cares of this life, and that Day come on you unexpectedly. [NKJV]
	
	"Watch out! Don't let me find you living in careless ease and drunkenness, and **filled with** the worries of this life. Don't let that day catch you unaware, [NLT]
	
	Προσέχετε δὲ ἑαυτοῖς, μήποτε **βαρυνθῶσιν** ὑμῶν αἱ καρδίαι ἐν κραιπάλῃ καὶ μέθῃ καὶ μερίμναις βιωτικαῖς, καὶ αἰφνίδιος ἐφ' ὑμᾶς ἐπιστῇ ἡ ἡμέρα ἐκείνη· [GNS]
	
	Προσέχετε δὲ ἑαυτοῖς μήποτε **βαρηθῶσιν** ὑμῶν αἱ καρδίαι ἐν κραιπάλῃ καὶ μέθῃ καὶ μερίμναις βιωτικαῖς καὶ ἐπιστῇ ἐφ' ὑμᾶς αἰφνίδιος ἡ ἡμέρα ἐκείνη [GNT]
		Heavy, weighed down, burdened, overloaded, filled up, indulged.
		
		### Practical Application
		The believer's heart is not to be weighed down with the worldliness described in this verse. Three worldly acts in particular are mentioned.
		1. Dissipation (*kraipale*). The word means to be light-hearted, silly, frivolous, giddy. Medically, it referred to drunken nausea or headaches. It is the kind of light-heartedness, silliness, frivolity, and giddiness that comes from partying and drinking.
		2. Drunkenness (*methei*). The word comes from the word meaning wine (*methu*). It means to be drunk with wine (or any other strong drink or drug), to be intoxicated.
		3. Anxieties of this life. This means to indulge one's cravings for more and more of the things of this world. Man too often gives his attention and focuses his mind upon more and more of this world. He desires far more than what he needs, more...
		• food and delicacies
		• clothes and the latest styles
		• houses and furnishings
		• property and holdings
		• cars and other vehicles
		• free time and recreation
		• money and wealth
		• recognition and esteem

#2812
## Overflow 	
 	
Abound–KJV
Abound–NASB
Overflow–NIV
Abound–NKJV
Overflow–NLT
 	
**POSB
REFERENCE**
(1 Th.3:12)
Note 2
	περισσεύσαι = *perisseusai*
	Pronunciation: [per-is-syoo'-sah-ee]
	Parsing (part of speech): verb
	  Mood—optative
	  Tense—aorist
	  Voice—active
	  Person—3rd person
	  Number—singular
	  Stem or root—from περισσεύω
	Concordance References:
	⇒ Strong's #4052 perisseuö
	⇒ NIV #4355 perisseuö
	⇒ NASB #4052 perisseuö
	
	### 1 Thes. 3:12
	And the Lord make you to increase and **abound** in love one toward another, and toward all men, even as we do toward you: [KJV]
		To increase; to overflow; to multiply; to abound; to be rampant. The word "overflow" (*perisseusai*) means to excel and overflow (Amplified New Testament).
		
		### Practical Application
		The great need is to grow in love—to overflow and multiply—to excel and overflow in love. But note the crucial point: the love being spoken about is not what the world means by love. This is seen in two significant points.
		1. The love that we must grow in is the love that makes us love *all men*, not just one another.
		2. The source of love is the Lord. There is no other source, not for the kind of love that can love *all men*. This is the reason Paul went

ENGLISH WORD	GREEK WORD AND VERSE	THE WORD MEANS...
	And may the Lord cause you to increase and **abound** in love for one another, and for all men, just as we also do for you; [NASB] May the Lord make your love increase and **overflow** for each other and for everyone else, just as ours does for you. [NIV] And may the Lord make you increase and **abound** in love to one another and to all, just as we do to you, [NKJV] And may the Lord make your love grow and **overflow** to each other and to everyone else, just as our love overflows toward you. [NLT] ὑμᾶς δὲ ὁ Κύριος πλεονάσαι καὶ **περισσεύσαι** τῇ ἀγάπῃ εἰς ἀλλήλους καὶ εἰς πάντας, καθάπερ καὶ ἡμεῖς εἰς ὑμᾶς, [GNS] ὑμᾶς δὲ ὁ κύριος πλεονάσαι καὶ **περισσεύσαι** τῇ ἀγάπῃ εἰς ἀλλήλους καὶ εἰς πάντας καθάπερ καὶ ἡμεῖς εἰς ὑμᾶς, [GNT]	before the Lord and requested such a love. Paul knew that it was impossible for him or the Thessalonians to work up the kind of love that could reach out and overflow toward all men.

#2813
Overlooked
 	
Winked–KJV
Overlooked–NASB
Overlooked–NIV
Overlooked–NKJV
Overlooked–NLT
 	
POSB REFERENCE
(Acts 17:29-30; esp. v.30)
Note 7, point 2
	ὑπεριδών = huperidōn
	Pronunciation: [hoop-er-i'-doawn]
	Parsing (part of speech): verb
	   Mood—participle
	   Tense—aorist
	   Voice—active
	   Case—nominative
	   Gender—masculine
	   Number—singular
	   Stem or root—from ὑπεροράω
	Concordance References:
	⇒ Strong's #5237 huperoraō
	⇒ NIV #5666 huperoraō
	⇒ NASB #5237 huperoraō
	
	Acts 17:30
	And the times of this ignorance God **winked** at; but now commandeth all men every where to repent: [KJV]
	
	"Therefore having **overlooked** the times of ignorance, God is now declaring to men that all everywhere should repent, [NASB]
	
	In the past God **overlooked** such ignorance, but now he commands all people everywhere to repent. [NIV]
	
	Truly, these times of ignorance God **overlooked**, but now commands all men everywhere to repent, [NKJV]
	
	God **overlooked** people's former ignorance about these things, but now he commands everyone everywhere to turn away from idols and turn to him. [NLT]
	
	τοὺς μὲν οὖν χρόνους τῆς ἀγνοίας **ὑπεριδὼν** ὁ Θεός, τὰ νῦν παραγγέλλει τοῖς ἀνθρώποις πᾶσι πανταχοῦ μετανοεῖν· [GNS]
	
	τοὺς μὲν οὖν χρόνους τῆς ἀγνοίας **ὑπεριδὼν** ὁ Θεὸς, τὰ νῦν παραγγέλλει τοῖς ἀνθρώποις πάντας πανταχοῦ μετανοεῖν, [GNT]
		To overlook; to wink; to disregard.
		
		Practical Application
		Before now God overlooked or winked at man's ignorance—not in the sense of closing His eyes or of condoning man's idolatry, but He overlooked man's ignorance until He could prepare man for the coming of His Son. Now God's Son has come, and God demands that all men repent (see POSB *Deeper Study* #1—Acts 17:29-30).

#2814
Overseer
 	
Bishop–KJV
Guardian–NASB
Overseer–NIV
Overseer–NKJV
Guardian–NLT
 	
POSB REFERENCE
(1 Pt.2:25)
Note 3, point 2
	ἐπίσκοπον = episkopon
	Pronunciation: [ep-is'-kop-on]
	Parsing (part of speech): noun
	   Case—accusative
	   Gender—masculine
	   Number—singular
	   Stem or root—from ἐπίσκοπος, ου
	Concordance References:
	⇒ Strong's #1985 episkopos
	⇒ NIV #2176 episkopos
	⇒ NASB #1985 episkopos
	
	1 Peter 2:25
	For ye were as sheep going astray; but are now returned unto the Shepherd and **Bishop** of your souls. [KJV]
	
	For you were continually straying like sheep, but now you have returned to the Shepherd and **Guardian** of your souls. [NASB]
		Overseer and caretaker, guardian, protector, guide, and director (William Barclay. *The Letters of James and Peter*, p.258).
		
		Practical Application
		It is the picture of Christ's watching over our souls and looking after them with the greatest of care. Jesus Christ is our Overseer, Caretaker, Guardian, Protector, Guide, and Director. When we come to Him, He takes complete charge of our lives.

ENGLISH WORD	GREEK WORD AND VERSE	THE WORD MEANS...
	For you were like sheep going astray, but now you have returned to the Shepherd and **Overseer** of your souls. [NIV] For you were like sheep going astray, but have now returned to the Shepherd and **Overseer** of your souls. [NKJV] Once you were wandering like lost sheep. But now you have turned to your Shepherd, the **Guardian** of your souls. [NLT] ἦτε γὰρ ὡς πρόβατα πλανώμενα· ἀλλ ἐπεστράφητε νῦν ἐπὶ τὸν ποιμένα καὶ **ἐπίσκοπον** τῶν ψυχῶν ὑμῶν. [GNS] ἦτε γὰρ ὡς πρόβατα πλανώμενοι, ἀλλὰ ἐπεστράφητε νῦν ἐπὶ τὸν ποιμένα καὶ **ἐπίσκοπον** τῶν ψυχῶν ὑμῶν. [GNT]	

#2815
Overseers
 	
Overseers–KJV
Overseers–NASB
Overseers–NIV
Overseers–NKJV
Elders–NLT
 	
POSB REFERENCE
(Acts 20:28-31; esp. v.28)
Note 2, point 2
	ἐπισκόπους = *episkopous*
	Pronunciation: [ep-is'-kop-oos]
	Parsing (part of speech): noun
	  Case—accusative
	  Gender—masculine
	  Number—plural
	  Stem or root—from **ἐπίσκοπος**, ου
	Concordance References:
	⇒ Strong's #1985 episkopos
	⇒ NIV #2176 episkopos
	⇒ NASB #1985 episkopos
	
	### Acts 20:28
	Take heed therefore unto yourselves, and to all the flock, over the which the Holy Ghost hath made you **overseers**, to feed the church of God, which he hath purchased with his own blood. [KJV]
	
	"Be on guard for yourselves and for all the flock, among which the Holy Spirit has made you **overseers**, to shepherd the church of God which He purchased with His own blood. [NASB]
	
	Keep watch over yourselves and all the flock of which the Holy Spirit has made you **overseers**. Be shepherds of the church of God, which he bought with his own blood. [NIV]
	
	Therefore take heed to yourselves and to all the flock, among which the Holy Spirit has made you **overseers**, to shepherd the church of God which He purchased with His own blood. [NKJV]
	
	"And now beware! Be sure that you feed and shepherd God's flock—his church—purchased with his blood—over whom the Holy Spirit has appointed you as **elders**. [NLT]
	
	προσέχετε οὖν ἑαυτοῖς καὶ παντὶ τῷ ποιμνίῳ, ἐν ᾧ ὑμᾶς τὸ Πνεῦμα τὸ Ἅγιον ἔθετο **ἐπισκόπους**, ποιμαίνειν τὴν ἐκκλησίαν τοῦ Θεοῦ, ἣν περιεποιήσατο διὰ τοῦ ἰδίου αἵματος. [GNS]
	
	προσέχετε ἑαυτοῖς καὶ παντὶ τῷ ποιμνίῳ, ἐν ᾧ ὑμᾶς τὸ πνεῦμα τὸ ἅγιον ἔθετο **ἐπισκόπους** ποιμαίνειν τὴν ἐκκλησίαν τοῦ θεοῦ, ἣν περιεποιήσατο διὰ τοῦ αἵματος τοῦ ἰδίου. [GNT]
		Overseers, elders, guardians, bishops.
		
		### Practical Application
		Note the terms are used interchangeably: elder (Acts 20:17), bishop (Acts 20:28), overseer or *episkopate* (Acts 20:28), and shepherd (feed, Acts 20:28). (See POSB *Deeper Study* #1, Elder—Titus 1:5-9 for discussion.)

#2816
Overseers
 	
Bishops–KJV
Overseers–NASB
Overseers–NIV
Bishops–NKJV
Elders–NLT
 	
POSB REFERENCE
(Philip.1:1)
Note 4, point 1
	ἐπισκόποις = *episkopois*
	Pronunciation: [ep-is'-kop-oys]
	Parsing (part of speech): noun
	  Case—dative
	  Gender—masculine
	  Number—plural
	  Stem or root—from **ἐπίσκοπος**, ου
	Concordance References:
	⇒ Strong's #1985 episkopos
	⇒ NIV #2176 episkopos
	⇒ NASB #1985 episkopos
	
	### Philip. 1:1
	Paul and Timotheus, the servants of Jesus Christ, to all the saints in Christ Jesus which are at Philippi, with the **bishops** and deacons: [KJV]
	
	Paul and Timothy, bond-servants of Christ Jesus, to all the saints in Christ Jesus who are in Philippi, including the
		To oversee, look after, manage, guard; to be an elder, a bishop.
		
		### Practical Application
		The overseers (*episkopois*) were apparently the same as the elders (*presbuteros*) or ministers of a church. The two words are used interchangeably to refer to the same men (Acts 20:17, 28; Titus 1:5, 7).
		
		The instructions in the Epistle of Titus say that his duties included primarily exhortation and overseeing the lives of the believers. The overseer was the person whom we call the minister of the church. (See POSB *Deeper Study* #1—Titus 1:5-9 for full discussion.)

ENGLISH WORD	GREEK WORD AND VERSE	THE WORD MEANS...
	overseers and deacons: [NASB] Paul and Timothy, servants of Christ Jesus, To all the saints in Christ Jesus at Philippi, together with the **overseers** and deacons: [NIV] Paul and Timothy, bondservants of Jesus Christ, To all the saints in Christ Jesus who are in Philippi, with the **bishops** and deacons: [NKJV] This letter is from Paul and Timothy, slaves of Christ Jesus. It is written to all of God's people in Philippi, who believe in Christ Jesus, and to the **elders** and deacons. [NLT] Παῦλος καὶ Τιμόθεος δοῦλοι Ἰησοῦ Χριστοῦ, πᾶσι τοῖς ἁγίοις ἐν Χριστῷ Ἰησοῦ τοῖς οὖσιν ἐν Φιλίπποις, σὺν **ἐπισκόποις** καὶ διακόνοις· [GNS] Παῦλος καὶ Τιμόθεος δοῦλοι Χριστοῦ Ἰησοῦ πᾶσιν τοῖς ἁγίοις ἐν Χριστῷ Ἰησοῦ τοῖς οὖσιν ἐν Φιλίπποις σὺν **ἐπισκόποις** καὶ διακόνοις, [GNT]	

#2817
Overwhelmed With Wonder
 	
Greatly amazed–KJV
Amazed–NASB
Overwhelmed with wonder–NIV
Greatly amazed–NKJV
In awe–NLT
 	
POSB REFERENCE
(Mk.9:15)
Deeper Study #1
	ἐξεθαμβήθησαν = *exethambēthēsan*
	Pronunciation: [ek-eh-tham-bayth'-ay-sahn]
	Parsing (part of speech): verb
	    Mood—indicative
	    Tense—aorist
	    Voice—passive
	    Person—3rd person
	    Number—plural
	    Stem or root—from ἐκθαμβέομαι
	Concordance References:
	  ⇒ Strong's #1568 ekthambeo
	  ⇒ NIV #1701 ekthambeö
	  ⇒ NASB #1568 ekthambeo
	
	Mark 9:15
	And straightway all the people, when they beheld him, were **greatly amazed**, and running to *him* saluted him. [KJV]
	And immediately, when the entire crowd saw Him, they were **amazed**, and *began* running up to greet Him. [NASB]
	As soon as all the people saw Jesus, they were **overwhelmed with wonder** and ran to greet him. [NIV]
	Immediately, when they saw Him, all the people were **greatly amazed**, and running to *Him,* greeted Him. [NKJV]
	The crowd watched Jesus **in awe** as he came toward them, and then they ran to greet him. [NLT]
	καὶ εὐθέως πᾶς ὁ ὄχλος ἰδὼν αὐτὸν **ἐξεθαμβήθη**, καὶ προστρέχοντες ἠσπάζοντο αὐτόν. [GNS]
	καὶ εὐθὺς πᾶς ὁ ὄχλος ἰδόντες αὐτὸν **ἐξεθαμβήθησαν** καὶ προστρέχοντες ἠσπάζοντο αὐτόν. [GNT]
		To be filled with wonder; to be overwhelmed with wonder and awe; to be amazed—greatly amazed.
		
		Practical Application
		What amazed the people when they "saw" Jesus?
		1. Perhaps Jesus retained some of the glory of the transfiguration. The people may have seen a glow, a majestic countenance about Jesus. (cp. Exodus 34:29 when Moses came down from the mountain after having been with God).
		2. Perhaps Jesus came at such an opportune time that the people were amazed to see Him, as though His timing were destined. He arrived just when His disciples needed help.
		3. Perhaps Jesus walked with a renewed aire, a more authoritative and decisive countenance than before. Just coming from the transfiguration was bound to instill a renewed confidence and authority within Him.

#2818
Own, On Its
 	
Of herself–KJV
By itself–NASB
All by itself–NIV
By itself–NKJV
On its own–NLT
 	
POSB REFERENCE
(Mk.4:28)
Note 4
	αὐτομάτη = *automate*
	Pronunciation: [ow-tom'-at-eh]
	Parsing (part of speech): adjective
	    Case—nominative
	    Gender—feminine
	    Number—singular
	    Stem or root—from αὐτόματος, η, ον
	Concordance References:
	  ⇒ Strong's #844 automatos
	  ⇒ NIV #897 automatos
	  ⇒ NASB #844 automatos
	
	Mark 4:28
	For the earth bringeth forth fruit **of herself**; first the blade, then the ear, after that the full corn in the ear. [KJV]
	"The soil produces crops **by itself**; first the blade, then the head, then the mature grain in the head. [NASB]
	All by itself the soil produces grain—first the stalk, then the head, then the full kernel in the head. [NIV]
	For the earth yields crops **by itself**: first the blade, then the head, after that the full grain in the head. [NKJV]
	Because the earth produces crops **on its own**. First a
		All by itself, on its own, of herself, automatically, spontaneously, of necessity, self-moving.
		
		Practical Application
		The idea is that the earth brings forth fruit automatically, by its very nature. Note two facts.
		1. Growth is sure, inevitable. But two conditions are essential. The ground must be "good soil" (Mark 4:20) and the seed must be sown in the ground. If these two conditions exist, then growth is both inevitable and unstoppable. Even a small blade of grass will find a crack in the pavement. Nothing can stop the seed from growing. (See POSB outline—Romans 8:28-39 and POSB notes—Romans 8:28-39 for more discussion.)
		2. Growth is constant, but it is gradual, ever so gradual. The seed is sown, and then day after day and night after night passes before the blade ever springs up. Then many more days

ENGLISH WORD	GREEK WORD AND VERSE	THE WORD MEANS...
	leaf blade pushes through, then the heads of wheat are formed, and finally the grain ripens. [NLT] αὐτομάτη γὰρ ἡ γῆ καρποφορεῖ, πρῶτον χόρτον, εἶτα στάχυν, εἶτα πλήρη σῖτον ἐν τῷ στάχυϊ. [GNS] αὐτομάτη ἡ γῆ καρποφορεῖ, πρῶτον χόρτον εἶτα στάχυν εἶτα πλήρη[ς] σῖτον ἐν τῷ στάχυϊ. [GNT]	and nights pass before the ear forms. It takes weeks before the full ear of corn appears. Growth does take place; it is constant—but growth is gradual. It does take time; it does not happen overnight.

ENGLISH WORD	GREEK WORD AND VERSE	THE WORD MEANS...

#2819
Paid
 	
Honour–KJV
Honor–NASB
Honor–NIV
Honor–NKJV
Paid–NLT
 	
**POSB
REFERENCE**
(1 Tim.5:17)
Note 1
 	
See also POSB REF:
(Rom.2:7)
Deeper Study #2
(Jn.4:44)
Note 2
(Rom.12:10)
Note 1, point 4
	τιμῆς = *timës*
	Pronunciation: [tee-mays']
	Parsing (part of speech): noun
	    Case—genitive
	    Gender—feminine
	    Number—singular
	    Stem or root—from τιμή, ῆς
	Concordance References:
	  ⇒ Strong's #5092 timë
	  ⇒ NIV #5507 timë
	  ⇒ NASB #5092 timë
	
	1 Tim. 5:17
	Let the elders that rule well be counted worthy of double **honour**, especially they who labour in the word and doctrine. [KJV]
	Let the elders who rule well be considered worthy of double **honor**, especially those who work hard at preaching and teaching. [NASB]
	The elders who direct the affairs of the church well are worthy of double **honor**, especially those whose work is preaching and teaching. [NIV]
	Let the elders who rule well be counted worthy of double **honor**, especially those who labor in the word and doctrine. [NKJV]
	Elders who do their work well should be **paid** well, especially those who work hard at both preaching and teaching. [NLT]
	Οἱ καλῶς προεστῶτες πρεσβύτεροι διπλῆς **τιμῆς** ἀξιούσθωσαν, μάλιστα οἱ κοπιῶντες ἐν λόγῳ καὶ διδασκαλίᾳ· [GNS]
	Οἱ καλῶς προεστῶτες πρεσβύτεροι διπλῆς **τιμῆς** ἀξιούσθωσαν, μάλιστα οἱ κοπιῶντες ἐν λόγῳ καὶ διδασκαλίᾳ. [GNT]
		To honor; to value; to fairly compensate. The word "paid" (*timës*) means more than just esteem and respect. It means to pay and bestow what is due.
		
		Practical Application
		A minister is due an honorarium; he is due compensation, some pay, some wage for his labor. And, if he performs his duty well—labors and labors and works and works—then he is to be paid well. Is this to be taken literally? Is the church to pay him a double salary? A.T. Robertson states that there are "numerous examples of Roman soldiers who received double pay for unusual services" (*Word Pictures in the New Testament*, Vol.4, p.588). One thing is sure: double pay means adequate, ample, sufficient, and generous financial support.

#2820
**Paid A Ransom
To Save You**
 	
Redeemed–KJV
Redeemed–NASB
Redeemed–NIV
Redeemed–NKJV
**Paid a ransom to
save you–NLT**
 	
**POSB
REFERENCE**
(1 Pt.1:18-20; esp.
v.18)
Note 4
	ἐλυτρώθητε = *elutröthëte*
	Pronunciation: [eh-loo-tro'-tahy-teh]
	Parsing (part of speech): verb
	    Mood—indicative
	    Tense—aorist
	    Voice—passive
	    Person—2nd person
	    Number—plural
	    Stem or root—from λυτρόομαι
	Concordance References:
	  ⇒ Strong's #3084 lutroö
	  ⇒ NIV #3390 lutroö
	  ⇒ NASB #3084 lutroö
	
	1 Peter 1:18
	Forasmuch as ye know that ye were not **redeemed** with corruptible things, as silver and gold, from your vain conversation received by tradition from your fathers; [KJV]
	Knowing that you were not **redeemed** with perishable things like silver or gold from your futile way of life inherited from your forefathers, [NASB]
	For you know that it was not with perishable things such as silver or gold that you were **redeemed** from the empty way of life handed down to you from your forefathers, [NIV]
	Knowing that you were not **redeemed** with corruptible things, *like* silver or gold, from your aimless conduct *received* by tradition from your fathers, [NKJV]
	For you know that God **paid a ransom to save you** from the empty life you inherited from your ancestors. And the ransom he paid was not mere gold or silver. [NLT]
	εἰδότες ὅτι οὐ φθαρτοῖς ἀργυρίῳ ἢ χρυσίῳ, **ἐλυτρώθητε** ἐκ τῆς ματαίας ὑμῶν ἀναστροφῆς πατροπαραδότου, [GNS]
	εἰδότες ὅτι οὐ φθαρτοῖς, ἀργυρίῳ ἢ χρυσίῳ, **ἐλυτρώθητε** ἐκ τῆς ματαίας ὑμῶν ἀναστροφῆς πατροπαραδότου [GNT]
		To redeem; to liberate; to set free or deliver by paying some ransom.
		
		Practical Application
		Note three significant points.
		1. We need to be redeemed, to be set free from the empty life that we have been taught to live by our forefathers.
		2. We are freely redeemed: redemption does not cost us a penny. We are not redeemed by silver and gold. Note why. Because they are corruptible; that is, silver and gold perish. Money passes away. Therefore, if we were able to buy redemption with money, our redemption would last only as long as our money lasted. When it deteriorated and passed away, the payment for our ransom would no longer exist. Therefore, God's righteousness and justice would no longer be able to accept us. Once again, we would stand guilty before Him. Why? Because God is eternal; therefore, the ransom demanded by His justice is an eternal ransom. If we are going to be delivered from this corruptible world and given eternal life, then the ransom paid for our release has to be an eternal ransom—a ransom that will last as long as we are going to be living. This is the reason silver and gold are totally inadequate in redeeming us.
		3. We are redeemed by the precious blood of Christ. A.T. Robertson says, "The blood of anyone is 'precious' [costly] far above gold or silver, but that of Jesus immeasurably more so" (A.T. Robertson. *Word Pictures in the New Testament*, Vol.6, p.90).

ENGLISH WORD	GREEK WORD AND VERSE	THE WORD MEANS...

#2821
Paid Close Attention
 	
Gave heed–KJV
Giving attention–NASB
Paid close attention–NIV
Heeded–NKJV
Listened intently–NLT
 	
POSB REFERENCE
(Acts 8:6)
Note 2, point 2
	προσεῖχον = *proseichon*
	Pronunciation: [pros-eekh'-on]
	Parsing (part of speech): verb
	    Mood—indicative
	    Tense—imperfect
	    Voice—active
	    Person—3rd person
	    Number—plural
	    Stem or root—from προσέχω
	Concordance References:
	⇒ Strong's #4337 prosechō
	⇒ NIV #4668 prosechō
	⇒ NASB #4337 prosechō
	
	Acts 8:6
	And the people with one accord **gave heed** unto those things which Philip spake, hearing and seeing the miracles which he did. [KJV]
	And the multitudes with one accord were **giving attention** to what was said by Philip, as they heard and saw the signs which he was performing. [NASB]
	When the crowds heard Philip and saw the miraculous signs he did, they all **paid close attention** to what he said. [NIV]
	And the multitudes with one accord **heeded** the things spoken by Philip, hearing and seeing the miracles which he did. [NKJV]
	Crowds **listened intently** to what he had to say because of the miracles he did. [NLT]
	προσεῖχον τὲ οἱ ὄχλοι τοῖς λεγομένοις ὑπὸ τοῦ Φιλίππου ὁμοθυμαδὸν, ἐν τῷ ἀκούειν αὐτοὺς καὶ βλέπειν τὰ σημεῖα ἃ ἐποίει. [GNS]
	προσεῖχον δὲ οἱ ὄχλοι τοῖς λεγομένοις ὑπὸ τοῦ Φιλίππου ὁμοθυμαδὸν ἐν τῷ ἀκούειν αὐτοὺς καὶ βλέπειν τὰ σημεῖα ἃ ἐποίει· [GNT]
		To pay close attention; to give attention; to listen intently; to heed.
		
		Practical Application
		The believer must "pay close attention"; must keep his mind and heart upon the message.

#2822
Paid No Attention
 	
Made light of it–KJV
Paid no attention–NASB
Paid no attention–NIV
Made light of it–NKJV
Ignored them–NLT
 	
POSB REFERENCE
(Mt.22:3-7; esp. v.5)
Note 2, point 3
	ἀμελήσαντες = *amelēsantes*
	Pronunciation: [am-el-ay'-sahn-tehs]
	Parsing (part of speech): verb
	    Mood—participle
	    Tense—aorist
	    Voice—active
	    Case—nominative
	    Gender—masculine
	    Number—plural
	    Stem or root—from ἀμελέω
	Concordance References:
	⇒ Strong's #272 ameleō
	⇒ NIV #288 ameleō
	⇒ NASB #272 ameleō
	
	Matthew 22:5
	But they **made light of it**, and went their ways, one to his farm, another to his merchandise: [KJV]
	"But they **paid no attention** and went their way, one to his own farm, another to his business, [NASB]
	"But they **paid no attention** and went off—one to his field, another to his business. [NIV]
	But they **made light of it** and went their ways, one to his own farm, another to his business. [NKJV]
	But the guests he had invited **ignored them** and went about their business, one to his farm, another to his store. [NLT]
	οἱ δὲ ἀμελήσαντες ἀπῆλθον, ὁ μὲν εἰς τὸν ἴδιον ἀγρόν, ὁ δὲ εἰς τὴν ἐμπορίαν αὐτοῦ· [GNS]
	οἱ δὲ ἀμελήσαντες ἀπῆλθον, ὃς μὲν εἰς τὸν ἴδιον ἀγρόν, ὃς δὲ ἐπὶ τὴν ἐμπορίαν αὐτοῦ· [GNT]
		To pay no attention; to make light of; to ignore; to care little if any; to be careless; to disregard; to neglect.
		
		Practical Application
		In the Greek this is an aorist participle: they subjects of the King were making light of the King's gracious invitation to attend His Son's wedding banquetit.
		They were definite in their decision not to attend the Great Wedding Banquet or Marriage Feast. They were careless and negligent about it. They were too busy to be concerned with the King's invitation, too busy with the world making a living and getting more and more for pleasure and comfort (cp. James 4:13).

#2823
Painful
	ἐν λύπῃ = *en lupē*
	Pronunciation: [en loo'-pay]
	Parsing *lupē* (part of speech): noun
	    Case—dative
	    Gender—feminine
		Painful; sorrow; in heaviness, grief, pain, regret.

ENGLISH WORD	GREEK WORD AND VERSE	THE WORD MEANS...
In heaviness–KJV Sorrow–NASB **Painful–NIV** Sorrow–NKJV **Painful–NLT** **POSB REFERENCE** (2 Cor.2:1) Note 2	Number—singular Stem or root—from λύπη, ης Concordance References: ⇒ Strong's #1722+3077 en lupë ⇒ NIV #1877+3383 en lupë ⇒ NASB #1722+3077 en lupë **2 Cor. 2:1** But I determined this with myself, that I would not come again to you **in heaviness**. [KJV] But I determined this for my own sake, that I would not come to you in **sorrow** again. [NASB] So I made up my mind that I would not make another **painful** visit to you. [NIV] But I determined this within myself, that I would not come again to you in **sorrow**. [NKJV] So I said to myself, "No, I won't do it. I won't make them unhappy with another **painful** visit." [NLT] ἔκρινα δὲ ἐμαυτῷ τοῦτο, τὸ μὴ πάλιν ἐλθεῖν **ἐν λύπῃ** πρὸς ὑμᾶς. [GNS] ἔκρινα γὰρ ἐμαυτῷ τοῦτο τὸ μὴ πάλιν **ἐν λύπῃ** πρὸς ὑμᾶς ἐλθεῖν. [GNT]	**Practical Application** It was best for the minister not to be the cause of pain. Note Paul's words, "So I made up my mind that I would not make another *painful* visit to you." [NIV] This just cannot apply to Paul's first visit to Corinth, for his first visit did not end in failure and rejection. When Paul first left Corinth, he was filled with joy over the great success God had given. Therefore, he must be speaking about some other visit when the church rejected him and cut his heart, causing great heaviness.
#2824 **Pains** **Pains–KJV** Agony–NASB Agony–NIV **Pains–NKJV** Horrors–NLT **POSB REFERENCE** (Acts 2:24) *Deeper Study* #4, point 2	**ὠδῖνας** = ödinas Pronunciation: [o-deen'-ahs] Parsing (part of speech): noun Case—accusative Gender—feminine Number—plural Stem or root—from ὠδίν Concordance References: ⇒ Strong's #5604 ödin ⇒ NIV #6047 ödin ⇒ NASB #5604 ödin **Acts 2:24** Whom God hath raised up, having loosed the **pains** of death: because it was not possible that he should be holden of it. [KJV] "And God raised Him up again, putting an end to the **agony** of death, since it was impossible for Him to be held in its power. [NASB] But God raised him from the dead, freeing him from the **agony** of death, because it was impossible for death to keep its hold on him. [NIV] Whom God raised up, having loosed the **pains** of death, because it was not possible that He should be held by it. [NKJV] However, God released him from the **horrors** of death and raised him back to life again, for death could not keep him in its grip. [NLT] ὃν ὁ Θεὸς ἀνέστησε, λύσας τὰς **ὠδῖνας** τοῦ θανάτου, καθότι οὐκ ἦν δυνατὸν κρατεῖσθαι αὐτὸν ὑπ' αὐτοῦ· [GNS] ὃν ὁ θεὸς ἀνέστησεν λύσας τὰς **ὠδῖνας** τοῦ θανάτου, καθότι οὐκ ἦν δυνατὸν κρατεῖσθαι αὐτὸν ὑπ' αὐτοῦ· [GNT]	Agony, pains, horrors, suffering, birth pangs. **Practical Application** For the unbeliever, there is great pain in death, pain such as that experienced by a woman in giving birth. But man no longer has to suffer the pain of death nor does he have to fear suffering through death. Christ has conquered and abolished death, made it completely harmless. Death is actually the most glorious and joyful experience for the believer, an experience that simply explodes human imagination. (Cp. John 5:24; Hebrews 2:14-15.) How can this be said? Because the believer actually never experiences death. Quicker than the eye can blink, God transfers the believer into His presence—to live with Him eternally.
#2825 **Panic** Terrified–KJV Terrified–NASB Frightened–NIV Terrified–NKJV **Panic–NLT** **POSB REFERENCE** (Lk.21:9-10; esp. v.9) Note 3, point 2	**πτοηθῆτε** = ptoëthëte Pronunciation: [pto-eh'-thay-teh] Parsing (part of speech): verb Mood—subjunctive OR imperative Tense—aorist Voice—passive Person—2nd person Number—plural Stem or root—from πτοέομαι Concordance References: ⇒ Strong's #4422 ptoeö ⇒ NIV #4765 ptoeö ⇒ NASB #4422 ptoeö	To be terrified; to be frightened; to panic; to be scared; to be startled. **Practical Application** Believers are not to "panic" (*ptoëthëte*). They are not to let their hearts "be troubled" (John 14:1). World violence can trouble people; but the believer's heart and life are to be centered upon God, trusting His presence, care, and security—eternally.

ENGLISH WORD	GREEK WORD AND VERSE	THE WORD MEANS...
Parade–NKJV Boastful–NLT **POSB** **REFERENCE** (1 Cor.13:4-7; esp. v.4) Note 2, point 4	Number—singular Stem or root—from περπερεύομαι Concordance References: ⇒ Strong's #4068 perpereuomai ⇒ NIV #4371 perpereuomai ⇒ NASB #4068 perpereuomai **1 Cor. 13:4** Charity suffereth long, and is kind; charity envieth not; charity **vaunteth** not itself, is not puffed up, [KJV] Love is patient, love is kind, and is not jealous; love does not **brag** and is not arrogant, [NASB] Love is patient, love is kind. It does not envy, it does not **boast**, it is not proud. [NIV] Love suffers long and is kind; love does not envy; love does not **parade** itself, is not puffed up; [NKJV] Love is patient and kind. Love is not jealous or **boastful** or proud [NLT] ἡ ἀγάπη μακροθυμεῖ, χρηστεύεται· ἡ ἀγάπη, οὐ ζηλοῖ· ἡ ἀγάπη οὐ **περπερεύεται**, οὐ φυσιοῦται, [GNS] Ἡ ἀγάπη μακροθυμεῖ, χρηστεύεται ἡ ἀγάπη, οὐ ζηλοῖ, [ἡ ἀγάπη] οὐ **περπερεύεται**, οὐ φυσιοῦται, [GNT]	honor, or applause from others. On the contrary, love seeks to give: to recognize, to honor, to applaud the other person.
#2829 **Paradise** **Paradise–KJV** **Paradise–NASB** **Paradise–NIV** **Paradise–NKJV** **Paradise–NLT** **POSB** **REFERENCE** (2 Cor.12:4) *Deeper Study #2*	παράδεισον = *paradeison* Pronunciation: [par-ad'-i-son] Parsing (part of speech): noun 　Case—accusative 　Gender—masculine 　Number—singular 　Stem or root—from παράδεισος, ου Concordance References: ⇒ Strong's #3857 paradeisos ⇒ NIV #4137 paradeisos ⇒ NASB #3857 paradeisos **2 Cor. 12:4** How that he was caught up into **paradise**, and heard unspeakable words, which it is not lawful for a man to utter. [KJV] Was caught up into **Paradise**, and heard inexpressible words, which a man is not permitted to speak. [NASB] Was caught up to **paradise**. He heard inexpressible things, things that man is not permitted to tell. [NIV] How he was caught up into **Paradise** and heard inexpressible words, which it is not lawful for a man to utter. [NKJV] But I do know that I was caught up into **paradise** and heard things so astounding that they cannot be told. [NLT] ὅτι ἡρπάγη εἰς τὸν **παράδεισον**, καὶ ἤκουσεν ἄρρητα ῥήματα, ἃ οὐκ ἐξὸν ἀνθρώπῳ λαλῆσαι. [GNS] ὅτι ἡρπάγη εἰς τὸν **παράδεισον** καὶ ἤκουσεν ἄρρητα ῥήματα ἃ οὐκ ἐξὸν ἀνθρώπῳ λαλῆσαι. [GNT]	Paradise; the other world, the unseen world, the spiritual world, the spiritual dimension of being. **Practical Application** 　Jesus Himself revealed that paradise is a place which is divided into two huge areas, sections, compartments, worlds, or dimensions of being. The two areas or worlds are separated by a great gulf that is impassable. One area or world is the place of sorrow, a place called hell. Hell is where unbelievers go. The other area or world is the place of paradise where believers go. Paradise is the picture of heaven, the place where God's presence and glory are fully manifested and experienced. (See POSB *Deeper Study #3*, Paradise—Luke 16:23 for more discussion.)
#2830 **Part–Partner** **Part–KJV** In common–NASB In common–NIV **Part–NKJV** **Partner–NLT** **POSB** **REFERENCE** (2 Cor.6:14-16; esp. v.15) Note 2, point 4	μερίς = *meris* Pronunciation: [mer-ece'] Parsing (part of speech): noun 　Case—nominative 　Gender—feminine 　Number—singular 　Stem or root—from μερίς, ίδος Concordance References: ⇒ Strong's #3310 meris ⇒ NIV #3535 meris ⇒ NASB #3310 meris **2 Cor. 6:15** And what concord hath Christ with Belial? or what **part** hath he that believeth with an infidel? [KJV] Or what harmony has Christ with Belial, or what has a believer **in common** with an unbeliever? [NASB] What harmony is there between Christ and Belial? What does a believer have **in common** with an unbeliever? [NIV]	In common, part, partner. It means a person's portion, lot, sphere, realm, or participation in life. **Practical Application** 　The believer's faith is pictured as changing his whole life: his belief causes him to move in a whole new sphere or realm of life. He may live among unbelievers, living and working next to them, but he moves in a different realm. His purpose and behavior upon earth is different: ⇒ The believer believes that Christ is the Son of God and the Savior of the world; the unbeliever does not. ⇒ The believer lives as Christ dictates; the unbeliever lives as he wishes. ⇒ The believer seeks to honor Christ by putting Christ first and serving Him; the

ENGLISH WORD	GREEK WORD AND VERSE	THE WORD MEANS...
	And what accord has Christ with Belial? Or what **part** has a believer with an unbeliever? [NKJV] What harmony can there be between Christ and the Devil? How can a believer be a **partner** with an unbeliever? [NLT] τίς δὲ συμφώνησις Χριστῷ πρὸς Βελιάλ; ἢ τίς **μερὶς** πιστῷ μετὰ ἀπίστου; [GNS] τίς δὲ συμφώνησις Χριστοῦ πρὸς Βελιάρ, ἢ τίς **μερὶς** πιστῷ μετὰ ἀπίστου; [GNT]	unbeliever lives for self and the world and its possessions. The very meaning, purpose, and significance of life differ radically between the believer and the unbeliever. The believer seeks Christ and the things of Christ, whereas the unbeliever focuses his life primarily upon this world and self.
#2831 **Partaken–** **Partakers Of** **Partakers of–KJV** Share–NASB Have–NIV **Partaken–NKJV** Not translated–NLT **POSB** **REFERENCE** (Heb.2:14-16; esp. v.14) Note 1, point 1	κεκοινώνηκεν = kekoinōnēken Pronunciation: [keh-koy-no-nay'-kehn] Parsing (part of speech): verb 　Mood—indicative 　Tense—perfect 　Voice—active 　Person—3rd person 　Number—singular 　Stem or root—from κοινωνέω Concordance References: ⇒ Strong's #2841 koinöneö ⇒ NIV #3125 koinöneö ⇒ NASB #2841 koinöneö **Hebrews 2:14** Forasmuch then as the children are **partakers** of flesh and blood, he also himself likewise took part of the same; that through death he might destroy him that had the power of death, that is, the devil; [KJV] Since then the children **share** in flesh and blood, He Himself likewise also partook of the same, that through death He might render powerless him who had the power of death, that is, the devil; [NASB] Since the children **have** flesh and blood, he too shared in their humanity so that by his death he might destroy him who holds the power of death—that is, the devil— [NIV] Inasmuch then as the children have **partaken** of flesh and blood, He Himself likewise shared in the same, that through death He might destroy him who had the power of death, that is, the devil, [NKJV] Because God's children are human beings—made of flesh and blood—Jesus also became flesh and blood by being born in human form. For only as a human being could he die, and only by dying could he break the power of the Devil, who had the power of death. [NLT]—Not Translated ἐπεὶ οὖν τὰ παιδία **κεκοινώνηκε** σαρκὸς καὶ αἵματος, καὶ αὐτὸς παραπλησίως μετέσχε τῶν αὐτῶν, ἵνα διὰ τοῦ θανάτου καταργήσῃ τὸν τὸ κράτος ἔχοντα τοῦ θανάτου, τοῦτ᾿ ἔστι τὸν διάβολον, [GNS] ἐπεὶ οὖν τὰ παιδία **κεκοινώνηκεν** αἵματος καὶ σαρκός, καὶ αὐτὸς παραπλησίως μετέσχεν τῶν αὐτῶν, ἵνα διὰ τοῦ θανάτου καταργήσῃ τὸν τὸ κράτος ἔχοντα τοῦ θανάτου, τοῦτ᾿ ἔστιν τὸν διάβολον, [GNT]	To have; to share; to be a partaker of; to participate; to be partners of a common human nature. **Practical Application** He deliberately determined and purposed to *take part* of human flesh and blood. He voluntarily took part of human nature—of a nature that was not a natural part of His being.
#2832 **Partakers** **Partakers–KJV** **Partakers–NASB** Shared in–NIV **Partakers–NKJV** Shared in–NLT **POSB** **REFERENCE** (Heb.6:4-5; esp. v.4) Note 1, point 3	μετόχους γενηθέντας = metochous genēthentas Pronunciation: [met'-okh-oos ghin'-ay-thehn-tahs] Parsing *metochous* (part of speech): pronominal adjective 　Case—accusative 　Gender—masculine 　Number—plural 　Stem or root—from μέτοχος, ου Parsing *genēthentas* (part of speech): verb 　Mood—participle 　Tense—aorist 　Voice—passive deponent 　Case—accusative 　Gender—masculine 　Number—plural 　Stem or root—from γίνομαι	To share in; partaker, companion, partner; to share as partners. **Practical Application** W.E. Vine says that it (*metochous*) means "the *fact of sharing*" (*Expository Dictionary of New Testament Words*, p.162). The Greek scholar A.T Robertson says, "These are all given as actual spiritual experiences" (*Word Pictures in the New Testament*, Vol. 5, p.375). These people were partakers in the Holy Spirit. It is very difficult to see how they can be said to be making a false profession without straining the Scripture.

ENGLISH WORD	GREEK WORD AND VERSE	THE WORD MEANS...
	Concordance References: ⇒ Strong's #1096+3353 ginomai metochos ⇒ NIV #1181+3581 ginomai metochos [shared in] ⇒ NASB #1096+3353 ginomai metochos **Hebrews 6:4** For it is impossible for those who were once enlightened, and have tasted of the heavenly gift, and were made **partakers** of the Holy Ghost, [KJV] For in the case of those who have once been enlightened and have tasted of the heavenly gift and have been made **partakers** of the Holy Spirit, [NASB] It is impossible for those who have once been enlightened, who have tasted the heavenly gift, who have **shared in** the Holy Spirit, [NIV] For *it is* impossible for those who were once enlightened, and have tasted the heavenly gift, and have become **partakers** of the Holy Spirit, [NKJV] For it is impossible to restore to repentance those who were once enlightened—those who have experienced the good things of heaven and **shared in** the Holy Spirit, [NLT] ἀδύνατον γὰρ τοὺς ἅπαξ φωτισθέντας, γευσαμένους τε τῆς δωρεᾶς τῆς ἐπουρανίου, καὶ **μετόχους γενηθέντας** Πνεύματος Ἁγίου, [GNS] Ἀδύνατον γὰρ τοὺς ἅπαξ φωτισθέντας, γευσαμένους τε τῆς δωρεᾶς τῆς ἐπουρανίου καὶ **μετόχους γενηθέντας** πνεύματος ἁγίου [GNT]	

#2833
Participation In Demonic Activities
 	
Witchcraft–KJV
Sorcery–NASB
Witchcraft–NIV
Sorcery–NKJV
Participation in demonic activities–NLT
 	
POSB REFERENCE
(Gal.5:19-21; esp. v.20)
Note 2
	φαρμακεία = *pharmakeia*
	Pronunciation: [far-mak-i'-ah]
	Parsing (part of speech): noun
	  Case—nominative
	  Gender—feminine
	  Number—singular
	  Stem or root—from φαρμακεία, ας
	Concordance References:
	⇒ Strong's #5331 pharmakeia
	⇒ NIV #5758 pharmakeia
	⇒ NASB #5331 pharmakeia
	
	Galatians 5:20
	Idolatry, **witchcraft**, hatred, variance, emulations, wrath, strife, seditions, heresies, [KJV]
	Idolatry, **sorcery**, enmities, strife, jealousy, outbursts of anger, disputes, dissensions, factions, [NASB]
	Idolatry and **witchcraft**; hatred, discord, jealousy, fits of rage, selfish ambition, dissensions, factions [NIV]
	Idolatry, **sorcery**, hatred, contentions, jealousies, outbursts of wrath, selfish ambitions, dissensions, heresies, [NKJV]
	Idolatry, **participation in demonic activities**, hostility, quarreling, jealousy, outbursts of anger, selfish ambition, divisions, the feeling that everyone is wrong except those in your own little group, [NLT]
	εἰδωλολατρία, **φαρμακεία**, ἔχθραι, ἔρεις, ζῆλοι, θυμοί, ἐριθεῖαι, διχοστασίαι, αἱρέσεις, [GNS]
	εἰδωλολατρία, **φαρμακεία**, ἔχθραι, ἔρις, ζῆλος, θυμοί, ἐριθεῖαι, διχοστασίαι, αἱρέσεις, [GNT]
		Witchcraft, sorcery, participation in demonic activities; the use of drugs or of evil spirits to gain control over the lives of others or over one's own life.
		
		Practical Application
		It would include all forms of seeking the control of one's fate through astrology, palm reading, seances, fortune telling, crystals, and other forms of witchcraft.

#2834
Parties
 	
Drinking–KJV
Drinking–NASB
Drinking–NIV
Drinking–NKJV
Parties–NLT
 	
POSB REFERENCE
(Mt.24:38)
Deeper Study #4
	πίνοντες = *pinontes*
	Pronunciation: [pee'-non-tes]
	Parsing (part of speech): verb
	  Mood—participle
	  Tense—present
	  Voice—active
	  Case—nominative
	  Gender—masculine
	  Number—plural
	  Stem or root— from πίνω
	Concordance References:
	⇒ Strong's #4095 pinō
	⇒ NIV #4403 pinō
	⇒ NASB #4095 pinō
		To drink; to participate in the partying spirit of drink; to participate in the abomination of drinking.
		
		Practical Application
		The idea is a habitual practice, drinking to excess (cp. Galatians 5:21; cp. Ephes. 5:18). The teaching from Scripture is clear:
		Drunkards "will not inherit the kingdom of God." (cp. 1 Cor.6:10). "Drunkards" (*methusoi*) are people who take drink and drugs to affect their senses for lust and pleasure; who seek to be

ENGLISH WORD	GREEK WORD AND VERSE	THE WORD MEANS...
	Matthew 24:38 For as in the days that were before the flood they were eating and **drinking**, marrying and giving in marriage, until the day that Noe entered into the ark, [KJV] "For as in those days which were before the flood they were eating and **drinking**, they were marrying and giving in marriage, until the day that Noah entered the ark, [NASB] For in the days before the flood, people were eating and **drinking**, marrying and giving in marriage, up to the day Noah entered the ark; [NIV] For as in the days before the flood, they were eating and **drinking**, marrying and giving in marriage, until the day that Noah entered the ark, [NKJV] In those days before the Flood, the people were enjoying banquets and **parties** and weddings right up to the time Noah entered his boat. [NLT] ὥσπερ γὰρ ἦσαν ἐν ταῖς ἡμέραις ταῖς πρὸ τοῦ κατακλυσμοῦ τρώγοντες καὶ **πίνοντες**, γαμοῦντες καὶ ἐκγαμίζοντες, ἄχρι ἧς ἡμέρας εἰσῆλθε Νῶε εἰς τὴν κιβωτόν, [GNS] ὡς γὰρ ἦσαν ἐν ταῖς ἡμέραις [ἐκείναις] ταῖς πρὸ τοῦ κατακλυσμοῦ τρώγοντες καὶ **πίνοντες**, γαμοῦντες καὶ γαμίζοντες, ἄχρι ἧς ἡμέρας εἰσῆλθεν Νῶε εἰς τὴν κιβωτόν, [GNT]	tipsy or intoxicated; who seek to loosen their moral restraints for the sake of bodily pleasure.

#2835
Parting
 	
Opened–KJV
Opening–NASB
Torn open–NIV
Parting–NKJV
Split open–NLT
 	
POSB
REFERENCE
(Mk.1:10)
Note 3
	σχιζομένους = *schizamenous*
	Pronunciation: [skhid'-zah-meh-noos]
	Parsing (part of speech): verb
	  Mood—participle
	  Tense—present
	  Voice—passive
	  Case—accusative
	  Gender—masculine
	  Number—plural
	  Stem or root—from σχίζω
	Concordance References:
	  ⇒ Strong's #4977 schizo
	  ⇒ NIV #5387 schizö
	  ⇒ NASB #4977 schizo
	
	Mark 1:10
	And straightway coming up out of the water, he saw the heavens **opened**, and the Spirit like a dove descending upon him: [KJV]
	And immediately coming up out of the water, He saw the heavens **opening**, and the Spirit like a dove descending upon Him; [NASB]
	As Jesus was coming up out of the water, he saw heaven being **torn open** and the Spirit descending on him like a dove. [NIV]
	And immediately, coming up from the water, He saw the heavens **parting** and the Spirit descending upon Him like a dove. [NKJV]
	And when Jesus came up out of the water, he saw the heavens **split open** and the Holy Spirit descending like a dove on him. [NLT]
	καὶ εὐθὺς ἀναβαίνων ἀπὸ τοῦ ὕδατος, εἶδε σχιζομένους τοὺς οὐρανοὺς, καὶ τὸ Πνεῦμα ὡσεὶ περιστερὰν καταβαῖνον ἐπ αὐτόν· [GNS]
	καὶ εὐθὺς ἀναβαίνων ἐκ τοῦ ὕδατος εἶδεν σχιζομένους τοὺς οὐρανοὺς καὶ τὸ πνεῦμα ὡς περιστερὰν καταβαῖνον εἰς αὐτόν· [GNT]
		Rent asunder, split open, parting, dividing, separating, or torn apart.
		
		Practical Application
		This could mean two things.
		1. It could mean a moment like the rays of sunlight breaking through the clouds ever so brilliantly after a thunderstorm.
		2. It could mean a moment when God miraculously tore apart the barrier between heaven and earth, and allowed Jesus to see into the glory of heaven from where He had come.

#2836
Partner–Partnership
 	
Fellowship–KJV
Partnership–NASB
In common–NIV
	μετοχή = *metochē*
	Pronunciation: [met-okh-ay']
	Parsing (part of speech): noun
	  Case—nominative
	  Gender—feminine
	  Number—singular
	  Stem or root—from μετοχή, ῆς
	Concordance References:
	  ⇒ Strong's #3352 metochē
		In common, sharing fellowship, partnership, and participation.
		
		Practical Application
		How can a believer who focuses his life upon the righteousness of Jesus Christ share and participate with unbelievers, unbelievers who care little if anything about Jesus Christ and His call

ENGLISH WORD	GREEK WORD AND VERSE	THE WORD MEANS...
Fellowship–NKJV **Partner–NLT** **POSB REFERENCE** (2 Cor.6:14-16; esp. v.14) Note 2, point 1c	⇒ NIV #3580 metochë ⇒ NASB #3352 metochë **2 Cor. 6:14** Be ye not unequally yoked together with unbelievers: for what **fellowship** hath righteousness with unrighteousness? and what communion hath light with darkness? [KJV] Do not be bound together with unbelievers; for what **partnership** have righteousness and lawlessness, or what fellowship has light with darkness? [NASB] Do not be yoked together with unbelievers. For what do righteousness and wickedness have **in common**? Or what fellowship can light have with darkness? [NIV] Do not be unequally yoked together with unbelievers. For what **fellowship** has righteousness with lawlessness? And what communion has light with darkness? [NKJV] Don't team up with those who are unbelievers. How can goodness be a **partner** with wickedness? How can light live with darkness? [NLT] Μὴ γίνεσθε ἑτεροζυγοῦντες ἀπίστοις· τίς γὰρ **μετοχὴ** δικαιοσύνῃ καὶ ἀνομίᾳ; τίς δὲ κοινωνία φωτὶ πρὸς σκότος; [GNS] Μὴ γίνεσθε ἑτεροζυγοῦντες ἀπίστοις· τίς γὰρ **μετοχὴ** δικαιοσύνῃ καὶ ἀνομίᾳ, η τίς κοινωνία φωτὶ πρὸς σκότος; [GNT]	to righteousness? Unbelievers do not obey God. They live and do as they wish, not as God says. says. Rejecting God and what He says, they go about doing their own thing. They rebel against God and His commandments, living lawless and unrighteous lives.

#2837
Partook
 	
Took part–KJV
Partook–NASB
Shared in–NIV
Shared in–NKJV
Became–NLT
 	
**POSB
REFERENCE**
(Heb.2:14-16; esp.
v.14)
Note 1, point 1
	μετέσχεν = *meteschen*
	Pronunciation: [met-es-khehn]
	Parsing (part of speech): verb
	  Mood—indicative
	  Tense—aorist
	  Voice—active
	  Person—3rd person
	  Number—singular
	  Stem or root—from μετέχω
	Concordance References:
	⇒ Strong's #3348 metochö
	⇒ NIV #3576 metochö
	⇒ NASB #3348 metochö
	
	Hebrews 2:14
	Forasmuch then as the children are partakers of flesh and blood, he also himself likewise **took part** of the same; that through death he might destroy him that had the power of death, that is, the devil; [KJV]
	Since then the children share in flesh and blood, He Himself likewise also **partook** of the same, that through death He might render powerless him who had the power of death, that is, the devil; [NASB]
	Since the children have flesh and blood, he too **shared in** their humanity so that by his death he might destroy him who holds the power of death—that is, the devil—[NIV]
	Inasmuch then as the children have partaken of flesh and blood, He Himself likewise **shared in** the same, that through death He might destroy him who had the power of death, that is, the devil, [NKJV]
	Because God's children are human beings—made of flesh and blood—Jesus also **became** flesh and blood by being born in human form. For only as a human being could he die, and only by dying could he break the power of the Devil, who had the power of death. [NLT]
	ἐπεὶ οὖν τὰ παιδία κεκοινώνηκε σαρκός καὶ αἵματος, καὶ αὐτὸς παραπλησίως **μετέσχε** τῶν αὐτῶν, ἵνα διὰ τοῦ θανάτου καταργήσῃ τὸν τὸ κράτος ἔχοντα τοῦ θανάτου, τοῦτ' ἔστι τὸν διάβολον, [GNS]
	ἐπεὶ οὖν τὰ παιδία κεκοινώνηκεν αἵματος καὶ σαρκός, καὶ αὐτὸς παραπλησίως **μετέσχεν** τῶν αὐτῶν, ἵνα διὰ τοῦ θανάτου καταργήσῃ τὸν τὸ κράτος ἔχοντα τοῦ θανάτου, τοῦτ' ἔστιν τὸν διάβολον, [GNT]
		To share in; to take part; to partake; to become; to hold with.
		
		Practical Application
		The word used of Christ is entirely different: Christ partook of or became (*meteschen*) human nature. The idea is that Christ became human nature and held human nature with man. He added human nature to His divine nature. His human nature was an addition to His divine nature. As God the Son, Jesus Christ had absolutely no part of flesh and blood, but as the Son of Man, He took hold of man's nature. The point is this: Jesus Christ became man, and as Man He became flesh and blood; willingly and voluntarily. Jesus Christ loves us so much that He would pay the ultimate price to deliver us. He would humble Himself to such a degree that He would leave heaven above in order to come to earth and live as a Man. (See POSB notes—Hebrews 2:17-18 for more discussion.) (Kenneth Wuest points this out in an excellent discussion and Marvin Vincent quotes the Biblical scholar B.F. Westcott as making the same point.)

ENGLISH WORD	GREEK WORD AND VERSE	THE WORD MEANS...

#2838
Passion
 	
Passion–KJV
Suffering–NASB
Suffering–NIV
Suffering–NKJV
Crucifixion–NLT
 	
POSB
REFERENCE
(Acts 1:3)
Note 3
	παθεῖν = *pathein*
	Pronunciation: [path'-een]
	Parsing (part of speech): verb
	    Mood—infinitive
	    Tense—aorist
	    Voice—active
	    Case—accusative
	    Stem or root—from πάσχω
	Concordance References:
	  ⇒ Strong's #3958 *paschö*
	  ⇒ NIV #4248 *paschö*
	  ⇒ NASB ##3958 *paschö*
	
	### Acts 1:3
	To whom also he showed himself alive after his **passion** by many infallible proofs, being seen of them forty days, and speaking of the things pertaining to the kingdom of God. [KJV]
	
	To these He also presented Himself alive, after His **suffering**, by many convincing proofs, appearing to them over a period of forty days, and speaking of the things concerning the kingdom of God. [NASB]
	
	After his **suffering**, he showed himself to these men and gave many convincing proofs that he was alive. He appeared to them over a period of forty days and spoke about the kingdom of God. [NIV]
	
	To whom He also presented Himself alive after His **suffering** by many infallible proofs, being seen by them during forty days and speaking of the things pertaining to the kingdom of God. [NKJV]
	
	During the forty days after his **crucifixion**, he appeared to the apostles from time to time and proved to them in many ways that he was actually alive. On these occasions he talked to them about the Kingdom of God. [NLT]
	
	οἷς καὶ παρέστησεν ἑαυτὸν ζῶντα μετὰ τὸ **παθεῖν** αὐτὸν ἐν πολλοῖς τεκμηρίοις, δι' ἡμερῶν τεσσεράκοντα ὀπτανόμενος αὐτοῖς, καὶ λέγων τὰ περὶ τῆς βασιλείας τοῦ Θεοῦ. [GNS]
	
	οἷς καὶ παρέστησεν ἑαυτὸν ζῶντα μετὰ τὸ **παθεῖν** αὐτὸν ἐν πολλοῖς τεκμηρίοις, δι' ἡμερῶν τεσσεράκοντα ὀπτανόμενος αὐτοῖς καὶ λέγων τὰ περὶ τῆς βασιλείας τοῦ Θεοῦ· [GNT]
		Suffering, passion, crucifixion.
		
		### Practical Application
		The word "passion" (*pathein*) refers to the sufferings or death of Christ. His death and resurrection assured the salvation of man.

#2839
Passion
 	
Inordinate affection–
KJV
Passion–NASB
Lust–NIV
Passion–NKJV
Lust–NLT
 	
POSB
REFERENCE
(Col.3:5-7; esp. v.5)
Note 1, point 1c
	πάθος = *pathos*
	Pronunciation: [path'-os]
	Parsing (part of speech): noun
	    Case—accusative
	    Gender—neuter
	    Number—singular
	    Stem or root—from πάθος, ους
	Concordance References:
	  ⇒ Strong's #3806 *pathos*
	  ⇒ NIV #4079 *pathos*
	  ⇒ NASB #3806 *pathos*
	
	### Col. 3:5
	Mortify therefore your members which are upon the earth; fornication, uncleanness, **inordinate affection**, evil concupiscence, and covetousness, which is idolatry: [KJV]
	
	Therefore consider the members of your earthly body as dead to immorality, impurity, **passion**, evil desire, and greed, which amounts to idolatry. [NASB]
	
	Put to death, therefore, whatever belongs to your earthly nature: sexual immorality, impurity, **lust**, evil desires and greed, which is idolatry. [NIV]
	
	Therefore put to death your members which are on the earth: fornication, uncleanness, **passion**, evil desire, and covetousness, which is idolatry. [NKJV]
	
	So put to death the sinful, earthly things lurking within you. Have nothing to do with sexual sin, impurity, **lust**,
		Lust; inordinate affection; lustful passion; craving; strong desire; intense arousal; a driving lust.
		
		### Practical Application
		It is, of course, a desire and craving for the wrong things such as the second and third helping of food, alcohol, drugs, nudity, pornography, suggestive and filthy literature, illicit affairs, extra-marital sex, etc and a host of other lusts.

ENGLISH WORD	GREEK WORD AND VERSE	THE WORD MEANS...
	and shameful desires. Don't be greedy for the good things of this life, for that is idolatry. [NLT] Νεκρώσατε οὖν τὰ μέλη ὑμῶν τὰ ἐπὶ τῆς γῆς, πορνείαν, ἀκαθαρσίαν, **πάθος**, ἐπιθυμίαν κακήν, καὶ τὴν πλεονεξίαν, ἥτις ἐστὶν εἰδωλολατρεία, [GNS] Νεκρώσατε οὖν τὰ μέλη τὰ ἐπὶ τῆς γῆς, πορνείαν ἀκαθαρσίαν **πάθος** ἐπιθυμίαν κακήν, καὶ τὴν πλεονεξίαν, ἥτις ἐστὶν εἰδωλολατρία, [GNT]	
#2840 **Passions** Lusts–KJV Lusts–NASB **Passions–NIV** Lusts–NKJV Desires–NLT **POSB REFERENCE** (Tit.3:3) Note 2 **See also POSB REF:** (Tit.2:12) Note 2, point 2d	ἐπιθυμίας = epithumias Pronunciation: [ep-ee-thoo-mee'-ahs] Parsing (part of speech): noun Case—accusative Gender—feminine Number—plural Stem or root—from ἐπιθυμία, ας Concordance References: ⇒ Strong's #1939 epithumia ⇒ NIV #2123 epithumia ⇒ NASB #1939 epithumia **Titus 3:3** For we ourselves also were sometimes foolish, disobedient, deceived, serving divers **lusts** and pleasures, living in malice and envy, hateful, and hating one another. [KJV] For we also once were foolish ourselves, disobedient, deceived, enslaved to various **lusts** and pleasures, spending our life in malice and envy, hateful, hating one another. [NASB] At one time we too were foolish, disobedient, deceived and enslaved by all kinds of **passions** and pleasures. We lived in malice and envy, being hated and hating one another. [NIV] For we ourselves were also once foolish, disobedient, deceived, serving various **lusts** and pleasures, living in malice and envy, hateful and hating one another. [NKJV] Once we, too, were foolish and disobedient. We were misled by others and became slaves to many wicked **desires** and evil pleasures. Our lives were full of evil and envy. We hated others, and they hated us. [NLT] ἦμεν γὰρ ποτε καὶ ἡμεῖς ἀνόητοι, ἀπειθεῖς, πλανώμενοι, δουλεύοντες **ἐπιθυμίαις** καὶ ἡδοναῖς ποικίλαις, ἐν κακίᾳ καὶ φθόνῳ διάγοντες, στυγητοί, μισοῦντες ἀλλήλους. [GNS] Ἦμεν γὰρ ποτε καὶ ἡμεῖς ἀνόητοι, ἀπειθεῖς, πλανώμενοι, δουλεύοντες **ἐπιθυμίαις** καὶ ἡδοναῖς ποικίλαις, ἐν κακίᾳ καὶ φθόνῳ διάγοντες, στυγητοί, μισοῦντες ἀλλήλους. [GNT]	Passions, lusts, desires, pleasures. It means desire, lust, loving to do evil things, a strong desire, a yearning passion for, an all-consuming craving. The word (epithumias) means passionate cravings, desires, and urges. **Practical Application** Man is enslaved by the things of the world, things that damage his body—that make him greedy and selfish—that destroy his spirit and doom him to destruction. But thanks be to God our Savior. He has saved us and delivered us from the enslavements of this world, the enslavements of lust and pleasure that destroy our bodies and souls. The wonderful news is that any person can be delivered from the destructive passions and pleasures of this world. How? Through our Lord Jesus Christ. If a person will turn away from the passions, lusts and pleasures and turn to Christ, God will deliver him. God will give him the power to conquer the passions and enslavements of this world.
#2841 **Past Feeling** **Past feeling–KJV** Having become callous–NASB Lost all sensitivity–NIV **Past feeling–NKJV** Don't care anymore about right and wrong–NLT **POSB REFERENCE** (Eph.4:17-19; esp. v.19) Note 1, point 4	ἀπηλγηκότες = apēlgēkotes Pronunciation: [ap-ayl'-gay'-ko-tehs] Parsing (part of speech): verb Mood—participle Tense—perfect Voice—active Case—nominative Gender—masculine Number—plural Stem or root—from ἀπαλγέω Concordance References: ⇒ Strong's #524 apalgeō ⇒ NIV #556 apalgeō ⇒ NASB #524 apalgeō **Ephes. 4:19** Who being **past feeling** have given themselves over unto lasciviousness, to work all uncleanness with greediness. [KJV] And they, **having become callous**, have given themselves over to sensuality, for the practice of every kind of impurity with greediness. [NASB] Having **lost all sensitivity**, they have given themselves over to sensuality so as to indulge in every kind of	To lose all sensitivity; to be past feeling; to become callous; not to care anymore about right and wrong; to become insensible, hardened. **Practical Application** Unbelievers reach a point where they lose all sensitivity for God and His standard of morality. The more a person walks without God, the more callous a person becomes to God. The more a person walks in sin, the more callous his conscience becomes to righteousness. Sin becomes more and more acceptable. The person's conscience no longer bothers him. He reaches a point of being past feeling. The believer is not to return to sin. He is not to walk as other men walk—in sin, becoming callous and insensitive to God.

ENGLISH WORD	GREEK WORD AND VERSE	THE WORD MEANS...
	impurity, with a continual lust for more. [NIV] Who, being **past feeling**, have given themselves over to lewdness, to work all uncleanness with greediness. [NKJV] They **don't care anymore about right and wrong**, and they have given themselves over to immoral ways. Their lives are filled with all kinds of impurity and greed. [NLT] οἵτινες **ἀπηλγηκότες** ἑαυτοὺς παρέδωκαν τῇ ἀσελγείᾳ, εἰς ἐργασίαν ἀκαθαρσίας πάσης ἐν πλεονεξίᾳ. [GNS] οἵτινες **ἀπηλγηκότες** ἑαυτοὺς παρέδωκαν τῇ ἀσελγείᾳ εἰς ἐργασίαν ἀκαθαρσίας πάσης ἐν πλεονεξίᾳ. [GNT]	
#2842 **Pastors** Pastors–KJV Pastors–NASB Pastors–NIV Pastors–NKJV Pastors–NLT **POSB** **REFERENCE** (Eph.4:11) Note 3, point 4	ποιμένας = *poimenas* Pronunciation: [poy-meh'-nahs] Parsing (part of speech): noun 　Case—accusative 　Gender—masculine 　Number—plural 　Stem or root—from ποιμήν, ένος Concordance References: ⇒　Strong's #4166 poimēn ⇒　NIV #4478 poimēn ⇒　NASB #4166 poimēn **Ephes. 4:11** And he gave some, apostles; and some, prophets; and some, evangelists; and some, **pastors** and teachers; [KJV] And He gave some as apostles, and some as prophets, and some as evangelists, and some as **pastors** and teachers, [NASB] It was he who gave some to be apostles, some to be prophets, some to be evangelists, and some to be **pastors** and teachers, [NIV] And He Himself gave some *to be* apostles, some prophets, some evangelists, and some **pastors** and teachers, [NKJV] He is the one who gave these gifts to the church: the apostles, the prophets, the evangelists, and the **pastors** and teachers. [NLT] καὶ αὐτὸς ἔδωκε τοὺς μὲν, ἀποστόλους, τοὺς δὲ, προφήτας, τοὺς δὲ, εὐαγγελιστάς, τοὺς δὲ, **ποιμένας** καὶ διδασκάλους, [GNS] καὶ αὐτὸς ἔδωκεν τοὺς μὲν ἀποστόλους, τοὺς δὲ προφήτας, τοὺς δὲ εὐαγγελιστάς, τοὺς δὲ **ποιμένας** καὶ διδασκάλους, [GNT]	Shepherd; pastor, minister, leader, navigator, guide, one who points and shows the way. **Practical Application** A.T. Robertson points out that the Lord Jesus told Peter to shepherd His sheep (John 21:16), that Peter told other ministers to shepherd the flock of God (1 Peter 5:2), and that Paul told the elders (ministers) of Ephesus to shepherd the church of God for which Christ had died (Acts 20:28) (*Word Pictures in the New Testament*, Vol.4, p.537.) The traits of a shepherd can be seen by looking at the references to Christ as the shepherd of believers. The pastor is an undershepherd to the Chief Shepherd, Christ Jesus our Lord. 1.　The shepherd knows the sheep; He knows each one by name. This is said to have been a fact among shepherds and their sheep in Jesus' day. Shepherds actually knew each sheep individually, even in large herds. The fact is certainly true with Christ and His sheep. 2.　The shepherd feeds the sheep even if He has to gather them in His arms and carry them to the feasting pasture. 3.　The shepherd guides the sheep to the pasture and away from the rough places and precipices. 4.　The shepherd seeks and saves the sheep who get lost. 5.　The shepherd protects the sheep. He even sacrifices His life for the sheep. 6.　The shepherd restores the sheep who go astray and return. 7.　The shepherd rewards the sheep for obedience and faithfulness. 8.　The shepherd will keep the sheep separate from the goats.
#2843 **Patience** Patience–KJV Endurance–NASB Endurance–NIV Patience–NKJV Endure–NLT **POSB** **REFERENCE** (2 Cor.6:4) Note 2	ὑπομονῇ = *hupomonē* Pronunciation: [hoop-om-on-ay'] Parsing (part of speech): noun 　Case—dative 　Gender—feminine 　Number—singular 　Stem or root—from ὑπομονή, ῆς Concordance References: ⇒　Strong's #5281 hupomonē ⇒　NIV #5705 hupomonē ⇒　NASB #5281 hupomonē **2 Cor. 6:4** But in all things approving ourselves as the ministers of God, in much **patience**, in afflictions, in necessities, in distresses, [KJV]	Endurance; steadfast endurance; patient endurance; perseverance; constancy; to stand firm. **Practical Application** Patience is the supreme quality, the very backbone of consistency. Unless a man endures, he will never be consistent, not in a corruptible and sinful world. A corruptible and sinful world presents obstacle after obstacle and sin after sin that have to be *endured and overcome* if a person is to live a consistent life. Steadfast endurance is the basic ingredient and force that a person must have to live a consistent life for the Lord Jesus. When trials, fatigue, temptations, or opposition

ENGLISH WORD	GREEK WORD AND VERSE	THE WORD MEANS...
	But in everything commending ourselves as servants of God, in much **endurance**, in afflictions, in hardships, in distresses, [NASB] Rather, as servants of God we commend ourselves in every way: in great **endurance**; in troubles, hardships and distresses; [NIV] But in all *things* we commend ourselves as ministers of God: in much **patience**, in tribulations, in needs, in distresses, [NKJV] In everything we do we try to show that we are true ministers of God. We patiently **endure** troubles and hardships and calamities of every kind. [NLT] ἀλλ' ἐν παντὶ συνίσταντες ἑαυτοὺς ὡς Θεοῦ διάκονοι, ἐν **ὑπομονῇ** πολλῇ, ἐν θλίψεσιν, ἐν ἀνάγκαις, ἐν στενοχωρίαις, [GNS] ἀλλ' ἐν παντὶ συνίσταντες ἑαυτοὺς ὡς θεοῦ διάκονοι, ἐν **ὑπομονῇ** πολλῇ, ἐν θλίψεσιν, ἐν ἀνάγκαις, ἐν στενοχωρίαις, [GNT]	confront the minister of God (or the believer), he must do all he can to endure.

#2844
## Patience 	
 	
Longsuffering–KJV
Patience–NASB
Patience–NIV
Longsuffering–NKJV
Patience–NLT
 	
**POSB
REFERENCE**
(Gal.5:22-23; esp. v.22)
Note 1
 	
See also POSB REF:
(2 Cor. 6:6-7; esp. v.6)
Note 5
	μακροθυμία = *makrothumia*
	Pronunciation: [mak-roth-oo-mee'-ah]
	Parsing (part of speech): noun
	    Case—nominative
	    Gender—feminine
	    Number—singular
	    Stem or root—from μακροθυμία, ας
	Concordance References:
	  ⇒ Strong's #3115 makrothumia
	  ⇒ NIV #3429 makrothumia
	  ⇒ NASB #3115 makrothumia
	
	### Galatians 5:22
	But the fruit of the Spirit is love, joy, peace, **longsuffering**, gentleness, goodness, faith, [KJV]
	
	But the fruit of the Spirit is love, joy, peace, **patience**, kindness, goodness, faithfulness, [NASB]
	
	But the fruit of the Spirit is love, joy, peace, **patience**, kindness, goodness, faithfulness, [NIV]
	
	But the fruit of the Spirit is love, joy, peace, **longsuffering**, kindness, goodness, faithfulness, [NKJV]
	
	But when the Holy Spirit controls our lives, he will produce this kind of fruit in us: love, joy, peace, **patience**, kindness, goodness, faithfulness, [NLT]
	
	ὁ δὲ καρπὸς τοῦ Πνεύματός ἐστιν ἀγάπη, χαρά, εἰρήνη, **μακροθυμία**, χρηστότης, ἀγαθωσύνη, πίστις, [GNS]
	
	Ὁ δὲ καρπὸς τοῦ πνεύματός ἐστιν ἀγάπη χαρά εἰρήνη, **μακροθυμία**, χρηστότης ἀγαθωσύνη, πίστις , [GNT]
		Patience, longsuffering; bearing and suffering a long time; perseverance; being constant, steadfast, and enduring.
		
		### Practical Application
		God's Spirit gives the believer a patience that never gives in; it is never broken no matter what attacks it.
		⇒ Pressure and hard work may fall upon us, but the Spirit of God helps us be patient under it all.
		⇒ Disease or accident or old age may afflict us, but the Spirit of God helps us to be patient under it.
		⇒ Discouragement and disappointment may attack us, but the Spirit of God helps us to be patient under it.
		⇒ People may do us wrong, abuse, slander, and injure us; but the Spirit of God helps us to be patient under it all.
		Two significant things need to be noted about patience.
		1. Patience never strikes back. Common sense tells us that a person who is attacked by others could strike back and retaliate. *But* the Christian believer is given the power of patience—the power to be patient with the situation or person for a long, long time.
		2. Patience is one of the great traits of God. As pointed out in this verse, it is a fruit of God's very own Spirit, a fruit that is to be in the life of the believer.

#2845
## Patience 	
 	
Patience–KJV
Steadfastness–NASB
Endurance–NIV
Patience–NKJV
Endurance–NLT
 	
**POSB
REFERENCE**
(Col.1:11)
Note 3, point 1
 	
See also POSB REF:
(2 Tim. 3:10)
	ὑπομονὴν = *hupomonēn*
	Pronunciation: [hoop-om-on-ayn']
	Parsing (part of speech): noun
	    Case—accusative
	    Gender—feminine
	    Number—singular
	    Stem or root—from ὑπομονή, ῆς
	Concordance References:
	  ⇒ Strong's #5281 hupomonē
	  ⇒ NIV #5705 hupomonē
	  ⇒ NASB #5281 hupomonē
	
	### Col. 1:11
	Strengthened with all might, according to his glorious power, unto all **patience** and longsuffering with joyfulness; [KJV]
	
	Strengthened with all power, according to His glorious might, for the attaining of all **steadfastness** and
		Endurance, patience, steadfastness, fortitude, constancy, perseverance.
		
		### Practical Application
		The word (*hupomonēn*) is not passive; it is active. It is not the spirit that sits back and puts up with the trials of life, taking whatever may come. Rather, it is the spirit that stands up and faces the trials of life, that actively goes about conquering and overcoming them. When trials confront a person who is truly justified, he is stirred to arise and face the trials head on. He immediately sets out to conquer and overcome them. He knows that God is allowing the trials in order to teach him more and more patience (endurance).

ENGLISH WORD	GREEK WORD AND VERSE	THE WORD MEANS...
Note 1, point 7 (2 Thes.1:4-5; esp. v.4) Note 6 (1 Tim.6:11) Note 2, point 5 (Heb.12:11) Note 2, point 2	patience; joyously [NASB] Being strengthened with all power according to his glorious might so that you may have great **endurance** and patience, and joyfully [NIV] Strengthened with all might, according to His glorious power, for all **patience** and longsuffering with joy; [NKJV] We also pray that you will be strengthened with his glorious power so that you will have all the patience and **endurance** you need. May you be filled with joy, [NLT] ἐν πάσῃ δυνάμει δυναμούμενοι κατὰ τὸ κράτος τῆς δόξης αὐτοῦ, εἰς πᾶσαν **ὑπομονὴν** καὶ μακροθυμίαν, μετὰ χαρᾶς· [GNS] ἐν πάσῃ δυνάμει δυναμούμενοι κατὰ τὸ κράτος τῆς δόξης αὐτοῦ εἰς πᾶσαν **ὑπομονὴν** καὶ μακροθυμίαν. μετὰ χαρᾶς [GNT]	The godly person follows the example of those who are actively patient, who endure by walking through the trials of life, conquering all for Christ.

#2846
Patience
 	
Patience–KJV
Endurance–NASB
To persevere–NIV
Endurance–NKJV
Patient endurance–NLT
 	
POSB REFERENCE
(Heb.10:32-39; esp. v.36)
Note 4
	ὑπομονῆς = *hupomonēs*
	Pronunciation: [hoop-om-on-ays']
	Parsing (part of speech): noun
	   Case—genitive
	   Gender—feminine
	   Number—singular
	   Stem or root—from ὑπομονή, ῆς
	Concordance References:
	  ⇒ Strong's #5281 hupomonë
	  ⇒ NIV #5705 hupomonë
	  ⇒ NASB #5281 hupomonë
	
	Hebrews 10:36
	For ye have need of **patience**, that, after ye have done the will of God, ye might receive the promise. [KJV]
	
	For you have need of **endurance**, so that when you have done the will of God, you may receive what was promised. [NASB]
	
	You need **to persevere** so that when you have done the will of God, you will receive what he has promised. [NIV]
	
	For you have need of **endurance**, so that after you have done the will of God, you may receive the promise: [NKJV]
	
	Patient endurance is what you need now, so you will continue to do God's will. Then you will receive all that he has promised. [NLT]
	
	ὑπομονῆς γὰρ ἔχετε χρείαν, ἵνα τὸ θέλημα τοῦ Θεοῦ ποιήσαντες, κομίσησθε τὴν ἐπαγγελίαν. [GNS]
	
	ὑπομονῆς γὰρ ἔχετε χρείαν ἵνα τὸ θέλημα τοῦ θεοῦ ποιήσαντες κομίσησθε τὴν ἐπαγγελίαν. [GNT]
		To persevere; to be patient; to have endurance; to be steadfast in doing the will of God.
		
		Practical Application
		The verses (Hebrews 10:35-37) state it well: endure and you will receive the promise of God's reward. For in just a little while Christ is coming, and He will not tarry. His coming is assured; and when He comes, He will come with His reward.

#2847
Patience
 	
Patience–KJV
Endurance–NASB
Perseverance–NIV
Endurance–NKJV
Endurance–NLT
 	
POSB REFERENCE
(Heb.12:1)
Note 2, point 2
	ὑπομονῆς = *hupomonēs*
	Pronunciation: [hoop-om-on-ays']
	Parsing (part of speech): noun
	   Case—genitive
	   Gender—feminine
	   Number—singular
	   Stem or root—from ὑπομονή, ῆς
	Concordance References:
	  ⇒ Strong's #5281 hupomonë
	  ⇒ NIV #5705 hupomonë
	  ⇒ NASB #5281 hupomonë
	
	Hebrews 12:1
	Wherefore seeing we also are compassed about with so great a cloud of witnesses, let us lay aside every weight, and the sin which doth so easily beset us, and let us run with **patience** the race that is set before us, [KJV]
	
	Therefore, since we have so great a cloud of witnesses surrounding us, let us also lay aside every encumbrance, and the sin which so easily entangles us, and let us run with **endurance** the race that is set before us, [NASB]
	
	Therefore, since we are surrounded by such a great cloud of witnesses, let us throw off everything that hinders and the sin that so easily entangles, and let us run
		To persevere; to be patient; to have endurance; to be steadfast in doing the will of God.
		
		Practical Application
		The word *patience* is not passive; it is active. It is not the spirit that just sits back and puts up with the trials of life, taking whatever may come. Rather, it is the spirit that stands up and faces the trials of life, that actively goes about conquering and overcoming them. When trials confront a man who is truly justified, he is stirred to arise and face the trials head on. He immediately sets out to conquer and overcome them. He knows that God is allowing the trials in order to teach him more and more endurance (patience).

ENGLISH WORD	GREEK WORD AND VERSE	THE WORD MEANS...
	with **perseverance** the race marked out for us. [NIV] Therefore we also, since we are surrounded by so great a cloud of witnesses, let us lay aside every weight, and the sin which so easily ensnares *us,* and let us run with **endurance** the race that is set before us, [NKJV] Therefore, since we are surrounded by such a huge crowd of witnesses to the life of faith, let us strip off every weight that slows us down, especially the sin that so easily hinders our progress. And let us run with **endurance** the race that God has set before us. [NLT] Τοιγαροῦν καὶ ἡμεῖς τοσοῦτον ἔχοντες περικείμενον ἡμῖν νέφος μαρτύρων, ὄγκον ἀποθέμενοι πάντα καὶ τὴν εὐπερίστατον ἁμαρτίαν, δι' **ὑπομονῆς** τρέχωμεν τὸν προκείμενον ἡμῖν ἀγῶνα, [GNS] Τοιγαροῦν καὶ ἡμεῖς τοσοῦτον ἔχοντες περικείμενον ἡμῖν νέφος μαρτύρων, ὄγκον ἀποθέμενοι πάντα καὶ τὴν εὐπερίστατον ἁμαρτίαν, δι' **ὑπομονῆς** τρέχωμεν τὸν προκείμενον ἡμῖν ἀγῶνα [GNT]	

#2848
Patience
 	
Patience–KJV
Perseverance–NASB
Perseverance–NIV
Perseverance–NKJV
Patient endurance–NLT
 	
POSB REFERENCE
(2 Pt.1:5-7; esp. v.6)
Note 1, point 4
	ὑπομονήν = *hupomonēn*
	Pronunciation: [hoop-om-on-ayn']
	Parsing (part of speech): noun
	    Case—accusative
	    Gender—feminine
	    Number—singular
	    Stem or root—from ὑπομονή, ῆς
	Concordance References:
	  ⇒ Strong's #5281 hupomonë
	  ⇒ NIV #5705 hupomonë
	  ⇒ NASB #5281 hupomonë
	
	2 Peter 1:6
	And to knowledge temperance; and to temperance **patience**; and to patience godliness; [KJV]
	
	And in your knowledge, self-control, and in your self-control, **perseverance**, and in your perseverance, godliness; [NASB]
	
	And to knowledge, self-control; and to self-control, **perseverance**; and to perseverance, godliness; [NIV]
	
	To knowledge self-control, to self-control perseverance, to **perseverance** godliness, [NKJV]
	
	Knowing God leads to self-control. Self-control leads to **patient endurance**, and patient endurance leads to godliness. [NLT]
	
	ἐν δὲ τῇ γνώσει τὴν ἐγκράτειαν, ἐν δὲ τῇ ἐγκρατείᾳ τὴν **ὑπομονήν**, ἐν δὲ τῇ ὑπομονῇ τὴν εὐσέβειαν, [GNS]
	
	ἐν δὲ τῇ γνώσει τὴν ἐγκράτειαν, ἐν δὲ τῇ ἐγκρατείᾳ τὴν **ὑπομονήν**, ἐν δὲ τῇ ὑπομονῇ τὴν εὐσέβειαν, [GNT]
		Perseverance, patience, patient endurance, fortitude, steadfastness, constancy.
		
		### Practical Application
		
		The word is not passive; it is active. It is not the spirit that just sits back and puts up with the trials of life, taking whatever may come. Rather it is the spirit that stands up and faces life's trials, that actively goes about conquering and overcoming them. When trials confront a man who is truly justified, he is stirred to arise and face the trials head on. He immediately sets out to conquer and overcome them. He knows that God is allowing the trials in order to teach him more and more patience (endurance).

#2849
Patience
 	
Patience–KJV
Endurance–NASB
Perseverance–NIV
Patience–NKJV
Endurance–NLT
 	
POSB REFERENCE
(Jas.1:2-4; esp. v.3)
Note 2, point 1
 	
See also POSB REF:
(Heb.10:32-39; esp. v.36)
Note 4
(2 Cor.6:4)
Note 2
(Rom.5:3-5; esp. v.3)
	ὑπομονήν = *hupomonēn*
	Pronunciation: [hoop-om-on-ayn']
	Parsing (part of speech): noun
	    Case—accusative
	    Gender—feminine
	    Number—singular
	    Stem or root—from ὑπομονή, ῆς
	Concordance References:
	  ⇒ Strong's #5281 hupomonë
	  ⇒ NIV #5705 hupomonë
	  ⇒ NASB #5281 hupomonë
	
	James 1:3
	Knowing this, that the trying of your faith worketh **patience**. [KJV]
	
	Knowing that the testing of your faith produces **endurance**. [NASB]
	
	Because you know that the testing of your faith develops **perseverance**. [NIV]
	
	Knowing that the testing of your faith produces **patience**. [NKJV]
	
	For when your faith is tested, your **endurance** has a chance to grow. [NLT]
		Perseverance, patience, endurance, steadfastness.
		
		### Practical Application
		
		We must know something: know that trials and temptations work patience (James 1:3). We must know that trials and temptations are not to defeat and discourage us, but to prove us, to make us much stronger and more pure and righteous. The believer is to know that the trials and temptations of life will make him more stedfast, more persevering, and more enduring. They will make him much stronger, not weaker. They will make him strong just like Jesus, and they will give him a pure and righteous character just like Jesus. When the believer keeps this fact in his mind, he can face trials and temptations much more positively. He can then begin to move toward the spirit of living joyfully in the face of trials and temptations.

ENGLISH WORD	GREEK WORD AND VERSE	THE WORD MEANS...
Note 5, point 1 (2 Pt.1:5-7; esp. v.6) Note 1, point 4	γινώσκοντες ὅτι τὸ δοκίμιον ὑμῶν τῆς πίστεως κατεργάζεται ὑπομονήν· [GNS] γινώσκοντες ὅτι τὸ δοκίμιον ὑμῶν τῆς πίστεως κατεργάζεται ὑπομονήν. [GNT]	

#2850
Patient
 	
Suffereth long–KJV
Patient–NASB
Patient–NIV
Suffers long–NKJV
Patient–NLT
 	
POSB
REFERENCE
(1 Cor.13:4-7; esp. v.4)
Note 2
	μακροθυμεῖ = *makrothumei*
	Pronunciation: [mak-roth-oo-meh'-ee]
	Parsing (part of speech): verb
	  Mood—indicative
	  Tense—present
	  Voice—active
	  Person—3rd person
	  Number—singular
	  Stem or root—from μακροθυμέω
	Concordance References:
	⇒ Strong's #3114 makrothumeö
	⇒ NIV #3428 makrothumeö
	⇒ NASB #3114 makrothumeö
	
	1 Cor. 13:4
	Charity **suffereth long**, and is kind; charity envieth not; charity vaunteth not itself, is not puffed up, [KJV]
	Love is **patient**, love is kind, and is not jealous; love does not brag and is not arrogant, [NASB]
	Love is **patient**, love is kind. It does not envy, it does not boast, it is not proud. [NIV]
	Love **suffers long** *and* is kind; love does not envy; love does not parade itself, is not puffed up; [NKJV]
	Love is **patient** and kind. Love is not jealous or boastful or proud [NLT]
	ἡ ἀγάπη **μακροθυμεῖ**, χρηστεύεται· ἡ ἀγάπη, οὐ ζηλοῖ· ἡ ἀγάπη οὐ περπερεύεται, οὐ φυσιοῦται, [GNS]
	Ἡ ἀγάπη **μακροθυμεῖ**, χρηστεύεται ἡ ἀγάπη, οὐ ζηλοῖ, [ἡ ἀγάπη] οὐ περπερεύεται, οὐ φυσιοῦται, [GNT]
		Patient, untiring, persevering; to suffer long; is patient with people.
		
		Practical Application
		The word always refers to being patient with people, not with circumstances (William Barclay. *The Letters to the Corinthians*, p.133).
		  Love is patient; it is patient a long, long time..
		• no matter the evil and injury done by a person.
		• no matter the neglect or ignoring by a loved one.
		
		Love is patient a long, long time without resentment, anger, or seeking revenge. Love controls itself in order to win the person and to help him live, work, and serve as he should.

#2851
Patient
 	
Patient–KJV
Persevering–NASB
Patient–NIV
Patient–NKJV
Patient–NLT
 	
POSB
REFERENCE
(Rom. 12:12)
Note 3, point 2
	ὑπομένοντες = *hupomenontes*
	Pronunciation: [hoop-om-en'-on-tehs]
	Parsing (part of speech): verb
	  Mood—participle (imperative sense)
	  Tense—present
	  Voice—active
	  Case—nominative
	  Gender—masculine
	  Person—2nd person
	  Number—plural
	  Stem or root—from ὑπομένω
	Concordance References:
	⇒ Strong's #5278 hupomenö
	⇒ NIV #5702 hupomenö
	⇒ NASB #5278 hupomenö
	
	Romans 12:12
	Be joyful in hope, **patient** in affliction, faithful in prayer. [NIV]
	Rejoicing in hope; **patient** in tribulation; continuing instant in prayer; [KJV]
	Rejoicing in hope, **persevering** in tribulation, devoted to prayer, [NASB]
	Rejoicing in hope, **patient** in tribulation, continuing steadfastly in prayer; [NKJV]
	Be glad for all God is planning for you. Be **patient** in trouble, and always be prayerful. [NLT]
	τῇ ἐλπίδι χαίροντες· τῇ θλίψει **ὑπομένοντες**· τῇ προσευχῇ προσκαρτεροῦντες· [GNS]
	τῇ ἐλπίδι χαίροντες, τῇ θλίψει **ὑπομένοντες**, τῇ προσευχῇ προσκαρτεροῦντες, [GNT]
		To be patient; to hold out; to stand firm; to bear; to put up with. It means to endure, remain, persevere, abide, bear up bravely.
		
		Practical Application
		The believer is to endure trials. The believer actually experiences a surge of fortitude from Christ when trials confront him.

#2852
Patient
 	
Patient–KJV
Gentle–NASB
Gentle–NIV
	ἐπιεικῆ = *epieikë*
	Pronunciation: [ep-eh-ee-kayn']
	Parsing (part of speech): adjective
	  Case—accusative
	  Gender—masculine
	  Number—singular
	  Stem or root—from ἐπιεικής, ές
		Gentle, patient, gracious, kind, forebearing, reasonable, soft, considerate, and tender.
		
		Practical Application
		The minister or bishop must be "patient" (*epieikë*). The word goes beyond treating some-

ENGLISH WORD	GREEK WORD AND VERSE	THE WORD MEANS...
Gentle–NKJV Gentle–NLT **POSB REFERENCE** (1 Tim.3:3; esp. v.3) Note 2, point 11	Concordance References: ⇒ Strong's #1933 epieikēs ⇒ NIV #2117 epieikēs ⇒ NASB #1933 epieikēs **1 Tim. 3:3** Not given to wine, no striker, not greedy of filthy lucre; but **patient**, not a brawler, not covetous; [KJV] Not addicted to wine or pugnacious, but **gentle**, uncontentious, free from the love of money. [NASB] Not given to drunkenness, not violent but **gentle**, not quarrelsome, not a lover of money. [NIV] Not given to wine, not violent, not greedy for money, but **gentle**, not quarrelsome, not covetous; [NKJV] He must not be a heavy drinker or be violent. He must be **gentle**, peace loving, and not one who loves money. [NLT] μὴ πάροινον, μὴ πλήκτην, μὴ αἰσχροκερδῆ, ἀλλ **ἐπιεικῆ**, ἄμαχον, ἀφιλάργυρον· [GNS] μὴ πάροινον μὴ πλήκτην, ἀλλὰ **ἐπιεικῆ** ἄμαχον ἀφιλάργυρον, [GNT]	one with justice: it treats a person graciously and tenderly. It reaches beyond justice and touches the person with a gentle hand. (See POSB note, Gentleness—Phil. 4:5 for more discussion.)

**#2853
Patient**
 	
Longsuffering–KJV
**Patient–NASB
Patient–NIV**
Longsuffering–NKJV
Patient–NLT
 	
**POSB
REFERENCE**
(2 Pt.3:9)
Note 2
	μακροθυμεῖ = *makrothumei*
	Pronunciation: [mak-roth-oo-meh'-ee]
	Parsing (part of speech): verb
	    Mood—indicative
	    Tense—present
	    Voice—active
	    Person—3rd person
	    Number—singular
	    Stem or root—from μακροθυμέω
	Concordance References:
	⇒ Strong's #3114 makrothumeō
	⇒ NIV #3428 makrothumeō
	⇒ NASB #3114 makrothumeō
	
	2 Peter 3:9
	The Lord is not slack concerning his promise, as some men count slackness; but is **longsuffering** to us-ward, not willing that any should perish, but that all should come to repentance. [KJV]
	The Lord is not slow about His promise, as some count slowness, but is **patient** toward you, not wishing for any to perish but for all to come to repentance. [NASB]
	The Lord is not slow in keeping his promise, as some understand slowness. He is **patient** with you, not wanting anyone to perish, but everyone to come to repentance. [NIV]
	The Lord is not slack concerning *His* promise, as some count slackness, but is **longsuffering** toward us, not willing that any should perish but that all should come to repentance. [NKJV]
	The Lord isn't really being slow about his promise to return, as some people think. No, he is being **patient** for your sake. He does not want anyone to perish, so he is giving more time for everyone to repent. [NLT]
	οὐ βραδύνει ὁ Κύριος τῆς ἐπαγγελίας, ὥς τινες βραδύτητα ἡγοῦνται· ἀλλὰ **μακροθυμεῖ** εἰς ἡμᾶς, μὴ βουλόμενός τινας ἀπολέσθαι ἀλλὰ πάντας εἰς μετάνοιαν χωρῆσαι. [GNS]
	οὐ βραδύνει κύριος τῆς ἐπαγγελίας, ὥς τινες βραδύτητα ἡγοῦνται, ἀλλὰ **μακροθυμεῖ** εἰς ὑμᾶς, μὴ βουλόμενός τινας ἀπολέσθαι ἀλλὰ πάντας εἰς μετάνοιαν χωρῆσαι. [GNT]
		To be patient; to be longsuffering; to wait patiently.
		
		Practical Application
		God is patient (*makrothumei*). The word means...
		• that God is patient with us.
		• that God bears and suffers a long time with us.
		• that God perseveres and is constant in suffering with us.
		• that God is steadfast and enduring in being patient with us.
		
		Very simply, God is slow to give in and to judge and condemn us. God loves and cares for us despite our sin and rebellion, cursing and rejection. This is the very reason He sent Christ to save us. He loves and cares for us; therefore, He is patient a long time with us.

**#2854
Patient**
 	
**Patient–KJV
Patient–NASB
Patient–NIV**
	Μακροθυμήσατε = *Makrothumēsate*
	Pronunciation: [mak-roth-oo-may'-sah-teh]
	Parsing (part of speech): verb
	    Mood—imperative
	    Tense—aorist
	    Voice—active
	    Person—2nd person
	    Number—plural
		To be patient, longsuffering, bearing and suffering, suffering a long time; persevering, waiting, being constant, steadfast, and enduring.
		
		Practical Application
		Note: this is a very special kind of patience—a spiritual patience that never gives in; it perse-

ENGLISH WORD	GREEK WORD AND VERSE	THE WORD MEANS...
Patient–NKJV **Patient–NLT** **POSB** **REFERENCE** (Jas.5:7) Note 1	Stem or root—from μακροθυμέω Concordance References: ⇒ Strong's #3114 makrothumeō ⇒ NIV #3428 makrothumeō ⇒ NASB #3114 makrothumeō **James 5:7** Be **patient** therefore, brethren, unto the coming of the Lord. Behold, the husbandman waiteth for the precious fruit of the earth, and hath long patience for it, until he receive the early and latter rain. [KJV] Be **patient**, therefore, brethren, until the coming of the Lord. Behold, the farmer waits for the precious produce of the soil, being patient about it, until it gets the early and late rains. [NASB] Be **patient**, then, brothers, until the Lord's coming. See how the farmer waits for the land to yield its valuable crop and how patient he is for the autumn and spring rains. [NIV] Therefore be **patient**, brethren, until the coming of the Lord. See *how* the farmer waits for the precious fruit of the earth, waiting patiently for it until it receives the early and latter rain. [NKJV] Dear brothers and sisters, you must be **patient** as you wait for the Lord's return. Consider the farmers who eagerly look for the rains in the fall and in the spring. They patiently wait for the precious harvest to ripen. [NLT] μακροθυμήσατε οὖν, ἀδελφοί, ἕως τῆς παρουσίας τοῦ Κυρίου. ἰδού, ὁ γεωργὸς ἐκδέχεται τὸν τίμιον καρπὸν τῆς γῆς, μακροθυμῶν ἐπ' αὐτῷ, ἕως ἂν λάβῃ ὑετὸν πρόϊμον καὶ ὄψιμον. [GNS] Μακροθυμήσατε οὖν, ἀδελφοί, ἕως τῆς παρουσίας τοῦ κυρίου. ἰδοὺ ὁ γεωργὸς ἐκδέχεται τὸν τίμιον καρπὸν τῆς γῆς μακροθυμῶν ἐπ' αὐτῷ ἕως λάβῃ πρόϊμον καὶ ὄψιμον. [GNT]	veres and suffers on and on no matter what attacks it. Two significant facts need to be noted about this spiritual patience. First, spiritual patience is *not a passive acceptance*. It does not just lay back and accept trials and temptations as though they are a part of life and nothing can be done about them. Spiritual patience is an active, fighting endurance that confronts trials and temptations and that sets out to conquer them. Gaining the victory is the very purpose for patiently confronting and standing fast against them. The believer patiently confronts them to conquer them, not to be defeated by them. Second, spiritual patience is a *fruit of the Spirit* (see POSB note, pt. 4—Galatians 5:22-23 for discussion). When the believer faces some trial or temptation, the Holy Spirit arouses the urge to combat the situation and to conquer it. The arousal or the urge is stirred by the Spirit of God. It is up to us to respond and follow the urge of the Spirit and to persevere. It is up to us to refuse to give in to the enslavement or discouragement and defeat. This kind of patience is a spiritual patience—a work of the Holy Spirit— and it can be had only by trusting the Spirit of God. Therefore, the believer must trust the Spirit of God to stir his heart to stand fast against the temptation and trial, and then he must exert his own will and energy to conquer the situation. When the Holy Spirit does His part, the believer is to do his part. The believer is to patiently combat the temptation or trial when the Spirit of God arouses his heart. The believer is to stand fast and not give in to the sin of the temptation or to the discouragement of the trial. He is to struggle and fight, persevere and endure— patiently suffer on and on against the temptation or trial—and all the while, he is to keep his eyes fixed on the goal and the end: the return of the Lord Jesus Christ. Keeping his eyes fixed upon the return of his wonderful Lord will stir the believer to follow the leadership and power of the Holy Spirit in combating all temptations and trials.
#2855 **Patient** **Continuance** **Patient continuance–** **KJV** Perseverance–NASB Persistence–NIV **Patient continuance–** **NKJV** Persist–NLT **POSB** **REFERENCE** (Romans 2:6-10; esp. v.7) Note 3, point 1b	ὑπομονήν = *hupomonēn* Pronunciation: [hoop-om-on-ayn'] Parsing (part of speech): noun Case—accusative Gender—feminine Number—singular Stem or root—from ὑπομονή, ῆς Concordance References: ⇒ Strong's #5281 hupomonē ⇒ NIV #5705 hupomonē ⇒ NASB #5281 hupomonē **Romans 2:7** To them who by **patient continuance** in well doing seek for glory and honour and immortality, eternal life: [KJV] to those who by **perseverance** in doing good seek for glory and honor and immortality, eternal life; [NASB] To those who by **persistence** in doing good seek glory, honor and immortality, he will give eternal life. [NIV] Eternal life to those who by **patient continuance** in doing good seek for glory, honor, and immortality; [NKJV]	Patient endurance, steadfastness, perseverance. The word means to be steadfast and constant; to endure, persevere, stick to, and continue **Practical Application** Note how the well-doer seeks: "by patient continuance" (*hupomonēn*). The word means to be stedfast and constant; to endure, persevere, stick to, and continue. The well-doer is faithful in doing good works. ⇒ He does not just start, he finishes. ⇒ He does not live an inconsistent, up-and-down life. He continues and keeps on doing good deeds. ⇒ He does not give in to hardships, difficulties, or opposition. He endures and perseveres, always doing good.

ENGLISH WORD	GREEK WORD AND VERSE	THE WORD MEANS...
	περὶ πάντα σεαυτὸν παρεχόμενος **τύπον** καλῶν ἔργων, ἐν τῇ διδασκαλίᾳ ἀδιαφθορίαν, σεμνότητα, ἀφθαρσαν, [GNS] περὶ πάντα, σεαυτὸν παρεχόμενος **τύπον** καλῶν ἔργων, ἐν τῇ διδασκαλίᾳ ἀφθορίαν, σεμνότητα, [GNT]	

#2860
 Pay
 	
 Pay–KJV
 Pay–NASB
 Pay–NIV
 Pay–NKJV
 Pay–NLT
 	
 POSB
 REFERENCE
 (Rom. 13:6-7)
 Note 4, point 3
	τελεῖτε = *teleite*
	 Pronunciation: [tel-ee'-teh]
	 Parsing (part of speech): verb
	   Mood—indicative
	   Tense—present
	   Voice—active
	   Person—2nd person
	   Number—plural
	   Stem or root—from τελέω
	 Concordance References:
	   ⇒ Strong's #5055 teleö
	   ⇒ NIV #5464 teleö
	   ⇒ NASB #5055 teleö
	
	 Romans 13:6
	 For for this cause **pay** ye tribute also: for they are God's ministers, attending continually upon this very thing. [KJV]
	 For because of this you also **pay** taxes, for rulers are servants of God, devoting themselves to this very thing. [NASB]
	 This is also why you **pay** taxes, for the authorities are God's servants, who give their full time to governing. [NIV]
	 For because of this you also **pay** taxes, for they are God's ministers attending continually to this very thing. [NKJV]
	 Pay your taxes, too, for these same reasons. For government workers need to be paid so they can keep on doing the work God intended them to do. [NLT]
	 διὰ τοῦτο γὰρ καὶ φόρους **τελεῖτε**· λειτουργοὶ γὰρ Θεοῦ εἰσιν, εἰς αὐτὸ τοῦτο προσκαρτεροῦντες. [GNS]
	 διὰ τοῦτο γὰρ καὶ φόρους **τελεῖτε**· λειτουργοὶ γὰρ θεοῦ εἰσιν εἰς αὐτὸ τοῦτο προσκαρτεροῦντες. [GNT]
		To pay (taxes), recompense, disburse; to fulfill or to complete; to accomplish.
		
		 Practical Application
		 The believer is not only to pay taxes, but he is to pay whatever is due to every man. The believer is to fulfill his obligations no matter what they are.
		   ⇒ If a nation is due tribute (taxes), he is to pay his tribute.
		   ⇒ If a civil authority is due custom (taxes), he is to pay his custom.
		   ⇒ If an authority or person is due fear, he is to reverence the authority or person.
		   ⇒ If an authority or person is due honor, he is to honor the authority or person.
		
		 Very simply, the believer is to live above reproach before all men, and this includes being a good citizen of his government.

#2861
 Pay...Attention, To
 	
 Heed–KJV
 Pay attention to–NASB
 Pay attention–NIV
 Heed–NKJV
 Listen to–NLT
 	
 POSB
 REFERENCE
 (Heb.2:1)
 Note 1
	προσέχειν = *prosechein*
	 Pronunciation: [pros-ekh'-een]
	 Parsing (part of speech): verb
	   Mood—infinitive
	   Tense—present
	   Voice—active
	   Stem or root—from προσέχω
	 Concordance References:
	   ⇒ Strong's #4337 prosechö
	   ⇒ NIV #4668 prosechö
	   ⇒ NASB #4337 prosechö
	
	 Hebrews 2:1
	 Therefore we ought to give the more earnest **heed** to the things which we have heard, lest at any time we should let them slip. [KJV]
	 For this reason we must **pay** much closer **attention to** what we have heard, lest we drift away from it. [NASB]
	 We must **pay** more careful **attention**, therefore, **to** what we have heard, so that we do not drift away. [NIV]
	 Therefore we must give the more earnest **heed** to the things we have heard, lest we drift away. [NKJV]
	 So we must **listen** very carefully **to** the truth we have heard, or we may drift away from it. [NLT]
	 Διὰ τοῦτο δεῖ περισσοτέρως ἡμᾶς **προσέχειν** τοῖς ἀκουσθεῖσι, μή ποτε παραρρυῶμεν. [GNS]
	 Διὰ τοῦτο δεῖ περισσοτέρως **προσέχειν** ἡμᾶς τοῖς ἀκουσθεῖσιν, μήποτε παραρυῶμεν. [GNT]
		To pay attention to; to heed; to listen to; to listen very carefully; to be careful; to be on guard.
		
		 Practical Application
		 Note how intense the warning is: we must pay attention to the gospel. We *must pay more careful attention* to the gospel. We are to pay the utmost attention to the gospel of salvation:
		   ⇒ to listen more closely than ever before.
		   ⇒ to pay more attention than ever before.

ENGLISH WORD	GREEK WORD AND VERSE	THE WORD MEANS...

#2862
Pay Close Attention
 	
Take heed–KJV
Pay close attention–NASB
Watch...closely–NIV
Take heed–NKJV
Keep a close watch–NLT
 	
POSB REFERENCE
(1 Tim.4:16)
Note 12
	ἔπεχε = epeche
	Pronunciation: [ep-ekh'-eh]
	Parsing (part of speech): verb
	  Mood—imperative
	  Tense—present
	  Voice—active
	  Person—2nd person
	  Number—singular
	  Stem or root—from ἐπέχω
	Concordance References:
	  ⇒ Strong's #1907 epechō
	  ⇒ NIV #2091 epechō
	  ⇒ NASB #1907 epechō
	
	1 Tim. 4:16
	Take heed unto thyself, and unto the doctrine; continue in them: for in doing this thou shalt both save thyself, and them that hear thee. [KJV]
	Pay close attention to yourself and to your teaching; persevere in these things; for as you do this you will insure salvation both for yourself and for those who hear you. [NASB]
	Watch your life and doctrine **closely**. Persevere in them, because if you do, you will save both yourself and your hearers. [NIV]
	Take heed to yourself and to the doctrine. Continue in them, for in doing this you will save both yourself and those who hear you. [NKJV]
	Keep a close watch on yourself and on your teaching. Stay true to what is right, and God will save you and those who hear you. [NLT]
	ἔπεχε σεαυτῷ καὶ τῇ διδασκαλίᾳ. ἐπίμενε αὐτοῖς· [GNS]
	ἔπεχε σεαυτῷ καὶ τῇ διδασκαλίᾳ, ἐπίμενε αὐτοῖς· τοῦτο γὰρ ποιῶν καὶ σεαυτὸν σώσεις καὶ τοὺς ἀκούοντάς σου. [GNT]
		To watch closely; to take heed; to pay close attention; to keep a close watch; to keep a strict eye upon or to keep on paying attention to oneself and to one's teaching.
		
		Practical Application
		The good minister guards himself and his teaching.
		⇒ He guards his body, keeps it both morally and physically fit. He flees the temptations that assault and seduce him, and he controls his thoughts and keeps them pure from the lusts of the world and flesh. He neither eats too much nor succumbs to immoral thoughts or acts. He neither gives in to greed nor seeks the possessions or wealth of the world.
		⇒ He guards his spirit and keeps it spiritually fit. He worships God every day and lives in God's Word and prayer all day long, and he shares the glorious gospel of Christ, witnessing to and exhorting people as he walks throughout the day.
		⇒ He guards his study and teaching, avoiding the profane doctrines, teachings, notions, philosophies, ideas, and fables of men.

#2863
Pay The Penalty
 	
Punished–KJV
Pay the penalty–NASB
Punished–NIV
Punished–NKJV
Punished–NLT
 	
POSB REFERENCE
(2 Thes.1:9)
Note 4, point 2
	δίκην τίσουσιν = dikēn tisousin
	Pronunciation: [dee'-kayn tee'-soo-sin]
	Parsing dikēn (part of speech): noun
	  Case—accusative
	  Gender—feminine
	  Number—singular
	  Stem or root—from δίκη, ης
	Parsing tisousin (part of speech): verb
	  Mood—indicative
	  Tense—future
	  Voice—active
	  Person—3rd person
	  Number—plural
	  Stem or root—from τίνω
	Concordance References:
	  ⇒ Strong's #1349+5099 dikē tinō
	  ⇒ NIV #1472+5514 dikē tinō
	  ⇒ NASB #1349+5099 dikē tinō
	
	2 Thes. 1:9
	Who shall be **punished** with everlasting destruction from the presence of the Lord, and from the glory of his power; [KJV]
	And these will **pay the penalty** of eternal destruction, away from the presence of the Lord and from the glory of His power, [NASB]
	They will be **punished** with everlasting destruction and shut out from the presence of the Lord and from the majesty of his power [NIV]
	These shall be **punished** with everlasting destruction from the presence of the Lord and from the glory of His power, [NKJV]
	They will be **punished** with everlasting destruction, forever separated from the Lord and from his glorious power [NLT]
	οἵτινες δίκην τίσουσιν, ὄλεθρον αἰώνιον ἀπὸ προσώπου τοῦ Κυρίου καὶ ἀπὸ τῆς δόξης τῆς ἰσχύος αὐτοῦ, [GNS]
	οἵτινες δίκην τίσουσιν ὄλεθρον αἰώνιον ἀπὸ προσώπου τοῦ κυρίου καὶ ἀπὸ τῆς δόξης τῆς ἰσχύος αὐτοῦ, [GNT]
		To undergo punishment, justice; to pay the penalty; to suffer punishment from God.
		
		Practical Application
		Matthew Henry says that "they did sin's work, and must receive sin's wages" (*Matthew Henry's Commentary*, Vol.6, p.795). Sinners may get away with their sin and rejection of God while on earth, but they will be punished in the final analysis.
		Note another fact about the punishment. Note the Greek word for pay the penalty (*dikēn*). It comes from the same root as righteous (*dikaios*). This means that the punishment will be righteous, just—exactly what the person deserves, no more, no less. A person will be measured an exact amount of punishment that he has earned while on earth. God's punishment will not be vindictive; it will be perfectly just, a punishment of retribution—a punishment that pays a person exactly what he deserves.

ENGLISH WORD	GREEK WORD AND VERSE	THE WORD MEANS...
		with everyone and to lead others to live in peace. The believer is to live at peace with all men. The believer is to work for as much peace as possible. Some level of harmony and concord can be achieved at least some of the time. The believer is never to give up, not as long as there is hope for some degree of peace. He is to achieve as much peace as possible. However remember, peace is not always possible—not with everyone.
#2868 **Peace Loving** Not a brawler–KJV Uncontentious–NASB Not quarrelsome–NIV Not quarrelsome–NKJV **Peace loving–NLT** **POSB** **REFERENCE** (1 Tim.3-2-3; esp. v.3) Note 2, point 12	ἄμαχον = amachon Pronunciation: [am'-akh-on] Parsing (part of speech): adjective 　Case—accusative 　Gender—masculine 　Number—singular 　Stem or root—from ἄμαχος, ον Concordance References: ⇒ Strong's #269 amachos ⇒ NIV #285 amachos ⇒ NASB #269 amachos **1 Tim. 3:3** Not given to wine, no striker, not greedy of filthy lucre; but patient, **not a brawler**, not covetous; [KJV] Not addicted to wine or pugnacious, but gentle, **uncontentious**, free from the love of money. [NASB] Not given to drunkenness, not violent but gentle, **not quarrelsome**, not a lover of money. [NIV] Not given to wine, not violent, not greedy for money, but gentle, **not quarrelsome**, not covetous; [NKJV] He must not be a heavy drinker or be violent. He must be gentle, **peace loving**, and not one who loves money. [NLT] μὴ πάροινον, μὴ πλήκτην, μὴ αἰσχροκερδῆ, ἀλλ ἐπιεικῆ, ἄμαχον, ἀφιλάργυρον· [GNS] μὴ πάροινον μὴ πλήκτην, ἀλλὰ ἐπιεικῆ ἄμαχον ἀφιλάργυρον, [GNT]	Not quarrelsome; not a brawler; not contentious or a fighter; to be peace loving, peaceable, peaceful. **Practical Application** The minister or elder must be peace loving (amachon): He must be a man of peace, a mild-mannered person, always under control. Again, this refers to the tongue as well as to the hands. He must be a man who is deeply touched when there is unrest, controversy, or disturbance in the church or among believers. He must be a person who is so touched that he will work and seek for peace.
#2869 **Peace, Be Still** **Peace, be still–KJV** Hush, be still–NASB Quiet! be still!–NIV **Peace, be still–NKJV** Quiet down!–NLT **POSB** **REFERENCE** (Mk.4:38-39; esp. v.39) Note 3	Σιώπα πεφίμωσο = siopa pephimoso Pronunciation: [see-o-pah' peh-fee-mo'-so] Parsing siopa (part of speech): verb 　Mood—imperative 　Tense—present 　Voice—active 　Person—2nd person 　Number—singular 　Stem or root—from σιωπάω Parsing pephimoso (part of speech): verb 　Mood—imperative 　Tense—perfect 　Voice—passive 　Person—2nd person 　Number—singular 　Stem or root—from φιμόω Concordance References: ⇒ Strong's #4623 siopaö + #5392 phimoö ⇒ NIV #4995 siöpaö [Quiet] + 5821 phimoö [still] ⇒ NASB #4623 siöpaö + #5392 phimoö **Mark 4:39** And he arose, and rebuked the wind, and said unto the sea, **Peace, be still**. And the wind ceased, and there was a great calm. [KJV] And being aroused, He rebuked the wind and said to the sea, "**Hush, be still**." And the wind died down and it became perfectly calm. [NASB] He got up, rebuked the wind and said to the waves, "**Quiet! Be still!**" Then the wind died down and it was completely calm. [NIV] Then He arose and rebuked the wind, and said to the sea, "**Peace, be still!**" And the wind ceased and there	Quiet! be still!; peace be still; be still; quiet down. Literally, it means to be muzzled; to hush, silence, suppress, quiet down; to be speechless. **Practical Application** The use of this word muzzled shows the fury and violence of the storm and stresses the dramatic act of Jesus.

ENGLISH WORD	GREEK WORD AND VERSE	THE WORD MEANS...
	was a great calm. [NKJV] When he woke up, he rebuked the wind and said to the water, "**Quiet down!**" Suddenly the wind stopped, and there was a great calm. [NLT] καὶ διεγερθεὶς ἐπετίμησε τῷ ἀνέμῳ καὶ εἶπε τῇ θαλάσσῃ, **Σιώπα, πεφίμωσο**. καὶ ἐκόπασεν ὁ ἄνεμος, καὶ ἐγένετο γαλήνη μεγάλη. [GNS] καὶ διεγερθεὶς ἐπετίμησεν τῷ ἀνέμῳ καὶ εἶπεν τῇ θαλάσσῃ, **Σιώπα, πεφίμωσο**. καὶ ἐκόπασεν ὁ ἄνεμος καὶ ἐγένετο γαλήνη μεγάλη. [GNT]	

#2870
Peace-Loving
 	
Peaceable–KJV
Peaceable–NASB
Peace-loving–NIV
Peaceable–NKJV
Peace loving–NLT
 	
POSB
REFERENCE
(Jas.3:17-18; esp. v.17)
Note 3, point 2b
	εἰρηνική = eirēnikē
	Pronunciation: [i-ray-nee-kay']
	Parsing (part of speech): adjective
	    Case—nominative
	    Gender—feminine
	    Number—singular
	    Stem or root—from εἰρηνικός, ή, όν
	Concordance References:
	  ⇒ Strong's #1516 eirēnikos
	  ⇒ NIV #1646 eirēnikos
	  ⇒ NASB #1516 eirēnikos
	
	James 3:17
	But the wisdom that is from above is first pure, then **peaceable**, gentle, and easy to be intreated, full of mercy and good fruits, without partiality, and without hypocrisy. [KJV]
	
	But the wisdom from above is first pure, then **peaceable**, gentle, reasonable, full of mercy and good fruits, unwavering, without hypocrisy. [NASB]
	
	But the wisdom that comes from heaven is first of all pure; then **pcace-loving**, considerate, submissive, full of mercy and good fruit, impartial and sincere. [NIV]
	
	But the wisdom that is from above is first pure, then **peaceable**, gentle, willing to yield, full of mercy and good fruits, without partiality and without hypocrisy. [NKJV]
	
	But the wisdom that comes from heaven is first of all pure. It is also **peace loving**, gentle at all times, and willing to yield to others. It is full of mercy and good deeds. It shows no partiality and is always sincere. [NLT]
	
	ἡ δὲ ἄνωθεν σοφία πρῶτον μὲν ἁγνή ἐστιν, ἔπειτα **εἰρηνική**, ἐπιεικής, εὐπειθής, μεστὴ ἐλέους καὶ καρπῶν ἀγαθῶν, ἀδιάκριτος καὶ ἀνυπόκριτος. [GNS]
	
	ἡ δὲ ἄνωθεν σοφία πρῶτον μὲν ἁγνή ἐστιν, ἔπειτα **εἰρηνική**, ἐπιεικής, εὐπειθής, μεστὴ ἐλέους καὶ καρπῶν ἀγαθῶν, ἀδιάκριτος, ἀνυπόκριτος. [GNT]
		Peace loving, peaceable. The word means to bind together; to join and weave together.
		
		Practical Application
		Truc wisdom is "peace-loving" (eirēnikē). It means that a wise teacher is bound, woven, and joined together...
		  • with himself
		  • with God
		  • with his fellow man
		And the wise teacher does all he can to keep the peace and to make peace where it has been broken, whether between two individuals or two groups, a family, a community, or a nation. A wise teacher, a teacher of true wisdom, works to reconcile people to God and to each other. He works to bring men closer to God and to each other.

#2871
Peaceable
 	
Peaceable–KJV
Peaceable–NASB
Peace-loving–NIV
Peaceable–NKJV
Peace loving–NLT
 	
POSB
REFERENCE
(Jas.3:17-18; esp. v.17)
Note 3, point 2b
	εἰρηνική = eirēnikē
	Pronunciation: [i-ray-nee-kay']
	Parsing (part of speech): adjective
	    Case—nominative
	    Gender—feminine
	    Number—singular
	    Stem or root—from εἰρηνικός, ή, όν
	Concordance References:
	  ⇒ Strong's #1516 eirēnikos
	  ⇒ NIV #1646 eirēnikos
	  ⇒ NASB #1516 eirēnikos
	
	James 3:17
	But the wisdom that is from above is first pure, then **peaceable**, gentle, and easy to be intreated, full of mercy and good fruits, without partiality, and without hypocrisy. [KJV]
	
	But the wisdom from above is first pure, then **peaceable**, gentle, reasonable, full of mercy and good fruits, unwavering, without hypocrisy. [NASB]
	
	But the wisdom that comes from heaven is first of all pure; then **peace-loving**, considerate, submissive, full of mercy and good fruit, impartial and sincere. [NIV]
	
	But the wisdom that is from above is first pure, then
		Peace loving, peaceable. The word means to bind together; to join and weave together.
		
		Practical Application
		True wisdom is "peaceable" (eirēnikē). It means that a wise teacher is bound, woven, and joined together...
		  • with himself
		  • with God
		  • with his fellow man
		
		And the wise teacher does all he can to keep the peace and to make peace where it has been broken, whether between two individuals or two groups, a family, a community, or a nation. A wise teacher, a teacher of true wisdom, works to reconcile people to God and to each other. He works to bring men closer to God and to each other.

ENGLISH WORD	GREEK WORD AND VERSE	THE WORD MEANS...
	peaceable, gentle, willing to yield, full of mercy and good fruits, without partiality and without hypocrisy. [NKJV] But the wisdom that comes from heaven is first of all pure. It is also **peace loving**, gentle at all times, and willing to yield to others. It is full of mercy and good deeds. It shows no partiality and is always sincere. [NLT] ἡ δὲ ἄνωθεν σοφία πρῶτον μὲν ἁγνή ἐστιν, ἔπειτα **εἰρηνική**, ἐπιεικής, εὐπειθής, μεστὴ ἐλέους καὶ καρπῶν ἀγαθῶν, ἀδιάκριτος καὶ ἀνυπόκριτος. [GNS] ἡ δὲ ἄνωθεν σοφία πρῶτον μὲν ἁγνή ἐστιν, ἔπειτα **εἰρηνική**, ἐπιεικής, εὐπειθής, μεστὴ ἐλέους καὶ καρπῶν ἀγαθῶν, ἀδιάκριτος, ἀνυπόκριτος. [GNT]	
#2872 **Peaceable** Brawlers–KJV Uncontentious–NASB **Peaceable–NIV** **Peaceable–NKJV** Quarreling–NLT **POSB** **REFERENCE** (Tit.3:2) Note 4	**ἄμάχους** = *amachous* Pronunciation: [ham'-akh-oos] Parsing (part of speech): adjective 　　Case—accusative 　　Gender—masculine 　　Number—plural 　　Stem or root—from **ἄμαχος**, ον Concordance References: ⇒　Strong's #269 amachos ⇒　NIV #285 amachos ⇒　NASB #269 amachos **Titus 3:2** To speak evil of no man, to be no **brawlers**, but gentle, showing all meekness unto all men. [KJV] To malign no one, to be **uncontentious**, gentle, showing every consideration for all men. [NASB] To slander no one, to be **peaceable** and considerate, and to show true humility toward all men. [NIV] to speak evil of no one, to be **peaceable**, gentle, showing all humility to all men. [NKJV] They must not speak evil of anyone, and they must avoid **quarreling**. Instead, they should be gentle and show true humility to everyone. [NLT] μηδένα βλασφημεῖν, **ἀμάχους** εἶναι, ἐπιεικεῖς, πᾶσαν ἐνδεικνυμένους πραότητα πρὸς πάντας ἀνθρώπους. [GNS] μηδένα βλασφημεῖν, **ἀμάχους** εἶναι, ἐπιεικεῖς, πᾶσαν ἐνδεικνυμένους πραΰτητα πρὸς πάντας ἀνθρώπους. [GNT]	To be peaceable; to be uncontentious; not to be quarreling or brawling. **Practical Application** The Christian is not to be a fighting, contentious person; not to be a person who is always walking around looking for an argument or fight; not to be a person who walks around with a chip on his shoulder looking for some controversy or argument; not to be so opinionated and stubborn that everyone else is always wrong; not to be a person who is always criticizing or talking about others, stirring up trouble and disturbing feelings and causing division. The Christian citizen is to be the very opposite: meek and peaceful. This, of course, does not mean that the Christian citizen does not speak up for what is right; he does. And he is strong in his stand, refusing to give in to the license and indulgence of evil. But he seeks peace where it is possible, and he seeks to lead others to be peaceable.
#2873 **Peacemakers** **Peacemakers–KJV** **Peacemakers–NASB** **Peacemakers–NIV** **Peacemakers–NKJV** Those who work for 　peace–NLT **POSB** **REFERENCE** (Mt.5:9) Note 8	**εἰρηνοποιοί** = *eirenopoios* Pronunciation: [i-ray-nop-oy-os] Parsing (part of speech): pronominal adjective 　　Case—nominative 　　Gender—masculine 　　Number—plural 　　Stem or root—from **εἰρηνοποιός**, ου Concordance References: ⇒　Strong's #1518 eirenopoios ⇒　NIV #1648 eirenopoios ⇒　NASB #1518 eirenopoios **Matthew 5:9** Blessed are the **peacemakers**: for they shall be called the children of God. [KJV] "Blessed are the **peacemakers**, for they shall be called sons of God. [NASB] Blessed are the **peacemakers**, for they will be called sons of God. [NIV] Blessed are the **peacemakers**, For they shall be called sons of God. [NKJV] God blesses **those who work for peace**, for they will be called the children of God. [NLT] Μακάριοι οἱ **εἰρηνοποιοί**· ὅτι αὐτοὶ υἱοὶ Θεοῦ κληθήσονται. [GNS] μακάριοι οἱ **εἰρηνοποιοί**, ὅτι αὐτοὶ υἱοὶ θεοῦ κληθήσονται. [GNT]	Peacemakers; to make peace; those who work for peace. **Practical Application** A peacemaker brings people together; but even more important than this, he makes peace between people and God. A peacemaker... • solves disputes and erases divisions. • reconciles differences and eliminates strife. • silences tongues and builds right relationships. Who is the peacemaker? 1. The person who strives to make peace with God (Romans 5:1; Ephes. 2:14-17). He conquers the inner struggle, settles the inner tension, handles the inner pressure. He takes the struggle within his heart between good and evil, and strives for the good and conquers the bad. 2. The person who strives at every opportunity to make peace *within* others. He seeks and leads others to make their peace with God—to conquer their inner struggle, to settle their inner tension, to handle their inner pressure. 3. The person who strives at every opportunity to make peace *between* others. He works to solve disputes and erase divisions, to reconcile differences and eliminate strife, to silence tongues and build relationships.

ENGLISH WORD	GREEK WORD AND VERSE	THE WORD MEANS...

#2874
Peculiar
 	
Peculiar–KJV
His...posession–NASB
His very own–NIV
His...people–NKJV
His very own–NLT
 	
**POSB
REFERENCE**
(Tit.2:14)
Note 4, point 2
	περιούσιον = periousion
	Pronunciation: [per-ee-oo'-see-on]
	Parsing (part of speech): adjective
	  Case—accusative
	  Gender—masculine
	  Number—singular
	  Stem or root—from περιούσιος, ον
	Concordance References:
	⇒ Strong's #4041 periousios
	⇒ NIV #4342 periousios
	⇒ NASB #4041 periousios
	
	Titus 2:14
	Who gave himself for us, that he might redeem us from all iniquity, and purify unto himself a **peculiar** people, zealous of good works. [KJV]
	Who gave Himself for us, that He might redeem us from every lawless deed and purify for Himself a people for **His** own **possession**, zealous for good deeds. [NASB]
	Who gave himself for us to redeem us from all wickedness and to purify for himself a people that are **his very own**, eager to do what is good. [NIV]
	Who gave Himself for us, that He might redeem us from every lawless deed and purify for Himself *His* own **special** people, zealous for good works. [NKJV]
	He gave his life to free us from every kind of sin, to cleanse us, and to make us **his very own** people, totally committed to doing what is right. [NLT]
	ὃς ἔδωκεν ἑαυτὸν ὑπὲρ ἡμῶν, ἵνα λυτρώσηται ἡμᾶς ἀπὸ πάσης ἀνομίας, καὶ καθαρίσῃ ἑαυτῷ λαὸν **περιούσιον**, ζηλωτὴν καλῶν ἔργων. [GNS]
	ὃς ἔδωκεν ἑαυτὸν ὑπὲρ ἡμῶν ἵνα λυτρώσηται ἡμᾶς ἀπὸ πάσης ἀνομίας καὶ καθαρίσῃ ἑαυτῷ λαὸν **περιούσιον**, ζηλωτὴν καλῶν ἔργων. [GNT]
		His very own; peculiar; His own possession, special, belonging only to Him. It means set apart, possessed over and above, especially selected and reserved for.
		
		Practical Application
		Christ died so that He might have a peculiar people, a very special people as His own possession. This is seen in the word "peculiar" (*periousion*). When a person really grasps what Jesus Christ has done for him, that person can only surrender all he is and has to Christ. The person wants to follow and serve Christ, to do all that Christ says. The person separates himself from the world, sets his life apart to follow Christ; then Christ sets the person apart to be His own very special possession. Through the death of Jesus Christ, the believer becomes the very special possession of the Lord Jesus Christ.

#2875
Peculiar People
 	
Peculiar people–KJV
People for God's own possession–NASB
People belonging to God–NIV
His own special people–NKJV
His very own possession–NLT
 	
**POSB
REFERENCE**
(1 Pt.2:9)
Note 1
	λαὸς εἰς περιποίησιν = laos eis peripoiēsin
	Pronunciation: [lah-os' ice per-ee-poy'-ay-sin]
	Parsing *laos* (part of speech): noun
	  Case—nominative
	  Gender—masculine
	  Number—singular
	  Stem or root—from λαός, οῦ
	Parsing *eis* (part of speech): preposition
	  Case—accusative
	  Stem or root—from εἰς
	Parsing *peripoiēsin* (part of speech): noun
	  Case—accusative
	  Gender—feminine
	  Number—singular
	  Stem or root—from περιποίησις, εως
	Concordance References:
	⇒ Strong's #2992 laos + 1519+4047 eis peripoiēsis
	⇒ NIV #3295 laos [people] + 1650+4348 eis peripoiēsis [belonging to God]
	⇒ NASB #2992 laos + 1519+4047 eis peripoiēsis
	
	1 Peter 2:9
	But ye are a chosen generation, a royal priesthood, an holy nation, a **peculiar people**; that ye should show forth the praises of him who hath called you out of darkness into his marvellous light: [KJV]
	But you are a chosen race, a royal priesthood, a HOLY NATION, a **people for God's own possession**, that you may proclaim the excellencies of Him who has called you out of darkness into His marvelous light; [NASB]
	But you are a chosen people, a royal priesthood, a holy nation, a **people belonging to God**, that you may declare the praises of him who called you out of darkness into his wonderful light. [NIV]
	But you *are* a chosen generation, a royal priesthood, a holy nation, **His own special people**, that you may pro-
		People belonging to God, peculiar people, people for God's own possession.
		
		Practical Application
		Believers become a "peculiar people" (*laos eis peripoiēsin*). The Greek means...
		• "a people for God's own possession" (A.T. Robertson. *Word Pictures in the New Testament*, Vol.6, p.98).
		• "the people to be His very own" (Charles B. Williams. *The New Testament in the Language of the People*. "The Four Translation New Testament").
		• "a people saved to be His own" (William F. Beck. *The New Testament in the Language of Today*. "The Four Translation New Testament").
		
		This is a most precious thought: that God makes us His very own people, a very special possession of His. Possession has the idea of value, of worth and preciousness. We are more precious to God than all the precious gems and treasures of the world. We are His *treasured possession*. Possession also has the idea of provision, protection, and security. We are God's possession, His very special people; therefore, He will provide for us and protect us to make us secure in every sense of the word.

ENGLISH WORD	GREEK WORD AND VERSE	THE WORD MEANS...

#2879
People
 	
People–KJV
People–NASB
People–NIV
People–NKJV
People–NLT
 	
**POSB
REFERENCE**
(Acts 15:13-21; esp.
v.14)
Note 4, point 1
	λαὸν = laon
	Pronunciation: [lah-on']
	Parsing (part of speech): noun
	  Case—accusative
	  Gender—masculine
	  Number—singular
	  Stem or root—from λαός, οῦ
	Concordance References:
	  ⇒ Strong's #2992 laos
	  ⇒ NIV #3295 laos
	  ⇒ NASB #2992 laos
	
	Acts 15:14
	Simeon hath declared how God at the first did visit the Gentiles, to take out of them a **people** for his name. [KJV]
	"Simeon has related how God first concerned Himself about taking from among the Gentiles a **people** for His name. [NASB]
	Simon has described to us how God at first showed his concern by taking from the Gentiles a **people** for himself. [NIV]
	Simon has declared how God at the first visited the Gentiles to take out of them a **people** for His name. [NKJV]
	Peter has told you about the time God first visited the Gentiles to take from them a **people** for himself. [NLT]
	Συμεὼν ἐξηγήσατο καθὼς πρῶτον ὁ Θεὸς ἐπεσκέψατο λαβεῖν ἐξ ἐθνῶν **λαὸν** ἐπὶ τῷ ὀνόματι αὐτοῦ. [GNS]
	Συμεὼν ἐξηγήσατο καθὼς πρῶτον ὁ θεὸς ἐπεσκέψατο λαβεῖν ἐξ ἐθνῶν **λαὸν** τῷ ὀνόματι αὐτοῦ. [GNT]
		People, nation.
		
		Practical Application
		The word "people" (laon) is the same word used of the Jewish people (cp. Acts 10:2). The point is that God was calling a new people out—a new body, a new nation, a new race—to be His chosen people, just as He had done with Abraham and the Jews. (See POSB Deeper Study #8, pt.6—Matthew 21:43; POSB note—Ephes. 2:11-18; POSB note—Ephes. 2:14-15; POSB note—Ephes. 2:19-22; and POSB note—Ephes. 4:17-19 for more discussion.)

#2880
**People
Belonging To
God**
 	
Peculiar people–KJV
People for God's own possession–NASB
People belonging to God–NIV
His own special people–NKJV
His very own possession–NLT
 	
**POSB
REFERENCE**
(1 Pt.2:9)
Note 1
	λαὸς εἰς περιποίησιν = laos eis peripoiësin
	Pronunciation: [lah-os' ice per-ee-poy'-ay-sin]
	Parsing laos (part of speech): noun
	  Case—nominative
	  Gender—masculine
	  Number—singular
	  Stem or root—from λαός, οῦ
	Parsing eis (part of speech): preposition
	  Case—accusative
	  Stem or root—from εἰς
	Parsing peripoiësin (part of speech): noun
	  Case—accusative
	  Gender—feminine
	  Number—singular
	  Stem or root—from περιποίησις, εως
	Concordance References:
	  ⇒ Strong's #2992 laos + 1519+4047 eis peripoiësis
	  ⇒ NIV #3295 laos [people] + 1650+4348 eis peripoiësis [belonging to God]
	  ⇒ NASB #2992 laos + 1519+4047 eis peripoiësis
	
	1 Peter 2:9
	But ye are a chosen generation, a royal priesthood, an holy nation, a **peculiar people**; that ye should show forth the praises of him who hath called you out of darkness into his marvellous light: [KJV]
	But you are a chosen race, a royal priesthood, a HOLY NATION, a **people for God's own possession**, that you may proclaim the excellencies of Him who has called you out of darkness into His marvelous light; [NASB]
	But you are a chosen people, a royal priesthood, a holy nation, a **people belonging to God**, that you may declare the praises of him who called you out of darkness into his wonderful light. [NIV]
	But you are a chosen generation, a royal priesthood, a holy nation, **His own special people**, that you may proclaim the praises of Him who called you out of darkness into His marvelous light; [NKJV]
	But you are not like that, for you are a chosen people. You are a kingdom of priests, God's holy nation, **his very**
		People belonging to God, peculiar people, people for God's own possession.
		
		Practical Application
		Believers become a "people belonging to God" (laos eis peripoiësin). The Greek means...
		• "a people for God's own possession" (A.T. Robertson. Word Pictures in the New Testament, Vol.6, p.98).
		• "the people to be His very own" (Charles B. Williams. The New Testament in the Language of the People. "The Four Translation New Testament").
		• "a people saved to be His own" (William F. Beck. The New Testament in the Language of Today. "The Four Translation New Testament").
		
		This is a most precious thought: that God makes us His very own people, a very special possession of His. Possession has the idea of value, of worth and preciousness. We are more precious to God than all the precious gems and treasures of the world. We are His treasured possession. Possession also has the idea of provision, protection, and security. We are God's possession, His very special people; therefore, He will provide for us and protect us and make us secure in every sense of the word.

ENGLISH WORD	GREEK WORD AND VERSE	THE WORD MEANS...
	own possession. This is so you can show others the goodness of God, for he called you out of the darkness into his wonderful light. [NLT] ὑμεῖς δὲ γένος ἐκλεκτόν, βασίλειον ἱεράτευμα, ἔθνος ἅγιον, **λαὸς εἰς περιποίησιν**, ὅπως τὰς ἀρετὰς ἐξαγγείλητε τοῦ ἐκ σκότους ὑμᾶς καλέσαντος εἰς τὸ θαυμαστὸν αὐτοῦ φῶς· [GNS] Ὑμεῖς δὲ γένος ἐκλεκτόν, βασίλειον ἱεράτευμα, ἔθνος ἅγιον, **λαὸς εἰς περιποίησιν**, ὅπως τὰς ἀρετὰς ἐξαγγείλητε τοῦ ἐκ σκότους ὑμᾶς καλέσαντος εἰς τὸ θαυμαστὸν αὐτοῦ φῶς· [GNT]	

#2881
People For God's Own Possession
 	
Peculiar people–KJV
People for God's own possession–NASB
People belonging to God–NIV
His own special people–NKJV
His very own possession–NLT
 	
POSB REFERENCE
(1 Pt.2:9)
Note 1
	λαὸς εἰς περιποίησιν = *laos eis peripoiësin*
	Pronunciation: [lah-os' ice per-ee-poy'-ay-sin]
	Parsing *laos* (part of speech): noun
	   Case—nominative
	   Gender—masculine
	   Number—singular
	   Stem or root—from **λαός**, οῦ
	Parsing *eis* (part of speech): preposition
	   Case—accusative
	   Stem or root—from **εἰς**
	Parsing *peripoiësin* (part of speech): noun
	   Case—accusative
	   Gender—feminine
	   Number—singular
	   Stem or root—from **περιποίησις**, εως
	Concordance References:
	  ⇒ Strong's #2992 laos + 1519+4047 eis peripoiësis
	  ⇒ NIV #3295 laos [people] + 1650+4348 eis peripoiësis [belonging to God]
	  ⇒ NASB #2992 laos + 1519+4047 eis peripoiësis
	
	1 Peter 2:9
	But ye are a chosen generation, a royal priesthood, an holy nation, a **peculiar people**; that ye should show forth the praises of him who hath called you out of darkness into his marvellous light: [KJV]
	But you are a chosen race, a royal priesthood, a HOLY NATION, a **people for God's own possession**, that you may proclaim the excellencies of Him who has called you out of darkness into His marvelous light; [NASB]
	But you are a chosen people, a royal priesthood, a holy nation, a **people belonging to God**, that you may declare the praises of him who called you out of darkness into his wonderful light. [NIV]
	But you *are* a chosen generation, a royal priesthood, a holy nation, **His own special people**, that you may proclaim the praises of Him who called you out of darkness into His marvelous light; [NKJV]
	But you are not like that, for you are a chosen people. You are a kingdom of priests, God's holy nation, **his very own possession**. This is so you can show others the goodness of God, for he called you out of the darkness into his wonderful light. [NLT]
	
	ὑμεῖς δὲ γένος ἐκλεκτόν, βασίλειον ἱεράτευμα, ἔθνος ἅγιον, **λαὸς εἰς περιποίησιν**, ὅπως τὰς ἀρετὰς ἐξαγγείλητε τοῦ ἐκ σκότους ὑμᾶς καλέσαντος εἰς τὸ θαυμαστὸν αὐτοῦ φῶς· [GNS]
	
	Ὑμεῖς δὲ γένος ἐκλεκτόν, βασίλειον ἱεράτευμα, ἔθνος ἅγιον, **λαὸς εἰς περιποίησιν**, ὅπως τὰς ἀρετὰς ἐξαγγείλητε τοῦ ἐκ σκότους ὑμᾶς καλέσαντος εἰς τὸ θαυμαστὸν αὐτοῦ φῶς· [GNT]
		People belonging to God, peculiar people, people for God's own possession.
		
		Practical Application
		Believers become a "people for God's own possession" (*laos eis peripoiësin*). The Greek means...
		• "a people for God's own possession" (A.T. Robertson. *Word Pictures in the New Testament*, Vol.6, p.98).
		• "the people to be His very own" (Charles B. Williams. *The New Testament in the Language of the People*. "The Four Translation New Testament").
		• "a people saved to be His own" (William F. Beck. *The New Testament in the Language of Today*. "The Four Translation New Testament").
		
		This is a most precious thought: that God makes us His very own people, a very special possession of His. Possession has the idea of value, of worth and preciousness. We are more precious to God than all the precious gems and treasures of the world. We are His *treasured possession*. Possession also has the idea of provision, protection, and security. We are God's possession, His very special people; therefore, He will provide for us and protect us and make us secure in every sense of the word.

#2882
People Who Aren't Christians
 	
Natural man–KJV
Natural man–NASB
	ψυχικός = *psuchikos*
	Pronunciation: [psoo-khee-kos']
	Parsing (part of speech): adjective
	   Case—nominative
	   Gender—masculine
	   Number—singular
	   Stem or root—from **ψυχικός**, ή, όν
	Concordance References:
	  ⇒ Strong's #5591 psuchikos
		Man without the Spirit; unspiritual; a natural man; a man who has physical life or who is living.
		
		Practical Application
		The root word is "soul" (*psuchikos*), which simply means the life of a man, the consciousness, the breath, the energy, the being of a man.

ENGLISH WORD	GREEK WORD AND VERSE	THE WORD MEANS...
Perfectly trained–NKJV Works hard–NLT **POSB REFERENCE** (Lk.6:40) Note 2, point 1	Number—singular Stem or root—from **καταρτίζω** Concordance References: ⇒ Strong's #2675 katartizō ⇒ NIV #2936 katartizō ⇒ NASB #2675 katartizō **Luke 6:40** The disciple is not above his master: but every one that is **perfect** shall be as his master. [KJV] "A pupil is not above his teacher; but everyone, after he has been **fully trained**, will be like his teacher. [NASB] A student is not above his teacher, but everyone who is **fully trained** will be like his teacher. [NIV] A disciple is not above his teacher, but everyone who is **perfectly trained** will be like his teacher. [NKJV] A student is not greater than the teacher. But the student who **works hard** will become like the teacher. [NLT] οὐκ ἔστι μαθητὴς ὑπὲρ τὸν διδάσκαλον αὐτοῦ· **κατηρτισμένος** δὲ πᾶς ἔσται ὡς ὁ διδάσκαλος αὐτοῦ. [GNS] οὐκ ἔστιν μαθητὴς ὑπὲρ τὸν διδάσκαλον· **κατηρτισμένος** δὲ πᾶς ἔσται ὡς ὁ διδάσκαλος αὐτοῦ. [GNT]	above his master" (see POSB note, pt.1—Matthew 10:24-25). The disciple is not better than his Lord; therefore, he cannot expect to be treated better, nor can he expect to receive more in this world than his Lord. The disciple cannot expect to be better by having more honor, praise, recognition, or esteem. He cannot expect to have more comfort, rest, or pleasure. The Lord suffered, humbled, and denied Himself for the sake of the world and its needs. The disciple, as a follower of the Lord, does the same; he denies himself in order to reach the world for his Lord (see POSB note—Luke 9:23 and POSB *Deeper Study* #1—Luke 9:23).
#2887 **Perfect** Perfect–KJV Adequate–NASB Thoroughly–NIV Thoroughly–NKJV Preparing us in every way–NLT **POSB REFERENCE** (2 Tim. 3:17) Note 5	**ἄρτιος** = *artios* Pronunciation: [ar'-tee-os] Parsing (part of speech): adjective Case—nominative Gender—masculine Number—singular Stem or root—from **ἄρτιος**, α, ον Concordance References: ⇒ Strong's #739 artios ⇒ NIV #787 artios ⇒ NASB #739 artios **2 Tim. 3:17** That the man of God may be **perfect**, throughly furnished unto all good works. [KJV] That the man of God may be **adequate**, equipped for every good work. [NASB] So that the man of God may be **thoroughly** equipped for every good work. [NIV] That the man of God may be complete, **thoroughly** equipped for every good work. [NKJV] It is God's way of **preparing us in every way**, fully equipped for every good thing God wants us to do. [NLT] ἵνα **ἄρτιος** ᾖ ὁ τοῦ Θεοῦ ἄνθρωπος, πρὸς πᾶν ἔργον ἀγαθὸν ἐξηρτισμένος. [GNS] ἵνα **ἄρτιος** ᾖ ὁ τοῦ θεοῦ ἄνθρωπος, πρὸς πᾶν ἔργον ἀγαθὸν ἐξηρτισμένος. [GNT]	To be thorough; to be perfect; to be adequate; to be prepared in every way. It means complete, matured, filled. **Practical Application** Scripture perfects a man and equips him for every good work. By "perfect" (*artios*) is meant complete, matured, perfect, filled. No person is complete or mature apart from Scripture. Man was made for God and he is to live by the Word of God. If he tries to live without God and His Word, man fails in life. He lives an incomplete, immature, and misfitted life. This is particularly true of the *man of God*, the person who claims to be a minister or teacher of God's Word.
#2888 **Perfect** Perfect–KJV Perfect–NASB Restore–NIV Perfect–NKJV Restore–NLT **POSB REFERENCE** (1 Pt.5:10) Note 2, point 1	**καταρτίσει** = *katartisei* Pronunciation: [kat-ar-tis'-ee] Parsing (part of speech): verb Mood—indicative Tense—future Voice—active Person—3rd person Number—singular Stem or root—from **καταρτίζω** Concordance References: ⇒ Strong's #2675 katartizō ⇒ NIV #2936 katartizō ⇒ NASB #2675 katartizō **1 Peter 5:10** But the God of all grace, who hath called us unto his eternal glory by Christ Jesus, after that ye have suffered a	To restore; to perfect; to make complete; to make fit or join together. **Practical Application** How does God keep and preserve the believer? The temptations and trials of life are severe and fierce. How does God make sure the believer makes it to heaven and its eternal glory? God does four wonderful things for the believer. Note: in the Greek the emphasis is upon God Himself doing these things. God Himself becomes actively involved in taking care of the believer, in keeping and preserving and taking the believer to heaven and its glory. God Himself uses the believer's suffering to perfect the believer. The Greek authority Marvin Vincent says:

ENGLISH WORD	GREEK WORD AND VERSE	THE WORD MEANS...
	while, make you **perfect**, stablish, strengthen, settle you. [KJV] And after you have suffered for a little while, the God of all grace, who called you to His eternal glory in Christ, will Himself **perfect**, confirm, strengthen and establish you. [NASB] And the God of all grace, who called you to his eternal glory in Christ, after you have suffered a little while, will himself **restore** you and make you strong, firm and steadfast. [NIV] But may the God of all grace, who called us to His eternal glory by Christ Jesus, after you have suffered a while, **perfect**, establish, strengthen, and settle *you*. [NKJV] In his kindness God called you to his eternal glory by means of Jesus Christ. After you have suffered a little while, he will **restore**, support, and strengthen you, and he will place you on a firm foundation. [NLT] ὁ δὲ Θεὸς πάσης χάριτος, ὁ καλέσας ὑμᾶς εἰς τὴν αἰώνιον αὐτοῦ δόξαν ἐν Χριστῷ Ἰησοῦ, ὀλίγον παθόντας αὐτὸς **καταρτίσει** ὑμᾶς, στηρίξει, σθενώσαι, θεμελιώσαι. [GNS] Ὁ δὲ θεὸς πάσης χάριτος, ὁ καλέσας ὑμᾶς εἰς τὴν αἰώνιον αὐτοῦ δόξαν ἐν Χριστῷ [Ἰησοῦ], ὀλίγον παθόντας αὐτὸς **καταρτίσει**, στηρίξει, σθενώσει, θεμελιώσει. [GNT]	⇒ "The radical notion of the verb is...*adjust-ment*—the putting of all the parts into right relation and connection. We find it used... • "of mending the nets (Matthew 4:21) • "of restoring an erring brother (Galatians 6:1) • "of framing the body and the worlds (Hebrews 10:5; Hebrews 11:3) • "of the union of members in the church (1 Cor. 1:10; 2 Cor. 13:11) "Out of this comes the general sense of *perfecting* (Matthew 21:16; Luke 6:40; 1 Thes. 3:10)." (*Word Studies in the New Testament*, Vol.1, p.671.) (Note: the paragraph has been outlined for simplicity.) God takes all the displaced joints and broken limbs of our lives and uses them to adjust our character. He uses all the trials and temptations, difficulties and persecutions—all the sufferings of life—and makes us more and more like Christ. If we are truly called of God and if we truly love God, then God will take all that ever happens to us and work it out for good. He will perfect us, fit all the parts of life together and lead us to glory. This is the glorious grace and call of God to eternal glory.
#2889 **Perfect** Perfect–KJV Perfect–NASB Mature–NIV Perfect–NKJV Fully developed–NLT **POSB REFERENCE** (Jas.1:4) Note 3 **See also POSB REF:** (1 Cor.2:6) Note 1	*τέλειοι* = *teleioi* Pronunciation: [tel'-i-oy] Parsing (part of speech): adjective Case—nominative Gender—masculine Number—plural Stem or root—from *τέλειος, α, ον* Concordance References: ⇒ Strong's #5046 teleios ⇒ NIV #5455 teleios ⇒ NASB #5046 teleios **James 1:4** But let patience have her perfect work, that ye may be **perfect** and entire, wanting nothing. [KJV] And let endurance have its perfect result, that you may be **perfect** and complete, lacking in nothing. [NASB] Perseverance must finish its work so that you may be **mature** and complete, not lacking anything. [NIV] But let patience have *its* perfect work, that you may be **perfect** and complete, lacking nothing. [NKJV] So let it grow, for when your endurance is **fully developed**, you will be strong in character and ready for anything. [NLT] ἡ δὲ ὑπομονὴ ἔργον τέλειον ἐχέτω, ἵνα ἦτε **τέλειοι** καὶ ὁλόκληροι, ἐν μηδενὶ λειπόμενοι. [GNS] ἡ δὲ ὑπομονὴ ἔργον τέλειον ἐχέτω, ἵνα ἦτε **τέλειοι** καὶ ὁλόκληροι ἐν μηδενὶ λειπόμενοι. [GNT]	Mature, perfect, fully developed; full grown, complete, whole. ### Practical Application A person becomes more perfect (*teleioi*). The word does not mean perfect in the sense of becoming a perfect person. The word means *perfection of purpose*. It has to do with an end, an aim, a goal, a purpose. It means fit, mature, fully grown at a particular stage of growth. For example, a fully grown child is a perfect child; he has reached his childhood and achieved the purpose of childhood. It does not mean perfection of character, that is, being without sin. It is fitness, maturity for task and purpose. It is full development, maturity of godliness. (See POSB note—Ephes. 4:12-13; cp. Phil. 3:12; 1 John 1:8, 10.) When a person stands against trials and temptations and conquers them... • he perfects the purpose God intended. That is, he becomes a stronger and more pure person—a person who is a little more like Jesus. • he perfects his task and purpose for being on earth a little bit more. God has a twofold purpose for every believer: to become more and more like Jesus and to do a specific task or job while on earth. When the believer perseveres against and conquers trials or temptations, he perfects both purposes a little bit more. He becomes more like Jesus, and he finishes his task a little more.
#2890 **Perfect– Perfected** Perfect–KJV Perfected–NASB	*τετελειωμένοι* = *teteleiōmenoi* Pronunciation: [teh-tel-i-o'-mehn-oy] Parsing (part of speech): verb Mood—participle Tense—perfect Voice—passive Case—nominative	To be complete; to be perfect; to finish; to accomplish some end; to reach a goal. ### Practical Application The idea of this word (*teteleiōmenoi*) is perfection of purpose. It has to do with an end, an aim, a goal, a purpose. It means fit, mature, fully

ENGLISH WORD	GREEK WORD AND VERSE	THE WORD MEANS...

Complete–NIV
Perfect–NKJV
Perfected–NLT

POSB
REFERENCE
(Jn.17:23)
Deeper Study #2

Gender—masculine
Number—plural
Stem or root—from τελειόω
Concordance References:
⇒ Strong's #5048 teleioo
⇒ NIV #5457 teleioo
⇒ NASB #5048 teleioo

John 17:23

I in them, and thou in me, that they may be made **perfect** in one; and that the world may know that thou hast sent me, and hast loved them, as thou hast loved me. [KJV]

I in them, and Thou in Me, that they may be **perfected** in unity, that the world may know that Thou didst send Me, and didst love them, even as Thou didst love Me. [NASB]

I in them and you in me. May they be brought to **complete** unity to let the world know that you sent me and have loved them even as you have loved me. [NIV]

I in them, and You in Me; that they may be made **perfect** in one, and that the world may know that You have sent Me, and have loved them as You have loved Me. [NKJV]

I in them and you in me, all being **perfected** into one. Then the world will know that you sent me and will understand that you love them as much as you love me. [NLT]

ἐγὼ ἐν αὐτοῖς καὶ σὺ ἐν ἐμοί, ἵνα ὦσι **τετελειωμένοι** εἰς ἕν, καὶ ἵνα γινώσκῃ ὁ κόσμος ὅτι σύ με ἀπέστειλας, καὶ ἠγάπησας αὐτοὺς, καθὼς ἐμὲ ἠγάπησας. [GNS]

ἐγὼ ἐν αὐτοῖς καὶ σὺ ἐν ἐμοί, ἵνα ὦσιν **τετελειωμένοι** εἰς ἕν, ἵνα γινώσκῃ ὁ κόσμος ὅτι σύ με ἀπέστειλας καὶ ἠγάπησας αὐτου [GNT]

grown at a particular stage of growth. For example, a fully grown child is a perfect child; he has reached the height of childhood, achieved the purpose of childhood. The word "perfect" does not mean completion or perfection of character, that is, being without sin. It is fitness, maturity for task and purpose. It is full development, maturity of godliness. (See POSB note—Ephes. 4:12-16; cp. Phil. 3:12; 1 John 1:8, 10.)

#2891
Perfect Leader

Captain–KJV
Author–NASB
Author–NIV
Captain–NKJV
Perfect leader–NLT

POSB
REFERENCE
(Heb.2:9-13; esp. v.10)
Note 3, point 2b

ἀρχηγὸν = archēgon
Pronunciation: [ar-khay-gon']
Parsing (part of speech): noun
    Case—accusative
    Gender—masculine
    Number—singular
    Stem or root—from ἀρχηγός, οῦ
Concordance References:
⇒ Strong's #747 archēgos
⇒ NIV #795 archēgos
⇒ NASB #747 archēgos

Hebrews 2:10

For it became him, for whom are all things, and by whom are all things, in bringing many sons unto glory, to make the **captain** of their salvation perfect through sufferings. [KJV]

For it was fitting for Him, for whom are all things, and through whom are all things, in bringing many sons to glory, to perfect the **author** of their salvation through sufferings. [NASB]

In bringing many sons to glory, it was fitting that God, for whom and through whom everything exists, should make the **author** of their salvation perfect through suffering. [NIV]

For it was fitting for Him, for whom are all things and by whom are all things, in bringing many sons to glory, to make the **captain** of their salvation perfect through sufferings. [NKJV]

And it was only right that God—who made everything and for whom everything was made—should bring his many children into glory. Through the suffering of Jesus, God made him a **perfect leader**, one fit to bring them into their salvation. [NLT]

ἔπρεπε γὰρ αὐτῷ, δι' ὃν τὰ πάντα καὶ δι' οὗ τὰ πάντα, πολλοὺς υἱοὺς εἰς δόξαν ἀγαγόντα, τὸν **ἀρχηγὸν**

Author, leader, pioneer, pathfinder, founder, originator, perfect leader. It means the one who blazes forth, cutting through something so that others may follow.

Practical Application

Jesus Christ opened up the way or trail to God. This He did by suffering all the experiences of man—perfectly. He remained perfect through all His sufferings. He never sinned; He never failed, not even once. He learned obedience by the things which He suffered—perfectly. And by such, He secured a perfect, eternal righteousness for man. He is the perfect pioneer who has cut the perfect path to God. He is the Ideal and Perfect Man who stands for and covers all persons...

- all who believe and trust Him to cover them.
- all who believe and trust Him to make them presentable to God.

ENGLISH WORD	GREEK WORD AND VERSE	THE WORD MEANS...
	τῆς σωτηρίας αὐτῶν διὰ παθημάτων τελειῶσαι· [GNS] Ἔπρεπεν γὰρ αὐτῷ, δι' ὃν τὰ πάντα καὶ δι' οὗ τὰ πάντα, πολλοὺς υἱοὺς εἰς δόξαν ἀγαγόντα τὸν **ἀρχηγὸν** τῆς σωτηρίας αὐτῶν διὰ παθημάτων τελειῶσαι. [GNT]	

#2892
 Perfect
  Understanding
 	
 Perfect understanding–KJV
 Investigated–NASB
 Investigated–NIV
 Perfect understanding–NKJV
 Investigated–NLT
 	
 POSB
 REFERENCE
 (Lk.1:3)
 Note 3, point 1
	παρηκολουθηκότι = *parëkolouthëkoti*
	 Pronunciation: [par-ak-ol-oo-thay'-ko-tee]
	 Parsing (part of speech): verb
	    Mood—participle
	    Tense—perfect
	    Voice—active
	    Case—dative
	    Gender—masculine
	    Person—1st person
	    Number—singular
	    Stem or root—from παρακολουθέω
	 Concordance References:
	 ⇒ Strong's #3877 parakoloutheō
	 ⇒ NIV #4158 parakoloutheō
	 ⇒ NASB #3877 parakoloutheō
	
	 Luke 1:3
	 It seemed good to me also, having had **perfect understanding** of all things from the very first, to write unto thee in order, most excellent Theophilus, [KJV]
	 It seemed fitting for me as well, having **investigated** everything carefully from the beginning, to write it out for you in consecutive order, most excellent Theophilus; [NASB]
	 Therefore, since I myself have carefully **investigated** everything from the beginning, it seemed good also to me to write an orderly account for you, most excellent Theophilus, [NIV]
	 It seemed good to me also, having had **perfect understanding** of all things from the very first, to write to you an orderly account, most excellent Theophilus, [NKJV]
	 Having carefully **investigated** all of these accounts from the beginning, I have decided to write a careful summary for you, [NLT]
	 ἔδοξε κἀμοὶ **παρηκολουθηκότι** ἄνωθεν πᾶσιν ἀκριβῶς, καθεξῆς σοι γράψαι, κράτιστε Θεόφιλε, [GNS]
	 ἔδοξε κἀμοὶ **παρηκολουθηκότι** ἄνωθεν πᾶσιν ἀκριβῶς καθεξῆς σοι γράψαι, κράτιστε Θεόφιλε, [GNT]
		To study; to follow up; to search out diligently; to investigate; to give careful attention; to trace accurately; to become acquainted with; to scrutinize.
		
		 Practical Application
		 Luke says that having been acquainted with and having perfect understanding of all things, he was determined to record the facts himself.

#2593
 Perfected
 	
 Perfected–KJV
 Reach goal–NASB
 Reach goal–NIV
 Perfected–NKJV
 Accomplish purpose–NLT
 	
 POSB
 REFERENCE
 (Lk.13:31-33; esp. v.32)
 Note 2, point 1
	τελειοῦμαι = *teleioumai*
	 Pronunciation: [tel-i-oo'-mah-ee]
	 Parsing (part of speech): verb
	    Mood—indicative
	    Tense—present
	    Voice—passive
	    Person—1st person
	    Number—singular
	    Stem or root—from τελειόω
	 Concordance References:
	 ⇒ Strong's #5048 teleioo
	 ⇒ NIV #5457 teleioō
	 ⇒ NASB #5048 teleioo
	
	 Luke 13:32
	 And he said unto them, Go ye, and tell that fox, Behold, I cast out devils, and I do cures to day and to morrow, and the third day I shall be **perfected**. [KJV]
	 And He said to them, "Go and tell that fox, 'Behold, I cast out demons and perform cures today and tomorrow, and the third day I **reach** My **goal**.' [NASB]
	 He replied, "Go tell that fox, 'I will drive out demons and heal people today and tomorrow, and on the third day I will **reach** my **goal**.' [NIV]
	 And He said to them, "Go, tell that fox, 'Behold, I cast out demons and perform cures today and tomorrow, and the third day I shall be **perfected**.' [NKJV]
	 Jesus replied, "Go tell that fox that I will keep on cast-
		To reach a goal; to complete an assignment; to accomplish a specific purpose; to finish a task.
		
		 Practical Application
		 His ministry of delivering men spiritually and physically (casting out evil spirits and healing) will not be stopped by any man, even rulers such as Herod.
		 The words "the third day I shall be perfected" mean that His witness and delivering power will be completed and finished. There is a definite time for it; then His witness will stop. It will be no more. But until that day, nothing can stop His ministry and witness. This is, of course, a reference to Jesus' death and His resurrection on the third day. Note that His resurrection is the perfection of His ministry. It is by arising from the dead that He conquered death and completed man's salvation.

ENGLISH WORD	GREEK WORD AND VERSE	THE WORD MEANS...
	ing out demons and doing miracles of healing today and tomorrow; and the third day I will **accomplish** my **purpose**. [NLT] καὶ εἶπεν αὐτοῖς, Πορευθέντες εἴπατε τῇ ἀλώπεκι ταύτῃ, Ἰδοὺ ἐκβάλλω δαιμόνια, καὶ ἰάσεις ἐπιτελῶ σήμερον καὶ αὔριον, καὶ τῇ τρίτῃ **τελειοῦμαι**. [GNS] καὶ εἶπεν αὐτοῖς, Πορευθέντες εἴπατε τῇ ἀλώπεκι ταύτῃ, Ἰδοὺ ἐκβάλλω δαιμόνια καὶ ἰάσεις ἀποτελῶ σήμερον καὶ αὔριον καὶ τῇ τρίτῃ **τελειοῦμαι**. [GNT]	

#2894
Perfected
 	
Made perfect–KJV
Perfected–NASB
Made complete–NIV
Made perfect–NKJV
Made complete–NLT
 	
**POSB
REFERENCE**
(Jas.2:21-24; esp.
v.22)
Note 5
	ἐτελειώθη = eteleiöthë
	Pronunciation: [eh-tel-i-o'-thay]
	Parsing (part of speech): verb
	  Mood—indicative
	  Tense—aorist
	  Voice—passive
	  Person—3rd person
	  Number—singular
	  Stem or root—from τελειόω
	Concordance References:
	  ⇒ Strong's #5048 teleioö
	  ⇒ NIV #5457 teleioö
	  ⇒ NASB #5048 teleioö
	
	James 2:22
	Seest thou how faith wrought with his works, and by works was faith **made perfect**? [KJV]
	
	You see that faith was working with his works, and as a result of the works, faith was **perfected**; [NASB]
	
	You see that his faith and his actions were working together, and his faith was **made complete** by what he did. [NIV]
	
	Do you see that faith was working together with his works, and by works faith was **made perfect**? [NKJV]
	
	You see, he was trusting God so much that he was willing to do whatever God told him to do. His faith was **made complete** by what he did—by his actions. [NLT]
	
	βλέπεις ὅτι ἡ πίστις συνήργει τοῖς ἔργοις αὐτοῦ, καὶ ἐκ τῶν ἔργων ἡ πίστις **ἐτελειώθη**; [GNS]
	
	βλέπεις ὅτι ἡ πίστις συνήργει τοῖς ἔργοις αὐτοῦ καὶ ἐκ τῶν ἔργων ἡ πίστις **ἐτελειώθη**, [GNT]
		Made complete, made perfect, perfected; to completely finish; carried to the end.
		
		Practical Application
		By his works Abraham's faith was perfected (*eteleiöthë*), that is, finished, completed, carried to the end. Abraham's faith was proven, shown to be a complete faith. A true and living faith works: it completes and finishes its course. If a faith does not work or act or complete or finish its course, it is a dead faith—an incomplete, unfinished, and unproven faith.

#2895
Perfected
 	
Consecrated–KJV
Made perfect–NASB
Made perfect–NIV
Perfected–NKJV
Made perfect–NLT
 	
**POSB
REFERENCE**
(Heb.7:28)
Note 4
	τετελειωμένον = teteleiömenon
	Pronunciation: [teh-tel-i-o'-mehn-on]
	Parsing (part of speech): verb
	  Mood—participle
	  Tense—perfect
	  Voice—passive
	  Case—accusative
	  Gender—masculine
	  Number—singular
	  Stem or root—from τελειόω
	Concordance References:
	  ⇒ Strong's #5048 teleioö
	  ⇒ NIV #5457 teleioö
	  ⇒ NASB #5048 teleioö
	
	Hebrews 7:28
	For the law maketh men high priests which have infirmity; but the word of the oath, which was since the law, maketh the Son, who is **consecrated** for evermore. [KJV]
	
	For the Law appoints men as high priests who are weak, but the word of the oath, which came after the Law, appoints a Son, **made perfect** forever. [NASB]
	
	For the law appoints as high priests men who are weak; but the oath, which came after the law, appointed the Son, who has been **made perfect** forever. [NIV]
	
	For the law appoints as high priests men who have weakness, but the word of the oath, which came after the law, *appoints* the Son who has been **perfected** forever. [NKJV]
	
	Those who were high priests under the law of Moses
		Made perfect, consecrated, perfected, make complete; to fulfill.
		
		Practical Application
		Jesus Christ is the High Priest with a perfect appointment. Men—mere men—are appointed to be priests by the law. The law can appoint no one else but men with infirmities and weaknesses—men who are imperfect, frail, sinful, and dying. But the glorious message of this passage offers eternal hope for man. Why? Because God has given us two wonderful things: God has given His Word, His precious promise that He will give us a perfect and eternal High Priest to save us, and God has sworn that He will fulfill His Word. God has assured us with a double surety. Jesus Christ, the Son of God, is consecrated forever more. Jesus Christ is the perfected and eternal High Priest promised and sworn by God to save man. What greater salvation and surety could we ask than to have God send His own Son to perfect us and to give us eternal life and the glorious privilege of living forever with Him—the glorious privilege of ruling and reigning with Him throughout all of eternity.

ENGLISH WORD	GREEK WORD AND VERSE	THE WORD MEANS...
	were limited by human weakness. But after the law was given, God appointed his Son with an oath, and his Son has been **made perfect** forever. [NLT] ὁ νόμος γὰρ ἀνθρώπους καθίστησιν ἀρχιερεῖς, ἔχοντας ἀσθένειαν· ὁ λόγος δὲ τῆς ὀρκωμοσίας τῆς μετὰ τὸν νόμον, υἱὸν εἰς τὸν αἰῶνα **τετελειωμένον**. [GNS] ὁ νόμος γὰρ ἀνθρώπους ἀθίστησιν ἀρχιερεῖς ἔχοντας ἀσθένειαν, ὁ λόγος δὲ τῆς ὀρκωμοσίας τῆς μετὰ τὸν νόμον υἱὸν εἰς τὸν αἰῶνα **τετελειωμένον**. [GNT]	

#2896
Perfecter
 	
Finisher–KJV
Perfecter–NASB
Perfecter–NIV
Finisher–NKJV
Finish–NLT
 	
POSB REFERENCE
(Heb.12:2)
Note 3
	τελειωτὴν = teleiōtēn
	Pronunciation: [tel-i-o'-tayn]
	Parsing (part of speech): noun
	    Case—accusative
	    Gender—masculine
	    Number—singular
	    Stem or root—from τελειωτής, οῦ
	Concordance References:
	  ⇒ Strong's #5051 teleiōtēs OR #5047 teleiotēs
	  ⇒ NIV #5460 teleiōtēs
	  ⇒ NASB #5051 teleiōtēs
	
	Hebrews 12:2
	Looking unto Jesus the author and **finisher** of our faith; who for the joy that was set before him endured the cross, despising the shame, and is set down at the right hand of the throne of God. [KJV]
	Fixing our eyes on Jesus, the author and **perfecter** of faith, who for the joy set before Him endured the cross, despising the shame, and has sat down at the right hand of God. [NASB]
	Let us fix our eyes on Jesus, the author and **perfecter** of our faith, who for the joy set before him endured the cross, scorning its shame, and sat down at the right hand of the throne of God. [NIV]
	Looking unto Jesus, the author and **finisher** of *our* faith, who for the joy that was set before Him endured the cross, despising the shame, and has sat down at the right hand of the throne of God. [NKJV]
	We do this by keeping our eyes on Jesus, on whom our faith depends from start to **finish**. He was willing to die a shameful death on the cross because of the joy he knew would be his afterward. Now he is seated in the place of highest honor beside God's throne in heaven. [NLT]
	
	ἀφορῶντες εἰς τὸν τῆς πίστεως ἀρχηγὸν καὶ **τελειωτὴν** Ἰησοῦν, ὃς ἀντὶ τῆς προκειμένης αὐτῷ χαρᾶς, ὑπέμεινε σταυρόν, αἰσχύνης καταφρονήσας, ἐν δεξιᾷ τε τοῦ θρόνου τοῦ Θεοῦ ἐκάθισεν. [GNS]
	
	ἀφορῶντες εἰς τὸν τῆς πίστεως ἀρχηγὸν καὶ **τελειωτὴν** Ἰησοῦν, ὃς ἀντὶ τῆς προκειμένης αὐτῷ χαρᾶς ὑπέμεινεν σταυρὸν αἰσχύνης καταφρονήσας ἐν δεξιᾷ τε τοῦ θρόνου τοῦ θεοῦ κεκάθικεν. [GNT]
		Perfecter, finisher; to finish. It means that He perfected, completed, and consummated the race. He ran the race to the finish.
		
		Practical Application
		The idea is that Jesus Christ ran the course of life perfectly. He was sinless, perfectly righteous, always obeying God in everything. He ran the race of faith—of utter obedience and trust in God—all through His life upon earth. He finished His course living a perfect and righteous life upon earth. Therefore, He created and authored and completed the Christian race for all believers. He is the blazing example of faith in God—of utter dependence and obedience—for the believer. The believer is always to be looking to Jesus the Author and Finisher of faith.

#2897
Perfecting
 	
Perfecting–KJV
Perfecting–NASB
Perfecting–NIV
Perfecting–NKJV
Work toward complete–NLT
 	
POSB REFERENCE
(2 Cor.7:1)
Note 4
	ἐπιτελοῦντες = epitelountes
	Pronunciation: [ep-ee-tel-oon-tace]
	Parsing (part of speech): verb
	    Mood—participle
	    Tense—present
	    Voice—active
	    Case—nominative
	    Gender—masculine
	    Person—1st person
	    Number—plural
	    Stem or root—from ἐπιτελέω
	Concordance References:
	  ⇒ Strong's #2005 epiteleō
	  ⇒ NIV #2200 epiteleō
	  ⇒ NASB #2005 epiteleō
	
	2 Cor. 7:1
	Having therefore these promises, dearly beloved, let us cleanse ourselves from all filthiness of the flesh and spirit, **perfecting** holiness in the fear of God. [KJV]
		Perfecting, completing, accomplishing, finishing.
		
		Practical Application
		God expects us to perfect holiness in the fear of God. Note that this is continuous action. The word "perfecting" (*epitelountes*) is an aggressive word demanding aggressive action. It means not only to practice but to finish and complete. The believer is, of course, to *practice holiness*. That is, he is to practice doing the things that will make him holy. But he is to do *much more*: he is to pursue holiness aggressively, seeking to perfect and complete holiness in his life. Of course, the believer can never become perfectly holy: he cannot become God. But he is to set his mind and heart upon becoming holy.

ENGLISH WORD	GREEK WORD AND VERSE	THE WORD MEANS...
	Therefore, having these promises, beloved, let us cleanse ourselves from all defilement of flesh and spirit, **perfecting** holiness in the fear of God. [NASB] Since we have these promises, dear friends, let us purify ourselves from everything that contaminates body and spirit, **perfecting** holiness out of reverence for God. [NIV] Therefore, having these promises, beloved, let us cleanse ourselves from all filthiness of the flesh and spirit, **perfecting** holiness in the fear of God. [NKJV] Because we have these promises, dear friends, let us cleanse ourselves from everything that can defile our body or spirit. And let us **work toward complete** purity because we fear God. [NLT] ταύτας οὖν ἔχοντες τὰς ἐπαγγελίας, ἀγαπητοί, καθαρίσωμεν ἑαυτοὺς ἀπὸ παντὸς μολυσμοῦ σαρκὸς καὶ πνεύματος, **ἐπιτελοῦντες** ἁγιωσύνην ἐν φόβῳ Θεοῦ. [GNS] ταύτας οὖν ἔχοντες τὰς ἐπαγγελίας, ἀγαπητοί, καθαρίσωμεν ἑαυτοὺς ἀπὸ παντὸς μολυσμοῦ σαρκὸς καὶ πνεύματος, **ἐπιτελοῦντες** ἁγιωσύνην ἐν φόβῳ θεοῦ. [GNT]	

#2898
Perfecting
 	
Perfecting–KJV
Equipping–NASB
Prepare–NIV
Equipping–NKJV
Equip–NLT
 	
POSB REFERENCE
(Eph.4:12-16; esp. v.12)
Note 4, point 1
	καταρτισμὸν = *katartismon*
	Pronunciation: [kat-ar-tis-mon']
	Parsing (part of speech): noun
	  Case—accusative
	  Gender—masculine
	  Number—singular
	  Stem or root—from καταρτισμός, οῦ
	Concordance References:
	  ⇒ Strong's #2677 katartismos
	  ⇒ NIV #2938 katartismos
	  ⇒ NASB #2677 katartismos
	
	Ephes. 4:12
	For the **perfecting** of the saints, for the work of the ministry, for the edifying of the body of Christ: [KJV]
	For the **equipping** of the saints for the work of service, to the building up of the body of Christ; [NASB]
	To **prepare** God's people for works of service, so that the body of Christ may be built up [NIV]
	For the **equipping** of the saints for the work of ministry, for the edifying of the body of Christ, [NKJV]
	Their responsibility is to **equip** God's people to do his work and build up the church, the body of Christ, [NLT]
	πρὸς τὸν **καταρτισμὸν** τῶν ἁγίων, εἰς ἔργον διακονίας, εἰς οἰκοδομὴν τοῦ σώματος τοῦ Χριστοῦ· [GNS]
	πρὸς τὸν **καταρτισμὸν** τῶν ἁγίων εἰς ἔργον διακονίας, εἰς οἰκοδομὴν τοῦ σώματος τοῦ Χριστοῦ, [GNT]
		To prepare; to perfect; to equip; to train; to equip for service and ministry.
		
		Practical Application
		There is an immediate purpose for the professional or office-bearing gifts in the church and among God's people. It is to equip believers to do the work of the ministry. This is critical to see, for the office bearer in the church is not to be the only one who goes about doing the work of the ministry. In fact, his *primary task* is to be an equipper, a person who makes disciples and prepares others to serve Christ (see POSB note, Discipleship—Matthew 28:19-20).
		Note another critical point: the very purpose for equipping laymen is so that the body of Christ, the church, may be built up. This is a significant point, for it means that the church cannot be built up without the members themselves doing the work of the ministry. All believers within a church must be involved in the work of the ministry. As Wuest says: "This is an order that the Body of Christ, the Church, might be built up, by additions to its membership in lost souls' being saved, and by the building up of individual saints." (Kenneth Wuest. *Ephesians and Colossians,* Vol.1, p.101.)

#2899
Perfection
 	
Perfection–KJV
Made complete–NASB
Perfection–NIV
Made complete–NKJV
Restoration to maturity–NLT
 	
POSB REFERENCE
(2 Cor.13:7-10; esp. v.9)
Note 2
	κατάρτισιν = *katartisin*
	Pronunciation: [kat-ar'-tis-in]
	Parsing (part of speech): noun
	  Case—accusative
	  Gender—feminine
	  Number—singular
	  Stem or root—from κατάρτισις, εως
	Concordance References:
	  ⇒ Strong's #2676 katartisis
	  ⇒ NIV #2937 katartisis
	  ⇒ NASB #2676 katartisis
	
	2 Cor. 13:9
	For we are glad, when we are weak, and ye are strong: and this also we wish, even your **perfection**. [KJV]
	For we rejoice when we ourselves are weak but you are strong; this we also pray for, that you be **made complete**. [NASB]
		Perfection, made complete, restoring to maturity; to repair what is broken and to restore it to a more perfect condition.
		
		Practical Application
		Paul was glad when the believers were strong in the Lord and he was able to appear weak, that is, when he did not have to be exercising authority and discipline. At such times, the believers and the church were growing toward perfection.
		What the Corinthian church needed was to become strong and perfected, that is, repaired and restored, to have its fellowship cleansed of critics and false teachers.

ENGLISH WORD	GREEK WORD AND VERSE	THE WORD MEANS...
	We are glad whenever we are weak but you are strong; and our prayer is for your **perfection**. [NIV] For we are glad when we are weak and you are strong. And this also we pray, that you may be **made complete**. [NKJV] We are glad to be weak, if you are really strong. What we pray for is your **restoration to maturity**. [NLT] χαίρομεν γὰρ ὅταν ἡμεῖς ἀσθενῶμεν, ὑμεῖς δὲ δυνατοὶ ἦτε· τοῦτο δὲ καὶ εὐχόμεθα, τὴν ὑμῶν **κατάρτισιν**. [GNS] χαίρομεν γὰρ ὅταν ἡμεῖς ἀσθενῶμεν, ὑμεῖς δὲ δυνατοὶ ἦτε· τοῦτο καὶ εὐχόμεθα, τὴν ὑμῶν **κατάρτισιν**. [GNT]	

#2900
Perfume
 	
Ointment–KJV
Perfume–NASB
Perfume–NIV
Oil–NKJV
Perfume–NLT
 	
POSB REFERENCE
(Jn.12:3)
Note 2, point 2
	μύρου = *murou*
	Pronunciation: [moo'-roo]
	Parsing (part of speech): noun
	    Case—genitive
	    Gender—neuter
	    Number—singular
	    Stem or root—from μύρον, ου
	Concordance References:
	  ⇒ Strong's #3464 muron
	  ⇒ NIV #3693 muron
	  ⇒ NASB #3464 muron
	
	John 12:3
	Then took Mary a pound of **ointment** of spikenard, very costly, and anointed the feet of Jesus, and wiped his feet with her hair: and the house was filled with the odour of the ointment. [KJV]
	
	Mary therefore took a pound of very costly **perfume** of pure nard, and anointed the feet of Jesus, and wiped His feet with her hair; and the house was filled with the fragrance of the perfume. [NASB]
	
	Then Mary took about a pint of pure nard, an expensive **perfume**; she poured it on Jesus' feet and wiped his feet with her hair. And the house was filled with the fragrance of the perfume. [NIV]
	
	Then Mary took a pound of very costly **oil** of spikenard, anointed the feet of Jesus, and wiped His feet with her hair. And the house was filled with the fragrance of the oil. [NKJV]
	
	Then Mary took a twelve-ounce jar of expensive **perfume** made from essence of nard, and she anointed Jesus' feet with it and wiped his feet with her hair. And the house was filled with fragrance. [NLT]
	
	ἡ οὖν Μαρία λαβοῦσα λίτραν **μύρου** νάρδου πιστικῆς πολυτίμου, ἤλειψε τοὺς πόδας τοῦ Ἰησοῦ, καὶ ἐξέμαξε ταῖς θριξὶν αὐτῆς τοὺς πόδας αὐτοῦ· ἡ δὲ οἰκία ἐπληρώθη ἐκ τῆς ὀσμῆς τοῦ **μύρου**. [GNS]
	
	ἡ οὖν Μαριὰμ λαβοῦσα λίτραν **μύρου** νάρδου πιστικῆς πολυτίμου ἤλειψεν τοὺς πόδας τοῦ Ἰησοῦ καὶ ἐξέμαξεν ταῖς θριξὶν αὐτῆς τοὺς πόδας αὐτοῦ· ἡ δὲ οἰκία ἐπληρώθη ἐκ τῆς ὀσμῆς τοῦ **μύρου**. [GNT]
		A sweet-smelling perfume, an ointment or oil.
		
		Practical Application
		
		This "perfume" (*murou*) was an especially-made mixture of sweet-smelling substances. It is important to note that the perfume Mary poured on Jesus' feet was of the highest quality—"an expensive perfume"—that filled the house with its fragrance. How expensive was this perfume (cp. Jn.12:5)?
		
		Three hundred pence or denarii equaled a year's wage (one denarii was the average pay for one day's labor). Just imagine the scene! A bottle of perfume worth a whole year's wage being poured upon the feet of Jesus. Think of the costly sacrifice being made. Perfume was the most precious thing to Eastern women. Mary was taking her most precious possession and giving it to her Lord.

#2901
Perish
 	
Perish–KJV
Perish–NASB
Perish–NIV
Perish–NKJV
Perish–NLT
 	
POSB REFERENCE
(Jn.3:16)
Deeper Study #2
 	
See also POSB REF:
(2 Thes.2:10)
	ἀπόληται = *apolētai*
	Pronunciation: [ap-ol'-lay-tah-ee]
	Parsing (part of speech): verb
	    Mood—subjunctive
	    Tense—aorist
	    Voice—middle
	    Person—3rd person
	    Number—singular
	    Stem or root—from ἀπόλλυμι
	Concordance References:
	  ⇒ Strong's #622 apollumi
	  ⇒ NIV #660 apollumi
	  ⇒ NASB #622 apollumi
	
	John 3:16
	For God so loved the world, that he gave his only begotten Son, that whosoever believeth in him should not **perish**, but have everlasting life. [KJV]
		To perish; to be lost; to be utterly destroyed; to lose eternal life; to be spiritually destitute; to be cut off.
		
		Practical Application
		1. Perishing means to be in a lost state in this world. It means to be...
		  • aging, deteriorating, decaying, dying. (See POSB *Deeper Study #2*—Matthew 8:17; POSB note—1 Cor. 15:50; POSB note—Col. 2:13; POSB *Deeper Study #1*—2 Peter 1:4.)
		  • without life (purpose, meaning, significance). (See POSB *Deeper Study #2*—John 1:4; POSB *Deeper Study #1*—John 10:10; POSB *Deeper Study #1*—John 17:2-3.)

ENGLISH WORD	GREEK WORD AND VERSE	THE WORD MEANS...
Note 1	"For God so loved the world, that He gave His only begotten Son, that whoever believes in Him should not **perish**, but have eternal life. [NASB] "For God so loved the world that he gave his one and only Son, that whoever believes in him shall not **perish** but have eternal life. [NIV] For God so loved the world that He gave His only begotten Son, that whoever believes in Him should not **perish** but have everlasting life. [NKJV] "For God so loved the world that he gave his only Son, so that everyone who believes in him will not **perish** but have eternal life. [NLT] Οὕτω γὰρ ἠγάπησεν ὁ Θεὸς τὸν κόσμον, ὥστε τὸν υἱὸν αὐτοῦ τὸν μονογενῆ ἔδωκεν, ἵνα πᾶς ὁ πιστεύων εἰς αὐτὸν μὴ **ἀπόληται** ἀλλ' ἔχῃ ζωὴν αἰώνιον. [GNS] Οὕτως γὰρ ἠγάπησεν ὁ θεὸς τὸν κόσμον, ὥστε τὸν υἱὸν τὸν μονογενῆ ἔδωκεν, ἵνα πᾶς ὁ πιστεύων εἰς αὐτὸν μὴ **ἀπόληται** ἀλλ' ἔχῃ ζωὴν αἰώνιον. [GNT]	• without peace (assurance, confidence, security in God's keeping). (See POSB note—John 14:27.) • without hope (of living forever). (See POSB *Deeper Study* #1—2 Tim. 4:18.) 2. Perishing means to be in a lost state in the world to come. It means... • having to die • facing judgment • being condemned • suffering separation from God and all loved ones • experiencing all that hell is (See POSB *Deeper Study* #2—Matthew 5:22; POSB *Deeper Study* #4—Luke 16:24; POSB *Deeper Study* #1—Hebrews 9:27.)
#2902 **Perishing** Lost–KJV **Perishing–NASB** **Perishing–NIV** **Perishing–NKJV** **Perishing–NLT** **POSB REFERENCE** (2 Cor.4:3-4; esp. v.3) Note 3	ἀπολλυμένοις = apollumenois Pronunciation: [ap-ol'-loo-mehn-oys] Parsing (part of speech): verb 　Mood—participle 　Tense—present 　Voice—middle or passive 　Case—dative 　Gender—masculine 　Number—plural 　Stem or root—from ἀπόλλυμι Concordance References: ⇒　Strong's #622 apollumi ⇒　NIV #660 apollumi ⇒　NASB #622 apollumi **2 Cor. 4:3** But if our gospel be hid, it is hid to them that are **lost**: [KJV] And even if our gospel is veiled, it is veiled to those who are **perishing**, [NASB] And even if our gospel is veiled, it is veiled to those who are **perishing**. [NIV] But even if our gospel is veiled, it is veiled to those who are **perishing**, [NKJV] If the Good News we preach is veiled from anyone, it is a sign that they are **perishing**. [NLT] εἰ δὲ καὶ ἔστι κεκαλυμμένον τὸ εὐαγγέλιον ἡμῶν, ἐν τοῖς **ἀπολλυμένοις** ἐστὶ κεκαλυμμένον· [GNS] εἰ δὲ καὶ ἔστιν κεκαλυμμένον τὸ εὐαγγέλιον ἡμῶν, ἐν τοῖς **ἀπολλυμένοις** ἐστὶν κεκαλυμμένον, [GNT]	Perishing; to be lost; to be in the process of being destroyed or ruined, corrupted and put to death; to be wasted; to be executed. **Practical Application** The gospel is "veiled" to men because they are "perishing" (*apollumenois*). Men are on the road to being lost, to perishing. They have turned away from God and are travelling in the opposite direction along the road that leads to perdition.
#2903 **Perplexed** **Perplexed–KJV** **Perplexed–NASB** **Perplexed–NIV** **Perplexed–NKJV** **Perplexed–NLT** **POSB REFERENCE** (2 Cor.4:7-9; esp. v.8) Note 2	ἀπορούμενοι = aporoumenoi Pronunciation: [ap-or-oo-mehn'-oy] Parsing (part of speech): verb 　Mood—participle 　Tense—present 　Voice—middle 　Case—nominative 　Gender—masculine 　Person—1st person 　Number—plural 　Stem or root—from ἀπορέω Concordance References: ⇒　Strong's #639 aporeö ⇒　NIV #679 aporeö ⇒　NASB #639 aporeö **2 Cor. 4:8** We are troubled on every side, yet not distressed; we are **perplexed**, but not in despair; [KJV] We are afflicted in every way, but not crushed; **perplexed**, but not despairing; [NASB] We are hard pressed on every side, but not crushed; **perplexed**, but not in despair; [NIV]	Perplexed; to be at a loss, to be doubting, not knowing, questioning, wondering which way to go, what to do, what to say; to be uncertain; to be disturbed. It means being perplexed and unable to find an answer. **Practical Application** The believer is often perplexed, not understanding why this or that happened, what should be done or said, how the situation should be handled, and on and on. Sometimes situations become so puzzling that he is almost stymied and the threat of despair faces him. There is the danger that his confidence and assurance will be shaken. But again, the presence and power of God steps in and saves the believer from despair. God gives him hope and stirs his confidence and shows him the way out. God never allows him to be overcome by despair.

ENGLISH WORD	GREEK WORD AND VERSE	THE WORD MEANS...
	We are hard pressed on every side, yet not crushed; *we are* **perplexed**, but not in despair; [NKJV] We are pressed on every side by troubles, but we are not crushed and broken. We are **perplexed**, but we don't give up and quit. [NLT] ἐν παντὶ θλιβόμενοι, ἀλλ' οὐ στενοχωρούμενοι· **ἀπορούμενοι** ἀλλ' οὐκ ἐξαπορούμενοι· [GNS] ἐν παντὶ θλιβόμενοι ἀλλ' οὐ στενοχωρούμενοι, **ἀπορούμενοι** ἀλλ' οὐκ ἐξαπορούμενοι, [GNT]	

#2904
Perplexed
 	
Doubted–KJV
Perplexed–NASB
Puzzled–NIV
Wondered–NKJV
Perplexed–NLT
 	
POSB REFERENCE
(Acts 5:21-25; esp. v.24)
Note 4, point 3
	διηπόρουν = *dieporoun*
	Pronunciation: [dee-ap-or-oon]
	Parsing (part of speech): verb
	    Mood—indicative
	    Tense—imperfect
	    Voice—active
	    Person—3rd person
	    Number—plural
	    Stem or root—from διαπορέω
	Concordance References:
	  ⇒ Strong's #1280 diaporeō
	  ⇒ NIV #1389 diaporeō
	  ⇒ NASB #1280 diaporeō
	
	Acts 5:24
	Now when the high priest and the captain of the temple and the chief priests heard these things, they **doubted** of them whereunto this would grow. [KJV]
	
	Now when the captain of the temple guard and the chief priests heard these words, they were greatly **perplexed** about them as to what would come of this. [NASB]
	
	On hearing this report, the captain of the temple guard and the chief priests were **puzzled**, wondering what would come of this. [NIV]
	
	Now when the high priest, the captain of the temple, and the chief priests heard these things, they **wondered** what the outcome would be. [NKJV]
	
	When the captain of the Temple guard and the leading priests heard this, they were **perplexed**, wondering where it would all end. [NLT]
	
	ὡς δὲ ἤκουσαν τοὺς λόγους τούτους ὅ τε ἱερεὺς καὶ ὁστρατηγὸς τοῦ ἱεροῦ καὶ οἱ ἀρχιερεῖς, **διηπόρουν** περὶ αὐτῶν, τί ἂν γένοιτο τοῦτο. [GNS]
	
	ὡς δὲ ἤκουσαν τοὺς λόγους τούτους ὅ τε στρατηγὸς τοῦ ἱεροῦ καὶ οἱ ἀρχιερεῖς, **διηπόρουν** περὶ αὐτῶν τί ἂν γένοιτο τοῦτο. [GNT]
		To be puzzled; to be perplexed; to be completely baffled; to be at a loss; to wonder about.
		
		Practical Application
		The religious leaders could not understand how the disciples could be delivered "out of their hand." They were apprehensive about the growth of the *new movement*.
		In the present situation, the authorities probably thought some of the guards had either willfully released the prisoners or else been careless while on duty.

#2905
Perplexed–Perplexity
 	
Doubt–KJV
Perplexity–NASB
Perplexed–NIV
Perplexed–NKJV
Perplexed–NLT
 	
POSB REFERENCE
(Acts 2:12-13; esp. v.12)
Note 6, point 1
	διηπόρουν = *dieporoun*
	Pronunciation: [dee-ayp-or-oon]
	Parsing (part of speech): verb
	    Mood—indicative
	    Tense—imperfect
	    Voice—active
	    Person—3rd person
	    Number—plural
	    Stem or root—from διαπορέω
	Concordance References:
	  ⇒ Strong's #1280 diaporeō
	  ⇒ NIV #1389 diaporeō
	  ⇒ NASB #1280 diaporeō
	
	Acts 2:12
	And they were all amazed, and were in **doubt**, saying one to another, What meaneth this? [KJV]
	
	And they all continued in amazement and great **perplexity**, saying to one another, "What does this mean?" [NASB]
	
	Amazed and **perplexed**, they asked one another, "What does this mean?" [NIV]
	
	So they were all amazed and **perplexed**, saying to one another, "Whatever could this mean?" [NKJV]
	
	They stood there amazed and **perplexed**. "What can
		To be perplexed; to doubt; to be puzzled; to be extremely confused.
		
		Practical Application
		Some were attracted, perplexed and wondering, at a loss as to what was happening. But they were attracted to seek meaning in it all.

ENGLISH WORD	GREEK WORD AND VERSE	THE WORD MEANS...
	this mean?" they asked each other. [NLT] ἐξίσταντο δὲ πάντες καὶ **διηπόρουν**, ἄλλος πρὸς ἄλλον λέγοντες, Τί ἂν θέλει τοῦτο εἶναι; [GNS] ἐξίσταντο δὲ πάντες καὶ **διηπόρουν**, ἄλλος πρὸς ἄλλον λέγοντες, Τί θέλει τοῦτο εἶναι; [GNT]	

#2906
Persecute
 	
Vex–KJV
Mistreat–NASB
Persecute–NIV
Harass–NKJV
Persecute–NLT
 	
POSB
REFERENCE
(Acts 12:1-4; esp. v.1)
Note 1, point 1
	κακῶσαί = *kakōsai*
	Pronunciation: [kak-o'-sah-ee]
	Parsing (part of speech): verb
	    Mood—infinitive
	    Tense—aorist
	    Voice—active
	    Stem or root—from **κακόω**
	Concordance References:
	  ⇒ Strong's #2559 kakoö
	  ⇒ NIV #2808 kakoö
	  ⇒ NASB #2559 kakoö
	
	Acts 12:1
	Now about that time Herod the king stretched forth his hands to **vex** certain of the church. [KJV]
	
	Now about that time Herod the king laid hands on some who belonged to the church, in order to **mistreat** them. [NASB]
	
	It was about this time that King Herod arrested some who belonged to the church, intending to **persecute** them. [NIV]
	
	Now about that time Herod the king stretched out *his* hand to **harass** some from the church. [NKJV]
	
	About that time King Herod Agrippa began to **persecute** some believers in the church. [NLT]
	
	Κατ' ἐκεῖνον δὲ τὸν καιρὸν ἐπέβαλεν Ἡρῴδης ὁ βασιλεὺς τὰς χεῖρας **κακῶσαί** τινας τῶν ἀπὸ τῆς ἐκκλησίας. [GNS]
	
	Κατ' ἐκεῖνον δὲ τὸν καιρὸν ἐπέβαλεν Ἡρῴδης ὁ βασιλεὺς τὰς χεῖρας **κακῶσαί** τινας τῶν ἀπὸ τῆς ἐκκλησίας. [GNT]
		To persecute; to mistreat; to vex; to harass; to oppress, torment, do evil against, harm; to be cruel.
		
		Practical Application
		Certain leaders in the church were arrested and imprisoned and apparently tortured. A person can just imagine believers' being man-handled and molested as the persecuted of every generation so often are with their homes and property being destroyed and confiscated or stolen.

#2907
Persecuted
 	
Persecuted–KJV
Persecuted–NASB
Persecuted–NIV
Persecuted–NKJV
Hunted down–NLT
 	
POSB
REFERENCE
(2 Cor.4:7-9; esp. v.9)
Note 2
 	
See also POSB REF:
(Mt.5:10-12; esp. v.10)
Note 9
	διωκόμενοι = *diōkomenoi*
	Pronunciation: [dee-o'-ko-mehn-oy]
	Parsing (part of speech): verb
	    Mood—participle
	    Tense—present
	    Voice—passive
	    Case—nominative
	    Gender—masculine
	    Person—1st person
	    Stem or root—from **διώκω**
	Concordance References:
	  ⇒ Strong's #1377 diökö
	  ⇒ NIV #1503 diökö
	  ⇒ NASB #1377 diökö
	
	2 Cor. 4:9
	Persecuted, but not forsaken; cast down, but not destroyed; [KJV]
	
	Persecuted, but not forsaken; struck down, but not destroyed; [NASB]
	
	Persecuted, but not abandoned; struck down, but not destroyed. [NIV]
	
	Persecuted, but not forsaken; struck down, but not destroyed—[NKJV]
	
	We are **hunted down**, but God never abandons us. We get knocked down, but we get up again and keep going. [NLT]
	
	διωκόμενοι ἀλλ' οὐκ ἐγκαταλειπόμενοι, καταβαλλόμενοι ἀλλ' οὐκ ἀπολλύμενοι· [GNS]
	
	διωκόμενοι ἀλλ' οὐκ ἐγκαταλειπόμενοι, καταβαλλόμενοι ἀλλ' οὐκ ἀπολλύμενοι, [GNT]
		Persecuted; to be hunted down; to drive away; to seek after.
		
		Practical Application
		The minister (or believer) may be persecuted, but he is not forsaken. Ministers are sometimes opposed, and sometimes the opposition is hot and severe. The persecution may be behind his back or to his face.
		
		The true believer will suffer persecution. Christ said so (cp. Jn.15:20). Christ suffered persecution; the early church suffered persecution; believers today will suffer persecution. It is inevitable.
		  ⇒ It may take the form of ridicule, abuse, anger, slander, gossip, mockery, cursing, isolation, or violence.
		  ⇒ It may take place in the market place, church, home, community, or school.
		
		What believers need is not deliverance from persecution, but victory and triumph through persecution. Believers need a conviction of mission, a conviction so strong that they become immovable.

#2908 **Perseverance**	**ὑπομονήν** = *hupomonēn* Pronunciation: [hoop-om-on-ayn'] Parsing (part of speech): noun Case—accusative	Patient endurance, steadfastness, perseverance. The word means to be steadfast and constant; to endure, persevere, stick to, and continue.

ENGLISH WORD	GREEK WORD AND VERSE	THE WORD MEANS...
Patient continuance– KJV **Perseverance–NASB** Persistence–NIV Patient continuance– NKJV Persist–NLT **POSB REFERENCE** (Romans 2:6-10; esp. v.7) Note 3, point 1b	Gender—feminine Number—singular Stem or root—from ὑπομονή, ῆς Concordance References: ⇒ Strong's #5281 hupomonë ⇒ NIV #5705 hupomonë ⇒ NASB #5281 hupomonë **Romans 2:7** To them who by **patient continuance** in well doing seek for glory and honour and immortality, eternal life: [KJV] to those who by **perseverance** in doing good seek for glory and honor and immortality, eternal life; [NASB] To those who by **persistence** in doing good seek glory, honor and immortality, he will give eternal life. [NIV] Eternal life to those who by **patient continuance** in doing good seek for glory, honor, and immortality; [NKJV] He will give eternal life to those who **persist** in doing what is good, seeking after the glory and honor and immortality that God offers. [NLT] τοῖς μὲν καθ' **ὑπομονὴν** ἔργου ἀγαθοῦ δόξαν καὶ τιμὴν καὶ ἀφθαρσίαν ζητοῦσι, ζωὴν αἰώνιον· [GNS] τοῖς μὲν καθ' **ὑπομονὴν** ἔργου ἀγαθοῦ δόξαν καὶ τιμὴν καὶ ἀφθαρσίαν ζητοῦσιν ζωὴν αἰώνιον, [GNT]	**Practical Application** Note how the well-doer seeks: by "perseverance" (*hupomonën*). The word means to be stedfast and constant; to endure, persevere, stick to, and continue. The well-doer is faithful in doing good works. ⇒ He does not just start, he finishes. ⇒ He does not live an inconsistent, up-and-down life. He continues and keeps on doing good deeds. ⇒ He does not give in to hardships, difficulties, or opposition. He endures and perseveres, always doing good.
#2909 **Perseverance** Patience–KJV Endurance–NASB **Perseverance–NIV** Endurance–NKJV Endurance–NLT **POSB REFERENCE** (Heb.12:1) Note 2, point 2	ὑπομονῆς = *hupomonës* Pronunciation: [hoop-om-on-ays'] Parsing (part of speech): noun Case—genitive Gender—feminine Number—singular Stem or root—from ὑπομονή, ῆς Concordance References: ⇒ Strong's #5281 hupomonë ⇒ NIV #5705 hupomonë ⇒ NASB #5281 hupomonë **Hebrews 12:1** Wherefore seeing we also are compassed about with so great a cloud of witnesses, let us lay aside every weight, and the sin which doth so easily beset us, and let us run with **patience** the race that is set before us, [KJV] Therefore, since we have so great a cloud of witnesses surrounding us, let us also lay aside every encumbrance, and the sin which so easily entangles us, and let us run with **endurance** the race that is set before us, [NASB] Therefore, since we are surrounded by such a great cloud of witnesses, let us throw off everything that hinders and the sin that so easily entangles, and let us run with **perseverance** the race marked out for us. [NIV] Therefore we also, since we are surrounded by so great a cloud of witnesses, let us lay aside every weight, and the sin which so easily ensnares *us,* and let us run with **endurance** the race that is set before us, [NKJV] Therefore, since we are surrounded by such a huge crowd of witnesses to the life of faith, let us strip off every weight that slows us down, especially the sin that so easily hinders our progress. And let us run with **endurance** the race that God has set before us. [NLT] Τοιγαροῦν καὶ ἡμεῖς τοσοῦτον ἔχοντες περικείμενον ἡμῖν νέφος μαρτύρων, ὄγκον ἀποθέμενοι πάντα καὶ τὴν εὐπερίστατον ἁμαρτίαν, δι' **ὑπομονῆς** τρέχωμεν τὸν προκείμενον ἡμῖν ἀγῶνα, [GNS] Τοιγαροῦν καὶ ἡμεῖς τοσοῦτον ἔχοντες περικείμενον ἡμῖν νέφος μαρτύρων, ὄγκον ἀποθέμενοι πάντα καὶ τὴν εὐπερίστατον ἁμαρτίαν, δι' **ὑπομονῆς** τρέχωμεν τὸν προκείμενον ἡμῖν ἀγῶνα [GNT]	To persevere; to be patient; to have endurance; to be steadfast in doing the will of God. **Practical Application** The word *perseverance* is not passive; it is active. It is not the spirit that just sits back and puts up with the trials of life, taking whatever may come. Rather, it is the spirit that stands up and faces the trials of life, that actively goes about conquering and overcoming them. When trials confront a man who is truly justified, he is stirred to arise and face the trials head on. He immediately sets out to conquer and overcome them. He knows that God is allowing the trials in order to teach him more and more endurance (patience).

ENGLISH WORD	GREEK WORD AND VERSE	THE WORD MEANS...
#2910 **Perseverance** Patience–KJV Endurance–NASB **Perseverance–NIV** Patience–NKJV Endurance–NLT **POSB REFERENCE** (Jas.1:2-4; esp. v.3) Note 2, point 1 **See also POSB REF:** (Heb.10:32-39; esp. v.36) Note 4 (2 Cor.6:4) Note 2 (Rom.5:3-5; esp. v.3) Note 5, point 1 (2 Pt.1:5-7; esp. v.6) Note 1, point 4	ὑπομονήν = hupomonën Pronunciation: [hoop-om-on-ayn'] Parsing (part of speech): noun 　Case—accusative 　Gender—feminine 　Number—singular 　Stem or root—from ὑπομονή, ῆς Concordance References: ⇒　Strong's #5281 hupomonë ⇒　NIV #5705 hupomonë ⇒　NASB #5281 hupomonë **James 1:3** Knowing this, that the trying of your faith worketh **patience**. [KJV] Knowing that the testing of your faith produces **endurance**. [NASB] Because you know that the testing of your faith develops **perseverance**. [NIV] Knowing that the testing of your faith produces **patience**. [NKJV] For when your faith is tested, your **endurance** has a chance to grow. [NLT] γινώσκοντες ὅτι τὸ δοκίμιον ὑμῶν τῆς πίστεως κατεργάζεται **ὑπομονήν**· [GNS] γινώσκοντες ὅτι τὸ δοκίμιον ὑμῶν τῆς πίστεως κατεργάζεται **ὑπομονήν**. [GNT]	Perseverance, patience, endurance, steadfastness. **Practical Application** We must know something: know that trials and temptations work patience (James 1:3). We must know that trials and temptations are not to defeat and discourage us, but to prove us, to make us much stronger and more pure and righteous. The believer is to know that the trials and temptations of life will make him more stedfast, more persevering, and more enduring. They will make him much stronger, not weaker. They will make him strong just like Jesus, and they will give him a pure and righteous character just like Jesus. When the believer keeps this fact in his mind, he can face trials and temptations much more positively. He can then begin to move toward the spirit of living joyfully in the face of trials and temptations.
#2911 **Persevere In** Continue–KJV **Persevere in–NASB** **Persevere in–NIV** Continue–NKJV Stay true–NLT **POSB REFERENCE** (1 Tim.4:16) Note 12 **See also POSB REF:** (Col.1:23) Note 4, point 1 (Rom.11:22) Note 4, point 2	ἐπίμενε = epimene Pronunciation: [ep-ee-men'-eh] Parsing (part of speech): verb 　Mood—imperative 　Tense—present 　Voice—active 　Person—2nd person 　Number—singular 　Stem or root—from ἐπιμένω Concordance References: ⇒　Strong's #1961 epimenö ⇒　NIV #2152 epimenö ⇒　NASB #1961 epimenö **1 Tim. 4:16** Take heed unto thyself, and unto the doctrine; **continue** in them: for in doing this thou shalt both save thyself, and them that hear thee. [KJV] Pay close attention to yourself and to your teaching; **persevere in** these things; for as you do this you will insure salvation both for yourself and for those who hear you. [NASB] Watch your life and doctrine closely. **Persevere in** them, because if you do, you will save both yourself and your hearers. [NIV] Take heed to yourself and to the doctrine. **Continue** in them, for in doing this you will save both yourself and those who hear you. [NKJV] Keep a close watch on yourself and on your teaching. **Stay true** to what is right, and God will save you and those who hear you. [NLT] ἔπεχε σεαυτῷ καὶ τῇ διδασκαλίᾳ. **ἐπίμενε** αὐτοῖς· τοῦτο γὰρ ποιῶν καὶ σεαυτὸν σώσεις καὶ τοὺς ἀκούοντάς σου. [GNS] ἔπεχε σεαυτῷ καὶ τῇ διδασκαλίᾳ, **ἐπίμενε** αὐτοῖς· τοῦτο γὰρ ποιῶν καὶ σεαυτὸν σώσεις καὶ τοὺς ἀκούοντάς σου. [GNT]	To persevere in; to persist in; to remain true; to continue; to stay true. The words "persevere in" (epimene) mean to "stay by them," "stick to them," "see them through" (A.T. Robertson. *Word Pictures in the New Testament*, Vol.4, p.582). **Practical Application** Note what he does. He perseveres in the instructions of the Word of God. Why? Because by persevering in them, he saves both himself and those who hear him.
#2912 **Persevere, To** Patience–KJV Endurance–NASB **To persevere–NIV**	ὑπομονῆς = hupomonës Pronunciation: [hoop-om-on-ays'] Parsing (part of speech): noun 　Case—genitive 　Gender—feminine 　Number—singular 　Stem or root—from ὑπομονή, ῆς	To persevere; to be patient; to have endurance; to be steadfast in doing the will of God. **Practical Application** The verses (Hebrews 10:35-37) state it well:

ENGLISH WORD	GREEK WORD AND VERSE	THE WORD MEANS...
Endurance–NKJV Patient endurance–NLT **POSB REFERENCE** (Heb.10:32-39; esp. v.36) Note 4	Concordance References: ⇒ Strong's #5281 hupomonë ⇒ NIV #5705 hupomonë ⇒ NASB #5281 hupomonë **Hebrews 10:36** For ye have need of **patience**, that, after ye have done the will of God, ye might receive the promise. [KJV] For you have need of **endurance**, so that when you have done the will of God, you may receive what was promised. [NASB] You need **to persevere** so that when you have done the will of God, you will receive what he has promised. [NIV] For you have need of **endurance**, so that after you have done the will of God, you may receive the promise: [NKJV] **Patient endurance** is what you need now, so you will continue to do God's will. Then you will receive all that he has promised. [NLT] ὑπομονῆς γὰρ ἔχετε χρείαν, ἵνα τὸ θέλημα τοῦ Θεοῦ ποιήσαντες, κομίσησθε τὴν ἐπαγγελίαν. [GNS] ὑπομονῆς γὰρ ἔχετε χρείαν ἵνα τὸ θέλημα τοῦ θεοῦ ποιήσαντες κομίσησθε τὴν ἐπαγγελίαν. [GNT]	endure and you will receive the promise of God's reward. For in just a little while Christ is coming, and He will not tarry. His coming is assured; and when He comes, He will come with His reward.

#2913
Perseveres
 	
Endureth–KJV
Endures–NASB
Perseveres–NIV
Endures–NKJV
Endures–NLT
 	
POSB REFERENCE
(1 Cor.13:4-7; esp. v.7)
Note 2, point 15
	ὑπομένει = hupomenei
	Pronunciation: [hoop-om-en'-ee]
	Parsing (part of speech): verb
	  Mood—indicative
	  Tense—present
	  Voice—active
	  Person—3rd person
	  Number—singular
	  Stem or root—from ὑπομένω
	Concordance References:
	⇒ Strong's #5278 hupomenō
	⇒ NIV #5702 hupomenō
	⇒ NASB #5278 hupomenō
	
	1 Cor. 13:7
	Beareth all things, believeth all things, hopeth all things, **endureth** all things. [KJV]
	Bears all things, believes all things, hopes all things, **endures** all things. [NASB]
	It always protects, always trusts, always hopes, always **perseveres**. [NIV]
	Bears all things, believes all things, hopes all things, **endures** all things. [NKJV]
	Love never gives up, never loses faith, is always hopeful, and **endures** through every circumstance. [NLT]
	πάντα στέγει, πάντα πιστεύει, πάντα ἐλπίζει, πάντα ὑπομένει. [GNS]
	πάντα στέγει, πάντα πιστεύει, πάντα ἐλπίζει, πάντα ὑπομένει. [GNT]
		To persevere; to endure; to be patient; to hold out; to stand firm; to stand ground; to put up with; to press on through opposition. The word "perseveres" (huopmenei) is a military word meaning to stand against the attack of an enemy.
		
		Practical Application
		Love actively fights and endures all attacks. Love is strong, full of fortitude and fight, and it struggles against any and every assault to buckle in to being unloving. Love conquers and triumphs—always—because it endures all things. No matter what attacks love, named or unnamed, it endures the attack and continues to love.

#2914
Persevering
 	
Patient–KJV
Persevering–NASB
Patient–NIV
Patient–NKJV
Patient–NLT
 	
POSB REFERENCE
(Rom. 12:12)
Note 3, point 2
	ὑπομένοντες = hupomenontes
	Pronunciation: [hoop-om-en'-on-tehs]
	Parsing (part of speech): verb
	  Mood—participle (imperative sense)
	  Tense—present
	  Voice—active
	  Case—nominative
	  Gender—masculine
	  Person—2nd person
	  Number—plural
	  Stem or root—from ὑπομένω
	Concordance References:
	⇒ Strong's #5278 hupomenō
	⇒ NIV #5702 hupomenō
	⇒ NASB #5278 hupomenō
	
	Romans 12:12
	Rejoicing in hope; **patient** in tribulation; continuing
		To be patient; to hold out; to stand firm; to put up with. It means to endure, remain, persevere, abide, bear up bravely.
		
		Practical Application
		The believer is to endure trials. The believer actually experiences a surge of fortitude from Christ when trials confront him.

ENGLISH WORD	GREEK WORD AND VERSE	THE WORD MEANS...

#2923
Persuasive
 	
Enticing–KJV
Persuasive–NASB
Persuasive–NIV
Persuasive–NKJV
Persuasive–NLT
 	
**POSB
REFERENCE**
(1 Cor.2:4)
Note 4, point 2
	πειθοῖ[ς] = peithois
	Pronunciation: [pee-thoys']
	Parsing (part of speech): adjective
	    Case—dative
	    Gender—masculine
	    Number—plural
	OR
	Parsing (part of speech): noun
	    Case—dative
	    Gender—feminine
	    Number—singular
	    Stem or root—from πειθός, ή, όν
	Concordance References:
	  ⇒ Strong's #3981 peithois
	  ⇒ NIV #4273 peithois
	  ⇒ NASB #3981 peithois
	
	1 Cor. 2:4
	And my speech and my preaching was not with **enticing** words of man's wisdom, but in demonstration of the Spirit and of power: [KJV]
	And my message and my preaching were not in **persuasive** words of wisdom, but in demonstration of the Spirit and of power, [NASB]
	My message and my preaching were not with wise and **persuasive** words, but with a demonstration of the Spirit's power, [NIV]
	And my speech and my preaching were not with **persuasive** words of human wisdom, but in demonstration of the Spirit and of power, [NKJV]
	And my message and my preaching were very plain. I did not use wise and **persuasive** speeches, but the Holy Spirit was powerful among you. [NLT]
	καὶ ὁ λόγος μου καὶ τὸ κήρυγμά μου οὐκ ἐν **πειθοῖς** ἀνθρωπίνης σοφίας λόγοις, ἀλλ' ἐν ἀποδείξει πνεύματος καὶ δυνάμεως· [GNS]
	καὶ ὁ λόγος μου καὶ τὸ κήρυγμά μου οὐκ ἐν **πειθοῖ[ς]** σοφίας [λόγοις] ἀλλ' ἐν ἀποδείξει πνεύματος καὶ δυνάμεως, [GNT]
		Persuasive, enticing, plausible, skillful.
		
		Practical Application
		Paul's witnessing and preaching were not based upon the enticing, persuasive, plausible arguments of man's wisdom and philosophy.

#2924
**Persuasive Argument–
Persuasive Arguments–
Persuasive Words**
 	
Enticing words–KJV
Persuasive argument–NASB
Fine-sounding arguments–NIV
Persuasive words–NKJV
Persuasive arguments–NLT
 	
**POSB
REFERENCE**
(Col.2:4)
Note 3
	πιθανολογία = pithanologia
	Pronunciation: [pith-an-ol-og-ee'-ah]
	Parsing (part of speech): noun
	    Case—dative
	    Gender—feminine
	    Number—singular
	    Stem or root—from πιθανολογία, ας
	Concordance References:
	  ⇒ Strong's #4086 pithanologia
	  ⇒ NIV #4391 pithanologia
	  ⇒ NASB #4086 pithanologia
	
	Col. 2:4
	And this I say, lest any man should beguile you with **enticing words**. [KJV]
	I say this in order that no one may delude you with **persuasive argument**. [NASB]
	I tell you this so that no one may deceive you by **fine-sounding arguments**. [NIV]
	Now this I say lest anyone should deceive you with **persuasive words**. [NKJV]
	I am telling you this so that no one will be able to deceive you with **persuasive arguments**. [NLT]
	τοῦτο δὲ λέγω, ἵνα μη τις ὑμᾶς παραλογίζηται ἐν πιθανολογίᾳ. [GNS]
	Τοῦτο λέγω ἵνα μηδεὶς ὑμᾶς παραλογίζηται ἐν πιθανολογίᾳ. [GNT]
		Fine-sounding arguments; enticing words; persuasive arguments.
		
		Practical Application
		A mature person resists seduction and deception. The word "deceive" (*paralogizetai*) means to mislead, delude, cheat, seduce, and lead someone astray. Note how the seduction takes place: by "persuasive words" [NKJV] (*pithanologia*), that is, by words that are enticing, appealing, eloquent, flowery, and attractive.

#2925
Persuasively
 	
Persuading–KJV
Persuading–NASB
	πείθων = peithön
	Pronunciation: [pi'-thown]
	Parsing (part of speech): verb
	    Mood—participle
	    Tense—present
		Persuasively; to persuade; to win favor; to convince.

ENGLISH WORD	GREEK WORD AND VERSE	THE WORD MEANS...
Persuasively–NIV Persuading–NKJV **Persuasively–NLT** **POSB REFERENCE** (Acts 19:2-9; esp. v.8) Note 2, point 2b	Voice—active Case—nominative Gender—masculine Number—singular Stem or root—from πείθω Concordance References: ⇒ Strong's #3982 peithö ⇒ NIV #4275 peithö ⇒ NASB #3982 peithö **Acts 19:8** And he went into the synagogue, and spake boldly for the space of three months, disputing and **persuading** the things concerning the kingdom of God. [KJV] And he entered the synagogue and continued speaking out boldly for three months, reasoning and **persuading** them about the kingdom of God. [NASB] Paul entered the synagogue and spoke boldly there for three months, arguing **persuasively** about the kingdom of God. [NIV] And he went into the synagogue and spoke boldly for three months, reasoning and **persuading** concerning the things of the kingdom of God. [NKJV] Then Paul went to the synagogue and preached boldly for the next three months, arguing **persuasively** about the Kingdom of God. [NLT] Εἰσελθὼν δὲ εἰς τὴν συναγωγὴν, ἐπαρρησιάζετο, ἐπὶ μῆνας τρεῖς διαλεγόμενος, καὶ **πείθων** τὰ περὶ τῆς βασιλείας τοῦ Θεοῦ. [GNS] Εἰσελθὼν δὲ εἰς τὴν συναγωγὴν ἐπαρρησιάζετο ἐπὶ μῆνας τρεῖς διαλεγόμενος καὶ **πείθων** [τὰ] περὶ τῆς βασιλείας τοῦ Θεοῦ. [GNT]	**Practical Application** Salvation necessitates a decision: a person either decides to accept Christ or else he automatically rejects Him. In the case of the audience who heard Paul, many rejected Christ. They just hardened their hearts and refused to believe. For three months Paul preached boldly in the synagogue of the Jews. Note four facts. 1. Paul disputed (*dialegomenos*) the gospel. The word means to reason, discuss, convince, and answer questions. He discussed the gospel, asking and answering questions, convincing all who were willing to be convinced. 2. He persuaded (*peithön*) men of the gospel. (See POSB note—Acts 18:4 for discussion.) 3. Paul's message concerned the Kingdom of God (see POSB *Deeper Study #3*, Kingdom of God—Matthew 19:23-24 for discussion). 4. Many were hardened and did not believe, being disobedient to the call of God to salvation (cp. Acts 19:9).

#2926
Perverse
 	
Untoward–KJV
Perverse–NASB
Corrupt–NIV
Perverse–NKJV
Astray–NLT
 	
**POSB
REFERENCE**
(Acts 2:40)
Note 5, point 2
	σκολιᾶς = *skolias*
	Pronunciation: [skol-ee-ahs']
	Parsing (part of speech): adjective
	    Case—genitive
	    Gender—feminine
	    Number—singular
	    Stem or root—from σκολιός, ά, όν
	Concordance References:
	⇒ Strong's #4646 skolios
	⇒ NIV #5021 skolios
	⇒ NASB #4646 skolios
	
	Acts 2:40
	And with many other words did he testify and exhort, saying, Save yourselves from this **untoward** generation. [KJV]
	And with many other words he solemnly testified and kept on exhorting them, saying, "Be saved from this **perverse** generation!" [NASB]
	With many other words he warned them; and he pleaded with them, "Save yourselves from this **corrupt** generation." [NIV]
	And with many other words he testified and exhorted them, saying, "Be saved from this **perverse** generation." [NKJV]
	Then Peter continued preaching for a long time, strongly urging all his listeners, "Save yourselves from this generation that has gone **astray**!" [NLT]
	ἑτέροις τε λόγοις πλείοσι διεμαρτύρετο καὶ παρεκάλει, λέγων, Σώθητε ἀπὸ τῆς γενεᾶς τῆς **σκολιᾶς** ταύτης. [GNS]
	ἑτέροις τε λόγοις πλείοσιν διεμαρτύρατο καὶ παρεκάλει αὐτοὺς λέγων, Σώθητε ἀπὸ τῆς γενεᾶς τῆς **σκολιᾶς** ταύτης. [GNT]
		To be corrupt; to be harsh; to be perverse; to go astray; to be crooked or bent out of shape.
		
		Practical Application
		    People are far from being straight and far from being in the shape intended by God. They are crooked and bent, unrighteous and ungodly, sinful and corrupt.

#2927
**Perverse–
Perverted**
	διεστραμμένη = *diestrammenë*
	Pronunciation: [dee-as-tram-mehn-ay]
	Parsing (part of speech): verb
	    Mood—participle
	    Tense—perfect
		To be perverse; to distort; to twist; to turn aside or away; to be torn in two; to be corrupted (cp. Acts 20:30; Phil. 2:15).

ENGLISH WORD	GREEK WORD AND VERSE	THE WORD MEANS...
Perverse–KJV **Perverse–NASB** **Perverse–NIV** **Perverse–NKJV** Stubborn–NLT **POSB REFERENCE** (Lk.9:41) *Deeper Study #3* **See also POSB REF:** (Mt.17:17) *Deeper Study #2*	Voice—passive Case—vocative Person—2nd person Number—singular Stem or root—from διαστρέφω Concordance References: ⇒ Strong's #1294 diastrephō ⇒ NIV #1406 diastrephō ⇒ NASB #1294 diastrephō **Luke 9:41** And Jesus answering said, O faithless and **perverse** generation, how long shall I be with you, and suffer you? Bring thy son hither. [KJV] And Jesus answered and said, "O unbelieving and **perverted** generation, how long shall I be with you, and put up with you? Bring your son here." [NASB] "O unbelieving and **perverse** generation," Jesus replied, "how long shall I stay with you and put up with you? Bring your son here." [NIV] Then Jesus answered and said, "O faithless and **perverse** generation, how long shall I be with you and bear with you? Bring your son here." [NKJV] "You **stubborn**, faithless people," Jesus said, "how long must I be with you and put up with you? Bring him here." [NLT] ἀποκριθεὶς δὲ ὁ Ἰησοῦς εἶπεν, Ὦ γενεὰ ἄπιστος καὶ **διεστραμμένη**, ἕως πότε ἔσομαι πρὸς ὑμᾶς, καὶ ἀνέξομαι ὑμῶν; προσάγαγε ὧδε τὸν υἱόν σου. [GNS] ἀποκριθεὶς δὲ ὁ Ἰησοῦς εἶπεν, Ὦ γενεὰ ἄπιστος καὶ **διεστραμμένη**, ἕως πότε ἔσομαι πρὸς ὑμᾶς καὶ ἀνέξομαι ὑμῶν; προσάγαγε ὧδε τὸν υἱόν σου. [GNT]	**Practical Application** In this Scripture, Jesus spoke to His whole generation. He enlarged His comments beyond the disciples. They had no power; neither did anyone else in His generation. What the disciples lacked was lacked by all. Their sins were the sins of all, the sins of being faithless and perverse.
#2928 **Pervert** **Pervert–KJV** Distort–NASB **Pervert–NIV** Pervert–NKJV Twist and change– NLT **POSB REFERENCE** (Gal.1:6-7; esp. v.7) Note 2	μεταστρέψαι = *metastrepsai* Pronunciation: [met-as-tref'-sah-ee] Parsing (part of speech): verb Mood—infinitive Tense—aorist Voice—active Stem or root—from μεταστρέφω Concordance References: ⇒ Strong's #3344 metastrephō ⇒ NIV #3570 metastrephō ⇒ NASB #3344 metastrephō **Galatians 1:7** Which is not another; but there be some that trouble you, and would **pervert** the gospel of Christ. [KJV] Which is really not another; only there are some who are disturbing you, and want to **distort** the gospel of Christ. [NASB] Which is really no gospel at all. Evidently some people are throwing you into confusion and are trying to **pervert** the gospel of Christ. [NIV] Which is not another; but there are some who trouble you and want to **pervert** the gospel of Christ. [NKJV] That pretends to be the Good News but is not the Good News at all. You are being fooled by those who **twist and change** the truth concerning Christ. [NLT] ὃ οὐκ ἔστιν ἄλλο, εἰ μή τινές εἰσιν οἱ ταράσσοντες ὑμᾶς καὶ θέλοντες **μεταστρέψαι** τὸ εὐαγγέλιον τοῦ Χριστοῦ. [GNS] ὃ οὐκ ἔστιν ἄλλο, εἰ μή τινές εἰσιν οἱ ταράσσοντες ὑμᾶς καὶ θέλοντες **μεταστρέψαι** τὸ εὐαγγέλιον τοῦ Χριστοῦ. [GNT]	To distort; to turn about; to pervert; to change completely; to twist and change; to alter. **Practical Application** The false teachers were taking the gospel of God's love as demonstrated in His Son, Jesus Christ, and changing it. The false teachers claimed to be Christians, followers of Christ. They even believed with Paul... • that God did love the world and sent His Son into the world. • that Jesus Christ was the Son of God who did actually come to earth. • that Jesus Christ did die and arise from the dead. However, the false teachers were adding to and taking away from the gospel, twisting its meaning and making it say something entirely different from the Holy Scripture.
#2929 **Perverted** Perverse–KJV **Perverted–NASB** Perverse–NIV	διεστραμμένη = *diestrammenē* Pronunciation: [dee-as-tram-mehn-ay] Parsing (part of speech): verb Mood—participle Tense—perfect Voice—passive Case—vocative	To be perverse; to be perverted; to distort; to twist; to turn aside or away; to be torn in two; to be corrupted (cp. Acts 20:30; Phil. 2:15). **Practical Application** In this Scripture, Jesus spoke to His whole

ENGLISH WORD	GREEK WORD AND VERSE	THE WORD MEANS...
Perverse–NKJV Stubborn–NLT **POSB REFERENCE** (Lk.9:41) *Deeper Study #3*	Person—2nd person Number—singular Stem or root—from διαστρέφω Concordance References: ⇒ Strong's #1294 diastrephō ⇒ NIV #1406 diastrephō ⇒ NASB #1294 diastrephō **Luke 9:41** And Jesus answering said, O faithless and **perverse** generation, how long shall I be with you, and suffer you? Bring thy son hither. [KJV] And Jesus answered and said, "O unbelieving and **perverted** generation, how long shall I be with you, and put up with you? Bring your son here." [NASB] "O unbelieving and **perverse** generation," Jesus replied, "how long shall I stay with you and put up with you? Bring your son here." [NIV] Then Jesus answered and said, "O faithless and **perverse** generation, how long shall I be with you and bear with you? Bring your son here." [NKJV] "You **stubborn**, faithless people," Jesus said, "how long must I be with you and put up with you? Bring him here." [NLT] ἀποκριθεὶς δὲ ὁ Ἰησοῦς εἶπεν, Ὦ γενεὰ ἄπιστος καὶ **διεστραμμένη**, ἕως πότε ἔσομαι πρὸς ὑμᾶς, καὶ ἀνέξομαι ὑμῶν; προσάγαγε ὧδε τὸν υἱόν σου. [GNS] ἀποκριθεὶς δὲ ὁ Ἰησοῦς εἶπεν, Ὦ γενεὰ ἄπιστος καὶ **διεστραμμένη**, ἕως πότε ἔσομαι πρὸς ὑμᾶς καὶ ἀνέξομαι ὑμῶν; προσάγαγε ὧδε τὸν υἱόν σου. [GNT]	generation. He enlarged His comments beyond the disciples. They had no power; neither did anyone else in His generation. What the disciples lacked was lacked by all. Their sins were the sins of all, the sins of being faithless and perverse.
#2930 Perverted Subverted–KJV **Perverted–NASB** Warped–NIV Warped–NKJV Turned away from the truth–NLT **POSB REFERENCE** (Tit.3:10-11; esp. v.11) Note 3	ἐξέστραπται = exestraptai Pronunciation: [ek-ehs'-trap-tah-ee] Parsing (part of speech): verb Mood—indicative Tense—perfect Voice—passive Person—3rd person Number—singular Stem or root— Concordance References: ⇒ Strong's #1612 ekstrephō ⇒ NIV #1750 ekstrephō ⇒ NASB #1612 ekstrephō **Titus 3:11** Knowing that he that is such is **subverted**, and sinneth, being condemned of himself. [KJV] Knowing that such a man is **perverted** and is sinning, being self-condemned. [NASB] You may be sure that such a man is **warped** and sinful; he is self-condemned. [NIV] Knowing that such a person is **warped** and sinning, being self-condemned. [NKJV] For people like that have **turned away from the truth**. They are sinning, and they condemn themselves. [NLT] εἰδὼς ὅτι **ἐξέστραπται** ὁ τοιοῦτος, καὶ ἁμαρτάνει, ων αὐτοκατάκριτος. [GNS] εἰδὼς ὅτι **ἐξέστραπται** ὁ τοιοῦτος καὶ ἁμαρτάνει ων αὐτοκατάκριτος. [GNT]	Perverted, corrupted, warped, turned away from the truth. It means the heretic is "perverted" (*exestraptai*): which means he is twisted or turned out and away from the truth of Christ and His Word. **Practical Application** Note that the heretic sins. The idea is that he sins greatly. Therefore, he condemns himself. He himself has chosen the path of unbelief, and he will be condemned for his unbelief.
#2931 Peter **Peter–KJV Peter–NASB Peter–NIV Peter–NKJV Peter–NLT**	Πέτρον = Petron Pronunciation: [pet'-ron] Parsing (part of speech): noun Case—accusative Gender—masculine Number—singular Stem or root—from Πέτρος, ου Concordance References: ⇒ Strong's #4074 Petros ⇒ NIV #4377 Petros ⇒ NASB #4074 Petros	Rock. Petron is the Greek translation of for the Aramaic word, Cephas. **Practical Application** What kind of man was this "rock"? Peter was a rough-hewn fisherman. He looked, acted, and spoke like any professional fisherman at the dock of a large lake or sea. Anyone who has been around a fisherman's dock or boat can picture Peter.

ENGLISH WORD	GREEK WORD AND VERSE	THE WORD MEANS...
POSB REFERENCE (Mk.3:16) *Deeper Study #4*	**Mark 3:16** And **Simon** he surnamed **Peter**; [KJV] And He appointed the twelve: **Simon** (to whom He gave the name **Peter**), [NASB] These are the twelve he appointed: **Simon** (to whom he gave the name **Peter**); [NIV] **Simon**, to whom He gave the name **Peter**; [NKJV] These are the names of the twelve he chose: **Simon** (he renamed him **Peter**), [NLT] Καὶ ἐπέθηκε τῷ Σίμωνι ὄνομα Πέτρον, [GNS] [καὶ ἐποίησεν τοὺς δώδεκα,] καὶ ἐπέθηκεν ὄνομα τῷ Σίμωνι Πέτρον, [GNT]	1. Peter had many commendable strengths. a. Peter was self-sacrificing, giving up all—even his home and business—to follow Jesus (see POSB notes—Mk. 1:16-18; POSB *Deeper Study #1*—Mt. 8:14). b. Peter was spiritual minded. He was the first to really grasp who Jesus was (Mt. 16:16-19). c. Peter was childlike and humble, often responding and leaping out to Jesus as a child does to his father (Mt. 14:26-29; Mk. 11:21; John 13:6-11). d. Peter was trusting, sometimes casting his whole being upon Jesus (Mt. 14:26-29). e. Peter was tenderhearted and loving, caring deeply for his Lord (Mt. 26:75; John 21:15-17). f. Peter was courageous, the only disciple who defended Jesus against arrest. He was also one of the two disciples who followed Jesus through His trials and crucifixion, although he followed afar off (Mt. 26:51; Mt. 26:58). g. Peter would have been judged a hard-working, industrious man by any society. 2. Peter had some glaring weaknesses. a. Peter was prideful and presumptuous, a man who thought he knew best and who sometimes lorded it over others. He was always depending upon human wisdom and strength, the arm of the flesh. ⇒ Peter thought he knew what was best for Jesus, insisting that Jesus did not have to die (Mt. 16:22-23). ⇒ Peter tried to prevent Jesus' arrest by drawing his sword and wounding one of the arresting party (Mt. 26:51; Mk. 14:47; Lk. 22:50). ⇒ Peter rebuked Jesus, overstepping the limits of his rights. When the crowd thronged Jesus, Jesus simply asked who had touched Him. Peter rebuked Jesus for asking such a question when there were so many people pressing in upon them (Lk. 8:45). ⇒ Peter, in a self-abasing pride, refused to let Jesus wash his feet (John 13:6-11). b. Peter was slow to learn and to understand truth (Mt. 15:15-16). c. Peter was self-seeking (Mt. 19:27). d. Peter was disbelieving (Mt. 14:30). e. Peter was overbearing, even to the point of instructing Jesus (Mt. 16:22-23). f. Peter had a weak, cowardly trait, being the only disciple to vocally deny Jesus (Mt. 26:69-74).

#2932
Petition
 	
Supplication–KJV
Supplication–NASB
Petition–NIV
Supplication–NKJV
What you need–NLT
	δεήσει = deësei
	Pronunciation: [deh'-ay-seh-ee]
	Parsing (part of speech): noun
	  Case—dative
	  Gender—feminine
	  Number—singular
	  Stem or root—from δέησις, εως
	Concordance References:
	  ⇒ Strong's #1162 deësis
	  ⇒ NIV #1255 deësis
	  ⇒ NASB #1162 deësis
		Petition, supplication, prayer, what you need.
		
		Practical Application
		  The word "petition" (*deësei*) refers to the prayers that focus upon special needs. We feel a deep, intense need, therefore, we go before God and *petition*, that is, pour out our soul to God. Need—great need—confronts us, and the only possible help and deliverance is God. Therefore, we come and lay our need before Him as a child: crying, pleading and begging for His help, com-

ENGLISH WORD	GREEK WORD AND VERSE	THE WORD MEANS...
POSB **REFERENCE** (Philip.4:6-7; esp. v.6) Note 1, point 2	**Philip. 4:6** Be careful for nothing; but in every thing by prayer and **supplication** with thanksgiving let your requests be made known unto God. [KJV] Be anxious for nothing, but in everything by prayer and **supplication** with thanksgiving let your requests be made known to God. [NASB] Do not be anxious about anything, but in everything, by prayer and **petition**, with thanksgiving, present your requests to God. [NIV] Be anxious for nothing, but in everything by prayer and **supplication**, with thanksgiving, let your requests be made known to God; [NKJV] Don't worry about anything; instead, pray about everything. Tell God **what you need**, and thank him for all he has done. [NLT] μηδὲν μεριμνᾶτε, ἀλλ' ἐν παντὶ τῇ προσευχῇ καὶ τῇ **δεήσει** μετὰ εὐχαριστίας τὰ αἰτήματα ὑμῶν γνωριζέσθω πρὸς τὸν θεόν, [GNS] μηδὲν μεριμνᾶτε, ἀλλ' ἐν παντὶ τῇ προσευχῇ καὶ τῇ **δεήσει** μετὰ εὐχαριστίας τὰ αἰτήματα ὑμῶν γνωριζέσθω πρὸς τὸν θεόν. [GNT]	fort, deliverance, and peace.

#2933
Petitions
 	
Intercessions–KJV
Petitions–NASB
Intercession–NIV
Intercessions–NKJV
Plead for God's mercy–NLT
 	
POSB
REFERENCE
(1 Tim.2:1)
Note 1, point 3
	ἐντεύξεις = *enteuxeis*
	Pronunciation: [ent'-yook-eh-ees]
	Parsing (part of speech): noun
	    Case—accusative
	    Gender—feminine
	    Number—plural
	    Stem or root—from ἔντευξις, εως
	Concordance References:
	  ⇒ Strong's #1783 enteuxis
	  ⇒ NIV #1950 enteuxis
	  ⇒ NASB #1783 enteuxis
	
	1 Tim. 2:1
	I exhort therefore, that, first of all, supplications, prayers, **intercessions**, and giving of thanks, be made for all men; [KJV]
	First of all, then, I urge that entreaties and prayers, **petitions** and thanksgivings, be made on behalf of all men, [NASB]
	I urge, then, first of all, that requests, prayers, **intercession** and thanksgiving be made for everyone— [NIV]
	Therefore I exhort first of all that supplications, prayers, **intercessions**, *and* giving of thanks be made for all men, [NKJV]
	I urge you, first of all, to pray for all people. As you make your requests, **plead for God's mercy** upon them, and give thanks. [NLT]
	Παρακαλῶ οὖν πρῶτον πάντων ποιεῖσθαι δεήσεις, προσευχάς, **ἐντεύξεις**, εὐχαριστίας, ὑπὲρ πάντων ἀνθρώπων· [GNS]
	Παρακαλῶ οὖν πρῶτον πάντων ποιεῖσθαι δεήσεις προσευχάς **ἐντεύξεις** εὐχαριστίας ὑπὲρ πάντων ἀνθρώπων, [GNT]
		Intercession, petition, prayer; to plead to God for another person.
		
		Practical Application
		This refers to bold praying; to standing before God in behalf of another person. Christ is our Intercessor, the One who stands between God and us in our behalf. But we are to intercede for men, to carry their names and lives before God and to boldly pray for them, expecting God to hear and answer—all in the name of Christ. We are to intercede for all men—to stand in the gap between them and God, boldly praying and asking God to be merciful and gracious in salvation and in deliverance.

#2934
Picked Up
 	
Gather–KJV
Gather–NASB
Picked up–NIV
Gather–NKJV
Gathered–NLT
 	
POSB
REFERENCE
(Jn.15:4-6; esp. v.6)
Note 4, point 4c
	συνάγουσιν = *sunagousin*
	Pronunciation: [soon-ahg'-oo-sin]
	Parsing (part of speech): verb
	    Mood—indicative
	    Tense—present
	    Voice—active
	    Person—3rd person
	    Number—plural
	    Stem or root—from συνάγω
	Concordance References:
	  ⇒ Strong's #4863 sunago
	  ⇒ NIV #5251 sunago
	  ⇒ NASB #4863 sunago
		To pick up; to gather; to collect; to assemble; to bring together; to invite in.
		
		Practical Application
		Note the purpose of this need for picking up the branches: the day of judgment arrived. In the Greek text, the person who picks up or gathers is not given. The Greek simply says, "they picked up." This is probably God having His angels pick up all the unattached branches, "everything that causes sin and all who do evil" (cp. Mt. 13:41). [NIV]

ENGLISH WORD	GREEK WORD AND VERSE	THE WORD MEANS...
	John 15:6 If a man abide not in me, he is cast forth as a branch, and is withered; and men **gather** them, and cast them into the fire, and they are burned. [KJV] "If anyone does not abide in Me, he is thrown away as a branch, and dries up; and they **gather** them, and cast them into the fire, and they are burned. [NASB] If anyone does not remain in me, he is like a branch that is thrown away and withers; such branches are **picked up**, thrown into the fire and burned. [NIV] If anyone does not abide in Me, he is cast out as a branch and is withered; and they **gather** them and throw *them* into the fire, and they are burned. [NKJV] Anyone who parts from me is thrown away like a useless branch and withers. Such branches are **gathered** into a pile to be burned. [NLT] ἐὰν μή τις μείνη ἐν ἐμοί, ἐβλήθη ἔξω ὡς τὸ κλῆμα, καὶ ἐξηράνθη, καὶ **συνάγουσιν** αὐτὰ, καὶ εἰς πῦρ βάλλουσι, καὶ καίεται. [GNS] ἐὰν μή τις μένη ἐν ἐμοί, ἐβλήθη ἔξω ὡς τὸ κλῆμα καὶ ἐξηράνθη καὶ **συνάγουσιν** αὐτὰ καὶ εἰς τὸ πῦρ βάλλουσιν καὶ καίεται. [GNT]	

#2935
Picture
 	
Figure–KJV
Corresponding–NASB
Symbolizes–NIV
Antitype–NKJV
Picture–NLT
 	
POSB REFERENCE
(1 Pt.3:21)
Note 1, point 3
	ἀντίτυπον = *antitupon*
	Pronunciation: [an-teet'-oo-pon]
	Parsing (part of speech): adjective adverb OR adjective
	    Case—nominative
	    Gender—neuter
	    Number—singular
	    Stem or root—from ἀντίτυπος, ον
	Concordance References:
	  ⇒ Strong's #499 antitupos
	  ⇒ NIV #531 antitupos
	  ⇒ NASB #499 antitupos
	
	1 Peter 3:21
	
	The like **figure** whereunto even baptism doth also now save us (not the putting away of the filth of the flesh, but the answer of a good conscience toward God,) by the resurrection of Jesus Christ: [KJV]
	
	And **corresponding** to that, baptism now saves you—not the removal of dirt from the flesh, but an appeal to God for a good conscience—through the resurrection of Jesus Christ, [NASB]
	
	And this water **symbolizes** baptism that now saves you also—not the removal of dirt from the body but the pledge of a good conscience toward God. It saves you by the resurrection of Jesus Christ, [NIV]
	
	There is also an **antitype** which now saves us—baptism (not the removal of the filth of the flesh, but the answer of a good conscience toward God), through the resurrection of Jesus Christ, [NKJV]
	
	And this is a **picture** of baptism, which now saves you by the power of Jesus Christ's resurrection. Baptism is not a removal of dirt from your body; it is an appeal to God from a clean conscience. [NLT]
	
	ᾧ καὶ ἡμᾶς **ἀντίτυπον** νῦν σώζει βάπτισμα, οὐ σαρκὸς ἀπόθεσις ῥύπου, ἀλλὰ συνειδήσεως ἀγαθῆς ἐπερώτημα εἰς Θεόν, δι' ἀναστάσεως Ἰησοῦ Χριστοῦ, [GNS]
	
	ὃ καὶ ὑμᾶς **ἀντίτυπον** νῦν σώζει βάπτισμα, οὐ σαρκὸς ἀπόθεσις ῥύπου ἀλλὰ συνειδήσεως ἀγαθῆς ἐπερώτημα εἰς Θεόν, δι' ἀναστάσεως Ἰησοῦ Χριστοῦ, [GNT]
		Symbolize, figure, copy, antitype.
		
		Practical Application
		
		Jesus Christ saves the believer through baptism: not the baptism by water, but the baptism of a good conscience wrought by the power of the resurrection of Jesus Christ (1 Peter 3:21).
		
		The water which saved Noah and his family is a type of the cleansing that saves us. The water...
		
		• bore up the ark and saved them through the judgment of God.
		• delivered them from the ridicule and mockery of evil men.
		• delivered them from the corruption of the world and led them to a new life.
		• put to death the old world and gave them the hope of a new world.
		• put to death their old life and gave them a new beginning.
		• saved the race of man and created a new people of God.
		• delivered them from the old world right into the new world.
		
		What is Peter saying? Note the word "picture" (*antitupon*). The figure or picture of baptism is just like the water that saved Noah and his family.
		
		⇒ The *flooding waters* of Noah's day picture the judgment of God upon sin. The flooding waters picture how man was saved from a corruptible world and carried into a new world.
		
		⇒ The *baptismal water* pictures the judgment of God upon Christ, a judgment of death that was due sinners. It pictures how man is saved from a corruptible life and world and carried into a new life and world by the resurrection of Christ.

#2936
Pierced
 	
Pricked–KJV
Pierced–NASB
Cut to–NIV
	κατενύγησαν = *katenugēsan*
	Pronunciation: [kat-en-oog'-ay-san]
	Parsing (part of speech): verb
	    Mood—indicative
	    Tense—aorist
	    Voice—passive
	    Person—3rd person
		To be cut to the heart; to be pricked; to be pierced; to be convicted deeply; to be stabbed. The word "pierced" (*katenugēsan*) means to convict, cut, sting, sense pain and hurt.

ENGLISH WORD	GREEK WORD AND VERSE	THE WORD MEANS...
Cut to–NKJV Convicted them deeply–NLT **POSB REFERENCE** (Acts 2:37) Note 1	Number—plural Stem or root—from **κατανύσσομαι** Concordance References: ⇒ Strong's #2660 katanussomai ⇒ NIV #2920 katanussomai ⇒ NASB #2660 katanussomai ### Acts 2:37 Now when they heard this, they were **pricked** in their heart, and said unto Peter and to the rest of the apostles, Men and brethren, what shall we do? [KJV] Now when they heard this, they were **pierced** to the heart, and said to Peter and the rest of the apostles, "Brethren, what shall we do?" [NASB] When the people heard this, they were **cut to** the heart and said to Peter and the other apostles, "Brothers, what shall we do?" [NIV] Now when they heard this, they were **cut to** the heart, and said to Peter and the rest of the apostles, "Men and brethren, what shall we do?" [NKJV] Peter's words **convicted them deeply**, and they said to him and to the other apostles, "Brothers, what should we do?" [NLT] Ἀκούσαντες δὲ **κατενύγησαν** τὴν καρδίαν, εἶπόν τε πρὸς τὸν Πέτρον καὶ τοὺς λοιποὺς ἀποστόλους, Τί ποιήσομεν, ἄνδρες ἀδελφοί; [GNS] Ἀκούσαντες δὲ **κατενύγησαν** τὴν καρδίαν εἶπόν τε πρὸς τὸν Πέτρον καὶ τοὺς λοιποὺς ἀποστόλους, Τί ποιήσωμεν, ἄνδρες ἀδελφοί; [GNT]	### Practical Application In this Scripture, we learn how the gospel affects the hearts of repentant sinners. The power of the gospel convicts people deeply.
#2937 **Piercing** **Piercing–KJV** **Piercing–NASB** Penetrates–NIV **Piercing–NKJV** Cutting deep–NLT **POSB REFERENCE** (Heb.4:11-13; esp. v.12) Note 5, point 2d	**διϊκνούμενος** = diiknoumenos Pronunciation: [dee-ik-noo'-mehn-os] Parsing (part of speech): verb Mood—participle Tense—present Voice—middle or passive deponent Case—nominative Gender—masculine Number—singular Stem or root—from **διϊκνέομαι** Concordance References: ⇒ Strong's #1338 diikneomai ⇒ NIV #1459 diikneomai ⇒ NASB #1338 diikneomai ### Hebrews 4:12 For the word of God is quick, and powerful, and sharper than any twoedged sword, **piercing** even to the dividing asunder of soul and spirit, and of the joints and marrow, and is a discerner of the thoughts and intents of the heart. [KJV] For the word of God is living and active and sharper than any two-edged sword, and **piercing** as far as the division of soul and spirit, of both joints and marrow, and able to judge the thoughts and intentions of the heart. [NASB] For the word of God is living and active. Sharper than any double-edged sword, it **penetrates** even to dividing soul and spirit, joints and marrow; it judges the thoughts and attitudes of the heart. [NIV] For the word of God is living and powerful, and sharper than any two-edged sword, **piercing** even to the division of soul and spirit, and of joints and marrow, and is a discerner of the thoughts and intents of the heart. [NKJV] For the word of God is full of living power. It is sharper than the sharpest knife, **cutting deep** into our innermost thoughts and desires. It exposes us for what we really are. [NLT] ζῶν γὰρ ὁ λόγος τοῦ Θεοῦ, καὶ ἐνεργής, καὶ τομώτερος ὑπὲρ πᾶσαν μάχαιραν δίστομον, καὶ **διϊκνούμενος**· ἄχρι μερισμοῦ ψυχῆς τὲ καὶ πνεύματος, ἀρμῶν τε καὶ μυελῶν, καὶ κριτικὸς ἐνθυμήσεων καὶ	Piercing; cutting deep; penetrating. ### Practical Application The Word of God is "piercing" (*diiknoumenos*). It goes right through to the soul and spirit of man. It is the Word of God that takes man's earthly, soulish nature and separates it from the spiritual call and promise of God. It pierces and separates a man's soul and spirit just as a sword pierces a man's joints and marrow. ⇒ It separates a proud soul from a humble spirit. ⇒ It separates a sinful soul from a righteous spirit. ⇒ It separates a rebellious soul from an obedient spirit. ⇒ It separates an unbelieving soul from a believing spirit.

ENGLISH WORD	GREEK WORD AND VERSE	THE WORD MEANS...
	ἐννοιῶν καρδίας. [GNS] Ζῶν γὰρ ὁ λόγος τοῦ θεοῦ καὶ ἐνεργὴς καὶ τομώτερος ὑπὲρ πᾶσαν μάχαιραν δίστομον καὶ **διϊκνούμενος** ἄχρι μερισμοῦ ψυχῆς καὶ πνεύματος, ἁρμῶν τε καὶ μυελῶν, καὶ κριτικὸς ἐνθυμήσεων καὶ ἐννοιῶν καρδίας· [GNT]	
#2938 **Pilgrims** Strangers–KJV Aliens–NASB Strangers–NIV **Pilgrims–NKJV** Foreigners–NLT **POSB REFERENCE** (1 Pt.1:1) Note 1	**παρεπιδήμοις** = *parepidēmois* Pronunciation: [par-ep-id'-ay-moys] Parsing (part of speech): pronominal adjective 　　Case—dative 　　Gender—masculine 　　Number—plural 　　Stem or root—from **παρεπίδημος**, ου Concordance References: ⇒　Strong's #3927 parepidēmos ⇒　NIV #4215 parepidēmos ⇒　NASB #3927 parepidēmos **1 Peter 1:1** 　Peter, an apostle of Jesus Christ, to the **strangers** scattered throughout Pontus, Galatia, Cappadocia, Asia, and Bithynia, [KJV] 　Peter, an apostle of Jesus Christ, to those who reside as **aliens**, scattered throughout Pontus, Galatia, Cappadocia, Asia, and Bithynia, who are chosen [NASB] 　Peter, an apostle of Jesus Christ, To God's elect, **strangers** in the world, scattered throughout Pontus, Galatia, Cappadocia, Asia and Bithynia, [NIV] 　Peter, an apostle of Jesus Christ, To the **pilgrims** of the Dispersion in Pontus, Galatia, Cappadocia, Asia, and Bithynia, [NKJV] 　This letter is from Peter, an apostle of Jesus Christ.I am writing to God's chosen people who are living as **foreigners** in the lands of Pontus, Galatia, Cappadocia, the province of Asia, and Bithynia. [NLT] 　Πέτρος, ἀπόστολος Ἰησοῦ Χριστοῦ, ἐκλεκτοῖς **παρεπιδήμοις** διασπορᾶς Πόντου, Γαλατίας, Καππαδοκίας, Ἀσίας, καὶ Βιθυνίας, [GNS] 　Πέτρος ἀπόστολος Ἰησοῦ Χριστοῦ ἐκλεκτοῖς **παρεπιδήμοις** διασπορᾶς Πόντου, Γαλατίας, Καππαδοκίας, Ἀσίας καὶ Βιθυνίας, [GNT]	Strangers, aliens, pilgrims, foreigners. The word means pilgrim, sojourner, refugee, visitor, or exile. **Practical Application** 　The chosen are believers, believers who are only pilgrims scattered over the earth. This is the descriptive picture being painted in 1 Peter 1:1. Believers are only pilgrims (*parepidēmois*) on earth. The idea is that of a person visiting a place for a while, but he is not a permanent resident. Believers are citizens of heaven; their home is in heaven *with God*, not on earth with the rulers of this world. The rulers and people of this earth may persecute believers, but believers are here on earth only temporarily—only as strangers, pilgrims, sojourners, and exiles.
#2939 **Pipe** **Pipe–KJV** Flute–NASB Flute–NIV Flute–NKJV Flute–NLT **POSB REFERENCE** (1 Cor.14:6-14 esp. v.7) Note 3	**αὐλός** = *aulos* Pronunciation: [ow-los'] Parsing (part of speech): noun 　　Case—nominative 　　Gender—masculine 　　Number—singular 　　Stem or root—from αὐλός, οῦ Concordance References: ⇒　Strong's #836 aulos ⇒　NIV #888 aulos ⇒　NASB #836 aulos **1 Cor. 14:7** 　And even things without life giving sound, whether **pipe** or harp, except they give a distinction in the sounds, how shall it be known what is piped or harped? [KJV] 　Yet even lifeless things, either **flute** or harp, in producing a sound, if they do not produce a distinction in the tones, how will it be known what is played on the flute or on the harp? [NASB] 　Even in the case of lifeless things that make sounds, such as the **flute** or harp, how will anyone know what tune is being played unless there is a distinction in the notes? [NIV] 　Even things without life, whether **flute** or harp, when they make a sound, unless they make a distinction in the sounds, how will it be known what is piped or played? [NKJV] 　Even musical instruments like the **flute** or the harp, though they are lifeless, are examples of the need for speaking in plain language. For no one will recognize the	Flute, pipe; wind instrument. **Practical Application** 　Pipes (*aulos*, wind instruments) and harps (*kithara*, string instruments) must have a distinctive sound or else their sound is meaningless, confused, and nonsense—just not understood. Musical instruments must communicate or else the music is unknown and fails to inspire the listeners. The point is striking: the believer who is zealous of spiritual gifts is to seek for the gifts that edify the church. Note: a believer's zeal is not to be dampened even if he has been misinformed and emphasizes the wrong gift. He is to straighten out his emphasis, keep his zeal, and direct his energy to edifying the church. The important gifts are those that build up people for Christ.

ENGLISH WORD	GREEK WORD AND VERSE	THE WORD MEANS...
	melody unless the notes are played clearly. [NLT] ὅμως τὰ ἄψυχα φωνὴν διδόντα, εἴτε **αὐλὸς**, εἴτε κιθάρα, ἐὰν διαστολὴν τοῖς φθόγγοις μὴ δῷ, πῶς γνωσθήσεται τὸ αὐλούμενον η τὸ κιθαριζόμενον; [GNS] ὅμως τὰ ἄψυχα φωνὴν διδόντα, εἴτε **αὐλὸς** εἴτε κιθάρα, ἐὰν διαστολὴν τοῖς φθόγγοις μὴ δῷ, πῶς γνωσθήσεται τὸ αὐλούμενον η τὸ κιθαριζόμενον; [GNT]	

#2940
Pitiful
 	
Pitiful–KJV
Kindhearted–NASB
Compassionate–NIV
Tenderhearted–NKJV
Tender hearts–NLT
 	
POSB
REFERENCE
(1 Pt.3:8)
Note 4
	εὔσπλαγχνοι = *eusplagchnoi*
	Pronunciation: [yoo'-splangkh-noy]
	Parsing (part of speech): adjective
	    Case—nominative
	    Gender—masculine
	    Number—plural
	    Stem or root—from εὔσπλαγχνος, ον
	Concordance References:
	  ⇒ Strong's #2155 cusplagchnos
	  ⇒ NIV #2359 eusplagchnos
	  ⇒ NASB #2155 eusplagchnos
	
	1 Peter 3:8
	Finally, be ye all of one mind, having compassion one of another, love as brethren, be **pitiful**, be courteous: [KJV]
	To sum up, let all be harmonious, sympathetic, brotherly, **kindhearted**, and humble in spirit; [NASB]
	Finally, all of you, live in harmony with one another; be sympathetic, love as brothers, be **compassionate** and humble. [NIV]
	Finally, all *of you be* of one mind, having compassion for one another; love as brothers, *be* **tenderhearted**, *be* courteous; [NKJV]
	Finally, all of you should be of one mind, full of sympathy toward each other, loving one another with **tender hearts** and humble minds. [NLT]
	
	Τὸ δὲ τέλος, πάντες ὁμόφρονες, συμπαθεῖς, φιλάδελφοι, **εὔσπλαγχνοι**, φιλόφρονες· [GNS]
	Τὸ δὲ τέλος πάντες ὁμόφρονες, συμπαθεῖς, φιλάδελφοι, **εὔσπλαγχνοι**, ταπεινόφρονες, [GNT]
		To be compassionate, to pity; to be kindhearted, to have a tender heart. It means to be tenderhearted; to be sensitive and affectionate toward the needs of others; to be moved with tender feelings over the pain and sufferings of others.
		
		### Practical Application
		We live in a world that desperately needs pity, a world of extreme suffering. So many suffer and continue to suffer without ever having their needs met. The means and resources to meet their needs exist, but so many within the world have become hardened to the sufferings of others. They bank, hoard, and build up asset after asset instead of sacrificing and reaching out to meet the needs of the world. But this is not to be true of the believer. Believers are to have pity upon the sufferings of others. Believers are to feel pity to the point that they are moved to act, sacrificing and reaching out to meet the needs of the suffering.
		Again, note how compassion leaves no room for selfishness. Compassion demands that a person deny himself and help others in their desperate needs and sufferings. Note also how pity draws people together. Helping and ministering to one another binds and knits people together. Having compassion—feeling for one another and sacrificing and reaching out to help one another—unites people together. A great bond is created between the believer and those to whom he ministers.

#2941
Pitiful
 	
Miserable–KJV
Miserable–NASB
Pitiful–NIV
Miserable–NKJV
Miserable–NLT
 	
POSB
REFERENCE
(Rev.3:16-17; esp. v.17)
Note 4, point 2b
	ἐλεεινός = *eleeinos*
	Pronunciation: [el-eh-i-nos']
	Parsing (part of speech): pronominal adjective
	    Case—nominative
	    Gender—masculine
	    Number—singular
	    Stem or root—from ἐλεεινός, ή, όν
	Concordance References:
	  ⇒ Strong's #1652 eleeinos
	  ⇒ NIV #1795 eleeinos
	  ⇒ NASB #1652 eleeinos
	
	Rev. 3:17
	Because thou sayest, I am rich, and increased with goods, and have need of nothing; and knowest not that thou art wretched, and **miserable**, and poor, and blind, and naked: [KJV]
	'Because you say, "I am rich, and have become wealthy, and have need of nothing," and you do not know that you are wretched and **miserable** and poor and blind and naked, [NASB]
	You say, 'I am rich; I have acquired wealth and do not need a thing.' But you do not realize that you are wretched, **pitiful**, poor, blind and naked. [NIV]
	Because you say, 'I am rich, have become wealthy, and have need of nothing'—and do not know that you are wretched, **miserable**, poor, blind, and naked [NKJV]
	You say, 'I am rich. I have everything I want. I don't need a thing!' And you don't realize that you are wretched and **miserable** and poor and blind and naked. [NLT]
		Pitiful, miserable, despicable, distressed, dismal.
		
		### Practical Application
		The church was spiritually "pitiful" (*eleeinos*). The believers felt self-sufficient and were carrying on all the works of the church, but they were doing it in their own strength. They were *missing out* on the greatest thing in all the world: the presence of Christ and the power of Christ. They were missing out on experiencing the power of Christ working in their lives and in the church. They were to be pitied. In God's eyes they were despicable, for they were ignoring and neglecting His Son.

ENGLISH WORD	GREEK WORD AND VERSE	THE WORD MEANS...

ὅτι λέγεις, ὅτι Πλούσιός εἰμι, καὶ πεπλούτηκα καὶ οὐδενὸς χρείαν ἔχω, καὶ οὐκ οἶδας ὅτι σὺ εἶ ὁ ταλαίπωρος καὶ **ἐλεεινὸς** καὶ πτωχὸς καὶ τυφλὸς καὶ γυμνός· [GNS]

ὅτι λέγεις ὅτι Πλούσιός εἰμι καὶ πεπλούτηκα καὶ οὐδὲν χρείαν ἔχω, καὶ οὐκ οἶδας ὅτι σὺ εἶ ὁ ταλαίπωρος καὶ **ἐλεεινὸς** καὶ πτωχὸς καὶ τυφλὸς καὶ γυμνός, [GNT]

#2942
Pity

Compassion–KJV
Compassion–NASB
Compassion–NIV
Compassion–NKJV
Pity–NLT

**POSB
REFERENCE**
(Mt.9:36)
Deeper Study #2

ἐσπλαγχνίσθη = *esplagchnisthē*
Pronunciation: [es-plangkh-ni'-sthee]
Parsing (part of speech): verb
    Mood—indicative
    Tense—aorist
    Voice—passive deponent
    Person—3rd person
    Number—singular
    Stem or root—from **σπλαγχνίζομαι**
Concordance References:
  ⇒ Strong's #4697 splagchnizomai
  ⇒ NIV #5072 splanchnizomai
  ⇒ NASB #4697 splagchnizomai

Matthew 9:36
But when he saw the multitudes, he was moved with **compassion** on them, because they fainted, and were scattered abroad, as sheep having no shepherd. [KJV]

And seeing the multitudes, He felt **compassion** for them, because they were distressed and downcast like sheep without a shepherd. [NASB]

When he saw the crowds, he had **compassion** on them, because they were harassed and helpless, like sheep without a shepherd. [NIV]

But when He saw the multitudes, He was moved with **compassion** for them, because they were weary and scattered, like sheep having no shepherd. [NKJV]

He felt great **pity** for the crowds that came, because their problems were so great and they didn't know where to go for help. They were like sheep without a shepherd. [NLT]

ἰδὼν δὲ τοὺς ὄχλους, **ἐσπλαγχνίσθη** περὶ αὐτῶν, ὅτι ἦσαν ἐκλελυμένοι καὶ ἐρριμμένοι ὡσεὶ πρόβατα μὴ ἔχοντα ποιμένα. [GNS]

Ἰδὼν δὲ τοὺς ὄχλους **ἐσπλαγχνίσθη** περὶ αὐτῶν, ὅτι ἦσαν ἐσκυλμένοι καὶ ἐρριμμένοι ὡ [GNT]

Compassion; to be moved inwardly; to yearn with tender mercy, affection, pity, and empathy.

Practical Application
Pity arises from the very depth of a person's affections. It is the deepest movement of emotions possible, being touched with the deepest feelings possible.

#2943
Place Of Leadership

Bishoprick–KJV
Office–NASB
Place of leadership–NIV
Office–NKJV
Position–NLT

**POSB
REFERENCE**
(Acts 1:16-20; esp. v.20)
Note 2, point 6a

ἐπισκοπὴν = *episkopēn*
Pronunciation: [ep-is-kop-ayn']
Parsing (part of speech): noun
    Case—accusative
    Gender—feminine
    Number—singular
    Stem or root—from **ἐπισκοπή**, ῆς
Concordance References:
  ⇒ Strong's #1984 episkopē
  ⇒ NIV #2175 episkopē
  ⇒ NASB #1984 episkopē

Acts 1:20
For it is written in the book of Psalms, Let his habitation be desolate, and let no man dwell therein: and his **bishoprick** let another take. [KJV]

"For it is written in the book of Psalms, 'Let his homestead be made desolate, And let no man dwell in it'; and, 'His OFFICE LET ANOTHER MAN TAKE.' [NASB]

"For," said Peter, "it is written in the book of Psalms, " 'May his place be deserted; let there be no one to dwell in it,' and, " 'May another take his **place of leadership**.' [NIV]

"For it is written in the book of Psalms: 'Let his dwelling place be desolate, And let no one live in it'; and, 'Let another take his **office**.' [NKJV]

Peter continued, "This was predicted in the book of Psalms, where it says, 'Let his home become desolate,

Place of leadership; office; position; place of service; overseership.

Practical Application
It is the word from which the office of overseer or bishop is taken. The idea is that Judas' office of overseeing the flock of God was to be filled by another person. Judas had lost his ministry completely.

ENGLISH WORD	GREEK WORD AND VERSE	THE WORD MEANS...

with no one living in it.' And again, 'Let his **position** be given to someone else.' [NLT]

γέγραπται γὰρ ἐν βίβλῳ Ψαλμῶν, Γενηθήτω ἡ ἔπαυλις αὐτοῦ ἔρημος, καὶ μὴ ἔστω ὁ κατοικῶν ἐν αὐτῇ· καί, Τὴν **ἐπισκοπὴν** αὐτοῦ λάβοι ἕτερος. [GNS]

Γέγραπται γὰρ ἐν βίβλῳ ψαλμῶν, Γενηθήτω ἡ ἔπαυλις αὐτοῦ ἔρημος καὶ μὴ ἔστω ὁ κατοικῶν ἐν αὐτῇ, καί, Τὴν **ἐπισκοπὴν** αὐτοῦ λαβέτω ἕτερος. [GNT]

#2944
Place Of The Dead, The

Hell–KJV
Hades–NASB
Hell–NIV
Hades–NKJV
The place of the dead–NLT

POSB REFERENCE
(Lk.16:23)
Deeper Study #3

ᾅδῃ = *hadë*
Pronunciation: [hah'-day]
Parsing (part of speech): noun
    Case—dative
    Gender—masculine
    Number—singular
    Stem or root—from ᾅδης, ου
Concordance References:
  ⇒ Strong's #86 hadës
  ⇒ NIV #87 hadës
  ⇒ NASB #86 hadës

Luke 16:23

And in **hell** he lift up his eyes, being in torments, and seeth Abraham afar off, and Lazarus in his bosom. [KJV]

"And in **Hades** he lifted up his eyes, being in torment, and saw Abraham far away, and Lazarus in his bosom. [NASB]

In **hell**, where he was in torment, he looked up and saw Abraham far away, with Lazarus by his side. [NIV]

And being in torments in **Hades**, he lifted up his eyes and saw Abraham afar off, and Lazarus in his bosom. [NKJV]

and his soul went to **the place of the dead**. There, in torment, he saw Lazarus in the far distance with Abraham. [NLT]

καὶ ἐν τῷ **ᾅδῃ** ἐπάρας τοὺς ὀφθαλμοὺς αὐτοῦ, ὑπάρχων ἐν βασάνοις, ὁρᾷ τὸν Ἀβραὰμ ἀπὸ μακρόθεν, καὶ Λάζαρον ἐν τοῖς κόλποις αὐτοῦ. [GNS]

καὶ ἐν τῷ **ᾅδῃ** ἐπάρας τοὺς ὀφθαλμοὺς αὐτοῦ, ὑπάρχων ἐν βασάνοις, ὁρᾷ Ἀβραὰμ ἀπὸ μακρόθεν καὶ Λάζαρον ἐν τοῖς κόλποις αὐτοῦ. [GNT]

Hades, hell, the place of the dead, the place of final and eternal punishment. The Greek word Hades is the same as the Hebrew word Sheol (see POSB *Deeper Study* #3—Genesis 37:35).

Practical Application

The picture of Hades, the place of the dead, revealed by Jesus is that of the other world: the unseen world, the spiritual world, the spiritual dimension of being.

Jesus says that Hades is a place which is divided into two huge areas or sections or compartments. The two areas are separated by a great gulf that is impassible (Luke 16:26). One area is the place of sorrow (Luke 16:23-24, 28). The other area is the place of Paradise where believers go. To say that a person is dead is to say that one is in hades, in the other world.

#2945
Place You On A Firm Foundation

Settle–KJV
Establish–NASB
Steadfast–NIV
Settle–NKJV
Place you on a firm foundation–NLT

POSB REFERENCE
(1 Pt.5:10)
Note 2, point 4

θεμελιώσει = *themeliösei*
Pronunciation: [them-el-ee-o'-seh-ee]
Parsing (part of speech): verb
    Mood—indicative
    Tense—future
    Voice—active
    Person—3rd person
    Number—singular
    Stem or root—from θεμελιόω
Concordance References:
  ⇒ Strong's #2311 themelioö
  ⇒ NIV #2530 themelioö
  ⇒ NASB #2311 themelioö

1 Peter 5:10

But the God of all grace, who hath called us unto his eternal glory by Christ Jesus, after that ye have suffered a while, make you perfect, stablish, strengthen, **settle** you. [KJV]

And after you have suffered for a little while, the God of all grace, who called you to His eternal glory in Christ, will Himself perfect, confirm, strengthen and **establish** you. [NASB]

And the God of all grace, who called you to his eternal glory in Christ, after you have suffered a little while, will himself restore you and make you strong, firm and **steadfast**. [NIV]

But may the God of all grace, who called us to His eternal glory by Christ Jesus, after you have suffered a while, perfect, establish, strengthen, and **settle** you. [NKJV]

To be steadfast; to settle; to establish; to place on a firm foundation; to secure as in a foundation; to ground with security.

Practical Application

God Himself will *place you on a firm foundation*. God is able to make us secure through all the sufferings of life, no matter what they are. He is able to settle and secure our nerves, thoughts, and fears—all the uneasy and unnerving emotions that disturb us. God can settle us if we will only do one thing: resist the devil and draw near to Him.

ENGLISH WORD	GREEK WORD AND VERSE	THE WORD MEANS...

In his kindness God called you to his eternal glory by means of Jesus Christ. After you have suffered a little while, he will restore, support, and strengthen you, and he will **place you on a firm foundation**. [NLT]

ὁ δὲ Θεὸς πάσης χάριτος, ὁ καλέσας ὑμᾶς εἰς τὴν αἰώνιον αὐτοῦ δόξαν ἐν Χριστῷ Ἰησοῦ, ὀλίγον παθόντας αὐτὸς καταρτίσει ὑμᾶς, στηρίξει, σθενώσαι, **θεμελιώσαι**. [GNS]

Ὁ δὲ θεὸς πάσης χάριτος, ὁ καλέσας ὑμᾶς εἰς τὴν αἰώνιον αὐτοῦ δόξαν ἐν Χριστῷ [Ἰησοῦ], ὀλίγον παθόντας αὐτὸς καταρτίσει, στηρίξει, σθενώσει, **θεμελιώσει**. [GNT]

#2946
Place, His

His habitation–KJV
His homestead–NASB
His place–NIV
His dwelling place–NKJV
His home–NLT

**POSB
REFERENCE**
(Acts 1:16-20; esp. v.20)
  Note 2, point 6a

ἡ ἔπαυλις αὐτοῦ = hë epaulis autou
Pronunciation: [ay ep'-ow-lis aw-too]
Parsing *epaulis* (part of speech): noun
  Case—nominative
  Gender—feminine
  Number—singular
  Stem or root—from ἔπαυλις, εως
Concordance References:
⇒ Strong's #3588 ho + 1886 epaulis + 846 autos
⇒ NIV #3836 ho [Not in English] + 2068 epaulis [place] + 899 autos [his]
⇒ NASB #3588 ho + 1886 epaulis + 846 autos

Acts 1:20

For it is written in the book of Psalms, Let **his habitation** be desolate, and let no man dwell therein: and his bishoprick let another take. [KJV]

"For it is written in the book of Psalms, 'Let **his homestead** be made desolate, And let no man dwell in it'; and, 'His OFFICE LET ANOTHER MAN TAKE.' [NASB]

"For," said Peter, "it is written in the book of Psalms, " 'May **his place** be deserted; let there be no one to dwell in it,' and, " 'May another take his place of leadership.' [NIV]

"For it is written in the book of Psalms: 'Let **his dwelling place** be desolate, And let no one live in it'; and, 'Let another take his office.' [NKJV]

Peter continued, "This was predicted in the book of Psalms, where it says, 'Let **his home** become desolate, with no one living in it.' And again, 'Let his position be given to someone else.' [NLT]

γέγραπται γὰρ ἐν βίβλῳ Ψαλμῶν, Γενηθήτω ἡ ἔπαυλις αὐτοῦ ἔρημος, καὶ μὴ ἔστω ὁ κατοικῶν ἐν αὐτῇ· καί, Τὴν ἐπισκοπὴν αὐτοῦ λάβοι ἕτερος. [GNS]

Γέγραπται γὰρ ἐν βίβλῳ ψαλμῶν, Γενηθήτω ἡ ἔπαυλις αὐτοῦ ἔρημος καὶ μὴ ἔστω ὁ κατοικῶν ἐν αὐτῇ, καί, Τὴν ἐπισκοπὴν αὐτοῦ λαβέτω ἕτερος. [GNT]

His place; His habitation; His homestead; His home.

Practical Application
The phrase "His place" (*hë epaulis autou*) is descriptive. It means a farm house or a place for sheep such as a pasture or sheep yard. The idea is that Judas would never again be allowed to be the farmer (husbandman) or shepherd for God.

#2947
Places Of
Honor At The
Table

Chief rooms–KJV
Places of honor at the table–NASB
Places of honor at the table–NIV
Best places–NKJV
Head of the table–NLT

**POSB
REFERENCE**
(Lk.14:7)
  Note 1

τὰς πρωτοκλισίας = tas prötoklisias
Pronunciation: [tas pro-tok-lis-ee'-ahs]
Parsing *prötoklisias* (part of speech): noun
  Case—accusative
  Gender—feminine
  Number—plural
  Stem or root—from πρωτοκλισία, ας
Concordance References:
⇒ Strong's #4411 prötoklisia
⇒ NIV #4752 prötoklisia
⇒ NASB #4411 prötoklisia

Luke 14:7

And he put forth a parable to those which were bidden, when he marked how they chose out the **chief rooms**; saying unto them, [KJV]

And He began speaking a parable to the invited guests when He noticed how they had been picking out the **places of honor at the table**; saying to them, [NASB]

When he noticed how the guests picked the **places of honor at the table**, he told them this parable: [NIV]

The places of honor at a table, the head of the table, the chief seats; the best places.

Practical Application
In this Scripture, it was time for everyone to be seated for the meal, and Jesus noticed how some guests scrambled for the places of honor at the table. Today, we usually place the names of the most honored guests at the plates. However, in Jesus' day the highest seat of honor was on the right of the host and the next highest on his left, and so the ranking continued alternating back and forth until the lowest ranked person sat the farthest away from the host. Very simply, the closer one sat to the host, the higher the honor. When Jesus saw how some quickly moved up close to the host, He saw an opportunity to teach the great importance of humility.

ENGLISH WORD	GREEK WORD AND VERSE	THE WORD MEANS...
	So He told a parable to those who were invited, when He noted how they chose the **best places**, saying to them: [NKJV] When Jesus noticed that all who had come to the dinner were trying to sit near the **head of the table**, he gave them this advice: [NLT] Ἔλεγε δὲ πρὸς τοὺς κεκλημένους παραβολήν, ἐπέχων πῶς **τὰς πρωτοκλισίας** ἐξελέγοντο, λέγων πρὸς αὐτούς, [GNS] Ἔλεγεν δὲ πρὸς τοὺς κεκλημένους παραβολήν, ἐπέχων πῶς **τὰς πρωτοκλισίας** ἐξελέγοντο, λέγων πρὸς αὐτούς, [GNT]	

#2948
Plainly
 	
Openly–KJV
Plainly–NASB
Plainly–NIV
Openly–NKJV
Openly–NLT
 	
POSB REFERENCE
(Mk.8:32-33; esp. v.32)
Note 2
	παρρησία = *parresia*
	Pronunciation: [par-rhay-see'-ah]
	Parsing (part of speech): noun
	    Case—dative
	    Gender—feminine
	    Number—singular
	    Stem or root—from παρρησία, ας
	Concordance References:
	⇒ Strong's #3954 parrhesia
	⇒ NIV #4244 parrēsia
	⇒ NASB #3954 parrēsia
	
	Mark 8:32
	And he spake that saying **openly**. And Peter took him, and began to rebuke him. [KJV]
	
	And He was stating the matter **plainly**. And Peter took Him aside and began to rebuke Him. [NASB]
	
	He spoke **plainly** about this, and Peter took him aside and began to rebuke him. [NIV]
	
	He spoke this word **openly**. And Peter took Him aside and began to rebuke Him. [NKJV]
	
	As he talked about this **openly** with his disciples, Peter took him aside and told him he shouldn't say things like that. [NLT]
	
	καὶ **παρρησία** τὸν λόγον ἐλάλει. καὶ προσλαβόμενος αὐτὸν ὁ Πέτρος, ἤρξατο ἐπιτιμᾶν αὐτῷ. [GNS]
	
	καὶ **παρρησία** τὸν λόγον ἐλάλει. καὶ προσλαβόμενος ὁ Πέτρος αὐτὸν ἤρξατο ἐπιτιμᾶν αὐτῷ. [GNT]
		Plainly, openly, unmistakably, frankly, without hesitation.
		
		Practical Application
		In this Scripture, Jesus literally indoctrinated His disciples with the fact and meaning of His death. He talked about it so much that it shook the apostles, so much so that they had Peter rebuke Christ.

#2949
Plan
 	
Fashion–KJV
Pattern–NASB
Pattern–NIV
Pattern–NKJV
Plan–NLT
 	
POSB REFERENCE
(Acts 7:42-53; esp. v.44)
Note 6, point 3a
	τύπον = *tupon*
	Pronunciation: [too'-pon]
	Parsing (part of speech): noun
	    Case—accusative
	    Gender—masculine
	    Number—singular
	    Stem or root—from τύπος, ου
	Concordance References:
	⇒ Strong's #5179 tupos
	⇒ NIV #5596 tupos
	⇒ NASB #5179 tupos
	
	Acts 7:44
	Our fathers had the tabernacle of witness in the wilderness, as he had appointed, speaking unto Moses, that he should make it according to the **fashion** that he had seen. [KJV]
	
	"Our fathers had the tabernacle of testimony in the wilderness, just as He who spoke to Moses directed him to make it according to the **pattern** which he had seen. [NASB]
	
	"Our forefathers had the tabernacle of the Testimony with them in the desert. It had been made as God directed Moses, according to the **pattern** he had seen. [NIV]
	
	"Our fathers had the tabernacle of witness in the wilderness, as He appointed, instructing Moses to make it according to the **pattern** that he had seen, [NKJV]
	
	"Our ancestors carried the Tabernacle with them through the wilderness. It was constructed in exact accordance with the **plan** shown to Moses by God. [NLT]
		A Pattern; a fashion; a plan; a form; a figure; a picture; an example; a model; a standard.
		
		Practical Application
		The people were inexcusable. Why? Because they were greatly blessed (Acts 7:44-47). God had blessed them with three particular things.
		1. God had blessed the people with the tabernacle of His presence and testimony. Note that God had shown Moses a "plan" (*tupon*), that is, a figure, a pattern, a picture of the tabernacle; and Moses had constructed it after the picture God had shown him.
		2. God had blessed the people with leaders. Joshua and David and Solomon are mentioned. All three had the favor and blessings of God upon their lives. Therefore, the people were greatly blessed through these leaders.
		3. God had blessed the people with the temple. David had desired to build the temple, but it was Solomon whom God appointed to construct it. (Cp. 1 Kings 6-8.) When the Jews returned from captivity to Jerusalem, Zerubbabel rebuilt the temple (516 B.C.). Sometime later, around 20 B.C., Herod the Great rebuilt the temple, making it one of the wonders of the world. It was this temple in which the Jews gloried.
		The point is this: by being so blessed, the

ENGLISH WORD	GREEK WORD AND VERSE	THE WORD MEANS...
	ἡ σκηνὴ τοῦ μαρτυρίου ἦν ἐν τοῖς πατράσιν ἡμῶν ἐν τῇ ἐρήμῳ, καθὼς διετάξατο ὁ λαλῶν τῷ Μωσῇ, ποιῆσαι αὐτὴν κατὰ τὸν **τύπον** ὃν ἑωράκει, [GNS] Ἡ σκηνὴ τοῦ μαρτυρίου ἦν τοῖς πατράσιν ἡμῶν ἐν τῇ ἐρήμῳ καθὼς διετάξατο ὁ λαλῶν τῷ Μωϋσῇ ποιῆσαι αὐτὴν κατὰ τὸν **τύπον** ὃν ἑωράκει [GNT]	people (Israel) were inexcusable in their rejection of God. They had every opportunity available, yet they still chose the world instead of God.

#2950
Plan
 	
Counsel–KJV
Plan–NASB
Purpose–NIV
Purpose–NKJV
Plan–NLT
 	
POSB
REFERENCE
(Acts 2:23)
Deeper Study #3,
point 2
	βουλή = *boulē*
	9Pronunciation: [boo-lay']
	Parsing (part of speech): noun
	  Case—dative
	  Gender—feminine
	  Number—singular
	  Stem or root—from βουλή, ῆς
	Concordance References:
	⇒ Strong's #1012 boulē
	⇒ NIV #1087 boulē
	⇒ NASB #1012 boulē
	
	Acts 2:23
	Him, being delivered by the determinate **counsel** and foreknowledge of God, ye have taken, and by wicked hands have crucified and slain: [KJV]
	This Man, delivered up by the predetermined **plan** and foreknowledge of God, you nailed to a cross by the hands of godless men and put Him to death. [NASB]
	This man was handed over to you by God's set **purpose** and foreknowledge; and you, with the help of wicked men, put him to death by nailing him to the cross. [NIV]
	Him, being delivered by the determined **purpose** and foreknowledge of God, you have taken by lawless hands, have crucified, and put to death; [NKJV]
	But you followed God's prearranged **plan**. With the help of lawless Gentiles, you nailed him to the cross and murdered him. [NLT]
	τοῦτον τῇ ὡρισμένῃ **βουλῇ** καὶ προγνώσει τοῦ Θεοῦ ἔκδοτον λαβόντες διὰ χειρῶν ἀνόμων προσπήξαντες ἀνείλατε, [GNS]
	τοῦτον τῇ ὡρισμένῃ **βουλῇ** καὶ προγνώσει τοῦ θεοῦ ἔκδοτον διὰ χειρὸς ἀνόμων προσπήξαντες ἀνείλατε, [GNT]
		Purpose, counsel, plan, intention, motive, design, will.
		
		Practical Application
		It carries the force of being willed and determined. Since God knows exactly what would happen in every situation, He plans for the best thing to happen. God takes counsel, puts all things under advisement, and chooses the best way.

#2951
Planted In
 	
Engrafted–KJV
Implanted–NASB
Planted in–NIV
Implanted–NKJV
Planted in–NLT
 	
POSB
REFERENCE
(Jas.1:19-21; esp.
v.21)
Note 1, point 5
	ἔμφυτον = *emphuton*
	Pronunciation: [em'-foo-ton]
	Parsing (part of speech): adjective
	  Case—accusative
	  Gender—masculine
	  Number—singular
	  Stem or root—from ἔμφυτος, ον
	Concordance References:
	⇒ Strong's #1721 emphutos
	⇒ NIV #1875 emphutos
	⇒ NASB #1721 emphutos
	
	James 1:21
	Wherefore lay apart all filthiness and superfluity of naughtiness, and receive with meekness the **engrafted** word, which is able to save your souls. [KJV]
	Therefore putting aside all filthiness and all that remains of wickedness, in humility receive the word **implanted**, which is able to save your souls. [NASB]
	Therefore, get rid of all moral filth and the evil that is so prevalent and humbly accept the word **planted in** you, which can save you. [NIV]
	Therefore lay aside all filthiness and overflow of wickedness, and receive with meekness the **implanted** word, which is able to save your souls. [NKJV]
	So get rid of all the filth and evil in your lives, and humbly accept the message God has **planted in** your hearts, for it is strong enough to save your souls. [NLT]
	διὸ ἀποθέμενοι πᾶσαν ῥυπαρίαν καὶ περισσείαν
		To be planted in; to be engrafted; to be implanted; to be born within.
		
		Practical Application
		When a person really listens to the Word of God, it is planted within his heart and life. What God says is actually born within his heart, and the man hears exactly what God says. The Word of God is born within his heart and life, and the person's soul is saved. He conquers and triumphs over all temptation, including the terrible temptation of rejecting God and doing his own thing and living like he wants. He is saved to live eternally with God. This is the first preparation that a person must make to withstand temptation: he must be quick to hear the Word of God.

ENGLISH WORD	GREEK WORD AND VERSE	THE WORD MEANS...
	κακίας, ἐν πραΰτητι δέξασθε τὸν ἔμφυτον λόγον, τὸν δυνάμενον σῶσαι τὰς ψυχὰς ὑμῶν. [GNS] διὸ ἀποθέμενοι πᾶσαν ῥυπαρίαν καὶ περισσείαν κακίας ἐν πραΰτητι, δέξασθε τὸν ἔμφυτον λόγον τὸν δυνάμενον σῶσαι τὰς ψυχὰς ὑμῶν. [GNT]	

#2952
Plead
 	
Beseech–KJV
Exhort–NASB
Appeal–NIV
Plead–NKJV
Appeal–NLT
 	
**POSB
REFERENCE**
(1 Cor.1:10)
Note 1
 	
See also POSB REF:
(1 Tim.5:1-2; esp. v.1)
Introduction
	Παρακαλῶ = Parakalō
	Pronunciation: [par-ak-al-o']
	Parsing (part of speech): verb
	  Mood—indicative
	  Tense—present
	  Voice—active
	  Person—1st person
	  Number—singular
	  Stem or root—from παρακαλέω
	Concordance References:
	  ⇒ Strong's #3870 parakaleō
	  ⇒ NIV #4151 parakaleō
	  ⇒ NASB #3870 parakaleō
	
	1 Cor. 1:10
	
	Now I **beseech** you, brethren, by the name of our Lord Jesus Christ, that ye all speak the same thing, and *that* there be no divisions among you; but *that* ye be perfectly joined together in the same mind and in the same judgment. [KJV]
	
	Now I **exhort** you, brethren, by the name of our Lord Jesus Christ, that you all agree, and there be no divisions among you, but you be made complete in the same mind and in the same judgment. [NASB]
	
	I **appeal** to you, brothers, in the name of our Lord Jesus Christ, that all of you agree with one another so that there may be no divisions among you and that you may be perfectly united in mind and thought. [NIV]
	
	Now I **plead** with you, brethren, by the name of our Lord Jesus Christ, that you all speak the same thing, and *that* there be no divisions among you, but *that* you be perfectly joined together in the same mind and in the same judgment. [NKJV]
	
	Now, dear brothers and sisters, I **appeal** to you by the authority of the Lord Jesus Christ to stop arguing among yourselves. Let there be real harmony so there won't be divisions in the church. I plead with you to be of one mind, united in thought and purpose. [NLT]
	
	Παρακαλῶ δὲ ὑμᾶς, ἀδελφοί, διὰ τοῦ ὀνόματος τοῦ Κυρίου ἡμῶν Ἰησοῦ Χριστοῦ, ἵνα τὸ αὐτὸ λέγητε πάντες, καὶ μὴ ᾖ ἐν ὑμῖν σχίσματα, ἦτε δὲ κατηρτισμένοι ἐν τῷ αὐτῷ νοῒ καὶ ἐν τῇ αὐτῇ γνώμῃ. [GNS]
	
	Παρακαλῶ δὲ ὑμᾶς, ἀδελφοί, διὰ τοῦ ὀνόματος τοῦ κυρίου ἡμῶν Ἰησοῦ Χριστοῦ, ἵνα τὸ αὐτὸ λέγητε πάντες καὶ μὴ ᾖ ἐν ὑμῖν σχίσματα, ἦτε δὲ κατηρτισμένοι ἐν τῷ αὐτῷ νοῒ καὶ ἐν τῇ αὐτῇ γνώμῃ. [GNT]
		To appeal; to ask; to exhort; to encourage; to beseech; to beg; to urge; to request; to summon; to call to one's side.
		
		Practical Application
		
		Paul says, "I call you to my side; come, let's share together, talk the matter over. I ask, plead, beg—hear what I have to say."

#2953
**Plead For
  God's Mercy**
 	
Intercessions–KJV
Petitions–NASB
Intercession–NIV
Intercessions–NKJV
**Plead for God's
  mercy–NLT**
 	
**POSB
REFERENCE**
(1 Tim.2:1)
Note 1, point 3
	ἐντεύξεις = enteuxeis
	Pronunciation: [ent'-yook-eh-ees]
	Parsing (part of speech): noun
	  Case—accusative
	  Gender—feminine
	  Number—plural
	  Stem or root—from ἔντευξις, εως
	Concordance References:
	  ⇒ Strong's #1783 enteuxis
	  ⇒ NIV #1950 enteuxis
	  ⇒ NASB #1783 enteuxis
	
	1 Tim. 2:1
	
	I exhort therefore, that, first of all, supplications, prayers, **intercessions**, and giving of thanks, be made for all men; [KJV]
	
	First of all, then, I urge that entreaties and prayers, **petitions** and thanksgivings, be made on behalf of all men, [NASB]
	
	I urge, then, first of all, that requests, prayers, **inter-**
		Intercession, petition, prayer; to plead to God for another person.
		
		Practical Application
		
		This refers to bold praying; to standing before God in behalf of another person. Christ is our Intercessor, the One who stands between God and us in our behalf. But we are to intercede for men, to carry their names and lives before God and to boldly pray for them, expecting God to hear and answer—all in the name of Christ. We are to intercede for all men—to stand in the gap between them and God, boldly praying and asking God to be merciful and gracious in salvation and in deliverance.

ENGLISH WORD	GREEK WORD AND VERSE	THE WORD MEANS...

#2965
Poor
 	
Poor–KJV
Poor–NASB
Poor–NIV
Poor–NKJV
Poor–NLT
 	
**POSB
REFERENCE**
(Lk.21:3)
Note 3
 	
See also POSB REF:
(Mk.12:42)
Note 2
(Rev.3:16-17; esp.
v.17)
Note 4
	πτωχὴ = ptöchë
	Pronunciation: [pto-khee']
	Parsing (part of speech): adjective
	    Case—nominative
	    Gender—feminine
	    Number—singular
	    Stem or root—from πτωχός, ή, όν
	Concordance References:
	  ⇒ Strong's #4434 ptochos
	  ⇒ NIV #4777 ptochos
	  ⇒ NASB #4434 ptochos
	
	### Luke 21:3
	And he said, Of a truth I say unto you, that this **poor** widow hath cast in more than they all: [KJV]
	And He said, "Truly I say to you, this **poor** widow put in more than all of them; [NASB]
	"I tell you the truth," he said, "this **poor** widow has put in more than all the others. [NIV]
	So He said, "Truly I say to you that this **poor** widow has put in more than all; [NKJV]
	"I assure you," he said, "this **poor** widow has given more than all the rest of them. [NLT]
	καὶ εἶπεν, Ἀληθῶς λέγω ὑμῖν, ὅτι ἡ χήρα ἡ **πτωχὴ** αὕτη πλεῖον πάντων ἔβαλεν· [GNS]
	καὶ εἶπεν, Ἀληθῶς λέγω ὑμῖν ὅτι ἡ χήρα αὕτη ἡ **πτωχὴ** πλεῖον πάντων ἔβαλεν [GNT]
		Pauper, indigent, pitiful, economically bankrupt, insolvent, dirt poor. It means having to beg in order to survive.
		
		### Practical Application
		The widow was not just poor, she was destitute, in deep poverty. Her poor dress and plain appearance showed her desperate plight. The coins were all she had, yet she gave them despite her own desperate need.
		Note what Jesus said. She "hath cast in more than they all." Jesus was not saying that she cast in more than any *one* of them, but she cast in more than *all of them put together*. This was shocking! How could He make such a statement, for some had cast in much more money than she? And all the rich combined had cast in an enormous sum. Very simply, God measured what was kept back, not how much was given.
		⇒ The widow had less remaining; the others still had much.
		⇒ The widow had given more of what she had; the others had given less of what they had.
		⇒ The widow had sacrificed more; the others had sacrificed less.
		In proportion to what she had, the widow gave a larger percent. The others gave a much smaller percent. After they had given they still had 85% or 95% to spend on themselves.

#2966
Poor
 	
Poor–KJV
Poor–NASB
Poor–NIV
Poor–NKJV
Poor–NLT
 	
**POSB
REFERENCE**
(Lk.21:2)
Note 2
	πενιχρὰν = penichran
	Pronunciation: [pen-tikh-rahn']
	Parsing (part of speech): adjective
	    Case—accusative
	    Gender—feminine
	    Number—singular
	    Stem or root—from πενιχρός, ά, όν
	Concordance References:
	  ⇒ Strong's #3998 penichros
	  ⇒ NIV #4293 penichros
	  ⇒ NASB #3998 penichros
	
	### Luke 21:2
	And he saw also a certain **poor** widow casting in thither two mites. [KJV]
	And He saw a certain **poor** widow putting in two small copper coins. [NASB]
	He also saw a **poor** widow put in two very small copper coins. [NIV]
	And He saw also a certain **poor** widow putting in two mites. [NKJV]
	Then a **poor** widow came by and dropped in two pennies. [NLT]
	εἶδε δέ καὶ τινα χήραν **πενιχρὰν** βάλλουσαν ἐκεῖ δύο λεπτὰ, [GNS]
	εἶδεν δέ τινα χήραν **πενιχρὰν** βάλλουσαν ἐκεῖ λεπτὰ δύο, [GNT]
		Poverty stricken; a meager, pitiful wage.
		
		### Practical Application
		The widow was not just poor, she was destitute, in deep poverty. Her poor dress and plain appearance showed her desperate plight. The coins were all she had, yet she gave them despite her own desperate need.
		Note: Jesus used two different words for "poor" to describe just how poor the woman really was. In verse two the word is *penichran* which means a person who earns only a meager, pitiful wage. In verse three the word is *ptöchë* which means abject poverty, utter destitution, poverty that is visible and unquestionable. It is the poverty that forces one to beg and seek alms in order to survive. In that day there was little work for a widow. Poor widows had to struggle for their very survival. Such was the case of this poor widow; she was desperately poor.

#2967
Position
 	
Bishoprick–KJV
Office–NASB
Place of leadership–
  NIV
Office–NKJV
Position–NLT
	ἐπισκοπὴν = episkopën
	Pronunciation: [ep-is-kop-ayn']
	Parsing (part of speech): noun
	    Case—accusative
	    Gender—feminine
	    Number—singular
	    Stem or root—from ἐπισκοπή, ῆς
	Concordance References:
	  ⇒ Strong's #1984 episkopë
	  ⇒ NIV #2175 episkopë
	  ⇒ NASB #1984 episkopë
		Place of leadership; office; position; place of service; overseership.
		
		### Practical Application
		It is the word from which the office of overseer or bishop is taken. The idea is that Judas' office of overseeing the flock of God was to be filled by another person. Judas had lost his ministry completely.

ENGLISH WORD	GREEK WORD AND VERSE	THE WORD MEANS...
POSB REFERENCE (Acts 1:16-20; esp. v.20) Note 2, point 6a	**Acts 1:20** For it is written in the book of Psalms, Let his habitation be desolate, and let no man dwell therein: and his **bishoprick** let another take. [KJV] "For it is written in the book of Psalms, 'Let his homestead be made desolate, And let no man dwell in it'; and, 'His **OFFICE** LET ANOTHER MAN TAKE.' [NASB] "For," said Peter, "it is written in the book of Psalms, " 'May his place be deserted; let there be no one to dwell in it,' and, " 'May another take his **place of leadership**.' [NIV] "For it is written in the book of Psalms: 'Let his dwelling place be desolate, And let no one live in it'; and, 'Let another take his **office**.' [NKJV] Peter continued, "This was predicted in the book of Psalms, where it says, 'Let his home become desolate, with no one living in it.' And again, 'Let his **position** be given to someone else.' [NLT] γέγραπται γὰρ ἐν βίβλῳ Ψαλμῶν, Γενηθήτω ἡ ἔπαυλις αὐτοῦ ἔρημος, καὶ μὴ ἔστω ὁ κατοικῶν ἐν αὐτῇ· καί, Τὴν **ἐπισκοπὴν** αὐτοῦ λαβέοι ἕτερος. [GNS] Γέγραπται γὰρ ἐν βίβλῳ ψαλμῶν, Γενηθήτω ἡ ἔπαυλις αὐτοῦ ἔρημος καὶ μὴ ἔστω ὁ κατοικῶν ἐν αὐτῇ, καί, Τὴν **ἐπισκοπὴν** αὐτοῦ λαβέτω ἕτερος. [GNT]	

#2968
 Pounds– Pounds Of Silver
 	
 Pounds–KJV
 Minas–NASB
 Minas–NIV
 Minas–NKJV
 Pounds of silver– NLT
 	
 POSB REFERENCE (Lk.19:13) *Deeper Study #1*
	μνᾶς = *mnas*
	 Pronunciation: [mn-ahs]
	 Parsing (part of speech): noun
	    Case—accusative
	    Gender—feminine
	    Number—plural
	    Stem or root—from μνᾶ, ᾶς
	 Concordance References:
	   ⇒ Strong's #3414 mna
	   ⇒ NIV #3641 mna
	   ⇒ NASB #3414 mna
	
	 Luke 19:13
	 And he called his ten servants, and delivered them ten **pounds**, and said unto them, Occupy till I come. [KJV]
	
	 "And he called ten of his slaves, and gave them ten **minas**, and said to them, 'Do business with this until I come back.' [NASB]
	
	 So he called ten of his servants and gave them ten **minas**. 'Put this money to work,' he said, 'until I come back.' [NIV]
	
	 So he called ten of his servants, delivered to them ten **minas**, and said to them, 'Do business till I come.' [NKJV]
	
	 Before he left, he called together ten servants and gave them ten **pounds of silver** to invest for him while he was gone. [NLT]
	
	 καλέσας δὲ δέκα δούλους ἑαυτοῦ, ἔδωκεν αὐτοῖς δέκα **μνᾶς**, καὶ εἶπε πρὸς αὐτούς, Πραγματεύσασθε ἕως ἔρχομαι. [GNS]
	
	 καλέσας δὲ δέκα δούλους ἑαυτοῦ ἔδωκεν αὐτοῖς δέκα **μνᾶς** καὶ εἶπεν πρὸς αὐτούς, Πραγματεύσασθε ἐν ᾧ ἔρχομαι. [GNT]
		Minas, pounds, pounds of silver.
		
		 Practical Application
		 The word in the Greek testament is *mnas* which was a Greek coin worth about one hundred drachmai. One drachmai was about one-day's wage for a laborer.

#2969
 Pour Forth– Pour Out
 	
 Pour out–KJV
 Pour forth–NASB
 Pour out–NIV
 Pour out–NKJV
 Pour out–NLT
	ἐκχέω = *ekcheō*
	 Pronunciation: [ek-kheh'-o]
	 Parsing (part of speech): verb
	    Mood—indicative
	    Tense—future
	    Voice—active
	    Person—1st person
	    Number—singular
	    Stem or root—from ἐκχέω and ἐκχύννω
	 Concordance References:
	   ⇒ Strong's #1632 ekcheō
	   ⇒ NIV #1772 ekcheō
	   ⇒ NASB #1632 ekcheō
		To pour out; to pour forth; to run out; to spill out; to shed forth.
		
		 Practical Application
		 It means that God gives His Spirit...
		 • to *dwell in* the believer (John 14:17; 1 Cor. 6:19-20).
		 • to *abide with* the believer forever (John 14:16).
		 • to fill, to overflow, to abundantly *fill* the believer (Ephes. 5:18).
		 • to give very special *manifestations* of Christ to the believer (John 14:21).

ENGLISH WORD	GREEK WORD AND VERSE	THE WORD MEANS...
POSB REFERENCE (Acts 2:17-21; esp. v.17) Note 2, point 1	**Acts 2:17** And it shall come to pass in the last days, saith God,I will **pour out** of my Spirit upon all flesh: and your sons and your daughters shall prophesy, and your young men shall see visions, and your old men shall dream dreams: [KJV] 'And it shall be in the last days,' God says, 'That I will **pour forth** of My Spirit upon all MANKIND; And your sons and your daughters shall prophesy, And your young men shall see visions, And your old men shall dream dreams; [NASB] "'In the last days, God says, I will **pour out** my Spirit on all people. Your sons and daughters will prophesy, your young men will see visions, your old men will dream dreams. [NIV] 'And it shall come to pass in the last days, says God, That I will **pour out** of My Spirit on all flesh; Your sons and your daughters shall prophesy, Your young men shall see visions, Your old men shall dream dreams.[NKJV] 'In the last days, God said, I will **pour out** my Spirit upon all people. Your sons and your daughters will prophesy, your young men will see visions, and your old men will dream dreams. [NLT] Καὶ ἔσται ἐν ταῖς ἐσχάταις ἡμέραις, -- λέγει ὁ Θεός -- **ἐκχεῶ** ἀπὸ τοῦ πνεύματός μου ἐπὶ πᾶσαν σάρκα· καὶ προφητεύσουσιν οἱ υἱοὶ ὑμῶν καὶ αἱ θυγατέρες ὑμῶν, καὶ οἱ *νεανίσκοι* ὑμῶν ὁράσεις ὄψονται, καὶ οἱ πρεσβύτεροι ὑμῶν ἐνυπνία ἐνυπνιασθήσονται· [GNS] Καὶ ἔσται ἐν ταῖς ἐσχάταις ἡμέραις, λέγει ὁ θεός, **ἐκχεῶ** ἀπὸ τοῦ πνεύματός μου ἐπὶ πᾶσαν σάρκα, καὶ προφητεύσουσιν οἱ υἱοὶ ὑμῶν καὶ αἱ θυγατέρες ὑμῶν καὶ οἱ *νεανίσκοι* ὑμῶν ὁράσεις ὄψονται καὶ οἱ πρεσβύτεροι ὑμῶν ἐνυπνίοις ἐνυπνιασθήσονται· [GNT]	

#2970
Poured Out As An Offering To God
 	
Offered–KJV
Poured out as a drink offering–NASB
Poured out like a drink offering–NIV
Poured out as a drink offering–NKJV
Poured out as an offering to God–NLT
 	
POSB REFERENCE
(2 Tim. 4:6)
Note 1, point 1
	σπένδομαι = *spendomai*
	Pronunciation: [spen'-do-mah-ee]
	Parsing (part of speech): verb
	  Mood—indicative
	  Tense—present
	  Voice—passive
	  Person—1st person
	  Number—singular
	  Stem or root—from σπένδομαι
	Concordance References:
	  ⇒ Strong's #4689 spendō
	  ⇒ NIV #5064 spendō
	  ⇒ NASB #4689 spendō
	
	2 Tim. 4:6
	For I am now ready to be **offered**, and the time of my departure is at hand. [KJV]
	
	For I am already being **poured out as a drink offering**, and the time of my departure has come. [NASB]
	
	For I am already being **poured out like a drink offering**, and the time has come for my departure. [NIV]
	
	For I am already being **poured out as a drink offering**, and the time of my departure is at hand. [NKJV]
	
	As for me, my life has already been **poured out as an offering to God**. The time of my death is near. [NLT]
	
	ἐγὼ γὰρ ἤδη **σπένδομαι**, καὶ ὁ καιρὸς τῆς ἐμῆς ἀναλύσεως ἐφέστηκε. [GNS]
	
	Ἐγὼ γὰρ ἤδη **σπένδομαι**, καὶ ὁ καιρὸς τῆς ἀναλύσεώς μου ἐφέστηκεν. [GNT]
		To be poured out like a drink offering; to be offered; poured out as an offering to God; to offer one's life as a sacrifice.
		
		Practical Application
		Paul says that his life is being offered and sacrificed to God in one last act—the act of death. What a view of death! Seeing death as an offering and sacrifice being presented to God. The Greek word for offering or sacrifice (*spendomai*) is striking: it refers to the drink offering that was presented to God. When a person wanted to make a sacrifice to God, he often took a cup of wine or oil and poured it out as an offering and sacrifice to God. The drink offering symbolized the Lord Jesus pouring out His soul—dying—for us.
		
		Paul is saying, "I am pouring out my soul through death for the Lord Jesus Christ. The life and blood of my body is being sacrificed for the preaching of God's Word. I am laying down my life as an offering to Christ Jesus my Lord—laying it down in the supreme act of sacrifice. I am dying for Him."

#2971
Poured Out As A Drink Offering–
	σπένδομαι = *spendomai*
	Pronunciation: [spen'-do-mah-ee]
	Parsing (part of speech): verb
	  Mood—indicative
	  Tense—present
	  Voice—passive
		To be poured out like a drink offering; to be offered; poured out as an offering to God; to offer one's life as a sacrifice.

ENGLISH WORD	GREEK WORD AND VERSE	THE WORD MEANS...
Poured Out Like a Drink Offering Offered–KJV **Poured out as a drink offering–NASB** **Poured out like a drink offering–NIV** **Poured out as a drink offering–NKJV** Poured out as an offering to God–NLT **POSB REFERENCE** (2 Tim. 4:6) Note 1, point 1	Person—1st person Number—singular Stem or root—from σπένδομαι Concordance References: ⇒ Strong's #4689 spendö ⇒ NIV #5064 spendö ⇒ NASB #4689 spendö **2 Tim. 4:6** For I am now ready to be **offered**, and the time of my departure is at hand. [KJV] For I am already being **poured out as a drink offering**, and the time of my departure has come. [NASB] For I am already being **poured out like a drink offering**, and the time has come for my departure. [NIV] For I am already being **poured out as a drink offering**, and the time of my departure is at hand. [NKJV] As for me, my life has already been **poured out as an offering to God**. The time of my death is near. [NLT] ἐγὼ γὰρ ἤδη **σπένδομαι**, καὶ ὁ καιρὸς τῆς ἐμῆς ἀναλύσεως ἐφέστηκε. [GNS] Ἐγὼ γὰρ ἤδη **σπένδομαι**, καὶ ὁ καιρὸς τῆς ἀναλύσεώς μου ἐφέστηκεν. [GNT]	**Practical Application** Paul says that his life is being offered and sacrificed to God in one last act—the act of death. What a view of death! Seeing death as an offering and sacrifice being presented to God. The Greek word for offering or sacrifice (*spendomai*) is striking: it refers to the drink offering that was presented to God. When a person wanted to make a sacrifice to God, he often took a cup of wine or oil and poured it out as an offering and sacrifice to God. The drink offering symbolized the Lord Jesus pouring out His soul—dying—for us. Paul is saying, "I am pouring out my soul through death for the Lord Jesus Christ. The life and blood of my body is being sacrificed for the preaching of God's Word. I am laying down my life as an offering to Christ Jesus my Lord—laying it down in the supreme act of sacrifice. I am dying for Him."
#2972 **Poverty** Lacked–KJV Needy–NASB Needy–NIV Lacked–NKJV **Poverty–NLT** **POSB REFERENCE** (Acts 4:34-37; esp. v.34) Note 3, point 1	ἐνδεής = endeës Pronunciation: [en-deh-ace'] Parsing (part of speech): pronominal adjective Case—nominative Gender—masculine Number— singular Stem or root—from ἐνδεής, ές Concordance References: ⇒ Strong's #1729 endees ⇒ NIV #1890 endeës ⇒ NASB #1729 endees **Acts 4:34** Neither was there any among them that **lacked**: for as many as were possessors of lands or houses sold them, and brought the prices of the things that were sold, [KJV] For there was not a **needy** person among them, for all who were owners of land or houses would sell them and bring the proceeds of the sales, [NASB] There were no **needy** persons among them. For from time to time those who owned lands or houses sold them, brought the money from the sales [NIV] Nor was there anyone among them who **lacked**; for all who were possessors of lands or houses sold them, and brought the proceeds of the things that were sold, [NKJV] There was no **poverty** among them, because people who owned land or houses sold them [NLT] οὐδὲ γὰρ **ἐνδεής** τις ὑπῆρχεν ἐν αὐτοῖς· ὅσοι γὰρ κτήτορες χωρίων η οἰκιῶν ὑπῆρχον, πωλοῦντες ἔφερον τὰς τιμὰς τῶν πιπρασκομένων, [GNS] οὐδὲ γὰρ **ἐνδεής** τις ἦν ἐν αὐτοῖς· ὅσοι γὰρ κτήτορες χωρίων η οἰκιῶν ὑπῆρχον, πωλοῦντες ἔφερον τὰς τιμὰς τῶν πιπρασκομένων [GNT]	Needy; the poor; the person who lacks and lives in poverty. **Practical Application** The idea is that no family, no man, no woman, no child was neglected. No one was left without the necessities of life; no one had to face a day without the food, clothing, or shelter that he needed to take care of himself or of his dear family. All of God's dear people were taken care of.
#2973 **Power** **Power–KJV** Authority–NASB Authority–NIV **Power–NKJV** Authority–NLT **POSB REFERENCE** (Mt.10:1) *Deeper Study #2*	ἐξουσίαν = exousia Pronunciation: [ex-oo-see'-ah] Parsing (part of speech): noun Case—accusative Gender—feminine Number—singular Stem or root—from ἐξουσία, ας Concordance References: ⇒ Strong's #1849 exousia ⇒ NIV #2026 exousia ⇒ NASB #1849 exousia **Matthew 10:1** And when he had called unto him his twelve disciples,	Authority, authorization, power, sanction. **Practical Application** In this Scripture, Christ was giving *His own power* to His messengers. They were being sent forth by Him on a very special mission; therefore, they were given His authority and power to minister. Notice that the power to save or convert the lost is not given. Why? Only God can save and penetrate the spiritual world or dimension. Man's power is limited to the physical world and dimension.

ENGLISH WORD	GREEK WORD AND VERSE	THE WORD MEANS...
		strength is not human, fleshly strength; it is not the strength of anything within this world. The believer's strength is found *in the Lord*—in a living, dynamic relationship with Him. The Lord is the source of the believer's strength. There is no other source that can give man the strength to overcome this world with all its trials and temptations and death.

#2977
Power
 	
Working–KJV
Power–NASB
Energy–NIV
Working–NKJV
Power–NLT
 	
POSB REFERENCE
(Col.1:29)
Note 5, point 2
	ἐνέργειαν = energeian
	Pronunciation: [en-erg'-i-ahn]
	Parsing (part of speech): noun
	    Case—accusative
	    Gender—feminine
	    Number—singular
	    Stem or root—from ἐνέργεια, ας
	Concordance References:
	  ⇒ Strong's #1753 energeia
	  ⇒ NIV #1918 energeia
	  ⇒ NASB #1753 energeia
	
	Col. 1:29
	Whereunto I also labour, striving according to his **working**, which worketh in me mightily. [KJV]
	And for this purpose also I labor, striving according to His **power**, which mightily works within me. [NASB]
	To this end I labor, struggling with all his **energy**, which so powerfully works in me. [NIV]
	To this *end* I also labor, striving according to His **working** which works in me mightily. [NKJV]
	I work very hard at this, as I depend on Christ's mighty **power** that works within me. [NLT]
	εἰς ὃ καὶ κοπιῶ, ἀγωνιζόμενος κατὰ τὴν ἐνέργειαν αὐτοῦ, τὴν ἐνεργουμένην ἐν ἐμοὶ ἐν δυνάμει. [GNS]
	εἰς ὃ καὶ κοπιῶ ἀγωνιζόμενος κατὰ τὴν ἐνέργειαν αὐτοῦ τὴν ἐνεργουμένην ἐν ἐμοὶ ἐν δυνάμει. [GNT]
		Energy, working, power. The word "energy" (*energeian*) means energy and efficiency and is only used of superhuman power (Kenneth Wuest. *Ephesians and Colossians,* Vol.1, p.195). In this case, it is the power of Christ.
		
		Practical Application
		When the minister has gone as far as he can, Christ steps in to infuse energy and power into his body—an energy and power that works in him powerfully. The minister who has truly labored to the point of exhaustion and experienced the energy and power of Christ knows how glorious the experience is. It is just tragic that there are too few who so labor and even fewer who consistently labor to the point that Christ has to step in with His energy and power. We seem to forget too easily
		  ⇒ as long as we have physical strength and energy left to labor, the energy and power of Christ are not needed.
		The only way we can experience the physical energy and power of Christ is to use up all of our own strength. When we are completely empty, then Christ has to step in or else leave us and abandon us and disregard the promise of His Word. And this He will never do. Therefore, when we have no more strength to walk and labor, it is then that He infuses us with His own supernatural energy and power.

#2978
Power
 	
Operation–KJV
Working–NASB
Power–NIV
Working–NKJV
Power–NLT
 	
POSB REFERENCE
(Col.2:11-12; esp. v.12)
Note 2, point 3
	ἐνέργείας = energeias
	Pronunciation: [en-erg'-i-ahs]
	Parsing (part of speech): noun
	    Case—genitive
	    Gender—feminine
	    Number—singular
	    Stem or root—from ἐνέργεια, ας
	Concordance References:
	  ⇒ Strong's #1753 energeia
	  ⇒ NIV #1918 energeia
	  ⇒ NASB #1753 energeia
	
	Col. 2:12
	Buried with him in baptism, wherein also ye are risen with him through the faith of the **operation** of God, who hath raised him from the dead. [KJV]
	Having been buried with Him in baptism, in which you were also raised up with Him through faith in the **working** of God, who raised Him from the dead. [NASB]
	Having been buried with him in baptism and raised with him through your faith in the **power** of God, who raised him from the dead. [NIV]
	Buried with Him in baptism, in which you also were raised with *Him* through faith in the **working** of God, who raised Him from the dead. [NKJV]
	For you were buried with Christ when you were baptized. And with him you were raised to a new life because you trusted the mighty **power** of God, who raised Christ from the dead. [NLT]
	συνταφέντες αὐτῷ ἐν τῷ βαπτίσματι, ἐν ᾧ καὶ
		Operation, working, power, energy.
		
		Practical Application
		Real religion is a power of God and a power of God alone. God has to perform the power or work upon a person if the person is to be acceptable to God. No person can operate upon any other person and make him acceptable to God. God alone has the ability and power to make a person acceptable to Him.

ENGLISH WORD	GREEK WORD AND VERSE	THE WORD MEANS...
	συνηγέρθητε διὰ τῆς πίστεως τῆς **ἐνεργείας** τοῦ Θεοῦ, τοῦ ἐγείραντος αὐτὸν ἐκ τῶν νεκρῶν. [GNS] συνταφέντες αὐτῷ ἐν τῷ βαπτισμῷ, ἐν ᾧ καὶ συνηγέρθητε διὰ τῆς πίστεως τῆς **ἐνεργείας** τοῦ θεοῦ τοῦ ἐγείραντος αὐτὸν ἐκ νεκρῶν· [GNT]	
#2979 **Power** Powerful–KJV Active–NASB Active–NIV Powerful–NKJV **Power–NLT** **POSB REFERENCE** (Heb.4:11-13; esp. v.12) Note 5, point 2a	**ἐνεργὴς** = energēs Pronunciation: [en-er-gace'] Parsing (part of speech): adjective 　Case—nominative 　Gender—masculine 　Number—singular 　Stem or root—from ἐνεργής, ές Concordance References: ⇒ Strong's #1756 energēs ⇒ NIV #1921 energēs ⇒ NASB #1756 energēs ### Hebrews 4:12 For the word of God is quick, and **powerful**, and sharper than any twoedged sword, piercing even to the dividing asunder of soul and spirit, and of the joints and marrow, and is a discerner of the thoughts and intents of the heart. [KJV] For the word of God is living and **active** and sharper than any two-edged sword, and piercing as far as the division of soul and spirit, of both joints and marrow, and able to judge the thoughts and intentions of the heart. [NASB] For the word of God is living and **active**. Sharper than any double-edged sword, it penetrates even to dividing soul and spirit, joints and marrow; it judges the thoughts and attitudes of the heart. [NIV] For the word of God is living and **powerful**, and sharper than any two-edged sword, piercing even to the division of soul and spirit, and of joints and marrow, and is a discerner of the thoughts and intents of the heart. [NKJV] For the word of God is full of living **power**. It is sharper than the sharpest knife, cutting deep into our innermost thoughts and desires. It exposes us for what we really are. [NLT] ζῶν γὰρ ὁ λόγος τοῦ Θεοῦ, καὶ **ἐνεργὴς**, καὶ τομώτερος ὑπὲρ πᾶσαν μάχαιραν δίστομον, καὶ διϊκνούμενος· ἄχρι μερισμοῦ ψυχῆς τὲ καὶ πνεύματος, ἁρμῶν τε καὶ μυελῶν, καὶ κριτικὸς ἐνθυμήσεων καὶ ἐννοιῶν καρδίας. [GNS] Ζῶν γὰρ ὁ λόγος τοῦ θεοῦ καὶ **ἐνεργὴς** καὶ τομώτερος ὑπὲρ πᾶσαν μάχαιραν δίστομον καὶ διϊκνούμενος ἄχρι μερισμοῦ ψυχῆς καὶ πνεύματος, ἁρμῶν τε καὶ μυελῶν, καὶ κριτικὸς ἐνθυμήσεων καὶ ἐννοιῶν καρδίας·. [GNT]	Active, powerful, effective. ### Practical Application God's word of promise, His rest of salvation, is active and powerful. It is not dormant and inactive. It is actually active and working, energizing the heart of the believer.
#2980 **Power– Power, Healing** Virtue–KJV **Power–NASB** **Power–NIV** **Power–NKJV** **Healing power–NLT** **POSB REFERENCE** (Lk.6:17-19; esp. v.19) Note 5, point 2c **See also POSB REF:** (Lk.8:43-48; esp. v.46) Note 3, point 4b	**δύναμις** = dunamis Pronunciation: [doo'-nam-is] Parsing (part of speech): noun 　Case—nominative 　Gender—feminine 　Number—singular 　Stem or root—from δύναμις, εως Concordance References: ⇒ Strong's #1411 dunamis ⇒ NIV #1539 dunamis ⇒ NASB #1411 dunamis ### Luke 6:19 And the whole multitude sought to touch him: for there went **virtue** out of him, and healed them all. [KJV] And all the multitude were trying to touch Him, for **power** was coming from Him and healing them all. [NASB] And the people all tried to touch him, because **power** was coming from him and healing them all. [NIV] And the whole multitude sought to touch Him, for	Power, healing power, spiritual power, virtue. ### Practical Application The people were touching Jesus in order to receive His power. Serving and helping others cost Jesus and cost Him dearly. Power (*dunamis*), spiritual power, flowed out from His being into the woman. It was that which healed her. Note that the disciples were unaware of what it cost Jesus to minister. They were insensitive to the spiritual energy He was exerting, ignorant of what Jesus was doing: ⇒ He was taking our infirmities upon Himself and bearing our sicknesses. ⇒ He was teaching that public confession of Him was essential. Note what the woman did when she "saw that she was not hid." She knew that He who had

ENGLISH WORD	GREEK WORD AND VERSE	THE WORD MEANS...
	power went out from Him and healed them all. [NKJV] Everyone was trying to touch him, because **healing power** went out from him, and they were all cured. [NLT] καὶ πᾶς ὁ ὄχλος ἐζήτει ἅπτεσθαι αὐτοῦ ὅτι **δύναμις** παρ' αὐτοῦ ἐξήρχετο καὶ ἰᾶτο πάντας. [GNS] καὶ πᾶς ὁ ὄχλος ἐζήτουν ἅπτεσθαι αὐτοῦ, ὅτι **δύναμις** παρ' αὐτοῦ ἐξήρχετο καὶ ἰᾶτο πάντας. [GNT]_	such power knew who had touched Him, so she came as all should come in approaching the Lord: "trembling and falling down before Him," confessing all.

#2981
Power, All
 	
All power–KJV
All authority–NASB
All authority–NIV
All authority–NKJV
Complete authority–NLT
 	
POSB REFERENCE
(Mt.28:18)
Note 2
	πᾶσα ἐξουσία = *pasa exousia*
	Pronunciation: [pas-ah ex-oo-see'-ah]
	Parsing *pasa* (part of speech): adjective
	    Case—nominative
	    Gender—feminine
	    Number—singular
	    Stem or root—from πᾶς, πᾶσα, πᾶν
	Parsing *exousia* (part of speech): noun
	    Case—nominative
	    Gender—feminine
	    Number—singular
	    Stem or root—from ἐξουσία, ας
	Concordance References:
	  ⇒ Strong's #3956 pas + 1849 exousia
	  ⇒ NIV #4246 pas [all] + #2026 exousia [authority]
	  ⇒ NASB #3956 pas + 1849 exousia
	
	Matthew 28:18
	And Jesus came and spake unto them, saying, **All power** is given unto me in heaven and in earth. [KJV]
	
	And Jesus came up and spoke to them, saying, "**All authority** has been given to Me in heaven and on earth. [NASB]
	
	Then Jesus came to them and said, "**All authority** in heaven and on earth has been given to me. [NIV]
	
	And Jesus came and spoke to them, saying, "**All authority** has been given to Me in heaven and on earth. [NKJV]
	
	Jesus came and told his disciples, "I have been given **complete authority** in heaven and on earth. [NLT]
	
	καὶ προσελθὼν ὁ Ἰησοῦς ἐλάλησεν αὐτοῖς λέγων, Ἐδόθη μοι **πᾶσα ἐξουσία** ἐν οὐρανῷ καὶ ἐπὶ τῆς γῆς. [GNS]
	
	καὶ προσελθὼν ὁ Ἰησοῦς ἐλάλησεν αὐτοῖς λέγων, Ἐδόθη μοι **πᾶσα ἐξουσία** ἐν οὐρανῷ καὶ ἐπὶ [τῆς] γῆς. [GNT]
		The ability, the power, the authority, the right to do something.
		
		### Practical Application
		God the Father entrusted Jesus Christ with this kind of power. Christ has been given complete freedom over *all*. This means...
		• all freedom to impose His power in heaven.
		• all freedom to impose His power on earth.
		• all freedom to impose His power over every disciple.
		• all freedom to impose His power over every person and every nation.
		
		On the basis of His power, believers are to go, and as we go we are to follow His instructions completely.

#2982
Powerful
 	
Demonstration–KJV
Demonstration–NASB
Demonstration–NIV
Demonstration–NKJV
Powerful–NLT
 	
POSB REFERENCE
(1 Cor.2:4)
Note 4, point 3
	ἀποδείξει = *apodeixei*
	Pronunciation: [ap-od'-eek-see]
	Parsing (part of speech): noun
	    Case—dative
	    Gender—feminine
	    Number—singular
	    Stem or root—from ἀπόδειξις, εως
	Concordance References:
	  ⇒ Strong's #585 apodeixis
	  ⇒ NIV #618 apodeixis
	  ⇒ NASB #585 apodeixis
	
	1 Cor. 2:4
	And my speech and my preaching was not with enticing words of man's wisdom, but in **demonstration** of the Spirit and of power: [KJV]
	
	And my message and my preaching were not in persuasive words of wisdom, but in **demonstration** of the Spirit and of power, [NASB]
	
	My message and my preaching were not with wise and persuasive words, but with a **demonstration** of the Spirit's power, [NIV]
	
	And my speech and my preaching were not with persuasive words of human wisdom, but in **demonstration** of the Spirit and of power, [NKJV]
	
	And my message and my preaching were very plain. I did not use wise and persuasive speeches, but the Holy
		Demonstration, proof, to show forth with the most rigorous evidence and proof.
		
		### Practical Application
		The idea is that the evidence is presented so strongly that the truth is clearly seen.

ENGLISH WORD	GREEK WORD AND VERSE	THE WORD MEANS...
	Spirit was **powerful** among you. [NLT] καὶ ὁ λόγος μου καὶ τὸ κήρυγμά μου οὐκ ἐν πειθοῖς ἀνθρωπίνης σοφίας λόγοις, ἀλλ᾽ ἐν **ἀποδείξει** πνεύματος καὶ δυνάμεως· [GNS] καὶ ὁ λόγος μου καὶ τὸ κήρυγμά μου οὐκ ἐν πειθοῖ[ς] σοφίας [λόγοις] ἀλλ᾽ ἐν **ἀποδείξει** πνεύματος καὶ δυνάμεως, [GNT]	

#2983
Powerful
 	
Powerful–KJV
Active–NASB
Active–NIV
Powerful–NKJV
Power–NLT
 	
**POSB
REFERENCE**
(Heb.4:11-13; esp.
v.12)
Note 5, point 2a
	ἐνεργὴς = energēs
	Pronunciation: [en-er-gace']
	Parsing (part of speech): adjective
	    Case—nominative
	    Gender—masculine
	    Number—singular
	    Stem or root—from ἐνεργής, ές
	Concordance References:
	⇒ Strong's #1756 energēs
	⇒ NIV #1921 energēs
	⇒ NASB #1756 energēs
	
	Hebrews 4:12
	For the word of God is quick, and **powerful**, and sharper than any twoedged sword, piercing even to the dividing asunder of soul and spirit, and of the joints and marrow, and is a discerner of the thoughts and intents of the heart. [KJV]
	For the word of God is living and **active** and sharper than any two-edged sword, and piercing as far as the division of soul and spirit, of both joints and marrow, and able to judge the thoughts and intentions of the heart. [NASB]
	For the word of God is living and **active**. Sharper than any double-edged sword, it penetrates even to dividing soul and spirit, joints and marrow; it judges the thoughts and attitudes of the heart. [NIV]
	For the word of God is living and **powerful**, and sharper than any two-edged sword, piercing even to the division of soul and spirit, and of joints and marrow, and is a discerner of the thoughts and intents of the heart. [NKJV]
	For the word of God is full of living **power**. It is sharper than the sharpest knife, cutting deep into our innermost thoughts and desires. It exposes us for what we really are. [NLT]
	
	ζῶν γὰρ ὁ λόγος τοῦ Θεοῦ, καὶ **ἐνεργὴς**, καὶ τομώτερος ὑπὲρ πᾶσαν μάχαιραν δίστομον, καὶ διϊκνούμενος· ἄχρι μερισμοῦ ψυχῆς τὲ καὶ πνεύματος, ἁρμῶν τε καὶ μυελῶν, καὶ κριτικὸς ἐνθυμήσεων καὶ ἐννοιῶν καρδίας. [GNS]
	
	Ζῶν γὰρ ὁ λόγος τοῦ θεοῦ καὶ **ἐνεργὴς** καὶ τομώτερος ὑπὲρ πᾶσαν μάχαιραν δίστομον καὶ διϊκνούμενος ἄχρι μερισμοῦ ψυχῆς καὶ πνεύματος, ἁρμῶν τε καὶ μυελῶν, καὶ κριτικὸς ἐνθυμήσεων καὶ ἐννοιῶν καρδίας·. [GNT]
		Active, powerful, effective.
		
		Practical Application
		God's word of promise, His rest of salvation, is active and powerful. It is not dormant and inactive. It is actually active and working, energizing the heart of the believer.

#2984
**Powerful–
Powerfully**
 	
Mightily–KJV
Powerfully–NASB
Vigorously–NIV
Vigorously–NKJV
Powerful–NLT
 	
**POSB
REFERENCE**
(Acts 18:27-28; esp.
v.28)
Note 8, point 2a
	εὐτόνως = eutonōs
	Pronunciation: [yoo-ton'-oce]
	Parsing (part of speech): adjective
	    Type— adverb
	    Stem or root—from εὐτόνως
	Concordance References:
	⇒ Strong's #2159 eutonōs
	⇒ NIV #2364 eutonōs
	⇒ NASB #2159 eutonōs
	
	Acts 18:28
	For he **mightily** convinced the Jews, and that publickly, showing by the scriptures that Jesus was Christ. [KJV]
	for he **powerfully** refuted the Jews in public, demonstrating by the Scriptures that Jesus was the Christ. [NASB]
	For he **vigorously** refuted the Jews in public debate, proving from the Scriptures that Jesus was the Christ. [NIV]
		Vigorously, mightily, powerfully.
		
		Practical Application
		The word "powerful" or "powerfully" (eutonōs) means that Apollos used the Scriptures with power, straining earnestly to prove that Jesus is the Christ, the true Messiah.

ENGLISH WORD	GREEK WORD AND VERSE	THE WORD MEANS...
	For he **vigorously** refuted the Jews publicly, showing from the Scriptures that Jesus is the Christ. [NKJV] He refuted all the Jews with **powerful** arguments in public debate. Using the Scriptures, he explained to them, "The Messiah you are looking for is Jesus." [NLT] εὐτόνως γὰρ τοῖς Ἰουδαίοις διακατηλέγχετο δημοσίᾳ ἐπιδεικνὺς διὰ τῶν γραφῶν εἶναι τὸν Χριστόν, Ἰησοῦν. [GNS] εὐτόνως γὰρ τοῖς Ἰουδαίοις διακατηλέγχετο δημοσίᾳ ἐπιδεικνὺς διὰ τῶν γραφῶν εἶναι τὸν Χριστὸν Ἰησοῦν. [GNT]	

#2985
Powerful Delusion
 	
Strong delusion–KJV
Deluding influence–NASB
Powerful delusion–NIV
Strong delusion–NKJV
Great deception–NLT
 	
POSB REFERENCE
(2 Thes.2:11)
Note 3
	ἐνέργειαν πλάνης = energeian planës
	Pronunciation: [en-erg'-i-ahn plan'-ace]
	Parsing (part of speech): noun
	    Case—accusative
	    Gender—feminine
	    Number—singular
	    Stem or root—from ἐνέργεια, ας
	Parsing (part of speech): noun
	    Case—genitive
	    Gender—feminine
	    Number—singular
	    Stem or root—from πλάνη, ης
	Concordance References:
	⇒ Strong's #1753 energeia + 4106 planë
	⇒ NIV #1918 energeia + 4415 planë
	⇒ NASB #1753 energeia + 4106 planë
	
	2 Thes. 2:11
	And for this cause God shall send them **strong delusion**, that they should believe a lie: [KJV]
	
	And for this reason God will send upon them a **deluding influence** so that they might believe what is false, [NASB]
	
	For this reason God sends them a **powerful delusion** so that they will believe the lie [NIV]
	
	And for this reason God will send them **strong delusion**, that they should believe the lie, [NKJV]
	
	So God will send **great deception** upon them, and they will believe all these lies. [NLT]
	
	καὶ διὰ τοῦτο πέμψει αὐτοῖς ὁ Θεὸς ἐνέργειαν πλάνης, εἰς τὸ πιστεῦσαι αὐτοὺς τῷ ψεύδει· [GNS]
	
	καὶ διὰ τοῦτο πέμπει αὐτοῖς ὁ θεὸς ἐνέργειαν πλάνης εἰς τὸ πιστεῦσαι αὐτοὺς τῷ ψεύδει, [GNT]
		Powerful delusion, strong delusion, deluding influence, great deception, great error, strong deceit, a working of error.
		
		Practical Application
		In the end time, people will work error after error, sin after sin, evil after evil. They will become stronger and stronger in their sin, harder and harder. They will become steeped in their rejection of the gospel more and more.

#2986
Powerful, More And More
 	
Increased the more in strength–KJV
Increasing in strength–NASB
More and more powerful–NIV
Increased all the more in strength–NKJV
More and more powerful–NLT
 	
POSB REFERENCE
(Acts 9:22)
Note 5, point 1
	μᾶλλον ἐνεδυναμοῦτο = mallon enedunamouto
	Pronunciation: [mal'-lon en-doo-nam-oo'-tow]
	Parsing mallon (part of speech): adjective adverb
	    Type—comparative
	    Stem or root—from μᾶλλον
	Parsing enedunamouto (part of speech): verb
	    Mood—indicative
	    Tense—imperfect
	    Voice—passive
	    Person—3rd person
	    Number—singular
	    Stem or root—from ἐνδυναμόω
	Concordance References:
	⇒ Strong's #3123 mallon + 1743 endunamoö
	⇒ NIV #3437 mallon [more and] + 1904 endunamoö [powerful]
	⇒ NASB #3123 mallon + 1743 endunamoö
	
	Acts 9:22
	But Saul **increased the more in strength**, and confounded the Jews which dwelt at Damascus, proving that this is very Christ. [KJV]
	
	But Saul kept **increasing in strength** and confounding the Jews who lived at Damascus by proving that this Jesus is the Christ. [NASB]
	
	Yet Saul grew **more and more powerful** and baf-
		More and more powerful; increasing in strength; to become strong within; to gain inner strength; to increase spiritually.
		
		Practical Application
		Note: the more Saul (or Paul) grew in the Lord, the more he was able to "baffle" (confuse) those who opposed and rebelled against the gospel. He was able to "prove" (affirm and confirm) it with more and more power as he grew and grew.

ENGLISH WORD	GREEK WORD AND VERSE	THE WORD MEANS...
	fled the Jews living in Damascus by proving that Jesus is the Christ. [NIV] But Saul **increased all the more in strength**, and confounded the Jews who dwelt in Damascus, proving that this *Jesus* is the Christ. [NKJV] Saul's preaching became **more and more powerful**, and the Jews in Damascus couldn't refute his proofs that Jesus was indeed the Messiah. [NLT] Σαῦλος δὲ **μᾶλλον ἐνεδυναμοῦτο**, καὶ συνέχυνε τοὺς Ἰουδαίους τοὺς κατοικοῦντας ἐν Δαμασκῷ, συμβιβάζων ὅτι οὗτός ἐστιν ὁ Χριστός. [GNS] Σαῦλος δὲ **μᾶλλον ἐνεδυναμοῦτο** καὶ συνέχυννεν [τοὺς] Ἰουδαίους τοὺς κατοικοῦντας ἐν Δαμασκῷ συμβιβάζων ὅτι οὗτός ἐστιν ὁ Χριστός. [GNT]	

#2987
 Powerless
 	
 Without strength–KJV
 Helpless–NASB
 Powerless–NIV
 Without strength– NKJV
 Helpless–NLT
 	
 POSB REFERENCE
 (Romans 5:6-7, esp. v.6)
 Note 1, point 1
	ἀσθενῶν = *asthenōn*
	 Pronunciation: [as-then-own']
	 Parsing (part of speech): adjective
	     Case—genitive
	     Gender—masculine
	     Number—plural
	     Stem or root—from ἀσθενής, ές
	 Concordance References:
	   ⇒ Strong's #772 asthenes
	   ⇒ NIV #820 astheneö
	   ⇒ NASB #772 asthenes
	
	 Romans 5:6
	 For when we were yet **without strength**, in due time Christ died for the ungodly. [KJV]
	
	 For while we were still **helpless**, at the right time Christ died for the ungodly. [NASB]
	
	 You see, at just the right time, when we were still **powerless**, Christ died for the ungodly. [NIV]
	
	 For when we were still **without strength**, in due time Christ died for the ungodly. [NKJV]
	
	 When we were utterly **helpless**, Christ came at just the right time and died for us sinners. [NLT]
	
	 ἔτι γὰρ Χριστὸς ὄντων ἡμῶν **ἀσθενῶν**, ἔτι κατὰ καιρὸν ὑπὲρ ἀσεβῶν ἀπέθανε. [GNS]
	
	 ἔτι γὰρ Χριστὸς ὄντων ἡμῶν **ἀσθενῶν** ἔτι κατὰ καιρὸν ὑπὲρ ἀσεβῶν ἀπέθανεν. [GNT]
		Sick; ill; diabled; weak; delicate; helpless; without strength powerless.
		
		 ### Practical Application
		 We were ungodly and without strength, yet Christ died for us. God's great love is seen in this unbelievable act. We were "powerless" (*asthenōn*), helpless, without strength. We were spiritually worthless and useless and unable to help ourselves.

#2988
 Powers
 	
 Powers–KJV
 Powers–NASB
 Authorities–NIV
 Powers–KJV
 Authorities–NLT
 	
 POSB REFERENCE
 (Eph.6:12)
 Note 3, point 5
	ἐξουσίας = *exousias*
	 Pronunciation: [ex-oo-see'-ahs]
	 Parsing (part of speech): noun
	     Case—accusative
	     Gender—feminine
	     Number—plural
	     Stem or root—from ἐξουσία, ας
	 Concordance References:
	   ⇒ Strong's #1849 exousia
	   ⇒ NIV #2026 exousia
	   ⇒ NASB #1849 exousia
	
	 Ephes. 6:12
	 For we wrestle not against flesh and blood, but against principalities, against **powers**, against the rulers of the darkness of this world, against spiritual wickedness in high places. [KJV]
	
	 For our struggle is not against flesh and blood, but against the rulers, against the **powers**, against the world forces of this darkness, against the spiritual forces of wickedness in the heavenly places. [NASB]
	
	 For our struggle is not against flesh and blood, but against the rulers, against the **authorities**, against the powers of this dark world and against the spiritual forces of evil in the heavenly realms. [NIV]
	
	 For we do not wrestle against flesh and blood, but against principalities, against **powers**, against the rulers of the darkness of this age, against spiritual hosts of wickedness in the heavenly places. [NKJV]
	
	 For we are not fighting against people made of flesh
		Authorities, powers, supernatural power, ruling power; the demons of Satan in the lower atmosphere who constitute his kingdom in the air.
		
		 ### Practical Application
		 Some persons have always scoffed at the idea of a personal devil or demons who actually exist in a so-called spiritual world. They feel they are too educated and intelligent to believe such nonsense. They proclaim that such ideas are outdated and belong to the dark ages of man's ignorance and superstitions. But note a significant fact: man is ever so conscious of what he terms...
		 • *sub-conscious horrors* that affect both his mind and body.
		 • *unseen and uncontrollable forces* that greatly affect his behavior.
		 • *unregulated behavior* that he cannot control even when he knows better and wills to do differently.
		 • *cosmic forces* that affect and determine his behavior.
		 • *blind fate* that controls his life like a puppet.

ENGLISH WORD	GREEK WORD AND VERSE	THE WORD MEANS...
	and blood, but against the evil rulers and **authorities** of the unseen world, against those mighty powers of darkness who rule this world, and against wicked spirits in the heavenly realms. [NLT] ὅτι οὐκ ἔστιν ἡμῖν ἡ πάλη πρὸς αἷμα καὶ σάρκα, ἀλλὰ πρὸς τὰς ἀρχάς, πρὸς τὰς **ἐξουσίας**, πρὸς τοὺς κοσμοκράτορας τοῦ σκότους τοῦ αἰῶνος τούτου, πρὸς τὰ πνευματικὰ τῆς πονηρίας ἐν τοῖς ἐπουρανίοις. [GNS] ὅτι οὐκ ἔστιν ἡμῖν ἡ πάλη πρὸς αἷμα καὶ σάρκα, ἀλλὰ πρὸς τὰς ἀρχάς, πρὸς τὰς **ἐξουσίας**, πρὸς τοὺς κοσμοκράτορας τοῦ σκότους τούτου, πρὸς τὰ πνευματικὰ τῆς πονηρίας ἐν τοῖς ἐπουρανίοις. [GNT]	

#2989
Powers Of...World
 	
Rulers...of...world–KJV
World forces–NASB
Powers of...world–NIV
Rulers..of...age–NKJV
Mighty powers...who rule this world–NLT
 	
POSB REFERENCE
(Eph.6:12)
Note 3, point 5
	κοσμοκράτορας = *kosmokratoras*
	Pronunciation: [kos-mok-rat'-ore-ahs]
	Parsing (part of speech): noun
	  Case—accusative
	  Gender—masculine
	  Number—plural
	  Stem or root—from **κοσμοκράτωρ**, ορος
	Concordance References:
	⇒ Strong's #2888 kosmokratör
	⇒ NIV #3179 kosmokratör
	⇒ NASB #2888 kosmokratör
	
	Ephes. 6:12
	For we wrestle not against flesh and blood, but against principalities, against powers, against the **rulers** of the darkness **of** this **world**, against spiritual wickedness in high places. [KJV]
	
	For our struggle is not against flesh and blood, but against the rulers, against the powers, against the **world forces** of this darkness, against the spiritual forces of wickedness in the heavenly places. [NASB]
	
	For our struggle is not against flesh and blood, but against the rulers, against the authorities, against the **powers of** this dark **world** and against the spiritual forces of evil in the heavenly realms. [NIV]
	
	For we do not wrestle against flesh and blood, but against principalities, against powers, against the **rulers** of the darkness **of** this **age**, against spiritual *hosts* of wickedness in the heavenly *places*. [NKJV]
	
	For we are not fighting against people made of flesh and blood, but against the evil rulers and authorities of the unseen world, against those **mighty powers** of darkness **who rule this world**, and against wicked spirits in the heavenly realms. [NLT]
	
	ὅτι οὐκ ἔστιν ἡμῖν ἡ πάλη πρὸς αἷμα καὶ σάρκα, ἀλλὰ πρὸς τὰς ἀρχάς, πρὸς τὰς ἐξουσίας, πρὸς τοὺς **κοσμοκράτορας** τοῦ σκότους τοῦ αἰῶνος τούτου, πρὸς τὰ πνευματικὰ τῆς πονηρίας ἐν τοῖς ἐπουρανίοις. [GNS]
	
	ὅτι οὐκ ἔστιν ἡμῖν ἡ πάλη πρὸς αἷμα καὶ σάρκα, ἀλλὰ πρὸς τὰς ἀρχάς, πρὸς τὰς ἐξουσίας, πρὸς τοὺς **κοσμοκράτορας** τοῦ σκότους τούτου, πρὸς τὰ πνευματικὰ τῆς πονηρίας ἐν τοῖς ἐπουρανίοις. [GNT]
		Powers of the world, rulers of the world, world forces, the mighty powers who rule this world.
		
		Practical Application
		Who is this? It refers to Satan and his demons. The forces of evil are the rulers of darkness, the rulers who blind the minds of men lest they believe the glorious gospel of eternal salvation.
		
		F.F. Bruce words it well:
		  Satan and his demonic forces *"rank among the highest angel-princes in the hierarchy of the heavenly places, yet all of them owe their existence to Christ, through whom they were created [Col. 1:16], and who is accordingly the head of all principality and power' [Col. 2:10]. But some at least of the principalities and powers have embarked upon rebellion against God and not only seek to force men to pay them the worship that is due to Him, but launched an assault upon the crucified Christ at a time when they thought they had Him at their mercy. But He, far from suffering their assault without resistance, grappled with them and overcame them, stripping them of their armour and driving them before Him in His triumphal procession [Col. 2:15]. Thus the hostile powers of evil which Christians must encounter are already vanquished powers, but it is only through faith-union with the victorious Christ that Christians can make His triumph theirs"* (The Epistle to the Ephesians, p.127f).

#2990
Practice
 	
Keep–KJV
Practice–NASB
Observe–NIV
Keep–NKJV
Obey–NLT
 	
POSB REFERENCE
(Romans 2:25-27; esp. v.25)
Note 3
	πράσσῃς = *prassës*
	Pronunciation: [pras'-sayce]
	Parsing (part of speech): verb
	  Mood—subjunctive
	  Tense—present
	  Voice—active
	  Person—2nd person
	  Number—singular
	  Stem or root—from **πράσσω**
	Concordance References:
	⇒ Strong's #4238 prassö
	⇒ NIV #4556 prassö
	⇒ NASB #4238 prassö
	
	Romans 2:25
	For circumcision verily profiteth, if thou **keep** the law: but if thou be a breaker of the law, thy circumcision
		Do, practice, keep, observe, obey, perform, play.
		
		Practical Application
		The religionist believes that a ritual is the way to secure God's praise or approval (for example, circumcision, baptism, and church membership). Just take the word circumcision and substitute whatever ritual a church says is essential for salvation and the meaning of the passage becomes clear. For example, take the ritual of church membership.
		
		"Church membership profits a man if he keeps the law: but if he breaks the law, his

ENGLISH WORD	GREEK WORD AND VERSE	THE WORD MEANS...
	is made uncircumcision. [KJV] For indeed circumcision is of value, if you **practice** the Law; but if you are a transgressor of the Law, your circumcision has become uncircumcision. [NASB] Circumcision has value if you **observe** the law, but if you break the law, you have become as though you had not been circumcised. [NIV] For circumcision is indeed profitable if you **keep** the law; but if you are a breaker of the law, your circumcision has become uncircumcision. [NKJV] The Jewish ceremony of circumcision is worth something only if you **obey** God's law. But if you don't obey God's law, you are no better off than an uncircumcised Gentile. [NLT] περιτομὴ μὲν γὰρ ὠφελεῖ, ἐὰν νόμον **πράσσῃς**· ἐὰν δὲ παραβάτης νόμου ᾖς, ἡ περιτομή σου ἀκροβυστία γέγονεν. [GNS] περιτομὴ μὲν γὰρ ὠφελεῖ ἐὰν νόμον **πράσσῃς**· ἐὰν δὲ παραβάτης νόμου ᾖς, ἡ περιτομή σου ἀκροβυστία γέγονεν. [GNT]	church membership is made or counted as unchurch membership." If a religionist does not practice (*prassës*) God's law and Word, then his ritual does not count. The man becomes... • unbaptized • unchurched • uncircumcised • unwhatever The point is obedience, not ritual. A person is acceptable to God because he lives for God and obeys Him, not because he has undergone some ritual.
#2991 **Practice Deceit–Practiced Deceit** Used deceit–KJV Keep deceiving–NASB **Practice deceit–NIV** **Practiced deceit–NKJV** Filled with lies–NLT **POSB REFERENCE** (Rom.3:13-14; esp. v.13) Note 3, point 2	ἐδολιοῦσαν = *edoliousan* Pronunciation: [eh-dol-ee-oo'-sahn] Parsing (part of speech): verb 　Mood—indicative 　Tense—imperfect 　Voice—active 　Person—3rd person 　Number—plural 　Stem or root—from δολιόω Concordance References: ⇒ Strong's #1387 dolioö ⇒ NIV #1514 dolioö ⇒ NASB #1387 dolioö **Romans 3:13** Their throat is an open sepulchre; with their tongues they have **used deceit**; the poison of asps is under their lips: [KJV] "Their throat is an open grave, With their tongues they **keep deceiving**," "The poison of asps is under their lips"; [NASB] "Their throats are open graves; their tongues **practice deceit**." "The poison of vipers is on their lips." [NIV] "Their throat is an open tomb; With their tongues they have **practiced deceit**"; "The poison of asps is under their lips"; [NKJV] "Their talk is foul, like the stench from an open grave. Their speech is **filled with lies**." "The poison of a deadly snake drips from their lips." [NLT] τάφος ἀνεῳγμένος ὁ λάρυγξ αὐτῶν, ταῖς γλώσσαις αὐτῶν **ἐδολιοῦσαν**· ἰὸς ἀσπίδων ὑπὸ τὰ χείλη αὐτῶν· [GNS] τάφος ἀνεῳγμένος ὁ λάρυγξ αὐτῶν, ταῖς γλώσσαις αὐτῶν **ἐδολιοῦσαν**, ἰὸς ἀσπίδων ὑπὸ τὰ χείλη αὐτῶν· [GNT]	To practice deceit; to be filled with lies; to be treacherous **Practical Application** A sinful tongue is deceitful (Romans 3:13; cp. Psalm 5:9): "They practice deceit." The Hebrew says, "They make smooth their tongue." A deceitful person has... • a false tongue • a lying tongue • a cheating tongue • a deluding tongue • a flattering tongue • a misleading tongue • a treacherous tongue • a beguiling tongue • a smooth talking tongue The word "deceit" (*edoliousan*) is continuous action: "They kept on practicing deceit." Man is not only guilty of deceiving, but of constantly deceiving. He is constantly hiding and camouflaging his true thoughts and feelings and behavior, seeking to protect himself or to get whatever he is after.
#2992 **Praise** Magnify–KJV Exalts–NASB Glorifies–NIV Magnifies–NKJV **Praise–NLT** **POSB REFERENCE** (Lk.1:46) Note 1, point 2	Μεγαλύνει = *Megalunei* Pronunciation: [meg-al-oo'-neh-ee] Parsing (part of speech): verb 　Mood—indicative 　Tense—present 　Voice—active 　Person—3rd person 　Number—singular 　Stem or root—from μεγαλύνω Concordance References: ⇒ Strong's #3170 megalunö ⇒ NIV #3486 megalunö ⇒ NASB #3170 megalunö **Luke 1:46** And Mary said, My soul doth **magnify** the Lord, [KJV]	To exalt; to magnify; to glorify; to praise; to declare the greatness of. **Practical Application** The idea is habitual; that is, it was the habit of Mary's soul to praise or glorify the Lord.

ENGLISH WORD	GREEK WORD AND VERSE	THE WORD MEANS...

#3008
Preached–
Preaching The
Word
 	
Preaching the word–
KJV
Preaching the word–
NASB
Preached the word–
NIV
Preaching the word–
NKJV
Preaching the good
news about
Jesus–NLT
 	
POSB
REFERENCE
(Acts 8:4)
Note 4, point 2
	εὐαγγελιζόμενοι τὸν λόγον = euaggelizomenoi ton logon
	Pronunciation: [yoo-ang-ghel-id'-zo-men-o-ee ton log'-on]
	Parsing euaggelizomenoi (part of speech): verb
	  Mood—participle
	  Tense—present
	  Voice—middle
	  Case—nominative
	  Gender—masculine
	  Number—plural
	  Stem or root—from εὐαγγελίζω
	Parsing logon (part of speech): noun
	  Case—accusative
	  Gender—masculine
	  Number—singular
	  Stem or root—from λόγος, ου
	Concordance References:
	⇒ Strong's #2097 euaggelizö + 3588 ho + 3056 logos
	⇒ NIV #2294 euaggelizö [preached] + 3836 ho [the] + 3364 logos [word]
	⇒ NASB #2097 euaggelizö + 3588 ho + 3056 logos
	
	Acts 8:4
	Therefore they that were scattered abroad went every where **preaching the word**. [KJV]
	Therefore, those who had been scattered went about **preaching the word**. [NASB]
	Those who had been scattered **preached the word** wherever they went. [NIV]
	Therefore those who were scattered went everywhere **preaching the word**. [NKJV]
	But the believers who had fled Jerusalem went every-where **preaching the Good News about Jesus**. [NLT]
	οἱ μὲν οὖν διασπαρέντες διῆλθον, **εὐαγγελιζόμενοι τὸν λόγον**. [GNS]
	Οἱ μὲν οὖν διασπαρέντες διῆλθον **εὐαγγελιζόμενοι τὸν λόγον**. [GNT]
		To preach the word; to preach the good news about Jesus Christ. It means to evangelize, to declare, to proclaim, to preach the Word of God, the gospel of the Lord Jesus Christ.
		
		Practical Application
		The lay believers who were scattered abroad went everywhere preaching Christ. Note two significant facts.
		1. The believers were "scattered abroad" (dias-parentes): dispersed, scattered about just as seed is sown or scattered throughout a field. God was using the evil of the world to spread His followers and message all over the world.
		2. Note that the scattered believers did not hide in secrecy and fearful silence. They preached the Word wherever they went. "Preaching the word" (euaggelizomenoi ton logon) means to evangelize, to declare, to proclaim, to preach the Word of God, the gospel of the Lord Jesus Christ. (See POSB Deeper Study #2, Preaching—Acts 11:19-30 for more discussion.)

#3009
Preached The
Gospel
 	
Preached the Gospel–
KJV
Preached the Gospel–
NASB
Preached the good
news–NIV
Preached the gospel–
NKJV
Preaching the Good
News–NLT
 	
POSB
REFERENCE
(Acts 14:21)
Note 1, point 1
	Εὐαγγελισάμενοί = Euaggelisamenoi
	Pronunciation: [yoo-ang-ghel-i-sah'-men-o-ee]
	Parsing (part of speech): verb
	  Mood—participle
	  Tense—aorist
	  Voice—middle
	  Case—nominative
	  Gender—masculine
	  Number—plural
	  Stem or root—from εὐαγγελίζω
	Concordance References:
	⇒ Strong's #2097 euaggelizö
	⇒ NIV #2294 euaggelizö
	⇒ NASB #2097 euaggelizö
	
	Acts 14:21
	And when they had **preached the gospel** to that city, and had taught many, they returned again to Lystra, and to Iconium, and Antioch, [KJV]
	And after they had **preached the gospel** to that city and had made many disciples, they returned to Lystra and to Iconium and to Antioch, [NASB]
	They **preached the good news** in that city and won a large number of disciples. Then they returned to Lystra, Iconium and Antioch, [NIV]
	And when they had **preached the gospel** to that city and made many disciples, they returned to Lystra, Iconium, and Antioch, [NKJV]
	After **preaching the Good News** in Derbe and making many disciples, Paul and Barnabas returned again
		To preach the good news; to preach the gospel.
		
		Practical Application
		Note two challenging facts.
		1. The ministry of the preachers (Paul and Barnabas) was to preach the gospel (Euaggelisamenoi). And that is exactly what they did.
		2. The ministry of the preachers (Paul and Barnabas) was to make disciples. The words "had taught many" (matheteusantes hikanous) mean had made many disciples. They not only preached, but they took the believers and made disciples out of them (see POSB note, Discipleship—Acts 13:5-6 for discussion).

ENGLISH WORD	GREEK WORD AND VERSE	THE WORD MEANS...
	to Lystra, Iconium, and Antioch of Pisidia, [NLT] εὐαγγελισάμενοί τε τὴν πόλιν ἐκείνην καὶ μαθητεύσαντες ἱκανούς, ὑπέστρεψαν εἰς τὴν Λύστραν καὶ Ἰκόνιον καὶ Ἀντιόχειαν, [GNS] Εὐαγγελισάμενοί τε τὴν πόλιν ἐκείνην καὶ μαθητεύσαντες ἱκανοὺς ὑπέστρεψαν εἰς τὴν Λύστραν καὶ εἰς Ἰκόνιον καὶ εἰς Ἀντιόχειαν [GNT]	

#3010
Preacher
 	
Preacher–KJV
Preacher–NASB
Herald–NIV
Preacher–NKJV
Preacher–NLT
 	
**POSB
REFERENCE**
(1 Tim.2:3-7; esp. v.7)
Note 3, point 5
	κῆρυξ = *kērux*
	Pronunciation: [kay'-roox]
	Parsing (part of speech): noun
	   Case—nominative
	   Gender—masculine
	   Number—singular
	   Stem or root—from κῆρυξ, υκος
	Concordance References:
	⇒ Strong's #2783 kērux
	⇒ NIV #3061 kērux
	⇒ NASB #2783 kērux
	
	1 Tim. 2:7
	Whereunto I am ordained a **preacher**, and an apostle, (I speak the truth in Christ, and lie not;) a teacher of the Gentiles in faith and verity. [KJV]
	And for this I was appointed a **preacher** and an apostle (I am telling the truth, I am not lying) as a teacher of the Gentiles in faith and truth. [NASB]
	And for this purpose I was appointed a **herald** and an apostle—I am telling the truth, I am not lying—and a teacher of the true faith to the Gentiles. [NIV]
	For which I was appointed a **preacher** and an apostle—I am speaking the truth in Christ *and* not lying—a teacher of the Gentiles in faith and truth. [NKJV]
	And I have been chosen—this is the absolute truth—as a **preacher** and apostle to teach the Gentiles about faith and truth. [NLT]
	εἰς ὃ ἐτέθην ἐγὼ **κῆρυξ** καὶ ἀπόστολος -- ἀλήθειαν λέγω ἐν Χριστῷ, οὐ ψεύδομαι -- διδάσκαλος ἐθνῶν ἐν πίστει καὶ ἀληθείᾳ. [GNS]
	εἰς ὃ ἐτέθην ἐγὼ **κῆρυξ** καὶ ἀπόστολος, ἀλήθειαν λέγω οὐ ψεύδομαι, διδάσκαλος ἐθνῶν ἐν πίστει καὶ ἀληθείᾳ. [GNT]
		Herald, preacher, an ambassador appointed by a king to go forth to proclaim the message of the king.
		
		Practical Application
		Ministers are ordained or appointed to proclaim the salvation of God. God had appointed Paul to be a preacher (*kērux*): a herald, an ambassador who was appointed by a king to go forth to proclaim the message of the king. The minister is a preacher who is sent forth by God to preach the truth about Jesus Christ...
		• that He is the Mediator between God and men.
		• that He has given Himself as a ransom for all.

#3011
Preaching
 	
Preaching–KJV
Proclaiming–NASB
Preaching–NIV
Preaching–NKJV
Announcing–NLT
 	
**POSB
REFERENCE**
(Mt.9:35)
Deeper Study #1
	κηρύσσων = *kērussōn*
	Pronunciation: [kay-roos'-sown]
	Parsing (part of speech): verb
	   Mood—participle
	   Tense—present
	   Voice—active
	   Case—nominative
	   Gender—masculine
	   Number—singular
	   Stem or root— from κηρύσσω
	Concordance References:
	⇒ Strong's #2784 kērussō
	⇒ NIV #3062 kērussō
	⇒ NASB #2784 kērussō
	
	Matthew 9:35
	And Jesus went about all the cities and villages, teaching in their synagogues, and **preaching** the gospel of the kingdom, and healing every sickness and every disease among the people. [KJV]
	And Jesus was going about all the cities and the villages, teaching in their synagogues, and **proclaiming** the gospel of the kingdom, and healing every kind of disease and every kind of sickness. [NASB]
	Jesus went through all the towns and villages, teaching in their synagogues, **preaching** the good news of the kingdom and healing every disease and sickness. [NIV]
	Then Jesus went about all the cities and villages, teaching in their synagogues, **preaching** the gospel of the kingdom, and healing every sickness and every dis-
		To proclaim, preach, announce, herald, publish.
		
		Practical Application
		The preacher is a herald who comes in the name of the King and who represents the King (cp. 2 Cor. 5:20). He comes to proclaim the message of the King and *only* the message of the King. He has no message of his own. If and when he begins to proclaim his own message, he is no longer the herald or the spokesman of the King.

ENGLISH WORD	GREEK WORD AND VERSE	THE WORD MEANS...
(1 Pt.5:8) Note 1, point 2	"Therefore **keep watch**, because you do not know on what day your Lord will come. [NIV] **Watch** therefore, for you do not know what hour your Lord is coming. [NKJV] So **be prepared**, because you don't know what day your Lord is coming. [NLT] γρηγορεῖτε οὖν, ὅτι οὐκ οἴδατε ποίᾳ ὥρᾳ ὁ Κύριος ὑμῶν ἔρχεται. [GNS] γρηγορεῖτε οὖν, ὅτι οὐκ οἴδατε ποίᾳ ἡμέρᾳ ὁ κύριος ὑμῶν ἔρχεται. [GNT]	

#3026
 Preparing Us In Every Way
 	
 Perfect–KJV
 Adequate–NASB
 Thoroughly–NIV
 Complete–NKJV
 Preparing us in every way–NLT
 	
 POSB REFERENCE
 (2 Tim. 3:17)
 Note 5
	ἄρτιος = *artios*
	 Pronunciation: [ar'-tee-os]
	 Parsing (part of speech): adjective
	     Case—nominative
	     Gender—masculine
	     Number—singular
	     Stem or root—from ἄρτιος, α, ον
	 Concordance References:
	 ⇒ Strong's #739 artios
	 ⇒ NIV #787 artios
	 ⇒ NASB #739 artios
	
	 2 Tim. 3:17
	 That the man of God may be **perfect**, throughly furnished unto all good works. [KJV]
	 That the man of God may be **adequate**, equipped for every good work. [NASB]
	 So that the man of God may be **thoroughly** equipped for every good work. [NIV]
	 That the man of God may be **complete**, thoroughly equipped for every good work. [NKJV]
	 It is God's way of **preparing us in every way**, fully equipped for every good thing God wants us to do. [NLT]
	 ἵνα ἄρτιος ᾖ ὁ τοῦ Θεοῦ ἄνθρωπος, πρὸς πᾶν ἔργον ἀγαθὸν ἐξηρτισμένος. [GNS]
	 ἵνα ἄρτιος ᾖ ὁ τοῦ θεοῦ ἄνθρωπος, πρὸς πᾶν ἔργον ἀγαθὸν ἐξηρτισμένος. [GNT]
		To be thorough; to be perfect; to be adequate; to be prepared in every way. It means complete, matured, filled.
		
		 Practical Application
		 Scripture perfects a man and equips him for every good work. "Preparing us in every way" (*artios*) means complete, matured, perfect, filled. No person is complete or mature apart from Scripture. Man was made for God and he is to live by the Word of God. If he tries to live without God and His Word, man fails in life. He lives an incomplete, immature, and misfitted life. This is particularly true of the *man of God*, the person who claims to be a minister or teacher of God's Word.

#3027
 Present– Presenting
 	
 Yield–KJV
 Presenting–NASB
 Offer–NIV
 Present–NKJV
 Let–NLT
 	
 POSB REFERENCE
 (Rom.6:13)
 Deeper Study #2
	παριστάνετε = *paristanete*
	 Pronunciation: [par-is'-tahn-eh-teh]
	 Parsing (part of speech): verb
	     Mood—imperative
	     Tense—present
	     Voice—active
	     Person—2nd person
	     Number—plural
	     Stem or root—from παρίστημι and παριστάνω
	 Concordance References:
	 ⇒ Strong's #3936 paristēmi
	 ⇒ NIV #4225 paristēmi
	 ⇒ NASB #3936 paristēmi
	
	 Romans 6:13
	 Neither **yield** ye your members as instruments of unrighteousness unto sin: but yield yourselves unto God, as those that are alive from the dead, and your members as instruments of righteousness unto God. [KJV]
	 And do not go on **presenting** the members of your body to sin as instruments of unrighteousness; but present yourselves to God as those alive from the dead, and your members as instruments of righteousness to God. [NASB]
	 Do not **offer** the parts of your body to sin, as instruments of wickedness, but rather offer yourselves to God, as those who have been brought from death to life; and offer the parts of your body to him as instruments of righteousness. [NIV]
	 And do not **present** your members *as* instruments of unrighteousness to sin, but present yourselves to God as being alive from the dead, and your members *as* instruments of righteousness to God. [NKJV]
	 Do not **let** any part of your body become a tool of
		To present; to bring into one's presence; to show; to yield; to dedicate; to provide; to send; to prove. It means to offer; to put at the disposal of; to give; to grant; to turn over to.
		
		 Practical Application
		 The believer must not present the members of his body to sin. The believer is not to present the members of his body to be instruments or tools of unrighteousness. If he takes a member of his body and uses it as an instrument or tool of unrighteousness, he sins. The members of a person's body refer to all the parts of the body: the eyes, ears, mouth, tongue, hands, feet, mind, or any of the covered and dressed parts. No believer is to offer or give any part of his body over to unrighteousness. To do so is to sin. The tense is present action, so the believer is to be constantly on guard against allowing any member of his body to be presented to sin. Note: the word "presenting" has the idea of struggling. It is a struggle to fight against sin and to control and protect the members of our bodies.

ENGLISH WORD	GREEK WORD AND VERSE	THE WORD MEANS...

wickedness, to be used for sinning. Instead, give your-selves completely to God since you have been given new life. And use your whole body as a tool to do what is right for the glory of God. [NLT]

μηδὲ **παριστάνετε** τὰ μέλη ὑμῶν ὅπλα ἀδικίας τῇ ἁμαρτίᾳ· ἀλλὰ παραστήσατε ἑαυτοὺς τῷ Θεῷ ὡς ἐκ νεκρῶν ζῶντας, καὶ τὰ μέλη ὑμῶν ὅπλα δικαιοσύνης τῷ Θεῷ. [GNS]

μηδὲ **παριστάνετε** τὰ μέλη ὑμῶν ὅπλα ἀδικίας τῇ ἁμαρτίᾳ, ἀλλὰ παραστήσατε ἑαυτοὺς τῷ θεῷ ὡσεὶ ἐκ νεκρῶν ζῶντας καὶ τὰ μέλη ὑμῶν ὅπλα δικαιοσύνης τῷ θεῷ. [GNT]

#3028
Present Form

Fashion–KJV
Form–NASB
Present form–NIV
Form–NKJV
All it contains–NLT

**POSB
REFERENCE**
(1 Cor.7:29-31; esp.
v.31)
Note 3

σχῆμα = schēma
Pronunciation: [skhay'-mah]
Parsing (part of speech): noun
   Case—nominative
   Gender—neuter
   Number—singular
   Stem or root—from σχῆμα, τος
Concordance References:
⇒ Strong's #4976 schēma
⇒ NIV #5386 schēma [present form]
⇒ NASB #4976 schēma

1 Cor. 7:31

And they that use this world, as not abusing it: for the **fashion** of this world passeth away. [KJV]

And those who use the world, as though they did not make full use of it; for the **form** of this world is passing away. [NASB]

Those who use the things of the world, as if not engrossed in them. For this world in its **present form** is passing away. [NIV]

And those who use this world as not misusing *it*. For the **form** of this world is passing away. [NKJV]

Those in frequent contact with the things of the world should make good use of them without becoming attached to them, for this world and **all it contains** will pass away. [NLT]

καὶ οἱ χρώμενοι τῷ κόσμῳ τοπύτῳ, ὡς μὴ καταχρώμενοι· παράγει γὰρ τὸ **σχῆμα** τοῦ κόσμου τούτου. [GNS]

καὶ οἱ χρώμενοι τὸν κόσμον ὡς μὴ καταχρώμενοι· παράγει γὰρ τὸ **σχῆμα** τοῦ κόσμου τούτου. [GNT]

Present form, fashion, likeness, appearance, nature, all it [the world] contains.

Practical Application

It is a word taken from the theater. The world is nothing more than the passing scenes of a film that will soon end. The world is destined to end in its present form or fashion. The present state of things will cease just as the scenes of a film cease. The believer must keep this in mind; he must not live for the passing fashion of this world. He must live for eternity, keeping before his mind that time is short, ever so short.

#3029
Present Time, The

The time–KJV
The time–NASB
The present time–NIV
The time–NKJV
Time–NLT

**POSB
REFERENCE**
(Romans 13:11)
Note 1

τὸν καιρόν = ton kairon
Pronunciation: [ton kahee-ron']
Parsing (part of speech): noun
   Case—accusative
   Gender—masculine
   Number—singular
   Stem or root—from καιρός, οῦ
Concordance References:
⇒ Strong's #3588 ho + 2540 kairos
⇒ NIV #3836 ho [the] + 2789 kairos [present time]
⇒ NASB #3588 ho + 2540 kairos

Romans 13:11

And that, knowing **the time**, that now it is high time to awake out of sleep: for now is our salvation nearer than when we believed. [KJV]

And this do, knowing **the time**, that it is already the hour for you to awaken from sleep; for now salvation is nearer to us than when we believed. [NASB]

And do this, understanding **the present time**. The hour has come for you to wake up from your slumber, because our salvation is nearer now than when we first believed. [NIV]

And *do* this, knowing **the time**, that now *it is* high time to awake out of sleep; for now our salvation *is* near-er than when we *first* believed. [NKJV]

Another reason for right living is that you know how

The last time; opportunity. Time (viewed as an occasion rather than an extent), appointed or proper time, season, age. It means the critical period; the strategic or special period of time.

Practical Application

The believer is to know the time. The word "understanding" (*eridotes*) means to make sure that you know; do not dare miss knowing.

What strategic or critical period of time is meant? What is the period of human history that we must not overlook?

⇒ The day of "our salvation," the day which is nearer than when we first believed.

⇒ The day which is at hand, the day when we will meet the Lord Jesus Christ face to face.

ENGLISH WORD	G[REEK WORD]	THE WORD MEANS...
	Him God h… and Savior, to g… sins. [NKJV] Then God … hand as **Princ**… of Israel an op… God so their s… τοῦτον ὁ Θ… αὐτοῦ, δοῦνα… ἁμαρτιῶν. [G… τοῦτον ὁ θ… αὐτοῦ [τοῦ] … ἁμαρτιῶν. [G…	To declare; to show forth; to proclaim; to …peak; to tell; to publish; to set forth. **Practical Application** The very task of the believer is to witness for …od, to share the glorious message of God. …hat is that message? The message that we are … share is the glorious message of salvation. …od will deliver man out of darkness into the …ght. This is what He has done for believers. …herefore, we are to proclaim the glorious truth …at God has saved us through the Light of the …orld, through Jesus Christ Himself. He has …ved us out of the darkness of sin and death and …livered us into the light of eternity. We shall …ve forever. We are to praise God, proclaim the …lorious message of His marvelous light or sal…ation.
#3042 **Principalities** **Principalities–KJV** Rulers–NASB Rulers–NIV **Principalities–NKJV** Evil rulers–NLT **POSB REFERENCE** (Eph.6:12) Note 3, point 5	*ἀρχάς* = *arc*… Pronunciatio… Parsing (part… Case… Gend… Numb… Stem… Concordanc… ⇒ Str… ⇒ NI… ⇒ NA… For we… **principal**… darkness … high place… For ou… against th… forces of … wickedne… For o… against t… powers o… of evil in… For … against … of the … wickedn… For … and blo… the uns… ness wh… heaven… ὅτι … πρὸς … κοσμοκ… πνευμα… ὅτι … πρὸς … κοσμο… τῆς πο… …ς …ος …τὰς …, τὸ …ἔθνος …ρετὰς …ις τὸ	
#3043 **Problems Were So Great** Fainted–KJV Distressed–NASB Harassed–NIV Weary–NKJV **Problems were so great–NLT** **POSB REFERENCE** (Mt.9:36) *Deeper Study* #3	*ἐσκυλ*… Pronun… Parsi… Con… ⇒… … Samaria, and	To proclaim, make known, tell, preach. **Practical Application** This is important to note: ⇒ the first great evangelistic thrust outside Jerusalem was carried out by a *layman*. ⇒ the first time the term *evangelist* is used, it is used with a layman (Acts 21:8). Philip proclaimed (*ekërussen*) and preached Christ. Later on, he is said to preach (*euaggelizomeno*), to announce the good news, "of the kingdom of God" (Acts 8:12) [NIV]. These two great words are used in the New Testament for proclaiming the gospel. Philip, the layman, was

THE WORD MEANS...

…unt; to make a reckoning; to set…

…ctical Application
…ocess" (*sunairein*) is simple, yet …and full of meaning. God is the … a very unusual King. He is a …stly as all kings should. But He …oving, compassionate, and for…s even more than these. He is …ve and compassion—so much …ves enormous debts, debts so …y are inconceivable. …s account of His servants. He …arying times. An accounting is …rsion and on those occasions … to evaluate our lives. …an account (Matthew 18:24). … check the province and the …vince: receipts and expendi…tal improvements. The king …est in what his servant had …fts and what he had used in

…o preach; to declare; to …known.

…al Application
…r is both a picture and ser…

…hrist died for us so that we … with Him. Therefore, His …hat He has done for us and …lo for us when He returns. …of both our past and pres…t is also a picture of our …n we will be conformed to …n.

ENGLISH WORD	GREEK WORD AND VERSE	THE WORD MEANS...
	And Philip went down to the city of Samaria and began **proclaiming** Christ to them. [NASB] Philip went down to a city in Samaria and **proclaimed** the Christ there. [NIV] Then Philip went down to the city of Samaria and **preached** Christ to them. [NKJV] Philip, for example, went to the city of Samaria and **told** the people there about the Messiah. [NLT] Φίλιππος δὲ κατελθὼν εἰς πόλιν τῆς Σαμαρείας, ἐκήρυσσεν αὐτοῖς τὸν Χριστόν. [GNS] Φίλιππος δὲ κατελθὼν εἰς [τὴν] πόλιν τῆς Σαμαρείας ἐκήρυσσεν αὐτοῖς τὸν Χριστόν. [GNT]	a true servant of the Lord, a lay believer who preached Christ. He was a layman who dedicated his time and energy to proclaiming the things concerning the kingdom of God.
#3048 **Proclaiming** Preaching–KJV **Proclaiming–NASB** Preaching–NIV Preaching–NKJV Announcing–NLT **POSB REFERENCE** (Mt.9:35) *Deeper Study #1*	κηρύσσων = *kērussōn* Pronunciation: [kay-roos'-sown] Parsing (part of speech): verb 　Mood—participle 　Tense—present 　Voice—active 　Case—nominative 　Gender—masculine 　Number—singular 　Stem or root— from κηρύσσω Concordance References: 　⇒　Strong's #2784 kērussō 　⇒　NIV #3062 kērussō 　⇒　NASB #2784 kērussō **Matthew 9:35** And Jesus went about all the cities and villages, teaching in their synagogues, and **preaching** the gospel of the kingdom, and healing every sickness and every disease among the people. [KJV] And Jesus was going about all the cities and the villages, teaching in their synagogues, and **proclaiming** the gospel of the kingdom, and healing every kind of disease and every kind of sickness. [NASB] Jesus went through all the towns and villages, teaching in their synagogues, **preaching** the good news of the kingdom and healing every disease and sickness. [NIV] Then Jesus went about all the cities and villages, teaching in their synagogues, **preaching** the gospel of the kingdom, and healing every sickness and every disease among the people. [NKJV] Jesus traveled through all the cities and villages of that area, teaching in the synagogues and **announcing** the Good News about the Kingdom. And wherever he went, he healed people of every sort of disease and illness. [NLT] Καὶ περιῆγεν ὁ Ἰησοῦς τὰς πόλεις πάσας καὶ τὰς κώμας, διδάσκων ἐν ταῖς συναγωγαῖς αὐτῶν, καὶ **κηρύσσων** τὸ εὐαγγέλιον τῆς βασιλείας, καὶ θεραπεύων πᾶσαν νόσον καὶ πᾶσαν μαλακίαν ἐν τῷ λαῷ. [GNS] Καὶ περιῆγεν ὁ Ἰησοῦς τὰς πόλεις πάσας καὶ τὰς κώμας διδάσκων ἐν ταῖς συναγωγαῖς αὐτῶν καὶ **κηρύσσων** τὸ εὐαγγέλιον τῆς βασιλείας καὶ θεραπεύων πᾶσαν νόσον καὶ πᾶσαν μαλακίαν. [GNT]	To proclaim, preach, announce, herald, publish. **Practical Application** 　The preacher is a herald who comes in the name of the King and who represents the King (cp. 2 Cor. 5:20). He comes to proclaim the message of the King and *only* the message of the King. He has no message of his own. If and when he begins to proclaim his own message, he is no longer the herald or the spokesman of the King.
#3049 **Proclaiming–Proclaiming The Good News** Preaching–KJV Proclaiming–NASB **Proclaiming the good news–NIV** Preaching–NKJV Announce–NLT	κηρύσσων = *kērussōn* Pronunciation: [kay-roos'-sown] Parsing (part of speech): verb 　Mood—participle 　Tense—present 　Voice—active 　Case—nominative 　Gender—masculine 　Number—singular 　Stem or root—from κηρύσσω Concordance References: 　⇒　Strong's #2784 kērussō 　⇒　NIV #3062 kērussō NOTE: Repeated Greek word. The NIV translates with NIV #2294 euaggelizō as "proclaiming the good news." See	To preach glad tidings: to announce glad tidings; to declare good news; to bring the glad tidings; to proclaim the gospel of Jesus Christ. **Practical Application** 　In this Scripture, Jesus began a tour of nearby cities and villages "proclaiming the good news." He had an ache, a compassion for all and was not willing that any should perish. He sought everyone within His reach. Note that He did not seek the limelight of the cities. He went out into the villages of the countryside as well. He had been sent to preach, and He preached anywhere and everywhere He could reach. The whole thrust of

ENGLISH WORD	GREEK WORD AND VERSE	THE WORD MEANS...
		Bible reveals how to live "soberly, righteously, and godly in this present world; looking for that blessed hope, and the glorious appearing of the great God and our Saviour Jesus Christ" (Tit.2:12-13). (Cp. 2 Tim.2:14-15; 1 Pet.2:2-3; Deut.1:18; Ps.119:11).

#3057
Prohibit
 	
Bind–KJV
Bind–NASB
Bind–NIV
Bind–NKJV
Prohibit–NLT
 	
POSB
REFERENCE
(Mt.18:17-18; esp. v.18)
Note 2, point 2
	δήσητε = dēsëte
	Pronunciation: [day'-say-teh]
	Parsing (part of speech): verb
	   Mood—subjunctive
	   Tense—aorist
	   Voice—active
	   Person—2nd person
	   Number—plural
	   Stem or root—from δέω
	Concordance References:
	  ⇒ Strong's #1210 deö
	  ⇒ NIV #1313 deö
	  ⇒ NASB #1210 deö
	
	Matthew 18:18
	Verily I say unto you, Whatsoever ye shall **bind** on earth shall be bound in heaven: and whatsoever ye shall loose on earth shall be loosed in heaven. [KJV]
	"Truly I say to you, whatever you shall **bind** on earth shall be bound in heaven; and whatever you loose on earth shall be loosed in heaven. [NASB]
	"I tell you the truth, whatever you **bind** on earth will be bound in heaven, and whatever you loose on earth will be loosed in heaven. [NIV]
	Assuredly, I say to you, whatever you **bind** on earth will be bound in heaven, and whatever you loose on earth will be loosed in heaven. [NKJV]
	I tell you this: Whatever you **prohibit** on earth is prohibited in heaven, and whatever you allow on earth is allowed in heaven. [NLT]
	Ἀμὴν λέγω ὑμῖν, ὅσα ἐὰν **δήσητε** ἐπὶ τῆς γῆς, ἔσται δεδεμένα ἐν τῷ οὐρανῷ· καὶ ὅσα ἐὰν λύσητε ἐπὶ τῆς γῆς, ἔσται λελυμένα ἐν τῷ οὐρανῷ. [GNS]
	Ἀμὴν λέγω ὑμῖν· ὅσα ἐὰν **δήσητε** ἐπὶ τῆς γῆς ἔσται δεδεμένα ἐν οὐρανῷ, καὶ ὅσα ἐὰν λύσητε ἐπὶ τῆς γῆς ἔσται λελυμένα ἐν οὐρανῷ. [GNT]
		To bind or tie as with a rope, chain, or cord; a loss of spiritual freedom.
		
		Practical Application
		What does it really mean to "prohibit" someone on earth? One thing is sure—it cannot mean that any man or any church has the power to forgive or not forgive sins. No man or church has the power to doom or save and set free a person.
		What it probably means is this: when a brother chooses sin and refuses to be reconciled after the church reaches out after him, he is lost to the church. There is no relationship between him and the church. The church failed to reach him; therefore, he is *prohibited on the earth* and to being treated as an outsider. Thus heaven—God Himself—will allow him to be prohibited by sin as an outsider just as the church prohibits (counts) him. Similarly, if he is ever reached by the church and "allowed to be free" from the bondage of sin, heaven will allow him to be free. God will receive him back as a redeemed brother, as an insider.

#3058
Prominent
 	
Honourable–KJV
Prominent–NASB
Prominent–NIV
Prominent–NKJV
Prominent–NLT
 	
POSB
REFERENCE
(Acts 17:12)
Note 6
	εὐσχημόνων = euschēmön
	Pronunciation: [yoo-skhay'-mown]
	Parsing (part of speech): adjective
	   Case—genitive
	   Gender—feminine
	   Number—plural
	   Stem or root—from εὐσχήμων, ον
	Concordance References:
	  ⇒ Strong's #2158 euschēmön
	  ⇒ NIV #2363 euschēmön
	  ⇒ NASB #2158 euschēmön
	
	Acts 17:12
	Therefore many of them believed; also of **honourable** women which were Greeks, and of men, not a few. [KJV]
	Many of them therefore believed, along with a number of **prominent** Greek women and men. [NASB]
	Many of the Jews believed, as did also a number of **prominent** Greek women and many Greek men. [NIV]
	Therefore many of them believed, and also not a few of the Greeks, **prominent** women as well as men. [NKJV]
	As a result, many Jews believed, as did some of the **prominent** Greek women and many men. [NLT]
	πολλοὶ μὲν οὖν ἐξ αὐτῶν ἐπίστευσαν, καὶ τῶν Ἑλληνίδων γυναικῶν τῶν **εὐσχημόνων** καὶ ἀνδρῶν οὐκ ὀλίγοι. [GNS]
	πολλοὶ μὲν οὖν ἐξ αὐτῶν ἐπίστευσαν καὶ τῶν Ἑλληνίδων γυναικῶν τῶν **εὐσχημόνων** καὶ ἀνδρῶν οὐκ ὀλίγοι. [GNT]
		Prominent, honorable; a person of high standing.
		
		Practical Application
		The word "prominent" means both good character and respectable and influential citizens.

ENGLISH WORD	GREEK WORD AND VERSE	THE WORD MEANS...
#3059 **Proof Of** Tried–KJV **Proof of–NASB** Proved genuine–NIV Tested–NKJV Tested–NLT **POSB REFERENCE** (1 Pt.1:7) Note 2, point 1	δοκίμιον = dokimion Pronunciation: [dok-im-ee'-on] Parsing (part of speech): noun Case—nominative Gender—neuter Number—singular Stem or root—from δοκίμιον, ου Concordance References: ⇒ Strong's #1383 dokimion ⇒ NIV #1510 dokimion ⇒ NASB #1383 dokimion **1 Peter 1:7** That the trial of your faith, being much more precious than of gold that perisheth, though it be **tried** with fire, might be found unto praise and honour and glory at the appearing of Jesus Christ: [KJV] That the **proof of** your faith, being more precious than gold which is perishable, even though tested by fire, may be found to result in praise and glory and honor at the revelation of Jesus Christ; [NASB] These have come so that your faith—of greater worth than gold, which perishes even though refined by fire—may be **proved genuine** and may result in praise, glory and honor when Jesus Christ is revealed. [NIV] That the genuineness of your faith, *being* much more precious than gold that perishes, though it is **tested** by fire, may be found to praise, honor, and glory at the revelation of Jesus Christ, [NKJV] These trials are only to test your faith, to show that it is strong and pure. It is being **tested** as fire tests and purifies gold—and your faith is far more precious to God than mere gold. So if your faith remains strong after being tried by fiery trials, it will bring you much praise and glory and honor on the day when Jesus Christ is revealed to the whole world. [NLT] ἵνα τὸ **δοκίμιον** ὑμῶν τῆς πίστεως πολυ τιμιώτερον χρυσίου τοῦ ἀπολλυμένου, διὰ πυρὸς δὲ δοκιμαζομένου, εὑρεθῇ εἰς ἔπαινον καὶ τιμὴν καὶ δόξαν, ἐν ἀποκαλύψει Ἰησοῦ Χριστοῦ· [GNS] ἵνα τὸ **δοκίμιον** ὑμῶν τῆς πίστεως πολυτιμότερον χρυσίου τοῦ ἀπολλυμένου διὰ πυρὸς δὲ δοκιμαζομένου, εὑρεθῇ εἰς ἔπαινον καὶ δόξαν καὶ τιμὴν ἐν ἀποκαλύψει Ἰησοῦ Χριστοῦ· [GNT]	Refined, tried, tested, proved genuine. The word "proof of" (*dokimion*) means to prove; to test; to strengthen; to show that your faith is genuine (A.T. Robertson. *Word Pictures in the New Testament*, Vol.6, p.83). **Practical Application** It is just like gold. Gold has to be put to the fire in order to clean out all the impurities and dross and to make it pure and clean. Now note what this verse says: we are much more precious than gold. Gold perishes, but not believers. Believers are to live forever. Therefore, if gold has to be put to the fire to be made clean and pure, how much more do we? The point is striking: God uses the fire of trials and temptations for a good purpose. He uses them to make us clean and pure and to make us trust Him more and more. ⇒ When we are faced with some trial or temptation, we draw nearer to God. We cry out to God more than when things go well. We even tend to clean up our lives in order to secure His help as we go through the trial. We just live more pure, clean, and righteous lives. In fact, the greater the trial and temptation, the more we see that we need God. And the more we see our need for God, the closer we usually draw to Him; and the closer we draw to Him, the cleaner we live. The fire of trials causes us to live more pure and clean lives and to learn to trust God more and more. This is a most wonderful point: our trials and temptations are purposeful. God uses them to make us much more pure and to stir us to draw closer and closer to Him and to trust Him more and more. We become stronger persons through trials—much stronger, much more steadfast, persevering, and enduring.
#3060 **Proofs, Convincing–Proofs–Proved** **Proofs–KJV** **Proofs–NASB** **Convincing proofs–NIV** **Proofs–NKJV** **Proved–NLT** **POSB REFERENCE** (Acts 1:3) Note 3, point 2a	τεκμηρίοις = tekmēriois Pronunciation: [tek-may'-ree-ois] Parsing (part of speech): noun Case—dative Gender—neuter Number—plural Stem or root—from τεκμήριον Concordance References: ⇒ Strong's #5039 tekmērion ⇒ NIV #5447 tekmērion ⇒ NASB #5039 tekmērion **Acts 1:3** To whom also he showed himself alive after his passion by many infallible **proofs**, being seen of them forty days, and speaking of the things pertaining to the kingdom of God: [KJV] To these He also presented Himself alive, after His suffering, by many convincing **proofs**, appearing to them over a period of forty days, and speaking of the things concerning the kingdom of God. [NASB] After his suffering, he showed himself to these men and gave many **convincing proofs** that he was alive. He appeared to them over a period of forty days and spoke about the kingdom of God. [NIV] To whom He also presented Himself alive after His suffering by many infallible **proofs**, being seen by them during forty days and speaking of the things pertaining to	Proofs, convincing proofs; to prove. **Practical Application** The word "convincing proofs" (*tekmēriois*) means positive proof; infallible proof; sure signs and ways.

ENGLISH WORD	GREEK WORD AND VERSE	THE WORD MEANS...
	the kingdom of God. [NKJV] During the forty days after his crucifixion, he appeared to the apostles from time to time and **proved** to them in many ways that he was actually alive. On these occasions he talked to them about the Kingdom of God. [NLT] οἷς καὶ παρέστησεν ἑαυτὸν ζῶντα μετὰ τὸ παθεῖν αὐτὸν ἐν πολλοῖς **τεκμηρίοις**, δι᾿ ἡμερῶν τεσσεράκοντα ὀπτανόμενος αὐτοῖς, καὶ λέγων τὰ περὶ τῆς βασιλείας τοῦ Θεοῦ. [GNS] οἷς καὶ παρέστησεν ἑαυτὸν ζῶντα μετὰ τὸ παθεῖν αὐτὸν ἐν πολλοῖς **τεκμηρίοις**, δι᾿ ἡμερῶν τεσσεράκοντα ὀπτανόμενος αὐτοῖς καὶ λέγων τὰ περὶ τῆς βασιλείας τοῦ θεοῦ· [GNT]	
#3061 **Properly** Honestly–KJV **Properly–NASB** Decently–NIV **Properly–NKJV** Decent and true–NLT **POSB REFERENCE** (Rom.13:13) Note 4	εὐσχημόνως = *euschēmonōs* Pronunciation: [yoo-skhay-mon'-oce] Parsing (part of speech): adjective adverb 　Stem or root—from εὐσχημόνως Concordance References: ⇒　NIV #2361 euschēmonōs ⇒　Strong's #2156 euschēmonōs ⇒　NASB #2156 euschēmonōs **Romans 13:13** Let us walk **honestly**, as in the day; not in rioting and drunkenness, not in chambering and wantonness, not in strife and envying. [KJV] Let us behave **properly** as in the day, not in carousing and drunkenness, not in sexual promiscuity and sensuality, not in strife and jealousy. [NASB] Let us behave **decently**, as in the daytime, not in orgies and drunkenness, not in sexual immorality and debauchery, not in dissension and jealousy. [NIV] Let us walk **properly**, as in the day, not in revelry and drunkenness, not in lewdness and lust, not in strife and envy. [NKJV] We should be **decent and true** in everything we do, so that everyone can approve of our behavior. Don't participate in wild parties and getting drunk, or in adultery and immoral living, or in fighting and jealousy. [NLT] ὡς ἐν ἡμέρᾳ, **εὐσχημόνως** περιπατήσωμεν, μὴ κώμοις καὶ μέθαις, μὴ κοίταις καὶ ἀσελγείαις, μὴ ἔριδι καὶ ζήλῳ. [GNS] ὡς ἐν ἡμέρᾳ **εὐσχημόνως** περιπατήσωμεν, μὴ κώμοις καὶ μέθαις, μὴ κοίταις καὶ ἀσελγείαις, μὴ ἔριδι καὶ ζήλῳ, [GNT]	Decently, honestly, properly; decent and true; honorable, noble, respectable. **Practical Application** The believer is to walk decently before God. He is to live a life of honesty, decency, and nobility. He is to live a life of honor and honesty before God. He is to walk in the day, not hiding nor trying to hide anything. This Scripture gives six sins in particular which the believer is to cast off and turn away from—forever.
#3062 **Prophesies– Prophesieth** Prophesieth–KJV Prophesies–NASB Prophesies–NIV Prophesies–NKJV Prophesies–NLT **POSB REFERENCE** (1 Cor.14:3) *Deeper Study #1*	προφητεύων = *prophēteuōn* Pronunciation: [prof-ate-yoo'-own] Parsing (part of speech): verb 　Mood—participle 　Tense—present 　Voice—active 　Case—nominative 　Gender—masculine 　Number—singular 　Stem or root—from προφητεύω Concordance References: ⇒　Strong's #4395 prophēteuō ⇒　NIV #4736 prophēteuō ⇒　NASB #4395 prophēteuō **1 Cor. 14:3** But he that **prophesieth** speaketh unto men to edification, and exhortation, and comfort. [KJV] But one who **prophesies** speaks to men for edification and exhortation and consolation. [NASB] But everyone who **prophesies** speaks to men for their strengthening, encouragement and comfort. [NIV] But he who **prophesies** speaks edification and exhortation and comfort to men. [NKJV] But one who **prophesies** is helping others grow in the Lord, encouraging and comforting them. [NLT] ὁ δὲ **προφητεύων** ἀνθρώποις λαλεῖ οἰκοδομὴν καὶ	To prophesy; to speak God's message with clarity; to proclaim God's Word; to preach; to make the truth known. **Practical Application** This is the gift of speaking under the inspiration of God's Spirit. In the Bible it includes both *prediction and proclamation*, and neither one should be minimized despite the abuse of the gift. There is no question... • the gift to predict events has been abused to the point of the ridiculous. However, the abuse of the gift does not eliminate the fact that the Spirit of God does sometimes give believers a glimpse into coming events in order to prepare and strengthen them to face the events. • the gift to proclaim the gospel has been abused to the point that most people's understanding of the gospel is tragically warped. However, the abuse of the gospel by false and immature prophets (ministers) does not eliminate the fact that God calls some men to proclaim His Word. The New Testament clearly states the purpose

ENGLISH WORD	GREEK WORD AND VERSE	THE WORD MEANS...
	παράκλησιν καὶ παραμυθίαν. [GNS] ὁ δὲ **προφητεύων** ἀνθρώποις λαλεῖ οἰκοδομὴν καὶ παράκλησιν καὶ παραμυθίαν. [GNT]	of prophecy in this verse: "everyone who *prophesies* speaks to men for their strengthening, encouragement and comfort." (1 Cor. 14:3) [NIV].

#3063
Prophetic Word
 	
Word of prophecy–KJV
Prophetic word–NASB
Word of the prophets–NIV
Prophetic word–NKJV
Message proclaimed by the prophets–NLT
 	
POSB REFERENCE
(2 Pt.1:19-21; esp. v.19)
Deeper Study #2
	προφητικὸν λόγον = *prophëtikon logon*
	Pronunciation: [prof-ay-tik-on' log'-on]
	Parsing *prophëtikon* (part of speech): adjective
	  Case—accusative
	  Gender—masculine
	  Number—singular
	  Stem or root—from **προφητικός**, ή, όν
	Parsing *logon* (part of speech): noun
	  Case—accusative
	  Gender—masculine
	  Number—singular
	  Stem or root—from **λόγος**, ου
	Concordance References:
	  ⇒ Strong's #4397 prophëtikos + 3056 logos
	  ⇒ NIV #4738 prophëtikos [of prophets] + 3364 [word]
	  ⇒ NASB #4397 prophëtikos + 3056 logos
	
	2 Peter 1:19
	We have also a more sure **word of prophecy**; whereunto ye do well that ye take heed, as unto a light that shineth in a dark place, until the day dawn, and the day star arise in your hearts: [KJV]
	And so we have the **prophetic word** made more sure, to which you do well to pay attention as to a lamp shining in a dark place, until the day dawns and the morning star arises in your hearts. [NASB]
	And we have the **word of the prophets** made more certain, and you will do well to pay attention to it, as to a light shining in a dark place, until the day dawns and the morning star rises in your hearts. [NIV]
	And so we have the **prophetic word** confirmed, which you do well to heed as a light that shines in a dark place, until the day dawns and the morning star rises in your hearts; [NKJV]
	Because of that, we have even greater confidence in the **message proclaimed by the prophets**. Pay close attention to what they wrote, for their words are like a light shining in a dark place—until the day Christ appears and his brilliant light shines in your hearts. [NLT]
	καὶ ἔχομεν βεβαιότερον·τὸν **προφητικὸν λόγον**, ᾧ καλῶς ποιεῖτε προσέχοντες ὡς λύχνῳ φαίνοντι ἐν αὐχμηρῷ τόπῳ, ἕως οὗ ἡμέρα διαυγάσῃ, καὶ φωσφόρος ἀνατείλῃ ἐν ταῖς καρδίαις ὑμῶν· [GNS]
	καὶ ἔχομεν βεβαιότερον τὸν **προφητικὸν λόγον**, ᾧ καλῶς ποιεῖτε προσέχοντες ὡς λύχνῳ φαίνοντι ἐν αὐχμηρῷ τόπῳ, ἕως οὗ ἡμέρα διαυγάσῃ καὶ φωσφόρος ἀνατείλῃ ἐν ταῖς καρδίαις ὑμῶν, [GNT]
		The word of the prophets; the word of prophecy; the prophetic word; the message proclaimed by the prophets.
		
		Practical Application
		The "prophetic word" (*prophëtikon logon*) refers to the whole prophetic message centered in Jesus Christ. The *prophetic word* did not begin or originate in the mind of man, but in the mind of God. However, God used men as instruments and authors to communicate His message to the world. Over a period of some 1500 years, He chose kings, soldiers, peasants, farmers, scholars, priests, statesmen—approximately thirty-five authors from different nations, professions, and social strata. The original manuscripts were written in three different languages—Hebrew, Aramaic, and Greek.
		1. The word "Bible" comes from the Greek word *biblos*, meaning *a book*. The Bible is also called "the Scriptures" (1 Cor. 15:3-4) and "the Word of God" (Hebrews 4:12). The Bible is divided into two parts:
		  ⇒ The first part, the *Old* Testament, was written before Christ.
		  ⇒ The second part, the *New* Testament, was written after Christ came. The word *testament* means a *covenant or an agreement*. Therefore, the Bible is God's covenant, an agreement He has made with man. The Old Testament is His covenant with man before Christ came, and the New Testament is His covenant with man after Christ came.
		2. The Old Testament has thirty-nine books which were designated as "the Law, the Prophets, and the Holy Writings or Psalms" (Luke 24:25-27). The books are sometimes divided as follows:
		  ⇒ Five Law Books: Genesis, Exodus, Leviticus, Numbers and Deuteronomy. These five are known as the Pentateuch.
		  ⇒ Twelve History Books: Joshua, Judges, Ruth, I and II Samuel, I and II Kings, I and II Chronicles, Ezra, Nehemiah, and Esther.
		  ⇒ Five Poetic Books: Job, Psalms, Proverbs, Ecclesiastes, and the Song of Solomon.
		  ⇒ Five Long or Major Prophetic Books: Isaiah, Jeremiah, Lamentations, Ezekiel, and Daniel.
		  ⇒ Twelve Short or Minor Prophetic Books: Hosea, Joel, Amos, Obadiah, Jonah, Micah, Nahum, Habakkuk, Zephaniah, Haggai, Zechariah, and Malachi.
		3. The New Testament has twenty-seven books which are sometimes divided as follows:
		  ⇒ Four Gospels which cover the life of Christ: Matthew, Mark, Luke, and John.
		  ⇒ One History Book which deals with the early believers and early church: Acts.
		  ⇒ Fourteen Pauline Letters or Epistles written to specific churches or individual

ENGLISH WORD	GREEK WORD AND VERSE	THE WORD MEANS...
		Christians: Romans, I and II Corinthians, Galatians, Ephesians, Philippians, Colossians, I and II Thessalonians, I and II Timothy, Titus, Philemon, and perhaps Hebrews.
		⇒ Seven General Letters or Epistles written by other men to specific groups, each bearing the author's name: James, I Peter, II Peter, I John, II John, III John, and Jude.
		⇒ One Prophetic Book: Revelation.
		4. The Bible has one central theme: Jesus Christ. He is the key to understanding what God reveals. He is the focal point of human history. In Him God reveals His purpose and program for the ages (Hebrews 1:1-2).
		5. The unity of the Bible is a miracle of God. Think of the facts: thirty-five different authors from so many diverse backgrounds wrote over a 1500-year period. Think of the number and diversity of subjects, yet look at the harmony of purpose and theme. There is only one explanation. God has spoken and has preserved an authoritative record of His message: "Holy men of God spoke as they were moved by the Holy Ghost" (1 Peter 1:21).
		6. The Bible claims to be the record of Jesus Christ (John 5:39), and it claims to be the written Word of God (2 Peter 1:21). As such it is inseparably linked with the living Word of God, Jesus Christ (Hebrews 4:12; 1 Peter 1:23). Jesus Christ is the *living Word of God* and the Bible is the *written Word of God*. The written Word testifies to the living Word even as the living Word [Christ Himself] testified to the written Word.

#3064
Prophets
 	
Prophets–KJV
Prophets–NASB
Prophets–NIV
Prophets–NKJV
Prophets–NLT
 	
POSB
REFERENCE
(Eph.4:11)
Note 3, point 2
	προφήτας = *prophētas*
	Pronunciation: [prof-ay'-tahs]
	Parsing (part of speech): noun
	    Case—accusative
	    Gender—masculine
	    Number—plural
	    Stem or root—from προφήτης, ου
	Concordance References:
	  ⇒ Strong's #4396 prophētēs
	  ⇒ NIV #4737 prophētēs
	  ⇒ NASB #4396 prophētēs
	
	Ephes. 4:11
	And he gave some, apostles; and some, **prophets**; and some, evangelists; and some, pastors and teachers; [KJV]
	
	And He gave some as apostles, and some as **prophets**, and some as evangelists, and some as pastors and teachers, [NASB]
	
	It was he who gave some to be apostles, some to be **prophets**, some to be evangelists, and some to be pastors and teachers, [NIV]
	
	And He Himself gave some *to be* apostles, some **prophets**, some evangelists, and some pastors and teachers, [NKJV]
	
	He is the one who gave these gifts to the church: the apostles, the **prophets**, the evangelists, and the pastors and teachers. [NLT]
	
	καὶ αὐτὸς ἔδωκε τοὺς μὲν, ἀποστόλους, τοὺς δὲ, **προφήτας**, τοὺς δὲ εὐαγγελιστάς, τοὺς δὲ, ποιμένας καὶ διδασκάλους, [GNS]
	
	καὶ αὐτὸς ἔδωκεν τοὺς μὲν ἀποστόλους, τοὺς δὲ **προφήτας**, τοὺς δὲ εὐαγγελιστάς, τοὺς δὲ ποιμένας καὶ διδασκάλους, [GNT]
		Prophet. This is the gift of speaking under the inspiration of God's Spirit. It includes both prediction and proclamation, and neither one should be minimized despite the abuse of the gift.
		
		Practical Application
		There is no question, the gift to predict events has been abused to the point of the ridiculous. However, the abuse of a gift does not eliminate the fact that the Spirit of God sometimes gives believers a glimpse into coming events in order to prepare and strengthen them to face the events.
		
		However, the major function of prophecy is clearly stated by Scripture, and the fact should be heeded by all believers:
		
		"But he that prophesieth speaketh unto men to edification, and exhortation, and comfort" (1 Cor. 14:3) [KJV].

ENGLISH WORD	GREEK WORD AND VERSE	THE WORD MEANS...

#3065
## Propitiation 	
 	
Propitiation–KJV
Propitiation–NASB
Sacrifice of atonement–NIV
Propitiation–NKJV
Punishment for our sins–NLT
 	
**POSB
REFERENCE**
(Romans 3:25)
Note 4
	ἱλαστήριον = hilastërion
	Pronunciation: [hil-as-tay'-ree-on]
	Parsing (part of speech): pronominal adjective
	    Case—accusative
	    Gender—neuter
	    Number—singular
	    Stem or root—from ἱλαστήριον, ου
	Concordance References:
	⇒ Strong's #2435 hilastërion
	⇒ NIV #2663 hilastërion
	⇒ NASB #2435 hilastërion
	
	### Romans 3:25
	Whom God hath set forth to be a **propitiation** through faith in his blood, to declare his righteousness for the remission of sins that are past, through the forbearance of God; [KJV]
	Whom God displayed publicly as a **propitiation** in His blood through faith. This was to demonstrate His righteousness, because in the forbearance of God He passed over the sins previously committed; [NASB]
	God presented him as a **sacrifice of atonement**, through faith in his blood. He did this to demonstrate his justice, because in his forbearance he had left the sins committed beforehand unpunished—[NIV]
	Whom God set forth *as* a **propitiation** by His blood, through faith, to demonstrate His righteousness, because in His forbearance God had passed over the sins that were previously committed, [NKJV]
	For God sent Jesus to take the **punishment for our sins** and to satisfy God's anger against us. We are made right with God when we believe that Jesus shed his blood, sacrificing his life for us. God was being entirely fair and just when he did not punish those who sinned in former times. [NLT]
	ὃν προέθετο ὁ Θεὸς **ἱλαστήριον** διὰ τῆς πίστεως, ἐν τῷ αὐτοῦ αἵματι, εἰς ἔνδειξιν τῆς δικαιοσύνης αὐτοῦ διὰ τὴν πάρεσιν τῶν προγεγονότων ἁμαρτημάτων [GNS]
	ὃν προέθετο ὁ θεὸς **ἱλαστήριον** διὰ [τῆς] πίστεως ἐν τῷ αὐτοῦ αἵματι εἰς ἔνδειξιν τῆς δικαιοσύνης αὐτοῦ διὰ τὴν πάρεσιν τῶν προγεγονότων ἁμαρτημάτων [GNT]
		To be a sacrifice, a covering, a satisfaction, a payment, an appeasement for sin. It means by which sins are forgiven.
		
		### Practical Application
		Righteousness is by an act of God alone, the act of propitiation. (See POSB note, Propitiation—1 John 2:1-2; POSB *Deeper Study* #1—1 John 2:2 for more discussion.)
		It is Christ Himself who is the propitiation for man's sins. But note: it is not His teachings, power, example, or life that make Christ the propitiation. It is His blood—His sacrifice, His death, His sufferings, His cross—that causes God to accept Jesus as the propitiation. It is the blood of Christ that God accepts as...
		• the *sacrifice* for our sins.
		• the *covering* for our sins.
		• the *satisfaction* for our sins.
		• the *payment* for the penalty of our sins.
		• the *appeasement* of His wrath against sin.
		
		What does the Bible mean by "the blood of Christ?" It means *the willingness* of Christ to die (shed His blood) for man. It means *the supreme sacrifice* Christ paid for man's sins. It means *the terrible sufferings* Christ underwent for man's sins. (See POSB note—Matthew 20:19.) It means *the voluntary laying down of His life* for man's sins (John 10:17-18).

#3066
## Propitiation 	
 	
Propitiation–KJV
Propitiation–NASB
Atoning sacrifice–NIV
Propitiation–NKJV
Sacrifice–NLT
 	
**POSB
REFERENCE**
(1 Jn.2:1-2; esp. v.2)
Note 3, point 2
 	
See also POSB REF:
(1 Jn.2:2)
Deeper Study #1
	ἱλασμός = hilasmos
	Pronunciation: [hil-as-mos']
	Parsing (part of speech): noun
	    Case—nominative
	    Gender—masculine
	    Number—singular
	    Stem or root—from ἱλασμός, οῦ
	Concordance References:
	⇒ Strong's #2434 hilasmos
	⇒ NIV #2662 hilasmos
	⇒ NASB #2434 hilasmos
	
	### 1 John 2:2
	And he is the **propitiation** for our sins: and not for ours only, but also for the sins of the whole world. [KJV]
	And He Himself is the **propitiation** for our sins; and not for ours only, but also for those of the whole world. [NASB]
	He is the **atoning sacrifice** for our sins, and not only for ours but also for the sins of the whole world. [NIV]
	And He Himself is the **propitiation** for our sins, and not for ours only but also for the whole world. [NKJV]
	He is the **sacrifice** for our sins. He takes away not only our sins but the sins of all the world. [NLT]
	καὶ αὐτὸς **ἱλασμός** ἐστι περὶ τῶν ἁμαρτιῶν ἡμῶν· οὐ περὶ τῶν ἡμετέρων δὲ μόνον, ἀλλὰ καὶ περὶ ὅλου τοῦ κόσμου. [GNS]
	καὶ αὐτὸς **ἱλασμός** ἐστιν περὶ τῶν ἁμαρτιῶν ἡμῶν, οὐ περὶ τῶν ἡμετέρων δὲ μόνον ἀλλὰ καὶ περὶ ὅλου τοῦ κόσμου. [GNT]
		Atoning sacrifice, propitiation. It means to be a sacrifice, a covering, a satisfaction, a payment, an appeasement for sin. It means to turn away anger or to make reconciliation between God and man.
		
		### Practical Application
		Jesus Christ is *the atoning sacrifice, the propitiation for our sins.* Remember: God is holy and just. He is perfect love, but He is also perfect holiness and justice. Therefore, He must execute justice against the sinner. He must judge and condemn sin. His justice must be perfectly satisfied. Now there is only one way God's justice can be perfectly satisfied: His justice has to be cast against the *perfect sacrifice*. If there were a Perfect and Ideal Man, that Man could accept the guilt and punishment for sin. The Perfect Man could step forward to bear the punishment for sin and satisfy the justice of God.
		This is the glorious gospel, the wonderful love and provision of God. Jesus Christ is the Ideal and Perfect Man. Therefore, He sacrificed His life for man and His sacrifice covered all men. As the Ideal Man, Jesus Christ accepted the guilt and punishment of sin for all men. He died for all men. When He died, He died as the perfect sacrifice for sins. Therefore, God accepts

ENGLISH WORD	GREEK WORD AND VERSE	THE WORD MEANS...
		His death... • as the *sacrifice* for our sins. • as the *covering* for our sins. • as the *satisfaction* for our sins. • as the *payment* for the penalty of our sins. • as the *appeasement* of His wrath against sin. When Jesus Christ carries a man's case before God, He pleads His own righteousness and death, and God accepts His righteousness and death for man. It is by this, by His sacrifice and death for our sins, that we become acceptable to God. Note one other point: Jesus Christ is the propitiation for the sins of the *whole world*. He is the eternal Son of God, the Ideal and Perfect Man. Therefore, all that He ever did covers eternity. His sacrifice for sin covers the first man ever born and spans all of time over to the last man, and then it continues right on throughout all of eternity. Jesus Christ paid the penalty of sin for all sinners of all generations. He died for the sins of all people, no matter who they are or what they have done. But note a critical fact: a person has to come to Jesus Christ, trusting Him to be his advocate before God. Jesus Christ is the only Person who has the right to stand as an advocate in the court of God's perfect justice. He is the only Person who can present man's case before God and have man declared righteous. Therefore, a person is not covered by the advocacy of Christ unless he comes to Christ and has Christ represent him before God.

#3067
## Proselyte 	
 	
Proselyte–KJV
Proselyte–NASB
Convert–NIV
Proselyte–NKJV
Convert–NLT
 	
POSB REFERENCE
(Mt.23:15)
Deeper Study #4
	προσήλυτον = *prosëluton*
	Pronunciation: [pros-ay'-loo-ton]
	Parsing (part of speech): noun
	  Case—accusative
	  Gender—masculine
	  Number—singular
	  Stem or root—from **προσήλυτος**, ου
	Concordance References:
	⇒ Strong's #4339 prosëlutos
	⇒ NIV #4670 prosëlutos
	⇒ NASB #4339 prosëlutos
	
	Matthew 23:15
	Woe unto you, scribes and Pharisees, hypocrites! for ye compass sea and land to make one **proselyte**, and when he is made, ye make him twofold more the child of hell than yourselves. [KJV]
	"Woe to you, scribes and Pharisees, hypocrites, because you travel about on sea and land to make one **proselyte**; and when he becomes one, you make him twice as much a son of hell as yourselves. [NASB]
	"Woe to you, teachers of the law and Pharisees, you hypocrites! You travel over land and sea to win a single **convert**, and when he becomes one, you make him twice as much a son of hell as you are. [NIV]
	Woe to you, scribes and Pharisees, hypocrites! For you travel land and sea to win one **proselyte**, and when he is won, you make him twice as much a son of hell as yourselves. [NKJV]
	Yes, how terrible it will be for you teachers of religious law and you Pharisees. For you cross land and sea to make one **convert**, and then you turn him into twice the son of hell as you yourselves are. [NLT]
	Οὐαὶ ὑμῖν, γραμματεῖς καὶ Φαρισαῖοι ὑποκριταί, ὅτι περιάγετε τὴν θάλασσαν καὶ τὴν ξηρὰν ποιῆσαι ἕνα
		A convert; a proselyte.
		
		### Practical Application
		It is a person who has actually approached and drawn near religion, that is, adopted the beliefs of religion. Note the tragedy of this portion of Scripture: The Jewish religious leaders went after the God-fearing and devout people who had already shown interest in religion (Judaism). Some of these people were so pleased with what Judaism offered them that when one really became a convert, he became extremely zealous for Judaism. He was so indoctrinated that he was made into a fanatic, more devoted than many of the Jews themselves. Thus the false teachers caused these converts to heap damnation upon themselves.
		
		One of the strongest lessons to be learned from the scribes and Pharisees is zeal in evangelism.
		1. They had a willingness to go. They who held to a false religion were so willing to go. Why are we, who know the truth, so unwilling to go? Where is our zeal to reach people?
		2. They were willing to go anyplace. They traveled worldwide to reach just one convert. Where is our willingness to go as missionaries? As witnesses? Where is our willingness to go even around the corner?

ENGLISH WORD	GREEK WORD AND VERSE	THE WORD MEANS...
	προσήλυτον, καὶ ὅταν γένηται ποιεῖτε αὐτὸν υἱὸν γεέννης διπλότερον ὑμῶν. [GNS] Οὐαὶ ὑμῖν, γραμματεῖς καὶ Φαρισαῖοι ὑποκριταί, ὅτι περιάγετε τὴν θάλασσαν καὶ τὴν ξηρὰν ποιῆσαι ἕνα προσήλυτον, καὶ ὅταν γένηται ποιεῖτε αὐτὸν υἱὸν γεέννης διπλότερον ὑμῶν. [GNT]	
#3068 **Protect** Keep–KJV **Protect–NASB** **Protect–NIV** Guard–NKJV Guard–NLT **POSB REFERENCE** (2 Thes.3:3-5; esp. v.3) Note 2, point 1	φυλάξει = phulaxei Pronunciation: [foo-lax'-eh-ee] Parsing (part of speech): verb Mood—indicative Tense—future Voice—active Person—3rd person Number—singular Stem or root—from φυλάσσω Concordance References: ⇒ Strong's #5442 phulassö ⇒ NIV #5875 phulassö ⇒ NASB #5442 phulassö **2 Thes. 3:3** But the Lord is faithful, who shall stablish you, and **keep** you from evil. [KJV] But the Lord is faithful, and He will strengthen and **protect** you from the evil one. [NASB] But the Lord is faithful, and he will strengthen and **protect** you from the evil one. [NIV] But the Lord is faithful, who will establish you and **guard** *you* from the evil one. [NKJV] But the Lord is faithful; he will make you strong and **guard** you from the evil one. [NLT] πιστὸς δέ ἐστι ὁ Κύριος, ὃς στηρίξει ὑμᾶς καὶ **φυλάξει** ἀπὸ τοῦ πονηροῦ. [GNS] πιστὸς δέ ἐστιν ὁ κύριος, ὃς στηρίξει ὑμᾶς καὶ **φυλάξει** ἀπὸ τοῦ πονηροῦ. [GNT]	To protect; to keep; to guard; to defend; to preserve; to cover; to insulate; to safeguard. **Practical Application** The point is this: the Lord is faithful, even if we fail to help one another. God will strengthen and guard us against Satan and his evil followers. In fact, the Lord will strenghten and guard us against all evil no matter what it is. Even if the evil seems to be conquering us, it will not—not in the final analysis.
#3069 **Protect– Protected** Kept–KJV **Protected–NASB** Shielded–NIV Kept–NKJV **Protect–NLT** **POSB REFERENCE** (1 Pt.1:5) Note 3, point 1	φρουρουμένους = phrouroumenous Pronunciation: [froo-roo-meh'-noos] Parsing (part of speech): verb Mood—participle Tense—present Voice—passive Case—accusative Gender—masculine Person—2nd person Number—plural Stem or root—from φρουρέω Concordance References: ⇒ Strong's #5432 phroureö ⇒ NIV #5864 phroureö ⇒ NASB #5432 phroureö **1 Peter 1:5** Who are **kept** by the power of God through faith unto salvation ready to be revealed in the last time. [KJV] Who are **protected** by the power of God through faith for a salvation ready to be revealed in the last time. [NASB] Who through faith are **shielded** by God's power until the coming of the salvation that is ready to be revealed in the last time. [NIV] Who are **kept** by the power of God through faith for salvation ready to be revealed in the last time. [NKJV] And God, in his mighty power, will **protect** you until you receive this salvation, because you are trusting him. It will be revealed on the last day for all to see. [NLT] τοὺς ἐν δυνάμει Θεοῦ **φρουρουμένους** διὰ πίστεως εἰς σωτηρίαν ἑτοίμην ἀποκαλυφθῆναι ἐν καιρῷ ἐσχάτῳ. [GNS] τοὺς ἐν δυνάμει θεοῦ **φρουρουμένους** διὰ πίστεως εἰς σωτηρίαν ἑτοίμην ἀποκαλυφθῆναι ἐν καιρῷ ἐσχάτῳ. [GNT]	Shielded; to keep; to protect; to guard; to garrison. **Practical Application** It is a military term; therefore it has the idea of might and strength. The might and strength of God's power protect us throughout our journey in life—through all the trials and temptations of life—and God will see to it that we will reach the glorious end of life: salvation. God Himself, in His sovereign and omnipotent power, will see to it that we receive eternal life and the inheritance that is being reserved for us.

ENGLISH WORD	GREEK WORD AND VERSE	THE WORD MEANS...
POSB REFERENCE (Rom. 12:2) Note 4, point 2	**Romans 12:2** And be not conformed to this world: but be ye transformed by the renewing of your mind, that ye may **prove** what is that good, and acceptable, and perfect, will of God. [KJV] And do not be conformed to this world, but be transformed by the renewing of your mind, that you may **prove** what the will of God is, that which is good and acceptable and perfect. [NASB] Do not conform any longer to the pattern of this world, but be transformed by the renewing of your mind. Then you will be able to **test and approve** what God's will is—his good, pleasing and perfect will. [NIV] And do not be conformed to this world, but be transformed by the renewing of your mind, that you may **prove** what *is* that good and acceptable and perfect will of God. [NKJV] Don't copy the behavior and customs of this world, but let God transform you into a new person by changing the way you think. Then you will know what God wants you to do, and you **will know** how good and pleasing and perfect his will really is. [NLT] καὶ μὴ συσχηματίζεσθε τῷ αἰῶνι τούτῳ, ἀλλὰ μεταμορφοῦσθε τῇ ἀνακαινώσει τοῦ νοὸς ὑμῶν, εἰς τὸ **δοκιμάζειν** ὑμᾶς τί τὸ θέλημα τοῦ Θεοῦ, τὸ ἀγαθὸν καὶ εὐάρεστον καὶ τέλειον. [GNS] καὶ μὴ συσχηματίζεσθε τῷ αἰῶνι τούτῳ, ἀλλὰ μεταμορφοῦσθε τῇ ἀνακαινώσει τοῦ νοὸς εἰς τὸ **δοκιμάζειν** ὑμᾶς τί τὸ θέλημα τοῦ θεοῦ, τὸ ἀγαθὸν καὶ εὐάρεστον καὶ τέλειον. [GNT]	and know the will of God? • how can the person ever follow or obey and do the will of God? The only conceivable way a person can ever find and follow God's will is to keep his mind focused upon God and upon the things of God.

#3075
Proved
 	
Proved–KJV
Testing–NASB
Tried–NIV
Tried–NKJV
Tried my patience–NLT
 	
POSB REFERENCE (Heb.3:7-11; esp. v.9) Note 1
	δοκιμασία = *dokimasia*
	Pronunciation: [dok-im-ahs-see-ah]
	Parsing (part of speech): noun
	  Case—dative
	  Gender—feminine
	  Number—singular
	  Stem or root—from δοκιμασία, ας
	Concordance References:
	⇒ Strong's #1381 dokimazo
	⇒ NIV #1508 dokimasia
	⇒ NASB #1381b dokimasia
	
	Hebrews 3:9
	When your fathers tempted me, **proved** me, and saw my works forty years. [KJV]
	
	Where your fathers tried Me by **testing** Me, And saw My works for FORTY YEARS. [NASB]
	
	Where your fathers tested and **tried** me and for forty years saw what I did. [NIV]
	
	Where your fathers tested Me, **tried** Me, And saw My works forty years. [NKJV]
	
	There your ancestors **tried my patience**, even though they saw my miracles for forty years. [NLT]
	
	οὗ ἐπείρασαν με οἱ πατέρες ὑμῶν, **ἐδοκίμασάν** με, καὶ εἶδον τὰ ἔργα μου τεσσεράκοντα ἔτη· [GNS]
	
	οὗ ἐπείρασαν οἱ πατέρες ὑμῶν ἐν **δοκιμασίᾳ** καὶ εἶδον τὰ ἔργα μου [GNT]
		Tried, proved, testing; to try God's patience; to test Him.
		
		Practical Application
		They proved (*dokimasia*) God. This means they tested Him, put Him to the test to see if He met their approval. If God would prove faithful, then He would be worthy of their obedience and loyalty. They wanted Him to prove Himself first, then they would follow Him.
		
		Note the unbelief and hardness of heart in all this. There is no belief or trust. They wanted God to prove Himself by giving the provision without any trial or suffering. They were unwilling to prove themselves, unwilling to show that they really believed and trusted God. They wanted God to prove Himself, that He was worthy of their trust and loyalty. What audacity! What an affront! What unbelief and hardness of heart—total disobedience.

#3076
Proved Genuine
 	
Tried–KJV
Proof of–NASB
Proved genuine–NIV
Tested–NKJV
Tested–NLT
	δοκίμιον = *dokimion*
	Pronunciation: [dok-im-ee'-on]
	Parsing (part of speech): noun
	  Case—nominative
	  Gender—neuter
	  Number—singular
	  Stem or root—from δοκίμιον, ου
	Concordance References:
	⇒ Strong's #1383 dokimion
	⇒ NIV #1510 dokimion
	⇒ NASB #1383 dokimion
	
	1 Peter 1:7
	That the trial of your faith, being much more precious
		Refined, tried, tested, proved genuine. The word "proved genuine" (*dokimion*) means to prove; to test; to strengthen; to show that your faith is genuine (A.T. Robertson. *Word Pictures in the New Testament*, Vol.6. Nashville, TN: Broadman Press, 1933, p.83).
		
		Practical Application
		It is just like gold. Gold has to be put to the fire in order to clean out all the impurities and dross and to make it pure and clean. Now note what this verse says: we are much more precious than gold. Gold perishes, but not believers.

ENGLISH WORD	GREEK WORD AND VERSE	THE WORD MEANS...
POSB REFERENCE (1 Pt.1:7) Note 2, point 1	than of gold that perisheth, though it be **tried** with fire, might be found unto praise and honour and glory at the appearing of Jesus Christ: [KJV] That the **proof of** your faith, being more precious than gold which is perishable, even though tested by fire, may be found to result in praise and glory and honor at the revelation of Jesus Christ; [NASB] These have come so that your faith—of greater worth than gold, which perishes even though refined by fire—may be **proved genuine** and may result in praise, glory and honor when Jesus Christ is revealed. [NIV] That the genuineness of your faith, *being* much more precious than gold that perishes, though it is **tested** by fire, may be found to praise, honor, and glory at the revelation of Jesus Christ, [NKJV] These trials are only to test your faith, to show that it is strong and pure. It is being **tested** as fire tests and purifies gold—and your faith is far more precious to God than mere gold. So if your faith remains strong after being tried by fiery trials, it will bring you much praise and glory and honor on the day when Jesus Christ is revealed to the whole world. [NLT] ἵνα τὸ **δοκίμιον** ὑμῶν τῆς πίστεως πολυ τιμιώτερον χρυσίου τοῦ ἀπολλυμένου, διὰ πυρὸς δὲ δοκιμαζομένου, εὑρεθῇ εἰς ἔπαινον καὶ τιμὴν καὶ δόξαν, ἐν ἀποκαλύψει Ἰησοῦ Χριστοῦ· [GNS] ἵνα τὸ **δοκίμιον** ὑμῶν τῆς πίστεως πολυτιμότερον χρυσίου τοῦ ἀπολλυμένου διὰ πυρὸς δὲ δοκιμαζομένου, εὑρεθῇ εἰς ἔπαινον καὶ δόξαν καὶ τιμὴν ἐν ἀποκαλύψει Ἰησοῦ Χριστοῦ· [GNT]	Believers are to live forever. Therefore, if gold has to be put to the fire to be made clean and pure, how much more do we? The point is striking: God uses the fire of trials and temptations for a good purpose. He uses them to make us clean and pure and to make us trust Him more and more. ⇒ When we are faced with some trial or temptation, we draw nearer to God. We cry out to God more than when things go well. We even tend to clean up our lives in order to secure His help as we go through the trial. We just live more pure, clean, and righteous lives. In fact, the greater the trial and temptation, the more we see that we need God. And the more we see our need for God, the closer we usually draw to Him; and the closer we draw to Him, the cleaner we live. The fire of trials causes us to live more pure and clean lives and to learn to trust God more and more. This is a most wonderful point: our trials and temptations are purposeful. God uses them to make us much more pure and to stir us to draw closer and closer to Him and to trust Him more and more. We become stronger persons through trials—much stronger, much more steadfast, persevering, and enduring.

#3077
Provide
 	
Provide–KJV
Respect–NASB
Careful–NIV
Have regard–NKJV
Do things in such a way–NLT
 	
POSB REFERENCE (Rom.12:17) Note 4, point 2
	προνοούμενοι = *pronooumenoi*
	Pronunciation: [pro-no-oo-meh'-noy]
	Parsing (part of speech): verb
	    Mood—participle (imperative sense)
	    Tense—present
	    Voice—middle
	    Case—nominative
	    Gender—masculine
	    Person—2nd person
	    Number—plural
	    Stem or root—from *προνοέω*
	Concordance References:
	  ⇒ Strong's #4306 pronoeō
	  ⇒ NIV #4629 pronoeō
	  ⇒ NASB #4306 pronoeō
	
	Romans 12:17
	Recompense to no man evil for evil. **Provide** things honest in the sight of all men. [KJV]
	
	Never pay back evil for evil to anyone. **Respect** what is right in the sight of all men. [NASB]
	
	Do not repay anyone evil for evil. Be **careful** to do what is right in the eyes of everybody. [NIV]
	
	Repay no one evil for evil. **Have regard** for good things in the sight of all men. [NKJV]
	
	Never pay back evil for evil to anyone. **Do things in such a way** that everyone can see you are honorable. [NLT]
	
	μηδενὶ κακὸν ἀντὶ κακοῦ ἀποδιδόντες. **προνοούμενοι** καλὰ ἐνώπιον πάντων ἀνθρώπων. [GNS]
	
	μηδενὶ κακὸν ἀντὶ κακοῦ ἀποδιδόντες, **προνοούμενοι** καλὰ ἐνώπιον πάντων ἀνθρώπων· [GNT]
		To be careful; to provide; to respect; to do things in such a way; to take care of; to think before acting; to take pains.
		
		The believer is to demonstrate good behavior in the sight of all men. The word "provide" (*pronooumenoi*) means to think before acting.
		
		Practical Application
		The idea is this: when someone does evil against the believer, the believer is to think before he acts. He is to think and pray through his behavior. Why? So that he can respond in the right and proper way. The believer needs to do what is right and noble, and the only way to do it is to think through the situation.

#3078
Provoke
 	
Provoke–KJV
Provoke–NASB
Exasperate–NIV
Provoke–NKJV
Treat–NLT
	παροργίζετε = *parorgizete*
	Pronunciation: [par-org-id'-zeh-teh]
	Parsing (part of speech): verb
	    Mood—imperative
	    Tense—present
	    Voice—active
	    Person—2nd person
	    Number—plural
	    Stem or root—from *παροργίζω*
		To exasperate; to provoke; to treat wrongly; to anger. The word "provoke" (*parorgizete*) means to arouse to wrath or anger, to provoke to the point of utter exasperation and resentment.
		
		Practical Application
		Parents are not to provoke their children to wrath. Parents are bound to upset and irritate

ENGLISH WORD	GREEK WORD AND VERSE	THE WORD MEANS...
POSB REFERENCE (Eph.6:4) Note 2	Concordance References: ⇒ Strong's #3949 parorgizō ⇒ NIV #4239 parorgizō ⇒ NASB #3949 parorgizō **Ephes. 6:4** And, ye fathers, **provoke** not your children to wrath: but bring them up in the nurture and admonition of the Lord. [KJV] And, fathers, do not **provoke** your children to anger; but bring them up in the discipline and instruction of the ord. [NASB] Fathers, do not **exasperate** your children; instead, bring them up in the training and instruction of the Lord. [NIV] And you, fathers, do not **provoke** your children to wrath, but bring them up in the training and admonition of the Lord. [NKJV] And now a word to you fathers. Don't make your children angry by the way you **treat** them. Rather, bring them up with the discipline and instruction approved by the Lord. [NLT] καὶ οἱ πατέρες, μὴ **παροργίζετε** τὰ τέκνα ὑμῶν, ἀλλ ἐκτρέφετε αὐτὰ ἐν παιδείᾳ καὶ νουθεσίᾳ Κυρίου. [GNS] Καὶ οἱ πατέρες, μὴ **παροργίζετε** τὰ τέκνα ὑμῶν ἀλλὰ ἐκτρέφετε αὐτὰ ἐν παιδείᾳ καὶ νουθεσίᾳ κυρίου. [GNT]	their children sometimes; we all upset and irritate people sometimes. Discipline, correction, and reproof are seldom enjoyable experiences. Their very nature is that of disturbance and irritation. This is not what this instruction means. Four things will provoke a child. 1. Failing to accept the fact that things do change. Time and generations do change. This does not mean that a child should participate in nor be allowed to do everything that his generation does. But it does mean that parents need to be alert to the changes between generations and allow the child to be a part of his own generation instead of trying to conform the child to the parent's childhood generation. The parent's childhood generation does not exist nor will it ever exist again. 2. Overcontrolling a child will also provoke a child to wrath. Overcontrol ranges all the way from stern restriction and discipline to child abuse. Disciplining and restricting a child too much will either stifle the growth of a child or stir him to react and rebel, causing the child to flee from the parent. What is too much discipline? How much should a child be restricted? Should he be allowed to do everything he wants? No! There is a limit, and the limit must be placed upon the child and discipline must be exercised when the limit is crossed. 3. Undercontrolling a child can provoke a child. It should be noted that this is the most prevalent problem in an industrialized society. There is a tendency for those with plenty or with wealth to pamper, indulge, and give a child everything imaginable—well beyond what a child needs and what is really best for him. 4. Living an inconsistent life before a child can provoke a child. A parent who tells a child one thing and then turns around and does the opposite thing himself is full of hypocrisy and false profession. Yet, how common! How many children are doing the following things because their parents do them... ⇒ drinking alcohol. ⇒ taking drugs. ⇒ watching sexual scenes on television or movies. ⇒ reading immoral stories. ⇒ looking at magazines exposing the human body. ⇒ eating too much. ⇒ wasting time. ⇒ dressing or exposing the body to attract attention. ⇒ attending socials or parties that are loose on decency, morality, marital faithfulness, and on and on.
#3079 Provoked Easily provoked–KJV **Provoked–NASB** Easily angered–NIV **Provoked–NKJV** Irritable–NLT	παροξύνεται = *paroxunetai* Pronunciation: [par-ox-oo'-neh-tah-ee] Parsing (part of speech): verb Mood—indicative Tense—present Voice—passive Person—3rd person Number—singular Stem or root—from παροξύνομαι	Seeing an inconsistent life in a parent can provoke children. To be easily angered; to be easily provoked; to be greatly distressed; to be irritable; to be greatly upset. **Practical Application** Love is not "provoked" (*paroxunetai*): not easily angered; not ready to take offence; not

ENGLISH WORD	GREEK WORD AND VERSE	THE WORD MEANS...
POSB REFERENCE (1 Cor.13:4-7; esp. v.5) Note 2, point 8	Concordance References: ⇒ Strong's #3947 paroxunō ⇒ NIV #4236 paroxunō ⇒ NASB #3947 paroxunō **1 Cor. 13:5** Doth not behave itself unseemly, seeketh not her own, is not **easily provoked**, thinketh no evil; [KJV] Does not act unbecomingly; it does not seek its own, is not **provoked**, does not take into account a wrong suffered, [NASB] It is not rude, it is not self-seeking, it is not **easily angered**, it keeps no record of wrongs. [NIV] Does not behave rudely, does not seek its own, is not **provoked**, thinks no evil; [NKJV] Or rude. Love does not demand its own way. Love is not **irritable**, and it keeps no record of when it has been wronged. [NLT] οὐκ ἀσχημονεῖ, οὐ ζητεῖ τὰ ἑαυτῆς, οὐ **παροξύνεται**, οὐ λογίζεται τὸ κακόν, [GNS] οὐκ ἀσχημονεῖ, οὐ ζητεῖ τὰ ἑαυτῆς, οὐ **παροξύνεται**, οὐ λογίζεται τὸ κακόν, [GNT]	quick tempered; not "touchy" (Phillips, as quoted by Leon Morris). It is not easily aroused to anger; does not become "exasperated" (Barclay). Love controls the emotions and never becomes angry without a cause (Romans 12:18).

#3080
Provoked
 	
Stirred–KJV
Provoked–NASB
Greatly distressed–NIV
Provoked–NKJV
Deeply troubled–NLT
 	
POSB REFERENCE (Acts 17:16) Note 1
	παρωξύνετο = parōxuneto
	Pronunciation: [par-ox-oo'-neh-tow]
	Parsing (part of speech): verb
	    Mood—indicative
	    Tense—imperfect
	    Voice—passive
	    Person—3rd person
	    Number—singular
	    Stem or root—from **παροξύνομαι**
	Concordance References:
	⇒ Strong's #3947 paroxunō
	⇒ NIV #4236 paroxunō
	⇒ NASB #3947 paroxunō
	
	Acts 17:16
	Now while Paul waited for them at Athens, his spirit was **stirred** in him, when he saw the city wholly given to idolatry. [KJV]
	Now while Paul was waiting for them at Athens, his spirit was being **provoked** within him as he was beholding the city full of idols. [NASB]
	While Paul was waiting for them in Athens, he was **greatly distressed** to see that the city was full of idols. [NIV]
	Now while Paul waited for them at Athens, his spirit was **provoked** within him when he saw that the city was given over to idols. [NKJV]
	While Paul was waiting for them in Athens, he was **deeply troubled** by all the idols he saw everywhere in the city. [NLT]
	Ἐν δὲ ταῖς Ἀθήναις ἐκδεχομένου αὐτοὺς τοῦ Παύλου, **παρωξύνετο** τὸ πνεῦμα αὐτοῦ ἐν αὐτῷ, θεωροῦντι κατείδωλον οὖσαν τὴν πόλιν. [GNS]
	Ἐν δὲ ταῖς Ἀθήναις ἐκδεχομένου αὐτοὺς τοῦ Παύλου **παρωξύνετο** τὸ πνεῦμα αὐτοῦ ἐν αὐτῷ θεωροῦντος κατείδωλον οὖσαν τὴν πόλιν. [GNT]
		To be greatly distressed; to be stirred; to be provoked; to be deeply troubled; to be aroused; to be agitated; to be irritated; to be greatly upset.
		
		Practical Application
		Paul was in Athens, the great intellectual and cultural center of the world. Paul was alone, and no doubt he did as anyone would do—he toured the city. But note: he was not swept off his feet by the majestic buildings and splendor of the architecture. Contrariwise, what gripped him was the idolatry. The city was "full of idols." Ancient writers estimate that the city had thousands and thousands of idols, one or more for every person in the city. The idols sat everywhere, lining the streets and buildings, within and without every home. Seeing such a sight "provoked" (*parōxuneto*) the spirit of Paul. Paul was aroused...
		• over the abuse of God's glory.
		• over the spiritual blindness of man's mind and reason.
		• against the devil's enslavement of lives.
		• with compassion for the souls of men.
		
		Note what happened: Paul could wait no longer. He had been waiting for Silas and Timothy, but he could not swallow the scene of idolatry anymore. He began to *reason* and *discuss* the gospel with men everywhere.

#3081
Prudence
 	
Prudence–KJV
Insight–NASB
Understanding–NIV
Prudence–NKJV
Understanding–NLT
	φρονήσει = phronēsei
	Pronunciation: [fron'-ay-see]
	Parsing (part of speech): noun
	    Case—dative
	    Gender—feminine
	    Number—singular
	    Stem or root—from **φρόνησις, εως**
	Concordance References:
	⇒ Strong's #5428 phronēsis
	⇒ NIV #5860 phronēsis
	⇒ NASB #5428 phronēsis
		Understanding, insight, wisdom, prudence, comprehension, discernment, intelligence, discretion, judgment.
		
		Practical Application
		The word "prudence" (*phronēsei*) means seeing how to use and do the truth. It is seeing the direction to take. It is understanding, insight, the ability to solve day-to-day problems. It is a down-to-earth practical understanding of things.

ENGLISH WORD	GREEK WORD AND VERSE	THE WORD MEANS...
POSB REFERENCE (Eph.1:8) Note 5, point 2	**Ephes. 1:8** Wherein he hath abounded toward us in all wisdom and **prudence**; [KJV] Which He lavished upon us. In all wisdom and **insight** [NASB] That he lavished on us with all wisdom and **understanding**. [NIV] Which He made to abound toward us in all wisdom and **prudence**, [NKJV] He has showered his kindness on us, along with all wisdom and **understanding**. [NLT] ἧς ἐπερίσσευσεν εἰς ἡμᾶς ἐν πάσῃ σοφίᾳ καὶ **φρονήσει**, [GNS] ἧς ἐπερίσσευσεν εἰς ἡμᾶς, ἐν πάσῃ σοφίᾳ καὶ **φρονήσει**, [GNT]	
#3082 Prudent Sober–KJV **Prudent–NASB** Self-controlled–NIV Sober-minded–NKJV Live wisely–NLT **POSB REFERENCE** (1 Tim.3:2; esp. v.2) Note 2, point 4	σώφρονα = *söphrona* Pronunciation: [so'-fron-ah] Parsing (part of speech): adjective Case—accusative Gender—masculine Number—singular Stem or root—from σώφρων, ον Concordance References: ⇒ Strong's #4998 söphrön ⇒ NIV #5409 söphrön ⇒ NASB #4998 söphrön **1 Tim. 3:2** A bishop then must be blameless, the husband of one wife, vigilant, **sober**, of good behaviour, given to hospitality, apt to teach; [KJV] An overseer, then, must be above reproach, the husband of one wife, temperate, **prudent**, respectable, hospitable, able to teach, [NASB] Now the overseer must be above reproach, the husband of but one wife, temperate, **self-controlled**, respectable, hospitable, able to teach, [NIV] A bishop then must be blameless, the husband of one wife, temperate, **sober-minded**, of good behavior, hospitable, able to teach; [NKJV] For an elder must be a man whose life cannot be spoken against. He must be faithful to his wife. He must exhibit self-control, **live wisely**, and have a good reputation. He must enjoy having guests in his home and must be able to teach. [NLT] δεῖ οὖν τὸν ἐπίσκοπον ἀνεπίλημπτον εἶναι, μιᾶς γυναικὸς ἄνδρα, νηφάλιον, **σώφρονα**, κόσμιον, φιλόξενον, διδακτικόν· [GNS] δεῖ οὖν τὸν ἐπίσκοπον ἀνεπίλημπτον εἶναι, μιᾶς γυναικὸς ἄνδρα, νηφάλιον **σώφρονα** κόσμιον φιλόξενον διδακτικόν, [GNT]	To be self-controlled; sober; prudent; to live wisely; to be sensible; to have a mind that is sound; sensible, controlled, disciplined, chaste, sober—a mind that has complete control over all sensual desires. **Practical Application** If the mind is controlled, a person's whole life—his body and behavior—is controlled. He lives wisely.
#3083 Prunes Purgeth–KJV **Prunes–NASB** **Prunes–NIV** **Prunes–NKJV** **Prunes–NLT** **POSB REFERENCE** (Jn.15:2-4; esp. v.2) Note 3, point 3	καθαίρει = *kathairei* Pronunciation: [kath-ah'ee-reh-ee] Parsing (part of speech): verb Mood—indicative Tense—present Voice—active Person—3rd person Number—singular Stem or root—from καθαίρω Concordance References: ⇒ Strong's #2508 kathairo ⇒ NIV #2748 kathairo ⇒ NASB #2508 kathairo **John 15:2** Every branch in me that beareth not fruit he taketh away: and every branch that beareth fruit, he **purgeth** it, that it may bring forth more fruit. [KJV] "Every branch in Me that does not bear fruit, He takes away; and every branch that bears fruit, He **prunes** it, that it may bear more fruit. [NASB]	To prune; to cut off; to lop off; to be purged and cleansed. **Practical Application** Note how the fruitful branches are pruned (*kathairei*) or purged and cleansed. There are three ways that God purges the believer... 1. Branches are cleansed by the words which Jesus has given to men, by the Word of the Lord Himself. The Word of God refines men by purging away all the dross and contamination, pollution and dirt that clings to them. When a man sincerely comes to the Word of God, the Word of God shows... • what he is doing and what he is not doing. • where he fails and how he fails. • the sins of commission and of omission.

ENGLISH WORD	GREEK WORD AND VERSE	THE WORD MEANS...
	He cuts off every branch in me that bears no fruit, while every branch that does bear fruit he **prunes** so that it will be even more fruitful. [NIV] Every branch in Me that does not bear fruit He takes away; and every *branch* that bears fruit He **prunes**, that it may bear more fruit. [NKJV] He cuts off every branch that doesn't produce fruit, and he **prunes** the branches that do bear fruit so they will produce even more. [NLT] πᾶν κλῆμα ἐν ἐμοὶ μὴ φέρον καρπόν, αἴρει αὐτό· καὶ πᾶν τὸ καρπὸν φέρον, **καθαίρει** αὐτό, ἵνα πλείονα καρπὸν φέρῃ. [GNS] πᾶν κλῆμα ἐν ἐμοὶ μὴ φέρον καρπόν αἴρει αὐτό, καὶ πᾶν τὸ καρπὸν φέρον **καθαίρει** αὐτὸ ἵνα καρπὸν πλείονα φέρῃ. [GNT]	2. Branches are cleansed by the mirror of the Word of God. When a man looks into the Word of God, he reflects both himself in his shortcomings and Christ in His perfection. The Word of God forces man to measure himself against Christ. (See POSB *Deeper Study* #1—Hebrews 4:12 for more discussion.) 3. Branches are cleansed by "abiding" in Jesus Christ (see POSB *Deeper Study* #2, Abide—John 15:4). Note exactly what Jesus said: "Abide [or remain] in me, and I in you." This can mean at least two things. ⇒ It can mean a promise: "Abide in me and I will abide in you." The believer is thereby cleansed by his position or by being in Christ (see POSB note, pt.4—John 13:6-11). ⇒ It can mean a command: "See to it that you abide in me, and I in you." The believer is cleansed by continuing in Christ and remaining faithful.

#3084
Published
 	
Published–KJV
Spread–NASB
Spread–NIV
Spread–NKJV
Spread–NLT
 	
POSB REFERENCE
(Acts 13:46-52; esp. v.49)
Note 2, point 2d
	διεφέρετο = *diephereto*
	Pronunciation: [di-eh-fehr'-eh-tow]
	Parsing (part of speech): verb
	  Mood—indicative
	  Tense—imperfect
	  Voice—passive
	  Person—3rd person
	  Number—singular
	  Stem or root—from διαφέρω
	Concordance References:
	⇒ Strong's #1308 diapherö
	⇒ NIV #1422 diapherö
	⇒ NASB #1308 diapherö
	
	Acts 13:49
	And the word of the Lord was **published** throughout all the region. [KJV]
	
	And the word of the Lord was being **spread** through the whole region. [NASB]
	
	The word of the Lord **spread** through the whole region. [NIV]
	
	And the word of the Lord was being **spread** throughout all the region. [NKJV]
	
	So the Lord's message **spread** throughout that region. [NLT]
	
	διεφέρετο δὲ ὁ λόγος τοῦ Κυρίου δι' ὅλης τῆς χώρας. [GNS]
	
	διεφέρετο δὲ ὁ λόγος τοῦ κυρίου δι' ὅλης τῆς χώρας. [GNT]
		To spread; to publish.
		
		Practical Application
		They published, that is, spread abroad and proclaimed the Word throughout all the region.

#3085
Puffed Up
 	
Puffed up–KJV
Become arrogant–NASB
Take pride–NIV
Puffed up–NKJV
Brag–NLT
 	
POSB REFERENCE
(1 Cor.4:6)
Note 1, point 2
	φυσιοῦσθε = *phusiousthe*
	Pronunciation: [foo-see-o'-oos-the]
	Parsing (part of speech): verb
	  Mood—indicative
	  Tense—present
	  Voice—passive
	  Person—2nd person
	  Number—plural
	  Stem or root—from φυσιόω
	Concordance References:
	⇒ Strong's #5448 phusioö
	⇒ NIV #5881 phusioö
	⇒ NASB #5448 phusioö
	
	1 Cor. 4:6
	And these things, brethren, I have in a figure transferred to myself and to Apollos for your sakes; that ye might learn in us not to think of men above that which is written, that no one of you be **puffed up** for one against another. [KJV]
		To take pride; to become arrogant; to brag; to be conceited; to be inflated; to be puffed up.
		
		Practical Application
		It is a picture of puffed up air bags. The point is, the judging of ministers and the feelings that one can judge ministers is nothing but hot air in *puffed up* or inflated balloons. It is meaningless. It means absolutely nothing to God. (Cp. 1 Cor. 4:18-19; 1 Cor. 5:2; 1 Cor. 8:1; 1 Cor. 13:4.)

ENGLISH WORD	GREEK WORD AND VERSE	THE WORD MEANS...
	Now these things, brethren, I have figuratively applied to myself and Apollos for your sakes, that in us you might learn not to exceed what is written, in order that no one of you might **become arrogant** in behalf of one against the other. [NASB] Now, brothers, I have applied these things to myself and Apollos for your benefit, so that you may learn from us the meaning of the saying, "Do not go beyond what is written." Then you will not **take pride** in one man over against another. [NIV] Now these things, brethren, I have figuratively transferred to myself and Apollos for your sakes, that you may learn in us not to think beyond what is written, that none of you may be **puffed up** on behalf of one against the other. [NKJV] Dear brothers and sisters, I have used Apollos and myself to illustrate what I've been saying. If you pay attention to the Scriptures, you won't **brag** about one of your leaders at the expense of another. [NLT] Ταῦτα δέ, ἀδελφοί, μετεσχημάτισα εἰς ἐμαυτὸν καὶ Ἀπολλῶν δι' ὑμᾶς, ἵνα ἐν ἡμῖν μάθητε τὸ μὴ ὑπὲρ ὃ γέγραπται φρονεῖν, ἵνα μὴ εἷς ὑπὲρ τοῦ ἑνὸς **φυσιοῦσθε** κατὰ τοῦ ἑτέρου. [GNS] Ταῦτα δέ, ἀδελφοί, μετεσχημάτισα εἰς ἐμαυτὸν καὶ Ἀπολλῶν δι' ὑμᾶς, ἵνα ἐν ἡμῖν μάθητε τὸ Μὴ ὑπὲρ ἃ γέγραπται, ἵνα μὴ εἷς ὑπὲρ τοῦ ἑνὸς **φυσιοῦσθε** κατὰ τοῦ ἑτέρου. [GNT]	
#3086 ## Puffed Up **Puffed up–KJV** Arrogant–NASB Proud–NIV **Puffed up–NKJV** Proud–NLT **POSB** **REFERENCE** (1 Cor.13:4-7; esp. v.4) Note 2, point 5	*φυσιοῦται = phusioutai* Pronunciation: [foo-see-oo'-tah-ee] Parsing (part of speech): verb 　　Mood—indicative 　　Tense—present 　　Voice—passive 　　Person—3rd person 　　Number—singular 　　Stem or root—from φυσιόω Concordance References: 　⇒　Strong's #5448 phusioö 　⇒　NIV #5881 phusioö 　⇒　NASB #5448 phusioö ### 1 Cor. 13:4 Charity suffereth long, and is kind; charity envieth not; charity vaunteth not itself, is not **puffed up**, [KJV] Love is patient, love is kind, and is not jealous; love does not brag and is not **arrogant**, [NASB] Love is patient, love is kind. It does not envy, it does not boast, it is not **proud**. [NIV] Love suffers long *and* is kind; love does not envy; love does not parade itself, is not **puffed up**; [NKJV] Love is patient and kind. Love is not jealous or boastful or **proud** [NLT] ἡ ἀγάπη μακροθυμεῖ, χρηστεύεται· ἡ ἀγάπη, οὐ ζηλοῖ· ἡ ἀγάπη οὐ περπερεύεται, οὐ **φυσιοῦται**, [GNS] Ἡ ἀγάπη μακροθυμεῖ, χρηστεύεται ἡ ἀγάπη, οὐ ζηλοῖ, [ἡ ἀγάπη] οὐ περπερεύεται, οὐ **φυσιοῦται**, [GNT]	Proud, puffed up, arrogant, conceited. ### Practical Application Love is not puffed up (*phusioutai*): prideful, arrogant, conceited; does not think nor act as though oneself is better or above others. Love is modest and humble and recognizes and honors others.
#3087 ## Puffed Up With Pride Highminded–KJV Conceited–NASB Conceited–NIV Haughty–NKJV **Puffed up with pride–NLT**	*τετυφωμένοι = tetuphömenoi* Pronunciation: [teh-toof-o'-mehn-oy] Parsing (part of speech): verb 　　Mood—participle 　　Tense—perfect 　　Voice—passive 　　Case—nominative 　　Gender—masculine 　　Number—plural 　　Stem or root—from τυφόομαι Concordance References: 　⇒　Strong's #5187 tuphoomai 　⇒　NIV #5605 tuphoomai 　⇒　NASB #5187 tuphoomai	To be conceited; to be highminded; to be haughty; to be puffed up with pride; to be swollen with pride, having feelings of self-importance. ### Practical Application It is a person who feels so educated, so scientific, so advanced, so high in position and authority, ability, and gifts that he feels completely self-sufficient. He feels no need for God. He is above God and above most people.

ENGLISH WORD	GREEK WORD AND VERSE	THE WORD MEANS...
POSB REFERENCE (2 Tim. 3:2-4; esp. v.4) Note 2, point 17	**2 Tim. 3:4** Traitors, heady, **highminded**, lovers of pleasures more than lovers of God; [KJV] Treacherous, reckless, **conceited**, lovers of pleasure rather than lovers of God; [NASB] Treacherous, rash, **conceited**, lovers of pleasure rather than lovers of God—[NIV] Traitors, headstrong, **haughty**, lovers of pleasure rather than lovers of God, [NKJV] They will betray their friends, be reckless, be **puffed up with pride**, and love pleasure rather than God. [NLT] προδόται, προπετεῖς, **τετυφωμένοι**, φιλήδονοι μᾶλλον η φιλόθεοι, [GNS] προδόται προπετεῖς **τετυφωμένοι**, φιλήδονοι μᾶλλον η φιλόθεοι, [GNT]	

#3088
Punished
 	
Punished–KJV
Pay the penalty–NASB
Punished–NIV
Punished–NKJV
Punished–NLT
 	
POSB REFERENCE (2 Thes.1:9) Note 4, point 2
	δίκην τίσουσιν = diken tisousin
	Pronunciation: [dee'-kayn tee'-soo-sin]
	Parsing *diken* (part of speech): noun
	    Case—accusative
	    Gender—feminine
	    Number—singular
	    Stem or root—from δίκη, ης
	Parsing *tisousin* (part of speech): verb
	    Mood—indicative
	    Tense—future
	    Voice—active
	    Person—3rd person
	    Number—plural
	    Stem or root—from τίνω
	Concordance References:
	⇒ Strong's #1349+5099 dike tino
	⇒ NIV #1472+5514 dike tino
	⇒ NASB #1349+5099 dike tino
	
	2 Thes. 1:9
	Who shall be **punished** with everlasting destruction from the presence of the Lord, and from the glory of his power; [KJV]
	And these will **pay the penalty** of eternal destruction, away from the presence of the Lord and from the glory of His power, [NASB]
	They will be **punished** with everlasting destruction and shut out from the presence of the Lord and from the majesty of his power [NIV]
	These shall be **punished** with everlasting destruction from the presence of the Lord and from the glory of His power, [NKJV]
	They will be **punished** with everlasting destruction, forever separated from the Lord and from his glorious power [NLT]
	οἵτινες **δίκην τίσουσιν**, ὄλεθρον αἰώνιον ἀπὸ προσώπου τοῦ Κυρίου καὶ ἀπὸ τῆς δόξης τῆς ἰσχύος αὐτοῦ, [GNS]
	οἵτινες **δίκην τίσουσιν** ὄλεθρον αἰώνιον ἀπὸ προσώπου τοῦ κυρίου καὶ ἀπὸ τῆς δόξης τῆς ἰσχύος αὐτοῦ, [GNT]
		To undergo punishment, justice; to pay the penalty; to suffer punishment from God.
		
		Practical Application
		Matthew Henry says that "they did sin's work, and must receive sin's wages" (*Matthew Henry's Commentary*, Vol.6, p.795). Sinners may get away with their sin and rejection of God while on earth, but they will be punished in the final analysis.
		Note another fact about the punishment. Note the Greek word for punishment (*diken*). It comes from the same root as righteous (*dikaios*). This means that the punishment will be righteous, just—exactly what the person deserves, no more, no less. A person will be measured an exact amount of punishment that he has earned while on earth. God's punishment will not be vindictive; it will be perfectly just, a punishment of retribution—a punishment that pays a person exactly what he deserves.

#3089
Punishment
 	
Vengeance–KJV
Vengeance–NASB
Punishment–NIV
Vengeance–NKJV
Vengeance–NLT
 	
POSB REFERENCE (Lk.21:22) *Deeper Study #1*
	ἐκδικήσεως = ekdikeseos
	Pronunciation: [ek-dik'-ay-seh-oce]
	Parsing (part of speech): noun
	    Case—genitive
	    Gender—feminine
	    Number—singular
	    Stem or root—from ἐκδίκησις, εως
	Concordance References:
	⇒ Strong's #1557 ekdikesis
	⇒ NIV #1689 ekdikesis
	⇒ NASB #1557 ekdikesis
	
	Luke 21:22
	For these be the days of **vengeance**, that all things
		Executing perfect justice, revenge, retribution, satisfaction.
		
		Practical Application
		It is judgment that flows out of righteousness and justice. It is not the retaliation that flows from human anger and hurt feelings. There is no self-gratification or selfish reaction in the word at all. It is judgment that executes perfect justice. It is judgment that makes things right, exactly as they should be.

ENGLISH WORD	GREEK WORD AND VERSE	THE WORD MEANS...
	which are written may be fulfilled. [KJV] 　　Because these are days of **vengeance**, in order that all things which are written may be fulfilled. [NASB] 　　For this is the time of **punishment** in fulfillment of all that has been written. [NIV] 　　For these are the days of **vengeance**, that all things which are written may be fulfilled. [NKJV] 　　For those will be days of God's **vengeance**, and the prophetic words of the Scriptures will be fulfilled. [NLT] 　　ὅτι ἡμέραι **ἐκδικήσεως** αὗταί εἰσι, τοῦ πληρωθῆναι πάντα τὰ γεγραμμένα. [GNS] 　　ὅτι ἡμέραι **ἐκδικήσεως** αὗταί εἰσιν τοῦ πλησθῆναι πάντα τὰ γεγραμμένα. [GNT]	
#3090 **Punishment** Damnation–KJV Condemnation–NASB Judgment–NIV Judgment–NKJV **Punishment–NLT** **POSB** **REFERENCE** (Rom.13:1-2; esp. v.2) Note 2, point 2 **See also POSB REF:** (1 Cor.11:27-30; esp. v.29) Note 4, point 2	κρίμα = *krima* Pronunciation: [kree'-mah] Parsing (part of speech): noun 　　Case—accusative 　　Gender—neuter 　　Number—singular 　　Stem or root—from κρίμα, τος Concordance References: 　⇒　Strong's #2917 krima 　⇒　NIV #3210 krima 　⇒　NASB #2917 krima **Romans 13:2** 　　Whosoever therefore resisteth the power, resisteth the ordinance of God: and they that resist shall receive to themselves **damnation**. [KJV] 　　Therefore he who resists authority has opposed the ordinance of God; and they who have opposed will receive **condemnation** upon themselves. [NASB] 　　Consequently, he who rebels against the authority is rebelling against what God has instituted, and those who do so will bring **judgment** on themselves. [NIV] 　　Therefore whoever resists the authority resists the ordinance of God, and those who resist will bring **judgment** on themselves. [NKJV] 　　So those who refuse to obey the laws of the land are refusing to obey God, and **punishment** will follow. [NLT] 　　ὥστε ὁ ἀντιτασσόμενος τῇ ἐξουσίᾳ, τῇ τοῦ Θεοῦ διαταγῇ ἀνθέστηκεν· οἱ δὲ ἀνθεστηκότες ἑαυτοῖς **κρίμα** λήμψονται. [GNS] 　　ὥστε ὁ ἀντιτασσόμενος τῇ ἐξουσίᾳ τῇ τοῦ θεοῦ διαταγῇ ἀνθέστηκεν, οἱ δὲ ἀνθεστηκότες ἑαυτοῖς **κρίμα** λήμψονται. [GNT]	Judgment, verdict; condemnation, punishment. **Practical Application** 　　The believer who resists the authorities will be condemned. The idea is that the disobedient believer will have to face the judgment of God if he disobeys the just laws of government. Some commentators think this refers to the judgment of the civil authorities. There is no question, if the believer is caught breaking the laws of the state, he will be punished. However, the civil authorities may never catch the believer. Yet, God knows every law broken by the believer; and by resisting the laws of the state, the believer has broken the law of God. Therefore, the believer stands guilty before God, and he will be judged by God.
#3091 **Punishment For Our Sins** Propitiation–KJV Propitiation–NASB Sacrifice of atonement–NIV Propitiation–NKJV **Punishment for our sins–NLT** **POSB** **REFERENCE** (Romans 3:25) Note 4	ἱλαστήριον = *hilastērion* Pronunciation: [hil-as-tay'-ree-on] Parsing (part of speech): pronominal adjective 　　Case—accusative 　　Gender—neuter 　　Number—singular 　　Stem or root—from ἱλαστήριον, ου Concordance References: 　⇒　Strong's #2435 hilastērion 　⇒　NIV #2663 hilastērion 　⇒　NASB #2435 hilastērion **Romans 3:25** 　　Whom God hath set forth to be a **propitiation** through faith in his blood, to declare his righteousness for the remission of sins that are past, through the forbearance of God; [KJV] 　　whom God displayed publicly as a **propitiation** in His blood through faith. This was to demonstrate His righteousness, because in the forbearance of God He passed over the sins previously committed; [NASB] 　　God presented him as a **sacrifice of atonement**, through faith in his blood. He did this to demonstrate his justice, because in his forbearance he had left the sins	To be a sacrifice, a covering, a satisfaction, a payment, an appeasement for sin. It means by which sins are forgiven. **Practical Application** 　　Righteousness is by an act of God alone, the act of propitiation. (See POSB note, Propitiation—1 John 2:1-2; POSB *Deeper Study* #1—1 John 2:2 for more discussion.) 　　It is Christ Himself who is the propitiation for man's sins. But note: it is not His teachings, power, example, or life that make Christ the propitiation. It is His blood—His sacrifice, His death, His sufferings, His cross—that causes God to accept Jesus as the propitiation. It is the blood of Christ that God accepts as... 　• the *sacrifice* for our sins. 　• the *covering* for our sins. 　• the *satisfaction* for our sins. 　• the *payment* for the penalty of our sins. 　• the *appeasement* of His wrath against sin.

ENGLISH WORD	GREEK WORD AND VERSE	THE WORD MEANS...
	committed beforehand unpunished—[NIV] Whom God set forth *as* a **propitiation** by His blood, through faith, to demonstrate His righteousness, because in His forbearance God had passed over the sins that were previously committed, [NKJV] For God sent Jesus to take the **punishment for our sins** and to satisfy God's anger against us. We are made right with God when we believe that Jesus shed his blood, sacrificing his life for us. God was being entirely fair and just when he did not punish those who sinned in former times. [NLT] ὃν προέθετο ὁ Θεὸς ἱλαστήριον διὰ τῆς πίστεως, ἐν τῷ αὐτοῦ αἵματι, εἰς ἔνδειξιν τῆς δικαιοσύνης αὐτοῦ διὰ τὴν πάρεσιν τῶν προγεγονότων ἁμαρτημάτων [GNS] ὃν προέθετο ὁ Θεὸς ἱλαστήριον διὰ [τῆς] πίστεως ἐν τῷ αὐτοῦ αἵματι εἰς ἔνδειξιν τῆς δικαιοσύνης αὐτοῦ διὰ τὴν πάρεσιν τῶν προγεγονότων ἁμαρτημάτων [GNT]	What does the Bible mean by "the blood of Christ"? It means *the willingness* of Christ to die (shed His blood) for man. It means *the supreme sacrifice* Christ paid for man's sins. It means *the terrible sufferings* Christ underwent for man's sins. (See POSB note—Matthew 20:19.) It means *the voluntary laying down of His life* for man's sins (John 10:17-18).

#3092
Purchase Freedom
 	
Ransom–KJV
Ransom–NASB
Ransom–NIV
Ransom–NKJV
Purchase freedom–NLT
 	
POSB REFERENCE
(1 Tim.2:3-7; esp. v 6)
Note 3, point 4
	ἀντίλυτρον = *antilutron*
	Pronunciation: [an-til'-oo-tron]
	Parsing (part of speech): noun
	    Case—accusative
	    Gender—neuter
	    Number—singular
	    Stem or root—from ἀντίλυτρον, ου
	Concordance References:
	  ⇒ Strong's #487 antilutron
	  ⇒ NIV #519 antilutron
	  ⇒ NASB #487 antilutron
	
	1 Tim. 2:6
	Who gave himself a **ransom** for all, to be testified in due time. [KJV]
	
	Who gave Himself as a **ransom** for all, the testimony borne at the proper time. [NASB]
	
	Who gave himself as a **ransom** for all men—the testimony given in its proper time. [NIV]
	
	Who gave Himself a **ransom** for all, to be testified in due time, [NKJV]
	
	He gave his life to **purchase freedom** for everyone. This is the message that God gave to the world at the proper time. [NLT]
	
	ὁ δοὺς ἑαυτὸν ἀντίλυτρον ὑπὲρ πάντων, τὸ μαρτύριον καιροῖς ἰδίοις, [GNS]
	
	ὁ δοὺς ἑαυτὸν ἀντίλυτρον ὑπὲρ πάντων, τὸ μαρτύριον καιροῖς ἰδίοις. [GNT]
		Ransom; to purchase freedom; to *exchange* something for something else.
		
		Practical Application
		The man Christ Jesus gave Himself to purchase freedom for all. The man Christ Jesus exchanged His life for the life of man; He gave up His life for the life of man. How? By the cross. Jesus Christ took the sin and condemnation of men upon Himself and bore their judgment for them. Christ died for man; He bore the judgment of God against sin for man.
		
		As the Ideal and Perfect Man, Christ could do this for man. Since He was the Ideal Man, His death was the ideal death. Therefore, His death can stand for and cover the death of all men. If a man really believes and trusts that the death of Jesus Christ is for him...
		
		• God counts the death of Christ for the man.
		• God actually *counts* the man as having already died in Christ.
		• God accepts the man as free from the guilt and condemnation of sin because Christ has already paid the ransom price for sin and death.

#3093
Purchased
 	
Purchased–KJV
Purchased–NASB
Bought–NIV
Purchased–NKJV
Purchased–NLT
 	
POSB REFERENCE
(Acts 20:28-31; esp. v.28)
Note 2, point 1b
	περιεποιήσατο = *periepoiësato*
	Pronunciation: [per-ee-poy-eh'-sah-tow]
	Parsing (part of speech): verb
	    Mood—indicative
	    Tense—aorist
	    Voice—middle
	    Person—3rd person
	    Number—singular
	    Stem or root—from περιποιέομαι
	Concordance References:
	  ⇒ Strong's #4046 peripoieö
	  ⇒ NIV #4347 peripoieö
	  ⇒ NASB #4046 peripoieö
	
	Acts 20:28
	Take heed therefore unto yourselves, and to all the flock, over the which the Holy Ghost hath made you overseers, to feed the church of God, which he hath **purchased** with his own blood. [KJV]
	
	"Be on guard for yourselves and for all the flock, among which the Holy Spirit has made you overseers, to shepherd the church of God which He **purchased** with His own blood. [NASB]
	
	Keep watch over yourselves and all the flock of which the Holy Spirit has made you overseers. Be shepherds of the church of God, which he **bought** with his own blood. [NIV]
		Bought, purchased, obtained, acquired.
		
		Practical Application
		Jesus "purchased" the church. He died as our substitute; He died for us: and because He died for us, we never have to die. This is what Scripture means when it says that Jesus Christ gave Himself for us. This is how God demonstrated His grace to the world: He gave His Son to die for the sins of men.

ENGLISH WORD	GREEK WORD AND VERSE	THE WORD MEANS...

Therefore take heed to yourselves and to all the flock, among which the Holy Spirit has made you overseers, to shepherd the church of God which He **purchased** with His own blood. [NKJV]

"And now beware! Be sure that you feed and shepherd God's flock—his church, **purchased** with his blood—over whom the Holy Spirit has appointed you as elders. [NLT]

προσέχετε οὖν ἑαυτοῖς καὶ παντὶ τῷ ποιμνίῳ, ἐν ᾧ ὑμᾶς τὸ Πνεῦμα τὸ Ἅγιον ἔθετο ἐπισκόπους, ποιμαίνειν τὴν ἐκκλησίαν τοῦ Θεοῦ, ἣν **περιεποιήσατο** διὰ τοῦ ἰδίου αἵματος. [GNS]

προσέχετε ἑαυτοῖς καὶ παντὶ τῷ ποιμνίῳ, ἐν ᾧ ὑμᾶς τὸ πνεῦμα τὸ ἅγιον ἔθετο ἐπισκόπους ποιμαίνειν τὴν ἐκκλησίαν τοῦ θεοῦ, ἣν **περιεποιήσατο** διὰ τοῦ αἵματος τοῦ ἰδίου. [GNT]

#3094

Purchased Our Freedom

Redemption–KJV
Redemption–NASB
Redemption–NIV
Redemption–NKJV
Purchased our freedom–NLT

**POSB
REFERENCE**
(Eph.1:7)
Note 4

ἀπολύτρωσιν = *apolutrōsin*
Pronunciation: [ap-ol-oo'-tro-sin]
Parsing (part of speech): noun
    Case—accusative
    Gender—feminine
    Number—singular
    Stem or root—from *ἀπολύτρωσις, εως*
Concordance References:
⇒ Strong's #629 apolutrōsis
⇒ NIV #667 apolutrōsis
⇒ NASB #629 apolutrōsis

Ephes. 1:7

In whom we have **redemption** through his blood, the forgiveness of sins, according to the riches of his grace; [KJV]

In Him we have **redemption** through His blood, the forgiveness of our trespasses, according to the riches of His grace, [NASB]

In him we have **redemption** through his blood, the forgiveness of sins, in accordance with the riches of God's grace [NIV]

In Him we have **redemption** through His blood, the forgiveness of sins, according to the riches of His grace [NKJV]

He is so rich in kindness that he **purchased our freedom** through the blood of his Son, and our sins are forgiven. [NLT]

ἐν ᾧ ἔχομεν τὴν **ἀπολύτρωσιν** διὰ τοῦ αἵματος αὐτοῦ, τὴν ἄφεσιν τῶν παραπτωμάτων, κατὰ τὸ πλοῦτον τῆς χάριτος αὐτοῦ, [GNS]

ἐν ᾧ ἔχομεν τὴν **ἀπολύτρωσιν** διὰ τοῦ αἵματος αὐτοῦ, τὴν ἄφεσιν τῶν παραπτωμάτων, κατὰ τὸ πλοῦτος τῆς χάριτος αὐτοῦ [GNT]

Redemption; atonement; ransom; purchased our freedom.

Practical Application

God has redeemed us and forgiven our sins. The word translated "purchased our freedom" (*apolutrōsin*) is one of the great words of the Bible. It conveys the idea of deliverance or setting a man free by paying a ransom. For example, a prisoner of war or a kidnapped person is ransomed or redeemed; or a convicted criminal is freed from the penalty of death. In every case the man is powerless to free himself. He cannot pay the penalty demanded to liberate himself from his situation or bondage. Note several significant facts.

1. Man has been captivated or kidnapped by several forces.
   a. The force of sin. All men sin and cannot help but sin. Man is sold under sin. Sin has captivated him (Rom.3:23; Rom.7:14).
   b. The force of corruption and death. The whole creation is corrupt (Romans 8:21). Everything wastes away; it deteriorates, decays, ages, and eventually dies. Corruption and death have captivated man. (Cp. 1 Cor.15:42, 50; Gal. 6:8; 2 Pet.1:4; 2 Pet.2:12, 19.)
   c. The force of Satan. All unbelievers are under the power and influence of Satan. He has blinded their minds to the gospel (2 Cor. 4:4). He works in the children of disobedience (Eph. 2:2). They are captivated by him (1 Jn.5:19).
2. Three key ideas are included in the concept of redemption.
   a. Man needs to be liberated, delivered, and set free.
   b. Man is unable to liberate himself. He has no energy, no power, no ability to free himself.
   c. God has redeemed man by the blood of His Son Jesus Christ. God Himself has paid the ransom for man's release—the ransom of a life for a life. God gave His own Son so that man might be set free. Man has been redeemed through the blood of Jesus Christ (cp. Lev.17:11; Mt.20:28; Rom.3:24; 1 Cor.6:20; 1 Cor.7:23; Col. 1:14; 1 Tim. 2:5-6; Heb.9:15; 1 Pet.1:18f; 2 Pet.2:1; Rev. 5:9; Rev.14:3-4). This is extremely important to note: when a man

ENGLISH WORD	GREEK WORD AND VERSE	THE WORD MEANS...
		truly calls upon the Lord to save him, God buys him right out of the marketplace of this corruptible life (Rom.10:13). God redeems him once for all, purchases and removes him from further sale. He is redeemed eternally (cp. Gal.3:13; Gal.4:5; Col. 4:5). 3. God redeems man because of the riches of His grace (see POSB note, Grace—Eph.2:8-9 for discussion). He loves man with an unbelievable love—a love so great that it spurs Him to do whatever is necessary to save man.

#3095
Pure
 	
Pure–KJV
Pure–NASB
Pure–NIV
Pure–NKJV
Pure–NLT
 	
POSB
REFERENCE
(Mt.5:8)
Note 7
	καθαροὶ = katharoi
	Pronunciation: [kath-ar-oy]
	Parsing (part of speech): pronominal adjective
	    Case—nominative
	    Gender—masculine
	    Number—plural
	    Stem or root—from καθαρός, ά, όν
	Concordance References:
	⇒ Strong's #2513 katharos
	⇒ NIV #2754 katharos
	⇒ NASB #2513 katharos
	
	Matthew 5:8
	Blessed are the **pure** in heart: for they shall see God. [KJV]
	"Blessed are the **pure** in heart, for they shall see God. [NASB]
	Blessed are the **pure** in heart, for they will see God. [NIV]
	Blessed are the **pure** in heart, For they shall see God. [NKJV]
	God blesses those whose hearts are **pure**, for they will see God. [NLT]
	Μακάριοι οἱ **καθαροὶ** τῇ καρδίᾳ· ὅτι αὐτοὶ τὸν Θεὸν ὄψονται. [GNS]
	μακάριοι οἱ **καθαροὶ** τῇ καρδίᾳ, ὅτι αὐτοὶ τὸν θεὸν ὄψονται. [GNT]
		To be pure, clean, unsoiled, innocent, unmixed, unpolluted.
		
		Practical Application
		In this Scripture it means to have a heart that has been cleansed, purged, forgiven. It means to be holy; to have a single purpose, that of God's glory.

#3096
Pure
 	
Sincere–KJV
Sincere–NASB
Pure–NIV
Sincere–NKJV
Pure–NLT
 	
POSB
REFERENCE
(Philip.1:9-10; esp.
v.9)
Note 7, point 2
	εἰλικρινεῖς = eilikrineis
	Pronunciation: [i-lik-ree-nees]
	Parsing (part of speech): adjective
	    Case—nominative
	    Gender—masculine
	    Number—plural
	    Stem or root—from εἰλικρινής, ές
	Concordance References:
	⇒ Strong's #1506 eilikrinēs
	⇒ NIV #1637 eilikrinēs
	⇒ NASB #1506 eilikrinēs
	
	Philip. 1:10
	That ye may approve things that are excellent; that ye may be **sincere** and without offence till the day of Christ; [KJV]
	So that you may approve the things that are excellent, in order to be **sincere** and blameless until the day of Christ; [NASB]
	So that you may be able to discern what is best and may be **pure** and blameless until the day of Christ, [NIV]
	That you may approve the things that are excellent, that you may be **sincere** and without offense till the day of Christ, [NKJV]
	For I want you to understand what really matters, so that you may live **pure** and blameless lives until Christ returns. [NLT]
	εἰς τὸ δοκιμάζειν ὑμᾶς τὰ διαφέροντα, ἵνα ἦτε **εἰλικρινεῖς** καὶ ἀπρόσκοποι εἰς ἡμέραν Χριστοῦ, [GNS]
	εἰς τὸ δοκιμάζειν ὑμᾶς τὰ διαφέροντα, ἵνα ἦτε **εἰλικρινεῖς** καὶ ἀπρόσκοποι εἰς ἡμέραν Χριστοῦ, [GNT]
		Pure, sincere, honest. It means to sift about through a sieve in order to make pure. Therefore, the word means pure, uncontaminated, untainted, not polluted.
		
		Practical Application
		A growing love is needed to be sincere and pure. Note that we are to stay pure until the return of Christ. Only a growing love will keep our eyes focused upon Christ. If we do not love Him, we will not look to Him. If we love Him, we will keep our eyes fastened upon Him, longing to see and be with Him. Only love—true love—will keep us pure waiting for His return.

ENGLISH WORD	GREEK WORD AND VERSE	THE WORD MEANS...

#3097
Pure
 	
Harmless–KJV
Innocent–NASB
Pure–NIV
Harmless–NKJV
Clean–NLT
 	
**POSB
REFERENCE**
(Philip.2:15)
Note 4, point 2
	ἀκέραιοι = *akeraioi*
	Pronunciation: [ak-er'-ah-ee-oy]
	Parsing (part of speech): adjective
	    Case—nominative
	    Gender—masculine
	    Number—plural
	    Stem or root—from ἀκέραιος, ον
	Concordance References:
	  ⇒ Strong's #185 akeraios
	  ⇒ NIV #193 akeraios
	  ⇒ NASB #185 akeraios
	
	Philip. 2:15
	That ye may be blameless and **harmless**, the sons of God, without rebuke, in the midst of a crooked and perverse nation, among whom ye shine as lights in the world; [KJV]
	That you may prove yourselves to be blameless and **innocent**, children of God above reproach in the midst of a crooked and perverse generation, among whom you appear as lights in the world, [NASB]
	So that you may become blameless and **pure**, children of God without fault in a crooked and depraved generation, in which you shine like stars in the universe [NIV]
	That you may become blameless and **harmless**, children of God without fault in the midst of a crooked and perverse generation, among whom you shine as lights in the world, [NKJV]
	So that no one can speak a word of blame against you. You are to live **clean**, innocent lives as children of God in a dark world full of crooked and perverse people. Let your lives shine brightly before them. [NLT]
	ἵνα γένησθε ἄμεμπτοι καὶ **ἀκέραιοι**, τέκνα Θεοῦ ἀμώμητα ἐν μέσῳ γενεᾶς σκολιᾶς καὶ διεστραμμένης, ἐν οἷς φαίνεσθε ὡς φωστῆρες ἐν κόσμῳ, [GNS]
	ἵνα γένησθε ἄμεμπτοι καὶ **ἀκέραιοι**, τέκνα θεοῦ ἄμωμα μέσον γενεᾶς σκολιᾶς καὶ διεστραμμένης, ἐν οἷς φαίνεσθε ὡς φωστῆρες ἐν κόσμῳ, [GNT]
		Pure, harmless, innocent, clean, without guile, unmixed and unadulterated.
		
		Practical Application
		Believers are to work at being pure (*akeraioi*). It is the idea of flour or grain passing through a sieve to separate the pure from the impure. It means that our thoughts and lives...
		• are not to be polluted by watching, reading, and listening to worldly and sexual attractions.
		• are not to be given over to worldly and sexual attractions.
		
		Our thoughts and lives are to be pure, clean, uncontaminated, and unpolluted.

#3098
Pure
 	
Pure–KJV
Pure–NASB
Pure–NIV
Pure–NKJV
Pure–NLT
 	
**POSB
REFERENCE**
(Philip.4:8-9; esp. v.8)
Note 2, point 1d
 	
See also POSB REF:
(Jas.3:17-18; esp. v.17)
Note 3
(Tit.2:4-5, esp. v.5)
Note 4
	ἁγνα = *hagna*
	Pronunciation: [hag-nah]
	Parsing (part of speech): adjective
	    Case—nominative
	    Gender—neuter
	    Number—plural
	    Stem or root—from ἁγνός, ή, όν
	Concordance References:
	  ⇒ Strong's #53 hagnos
	  ⇒ NIV #54 hagnos
	  ⇒ NASB #53 hagnos
	
	Philip. 4:8
	Finally, brethren, whatsoever things are true, whatsoever things are honest, whatsoever things are just, whatsoever things are **pure**, whatsoever things are lovely, whatsoever things are of good report; if there be any virtue, and if there be any praise, think on these things. [KJV]
	Finally, brethren, whatever is true, whatever is honorable, whatever is right, whatever is **pure**, whatever is lovely, whatever is of good repute, if there is any excellence and if anything worthy of praise, let your mind dwell on these things. [NASB]
	Finally, brothers, whatever is true, whatever is noble, whatever is right, whatever is **pure**, whatever is lovely, whatever is admirable—if anything is excellent or praiseworthy—think about such things. [NIV]
	Finally, brethren, whatever things are true, whatever things *are* noble, whatever things *are* just, whatever things *are* **pure**, whatever things *are* lovely, whatever things *are* of good report, if *there is* any virtue and if *there is* anything praiseworthy—meditate on these things. [NKJV]
		Pure, morally clean, spotless, stainless, chaste, undefiled, free from moral pollution, filth, dirt, and impurities. The word means to be pure from fault and defilement; it means moral purity; to be completely separated from impurity and wrongdoing and set apart unto God. It is not being half good and half bad, but totally pure and clean (A.T. Robertson. *Word Pictures in the New Testament*, Vol. 6, p.47). A person who has true wisdom lives a clean and pure life.
		
		Practical Application
		The believer's mind and thoughts are to be pure—every thought.
		⇒ A truly wise person keeps his body pure. He does not damage himself by overeating, drinking, taking drugs, smoking, and letting himself become flabbly. He disciplines himself in all things and keeps himself fit in order to get maximum use out of life.
		⇒ A truly wise person keeps his relationships pure. He lives a moral and just life, protecting his spouse, his children, his family, his loved ones, the name of Christ, and his own testimony and ministry.
		⇒ A truly wise person keeps himself pure before God so that his relationship with God is always open and so that God can use him as much as He wishes.

ENGLISH WORD	GREEK WORD AND VERSE	THE WORD MEANS...
	And now, dear brothers and sisters, let me say one more thing as I close this letter. Fix your thoughts on what is true and honorable and right. Think about things that are **pure** and lovely and admirable. Think about things that are excellent and worthy of praise. [NLT] Τὸ λοιπόν, ἀδελφοί, ὅσα ἐστὶν ἀληθῆ, ὅσα σεμνά, ὅσα δίκαια, ὅσα **ἁγνά**, ὅσα προσφιλῆ, ὅσα εὔφημα, εἴ τις ἀρετὴ καὶ εἴ τις ἔπαινος, ταῦτα λογίζεσθε· [GNS] Τὸ λοιπόν, ἀδελφοί, ὅσα ἐστὶν ἀληθῆ, ὅσα σεμνά, ὅσα δίκαια, ὅσα **ἁγνά**, ὅσα προσφιλῆ, ὅσα εὔφημα, εἴ τις ἀρετὴ καὶ εἴ τις ἔπαινος, ταῦτα λογίζεσθε· [GNT]	

#3099
Pure
 	
Incorruptible–KJV
Imperishable–NASB
That can never perish–NIV
Incorruptible–NKJV
Pure–NLT
 	
POSB
REFERENCE
(1 Pt.1:4)
Note 2, point 1
	ἄφθαρτον = aphtharton
	Pronunciation: [af'-thar-ton]
	Parsing (part of speech): adjective
	   Case—accusative
	   Gender—feminine
	   Number—singular
	   Stem or root—from **ἄφθαρτος**, ον
	Concordance References:
	  ⇒ Strong's #862 aphtartos
	  ⇒ NIV #915 aphtartos
	  ⇒ NASB #862 aphtartos
	
	1 Peter 1:4
	To an inheritance **incorruptible**, and undefiled, and that fadeth not away, reserved in heaven for you, [KJV]
	To obtain an inheritance which is **imperishable** and undefiled and will not fade away, reserved in heaven for you, [NASB]
	And into an inheritance **that can never perish**, spoil or fade—kept in heaven for you, [NIV]
	To an inheritance **incorruptible** and undefiled and that does not fade away, reserved in heaven for you, [NKJV]
	For God has reserved a priceless inheritance for his children. It is kept in heaven for you, **pure** and undefiled, beyond the reach of change and decay. [NLT]
	εἰς κληρονομίαν **ἄφθαρτον** καὶ ἀμίαντον καὶ ἀμάραντον, τετηρημένην ἐν οὐρανοῖς εἰς ὑμᾶς [GNS]
	εἰς κληρονομίαν **ἄφθαρτον** καὶ ἀμίαντον καὶ ἀμάραντον, τετηρημένην ἐν οὐρανοῖς εἰς ὑμᾶς [GNT]
		Incorruptible, immortal, imperishable, pure, that can never perish; it does not age, deteriorate, or die; it does not have the seed of corruption within it.
		
		Practical Application
		Matthew Henry points out that everything on earth changes from better to worse, but not our inheritance. It is perfect and incorruptible. It never changes, and it will never cease to be the most perfect inheritance and gift imaginable (*Matthew Henry's Commentary*, Vol.6, p.1005).

#3100
Pure
 	
Sincere–KJV
Pure–NASB
Pure–NIV
Pure–NKJV
Pure–NLT
 	
POSB
REFERENCE
(1 Pt.2:2-3; esp. v.2)
Note 2, point 1b
	ἄδολον = adolon
	Pronunciation: [ad'-ol-on]
	Parsing (part of speech): adjective
	   Case—accusative
	   Gender—neuter
	   Number—singular
	   Stem or root—from **ἄδολος**, ον
	Concordance References:
	  ⇒ Strong's #97 adolos
	  ⇒ NIV #100 adolos
	  ⇒ NASB #97 adolos
	
	1 Peter 2:2
	As newborn babes, desire the **sincere** milk of the word, that ye may grow thereby: [KJV]
	Like newborn babes, long for the **pure** milk of the word, that by it you may grow in respect to salvation, [NASB]
	Like newborn babies, crave **pure** spiritual milk, so that by it you may grow up in your salvation, [NIV]
	As newborn babes, desire the **pure** milk of the word, that you may grow thereby, [NKJV]
	You must crave **pure** spiritual milk so that you can grow into the fullness of your salvation. Cry out for this nourishment as a baby cries for milk, [NLT]
	ὡς ἀρτιγέννητα βρέφη, τὸ λογικὸν **ἄδολον** γάλα ἐπιποθήσατε, ἵνα ἐν αὐτῷ αὐξηθῆτε, [GNS]
	ὡς ἀρτιγέννητα βρέφη τὸ λογικὸν **ἄδολον** γάλα ἐπιποθήσατε, ἵνα ἐν αὐτῷ αὐξηθῆτε εἰς σωτηρίαν, [GNT]
		Pure, sincere, unadulterated, unmixed with anything else.
		
		Practical Application
		Men may seek the milk of other things; they may seek to be fed and satisfied by such things as...
		  • religion
		  • philosophy
		  • education
		  • possessions
		  • pleasure
		  • power
		  • fortune
		  • psychology
		  • counseling
		  • health
		  • science
		  • fame
		  • comfort
		
		But none of these are pure. There are specks and dust and particles within every pursuit on earth—particles that make everything on earth weak and infirmed and to some degree harmful. In addition and most tragic of all, every pursuit of man is doomed to pass away when man passes away. But there is one thing that is unadulter-

ENGLISH WORD	GREEK WORD AND VERSE	THE WORD MEANS...
		ated; one thing that is completely and perfectly pure with no mixture whatsoever, and that is the Word of God. The Word of God lives and abides forever; therefore, we must crave and yearn for the Word of God. It is our only hope of enduring forever.
#3101 **Pure** Undefiled–KJV Undefiled–NASB **Pure–NIV** Undefiled–NKJV Unstained by sin–NLT **POSB** **REFERENCE** (Heb.7:26) Note 2	ἀμίαντος = amiantos Pronunciation: [am-ee'-an-tos] Parsing (part of speech): adjective 　　Case—nominative 　　Gender—masculine 　　Number—singular 　　Stem or root—from ἀμίαντος, ον Concordance References: 　⇒　Strong's #283 amiantos 　⇒　NIV #299 amiantos 　⇒　NASB #283 amiantos **Hebrews 7:26** For such an high priest became us, who is holy, harmless, **undefiled**, separate from sinners, and made higher than the heavens; [KJV] For it was fitting that we should have such a high priest, holy, innocent, **undefiled**, separated from sinners and exalted above the heavens; [NASB] Such a high priest meets our need—one who is holy, blameless, **pure**, set apart from sinners, exalted above the heavens. [NIV] For such a High Priest was fitting for us, *who is* holy, harmless, **undefiled**, separate from sinners, and has become higher than the heavens; [NKJV] He is the kind of high priest we need because he is holy and blameless, **unstained by sin**. He has now been set apart from sinners, and he has been given the highest place of honor in heaven. [NLT] Τοιοῦτος γὰρ ἡμῖν ἔπρεπεν ἀρχιερεύς, ὅσιος, ἄκακος, ἀμίαντος, κεχωρισμένος ἀπὸ τῶν ἁμαρτωλῶν, καὶ ὑψηλότερος τῶν οὐρανῶν γενόμενος· [GNS] Τοιοῦτος γὰρ ἡμῖν καὶ ἔπρεπεν ἀρχιερεύς, ὅσιος ἄκακος ἀμίαντος, κεχωρισμένος ἀπὸ τῶν ἁμαρτωλῶν καὶ ὑψηλότερος τῶν οὐρανῶν γενόμενος, [GNT]	Pure, undefiled, unstained by sin. **Practical Application** Jesus Christ is "pure" (*amiantos*): unstained by sin; absolutely free from all moral impurity, uncleanness, and defilement. Jesus Christ was completely free from anything that would keep Him from approaching God. He is absolutely *pure*.
#3102 **Pure** Undefiled–KJV Undefiled–NASB **Pure–NIV** Undefiled–NKJV Faithful–NLT **POSB** **REFERENCE** (Heb.13:4) Note 4	ἀμίαντος = amiantos Pronunciation: [am-ee'-ahn-tos] Parsing (part of speech): adjective 　　Case—nominative 　　Gender—feminine 　　Number—singular 　　Stem or root—from ἀμίαντος, ον Concordance References: 　⇒　Strong's #283 amiantos 　⇒　NIV #299 amiantos 　⇒　NASB #283 amiantos **Hebrews 13:4** Marriage is honourable in all, and the bed **undefiled**: but whoremongers and adulterers God will judge. [KJV] Let marriage be held in honor among all, and let the marriage bed be **undefiled**; for fornicators and adulterers God will judge. [NASB] Marriage should be honored by all, and the marriage bed kept **pure**, for God will judge the adulterer and all the sexually immoral. [NIV] Marriage *is* honorable among all, and the bed **undefiled**; but fornicators and adulterers God will judge. [NKJV] Give honor to marriage, and remain **faithful** to one another in marriage. God will surely judge people who are immoral and those who commit adultery. [NLT] τίμιος ὁ γάμος ἐν πᾶσι, καὶ ἡ κοίτη ἀμίαντος· πόρνους δὲ καὶ μοιχοὺς κρινεῖ ὁ Θεός. [GNS] Τίμιος ὁ γάμος ἐν πᾶσιν καὶ ἡ κοίτη ἀμίαντος, πόρνους γὰρ καὶ μοιχοὺς κρινεῖ ὁ θεός. [GNT]	Pure, undefiled, faithful, faultless, unstained, devoted, reliable, constant, unswerving, allegiant, unwavering, scrupulous. **Practical Application** The word "pure" (*amiantos*) means that the bed is unstained by sin, absolutely free from all moral impurity, uncleanness, and defilement. This is saying at least three things. ⇒First, husband and wife are free and encouraged to be close in bed. Closeness and intimacy are a gift from God; it is even a type of the church (cp. Ephes. 5:22f). ⇒ Second, the closeness in bed between husband and wife will prevent unfaithfulness. ⇒ Third, the bed is to be kept pure. Only husband and wife are to be close in bed, and only with each other. There is absolutely no place for anyone else in the bed. The importance of the bed in marriage cannot be overemphasized. God's Word says that it is so important that husband and wife are not to separate for any period of time except for fasting and prayer, and even then separation is not to occur unless it is by mutual consent.

ENGLISH WORD	GREEK WORD AND VERSE	THE WORD MEANS...

#3103
Pure
 	
Chaste–KJV
Chaste–NASB
Purity–NIV
Chaste–NKJV
Pure–NLT
 	
POSB
REFERENCE
(1 Pt.3:2)
Note 2
	ἁγνήν = *hagnēn*
	Pronunciation: [hag-nayn']
	Parsing (part of speech): adjective
	    Case—accusative
	    Gender—feminine
	    Number—singular
	    Stem or root—from ἁγνός, ή, όν
	Concordance References:
	  ⇒ Strong's #53 hagnos
	  ⇒ NIV #54 hagnos
	  ⇒ NASB #53 hagnos
	
	1 Peter 3:2
	While they behold your **chaste** conversation coupled with fear. [KJV]
	As they observe your **chaste** and respectful behavior. [NASB]
	When they see the **purity** and reverence of your lives. [NIV]
	When they observe your **chaste** conduct *accompanied* by fear. [NKJV]
	By watching your **pure**, godly behavior. [NLT]
	ἐποπτεύσαντες τὴν ἐν φόβῳ ἁγνὴν ἀναστροφὴν ὑμῶν. [GNS]
	ἐποπτεύσαντες τὴν ἐν φόβῳ ἁγνὴν ἀναστροφὴν ὑμῶν. [GNT]
		Pure, chaste. The word "pure" (*hagnēn*) means to be pure from all fault; to be clean and holy and free from all defilement; to act and behave in the most pure and modest way possible.
		
		Practical Application
		When a woman marries a man, she sets herself apart for him and him alone. She keeps herself clean and pure for him and for him alone. Note that the verse says, "Wives, must accept the authority of your *husbands*" (3:1). She does not subject or give herself to some other husband or man. She is her husband's and his alone.
		A dirty wife or husband is never to be named among Christian believers. Nothing destroys the testimony of believers any more than sexual impurity. And nothing affects the love and the trust that couples can put in one another any more than sexual impurity. For this reason, the Christian wife is to subject herself to her own husband by living a pure life.

#3104
Pure And Holy
 	
Sanctify–KJV
Sanctify–NASB
Sanctify–NIV
Sanctify–NKJV
Pure and holy–NLT
 	
POSB
REFERENCE
(Jn.17:17)
Deeper Study #4
 	
See also POSB REF:
(1 Cor.1:2)
Deeper Study #1
	ἁγίασον = *hagiason*
	Pronunciation: [hag-ee-ah'-son]
	Parsing (part of speech): verb
	    Mood—imperative
	    Tense—aorist
	    Voice—active
	    Person—2nd person
	    Number—singular
	    Stem or root—from ἁγιάζω
	Concordance References:
	  ⇒ Strong's #37 hagiazo
	  ⇒ NIV #39 hagiazo
	  ⇒ NASB #37 hagiazo
	
	John 17:17
	Sanctify them through thy truth: thy word is truth. [KJV]
	"**Sanctify** them in the truth; Thy word is truth. [NASB]
	Sanctify them by the truth; your word is truth. [NIV]
	Sanctify them by Your truth. Your word is truth. [NKJV]
	Make them **pure and holy** by teaching them your words of truth. [NLT]
	ἁγίασον αὐτοὺς ἐν τῇ ἀληθείᾳ σου· ὁ λόγος ὁ σὸς ἀλήθειά ἐστι. [GNS]
	ἁγίασον αὐτοὺς ἐν τῇ ἀληθείᾳ· ὁ λόγος ὁ σὸς ἀλήθειά ἐστιν. [GNT]
		To be set apart, to be separated; to be pure and holy; to be consecrated. (cp. 1 Peter 1:15-16).
		
		Practical Application
		There are three stages of sanctification.
		1. There is *initial or positional sanctification*. When a person believes in Jesus Christ, he is immediately set apart for God permanently, once-for-all (Hebrews 3:1; cp. Hebrews 10:10).
		2. There is *progressive sanctification*. The true believer makes a determined and disciplined effort to allow the Spirit of God to set him apart day by day. The Spirit of God takes him and conforms him to the image of Christ more and more. This growth takes place as long as the believer walks upon this earth (cp. John 17:17; 2 Cor. 3:18; Ephes. 5:25-26; 1 Thes. 5:23-24).
		3. There is *eternal sanctification*. The day is coming when the believer will be perfectly set apart unto God and His service—without any sin or failure whatsoever. That day will be the great and glorious day of the believer's eternal redemption (Ephes. 5:27; 1 John 3:2).

#3105
Pure Minds
 	
Pure minds–KJV
Sincere mind–NASB
Wholesome thinking–NIV
Pure minds–NKJV
Wholesome thinking–NLT
 	
POSB
REFERENCE
(2 Pt.3:1-2; esp. v.1)
Note 1
	εἰλικρινῆ διάνοιαν = *eilikrinē dianoian*
	Pronunciation: [i-lik-ree-nay' dee-an'-oy-ahn]
	Parsing *eilikrinē* (part of speech): adjective
	    Case—accusative
	    Gender—feminine
	    Number—singular
	    Stem or root—from εἰλικρινής, ές
	Parsing *dianoian* (part of speech): noun
	    Case—accusative
	    Gender—feminine
	    Number—singular
	    Stem or root—from διάνοια, ας
	Concordance References:
	  ⇒ Strong's #1506 eilikrinēs + 1271 dianoia
	  ⇒ NIV #1637 eilikrinēs [wholesome] + 1379 dianoia [thinking]
	  ⇒ NASB #1506 eilikrinēs + 1271 dianoia
		Wholesome thinking, pure minds, sincere mind, thoughts, attitudes. The phrase "pure minds" (*eilikrinē dianoian*) means to have a clear, pure, unmixed, uncontaminated, focused, and concentrating mind.
		
		Practical Application
		It is the picture of thoughts being sifted just like wheat is sifted in order to be separated from the chaff. Thoughts are to be sifted in order to separate the true and pure from the untrue and impure. There is always so much false teaching about the end time that the mind must be pure in order to sift the true teaching from the false. The picture of a pure mind is this: the mind must be exposed to the light of the sun and be found

ENGLISH WORD	GREEK WORD AND VERSE	THE WORD MEANS...
POSB REFERENCE (2 Cor.6:6-7; esp. v.6) Note 5	**2 Cor. 6:6** By **pureness**, by knowledge, by longsuffering, by kindness, by the Holy Ghost, by love unfeigned, [KJV] In **purity**, in knowledge, in patience, in kindness, in the Holy Spirit, in genuine love, [NASB] In **purity**, understanding, patience and kindness; in the Holy Spirit and in sincere love; [NIV] By **purity**, by knowledge, by longsuffering, by kindness, by the Holy Spirit, by sincere love, [NKJV] We have proved ourselves by our **purity**, our understanding, our patience, our kindness, our sincere love, and the power of the Holy Spirit. [NLT] ἐν ἁγνότητι, ἐν γνώσει, ἐν μακροθυμίᾳ, ἐν χρηστότητι, ἐν Πνεύματι Ἁγίῳ, ἐν ἀγάπῃ ἀνυποκρίτῳ, [GNS] sἐν ἁγνότητι, ἐν γνώσει, ἐν μακροθυμίᾳ, ἐν χρηστότητι, ἐν πνεύματι ἁγίῳ, ἐν ἀγάπῃ ἀνυποκρίτῳ, [GNT]	

#3110
Purity
 	
Chaste–KJV
Chaste–NASB
Purity–NIV
Chaste–NKJV
Pure–NLT
 	
POSB REFERENCE (1 Pt.3:2) Note 2
	ἁγνὴν = *hagnēn*
	Pronunciation: [hag-nayn']
	Parsing (part of speech): adjective
	   Case—accusative
	   Gender—feminine
	   Number—singular
	   Stem or root—from ἁγνός, ή, όν
	Concordance References:
	⇒ Strong's #53 hagnos
	⇒ NIV #54 hagnos
	⇒ NASB #53 hagnos
	
	1 Peter 3:2
	While they behold your **chaste** conversation coupled with fear. [KJV]
	As they observe your **chaste** and respectful behavior. [NASB]
	When they see the **purity** and reverence of your lives. [NIV]
	When they observe your **chaste** conduct *accompanied* by fear. [NKJV]
	By watching your **pure**, godly behavior. [NLT]
	ἐποπτεύσαντες τὴν ἐν φόβῳ ἁγνὴν ἀναστροφὴν ὑμῶν. [GNS]
	ἐποπτεύσαντες τὴν ἐν φόβῳ ἁγνὴν ἀναστροφὴν ὑμῶν. [GNT]
		Pure, chaste. The word "purity" (*hagnēn*) means to be pure from all fault; to be clean and holy and free from all defilement; to act and behave in the most pure and modest way possible.
		
		Practical Application
		When a woman marries a man, she sets herself apart for him and him alone. She keeps herself clean and pure for him and for him alone. Note that the verse says, "Wives, in the same way be submissive to your *husbands*" (3.1). She does not subject or give herself to some other husband or man. She is her husband's and his alone.
		A dirty wife or husband is never to be named among Christian believers. Nothing destroys the testimony of believers any more than sexual impurity. And nothing affects the love and the trust that couples can put in one another any more than sexual impurity. For this reason, the Christian wife is to subject herself to her own husband by living a chaste life.

#3111
Purpose
 	
Counsel–KJV
Plan–NASB
Purpose–NIV
Purpose–NKJV
Plan–NLT
 	
POSB REFERENCE (Acts 2:23) *Deeper Study* #3, point 2
	βουλῇ = *boulē*
	Pronunciation: [boo-lay']
	Parsing (part of speech): noun
	   Case—dative
	   Gender—feminine
	   Number—singular
	   Stem or root—from βουλή, ῆς
	Concordance References:
	⇒ Strong's #1012 boulē
	⇒ NIV #1087 boulē
	⇒ NASB #1012 boulē
	
	Acts 2:23
	Him, being delivered by the determinate **counsel** and foreknowledge of God, ye have taken, and by wicked hands have crucified and slain: [KJV]
	This Man, delivered up by the predetermined **plan** and foreknowledge of God, you nailed to a cross by the hands of godless men and put Him to death. [NASB]
	This man was handed over to you by God's set **purpose** and foreknowledge; and you, with the help of wicked men, put him to death by nailing him to the cross. [NIV]
	Him, being delivered by the determined **purpose** and foreknowledge of God, you have taken by lawless hands, have crucified, and put to death; [NKJV]
	But you followed God's prearranged **plan**. With the
		Purpose, counsel, plan, intention, motive, design, will.
		
		Practical Application
		It carries the force of being willed and determined. Since God knows exactly what would happen in every situation, He plans for the best thing to happen. God takes purpose, puts all things under advisement, and chooses the best way.

ENGLISH WORD	GREEK WORD AND VERSE	THE WORD MEANS...
	help of lawless Gentiles, you nailed him to the cross and murdered him. [NLT] τοῦτον τῇ ὡρισμένῃ **βουλῇ** καὶ προγνώσει τοῦ Θεοῦ ἔκδοτον λαβόντες διὰ χειρῶν ἀνόμων προσπήξαντες ἀνείλατε, [GNS] τοῦτον τῇ ὡρισμένῃ **βουλῇ** καὶ προγνώσει τοῦ θεοῦ ἔκδοτον διὰ χειρὸς ἀνόμων προσπήξαντες ἀνείλατε, [GNT]	
#3112 **Purse** **Purse–KJV** **Purse–NASB** **Purse-NIV** Money bag–NKJV Not translated–NLT **POSB REFERENCE** (Lk.10:4) Note 4, point 1	βαλλάντιον = *ballantion* Pronunciation: [bal-an'-tee-on] Parsing (part of speech): noun 　　Case—accusative 　　Gender—neuter 　　Number—singular 　　Stem or root—from βαλλάντιον, ου Concordance References: 　⇒　Strong's #905 balantion 　⇒　NIV #964 balantion 　⇒　NASB #905 balantion **Luke 10:4** Carry neither **purse**, nor scrip, nor shoes: and salute no man by the way. [KJV] "Carry no **purse**, no bag, no shoes; and greet no one on the way. [NASB] Do not take a **purse** or bag or sandals; and do not greet anyone on the road. [NIV] Carry neither **money bag**, knapsack, nor sandals; and greet no one along the road. [NKJV] Don't take along any money, or a traveler's bag, or even an extra pair of sandals. And don't stop to greet anyone on the road. [NLT] NOT TRANSLATED μὴ βαστάζετε **βαλάντιον**, μὴ πήραν, μὴ ὑποδήματα· καὶ μηδένα κατὰ τὴν ὁδὸν ἀσπάσησθε. [GNS] μὴ βαστάζετε **βαλλάντιον**, μὴ πήραν, μὴ ὑποδήματα, καὶ μηδένα κατὰ τὴν ὁδὸν ἀσπάσησθε. [GNT]	Purse, money bag, money pouch. **Practical Application** 　What did a money pouch have to do with a believer's life? In this Scripture, they were not to carry a money bag, purse, (*ballantion*) or a traveller's bag (*pera*) or two pair of sandals. They were to trust God for provisions, not worrying about money for food, housing, or clothing (Matthew 6:24-34). Worrying about such things would be cumbersome, taking away precious time that should be spent in ministering. Also, they were preaching a message of faith and trust in God. They needed to live what they were preaching and become a living picture of the dependency that God wants from every man.
#3113 **Pursue** Follow–KJV **Pursue–NASB** Follow–NIV **Pursue–NKJV** Highest goal–NLT **POSB REFERENCE** (1 Cor.14:1) Note 1	Διώκετε = *Diōkete* Pronunciation: [dee-o'-keh-teh] Parsing (part of speech): verb 　　Mood—imperative 　　Tense—present 　　Voice—active 　　Person—2nd person 　　Number—plural 　　Stem or root—from διώκω Concordance References: 　⇒　Strong's #1377 diōkō 　⇒　NIV #1503 diōkō 　⇒　NASB #1377 diōkō **1 Cor. 14:1** **Follow** after charity, and desire spiritual gifts, but rather that ye may prophesy. [KJV] **Pursue** love, yet desire earnestly spiritual gifts, but especially that you may prophesy. [NASB] **Follow** the way of love and eagerly desire spiritual gifts, especially the gift of prophecy. [NIV] **Pursue** love, and desire spiritual *gifts,* but especially that you may prophesy. [NKJV] Let love be your **highest goal**, but also desire the special abilities the Spirit gives, especially the gift of prophecy. [NLT] Διώκετε τὴν ἀγάπην· ζηλοῦτε δὲ τὰ πνευματικά, μᾶλλον δὲ ἵνα προφητεύητε. [GNS] Διώκετε τὴν ἀγάπην, ζηλοῦτε δὲ τὰ πνευματικά, μᾶλλον δὲ ἵνα προφητεύητε. [GNT]	To follow; to pursue, to persist; to seek after; to strive for; to continue on and on, never giving up until love is possessed. **Practical Application** 　Love is to be pursued above all else in life. Gifts, abilities, and service are important; but they pale into insignificance in comparison with love. Love is the greatest need and the supreme answer to all the needs of men. It is when we love a person that we meet the needs of a person. In fact, if we truly love a person, then we will do all we can to meet all the needs of that person.
#3114 **Pursue** Follow–KJV **Pursue–NASB**	δίωκε = *dioke* Pronunciation: [dee-o'-keh] Parsing (part of speech): verb 　　Mood—imperative 　　Tense—present 　　Voice—active	To pursue; to follow; to seek after. The word "pursue" (*dioke*) is strong. It means to run after; to run swiftly after; to hotly pursue; to seek eagerly and earnestly.

ENGLISH WORD	GREEK WORD AND VERSE	THE WORD MEANS...
Pursue–NIV **Pursue–NKJV** **Pursue–NLT** **POSB REFERENCE** (1 Tim.6:11) Note 2, point 2 **See also POSB REF:** (Heb.12:14) Note 1	Person—2nd person Number—singular Stem or root—from διώκω Concordance References: ⇒ Strong's #1377 diökö ⇒ NIV #1503 diökö ⇒ NASB #1377 diökö **1 Tim. 6:11** But thou, O man of God, flee these things; and **follow** after righteousness, godliness, faith, love, patience, meekness. [KJV] But flee from these things, you man of God; and **pursue** righteousness, godliness, faith, love, perseverance and gentleness. [NASB] But you, man of God, flee from all this, and **pursue** righteousness, godliness, faith, love, endurance and gentleness. [NIV] But you, O man of God, flee these things and **pursue** righteousness, godliness, faith, love, patience, gentleness. [NKJV] But you, Timothy, belong to God; so run from all these evil things, and follow what is right and good. **Pursue** a godly life, along with faith, love, perseverance, and gentleness. [NLT] Σὺ δέ ὦ ἄνθρωπε τοῦ Θεοῦ, ταῦτα φεῦγε· **δίωκε** δὲ δικαιοσύνην, εὐσέβειαν, πίστιν, ἀγάπην, ὑπομονήν, πραόπατητα· [GNS] Σὺ δέ, ὦ ἄνθρωπε θεοῦ, ταῦτα φεῦγε· **δίωκε** δὲ δικαιοσύνην εὐσέβειαν πίστιν, ἀγάπην ὑπομονήν πραϋπαθίαν. [GNT]	**Practical Application** It has the idea of aiming at and pursuing until something is gained; of never giving up until we have reached our goal.
#3115 **Pursue** Ensue–KJV **Pursue–NASB** **Pursue–NIV** **Pursue–NKJV** Work hard–NLT **POSB REFERENCE** (1 Pt.3:11) Note 3	διωξάτω = diöxatö Pronunciation: [dee-o'-kaht-o'] Parsing (part of speech): verb Mood—imperative Tense—aorist Voice—active Person—3rd person Number—singular Stem or root—from διώκω Concordance References: ⇒ Strong's #1377 diökö ⇒ NIV #1503 diökö ⇒ NASB #1377 diökö **1 Peter 3:11** Let him eschew evil, and do good; let him seek peace, and **ensue** it. [KJV] "And let him turn away from evil and do good; Let him seek peace and **pursue** it. [NASB] He must turn from evil and do good; he must seek peace and **pursue** it. [NIV] Let him turn away from evil and do good; Let him seek peace and **pursue** it. [NKJV] Turn away from evil and do good. **Work hard** at living in peace with others. [NLT] ἐκκλινάτω ἀπὸ κακοῦ, καὶ ποιησάτω ἀγαθόν· ζητησάτω εἰρήνην, καὶ **διωξάτω** αὐτήν. [GNS] ἐκκλινάτω δὲ ἀπὸ κακοῦ καὶ ποιησάτω ἀγαθόν, ζητησάτω εἰρήνην καὶ **διωξάτω** αὐτήν· [GNT]	To pursue; to ensue; to work hard; to strive for; to seek after. The word "pursue" (*diöxatö*) means to run after, chase after, press after, and to pursue. It has the idea of swiftness and endurance—of hotly pursuing and staying after peace. **Practical Application** Believers are not only to desire peace, but they are to actively pursue and go after it. We live in a world that is full of corruptible and evil people who could care less about peace and holiness just so they get what they are after. However, the believer must not give up, for peace is the very reason he is on earth. The believer is to follow after peace (*eirenen*) with all men. The fact that he has to follow after peace means that peace is not always possible. ⇒ Some persons within the church are troublemakers: grumblers, complainers, gossipers, criticizers; some are self-centered leaders full of pride; some people within the church are just selfish and self-centered and care more about pushing themselves forward and getting their own way than they do about peace. Self is put before Christ and the church and its mission. ⇒ Some persons within the world are troublemakers and they cause great trouble for the believer. They oppose the believer: ridicule, mock, poke fun at, curse, abuse, persecute, ignore, and isolate him. ⇒ Some persons within the world are troublemakers for the world at large: dissenters, dividers, fighters, egotists, power-builders, and warmongers. Some people

ENGLISH WORD	GREEK WORD AND VERSE	THE WORD MEANS...
		have no interest in peace whatever unless they can have their own way. The point is this: the believer is to follow after peace with *all men*—no matter who they are. The very purpose for the believer being on earth is to bring peace between men and God and between men and all other men. Therefore, the believer is to do all he can to live at peace with everyone and to lead others to live in peace.

#3116
Push
 	
Hold–KJV
Suppress–NASB
Suppress–NIV
Suppress–NKJV
Push–NLT
 	
**POSB
REFERENCE**
(Romans 1:18)
Note 1, point 3b
	κατεχόντων = *katechontōn*
	Pronunciation: [kat-ech'-own-town]
	Parsing (part of speech): verb
	    Mood—participle
	    Tense—active
	    Case—genitive
	    Gender—masculine
	    Number—plural
	    Stem or root—from κατέχω
	Concordance References:
	  ⇒ Strong's #2722 katechō
	  ⇒ NIV #2988 katechō
	  ⇒ NASB #2722 katechō
	
	Romans 1:18
	For the wrath of God is revealed from heaven against all ungodliness and unrighteousness of men, who **hold** the truth in unrighteousness; [KJV]
	For the wrath of God is revealed from heaven against all ungodliness and unrighteousness of men, who **suppress** the truth in unrighteousness, [NASB]
	The wrath of God is being revealed from heaven against all the godlessness and wickedness of men who **suppress** the truth by their wickedness, [NIV]
	For the wrath of God is revealed from heaven against all ungodliness and unrighteousness of men, who **suppress** the truth in unrighteousness, [NKJV]
	But God shows his anger from heaven against all sinful, wicked people who **push** the truth away from themselves. [NLT]
	Ἀποκαλύπτεται γὰρ ὀργὴ Θεοῦ ἀπ' οὐρανοῦ ἐπὶ πᾶσαν ἀσέβειαν καὶ ἀδικίαν ἀνθρώπων τῶν τὴν ἀλήθειαν ἐν ἀδικίᾳ **κατεχόντων**, [GNS]
	Ἀποκαλύπτεται γὰρ ὀργὴ θεοῦ ἀπ' οὐρανοῦ ἐπὶ πᾶσαν ἀσέβειαν καὶ ἀδικίαν ἀνθρώπων τῶν τὴν ἀλήθειαν ἐν ἀδικίᾳ **κατεχόντων**, [GNT]
		To hold fast; to keep; to take; to possess; to hold back; to restrain; to suppress. It means to hold down, suppress, repress, stifle, hinder.
		
		Practical Application
		Men know the truth from three sources:
		⇒ from nature (cp. Romans 1:20).
		⇒ from reason and conscience (cp. Romans 1:18; Romans 2:15).
		⇒ from Scripture (John 5:39; 2 Tim. 3:16).
		
		Yet despite having access to the truth, they ignore, neglect, and even push the truth aside, doing all they can to avoid and get rid of it. Why? Because they want to live as they wish and not as God says. They want to live unrighteous lives, to taste and feel and see and have all the stimulating things they want.
		But note what Scripture says: they "suppress the truth in unrighteousness"; [NASB] that is, they know the truth while they go about living in unrighteousness. They are without excuse.

#3117
Put Aside
 	
Deny–KJV
Deny–NASB
Deny–NIV
Deny–NKJV
Put aside–NLT
 	
**POSB
REFERENCE**
(Mt.16:24)
Note 2, point 2
 	
See also POSB REF:
(Mk.8:34)
Deeper Study #2
	ἀπαρνησάσθω = *aparnēsasthō*
	Pronunciation: [ap-ar-neh'-sas-tho]
	Parsing (part of speech): verb
	    Mood—imperative
	    Tense—aorist
	    Voice—middle deponent
	    Person—3rd person
	    Number—singular
	    Stem or root—from ἀπαρνέομαι
	Concordance References:
	  ⇒ Strong's #533 aparneomai
	  ⇒ NIV #565 aparneomai
	  ⇒ NASB #533 aparneomai
	
	Matthew 16:24
	Then said Jesus unto his disciples, If any man will come after me, let him **deny** himself, and take up his cross, and follow me. [KJV]
	Then Jesus said to His disciples, "If anyone wishes to come after Me, let him **deny** himself, and take up his cross, and follow Me. [NASB]
	Then Jesus said to his disciples, "If anyone would come after me, he must **deny** himself and take up his cross and follow me. [NIV]
	Then Jesus said to His disciples, "If anyone desires to
		To disown, disregard, deny, put aside, forsake, renounce, reject, refuse, restrain, disclaim. It means to subdue, to disregard one's self and one's interest. Very simply, it means to say "no."
		
		Practical Application
		But note: the call is not to say "no" to some behavior or thing, but to self. A person is to put aside self; and this means much more than just being negative, that is, giving up something and doing without something. It means that we are to act positively, to say "yes" to Christ and "no" to self. It means to let Christ rule and reign in our hearts and lives, to let Christ have His way completely. Of course, if a person allows Christ to rule in his life, all negative as well as positive behavior is taken care of (see POSB note and *Deeper Study #1*—Mark 8:34, POSB *Deeper Study #2*—Mark 8:34, POSB *Deeper Study #3*—Mark 8:34). In the Greek the word "put aside" is an ingressive aorist which means that the person enters a new state or condition. It means, "Let him at once begin to put aside self."

ENGLISH WORD	GREEK WORD AND VERSE	THE WORD MEANS...
	come after Me, let him **deny** himself, and take up his cross, and follow Me. [NKJV] Then Jesus said to the disciples, "If any of you wants to be my follower, you must **put aside** your selfish ambition, shoulder your cross, and follow me. [NLT] τότε ὁ Ἰησοῦς εἶπε τοῖς μαθηταῖς αὐτοῦ, Εἴ τις θέλει ὀπίσω μου ἐλθεῖν, **ἀπαρνησάσθω** ἑαυτὸν, καὶ ἀράτω τὸν σταυρὸν αὐτοῦ καὶ ἀκολουθείτω μοι. [GNS] Τότε ὁ Ἰησοῦς εἶπεν τοῖς μαθηταῖς αὐτοῦ, Εἴ τις θέλει ὀπίσω μου ἐλθεῖν, **ἀπαρνησάσθω** ἑαυτὸν καὶ ἀράτω τὸν σταυρὸν αὐτοῦ καὶ ἀκολουθείτω μοι. [GNT]	

#3118
Put Away
 	
Put away–KJV
Rejected–NASB
Rejected–NIV
Rejected–NKJV
Deliberately violated–NLT
 	
**POSB
REFERENCE**
(1 Tim.1:19-20; esp. v.19)
Note 3
	ἀπωσάμενοι = *apōsamenoi*
	Pronunciation: [ap-o'-sah-mehn-oy]
	Parsing (part of speech): verb
	    Mood—participle
	    Tense—aorist
	    Voice—middle deponent
	    Case—nominative
	    Gender—masculine
	    Number—plural
	    Stem or root—from **ἀπωθέομαι**
	Concordance References:
	⇒ Strong's #683 apötheō
	⇒ NIV #723 apötheō
	⇒ NASB #683 apötheō
	
	1 Tim. 1:19
	Holding faith, and a good conscience; which some having **put away** concerning faith have made shipwreck: [KJV]
	Keeping faith and a good conscience, which some have **rejected** and suffered shipwreck in regard to their faith. [NASB]
	Holding on to faith and a good conscience. Some have **rejected** these and so have shipwrecked their faith. [NIV]
	Having faith and a good conscience, which some having **rejected**, concerning the faith have suffered shipwreck, [NKJV]
	Cling tightly to your faith in Christ, and always keep your conscience clear. For some people have **deliberately violated** their consciences; as a result, their faith has been shipwrecked. [NLT]
	ἔχων πίστιν καὶ ἀγαθὴν συνείδησιν, ἥν τινες **ἀπωσάμενοι**, περὶ τὴν πίστιν ἐναυάγησαν· [GNS]
	ἔχων πίστιν καὶ ἀγαθὴν συνείδησιν, ἥν τινες **ἀπωσάμενοι** περὶ τὴν πίστιν ἐναυάγησαν, [GNT]
		To reject; to put away; to deliberately violate; to push aside; to push away with force.
		
		Practical Application
		It is a willful and deliberate pushing away of conscience. Conscience says that something is wrong and should not be done, but conscience is ignored and subdued, turned away from and denied.
		When a person *continues to push his conscience away*, something terrible happens: his faith is shipwrecked. His faith is broken to pieces and destroyed. A person must live as Scripture dictates: righteously and godly. If he does not live righteously and godly, then he weakens his faith and soon dashes it upon the storms of evil, worldliness, and false doctrine. His faith is shipwrecked—because he pushed his conscience aside refusing to listen to its call to live righteously and godly.

#3119
**Put In Charge
As A
Manager**
 	
Stewards–KJV
Stewards–NASB
Given a trust–NIV
Stewards–NKJV
**Put in charge as a
manager–NLT**
 	
**POSB
REFERENCE**
(1 Cor.4:1-2; esp. v.2)
Note 1, point 2
	ἐν οἰκονόμοις = *en oikonomois*
	Pronunciation: [en oy-kon-om'-oys]
	Parsing *oikonomois* (part of speech): noun
	    Case—dative
	    Gender—masculine
	    Number—plural
	    Stem or root—from **οἰκονόμος**, ου
	Concordance References:
	⇒ Strong's #1722+3623 en oikonomos
	⇒ NIV #1877+3874 en oikonomos [given a trust]
	⇒ NASB #1722+3623 en oikonomos
	
	1 Cor. 4:2
	Moreover it is required in **stewards**, that a man be found faithful. [KJV]
	In this case, moreover, it is required of **stewards** that one be found trustworthy. [NASB]
	Now it is required that those who have been **given a trust** must prove faithful. [NIV]
	Moreover it is required in **stewards** that one be found faithful. [NKJV]
	Now, a person who is **put in charge as a manager** must be faithful. [NLT]
	ὃ δὲ λοιπὸν, ζητεῖται **ἐν** τοῖς **οἰκονόμοις**, ἵνα πιστός τις εὑρεθῇ. [GNS]
	ὧδε λοιπὸν ζητεῖται **ἐν** τοῖς **οἰκονόμοις**, ἵνα πιστός τις εὑρεθῇ. [GNT]
		To be given a trust; to be put in charge as a manager; to be a steward; to be a trustee; to be the overseer of an estate.
		
		Practical Application
		The steward or manager was always a slave, subject to a master, but he was *placed in charge* of the other slaves throughout the master's house or estate. He controlled the staff and ran the whole operation for the master. He was set over others, yet he himself was still a slave of the master. His work was not closely supervised; therefore, he had to be trustworthy and responsible. Note what the minister is given a trust over: the mysteries of God. A mystery is not something hard to understand. Rather, it is something that has been hidden and kept secret. It is something that was undiscoverable by human reason, but now is revealed by God. It is crystal clear to those to whom it is revealed, but it is completely alien to those who do not receive it. What are the mysteries of God? They are the truths—the glorious truths—of God's Word. Who are the ones to whom the mysteries are revealed? The stewards, the ministers, the believing servants or managers of Christ.

ENGLISH WORD	GREEK WORD AND VERSE	THE WORD MEANS...

#3120
Put In Charge To Lead
 	
Schoolmaster–KJV
Tutor–NASB
Put in charge to lead–NIV
Tutor–NKJV
Guardian and teacher–NLT
 	
POSB REFERENCE
(Gal.3:23-25; esp. v.24)
Note 1
	παιδαγωγός = paidagögos
	Pronunciation: [pahee-dag-o-gos']
	Parsing (part of speech): noun
	    Case—nominative
	    Gender—masculine
	    Number—singular
	    Stem or root—from παιδαγωγός, οῦ
	Concordance References:
	  ⇒ Strong's #3807 paidagögos
	  ⇒ NIV #4080 paidagögos
	  ⇒ NASB #3807 paidagögos
	
	Galatians 3:24
	Wherefore the law was our **schoolmaster** to bring us unto Christ, that we might be justified by faith. [KJV]
	Therefore the Law has become our **tutor** to lead us to Christ, that we may be justified by faith. [NASB]
	So the law was **put in charge to lead** us to Christ that we might be justified by faith. [NIV]
	Therefore the law was our **tutor** *to bring us* to Christ, that we might be justified by faith. [NKJV]
	Let me put it another way. The law was our **guardian and teacher** to lead us until Christ came. So now, through faith in Christ, we are made right with God. [NLT]
	ὥστε ὁ νόμος **παιδαγωγὸς** ἡμῶν γέγονεν εἰς Χριστόν, ἵνα ἐκ πίστεως δικαιωθῶμεν· [GNS]
	ὥστε ὁ νόμος **παιδαγωγὸς** ἡμῶν γέγονεν εἰς Χριστόν, ἵνα ἐκ πίστεως δικαιωθῶμεν· [GNT]
		Put in charge to lead, tutor, teacher, instructor, guide, supervisor.
		
		Practical Application
		The law was man's guardian to lead him to see his need for Christ. The *paidagögos* was usually a trusted slave who was in charge of a child's moral welfare, but he had one particular duty to which Paul was referring. Every day the guardian took the child to school and delivered him to the teacher. And then at the end of the day, he returned for the child and brought him safely back home. This was what the law was to do. The law was to lead man to Christ, the true Teacher. The law does this by showing man that he is utterly unable to secure righteousness by himself. He must look to Christ, the real Teacher, for righteousness and acceptance by God, that is, for justification by faith. And once Christ (faith in Him) has come, there is no need for the law nor for any other guardian, for Jesus Christ brings us face to face with God.

#3121
Put...In Remembrance
 	
Put...in remembrance–KJV
Pointing out–NASB
Point...out–NIV
Instruct–NKJV
Explain–NLT
 	
POSB REFERENCE
(1 Tim.4:6)
Note 1
	ὑποτιθέμενος = hupotithemenos
	Pronunciation: [hoop-ot-ith'-eh-mehn-os]
	Parsing (part of speech): verb
	    Mood—participle
	    Tense—present
	    Voice—middle
	    Case—nominative
	    Gender—masculine
	    Person—2nd person
	    Number—singular
	    Stem or root—from ὑποτίθημι
	Concordance References:
	  ⇒ Strong's #5294 hupotithëmi
	  ⇒ NIV #5719 hupotithëmi
	  ⇒ NASB #5294 hupotithëmi
	
	1 Tim. 4:6
	If thou **put** the brethren **in remembrance** of these things, thou shalt be a good minister of Jesus Christ, nourished up in the words of faith and of good doctrine, whereunto thou hast attained. [KJV]
	In **pointing out** these things to the brethren, you will be a good servant of Christ Jesus, constantly nourished on the words of the faith and of the sound doctrine which you have been following. [NASB]
	If you **point** these things **out** to the brothers, you will be a good minister of Christ Jesus, brought up in the truths of the faith and of the good teaching that you have followed. [NIV]
	If you **instruct** the brethren in these things, you will be a good minister of Jesus Christ, nourished in the words of faith and of the good doctrine which you have carefully followed. [NKJV]
	If you **explain** this to the brothers and sisters, you will be doing your duty as a worthy servant of Christ Jesus, one who is fed by the message of faith and the true teaching you have followed. [NLT]
	Ταῦτα **ὑποτιθέμενος** τοῖς ἀδελφοῖς καλὸς ἔσῃ διάκονος Ἰησοῦ Χριστοῦ, ἐντρεφόμενος τοῖς λόγοις τῆς πίστεως, καὶ τῆς καλῆς διδασκαλίας ᾗ παρηκολούθηκας. [GNS]
	Ταῦτα **ὑποτιθέμενος** τοῖς ἀδελφοῖς καλὸς ἔσῃ διάκονος Χριστοῦ Ἰησοῦ, ἐντρεφόμενος τοῖς λόγοις τῆς πίστεως καὶ τῆς καλῆς διδασκαλίας ᾗ παρηκολούθηκας· [GNT]
		To point out; to put in remembrance; to explain; to teach. The Greek word "put...in remembrance" (*hupotithemenos*) means to place under, suggest, counsel, advise.
		
		Practical Application
		The point is this: false teaching is such a threat to the church and believers that the good minister of Jesus Christ will use every method of communication he can to instruct and protect his flock from being seduced by false teachers.

ENGLISH WORD	GREEK WORD AND VERSE	THE WORD MEANS...

#3122
Put Into Action

Work out–KJV
Work out–NASB
Work out–NIV
Work out–NKJV
Put into action–NLT

**POSB
REFERENCE**
(Philip.2:12)
Note 1

κατεργάζεσθε = *katergazesthe*
Pronunciation: [kat-er-gad'-zehs-theh]
Parsing (part of speech): verb
  Mood—imperative
  Tense—present
  Voice—middle or passive deponent
  Person—2nd person
  Number—plural
  Stem or root—from κατεργάζομαι
Concordance References:
⇒ Strong's #2716 katergazomai
⇒ NIV #2981 katergazomai
⇒ NASB #2716 katergazomai

Philip. 2:12

Wherefore, my beloved, as ye have always obeyed, not as in my presence only, but now much more in my absence, **work out** your own salvation with fear and trembling. [KJV]

So then, my beloved, just as you have always obeyed, not as in my presence only, but now much more in my absence, **work out** your salvation with fear and trembling; [NASB]

Therefore, my dear friends, as you have always obeyed—not only in my presence, but now much more in my absence—continue to **work out** your salvation with fear and trembling, [NIV]

Therefore, my beloved, as you have always obeyed, not as in my presence only, but now much more in my absence, **work out** your own salvation with fear and trembling; [NKJV]

Dearest friends, you were always so careful to follow my instructions when I was with you. And now that I am away you must be even more careful to **put into action** God's saving work in your lives, obeying God with deep reverence and fear. [NLT]

Ὥστε, ἀγαπητοί μου, καθὼς πάντοτε ὑπηκούσατε, μὴ ὡς ἐν τῇ παρουσίᾳ μου μόνον, ἀλλὰ νῦν πολλῷ μᾶλλον ἐν τῇ ἀπουσίᾳ μου, μετὰ φόβου καὶ τρόμου τὴν ἑαυτῶν σωτηρίαν **κατεργάζεσθε**· [GNS]

Ὥστε, ἀγαπητοί μου, καθὼς πάντοτε ὑπηκούσατε, μὴ ὡς ἐν τῇ παρουσίᾳ μου μόνον ἀλλὰ νῦν πολλῷ μᾶλλον ἐν τῇ ἀπουσίᾳ μου, μετὰ φόβου καὶ τρόμου τὴν ἑαυτῶν σωτηρίαν **κατεργάζεσθε**· [GNT]

To work out; to put into action; to produce; to carry out. It means to work on to the finish, to completion, to perfection.

Practical Application

It always means to complete the effort and the work begun; to accomplish it perfectly; to bring it to completion. The point is: do not go halfway in salvation. Do not take bits and pieces when there is a whole parcel. Do not be satisfied with a little when you can have much. Go on, grow until salvation is completed in you. It is your own salvation. No friend, no pastor can work it out for you. You alone must do it.

The point is clearly stated: once God has saved a person, that person is to get busy obeying God. He is to take hold of the new life and salvation God has given him, and he is to work on it until it is completed and finished, that is, until God takes him home and perfects him.

#3123
Put Into Effect

Dispensation–KJV
Administration–NASB
Put into effect–NIV
Dispensation–NKJV
This is his plan–NLT

**POSB
REFERENCE**
(Eph.1:9-10; esp. v.10)
Note 6, point 3

οἰκονομίαν = *oikonomian*
Pronunciation: [oy-kon-om-ee'-ahn]
Parsing (part of speech): noun
  Case—accusative
  Gender—feminine
  Number—singular
  Stem or root—from οἰκονομία, ας
Concordance References:
⇒ Strong's #3622 oikonomia
⇒ NIV #3873 oikonomia
⇒ NASB #3622 oikonomia

Ephes. 1:10

That in the **dispensation** of the fulness of times he might gather together in one all things in Christ, both which are in heaven, and which are on earth; even in him: [KJV]

With a view to an **administration** suitable to the fulness of the times, that is, the summing up of all things in Christ, things in the heavens and things upon the earth. In Him [NASB]

To be **put into effect** when the times will have reached their fulfillment—to bring all things in heaven and on earth together under one head, even Christ. [NIV]

That in the **dispensation** of the fullness of the times He might gather together in one all things in Christ, both which are in heaven and which are on earth—in Him. [NKJV]

To put into effect; administration; job, commission, management, dispensation; to have a plan. The word Paul uses literally means "household arrangement."

Practical Application

The idea is that the universe is a house under the management of God. God is handling, planning, arranging, and administering all things toward a climactic consummation for Christ and His followers. In that climactic day all disharmony and division and evil will be subjected and harmonized (*anakephalaioo*) under Christ. A new and perfect and eternal creation will be established for the Lord and His followers throughout the universe.

ENGLISH WORD	GREEK WORD AND VERSE	THE WORD MEANS...
	And **this is his plan**: At the right time he will bring everything together under the authority of Christ—everything in heaven and on earth. [NLT] εἰς **οἰκονομίαν** τοῦ πληρώματος τῶν καιρῶν, ἀνακεφαλαιώσασθαι τὰ πάντα ἐν τῷ Χριστῷ, τὰ τε ἐν τοῖς οὐρανοῖς καὶ τὰ ἐπὶ τῆς γῆς· ἐν αὐτῷ, [GNS] εἰς **οἰκονομίαν** τοῦ πληρώματος τῶν καιρῶν, ἀνακεφαλαιώσασθαι τὰ πάντα ἐν τῷ Χριστῷ, τὰ ἐπὶ τοῖς οὐρανοῖς καὶ τὰ ἐπὶ τῆς γῆς ἐν αὐτῷ. [GNT]	

#3124
Put On
 	
Put...on–KJV
Put on–NASB
Clothe...with–NIV
Put on–NKJV
Take control–NLT
 	
POSB REFERENCE
(Rom.13:14)
Deeper Study #2
 	
See also POSB REF:
(Col.3:12-14; esp. v.12)
Note 1
	ἐνδύσασθε = *endusasthe*
	Pronunciation: [en-doo'-sahs-theh]
	Parsing (part of speech): verb
	    Mood—imperative
	    Tense—aorist
	    Voice—middle
	    Person—2nd person
	    Number—plural
	    Stem or root—from ἐνδύω
	Concordance References:
	  ⇒ Strong's #1746 enduö
	  ⇒ NIV #1907 enduö
	  ⇒ NASB #1746 enduö
	
	Romans 13:14
	But **put** ye **on** the Lord Jesus Christ, and make not provision for the flesh, to fulfil the lusts thereof. [KJV]
	But **put on** the Lord Jesus Christ, and make no provision for the flesh in regard to its lusts. [NASB]
	Rather, **clothe** yourselves **with** the Lord Jesus Christ, and do not think about how to gratify the desires of the sinful nature. [NIV]
	But **put on** the Lord Jesus Christ, and make no provision for the flesh, to fulfill its lusts. [NKJV]
	But let the Lord Jesus Christ **take control** of you, and don't think of ways to indulge your evil desires. [NLT]
	ἀλλ᾽ **ἐνδύσασθε** τὸν Κύριον Ἰησοῦν Χριστόν, καὶ τῆς σαρκὸς πρόνοιαν μὴ ποιεῖσθε, εἰς ἐπιθυμίας. [GNS]
	ἀλλὰ **ἐνδύσασθε** τὸν κύριον Ἰησοῦν Χριστόν καὶ τῆς σαρκὸς πρόνοιαν μὴ ποιεῖσθε εἰς ἐπιθυμίας. [GNT]
		To clothe with; to put on; to wear; to dress; to take control.
		
		Practical Application
		Scripture lists seven things that the believer is to put on or with which he is to clothe himself.
		1. The believer is to put on and be "endued or clothed" (*endusesthe*) with the Holy Spirit (Luke 24:49).
		2. The believer is to put on and be clothed with the Lord Jesus Christ (Romans 13:14; Galatians 3:27).
		3. The believer is to put on and be clothed with immortality (1 Cor. 15:53-54; 2 Cor. 5:3).
		4. The believer is to put on and be clothed with the new man (Ephes. 4:24; Col. 3:10).
		5. The believer is to put on and be clothed with the nature of God (Col. 3:12).
		6. The believer is to put on and be clothed with the armour of light and of God (Romans 13:14; Ephes. 6:11f).
		7. The believer is to put on and be clothed with love (Col. 3:14).

#3125
Put On Display
 	
Set forth–KJV
Exhibited–NASB
Put...on display–NIV
Displayed–NKJV
Put...on display–NLT
 	
POSB REFERENCE
(1 Cor.4:9-10; esp. v.9)
Note 4
	ἀπέδειξεν = *apedeixen*
	Pronunciation: [ap-ed'-eek-zehn]
	Parsing (part of speech): verb
	    Mood—indicative
	    Tense—aorist
	    Voice—active
	    Person—3rd person
	    Number—singular
	    Stem or root—from ἀποδείκνυμι
	Concordance References:
	  ⇒ Strong's #584 apodeiknumi
	  ⇒ NIV #617 apodeiknumi
	  ⇒ NASB #584 apodeiknumi
	
	1 Cor. 4:9
	For I think that God hath **set forth** us the apostles last, as it were appointed to death: for we are made a spectacle unto the world, and to angels, and to men. [KJV]
	For, I think, God has **exhibited** us apostles last of all, as men condemned to death; because we have become a spectacle to the world, both to angels and to men. [NASB]
	For it seems to me that God has **put** us apostles **on display** at the end of the procession, like men condemned to die in the arena. We have been made a spectacle to the whole universe, to angels as well as to men. [NIV]
	For I think that God has **displayed** us, the apostles, last, as men condemned to death; for we have been made a spectacle to the world, both to angels and to men. [NKJV]
	But sometimes I think God has **put** us apostles **on display**, like prisoners of war at the end of a victor's
		To put on display; to set forth; to exhibit; to proclaim; to prove.
		
		Practical Application
		The phrase "put on display" (*apedeixen*) means more than to be seen or exhibited. The picture is that of doomed gladiators being taken to the arena. God has put on display the minister as a doomed gladiator to serve the world no matter the cost.

ENGLISH WORD	GREEK WORD AND VERSE	THE WORD MEANS...
	parade, condemned to die. We have become a spectacle to the entire world—to people and angels alike. [NLT] δοκῶ γάρ, ὅτι ὁ Θεὸς ἡμᾶς τοὺς ἀποστόλους ἐσχάτους **ἀπέδειξεν** ὡς ἐπιθανατίους· ὅτι θέατρον ἐγενήθημεν τῷ κόσμῳ, καὶ ἀγγέλοις καὶ ἀνθρώποις. [GNS] δοκῶ γάρ, ὁ θεὸς ἡμᾶς τοὺς ἀποστόλους ἐσχάτους **ἀπέδειξεν** ὡς ἐπιθανατίους, ὅτι θέατρον ἐγενήθημεν τῷ κόσμῳ καὶ ἀγγέλοις καὶ ἀνθρώποις. [GNT]	
#3126 **Put To Death– Putting To Death** Mortify–KJV **Putting to death– NASB** **Put to death–NIV** **Put to death–NKJV** Turn from–NLT **POSB REFERENCE** (Romans 8:12-13, esp. v.13) Note 6, point 2c	θανατοῦτε = *thanatoute* Pronunciation: [than-at-oo'-teh] Parsing (part of speech): verb Mood—indicative Tense—present Voice—active Person—2nd person Number—plural Stem or root—from θανατόω Concordance References: ⇒ Strong's #2289 thanatoö ⇒ NIV #2506 thanatoö ⇒ NASB #2289 thanatoö **Romans 8:13** For if ye live after the flesh, ye shall die: but if ye through the Spirit do **mortify** the deeds of the body, ye shall live. [KJV] For if you are living according to the flesh, you must die; but if by the Spirit you are **putting to death** the deeds of the body, you will live. [NASB] For if you live according to the sinful nature, you will die; but if by the Spirit you **put to death** the misdeeds of the body, you will live, [NIV] For if you live according to the flesh you will die; but if by the Spirit you **put to death** the deeds of the body, you will live. [NKJV] For if you keep on following it, you will perish. But if through the power of the Holy Spirit you **turn from** it and its evil deeds, you will live. [NLT] εἰ γὰρ κατὰ σάρκα ζῆτε, μέλλετε ἀποθνήσκειν· εἰ δὲ πνεύματι τὰς πράξεις τοῦ σώματος **θανατοῦτε**, ζήσεσθε. [GNS] εἰ γὰρ κατὰ σάρκα ζῆτε, μέλλετε ἀποθνήσκειν· εἰ δὲ πνεύματι τὰς πράξεις τοῦ σώματος **θανατοῦτε**, ζήσεσθε. [GNT]	To put to death; to mortify; to turn from. The idea is that of denying, subjecting, subduing, deadening, destroying the strength of. **Practical Application** The power to put to death the evil deeds of the body comes "through the Spirit." However, note this: we deny the evil deeds, and then the Spirit gives the strength to deaden and to subdue their strength. We are involved just as the Spirit is involved. We cannot destroy the strength of sin unless we exercise our will and work to destroy it ourselves, and we cannot will and work at it apart from Him. Both the Spirit and ourselves have to be involved, each doing his part if we wish the evil deeds of the body to be put to death. To repeat the point above: we exercise our will to deny the evil deeds, and then the Spirit immediately steps in to deaden the pull and strength of the evil deed. If we do not want the evil deeds of our body destroyed, if we want to continue living in the sins of the flesh, if we want nothing to do with the Spirit—then the Spirit can do nothing for us. God loves us too much to force us; He will not override our choices. But if we honestly will to follow the Spirit and honestly desire to destroy the evil deeds of our body, the Spirit will step in and give the power to do so. He will break the power of sin: He will deaden and subdue the strength of it.
#3127 **Put...To Work** Occupy–KJV Do business–NASB **Put...to work–NIV** Do business–NKJV Invest–NLT **POSB REFERENCE** (Lk.19:13) Note 3, point 2 *Deeper Study #2*	Πραγματεύσασθε = *Pragmateusasthe* Pronunciation: [prag-mat-yoo'-sahs-theh] Parsing (part of speech): verb Mood—imperative Tense—aorist Voice—middle deponent Person—2nd person Number—plural Stem or root—from πραγματεύομαι Concordance References: ⇒ Strong's #4231 pragmateuomai ⇒ NIV #4549 pragmateuomai ⇒ NASB #4231 pragmateuomai **Luke 19:13** And he called his ten servants, and delivered them ten pounds, and said unto them, **Occupy** till I come. [KJV] "And he called ten of his slaves, and gave them ten minas, and said to them, '**Do business** with this until I come back.' [NASB] So he called ten of his servants and gave them ten minas. '**Put** this money **to work**,' he said, 'until I come back.' [NIV] So he called ten of his servants, delivered to them ten minas, and said to them, '**Do business** till I come.' [NKJV] Before he left, he called together ten servants and gave	To invest; to do business; to put to work; to trade; to occupy. **Practical Application** The words *put to work (Pragmateusasthe)* are words of diligent action. It is from the root word meaning to walk, to set in motion, and to continue in motion. The servant is to labor diligently, never letting up but using all the Lord has given him to look after. This is the only time the word is used in the New Testament (cp. Isaiah 35:3; Hebrews 12:28; Hebrews 12:12).

ENGLISH WORD	GREEK WORD AND VERSE	THE WORD MEANS...
	them ten pounds of silver to **invest** for him while he was gone. [NLT] καλέσας δὲ δέκα δούλους ἑαυτοῦ, ἔδωκεν αὐτοῖς δέκα μνᾶς, καὶ εἶπε πρὸς αὐτούς, **Πραγματεύσασθε** ἕως ἔρχομαι. [GNS] καλέσας δὲ δέκα δούλους ἑαυτοῦ ἔδωκεν αὐτοῖς δέκα μνᾶς καὶ εἶπεν πρὸς αὐτούς, **Πραγματεύσασθε** ἐν ᾧ ἔρχομαι. [GNT]	

#3128
Put Together
 	
Tempered–KJV
Composed–NASB
Combined–NIV
Composed–NKJV
Put...together–NLT
 	
**POSB
REFERENCE**
(1 Cor.12:24-26; esp.
v.24)
Note 4
	συνεκέρασεν = sunekerasen
	Pronunciation: [soon-eh-ker'-ahn-sehn]
	Parsing (part of speech): verb
	   Mood—indicative
	   Tense—aorist
	   Voice—active
	   Person—3rd person
	   Number—singular
	   Stem or root—from συγκεράννυμι
	Concordance References:
	⇒ Strong's #4786 sugkerannumi
	⇒ NIV #5166 sugkerannumi
	⇒ NASB #4786 sugkerannumi
	
	1 Cor. 12:24
	For our comely parts have no need: but God hath **tempered** the body together, having given more abundant honour to that part which lacked: [KJV]
	
	Whereas our seemly members have no need of it. But God has so **composed** the body, giving more abundant honor to that member which lacked, [NASB]
	
	While our presentable parts need no special treatment. But God has **combined** the members of the body and has given greater honor to the parts that lacked it, [NIV]
	
	But our presentable parts have no need. But God **composed** the body, having given greater honor to that part which lacks it, [NKJV]
	
	While other parts do not require this special care. So God has **put** the body **together** in such a way that extra honor and care are given to those parts that have less dignity. [NLT]
	
	τὰ δὲ εὐσχήμονα ἡμῶν οὐ χρείαν ἔχει· ἀλλ ὁ Θεὸς **συνεκέρασε** τὸ σῶμα, τῷ ὑστερουντι περισσοτέραν δοὺς τιμήν, [GNS]
	
	τὰ δὲ εὐσχήμονα ἡμῶν οὐ χρείαν ἔχει. ἀλλὰ ὁ θεὸς **συνεκέρασεν** τὸ σῶμα τῷ ὑστερουμένῳ περισσοτέραν δοὺς τιμήν, [GNT]
		To mix; to combine; to unite; to put together; to arrange and blend together.
		
		Practical Application
		God has arranged the church as it is: the gifted and less gifted mix, combine, and blend together. And He has done it in such a manner that more honor really belongs to those who are not as gifted. The prayer warrior is much more essential than the soloist who is out before the people. The lay witness for Christ is more necessary than the preacher who stands in the pulpit. The person who ministers to the sick or elderly is more honorable than the committee chairman who leads the whole congregation in administrative matters.

#3129
Put Your Trust
 	
Believe–KJV
Believe–NASB
Put your trust–NIV
Believe–NKJV
Believe–NLT
 	
**POSB
REFERENCE**
(Jn.12:34-36; esp.
v.36)
Note 5, point 2
	πιστεύετε = pisteuete
	Pronunciation: [pist-yoo'-eh-teh]
	Parsing (part of speech): verb
	   Mood—imperative
	   Tense—present
	   Voice—active
	   Person—2nd person
	   Number—plural
	   Stem or root—from πιστεύω
	Concordance References:
	⇒ Strong's #4100 pisteuo
	⇒ NIV #4409 pisteuo
	⇒ NASB #4100 pisteuo
	
	John 12:36
	While ye have light, **believe** in the light, that ye may be the children of light. These things spake Jesus, and departed, and did hide himself from them. [KJV]
	
	"While you have the light, **believe** in the light, in order that you may become sons of light." These things Jesus spoke, and He departed and hid Himself from them. [NASB]
	
	Put your trust in the light while you have it, so that you may become sons of light." When he had finished speaking, Jesus left and hid himself from them. [NIV]
	
	While you have the light, **believe** in the light, that you
		To believe; to put trust in; to be convinced; to have no doubt; to be certain of.
		
		Practical Application
		Note this important grammatical form of the phrase "put your trust" (pisteuete): it is continuous action. A person who truly sees Jesus Christ as the Light of the world believes and continues to believe. And the very moment his heart leaps toward Christ in belief, he becomes a child of the Light, a child of God Himself. The person sees the Light and begins to walk in the Light, living the kind of life he should.

ENGLISH WORD	GREEK WORD AND VERSE	THE WORD MEANS...

| | For I am afraid that when I come to visit you I won't like what I find, and then you won't like my response. I am afraid that I will find **quarreling**, jealousy, outbursts of anger, selfishness, backstabbing, gossip, conceit, and disorderly behavior. [NLT]

φοβοῦμαι γὰρ μή πως ἐλθὼν οὐχ οἵους θέλω εὕρω ὑμᾶς, κἀγὼ εὑρεθῶ ὑμῖν οἷον οὐ θέλετε· μή πως **ἔρις**, ζῆλοι, θυμοί, ἐριθεῖαι, καταλαλιαί, ψιθυρισμοί, φυσιώσεις, ἀκαταστασίαι· [GNS]

φοβοῦμαι γὰρ μή πως ἐλθὼν οὐχ οἵους θέλω εὕρω ὑμᾶς κἀγὼ εὑρεθῶ ὑμῖν οἷον οὐ θέλετε· μή πως **ἔρις**, ζῆλος, θυμοί, ἐριθεῖαι, καταλαλιαί, ψιθυρισμοί, fusiώσεις, ἀκαταστασίαι· [GNT] | |

| **#3134**
Quarreling

Variance–KJV
Strife–NASB
Discord–NIV
Contentions–NKJV
Quarreling–NLT

POSB
REFERENCE
(Gal.5:19-21; esp.
v.20)
Note 2 | **ἔρις** = eris
Pronunciation: [er'-is]
Parsing (part of speech): noun
    Case—nominative
    Gender—feminine
    Number—singular
    Stem or root—from ἔρις, ιδος
Concordance References:
  ⇒ Strong's #2054 eris
  ⇒ NIV #2251 eris
  ⇒ NASB #2054 eris

Galatians 5:20
Idolatry, witchcraft, hatred, **variance**, emulations, wrath, strife, seditions, heresies, [KJV]
Idolatry, sorcery, enmities, **strife**, jealousy, outbursts of anger, disputes, dissensions, factions, [NASB]
Idolatry and witchcraft; hatred, **discord**, jealousy, fits of rage, selfish ambition, dissensions, factions [NIV]
Idolatry, sorcery, hatred, **contentions**, jealousies, outbursts of wrath, selfish ambitions, dissensions, heresies, [NKJV]
Idolatry, participation in demonic activities, hostility, **quarreling**, jealousy, outbursts of anger, selfish ambition, divisions, the feeling that everyone is wrong except those in your own little group, [NLT]
εἰδωλολατρία, φαρμακεία, ἔχθραι, **ἔρεις**, ζῆλοι, θυμοί, ἐριθεῖαι, διχοστασίαι, αἱρέσεις, [GNS]
εἰδωλολατρία, φαρμακεία, ἔχθραι, **ἔρις**, ζῆλος, θυμοί, ἐριθεῖαι, διχοστασίαι, αἱρέσεις, [GNT] | Discord, variance, strife, quarreling, contention, fighting, struggling, dissension, wrangling, selfish rivalry.

Practical Application
It means that a person fights against another person in order to get something: position, promotion, property, honor, recognition. He deceives, doing whatever has to be done to get what he is after. |

| **#3135**
Quarreling

Brawlers–KJV
Uncontentious–NASB
Peaceable–NIV
Peaceable–NKJV
Quarreling–NLT

POSB
REFERENCE
(Tit.3:2)
Note 4 | **ἀμάχους** = amachous
Pronunciation: [am'-akh-oos]
Parsing (part of speech): adjective
    Case—accusative
    Gender—masculine
    Number—plural
    Stem or root—from ἄμαχος, ον
Concordance References:
  ⇒ Strong's #269 amachos
  ⇒ NIV #285 amachos
  ⇒ NASB #269 amachos

Titus 3:2
To speak evil of no man, to be no **brawlers**, *but* gentle, shewing all meekness unto all men. [KJV]
To malign no one, to be **uncontentious**, gentle, showing every consideration for all men. [NASB]
To slander no one, to be **peaceable** and considerate, and to show true humility toward all men. [NIV]
To speak evil of no one, to be **peaceable**, gentle, showing all humility to all men. [NKJV]
They must not speak evil of anyone, and they must avoid **quarreling**. Instead, they should be gentle and show true humility to everyone. [NLT]
μηδένα βλασφημεῖν, **ἀμάχους** εἶναι, ἐπιεικεῖς, πᾶσαν ἐνδεικνυμένους πρᾳότητα πρὸς πάντας ἀνθρώπους. [GNS]
μηδένα βλασφημεῖν, **ἀμάχους** εἶναι, ἐπιεικεῖς, πᾶσαν ἐνδεικνυμένους πραΰτητα πρὸς πάντας ἀνθρώπους. [GNT] | To be peaceable; to be uncontentious; not to be quarreling or brawling.

Practical Application
The Christian is not to be a fighting, contentious person; not to be a person who is always walking around looking for an argument or fight; not to be a person who walks around with a chip on his shoulder looking for some controversy or argument; not to be so opinionated and stubborn that everyone else is always wrong; not to be a person who is always criticizing or talking about others, stirring up trouble and disturbing feelings and causing division. The Christian citizen is to be the very opposite: meek and peaceful. This, of course, does not mean that the Christian citizen does not speak up for what is right; he does. And he is strong in his stand, refusing to give in to the license and indulgence of evil. But he seeks peace where it is possible, and he seeks to lead others to be peaceable. |

ENGLISH WORD	GREEK WORD AND VERSE	THE WORD MEANS...

#3136
Quarreling,
Been
 	
Was...displeased–KJV
Was very angry–NASB
Been quarreling–NIV
Had been very angry–NKJV
Was very angry–NLT
 	
POSB
REFERENCE
(Acts 12:18-23; esp. v.20)
Note 3, point 1
	Ἦν θυμομαχῶν = *Ēn thumomachön*
	Pronunciation: [ayne thoo-mom-ach-on]
	Parsing *thumomachön* (part of speech): verb
	    Mood—participle
	    Tense—present
	    Voice—active
	    Case—nominative
	    Gender—masculine
	    Number—singular
	    Stem or root—from θυμομαχέω
	Concordance References:
	⇒ Strong's #1510 eimi + 2371 thumomacheö
	⇒ NIV #1639 eimi [been] + 2595 thumomacheö [quarreling]
	⇒ NASB #1510 eimi + 2371thumomacheö
	
	Acts 12:20
	And Herod **was** highly **displeased** with them of Tyre and Sidon: but they came with one accord to him, and, having made Blastus the king's chamberlain their friend, desired peace; because their country was nourished by the king's *country.* [KJV]
	Now he **was very angry** with the people of Tyre and Sidon; and with one accord they came to him, and having won over Blastus the king's chamberlain, they were asking for peace, because their country was fed by the king's country. [NASB]
	He had **been quarreling** with the people of Tyre and Sidon; they now joined together and sought an audience with him. Having secured the support of Blastus, a trusted personal servant of the king, they asked for peace, because they depended on the king's country for their food supply. [NIV]
	Now Herod **had been very angry** with the people of Tyre and Sidon; but they came to him with one accord, and having made Blastus the king's personal aide their friend, they asked for peace, because their country was supplied with food by the king's *country.* [NKJV]
	Now Herod **was very angry** with the people of Tyre and Sidon. So they sent a delegation to make peace with him because their cities were dependent upon Herod's country for their food. They made friends with Blastus, Herod's personal assistant, [NLT]
	Ἦν δὲ ὁ Ἡρώδης **θυμομαχῶν** Τυρίοις καὶ Σιδωνίοις· τὴν ὁμοθυμαδὸν δὲ παρῆσαν πρὸς αὐτόν, καὶ πείσαντες Βλάστον τὸν ἐπὶ τοῦ κοιτῶνος τοῦ βασιλέως, ἠτοῦντο εἰρήνην, διὰ τὸ τρέφεσθαι αὐτῶν τὴν χώραν ἀπὸ τῆς βασιλικῆς. [GNS]
	Ἦν δὲ **θυμομαχῶν** Τυρίοις καὶ Σιδωνίοις· ὁμοθυμαδὸν δὲ παρῆσαν πρὸς αὐτόν καὶ πείσαντες Βλάστον, τὸν ἐπὶ τοῦ κοιτῶνος τοῦ βασιλέως, ἠτοῦντο εἰρήνην διὰ τὸ τρέφεσθαι αὐτῶν τὴν χώραν ἀπὸ τῆς βασιλικῆς. [GNT]
		To be very angry; to be displeased; to quarrel in an irate way.
		
		Practical Application
		Herod's nature is seen in the word "Been quarreling" (*Ēn thumomachön*). The word means to be inflamed; to be filled with violent hostility. It is very hot anger, an emotion that should never characterize the leader of a nation.

#3137
Quarrels
 	
Contentions–KJV
Quarrels–NASB
Quarrels–NIV
Contentions–NKJV
Arguments–NLT
 	
POSB
REFERENCE
(1 Cor.1:11)
Note 2
	ἔριδες = *erides*
	Pronunciation: [er'-i-des]
	Parsing (part of speech): noun
	    Case—nominative
	    Gender—feminine
	    Number—plural
	    Stem or root—from ἔρις, ιδος
	Concordance References:
	⇒ Strong's #2054 eris
	⇒ NIV #2251 eris
	⇒ NASB #2054 eris
	
	1 Cor. 1:11
	For it hath been declared unto me of you, my brethren, by them *which are of the house* of Chloe, that there are **contentions** among you. [KJV]
	For I have been informed concerning you, my brethren, by Chloe's *people,* that there are **quarrels**
		Wranglings, strifes, quarrels, disregard, rivalries, fightings, factions.
		
		Practical Application
		Note: the nature of division is more clearly defined by the word. The church was arguing and splitting into groups, contending and quarreling over something. There was a severe strife between factions and cliques in the church.

ENGLISH WORD	GREEK WORD AND VERSE	THE WORD MEANS...
	among you. [NASB] My brothers, some from Chloe's household have informed me that there are **quarrels** among you. [NIV] For it has been declared to me concerning you, my brethren, by those of Chloe's *household,* that there are **contentions** among you. [NKJV] For some members of Chloe's household have told me about your **arguments**, dear brothers and sisters. [NLT] ἐδηλώθη γάρ μοι περὶ ὑμῶν, ἀδελφοί μου, ὑπὸ τῶν Χλόης ὅτι **ἔριδες** ἐν ὑμῖν εἰσι. [GNS] ἐδηλώθη γάρ μοι περὶ ὑμῶν, ἀδελφοί μου, ὑπὸ τῶν Χλόης ὅτι **ἔριδες** ἐν ὑμῖν εἰσιν. [GNT]	

#3138
 Quarrelsome, Not
 	
 Not a brawler–KJV
 Uncontentious–NASB
 Not quarrelsome–NIV
 Not quarrelsome–NKJV
 Peace loving–NLT
 	
 POSB REFERENCE
 (1 Tim.3-2-3; esp. v.3)
 Note 2, point 12
	ἄμαχον = *amachon*
	 Pronunciation: [am'-akh-on]
	 Parsing (part of speech): adjective
	     Case—accusative
	     Gender—masculine
	     Number—singular
	     Stem or root—from **ἄμαχος**, ον
	 Concordance References:
	 ⇒ Strong's #269 amachos
	 ⇒ NIV #285 amachos
	 ⇒ NASB #269 amachos
	
	 1 Tim. 3:3
	 Not given to wine, no striker, not greedy of filthy lucre; but patient, **not a brawler**, not covetous; [KJV]
	
	 Not addicted to wine or pugnacious, but gentle, **uncontentious**, free from the love of money. [NASB]
	
	 Not given to drunkenness, not violent but gentle, **not quarrelsome**, not a lover of money. [NIV]
	
	 Not given to wine, not violent, not greedy for money, but gentle, **not quarrelsome**, not covetous; [NKJV]
	
	 He must not be a heavy drinker or be violent. He must be gentle, **peace loving**, and not one who loves money. [NLT]
	
	 μὴ πάροινον, μὴ πλήκτην, μὴ αἰσχροκερδῆ, ἀλλ ἐπιεικῆ, **ἄμαχον**, ἀφιλάργυρον· [GNS]
	
	 μὴ πάροινον μὴ πλήκτην, ἀλλὰ ἐπιεικῆ **ἄμαχον** ἀφιλάργυρον, [GNT]
		Not quarrelsome; not a brawler; not contentious or a fighter; to be peace loving, peaceable, peaceful.
		
		 Practical Application
		 The minister or elder must not be quarrelsome (*amachon*): He must be a man of peace, a mild-mannered person, always under control. Again, this refers to the tongue as well as to the hands. He must be a man who is deeply touched when there is unrest, controversy, or disturbance in the church or among believers. He must be a person who is so touched that he will work and seek for peace.

#3139
 Quick
 	
 Quick–KJV
 Living–NASB
 Living–NIV
 Living–NKJV
 Living–NLT
 	
 POSB REFERENCE
 (Heb.4:11-13; esp. v.12)
 Note 5, point 2a
	Ζῶν = *Zön*
	 Pronunciation: [zone]
	 Parsing (part of speech): verb
	     Mood—participle
	     Tense—present
	     Voice—active
	     Case—nominative
	     Gender—masculine
	     Number—singular
	     Stem or root—from ζάω
	 Concordance References:
	 ⇒ Strong's #2198 zaö
	 ⇒ NIV #2409 zaö
	 ⇒ NASB #2198 zaö
	
	 Hebrews 4:12
	 For the word of God *is* **quick**, and powerful, and sharper than any twoedged sword, piercing even to the dividing asunder of soul and spirit, and of the joints and marrow, and *is* a discerner of the thoughts and intents of the heart. [KJV]
	
	 For the word of God is **living** and active and sharper than any two-edged sword, and piercing as far as the division of soul and spirit, of both joints and marrow, and able to judge the thoughts and intentions of the heart. [NASB]
	
	 For the word of God is **living** and active. Sharper than any double-edged sword, it penetrates even to dividing soul and spirit, joints and marrow; it judges the thoughts and attitudes of the heart. [NIV]
	
	 For the word of God *is* **living** and powerful, and sharper than any two-edged sword, piercing even to the
		Living, quick, alive; coming to life; bringing to life.
		
		 Practical Application
		 The Word of God is "quick" (*Zön*): alive and living. The idea is that the Word of God is always alive and active; it is always working and quickening its message to the human heart. Therefore, God's word of rest is not a dead and meaningless promise; it is living and full of life to the heart of the believer.

ENGLISH WORD	GREEK WORD AND VERSE	THE WORD MEANS...
	division of soul and spirit, and of joints and marrow, and is a discerner of the thoughts and intents of the heart. [NKJV] For the word of God is full of **living** power. It is sharper than the sharpest knife, cutting deep into our innermost thoughts and desires. It exposes us for what we really are. [NLT] ζῶν γὰρ ὁ λόγος τοῦ Θεοῦ, καὶ ἐνεργὴς, καὶ τομώτερος ὑπὲρ πᾶσαν μάχαιραν δίστομον, καὶ διϊκνούμενος· ἄχρι μερισμοῦ ψυχῆς τὲ καὶ πνεύματος, ἁρμῶν τε καὶ μυελῶν, καὶ κριτικὸς ἐνθυμήσεων καὶ ἐννοιῶν καρδίας. [GNS] Ζῶν γὰρ ὁ λόγος τοῦ θεοῦ καὶ ἐνεργὴς καὶ τομώτερος ὑπὲρ πᾶσαν μάχαιραν δίστομον καὶ διϊκνούμενος ἄχρι μερισμοῦ ψυχῆς καὶ πνεύματος, ἁρμῶν τε καὶ μυελῶν, καὶ κριτικὸς ἐνθυμήσεων καὶ ἐννοιῶν καρδίας. [GNT]	

#3140
 	
Quick Tempered
 	
Soon angry–KJV
Quick-tempered– NASB
Quick-tempered–NIV
Quick-tempered– NKJV
Quick-tempered– NLT
 	
POSB REFERENCE
(Tit.1:7-8; esp. v.7)
Note 3, point 1b
	ὀργίλον = orgilon
	Pronunciation: [org-ee'-lon]
	Parsing (part of speech): adjective
	    Case—accusative
	    Gender—masculine
	    Number—singular
	    Stem or root—from ὀργίλος, η, ον
	Concordance References:
	  ⇒ Strong's #3711 orgilos
	  ⇒ NIV #3975 orgilos
	  ⇒ NASB #3711 orgilos
	
	Titus 1:7
	For a bishop must be blameless, as the steward of God; not selfwilled, not **soon angry**, not given to wine, no striker, not given to filthy lucre; [KJV]
	
	For the overseer must be above reproach as God's steward, not self-willed, not **quick-tempered**, not addicted to wine, not pugnacious, not fond of sordid gain, [NASB]
	
	Since an overseer is entrusted with God's work, he must be blameless—not overbearing, not **quick-tempered**, not given to drunkenness, not violent, not pursuing dishonest gain. [NIV]
	
	For a bishop must be blameless, as a steward of God, not self-willed, not **quick-tempered**, not given to wine, not violent, not greedy for money, [NKJV]
	
	An elder must live a blameless life because he is God's minister. He must not be arrogant or **quick-tempered**; he must not be a heavy drinker, violent, or greedy for money. [NLT]
	
	δεῖ γὰρ τὸν ἐπίσκοπον ἀνέγκλητον εἶναι, ὡς Θεοῦ οἰκονόμον· μὴ αὐθάδη, μὴ **ὀργίλον**, μὴ πάροινον, μὴ πλήκτην, μὴ αἰσχροκερδῆ, [GNS]
	
	δεῖ γὰρ τὸν ἐπίσκοπον ἀνέγκλητον εἶναι ὡς θεοῦ οἰκονόμον, μὴ αὐθάδη, μὴ **ὀργίλον**, μὴ πάροινον, μὴ πλήκτην, μὴ αἰσχροκερδῆ, [GNT]
		To be quick tempered, soon angry. It is a long-lasting anger; an anger that is deeply rooted and has been held for a long time; an anger against someone that a person just refuses to let go; the person refuses to forgive the other person.
		
		Practical Application
		The minister must not be quick-tempered or hot-headed, nor given over to long-lasting anger.

#3141
 	
Quicken
 	
Quicken–KJV
Give life–NASB
Give life–NIV
Give life–NKJV
Give life–NLT
 	
POSB REFERENCE
(Rom.8:10-11; esp. v.11)
Note 5, point 2a
	ζῳοποιήσει = zōopoiēsei
	Pronunciation: [dzo-op-oy-ay'-seh-ee]
	Parsing (part of speech): verb
	    Mood—indicative
	    Tense—future
	    Voice—active
	    Person—3rd person
	    Number—singular
	    Stem or root—from ζῳοποιέω
	Concordance References:
	  ⇒ Strong's #2227 zōopoieō
	  ⇒ NIV #2443 zōopoieō
	  ⇒ NASB #2227 zōopoieō
	
	Romans 8:11
	But if the Spirit of him that raised up Jesus from the dead dwell in you, he that raised up Christ from the dead shall also **quicken** your mortal bodies by his Spirit that
		To make alive, to cause to live, to renew and remake life.
		
		Practical Application
		The Spirit of Christ quickens the mortal body *in the future*, in the great day of redemption. The "mortal body" will be quickened and made alive.
		  ⇒ The mortal body is the same body that died. The person is the very same person.
		  ⇒ The mortal body is given a totally new life; its elements are recreated and remade into a perfect and eternal body. The new body is to be given the power and energy of eternal elements, eternal molecules and atoms or whatever the most minute elements are. All will be arranged so that the mortal body becomes an immortal body.

ENGLISH WORD	GREEK WORD AND VERSE	THE WORD MEANS...
You fool–NKJV You idiot–NLT **POSB REFERENCE** (Mt.5:22) Note 3, point 2	Concordance References: ⇒ Strong's #4469 hraka ⇒ NIV #4819 hraka ⇒ NASB #4469 hraka **Matthew 5:22** But I say unto you, That whosoever is angry with his brother without a cause shall be in danger of the judgment: and whosoever shall say to his brother, **Raca**, shall be in danger of the council: but whosoever shall say, Thou fool, shall be in danger of hell fire. [KJV] "But I say to you that everyone who is angry with his brother shall be guilty before the court; and whoever shall say to his brother, '**Raca**,' shall be guilty before the supreme court; and whoever shall say, 'You fool,' shall be guilty enough to go into the fiery hell. [NASB] But I tell you that anyone who is angry with his brother will be subject to judgment. Again, anyone who says to his brother, '**Raca**,' is answerable to the Sanhedrin. But anyone who says, 'You fool!' will be in danger of the fire of hell. [NIV] But I say to you that whoever is angry with his brother without a cause shall be in danger of the judgment. And whoever says to his brother, '**Raca**!' shall be in danger of the council. But whoever says, '**You fool**!' shall be in danger of hell fire. [NKJV] But I say, if you are angry with someone, you are subject to judgment! If you say to your friend, '**You idiot**,' you are in danger of being brought before the court. And if you curse someone, you are in danger of the fires of hell. [NLT] ἐγὼ δὲ λέγω ὑμῖν ὅτι πᾶς ὁ ὀργιζόμενος τῷ ἀδελφῷ αὐτοῦ εἰκῆ ἔνοχος ἔσται τῇ κρίσει· ὃς δ' ἂν εἴπῃ τῷ ἀδελφῷ αὐτοῦ, '**ρακά**, ἔνοχος ἔσται τῷ συνεδρίῳ· ὃς δ' ἂν εἴπῃ, Μωρέ, ἔνοχος ἔσται εἰς τὴν γέενναν τοῦ πυρός. [GNS] ἐγὼ δὲ λέγω ὑμῖν ὅτι πᾶς ὁ ὀργιζόμενος τῷ ἀδελφῷ αὐτοῦ ἔνοχος ἔσται τῇ κρίσει· ὃς δ' ἂν εἴπῃ τῷ ἀδελφῷ αὐτοῦ, '**Ρακά**, ἔνοχος ἔσται τῷ συνεδρίῳ· ὃς δ' ἂν εἴπῃ, Μωρέ, ἔνοχος ἔσται εἰς τὴν γέενναν τοῦ πυρός. [GNT]	

**#3152
Radiant**
 	
Shining–KJV
Radiant–NASB
Dazzling–NIV
Shining–NKJV
Dazzling–NLT
 	
**POSB
REFERENCE**
(Mk.9:2-3; esp. v.3)
Deeper Study #2,
point 1
	στίλβοντα λίαν = stilbonta lian
	Pronunciation: [stil'-bon-tah lee'-ahn]
	Parsing *stilbonta* (part of speech): verb
	  Mood—participle
	  Tense—present
	  Voice—active
	  Case—nominative
	  Gender—neuter
	  Number—plural
	  Stem or root—from στίλβω
	Parsing *lian* (part of speech): adjective adverb
	  Stem or root—from λίαν
	Concordance References:
	⇒ Strong's #3029+4744 lian stilbō
	⇒ NIV #3336+5118 lian stilbō
	⇒ NASB #3029+4744 lian stilbō
	
	Mark 9:3
	And his raiment became **shining**, exceeding white as snow; so as no fuller on earth can white them. [KJV]
	And His garments became **radiant** and exceedingly white, as no launderer on earth can whiten them. [NASB]
	His clothes became **dazzling** white, whiter than anyone in the world could bleach them. [NIV]
	His clothes became **shining**, exceedingly white, like snow, such as no launderer on earth can whiten them. [NKJV]
	And his clothing became **dazzling** white, far whiter than any earthly process could ever make it. [NLT]
	καὶ τὰ ἱμάτια αὐτοῦ ἐγένετο στίλβοντα, λευκὰ λίαν
		To be dazzling, radiant, brilliant, shining, awe inspiring; to glisten very much.
		
		Practical Application
		The word "radiant" (*stilbonta*) is a Greek participle which means the shining is active. The transfiguration was a real, active experience. It was no illusion, no dream; it was not of the imagination. It was not a reflection of the sun shining off some rock, glass, or lake. "His [own] face did shine." The radiant glory was the glory of the Lord's inner nature, of His Godly nature actively shining right through His being.

ENGLISH WORD	GREEK WORD AND VERSE	THE WORD MEANS...
	ὡς χιών, οἷα γναφεὺς ἐπὶ τῆς γῆς οὐ δύναται λευκᾶναι. [GNS] καὶ τὰ ἱμάτια αὐτοῦ ἐγένετο **στίλβοντα** λευκὰ **λίαν** οἷα γναφεὺς ἐπὶ τῆς γῆς οὐ δύναται οὕτως λευκᾶναι. [GNT]	
#3153 **Rage** Rage–KJV Rage–NASB Rage–NIV Rage–NKJV Rage–NLT **POSB REFERENCE** (Acts 4:25-28; esp. v.25) Note 3, point 1a	**ἐφρύαξαν** = ephruaxan Pronunciation: [eh-froo-ahx'-ahn] Parsing (part of speech): verb 　Mood—indicative 　Tense—aorist 　Voice—active 　Person—3rd person 　Number—plural 　Stem or root—from **φρυάσσω** Concordance References: ⇒ Strong's #5433 phruassö ⇒ NIV #5865 phruassö ⇒ NASB #5433 phruassö **Acts 4:25** Who by the mouth of thy servant David hast said, Why did the heathen **rage**, and the people imagine vain things? [KJV] Who by the Holy Spirit, *through* the mouth of our father David Thy servant, didst say, 'WHY DID THE GENTILES **RAGE**, AND THE PEOPLES DEVISE FUTILE THINGS? [NASB] You spoke by the Holy Spirit through the mouth of your servant, our father David: " 'Why do the nations **rage** and the peoples plot in vain? [NIV] Who by the mouth of Your servant David have said: *'Why did the nations* **rage**, *And the people plot vain things?* [NKJV] You spoke long ago by the Holy Spirit through our ancestor King David, your servant, saying, 'Why did the nations **rage**? Why did the people waste their time with futile plans? [NLT] ὁ διὰ στόματος, Δαβὶδ τοῦ παιδός σου εἰπὼν τοῦ πατρός σου, Ἱνατί **ἐφρύαξαν** ἔθνη, καὶ λαοὶ ἐμελέτησαν κενά; [GNS] ὁ τοῦ πατρὸς ἡμῶν διὰ πνεύματος ἁγίου στόματος Δαυὶδ παιδός σου εἰπών, Ἱνατί **ἐφρύαξαν** ἔθνη καὶ λαοὶ ἐμελέτησαν κενά; [GNT]	Rage; to be furious. It means to neigh, stomp the ground like a fierce horse; to act untamed, haughty, unruly. **Practical Application** Men will oppose God. God through David foretold their opposition in Scripture (cp. Psalm 2:1-2). 1. The heathen, that is, the *lost* of the world, "rage" (*ephruaxan*). 2. The people, that is, the *worldly*, "imagine vain things": to be anxious over *empty* things; to focus one's life, time and energy upon *meaningless* possessions and *material things*—the empty, unsatisfying things of the world. 3. The *kings and rulers* stand up and gather together against God and His Christ, the Messiah. They stand against; stand in an opposite direction; stand in opposition and hostility to God and Christ.
#3154 **Rage** Wrath–KJV Wrath–NASB Rage–NIV Wrath–NKJV Rage–NLT **POSB REFERENCE** (Eph.4:31) Note 6, point 2 **See also POSB REF:** (Col.3:8-11; esp. v.8) Note 2, point 1b	**θυμός** = thumos Pronunciation: [thoo-mos'] Parsing (part of speech): noun 　Case—nominative 　Gender—masculine 　Number—singular 　Stem or root—from **θυμός**, ου Concordance References: ⇒ Strong's #2372 thumos ⇒ NIV #2596 thumos ⇒ NASB #2372 thumos **Ephes. 4:31** Let all bitterness, and **wrath**, and anger, and clamour, and evil speaking, be put away from you, with all malice: [KJV] Let all bitterness and **wrath** and anger and clamor and slander be put away from you, along with all malice. [NASB] Get rid of all bitterness, **rage** and anger, brawling and slander, along with every form of malice. [NIV] Let all bitterness, **wrath**, anger, clamor, and evil speaking be put away from you, with all malice. [NKJV] Get rid of all bitterness, **rage**, anger, harsh words, and slander, as well as all types of malicious behavior. [NLT] πᾶσα πικρία καὶ **θυμὸς** καὶ ὀργὴ καὶ κραυγὴ καὶ βλασφημία ἀρθήτω ἀφ' ὑμῶν, σὺν πάσῃ κακίᾳ [GNS] πᾶσα πικρία καὶ **θυμὸς** καὶ ὀργὴ καὶ κραυγὴ καὶ βλασφημία ἀρθήτω ἀφ' ὑμῶν σὺν πάσῃ κακίᾳ. [GNT]	Rage, wrath, intense anger, fury. **Practical Application** This kind of rage (*thumos*) is bursts of anger. It is indignation, a violent, explosive temper. It is being quick-tempered, having explosive reactions that arise from stirred and boiling emotions. But it is anger which fades away just as quickly as it arose. It is not anger that lasts.

ENGLISH WORD	GREEK WORD AND VERSE	THE WORD MEANS...
#3155 **Rage, Filled With–** **Rage, Wild With** Filled with madness–KJV **Filled with rage–NASB** Furious–NIV **Filled with rage–NKJV** Wild with rage–NLT **POSB REFERENCE** (Lk.6:6-11; esp. v.11) Note 3, point 5	*ἐπλήσθησαν ἀνοίας* = *eplēsthēsan anoias* Pronunciation: [eh-playce'-thay-san' an-oy-ahs] Parsing *eplēsthēsan* (part of speech): verb 　Mood—indicative 　Tense—aorist 　Voice—passive 　Person—3rd person 　Number—plural 　Stem or root—from πίμπλημι Parsing *anoias* (part of speech): noun 　Case—genitive 　Gender—feminine 　Number—singular 　Stem or root—from ἄνοια, ας Concordance References: ⇒　Strong's #454+4130 anoia pletho ⇒　NIV #486+4398 anoia pimplēmi [furious] ⇒　NASB #454+4130 anoia pletho **Luke 6:11** And they were **filled with madness**; and communed one with another what they might do to Jesus. [KJV] But they themselves were **filled with rage**, and discussed together what they might do to Jesus. [NASB] But they were **furious** and began to discuss with one another what they might do to Jesus. [NIV] But they were **filled with rage**, and discussed with one another what they might do to Jesus. [NKJV] At this, the enemies of Jesus were **wild with rage** and began to discuss what to do with him. [NLT] αὐτοὶ δὲ **ἐπλήσθησαν ἀνοίας**· καὶ διελάλουν πρὸς ἀλλήλους, τί ἂν ποιήσειαν τῷ Ἰησοῦ. [GNS] αὐτοὶ δὲ **ἐπλήσθησαν ἀνοίας** καὶ διελάλουν πρὸς ἀλλήλους τί ἂν ποιήσαιεν τῷ Ἰησοῦ. [GNT]	To be furious; to be filled with wild, insane rage; to be controlled by foolishness, stupidity. **Practical Application** Jesus had confronted the religionists with the truth. They had been shown unmistakably what true religion is. They were now faced with the dilemma: they had to either accept true religion, Jesus and His teaching, or else oppose Him. They chose to oppose Him, but they needed political help, so they went out to form an alliance with the Herodians (see POSB *Deeper Study* #2—Matthew 22:16). Note a significant fact: despite enormous philosophical differences, there was no difference between the religious and political leaders in behavior (the Pharisees and the Herodians). Position, power, and security had corrupted their hearts and minds. They both plotted to destroy a person (Jesus) who opposed them.
#3156 **Railer** **Railer–KJV** Reviler–NASB Slanderer–NIV Reviler–NKJV Abusive–NLT **POSB REFERENCE** (1 Cor.5:11) Note 5	*λοίδορος* = *loidoros* Pronunciation: [loy'-dor-os] Parsing (part of speech): noun 　Case—nominative 　Gender—masculine 　Number—singular 　Stem or root—from λοίδορος, ου Concordance References: ⇒　Strong's #3060 loidoros ⇒　NIV #3368 loidoros ⇒　NASB #3060 loidoros **1 Cor. 5:11** But now I have written unto you not to keep company, if any man that is called a brother be a fornicator, or covetous, or an idolater, or a **railer**, or a drunkard, or an extortioner; with such an one no not to eat. [KJV] But actually, I wrote to you not to associate with any so-called brother if he should be an immoral person, or covetous, or an idolater, or a **reviler**, or a drunkard, or a swindler—not even to eat with such a one. [NASB] But now I am writing you that you must not associate with anyone who calls himself a brother but is sexually immoral or greedy, an idolater or a **slanderer**, a drunkard or a swindler. With such a man do not even eat. [NIV] But now I have written to you not to keep company with anyone named a brother, who is sexually immoral, or covetous, or an idolater, or a **reviler**, or a drunkard, or an extortioner—not even to eat with such a person. [NKJV] What I meant was that you are not to associate with anyone who claims to be a Christian yet indulges in sexual sin, or is greedy, or worships idols, or is **abusive**, or a drunkard, or a swindler. Don't even eat with such people. [NLT] νυνὶ δὲ ἔγραψα ὑμῖν μὴ συναναμίγνυσθαι, ἐάν τις ἀδελφὸς ὀνομαζόμενος ᾖ πόρνος, ἢ πλεονέκτης, ἢ εἰδωλολάτρης, ἢ **λοίδορος**, ἢ μέθυσος ἢ ἅρπαξ· τῷ	Someone who is a slanderer; railer; reviler; an abusive person. **Practical Application** The railer (*loidoros*) is a person who rants and scolds; reviles and abuses; uses insolent, abusive, and slanderous language.

ENGLISH WORD	GREEK WORD AND VERSE	THE WORD MEANS...
	τοιούτῳ μηδὲ συνεσθίειν. [GNS] νῦν δὲ ἔγραψα ὑμῖν μὴ συναναμίγνυσθαι ἐάν τις ἀδελφὸς ὀνομαζόμενος ἦ πόρνος η πλεονέκτης η εἰδωλολάτρης η **λοίδορος** η μέθυσος η ἅρπαξ, τῷ τοιούτῳ μηδὲ συνεσθίειν. [GNT]	
#3157 **Raised...From The Dead Along With** Raised...up together–KJV Raised...up with–NASB Raised...up with–NIV Raised...up together–NKJV **Raised...from the dead along with–NLT** **POSB REFERENCE** (Eph.2:6) Note 3	*συνήγειρεν* = sunēgeiren Pronunciation: [soon-eg-i'-rehn] Parsing (part of speech): verb 　　Mood—indicative 　　Tense—aorist 　　Voice—active 　　Person—3rd person 　　Number—singular 　　Stem or root—from συνεγείρω Concordance References: ⇒　Strong's #4891 sunegeirō ⇒　NIV #5283 sunegeirō ⇒　NASB #4891 sunegeirō **Ephes. 2:6** And hath **raised** us **up together**, and made us sit together in heavenly places in Christ Jesus: [KJV] And **raised** us **up with** Him, and seated us with Him in the heavenly places, in Christ Jesus, [NASB] And God **raised** us **up with** Christ and seated us with him in the heavenly realms in Christ Jesus, [NIV] And **raised** *us* **up together**, and made *us* sit together in the heavenly *places* in Christ Jesus, [NKJV] For he **raised** us **from the dead along with** Christ, and we are seated with him in the heavenly realms—all because we are one with Christ Jesus. [NLT] καὶ *συνήγειρε*, καὶ συνεκάθισεν ἐν τοῖς ἐπουρανίοις ἐν Χριστῷ Ἰησοῦ· [GNS] καὶ *συνήγειρεν* καὶ συνεκάθισεν ἐν τοῖς ἐπουρανίοις ἐν Χριστῷ ἰησοῦ, [GNT]	Raised up with; raised up together; raised from the dead along with. **Practical Application** 　The believer's salvation, his resurrection and exaltation, is an accomplished fact. In the words "raised with" (*sunēgeiren*) or "with Him" (RV), a profound truth is unfolded. 1. God's unsurpassing power is said to have raised Christ from the dead and made Him to sit at God's right hand in the heavenly places (Eph.1:20). 2. Believers are said to have been raised *with Christ* and are urged to "set your sights on the realities of heaven, where Christ sits at God's right hand...." (Col.2:12; Col.3:1, 3). 3. It is said that believers are already raised from the dead with Christ and already seated *with Christ* at the right hand of God. The words "made alive" and "raised" and "seated" are all in the Greek aorist tense. They express what God has already done for the believers in Christ. Christ has already died and been raised and exalted to live in heaven with God forever. God sees all things as they really are. Therefore, He sees believers as having already been raised and exalted to live eternally with Him—all because He sees them in Christ Jesus. He sees their faith and counts them—considers them, looks upon them—as being in Christ. (Cp. Acts 1:10-11; Phil.2:9; 1 Pet.2:9; Rev.1:6; Rev.5:10.)
#3158 **Raised...Up** **Raised...up–KJV** **Raised...up–NASB** **Raised...up–NIV** **Raised...up–NKJV** Appointed–NLT **POSB REFERENCE** (Rom.9:15-18; esp. v.17) Note 2, point 2a	*ἐξήγειρά* = exēgeira Pronunciation: [ex-eg-i'-rah] Parsing (part of speech): verb 　　Mood—indicative 　　Tense—aorist 　　Voice—active 　　Person—1st person 　　Number—singular 　　Stem or root—from ἐξεγείρω Concordance References: ⇒　Strong's #1825 exegeirō ⇒　NIV #1995 exegeirō ⇒　NASB #1825 exegeirō **Romans 9:17** For the scripture saith unto Pharaoh, Even for this same purpose have I **raised** thee **up**, that I might show my power in thee, and that my name might be declared throughout all the earth. [KJV] For the Scripture says to Pharaoh, "For this very purpose I **raised** you **up**, to demonstrate My power in you, and that My name might be proclaimed THROUGHOUT THE WHOLE EARTH." [NASB] For the Scripture says to Pharaoh: "I **raised** you **up** for this very purpose, that I might display my power in you and that my name might be proclaimed in all the earth." [NIV] For the Scripture says to Pharaoh, *"For this very purpose I have* **raised** *you* **up**, *that I may show My power in you, and that My name may be declared in all the earth."* [NKJV] For the Scriptures say that God told Pharaoh, "I have	To be raised up; to be appointed. **Practical Application** 　God shows justice as He wills. Scripture says that God "raised up" (*exēgeira*) Pharaoh. This means that God allowed Pharaoh to appear, brought him forth upon the scene of world history. We must always remember the teaching of Scripture: ***"...there is no authority except that which God has established. The authorities that exist have been established by God." (Romans 13:1) [NIV]***

ENGLISH WORD	GREEK WORD AND VERSE	THE WORD MEANS...

#3163
Rash
 	
Heady–KJV
Reckless–NASB
Rash–NIV
Headstrong–NKJV
Reckless–NLT
 	
POSB
REFERENCE
(2 Tim. 3:2-4; esp. v.4)
Note 2, point 16
	προπετεῖς = *propeteis*
	Pronunciation: [prop-et-eh-ees]
	Parsing (part of speech): adjective
	    Case—nominative
	    Gender—masculine
	    Number—plural
	    Stem or root—from προπετής, ές
	Concordance References:
	  ⇒ Strong's #4312 propetës
	  ⇒ NIV #4637 propetës
	  ⇒ NASB #4312 propetës
	
	2 Tim. 3:4
	Traitors, **heady**, highminded, lovers of pleasures more than lovers of God; [KJV]
	Treacherous, **reckless**, conceited, lovers of pleasure rather than lovers of God; [NASB]
	Treacherous, **rash**, conceited, lovers of pleasure rather than lovers of God—[NIV]
	Traitors, **headstrong**, haughty, lovers of pleasure rather than lovers of God, [NKJV]
	They will betray their friends, be **reckless**, be puffed up with pride, and love pleasure rather than God. [NLT]
	προδόται, **προπετεῖς**, τετυφωμένοι, φιλήδονοι μᾶλλον ἢ φιλόθεοι, [GNS]
	προδόται **προπετεῖς** τετυφωμένοι, φιλήδονοι μᾶλλον ἢ φιλόθεοι, [GNT]
		Rash, heady, reckless, headstrong, hasty. Without giving thought to the consequences. Reckless is probably the best description.
		
		Practical Application
		A rash person is a person who thinks he knows best and can live and act rashly, without paying any attention to the consequences. The rash person thinks little about what he is doing; he just enjoys the feeling and pleasure. He enjoys the stimulation and excitement; the consequences matter little in the midst of the pleasure and excitement.
		Think how much hurt and damage is done when a person lives for the pleasure of the moment. Think of the hurt and damage done because of the pleasure of...
		• reckless driving and boating
		• reckless work and recreation
		• reckless passion and lust
		• reckless eating and drinking
		
		Being rash—thinking that one knows best and can live and act recklessly without consequence—has led to more hurt, accidents, damaged bodies, and death than could ever be imagined.

#3164
Ravaging
 	
Havock–KJV
Ravaging–NASB
Began [to] destroy–
NIV
Havoc–NKJV
Devastate–NLT
 	
POSB
REFERENCE
(Acts 8:3)
Note 3
	ἐλυμαίνετο = *elumaineto*
	Pronunciation: [loo-mah'ee-neh-tow]
	Parsing (part of speech): verb
	    Mood—indicative
	    Tense—imperfect
	    Voice—middle
	    Person—3rd person
	    Number—singular
	    Stem or root—from λυμαίνομαι
	Concordance References:
	  ⇒ Strong's #3075 lumainomai
	  ⇒ NIV #3381 lumainö
	  ⇒ NASB #3075 lumainomai
	
	Acts 8:3
	As for Saul, he made **havock** of the church, entering into every house, and haling men and women committed them to prison. [KJV]
	But Saul began **ravaging** the church, entering house after house; and dragging off men and women, he would put them in prison. [NASB]
	But Saul **began to destroy** the church. Going from house to house, he dragged off men and women and put them in prison. [NIV]
	As for Saul, he made **havoc** of the church, entering every house, and dragging off men and women, committing *them* to prison. [NKJV]
	Saul was going everywhere to **devastate** the church. He went from house to house, dragging out both men and women to throw them into jail. [NLT]
	Σαῦλος δὲ **ἐλυμαίνετο** τὴν ἐκκλησίαν, κατὰ τοὺς οἴκους εἰσπορευόμενος, σύρων τε ἄνδρας καὶ γυναῖκας παρεδίδου εἰς φυλακήν. [GNS]
	Σαῦλος δὲ **ἐλυμαίνετο** τὴν ἐκκλησίαν κατὰ τοὺς οἴκους εἰσπορευόμενος, σύρων τε ἄνδρας καὶ γυναῖκας παρεδίδου εἰς φυλακήν. [GNT]
		To destroy; to devastate; to ravage; to ruin; to wipe out.
		
		Practical Application
		The mercy and grace of God are fully demonstrated in the life of Paul. God's mercy is available to all of us, no matter how terribly we have sinned. There is hope, forgiveness, and a glorious ministry for any of us, no matter who we are or what we have done—if we will repent and surrender ourselves to the Lord Jesus, to follow and obey Him.

#3165
Ravening
 	
Ravening–KJV
Robbery–NASB
	ἁρπαγῆς = *harpagës*
	Pronunciation: [ar-pag-ays']
	Parsing (part of speech): noun
	    Case–genitive
	    Gender–feminine
	    Number–singular
	    Stem or root–from ἁρπαγή, ῆς
		Greed, robbery; a spirit of taking by violent force; plunder, seizing, extortion.
		
		Practical Application
		What did Jesus mean? A religionist is plundering the way of God, trying to seize God's

ENGLISH WORD	GREEK WORD AND VERSE	THE WORD MEANS...
Greed–NIV Greed–NKJV Greed–NLT **POSB REFERENCE** (Lk.11:39-41; esp. v.39) Note 2, point 1	Concordance References: ⇒ Strong's #724 harpagë ⇒ NIV #771 harpagë ⇒ NASB #724 harpagë ### Luke 11:39 And the Lord said unto him, Now do ye Pharisees make clean the outside of the cup and the platter; but your inward part is full of **ravening** and wickedness. [KJV] But the Lord said to him, "Now you Pharisees clean the outside of the cup and of the platter; but inside of you, you are full of **robbery** and wickedness. [NASB] Then the Lord said to him, "Now then, you Pharisees clean the outside of the cup and dish, but inside you are full of **greed** and wickedness. [NIV] Then the Lord said to him, "Now you Pharisees make the outside of the cup and dish clean, but your inward part is full of **greed** and wickedness. [NKJV] Then the Lord said to him, "You Pharisees are so careful to clean the outside of the cup and the dish, but inside you are still filthy–full of **greed** and wickedness! [NLT] εἶπε δὲ ὁ Κύριος πρὸς αὐτόν, Νῦν ὑμεῖς οἱ Φαρισαῖοι τὸ ἔξωθεν τοῦ ποτηρίου καὶ τοῦ πίνακος καθαρίζετε, τὸ δὲ ἔσωθεν ὑμῶν γέμει **ἁρπαγῆς** καὶ πονηρίας. [GNS] εἶπεν δὲ ὁ κύριος πρὸς αὐτόν, Νῦν ὑμεῖς οἱ Φαρισαῖοι τὸ ἔξωθεν τοῦ ποτηρίου καὶ τοῦ πίνακος καθαρίζετε, τὸ δὲ ἔσωθεν ὑμῶν γέμει **ἁρπαγῆς** καὶ πονηρίας. [GNT]	kingdom his own way instead of following the way of God. He is committing extortion against God by robbing God of the salvation He has set up.

#3166
 	
## Reach...Goal 	
 	
Perfected–KJV
Reach...goal–NASB
Reach...goal–NIV
Perfected–NKJV
Accomplish...purpose–
NLT
 	
**POSB
REFERENCE**
(Lk.13:31-33; esp.
v.32)
Note 2, point 1
	τελειοῦμαι = *teleioumai*
	Pronunciation: [tel-i-oo'-mah-ee]
	Parsing (part of speech): verb
	    Mood—indicative
	    Tense—present
	    Voice—passive
	    Person—1st person
	    Number—singular
	    Stem or root—from τελειόω
	Concordance References:
	⇒ Strong's #5048 teleioo
	⇒ NIV #5457 teleioö
	⇒ NASB #5048 teleioo
	
	### Luke 13:32
	And he said unto them, Go ye, and tell that fox, Behold, I cast out devils, and I do cures to day and to morrow, and the third *day* I shall be **perfected**. [KJV]
	And He said to them, "Go and tell that fox, 'Behold, I cast out demons and perform cures today and tomorrow, and the third *day* I **reach** My **goal**.' [NASB]
	He replied, "Go tell that fox, 'I will drive out demons and heal people today and tomorrow, and on the third day I will **reach** my **goal**.' [NIV]
	And He said to them, "Go, tell that fox, 'Behold, I cast out demons and perform cures today and tomorrow, and the third *day* I shall be **perfected**.' [NKJV]
	Jesus replied, "Go tell that fox that I will keep on casting out demons and doing miracles of healing today and tomorrow; and the third day I will **accomplish** my **purpose**. [NLT]
	καὶ εἶπεν αὐτοῖς, Πορευθέντες εἴπατε τῇ ἀλώπεκι ταύτῃ, Ἰδοὺ ἐκβάλλω δαιμόνια, καὶ ἰάσεις ἐπιτελῶ σήμερον καὶ αὔριον, καὶ τῇ τρίτῃ **τελειοῦμαι**. [GNS]
	καὶ εἶπεν αὐτοῖς, Πορευθέντες εἴπατε τῇ ἀλώπεκι ταύτῃ, Ἰδοὺ ἐκβάλλω δαιμόνια καὶ ἰάσεις ἀποτελῶ σήμερον καὶ αὔριον καὶ τῇ τρίτῃ **τελειοῦμαι**. [GNT]
		To reach a goal; to complete an assignment; to accomplish a specific purpose; to finish a task.
		
		### Practical Application
		His ministry of delivering men spiritually and physically (casting out evil spirits and healing) will not be stopped by any man, even rulers such as Herod.
		The words "the third day I will accomplish my purpose" mean that His witness and delivering power will be completed and finished. There is a definite time for it; then His witness will stop. It will be no more. But until that day, nothing can stop His ministry and witness. This is, of course, a reference to Jesus' death and His resurrection on the third day. Note that His resurrection is the perfection of His ministry. It is by arising from the dead that He conquered death and completed man's salvation.

#3167
 	
## Readiness, 	
## With All– 	
	μετὰ πάσης προθυμίας = *meta pasës prothumias*
	Pronunciation: [meh-tah pah-sace thro-thoo-me-ahs]
	Parsing *pasës* (part of speech): adjective
	    Case—genitive
	    Gender—feminine
		With great eagerness; with all readiness of mind; with willingness; eagerly; with zeal. It means to have a willing desire, an eagerness, a hunger, a thirst to know the truth.

ENGLISH WORD	GREEK WORD AND VERSE	THE WORD MEANS...

#3175
Reasoned–
Reasoning
 	
Disputed–KJV
Reasoning–NASB
Reasoned–NIV
Reasoned–NKJV
Debate–NLT
 	
POSB
REFERENCE
(Acts 17:17)
Note 2
 	
See also POSB REF:
(Acts 18:4)
Note 4, point 1
	διελέγετο = *dielegeto*
	Pronunciation: [dee-ehl-eg'-eh-tow]
	Parsing (part of speech): verb
	    Mood—indicative
	    Tense—imperfect
	    Voice—middle or passive deponent
	    Person—3rd person
	    Number—singular
	    Stem or root—from διαλέγομαι
	Concordance References:
	  ⇒ Strong's #1256 dialegomai
	  ⇒ NIV #1363 dialegomai
	  ⇒ NASB #1256 dialegomai
	
	Acts 17:17
	Therefore **disputed** he in the synagogue with the Jews, and with the devout persons, and in the market daily with them that met with him. [KJV]
	So he was **reasoning** in the synagogue with the Jews and the God-fearing Gentiles, and in the market place every day with those who happened to be present. [NASB]
	So he **reasoned** in the synagogue with the Jews and the God-fearing Greeks, as well as in the marketplace day by day with those who happened to be there. [NIV]
	Therefore he **reasoned** in the synagogue with the Jews and with the *Gentile* worshipers, and in the marketplace daily with those who happened to be there. [NKJV]
	He went to the synagogue to **debate** with the Jews and the God-fearing Gentiles, and he spoke daily in the public square to all who happened to be there. [NLT]
	διελέγετο μὲν οὖν ἐν τῇ συναγωγῇ τοῖς Ἰουδαίοις καὶ τοῖς σεβομένοις καὶ ἐν τῇ ἀγορᾷ κατὰ πᾶσαν ἡμέραν πρὸς τοὺς παρατυγχάνοντας. [GNS]
	διελέγετο μὲν οὖν ἐν τῇ συναγωγῇ τοῖς Ἰουδαίοις καὶ τοῖς σεβομένοις καὶ ἐν τῇ ἀγορᾷ κατὰ πᾶσαν ἡμέραν πρὸς τοὺς παρατυγχάνοντας. [GNT]
		Reasoning, addressing, dispute, debate, discussion.
		
		Practical Application
		Paul proclaimed the gospel daily. The idea is twofold.
		1. He was zealous, full of fervor and passion, eagerly grasping every moment and opportunity.
		2. He knew the stakes were high. The destiny of everyone he passed and saw lay in the balance. They were all lost and doomed unless he could reach them with the gospel. Therefore, no matter the cost, he had to do all he could to reach and help them in their search for the truth. He reasoned, argued, debated for the gospel and the salvation of souls.

#3176
Reasoning
 	
Disputing–KJV
Reasoning–NASB
Arguing–NIV
Reasoning–NKJV
Arguing–NLT
 	
POSB
REFERENCE
(Acts 19:2-9; esp. v.8)
Note 2, point 2a
	διαλεγόμενος = *dialegomenos*
	Pronunciation: [dee-al-eg'-om-ehn-os]
	Parsing (part of speech): verb
	    Mood—participle
	    Tense—present
	    Voice—middle or passive deponent
	    Case—nominative
	    Gender—masculine
	    Number—singular
	    Stem or root—from διαλέγομαι
	Concordance References:
	  ⇒ Strong's #1256 dialegomai
	  ⇒ NIV #1363 dialegomai
	  ⇒ NASB #1256 dialegomai
	
	Acts 19:8
	And he went into the synagogue, and spake boldly for the space of three months, **disputing** and persuading the things concerning the kingdom of God. [KJV]
	And he entered the synagogue and continued speaking out boldly for three months, **reasoning** and persuading *them* about the kingdom of God. [NASB]
	Paul entered the synagogue and spoke boldly there for three months, **arguing** persuasively about the kingdom of God. [NIV]
	And he went into the synagogue and spoke boldly for three months, **reasoning** and persuading concerning the things of the kingdom of God. [NKJV]
	Then Paul went to the synagogue and preached boldly for the next three months, **arguing** persuasively about the Kingdom of God. [NLT]
	Εἰσελθὼν δὲ εἰς τὴν συναγωγὴν, ἐπαρρησιάζετο, ἐπὶ μῆνας τρεῖς **διαλεγόμενος**, καὶ πείθων τὰ περὶ τῆς
		To argue; to dispute; to reason; to discuss; to convince; to debate; to answer questions.
		
		Practical Application
		Paul preached boldly in the synagogue of the Jews. He discussed the gospel, asking and answering questions, convincing all who were willing to be convinced.

ENGLISH WORD	GREEK WORD AND VERSE	THE WORD MEANS...
	βασιλείας τοῦ Θεοῦ. [GNS] Εἰσελθὼν δὲ εἰς τὴν συναγωγὴν ἐπαρρησιάζετο ἐπὶ μῆνας τρεῖς **διαλεγόμενος** καὶ πείθων [τὰ] περὶ τῆς βασιλείας τοῦ Θεοῦ. [GNT]	

#3177
Rebel–Rebellious
 	
Unruly–KJV
Rebellious–NASB
Rebellious–NIV
Insubordinate–NKJV
Rebel–NLT
 	
POSB REFERENCE
(Tit.1:10-12; esp. v.10
Note 1, point 1
	ἀνυπότακτοι = anupotaktoi
	Pronunciation: [an-oo-pot'-ak-toy]
	Parsing (part of speech): pronominal adjective
	    Case—nominative
	    Gender—masculine
	    Number—plural
	    Stem or root—from **ἀνυπότακτος**, ον
	Concordance References:
	⇒ Strong's #506 anupotaktos
	⇒ NIV #538 anupotaktos
	⇒ NASB #506 anupotaktos
	
	Titus 1:10
	For there are many **unruly** and vain talkers and deceivers, specially they of the circumcision: [KJV]
	For there are many **rebellious** men, empty talkers and deceivers, especially those of the circumcision, [NASB]
	For there are many **rebellious** people, mere talkers and deceivers, especially those of the circumcision group. [NIV]
	For there are many **insubordinate**, both idle talkers and deceivers, especially those of the circumcision, [NKJV]
	For there are many who **rebel** against right teaching; they engage in useless talk and deceive people. This is especially true of those who insist on circumcision for salvation. [NLT]
	Εἰσὶ γὰρ πολλοὶ καὶ **ἀνυπότακτοι**, ματαιολόγοι καὶ φρεναπάται, μάλιστα οἱ ἐκ τῆς περιτομῆς, [GNS]
	Εἰσὶν γὰρ πολλοὶ [καὶ] **ἀνυπότακτοι**, ματαιολόγοι καὶ φρεναπάται, μάλιστα οἱ ἐκ τῆς περιτομῆς, [GNT]
		Rebellious, unruly, insubordinate; to rebel.
		
		Practical Application
		They were "rebellious" (*anupotaktoi*): undisciplined, unruly, disloyal, insubordinate against God and the truth. They refused to submit to God and to the truth of the gospel and of God's Word.

#3178
Rebirth
 	
Regeneration–KJV
Regeneration–NASB
Rebirth–NIV
Regeneration–NKJV
New life–NLT
 	
POSB REFERENCE
(Tit.3:5)
Note 2, point 1
 	
See also POSB REF:
(Mt.19:28)
Note 2
	παλιγγενεσίας = paliggenesias
	Pronunciation: [pal-ing-ghen'-es-ee' ahs]
	Parsing (part of speech): noun
	    Case—genitive
	    Gender—feminine
	    Number—singular
	    Stem or root—from **παλιγγενεσία**, ας
	Concordance References:
	⇒ Strong's #3824 paliggenesia
	⇒ NIV #4098 paliggenesia
	⇒ NASB #3824 paliggenesia
	
	Titus 3:5
	Not by works of righteousness which we have done, but according to his mercy he saved us, by the washing of **regeneration**, and renewing of the Holy Ghost; [KJV]
	He saved us, not on the basis of deeds which we have done in righteousness, but according to His mercy, by the washing of **regeneration** and renewing by the Holy Spirit, [NASB]
	He saved us, not because of righteous things we had done, but because of his mercy. He saved us through the washing of **rebirth** and renewal by the Holy Spirit, [NIV]
	Not by works of righteousness which we have done, but according to His mercy He saved us, through the washing of **regeneration** and renewing of the Holy Spirit, [NKJV]
	He saved us, not because of the good things we did, but because of his mercy. He washed away our sins and gave us a **new life** through the Holy Spirit. [NLT]
	οὐκ ἐξ ἔργων τῶν ἐν δικαιοσύνῃ ὧν ἐποιήσαμεν ἡμεῖς, ἀλλὰ κατὰ τὸν αὐτοῦ ἔλεον ἔσωσεν ἡμᾶς, διὰ λουτροῦ **παλιγγενεσίας** καὶ ἀνακαινώσεως Πνεύματος Ἁγίου, [GNS]
	οὐκ ἐξ ἔργων τῶν ἐν δικαιοσύνῃ ἃ ἐποιήσαμεν ἡμεῖς ἀλλὰ κατὰ τὸ αὐτοῦ ἔλεος ἔσωσεν ἡμᾶς διὰ λουτροῦ **παλιγγενεσίας** καὶ ἀνακαινώσεως πνεύματος ἁγίου, [GNT]
		Rebirth, regeneration, new life. It means to be regenerated or given new life; to be given a new birth; to be renewed or revived; to be spiritually reborn or converted.
		
		Practical Application
		Salvation is a spiritual rebirth; it is a person being *born again* by the Spirit of God.

ENGLISH WORD	GREEK WORD AND VERSE	THE WORD MEANS...

#3179
Rebuke
 	
Rebuke–KJV
Sharply rebuke–NASB
Rebuke...harshly–NIV
Rebuke–NKJV
Speak harshly–NLT
 	
POSB
REFERENCE
(1 Tim.5:1-3; esp. v.1)
Introduction
	ἐπιπλήξῃς = *epiplëxës*
	Pronunciation: [ep-ee-playk'-ays]
	Parsing (part of speech): verb
	    Mood—subjunctive OR imperative
	    Tense—aorist
	    Voice—active
	    Person—2nd person
	    Number—singular
	    Stem or root—from ἐπιπλήσσω
	Concordance References:
	⇒ Strong's #1969 epiplëssö
	⇒ NIV #2159 epiplëssö
	⇒ NASB #1969 epiplëssö
	
	1 Tim. 5:1
	Rebuke not an elder, but intreat him as a father; and the younger men as brethren; [KJV]
	Do not **sharply rebuke** an older man, but rather appeal to him as a father, to the younger men as brothers, [NASB]
	Do not **rebuke** an older man **harshly**, but exhort him as if he were your father. Treat younger men as brothers, [NIV]
	Do not **rebuke** an older man, but exhort *him* as a father, younger men as brothers, [NKJV]
	Never **speak harshly** to an older man, but appeal to him respectfully as though he were your own father. Talk to the younger men as you would to your own brothers. [NLT]
	Πρεσβυτέρῳ μὴ **ἐπιπλήξῃς**, ἀλλὰ παρακάλει ὡς πατέρα· νεωτέρους, ὡς ἀδελφούς· [GNS]
	Πρεσβυτέρῳ μὴ **ἐπιπλήξῃς** ἀλλὰ παρακάλει ὡς πατέρα, νεωτέρους ὡς ἀδελφούς, [GNT]
		To rebuke harshly; to sharply rebuke; to speak harshly; to be severely censured, angrily reprimanded, violently reproached.
		
		Practical Application
		The instructions are clear: the members of a church are to treat each other as family members. In no sense is any member to be "rebuked" (*epiplëxës*). When a family church member needs to be corrected, there is to be no severity, anger, or violence involved; no contempt or disgust. A church member is to be corrected and disciplined through entreaty (*parakalei*), that is, through exhortation and encouragement, through appeal and pleading. This passage deals with the spirit and discipline of various relationships within the church.

#3180
Rebuke
 	
Rebuke–KJV
Rebuke–NASB
Rebuke–NIV
Rebuke–NKJV
Corrected–NLT
 	
POSB
REFERENCE
(Mt.16:21-23; esp. v.22)
Note 1, point 2
 	
See also POSB REF:
(2 Tim. 4:2)
Note 2, point 4
	ἐπιτιμᾶν = *epitiman*
	Pronunciation: [ep-ee-tee-mahn']
	Parsing (part of speech): verb
	    Mood—infinitive
	    Tense—present
	    Voice—active
	    Stem or root—from ἐπιτιμάω
	Concordance References:
	⇒ Strong's #2008 epitimaö
	⇒ NIV #2203 epitimaö
	⇒ NASB #2008 epitimaö
	
	Matthew 16:22
	Then Peter took him, and began to **rebuke** him, saying, Be it far from thee, Lord: this shall not be unto thee. [KJV]
	And Peter took Him aside and began to **rebuke** Him, saying, "God forbid it, Lord! This shall never happen to You." [NASB]
	Peter took him aside and began to **rebuke** him. "Never, Lord!" he said. "This shall never happen to you!" [NIV]
	Then Peter took Him aside and began to **rebuke** Him, saying, "Far be it from You, Lord; this shall not happen to You!" [NKJV]
	But Peter took him aside and **corrected** him. "Heaven forbid, Lord," he said. "This will never happen to you!" [NLT]
	καὶ προσλαβόμενος αὐτὸν ὁ Πέτρος ἤρξατο **ἐπιτιμᾶν** αὐτῷ, λέγων, Ἴλεώς σοι, Κύριε· οὐ μὴ ἔσται σοι τοῦτο. [GNS]
	καὶ προσλαβόμενος αὐτὸν ὁ Πέτρος ἤρξατο **ἐπιτιμᾶν** αὐτῷ λέγων, Ἴλεώς σοι, κύριε· οὐ μὴ ἔσται σοι τοῦτο. [GNT]
		To rebuke; to censure; to order; to correct; to scold; to strongly disapprove of; to give a command.
		
		Practical Application
		It is not just a wish, but a forcible attempt to stop the idea of the suffering Savior. "This shall never happen to you!" This must not and cannot happen to you. God forbid it is the equivalent idea. The point is this: Peter was out to stop the cross. He was urging Christ to be the Messiah of power, fame, and sensation whom the Jews were expecting.

#3181 **Rebuke...** **Harshly**	ἐπιπλήξῃς = *epiplëxës* Pronunciation: [ep-ee-playk'-ays] Parsing (part of speech): verb Mood—subjunctive OR imperative	To rebuke harshly; to sharply rebuke; to speak harshly; to be severely censured, angrily reprimanded, violently reproached.

ENGLISH WORD	GREEK WORD AND VERSE	THE WORD MEANS...
Rebuke–KJV Sharply rebuke–NASB **Rebuke...harshly–NIV** Rebuke–NKJV Speak harshly–NLT **POSB REFERENCE** (1 Tim.5:1-3; esp. v.1) Introduction	Tense—aorist Voice—active Person—2nd person Number—singular Stem or root—from ἐπιπλήσσω Concordance References: ⇒ Strong's #1969 epiplёssö ⇒ NIV #2159 epiplёssö ⇒ NASB #1969 epiplёssö **1 Tim. 5:1** **Rebuke** not an elder, but intreat him as a father; and the younger men as brethren; [KJV] Do not **sharply rebuke** an older man, but rather appeal to him as a father, to the younger men as brothers, [NASB] Do not **rebuke** an older man **harshly**, but exhort him as if he were your father. Treat younger men as brothers, [NIV] Do not **rebuke** an older man, but exhort *him* as a father, younger men as brothers, [NKJV] Never **speak harshly** to an older man, but appeal to him respectfully as though he were your own father. Talk to the younger men as you would to your own brothers. [NLT] Πρεσβυτέρῳ μὴ **ἐπιπλήξῃς**, ἀλλὰ παρακάλει ὡς πατέρα· νεωτέρους, ὡς ἀδελφούς· [GNS] Πρεσβυτέρῳ μὴ **ἐπιπλήξῃς** ἀλλὰ παρακάλει ὡς πατέρα, νεωτέρους ὡς ἀδελφούς, [GNT]	**Practical Application** The instructions are clear: the members of a church are to treat each other as family members. In no sense is any member to be "rebuked harshly" (*epiplëxës*). When a family church member needs to be corrected, there is to be no severity, anger, or violence involved; no contempt or disgust. A church member is to be corrected and disciplined through entreaty (*parakalei*), that is, through exhortation and encouragement, through appeal and pleading. This passage deals with the spirit and discipline of various relationships within the church.
#3182 Rebuked... Harshly Murmured against–KJV Scolding–NASB **Rebuked...harshly–NIV** Criticized...sharply–NKJV Scolded...harshly–NLT **POSB REFERENCE** (Mk.14:4-5; esp. v.5) Note 2	ἐνεβριμῶντο = eneboimonto Pronunciation: [en-eh-brim-own'-tow] Parsing (part of speech): verb Mood—indicative Tense—imperfect Voice—middle or passive deponent Person—3rd person Number—plural Stem or root—from ἐμβριμάομαι Concordance References: ⇒ Strong's #1690 embrimaomai ⇒ NIV #1839 embrimaomai ⇒ NASB #1690 embrimaomai **Mark 14:5** For it might have been sold for more than three hundred pence, and have been given to the poor. And they **murmured against** her. [KJV] "For this perfume might have been sold for over three hundred denarii, and the money given to the poor." And they were **scolding** her. [NASB] It could have been sold for more than a year's wages and the money given to the poor." And they **rebuked** her **harshly**. [NIV] For it might have been sold for more than three hundred denarii and given to the poor." And they **criticized** her **sharply**. [NKJV] "She could have sold it for a small fortune and given the money to the poor!" And they **scolded** her **harshly**. [NLT] ἠδύνατο γὰρ τοῦτο πραθῆναι ἐπάνω τριακοσίων δηναρίων, καὶ δοθῆναι τοῖς πτωχοῖς. καὶ **ἐνεβριμῶντο** αὐτῇ. [GNS] 'δύνατο γὰρ τοῦτο τὸ μύρον πραθῆναι ἐπάνω δηναρίων τριακοσίων καὶ δοθῆναι τοῖς πτωχοῖς· καὶ **ἐνεβριμῶντο** αὐτῇ. [GNT]	To growl, rebuke, murmur against, scold; to speak harshly against. **Practical Application** In this Scripture, what disturbed the disciples was not the fact that Mary anointed Jesus. Anointing Him was easy enough to understand since it was a common custom of the day. What disturbed them was the gift she gave. The gift... • seemed too valuable and priceless. • seemed unnecessary and thoughtless. • seemed misplaced and wasted. • seemed too costly and sacrificial. • seemed to be a foolish and senseless act.
#3183 Receive **Receive–KJV** Accept–NASB	προσλαμβάνεσθε = proslambanesthe Pronunciation: [pros-lam-ban'-ehs-theh] Parsing (part of speech): verb Mood—imperative Tense—present Voice—middle	To accept; to receive; to welcome; to take to oneself.

ENGLISH WORD	GREEK WORD AND VERSE	THE WORD MEANS...
		order to secure the help we need. But Christ knows and understands. He has been to earth and suffered just as we suffer. Therefore, He knows how to intercede for us and how to deliver us. 4. It means the *Exalted Lord*. Christ has ascended to be exalted, to rule and reign over the universe for God. There is a great day of judgment coming upon the world, a day when all men will bow the knee and acknowledge that Jesus is Lord, the Son of the living God.

#3191
Receiveth Not–Receive, Not
 	
Receiveth not–KJV
Not accept–NASB
Not accept–NIV
Not receive–NKJV
Can't understand–NLT
 	
POSB REFERENCE
(1 Cor.2:14)
Note 1, point 1
	οὐ δέχεται = *ou dechetai*
	Pronunciation: [oo dekh'-eh-tah-ee]
	Parsing *dechetai* (part of speech): verb
	  Mood—indicative
	  Tense—present
	  Voice—middle or passive deponent
	  Person—3rd person
	  Number—singular
	  Stem or root—from δέχομαι
	Concordance References:
	  ⇒ Strong's #3756 ou + 1209 dechomai
	  ⇒ NIV #4024 ou [not] + 1312 dechomai [accept]
	  ⇒ NASB #3756 ou + 1209 dechomai
	
	1 Cor. 2:14
	But the natural man **receiveth not** the things of the Spirit of God: for they are foolishness unto him: neither can he know them, because they are spiritually discerned. [KJV]
	But a natural man does **not accept** the things of the Spirit of God; for they are foolishness to him, and he cannot understand them, because they are spiritually appraised. [NASB]
	The man without the Spirit does **not accept** the things that come from the Spirit of God, for they are foolishness to him, and he cannot understand them, because they are spiritually discerned. [NIV]
	But the natural man does **not receive** the things of the Spirit of God, for they are foolishness to him; nor can he know them, because they are spiritually discerned. [NKJV]
	But people who aren't Christians **can't understand** these truths from God's Spirit. It all sounds foolish to them because only those who have the Spirit can understand what the Spirit means. [NLT]
	ψυχικὸς δὲ ἄνθρωπος **οὐ δέχεται** τὰ τοῦ Πνεύματος τοῦ Θεοῦ· μωρία γὰρ αὐτῷ ἐστι, καὶ οὐ δύναται γνῶναι, ὅτι πνευματικῶς ἀνακρίνεται· [GNS]
	ψυχικὸς δὲ ἄνθρωπος **οὐ δέχεται** τὰ τοῦ πνεύματος τοῦ θεοῦ, μωρία γὰρ αὐτῷ ἐστιν, καὶ οὐ δύναται γνῶναι, ὅτι πνευματικῶς ἀνακρίνεται· [GNT]
		Not receive; not accept; not take; not welcome; not bear with; to refuse and regret; not obtain.
		
		### Practical Application
		The man without the Spirit is the natural man. He does not accept the things that come from the Spirit of God. The phrase "receiveth not" or "not receive" (*dechetai*) means that spiritual things are not welcomed as a guest, are not accepted. It means to refuse and reject. Spiritual things are of little, if any, concern to the natural man. His mind is primarily upon this world, upon...
		  • bigger and better things
		  • acquiring more and more
		  • desires and feelings
		  • wants and cravings
		  • position and wealth
		  • attention and recognition
		  • ambition and promotion
		  • socials and parties
		  • play and recreation
		  • comfort and ease
		  • drinking and eating
		  • dress and appearance
		
		The natural man's life and mind are spent focusing upon the natural, upon this world and not upon the spiritual; therefore, in God's eyes he is classified as the natural man. His heart welcomes only the world; it is closed to God. As stated, God is not welcomed into his life. Therefore, he does not accept the things that come from the Spirit of God.

#3192
Reckless
 	
Heady–KJV
Reckless–NASB
Rash–NIV
Headstrong–NKJV
Reckless–NLT
 	
POSB REFERENCE
(2 Tim. 3:2-4; esp. v.4)
Note 2, point 16
	προπετεῖς = *propeteis*
	Pronunciation: [prop-et-eh-ees]
	Parsing (part of speech): adjective
	  Case—nominative
	  Gender—masculine
	  Number—plural
	  Stem or root—from προπετής, ές
	Concordance References:
	  ⇒ Strong's #4312 propetēs
	  ⇒ NIV #4637 propetēs
	  ⇒ NASB #4312 propetēs
	
	2 Tim. 3:4
	Traitors, **heady**, highminded, lovers of pleasures more than lovers of God; [KJV]
	Treacherous, **reckless**, conceited, lovers of pleasure rather than lovers of God; [NASB]
	Treacherous, **rash**, conceited, lovers of pleasure
		Rash, heady, reckless, headstrong, hasty. It means without giving thought to the consequences. Reckless is probably the best description.
		
		### Practical Application
		A reckless person is a person who thinks he knows best and can live and act recklessly, without paying any attention to the consequences. The reckless person thinks little about what he is doing; he just enjoys the feeling and pleasure. He enjoys the stimulation and excitement; the consequences matter little in the midst of the pleasure and excitement.
		Think how much hurt and damage is done when a person lives for the pleasure of the moment. Think of the hurt and damage done

ENGLISH WORD	GREEK WORD AND VERSE	THE WORD MEANS...
	rather than lovers of God—[NIV] Traitors, **headstrong**, haughty, lovers of pleasure rather than lovers of God, [NKJV] They will betray their friends, be **reckless**, be puffed up with pride, and love pleasure rather than God. [NLT] προδόται, **προπετεῖς**, τετυφωμένοι, φιλήδονοι μᾶλλον ἢ φιλόθεοι, [GNS] προδόται, **προπετεῖς** τετυφωμένοι, φιλήδονοι μᾶλλον ἢ φιλόθεοι, [GNT]	because of the pleasure of... • reckless driving and boating • reckless work and recreation • reckless passion and lust • reckless eating and drinking Being reckless—thinking that one knows best and can live and act recklessly without consequence—has led to more hurt, accidents, damaged bodies, and death than could ever be imagined.

#3193
Reckon
 	
Reckon–KJV
Settle–NASB
Settlement–NIV
Settle–NKJV
Process–NLT
 	
**POSB
REFERENCE**
(Mt.18:23-27; esp.
v.24)
Note 2, point 1
	συναίρειν = sunairein
	Pronunciation: [soon-ah'ee-reen]
	Parsing (part of speech): verb
	    Mood—infinitive
	    Tense—present
	    Voice—active
	    Stem or root—from συναίρω
	Concordance References:
	⇒ Strong's #4868 sunairō
	⇒ NIV #5256 sunairō
	⇒ NASB #4868 sunairō
	
	Matthew 18:24
	And when he had begun to **reckon**, one was brought unto him, which owed him ten thousand talents. [KJV]
	"And when he had begun to **settle** them, there was brought to him one who owed him ten thousand talents. [NASB]
	As he began the **settlement**, a man who owed him ten thousand talents was brought to him. [NIV]
	And when he had begun to **settle** accounts, one was brought to him who owed him ten thousand talents. [NKJV]
	In the **process**, one of his debtors was brought in who owed him millions of dollars. [NLT]
	ἀρξαμένου δὲ αὐτοῦ **συναίρειν**, προσηνέχθη αὐτῷ εἷς ὀφειλέτης μυρίων ταλάντων. [GNS]
	ἀρξαμένου δὲ αὐτοῦ **συναίρειν** προσηνέχθη αὐτῷ εἷς ὀφειλέτης μυρίων ταλάντων. [GNT]
		To take account; to make a reckoning; to settle accounts.
		
		Practical Application
		The word "reckon" (*sunairein*) is simple, yet very descriptive and full of meaning. God is the King, but He is a very unusual King. He is a King who rules justly as all kings should. But He is more. He is loving, compassionate, and forgiving; and He is even more than these. He is consumed with love and compassion—so much so that He forgives enormous debts, debts so enormous that they are inconceivable.
		The King takes account of His servants. He takes account at varying times. An accounting is required at conversion and on those occasions when God leads us to evaluate our lives.
		All must give an account (Matthew 18:24). The king began to check the province and the ledgers of his province: receipts and expenditures and the capital improvements. The king had a critical interest in what his servant had received through gifts and what he had used in the ministry.

#3194
Reckon
 	
Reckon–KJV
Consider–NASB
Count–NIV
Reckon–NKJV
Consider–NLT
 	
**POSB
REFERENCE**
(Rom.6:11)
Deeper Study #1
	λογίζεσθε = logizesthe
	Pronunciation: [log-id'-zehs-theh]
	Parsing (part of speech): verb
	    Mood—imperative
	    Tense—present
	    Voice—middle or passive deponent
	    Person—2nd person
	    Number—plural
	    Stem or root—from λογίζομαι
	Concordance References:
	⇒ Strong's #3049 logizomai
	⇒ NIV #3357 logizomai
	⇒ NASB #3049 logizomai
	
	Romans 6:11
	Likewise **reckon** ye also yourselves to be dead indeed unto sin, but alive unto God through Jesus Christ our Lord. [KJV]
	Even so **consider** yourselves to be dead to sin, but alive to God in Christ Jesus. [NASB]
	In the same way, **count** yourselves dead to sin but alive to God in Christ Jesus. [NIV]
	Likewise you also, **reckon** yourselves to be dead indeed to sin, but alive to God in Christ Jesus our Lord. [NKJV]
	So you should **consider** yourselves dead to sin and able to live for the glory of God through Christ Jesus. [NLT]
	οὕτω καὶ ὑμεῖς **λογίζεσθε** ἑαυτοὺς νεκροὺς μὲν εἶναι τῇ ἁμαρτίᾳ, ζῶντας δὲ τῷ Θεῷ ἐν Χριστῷ Ἰησοῦ τῷ Κυρίῳ ἡμῶν. [GNS]
	οὕτως καὶ ὑμεῖς **λογίζεσθε** ἑαυτοὺς [εἶναι] νεκροὺς μὲν τῇ ἁμαρτίᾳ ζῶντας δὲ τῷ Θεῷ ἐν Χριστῷ Ἰησοῦ. [GNT]
		To count; to consider; to reckon; to credit; to set to one's account; to lay to one's charge; to impute; to judge; to treat; to compute. It is an accounting word; it implies something put to a man's credit. It is used many times throughout Romans, about eleven times in Romans 4 alone. It is an extremely important idea in Scripture.
		
		Practical Application
		The believer's first step in conquering sin is to reckon himself dead to sin, but alive to God. The believer must *know and live out* his position, the glorious life God has given him in the death and resurrection of Jesus Christ our Lord. The believer who keeps his mind and thoughts upon *his position* in Christ's death and resurrection will conquer sin—every time.

ENGLISH WORD	GREEK WORD AND VERSE	THE WORD MEANS...

#3195
Reckoned
 	
Reckoned–KJV
Reckoned–NASB
Credited–NIV
Accounted–NKJV
Declared–NLT
 	
POSB
REFERENCE
(Rom.4:9)
Note 2
	Ἐλογίσθη = *elogisthë*
	Pronunciation: [eh-log-ees'-thay]
	Parsing (part of speech): verb
	    Mood—indicative
	    Tense—aorist
	    Voice—passive
	    Person—3rd person
	    Number—singular
	    Stem or root—from λογίζομαι
	Concordance References:
	  ⇒ Strong's #3049 logizomai
	  ⇒ NIV #3357 logizomai
	  ⇒ NASB #3049 logizomai
	
	Romans 4:9
	Cometh this blessedness then upon the circumcision only, or upon the uncircumcision also? for we say that faith was **reckoned** to Abraham for righteousness. [KJV]
	Is this blessing then upon the circumcised, or upon the uncircumcised also? For we say, "Faith was **reckoned** to Abraham as righteousness." [NASB]
	Is this blessedness only for the circumcised, or also for the uncircumcised? We have been saying that Abraham's faith was **credited** to him as righteousness. [NIV]
	Does this blessedness then come upon the circumcised only, or upon the uncircumcised also? For we say that faith was **accounted** to Abraham for righteousness. [NKJV]
	Now then, is this blessing only for the Jews, or is it for Gentiles, too? Well, what about Abraham? We have been saying he was **declared** righteous by God because of his faith. [NLT]
	ὁ μακαρισμὸς οὖν οὗτος ἐπὶ τὴν περιτομὴν ἡ καὶ ἐπὶ τὴν ἀκροβυστίαν; λέγομεν γάρ ὅτι Ἐλογίσθη τῷ Ἀβραὰμ ἡ πίστις εἰς δικαιοσύνην. [GNS]
	ὁ μακαρισμὸς οὖν οὗτος ἐπὶ τὴν περιτομὴν ἡ καὶ ἐπὶ τὴν ἀκροβυστίαν; λέγομεν γάρ, Ἐλογίσθη τῷ Ἀβραὰμ ἡ πίστις εἰς δικαιοσύνην. [GNT]
		Credited, reckoned, declared; to count; to deposit; to put to one's account; to impute; to consider; to evaluate; to calculate.
		
		Practical Application
		Abraham's faith was counted for righteousness or credited as righteousness (see POSB note, Justification—Romans 4:1-3; POSB note—Romans 4:6-8; POSB *Deeper Study* #1—Romans 4:22; POSB *Deeper Study* #2—Romans 4:22; POSB note—Romans 5:1 for more discussion).
		Note that Abraham was justified or counted righteous by faith; he was not justified...
		• by being religious.
		• by performing good deeds.
		• by doing some good work.
		• by being good and virtuous.
		• by submitting to a ritual.
		• by joining some body of believers.

#3196
Reckoned
 	
Imputed–KJV
Reckoned–NASB
Credited–NIV
Accounted–NKJV
Declared–NLT
 	
POSB
REFERENCE
(Rom.4:22)
Deeper Study #1
	ἐλογίσθη = *elogisthë*
	Pronunciation: [eh-log-ees'-thay]
	Parsing (part of speech): verb
	    Mood—indicative
	    Tense—aorist
	    Voice—passive
	    Person—3rd person
	    Number—singular
	    Stem or root—from λογίζομαι
	Concordance References:
	  ⇒ Strong's #3049 logizomai
	  ⇒ NIV #3357 logizomai
	  ⇒ NASnB #3049 logizomai
	
	Romans 4:22
	And therefore it was **imputed** to him for righteousness. [KJV]
	Therefore also it was **reckoned** to him as righteousness. [NASB]
	This is why "it was **credited** to him as righteousness." [NIV]
	And therefore "it was **accounted** to him for righteousness." [NKJV]
	And because of Abraham's faith, God **declared** him to be righteous. [NLT]
	διὸ καὶ ἐλογίσθη αὐτῷ εἰς δικαιοσύνην. [GNS]
	διὸ [καὶ] ἐλογίσθη αὐτῷ εἰς δικαιοσύνην. [GNT]
		Imputed (*elogisthe*): means to reckon, to credit, to count, to compute, to ascribe, to deposit, to put to one's account.
		
		Practical Application
		Abraham's faith was counted for righteousness. (See POSB *Deeper Study* #1, Reckon—Romans 6:11 for a fuller discussion.) Abraham deposited his faith with God, and God credited Abraham's faith as righteousness.

#3197
Reckons
 	
Imputeth–KJV
Reckons–NASB
	λογίζεται = *logizetai*
	Pronunciation: [log-id'-zeh-ahee]
	Parsing (part of speech): verb
	    Mood—indicative
	    Tense—present
	    Voice—middle or passive deponent
		To credit; to impute; to reckon; to declare; to count; to put to one's account; to deposit.
		
		Practical Application
		The blessed man is the man who is counted righteous without works. Just think for a

ENGLISH WORD	GREEK WORD AND VERSE	THE WORD MEANS...
Credits–NIV Imputes–NKJV Declared–NLT **POSB REFERENCE** (Rom.4:6-8; esp. v.6) Note 3, point 1	Person—3rd person Number—singular Stem or root—from λογίζομαι Concordance References: ⇒ Strong's #3049 logizomai ⇒ NIV #3357 logizomai ⇒ NASB #3049 logizomai **Romans 4:6** Even as David also describeth the blessedness of the man, unto whom God **imputeth** righteousness without works, [KJV] Just as David also speaks of the blessing upon the man to whom God **reckons** righteousness apart from works: [NASB] David says the same thing when he speaks of the blessedness of the man to whom God **credits** righteousness apart from works: [NIV] Just as David also describes the blessedness of the man to whom God **imputes** righteousness apart from works: [NKJV] King David spoke of this, describing the happiness of an undeserving sinner who is **declared** to be righteous: [NLT] καθάπερ καὶ Δαβὶδ λέγει τὸν μακαρισμὸν τοῦ ἀνθρώπου, ᾧ ὁ Θεὸς **λογίζεται** δικαιοσύνην χωρὶς ἔργων, [GNS] καθάπερ καὶ Δαυὶδ λέγει τὸν μακαρισμὸν τοῦ ἀνθρώπου ᾧ ὁ θεὸς **λογίζεται** δικαιοσύνην χωρὶς ἔργων, [GNT]	moment. If God credits and counts a man righteous "without works," then we know something: Man is not justified by works, but by faith. (See POSB *Deeper Study* #1, Reckon—Romans 6:11 for more discussion.)
#3198 **Recognize** Know–KJV Appreciate–NASB Respect–NIV **Recognize–NKJV** Honor–NLT **POSB REFERENCE** (1 Thes.5:12-13; esp.v.12) Note 1, point 1	εἰδέναι = eidenai Pronunciation: [i'-dehn-ah-ee] Parsing (part of speech): verb Mood—infinitive Tense—perfect Voice—active Stem or root—from οἶδα Concordance References: ⇒ Strong's #1492 eido ⇒ NIV #3857 oida ⇒ NASB #3609a oida **1 Thes. 5:12** And we beseech you, brethren, to **know** them which labour among you, and are over you in the Lord, and admonish you; [KJV] But we request of you, brethren, that you **appreciate** those who diligently labor among you, and have charge over you in the Lord and give you instruction, [NASB] Now we ask you, brothers, to **respect** those who work hard among you, who are over you in the Lord and who admonish you. [NIV] And we urge you, brethren, to **recognize** those who labor among you, and are over you in the Lord and admonish you, [NKJV] Dear brothers and sisters, **honor** those who are your leaders in the Lord's work. They work hard among you and warn you against all that is wrong. [NLT] Ἐρωτῶμεν δὲ ὑμᾶς, ἀδελφοί, **εἰδέναι** τοὺς κοπιῶντας ἐν ὑμῖν, καὶ προϊσταμένους ὑμῶν ἐν Κυρίῳ, καὶ νουθετοῦν τας ὑμᾶς, [GNS] Ἐρωτῶμεν δὲ ὑμᾶς, ἀδελφοί, **εἰδέναι** τοὺς κοπιῶντας ἐν ὑμῖν καὶ προϊσταμένους ὑμῶν ἐν κυρίῳ καὶ νουθετοῦντας ὑμᾶς [GNT]	To respect; to know; to appreciate; to recognize; to honor; to be acquainted with; to acknowledge; know the value of. **Practical Application** Believers are to respect the leaders of their church. Few people labor as much as a committed church leader.
#3199 **Recognizing** Discerning–KJV Judge...rightly–NASB **Recognizing–NIV**	διακρίνων = diakrinōn Pronunciation: [dee-ak-ree'-noan] Parsing (part of speech): verb Mood—participle Tense—present Voice—active Case—nominative	To recognize; to discriminate; to distinguish; to evaluate; to judge rightly. **Practical Application** The person who eats the bread and drinks the cup unworthily just fails to think about what he

ENGLISH WORD	GREEK WORD AND VERSE	THE WORD MEANS...
Redeemed–NIV **Redeemed–NKJV** Paid a ransom to save you–NLT **POSB** **REFERENCE** (1 Pt.1:18-20; esp. v.18) Note 4	Person—2nd person Number—plural Stem or root—from λυτρόομαι Concordance References: ⇒ Strong's #3084 lutroö ⇒ NIV #3390 lutroö ⇒ NASB #3084 lutroö **1 Peter 1:18** Forasmuch as ye know that ye were not **redeemed** with corruptible things, as silver and gold, from your vain conversation received by tradition from your fathers; [KJV] Knowing that you were not **redeemed** with perishable things like silver or gold from your futile way of life inherited from your forefathers, [NASB] For you know that it was not with perishable things such as silver or gold that you were **redeemed** from the empty way of life handed down to you from your forefathers, [NIV] Knowing that you were not **redeemed** with corruptible things, *like* silver or gold, from your aimless conduct *received* by tradition from your fathers, [NKJV] For you know that God **paid a ransom to save you** from the empty life you inherited from your ancestors. And the ransom he paid was not mere gold or silver. [NLT] εἰδότες ὅτι οὐ φθαρτοῖς ἀργυρίῳ η χρυσίῳ, **ἐλυτρώθητε** ἐκ τῆς ματαίας ὑμῶν ἀναστροφῆς πατροπαραδότου, [GNS] εἰδότες ὅτι οὐ φθαρτοῖς, ἀργυρίῳ η χρυσίῳ, **ἐλυτρώθητε** ἐκ τῆς ματαίας ὑμῶν ἀναστροφῆς πατροπαραδότου [GNT]	1. We need to be redeemed, to be set free from the empty life that we have been taught to live by our forefathers. 2. We are freely redeemed: redemption does not cost us a penny. We are not redeemed by silver and gold. Note why. Because they are corruptible; that is, silver and gold perish. Money passes away. Therefore, if we were able to buy redemption with money, our redemption would last only as long as our money lasted. When it deteriorated and passed away, the payment for our ransom would no longer exist. Therefore, God's righteousness and justice would no longer be able to accept us. Once again, we would stand guilty before Him. Why? Because God is eternal; therefore, the ransom demanded by His justice is an eternal ransom. If we are going to be delivered from this corruptible world and given eternal life, then the ransom paid for our release has to be an eternal ransom—a ransom that will last as long as we are going to be living. This is the reason silver and gold are totally inadequate in redeeming us. 3. We are redeemed by the precious blood of Christ. A.T. Robertson says, "The blood of anyone is 'precious' [costly] far above gold or silver, but that of Jesus immeasurably more so" (A.T. Robertson. *Word Pictures in the New Testament*, Vol.6, p.90).

#3208
Redemption
 	
Redemption–KJV
Redemption–NASB
Redemption–NIV
Redemption–NKJV
Purchased our freedom–NLT
 	
POSB
REFERENCE
(Eph.1:7)
Note 4
	ἀπολύτρωσιν = *apolutrösin*
	Pronunciation: [ap-ol-oo'-tro-sin]
	Parsing (part of speech): noun
	Case—accusative
	Gender—feminine
	Number—singular
	Stem or root—from ἀπολύτρωσις, εως
	Concordance References:
	⇒ Strong's #629 apolutrösis
	⇒ NIV #667 apolutrösis
	⇒ NASB #629 apolutrösis
	
	Ephes. 1:7
	In whom we have **redemption** through his blood, the forgiveness of sins, according to the riches of his grace; [KJV]
	In Him we have **redemption** through His blood, the forgiveness of our trespasses, according to the riches of His grace, [NASB]
	In him we have **redemption** through his blood, the forgiveness of sins, in accordance with the riches of God's grace [NIV]
	In Him we have **redemption** through His blood, the forgiveness of sins, according to the riches of His grace [NKJV]
	He is so rich in kindness that he **purchased our freedom** through the blood of his Son, and our sins are forgiven. [NLT]
	ἐν ᾧ ἔχομεν τὴν **ἀπολύτρωσιν** διὰ τοῦ αἵματος αὐτοῦ, τὴν ἄφεσιν τῶν παραπτωμάτων, κατὰ τὸ πλοῦτον τῆς χάριτος αὐτοῦ, [GNS]
	ἐν ᾧ ἔχομεν τὴν **ἀπολύτρωσιν** διὰ τοῦ αἵματος αὐτοῦ, τὴν ἄφεσιν τῶν παραπτωμάτων, κατὰ τὸ πλοῦτος τῆς χάριτος αὐτοῦ [GNT]
		Redemption; atonement; ransom; purchased our freedom.
		
		Practical Application
		God has redeemed us and forgiven our sins. The word translated "redemption" (*apolutrösin*) is one of the great words of the Bible. It conveys the idea of deliverance or setting a man free by paying a ransom. For example, a prisoner of war or a kidnapped person is ransomed or redeemed; or a convicted criminal is freed from the penalty of death. In every case the man is powerless to free himself. He cannot pay the penalty demanded to liberate himself from his situation or bondage. Note several significant facts.
		1. Man has been captivated or kidnapped by several forces.
		  a. The force of sin. All men sin and cannot help but sin. Man is sold under sin. Sin has captivated him (Rom.3:23; Rom.7:14).
		  b. The force of corruption and death. The whole creation is corrupt (Romans 8:21). Everything wastes away; it deteriorates, decays, ages, and eventually dies. Corruption and death have captivated man. (Cp. 1 Cor.15:42, 50; Gal. 6:8; 2 Pet.1:4; 2 Pet.2:12, 19.)
		  c. The force of Satan. All unbelievers are under the power and influence of Satan. He has blinded their minds to the gospel (2 Cor. 4:4). He works in the children of disobedience (Eph. 2:2). They are captivated by him (1 Jn.5:19).
		2. Three key ideas are included in the concept of redemption.
		  a. Man needs to be liberated, delivered, and set free.

ENGLISH WORD	GREEK WORD AND VERSE	THE WORD MEANS...
		b. Man is unable to liberate himself. He has no energy, no power, no ability to free himself. c. God has redeemed man by the blood of His Son Jesus Christ. God Himself has paid the ransom for man's release—the ransom of a life for a life. God gave His own Son so that man might be set free. Man has been redeemed through the blood of Jesus Christ (cp. Lev.17:11; Mt.20:28; Rom.3:24; 1 Cor.6:20; 1 Cor.7:23; Col. 1:14; 1 Tim. 2:5-6; Heb.9:15; 1 Pet.1:18f; 2 Pet.2:1; Rev. 5:9; Rev.14:3-4). This is extremely important to note: when a man truly calls upon the Lord to save him, God buys him right out of the marketplace of this corruptible life (Rom.10:13). God redeems him once for all, purchases and removes him from further sale. He is redeemed eternally (cp. Gal.3:13; Gal.4:5; Col. 4:5). 3. God redeems man because of the riches of His grace (see POSB note, Grace—Eph.2:8-9 for discussion). He loves man with an unbelievable love—a love so great that it spurs Him to do whatever is necessary to save man.
#3209 **Redemption** **Redemption–KJV** **Redemption–NASB** **Redemption–NIV** **Redemption–NKJV** Freed us by taking away our sins–NLT **POSB REFERENCE** (Rom.3:24) *Deeper Study #2*	*ἀπολυτρώσεως* = *apolutröseös* Pronunciation: [ap-ol-oo'-tro-seh-os] Parsing (part of speech): noun 　Case—genitive 　Gender—feminine 　Number—singular 　Stem or root—from *ἀπολύτρωσις, εως* Concordance References: 　⇒　Strong's #629 apolutrösis 　⇒　NIV #667 apolutrösis 　⇒　NASB #629 apolutrösis **Romans 3:24** Being justified freely by his grace through the **redemption** that is in Christ Jesus: [KJV] Being justified as a gift by His grace through the **redemption** which is in Christ Jesus; [NASB] And arc justified freely by his grace through the **redemption** that came by Christ Jesus. [NIV] Being justified freely by His grace through the **redemption** that is in Christ Jesus, [NKJV] Yet now God in his gracious kindness declares us not guilty. He has done this through Christ Jesus, who has **freed us by taking away our sins**. [NLT] δικαιούμενοι δωρεὰν τῇ αὐτοῦ χάριτι διὰ τῆς **ἀπολυτρώσεως** τῆς ἐν Χριστῷ Ἰησοῦ· [GNS] δικαιούμενοι δωρεὰν τῇ αὐτοῦ χάριτι διὰ τῆς **ἀπολυτρώσεως** τῆς ἐν Χριστῷ Ἰησοῦ· [GNT]	Redemption; to deliver by paying a price; to set free, deliver, release; to be freed by taking away sins. **Practical Application** The word "redemption" (*apolutröseös*) is used three ways in the New Testament. 1. It means to redeem (*agorazo*): to deliver; to set free from the slave market of sin, death, and hell. 2. It means to redeem out of (*exagorazo*): to deliver out of the enslavement to sin, death, and hell. It means to be delivered out of and never returned. 3. It means to redeem (*lutroo*): to deliver by paying a price; to buy.
#3210 **Refuse–** **Refused** Received–KJV Receive–NASB **Refused–NIV** Receive–NKJV **Refuse–NLT** **POSB REFERENCE** (2 Thes.2:10) Note 2	*οὐκ ἐδέξαντο* = *ouk edexanto* Pronunciation: [ook eh-dekh'-ahn-tow] Parsing *edexanto* (part of speech): verb 　Mood—indicative 　Tense—aorist 　Voice—middle deponent 　Person—3rd person 　Number—plural 　Stem or root—from δέχομαι Concordance References: 　⇒　Strong's #1209+3756 dechomai ou 　⇒　NIV #1312+4024 dechomai ou [refused] 　⇒　NASB #1209+3756 dechomai ou **2 Thes. 2:10** And with all deceivableness of unrighteousness in	Refused, received; to welcome. **Practical Application** The followers of the antichrist are the persons who do not receive the truth. Note what it is that they do not welcome: the truth, the love of the truth. By truth is meant the truth of the gospel. They do not welcome the love of the gospel; they do not love the gospel. What a terrible indictment against the followers of the antichrist. They reject the love of God. God has provided... ● the way for them to be saved. ● the way for them to escape death.

ENGLISH WORD	GREEK WORD AND VERSE	THE WORD MEANS...
	them that perish; because they **received** not the love of the truth, that they might be saved. [KJV] And with all the deception of wickedness for those who perish, because they did not **receive** the love of the truth so as to be saved. [NASB] And in every sort of evil that deceives those who are perishing. They perish because they **refused** to love the truth and so be saved. [NIV] And with all unrighteous deception among those who perish, because they did not **receive** the love of the truth, that they might be saved. [NKJV] He will use every kind of wicked deception to fool those who are on their way to destruction because they **refuse** to believe the truth that would save them. [NLT] καὶ ἐν πάσῃ ἀπάτῃ τῆς ἀδικίας ἐν τοῖς ἀπολλυμένοις, ἀνθ' ὧν τὴν ἀγάπην τῆς ἀληθείας **οὐκ ἐδέξαντο** εἰς τὸ σωθῆναι αὐτούς. [GNS] καὶ ἐν πάσῃ ἀπάτῃ ἀδικίας τοῖς ἀπολλυμένοις, ἀνθ' ὧν τὴν ἀγάπην τῆς ἀληθείας **οὐκ ἐδέξαντο** εἰς τὸ σωθῆναι αὐτούς. [GNT]	• the way for them to live eternally. • the way for them to live victoriously over the trials and sufferings of this life. But despite all this, they do not love the truth of the gospel. And the result is terrible: they are not saved. The followers of the antichrist will be those who have not welcomed the love of the truth—those who have rejected the love of the gospel.
#3211 **Refuse-Refused** Refuse–KJV Refuse–NASB Refuse–NIV Refuse–NKJV Refused–NLT **POSB REFERENCE** (Heb.12:25-29; esp. v.25) Introduction	**παραιτήσησθε** = *paraitēsesthe* Pronunciation: [par-ahee-tay'-says-theh] Parsing (part of speech): verb Mood—subjunctive Tense—aorist Voice—middle deponent Person—2nd person Number—plural Stem or root—from **παραιτέομαι** Concordance References: ⇒ Strong's #3868 paraiteomai ⇒ NIV #4148 paraiteomai ⇒ NASB #3868 paraiteomai **Hebrews 12:25** See that ye **refuse** not him that speaketh. For if they escaped not who refused him that spake on earth, much more shall not we escape, if we turn away from him that speaketh from heaven: [KJV] See to it that you do not **refuse** Him who is speaking. For if those did not escape when they refused him who warned them on earth, much less shall we escape who turn away from Him who warns from heaven. [NASB] See to it that you do not **refuse** him who speaks. If they did not escape when they refused him who warned them on earth, how much less will we, if we turn away from him who warns us from heaven? [NIV] See that you do not **refuse** Him who speaks. For if they did not escape who refused Him who spoke on earth, much more *shall we not escape* if we turn away from Him who *speaks* from heaven, [NKJV] See to it that you obey God, the one who is speaking to you. For if the people of Israel did not escape when they **refused** to listen to Moses, the earthly messenger, how terrible our danger if we reject the One who speaks to us from heaven! [NLT] βλέπετε μὴ **παραιτήσησθε** τὸν λαλοῦντα. εἰ γὰρ ἐκεῖνοι οὐκ ἔφυγον, τὸν ἐπὶ τῆς γῆς παραιτησάμενοι χρηματίζοντα, πολλῷ μᾶλλον ἡμεῖς οἱ τὸν ἀπ' οὐρανῶν ἀποστρεφόμενοι [GNS] βλέπετε μὴ **παραιτήσησθε** τὸν λαλοῦντα· εἰ γὰρ ἐκεῖνοι οὐκ ἐξέφυγον ἐπὶ γῆς παραιτησάμενοι τὸν χρηματίζοντα, πολὺ μᾶλλον ἡμεῖς οἱ τὸν ἀπ' οὐρανῶν ἀποστρεφόμενοι, [GNT]	To refuse; to have nothing to do with. The word "refuse" (*paraitēsesthe*) means to reject, decline, turn down, deny, disavow (Kenneth Wuest. *Hebrews*, Vol. 2, p.229). **Practical Application** There are three reasons why a person must not refuse Jesus Christ and His message. 1. There will be no escape whatsoever for the close-minded (v.25). 2. God warns about a great shaking and judgment of heaven and earth in the future (v.26-27). 3. Think: an unshakeable kingdom can be received (v.28-29).
#3212 **Refused To Believe** Unbelieving–KJV Disbelieved–NASB	**ἀπειθήσαντες** = *apeithēsantes* Pronunciation: [ap-i-thoon'-tace] Parsing (part of speech): verb Mood—participle Tense—aorist Voice—active Case—nominative	Refused to believe; unbelieving; disbelieved; to spurn God's message; to be disobedient; to be an unbeliever. **Practical Application** The idea is they were unwilling to believe or

ENGLISH WORD	GREEK WORD AND VERSE	THE WORD MEANS...
Refused to believe–NIV Unbelieving–NKJV Spurned God's message–NLT **POSB REFERENCE** (Acts 14:2) Note 4, point 1	Gender—masculine Number—plural Stem or root—from ἀπειθέω Concordance References: ⇒ Strong's #544 apeitheö ⇒ NIV #578 apeitheö ⇒ NASB #544 apeitheö **Acts 14:2** But the **unbelieving** Jews stirred up the Gentiles, and made their minds evil affected against the brethren. [KJV] But the Jews who **disbelieved** stirred up the minds of the Gentiles, and embittered them against the brethren. [NASB] But the Jews who **refused to believe** stirred up the Gentiles and poisoned their minds against the brothers. [NIV] But the **unbelieving** Jews stirred up the Gentiles and poisoned their minds against the brethren. [NKJV] But the Jews who **spurned God's message** stirred up distrust among the Gentiles against Paul and Barnabas, saying all sorts of evil things about them. [NLT] οἱ δὲ ἀπειθοῦντες Ἰουδαῖοι ἐπήγειραν καὶ ἐκάκωσαν τὰς ψυχὰς τῶν ἐθνῶν κατὰ τῶν ἀδελφῶν. [GNS] οἱ δὲ ἀπειθήσαντες Ἰουδαῖοι ἐπήγειραν καὶ ἐκάκωσαν τὰς ψυχὰς τῶν ἐθνῶν κατὰ τῶν ἀδελφῶν. [GNT]	be persuaded. They deliberately withheld belief, disobeying God.
#3213 **Refused To Believe** Believed not–KJV Disobedient–NASB **Refused to believe–NIV** Did not believe–NKJV Rejected–NLT **POSB REFERENCE** (Acts 19:2-9; esp. v.9) Note 2, point 2d	ἠπείθουν = ëpeithoun Pronunciation: [ayp-i-thoon'] Parsing (part of speech): verb Mood—indicative Tense—imperfect Voice—active Person—3rd person Number—plural Stem or root—from ἀπειθέω Concordance References: ⇒ Strong's #544 apeitheö ⇒ NIV #578 apeitheö ⇒ NASB #544 apeitheö **Acts 19:9** But when divers were hardened, and **believed not**, but spake evil of that way before the multitude, he departed from them, and separated the disciples, disputing daily in the school of one Tyrannus. [KJV] But when some were becoming hardened and **disobedient**, speaking evil of the Way before the multitude, he withdrew from them and took away the disciples, reasoning daily in the school of Tyrannus. [NASB] But some of them became obstinate; they **refused to believe** and publicly maligned the Way. So Paul left them. He took the disciples with him and had discussions daily in the lecture hall of Tyrannus. [NIV] But when some were hardened and **did not believe**, but spoke evil of the Way before the multitude, he departed from them and withdrew the disciples, reasoning daily in the school of Tyrannus. [NKJV] But some **rejected** his message and publicly spoke against the Way, so Paul left the synagogue and took the believers with him. Then he began preaching daily at the lecture hall of Tyrannus. [NLT] ὡς δέ τινες ἐσκληρύνοντο καὶ ἠπείθουν, κακολογοῦντες τὴν ὁδὸν ἐνώπιον τοῦ πλήθους, ἀποστὰς ἀπ' αὐτῶν ἀφώρισε τοὺς μαθητάς, καθ' ἡμέραν διαλεγόμενος ἐν τῇ σχολῇ τυράννου τινός. [GNS] ὡς δέ τινες ἐσκληρύνοντο καὶ ἠπείθουν κακολογοῦντες τὴν ὁδὸν ἐνώπιον τοῦ πλήθους, ἀποστὰς ἀπ' αὐτῶν ἀφώρισεν τοὺς μαθητὰς καθ' ἡμέραν διαλεγόμενος ἐν τῇ σχολῇ Τυράννου. [GNT]	To refuse to believe; to be disobedient; to reject. **Practical Application** Take note of this, for rejecting the gospel is not just unbelief. It is much worse: it is disobeying God. God demands that men believe in His Son Jesus Christ. Refusing to believe is an act of outright disobedience, an affront to God, an act of rebellion and hostility against His commandment.

ENGLISH WORD	GREEK WORD AND VERSE	THE WORD MEANS...

#3213
Regarding, Not
 	
Not regarding–KJV
Risking–NASB
Risking–NIV
Not regarding–NKJV
Risked–NLT
 	
POSB REFERENCE
(Philip.2:28-30; esp. v.30)
Note 4
	παραβολευσάμενος = paraboleusamenos
	Pronunciation: [par-ab-ool-yoo'-sah-mehn-os]
	Parsing (part of speech): verb
	  Mood—participle
	  Tense—aorist
	  Voice—middle deponent
	  Case—nominative
	  Gender—masculine
	  Number—singular
	  Stem or root—from παραβολεύομαι
	Concordance References:
	⇒ Strong's #3851 paraboleuomai
	⇒ NIV #4129 paraboleuomai
	⇒ NASB #3851 paraboleuomai
	
	Philip. 2:30
	Because for the work of Christ he was nigh unto death, **not regarding** his life, to supply your lack of service toward me. [KJV]
	Because he came close to death for the work of Christ, **risking** his life to complete what was deficient in your service to me. [NASB]
	Because he almost died for the work of Christ, **risking** his life to make up for the help you could not give me. [NIV]
	Because for the work of Christ he came close to death, **not regarding** his life, to supply what was lacking in your service toward me. [NKJV]
	For he **risked** his life for the work of Christ, and he was at the point of death while trying to do for me the things you couldn't do because you were far away. [NLT]
	ὅτι διὰ τὸ ἔργον τοῦ Χριστοῦ μέχρι θανάτου ἤγγισε, **παραβολευσάμενος** τῇ ψυχῇ, ἵνα ἀναπληρώσῃ τὸ ὑμῶν ὑστέρημα τῆς πρός με λειτουργίας. [GNS]
	ὅτι διὰ τὸ ἔργον τοῦ Χριστοῦ μέχρι θανάτου ἤγγισεν **παραβολευσάμενος** τῇ ψυχῇ, ἵνα ἀναπληρώσῃ τὸ ὑμῶν ὑστέρημα τῆς πρός με λειτουργίας. [GNT]
		Risk, not regarding. It means to take a chance, a venture, a dare, a hazard.
		
		Practical Application
		A.T. Robertson points out that this is a gambling word, that it means to gamble one's life; to stake everything; to chance everything; to recklessly gamble. Epaphroditus staked his life for the ministry of Christ. He courageously risked his life. (*Word Pictures in the New Testament*, Vol.4, p.449.)
		Epaphroditus both challenges and rebukes a soft, easy going Christianity and ministry. His life shows that Christianity is stern and demanding. It calls for self-denial and self-effacing sacrifice. It gives little thought to personal comfort and safety.

#3214
Refute
 	
Convince–KJV
Refute–NASB
Refute–NIV
Convict–NKJV
Show–NLT
 	
POSB REFERENCE
(Tit.1:9)
Note 4, point 2
	ἐλέγχειν = elegchein
	Pronunciation: [el-eng'-kheen]
	Parsing (part of speech): verb
	  Mood—infinitive
	  Tense—present
	  Voice—active
	  Stem or root—from ἐλέγχω
	Concordance References:
	⇒ Strong's #1651 elegchō
	⇒ NIV #1794 elegchō
	⇒ NASB #1651 elegchō
	
	Titus 1:9
	Holding fast the faithful word as he hath been taught, that he may be able by sound doctrine both to exhort and to **convince** the gainsayers. [KJV]
	Holding fast the faithful word which is in accordance with the teaching, that he may be able both to exhort in sound doctrine and to **refute** those who contradict. [NASB]
	He must hold firmly to the trustworthy message as it has been taught, so that he can encourage others by sound doctrine and **refute** those who oppose it. [NIV]
	Holding fast the faithful word as he has been taught, that he may be able, by sound doctrine, both to exhort and **convict** those who contradict. [NKJV]
	He must have a strong and steadfast belief in the trustworthy message he was taught; then he will be able to encourage others with right teaching and **show** those who oppose it where they are wrong. [NLT]
	ἀντεχόμενον τοῦ κατὰ τὴν διδαχὴν πιστοῦ λόγου, ἵνα δυνατὸς ᾖ καὶ παρακαλεῖν ἐν τῇ διδασκαλίᾳ τῇ ὑγιαινούσῃ, καὶ τοὺς ἀντιλέγοντας **ἐλέγχειν**. [GNS]
	ἀντεχόμενον τοῦ κατὰ τὴν διδαχὴν πιστοῦ λόγου, ἵνα
		To convict of guilt; to reprove; to convince; to show a person his error; to rebuke; to refute.
		
		Practical Application
		There is a strong reason why the overseer, elder, bishop or minister must hold firmly to the Word of God: he must be able to exhort and to convert those who oppose God and Christ.
		⇒ People need to be exhorted, that is, encouraged to trust Christ and to follow Him.
		⇒ People need to be convicted, especially those who stand opposed to God and curse him refusing to surrender to Him. The word "refute" (*elegchein*) means *"to rebuke a man in such a way that he is compelled to see and to admit the error of his ways. Trench says that it means 'to rebuke another, with such an effectual wielding of the victorious arms of the truth, as to bring him, if not always to a confession, yet at least to a conviction of his sin'....Christian rebuke means far more than 'giving a man a row'...means far more than merely speaking to him in such a way that he sees the error of his ways and accepts the truth. The aim of Christian rebuke is not to humiliate a man, but to enable him to see and recognize and admit the duty and the truth to which he has been either blind or disobedient"* (William Barclay. *The Letters to*

ENGLISH WORD	GREEK WORD AND VERSE	THE WORD MEANS...
	δυνατὸς ᾖ καὶ παρακαλεῖν ἐν τῇ διδασκαλίᾳ τῇ ὑγιαινούσῃ καὶ τοὺς ἀντιλέγοντας **ἐλέγχειν**. [GNT]	*Timothy, Titus, and Philemon*, p.274). Note how the minister of God is to exhort and convince people: "by sound doctrine." And note the word "can": he is to be so grounded in God's Word that he can exhort and convict people *out of God's Word*.

#3215
Refuted
 	
Convinced–KJV
Refuted–NASB
Refuted–NIV
Refuted–NKJV
Arguments–NLT
 	
POSB REFERENCE
(Acts 18:27-28; esp. v.28)
Note 8, point 2b
	διακατηλέγχετο = *diakatēlegcheto*
	Pronunciation: [dee-ak-at-el-eng'-cheh-tow]
	Parsing (part of speech): verb
	    Mood—indicative
	    Tense—imperfect
	    Voice—middle or passive deponent
	    Person—3rd person
	    Number—singular
	    Stem or root—from **διακατελέγχομαι**
	Concordance References:
	  ⇒ Strong's #1246 diakatelegchomai
	  ⇒ NIV #1352 diakatelegchomai
	  ⇒ NASB #1246 diakatelegchomai
	
	Acts 18:28
	For he mightily **convinced** the Jews, *and that* publickly, showing by the scriptures that Jesus was Christ. [KJV]
	For he powerfully **refuted** the Jews in public, demonstrating by the Scriptures that Jesus was the Christ. [NASB]
	For he vigorously **refuted** the Jews in public debate, proving from the Scriptures that Jesus was the Christ. [NIV]
	For he vigorously **refuted** the Jews publicly, showing from the Scriptures that Jesus is the Christ. [NKJV]
	He refuted all the Jews with powerful **arguments** in public debate. Using the Scriptures, he explained to them, "The Messiah you are looking for is Jesus." [NLT]
	εὐτόνως γὰρ τοῖς Ἰουδαίοις **διακατηλέγχετο** δημοσίᾳ ἐπιδεικνὺς διὰ τῶν γραφῶν εἶναι τὸν Χριστὸν, Ἰησοῦν. [GNS]
	εὐτόνως γὰρ τοῖς Ἰουδαίοις **διακατηλέγχετο** δημοσίᾳ ἐπιδεικνὺς διὰ τῶν γραφῶν εἶναι τὸν Χριστὸν Ἰησοῦν. [GNT]
		Refuted to the very last point, confronted, defeated in argument; to be argued down.
		
		Practical Application
		Apollos refuted the Jews publicly. But note: he was not using human reason to argue; he was using the Scripture. And his purpose was to prove that Jesus is the Messiah. (See POSB *Deeper Study* #2—Matthew 1:18 for discussion.)

#3216
Regard With Contempt
 	
Despise–KJV
Regard with contempt–NASB
Look down on–NIV
Judge–NKJV
Look down on–NLT
 	
POSB REFERENCE
(Rom.14:3-4, esp. v.3)
Note 2
	ἐξουθενείτω = *exoutheneitō*
	Pronunciation: [ex-oo-then-ee'-tow]
	Parsing (part of speech): verb
	    Mood—imperative
	    Tense—present
	    Voice—active
	    Person—3rd person
	    Number—singular
	    Stem or root—from **ἐξουθενέω**
	Concordance References:
	  ⇒ Strong's #1848 exoutheneō
	  ⇒ NIV #2024 exoutheneō
	  ⇒ NASB #1848 exoutheneō
	
	Romans 14:3
	Let not him that eateth **despise** him that eateth not; and let not him which eateth not judge him that eateth: for God hath received him. [KJV]
	Let not him who eats **regard with contempt** him who does not eat, and let not him who does not eat judge him who eats, for God has accepted him. [NASB]
	The man who eats everything must not **look down on** him who does not, and the man who does not eat everything must not condemn the man who does, for God has accepted him. [NIV]
	Let not him who eats despise him who does not eat, and let not him who does not eat **judge** him who eats; for God has received him. [NKJV]
	Those who think it is all right to eat anything must not
		To look down on; to despise; to refuse to accept; to regard with contempt; to hold in contempt; to reject; to treat as meaningless and utterly wrong.
		
		Practical Application
		Three reasons are given for not looking down on and judging one another, three reasons that stand as a warning to believers.
		1. God Himself has received the strong believer. The believer who walks in the liberty of Christ and does not live a strict life has been accepted by God, no matter what the more legalistic believer may think. There may be some man-made religious rules which he does not observe, but he has trusted Christ, and he obeys the Word of God. Therefore, he is not to be criticized and judged, but he is to be accepted into the fellowship of the more legalistic believer.
		2. No one has the *right* to judge the Lord's servant. Note: both believers belong to the Lord; both are the servants of the Lord. Therefore, the Lord alone has the right to judge them. Believers do not have the *right to play God* by judging each other. They have no right to condemn and pass judgment upon one anoth-

ENGLISH WORD	GREEK WORD AND VERSE	THE WORD MEANS...
	look down on those who won't. And those who won't eat certain foods must not condemn those who do, for God has accepted them. [NLT] ὁ ἐσθίων τὸν μὴ ἐσθίοντα μὴ **ἐξουθενείτω**, καὶ ὁ μὴ ἐσθίων τὸν ἐσθίοντα μὴ κρινέτω· ὁ Θεὸς γὰρ αὐτὸν προσελάβετο. [GNS] ὁ ἐσθίων τὸν μὴ ἐσθίοντα μὴ **ἐξουθενείτω**, ὁ δὲ μὴ ἐσθίων τὸν ἐσθίοντα μὴ κρινέτω, ὁ θεὸς γὰρ αὐτὸν προσελάβετο. [GNT]	er's each other's behavior and works, for they do not belong to eachone another. They each belong to Christ; therefore, He alone determines whether or not they stand or fall and are accepted or rejected. 3. God *will make* the believer stand. There is no question about the matter: the believer will stand, for God is able to make him stand (Rom.14:4).

#3217
Regard, Have
 	
Provide–KJV
Respect–NASB
Careful–NIV
Have regard–NKJV
Do things in such a way–NLT
 	
POSB REFERENCE
(Rom.12:17)
Note 4, point 2
	προνοούμενοι = *pronooumenoi*
	Pronunciation: [pro-no-oo-meh'-noy]
	Parsing (part of speech): verb
	   Mood—participle (imperative sense)
	   Tense—present
	   Voice—middle
	   Case—nominative
	   Gender—masculine
	   Person—2nd person
	   Number—plural
	   Stem or root—from προνοέω
	Concordance References:
	  ⇒ Strong's #4306 pronoeö
	  ⇒ NIV #4629 pronoeö
	  ⇒ NASB #4306 pronoeö
	
	Romans 12:17
	Recompense to no man evil for evil. **Provide** things honest in the sight of all men. [KJV]
	Never pay back evil for evil to anyone. **Respect** what is right in the sight of all men. [NASB]
	Do not repay anyone evil for evil. Be **careful** to do what is right in the eyes of everybody. [NIV]
	Repay no one evil for evil. **Have regard** for good things in the sight of all men. [NKJV]
	Never pay back evil for evil to anyone. **Do things in such a way** that everyone can see you are honorable. [NLT]
	μηδενὶ κακὸν ἀντὶ κακοῦ ἀποδιδόντες. **προνοούμενοι** καλὰ ἐνώπιον πάντων ἀνθρώπων. [GNS]
	μηδενὶ κακὸν ἀντὶ κακοῦ ἀποδιδόντες, **προνοούμενοι** καλὰ ἐνώπιον πάντων ἀνθρώπων· [GNT]
		To be careful; to provide; to respect; to do things in such a way; to take care of; to think before acting; to take pains.
		
		Practical Application
		The idea is this: when someone does evil against the believer, the believer is to think before he acts. He is to think and pray through his behavior. Why? So that he can respond in the right and proper way. The believer needs to do what is right and noble, and the only way to do it is to think through the situation.

#3219
Regeneration
 	
Regeneration–KJV
Regeneration–NASB
Rebirth–NIV
Regeneration–NKJV
New life–NLT
 	
POSB REFERENCE
(Tit.3:5)
Note 2, point 1
 	
See also POSB REF:
(Mt.19:28)
Note 2
	παλιγγενεσίας = *paliggenesias*
	Pronunciation: [pal-ing-ghen-es-ee'-ahs]
	Parsing (part of speech): noun
	   Case—genitive
	   Gender—feminine
	   Number—singular
	   Stem or root—from παλιγγενεσία, ας
	Concordance References:
	  ⇒ Strong's #3824 paliggenesia
	  ⇒ NIV #4098 paliggenesia
	  ⇒ NASB #3824 paliggenesia
	
	Titus 3:5
	Not by works of righteousness which we have done, but according to his mercy he saved us, by the washing of **regeneration**, and renewing of the Holy Ghost; [KJV]
	He saved us, not on the basis of deeds which we have done in righteousness, but according to His mercy, by the washing of **regeneration** and renewing by the Holy Spirit, [NASB]
	He saved us, not because of righteous things we had done, but because of his mercy. He saved us through the washing of **rebirth** and renewal by the Holy Spirit, [NIV]
	Not by works of righteousness which we have done, but according to His mercy He saved us, through the washing of **regeneration** and renewing of the Holy Spirit, [NKJV]
	He saved us, not because of the good things we did, but because of his mercy. He washed away our sins and
		Rebirth, regeneration, new life. It means to be regenerated or given new life; to be given a new birth; to be renewed or revived; to be spiritually reborn or converted.
		
		Practical Application
		Salvation is a spiritual rebirth; it is a person being *born again* by the Spirit of God.

ENGLISH WORD	GREEK WORD AND VERSE	THE WORD MEANS...
	gave us a **new life** through the Holy Spirit. [NLT] οὐκ ἐξ ἔργων τῶν ἐν δικαιοσύνῃ ὧν ἐποιήσαμεν ἡμεῖς, ἀλλὰ κατὰ τὸν αὐτοῦ ἔλεον ἔσωσεν ἡμᾶς, διὰ λουτροῦ **παλιγγενεσίας** καὶ ἀνακαινώσεως Πνεύματος Ἁγίου, [GNS] οὐκ ἐξ ἔργων τῶν ἐν δικαιοσύνῃ ἃ ἐποιήσαμεν ἡμεῖς ἀλλὰ κατὰ τὸ αὐτοῦ ἔλεος ἔσωσεν ἡμᾶς διὰ λουτροῦ **παλιγγενεσίας** καὶ ἀνακαινώσεως πνεύματος ἁγίου, [GNT]	

#3220
Reign
 	
Reign–KJV
Reign–NASB
Reign–NIV
Reign–NKJV
Control–NLT
 	
**POSB
REFERENCE**
(Rom.6:12)
Note 2, point 1
	βασιλευέτω = basileuetö
	Pronunciation: [bas-il-yoo'-eh-tow]
	Parsing (part of speech): verb
	   Mood—imperative
	   Tense—present
	   Voice—active
	   Person—3rd person
	   Number—singular
	   Stem or root—from βασιλεύω
	Concordance References:
	  ⇒ Strong's #936 basileuö
	  ⇒ NIV #996 basileuö
	  ⇒ NASB #936 basileuö
	
	Romans 6:12
	Let not sin therefore **reign** in your mortal body, that ye should obey it in the lusts thereof. [KJV]
	Therefore do not let sin **reign** in your mortal body that you should obey its lusts, [NASB]
	Therefore do not let sin **reign** in your mortal body so that you obey its evil desires. [NIV]
	Therefore do not let sin reign in your mortal body, that you should obey it in its lusts. [NKJV]
	Therefore do not let sin **reign** in your mortal body, that you should obey it in its lusts. [NKJV]
	Do not let sin **control** the way you live; do not give in to its lustful desires. [NLT]
	Μὴ οὖν **βασιλευέτω** ἡ ἁμαρτία ἐν τῷ θνητῷ ὑμῶν σώματι, εἰς τὸ ὑπακούειν ταῖς ἐπιθυμίαις αὐτοῦ· [GNS]
	Μὴ οὖν **βασιλευέτω** ἡ ἁμαρτία ἐν τῷ θνητῷ ὑμῶν σώματι εἰς τὸ ὑπακούειν ταῖς ἐπιθυμίαις αὐτοῦ, [GNT
		To rule; to reign; to become like a king; to have authority; to control; to occupy; to hold sway; to prevail over.
		
		Practical Application
		The believer must resist sin. This is an imperative—a forceful command. It is up to the believer to resist sin; he is responsible for resisting it.
		He must not let sin have reign (*basileueto*): have authority, rule, control, occupy, hold sway, prevail over him. The present tense is used, so the idea is a continuous attitude and behavior. The believer is always to keep his mind off sin. He is to keep his mind under control by keeping his mind off...
		• wealth and material things
		• position and power
		• recognition and fame
		• the lust of the eyes
		• the lust of the flesh
		• the pride of life
		• parties and sex
		• appearance and clothes
		The believer is not to let sin dominate, control, and reign in his mortal body. Sin is not to dominate his thoughts and life. He is to resist sin by standing against it and by rebuking and fighting against it. He is to oppose sin with all his might.

#3221
**Reject–
Rejected**
 	
Cast away–KJV
Rejected–NASB
Reject–NIV
Cast away–NKJV
Rejected–NLT
 	
**POSB
REFERENCE**
(Rom.11:1)
Note 1
	ἀπώσατο = apösato
	Pronunciation: [ap-o-sah-tow]
	Parsing (part of speech): verb
	   Mood—indicative
	   Tense—aorist
	   Voice—middle deponent
	   Person—3rd person
	   Number—singular
	   Stem or root—from ἀπωθέομαι
	Concordance References:
	  ⇒ Strong's #683 apötheömai
	  ⇒ NIV #723 apötheö
	  ⇒ NASB #683 apötheömai
	
	Romans 11:1
	I say then, Hath God **cast away** his people? God forbid. For I also am an Israelite, of the seed of Abraham, of the tribe of Benjamin. [KJV]
	I say then, God has not **rejected** His people, has He? May it never be! For I too am an Israelite, a descendant of Abraham, of the tribe of Benjamin. [NASB]
	I ask then: Did God **reject** his people? By no means! I am an Israelite myself, a descendant of Abraham, from the tribe of Benjamin. [NIV]
	I say then, has God **cast away** His people? Certainly not! For I also am an Israelite, of the seed of Abraham, *of* the tribe of Benjamin. [NKJV]
	I ask, then, has God **rejected** his people, the Jews? Of course not! Remember that I myself am a Jew, a descendant of Abraham and a member of the tribe of Benjamin. [NLT]
		To cast away; to push away, to thrust away; to repel; to repudiate; to push aside; to reject; to fail to listen to (one's conscience)
		
		Practical Application
		The idea is to utterly and totally and finally reject. Has God utterly rejected Jews? Paul shouts: "May it never be!" (*me genoito*). It is impossible! It must never be! It can never be! God has not broken and violated His Word to Israel. God's promises to Israel did not mean that all Jews were locked in to salvation no matter how sinful and disobedient they were. It did not mean that an unbelieving and disobedient Jew was acceptable to God simply because he had been born a Jew. God's promises were intended for those who believed and obeyed Him. The people who believed and obeyed Him have always been "His people."

ENGLISH WORD	GREEK WORD AND VERSE	THE WORD MEANS...
	Λέγω οὖν, Μὴ **ἀπώσατο** ὁ Θεὸς τὸν λαὸν αὐτοῦ; μὴ γένοιτο. καὶ γὰρ ἐγὼ Ἰσραηλίτης εἰμί, ἐκ σπέρματος Ἀβραάμ, φυλῆς Βενϊαμίν. [GNS] Λέγω οὖν, μὴ **ἀπώσατο** ὁ θεὸς τὸν λαὸν αὐτοῦ; μὴ γένοιτο· καὶ γὰρ ἐγὼ Ἰσραηλίτης εἰμί, ἐκ σπέρματος Ἀβραάμ, φυλῆς Βενιαμίν. [GNT]	
#3222 **Rejected** Believed not–KJV Disobedient–NASB Refused to believe–NIV Did not believe–NKJV **Rejected–NLT** **POSB REFERENCE** (Acts 19:2-9; esp. v.9) Note 2, point 2d	*ἠπείθουν* = *ëpeithoun* Pronunciation: [ayp-i-thoon'] Parsing (part of speech): verb 　Mood—indicative 　Tense—imperfect 　Voice—active 　Person—3rd person 　Number—plural 　Stem or root—from **ἀπειθέω** Concordance References: ⇒　Strong's #544 apeitheö ⇒　NIV #578 apeitheö ⇒　NASB #544 apeitheö **Acts 19:9** But when divers were hardened, and **believed not**, but spake evil of that way before the multitude, he departed from them, and separated the disciples, disputing daily in the school of one Tyrannus. [KJV] But when some were becoming hardened and **disobedient**, speaking evil of the Way before the multitude, he withdrew from them and took away the disciples, reasoning daily in the school of Tyrannus. [NASB] But some of them became obstinate; they **refused to believe** and publicly maligned the Way. So Paul left them. He took the disciples with him and had discussions daily in the lecture hall of Tyrannus. [NIV] But when some were hardened and **did not believe**, but spoke evil of the Way before the multitude, he departed from them and withdrew the disciples, reasoning daily in the school of Tyrannus. [NKJV] But some **rejected** his message and publicly spoke against the Way, so Paul left the synagogue and took the believers with him. Then he began preaching daily at the lecture hall of Tyrannus. [NLT] ὡς δέ τινες ἐσκληρύνοντο καὶ **ἠπείθουν**, κακολογοῦντες τὴν ὁδὸν ἐνώπιον τοῦ πλήθους, ἀποστὰς ἀπ' αὐτῶν ἀφώρισε τοὺς μαθητάς, καθ' ἡμέραν διαλεγόμενος ἐν τῇ σχολῇ τυράννου τινός. [GNS] ὡς δέ τινες ἐσκληρύνοντο καὶ **ἠπείθουν** κακολογοῦντες τὴν ὁδὸν ἐνώπιον τοῦ πλήθους, ἀποστὰς ἀπ' αὐτῶν ἀφώρισεν τοὺς μαθητὰς καθ' ἡμέραν διαλεγόμενος ἐν τῇ σχολῇ Τυράννου. [GNT]	To refuse to believe; to be disobedient; to reject. **Practical Application** Take note of this, for rejecting the gospel is not just unbelief. It is much worse: it is disobeying God. God demands that men believe in His Son Jesus Christ. Not believing is outright disobedience, an affront to God, an act of rebellion and hostility against His commandment.
#3223 **Rejected** Hardened–KJV Hardened–NASB Obstinate–NIV Hardened–NKJV **Rejected–NLT** **POSB REFERENCE** (Acts 19:2-9; esp. v.9) Note 2, point 2d	*ἐσκληρύνοντο* = *esklërunonto* Pronunciation: [es-sklay-roo'-non-tow] Parsing (part of speech): verb 　Mood—indicative 　Tense—imperfect 　Voice—passive 　Person—3rd person 　Number—plural 　Stem or root—from **σκληρύνω** Concordance References: ⇒　Strong's #4645 sklërunö ⇒　NIV #5020 sklërunö ⇒　NASB #4645 sklërunö **Acts 19:9** But when divers were **hardened**, and believed not, but spake evil of that way before the multitude, he departed from them, and separated the disciples, disputing daily in the school of one Tyrannus. [KJV] But when some were becoming **hardened** and disobedient, speaking evil of the Way before the multitude, he withdrew from them and took away the disciples, reasoning daily in the school of Tyrannus. [NASB]	To be obstinate, to be hardened, to be rejected; to be stubborn. It means to be as hard as a stone; to be unfeeling and difficult, standing in opposition. **Practical Application** Many were hardened and did not believe, being disobedient to the call of God to salvation.

ENGLISH WORD	GREEK WORD AND VERSE	THE WORD MEANS...
	But some of them became **obstinate**; they refused to believe and publicly maligned the Way. So Paul left them. He took the disciples with him and had discussions daily in the lecture hall of Tyrannus. [NIV] But when some were **hardened** and did not believe, but spoke evil of the Way before the multitude, he departed from them and withdrew the disciples, reasoning daily in the school of Tyrannus. [NKJV] But some **rejected** his message and publicly spoke against the Way, so Paul left the synagogue and took the believers with him. Then he began preaching daily at the lecture hall of Tyrannus. [NLT] ὡς δέ τινες **ἐσκληρύνοντο** καὶ ἠπείθουν, κακολογοῦντες τὴν ὁδὸν ἐνώπιον τοῦ πλήθους, ἀποστὰς ἀπ' αὐτῶν ἀφώρισε τοὺς μαθητάς, καθ' ἡμέραν διαλεγόμενος ἐν τῇ σχολῇ τυράννου τινός. [GNS] ὡς δέ τινες **ἐσκληρύνοντο** καὶ ἠπείθουν κακολογοῦντες τὴν ὁδὸν ἐνώπιον τοῦ πλήθους, ἀποστὰς ἀπ' αὐτῶν ἀφώρισεν τοὺς μαθητάς καθ' ἡμέραν διαλεγόμενος ἐν τῇ σχολῇ Τυράννου. [GNT]	

#3224
Rejected
 	
Put away–KJV
Rejected–NASB
Rejected–NIV
Rejected–NKJV
Deliberately violated–NLT
 	
POSB REFERENCE
(1 Tim.1:19-20; esp. v.19)
Note 3
	ἀπωσάμενοι = apōsamenoi
	Pronunciation: [ap-o'-sah-mehn-oy]
	Parsing (part of speech): verb
	  Mood—participle
	  Tense—aorist
	  Voice—middle deponent
	  Case—nominative
	  Gender—masculine
	  Number—plural
	  Stem or root—from ἀπωθέομαι
	Concordance References:
	⇒ Strong's #683 apōtheō
	⇒ NIV #723 apōtheō
	⇒ NASB #683 apōtheō
	
	1 Tim. 1:19
	Holding faith, and a good conscience; which some having **put away** concerning faith have made shipwreck: [KJV]
	
	Keeping faith and a good conscience, which some have **rejected** and suffered shipwreck in regard to their faith. [NASB]
	
	Holding on to faith and a good conscience. Some have **rejected** these and so have shipwrecked their faith. [NIV]
	
	Having faith and a good conscience, which some having **rejected**, concerning the faith have suffered shipwreck, [NKJV]
	
	Cling tightly to your faith in Christ, and always Keep your conscience clear. For some people have **deliberately violated** their consciences; as a result, their faith has been shipwrecked. [NLT]
	
	ἔχων πίστιν καὶ ἀγαθὴν συνείδησιν, ἥν τινες **ἀπωσάμενοι**, περὶ τὴν πίστιν ἐναυάγησαν· [GNS]
	
	ἔχων πίστιν καὶ ἀγαθὴν συνείδησιν, ἥν τινες **ἀπωσάμενοι** περὶ τὴν πίστιν ἐναυάγησαν, [GNT]
		To reject; to put away; to deliberately violate; to push aside; to push away with force.
		
		Practical Application
		It is a willful and deliberate pushing away of conscience. Conscience says that something is wrong and should not be done, but conscience is ignored and subdued, turned away from and denied.
		
		When a person *continues to push his conscience away*, something terrible happens: his faith is shipwrecked. His faith is broken to pieces and destroyed. A person must live as Scripture dictates: righteously and godly. If he does not live righteously and godly, then he weakens his faith and soon dashes it upon the storms of evil, worldliness, and false doctrine. His faith is shipwrecked—because he pushed his conscience aside refusing to listen to its call to live righteously and godly.

#3225
Rejoice
 	
Hail–KJV
Greeted–NASB
Greetings–NIV
Rejoice–NKJV
Greetings–NLT
 	
POSB REFERENCE
(Mt.28:9)
Deeper Study #2
	Χαίρετε. = Chairete
	Pronunciation: [khah'ee-reh-teh]
	Parsing (part of speech): verb
	  Mood—imperative
	  Tense—present
	  Voice—active
	  Person—2nd person
	  Number—plural
	  Stem or root—from χαίρω
	OR
	Parsing (part of speech): particle
	  Type—sentence
	  Stem or root—from χαίρω
		To be greeted, hailed, to rejoice.
		
		Practical Application
		It is significant that the risen Christ used this every day, common greeting to proclaim the extraordinary news of His resurrection.

ENGLISH WORD	GREEK WORD AND VERSE	THE WORD MEANS...
	Concordance References: ⇒ Strong's #5463 chairö ⇒ NIV #5897 chairö ⇒ NASB #5463 chairö **Matthew 28:9** And as they went to tell his disciples, behold, Jesus met them, saying, All **hail**. And they came and held him by the feet, and worshipped him. [KJV] And behold, Jesus met them and **greeted** them. And they came up and took hold of His feet and worshiped Him. [NASB] Suddenly Jesus met them. "**Greetings**," he said. They came to him, clasped his feet and worshiped him. [NIV] And as they went to tell His disciples, behold, Jesus met them, saying, "**Rejoice**!" So they came and held Him by the feet and worshiped Him. [NKJV] And as they went, Jesus met them. "**Greetings**!" he said. And they ran to him, held his feet, and worshiped him. [NLT] ὡς δὲ ἐπορεύοντο ἀπαγγεῖλαι τοῖς μαθηταῖς αὐτοῦ, καὶ ἰδού, ὁ Ἰησοῦς ἀπήντησεν αὐταῖς, λέγων, **Χαίρετε**. αἱ δὲ προσελθοῦσαι ἐκράτησαν αὐτοῦ τοὺς πόδας καὶ προσεκύνησαν αὐτῷ. [GNS] καὶ ἰδοὺ Ἰησοῦς ὑπήντησεν αὐταῖς λέγων, **Χαίρετε**. αἱ δὲ προσελθοῦσαι ἐκράτησαν αὐτοῦ τοὺς πόδας καὶ προσεκύνησαν αὐτῷ. [GNT]	
#3226 **Rejoice–** **Rejoiced** **Rejoice–KJV** **Rejoiced–NASB** Glad–NIV **Rejoice–NKJV** Happy–NLT **POSB** **REFERENCE** (Jn.14:28-29; esp. v.28) Note 2	ἐχάρητε = echarëte Pronunciation: [eh-chah'-ray-teh] Parsing (part of speech): verb 　Mood—indicative 　Tense—aorist 　Voice—passive deponent 　Person—2nd person 　Number—plural 　Stem or root—from χαίρω Concordance References: ⇒ Strong's #5463 chairo ⇒ NIV #5897 chairo ⇒ NASB #5463 chairo **John 14:28** Ye have heard how I said unto you, I go away, and come again unto you. If ye loved me, ye would **rejoice**, because I said, I go unto the Father: for my Father is greater than I. [KJV] "You heard that I said to you, 'I go away, and I will come to you.' If you loved Me, you would have **rejoiced**, because I go to the Father; for the Father is greater than I. [NASB] "You heard me say, 'I am going away and I am coming back to you.' If you loved me, you would be **glad** that I am going to the Father, for the Father is greater than I. [NIV] You have heard Me say to you, 'I am going away and coming *back* to you.' If you loved Me, you would **rejoice** because I said, 'I am going to the Father,' for My Father is greater than I. [NKJV] Remember what I told you: I am going away, but I will come back to you again. If you really love me, you will be very **happy** for me, because now I can go to the Father, who is greater than I am. [NLT] ἠκούσατε ὅτι ἐγὼ εἶπον ὑμῖν, Ὑπάγω καὶ ἔρχομαι πρὸς ὑμᾶς. εἰ ἠγαπᾶτέ με, **ἐχάρητε** ἄν ὅτι εἶπον, Πορεύομαι πρὸς τὸν πατέρα· ὅτι ὁ πατὴρ μού μείζων ἐστί. [GNS] ἠκούσατε ὅτι ἐγὼ εἶπον ὑμῖν, Ὑπάγω καὶ ἔρχομαι πρὸς ὑμᾶς. εἰ ἠγαπᾶτέ με **ἐχάρητε** ἄν ὅτι πορεύομαι πρὸς τὸν πατέρα, ὅτι ὁ πατὴρ μείζων μού ἐστιν. [GNT]	To rejoice; to have great joy; to be glad; to be delighted; to be satisfied. Joy (*chara*) and rejoicing (*echarete*, the same root word as joy) mean an inner gladness and a deep seated pleasure. It is a depth of assurance and confidence that ignites a cheerful heart. It is a cheerful heart that leads to cheerful behavior. **Practical Application** The source of joy is threefold. (See POSB *Deeper Study* #1–John 15:11 for more discussion.) 1. The return of Jesus to the Father causes believers to be glad. "I am going away, and I am coming back to you" is a reference to His death, resurrection, and ascension. 　a. The death or cross of Christ attracts and causes men to joy and rejoice. The cross is the source of their deliverance from sin, death, and hell (see POSB *Deeper Study* #4–John 12:32). 　b. The resurrection and ascension of Christ attracts and causes men to joy and rejoice. The resurrection and ascension are the sources of their new life and hope for eternity (see POSB notes, Resurrection–John 14:6; POSB note–John 7:33-34; POSB note–Mark 16:19-20). 2. The Father's greatness causes believers to be glad. The Father demonstrated His great love and power by releasing Jesus ... ⇒ from the flesh: in all its limitations and weaknesses. ⇒ from the world: in all its trials and tensions. ⇒ from the devil: in all his oppressions and attacks. ⇒ from the pressure of men: in all their needful demands and, in some cases, terrible threats and attacks. 　The Father took Jesus home, back from where He had come; and He restored Him to His seat of glory, exalting Him above every

ENGLISH WORD	GREEK WORD AND VERSE	THE WORD MEANS...
		name that is named (Phil. 2:9-11). The believer joys and rejoices in the phenomenal power of the Father's greatness.
		3. A confirmed faith causes believers to be glad. The claims of Jesus have been proven and verified. Just as He told His disciples, all that He predicted has come to pass. ⇒ He did leave (die). ⇒ He did go to His Father (the ascension). ⇒ He did return (the resurrection). ⇒ He did send the Holy Spirit. Note: by foretelling these things, Jesus strengthened the faith of believers enormously. (In fact, think about it: He could have chosen no better way to strengthen the faith of believers.)
#3227 **Rejoice–** **Rejoiced** **Rejoice–KJV** Glad–NASB Glad–NIV **Rejoiced–NKJV** Joy–NLT **POSB REFERENCE** (Acts 2:25-28; esp. v.26) Note 1, point 1b	ηὐφράνθη = ëuphranthë Pronunciation: [yoo-frahn'-thay] Parsing (part of speech): verb Mood—indicative Tense—aorist Voice—passive Person—3rd person Number—singular Stem or root—from εὐφραίνω Concordance References: ⇒ Strong's #2165 euphrainö ⇒ NIV #2370 euphrainö ⇒ NASB #2165 euphrainö **Acts 2:26** Therefore did my heart **rejoice**, and my tongue was glad; moreover also my flesh shall rest in hope: [KJV] 'Therefore my heart was **glad** and my tongue exulted; Moreover my flesh also will abide in hope; [NASB] Therefore my heart is **glad** and my tongue rejoices; my body also will live in hope, [NIV] *Therefore my hart **rejoiced**, and my tongue was **glad**;Moreover my flesh also will rest in hope.* [NKJV] No wonder my heart is filled with **joy**, and my mouth shouts his praises! My body rests in hope. [NLT] Διὰ τοῦτο **εὐφράνθη** ἡ καρδία μου, καὶ ἠγαλλιάσατο ἡ γλῶσσά μου· ἔτι δὲ καὶ ἡ σάρξ μου κατασκηνώσει ἐπ' ἐλπίδι· [GNS] διὰ τοῦτο **ηὐφράνθη** ἡ καρδία μου καὶ ἠγαλλιάσατο ἡ γλῶσσά μου, ἔτι δὲ καὶ ἡ σάρξ μου κατασκηνώσει ἐπ' ἐλπίδι, [GNT]	To be glad; to rejoice; to celebrate; to be merry. It means to be joyful and full of euphoria, full of God's presence and glory. **Practical Application** Peter said that "David [spoke] concerning Christ" (Psalm 16:8-11). What David said was a prophecy of the Lord's experience upon earth (Acts 2:25-28). David's prophecy concerned Jesus' daily experience or life. 1. Jesus experienced God's constant presence and power. ⇒ Jesus always saw God before His face. Jesus looked and kept His gaze upon God. He thought upon God, focused His mind and attention upon God. He concentrated and stayed His mind upon Him. The idea is that Jesus always practiced and was always conscious of God's presence—"captivating every thought" (cp. 2 Cor. 10:5). ⇒ Jesus always had God on His right hand, that He should not be moved. God was right there as an advocate and as a protector and defender. God was a provider looking after Christ, strengthening, guiding, upholding, seeing that He was not moved nor shaken. The picture is that of a defender in court or of a soldier on the battlefield standing at a person's right hand, protecting, looking after, and providing for his welfare. (Cp. Psalm 109:31 for this picture.) 2. Jesus' heart rejoiced and His tongue praised God. Such a consciousness of God's presence was bound to cause... ⇒ the heart to rejoice (*ëuphranthë*): to be joyful and full of euphoria, full of God's presence and glory. ⇒ the tongue to be glad (*ëgalliasato*): to leap for joy and break forth with praise and song. 3. Jesus' flesh rested in hope. The phrase "shall rest" (*kataskenosei*) means *shall tabernacle* or pitch a tent. Jesus' *flesh* rested, tabernacled, pitched its tent, encamped and made its abode upon hope—the hope of conquering death, of being resurrected. Hope of living forever was the basis and foundation of Jesus' life, that for which He lived. He focused His whole life and being upon the hope of the glorious resurrection (cp. Paul's testimony—Phil. 3:7-16, esp. Phil. 3:11).

ENGLISH WORD	GREEK WORD AND VERSE	THE WORD MEANS...
#3228 **Rejoiced** **Rejoiced–KJV** **Rejoiced–NASB** Glad–NIV **Rejoiced–NKJV** Great joy–NLT **POSB** **REFERENCE** (Acts 15:30-35; esp. v.31) Note 5, point 1	ἐχάρησαν = echarēsan Pronunciation: [eh-chah'ray-sahn] Parsing (part of speech): verb 　Mood—indicative 　Tense—aorist 　Voice—passive deponent 　Person—3rd person 　Number—plural 　Stem or root—from χαίρω Concordance References: 　⇒　Strong's #5463 chairö 　⇒　NIV #5897 chairö 　⇒　NASB #5463 chairö **Acts 15:31** Which when they had read, they **rejoiced** for the consolation. [KJV] 　And when they had read it, they **rejoiced** because of its encouragement. [NASB] 　The people read it and were **glad** for its encouraging message. [NIV] 　When they had read it, they **rejoiced** over its encouragement. [NKJV] 　And there was **great joy** throughout the church that day as they read this encouraging message. [NLT] ἀναγνόντες δὲ, **ἐχάρησαν** ἐπὶ τῇ παρακλήσει. [GNS] ἀναγνόντες δὲ **ἐχάρησαν** ἐπὶ τῇ παρακλήσει. [GNT]	Gladness; rejoiced; to have great joy; to be delighted; to be happy. **Practical Application** When the four men arrived in Antioch, the whole church was called together and the great decree on salvation was read. When it was read, four great results occurred. Note how God took the dissension and its subsequent events to work it all out for the good of the Antioch church and for the cause of Christ. The results were fourfold. 1. There was great *"rejoicing"* (*echarēsan*). 2. There was great *"exhortation"* (v.32). 3. There was the discovery of the great missionary, Silas (v.32). 4. A great teaching ministry grew within the church (v.35).
#3229 **Rejoices** Glad–KJV Exulted–NASB **Rejoices–NIV** Glad–NKJV Shouts his praises–NLT **POSB** **REFERENCE** (Acts 2:25-28; esp. v.26) Note 1, point 1b	ἠγαλλιάσατο = ëgalliasato Pronunciation: [ayg-al-lee-ah'-sah-tow] Parsing (part of speech): verb 　Mood—indicative 　Tense—aorist 　Voice—middle 　Person—3rd person 　Number—singular 　Stem or root—from ἀγαλλιάω Concordance References: 　⇒　Strong's #21 agalliaö 　⇒　NIV #22 agalliaö 　⇒　NASB #21 agalliaö **Acts 2:26** Therefore did my heart rejoice, and my tongue was **glad**; moreover also my flesh shall rest in hope: [KJV] 　'Therefore my heart was glad and my tongue **exulted**; Moreover my flesh also will abide in hope; [NASB] 　Therefore my heart is glad and my tongue **rejoices**; my body also will live in hope, [NIV] 　*Therefore my heart rejoiced, and my tongue was **glad**; Moreover my flesh also will rest in hope.* [NKJV] 　No wonder my heart is filled with joy, and my mouth **shouts his praises**! My body rests in hope. [NLT] Διὰ τοῦτο εὐφράνθη ἡ καρδία μου, καὶ **ἠγαλλιάσατο** ἡ γλῶσσά μου· ἔτι δὲ καὶ ἡ σάρξ μου κατασκηνώσει ἐπ' ἐλπίδι· [GNS] διὰ τοῦτο ηὐφράνθη ἡ καρδία μου καὶ **Ἠγαλλιάσατο** ἡ γλῶσσά μου, ἔτι δὲ καὶ ἡ σάρξ μου κατασκηνώσει ἐπ' ἐλπίδι, [GNT]	Rejoices, glad, exulting, rejoicing, filled with joy; greatly rejoicing; to shout God's praises; to be extremely joyful. It means to leap for joy and break forth with praise and song. **Practical Application** Peter said that "David [spoke] about Christ" (Psalm 16:8-11). What David said was a prophecy of the Lord's experience upon earth (Acts 2:25-28). David's prophecy concerned Jesus' daily experience or life. 1. Jesus experienced God's constant presence and power. 　⇒　Jesus always saw God before His face. Jesus looked and kept His gaze upon God. He thought upon God, focused His mind and attention upon God. He concentrated and stayed His mind upon Him. The idea is that Jesus always practiced and was always conscious of God's presence—"taking captive every thought" (cp. 2 Cor. 10:5). 　⇒　Jesus always had God on His right hand, that He should not be moved. God was right there as an advocate and as a protector and defender. God was a provider looking after Christ, strengthening, guiding, upholding, seeing that He was not moved nor shaken. The picture is that of a defender in court or of a soldier on the battlefield standing at a person's right hand, protecting, looking after, and providing for his welfare. (Cp. Psalm 109:31 for this picture.) 2. Jesus' heart rejoiced and His tongue praised God. Such a consciousness of God's presence was bound to cause... 　⇒　the heart to be glad (*ëuphranthë*): to be joyful and full of euphoria, full of God's presence and glory. 　⇒　the tongue to rejoice (*ëgalliasato*): to leap for joy and break forth with praise and song.

ENGLISH WORD	GREEK WORD AND VERSE	THE WORD MEANS...
		3. Jesus' body rested in hope. The phrase "will live" or "abide" (*kataskenosei*) means *shall tabernacle* or pitch a tent. Jesus' *body* rested, tabernacled, pitched its tent, encamped and made its abode upon hope—the hope of conquering death, of being resurrected. Hope of living forever was the basis and foundation of Jesus' life, that for which He lived. He focused His whole life and being upon the hope of the glorious resurrection (cp. Paul's testimony—Phil. 3:7-16, esp. Phil. 3:11).
#3230 **Relative** Kinsman–KJV Kinsman–NASB **Relative–NIV** Countryman–NKJV **Relative–NLT** **POSB** **REFERENCE** (Rom.16:11) Note 11	*συγγενη* = *suggenē* Pronunciation: [soong-ghen-ay'] Parsing (part of speech): pronominal adjective 　　Case—accusative 　　Gender—masculine 　　Number—singular 　　Stem or root—from συγγενής, οῦς Concordance References: ⇒　Strong's #4773 suggenēs ⇒　NIV #5150 suggenēs ⇒　NASB #4773 suggenēs **Romans 16:11** Salute Herodion my **kinsman**. Greet them that be of the household of Narcissus, which are in the Lord. [KJV] Greet Herodion, my **kinsman**. Greet those of the household of Narcissus, who are in the Lord. [NASB] Greet Herodion, my **relative**. Greet those in the household of Narcissus who are in the Lord [NIV] Likewise you also, reckon yourselves to be dead indeed to sin, but alive to God in Christ Jesus our Lord. [NKJV] Greet Herodion, my **countryman**. Greet those who are of the *household* of Narcissus who are in the Lord. [NKJV] Greet Herodion, my **relative**. Greet the Christians in the household of Narcissus. [NLT] ἀσπάσασθε Ἡρῳδίωνα τὸν **συγγενῆ** μου. ἀσπάσασθε τοὺς ἐκ τῶν Ναρκίσσου, τοὺς ὄντας ἐν Κυρίῳ. [GNS] ἀσπάσασθε Ἡρῳδίωνα τὸν **συγγενῆ** μου. ἀσπάσασθε τοὺς ἐκ τῶν Ναρκίσσου τοὺς ὄντας ἐν κυρίῳ. [GNT]	Relative, kinsman; fellow countryman. **Practical Application** Herodion was another relative of Paul who was a believer (cp. Romans 16:7). There is no reason for translating kinsman (*suggenē*) as fellow countryman instead of relative. Others who are mentioned were Jews, but are not called kinsmen by Paul. What effect did this relative have upon Paul's conversion? Again the answer is unknown, but the fact that we should be witnessing to our relatives is driven home to our hearts and minds.
#3231 **Released** Delivered–KJV **Released–NASB** **Released–NIV** Delivered–NKJV **Released–NLT** **POSB** **REFERENCE** (Rom.7:6) Note 4	*κατηργήθημεν* = *katērgēthēmen* Pronunciation: [kat-ayrg-ay'-thay-mehn] Parsing (part of speech): verb 　　Mood—indicative 　　Tense—aorist 　　Voice—passive 　　Person—1st person 　　Number—plural 　　Stem or root—from καταργέω Concordance References: ⇒　Strong's #2673 katargeō ⇒　NIV #2934 katargeō ⇒　NASB #2673 katargeō **Romans 7:6** But now we are **delivered** from the law, that being dead wherein we were held; that we should serve in newness of spirit, and not in the oldness of the letter. [KJV] But now we have been **released** from the Law, having died to that by which we were bound, so that we serve in newness of the Spirit and not in oldness of the letter. [NASB] But now, by dying to what once bound us, we have been **released** from the law so that we serve in the new way of the Spirit, and not in the old way of the written code. [NIV] But now we have been **delivered** from the law, having died to what we were held by, so that we should serve	To be released; to be delivered; to be discharged. **Practical Application** Believers are "released" (*katērgēthēmen*), that is, have been discharged from the law. How? By their death "in" Christ (see POSB note, Jesus Christ, Redemption—Romans 7:4 for discussion).

ENGLISH WORD	GREEK WORD AND VERSE	THE WORD MEANS...
	in the newness of the Spirit and not *in* the oldness of the letter. [NKJV] But now we have been **released** from the law, for we died with Christ, and we are no longer captive to its power. Now we can really serve God, not in the old way by obeying the letter of the law, but in the new way, by the Spirit. [NLT] νυνὶ δὲ **κατηργήθημεν** ἀπὸ τοῦ νόμου, ἀποθανόντες ἐν ᾧ κατειχόμεθα, ὥστε δουλεύειν ἡμᾶς ἐν καινότητι πνεύματος, καὶ οὐ παλαιότητι γράμματος. [GNS] νυνὶ δὲ **κατηργήθημεν** ἀπὸ τοῦ νόμου ἀποθανόντες ἐν ᾧ κατειχόμεθα, ὥστε δουλεύειν ἡμᾶς ἐν καινότητι πνεύματος καὶ οὐ παλαιότητι γράμματος. [GNT]	

#3232
Released
 	
Washed–KJV
Released–NASB
Freed–NIV
Washed–NKJV
Freed–NLT
 	
**POSB
REFERENCE**
(Rev.1:5-6; esp.v.5)
Note 2, point 4
	λύσαντι = *lusanti*
	Pronunciation: [loo'-sahn-tee]
	Parsing (part of speech): verb
	    Mood—participle
	    Tense—aorist
	    Voice—active
	    Case—dative
	    Gender—masculine
	    Number—singular
	    Stem or root—from λύω
	Concordance References:
	  ⇒ Strong's #3089 luö
	  ⇒ NIV #3395 luö
	  ⇒ NASB #3089 luö
	
	Rev. 1:5
	And from Jesus Christ, who is the faithful witness, and the first begotten of the dead, and the prince of the kings of the earth. Unto him that loved us, and **washed** us from our sins in his own blood, [KJV]
	
	And from Jesus Christ, the faithful witness, the first-born of the dead, and the ruler of the kings of the earth. To Him who loves us, and **released** us from our sins by His blood, [NASB]
	
	And from Jesus Christ, who is the faithful witness, the firstborn from the dead, and the ruler of the kings of the earth. To him who loves us and has **freed** us from our sins by his blood, [NIV]
	
	And from Jesus Christ, the faithful witness, the first-born from the dead, and the ruler over the kings of the earth. To Him who loved us and **washed** us from our sins in His own blood, [NKJV]
	
	And from Jesus Christ, who is the faithful witness to these things, the first to rise from the dead, and the commander of all the rulers of the world. All praise to him who loves us and has **freed** us from our sins by shedding his blood for us. [NLT]
	
	καὶ ἀπὸ Ἰησοῦ Χριστοῦ, ὁ μάρτυς ὁ πιστός, ὁ πρωτότοκος τῶν νεκρῶν καὶ ὁ ἄρχων τῶν βασιλέων τῆς γῆς. τῷ ἀγαπήσαντι ἡμᾶς, καὶ **λούσαντι** ἡμᾶς ἀπὸ τῶν ἁμαρτιῶν ἡμῶν ἐν τῷ αἵματι αὐτοῦ· [GNS]
	
	καὶ ἀπὸ Ἰησοῦ Χριστοῦ, ὁ μάρτυς ὁ πιστός, ὁ πρωτότοκος τῶν νεκρῶν καὶ ὁ ἄρχων τῶν βασιλέων τῆς γῆς. Τῷ ἀγαπῶντι ἡμᾶς καὶ **λύσαντι** ἡμᾶς ἐκ τῶν ἁμαρτιῶν ἡμῶν ἐν τῷ αἵματι αὐτοῦ, [GNT]
		To be freed, washed, loosed, set free, and released from sin.
		
		Practical Application
		Jesus Christ has redeemed us. He *"loves us and has washed us from our sins in His own blood"* (Rev. 1:5). The word *love* is in the present tense in the Greek. This means that Jesus Christ *always loves* us. He loves us today just as He has loved us in the past. How did the blood of Jesus Christ set us free from sin?
		
		Jesus Christ took our sins and died for them. He had lived a sinless and perfect life as a Man upon earth. Therefore, He was able to present Himself as the Ideal and Perfect Man before God. He was able to die as the Ideal and Perfect Sacrifice. He was able to take our sins—the guilt and the judgment of our sins—upon Himself to bear the punishment for them. He was the Ideal and Perfect Man; therefore, God is able to accept His death as the Ideal and Perfect Sacrifice for sin.
		
		The point is this: Jesus Christ died for our sins. He actually took our sins off of us, removed them, and died for them. Therefore, we are free and loosed from sin. Sin has been removed from us. We stand before God free of sin and acceptable to Him. But remember how: by the shed blood of Jesus Christ upon the cross. It is the shed blood of Christ upon the cross—His dying for our sins—that frees us from sin.

#3233
Reliable
 	
Faithful–KJV
Faithful–NASB
Reliable–NIV
Faithful–NKJV
Trustworthy–NLT
	πιστοῖς = *pistois*
	Pronunciation: [pis-toys']
	Parsing (part of speech): adjective
	    Case—dative
	    Gender—masculine
	    Number—plural
	    Stem or root— from πιστός, ή, όν
	Concordance References:
	  ⇒ Strong's #4103 pistos
	  ⇒ NIV #4412 pistos
	  ⇒ NASB #4103 pistos
		Reliable, faithful, trustworthy, unfailing.
		
		Practical Application
		By reliable (*pistois*) is meant a person...
		• who *believes* in Christ and in the Word of God.
		• who is loyal, reliable, dependable, and trustworthy.
		
		Naturally, a person who does not believe in God or in God's Word cannot be said to be reliable to God. He is unfaithful and disloyal. God

ENGLISH WORD	GREEK WORD AND VERSE	THE WORD MEANS...
POSB REFERENCE (2 Tim.2:2) Note 2, point 2	**2 Tim. 2:2** And the things that thou hast heard of me among many witnesses, the same commit thou to **faithful** men, who shall be able to teach others also. [KJV] And the things which you have heard from me in the presence of many witnesses, these entrust to **faithful** men, who will be able to teach others also. [NASB] And the things you have heard me say in the presence of many witnesses entrust to **reliable** men who will also be qualified to teach others. [NIV] And the things that you have heard from me among many witnesses, commit these to **faithful** men who will be able to teach others also. [NKJV] You have heard me teach many things that have been confirmed by many reliable witnesses. Teach these great truths to **trustworthy** people who are able to pass them on to others. [NLT] καὶ ἃ ἤκουσας παρ' ἐμοῦ διὰ πολλῶν μαρτύρων, ταῦτα παράθου **πιστοῖς** ἀνθρώποις, οἵτινες ἱκανοὶ ἔσονται καὶ ἑτέρους διδάξαι. [GNS] καὶ ἃ ἤκουσας παρ' ἐμοῦ διὰ πολλῶν μαρτύρων, ταῦτα παράθου **πιστοῖς** ἀνθρώποις, οἵτινες ἱκανοὶ ἔσονται καὶ ἑτέρους διδάξαι. [GNT]	cannot trust or rely on him. The point is this: a strong teacher will not commit the truth to an unreliable person. The strong teacher will look for reliable people and commit the truth to them.

#3234 Religion
 	
Religion–KJV
Religion–NASB
Religion–NIV
Religion–NKJV
Religion–NLT
 	
POSB REFERENCE (Jas.1:26) Note 3
	θρησκεία = *thrēskeia*
	Pronunciation: [thrace-ki'-ah]
	Parsing (part of speech): noun
	    Case—nominative
	    Gender—feminine
	    Number—singular
	    Stem or root—from θρησκεία, ας
	Concordance References:
	⇒ Strong's #2356 thrēskeia
	⇒ NIV #2579 thrēskeia
	⇒ NASB #2356 thrēskeia
	
	James 1:26
	If any man among you seem to be religious, and bridleth not his tongue, but deceiveth his own heart, this man's **religion** is vain. [KJV]
	If anyone thinks himself to be religious, and yet does not bridle his tongue but deceives his own heart, this man's **religion** is worthless. [NASB]
	If anyone considers himself religious and yet does not keep a tight rein on his tongue, he deceives himself and his **religion** is worthless. [NIV]
	If anyone among you thinks he is religious, and does not bridle his tongue but deceives his own heart, this one's **religion** *is* useless. [NKJV]
	If you claim to be religious but don't control your tongue, you are just fooling yourself, and your **religion** is worthless. [NLT]
	εἴ τις δοκεῖ θρησκὸς εἶναι ἐν ὑμῖν, μὴ χαλιναγωγῶν γλῶσσαν αὐτοῦ, ἀλλ ἀπατῶν καρδίαν αὐτοῦ, τούτου μάταιος ἡ **θρησκεία**. [GNS]
	Εἴ τις δοκεῖ θρησκὸς εἶναι μὴ χαλιναγωγῶν γλῶσσαν αὐτοῦ ἀλλὰ ἀπατῶν καρδίαν αὐτοῦ, τούτου μάταιος ἡ **θρησκεία**. [GNT]
		Religion, creed, worship, belief system, persuasion.
		
		Practical Application
		If a person thinks that he is religious, that is, acceptable to God, and he does not bridle his tongue, he deceives himself. No matter what he thinks or professes, his religion is empty. And note: the word religious (*thrēskos*) and religion (*thrēskeia*) describes a person who is very religious, who gives great attention to religion (RVG Tasker. *The General Epistle of James.* "Tyndale New Testament Commentaries," p.54). The person is actively religious, very faithful in his religious worship and service. But he is loose with his tongue...
		• interrupting and dominating the coversation
		• being easily provoked and lashing out at others
		• gossiping and telling tales
		• criticizing and murmuring
		• judging and condemning others
		• using slang and cursing
		• engaging in suggestive and off-colored talk
		• talking about and running down others
		As stated, no matter what a person thinks—no matter how religious he is—if he does not bridle his tongue, he deceives himself. His religion is empty. He does not please God and is thereby unacceptable to God. For a person to withstand and to conquer temptation, he must bridle his tongue. This is the third preparation necessary to conquer temptations.

#3235 Religious, Are Very
 	
Are too superstitious– KJV
 	
Are very religious– NASB
 	
Are very religious– NIV
 	
Are very religious– NKJV
	ὡς δεισιδαιμονεστέρους = *hōs deisidaimonesterous*
	Pronunciation: [hos dice-ee-dahee-mon-es'-ter-oos]
	Parsing (part of speech): adjective
	    Type—comparative
	    Case—accusative
	    Gender—masculine
	    Number—plural
	    Stem or root—from δεισιδαίμων
	Concordance References:
	⇒ Strong's #5613 hōs + 1174 deisidaimōn
	⇒ NIV #6055 hōs [are] + 1273 deisidaimonester-ous [very religious]
	⇒ NASB #5613 hōs + 1174 deisidaimōn
		To be very religious; to be superstitious.
		
		Practical Application
		The word can be equally translated either way (to be very religious; to be superstitious). The fact that man is religious and superstitious reveals he is searching for God. Men worship because they seek God. Their hearts...
		• are restless, searching for peace and life with God.
		• are hungry, seeking to have God's care and provision.
		• are fearful, seeking to have God's protection.

ENGLISH WORD	GREEK WORD AND VERSE	THE WORD MEANS...
Are very religious–NLT **POSB REFERENCE** (Acts 17:22) Note 2	**Acts 17:22** Then Paul stood in the midst of Mars' hill, and said, *Ye* men of Athens, I perceive that in all things ye **are too superstitious**. [KJV] And Paul stood in the midst of the Areopagus and said, "Men of Athens, I observe that you **are very religious** in all respects. [NASB] Paul then stood up in the meeting of the Areopagus and said: "Men of Athens! I see that in every way you **are very religious**. [NIV] Then Paul stood in the midst of the Areopagus and said, "Men of Athens, I perceive that in all things you **are very religious**; [NKJV] So Paul, standing before the Council, addressed them as follows: "Men of Athens, I notice that you **are very religious**, [NLT] σταθεὶς δὲ ὁ Παῦλος ἐν μέσῳ τοῦ Ἀρείου Πάγου, ἔφη, Ἄνδρες Ἀθηναῖοι, κατὰ πάντα **ὡς δεισιδαιμονεστέρους** ὑμᾶς θεωρῶ. [GNS] Σταθεὶς δὲ [ὁ] Παῦλος ἐν μέσῳ τοῦ Ἀρείου Πάγου ἔφη, Ἄνδρες Ἀθηναῖοι, κατὰ πάντα **ὡς δεισιδαιμονεστέρους** ὑμᾶς θεωρῶ. [GNT]	
#3236 **Remain** Abide–KJV Abide–NASB **Remain–NIV** Abide–NKJV **Remain–NLT** **POSB REFERENCE** (Jn.15:4) *Deeper Study* #2 **See also POSB REF:** (1 Jn.2:24) Note 1	μείνατε = *meinate* Pronunciation: [meh-een'-ah-teh] Parsing (part of speech): verb 　Mood—imperative 　Tense—aorist 　Voice—active 　Person—2nd person 　Number—plural 　Stem or root—from μένω Concordance References: ⇒　Strong's #3306 meno ⇒　NIV #3531 meno ⇒　NASB #3306 meno **John 15:4** **Abide** in me, and I in you. As the branch cannot bear fruit of itself, except it abide in the vine; no more can ye, except ye abide in me. [KJV] "**Abide** in Me, and I in you. As the branch cannot bear fruit of itself, unless it abides in the vine, so neither *can* you, unless you abide in Me. [NASB] **Remain** in me, and I will remain in you. No branch can bear fruit by itself; it must remain in the vine. Neither can you bear fruit unless you remain in me [NIV] **Abide** in Me, and I in you. As the branch cannot bear fruit of itself, unless it abides in the vine, neither can you, unless you abide in Me. [NKJV] **Remain** in me, and I will remain in you. For a branch cannot produce fruit if it is severed from the vine, and you cannot be fruitful apart from me. [NLT] **μείνατε** ἐν ἐμοί, κἀγὼ ἐν ὑμῖν. καθὼς τὸ κλῆμα οὐ δύναται καρπὸν φέρειν ἀφ' ἑαυτοῦ, ἐὰν μὴ μείνῃ ἐν τῇ ἀμπέλῳ, οὕτως οὐδὲ ὑμεῖς, ἐὰν μὴ ἐν ἐμοὶ μένητε. [GNS] **μείνατε** ἐν ἐμοί, κἀγὼ ἐν ὑμῖν. καθὼς τὸ κλῆμα οὐ δύναται καρπὸν φέρειν ἀφ' ἑαυτοῦ ἐὰν μὴ μένῃ ἐν τῇ ἀμπέλῳ, οὕτως οὐδὲ ὑμεῖς ἐὰν μὴ ἐν ἐμοὶ μένητε. [GNT]	To hold; to continue; to abide; to remain; to keep on obeying. It means to dwell, continue, stay, sojourn, rest in or upon; to live; to rest; to nest. **Practical Application** It is being set and fixed and remaining there. It is continuing on and on in a fixed state, condition, or being. (See POSB *Deeper Study* #1, Abide—John 15:1-8; POSB note—John 6:56.) The more a branch abides in the vine, that is, the closer the branch abides to the heart of the vine, the more nourishment a branch draws from the vine and the more fruit it bears.
#3237 **Remain–Remains** Dwelleth–KJV Abides–NASB **Remains–NIV** Abides–NKJV **Remain–NLT**	μένει = *menei* Pronunciation: [mehn'-ee] Parsing (part of speech): verb 　Mood—indicative 　Tense—present 　Voice—active 　Number—3rd person singular 　Stem or root—from μένω Concordance References: ⇒　Strong's #3306 meno ⇒　NIV #3531 menö ⇒　NASB #3306 meno	To hold; to continue; to abide; to remain; to keep on obeying. It means to dwell, stay, sojourn, rest in or upon; to live; to rest; to nest. **Practical Application** It is being fixed and set and remaining there, continuing on and on. Such is the state and condition and being of the person who receives Christ. The person receives Christ into his being, and Christ enters the person's life and abides within him. The person is also taken and placed into Christ, that is, placed with all other believers into the spiritual body of Christ.

ENGLISH WORD	GREEK WORD AND VERSE	THE WORD MEANS...
POSB **REFERENCE** (Jn.6:56) Note 4	**John 6:56** He that eateth my flesh, and drinketh my blood, **dwelleth** in me, and I in him. [KJV] "He who eats My flesh and drinks My blood **abides** in Me, and I in him. [NASB] Whoever eats my flesh and drinks my blood **remains** in me, and I in him. [NIV] He who eats My flesh and drinks My blood **abides** in Me, and I in him. [NKJV] All who eat my flesh and drink my blood **remain** in me, and I in them. [NLT] ὁ τρώγων μου τὴν σάρκα, καὶ πίνων μου τὸ αἷμα, ἐν ἐμοὶ **μένει**, κἀγὼ ἐν αὐτῷ. [GNS] ὁ τρώγων μου τὴν σάρκα καὶ πίνων μου τὸ αἷμα ἐν ἐμοὶ **μένει** κἀγὼ ἐν αὐτῷ. [GNT]	

#3238
Remain Faithful
 	
Continue–KJV
Continue–NASB
Continue–NIV
Continue–NKJV
Remain faithful–NLT
 	
POSB
REFERENCE
(2 Tim. 3:14)
Note 1
	μένε = *mene*
	Pronunciation: [men'-eh]
	Parsing (part of speech): verb
	  Mood—imperative
	  Tense—present
	  Voice—active
	  Person—2nd person
	  Number—singular
	  Stem or root—from μένω
	Concordance References:
	  ⇒ Strong's #3306 menö
	  ⇒ NIV #3531 menö
	  ⇒ NASB #3306 menö
	
	2 Tim. 3:14
	But **continue** thou in the things which thou hast learned and hast been assured of, knowing of whom thou hast learned them; [KJV]
	You, however, **continue** in the things you have learned and become convinced of, knowing from whom you have learned them; [NASB]
	But as for you, **continue** in what you have learned and have become convinced of, because you know those from whom you learned it, [NIV]
	But you must **continue** in the things which you have learned and been assured of, knowing from whom you have learned *them,* [NKJV]
	But you must **remain faithful** to the things you have been taught. You know they are true, for you know you can trust those who taught you. [NLT]
	σὺ δὲ **μένε** ἐν οἷς ἔμαθες καὶ ἐπιστώθης, εἰδὼς παρὰ τίνος ἔμαθες, [GNS]
	σὺ δὲ **μένε** ἐν οἷς ἔμαθες καὶ ἐπιστώθης, εἰδὼς παρὰ τίνων ἔμαθες, [GNT]
		To continue; to remain faithful; to abide, dwell, remain, and stay in the Scripture.
		
		Practical Application
		Simply stated, Timothy had to *live* in the Scripture—live, move, and have his being in the Scripture. And more, he had to *live out* the Scripture—remain faithful to walk and live in the truths of the Scripture. He had to do what Scripture said.

#3239
Remained
 	
Tarried–KJV
Spending time–NASB
Spent some time–NIV
Remained–NKJV
Stayed–NLT
 	
POSB
REFERENCE
(Jn.3:22-26; esp. v.22)
Note 1, point 1
	διέτριβεν = *dietriben*
	Pronunciation: [dee-eht-ree'-behn]
	Parsing (part of speech): verb
	  Mood—indicative
	  Tense—imperfect
	  Voice—active
	  Person—3rd person
	  Number—singular
	  Stem or root—from διατρίβω
	Concordance References:
	  ⇒ Strong's #1304 diatribö
	  ⇒ NIV #1417 diatribö
	  ⇒ NASB #1304 diatribö
	
	John 3:22
	After these things came Jesus and his disciples into the land of Judaea; and there he **tarried** with them, and baptized. [KJV]
	After these things Jesus and His disciples came into the land of Judea, and there He was **spending time** with them and baptizing. [NASB]
	After this, Jesus and his disciples went out into the
		To spend time with; to tarry; to remain; to stay. It has the idea of spending much time in sharing and ministering.
		
		Practical Application
		We can learn from Christ's example by spending time—quality time—with other believers. The fellowship wrought by the Spirit of God means more than the association existing in secular groups such as civic clubs and community bodies. There is a vast difference between *community participation* and *spiritual participation. Community participation* is based upon neighborly association. *Spiritual participation* is based upon a spiritual union wrought by the Spirit of God.
		The distinctiveness is this: the Holy Spirit is within the Christian believer. The Holy Spirit creates a spiritual union by melting and molding the heart of the Christian believer to the hearts of

ENGLISH WORD	GREEK WORD AND VERSE	THE WORD MEANS...
	Judean countryside, where he **spent some time** with them, and baptized. [NIV] After these things Jesus and His disciples came into the land of Judea, and there He **remained** with them and baptized. [NKJV] Afterward Jesus and his disciples left Jerusalem, but they **stayed** in Judea for a while and baptized there. [NLT] Μετὰ ταῦτα ἦλθεν ὁ Ἰησοῦς καὶ οἱ μαθηταὶ αὐτοῦ εἰς τὴν Ἰουδαίαν γῆν· καὶ ἐκεῖ **διέτριβε** μετ' αὐτῶν καὶ ἐβάπτιζεν. [GNS] Μετὰ ταῦτα ἦλθεν ὁ Ἰησοῦς καὶ οἱ μαθηταὶ αὐτοῦ εἰς τὴν Ἰουδαίαν γῆν καὶ ἐκεῖ **διέτριβεν** μετ' αὐτῶν καὶ ἐβάπτιζεν. [GNT]	other believers. He attaches the life of one believer to the lives of other believers. Through the Spirit of God, believers become one in life and purpose. They have a joint life sharing their blessings and needs and gifts together.

#3240
Remember
 	
Remember–KJV
Remember–NASB
Remember–NIV
Remember–NKJV
Remember–NLT
 	
POSB REFERENCE
(Heb.13:7)
Note 6
	Μνημονεύετε = *Mnēmoneuete*
	Pronunciation: [mnay-mon-yoo'-eh-teh]
	Parsing (part of speech): verb
	    Mood—imperative
	    Tense—present
	    Voice—active
	    Person—2nd person
	    Number—plural
	    Stem or root—from μνημονεύω
	Concordance References:
	  ⇒ Strong's #3421 mnēmoneuō
	  ⇒ NIV #3648 mnēmoneuō
	  ⇒ NASB #3421 mnēmoneuō
	
	Hebrews 13:7
	Remember them which have the rule over you, who have spoken unto you the word of God: whose faith follow, considering the end of their conversation. [KJV]
	
	Remember those who led you, who spoke the word of God to you; and considering the result of their conduct, imitate their faith. [NASB]
	
	Remember your leaders, who spoke the word of God to you. Consider the outcome of their way of life and imitate their faith. [NIV]
	
	Remember those who rule over you, who have spoken the word of God to you, whose faith follow, considering the outcome of *their* conduct. [NKJV]
	
	Remember your leaders who first taught you the word of God. Think of all the good that has come from their lives, and trust the Lord as they do. [NLT]
	
	Μνημονεύετε τῶν ἡγουμένων ὑμῶν, οἵτινες ἐλάλησαν ὑμῖν τὸν λόγον τοῦ Θεοῦ· ὧν ἀναθεωροῦντες τὴν ἔκβασιν τῆς ἀναστροφῆς, μιμεῖσθε τὴν πίστιν. [GNS]
	
	Μνημονεύετε τῶν ἡγουμένων ὑμῶν, οἵτινες ἐλάλησαν ὑμῖν τὸν λόγον τοῦ θεοῦ, ὧν ἀναθεωροῦντες τὴν ἔκβασιν τῆς ἀναστροφῆς μιμεῖσθε τὴν πίστιν. [GNT]
		To remember; to be mindful; to think; to keep in mind.
		
		### Practical Application
		The idea is continuous remembrance. Leaders are never to be forgotten. But note who the leaders are that are to be remembered: those who have proclaimed the Word of God. If a person has been faithful in proclaiming and teaching God's Word, we are to remember them and never forget them. Note why: *so that we can follow their faith.* A leader who faithfully proclaims God's Word is a leader to follow. As the Amplified New Testament says:
		
		"Remember your leaders and superiors in authority, [for it was they] who brought to you the Word of God. Observe attentively and consider their manner of living—the outcome of their well-spent lives—and imitate their faith [that is, their conviction that God exists and is the Creator and Ruler of all things, the Provider and Bestower of eternal salvation through Christ; and their leaning of the entire human personality on God in absolute trust and confidence in His power, wisdom and goodness]."

#3241
Remind
 	
Declare–KJV
Make known–NASB
Remind–NIV
Declare–NKJV
Remind–NLT
 	
POSB REFERENCE
(1 Cor.15:1-2; esp. v.1)
Note 1
	Γνωρίζω = *Gnōrizō*
	Pronunciation: [gno-rid'-zo]
	Parsing (part of speech): verb
	    Mood—indicative
	    Tense—present
	    Voice—active
	    Person—1st person
	    Number—singular
	    Stem or root—from γνωρίζω
	Concordance References:
	  ⇒ Strong's #1107 gnōrizō
	  ⇒ NIV #1192 gnōrizō
	  ⇒ NASB #1107 gnōrizō
	
	1 Cor. 15:1
	Moreover, brethren, I **declare** unto you the gospel which I preached unto you, which also ye have received, and wherein ye stand; [KJV]
	
	Now I **make known** to you, brethren, the gospel which I preached to you, which also you received, in
		To remind; to declare; to tell; to present; to make known.
		
		### Practical Application
		Paul is not reminding the Corinthians of the gospel, he is...
		• declaring it as though they had never heard it.
		• proclaiming it as though they had never sat before it.
		• making it known as though they had never known it.

ENGLISH WORD	GREEK WORD AND VERSE	THE WORD MEANS...

	which also you stand, [NASB]
	    Now, brothers, I want to **remind** you of the gospel I preached to you, which you received and on which you have taken your stand. [NIV]
	    Moreover, brethren, I **declare** to you the gospel which I preached to you, which also you received and in which you stand, [NKJV]
	    Now let me **remind** you, dear brothers and sisters, of the Good News I preached to you before. You welcomed it then and still do now, for your faith is built on this wonderful message. [NLT]
	    Γνωρίζω δὲ ὑμῖν, ἀδελφοί, τὸ εὐαγγέλιον ὃ εὐηγγελισάμην ὑμῖν, ὃ καὶ παρελάβετε, ἐν ᾧ καὶ ἑστήκατε, [GNS]
	    Γνωρίζω δὲ ὑμῖν, ἀδελφοί, τὸ εὐαγγέλιον ὃ εὐηγγελισάμην ὑμῖν, ὃ καὶ παρελάβετε, ἐν ᾧ καὶ ἑστήκατε, [GNT]	

#3242
Remission
 	
Remission–KJV
Forgiveness–NASB
Forgiveness–NIV
Remission–NKJV
Forgive–NLT
 	
POSB
REFERENCE
(Mt.26:28)
Deeper Study #4
 	
See also POSB REF:
(Acts 2:38)
Deeper Study #2
	ἄφεσιν = aphesin
	Pronunciation: [af'-es-in]
	Parsing (part of speech): noun
	    Case—accusative
	    Gender—feminine
	    Number—singular
	    Stem or root—from ἄφεσις, εως
	Concordance References:
	  ⇒ Strong's #859 aphesis
	  ⇒ NIV #912 aphesis
	  ⇒ NASB #859 aphesis
	
	Matthew 26:28
	    For this is my blood of the new testament, which is shed for many for the **remission** of sins. [KJV]
	    For this is My blood of the covenant, which is poured out for many for **forgiveness** of sins. [NASB]
	    This is my blood of the covenant, which is poured out for many for the **forgiveness** of sins. [NIV]
	    For this is My blood of the new covenant, which is shed for many for the **remission** of sins. [NKJV]
	    For this is my blood, which seals the covenant between God and his people. It is poured out to **forgive** the sins of many. [NLT]
	    τοῦτο γάρ ἐστι τὸ αἷμά μου, τὸ τῆς καινῆς διαθήκης, τὸ περὶ πολλῶν ἐκχυννόμενον εἰς ἄφεσιν ἁμαρτιῶν. [GNS]
	    τοῦτο γάρ ἐστιν τὸ αἷμά μου τῆς διαθήκης τὸ περὶ πολλῶν ἐκχυννόμενον εἰς ἄφεσιν ἁμαρτιῶν. [GNT]
		Forgiveness, remission; to forgive; to send off; to send away. The wrong is cut out, sent off, and sent away from the wrongdoer. The sin is separated from the sinner.
		
		Practical Application
		    There are four main ideas in the Biblical concept of forgiveness or remission.
		1. There is the idea of why forgiveness or remission is needed. Forgiveness is needed because of wrongdoing and guilt and the penalty arising from both (cp. Romans 3:23; Romans 6:23; Romans 8:1).
		2. There is the idea of a *once-for-all* forgiveness, a total forgiveness. A man is *once-for-all* forgiven when he receives Jesus Christ as his Savior. Belief in Jesus Christ is the only condition for being forgiven *once-for-all* (Ephes. 1:7; Romans 4:5-8).
		3. There is the idea of forgiveness that maintains fellowship. Fellowship exists between God as Father and the believer as His child. When the child does wrong, the fellowship is disturbed and broken. The condition for restoring the fellowship is confessing and forsaking the sin (Psalm 66:18; Proverbs 28:13; 1 John 1:7).
		4. There is the idea of a *releasing from guilt*. This is one of the differences between man's forgiving a man and God's forgiving a man. A man may forgive a person for wronging him, but he can never remove the guilt that his friend feels. And often he cannot remove the resentment he feels within his own heart. Only God can remove the guilt and assure the removal of resentment, and God does both. God forgives and erases the guilt and resentment (Psalm 51:2, 7-12; Psalm 103:12; 1 John 1:9).

#3243
Removed
 	
Bare–KJV
Carried–NASB
Carried–NIV
Bore–NKJV
Removed–NLT
 	
POSB
REFERENCE
(Mt.8:17)
Note 3
	ἐβάστασεν = ebastasen
	Pronunciation: [eh-bas-ta'-sen]
	Parsing (part of speech): verb
	    Mood—indicative
	    Tense—aorist
	    Voice—active
	    Person—3rd person
	    Number—singular
	    Stem or root—from βαστάζω
	Concordance References:
	  ⇒ Strong's #941 bastazō
	  ⇒ NIV #1002 bastazō
	  ⇒ NASB #941 bastazō
		To bear; to bear with; to endure; to take up; to carry; to support; to sustain; to remove; to endure hardship.
		
		Practical Application
		    In this Scripture, Christ did not just heal our sicknesses as any other minister, but He "Himself took [*elaben*] our sicknesses, and removed [*ebastasen*] our diseases." This means at least two things.
		1. He carried our sicknesses and diseases to the ultimate degree when He died on the cross for us. It was there that He bore them (see POSB

ENGLISH WORD	GREEK WORD AND VERSE	THE WORD MEANS...
	Matthew 8:17 That it might be fulfilled which was spoken by Esaias the prophet, saying, Himself took our infirmities, and **bare** our sicknesses. [KJV] In order that what was spoken through Isaiah the prophet might be fulfilled, saying, "He Himself took our infirmities, and **CARRIED** AWAY OUR DISEASES." [NASB] This was to fulfill what was spoken through the prophet Isaiah: "He took up our infirmities and **carried** our diseases." [NIV] That it might be fulfilled which was spoken by Isaiah the prophet, saying: "He Himself took our infirmities And **bore** our sicknesses." [NKJV] This fulfilled the word of the Lord through Isaiah, who said, "He took our sicknesses and **removed** our diseases." [NLT] ὅπως πληρωθῇ τὸ ῥηθὲν διὰ Ἠσαΐου τοῦ προφήτου, λέγοντος, Αὐτὸς τὰς ἀσθενείας ἡμῶν ἔλαβε, καὶ τὰς νόσους **ἐβάστασεν**. [GNS] ὅπως πληρωθῇ τὸ ῥηθὲν διὰ Ἠσαΐου τοῦ προφήτου λέγοντος, Αὐτὸς τὰς ἀσθενείας ἡμῶν ἔλαβεν καὶ τὰς νόσους **ἐβάστασεν**. [GNT]	*Deeper Study #2*—Mt.8:17 for discussion). (Cp. Jn.1:29.) 2. He carried each fresh illness in a way that will never be understood. a. Each need that stood before Him was a reminder that He had to bear the sin of the world. And He knew what this meant and all that it was to include. Seeing the needs of people standing before Him reminded Him of the suffering He was to bear. b. Each need that He met was a foretaste of the cross. The thought of what He had to bear was upon His mind day by day and hour by hour as He went about ministering. This was bound to weigh ever so heavily upon Him.
#3244 **Removed** **Removed–KJV** Deserting–NASB Deserting–NIV Turning away–NKJV Turning away–NLT **POSB REFERENCE** (Gal.1:6-7; esp. v.6) Note 2, point 1	**μετατίθεσθε ἀπὸ** = *metatithesthe apo* Pronunciation: [met-at-ith'-ehs-the ah-po] Parsing *metatithesthe* (part of speech): verb 　　Mood—indicative 　　Tense—present 　　Voice—middle or passive 　　Person—2nd person 　　Number—plural 　　Stem or root—from μετατίθημι Parsing *apo* (part of speech): preposition 　　Case—genitive 　　Stem or root—from **ἀπό** Concordance References: ⇒　Strong's #575+3346 apo metatithēmi ⇒　NIV #608+3572 apo metatithēmi [deserting] ⇒　NASB #575+3346 apo metatithēmi **Galatians 1:6** I marvel that ye are so soon **removed** from him that called you into the grace of Christ unto another gospel: [KJV] I am amazed that you are so quickly **deserting** Him who called you by the grace of Christ, for a different gospel; [NASB] I am astonished that you are so quickly **deserting** the one who called you by the grace of Christ and are turning to a different gospel [NIV] I marvel that you are **turning away** so soon from Him who called you in the grace of Christ, to a different gospel, [NKJV] I am shocked that you are **turning away** so soon from God, who in his love and mercy called you to share the eternal life he gives through Christ. You are already following a different way [NLT] Θαυμάζω ὅτι οὕτω ταχέως **μετατίθεσθε ἀπὸ** τοῦ καλέσαντος ὑμᾶς ἐν χάριτι Χριστοῦ εἰς ἕτερον εὐαγγέλιον· [GNS] Θαυμάζω ὅτι οὕτως ταχέως **μετατίθεσθε ἀπὸ** τοῦ καλέσαντος ὑμᾶς ἐν χάριτι [Χριστοῦ] εἰς ἕτερον εὐαγγέλιον, [GNT]	To desert; to remove; to turn away; to change places; to transfer elsewhere. **Practical Application** 　The believers were deserting God, removing themselves away from God. The tense of the verb (*metatithesthe*) is present tense which means the Galatians were in the process of turning; they had not yet fully turned. There was still hope for them to repent and return to God.
#3245 **Render Powerless** Destroy–KJV **Render powerless– NASB**	**καταργήσῃ** = *katargēsē* Pronunciation: [kat-arg-ay'-say] Parsing (part of speech): verb 　　Mood—subjunctive 　　Tense—aorist 　　Voice—active 　　Person—3rd person 　　Number—singular	To destroy; to render powerless; to break; to abolish; to render ineffective; to cancel; to nullify; to bring to nothing; to do away; to make inoperative. **Practical Application** Jesus Christ alone has broken and destroyed

ENGLISH WORD	GREEK WORD AND VERSE	THE WORD MEANS...
Destroy–NIV Destroy–NKJV Break–NLT **POSB REFERENCE** (Heb.2:14-16; esp. v.14) Note 1, point 3	Stem or root—from **καταργέω** Concordance References: ⇒ Strong's #2673 katargeö ⇒ NIV #2934 katargeö ⇒ NASB #2673 katargeö **Hebrews 2:14** Forasmuch then as the children are partakers of flesh and blood, he also himself likewise took part of the same; that through death he might **destroy** him that had the power of death, that is, the devil; [KJV] Since then the children share in flesh and blood, He Himself likewise also partook of the same, that through death He might **render powerless** him who had the power of death, that is, the devil; [NASB] Since the children have flesh and blood, he too shared in their humanity so that by his death he might **destroy** him who holds the power of death—that is, the devil—[NIV] Inasmuch then as the children have partaken of flesh and blood, He Himself likewise shared in the same, that through death He might **destroy** him who had the power of death, that is, the devil, [NKJV] Because God's children are human beings—made of flesh and blood—Jesus also became flesh and blood by being born in human form. For only as a human being could he die, and only by dying could he **break** the power of the Devil, who had the power of death. [NLT] ἐπεὶ οὖν τὰ παιδία κεκοινώνηκε σαρκός καὶ αἵματος, καὶ αὐτὸς παραπλησίως μετέσχε τῶν αὐτῶν, ἵνα διὰ τοῦ θανάτου **καταργήσῃ** τὸν τὸ κράτος ἔχοντα τοῦ θανάτου, τοῦτ᾽ ἔστι τὸν διάβολον, [GNS] ἐπεὶ οὖν τὰ παιδία κεκοινώνηκεν αἵματος καὶ σαρκός, καὶ αὐτὸς παραπλησίως μετέσχεν τῶν αὐτῶν, ἵνα διὰ τοῦ θανάτου **καταργήσῃ** τὸν τὸ κράτος ἔχοντα τοῦ θανάτου, τοῦτ᾽ ἔστιν τὸν διάβολον, [GNT]	the power of Satan over sin and death. Satan's power over sin and death functions and operates within man, and what a power it is—the awesome power to separate men from God for eternity. But Jesus Christ has broken that power. He has made the power of Satan ineffective and inoperative. Man no longer has to be enslaved by sin and its guilt nor by death. He is delivered from death because Jesus Christ has broken Satan's power over death.

#3246
**Renewal–
Renewing**
 	
Renewing–KJV
Renewing–NASB
Renewal–NIV
Renewing–NKJV
Not translated–NLT
 	
**POSB
REFERENCE**
(Tit.3:5)
Note 2, point 2
	ἀνακαινώσεως = anakainöseös
	Pronunciation: [an-ak-ah'een-o-seh-os]
	Parsing (part of speech): noun
	  Case—genitive
	  Gender—feminine
	  Number—singular
	  Stem or root—from **ἀνακαίνωσις, εως**
	Concordance References:
	⇒ Strong's #342 anakainösis
	⇒ NIV #364 anakainösis
	⇒ NASB #342 anakainösis
	
	Titus 3:5
	Not by works of righteousness which we have done, but according to his mercy he saved us, by the washing of regeneration, and **renewing** of the Holy Ghost; [KJV]
	He saved us, not on the basis of deeds which we have done in righteousness, but according to His mercy, by the washing of regeneration and **renewing** by the Holy Spirit, [NASB]
	He saved us, not because of righteous things we had done, but because of his mercy. He saved us through the washing of rebirth and **renewal** by the Holy Spirit, [NIV]
	Not by works of righteousness which we have done, but according to His mercy He saved us, through the washing of regeneration and **renewing** of the Holy Spirit, [NKJV]
	He saved us, not because of the good things we did, but because of his mercy. He washed away our sins and gave us a new life through the Holy Spirit. [NLT]—Not Translated
	οὐκ ἐξ ἔργων τῶν ἐν δικαιοσύνῃ ὧν ἐποιήσαμεν ἡμεῖς, ἀλλὰ κατὰ τὸν αὐτοῦ ἔλεον ἔσωσεν ἡμᾶς, διὰ λουτροῦ παλιγγενεσίας καὶ **ἀνακαινώσεως** Πνεύματος Ἁγίου, [GNS]
		Renewal, renewing, regeneration, a new start. The word "renewing" (*anakainöseös*) means to make new again; to renew again; to revive again; to make new spiritually; to begin all over again; to adjust again.
		
		Practical Application
		Salvation is the Holy Spirit adjusting a person and renewing him all over again. It is the Spirit of God taking a person, readjusting his life and reviving him spiritually. Note that the renewing is done by the Spirit of God just as regeneration is.
		⇒ W.E. Vine says that the stress is "the continual operation of the indwelling Spirit of God" (*Expository Dictionary of New Testament Words*).
		⇒ Kenneth Wuest says, "This is the work of the Holy Spirit in sanctification" (*Word Studies in the Greek New Testament*).
		
		The point is a most wonderful truth. The Holy Spirit not only regenerates a person and gives him a new birth and a new life, but He does much, much more. He renews and revives a person *day-by-day*.

ENGLISH WORD	GREEK WORD AND VERSE	THE WORD MEANS...
	οὐκ ἐξ ἔργων τῶν ἐν δικαιοσύνῃ ἃ ἐποιήσαμεν ἡμεῖς ἀλλὰ κατὰ τὸ αὐτοῦ ἔλεος ἔσωσεν ἡμᾶς διὰ λουτροῦ παλιγγενεσίας καὶ **ἀνακαινώσεως** πνεύματος ἁγίου, [GNT]	
#3247 **Renewed** **Renewed–KJV** **Renewed–NASB** Made new–NIV **Renewed–NKJV** Spiritual renewal–NLT **POSB REFERENCE** (Eph.4:23) *Deeper Study #2*	**ἀνανεοῦσθαι** = *ananeousthai* Pronunciation: [an-an-eh-oos-tha-ee] Parsing (part of speech): verb 　　Mood—infinitive 　　Tense—present 　　Voice—passive 　　Stem or root—from **ἀνανεόω** Concordance References: ⇒　Strong's #365 ananeoomai ⇒　NIV #391 ananeoomai ⇒　NASB #365 ananeoomai **Ephes. 4:23** And be **renewed** in the spirit of your mind; [KJV] And that you be **renewed** in the spirit of your mind, [NASB] To be **made new** in the attitude of your minds; [NIV] And be **renewed** in the spirit of your mind, [NKJV] Instead, there must be a **spiritual renewal** of your thoughts and attitudes. [NLT] **ἀνανεοῦσθαι** δὲ τῷ πνεύματι τοῦ νοὸς ὑμῶν, [GNS] **ἀνανεοῦσθαι** δὲ τῷ πνεύματι τοῦ νοὸς ὑμῶν [GNT]	Renewed; made new, readjusted, changed, turned around, and regenerated. It is spiritual renewal. **Practical Application** 　The mind of man has been affected by sin. It desperately needs to be renewed. The mind is far from perfect. It is *basically worldly*, that is... • selfish • self-centered • self-seeking • centered on this world • centered on the flesh • centered on this life
#3248 **Renewed** Flourished again–KJV Revived–NASB **Renewed–NIV** Flourished again–NKJV Again–NLT **POSB REFERENCE** (Philip.4:10) Note 1	**ἀνεθάλετε** = *anethalete* Pronunciation: [an-ath-al'-eh-teh] Parsing (part of speech): verb 　　Mood—indicative 　　Tense—aorist 　　Voice—active 　　Person—2nd person 　　Number—plural 　　Stem or root—from **ἀναθάλλω** Concordance References: ⇒　Strong's #330 anathallo ⇒　NIV #352 anathallo ⇒　NASB #330 anathallo **Philip. 4:10** But I rejoiced in the Lord greatly, that now at the last your care of me hath **flourished again**; wherein ye were also careful, but ye lacked opportunity. [KJV] But I rejoiced in the Lord greatly, that now at last you have **revived** your concern for me; indeed, you were concerned before, but you lacked opportunity. [NASB] I rejoice greatly in the Lord that at last you have **renewed** your concern for me. Indeed, you have been concerned, but you had no opportunity to show it. [NIV] But I rejoiced in the Lord greatly that now at last your care for me has **flourished again**; though you surely did care, but you lacked opportunity. [NKJV] How grateful I am, and how I praise the Lord that you are concerned about me **again**. I know you have always been concerned for me, but for a while you didn't have the chance to help me. [NLT] Ἐχάρην δὲ ἐν Κυρίῳ μεγάλως, ὅτι ἤδη ποτὲ **ἀνεθάλετε** τὸ ὑπὲρ ἐμοῦ φρονεῖν, ἐφ' ᾧ καὶ ἐφρονεῖτε, ἠκαιρεῖσθε δέ. [GNS] Ἐχάρην δὲ ἐν κυρίῳ μεγάλως ὅτι ἤδη ποτὲ **ἀνεθάλετε** τὸ ὑπὲρ ἐμοῦ φρονεῖν, ἐφ' ᾧ καὶ ἐφρονεῖτε, ἠκαιρεῖσθε δέ. [GNT]	To renew; to flourish again; to revive again. **Practical Application** 　It is the picture of plants and flowers sprouting, shooting up, and blossoming *again*. The key word is *again*. When the church had been founded, the believers had supported Paul and his mission work on a regular basis. But for some reason, they had dropped their mission support. That had probably been over ten to twelve years before (Strauss). Why they had stopped sending support to Paul is not known. However, the point is the glorious revival of mission support that took place in the church. They picked up the support of Paul once again, and their giving flourished and blossomed anew. The joy and rejoicing of Paul's heart can just be imagined. He says, "I rejoice greatly in the Lord."
#3249 **Renewing** Renewing–KJV Renewing–NASB	**ἀνακαινώσει** = *anakainōsei* Pronunciation: [an-ak-ah'ee-no-seh-ee] Parsing (part of speech): noun 　　Case—dative 　　Gender—feminine 　　Number—singular	Renewing, changing; to be renewed; to to be made new, readjusted, changed, turned around, regenerated.

ENGLISH WORD	GREEK WORD AND VERSE	THE WORD MEANS...
Renewing–NIV **Renewing–NKJV** Changing–NLT **POSB REFERENCE** (Rom.12:2) Note 4, point 1	Stem or root—from ἀνακαίνωσις Concordance References: ⇒ Strong's #342 anakainōsis ⇒ NIV #364 anakainōsis ⇒ NASB #342 anakainōsis **Romans 12:2** And be not conformed to this world: but be ye transformed by the **renewing** of your mind, that ye may prove what is that good, and acceptable, and perfect, will of God. [KJV] And do not be conformed to this world, but be transformed by the **renewing** of your mind, that you may prove what the will of God is, that which is good and acceptable and perfect. [NASB] Do not conform any longer to the pattern of this world, but be transformed by the **renewing** of your mind. Then you will be able to test and approve what God's will is—his good, pleasing and perfect will. [NIV] And do not be conformed to this world, but be transformed by the **renewing** of your mind, that you may prove what is that good and acceptable and perfect will of God. [NKJV] Don't copy the behavior and customs of this world, but let God transform you into a new person by **changing** the way you think. Then you will know what God wants you to do, and you will know how good and pleasing and perfect his will really is. [NLT] καὶ μὴ συσχηματίζεσθε τῷ αἰῶνι τούτῳ, ἀλλὰ μεταμορφοῦσθε τῇ **ἀνακαινώσει** τοῦ νοός ὑμῶν, εἰς τὸ δοκιμάζειν ὑμᾶς τί τὸ θέλημα τοῦ Θεοῦ, τὸ ἀγαθὸν καὶ εὐάρεστον καὶ τέλειον. [GNS] αἱ μὴ συσχηματίζεσθε τῷ αἰῶνι τούτῳ, ἀλλὰ μεταμορφοῦσθε τῇ **ἀνακαινώσει** τοῦ νοός εἰς τὸ δοκιμάζειν ὑμᾶς τί τὸ θέλημα τοῦ θεοῦ, τὸ ἀγαθὸν καὶ εὐάρεστον καὶ τέλειον. [GNT]	**Practical Application** How is a man transformed within his inner person? The Bible declares as simply as can be stated, "by the renewing of your mind." The believer's mind is to be renewed (*anakainōsei*), which means to be made new, readjusted, changed, turned around, regenerated. The mind of man has been affected by sin. It desperately needs to be renewed. The mind is far from perfect. It is basically worldly, that is... • selfish • self-centered • self-seeking • centered on this world • centered on the flesh • centered on this life Scripture is clear about the corruption of man's mind. The human mind has been tragically corrupted by man's selfishness and sin.

#3250
Repent
 	
Repent–KJV
Repent–NASB
Repent–NIV
Repent–NKJV
Turn from your sins–NLT
 	
**POSB
REFERENCE**
(Mt.3:2-6; esp. v.2)
Note 1
	Μετανοεῖτε = *Metanoeite*
	Pronunciation: [met-an-o-ee'-teh]
	Parsing (part of speech): verb
	  Mood—imperative
	  Tense—present
	  Voice—active
	  Person—2nd person
	  Number—plural
	  Stem or root—from μετανοέω
	Concordance References:
	⇒ Strong's #3340 metanoeō
	⇒ NIV #3566 metanoeō
	⇒ NASB #3340 metanoeō
	
	Matthew 3:2
	And saying, **Repent** ye: for the kingdom of heaven is at hand. [KJV]
	"**Repent**, for the kingdom of heaven is at hand." [NASB]
	And saying, "**Repent**, for the kingdom of heaven is near." [NIV]
	And saying, "**Repent**, for the kingdom of heaven is at hand!" [NKJV]
	"**Turn from your sins** and turn to God, because the Kingdom of Heaven is near." [NLT]
	καὶ λέγων, **Μετανοεῖτε**, ἤγγικε γὰρ ἡ βασιλεία τῶν οὐρανῶν. [GNS]
	[καὶ] λέγων, **Μετανοεῖτε**· ἤγγικεν γὰρ ἡ βασιλεία τῶν οὐρανῶν. [GNT]
		To repent; to turn from one's sins; to change; to turn; to change one's mind; to turn one's life around.
		
		Practical Application
		In this Scripture, repentance is a turning away from sin and turning toward God. It is a change of mind, a forsaking of sin. It is putting sin out of one's thoughts and behavior. It is resolving never to think or do a thing again. (Cp. Mt.3:2; Lk.13:2-3; Acts 2:38; Acts 3:19; Acts 8:22; Acts 26:20.) The change is turning away from lying, stealing, cheating, immorality, cursing, drunkenness, and the other so-called glaring sins of the flesh. But the change is also turning away from the silent sins of the spirit such as self-centeredness, selfishness, envy, bitterness, pride, covetousness, anger, evil thoughts, hopelessness, laziness, jealousy, lust.
		1. Repentance involves two turns. There is a negative turn away from sin and a positive turn toward God. It is a turning to God away from sin, whether sins of thought or action. (See POSB note, Repentance—Lk.3:3. Cp. 1 Thes. 1:9; Acts 14:15.)
		2. Repentance is more than sorrow. Sorrow may or may not be involved in repentance. A person may repent simply because he wills and acts to change; or a person may repent because he senses an agonizing sorrow within. But the sense or feeling of sorrow is not repentance. Repentance is both the change of mind and the actual turning of one's life away from sin and toward God. (See POSB *Deeper Study* #1—2 Cor. 7:10.)

ENGLISH WORD	GREEK WORD AND VERSE	THE WORD MEANS...

#3251
 	
Repented And Turned
 	
Converted–KJV
Turned again–NASB
Turned back–NIV
Returned–NKJV
Repented and turned–NLT
 	
POSB REFERENCE
(Lk.22:32)
Note 2, point 2
	ἐπιστρέψας = epistrepsas
	Pronunciation: [ep-ee-stref'-ahs]
	Parsing (part of speech): verb
	  Mood—participle
	  Tense—aorist
	  Voice—active
	  Case—nominative
	  Gender—masculine
	  Person—2nd person
	  Number—singular
	  Stem or root—from ἐπιστρέφω
	Concordance References:
	  ⇒ Strong's #1994 epistrephō
	  ⇒ NIV #2188 epistrephō
	  ⇒ NASB #1994 epistrephō
	
	Luke 22:32
	But I have prayed for thee, that thy faith fail not: and when thou art **converted**, strengthen thy brethren." [KJV]
	But I have prayed for you, that your faith may not fail; and you, when once you have **turned again**, strengthen your brothers." [NASB]
	But I have prayed for you, Simon, that your faith may not fail. And when you have **turned back**, strengthen your brothers." [NIV]
	But I have prayed for you, that your faith should not fail; and when you have **returned** to *Me,* strengthen your brethren." [NKJV]
	But I have pleaded in prayer for you, Simon, that your faith should not fail. So when you have **repented and turned** to me again, strengthen and build up your brothers." [NLT]
	ἐγὼ δὲ ἐδεήθην περὶ σοῦ, ἵνα μὴ ἐκλείπῃ ἡ πίστις σου· καὶ σύ ποτε **ἐπιστρέψας**, στήριξον τοὺς ἀδελφούς σου. [GNS]
	ἐγὼ δὲ ἐδεήθην περὶ σοῦ ἵνα μὴ ἐκλίπῃ ἡ πίστις σου· καὶ σύ ποτε **ἐπιστρέψας** στήρισον τοὺς ἀδελφούς σου. [GNT]
		To turn around; to convert; to turn back to; to repent and turn; to turn again.
		
		Practical Application
		It is a turning away from sin and turning toward God. It is a change of mind, a forsaking of sin. It is putting sin out of one's thoughts and behavior. It is resolving never to think or do a thing again. (See POSB note—Acts 17:29-30 and POSB *Deeper Study* #1, Repentance—Acts 17:29-30.)

#3252
 	
Represents God Exactly
 	
Express image–KJV
Exact representation–NASB
Exact representation–NIV
Express image–NKJV
Represents God exactly–NLT
 	
POSB REFERENCE
(Heb.1:3)
Note 5
	χαρακτήρ = charaktër
	Pronunciation: [khar-ak-tare']
	Parsing (part of speech): noun
	  Case—nominative
	  Gender—masculine
	  Number—singular
	  Stem or root—from χαρακτήρ, ῆρος
	Concordance References:
	  ⇒ Strong's #5481 charaktër
	  ⇒ NIV #5917 charaktër
	  ⇒ NASB #5481 charaktër
	
	Hebrews 1:3
	Who being the brightness of his glory, and the **express image** of his person, and upholding all things by the word of his power, when he had by himself purged our sins, sat down on the right hand of the Majesty on high; [KJV]
	And He is the radiance of His glory and the **exact representation** of His nature, and upholds all things by the word of His power. When He had made purification of sins, He sat down at the right hand of the Majesty on high; [NASB]
	The Son is the radiance of God's glory and the **exact representation** of his being, sustaining all things by his powerful word. After he had provided purification for sins, he sat down at the right hand of the Majesty in heaven. [NIV]
	Who being the brightness of *His* glory and the **express image** of His person, and upholding all things by the word of His power, when He had by Himself purged our sins, sat down at the right hand of the Majesty
		Exact representation, express image; an exact likeness represents God exactly. The phrase "represents God exactly" (*charaktër*) means the very stamp, mark, and impression—the very reproduction of God.
		
		Practical Application
		Jesus Christ is "the perfect imprint and very image of [God's] nature." Jesus Christ represents God exactly. When Jesus Christ came to earth, men were able to see God, to see exactly what God is like:
		⇒ loving, compassionate, caring
		⇒ healing, restoring, saving
		⇒ correcting, disciplining, controlling
		⇒ holy, righteous, just
		
		A person could look at Jesus Christ and see exactly what God is like.

ENGLISH WORD	GREEK WORD AND VERSE	THE WORD MEANS...
	on high, [NKJV] The Son reflects God's own glory, and everything about him **represents God exactly**. He sustains the universe by the mighty power of his command. After he died to cleanse us from the stain of sin, he sat down in the place of honor at the right hand of the majestic God of heaven. [NLT] ὃς ων ἀπαύγασμα τῆς δόξης, καὶ **χαρακτὴρ** τῆς ὑποστάσεως αὐτοῦ, φέρων τε τὰ πάντα τῷ ῥήματι τῆς δυνάμεως αὐτοῦ, δι' εαυτοῦ καθαρισμὸν ποιησάμενος τῶν ἁμαρτιῶν ημῶν, ἐκάθισεν ἐν δεξιᾷ τῆς μεγαλωσύνης ἐν ὑψηλοῖς, [GNS] ὃς ων ἀπαύγασμα τῆς δόξης καὶ **χαρακτὴρ** τῆς ὑποστάσεως αὐτοῦ, φέρων τε τὰ πάντα τῷ ῥήματι τῆς δυνάμεως αὐτοῦ, καθαρισμὸν τῶν ἁμαρτιῶν ποιησάμενος ἐκάθισεν ἐν δεξιᾷ τῆς μεγαλωσύνης ἐν ὑψηλοῖς, [GNT]	

#3253
Reprobate Mind
 	
Reprobate mind–KJV
Depraved mind–NASB
Depraved mind–NIV
Debased mind–NKJV
Evil minds–NLT
 	
POSB REFERENCE
(Rom.1:28-31; esp. v.28)
Note 4, point 1
	ἀδόκιμον νοῦν = adokimon noun
	Pronunciation: [ad-ok'-ee-mon noon]
	Parsing *adokimon* (part of speech): adjective
	  Case—accusative
	  Gender—masculine
	  Number—singular
	  Stem or root—from *ἀδόκιμος*, ον
	Parsing *noun* (part of speech): noun
	  Case—accusative
	  Gender—masculine
	  Number—singular
	  Stem or root—from *νοῦς*, νοός, νοΐ, νοῦν
	Concordance References:
	⇒ Strong's #96 adokimos + 3563 nous
	⇒ NIV #99 adokimos [depraved] + 3808 nous [mind]
	⇒ NASB #96 adokimos + 3563 nous
	
	Romans 1:28
	And even as they did not like to retain God in their knowledge, God gave them over to a **reprobate mind**, to do those things which are not convenient; [KJV]
	
	And just as they did not see fit to acknowledge God any longer, God gave them over to a **depraved mind**, to do those things which are not proper, [NASB]
	
	Furthermore, since they did not think it worthwhile to retain the knowledge of God, he gave them over to a **depraved mind**, to do what ought not to be done. [NIV]
	
	And even as they did not like to retain God in their knowledge, God gave them over to a **debased mind**, to do those things which are not fitting; [NKJV]
	
	When they refused to acknowledge God, he abandoned them to their **evil minds** and let them do things that should never be done. [NLT]
	
	Καὶ καθὼς οὐκ ἐδοκίμασαν τὸν Θεὸν ἔχειν ἐν ἐπιγνώσει, παρέδωκεν αὐτοὺς ὁ Θεὸς εἰς **ἀδόκιμον νοῦν**, ποιεῖν τὰ μὴ καθήκοντα, [GNS]
	
	καὶ καθὼς οὐκ ἐδοκίμασαν τὸν θεὸν ἔχειν ἐν ἐπιγνώσει, παρέδωκεν αὐτοὺς ὁ θεὸς εἰς **ἀδόκιμον νοῦν**, ποιεῖν τὰ μὴ καθήκοντα, [GNT]
		Failing to meet the test; disqualified; worthless; corrupted (mind); mind, thought, reason; attitude, intention, purpose; understanding, discernment.
		
		Practical Application
		God shows wrath by giving men up to reprobate, depraved minds. The term "reprobate mind" (*adokimon noun*) means a mind that is rejected, disapproved, degraded, depraved; a mind that cannot stand the test of judgment.
		
		The reason God gives men up to reprobate minds is because men reject God. They know God, but they do not "like to retain God in their knowledge." They...
		• do not like to approve God.
		• do not like to recognize God.
		• do not like to acknowledge God.
		
		They simply do not want God to have anything to do with their lives; therefore, they push Him out of their minds. They ignore and refuse to accept God's presence.

#3254
Reprobates
 	
Reprobates–KJV
Fail the test–NASB
Fail the test–NIV
Disqualified–NKJV
Failed the test–NLT
 	
POSB REFERENCE
(2 Cor.13:1-6; esp. v.5)
Note 1
	ἀδόκιμοί ἐστε = adokimoi este
	Pronunciation: [ad-ok'-ee-moy hes-teh]
	Parsing *adokimoi* (part of speech): adjective
	  Case—nominative
	  Gender—masculine
	  Number—plural
	  Stem or root—from *ἀδόκιμος*, ον
	Concordance References:
	⇒ Strong's #96 adokimos
	⇒ NIV #99+1639 adokimos eimi [fail the test]
	⇒ NASB #96b adokimos
	
	2 Cor. 13:5
	Examine yourselves, whether ye be in the faith; prove
		To fail the test; to be a reprobate; to be tested and found worthless; to be tested and disqualified and rejected; to be found unfit and disapproved; to be doomed and condemned to perdition.
		
		Practical Application
		The believers had to examine themselves to make sure they were in the faith.
		⇒ They needed to make sure they were genuine. Living in sin makes a person's faith suspect. Some were living in sin: "Examine yourselves *as to* whether you

ENGLISH WORD	GREEK WORD AND VERSE	THE WORD MEANS...
	your own selves. Know ye not your own selves, how that Jesus Christ is in you, except ye be **reprobates**? [KJV] Test yourselves to see if you are in the faith; examine yourselves! Or do you not recognize this about yourselves, that Jesus Christ is in you— unless indeed you **fail the test**? [NASB] Examine yourselves to see whether you are in the faith; test yourselves. Do you not realize that Christ Jesus is in you—unless, of course, you **fail the test**? [NIV] Examine yourselves *as to* whether you are in the faith. Test yourselves. Do you not know yourselves, that Jesus Christ is in you?—unless indeed you are **disqualified**. [NKJV] Examine yourselves to see if your faith is really genuine. Test yourselves. If you cannot tell that Jesus Christ is among you, it means you have **failed the test**. [NLT] ἑαυτοὺς πειράζετε εἰ ἐστὲ ἐν τῇ πίστει, ἑαυτοὺς δοκιμάζετε. ἠ οὐκ ἐπιγινώσκετε ἑαυτοὺς ὅτι Ἰησοῦς Χριστὸς ἐν ὑμῖν; εἰ μή τι **ἀδόκιμοί ἐστε**. [GNS] Ἑαυτοὺς πειράζετε εἰ ἐστὲ ἐν τῇ πίστει, ἑαυτοὺς δοκιμάζετε· ἠ οὐκ ἐπιγινώσκετε ἑαυτοὺς ὅτι Ἰησοῦς Χριστὸς ἐν ὑμῖν; εἰ μήτι **ἀδόκιμοί ἐστε**. [GNT]	are in the faith. Test yourselves." ⇒ They needed to make sure that *Jesus Christ was in them* and that they were *not* "reprobates" (*adokimoi este*). (see POSB note, Castaway—1 Cor. 9:27—for more discussion.) ⇒ They needed to know that Paul was not disqualified. The only way the Corinthians could know these things was to examine themselves.
#3255 **Reprove** **Reprove–KJV** Expose–NASB Expose–NIV Expose–NKJV Expose–NLT **POSB REFERENCE** (Eph.5:11-12; esp. v.11) Note 4, point 2	ἐλέγχετε = *elegchete* Pronunciation: [el-eng'-ckeh-teh] Parsing (part of speech): verb 　　Mood—imperative 　　Tense—present 　　Voice—active 　　Person—2nd person 　　Number—plural 　　Stem or root—from ἐλέγχω Concordance References: ⇒ Strong's #1651 elegchō ⇒ NIV #1794 elegchō ⇒ NASB #1651 elegchō **Ephes. 5:11** And have no fellowship with the unfruitful works of darkness, but rather **reprove** them. [KJV] And do not participate in the unfruitful deeds of darkness, but instead even **expose** them; [NASB] Have nothing to do with the fruitless deeds of darkness, but rather **expose** them. [NIV] And have no fellowship with the unfruitful works of darkness, but rather **expose** *them*. [NKJV] Take no part in the worthless deeds of evil and darkness; instead, rebuke and **expose** them. [NLT] καὶ μὴ συγκοινωνεῖτε τοῖς ἔργοις τοῖς ἀκάρποις τοῦ σκότους, μᾶλλον δὲ καὶ **ἐλέγχετε**· [GNS] καὶ μὴ συγκοινωνεῖτε τοῖς ἔργοις τοῖς ἀκάρποις τοῦ σκότους, μᾶλλον δὲ καὶ **ἐλέγχετε**. [GNT]	To expose; to reprove; to rebuke; to condemn; to convict; to correct; to prove guilty. **Practical Application** The believer's task on earth is striking: he is not to fellowship with the works of darkness; he is to live in so much light that his life reproves (*elegchete*, that is, exposes, rebukes, and convicts) people of their sins or dark works. Sin is never to be taken lightly. The very fact that we are charged to reprove it is clear evidence. Our task is to reflect so much light that all the works of darkness around us are exposed and expelled. Remember when light appears, the darkness is always extinguished. But if the light leaves or is turned off, the darkness reappears.
#3256 **Reprove** **Reprove–KJV** **Reprove–NASB** Correct–NIV Rebuke–NKJV Correct–NLT **POSB REFERENCE** (2 Tim. 4:2) Note 2, point 3	ἔλεγξον = *elegxon* Pronunciation: [el-eng'-khon] Parsing (part of speech): verb 　　Mood—imperative 　　Tense—aorist 　　Voice—active 　　Person—2nd person 　　Number—singular 　　Stem or root—from ἐλέγχω Concordance References: ⇒ Strong's #1651 elegchō ⇒ NIV #1794 elegchō ⇒ NASB #1651 elegchō **2 Tim. 4:2** Preach the word; be instant in season, out of season; **reprove**, rebuke, exhort with all longsuffering and doctrine. [KJV]	To correct; to reprove; to rebuke; to convince; to show fault; to prove guilty. **Practical Application** The word means to stir a person to prove himself; to put a person under conviction; to lead a person to see his sin and to feel guilt over it. It means to put a person under conviction of sin and to lead him to confession and repentance.

ENGLISH WORD	GREEK WORD AND VERSE	THE WORD MEANS...
	Preach the word; be ready in season and out of season; **reprove**, rebuke, exhort, with great patience and instruction. [NASB] Preach the Word; be prepared in season and out of season; **correct**, rebuke and encourage—with great patience and careful instruction. [NIV] Preach the word! Be ready in season *and* out of season. Convince, **rebuke**, exhort, with all longsuffering and teaching. [NKJV] Preach the word of God. Be persistent, whether the time is favorable or not. Patiently **correct**, rebuke, and encourage your people with good teaching. [NLT] κήρυξον τὸν λόγον, ἐπίστηθι εὐκαίρως, ἀκαίρως, **ἔλεγξον**, ἐπιτίμησον, παρακάλεσον, ἐν πάσῃ μακροθυμίᾳ καὶ διδαχῇ. [GNS] κήρυξον τὸν λόγον, ἐπίστηθι εὐκαίρως ἀκαίρως, **ἔλεγξον**, ἐπιτίμησον, παρακάλεσον, ἐν πάσῃ μακροθυμίᾳ καὶ διδαχῇ. [GNT]	

#3257
Reprove
 	
Reprove–KJV
Convict–NASB
Convict...of guilt–NIV
Convict–NKJV
Convince–NLT
 	
POSB
REFERENCE
(Jn.16:8-11; esp. v.8)
Note 2
	ἐλέγξει = *elegxei*
	Pronunciation: [el-eng'-cheh-ee]
	Parsing (part of speech): verb
	    Mood—indicative
	    Tense—future
	    Voice—active
	    Person—3rd person
	    Number—singular
	    Stem or root—from ἐλέγχω
	Concordance References:
	 ⇒ Strong's #1651 elegcho
	 ⇒ NIV #1794 elegcho
	 ⇒ NASB #1651 elegcho
	
	John 16:8
	And when he is come, he will **reprove** the world of sin, and of righteousness, and of judgment: [KJV]
	
	"And He, when He comes, will **convict** the world concerning sin, and righteousness, and judgment; [NASB]
	
	When he comes, he will **convict** the world **of guilt** in regard to sin and righteousness and judgment: [NIV]
	
	And when He has come, He will **convict** the world of sin, and of righteousness, and of judgment: [NKJV]
	
	And when he comes, he will **convince** the world of its sin, and of God's righteousness, and of the coming judgment. [NLT]
	
	καὶ ἐλθὼν ἐκεῖνος **ἐλέγξει** τὸν κόσμον περὶ ἁμαρτίας καὶ περὶ δικαιοσύνης καὶ περὶ κρίσεως. [GNS]
	
	καὶ ἐλθὼν ἐκεῖνος **ἐλέγξει** τὸν κόσμον περὶ ἁμαρτίας καὶ περὶ δικαιοσύνης καὶ περὶ κρίσεως· [GNT]
		To convict of guilt; to reprove; to correct; to convince; to condemn; to prove guilty; to show a person his error.
		
		Practical Application
		It means both to convict and to convince a person of his fault.
		 ⇒ Convict means to prick a person's heart until he senses and knows he is guilty. He has done wrong or failed to do right.
		 ⇒ Convince means to hammer and drive at a person's heart until he knows the fact is true.

#3258
Reputation
 	
Reputation–KJV
Emptied–NASB
Made...nothing–NIV
Reputation–NKJV
Made...nothing–NLT
 	
POSB
REFERENCE
(Philip.2:7)
Note 3, point 1
	ἐκένωσεν = *ekenösen*
	Pronunciation: [eh-ken-o'-sehn]
	Parsing (part of speech): verb
	    Mood—indicative
	    Tense—aorist
	    Voice—active
	    Person—3rd person
	    Number—singular
	    Stem or root—from κενόω
	Concordance References:
	 ⇒ Strong's #2758 kenoö
	 ⇒ NIV #3033 kenoö
	 ⇒ NASB #2758 kenoö
	
	Philip. 2:7
	But made himself of no **reputation**, and took upon him the form of a servant, and was made in the likeness of men: [KJV]
	
	But **emptied** Himself, taking the form of a bond-servant, and being made in the likeness of men. [NASB]
	
	But **made** himself **nothing**, taking the very nature of a servant, being made in human likeness. [NIV]
		Made [himself] nothing; to have no reputation; to empty oneself; to be completely empty.
		
		Practical Application
		Jesus Christ made Himself of no *reputation*; that is, He *emptied Himself*. It is the picture of pouring water out of a glass until it is empty or of dumping something until it is all removed (William Barclay. *The Letters to the Philippians, Colossians, and Thessalonians*, p.44). The very picture of being completely empty stirs a feeling of just how far Christ went in humbling Himself for us. What was it that was poured or emptied out of Jesus Christ when He left heaven and came to earth? (This is what theologians call the *kenosis theory*.) Note that this passage does not say. It only says that Christ *emptied Himself*. Other Scriptures, however, give some indication. (See POSB note, pt.4—Mark 13:32 for more discussion.)

ENGLISH WORD	GREEK WORD AND VERSE	THE WORD MEANS...
	But made Himself of no **reputation**, taking the form of a bondservant, *and* coming in the likeness of men. [NKJV] He **made** himself **nothing**; he took the humble position of a slave and appeared in human form. [NLT] ἀλλ ἑαυτὸν **ἐκένωσε**, μορφὴν δούλου λαβών, ἐν ὁμοιώματι ἀνθρώπων γενόμενος· καὶ σχήματι εὑρεθεὶς ὡς ἄνθρωπος, [GNS] ἀλλὰ ἑαυτὸν **ἐκένωσεν** μορφὴν δούλου λαβών, ἐν ὁμοιώματι ἀνθρώπων γενόμενος· καὶ σχήματι εὑρεθεὶς ὡς ἄνθρωπος [GNT]	1. Christ did not lay aside His deity when He came to earth. He could not cease to be who He was: God. No person can ever cease to be who he is. A person may take on different traits and behave differently; a person may change his behavior and looks, but he is the same person in being, nature, and essence. Jesus Christ is God; therefore, He is always God—He always possesses the nature of God (See POSB notes—John 1:1-2 for more discussion.) 2. Christ laid aside some of His rights as God: ⇒ He laid aside His right *to experience only the glory* and majesty, honor and worship of heaven. In coming to earth as a man, He was to experience anything but glory and majesty, honor and worship. Men would treat Him far differently than they would a heavenly being. ⇒ He laid aside His right *to appear only in heaven* and to appear only as the Sovereign God of heaven. In coming to earth as a man, He was, of course, to appear as a man on earth.

#3259
Request
 	
Beseech–KJV
Request–NASB
Ask–NIV
Urge–NKJV
Not translated–NLT
 	
POSB REFERENCE
(1 Thes.4:1-2; esp. v.1)
Note 1, point 1
	ἐρωτῶμεν = *erōtōmen*
	Pronunciation: [er-o-to'-mehn]
	Parsing (part of speech): verb
	  Mood—indicative
	  Tense—present
	  Voice—active
	  Person—1st person
	  Number—plural
	  Stem or root—from ἐρωτάω
	Concordance References:
	⇒ Strong's #2065 erōtaō
	⇒ NIV #2263 erōtaō
	⇒ NASB #2065 erōtaō
	
	1 Thes. 4:1
	Furthermore then we **beseech** you, brethren, and exhort you by the Lord Jesus, that as ye have received of us how ye ought to walk and to please God, so ye would abound more and more. [KJV]
	
	Finally then, brethren, we **request** and exhort you in the Lord Jesus, that, as you received from us instruction as to how you ought to walk and please God (just as you actually do walk), that you may excel still more. [NASB]
	
	Finally, brothers, we instructed you how to live in order to please God, as in fact you are living. Now we **ask** you and urge you in the Lord Jesus to do this more and more. [NIV]
	
	Finally then, brethren, we **urge** and exhort in the Lord Jesus that you should abound more and more, just as you received from us how you ought to walk and to please God; [NKJV]
	
	Finally, dear brothers and sisters, we urge you in the name of the Lord Jesus to live in a way that pleases God, as we have taught you. You are doing this already, and we encourage you to do so more and more. [NLT]—NOT TRANSLATED
	
	Τὸ λοιπὸν οὖν, ἀδελφοί, **ἐρωτῶμεν** ὑμᾶς καὶ παρακαλοῦμεν ἐν Κυρίῳ Ἰησοῦ, καθὼς παρελάβετε παρ' ἡμῶν τὸ πῶς δεῖ ὑμᾶς περιπατεῖν καὶ ἀρέσκειν Θεῷ, ἵνα περισσεύητε μᾶλλον. [GNS]
	
	Λοιπὸν οὖν, ἀδελφοί, **ἐρωτῶμεν** ὑμᾶς καὶ παρακαλοῦμεν ἐν κυρίῳ Ἰησοῦ, ἵνα καθὼς παρελάβετε παρ' ἡμῶν τὸ πῶς δεῖ ὑμᾶς περιπατεῖν καὶ ἀρέσκειν θεῷ, καθὼς καὶ περιπατεῖτε, ἵνα περισσεύητε μᾶλλον. [GNT]
		To ask; to beseech; to invite; to request; to beg; to urge.
		
		Practical Application
		This word always has a sense of urgency about it. Paul was tenderly requesting his dear brothers to continue to please God in their daily walk, but it was an urgent request. Their walking to please God was an absolute necessity, a necessity that carried with it great blessings for obedience and terrible judgment for disobedience (the displeasure of God).

ENGLISH WORD	GREEK WORD AND VERSE	THE WORD MEANS...

#3260
Requesting
 	
Besought–KJV
Requesting–NASB
Begged–NIV
Implored–NKJV
Begged–NLT
 	
POSB
REFERENCE
(Jn.4:46-47; esp. v.47)
Note 1, point 4
	ἡρώτα = ērōta
	Pronunciation: [ay-ro-tah']
	Parsing (part of speech): verb
	    Mood—indicative
	    Tense—imperfect
	    Voice—active
	    Person—3rd person
	    Number—singular
	    Stem or root—from ἐρωτάω
	Concordance References:
	⇒ Strong's #2065 erōtaō
	⇒ NIV #2263 erōtaō
	⇒ NASB #2065 erōtaō
	
	John 4:47
	When he heard that Jesus was come out of Judaea into Galilee, he went unto him, and **besought** him that he would come down, and heal his son: for he was at the point of death. [KJV]
	When he heard that Jesus had come out of Judea into Galilee, he went to Him, and was **requesting** Him to come down and heal his son; for he was at the point of death. [NASB]
	When this man heard that Jesus had arrived in Galilee from Judea, he went to him and **begged** him to come and heal his son, who was close to death. [NIV]
	When he heard that Jesus had come out of Judea into Galilee, he went to Him and **implored** Him to come down and heal his son, for he was at the point of death. [NKJV]
	When he heard that Jesus had come from Judea and was traveling in Galilee, he went over to Cana. He found Jesus and **begged** him to come to Capernaum with him to heal his son, who was about to die. [NLT]
	οὗτος ἀκούσας ὅτι Ἰησοῦς ἥκει ἐκ τῆς Ἰουδαίας εἰς τὴν Γαλιλαίαν, ἀπῆλθε πρὸς αὐτὸν, καὶ **ἡρώτα** αὐτὸν ἵνα καταβῇ καὶ ἰάσηται αὐτοῦ τὸν υἱόν· ἤμελλε γὰρ ἀποθνῄσκειν. [GNS]
	οὗτος ἀκούσας ὅτι Ἰησοῦς ἥκει ἐκ τῆς Ἰουδαίας εἰς τὴν Γαλιλαίαν ἀπῆλθεν πρὸς αὐτὸν καὶ **ἡρώτα** ἵνα καταβῇ καὶ ἰάσηται αὐτοῦ τὸν υἱόν, ἤμελλεν γὰρ ἀποθνῄσκειν. [GNT]
		To ask; to request; to implore; to plead desperately; to urge; to beseech; to appeal; to supplicate; to pray for immediate help.
		
		Practical Application
		Note an important lesson from this Scripture: The man did not let his high position keep him from Jesus. He did not wrap himself in pride, nor did he allow what others might say keep him from Jesus. He swallowed his pride and confessed his need in the face of all who ridiculed, and he went to Jesus.

#3261
Requests
 	
Requests–KJV
Requests–NASB
Requests–NIV
Requests–NKJV
Tell God–NLT
 	
POSB
REFERENCE
(Philip.4:6-7; esp. v.6)
Note 1, point 2
	αἰτήματα = aitēmata
	Pronunciation: [ah'ee-tay-mah-tah]
	Parsing (part of speech): noun
	    Case—nominative
	    Gender—neuter
	    Number—plural
	    Stem or root— from αἴτημα, τος
	Concordance References:
	⇒ Strong's #155 aitēma
	⇒ NIV #161 aitēma
	⇒ NASB #155 aitēma
	
	Philip. 4:6
	Be careful for nothing; but in every thing by prayer and supplication with thanksgiving let your **requests** be made known unto God. [KJV]
	Be anxious for nothing, but in everything by prayer and supplication with thanksgiving let your **requests** be made known to God. [NASB]
	Do not be anxious about anything, but in everything, by prayer and petition, with thanksgiving, present your **requests** to God. [NIV]
	Be anxious for nothing, but in everything by prayer and supplication, with thanksgiving, let your **requests** be made known to God; [NKJV]
	Don't worry about anything; instead, pray about everything. **Tell God** what you need, and thank him for all he has done. [NLT]
	μηδὲν μεριμνᾶτε, ἀλλ' ἐν παντὶ τῇ προσευχῇ καὶ τῇ
		To request; to tell God; to solicit; to ask; to demand. It means specific and definite requests.
		
		Practical Application
		Our praying is not to be general, but specific. We are to lay before God exactly what is needed, and we are not to fear that we are being too detailed with God or bothering God. Neither are we to hold back from asking because we fear He will not answer something so specific. Too often believers fear not receiving the answer to a specific request, fear that it will show how weak they are spiritually if the request is not granted.
		Note what Scripture says: "In everything" pray like this—use all four ways of praying and use them in praying for everything.

ENGLISH WORD	GREEK WORD AND VERSE	THE WORD MEANS...
	δεήσει μετὰ εὐχαριστίας τὰ **αἰτήματα** ὑμῶν γνωριζέσθω πρὸς τὸν Θεόν, [GNS] μηδὲν μεριμνᾶτε, ἀλλ' ἐν παντὶ τῇ προσευχῇ καὶ τῇ δεήσει μετὰ εὐχαριστίας τὰ **αἰτήματα** ὑμῶν γνωριζέσθω πρὸς τὸν θεόν. [GNT]	
#3262 **Requests** Supplications–KJV Entreaties–NASB **Requests–NIV** Supplications–NKJV **Requests–NLT** **POSB REFERENCE** (1 Tim.2:1) Note 1, point 1	**δεήσεις** = *deēseis* Pronunciation: [deh'-ay-seh-is] Parsing (part of speech): noun 　　Case—accusative 　　Gender—feminine 　　Number—plural 　　Stem or root—from **δέησις**, εως Concordance References: ⇒　Strong's #1162 deēsis ⇒　NIV #1255 deēsis ⇒　NASB #1162 deēsis **1 Tim. 2:1** 　　I exhort therefore, that, first of all, **supplications**, prayers, intercessions, and giving of thanks, be made for all men; [KJV] 　　First of all, then, I urge that **entreaties** and prayers, petitions and thanksgivings, be made on behalf of all men, [NASB] 　　I urge, then, first of all, that **requests**, prayers, intercession and thanksgiving be made for everyone [NIV] 　　Therefore I exhort first of all that **supplications**, prayers, intercessions, *and* giving of thanks be made for all men, [NKJV] 　　I urge you, first of all, to pray for all people. As you make your **requests**, plead for God's mercy upon them, and give thanks. [NLT] 　　Παρακαλῶ οὖν πρῶτον πάντων ποιεῖσθαι **δεήσεις**, προσευχάς, ἐντεύξεις, εὐχαριστίας, ὑπὲρ πάντων ἀνθρώπων· [GNS] 　　Παρακαλῶ οὖν πρῶτον πάντων ποιεῖσθαι **δεήσεις** προσευχάς ἐντεύξεις εὐχαριστίας ὑπὲρ πάντων ἀνθρώπων, [GNT]	Requests, supplications, entreaties, petitions, specific prayers. **Practical Application** 　　This refers to the prayers that focus upon special needs—deep and intense needs. When we see special needs in the life of a person, we are to supplicate for them. That is, we are to be carrying the needs before God with a great sense of urgency and plead and beg for the person or persons. The idea is that of intense and deep brokenness before God in behalf of another person—that God would help and save the person.
#3263 **Rescue** Deliver–KJV Deliver–NASB **Rescue–NIV** Deliver–NKJV **Rescue–NLT** **POSB REFERENCE** (Gal.1:4-5; esp. v.4) Note 4, point 2	**ἐξέληται** = *exelētai* Pronunciation: [ex-eh-lay'-tah-ee] Parsing (part of speech): verb 　　Mood—subjunctive 　　Tense—aorist 　　Voice—middle 　　Person—3rd person 　　Number—singular 　　Stem or root—from **ἐξαιρέω** Concordance References: ⇒　Strong's #1807 exaireō ⇒　NIV #1975 exaireō ⇒　NASB #1807 exaireō **Galatians 1:4** 　　Who gave himself for our sins, that he might **deliver** us from this present evil world, according to the will of God and our Father: [KJV] 　　Who gave Himself for our sins, that He might **deliver** us out of this present evil age, according to the will of our God and Father, [NASB] 　　Who gave himself for our sins to **rescue** us from the present evil age, according to the will of our God and Father, [NIV] 　　Who gave Himself for our sins, that He might **deliver** us from this present evil age, according to the will of our God and Father, [NKJV] 　　He died for our sins, just as God our Father planned, in order to **rescue** us from this evil world in which we live. [NLT] 　　τοῦ δόντος ἑαυτὸν ὑπὲρ τῶν ἁμαρτιῶν ἡμῶν ὅπως **ἐξέληται** ἡμᾶς ἐκ τοῦ ἐνεστῶτος αἰῶνος πονηροῦ, κατὰ τὸ θέλημα τοῦ Θεοῦ καὶ πατρὸς ἡμῶν· [GNS] 　　τοῦ δόντος ἑαυτὸν ὑπὲρ τῶν ἁμαρτιῶν ἡμῶν, ὅπως **ἐξέληται** ἡμᾶς ἐκ τοῦ αἰῶνος τοῦ ἐνεστῶτος πονηροῦ κατὰ τὸ θέλημα τοῦ θεοῦ καὶ πατρὸς ἡμῶν, [GNT]	To deliver; to rescue and to pluck out; to save; to set free. **Practical Application** 　　But note the point: this was the very purpose for Jesus' death. He died to deliver us from this present evil world. The word "rescue" (*exelētai*) means to deliver and to pluck out. Jesus Christ died to rescue and to pluck us out of this present evil world. How? As stated above, "He gave Himself for our sins." He delivers or rescues us from both *the power and the fate of the world*. The believer experiences both abundant and eternal life now and forever.

ENGLISH WORD	GREEK WORD AND VERSE	THE WORD MEANS...
#3264 **Rescued** Delivered–KJV Delivered–NASB **Rescued–NIV** Delivered–NKJV **Rescued–NLT** **POSB REFERENCE** (Col.1:13) Note 2, point 2	ἐρρύσατο = *errusato* Pronunciation: [eh-rhoo'-sah-to] Parsing (part of speech): verb 　Mood—indicative 　Tense—aorist 　Voice—middle deponent 　Person—3rd person 　Number—singular 　Stem or root—from ῥύομαι Concordance References: 　⇒　Strong's #4506 hruomai 　⇒　NIV #4861 hruomai 　⇒　NASB #4506 hruomai **Col. 1:13** Who hath **delivered** us from the power of darkness, and hath translated us into the kingdom of his dear Son: [KJV] For He **delivered** us from the domain of darkness, and transferred us to the kingdom of His beloved Son, [NASB] For he has **rescued** us from the dominion of darkness and brought us into the kingdom of the Son he loves, [NIV] He has **delivered** us from the power of darkness and conveyed *us* into the kingdom of the Son of His love, [NKJV] For he has **rescued** us from the one who rules in the kingdom of darkness, and he has brought us into the Kingdom of his dear Son. [NLT] ὃς ἐρρύσατο ἡμᾶς ἐκ τῆς ἐξουσίας τοῦ σκότους, καὶ μετέστησεν εἰς τὴν βασιλείαν τοῦ υἱοῦ τῆς ἀγάπης αὐτοῦ, [GNS] ὃς ἐρρύσατο ἡμᾶς ἐκ τῆς ἐξουσίας τοῦ σκότους καὶ μετέστησεν εἰς τὴν βασιλείαν τοῦ υἱοῦ τῆς ἀγάπης αὐτοῦ, [GNT]	To be rescued; to be delivered; to be saved. The word "rescued" (*errusato*) means to rescue or snatch from darkness. **Practical Application** 　Note that it is God Himself who has rescued us from darkness. A person lost in pitch black darkness is hopeless unless someone rescues him. And note: he cannot be rescued by those who are lost in the same darkness as he is. No person who is in the world of darkness has light, or else he would use the light to get out of the darkness. This is the very reason God had to rescue man. He alone is light; therefore, He alone could reach down and snatch man from the darkness. How did He do this? The answer is given in the next paragraph. 　God brought us into the kingdom of His dear Son, into the kingdom of the Lord Jesus Christ. We must always remember that the kingdom of Christ already exists. 　⇒　His rule and reign already exists in the spiritual world or spiritual dimension of being, that is, in heaven. 　⇒　His rule and reign already exists in the hearts and lives of believers in this physical world or physical dimension of being. 　The message of the glorious gospel is that God has brought the believer from the power of darkness into the kingdom of His dear Son. (See POSB *Deeper Study* #3, Kingdom of Heaven—Matthew 19:23-24 for more discussion.)
#3265 **Resist** **Resist–KJV** **Resist–NASB** **Resist–NIV** **Resist–NKJV** Take a firm stand– 　NLT **POSB REFERENCE** (1 Pt.5:9) Note 3, point 1 **See also POSB REF:** (Jas.4:7) Note 1	ἀντίστητε = *antistēte* Pronunciation: [an-tis'-tay-teh] Parsing (part of speech): verb 　Mood—imperative 　Tense—aorist 　Voice—active 　Person—2nd person 　Number—plural 　Stem or root—from ἀνθίστημι Concordance References: 　⇒　Strong's #436 anthistēmi 　⇒　NIV #468 anthistēmi 　⇒　NASB #436 anthistēmi **1 Peter 5:9** Whom **resist** stedfast in the faith, knowing that the same afflictions are accomplished in your brethren that are in the world. [KJV] But **resist** him, firm in your faith, knowing that the same experiences of suffering are being accomplished by your brethren who are in the world. [NASB] **Resist** him, standing firm in the faith, because you know that your brothers throughout the world are undergoing the same kind of sufferings. [NIV] **Resist** him, steadfast in the faith, knowing that the same sufferings are experienced by your brotherhood in the world. [NKJV] **Take a firm stand** against him, and be strong in your faith. Remember that your Christian brothers and sisters all over the world are going through the same kind of suffering you are. [NLT] ᾧ ἀντίστητε στερεοὶ τῇ πίστει, εἰδότες τὰ αὐτὰ τῶν παθημάτων τῇ ἐν τῷ κόσμῳ ὑμῶν ἀδελφότητι ἐπιτελεῖσθαι. [GNS] ᾧ ἀντίστητε στερεοὶ τῇ πίστει εἰδότες τὰ αὐτὰ τῶν	To resist; to take a firm stand; to hold one's ground; to oppose. It means to withstand the devil; to stand firm against him; to strive and struggle against him. **Practical Application** 　We must resist the devil. Note that we must be steadfast in our resistance. We must not... ● let our guard down ● slip one step ● look one time ● touch at all ● taste a single bite ● listen to one word ● think a single thought ● give way to any desire ● loosen the restraint It might look good, taste good, and feel good, but we must resist the desire and lust and be steadfast in our resistance. We must not give in at all. Giving in one step leads to a second step, and before we know it, we have caved in and are engaged in the sin. Satan has devoured us. 　Our duty is to resist the devil and to be steadfast in our resistance. Note what it is that Satan is after: the believer's faith. He wants the believer to deny his faith, to turn away from Christ. The devil's crowd may say... ● "Oh come on! It won't hurt you." ● "Do your own thing." ● "You're a fool if you don't get all you can." ● "Live, drink, and be merry."

ENGLISH WORD	GREEK WORD AND VERSE	THE WORD MEANS...
	παθημάτων τῇ ἐν [τῷ] κόσμῳ ὑμῶν ἀδελφότητι ἐπιτελεῖσθαι. [GNT]	A person's desires and lusts may want more and more of the possessions and pleasures of this world. The temptation will always be there to turn away from Christ and His righteousness, to turn away from one's faith and to return to the world and its ways. Our duty is to resist the devil steadfastly in the faith, trusting God for the necessary strength to conquer the temptation.
#3266 **Resisteth–Resists** **Resisteth–KJV** Opposed–NASB Opposes–NIV **Resists–NKJV** Sets...against–NLT **POSB REFERENCE** (1 Pt.5:5) Note 2, point 3a	*ἀντιτάσσεται* = *antitassetai* Pronunciation: [an-tee-tahs'-seh-tah-ee] Parsing (part of speech): verb 　　Mood—indicative 　　Tense—present 　　Voice—middle 　　Person—3rd person 　　Number—singular 　　Stem or root—from *ἀντιτάσσομαι* Concordance References: 　⇒　Strong's #498 antitassomai 　⇒　NIV #530 antitassō 　⇒　NASB #498 antitassō **1 Peter 5:5** Likewise, ye younger, submit yourselves unto the elder. Yea, all of you be subject one to another, and be clothed with humility: for God **resisteth** the proud, and giveth grace to the humble. [KJV] You younger men, likewise, be subject to your elders; and all of you, clothe yourselves with humility toward one another, for God is **opposed** to the proud, but gives grace to the humble. [NASB] Young men, in the same way be submissive to those who are older. All of you, clothe yourselves with humility toward one another, because, "God **opposes** the proud but gives grace to the humble." [NIV] Likewise you younger people, submit yourselves to your elders. Yes, all of you be submissive to one another, and be clothed with humility, for "God **resists** the proud, But gives grace to the humble." [NKJV] You younger men, accept the authority of the elders. And all of you, serve each other in humility, for "God **sets** himself **against** the proud, but he shows favor to the humble." [NLT] ὁμοίως, νεώτεροι, ὑποτάγητε πρεσβυτέροις· πάντες δὲ ἀλλήλοις ὑποτασσόμενοι, τὴν ταπεινοφροσύνην ἐγκομβώσασθε· ὅτι ὁ Θεὸς ὑπερηφάνοις **ἀντιτάσσεται**, ταπεινοῖς δὲ δίδωσι χάριν. [GNS] Ὁμοίως, νεώτεροι, ὑποτάγητε πρεσβυτέροις· πάντες δὲ ἀλλήλοις τὴν ταπεινοφροσύνην ἐγκομβώσασθε, ὅτι [Ὁ] θεὸς ὑπερηφάνοις **ἀντιτάσσεται**, ταπεινοῖς δὲ δίδωσιν χάριν. [GNT]	Opposes, resist, sets against; rebels against. **Practical Application** Note why we are to subject to one another and to clothe ourselves with humility: because God resists the proud and gives grace to the humble (cp. Proverbs 3:34). God resists the proud. He stands against all... • who look down upon others • who feel superior to others • who discriminate against others • who are prejudiced • who are boastful • who are haughty God resists the proud—all who oppress others—no matter who they are. The word "resist" (*antitassetai*) is a strong word. It is the picture of an army being set and arrayed against the enemy. Marvin Vincent says that "pride calls out God's armies. No wonder, therefore, that it 'goeth before destruction'" (*Word Studies in the New Testament*, Vol.1, p.668). Those who walk upon this earth exalting themselves above others shall be destroyed by God Himself.
#3267 **Respect** Provide–KJV **Respect–NASB** Careful–NIV Have regard–NKJV Do things in such a way–NLT **POSB REFERENCE** (Rom.12:17) Note 4, point 2	*προνοούμενοι* = *pronooumenoi* Pronunciation: [pro-no-oo-meh'-noy] Parsing (part of speech): verb 　　Mood—participle (imperative sense) 　　Tense—present 　　Voice—middle 　　Case—nominative 　　Gender—masculine 　　Person—2nd person 　　Number—plural 　　Stem or root—from *προνοέω* Concordance References: 　⇒　Strong's #4306 pronoeō 　⇒　NIV #4629 pronoeō 　⇒　NASB #4306 pronoeō **Romans 12:17** Recompense to no man evil for evil. **Provide** things honest in the sight of all men. [KJV] Never pay back evil for evil to anyone. **Respect** what	To be careful; to provide; to respect; to do things in such a way; take care of; to think before acting; taking pains. The believer is to demonstrate good behavior in the sight of all men. The word "respect" (*pronooumenoi*) means to think before acting. **Practical Application** The idea is this: when someone does evil against the believer, the believer is to think before he acts. He is to think and pray through his behavior. Why? So that he can respond in the right and proper way. The believer needs to do what is right and noble, and the only way to do it is to think the situation through.

ENGLISH WORD	GREEK WORD AND VERSE	THE WORD MEANS...
	is right in the sight of all men. [NASB] Do not repay anyone evil for evil. Be **careful** to do what is right in the eyes of everybody. [NIV] Repay no one evil for evil. **Have regard** for good things in the sight of all men. [NKJV] Never pay back evil for evil to anyone. **Do things in such a way** that everyone can see you are honorable. [NLT] μηδενὶ κακὸν ἀντὶ κακοῦ ἀποδιδόντες. **προνοούμενοι** καλὰ ἐνώπιον πάντων ἀνθρώπων. [GNS] μηδενὶ κακὸν ἀντὶ κακοῦ ἀποδιδόντες, **προνοούμενοι** καλὰ ἐνώπιον πάντων ἀνθρώπων· [GNT]	

#3268
Respect
 	
Gravity–KJV
Dignity–NASB
Respect–NIV
Reverence–NKJV
Respect–NLT
 	
**POSB
REFERENCE**
(1 Tim.3:4-5; esp. v.4)
Note 3
	σεμνότητος = semnotētos
	Pronunciation: [sem-no-tay-tos]
	Parsing (part of speech): noun
	    Case—genitive
	    Gender—feminine
	    Number—singular
	    Stem or root—from σεμνότης, ητος
	Concordance References:
	  ⇒ Strong's #4587 semnotēs
	  ⇒ NIV #4949 semnotēs
	  ⇒ NASB #4587 semnotēs
	
	1 Tim. 3:4
	One that ruleth well his own house, having his children in subjection with all **gravity**; [KJV]
	
	He must be one who manages his own household well, keeping his children under control with all **dignity** [NASB]
	
	He must manage his own family well and see that his children obey him with proper **respect**. [NIV]
	
	One who rules his own house well, having *his* children in submission with all **reverence** [NKJV]
	
	He must manage his own family well, with children who **respect** and obey him. [NLT]
	
	τοῦ ἰδίου οἴκου καλῶς προϊστάμενον, τέκνα ἔχοντα ἐν ὑποταγῇ μετὰ πάσης **σεμνότητος**· [GNS]
	
	τοῦ ἰδίου οἴκου καλῶς προϊστάμενον, τέκνα ἔχοντα ἐν ὑποταγῇ, μετὰ πάσης **σεμνότητος** [GNT]
		Respect, gravity, dignity, reverence, respectability, seriousness.
		
		Practical Application
		The minister must manage his home with dignity, respect, and love. As the Amplified New Testament says: "With true dignity, commanding their respect in every way and keeping them respectful."
		
		As Scripture says, "If anyone does not know how to manage his own family, how can he take care of God's church?" (1 Tim. 3:5) [NIV]

#3269
Respect
 	
Honour–KJV
Honor–NASB
Respect–NIV
Honor–NKJV
Honor–NLT
 	
**POSB
REFERENCE**
(1 Pt.3:7)
Note 3
	τιμήν = timēn
	Pronunciation: [tee-mayn']
	Parsing (part of speech): noun
	    Case—accusative
	    Gender—feminine
	    Number—singular
	    Stem or root—from τιμή, ῆς
	Concordance References:
	  ⇒ Strong's #5092 timē
	  ⇒ NIV #5507 timē
	  ⇒ NASB #5092 timē
	
	1 Peter 3:7
	Likewise, ye husbands, dwell with them according to knowledge, giving **honour** unto the wife, as unto the weaker vessel, and as being heirs together of the grace of life; that your prayers be not hindered. [KJV]
	
	You husbands likewise, live with your wives in an understanding way, as with a weaker vessel, since she is a woman; and grant her **honor** as a fellow heir of the grace of life, so that your prayers may not be hindered. [NASB]
	
	Husbands, in the same way be considerate as you live with your wives, and treat them with **respect** as the weaker partner and as heirs with you of the gracious gift of life, so that nothing will hinder your prayers. [NIV]
	
	Husbands, likewise, dwell with *them* with understanding, giving **honor** to the wife, as to the weaker vessel, and as *being* heirs together of the grace of life, that your prayers may not be hindered. [NKJV]
	
	In the same way, you husbands must give **honor** to
		To give respect; to honor. It means to value; to esteem; to prize; to count as precious.
		
		Practical Application
		Husbands are to respect their wives. A husband is to count his wife as a precious gem, as a prize of extreme value. He is to highly esteem her, set her up on a pedestal before his very eyes. Note three points.
		1. The husband is to respect his wife as the weaker vessel. By nature, the wife is just more delicate and frail. This means that the husband is...
		   • to protect her.
		   • to be the primary provider.
		   • to take the lead.
		   • to oversee the family and its welfare.
		   • to be the driving force.
		   • to plow the way.
		   • to be the initiator.
		   Husbands are to respect their wives by loving and tenderly taking care of them. They are to look after and care for them with warmth and tenderness, treating them in the most precious of spirits and esteeming them ever so highly.
		2. The husband is to respect his wife as a *joint heir* of the grace of life. Note this point: in God's eyes men and women are joint or equal heirs. The husband is not above the wife nor

ENGLISH WORD	GREEK WORD AND VERSE	THE WORD MEANS...
	your wives. Treat her with understanding as you live together. She may be weaker than you are, but she is your equal partner in God's gift of new life. If you don't treat her as you should, your prayers will not be heard. [NLT] Οἱ ἄνδρες ὁμοίως, συνοικοῦντες κατὰ γνῶσιν, ὡς ἀσθενεστέρῳ σκεύει τῷ γυναικείῳ ἀπονέμοντες **τιμήν**, ὡς καὶ συγκληρονόμοι χάριτος ζωῆς, εἰς τὸ μὴ ἐκκόπτεσθαι τὰς προσευχὰς ὑμῶν. [GNS] ἄνδρες ὁμοίως, συνοικοῦντες κατὰ γνῶσιν ὡς ἀσθενεστέρῳ σκεύει τῷ γυναικείῳ, ἀπονέμοντες **τιμήν** ὡς καὶ συγκληρονόμοις χάριτος ζωῆς εἰς τὸ μὴ ἐγκόπτεσθαι τὰς προσευχὰς ὑμῶν. [GNT]	the wife above the husband. God has no favorites. Spiritual gifts and rights are given equally to wives and husbands. Women receive the spiritual gifts of God just as readily as men do. 　The point is well made: husbands are to respect their wives as being equal in life. Life is a grace; it is an undeserved gift of God. Therefore in life, the husband is to treat the wife as an equal. He is not to be a tyrant, not to dominate and enslave her to serve and to meet his needs and wants. He is to be understanding, loving, gentle, and considerate. He is to respect her as a fellow heir of life, of the wonderful grace and gift of life that God has given us all. 3. Failure to respect the wife hinders the prayers of the husband. God will not answer the prayers of any husband who fails to respect his wife, no matter who he is or how much he professes Christ. What God hears is the sigh of the wife, not the prayers of a mean and domineering husband. The husband can cry out to God all he wants, but God's back is turned away from him and toward the sigh of the wife. God is going to hear the broken and contrite heart, not the prayers of the arrogant and dominating spirit. Both husband and wife must love one another and live as God says to live, both fulfilling their duty to one another, if they wish God to answer their prayers.
#3270 **Respect** Know–KJV Appreciate–NASB **Respect–NIV** Recognize–NKJV Honor–NLT **POSB REFERENCE** (1 Thes.5:12-13; esp.v.12) Note 1, point 1	εἰδέναι = *eidenai* Pronunciation: [i'-dehn-ah-ee] Parsing (part of speech): verb 　Mood—infinitive 　Tense—perfect 　Voice—active 　Stem or root—from οἶδα Concordance References: ⇒　Strong's #1492 eido ⇒　NIV #3857 oida ⇒　NASB #3609a oida **1 Thes. 5:12** And we beseech you, brethren, to **know** them which labour among you, and are over you in the Lord, and admonish you; [KJV] 　But we request of you, brethren, that you **appreciate** those who diligently labor among you, and have charge over you in the Lord and give you instruction, [NASB] 　Now we ask you, brothers, to **respect** those who work hard among you, who are over you in the Lord and who admonish you. [NIV] 　And we urge you, brethren, to **recognize** those who labor among you, and are over you in the Lord and admonish you, [NKJV] 　Dear brothers and sisters, **honor** those who are your leaders in the Lord's work. They work hard among you and warn you against all that is wrong. [NLT] Ἐρωτῶμεν δὲ ὑμᾶς, ἀδελφοί, **εἰδέναι** τοὺς κοπιῶντας ἐν ὑμῖν, καὶ προϊσταμένους ὑμῶν ἐν Κυρίῳ, καὶ νουθετοῦν τας ὑμᾶς, [GNS] Ἐρωτῶμεν δὲ ὑμᾶς, ἀδελφοί, **εἰδέναι** τοὺς κοπιῶντας ἐν ὑμῖν καὶ προϊσταμένους ὑμῶν ἐν κυρίῳ καὶ νουθετοῦντας ὑμᾶς [GNT]	To respect; to know; to appreciate; to recognize; to honor; to be acquainted with; to acknowledge; to know the value of. **Practical Application** Believers are to repect the leaders of their church. Few people labor as much as a committed church leader.
#3271 **Respectable** Good behaviour–KJV **Respectable–NASB**	κόσμιον = *kosmion* Pronunciation: [kos'-mee-on] Parsing (part of speech): adjective 　Case—accusative 　Gender—masculine 　Number—singular	Respectable, good behavior, good reputation, well-behaved, modest, orderly, composed, solid, and honest.

ENGLISH WORD	GREEK WORD AND VERSE	THE WORD MEANS...
Respectable–NIV Good behavior–NKJV Good reputation–NLT **POSB REFERENCE** (1 Tim.3:2-3; esp. v.2) Note 2, point 5	Stem or root—from **κόσμιος**, ον Concordance References: ⇒ Strong's #2887 kosmios ⇒ NIV #3177 kosmios ⇒ NASB #2887 kosmios **1 Tim. 3:2** A bishop then must be blameless, the husband of one wife, vigilant, sober, of **good behaviour**, given to hospitality, apt to teach; [KJV] An overseer, then, must be above reproach, the husband of one wife, temperate, prudent, **respectable**, hospitable, able to teach, [NASB] Now the overseer must be above reproach, the husband of but one wife, temperate, self-controlled, **respectable**, hospitable, able to teach, [NIV] A bishop then must be blameless, the husband of one wife, temperate, sober-minded, of **good behavior**, hospitable, able to teach; [NKJV] For an elder must be a man whose life cannot be spoken against. He must be faithful to his wife. He must exhibit self-control, live wisely, and have a **good reputation**. He must enjoy having guests in his home and must be able to teach. [NLT] δεῖ οὖν τὸν ἐπίσκοπον ἀνεπίλημπτον εἶναι, μιᾶς γυναικὸς ἄνδρα, νηφάλιον, σώφρονα, **κόσμιον**, φιλόξενον, διδακτικόν· [GNS] δεῖ οὖν τὸν ἐπίσκοπον ἀνεπίλημπτον εἶναι, μιᾶς γυναικὸς ἄνδρα, νηφάλιον σώφρονα **κόσμιον** φιλόξενον διδακτικόν, [GNT]	**Practical Application** The minister or overseer must be of "respectable" (*kosmion*). It is a person who has good conduct, whose character and behavior stand as the ideal and pattern for others.

#3272
Respected
 	
Grave–KJV
Dignity–NASB
Worthy of respect–
NIV
Reverent–NKJV
Respected–NLT
 	
**POSB
REFERENCE**
(1 Tim.3:8)
Note 1, point 1
 	
See also POSB REF:
(1 Tim.3:11-12)
Note 3
(Tit.2:2)
Note 2
	σεμνούς = *semnous*
	Pronunciation: [sem-noos']
	Parsing (part of speech): adjective
	  Case—accusative
	  Gender—masculine
	  Number—plural
	  Stem or root—from **σεμνός**, ή, όν
	Concordance References:
	⇒ Strong's #4586 semnos
	⇒ NIV #4948 semnos
	⇒ NASB #4586 semnos
	
	1 Tim. 3:8
	Likewise must the deacons be **grave**, not double-tongued, not given to much wine, not greedy of filthy lucre; [KJV]
	Deacons likewise must be men of **dignity**, not double-tongued, or addicted to much wine or fond of sordid gain, [NASB]
	Deacons, likewise, are to be men **worthy of respect**, sincere, not indulging in much wine, and not pursuing dishonest gain. [NIV]
	Likewise deacons *must be* **reverent**, not double-tongued, not given to much wine, not greedy for money, [NKJV]
	In the same way, deacons must be people who are **respected** and have integrity. They must not be heavy drinkers and must not be greedy for money. [NLT]
	διακόνους ὡσαύτως **σεμνούς**, μὴ διλόγους, μὴ οἴνῳ πολλῷ προσέχοντας, μὴ αἰσχροκερδεῖς, [GNS]
	Διακόνους ὡσαύτως **σεμνούς**, μὴ διλόγους, μὴ οἴνῳ πολλῷ προσέχοντας, μὴ αἰσχροκερδεῖς, [GNT]
		Worthy of respect, grave, dignity, highly respected, serious, honorable, worthy, revered, noble.
		
		Practical Application
		It is being serious-minded, the very opposite...
		• of being flippant.
		• of dishonoring oneself.
		• of being shallow by being over-talkative.
		• of having little respect because one is not grave or serious enough.
		• of having a surface religion only.
		
		However, this does not mean that the deacon is to walk around with a long face, never smiling, joking, or having fun. It simply means that he is to be serious-minded and committed to Christ and to the mission of the church: the mission of reaching the lost and meeting the desperate needs of the world.

#3273
Respector Of Persons
 	
Respector of persons–KJV
Show partiality–NASB
	ἔστιν προσωπολήμπτης = *estin prosöpolëmptës*
	Pronunciation: [es-tin pros-o-pol-ape'-tace]
	Parsing *estin* (part of speech): verb
	  Mood—indicative
	  Tense—present
	  Voice—active
	  Person—3rd person
	  Number—singular
	  Stem or root—from **εἰμί**
		To show favoritism; to show partiality. It means to regard with partiality and favoritism; to favor a person because of looks, position, or circumstances.
		
		Practical Application
		The great point of this chapter is that God has no favorites and no prejudice against anyone. He

ENGLISH WORD	GREEK WORD AND VERSE	THE WORD MEANS...

Show favoritism–NIV
Shows...partiality–NKJV
Show partiality–NLT
 	
**POSB
REFERENCE**
(Acts 10:34-35; esp. v.34)
Note 1
	Parsing *prosöpolëmptës* (part of speech): noun
	    Case—nominative
	    Gender—masculine
	    Number—singular
	    Stem or root—from προσωπολήμπτης, ου
	Concordance References:
	⇒ Strong's #1488 + 4381 eimi prosöpolëmptës [show favoritism]
	⇒ NIV #1639 + 4720 eimi prosöpolëmptës
	⇒ NASB #1488 + 4381 eimi prosöpolëmptës
	
	### Acts 10:34
	Then Peter opened *his* mouth, and said, Of a truth I perceive that God is no **respecter of persons**: [KJV]
	
	And opening his mouth, Peter said:"I most certainly understand *now* that God is not one to **show partiality**, [NASB]
	
	Then Peter began to speak: "I now realize how true it is that God does not **show favoritism** [NIV]
	
	Then Peter opened *his* mouth and said: "In truth I perceive that God **shows** no **partiality**. [NKJV]
	
	Then Peter replied, "I see very clearly that God doesn't **show partiality**. [NLT]
	
	' Ανοίξας δὲ Πέτρος τὸ στόμα, εἶπεν, 'Επ' ἀληθείας καταλαμβάνομαι ὅτι οὐκ **ἔστι προσωπολήμπτης** ὁ Θεός, [GNS]
	
	'Ανοίξας δὲ Πέτρος τὸ στόμα εἶπεν, 'Επ' ἀληθείας καταλαμβάνομαι ὅτι οὐκ **ἔστιν προσωπολήμπτης** ὁ θεός, [GNT]
		shows no partiality or discrimination whatsoever. He does not accept a person because of nationality, race, caste, social standing, or class. God does not favor a man because of...
		• who he is
		• what he does
		• what he has
		
		Person or appearance, possessions or position, abilities or works, health or stature—these things do not make a person acceptable to God. "God is no respecter of persons." He has always said so, but men, including Peter, had not paid attention to Him (cp. Deut. 10:17; 2 Chron. 19:7; Job 34:10; Romans 2:11; Ephes. 6:9; Col. 3:25; James 2:1; 1 Peter 1:17). They just went right on ignoring the truth of God's Word and feeding their prejudices. Note that Peter said...
		• God is no respecter of persons (Acts 10:34).
		• God is no respecter of nations (Acts 10:35. Cp. Romans 2:27-29).

#3274
## Responsibility 	
 	
Dispensation–KJV
Stewardship–NASB
Commission–NIV
Stewardship–NKJV
Responsibility–NLT
 	
**POSB
REFERENCE**
(Col.1:25)
Note 2
	οἰκονομίαν = oikonomian
	Pronunciation: [oy-kon-om-ee'-ahn]
	Parsing (part of speech): noun
	    Case—accusative
	    Gender—feminine
	    Number—singular
	    Stem or root—from οἰκονομία, ας
	Concordance References:
	⇒ Strong's #3622 oikonomia
	⇒ NIV #3873 oikonomia
	⇒ NASB #3622 oikonomia
	
	### Col. 1:25
	Whereof I am made a minister, according to the **dispensation** of God which is given to me for you, to fulfil the word of God; [KJV]
	
	Of this church I was made a minister according to the **stewardship** from God bestowed on me for your benefit, that I might fully carry out the preaching of the word of God, [NASB]
	
	I have become its servant by the **commission** God gave me to present to you the word of God in its fullness [NIV]
	
	Of which I became a minister according to the **stewardship** from God which was given to me for you, to fulfill the word of God, [NKJV]
	
	God has given me the **responsibility** of serving his church by proclaiming his message in all its fullness to you Gentiles. [NLT]
	
	ἧς ἐγενόμην ἐγὼ διάκονος, κατὰ τὴν **οἰκονομίαν** τοῦ Θεοῦ τὴν δοθεῖσάν μοι εἰς ὑμᾶς, πληρῶσαι τὸν λόγον τοῦ Θεοῦ, [GNS]
	
	ἧς ἐγενόμην ἐγὼ διάκονος κατὰ τὴν **οἰκονομίαν** τοῦ θεοῦ τὴν δοθεῖσάν μοι εἰς ὑμᾶς πληρῶσαι τὸν λόγον τοῦ θεοῦ, [GNT]
		Commission, dispensation, stewardship, responsibility; management of; responsibility of, duty of.
		
		### Practical Application
		The word "responsibility" (*oikonomian*) refers to the steward who oversees the household and property of the owner. The minister is the steward of God, the person chosen to oversee the house or church of God. This fact is almost unbelievable, but it is true: God has actually chosen some persons to oversee His affairs for Him. The minister has actually been chosen by God to be the steward of His world and church and people. God has literally taken His church and people and placed them into the hands of His ministers, into...
		• their stewardship
		• their supervision
		• their administration
		• their ministry
		• their responsibility
		• their management
		• their care
		• their lives
		• their love
		
		What an enormous call and responsibility, yet it comes from God; therefore, it must be fulfilled.

#3275
## Rest 	
 	
Rest–KJV
Rest–NASB
Rest–NIV
	ἀνάπαυσιν = anapausin
	Pronunciation: [an-ap'-ow-sin]
	Parsing (part of speech): noun
	    Case—accusative
	    Gender—feminine
	    Number—singular
	    Stem or root—from ἀνάπαυσις, εως
		To cease from labor, to pause, to rest; to stop.
		
		### Practical Application
		Note the difference between the two rests promised by Jesus Christ. They are the two greatest *rests* imaginable. (Also see POSB

ENGLISH WORD	GREEK WORD AND VERSE	THE WORD MEANS...

Rest–NKJV
Rest–NLT
 	
POSB
REFERENCE
(Mt.11:29)
Note 2
Deeper Study #1
	Concordance References:
	⇒ Strong's #372 anapausis
	⇒ NIV #398 anapausis
	⇒ NASB #372 anapausis
	
	Matthew 11:29
	Take my yoke upon you, and learn of me; for I am meek and lowly in heart: and ye shall find **rest** unto your souls. [KJV]
	"Take My yoke upon you, and learn from Me, for I am gentle and humble in heart; and you shall find **rest** for your souls. [NASB]
	Take my yoke upon you and learn from me, for I am gentle and humble in heart, and you will find **rest** for your souls. [NIV]
	Take My yoke upon you and learn from Me, for I am gentle and lowly in heart, and you will find **rest** for your souls. [NKJV]
	Take my yoke upon you. Let me teach you, because I am humble and gentle, and you will find **rest** for your souls. [NLT]
	ἄρατε τὸν ζυγόν μου ἐφ' ὑμᾶς καὶ μάθετε ἀπ' ἐμοῦ, ὅτι πρᾷός εἰμι καὶ ταπεινὸς τῇ καρδίᾳ· καὶ εὑρήσετε **ἀνάπαυσιν** ταῖς ψυχαῖς ὑμῶν· [GNS]
	ἄρατε τὸν ζυγόν μου ἐφ' ὑμᾶς καὶ μάθετε ἀπ' ἐμοῦ, ὅτι πραΰς εἰμι καὶ ταπεινὸς τῇ καρδίᾳ, καὶ εὑρήσετε **ἀνάπαυσιν** ταῖς ψυχαῖς ὑμῶν· [GNT]
		notes—Heb.4:1-13 for more discussion.)
		1. "I will give you rest (*anapausin*)" (Mt.11:28). First, there is the rest of salvation or justification. This is the rest of deliverance from the slavery and bondage of sin, the power of Christ to conquer the enslaving habits that damage the human body and destroy the human soul. It is the rest of conscience that comes to a person's soul when he ceases his struggle in the wilderness of sin. It is the rest of conquest and triumph which a person experiences when he conquers the enemies of sin and evil through the power of Christ—day-by-day. It is the rest of victory through the daily storms of life (see POSB *Deeper Study #1*—Ro.4:22; POSB *Deeper Study #2*—Ro.4:22; POSB note—Ro.5:1; cp. Ro.4:5; Ro.4:1-3; Ro.4:1-25).
		2. "You will find rest (*anapausin*) for your souls" (Mt.11:29). Second, there is the rest of sanctification, of being set apart to live a pure and holy life while completing one's task throughout life. This might be called the rest of purpose and satisfaction, of confidence and completeness. The rest is not a rest of inactivity, of no work, of an endless slumber, of the right to laziness. It is a rest of three things.
		  a. It is a rest of refreshment: a rest of refreshing one's body, mind, and spirit with the presence and guidance of God day by day.
		  b. It is a rest that fits one for life: a rest that infuses a person with true purpose, meaning, and significance.
		  c. It is a rest of encouragement and motivation of soul: a rest that stirs a person to live and undertake his God-given task with enthusiasm and vigor and endurance.

#3276
Rest
 	
Rest–KJV
Peace–NASB
Peace–NIV
Peace–NKJV
Peace–NLT
 	
POSB
REFERENCE
(Acts 9:31)
Note 1
	εἰρήνην = eirēnēn
	Pronunciation: [ee-ray-nayn]
	Parsing (part of speech): noun
	  Case—accusative
	  Gender—feminine
	  Number—singular
	  Stem or root—from εἰρήνη, ης
	Concordance References:
	⇒ Strong's #1515 eirēnē
	⇒ NIV #1645 cirēnē
	⇒ NASB #1515 eirēnē
	
	Acts 9:31
	Then had the churches **rest** throughout all Judaea and Galilee and Samaria, and were edified; and walking in the fear of the Lord, and in the comfort of the Holy Ghost, were multiplied. [KJV]
	So the church throughout all Judea and Galilee and Samaria enjoyed **peace**, being built up; and, going on in the fear of the Lord and in the comfort of the Holy Spirit, it continued to increase. [NASB]
	Then the church throughout Judea, Galilee and Samaria enjoyed a time of **peace**. It was strengthened; and encouraged by the Holy Spirit, it grew in numbers, living in the fear of the Lord. [NIV]
	Then the churches throughout all Judea, Galilee, and Samaria had **peace** and were edified. And walking in the fear of the Lord and in the comfort of the Holy Spirit, they were multiplied. [NKJV]
	The church then had **peace** throughout Judea, Galilee, and Samaria, and it grew in strength and numbers. The
		Peace, rest, harmony; the opposite of chaos and disorder.
		
		### Practical Application
		The church was in a continuous state of peace or rest. It had been going through a most troublesome time, but now the trouble had been handled and peace reigned. Calm and rest settled in and took control. The idea is that the believers were now joying and rejoicing in the peace and deliverance God had given from their great trial. The problem had been severe persecution (see POSB outline—Acts 8:1-4; POSB notes—Acts 8:1-4; POSB outline—Acts 9:1-2; and POSB note—POSB Acts 9:1-2 for discussion). But now the storm had settled, and peace and calm, quiet and rest prevailed.

ENGLISH WORD	GREEK WORD AND VERSE	THE WORD MEANS...
	believers were walking in the fear of the Lord and in the comfort of the Holy Spirit. [NLT] Αἱ μὲν οὖν ἐκκλησίαι καθ᾽ ὅλης τῆς Ἰουδαίας καὶ Γαλιλαίας καὶ Σαμαρείας εἶχον **εἰρήνην**, οἰκοδομούμεναι καὶ πορευόμεναι τῷ φόβῳ τοῦ Κυρίου, καὶ τῇ παρακλήσει τοῦ Ἁγίου Πνεύματος ἐπληθύνετο. [GNS] Ἡ μὲν οὖν ἐκκλησία καθ᾽ ὅλης τῆς Ἰουδαίας καὶ Γαλιλαίας καὶ Σαμαρείας εἶχεν **εἰρήνην** οἰκοδομουμένη καὶ πορευομένη τῷ φόβῳ τοῦ κυρίου καὶ τῇ παρακλήσει τοῦ ἁγίου πνεύματος ἐπληθύνετο. [GNT]	

#3277
Rest
 	
Rest–KJV
Rest–NASB
Rest–NIV
Rest–NKJV
Rest–NLT
 	
**POSB
REFERENCE**
(Rev.14:13)
Note 2, point 1
	ἀναπαήσονται = *anapaësontai*
	Pronunciation: [an-ap-ah-ay-son-tah-ee]
	Parsing (part of speech): verb
	    Mood—indicative
	    Tense—future
	    Voice—passive
	    Person—3rd person
	    Number—plural
	    Stem or root—from ἀναπαύω
	Concordance References:
	  ⇒ Strong's #373 anapauō
	  ⇒ NIV #399 anapauō
	  ⇒ NASB #373 anapauō
	
	Rev. 14:13
	And I heard a voice from heaven saying unto me, Write, Blessed are the dead which die in the Lord from henceforth: Yea, saith the Spirit, that they may **rest** from their labours; and their works do follow them. [KJV]
	And I heard a voice from heaven, saying, "Write, 'Blessed are the dead who die in the Lord from now on!' " "Yes," says the Spirit, "that they may **rest** from their labors, for their deeds follow with them." [NASB]
	Then I heard a voice from heaven say, "Write: Blessed are the dead who die in the Lord from now on." "Yes," says the Spirit, "they will **rest** from their labor, for their deeds will follow them." [NIV]
	Then I heard a voice from heaven saying to me, "Write: 'Blessed *are* the dead who die in the Lord from now on.'" "Yes," says the Spirit, "that they may **rest** from their labors, and their works follow them." [NKJV]
	And I heard a voice from heaven saying, "Write this down: Blessed are those who die in the Lord from now on. Yes, says the Spirit, they are blessed indeed, for they will **rest** from all their toils and trials; for their good deeds follow them!" [NLT]
	
	Καὶ ἤκουσα φωνῆς ἐκ τοῦ οὐρανοῦ λεγούσης μοι, Γράψον, Μακάριοι οἱ νεκροὶ οἱ ἐν Κυρίῳ ἀποθνήσκοντες ἀπ᾽ ἄρτι· ναί, λέγει τὸ Πνεῦμα, ἵνα **ἀναπαύσωνται** ἐκ τῶν κόπων αὐτῶν· τὰ δὲ ἔργα αὐτῶν ἀκολουθεῖ μετ᾽ αὐτῶν. [GNS]
	
	Καὶ ἤκουσα φωνῆς ἐκ τοῦ οὐρανοῦ λεγούσης, Γράψον· Μακάριοι οἱ νεκροὶ οἱ ἐν κυρίῳ ἀποθνήσκοντες ἀπ᾽ ἄρτι. ναί, λέγει τὸ πνεῦμα, ἵνα **ἀναπαήσονται** ἐκ τῶν κόπων αὐτῶν, τὰ γὰρ ἔργα αὐτῶν ἀκολουθεῖ μετ᾽ αὐτῶν. [GNT]
		To rest; to relax; to repose. It means to be refreshed, revitalized, restirred, recharged, and rejuvinated. It means to be free of all temptations and trials, to be comforted and relaxed while being refreshed and recharged.
		
		Practical Application
		When we get to heaven, we will be free from all the temptations and trials and labors of this earth. We will also be perfected in body, free from ever getting tired, from aching muscles and headaches and heavy eyes; free from ever becoming exhausted and weary again. We will be perfected: we will live in a perfect society of godliness and righteousness forever and ever. In that glorious day we will rest from all our labors and struggles in this corruptible world.

#3278
Rest–Rests
 	
Rest–KJV
Abide–NASB
Live–NIV
Rest–NKJV
Rests–NLT
	κατασκηνώσει = *kataskēnōsei*
	Pronunciation: [ka-tah-skay-no-seh-ee]
	Parsing (part of speech): verb
	    Mood—indicative
	    Tense—future
	    Voice—active
	    Person—3rd person
	    Number—singular
	    Stem or root—from κατασκηνόω
		To hold; to continue; to abide; to remain; to keep on obeying. It means to dwell, continue, stay, sojourn, rest in or upon; to live; to rest; to nest.
		
		Practical Application
		The word "rest" means to tabernacle or pitch a tent. Jesus' flesh rested, tabernacled, pitched its tent, encamped and made its abode upon hope—the hope of conquering death, of being resurrected. Hope of living forever was the basis

ENGLISH WORD	GREEK WORD AND VERSE	THE WORD MEANS...
POSB REFERENCE (Acts 2:25-28; esp. v.26) Note 1, point 1c	Concordance References: ⇒ Strong's #2681 kataskënöö ⇒ NIV #2942 kataskënöö ⇒ NASB #2681 kataskënöö **Acts 2:26** Therefore did my heart rejoice, and my tongue was glad; moreover also my flesh shall **rest** in hope: [KJV] 'THEREFORE MY HEART WAS GLAD AND MY TONGUE EXULTED; MOREOVER MY FLESH ALSO WILL **ABIDE** IN HOPE; [NASB] Therefore my heart is glad and my tongue rejoices; my body also will **live** in hope, [NIV] *Therefore my heart rejoiced, and my tongue was glad; Moreover my flesh also will* **rest** *in hope.* [NKJV] No wonder my heart is filled with joy, and my mouth shouts his praises! My body **rests** in hope. [NLT] Διὰ τοῦτο εὐφράνθη ἡ καρδία μου, καὶ ἠγαλλιάσατο ἡ γλῶσσά μου· ἔτι δὲ καὶ ἡ σάρξ μου **κατασκηνώσει** ἐπ' ἐλπίδι· [GNS] διὰ τοῦτο ηὐφράνθη ἡ καρδία μου καὶ ἠγαλλιάσατο ἡ γλῶσσά μου, ἔτι δὲ καὶ ἡ σάρξ μου **κατασκηνώσει** ἐπ' ἐλπίδι, [GNT]	and foundation of Jesus' life, that for which He lived. He focused His whole life upon the hope of the cross and of the glorious resurrection from the dead (cp. Paul's testimony—Phil. 3:7-16, esp. Phil. 3:11).
#3279 **Rest On–** **Rest Upon** **Rest upon–KJV** Dwell in–NASB **Rest on–NIV** **Rest upon–NKJV** Work through–NLT **POSB REFERENCE** (2 Cor.12:7-10; esp. v.9) Note 3, point 3b	*ἐπισκηνώσῃ ἐπ'* = episkënösë ep' Pronunciation: [ep-ee-skay-no'-say ep] Parsing episkënösë (part of speech): verb Mood—subjunctive Tense—aorist Voice—active Person—3rd person Number—singular Stem or root—from ἐπισκηνόω Concordance References: ⇒ Strong's #1909+1981 epi episkënöö ⇒ NIV #2093+2172 epi episkënoo [rest on] ⇒ NASB #1909+1981 epi episkënöö **2 Cor. 12:9** And he said unto me, My grace is sufficient for thee: for my strength is made perfect in weakness. Most gladly therefore will I rather glory in my infirmities, that the power of Christ may **rest upon** me. [KJV] And He has said to me, "My grace is sufficient for you, for power is perfected in weakness." Most gladly, therefore, I will rather boast about my weaknesses, that the power of Christ may **dwell in** me. [NASB] But he said to me, "My grace is sufficient for you, for my power is made perfect in weakness." Therefore I will boast all the more gladly about my weaknesses, so that Christ's power may **rest on** me. [NIV] And He said to me, "My grace is sufficient for you, for My strength is made perfect in weakness." Therefore most gladly I will rather boast in my infirmities, that the power of Christ may **rest upon** me. [NKJV] Each time he said, "My gracious favor is all you need. My power works best in your weakness." So now I am glad to boast about my weaknesses, so that the power of Christ may **work through** me. [NLT] καὶ εἴρηκέ μοι, Ἀρκεῖ σοι ἡ χάρις μου· ἡ γὰρ δύναμις μου ἐν ἀσθενείᾳ τελειοῦται. ἥδιστα οὖν μᾶλλον καυχήσομαι ἐν ταῖς ἀσθενείαις μου, ἵνα **ἐπισκηνώσῃ ἐπ'** ἐμὲ ἡ δύναμις τοῦ Χριστοῦ. [GNS] καὶ εἴρηκέν μοι· Ἀρκεῖ σοι ἡ χάρις μου, ἡ γὰρ δύναμις ἐν ἀσθενείᾳ τελεῖται. ἥδιστα οὖν μᾶλλον καυχήσομαι ἐν ταῖς ἀσθενείαις μου, ἵνα **ἐπισκηνώσῃ ἐπ'** ἐμὲ ἡ δύναμις τοῦ Χριστοῦ. [GNT]	To rest on; to rest upon; to dwell in; to live in; to work through; to fix a tent upon. **Practical Application** The idea is that the power of Christ rests upon the suffering believer just as the Shekinah glory dwelt in the holy place of the tabernacle. What a glorious thought! The strength of Christ fixes itself upon and dwells within the believer—filling him with the Shekinah glory of God—when he suffers.
#3280 **Rest, Came To**	*ἐκάθισεν* = ekathisen Pronunciation: [eh-kath-i'-sen] Parsing (part of speech): verb Mood—indicative	Came to rest; to sit upon; to rest upon; to settle upon.

ENGLISH WORD	GREEK WORD AND VERSE	THE WORD MEANS...
Sat–KJV Rested–NASB **Came to rest–NIV** Sat–NKJV Settled–NLT **POSB REFERENCE** (Acts 2:2-4; esp. v.3) Note 4, point 2b	Tense—aorist Voice—active Person—3rd person Number—singular Stem or root—from **καθίζω** Concordance References: ⇒ Strong's #2523 kathizö ⇒ NIV #2767 kathizö ⇒ NASB #2523 kathizö **Acts 2:3** And there appeared unto them cloven tongues like as of fire, and it **sat** upon each of them. [KJV] And there appeared to them tongues as of fire distributing themselves, and they **rested** on each one of them. [NASB] They saw what seemed to be tongues of fire that separated and **came to rest** on each of them. [NIV] Then there appeared to them divided tongues, as of fire, and *one* **sat** upon each of them. [NKJV] Then, what looked like flames or tongues of fire appeared and **settled** on each of them. [NLT] καὶ ὤφθησαν αὐτοῖς διαμεριζόμεναι γλῶσσαι ὡσεὶ πυρός, καὶ **ἐκάθισε** τε ἐφ' ἕνα ἕκαστο αὐτῶν. [GNS] καὶ ὤφθησαν αὐτοῖς διαμεριζόμεναι γλῶσσαι ὡσεὶ πυρός καὶ **ἐκάθισεν** ἐφ' ἕνα ἕκαστον αὐτῶν, [GNT]	**Practical Application** The word is singular, not plural; The Holy Spirit Himself was descending and resting upon each of the disciples. They were not receiving "tongues of fire," but the Spirit of God. Note also that the Spirit appeared in the form of a tongue of fire. The tongue symbolizes the instrument of speaking and preaching and sharing the gospel. The Holy Spirit was to be the burning power of the tongue, of the convicting message to be proclaimed.
#3281 Rested Sat–KJV **Rested–NASB** Came to rest–NIV Sat–NKJV Settled–NLT **POSB REFERENCE** (Acts 2:2-4; esp. v.3) Note 4, point 2b	**ἐκάθισεν** = *ekathisen* Pronunciation: [eh-kath-i'-sen] Parsing (part of speech): verb Mood—indicative Tense—aorist Voice—active Person—3rd person Number—singular Stem or root—from **καθίζω** Concordance References: ⇒ Strong's #2523 kathizö ⇒ NIV #2767 kathizö ⇒ NASB #2523 kathizö **Acts 2:3** And there appeared unto them cloven tongues like as of fire, and it **sat** upon each of them. [KJV] And there appeared to them tongues as of fire distributing themselves, and they **rested** on each one of them. [NASB] They saw what seemed to be tongues of fire that separated and **came to rest** on each of them. [NIV] Then there appeared to them divided tongues, as of fire, and *one* **sat** upon each of them. [NKJV] Then, what looked like flames or tongues of fire appeared and **settled** on each of them. [NLT] καὶ ὤφθησαν αὐτοῖς διαμεριζόμεναι γλῶσσαι ὡσεὶ πυρός, καὶ **ἐκάθισε** τε ἐφ' ἕνα ἕκαστο αὐτῶν. [GNS] καὶ ὤφθησαν αὐτοῖς διαμεριζόμεναι γλῶσσαι ὡσεὶ πυρός καὶ **ἐκάθισεν** ἐφ' ἕνα ἕκαστον αὐτῶν, [GNT]	Came to rest; to sit upon; to rest upon; to settle upon. **Practical Application** The word is singular, not plural; The Holy Spirit Himself was descending and resting upon each of the disciples. They were not receiving "tongues of fire," but the Spirit of God. Note also that the Spirit appeared in the form of a tongue of fire. The tongue symbolizes the instrument of speaking and preaching and sharing the gospel. The Holy Spirit was to be the burning power of the tongue, of the convicting message to be proclaimed.
#3282 Restitution **Restitution–KJV** Restoration–NASB Restore–NIV Restoration–NKJV Restoration–NLT **POSB REFERENCE** (Acts 3:21) *Deeper Study* #3	**ἀποκαταστάσεως** = *apokatastaseös* Pronunciation: [ap-ok-at-as'-tas-eh-os] Parsing (part of speech): noun Case—genitive Gender—feminine Number—singular Stem or root—from **ἀποκατάστασις**, εως Concordance References: ⇒ Strong's #605 apokatastasis ⇒ NIV #640 apokatastasis ⇒ NASB #605 apokatastasis **Acts 3:21** Whom the heaven must receive until the times of **restitution** of all things, which God hath spoken by the mouth of all his holy prophets since the world began. [KJV]	To restore; restitution, restoration, compensation. **Practical Application** It means to set in order again; to bring back to a former condition or state of being; to restore; to recreate or remake or renew all over again. (See POSB note, Regeneration—Matthew 19:28 for more discussion.)

ENGLISH WORD	GREEK WORD AND VERSE	THE WORD MEANS...
	Whom heaven must receive until *the* period of **restoration** of all things about which God spoke by the mouth of His holy prophets from ancient time. [NASB] He must remain in heaven until the time comes for God to **restore** everything, as he promised long ago through his holy prophets. [NIV] Whom heaven must receive until the times of **restoration** of all things, which God has spoken by the mouth of all His holy prophets since the world began. [NKJV] For he must remain in heaven until the time for the final **restoration** of all things, as God promised long ago through his prophets. [NLT] ὃν δεῖ οὐρανὸν μὲν δέξασθαι ἄχρι χρόνων **ἀποκαταστάσεως** πάντων, ὧν ἐλάλησεν ὁ Θεὸς διὰ στόματος πάντων ἁγίων αὐτοῦ προφητῶν ἀπ' αἰῶνος. [GNS] ὃν δεῖ οὐρανὸν μὲν δέξασθαι ἄχρι χρόνων **ἀποκαταστάσεως** πάντων ὧν ἐλάλησεν ὁ θεὸς διὰ στόματος τῶν ἁγίων ἀπ' αἰῶνος αὐτοῦ προφητῶν. [GNT]	

#3283
Restless
 	
Unruly–KJV
Restless–NASB
Restless–NIV
Unruly–NKJV
Uncontrollable–NLT
 	
POSB REFERENCE
(Jas 3:7-12; esp. v.8)
Note 5, point 3
	ἀκατάστατον = *akatastaton*
	Pronunciation: [ak-at-as'-tah-ton]
	Parsing (part of speech): adjective
	    Case—nominative
	    Gender—neuter
	    Number—singular
	    Stem or root—from ἀκατάστατος, ον
	Concordance References:
	  ⇒ Strong's #183 akataschetos
	  ⇒ NIV #190 akatastatos
	  ⇒ NASB #182 akatastatos
	
	James 3:8
	But the tongue can no man tame; it is an **unruly** evil, full of deadly poison. [KJV]
	
	But no one can tame the tongue; it is a **restless** evil and full of deadly poison. [NASB]
	
	But no man can tame the tongue. It is a **restless** evil, full of deadly poison. [NIV]
	
	But no man can tame the tongue. *It is* an **unruly** evil, full of deadly poison. [NKJV]
	
	But no one can tame the tongue. It is an **uncontrollable** evil, full of deadly poison. [NLT]
	
	τὴν δὲ γλῶσσαν οὐδεὶς δύναται ἀνθρώπων δαμάσαι· **ἀκατάσχετον** κακόν, μεστὴ ἰοῦ θανατηφόρου. [GNS]
	
	τὴν δὲ γλῶσσαν οὐδεὶς δαμάσαι δύναται ἀνθρώπων, **ἀκατάστατον** κακόν, μεστὴ ἰοῦ θανατηφόρου. [GNT]
		Restless, unruly, uncontrollable, nervous, jittery, unsettled.
		
		Practical Application
		The tongue is "restless" (*akatastaton*), that is, unruly, uneasy, unstable, always roaming about. And it is full of deadly poison. It can bless God in one breath and curse men in the next, men who are made in the image of God. Note how inconsistent the tongue is: it blesses God and curses men. Imagine! The very same tongue that blesses is the same tongue that curses. How many sit in church on Sunday or at meals blessing God and then turn around on Monday and curse or use foul and off-colored language? It is the same tongue that does both. How restless it is! It is just difficult to hold the tongue still, and when it speaks, it is just as liable to speak some curse word as it is to speak some blessing.

#3284
Restoration To Maturity
 	
Perfection–KJV
Made complete–NASB
Perfection–NIV
Made complete–NKJV
Restoration to maturity–NLT
 	
POSB REFERENCE
(2 Cor.13:7-10; esp. v.9)
Note 2
	κατάρτισιν = *katartisin*
	Pronunciation: [kat-ar'-tis-in]
	Parsing (part of speech): noun
	    Case—accusative
	    Gender—feminine
	    Number—singular
	    Stem or root—from κατάρτισις, εως
	Concordance References:
	  ⇒ Strong's #2676 katartisis
	  ⇒ NIV #2937 katartisis
	  ⇒ NASB #2676 katartisis
	
	2 Cor. 13:9
	For we are glad, when we are weak, and ye are strong: and this also we wish, even your **perfection**. [KJV]
	
	For we rejoice when we ourselves are weak but you are strong; this we also pray for, that you be **made complete**. [NASB]
	
	We are glad whenever we are weak but you are strong; and our prayer is for your **perfection**. [NIV]
	
	For we are glad when we are weak and you are strong. And this also we pray, that you may be **made complete**. [NKJV]
		Perfection; excellence; made whole; made complete, restoring to maturity; to repair what is broken and to restore it to a more perfect condition.
		
		Practical Application
		Paul was glad when the believers were strong in the Lord and he was able to appear weak, that is, when he did not have to be exercising authority and discipline. At such times, the believers and the church were growing toward perfection.
		
		What the Corinthian church needed was to become strong and perfected, that is, repaired and restored, to have its fellowship cleansed of critics and false teachers.

ENGLISH WORD	GREEK WORD AND VERSE	THE WORD MEANS...
	We are glad to be weak, if you are really strong. What we pray for is your **restoration to maturity**. [NLT] χαίρομεν γὰρ ὅταν ἡμεῖς ἀσθενῶμεν, ὑμεῖς δὲ δυνατοὶ ἦτε· τοῦτο δὲ καὶ εὐχόμεθα, τὴν ὑμῶν **κατάρτισιν**. [GNS] χαίρομεν γὰρ ὅταν ἡμεῖς ἀσθενῶμεν, ὑμεῖς δὲ δυνατοὶ ἦτε· τοῦτο δὲ καὶ εὐχόμεθα, τὴν ὑμῶν **κατάρτισιν**. [GNT]	

#3285
Restore
 	
Restore–KJV
Restore–NASB
Restore–NIV
Restore–NKJV
Help that person back onto the right path–NLT
 	
POSB REFERENCE
(Gal.6:1-5; esp. v.1)
Introduction
	κατάρτιζετε = *katartizete*
	Pronunciation: [kat-ar-tidz'-eh-teh]
	Parsing (part of speech): verb
	    Mood—imperative
	    Tense—present
	    Voice—active
	    Person—2nd person
	    Number—plural
	    Stem or root—from κατάρτιζω
	Concordance References:
	  ⇒ Strong's #2675 katartizō
	  ⇒ NIV #2936 katartizō
	  ⇒ NASB #2675 katartizō
	
	Galatians 6:1
	Brethren, if a man be overtaken in a fault, ye which are spiritual, **restore** such an one in the spirit of meekness; considering thyself, lest thou also be tempted. [KJV]
	
	Brethren, even if a man is caught in any trespass, you who are spiritual, **restore** such a one in a spirit of gentleness; each one looking to yourself, lest you too be tempted. [NASB]
	
	Brothers, if someone is caught in a sin, you who are spiritual should **restore** him gently. But watch yourself, or you also may be tempted. [NIV]
	
	Brethren, if a man is overtaken in any trespass, you who *are* spiritual **restore** such a one in a spirit of gentleness, considering yourself lest you also be tempted. [NKJV]
	
	Dear brothers and sisters, if another Christian is overcome by some sin, you who are godly should gently and humbly **help that person back onto the right path**. And be careful not to fall into the same temptation yourself. [NLT]
	
	Ἀδελφοί, ἐὰν καὶ προληφθῇ ἄνθρωπος ἔν τινι παραπτώματι, ὑμεῖς οἱ πνευματικοὶ **καταρτίζετε** τὸν τοιοῦτον ἐν πνεύματι πραΰτητος, σκοπῶν σεαυτόν, μὴ καὶ σὺ πειρασθῇς. [GNS]
	
	Ἀδελφοί, ἐὰν καὶ προλημφθῇ ἄνθρωπος ἔν τινι παραπτώματι, ὑμεῖς οἱ πνευματικοὶ **καταρτίζετε** τὸν τοιοῦτον ἐν πνεύματι πραΰτητος, σκοπῶν σεαυτόν μὴ καὶ σὺ πειρασθῇς. [GNT]
		To restore; to be unruly; help that person back onto the right path.
		
		Practical Application
		When a brother is caught in sin and slips and falls, what should be done? Scripture is clear: Christian brothers are to restore him. The word "restore" (*katartizete*) is a word that is used for setting a broken arm or leg or for mending nets or for cutting some growth out of a body (William Barclay. *The Letters to the Galatians and Ephesians*, p.58). Believers are to help the brother:
		
		• set him right
		• restore him
		• help cut the sin out
		• mend him
		• lead him back
		
		However, there is a right way and a wrong way to help the fallen brother. This is the point that is being stressed and that is desperately needed by believers and the church. All believers are mere men of like passions with all other men, and there are always some being overtaken by sin. This, of course, means that we need to constantly stay alert and available to fallen brothers.

#3286
Restore
 	
Perfect–KJV
Perfect–NASB
Restore–NIV
Perfect–NKJV
Restore–NLT
 	
POSB REFERENCE
(1 Pt.5:10)
Note 2, point 1
	καταρτίσει = *katartisei*
	Pronunciation: [kat-ar-tis'-ee]
	Parsing (part of speech): verb
	    Mood—indicative
	    Tense—future
	    Voice—active
	    Person—3rd person
	    Number—singular
	    Stem or root—from κατάρτιζω
	Concordance References:
	  ⇒ Strong's #2675 katartizō
	  ⇒ NIV #2936 katartizō
	  ⇒ NASB #2675 katartizō
	
	1 Peter 5:10
	But the God of all grace, who hath called us unto his eternal glory by Christ Jesus, after that ye have suffered a while, make you **perfect**, stablish, strengthen, settle you. [KJV]
	
	And after you have suffered for a little while, the God of all grace, who called you to His eternal glory in Christ, will Himself **perfect**, confirm, strengthen and establish
		To restore; to perfect; to make complete; to equip fully; to fully train; to make fit or join together.
		
		Practical Application
		How does God keep and preserve the believer? The temptations and trials of life are severe and fierce. How does God make sure the believer makes it to heaven and its eternal glory? God does four wonderful things for the believer. Note: in the Greek the emphasis is upon God Himself doing these things. God Himself becomes actively involved in taking care of the believer, in keeping and preserving and taking the believer to heaven and its glory.
		
		God Himself uses the believer's suffering to perfect the believer. The Greek authority Marvin Vincent says:
		
		⇒ "The radical notion of the verb is...*adjustment*—the putting of all the parts into

ENGLISH WORD	GREEK WORD AND VERSE	THE WORD MEANS...
	you. [NASB] And the God of all grace, who called you to his eternal glory in Christ, after you have suffered a little while, will himself **restore** you and make you strong, firm and steadfast. [NIV] But may the God of all grace, who called us to His eternal glory by Christ Jesus, after you have suffered a while, **perfect**, establish, strengthen, and settle *you.* [NKJV] In his kindness God called you to his eternal glory by means of Jesus Christ. After you have suffered a little while, he will **restore**, support, and strengthen you, and he will place you on a firm foundation. [NLT] ὁ δὲ Θεὸς πάσης χάριτος, ὁ καλέσας ὑμᾶς εἰς τὴν αἰώνιον αὐτοῦ δόξαν ἐν Χριστῷ Ἰησοῦ, ὀλίγον παθόντας αὐτὸς **καταρτίσει** ὑμᾶς, στηρίξει, σθενώσαι, θεμελιώσαι. [GNS] Ὁ δὲ θεὸς πάσης χάριτος, ὁ καλέσας ὑμᾶς εἰς τὴν αἰώνιον αὐτοῦ δόξαν ἐν Χριστῷ [Ἰησοῦ], ὀλίγον παθόντας αὐτὸς **καταρτίσει**, στηρίξει, σθενώσει, θεμελιώσει. [GNT]	right relation and connection. We find it used.... - "of mending the nets (Matthew 4:21). - "of restoring an erring brother (Galatians 6:1) - "of framing the body and the worlds (Hebrews 10:5; Hebrews 11:3). - "of the union of members in the church (1 Cor. 1:10; 2 Cor. 13:11). "Out of this comes the general sense of *perfecting* (Matthew 21:16; Luke 6:40; 1 Thes. 3:10)" (*Word Studies in the New Testament*, Vol.1, p.671). (Note: the paragraph has been outlined for simplicity). God takes all the displaced joints and broken limbs of our lives and uses them to adjust our character. He uses all the trials and temptations, difficulties and persecutions—all the sufferings of life—and makes us more and more like Christ. If we are truly called of God and if we truly love God, then God will take all that ever happens to us and work it out for good. He will perfect us, fit all the parts of life together and lead us to glory. This is the glorious grace and call of God to eternal glory.

#3287
Restore–
Restoration
 	
Restitution–KJV
Restoration–NASB
Restore–NIV
Restoration–NKJV
Restoration–NLT
 	
POSB
REFERENCE
(Acts 3:21)
Deeper Study #3
	ἀποκαταστάσεως = *apokatastaseōs*
	Pronunciation: [ap-ok-at-as'-tas-eh-os]
	Parsing (part of speech): noun
	    Case—genitive
	    Gender—feminine
	    Number—singular
	    Stem or root—from *ἀποκατάστασις, εως*
	Concordance References:
	⇒ Strong's #605 apokatastasis
	⇒ NIV #640 apokatastasis
	⇒ NASB #605 apokatastasis
	
	Acts 3:21
	Whom the heaven must receive until the times of **restitution** of all things, which God hath spoken by the mouth of all his holy prophets since the world began. [KJV]
	
	Whom heaven must receive until *the* period of **restoration** of all things about which God spoke by the mouth of His holy prophets from ancient time. [NASB]
	
	He must remain in heaven until the time comes for God to **restore** everything, as he promised long ago through his holy prophets. [NIV]
	
	Whom heaven must receive until the times of **restoration** of all things, which God has spoken by the mouth of all His holy prophets since the world began. [NKJV]
	
	For he must remain in heaven until the time for the final **restoration** of all things, as God promised long ago through his prophets. [NLT]
	
	ὃν δεῖ οὐρανὸν μὲν δέξασθαι ἄχρι χρόνων **ἀποκαταστάσεως** πάντων, ὧν ἐλάλησεν ὁ Θεὸς διὰ στόματος πάντων ἁγίων αὐτοῦ προφητῶν ἀπ' αἰῶνος. [GNS]
	
	ὃν δεῖ οὐρανὸν μὲν δέξασθαι ἄχρι χρόνων **ἀποκαταστάσεως** πάντων ὧν ἐλάλησεν ὁ θεὸς διὰ στόματος τῶν ἁγίων ἀπ' αἰῶνος αὐτοῦ προφητῶν. [GNT]
		To restore; restitution, restoration, compensation.
		
		Practical Application
		It means to set in order again; to bring back to a former condition or state of being; to restore; to recreate or remake or renew all over again. (See POSB note, Regeneration—Matthew 19:28 for more discussion.)

#3288
Restored To
Friendship
 	
Reconciled–KJV
Reconciled–NASB
	κατηλλάγημεν = *katēllagēmen*
	Pronunciation: [kat-ayl-lahg'-ay-mehn]
	Parsing (part of speech): verb
	    Mood—indicative
	    Tense—aorist
	    Voice—passive
	    Person—1st person
		To reconcile; to restore to friendship; to change; to change thoroughly; to exchange; to change from enmity to friendship; to bring together, restore.

ENGLISH WORD	GREEK WORD AND VERSE	THE WORD MEANS...
Reconciled–NIV Reconciled–NKJV **Restored to friendship–NLT** **POSB REFERENCE** (Romans 5:10) *Deeper Study #1*	Number—plural Stem or root—from καταλλάσσω Concordance References: ⇒ Strong's #2644 katallassö ⇒ NIV #2904 katallassö ⇒ NASB #2644 katallassö **Romans 5:10** For if, when we were enemies, we were **reconciled** to God by the death of his Son, much more, being reconciled, we shall be saved by his life. [KJV] For if while we were enemies, we were **reconciled** to God through the death of His Son, much more, having been reconciled, we shall be saved by His life. [NASB] For if, when we were God's enemies, we were **reconciled** to him through the death of his Son, how much more, having been reconciled, shall we be saved through his life! [NIV] For if when we were enemies we were **reconciled** to God through the death of His Son, much more, having been reconciled, we shall be saved by His life. [NKJV] For since we were **restored to friendship** with God by the death of his Son while we were still his enemies, we will certainly be delivered from eternal punishment by his life. [NLT] εἰ γὰρ ἐχθροὶ ὄντες **κατηλλάγημεν** τῷ Θεῷ διὰ τοῦ θανάτου τοῦ υἱοῦ αὐτοῦ, πολλῷ μᾶλλον καταλλαγέντες σωθησόμεθα ἐν τῇ ζωῇ αὐτοῦ· [GNS] εἰ γὰρ ἐχθροὶ ὄντες **κατηλλάγημεν** τῷ θεῷ διὰ τοῦ θανάτου τοῦ υἱοῦ αὐτοῦ, πολλῷ μᾶλλον καταλλαγέντες σωθησόμεθα ἐν τῇ ζωῇ αὐτοῦ· [GNT]	**Practical Application** The idea is that two persons who should have been together all along are brought together; two persons who had something between them are restored and reunited.
#3289 **Restrained** Straitened–KJV **Restrained–NASB** Withholding–NIV Restricted–NKJV Withheld–NLT **POSB REFERENCE** (2 Cor.6:11-13; esp. v.12) Note 1	στενοχωρεῖσθε = *stenochöreisthe* Pronunciation: [sten-okh-o-reh'-ees-the] Parsing (part of speech): verb Mood—indicative Tense—present Voice—passive Person—2nd person Number—plural Stem or root—from στενοχωρέομαι Concordance References: ⇒ Strong's #4729 stenochöreö ⇒ NIV #5102 stenochöreö ⇒ NASB #4729 stenochöreö **2 Cor. 6:12** Ye are not **straitened** in us, but ye are **straitened** in your own bowels. [KJV] You are not **restrained** by us, but you are **restrained** in your own affections. [NASB] We are not **withholding** our affection from you, but you are **withholding** yours from us. [NIV] You are not **restricted** by us, but you are **restricted** by your own affections. [NKJV] If there is a problem between us, it is not because of a lack of love on our part, but because you have **withheld** your love from us. [NLT] οὐ **στενοχωρεῖσθε** ἐν ἡμῖν, **στενοχωρεῖσθε** δὲ ἐν τοῖς σπλάγχνοις ὑμῶν. [GNS] οὐ **στενοχωρεῖ**sqe ἐν ἡμῖν, **στενοχωρεῖσθε** δὲ ἐν τοῖς σπλάγχνοις ὑμῶν· [GNT]	To withhold; to be restrained; to be restricted; to lack room; to be held in check; to be pressed or distressed; to be in anguish or straits. **Practical Application** Paul says there was no lack of room in his heart for the church; no restraint against the Corinthians. He held nothing against them. His heart was wide open to receive them.
#3290 **Restricted** Straitened–KJV Restrained–NASB Withholding–NIV **Restricted–NKJV** Withheld–NLT	στενοχωρεῖσθε = *stenochöreisthe* Pronunciation: [sten-okh-o-reh'-ees-the] Parsing (part of speech): verb Mood—indicative Tense—present Voice—passive Person—2nd person Number—plural Stem or root—from στενοχωρέομαι	To withhold; to be restrained; to be restricted; to lack room; to be held in check; to be pressed or distressed; to be in anguish or straits. **Practical Application** Paul says there was no lack of room in his heart for the church; no restriction against the Corinthians. He held nothing against them. His heart was wide open to receive them.

ENGLISH WORD	GREEK WORD AND VERSE	THE WORD MEANS...
POSB REFERENCE (2 Cor.6:11-13; esp. v.12) Note 1	Concordance References: ⇒ Strong's #4729 stenochōreō ⇒ NIV #5102 stenochōreō ⇒ NASB #4729 stenochōreō **2 Cor. 6:12** Ye are not **straitened** in us, but ye are **straitened** in your own bowels. [KJV] You are not **restrained** by us, but you are **restrained** in your own affections. [NASB] We are not **withholding** our affection from you, but you are **withholding** yours from us. [NIV] You are not **restricted** by us, but you are **restricted** by your own affections. [NKJV] If there is a problem between us, it is not because of a lack of love on our part, but because you have **withheld** your love from us. [NLT] οὐ **στενοχωρεῖσθε** ἐν ἡμῖν, **στενοχωρεῖσθε** δὲ ἐν τοῖς σπλάγχνοις ὑμῶν. [GNS] οὐ **στενοχωρεῖ**sqe ἐν ἡμῖν, **στενοχωρεῖσθε** δὲ ἐν τοῖς σπλάγχνοις ὑμῶν· [GNT]	

#3291
Return
 	
Received up–KJV
Ascension–NASB
Taken up–NIV
Received up–NKJV
Return–NLT
 	
POSB REFERENCE (Lk.9:51) *Deeper Study* #1
	ἀναλήμψεως = analēmpseōs
	Pronunciation: [an-al'-aimp-se-os]
	Parsing (part of speech): noun
	  Case—genitive
	  Gender—feminine
	  Number—singular
	  Stem or root—from ἀνάλημψις, εως
	Concordance References:
	⇒ Strong's #354 analepsis
	⇒ NIV #378 analēmpsis
	⇒ NASB #354 analēmpsis
	
	Luke 9:51
	And it came to pass, when the time was come that he should be **received up**, he stedfastly set his face to go to Jerusalem, [KJV]
	And it came about, when the days were approaching for His **ascension**, that He resolutely set His face to go to Jerusalem; [NASB]
	As the time approached for him to be **taken up** to heaven, Jesus resolutely set out for Jerusalem. [NIV]
	Now it came to pass, when the time had come for Him to be **received up**, that He steadfastly set His face to go to Jerusalem, [NKJV]
	As the time drew near for his **return** to heaven, Jesus resolutely set out for Jerusalem. [NLT]
	Ἐγένετο δὲ ἐν τῷ συμπληροῦσθαι τὰς ἡμέρας τῆς **ἀναλήμψεως** αὐτοῦ, καὶ αὐτὸς τὸ πρόσωπον αὐτοῦ ἐστήριξε τοῦ πορεύεσθαι εἰς ‘ιερουσαλήμ, [GNS]
	Ἐγένετο δὲ ἐν τῷ συμπληροῦσθαι τὰς ἡμέρας τῆς **ἀναλήμψεως** αὐτοῦ καὶ αὐτὸς τὸ πρόσωπον ἐστήρισεν τοῦ πορεύεσθαι εἰς Ἰερουσαλήμ. [GNT]
		Taken up, ascension, received up, returned.
		
		Practical Application
		This word refers to the ascension of Christ (cp. *analambano*, Acts 1:2, 11, 22; 1 Tim. 3:16). Salvation was to be secured by the ascension of Christ. How? The Ascended Lord means at least four things.
		1. It means the *Risen Lord*. The ascension means that Christ arose from the dead. If He had remained in the grave, He would still be there in the form of dust. He could not have ascended. If He was to be "received up" He had to be raised up—quickened—made alive—taken up. No one can be taken up without first being raised up. Therefore, to speak of the ascension is to mean that Christ is risen. Death is conquered; man can now be saved from death.
		2. It means the *Advocate* or *Representative* Lord. On earth, Christ lived a perfect life; He was without sin (2 Cor. 5:21; Hebrews 4:15; 1 Peter 1:19; 1 Peter 2:22; John 8:46). He was "obedient unto death, even the death of the cross. Wherefore God also hath highly exalted Him" (Phil. 2:8-9). He is "sitting on the right hand of God (Col. 3:1). He is "Jesus Christ the righteous"; therefore, He is our "advocate with the Father" (1 John 2:1). He is able to represent us before God because He has lived upon earth and secured a perfect righteousness. He is the Ideal Man (see note—Matthew 5:17-18), our advocate, the One who is qualified to plead our case before God and see to it that we are saved.
		3. It means the *Priestly* or *Intercessory Lord*. Every man suffers while on earth: suffers pain, trial, need, want, temptation, loss, illness, and eventually death. We are incapable of even knowing how to pray as we ought in order to secure the help we need. But Christ knows and understands. He has been to earth and suffered just as we suffer. Therefore, He knows how to intercede for us and how to deliver us.
		4. It means the *Exalted Lord*. Christ has ascended to be exalted, to rule and reign over the

ENGLISH WORD	GREEK WORD AND VERSE	THE WORD MEANS...
POSB REFERENCE (Jn.14:21) *Deeper Study #3*	Concordance References: ⇒ Strong's #1718 emphanizo ⇒ NIV #1872 emphanizo ⇒ NASB #1718 emphanizo **John 14:21** He that hath my commandments, and keepeth them, he it is that loveth me: and he that loveth me shall be loved of my Father, and I will love him, and will **manifest** myself to him. [KJV] "He who has My commandments and keeps them, he it is who loves Me; and he who loves Me shall be loved by My Father, and I will love him, and will **disclose** Myself to him." [NASB] Whoever has my commands and obeys them, he is the one who loves me. He who loves me will be loved by my Father, and I too will love him and **show** myself to him." [NIV] He who has My commandments and keeps them, it is he who loves Me. And he who loves Me will be loved by My Father, and I will love him and **manifest** Myself to him." [NKJV] Those who obey my commandments are the ones who love me. And because they love me, my Father will love them, and I will love them. And I will **reveal** myself to each one of them." [NLT] ὁ ἔχων τὰς ἐντολάς μου καὶ τηρῶν αὐτάς, ἐκεῖνός ἐστιν ὁ ἀγαπῶν με· ὁ δὲ ἀγαπῶν με, ἀγαπηθήσεται ὑπὸ τοῦ πατρός μου· καὶ ἐγὼ ἀγαπήσω αὐτόν, καὶ **ἐμφανίσω** αὐτῷ ἐμαυτόν. [GNS] ὁ ἔχων τὰς ἐντολάς μου καὶ τηρῶν αὐτὰς ἐκεῖνός ἐστιν ὁ ἀγαπῶν με· ὁ δὲ ἀγαπῶν με ἀγαπηθήσεται ὑπὸ τοῦ πατρός μου, κἀγὼ ἀγαπήσω αὐτὸν καὶ **ἐμφανίσω** αὐτῷ ἐμαυτόν. [GNT]	is something that cannot be discovered by man's reason or wisdom. It is a mystery that is hidden from man and beyond his grasp. Here in John 14:21-22, it means that Jesus' presence is revealed (brought to light), illuminated, manifested, quickened in the life of the believer. It means that He manifests Himself to His disciples in a very special way. He discloses His person, His nature, His goodness. He illuminates Himself within their hearts and lives. He gives a very special consciousness within their souls. (See POSB note—John 14:21-22; POSB *Deeper Study #1*—Acts 2:1-4.)

#3296 Revealed
 	
Revealed–KJV
Revealed–NASB
Revealed–NIV
Revealed–NKJV
Appears–NLT
 	
POSB REFERENCE (2 Thes.1:7-8; esp. v.7) Note 2, point 1
	ἀποκαλύψει = apokalupsei
	Pronunciation: [ap-ok-al'-oop-seh-ee]
	Parsing (part of speech): noun
	    Case—dative
	    Gender—feminine
	    Number—singular
	    Stem or root—from ἀποκάλυψις, εως
	Concordance References:
	⇒ Strong's #602 apokalupsis
	⇒ NIV #637 apokalupsis
	⇒ NASB #602 apokalupsis
	
	2 Thes. 1:7
	And to you who are troubled rest with us, when the Lord Jesus shall be **revealed** from heaven with his mighty angels, [KJV]
	And to give relief to you who are afflicted and to us as well when the Lord Jesus shall be **revealed** from heaven with His mighty angels in flaming fire, [NASB]
	And give relief to you who are troubled, and to us as well. This will happen when the Lord Jesus is **revealed** from heaven in blazing fire with his powerful angels. [NIV]
	And to *give* you who are troubled rest with us when the Lord Jesus is **revealed** from heaven with His mighty angels, [NKJV]
	And God will provide rest for you who are being persecuted and also for us when the Lord Jesus **appears** from heaven. He will come with his mighty angels, [NLT]
	καὶ ὑμῖν τοῖς θλιβομένοις ἄνεσιν μεθ' ἡμῶν, ἐν τῇ **ἀποκαλύψει** τοῦ Κυρίου Ἰησοῦ ἀπ' οὐρανοῦ μετ' ἀγγέλων δυνάμεως αὐτοῦ, [GNS]
	καὶ ὑμῖν τοῖς θλιβομένοις ἄνεσιν μεθ' ἡμῶν, ἐν τῇ **ἀποκαλύψει** τοῦ κυρίου Ἰησοῦ ἀπ' οὐρανοῦ μετ' ἀγγέλων δυνάμεως αὐτοῦ [GNT]
		To reveal, revelation; to appear; to be unveiled and uncovered.
		
		Practical Application
		Jesus' return in judgment shall be a spectacular appearance from heaven. The day is coming when Jesus Christ shall rent the heavens and return to earth in judgment. As Matthew Henry says, "He will come in all the pomp and power of the upper world" (*Matthew Henry's Commentary*, Vol.6, p.794). He will be revealed as the Supreme Majesty and Judge of the world.

ENGLISH WORD	GREEK WORD AND VERSE	THE WORD MEANS...

#3297
Revelation

Revelation–KJV
Revelation–NASB
Revelation–NIV
Revelation–NKJV
Understanding–NLT

**POSB
REFERENCE**
(Eph.1:17-18; esp.
v.17)
Note 2, point 2

ἀποκαλύψεως = *apokalupseōs*
Pronunciation: [ap-ok-al'-oop-seh-os]
Parsing (part of speech): noun
    Case—genitive
    Gender—feminine
    Number—singular
    Stem or root—from ἀποκάλυψις, εως
Concordance References:
  ⇒ Strong's #602 apokalupsis
  ⇒ NIV #637 apokalupsis
  ⇒ NASB #602 apokalupsis

Ephes. 1:17

That the God of our Lord Jesus Christ, the Father of glory, may give unto you the spirit of wisdom and **revelation** in the knowledge of him: [KJV]

That the God of our Lord Jesus Christ, the Father of glory, may give to you a spirit of wisdom and of **revelation** in the knowledge of Him. [NASB]

I keep asking that the God of our Lord Jesus Christ, the glorious Father, may give you the Spirit of wisdom and **revelation**, so that you may know him better. [NIV]

That the God of our Lord Jesus Christ, the Father of glory, may give to you the spirit of wisdom and **revelation** in the knowledge of Him, [NKJV]

Asking God, the glorious Father of our Lord Jesus Christ, to give you spiritual wisdom and **understanding**, so that you might grow in your knowledge of God. [NLT]

ἵνα ὁ Θεὸς τοῦ Κυρίου ἡμῶν Ἰησοῦ Χριστοῦ, ὁ πατὴρ τῆς δόξης, δώῃ ὑμῖν πνεῦμα σοφίας καὶ ἀποκαλύψεως, ἐν ἐπιγνώσει αὐτοῦ· [GNS]

ἵνα ὁ θεὸς τοῦ κυρίου ἡμῶν Ἰησοῦ Χριστοῦ, ὁ πατὴρ τῆς δόξης, δώῃ ὑμῖν πνεῦμα σοφίας καὶ ἀποκαλύψεως ἐν ἐπιγνώσει αὐτοῦ, [GNT]

Revelation, understanding. It means to manifest; to reveal; to unveil; to uncover; to open.

Practical Application

It is the work of the Holy Spirit to reveal the knowledge of God to Christians. In fact, it is the work of the Holy Spirit to reveal the meaning of all truth to the Christian (John 14:26; John 16:12-15). This is clearly seen in 1 Cor. 1:9-16 where the wisdom of the world is contrasted with the wisdom of God. A spiritual Christian sees (through the Spirit revealing to him) the meaning behind world events as well as day-to-day experiences. He understands who and what is behind the events of history and human experience. Therefore, he gains a growing knowledge of God day-by-day.

#3298
Revelation

Revelation–KJV
Revelation–NASB
Revelation–NIV
Revelation–NKJV
Revelation–NLT

**POSB
REFERENCE**
(Rev.1:1-3; esp. v.1)
Introduction

Ἀποκάλυψις = *Apokalupsis*
Pronunciation: [ap-ok-al'-oop-sis]
Parsing (part of speech): noun
    Case—nominative
    Gender—feminine
    Number—singular
    Stem or root—from ἀποκάλυψις, εως
Concordance References:
  ⇒ Strong's #602 apokalupsis
  ⇒ NIV #637 apokalupsis
  ⇒ NASB #602 apokalupsis

Rev. 1:1

The **Revelation** of Jesus Christ, which God gave unto him, to show unto his servants things which must shortly come to pass; and he sent and signified it by his angel unto his servant John: [KJV]

The **Revelation** of Jesus Christ, which God gave Him to show to His bond-servants, the things which must shortly take place; and He sent and communicated it by His angel to His bond-servant John, [NASB]

The **revelation** of Jesus Christ, which God gave him to show his servants what must soon take place. He made it known by sending his angel to his servant John, [NIV]

The **Revelation** of Jesus Christ, which God gave Him to show His servants—things which must shortly take place. And He sent and signified *it* by His angel to His servant John, [NKJV]

This is a **revelation** from Jesus Christ, which God gave him concerning the events that will happen soon. An angel was sent to God's servant John so that John could share the revelation with God's other servants. [NLT]

Ἀποκάλυψις Ἰησοῦ Χριστοῦ, ἣν ἔδωκεν αὐτῷ ὁ Θεός, δεῖξαι τοῖς δούλοις αὐτοῦ, ἃ δεῖ γενέσθαι ἐν τάχει, καὶ ἐσήμανεν ἀποστείλας διὰ τοῦ ἀγγέλου αὐτοῦ τῷ δούλῳ αὐτοῦ Ἰωάννῃ, [GNS]

Revelation; to uncover and unveil. It means to pull back a covering or a veil that is hiding something. It means to make known something; to reveal something that a person could not find out for himself. It is a revelation of truth that man could never discover for himself.

Practical Application

This is what the book of Revelation is: it is the great revelation of Jesus Christ to His servants or followers. This means a most wonderful fact: it means that there are some things that God wants us to know, some things that we could never know if we were left on our own. It means that God cares about us, that He loves us enough to reveal some things to us. And note: God cares so much for us that He has revealed a whole book of events to us. What are these events? They are events or truths that lie out in the future, that concern the end of the world.

ENGLISH WORD	GREEK WORD AND VERSE	THE WORD MEANS...
	drinking parties and abominable idolatries. [NASB] For you have spent enough time in the past doing what pagans choose to do—living in debauchery, lust, drunkenness, **orgies**, carousing and detestable idolatry. [NIV] For we have spent enough of our past lifetime in doing the will of the Gentiles—when we walked in lewdness, lusts, drunkenness, **revelries**, drinking parties, and abominable idolatries. [NKJV] You have had enough in the past of the evil things that godless people enjoy—their immorality and lust, their **feasting** and drunkenness and wild parties, and their terrible worship of idols. [NLT] ἀρκετὸς γὰρ ἡμῖν ὁ παρεληλυθὼς χρόνος τὸ βίου τὸ θέλημα τῶν ἐθνῶν κατεργάσασθαι, πεπορευμένους ἐν ἀσελγείαις, ἐπιθυμίαις, οἰνοφλυγίαις, **κώμοις**, πότοις, καὶ ἀθεμίτοις εἰδωλολατρείαις· [GNS] ἀρκετὸς γὰρ ὁ παρεληλυθὼς χρόνος τὸ βούλημα τῶν ἐθνῶν κατειργάσθαι πεπορευμένους ἐν ἀσελγείαις, ἐπιθυμίαις, οἰνοφλυγίαις, **κώμοις**, πότοις καὶ ἀθεμίτοις εἰδωλολατρίαις. [GNT]	

#3303
Reverence
 	
Gravity–KJV
Dignity–NASB
Respect–NIV
Reverence–NKJV
Respect–NLT
 	
**POSB
REFERENCE**
(1 Tim.3:4-5; esp. v.4)
Note 3
	σεμνότητος = semnotētos
	Pronunciation: [sem-no-tay-tos]
	Parsing (part of speech): noun
	    Case—genitive
	    Gender—feminine
	    Number—singular
	    Stem or root—from σεμνότης, ητος
	Concordance References:
	  ⇒ Strong's #4587 semnotēs
	  ⇒ NIV #4949 semnotēs
	  ⇒ NASB #4587 semnotēs
	
	1 Tim. 3:4
	One that ruleth well his own house, having his children in subjection with all **gravity**; [KJV]
	
	He must be one who manages his own household well, keeping his children under control with all **dignity** [NASB]
	
	He must manage his own family well and see that his children obey him with proper **respect**. [NIV]
	
	One who rules his own house well, having *his* children in submission with all **reverence** [NKJV]
	
	He must manage his own family well, with children who **respect** and obey him. [NLT]
	
	τοῦ ἰδίου οἴκου καλῶς προϊστάμενον, τέκνα ἔχοντα ἐν ὑποταγῇ μετὰ πάσης **σεμνότητος**· [GNS]
	
	τοῦ ἰδίου οἴκου καλῶς προϊστάμενον, τέκνα ἔχοντα ἐν ὑποταγῇ, μετὰ πάσης **σεμνότητος** [GNT]
		Respect, gravity, dignity, reverence, respectability, seriousness.
		
		Practical Application
		The minister must rule his home with dignity, respect, and love. As the Amplified New Testament says: "With true dignity, commanding their respect in every way and keeping them respectful."
		
		As Scripture says, "for if a man does not know how to rule his own house, how will he take care of the church of God?; (1 Tim. 3:5) [NKJV].

#3304
Reverence
 	
Reverence–KJV
Reverence–NASB
Reverence–NIV
Reverence–NKJV
Holy fear–NLT
 	
**POSB
REFERENCE**
(Heb.12:28-29; esp. v.28)
Note 3, point 2
	εὐλαβείας = eulabeias
	Pronunciation: [yoo-lab'-i-ahs]
	Parsing (part of speech): noun
	    Case—genitive
	    Gender—feminine
	    Number—singular
	    Stem or root—from εὐλάβεια, ας
	Concordance References:
	  ⇒ Strong's #2124 eulabeia
	  ⇒ NIV #2325 eulabeia
	  ⇒ NASB #2124 eulabeia
	
	Hebrews 12:28
	Wherefore we receiving a kingdom which cannot be moved, let us have grace, whereby we may serve God acceptably with **reverence** and godly fear: [KJV]
	
	Therefore, since we receive a kingdom which cannot be shaken, let us show gratitude, by which we may offer to God an acceptable service with **reverence** and awe; [NASB]
	
	Therefore, since we are receiving a kingdom that cannot be shaken, let us be thankful, and so worship God acceptably with **reverence** and awe, [NIV]
		Reverence, holy fear. The word "reverence" means with caution, carefully, with discretion and circumspection (Kenneth Wuest. *Hebrews*, Vol. 2, p.231).
		
		Practical Application
		A person must do exactly what this verse says: *serve God acceptably* with reverence and godly fear. God must be feared, for He is Lord. A person must serve God in an acceptable way.

ENGLISH WORD	GREEK WORD AND VERSE	THE WORD MEANS...
	Therefore, since we are receiving a kingdom which cannot be shaken, let us have grace, by which we may serve God acceptably with **reverence** and godly fear. [NKJV] Since we are receiving a kingdom that cannot be destroyed, let us be thankful and please God by worshiping him with **holy fear** and awe. [NLT] διὸ βασιλείαν ἀσάλευτον παραλαμβάνοντες, ἔχωμεν χάριν δι' ἧς λατρεύωμεν εὐαρέστως τῷ Θεῷ μετὰ αἰδοῦς καὶ **εὐλαβείας**· [GNS] Διὸ βασιλείαν ἀσάλευτον παραλαμβάνοντες ἔχωμεν χάριν, δι' ἧς λατρεύωμεν εὐαρέστως τῷ θεῷ μετὰ **εὐλαβείας** καὶ δέους· [GNT]	

#3305
Reverence
 	
Fear–KJV
Reverence–NASB
Holy fear–NIV
Godly fear–NKJV
Obeyed–NLT
 	
**POSB
REFERENCE**
(Heb.11:7)
Note 1, point 1
	εὐλαβηθείς = eulabētheis
	Pronunciation: [yoo-lab-ay'-theh-ees]
	Parsing (part of speech): verb
	    Mood—participle
	    Tense—aorist
	    Voice—passive deponent
	    Case—nominative
	    Gender—masculine
	    Number—singular
	    Stem or root—from **εὐλαβέομαι**
	Concordance References:
	⇒ Strong's #2125 eulabeomai
	⇒ NIV #2326 eulabeomai
	⇒ NASB #2125 eulabeomai
	
	Hebrews 11:7
	By faith Noah, being warned of God of things not seen as yet, moved with **fear**, prepared an ark to the saving of his house; by the which he condemned the world, and became heir of the righteousness which is by faith. [KJV]
	
	By faith Noah, being warned by God about things not yet seen, in **reverence** prepared an ark for the salvation of his household, by which he condemned the world, and became an heir of the righteousness which is according to faith. [NASB]
	
	By faith Noah, when warned about things not yet seen, in **holy fear** built an ark to save his family. By his faith he condemned the world and became heir of the righteousness that comes by faith. [NIV]
	
	By faith Noah, being divinely warned of things not yet seen, moved with **godly fear**, prepared an ark for the saving of his household, by which he condemned the world and became heir of the righteousness which is according to faith. [NKJV]
	
	It was by faith that Noah built an ark to save his family from the flood. He **obeyed** God, who warned him about something that had never happened before. By his faith he condemned the rest of the world and was made right in God's sight. [NLT]
	
	Πίστει χρηματισθεὶς Νῶε περὶ τῶν μηδέπω βλεπομένων, **εὐλαβηθείς**, κατεσκεύασε κιβωτὸν εἰς σωτηρίαν τοῦ οἴκου αὐτοῦ· δι' ἧς κατέκρινε τὸν κόσμον, καὶ τῆς κατὰ πίστιν δικαιοσύνης ἐγένετο κληρονόμος. [GNS]
	
	Πίστει χρηματισθεὶς Νῶε περὶ τῶν μηδέπω βλεπομένων, **εὐλαβηθείς** κατεσκεύασεν κιβωτὸν εἰς σωτηρίαν τοῦ οἴκου αὐτοῦ δι' ἧς κατέκρινεν τὸν κόσμον, καὶ τῆς κατὰ πίστιν δικαιοσύνης ἐγένετο κληρονόμος. [GNT]
		Fear, holy fear; to reverence; to obey; to be moved with fear. The word "reverence" (*eulabētheis*) means with godly fear (A.T. Robertson. *Word Pictures in the New Testament*, Vol. 5, p.421). It has the idea of...
		• reverence.
		• standing in awe of God and His warning.
		• taking heed lest one fall under God's judgment.
		• diligently taking God at His Word.
		• immediately acting upon what God says.
		
		Practical Application
		There was a time in world history when the earth had become so wicked that it was filled with corruption and violence. It was so corrupt that every imagination of man's heart was corrupt and evil. Man had reached the point of no return; he would never repent and return to God. God was left with no choice: the earth had to be destroyed. But there was one man on earth who was godly—Noah. Noah worshipped and honored God in his life. Therefore, God warned Noah of the coming judgment upon the earth.
		⇒ God told Noah to prepare an ark and the ark would save him, his family, and two of every animal.
		⇒ God also told Noah to warn the world of coming judgment.
		
		Noah believed God's warning of coming judgment, and he began to build the ark with a godly fear and reverence, knowing that what God said would come true. God's judgment would fall upon the earth; Noah believed it and knew it by faith.

#3306
Reverent
 	
Grave–KJV
Dignity–NASB
Worthy of respect–NIV
Reverent–NKJV
Respected–NLT
	σεμνούς = semnous
	Pronunciation: [sem-noos']
	Parsing (part of speech): adjective
	    Case—accusative
	    Gender—masculine
	    Number—plural
	    Stem or root—from **σεμνός**, ή, όν
	Concordance References:
	⇒ Strong's #4586 semnos
		Worthy of respect, grave, dignity, highly respected, serious, honorable, worthy, revered, noble.
		
		Practical Application
		It is being serious-minded, the very opposite...

ENGLISH WORD	GREEK WORD AND VERSE	THE WORD MEANS...

POSB REFERENCE
(1 Tim.3:8)
Note 1, point 1

See also POSB REF:
(1 Tim.3:11-12)
Note 3
(Tit.2:2)
Note 2

⇒ NIV #4948 semnos
⇒ NASB #4586 semnos

1 Tim. 3:8
Likewise must the deacons be **grave**, not double-tongued, not given to much wine, not greedy of filthy lucre; [KJV]

Deacons likewise must be men of **dignity**, not double-tongued, or addicted to much wine or fond of sordid gain, [NASB]

Deacons, likewise, are to be men **worthy of respect**, sincere, not indulging in much wine, and not pursuing dishonest gain. [NIV]

Likewise deacons must be **reverent**, not double-tongued, not given to much wine, not greedy for money, [NKJV]

In the same way, deacons must be people who are **respected** and have integrity. They must not be heavy drinkers and must not be greedy for money. [NLT]

διακόνους ὡσαύτως **σεμνούς**, μὴ διλόγους, μὴ οἴνῳ πολλῷ προσέχοντας, μὴ αἰσχροκερδεῖς, [GNS]

Διακόνους ὡσαύτως **σεμνούς**, μὴ διλόγους, μὴ οἴνῳ πολλῷ προσέχοντας, μὴ αἰσχροκερδεῖς, [GNT]

- of being flippant.
- of dishonoring oneself.
- of being shallow by being over-talkative.
- of having little respect because one is not grave or serious enough.
- of having a surface religion only.

However, this does not mean that the deacon is to walk around with a long face, never smiling, joking, or having fun. It simply means that he is to be serious-minded and committed to Christ and to the mission of the church: the mission of reaching the lost and meeting the desperate needs of the world.

#3307
Reverent

Holiness–KJV
Reverent–NASB
Reverent–NIV
Reverent–NKJV
Appropriate–NLT

POSB REFERENCE
(Tit.2:3)
Note 3, point 1

ἱεροπρεπεῖς = *hieroprepeis*
Pronunciation: [hee-er-op-rep-ice']
Parsing (part of speech): adjective
  Case—accusative
  Gender—feminine
  Number—plural
  Stem or root—from ἱεροπρεπής, ές
Concordance References:
⇒ Strong's #2412 hieroprepēs
⇒ NIV #2640 hieroprepēs
⇒ NASB #2412 hieroprepēs

Titus 2:3
The aged women likewise, that they be in behaviour as becometh **holiness**, not false accusers, not given to much wine, teachers of good things; [KJV]

Older women likewise are to be **reverent** in their behavior, not malicious gossips, nor enslaved to much wine, teaching what is good, [NASB]

Likewise, teach the older women to be **reverent** in the way they live, not to be slanderers or addicted to much wine, but to teach what is good. [NIV]

The older women likewise, that they be **reverent** in behavior, not slanderers, not given to much wine, teachers of good things— [NKJV]

Similarly, teach the older women to live in a way that is **appropriate** for someone serving the Lord. They must not go around speaking evil of others and must not be heavy drinkers. Instead, they should teach others what is good. [NLT]

Πρεσβύτιδας ὡσαύτως ἐν καταστήματι **ἱεροπρεπεῖς**, μὴ διαβόλους, μὴ οἴνῳ πολλῷ δεδουλωμένας, καλοδιδασκάλους, [GNS]

πρεσβύτιδας ὡσαύτως ἐν καταστήματι **ἱεροπρεπεῖς**, μὴ διαβόλους μηδὲ οἴνῳ πολλῷ δεδουλωμένας, καλοδιδασκάλους, [GNT]

Reverent, devout, holy, different and set apart in purity of behavior and thought.

Practical Application
Elderly women are to live and move about in a spirit of holiness and be focused upon sacred things. Matthew Henry says that elderly women are to keep "a pious [holy] decency and decorum in clothing and gesture, in looks and speech, and in all their deportment [behavior]" (*Matthew Henry's Commentary*, p.862).

#3308
Reverent Fear

Fear–KJV
Fear–NASB
Reverent fear–NIV
Fear–NKJV
Reverent fear–NLT

φόβῳ = *phobō*
Pronunciation: [fob'-o]
Parsing (part of speech): noun
  Case—dative
  Gender—masculine
  Number—singular
  Stem or root—from φόβος, ου
Concordance References:
⇒ Strong's #5401 phobos
⇒ NIV #5832 phobos
⇒ NASB #5401 phobos

Fear, reverent fear; respect; awe; wonder; amazement.

Practical Application
Believers are to reverence God because *God will judge the world*. Note that the term "reverent fear" (*phobō*) is used. It means to hold God in reverence and awe. The judgment of God should strike fear, dread and terror within us, for it is to be the most fearful, dreaded and terrorizing experience imaginable. In fact, the human

ENGLISH WORD	GREEK WORD AND VERSE	THE WORD MEANS...
POSB REFERENCE (1 Pt.1:17) Note 2	**1 Peter 1:17** And if ye call on the Father, who without respect of persons judgeth according to every man's work, pass the time of your sojourning here in **fear**: [KJV] And if you address as Father the One who impartially judges according to each man's work, conduct yourselves in **fear** during the time of your stay upon earth; [NASB] Since you call on a Father who judges each man's work impartially, live your lives as strangers here in **reverent fear**. [NIV] And if you call on the Father, who without partiality judges according to each one's work, conduct yourselves throughout the time of your stay *here* in **fear**; [NKJV] And remember that the heavenly Father to whom you pray has no favorites when he judges. He will judge or reward you according to what you do. So you must live in **reverent fear** of him during your time as foreigners here on earth. [NLT] καὶ εἰ πατέρα ἐπικαλεῖσθε τὸν ἀπροσωπολήπτως κρίνοντα κατὰ τὸ ἑκάστου ἔργον, ἐν **φόβῳ** τὸν τῆς παροικίας ὑμῶν χρόνον ἀναστράφητε· [GNS] Καὶ εἰ πατέρα ἐπικαλεῖσθε τὸν ἀπροσωπολήμπτως κρίνοντα κατὰ τὸ ἑκάστου ἔργον, ἐν **φόβῳ** τὸν τῆς παροικίας ὑμῶν χρόνον ἀναστράφητε, [GNT]	mind cannot even picture how awful and frightening it will be to be judged and cut off from God for eternity. Two things are said about the judgment of God. 1. Every person is going to be judged. No one will escape. Every person will come to the day when he will stand all alone in a private interview with God. In that moment, he will stand face to face with God for one purpose and one purpose alone: to be judged. 2. It is the works of a person that are to be judged. No false profession will stand in that day. When God reveals the person's works, his works will show that he never really trusted in Christ. He only said that he believed Christ, but his life and works will prove differently. It will be seen that he lived a lie. His life and works will show that he lived for the world and its possessions and pleasure.
#3309 Reviler Railer–KJV **Reviler–NASB** Slanderer–NIV **Reviler–NKJV** Abusive–NLT **POSB REFERENCE** (1 Cor.5:11) Note 5	λοίδορος = *loidoros* Pronunciation: [loy'-dor-os] Parsing (part of speech): noun Case—nominative Gender—masculine Number—singular Stem or root—from λοίδορος, ου Concordance References: ⇒ Strong's #3060 loidoros ⇒ NIV #3368 loidoros ⇒ NASB #3060 loidoros **1 Cor. 5:11** But now I have written unto you not to keep company, if any man that is called a brother be a fornicator, or covetous, or an idolater, or a **railer**, or a drunkard, or an extortioner; with such an one no not to eat. [KJV] But actually, I wrote to you not to associate with any so-called brother if he should be an immoral person, or covetous, or an idolater, or a **reviler**, or a drunkard, or a swindler—not even to eat with such a one. [NASB] But now I am writing you that you must not associate with anyone who calls himself a brother but is sexually immoral or greedy, an idolater or a **slanderer**, a drunkard or a swindler. With such a man do not even eat. [NIV] But now I have written to you not to keep company with anyone named a brother, who is sexually immoral, or covetous, or an idolater, or a **reviler**, or a drunkard, or an extortioner—not even to eat with such a person. [NKJV] What I meant was that you are not to associate with anyone who claims to be a Christian yet indulges in sexual sin, or is greedy, or worships idols, or is **abusive**, or a drunkard, or a swindler. Don't even eat with such people. [NLT] νυνὶ δὲ ἔγραψα ὑμῖν μὴ συναναμίγνυσθαι, ἐάν τις ἀδελφὸς ὀνομαζόμενος ᾖ πόρνος, ἢ πλεονέκτης, ἢ εἰδωλολάτρης, ἢ **λοίδορος**, ἢ μέθυσος ἢ ἅρπαξ· τῷ τοιούτῳ μηδὲ συνεσθίειν. [GNS] νῦν δὲ ἔγραψα ὑμῖν μὴ συναναμίγνυσθαι ἐάν τις ἀδελφὸς ὀνομαζόμενος ᾖ πόρνος ἢ πλεονέκτης ἢ εἰδωλολάτρης ἢ **λοίδορος** ἢ μέθυσος ἢ ἅρπαξ, τῷ τοιούτῳ μηδὲ συνεσθίειν. [GNT]	Someone who is a slanderer; railer; reviler; an abusive person. **Practical Application** The reviler (*loidoros*) is a person who rants and scolds; reviles and abuses; uses insolent, abusive, and slanderous language.
#3310 Revilers	βλάσφημοι = *blasphēmoi* Pronunciation: [blas'-fay-moy] Parsing (part of speech): adjective Case—nominative	To be verbally abusive; to blaspheme; to revile; to openly scoff at God; to slander, insult, rail, reproach, curse.

ENGLISH WORD	GREEK WORD AND VERSE	THE WORD MEANS...
Blasphemers–KJV **Revilers–NASB** Abusive–NIV Blasphemers–NKJV Scoffing at God–NLT **POSB REFERENCE** (2 Tim.3:2-4; esp. v.2) Note 2, point 5	Gender—masculine Number—plural Stem or root—from βλάσφημος, ον Concordance References: ⇒ Strong's #989 blasphēmos ⇒ NIV #1061 blasphēmos ⇒ NASB #989 blasphēmos **2 Tim. 3:2** For men shall be lovers of their own selves, covetous, boasters, proud, **blasphemers**, disobedient to parents, unthankful, unholy, [KJV] For men will be lovers of self, lovers of money, boastful, arrogant, **revilers**, disobedient to parents, ungrateful, unholy, [NASB] People will be lovers of themselves, lovers of money, boastful, proud, **abusive**, disobedient to their parents, ungrateful, unholy, [NIV] For men will be lovers of themselves, lovers of money, boasters, proud, **blasphemers**, disobedient to parents, unthankful, unholy, [NKJV] For people will love only themselves and their money. They will be boastful and proud, **scoffing at God**, disobedient to their parents, and ungrateful. They will consider nothing sacred. [NLT] ἔσονται γὰρ οἱ ἄνθρωποι φίλαυτοι, φιλάργυροι, ἀλαζόνες, ὑπερήφανοι, **βλάσφημοι**, γονεῦσιν ἀπειθεῖς, ἀχάριστοι, ἀνόσιοι, [GNS] ἔσονται γὰρ οἱ ἄνθρωποι φίλαυτοι φιλάργυροι ἀλαζόνες ὑπερήφανοι **βλάσφημοι**, γονεῦσιν ἀπειθεῖς, ἀχάριστοι ἀνόσιοι [GNT]	**Practical Application** The word "revilers" or "blasphemy" (*blasphēmoi*) is usually thought to be against God, and it is. But it is also a sin against men. Men can blaspheme men. Think of the cursing and insults that will be thrown against God and men today. Practically everyone is cursing and reviling others: mothers, fathers, children, teachers, professionals, actors, comedians, politicians, even some professing religionists feel the need to occasionally curse in order to be acceptable. Why is there so much cursing and profanity today? Because there is a loss of respect for both self and others, for both position and authority. People rail, revile, insult, reproach, and curse when they are disturbed within—when they sense dissatisfaction, disapproval, unacceptance, bitterness, emptiness, loneliness, and reaction within their heart. A disturbed and dissatisfied heart causes people to blaspheme God and man, including themselves (blaming and cursing themselves when they fail and come ever so short).
#3311 **Revilers** **Revilers–KJV** **Revilers–NASB** Slanderers–NIV **Revilers–NKJV** Abusers–NLT **POSB REFERENCE** (1 Cor.6:10) Note 3, point 4	*λοίδοροι = loidoroi* Pronunciation: [loy'-dor-oy-ee] Parsing (part of speech): noun Case—nominative Gender—masculine Number—plural Stem or root—from λοίδορος, ου Concordance References: ⇒ Strong's #3060 loidoros ⇒ NIV #3368 loidoros ⇒ NASB #3060 loidoros **1 Cor. 6:10** Nor thieves, nor covetous, nor drunkards, nor **revilers**, nor extortioners, shall inherit the kingdom of God. [KJV] Nor thieves, nor the covetous, nor drunkards, nor **revilers**, nor swindlers, shall inherit the kingdom of God. [NASB] Nor thieves nor the greedy nor drunkards nor **slanderers** nor swindlers will inherit the kingdom of God. [NIV] Nor thieves, nor covetous, nor drunkards, nor **revilers**, nor extortioners will inherit the kingdom of God. [NKJV] Thieves, greedy people, drunkards, **abusers**, and swindlers—none of these will have a share in the Kingdom of God. [NLT] οὔτε κλέπται, οὔτε πλεονέκται, οὐ μέθυσοι, οὐ **λοίδοροι**, οὐχ ἅρπαγες, βασιλείαν Θεοῦ οὐ κληρονομήσουσι. [GNS] οὔτε κλέπται οὔτε πλεονέκται, οὐ μέθυσοι, οὐ **λοίδοροι**, οὐχ ἅρπαγες βασιλείαν θεοῦ κληρονομήσουσιν. [GNT]	Slanderers, revilers, abusers. **Practical Application** Revilers (*blasphēmoi*) are people who abuse others through scolding, ranting and raving, insolent and abusive language, cursing and slanderous language.
#3312 **Revived** Flourished again–KJV **Revived–NASB**	*ἀνεθάλετε = anethalete* Pronunciation: [an-ath-al'-eh-teh] Parsing (part of speech): verb Mood—indicative Tense—aorist Voice—active	To renew; to flourish again; to revive again. **Practical Application** It is the picture of plants and flowers sprouting, shooting up, and blossoming *again*. The key

ENGLISH WORD	GREEK WORD AND VERSE	THE WORD MEANS...
Renewed–NIV Flourished again– NKJV Again–NLT **POSB** **REFERENCE** (Philip.4:10) Note 1	Person—2nd person Number—plural Stem or root—from ἀναθάλλω Concordance References: ⇒ Strong's #330 anathallö ⇒ NIV #352 anathallö ⇒ NASB #330 anathallö **Philip. 4:10** But I rejoiced in the Lord greatly, that now at the last your care of me hath **flourished again**; wherein ye were also careful, but ye lacked opportunity. [KJV] But I rejoiced in the Lord greatly, that now at last you have **revived** your concern for me; indeed, you were concerned *before,* but you lacked opportunity. [NASB] I rejoice greatly in the Lord that at last you have **renewed** your concern for me. Indeed, you have been concerned, but you had no opportunity to show it. [NIV] But I rejoiced in the Lord greatly that now at last your care for me has **flourished again**; though you surely did care, but you lacked opportunity. [NKJV] How grateful I am, and how I praise the Lord that you are concerned about me **again**. I know you have always been concerned for me, but for a while you didn't have the chance to help me. [NLT] Ἐχάρην δὲ ἐν Κυρίῳ μεγάλως, ὅτι ἤδη ποτὲ **ἀνεθάλετε** τὸ ὑπὲρ ἐμοῦ φρονεῖν,, ἐφ' ᾧ καὶ ἐφρονεῖτε, ἠκαιρεῖσθε δέ. [GNS] Ἐχάρην δὲ ἐν κυρίῳ μεγάλως ὅτι ἤδη ποτὲ **ἀνεθάλετε** τὸ ὑπὲρ ἐμοῦ φρονεῖν, ἐφ' ᾧ καὶ ἐφρονεῖτε, ἠκαιρεῖσθε δέ. [GNT]	word is *again.* When the church had been founded, the believers had supported Paul and his mission work on a regular basis. But for some reason, they had dropped their mission support. That had probably been over ten to twelve years before (Strauss). Why they had stopped sending support to Paul is not known. However, the point is the glorious revival of mission support that took place in the church. They picked up the support of Paul once again, and their giving flourished and blossomed anew. The joy and rejoicing of Paul's heart can just be imagined. He says, "I rejoiced greatly in the Lord."
#3313 **Revolutions** Commotions–KJV Disturbances–NASB **Revolutions–NIV** Commotions–NKJV Insurrections–NLT **POSB** **REFERENCE** (Lk.21:9-10; esp. v.9) Note 3, point 1	*ἀκαταστασίας* = akatastasias Pronunciation: [ak-at-as-tah-see'-ahs] Parsing (part of speech): noun Case—accusative Gender—feminine Number—plural Stem or root—from ἀκαταστασία, ας Concordance References: ⇒ Strong's #181 akatastasia ⇒ NIV #189 akatastasia ⇒ NASB #181 akatastasia **Luke 21:9** But when ye shall hear of wars and **commotions**, be not terrified: for these things must first come to pass; but the end is not by and by. [KJV] "And when you hear of wars and **disturbances**, do not be terrified; for these things must take place first, but the end does not follow immediately." [NASB] When you hear of wars and **revolutions**, do not be frightened. These things must happen first, but the end will not come right away." [NIV] But when you hear of wars and **commotions**, do not be terrified; for these things must come to pass first, but the end *will not come* immediately." [NKJV] And when you hear of wars and **insurrections**, don't panic. Yes, these things must come, but the end won't follow immediately." [NLT] ὅταν δὲ ἀκούσητε πολέμους καὶ **ἀκαταστασίας**, μὴ πτοηθῆτε· δεῖ γὰρ ταῦτα γενέσθαι πρῶτον, ἀλλ' οὐκ εὐθέως τὸ τέλος. [GNS] ὅταν δὲ ἀκούσητε πολέμους καὶ **ἀκαταστασίας**, μὴ πτοηθῆτε· δεῖ γὰρ ταῦτα γενέσθαι πρῶτον, ἀλλ' οὐκ εὐθέως τὸ τέλος. [GNT]	Revolutions, disturbances, insurrections, commotions, anarchy, rebellion, tumults, uproars, riots, terrorism; mob violence; treason against and confusion within governments. **Practical Application** Believers can become extremely disturbed over the news. But, believers are not to be "frightened" (*ptoethete*). They are not to let their hearts "be troubled" (John 14:1). World violence can trouble people; but the believer's heart and life are to be centered upon God, trusting His presence, care, and security—eternally.
#3314 **Rich Blessing** Fulness–KJV Fullness–NASB	*πληρώματος* = plërömatos Pronunciation: [play'-ro-mah-tos] Parsing (part of speech): noun Case—genitive Gender—neuter Number—singular	Fullness, that which fills, the sum total, the totality. It is the sum total of all that is in God (Col. 1:19). It is rich blessings from God.

ENGLISH WORD	GREEK WORD AND VERSE	THE WORD MEANS...
Fullness–NIV Fullness–NKJV **Rich blessings–NLT** **POSB REFERENCE** (Jn.1:16-17; esp. v.16) Note 4	Stem or root—from πλήρωμα, τος Concordance References: ⇒ Strong's #4138 plërōma ⇒ NIV #4445 plērōma ⇒ NASB #4138 plërōma **John 1:16** And of his **fulness** have all we received, and grace for grace. [KJV] For of His **fulness** we have all received, and grace upon grace. [NASB] From the **fullness** of his grace we have all received one blessing after another. [NIV] And of His **fullness** we have all received, and grace for grace. [NKJV] We have all benefited from the **rich blessings** he brought to us—one gracious blessing after another. [NLT] καὶ ἐκ τοῦ **πληρώματος** αὐτοῦ ἡμεῖς πάντες ἐλάβομεν, καὶ χάριν ἀντὶ χάριτος· [GNS] ὅτι ἐκ τοῦ **πληρώματος** αὐτοῦ ἡμεῖς πάντες ἐλάβομεν καὶ χάριν ἀντὶ χάριτος· [GNT]	**Practical Application** All that Christ is, the very fullness of His being, is given to us who believe—all His "love, joy, peace, patience, kindness, goodness, faithfulness, gentleness, self-control" (Galatians 5:22-23). We are complete in Him.

#3315
Rid Of–
Rid Of, Get
 	
Laying aside–KJV
Putting aside–NASB
Rid...of–NIV
Laying aside–NKJV
Get rid of–NLT
 	
**POSB
REFERENCE**
(1 Pt.2:1)
Note 1
	Ἀποθέμενοι = Apothemenoi
	Pronunciation: [ap-oth-eh'-mehn-oy]
	Parsing (part of speech): verb
	    Mood—participle (imperative sense)
	    Tense—aorist
	    Voice—middle
	    Case—nominative
	    Gender—masculine
	    Person—2nd person
	    Number—plural
	    Stem or root—from ἀποτίθημι
	Concordance References:
	⇒ Strong's #659 apotithëmi
	⇒ NIV #700 apotithëmi
	⇒ NASB #659 apotithëmi
	
	1 Peter 2:1
	Wherefore **laying aside** all malice, and all guile, and hypocrisies, and envies, and all evil speakings, [KJV]
	Therefore, **putting aside** all malice and all guile and hypocrisy and envy and all slander, [NASB]
	Therefore, **rid** yourselves **of** all malice and all deceit, hypocrisy, envy, and slander of every kind. [NIV]
	Therefore, **laying aside** all malice, all deceit, hypocrisy, envy, and all evil speaking, [NKJV]
	So **get rid of** all malicious behavior and deceit. Don't just pretend to be good! Be done with hypocrisy and jealousy and backstabbing. [NLT]
	Ἀποθέμενοι οὖν πᾶσαν κακίαν καὶ πάντα δόλον καὶ ὑποκρίσεις καὶ φθόνους καὶ πάσας καταλαλιάς, [GNS]
	Ἀποθέμενοι οὖν πᾶσαν κακίαν καὶ πάντα δόλον καὶ ὑποκρίσεις καὶ φθόνους καὶ πάσας καταλαλιάς, [GNT]
		To get rid of; to lay aside; to put aside.
		
		Practical Application
		The Greek word for "rid of" (Apothemenoi) means to put off one's clothing; to cleanse oneself of those things that defile. Both meanings are applicable in this verse (A.T. Robertson. *Word Pictures in the New Testament*, Vol.6, p.94). There are some things that defile the believer. He is to take these things and strip them off just as he would strip off his clothes; he is to cleanse himself from all that defiles him. Five things in particular are mentioned, and note: all five have to do with what has just been said in the former passage. We are to love one another fervently with a pure heart. The very things that we are to strip off are the things that dirty and soil our love. They have to do with how we treat one another, with our behavior toward our Christian brothers and sisters.

#3316
Ridiculed–
Ridiculing
 	
Nought–KJV
Contempt–NASB
Ridiculed–NIV
Contempt–NKJV
Ridiculing–NLT
 	
**POSB
REFERENCE**
(Lk.23:8-11; esp. v.11)
Note 3, point 4
	ἐξουθενήσας = exouthenësas
	Pronunciation: [ex-oo-then-eh'-sas]
	Parsing (part of speech): verb
	    Mood—participle
	    Tense—aorist
	    Voice—active
	    Case—nominative
	    Gender—masculine
	    Number—singular
	    Stem or root—from ἐξουθενέω
	Concordance References:
	⇒ Strong's #1848 exoutheneō
	⇒ NIV #2024 exoutheneō
	⇒ NASB #1848 exoutheneō
	
	Luke 23:11
	And Herod with his men of war set him at **nought**, and mocked him, and arrayed him in a gorgeous robe, and
		To ridicule; to count as nothing; to make nothing of; to despise; to look down upon; to reject; to think something is unimportant; to count as zero—therefore, to treat with utter contempt.
		
		Practical Application
		Note the contrast in the verse. Herod sat there as King with "his soldiers" surrounding him, and Jesus stood there beaten and battered in torn, ragged clothes. Herod, judging by appearance, counted the Man who claimed to be the Son of God as nothing. This Man and His claim did not matter, not to Herod.

ENGLISH WORD	GREEK WORD AND VERSE	THE WORD MEANS...

	sent him again to Pilate. [KJV]
	    And Herod with his soldiers, after treating Him with **contempt** and mocking Him, dressed Him in a gorgeous robe and sent Him back to Pilate. [NASB]
	    Then Herod and his soldiers **ridiculed** and mocked him. Dressing him in an elegant robe, they sent him back to Pilate. [NIV]
	    Then Herod, with his men of war, treated Him with **contempt** and mocked *Him,* arrayed Him in a gorgeous robe, and sent Him back to Pilate. [NKJV]
	    Now Herod and his soldiers began mocking and **ridiculing** Jesus. Then they put a royal robe on him and sent him back to Pilate. [NLT]
	    ἐξουθενήσας δὲ αὐτὸν ὁ Ἡρώδης σὺν τοῖς στρατεύμασιν αὐτοῦ, καὶ ἐμπαίξας, περιβαλὼν αὐτὸν ἐσθῆτα λαμπρὰν, ἀνέπεμψεν αὐτὸν τῷ Πιλάτῳ. [GNS]
	    ἐξουθενήσας δὲ αὐτὸν [καὶ] ὁ Ἡρώδης σὺν τοῖς στρατεύμασιν αὐτοῦ καὶ ἐμπαίξας περιβαλὼν ἐσθῆτα λαμπρὰν ἀνέπεμψεν αὐτὸν τῷ Πιλάτῳ. [GNT]	

#3317
Right
 	
Just–KJV
Right–NASB
Right–NIV
Just–NKJV
Right–NLT
 	
POSB
REFERENCE
(Philip.4:8-9; esp. v.8)
Note 2, point 1c
	δίκαια = dikaia
	Pronunciation: [dik'-ah-ee-ah]
	Parsing (part of speech): adjective
	        Case—nominative
	        Gender—neuter
	        Number—plural
	        Stem or root—from δίκαιος, α, ον
	Concordance References:
	    ⇒ Strong's #1342 dikaios
	    ⇒ NIV #1465 dikaios
	    ⇒ NASB #1342 dikaios
	
	Philip. 4:8
	    Finally, brethren, whatsoever things are true, whatsoever things are honest, whatsoever things are **just**, whatsoever things are pure, whatsoever things are lovely, whatsoever things are of good report; if there be any virtue, and if there be any praise, think on these things. [KJV]
	    Finally, brethren, whatever is true, whatever is honorable, whatever is **right**, whatever is pure, whatever is lovely, whatever is of good repute, if there is any excellence and if anything worthy of praise, let your mind dwell on these things. [NASB]
	    Finally, brothers, whatever is true, whatever is noble, whatever is **right**, whatever is pure, whatever is lovely, whatever is admirable—if anything is excellent or praiseworthy—think about such things. [NIV]
	    Finally, brethren, whatever things are true, whatever things *are* noble, whatever things *are* **just**, whatever things *are* pure, whatever things *are* lovely, whatever things *are* of good report, if *there is* any virtue and if *there is* anything praiseworthy—meditate on these things. [NKJV]
	    And now, dear brothers and sisters, let me say one more thing as I close this letter. Fix your thoughts on what is true and honorable and **right**. Think about things that are pure and lovely and admirable. Think about things that are excellent and worthy of praise. [NLT]
	    Τὸ λοιπόν, ἀδελφοί, ὅσα ἐστὶν ἀληθῆ, ὅσα σεμνά, ὅσα **δίκαια**, ὅσα ἁγνά, ὅσα προσφιλῆ, ὅσα εὔφημα, εἴ τις ἀρετὴ καὶ εἴ τις ἔπαινος, ταῦτα λογίζεσθε· [GNS]
	    Τὸ λοιπόν, ἀδελφοί, ὅσα ἐστὶν ἀληθῆ, ὅσα σεμνά, ὅσα **δίκαια**, ὅσα ἁγνά, ὅσα προσφιλῆ, ὅσα εὔφημα, εἴ τις ἀρετὴ καὶ εἴ τις ἔπαινος, ταῦτα λογίζεσθε· [GNT]
		Right, just, righteous, proper, innocent, honest, fair. It is righteous behavior. It has to do with right behavior toward man and God.
		
		Practical Application
		    The believer is to keep his thoughts upon his duty toward men and God—upon doing what is right toward both. Man is to be a responsible being while on earth. He is responsible for the earth and his fellow human beings, and he is to be held accountable by God for both. Therefore, he is not to focus his thoughts upon comfort and selfish pleasures and pursuits. He is to focus his thoughts upon the things that are *righteous.* He owes his thoughts and mind to the world and to his fellow men and especially to God. He owes whatever contribution he can make to the world and to God. A mind filled with *right* thoughts will know peace.

#3318
Right
 	
Sound–KJV
Sound–NASB
Sound–NIV
	ὑγιαινόντων = hugiainontōn
	Pronunciation: [hoog-ee-ah'ee-non-tone]
	Parsing (part of speech): verb
	        Mood—participle
	        Tense—present
	        Voice—active
	        Case—genitive
		Sound, right, well. It means healthful, health giving. It means wholesome and healthy doctrine and teaching.
		
		Practical Application
		    Believers must hold fast to right, health giv-

ENGLISH WORD	GREEK WORD AND VERSE	THE WORD MEANS...
	παιδεύουσα ἡμᾶς ἵνα, ἀρνησάμενοι τὴν ἀσέβειαν καὶ τὰς κοσμικὰς ἐπιθυμίας σωφρόνως καὶ **δικαίως** καὶ εὐσεβῶς ζήσωμεν ἐν τῷ νῦν αἰῶνι, [GNS] παιδεύουσα ἡμᾶς, ἵνα ἀρνησάμενοι τὴν ἀσέβειαν καὶ τὰς κοσμικὰς ἐπιθυμίας σωφρόνως καὶ **δικαίως** καὶ εὐσεβῶς ζήσωμεν ἐν τῷ νῦν αἰῶνι, [GNT]	

#3322
Right Time
 	
Due time–KJV
Right time–NASB
Right time–NIV
Due time–NKJV
Right time–NLB
 	
POSB REFERENCE
(Romans 5:6-7; esp. v.6)
Note 1, point 3
	κατὰ καιρὸν = kata kairon
	Pronunciation: [ah-tah kahee-ron']
	Parsing *kairon* (part of speech): noun
	  Case—accusative
	  Gender—masculine
	  Number—singular
	  Stem or root—from **καιρός**, οῦ
	Concordance References:
	⇒ Strong's #2596 kata + 2540 kairos
	⇒ NIV #2848 kata [at] + 2789 kairos [right time]
	⇒ NASB #2596 kata + 2540 kairos
	
	Romans 5:6
	  For when we were yet without strength, in **due time** Christ died for the ungodly. [KJV]
	  For while we were still helpless, at the **right time** Christ died for the ungodly. [NASB]
	  You see, at just the **right time**, when we were still powerless, Christ died for the ungodly. [NIV]
	  For when we were still without strength, in **due time** Christ died for the ungodly. [NKJV]
	  When we were utterly helpless, Christ came at just the **right time** and died for us sinners. [NLT]
	  ἔτι γὰρ Χριστὸς ὄντων ἡμῶν ἀσθενῶν, ἔτι **κατὰ καιρὸν** ὑπὲρ ἀσεβῶν ἀπέθανε. [GNS]
	  ἔτι γὰρ Χριστὸς ὄντων ἡμῶν ἀσθενῶν ἔτι **κατὰ καιρὸν** ὑπὲρ ἀσεβῶν ἀπέθανεν. [GNT]
		Appointed or proper time, season, age opportunity; the last times
		
		Practical Application
		  It was in "right time" (*kata kairon*) that Christ died for us. It was in God's appointed time: His destined time, appropriate time. Men had to be prepared for Christ before God could send Him into the world. Men had to learn that they were without strength and ungodly, that they needed a Savior. (This was the purpose of the Old Testament and the law, to show men that they were sinful. See POSB outline—Romans 4:14-15 and POSB note—Romans 4:14-15.)

#3323
Right, What [Is]
 	
Which [is] honest–KJV
What [is] right–NASB
What [is] right–NIV
What [is] honorable–NKJV
Right–NLT
 	
POSB REFERENCE
(2 Cor.13:7-10; esp. v.7)
Note 2
	τὸ καλὸν = to kalon
	Pronunciation: [to kal-on']
	Parsing *kalon* (part of speech): pronominal adjective
	  Case—accusative
	  Gender—neuter
	  Number—singular
	  Stem or root—from **καλός**, ή, όν
	Concordance References:
	⇒ Strong's #3588 ho + 2570 kalos
	⇒ NIV #3836 ho [what] + 2819 kalos [right]
	⇒ NASB #3588 ho + 2570 kalos
	
	2 Cor. 13:7
	  Now I pray to God that ye do no evil; not that we should appear approved, but that ye should do that **which** is **honest**, though we be as reprobates. [KJV]
	  Now we pray to God that you do no wrong; not that we ourselves may appear approved, but that you may do **what** is **right**, even though we should appear unapproved. [NASB]
	  Now we pray to God that you will not do anything wrong. Not that people will see that we have stood the test but that you will do **what** is **right** even though we may seem to have failed. [NIV]
	  Now I pray to God that you do no evil, not that we should appear approved, but that you should do **what** is **honorable**, though we may seem disqualified. [NKJV]
	  We pray to God that you will not do anything wrong. We pray this, not to show that our ministry to you has been successful, but because we want you to do **right** even if we ourselves seem to have failed. [NLT]
	  εὐχόμαι δὲ πρὸς τὸν Θεὸν, μὴ ποιῆσαι ὑμᾶς κακὸν μηδέν, οὐχ ἵνα ἡμεῖς δόκιμοι φανῶμεν, ἀλλ' ἵνα ὑμεῖς **τὸ καλὸν** ποιῆτε, ἡμεῖς δὲ ὡς ἀδόκιμοι ὦμεν. [GNS]
	  εὐχόμεθα δὲ πρὸς τὸν θεὸν μὴ ποιῆσαι ὑμᾶς κακὸν μηδέν, οὐχ ἵνα ἡμεῖς δόκιμοι φανῶμεν, ἀλλ' ἵνα ὑμεῖς **τὸ καλὸν** ποιῆτε, ἡμεῖς δὲ ὡς ἀδόκιμοι ὦμεν. [GNT]
		Right, noble, honest, proper, good, pleasing.
		
		Practical Application
		  Paul was under attack and suffered the tension and pressure of the attack, but that was not the reason he wanted his critics to repent. His purpose was not selfish or self-centered: he wanted his critics to repent for the sake of righteousness, that the good and right thing might be done. He wanted this despite the fact that they treated him as a reprobate. They might not love him, but he loved them and wanted only the best for them. He did not want to discipline them; he wanted them to repent before he arrived.

ENGLISH WORD	GREEK WORD AND VERSE	THE WORD MEANS...

#3324
Righteous Acts
 	
Righteousness–KJV
Righteous acts–
NASB
Righteous acts–NIV
Righteous acts–
NKJV
Good deeds done–
NLT
 	
POSB
REFERENCE
(Rev.19:7-8; esp.v.8)
Note 3, point 2
	δικαιώματα = dikaiōmata
	Pronunciation: [dik-ah'-ee-yo-mah-tah]
	Parsing (part of speech): noun
	  Case—nominative
	  Gender—neuter
	  Number—plural
	  Stem or root—from δικαίωμα, τος
	Concordance References:
	⇒ Strong's #1345 dikaiōma
	⇒ NIV #1468 dikaiōma
	⇒ NASB #1345 dikaiōma
	
	Rev. 19:8
	And to her was granted that she should be arrayed in fine linen, clean and white: for the fine linen is the **righteousness** of saints. [KJV]
	And it was given to her to clothe herself in fine linen, bright and clean; for the fine linen is the **righteous acts** of the saints. [NASB]
	Fine linen, bright and clean, was given her to wear." (Fine linen stands for the **righteous acts** of the saints.) [NIV]
	And to her it was granted to be arrayed in fine linen, clean and bright, for the fine linen is the **righteous acts** of the saints. [NKJV]
	She is permitted to wear the finest white linen." (Fine linen represents the **good deeds done** by the people of God.) [NLT]
	καὶ ἐδόθη αὐτῇ ἵνα περιβάληται βύσσινον καθαρόν καὶ λαμπρόν· τὸ γὰρ βύσσινον τὰ **δικαιώματα** ἐστι τῶν ἀγίων. [GNS]
	καὶ ἐδόθη αὐτῇ ἵνα περιβάληται βύσσινον λαμπρὸν καθαρόν· τὸ γὰρ βύσσινον τὰ **δικαιώματα** τῶν ἀγίων ἐστίν. [GNT]
		Righteous acts, righteousness, good deeds done.
		
		Practical Application
		A believer prepares himself by righteous deeds or acts (Rev. 19:8). This would mean two things.
		1. The believer acts righteously, *does the right thing* when he receives Jesus Christ as his Savior. It is then that God accepts the belief of the person *as righteousness*. God actualy takes a person's faith in His Son and *counts his faith as righteousness*. Why? Because the person believes that the sacrifice of the Lamb, the death of the Lord Jesus Christ, was for the sins of the world. The person believes that Jesus Christ died for his sins, as his sacrifice, as his substitute. He believes that the penalty and judgment of his sins have been paid for by Christ. Therefore, he is free of sin and made acceptable to God. God takes his faith and *counts his faith as righteousness*. God counts him righteous in the righteousness of Jesus Christ. This is what is called *imputed* righteousness, righteousness that is given or put to one's account before God. It is a righteousness that is counted and credited to the believer. Therefore, when the believer is ready to attend the great *Marriage Supper of the Lamb*, he will be given the clean and white clothing necessary to enter the supper. Note: the fine clothing is actually said to be the righteousness or righteous deeds of the saints.
		  Now, this is the first righteous deed that a person is to do. If he does this righteous deed, then he will be accepted into the great *Marriage Supper of the Lamb*.
		2. The believer is also to do other righteous deeds. He is to serve the Lamb of God to the fullest degree possible. Every believer is aware that not all believers do this; not all believers serve God with all their heart, soul, and body. In fact, some believers do little for Christ. Therefore, note verse eight carefully: the bride of Christ—all believers—will be in heaven. They will be accepted and made perfect in the righteousness of Christ. They have robes that are white and pure. But note: when they get ready to attend the great *Marriage Supper of the Lamb*, God will give believers another garment that is made of fine linen that will be clean and white. What is the other garment? It is...
		• the garment of righteous deeds and acts.
		• the garment of reward.
		• the garment that shows position and responsibility.
		• the garment that rewards one for faithfulness.

#3325
Righteous
Judgment
 	
Righteous judgment–
KJV
	δικαιοκρισίας = dikaiokrisias
	Pronunciation: [dik-ah-yok-ris-ee'-ahs]
	Parsing (part of speech): noun
	  Case—genitive
	  Gender—feminine
	  Number—singular
	  Stem or root—from δικαιοκρισία, ας
		Righteous judgment; just judge (God). It means just, fair, impartial, correct, exact.
		
		Practical Application
		God's judgment is a judgment that should be, that should and will take place. In fact, God must judge, for God is love. As love, He must

ENGLISH WORD	GREEK WORD AND VERSE	THE WORD MEANS...
Righteous judgment– NASB **Righteous judgment– NIV** **Righteous judgment– NKJV** Just judge–NLT **POSB REFERENCE** (Rom.2:2-5; esp. v.5) Note 2, point 4	Concordance References: ⇒ Strong's #1341 dikaiokrisia ⇒ NIV #1464 dikaiokrisia ⇒ NASB #1341 dikaiokrisia **Romans 2:5** But after thy hardness and impenitent heart treasurest up unto thyself wrath against the day of wrath and revelation of the **righteous judgment** of God; [KJV] But because of your stubbornness and unrepentant heart you are storing up wrath for yourself in the day of wrath and revelation of the **righteous judgment** of God, [NASB] But because of your stubbornness and your unrepentant heart, you are storing up wrath against yourself for the day of God's wrath, when his **righteous judgment** will be revealed. [NIV] But in accordance with your hardness and your impenitent heart you are treasuring up for yourself wrath in the day of wrath and revelation of the **righteous judgment** of God, [NKJV] But no, you won't listen. So you are storing up terrible punishment for yourself because of your stubbornness in refusing to turn from your sin. For there is going to come a day of judgment when God, the **just judge** of all the world, [NLT] κατὰ δὲ τὴν σκληρότητά σου καὶ ἀμετανόητον καρδίαν θησαυρίζεις σεαυτῷ ὀργὴν ἐν ἡμέρᾳ ὀργῆς καὶ ἀποκαλύψεως **δικαιοκρισίας** τοῦ Θεοῦ, [GNS] κατὰ δὲ τὴν σκληρότητά σου καὶ ἀμετανόητον καρδίαν θησαυρίζεις σεαυτῷ ὀργὴν ἐν ἡμέρᾳ ὀργῆς καὶ ἀποκαλύψεως **δικαιοκρισίας** τοῦ θεοῦ [GNT]	straighten out all the injustices on earth. He must right the wrongs and correct all the injustices of men. He must judge men with a perfect and "righteous judgment."

#3326
Righteously
 	
Righteously–KJV
Righteously–NASB
Upright–NIV
Righteously–NKJV
Right conduct–NLT
 	
POSB REFERENCE
(Tit.2:12)
Note 2, point 2b
	δικαίως = *dikaiōs*
	Pronunciation: [dik-ah'-yoce]
	Parsing (part of speech): adjective
	    Type—adverb
	    Stem or root—from δικαίως
	Concordance References:
	⇒ Strong's #1346 dikaiōs
	⇒ NIV #1469 dikaiōs
	⇒ NASB #1346 dikaiōs
	
	Titus 2:12
	Teaching us that, denying ungodliness and worldly lusts, we should live soberly, **righteously**, and godly, in this present world; [KJV]
	Instructing us to deny ungodliness and worldly desires and to live sensibly, **righteously** and godly in the present age, [NASB]
	It teaches us to say "No" to ungodliness and worldly passions, and to live self-controlled, **upright** and godly lives in this present age, [NIV]
	Teaching us that, denying ungodliness and worldly lusts, we should live soberly, **righteously**, and godly in the present age, [NKJV]
	And we are instructed to turn from godless living and sinful pleasures. We should live in this evil world with self-control, **right conduct**, and devotion to God, [NLT]
	παιδεύουσα ἡμᾶς, ἵνα, ἀρνησάμενοι τὴν ἀσέβειαν καὶ τὰς κοσμικὰς ἐπιθυμίας σωφρόνως καὶ **δικαίως** καὶ εὐσεβῶς ζήσωμεν ἐν τῷ νῦν αἰῶνι, [GNS]
	παιδεύουσα ἡμᾶς, ἵνα ἀρνησάμενοι τὴν ἀσέβειαν καὶ τὰς κοσμικὰς ἐπιθυμίας σωφρόνως καὶ **δικαίως** καὶ εὐσεβῶς ζήσωμεν ἐν τῷ νῦν αἰῶνι, [GNT]
		Righteously, doing right, treating others like one should, doing good to them, giving them their due share, right conduct.
		
		Practical Application
		What an indictment! How selfish we are in our hoarding and banking while a world dies from starvation, disease, war, evil, and sin. Every person is due his share. We are to live righteously, giving and seeing to it that every man is treated right, that every man receives his due share. If they are well-off physically and materially, we are to treat them righteously, just like we would want to be treated. If they are needy, poor, destitute, hungry, diseased, lonely, bedridden, and sinful, we are to do right toward them and meet their needs. They are to receive their due share of this earth just as we are.

#3327
Righteousness
 	
Righteousness–KJV
Righteousness–NASB
Righteousness–NIV
	δικαιοσύνη = *dikaiosunē*
	Pronunciation: [dik-ah-yos-oo'-nay]
	Parsing (part of speech): noun
	    Case—dative
	    Gender—feminine
	    Number—singular
	    Stem or root—from δικαιοσύνη, ης
		Righteousness, good and right. Righteousness (*dikaiosunē*) means two simple but profound things. It means both *to be right and to do right*. (See *Deeper Study* #5, Righteousness—Matthew 5:6 for more discussion.)

ENGLISH WORD	GREEK WORD AND VERSE	THE WORD MEANS...

Righteousness–NKJV
Good and right–NLT
 	
**POSB
REFERENCE**
(Eph.5:9)
Deeper Study #1
 	
See also POSB REF:
(1 Tim.6:11-16; esp.
v.11)
Note 2, point 1
	Concordance References:
	⇒ Strong's #1343 dikaiosunë
	⇒ NIV #1466 dikaiosunë
	⇒ NASB #1343 dikaiosunë
	
	Ephes. 5:9
	(For the fruit of the Spirit is in all goodness and **right-eousness** and truth;) [KJV]
	(For the fruit of the light consists in all goodness and **righteousness** and truth), [NASB]
	(For the fruit of the light consists in all goodness, **righteousness** and truth) [NIV]
	(For the fruit of the Spirit is in all goodness, **right-eousness**, and truth), [NKJV]
	For this light within you produces only what is **good and right** and true. [NLT]
	-- ὁ γὰρ καρπὸς τοῦ Πνεύματος ἐν πάσῃ ἀγαθωσύνῃ καὶ **δικαιοσύνῃ** καὶ ἀληθείᾳ [GNS]
	ὁ γὰρ καρπὸς τοῦ φωτὸς ἐν πάσῃ ἀγαθωσύνῃ καὶ **δικαιοσύνῃ** καὶ ἀληθείᾳ [GNT]
		Practical Application
		1. There are those who stress *being righteous but neglect doing righteousness*. This leads to two serious errors.
		a. False security. It causes a person to stress that he is saved and acceptable to God because he has *believed in* Jesus Christ. But he neglects doing good and living as he should. He neglects obeying God and serving man.
		b. Loose living. It allows one to go out and do pretty much as he desires. He feels secure and comfortable in his *faith in Christ*. He knows that what he does may affect his fellowship with God and other believers, but he thinks his behavior will not affect his salvation. He thinks that no matter what he does he is still acceptable to God.
		    The problem with this stress is that it is a false righteousness. Righteousness in the Bible means *being righteous*, but it also means *doing righteousness*. The Bible knows nothing about being righteous without living righteously.
		2. There are those who stress *doing righteousness but neglect being righteous*. This also leads to two serious errors.
		a. Self-righteousness and legalism. It causes a person to stress that he is saved and acceptable to God because he does good. He works and behaves morally and keeps certain rules and regulations. He does the things a Christian should do by obeying the main laws of God. But he neglects the basic law: the law of love and acceptance—that God does not love him and accept him because he does good, but because he loves and trusts the righteousness of Christ (see POSB *Deeper Study* #5—Matthew 5:6).
		b. Being judgmental and fault-finding. A person who stresses that he is righteous (acceptable to God) because he keeps certain laws often judges and finds fault with others. He feels that rules and regulations can be kept, he keeps them. Therefore, anyone who fails to keep them is judged, criticized, and censored.
		    The problem with this stress is that it, too, is a false righteousness. Again, righteousness in the Bible is *being righteous as well as doing righteousness*. The Bible knows nothing of being acceptable to God without *being made righteous in Christ Jesus* (see POSB *Deeper Study* #5—Matthew 5:6; POSB note—Romans 5:1 for more discussion. Cp. 2 Cor. 5:21.)

#3328
Righteousness
 	
Righteousness–KJV
Righteous acts–NASB
Righteous acts–NIV
Righteous acts–NKJV
Good deeds done–
   NLT
	δικαιώματα = dikaiömata
	Pronunciation: [dik-ah'-ee-yo-mah-tah]
	Parsing (part of speech): noun
	   Case—nominative
	   Gender—neuter
	   Number—plural
	   Stem or root—from δικαίωμα, τος
	Concordance References:
	⇒ Strong's #1345 dikaiöma
	⇒ NIV #1468 dikaiöma
	⇒ NASB #1345 dikaiöma
		Righteous acts, righteousness, justification, good deeds done. The word "righteousness" (*dikaiömata*) here means righteous deeds or acts.
		
		Practical Application
		A believer prepares himself by righteous deeds or acts (Rev. 19:8). This would mean two things.
		1. The believer acts righteously, *does the right thing* when he receives Jesus Christ as his Savior. It is then that God accepts the belief

ENGLISH WORD	GREEK WORD AND VERSE	THE WORD MEANS...
POSB REFERENCE (Rev.19:7-8; esp.v.8) Note 3, point 2	**Rev. 19:8** And to her was granted that she should be arrayed in fine linen, clean and white: for the fine linen is the **righteousness** of saints. [KJV] And it was given to her to clothe herself in fine linen, bright and clean; for the fine linen is the **righteous acts** of the saints. [NASB] Fine linen, bright and clean, was given her to wear." (Fine linen stands for the **righteous acts** of the saints.) [NIV] And to her it was granted to be arrayed in fine linen, clean and bright, for the fine linen is the **righteous acts** of the saints. [NKJV] She is permitted to wear the finest white linen." (Fine linen represents the **good deeds done** by the people of God.) [NLT] καὶ ἐδόθη αὐτῇ ἵνα περιβάληται βύσσινον καθαρόν καὶ λαμπρόν· τὸ γὰρ βύσσινον τὰ **δικαιώματα** ἐστι τῶν ἁγίων. [GNS] καὶ ἐδόθη αὐτῇ ἵνα περιβάληται βύσσινον λαμπρὸν καθαρόν· τὸ γὰρ βύσσινον τὰ **δικαιώματα** τῶν ἁγίων ἐστίν. [GNT]	of the person *as righteousness*. God actualy takes a person's faith in His Son and *counts his faith as righteousness*. Why? Because the person believes that the sacrifice of the Lamb, the death of the Lord Jesus Christ, was for the sins of the world. The person believes that Jesus Christ died for his sins, as his sacrifice, as his substitute. He believes that the penalty and judgment of his sins have been paid for by Christ. Therefore, he is free of sin and made acceptable to God. God takes his faith and *counts his faith as righteousness*. God counts him righteous in the righteousness of Jesus Christ. This is what is called *imputed* righteousness, righteousness that is given or put to one's account before God. It is a righteousness that is counted and credited to the believer. Therefore, when the believer is ready to attend the great *Marriage Supper of the Lamb*, he will be given the clean and white clothing necessary to enter the supper. Note: the fine clothing is actually said to be the righteousness or righteous deeds of the saints. Now, this is the first righteous deed that a person is to do. If he does this righteous deed, then he will be accepted into the great *Marriage Supper of the Lamb*. 2. The believer is also to do other righteous deeds. He is to serve the Lamb of God to the fullest degree possible. Every believer is aware that not all believers do this; not all believers serve God with all their heart, soul, and body. In fact, some believers do little for Christ. Therefore, note verse eight carefully: the bride of Christ—all believers—will be in heaven. They will be accepted and made perfect in the righteousness of Christ. They have robes that are white and pure. But note: when they get ready to attend the great *Marriage Supper of the Lamb*, God will give believers another garment that is made of fine linen that will be clean and white. What is the other garment? It is... • the garment of righteous deeds and acts. • the garment of reward. • the garment that shows position and responsibility. • the garment that rewards one for faithfulness.

#3329
 Righteousness
 	
 Righteousness–KJV
 Righteousness–NASB
 Righteousness–NIV
 Righteousness–NKJV
 Made right in God's sight–NLT
 	
 POSB REFERENCE (Heb.11:7) Note 2, point 3
	δικαιοσύνης = *dikaiosunēs*
	 Pronunciation: [dik-ah-ee-os-soo'-nays]
	 Parsing (part of speech): noun
	     Case—genitive
	     Gender—feminine
	     Number—singular
	     Stem or root—from δικαιοσύνη, ης
	 Concordance References:
	 ⇒ Strong's #1343 dikaiosune
	 ⇒ NIV #1466 dikaiosune
	 ⇒ NASB #1343 dikaiosune
	
	 Hebrews 11:7
	 By faith Noah, being warned of God of things not seen as yet, moved with fear, prepared an ark to the saving of his house; by the which he condemned the world, and became heir of the **righteousness** which is by faith. [KJV]
	 By faith Noah, being warned by God about things not yet seen, in reverence prepared an ark for the salvation of
		Righteousness; to be made right in God's sight.
		
		 Practical Application
		 Noah was counted righteous (*dikaiosunēs*). Noah believed God and God counted his faith as righteousness. He "became heir of the righteousness *which is by faith.*" As Matthew Henry says, Noah had faith in the *promised Seed*, the Savior whom God was someday going to send to earth (*Matthew Henry's Commentary*, Vol. 6, p.941). There is nothing else upon earth that can cause God to count a man righteous but faith—faith in the *promised Seed*, the Savior of the world, even the Lord Jesus Christ.

ENGLISH WORD	GREEK WORD AND VERSE	THE WORD MEANS...
	his household, by which he condemned the world, and became an heir of the **righteousness** which is according to faith. [NASB] By faith Noah, when warned about things not yet seen, in holy fear built an ark to save his family. By his faith he condemned the world and became heir of the **righteousness** that comes by faith. [NIV] By faith Noah, being divinely warned of things not yet seen, moved with godly fear, prepared an ark for the saving of his household, by which he condemned the world and became heir of the **righteousness** which is according to faith. NKJV It was by faith that Noah built an ark to save his family from the flood. He obeyed God, who warned him about something that had never happened before. By his faith he condemned the rest of the world and was **made right in God's sight**. [NLT] πίστει χρηματισθεὶς Νῶε περὶ τῶν μηδέπω βλεπομένων, εὐλαβηθείς, κατεσκεύασε κιβωτὸν εἰς σωτηρίαν τοῦ οἴκου αὐτοῦ· δι᾽ ἧς κατέκρινε τὸν κόσμον, καὶ τῆς κατὰ πίστιν **δικαιοσύνης** ἐγένετο κληρονόμος. [GNS] Πίστει χρηματισθεὶς Νῶε περὶ τῶν μηδέπω βλεπομένων, εὐλαβηθεὶς κατεσκεύασεν κιβωτὸν εἰς σωτηρίαν τοῦ οἴκου αὐτοῦ δι᾽ ἧς κατέκρινεν τὸν κόσμον, καὶ τῆς κατὰ πίστιν **δικαιοσύνης** ἐγένετο κληρονόμος. [GNT]	

#3330
Rightly
 	
Truth–KJV
Rightly–NASB
Truth–NIV
Truth–NKJV
Justice–NLT
 	
POSB REFERENCE
(Rom.2:2-5; esp. v.2)
Note 2
	ἀλήθειαν = *alëtheian*
	Pronunciation: [al-ay'-thi-ahn]
	Parsing (part of speech): noun
	    Case—accusative
	    Gender—feminine
	    Number—singular
	    Stem or root—from **ἀλήθεια**, ας
	Concordance References:
	  ⇒ Strong's #225 alëtheia
	  ⇒ NIV #237 alëtheia
	  ⇒ NASB #2596 kata + 225 alëtheia
	
	      Romans 2:2
	But we are sure that the judgment of God is according to **truth** against them which commit such things. [KJV]
	And we know that the judgment of God **rightly** falls upon those who practice such things. [NASB]
	Now we know that God's judgment against those who do such things is based on **truth**. [NIV]
	But we know that the judgment of God is according to **truth** against those who practice such things. [NKJV]
	And we know that God, in his **justice**, will punish anyone who does such things. [NLT]
	οἴδαμεν δὲ ὅτι τὸ κρίμα τοῦ Θεοῦ ἐστι κατὰ **ἀλήθειαν** ἐπὶ τοὺς τὰ τοιαῦτα πράσσοντας. [GNS]
	οἴδαμεν δὲ ὅτι τὸ κρίμα τοῦ θεοῦ ἐστιν κατὰ **ἀλήθειαν** ἐπὶ τοὺς τὰ τοιαῦτα πράσσοντας. [GNT]
		Often truly, to be sure; with right motives (Ph.1:18).
		
		Practical Application
		The judgment of God—of the only living and true God—is according to truth. God's judgment will be executed in perfect justice. The word "rightly" (*alëtheian*) means true as opposed to false. It means what really is; what actually exists; what exactly takes place. God's judgment is perfectly just, exactly what it should be, nothing more and nothing less. His judgment is based upon...
		• what really happens
		• what the facts are
		• what actually takes place
		• what a person really is within his heart
		• what the person actually did

#3331
Rightly Dividing
 	
Rightly dividing–KJV
Handling accurately–NASB
Correctly handles–NIV
Rightly dividing–NKJV
Correctly explains–NLT
	ὀρθοτομοῦντα = *orthotomounta*
	Pronunciation: [or-tho-tow-moon-tah]
	Parsing (part of speech): verb
	    Mood—participle (imperative sense)
	    Tense—present
	    Voice—active
	    Case—accusative
	    Gender—masculine
	    Person—2nd person
	    Number—singular
	    Stem or root—from **ὀρθοτομέω**
	Concordance References:
	  ⇒ Strong's #3718 orthotomeö
	  ⇒ NIV #3982 orthotomeö
	  ⇒ NASB #3718 orthotomeö
		To correctly handle; to rightly divide; to handle accurately; to correctly explain; to interpret correctly; to cut straight.
		
		Practical Application
		Believers are to cut straight to the truth; they are not to take crooked paths and side tracks to the truth. We are to study the truth and correctly handle it. Once we have studied and learned the Word of God, we are to *accurately teach* the Word of God. We are not to teach...
		• our own ideas
		• the theories of other people
		• what we think
		• what other men think

ENGLISH WORD	GREEK WORD AND VERSE	THE WORD MEANS...
POSB REFERENCE (2 Tim. 2:15) Note 2	**2 Tim. 2:15** Study to show thyself approved unto God, a workman that needeth not to be ashamed, **rightly dividing** the word of truth. [KJV] Be diligent to present yourself approved to God as a workman who does not need to be ashamed, **handling accurately** the word of truth. [NASB] Do your best to present yourself to God as one approved, a workman who does not need to be ashamed and who **correctly handles** the word of truth. [NIV] Be diligent to present yourself approved to God, a worker who does not need to be ashamed, **rightly dividing** the word of truth. [NKJV] Work hard so God can approve you. Be a good worker, one who does not need to be ashamed and who **correctly explains** the word of truth. [NLT] σπούδασον σεαυτὸν δόκιμον παραστῆσαι τῷ Θεῷ, ἐργάτην ἀνεπαίσχυντον, **ὀρθοτομοῦντα** τὸν λόγον τῆς ἀληθείας. [GNS] σπούδασον σεαυτὸν δόκιμον παραστῆσαι τῷ θεῷ, ἐργάτην ἀνεπαίσχυντον, **ὀρθοτομοῦντα** τὸν λόγον τῆς ἀληθείας. [GNT]	We are not to mishandle the Word of God: twist it to fit what we think or want it to say; over emphasize or under emphasize its teachings; add to or take away from it. Any person who mishandles God's Word is not approved of God. This is the point of this verse: if we want God's approval—if we want to be acceptable to God—we must study, rush and seek to be a true teacher of God's Word. We must be *workmen* who study God's Word, workmen who study diligently: *who correctly analyze and accurately divide—rightly handle and skillfully teach—the Word of Truth* (Amplified New Testament). This is the believer who will not be ashamed when he faces the Lord Jesus Christ in the great day of judgment.

#3332
Rights
 	
Equal–KJV
Equality–NASB
Equality–NIV
Equal–NKJV
Rights–NLT
 	
POSB REFERENCE (Philip.2:6) Note 2, point 3
	τὸ εἶναι ἴσα = *to einai isa*
	Pronunciation: [to i-nah-ee' ee'-sah]
	Parsing *einai* (part of speech): verb
	  Mood—infinitive
	  Tense—present
	  Voice—active
	  Case—accusative
	  Stem or root—from εἰμί
	Parsing *isa* (part of speech): adjective
	  Type—adverb
	  Stem or root—from ἴσος, η, ον
	Concordance References:
	⇒ Strong's #1510+2470+3588 eimi isos ho
	⇒ NIV #1639+2698+3836 eimi isos ho [equality]
	⇒ NASB #1510+2470+3588 eimi isos ho
	
	Philip. 2:6
	Who, being in the form of God, thought it not robbery to be **equal** with God: [KJV]
	Who, although He existed in the form of God, did not regard **equality** with God a thing to be grasped, [NASB]
	Who, being in very nature God, did not consider **equality** with God something to be grasped, [NIV]
	Who, being in the form of God, did not consider it robbery to be **equal** with God, [NKJV]
	Though he was God, he did not demand and cling to his **rights** as God. [NLT]
	ὃς ἐν μορφῇ Θεοῦ ὑπάρχων, οὐχ ἁρπαγμὸν ἡγήσατο τὸ εἶναι ἴσα Θεῷ, [GNS]
	ὃς ἐν μορφῇ θεοῦ ὑπάρχων οὐχ ἁρπαγμὸν ἡγήσατο τὸ εἶναι ἴσα θεῷ, [GNT]
		Equal, equality, same. Jesus Christ is "equal with God" (Greek). It means to be *on an equal basis with God*; to possess all the being, qualities and attributes of God Himself.
		
		Practical Application
		Note also the word "robbery" [KJV, NKJV] (*arpagmon*). It is the picture of a thief's seeking to snatch or take something that is not his. When Jesus Christ was on earth, He was constantly claiming...
		• to be God.
		• to be the Son of God.
		• to have the nature of God.
		• to be one with God.
		• to be *on an equal basis with God.*
		Was He a thief? Was He robbing and snatching the title of God or was He truly God?
		The answer is a most glorious truth. Jesus Christ did not have to rob or snatch at equality with God. He did not have to rob and grasp after the deity of God; He was already on an equal basis with God.

#3333
Riots
 	
Tumults–KJV
Tumults–NASB
Riots–NIV
Tumults–NKJV
Faced angry mobs– NLT
 	
POSB REFERENCE (2 Cor.6:4-5; esp. v.5) Note 3
	ἀκαταστασίαις = *akatastasiais*
	Pronunciation: [ak-at-as-tah-see'-ah-ees]
	Parsing (part of speech): noun
	  Case—dative
	  Gender—feminine
	  Number—plural
	  Stm or root—from ἀκαταστασία, ας
	Concordance References:
	⇒ Strong's #181 akatastasia
	⇒ NIV #189 akatastasia
	⇒ NASB #181 akatastasia
	
	2 Cor. 6:5
	In stripes, in imprisonments, in **tumults**, in labours, in watchings, in fastings; [KJV]
	In beatings, in imprisonments, in **tumults**, in labors, in sleeplessness, in hunger, [NASB]
	In beatings, imprisonments and **riots**; in hard work,
		Riots, tumults, disorder, revolutions, insurrection; to face angry mob uprisings and attacks.
		
		Practical Application
		Paul often faced angered mobs: at Antioch of Pisidia (Acts 13:50); Lystra (Acts 14:19); Philippi (Acts 16:19); Ephesus (Acts 19:29); and at Jerusalem (Acts 21:30). Mob uprisings present one of the most difficult and frightening situations imaginable for a believer, for a mob cannot be controlled by reason. The believer is unable to be heard, so speech is useless. Believers often face the abuse and ridicule of crowds because of the righteous lives they live and because they refuse to join in the worldly pleasures and indulgences of life. At such times

ENGLISH WORD	GREEK WORD AND VERSE	THE WORD MEANS...
	sleepless nights and hunger; [NIV] 　In stripes, in imprisonments, in **tumults**, in labors, in sleeplessness, in fastings; [NKJV] 　We have been beaten, been put in jail, **faced angry mobs**, worked to exhaustion, endured sleepless nights, and gone without food. [NLT] 　ἐν πληγαῖς, ἐν φυλακαῖς, ἐν **ἀκαταστασίαις**, ἐν κόποις, ἐν ἀγρυπνίαις, ἐν νηστείαις, [GNS] 　ἐν πληγαῖς, ἐν φυλακαῖς, ἐν **ἀκαταστασίαις**, ἐν κόποις, ἐν ἀγρυπνίαις, ἐν νηστείαις, [GNT]	the believer must be consistent in his testimony—no matter the temptation to go along with the crowd. The true believer, layman and minister alike, must steadfastly endure.
#3334 **Rise And Come** Stand forth–KJV **Rise and come– NASB** Stand up–NIV Step forward–NKJV Come and stand–NLT **POSB REFERENCE** (Mk.3:3) Note 2	῎Εγειρε = *Egeire* Pronunciation: [eg-i'-reh] Parsing (part of speech): verb 　Mood—imperative 　Tense—present 　Voice—active 　Person—2nd person 　Number—singular 　Stem or root—from ἐγείρω Concordance References: ⇒　Strong's #1453 egeirō ⇒　NIV #1586 egeirō ⇒　NASB #1453 egeirō **Mark 3:3** 　And he saith unto the man which had the withered hand, **Stand forth**. [KJV] 　And He said to the man with the withered hand, "**Rise and come** forward!" [NASB] 　Jesus said to the man with the shriveled hand, "**Stand up** in front of everyone." [NIV] 　And He said to the man who had the withered hand, "**Step forward**." [NKJV] 　Jesus said to the man, "**Come and stand** in front of everyone." [NLT] 　καὶ λέγει τῷ ἀνθρώπῳ τῷ ἐξηραμμένην ἔχοντι, τὴν χεῖρα ῎Εγειρε εἰς τὸ μέσον. [GNS] 　καὶ λέγει τῷ ἀνθρώπῳ τῷ τὴν ξηρὰν χεῖρα ἔχοντι, ῎Εγειρε εἰς τὸ μέσον. [GNT]	To stand up; to rise and come; to get up. **Practical Application** 　The words "rise and come" (*egeirai eis to meson*) actually say, "Rise up, stand up in the midst." Jesus was calling for the man's will—his willingness to do exactly what the Messiah was saying. The man had to want help enough to be willing to stand before the audience and before the scornful religionists. By such a stand he would be confessing his faith in Jesus and in His power to save and heal.
#3335 **Risked– Risking** Not regarding–KJV **Risking–NASB** **Risking–NIV** Not regarding–NKJV **Risked–NLT** **POSB REFERENCE** (Philip.2:28-30; esp. v.30) Note 4	παραβολευσάμενος = *paraboleusamenos* Pronunciation: [par-ab-ool-yoo'-sah-mehn-os] Parsing (part of speech): verb 　Mood—participle 　Tense—aorist 　Voice—middle deponent 　Case—nominative 　Gender—masculine 　Number—singular 　Stem or root—from παραβολεύομαι Concordance References: ⇒　Strong's #3851 paraboleuomai ⇒　NIV #4129 paraboleuomai ⇒　NASB #3851 paraboleuomai **Philip. 2:30** 　Because for the work of Christ he was nigh unto death, **not regarding** his life, to supply your lack of service toward me. [KJV] 　Because he came close to death for the work of Christ, **risking** his life to complete what was deficient in your service to me. [NASB] 　Because he almost died for the work of Christ, **risking** his life to make up for the help you could not give me. [NIV] 　Because for the work of Christ he came close to death, **not regarding** his life, to supply what was lacking in your service toward me. [NKJV] 　For he **risked** his life for the work of Christ, and he was at the point of death while trying to do for me the things you couldn't do because you were far away. [NLT] 　ὅτι διὰ τὸ ἔργον τοῦ Χριστοῦ μέχρι θανάτου ἤγγισε,	Risk, not regarding. It means to take a chance, a venture, a dare, a hazard. **Practical Application** 　A.T. Robertson points out that this is a gambling word, that it means to gamble one's life; to stake everything; to chance everything; to recklessly gamble. Epaphroditus staked his life for the ministry of Christ. He courageously risked his life. (*Word Pictures in the New Testament*, Vol.4, p.449.) 　Epaphroditus both challenges and rebukes a soft, easy going Christianity and ministry. His life shows that Christianity is stern and demanding. It calls for self-denial and self-effacing sacrifice. It gives little thought to personal comfort and safety.

ENGLISH WORD	GREEK WORD AND VERSE	THE WORD MEANS...
	δὲ μή, εἶπον ἀν ὑμῖν; πορεύομαι ἑτοιμάσαι τόπον ὑμῖν. [GNS] ἐν τῇ οἰκίᾳ τοῦ πατρός μου **μοναὶ** πολλαί εἰσιν· εἰ δὲ μή, εἶπον ἀν ὑμῖν ὅτι πορεύομαι ἑτοιμάσαι τόπον ὑμῖν; [GNT]	
#3340 **Rose Up** Arose–KJV **Rose up–NASB** Opposition arose–NIV Arose–NKJV Started–NLT **POSB REFERENCE** (Acts 6:9-10; esp. v.9) Note 2, point 2	ἀνέστησαν = anestēsan Pronunciation: [an-is'-tay-san] Parsing (part of speech): verb 　　Mood—indicative 　　Tense—aorist 　　Voice—active 　　Person—3rd person 　　Number—plural 　　Stem or root—from ἀνίστημι Concordance References: ⇒　Strong's #450 anistemi ⇒　NIV #482 anistēmi ⇒　NASB #450 anistemi **Acts 6:9** Then there **arose** certain of the synagogue, which is called the synagogue of the Libertines, and Cyrenians, and Alexandrians, and of them of Cilicia and of Asia, disputing with Stephen. [KJV] But some men from what was called the Synagogue of the Freedmen, including both Cyrenians and Alexandrians, and some from Cilicia and Asia, **rose up** and argued with Stephen. [NASB] **Opposition arose**, however, from members of the Synagogue of the Freedmen (as it was called)—Jews of Cyrene and Alexandria as well as the provinces of Cilicia and Asia. These men began to argue with Stephen, [NIV] Then there **arose** some from what is called the Synagogue of the Freedmen (Cyrenians, Alexandrians, and those from Cilicia and Asia), disputing with Stephen. [NKJV] But one day some men from the Synagogue of Freed Slaves, as it was called, **started** to debate with him. They were Jews from Cyrene, Alexandria, Cilicia, and the province of Asia. [NLT] ἀνέστησαν δέ τινες τῶν ἐκ τῆς συναγωγῆς τῆς λεγομένης Λιβερτίνων, καὶ Κυρηναίων, καὶ Ἀλεξανδρέων, καὶ τῶν ἀπὸ Κιλικίας καὶ Ἀσίας, συζητοῦντες τῷ Στεφάνῳ. [GNS] ἀνέστησαν δέ τινες τῶν ἐκ τῆς συναγωγῆς τῆς λεγομένης Λιβερτίνων καὶ Κυρηναίων καὶ Ἀλεξανδρέων καὶ τῶν ἀπὸ Κιλικίας καὶ Ἀσίας συζητοῦντες τῷ Στεφάνῳ, [GNT]	Opposition arose; stood up. **Practical Application** 　Five synagogues in particular stood up against Stephen. They opposed what he was preaching. There was a strong reason for the opposition of the Grecian Jews. They and their forefathers had been forcibly deported out of their homeland and scattered across the world by the Romans. While living in the foreign lands of the world, they had remained faithful to their Jewish religion. The message of Jesus Christ was a threat to them and their religion.
#3341 **Rot In The Grave** Corruption–KJV Decay–NASB Decay–NIV Corruption–NKJV **Rot in the grave–NLT** **POSB REFERENCE** (Acts 2:25-28; esp. v.27) Note 1, point 2c (Acts 2:27) *Deeper Study* #1, point 2	διαφθοράν = diaphthoran Pronunciation: [dee-af-thor-ahn'] Parsing (part of speech): noun 　　Case—accusative 　　Gender—feminine 　　Number—singular 　　Stem or root—from διαφθορά, ᾶς Concordance References: ⇒　Strong's #1312 diaphthora ⇒　NIV #1426 diaphthora ⇒　NASB #1312 diaphthora **Acts 2:27** Because thou wilt not leave my soul in hell, neither wilt thou suffer thine Holy One to see **corruption**. [KJV] Because Thou wilt not abandon my soul to Hades, Nor ALLOW Thy Holy One to UNDERGO **DECAY**. [NASB] Because you will not abandon me to the grave, nor will you let your Holy One see **decay**. [NIV] *For You will not leave my soul in Hades, Nor will You allow Your Holy One to see* **corruption**. [NKJV] For you will not leave my soul among the dead or allow your Holy One to **rot in the grave**. [NLT]	Decay; corrupt; deteriorate, putrefy, perish. It speaks of the grave and the rotting of a dead body. **Practical Application** 　In no place does Christ promise a new body to the unbeliever, to the unsaved and lost. A person's body and flesh can be destroyed forever. (This is a fact seldom pointed out.)

ENGLISH WORD	GREEK WORD AND VERSE	THE WORD MEANS...
See also POSB REF: (Acts 13:32-37; esp. v.34) *Deeper Study #4*	ὅτι οὐκ ἐγκαταλείψεις τὴν ψυχήν μου εἰς ᾅδου, οὐδὲ δώσεις τὸν ὅσιόν σου ἰδεῖν **διαφθοράν**. [GNS] ὅτι οὐκ ἐγκαταλείψεις τὴν ψυχήν μου εἰς ᾅδην οὐδὲ δώσεις τὸν ὅσιόν σου ἰδεῖν **διαφθοράν**. [GNT]	

#3342
 Rotted– Rotting Away
 	
 Corrupted–KJV
 Rotted–NASB
 Rotted–NIV
 Corrupted–NKJV
 Rotting away–NLT
 	
 POSB REFERENCE
 (Jas.5:2-3; esp. v.2)
 Note 2
	σέσηπεν = sesëpen
	 Pronunciation: [seh-say'-pehn]
	 Parsing (part of speech): verb
	     Mood—indicative
	     Tense—perfect
	     Voice—active
	     Person—3rd person
	     Number—singular
	     Stem or root—from σήπω
	 Concordance References:
	 ⇒ Strong's #4595 sëpö
	 ⇒ NIV #4960 sëpö
	 ⇒ NASB #4595 sëpö
	
	 James 5:2
	 Your riches are **corrupted**, and your garments are motheaten. [KJV]
	 Your riches have **rotted** and your garments have become moth-eaten. [NASB]
	 Your wealth has **rotted**, and moths have eaten your clothes. [NIV]
	 Your riches are **corrupted**, and your garments are moth-eaten. [NKJV]
	 Your wealth is **rotting away**, and your fine clothes are moth-eaten rags. [NLT]
	 ὁ πλοῦτος ὑμῶν **σέσηπε**, καὶ τὰ ἱμάτια ὑμῶν σητόβρωτα γέγονεν· [GNS]
	 ὁ πλοῦτος ὑμῶν **σέσηπεν** καὶ τὰ ἱμάτια ὑμῶν σητόβρωτα γέγονεν, [GNT]
		Rotted, corrupted.
		
		 Practical Application
		 This (wealth or riches) would refer to such things as farm produce like wheat and vegetables or building products like wood or wallboard. Many a person gains a comfortable and lavish living and, in some cases, wealth through an industry (like farming or construction) whose products eventually rot away.

#3343
 Roused
 	
 Stirred up–KJV
 Stirred up–NASB
 Stirred up–NIV
 Stirred up–NKJV
 Roused–NLT
 	
 POSB REFERENCE
 (Acts 6:11-14, esp. v.12)
 Note 3, point 1
	συνεκίνησάν = sunekinësan
	 Pronunciation: [soon-eh-kin-eh'-san]
	 Parsing (part of speech): verb
	     Mood—indicative
	     Tense—aorist
	     Voice—active
	     Person—3rd person
	     Number—plural
	     Stem or root—from συγκινέω
	 Concordance References:
	 ⇒ Strong's #4787 sugkineo
	 ⇒ NIV #5167 sugkineö
	 ⇒ NASB #4787 sugkineo
	
	 Acts 6:12
	 And they **stirred up** the people, and the elders, and the scribes, and came upon *him,* and caught him, and brought *him* to the council, [KJV]
	 And they **stirred up** the people, the elders and the scribes, and they came upon him and dragged him away, and brought him before the Council. [NASB]
	 So they **stirred up** the people and the elders and the teachers of the law. They seized Stephen and brought him before the Sanhedrin. [NIV]
	 And they **stirred up** the people, the elders, and the scribes; and they came upon *him,* seized him, and brought *him* to the council. [NKJV]
	 Naturally, this **roused** the crowds, the elders, and the teachers of religious law. So they arrested Stephen and brought him before the high council. [NLT]
	 συνεκίνησάν τε τὸν λαὸν καὶ τοὺς πρεσβυτέρους καὶ τοὺς γραμματεῖς, καὶ ἐπιστάντες συνήρπασαν αὐτόν, καὶ ἤγαγον εἰς τὸ συνέδριον, [GNS]
	 συνεκίνησάν τε τὸν λαὸν καὶ τοὺς πρεσβυτέρους καὶ τοὺς γραμματεῖς, καὶ ἐπιστάντες συνήρπασαν αὐτὸν καὶ ἤγαγον εἰς τὸ συνέδριον, [GNT]
		To stir up, arouse.
		
		 Practical Application
		 It means to shake as a volcano; to move and rock together as with a violent shaking. This was the first time the people themselves were aroused against the disciples.

ENGLISH WORD	GREEK WORD AND VERSE	THE WORD MEANS...

#3344
Royal Official
 	
Nobleman–KJV
Royal official–NASB
Royal official–NIV
Nobleman–NKJV
Government official–
NLT
 	
POSB
REFERENCE
(Jn.4:46-47; esp. v.46)
Note 1
	βασιλικός = basilikos
	Pronunciation: [bas-il-ee-kos']
	Parsing (part of speech): pronominal adjective
	    Case—nominative
	    Gender—masculine
	    Number—singular
	    Stem or root—from βασιλικός, ή, όν
	Concordance References:
	  ⇒ Strong's #937 basilikos
	  ⇒ NIV #997 basilikos
	  ⇒ NASB #937 basilikos
	
	John 4:46
	So Jesus came again into Cana of Galilee, where he made the water wine. And there was a certain **nobleman**, whose son was sick at Capernaum. [KJV]
	He came therefore again to Cana of Galilee where He had made the water wine. And there was a certain **royal official**, whose son was sick at Capernaum. [NASB]
	Once more he visited Cana in Galilee, where he had turned the water into wine. And there was a certain **royal official** whose son lay sick at Capernaum. [NIV]
	So Jesus came again to Cana of Galilee where He had made the water wine. And there was a certain **nobleman** whose son was sick at Capernaum. [NKJV]
	In the course of his journey through Galilee, he arrived at the town of Cana, where he had turned the water into wine. There was a **government official** in the city of Capernaum whose son was very sick. [NLT]
	Ἦλθεν οὖν ὁ Ἰησοῦς πάλιν εἰς τὴν Κανὰ τῆς Γαλιλαίας, ὅπου ἐποίησε τὸ ὕδωρ οἶνον. καὶ ἦν τις **βασιλικός**. οὗ ὁ υἱὸς ἠσθένει ἐν Καπερναούμ· [GNS]
	Ἦλθεν οὖν πάλιν εἰς τὴν Κανὰ τῆς Γαλιλαίας, ὅπου ἐποίησεν τὸ ὕδωρ οἶνον. καὶ ἦν τις **βασιλικός** οὗ ὁ υἱὸς ἠσθένει ἐν Καφαρναούμ. [GNT]
		A royal official; a nobleman; a government official; a secular leader. This man was an official of the King's royal court.
		
		Practical Application
		Needs confront every human being. Eventually the severe needs arising from accident, illness, disease, suffering, and death strike everyone. No one is exempt. One may be an official in government or even the King himself—it does not matter. The day eventually comes when every person needs help. The severe disasters of life are beyond any person's control.

#3345
Rude
 	
Behave itself unseemly–KJV
Act unbecomingly–NASB
Rude–NIV
Behave rudely–NKJV
Rude–NLT
 	
POSB
REFERENCE
(1 Cor.13:4-7; esp. v.5)
Note 2, point 6
	ἀσχημονεῖ = aschēmonei
	Pronunciation: [as-kay-mon-ee']
	Parsing (part of speech): verb
	    Mood—indicative
	    Tense—present
	    Voice—active
	    Person—3rd person
	    Number—singular
	    Stem or root—from ἀσχημονέω
	Concordance References:
	  ⇒ Strong's #807 aschēmoneō
	  ⇒ NIV #858 aschēmoneō
	  ⇒ NASB #809 aschēmoneō
	
	1 Cor. 13:5
	Doth not **behave itself unseemly**, seeketh not her own, is not easily provoked, thinketh no evil; [KJV]
	Does not **act unbecomingly**; it does not seek its own, is not provoked, does not take into account a wrong suffered, [NASB]
	It is not **rude**, it is not self-seeking, it is not easily angered, it keeps no record of wrongs. [NIV]
	Does not **behave rudely**, does not seek its own, is not provoked, thinks no evil; [NKJV]
	Or **rude**. Love does not demand its own way. Love is not irritable, and it keeps no record of when it has been wronged. [NLT]
	οὐκ **ἀσχημονεῖ**, οὐ ζητεῖ τὰ ἑαυτῆς, οὐ παροξύνεται, οὐ λογίζεται τὸ κακόν, [GNS]
	οὐκ **ἀσχημονεῖ**, οὐ ζητεῖ τὰ ἑαυτῆς, οὐ παροξύνεται, οὐ λογίζεται τὸ κακόν, [GNT]
		Unbecomingly, rudely, indecently, unmannerly, disgracefully.
		
		Practical Application
		Love does nothing to shame oneself. Love is orderly and controlled, and it behaves and treats all persons with respect, honoring and respecting who they are.

#3346
Rudiments
	στοιχείων = stoicheiōn
	Pronunciation: [stoy-khi'-on]
	Parsing (part of speech): noun
	    Case—genitive
	    Gender—neuter
		Basic principles; rudiments; elements; elementary principles; first lessons; evil powers.

ENGLISH WORD	GREEK WORD AND VERSE	THE WORD MEANS...

Rudiments–KJV
Elementary princi-
ples–NASB
Basic principles–NIV
Basic principles–
NKJV
Evil powers–NLT
 	
**POSB
REFERENCE**
(Col.2:20)
Note 1
	Number—plural
	Stem or root—from στοιχεῖα, ων
	Concordance References:
	⇒ Strong's #4747 stoicheion
	⇒ NIV #5122 stoicheion
	⇒ NASB #4747 stoicheion
	
	Col. 2:20
	Wherefore if ye be dead with Christ from the **rudiments** of the world, why, as though living in the world, are ye subject to ordinances, [KJV]
	
	If you have died with Christ to the **elementary principles** of the world, why, as if you were living in the world, do you submit yourself to decrees, such as, [NASB]
	
	Since you died with Christ to the **basic principles** of this world, why, as though you still belonged to it, do you submit to its rules: [NIV]
	
	Therefore, if you died with Christ from the **basic principles** of the world, why, as though living in the world, do you subject yourselves to regulations— [NKJV]
	
	You have died with Christ, and he has set you free from the **evil powers** of this world. So why do you keep on following rules of the world, such as, [NLT]
	
	Εἰ οὖν ἀπεθάνετε σὺν τῷ Χριστῷ, ἀπὸ τῶν **στοιχείων** τοῦ κόσμου, τί ὡς ζῶντες ἐν κόσμῳ δογματίζεσθε, [GNS]
	
	Εἰ ἀπεθάνετε σὺν Χριστῷ ἀπὸ τῶν **στοιχείων** τοῦ κόσμου, τί ὡς ζῶντες ἐν κόσμῳ δογματίζεσθε; [GNT]
		Practical Application
		The word "rudiments" (*stoicheïon*) means two things and Christ saves us from both. (See POSB note, Philosophy—Col. 2:8 for more discussion.)
		1. *Rudiments* means crude notions of men about the universe—that is, about God, reality, and truth. It is man's ideas and philosophies, their elementary or rudimentary teachings, their ABC understanding of God and the universe, reality, and truth. When men think of God, they come up with all kinds of ways and laws to reach Him and to secure His approval and acceptance. However, there are three basic problems with man's approach to God.
		  a. First, we cannot keep rules and laws—not in a perfect sense. No matter what way we choose to reach God, we cannot walk a straight path to Him.
		  b. Second, once we have broken a rule or law, we stand guilty before God. Therefore, we must be judged, condemned, and punished for having broken the law. A law breaker is guilty and unacceptable, and the punishment must be borne. Therefore, rules and laws cannot make us acceptable to God. They can only lead to guilt and condemnation.
		  c. Third, we die; we do not live forever. Moreover, there is no law or force on this earth that can give us the energy and power to live forever. Rules and laws only condemn us when we break them. They have no power to save us from death nor to give us eternal life. Because of this, rules and laws cannot be the way to approach God.
		    How then can we approach God? If the best thinking of men about the universe and God are not the way to approach God, what is the way? The answer will be discussed in a moment, but first look at the second meaning of the term *rudiments*.
		2. *Rudiments* means the basic elements or materials of the universe, the things that men say lie behind the universe or at the very base of reality. Down through the centuries, men have posed all kinds of forces, energies, powers, principalities, spirits, angels, and beings as standing behind the universe and life. As a result, men have committed their lives to and worshipped all sorts of creatures and forces or elements and materials. However, there is a critical problem with this approach to God, a problem that dooms all who seek truth and who approach God through the elements of this universe or through the spirits of the spiritual world.
		  a. First, there is the problem of corruption. Everything in the universe is corruptible, aging, dying, deteriorating, and decaying. Therefore, there is nothing in the universe that can save man, for the way of all things—all elements and all materials—is the way of change and death.
		  b. Second, there is a problem with seeking truth and God through the spirits or angels of a spiritual world.
		    ⇒ First, man cannot penetrate the spiritual world. He is physical, and the physi-

ENGLISH WORD	GREEK WORD AND VERSE	THE WORD MEANS...
		cal just cannot move over into the world of the spiritual no matter what any person claims. If the spiritual world is ever to be known, then the spiritual has to reveal itself to us. ⇒ Second, any person who claims to have been given visions or revelations by the spiritual world still has the same problems that everyone else has: the problems of imperfection (unrighteousness), death, and eternal life. No angel, spirit, or any other intermediary has ever taken care of the problem of sin and death and of eternal life for us. We have already sinned, and we are already imperfect. Therefore, someone, someplace must *bear our sin* or punishment for us or else we have to pay for it ourselves. And, in addition, someone has to go through the experience of death to conquer it and tell us how to do the same or else we are going to die and never reach God. This is the glorious message of the gospel. God is love, eternal and infinite love, so He has done all this for us. He did it through His Son, Jesus Christ.

#3347
Ruin, Don't
 	
Destroy not–KJV
Do not destroy–NASB
Do not...destroy–NIV
Do not destroy–NKJV
Don't...ruin–NLT
 	
**POSB
REFERENCE**
(Rom.14:13-15; esp.
v.15)
Note 6, point 2
	μὴ ἀπόλλυε = *më apollue*
	Pronunciation: [may hap-ol'-loo-eh]
	Parsing *apollue* (part of speech): verb
	   Mood—imperative
	   Tense—present
	   Voice—active
	   Person—2nd person
	   Number—singular
	   Stem or root—from ἀπόλλυμι
	Concordance References:
	⇒ Strong's #3361 më + 622 apollumi
	⇒ NIV #3590 më [not] + 660 apollumi [destroy]
	⇒ NASB #3361 më + 622 apollumi
	
	Romans 14:15
	But if thy brother be grieved with thy meat, now walkest thou not charitably. **Destroy not** him with thy meat, for whom Christ died. [KJV]
	For if because of food your brother is hurt, you are no longer walking according to love. **Do not destroy** with your food him for whom Christ died. [NASB]
	If your brother is distressed because of what you eat, you are no longer acting in love. **Do not** by your eating **destroy** your brother for whom Christ died. [NIV]
	Yet if your brother is grieved because of *your* food, you are no longer walking in love. **Do not destroy** with your food the one for whom Christ died. [NKJV]
	And if another Christian is distressed by what you eat, you are not acting in love if you eat it. **Don't** let your eating **ruin** someone for whom Christ died. [NLT]
	εἰ δὲ διὰ βρῶμα ὁ ἀδελφός σου λυπεῖται, οὐκέτι κατὰ ἀγάπην περιπατεῖς. **μὴ** τῷ βρώματί σου ἐκεῖνον **ἀπόλλυε**, ὑπὲρ οὗ Χριστὸς ἀπέθανε. [GNS]
	εἰ γὰρ διὰ βρῶμα ὁ ἀδελφός σου λυπεῖται, οὐκέτι κατὰ ἀγάπην περιπατεῖς· **μὴ** τῷ βρώματί σου ἐκεῖνον **ἀπόλλυε** ὑπὲρ οὗ Χριστὸς ἀπέθανεν. [GNT]
		Do not destroy, don't ruin; to not spoil; to hurt and wound to the point of ruining.
		
		Practical Application
		We are to do nothing that would destroy a brother. This is a forceful command: "Do not don't ruin (*më apollue*)." Such behavior is absolutely forbidden of the Christian believer. We are to do absolutely nothing that would destroy or ruin our brother.

#3348
Ruins
 	
Defile–KJV
Destroys–NASB
Destroys–NIV
	φθερεῖ = *phtheirei*
	Pronunciation: [fthee'-ree]
	Parsing (part of speech): verb
	   Mood—indicative
	   Tense—future
	   Voice—active
	   Person—3rd person
	   Number—singular
		To destroy; to defile; to ruin; to corrupt; to lead astray.
		
		Practical Application
		The person who ruins the church shall face terrible judgment. The point is striking: the person who troubles the church will suffer the same

ENGLISH WORD	GREEK WORD AND VERSE	THE WORD MEANS...
Defiles–NKJV Ruins–NLT **POSB REFERENCE** (1 Cor.3:17) Note 7	Stem or root—from φθείρω Concordance References: ⇒ Strong's #5351 phtheirō ⇒ NIV #5780 phtheirō ⇒ NASB #5351 phtheirō **1 Cor. 3:17** If any man **defile** the temple of God, him shall God destroy; for the temple of God is holy, which temple ye are. [KJV] If any man **destroys** the temple of God, God will destroy him, for the temple of God is holy, and that is what you are. [NASB] If anyone **destroys** God's temple, God will destroy him; for God's temple is sacred, and you are that temple. [NIV] If anyone **defiles** the temple of God, God will destroy him. For the temple of God is holy, which temple you are. [NKJV] God will bring ruin upon anyone who **ruins** this temple. For God's temple is holy, and you Christians are that temple. [NLT] εἴ τις τὸν ναὸν τοῦ Θεοῦ φθείρει, **φθερεῖ** τοῦτον ὁ Θεός· ὁ γὰρ ναὸς τοῦ Θεοῦ ἅγιός ἐστιν, οἵτινές ἐστε ὑμεῖς. [GNS] εἴ τις τὸν ναὸν τοῦ θεοῦ φθείρει, **φθερεῖ** τοῦτον ὁ θεός· ὁ γὰρ ναὸς τοῦ θεοῦ ἅγιός ἐστιν, οἵτινές ἐστε ὑμεῖς. [GNT]	kind of trouble himself. Whatever he sows, he is definitely going to reap. Troublemaking within the church destroys the spirit of unity and love within the church. To corrupt and destroy the church is to invite God to corrupt and destroy the troublemaker. Note that the punishment is not specifically described. It is simply made clear that he who does such a terrible thing as trouble a church will suffer a terrible punishment. He will be ruined: destroyed, wrecked, torn apart, ripped, devastated.

#3349
Rule
 	
Rule–KJV
Rule–NASB
Direct–NIV
Rule–NKJV
Do their work–NLT
 	
**POSB
REFERENCE**
(1 Tim.5:17-18;esp.
v.17)
Note 1
	προεστῶτες = proestōtes
	Pronunciation: [pro-ehst'-o-tehs]
	Parsing (part of speech): verb
	  Mood—participle
	  Tense—perfect
	  Voice—active
	  Case—nominative
	  Gender—plural
	  Stem or root—from προΐστημι
	Concordance References:
	⇒ Strong's #4291 proistēmi
	⇒ NIV #4613 proistēmi
	⇒ NASB #4291 proistēmi
	
	1 Tim. 5:17
	Let the elders that **rule** well be counted worthy of double honour, especially they who labour in the word and doctrine. [KJV]
	Let the elders who **rule** well be considered worthy of double honor, especially those who work hard at preaching and teaching. [NASB]
	The elders who **direct** the affairs of the church well are worthy of double honor, especially those whose work is preaching and teaching. [NIV]
	Let the elders who **rule** well be counted worthy of double honor, especially those who labor in the word and doctrine. [NKJV]
	Elders who **do their work** well should be paid well, especially those who work hard at both preaching and teaching. [NLT]
	Οἱ καλῶς **προεστῶτες** πρεσβύτεροι διπλῆς τιμῆς ἀξιούσθωσαν, μάλιστα οἱ κοπιῶντες ἐν λόγῳ καὶ διδασκαλίᾳ· [GNS]
	Οἱ καλῶς **προεστῶτες** πρεσβύτεροι διπλῆς τιμῆς ἀξιούσθωσαν, μάλιστα οἱ κοπιῶντες ἐν λόγῳ καὶ διδασκαλίᾳ. [GNT]
		To direct; to rule; to do their work; to be a manager; to be a leader; to have authority over. The word (proestōtes) is a general word meaning to oversee, supervise, and look after.
		
		Practical Application
		There is a condition attached to honoring the minister. The minister to be honored is one who "rules well." The minister who is worthy of double honor is the minister who labors and labors and works and works. If he is to receive double honor, then he must demonstrate a double commitment to Christ and the church.
		Note also that the whole ministerial staff is covered by this charge. All the ministers of a church staff are to be counted worthy of double honor. But there is one minister who is singled out: the minister who labors in the Word and doctrine, that is, who preaches and teaches. It is he upon whom so much responsibility lies: he is the minister who takes the lead in edifying and building up the believer and the church. He is the one who has to spend hours on his face before God and in the Word in order to preach and teach—this in addition to taking the lead in all the other duties and ministries of the church. If he is a committed minister, a minister who labors and labors for Christ and works and works for the church, then he is worthy of double honor.

#3350
Rulers
 	
Principalities–KJV
Rulers–NASB
Rulers–NIV
	ἀρχάς = archas
	Pronunciation: [ar-khas']
	Parsing (part of speech): noun
	  Case—accusative
	  Gender—feminine
	  Number—plural
	  Stem or root—from ἀρχή, ῆς
		Rulers, principalities, evil rulers, ruling powers.
		
		Practical Application
		The great Greek scholar Kenneth Wuest identifies the forces of evil as follows:
		⇒ The principalities (archas): "the first ones,

ENGLISH WORD	GREEK WORD AND VERSE	THE WORD MEANS...

#3354
Sabbath
 	
Sabbath–KJV
Sabbath–NASB
Sabbath–NIV
Sabbath–NKJV
Sabbath–NLT
 	
POSB
REFERENCE
(Mt.12:1)
Deeper Study #1
	σάββασιν = *sabbasin*
	Pronunciation: [sab'-bah-sin]
	Parsing (part of speech): noun
	    Case—dative
	    Gender—neuter
	    Number—plural
	    Stem or root—from σάββατον, ου
	Concordance References:
	  ⇒ Strong's #4521 sabbaton
	  ⇒ NIV #4879 sabbaton
	  ⇒ NASB #4521 sabbaton
	
	Matthew 12:1
	At that time Jesus went on the **sabbath** day through the corn; and his disciples were an hungred, and began to pluck the ears of corn, and to eat. [KJV]
	At that time Jesus went on the **Sabbath** through the grainfields, and His disciples became hungry and began to pick the heads of grain and eat. [NASB]
	At that time Jesus went through the grainfields on the **Sabbath**. His disciples were hungry and began to pick some heads of grain and eat them. [NIV]
	At that time Jesus went through the grainfields on the **Sabbath**. And His disciples were hungry, and began to pluck heads of grain and to eat. [NKJV]
	At about that time Jesus was walking through some grainfields on the **Sabbath**. His disciples were hungry, so they began breaking off heads of wheat and eating the grain. [NLT]
	Ἐν ἐκείνῳ τῷ καιρῷ ἐπορεύθη ὁ Ἰησοῦς τοῖς **σάββασι** διὰ τῶν σπορίμων· οἱ δὲ μαθηταὶ αὐτοῦ ἐπείνασαν, καὶ ἤρξαντο τίλλειν στάχυας καὶ ἐσθίειν. [GNS]
	Ἐν ἐκείνῳ τῷ καιρῷ ἐπορεύθη ὁ Ἰησοῦς τοῖς **σάββασιν** διὰ τῶν σπορίμων· οἱ δὲ μαθηταὶ αὐτοῦ ἐπείνασαν καὶ ἤρξαντο τίλλειν στάχυας καὶ ἐσθίειν. [GNT]
		Rest, cessation of labor, the sacred Jewish day of worship and rest.
		
		Practical Application
		The Sabbath is the seventh day of each week (Saturday). It was the day Israel celebrated by resting and doing absolutely no work. It was based upon the seventh day when God rested following His six days of creation (Gen.2:2-3). Jewish law prohibited work on the sabbath, allowing no activity whatsoever, not even the plucking of corn if one was hungry.

#3355
Sacred Trust
 	
Dispensation–KJV
Stewardship–NASB
Trust–NIV
Stewardship–NKJV
Sacred trust–NLT
 	
POSB
REFERENCE
(1 Cor.9:16-17; esp.
v.17)
Note 2
	οἰκονομίαν = *oikonomian*
	Pronunciation: [oy-kon-om-ee'-ahn]
	Parsing (part of speech): noun
	    Case—accusative
	    Gender—feminine
	    Number—singular
	    Stem or root—from οἰκονομία, ας
	Concordance References:
	  ⇒ Strong's #3622 oikonomia
	  ⇒ NIV #3873 oikonomia
	  ⇒ NASB #3622 oikonomia
	
	1 Cor. 9:17
	For if I do this thing willingly, I have a reward: but if against my will, a **dispensation** of the gospel is committed unto me. [KJV]
	For if I do this voluntarily, I have a reward; but if against my will, I have a **stewardship** entrusted to me. [NASB]
	If I preach voluntarily, I have a reward; if not voluntarily, I am simply discharging the **trust** committed to me. [NIV]
	For if I do this willingly, I have a reward; but if against my will, I have been entrusted with a **stewardship**. [NKJV]
	If I were doing this of my own free will, then I would deserve payment. But God has chosen me and given me this **sacred trust**, and I have no choice. [NLT]
	εἰ γὰρ ἑκὼν τοῦτο πράσσω, μισθὸν ἔχω· εἰ δὲ ἄκων, **οἰκονομίαν** πεπίστευμαι. [GNS]
	εἰ γὰρ ἑκὼν τοῦτο πράσσω, μισθὸν ἔχω· εἰ δὲ ἄκων, **οἰκονομίαν**, πεπίστευμαι. [GNT]
		A stewardship; a sacred trust; a commission; a responsibility.
		
		Practical Application
		The steward was the manager of a large household or estate. The minister of God is the manager of God's household and estate (church).
		Once God had called Paul to preach, the stewardship and sacred trust of preaching was his. Whether he followed through and preached did not matter; he was still responsible for preaching. There was no release from the call and duty. He would stand accountable for preaching the gospel, or he would stand accountable for not preaching the gospel.
		The call to preach the gospel is an awesome responsibility. God places the sacred trust of the gospel into the hands of the person He calls. Just think about it: whatever these persons do with the gospel is all that will be done with the gospel—nothing more, nothing less. God has placed His gospel—the sacred trust of it—into the hands of the persons He calls. Only what they do with the gospel will be done. What an awesome responsibility!

ENGLISH WORD	GREEK WORD AND VERSE	THE WORD MEANS...

#3356
Sacrifice
 	
Propitiation–KJV
Propitiation–NASB
Atoning sacrifice–NIV
Propitiation–NKJV
Sacrifice–NLT
 	
**POSB
REFERENCE**
(1 Jn.2:1-2; esp. v.2)
Note 3, point 2
 	
See also POSB REF:
(1 Jn.2:2)
Deeper Study #1
	ἱλασμός = *hilasmos*
	Pronunciation: [hil-as-mos']
	Parsing (part of speech): noun
	    Case—nominative
	    Gender—masculine
	    Number—singular
	    Stem or root—from ἱλασμός, οῦ
	Concordance References:
	  ⇒ Strong's #2434 hilasmos
	  ⇒ NIV #2662 hilasmos
	  ⇒ NASB #2434 hilasmos
	
	1 John 2:2
	And he is the **propitiation** for our sins: and not for ours only, but also for the sins of the whole world. [KJV]
	
	And He Himself is the **propitiation** for our sins; and not for ours only, but also for those of the whole world. [NASB]
	
	He is the **atoning sacrifice** for our sins, and not only for ours but also for the sins of the whole world. [NIV]
	
	And He Himself is the **propitiation** for our sins, and not for ours only but also for the whole world. [NKJV]
	
	He is the **sacrifice** for our sins. He takes away not only our sins but the sins of all the world. [NLT]
	
	καὶ αὐτὸς ἱλασμός ἐστι περὶ τῶν ἁμαρτιῶν ἡμῶν· οὐ περὶ τῶν ἡμετέρων δὲ μόνον, ἀλλὰ καὶ περὶ ὅλου τοῦ κόσμου. [GNS]
	
	καὶ αὐτὸς ἱλασμός, ἐστιν περὶ τῶν ἁμαρτιῶν ἡμῶν, οὐ περὶ τῶν ἡμετέρων δὲ μόνον ἀλλὰ καὶ περὶ ὅλου τοῦ κόσμου. [GNT]
		Atoning sacrifice, propitiation. It means to be a sacrifice, a covering, a satisfaction, a payment, an appeasement for sin. It means to turn away anger or to make reconciliation between God and man.
		
		Practical Application
		Jesus Christ is *the atoning sacrifice, the propitiation for our sins.* Remember: God is holy and just. He is perfect love, but He is also perfect holiness and justice. Therefore, He must execute justice against the sinner. He must judge and condemn sin. His justice must be perfectly satisfied. Now there is only one way God's justice can be perfectly satisfied: His justice has to be cast against the *perfect sacrifice.* If there were a Perfect and Ideal Man, that Man could accept the guilt and punishment for sin. The Perfect Man could step forward to bear the punishment for sin and satisfy the justice of God.
		
		This is the glorious gospel, the wonderful love and provision of God. Jesus Christ is the Ideal and Perfect Man. Therefore, He sacrificed His life for man and His sacrifice covered all men. As the Ideal Man, Jesus Christ accepted the guilt and punishment of sin for all men. He died for all men. When He died, He died as the perfect sacrifice for sins. Therefore, God accepts His death...
		• as the *sacrifice* for our sins.
		• as the *covering* for our sins.
		• as the *satisfaction* for our sins.
		• as the *payment* for the penalty of our sins.
		• as the *appeasement* of His wrath against sin.
		
		When Jesus Christ carries a man's case before God, He pleads His own righteousness and death, and God accepts His righteousness and death for man. It is by this, by His sacrifice and death for our sins, that we become acceptable to God.
		
		Note one other point: Jesus Christ is the sacrifice for the sins of the *whole world.* He is the eternal Son of God, the Ideal and Perfect Man. Therefore, all that He ever did covers eternity. His sacrifice for sin covers the first man ever born and spans all of time over to the last man, and then continues right on throughout all of eternity. Jesus Christ paid the penalty of sin for all sinners of all generations. He died for the sins of all people, no matter who they are or what they have done.
		
		But note a critical fact: a person has to come to Jesus Christ and trust Him to be his advocate before God. Jesus Christ is the only Person who has the right to stand as an advocate in the court of God's perfect justice. He is the only Person who can present man's case before God and have man declared righteous. Therefore, a person is not covered by the advocacy of Christ unless he comes to Christ and has Christ represent him before God.

#3357
**Sacrifice Of
Atonement**
	ἱλαστήριον = *hilastērion*
	Pronunciation: [hil-as-tay'-ree-on]
	Parsing (part of speech): pronominal adjective
	    Case—accusative
	    Gender—neuter
		To be a sacrifice, a covering, a satisfaction, a payment, an appeasement for sin. It means by which sins are forgiven.

ENGLISH WORD	GREEK WORD AND VERSE	THE WORD MEANS...
Propitiation–KJV Propitiation–NASB **Sacrifice of atonement–NIV** Propitiation–NKJV Punishment for our sins–NLT **POSB REFERENCE** (Rom.3:25) Note 4	Number—singular Stem or root—from ἱλαστήριον, ου Concordance References: ⇒ Strong's #2435 hilastērion ⇒ NIV #2663 hilastērion ⇒ NASB #2435 hilastērion **Romans 3:25** Whom God hath set forth to be a **propitiation** through faith in his blood, to declare his righteousness for the remission of sins that are past, through the forbearance of God; [KJV] Whom God displayed publicly as a **propitiation** in His blood through faith. This was to demonstrate His righteousness, because in the forbearance of God He passed over the sins previously committed; [NASB] God presented him as a **sacrifice of atonement**, through faith in his blood. He did this to demonstrate his justice, because in his forbearance he had left the sins committed beforehand unpunished. [NIV] Whom God set forth *as* a **propitiation** by His blood, through faith, to demonstrate His righteousness, because in His forbearance God had passed over the sins that were previously committed, [NKJV] For God sent Jesus to take the **punishment for our sins** and to satisfy God's anger against us. We are made right with God when we believe that Jesus shed his blood, sacrificing his life for us. God was being entirely fair and just when he did not punish those who sinned in former times. [NLT] ὃν προέθετο ὁ Θεὸς ἱλαστήριον διὰ τῆς πίστεως, ἐν τῷ αὐτοῦ αἵματι, εἰς ἔνδειξιν τῆς δικαιοσύνης αὐτοῦ διὰ τὴν πάρεσιν τῶν προγεγονότων ἁμαρτημάτων [GNS] ὃν προέθετο ὁ θεὸς ἱλαστήριον διὰ [τῆς] πίστεως ἐν τῷ αὐτοῦ αἵματι εἰς ἔνδειξιν τῆς δικαιοσύνης αὐτοῦ διὰ τὴν πάρεσιν τῶν προγεγονότων ἁμαρτημάτων [GNT]	**Practical Application** Righteousness is by an act of God alone, the act of propitiation. (See note, Propitiation—1 John 2:1-2; *Deeper Study #1*—1 John 2:2 for more discussion.) Sacrifice of Atonement (*hilasterion*) means to be a sacrifice, a covering, a satisfaction, a payment, an appeasement for sin. It is Christ Himself who is the propitiation for man's sins. But note: it is not His teachings, power, example, or life that make Christ the propitiation. It is His blood—His sacrifice, His death, His sufferings, His cross—that causes God to accept Jesus as the propitiation. It is the blood of Christ that God accepts as... • the *sacrifice* for our sins. • the *covering* for our sins. • the *satisfaction* for our sins. • the *payment* for the penalty of our sins. • the *appeasement* of His wrath against sin. What does the Bible mean by "the blood of Christ"? It means *the willingness* of Christ to die (shed His blood) for man. It means *the supreme sacrifice* Christ paid for man's sins. It means *the terrible sufferings* Christ underwent for man's sins. (See POSB note—Matthew 20:19.) It means *the voluntary laying down of His life* for man's sins (John 10:17-18).

#3358
Sacrilegious Object That Causes Desecration
 	
Abomination of desolation–KJV
Abomination of desolation–NASB
Abomination that causes desolation–NIV
Abomination of desolation–NKJV
Sacrilegious object that causes desecration–NLT
 	
POSB REFERENCE
(Mt.24:15)
Deeper Study #1
 	
See also POSB REF:
(Mk.13:14)
Deeper Study #1
	βδέλυγμα ἐρημώσεως = *bdelugma erēmōseōs*
	Pronunciation: [bdel'-oog-mah er-ay'-mo-say'-os]
	Parsing *bdelugma* (part of speech): noun
	  Case—accusative
	  Gender—neuter
	  Number—singular
	  Stem or root—from βδέλυγμα, τος
	Parsing *erēmōseōs* (part of speech): noun
	  Case—genitive
	  Gender—feminine
	  Number—singular
	  Stem or root—from ἐρήμωσις, εως
	Concordance References:
	⇒ Strong's #946 bdelugma + 2050 eremosis
	⇒ NIV #1007 bdelugma [abomination] + 3836 ho + 2247 erēmōsis [desolation]
	⇒ NASB #946 bdelugma + 2050 erēmōsis
	
	Matthew 24:15
	When ye therefore shall see the **abomination of desolation**, spoken of by Daniel the prophet, stand in the holy place, (whoso readeth, let him understand:) [KJV]
	"Therefore when you see the **abomination of desolation** which was spoken of through Daniel the prophet, standing in the holy place (let the reader understand), [NASB]
	"So when you see standing in the holy place 'the **abomination that causes desolation**,' spoken of through the prophet Daniel—let the reader understand—[NIV]
	"Therefore when you see the '**abomination of desolation**,' spoken of by Daniel the prophet, standing in the holy place" (whoever reads, let him understand), [NKJV]
	"The time will come when you will see what Daniel the prophet spoke about: the **sacrilegious object that**
		To detest or detestable.
		
		Practical Application
		It is a picture of becoming sick with nausea. The abomination that causes desolation is translated three other times as "abomination" or "abominable" or "obscenities"—[NLT] in the New Testament (See Mark 13:14 and Rev.17:4-5).
		The word "desecration" comes from the Greek word *erēmōsis* and means a wilderness or a desert and, in this context, a wasted, desolate place.

ENGLISH WORD	GREEK WORD AND VERSE	THE WORD MEANS...
	causes desecration standing in the holy place"—reader, pay attention! [NLT] Ὅταν οὖν ἴδητε τὸ **βδέλυγμα** τῆς **ἐρημώσεως** τὸ ῥηθὲν διὰ Δανιὴλ τοῦ προφήτου ἑστὼς ἐν τόπῳ ἁγίῳ, -- ὁ ἀναγινώσκων νοείτω, -- [GNS] Ὅταν οὖν ἴδητε τὸ **βδέλυγμα** τῆς **ἐρημώσεως** τὸ ῥηθὲν διὰ Δανιὴλ τοῦ προφήτου ἑστὸς ἐν τόπῳ ἁγίῳ, ὁ ἀναγινώσκων νοείτω, [GNT]	

#3359
Sad–Sadness
 	
Sad–KJV
Sad–NASB
Downcast–NIV
Sad–NKJV
Sadness–NLT
 	
POSB REFERENCE
(Lk.24:15-27; esp. v.17)
Note 2, point 1
	σκυθρωποί = *skuthröpoi*
	Pronunciation: [skoo-thro-po-ee']
	Parsing (part of speech): adjective
	   Case—nominative
	   Gender—masculine
	   Number—plural
	   Stem or root—from σκυθρωπός, ή, όν
	Concordance References:
	  ⇒ Strong's #4659 skuthröpos
	  ⇒ NIV #5034 skuthröpos
	  ⇒ NASB #4659 skuthröpos
	
	Luke 24:17
	And he said unto them, What manner of communications are these that ye have one to another, as ye walk, and are **sad**? [KJV]
	
	And He said to them, "What are these words that you are exchanging with one another as you are walking?" And they stood still, looking **sad**. [NASB]
	
	He asked them, "What are you discussing together as you walk along?"They stood still, their faces **downcast**. [NIV]
	
	And He said to them, "What kind of conversation is this that you have with one another as you walk and are **sad**?" [NKJV]
	
	"You seem to be in a deep discussion about something," he said. "What are you so concerned about?"They stopped short, **sadness** written across their faces. [NLT]
	
	εἶπε δὲ πρὸς αὐτούς, Τίνες οἱ λόγοι οὗτοι οὓς ἀντιβάλλετε πρὸς ἀλλήλους περιπατοῦντες, καὶ ἐστὲ **σκυθρωποί**; [GNS]
	
	εἶπεν δὲ πρὸς αὐτούς, Τίνες οἱ λόγοι οὗτοι οὓς ἀντιβάλλετε πρὸς ἀλλήλους περιπατοῦντες; καὶ ἐστάθησαν **σκυθρωποί**, [GNT]
		Sad, downcast, gloomy, dejected, despondent, sullen, overcast, grim, helpless.
		
		Practical Application
		Jesus could see sadness and despair written all over their faces. Why were these two so sad? Cleopas was surprised that the stranger did not know. "How could anyone be in Jerusalem and not know why we are sad and despairing?" he asked. Terrible things had happened. These two were seeking to understand the death and empty tomb of Christ. Christ was the subject of their conversation. They were seeking the truth; therefore, Christ drew near them.

#3360
Saints
 	
Saints–KJV
Saints–NASB
Holy–NIV
Saints–NKJV
Holy–NLT
 	
POSB REFERENCE
(1 Cor.1:2)
Deeper Study #2
	ἁγίοις = *hagiois*
	Pronunciation: [hag'-ee-os]
	Parsing (part of speech): adjective
	   Case—dative
	   Gender—masculine
	   Number—plural
	   Stem or root—from ἅγιος, α, ον
	Concordance References:
	  ⇒ Strong's #40 hagios
	  ⇒ NIV #41 hagios
	  ⇒ NASB #40 hagios
	
	1 Cor. 1:2
	Unto the church of God which is at Corinth, to them that are sanctified in Christ Jesus, called to be **saints**, with all that in every place call upon the name of Jesus Christ our Lord, both theirs and ours: [KJV]
	
	To the church of God which is at Corinth, to those who have been sanctified in Christ Jesus, **saints** by calling, with all who in every place call upon the name of our Lord Jesus Christ, their Lord and ours: [NASB]
	
	To the church of God in Corinth, to those sanctified in Christ Jesus and called to be **holy**, together with all those everywhere who call on the name of our Lord Jesus Christ—their Lord and ours: [NIV]
	
	To the church of God which is at Corinth, to those who are sanctified in Christ Jesus, called *to be* **saints**, with all who in every place call on the name of Jesus Christ our Lord, both theirs and ours: [NKJV]
		Set apart by God, consecrated, sacred, and holy.
		
		Practical Application
		A saint, a holy person, is a follower of the Lord Jesus Christ who has been set apart to live for God. The saint has given himself to live a consecrated, sacred, and holy life—all for the glory of God. Note that believers are saints in both senses:
		1. Believers are saints in the sense that they have been given a new heart by God: a heart that is renewed and recreated in righteousness and true holiness.
		2. Believers are saints in the sense that they are set apart to live consecrated and holy lives in this world.

ENGLISH WORD	GREEK WORD AND VERSE	THE WORD MEANS...
	We are writing to the church of God in Corinth, you who have been called by God to be his own holy people. He made you **holy** by means of Christ Jesus, just as he did all Christians everywhere—whoever calls upon the name of Jesus Christ, our Lord and theirs. [NLT] τῇ ἐκκλησίᾳ τοῦ Θεοῦ τῇ οὔσῃ ἐν Κορίνθῳ, ἡγιασμένοις ἐν Χριστῷ Ἰησοῦ, κλητοῖς **ἁγίοις**, σὺν πᾶσι τοῖς ἐπικαλουμένοις τὸ ὄνομα τοῦ Κυρίου ἡμῶν Ἰησοῦ Χριστοῦ ἐν παντὶ τόπῳ, αὐτῶν τε καὶ ἡμῶν· [GNS]· τῇ ἐκκλησίᾳ τοῦ θεοῦ τῇ οὔσῃ ἐν Κορίνθῳ, ἡγιασμένοις ἐν Χριστῷ Ἰησοῦ, κλητοῖς **ἁγίοις**, σὺν πᾶσιν τοῖς ἐπικαλουμένοις τὸ ὄνομα τοῦ κυρίου ἡμῶν Ἰησοῦ Χριστοῦ ἐν παντὶ τόπῳ, αὐτῶν καὶ ἡμῶν· [GNT]	
#3361 **Saints** Saints–KJV Saints–NASB Saints–NIV Saints–NKJV Christians in Jerusalem–NLT **POSB REFERENCE** (2 Cor.9:1-2; esp. v.1) Note 1	**ἁγίους** = hagious Pronunciation: [hag'-ee-oys] Parsing (part of speech): pronominal adjective Case—accusative Gender—masculine Number—plural Stem or root—from **ἅγιος**, α, ον Concordance References: ⇒ Strong's #40 hagios ⇒ NIV #41 hagios ⇒ NASB #40 hagios **2 Cor. 9:1** For as touching the ministering to the **saints**, it is superfluous for me to write to you: [KJV] For it is superfluous for me to write to you about this ministry to the **saints**; [NASB] There is no need for me to write to you about this service to the **saints**. [NIV] Now concerning the ministering to the **saints**, it is superfluous for me to write to you; [NKJV] I really don't need to write to you about this gift for the **Christians in Jerusalem**. [NLT] Περὶ μὲν γὰρ τῆς διακονίας τῆς εἰς τοὺς **ἁγίους** περισσόν μοί ἐστι τὸ γράφειν ὑμῖν· [GNS] Περὶ μὲν γὰρ τῆς διακονίας τῆς εἰς τοὺς **ἁγίους** περισσόν μοί ἐστιν τὸ γράφειν ὑμῖν· [GNT]	Saints, consecrated, pure, upright, those who are set apart and devoted to God. It is a term referring to genuine believers. **Practical Application** The point is striking. Some fellow believers were in desperate need. The churches in Judea were poor and desperately needed help; therefore the Corinthians were expected to help them. In fact, the expectation was so strong there was little need to even say anything about it.
#3362 **Saints** Saints–KJV Saints–NASB Saints–NIV Saints–NKJV God's holy people– NLT **POSB REFERENCE** (Eph.1:1-2; esp. v.1) Note 2 **See also POSB REF:** (Philip.4:21-22; esp. v.21) Note 2	**ἁγίοις** = hagiois Pronunciation: [hag'-ee-oys] Parsing (part of speech): pronominal adjective Case—dative Gender—masculine Number—plural Stem or root—from **ἅγιος** α, ον Concordance References: ⇒ Strong's #40 hagios ⇒ NIV #41 hagios ⇒ NASB #40 hagios **Ephes. 1:1** Paul, an apostle of Jesus Christ by the will of God, to the **saints** which are at Ephesus, and to the faithful in Christ Jesus: [KJV] Paul, an apostle of Christ Jesus by the will of God, to the **saints** who are at Ephesus, and who are faithful in Christ Jesus: [NASB] Paul, an apostle of Christ Jesus by the will of God, To the **saints** in Ephesus, the faithful in Christ Jesus: [NIV] Paul, an apostle of Jesus Christ by the will of God, To the **saints** who are in Ephesus, and faithful in Christ Jesus: [NKJV] This letter is from Paul, chosen by God to be an apostle of Christ Jesus. It is written to **God's holy people** in Ephesus, who are faithful followers of Christ Jesus. [NLT] Παῦλος ἀπόστολος Ἰησοῦ Χριστοῦ διὰ θελήματος Θεοῦ, τοῖς **ἁγίοις** τοῖς οὖσιν ἐν Ἐφέσῳ, καὶ πιστοῖς ἐν Χριστῷ Ἰησοῦ· [GNS] Παῦλος ἀπόστολος Χριστοῦ Ἰησοῦ διὰ θελήματος θεοῦ τοῖς **ἁγίοις** τοῖς οὖσιν [ἐν Ἐφέσῳ] καὶ πιστοῖς ἐν Χριστῷ Ἰησοῦ, [GNT]	Saint; to be God's holy people; to be set apart; to be consecrated, sacred, devoted and holy. **Practical Application** In the Bible the word "saint" does not refer to just a few people who have done great works for God. It refers to all people. A saint is a follower of the Lord Jesus Christ who has been set apart to live for God. The saint has given himself to live a consecrated, sacred, and holy life—all for the glory of God. Note that believers are *saints* in both senses: ⇒ Believers are *saints* in the sense that they have been given a new heart by God: a heart that is renewed and recreated in righteousness and true holiness. ⇒ Believers are *saints* in the sense that they are set apart to live consecrated and holy lives in this world.

ENGLISH WORD	GREEK WORD AND VERSE	THE WORD MEANS...

#3363
Saints

Saints–KJV
Saints–NASB
Holy–NIV
Saints–NKJV
God's holy people–
NLT

**POSB
REFERENCE**
(Col.1:2)
Note 3, point 1

See also POSB REF:
(Eph.1:4)
Note 2, point 1
(Eph.5:25-33; esp.
v.25)
Note 2, point 1
(Col.1:22)
Note 3, point 1
(Col.3:12-14; esp.
v.12)
Note 1

ἀγίοις = hagiois
Pronunciation: [hag'-ee-oys]
Parsing (part of speech): adjective
    Case—dative
    Gender—masculine
    Number—plural
    Stem or root—from ἄγιος, α, ον
Concordance References:
⇒ Strong's #40 hagios
⇒ NIV #41 hagios
⇒ NASB #40 hagios

Col. 1:2

To the **saints** and faithful brethren in Christ which are at Colosse: Grace be unto you, and peace, from God our Father and the Lord Jesus Christ. [KJV]

To the **saints** and faithful brethren in Christ who are at Colossae: Grace to you and peace from God our Father. [NASB]

To the **holy** and faithful brothers in Christ at Colosse: Grace and peace to you from God our Father. [NIV]

To the **saints** and faithful brethren in Christ who are in Colosse: Grace to you and peace from God our Father and the Lord Jesus Christ. [NKJV]

It is written to **God's holy people** in the city of Colosse, who are faithful brothers and sisters in Christ.May God our Father give you grace and peace. [NLT]

τοῖς ἐν Κολοσσαῖς ἀγίοις καὶ πιστοῖς ἀδελφοῖς ἐν Χριστῷ· χάρις ὑμῖν καὶ εἰρήνη ἀπὸ Θεοῦ πατρὸς ἡμῶν καὶ Κυρίου Ἰησοῦ Χριστοῦ. [GNS]

τοῖς ἐν Κολοσσαῖς ἀγίοις καὶ πιστοῖς ἀδελφοῖς ἐν Χριστῷ, χάρις ὑμῖν καὶ εἰρήνη ἀπὸ θεοῦ πατρὸς ἡμῶν. [GNT]

To be holy; to be morally pure. It means to be set apart and consecrated to God.

Practical Application

There are the *carnal saints or believers* within the church. This refers to those who in the past had set their lives apart to follow the Lord Jesus. They *had separated* themselves from the world and *had turned* to the Lord Jesus to save them. However, a saint or believer may or may not *continue on* with the Lord Jesus. Some in the Colossian church *were not continuing on*. They were not fully committed. Their commitment to the Lord Jesus Christ was lacking. Therefore, they were running the risk of falling into the error of false teaching and turning away from Christ. The point is this: a person can be a carnal believer or carnal "saint" within the church. Just because a person has made a profession and given some semblance of following Christ does not mean he is safe and secure forever—that he is automatically mature in Christ. When a person truly comes to know Christ, he is just beginning a journey with Christ, a journey that has a much higher level of spiritual growth to reach.

There are faithful saints or believers in the church. This refers to those who had set their lives apart to Christ and had continued on. They were loyal and steadfast in their allegiance, and they held firm against the attacks of worldliness and false teaching. They were not shaken by the temptations of the devil nor by the urges of the flesh. They were faithful against all foes.

The point is this: once a person has become a saint, that is, set his life apart to follow Christ, he is to be faithful. And he is to grow in his faithfulness. In fact, the highest level of spiritual maturity is that of faithfulness. Being faithful or obedient to Christ is the one thing that pleases Christ above all else.

⇒ We must live lives that are set apart to Christ, to the belief that He died for our reconciliation and that His death covers us.
⇒ We must live lives that are separated from worldliness and selfishness and from the flesh and its sins.
⇒ We must live lives that are set apart and consecrated to God and His service, lives that live for His cause.

#3364
Salvation

Salvation–KJV
Salvation–NASB
Salvation–NIV
Salvation–NKJV
Salvation–NLT

**POSB
REFERENCE**
(Jn.4:22)
Note 3, point 1

See also POSB REF:
(Rom.1:16)
Deeper Study #1

ἡ σωτηρία = hē sōtēria
Pronunciation: [ay so-tay-ree'-ah]
Parsing *sōtēria* (part of speech): noun
    Case—nominative
    Gender—feminine
    Number—singular
    Stem or root—from σωτηρία, ας
Concordance References:
⇒ Strong's #3588 ho + 4991 sōtēria
⇒ NIV #3836 ho [Not in English] + 5401 sōtēria [salvation]
⇒ NASB #3588 ho + 4991 sōtēria

John 4:22

Ye worship ye know not what: we know what we worship: for **salvation** is of the Jews. [KJV]

"You worship that which you do not know; we worship that which we know, for **salvation** is from the Jews.

To deliver; to be made whole. It means preservation, salvation, salvation from certain destruction; salvation and deliverance from one's enemies. The word "salvation" in the Greek has the definite article, "the (*hē*) salvation" (*sōtēria*); salvation from sin and its penalty of death and eternal damnation.

Practical Application

The Messiah, who is the salvation of all men, comes through the Jews, not from any other source. The great word *salvation* is used in Scripture to describe at least three experiences for the believer.

1. The *once-for-all experience* of salvation. It is an experience that has happened sometime

ENGLISH WORD	GREEK WORD AND VERSE	THE WORD MEANS...

[NASB]
You Samaritans worship what you do not know; we worship what we do know, for **salvation** is from the Jews. [NIV]

You worship what you do not know; we know what we worship, for **salvation** is of the Jews. [NKJV]

You Samaritans know so little about the one you worship, while we Jews know all about him, for **salvation** comes through the Jews. [NLT]

ὑμεῖς προσκυνεῖτε ὃ οὐκ οἴδατε· ἡμεῖς προσκυνοῦμεν ὃ οἴδαμεν· ὅτι **ἡ σωτηρία** ἐκ τῶν Ἰουδαίων ἐστίν. [GNS]

ὑμεῖς προσκυνεῖτε ὃ οὐκ οἴδατε· ἡμεῖς προσκυνοῦμεν ὃ οἴδαμεν, ὅτι **ἡ σωτηρία** ἐκ τῶν Ἰουδαίων ἐστίν. [GNT]

in the past: "You have been saved" (Luke 7:50). It is the initial act of faith in the Lord Jesus Christ. It is receiving Christ into one's heart and life as Lord. It means being saved or delivered from sin, death, and hell; and being given the assurance that one will never be separated from God—either in this life or in the world to come. (See POSB *Deeper Study* #2—John 1:4; POSB *Deeper Study* #1—John 10:10; POSB *Deeper Study* #1—John 17:2-3.)

2. The *continuous experience* of salvation. It is an experience that is occurring right now, in the present: "You are being saved" (1 Cor. 1:18). It is a description of God's work day by day in the believer's life. It is the Holy Spirit of God working within the believer. (Cp. Romans 6:14; Romans 8:2; 2 Cor. 3:18; Galatians 2:20; Phil. 1:19; Phil. 2:12-13; 2 Thes. 2:13.)

3. The *redemptive experience* of salvation that is to occur in the future. "Our salvation is nearer now than when we first believed" (Romans 13:11). This future reference to salvation points to the day of redemption—to the day of Christ's kingdom—to the day when Christ will usher in His kingdom upon this earth—to the day when God will create a new heavens and earth and bring about His perfect will and rule throughout the universe.

#3365
Same Kind

Like precious–KJV
Same kind–NASB
As precious as–NIV
Like precious–NKJV
Same precious–NLT

**POSB
REFERENCE**
(2 Pt.1:1)
Note 2

ἰσότιμον = isotimon
Pronunciation: [ee-sot'-ee-mon]
Parsing (part of speech): adjective
    Case—accusative
    Gender—feminine
    Number—singular
    Stem or root—from ἰσότιμος, ον
Concordance References:
⇒ Strong's #2472 isotimos
⇒ NIV #2700 isotimos
⇒ NASB #2472 isotimos

2 Peter 1:1
Simon Peter, a servant and an apostle of Jesus Christ, to them that have obtained **like precious** faith with us through the righteousness of God and our Saviour Jesus Christ: [KJV]

Simon Peter, a bond-servant and apostle of Jesus Christ, to those who have received a faith of the **same kind** as ours, by the righteousness of our God and Savior, Jesus Christ: [NASB]

Simon Peter, a servant and apostle of Jesus Christ, To those who through the righteousness of our God and Savior Jesus Christ have received a faith **as precious as** ours: [NIV]

Simon Peter, a bondservant and apostle of Jesus Christ, To those who have obtained **like precious** faith with us by the righteousness of our God and Savior Jesus Christ: [NKJV]

This letter is from Simon Peter, a slave and apostle of Jesus Christ. I am writing to all of you who share the **same precious** faith we have, faith given to us by Jesus Christ, our God and Savior, who makes us right with God. [NLT]

Σίμων Πέτρος, δοῦλος καὶ ἀπόστολος Ἰησοῦ Χριστοῦ, τοῖς **ἰσότιμον** ἡμῖν λαχοῦσι πίστιν ἐν δικαιοσύνῃ τοῦ Θεοῦ ἡμῶν καὶ σωτῆρος ἡμῶν Ἰησοῦ Χριστοῦ· [GNS]

Συμεὼν Πέτρος δοῦλος καὶ ἀπόστολος Ἰησοῦ Χριστοῦ τοῖς **ἰσότιμον** ἡμῖν λαχοῦσιν πίστιν ἐν δικαιοσύνῃ τοῦ θεοῦ ἡμῶν καὶ σωτῆρος Ἰησοῦ Χριστοῦ, [GNT]

As precious as; equally valuable; of the same kind.

Practical Application
Note this: the faith of Jesus Christ is the *same kind* of faith that is given to all believers. The Greek word that Peter uses for "kind" (*isotimos*) is an unusual word. This is the only time it is used in the New Testament. It is really a double word. The *isos* means *equal*, and *time* means *honor* (A.T. Robertson. *Word Pictures in the New Testament*, Vol.6, p.147). Therefore, by *same kind* of faith is meant *like faith*, a faith that is like everyone else's faith. This is a most wonderful thing. It means that we are all given the very same faith; we are all equal in value and honor and privilege before God. God does not discriminate; He does not have favorites. God loves us all equally and He values and honors us all as much as He did Peter and James and John and Paul.

ENGLISH WORD	GREEK WORD AND VERSE	THE WORD MEANS...

#3366
Same Nature
 	
Like passions–KJV
Same nature–NASB
Human like–NIV
Same nature–NKJV
Human beings like–NLT
 	
POSB
REFERENCE
(Acts 14:14-18; esp. v.15)
Note 3, point 1
	ὁμοιοπαθεῖς = homoiopatheis
	Pronunciation: [hom-oy-op-ath-ice']
	Parsing (part of speech): adjective
	    Case—nominative
	    Gender—masculine
	    Number—plural
	    Stem or root—from ὁμοιοπαθής, ές
	Concordance References:
	  ⇒ Strong's #3663 homoiopathës
	  ⇒ NIV #3926 homoiopathës
	  ⇒ NASB #3663 homoiopathës
	
	Acts 14:15
	And saying, Sirs, why do ye these things? We also are men of **like passions** with you, and preach unto you that ye should turn from these vanities unto the living God, which made heaven, and earth, and the sea, and all things that are therein: [KJV]
	And saying, "Men, why are you doing these things? We are also men of the **same nature** as you, and preach the gospel to you in order that you should turn from these vain things to a living God, who made the heaven and the earth and the sea, and all that is in them. [NASB]
	"Men, why are you doing this? We too are only men, **human like** you. We are bringing you good news, telling you to turn from these worthless things to the living God, who made heaven and earth and sea and everything in them. [NIV]
	And saying, "Men, why are you doing these things? We also are men with the **same nature** as you, and preach to you that you should turn from these useless things to the living God, who made the heaven, the earth, the sea, and all things that are in them, [NKJV]
	"Friends, why are you doing this? We are merely **human beings like** yourselves! We have come to bring you the Good News that you should turn from these worthless things to the living God, who made heaven and earth, the sea, and everything in them. [NLT]
	καὶ λέγοντες, Ἄνδρες, τί ταῦτα ποιεῖτε; καὶ ἡμεῖς **ὁμοιοπαθεῖς** ἐσμεν ὑμῖν ἄνθρωποι, εὐαγγελιζόμενοι ὑμᾶς ἀπὸ τούτων τῶν ματαίων ἐπιστρέφειν ἐπὶ τὸν Θεὸν ζῶντα, ὃς ἐποίησε τὸν οὐρανὸν καὶ τὴν γῆν καὶ τὴν θάλασσαν, καὶ πάντα τὰ ἐν αὐτοῖς· [GNS]
	καὶ λέγοντες, Ἄνδρες, τί ταῦτα ποιεῖτε; καὶ ἡμεῖς **ὁμοιοπαθεῖς** ἐσμεν ὑμῖν ἄνθρωποι εὐαγγελιζόμενοι ὑμᾶς ἀπὸ τούτων τῶν ματαίων ἐπιστρέφειν ἐπὶ θεὸν ζῶντα, ὃς ἐποίησεν τὸν οὐρανὸν καὶ τὴν γῆν καὶ τὴν θάλασσαν καὶ πάντα τὰ ἐν αὐτοῖς· [GNT]
		Like, passions, same; to like in every way. It means the same nature.
		
		Practical Application
		It means that all men have the same...
		• heart (Psalm 33:15)
		• feelings
		• infirmities
		• temptations (1 Cor. 10-13)
		• sufferings
		• aging and dying bodies (Hebrews 9:27)

#3367
Same Precious
 	
Like precious–KJV
Same kind–NASB
As precious as–NIV
Like precious–NKJV
Same precious–NLT
 	
POSB
REFERENCE
(2 Pt.1:1)
Note 2
	ἰσότιμον = isotimon
	Pronunciation: [ee-sot'-ee-mon]
	Parsing (part of speech): adjective
	    Case—accusative
	    Gender—feminine
	    Number—singular
	    Stem or root—from ἰσότιμος, ον
	Concordance References:
	  ⇒ Strong's #2472 isotimos
	  ⇒ NIV #2700 isotimos
	  ⇒ NASB #2472 isotimos
	
	2 Peter 1:1
	Simon Peter, a servant and an apostle of Jesus Christ, to them that have obtained **like precious** faith with us through the righteousness of God and our Saviour Jesus Christ: [KJV]
	Simon Peter, a bond-servant and apostle of Jesus Christ, to those who have received a faith of the **same kind** as ours, by the righteousness of our God and Savior, Jesus Christ: [NASB]
	Simon Peter, a servant and apostle of Jesus Christ, To
		As precious as; equally valuable; of the same kind.
		
		Practical Application
		Note this: the faith of Jesus Christ is the *same precious faith* that is given to all believers. The Greek word that Peter uses for "precious" (*isotimos*) is an unusual word. This is the only time it is used in the New Testament. It is really a double word. The *isos* means *equal*, and *time* means *honor* (A.T. Robertson. *Word Pictures in the New Testament*, Vol.6, p.147). Therefore, by *precious faith* is meant *like faith*, a faith that is like everyone else's faith. This is a most wonderful thing. It means that we are all given the very same faith; we are all equal in value and honor and privilege before God. God does not discriminate; He does not have favorites. God loves us all equally and He values and honors us all as much as He did Peter and James and John and Paul.

ENGLISH WORD	GREEK WORD AND VERSE	THE WORD MEANS...
	those who through the righteousness of our God and Savior Jesus Christ have received a faith **as precious as** ours: [NIV] Simon Peter, a bondservant and apostle of Jesus Christ, To those who have obtained **like precious** faith with us by the righteousness of our God and Savior Jesus Christ: [NKJV] This letter is from Simon Peter, a slave and apostle of Jesus Christ. I am writing to all of you who share the **same precious** faith we have, faith given to us by Jesus Christ, our God and Savior, who makes us right with God. [NLT] Σίμων Πέτρος, δοῦλος καὶ ἀπόστολος Ἰησοῦ Χριστοῦ, τοῖς **ἰσότιμον** ἡμῖν λαχοῦσι πίστιν ἐν δικαιοσύνῃ τοῦ Θεοῦ ἡμῶν καὶ σωτῆρος ἡμῶν Ἰησοῦ Χριστοῦ· [GNS] Συμεὼν Πέτρος δοῦλος καὶ ἀπόστολος Ἰησοῦ Χριστοῦ τοῖς **ἰσότιμον** ἡμῖν λαχοῦσιν πίστιν ἐν δικαιοσύνῃ τοῦ θεοῦ ἡμῶν καὶ σωτῆρος Ἰησοῦ Χριστοῦ, [GNT]	

#3368
Sanctification
 	
Sanctification–KJV
Sanctifying–NASB
Sanctifying–NIV
Sanctification–NKJV
Holy–NLT
 	
POSB REFERENCE
(1 Pt.1:2)
Note 2
 	
See also POSB REF:
(Heb.12:14)
Note 1, point 2
	ἁγιασμῷ = hagiasmō
	Pronunciation: [hag-ee-ahs-mo']
	Parsing (part of speech): noun
	    Case—dative
	    Gender—masculine
	    Number—singular
	    Stem or root—from ἁγιασμός, οῦ
	Concordance References:
	⇒ Strong's #38 hagiasmos
	⇒ NIV #40 hagiasmos
	⇒ NASB #38 hagiasmos
	
	1 Peter 1:2
	Elect according to the foreknowledge of God the Father, through **sanctification** of the Spirit, unto obedience and sprinkling of the blood of Jesus Christ: Grace unto you, and peace, be multiplied. [KJV]
	
	According to the foreknowledge of God the Father, by the **sanctifying** work of the Spirit, that you may obey Jesus Christ and be sprinkled with His blood: May grace and peace be yours in fullest measure. [NASB]
	
	Who have been chosen according to the foreknowledge of God the Father, through the **sanctifying** work of the Spirit, for obedience to Jesus Christ and sprinkling by his blood: Grace and peace be yours in abundance. [NIV]
	
	Elect according to the foreknowledge of God the Father, in **sanctification** of the Spirit, for obedience and sprinkling of the blood of Jesus Christ: Grace to you and peace be multiplied. [NKJV]
	
	God the Father chose you long ago, and the Spirit has made you **holy**. As a result, you have obeyed Jesus Christ and are cleansed by his blood. May you have more and more of God's special favor and wonderful peace. [NLT]
	
	κατὰ πρόγνωσιν Θεοῦ πατρός, ἐν **ἁγιασμῷ** Πνεύματος, εἰς ὑπακοὴν καὶ ῥαντισμὸν αἵματος Ἰησοῦ Χριστοῦ· χάρις ὑμῖν καὶ εἰρήνη πληθυνθείη. [GNS]
	
	κατὰ πρόγνωσιν θεοῦ πατρὸς ἐν **ἁγιασμῷ** πνεύματος εἰς ὑπακοὴν καὶ ῥαντισμὸν αἵματος Ἰησοῦ Χριστοῦ, χάρις ὑμῖν καὶ εἰρήνη πληθυνθείη. [GNT]
		Sanctifying, sanctification; holiness, dedication, consecration. It means separated or set apart.
		
		Practical Application
		The chosen are elected by God. They are actually called the elect, a people who had been elected or chosen by God. This means a most wonderful thing. It means that believers have the highest position in all the world, the position of being *God's own holy and beloved children* (cp. Col. 3:12).
		
		Believers have been elected to be *holy*. God called believers out of the world and away from the old life it offered, the old life of sin and death. He called believers to be separated and set apart to Himself and the new life He offers, the new life of righteousness and eternity.

#3369
Sanctification
 	
Holiness–KJV
Sanctification–NASB
Holiness–NIV
Holiness–NKJV
Holy–NLT
 	
POSB REFERENCE
(Rom.6:19-20, esp. v.19)
	ἁγιασμόν = hagiasmon
	Pronunciation: [hag-ee-ahs-mown']
	Parsing (part of speech): noun
	    Case—accusative
	    Gender—masculine
	    Number—singular
	    Stem or root—from ἁγιασμός, οῦ
	Concordance References:
	⇒ Strong's #38 hagiasmos
	⇒ NIV #40 hagiasmos
	⇒ NASB #38 hagiasmos
		Consecration, dedication, sanctification, holiness.
		
		Practical Application
		The believer is to let righteousness work holiness (*hagiasmon*). The word means sanctification or holiness. The believer is to yield the parts of his body to serve righteousness, and he is to let righteousness sanctify him more and more. He is to live righteously and become more and more holy like God. (See POSB *Deeper Study* #1, Holy—1 Peter 1:15-16 for more discussion.)

ENGLISH WORD	GREEK WORD AND VERSE	THE WORD MEANS...
See also POSB REF: (Heb.12:14) Note 1, point 2	**Romans 6:19** I speak after the manner of men because of the infirmity of your flesh: for as ye have yielded your members servants to uncleanness and to iniquity unto iniquity; even so now yield your members servants to righteousness unto **holiness**. [KJV] I am speaking in human terms because of the weakness of your flesh. For just as you presented your members as slaves to impurity and to lawlessness, resulting in further lawlessness, so now present your members as slaves to righteousness, resulting in **sanctification**. [NASB] I put this in human terms because you are weak in your natural selves. Just as you used to offer the parts of your body in slavery to impurity and to ever-increasing wickedness, so now offer them in slavery to righteousness leading to **holiness**. [NIV] I speak in human *terms* because of the weakness of your flesh. For just as you presented your members *as* slaves of uncleanness, and of lawlessness *leading* to *more* lawlessness, so now present your members *as* slaves *of* righteousness for **holiness**. [NKJV] I speak this way, using the illustration of slaves and masters, because it is easy to understand. Before, you let yourselves be slaves of impurity and lawlessness. Now you must choose to be slaves of righteousness so that you will become **holy**. [NLT] ἀνθρώπινον λέγω διὰ τὴν ἀσθένειαν τῆς σαρκὸς ὑμῶν. ὥσπερ γὰρ παρεστήσατε τὰ μέλη ὑμῶν δοῦλα τῇ ἀκαθαρσίᾳ καὶ τῇ ἀνομίᾳ εἰς τὴν ἀνομίαν, οὕτω νῦν παραστήσατε τὰ μέλη ὑμῶν δοῦλα τῇ δικαιοσύνῃ εἰς **ἁγιασμόν**. [GNS] ἀνθρώπινον λέγω διὰ τὴν ἀσθένειαν τῆς σαρκὸς ὑμῶν. ὥσπερ γὰρ παρεστήσατε τὰ μέλη ὑμῶν δοῦλα τῇ ἀκαθαρσίᾳ καὶ τῇ ἀνομίᾳ εἰς τὴν ἀνομίαν, οὕτως νῦν παραστήσατε τὰ μέλη ὑμῶν δοῦλα τῇ δικαιοσύνῃ εἰς **ἁγιασμόν** [GNT]	The believer is to follow after "holiness" (*hagiasmon*). The word means sanctification, consecration, and separation. It means to be set apart and different. The root meaning of holiness is to be different. The believer is to be different from the unbelievers of the world in that he... • is set apart to God and to Him alone. • is separated from the world and its pleasures and possessions. The believer, of course, *lives in the world*. He walks and moves within the world; buys, eats, and sleeps in the world; works, plays, and is housed in the world; relates, associates, and fellowships in the world. However, the believer is *not to be of the world*. He is not to be possessed by the world, enslaved to its pleasures and possessions. What does this mean? In very simple terms, the believer is not to indulge and give license to his flesh: ⇒ He is not to buy and buy; he is not to be a materialist. ⇒ He is not to eat and eat; he is not to be a glutton. ⇒ He is not to sleep and sleep; he is not to be slothful. ⇒ He is not to work and work; he is not to be a workaholic. ⇒ He is not to play and play; he is not to over emphasize recreation. ⇒ He is not to have house after house; he is not to hoard riches in a world of desperate needs. ⇒ He is not to fellowship and fellowship; he is not to neglect duty. The believer is to be separated from the world and its pleasures and possessions. He is to be set apart to God, living for God and serving Him in His great mission. The believer is to meet the needs of a desperate world that is dying from sin, disease, hunger, and war. The believer is to be different from the rest of the world; he is to follow after holiness. Note: this verse declares that no person will ever see the Lord unless he is holy. Holiness is an absolute essential if a person is to live with God (See POSB *Deeper Study* #1, Holy—1 Peter 1:15-16 for more discussion.)

#3370
Sanctified
 	
Sanctified–KJV
Sanctified–NASB
Sanctified–NIV
Sanctified–NKJV
Holy–NLT
 	
POSB REFERENCE
(1 Cor.1:2)
Deeper Study #1
	οὖσῃ ἡγιασμένοις = *ousē hēgiasmenois*
	Pronunciation: [hayg-ee-ahs-meh'-nois]
	Parsing *hēgiasmenois* (part of speech): verb
	  Mood—participle
	  Tense—perfect
	  Voice—passive
	  Case—dative
	  Gender—masculine
	  Person—2nd person
	  Number—plural
	  Stem or root—from ἁγιάζω
	Concordance References:
	⇒ Strong's #37+1510 hagiazō eimi
	⇒ NIV #39+1639 hagiazō eimi [sanctified]
	⇒ NASB #37+1510 hagiazō eimi
	
	1 Cor. 1:2
	Unto the church of God which is at Corinth, to them that are **sanctified** in Christ Jesus, called to be saints, with all that in every place call upon the name of Jesus
		To be sanctified; to be set apart; to be made holy; to be consecrated; to be separated (cp. 1 Peter 1:15-16).
		
		Practical Application
		There are three stages of sanctification.
		1. There is initial or positional sanctification. When a person believes in Jesus Christ, he is immediately set apart for God. This is a permanent, once-for-all act (Hebrews 3:1; cp. Hebrews 10:10).
		2. There is progressive sanctification. The true believer makes a determined and disciplined effort to allow the Spirit of God to set him apart day by day. The Spirit of God takes him and conforms him to the image of Christ more and more. This growth takes place as long as the believer walks upon this earth (cp.

ENGLISH WORD	GREEK WORD AND VERSE	THE WORD MEANS...

Christ our Lord, both theirs and ours: [KJV]

To the church of God which is at Corinth, to those who have been **sanctified** in Christ Jesus, saints by calling, with all who in every place call upon the name of our Lord Jesus Christ, their Lord and ours: [NASB]

To the church of God in Corinth, to those **sanctified** in Christ Jesus and called to be holy, together with all those everywhere who call on the name of our Lord Jesus Christ—their Lord and ours: [NIV]

To the church of God which is at Corinth, to those who are **sanctified** in Christ Jesus, called *to be* saints, with all who in every place call on the name of Jesus Christ our Lord, both theirs and ours: [NKJV]

We are writing to the church of God in Corinth, you who have been called by God to be his own holy people. He made you **holy** by means of Christ Jesus, just as he did all Christians everywhere—whoever calls upon the name of Jesus Christ, our Lord and theirs. [NLT]

τῇ ἐκκλησίᾳ τοῦ Θεοῦ τῇ **οὔσῃ** ἐν Κορίνθῳ, **ἡγιασμένοις** ἐν Χριστῷ Ἰησοῦ, κλητοῖς ἁγίοις, σὺν πᾶσι τοῖς ἐπικαλουμένοις τὸ ὄνομα τοῦ Κυρίου ἡμῶν Ἰησοῦ Χριστοῦ ἐν παντὶ τόπῳ, αὐτῶν τε καὶ ἡμῶν· [GNS]

τῇ ἐκκλησίᾳ τοῦ θεοῦ τῇ **οὔσῃ** ἐν Κορίνθῳ, **ἡγιασμένοις** ἐν Χριστῷ Ἰησοῦ, κλητοῖς ἁγίοις, σὺν πᾶσι τοῖς ἐπικαλουμένοις τὸ ὄνομα τοῦ κυρίου ἡμῶν Ἰησοῦ Χριστοῦ ἐν παντὶ τόπῳ, αὐτῶν καὶ ἡμῶν· [GNT]

John 17:17; 2 Cor. 3:18; Ephes. 5:25-26; 1 Thes. 5:23-24).

3. There is eternal sanctification. The day is coming when the believer will be perfectly set apart unto God and His service—without any sin or failure whatsoever. That day will be the great and glorious day of the believer's eternal redemption (Ephes. 5:27; 1 John 3:2).

#3371
Sanctify

Sanctify–KJV
Sanctify–NASB
Sanctify–NIV
Sanctify–NKJV
Pure and holy–NLT

POSB REFERENCE
(Jn.17:17)
Deeper Study #4

See also POSB REF:
(1 Cor.1:2)
Deeper Study #1

ἁγίασον = *hagiason*
Pronunciation: [hag-ee-ah'-son]
Parsing (part of speech): verb
    Mood—imperative
    Tense—aorist
    Voice—active
    Person—2nd person
    Number—singular
    Stem or root—from ἁγιάζω
Concordance References:
⇒ Strong's #37 hagiazo
⇒ NIV #39 hagiazo
⇒ NASB #37 hagiazo

John 17:17
Sanctify them through thy truth: thy word is truth. [KJV]

"**Sanctify** them in the truth; Thy word is truth. [NASB]

Sanctify them by the truth; your word is truth. [NIV]

Sanctify them by Your truth. Your word is truth. [NKJV]

Make them **pure and holy** by teaching them your words of truth. [NLT]

ἁγίασον αὐτοὺς ἐν τῇ ἀληθείᾳ σου· ὁ λόγος ὁ σὸς ἀλήθειά ἐστι. [GNS]

ἁγίασον αὐτοὺς ἐν τῇ ἀληθείᾳ· ὁ λόγος ὁ σὸς ἀλήθειά ἐστιν. [GNT]

To be set apart, to be separated; to be pure and holy; to be consecrated. (cp. 1 Peter 1:15-16).

Practical Application
There are three stages of sanctification.
1. There is *initial or positional sanctification*. When a person believes in Jesus Christ, he is immediately set apart for God permanently, once-for-all (Hebrews 3:1; cp. Hebrews 10:10).
2. There is *progressive sanctification*. The true believer makes a determined and disciplined effort to allow the Spirit of God to set him apart day by day. The Spirit of God takes him and conforms him to the image of Christ more and more. This growth takes place as long as the believer walks upon this earth (cp. John 17:17; 2 Cor. 3:18; Ephes. 5:25-26; 1 Thes. 5:23-24).
3. There is *eternal sanctification*. The day is coming when the believer will be perfectly set apart unto God and His service—without any sin or failure whatsoever. That day will be the great and glorious day of the believer's eternal redemption (Ephes. 5:27; 1 John 3:2).

#3372
Sanctifying

Sanctification–KJV
Sanctifying–NASB
Sanctifying–NIV
Sanctification–NKJV
Holy–NLT

POSB REFERENCE
(1 Pt.1:2)
Note 2

ἁγιασμῷ = *hagiasmō*
Pronunciation: [hag-ee-ahs-mo']
Parsing (part of speech): noun
    Case—dative
    Gender—masculine
    Number—singular
    Stem or root—from ἁγιασμός, οῦ
Concordance References:
⇒ Strong's #38 hagiasmos
⇒ NIV #40 hagiasmos
⇒ NASB #38 hagiasmos

1 Peter 1:2
Elect according to the foreknowledge of God the Father, through **sanctification** of the Spirit, unto obe-

Sanctifying, sanctification; holiness, dedication, consecration. It means separated or set apart.

Practical Application
The chosen are elected by God. They are actually called the elect, a people who had been elected or chosen by God. This means a most wonderful thing. It means that believers have the highest position in all the world, the position of being *God's own holy and beloved children* (cp. Col. 3:12).

Believers have been elected to be *holy*. God called believers out of the world and away from the old life it offered, the old life of sin and

ENGLISH WORD	GREEK WORD AND VERSE	THE WORD MEANS...
See also POSB REF: (Heb.12:14) Note 1, point 2	dience and sprinkling of the blood of Jesus Christ: Grace unto you, and peace, be multiplied. [KJV] According to the foreknowledge of God the Father, by the **sanctifying** work of the Spirit, that you may obey Jesus Christ and be sprinkled with His blood: May grace and peace be yours in fullest measure. [NASB] Who have been chosen according to the foreknowledge of God the Father, through the **sanctifying** work of the Spirit, for obedience to Jesus Christ and sprinkling by his blood: Grace and peace be yours in abundance. [NIV] Elect according to the foreknowledge of God the Father, in **sanctification** of the Spirit, for obedience and sprinkling of the blood of Jesus Christ: Grace to you and peace be multiplied. [NKJV] God the Father chose you long ago, and the Spirit has made you **holy**. As a result, you have obeyed Jesus Christ and are cleansed by his blood. May you have more and more of God's special favor and wonderful peace. [NLT] κατὰ πρόγνωσιν Θεοῦ πατρός, ἐν **ἁγιασμῷ** Πνεύματος, εἰς ὑπακοὴν καὶ ῥαντισμὸν αἵματος Ἰησοῦ Χριστοῦ· χάρις ὑμῖν καὶ εἰρήνη πληθυνθείη. [GNS] κατὰ πρόγνωσιν θεοῦ πατρός ἐν **ἁγιασμῷ** πνεύματος εἰς ὑπακοὴν καὶ ῥαντισμὸν αἵματος Ἰησοῦ Χριστοῦ, χάρις ὑμῖν καὶ εἰρήνη πληθυνθείη. [GNT]	death. He called believers to be separated and set apart to Himself and the new life He offers, the new life of righteousness and eternity.

#3373
Sat
 	
Sat–KJV
Rested–NASB
Came to rest–NIV
Sat–NKJV
Settled–NLT
 	
POSB REFERENCE
(Acts 2:2-4; esp. v.3)
Note 4, point 2b
	ἐκάθισεν = ekathisen
	Pronunciation: [eh-kath-i'-sen]
	Parsing (part of speech): verb
	    Mood—indicative
	    Tense—aorist
	    Voice—active
	    Person—3rd person
	    Number—singular
	    Stem or root—from καθίζω
	Concordance References:
	  ⇒ Strong's #2523 kathizö
	  ⇒ NIV #2767 kathizö
	  ⇒ NASB #2523 kathizö
	
	Acts 2:3
	And there appeared unto them cloven tongues like as of fire, and it **sat** upon each of them. [KJV]
	
	And there appeared to them tongues as of fire distributing themselves, and they **rested** on each one of them. [NASB]
	
	They saw what seemed to be tongues of fire that separated and **came to rest** on each of them. [NIV]
	
	Then there appeared to them divided tongues, as of fire, and *one* **sat** upon each of them. [NKJV]
	
	Then, what looked like flames or tongues of fire appeared and **settled** on each of them. [NLT]
	
	καὶ ὤφθησαν αὐτοῖς διαμεριζόμεναι γλῶσσαι ὡσεὶ πυρός, καὶ **ἐκάθισε** τε ἐφ' ἕνα ἕκαστο αὐτῶν. [GNS]
	
	καὶ ὤφθησαν αὐτοῖς διαμεριζόμεναι γλῶσσαι ὡσεὶ πυρός καὶ **ἐκάθισεν** ἐφ' ἕνα ἕκαστον αὐτῶν, [GNT]
		Came to rest; to sit upon; to rest upon; to settle upon.
		
		### Practical Application
		The word is singular, not plural; The Holy Spirit Himself was descending and resting upon each of the disciples. They were not receiving "tongues of fire," but the Spirit of God.
		
		Note also that the Spirit appeared in the form of a tongue of fire. The tongue symbolizes the instrument of speaking and preaching and sharing the gospel. The Holy Spirit was to be the burning power of the tongue, of the convicting message to be proclaimed.

#3374
Satan
 	
Satan–KJV
Satan–NASB
Satan–NIV
Satan–NKJV
Satan–NLT
 	
POSB REFERENCE
(Rev.12:9)
Note 1
Deeper Study #1
	Σατανᾶς = Satanas
	Pronunciation: [sat-an-as']
	Parsing (part of speech): noun
	    Case—nominative
	    Gender—masculine
	    Number—singular
	    Stem or root—from Σατανᾶς, ᾶ
	Concordance References:
	  ⇒ Strong's #4567 Satanas
	  ⇒ NIV #4928 Satanas
	  ⇒ NASB #4567 Satanas
	
	Rev. 12:9
	And the great dragon was cast out, that old serpent, called the Devil, and **Satan**, which deceiveth the whole world: he was cast out into the earth, and his angels were
		Satan, the Adversary.
		
		### Practical Application
		Satan is called "the great dragon...that old serpent." His name is *Lucifer*. He was probably one of the highest angels ever created by God, but he fell because of selfishness and pride (Isaiah 14:12; cp. 1 Tim. 3:6. See POSB note—Rev. 12:3-4; POSB *Deeper Study #1*—2 Cor. 4:4; POSB note—2 Cor. 11:13-15; POSB note—1 Peter 5:8.) He is "an angel of light" with such deceptive and seductive power that even some ministers follow him, ministers who are "transformed as the ministers of righteousness" (2 Cor.

ENGLISH WORD	GREEK WORD AND VERSE	THE WORD MEANS...
	cast out with him. [KJV] And the great dragon was thrown down, the serpent of old who is called the devil and **Satan**, who deceives the whole world; he was thrown down to the earth, and his angels were thrown down with him. [NASB] The great dragon was hurled down—that ancient serpent called the devil, or **Satan**, who leads the whole world astray. He was hurled to the earth, and his angels with him. [NIV] So the great dragon was cast out, that serpent of old, called the Devil and **Satan**, who deceives the whole world; he was cast to the earth, and his angels were cast out with him. [NKJV] This great dragon—the ancient serpent called the Devil, or **Satan**, the one deceiving the whole world—was thrown down to the earth with all his angels. [NLT] καὶ ἐβλήθη ὁ δράκων ὁ μέγας, ὁ ὄφις ὁ ἀρχαῖος, ὁ καλούμενος διάβολος καὶ ὁ **Σατανᾶς**, ὁ πλανῶν τὴν οἰκουμένην ὅλην· ἐβλήθη εἰς τὴν γῆν, καὶ οἱ ἄγγελοι αὐτοῦ μετ' αὐτοῦ ἐβλήθησαν. [GNS] καὶ ἐβλήθη ὁ δράκων ὁ μέγας, ὁ ὄφις ὁ ἀρχαῖος, ὁ καλούμενος Διάβολος καὶ ὁ **Σατανᾶς**, ὁ πλανῶν τὴν οἰκουμένην ὅλην, ἐβλήθη εἰς τὴν γῆν, καὶ οἱ ἄγγελοι αὐτοῦ μετ' αὐτοῦ ἐβλήθησαν. [GNT]	11:14-15). Throughout Scripture Satan is described as follows: 1. He is "the god of this world" who blinds men's minds (2 Cor. 4:4). 2. He is "the prince of this world" (John 12:31; John 14:20; John 16:11) and "the prince of the power of the air" (Ephes. 2:2; Ephes. 6:12). 3 He is satan, which means the adversary (1 Chron. 21:1; Job 1:6; Job 2:1-6; Zech. 3:1; Matthew 4:10; Mark 1:13; Luke 4:8; John 13:27; Acts 5:3; Acts 26:18; Romans 16:20). 4. He is the devil, which means the slanderer (Matthew 4:1, 5, 8, 11; Luke 4:2-6, 13; 1 Peter 5:8; Rev. 20:2). 5. He is the deceiver of the whole world (2 Cor. 11:3; Rev. 12:9). 6. He is the tempter (Matthew 4:3; 1 Thes. 3:5). 7. He is the evil one (Matthew 6:13; Matthew 13:19, 38). 8. He is the father of lies (John 8:44). 9. He is the accuser of the brethren (Rev. 12:10). 10. He is a murderer (John 8:44). 11. He is called Beelzebub (Matthew 12:24; Mark 3:22; Luke 11:15). 12. He is called Belial (2 Cor. 6:15). 13. He is called Abaddon (Rev. 9:11). 14. He is called the angel of the bottomless pit (Rev. 9:11). 15. He is called Apollyon (Rev. 9:11). 16. He is called the enemy (Matthew 13:39). 17. He is called the gates of hell (Matthew 16:18). 18. He is called the great red dragon (Rev. 12:3). 19. He is called a lying spirit (1 Kings 22:22). 20. He is called that old serpent (Rev. 12:9; Rev. 20:2; cp. Genesis 3:4, 14; 2 Cor. 11:3). 21. He is called the power of darkness (Col. 1:13). 22. He called the prince of devils (Matthew 12:24). 23. He is called the ruler of the darkness of this world (Ephes. 6:12). 24. He is called the spirit that works in the children of disobedience (Ephes. 2:2). 25. He is called the unclean spirit (Matthew 12:43). 26. He is called the wicked one (Matthew 13:19, 38). (See POSB note—Luke 22:3; POSB *Deeper Study* #1—2 Cor. 4:4; POSB note—Col. 2:15; POSB note—James 4:7 and POSB *Deeper Study* #1—James 4:7; POSB note—1 Peter 5:8; POSB note—Rev. 12:3-4 for more discussion.) Satan's purpose in making war against God is twofold. 1. Satan's purpose is power and worship, to receive as much of the power and worship of the universe as possible (Isaiah 14:12-17; Ezekiel 28:11-17). He goes about this in three ways. ⇒ He opposes and disturbs God's work in the world (Isaiah 14:12-17; Ezekiel 28:11-17; Job 1:6; Job 2:1-6; Matthew 4:10; Mark 1:13; Luke 4:8; Rev. 12:7-9). ⇒ He discourages believers through various

ENGLISH WORD	GREEK WORD AND VERSE	THE WORD MEANS...
		strategies (see POSB note—Luke 22:31; POSB notes—Ephes. 6:10-12). ⇒ He arouses God's justice against people by leading people to sin and to deny and rebel against God. And when they do, God's justice has to act and judge people to the fate of their choice: that of living with Satan eternally (see POSB note—Matthew 12:25-26;John 13:31-32). 2. Satan's purpose is to hurt and cut the heart of God. Why? Because God has judged and condemned him for rebelling against God. Therefore, Satan does all he can to get back at God. The best way he can do this is to turn the hearts of people away from God and lead them to sin and to follow the way of evil. (See POSB notes, pt.3—Rev. 12:3-4; pt.2—Rev. 12:7-9; pt.2—Rev. 12:10-11 for more discussion.) 　　However, Christ has broken Satan's power by two acts (see POSB note—John 12:31-32; POSB *Deeper Study* #1—John 16:11; POSB note—John 8:44; POSB note—Col. 2:15). 　a. By never giving in to the devil's temptation (Matthew 4:1-11) and by never sinning (2 Cor. 5:21). Christ overcame sin. He was righteous; He was perfect. 　b. By destroying the devil's power of death. Christ was not held by physical or spiritual death (Hebrews 2:14-15). He arose and ascended to God's right hand. 　　It is for this reason that the Bible says "greater is he that is in you, than he that is in the world" (1 John 4:4); and again, "If God be for us, who can be against us?" (Romans 8:31).
#3375 **Save** Save–KJV Save–NASB Save–NIV Save–NKJV Save–NLT **POSB** **REFERENCE** (Mt.1:20-21; esp. v.21) *Deeper Study* #6 **See also POSB REF:** (Acts 2:40) 　Note 5, point 1	σώσει = *sösei* Pronunciation: [so'-seh-ee] Parsing (part of speech): verb 　Mood—indicative 　Tense—future 　Voice—active 　Person—3rd person 　Number—singular 　Stem or root—from σώζω Concordance References: 　⇒ Strong's #4982 sözö 　⇒ NIV #5392 sözö 　⇒ NASB #4982 sözö **Matthew 1:21** 　And she shall bring forth a son, and thou shalt call his name Jesus: for he shall **save** his people from their sins. [KJV] 　"And she will bear a Son; and you shall call His name Jesus, for it is He who will **save** His people from their sins." [NASB] 　She will give birth to a son, and you are to give him the name Jesus, because he will **save** his people from their sins." [NIV] 　And she will bring forth a Son, and you shall call His name Jesus, for He will **save** His people from their sins." [NKJV] 　And she will have a son, and you are to name him Jesus, for he will **save** his people from their sins." [NLT] 　τέξεται δὲ υἱὸν καὶ καλέσεις τὸ ὄνομα αὐτοῦ Ἰησοῦν, αὐτὸς γὰρ **σώσει** τὸν λαὸν αὐτοῦ ἀπὸ τῶν ἁμαρτιῶν αὐτῶν. [GNS]	To deliver, to save; to cure; to make well; to preserve. **Practical Application** 　This Scripture emphatically declares that it is Jesus Christ, the promised Messiah, who saves. The great word salvation is used in Scripture to describe at least three experiences for the believer. 1. The *once-for-all experience* of salvation. For the believer, salvation is an experience that has happened sometime in the past: "Your faith has saved you" (Lk.7:50). This is the initial act of faith in the Lord Jesus Christ, a once-for-all, one time experience. It is receiving Christ into one's heart and life as Lord. It means being saved or delivered from sin, death, and hell; and being given the assurance that one will never be separated from God—neither in this life nor in the world to come. (See POSB *Deeper Study* #2—Jn.1:4; POSB *Deeper Study* #1—Jn.10:10; POSB *Deeper Study* #1—Jn.17:2-3.) 2. The *continuous experience* of salvation. It is an experience that is occurring right now, in the present. "You are being saved" (1 Cor. 1:18). It is a description of God's work day by day in the believer's life. It is the Holy Spirit of God working within the believer. ⇒ To guide and teach him and to deliver him

ENGLISH WORD	GREEK WORD AND VERSE	THE WORD MEANS...
	τέξεται δὲ υἱὸν, καὶ καλέσεις τὸ ὄνομα αὐτοῦ Ἰησοῦν· αὐτὸς γὰρ **σώσει** τὸν λαὸν αὐτοῦ ἀπὸ τῶν ἁμαρτιῶν αὐτῶν. [GNT]	through all the trials and problems of life. ⇒ To fill him with a heart of love, joy, and peace—all the fruit and resources necessary to live life to the fullest. ⇒ To conform him more and more to the image of Christ. ⇒ To stir and equip him to live and witness for Christ day by day and hour by hour. (Cp. Ro.6:14; Ro.8:2; 2 Cor. 3:18; Gal.2:20; Ph.1:19; Ph.2:12-13; 2 Thes. 2:13.) 3. The *redemptive experience* of salvation that is to occur in the future. "Our salvation is nearer now than when we first believed" (Ro.13:11). This future reference to salvation points to the day of redemption—to the day of Christ's kingdom, to the day when Christ will usher in His kingdom upon this earth—to the day when God will create a new heavens and earth and bring about His perfect will and rule throughout the universe.

#3376
Saved
 	
Saved–KJV
Saved–NASB
Saved–NIV
Saved–NKJV
Saved–NLT
 	
POSB REFERENCE
(Acts 2:46-47; esp. v.47)
Note 6, point 5
	σῳζομένους = *sōzomenous*
	Pronunciation: [sode'-zo-men-oos]
	Parsing (part of speech): verb
	    Mood—participle
	    Tense—present
	    Voice—passive
	    Case—accusative
	    Gender—masculine
	    Number—plural
	    Stem or root—from σῴζω
	Concordance References:
	⇒ Strong's #4982 sōzō
	⇒ NIV #5392 sōzō
	⇒ NASB #4982 sōzō
	
	Acts 2:47
	Praising God, and having favour with all the people. And the Lord added to the church daily such as should be **saved**. [KJV]
	Praising God, and having favor with all the people. And the Lord was adding to their number day by day those who were being **saved**. [NASB]
	Praising God and enjoying the favor of all the people. And the Lord added to their number daily those who were being **saved**. [NIV]
	Praising God and having favor with all the people. And the Lord added to the church daily those who were being **saved**. [NKJV]
	All the while praising God and enjoying the goodwill of all the people. And each day the Lord added to their group those who were being **saved**. [NLT]
	αἰνοῦντες τὸν Θεὸν καὶ ἔχοντες χάριν πρὸς ὅλον τὸν λαόν. ὁ δὲ Κύριος προσετίθει τοὺς **σῳζομένους** καθ' ἡμέραν τῇ ἐκκλησίᾳ. [GNS]
	αἰνοῦντες τὸν θεὸν καὶ ἔχοντες χάριν πρὸς ὅλον τὸν λαόν. ὁ δὲ κύριος προσετίθει τοὺς **σῳζομένους** καθ' ἡμέραν ἐπὶ τὸ αὐτό. [GNT]
		Saved; to rescue; to preserve; to keep safe.
		
		Practical Application
		The word "saved." (*sōzomenous*) is in the present tense, "those who were being **saved**." Salvation is a present experience of the believer as well as past and future (see POSB *Deeper Study* #1—1 Cor. 1:18 for discussion).

#3377
Savior–
Saviour
 	
Saviour–KJV
Savior–NASB
Savior–NIV
Savior–NKJV
Savior–NLT
	σωτήρ = *sōtēr*
	Pronunciation: [so-tayre']
	Parsing (part of speech): noun
	    Case—nominative
	    Gender—masculine
	    Number—singular
	    Stem or root—from σωτήρ, ῆρος
	Concordance References:
	⇒ Strong's #4990 sōtēr
	⇒ NIV #5400 sōtēr
	⇒ NASB #4990 sōtēr
		A Deliverer, a Preserver, a Savior, a Redeemer. It has the idea of a Deliverer, a Savior who snatches a person from some terrible disaster that leads to perishing (cp. John 3:16). (See POSB *Deeper Study* #6, Salvation—Matthew 1:21 for more discussion.)
		
		Practical Application
		1. Jesus Christ is said to be the Savior (Luke 2:11; John 4:42; Acts 5:31; Acts 13:23; Ephes. 5:23; Phil. 3:20; 2 Tim. 1:10; Titus 1:4; Titus 2:13; Titus 3:6; 2 Peter 1:1, 11;

ENGLISH WORD	GREEK WORD AND VERSE	THE WORD MEANS...
Saw–KJV Saw–NASB Saw–NIV Saw–NKJV Saw–NLT **POSB REFERENCE** (Jn.20:20) *Deeper Study #2*	Tense—aorist Voice—active Case—nominative Gender—masculine Number—plural Stem or root—from εἶδος, ους Concordance References: ⇒ Strong's #1492 eido ⇒ NIV #3972 horaö ⇒ NASB #3708 horaö **John 20:20** And when he had so said, he shewed unto them his hands and his side. Then were the disciples glad, when they **saw** the Lord. [KJV] And when He had said this, He showed them both His hands and His side. The disciples therefore rejoiced when they **saw** the Lord. [NASB] After he said this, he showed them his hands and side. The disciples were overjoyed when they **saw** the Lord. [NIV] When He had said this, He showed them *His* hands and His side. Then the disciples were glad when they **saw** the Lord. [NKJV] As he spoke, he held out his hands for them to see, and he showed them his side. They were filled with joy when they **saw** their Lord! [NLT] καὶ τοῦτο εἰπὼν ἔδειξεν αὐτοῖς τὰς χεῖρας καὶ τὴν πλευρὰν αὐτοῦ. ἐχάρησαν οὖν οἱ μαθηταὶ **ἰδόντες** τὸν Κύριον. [GNS] καὶ τοῦτο εἰπὼν ἔδειξεν τὰς χεῖρας καὶ τὴν πλευρὰν αὐτοῖς. ἐχάρησαν οὖν οἱ μαθηταὶ **ἰδόντες** τὸν κύριον. [GNT]	**Practical Application** After the disciples saw the Lord, note what happened: The effect upon the disciples was unbelievable joy and gladness (cp. Luke 24:41). Their spirits and attitudes were charged with joy and were transformed from the lowest point of dejection to the highest point of triumphant conviction. They now knew what Jesus meant, that He was truly... • the Way to God • the Truth of God • the Life of God In Him was life—His words were *literally* true. He had meant exactly what He had said. They had just spiritualized His words, twisted them to mean what they had wanted. But now they knew. ⇒ When He had said that He was going to die, He meant He was going to die. ⇒ When He had said that He was going to arise, He meant He was going to arise. And here He was standing before them, revealing the most glorious truth in all the universe. Man could now conquer sin and death and live forever. He had actually come "that they might have life, and that they might have it more abundantly" (John 10:10. Cp. John 10:38.) They now saw and understood (see POSB *Deeper Study # 2*, See—John 20:20).
#3382 Saw Looked upon–KJV Beheld–NASB Looked at–NIV Looked upon–NKJV **Saw–NLT** **POSB REFERENCE** (1 Jn.1:1) Note 2, point 3	**ἐθεασάμεθα** = *etheasametha* Pronunciation: [eh-theh-ahs'-ah-meh-tha] Parsing (part of speech): verb Mood—indicative Tense—aorist Voice—middle dep Person—1st person Number—plural Stem or root—from θεάομαι Concordance References: ⇒ Strong's #2300 theaomai ⇒ NIV #2517 theaomai ⇒ NASB #2300 theaomai **1 John 1:1** That which was from the beginning, which we have heard, which we have seen with our eyes, which we have **looked upon**, and our hands have handled, of the Word of life; [KJV] What was from the beginning, what we have heard, what we have seen with our eyes, what we **beheld** and our hands handled, concerning the Word of Life— [NASB] That which was from the beginning, which we have heard, which we have seen with our eyes, which we have **looked at** and our hands have touched—this we proclaim concerning the Word of life. [NIV] That which was from the beginning, which we have heard, which we have seen with our eyes, which we have **looked upon,** and our hands have handled, concerning the Word of life— [NKJV] The one who existed from the beginning is the one we have heard and seen. We **saw** him with our own eyes and touched him with our own hands. He is Jesus Christ, the Word of life. [NLT] Ὃ ἦν ἀπ' ἀρχῆς, ὃ ἀκηκόαμεν, ὃ ἑωράκαμεν τοῖς ὀφθαλμοῖς ἡμῶν, ὃ **ἐθεασάμεθα**, καὶ αἱ χεῖρες ἡμῶν ἐψηλάφησαν, περὶ τοῦ λόγου τῆς ζωῆς [GNS]	To look at; to look upon; to behold; to see; to gaze and look upon for a long time in order to study and understand and grasp. It means to look intensely and earnestly; it means to grasp the meaning and significance of a person. **Practical Application** John is testifying that he and the other apostles and believers looked and gazed upon Jesus Christ in order... • to study and understand Him. • to seek and grasp the meaning and significance of His person. A person will never see and understand who Christ is by just glancing at Him. If a person wants to know Christ, he has to look intensely and seriously; he has to seek to understand if Christ really is who John and other believers claim He is.

ENGLISH WORD	GREEK WORD AND VERSE	THE WORD MEANS...
	Ὁ ἦν ἀπ᾽ ἀρχῆς, ὃ ἀκηκόαμεν, ὃ ἑωράκαμεν τοῖς ὀφθαλμοῖς ἡμῶν, ὃ **ἐθεασάμεθα** καὶ αἱ χεῖρες ἡμῶν ἐψηλάφησαν περὶ τοῦ λόγου τῆς ζωῆς [GNT]	
#3383 **Scattered–** **Scattered** **Abroad** Scattered abroad– KJV Scattered–NASB Scattered–NIV Scattered–NKJV Fled–NLT **POSB** **REFERENCE** (Acts 8:4) Note 4, point 1	**διασπαρέντες** = *diasparentes* Pronunciation: [dee-as-pah'-rehn-tehs] Parsing (part of speech): verb Mood—participle Tense—aorist Voice—passive Case—nominative Number—plural Stem or root—from διασπείρω Concordance References: ⇒ Strong's #1289 diaspeirö ⇒ NIV #1401 diaspeirö ⇒ NASB #1289 diaspeirö **Acts 8:4** Therefore they that were **scattered abroad** went every where preaching the word. [KJV] Therefore, those who had been **scattered** went about preaching the word. [NASB] Those who had been **scattered** preached the word wherever they went. [NIV] Therefore those who were **scattered** went everywhere preaching the word. [NKJV] But the believers who had **fled** Jerusalem went everywhere preaching the Good News about Jesus. [NLT] οἱ μὲν οὖν **διασπαρέντες** διῆλθον, εὐαγγελιζόμενοι τὸν λόγον. [GNS] Οἱ μὲν οὖν **διασπαρέντες** διῆλθον εὐαγγελιζόμενοι τὸν λόγον. [GNT]	To scatter; to scatter abroad; to broadcast; to flee. **Practical Application** The believers were dispersed, "scattered about," just as seed is sown or scattered throughout a field.
#3384 **Scattered–** **Scattered** **Abroad** Scattered abroad– KJV Downcast–NASB Helpless–NIV Scattered–NKJV Didn't know where to go for help–NLT **POSB** **REFERENCE** (Mt.9:36) *Deeper Study #4*	**ἐρριμμένοι** = *errimmenoi* Pronunciation: [hrim-me'-noi] Parsing (part of speech): verb Mood—participle Tense—perfect Voice—passive Case—nominative Gender—masculine Number—plural Stem or root—from ῥίπτω and ῥιπτέω Concordance References: ⇒ Strong's #4496 hriptö ⇒ NIV #4849 hriptö ⇒ NASB #4496 hriptö **Matthew 9:36** But when he saw the multitudes, he was moved with compassion on them, because they fainted, and were **scattered abroad**, as sheep having no shepherd. [KJV] And seeing the multitudes, He felt compassion for them, because they were distressed and **downcast** like sheep without a shepherd. [NASB] When he saw the crowds, he had compassion on them, because they were harassed and **helpless**, like sheep without a shepherd. [NIV] But when He saw the multitudes, He was moved with compassion for them, because they were weary and **scattered**, like sheep having no shepherd. [NKJV] He felt great pity for the crowds that came, because their problems were so great and they **didn't know where to go for help**. They were like sheep without a shepherd. [NLT] ἰδὼν δὲ τοὺς ὄχλους, ἐσπλαγχνίσθη περὶ αὐτῶν, ὅτι ἦσαν ἐκλελυμένοι καὶ **ἐρριμμένοι** ὡσεὶ πρόβατα μὴ ἔχοντα ποιμένα. [GNS] Ἰδὼν δὲ τοὺς ὄχλους ἐσπλαγχνίσθη περὶ αὐτῶν, ὅτι ἦσαν ἐσκυλμένοι καὶ **ἐρριμμένοι** ὡσεὶ πρόβατα μὴ ἔχοντα ποιμένα. [GNT]	To be helpless, hopeless, scattered, downcast; to be cast out, laid low, thrown down, prostrated, dejected and hopeless. **Practical Application** Being scattered may come from experiences such as drunkenness, or struggling and fighting within and without, or being so weary that a person is just cast down. It is being prostrated by forces within oneself or laid low by forces outside of oneself.

ENGLISH WORD	GREEK WORD AND VERSE	THE WORD MEANS...

#3385
Scattered
Abroad
 	
Scattered abroad–KJV
 	
Dispersed abroad–NASB
 	
Scattered among the nations–NIV
 	
Scattered abroad–NKJV
 	
Scattered among the nations–NLT
 	
POSB
REFERENCE
(Jas.1:1)
Note 2, point 2
	διασπορᾷ = diaspora
	Pronunciation: [dee-as-por-ah']
	Parsing (part of speech): noun
	    Case—dative
	    Gender—feminine
	    Number—singular
	    Stem or root—from **διασπορα**, ας
	Concordance References:
	  ⇒ Strong's #1290 diaspora
	  ⇒ NIV #1402 diaspora
	  ⇒ NASB #1290 diaspora
	
	James 1:1
	James, a servant of God and of the Lord Jesus Christ, to the twelve tribes which are **scattered abroad**, greeting. [KJV]
	James, a bond-servant of God and of the Lord Jesus Christ, to the twelve tribes who are **dispersed abroad**, greetings. [NASB]
	James, a servant of God and of the Lord Jesus Christ, To the twelve tribes **scattered among the nations**: Greetings. [NIV]
	James, a bondservant of God and of the Lord Jesus Christ, To the twelve tribes which are **scattered abroad**: Greetings. [NKJV]
	This letter is from James, a slave of God and of the Lord Jesus Christ.It is written to Jewish Christians **scattered among the nations**.Greetings! [NLT]
	Ἰάκωβος, Θεοῦ καὶ Κυρίου Ἰησοῦ Χριστοῦ δοῦλος, ταῖς δώδεκα φυλαῖς ταῖς ἐν τῇ **διασπορᾷ**, χαίρειν. [GNS]
	Ἰάκωβος θεοῦ καὶ κυρίου Ἰησοῦ Χριστοῦ δοῦλος ταῖς δώδεκα φυλαῖς ταῖς ἐν τῇ **διασπορᾷ** χαίρειν. [GNT]
		Scattered among the nations, scattered abroad, dispersed abroad. *Diaspora* is simply a Greek word that means all the millions of Jews scattered all over the world.
		
		Practical Application
		James loved his people with an unusual love. They were deeply rooted in his heart, and he felt a strong calling to reach and exhort them in the Lord. This is the very reason he was writing them. Just think what an awesome task it must have been to draw up the plans by which his letter could be passed from church to church and from synagogue to synagogue all over the world. James either laid out the plans and followed through in seeing that the plans were carried out or else the Holy Spirit gave him assurance that his letter would be spread to all the Jews scattered all over the world. James had some indication that he would be reaching all Jews—the twelve tribes scattered all over. His heart longed to reach the millions of the *diaspora*.
		The point to see is the love and the evangelistic heart that James had for his people. True, he is writing primarily to Jewish believers, but he is also doing what he says: sending greetings to the twelve tribes of the diaspora—all the millions who are scattered all over the world. What he says is applicable to all believers of all generations.
		What a dynamic example in love and evangelism for us. What would happen if our hearts beat with the same degree of love and evangelism—the compassion to reach the lost and suffering people of our communities, cities, and nations?

#3386
Scattered
Among The
Nations
 	
Scattered abroad–KJV
 	
Dispersed abroad–NASB
 	
Scattered among the nations–NIV
 	
Scattered abroad–NKJV
 	
Scattered among the nations–NLT
 	
POSB
REFERENCE
(Jas.1:1)
Note 2, point 2
	διασπορᾷ = diaspora
	Pronunciation: [dee-as-por-ah']
	Parsing (part of speech): noun
	    Case—dative
	    Gender—feminine
	    Number—singular
	    Stem or root—from **διασπορα,,** ας
	Concordance References:
	  ⇒ Strong's #1290 diaspora
	  ⇒ NIV #1402 diaspora
	  ⇒ NASB #1290 diaspora
	
	James 1:1
	James, a servant of God and of the Lord Jesus Christ, to the twelve tribes which are **scattered abroad**, greeting. [KJV]
	James, a bond-servant of God and of the Lord Jesus Christ, to the twelve tribes who are **dispersed abroad**, greetings. [NASB]
	James, a servant of God and of the Lord Jesus Christ, To the twelve tribes **scattered among the nations**: Greetings. [NIV]
	James, a bondservant of God and of the Lord Jesus Christ, To the twelve tribes which are **scattered abroad**: Greetings. [NKJV]
	This letter is from James, a slave of God and of the Lord Jesus Christ.It is written to Jewish Christians **scattered among the nations**.Greetings! [NLT]
	Ἰάκωβος, Θεοῦ καὶ Κυρίου Ἰησοῦ Χριστοῦ δοῦλος, ταῖς δώδεκα φυλαῖς ταῖς ἐν τῇ **διασπορᾷ**, χαίρειν. [GNS]
	Ἰάκωβος θεοῦ καὶ κυρίου Ἰησοῦ Χριστοῦ δοῦλος ταῖς δώδεκα φυλαῖς ταῖς ἐν τῇ **διασπορᾷ** χαίρειν. [GNT]
		Scattered among the nations, scattered abroad, dispersed abroad. *Diaspora* is simply a Greek word that means all the millions of Jews scattered all over the world.
		
		Practical Application
		James loved his people with an unusual love. They were deeply rooted in his heart, and he felt a strong calling to reach and exhort them in the Lord. This is the very reason he was writing them. Just think what an awesome task it must have been to draw up the plans by which his letter could be passed from church to church and from synagogue to synagogue all over the world. James either laid out the plans and followed through in seeing that the plans were carried out or else the Holy Spirit gave him assurance that his letter would be spread to all the Jews scattered all over the world. James had some indication that he would be reaching all Jews—the twelve tribes scattered all over. His heart longed to reach the millions of the *diaspora*.
		(See **Scattered Abroad**, for more discussion).

ENGLISH WORD	GREEK WORD AND VERSE	THE WORD MEANS...

#3387
Schemes
 	
Wiles–KJV
Schemes–NASB
Schemes–NIV
Wiles–NKJV
Strategies and tricks–NLT
 	
POSB REFERENCE
(Eph.6:11)
Note 2
	μεθοδείας = *methodeias*
	Pronunciation: [meth-od-i'-ahs]
	Parsing (part of speech): noun
	    Case—accusative
	    Gender—feminine
	    Number—plural
	    Stem or root—from μεθοδεία, ας
	Concordance References:
	⇒ Strong's #3180 methodeia
	⇒ NIV #3497 methodeia
	⇒ NASB #3180 methodeiat
	
	Ephes. 6:11
	Put on the whole armour of God, that ye may be able to stand against the **wiles** of the devil. [KJV]
	Put on the full armor of God, that you may be able to stand firm against the **schemes** of the devil. [NASB]
	Put on the full armor of God so that you can take your stand against the devil's **schemes**. [NIV]
	Put on the whole armor of God, that you may be able to stand against the **wiles** of the devil. [NKJV]
	Put on all of God's armor so that you will be able to stand firm against all **strategies and tricks** of the Devil. [NLT]
	ἐνδύσασθε τὴν πανοπλίαν τοῦ Θεοῦ, πρὸς τὸ δύνασθαι ὑμᾶς στῆναι πρὸς τὰς **μεθοδείας** τοῦ διαβόλου· [GNS]
	ἐνδύσασθε τὴν πανοπλίαν τοῦ θεοῦ πρὸς τὸ δύνασθαι ὑμᾶς στῆναι πρὸς τὰς **μεθοδεία** τοῦ διαβόλου· [GNT]
		Schemes, wiles, strategies and tricks; trickery. It means the deceits, craftiness, trickery, methods, and strategies which the devil uses to wage war against the believer.
		
		Practical Application
		The enemy is the devil and his schemes. He will do everything he can to deceive and capture the believer.

#3388
Schoolmaster
 	
Schoolmaster–KJV
Tutor–NASB
Put in charge to lead–NIV
Tutor–NKJV
Guardian and teacher–NLT
 	
POSB REFERENCE
(Gal.3:23-25; esp. v.24)
Note 1
 	
See also POSB REF:
(1 Cor.4:15)
Note 2
	παιδαγωγὸς = *paidagōgos*
	Pronunciation: [pahee-dag-o-gos']
	Parsing (part of speech): noun
	    Case—nominative
	    Gender—masculine
	    Number—singular
	    Stem or root—from παιδαγωγός, οῦ
	Concordance References:
	⇒ Strong's #3807 paidagōgos
	⇒ NIV #4080 paidagōgos
	⇒ NASB #3807 paidagōgos
	
	Galatians 3:24
	Wherefore the law was our **schoolmaster** to bring us unto Christ, that we might be justified by faith. [KJV]
	Therefore the Law has become our **tutor** to lead us to Christ, that we may be justified by faith. [NASB]
	So the law was **put in charge to lead** us to Christ that we might be justified by faith. [NIV]
	Therefore the law was our **tutor** *to bring us* to Christ, that we might be justified by faith. [NKJV]
	Let me put it another way. The law was our **guardian and teacher** to lead us until Christ came. So now, through faith in Christ, we are made right with God. [NLT]
	ὥστε ὁ νόμος **παιδαγωγὸς** ἡμῶν γέγονεν εἰς Χριστόν, ἵνα ἐκ πίστεως δικαιωθῶμεν· [GNS]
	ὥστε ὁ νόμος **παιδαγωγὸς** ἡμῶν γέγονεν εἰς Χριστόν, ἵνα ἐκ πίστεως δικαιωθῶμεν· [GNT]
		Put in charge to lead, tutor, teacher, instructor, guide.
		
		Practical Application
		The law was man's schoolmaster to lead him to see his need for Christ. The *paidagogos* was usually a trusted slave who was in charge of a child's moral welfare, but he had one particular duty to which Paul was referring. Every day the guardian took the child to school to deliver him to the teacher. And then at the end of the day, he returned for the child and brought him safely back home. This was what the law was to do. The law is to lead man to Christ, the true Teacher. The law does this by showing man that he is utterly unable to secure righteousness by himself. He must look to Christ, the real Teacher, for righteousness and acceptance by God, that is, for justification by faith. And once Christ (faith in Him) has come, there is no need for the law nor for any other schoolmaster, for Jesus Christ brings us face to face with God.

#3389
Scoffers
 	
Despisers–KJV
Scoffers–NASB
Scoffers–NIV
Despisers–NKJV
Mockers–NLT
 	
POSB REFERENCE
(Acts 13:23-41; esp. v.41)
Note 3, point 7
	καταφρονηταί = *kataphronētai*
	Pronunciation: [kat-af-ron-ay-tah-ee]
	Parsing (part of speech): noun
	    Case—vocative
	    Gender—masculine
	    Number—plural
	    Stem or root—from καταφρονητής, οῦ
	Concordance References:
	⇒ Strong's #2707 kataphronētēs
	⇒ NIV #2970 kataphronētēs
	⇒ NASB #2707 kataphronētēs
	
	Acts 13:41
	Behold, ye **despisers**, and wonder, and perish: for I
		Scoffers; scorners; mockers; cynics; mimics. It means to look down upon; think lightly of; act against.
		
		Practical Application
		The Savior brings judgment upon men. Since He has come, men must beware lest what the prophet declared come upon them (Habakkuk 1:5).
		⇒ They can be "scoffers" (*kataphronētai*).
		⇒ They can wonder and perish. The idea is that a man can perish wondering if Jesus is truly the Savior and if the Word preached

ENGLISH WORD	GREEK WORD AND VERSE	THE WORD MEANS...
	work a work in your days, a work which ye shall in no wise believe, though a man declare it unto you. [KJV] 'Behold, you **scoffers**, and marvel, and perish; For I am accomplishing a work in your days, A work which you will never believe, though someone should describe it to you.' [NASB] " 'Look, you **scoffers**, wonder and perish, for I am going to do something in your days that you would never believe, even if someone told you.'" [NIV] "Behold, you **despisers**, Marvel and perish! For I work a work in your days, A work which you will by no means believe, Though one were to declare it to you.' [NKJV] 'Look you **mockers**, be amazed and die! For I am doing something in your own day, something you wouldn't believe even if someone told you about it.' [NLT] Ἴδετε, οἱ **καταφρονηταί**, καὶ θαυμάσατε καὶ ἀφανίσθητε· ὅτι ἔργον ἐγὼ ἐργάζομαι ἐν ταῖς ἡμέραις ὑμῶν, ἔργον ᾧ οὐ μὴ πιστεύσητε ἐάν τις ἐκδιηγῆται ὑμῖν. [GNS] Ἴδετε, οἱ **καταφρονητής**, καὶ θαυμάσατε καὶ ἀφανίσθητε, ὅτι ἔργον ἐργάζομαι ἐγὼ ἐν ταῖς ἡμέραις ὑμῶν, ἔργον ὃ οὐ μὴ πιστεύσητε ἐάν τις ἐκδιηγῆται ὑμῖν. [GNT]	is true (Acts 13:38-39). (See POSB *Deeper Study #2*, Perish—John 3:16.)

#3390
Scoffing At God
 	
Blasphemers–KJV
Revilers–NASB
Abusive–NIV
Blasphemers–NKJV
Scoffing at God–NLT
 	
POSB REFERENCE
(2 Tim.3:2-4; esp. v.2)
Note 2, point 5
	βλάσφημοι = *blasphēmoi*
	Pronunciation: [blas'-fay-moy]
	Parsing (part of speech): adjective
	    Case—nominative
	    Gender—masculine
	    Number—plural
	    Stem or root—from **βλάσφημος** , ον
	Concordance References:
	  ⇒ Strong's #989 blasphēmos
	  ⇒ NIV #1061 blasphēmos
	  ⇒ NASB #989 blasphēmos
	
	2 Tim. 3:2
	For men shall be lovers of their own selves, covetous, boasters, proud, **blasphemers**, disobedient to parents, unthankful, unholy, [KJV]
	
	For men will be lovers of self, lovers of money, boastful, arrogant, **revilers**, disobedient to parents, ungrateful, unholy, [NASB]
	
	People will be lovers of themselves, lovers of money, boastful, proud, **abusive**, disobedient to their parents, ungrateful, unholy, [NIV]
	
	For men will be lovers of themselves, lovers of money, boasters, proud, **blasphemers**, disobedient to parents, unthankful, unholy, [NKJV]
	
	For people will love only themselves and their money. They will be boastful and proud, **scoffing at God**, disobedient to their parents, and ungrateful. They will consider nothing sacred. [NLT]
	
	ἔσονται γὰρ οἱ ἄνθρωποι φίλαυτοι, φιλάργυροι, ἀλαζόνες, ὑπερήφανοι, **βλάσφημοι**, γονεῦσιν ἀπειθεῖς, ἀχάριστοι, ἀνόσιοι, [GNS]
	
	ἔσονται γὰρ οἱ ἄνθρωποι φίλαυτοι φιλάργυροι ἀλαζόνες ὑπερήφανοι **βλάσφημοι**, γονεῦσιν ἀπειθεῖς, ἀχάριστοι ἀνόσιοι [GNT]
		To be verbally abusive; to blaspheme; to revile; to openly scoff at God; to slander, insult, rail, reproach, curse.
		
		Practical Application
		The phrase "scoffing at God" (*blasphēmoi*) is usually thought to be against God, and it is. But it is also a sin against men. Men can blaspheme men. Think of the cursing and insults that will be thrown against God and men today. Practically everyone is cursing and reviling others: mothers, fathers, children, teachers, professionals, actors, comedians, politicians, even some professing religionists feel the need to occasionally curse in order to be acceptable.
		
		Why is there so much cursing and profanity today? Because there is a loss of respect for both self and others, for both position and authority. People rail, revile, insult, reproach, and curse when they are disturbed within—when they sense dissatisfaction, disapproval, unacceptance, bitterness, emptiness, loneliness, and reaction within their heart. A disturbed and dissatisfied heart causes people to scoff God and man, including themselves (blaming and cursing themselves when they fail and come ever so short).

#3391
Scolded Harshly
 	
Murmured against–KJV
Scolding–NASB
Rebuked...harshly–NIV
Criticized...sharply–NKJV
Scolded...harshly–NLT
	ἐνεβριμῶντο = *eneboimonto*
	Pronunciation: [en-eh-brim-own'-tow]
	Parsing (part of speech): verb
	    Mood—indicative
	    Tense—imperfect
	    Voice—middle or passive deponent
	    Person—3rd person
	    Number—plural
	    Stem or root—from ἐμβριμάομαι
	Concordance References:
	  ⇒ Strong's #1690 embrimaomai
	  ⇒ NIV #1839 embrimaomai
	  ⇒ NASB #1690 embrimaomai
		To growl, rebuke, murmur against, scold; to speak harshly against.
		
		Practical Application
		In this Scripture, what disturbed the disciples was not the fact that Mary anointed Jesus. Anointing Him was easy enough to understand since it was a common custom of the day. What disturbed them was the gift she gave. The gift...
		• seemed too valuable and priceless.
		• seemed unnecessary and thoughtless.

ENGLISH WORD	GREEK WORD AND VERSE	THE WORD MEANS...
POSB REFERENCE (Mk.14:4-5; esp. v.5) Note 2	**Mark 14:5** For it might have been sold for more than three hundred pence, and have been given to the poor. And they **murmured against** her. [KJV] "For this perfume might have been sold for over three hundred denarii, and the money given to the poor." And they were **scolding** her. [NASB] It could have been sold for more than a year's wages and the money given to the poor." And they **rebuked** her **harshly**. [NIV] For it might have been sold for more than three hundred denarii and given to the poor." And they **criticized** her **sharply**. [NKJV] "She could have sold it for a small fortune and given the money to the poor!" And they **scolded** her **harshly**. [NLT] ἠδύνατο γὰρ τοῦτο πραθῆναι ἐπάνω τριακοσίων δηναρίων, καὶ δοθῆναι τοῖς πτωχοῖς. καὶ **ἐνεβριμῶντο** αὐτῇ. [GNS] ἠδύνατο γὰρ τοῦτο τὸ μύρον πραθῆναι ἐπάνω δηναρίων τριακοσίων καὶ δοθῆναι τοῖς πτωχοῖς· καὶ **ἐνεβριμῶντο** αὐτῇ. [GNT]	• seemed misplaced and wasted. • seemed too costly and sacrificial. • seemed ton be a foolish and senseless act.

#3392
Scolding
 	
Murmured against–KJV
Scolding–NASB
Rebuked...harshly–NIV
Criticized...sharply–NKJV
Scolded...harshly–NLT
 	
POSB REFERENCE (Mk.14:4-5; esp. v.5) Note 2
	ἐνεβριμῶντο = *eneboimonto*
	Pronunciation: [en-eh-brim-own'-tow]
	Parsing (part of speech): verb
	    Mood—indicative
	    Tense—imperfect
	    Voice—middle or passive deponent
	    Person—3rd person
	    Number—plural
	    Stem or root—from ἐμβριμάομαι
	Concordance References:
	⇒ Strong's #1690 embrimaomai
	⇒ NIV #1839 embrimaomai
	⇒ NASB #1690 embrimaomai
	
	Mark 14:5
	For it might have been sold for more than three hundred pence, and have been given to the poor. And they **murmured against** her. [KJV]
	"For this perfume might have been sold for over three hundred denarii, and the money given to the poor." And they were **scolding** her. [NASB]
	It could have been sold for more than a year's wages and the money given to the poor." And they **rebuked** her **harshly**. [NIV]
	For it might have been sold for more than three hundred denarii and given to the poor." And they **criticized** her **sharply**. [NKJV]
	"She could have sold it for a small fortune and given the money to the poor!" And they **scolded** her **harshly**. [NLT]
	ἠδύνατο γὰρ τοῦτο πραθῆναι ἐπάνω τριακοσίων δηναρίων, καὶ δοθῆναι τοῖς πτωχοῖς. καὶ **ἐνεβριμῶντο** αὐτῇ. [GNS]
	ἠδύνατο γὰρ τοῦτο τὸ μύρον πραθῆναι ἐπάνω δηναρίων τριακοσίων καὶ δοθῆναι τοῖς πτωχοῖς· καὶ **ἐνεβριμῶντο** αὐτῇ. [GNT]
		To growl, rebuke, murmur against, scold; to speak harshly against.
		
		### Practical Application
		In this Scripture, what disturbed the disciples was not the fact that Mary anointed Jesus. Anointing Him was easy enough to understand since it was a common custom of the day. What disturbed them was the gift she gave. The gift...
		• seemed too valuable and priceless.
		• seemed unnecessary and thoughtless.
		• seemed misplaced and wasted.
		• seemed too costly and sacrificial.
		• seemed to be a foolish and senseless act.

#3393
Scorned
 	
Despised–KJV
Viewed others with contempt–NASB
Looked down on–NIV
Despised–NKJV
Scorned–NLT
	ἐξουθενοῦντας = *exouthenountas*
	Pronunciation: [ex-oo-then-oon'-tas]
	Parsing (part of speech): verb
	    Mood—participle
	    Tense—present
	    Voice—active
	    Case—accusative
	    Gender—masculine
	    Number—plural
	    Stem or root—from ἐξουθενέω
	Concordance References:
	⇒ Strong's #1848 exoutheneō
	⇒ NIV #2024 exoutheneō
	⇒ NASB #1848 exoutheneō
		To despise; to view others with contempt; to look down on; to scorn; to set at naught; to count as nothing, as unimportant and insignificant.
		
		### Practical Application
		Such persons feel and act as though they are above and better, more important and significant, than others. They shy away from, ignore and neglect, pass by and downgrade, criticize and talk about...
		• the poor
		• the unfortunate

ENGLISH WORD	GREEK WORD AND VERSE	THE WORD MEANS...
POSB REFERENCE (Lk.18:9) Note 1, point 3	**Luke 18:9** And he spake this parable unto certain which trusted in themselves that they were righteous, and **despised** others: [KJV] And He also told this parable to certain ones who trusted in themselves that they were righteous, and **viewed others with contempt**: [NASB] To some who were confident of their own righteousness and **looked down on** everybody else, Jesus told this parable: [NIV] Also He spoke this parable to some who trusted in themselves that they were righteous, and **despised** others: [NKJV] Then Jesus told this story to some who had great self-confidence and **scorned** everyone else: [NLT] Εἶπε δὲ καὶ πρός τινας τοὺς πεποιθότας ἐφ᾿ ἑαυτοῖς ὅτι εἰσὶ δίκαιοι, καὶ **ἐξουθενοῦντας** τοὺς λοιποὺς, τὴν παραβολὴν ταύτην· [GNS] Εἶπεν δὲ καὶ πρός τινας τοὺς πεποιθότας ἐφ᾿ ἑαυτοῖς ὅτι εἰσὶν δίκαιοι καὶ **ἐξουθενοῦντας** τοὺς λοιποὺς τὴν παραβολὴν ταύτην· [GNT]	• the poorly dressed • the homeless • the downcast • the derelict • the undernourished

#3394
Scourged
 	
Scourged–KJV
Scourged–NASB
Had...flogged–NIV
Scourged–NKJV
Flogged–NLT
 	
POSB REFERENCE (Mt.27:26-38; esp. v.26) Note 2, point 1
	φραγελλώσας = *phragellōsas*
	Pronunciation: [frag-el-lo'-sahs]
	Parsing (part of speech): verb
	    Mood—participle
	    Tense—aorist
	    Voice—active
	    Case—nominative
	    Gender—masculine
	    Number—singular
	    Stem or root—from φραγελλόω
	Concordance References:
	⇒ Strong's #5417 phragelloo
	⇒ NIV #5849 phragelloö
	⇒ NASB #5417 phragelloo
	
	Matthew 27:26
	Then released he Barabbas unto them: and when he had **scourged** Jesus, he delivered him to be crucified. [KJV]
	Then he released Barabbas for them; but after having Jesus **scourged**, he delivered Him to be crucified. [NASB]
	Then he released Barabbas to them. But he **had** Jesus **flogged**, and handed him over to be crucified. [NIV]
	Then he released Barabbas to them; and when he had **scourged** Jesus, he delivered Him to be crucified. [NKJV]
	So Pilate released Barabbas to them. He ordered Jesus **flogged** with a lead-tipped whip, then turned him over to the Roman soldiers to crucify him. [NLT]
	τότε ἀπέλυσεν αὐτοῖς τὸν Βαραββᾶν· τὸν δὲ Ἰησοῦν **φραγελλώσας** παρέδωκεν ἵνα σταυρωθῇ. [GNS]
	τότε ἀπέλυσεν αὐτοῖς τὸν Βαραββᾶν, τὸν δὲ Ἰησοῦν **φραγελλώσας** παρέδωκεν ἵνα σταυρωθῇ. [GNT]
		To flog; to scourge; to lash or beat with a whip.
		
		Practical Application
		The whip that was used to flog Jesus was made of leather straps with two small balls attached to the end of each strap. The balls of rough lead or sharp bones or spikes would cut deeply into the flesh. His hands were tied to a post above His head as He was scourged (John 19:1). It was the custom for the prisoner to be lashed until he was judged near death by the presiding centurion (Jewish trials allowed only forty lashes [Dt.25:2-3] less one, cp. 2 Cor. 11:24). The criminal's back was, of course, nothing more than an unrecognizable mass of torn flesh.

#3395
Scribes
 	
Scribes–KJV
Scribes–NASB
Teachers of the law–NIV
Scribes–NKJV
Teachers of religious law–NLT
	γραμματέων = *grammateōn*
	Pronunciation: [gram-mat-eh-own']
	Parsing (part of speech): noun
	    Case—genitive
	    Gender—masculine
	    Number—plural
	    Stem or root—from γραμματεύς έως
	Concordance References:
	⇒ Strong's #1122 grammateus
	⇒ NIV #1208 grammateus
	⇒ NASB #1122 grammateus
	
	Mark 12:28
	And one of the **scribes** came, and having heard them
		Teachers of the law, teachers of religious law, scribes, scholars.
		
		Practical Application
		This word (*grammateōn*) describes a profession of laymen who studied, taught, interpreted, and dealt with the practical questions of Jewish law. They were a specialization within the profession commonly called Scribes (cp. Matthew 22:35). They functioned both in the court and synagogues (cp. Luke 7:30; Luke 10:25; Luke 11:45, 46, 52; Luke 14:3; Titus 3:13). They were apparently a specialization dealing more with the study and interpretation of the law.

ENGLISH WORD	GREEK WORD AND VERSE	THE WORD MEANS...
POSB REFERENCE (Mk.12:28) *Deeper Study #1*	reasoning together, and perceiving that he had answered them well, asked him, Which is the first commandment of all? [KJV] And one of the **scribes** came and heard them arguing, and recognizing that He had answered them well, asked Him, "What commandment is the foremost of all?" [NASB] One of the **teachers of the law** came and heard them debating. Noticing that Jesus had given them a good answer, he asked him, "Of all the commandments, which is the most important?" [NIV] Then one of the **scribes** came, and having heard them reasoning together, perceiving that He had answered them well, asked Him, "Which is the first commandment of all?" [NKJV] One of the **teachers of religious law** was standing there listening to the discussion. He realized that Jesus had answered well, so he asked, "Of all the commandments, which is the most important?" [NLT] Καὶ προσελθὼν εἷς τῶν **γραμματέων**, ἀκούσας αὐτῶν συζητούντων, εἰδὼς ὅτι καλῶς αὐτοῖς ἀπεκρίθη, ἐπηρώτησεν αὐτόν, Ποία ἐστὶ πρώτη πάντων ἐντολή; [GNS] Καὶ προσελθὼν εἷς τῶν **γραμματέων** ἀκούσας αὐτῶν συζητούντων, ἰδὼν ὅτι καλῶς ἀπεκρίθη αὐτοῖς ἐπηρώτησεν αὐτόν, Ποία ἐστὶν ἐντολὴ πρώτη πάντων; [GNT]	

#3396
Scrip
 	
Scrip–KJV
Bag–NASB
Bag–NIV
Knapsack–NKJV
Traveler's bag–NLT
 	
POSB REFERENCE (Lk.10:4) Note 4, point 1
	πήραν = *përan*
	Pronunciation: [pay'-rahn]
	Parsing (part of speech): noun
	  Case—accusative
	  Gender—feminine
	  Number—singular
	  Stem or root—from πήρα, ας
	Concordance References:
	  ⇒ Strong's #4082 përa
	  ⇒ NIV #4385 përa
	  ⇒ NASB #4082 përa
	
	Luke 10:4
	Carry neither purse, nor **scrip**, nor shoes: and salute no man by the way. [KJV]
	
	"Carry no purse, no **bag**, no shoes; and greet no one on the way. [NASB]
	
	Do not take a purse or **bag** or sandals; and do not greet anyone on the road. [NIV]
	
	Carry neither money bag, **knapsack**, nor sandals; and greet no one along the road. [NKJV]
	
	Don't take along any money, or a **traveler's bag**, or even an extra pair of sandals. And don't stop to greet anyone on the road. [NLT]
	
	μὴ βαστάζετε βαλάντιον, μὴ **πήραν**, μὴ ὑποδήματα· καὶ μηδένα κατὰ τὴν ὁδὸν ἀσπάσησθε. [GNS]
	
	μὴ βαστάζετε βαλλάντιον, μὴ **πήραν**, μὴ ὑποδήματα, καὶ μηδένα κατὰ τὴν ὁδὸν ἀσπάσησθε. [GNT]
		A traveler's bag, wallet, or sack usually made of animal skin (leather). This bag was used to carry the possessions that a traveler would need for his journey.
		
		Practical Application
		Note Jesus' clear instructions: they were not to carry a money-bag (purse, *ballantion*) or a scrip (*pera*) or two pair of shoes. They were to trust God for provisions, not worrying about money for food, housing, or clothing (Matthew 6:24-34). Worrying about such things would be cumbersome, taking away precious time that should be spent in ministering. Also, they were preaching a message of faith and trust in God. They needed to live what they were preaching and become a living picture of the dependency that God wants from every man.

#3397
Sealed
 	
Sealed–KJV
Sealed–NASB
Set...seal of ownership on–NIV
Sealed–NKJV
Identified us as his own–NLT
	σφραγισάμενος = *sphragisamenos*
	Pronunciation: [sfrag-is'-ah-mehn-os]
	Parsing (part of speech): verb
	  Mood—participle
	  Tense—aorist
	  Voice—middle
	  Case—nominative
	  Gender—masculine
	  Number—singular
	  Stem or root—from σφραγίζω
	Concordance References:
	  ⇒ Strong's #4972 sphragizō
	  ⇒ NIV #5381 sphragizō
	  ⇒ NASB #4972 sphragizō
		To set a seal of ownership on; to mark; to stamp; to set apart by a seal; to place a seal upon.
		
		Practical Application
		God places His seal, His stamp, His mark upon believers. Paul was just as much in Christ and anointed as others. The word "us" refers primarily to Paul. He is comparing himself with the Corinthians, and he is also including those who oppose him. In no uncertain terms, Paul says that the same God who has worked in the Corinthians has also worked in him.

ENGLISH WORD	GREEK WORD AND VERSE	THE WORD MEANS...
POSB REFERENCE (2 Cor.1:21-22; esp. v.22) Note 5	**2 Cor. 1:22** Who hath also **sealed** us, and given the earnest of the Spirit in our hearts. [KJV] Who also **sealed** us and gave us the Spirit in our hearts as a pledge. [NASB] **Set** his **seal of ownership on** us, and put his Spirit in our hearts as a deposit, guaranteeing what is to come. [NIV] Who also has **sealed** us and given us the Spirit in our hearts as a guarantee. [NKJV] And he has **identified us as his own** by placing the Holy Spirit in our hearts as the first installment of everything he will give us. [NLT] ὁ καὶ **σφραγισάμενος** ἡμᾶς, καὶ δοὺς τὸν ἀρραβῶνα τοῦ Πνεύματος ἐν ταῖς καρδίαις ἡμῶν. [GNS] ὁ καὶ **σφραγισάμενος** ἡμᾶς καὶ δοὺς τὸν ἀρραβῶνα τοῦ πνεύματος ἐν ταῖς καρδίαις ἡμῶν. [GNT]	

#3398
Search
 	
Search–KJV
Search–NASB
Diligently study–NIV
Search–NKJV
Search–NLT
 	
POSB REFERENCE (Jn.5:39) Note 6, point 1
	ἐραυνᾶτε = *eraunate*
	Pronunciation: [eh-rah-oon-ah'-teh]
	Parsing (part of speech): verb
	    Mood—indicative or imperative
	    Tense—present
	    Voice—active
	    Person—2nd person
	    Number—plural
	    Stem or root—from ἐραυνάω
	Concordance References:
	  ⇒ Strong's #2045 eraunaō
	  ⇒ NIV #2236 eraunaō
	  ⇒ NASB #2045 eraunaō
	
	John 5:39
	Search the scriptures; for in them ye think ye have eternal life: and they are they which testify of me. [KJV]
	"You **search** the Scriptures, because you think that in them you have eternal life; and it is these that bear witness of Me; [NASB]
	You **diligently study** the Scriptures because you think that by them you possess eternal life. These are the Scriptures that testify about me, [NIV]
	You **search** the Scriptures, for in them you think you have eternal life; and these are they which testify of Me. [NKJV]
	"You **search** the Scriptures because you believe they give you eternal life. But the Scriptures point to me! [NLT]
	ἐρευνᾶτε τὰς γραφάς, ὅτι ὑμεῖς δοκεῖτε ἐν αὐταῖς ζωὴν αἰώνιον ἔχειν, καὶ ἐκεῖναί εἰσιν αἱ μαρτυροῦσαι περὶ ἐμοῦ· [GNS]
	ἐραυνᾶτε τὰς γραφάς, ὅτι ὑμεῖς δοκεῖτε ἐν αὐταῖς ζωὴν αἰώνιον ἔχειν· καὶ ἐκεῖναί εἰσιν αἱ μαρτυροῦσαι περὶ ἐμοῦ· [GNT]
		To diligently study; to search; to inquire; to investigate; to closely examine; to explore; to thoroughly search; to research; to delve into.
		
		Practical Application
		The word "search," can be either a fact, that "you search the Scriptures," or a command, "search the Scriptures." It seems that the words "for you think that by them" point toward the meaning being a statement of fact. The religionists do "diligently study the Scriptures," for they think they have eternal life "in their diligently study." But note this most important fact:
		The Scriptures *proclaim* the message of eternal life and show us how to secure eternal life, but the Scriptures do not impart or give eternal life. Only Christ can give eternal life. A person does not secure eternal life...
		• by reading the Scripture, no matter how much he reads.
		• by knowing the Scripture, no matter how much he knows.
		• by being religious, no matter how religious he is.
		• by doing religious works, no matter how much good he does.
		A person receives eternal life only by believing and giving his heart and life to Jesus Christ. (See POSB *Deeper Study #2—John 2:24*.)

#3399
Seasons
 	
Seasons–KJV
Time–NASB
Time–NIV
Day–NKJV
Day...now–NLT
 	
POSB REFERENCE (Acts 20:18-19; esp. v.18) Note 2, point 1
	χρόνον = *chronon*
	Pronunciation: [khron'-on]
	Parsing (part of speech): noun
	    Case—accusative
	    Gender—masculine
	    Number—singular
	    Stem or root— from χρόνος, ου
	Concordance References:
	  ⇒ Strong's #5550 chronos
	  ⇒ NIV #5989 chronos
	  ⇒ NASB #5550 chronos
	
	Acts 20:18
	And when they were come to him, he said unto them, Ye know, from the first day that I came into Asia, after what manner I have been with you at all **seasons**, [KJV]
	And when they had come to him, he said to them, "You yourselves know, from the first day that I set foot in Asia, how I was with you the whole **time**, [NASB]
		Time, seasons, day as in a moment of time.
		
		Practical Application
		Paul was totally devoted "at all seasons" (*chronon*) and in "after what manner," [KJV] that is, through all kinds of situations and circumstances.

ENGLISH WORD	GREEK WORD AND VERSE	THE WORD MEANS...
	When they arrived, he said to them: "You know how I lived the whole **time** I was with you, from the first day I came into the province of Asia. [NIV] And when they had come to him, he said to them: "You know, from the first **day** that I came to Asia, in what manner I always lived among you, [NKJV] When they arrived he declared, "You know that from the **day** I set foot in the province of Asia until **now** [NLT] ὡς δὲ παρεγένοντο πρὸς αὐτόν, εἶπεν αὐτοῖς, Ὑμεῖς ἐπίστασθε, ἀπὸ πρώτης ἡμέρας ἀφ' ἧς ἐπέβην εἰς τὴν Ἀσίαν, πῶς μεθ' ὑμῶν τὸν πάντα **χρόνον** ἐγενόμην, [GNS] ὡς δὲ παρεγένοντο πρὸς αὐτὸν εἶπεν αὐτοῖς, Ὑμεῖς ἐπίστασθε, ἀπὸ πρώτης ἡμέρας ἀφ' ἧς ἐπέβην εἰς τὴν Ἀσίαν πῶς μεθ' ὑμῶν τὸν πάντα **χρόνος** ἐγενόμην, [GNT]	

#3400
Secret
 	
Mystery–KJV
Mystery–NASB
Secret–NIV
Mystery–NKJV
Secret–NLT
 	
POSB
REFERENCE
(1 Cor.2:7)
Deeper Study #1
	ἐν μυστηρίῳ = *en mustēriō*
	Pronunciation: [en moos-tay'-ree-o]
	Parsing (part of speech): noun
	    Case—dative
	    Gender—neuter
	    Number—singular
	Stem or root—from μυστήριον ου
	Concordance References:
	⇒ Strong's #1722+3466 en mustērion
	⇒ NIV #1877+3696 en mustērion [secret]
	⇒ NASB #1722+3466 en mustērion
	
	1 Cor. 2:7
	But we speak the wisdom of God in a **mystery**, even the hidden wisdom, which God ordained before the world unto our glory: [KJV]
	
	But we speak God's wisdom in a **mystery**, the hidden wisdom, which God predestined before the ages to our glory; [NASB]
	
	No, we speak of God's **secret** wisdom, a wisdom that has been hidden and that God destined for our glory before time began. [NIV]
	
	But we speak the wisdom of God in a **mystery**, the hidden *wisdom* which God ordained before the ages for our glory, [NKJV]
	
	No, the wisdom we speak of is the **secret** wisdom of God, which was hidden in former times, though he made it for our benefit before the world began. [NLT]
	
	ἀλλὰ λαλοῦμεν σοφίαν Θεοῦ **ἐν μυστηρίῳ**, τὴν ἀποκεκρυμμένην, ἣν προώρισεν ὁ Θεὸς πρὸ τῶν αἰώνων εἰς δόξαν ἡμῶν· [GNS]
	
	ἀλλὰ λαλοῦμεν θεοῦ σοφίαν **ἐν μυστηρίῳ**, τὴν ἀποκεκρυμμένην, ἣν προώρισεν ὁ θεὸς πρὸ τῶν αἰώνων εἰς δόξαν ἡμῶν· [GNT]
		A secret; a mystery; a fact or truth that man is unable to discover by himself; a fact or truth that has to be revealed to man.
		
		Practical Application
		
		It is a fact or truth that had been hidden and kept secret by God until it was time for it to be revealed. It does not mean something hard to understand or something strange and mysterious as a magical trick. It does not mean that there is something mysterious about God. It means some fact or truth...
		
		• that is known only by God.
		• that God reveals to man because He loves man and man desperately needs to know the truth.
		
		There are several important mysteries or secrets revealed in the Bible.
		
		1. The secret of the gospel, that is, God's wisdom which is Christ crucified.
		2. The secrets of the Kingdom of heaven. (See POSB note—Matthew 13:10-11; cp. Matthew 13:1-52.)
		3. The secret of Israel's blindness and restoration.
		4. The secret of the believers' resurrection, which will enable them to live an incorruptible life with God.
		5. The secret of God's will: that He is to gather together and unify all things in Christ—unify them in a spirit of peace and harmony—all things, both visible and invisible.
		6. The secret of the church and of God's universal love: that both Jew and Gentile are included in the church.
		7. The secret of the church: that the church is the bride and body of Christ.
		8. The secret of the indwelling Christ, of "Christ in you, the hope of glory."
		9. The secret of godliness or of Christ; of God coming to earth in human flesh in the person of Jesus Christ.
		10. The secret of iniquity and of sin in the world and of man's disobedience to God.
		11. The secret of the seven stars or local churches and pastors.
		12. The secret of Babylon in the end time.

ENGLISH WORD	GREEK WORD AND VERSE	THE WORD MEANS...
See to it–NIV Looking carefully–NKJV Look after–NLT **POSB REFERENCE** (Heb.12:15-17; esp. v.15) Note 2	Gender—masculine Person—2nd person Number—plural Stem or root—from ἐπισκοπέω Concordance References: ⇒ Strong's #1983 episkopeō ⇒ NIV #2174 episkopeō ⇒ NASB #1983 episkopeō ### Hebrews 12:15 **Looking diligently** lest any man fail of the grace of God; lest any root of bitterness springing up trouble you, and thereby many be defiled; [KJV] **See to it** that no one comes short of the grace of God; that no root of bitterness springing up causes trouble, and by it many be defiled; [NASB] **See to it** that no one misses the grace of God and that no bitter root grows up to cause trouble and defile many. [NIV] **Looking carefully** lest anyone fall short of the grace of God; lest any root of bitterness springing up cause trouble, and by this many become defiled; [NKJV] **Look after** each other so that none of you will miss out on the special favor of God. Watch out that no bitter root of unbelief rises up among you, for whenever it springs up, many are corrupted by its poison. [NLT] ἐπισκοποῦντες μή τις ὑστερῶν ἀπὸ τῆς χάριτος τοῦ Θεοῦ· μή τις ῥίζα πικρίας ἄνω φύουσα ἐνοχλῇ, καὶ διὰ ταύτης μιανθῶσι πολλοί· [GNS] ἐπισκοποῦντες μή τις ὑστερῶν ἀπὸ τῆς χάριτος τοῦ θεοῦ, μή τις ῥίζα πικρίας ἄνω φύουσα ἐνοχλῇ καὶ δι' αὐτῆς μιανθῶσιν πολλοί, [GNT]	believers. Therefore, believers must look diligently after themselves and after others. It is of utmost importance, of a critical nature. Therefore, be on the lookout and search diligently lest one fall into one of these dangers and fail to lay hold of the grace of God [salvation].
#3410 **Seeing Things Merely From A Human Point Of View** Savourest not–KJV Not setting your mind–NASB Not have in mind–NIV Not mindful–NKJV Seeing things merely from a human point of view–NLT **POSB REFERENCE** (Mk.8:32-33; esp. v.33) Note 2, point 3 **See also POSB REF:** (Mt.16:21-23; 3sp. v.23) Note 1, point 4	οὐ φρονεῖς = ou phroneis Pronunciation: [oo fron-eh'-ees] Parsing phroneis (part of speech): verb Mood—indicative Tense—present Voice—active Person—2nd person Number—singular Stem or root—from φρονέω Concordance References: ⇒ Strong's #3756 ou + #5426 phroneō ⇒ NIV #4024 ou [not] + 5858 phroneō [have in mind] ⇒ NASB #3756 ou + #5426 phroneō ### Mark 8:33 But when he had turned about and looked on his disciples, he rebuked Peter, saying, Get thee behind me, Satan: for thou **savourest not** the things that be of God, but the things that be of men. [KJV] But turning around and seeing His disciples, He rebuked Peter, and said, "Get behind Me, Satan; for you are **not setting your mind** on God's interests, but man's." [NASB] But when Jesus turned and looked at his disciples, he rebuked Peter. "Get behind me, Satan!" he said. "You do **not have in mind** the things of God, but the things of men." [NIV] But when He had turned around and looked at His disciples, He rebuked Peter, saying, "Get behind Me, Satan! For you are **not mindful** of the things of God, but the things of men." [NKJV] Jesus turned and looked at his disciples and then said to Peter very sternly, "Get away from me, Satan! You are **seeing things merely from a human point of view**, not from God's." [NLT] ὁ δὲ ἐπιστραφείς, καὶ ἰδὼν τοὺς μαθητὰς αὐτοῦ ἐπετίμησε τῷ Πέτρῳ, λέγει, Ὕπαγε ὀπίσω μου, Σατανᾶ·	To think; to mind; to have a certain mindset; to see things merely from a human point of view. **Practical Application** It is a word that is governed by human choice, an act of a person's will. Peter did not have his mind, his thinking, in line with God's mind and thoughts. His tastes were different from God's tastes. Peter's thoughts and tastes were worldly and self-pleasing, not spiritual and pleasing to God. He was using human reasoning, not God's reasoning. The thought that God's Son had to die and shed His blood for the sins of the world was disgraceful to Peter. In his mind such a concept was unfit for God.

ENGLISH WORD	GREEK WORD AND VERSE	THE WORD MEANS...
	ὅτι **οὐ φρονεῖς** τὰ τοῦ Θεοῦ, ἀλλὰ τὰ τῶν ἀνθρώπων. [GNS] ὁ δὲ ἐπιστραφεὶς καὶ ἰδὼν τοὺς μαθητὰς αὐτοῦ ἐπετίμησεν Πέτρῳ καὶ λέγει, Ὕπαγε ὀπίσω μου, σατανᾶ, ὅτι **οὐ φρονεῖς** τὰ τοῦ θεοῦ ἀλλὰ τὰ τῶν ἀνθρώπων. [GNT]	

#3411
Seek
 	
Seek–KJV
Seek–NASB
Seek–NIV
Seek–NKJV
Primary concern–NLT
 	
POSB REFERENCE
(Mt.6:33)
Note 7
	ζητεῖτε = zēteite
	Pronunciation: [dzay-teh'-ee-teh]
	Parsing (part of speech): verb
	    Mood—imperative
	    Tense—present
	    Voice—active
	    Person—2nd person
	    Number—plural
	    Stem or root—from ζητέω
	Concordance References:
	⇒ Strong's #2212 zēteō
	⇒ NIV #2426 zēteō
	⇒ NASB #2212 zēteō
	
	Matthew 6:33
	But **seek** ye first the kingdom of God, and his righteousness; and all these things shall be added unto you. [KJV]
	"But **seek** first His kingdom and His righteousness; and all these things shall be added to you. [NASB]
	But **seek** first his kingdom and his righteousness, and all these things will be given to you as well. [NIV]
	But **seek** first the kingdom of God and His righteousness, and all these things shall be added to you. [NKJV]
	And he will give you all you need from day to day if you live for him and make the Kingdom of God your **primary concern**. [NLT]
	ζητεῖτε δὲ πρῶτον τὴν βασιλείαν τοῦ Θεοῦ καὶ τὴν δικαιοσύνην αὐτοῦ, καὶ ταῦτα πάντα προστεθήσεται ὑμῖν. [GNS]
	ζητεῖτε δὲ πρῶτον τὴν βασιλείαν [τοῦ θεοῦ] καὶ τὴν δικαιοσύνην αὐτοῦ, καὶ ταῦτα πάντα προστεθήσεται ὑμῖν. [GNT]
		To seek; to go after; to strive; to pursue; to desire; to aim at; to search for; to endeavor to get; to make that which is most important your primary concern.
		
		Practical Application
		Zeal and enthusiasm for Christ are so desperately lacking. People should be flocking to Him—seeking Him—by the multitudes, but they are not. Why?
		⇒ Do they love the world and the things of the world too much (1 Jn.2:15-16)?
		⇒ Do they love the flesh and its feelings too much?
		⇒ Do they love pride and fame and power too much?
		⇒ Do they just not know? Have they not heard (Ro.10:14-15)?
		⇒ Are the witness and life of believers too weak (Eph. 4:17:24)?

#3412
Seek
 	
Seek–KJV
Look for–NASB
Look for–NIV
Seek–NKJV
Find–NLT
 	
POSB REFERENCE
(Acts 11:25-26; esp. v.25)
Note 3
	ἀναζητῆσαι = anazēteō
	Pronunciation: [an-ad-zay-teh'-sah-ee]
	Parsing (part of speech): verb
	    Mood—infinitive
	    Tense—aorist
	    Voice—active
	    Stem or root—from ἀναζητέω
	Concordance References:
	⇒ Strong's #327 anazēteō
	⇒ NIV #349 anazēteō
	⇒ NASB #327 anazēteō
	
	Acts 11:25
	Then departed Barnabas to Tarsus, for to **seek** Saul: [KJV]
	And he left for Tarsus to **look for** Saul; [NASB]
	Then Barnabas went to Tarsus to **look for** Saul, [NIV]
	Then Barnabas departed for Tarsus to **seek** Saul. [NKJV]
	Then Barnabas went on to Tarsus to **find** Saul. [NLT]
	ἐξῆλθε δὲ εἰς Ταρσὸν ὁ Βαρνάβας **ἀναζητῆσαι** Σαῦλον, [GNS]
	ἐξῆλθεν δὲ εἰς Ταρσὸν **ἀναζητῆσαι** Σαῦλον, [GNT]
		To look for; to seek; to find; to search after. It means to search for, to search back and forth, up and down; to make a thorough search.
		
		Practical Application
		The church sought additional staff—to have an adequate teaching staff. Barnabas is the one who is the focus of attention in this point, but the church was bound to have sensed the need for additional staff and given its approval. The point is this: the need was sensed, and the decision was made to seek for help. The only question was who should be secured. A unique person was needed, a person who not only had a Jewish background, but who knew the Greek language and culture and could relate to both Gentile and Jew alike. The person also needed to be fearless and bold in his witness for Christ because of the godless, immoral society of Antioch.
		Barnabas knew such a man: Saul of Tarsus. So he set out to find him. Paul had been busy throughout Syria and Cilicia preaching Christ (Galatians 1:21). Apparently, Barnabas had difficulty finding him. But note: he knew God's will, so he did not give up the search. He kept searching until he found God's choice. What a dynamic lesson for all churches in seeking help and in building a church staff!

ENGLISH WORD	GREEK WORD AND VERSE	THE WORD MEANS...

#3413
Seek
 	
Diligently seek–KJV
Seek–NASB
Earnestly seek–NIV
Seek–NKJV
Sincerely seek–NLT
 	
POSB REFERENCE
(Heb.11:6)
Note 5, point 2b
	ἐκζητοῦσιν = ekzētousin
	Pronunciation: [ek-zay-too-sin]
	Parsing (part of speech): verb
	   Mood—participle
	   Tense—present
	   Voice—active
	   Case—dative
	   Gender—masculine
	   Number—plural
	   Stem or root—from ἐκζητέω
	Concordance References:
	⇒ Strong's #1567 ekzēteō
	⇒ NIV #1699 ekzēteō
	⇒ NASB #1567 ekzēteō
	
	### Hebrews 11:6
	But without faith it is impossible to please him: for he that cometh to God must believe that he is, and that he is a rewarder of them that **diligently seek** him. [KJV]
	And without faith it is impossible to please Him, for he who comes to God must believe that He is, and that He is a rewarder of those who **seek** Him. [NASB]
	And without faith it is impossible to please God, because anyone who comes to him must believe that he exists and that he rewards those who **earnestly seek** him. [NIV]
	But without faith *it is* impossible to please *Him,* for he who comes to God must believe that He is, and *that* He is a rewarder of those who diligently **seek** Him. [NKJV]
	So, you see, it is impossible to please God without faith. Anyone who wants to come to him must believe that there is a God and that he rewards those who **sincerely seek** him. [NLT]
	χωρὶς δὲ πίστεως ἀδύνατον εὐαρεστῆσαι· πιστεῦσαι γὰρ δεῖ τὸν προσερχόμενον τῷ Θεῷ, ὅτι ἔστι, καὶ τοῖς ἐκζητοῦσιν αὐτὸν μισθαποδότης γίνεται. [GNS]
	χωρὶς δὲ πίστεως ἀδύνατον εὐαρεστῆσαι· πιστεῦσαι γὰρ δεῖ τὸν προσερχόμενον τῷ θεῷ ὅτι ἔστιν καὶ τοῖς ἐκζητοῦσιν αὐτὸν μισθαποδότης γίνεται. [GNT]
		To earnestly seek; to diligently seek; to sincerely seek. It means to *seek out God*; to diligently seek to find Him and to follow Him.
		
		### Practical Application
		God does not reward the sleepy eyed, the complacent, the non-thinker, the half-interested, the worldly-minded, the pleasure seeker. God rewards those who seek to know and follow Him. The idea is that we must be in earnest and persevere, enduring to the end. What is the reward to those who seek God? It is the same reward given to Abel and Enoch: righteousness and God's care in this life and deliverance from death to live eternally with God.

#3414
Seeketh Not Her Own
 	
Seeketh not her own–KJV
Seeks its own–NASB
Self-seeking–NIV
Seek its own–NKJV
Demands its own way–NLT
 	
POSB REFERENCE
(1 Cor.13:4-7; esp. v.5)
Note 2, point 7
	ζητεῖ τὰ ἑαυτῆς = zētei ta heautēs
	Pronunciation: [dzay-teh'-ee tah yoo-tace']
	Parsing *zētei* (part of speech): verb
	   Mood—indicative
	   Tense—present
	   Voice—active
	   Person—3rd person
	   Number—singular
	   Stem or root—from ζητέω
	Concordance References:
	⇒ Strong's #1438+2212+3588 heautou zēteō ho
	⇒ NIV #1571+2426+3836 heautou zēteō ho [self seeking]
	⇒ NASB #1438+2212+3588 heautou zēteō ho
	
	### 1 Cor. 13:5
	Doth not behave itself unseemly, **seeketh not her own**, is not easily provoked, thinketh no evil; [KJV]
	Does not act unbecomingly; it does not **seek its own**, is not provoked, does not take into account a wrong suffered, [NASB]
	It is not rude, it is not **self-seeking**, it is not easily angered, it keeps no record of wrongs. [NIV]
	Does not behave rudely, does not **seek its own**, is not provoked, thinks no evil; [NKJV]
	Or rude. Love does not **demand its own way**. Love is not irritable, and it keeps no record of when it has been wronged. [NLT]
	οὐκ ἀσχημονεῖ, οὐ **ζητεῖ τὰ ἑαυτῆς**, οὐ παροξύνεται, οὐ λογίζεται τὸ κακόν, [GNS]
	οὐκ ἀσχημονεῖ, οὐ **ζητεῖ τὰ ἑαυτῆς** οὐ παροξύνεται, οὐ λογίζεται τὸ κακόν, [GNT]
		Self-seeking; demanding one's own way; to strive for one's own interest—ignoring the feelings of other people.
		
		### Practical Application
		Love seeks not her own: is not selfish; does not insist upon its own rights (Williams). Love is not focused upon who one is nor upon what one has done. Love seeks to serve, not have others serving oneself. Love is acknowledging others, not insisting that others acknowledge oneself; it is giving to others, not insisting that others give to oneself.

ENGLISH WORD	GREEK WORD AND VERSE	THE WORD MEANS...
#3415 **Seeks, For, After–Seeketh After–Seeking** Seeketh after–KJV Seeks for–NASB Seeks–NIV Seeks after–NKJV Seeking –NLT **POSB REFERENCE** (Rom.3:10-12; esp. v.11) Note, point 3	ἐκζητῶν = ekzëtön Pronunciation: [ek-zay-tone] Parsing (part of speech): verb 　Mood—participle 　Tense—present 　Voice—active 　Gender—masculine 　Number—singular 　Stem or root—from ἐκζητέω Concordance References: ⇒　Strong's #1567 ekzëteö ⇒　NIV #1699 ekzëteö ⇒　NASB #1567 ekzëteö **Romans 3:11** There is none that understandeth, there is none that **seeketh after** God. [KJV] There is none who understands, There is none who **seeks for** God; [NASB] There is no one who understands, no one who **seeks** God. [NIV] There is none who understands; There is none who **seeks after** God. [NKJV] No one has real understanding; no one is **seeking** God. [NLT] οὐκ ἔστιν ὁ συνίων, οὐκ ἔστιν ὁ **ἐκζητῶν** τὸν Θεόν· [GNS] οὐκ ἔστιν ὁ συνίων, οὐκ ἔστιν ὁ **ἐκζητῶν** τὸν θεόν. [GNT]	To seek or search diligently. **Practical Application** A sinful nature is indifferent and selfish (Romans 3:11; cp. Psalm 14:2): "There is none that seeks after God." The word "seek after" (ekzëtön) means to seek out and search for. The idea is that of a diligent, careful, determined seeking and searching. No one searches and seeks after God, not after the only living and true God, not with so careful and determined a spirit. Why? Because men are indifferent and selfish. Men want gods that allow them to do their own thing.
#3416 **Seeks Its Own–Seek Its Own** Seeketh not her own–KJV **Seeks its own–NASB** Self-seeking–NIV **Seek its own–NKJV** Demands its own way–NLT **POSB REFERENCE** (1 Cor.13:4-7; esp. v.5) Note 2, point 7	ζητεῖ τὰ ἑαυτῆς = zëtei ta heautës Pronunciation: [dzay-teh'-ee tah yoo-tace'] Parsing zëtei (part of speech): verb 　Mood—indicative 　Tense—present 　Voice—active 　Person—3rd person 　Number—singular 　Stem or root—from ζητέω Concordance References: ⇒　Strong's #1438+2212+3588 heautou zëteö ho ⇒　NIV #1571+2426+3836 heautou zëteö ho [self seeking] ⇒　NASB #1438+2212+3588 heautou zëteö ho **1 Cor. 13:5** Doth not behave itself unseemly, **seeketh not her own**, is not easily provoked, thinketh no evil; [KJV] Does not act unbecomingly; it does not **seek its own**, is not provoked, does not take into account a wrong suffered, [NASB] It is not rude, it is not **self-seeking**, it is not easily angered, it keeps no record of wrongs. [NIV] Does not behave rudely, does not **seek its own**, is not provoked, thinks no evil; [NKJV] Or rude. Love does not **demand its own way**. Love is not irritable, and it keeps no record of when it has been wronged. [NLT] οὐκ ἀσχημονεῖ, οὐ **ζητεῖ τὰ ἑαυτῆς**, οὐ παροξύνεται, οὐ λογίζεται τὸ κακόν, [GNS] οὐκ ἀσχημονεῖ, οὐ **ζητεῖ τὰ ἑαυτῆς**, οὐ παροξύνεται, οὐ λογίζεται τὸ κακόν, [GNT]	Self-seeking; demanding one's own way; to strive for one's own interest—ignoring the feelings of other people. **Practical Application** Love seeks not her own: is not selfish; does not insist upon its own rights (Williams). Love is not focused upon who one is nor upon what one has done. Love seeks to serve, not have others serving oneself. Love is acknowledging others, not insisting that others acknowledge oneself; it is giving to others, not insisting that others give to oneself.
#3417 **Seen** Beheld–KJV Beheld–NASB **Seen–NIV** Beheld–NKJV **Seen–NLT**	ἐθεασάμεθα = etheasametha Pronunciation: [eh-theh-ah-sah'-meh-thah] Parsing (part of speech): verb 　Mood—indicative 　Tense—aorist 　Voice—middle deponent 　Person—1st person 　Number—plural 　Stem or root—from θεάομαι	Seen, beheld; to notice; to look at; to observe. **Practical Application** The word actually means seeing with the human eye. It is used about twenty times in the New Testament. There is no room whatever for saying that God's becoming a man was merely a vision of some man's mind or imagination. John was saying that he and others actually saw the

ENGLISH WORD	GREEK WORD AND VERSE	THE WORD MEANS...
POSB REFERENCE (Jn.1:14) Note 1	Concordance References: ⇒ Strong's #2300 theaomai ⇒ NIV #2517 theaomai ⇒ NASB #2300 theaomai **John 1:14** And the Word was made flesh, and dwelt among us, (and we **beheld** his glory, the glory as of the only begotten of the Father,) full of grace and truth. [KJV] And the Word became flesh, and dwelt among us, and we **beheld** His glory, glory as of the only begotten from the Father, full of grace and truth. [NASB] The Word became flesh and made his dwelling among us. We have **seen** his glory, the glory of the One and Only, who came from the Father, full of grace and truth. [NIV] And the Word became flesh and dwelt among us, and we **beheld** His glory, the glory as of the only begotten of the Father, full of grace and truth. [NKJV] So the Word became human and lived here on earth among us. He was full of unfailing love and faithfulness. And we have **seen** his glory, the glory of the only Son of the Father. [NLT] καὶ ὁ λόγος σὰρξ ἐγένετο, καὶ ἐσκήνωσεν ἐν ἡμῖν, -- καὶ **ἐθεασάμεθα** τὴν δόξαν αὐτοῦ, δόξαν ὡς μονογενοῦς παρὰ πατρός -- , πλήρης χάριτος καὶ ἀληθείας. [GNS] Καὶ ὁ λόγος σὰρξ ἐγένετο καὶ ἐσκήνωσεν ἐν ἡμῖν, καὶ **ἐθεασάμεθα** τὴν δόξαν αὐτοῦ, δόξαν ὡς μονογενοῦς παρὰ πατρός, πλήρης χάριτος καὶ ἀληθείας. [GNT]	Word made flesh. Jesus Christ was beyond question God Himself who became man, who partook of the very same flesh as all other men. (Cp. 1 John 1:1-4.) (See POSB *Deeper Study* #1, Flesh—John 1:14 for the meaning of "flesh" and why Jesus Christ had to become flesh. Also see POSB *Deeper Study* #1, Flesh—1 Cor. 3:1-4 for more discussion.)
#3418 **Seen, Be** Showed...openly–KJV Become visible–NASB **Be seen–NIV** Showed...openly–NKJV To appear–NLT **POSB REFERENCE** (Acts 10:40-41; esp. v.40) Note 6, point 1	ἐμφανῆ γενέσθαι = emphanë genesthai Pronunciation: [em-fan-ay' ghin'-es-tha-ee] Parsing emphanë (part of speech): adjective 　Case—accusative 　Gender—masculine 　Number—singular 　Stem or root—from ἐμφανής Parsing genesthai (part of speech): verb 　Mood—infinitive 　Tense—aorist 　Voice—middle deponent 　Stem or root—from γίνομαι Concordance References: ⇒ Strong's #1717 emphanës + 1096 ginomai ⇒ NIV #1871 [seen] emphanës + 1181 ginomai [be] ⇒ NASB #1717 emphanës + 1096 ginomai **Acts 10:40** Him God raised up the third day, and **showed** him **openly**; [KJV] "God raised Him up on the third day, and granted that He should **become visible**, [NASB] But God raised him from the dead on the third day and caused him to **be seen**. [NIV] Him God raised up on the third day, and **showed** Him **openly**, [NKJV] But God raised him to life three days later. Then God allowed him **to appear**, [NLT] Τοῦτον ὁ Θεὸς ἤγειρε τῇ τρίτῃ ἡμέρᾳ, καὶ ἔδωκεν αὐτὸν **ἐμφανῆ γενέσθαι**, [GNS] τοῦτον ὁ θεὸς ἤγειρεν [ἐν] τῇ τρίτῃ ἡμέρᾳ καὶ ἔδωκεν αὐτὸν **ἐμφανῆ γενέσθαι**, [GNT]	To be seen; to become visible; to appear; to show openly; to be revealed. **Practical Application** God showed Jesus openly—He allowed Him to appear—which means that God set Jesus before people so that He could be visibly, openly, and publicly seen. God manifested, showed, and set Him forth as the Risen Lord. (See POSB note—Acts 1:3 and POSB *Deeper Study* #1, Jesus, Resurrection—Acts 1:3 for more discussion.)
#3419 **Seized** Caught–KJV Dragged..away–NASB **Seized–NIV** **Seized–NKJV** Brought–NLT	συνήρπασαν = sunërpasan Pronunciation: [soon-ayr-pa'-sahn] Parsing (part of speech): verb 　Mood—indicative 　Tense—aorist 　Voice—active 　Person—3rd person 　Number—plural 　Stem or root—from συναρπάζω Concordance References: ⇒ Strong's #4884 sunarpazo	To seize; to catch; to drag away; to bring; to lay hold of; to carry off. **Practical Application** The word "seized" (sunërpasan) means to seize with violence. The picture is that they seized and literally dragged him to court (cp. Luke 8:29; Acts 19:29; Acts 27:15).

ENGLISH WORD	GREEK WORD AND VERSE	THE WORD MEANS...

POSB REFERENCE
(Acts 6:11-14; esp. v.12)
Note 3, point 3

⇒ NIV #5275 sunarpazö
⇒ NASB #4884 sunarpazo

Acts 6:12

And they stirred up the people, and the elders, and the scribes, and came upon him, and **caught** him, and brought him to the council, [KJV]

And they stirred up the people, the elders, and the scribes, and they came upon him and **dragged** him **away**, and brought him before the Council. [NASB]

So they stirred up the people and the elders and the teachers of the law. They **seized** Stephen and brought him before the Sanhedrin. [NIV]

And they stirred up the people, the elders, and the scribes; and they came upon *him*, **seized** him, and brought *him* to the council. [NKJV]

Naturally, this roused the crowds, the elders, and the teachers of religious law. So they arrested Stephen and **brought** him before the high council. [NLT]

συνεκίνησάν τε τὸν λαὸν καὶ τοὺς πρεσβυτέρους καὶ τοὺς γραμματεῖς, καὶ ἐπιστάντες **συνήρπασαν** αὐτόν, καὶ ἤγαγον εἰς τὸ συνέδριον, [GNS]

συνεκίνησάν τε τὸν λαὸν καὶ τοὺς πρεσβυτέρους καὶ τοὺς γραμματεῖς, καὶ ἐπιστάντες **συνήρπασαν** αὐτὸν καὶ ἤγαγον εἰς τὸ συνέδριον. [GNT]

#3420
Selected

Ordained–KJV
Appointed–NASB
Appointed–NIV
Appointed–NKJV
Selected–NLT

POSB REFERENCE
(Mk.3:14)
Deeper Study #1

ἐποίησεν = epoiesen
Pronunciation: [eh-poy-eh'-sen]
Parsing (part of speech): verb
    Mood—indicative
    Tense—aorist
    Voice—active
    Person—3rd person
    Number—singular
    Stem or root—from ποιέω
Concordance References:
⇒ Strong's #4160 poieö
⇒ NIV #4472 poieö
⇒ NASB #4160 poieö

Mark 3:14

And he **ordained** twelve, that they should be with him, and that he might send them forth to preach, [KJV]

And He **appointed** twelve, that they might be with Him, and that He might send them out to preach, [NASB]

He **appointed** twelve—designating them apostles—that they might be with him and that he might send them out to preach [NIV]

Then He **appointed** twelve, that they might be with Him and that He might send them out to preach, [NKJV]

Then he **selected** twelve of them to be his regular companions, calling them apostles. He sent them out to preach, [NLT]

καὶ **ἐποίησε** δώδεκα, ἵνα ὦσι μετ' αὐτοῦ, καὶ ἵνα ἀποστέλλῃ αὐτοὺς κηρύσσειν, [GNS]

καὶ **ἐποίησεν** δώδεκα [οὓς καὶ ἀποστόλους ὠνόμασεν] ἵνα ὦσιν μετ' αὐτοῦ καὶ ἵνα ἀποστέλλῃ αὐτοὺς κηρύσσειν [GNT]

To be ordained, chosen, designated, commissioned, picked, elected, selected, or appointed.

Practical Application

The word is taken from the Greek root word *poieö* which means to do, to make, to appoint with credentials. The word is often used to refer to a person's being appointed to some high position or office. The picture is that of Jesus Christ, the future King of the universe, taking twelve men and selecting them to be His. He selected (ordained) them to the *office* of being His ministers and representatives on earth.

#3421
Self-Confidence

Trusted–KJV
Trusted–NASB
Confident–NIV
Trusted–NKJV
Self-confidence–NLT

πεποιθότας = pepoithotas
Pronunciation: [peh-poy'-tho-tahs]
Parsing (part of speech): verb
    Mood—participle
    Tense—perfect
    Voice—active
    Case—accusative
    Gender—masculine
    Number—plural
    Stem or root—from πείθω
Concordance References:
⇒ Strong's #3982 peithö
⇒ NIV #4275 peithö
⇒ NASB #3982 peithö

To be confident; to trust in one's own self; to have self-confidence; to rely upon oneself.

Practical Application

It means those who trust in themselves; that is, those who feel they are completely self-sufficient and have no need for anyone else. They feel all they need dwells within their own bodies and minds. There is a feeling that neither God nor anyone else is really needed—not too often, if ever—as one ploughs through life.

ENGLISH WORD	GREEK WORD AND VERSE	THE WORD MEANS...

#3430
Self-Discipline
 	
Sound mind–KJV
Discipline–NASB
Self-discipline–NIV
Sound mind–NKJV
Self-discipline–NLT
 	
POSB
REFERENCE
(2 Tim. 1:7)
Note 2, point 3
	σωφρονισμοῦ = sōphronismou
	Pronunciation: [so-fron-is-moo']
	Parsing (part of speech): noun
	    Case—genitive
	    Gender—masculine
	    Number—singular
	    Stem or root—from σωφρονισμός οῦ
	Concordance References:
	  ⇒ Strong's #4995 sōphronismos
	  ⇒ NIV #5406 sōphronismos
	  ⇒ NASB #4995 sōphronismos
	
	2 Tim. 1:7
	For God hath not given us the spirit of fear; but of power, and of love, and of a **sound mind**. [KJV]
	For God has not given us a spirit of timidity, but of power and love and **discipline**. [NASB]
	For God did not give us a spirit of timidity, but a spirit of power, of love and of **self-discipline**. [NIV]
	For God has not given us a spirit of fear, but of power and of love and of a **sound mind**. [NKJV]
	For God has not given us a spirit of fear and timidity, but of power, love, and **self-discipline**. [NLT]
	οὐ γὰρ ἔδωκεν ἡμῖν ὁ Θεὸς πνεῦμα δειλίας, ἀλλὰ δυνάμεως καὶ ἀγάπης καὶ **σωφρονισμοῦ**. [GNS]
	οὐ γὰρ ἔδωκεν ἡμῖν ὁ θεὸς πνεῦμα δειλίας ἀλλὰ δυνάμεως καὶ ἀγάπης καὶ **σωφρονισμοῦ**. [GNT]
		Self-discipline, sound mind, discipline, self-control; the ability to control one's emotions, feelings, and thoughts in the midst of trials and circumstances, no matter how severe and stressful; to have sound judgment.
		
		Practical Application
		The Holy Spirit infuses self-discipline into the believer's spirit. It is just as the verse says, self-discipline—the mastery over one's mind, over one's heart and life despite the trial or opposition. When the believer begins to live and bear testimony for Christ, the Holy Spirit gives him self-discipline—a most glorious gift.

#3431
Self-seeking
 	
Seeketh not her own–KJV
Seeks its own–NASB
Self-seeking–NIV
Seek its own–NKJV
Demands its own way–NLT
 	
POSB
REFERENCE
(1 Cor. 13:4-7; esp. v.5)
Note 2, point 7
	ζητεῖ τὰ ἑαυτῆς = zētei ta heautēs
	Pronunciation: [dzay-teh'-ee tah yoo-tace']
	Parsing zētei (part of speech): verb
	    Mood—indicative
	    Tense—present
	    Voice—active
	    Person—3rd person
	    Number—singular
	    Stem or root—from ζητέω
	Concordance References:
	  ⇒ Strong's #1438+2212+3588 heautou zēteō ho
	  ⇒ NIV #1571+2426+3836 heautou zēteō ho [self seeking]
	  ⇒ NASB #1438+2212+3588 heautou zēteō ho
	
	1 Cor. 13:5
	Doth not behave itself unseemly, **seeketh not her own**, is not easily provoked, thinketh no evil; [KJV]
	Does not act unbecomingly; it does not **seek its own**, is not provoked, does not take into account a wrong suffered, [NASB]
	It is not rude, it is not **self-seeking**, it is not easily angered, it keeps no record of wrongs. [NIV]
	Does not behave rudely, does not **seek its own**, is not provoked, thinks no evil; [NKJV]
	Or rude. Love does not **demand its own way**. Love is not irritable, and it keeps no record of when it has been wronged. [NLT]
	οὐκ ἀσχημονεῖ, οὐ **ζητεῖ τὰ ἑαυτῆς**, οὐ παροξύνεται, οὐ λογίζεται τὸ κακόν, [GNS]
	οὐκ ἀσχημονεῖ, οὐ **ζητεῖ τὰ ἑαυτῆς**, οὐ παροξύνεται, οὐ λογίζεται τὸ κακόν, [GNT]
		Self-seeking; demanding one's own way; to strive for one's own interest—ignoring the feelings of other people.
		
		Practical Application
		Love seeks not her own: is not selfish; does not insist upon its own rights (Williams). Love is not focused upon who one is nor upon what one has done. Love seeks to serve, not have others serving oneself. Love is acknowledging others, not insisting that others acknowledge oneself; it is giving to others, not insisting that others give to oneself.

#3432
Self-seeking
 	
Contentious–KJV
Selfishly ambitious–NASB
Self-seeking–NIV
Self-seeking–NKJV
Live for themselves–NLT
	ἐριθείας = eritheias
	Pronunciation: [her-ith-i'-ahs]
	Parsing (part of speech): noun
	    Case—genitive
	    Gender—feminine
	    Number—singular
	    Stem or root—from ἐριθεία, ας
	Concordance References:
	  ⇒ Strong's #1537 ek + 2052 eritheia
	  ⇒ NIV #2249 eritheia
	  ⇒ NASB #2052 eritheia
		To strive; to struggle; to fight; to quarrel; to wrangle; to argue; to debate; to be divisive, factious, contentious, argumentative, and belligerent; selfish rivalry; selfish ambition.
		
		Practical Application
		The evil-doer does not like what God says; therefore, he strives against it. He wrangles and wrestles, struggles and fights against God. He refuses to buckle under and surrender to God's will. When dealing with God, the evil-doer is contentious.

ENGLISH WORD	GREEK WORD AND VERSE	THE WORD MEANS...
POSB REFERENCE (Rom.2:8) *Deeper Study #4*	**Romans 2:8** But unto them that are **contentious**, and do not obey the truth, but obey unrighteousness, indignation and wrath, [KJV] But to those who are **selfishly ambitious** and do not obey the truth, but obey unrighteousness, wrath and indignation. [NASB] But for those who are **self-seeking** and who reject the truth and follow evil, there will be wrath and anger. [NIV] But to those who are **self-seeking** and do not obey the truth, but obey unrighteousness—indignation and wrath, [NKJV] But he will pour out his anger and wrath on those who **live for themselves**, who refuse to obey the truth and practice evil deeds. [NLT] τοῖς δὲ ἐξ **ἐριθείας**, καὶ ἀπειθοῦσι μὲν τῇ ἀληθείᾳ πειθομένοις δὲ τῇ ἀδικίᾳ, θυμός καὶ ὀργὴ, [GNS] τοῖς δὲ ἐξ **ἐριθείας** καὶ ἀπειθοῦσι τῇ ἀληθείᾳ πειθομένοις δὲ τῇ ἀδικίᾳ ὀργὴ καὶ θυμός. [GNT]	
#3433 **Selfish Ambitions** Strifes–KJV Disputes–NASB Factions–NIV **Selfish ambitions–NKJV** Selfishness–NLT **POSB REFERENCE** (2 Cor.12:19-21; esp. v.20) Note 3, point 2 **See also POSB REF:** (Gal.5:19-21; esp. v.20) Note 2 (Jas.3:14-16) Note 2, point 1b	**ἐριθείαι** = eritheiai Pronunciation: [er-ith-i'-ah-ee] Parsing (part of speech): noun 　　Case—nominative 　　Gender—feminine 　　Number—plural 　　Stem or root—from ἐριθεία ας Concordance References: ⇒ Strong's #2052 eritheia ⇒ NIV #2249 eritheia ⇒ NASB #2052 eritheia **2 Cor. 12:20** For I fear, lest, when I come, I shall not find you such as I would, and that I shall be found unto you such as ye would not: lest there be debates, envyings, wraths, **strifes**, backbitings, whisperings, swellings, tumults: [KJV] For I am afraid that perhaps when I come I may find you to be not what I wish and may be found by you to be not what you wish; that perhaps there may be strife, jealousy, angry tempers, **disputes**, slanders, gossip, arrogance, disturbances; [NASB] For I am afraid that when I come I may not find you as I want you to be, and you may not find me as you want me to be. I fear that there may be quarreling, jealousy, outbursts of anger, **factions**, slander, gossip, arrogance and disorder. [NIV] For I fear lest, when I come, I shall not find you such as I wish, and that I shall be found by you such as you do not wish; lest there be contentions, jealousies, outbursts of wrath, **selfish ambitions**, backbitings, whisperings, conceits, tumults; [NKJV] For I am afraid that when I come to visit you I won't like what I find, and then you won't like my response. I am afraid that I will find quarreling, jealousy, outbursts of anger, **selfishness**, backstabbing, gossip, conceit, and disorderly behavior. [NLT] φοβοῦμαι γὰρ μή πως ἐλθὼν οὐχ οἵους θέλω εὕρω ὑμᾶς, κἀγὼ εὑρεθῶ ὑμῖν οἷον οὐ θέλετε· μή πως ἔρις, ζῆλοι, θυμοί, **ἐριθεῖαι**, καταλαλιαί, ψιθυρισμοί, φυσιώσεις, ἀκαταστασίαι [GNS] φοβοῦμαι γὰρ μή πως ἐλθὼν οὐχ οἵους θέλω εὕρω ὑμᾶς κἀγὼ εὑρεθῶ ὑμῖν οἷον οὐ θέλετε· μή πως ἔρις, ζῆλος, θυμοί, **ἐριθεῖαι**, καταλαλιαί, ψιθυρισμοί, φυσιώσεις, ἀκαταστασίαι [GNT]	Factions, envying, disputes, selfishness; selfish ambitions; an envious spirit or clique that stands as a rival to others; a factious spirit caused by selfishness or self-seeking; to pay attention to; to fix thoughts on; to look more closely. **Practical Application** Paul was stricken with fear, fear lest the church fail to be what it should be and reject him and his ministry. Paul feared that the church would fail to deal with the carnal critics and continue putting up with their evil attacks against him. He lists eight evils—including selfish ambitions (*eritheiai*), that were and still are characteristic of divisive critics in the church.
#3434 **Selfishly Ambitious**	**ἐριθείας** = eritheias Pronunciation: [er-ith-i'-ahs] Parsing (part of speech): noun 　　Case—genitive 　　Gender—feminine	To strive; to struggle; to fight; to quarrel; to wrangle; to argue; to debate; to be divisive, factious, contentious, argumentative, and belligerent; selfish rivalry; selfish ambition.

ENGLISH WORD	GREEK WORD AND VERSE	THE WORD MEANS...
Contentious–KJV **Selfishly ambitious–NASB** Self-seeking–NIV Self-seeking–NKJV Live for themselves–NLT **POSB REFERENCE** (Rom.2:8) *Deeper Study #4*	Number—singular Stem or root—from ἐριθεία, ας Concordance References: ⇒ Strong's #1537 ek + 2052 eritheia ⇒ NIV #2249 eritheia ⇒ NASB #2052 eritheia **Romans 2:8** But unto them that are **contentious**, and do not obey the truth, but obey unrighteousness, indignation and wrath, [KJV] But to those who are **selfishly ambitious** and do not obey the truth, but obey unrighteousness, wrath and indignation. [NASB] But for those who are **self-seeking** and who reject the truth and follow evil, there will be wrath and anger. [NIV] But to those who are **self-seeking** and do not obey the truth, but obey unrighteousness—indignation and wrath, [NKJV] But he will pour out his anger and wrath on those who **live for themselves**, who refuse to obey the truth and practice evil deeds. [NLT] τοῖς δὲ ἐξ **ἐριθείας**, καὶ ἀπειθοῦσι μὲν τῇ ἀληθείᾳ πειθομένοις δὲ τῇ ἀδικίᾳ, θυμός καὶ ὀργὴ, [GNS] τοῖς δὲ ἐξ **ἐριθείας** καὶ ἀπειθοῦσι τῇ ἀληθείᾳ πειθομένοις δὲ τῇ ἀδικίᾳ ὀργὴ καὶ θυμός. [GNT]	**Practical Application** The evil-doer does not like what God says; therefore, he strives against it. He wrangles and wrestles, struggles and fights against God. He refuses to buckle under and surrender to God's will. When dealing with God, the evil-doer is selfishly ambitious.

#3435
Selfishness
 	
Strifes–KJV
Disputes–NASB
Factions–NIV
Selfish ambitions–NKJV
Selfishness–NLT
 	
POSB REFERENCE
(2 Cor.12:19-21; esp. v.20)
Note 3, point 2
 	
See also POSB REF:
(Gal.5:19-21; esp. v.20)
Note 2
(Jas.3:14-16)
Note 2, point 1b
	ἐριθείαι = *eritheiai*
	Pronunciation: [er-ith-i'-ah-ee]
	Parsing (part of speech): noun
	  Case—nominative
	  Gender—feminine
	  Number—plural
	  Stem or root—from ἐριθεία, ας
	Concordance References:
	⇒ Strong's #2052 eritheia
	⇒ NIV #2249 eritheia
	⇒ NASB #2052 eritheia
	
	2 Cor. 12:20
	For I fear, lest, when I come, I shall not find you such as I would, and that I shall be found unto you such as ye would not: lest there be debates, envyings, wraths, **strifes**, backbitings, whisperings, swellings, tumults: [KJV]
	For I am afraid that perhaps when I come I may find you to be not what I wish and may be found by you to be not what you wish; that perhaps there may be strife, jealousy, angry tempers, **disputes**, slanders, gossip, arrogance, disturbances; [NASB]
	For I am afraid that when I come I may not find you as I want you to be, and you may not find me as you want me to be. I fear that there may be quarreling, jealousy, outbursts of anger, **factions**, slander, gossip, arrogance and disorder. [NIV]
	For I fear lest, when I come, I shall not find you such as I wish, and *that* I shall be found by you such as you do not wish; lest *there be* contentions, jealousies, outbursts of wrath, **selfish ambitions**, backbitings, whisperings, conceits, tumults; [NKJV]
	For I am afraid that when I come to visit you I won't like what I find, and then you won't like my response. I am afraid that I will find quarreling, jealousy, outbursts of anger, **selfishness**, backstabbing, gossip, conceit, and disorderly behavior. [NLT]
	φοβοῦμαι γὰρ μή πως ἐλθὼν οὐχ οἵους θέλω εὕρω ὑμᾶς, κἀγὼ εὑρεθῶ ὑμῖν οἷον οὐ θέλετε· μή πως ἔρις, ζῆλοι, θυμοί, **ἐριθείαι**, καταλαλιαί, ψιθυρισμοί, φυσιώσεις, ἀκαταστασίαι [GNS]
	φοβοῦμαι γὰρ μή πως ἐλθὼν οὐχ οἵους θέλω εὕρω ὑμᾶς κἀγὼ εὑρεθῶ ὑμῖν οἷον οὐ θέλετε· μή πως ἔρις, ζῆλος, θυμοί, **ἐριθεία**,, καταλαλιαί, ψιθυρισμοί, φυσιώσεις, ἀκαταστασίαι [GNT]
		Factions, envying, disputes, selfishness; selfish ambitions; an envious spirit or clique that stands as a rival to others; a factious spirit caused by selfishness or self-seeking; to pay attention to; to fix thoughts on; to look more closely.
		
		Practical Application
		Paul was stricken with fear, fear lest the church fail to be what it should be and reject him and his ministry. Paul feared that the church would fail to deal with the carnal critics and continue putting up with their evil attacks against him. He lists eight evils—including selfishness (*eritheiai*), that were and still are characteristic of divisive critics in the church.

ENGLISH WORD	GREEK WORD AND VERSE	THE WORD MEANS...

#3436
Selfwilled

Selfwilled–KJV
Self-willed–NASB
Overbearing–NIV
Self-willed–NKJV
Arrogant–NLT

**POSB
REFERENCE**
(Tit.1:7-8; esp. v.7)
Note 3, point 1a

αὐθάδη = authadë
Pronunciation: [ow-thad'-ay]
Parsing (part of speech): adjective
    Case—accusative
    Gender—masculine
    Number—singular
    Stem or root—from αὐθάδης, ες
Concordance References:
⇒ Strong's #829 authadës
⇒ NIV #881 authadës
⇒ NASB #829 authadës

Titus 1:7

For a bishop must be blameless, as the steward of God; not **selfwilled**, not soon angry, not given to wine, no striker, not given to filthy lucre; [KJV]

For the overseer must be above reproach as God's steward, not **self-willed**, not quick-tempered, not addicted to wine, not pugnacious, not fond of sordid gain, [NASB]

Since an overseer is entrusted with God's work, he must be blameless—not **overbearing**, not quick-tempered, not given to drunkenness, not violent, not pursuing dishonest gain. [NIV]

For a bishop must be blameless, as a steward of God, not **self-willed**, not quick-tempered, not given to wine, not violent, not greedy for money, [NKJV]

An elder must live a blameless life because he is God's minister. He must not be **arrogant** or quick-tempered; he must not be a heavy drinker, violent, or greedy for money. [NLT]

δεῖ γὰρ τὸν ἐπίσκοπον ἀνέγκλητον εἶναι, ὡς Θεοῦ οἰκονόμον· μὴ **αὐθάδη**, μὴ ὀργίλον, μὴ πάροινον, μὴ πλήκτην, μὴ αἰσχροκερδῆ, [GNS]

δεῖ γὰρ τὸν ἐπίσκοπον ἀνέγκλητον εἶναι ὡς θεοῦ οἰκονόμον, μὴ **αὐθάδη**, μὴ ὀργίλον, μὴ πάροινον, μὴ πλήκτην, μὴ αἰσχροκερδῆ, [GNT]

Overbearing, self-willed, self-pleasing, arrogant, haughty, and self-centered.

Practical Application

It is a person who thinks too highly of himself, who looks at his own things and ignores or neglects the things of others. It is a person who is harsh to others; who criticizes, grumbles, and condemns others; who downs others and elevates himself in his own mind.

#3437
**Seller Of
Purple,
Fabrics**

Seller of purple–KJV
Seller of purple fabrics–NASB
Dealer in purple cloth–NIV
Seller of purple–NKJV
Merchant of expensive purple cloth–NLT

**POSB
REFERENCE**
(Acts 16:14)
Note 2

πορφυρόπωλις = porphuropölis
Pronunciation: [por-foo-rop'-o-lis]
Parsing (part of speech): noun
    Case—nominative
    Gender—feminine
    Number—singular
    Stem or root— from πορφυρόπωλις, ιδος
Concordance References:
⇒ Strong's #4211 porphuropölis
⇒ NIV #4527 porphuropölis
⇒ NASB #4211 porphuropölis

Acts 16:14

And a certain woman named Lydia, a **seller of purple**, of the city of Thyatira, which worshipped God, heard us: whose heart the Lord opened, that she attended unto the things which were spoken of Paul. [KJV]

And a certain woman named Lydia, from the city of Thyatira, a **seller of purple fabrics**, a worshiper of God, was listening; and the Lord opened her heart to respond to the things spoken by Paul. [NASB]

One of those listening was a woman named Lydia, a **dealer in purple cloth** from the city of Thyatira, who was a worshiper of God. The Lord opened her heart to respond to Paul's message. [NIV]

Now a certain woman named Lydia heard us. She was a **seller of purple** from the city of Thyatira, who worshiped God. The Lord opened her heart to heed the things spoken by Paul. [NKJV]

One of them was Lydia from Thyatira, a **merchant of expensive purple cloth**. She was a worshiper of God. As she listened to us, the Lord opened her heart, and she accepted what Paul was saying. [NLT]

καί τις γυνὴ ὀνόματι Λυδία, **πορφυρόπωλις**, πόλεως

Dealer in purple cloth; seller of purple; seller of purple fabrics; merchant of expensive purple cloth.

Practical Application

Purple fabrics were in great demand in the Roman world. Purple was used on the toga or outer garments by the royalty of Rome. Therefore, as in every society, even the lower classes desired what the upper class had. Royal purple always has been and still is a common term.

ENGLISH WORD	GREEK WORD AND VERSE	THE WORD MEANS...
	Likewise urge the young men to be **sensible**; [NASB] Similarly, encourage the young men to be **self-controlled**. [NIV] Young men likewise exhort to be **sober minded**. [NKJV] In the same way, encourage the young men to **live wisely** in all they do. [NLT] Τοὺς νεωτέρους ὡσαύτως παρακάλει **σωφρονεῖν·** [GNS] τοὺς νεωτέρους ὡσαύτως παρακάλει **σωφρονεῖν** [GNT]	

#3443
Sensibly
 	
Soberly–KJV
Sensibly–NASB
Self controlled–NIV
Soberly–NKJV
Self-control–NLT
 	
**POSB
REFERENCE**
(Tit.2:12)
Note 2, point 2
	σωφρόνως = *sōphronōs*
	Pronunciation: [so-fron'-oce]
	Parsing (part of speech): adjective
	    Type—adverb
	    Stem or root—from
	Concordance References:
	  ⇒ Strong's #4996 sōphronōs
	  ⇒ NIV #5407 sōphronōs
	  ⇒ NASB #4996 sōphronōs
	
	Titus 2:12
	Teaching us that, denying ungodliness and worldly lusts, we should live **soberly**, righteously, and godly, in this present world; [KJV]
	Instructing us to deny ungodliness and worldly desires and to live **sensibly**, righteously and godly in the present age, [NASB]
	It teaches us to say "No" to ungodliness and worldly passions, and to live **self-controlled**, upright and godly lives in this present age, [NIV]
	Teaching us that, denying ungodliness and worldly lusts, we should live **soberly**, righteously, and godly, in this present world; [NKJV]
	And we are instructed to turn from godless living and sinful pleasures. We should live in this evil world with **self-control**, right conduct, and devotion to God, [NLT]
	παιδεύουσα ἡμᾶς ἵνα, ἀρνησάμενοι τὴν ἀσέβειαν καὶ τὰς κοσμικὰς ἐπιθυμίας **σωφρόνως** καὶ δικαίως καὶ εὐσεβῶς ζήσωμεν ἐν τῷ νῦν αἰῶνι, [GNS]
	παιδεύουσα ἡμᾶς, ἵνα ἀρνησάμενοι τὴν ἀσέβειαν καὶ τὰς κοσμικὰς ἐπιθυμίας **σωφρόνως** καὶ δικαίως καὶ εὐσεβῶς ζήσωμεν ἐν τῷ νῦν αἰῶνι, [GNT]
		To be self controlled; to live soberly, sensibly, temperate, and disciplined.
		
		Practical Application
		It is restraining desires, lusts, and appetites. It is never giving in to excess—to the lust for more and more. It is controlling everything and using it for its proper purpose:
		  ⇒ It is controlling the desire for sex and using it for marriage.
		  ⇒ It is controlling the desire for food and using it for health.
		  ⇒ It is controlling the desire for material things and using it to meet both the needs of one's own family and the desperate needs of the world.

#3444
Sensuality
 	
Lasciviousness–KJV
Sensuality–NASB
Lewdness–NIV
Lewdness–NKJV
Eagerness for lustful
  pleasure–NLT
 	
**POSB
REFERENCE**
(Mk.7:22)
Deeper Study #11
 	
See also POSB REF:
(2 Cor.12:19-21; esp.
  v.21)
  Note 3, point 2
(Gal.5:19-21; esp.
  v.19)
  Note 2
(1 Pt.4:3)
  Note 3, point 1
	ἀσέλγεια = *aselgeia*
	Pronunciation: [as-elg'-i-a]
	Parsing (part of speech): noun
	    Case—nominative
	    Gender—feminine
	    Number—singular
	    Stem or root—from **ἀσέλγεια**, ας
	Concordance References:
	  ⇒ Strong's #766 aselgeia
	  ⇒ NIV #816 aselgeia
	  ⇒ NASB #766 aselgeia
	
	Mark 7:22
	Thefts, covetousness, wickedness, deceit, **lasciviousness**, an evil eye, blasphemy, pride, foolishness: [KJV]
	Deeds of coveting and wickedness, as well as deceit, **sensuality**, envy, slander, pride and foolishness. [NASB]
	Greed, malice, deceit, **lewdness**, envy, slander, arrogance and folly. [NIV]
	Thefts, covetousness, wickedness, deceit, **lewdness**, an evil eye, blasphemy, pride, foolishness: [NKJV]
	Adultery, greed, wickedness, deceit, **eagerness for lustful pleasure**, envy, slander, pride, and foolishness. [NLT]
	πλεονεξίαι, πονηρίαι, δόλος, **ἀσέλγεια**, ὀφθαλμὸς πονηρός, βλασφημία, ὑπερηφανία, ἀφροσύνη· [GNS]
	μοιχεῖαι, πλεονεξίαι, πονηρίαι, δόλος, **ἀσέλγεια**, ὀφθαλμὸς πονηρός, βλασφημία, ὑπερηφανία, ἀφροσύνη· [GNT]
		Debauchery; lasciviousness; lewdness; eagerness for lustful pleasure; sensuality and indecency; shamelessness; uncontrolled, undisciplined, and unrestrained lust and passion.
		
		Practical Application
		A chief characteristic of the behavior is open and shameless indecency. It means unrestrained evil thoughts and behavior. It is giving in to brutish and lustful desires, a readiness for any pleasure. It is a person who knows no restraint, an individual who has sinned so much that he no longer cares what people say or think. It is something far more distasteful than just doing wrong. The person who misbehaves usually tries to hide his wrong, but a lascivious man does not care who knows about his exploits or shame. He wants; therefore, he seeks to take and gratify. Decency and opinion do not matter. When he initially began to sin, he did as all people do: he misbehaved in secret. But eventually, the sin got the best of him—to the point that he no longer cared who saw or knew. He became the subject of a master—the master of habit, of the thing itself. People become the slaves of such things as unbridled lust, wantonness, licentiousness, out-

ENGLISH WORD	GREEK WORD AND VERSE	THE WORD MEANS...
		rageousness, shamelessness, insolence (Mark 7:22), wanton manners, filthy words, indecent body movements, immoral handling of males and females (Romans 13:13), carnality, gluttony, and sexual immorality (1 Peter 4:3; 2 Peter 2:2, 18). (Cp. 2 Cor. 12:21; Galatians 5:19; Ephes. 4:19; 2 Peter 2:7.)

#3445
Sensuality
 	
Wantonness–KJV
Sensuality–NASB
Debauchery–NIV
Lust–NKJV
Immoral living–NLT
 	
POSB REFERENCE
(Rom.13:13)
Note 4, point 4
	ἀσελγείαις = aselgeiais
	Pronunciation: [as-elg'-i-ah-is]
	Parsing (part of speech): noun
	  Case—dative
	  Gender—feminine
	  Number—plural
	  Stem or root—from ἀσέλγεια, ας
	Concordance References:
	⇒ Strong's #766 aselgeia
	⇒ NIV #816 aselgeia
	⇒ NASB #766 aselgeia
	
	Romans 13:13
	Let us walk honestly, as in the day; not in rioting and drunkenness, not in chambering and **wantonness**, not in strife and envying. [KJV]
	Let us behave properly as in the day, not in carousing and drunkenness, not in sexual promiscuity and **sensuality**, not in strife and jealousy. [NASB]
	Let us behave decently, as in the daytime, not in orgies and drunkenness, not in sexual immorality and **debauchery**, not in dissension and jealousy. [NIV]
	Let us walk properly, as in the day, not in revelry and drunkenness, not in lewdness and **lust**, not in strife and envy. [NKJV]
	We should be decent and true in everything we do, so that everyone can approve of our behavior. Don't participate in wild parties and getting drunk, or in adultery and **immoral living**, or in fighting and jealousy. [NLT]
	ὡς ἐν ἡμέρα, εὐσχημόνως περιπατήσωμεν, μὴ κώμοις καὶ μέθαις, μὴ κοίταις καὶ **ἀσελγείαις**, μὴ ἔριδι καὶ ζήλῳ. [GNS]
	ὡς ἐν ἡμέρα εὐσχημόνως περιπατήσωμεν, μὴ κώμοις καὶ μέθαις, μὴ κοίταις καὶ **ἀσελγείαις**, μὴ ἔριδι καὶ ζήλῳ, [GNT]
		Debauchery; sensuality; lust; running wild; licentiousness; wantonness; homosexuality; lasciviousness; living a wild, partying, and immoral life.
		
		Practical Application
		It is excess lust, unbridled lust that consumes one's thoughts and behavior through...
		• looks and dress
		• films and pictures
		• dances and parties
		• suggestions and gestures
		• books and pamphlets
		• songs and music
		• talk and jokes
		• touch and behavior
		• sensuality, indecency, vice

#3446
Sensuality
 	
Lasciviousness–KJV
Sensuality–NASB
Debauchery–NIV
Lewdness–NKJV
Immorality–NLT
 	
POSB REFERENCE
(1 Pt.4:3)
Note 3, point 1
	ἀσελγείαις = aselgeiais
	Pronunciation: [as-elg'-i-ah-is]
	Parsing (part of speech): noun
	  Case—dative
	  Gender—feminine
	  Number—plural
	  Stem or root—from ἀσέλγεια, ας
	Concordance References:
	⇒ Strong's #766 aselgeia
	⇒ NIV #816 aselgeia
	⇒ NASB #766 aselgeia
	
	1 Peter 4:3
	For the time past of our life may suffice us to have wrought the will of the Gentiles, when we walked in **lasciviousness**, lusts, excess of wine, revellings, banquetings, and abominable idolatries: [KJV]
	For the time already past is sufficient for you to have carried out the desire of the Gentiles, having pursued a course of **sensuality**, lusts, drunkenness, carousals, drinking parties and abominable idolatries. [NASB]
	For you have spent enough time in the past doing what pagans choose to do—living in **debauchery**, lust, drunkenness, orgies, carousing and detestable idolatry. [NIV]
	For we *have spent* enough of our past lifetime in doing the will of the Gentiles—when we walked in **lewdness**, lusts, drunkenness, revelries, drinking parties, and abominable idolatries. [NKJV]
		Debauchery, lasciviousness, sensuality, immorality, vice, filthiness, indecency, shamelessness, license, lustful desire; without restraint; lewdness.
		
		Practical Application
		A chief characteristic of the behavior is open and shameless indecency. It means unrestrained evil thoughts and behavior. It is giving in to brutish and lustful desires, a readiness for any pleasure. It is a man who knows no restraint, a man who has sinned so much that he no longer cares what people say or think. It is something far more distasteful than just doing wrong. The man who misbehaves usually tries to hide his wrong, but a sensual man does not care who knows about his exploits or shame. He wants; therefore he seeks to take and gratify. Decency and opinion do not matter. Initially when he began to sin, he did as all men do: he misbehaved in secret. But eventually, the sin got the best of him—to the point that he no longer cared who saw or knew. He became the subject of a master—the master of habit, of the thing itself.

ENGLISH WORD	GREEK WORD AND VERSE	THE WORD MEANS...
	Παῦλος δοῦλος Ἰησοῦ Χριστοῦ, κλητὸς ἀπόστολος, ἀφωρισμένος εἰς εὐαγγέλιον Θεοῦ, [GNS] Παῦλος δοῦλος Χριστοῦ Ἰησοῦ, κλητὸς ἀπόστολος ἀφωρισμένος εἰς εὐαγγέλιον θεοῦ, [GNT]	

#3451
Separate
 	
Sever–KJV
Take out–NASB
Separate–NIV
Separate–NKJV
Separate–NLT
 	
POSB REFERENCE
(Mt.13:49)
Deeper Study #3
	ἀφοριοῦσιν = aphoriousin
	Pronunciation: [af-or-i-oo'-sin]
	Parsing (part of speech): verb
	  Mood—indicative
	  Tense—future
	  Voice—active
	  Person—3rd person
	  Number—plural
	  Stem or root—from ἀφορίζω
	Concordance References:
	⇒ Strong's #873 aphorizö
	⇒ NIV #928 aphorizö
	⇒ NASB #873 aphorizö
	
	Matthew 13:49
	So shall it be at the end of the world: the angels shall come forth, and **sever** the wicked from among the just, [KJV]
	"So it will be at the end of the age; the angels shall come forth, and **take out** the wicked from among the righteous, [NASB]
	This is how it will be at the end of the age. The angels will come and **separate** the wicked from the righteous [NIV]
	So it will be at the end of the age. The angels will come forth, **separate** the wicked from among the just, [NKJV]
	That is the way it will be at the end of the world. The angels will come and **separate** the wicked people from the godly, [NLT]
	οὕτως ἔσται ἐν τῇ συντελείᾳ τοῦ αἰῶνος· ἐξελεύσονται οἱ ἄγγελοι, καὶ **ἀφοριοῦσι** τοὺς πονηροὺς ἐκ μέσου τῶν δικαίων, [GNS]
	οὕτως ἔσται ἐν τῇ συντελείᾳ τοῦ αἰῶνος· ἐξελεύσονται οἱ ἄγγελοι καὶ **ἀφοριοῦσιν** τοὺς πονηροὺς ἐκ μέσου τῶν δικαίων [GNT]
		To separate; to sever; to take out; to exclude; to set off by bounds; to set apart.
		
		Practical Application
		In this Scripture, the wicked are to be taken completely away. They are taken and cast completely out of the presence of the good.

#3452
Separated
 	
Separated–KJV
Set apart–NASB
Set apart–NIV
Separated–NKJV
Sent out–NLT
 	
POSB REFERENCE
(Rom.1:1-4; esp. v.1)
Note 3
	ἀφωρισμένος = aphörismenos
	Pronunciation: [af-or-is'-mehn-os]
	Parsing (part of speech): verb
	  Mood—participle
	  Tense—perfect
	  Voice—passive
	  Case—nominative
	  Gender—masculine
	  Person—1st person
	  Number—singular
	  Stem or root—from ἀφορίζω
	Concordance References:
	⇒ Strong's #873 aphorizö
	⇒ NIV #928 aphorizö
	⇒ NASB #873 aphorizö
	
	Romans 1:1
	Paul, a servant of Jesus Christ, called to be an apostle, **separated** unto the gospel of God, [KJV]
	Paul, a bond-servant of Christ Jesus, called as an apostle, **set apart** for the gospel of God, [NASB]
	Paul, a servant of Christ Jesus, called to be an apostle and **set apart** for the gospel of God—[NIV]
	Paul, a bondservant of Jesus Christ, called *to be* an apostle, **separated** to the gospel of God [NKJV]
	This letter is from Paul, Jesus Christ's slave, chosen by God to be an apostle and **sent out** to preach his Good News. [NLT]
	Παῦλος δοῦλος Ἰησοῦ Χριστοῦ, κλητὸς ἀπόστολος, **ἀφωρισμένος** εἰς εὐαγγέλιον Θεοῦ, [GNS]
	Παῦλος δοῦλος Χριστοῦ Ἰησοῦ, κλητὸς ἀπόστολος **ἀφωρισμένος** εἰς εὐαγγέλιον θεοῦ, [GNT]
		To separate; to take away; to exclude (from one's company); to set apart; to appoint.
		
		Practical Application
		Paul was set apart to the gospel of God. This is the reason God called Paul: that Paul might be separated (*aphörismenos*) or marked and set apart to the gospel of God. The word "gospel" simply means the good news of God.
		⇒ Paul did not say he was called and set apart to a man-made religion, denomination, or sect; nor was he called primarily to a gospel of social justice and welfare, as important as these calls are.
		⇒ Paul said he was set apart to the gospel, to "God's Good News (cp. 1 Thes. 2:2-13).

ENGLISH WORD	GREEK WORD AND VERSE	THE WORD MEANS...

#3453
Separated
 	
Cloven–KJV
Distributing–NASB
Separated–NIV
Divided–NKJV
Not translated–NLT
 	
**POSB
REFERENCE**
(Acts 2:2-4; esp. v.3)
Note 4, point 2
	διαμεριζόμεναι = *diamerizomenai*
	Pronunciation: [dee-am-er-id'-zo-men-ah-ee]
	Parsing (part of speech): verb
	    Mood—participle
	    Tense—present
	    Voice—middle or passive
	    Case—nominative
	    Gender—feminine
	    Number—plural
	    Stem or root—from διαμερίζω
	Concordance References:
	⇒ Strong's #1266 diamerizö
	⇒ NIV #1374 diamerizö
	⇒ NASB #1266 diamerizö
	
	Acts 2:3
	And there appeared unto them **cloven** tongues like as of fire, and it sat upon each of them. [KJV]
	And there appeared to them tongues as of fire **distributing** themselves, and they rested on each one of them. [NASB]
	They saw what seemed to be tongues of fire that **separated** and came to rest on each of them. [NIV]
	Then there appeared to them **divided** tongues, as of fire, and *one* sat upon each of them. [NKJV]
	Then, what looked like flames or tongues of fire appeared and settled on each of them. [NLT]—NOT TRANSLATED
	καὶ ὤφθησαν αὐτοῖς **διαμεριζόμεναι** γλῶσσαι ὡσεὶ πυρός, καὶ ἐκάθισε τε ἐφ' ἕνα ἕκαστο αὐτῶν. [GNS]
	καὶ ὤφθησαν αὐτοῖς **διαμεριζόμεναι** γλῶσσαι ὡσεὶ πυρὸς καὶ ἐκάθισεν ἐφ' ἕνα ἕκαστον αὐτῶν, [GNT]
		Separated, distributed; divided.
		
		Practical Application
		The Greek means a tongue that was separated, that is, parted asunder. The idea is that a single tongue appeared and then began to split and divide itself, resting upon each of the disciples.

#3454
Serious
 	
Sober–KJV
Sound judgment–
  NASB
Clear minded–NIV
Serious–NKJV
Earnest–NLT
 	
**POSB
REFERENCE**
(1 Pt.4:7)
Note 1
	σωφρονήσατε = *söphronësate*
	Pronunciation: [so-fron-ay'-sah-teh]
	Parsing (part of speech): verb
	    Mood—imperative
	    Tense—aorist
	    Voice—active
	    Person—2nd person
	    Number—plural
	    Stem or root—from σωφρονέω
	Concordance References:
	⇒ Strong's #4993 söphroneö
	⇒ NIV #5404 söphroneö
	⇒ NASB #4993 söphroneö
	
	1 Peter 4:7
	But the end of all things is at hand: be ye therefore **sober**, and watch unto prayer. [KJV]
	The end of all things is at hand; therefore, be of **sound judgment** and sober *spirit* for the purpose of prayer. [NASB]
	The end of all things is near. Therefore be **clear minded** and self-controlled so that you can pray. [NIV]
	But the end of all things is at hand; therefore be **serious** and watchful in your prayers. [NKJV]
	The end of the world is coming soon. Therefore, be **earnest** and disciplined in your prayers. [NLT]
	Πάντων δὲ τὸ τέλος ἤγγικε· **σωφρονήσατε** οὖν καὶ νήψατε εἰς τὰς προσευχάς· [GNS]
	Πάντων δὲ τὸ τέλος ἤγγικεν. **σωφρονήσατε** οὖν καὶ νήψατε εἰς προσευχάς· [GNT]
		To be clear minded; to be sober; to exhibit sound judgment; to be earnest. This means to be serious and to have a sound mind; to be in control of oneself and to be self-restrained; to be calm and sensible.
		
		Practical Application
		The believer lives under the climax of history; he keeps his mind upon the return of Christ by doing three things.
		1. He keeps a serious and sound mind about everything. He is not a jolly, back slapping, frivolous type of person. He takes life seriously, knowing that man has a purpose for being on earth, that life is the most meaningful and significant possession that man has. Therefore, he measures the importance of things. He measures all things in light of eternity as well as time. He considers the future as well as the present. He knows that his life could be snatched from him overnight by some accident or by the news of some disease. The believer who keeps his mind upon the climax of history, upon the return of the Lord Jesus Christ, is a sober person; he is a serious and sound-minded person.
		2. He controls and restrains his desires and lusts and appetites. He never gives in to excess—to the lust for more and more. He controls sex and uses it for marriage. He controls desire for food and uses it for health. He controls the desire for material possessions and uses it to meet the needs of his family and the desperate needs of the world.
		3. He is calm and sensible about all things. He is not overly shaken by trouble, problems, or

ENGLISH WORD	GREEK WORD AND VERSE	THE WORD MEANS...
		circumstances that arise within his family, employment, society, or world. Family problems and world events just do not shake him. He is concerned but not shaken. He does not get overly excited with recreation, sports, or any other happening of life. He enjoys the happenings and experiences of life, but he keeps a sensible perspective of all things and gives each thing its proper place.

#3455
Seriously
 	
Diligence–KJV
Diligence–NASB
Diligently–NIV
Diligence–NKJV
Seriously–NLT
 	
POSB REFERENCE
(Rom.12:6-8; esp. v.8)
Note 2, point 6
	ἐν σπουδῇ = *en spoudë*
	Pronunciation: [ehn spoo-day']
	Parsing *spoudë* (part of speech): noun
	    Case—dative
	    Gender—feminine
	    Number—singular
	    Stem or root—from σπουδή, ῆς
	Concordance References:
	⇒ Strong's #1722 + 4710 en spoudë
	⇒ NIV #1877 + 5082 en spoudë [diligently]
	⇒ NASB #1722 + 4710 en spoudë
	
	Romans 12:8
	Or he that exhorteth, on exhortation: he that giveth, let him do it with simplicity; he that ruleth, with **diligence**; he that sheweth mercy, with cheerfulness. [KJV]
	Or he who exhorts, in his exhortation; he who gives, with liberality; he who leads, with **diligence**; he who shows mercy, with cheerfulness. [NASB]
	If it is encouraging, let him encourage; if it is contributing to the needs of others, let him give generously; if it is leadership, let him govern **diligently**; if it is showing mercy, let him do it cheerfully. [NIV]
	He who exhorts, in exhortation; he who gives, with liberality; he who leads, with **diligence**; he who shows mercy, with cheerfulness. [NKJV]
	If your gift is to encourage others, do it! If you have money, share it generously. If God has given you leadership ability, take the responsibility **seriously**. And if you have a gift for showing kindness to others, do it gladly. [NLT]
	εἴτε ὁ παρακαλῶν, ἐν τῇ παρακλήσει· ὁ μεταδιδοὺς ἐν ἁπλότητι, ὁ προϊστάμενος **ἐν σπουδῇ**· ὁ ἐλεῶν ἐν ἱλαρότητι. [GNS]
	εἴτε ὁ παρακαλῶν ἐν τῇ παρακλήσει· ὁ μεταδιδοὺς ἐν ἁπλότητι, ὁ προϊστάμενος **ἐν σπουδη** ὁ ἐλεῶν ἐν ἱλαρότητι. [GNT]
		Earnestness, diligence, eagerness, zeal, effort.
		
		Practical Application
		There is the gift of ruling (*proistemi*). This means the ability of leadership, authority, administration, government. Note that this person is to lead with seriousness (*spoudë*): diligence, haste, zeal, desire, and concentrated attention. There is no room for laziness, complacency, and irresponsibility in the Kingdom of God and His church. The leaders are the ones who are to blaze the path for the flock of God, and they are to do it with zeal, hard work, and iron determination.

#3456
Servant
 	
Servant–KJV
Slave–NASB
Slave–NIV
Slave–NKJV
Slave–NLT
 	
POSB REFERENCE
(Mt.20:23-28; esp. v.27)
  Note 3, point 3
 	
See also POSB REF:
(Lk.12:41-48; esp. v.43)
  Note 2, point 2b
(Jn.8:34-36; esp. v.34)
  Note 2
	δοῦλος = *doulos*
	Pronunciation: [doo'-los]
	Parsing (part of speech): noun
	    Case—nominative
	    Gender—masculine
	    Number—singular
	    Stem or root—from δοῦλος η, ον
	Concordance References:
	⇒ Strong's #1401 doulos
	⇒ NIV #1528 doulos1
	⇒ NASB #1401 doulos
	
	Matthew 20:27
	And whosoever will be chief among you, let him be your **servant**: [KJV]
	And whoever wishes to be first among you shall be your **slave**; [NASB]
	And whoever wants to be first must be your **slave**—[NIV]
	And whoever desires to be first among you, let him be your **slave**—[NKJV]
	And whoever wants to be first must become your **slave**. [NLT]
	καὶ ὃς ἐὰν θέλῃ ἐν ὑμῖν εἶναι πρῶτος ἔστω ὑμῶν **δοῦλος**· [GNS]
	καὶ ὃς ἂν θέλῃ ἐν ὑμῖν εἶναι πρῶτος ἔσται ὑμῶν **δοῦλος**· [GNT]
		To serve as a slave, submitting one's own will to his master.
		
		Practical Application
		Throughout society many of us hold positions of authority. Far too often we forget that with authority comes great responsibility. And when we forget to fulfill our responsibility, we usually abuse the power of our position. And when power is abused, those who are under our control usually catch the brunt of our frustration or anger (Exodus 21:26-27). God has called every believer to be a good and faithful steward. To be a good and faithful steward...
		• we must acknowledge that God Himself is the owner of all things
		• we must act like managers not owners
		• we must seek the best for God and others not for ourselves
		• we must think about the possible consequences before we act
		• we must keep an open heart for communication, not a clenched fist for retaliation
		• we must minister to others as Jesus would and not as our fallen natures desire

ENGLISH WORD	GREEK WORD AND VERSE	THE WORD MEANS...

#3457
Servant
 	
Handmaid–KJV
Bondslave–NASB
Servant–NIV
Maidservant–NKJV
Servant–NLT
 	
POSB REFERENCE
(Lk.1:38)
Note 8
	δούλη = doulë
	Pronunciation: [doo'-lay]
	Parsing (part of speech): noun
	  Case—nominative
	  Gender—feminine
	  Number—singular
	  Stem or root—from δούλη, ης
	Concordance References:
	⇒ Strong's #1399 doulë
	⇒ NIV #1527 doulë
	⇒ NASB #1399 doulë
	
	Luke 1:38
	And Mary said, Behold the **handmaid** of the Lord; be it unto me according to thy word. And the angel departed from her. [KJV]
	And Mary said, "Behold, the **bondslave** of the Lord; be it done to me according to your word." And the angel departed from her. [NASB]
	"I am the Lord's **servant**," Mary answered. "May it be to me as you have said." Then the angel left her. [NIV]
	Then Mary said, "Behold the **maidservant** of the Lord! Let it be to me according to your word." And the angel departed from her. [NKJV]
	Mary responded, "I am the Lord's **servant**, and I am willing to accept whatever he wants. May everything you have said come true." And then the angel left. [NLT]
	εἶπε δὲ Μαριάμ, Ἰδοὺ ἡ **δούλη** Κυρίου· γένοιτό μοι κατὰ τὸ ῥῆμά σου. καὶ ἀπῆλθεν ἀπ' αὐτῆς ὁ ἄγγελος. [GNS]
	εἶπεν δὲ Μαριάμ, Ἰδοὺ ἡ **δούλη**, κυρίου· γένοιτό μοι κατὰ τὸ ῥῆμά σου. καὶ ἀπῆλθεν ἀπ' αὐτῆς ὁ ἄγγελος. [GNT]
		Slave girl; a handmaid; a maidservant; a female servant; a bondslave.
		
		Practical Application
		Mary was saying that she was a bondslave, willing to sell herself out completely to God. She would possess herself no longer but would give herself completely to God.

#3458
Servant
 	
Serve–KJV
Servant–NASB
Serves–NIV
Serves–NKJV
Servant–NLT
 	
POSB REFERENCE
(Lk.22:26-27 esp. v.26)
Note 3, point 2
	διακονῶν = diakonön
	Pronunciation: [dee-ak-o-known]
	Parsing (part of speech): verb
	  Mood—participle
	  Tense—present
	  Voice—active
	  Case—nominative
	  Gender—masculine
	  Number—singular
	  Stem or root—from διακονέω
	Concordance References:
	⇒ Strong's #1247 diakoneö
	⇒ NIV #1354 diakoneö
	⇒ NASB #1247 diakoneö
	
	Luke 22:26
	But ye shall not be so: but he that is greatest among you, let him be as the younger; and he that is chief, as he that doth **serve**. [KJV]
	"But not so with you, but let him who is the greatest among you become as the youngest, and the leader as the **servant**. [NASB]
	But you are not to be like that. Instead, the greatest among you should be like the youngest, and the one who rules like the one who **serves**. [NIV]
	But not so *among* you; on the contrary, he who is greatest among you, let him be as the younger, and he who governs as he who **serves**. [NKJV]
	But among you, those who are the greatest should take the lowest rank, and the leader should be like a **servant**. [NLT]
	ὑμεῖς δὲ οὐχ οὕτως· ἀλλ' ὁ μείζων ἐν ὑμῖν, γινέσθω ὡς ὁ νεώτερος· καὶ ὁ ἡγούμενος ὡς ὁ **διακ-ονῶν**. [GNS]
	ὑμεῖς δὲ οὐχ οὕτως, ἀλλ' ὁ μείζων ἐν ὑμῖν γινέσθω ὡς ὁ νεώτερος καὶ ὁ ἡγούμενος ὡς ὁ **διακ-ονῶν**. [GNT]
		Servant, deacon, one who serves voluntarily, to wait upon; to care for.
		
		Practical Application
		The truly great man will serve others just as a table waiter serves the guests at a banquet. The table waiter in Jesus' day was a bond-slave (*doulos*). The bond-slave was bound every moment of his life, always serving, no matter the hour or call or difficulty (see POSB note, Slave—Romans 1:1).
		The truly great person looks for people to help and for ways to help them, whether at work, home, play, or church. He is always seeking those who need a visit, care, attention, company, food, clothing, shelter, money. He seeks for the sake of ministering (cp. Matthew 25:34-40).

ENGLISH WORD	GREEK WORD AND VERSE	THE WORD MEANS...
	"Then the king said to the **servants**, 'Bind him hand and foot, and cast him into the outer darkness; in that place there shall be weeping and gnashing of teeth.' [NASB] "Then the king told the **attendants**, 'Tie him hand and foot, and throw him outside, into the darkness, where there will be weeping and gnashing of teeth.' [NIV] Then the king said to the **servants**, 'Bind him hand and foot, take him away, and cast him into outer darkness; there will be weeping and gnashing of teeth.' [NKJV] Then the king said to his **aides**, 'Bind him hand and foot and throw him out into the outer darkness, where there is weeping and gnashing of teeth.' [NLT] τότε εἶπεν ὁ βασιλεὺς τοῖς **διακόνοις**, Δήσαντες αὐτοῦ πόδας καὶ χεῖρας, ἄρατε αὐτὸν καὶ ἐκβάλετε εἰς τὸ σκότος τὸ ἐξώτερον· ἐκεῖ ἔσται ὁ κλαυθμὸς καὶ ὁ βρυγμὸς τῶν ὀδόντων. [GNS] τότε ὁ βασιλεὺς εἶπεν τοῖς **διακόνοις**, Δήσαντες αὐτοῦ πόδας καὶ χεῖρας ἐκβάλετε αὐτὸν εἰς τὸ σκότος τὸ ἐξώτερον· ἐκεῖ ἔσται ὁ κλαυθμὸς καὶ ὁ βρυγμὸς τῶν ὀδόντων. [GNT]	1. The man was bound hand and foot. The hand and foot are usually the bodily parts used by man to sin. The hands are bound, so there is no resistance. The feet are bound, so there is no escape. Whatever the King says is done in the Great Day of the Feast. No man can resist or flee. 2. The man was taken away, out of the King's presence and out of the presence of His Son and of the other guests. He was not allowed to share in the joy and bounty of the occasion. 3. He was cast into outer darkness, far, far away from everyone else. He was not only cut off from the sharing of the occasion but from ever seeing the occasion. Whatever light and splendor there was in the Great Wedding Feast, he was cast into the *outer* regions of darkness, never to glimpse the light.

#3463
Servants
 	
Ministers–KJV
Servants–NASB
Servants–NIV
Ministers–NKJV
Servants–NLT
 	
**POSB
REFERENCE**
(1 Cor.3:5)
Note 1
	διάκονοι = *diakonoi*
	Pronunciation: [dee-ak'-on-oy]
	Parsing (part of speech): noun
	    Case—nominative
	    Gender—masculine
	    Number—plural
	    Stem or root—from διακόνοις, ου
	Concordance References:
	  ⇒ Strong's #1249 diakonos
	  ⇒ NIV #1356 diakonos
	  ⇒ NASB #1249 diakonos
	
	1 Cor. 3:5
	Who then is Paul, and who is Apollos, but **ministers** by whom ye believed, even as the Lord gave to every man? [KJV]
	
	What then is Apollos? And what is Paul? **Servants** through whom you believed, even as the Lord gave opportunity to each one. [NASB]
	
	What, after all, is Apollos? And what is Paul? Only **servants**, through whom you came to believe—as the Lord has assigned to each his task. [NIV]
	
	Who then is Paul, and who *is* Apollos, but **ministers** through whom you believed, as the Lord gave to each one? [NKJV]
	
	Who is Apollos, and who is Paul, that we should be the cause of such quarrels? Why, we're only **servants**. Through us God caused you to believe. Each of us did the work the Lord gave us. [NLT]
	
	τίς οὖν ἐστι Παῦλος; τίς δέ Ἀπολλώς; ἀλλ η **διάκονοι** δι' ὧν ἐπιστεύσατε, καὶ ἑκάστω ὡς ὁ Κύριος ἔδωκεν, [GNS]
	
	τί οὖν ἐστιν Ἀπολλῶς; τί δέ ἐστιν Παῦλος; **διάκονοι** δι' ὧν ἐπιστεύσατε, καὶ ἑκάστῳ ὡς ὁ κύριος ἔδωκεν. [GNT]
		A servant, an attendant, a helper, or a waiter on tables.
		
		Practical Application
		The stress is upon the lowly status of the service. Servants; yes, even all believers, are not *lords* over God's flock and church; they are the lowly servants. They are the servants of God and the servants of God's people.

#3464
Servants
 	
Ministers–KJV
Servants–NASB
Servants–NIV
Servants–NKJV
Servants–NLT
 	
**POSB
REFERENCE**
(1 Cor.4:1-2; esp. v.1)
Note 1
	ὑπηρέτας = *hupēretas*
	Pronunciation: [hoop-ay-ret'-ahs]
	Parsing (part of speech): noun
	    Case—accusative
	    Gender—masculine
	    Number—plural
	    Stem or root—from ὑπηρέτης, ου
	Concordance References:
	  ⇒ Strong's #5257 hupēretēs
	  ⇒ NIV #5677 hupēretēs
	  ⇒ NASB #5257 hupēretēs
	
	1 Cor. 4:1
	Let a man so account of us, as of the **ministers** of Christ, and stewards of the mysteries of God. [KJV]
		Servants, attendants, helper, an under-rower.
		
		Practical Application
		It refers to the slaves who sat in the belly of the large ships and pulled at the great oars to carry the boat through the sea. Christ is the Master of the ship and each believer is *one of the slaves of Christ*. Note: he is only one of many under-rowing servants. Remember also that slaves in the belly of the ship were bound by chains. They were allowed to do nothing but serve the master of the ship. The believer is a bound slave of Christ: he exists only to row for

ENGLISH WORD	GREEK WORD AND VERSE	THE WORD MEANS...
	Let a man regard us in this manner, as **servants** of Christ, and stewards of the mysteries of God. [NASB] So then, men ought to regard us as **servants** of Christ and as those entrusted with the secret things of God. [NIV] Let a man so consider us, as **servants** of Christ and stewards of the mysteries of God. [NKJV] So look at Apollos and me as mere **servants** of Christ who have been put in charge of explaining God's secrets. [NLT] Οὕτως ἡμᾶς λογιζέσθω ἄνθρωπος ὡς **ὑπηρέτας** Χριστοῦ καὶ οἰκονόμους μυστηρίων Θεοῦ. [GNS] Οὕτως ἡμᾶς λογιζέσθω ἄνθρωπος ὡς **ὑπηρέτας** Χριστοῦ καὶ οἰκονόμους μυστηρίων θεοῦ. [GNT]	the Master. He does not and cannot serve anyone else.
#3465 **Servants** **Servants–KJV** Slaves–NASB Slaves–NIV Slaves–NKJV Whatever you choose to obey–NLT **POSB REFERENCE** (Rom.6:16) Note 2	*δούλους = doulous* Pronunciation: [doo'-loos] Parsing (part of speech): noun 　Case—accusative 　Gender—masculine 　Number—plural 　Stem or root—from δοῦλος, η, ον Concordance References: ⇒ Strong's #1401 doulos ⇒ NIV #1528 doulos1 ⇒ NASB #1401 doulos **Romans 6:16** Know ye not, that to whom ye yield yourselves **servants** to obey, his servants ye are to whom ye obey; whether of sin unto death, or of obedience unto righteousness? [KJV] Do you not know that when you present yourselves to someone as **slaves** for obedience, you are slaves of the one whom you obey, either of sin resulting in death, or of obedience resulting in righteousness? [NASB] Don't you know that when you offer yourselves to someone to obey him as **slaves**, you are slaves to the one whom you obey—whether you are slaves to sin, which leads to death, or to obedience, which leads to righteousness? [NIV] Do you not know that to whom you present yourselves **slaves** to obey, you are that one's slaves whom you obey, whether of sin leading to death, or of obedience leading to righteousness? [NKJV] Don't you realize that **whatever you choose to obey** becomes your master? You can choose sin, which leads to death, or you can choose to obey God and receive his approval. [NLT] οὐκ οἴδατε ὅτι ᾧ παριστάνετε ἑαυτοὺς **δούλους** εἰς ὑπακοήν, δοῦλοί ἐστε ᾧ ὑπακούετε, ἤτοι ἁμαρτίας εἰς θάνατον, ἢ ὑπακοῆς εἰς δικαιοσύνην; [GNS] οὐκ οἴδατε ὅτι ᾧ παριστάνετε ἑαυτοὺς **δούλους** εἰς ὑπακοήν, δοῦλοί ἐστε ᾧ ὑπακούετε, ἤτοι ἁμαρτίας εἰς θάνατον ἢ ὑπακοῆς εἰς δικαιοσύνην; [GNT]	Slaves, servants; whatever you choose to obey. **Practical Application** A person is either the slave of sin or of God, and there is a very simple test to tell which master a person serves. ⇒ Do you yield to sin, that is, serve sin? ⇒ Do you yield to God, that is, serve God? If you yield to sin, you will die. If you yield to God and obey Him, you will be counted righteous and live. Now note a crucial point. Either sin is your master or God is your Master. You either yield to sin or you yield to God. This does not mean that you become sinless and perfect, but that... • you do not plan to sin. • you hate sin and fight against it. • you struggle to please God by not sinning. • you diligently seek to make God the Master of your life by obeying Him. • you study God's Word so that you will know His commandments and can obey Him. • you immediately seek God's forgiveness when you do sin and you repent—you turn away from the sin (1 John 1:9; 1 John 2:1-2). • you walk in open confession before God, talking to Him all day long, ever gaining an unbroken fellowship with Him as the Master of your life. Again, note the results, for whom we serve determines our destiny. If we yield to sin, we will die; but if we yield to God, we will be counted righteous and live eternally.
#3466 **Servants** **Servants–KJV** Bond-servants–NASB **Servants–NIV** **Servants–NKJV** **Servants–NLT** **POSB REFERENCE** (Acts 4:29-30; esp. v.29) Note 4, point 1c	*δούλοις = doulois* Pronunciation: [doo'-lo-ees] Parsing (part of speech): noun 　Case—dative 　Gender—masculine 　Number—plural 　Stem or root—from δοῦλος, η, ον Concordance References: ⇒ Strong's #1401 doulos ⇒ NIV #1528 doulos1 ⇒ NASB #1401 doulos **Acts 4:29** And now, Lord, behold their threatenings: and grant unto thy **servants**, that with all boldness they may speak thy word, [KJV] "And now, Lord, take note of their threats, and grant	To be a servant; to be a bond-servant; to be as a slave. **Practical Application** The word "servants" (*doulois*) is the word for bond-slaves. The church was saying that they were the slaves of the Lord, to do His will, to share and speak God's Word despite persecution.

ENGLISH WORD	GREEK WORD AND VERSE	THE WORD MEANS...

and all of you, **clothe** yourselves **with** humility toward one another, for God is opposed to the proud, but gives grace to the humble. [NASB]

Young men, in the same way be submissive to those who are older. All of you, **clothe** yourselves **with** humility toward one another, because, "God opposes the proud but gives grace to the humble." [NIV]

Likewise you younger people, submit yourselves to your elders. Yes, all of you be submissive to one another, and be **clothed with** humility, for "God resists the roud, But gives grace to the humble." [NKJV]

You younger men, accept the authority of the elders. And all of you, **serve each other** in humility, for "God sets himself against the proud, but he shows favor to the humble." [NLT]

ὁμοίως, νεώτεροι, ὑποτάγητε πρεσβυτέροις· πάντες δὲ ἀλλήλοις ὑποτασσόμενοι, τὴν ταπεινοφροσύνην **ἐγκομβώσασθε·** ὅτι ὁ Θεὸς ὑπερηφάνοις ἀντιτάσσεται, ταπεινοῖς δὲ δίδωσι χάριν. [GNS]

Ὁμοίως, νεώτεροι, ὑποτάγητε πρεσβυτέροις· πάντες δὲ ἀλλήλοις τὴν ταπεινοφροσύνην **ἐγκομβώσασθε,** ὅτι [Ο] θεὸς ὑπερηφάνοις ἀντιτάσσεται, ταπεινοῖς δὲ δίδωσιν χάριν. [GNT]

#3471
Served–Serving The Lord

Serving the Lord–KJV
Serving the Lord–NASB
Served the Lord–NIV
Serving the Lord–NKJV
Done the Lord's work–NLT

POSB REFERENCE
(Acts 20:18-19; esp. v.19)
Note 2, point 2

δουλεύων τῷ κυρίῳ = *douleuōn tō kuriō*
Pronunciation: [dool-yoo'-own tow koo'-ree-o]
Parsing *douleuōn* (part of speech): verb
  Mood—participle
  Tense—present
  Voice—active
  Case—nominative
  Gender—masculine
  Person—1st person
  Number—singular
  Stem or root—from δουλεύω
Concordance References:
⇒ Strong's #1398 douleuö +3588 ho + 2962 kurios
⇒ NIV #1526 douleuö [served] + 3836 ho [the] + 3261 kurios [Lord]
⇒ NASB #1398 douleuö +3588 ho +2962 kurios

Acts 20:19
Serving the Lord with all humility of mind, and with many tears, and temptations, which befell me by the lying in wait of the Jews: [KJV]

Serving the Lord with all humility and with tears and with trials which came upon me through the plots of the Jews; [NASB]

I **served the Lord** with great humility and with tears, although I was severely tested by the plots of the Jews. [NIV]

Serving the Lord with all humility, with many tears and trials which happened to me by the plotting of the Jews; [NKJV]

I have **done the Lord's work** humbly—yes, and with tears. I have endured the trials that came to me from the plots of the Jews. [NLT]

δουλεύων τῷ Κυρίῳ μετὰ πάσης ταπεινοφροσύνης καὶ δακρύων καὶ πολλῶν πειρασμῶν τῶν συμβάντων μοι ἐν ταῖς ἐπιβουλαῖς τῶν Ἰουδαίων· [GNS]

δουλεύων τῷ κυρίῳ μετὰ πάσης ταπεινοφροσύνης καὶ δακρύων καὶ πειρασμῶν τῶν συμβάντων μοι ἐν ταῖς ἐπιβουλαῖς τῶν Ἰουδαίων, [GNT]

To have served the Lord; to have done the Lord's work; to have served as a slave.

Practical Application
The word "serve" (*douleuōn*) is taken from the word bond-slave (*doulos*). Paul constantly called himself the slave of Jesus Christ (see POSB note—Romans 1:1 for discussion).

#3472
Service

Service–KJV
Service of worship–NASB
Act of worship–NIV

λατρείαν = *latreian*
Pronunciation: [lat-ri'-ahn]
Parsing (part of speech): noun
  Case—accusative
  Gender—feminine
  Number—singular
  Stem or root—from λατρεία, ας
Concordance References:
⇒ Strong's #2999 latreia

An act of worship; a service of worship; a ministry; a service.

Practical Application
The believer is to use his mind in dedicating his body to the service of God. He is to study the Scriptures, and intelligently think about how to best serve God as he walks through life day by day.

ENGLISH WORD	GREEK WORD AND VERSE	THE WORD MEANS...

Service–NKJV
Not translated–NLT
 	
POSB
REFERENCE
(Rom.12:1)
    Note 2, point 2b
	⇒ NIV #3301 latreia
	⇒ NASB #2999 latreia
	
	Romans 12:1
	    I beseech you therefore, brethren, by the mercies of God, that ye present your bodies a living sacrifice, holy, acceptable unto God, which is your reasonable **service**. [KJV]
	    I urge you therefore, brethren, by the mercies of God, to present your bodies a living and holy sacrifice, acceptable to God, which is your spiritual **service of worship**. [NASB]
	    Therefore, I urge you, brothers, in view of God's mercy, to offer your bodies as living sacrifices, holy and pleasing to God—this is your spiritual **act of worship**. [NIV]
	    I beseech you therefore, brethren, by the mercies of God, that you present your bodies a living sacrifice, holy, acceptable to God, which is your reasonable **service**. [NKJV]
	    And so, dear brothers and sisters, I plead with you to give your bodies to God. Let them be a living and holy sacrifice—the kind he will accept. When you think of what he has done for you, is this too much to ask? [NLT]—NOT TRANSLATED
	    Παρακαλῶ οὖν ὑμᾶς, ἀδελφοί, διὰ τῶν οἰκτιρμῶν τοῦ Θεοῦ, παραστῆσαι τὰ σώματα ὑμῶν θυσίαν ζῶσαν, ἁγίαν εὐάρεστον τῷ Θεῷ, τὴν λογικὴν **λατρείαν** ὑμῶν. [GNS]
	    Παρακαλῶ οὖν ὑμᾶς, ἀδελφοί, διὰ τῶν οἰκτιρμῶν τοῦ θεοῦ παραστῆσαι τὰ σώματα ὑμῶν θυσίαν ζῶσαν ἁγίαν εὐάρεστον τῷ θεῷ, τὴν λογικὴν **λατρεία**, ὑμῶν· [GNT]	

#3473
Service
 	
Ministry–KJV
Service–NASB
Serving–NIV
Ministry–NKJV
Serving–NLT
 	
POSB
REFERENCE
(Rom.12:6-8; esp. v.7)
    Note 2, point 2
	διακονίαν = diakonian
	Pronunciation: [dee-ak-on-ee'-ahn]
	Parsing (part of speech): noun
	    Case—accusative
	    Gender—feminine
	    Number—singular
	    Stem or root—from **διακονία**, ας
	Concordance References:
	⇒ Strong's #1248 diakonia
	⇒ NIV #1355 diakonia
	⇒ NASB #1248 diakonia
	
	Romans 12:7
	    Or **ministry**, let us wait on our ministering: or he that teacheth, on teaching; [KJV]
	    If **service**, in his serving; or he who teaches, in his teaching; [NASB]
	    If it is **serving**, let him serve; if it is teaching, let him teach; [NIV]
	    Or **ministry**, *let us use it* in *our* ministering; he who teaches, in teaching; [NKJV]
	    If your gift is that of **serving** others, serve them well. If you are a teacher, do a good job of teaching. [NLT]
	    εἴτε **διακονίαν**, ἐν τῇ διακονίᾳ· εἴτε ὁ διδάσκων, ἐν τῇ διδασκαλίᾳ· [GNS]
	    εἴτε **διακονίαν** ἐν τῇ διακονίᾳ, εἴτε ὁ διδάσκων ἐν τῇ διδασκαλίᾳ, [GNT]
		Service; ministry, contribution, help, support, mission; perhaps office of deacon or authority (Ro.12:7)
		
		Practical Application
		    The word is often used of a servant or of a person who serves and ministers to others in the most practical ways. Therefore, the meaning would be the very special ability to serve, minister, aid, help and assist others—to assist them in such a way that they are built up and truly helped. It is the most practical of gifts. Most of us know a few people who are always willing and who are unusually gifted to help others when help is needed. All of us can help, and all of us can develop our willingness and ability to help, but there are some believers who are unusually gifted with the very special gift of ministry.

#3474
Service Of
Worship
 	
Service–KJV
Service of worship–
NASB
Act of worship–NIV
Service–NKJV
Not translated–NLT
	λατρείαν = latreian
	Pronunciation: [lat-ri'-ahn]
	Parsing (part of speech): noun
	    Case—accusative
	    Gender—feminine
	    Number—singular
	    Stem or root—from **λατρεία**, ας
	Concordance References:
	⇒ Strong's #2999 latreia
	⇒ NIV #3301 latreia
	⇒ NASB #2999 latreia
		An act of worship; a service of worship; a ministry; a service.
		
		Practical Application
		    The idea is that the believer is to use his mind in dedicating his body to the service of God. He is to study the Scriptures and intelligently think about how to best serve God as he walks through life day by day.

ENGLISH WORD	GREEK WORD AND VERSE	THE WORD MEANS...
POSB REFERENCE (Rom.12:1) Note 2, point 2b	**Romans 12:1** I beseech you therefore, brethren, by the mercies of God, that ye present your bodies a living sacrifice, holy, acceptable unto God, which is your reasonable **service**. [KJV] I urge you therefore, brethren, by the mercies of God, to present your bodies a living and holy sacrifice, acceptable to God, which is your spiritual **service of worship**. [NASB] Therefore, I urge you, brothers, in view of God's mercy, to offer your bodies as living sacrifices, holy and pleasing to God—this is your spiritual **act of worship**. [NIV] I beseech you therefore, brethren, by the mercies of God, that you present your bodies a living sacrifice, holy, acceptable to God, which is your reasonable **service**. [NKJV] And so, dear brothers and sisters, I plead with you to give your bodies to God. Let them be a living and holy sacrifice—the kind he will accept. When you think of what he has done for you, is this too much to ask? [NLT]—NOT TRANSLATED Παρακαλῶ οὖν ὑμᾶς, ἀδελφοί, διὰ τῶν οἰκτιρμῶν τοῦ Θεοῦ, παραστῆσαι τὰ σώματα ὑμῶν θυσίαν ζῶσαν, ἁγίαν εὐάρεστον τῷ Θεῷ, τὴν λογικὴν **λατρείαν** ὑμῶν. [GNS] Παρακαλῶ οὖν ὑμᾶς, ἀδελφοί, διὰ τῶν οἰκτιρμῶν τοῦ θεοῦ παραστῆσαι τὰ σώματα ὑμῶν θυσίαν ζῶσαν ἁγίαν εὐάρεστον τῷ θεῷ, τὴν λογικὴν **λατρείαν** ὑμῶν· [GNT]	

#3475
 Serving
 	
 Ministry–KJV
 Service–NASB
 Serving–NIV
 Ministry–NKJV
 Serving–NLT
 	
 POSB REFERENCE (Rom.12:6-8; esp. v.7) Note 2, point 2
	διακονίαν = *diakonian*
	 Pronunciation: [dee-ak-on-ee'-ahn]
	 Parsing (part of speech): noun
	     Case—accusative
	     Gender—feminine
	     Number—singular
	     Stem or root—from διακονία, ας
	 Concordance References:
	   ⇒ Strong's #1248 diakonia
	   ⇒ NIV #1355 diakonia
	   ⇒ NASB #1248 diakonia
	
	 Romans 12:7
	 Or **ministry**, let us wait on our ministering: or he that teacheth, on teaching; [KJV]
	 If **service**, in his serving; or he who teaches, in his teaching; [NASB]
	 If it is **serving**, let him serve; if it is teaching, let him teach; [NIV]
	 Or **ministry**, *let us use it* in *our* ministering; he who teaches, in teaching; [NKJV]
	 If your gift is that of **serving** others, serve them well. If you are a teacher, do a good job of teaching. [NLT]
	 εἴτε **διακονίαν**, ἐν τῇ διακονίᾳ· εἴτε ὁ διδάσκων, ἐν τῇ διδασκαλίᾳ· [GNS]
	 εἴτε **διακονίαν** ἐν τῇ διακονίᾳ, εἴτε ὁ διδάσκων ἐν τῇ διδασκαλίᾳ, [GNT]
		Service; ministry, contribution, help, support, mission; perhaps office of deacon or authority (Ro.12.7)
		
		 Practical Application
		 The word is often used of a servant or of a person who serves and ministers to others in the most practical ways. Therefore, the meaning would be the very special ability to serve, minister, aid, help and assist others—to assist them in such a way that they are built up and truly helped. It is the most practical of gifts. Most of us know a few people who are always willing and who are unusually gifted to help others when help is needed. All of us can help, and all of us can develop our willingness and ability to help, but there are some believers who are unusually gifted with the very special gift of ministry.

#3476
 Set
 	
 Determinate–KJV
 Predetermined–NASB
 Set–NIV
 Determined–NKJV
 Prearranged–NLT
 	
 POSB REFERENCE (Acts 2:23) *Deeper Study #3,* point 2
	ὡρισμένη = *hōrismenē*
	 Pronunciation: [hor-is'-meh-nay]
	 Parsing (part of speech): verb
	     Mood—participle
	     Tense—perfect
	     Voice—passive
	     Case—dative
	     Gender—feminine
	     Number—singular
	     Stem or root—from ὁρίζω
	 Concordance References:
	   ⇒ Strong's #3724 horizō
	   ⇒ NIV #3988 horizō
	   ⇒ NASB #3724 horizō
	
	 Acts 2:23
	 Him, being delivered by the **determinate** counsel
		Set, predetermined, prearranged, appointed, decreed, ordained, planned, purposed.
		
		 Practical Application
		 The word "set" (*hōrismenē*) means pre-determined, appointed, decreed, ordained, planned, purposed. It is a plan set within bounds, within a certain boundary. It is a purpose that is set, marked out, determined, decreed to happen.

ENGLISH WORD	GREEK WORD AND VERSE	THE WORD MEANS...
	and foreknowledge of God, ye have taken, and by wicked hands have crucified and slain: [KJV] This Man, delivered up by the **predetermined** plan and foreknowledge of God, you nailed to a cross by the hands of godless men and put Him to death. [NASB] This man was handed over to you by God's **set** purpose and foreknowledge; and you, with the help of wicked men, put him to death by nailing him to the cross. [NIV] Him, being delivered by the **determined** purpose and foreknowledge of God, you have taken by lawless hands, have crucified, and put to death; [NKJV] But you followed God's **prearranged** plan. With the help of lawless Gentiles, you nailed him to the cross and murdered him. [NLT] τοῦτον τῇ **ὡρισμένῃ** βουλῇ καὶ προγνώσει τοῦ Θεοῦ ἔκδοτον λαβόντες διὰ χειρῶν ἀνόμων προσπήξαντες ἀνείλατε, [GNS] τοῦτον τῇ **ὡρισμένῃ** βουλῇ καὶ προγνώσει τοῦ θεοῦ ἔκδοτον διὰ χειρὸς ἀνόμων προσπήξαντες ἀνείλατε, [GNT]	

#3477
Set Apart
 	
Separated–KJV
Set apart–NASB
Set apart–NIV
Separated–NKJV
Sent out–NLT
 	
POSB REFERENCE
(Rom.1:1-4; esp. v.1)
Note 3
	ἀφωρισμένος = aphōrismenos
	Pronunciation: [af-or-is'-mehn-os]
	Parsing (part of speech): verb
	    Mood—participle
	    Tense—perfect
	    Voice—passive
	    Case—nominative
	    Gender—masculine
	    Person—1st person
	    Number—singular
	    Stem or root—from **ἀφορίζω**
	Concordance References:
	  ⇒ Strong's #873 aphorizō
	  ⇒ NIV #928 aphorizō
	  ⇒ NASB #873 aphorizō
	
	Romans 1:1
	Paul, a servant of Jesus Christ, called to be an apostle, **separated** unto the gospel of God, [KJV]
	
	Paul, a bond-servant of Christ Jesus, called as an apostle, **set apart** for the gospel of God, [NASB]
	
	Paul, a servant of Christ Jesus, called to be an apostle and **set apart** for the gospel of God— [NIV]
	
	Paul, a bondservant of Jesus Christ, called *to be* an apostle, **separated** to the gospel of od [NKJV]
	
	This letter is from Paul, Jesus Christ's slave, chosen by God to be an apostle and **sent out** to preach his Good News. [NLT]
	
	Παῦλος δοῦλος Ἰησοῦ Χριστοῦ, κλητὸς ἀπόστολος, **ἀφωρισμένος** εἰς εὐαγγέλιον Θεοῦ, [GNS]
	
	Παῦλος δοῦλος Χριστοῦ Ἰησοῦ, κλητὸς ἀπόστολος **ἀφωρισμένος** εἰς εὐαγγέλιον θεοῦ, [GNT]
		To separate; to take away; to exclude (from one's company); to set apart.
		
		Practical Application
		Paul was set apart for the gospel of God. This is the reason God called Paul: that Paul might be set apart (*aphōrismenos*) or marked and set apart to the gospel of God. The word "gospel" simply means the good news of God.
		  ⇒ Paul did not say he was called and set apart to a man-made religion, denomination, or sect; nor was he called primarily to a gospel of social justice and welfare, as important as these calls are.
		  ⇒ Paul said he was set apart to the gospel, the "God's Good News" (cp. 1 Thes. 2:2-13).

#3478
Set Aside
 	
Frustrate–KJV
Nullify–NASB
Set aside–NIV
Set aside–NKJV
Meaningless–NLT
 	
POSB REFERENCE
(Gal.2:19-21; esp. v.21)
Note 5
	ἀθετῶ = athetō
	Pronunciation: [ath-eh-tow]
	Parsing (part of speech): verb
	    Mood—indicative
	    Tense—present
	    Voice—active
	    Person—1st person
	    Number—singular
	    Stem or root—from **ἀθετέω**
	Concordance References:
	  ⇒ Strong's #114 atheteō
	  ⇒ NIV #119 atheteō
	  ⇒ NASB #114 atheteō
	
	Galatians 2:21
	I do not **frustrate** the grace of God: for if righteousness come by the law, then Christ is dead in vain. [KJV]
	
	"I do not **nullify** the grace of God; for if righteousness comes through the Law, then Christ died needlessly." [NASB]
		To set aside, void, invalidate, ignore, make ineffective, and nullify; to frustrate; to reject; to refuse; to be meaningless.
		
		Practical Application
		If a man sets aside the grace of God and seeks righteousness by the law, then Christ died in vain. The person who preaches that a man can be good enough—that he can work enough and keep enough law—to become righteous and acceptable to God...
		  • voids and does away with the love and grace of God.
		  • makes the death of Christ empty and meaningless.
		
		The only way a man can live for God is by trusting the grace and love of God, that is, by

ENGLISH WORD	GREEK WORD AND VERSE	THE WORD MEANS...
	I do not **set aside** the grace of God, for if righteousness could be gained through the law, Christ died for nothing!" [NIV] I do not **set aside** the grace of God; for if righteousness *comes* through the law, then Christ died in vain." [NKJV] I am not one of those who treats the grace of God as **meaningless**. For if we could be saved by keeping the law, then there was no need for Christ to die. [NLT] οὐκ **ἀθετῶ** τὴν χάριν τοῦ Θεοῦ· εἰ γὰρ διὰ νόμου δικαιοσύνη, ἄρα Χριστὸς δωρεὰν ἀπέθανεν. [GNS] οὐκ **ἀθετέω** τὴν χάριν τοῦ Θεοῦ· εἰ γὰρ διὰ νόμου δικαιοσύνη, ἄρα Χριστὸς δωρεὰν ἀπέθανεν. [GNT]	trusting the death of Jesus Christ for His righteousness.

#3479
Set Forth
 	
Set forth–KJV
Exhibited–NASB
Put...on display–NIV
Displayed–NKJV
Put...on...display–NLT
 	
POSB REFERENCE
(1 Cor.4:9-10; esp. v.9)
Note 4
	ἀπέδειξεν = apedeixen
	Pronunciation: [ap-ed'-eek-zehn]
	Parsing (part of speech): verb
	    Mood—indicative
	    Tense—aorist
	    Voice—active
	    Person—3rd person
	    Number—singular
	    Stem or root—from **ἀποδείκνυμι**
	Concordance References:
	⇒ Strong's #584 apodeiknumi
	⇒ NIV #617 apodeiknumi
	⇒ NASB #584 apodeiknumi
	
	1 Cor. 4:9
	For I think that God hath **set forth** us the apostles last, as it were appointed to death: for we are made a spectacle unto the world, and to angels, and to men. [KJV]
	
	For, I think, God has **exhibited** us apostles last of all, as men condemned to death; because we have become a spectacle to the world, both to angels and to men. [NASB]
	
	For it seems to me that God has **put** us apostles **on display** at the end of the procession, like men condemned to die in the arena. We have been made a spectacle to the whole universe, to angels as well as to men. [NIV]
	
	For I think that God has **displayed** us, the apostles, last, as men condemned to death; for we have been made a spectacle to the world, both to angels and to men. [NKJV]
	
	But sometimes I think God has **put** us apostles **on display**, like prisoners of war at the end of a victor's parade, condemned to die. We have become a spectacle to the entire world—to people and angels alike. [NLT]
	
	δοκῶ γάρ, ὅτι ὁ Θεὸς ἡμᾶς τοὺς ἀποστόλους ἐσχάτους **ἀπέδειξεν** ὡς ἐπιθανατίους· ὅτι θέατρον ἐγενήθημεν τῷ κόσμῳ, καὶ ἀγγέλοις καὶ ἀνθρώποις. [GNS]
	
	δοκῶ γάρ, ὁ θεὸς ἡμᾶς τοὺς ἀποστόλους ἐσχάτους **ἀπέδειξεν** ὡς ἐπιθανατίους, ὅτι θέατρον ἐγενήθημεν τῷ κόσμῳ καὶ ἀγγέλοις καὶ ἀνθρώποις. [GNT]
		To put on display; to set forth; to exhibit; to proclaim; to prove.
		
		Practical Application
		The phrase "set forth" (*apedeixen*) means more than to be seen or exhibited. The picture is that of doomed gladiators being taken to the arena. God has put on display the minister as a doomed gladiator to serve the world no matter the cost.

#3480
Set Forth
 	
Set forth–KJV
Displayed publicly–NASB
Presented–NIV
Set forth–NKJV
Sent–NLT
 	
POSB REFERENCE
(Rom.3:25)
Note 4, point 1a
	προέθετο = proetheto
	Pronunciation: [pro-eth'-eh-tow]
	Parsing (part of speech): verb
	    Mood—indicative
	    Tense—aorist
	    Voice—middle
	    Person—3rd person
	    Number—singular
	    Stem or root—from **προτίθεμαι**
	Concordance References:
	⇒ Strong's #4388 protithēmi
	⇒ NIV #4729 protithēmi
	⇒ NASB #4388 protithēmi
	
	Romans 3:25
	Whom God hath **set forth** to be a propitiation through faith in his blood, to declare his righteousness for the remission of sins that are past, through the forbearance of
		To set forth; to send; to display publicly; to present; to plan; to purpose; to intend.
		
		Practical Application
		God is the One who appointed Christ to be "set forth" (*proetheto*) to be the propitiation for man's sins.
		
		God purposed to *set forth* Christ: God determined, resolved, ordained Christ to be the propitiation or the sacrifice for man's sins.
		
		God set Christ "before" (*pro*) the world as the propitiation for the world's sins. The "pro" in the Greek word proetheto (set forth) indicates this fact.
		
		⇒ God set Christ before Himself, purposed that He be the propitiation or the sacrifice for man's sin.

ENGLISH WORD	GREEK WORD AND VERSE	THE WORD MEANS...

	God; [KJV]
	    Whom God **displayed publicly** as a propitiation in His blood through faith. This was to demonstrate His righteousness, because in the forbearance of God He passed over the sins previously committed; [NASB]
	    God **presented** him as a sacrifice of atonement, through faith in his blood. He did this to demonstrate his justice, because in his forbearance he had left the sins committed beforehand unpunished— [NIV]
	    Whom God **set forth** *as* a propitiation by His blood, through faith, to demonstrate His righteousness, because in His forbearance God had passed over the sins that were previously committed, [NKJV]
	    For God **sent** Jesus to take the punishment for our sins and to satisfy God's anger against us. We are made right with God when we believe that Jesus shed his blood, sacrificing his life for us. God was being entirely fair and just when he did not punish those who sinned in former times. [NLT]
	    ὃν **προέθετο** ὁ Θεὸς ἱλαστήριον διὰ τῆς πίστεως, ἐν τῷ αὐτοῦ αἵματι, εἰς ἔνδειξιν τῆς δικαιοσύνης αὐτοῦ διὰ τὴν πάρεσιν τῶν προγεγονότων ἁμαρτημάτων [GNS]
	    ὃν **προέθετο** ὁ θεὸς ἱλαστήριον διὰ [τῆς] πίστεως ἐν τῷ αὐτοῦ αἵματι εἰς ἔνδειξιν τῆς δικαιοσύνης αὐτοῦ διὰ τὴν πάρεσιν τῶν προγεγονότων ἁμαρτημάτων [GNT]
		⇒ God set Christ publicly before the world, showing that He is definitely the propitiation for the world's sins.

#3481
Set Seal Of Ownership On Us
 	
Sealed–KJV
Sealed–NASB
Set...seal of ownership on us–NIV
Sealed–NKJV
Identified us as his own–NLT
 	
POSB REFERENCE
(2 Cor.1:21-22; esp. v.22)
Note 5
	σφραγισάμενος = *sphragisamenos*
	Pronunciation: [sfrag-is'-ah-mehn-os]
	Parsing (part of speech): verb
	  Mood—participle
	  Tense—aorist
	  Voice—middle
	  Case—nominative
	  Gender—masculine
	  Number—singular
	  Stem or root—from σφραγίζω
	Concordance References:
	  ⇒ Strong's #4972 sphragizö
	  ⇒ NIV #5381 sphragizö
	  ⇒ NASB #4972 sphragizö
	
	2 Cor. 1:22
	    Who hath also **sealed** us, and given the earnest of the Spirit in our hearts. [KJV]
	    Who also **sealed** us and gave us the Spirit in our hearts as a pledge. [NASB]
	    Set his **seal of ownership on** us, and put his Spirit in our hearts as a deposit, guaranteeing what is to come. [NIV]
	    Who also has **sealed** us and given us the Spirit in our hearts as a guarantee. [NKJV]
	    And he has **identified us as his own** by placing the Holy Spirit in our hearts as the first installment of everything he will give us. [NLT]
	    ὁ καὶ **σφραγισάμενος** ἡμᾶς, καὶ δοὺς τὸν ἀρραβῶνα τοῦ Πνεύματος ἐν ταῖς καρδίαις ἡμῶν. [GNS]
	    ὁ καὶ **σφραγισάμενος** ἡμᾶς καὶ δοὺς τὸν ἀρραβῶνα τοῦ πνεύματος ἐν ταῖς καρδίαις ἡμῶν. [GNT]
		To set a seal of ownership on; to mark; to stamp; to set apart by a seal; to place a seal upon.
		
		Practical Application
		    God places His seal, His stamp, His mark upon believers. Paul was just as much in Christ and anointed as others. The word "us" refers primarily to Paul. He is comparing himself with the Corinthians, and he is also including those who oppose him. In no uncertain terms, Paul says that the same God who has worked in the Corinthians has also worked in him.

#3482
Sets Against
 	
Resisteth–KJV
Opposed–NASB
Opposes–NIV
Resists–NKJV
Sets...against–NLT
 	
POSB REFERENCE
(1 Pt.5:5)
Note 2, point 3a
	ἀντιτάσσεται = *antitassetai*
	Pronunciation: [an-tee-tahs'-seh-tah-ee]
	Parsing (part of speech): verb
	  Mood—indicative
	  Tense—present
	  Voice—middle
	  Person—3rd person
	  Number—singular
	  Stem or root—from ἀντιτάσσομαι
	Concordance References:
	  ⇒ Strong's #498 antitassomai
	  ⇒ NIV #530 antitassö
	  ⇒ NASB #498 antitassö
		Opposes, resist, sets against; rebels against.
		
		Practical Application
		    Note why we are to subject to one another and to clothe ourselves with humility: because God sets Himself against the proud and shows favor to the humble (cp. Proverbs 3:34).
		    God sets Himself against the proud. He stands against all...
		• who look down upon others
		• who feel superior to others
		• who discriminate against others
		• who are prejudiced

ENGLISH WORD	GREEK WORD AND VERSE	THE WORD MEANS...
	1 Peter 5:5 Likewise, ye younger, submit yourselves unto the elder. Yea, all of you be subject one to another, and be clothed with humility: for God **resisteth** the proud, and giveth grace to the humble. [KJV] You younger men, likewise, be subject to your elders; and all of you, clothe yourselves with humility toward one another, for God is **opposed** to the proud, but gives grace to the humble. [NASB] Young men, in the same way be submissive to those who are older. All of you, clothe yourselves with humility toward one another, because, "God **opposes** the proud but gives grace to the humble." [NIV] Likewise you younger people, submit yourselves to your elders. Yes, all of you be submissive to one another, and be clothed with humility, for "God **resists** the proud, But gives grace to the humble." [NKJV] You younger men, accept the authority of the elders. And all of you, serve each other in humility, for "God **sets** himself **against** the proud, but he shows favor to the humble." [NLT] ὁμοίως, νεώτεροι, ὑποτάγητε πρεσβυτέροις· πάντες δὲ ἀλλήλοις ὑποτασσόμενοι, τὴν ταπεινοφροσύνην ἐγκομβώσασθε· ὅτι ὁ Θεὸς ὑπερηφάνοις **ἀντιτάσσεται**, ταπεινοῖς δὲ δίδωσι χάριν. [GNS] Ὁμοίως, νεώτεροι, ὑποτάγητε πρεσβυτέροις· πάντες δὲ ἀλλήλοις τὴν ταπεινοφροσύνην ἐγκομβώσασθε, ὅτι [Ο] Θεὸς ὑπερηφάνοις **ἀντιτάσσομαι**, ταπεινοῖς δὲ δίδωσιν χάριν. [GNT]	• who are boastful • who are haughty God sets Himself against the proud—all who oppress others—no matter who they are. The phrase "sets against" (*antitassetai*) is a strong word. It is the picture of an army being set and arrayed against the enemy. Marvin Vincent says that "pride calls out God's armies. No wonder, therefore, that it 'goeth before destruction'" (*Word Studies In The New Testament*, Vol.1, p.668). Those who walk upon this earth exalting themselves above others shall be destroyed by God Himself.
#3483 **Sets Its Desire Against** Lusteth–KJV **Sets its desire against–NASB** Desires...contrary to–NIV Lusts–NKJV Loves to do evil–NLT **POSB REFERENCE** (Gal.5:16-18; esp. v.17) Note 1	**ἐπιθυμεῖ κατὰ** = *epithumei kata* Pronunciation: [ep-ee-thoo-mee' kat-ah'] Parsing *epithumei* (part of speech): verb 　　Mood—indicative 　　Tense—present 　　Voice—active 　　Person—3rd person 　　Number—singular 　　Stem or root—from **ἐπιθυμέω** Parsing *kata* (part of speech): preposition 　　Case—genitive 　　Stem or root—from **κατά** Concordance References: ⇒ Strong's #1937 epithumeö + 2596 kata ⇒ NIV #2121 epithumeö [desires] + 2848 kata [contrary to] ⇒ NASB #1937 epithumeö + 2596 kata **Galatians 5:17** For the flesh **lusteth** against the Spirit, and the Spirit against the flesh: and these are contrary the one to the other: so that ye cannot do the things that ye would. [KJV] For the flesh **sets its desire against** the Spirit, and the Spirit against the flesh; for these are in opposition to one another, so that you may not do the things that you please. [NASB] For the sinful nature **desires** what is **contrary to** the Spirit, and the Spirit what is contrary to the sinful nature. They are in conflict with each other, so that you do not do what you want. [NIV] For the flesh **lusts** against the Spirit, and the Spirit against the flesh; and these are contrary to one another, so that you do not do the things that you wish. [NKJV] The old sinful nature **loves to do evil**, which is just opposite from what the Holy Spirit wants. And the Spirit gives us desires that are opposite from what the sinful nature desires. These two forces are constantly fighting each other, and your choices are never free from this conflict. [NLT] ἡ γὰρ σὰρξ **ἐπιθυμεῖ κατὰ** τοῦ Πνεύματος, τὸ δὲ Πνεῦμα κατὰ τῆς σαρκός· ταῦτα δὲ ἀντίκειται ἀλλήλοις, ἵνα μὴ ἃ ἐὰν θέλητε, ταῦτα ποιῆτε. [GNS]	A yearning passion for; a love to do evil; to long for; to desire; to lust for. **Practical Application** The flesh fights for dominance. It lusts against the Spirit, struggles and fights to control the man. The picture is that of a tug of war (A.T. Robertson. *Word Pictures in the New Testament*, Vol.4, p.311). The flesh stands contrary to the Spirit—toe to toe, face to face—and it seeks to control man. Every person has experienced the flesh's... • yearning • pulling • desiring • wanting • grasping • grabbing • craving • hungering • thirsting • longing • taking Every person knows what it is to have his sinful nature lusting after something, to have it yearning and yearning to lay hold of something. The sinful nature is very strong and difficult to control. This is the first reason why a believer's only hope to control the sinful nature is the Spirit of God.

ENGLISH WORD	GREEK WORD AND VERSE	THE WORD MEANS...

ἡ γὰρ σὰρξ **ἐπιθυμεῖ κατὰ.** τοῦ πνεύματος, τὸ δὲ πνεῦμα κατὰ τῆς σαρκός, ταῦτα γὰρ ἀλλήλοις ἀντίκειται, ἵνα μὴ ἃ ἐὰν θέλητε ταῦτα ποιῆτε. [GNT]

#3484
Settle

Settle–KJV
Establish–NASB
Steadfast–NIV
Establish–NKJV
Place you on a firm foundation–NLT

POSB REFERENCE
(1 Pt.5:10)
Note 2, point 4

θεμελιώσει = *themeliösei*
Pronunciation: [them-el-ee-o'-seh-ee]
Parsing (part of speech): verb
    Mood—indicative
    Tense—future
    Voice—active
    Person—3rd person
    Number—singular
    Stem or root—from θεμελιόω
Concordance References:
⇒ Strong's #2311 themelioö
⇒ NIV #2530 themelioö
⇒ NASB #2311 themelioö

1 Peter 5:10
But the God of all grace, who hath called us unto his eternal glory by Christ Jesus, after that ye have suffered a while, make you perfect, stablish, strengthen, **settle** you. [KJV]

And after you have suffered for a little while, the God of all grace, who called you to His eternal glory in Christ, will Himself perfect, confirm, strengthen and **establish** you. [NASB]

And the God of all grace, who called you to his eternal glory in Christ, after you have suffered a little while, will himself restore you and make you strong, firm and **steadfast**. [NIV]

But may the God of all grace, who called us to His eternal glory by Christ Jesus, after you have suffered a while, perfect, **establish**, strengthen, and settle *you.* [NKJV]

In his kindness God called you to his eternal glory by means of Jesus Christ. After you have suffered a little while, he will restore, support, and strengthen you, and he will **place you on a firm foundation**. [NLT]

ὁ δὲ Θεὸς πάσης χάριτος, ὁ καλέσας ὑμᾶς εἰς τὴν αἰώνιον αὐτοῦ δόξαν ἐν Χριστῷ Ἰησοῦ, ὀλίγον παθόντας αὐτὸς καταρτίσει ὑμᾶς, στηρίξει, σθενώσαι, **θεμελιώσαι.** [GNS]

Ὁ δὲ Θεὸς πάσης χάριτος, ὁ καλέσας ὑμᾶς εἰς τὴν αἰώνιον αὐτοῦ δόξαν ἐν Χριστῷ [Ἰησοῦ], ὀλίγον παθόντας αὐτὸς καταρτίσει, στηρίξει, σθενώσει, **θεμελιώσει.** [GNT]

To be steadfast; to settle; to establish; to place on a firm foundation; to secure as in a foundation; to ground with security.

Practical Application
God Himself will *settle us*. God is able to make us secure through all the sufferings of life, no matter what they are. He is able to settle and secure our nerves, thoughts, and fears—all the uneasy and unnerving emotions that disturb us. God can settle us if we will only do one thing: resist the devil and draw near to Him.

#3485
Settle–Settlement

Reckon–KJV
Settle–NASB
Settlement–NIV
Settle–NKJV
Process–NLT

POSB REFERENCE
(Mt.18:23-27; esp. v.24)
Note 2, point 1

συναίρειν = *sunairein*
Pronunciation: [soon-ah'ee-reen]
Parsing (part of speech): verb
    Mood—infinitive
    Tense—present
    Voice—active
    Stem or root—from συναίρω
Concordance References:
⇒ Strong's #4868 sunairô
⇒ NIV #5256 sunairô
⇒ NASB #4868 sunairô

Matthew 18:24
And when he had begun to **reckon**, one was brought unto him, which owed him ten thousand talents. [KJV]

"And when he had begun to **settle** them, there was brought to him one who owed him ten thousand talents. [NASB]

As he began the **settlement**, a man who owed him ten thousand talents was brought to him. [NIV]

And when he had begun to **settle** accounts, one was brought to him who owed him ten thousand talents. [NKJV]

In the **process**, one of his debtors was brought in who owed him millions of dollars. [NLT]

To take account; to make a reckoning; to settle accounts.

Practical Application
The word "settle or settlement" (*sunairein*) is simple, yet very descriptive and full of meaning. God is the King, but He is a very unusual King. He is a King who rules justly as all kings should. But He is more. He is loving, compassionate, and forgiving; and He is even more than these. He is consumed with love and compassion—so much so that He forgives enormous debts, debts so enormous that they are inconceivable.

The King takes account of His servants. He takes account at varying times. An accounting is required at conversion and on those occasions when God leads us to evaluate our lives.

All must give an account (Matthew 18:24). The king began to check the province and the ledgers of his province: receipts and expenditures and the capital improvements. The king had a critical interest in what his servant had received through gifts and what he had used in the ministry.

ENGLISH WORD	GREEK WORD AND VERSE	THE WORD MEANS...
	And after taking some food, he regained his strength. Saul spent **several days** with the disciples in Damascus. [NIV] So when he had received food, he was strengthened. Then Saul spent **some days** with the disciples at Damascus. [NKJV] Afterward he ate some food and was strengthened. Saul stayed with the believers in Damascus for a **few days**. [NLT] καὶ λαβὼν τροφὴν ἐνίσχυσεν. Ἐγένετο δὲ ὁ Σαῦλος μετὰ τῶν ἐν Δαμασκῷ μαθητῶν **ἡμέρας τινάς**. [GNS] καὶ λαβὼν τροφὴν ἐνίσχυσεν. Ἐγένετο δὲ μετὰ τῶν ἐν Δαμασκῷ μαθητῶν **ἡμέρας τινάς** [GNT]	• their witness and service. Saul (or Paul) associated and became identified with the church so that the world might know that he was a believer. He wanted to openly and publicly declare that he was now... • a new creature in Christ Jesus. • a follower of "the Way" which he had opposed and persecuted. • a true disciple of the Lord Jesus.
#3490 **Severe–** **Severity** Severity–KJV Severity–NASB Sternness–NIV Severity–NKJV Severe–NLT **POSB** **REFERENCE** (Rom.11:22) Note 4, point 1	*ἀποτομίαν = apotomian* Pronunciation: [ap-ot-om-ee´-ahn] Parsing (part of speech): noun 　Case—accusative 　Gender—feminine 　Number—singular 　Stem or root—from ἀποτομία, ας Concordance References: ⇒ Strong's #663 apotomia ⇒ NIV #704 apotomia ⇒ NASB #663 apotomia **Romans 11:22** Behold therefore the goodness and **severity** of God: on them which fell, severity; but toward thee, goodness, if thou continue in his goodness: otherwise thou also shalt be cut off. [KJV] Behold then the kindness and **severity** of God; to those who fell, severity, but to you, God's kindness, if you continue in His kindness; otherwise you also will be cut off. [NASB] Consider therefore the kindness and **sternness** of God: sternness to those who fell, but kindness to you, provided that you continue in his kindness. Otherwise, you also will be cut off. [NIV] Therefore consider the goodness and **severity** of God: on those who fell, severity; but toward you, goodness, if you continue in *His* goodness. Otherwise you also will be cut off. [NKJV] Notice how God is both kind and **severe**. He is severe to those who disobeyed, but kind to you as you continue to trust in his kindness. But if you stop trusting, you also will be cut off. [NLT] ἴδε οὖν χρηστότητα καὶ **ἀποτομίαν** Θεοῦ· ἐπὶ μὲν τοὺς πεσόντας, ἀποτομίαν· ἐπὶ δὲ σέ, χρηστότητα, ἐὰν ἐπιμένῃς τῇ χρηστότητι· ἐπεὶ καὶ σὺ ἐκκοπήσῃ. [GNS] ἴδε οὖν χρηστότητα καὶ **ἀποτομίαν** θεοῦ· ἐπὶ μὲν τοὺς πεσόντας ἀποτομία, ἐπὶ δὲ σὲ χρηστότης θεοῦ, ἐὰν ἐπιμένῃς τῇ χρηστότητι, ἐπεὶ καὶ σὺ ἐκκοπήσῃ. [GNT]	Severity, sternness, harshness, hardness, grievousness, strictness. **Practical Application** The severity of God is seen in the spiritual fall of Israel. The Jews had committed the very sins the Gentiles are being warned about in this passage. The Jews... ⇒ had developed an attitude of arrogance and boasting toward other people, refusing to carry the Word of God to them. ⇒ had felt highminded and complacent, feeling safe and secure, thinking themselves to be more acceptable to God than other people. In addition to these gross sins, the Jews had rejected God's prophets down through the centuries until they eventually killed God's very own Son. In one brief word, their sin was unbelief. The vast majority of the Jews never did believe God, not to the point that they loved God supremely. As a result, the judgment and severity of God fell upon them (see POSB *Deeper Study* #2, Judgment—Romans 11:7-10 for more discussion).
#3491 **Sexual** **Immorality** Fornication–KJV Not translated–NASB Not translated–NIV **Sexual immorality–** **NKJV** Not translated–NLT **POSB** **REFERENCE** (Rom.1:29) *Deeper Study* #2	*πορνεία = porneiai* Pronunciation: [por-ni´-ah] (Special Note: KJV & NKJV term only) Parsing (part of speech): noun 　Case—dative 　Gender—feminine 　Number—singular 　Stem or root—from πονηρία, ας Concordance References: ⇒ Strong's #4202 porneiai ⇒ NIV #Not Found In NIV ⇒ NASB #Not Found In NASB **Romans 1:29** Being filled with all unrighteousness, **fornication**, wickedness, covetousness, maliciousness; full of envy, murder, debate, deceit, malignity; whisperers, [KJV] Being filled with all unrighteousness, wickedness, greed, evil; full of envy, murder, strife, deceit, malice;	Fornication, sexual immorality, wickedness. **Practical Application** This is a broad word including all forms and kinds of immoral and sexual acts. It is pre-marital sex, adultery, and abnormal sex—all kinds of sexual vice.

ENGLISH WORD	GREEK WORD AND VERSE	THE WORD MEANS...
	they are gossips, [NASB]– NOT TRANSLATED They have become filled with every kind of wickedness, evil, greed and depravity. They are full of envy, murder, strife, deceit and malice. They are gossips, [NIV]–NOT TRANSLATED Being filled with all unrighteousness, **sexual immorality**, wickedness, covetousness, maliciousness; full of envy, murder, strife, deceit, evil-mindedness; *they are* whisperers, [NKJV] Their lives became full of every kind of wickedness, sin, greed, hate, envy, murder, fighting, deception, malicious behavior, and gossip. [NLT] NOT TRANSLATED πεπληρωμένους πάσῃ ἀδικίᾳ **πορνείᾳ**, πονηρίᾳ πλεονεξίᾳ κακίᾳ· μεστοὺς φθόνου, φόνου, ἔριδος, δόλου, κακοηθείας·[GNS] πεπληρωμένους πάσῃ ἀδικίᾳ πονηρίᾳ πλεονεξίᾳ κακίᾳ, μεστοὺς φθόνου φόνου ἔριδος δόλου κακοηθείας, ψιθυριστάς [GNT]	

#3492
Sexual Immorality
 	
Chambering–KJV
Sexual promiscuity–NASB
Sexual immorality–NIV
Lewdness–NKJV
Adultery–NLT
 	
POSB REFERENCE
(Rom.13:13)
Note 4, point 3
	κοίταις = *koitais*
	Pronunciation: [koy'-tays]
	Parsing (part of speech): noun
	  Case—dative
	  Gender—feminine
	  Number—plural
	  Stem or root—from κοίτη, ης
	Concordance References:
	  ⇒ Strong's #2845 koitë
	  ⇒ NIV #3130 koitë
	  ⇒ NASB #2845 koitë
	
	Romans 13:13
	Let us walk honestly, as in the day; not in rioting and drunkenness, not in **chambering** and wantonness, not in strife and envying. [KJV]
	Let us behave properly as in the day, not in carousing and drunkenness, not in **sexual promiscuity** and sensuality, not in strife and jealousy. [NASB]
	Let us behave decently, as in the daytime, not in orgies and drunkenness, not in **sexual immorality** and debauchery, not in dissension and jealousy. [NIV]
	Let us walk properly, as in the day, not in revelry and drunkenness, not in **lewdness** and lust, not in strife and envy. [NKJV]
	We should be decent and true in everything we do, so that everyone can approve of our behavior. Don't participate in wild parties and getting drunk, or in **adultery** and immoral living, or in fighting and jealousy. [NLT]
	ὡς ἐν ἡμέρᾳ, εὐσχημόνως περιπατήσωμεν, μὴ κώμοις καὶ μέθαις, μὴ **κοίταις** καὶ ἀσελγείαις, μὴ ἔριδι καὶ ζήλῳ. [GNS]
	ὡς ἐν ἡμέρᾳ εὐσχημόνως περιπατήσωμεν, μὴ κώμοις καὶ μέθαις, μὴ **κοίταις** καὶ ἀσελγείαις, μὴ ἔριδι καὶ ζήλῳ, [GNT]
		Sexual immorality; sexual promiscuity; sexual impurity; adultery, lewdness, fornication (premarital sex).
		
		Practical Application
		The charge is straightforward. The believer is not to participate...
		• in wild parties
		• in getting drunk
		• in adultery
		• in immoral living
		• in jealousy

#3493
Sexual Immorality
 	
Fornication–KJV
Immorality–NASB
Sexual immorality–NIV
Fornication–NKJV
Sexual immorality–NLT
 	
POSB REFERENCE
(Gal.5:19-21; esp. v.19)
Note 2
	πορνεία = *porneia*
	Pronunciation: [por-ni'-ah]
	Parsing (part of speech): noun
	  Case—nominative
	  Gender—feminine
	  Number—singular
	  Stem or root—from πορνεία, ας
	Concordance References:
	  ⇒ Strong's #4202 porneia
	  ⇒ NIV #4518 porneia
	  ⇒ NASB #4202 porneia
	
	Galatians 5:19
	Now the works of the flesh are manifest, which are these; Adultery, **fornication**, uncleanness, lasciviousness, [KJV]
	Now the deeds of the flesh are evident, which are: **immorality**, impurity, sensuality, [NASB]
		Sexual immorality, fornication, adulteries.
		
		Practical Application
		This a broad word including all forms of immoral and sexual acts. It is premarital sex and adultery; it is abnormal sex, all kinds of sexual vice.

ENGLISH WORD	GREEK WORD AND VERSE	THE WORD MEANS...
See also POSB REF: (Mk.7:21) *Deeper Study #5* (2 Cor.12:19-21; esp. v.21) Note 3, point 2 (Col.3:5-7; esp. v.5) Note 1 (Rev.9:20-21; esp.v.21) Note 4, point 2d	The acts of the sinful nature are obvious: **sexual immorality**, impurity and debauchery; [NIV] Now the works of the flesh are evident, which are: adultery, **fornication**, uncleanness, lewdness, [NKJV] When you follow the desires of your sinful nature, your lives will produce these evil results: **sexual immorality**, impure thoughts, eagerness for lustful pleasure, [NLT] φανερὰ δέ ἐστι τὰ ἔργα τῆς σαρκός, ἅτινά ἐστι μοιχεία, **πορνεία**, ἀκαθαρσία, ἀσέλγεια, [GNS] φανερὰ δέ ἐστιν τὰ ἔργα τῆς σαρκός, ἅτινά ἐστιν **πορνεία**, ἀκαθαρσία, ἀσέλγεια, [GNT]	

#3494
Sexual Impurity
 	
Uncleanness–KJV
Impurity–NASB
Sexual impurity–NIV
Uncleanness–NKJV
Shameful things–NLT
 	
**POSB
REFERENCE**
(Rom.1:24-25; esp.
v.24)
Note 2
	ἀκαθαρσίαν = akatharsian
	Pronunciation: [ak-ath-ar-see'-ahn]
	Parsing (part of speech): noun
	   Case—accusative
	   Gender—feminine
	   Number—singular
	   Stem or root—from ἀκαθαρσία, ας
	Concordance References:
	⇒ Strong's #167 akatharsia
	⇒ NIV #174 akatharsia
	⇒ NASB #167 akatharsia
	
	Romans 1:24
	Wherefore God also gave them up to **uncleanness** through the lusts of their own hearts, to dishonour their own bodies between themselves: [KJV]
	Therefore God gave them over in the lusts of their hearts to **impurity**, that their bodies might be dishonored among them. [NASB]
	Therefore God gave them over in the sinful desires of their hearts to **sexual impurity** for the degrading of their bodies with one another. [NIV]
	Therefore God also gave them up to **uncleanness**, in the lusts of their hearts, to dishonor their bodies among themselves, [NKJV]
	So God let them go ahead and do whatever **shameful things** their hearts desired. As a result, they did vile and degrading things with each other's bodies. [NLT]
	Διὸ καὶ παρέδωκεν αὐτοὺς ὁ Θεὸς ἐν ταῖς ἐπιθυμίαις τῶν καρδιῶν αὐτῶν εἰς **ἀκαθαρσίαν** τοῦ ἀτιμάζεσθαι τὰ σώματα αὐτῶν ἐν αὐτοῖς· [GNS]
	Διὸ παρέδωκεν αὐτοὺς ὁ θεὸς ἐν ταῖς ἐπιθυμίαις τῶν καρδιῶν αὐτῶν εἰς **ἀκαθαρσίαν** τοῦ ἀτιμάζεσθαι τὰ σώματα αὐτῶν ἐν αὐτοῖς· [GNT]
		Impurity, immorality; impure motive; rottenness, filthiness, defilement, dirt, pollution, contamination, infection.
		
		Practical Application
		God—the only living and true God—shows wrath by giving men up to sexual impurity. When men turn from God—abandon God to live sexually impure and immoral lives—God leaves men. He abandons them to their choice. God lets men wallow around in their filthiness. Men are judged and condemned to uncleanness.

#3495
Sexual Intimacy
 	
Due–KJV
His duty–NASB
His marital duty–NIV
Render–NKJV
Sexual intimacy–NLT
 	
**POSB
REFERENCE**
(1 Cor.7:3)
Note 3
	τὴν ὀφειλὴν = tēn opheilēn
	Pronunciation: [tayn of-i'-layn]
	Parsing *opheilēn* (part of speech): noun
	   Case—accusative
	   Gender—feminine
	   Number—singular
	   Stem or root—from ὀφειλή, ῆς
	Concordance References:
	⇒ Strong's #3588 ho + 3784 opheilo
	⇒ NIV #3836 ho [his] + 4051 opheilē [marital duty]
	⇒ NASB #3588 ho + 3782 opheilē
	
	1 Cor. 7:3
	Let the husband render unto the wife **due** benevolence: and likewise also the wife unto the husband. [KJV]
	Let the husband fulfill **his duty** to his wife, and likewise also the wife to her husband. [NASB]
	The husband should fulfill **his marital duty** to his wife, and likewise the wife to her husband. [NIV]
	Let the husband **render** to his wife the affection due her, and likewise also the wife to her husband. [NKJV]
	The husband should not deprive his wife of **sexual intimacy**, which is her right as a married woman, nor should the wife deprive her husband. [NLT]
		Marital duty; the debt; to owe; to render what is due.
		
		Practical Application
		The husband and wife owe some things to the other.
		⇒ Both have rights; each can expect to receive some things from the other.
		⇒ Both have responsibilities; each can expect to pay to the other exactly what is due.

ENGLISH WORD	GREEK WORD AND VERSE	THE WORD MEANS...
	τῇ γυναικὶ ὁ ἀνὴρ **τὴν ὀφειλομένην** εὔνοιαν ἀποδιδότω· ὁμοίως δὲ καὶ ἡ γυνὴ τῷ ἀνδρί. [GNS] τῇ γυναικὶ ὁ ἀνὴρ **τὴν ὀφειλὴν** ἀποδιδότω, ὁμοίως δὲ καὶ ἡ γυνὴ τῷ ἀνδρί. [GNT]	

#3496
Sexual Promiscuity
 	
Chambering–KJV
Sexual promiscu-ity–NASB
Sexual immorality–NIV
Lewdness–NKJV
Adultery–NLT
 	
POSB REFERENCE
(Rom.13:13)
Note 4, point 3
	κοίταις = *koitais*
	Pronunciation: [koy'-tays]
	Parsing (part of speech): noun
	    Case—dative
	    Gender—feminine
	    Number—plural
	    Stem or root—from κοίτη ης
	Concordance References:
	  ⇒ Strong's #2845 koitë
	  ⇒ NIV #3130 koitë
	  ⇒ NASB #2845 koitë
	
	Romans 13:13
	Let us walk honestly, as in the day; not in rioting and drunkenness, not in **chambering** and wantonness, not in strife and envying. [KJV]
	Let us behave properly as in the day, not in carousing and drunkenness, not in **sexual promiscuity** and sensuality, not in strife and jealousy. [NASB]
	Let us behave decently, as in the daytime, not in orgies and drunkenness, not in **sexual immorality** and debauchery, not in dissension and jealousy. [NIV]
	Let us walk properly, as in the day, not in revelry and drunkenness, not in **lewdness** and lust, not in strife and envy. [NKJV]
	We should be decent and true in everything we do, so that everyone can approve of our behavior. Don't participate in wild parties and getting drunk, or in **adultery** and immoral living, or in fighting and jealousy. [NLT]
	ὡς ἐν ἡμέρᾳ, εὐσχημόνως περιπατήσωμεν, μὴ κώμοις καὶ μέθαις, μὴ **κοίταις** καὶ ἀσελγείαις, μὴ ἔριδι καὶ ζήλῳ. [GNS]
	ὡς ἐν ἡμέρᾳ εὐσχημόνως περιπατήσωμεν, μὴ κώμοις καὶ μέθαις, μὴ **κοίταις** καὶ ἀσελγείαις, μὴ ἔριδι καὶ ζήλῳ, [GNT]
		Sexual immorality; sexual promiscuity; sexual impurity; adultery, lewdness, fornication (premarital sex).
		
		Practical Application
		The charge is straightforward. The believer is not to participate...
		• in wild parties
		• in getting drunk
		• in adultery
		• in immoral living
		• in jealousy

#3497
Sexually Immoral
 	
Fornicator–KJV
Immoral–NASB
Sexually immoral–NIV
Fornicator–NKJV
Immoral–NLT
 	
POSB REFERENCE
(Heb.12:15-17; esp. v.16)
Note 2, point 3
 	
See also POSB REF:
(1 Cor.6:9)
Note 2
	πόρνος = *pornos*
	Pronunciation: [por'-nos]
	Parsing (part of speech): noun
	    Case—nominative
	    Gender—masculine
	    Number—singular
	    Stem or root—from πόρνος, ου
	Concordance References:
	  ⇒ Strong's #4205 pornos
	  ⇒ NIV #4521 pornos
	  ⇒ NASB #4205 pornos
	
	Hebrews 12:16
	Lest there be any **fornicator**, or profane person, as Esau, who for one morsel of meat sold his birthright. [KJV]
	That there be no **immoral** or godless person like Esau, who sold his own birthright for a single meal. [NASB]
	See that no one is **sexually immoral**, or is godless like Esau, who for a single meal sold his inheritance rights as the oldest son. [NIV]
	Lest there *be* any **fornicator** or profane person like Esau, who for one morsel of food sold his birthright. [NKJV]
	Make sure that no one is **immoral** or godless like Esau. He traded his birthright as the oldest son for a single meal. [NLT]
	μή τις **πόρνος** η βέβηλος, ὡς Ἠσαῦ, ὃς ἀντὶ βρώσεως μιᾶς ἀπέδετο τὰ πρωτοτόκια ἀτοῦ. [GNS]
	μή τις **πόρνος** η βέβηλος ὡς Ἠσαῦ, ὃς ἀντὶ βρώσεως μιᾶς ἀπέδετο τὰ πρωτοτόκια ἑαυτοῦ. [GNT]
		To be sexually immoral; to be a fornicator; to be an adulterer. The word is a broad word including all forms of immoral and sexual acts. It is premarital sex and adultery; it is homosexuality and abnormal sex; it is all kinds of sexual vice, whether married or unmarried.
		
		Practical Application
		Immorality is not only committed by the act. A person is guilty of immorality when he looks in order to lust. Looking at and lusting after the opposite sex—whether in person, in magazines, in books, on beaches, or anywhere else—is committing fornication. Imagining and lusting within the mind is the very same as committing the act in the eyes of God.

ENGLISH WORD	GREEK WORD AND VERSE	THE WORD MEANS...

#3498
Sexually Immoral People
 	
Fornicators–KJV
Immoral people–NASB
Sexually immoral people–NIV
Sexually immoral people–NKJV
People who indulge in sexual sin–NLT
 	
POSB REFERENCE
(1 Cor.5:9-10; esp. v.9)
Note 4
	πόρνοις = pornois
	Pronunciation: [por'-noys]
	Parsing (part of speech): noun
	    Case—dative
	    Gender—masculine
	    Number—plural
	    Stem or root—from πόρνος ου
	Concordance References:
	  ⇒ Strong's #4205 pornos
	  ⇒ NIV #4521 pornos
	  ⇒ NASB #4205 pornos
	
	1 Cor. 5:9
	I wrote unto you in an epistle not to company with **fornicators**: [KJV]
	I wrote you in my letter not to associate with **immoral people**; [NASB]
	I have written you in my letter not to associate with **sexually immoral people**— [NIV]
	I wrote to you in my epistle not to keep company with **sexually immoral people**. [NKJV]
	When I wrote to you before, I told you not to associate with **people who indulge in sexual sin**. [NLT]
	Ἔγραψα ὑμῖν ἐν τῇ ἐπιστολῇ μὴ συναναμίγνυσθαι **πόρνοις**· [GNS]
	Ἔγραψα ὑμῖν ἐν τῇ ἐπιστολῇ μὴ συναναμίγνυσθαι **πόρνοις**, [GNT]
		Sexually immoral people, fornicators, adulterers; people who indulge in sexual sin.
		
		Practical Application
		The phrase "sexually immoral people (pornois) means all kinds of immoral sexual acts. It includes adultery, premarital sex, homosexuality, and all forms of sexual deviation. Those who practice immorality are not to be part of the fellowship of the church. Believers are not to keep close fellowship with them.

#3499
Shadow
 	
Shadow–KJV
Shadow–NASB
Shadow–NIV
Shadow–NKJV
Shadow–NLT
 	
POSB REFERENCE
(Heb.10:1-4, esp. v.1)
Note 1, point 1
	Σκιὰν = Skian
	Pronunciation: [skee'-ahn]
	Parsing (part of speech): noun
	    Case—accusative
	    Gender—feminine
	    Number—singular
	    Stem or root—from σκιά, ᾶς
	Concordance References:
	  ⇒ Strong's #4639 skia
	  ⇒ NIV #5014 skia
	  ⇒ NASB #4639 skia
	
	Hebrews 10:1
	For the law having a **shadow** of good things to come, and not the very image of the things, can never with those sacrifices which they offered year by year continually make the comers thereunto perfect. [KJV]
	For the Law, since it has only a **shadow** of the good things to come and not the very form of things, can never by the same sacrifices year by year, which they offer continually, make perfect those who draw near. [NASB]
	The law is only a **shadow** of the good things that are coming—not the realities themselves. For this reason it can never, by the same sacrifices repeated endlessly year after year, make perfect those who draw near to worship. [NIV]
	For the law, having a **shadow** of the good things to come, *and* not the very image of the things, can never with these same sacrifices, which they offer continually year by year, make those who approach perfect. [NKJV]
	The old system in the law of Moses was only a **shadow** of the things to come, not the reality of the good things Christ has done for us. The sacrifices under the old system were repeated again and again, year after year, but they were never able to provide perfect cleansing for those who came to worship. [NLT]
	Σκιὰν γὰρ ἔχων ὁ νόμος τῶν μελλόντων ἀγαθῶν, οὐκ αὐτὴν τὴν εἰκόνα τῶν πραγμάτων, κατ' ἐνιαυτὸν ταῖς αὐταῖς θυσίαις ἃς προσφέρουσιν εἰς τὸ διηνεκὲς, οὐδέποτε δύναται τοὺς προσερχομένους τελειῶσαι. [GNS]
	Σκιὰν, γὰρ ἔχων ὁ νόμος τῶν μελλόντων ἀγαθῶν, οὐκ αὐτὴν τὴν εἰκόνα τῶν πραγμάτων, κατ' ἐνιαυτὸν ταῖς αὐταῖς θυσίαις ἃς προσφέρουσιν εἰς τὸ διηνεκὲς οὐδέποτε δύναται τοὺς προσερχομένους τελειῶσαι· [GNT]
		Shadow, symbol, outline, hint, foreshadowing.
		
		Practical Application
		The old covenant, the law, was only a shadow of good things to come (Hebrews 10:1). It was the law of the Old Testament that spelled out that animal sacrifices were to be offered for the sins of men. But note: the law was only a *shadow* of good things. The law was not the embodiment of the perfection that was to come. It was only a "shadow" (*Skian*). The word means a dim outline, a reflection of the perfection that was to come. The word even has the idea of foreshadowing, of pointing forward. That is, a *shadow* means that there is reality behind the shadow. When we see a shadow, there is something real someplace that is reflecting the shadow (cp. the shadow of a tree).
		
		The point is this: the shadow is not the real thing; it is only an imperfect reflection of the real thing. This was the law of the Old Testament. It and its sacrifices for sin were only a shadow of better things. The law and its sacrifices did not possess the perfection or power necessary to forgive sins. But they did reflect and point to the perfection and power that were to come in the Lord Jesus Christ.

#3500 **Shame**	κατ αισχύνῃ = kataischunē Pronunciation: [kat-ahee-skhoo'-nay] Parsing (part of speech): verb Mood—subjunctive	To shame; to confound; to humiliate; to disgrace; to disappoint; to embarrass.

ENGLISH WORD	GREEK WORD AND VERSE	THE WORD MEANS...
Confound–KJV **Shame–NASB** **Shame–NIV** **Shame–NKJV** **Shame–NLT** **POSB REFERENCE** (1 Cor.1:27-28; esp. v.27) Note 2, point 1	Tense—present Voice—active Person—3rd person Number—singular Stem or root—from καταισχύνω Concordance References: ⇒ Strong's #2617 kataischunö ⇒ NIV #2875 kataischunö ⇒ NASB #2617 kataischunö **1 Cor. 1:27** But God hath chosen the foolish things of the world to **confound** the wise; and God hath chosen the weak things of the world to confound the things which are mighty; [KJV] But God has chosen the foolish things of the world to shame the wise, and God has chosen the weak things of the world to **shame** the things which are strong, [NASB] But God chose the foolish things of the world to shame the wise; God chose the weak things of the world to **shame** the strong. [NIV] But God has chosen the foolish things of the world to put to shame the wise, and God has chosen the weak things of the world to put to **shame** the things which are mighty; [NKJV] Instead, God deliberately chose things the world considers foolish in order to **shame** those who think they are wise. And he chose those who are powerless to shame those who are powerful. [NLT] ἀλλὰ τὰ μωρὰ τοῦ κόσμου ἐξελέξατο ὁ Θεός, ἵνα τοὺς σοφούς, **καταισχύνη**· καὶ τὰ ἀσθενῆ τοῦ κόσμου ἐξελέξατο ὁ Θεός, ἵνα καταισχύνη τὰ ἰσχυρά· [GNS] ἀλλὰ τὰ μωρὰ τοῦ κόσμου ἐξελέξατο ὁ θεός, ἵνα **καταισχύνη** τοὺς σοφούς, καὶ τὰ ἀσθενῆ τοῦ κόσμου ἐξελέξατο ὁ θεός, ἵνα καταισχύνη τὰ ἰσχυρά, [GNT]	**Practical Application** The wise feel self-sufficient in their education, knowledge, and wisdom. They feel little if any need for God and often question if there is a living and true God who is sovereign. Common sense and logic tell us that such an attitude of arrogance could never be acceptable to God. Not because He denies men the right to ask and think through legitimate questions, but because most of the wise of this world are not sincere enough to genuinely study the truth of God which has been revealed in Christ and in the Holy Scriptures. And, too often, the few who might seek the truth study secondary sources (books about the Bible) instead of studying the primary source, the Bible itself. Too many seek for God through what men say instead of letting God speak for Himself. It is because of such pride, arrogance, and close-mindedness that God chooses few of the wise in this world. In fact, God does exactly what most men would do: He chooses those who humble themselves before Him, confessing Him to be God and asking Him to save them. The result, of course, is that the wise of this world are shamed, and their shame will become ever so visible and embarrassing when judgment comes.
#3501 **Shame** Ashamed–KJV **Shame–NASB** Unashamed–NIV Ashamed–NKJV **Shame–NLT** **POSB REFERENCE** (1 Jn.2:28) Note 2	**μὴ αἰσχυνθῶμεν = mē aischunthōmen** Pronunciation: [may ahee-skhoo'-tho-mehn] Parsing (part of speech): verb Mood—subjunctive Tense—aorist Voice—passive deponent Person—1st person Number—plural Stem or root—from αἰσχύνομαι Concordance References: ⇒ Strong's #153 + 3361 aischunomai mē ⇒ NIV #159 + 3590 aischunomai mē [unashamed] ⇒ NASB #153 + 3361 aischunomai mē **1 John 2:28** And now, little children, abide in him; that, when he shall appear, we may have confidence, and not be **ashamed** before him at his coming. [KJV] And now, little children, abide in Him, so that when He appears, we may have confidence and not shrink away from Him in **shame** at His coming. [NASB] And now, dear children, continue in him, so that when he appears we may be confident and **unashamed** before him at his coming. [NIV] And now, little children, abide in Him, that when He appears, we may have confidence and not be **ashamed** before Him at His coming. [NKJV] And now, dear children, continue to live in fellowship with Christ so that when he returns, you will be full of courage and not shrink back from him in **shame**. [NLT] καὶ νῦν, τεκνία, μένετε ἐν αὐτῷ· ἵνα ὅταν φανερωθῇ ἔχωμεν παρρησίαν, καὶ **μὴ αἰσχυνθῶμεν** ἀπ' αὐτοῦ, ἐν τῇ παρουσίᾳ αὐτοῦ. [GNS] Καὶ νῦν, τεκνία, μένετε ἐν αὐτῷ, ἵνα ἐὰν φανερωθῇ σχῶμεν παρρησίαν καὶ **μὴ αἰσχυνθῶμεν** ἀπ' αὐτοῦ ἐν τῇ παρουσίᾳ αὐτοῦ. [GNT]	Ashamed, shame. It means not to shrink back; to sense guilt and disgrace; to feel embarrassment. **Practical Application** If we do not abide in Christ, we will be ashamed when Jesus Christ returns to earth. Note a fact that is so often ignored by believers, a fact that is seldom if ever thought about. There will be shame, disgrace, and embarrassment when Christ returns. Some believers will shrink back from Christ. The picture of nothing but joy and rejoicing when Christ returns is not a true picture. There is going to be judgment: the judgment of every man's works no matter what the works are, and there will be the judgement of sinners no matter who they are, all unbelievers. There will be joy and rejoicing for some believers, for those who have been abiding in Christ. But there will be shame, guilt, disgrace, and embarrassment—a shrinking back—for those who have been walking unfaithfully.
#3502 **Shame**	**αἰσχύνης = aischunēs** Pronunciation: [ahee-skhoo'-nays] Parsing (part of speech): noun Case—genitive	Shame, shameful, disgrace, humiliate; scandal.

ENGLISH WORD	GREEK WORD AND VERSE	THE WORD MEANS...
	Col. 3:5 Mortify therefore your members which are upon the earth; fornication, uncleanness, inordinate affection, **evil concupiscence**, and covetousness, which is idolatry: [KJV] Therefore consider the members of your earthly body as dead to immorality, impurity, passion, **evil desire**, and greed, which amounts to idolatry. [NASB] Put to death, therefore, whatever belongs to your earthly nature: sexual immorality, impurity, lust, **evil desires** and greed, which is idolatry. [NIV] Therefore put to death your members which are on the earth: fornication, uncleanness, passion, **evil desire**, and covetousness, which is idolatry. [NKJV] So put to death the sinful, earthly things lurking within you. Have nothing to do with sexual sin, impurity, lust, and **shameful desires**. Don't be greedy for the good things of this life, for that is idolatry. [NLT] Νεκρώσατε οὖν τὰ μέλη ὑμῶν τὰ ἐπὶ τῆς γῆς, πορνείαν, ἀκαθαρσίαν, πάθος, **ἐπιθυμίαν κακήν**, καὶ τὴν πλεονεξίαν, ἥτις ἐστὶν εἰδωλολατρεία, [GNS] Νεκρώσατε οὖν τὰ μέλη τὰ ἐπὶ τῆς γῆς, πορνείαν ἀκαθαρσίαν πάθος **ἐπιθυμίαν κακήν**, καὶ τὴν πλεονεξίαν, ἥτις ἐστὶν εἰδωλολατρία, [GNT]	

#3506
Shameful Lusts
 	
Vile affections–KJV
Degrading passions–NASB
Shameful lusts–NIV
Vile passions–NKJV
Shameful desires–NLT
 	
POSB REFERENCE
(Rom.1:26-27; esp. v.26)
Note 3, point 1
	πάθη ἀτιμίας = *pathë atimias*
	Pronunciation: [path'-ay hat-ee-mee'-ahs]
	Parsing *pathë* (part of speech): noun
	    Case—accusative
	    Gender—neuter
	    Number—plural
	    Stem or root—from πάθος, ους
	Parsing *atimias* (part of speech): noun
	    Case—genitive
	    Gender—feminine
	    Number—singular
	    Stem or root—from ἀτιμία, ας
	Concordance References:
	⇒ Strong's #3806 pathos + 819 atimia
	⇒ NIV #4079 pathos [lusts] + 871 atimia [shameful]
	⇒ NASB #3806 pathos + 819 atimia
	
	Romans 1:26
	For this cause God gave them up unto **vile affections**: for even their women did change the natural use into that which is against nature: [KJV]
	For this reason God gave them over to **degrading passions**; for their women exchanged the natural function for that which is unnatural, [NASB]
	Because of this, God gave them over to **shameful lusts**. Even their women exchanged natural relations for unnatural ones. [NIV]
	For this reason God gave them up to **vile passions**. For even their women exchanged the natural use for what is against nature. [NKJV]
	That is why God abandoned them to their **shameful desires**. Even the women turned against the natural way to have sex and instead indulged in sex with each other. [NLT]
	Διὰ τοῦτο παρέδωκεν αὐτοὺς ὁ Θεὸς εἰς **πάθη ἀτιμίας**· αἵ τε γὰρ θήλειαι αὐτῶν μετήλλαξαν τὴν φυσικὴν χρῆσιν εἰς τὴν παρὰ φύσιν· [GNS]
	διὰ τοῦτο παρέδωκεν αὐτοὺς ὁ Θεὸς εἰς **πάθη ἀτιμίας**, αἵ τε γὰρ θήλειαι αὐτῶν μετήλλαξαν τὴν φυσικὴν χρῆσιν εἰς τὴν παρὰ φύσιν, [GNT]
		Shameful lusts, vile affections, degrading passions, shameful desires. It means to be dishonored, disgraced, shamed, and degraded. It means passions that cannot be controlled or governed, that run loose and wild, no matter how much a person tries to control them.
		
		Practical Application
		The reason God gives men up to shameful lusts (*pathë atimias*) is because of their unnatural passion. Men lust and lust, craving the illegitimate and unlawful. They burn in their lust one for another. And note what Scripture is talking about: unnatural affection, that is, homosexuality.
		⇒ Women burn and lust and exchange the "natural relations for unnatural ones." [NIV] And note, it is unnatural.
		⇒ Men "were inflamed with lust for one another. Men committed indecent acts with other men." (Rom.1:27) [NIV]

#3507
Shameful Things
	ἀκαθαρσίαν = *akatharsian*
	Pronunciation: [ak-ath-ar-see'-ahn]
	Parsing (part of speech): noun
	    Case—accusative
	    Gender—feminine
	    Number—singular
		Impurity, immorality; impure motive; rottenness, filthiness, defilement, dirt, pollution, contamination, infection.

ENGLISH WORD	GREEK WORD AND VERSE	THE WORD MEANS...
Uncleanness–KJV Impurity–NASB Sexual impurity–NIV Uncleanness–NKJV **Shameful things– NLT** **POSB REFERENCE** (Rom.1:24-25; esp. v.24) Note 2	Stem or root—from ἀκαθαρσία, ας Concordance References: ⇒ Strong's #167 akatharsia ⇒ NIV #174 akatharsia ⇒ NASB #167 akatharsia **Romans 1:24** Wherefore God also gave them up to **uncleanness** through the lusts of their own hearts, to dishonour their own bodies between themselves: [KJV] Therefore God gave them over in the lusts of their hearts to **impurity**, that their bodies might be dishonored among them. [NASB] Therefore God gave them over in the sinful desires of their hearts to **sexual impurity** for the degrading of their bodies with one another. [NIV] Therefore God also gave them up to **uncleanness**, in the lusts of their hearts, to dishonor their bodies among themselves, [NKJV] So God let them go ahead and do whatever **shameful things** their hearts desired. As a result, they did vile and degrading things with each other's bodies. [NLT] Διὸ καὶ παρέδωκεν αὐτοὺς ὁ Θεὸς ἐν ταῖς ἐπιθυμίαις τῶν καρδιῶν αὐτῶν εἰς **ἀκαθαρσίαν** τοῦ ἀτιμάζεσθαι τὰ σώματα αὐτῶν ἐν αὐτοῖς· [GNS] Διὸ παρέδωκεν αὐτοὺς ὁ θεὸς ἐν ταῖς ἐπιθυμίαις τῶν καρδιῶν αὐτῶν εἰς **ἀκαθαρσίαν** τοῦ ἀτιμάζεσθαι τὰ σώματα αὐτῶν ἐν αὐτοῖς· [GNT]	**Practical Application** God—the only living and true God—shows wrath by giving men up to shameful things. When men turn from God—abandon God to live shameful and immoral lives—God leaves men. He abandons them to their choice. God lets men wallow around in their filthiness. Men are judged and condemned to shameful things.

**#3508
Share**
 	
Obtained–KJV
Received–NASB
Received–NIV
Obtained–NKJV
Share–NLT
 	
**POSB
REFERENCE**
(2 Pt.1:1)
Note 2, point 2
	λαχοῦσιν = lachousin
	Pronunciation: [la-khoo'-sin]
	Parsing (part of speech): verb
	    Mood—participle
	    Tense—aorist
	    Voice—active
	    Case—dative
	    Gender—masculine
	    Person—2nd person
	    Number—plural
	    Stem or root—from λαγχάνω
	Concordance References:
	⇒ Strong's #2975 lagchanö
	⇒ NIV #3275 lagchanö
	⇒ NASB #2975 lagchanö
	
	2 Peter 1:1
	Simon Peter, a servant and an apostle of Jesus Christ, to them that have **obtained** like precious faith with us through the righteousness of God and our Saviour Jesus Christ: [KJV]
	Simon Peter, a bond-servant and apostle of Jesus Christ, to those who have **received** a faith of the same kind as ours, by the righteousness of our God and Savior, Jesus Christ: [NASB]
	Simon Peter, a servant and apostle of Jesus Christ, To those who through the righteousness of our God and Savior Jesus Christ have **received** a faith as precious as ours: [NIV]
	Simon Peter, a bondservant and apostle of Jesus Christ, To those who have **obtained** like precious faith with us by the righteousness of our God and Savior Jesus Christ: [NKJV]
	This letter is from Simon Peter, a slave and apostle of Jesus Christ.I am writing to all of you who **share** the same precious faith we have, faith given to us by Jesus Christ, our God and Savior, who makes us right with God. [NLT]
	Σίμων Πέτρος, δοῦλος καὶ ἀπόστολος Ἰησοῦ Χριστοῦ, τοῖς ἰσότιμον ἡμῖν **λαχοῦσι** πίστιν ἐν δικαιοσύνῃ τοῦ Θεοῦ ἡμῶν καὶ σωτῆρος ἡμῶν Ἰησοῦ Χριστοῦ· [GNS]
	Συμεὼν Πέτρος δοῦλος καὶ ἀπόστολος Ἰησοῦ Χριστοῦ τοῖς ἰσότιμον ἡμῖν **λαχοῦσιν** πίστιν ἐν δικαιοσύνῃ τοῦ θεοῦ ἡμῶν καὶ σωτῆρος Ἰησοῦ Χριστοῦ, [GNT]
		Received, obtained, share. It means to secure by lot; to receive by allotment; to be given a share or a portion.
		
		Practical Application
		The faith of Jesus Christ is shared not earned. No person deserves the precious faith of Jesus Christ. No person can work and earn it. It is a gift of God, a free gift that is given to every person who believes in Jesus Christ.

ENGLISH WORD	GREEK WORD AND VERSE	THE WORD MEANS...

#3509
Share
 	
Partakers–KJV
Share–NASB
Have–NIV
Partaken–NKJV
Not translated–NLT
 	
POSB REFERENCE
(Heb.2:14-16; esp. v.14)
Note 1, point 1
	κεκοινώνηκεν = kekoinönëken
	Pronunciation: [keh-koy-no-nay'-kehn]
	Parsing (part of speech): verb
	    Mood—indicative
	    Tense—perfect
	    Voice—active
	    Person—3rd person
	    Number—singular
	    Stem or root—from κοινωνέω
	Concordance References:
	⇒ Strong's #2841 koinöneö
	⇒ NIV #3125 koinöneö
	⇒ NASB #2841 koinöneö
	
	Hebrews 2:14
	Forasmuch then as the children are **partakers** of flesh and blood, he also himself likewise took part of the same; that through death he might destroy him that had the power of death, that is, the devil; [KJV]
	
	Since then the children **share** in flesh and blood, He Himself likewise also partook of the same, that through death He might render powerless him who had the power of death, that is, the devil; [NASB]
	
	Since the children **have** flesh and blood, he too shared in their humanity so that by his death he might destroy him who holds the power of death—that is, the devil— [NIV]
	
	Inasmuch then as the children have **partaken** of flesh and blood, He Himself likewise shared in the same, that through death He might destroy him who had the power of death, that is, the devil, [NKJV]
	
	Because God's children are human beings—made of flesh and blood—Jesus also became flesh and blood by being born in human form. For only as a human being could he die, and only by dying could he break the power of the Devil, who had the power of death. [NLT]—NOT TRANSLATED
	
	ἐπεὶ οὖν τὰ παιδία **κεκοινώνηκε** σαρκός καὶ αἵματος, καὶ αὐτὸς παραπλησίως μετέσχε τῶν αὐτῶν, ἵνα διὰ τοῦ θανάτου καταργήσῃ τὸν τὸ κράτος ἔχοντα τοῦ θανάτου, τοῦτ᾿ ἐστι τὸν διάβολον, [GNS]
	
	ἐπεὶ οὖν τὰ παιδία **κεκοινώνηκεν** αἵματος καὶ σαρκός, καὶ αὐτὸς παραπλησίως μετέσχεν τῶν αὐτῶν, ἵνα διὰ τοῦ θανάτου καταργήσῃ τὸν τὸ κράτος ἔχοντα τοῦ θανάτου, τοῦτ᾿ ἔστιν τὸν διάβολον, [GNT]
		To have; to share; to be a partaker of; to participate; to be partners of a common human nature.
		
		Practical Application
		He deliberately determined and purposed to *take part* of human flesh and blood. He voluntarily took part of human nature—of a nature that was not a natural part of His being.

#3510
Share It
 	
Giveth–KJV
Gives–NASB
Contributing to the needs of others–NIV
Gives–NKJV
Share it–NLT
 	
POSB REFERENCE
(Rom.12:6-8; esp. v.8)
Note 2, point 5
	μεταδιδοὺς = metadidous
	Pronunciation: [met-ad-id'-oos]
	Parsing (part of speech): verb
	    Mood—participle
	    Tense—present
	    Voice—active
	    Case—nominative
	    Gender—masculine
	    Number—singular
	    Stem or root—from μεταδίδωμι
	Concordance References:
	⇒ Strong's #3330 metadidömi
	⇒ NIV #3556 metadidömi
	⇒ NASB #3330 metadidömi
	
	Romans 12:8
	Or he that exhorteth, on exhortation: he that **giveth**, let him do it with simplicity; he that ruleth, with diligence; he that sheweth mercy, with cheerfulness. [KJV]
	
	Or he who exhorts, in his exhortation; he who **gives**, with liberality; he who leads, with diligence; he who shows mercy, with cheerfulness. [NASB]
	
	If it is encouraging, let him encourage; if it is **contributing to the needs of others**, let him give generously; if it is leadership, let him govern diligently; if it is showing mercy, let him do it cheerfully. [NIV]
		To contribute to the needs of others; to give; to share; to impart.
		
		Practical Application
		There is the gift of sharing (*metadidous*). This simply means the giving of one's earthly possessions such as money, clothing, and food. Note that in listing this particular gift, Scripture adds a point: it tells how the person is to give. He is to share "generously" (*haplotetes*).

ENGLISH WORD	GREEK WORD AND VERSE	THE WORD MEANS...
	He who exhorts, in exhortation; he who **gives**, with liberality; he who leads, with diligence; he who shows mercy, with cheerfulness. [NKJV] If your gift is to encourage others, do it! If you have money, **share it** generously. If God has given you leadership ability, take the responsibility seriously. And if you have a gift for showing kindness to others, do it gladly. [NLT] εἴτε ὁ παρακαλῶν, ἐν τῇ παρακλήσει· ὁ **μεταδιδοὺς** ἐν ἁπλότητι, ὁ προϊστάμενος, ἐν σπουδῇ· ὁ ἐλεῶν ἐν ἱλαρότητι. [GNS] εἴτε ὁ παρακαλῶν ἐν τῇ παρακλήσει· ὁ **μεταδιδοὺς** ἐν ἁπλότητι, ὁ προϊστάμενος ἐν σπουδῇ, ὁ ἐλεῶν ἐν ἱλαρότητι. [GNT]	

#3511
Share With
 	
Distributing–KJV
Contributing–NASB
Share with–NIV
Distributing–NKJV
Help them–NLT
 	
POSB REFERENCE
(Rom.12:13)
Note 4, point 1
	κοινωνοῦντες = koinōnountes
	Pronunciation: [koy-no-noon'-tehs]
	Parsing (part of speech): verb
	    Mood—participle (imperative sense)
	    Tense—present
	    Voice—active
	    Case—nominative
	    Gender—masculine
	    Person—2nd person
	    Number—plural
	    Stem or root—from κοινωνέω
	Concordance References:
	⇒ Strong's #2841 koinōneō
	⇒ NIV #3125 koinōneō
	⇒ NASB #2841 koinōneō
	
	Romans 12:13
	Distributing to the necessity of saints; given to hospitality. [KJV]
	Contributing to the needs of the saints, practicing hospitality. [NASB]
	Share with God's people who are in need. Practice hospitality. [NIV]
	Distributing to the needs of the saints, given to hospitality. [NKJV]
	When God's children are in need, be the one to **help them** out. And get into the habit of inviting guests home for dinner or, if they need lodging, for the night. [NLT]
	ταῖς χρείαις τῶν ἁγίων **κοινωνοῦντες**· τὴν φιλοξενίαν διώκοντες. [GNS]
	ταῖς χρείαις τῶν ἁγίων **κοινωνοῦντες**, τὴν φιλοξενίαν διώκοντες. [GNT]
		To share; to help; to contribute; to give.
		
		Practical Application
		The believer is to meet the needs of people unselfishly. The believer is to give generously; to share with those in need. He is to "share with" (koinōnountes), that is, to give and share in order to meet their needs.

#3512
Shared In
 	
Took part–KJV
Partook–NASB
Shared in–NIV
Shared in–NKJV
Became–NLT
 	
POSB REFERENCE
(Heb.2:14-16; esp. v.14)
Note 1, point 1
	μετέσχεν = meteschen
	Pronunciation: [met-es-khehn]
	Parsing (part of speech): verb
	    Mood—indicative
	    Tense—aorist
	    Voice—active
	    Person—3rd person
	    Number—singular
	    Stem or root—from μετέχω
	Concordance References:
	⇒ Strong's #3348 metechō
	⇒ NIV #3576 metechō
	⇒ NASB #3348 metechō
	
	Hebrews 2:14
	Forasmuch then as the children are partakers of flesh and blood, he also himself likewise **took part** of the same; that through death he might destroy him that had the power of death, that is, the devil; [KJV]
	Since then the children share in flesh and blood, He Himself likewise also **partook** of the same, that through death He might render powerless him who had the power of death, that is, the devil; [NASB]
	Since the children have flesh and blood, he too **shared in** their humanity so that by his death he might
		To share in; to take part of; to partake of; to become; to hold with.
		
		Practical Application
		Christ "shared in" or became (meteschen) human nature. The idea is that Christ became human nature and held human nature with man. He added human nature to His divine nature. His human nature was an addition to His divine nature. As God the Son, Jesus Christ had absolutely no part of flesh and blood; but as the Son of Man, He took hold of man's nature. The point is this: Jesus Christ became man, and as Man He became flesh and blood, willingly and voluntarily. Jesus Christ loves us so much that He would pay the ultimate price to deliver us. He would humble Himself to such a degree that He would leave heaven above in order to come to earth and live as a Man. (See POSB notes—Hebrews 2:17-18 for more discussion.) (Kenneth Wuest points this out in an excellent discussion and Marvin Vincent quotes the Biblical scholar B.F. Westcott as making the

ENGLISH WORD	GREEK WORD AND VERSE	THE WORD MEANS...
	destroy him who holds the power of death—that is, the devil— [NIV]	same point.)
	Inasmuch then as the children have partaken of flesh and blood, He Himself likewise **shared in** the same, that through death He might destroy him who had the power of death, that is, the devil, [NKJV]	
	Because God's children are human beings—made of flesh and blood—Jesus also **became** flesh and blood by being born in human form. For only as a human being could he die, and only by dying could he break the power of the Devil, who had the power of death. [NLT]	
	ἐπεὶ οὖν τὰ παιδία κεκοινώνηκε σαρκός καὶ αἵματος, καὶ αὐτὸς παραπλησίως **μετέσχε** τῶν αὐτῶν, ἵνα διὰ τοῦ θανάτου καταργήσῃ τὸν τὸ κράτος ἔχοντα τοῦ θανάτου, τοῦτ' ἔστι τὸν διάβολον, [GNS]	
	ἐπεὶ οὖν τὰ παιδία κεκοινώνηκεν αἵματος καὶ σαρκός, καὶ αὐτὸς παραπλησίως **μετέσχεν** τῶν αὐτῶν, ἵνα διὰ τοῦ θανάτου καταργήσῃ τὸν τὸ κράτος ἔχοντα τοῦ θανάτου, τοῦτ' ἔστιν τὸν διάβολον, [GNT]	

#3513
Shared In
 	
Partakers–KJV
Partakers–NASB
Shared in–NIV
Partakers–NKJV
Shared in–NLT
 	
POSB
REFERENCE
(Heb.6:4-5; esp. v.4)
Note 1, point 3
	μετόχους γενηθέντας = *metochous genēthentas*
	Pronunciation: [met'-okh-oos ghin'-ay-thehn-tahs]
	Parsing *metochous* (part of speech): pronominal adjective
	    Case—accusative
	    Gender—masculine
	    Number—plural
	    Stem or root—from **μέτοχος**, ου
	Parsing *genēthentas* (part of speech): verb
	    Mood—participle
	    Tense—aorist
	    Voice—passive deponent
	    Case—accusative
	    Gender—masculine
	    Number—plural
	    Stem or root—from **γίνομαι**
	Concordance References:
	  ⇒ Strong's #1096+3353 ginomai metochos
	  ⇒ NIV #1181+3581 ginomai metochos [shared in]
	  ⇒ NASB #1096+3353 ginomai metochos
	
	Hebrews 6:4
	For it is impossible for those who were once enlightened, and have tasted of the heavenly gift, and were made **partakers** of the Holy Ghost, [KJV]
	For in the case of those who have once been enlightened and have tasted of the heavenly gift and have been made **partakers** of the Holy Spirit, [NASB]
	It is impossible for those who have once been enlightened, who have tasted the heavenly gift, who have **shared in** the Holy Spirit, [NIV]
	For *it is* impossible for those who were once enlightened, and have tasted the heavenly gift, and have become **partakers** of the Holy Spirit, [NKJV]
	For it is impossible to restore to repentance those who were once enlightened—those who have experienced the good things of heaven and **shared in** the Holy Spirit, [NLT]
	ἀδύνατον γὰρ τοὺς ἅπαξ φωτισθέντας, γευσαμένους τε τῆς δωρεᾶς τῆς ἐπουρανίου, καὶ **μετόχους γενηθέντας** Πνεύματος Ἁγίου, [GNS]
	Ἀδύνατον γὰρ τοὺς ἅπαξ φωτισθέντας, γευσαμένους τε τῆς δωρεᾶς τῆς ἐπουρανίου καὶ **μετόχους γενηθέντας** πνεύματος ἁγίου [GNT]
		To share in; partaker, companion, partner; to share as partners.
		
		### Practical Application
		W.E. Vine says that it (*metochous*) means "the *fact of sharing*" (*Expository Dictionary of New Testament Words*, p.162). The Greek scholar A.T Robertson says, "These are all given as actual spiritual experiences" (*Word Pictures in the New Testament*, Vol. 5, p.375). These people were sharers in the Holy Spirit. It is very difficult to see how they can be said to be making a false profession without straining the Scripture.

#3514
Sharp Disagreement
 	
Contention–KJV
Sharp disagreement–NASB
	παροξυσμός = *paroxusmos*
	Pronunciation: [par-ox-oos-mos']
	Parsing (part of speech): noun
	    Case—nominative
	    Gender—masculine
	    Number—singular
	    Stem or root—from **παροξυσμός**, οῦ
		A sharp disagreement; a contention; a debate; a struggle; a conflict.
		
		### Practical Application
		The idea is that of differing to the point of suffering pain. Contrary to the picture usually

ENGLISH WORD	GREEK WORD AND VERSE	THE WORD MEANS...
Sharp disagreement–NIV Contention–NKJV Disagreement–NLT **POSB REFERENCE** (Acts 15:39) Note 2, point 1	Concordance References: ⇒ Strong's #3948 paroxusmos ⇒ NIV #4237 paroxusmos ⇒ NASB #3948 paroxusmos ### Acts 15:39 And the **contention** was so sharp between them, that they departed asunder one from the other: and so Barnabas took Mark, and sailed unto Cyprus; [KJV] And there arose such a **sharp disagreement** that they separated from one another, and Barnabas took Mark with him and sailed away to Cyprus. [NASB] They had such a **sharp disagreement** that they parted company. Barnabas took Mark and sailed for Cyprus, [NIV] Then the **contention** became so sharp that they parted from one another. And so Barnabas took Mark and sailed to Cyprus; [NKJV] Their **disagreement** over this was so sharp that they separated. Barnabas took John Mark with him and sailed for Cyprus. [NLT] ἐγένετο οὖν **παροξυσμὸς**, ὥστε ἀποχωρισθῆναι αὐτοὺς ἀπ' ἀλλήλων, τόν τε Βαρναβᾶν παραλαβόντα τὸν Μᾶρκον, ἐκπλεῦσαι εἰς Κύπρον· [GNS] ἐγένετο δὲ **παροξυσμὸς** ὥστε ἀποχωρισθῆναι αὐτοὺς ἀπ' ἀλλήλων, τόν τε Βαρναβᾶν παραλαβόντα τὸν Μᾶρκον ἐκπλεῦσαι εἰς Κύπρον, [GNT]	painted of the conflict, the picture seems to be that both men were hurting. The difference was sharp and both hearts were cut deeply. Each man was thoroughly convinced that he was right before the Lord; therefore, each argued strongly for his position. This does not mean that they were cutting each other with sharp and ugly words. This is important to note, for sharp words should never be spoken among believers. But the opposing positions and convictions cut and hurt both hearts. They loved and respected each other, and their sharp conflict seemed irreconcilable.

#3515
Sharper
 	
Sharper–KJV
Sharper–NASB
Sharper–NIV
Sharper–NKJV
Sharper–NLT
 	
POSB REFERENCE
(Heb.4:11-13; esp. v.12)
Note 5, point 2c
	τομώτερος = tomōteros
	Pronunciation: [tom-o'-ter-os]
	Parsing (part of speech): adjective
	    Type—comparative
	    Case—nominative
	    Gender—masculine
	    Number—singular
	    Stem or root—from τομός, ή, όν
	Concordance References:
	⇒ Strong's #5114 tomos
	⇒ NIV #5533 tomos
	⇒ NASB #5114 tomos
	
	### Hebrews 4:12
	For the word of God is quick, and powerful, and **sharper** than any twoedged sword, piercing even to the dividing asunder of soul and spirit, and of the joints and marrow, and is a discerner of the thoughts and intents of the heart. [KJV]
	
	For the word of God is living and active and **sharper** than any two-edged sword, and piercing as far as the division of soul and spirit, of both joints and marrow, and able to judge the thoughts and intentions of the heart. [NASB]
	
	For the word of God is living and active. **Sharper** than any double-edged sword, it penetrates even to dividing soul and spirit, joints and marrow; it judges the thoughts and attitudes of the heart. [NIV]
	
	For the word of God is living and powerful, and **sharper** than any two-edged sword, piercing even to the division of soul and spirit, and of joints and marrow, and is a discerner of the thoughts and intents of the heart. [NKJV]
	
	For the word of God is full of living power. It is **sharper** than the sharpest knife, cutting deep into our innermost thoughts and desires. It exposes us for what we really are. [NLT]
	
	ζῶν γὰρ ὁ λόγος τοῦ Θεοῦ, καὶ ἐνεργής, καὶ **τομώτερος** ὑπὲρ πᾶσαν μάχαιραν δίστομον, καὶ διϊκνούμενος· ἄχρι μερισμοῦ ψυχῆς τε καὶ πνεύματος, ἁρμῶν τε καὶ μυελῶν, καὶ κριτικὸς ἐνθυμήσεων καὶ ἐννοιῶν καρδίας. [GNS]
	
	Ζῶν γὰρ ὁ λόγος τοῦ θεοῦ καὶ ἐνεργὴς καὶ **τομώτερος** ὑπὲρ πᾶσαν μάχαιραν δίστομον καὶ διϊκνούμενος ἄχρι μερισμοῦ ψυχῆς καὶ πνεύματος, ἁρμῶν τε καὶ μυελῶν, καὶ κριτικὸς ἐνθυμήσεων καὶ ἐννοιῶν καρδίας [GNT]
		To cut; sharper, cutting, knifelike, piercing.
		
		Practical Application
		The Word of God is "sharper" than any two edged sword." It is penetrating and convicting. It does not leave a soul alone. The Word of God will not let a soul who hears it ignore God's promise of rest.

ENGLISH WORD	GREEK WORD AND VERSE	THE WORD MEANS...
#3523 **Shielded** Kept–KJV Protected–NASB **Shielded–NIV** Kept–NKJV Protect–NLT **POSB REFERENCE** (1 Pt.1:5) Note 3, point 1	φρουρουμένους = phrouroumenous Pronunciation: [froo-roo-meh'-noos] Parsing (part of speech): verb 　Mood—participle 　Tense—present 　Voice—passive 　Case—accusative 　Gender—masculine 　Person—2nd person 　Number—plural 　Stem or root—from φρουρέω Concordance References: ⇒　Strong's #5432 phroureö ⇒　NIV #5864 phroureö ⇒　NASB #5432 phroureö **1 Peter 1:5** Who are **kept** by the power of God through faith unto salvation ready to be revealed in the last time. [KJV] Who are **protected** by the power of God through faith for a salvation ready to be revealed in the last time. [NASB] Who through faith are **shielded** by God's power until the coming of the salvation that is ready to be revealed in the last time. [NIV] Who are **kept** by the power of God through faith for salvation ready to be evealed in the last time. [NKJV] And God, in his mighty power, will **protect** you until you receive this salvation, because you are trusting him. It will be revealed on the last day for all to see. [NLT] τοὺς ἐν δυνάμει Θεοῦ **φρουρουμένους** διὰ πίστεως εἰς σωτηρίαν ἑτοίμην ἀποκαλυφθῆναι ἐν καιρῷ ἐσχάτῳ. [GNS] τοὺς ἐν δυνάμει Θεοῦ **φρουρουμένους** διὰ πίστεως εἰς σωτηρίαν ἑτοίμην ἀποκαλυφθῆναι ἐν καιρῷ ἐσχάτῳ. [GNT]	Shielded; to keep; to protect; to guard; to garrison. **Practical Application** It is a military term; therefore it has the idea of might and strength. The might and strength of God's power shield us throughout our journey in life—through all the trials and temptations of life—and God will see to it that we will reach the glorious end of life: salvation. God Himself, in His sovereign and omnipotent power, will see to it that we receive eternal life and the inheritance that is being reserved for us.
#3524 **Shining** **Shining–KJV** Radiant–NASB Dazzling–NIV **Shining–NKJV** Dazzling–NLT **POSB REFERENCE** (Mk.9:2-3; esp. v.3) *Deeper Study #2,* point 1	στίλβοντα λίαν = stilbonta lian Pronunciation: [stil'-bon-tah lee'-an] Parsing *stilbonta* (part of speech): verb 　Mood—participle 　Tense—present 　Voice—active 　Case—nominative 　Gender—neuter 　Number—plural 　Stem or root—from στίλβω Parsing *lian* (part of speech): adjective adverb 　Stem or root—from λίαν Concordance References: ⇒　Strong's #3029+4744 lian stilbö ⇒　NIV #3336+5118 lian stilbö ⇒　NASB #3029+4744 lian stilbö **Mark 9:3** And his raiment became **shining**, exceeding white as snow; so as no fuller on earth can white them. [KJV] And His garments became **radiant** and exceedingly white, as no launderer on earth can whiten them. [NASB] His clothes became **dazzling** white, whiter than anyone in the world could bleach them. [NIV] His clothes became **shining**, exceedingly white, like snow, such as no launderer on earth can whiten them. [NKJV] And his clothing became **dazzling** white, far whiter than any earthly process could ever make it. [NLT] καὶ τὰ ἱμάτια αὐτοῦ ἐγένετο **στίλβοντα**, λευκὰ **λίαν** ὡς χιών, οἷα γναφεὺς ἐπὶ τῆς γῆς οὐ δύναται λευκᾶναι. [GNS] καὶ τὰ ἱμάτια αὐτοῦ ἐγένετο **στίλβοντα** λευκὰ **λίαν** οἷα γναφεὺς ἐπὶ τῆς γῆς οὐ δύναται οὕτως λευκᾶναι. [GNT]	To be dazzling, radiant, brilliant, shining, awe inspiring; to glisten very much. **Practical Application** The word "shining" (*stilbonta*) is a Greek participle which means the shining is active. The transfiguration was a real, active experience. It was no illusion, no dream; it was not of the imagination. It was not a reflection of the sun shining off some rock, glass, or lake. "His [own] face did shine." The glory that was "shining" was the glory of the Lord's inner nature, of His Godly nature actively shining right through His being.

ENGLISH WORD	GREEK WORD AND VERSE	THE WORD MEANS...

#3525
Shook
 	
Gnashed–KJV
Gnashing–NASB
Gnashed–NIV
Gnashed–NKJV
Shook–NLT
 	
POSB
REFERENCE
(Acts 7:54)
Note 1, point 3
	ἔβρυχον = *ebruchon*
	Pronunciation: [eh-broo'-khon]
	Parsing (part of speech): verb
	    Mood—indicative
	    Tense—imperfect
	    Voice—active
	    Person—3rd person
	    Number—plural
	    Stem or root—from βρύχω
	Concordance References:
	⇒ Strong's #1031 bruchö
	⇒ NIV #1107 bruchö
	⇒ NASB #1031 bruchö
	
	Acts 7:54
	When they heard these things, they were cut to the heart, and they **gnashed** on him with their teeth. [KJV]
	Now when they heard this, they were cut to the quick, and they began **gnashing** their teeth at him. [NASB]
	When they heard this, they were furious and **gnashed** their teeth at him. [NIV]
	When they heard these things they were cut to the heart, and they **gnashed** at him with their teeth. [NKJV]
	The Jewish leaders were infuriated by Stephen's accusation, and they **shook** their fists in rage. [NLT]
	Ἀκούοντες δὲ ταῦτα, διεπρίοντο ταῖς καρδίαις αὐτῶν, καὶ **ἔβρυχον** τοὺς ὀδόντας ἐπ' αὐτόν. [GNS]
	Ἀκούοντες δὲ ταῦτα διεπρίοντο ταῖς καρδίαις αὐτῶν καὶ **ἔβρυχον** τοὺς ὀδόντας ἐπ' αὐτόν. [GNT]
		To gnash, grind, shake, oppress.
		
		Practical Application
		The word means to bite; to grind; to gnash the teeth just like a pack of snarling dogs. The people were in a rage, filled with anger and malice, ready to do violence, ready to unleash the fury of their emotions.

#3526
Shook Violently
 	
Torn–KJV
Throwing...into convulsions–NASB
Shook...violently–NIV
Convulsed–NKJV
Threw...into a convulsion–NLT
 	
POSB
REFERENCE
(Mk.1:25-26; esp.
v.26)
Note 2, point 2
	σπαράξαν = *sparaxan*
	Pronunciation: [spar-ach'-zahn]
	Parsing (part of speech): verb
	    Mood—participle
	    Tense—aorist
	    Voice—active
	    Case—nominative
	    Gender—neuter
	    Number—singular
	    Stem or root—from σπαράσσω
	Concordance References:
	⇒ Strong's #4682 sparassö
	⇒ NIV #5057 sparassö
	⇒ NASB #4682 sparassö
	
	Mark 1:26
	And when the unclean spirit had **torn** him, and cried with a loud voice, he came out of him. [KJV]
	And **throwing** him **into convulsions**, the unclean spirit cried out with a loud voice, and came out of him. [NASB]
	The evil spirit **shook** the man **violently** and came out of him with a shriek. [NIV]
	And when the unclean spirit had **convulsed** him and cried out with a loud voice, he came out of him. [NKJV]
	At that, the evil spirit screamed and **threw** the man **into a convulsion**, but then he left him. [NLT]
	καὶ **σπαράξαν** αὐτὸν τὸ πνεῦμα τὸ ἀκάθαρτον καὶ κράξαν φωνῇ μεγάλῃ, ἐξῆλθεν ἐξ αὐτοῦ. [GNS]
	καὶ **σπαράξαν** αὐτὸν τὸ πνεῦμα τὸ ἀκάθαρτον καὶ φωνῆσαν φωνῇ μεγάλῃ ἐξῆλθεν ἐξ αὐτοῦ. [GNT]
		To be shaken violently; to be convulsed; to be thrown into convulsions; to jolt, jar, or shake up.
		
		Practical Application
		Apparently the man had a convulsion, jerking to and fro and crying out with a loud voice.

#3527
Should
 	
Ought–KJV
Ought–NASB
Should–NIV
Ought–NKJV
Must–NLT
	δεῖν = *dein*
	Pronunciation: [dine]
	Parsing (part of speech): verb
	    Mood—infinitive
	    Tense—present
	    Voice—active
	    Case—accusative
	    Stem or root—from δεῖ
	Concordance References:
	⇒ Strong's #1163 dei
	⇒ NIV #1256 dei
	⇒ NASB #1163 dei
		Must, should, ought. It means a strong sense of duty and responsibility.
		
		Practical Application
		The words "should always pray" have the idea of necessity. It is absolutely necessary that men persevere in prayer.

ENGLISH WORD	GREEK WORD AND VERSE	THE WORD MEANS...
POSB REFERENCE (Lk.18:1) Note 1, point 2	**Luke 18:1** And he spake a parable unto them to this end, that men **ought** always to pray, and not to faint; [KJV] Now He was telling them a parable to show that at all times they **ought** to pray and not to lose heart, [NASB] Then Jesus told his disciples a parable to show them that they **should** always pray and not give up. [NIV] Then He spoke a parable to them, that men always **ought** to pray and not lose heart, [NKJV] One day Jesus told his disciples a story to illustrate their need for constant prayer and to show them that they **must** never give up. [NLT] Ἔλεγε δὲ καὶ παραβολὴν αὐτοῖς πρὸς τὸ **δεῖν** πάντοτε προσεύχεσθαι, καὶ μὴ ἐκκακεῖν, [GNS] Ἔλεγεν δὲ παραβολὴν αὐτοῖς πρὸς τὸ **δεῖν** πάντοτε προσεύχεσθαι αὐτοὺς καὶ μὴ ἐγκακεῖν, [GNT]	

#3528 Shouted
 	
Cried–KJV
Cried out–NASB
A loud voice–NIV
Cried out–NKJV
Shouted–NLT
 	
POSB REFERENCE (Jn.7:37-39; esp. v.37) Note 2
	ἔκραξεν = ekraxen
	Pronunciation: [eh-krahd'-zehn]
	Parsing (part of speech): verb
	    Mood—indicative
	    Tense—aorist
	    Voice—active
	    Person—3rd person
	    Number—singular
	    Stem or root—from **κράζω**
	Concordance References:
	⇒ Strong's #2896 krazö
	⇒ NIV #3189 krazö
	⇒ NASB #2896 krazö
	
	John 7:37
	In the last day, that great day of the feast, Jesus stood and **cried**, saying, If any man thirst, let him come unto me, and drink. [KJV]
	Now on the last day, the great day of the feast, Jesus stood and **cried out**, saying, "If any man is thirsty, let him come to Me and drink. [NASB]
	On the last and greatest day of the Feast, Jesus stood and said in **a loud voice**, "If anyone is thirsty, let him come to me and drink. [NIV]
	On the last day, that great *day* of the feast, Jesus stood and **cried out**, saying, "If anyone thirsts, let him come to Me and drink. [NKJV]
	On the last day, the climax of the festival, Jesus stood and **shouted** to the crowds, "If you are thirsty, come to me! [NLT]
	Ἐν δὲ τῇ ἐσχάτῃ ἡμέρᾳ τῇ μεγάλῃ τῆς ἑορτῆς εἱστήκει ὁ Ἰησοῦς, καὶ **ἔκραξε**, λέγων, Ἐάν τις διψᾷ ἐρχέσθω πρός με, καὶ πινέτω. [GNS]
	Ἐν δὲ τῇ ἐσχάτῃ ἡμέρᾳ τῇ μεγάλῃ τῆς ἑορτῆς εἱστήκει ὁ Ἰησοῦς καὶ **ἔκραξεν** λέγων, Ἐάν τις διψᾷ ἐρχέσθω πρός με καὶ πινέτω. [GNT]
		To cry out with a loud voice; to shout in order to be heard.
		
		Practical Application
		It was on "the last day, the climax of the festival," the day when the people marched in the processional seven times that Jesus made His phenomenal claim. Some imagine Jesus' shouting His claim just as the people finished saying, "Please give us success" (Psalm 118:25).
		Imagine the scene: Jesus did two unusual things. He "stood" (a teacher always sat in that day), and He "shouted" (*ekrazen*), shouting loudly. Both actions would startle and shock the people to attention. Picture thousands of voices praying to God for the fruitful rains in the coming season, reciting: "Please give us success." Then all of a sudden piercing the air, comes the thundering cry:
		
		"On the last day, the climax of the festival, Jesus stood and shouted to the crowds, "If you are thirsty, come to me! If you believe in me, come and drink! For the Scriptures declare that rivers of living water will flow out from within." (John 7:37-38) [NLT]
		
		Jesus made three phenomenal claims.
		1. Jesus Christ is the source of life: He is the One who can quench the real thirst of man's being, who can meet the desperate need of man for prosperity, the real fruit and bounty of life.
		2. Jesus Christ is the source of abundant life. Streams of *living water* can flow out from a person. An abundance of life can be experienced (see POSB *Deeper Study* #1—John 1:4; POSB *Deeper Study* #1—John 10:10).
		3. Jesus Christ is the source of the Holy Spirit. Streams of living water refer to the Holy Spirit. This is a crucial verse, for it is the only place "living waters" is defined. When Jesus spoke of giving "living water," He meant He would give the Holy Spirit to a person. The presence of the Holy Spirit, of course, meant the experience of abundant and eternal life.
		Note: it is only the believer in Christ who receives the Holy Spirit. Belief in Him is essential. Christ is the Giver of the Spirit. (See POSB note—John 4:13-14 for more discussion.)

ENGLISH WORD	GREEK WORD AND VERSE	THE WORD MEANS...

#3529
Shouts His Praises
 	
Glad–KJV
Exulted–NASB
Rejoices–NIV
Glad–NKJV
Shouts his praises– NLT
 	
POSB REFERENCE
(Acts 2:25-28; esp. v.26)
Note 1, point 1b
	ἠγαλλιάσατο = *ëgalliasato*
	Pronunciation: [ag-al-lee-ah'-sah-tow]
	Parsing (part of speech): verb
	  Mood—indicative
	  Tense—aorist
	  Voice—middle
	  Person—3rd person
	  Number—singular
	  Stem or root—from ἀγαλλιάω
	Concordance References:
	  ⇒ Strong's #21 agalliaö
	  ⇒ NIV #22 agalliaö
	  ⇒ NASB #21 agalliaö
	
	Acts 2:26
	Therefore did my heart rejoice, and my tongue was **glad**; moreover also my flesh shall rest in hope: [KJV]
	'Therefore my heart was glad and my tongue **exulted**; Moreover my flesh also will abide in hope; [NASB]
	Therefore my heart is glad and my tongue **rejoices**; my body also will live in hope, [NIV]
	Therefore my heart rejoiced, and my tongue was **glad**; Moreover my flesh also will rest in hope. [NKJV]
	No wonder my heart is filled with joy, and my mouth **shouts his praises**! My body rests in hope. [NLT]
	Διὰ τοῦτο εὐφράνθη ἡ καρδία μου, καὶ **ἠγαλλιάσατο** ἡ γλῶσσά μου· ἔτι δὲ καὶ ἡ σάρξ μου κατασκηνώσει ἐπ' ἐλπίδι [GNS]
	διὰ τοῦτο ηὐφράνθη ἡ καρδία μου καὶ **ἠγαλλιάσατο** ἡ γλῶσσά μου, ἔτι δὲ καὶ ἡ σάρξ μου κατασκηνώσει ἐπ' ἐλπίδι, [GNT]
		Rejoices, glad, exulting, rejoicing, filled with joy; greatly rejoicing; to shout God's praises; to be extremely joyful. It means to leap for joy and break forth with praise and song.
		
		Practical Application
		Peter said that "David [spoke] concerning Christ" (Psalm 16:8-11). What David said was a prophecy of the Lord's experience upon earth (Acts 2:25-28). David's prophecy concerned Jesus' daily experience or life.
		1. Jesus experienced God's constant presence and power.
		  ⇒ Jesus always saw God before His face. Jesus looked and kept His gaze upon God. He thought upon God, focused His mind and attention upon God. He concentrated and stayed His mind upon Him. The idea is that Jesus always practiced and was always conscious of God's presence— "conquering rebellious ideas" (cp. 2 Cor. 10:5).
		  ⇒ Jesus always had God on His right hand, that He should not be moved. God was right there as an advocate and as a protector and defender. God was a provider looking after Christ, strengthening, guiding, upholding, seeing that He was not moved nor shaken. The picture is that of a defender in court or of a soldier on the battlefield standing at a person's right hand, protecting, looking after, and providing for his welfare. (Cp. Psalm 109:31 for this picture.)
		
		2. Jesus' heart rejoiced, and His tongue praised God. Such a consciousness of God's presence was bound to cause...
		  • the heart to be filled with joy (*ëuphranthë*): to be joyful and full of euphoria, full of God's presence and glory.
		  • the mouth to shout His praises (*ëgalliasato*): to leap for joy and break forth with praise and song.
		
		3. Jesus' body rested in hope. The word "rest" or "abide" (*kataskenosei*) means *shall tabernacle* or pitch a tent. Jesus' *body* rested, tabernacled, pitched its tent, encamped and made its abode upon hope—the hope of conquering death, of being resurrected. Hope of living forever was the basis and foundation of Jesus' life, that for which He lived. He focused His whole life and being upon the hope of the glorious resurrection (cp. Paul's testimony—Phil. 3:7-16, esp. Phil. 3:11).

#3530
Show
 	
Manifest–KJV
Disclose–NASB
Show–NIV
Manifest–NKJV
Reveal–NLT
	ἐμφανίσω = *emphanisö*
	Pronunciation: [em-fahn-ee'-so]
	Parsing (part of speech): verb
	  Mood—indicative
	  Tense—future
	  Voice—active
	  Person—1st person
	  Number—singular
	  Stem or root—from ἐμφανίζω
	Concordance References:
	  ⇒ Strong's #1718 emphanizo
		To show; to manifest; to disclose; to reveal; to appear; to make known.
		
		Practical Application
		When "show" (*emphanisö*) is used in the sense of an unveiling or revelation, it suggests that a new thing has come to light, that something never known by man before is made known. Some mystery has now been revealed. It is something that cannot be discovered by man's

ENGLISH WORD	GREEK WORD AND VERSE	THE WORD MEANS...
POSB REFERENCE (Jn.14:21) *Deeper Study* #3	⇒ NIV #1872 emphanizo ⇒ NASB #1718 emphanizo **John 14:21** He that hath my commandments, and keepeth them, he it is that loveth me: and he that loveth me shall be loved of my Father, and I will love him, and will **manifest** myself to him. [KJV] "He who has My commandments and keeps them, he it is who loves Me; and he who loves Me shall be loved by My Father, and I will love him, and will **disclose** Myself to him." [NASB] Whoever has my commands and obeys them, he is the one who loves me. He who loves me will be loved by my Father, and I too will love him and **show** myself to him." [NIV] He who has My commandments and keeps them, it is he who loves Me. And he who loves Me will be loved by My Father, and I will love him and **manifest** Myself to him." [NKJV] Those who obey my commandments are the ones who love me. And because they love me, my Father will love them, and I will love them. And I will **reveal** myself to each one of them." [NLT] ὁ ἔχων τὰς ἐντολάς μου καὶ τηρῶν αὐτάς, ἐκεῖνός ἐστιν ὁ ἀγαπῶν με· ὁ δὲ ἀγαπῶν με, ἀγαπηθήσεται ὑπὸ τοῦ πατρός μου· καὶ ἐγὼ ἀγαπήσω αὐτόν, καὶ **ἐμφανίσω** αὐτῷ ἐμαυτόν. [GNS] ὁ ἔχων τὰς ἐντολάς μου καὶ τηρῶν αὐτὰς ἐκεῖνός ἐστιν ὁ ἀγαπῶν με· ὁ δὲ ἀγαπῶν με ἀγαπηθήσεται ὑπὸ τοῦ πατρός μου, κἀγὼ ἀγαπήσω αὐτὸν καὶ **ἐμφανίσω** αὐτῷ ἐμαυτόν. [GNT]	reason or wisdom. It is a mystery that is hidden from man and beyond his grasp. Here in John 14:21-22, it means that Jesus' presence is revealed (brought to light), illuminated, manifested, quickened in the life of the believer. It means that He manifests Himself to His disciples in a very special way. He discloses His person, His nature, His goodness. He illuminates Himself within their hearts and lives. He gives a very special consciousness within their souls. (See POSB note—John 14:21-22; POSB *Deeper Study* #1—Acts 2:1-4.)

#3531
Show
 	
Show–KJV
Proclaim–NASB
Proclaim–NIV
Proclaim–NKJV
Announcing–NLT
 	
POSB REFERENCE (1 Cor.11:23-26; esp. v.26) Note 3, point 3
	καταγγέλλετε = *kataggellete*
	Pronunciation: [kat-ang-gel'-leh-teh]
	Parsing (part of speech): verb
	  Mood—indicative
	  Tense—present
	  Voice—active
	  Person—2nd person
	  Number—plural
	  Stem or root—from καταγγέλλω
	Concordance References:
	⇒ Strong's #2605 kataggellö
	⇒ NIV #2859 kataggellö
	⇒ NASB #2605 kataggellö
	
	1 Cor. 11:26
	For as often as ye eat this bread, and drink this cup, ye do **show** the Lord's death till he come. [KJV]
	For as often as you eat this bread and drink the cup, you **proclaim** the Lord's death until He comes. [NASB]
	For whenever you eat this bread and drink this cup, you **proclaim** the Lord's death until he comes. [NIV]
	For as often as you eat this bread and drink this cup, you **proclaim** the Lord's death till He comes. [NKJV]
	For every time you eat this bread and drink this cup, you are **announcing** the Lord's death until he comes again. [NLT]
	ὁσάκις γὰρ ἂν ἐσθίητε τὸν ἄρτον τοῦτον, καὶ τὸ ποτήριον τοῦτο πίνητε, τὸν θάνατον τοῦ Κυρίου **καταγγέλλετε** ἄχρις οὗ ἂν ἔλθῃ. [GNS]
	ὁσάκις γὰρ ἐὰν ἐσθίητε τὸν ἄρτον τοῦτον καὶ τὸ ποτήριον πίνητε, τὸν θάνατον τοῦ κυρίου **καταγγέλλετε** ἄχρις οὗ ἔλθῃ. [GNT]
		To proclaim; to preach; to declare; to announce; to make known.
		
		Practical Application
		The Lord's Supper is both a picture and sermon which proclaims...
		• the Lord's death
		• the Lord's return
		
		The point is this: Christ died for us so that we might live eternally with Him. Therefore, His death pictures both what He has done for us and what He is going to do for us when He returns. His death is a picture of both our past and present redemption. But it is also a picture of our future redemption when we will be conformed to His image of perfection.

#3532
Show
 	
Manifest–KJV
Disclose–NASB
Show–NIV
	ἐμφανίσω = *emphanisö*
	Pronunciation: [em-fahn-ee'-so]
	Parsing (part of speech): verb
	  Mood—indicative
	  Tense—future
	  Voice—active
	  Person—1st person
		To show; to manifest; to disclose; to reveal; to make known.
		
		Practical Application
		When *emphanisö* is used in the sense of an unveiling or revelation, it suggests that a new

ENGLISH WORD	GREEK WORD AND VERSE	THE WORD MEANS...
Manifest–NKJV Reveal–NLT **POSB REFERENCE** (Jn.14:21) *Deeper Study #3*	Number—singular Stem or root—from ἐμφανίζω Concordance References: ⇒ Strong's #1718 emphanizo ⇒ NIV #1872 emphanizo ⇒ NASB #1718 emphanizo **John 14:21** He that hath my commandments, and keepeth them, he it is that loveth me: and he that loveth me shall be loved of my Father, and I will **manifest** myself to him. [KJV] "He who has My commandments and keeps them, he it is who loves Me; and he who loves Me shall be loved by My Father, and I will love him, and will **disclose** Myself to him." [NASB] Whoever has my commands and obeys them, he is the one who loves me. He who loves me will be loved by my Father, and I too will love him and **show** myself to him." [NIV] He who has My commandments and keeps them, it is he who loves Me. And he who loves Me will be loved by My Father, and I will love him and **manifest** Myself to him." [NKJV] Those who obey my commandments are the ones who love me. And because they love me, my Father will love them, and I will love them. And I will **reveal** myself to each one of them." [NLT] ὁ ἔχων τὰς ἐντολάς μου καὶ τηρῶν αὐτάς, ἐκεῖνός ἐστιν ὁ ἀγαπῶν με· ὁ δὲ ἀγαπῶν με, ἀγαπηθήσεται ὑπὸ τοῦ πατρός μου· καὶ ἐγὼ ἀγαπήσω αὐτὸν, καὶ **ἐμφανίσω** αὐτῷ ἐμαυτόν. [GNS] ὁ ἔχων τὰς ἐντολάς μου καὶ τηρῶν αὐτὰς ἐκεῖνός ἐστιν ὁ ἀγαπῶν με· ὁ δὲ ἀγαπῶν με ἀγαπηθήσεται ὑπὸ τοῦ πατρός μου, κἀγὼ ἀγαπήσω αὐτὸν καὶ **ἐμφανίσω** αὐτῷ ἐμαυτόν. [GNT]	thing has come to light; that something never known by man before is made known. Some mystery has now been revealed. It is something that cannot be discovered by man's reason or wisdom. It is a mystery that is hidden from man and beyond his grasp. Here in John 14:21-22, it means that Jesus' presence is revealed (brought to light), illuminated, manifested, quickened in the life of the believer. It means that He manifests Himself to His disciples in a very special way. He discloses His person, His nature, His goodness. He illuminates Himself within their hearts and lives. He gives a very special consciousness within their souls. (See POSB note—John 14:21-22; POSB *Deeper Study #1*—Acts 2:1-4.)

#3533
Show
 	
Show forth–KJV
Proclaim–NASB
That...declare–NIV
Proclaim–NKJV
Show–NLT
 	
**POSB
REFERENCE**
(1 Pt.2:9)
Note 2
	ὅπως ἐξαγγείλητε = *hopōs exaggeilēte*
	Pronunciation: [hop'-oce ex-ang-eel'-lay-teh]
	Parsing (part of speech): verb
	  Mood—subjunctive
	  Tense—aorist
	  Voice—active
	  Person—2nd person
	  Number—plural
	  Stem or root—from ἐξαγγέλλω
	Concordance References:
	⇒ Strong's #3704 hopōs + 1804 exaggellō
	⇒ NIV #3968 hopōs [that] + 1972 exaggellō [declare]
	⇒ NASB #3704 hopōs + 1804 exaggellō
	
	1 Peter 2:9
	But ye are a chosen generation, a royal priesthood, an holy nation, a peculiar people; that ye should **show forth** the praises of him who hath called you out of darkness into his marvellous light: [KJV]
	But you are a chosen race, a royal priesthood, a HOLY NATION, a people for God's own possession, that you may **proclaim** the excellencies of Him who has called you out of darkness into His marvelous light; [NASB]
	But you are a chosen people, a royal priesthood, a holy nation, a people belonging to God, **that** you may **declare** the praises of him who called you out of darkness into his wonderful light. [NIV]
	But you *are* a chosen generation, a royal priesthood, a holy nation, His own special people, that you may **proclaim** the praises of Him who called you out of darkness into His marvelous light; [NKJV]
	But you are not like that, for you are a chosen people. You are a kingdom of priests, God's holy nation, his very own possession. This is so you can **show** others the good-
		To declare; to show forth; to proclaim; to speak; to tell; to publish; to set forth.
		
		Practical Application
		The very task of the believer is to witness for God, to share the glorious message of God. What is that message? The message that we are to share is the glorious message of salvation. God will deliver man out of darkness into the light. This is what He has done for believers. Therefore, we are to proclaim the glorious truth that God has saved us through the Light of the world, through Jesus Christ Himself. He has saved us out of the darkness of sin and death and delivered us into the light of eternity. We shall live forever. We are to praise God, proclaim the glorious message of His marvelous light or salvation.

ENGLISH WORD	GREEK WORD AND VERSE	THE WORD MEANS...
	Acts 1:3	
	To whom also he **showed** himself alive after his passion by many infallible proofs, being seen of them forty days, and speaking of the things pertaining to the kingdom of God: [KJV] To these He also **presented** Himself alive, after His suffering, by many convincing proofs, appearing to them over a period of forty days, and speaking of the things concerning the kingdom of God. [NASB] After his suffering, he **showed** himself to these men and gave many convincing proofs that he was alive. He appeared to them over a period of forty days and spoke about the kingdom of God. [NIV] To whom He also **presented** Himself alive after His suffering by many infallible proofs, being seen by them during forty days and speaking of the things pertaining to the kingdom of God. [NKJV] During the forty days after his crucifixion, he **appeared** to the apostles from time to time and proved to them in many ways that he was actually alive. On these occasions he talked to them about the Kingdom of God. [NLT] οἷς καὶ **παρέστησεν** ἑαυτὸν ζῶντα μετὰ τὸ παθεῖν αὐτὸν ἐν πολλοῖς τεκμηρίοις, δι' ἡμερῶν τεσσεράκοντα ὀπτανόμενος αὐτοῖς, καὶ λέγων τὰ περὶ τῆς βασιλείας τοῦ Θεοῦ. [GNS] οἷς καὶ **παρέστησεν** ἑαυτὸν ζῶντα μετὰ τὸ παθεῖν αὐτὸν ἐν πολλοῖς τεκμηρίοις, δι' ἡμερῶν τεσσεράκοντα ὀπτανόμενος αὐτοῖς καὶ λέγων τὰ περὶ τῆς βασιλείας τοῦ θεοῦ· [GNT]	

#3541
Showed
 	
Commendeth–KJV
Demonstrates–NASB
Demonstrates–NIV
Demonstrates–NKJV
Showed–NLT
 	
**POSB
REFERENCE**
(Rom.5:8-9; esp. v.8)
Note 2
	συνίστησιν = sunistēsin
	Pronunciation: [soon-is-tay'-sin]
	Parsing (part of speech): verb
	   Mood—indicative
	   Tense—present
	   Voice—active
	   Person—3rd person
	   Number—singular
	   Stem or root—from συνίστημι and συνιστάνω
	Concordance References:
	  ⇒ Strong's #4921 sunistēmi
	  ⇒ NIV #5319 sunistēmi
	  ⇒ NASB #4921 sunistēmi
	
	Romans 5:8
	But God **commendeth** his love toward us, in that, while we were yet sinners, Christ died for us. [KJV]
	
	But God **demonstrates** His own love toward us, in that while we were yet sinners, Christ died for us. [NASB]
	
	But God **demonstrates** his own love for us in this: While we were still sinners, Christ died for us. [NIV]
	
	But God **demonstrates** His own love toward us, in that while we were still sinners, Christ died for us. [NKJV]
	
	But God **showed** his great love for us by sending Christ to die for us while we were still sinners. [NLT]
	
	συνίστησι δὲ τὴν ἑαυτοῦ ἀγάπην εἰς ἡμᾶς ὁ Θεὸς ὅτι ἔτι ἁμαρτωλῶν ὄντων ἡμῶν Χριστὸς ὑπὲρ ἡμῶν ἀπέθανε. [GNS]
	
	συνίστησιν δὲ τὴν ἑαυτοῦ ἀγάπην εἰς ἡμᾶς ὁ θεός, ὅτι ἔτι ἁμαρτωλῶν ὄντων ἡμῶν Χριστὸς ὑπὲρ ἡμῶν ἀπέθανεν. [GNT]
		Recommends, commends; gives approval to; demonstrates, shows, proves, exhibits.
		
		Practical Application
		We were sinners, yet God proved His love to us. The word "showed" (sunistēsin) means to show, prove, exhibit. It is the present tense: God is always showing and proving His love to us.

#3542
Showed
 	
Showed–KJV
Presented–NASB
Showed–NIV
Presented–NKJV
Appeared–NLT
	παρέστησεν = parestēsen
	Pronunciation: [par-is'-tay-sen]
	Parsing (part of speech): verb
	   Mood—indicative
	   Tense—aorist
	   Voice—active
	   Person—3rd person
	   Number—singular
	   Stem or root—from παρίστημι
		To show; to present; to appear.
		
		Practical Application
		Jesus showed, presented Himself alive. Note the exciting facts in this Scripture during the forty days after His crucifixion:
		⇒ He personally appeared to the apostles.
		⇒ He proved to them in many ways that He was

ENGLISH WORD	GREEK WORD AND VERSE	THE WORD MEANS...
POSB REFERENCE (Acts 1:3) Note 3, point 1	Concordance References: ⇒ Strong's #3936 paristēmi ⇒ NIV #4225 paristēmi ⇒ NASB ##3936 paristēmi ### Acts 1:3 To whom also he **showed** himself alive after his passion by many infallible proofs, being seen of them forty days, and speaking of the things pertaining to the kingdom of God: [KJV] To these He also **presented** Himself alive, after His suffering, by many convincing proofs, appearing to them over a period of forty days, and speaking of the things concerning the kingdom of God. [NASB] After his suffering, he **showed** himself to these men and gave many convincing proofs that he was alive. He appeared to them over a period of forty days and spoke about the kingdom of God. [NIV] To whom He also **presented** Himself alive after His suffering by many infallible proofs, being seen by them during forty days and speaking of the things pertaining to the kingdom of God. [NKJV] During the forty days after his crucifixion, he **appeared** to the apostles from time to time and proved to them in many ways that he was actually alive. On these occasions he talked to them about the Kingdom of God. [NLT] οἷς καὶ **παρέστησεν** ἑαυτὸν ζῶντα μετὰ τὸ παθεῖν αὐτὸν ἐν πολλοῖς τεκμηρίοις, δι' ἡμερῶν τεσσεράκοντα ὀπτανόμενος αὐτοῖς, καὶ λέγων τὰ περὶ τῆς βασιλείας τοῦ Θεοῦ. [GNS] οἷς καὶ **παρέστησεν** ἑαυτὸν ζῶντα μετὰ τὸ παθεῖν αὐτὸν ἐν πολλοῖς τεκμηρίοις, δι' ἡμερῶν τεσσεράκοντα ὀπτανόμενος αὐτοῖς καὶ λέγων τὰ περὶ τῆς βασιλείας τοῦ θεοῦ· [GNT]	actually alive. ⇒ He talked to them about the Kingdom of God.

#3543
Showed Concern
 	
Visit–KJV
Concerned–NASB
Showed...concern–NIV
Visited–NKJV
Visited–NLT
 	
POSB REFERENCE (Acts 15:13-21; esp. v.14) Note 4, point 1
	ἐπεσκέψατο = *epeskepsato*
	Pronunciation: [ep eh-skcp'-sah-tow]
	Parsing (part of speech): verb
	  Mood—indicative
	  Tense—aorist
	  Voice—middle dep
	  Person—3rd person
	  Number—singular
	  Stem or root—from ἐπισκέπτομαι
	Concordance References:
	⇒ Strong's #1980 episkeptomai
	⇒ NIV #2170 episkeptomai
	⇒ NASB #1980a episkeptomai
	
	### Acts 15:14
	Simeon hath declared how God at the first did **visit** the Gentiles, to take out of them a people for his name. [KJV]
	
	"Simeon has related how God first **concerned** Himself about taking from among the Gentiles a people for His name. [NASB]
	
	Simon has described to us how God at first **showed** his **concern** by taking from the Gentiles a people for himself. [NIV]
	
	Simon has declared how God at the first **visited** the Gentiles to take out of them a people for His name. [NKJV]
	
	Peter has told you about the time God first **visited** the Gentiles to take from them a people for himself. [NLT]
	
	Συμεὼν ἐξηγήσατο καθὼς πρῶτον ὁ Θεὸς **ἐπεσκέψατο** λαβεῖν ἐξ ἐθνῶν λαὸν ἐπὶ τῷ ὀνόματι αὐτοῦ. [GNS]
	
	Συμεὼν ἐξηγήσατο καθὼς πρῶτον ὁ Θεὸς **ἐπεσκέψατο** λαβεῖν ἐξ ἐθνῶν λαὸν τῷ ὀνόματι αὐτοῦ. [GNT]
		To show concern; to visit; to care for; to look after.
		
		### Practical Application
		James supported Peter's great declaration. The way James worded his support is significant.
		⇒ "God...did show concern (*epeskepsato*) for the Gentiles."
		⇒ "to take *from among the Gentiles* a people": to choose; to appoint; to remove them from the Gentile nations and select a chosen people. The word "people" (*laon*) is the same word used of the Jewish people (cp. Acts 10:2). The point is that God was calling *a new people out*—a new body, a new nation, a new race—to be His chosen people, just as He had done with Abraham and the Jews. (See POSB *Deeper Study #8*, pt.6—Matthew 21:43; POSB note—Ephes. 2:11-18; POSB note—Ephes. 2:14-15; POSB note—Ephes. 2:19-22; and POSB note—Ephes. 4:17-19 for more discussion.)
		⇒ "For His name": two verses clearly show what God means by choosing a people "for His name."
		
		"You are my witnesses," declares the Lord, "and my servant whom I have chosen, so that you may know and believe me and understand that I am he. Before me no god was formed, nor will there be one after me. (Isaiah 43:10) [NIV]
		
		For as a belt is bound around a man's waist,

ENGLISH WORD	GREEK WORD AND VERSE	THE WORD MEANS...
		so I bound the whole house of Israel and the whole house of Judah to me,' declares the Lord, 'to be my people for my renown and praise and honor. But they have not listened.' (Jeremiah 13:11) [NIV]

#3544
Showed Openly
 	
Showed...openly–KJV
Become visible–NASB
Be seen–NIV
Showed...openly–NKJV
To appear–NLT
 	
POSB REFERENCE
(Acts 10:40-41; esp. v.40)
Note 6, point 1
	ἐμφανῆ γενέσθαι = emphanë genesthai
	Pronunciation: [em-fan-ay' ghin'-es-tha-ee]
	Parsing *emphanë* (part of speech): adjective
	  Case—accusative
	  Gender—masculine
	  Number—singular
	  Stem or root—from ἐμφανής
	Parsing *genesthai* (part of speech): verb
	  Mood—infinitive
	  Tense—aorist
	  Voice—middle deponent
	  Stem or root—from γίνομαι
	Concordance References:
	⇒ Strong's #1717 emphanës + 1096 ginomai
	⇒ NIV #1871 [seen] emphanës + 1181 genesthai [be]
	⇒ NASB #1717 emphanës + 1096 ginomai
	
	Acts 10:40
	Him God raised up the third day, and **showed** him **openly**; [KJV]
	"God raised Him up on the third day, and granted that He should **become visible**, [NASB]
	But God raised him from the dead on the third day and caused him to **be seen**. [NIV]
	Him God raised up on the third day, and **showed** Him **openly**, [NKJV]
	But God raised him to life three days later. Then God allowed him **to appear**, [NLT]
	Τοῦτον ὁ Θεὸς ἤγειρε τῇ τρίτῃ ἡμέρα, καὶ ἔδωκεν αὐτὸν ἐμφανῆ γενέσθαι, [GNS]
	τοῦτον ὁ θεὸς ἤγειρεν [ἐν] τῇ τρίτῃ ἡμέρᾳ καὶ ἔδωκεν αὐτὸν ἐμφανῆ γενέσθαι, [GNT]
		To be seen; to become visible; to appear; to show openly.
		
		Practical Application
		God showed Jesus openly, which means that God set Jesus before people, so that He could be visibly, openly, and publicly seen. God manifested, showed, and set Him forth as the Risen Lord. (See POSB note—Acts 1:3 and POSB *Deeper Study #1*, Jesus, Resurrection—Acts 1:3 for more discussion.)

#3545
Showeth Mercy
 	
Showeth mercy–KJV
Shows mercy–NASB
Showing mercy–NIV
Shows mercy–NKJV
Showing kindness–NLT
 	
POSB REFERENCE
(Rom.12:6-8; esp. v.8)
Note 2, point 7
	ἐλεῶν = eleön
	Pronunciation: [el-eh-own]
	Parsing (part of speech): verb
	  Mood—participle
	  Tense—present
	  Voice—active
	  Case—nominative
	  Gender—masculine
	  Number—singular
	  Stem or root—from ἐλεέω
	Concordance References:
	⇒ Strong's #1653 eleeö
	⇒ NIV #1796 eleeö
	⇒ NASB #1653 eleeö
	
	Romans 12:8
	Or he that exhorteth, on exhortation: he that giveth, let him do it with simplicity; he that ruleth, with diligence; he that **showeth mercy**, with cheerfulness. [KJV]
	Or he who exhorts, in his exhortation; he who gives, with liberality; he who leads, with diligence; he who **shows mercy**, with cheerfulness. [NASB]
	If it is encouraging, let him encourage; if it is contributing to the needs of others, let him give generously; if it is leadership, let him govern diligently; if it is **showing mercy**, let him do it cheerfully. [NIV]
	He who exhorts, in exhortation; he who gives, with liberality; he who leads, with diligence; he who **shows mercy**, with cheerfulness. [NKJV]
	If your gift is to encourage others, do it! If you have money, share it generously. If God has given you leadership ability, take the responsibility seriously. And if you
		Shows mercy, shows kindness.
		
		Practical Application
		There is the gift of mercy (*eleon*). This is a person who is full of forgiveness and compassion, pity and kindness toward others. Note that the merciful person is to show mercy with a cheerful (*hilarotes*) heart.

ENGLISH WORD	GREEK WORD AND VERSE	THE WORD MEANS...
	have a gift for **showing kindness** to others, do it gladly. [NLT] εἴτε ὁ παρακαλῶν, ἐν τῇ παρακλήσει· ὁ μεταδιδοὺς ἐν ἁπλότητι, ὁ προϊστάμενος, ἐν σπουδῇ· ὁ ἐλεῶν ἐν ἱλαρότητι. [GNS] εἴτε ὁ παρακαλῶν ἐν τῇ παρακλήσει· ὁ μεταδιδοὺς ἐν ἁπλότητι, ὁ προϊστάμενος ἐν σπουδῇ, ὁ ἐλεῶν ἐν ἱλαρότητι. [GNT]	
#3546 **Showing** Showing–KJV Showing–NASB Showing–NIV Showing–NKJV Showing–KJV **POSB REFERENCE** (Acts 9:36-39; esp. v.39) Note 2, point 5	ἐπιδεικνύμεναι = epideiknumenai Pronunciation: [ep-ee-dike'-noo-men-ah-ee] Parsing (part of speech): verb 　Mood—participle 　Tense—present 　Voice—middle 　Case—nominative 　Gender—feminine 　Number—plural 　Stem or root—from ἐπιδείκνυμι Concordance References: ⇒　Strong's #1925 epideiknumi ⇒　NIV #2109 epideiknumi ⇒　NASB #1925 epideiknumi **Acts 9:39** Then Peter arose and went with them. When he was come, they brought him into the upper chamber: and all the widows stood by him weeping, and **showing** the coats and garments which Dorcas made, while she was with them. [KJV] And Peter arose and went with them. And when he had come, they brought him into the upper room; and all the widows stood beside him weeping, and **showing** all the tunics and garments that Dorcas used to make while she was with them. [NASB] Peter went with them, and when he arrived he was taken upstairs to the room. All the widows stood around him, crying and **showing** him the robes and other clothing that Dorcas had made while she was still with them. [NIV] Then Peter arose and went with them. When he had come, they brought *him* to the upper room. And all the widows stood by him weeping, **showing** the tunics and garments which Dorcas had made while she was with them. [NKJV] So Peter returned with them; and as soon as he arrived, they took him to the upstairs room. The room was filled with widows who were weeping and **showing** him the coats and other garments Dorcas had made for them. [NLT] ἀναστὰς δὲ Πέτρος συνῆλθεν αὐτοῖς· ὃν παραγενόμενον ἀνήγαγον εἰς τὸ ὑπερῷον, καὶ παρέστησαν αὐτῷ πᾶσαι αἱ χῆραι κλαίουσαι καὶ **ἐπιδεικνύμεναι** χιτῶνας καὶ ἱμάτια ὅσα ἐποίει μετ' αὐτῶν οὖσα ἡ Δορκάς. [GNS] ἀναστὰς δὲ Πέτρος συνῆλθεν αὐτοῖς· ὃν παραγενόμενον ἀνήγαγον εἰς τὸ ὑπερῷον καὶ παρέστησαν αὐτῷ πᾶσαι αἱ χῆραι κλαίουσαι καὶ **ἐπιδεικνύμεναι** χιτῶνας καὶ ἱμάτια ὅσα ἐποίει μετ' αὐτῶν οὖσα ἡ Δορκάς. [GNT]	Showing; to point out. **Practical Application** The word "showing" (*epideiknumenai*, middle voice) means they were pointing to the clothes. They were actually wearing the clothes she had made either to honor her or because they had few or no other clothes decent enough to wear publicly.
#3547 **Showing Kindness** Showeth mercy–KJV Shows mercy–NASB Showing mercy–NIV Shows mercy–NKJV **Showing kindness–NLT**	ἐλεῶν = eleön Pronunciation: [el-eh-own] Parsing (part of speech): verb 　Mood—participle 　Tense—present 　Voice—active 　Case—nominative 　Gender—masculine 　Number—singular 　Stem or root—from ἐλεέω Concordance References: ⇒　Strong's #1653 eleeö	Show kindness; show mercy. **Practical Application** There is the gift of kindness (*eleön*). This is a person who is full of forgiveness and compassion, pity and kindness toward others. Note that the merciful person is to show mercy with a glad (*hilarotes*) heart.

ENGLISH WORD	GREEK WORD AND VERSE	THE WORD MEANS...
POSB REFERENCE (Rom.12:6-8; esp. v.8) Note 2, point 7	⇒ NIV #1796 eleeö ⇒ NASB #1653 eleeö **Romans 12:8** Or he that exhorteth, on exhortation: he that giveth, let him do it with simplicity; he that ruleth, with diligence; he that **showeth mercy**, with cheerfulness. [KJV] Or he who exhorts, in his exhortation; he who gives, with liberality; he who leads, with diligence; he who **shows mercy**, with cheerfulness. [NASB] If it is encouraging, let him encourage; if it is contributing to the needs of others, let him give generously; if it is leadership, let him govern diligently; if it is **showing mercy**, let him do it cheerfully. [NIV] He who exhorts, in exhortation; he who gives, with liberality; he who leads, with diligence; he who **shows mercy**, with cheerfulness. [NKJV] If your gift is to encourage others, do it! If you have money, share it generously. If God has given you leadership ability, take the responsibility seriously. And if you have a gift for **showing kindness** to others, do it gladly. [NLT] εἴτε ὁ παρακαλῶν, ἐν τῇ παρακλήσει· ὁ μεταδιδοὺς ἐν ἁπλότητι, ὁ προϊστάμενος, ἐν σπουδῇ· ὁ **ἐλεῶν** ἐν ἱλαρότητι. [GNS] εἴτε ὁ παρακαλῶν ἐν τῇ παρακλήσει· ὁ μεταδιδοὺς ἐν ἁπλότητι, ὁ προϊστάμενος ἐν σπουδῇ, ὁ **ἐλεῶν** ἐν ἱλαρότητι. [GNT]	

#3548
 Showing Mercy– Shows Mercy
 	
 Showeth mercy–KJV
 Shows mercy–NASB
 Showing mercy–NIV
 Shows mercy–NKJV
 Showing kindness– NLT
 	
 POSB REFERENCE (Rom.12:6-8; esp. v.8) Note 2, point 7
	ἐλεῶν = eleön
	 Pronunciation: [el-eh-own]
	 Parsing (part of speech): verb
	   Mood—participle
	   Tense—present
	   Voice—active
	   Case—nominative
	   Gender—masculine
	   Number—singular
	   Stem or root—from ἐλεέω
	 Concordance References:
	 ⇒ Strong's #1653 eleeö
	 ⇒ NIV #1796 eleeö
	 ⇒ NASB #1653 eleeö
	
	 Romans 12:8
	 Or he that exhorteth, on exhortation: he that giveth, let him do it with simplicity; he that ruleth, with diligence; he that **showeth mercy**, with cheerfulness. [KJV]
	 Or he who exhorts, in his exhortation; he who gives, with liberality; he who leads, with diligence; he who **shows mercy**, with cheerfulness. [NASB]
	 If it is encouraging, let him encourage; if it is contributing to the needs of others, let him give generously; if it is leadership, let him govern diligently; if it is **showing mercy**, let him do it cheerfully. [NIV]
	 He who exhorts, in exhortation; he who gives, with liberality; he who leads, with diligence; he who **shows mercy**, with cheerfulness. [NKJV]
	 If your gift is to encourage others, do it! If you have money, share it generously. If God has given you leadership ability, take the responsibility seriously. And if you have a gift for **showing kindness** to others, do it gladly. [NLT]
	 εἴτε ὁ παρακαλῶν, ἐν τῇ παρακλήσει· ὁ μεταδιδοὺς ἐν ἁπλότητι, ὁ προϊστάμενος, ἐν σπουδῇ· ὁ **ἐλεῶν** ἐν ἱλαρότητι. [GNS]
	 εἴτε ὁ παρακαλῶν ἐν τῇ παρακλήσει· ὁ μεταδιδοὺς ἐν ἁπλότητι, ὁ προϊστάμενος ἐν σπουδῇ, ὁ **ἐλεῶν** ἐν ἱλαρότητι. [GNT]
		Show kindness; show mercy.
		
		 Practical Application
		 There is the gift of mercy (*eleon*). This is a person who is full of forgiveness and compassion, pity and kindness toward others. Note that the merciful person is to show mercy with a cheerful (*hilarotes*) heart.

ENGLISH WORD	GREEK WORD AND VERSE	THE WORD MEANS...

#3549
Showing The Glad Tidings
 	
Showing the glad tidings–KJV
Preaching–NASB
Proclaiming the good news–NIV
Bringing the glad tidings–NKJV
Announce the Good News–NLT
 	
POSB REFERENCE
(Lk.8:1)
Deeper Study #2
	εὐαγγελιζόμενος = *euaggelizomenos*
	Pronunciation: [yoo-ang-ghel-id'-zo-men-os]
	Parsing (part of speech): verb
	  Mood—participle
	  Tense—present
	  Voice—middle
	  Case—nominative
	  Gender—masculine
	  Number—plural
	  Stem or root—from εὐαγγελίζω
	Concordance References:
	  ⇒ Strong's #2097 euaggelizō
	  ⇒ NIV #2294 euaggelizō
	  ⇒ NASB #2097 euaggelizō
	
	Luke 8:1
	And it came to pass afterward, that he went throughout every city and village, preaching and **showing the glad tidings** of the kingdom of God: and the twelve were with him, [KJV]
	And it came about soon afterwards, that He began going about from one city and village to another, proclaiming and **preaching** the kingdom of God; and the twelve were with Him, [NASB]
	After this, Jesus traveled about from one town and village to another, **proclaiming the good news** of the kingdom of God. The Twelve were with him, [NIV]
	Now it came to pass, afterward, that He went through every city and village, preaching and **bringing the glad tidings** of the kingdom of God. And the twelve were with Him, [NKJV]
	Not long afterward Jesus began a tour of the nearby cities and villages to **announce the Good News** concerning the Kingdom of God. He took his twelve disciples with him, [NLT]
	Καὶ ἐγένετο ἐν τῷ καθεξῆς, καὶ αὐτὸς διώδευε κατὰ πόλιν καὶ κώμην, κηρύσσων καὶ **εὐαγγελιζόμενος** τὴν βασιλείαν τοῦ Θεοῦ· καὶ οἱ δώδεκα σὺν αὐτῷ, [GNS]
	Καὶ ἐγένετο ἐν τῷ καθεξῆς καὶ αὐτὸς διώδευεν κατὰ πόλιν καὶ κώμην κηρύσσων καὶ **εὐαγγελιζόμενος** τὴν βασιλείαν τοῦ θεοῦ καὶ οἱ δώδεκα σὺν αὐτῷ, [GNT]
		To preach glad tidings: to announce glad tidings; to declare good news; to proclaim the gospel of Jesus Christ.
		
		Practical Application
		Note the Greek word, how it resembles the word *evangelism*. The English word *evangelism* comes from it. By the very nature of his work, the preacher is an evangelist. He is a herald who comes in the name of the King, representing the King (cp. 2 Cor. 5:20). He announces *only* the message of the King; he has no message of his own. If and when he begins to announce his own message, he is no longer the representative or the spokesman of the King.

#3550
Shrines
 	
Tabernacles–KJV
Tabernacles–NASB
Shelters–NIV
Tabernacles–NKJV
Shrines–NLT
 	
POSB REFERENCE
(Mt.17:4)
  Note 4, point 1
 	
See also POSB REF:
(Mk.9:5)
  Note 3, point 2a
(Lk.9:32-33; esp. v.33)
  Note 5, point 1
	σκηνάς = *skēnas*
	Pronunciation: [skay-nas]
	Parsing (part of speech): noun
	  Case—accusative
	  Gender—feminine
	  Number—plural
	  Stem or root—from σκηνη,, ῆς
	Concordance References:
	  ⇒ Strong's #4633 skēnē
	  ⇒ NIV #5008 skēnē
	  ⇒ NASB #4633 skēnē
	
	Matthew 17:4
	Then answered Peter, and said unto Jesus, Lord, it is good for us to be here: if thou wilt, let us make here three **tabernacles**; one for thee, and one for Moses, and one for Elias. [KJV]
	And Peter answered and said to Jesus, "Lord, it is good for us to be here; if You wish, I will make three **tabernacles** here, one for You, and one for Moses, and one for Elijah." [NASB]
	Peter said to Jesus, "Lord, it is good for us to be here. If you wish, I will put up three **shelters**—one for you, one for Moses and one for Elijah." [NIV]
	Then Peter answered and said to Jesus, "Lord, it is good for us to be here; if You wish, let us make here three **tabernacles**: one for You, one for Moses, and one for Elijah." [NKJV]
	Peter blurted out, "Lord, this is wonderful! If you want
		A temporary shelter, tent, tabernacle, shrine, or dwelling.
		
		Practical Application
		These shrines or shelters were made of branches and grass which could be quickly built, the kind often built by travellers on their stops along the road night by night. Why did Peter want to build these shrines or tabernacles? He hoped to extend the stay of the heavenly guests and the glorious experience.

ENGLISH WORD	GREEK WORD AND VERSE	THE WORD MEANS...
	Now while he was in Jerusalem at the Passover Feast, many people saw the **miraculous signs** he was doing and believed in his name. [NIV] Now when He was in Jerusalem at the Passover, during the feast, many believed in His name when they saw the **signs** which He did. [NKJV] Because of the **miraculous signs** he did in Jerusalem at the Passover celebration, many people were convinced that he was indeed the Messiah. [NLT] Ὡς δὲ ἦν ἐν Ἱεροσολύμοις ἐν τῷ πάσχα ἐν τῇ ἑορτῇ, πολλοὶ ἐπίστευσαν εἰς τὸ ὄνομα αὐτοῦ, θεωροῦντες αὐτοῦ τὰ **σημεῖα** ἃ ἐποίει. [GNS] Ὡς δὲ ἦν ἐν τοῖς Ἱεροσολύμοις ἐν τῷ πάσχα ἐν τῇ ἑορτῇ, πολλοὶ ἐπίστευσαν εἰς τὸ ὄνομα αὐτοῦ θεωροῦντες αὐτοῦ τὰ **σημεῖα** ἃ ἐποίει· [GNT]	Many believed and followed Jesus because it made them feel good and comfortable and secure. Such belief is weak and often fails. This word is never used by itself to initiate faith in the Lord Jesus. If a person is to have genuine faith in the Lord Jesus, he must have some basis other than the spectacular sign (*teras*). 2. *Dunamis* means power—unusual, extraordinary power; effective, explosive power. There were those who were attracted to Jesus because of the unusual power (*dunamis*) they witnessed. They believed because of the power. Such is a legitimate belief and leads to salvation for everyone who believes. 3. *Ergon* means distinctive works, deeds, and miracles. Such works come from God (John 14:10) and bear witness to Christ. They point men to Christ (John 5:36; John 10:25). Some men look at the very special works of Christ and believe because of the works (*ergon*). 4. *Semeion* (*sēmeia*) means a sign that characterizes the person, his nature and character. A few throughout Jesus' ministry did believe because they saw in the miracles exactly who He was, the very Son of God. However, the word "semeion" is also used of those who believed the signs, but did not have the highest or right kind of faith. Their faith was not a faith that committed itself (see POSB *Deeper Study #2—John 2:24*).
#3559 **Signs** Signs–KJV Signs–NASB Signs–NIV Signs–NKJV Signs–NLT **POSB REFERENCE** (2 Cor. 12:11-12; esp. v.12) Note 1 **See also POSB REF:** (Acts 2:19-20; esp. v.19) *Deeper Study #1*, point 1b	σημείοις = *sēmeiois* Pronunciation: [say-mah-ee'-oys] Parsing (part of speech): noun 　　Case—dative 　　Gender—neuter 　　Number—plural 　　Stem or root—from σημεῖον, ου Concordance References: 　⇒　Strong's #4592 *sēmeion* 　⇒　NIV #4956 *sēmeion* 　⇒　NASB #4592 *sēmeion* ### 2 Cor. 12:12 Truly the signs of an apostle were wrought among you in all patience, in **signs**, and wonders, and mighty deeds. [KJV] The signs of a true apostle were performed among you with all perseverance, by **signs** and wonders and miracles. [NASB] The things that mark an apostle—**signs**, wonders and miracles—were done among you with great perseverance. [NIV] Truly the signs of an apostle were accomplished among you with all perseverance, in **signs** and wonders and mighty deeds. [NKJV] When I was with you, I certainly gave you every proof that I am truly an apostle, sent to you by God himself. For I patiently did many **signs** and wonders and miracles among you. [NLT] τὰ μὲν σημεῖα τοῦ ἀποστόλου κατειργάσθη ἐν ὑμῖν ἐν πάσῃ ὑπομονῇ, ἐν **σημείοις** καὶ τέρασι καὶ δυνάμεσι. [GNS] τὰ μὲν σημεῖα τοῦ ἀποστόλου κατειργάσθη ἐν ὑμῖν ἐν πάσῃ ὑπομονῇ, **σημείοις** τε καὶ τέρασιν καὶ δυνάμεσιν. [GNT]	Signs, miraculous signs, a mark, a signal; a warning sign. ### Practical Application Paul was equal to any apostle or minister, and his ministry among the church proved it. The signs of an apostle were done among the church. And note: they had been done under the most *severe circumstances* requiring great patience (endurance, perseverance, constancy).
#3560 **Silence**	ἡσυχία = *hēsuchia* Pronunciation: [hay-soo-khee'-ah] Parsing (part of speech): noun 　　Case—dative	Quietness, silence.

ENGLISH WORD	GREEK WORD AND VERSE	THE WORD MEANS...
Silence–KJV Quietly–NASB Quietness–NIV **Silence–NKJV** Quietly–NLT **POSB REFERENCE** (1 Tim.2:11-14; esp. v.11) Note 2	Gender—feminine Number—singular Stem or root—from ἡσυχία, ας Concordance References: ⇒ Strong's #2271 hësuchia ⇒ NIV #2484 hësuchia ⇒ NASB #2271 hësuchia **1 Tim. 2:11** Let the woman learn in **silence** with all subjection. [KJV] Let a woman **quietly** receive instruction with entire submissiveness. [NASB] A woman should learn in **quietness** and full submission. [NIV] Let a woman learn in **silence** with all submission. [NKJV] Women should listen and learn **quietly** and submissively. [NLT] γυνὴ ἐν ἡσυχίᾳ μανθανέτω ἐν πάσῃ ὑποταγῇ. [GNS] γυνὴ ἐν ἡσυχίᾳ μανθανέτω ἐν πάσῃ ὑποταγῇ· [GNT]	**Practical Application** In church women are to learn in silence and submissiveness. Two striking points are given in these verses. Remember: this passage is being written to genuine Christian women, women who truly love and wish to honor the Lord and to have a strong testimony for Him. The woman who is a true Christian wants to guard her behavior in church as well as in public. The Christian woman is a follower of Christ, a true believer; therefore, she is to learn all she can about Christ. She is to attend church and read, listen, and study. She is to show and demonstrate her love for the Lord by learning all she can about Him. And note the spirit in which she is to learn. She is to learn... • in a spirit of "silence" (*hës1uchia*) which means quietness. • in a spirit of "subjection" which means submissiveness.
#3561 ## Silenced Stopped–KJV **Silenced–NASB** **Silenced–NIV** Stopped–NKJV **Silenced–NLT** **POSB REFERENCE** (Tit.1:10-12; esp. v.11) Note 1, point 5	ἐπιστομίζειν = epistomizein Pronunciation: [ep-ees-to-miz'-eh-een] Parsing (part of speech): verb Mood—infinitive Tense—present Voice—active Stem or root—from ἐπιστομίζω Concordance References: ⇒ Strong's #1993 epistomizö ⇒ NIV #2187 epistomizö ⇒ NASB #1993 epistomizö **Titus 1:11** Whose mouths must be **stopped**, who subvert whole houses, teaching things which they ought not, for filthy lucre's sake. [KJV] Who must be **silenced** because they are upsetting whole families, teaching things they should not teach, for the sake of sordid gain. [NASB] They must be **silenced**, because they are ruining whole households by teaching things they ought not to teach—and that for the sake of dishonest gain. [NIV] Whose mouths must be **stopped**, who subvert whole households, teaching things which they ought not, for the sake of dishonest gain. [NKJV] They must be **silenced**. By their wrong teaching, they have already turned whole families away from the truth. Such teachers only want your money. [NLT] οὓς δεῖ ἐπιστομίζειν· οἵτινες ὅλους οἴκους ἀνατρέπουσι, διδάσκοντες ἃ μὴ δεῖ, αἰσχροῦ κέρδους χάριν. [GNS] οὓς δεῖ ἐπιστομίζειν, οἵτινες ὅλους οἴκους ἀνατρέπουσιν διδάσκοντες ἃ μὴ δεῖ αἰσχροῦ κέρδους χάριν. [GNT]	Silenced, stopped. It means to muzzle or bridle, but it should be by reason and argument, not by physical force. **Practical Application** The false teachers had mouths that needed to be silenced. Their false teaching needed to be stopped, but not by physical force. False teachers must always be stopped. Their teaching is misleading and erroneous; therefore, their teaching must be restrained, stopped dead in its tracks. Their tongues must be silenced. False teachers must not be allowed to sow the seeds of their error.
#3562 ## Silly Talk Foolish talking–KJV **Silly talk–NASB** Foolish talk–NIV Foolish talking–NKJV Foolish talk–NLT **POSB REFERENCE** (Eph.5:4) Note 4, point 21	μωρολογία = mörologia Pronunciation: [mo-rol-og-ee'-ah] Parsing (part of speech): noun Case—nominative Gender—feminine Number—singular Stem or root—from μωρολογία, ας Concordance References: ⇒ Strong's #3473 mörologia ⇒ NIV #3703 mörologia ⇒ NASB #3473 mörologia **Ephes. 5:4** Neither filthiness, nor **foolish talking**, nor jesting, which are not convenient: but rather giving of thanks. [KJV]	Foolish talk, silly talk, purposeless talk. **Practical Application** The believer is never once to engage in "silly talk" (*mörologia*): empty, unthoughtful, senseless, wasted, idle, aimless, or purposeless talk; talk that fritters away and wastes time, that has absolutely no purpose to it. It also means sinful, foolish, silly and corrupt talk.

ENGLISH WORD	GREEK WORD AND VERSE	THE WORD MEANS...
	And there must be no filthiness and **silly talk**, or coarse jesting, which are not fitting, but rather giving of thanks. [NASB] Nor should there be obscenity, **foolish talk** or coarse joking, which are out of place, but rather thanksgiving. [NIV] Neither filthiness, nor **foolish talking**, nor coarse jesting, which are not fitting, but rather giving of thanks. [NKJV] Obscene stories, **foolish talk**, and coarse jokes—these are not for you. Instead, let there be thankfulness to God. [NLT] καὶ αἰσχρότης, καὶ **μωρολογία**, ἡ εὐτραπελία, τὰ οὐκ ἀνήκοντα· ἀλλὰ μᾶλλον εὐχαριστία. [GNS] καὶ αἰσχρότης καὶ **μωρολογία** ἡ εὐτραπελία, ἃ οὐκ ἀνῆκεν, ἀλλὰ μᾶλλον εὐχαριστία. [GNT]	

#3563
Silly Women
 	
Silly women–KJV
Weak women–NASB
Weak-willed women–NIV
Gullible women–NKJV
Vulnerable women–NLT
 	
POSB REFERENCE
(2 Tim. 3:6-9; esp. v.6)
Note 4, point 1
	γυναικάρια = gunaikaria
	Pronunciation: [goo-nahee-kar'-ee-ah]
	Parsing (part of speech): noun
	    Case—accusative
	    Gender—neuter
	    Number—plural
	    Stem or root—from *γυναικάριον*, ου
	Concordance References:
	  ⇒ Strong's #1133 gunaikarion
	  ⇒ NIV #1220 gunaikarion
	  ⇒ NASB #1133 gunaikarion
	
	2 Tim. 3:6
	For of this sort are they which creep into houses, and lead captive **silly women** laden with sins, led away with divers lusts, [KJV]
	
	For among them are those who enter into households and captivate **weak women** weighed down with sins, led on by various impulses, [NASB]
	
	They are the kind who worm their way into homes and gain control over **weak-willed women**, who are loaded down with sins and are swayed by all kinds of evil desires, [NIV]
	
	For of this sort are those who creep into households and make captives of **gullible women** loaded down with sins, led away by various lusts, [NKJV]
	
	They are the kind who work their way into people's homes and win the confidence of **vulnerable women** who are burdened with the guilt of sin and controlled by many desires. [NLT]
	
	ἐκ τούτων γάρ εἰσιν οἱ ἐνδύνοντες εἰς τὰς οἰκίας, καὶ αἰχμαλωτεύοντες τὰ **γυναικάρια** σεσωρευμένα ἁμαρτίαις, ἀγόμενα ἐπιθυμίαις ποικίλαις, [GNS]
	
	ἐκ τούτων γάρ εἰσιν οἱ ἐνδύνοντες εἰς τὰς οἰκίας καὶ αἰχμαλωτίζοντες **γυναικάρια** σεσωρευμένα ἁμαρτίαις, ἀγόμενα ἐπιθυμίαις ποικίλαις, [GNT]
		Weak-willed women, silly women, vulnerable women, morally weak women. The Greek word means *little women*, *little* in the sense of being spiritually dead, weak, immature, and unstable. However, it should always be remembered that men are just as gullible as women, just as spiritually dead, weak, immature, and unstable.
		
		Practical Application
		The present passage zeros in on women because of the local situation in Ephesus; some of the women in the Ephesian church were following the corrupt ministers. But the warning is applicable to us all: both men and women must guard against corrupt ministers.
		
		Note what the corrupt minister does. He seeks after people...
		
		• who are laden or burdened down with sins and guilt.
		• who are easily swayed and led away by all kinds of desires and lusts.
		• who are seeking after truth—who are listening and learning all they can from anybody who claims to have the truth.
		
		This is the person the false minister goes after and eventually captivates. When a person begins to seek the truth because he senses a need in his life, senses that he has been living only for his own selfish desires and lusts—that person is wide open for a corrupt minister to step in and lead him astray. Unfortunately, this is exactly what happens ever too often. And note the great tragedy: the person never comes to the knowledge of the truth. Why? Because he never seeks the truth in Christ. He only seeks a "form of godliness," not true godliness. True godliness is found in Christ alone and nowhere else.

#3564
Simple
 	
Simple–KJV
Innocent–NASB
Innocent–NIV
Simple–NKJV
Innocent–NLT
	ἀκεραίους = akeraious
	Pronunciation: [ak-er'-ah-yoos]
	Parsing (part of speech): adjective
	    Case—accusative
	    Gender—masculine
	    Number—plural
	    Stem or root—from *ἀκέραιος*, ον
	Concordance References:
	  ⇒ Strong's #185 akeraios
	  ⇒ NIV #193 akeraios
	  ⇒ NASB #185 akeraios
	
	Romans 16:19
	For your obedience is come abroad unto all men. I am
		Unmixed, unadulterated, pure, guileless, innocent, without any mixture of evil.
		
		Practical Application
		The idea is that the believers of a strong church must constantly mark, focus, and concentrate upon what is good in order to keep the bad out of its fellowship. The way to keep evil out of a church is to focus upon the good. The way to demonstrate spiritual wisdom is to concentrate upon the good; then evil will be recognized for what it is, and it will be rejected.

ENGLISH WORD	GREEK WORD AND VERSE	THE WORD MEANS...
POSB REFERENCE (Rom.16:19-20; esp. v.19) Note 2, point 2	glad therefore on your behalf: but yet I would have you wise unto that which is good, and **simple** concerning evil. [KJV] For the report of your obedience has reached to all; therefore I am rejoicing over you, but I want you to be wise in what is good, and **innocent** in what is evil. [NASB] Everyone has heard about your obedience, so I am full of joy over you; but I want you to be wise about what is good, and **innocent** about what is evil. [NIV] For your obedience has become known to all. Therefore I am glad on your behalf; but I want you to be wise in what is good, and **simple** concerning evil. [NKJV] But everyone knows that you are obedient to the Lord. This makes me very happy. I want you to see clearly what is right and to stay **innocent** of any wrong. [NLT] ἡ γὰρ ὑμῶν ὑπακοὴ εἰς πάντας ἀφίκετο. χαίρω οὖν τὸ ἐφ᾽ ὑμῖν, θέλω δὲ ὑμᾶς σοφοὺς εἶναι εἰς τὸ ἀγαθόν, **ἀκεραίους** δὲ εἰς τὸ κακόν. [GNS] ἡ γὰρ ὑμῶν ὑπακοὴ εἰς πάντας ἀφίκετο· ἐφ᾽ ὑμῖν οὖν χαίρω, θέλω δὲ ὑμᾶς σοφοὺς εἶναι εἰς τὸ ἀγαθόν, **ἀκεραίους** δὲ εἰς τὸ κακόν. [GNT]	The point is this: a strong church must not only avoid evil (Romans 16:17); it must not allow evil to penetrate its fellowship. It must not allow a divisive person to stir up the "simple" (unsuspecting and innocent) believers of the church. A church must be wise: it must mark and focus upon what is good and untainted with evil. It must be wise enough to spot evil and to stop its penetration into the fellowship.

#3565
Simple Devotion
 	
Simplicity–KJV
Simplicity–NASB
Sincere...devotion–NIV
Simplicity–NKJV
Simple devotion–NLT
 	
POSB REFERENCE
(2 Cor.11:3)
Note 2
	ἁπλότητος = *haplotëtos*
	Pronunciation: [hap-lot'-ay-tos]
	Parsing (part of speech): noun
	   Case—genitive
	   Gender—feminine
	   Number—singular
	   Stem or root—from ἁπλότης, ητος
	Concordance References:
	⇒ Strong's #572 haplotēs
	⇒ NIV #605 haplotēs
	⇒ NASB #572 haplotēs
	
	2 Cor. 11:3
	But I fear, lest by any means, as the serpent beguiled Eve through his subtilty, so your minds should be corrupted from the **simplicity** that is in Christ. [KJV]
	
	But I am afraid, lest as the serpent deceived Eve by his craftiness, your minds should be led astray from the **simplicity** and purity of devotion to Christ. [NASB]
	
	But I am afraid that just as Eve was deceived by the serpent's cunning, your minds may somehow be led astray from your **sincere** and pure **devotion** to Christ. [NIV]
	
	But I fear, lest somehow, as the serpent deceived Eve by his craftiness, so your minds may be corrupted from the **simplicity** that is in Christ. [NKJV]
	
	But I fear that somehow you will be led away from your pure and **simple devotion** to Christ, just as Eve was deceived by the serpent. [NLT]
	
	φοβοῦμαι δὲ μή πως, ὡς ὁ ὄφις Εὕαν ἐξηπάτησεν ἐν τῇ πανουργίᾳ αὐτοῦ, οὕτω φθαρῇ τὰ νοήματα ὑμῶν ἀπὸ τῆς **ἁπλότητος** τῆς τῆς εἰς τὸν Χριστόν. [GNS]
	
	φοβοῦμαι δὲ μή πως, ὡς ὁ ὄφις ἐξηπάτησεν Εὕαν ἐν τῇ πανουργίᾳ αὐτοῦ, φθαρῇ τὰ νοήματα ὑμῶν ἀπὸ τῆς **ἁπλότητος** [καὶ τῆς ἁγνότητος] τῆς εἰς τὸν Χριστόν. [GNT]
		Sincere devotion, simple devotion, single-hearted devotion. It means devotion, loyalty, and commitment to Christ.
		
		### Practical Application
		Believers are to have their minds and lives focused upon Christ and upon Him alone. There was great danger that the false teachers would break the loyalty and focus of some believers in Christ and lead them to focus upon...
		
		- some false belief or doctrine.
		- some new idea or position.
		- some ritual or ceremony.
		- some emphasis or program.
		- some person or preacher.

#3566
Simplicity
 	
Singleness–KJV
Sincerity–NASB
Sincere–NIV
Simplicity–NKJV
Generosity–NLT
	ἀφελότητι = *aphelotëti*
	Pronunciation: [af-el-ot'-ay-tee]
	Parsing (part of speech): noun
	   Case—dative
	   Gender—feminine
	   Number—singular
	   Stem or root—from ἁπλότης, ητος
	Concordance References:
	⇒ Strong's #858 aphelotēs
	⇒ NIV #911 aphelotēs
	⇒ NASB #858 aphelotēs
		To be sincere, without hardness; to be generous.
		
		### Practical Application
		Their hearts were soft and tender, easily touched and giving. There was no selfishness or withholding on their part. Where there was need, they gave.

ENGLISH WORD	GREEK WORD AND VERSE	THE WORD MEANS...
POSB REFERENCE (Acts 2:46-47; esp. v.46) Note 6, point 3	**Acts 2:46** And they, continuing daily with one accord in the temple, and breaking bread from house to house, did eat their meat with gladness and **singleness** of heart, [KJV] And day by day continuing with one mind in the temple, and breaking bread from house to house, they were taking their meals together with gladness and **sincerity** of heart, [NASB] Every day they continued to meet together in the temple courts. They broke bread in their homes and ate together with glad and **sincere** hearts, [NIV] So continuing daily with one accord in the temple, and breaking bread from house to house, they ate their food with gladness and **simplicity** of heart, [NKJV] They worshiped together at the Temple each day, met in homes for the Lord's Supper, and shared their meals with great joy and **generosity** [NLT] καθ' ἡμέραν τε προσκαρτεροῦντες ὁμοθυμαδὸν ἐν τῷ ἱερῷ, κλῶντές τε κατ' οἶκον ἄρτον, μετελάμβανον τροφῆς ἐν ἀγαλλιάσει καὶ **ἀφελότητι** καρδίας, [GNS] καθ' ἡμέραν τε προσκαρτεροῦντες ὁμοθυμαδὸν ἐν τῷ ἱερῷ, κλῶντές τε κατ' οἶκον ἄρτον, μετελάμβανον τροφῆς ἐν ἀγαλλιάσει καὶ **ἀφελότητι** καρδίας, [GNT]	

#3567
Simplicity
 	
Simplicity–KJV
Simplicity–NASB
Sincere...devotion–NIV
Simplicity–NKJV
Simple devotion–NLT
 	
POSB REFERENCE
(2 Cor.11:3)
Note 2
 	
See also POSB REF:
(2 Cor.1:12; esp. v.2)
Note 1
	ἁπλότητος = haplotētos
	Pronunciation: [hap-lot'-ay-tos]
	Parsing (part of speech): noun
	    Case—genitive
	    Gender—feminine
	    Number—singular
	    Stem or root—from ἁπλότης, ητος
	Concordance References:
	⇒ Strong's #572 haplotēs
	⇒ NIV #605 haplotēs
	⇒ NASB #572 haplotēs
	
	2 Cor. 11:3
	But I fear, lest by any means, as the serpent beguiled Eve through his subtilty, so your minds should be corrupted from the **simplicity** that is in Christ. [KJV]
	But I am afraid, lest as the serpent deceived Eve by his craftiness, your minds should be led astray from the **simplicity** and purity of devotion to Christ. [NASB]
	But I am afraid that just as Eve was deceived by the serpent's cunning, your minds may somehow be led astray from your **sincere** and pure **devotion** to Christ. [NIV]
	But I fear, lest somehow, as the serpent deceived Eve by his craftiness, so your minds may be corrupted from the **simplicity** that is in Christ. [NKJV]
	But I fear that somehow you will be led away from your pure and **simple devotion** to Christ, just as Eve was deceived by the serpent. [NLT]
	φοβοῦμαι δὲ μή πως, ὡς ὁ ὄφις Εὕαν ἐξηπάτησεν ἐν τῇ πανουργίᾳ αὐτοῦ, οὕτω φθαρῇ τὰ νοήματα ὑμῶν ἀπὸ τῆς **ἁπλότητος** τῆς τῆς εἰς τὸν Χριστόν. [GNS]
	φοβοῦμαι δὲ μή πως, ὡς ὁ ὄφις ἐξηπάτησεν Εὕαν ἐν τῇ πανουργίᾳ αὐτοῦ, φθαρῇ τὰ νοήματα ὑμῶν ἀπὸ τῆς **ἁπλότητος** [καὶ τῆς ἁγνότητος] τῆς εἰς τὸν Χριστόν. [GNT]
		Sincere devotion, simple devotion, single-hearted devotion. It means devotion, loyalty, and commitment to Christ.
		
		Practical Application
		Believers are to have their minds and lives focused upon Christ and upon Him alone. There was great danger that the false teachers would break the loyalty and focus of some believers in Christ and lead them to focus upon...
		• some false belief or doctrine.
		• some new idea or position.
		• some ritual or ceremony.
		• some emphasis or program.
		• some person or preacher.

#3568
Simplicity
 	
Simplicity–KJV
Liberality–NASB
Generously–NIV
Liberality–NKJV
Generously–NLT
	ἐν ἁπλότητι = en haplotēti
	Pronunciation: [en hap-lot'-ay-tee]
	Parsing haplotēti (part of speech): noun
	    Case—dative
	    Gender—feminine
	    Number—from ἁπλότης, ητος
	Concordance References:
	⇒ Strong's #572 + 1722 haplotēs en
	⇒ NIV #605 + 1877 haplotēs en [generously]
	⇒ NASB #572 + 1722 haplotēs en
		Generosity; simplicity; sincerity; singlehearted devotion
		
		Practical Application
		The word has several ideas. It means...
		• to give with sincerity and in simplicity.
		• to give with singleness of heart and without show.
		• to give liberally and generously.

ENGLISH WORD	GREEK WORD AND VERSE	THE WORD MEANS...
POSB REFERENCE (Rom.12:6-8; esp. v.8) Note 2, point 5	**Romans 12:8** Or he that exhorteth, on exhortation: he that giveth, let him do it with **simplicity**; he that ruleth, with diligence; he that sheweth mercy, with cheerfulness. [KJV] Or he who exhorts, in his exhortation; he who gives, with **liberality**; he who leads, with diligence; he who shows mercy, with cheerfulness. [NASB] If it is encouraging, let him encourage; if it is contributing to the needs of others, let him give **generously**; if it is leadership, let him govern diligently; if it is showing mercy, let him do it cheerfully. [NIV] He who exhorts, in exhortation; he who gives, with **liberality**; he who leads, with diligence; he who shows mercy, with cheerfulness. [NKJV] If your gift is to encourage others, do it! If you have money, share it **generously**. If God has given you leadership ability, take the responsibility seriously. And if you have a gift for showing kindness to others, do it gladly. [NLT] εἴτε ὁ παρακαλῶν, ἐν τῇ παρακλήσει· ὁ μεταδιδοὺς **ἐν ἁπλότητι**, ὁ προϊστάμενος, ἐν σπουδῇ· ὁ ἐλεῶν ἐν ἱλαρότητι. [GNS] εἴτε ὁ παρακαλῶν ἐν τῇ παρακλήσει· ὁ μεταδιδοὺς **ἐν ἁπλότητι**, ὁ προϊστάμενος ἐν σπουδῇ, ὁ ἐλεῶν ἐν ἱλαρότητι. [GNT]	The point is this: God gives some persons the special gift to make money in order to have plenty to help others and to spread the gospel around the world. These persons... <ul><li>must give generously. God gave them the gift of making money in order to have enough to fulfill the will of God for the world. Therefore, they must give liberally.</li><li>must not hoard and bank and misuse their gift of wealth.</li><li>must not give grudgingly and complaining about having to give.</li><li>must not give to attract attention or to heap honor upon themselves.</li><li>must not give to boost their own egos and pride.</li></ul>
#3569 **Sin** Trespasses–KJV Transgressions–NASB Sin against–NIV Trespasses–NKJV **Sin–NLT** **POSB REFERENCE** (Mt.6:14) Note 1	παραπτώματα = *paraptömata* Pronunciation: [par-ap'-to-mah-tah] Parsing (part of speech): noun Case—accusative Gender—neuter Number—plural Stem or root—from παράπτωμα, τος Concordance References: ⇒ Strong's #3900 paraptöma ⇒ NIV #4183 paraptöma ⇒ NASB #3900 paraptöma **Matthew 6:14** For if ye forgive men their **trespasses**, your heavenly Father will also forgive you: [KJV] "For if you forgive men for their **transgressions**, your heavenly Father will also forgive you. [NASB] For if you forgive men when they **sin against** you, your heavenly Father will also forgive you. [NIV] "For if you forgive men their **trespasses**, your heavenly Father will also forgive you. [NKJV] "If you forgive those who **sin** against you, your heavenly Father will forgive you. [NLT] ἐὰν γὰρ ἀφῆτε τοῖς ἀνθρώποις τὰ **παραπτώματα** αὐτῶν, ἀφήσει καὶ ὑμῖν ὁ πατὴρ ὑμῶν ὁ οὐράνιος· [GNS] Ἐὰν γὰρ ἀφῆτε τοῖς ἀνθρώποις τὰ **παραπτώματα** αὐτῶν, ἀφήσει καὶ ὑμῖν ὁ πατὴρ ὑμῶν ὁ οὐράνιος· [GNT]	To sin; to trespass or to transgress; to stumble; to fall; to slip; to blunder; to deviate from righteousness and truth. **Practical Application** ⇒ Sin is the transgression of the law. It is violating the law of God. ⇒ Sin is choosing to go one's own way in life, doing one's own thing instead of doing what God says. ⇒ Sin is living like one wants instead of living like God says. ⇒ Sin is disobeying God, not doing what God says to do and doing what God says not to do. ⇒ Sin is disbelieving God instead of believing what God says. ⇒ Sin is ignoring God and neglecting God instead of following and worshipping Him as He says. ⇒ Sin is rebelling against God instead of doing what God says. ⇒ Sin is rejecting God and denying God instead of confessing God and becoming a follower of God.
#3570 **Sin** Sin–KJV Sin–NASB Sin–NIV Sin–NKJV Sin–NLT **POSB REFERENCE** (Jn.1:29) Note 1, point 4b	ἁμαρτίαν = *hamartian* Pronunciation: [ham-ar-tee'-ahn] Parsing (part of speech): noun Case—accusative Gender—feminine Number—singular Stem or root—from ἁμαρτία, ας Concordance References: ⇒ Strong's #266 hamartia ⇒ NIV #281 hamartia ⇒ NASB #266 hamartia **John 1:29** The next day John seeth Jesus coming unto him, and saith, Behold the Lamb of God, which taketh away the **sin** of the world. [KJV] The next day he saw Jesus coming to him, and said,	To sin; to miss the mark; to offend God. Sin is the *transgression of the law*. It is violating the law of God. **Practical Application** ⇒ Sin is choosing to go one's own way in life, doing one's own thing instead of doing what God says. ⇒ Sin is living like one wants instead of living like God says. ⇒ Sin is disobeying God, not doing what God says to do and doing what God says not to do. ⇒ Sin is disbelieving God instead of believing what God says.

ENGLISH WORD	GREEK WORD AND VERSE	THE WORD MEANS...
See also POSB REF: (Jn.8:21-22; esp. v.21) Note 1, point 2	"Behold, the Lamb of God who takes away the **sin** of the world! [NASB] The next day John saw Jesus coming toward him and said, "Look, the Lamb of God, who takes away the **sin** of the world! [NIV] The next day John saw Jesus coming toward him, and said, "Behold! The Lamb of God who takes away the **sin** of the world! [NKJV] The next day John saw Jesus coming toward him and said, "Look! There is the Lamb of God who takes away the **sin** of the world! [NLT] Τῇ ἐπαύριον βλέπει ὁ Ἰωάννης τὸν Ἰησοῦν ἐρχόμενον πρὸς αὐτόν, καὶ λέγει, Ἴδε ὁ ἀμνὸς τοῦ Θεοῦ, ὁ αἴρων τὴν **ἁμαρτίαν** τοῦ κόσμου. [GNS] Τῇ ἐπαύριον βλέπει τὸν Ἰησοῦν ἐρχόμενον πρὸς αὐτόν καὶ λέγει, Ἴδε ὁ ἀμνὸς τοῦ θεοῦ ὁ αἴρων τὴν **ἁμαρτίαν** τοῦ κόσμου. [GNT]	⇒ Sin is ignoring God and neglecting God instead of following and worshipping Him as He says. ⇒ Sin is rebelling against God instead of doing what God says. ⇒ Sin is rejecting God and denying God instead of confessing God and becoming a follower of God. The word "sin" is singular, not plural. All the sins of the world are taken and placed into one package. The whole package of sin—all the sin of every man who has ever lived—was laid upon and borne by Christ.

#3571
Sin
 	
Wickedness–KJV
Evil–NASB
Evil–NIV
Wickedness–NKJV
Sin–NLT
 	
POSB REFERENCE
(Rom.1:29)
Deeper Study #3
	πονηρία = *ponēria*
	Pronunciation: [pon-ay-ree'-ah]
	Parsing (part of speech): noun
	   Case—dative
	   Gender—feminine
	   Number—singular
	   Stem or root—from πονηρία, ας
	Concordance References:
	  ⇒ Strong's #4189 ponēria
	  ⇒ NIV #4504 ponēria
	  ⇒ NASB #4189 ponēria
	
	Romans 1:29
	Being filled with all unrighteousness, fornication, **wickedness**, covetousness, maliciousness; full of envy, murder, debate, deceit, malignity; whisperers, [KJV]
	
	Being filled with all unrighteousness, wickedness, greed, **evil**; full of envy, murder, strife, deceit, malice; they are gossips, [NASB]
	
	They have become filled with every kind of wickedness, **evil**, greed and depravity. They are full of envy, murder, strife, deceit and malice. They are gossips, [NIV]
	
	Being filled with all unrighteousness, sexual immorality, **wickedness**, covetousness, maliciousness; full of envy, murder, strife, deceit, evil-mindedness; *they are* whisperers, [NKJV]
	
	Their lives became full of every kind of wickedness, **sin**, greed, hate, envy, murder, fighting, deception, malicious behavior, and gossip. [NLT]
	
	πεπληρωμένους πάσῃ ἀδικίᾳ **πορνείᾳ**, πονηρίᾳ πλεονεξίᾳ κακίᾳ· μεστοὺς φθόνου, φόνου, ἔριδος, δόλου, κακοηθείας· [GNS]
	
	πεπληρωμένους πάσῃ ἀδικίᾳ **πονηρίᾳ** πλεονεξίᾳ κακίᾳ, μεστοὺς φθόνου φόνου ἔριδος δόλου κακοηθείας, ψιθυριστάς [GNT]
		To be depraved; to be actively evil; to do mischief; to trouble others and cause harm; to be malicious; to be dangerous and destructive. It is malice, wickedness, sin, hatred, evil intention and ill will.
		
		Practical Application
		It is an active evil or wickedness, a desire within the heart to do harm and to corrupt people. It is a person who actually pursues others to seduce or to injure them.

#3572
Sin
 	
Sin–KJV
Sin–NASB
Sin–NIV
Sin–NKJV
Sin–NLT
 	
POSB REFERENCE
(1 Jn.3:4)
Deeper Study #1
	ἁμαρτία = *hamartia*
	Pronunciation: [ham-ar-tee'-ah]
	Parsing (part of speech): noun
	   Case—nominative
	   Gender—feminine
	   Number—singular
	   Stem or root—from ἁμαρτία, ας
	Concordance References:
	  ⇒ Strong's #266 hamartia
	  ⇒ NIV #281 hamartia
	  ⇒ NASB #266 hamartia
	
	1 John 3:4
	Whosoever committeth sin transgresseth also the law: for **sin** is the transgression of the law. [KJV]
	
	Everyone who practices sin also practices lawlessness; and **sin** is lawlessness. [NASB]
	
	Everyone who sins breaks the law; in fact, **sin** is lawlessness. [NIV]
		To sin; to miss the mark; to offend God. Sin is the *transgression of the law*. It is violating the law of God.
		
		Practical Application
		There are a number of Hebrew words and a number of Greek words for sin in the Bible. A literal translation of the major words will show the meaning of sin.
		1. Sin is unbelief, the failure to believe God (Matthew 13:58; Matthew 17:20; Romans 3:3; Romans 4:20; Romans 11:20, 23; 1 Tim. 1:13; Hebrews 3:12, 19).
		2. Sin is missing the mark, coming short of the glory of God (see *Deeper Study #1*—Romans 3:23).
		3. Sin is error, making a mistake; a wandering

ENGLISH WORD	GREEK WORD AND VERSE	THE WORD MEANS...

Whoever commits sin also commits lawlessness, and **sin** is lawlessness. [NKJV]

Those who sin are opposed to the law of God, for all **sin** opposes the law of God. [NLT]

πᾶς ὁ ποιῶν τὴν ἁμαρτίαν, καὶ τὴν ἀνομίαν ποιεῖ· καὶ ἡ **ἁμαρτία** ἐστὶν ἡ ἀνομία. [GNS]

Πᾶς ὁ ποιῶν τὴν ἁμαρτίαν καὶ τὴν ἀνομίαν ποιεῖ, καὶ ἡ **ἁμαρτία** ἐστὶν ἡ ἀνομία. [GNT]

off of the right path (Romans 1:27; James 5:20; 2 Peter 2:18; 2 Peter 3:17; Jude 11).

4. Sin is ungodliness and unrighteousness (Romans 1:18; Romans 11:26; 2 Tim. 2:16; Titus 2:12; Jude 15, 18).
5. Sin is transgression, a stepping outside the law (Romans 3:23; Romans 4:15; Romans 5:13, 20; Hebrews 2:2; Hebrews 9:15).
6. Sin is trespassing, intruding where one should not go (see note—Ephes. 2:1).
7. Sin is disobedience, a refusal to listen and hear and do the commandments of God (Ephes. 2:2; Ephes. 5:6; Col. 3:6).
8. Sin is lawlessness, rebellion, a rejection of God's will and law (1 John 3:4).
9. Sin is iniquity, an inward contempt that leads to the continual practice of sin (Matthew 7:23; Romans 6:19; 2 Thes. 2:3. Cp. Romans 1:21-23.)

All men have sinned (Romans 3:23). Sin first entered the world through Adam (Romans 5:12). Because of sin, all men are spiritually dead, forever, and are destined to die physically (Romans 6:23; cp. Genesis 2:17; Genesis 3:19; Ezekiel 18:4, 20). But there is a deliverance from sin and from its penalty—the sacrificial death of Jesus Christ (Acts 4:12; Hebrews 9:26). (See *Deeper Study* #1—2 Peter 1:4.)

#3573

Sin Against

Trespasses-KJV
Transgressions—NASB
Sin against—NIV
Trespasses—NKJV
Sin—NLT

POSB REFERENCE
(Mt.6:14)
Note 1

παραπτώματα = paraptōmata
Pronunciation: [par-ap'-to-mah-tah]
Parsing (part of speech): noun
 Case—accusative
 Gender—neuter
 Number—plural
 Stem or root—from παράπτωμα, τος
Concordance References:
⇒ Strong's #3900 paraptōma
⇒ NIV #4183 paraptōma
⇒ NASB #3900 paraptōma

Matthew 6:14

For if ye forgive men their **trespasses**, your heavenly Father will also forgive you: [KJV]

"For if you forgive men for their **transgressions**, your heavenly Father will also forgive you. [NASB]

For if you forgive men when they **sin against** you, your heavenly Father will also forgive you. [NIV]

"For if you forgive men their **trespasses**, your heavenly Father will also forgive you. [NKJV]

"If you forgive those who **sin** against you, your heavenly Father will forgive you. [NLT]

ἐὰν γὰρ ἀφῆτε τοῖς ἀνθρώποις τὰ **παραπτώματα** αὐτῶν, ἀφήσει καὶ ὑμῖν ὁ πατὴρ ὑμῶν ὁ οὐράνιος· [GNS]

Ἐὰν γὰρ ἀφῆτε τοῖς ἀνθρώποις τὰ **παραπτώματα** αὐτῶν, ἀφήσει καὶ ὑμῖν ὁ πατὴρ ὑμῶν ὁ οὐράνιος· [GNT]

To sin; to trespass or to transgress; to stumble; to fall; to slip; to blunder; to deviate from righteousness and truth.

Practical Application

Sin is the transgression of the law. It is violating the law of God.

⇒ Sin is choosing to go one's own way in life, doing one's own thing instead of doing what God says.
⇒ Sin is living like one wants instead of living like God says.
⇒ Sin is disobeying God, not doing what God says to do and doing what God says not to do.
⇒ Sin is disbelieving God instead of believing what God says.
⇒ Sin is ignoring God and neglecting God instead of following and worshipping Him as He says.
⇒ Sin is rebelling against God instead of doing what God says.
⇒ Sin is rejecting God and denying God instead of confessing God and becoming a follower of God.

#3574

Sin Will Be Rampant

Iniquity–KJV
Lawlessness–NASB
Wickedness–NIV
Lawlessness–NKJV
Sin will be rampant–NLT

ἀνομίαν = anomian
Pronunciation: [an-om-ee'-ahn]
Parsing (part of speech): noun
 Case—accusative
 Gender—feminine
 Number—singular
 Stem or root—from ἀνομία, ας
Concordance References:
⇒ Strong's #458 anomia
⇒ NIV #490 anomia
⇒ NASB #458 anomia

Lawlessness, wickedness, iniquity, unrighteousness; sin that is rampant; a gross transgression of the law; unauthorized acts or conduct; evil-doing.

Practical Application

Unbelievers do not obey God. They live and do as they wish, not as God says. Rejecting God and what He says they go about doing their own thing. They rebel against God and His commandments, living lawless and unrighteous

ENGLISH WORD	GREEK WORD AND VERSE	THE WORD MEANS...
POSB REFERENCE (Mt.24:12) *Deeper Study #6* **See also POSB REF:** (Mt.7:23) Note 3, point 2 (2 Cor.6:14-16; esp. v.14) Note 2	**Matthew 24:12** And because **iniquity** shall abound, the love of many shall wax cold. [KJV] "And because **lawlessness** is increased, most people's love will grow cold. [NASB] Because of the increase of **wickedness**, the love of most will grow cold, [NIV] And because **lawlessness** will abound, the love of many will grow cold. [NKJV] **Sin will be rampant** everywhere, and the love of many will grow cold. [NLT] καὶ διὰ τὸ πληθυνθῆναι τὴν **ἀνομίαν** ψυγήσεται ἡ ἀγάπη τῶν πολλῶν· [GNS] καὶ διὰ τὸ πληθυνθῆναι τὴν **ἀνομίαν** ψυγήσεται ἡ ἀγάπη τῶν πολλῶν. [GNT]	lives. What is lawlessness? It is taking license... • with the law and righteousness • with morality and discipline It is neglect of or opposition to the law of God; it is substituting the will of self in the place of God's will (1 John 3:4). It is looking to self or to the world instead of looking to God. It is following the course of self and the desires of self instead of following the course of God. (See POSB *Deeper Study #1*—Matthew 7:23 for discussion).
#3575 **Sincere** Godly sincerity–KJV Godly sincerity– NASB Sincerity...from God– NIV Godly sincerity–NKJV **Sincere–NLT** **POSB REFERENCE** (2 Cor.1:12) Note 1	*εἰλικρινείᾳ τοῦ θεοῦ = eilikrineia too theou* Pronunciation: [hi-lik-ree'-ni-ah too theh-oo] Parsing *eilikrineia* (part of speech): noun Case—dative Gender—feminine Number—singular Stem or root—from εἰλικρίνεια, ας Concordance References: ⇒ Strong's #1505 eilikrineia ⇒ NIV #1636 eilikrineia [sincerity] ⇒ NASB #1505 eilikrineia **2 Cor. 1:12** For our rejoicing is this, the testimony of our conscience, that in simplicity and **godly sincerity**, not with fleshly wisdom, but by the grace of God, we have had our conversation in the world, and more abundantly to youward. [KJV] For our proud confidence is this, the testimony of our conscience, that in holiness and **godly sincerity**, not in fleshly wisdom but in the grace of God, we have conducted ourselves in the world, and especially toward you. [NASB] Now this is our boast: Our conscience testifies that we have conducted ourselves in the world, and especially in our relations with you, in the holiness and **sincerity** that are **from God**. We have done so not according to worldly wisdom but according to God's grace. [NIV] For our boasting is this: the testimony of our conscience that we conducted ourselves in the world in simplicity and **godly sincerity**, not with fleshly wisdom but by the grace of God, and more abundantly toward you. [NKJV] We can say with confidence and a clear conscience that we have been honest and **sincere** in all our dealings. We have depended on God's grace, not on our own earthly wisdom. That is how we have acted toward everyone, and especially toward you. [NLT] Ἡ γὰρ καύχησις ἡμῶν αὕτη ἐστί, τὸ μαρτύριον τῆς συνειδήσεως ἡμῶν, ὅτι ἐν ἁπλότητι καὶ **εἰ-λικρινείᾳ Θεοῦ**, οὐκ ἐν σοφίᾳ σαρκικῇ ἀλλ' ἐν χάριτι Θεοῦ, ἀνεστράφημεν ἐν τῷ κόσμῳ, περισσοτέρως δὲ πρὸς ὑμᾶς. [GNS] Ἡ γὰρ καύχησις ἡμῶν αὕτη ἐστίν, τὸ μαρτύριον τῆς συνειδήσεως ἡμῶν, ὅτι ἐν ἁπλότητι καὶ **εἰ-λικρινείᾳ τοῦ θεου**, [καὶ] οὐκ ἐν σοφίᾳ σαρκικῇ ἀλλ' ἐν χάριτι θεοῦ, ἀνεστράφημεν ἐν τῷ κόσμῳ, περισσοτέρως δὲ πρὸς ὑμᾶς. [GNT]	Godly sincerity, purity. It is the unadulterated, the pure that has been shaken and rolled through a sieve. It means the unadulterated, the pure that shows up unstained and untainted when examined in the sunlight. **Practical Application** Paul is saying that he is pure, unstained, untainted, unadulterated in his conduct and behavior. 1 Cor. 5:8 is the only other time Paul uses this word in his writings.
#3576 **Sincere** Without dissimulation– tion–KJV	*ἀνυπόκριτος = anupokritos* Pronunciation: [an-oo-pok'-ree-tos] Parsing (part of speech): adjective Case—nominative Gender—feminine Number—singular Stem or root—from ἀνυπόκριτος, ον	To be sincere; to be genuine. It means without hypocrisy, without play-acting. This means to be free from insincerity, hypocrisy, play-acting, and wearing a mask. **Practical Application** The believer is to love sincerely without

ENGLISH WORD	GREEK WORD AND VERSE	THE WORD MEANS...
Without hypocrisy–NASB **Sincere–NIV** Without hypocrisy–NKJV Don't just pretend–NLT **POSB REFERENCE** (Rom.12:9-10; esp. v.9) Note 1 See also POSB REF: (1 Pt.1:22-25; esp. v.22) Note 1 (Jas.3:17-18; esp. v.17) Note 3	Concordance References: ⇒ Strong's #505 anupokritos ⇒ NIV #537 anupokritos ⇒ NASB #505 anupokritos **Romans 12:9** Let love be **without dissimulation**. Abhor that which is evil; cleave to that which is good. [KJV] Let love be **without hypocrisy**. Abhor what is evil; cling to what is good. [NASB] Love must be **sincere**. Hate what is evil; cling to what is good. [NIV] *Let* love *be* **without hypocrisy**. Abhor what is evil. Cling to what is good. [NKJV] **Don't just pretend** that you love others. Really love them. Hate what is wrong. Stand on the side of the good. [NLT] Ἡ ἀγάπη **ἀνυπόκριτος**. ἀποστυγοῦντες τὸ πονηρόν, κολλώμενοι τῷ ἀγαθῷ. [GNS] Ἡ ἀγάπη **ἀνυπόκριτος**. ἀποστυγοῦντες τὸ πονηρόν, κολλώμενοι τῷ ἀγαθῷ, [GNT]	hypocrisy. It means that a person does not just say "I love you," but he actually loves. He sincerely loves; he honestly and truthfully loves. The love being spoken about is love for all men and not only for believers. The believer must never pretend, be hypocritical, play-act, or have an ulterior motive when dealing with others. He must show love and respect, interest and attention, care and concern; but he must not show it from an impure motive:
#3577 **Sincere** Singleness–KJV Sincerity–NASB **Sincere–NIV** Simplicity–NKJV Generosity–NLT **POSB REFERENCE** (Acts 2:46-47; esp. v.46) Note 6, point 3	ἀφελότητι = aphelotëti Pronunciation: [af-el-ot'-ay-tee] Parsing (part of speech): noun 　　Case—dative 　　Gender—feminine 　　Number—singular 　　Stem or root—from ἀφελότης, ητος Concordance References: ⇒ Strong's #858 aphelotës ⇒ NIV #911 aphelotës ⇒ NASB #858 aphelotës **Acts 2:46** And they, continuing daily with one accord in the temple, and breaking bread from house to house, did eat their meat with gladness and **singleness** of heart, [KJV] And day by day continuing with one mind in the temple, and breaking bread from house to house, they were taking their meals together with gladness and **sincerity** of heart, [NASB] Every day they continued to meet together in the temple courts. They broke bread in their homes and ate together with glad and **sincere** hearts, [NIV] So continuing daily with one accord in the temple, and breaking bread from house to house, they ate their food with gladness and **simplicity** of heart, [NKJV] They worshiped together at the Temple each day, met in homes for the Lord's Supper, and shared their meals with great joy and **generosity** [NLT] καθ' ἡμέραν τε προσκαρτεροῦντες ὁμοθυμαδὸν ἐν τῷ ἱερῷ, κλῶντές τε κατ' οἶκον ἄρτον, μετελάμβανον τροφῆς ἐν ἀγαλλιάσει καὶ **ἀφελότητι** καρδίας, [GNS] καθ' ἡμέραν τε προσκαρτεροῦντες ὁμοθυμαδὸν ἐν τῷ ἱερῷ, κλῶντές τε κατ' οἶκον ἄρτον, μετελάμβανον τροφῆς ἐν ἀγαλλιάσει καὶ **ἀφελότητι** καρδίας, [GNT]	To be sincere, without hardness; to be generous. **Practical Application** Their hearts were soft and tender, easily touched and giving. There was no selfishness or withholding on their part. Where there was need, they gave.
#3578 **Sincere** **Sincere–KJV** **Sincere–NASB** Pure–NIV **Sincere–NKJV** Pure–NLT **POSB REFERENCE** (Philip.1:9-10; esp. v.9) Note 7, point 2	εἰλικρινεῖς = eilikrineis Pronunciation: [i-lik-ree-nees] Parsing (part of speech): adjective 　　Case—nominative 　　Gender—masculine 　　Number—plural 　　Stem or root—from εἰλικρινής, ές Concordance References: ⇒ Strong's #1506 eilikrinës ⇒ NIV #1637 eilikrinës ⇒ NASB #1506 eilikrinës **Philip. 1:10** That ye may approve things that are excellent; that ye may be **sincere** and without offence till the day of Christ; [KJV]	Pure, sincere, honest. It means to sift about through a sieve in order to make pure. Therefore, the word means pure, uncontaminated, untainted, not polluted. **Practical Application** A growing love is needed to be sincere and pure. Note that we are to stay pure until the return of Christ. Only a growing love will keep our eyes focused upon Christ. If we do not love Him, we will not look to Him. If we love Him, we will keep our eyes fastened upon Him, longing to see and be with Him. Only love—true love—will keep us pure waiting for His return.

ENGLISH WORD	GREEK WORD AND VERSE	THE WORD MEANS...
	This is now, beloved, the second letter I am writing to you in which I am stirring up your **sincere mind** by way of reminder, [NASB] Dear friends, this is now my second letter to you. I have written both of them as reminders to stimulate you to **wholesome thinking**. [NIV] Beloved, I now write to you this second epistle (in *both of* which I stir up your **pure minds** by way of reminder), [NKJV] This is my second letter to you, dear friends, and in both of them I have tried to stimulate your **wholesome thinking** and refresh your memory. [NLT] Ταύτην ἤδη, ἀγαπητοί, δευτέραν ὑμῖν γράφω ἐπιστολήν, ἐν αἷς διεγείρω ὑμῶν ἐν ὑπομνήσει τὴν **εἰλικρινῆ διάνοιαν**, [GNS] Ταύτην ἤδη, ἀγαπητοί, δευτέραν ὑμῖν γράφω ἐπιστολήν, ἐν αἷς διεγείρω ὑμῶν ἐν ὑπομνήσει τὴν **εἰλικρινῆ διάνοιαν** [GNT]	

#3583
Sincerely
 	
Naturally–KJV
Genuinely–NASB
Genuine–NIV
Sincerely–NKJV
Genuinely–NLT
 	
POSB
REFERENCE
(Philip.2:20)
Note 1
	γνησίως = *gnēsiōs*
	Pronunciation: [gnay'-see-os]
	Parsing (part of speech): adjective
	    Type—adverb
	    Stem or root—from γνησίως
	Concordance References:
	  ⇒ Strong's #1104 gnēsiōs
	  ⇒ NIV #1189 gnēsiōs
	  ⇒ NASB #1104 gnēsiōs
	
	Philip. 2:20
	For I have no man likeminded, who will **naturally** care for your state. [KJV]
	
	For I have no one else of kindred spirit who will **genuinely** be concerned for your welfare. [NASB]
	
	I have no one else like him, who takes a **genuine** interest in your welfare. [NIV]
	
	For I have no one like-minded, who will **sincerely** care for your state. [NKJV]
	
	I have no one else like Timothy, who **genuinely** cares about your welfare. [NLT]
	
	οὐδένα γὰρ ἔχω ἰσόψυχον, ὅστις **γνησίως** τὰ περὶ ὑμῶν μεριμνήσει, [GNS]
	
	οὐδένα γὰρ ἔχω ἰσόψυχον, ὅστις **γνησίως** τὰ περὶ ὑμῶν μεριμνήσει· [GNT]
		Genuine, naturally, sincere, authentic, real, actual, certified.
		
		Practical Application
		Timothy had a kindred, brotherly spirit in caring for others. In fact, he was unequaled. There were many excellent ministers of the gospel, but Timothy's spirit came closest to Paul's than all the others. Timothy cared for the churches and their believers just as Paul cared. His heart was sincere (*gnēsiōs*). His care or interest arose from deep within: it was natural and sincere—the same kind of care that a genuine brother would have. Timothy's ministry—his care and concern for the believers—would be deep and genuine, a true concern.

#3584
Sincerely Seek
 	
Diligently seek–KJV
Seek–NASB
Earnestly seek–NIV
Seek–NKJV
Sincerely seek–NLT
 	
POSB
REFERENCE
(Heb.11:6)
Note 5, point 2b
	ἐκζητοῦσιν = *ekzētousin*
	Pronunciation: [ek-zay-too-sin]
	Parsing (part of speech): verb
	    Mood—participle
	    Tense—present
	    Voice—active
	    Case—dative
	    Gender—masculine
	    Number—plural
	    Stem or root—from ἐκζητέω
	Concordance References:
	  ⇒ Strong's #1567 ekzēteō
	  ⇒ NIV #1699 ekzēteō
	  ⇒ NASB #1567 ekzēteō
	
	Hebrews 11:6
	But without faith it is impossible to please him: for he that cometh to God must believe that he is, and that he is a rewarder of them that **diligently seek** him. [KJV]
	
	And without faith it is impossible to please Him, for he who comes to God must believe that He is, and that He is a rewarder of those who **seek** Him. [NASB]
	
	And without faith it is impossible to please God, because anyone who comes to him must believe that he exists and that he rewards those who **earnestly seek** him. [NIV]
	
	But without faith *it is* impossible to please *Him,* for he
		To earnestly seek; to diligently seek; to sincerely seek. It means to *seek out God*; to diligently seek to find Him and to follow Him.
		
		Practical Application
		God does not reward the sleepy eyed, the complacent, the non-thinker, the half-interested, the worldly-minded, the pleasure seeker. God rewards those who sincerely seek to know and follow Him. The idea is that we must be in earnest and persevere, enduring to the end. What is the reward to those who sincerely seek God? It is the same reward given to Abel and Enoch: righteousness and God's care in this life and deliverance from death to live eternally with God.

ENGLISH WORD	GREEK WORD AND VERSE	THE WORD MEANS...
	who comes to God must believe that He is, and *that* He is a rewarder of those who diligently **seek** Him. [NKJV] So, you see, it is impossible to please God without faith. Anyone who wants to come to him must believe that there is a God and that he rewards those who **sincerely seek** him. [NLT] χωρὶς δὲ πίστεως ἀδύνατον εὐαρεστῆσαι· πιστεῦσαι γὰρ δεῖ τὸν προσερχόμενον τῷ Θεῷ, ὅτι ἔστι, καὶ τοῖς **ἐκζητοῦσιν** αὐτὸν μισθαποδότης γίνεται. [GNS] χωρὶς δὲ πίστεως ἀδύνατον εὐαρεστῆσαι· πιστεῦσαι γὰρ δεῖ τὸν προσερχόμενον τῷ θεῷ ὅτι ἔστιν καὶ τοῖς **ἐκζητοῦσιν** αὐτὸν μισθαποδότης γίνεται. [GNT]	

#3585
Sincerity
 	
Sincerity–KJV
Sincerity–NASB
Sincerity–NIV
Sincerity–NKJV
Sincerity–NLT
 	
POSB REFERENCE
(2 Cor.2:16-17; esp. v.17)
Note 4
 	
See also POSB REF:
(1 Cor.5:8)
Note 3
	εἰλικρινείας = *eilikrineias*
	Pronunciation: [i-lik-ree'-ni-ahs]
	Parsing (part of speech): noun
	    Case—genitive
	    Gender—feminine
	    Number—singular
	    Stem or root—from εἰλικρίνεια, ας
	Concordance References:
	  ⇒ Strong's #1505 eilikrineia
	  ⇒ NIV #1636 eilikrineia
	  ⇒ NASB #1505 eilikrineia
	
	2 Cor. 2:17
	For we are not as many, which corrupt the word of God: but as of **sincerity**, but as of God, in the sight of God speak we in Christ. [KJV]
	
	For we are not like many, peddling the word of God, but as from **sincerity**, but as from God, we speak in Christ in the sight of God. [NASB]
	
	Unlike so many, we do not peddle the word of God for profit. On the contrary, in Christ we speak before God with **sincerity**, like men sent from God. [NIV]
	
	For we are not, as so many, peddling the word of God; but as of **sincerity**, but as from God, we speak in the sight of God in Christ. [NKJV]
	
	You see, we are not like those hucksters—and there are many of them—who preach just to make money. We preach God's message with **sincerity** and with Christ's authority. And we know that the God who sent us is watching us. [NLT]
	
	οὐ γάρ ἐσμεν ὡς οἱ πολλοί, καπηλεύοντες τὸν λόγον τοῦ Θεοῦ· ἀλλ' ὡς ἐξ **εἰλικρινείας**, ἀλλ' ὡς ἐκ Θεοῦ κατενώπιον τοῦ Θεοῦ, ἐν Χριστῷ λαλοῦμεν. [GNS]
	
	οὐ γάρ ἐσμεν ὡς οἱ πολλοὶ καπηλεύοντες τὸν λόγον τοῦ θεοῦ, ἀλλ' ὡς ἐξ **εἰλικρινείας**, ἀλλ' ὡς ἐκ θεοῦ κατέναντι θεοῦ ἐν Χριστῷ λαλοῦμεν. [GNT]
		To be sincere; sincerity.
		
		Practical Application
		The qualified man is "sincere" (*eilikrineias*). This means that the minister and his motives are pure and unadulterated, that he and his motives have been shaken and rolled through a sieve. The minister is unstained and untainted when inspected. He is in the ministry to serve God and to help people. He is not in the ministry because he respects it as a profession nor for any other reason. God has called him, and he is gripped by the necessity to serve God.

#3586
Sincerity
 	
Singleness–KJV
Sincerity–NASB
Sincere–NIV
Simplicity–NKJV
Generosity–NLT
 	
POSB REFERENCE
(Acts 2:46-47; esp. v.46)
Note 6, point 3
	ἀφελότητι = *apheloteti*
	Pronunciation: [af-el-ot'-ay-tee]
	Parsing (part of speech): noun
	    Case—dative
	    Gender—feminine
	    Number—singular
	    Stem or root—from ἀφελότης, ητος
	Concordance References:
	  ⇒ Strong's #858 aphelotes
	  ⇒ NIV #911 aphelotes
	  ⇒ NASB #858 aphelotes
	
	Acts 2:46
	And they, continuing daily with one accord in the temple, and breaking bread from house to house, did eat their meat with gladness and **singleness** of heart, [KJV]
	
	And day by day continuing with one mind in the temple, and breaking bread from house to house, they were taking their meals together with gladness and **sincerity** of heart, [NASB]
	
	Every day they continued to meet together in the temple courts. They broke bread in their homes and ate together with glad and **sincere** hearts, [NIV]
		To be sincere, without hardness; to be generous.
		
		Practical Application
		Their hearts were soft and tender, easily touched and giving. There was no selfishness or withholding on their part. Where there was need, they gave.

ENGLISH WORD	GREEK WORD AND VERSE	THE WORD MEANS...
	So continuing daily with one accord in the temple, and breaking bread from house to house, they ate their food with gladness and **simplicity** of heart, [NKJV] They worshiped together at the Temple each day, met in homes for the Lord's Supper, and shared their meals with great joy and **generosity** [NLT] καθ' ἡμέραν τε προσκαρτεροῦντες ὁμοθυμαδὸν ἐν τῷ ἱερῷ, κλῶντές τε κατ' οἶκον ἄρτον, μετελάμβανον τροφῆς ἐν ἀγαλλιάσει καὶ **ἀφελότητι** καρδίας, [GNS] καθ' ἡμέραν τε προσκαρτεροῦντες ὁμοθυμαδὸν ἐν τῷ ἱερῷ, κλῶντές τε κατ' οἶκον ἄρτον, μετελάμβανον τροφῆς ἐν ἀγαλλιάσει καὶ **ἀφελότητι** καρδίας, [GNT]	

#3587
Sincerity From God
 	
Godly sincerity–KJV
Godly sincerity–NASB
Sincerity...from God–NIV
Godly sincerity–NKJV
Sincere–NLT
 	
POSB REFERENCE
(2 Cor.1:12)
Note 1
	εἰλικρινείᾳ τοῦ θεοῦ = *eilikrineia too theou*
	Pronunciation: [hi-lik-ree'-ni-ah too theh-oo]
	Parsing *eilikrineia* (part of speech): noun
	  Case—dative
	  Gender—feminine
	  Number—singular
	  Stem or root—from **εἰλικρίνεια**, ας
	Concordance References:
	⇒ Strong's #1505 eilikrineia
	⇒ NIV #1636 eilikrineia [sincerity]
	⇒ NASB #1505 eilikrineia
	
	<div align="center">**2 Cor. 1:12**</div>For our rejoicing is this, the testimony of our conscience, that in simplicity and **godly sincerity**, not with fleshly wisdom, but by the grace of God, we have had our conversation in the world, and more abundantly to you-ward. [KJV]
	
	For our proud confidence is this, the testimony of our conscience, that in holiness and **godly sincerity**, not in fleshly wisdom but in the grace of God, we have conducted ourselves in the world, and especially toward you. [NASB]
	
	Now this is our boast: Our conscience testifies that we have conducted ourselves in the world, and especially in our relations with you, in the holiness and **sincerity** that are **from God**. We have done so not according to worldly wisdom but according to God's grace. [NIV]
	
	For our boasting is this: the testimony of our conscience that we conducted ourselves in the world in simplicity and **godly sincerity**, not with fleshly wisdom but by the grace of God, and more abundantly toward you. [NKJV]
	
	We can say with confidence and a clear conscience that we have been honest and **sincere** in all our dealings. We have depended on God's grace, not on our own earthly wisdom. That is how we have acted toward everyone, and especially toward you. [NLT]
	
	Ἡ γὰρ καύχησις ἡμῶν αὕτη ἐστί, τὸ μαρτύριον τῆς συνειδήσεως ἡμῶν, ὅτι ἐν ἁπλότητι καὶ **εἰλικρινείᾳ Θεοῦ**, οὐκ ἐν σοφίᾳ σαρκικῇ ἀλλ' ἐν χάριτι Θεοῦ, ἀνεστράφημεν ἐν τῷ κόσμῳ, περισσοτέρως δὲ πρὸς ὑμᾶς. [GNS]
	
	Ἡ γὰρ καύχησις ἡμῶν αὕτη ἐστίν, τὸ μαρτύριον τῆς συνειδήσεως ἡμῶν, ὅτι ἐν ἁπλότητι καὶ **εἰλικρινείᾳ τοῦ θεοῦ**, [καὶ] οὐκ ἐν σοφίᾳ σαρκικῇ ἀλλ' ἐν χάριτι θεοῦ, ἀνεστράφημεν ἐν τῷ κόσμῳ, περισσοτέρως δὲ πρὸς ὑμᾶς. [GNT]
		Godly sincerity, purity. It is the unadulterated, the pure that has been shaken and rolled through a sieve. It means the unadulterated, the pure that shows up unstained and untainted when examined in the sunlight.
		
		### Practical Application
		Paul is saying that he is pure, unstained, untainted, unadulterated in his conduct and behavior. 1 Cor. 5:8 is the only other time Paul uses this word in his writings.

#3588
Sinful
 	
Ungodliness–KJV
Ungodliness–NASB
Godlessness–NIV
Ungodliness–NKJV
Sinful–NLT
	ἀσέβειαν = *asebeian*
	Pronunciation: [as-eb'-i-ahn]
	Parsing (part of speech): noun
	  Case—accusative
	  Gender—feminine
	  Number—singular
	  Stem or root—from **ἀσέβεια**, ας
	Concordance References:
	⇒ Strong's #763 asebeia
	⇒ NIV #813 asebeia
	⇒ NASB #763 asebeia
		Godlessness, ungodliness; sinful, wicked behavior that is contrary to God's nature.
		
		### Practical Application
		The sinful (*asebeian*) fail to love and obey God. They are those who do not live as God lives. They are not like God, not holy and righteous and pure. They do not work at developing a godly nature, do not honor God by word or deed, do not worship and obey God as the only living

ENGLISH WORD	GREEK WORD AND VERSE	THE WORD MEANS...
POSB REFERENCE (Rom.1:18) Note 1, point 3a	**Romans 1:18** For the wrath of God is revealed from heaven against all **ungodliness** and unrighteousness of men, who hold the truth in unrighteousness; [KJV] For the wrath of God is revealed from heaven against all **ungodliness** and unrighteousness of men, who suppress the truth in unrighteousness, [NASB] The wrath of God is being revealed from heaven against all the **godlessness** and wickedness of men who suppress the truth by their wickedness, [NIV] For the wrath of God is revealed from heaven against all **ungodliness** and unrighteousness of men, who suppress the truth in unrighteousness, [NKJV] But God shows his anger from heaven against all **sinful**, wicked people who push the truth away from themselves. [NLT] Ἀποκαλύπτεται γὰρ ὀργὴ Θεοῦ ἀπ' οὐρανοῦ ἐπὶ πᾶσαν **ἀσέβειαν** καὶ ἀδικίαν ἀνθρώπων τῶν τὴν ἀλήθειαν ἐν ἀδικίᾳ κατεχόντων, [GNS] Ἀποκαλύπτεται γὰρ ὀργὴ θεοῦ ἀπ' οὐρανοῦ ἐπὶ πᾶσαν **ἀσέβειαν** καὶ ἀδικίαν ἀνθρώπων τῶν τὴν ἀλήθειαν ἐν ἀδικίᾳ κατεχόντων, [GNT]	and true God, do not reverence Him by doing what He says. On the contrary, the sinful are those who do what they want when they want, who may give lip service to God, but who ignore Him in their day-to-day lives.

#3589 Sinful
 	
Worldly–KJV
Worldly–NASB
Worldly–NIV
Worldly–NKJV
Sinful–NLT
 	
POSB REFERENCE (Tit.2:12) Note 2, point 1b
	κοσμικὰς = kosmikas
	Pronunciation: [kos-mee-kahs']
	Parsing (part of speech): adjective
	  Case—accusative
	  Gender—feminine
	  Number—plural
	  Stem or root—from κοσμικός ή, όν
	Concordance References:
	⇒ Strong's #2886 kosmikos
	⇒ NIV #3176 kosmikos
	⇒ NASB #2886 kosmikos
	
	Titus 2:12
	Teaching us that, denying ungodliness and **worldly** lusts, we should live soberly, righteously, and godly, in this present world; [KJV]
	Instructing us to deny ungodliness and **worldly** desires and to live sensibly, righteously and godly in the present age, [NASB]
	It teaches us to say "No" to ungodliness and **worldly** passions, and to live self-controlled, upright and godly lives in this present age, [NIV]
	Teaching us that, denying ungodliness and **worldly** lusts, we should live soberly, righteously, and godly, in the present age, [NKJV]
	And we are instructed to turn from godless living and **sinful** pleasures. We should live in this evil world with self-control, right conduct, and devotion to God, [NLT]
	παιδεύουσα ἡμᾶς ἵνα, ἀρνησάμενοι τὴν ἀσέβειαν καὶ τὰς **κοσμικὰς** ἐπιθυμίας σωφρόνως καὶ δικαίως καὶ εὐσεβῶς ζήσωμεν ἐν τῷ νῦν αἰῶνι, [GNS]
	παιδεύουσα ἡμᾶς, ἵνα ἀρνησάμενοι τὴν ἀσέβειαν καὶ τὰς **κοσμικὰς** ἐπιθυμίας σωφρόνως καὶ δικαίως καὶ εὐσεβῶς ζήσωμεν ἐν τῷ νῦν αἰῶνι, [GNT]
		Worldly, sinful; all the desires of this world that are not fit for heaven and could not be presented to God; all the desires that push us away from God.
		
		Practical Application
		It means all the desires and lusts of the world that stir us...
		• to look when we should not look.
		• to do when we should not do.
		• to get more when we should give more.
		• to be selfish and vicious when we should be sacrificial and kind.
		• to be sensual and immoral when we should be disciplined and pure.
		• to seek the recognition of men when we should seek the recognition of God.

#3590 Sinful Desires
 	
Lusts–KJV
Lusts–NASB
Sinful desires–NIV
Lusts–NKJV
Desired–NLT
 	
POSB REFERENCE (Rom.1:24-25; esp. v.24) Note 2, point 1
	ἐπιθυμίαις = epithumiais
	Pronunciation: [ep-ee-thoo-mee'-ah-ees]
	Parsing (part of speech): noun
	  Case—dative
	  Gender—feminine
	  Number—plural
	  Stem or root—from ἐπιθυμία, ας
	Concordance References:
	⇒ Strong's #1939 epithumia
	⇒ NIV #2123 epithumia
	⇒ NASB #1939 epithumia
	
	Romans 1:24
	Wherefore God also gave them up to uncleanness
		Desire, longing; lust, passion; covetousness; sinful desires.
		
		Practical Application
		Their hearts are filled with lusts or "shameful...desires" (*epithumiais*), that is, passionate cravings and urges. They long after things that displease God and that dishonor their bodies. God cares deeply about the human body, and he judges any person who abuses the body. (See POSB outline—Matthew 6:11 and POSB *Deeper Study* #6—Matthew 6:11; POSB note— 1 Cor. 3:16; POSB note—1 Cor. 3:17; POSB

ENGLISH WORD	GREEK WORD AND VERSE	THE WORD MEANS...
#3594 **Sinful Nature Controls Your Mind** To be carnally minded–KJV The mind set on the flesh–NASB The mind of sinful man–NIV To be carnally minded–NKJV **Sinful nature controls your mind–NLT** **POSB REFERENCE** (Rom.8:5-8; esp. v.6) Note 3, point 1	τὸ φρόνημα τῆς σαρκὸς = to phronēma tēs sarkos Pronunciation: [to fron'-ay-mah tace sar-kos] Parsing *phronēma* (part of speech): noun 　Case—nominative 　Gender—neuter 　Number—singular 　Stem or root—from φρόνημα, τος Parsing *sarkos* (part of speech): noun 　Case—genitive 　Gender—feminine 　Number—singular 　Stem or root—from σάρξ Concordance References: ⇒　Strong's #3588 ho + 5427 phronēma + 3588 ho + 4561 sarx ⇒　NIV #3836 ho [The] + 5859 phronēma [mind] + 3836 ho [Not in English] + 4922 sarx [sinful man] ⇒　NASB #3588 ho + 5427 phronēma + 3588 ho + 4561 sarx **Romans 8:6** 　For **to be carnally minded** is death; but to be spiritually minded is life and peace. [KJV] 　For **the mind set on the flesh** is death, but the mind set on the Spirit is life and peace, [NASB] 　**The mind of sinful man** is death, but the mind controlled by the Spirit is life and peace; [NIV] 　For **to be carnally minded** is death, but to be spiritually minded is life and peace. [NKJV] 　If your **sinful nature controls your mind**, there is death. But if the Holy Spirit controls your mind, there is life and peace. [NLT] 　τὸ γὰρ φρόνημα τῆς σαρκὸς θάνατος· τὸ δὲ φρόνημα τοῦ πνεύματος ζωὴ καὶ εἰρήνη· [GNS] 　τὸ. γὰρ φρόνημα τῆς σαρκὸς θάνατος, τὸ δὲ φρόνημα τοῦ πνεύματος ζωὴ καὶ εἰρήνη· [GNT]	To have a worldly, carnal, fleshly, mind and thoughts; to be controlled by your own sinful desires; to be unspiritual. **Practical Application** This is one of the most important passages in all of Scripture, for it discusses the human mind: *"Eat and drink,' they say, but they don't mean it. They are always thinking about how much it costs" (Proverbs 23:7) [NLT]* *"As [a man] thinketh in his heart, so is he" (Proverbs 23:7).* Where a man keeps his mind and what he thinks about determine who he is and what he does. If a man keeps his mind and thoughts in the gutter, he becomes part of the filth in the gutter. If he keeps his mind upon the *good*, he becomes good. If he focuses upon achievement and success, he achieves and succeeds. If his mind is filled with religious thoughts, he becomes religious. If his thoughts are focused upon God and righteousness, he becomes godly and righteous. A man becomes and does what he thinks. It is the law of the mind.
#3595 **Sinful Passions** Motions of sins, the–KJV **Sinful passions, the–NASB** **Sinful passions, the–NIV** **Sinful passions, the–NKJV** Sinful desires–NLT **POSB REFERENCE** (Rom.7:5) Note 3, point 1b	τὰ παθήματα τῶν ἁμαρτιῶν = ta pathēmata tōn hamartiōn Pronunciation: [tah pah-thay-mah-tah tone ha-mar-tee-own] Parsing *pathēmata* (part of speech): noun 　Case—nominative 　Gender—neuter 　Number—plural 　Stem or root—from πάθημα, τος Parsing *hamartiōn* (part of speech): noun 　Case—genitive 　Gender—feminine 　Number—plural 　Stem or root—from ἁμαρτία ας Concordance References: ⇒　Strong's #3588 ho + 3804 pathēma + 3588 ho + 266 hamartia ⇒　NIV #3836 ho [Not in English] + 4077 pathēma [passions] + 3836 ho [the] + 281 hamartia [sinful] ⇒　NASB #3588 ho + 3804 pathēma + 3588 ho + 266 hamartia **Romans 7:5** 　For when we were in the flesh, **the motions of sins**, which were by the law, did work in our members to bring forth fruit unto death. [KJV] 　For while we were in the flesh, **the sinful passions**, which were aroused by the Law, were at work in the members of our body to bear fruit for death. [NASB] 　For when we were controlled by the sinful nature, **the sinful passions** aroused by the law were at work in our bodies, so that we bore fruit for death. [NIV] 　For when we were in the flesh, **the sinful passions** which were aroused by the law were at work in our mem-	Sinful passions; motions of sins; sinful desires. **Practical Application** 　It is alive and active in that it arouses sinful passions or "the sinful passions" (*ta pathēmata tōn hamartiōn*). The law not only points out sin, it actually arouses feelings and stirs the emotions to do the forbidden.

ENGLISH WORD	GREEK WORD AND VERSE	THE WORD MEANS...
	bers to bear fruit to death. [NKJV] When we were controlled by our old nature, **sinful desires** were at work within us, and the law aroused these evil desires that produced sinful deeds, resulting in death. [NLT] ὅτε γὰρ ἦμεν ἐν τῇ σαρκί, **τὰ παθήματα τῶν ἁμαρτιῶν** τὰ διὰ τοῦ νόμου ἐνηργεῖτο ἐν τοῖς μέλεσιν ἡμῶν εἰς τὸ καρποφορῆσαι τῷ θανάτῳ, [GNS] ὅτε γὰρ ἦμεν ἐν τῇ σαρκί, **τὰ παθήματα τῶν ἁμαρτιῶν** τὰ διὰ τοῦ νόμου ἐνηργεῖτο ἐν τοῖς μέλεσιν ἡμῶν, εἰς τὸ καρποφορῆσαι τῷ θανάτῳ· [GNT]	

#3596
Singleness
 	
Singleness–KJV
Sincerity–NASB
Sincere–NIV
Simplicity–NKJV
Generosity–NLT
 	
**POSB
REFERENCE**
(Acts 2:46-47; esp. v.46)
Note 6, point 3
	ἀφελότητι = *aphelotëti*
	Pronunciation: [af-el-ot'-ay-tee]
	Parsing (part of speech): noun
	    Case—dative
	    Gender—feminine
	    Number—singular
	    Stem or root—from ἀφελότης, ητος
	Concordance References:
	  ⇒ Strong's #858 aphelotës
	  ⇒ NIV #911 aphelotës
	  ⇒ NASB #858 aphelotës
	
	### Acts 2:46
	And they, continuing daily with one accord in the temple, and breaking bread from house to house, did eat their meat with gladness and **singleness** of heart, [KJV]
	
	And day by day continuing with one mind in the temple, and breaking bread from house to house, they were taking their meals together with gladness and **sincerity** of heart, [NASB]
	
	Every day they continued to meet together in the temple courts. They broke bread in their homes and ate together with glad and **sincere** hearts, [NIV]
	
	So continuing daily with one accord in the temple, and breaking bread from house to house, they ate their food with gladness and **simplicity** of heart, [NKJV]
	
	They worshiped together at the Temple each day, met in homes for the Lord's Supper, and shared their meals with great joy and **generosity** [NLT]
	
	καθ' ἡμέραν τε προσκαρτεροῦντες ὁμοθυμαδὸν ἐν τῷ ἱερῷ, κλῶντές τε κατ' οἶκον ἄρτον, μετελάμβανον τροφῆς ἐν ἀγαλλιάσει καὶ **ἀφελότητι** καρδίας, [GNS]
	
	καθ' ἡμέραν τε προσκαρτεροῦντες ὁμοθυμαδὸν ἐν τῷ ἱερῷ, κλῶντές τε κατ' οἶκον ἄρτον, μετελάμβανον τροφῆς ἐν ἀγαλλιάσει καὶ **ἀφελότητι** καρδίας, [GNT]
		To be sincere, without hardness; to be generous.
		
		### Practical Application
		Their hearts were soft and tender, easily touched and giving. There was no selfishness or withholding on their part. Where there was need, they gave.

#3597
Sinned
 	
Sinned–KJV
Sinned–NASB
Sinned–NIV
Sinned–NKJV
Sinned–NLT
 	
**POSB
REFERENCE**
(Rom.3:22-23; esp. v.23)
Note 2, point 2a
	ἥμαρτον = *hëmarton*
	Pronunciation: [haym-ar-ton']
	Parsing (part of speech): verb
	    Mood—indicative
	    Tense—aorist
	    Voice—active
	    Person—3rd person
	    Number—plural
	    Stem or root—from ἁμαρτάνω
	Concordance References:
	  ⇒ Strong's #264 hamartanö
	  ⇒ NIV #279 hamartanö
	  ⇒ NASB #264 hamartanö
	
	### Romans 3:23
	For all have **sinned**, and come short of the glory of God; [KJV]
	
	For all have **sinned** and fall short of the glory of God, [NASB]
	
	For all have **sinned** and fall short of the glory of God, [NIV]
	
	For all have **sinned** and fall short of the glory of God, [NKJV]
	
	For all have **sinned**; all fall short of God's glorious standard. [NLT]
		Sinned; to miss the mark; to offend.
		
		### Practical Application
		All men are sinners. The word "sinned" (*hëmarton*) is in the Greek aorist tense; that is, it is a once-for-all happening. It looks back to the historical entrance of sin into the world. This means that all men...
		• inherited the nature of their sinful fathers and mothers.
		• have sinned and are sinners.
		• cannot keep from sinning and will sin.

ENGLISH WORD	GREEK WORD AND VERSE	THE WORD MEANS...
Slander–NIV Evil speaking–NKJV **Slander–NLT** **POSB REFERENCE** (Eph.4:31) Note 6, point 5	Stem or root—from βλασφημία ας Concordance References: ⇒ Strong's #988 blasphēmia ⇒ NIV #1060 blasphēmia ⇒ NASB #988 blasphēmia **Ephes. 4:31** Let all bitterness, and wrath, and anger, and clamour, and **evil speaking**, be put away from you, with all malice: [KJV] Let all bitterness and wrath and anger and clamor and **slander** be put away from you, along with all malice. [NASB] Get rid of all bitterness, rage and anger, brawling and **slander**, along with every form of malice. [NIV] Let all bitterness, wrath, anger, clamor, and **evil speaking** be put away from you, with all malice. [NKJV] Get rid of all bitterness, rage, anger, harsh words, and **slander**, as well as all types of malicious behavior. [NLT] πᾶσα πικρία καὶ θυμὸς καὶ ὀργὴ καὶ κραυγὴ καὶ **βλασφημία** ἀρθήτω ἀφ' ὑμῶν, σὺν πάσῃ κακίᾳ· [GNS] πᾶσα πικρία καὶ θυμὸς καὶ ὀργὴ καὶ κραυγὴ καὶ **βλασφημία** ἀρθήτω ἀφ' ὑμῶν σὺν πάσῃ κακίᾳ. [GNT]	**Practical Application** The Christian citizen is *not to slander any person*. No citizen is to be slandered or verbally abused and torn down. God's ideal for society is this: all citizens working to build up and enrich the lives of each other and their community and nation. If a person, ruler or citizen, is working to build us up, why would we slander him? We know that in day-to-day practical living, we live in an evil world where some citizens are selfish and greedy and others commit some terrible and atrocious acts. It is this that causes chaos in society. But note: the Christian citizen is not to slander any citizen, not even an evil ruler. The answer to reaching evil people is not cursing, reviling, slandering, criticizing, and tearing them down. Verbal abuse only causes more evil—active retaliation. The only answer to reaching an evil citizen is to reach out to him in kindness, trying to lead him to change and live the way he should as a contributing citizen to the community. But note this: reaching out to evil people and not slandering them does not mean that we do not use firm, strong, and warning words. We are never to give license to evil, nor to indulge the selfish and sinful acts of people. We are to speak with authority and strength against evil and untruth. We are to warn, and the community is to back up the warning with *just control*, even if it means imprisonment. The point is this; there is no place in a just society for citizens slandering each other. Cursing, reviling, slandering, and railing at each other is not the way to help those in rebellion against God, government, and man. The way to help is to reach out with kindness, and then if kindness fails, to reach out with strong, authoritative warnings—and then back up the warning. There is never a place for slander. Christian citizens are to take the lead in speaking kind and strong words, words that warn against selfish and evil behavior.

#3607
Slander
 	
False accusers–KJV
Malicious gossips–NASB
Slanderous–NIV
Slanderers–NKJV
Slander–NLT
 	
**POSB
REFERENCE**
(2 Tim. 3:2-4; esp. v.3)
Note 2, point 11
	διάβολοι = diaboloi
	Pronunciation: [dee-ab'-ol-oy]
	Parsing (part of speech): adjective
	  Case—nominative
	  Gender—masculine
	  Number—plural
	  Stem or root—from διάβολος, ου
	Concordance References:
	⇒ Strong's #1228 diabolos
	⇒ NIV #1333 diabolos
	⇒ NASB #1228 diabolos
	
	2 Tim. 3:3
	Without natural affection, trucebreakers, **false accusers**, incontinent, fierce, despisers of those that are good, [KJV]
	Unloving, irreconcilable, **malicious gossips**, without self-control, brutal, haters of good, [NASB]
	Without love, unforgiving, **slanderous**, without self-control, brutal, not lovers of the good, [NIV]
	Unloving, unforgiving, **slanderers**, without self-control, brutal, despisers of good, [NKJV]
	They will be unloving and unforgiving; they will **slander** others and have no self-control; they will be cruel and have no interest in what is good. [NLT]
		Slanderous, false accusers, malicious gossips, to slander.
		
		Practical Application
		Note that the Greek word is *diabolos*, the very word for the devil.

ENGLISH WORD	GREEK WORD AND VERSE	THE WORD MEANS...

ἄστοργοι, ἄσπονδοι, **διάβολοι**, ἀκρατεῖς, ἀνήμεροι, ἀφιλάγαθοι, [GNS]

ἄστοργοι ἄσπονδοι **διάβολοι** ἀκρατεῖς ἀνήμεροι ἀφιλάγαθοι [GNT]

#3608
Slander

Speak...evil–KJV
Speak against–NASB
Slander–NIV
Speak evil–NKJV
Speak evil–NLT

POSB REFERENCE
(Jas.4:11)
  Note 1, point 1

κατalαλεῖτε = *katalaleite*
Pronunciation: [kat-al-al-eh'-ee-teh]
Parsing (part of speech): verb
  Mood—imperative
  Tense—present
  Voice—active
  Person—2nd person
  Number—plural
  Stem or root—from καταλαλέω
Concordance References:
  ⇒ Strong's #2635 katalaleō
  ⇒ NIV #2895 katalaleō
  ⇒ NASB #2635 katalaleō

James 4:11

Speak not **evil** one of another, brethren. He that speaketh evil of his brother, and judgeth his brother, speaketh evil of the law, and judgeth the law: but if thou judge the law, thou art not a doer of the law, but a judge. [KJV]

Do not **speak against** one another, brethren. He who speaks against a brother, or judges his brother, speaks against the law, and judges the law; but if you judge the law, you are not a doer of the law, but a judge of it. [NASB]

Brothers, do not **slander** one another. Anyone who speaks against his brother or judges him speaks against the law and judges it. When you judge the law, you are not keeping it, but sitting in judgment on it. [NIV]

Do not **speak evil** of one another, brethren. He who speaks evil of a brother and judges his brother, speaks evil of the law and judges the law. But if you judge the law, you are not a doer of the law but a judge. [NKJV]

Don't **speak evil** against each other, my dear brothers and sisters. If you criticize each other and condemn each other, then you are criticizing and condemning God's law. But you are not a judge who can decide whether the law is right or wrong. Your job is to obey it. [NLT]

Μὴ **καταλαλεῖτε** ἀλλήλων, ἀδελφοί. ὁ καταλαλῶν ἀδελφοῦ, καὶ κρίνων τὸν ἀδελφὸν αὐτοῦ, καταλαλεῖ νόμου, καὶ κρίνει νόμον· εἰ δὲ νόμον κρίνεις, οὐκ εἶ ποιητὴς νόμου, ἀλλὰ κριτής. [GNS]

Μὴ **καταλαλεῖτε** ἀλλήλων, ἀδελφοί. ὁ καταλαλῶν ἀδελφοῦ η κρίνων τὸν ἀδελφὸν αὐτοῦ καταλαλεῖ νόμου καὶ κρίνει νόμον· εἰ δὲ νόμον κρίνεις, οὐκ εἶ ποιητὴς νόμου ἀλλὰ κριτής. [GNT]

To slander; to speak evil of; to speak against; to say bad things about a person. It means to criticize, judge, backbite, gossip, censor, condemn, and grumble against another person.

Practical Application
It means to talk about and to tear down another person; to share things about another person that cut and hurt him and that lower his image and reputation in the eyes of others. The word usually means to talk about a person behind his back when he is not present.

#3609
Slander–Slanders

Backbitings–KJV
Slanders–NASB
Slander–NIV
Backbitings–NKJV
Backstabbing–NLT

POSB REFERENCE
(2 Cor.12:19-21; esp. v.20)
  Note 3, point 2

See also POSB REF:
(1 Pt.2:1)
  Note 1, point 5

καταλαλιαι = *katalaliai*
Pronunciation: [kat-al-al-ee'-ah-ee]
Parsing (part of speech): noun
  Case—nominative
  Gender—feminine
  Number—plural
  Stem or root—from καταλαλιά, ᾶς
Concordance References:
  ⇒ Strong's #2636 katalalia
  ⇒ NIV #2896 katalalia
  ⇒ NASB #2636 katalalia

2 Cor. 12:20

For I fear, lest, when I come, I shall not find you such as I would, and that I shall be found unto you such as ye would not: lest there be debates, envyings, wraths, strifes, **backbitings**, whisperings, swellings, tumults: [KJV]

For I am afraid that perhaps when I come I may find you to be not what I wish and may be found by you to be not what you wish; that perhaps there may be strife, jealousy, angry tempers, disputes, **slanders**, gossip, arro-

Slander, backbiting, insult, vilification, verbal attack.

Practical Application
This means to criticize, judge, backbite, gossip, censor, condemn, and grumble against another person. It means to talk about and tear down another person; to spread tales about another person that cut and hurt him and that lower his image and reputation in the eyes of others.

When we criticize a brother or sister in Christ, we are slandering one of God's own children. Just think: we are actually slandering a son or daughter of God. This alone should keep us from backbiting another believer.

ENGLISH WORD	GREEK WORD AND VERSE	THE WORD MEANS...
POSB REFERENCE (Tit.2:3) Note 3, point 2 **See also POSB REF:** (2 Tim.3:2-4; esp. v.3) Note 2, point 11	**Titus 2:3** The aged women likewise, that they be in behaviour as becometh holiness, not **false accusers**, not given to much wine, teachers of good things; [KJV] Older women likewise are to be reverent in their behavior, not **malicious gossips**, nor enslaved to much wine, teaching what is good, [NASB] Likewise, teach the older women to be reverent in the way they live, not to be **slanderers** or addicted to much wine, but to teach what is good. [NIV] The older women likewise, that they be reverent in behavior, not **slanderers**, not given to much wine, teachers of good things—[NKJV] Similarly, teach the older women to live in a way that is appropriate for someone serving the Lord. They must not go around **speaking evil of others** and must not be heavy drinkers. Instead, they should teach others what is good. [NLT] Πρεσβύτιδας ὡσαύτως ἐν καταστήματι ἱεροπρεπεῖς, μὴ **διαβόλους**, μὴ οἴνῳ πολλῷ δεδουλωμένας, καλοδιδασκάλους, [GNS] πρεσβύτιδας ὡσαύτως ἐν καταστήματι ἱεροπρεπεῖς, μὴ **διαβόλους** μηδὲ οἴνῳ πολλῷ δεδουλωμένας, καλοδιδασκάλους, [GNT]	

#3614
 Slapped
 	
 Smote–KJV
 Slapped–NASB
 Slapped–NIV
 Struck–NKJV
 Slapped–NLT
 	
 POSB REFERENCE (Mt.26:67-68; esp. v.67) Note 8, point 1
	ἐράπισαν = erapisan
	 Pronunciation: [eh-rap-id'-san]
	 Parsing (part of speech): verb
	   Mood—indicative
	   Tense—aorist
	   Voice—active
	   Person—3rd person
	   Number—plural
	   Stem or root—from ῥαπίζω
	 Concordance References:
	 ⇒ Strong's #4474 hrapizö
	 ⇒ NIV #4824 hrapizö
	 ⇒ NASB #4474 hrapizö
	
	 Matthew 26:67
	 Then did they spit in his face, and buffeted him; and others **smote** him with the palms of their hands, [KJV]
	 Then they spat in His face and beat Him with their fists; and others **slapped** Him, [NASB]
	 Then they spit in his face and struck him with their fists. Others **slapped** him [NIV]
	 Then they spat in His face and beat Him; and others **struck** Him with the palms of their hands, [NKJV]
	 Then they spit in Jesus' face and hit him with their fists. And some **slapped** him, [NLT]
	 τότε ἐνέπτυσαν εἰς τὸ πρόσωπον αὐτοῦ καὶ ἐκολάφισαν αὐτόν, οἱ δὲ **ἐρράπισαν**, [GNS]
	 Τότε ἐνέπτυσαν εἰς τὸ πρόσωπον αὐτοῦ καὶ ἐκολάφισαν αὐτόν, οἱ δὲ **ἐράπισαν** [GNT]
		To slap; to smote; to hit; to strike the face with an open hand.
		
		 Practical Application
		 This was an outburst of the inner bitterness within the heart. A person's hatred of Christ will cause bitterness. Too many harbor an inner bitterness against God and Christ. Too many have allowed their rejection and opposition and the events which happened to them to grow into bitterness. Thus when opportunity arises, they vent their feelings and hostility. Too many believers, in rejecting or opposing Christ, allow bitterness to seep into their hearts. Too many vent their feelings and bitterness when they have a chance to attack some movement of God or some true believer who faithfully follows Christ day by day.

#3615
 Slave
 	
 Servant–KJV
 Slave–NASB
 Slave–NIV
 Slave–NKJV
 Slave–NLT
 	
 POSB REFERENCE (Mt.20:23-28; esp. v.27) Note 3, point 3
	δοῦλος = doulos
	 Pronunciation: [doo'-los]
	 Parsing (part of speech): noun
	   Case—nominative
	   Gender—masculine
	   Number—singular
	   Stem or root—from δοῦλος, η, ον
	 Concordance References:
	 ⇒ Strong's #1401 doulos
	 ⇒ NIV #1528 doulos1
	 ⇒ NASB #1401 doulos
	
	 Matthew 20:27
	 And whosoever will be chief among you, let him be your **servant**: [KJV]
	 And whoever wishes to be first among you shall be your **slave**; [NASB]
	 And whoever wants to be first must be your
		To serve as a slave, submitting one's own will to his master.
		
		 Practical Application
		 Throughout society many of us hold positions of authority. Far too often we forget that with authority comes great responsibility. And when we forget to fulfill our responsibility, we usually abuse the power of our position. And when power is abused, those who are under our control usually catch the brunt of our frustration or anger (Exodus 21:26-27). God has called every believer to be a good and faithful steward. To be a good and faithful steward...
		 • we must acknowledge that God Himself is the owner of all things

ENGLISH WORD	GREEK WORD AND VERSE	THE WORD MEANS...
	slave [NIV] And whoever desires to be first among you, let him be your slave [NKJV] And whoever wants to be first must become your slave. [NLT] καὶ ὃς ἐὰν θέλη ἐν ὑμῖν εἶναι πρῶτος ἔστω ὑμῶν δοῦλος· [GNS] καὶ ὃς ἂν θέλη ἐν ὑμῖν εἶναι πρῶτος ἔσται ὑμῶν δοῦλος· [GNT]	• we must act like managers not owners • we must seek the best for God and others not for ourselves • we must think about the possible consequences before we act • we must keep an open heart for communication not a clenched fist for retaliation • we must minister to others as Jesus would and not as our fallen natures desire

#3616
Slave
 	
Servant–KJV
Bond-servant–NASB
Servant–NIV
Bondservant–NKJV
Slave–NLT
 	
POSB
REFERENCE
(Jas.1:1)
Note 1, point 1
 	
See also POSB REF:
(Rom.1:1)
Note 1
(Gal.1:10)
Note 1
(2 Cor.4:5)
Note 4
(2 Pt.1:1)
Note 1, point 1
(Philip.1:1)
Note 2
	δοῦλος = doulos
	Pronunciation: [doo'-los]
	Parsing (part of speech): noun
	  Case—nominative
	  Gender—masculine
	  Number—singular
	  Stem or root—from δοῦλος, η, ον
	Concordance References:
	⇒ Strong's #1401 doulos
	⇒ NIV #1528 doulos1
	⇒ NASB #1401 doulos
	
	James 1:1
	James, a **servant** of God and of the Lord Jesus Christ, to the twelve tribes which are scattered abroad, greeting. [KJV]
	James, a **bond-servant** of God and of the Lord Jesus Christ, to the twelve tribes who are dispersed abroad, greetings. [NASB]
	James, a **servant** of God and of the Lord Jesus Christ, To the twelve tribes scattered among the nations: Greetings. [NIV]
	James, a **bondservant** of God and of the Lord Jesus Christ, To the twelve tribes which are scattered abroad: Greetings. [NKJV]
	This letter is from James, a **slave** of God and of the Lord Jesus Christ.It is written to Jewish Christians scattered among the nations.Greetings! [NLT]
	Ἰάκωβος, Θεοῦ καὶ Κυρίου Ἰησοῦ Χριστοῦ δοῦλος, ταῖς δώδεκα φυλαῖς ταῖς ἐν τῇ διασπορᾷ, χαίρειν. [GNS]
	Ἰάκωβος θεοῦ καὶ κυρίου Ἰησοῦ Χριστοῦ δοῦλος ταῖς δώδεκα φυλαῖς ταῖς ἐν τῇ διασπορᾷ χαίρειν. [GNT]
		A servant; to be a bond-servant; to be as a slave.
		
		Practical Application
		The word "slave" (doulos) in the Greek means far more than just a servant. It means a slave totally possessed by the master. It means a bond-servant bound by law to a master. A look at the slave market of James's day shows more clearly what James meant when he said he was a "slave of Jesus Christ."
		1. The slave was owned by his master; he was totally possessed by his master. This is what James meant. James was purchased and possessed by Christ, the Son of the living God. Christ had looked upon him and had seen his rebellious and needful condition. And when Christ looked, the most wonderful thing happened: Christ loved him and bought him; therefore, he was now the possession of Christ.
		2. The slave existed for his master, and he had no other reason for existence. He had no personal rights whatsoever. The same was true with James: he existed only for Christ. His rights were the rights of Christ only.
		3. The slave served his master, and he existed only for the purpose of service. He was at the master's disposal any hour of the day. So it was with James: he lived only to serve Christ—hour by hour and day by day.
		4. The slave's will belonged to his master. He was allowed no will and no ambition other than the will and ambition of the master. He was completely subservient to the master, owing total obedience to the will of the master. James belonged to Christ. In fact, he fought and struggled to bring "every thought into captivity to the obedience of Christ" (2 Cor. 10:3-5, esp. 2 Cor. 10:5).
		5. There is a fifth and most precious thing that James meant by "a slave of Jesus Christ." He meant that he had the highest and most honored and kingly profession in all the world. Men of God, the greatest men of history, have always been called "the servants of God." It was the highest title of honor. The believer's slavery to Jesus Christ is no cringing, cowardly, shameful subjection. It is the position of honor—the honor that bestows upon a man the privileges and responsibilities of serving the King of kings and Lord of lords.

#3617
Slaves
 	
Servants–KJV
Slaves–NASB
	δοῦλους = doulous
	Pronunciation: [doo'-loos]
	Parsing (part of speech): noun
	  Case—accusative
	  Gender—masculine
	  Number—plural
	  Stem or root—from δοῦλος η, ον
		Slaves, servants; whatever you choose to obey.
		
		Practical Application
		A person is either the slave of sin or of God, and there is a very simple test to tell which mas-

ENGLISH WORD	GREEK WORD AND VERSE	THE WORD MEANS...
	things we have heard, lest we **drift away**. [NKJV] So we must listen very carefully to the truth we have heard, or we may **drift away** from it. [NLT] Διὰ τοῦτο δεῖ περισσοτέρως ἡμᾶς προσέχειν τοῖς ἀκουσθεῖσι, μή ποτε **παραρρυῶμεν**. [GNS] Διὰ τοῦτο δεῖ περισσοτέρως προσέχειν ἡμᾶς τοῖς ἀκουσθεῖσιν, μήποτε **παραρυῶμεν** [GNT]	• miscalculations • lethargy and complacency • sleepiness • carelessness • in attentiveness • drunkenness An innumerable list of things could be given as to why the captain would drift away from the safety of the harbor. But the point is well made: we must all anchor our lives to the truths of salvation. We must earnestly heed them. We must heed them lest the ship of our lives drift away from the safety of salvation.
#3622 **Slothful** **Slothful–KJV** Lagging behind– NASB Lacking–NIV Lagging–NKJV Lazy–NLT **POSB REFERENCE** (Rom.12:11) Note 2, point 1.	ὀκνηροί = oknëroi Pronunciation: [ok-nay-roy'] Parsing (part of speech): adjective 　Case—nominative 　Gender—masculine 　Number—plural 　Stem or root—from ὀκνηρός ά, όν Concordance References: ⇒ Strong's #3636 oknëros ⇒ NIV #3891 oknëros ⇒ NASB #3636 oknëros **Romans 12:11** Not **slothful** in business; fervent in spirit; serving the Lord; [KJV] Not **lagging behind** in diligence, fervent in spirit, serving the Lord; [NASB] Never be **lacking** in zeal, but keep your spiritual fervor, serving the Lord. [NIV] Not **lagging** in diligence, fervent in spirit, serving the Lord; [NKJV] Never be **lazy** in your work, but serve the Lord enthusiastically. [NLT] τῇ σπουδῇ μὴ **ὀκνηροί**· τῷ πνεύματι ζέοντες· τῷ Κυρίῳ δουλεύοντες· [GNS] τῇ σπουδῇ μὴ **ὀκνηροί**, τῷ πνεύματι ζέοντες, τῷ κυρίῳ δουλέοντες, [GNT]	To be lazy, slow moving, sluggish, slothful, lethargic, complacent, hesitating, delaying, a lagging behind. **Practical Application** The believer is to serve the Lord. The charge is twofold. Do not be slothful in zeal; do not be slothful in diligence. The exhortation is clear: the believer must... • not be lazy or slow moving in zeal. • not be sluggish or lethargic in diligence. • not be hesitating or delaying in earnestness. • not ben lagging behind. The believer cannot approach life in a lackadaisical, easy-going, slow-moving fashion. The world is reeling in pain, with millions starving and suffering due to man's selfishness and sin, hoarding, disease, war, death—and the list could go on and on. The believer must not give in to sluggishness and complacency. He must serve the Lord with all diligence and zeal and earnestness. He must be enthusiastic in his service.
#3623 **Slow** Dull–KJV Dull–NASB **Slow–NIV** Dull–NKJV Hard–NLT **POSB REFERENCE** (Heb.5:11) Note 1	νωθροί = nöthroi Pronunciation: [no-throy'] Parsing (part of speech): adjective 　Case—nominative 　Gender—masculine 　Number—plural 　Stem or root—from νωθρός, ά, όν Concordance References: ⇒ Strong's #3576 nöthros ⇒ NIV #3821 nöthros ⇒ NASB #3576 nöthros **Hebrews 5:11** Of whom we have many things to say, and hard to be uttered, seeing ye are **dull** of hearing. [KJV] Concerning him we have much to say, and it is hard to explain, since you have become **dull** of hearing. [NASB] We have much to say about this, but it is hard to explain because you are **slow** to learn. [NIV] Of whom we have much to say, and hard to explain, since you have become **dull** of hearing. [NKJV] There is so much more we would like to say about this. But you don't seem to listen, so it's **hard** to make you understand. [NLT] Περὶ οὗ πολὺς ἡμῖν ὁ λόγος καὶ δυσερμήνευτος λέγειν, ἐπεὶ **νωθροί** γεγόνατε ταῖς ἀκοαῖς. [GNS] Περὶ οὗ πολὺς ἡμῖν ὁ λόγος καὶ δυσερμήνευτος λέγειν, ἐπεὶ **νωθροί**. γεγόνατε ταῖς ἀκοαῖς. [GNT]	Slow, dull, hard of hearing. It means sluggish, slow, lazy, lethargic, forgetful. **Practical Application** A person becomes immature because of slow hearing. The writer to the Hebrews had much that he wanted to teach, especially about the Lord Jesus Christ and His Priestly ministry, but he was unable. Why? Because the Christian faith—the Word of God and the Bible—is difficult to understand. No person can grasp the Word of God and its truths by simply reading it. A person must study, meditate, and practice the Word of God in order to understand it. 　The Hebrew believers had become mentally lazy and sluggish and spiritually complacent and slothful. Even though they were sitting and listening to the preachers and teachers and reading the Scriptures, they were not listening or paying attention. Their minds, wandering about, were unwilling to exert the energy to concentrate and study. 　Note: some of the Hebrew believers were already slow of hearing. Some had already become immature; they had already fallen and were no longer growing spiritually.

ENGLISH WORD	GREEK WORD AND VERSE	THE WORD MEANS...

#3624
Slows [Us] Down
 	
Easily beset–KJV
Easily entangles–NASB
Easily entangles–NIV
Easily ensnares–NKJV
Slows [us] down–NLT
 	
POSB REFERENCE
(Heb.12:1)
Note 2, point 1b
	εὐπερίστατον = *euperistaton*
	Pronunciation: [yoo-per-is'-taht-on]
	Parsing (part of speech): adjective
	    Case—accusative
	    Gender—feminine
	    Number—singular
	    Stem or root—from εὐπερίστατος, ον
	Concordance References:
	⇒ Strong's #2139 euperistatos
	⇒ NIV #2342 euperistatos
	⇒ NASB #2139 euperistatos
	
	Hebrews 12:1
	Wherefore seeing we also are compassed about with so great a cloud of witnesses, let us lay aside every weight, and the sin which doth so **easily beset** us, and let us run with patience the race that is set before us, [KJV]
	Therefore, since we have so great a cloud of witnesses surrounding us, let us also lay aside every encumbrance, and the sin which so **easily entangles** us, and let us run with endurance the race that is set before us, [NASB]
	Therefore, since we are surrounded by such a great cloud of witnesses, let us throw off everything that hinders and the sin that so **easily entangles**, and let us run with perseverance the race marked out for us. [NIV]
	Therefore we also, since we are surrounded by so great a cloud of witnesses, let us lay aside every weight, and the sin which so **easily ensnares** *us,* and let us run with endurance the race that is set before us, [NKJV]
	Therefore, since we are surrounded by such a huge crowd of witnesses to the life of faith, let us strip off every weight that **slows us down**, especially the sin that so easily hinders our progress. And let us run with endurance the race that God has set before us. [NLT]
	Τοιγαροῦν καὶ ἡμεῖς τοσοῦτον ἔχοντες περικείμενον ἡμῖν νέφος μαρτύρων, ὄγκον ἀποθέμενοι πάντα καὶ τὴν **εὐπερίστατον** ἁμαρτίαν, δι' ὑπομονῆς τρέχωμεν τὸν προκείμενον ἡμῖν ἀγῶνα, [GNS]
	Τοιγαροῦν καὶ ἡμεῖς τοσοῦτον ἔχοντες περικείμενον ἡμῖν νέφος μαρτύρων, ὄγκον ἀποθέμενοι πάντα καὶ τὴν **εὐπερίστατον** ἁμαρτίαν, δι' ὑπομονῆς τρέχωμεν τὸν προκείμενον ἡμῖν ἀγῶνα [GNT]
		To easily entangle, easily beset, slow us down. The words "slows us down" (*euperistaton*) mean the sin that clings, distracts, entangles, and trips up the Christian runner.
		
		Practical Application
		The Christian runner must strip off the sin which so easily trips or besets him. It is the picture of clothing flapping around a person while he is running: it entangles and trips him and he falls. What is the sin that entangles and trips believers? Various sins have been suggested as common to all believers. However, the exhortation speaks strongly to any *particular sin* that entangles and throws that believer. Each one of us must ask: What is the sin that so easily trips me? Pleasure, indulgence, the tongue, the flesh, pride, possessions, worldly friends, television, sports—what is it that consumes my energy, keeping me from following God fully and wholly—that trips me up far, far too often. We must strip it off or else it will entangle us and trip us up, and we will never finish the race.

#3625
Slumbered
 	
Slumbered–KJV
Drowsy–NASB
Drowsy–NIV
Slumbered–NKJV
Lay down–NLT
 	
POSB REFERENCE
(Mt.25:5)
Deeper Study #3
	ἐνύσταξαν = *enustaxan*
	Pronunciation: [noos-tadz'-an]
	Parsing (part of speech): verb
	    Mood—indicative
	    Tense—aorist
	    Voice—active
	    Person—3rd person
	    Number—plural
	    Stem or root—from νυστάζω
	Concordance References:
	⇒ Strong's #3573 nustazō
	⇒ NIV #3818 nustazō
	⇒ NASB #3573 nustazō
	
	Matthew 25:5
	While the bridegroom tarried, they all **slumbered** and slept. [KJV]
	"Now while the bridegroom was delaying, they all got **drowsy** and began to sleep. [NASB]
	The bridegroom was a long time in coming, and they all became **drowsy** and fell asleep. [NIV]
	But while the bridegroom was delayed, they all **slumbered** and slept. [NKJV]
	When the bridegroom was delayed, they all **lay down** and slept. [NLT]
	χρονίζοντος δὲ τοῦ νυμφίου **ἐνύσταξαν** πᾶσαι καὶ ἐκάθευδον. [GNS]
	χρονίζοντος δὲ τοῦ νυμφίου **ἐνύσταξαν** πᾶσαι καὶ ἐκάθευδον. [GNT]
		To grow drowsy; to slumber; to lay down to sleep; to nod; to nap; to drift off to sleep.
		
		Practical Application
		Note that the bridesmaids allowed themselves to lay down, then laying down led to sleep. We must guard against laying down, against cooling off. Laying down will lead to a cooling of fervor. A little loss of fervor may not seem too serious; but the first step, as small as it may seem, leads to heavy eyelids.

ENGLISH WORD	GREEK WORD AND VERSE	THE WORD MEANS...

#3626
Smote
 	
Smote–KJV
Beat–NASB
Struck–NIV
Struck–NKJV
Beat–NLT
 	
POSB
REFERENCE
(Mt.27:26-38; esp.
v.30)
Note 2, point 7
	ἔτυπτον = *etupton*
	Pronunciation: [eh-toop'-ton]
	Parsing (part of speech): verb
	   Mood—indicative
	   Tense—imperfect
	   Voice—active
	   Person—3rd person
	   Number—plural
	   Stem or root—from τύπτω
	Concordance References:
	⇒ Strong's #5180 tuptö
	⇒ NIV #5597 tuptö
	⇒ NASB #5180 tuptö
	
	Matthew 27:30
	And they spit upon him, and took the reed, and **smote** him on the head. [KJV]
	And they spat on Him, and took the reed and began to **beat** Him on the head. [NASB]
	They spit on him, and took the staff and **struck** him on the head again and again. [NIV]
	Then they spat on Him, and took the reed and **struck** Him on the head. [NKJV]
	And they spit on him and grabbed the stick and **beat** him on the head with it. [NLT]
	καὶ ἐμπτύσαντες εἰς αὐτὸν ἔλαβον τὸν κάλαμον καὶ ἔτυπτον εἰς τὴν κεφαλὴν αὐτοῦ. [GNS]
	καὶ ἐμπτύσαντες εἰς αὐτὸν ἔλαβον τὸν κάλαμον καὶ ἔτυπτον εἰς τὴν κεφαλὴν αὐτοῦ. [GNT]
		Struck, smote, hit, wound, beat; injure. It means to literally strike with the fist, to beat and injure.
		
		Practical Application
		In the context of this Scripture, they kept on beating Christ. They took the staff, the mock scepter, and used it as a weapon beating Him on the head continuously. They probably passed the staff from one soldier to another, giving many an opportunity to vent their folly and spite. He was bruised and bleeding, a horrible sight.

#3627
Smote
 	
Smote–KJV
Slapped–NASB
Slapped–NIV
Struck–NKJV
Slapped–NLT
 	
POSB
REFERENCE
(Mt.26:67-68; esp.
v.67)
Note 8, point 1
	ἐράπισαν = *erapisan*
	Pronunciation: [eh-rap-id'-san]
	Parsing (part of speech): verb
	   Mood—indicative
	   Tense—aorist
	   Voice—active
	   Person—3rd person
	   Number—plural
	   Stem or root—from ῥαπίζω
	Concordance References:
	⇒ Strong's #4474 hrapizö
	⇒ NIV #4824 hrapizö
	⇒ NASB #4474 hrapizö
	
	Matthew 26:67
	Then did they spit in his face, and buffeted him; and others **smote** him with the palms of their hands, [KJV]
	Then they spat in His face and beat Him with their fists; and others **slapped** Him, [NASB]
	Then they spit in his face and struck him with their fists. Others **slapped** him [NIV]
	Then they spat in His face and beat Him; and others **struck** Him with the palms of their hands, [NKJV]
	Then they spit in Jesus' face and hit him with their fists. And some **slapped** him, [NLT]
	τότε ἐνέπτυσαν εἰς τὸ πρόσωπον αὐτοῦ καὶ ἐκολάφισαν αὐτόν, οἱ δὲ ἐρράπισαν, [GNS]
	Τότε ἐνέπτυσαν εἰς τὸ πρόσωπον αὐτοῦ καὶ ἐκολάφισαν αὐτόν, οἱ δὲ ἐράπισαν [GNT]
		To slap; to smote; to hit; to strike the face with an open hand.
		
		Practical Application
		This was an outburst of the inner bitterness within the heart. A person's hatred of Christ will cause bitterness. Too many harbor an inner bitterness against God and Christ. Too many have allowed their rejection and opposition and the events which happened to them to grow into bitterness. Thus when opportunity arises, they vent their feelings and hostility. Too many believers, in rejecting or opposing Christ, allow bitterness to seep into their hearts. Too many vent their feelings and bitterness when they have a chance to attack some movement of God or some true believer who faithfully follows Christ day by day.

#3628
Snare
 	
Snare–KJV
Trap–NASB
Trap–NIV
Snare–NKJV
Trap–NLT
 	
POSB
REFERENCE
(Lk.21:35)
Deeper Study #1
	παγίς = *pagis*
	Pronunciation: [pag-ece']
	Parsing (part of speech): noun
	   Case—nominative
	   Gender—feminine
	   Number—singular
	   Stem or root—from παγίς, ίδος
	Concordance References:
	⇒ Strong's #3803 pagis
	⇒ NIV #4075 pagis
	⇒ NASB #3803 pagis
	
	Luke 21:34-35
	(Note: *pagis* is translated in vs. 34 in the NASB & NIV)
		To snare or trap as in a net.
		
		Practical Application
		That day, the end time, is going to catch the whole world unprepared. The terrible events and calamities of the end times are going to fall upon the earth and entrap all. All who dwell upon the earth will be caught in the disastrous events, the destruction and devastation, distress and misery, misfortune and loss, suffering and affliction. (See POSB outline—Luke 21:5-33 and POSB notes—Luke 21:5-33.)

ENGLISH WORD	GREEK WORD AND VERSE	THE WORD MEANS...
	For as a **snare** shall it come on all them that dwell on the face of the whole earth. [KJV]—**Luke 21:35** "Be on guard, that your hearts may not be weighted down with dissipation and drunkenness and the worries of life, and that day come on you suddenly like a **trap**; [NASB]—**Luke 21:34** For it will come upon all those who dwell on the face of all the earth. [NASB]—**Luke 21:35** "Be careful, or your hearts will be weighed down with dissipation, drunkenness and the anxieties of life, and that day will close on you unexpectedly like a **trap**. [NIV]—**Luke 21:34** For it will come upon all those who live on the face of the whole earth. [NIV]—**Luke 21:35** For it will come as a **snare** on all those who dwell on the face of the whole earth. [NKJV]—**Luke 21:35** As in a **trap**. For that day will come upon everyone living on the earth. [NLT]—**Luke 21:35** ὡς παγὶς γὰρ ἐπελεύσεται ἐπὶ πάντας τοὺς καθημένους ἐπὶ πρόσωπον πάσης τῆς γῆς. [GNS]—**Luke 21:35** ὡς παγίς· ἐπεισελεύσεται γὰρ ἐπὶ πάντας τοὺς καθημένους ἐπὶ πρόσωπον πάσης τῆς γῆς. [GNT]—**Luke 21:35**	
#3629 **Snatched... Away** Caught away–KJV **Snatched...away–NASB** Suddenly took...away–NIV Caught...away–NKJV Caught away–NLT **POSB REFERENCE** (Acts 8:39-40; esp. v.39) Note 7, point 1	ἥρπασεν = hërpasen Pronunciation: [heyr-pah'-sehn] Parsing (part of speech): verb Mood—indicative Tense—aorist Voice—active Person—3rd person Number—singular Stem or root—from ἁρπάζω Concordance References: ⇒ Strong's #726 harpazö ⇒ NIV #773 harpazö ⇒ NASB #726 harpazö **Acts 8:39** And when they were come up out of the water, the Spirit of the Lord **caught away** Philip, that the eunuch saw him no more: and he went on his way rejoicing. [KJV] And when they came up out of the water, the Spirit of the Lord **snatched** Philip **away**; and the eunuch saw him no more, but went on his way rejoicing. [NASB] When they came up out of the water, the Spirit of the Lord **suddenly took** Philip **away**, and the eunuch did not see him again, but went on his way rejoicing. [NIV] Now when they came up out of the water, the Spirit of the Lord **caught** Philip **away**, so that the eunuch saw him no more; and he went on his way rejoicing. [NKJV] When they came up out of the water, the Spirit of the Lord **caught** Philip **away**. The eunuch never saw him again but went on his way rejoicing. [NLT] ὅτε δὲ ἀνέβησαν ἐκ τοῦ ὕδατος, Πνεῦμα Κυρίου ἥρπασε τὸν Φίλιππον· καὶ οὐκ εἶδεν αὐτὸν οὐκέτι ὁ εὐνοῦχος, ἐπορεύετο γὰρ τὴν ὁδὸν αὐτοῦ χαίρων. [GNS] ὅτε δὲ ἀνέβησαν ἐκ τοῦ ὕδατος, πνεῦμα κυρίου ἥρπασεν τὸν Φίλιππον· καὶ οὐκ εἶδεν αὐτὸν οὐκέτι ὁ εὐνοῦχος, ἐπορεύετο γὰρ τὴν ὁδὸν αὐτοῦ χαίρων. [GNT]	To be suddenly taken away; to be caught away; to be snatched away; to be taken by force. **Practical Application** The word for "snatched away" (hërpasen) is strong. It means to be snatched away quickly, immediately, miraculously. It is the same word used for the rapture of the church. It means to catch up into heaven during the rapture.
#3630 **Sneaks Over** Some other way–KJV Some other way–NASB Other way–NIV	ἀλλαχόθεν = allachothen Pronunciation: [al-lach-oth'-ehn] Parsing (part of speech): adjective Type—adverb Stem or root—from ἀλλαχόθεν Concordance References: ⇒ Strong's #237 allachothen ⇒ NIV #249 allachothen ⇒ NASB #237 allachothen	To come from elsewhere; to come from some other way; to sneak over. **Practical Application** Some shepherds "sneak over the wall (allachothen) of a sheepfold." The word from is important. It indicates origin. The false shepherd comes from and originates from...

ENGLISH WORD	GREEK WORD AND VERSE	THE WORD MEANS...
	work of an evangelist, make full proof of thy ministry. [KJV] But you, be **sober** in all things, endure hardship, do the work of an evangelist, fulfill your ministry. [NASB] But you, **keep** your **head** in all situations, endure hardship, do the work of an evangelist, discharge all the duties of your ministry. [NIV] But you be **watchful** in all things, endure afflictions, do the work of an evangelist, fulfill your ministry. [NKJV] But you should **keep** a **clear mind** in every situation. Don't be afraid of suffering for the Lord. Work at bringing others to Christ. Complete the ministry God has given you. [NLT] σὺ δὲ **νῆφε** ἐν πᾶσι, κακοπάθησον, ἔργον ποίησον εὐαγγελιστοῦ, τὴν διακονίαν σου πληροφόρησον. [GNS] σὺ δὲ **νῆφε** ἐν πᾶσιν, κακοπάθησον, ἔργον ποίησον εὐαγγελιστοῦ, τὴν διακονίαν σου πληροφόρησον. [GNT]	

#3635
Sober
 	
Sober–KJV
Sound judgment–
    NASB
Clear minded–NIV
Serious–NKJV
Earnest–NLT
 	
POSB
REFERENCE
(1 Pt.4:7)
Note 1
	σωφρονήσατε = sōphronēsate
	Pronunciation: [so-fron-ay'-sah-teh]
	Parsing (part of speech): verb
	    Mood—imperative
	    Tense—aorist
	    Voice—active
	    Person—2nd person
	    Number—plural
	    Stem or root—from σωφρονέω
	Concordance References:
	⇒ Strong's #4993 sōphroneō
	⇒ NIV #5404 sōphroneō
	⇒ NASB #4993 sōphroneō
	
	1 Peter 4:7
	But the end of all things is at hand: be ye therefore **sober**, and watch unto prayer. [KJV]
	
	The end of all things is at hand; therefore, be of **sound judgment** and sober spirit for the purpose of prayer. [NASB]
	
	The end of all things is near. Therefore be **clear minded** and self-controlled so that you can pray. [NIV]
	
	But the end of all things is at hand; therefore be **serious** and watchful in your prayers. [NKJV]
	
	The end of the world is coming soon. Therefore, be **earnest** and disciplined in your prayers. [NLT]
	
	Πάντων δὲ τὸ τέλος ἤγγικε· **σωφρονήσατε** οὖν καὶ νήψατε εἰς τὰς προσευχάς· [GNS]
	
	Πάντων δὲ τὸ τέλος ἤγγικεν. **σωφρονήσατε** οὖν καὶ νήψατε εἰς προσευχάς· [GNT]
		To be clear minded; to be sober; to exhibit sound judgment; to be earnest. This means to be serious and to have a sound mind; to be in control of oneself and to be self-restrained; to be calm and sensible.
		
		Practical Application
		The believer lives under the climax of history; he keeps his mind upon the return of Christ by doing three things.
		1. He keeps a serious and sober mind about everything. He is not a jolly, back slapping, frivolous type of person. He takes life seriously, knowing that man has a purpose for being on earth, that life is the most meaningful and significant possession that man has. Therefore, he measures the importance of things. He measures all things in light of eternity as well as time. He considers the future as well as the present. He knows that his life could be snatched from him overnight by some accident or by the news of some disease. The believer who keeps his mind upon the climax of history, upon the return of the Lord Jesus Christ, is a sober person; he is a serious and sober-minded person.
		2. He controls and restrains his desires and lusts and appetites. He never gives in to excess—to the lust for more and more. He controls sex and uses it for marriage. He controls desire for food and uses it for health. He controls the desire for material possessions and uses it to meet the needs of his family and the desperate needs of the world.
		3. He is calm and sensible about all things. He is not overly shaken by trouble, problems, or circumstances that arise within his family, employment, society, or world. Family problems and world events just do not shake him. He is concerned but not shaken. He does not get overly excited with recreation, sports, or any other happening of life. He enjoys the happenings and experiences of life, but he keeps a sensible perspective of all things and gives each thing its proper place.

ENGLISH WORD	GREEK WORD AND VERSE	THE WORD MEANS...

#3636
Sober
 	
Sober–KJV
Temperate–NASB
Temperate–NIV
Sober–NKJV
Exercise self control–NLT
 	
POSB REFERENCE
(Tit.2:2)
Note 2, point 1
	νηφαλίους = *nēphalious*
	Pronunciation: [nay-fal'-ee'-oos]
	Parsing (part of speech): adjective
	  Case—accusative
	  Gender—masculine
	  Number—plural
	  Stem or root—from *νηφάλιος*, α, ον
	Concordance References:
	⇒ Strong's #3524 nēphalios
	⇒ NIV #3767 nēphalios
	⇒ NASB #3524 nēphalios
	
	Titus 2:2
	That the aged men be **sober**, grave, temperate, sound in faith, in charity, in patience. [KJV]
	Older men are to be **temperate**, dignified, sensible, sound in faith, in love, in perseverance. [NASB]
	Teach the older men to be **temperate**, worthy of respect, self-controlled, and sound in faith, in love and in endurance. [NIV]
	That the older men be **sober**, reverent, temperate, sound in faith, in love, in patience; [NKJV]
	Teach the older men to **exercise self-control**, to be worthy of respect, and to live wisely. They must have strong faith and be filled with love and patience. [NLT]
	πρεσβύτας *νηφαλίους* εἶναι, σεμνούς, σώφρονας, ὑγιαίνοντας τῇ πίστει, τῇ ἀγάπῃ, τῇ ὑπομονῇ· [GNS]
	πρεσβύτας *νηφαλίους* εἶναι, σεμνούς, σώφρονας, ὑγιαίνοντας τῇ πίστει, τῇ ἀγάπῃ, τῇ ὑπομονῇ· [GNT]
		To be temperate; to be sober; to exercise self-control; to be moderate.
		
		Practical Application
		It is the opposite of over indulgence in anything such as eating, drinking, recreation, or whatever.

#3637
Sober–
Sober Spirit
 	
Sober–KJV
Sober spirit–NASB
Self-controlled–NIV
Sober–NKJV
Careful–NLT
 	
POSB REFERENCE
(1 Pt.5:8)
Note 1
	Νήψατε = *Nēpsate*
	Pronunciation: [nay'-psah-teh]
	Parsing (part of speech): verb
	  Mood—imperative
	  Tense—aorist
	  Voice—active
	  Person—2nd person
	  Number—plural
	  Stem or root—from *νήφω*
	Concordance References:
	⇒ Strong's #3525 nēphō
	⇒ NIV #3768 nēphō
	⇒ NASB #3525 nēphō
	
	1 Peter 5:8
	Be **sober**, be vigilant; because your adversary the devil, as a roaring lion, walketh about, seeking whom he may devour: [KJV]
	Be of **sober spirit**, be on the alert. Your adversary, the devil, prowls about like a roaring lion, seeking someone to devour. [NASB]
	Be **self-controlled** and alert. Your enemy the devil prowls around like a roaring lion looking for someone to devour. [NIV]
	Be **sober**, be vigilant; because your adversary the devil walks about like a roaring lion, seeking whom he may devour. [NKJV]
	Be **careful**! Watch out for attacks from the Devil, your great enemy. He prowls around like a roaring lion, looking for some victim to devour. [NLT]
	νήψατε, γρηγορήσατε, ὅτι ὁ ἀντίδικος ὑμῶν διάβολος, ὡς λέων ὠρυόμενος περιπατεῖ ζητῶν τινα καταπίῃ· [GNS]
	Νήψατε, γρηγορήσατε. ὁ ἀντίδικος ὑμῶν διάβολος ὡς λέων ὠρυόμενος περιπατεῖ ζητῶν [τινα] καταπιεῖν· [GNT]
		To be self-controlled; to be sober in mind and behavior; to live a strong life; to keep head.
		
		Practical Application
		How can we stand against the attacks and temptations of the devil? There is only one way: we must be sober, be vigilant. The word means...
		• not to become intoxicated with drugs or alcohol of any kind.
		• to be sober in mind and behavior; to be controlled in all things; not given over to indulgence, license, or extravagance. It is the opposite of indulgence in anything such as eating, drinking, and recreation. It means to live a sober, solid, controlled, and strong life.
		The believer has to be careful as he watches for the attacks of the devil. If he is not sober, he will not be alert enough to conquer the attacks and the temptations of the devil. The believer will be overcome and led into sin and destruction. And no believer can be alert enough to stand up against the devil if he indulges and gratifies his flesh in...
		• sex
		• food
		• sleep
		• relaxation
		• alcohol and drugs
		• recognition
		• pornography
		• position
		• clothing
		• possessions
		• power
		The believer is to live a careful and controlled life. He is to stay alert to the devil and his temptations at all times. He must be alert enough to see the temptations and attacks coming and have a mind and spirit strong enough to stand against the temptations and attacks.

ENGLISH WORD	GREEK WORD AND VERSE	THE WORD MEANS...
	ἀλλὰ φρονεῖν εἰς τὸ **σωφρονεῖν**, ἑκάστῳ ὡς ὁ Θεὸς ἐμέρισε μέτρον πίστεως. [GNS] Λέγω γὰρ διὰ τῆς χάριτος τῆς δοθείσης μοι παντὶ τῷ ὄντι ἐν ὑμῖν μὴ ὑπερφρονεῖν παρ' ὃ δεῖ φρονεῖν ἀλλὰ φρονεῖν εἰς τὸ **σωφρονεῖν**, ἑκάστῳ ὡς ὁ θεὸς ἐμέρισεν μέτρον πίστεως. [GNT]	

#3642
Soberly
 	
Soberly–KJV
Sensibly–NASB
Self controlled–NIV
Soberly–NKJV
Self-control–NLT
 	
**POSB
REFERENCE**
(Tit.2:12)
Note 2, point 2
	σωφρόνως = söphronös
	Pronunciation: [so-fron'-oce]
	Parsing (part of speech): adjective
	    Type—adverb
	    Stem or root—from **σωφρόνως**
	Concordance References:
	  ⇒ Strong's #4996 söphronös
	  ⇒ NIV #5407 söphronös
	  ⇒ NASB #4996 söphronös
	
	Titus 2:12
	Teaching us that, denying ungodliness and worldly lusts, we should live **soberly**, righteously, and godly, in this present world; [KJV]
	Instructing us to deny ungodliness and worldly desires and to live **sensibly**, righteously and godly in the present age, [NASB]
	It teaches us to say "No" to ungodliness and worldly passions, and to live **self-controlled**, upright and godly lives in this present age, [NIV]
	Teaching us that, denying ungodliness and worldly lusts, we should live **soberly**, righteously, and godly in the present age, [NKJV]
	And we are instructed to turn from godless living and sinful pleasures. We should live in this evil world with **self-control**, right conduct, and devotion to God, [NLT]
	παιδεύουσα ἡμᾶς ἵνα, ἀρνησάμενοι τὴν ἀσέβειαν καὶ τὰς κοσμικὰς ἐπιθυμίας **σωφρόνως** καὶ δικαίως καὶ εὐσεβῶς ζήσωμεν ἐν τῷ νῦν αἰῶνι, [GNS]
	παιδεύουσα ἡμᾶς, ἵνα ἀρνησάμενοι τὴν ἀσέβειαν καὶ τὰς κοσμικὰς ἐπιθυμίας **σωφρόνως** καὶ δικαίως καὶ εὐσεβῶς ζήσωμεν ἐν τῷ νῦν αἰῶνι, [GNT]
		To be self controlled; to live soberly, sensibly, temperate, and disciplined.
		
		Practical Application
		It is restraining desires, lusts, and appetites. It is never giving in to excess—to the lust for more and more. It is controlling everything and using it for its proper purpose:
		⇒ It is controlling the desire for sex and using it for marriage.
		⇒ It is controlling the desire for food and using it for health.
		⇒ It is controlling the desire for material things and using it to meet both the needs of one's own family and the desperate needs of the world.

#3643
Sodomites
 	
Abusers of themselves
  with mankind–KJV
Homosexuals–NASB
Homosexual offend-
  ers–NIV
Sodomites–NKJV
Homosexuals–NLT
 	
**POSB
REFERENCE**
(1 Cor.6:9)
Note 2, point 4
	ἀρσενοκοῖται = arsenokoitai
	Pronunciation: [ar-sen-ok-oy'-tah-ee]
	Parsing (part of speech): noun
	    Case—nominative
	    Gender—masculine
	    Number—plural
	    Stem or root—from **ἀρσενοκοίτης**, ου
	Concordance References:
	  ⇒ Strong's #733 arsenokoitës
	  ⇒ NIV #780 arsenokoitës
	  ⇒ NASB #733 arsenokoitës
	
	1 Cor. 6:9
	Know ye not that the unrighteous shall not inherit the kingdom of God? Be not deceived: neither fornicators, nor idolaters, nor adulterers, nor effeminate, nor **abusers of themselves with mankind**, [KJV]
	Or do you not know that the unrighteous shall not inherit the kingdom of God? Do not be deceived; neither fornicators, nor idolaters, nor adulterers, nor effeminate, nor **homosexuals**, [NASB]
	Do you not know that the wicked will not inherit the kingdom of God? Do not be deceived: Neither the sexually immoral nor idolaters nor adulterers nor male prostitutes nor **homosexual offenders** [NIV]
	Do you not know that the unrighteous will not inherit the kingdom of God? Do not be deceived. Neither fornicators, nor idolaters, nor adulterers, nor homosexuals, nor **sodomites**, [NKJV]
	Don't you know that those who do wrong will have no share in the Kingdom of God? Don't fool yourselves. Those who indulge in sexual sin, who are idol worshipers,
		Homosexual offenders; sodomites, perverts; the abusers of themselves with mankind.
		
		Practical Application
		The warning is clear and sober: the practicing homosexual, those who are "Sodomites" (*arsenokoitai*), shall not inherit the kingdom of God.

ENGLISH WORD	GREEK WORD AND VERSE	THE WORD MEANS...
	adulterers, male prostitutes, **homosexuals**, [NLT] η οὐκ οἴδατε ὅτι ἄδικοι βασιλείαν Θεοῦ οὐ κληρονομήσουσι; μὴ πλανᾶσθε· οὔτε πόρνοι, οὔτε εἰδωλολάτραι, οὔτε μοιχοί, οὔτε μαλακοί, οὔτε **ἀρσενοκοῖται**, [GNS] η οὐκ οἴδατε ὅτι ἄδικοι θεοῦ βασιλείαν οὐ κληρονομήσουσιν; μὴ πλανᾶσθε· οὔτε πόρνοι οὔτε εἰδωλολάτραι οὔτε μοιχοὶ οὔτε μαλακοὶ οὔτε **ἀρσενοκοῖται** [GNT]	

#3644
Sojourning
 	
Sojourning–KJV
Stay–NASB
Strangers–NIV
Stay–NKJV
Foreigners–NLT
 	
POSB
REFERENCE
(1 Pt.1:17)
Note 3
	παροικίας = *paroikias*
	Pronunciation: [par-oy-kee'-ahs]
	Parsing (part of speech): noun
	    Case—genitive
	    Gender—feminine
	    Number—singular
	    Stem or root—from *παροικία ας*
	Concordance References:
	  ⇒ Strong's #3940 paroikia
	  ⇒ NIV #4229 paroikia
	  ⇒ NASB #3940 paroikia
	
	1 Peter 1:17
	And if ye call on the Father, who without respect of persons judgeth according to every man's work, pass the time of your **sojourning** here in fear: [KJV]
	And if you address as Father the One who impartially judges according to each man's work, conduct yourselves in fear during the time of your **stay** upon earth; [NASB]
	Since you call on a Father who judges each man's work impartially, live your lives as **strangers** here in reverent fear. [NIV]
	And if you call on the Father, who without partiality judges according to each one's work, conduct yourselves throughout the time of your **stay** *here* in fear; [NKJV]
	And remember that the heavenly Father to whom you pray has no favorites when he judges. He will judge or reward you according to what you do. So you must live in reverent fear of him during your time as **foreigners** here on earth. [NLT]
	καὶ εἰ πατέρα ἐπικαλεῖσθε τὸν ἀπροσωπολήπτως κρίνοντα κατὰ τὸ ἑκάστου ἔργον, ἐν φόβῳ τὸν τῆς **παροικίας** ὑμῶν χρόνον ἀναστράφητε· [GNS]
	Καὶ εἰ πατέρα ἐπικαλεῖσθε τὸν ἀπροσωπολήμπτως κρίνοντα κατὰ τὸ ἑκάστου ἔργον, ἐν φόβῳ τὸν τῆς **παροικίας** ὑμῶν χρόνον ἀναστράφητε, [GNT]
		Strangers, foreigners, sojourning, staying. The word "sojournings" (*paroikias*) means to dwell alongside; to be passing by.
		
		Practical Application
		It is the picture of a pilgrim or stranger who is only dwelling in or passing by a foreign country for a brief time. This is the believer here on earth. He is not a permanent resident on earth. He is only passing through the earth to a better world. This means a most wonderful thing: when a person is a stranger or pilgrim in a foreign land, his mind and heart are home. He lives in a consciousness of home. So it is with the believer: his thoughts are home. He lives and walks in the consciousness of being in heaven with God. This is his attitude and his thoughts as he walks through his pilgrimage upon earth. He travels through life with his mind and heart upon heaven, his permanent home.

#3645
Solemnly Assure
 	
Certify–KJV
Know–NASB
Know–NIV
Make known–NKJV
Solemnly assure–
NLT
 	
POSB
REFERENCE
(Gal.1:11-12; esp.
v.11)
Note 2
	Γνωρίζω = *Gnōrizō*
	Pronunciation: [gno-rid'-zo]
	Parsing (part of speech): verb
	    Mood—indicative
	    Tense—present
	    Voice—active
	    Person—1st person
	    Number—singular
	    Stem or root—from *γνωρίζω*
	Concordance References:
	  ⇒ Strong's #1107 gnōrizō
	  ⇒ NIV #1192 gnōrizō
	  ⇒ NASB #1107 gnōrizō
	
	Galatians 1:11
	But I **certify** you, brethren, that the gospel which was preached of me is not after man. [KJV]
	For I would have you **know**, brethren, that the gospel which was preached by me is not according to man. [NASB]
	I want you to **know**, brothers, that the gospel I preached is not something that man made up. [NIV]
	But I **make known** to you, brethren, that the gospel which was preached by me is not according to man. [NKJV]
	Dear brothers and sisters, I **solemnly assure** you that the Good News of salvation which I preach is not based
		To certify; to make known; to solemnly assure.
		
		Practical Application
		The minister proclaimed the gospel. Some critics of Paul were saying that he was not a true apostle of the Lord Jesus because he had not been a follower of the Lord when the Lord was upon the earth. Therefore, what he was teaching was a man-made gospel taught by mistaken and misguided men.
		Note that the word "solemnly assure" (*gnorizo*) is a solemn word, a strong declaration that what follows is of crucial importance and needs to be heard.

ENGLISH WORD	GREEK WORD AND VERSE	THE WORD MEANS...
	on mere human reasoning or logic. [NLT] Γνωρίζω δὲ ὑμῖν, ἀδελφοί, τὸ εὐαγγέλιον τὸ εὐαγγελισθὲν ὑπ' ἐμοῦ, ὅτι οὐκ ἔστι κατὰ ἄνθρωπον. [GNS] Γνωρίζω γὰρ ὑμῖν, ἀδελφοί, τὸ εὐαγγέλιον τὸ εὐαγγελισθὲν ὑπ' ἐμοῦ ὅτι οὐκ ἔστιν κατὰ ἄνθρωπον· [GNT]	
#3646 **Some Days** Certain days–KJV Several days–NASB Several days–NIV **Some days–NKJV** Few days–NLT **POSB REFERENCE** (Acts 9:23) *Deeper Study #1*	ἡμέρας τινάς = *hēmeras tinas* Pronunciation: [hay-mer'-ahs ti'-nahs] Parsing *hēmeras* (part of speech): noun 　Case—accusative 　Gender—feminine 　Number—plural 　Stem or root—from ἡμέρα, ας Parsing *tinas* (part of speech): adjective indefinite 　Case—accusative 　Gender—feminine 　Number—plural 　Stem or root—from τὶς, τὶ Concordance References: ⇒ Strong's #2250 hēmera + 5100 tis ⇒ NIV #2465 hēmera [days] + 5516 tis [several] ⇒ NASB #2250 hēmera + 5100 tis **Acts 9:19** And when he had received meat, he was strengthened. Then was Saul **certain days** with the disciples which were at Damascus. [KJV] And he took food and was strengthened. Now for **several days** he was with the disciples who were at Damascus, [NASB] And after taking some food, he regained his strength. Saul spent **several days** with the disciples in Damascus. [NIV] So when he had received food, he was strengthened. Then Saul spent **some days** with the disciples at Damascus. [NKJV] Afterward he ate some food and was strengthened. Saul stayed with the believers in Damascus for a **few days**. [NLT] καὶ λαβὼν τροφὴν ἐνίσχυσεν. Ἐγένετο δὲ ὁ Σαῦλος μετὰ τῶν ἐν Δαμασκῷ μαθητῶν **ἡμέρας τινάς**. [GNS] καὶ λαβὼν τροφὴν ἐνίσχυσεν. Ἐγένετο δὲ μετὰ τῶν ἐν Δαμασκῷ μαθητῶν **ἡμέρας τινάς** [GNT]	Several days; a few days; certain days. It is a term indicating a short time. **Practical Application** Paul joined and became associated and identified with other believers. What happened is important to note, for it holds a much needed lesson for every generation. Paul joined the other believers at Damascus because he was a *true* believer. His old nature, the old man, had truly died; and he now had the new nature of believers. He was *bound* to join those who had the same nature as he. It was their presence he desired. He wanted to share in... • their companionship and fellowship (see POSB *Deeper Study #3*—Acts 2:42 for more discussion) • their love, concern, and care • their beliefs and principles • their study of the Word • their growth in Christ • their edifying and building up of each other • their witness and service Saul (or Paul) associated and became identified with the church so that the world might know that he was a believer. He wanted to openly and publicly declare that he was now... • a new creation in Christ Jesus. • a follower of "the Way" which he had opposed and persecuted. • a true disciple of the Lord Jesus.
#3647 **Someone Else** Another–KJV Another–NASB Another–NIV Another–NKJV **Someone else–NLT** **POSB REFERENCE** (Jn.5:32) Note 2	ἄλλος = *allos* Pronunciation: [al'-los] Parsing (part of speech): adjective 　Case—nominative 　Gender—masculine 　Number—singular 　Stem or root— from ἄλλος, η Concordance References: ⇒ Strong's #243 allos ⇒ NIV #257 allos ⇒ NASB #243 allos **John 5:32** There is **another** that beareth witness of me; and I know that the witness which he witnesseth of me is true. [KJV] "There is **another** who bears witness of Me, and I know that the testimony which He bears of Me is true. [NASB] There is **another** who testifies in my favor, and I know that his testimony about me is valid. [NIV] There is **another** who bears witness of Me, and I know that the witness which He witnesses of Me is true. [NKJV] But **someone else** is also testifying about me, and I can assure you that everything he says about me is true. [NLT]	Another, someone else, some other, different one. **Practical Application** Christ did not identify who He meant by "someone else" (*allos*). (Cp. John 14:16.) Most commentators believe He was referring to God Himself. However, there are three reasons why the Holy Spirit is thought to be the One to whom Christ was referring. 1. The Holy Spirit had already been given to Christ "without measure or limit" (see POSB note—John 3:34). He was, of course, very conscious of the witness of the Spirit both within and without Him. The Spirit was empowering Him and doing the works of God through Him. 2. The Holy Spirit is One of the witnesses that bears witness to Christ (cp. 1 John 5:6-12). When John the apostle discusses the witness to Christ in his epistle, he mentions the Spirit. If the present verse is not referring to the Spirit, then the Spirit is not listed as one of the witnesses in the present passage. This would be most unlikely, especially since the

ENGLISH WORD	GREEK WORD AND VERSE	THE WORD MEANS...
	ἄλλος ἐστὶν ὁ μαρτυρῶν περὶ ἐμοῦ, καὶ οἶδα ὅτι ἀληθής ἐστιν ἡ μαρτυρία ἣν μαρτυρεῖ περὶ ἐμοῦ. [GNS] ἄλλος ἐστὶν ὁ μαρτυρῶν περὶ ἐμοῦ, καὶ οἶδα ὅτι ἀληθής ἐστιν ἡ μαρτυρία ἣν μαρτυρεῖ περὶ ἐμοῦ. [GNT]	witness of the Father is covered in John 5:37-38, and the ministry and witness of the Spirit is covered so thoroughly in this Gospel. (See POSB outline and notes—John 14:15-26; POSB notes—John 16:7-15.) 3. Note how the verse reads. Christ seems to be talking about an inner witness, the witness of a Presence which He senses within His innermost Being, a Power that works in and through Him. This of course could be God; but again, it could also be the Spirit which would seem to fit more naturally in the context. Note the Lord's words, "I can assure you that everything he says about me is true." [NLT] The Lord meant at least two things. 1. He knew the truth of the witness within His own heart and life. He had the consciousness, the sense, the awareness, the personal knowledge of the Spirit's witness within His own inner Being. The Spirit bore witness with Jesus' own Spirit that He was the Son of God Himself. 2. He knew that the witness and the work of the Holy Spirit, in and through Him, was true. The Spirit was convicting men, working in their hearts and lives, convincing them of the claims of Christ. (See POSB outline and notes—John 16:7-15 for the Lord's discussion of the Spirit's work.)

#3648
Someone To Plead For You
 	
Advocate–KJV
Advocate–NASB
Speaks...in...defense–NIV
Advocate–NKJV
Someone to plead for you–NLT
 	
POSB REFERENCE
(1 Jn.2:1-2; esp. v.1) Note 3, point 1
	παράκλητον = paraklēton
	Pronunciation: [par-ak'-lay-ton]
	Parsing (part of speech): noun
	  Case—accusative
	  Gender—masculine
	  Number—singular
	  Stem or root—from παράκλητος, ου
	Concordance References:
	⇒ Strong's #3875 paraklētos
	⇒ NIV #4156 paraklētos
	⇒ NASB #3875 paraklētos
	
	1 John 2:1
	My little children, these things write I unto you, that ye sin not. And if any man sin, we have an **advocate** with the Father, Jesus Christ the righteous: [KJV]
	My little children, I am writing these things to you that you may not sin. And if anyone sins, we have an **Advocate** with the Father, Jesus Christ the righteous; [NASB]
	My dear children, I write this to you so that you will not sin. But if anybody does sin, we have one who **speaks** to the Father **in** our **defense**—Jesus Christ, the Righteous One. [NIV]
	My little children, these things I write to you, so that you may not sin. And if anyone sins, we have an **Advocate** with the Father, Jesus Christ the righteous. [NKJV]
	My dear children, I am writing this to you so that you will not sin. But if you do sin, there is **someone to plead for you** before the Father. He is Jesus Christ, the one who pleases God completely. [NLT]
	Τεκνία μου, ταῦτα γράφω ὑμῖν, ἵνα μὴ ἁμάρτητε. καὶ ἐάν τις ἁμάρτῃ, **παράκλητον** ἔχομεν πρὸς τὸν πατέρα, Ἰησοῦν Χριστὸν δίκαιον· [GNS]
	Τεκνία μου, ταῦτα γράφω ὑμῖν ἵνα μὴ ἁμάρτητε. καὶ ἐάν τις ἁμάρτῃ, **παράκλητον** ἔχομεν πρὸς τὸν πατέρα Ἰησοῦν Χριστὸν δίκαιον· [GNT]
		One who speaks in defense; an advocate; someone who pleads for you; a Helper; an Intercessor. This word is associated with Christ and the Holy Spirit.
		
		Practical Application
		Jesus Christ is "someone to plead for you" (parakleton). The term means someone who is called in to stand by the side of another. The purpose is to help in any way possible. This is the word [parakletos] used of the Holy Spirit. (See Deeper Study #1—John 14:16 for discussion.)
		⇒ There is the picture of a friend called in to help a person who is troubled or distressed or confused.
		⇒ There is the picture of a commander called in to help a discouraged and dispirited army.
		⇒ There is the picture of a lawyer, an advocate called in to help a defendant who needs his case pleaded.
		
		There is no one word that can adequately translate paracletos. The word that probably comes closest is simply helper. Sin causes the believer to be distressed and confused, discouraged and dispirited. Sin separates the believer from God, making him guilty of transgression and worthy of condemnation and punishment. But Jesus Christ is the believer's Helper—his Advocate, the One who pleads for you. Jesus Christ stands before God to plead the case of the believer.

ENGLISH WORD	GREEK WORD AND VERSE	THE WORD MEANS...

#3649
Son
 	
Son–KJV
Son–NASB
Son–NIV
Son–NKJV
Son–NLT
 	
**POSB
REFERENCE**
(Mk.2:5)
Note 3, point 2b
	Τέκνον = *teknon*
	Pronunciation: [tek'-non]
	Parsing (part of speech): noun
	  Case—vocative
	  Gender—neuter
	  Number—singular
	  Stem or root—from τέκνον, ου
	Concordance References:
	  ⇒ Strong's #5043 teknon
	  ⇒ NIV #5451 teknon
	  ⇒ NASB #5043 teknon
	
	Mark 2:5
	When Jesus saw their faith, he said unto the sick of the palsy, **Son**, thy sins be forgiven thee. [KJV]
	And Jesus seeing their faith said to the paralytic, "My **son**, your sins are forgiven." [NASB]
	When Jesus saw their faith, he said to the paralytic, "**Son**, your sins are forgiven." [NIV]
	When Jesus saw their faith, He said to the paralytic, "**Son**, your sins are forgiven you." [NKJV]
	Seeing their faith, Jesus said to the paralyzed man, "My **son**, your sins are forgiven." [NLT]
	ἰδὼν δὲ ὁ Ἰησοῦς τὴν πίστιν αὐτῶν, λέγει τῷ παραλυτικῷ, **Τέκνον**, ἀφέωνταί σοι αἱ ἁμαρτίαι σου. [GNS]
	καὶ ἰδὼν ὁ Ἰησοῦς τὴν πίστιν αὐτῶν λέγει τῷ παραλυτικῷ, **Τέκνον**, ἀφίενταί σου αἱ ἁμαρτίαι. [GNT]
		Son or child.
		
		Practical Application
		Jesus used this word "son" (*teknon*) to convey a tender, kind form of personal address. Jesus proclaimed forgiveness in tenderness and compassion. When a person comes to Jesus for forgiveness, Jesus does not...
		• accuse the person of past sins.
		• find fault with the person: what he has done—why he has come—from where he has come.
		• begrudge or hesitate in forgiving the person.
		
		When a person comes to Jesus, Jesus responds tenderly and compassionately. This is seen in the word "son." Looking upon the man lying at His feet, Jesus saw a child, and Jesus responded to the man just as any of us would respond to a child lying helpless at our feet—tenderly and compassionately.

#3650
Son
 	
Son–KJV
Servant–NASB
Servant–NIV
Servant–NKJV
Servant–NLT
 	
**POSB
REFERENCE**
(Acts 3:12-13; esp. v.13)
Note 2, point 2c
	τὸν παῖδα = *ton paida*
	Pronunciation: [ton pah-ee-dah]
	Parsing *paida* (part of speech): noun
	  Case—accusative
	  Gender—masculine
	  Number—singular
	  Stem or root—from παῖς, παιδός
	Concordance References:
	  ⇒ Strong's #3588 ho + 3816 pais
	  ⇒ NIV #3836 ho + 4090 pais
	  ⇒ NASB #3588 ho + 3816 pais
	
	Acts 3:13
	The God of Abraham, and of Isaac, and of Jacob, the God of our fathers, hath glorified his **Son** Jesus; whom ye delivered up, and denied him in the presence of Pilate, when he was determined to let him go. [KJV]
	"The God of Abraham, Isaac, and Jacob, the God of our fathers, has glorified His **servant** Jesus, the one whom you delivered up, and disowned in the presence of Pilate, when he had decided to release Him. [NASB]
	The God of Abraham, Isaac and Jacob, the God of our fathers, has glorified his **servant** Jesus. You handed him over to be killed, and you disowned him before Pilate, though he had decided to let him go. [NIV]
	The God of Abraham, Isaac, and Jacob, the God of our fathers, glorified His **Servant** Jesus, whom you delivered up and denied in the presence of Pilate, when he was determined to let *Him* go. [NKJV]
	For it is the God of Abraham, the God of Isaac, the God of Jacob, the God of all our ancestors who has brought glory to his **servant** Jesus by doing this. This is the same Jesus whom you handed over and rejected before Pilate, despite Pilate's decision to release him. [NLT]
	ὁ Θεὸς Ἀβραὰμ καὶ Ἰσαὰκ καὶ Ἰακώβ, ὁ Θεὸς τῶν πατέρων ἡμῶν, ἐδόξασε **τὸν παῖδα** αὐτοῦ Ἰησοῦν· ὃν ὑμεῖς παρεδώκατε καὶ ἠρνήσασθε κατὰ πρόσωπον Πιλάτου, κρίναντος ἐκείνου ἀπολύειν. [GNS]
	ὁ θεὸς Ἀβραὰμ καὶ [ὁ θεὸς] Ἰσαὰκ καὶ [ὁ θεὸς] Ἰακώβ, ὁ θεὸς τῶν πατέρων ἡμῶν, ἐδόξασεν **τὸν παῖδα**, αὐτοῦ Ἰησοῦν ὃν ὑμεῖς μὲν παρεδώκατε καὶ ἠρνήσασθε κατὰ πρόσωπον Πιλάτου, κρίναντος ἐκείνου ἀπολύειν· [GNT]
		Servant, slave.
		
		Practical Application
		It is a name or title for the Messiah (Isaiah 42:1-4; Isaiah 52:13). The Messiah was to be the "Servant of the Lord" (cp. Isaiah 50-53). Peter was declaring that "the God of Abraham, and of Isaac, and of Jacob, the God of our Fathers" has done this miracle. He has glorified His Son, that is, His Servant the Messiah.

ENGLISH WORD	GREEK WORD AND VERSE	THE WORD MEANS...

#3651
Sons
 	
Children–KJV
Sons–NASB
Sons–NIV
Sons–NKJV
Children–NLT
 	
POSB
REFERENCE
(Jn.12:34-36; esp.
v.36)
Note 5, point 2
	υἱοί = huioi
	Pronunciation: [hwee-o-ee']
	Parsing (part of speech): noun
	  Case—nominative
	  Gender—masculine
	  Number—plural
	  Stem or root—from υἱός, οῦ
	Concordance References:
	⇒ Strong's #5207 huios
	⇒ NIV #5626 huios
	⇒ NASB #5207 huios
	
	John 12:36
	While ye have light, believe in the light, that ye may be the **children** of light. These things spake Jesus, and departed, and did hide himself from them. [KJV]
	"While you have the light, believe in the light, in order that you may become **sons** of light." These things Jesus spoke, and He departed and hid Himself from them. [NASB]
	Put your trust in the light while you have it, so that you may become **sons** of light." When he had finished speaking, Jesus left and hid himself from them. [NIV]
	While you have the light, believe in the light, that you may become **sons** of light." These things Jesus spoke, and departed, and was hidden from them. [NKJV]
	Believe in the light while there is still time; then you will become **children** of the light." After saying these things, Jesus went away and was hidden from them. [NLT]
	ἕως τὸ φῶς ἔχετε, πιστεύετε εἰς τὸ φῶς, ἵνα υἱοὶ φωτὸς γένησθε. Ταῦτα ἐλάλησεν ὁ Ἰησοῦς, καὶ ἀπελθὼν ἐκρύβη ἀπ' αὐτῶν. [GNS]
	ὡς τὸ φῶς ἔχετε, πιστεύετε εἰς τὸ φῶς, ἵνα υἱοὶ φωτὸς γένησθε. Ταῦτα ἐλάλησεν Ἰησοῦς, καὶ ἀπελθὼν ἐκρύβη ἀπ' αὐτῶν. [GNT]
		Sons, children, descendants, offsprings, heirs, followers.
		
		Practical Application
		A person must believe in the Light. If people believe, something significant will happen. They will become children (*huioi*, sons) of the Light.
		⇒ "Believe" (*pisteuete*) is continuous action.
		⇒ "Become" (*genesthe*) is a once-for-all act, a personal experience that happens all at once.
		
		A person who truly sees Jesus Christ as the Light of the world believes and continues to believe. And the very moment his heart leaps toward Christ in belief, he becomes a child of the Light, a child of God Himself. The person sees the Light and begins to walk in the Light, living the kind of life he should.

#3652
Sons Of God
 	
Sons of God–KJV
Children of God–
  NASB
Children of God–NIV
Children of God–
  NKJV
Children of God–NLT
 	
POSB
REFERENCE
(Jn.1:12-13; esp. v.12)
Note 3, point 2
	τέκνα θεοῦ = tekna theou
	Pronunciation: [tek'-nah theh'-oo]
	Parsing *tekna* (part of speech): noun
	  Case—accusative
	  Gender—neuter
	  Number—plural
	  Stem or root—from τέκνον, ου
	Concordance References:
	⇒ Strong's #5043 teknon + 2316 theos
	⇒ NIV #5451 teknon [children] + 2536 theos [God]
	⇒ NASB #5043 teknon + 2316 theos
	
	John 1:12
	But as many as received him, to them gave he power to become the **sons of God**, even to them that believe on his name: [KJV]
	But as many as received Him, to them He gave the right to become **children of God**, even to those who believe in His name, [NASB]
	Yet to all who received him, to those who believed in his name, he gave the right to become **children of God** [NIV]
	But as many as received Him, to them He gave the right to become **children of God**, to those who believe in His name: [NKJV]
	But to all who believed him and accepted him, he gave the right to become **children of God**. [NLT]
	ὅσοι δὲ ἔλαβον αὐτόν, ἔδωκεν αὐτοῖς ἐξουσίαν τέκνα θεοῦ γενέσθαι, τοῖς πιστεύουσιν εἰς τὸ ὄνομα αὐτοῦ· [GNS]
	ὅσοι δὲ ἔλαβον αὐτόν, ἔδωκεν αὐτοῖς ἐξουσίαν τέκνα θεοῦ γενέσθαι, τοῖς πιστεύουσιν εἰς τὸ ὄνομα αὐτοῦ, [GNT]
		Children, people, descendants—male or female—of God; sons of God.
		
		Practical Application
		It is important to understand how a person becomes a child of God. There is only one way—the way of adoption. The picture of adoption is a beautiful picture of what God does for the Christian believer. In the ancient world the family was based on a Roman law called "patria potestas," the father's power. The law gave the father absolute authority over his children so long as the father lived. He could work, enslave, sell; and, if he wished, he could pronounce the death penalty. Regardless of the child's adult age, the father held all power over personal and property rights.
		Therefore, adoption was a serious matter. Yet, it was a common practice to ensure that a family would not become extinct by having no male children. And when a child was adopted, three legal steps were taken.
		1. The adopted son was adopted permanently. He could not be adopted today and disinherited tomorrow. He became a son of the father—forever. He was eternally secure as a son.
		2. The adopted son immediately had all the rights of a legitimate son in the new family.
		3. The adopted son completely lost all rights in his old family. The adopted son was looked upon as a new person—so new that old debts and obligations connected with his former family were canceled out and abolished as if they never existed.

ENGLISH WORD	GREEK WORD AND VERSE	THE WORD MEANS...

#3653
Soon Angry
 	
Soon angry–KJV
Quick-tempered–NASB
Quick-tempered–NIV
Quick-tempered–NKJV
Quick-tempered–NLT
 	
POSB
REFERENCE
(Tit.1:7-8; esp. v.7)
Note 3, point 1b
	ὀργίλον = orgilon
	Pronunciation: [org-ee'-lon]
	Parsing (part of speech): adjective
	  Case—accusative
	  Gender—masculine
	  Number—singular
	  Stem or root—from ὀργίλος, η, ον
	Concordance References:
	  ⇒ Strong's #3711 orgilos
	  ⇒ NIV #3975 orgilos
	  ⇒ NASB #3711 orgilos
	
	Titus 1:7
	For a bishop must be blameless, as the steward of God; not selfwilled, not **soon angry**, not given to wine, no striker, not given to filthy lucre; [KJV]
	For the overseer must be above reproach as God's steward, not self-willed, not **quick-tempered**, not addicted to wine, not pugnacious, not fond of sordid gain, [NASB]
	Since an overseer is entrusted with God's work, he must be blameless—not overbearing, not **quick-tempered**, not given to drunkenness, not violent, not pursuing dishonest gain. [NIV]
	For a bishop must be blameless, as a steward of God, not self-willed, not **quick-tempered**, not given to wine, not violent, not greedy for money, [NKJV]
	An elder must live a blameless life because he is God's minister. He must not be arrogant or **quick-tempered**; he must not be a heavy drinker, violent, or greedy for money. [NLT]
	δεῖ γὰρ τὸν ἐπίσκοπον ἀνέγκλητον εἶναι, ὡς Θεοῦ οἰκονόμον· μὴ αὐθάδη, μὴ **ὀργίλον**, μὴ πάροινον, μὴ πλήκτην, μὴ αἰσχροκερδῆ, [GNS]
	δεῖ γὰρ τὸν ἐπίσκοπον ἀνέγκλητον εἶναι ὡς θεοῦ οἰκονόμον, μὴ αὐθάδη, μὴ **ὀργίλον**, μὴ πάροινον, μὴ πλήκτην, μὴ αἰσχροκερδῆ, [GNT]
		To be quick tempered, soon angry. It is a long-lasting anger; an anger that is deeply rooted and has been held for a long time; an anger against someone that a person just refuses to let go; the person refuses to forgive the other person.
		
		Practical Application
		The minister must not be quick tempered or hot-headed, nor given over to long-lasting anger.

#3654
Sorceries
 	
Sorceries–KJV
Sorceries–NASB
Magic arts–NIV
Sorceries–NKJV
Witchcraft–NLT
 	
POSB
REFERENCE
(Rev.9:20-21; esp. v.21)
Note 4, point 2c
	φαρμάκων = pharmakön
	Pronunciation: [far-mak-own']
	Parsing (part of speech): noun
	  Case—genitive
	  Gender—neuter
	  Number—plural
	  Stem or root—from φάρμακον, ου
	Concordance References:
	  ⇒ Strong's #5331 pharmakon
	  ⇒ NIV #5760 pharmakon
	  ⇒ NASB #5331 pharmakon
	Rev. 9:21
	Neither repented they of their murders, nor of their **sorceries**, nor of their fornication, nor of their thefts. [KJV]
	And they did not repent of their murders nor of their **sorceries** nor of their immorality nor of their thefts. [NASB]
	Nor did they repent of their murders, their **magic arts**, their sexual immorality or their thefts. [NIV]
	And they did not repent of their murders or their **sorceries** or their sexual immorality or their thefts. [NKJV]
	And they did not repent of their murders or their **witchcraft** or their immorality or their thefts. [NLT]
	καὶ οὐ μετενόησαν ἐκ τῶν φόνων αὐτῶν, οὔτε ἐκ τῶν **φαρμακειῶν** αὐτῶν, οὔτε ἐκ τῆς πορνείας αὐτῶν, οὔτε ἐκ τῶν κλεμμάτων αὐτῶν. [GNS]
	καὶ οὐ μετενόησαν ἐκ τῶν φόνων αὐτῶν οὔτε ἐκ τῶν **φαρμάκων** αὐτῶν οὔτε ἐκ τῆς πορνείας αὐτῶν οὔτε ἐκ τῶν κλεμμάτων αὐτῶν. [GNT]
		Magic arts, sorceries, witchcraft.
		
		Practical Application
		Note that the Greek word is close to the spelling of the English word *pharmacy*, that is, a place that handles drugs. Sorcery includes all kinds of witchcraft, the use of drugs or of evil spirits to gain control over the lives of others or over one's own life. In the present context, it would include all forms of sorcery including astrology, palm reading, seances, fortune telling, crystals, and other forms of witchcraft.

#3655 **Sorcery**	φαρμακεία = pharmakeia Pronunciation: [far-mak-i'-ah] Parsing (part of speech): noun Case—nominative	Witchcraft, sorcery, participation in demonic activities; the use of drugs or of evil spirits to gain control over the lives of others or over one's own life.

ENGLISH WORD	GREEK WORD AND VERSE	THE WORD MEANS...
Witchcraft–KJV **Sorcery–NASB** Witchcraft–NIV **Sorcery–NKJV** Participation in demonic activities–NLT **POSB REFERENCE** (Gal.5:19-21; esp. v.20) Note 2	Gender—feminine Number—singular Stem or root—from φαρμακεία, ας Concordance References: ⇒ Strong's #5331 pharmakeia ⇒ NIV #5758 pharmakeia ⇒ NASB #5331 pharmakeia **Galatians 5:20** Idolatry, **witchcraft**, hatred, variance, emulations, wrath, strife, seditions, heresies, [KJV] Idolatry, **sorcery**, enmities, strife, jealousy, outbursts of anger, disputes, dissensions, factions, [NASB] Idolatry and **witchcraft**; hatred, discord, jealousy, fits of rage, selfish ambition, dissensions, factions [NIV] Idolatry, **sorcery**, hatred, contentions, jealousies, outbursts of wrath, selfish ambitions, dissensions, heresies, [NKJV] Idolatry, **participation in demonic activities**, hostility, quarreling, jealousy, outbursts of anger, selfish ambition, divisions, the feeling that everyone is wrong except those in your own little group, [NLT] εἰδωλολατρία, **φαρμακεία**, ἔχθραι, ἔρεις, ζῆλοι, θυμοί, ἐριθείαι, διχοστασίαι, αἱρέσεις, [GNS] εἰδωλολατρία, **φαρμακεία**, ἔχθραι, ἔρις, ζῆλος, θυμοί, ἐριθείαι, διχοστασίαι, αἱρέσεις, [GNT]	**Practical Application** It would include all forms of seeking the control of one's fate through astrology, palm reading, seances, fortune telling, crystals, and other forms of witchcraft.
#3656 **Sordid Gain, Not For** Not for filthy lucre–KJV **Not for sordid gain–NASB** Not greedy for money–NIV Not for dishonest gain–NKJV Not grudgingly–NLT **POSB REFERENCE** (1 Pt.5:2-3; esp. v.2) Note 2, point 2	μηδὲ αἰσχροκερδῶς = mēde aischrokerdōs Pronunciation: [may-deh' ahee-skhrok-er-doce'] Parsing aischrokerdōs (part of speech): adjective 　Type—adverb 　Stem or root—from αἰσχροκερδῶς Concordance References: ⇒ Strong's #3366 mēde + 147 aischrokerdōs ⇒ NIV #3593 mēde [not] +154 aischrokerdōs [greedy for money] ⇒ NASB #3366 mēde + 147 aischrokerdōs **1 Peter 5:2** Feed the flock of God which is among you, taking the oversight thereof, not by constraint, but willingly; **not for filthy lucre**, but of a ready mind; [KJV] Shepherd the flock of God among you, exercising oversight not under compulsion, but voluntarily, according to the will of God; and **not for sordid gain**, but with eagerness; [NASB] Be shepherds of God's flock that is under your care, serving as overseers—not because you must, but because you are willing, as God wants you to be; **not greedy for money**, but eager to serve; [NIV] Shepherd the flock of God which is among you, serving as overseers, not by compulsion but willingly, **not for dishonest gain** but eagerly; [NKJV] Care for the flock of God entrusted to you. Watch over it willingly, **not grudgingly**—not for what you will get out of it, but because you are eager to serve God. [NLT] ποιμάνατε τὸ ἐν ὑμῖν ποίμνιον τοῦ θεοῦ, ἐπισκοποῦντες μὴ ἀναγκαστῶς, ἀλλ ἑκουσίως· **μηδὲ αἰσχροκερδῶς**, ἀλλὰ προθύμως, [GNS] ποιμάνατε τὸ ἐν ὑμῖν ποίμνιον τοῦ θεοῦ [ἐπισκοποῦντες] μὴ ἀναγκαστῶς ἀλλὰ ἑκουσίως κατὰ Θεόν, **μηδὲ αἰσχροκερδῶς** ἀλλὰ προθύμως, [GNT]	Not greedy for money; not greedy for sordid gain; not grudgingly; not greedy for material gain. **Practical Application** The elder or minister must take the oversight of the flock not for personal profit and gain, but with a ready mind. The Greek says that no person is to enter the ministry for "sordid gain" (aischrokerdōs), that is, for base gain, or for some soiled and dirty advantage. No person should ever enter the ministry... • as a profession. • as a means of livelihood. • as a means to serve mankind. • because people say he has the gifts for it. • because people say he would make a good minister. • because family and friends encourage him to enter the ministry. All of these reasons usually surround a person's entrance into the ministry. But they must never be *the reasons* why a person enters the ministry and cares for God's people. The ministry is a *call from God*, and no person dare enter the ministry without a personal call to the ministry. But note: when the call comes, the person is to have a ready mind. He is to minister to God's people; he is to readily feed the flock of God.
#3657 **Sore Amazed** Sore amazed–KJV Very distressed–NASB Deeply distressed–NIV	ἐκθαμβεῖσθαι = ekthambeisthai Pronunciation: [ehk-tham-be-ees-tha-ee] Parsing (part of speech): verb 　Mood—infinitive 　Tense—present 　Voice—passive 　Stem or root—from ἐκθαμβέομαι Concordance References: ⇒ Strong's #1568 ekthambeō	To be deeply distressed, to be filled with utter and extreme fright, horror, terror, bewilderment, and amazement. **Practical Application** Jesus "began" to experience extreme agony and pressure beyond imagination. The words "sore amazed" (ekthambeisthai) are very strong

ENGLISH WORD	GREEK WORD AND VERSE	THE WORD MEANS...
Deeply distressed– NKJV Filled with horror– NLT **POSB REFERENCE** (Mk.14:33-34; esp. v.33) Note 2	⇒ NIV #1701 ekthambeō ⇒ NASB #1568 ekthambeō **Mark 14:33** And he taketh with him Peter and James and John, and began to be **sore amazed**, and to be very heavy; [KJV] And He took with Him Peter and James and John, and began to be **very distressed** and troubled. [NASB] He took Peter, James and John along with him, and he began to be **deeply distressed** and troubled. [NIV] And He took Peter, James, and John with Him, and He began to be troubled and **deeply distressed**. . [NKJV] He took Peter, James, and John with him, and he began to be **filled with horror** and deep distress. [NLT] καὶ παραλαμβάνει τὸν Πέτρον καὶ τὸν Ἰάκωβον καὶ Ἰωάννην μετ' αὐτοῦ, καὶ ἤρξατο **ἐκθαμβεῖσθαι** καὶ ἀδημονεῖν. [GNS] καὶ παραλαμβάνει τὸν Πέτρον καὶ [τὸν] Ἰάκωβον καὶ [τὸν] Ἰωάννην μετ' αὐτοῦ καὶ ἤρξατο **ἐκθαμ-βεῖσθαι** καὶ ἀδημονεῖν [GNT]	words in the Greek. Jesus was staggering under the "horror of great darkness," something like what fell upon Abraham, except Jesus' horror was much, much worse (Genesis 15:12).
#3658 **Sorrow** In heaviness–KJV **Sorrow–NASB** Painful–NIV **Sorrow–NKJV** Painful–NLT **POSB REFERENCE** (2 Cor.2:1) Note 2	ἐν λύπῃ = en lupē Pronunciation: [en loo'-pay] Parsing *lupē* (part of speech): noun 　Case—dative 　Gender—feminine 　Number—singular 　Stem or root—from λύπη, ης Concordance References: ⇒ Strong's #1722+3077 en lupē ⇒ NIV #1877+3383 en lupē ⇒ NASB #1722+3077 en lupē **2 Cor. 2:1** But I determined this with myself, that I would not come again to you **in heaviness**. [KJV] But I determined this for my own sake, that I would not come to you in **sorrow** again. [NASB] So I made up my mind that I would not make another **painful** visit to you. [NIV] But I determined this within myself, that I would not come again to you in **sorrow**. [NKJV] So I said to myself, "No, I won't do it. I won't make them unhappy with another **painful** visit." [NLT] ἔκρινα δὲ ἐμαυτῷ τοῦτο, τὸ μὴ πάλιν ἐλθεῖν **ἐν λύπῃ** πρὸς ὑμᾶς. [GNS] ἔκρινα γὰρ ἐμαυτῷ τοῦτο τὸ μὴ πάλιν **ἐν λύπῃ** πρὸς ὑμᾶς ἐλθεῖν. [GNT]	Painful; sorrow; in heaviness, grief, pain, regret. **Practical Application** It was best for the minister not to be the cause of pain. Note Paul's words, "But I determined this for my own sake, that I would not come to you in *sorrow* again." [NASB] This just cannot apply to Paul's first visit to Corinth, for his first visit did not end in failure and rejection. When Paul first left Corinth, he was filled with joy over the great success God had given. Therefore, he must be speaking about some other visit when the church rejected him and cut his heart, causing great sorrow.
#3659 **Sorrow** Heaviness–KJV **Sorrow–NASB** **Sorrow–NIV** **Sorrow–NKJV** **Sorrow–NLT** **POSB REFERENCE** (Rom.9:1-3; esp. v.2) Note 1, point 2	λύπη = lupē Pronunciation: [loo'-pay] Parsing (part of speech): noun 　Case—nominative 　Gender—feminine 　Number—singular 　Stem or root—from λύπη ης Concordance References: ⇒ Strong's #3077 lupē ⇒ NIV #3383 lupē ⇒ NASB #3077 lupē **Romans 9:2** That I have great **heaviness** and continual sorrow in my heart. [KJV] That I have great **sorrow** and unceasing grief in my heart. [NASB] I have great **sorrow** and unceasing anguish in my heart. [NIV] That I have great **sorrow** and continual grief in my heart. [NKJV] My heart is filled with bitter **sorrow** and unending grief [NLT] ὅτι **λύπη** μοί ἐστι μεγάλη, καὶ ἀδιάλειπτος ὀδύνη τῇ	Grief, sorrow, heaviness; mourning; pain; reluctantly; with regret. **Practical Application** Just how deeply Paul's heart was distressed over his kinsmen is clearly seen in the description of his heart. "I have great sorrow" (*lupē*): pain, grief, mourning.

ENGLISH WORD	GREEK WORD AND VERSE	THE WORD MEANS...
	power, and of love, and of a **sound mind**. [KJV] For God has not given us a spirit of timidity, but of power and love and **discipline**. [NASB] For God did not give us a spirit of timidity, but a spirit of power, of love and of **self-discipline**. [NIV] For God has not given us a spirit of fear, but of power and of love and of a **sound mind**. [NKJV] For God has not given us a spirit of fear and timidity, but of power, love, and **self-discipline**. [NLT] οὐ γὰρ ἔδωκεν ἡμῖν ὁ Θεὸς πνεῦμα δειλίας, ἀλλὰ δυνάμεως καὶ ἀγάπης καὶ **σωφρονισμοῦ**. [GNS] οὐ γὰρ ἔδωκεν ἡμῖν ὁ Θεὸς πνεῦμα δειλίας ἀλλὰ δυνάμεως καὶ ἀγάπης καὶ **σωφρονισμοῦ**. [GNT]	testimony for Christ, the Holy Spirit gives him a sound mind—a most glorious gift.
#3668 **Sound** **Occurred** Noised abroad–KJV **Sound occurred–** **NASB** Heard...sound–NIV **Sound occurred–** **NKJV** Heard...sound–NLT **POSB** **REFERENCE** (Acts 2:5-11; esp. v.6) Note 5, point 2	*γενομένης φωνῆς* = *genomenēs phōnēs* Pronunciation: [ghin'-om-eh-nace fo-nays'] Parsing *genomenēs* (part of speech): verb Mood—participle Tense—aorist Voice—middle deponent Case—genitive Gender—feminine Number—singular Stem or root—from *γίνομαι* Parsing *phōnēs* (part of speech): noun Case—genitive Gender—feminine Number—singular Stem or root—from *φωνη*, ῆς Concordance References: ⇒ Strong's #1096 ginomai + 5456 phōnē ⇒ NIV #1181 ginomai [heard] + 5889 phōnē [sound] ⇒ NASB ##1096 ginomai + 5456 phōnē **Acts 2:6** Now when this was **noised abroad**, the multitude came together, and were confounded, because that every man heard them speak in his own language. [KJV] And when this **sound occurred**, the multitude came together, and were bewildered, because they were each one hearing them speak in his own language. [NASB] When they **heard** this **sound**, a crowd came together in bewilderment, because each one heard them speaking in his own language. [NIV] And when this **sound occurred**, the multitude came together, and were confused, because everyone heard them speak in his own language. [NKJV] When they **heard** this **sound**, they came running to see what it was all about, and they were bewildered to hear their own languages being spoken by the believers. [NLT] *γενομένης* δὲ τῆς *φωνῆς* ταύτης, συνῆλθε τὸ πλῆθος, καὶ συνεχύθη, ὅτι ἤκουον εἷς ἕκαστος τῇ ἰδίᾳ διαλέκτῳ λαλούντων αὐτῶν. [GNS] *γίνομαι* δὲ τῆς *φωνη* ταύτης συνῆλθεν τὸ πλῆθος καὶ συνεχύθη, ὅτι ἤκουον εἷς ἕκαστος τῇ ἰδίᾳ διαλέκτῳ λαλούντων αὐτῶν. [GNT]	To hear a sound, noise, roar. **Practical Application** The Greek says, "When this sound was heard." It was apparently the sound of the thunderous blast caused by God that brought the people rushing to the scene.
#3669 **Soundness,** **Perfect** **Perfect soundness–** **KJV** Perfect health–NASB Complete healing– NIV **Perfect soundness–** **NKJV** Healing–NLT	*ὁλοκληρίαν* = *holoklērian* Pronunciation: [hol-ok-lay-ree'-ahn] Parsing (part of speech): noun Case—accusative Gender—feminine Number—singular Stem or root—from *ὁλοκληρία* Concordance References: ⇒ Strong's #3647 holoklēria ⇒ NIV #3907 holoklēria ⇒ NASB #3647 holoklēria **Acts 3:16** And his name through faith in his name hath made this	Complete healing, perfect soundness, perfect health. **Practical Application** It means to be whole: to be perfectly sound in *all* of one's parts; to be perfectly complete and entire. It means the man was perfectly sound in both body and soul.

ENGLISH WORD	GREEK WORD AND VERSE	THE WORD MEANS...
	Do not **speak against** one another, brethren. He who speaks against a brother, or judges his brother, speaks against the law, and judges the law; but if you judge the law, you are not a doer of the law, but a judge of it. [NASB] Brothers, do not **slander** one another. Anyone who speaks against his brother or judges him speaks against the law and judges it. When you judge the law, you are not keeping it, but sitting in judgment on it. [NIV] Do not **speak evil** of one another, brethren. He who speaks evil of a brother and judges his brother, speaks evil of the law and judges the law. But if you judge the law, you are not a doer of the law but a judge. [NKJV] Don't **speak evil** against each other, my dear brothers and sisters. If you criticize each other and condemn each other, then you are criticizing and condemning God's law. But you are not a judge who can decide whether the law is right or wrong. Your job is to obey it. [NLT] Μὴ **καταλαλεῖτε** ἀλλήλων, ἀδελφοί. ὁ καταλαλῶν ἀδελφοῦ, καὶ κρίνων τὸν ἀδελφὸν αὐτοῦ, καταλαλεῖ νόμου, καὶ κρίνει νόμον· εἰ δὲ νόμον κρίνεις, οὐκ εἶ ποιητὴς νόμου, ἀλλὰ κριτής. [GNS] Μὴ **καταλαλεῖτε** ἀλλήλων, ἀδελφοί. ὁ καταλαλῶν ἀδελφοῦ ἢ κρίνων τὸν ἀδελφὸν αὐτοῦ καταλαλεῖ νόμου καὶ κρίνει νόμον· εἰ δὲ νόμον κρίνεις, οὐκ εἶ ποιητὴς νόμου ἀλλὰ κριτής. [GNT]	

#3677
Speak Evil
 	
Speak...evil–KJV
Speak against–NASB
Slander–NIV
Speak evil–NKJV
Speak evil–NLT
 	
POSB
REFERENCE
(Jas.4:11)
Note 1, point 1
	καταλαλεῖτε = *katalaleite*
	Pronunciation: [kat-al-al-eh'-ee-teh]
	Parsing (part of speech): verb
	    Mood—imperative
	    Tense—present
	    Voice—active
	    Person—2nd person
	    Number—plural
	    Stem or root—from **καταλαλέω**
	Concordance References:
	⇒ Strong's #2635 katalaleö
	⇒ NIV #2895 katalaleö
	⇒ NASB #2635 katalaleö
	
	James 4:11
	
	Speak not **evil** one of another, brethren. He that speaketh evil of his brother, and judgeth his brother, speaketh evil of the law, and judgeth the law: but if thou judge the law, thou art not a doer of the law, but a judge. [KJV]
	
	Do not **speak against** one another, brethren. He who speaks against a brother, or judges his brother, speaks against the law, and judges the law; but if you judge the law, you are not a doer of the law, but a judge of it. [NASB]
	
	Brothers, do not **slander** one another. Anyone who speaks against his brother or judges him speaks against the law and judges it. When you judge the law, you are not keeping it, but sitting in judgment on it. [NIV]
	
	Do not **speak evil** of one another, brethren. He who speaks evil of a brother and judges his brother, speaks evil of the law and judges the law. But if you judge the law, you are not a doer of the law but a judge. [NKJV]
	
	Don't **speak evil** against each other, my dear brothers and sisters. If you criticize each other and condemn each other, then you are criticizing and condemning God's law. But you are not a judge who can decide whether the law is right or wrong. Your job is to obey it. [NLT]
	
	Μὴ **καταλαλεῖτε** ἀλλήλων, ἀδελφοί. ὁ καταλαλῶν ἀδελφοῦ, καὶ κρίνων τὸν ἀδελφὸν αὐτοῦ, καταλαλεῖ νόμου, καὶ κρίνει νόμον· εἰ δὲ νόμον κρίνεις, οὐκ εἶ ποιητὴς νόμου, ἀλλὰ κριτής. [GNS]
	
	Μὴ **καταλαλεῖτε** ἀλλήλων, ἀδελφοί. ὁ καταλαλῶν ἀδελφοῦ ἢ κρίνων τὸν ἀδελφὸν αὐτοῦ καταλαλεῖ νόμου καὶ κρίνει νόμον· εἰ δὲ νόμον κρίνεις, οὐκ εἶ ποιητὴς νόμου ἀλλὰ κριτής. [GNT]
		To slander; to speak evil of; to speak against; to say bad things about a person. To "speak against" (*katalaleite*) means to criticize, judge, backbite, gossip, censor, condemn, and grumble against another person.
		
		Practical Application
		
		It means to talk about and to tear down another person; to share things about another person that cut and hurt him and that lower his image and reputation in the eyes of others. The word usually means to talk about a person behind his back when he is not present.

ENGLISH WORD	GREEK WORD AND VERSE	THE WORD MEANS...

#3678
Speak Harshly
 	
Rebuke–KJV
Sharply rebuke–NASB
Rebuke...harshly–NIV
Rebuke–NKJV
Speak harshly–NLT
 	
**POSB
REFERENCE**
(1 Tim.5:1-3; esp. v.1)
Introduction
	ἐπιπλήξης = epiplëxës
	Pronunciation: [ep-ee-playk'-ays]
	Parsing (part of speech): verb
	   Mood—subjunctive OR imperative
	   Tense—aorist
	   Voice—active
	   Person—2nd person
	   Number—singular
	   Stem or root—from ἐπιπλήσσω
	Concordance References:
	⇒ Strong's #1969 epiplëssö
	⇒ NIV #2159 epiplëssö
	⇒ NASB #1969 epiplëssöt
	
	1 Tim. 5:1
	Rebuke not an elder, but intreat him as a father; and the younger men as brethren; [KJV]
	Do not **sharply rebuke** an older man, but rather appeal to him as a father, to the younger men as brothers, [NASB]
	Do not **rebuke** an older man **harshly**, but exhort him as if he were your father. Treat younger men as brothers, [NIV]
	Do not **rebuke** an older man, but exhort *him* as a father, younger men as brothers, [NKJV]
	Never **speak harshly** to an older man, but appeal to him respectfully as though he were your own father. Talk to the younger men as you would to your own brothers. [NLT]
	Πρεσβυτέρῳ μὴ **ἐπιπλήξης**, ἀλλὰ παρακάλει ὡς πατέρα· νεωτέρους, ὡς ἀδελφούς· [GNS]
	Πρεσβυτέρῳ μὴ **ἐπιπλήξης** ἀλλὰ παρακάλει ὡς πατέρα, νεωτέρους ὡς ἀδελφούς, [GNT]
		To rebuke harshly; to sharply rebuke; to speak harshly; to be severely censured, angrily reprimanded, violently reproached.
		
		Practical Application
		The instructions are clear: the members of a church are to treat each other as family members. In no sense is any member to be "spoken harshly to" (*epiplëxës*). When a family church member needs to be corrected, there is to be no severity, anger, or violence involved; no contempt or disgust. A church member is to be corrected and disciplined through entreaty (*parakalei*), that is, through exhortation and encouragement, through appeal and pleading. This passage deals with the spirit and discipline of various relationships within the church.

#3679
**Speaking Evil
Of Others**
 	
False accusers–KJV
Malicious gossips–
  NASB
Slanderers–NIV
Slanderers–NKJV
Speaking evil of others–NLT
 	
**POSB
REFERENCE**
(Tit.2:3)
Note 3, point 2
 	
See also POSB REF:
(2 Tim. 3:2-4; esp. v.3)
Note 2, point 11
	διαβόλους = diabolous
	Pronunciation: [dee-ab'-ol-oos]
	Parsing (part of speech): adjective
	   Case—accusative
	   Gender—feminine
	   Number—plural
	   Stem or root—from διάβολος, ου
	Concordance References:
	⇒ Strong's #1228 diabolos
	⇒ NIV #1333 diabolos
	⇒ NASB #1228 diabolos
	
	Titus 2:3
	The aged women likewise, that they be in behaviour as becometh holiness, not **false accusers**, not given to much wine, teachers of good things; [KJV]
	Older women likewise are to be reverent in their behavior, not **malicious gossips**, nor enslaved to much wine, teaching what is good, [NASB]
	Likewise, teach the older women to be reverent in the way they live, not to be **slanderers** or addicted to much wine, but to teach what is good. [NIV]
	The older women likewise, that they be reverent in behavior, not **slanderers**, not given to much wine, teachers of good things—[NKJV]
	Similarly, teach the older women to live in a way that is appropriate for someone serving the Lord. They must not go around **speaking evil of others** and must not be heavy drinkers. Instead, they should teach others what is good. [NLT]
	Πρεσβύτιδας ὡσαύτως ἐν καταστήματι ἱεροπρεπεῖς, μὴ **διαβόλους**, μὴ οἴνῳ πολλῷ δεδουλωμένας, καλοδιδασκάλους, [GNS]
	πρεσβύτιδας ὡσαύτως ἐν καταστήματι ἱεροπρεπεῖς, μὴ **διαβόλους** μηδὲ οἴνῳ πολλῷ δεδουλωμένας, καλοδιδασκάλους, [GNT]
		Slanderers, false accusers, malicious gossips, speaking evil of others, talebearers, gossipers, a person who goes about talking about others, stirring up mischief and disturbance.
		
		Practical Application
		This is so terrible a sin that the devil himself is called *the slanderer* (*diabolous*). This—slanderer, the one who speaks evil of others (*diabolous*)—is one of the very names of the devil.

#3680 **Speaking Perverse Things**	λαλοῦντες διεστραμμένα = lalountes diestrammena Pronunciation: [lal-oon'-tehs dee-as-tram'-mehn-ah] Parsing *lalountes* (part of speech): verb Mood—participle	To distort the truth; to speak perverse things; to pervert; to turn away; to mislead; to lead astray.

ENGLISH WORD	GREEK WORD AND VERSE	THE WORD MEANS...
Speaking perverse things–KJV **Speaking perverse things–NASB** Distort the truth–NIV **Speaking perverse things–NKJV** Distort the truth–NLT **POSB REFERENCE** (Acts 20:29-30; esp. v.30) *Deeper Study #2,* point 3	Tense—present Voice—active Case—nominative Gender—masculine Number—plural Stem or root—from λαλέω Parsing *diestrammena* (part of speech): verb Mood—participle Tense—perfect Voice—passive Case—accusative Gender—neuter Number—plural Stem or root—from διαστρέφω Concordance References: ⇒ Strong's #1294 + 2980 diastrephō laleō ⇒ NIV #1406 + 3281 diastrephō laleō [distort the truth] ⇒ NASB #1294 + 2980 diastrephō laleō **Acts 20:30** Also of your own selves shall men arise, **speaking perverse things**, to draw away disciples after them. [KJV] And from among your own selves men will arise, **speaking perverse things**, to draw away the disciples after them. [NASB] Even from your own number men will arise and **distort the truth** in order to draw away disciples after them. [NIV] Also from among yourselves men will rise up, **speaking perverse things**, to draw away the disciples after themselves. [NKJV] Even some of you will **distort the truth** in order to draw a following. [NLT] καὶ ἐξ ὑμῶν αὐτῶν ἀναστήσονται ἄνδρες **λαλοῦντες διεστραμμένα**, τοῦ ἀποσπᾶν τοὺς μαθητὰς ὀπίσω αὐτῶν. [GNS] καὶ ἐξ ὑμῶν αὐτῶν ἀναστήσονται ἄνδρες **λαλοῦντες διεστραμμένα** τοῦ ἀποσπᾶν τοὺς μαθητὰς ὀπίσω αὐτῶν. [GNT]	**Practical Application** The term "speaking perverse things" (*lalountes diestrammena*) means turned aside, twisted, distorted. What they teach has some truth and some error. They take the truth and pervert it, coming up with a twisted truth. They teach "perverse things" that are not of God, not of His Word or will. (See POSB note—Matthew 7:17; POSB note—Matthew 7:18 for more discussion.)
#3681 **Speaks– Speaketh– Speaking** **Speaketh–KJV** **Speaking–NASB** **Speaks–NIV** **Speaks–NKJV** **Speaking–NLT** **POSB REFERENCE** (Heb.12:25) Note 1	λαλοῦντα = *lalounta* Pronunciation: [lal-oon-tah] Parsing (part of speech): verb Mood—participle Tense—present Case—accusative Gender—masculine Number—singular Stem or root—from λαλέω Concordance References: ⇒ Strong's #2980 laleō ⇒ NIV #3281 laleō ⇒ NASB #2980 laleō **Hebrews 12:25** See that ye refuse not him that **speaketh**. For if they escaped not who refused him that spake on earth, much more shall not we escape, if we turn away from him that speaketh from heaven: [KJV] See to it that you do not refuse Him who is **speaking**. For if those did not escape when they refused him who warned them on earth, much less shall we escape who turn away from Him who warns from heaven. [NASB] See to it that you do not refuse him who **speaks**. If they did not escape when they refused him who warned them on earth, how much less will we, if we turn away from him who warns us from heaven? [NIV] See that you do not refuse Him who **speaks**. For if they did not escape who refused Him who spoke on earth, much more *shall we not escape* if we turn away from Him	To speak; to proclaim; to talk; to address; to tell. **Practical Application** Note that Jesus Christ *speaks from heaven*. It (*lalounta*) means the very voice of God. Jesus Christ spoke as God Himself. He was the heavenly voice of God Himself. The point is critical for people today: we are held much more accountable and will face much greater judgment. Just think for a moment. Moses, a mere man, spoke and gave the law of God to man. When the people broke the law given by Moses, not a single one escaped the judgment and punishment. Every person bore the guilt and punishment when he broke the Word of God.

ENGLISH WORD	GREEK WORD AND VERSE	THE WORD MEANS...

who *speaks* from heaven, [NKJV]

See to it that you obey God, the one who is **speaking** to you. For if the people of Israel did not escape when they refused to listen to Moses, the earthly messenger, how terrible our danger if we reject the One who speaks to us from heaven! [NLT]

βλέπετε μὴ παραιτήσησθε τὸν **λαλοῦντα**. εἰ γὰρ ἐκεῖνοι οὐκ ἔφυγον, τὸν ἐπὶ τῆς γῆς παραιτησάμενοι χρηματίζοντα, πολλῷ μᾶλλον ἡμεῖς οἱ τὸν ἀπ' οὐρανῶν ἀποστρεφόμενοι· [GNS]

Βλέπετε μὴ παραιτήσησθε τὸν **λαλοῦντα** · εἰ γὰρ ἐκεῖνοι οὐκ ἐξέφυγον ἐπὶ γῆς παραιτησάμενοι τὸν χρηματίζοντα, πολὺ μᾶλλον ἡμεῖς οἱ τὸν ἀπ' οὐρανῶν ἀποστρεφόμενοι, [GNT]

#3682

Speaks In Defense

Advocate–KJV
Advocate–NASB
Speaks...in...defense–NIV
Advocate–NKJV
Someone to plead for you–NLT

POSB REFERENCE
(1 Jn.2:1-2; esp. v.1)
Note 3, point 1

παράκλητον = *parakléton*
Pronunciation: [par-ak'-lay-ton]
Parsing (part of speech): noun
   Case—accusative
   Gender—masculine
   Number—singular
   Stem or root—from παράκλητος, ου
Concordance References:
  ⇒ Strong's #3875 paraklētos
  ⇒ NIV #4156 paraklētos
  ⇒ NASB #3875 paraklētos

1 John 2:1

My little children, these things write I unto you, that ye sin not. And if any man sin, we have an **advocate** with the Father, Jesus Christ the righteous: [KJV]

My little children, I am writing these things to you that you may not sin. And if anyone sins, we have an **Advocate** with the Father, Jesus Christ the righteous; [NASB]

My dear children, I write this to you so that you will not sin. But if anybody does sin, we have one who **speaks** to the Father **in** our **defense**—Jesus Christ, the Righteous One. [NIV]

My little children, these things I write to you, so that you may not sin. And if anyone sins, we have an **Advocate** with the Father, Jesus Christ the righteous. [NKJV]

My dear children, I am writing this to you so that you will not sin. But if you do sin, there is **someone to plead for you** before the Father. He is Jesus Christ, the one who pleases God completely. [NLT]

Τεκνία μου, ταῦτα γράφω ὑμῖν, ἵνα μὴ ἁμάρτητε. καὶ ἐάν τις ἁμάρτῃ, **παράκλητον** ἔχομεν πρὸς τὸν πατέρα, Ἰησοῦν Χριστὸν δίκαιον· [GNS]

Τεκνία μου, ταῦτα γράφω ὑμῖν ἵνα μὴ ἁμάρτητε. καὶ ἐάν τις ἁμάρτῃ, **παράκλητον** ἔχομεν πρὸς τὸν πατέρα Ἰησοῦν Χριστὸν δίκαιον· [GNT]

One who speaks in defense; an advocate; someone who pleads for you; a Helper; an Intercessor. This word is associated with Christ and the Holy Spirit.

Practical Application

Jesus Christ "speaks in our defense" (*parakléton*). The word means someone who is called in to stand by the side of another. The purpose is to help in any way possible. This is the word [*parakletos*] used of the Holy Spirit. (See *Deeper Study* #1—John 14:16 for discussion.)

⇒ There is the picture of a friend called in to help a person who is troubled or distressed or confused.

⇒ There is the picture of a commander called in to help a discouraged and dispirited army.

⇒ There is the picture of a lawyer, an advocate called in to help a defendant who needs his case pleaded.

There is no one word that can adequately translate *paracletos*. The word that probably comes closest is simply *helper*. Sin causes the believer to be distressed and confused, discouraged and dispirited. Sin separates the believer from God, making him guilty of transgression and worthy of condemnation and punishment. But Jesus Christ is the believer's Helper—his *Advocate, the one who speaks in our defense*. Jesus Christ stands before God to plead the case of the believer.

#3683

Special Bread

Shewbread–KJV
Consecrated bread–NASB
Consecrated bread–NIV
Showbread–NKJV
Special bread–NLT

POSB REFERENCE
(Lk.6:4)
Deeper Study #2

ἄρτους τῆς προθέσεως = *artous tace prothéseōs*
Pronunciation: [ar'-tos tace proth'-es-eh-os]
Parsing *artous* (part of speech): noun
   Case—accusative
   Gender—masculine
   Number—plural
   Stem or root—from ἄρτος, ου
Parsing *prothéseōs* (part of speech): noun
   Case—genitive
   Gender—feminine
   Number—singular
   Stem or root—from πρόθεσις, εως
Concordance References:
  ⇒ Strong's #4286 prothesis +740 artos
  ⇒ NIV #4606 prothesis [consecrated] +788 artos [bread]
  ⇒ NASB #4286 prothesis +740 artos

Consecrated bread, special bread, showbread, the bread of the face or the bread of the Presence.

Practical Application

What the table of special bread taught:
1. The twelve loaves of consecrated bread represented an offering from each tribe of Israel, an offering of thanksgiving to God. Each tribe was represented as thanking God for the bread and food He provided, for meeting their physical needs.
2. The twelve loaves also represented the people's dependence upon God. Note that the loaves sat in God's presence, before His very face. The people were to acknowledge their dependence upon God, acknowledge that

ENGLISH WORD	GREEK WORD AND VERSE	THE WORD MEANS...
	Luke 6:4 How he went into the house of God, and did take and eat the **shewbread**, and gave also to them that were with him; which it is not lawful to eat but for the priests alone? [KJV] How he entered the house of God, and took and ate the **consecrated bread** which is not lawful for any to eat except the priests alone, and gave it to his companions?" [NASB] He entered the house of God, and taking the **consecrated bread**, he ate what is lawful only for priests to eat. And he also gave some to his companions." [NIV] How he went into the house of God, took and ate the **showbread**, and also gave some to those with him, which is not lawful for any but the priests to eat?" [NKJV] He went into the house of God, ate the **special bread** reserved for the priests alone, and then gave some to his friends. That was breaking the law, too." [NLT] ὡς εἰσῆλθεν εἰς τὸν οἶκον τοῦ Θεοῦ, καὶ τοὺς **ἄρτους τῆς προθέσεως** ἔλαβε, καὶ ἔφαγε, καὶ ἔδωκε καὶ τοῖς μετ' αὐτοῦ, οὓς οὐκ ἔξεστι φαγεῖν εἰ μὴ μόνους τοὺς ἱερεῖς; [GNS] [ὡς] εἰσῆλθεν εἰς τὸν οἶκον τοῦ θεοῦ καὶ τοὺς **ἄρτους τῆς προθέσεως** λαβὼν ἔφαγεν καὶ ἔδωκεν τοῖς μετ' αὐτοῦ, οὓς οὐκ ἔξεστιν φαγεῖν εἰ μὴ μόνους τοὺς ἱερεῖς; [GNT]	they needed His provision. They needed His watchful eye upon the bread, upon them as His followers. They needed Him to continue to provide their bread and food, continue to look after and care for them. Their dependence upon God as the Provision of life was symbolized in the consecrated bread as well as their offering of thanksgiving. 3. The twelve loaves also acknowledged their trust of God. By setting the bread before God, they were declaring their belief and trust that He would continue to meet their physical needs. 4. The special bread also pointed to Jesus Christ as the Bread of Life. Scripture declares that He is the Living Bread that came *out of* heaven to satisfy the hunger of a person's soul. 5. The special bread pointed to God Himself as the nourishment that man really needs. Far too often, man tries to live his life apart from God's provision and presence. 6. The special bread pointed to the great need of people for the bread of God's presence and worship. A constant diet of unhealthy things will cause a person to become sick and unhealthy. 7. The special bread pointed to the bread that we all desperately need, the bread... • that satisfies the hunger of our hearts • that supplies our needs • that provides for us • that nourishes fellowship among us (cp. 1 Jn.1:3; Rev.3:20) The special bread pointed to the spiritual needs of man. This is seen in that the showbread sat in the Tabernacle itself, the very place where spiritual needs were met. This truth was dictated by both God and His Son, the Lord Jesus Christ.

#3684
Special Favor
 	
Blessed–KJV
Blessed–NASB
Good–NIV
Blessed–NKJV
Special favor–NLT
 	
POSB REFERENCE
(Lk.12:35-40; esp. v.37)
Note 1, point 3
	μακάριοι = *makarioi*
	Pronunciation: [mak-ar'-ee-o-ee]
	Parsing (part of speech): adjective
	    Case—nominative
	    Gender—masculine
	    Number—plural
	    Stem or root—from μακάριος, α, ον
	Concordance References:
	⇒ Strong's #3107 makarios
	⇒ NIV #3421 makarios
	⇒ NASB #3107 makarios
	
	Luke 12:37
	Blessed are those servants, whom the lord when he cometh shall find watching: verily I say unto you, that he shall gird himself, and make them to sit down to meat, and will come forth and serve them. [KJV]
	
	"**Blessed** are those slaves whom the master shall find on the alert when he comes; truly I say to you, that he will gird himself to serve, and have them recline at the table, and will come up and wait on them. [NASB]
	
	It will be **good** for those servants whose master finds them watching when he comes. I tell you the truth, he will dress himself to serve, will have them recline at the table and will come and wait on them. [NIV]
	
	Blessed are those servants whom the master, when he comes, will find watching. Assuredly, I say to you that he will gird himself and have them sit down to eat, and will come and serve them. [NKJV]
	
	There will be **special favor** for those who are ready
		Good, blessed; to have special favor; to pronounce a person happy, fortunate or blessed.
		
		Practical Application
		It is a judgment that affirms a person's condition as having "special favor." The idea is that Christ is going to bestow special favor upon the believer to make him happy and blessed. Happiness and blessedness will become a state of being, the constant experience of the believer.

ENGLISH WORD	GREEK WORD AND VERSE	THE WORD MEANS...
	and waiting for his return. I tell you, he himself will seat them, put on an apron, and serve them as they sit and eat! [NLT] μακάριοι οἱ δοῦλοι ἐκεῖνοι, οὓς ἐλθὼν ὁ κύριος εὑρήσει γρηγοροῦντας· ἀμὴν λέγω ὑμῖν ὅτι περιζώσεται καὶ ἀνακλινεῖ αὐτοὺς, καὶ παρελθὼν διακονήσει αὐτοῖς. [GNS] μακάριοι οἱ δοῦλοι ἐκεῖνοι, οὓς ἐλθὼν ὁ κύριος εὑρήσει γρηγοροῦντας· ἀμὴν λέγω ὑμῖν ὅτι περιζώσεται καὶ ἀνακλινεῖ αὐτοὺς, καὶ παρελθὼν διακονήσει αὐτοῖς. [GNT]	
#3685 **Special Messenger** Minister–KJV Minister–NASB Minister–NIV Minister–NKJV **Special messenger–NLT** **POSB REFERENCE** (Rom.15:16) Note 3	λειτουργὸν = leitourgon Pronunciation: [li-toorg-own'] Parsing (part of speech): noun 　　Case—accusative 　　Gender—masculine 　　Number—singular 　　Stem or root—from λειτουργός, οῦ Concordance References: 　⇒　Strong's #3011 leitourgos 　⇒　NIV #3313 leitourgos 　⇒　NASB #3011 leitourgos **Romans 15:16** 　　That I should be the **minister** of Jesus Christ to the Gentiles, ministering the gospel of God, that the offering up of the Gentiles might be acceptable, being sanctified by the Holy Ghost. [KJV] 　　To be a **minister** of Christ Jesus to the Gentiles, ministering as a priest the gospel of God, that my offering of the Gentiles might become acceptable, sanctified by the Holy Spirit. [NASB] 　　To be a **minister** of Christ Jesus to the Gentiles with the priestly duty of proclaiming the gospel of God, so that the Gentiles might become an offering acceptable to God, sanctified by the Holy Spirit. [NIV] 　　That I might be a **minister** of Jesus Christ to the Gentiles, ministering the gospel of God, that the offering of the Gentiles might be acceptable, sanctified by the Holy Spirit. [NKJV] 　　A **special messenger** from Christ Jesus to you Gentiles. I bring you the Good News and offer you up as a fragrant sacrifice to God so that you might be pure and pleasing to him by the Holy Spirit. [NLT] εἰς τὸ εἶναί με **λειτουργὸν** Ἰησοῦ Χριστοῦ εἰς τὰ ἔθνη, ἱερουργοῦντα τὸ εὐαγγέλιον τοῦ Θεοῦ, ἵνα γένηται ἡ προσφορὰ τῶν ἐθνῶν εὐπρόσδεκτος, ἡγιασμένη ἐν Πνεύματι Ἁγίῳ. [GNS] εἰς τὸ εἶναί με **λειτουργὸν** Χριστοῦ Ἰησοῦ εἰς τὰ ἔθνη, ἱερουργοῦντα τὸ εὐαγγέλιον τοῦ θεοῦ, ἵνα γένηται ἡ προσφορὰ τῶν ἐθνῶν εὐπρόσδεκτος, ἡγιασμένη ἐν πνεύματι ἁγίῳ. [GNT]	Servant, minister, special messenger. **Practical Application** 　　The minister of God is called to minister the gospel of God. When Paul called himself a minister (*leitourgon*), the Greek word was often used to refer to the priests of the Old Testament. 　　This is a beautiful passage describing the nature of the Christian ministry. The Christian ministry is seen as a priestly ministry. However, we must always remember that the ministry is not an office to make atonement for sin, nor to offer a propitiatory sacrifice to God. It is a ministry of preaching the gospel under the influence of the Holy Spirit. The purpose of the ministry is this: to bring men to the point where they will offer themselves as living sacrifices, holy, acceptable to God (cp. Romans 12:1-2). A minister's only priesthood is the preaching of the gospel, and his only offering is the offering of redeemed and sanctified men to God. He is not a mediator between God and men; he does not offer propitiatory sacrifices. He is only an instrument which God uses to share the gospel of salvation with men. He is a priest only in the sense that he serves the gospel of God to men and brings men to God through the gospel of God. 　　Note what the "offering" was that God wanted Paul to make: the offering of the Gentiles, of human lives. God wanted Paul to bring people to Him. This is the task of ministers: to offer the lives of men, women, boys, and girls to God.
#3686 **Special Ministry** Dispensation–KJV Stewardship–NASB Administration–NIV Dispensation–NKJV **Special ministry–NLT** **POSB REFERENCE** (Eph.3:2) Note 1, point 2	οἰκονομίαν = oikonomian Pronunciation: [oy-kon-om-ee'-ahn] Parsing (part of speech): noun 　　Case—accusative 　　Gender—feminine 　　Number—singular 　　Stem or root—from οἰκονομία, ας Concordance References: 　⇒　Strong's #3622 oikonomia 　⇒　NIV #3873 oikonomia 　⇒　NASB #3622 oikonomia **Ephes. 3:2** 　　If ye have heard of the **dispensation** of the grace of God which is given me to youward: [KJV] 　　If indeed you have heard of the **stewardship** of God's grace which was given to me for you; [NASB] 　　Surely you have heard about the **administration** of God's grace that was given to me for you, [NIV]	Administration, stewardship, management, ownership; to have a special ministry. **Practical Application** 　　Paul existed to be a steward of God. Paul was given the duty to oversee and administer the grace of God to the world.

ENGLISH WORD	GREEK WORD AND VERSE	THE WORD MEANS...
	If indeed you have heard of the **dispensation** of the grace of God which was given to me for you, [NKJV] As you already know, God has given me this **special ministry** of announcing his favor to you Gentiles. [NLT] εἴγε ἠκούσατε τὴν **οἰκονομίαν** τῆς χάριτος τοῦ Θεοῦ τῆς δοθείσης μοι εἰς ὑμᾶς, [GNS] εἴ γε ἠκούσατε τὴν **οἰκονομίαν** τῆς χάριτος τοῦ θεοῦ τῆς δοθείσης μοι εἰς ὑμᾶς, [GNT]	
#3687 **Special Miracles** **Special miracles–KJV** Extraordinary miracles–NASB Extraordinary miracles–NIV Unusual miracles–NKJV Unusual miracles–NLT **POSB REFERENCE** (Acts 19:10-20; esp. v.11) Note 3, point 2	*Δυνάμεις τε οὐ τὰς τυχούσας = Dunameis te ou tas tuchousas* Pronunciation: [doo'-nam-eh-is the oo tahs too-choo'-sahs] Parsing *Dunameis* (part of speech): noun 　　Case—accusative 　　Gender—feminine 　　Number—plural 　　Stem or root—from δύναμις, εως Parsing *tuchousas* (part of speech): verb 　　Mood—participle 　　Tense—aorist 　　Voice—active 　　Case—accusative 　　Gender—feminine 　　Number—plural 　　Stem or root—from τυγχάνω Concordance References: ⇒　Strong's #1411 dunamis + 5037 te + 3588 + 3756 + 5177 ho ou tugchanö ⇒　NIV #1539 dunamis [miracles] + 5445 te + 3836 + 4024 + 5593 ho ou tugchanö [extraordinary] ⇒　NASB #1411 dunamis + 5037 te + 3588 + 3756 + 5177 ho ou tugchanö **Acts 19:11** And God wrought **special miracles** by the hands of Paul: [KJV] And God was performing **extraordinary miracles** by the hands of Paul, [NASB] God did **extraordinary miracles** through Paul, [NIV] Now God worked **unusual miracles** by the hands of Paul, [NKJV] God gave Paul the power to do **unusual miracles**, [NLT] **δυνάμεις τε οὐ τὰς τυχούσας** ἐποίει ὁ Θεὸς διὰ τῶν χειρῶν Παύλου, [GNS] **Δυνάμεις τε οὐ τὰς τυχούσας** ὁ θεὸς ἐποίει διὰ τῶν χειρῶν Παύλου, [GNT]	Extraordinary miracles; special miracles; unusual miracles; supernatural miracles. **Practical Application** The phrase actually means two things: ⇒　They were miracles, powers that were not regular happenings; powers that were not the day-to-day experiences of men. ⇒　They were miracles that were extraordinary; that were usually not seen; that were uncommon; that were usually not performed. Even the disciples had not witnessed such miracles, not on a regular basis.
#3688 **Speculations** Imaginations–KJV **Speculations–NASB** Arguments–NIV Arguments–NKJV Every proud argument–NLT **POSB REFERENCE** (2 Cor.10:3-5; esp. v.5) Note 2	*λογισμοὺς = logismous* Pronunciation: [log-is-moos'] Parsing (part of speech): noun 　　Case—accusative 　　Gender—masculine 　　Number—plural 　　Stem or root—from λογισμός, οῦ **Note: this comes from verse 4 in the Greek, but is translated in the English Bible in verse 5** Concordance References: ⇒　Strong's #3053 logismos ⇒　NIV #3361 logismos ⇒　NASB #3053 logismos **2 Cor. 10:5** Casting down **imaginations**, and every high thing that exalteth itself against the knowledge of God, and bringing into captivity every thought to the obedience of Christ; [KJV] *We are* destroying **speculations** and every lofty thing raised up against the knowledge of God, and *we are* taking every thought captive to the obedience of Christ, [NASB]	Arguments, speculations, false reasoning. **Practical Application** The believer is to *destroy speculations*: thoughts and imaginations that are uncontrolled, wild, evil, lustful, immoral, unjust, wrong, untrue, devilish, and set against God.

ENGLISH WORD	GREEK WORD AND VERSE	THE WORD MEANS...
	We demolish **arguments** and every pretension that sets itself up against the knowledge of God, and we take captive every thought to make it obedient to Christ. [NIV] Casting down **arguments** and every high thing that exalts itself against the knowledge of God, bringing every thought into captivity to the obedience of Christ, [NKJV] With these weapons we break down **every proud argument** that keeps people from knowing God. With these weapons we conquer their rebellious ideas, and we teach them to obey Christ. [NLT] -- τὰ γὰρ ὅπλα τῆς στρατείας ἡμῶν οὐ σαρκικά, ἀλλὰ δυνατὰ τῷ Θεῷ πρὸς καθαίρεσιν ὀχυρωμάτων, **λογισμοὺς** καθαιροῦντες [GNS] **2 Cor. 10:4** καὶ πᾶν ὕψωμα ἐπαιρόμενον κατὰ τῆς γνώσεως τοῦ Θεοῦ, καὶ αἰχμαλωτίζοντες πᾶν νόημα εἰς τὴν ὑπακοὴν τοῦ Χριστοῦ, [GNS] **2 Cor. 10:5** τὰ γὰρ ὅπλα τῆς στρατείας ἡμῶν οὐ σαρκικὰ ἀλλὰ δυνατὰ τῷ θεῷ πρὸς καθαίρεσιν ὀχυρωμάτων, **λογισμοὺς** καθαροῦντες [GNT] **2 Cor. 10:4** καὶ πᾶν ὕψωμα ἐπαιρόμενον κατὰ τῆς γνώσεως τοῦ θεοῦ, καὶ αἰχμαλωτίζοντες πᾶν νόημα eivj τὴν ὑπακοὴν τοῦ Χριστοῦ, [GNT] **2 Cor. 10:5**	

#3689
Speculations
 	
Imaginations–KJV
Speculations–NASB
Thinking–NIV
Thoughts–NKJV
Ideas–NLT
 	
**POSB
REFERENCE**
(Rom.1:21)
Note 4, point 1
	διαλογισμοῖς = *dialogismois*
	Pronunciation: [dee-al-og-is-mo-ees']
	Parsing (part of speech): noun
	    Case—dative
	    Gender—masculine
	    Number—plural
	    Stem or root—from *διαλογισμός, οῦ*
	Concordance References:
	  ⇒ Strong's #1261 dialogismos
	  ⇒ NIV #1369 dialogismos
	  ⇒ NASB #1261 dialogismos
	
	Romans 1:21
	Because that, when they knew God, they glorified him not as God, neither were thankful; but became vain in their **imaginations**, and their foolish heart was darkened. [KJV]
	
	For even though they knew God, they did not honor Him as God, or give thanks; but they became futile in their **speculations**, and their foolish heart was darkened. [NASB]
	
	For although they knew God, they neither glorified him as God nor gave thanks to him, but their **thinking** became futile and their foolish hearts were darkened. [NIV]
	
	Because, although they knew God, they did not glorify *Him* as God, nor were thankful, but became futile in their **thoughts**, and their foolish hearts were darkened. [NKJV]
	
	Yes, they knew God, but they wouldn't worship him as God or even give him thanks. And they began to think up foolish **ideas** of what God was like. The result was that their minds became dark and confused. [NLT]
	διότι γνόντες τὸν Θεὸν οὐχ ὡς Θεὸν ἐδόξασαν η ηὐχαρίστησαν, ἀλλ' ἐματαιώθησαν ἐν τοῖς **διαλογισμοῖς** αὐτῶν, καὶ ἐσκοτίσθη ἡ ἀσύνετος αὐτῶν καρδία. [GNS]
	
	διότι γνόντες τὸν θεὸν οὐχ ὡς θεὸν ἐδόξασαν η ηὐχαρίστησαν, ἀλλ' ἐματαιώθησαν ἐν τοῖς **διαλογισμοῖς** αὐτῶν καὶ ἐσκοτίσθη ἡ ἀσύνετος αὐτῶν καρδία. [GNT]
		Thoughts, opinions, motives, reasonings; doubts, questions; arguments, disputes, deliberations, conclusions, speculations.
		
		Practical Application
		When men push God out of their minds, their minds are void and empty of God. God is not in their thoughts. (Cp. Psalm 10:4.) Their minds are ready to be *filled* with some other *god* or *supremacy*.

#3690
Speechless
 	
Speechless–KJV
Speechless–NASB
Speechless–NIV
Speechless–NKJV
No reply–NLT
	ἐφιμώθη = *ephimōthē*
	Pronunciation: [eh-fee-mo'-thay]
	Parsing (part of speech): verb
	    Mood—indicative
	    Tense—aorist
	    Voice—passive
	    Person—3rd person
	    Number—singular
	    Stem or root—from *φιμόω*
		Muzzled, muted, speechless, silenced, tongue-tied, closed-mouthed; not able to reply.
		
		Practical Application
		The man was speechless (*ephimōthē*). He had no excuse. He stood guilty of disrespect and dishonor for wearing the wrong wedding clothes, a garment that was not right for a kingly occasion. The wedding clothes were unclean.

ENGLISH WORD	GREEK WORD AND VERSE	THE WORD MEANS...
POSB REFERENCE (Mt.22:11-14; esp. v.12) Note 4, point 1c	Concordance References: ⇒ Strong's #5392 phimoö ⇒ NIV #5821 phimoö ⇒ NASB #5392 phimoö **Matthew 22:12** And he saith unto him, Friend, how camest thou in hither not having a wedding garment? And he was **speechless**. [KJV] And he said to him, 'Friend, how did you come in here without wedding clothes?' And he was **speechless**. [NASB] 'Friend,' he asked, 'how did you get in here without wedding clothes?' The man was **speechless**. [NIV] So he said to him, 'Friend, how did you come in here without a wedding garment?' And he was **speechless**. [NKJV] 'Friend,' he asked, 'how is it that you are here without wedding clothes?' And the man had **no reply**. [NLT] καὶ λέγει αὐτῷ, Ἑταῖρε, πῶς εἰσῆλθες ὧδε μὴ ἔχων ἔνδυμα γάμου; ὁ δὲ **ἐφιμώθη**. [GNS] καὶ λέγει αὐτῷ, Ἑταῖρε, πῶς εἰσῆλθες ὧδε μὴ ἔχων ἔνδυμα γάμου; ὁ δὲ **ἐφιμώθη**. [GNT]	

#3691
Speed
 	
Hasting–KJV
Hastening–NASB
Speed–NIV
Hastening–NKJV
Hurry–NLT
 	
POSB REFERENCE (2 Pt.3:12) Note 2, point 2
	σπεύδοντας = *speudontas*
	Pronunciation: [spyoo'-don-tahs]
	Parsing (part of speech): verb
	  Mood—participle
	  Tense—present
	  Voice—active
	  Case—accusative
	  Gender—masculine
	  Person—2nd person
	  Number—plural
	  Stem or root—from σπεύδω
	Concordance References:
	⇒ Strong's #4692 speudö
	⇒ NIV #5067 speudö
	⇒ NASB #4692 speudö
	
	2 Peter 3:12
	Looking for and **hasting** unto the coming of the day of God, wherein the heavens being on fire shall be dissolved, and the elements shall melt with fervent heat? [KJV]
	Looking for and **hastening** the coming of the day of God, on account of which the heavens will be destroyed by burning, and the elements will melt with intense heat! [NASB]
	As you look forward to the day of God and **speed** its coming. That day will bring about the destruction of the heavens by fire, and the elements will melt in the heat. [NIV]
	Looking for and **hastening** the coming of the day of God, because of which the heavens will be dissolved, being on fire, and the elements will melt with fervent heat? [NKJV]
	You should look forward to that day and **hurry** it along—the day when God will set the heavens on fire and the elements will melt away in the flames. [NLT]
	προσδοκῶντας καὶ **σπεύδοντας** τὴν παρουσίαν τῆς τοῦ Θεοῦ ἡμέρας, δι' ἣν οὐρανοὶ πυρούμενοι λυθήσονται, καὶ στοιχεῖα καυσούμενα τήκεται; [GNS]
	προσδοκῶντας καὶ **σπεύδοντας** τὴν παρουσίαν τῆς τοῦ Θεοῦ ἡμέρας δι' ἣν οὐρανοὶ πυρούμενοι λυθήσονται καὶ στοιχεῖα καυσούμενα τήκεται. [GNT]
		Speed; to hasten; to hurry; to strive for.
		
		Practical Application
		The believer is to *speed* the day of God. The word "speed" (*speudontas*) can mean two things.
		1. *To speed* can mean *to hurry after*; to earnestly desire; to rush toward. The believer is to live a holy and godly life looking for and hastening toward the day of God. Keeping his eyes upon that terrible day of judgment is to *arouse him* to live a holy and godly life. Every day that he lives upon earth is to be a day in which he hastens toward the judgment of God; he should never take his eyes off the terrible day of God that is coming. If he takes his eyes off that day, if he fails to direct his life toward the day of God, then he will most likely slip into unholiness and ungodliness. He must, therefore, stay focused upon the day of God, the day of the terrible judgment to come upon the heavens and earth.
		2. *To speed* can also mean *to speed on* the day of God; to rush the coming of Christ; to cause the day of God to come sooner. The believer has a part in bringing about the eternal kingdom of God; he has a part in bringing about the return of Christ and the great day of God. How? God is "longsuffering...not willing that any should perish" (2 Peter 3:9). This is the reason He is delaying the return of Christ. Apparently, God has a certain number of believers that He has ordained to be brothers and sisters of His dear Son; apparently, there are to be a certain number of believers to rule and manage the new heavens and earth for Christ. In His eternal knowledge, God certainly knows the number who will be saved and serving His dear Son. Whatever the number and whatever the case, that number has to be reached before Christ can come and before the great day of God can destroy the universe and make a new heavens and earth. This much is known for sure:
		⇒ God does have a certain number of believers in mind. Being God, He has purposed that His Son have many brothers who will

ENGLISH WORD	GREEK WORD AND VERSE	THE WORD MEANS...
		reign with Him and who will worship and serve God through all eternity (cp. Romans 8:28-29 where God will allow nothing to stop Him from giving Christ "many brothers.") ⇒ This Scripture tells us that we are *to speed* on, to help bring about the day of God.
#3692 **Spend Our Time** Give ourselves–KJV Devote ourselves–NASB Give...attention–NIV Give ourselves–NKJV **Spend our time–NLT** **POSB REFERENCE** (Acts 6:4) Note 4, point 2	προσκαρτερήσομεν = *proskarterësomen* Pronunciation: [pros-kar-ter-eh'-so-men] Parsing (part of speech): verb 　Mood—indicative 　Tense—future 　Voice—active 　Person—1st person 　Number—plural 　Stem or root—from προσκαρτερέ Concordance References: ⇒　Strong's #4342 proskartereo ⇒　NIV #4674 proskartereö ⇒　NASB #4342 proskartereo **Acts 6:4** But we will **give ourselves** continually to prayer, and to the ministry of the word. [KJV] "But we will **devote ourselves** to prayer, and to the ministry of the word." [NASB] And will **give** our **attention** to prayer and the ministry of the word." [NIV] But we will **give ourselves** continually to prayer and to the ministry of the word." [NKJV] Then we can **spend our time** in prayer and preaching and teaching the word." [NLT] ἡμεῖς δὲ τῇ προσευχῇ καὶ τῇ διακονίᾳ τοῦ λόγου **προσκαρτερήσομεν**. [GNS] ἡμεῖς δὲ τῇ προσευχῇ καὶ τῇ διακονίᾳ τοῦ λόγου **προσκαρτερήσομεν**. [GNT]	To give attention; to give ourselves; to devote ourselves; to spend our time. It means to continue steadfastly; to persevere; to continue on and on, sticking to it. **Practical Application** The minister is to pray and pray and study and study and share and share, preaching and teaching the Word—without letting up. He is to be steadfast, persevering, continuing on and on in both prayer and in the Word.
#3693 **Spending Their Lives** Addicted–KJV Devoted–NASB Devoted–NIV Devoted–NKJV **Spending their lives–NLT** **POSB REFERENCE** (1 Cor.16:15-18; esp. v.15) Note 5	ἔταξαν = *etaxan* Pronunciation: [eh-taxs'-ahn] Parsing (part of speech): verb 　Mood—indicative 　Tense—aorist 　Voice—active 　Person—3rd person 　Number—plural 　Stem or root—from τάσσω Concordance References: ⇒　Strong's #5021 tassö ⇒　NIV #5435 tassö ⇒　NASB #5021 tassö **1 Cor. 16:15** I beseech you, brethren, (ye know the house of Stephanas, that it is the firstfruits of Achaia, and that they have **addicted** themselves to the ministry of the saints,) [KJV] Now I urge you, brethren (you know the household of Stephanas, that they were the first fruits of Achaia, and that they have **devoted** themselves for ministry to the saints), [NASB] You know that the household of Stephanas were the first converts in Achaia, and they have **devoted** themselves to the service of the saints. I urge you, brothers, [NIV] I urge you, brethren—you know the household of Stephanas, that it is the firstfruits of Achaia, and that they have **devoted** themselves to the ministry of the saints— [NKJV] You know that Stephanas and his household were the first to become Christians in Greece, and they are **spending their lives** in service to other Christians. I urge you,	Devoted, addicted, loyal, faithful, devout, dutiful, established; spending their lives. **Practical Application** It means they [Stephanas and his household] devoted themselves, appointed themselves, diligently gave themselves to meeting the day-to-day needs of the believers. They not only ministered to others; they were spending their lives to meeting the needs of believers.

ENGLISH WORD	GREEK WORD AND VERSE	THE WORD MEANS...
	dear brothers and sisters, [NLT] Παρακαλῶ δὲ ὑμᾶς, ἀδελφοί· -- οἴδατε τὴν οἰκίαν Στεφανᾶ, ὅτι ἐστὶν ἀπαρχὴ τῆς Ἀχαΐας, καὶ εἰς διακονίαν τοῖς ἁγίοις **ἔταξαν** ἑαυτούς -- , [GNS] Παρακαλῶ δὲ ὑμᾶς, ἀδελφοί· οἴδατε τὴν οἰκίαν Στεφανᾶ, ὅτι ἐστὶν ἀπαρχὴ τῆς Ἀχαΐας καὶ εἰς διακονίαν τοῖς ἁγίοις **ἔταξαν** ἑαυτούς·[GNT]	

#3694
Spending Time
 	
Tarried–KJV
Spending time–NASB
Spent some time–NIV
Remained–NKJV
Stayed–NLT
 	
POSB REFERENCE
(Jn.3:22-26; esp. v.22)
Note 1, point 1
	διέτριβεν = dietriben
	Pronunciation: [dee-eht-ree'-behn]
	Parsing (part of speech): verb
	    Mood—indicative
	    Tense—imperfect
	    Voice—active
	    Person—3rd person
	    Number—singular
	    Stem or root—from **διατρίβω**
	Concordance References:
	  ⇒ Strong's #1304 diatribō
	  ⇒ NIV #1417 diatribō
	  ⇒ NASB #1304 diatribō
	
	John 3:22
	After these things came Jesus and his disciples into the land of Judaea; and there he **tarried** with them, and baptized. [KJV]
	After these things Jesus and His disciples came into the land of Judea, and there He was **spending time** with them and baptizing. [NASB]
	After this, Jesus and his disciples went out into the Judean countryside, where he **spent some time** with them, and baptized. [NIV]
	After these things Jesus and His disciples came into the land of Judea, and there He **remained** with them and baptized. [NKJV]
	Afterward Jesus and his disciples left Jerusalem, but they **stayed** in Judea for a while and baptized there. [NLT]
	Μετὰ ταῦτα ἦλθεν ὁ Ἰησοῦς καὶ οἱ μαθηταὶ αὐτοῦ εἰς τὴν Ἰουδαίαν γῆν· καὶ ἐκεῖ **διέτριβε** μετ' αὐτῶν καὶ ἐβάπτιζεν. [GNS]
	Μετὰ ταῦτα ἦλθεν ὁ Ἰησοῦς καὶ οἱ μαθηταὶ αὐτοῦ εἰς τὴν Ἰουδαίαν γῆν καὶ ἐκεῖ **διέτριβεν** μετ' αὐτῶν καὶ ἐβάπτιζεν. [GNT]
		To spend time with; to tarry; to remain; to stay. It has the idea of spending much time in sharing and ministering.
		
		Practical Application
		We can learn from Christ's example by spending time—quality time—with other believers. The fellowship wrought by the Spirit of God means more than the association existing in secular groups such as civic clubs and community bodies. There is a vast difference between *community participation* and *spiritual participation. Community participation* is based upon neighborly association. *Spiritual participation* is based upon a spiritual union wrought by the Spirit of God.
		The distinctiveness is this: the Holy Spirit is within the Christian believer. The Holy Spirit creates a spiritual union by melting and molding the heart of the Christian believer to the hearts of other believers. He attaches the life of one believer to the lives of other believers. Through the Spirit of God, believers become one in life and purpose. They have a joint life sharing their blessings and needs and gifts together.

#3695
Spent Some Time
 	
Tarried–KJV
Spending time–NASB
Spent some time–NIV
Remained–NKJV
Stayed–NLT
 	
POSB REFERENCE
(Jn.3:22-26; esp. v.22)
Note 1, point 1
	διέτριβεν = dietriben
	Pronunciation: [dee-eht-ree'-behn]
	Parsing (part of speech): verb
	    Mood—indicative
	    Tense—imperfect
	    Voice—active
	    Person—3rd person
	    Number—singular
	    Stem or root—from **διατρίβω**
	Concordance References:
	  ⇒ Strong's #1304 diatribō
	  ⇒ NIV #1417 diatribō
	  ⇒ NASB #1304 diatribō
	
	John 3:22
	After these things came Jesus and his disciples into the land of Judaea; and there he **tarried** with them, and baptized. [KJV]
	After these things Jesus and His disciples came into the land of Judea, and there He was **spending time** with them and baptizing. [NASB]
	After this, Jesus and his disciples went out into the Judean countryside, where he **spent some time** with them, and baptized. [NIV]
	After these things Jesus and His disciples came into the land of Judea, and there He **remained** with them and baptized. [NKJV]
	Afterward Jesus and his disciples left Jerusalem, but they **stayed** in Judea for a while and baptized there. [NLT]
		To spend time with; to tarry; to remain; to stay. It has the idea of spending much time in sharing and ministering.
		
		Practical Application
		We can learn from Christ's example by spending time—quality time—with other believers. The fellowship wrought by the Spirit of God means more than the association existing in secular groups such as civic clubs and community bodies. There is a vast difference between *community participation* and *spiritual participation. Community participation* is based upon neighborly association. *Spiritual participation* is based upon a spiritual union wrought by the Spirit of God.
		The distinctiveness is this: the Holy Spirit is within the Christian believer. The Holy Spirit creates a spiritual union by melting and molding the heart of the Christian believer to the hearts of other believers. He attaches the life of one believer to the lives of other believers. Through the Spirit of God, believers become one in life and purpose. They have a joint life sharing their blessings and needs and gifts together.

ENGLISH WORD	GREEK WORD AND VERSE	THE WORD MEANS...
	Μετὰ ταῦτα ἦλθεν ὁ Ἰησοῦς καὶ οἱ μαθηταὶ αὐτοῦ εἰς τὴν Ἰουδαίαν γῆν· καὶ ἐκεῖ **διέτριβε** μετ' αὐτῶν καὶ ἐβάπτιζεν. [GNS] Μετὰ ταῦτα ἦλθεν ὁ Ἰησοῦς καὶ οἱ μαθηταὶ αὐτοῦ εἰς τὴν Ἰουδαίαν γῆν· καὶ ἐκεῖ **διέτριβεν** μετ' αὐτῶν καὶ ἐβάπτιζεν. [GNT]	
#3696 **Spirit** Spirit–KJV Breath–NASB Breath–NIV Breath–NKJV Breath–NLT **POSB** **REFERENCE** (2 Thes.2:8) Note 4, point 1	πνεύματι = pneumati Pronunciation: [pnyoo'-mah-tee] Parsing (part of speech): noun 　　Case—dative 　　Gender—neuter 　　Number—singular 　　Stem or root—from πνεῦμα τος Concordance References: ⇒　Strong's #4151 pneuma ⇒　NIV #4460 pneuma ⇒　NASB #4151 pneuma **2 Thes. 2:8** And then shall that Wicked be revealed, whom the Lord shall consume with the **spirit** of his mouth, and shall destroy with the brightness of his coming: [KJV] And then that lawless one will be revealed whom the Lord will slay with the **breath** of His mouth and bring to an end by the appearance of His coming; [NASB] And then the lawless one will be revealed, whom the Lord Jesus will overthrow with the **breath** of his mouth and destroy by the splendor of his coming. [NIV] And then the lawless one will be revealed, whom the Lord will consume with the **breath** of His mouth and destroy with the brightness of His coming. [NKJV] Then the man of lawlessness will be revealed, whom the Lord Jesus will consume with the **breath** of his mouth and destroy by the splendor of his coming. [NLT] καὶ τότε ἀποκαλυφθήσεται ὁ ἄνομος, ὃν ὁ Κύριος ἀναλώσει τῷ **πνεύματι** τοῦ στόματος αὐτοῦ, καὶ καταργήσει τῇ ἐπιφανείᾳ τῆς παρουσίας αὐτοῦ· [GNS] καὶ τότε ἀποκαλυφθήσεται ὁ ἄνομος, ὃν ὁ κύριος [Ἰησοῦς] ἀνελεῖ τῷ **πνεύματι** τοῦ στόματος αὐτοῦ καὶ καταργήσει τῇ ἐπιφανείᾳ τῆς παρουσίας αὐτοῦ, [GNT]	Breath, the Spirit of God, wind. **Practical Application** The Lord Jesus will slay the antichrist with the spirit of His mouth. What is *the spirit of Jesus' mouth*? It is the spirit of truth, holiness, and unlimited power. When Jesus speaks, what He says is of God and unstoppable. When He rents the sky to slay the antichrist, there will be no battle, for all the forces of heaven and earth combined would be as nonexistent against the Lord God of the universe. Christ will speak the Word, and the antichrist will be slain. It will be like the blowing of a little breath and the dust particle is removed never to return.
#3697 **Spirit Of Divination** Spirit of divination–KJV Spirit of divination–NASB Spirit...which..predicited the future–NIV Spirit of divination–NKJV Demon-possessed–NLT **POSB** **REFERENCE** (Acts 16:16-17; esp. v.16) Note 1, point 1	πνεῦμα πύθωνα = pneuma puthöna Pronunciation: [pnyoo'-mah poo'-thone-ah] Parsing *pneuma* (part of speech): noun 　　Case—accusative 　　Gender—neuter 　　Number—singular 　　Stem or root—from πνεῦμα, τος Parsing *puthöna* (part of speech): noun 　　Case—accusative 　　Gender—masculine 　　Number—plural 　　Stem or root—from πύθων, ωνος Concordance References: ⇒　Strong's #4151 + 4436 pneuma puthön ⇒　NIV #4460 + 4780 pneuma puthön [spirit which predicted the future] ⇒　NASB #4151 + 4436 pneuma puthön **Acts 16:16** And it came to pass, as we went to prayer, a certain damsel possessed with a **spirit of divination** met us, which brought her masters much gain by soothsaying: [KJV] And it happened that as we were going to the place of prayer, a certain slave-girl having a **spirit of divination** met us, who was bringing her masters much profit by fortunetelling. [NASB] Once when we were going to the place of prayer, we were met by a slave girl who had a **spirit** by **which** she	Spirit which predicted the future; spirit of divination; spirit that is demon possessed; spirit of foretelling the future and fate of people; to be a fortuneteller. **Practical Application** The Greek word *puthön* which is our English word python, refers to the large python serpent. In ancient myth the Greek god Apollo was said to have slain the great serpent or dragon python. As a result Apollo took both his great gift of predictions and his name. Apollo became known as "puthios Apollo" or "Python Apollo." The young slave girl is said to have the spirit of "python" (*puthöna*); that is, the people thought she was the voice, the oracle of the great Greek god Apollo. There were also ventriloquists who were thought to be empowered with the spirit of Apollo.

ENGLISH WORD	GREEK WORD AND VERSE	THE WORD MEANS...
	Ἰησοῦς δὲ Πνεύματος Ἁγίου πλήρης ὑπέστρεψεν ἀπὸ τοῦ Ἰορδάνου, καὶ **ἤγετο ἐν τῷ πνεύματι** εἰς τῇ ἐρήμου [GNS] Ἰησοῦς δὲ πλήρης πνεύματος ἁγίου ὑπέστρεψεν ἀπὸ τοῦ Ἰορδάνου καὶ **ἤγετο ἐν τῷ πνεύματι** ἐν τῇ ἐρήμῳ [GNT]	

#3701
Spirit, The
 	
The Spirit–KJV
The Spirit of Jesus–NASB
The Spirit of Jesus–NIV
The Spirit–NKJV
The Spirit of Jesus–NLT
 	
POSB REFERENCE
(Acts 16:7)
Deeper Study #1
	τὸ πνεῦμα Ἰησου = *to pneuma Iēsou*
	Pronunciation: [to pnyoo'-mah hey-soo]
	Parsing *pneuma* (part of speech): noun
	  Case—nominative
	  Gender—neuter
	  Number—singular
	  Stem or root—from πνεῦμα, τος
	Parsing *Iēsou* (part of speech): noun
	  Case—genitive
	  Gender—masculine
	  Number—singular
	  Stem or root—from Ἰησοῦς
	Concordance References:
	⇒ Strong's #3588 ho +4151 pneuma + 2424 Iēsous
	⇒ NIV #3836 ho [the] + 4460 pneuma [Spirit] + 2652 Iēsous [Jesus]
	⇒ NASB #3588 ho + 4151 pneuma + 2424 Iēsous
	
	Acts 16:7
	After they were come to Mysia, they assayed to go into Bithynia: but **the Spirit** suffered them not. [KJV]
	And when they had come to Mysia, they were trying to go into Bithynia, and **the Spirit of Jesus** did not permit them; [NASB]
	When they came to the border of Mysia, they tried to enter Bithynia, but **the Spirit of Jesus** would not allow them to. [NIV]
	After they had come to Mysia, they tried to go into Bithynia, but **the Spirit** did not permit them. [NKJV]
	Then coming to the borders of Mysia, they headed for the province of Bithynia, but again **the Spirit of Jesus** did not let them go. [NLT]
	ἐλθόντες δὲ κατὰ τὴν Μυσίαν ἐπείραζον κατὰ τὴν Βιθυνίαν πορεύεσθαι· καὶ οὐκ εἴασεν αὐτοὺς **τὸ Πνεῦμα**. [GNS]
	ἐλθόντες δὲ κατὰ τὴν Μυσίαν ἐπείραζον εἰς τὴν Βιθυνίαν πορευθῆναι, καὶ οὐκ εἴασεν αὐτοὺς **τὸ πνεῦμα** Ἰησοῦ· [GNT]
		The Spirit of Jesus.
		
		Practical Application
		There is a close identity between the Holy Spirit and Jesus in these two verses (Acts 16:6-7). Both are distinct persons, yet they are God; that is, they possess the very nature and power of God in dealing with Paul in these verses.

#3702
Spiritual
 	
Spiritual–KJV
Spiritual–NASB
Spiritual–NIV
Spiritual–NKJV
Who have the Spirit–NLT
 	
POSB REFERENCE
(1 Cor.2:15-16; esp. v.15)
Note 2
	πνευματικός = *pneumatikos*
	Pronunciation: [pnyoo-mat-ik-os']
	Parsing (part of speech): pronominal adjective
	  Case—nominative
	  Gender—masculine
	  Number—singular
	  Stem or root—from πνευματικός, ή, όν
	Concordance References:
	⇒ Strong's #4152 pneumatikos
	⇒ NIV #4461 pneumatikos
	⇒ NASB #4152 pneumatikos
	
	1 Cor. 2:15
	But he that is **spiritual** judgeth all things, yet he himself is judged of no man. [KJV]
	But he who is **spiritual** appraises all things, yet he himself is appraised by no man. [NASB]
	The **spiritual** man makes judgments about all things, but he himself is not subject to any man's judgment: [NIV]
	But he who is **spiritual** judges all things, yet he himself is rightly judged by no one. [NKJV]
	We **who have the Spirit** understand these things, but others can't understand us at all. [NLT]
	ὁ δὲ **πνευματικὸς** ἀνακρίνει μὲν πάντα, αὐτὸς δὲ ὑπ' οὐδενὸς ἀνακρίνεται. [GNS]
	ὁ δὲ **πνευματικὸς** ἀνακρίνει [τὰ] πάντα, αὐτὸς δὲ ὑπ' οὐδενὸς ἀνακρίνεται. [GNT]
		Spiritual; the person who has the Spirit.
		
		Practical Application
		A man is spiritual because the Holy Spirit dwells in him. He is not spiritual because he...
		• has received some superior, human gift
		• has received some unusual ability
		• has become more intelligent than before
		• has become greater than he was before
		• has become better than he was before
		
		A man becomes spiritual because he has received the Spirit of God and is living under the influence of the Spirit of God.

ENGLISH WORD	GREEK WORD AND VERSE	THE WORD MEANS...

#3703
Spiritual
 	
Spiritual–KJV
Spiritual–NASB
Spiritual–NIV
Spiritual–NKJV
Good–NLT
 	
**POSB
REFERENCE**
(Rom.7:14)
Note 1, point 1
	πνευματικός = *pneumatikos*
	Pronunciation: [pnyoo-mat-ik-os']
	Parsing (part of speech): adjective
	    Case—nominative
	    Gender—masculine
	    Number—singular
	    Stem or root—from πνευματικός, ή, όν
	Concordance References:
	  ⇒ Strong's #4152 pneumatikos
	  ⇒ NIV #4461 pneumatikos
	  ⇒ NASB #4152 pneumatikos
	
	Romans 7:14
	    For we know that the law is **spiritual**: but I am carnal, sold under sin. [KJV]
	    For we know that the Law is **spiritual**; but I am of flesh, sold into bondage to sin. [NASB]
	    We know that the law is **spiritual**; but I am unspiritual, sold as a slave to sin. [NIV]
	    For we know that the law is **spiritual**, but I am carnal, sold under sin. [NKJV]
	    The law is **good**, then. The trouble is not with the law but with me, because I am sold into slavery, with sin as my master. [NLT]
	    οἴδαμεν γὰρ ὅτι ὁ νόμος **πνευματικός** ἐστιν· ἐγὼ δὲ σάρκικός εἰμι, πεπραμένος ὑπὸ τὴν ἁμαρτίαν. [GNS]
	    οἴδαμεν γὰρ ὅτι ὁ νόμος **πνευματικός** ἐστιν, ἐγὼ δὲ σάρκινός εἰμι πεπραμένος ὑπὸ τὴν ἁμαρτίαν. [GNT]
		Spiritual; good; pertaining to the spirit.
		
		Practical Application
		    The law is spiritual. It is spiritual in at least three senses.
		1. The law was given to man by the Spirit of God (*pneumatikos*). The Greek word used is the very name of the Holy Spirit. The Holy Spirit is the source of the law.
		2. The law is the expression of the will and nature of God. The law is spiritual because it describes the will of God and tells man just what God is like. The rules of the law reveal both the mind and nature of God.
		3. The law is spiritual because of its purposes (see POSB note, Law, Purpose—Romans 7:12 for discussion. Also cp. POSB outline—Romans 7:7-13 and POSB notes—Romans 7:7-13 for more discussion.)

#3704
Spiritual
 	
Reasonable–KJV
Spiritual–NASB
Spiritual–NIV
Reasonable–NKJV
Not translated–NLT
 	
**POSB
REFERENCE**
(Rom.12:1)
Note 2, point 2b
	λογικήν = *logikën*
	Pronunciation: [log-ik-ayn']
	Parsing (part of speech): adjective
	    Case—accusative
	    Gender—feminine
	    Number—singular
	    Stem or root—from λογικός, ή, όν
	Concordance References:
	  ⇒ Strong's #3050 logikos
	  ⇒ NIV #3358 logikos
	  ⇒ NASB #3050 logikos
	
	Romans 12:1
	    I beseech you therefore, brethren, by the mercies of God, that ye present your bodies a living sacrifice, holy, acceptable unto God, which is your **reasonable** service. [KJV]
	    I urge you therefore, brethren, by the mercies of God, to present your bodies a living and holy sacrifice, acceptable to God, which is your **spiritual** service of worship. [NASB]
	    Therefore, I urge you, brothers, in view of God's mercy, to offer your bodies as living sacrifices, holy and pleasing to God—this is your **spiritual** act of worship. [NIV]
	    I beseech you therefore, brethren, by the mercies of God, that you present your bodies a living sacrifice, holy, acceptable to God, *which is* your **reasonable** service. [NKJV]
	    And so, dear brothers and sisters, I plead with you to give your bodies to God. Let them be a living and holy sacrifice—the kind he will accept. When you think of what he has done for you, is this too much to ask? [NLT]—NOT TRANSLATED
	    Παρακαλῶ οὖν ὑμᾶς, ἀδελφοί, διὰ τῶν οἰκτιρμῶν τοῦ Θεοῦ, παραστῆσαι τὰ σώματα ὑμῶν θυσίαν ζῶσαν, ἁγίαν εὐάρεστον τῷ Θεῷ, τὴν **λογικὴν** λατρείαν ὑμῶν. [GNS]
	    Παρακαλῶ οὖν ὑμᾶς, ἀδελφοί, διὰ τῶν οἰκτιρμῶν τοῦ θεοῦ παραστῆσαι τὰ σώματα ὑμῶν θυσίαν ζῶσαν ἁγίαν εὐάρεστον τῷ θεῷ, τὴν **λογικὴν** λατρείαν ὑμῶν· [GNT]
		Rational, spiritual, intelligent, logical, fair, sensible, just, right, wise.
		
		Practical Application
		    The dedication of the body to God is the believer's spiritual service. It is an act of the mind thinking and figuring out what and how to do something.

#3705
Spiritual
	λογικὸν = *logikon*
	Pronunciation: [log-ik-on']
	Parsing (part of speech): adjective
	    Case—accusative
	    Gender—neuter
		Spiritual, word, rational.
		
		Practical Application
		    The Greek word that is translated "spiritual"

ENGLISH WORD	GREEK WORD AND VERSE	THE WORD MEANS...
Mind set on the Spirit–NASB Mind controlled by the Spirit–NIV **Spiritually minded– NKJV** Holy Spirit controls your mind–NLT **POSB REFERENCE** (Rom.8:5-8, esp. v.6) Note 3, point 2	Stem or root—from φρόνημα, τος Parsing *pneumatos* (part of speech): noun Case—genitive Gender—neuter Number—singular Stem or root—from πνεῦμα, τος Concordance References: ⇒ Strong's #3588 ho + 5427 phronēma + 3588 ho + 4151 pneuma ⇒ NIV #3836 ho [the] + 5859 phronēma [mind] + 3836 ho [the] + 4460 pneuma [Spirit] ⇒ NASB #3588 ho + 5427 phronēma + 3588 ho + 4151 pneuma **Romans 8:6** For to be carnally minded is death; but to be **spiritually minded** is life and peace. [KJV] For the mind set on the flesh is death, but **the mind set on the Spirit** is life and peace, [NASB] The mind of sinful man is death, but **the mind controlled by the Spirit** is life and peace; [NIV] For to be carnally minded *is* death, but to be **spiritually minded** *is* life and peace. [NKJV] If your sinful nature controls your mind, there is death. But if **the Holy Spirit controls your mind**, there is life and peace. [NLT] τὸ γὰρ φρόνημα τῆς σαρκὸς θάνατος· τὸ δὲ **φρόνημα τοῦ πνεύματος** ζωὴ καὶ εἰρήνη. [GNS] τὸ γὰρ φρόνημα τῆς σαρκὸς θάνατος,τὸ. δὲ **φρόνημα τοῦ πνεύματος** ζωὴ καὶ εἰρήνη. [GNT]	Spirit or to be controlled and dominated by the Spirit. It means that the man who walks after the Spirit minds "the things of the Spirit" day by day. And note: it is the Spirit of God who draws the believer's mind to focus upon spiritual things. The Spirit of God lives within the believer. He is there to work within the believer, both to will and to do God's pleasure. He is there to keep the mind and thoughts of the believer focused upon spiritual things.
#3712 **Spitefully Entreated** **Spitefully entreated– KJV** Mistreated–NASB Insult–NIV Insulted–NKJV Treated shamefully– NLT **POSB REFERENCE** (Lk.18:32-33; esp. v.32) Note 2, point 1b	ὑβρισθήσεται = *hubristhēsetai* Pronunciation: [hoo-bris'-thay-seh-tah-ee] Parsing (part of speech): verb Mood—indicative Tense—future Voice—passive Person—3rd person Number—singular Stem or root—from ὑβρίζω Concordance References: ⇒ Strong's #5195 hubrizo ⇒ NIV #5614 hubrizo ⇒ NASB #5195 hubrizo **Luke 18:32** For he shall be delivered unto the Gentiles, and shall be mocked, and **spitefully entreated**, and spitted on: [KJV] "For He will be delivered to the Gentiles, and will be mocked and **mistreated** and spit upon, [NASB] He will be handed over to the Gentiles. They will mock him, **insult** him, spit on him, flog him and kill him. [NIV] For He will be delivered to the Gentiles and will be mocked and **insulted** and spit upon. [NKJV] He will be handed over to the Romans to be mocked, **treated shamefully**, and spit upon. [NLT] παραδοθήσεται γὰρ τοῖς ἔθνεσι, καὶ ἐμπαιχθήσεται, καὶ **ὑβρισθήσεται**, καὶ ἐμπτυσθήσεται, [GNS] παραδοθήσεται γὰρ τοῖς ἔθνεσιν καὶ ἐμπαιχθήσεται καὶ **ὑβρισθήσεται** καὶ ἐμπτυσθήσεται [GNT]	To insult; to reproach; to treat with insolence and contempt; to be outraged; to mistreat; to treat disgracefully; to treat shamefully and despitefully. **Practical Application** Jesus was to be delivered to the Gentiles, and the Jews were going to be the ones to deliver Him into Gentile hands. This fact was to symbolize both the religionists and the world—both were going to reject God's Son and put Him to death. Neither could accept Him and His message of total self-denial.
#3713 **Splendor** Brightness–KJV Appearance–NASB **Splendor–NIV** Brightness–NKJV **Splendor–NLT**	ἐπιφανεία = *epiphaneia* Pronunciation: [ep-if-an'-ee-ah] Parsing (part of speech): noun Case—dative Gender—feminine Number—singular Stem or root—from ἐπιφάνεια, ας Concordance References: ⇒ Strong's #2015 epiphaneia ⇒ NIV #2211 epiphaneia ⇒ NASB #2015 epiphaneia	Splendor, brightness, appearance. **Practical Application** The Lord of glory will destroy the antichrist with the brightness of His coming. The word "splendor" (*epiphaneia*) is a very special word. It is a word chosen by the New Testament to refer only to the coming (*parousia*) of the Lord. It is used only five times in all the New Testament, and in every instance it refers to the

ENGLISH WORD	GREEK WORD AND VERSE	THE WORD MEANS...
POSB REFERENCE (2 Thes.2:8) Note 4, point 2	**2 Thes. 2:8** And then shall that Wicked be revealed, whom the Lord shall consume with the spirit of his mouth, and shall destroy with the **brightness** of his coming: [KJV] And then that lawless one will be revealed whom the Lord will slay with the breath of His mouth and bring to an end by the **appearance** of His coming; [NASB] And then the lawless one will be revealed, whom the Lord Jesus will overthrow with the breath of his mouth and destroy by the **splendor** of his coming. [NIV] And then the lawless one will be revealed, whom the Lord will consume with the breath of His mouth and destroy with the **brightness** of His coming. [NKJV] Then the man of lawlessness will be revealed, whom the Lord Jesus will consume with the breath of his mouth and destroy by the **splendor** of his coming. [NLT] καὶ τότε ἀποκαλυφθήσεται ὁ ἄνομος, ὃν ὁ Κύριος ἀναλώσει τῷ πνεύματι τοῦ στόματος αὐτοῦ, καὶ καταργήσει τῇ **ἐπιφανείᾳ** τῆς παρουσίας αὐτοῦ· [GNS] καὶ τότε ἀποκαλυφθήσεται ὁ ἄνομος, ὃν ὁ κύριος [Ἰησοῦς] ἀνελεῖ τῷ πνεύματι τοῦ στόματος αὐτοῦ καὶ καταργήσει τῇ **ἐπιφανείᾳ** τῆς παρουσίας αὐτοῦ, [GNT]	Lord's coming into the world. It refers once to His first coming (2 Tim. 1:10) and four times to His second coming (1 Tim. 6:14; 2 Tim. 4:1, 8; Titus 2:13). The whole idea of *splendor* is brightness, radiance, glory, and light. Someone has pointed out that when Jesus Christ returns to earth, there will be such a spectacular display of glory and splendor that the explosion of every star in the universe could not match the sight of the Lord (source unknown). When Christ first appears, there will apparently be the energizing of a laser beam of glory zeroed in on the antichrist, and he will be immediately destroyed by the radiance of the Lord's glory and light— quicker than we could blink an eye. Simply by showing Himself, the Lord will destroy the antichrist. Note: the word "destroy" does not mean to annihilate but to make inoperative; to make powerless; to end; to put a stop to his evil work.
#3714 **Splendor, In** Sumptuously–KJV **In splendor–NASB** In luxury–NIV Sumptuously–NKJV In luxury–NLT **POSB REFERENCE** (Lk.16:19-21; esp. v.19) *Deeper Study* #1 point 1	λαμπρῶς = *lamprōs* Pronunciation: [lamp-rows] Parsing (part of speech): adjective Type—adverb Stem or root—from λαμπρῶς Concordance References: ⇒ Strong's #2983 lambano ⇒ NIV #3289 lamprōs ⇒ NASB #2988 lamprōs **Luke 16:19** There was a certain rich man, which was clothed in purple and fine linen, and fared **sumptuously** every day: [KJV] "Now there was a certain rich man, and he habitually dressed in purple and fine linen, gaily living **in splendor** every day. [NASB] "There was a rich man who was dressed in purple and fine linen and lived **in luxury** every day. [NIV] "There was a certain rich man who was clothed in purple and fine linen and fared **sumptuously** every day. [NKJV] Jesus said, "There was a certain rich man who was splendidly clothed and who lived each day **in luxury**. [NLT] Ἄνθρωπος δέ τις ἦν πλούσιος, καὶ ἐνεδιδύσκετο πορφύραν καὶ βύσσον, εὐφραινόμενος καθ᾽ ἡμέραν **λαμπρῶς**. [GNS] Ἄνθρωπος δέ τις ἦν πλούσιος, καὶ ἐνεδιδύσκετο πορφύραν καὶ βύσσον εὐφραινόμενος καθ᾽ ἡμέραν **λαμπρῶς**. [GNT]	To live in luxury; to live in splendor. The word means that the rich man was flamboyant, displaying his wealth in materialistic ways. ### Practical Application His sin was *self-indulgence*, *comfort*, *ease*, *luxury*, *extravagant living*. He sought the things and pleasures of this world. He was complacent, hoarding and allowing money to lie around making more and more for himself and his estate while needs lay all around him—right at his gate. He neglected and ignored others, most significantly, Lazarus. The needs of a degenerate world concerned him little, if at all. He wanted what others in the world had, plenty for themselves and more. The world acknowledged and honored those who had plenty, and he wanted such recognition and honor for himself. He wanted what others had, and he wanted to keep up with them.
#3715 **Spoil** **Spoil–KJV** Captive–NASB Captive–NIV Cheat–NKJV Astray–NLT **POSB REFERENCE** (Col.2:8) Note 1	ἔσται συλαγωγῶν = *estai sulagōgōn* Pronunciation: [es-tah-ee soo-lag-og-o'-gon'] Parsing *sulagōgōn* (part of speech): verb Mood—participle Tense—present Voice—active Case—nominative Gender—masculine Number—singular Stem or root—from συλαγωγέω Concordance References: ⇒ Strong's #1510 eimi + 4812 sulagōgeō ⇒ NIV #1639+5194 eimi sulagōgeō [takes captive] ⇒ NASB #1510 eimi + 4812 sulagōgeō **Col. 2:8** Beware lest any man **spoil** you through philosophy and vain deceit, after the tradition of men, after the rudi-	To take captive; to lead astray; to lead into captivity or slavery; to cheat. ### Practical Application Some men are in a genuine search for truth and reality. They seek to learn the truth and reality of the universe and the problems that face them, but they limit themselves to the universe. Other persons have novel ideas or philosophies about truth and reality, but they become more interested in their positions than the truth. They need others to accept their positions or else their ideas die. Therefore, they have to present and persuade people of their ideas and philosophies whether they are sound or not. Believers must, therefore, beware and guard

ENGLISH WORD	GREEK WORD AND VERSE	THE WORD MEANS...
	ments of the world, and not after Christ. [KJV] See to it that no one takes you **captive** through philosophy and empty deception, according to the tradition of men, according to the elementary principles of the world, rather than according to Christ. [NASB] See to it that no one takes you **captive** through hollow and deceptive philosophy, which depends on human tradition and the basic principles of this world rather than on Christ. [NIV] Beware lest anyone **cheat** you through philosophy and empty deceit, according to the tradition of men, according to the basic principles of the world, and not according to Christ. [NKJV] Don't let anyone lead you **astray** with empty philosophy and high-sounding nonsense that come from human thinking and from the evil powers of this world, and not from Christ. [NLT] βλέπετε μή τις ὑμᾶς **ἔσται** ὁ **συλαγωγῶν** διὰ τῆς φιλοσοφίας καὶ κενῆς ἀπάτης, κατὰ τὴν παράδοσιν τῶν ἀνθρώπων, κατὰ τὰ στοιχεῖα τοῦ κόσμου, καὶ οὐ κατὰ Χριστόν·[GNS] βλέπετε μή τις ὑμᾶς **ἔσται** ὁ **συλαγωγῶν** διὰ τῆς φιλοσοφίας καὶ κενῆς ἀπάτης κατὰ τὴν παράδοσιν τῶν ἀνθρώπων, κατὰ τὰ στοιχεῖα τοῦ κόσμου καὶ οὐ κατὰ Χριστόν· [GNT]	against worldly philosophies and ideas lest they become ensnared and enslaved.

#3716
Spoil
 	
Undefiled–KJV
Undefiled–NASB
Spoil–NIV
Undefiled–NKJV
Undefiled–NLT
 	
POSB
REFERENCE
(1 Pt.1:4)
Note 2, point 2
	ἀμάραντον = amianton
	Pronunciation: [am-ee'-an-ton]
	Parsing (part of speech): adjective
	    Case—accusative
	    Gender—feminine
	    Number—singular
	    Stem or root—from *ἀμίαντος, ον*
	Concordance References:
	  ⇒ Strong's #283 amiantos
	  ⇒ NIV #299 amiantos
	  ⇒ NASB #283 amiantos
	
	1 Pet. 1:4
	To an inheritance incorruptible, and **undefiled**, and that fadeth not away, reserved in heaven for you, [KJV]
	
	To obtain an inheritance which is imperishable and **undefiled** and will not fade away, reserved in heaven for you, [NASB]
	
	And into an inheritance that can never perish, **spoil** or fade—kept in heaven for you, [NIV]
	
	To an inheritance incorruptible and **undefiled** and that does not fade away, reserved in heaven for you, [NKJV]
	
	For God has reserved a priceless inheritance for his children. It is kept in heaven for you, pure and **undefiled**, beyond the reach of change and decay. [NLT]
	
	εἰς κληρονομίαν ἄφθαρτον καὶ ἀμίαντον καὶ **ἀμάραντον**, τετηρημένην ἐν οὐρανοῖς εἰς ὑμᾶς [GNS]
	
	εἰς κληρονομίαν ἄφθαρτον καὶ ἀμίαντον καὶ **ἀμάραντον**, τετηρημένην ἐν οὐρανοῖς εἰς ὑμᾶς [GNT]
		Not spoiled, undefiled, unstained, pure.
		
		Practical Application
		The word means that it cannot be polluted or defiled, dirtied or infected. It means that our inheritance will be without any flaw or defect; it will be perfectly free from sickness, disease, infections, accident, pollution, dirt—from any spoilage whatsoever. There will never be any tears over what happens to oneself or over the damage or loss of some possession.

#3717
Spoke
 	
Spake–KJV
Speaking–NASB
Speak–NIV
Spoke–NKJV
Not translated–NLT
 	
POSB
REFERENCE
(Acts 11:19-30; esp. v.20)
Deeper Study #2,
point 1
	ἐλάλουν = elaloun
	Pronunciation: [eh-lah-loon]
	Parsing (part of speech): verb
	    Mood—indicative
	    Tense—imperfect
	    Voice—active
	    Person—3rd person
	    Number—plural
	    Stem or root—from *λαλέω*
	Concordance References:
	  ⇒ Strong's #2980 laleö
	  ⇒ NIV #3281 laleö
	  ⇒ NASB #2980 laleö
	
	Acts 11:20
	And some of them were men of Cyprus and Cyrene,
		To speak; to proclaim; to tell.
		
		Practical Application
		It is the simple sharing of conversation among people. As the believers scattered and travelled about, they "spoke the Word," shared Christ in ordinary conversation. The picture is that of witnessing one on one, of scattering the seed wherever they went. Christ was the topic of their conversation.

ENGLISH WORD	GREEK WORD AND VERSE	THE WORD MEANS...
	which, when they were come to Antioch, **spake** unto the Grecians, preaching the Lord Jesus. [KJV] But there were some of them, men of Cyprus and Cyrene, who came to Antioch and began **speaking** to the Greeks also, preaching the Lord Jesus. [NASB] Some of them, however, men from Cyprus and Cyrene, went to Antioch and began to **speak** to Greeks also, telling them the good news about the Lord Jesus. [NIV] But some of them were men from Cyprus and Cyrene, who, when they had come to Antioch, **spoke** to the Hellenists, preaching the Lord Jesus. [NKJV] However, some of the believers who went to Antioch from Cyprus and Cyrene began preaching to Gentiles about the Lord Jesus. [NLT]—NOT TRANSLATED ἦσαν δέ τινες ἐξ αὐτῶν ἄνδρες Κύπριοι καὶ Κυρηναῖοι, οἵτινες ἐλθόντες εἰς Ἀντιόχειαν, **ἐλάλουν** πρὸς τοὺς Ἑλληνιστάς, εὐαγγελιζόμενοι τὸν Κύριον Ἰησοῦν. [GNS] ἦσαν δέ τινες ἐξ αὐτῶν ἄνδρες Κύπριοι καὶ Κυρηναῖοι, οἵτινες ἐλθόντες εἰς Ἀντιόχειαν **ἐλάλουν** καὶ πρὸς τοὺς Ἑλληνιστάς εὐαγγελιζόμενοι τὸν κύριον Ἰησοῦν. [GNT]	

#3718
Spoke On
 	
Spoke on–KJV
Warned–NASB
Warned–NIV
Spoke on–NKJV
Not translated–NLT
 	
**POSB
REFERENCE**
(Heb.12:25)
Note 1
	χρηματίζοντα = *chrēmatizonta*
	Pronunciation: [khray-mat-id'-zon-tah]
	Parsing (part of speech): verb
	    Mood—participle
	    Tense—present
	    Voice—active
	    Case—accusative
	    Gender—masculine
	    Number—singular
	    Stem or root—from χρηματίζω
	Concordance References:
	  ⇒ Strong's #5537 chrēmatizō
	  ⇒ NIV #5976 chrēmatizō
	  ⇒ NASB #5537 chrēmatizō
	
	Hebrews 12:25
	See that ye refuse not him that speaketh. For if they escaped not who refused him that **spake on** earth, much more shall not we escape, if we turn away from him that speaketh from heaven: [KJV]
	
	See to it that you do not refuse Him who is speaking. For if those did not escape when they refused him who **warned** them on earth, much less shall we escape who turn away from Him who warns from heaven. [NASB]
	
	See to it that you do not refuse him who speaks. If they did not escape when they refused him who **warned** them on earth, how much less will we, if we turn away from him who warns us from heaven? [NIV]
	
	See that you do not refuse Him who speaks. For if they did not escape who refused Him who **spoke on** earth, much more *shall we not escape* if we turn away from Him who *speaks* from heaven, [NKJV]
	
	See to it that you obey God, the one who is speaking to you. For if the people of Israel did not escape when they refused to listen to Moses, the earthly messenger, how terrible our danger if we reject the One who speaks to us from heaven! [NLT]—NOT TRANSLATED
	
	βλέπετε μὴ παραιτήσησθε τὸν λαλοῦντα. εἰ γὰρ ἐκεῖνοι οὐκ ἔφυγον, τὸν ἐπὶ τῆς γῆς παραιτησάμενοι **χρηματίζοντα**, πολλῷ μᾶλλον ἡμεῖς οἱ τὸν ἀπ' οὐρανῶν ἀποστρεφόμενοι· [GNS]
	
	Βλέπετε μὴ παραιτήσησθε τὸν λαλοῦντα· εἰ γὰρ ἐκεῖνοι οὐκ ἐξέφυγον ἐπὶ γῆς παραιτησάμενοι τὸν **χρηματίζοντα**, πολὺ μᾶλλον ἡμεῖς οἱ τὸν ἀπ' οὐρανῶν ἀποστρεφόμενοι, [GNT]
		To warn; to speak; to disclose; to reveal. It means transmitter or mouthpiece (William Barclay. *The Letter to the Hebrews*, p.215).
		
		Practical Application
		There shall be no escape whatsoever for the close-minded. Moses is the person who spoke on earth and gave the law of God to man, but Jesus Christ is the One who spoke and brought the Word of God down *out of* heaven.

ENGLISH WORD	GREEK WORD AND VERSE	THE WORD MEANS...

#3719
Spots
 	
Spots–KJV
Hidden reefs–NASB
Blemishes–NIV
Spots–NKJV
Dangerous reefs–NLT
 	
POSB
REFERENCE
(Jude 1:12)
Note 14
	σπιλάδες = *spilades*
	Pronunciation: [spee-la-des']
	Parsing (part of speech): noun
	    Case—nominative
	    Gender—feminine
	    Number—plural
	    Stem or root—from σπιλάς, άδος
	Concordance References:
	⇒ Strong's #4694 spilas
	⇒ NIV #5069 spilas
	⇒ NASB #4694 spilas
		Blemishes, spots, hidden reefs, dangerous reefs; anything that poses a dangerous threat.

Jude 1:12

These are **spots** in your feasts of charity, when they feast with you, feeding themselves without fear: clouds they are without water, carried about of winds; trees whose fruit withereth, without fruit, twice dead, plucked up by the roots; [KJV]

These men are those who are **hidden reefs** in your love feasts when they feast with you without fear, caring for themselves; clouds without water, carried along by winds; autumn trees without fruit, doubly dead, uprooted; [NASB]

These men are **blemishes** at your love feasts, eating with you without the slightest qualm—shepherds who feed only themselves. They are clouds without rain, blown along by the wind; autumn trees, without fruit and uprooted—twice dead. [NIV]

These are **spots** in your love feasts, while they feast with you without fear, serving only themselves. They are clouds without water, carried about by the winds; late autumn trees without fruit, twice dead, pulled up by the roots; [NKJV]

When these people join you in fellowship meals celebrating the love of the Lord, they are like **dangerous reefs** that can shipwreck you. They are shameless in the way they care only about themselves. They are like clouds blowing over dry land without giving rain, promising much but producing nothing. They are like trees without fruit at harvesttime. They are not only dead but doubly dead, for they have been pulled out by the roots. [NLT]

οὗτοί εἰσιν ἐν ταῖς ἀγάπαις ὑμῶν **σπιλάδες**, συνευωχούμενοι ὑμῖν, ἀφόβως ἑαυτοὺς ποιμαίνοντες· νεφέλαι ἄνυδροι, ὑπὸ ἀνέμων περιφερόμεναι· δένδρα φθινοπωρινά, ἄκαρπα, δὶς ἀποθανόντα, ἐκριζωθέντα· [GNS]

οὗτοί εἰσιν οἱ ἐν ταῖς ἀγάπαις ὑμῶν **σπιλάδες** συνευωχούμενοι ἀφόβως, ἑαυτοὺς ποιμαίνοντες, νεφέλαι ἄνυδροι ὑπὸ ἀνέμων παραφερόμεναι, δένδρα φθινοπωρινὰ ἄκαρπα δὶς ἀποθανόντα ἐκριζωθέντα, [GNT]

Practical Application

False teachers are *spots and blemishes* upon the fellowship of the church. The Greek word for "spots" (*spilades*) can mean *submerged rocks or hidden reefs* that can wreck a ship. False teachers are reefs within the church that can wreck the fellowship of the church. Translators differ as to which meaning Jude intended. Perhaps he meant both, for both are certainly true.

The *love feasts* referred to were called *love feasts* by the early church. They were fellowship meals that the church celebrated after the services on the Lord's Day. Each family brought what food they could. This, of course, meant that the wealthy brought plenty and the poor brought little or nothing. Remember that many of the believers were slaves in that day, so some of them would not be able to bring any food whatsoever. Some churches had the most joyful fellowship around the love feasts. It provided a time when the believers could share the warmth of their hearts and grow in fellowship together. It was a time when the Holy Spirit could draw the hearts of believers together in love and joy and care and sharing. It was a time that the Holy Spirit could use to bind believers together in feelings for one another and in warmth and tenderness.

The point is this: fellowship among believers is a most wonderful time, a unique opportunity to grow and share together. But when false teachers are present, the scene is entirely different.

⇒ False teachers are spots or blemishes upon the fellowship of believers. They dirty and soil the name of Christ and the testimony of the church. They profess to be believers and are even teachers of God's Word, but they are not pure. Their false teaching disturbs genuine believers and causes division within the fellowship of the church. Those who are not rooted in Christ and in God's Word follow and support the false teacher; those who are rooted in Christ and in God's Word reject the false teacher. False teachers always spot and dirty the fellowship of the church because they cause division among the people and destroy the Spirit of Christ among them.

⇒ False teachers are reefs or submerged rocks that wreck the fellowship of the church. Their teaching is often injected into the church quietly and insidiously, completely unknown to the general membership. Therefore, the fellowship is subject to being shipwrecked upon the reefs of false teaching.

Note that the false teachers feed themselves—that is, they fellowship with believers—without fear. There is no fear of God nor thought about the damage they are doing to the fellowship of the church. Their interest is to boost themselves forward; to be recognized as excellent teachers or preachers, persons of unusual gifts, teachers with new insights, teachers who are progressive, who are a notch above others.

ENGLISH WORD	GREEK WORD AND VERSE	THE WORD MEANS...

#3720
Spread
 	
Published–KJV
Spread–NASB
Spread–NIV
Spread–NKJV
Spread–NLT
 	
**POSB
REFERENCE**
(Acts 13:46-52; esp.
v.49)
Note 2, point 2d
	διεφέρετο = *diephereto*
	Pronunciation: [di-eh-fehr'-eh-tow]
	Parsing (part of speech): verb
	    Mood—indicative
	    Tense—imperfect
	    Voice—passive
	    Person—3rd person
	    Number—singular
	    Stem or root—from διαφέρω
	Concordance References:
	⇒ Strong's #1308 diapherö
	⇒ NIV #1422 diapherö
	⇒ NASB #1308 diapherö
	
	Acts 13:49
	And the word of the Lord was **published** throughout all the region. [KJV]
	And the word of the Lord was being **spread** through the whole region. [NASB]
	The word of the Lord **spread** through the whole region. [NIV]
	And the word of the Lord was being **spread** throughout all the region. [NKJV]
	So the Lord's message **spread** throughout that region. [NLT]
	διεφέρετο δὲ ὁ λόγος τοῦ Κυρίου δι' ὅλης τῆς χώρας. [GNS]
	διεφέρετο δὲ ὁ λόγος τοῦ κυρίου δι' ὅλης τῆς χώρας. [GNT]
		To spread; to publish.
		
		Practical Application
		They published, that is, spread abroad and proclaimed the Word throughout all the region.

#3721
Spreading Rapidly
 	
Grew and multiplied–KJV
Grow and to be multiplied–NASB
Increase and spread–NIV
Grew and multiplied–NKJV
Spreading rapidly–NLT
 	
**POSB
REFERENCE**
(Acts 12:24-25; esp.
v.24)
Note 4, point 1
	ηὔξανεν καὶ ἐπληθύνετο = *ëuxanen kai eplëthuneto*
	Pronunciation: [yoowx-ahn'-ehn ky eh-play-thoo'-neh-tow]
	Parsing *ëuxanen* (part of speech): verb
	    Mood—indicative
	    Tense—imperfect
	    Voice—active
	    Person—3rd person
	    Number—singular
	    Stem or root—from αὐξάνω
	Parsing *eplëthuneto* (part of speech): verb
	    Mood—indicative
	    Tense—imperfect
	    Voice—passive
	    Person—3rd person
	    Number—singular
	    Stem or root—from πληθύνω
	Concordance References:
	⇒ Strong's #837 auxanö + 2532 kai + 4129 plëthunö
	⇒ NIV #889 auxanö [increase] + 2779 kai [and] + 4437 plëthunö [spread]
	⇒ NASB #837 auxanö + 2532 kai + 4129 plëthunöt
	
	Acts 12:24
	But the word of God **grew and multiplied**. [KJV]
	But the word of the Lord continued to **grow and to be multiplied**. [NASB]
	But the word of God continued to **increase and spread**. [NIV]
	But the word of God **grew and multiplied**. [NKJV]
	But God's Good News was **spreading rapidly**, and there were many new believers. [NLT]
	Ὁ δὲ λόγος τοῦ Θεοῦ ηὔξανε καὶ ἐπληθύνετο. [GNS]
	Ὁ δὲ λόγος τοῦ θεοῦ ηὔξανεν καὶ Ἐπληθύνετο [GNT]
		To increase and spread; to grow and multiply; to spread rapidly.
		
		Practical Application
		The words "spreading rapidly" (*ëuxanen kai eplëthuneto*) mean that the church kept on growing and multiplying. The progress of God's Word could not be stopped. Men and governments might try to stop it. They might persecute, imprison, and kill those who proclaim God's Word, but their efforts to silence the Word will always be to no avail. God overrules all and always will.

#3722
Spurned God's Message
	ἀπειθήσαντες = *apeithësantes*
	Pronunciation: [ap-i-thoon'-tace]
	Parsing (part of speech): verb
	    Mood—participle
	    Tense—aorist
		Refused to believe; unbelieving; disbelieved; to spurn God's message; to be disobedient; to be an unbeliever.

ENGLISH WORD	GREEK WORD AND VERSE	THE WORD MEANS...
Unbelieving–KJV Disbelieved–NASB Refused to believe–NIV Unbelieving–NKJV **Spurned God's message–NLT** **POSB REFERENCE** (Acts 14:2) Note 4, point 1	Voice—active Case—nominative Gender—masculine Number—plural Stem or root—from ἀπειθέω Concordance References: ⇒ Strong's #544 apeitheö ⇒ NIV #578 apeitheö ⇒ NASB #544 apeitheö **Acts 14:2** But the **unbelieving** Jews stirred up the Gentiles, and made their minds evil affected against the brethren. [KJV] But the Jews who **disbelieved** stirred up the minds of the Gentiles, and embittered them against the brethren. [NASB] But the Jews who **refused to believe** stirred up the Gentiles and poisoned their minds against the brothers. [NIV] But the **unbelieving** Jews stirred up the Gentiles and poisoned their minds against the brethren. [NKJV] But the Jews who **spurned God's message** stirred up distrust among the Gentiles against Paul and Barnabas, saying all sorts of evil things about them. [NLT] οἱ δὲ **ἀπειθοῦντες** Ἰουδαῖοι ἐπήγειραν καὶ ἐκάκωσαν τὰς ψυχὰς τῶν ἐθνῶν κατὰ τῶν ἀδελφῶν. [GNS] οἱ δὲ **ἀπειθήσαντες** Ἰουδαῖοι ἐπήγειραν καὶ ἐκάκωσαν τὰς ψυχὰς τῶν ἐθνῶν κατὰ τῶν ἀδελφῶν. [GNT]	**Practical Application** The idea is they were unwilling to believe or be persuaded. They deliberately withheld belief, disobeying God.
#3723 **Stability** Stedfastness–KJV **Stability–NASB** Firm–NIV Steadfastness–NKJV Strong–NLT **POSB REFERENCE** (Col.2:5) Note 4	στερέωμα = stereöma Pronunciation: [ster-eh'-o-mah] Parsing (part of speech): noun Case—accusative Gender—neuter Number—singular Stem or root—from στερέωμα, τος Concordance References: ⇒ Strong's #4733 stereöma ⇒ NIV #5106 stereöma ⇒ NASB #4733 stereöma **Col. 2:5** For though I be absent in the flesh, yet am I with you in the spirit, joying and beholding your order, and the **stedfastness** of your faith in Christ. [KJV] For even though I am absent in body, nevertheless I am with you in spirit, rejoicing to see your good discipline and the **stability** of your faith in Christ. [NASB] For though I am absent from you in body, I am present with you in spirit and delight to see how orderly you are and how **firm** your faith in Christ is. [NIV] For though I am absent in the flesh, yet I am with you in spirit, rejoicing to see your *good* order and the **steadfastness** of your faith in Christ. [NKJV] For though I am far away from you, my heart is with you. And I am very happy because you are living as you should and because of your **strong** faith in Christ. [NLT] εἰ γὰρ καὶ τῇ σαρκὶ ἄπειμι, ἀλλὰ τῷ πνεύματι σὺν ὑμῖν εἰμι, χαίρων καὶ βλέπων ὑμῶν τὴν τάξιν καὶ τὸ **στερέωμα** τῆς εἰς Χριστὸν πίστεως ὑμῶν. [GNS] εἰ γὰρ καὶ τῇ σαρκὶ ἄπειμι, ἀλλὰ τῷ πνεύματι σὺν ὑμῖν εἰμι, χαίρων καὶ βλέπων ὑμῶν τὴν τάξιν καὶ τὸ **στερέωμα** τῆς εἰς Χριστὸν πίστεως ὑμῶν. [GNT]	To be firm, steadfast, stable, strong. It means to stand fast and persevere; to be immovable, steady, and unyielding; to never crack, give in, or back up. **Practical Application** A mature people maintain discipline—order and steadfastness. ⇒ The word "orderly" (*taxin*) means to maintain military discipline, array, and arrangement; to hold a solid front (The Amplified New Testament); to hold the military line unbroken and intact (A.T. Robertson, *Word Pictures in the New Testament*, Vol.4, p.489). ⇒ The word "stability" (*stereöma*) is also a military word. A.T. Robertson says that it is "the solid part of the line which can and does stand the attack" of the seduction. Note that the believers of the Colossian church were being attacked by false teaching even as Paul was writing to them. But they were responding like a victorious army. They were maintaining their discipline and holding their order and standing fast. Note also the importance of the minister's encouragement: Paul says that he was with them *in spirit*, joying and watching them gain the victory over the false teachers.
#3724 **Stablish** Stablish–KJV Establish–NASB Establish–NIV	στηρίξαι = stërixai Pronunciation: [stay-rich'-ah-ee] Parsing (part of speech): verb Mood—infinitive Tense—aorist Voice—active Stem or root—from στηρίζω	To strengthen; to make firm; to establish; to fix; to set up. It means to strengthen, secure, make stable, set fast, and make firm. **Practical Application** God is able to stablish the believer. The one thing people long for is to be secure, strong, and

ENGLISH WORD	GREEK WORD AND VERSE	THE WORD MEANS...
Establish–NKJV Make strong–NLT **POSB REFERENCE** (Rom.16:25-27, esp. v.25) Introduction	Concordance References: ⇒ Strong's #4741 stërizö ⇒ NIV #5114 stërizö ⇒ NASB #4741 stërizö **Romans 16:25** Now to him that is of power to **stablish** you according to my gospel, and the preaching of Jesus Christ, according to the revelation of the mystery, which was kept secret since the world began, [KJV] Now to Him who is able to **establish** you according to my gospel and the preaching of Jesus Christ, according to the revelation of the mystery which has been kept secret for long ages past, [NASB] Now to him who is able to **establish** you by my gospel and the proclamation of Jesus Christ, according to the revelation of the mystery hidden for long ages past, [NIV] Now to Him who is able to **establish** you according to my gospel and the preaching of Jesus Christ, according to the revelation of the mystery kept secret since the world began [NKJV] God is able to **make** you **strong**, just as the Good News says. It is the message about Jesus Christ and his plan for you Gentiles, a plan kept secret from the beginning of time. [NLT] Τῷ δὲ δυναμένῳ ὑμᾶς **στηρίξαι** κατὰ τὸ εὐαγγέλιόν μου καὶ τὸ κήρυγμα Ἰησοῦ Χριστοῦ, κατὰ ἀποκάλυψιν μυστηρίου χρόνοις αἰωνίοις σεσιγημένου [GNS] [Τῷ δὲ δυναμένῳ ὑμᾶς **στηρίξαι** κατὰ τὸ εὐαγγέλιόν μου καὶ τὸ κήρυγμα Ἰησοῦ Χριστοῦ, κατὰ ἀποκάλυψιν μυστηρίου χρόνοις αἰωνίοις σεσιγημένου, [GNT]	firmly established in life. God is able to fulfill this longing. God is able to establish and strengthen people and to give them a strong life.
#3725 Stablish **Stablish–KJV** Strengthen–NASB Strengthen–NIV Establish–NKJV Strength–NLT **POSB REFERENCE** (2 Thes.2:16-17; esp. v.17) Note 5, point 5 **See also POSB REF:** (2 Thes.3:3-5; esp. v.3) Note 2, point 1	**στηρίξαι = stërixai** Pronunciation: [stay-rix'-ah-ee] Parsing (part of speech): verb 　Mood—optative 　Tense—aorist 　Voice—active 　Person—3rd person 　Number—singular 　Stem or root—from στηρίζω Concordance References: ⇒ Strong's #4741 stërizö ⇒ NIV #5114 stërizö ⇒ NASB #4741 stërizö **2 Thes. 2:17** Comfort your hearts, and **stablish** you in every good word and work. [KJV] Comfort and **strengthen** your hearts in every good work and word. [NASB] Encourage your hearts and **strengthen** you in every good deed and word. [NIV] Comfort your hearts and **establish** you in every good word and work. [NKJV] Comfort your hearts and give you **strength** in every good thing you do and say. [NLT] παρακαλέσαι ὑμῶν τὰς καρδίας, καὶ **στηρίξαι** ὑμᾶς ἐν παντὶ λόγῳ καὶ ἔργῳ ἀγαθῷ. [GNS] παρακαλέσαι ὑμῶν τὰς καρδίας καὶ **στηρίξαι** ἐν παντὶ ἔργῳ καὶ λόγῳ ἀγαθῷ. [GNT]	To strengthen, secure, establish, make stable, set fast, and make firm. ### Practical Application The person who is saved is stablished in every good word and work. The one thing men long for is to be secure, strong, and firmly established in life. God is able to fulfill this longing. God is able to establish and strengthen man and to give him a strong life.
#3726 Stablish **Stablish–KJV** Confirm–NASB Make strong–NIV Establish–NKJV Support–NLT	**στηρίζει = stërixei** Pronunciation: [stay-rich'-eh-ee] Parsing (part of speech): veerb 　Mood—indicative 　Tense—future 　Voice—active 　Person—3rd person 　Number—singular 　Stem or root—from στηρίζω Concordance References: ⇒ Strong's #4741 stërizö	To make strong; to confirm; to stablish; to support. It means to make steadfast, firm, and solid. It means to be firmly set, as firmly as if one were set in reinforced concrete. It means to be immovable. ### Practical Application God Himself uses the believer's sufferings to establish the believer. God is able to attach us to Himself to such a degree that we will be immov-

ENGLISH WORD	GREEK WORD AND VERSE	THE WORD MEANS...
POSB REFERENCE (1 Pt.5:10) Note 2, point 2	⇒ NIV #5114 stërizö ⇒ NASB #4741 stërizö **1 Peter 5:10** But the God of all grace, who hath called us unto his eternal glory by Christ Jesus, after that ye have suffered a while, make you perfect, **stablish**, strengthen, settle you. [KJV] And after you have suffered for a little while, the God of all grace, who called you to His eternal glory in Christ, will Himself perfect, **confirm**, strengthen and establish you. [NASB] And the God of all grace, who called you to his eternal glory in Christ, after you have suffered a little while, will himself restore you and **make** you **strong**, firm and steadfast. [NIV] But may the God of all grace, who called us to His eternal glory by Christ Jesus, after you have suffered a while, perfect, **establish**, strengthen, and settle *you*. [NKJV] In his kindness God called you to his eternal glory by means of Jesus Christ. After you have suffered a little while, he will restore you, **support**, and strengthen you, and he will place you on a firm foundation. [NLT] ὁ δὲ Θεὸς πάσης χάριτος, ὁ καλέσας ὑμᾶς εἰς τὴν αἰώνιον αὐτοῦ δόξαν ἐν Χριστῷ Ἰησοῦ, ὀλίγον παθόντας αὐτὸς καταρτίσει ὑμᾶς, **στηρίξει**, σθενώσαι, θεμελιώσαι. [GNS] Ὁ δὲ θεὸς πάσης χάριτος, ὁ καλέσας ὑμᾶς εἰς τὴν αἰώνιον αὐτοῦ δόξαν ἐν Χριστῷ [Ἰησοῦ], ὀλίγον παθόντας αὐτὸς καταρτίσει, **στηρίξει**, σθενώσει, θεμελιώσει. [GNT]	able, no matter how severe the attack of temptation or suffering. But remember our duty: we must resist the devil and resist him steadfastly (1 Peter 5:8). The promise is clear: if we resist the devil and draw near God, He will draw near us (James 4:7-8).

#3727
Stablish
 	
Stablish–KJV
Strengthen–NASB
Stand firm–NIV
Establish–NKJV
Take courage–NLT
 	
POSB REFERENCE
(James 5:7-9; esp. v.8) Note 2, point 1
	στηρίξατε τὰς καρδίας = stërixate tas kardias
	Pronunciation: [stay-rid'-zah-teh tas kar-dee'-ahs]
	Parsing *stërixate* (part of speech): verb
	    Mood—imperative
	    Tense—aorist
	    Voice—active
	    Person—2nd person
	    Number—plural
	    Stem or root— from στηρίζω
	Parsing *kardias* (part of speech): noun
	    Case—accusative
	    Gender—feminine
	    Number—plural
	    Stem or root—from καρδία ας
	Concordance References:
	⇒ Strong's #2588+3588+4741 kardia ho stërizo
	⇒ NIV #2840+3836+5114 kardia ho stërizo [stand firm]
	⇒ NASB #2588+3588+4741 kardia ho stërizo
	
	James 5:8
	Be ye also patient; **stablish** your hearts: for the coming of the Lord draweth nigh. [KJV]
	You too be patient; **strengthen** your hearts, for the coming of the Lord is at hand. [NASB]
	You too, be patient and **stand firm**, because the Lord's coming is near. [NIV]
	You also be patient. **Establish** your hearts, for the coming of the Lord is at hand. [NKJV]
	You, too, must be patient. And **take courage**, for the coming of the Lord is near. [NLT]
	μακροθυμήσατε καὶ ὑμεῖς, **στηρίξατε τὰς καρδίας** ὑμῶν, ὅτι ἡ παρουσία τοῦ Κυρίου ἤγγικε. [GNS]
	μακροθυμήσατε καὶ ὑμεῖς, **στηρίξατε τὰς καρδίας** ὑμῶν, ὅτι ἡ παρουσία τοῦ κυρίου ἤγγικεν. [GNT]
		To stand firm; to stablish; to strengthen; to take courage; to stand firm in one's mind, his inner self, his heart.
		
		Practical Application
		Believers must "stablish" (*stërixate*) their hearts. The word means to set upon; to fix upon; to make fast (W.E. Vine. *Expository Dictionary of New Testament Words*, p.41). We must set our hearts upon the Lord's coming, for His coming is near. The idea is that it is drawing ever so close and can happen at any moment. We must focus and set our hearts upon His return—be looking for it every day just as the farmer looks for his great day of harvest. Looking for the great day of redemption—for the Lord's glorious return—will stir us to combat temptation and trial step by step. It will stir us to patiently endure no matter the situation, and by patiently enduring we shall gain the victory over all—no matter how bad the situation may be.

#3728 **Stablisheth**	βεβαιῶν = bebaiön Pronunciation: [beb-ah-yi'-own] Parsing (part of speech): verb Mood—participle	To establish; to confirm; to sustain; to keep strong; to strengthen, to make firm, steadfast, and constant.

ENGLISH WORD	GREEK WORD AND VERSE	THE WORD MEANS...
Stablisheth–KJV Establishes–NASB Makes...stand firm–NIV Establishes–NKJV Stand firm–NLT **POSB REFERENCE** (2 Cor.1:21-22; esp. v.21) Note 5	Tense—present Voice—active Case—nominative Gender—masculine Number—singular Stem or root—from βεβαιόω Concordance References: ⇒ Strong's #950 bebaioö ⇒ NIV #1011 bebaioö ⇒ NASB #950 bebaioö **2 Cor. 1:21** Now he which **stablisheth** us with you in Christ, and hath anointed us, is God; [KJV] Now He who **establishes** us with you in Christ and anointed us is God, [NASB] Now it is God who **makes** both us and you **stand firm** in Christ. He anointed us, [NIV] Now He who **establishes** us with you in Christ and has anointed us *is* God, [NKJV] It is God who gives us, along with you, the ability to **stand firm** for Christ. He has commissioned us, [NLT] ὁ δὲ **βεβαιῶν** ἡμᾶς σὺν ὑμῖν εἰς Χριστὸν, καὶ χρίσας ἡμᾶς, Θεός, [GNS] ὁ δὲ **βεβαιῶν** ἡμᾶς σὺν ὑμῖν εἰς Χριστὸν καὶ χρίσας ἡμᾶς θεός, [GNT]	**Practical Application** The word "us" refers primarily to Paul. He is comparing himself with the Corinthians, and he is also including those who oppose him. In no uncertain terms, Paul says that the same God who has worked in the Corinthians has also worked in him.
#3729 **Staggered** **Staggered–KJV** Waver–NASB Waver–NIV Waver–NKJV Wavered–NLT **POSB REFERENCE** (Rom.4:18-22; esp. v.20) Note 2, point 1b	διεκρίθη = *diekrithē* Pronunciation: [dee-ek-ree'-thay] Parsing (part of speech): verb Mood—indicative Tense—aorist Voice—passive Person—3rd person Number—singular Stem or root—from διακρίνω Concordance References: ⇒ Strong's #1252 diakrinö ⇒ NIV #1359 diakrinö ⇒ NASB #1252 diakrinö **Romans 4:20** He **staggered** not at the promise of God through unbelief; but was strong in faith, giving glory to God; [KJV] Yet, with respect to the promise of God, he did not **waver** in unbelief, but grew strong in faith, giving glory to God, [NASB] Yet he did not **waver** through unbelief regarding the promise of God, but was strengthened in his faith and gave glory to God, [NIV] He did not **waver** at the promise of God through unbelief, but was strengthened in faith, giving glory to God, [NKJV] Abraham never **wavered** in believing God's promise. In fact, his faith grew stronger, and in this he brought glory to God. [NLT] εἰς δὲ τὴν ἐπαγγελίαν τοῦ Θεοῦ οὐ **διεκρίθη** τῇ ἀπιστίᾳ, ἀλλ' ἐνεδυναμώθη τῇ πίστει, δοὺς δόξαν τῷ Θεῷ, [GNS] εἰς δὲ τὴν ἐπαγγελίαν τοῦ θεοῦ οὐ **διεκρίθη** τῇ ἀπιστίᾳ ἀλλ' ἐνεδυναμώθη τῇ πίστει, δοὺς δόξαν τῷ θεῷ [GNT]	To waver; to stagger; to fluctuate; to take issue; to doubt. **Practical Application** Abraham was strong in faith—not staggering at the promise of God. Instead he walked about glorifying and praising God for His glorious promise. The word "staggered" (*diakrino*) means he did not waver, did not vacillate, did not question God's ability to fulfill His promise.
#3730 **Stand Fast** **Stand fast–KJV** Stand firm–NASB Stand firm–NIV **Stand fast–NKJV** Stay true–NLT	στήκετε = *stēkete* Pronunciation: [stay'-keh-teh] Parsing (part of speech): verb Mood—imperative Tense—present Voice—active Person—2nd person Number—plural Stem or root—from στήκω	To stand firm; to stand fast; to persist; to persevere; to stay true. **Practical Application** It is the picture of a soldier standing fast against the onslaught of an enemy. He refuses to give ground no matter the pressure and strength of attack. He does not flinch; he is not unstable,

ENGLISH WORD	GREEK WORD AND VERSE	THE WORD MEANS...
POSB REFERENCE (Philip.4:1) Note 1	Concordance References: ⇒ Strong's #4739 stëkö ⇒ NIV #5112 stëkö ⇒ NASB #4739 stëkö **Philip. 4:1** Therefore, my brethren dearly beloved and longed for, my joy and crown, so **stand fast** in the Lord, my dearly beloved. [KJV] Therefore, my beloved brethren whom I long to see, my joy and crown, so **stand firm** in the Lord, my beloved. [NASB] Therefore, my brothers, you whom I love and long for, my joy and crown, that is how you should **stand firm** in the Lord, dear friends! [NIV] Therefore, my beloved and longed-for brethren, my joy and crown, so **stand fast** in the Lord, beloved. [NKJV] Dear brothers and sisters, I love you and long to see you, for you are my joy and the reward for my work. So please **stay true** to the Lord, my dear friends. [NLT] Ὥστε, ἀδελφοί μου ἀγαπητοὶ καὶ ἐπιπόθητοι, χαρὰ καὶ στέφανός μου, οὕτω **στήκετε** ἐν Κυρίῳ, ἀγαπητοί. [GNS] Ὥστε, ἀδελφοί μου ἀγαπητοὶ καὶ ἐπιπόθητοι, χαρὰ καὶ στέφανός μου, οὕτως **στήκετε** ἐν κυρίῳ, ἀγαπητοί. [GNT]	and he is never defeated. The Christian believer is to stand fast... • no matter how great the trial. • no matter the pressure of the temptation. • no matter the influence, offer, and allurement made by others. But how does a believer stand fast? When the temptation to surrender is so appealing and the trial is so terrible, where can the believer find the strength to stand fast? There are two places. 1. There is the believer's source of strength: the Lord Himself. 2. There is the encouragement: a minister or brother who loves and cares about his fellow-believer's standing fast.

#3731 **Stand Firm**
 	
Stedfast–KJV
Steadfast–NASB
Stand firm–NIV
Steadfast–NKJV
Strong–NLT
 	
POSB REFERENCE (1 Cor.15:58) Note 6, point 2
	ἑδραῖοι γίνεσθε = *hedraioi ginesthe*
	Pronunciation: [hed-rah'-ee-yoy gin-es-theh]
	Parsing *hedraioi* (part of speech): adjective
	    Case—nominative
	    Gender—masculine
	    Number—plural
	    Stem or root—from ἑδραῖος, α, ον
	Concordance References:
	⇒ Strong's #1096+1476 ginomai hedraios
	⇒ NIV #1181+1612 ginomai hedraios [stand firm]
	⇒ NASB #1096+1476 ginomai hedraios
	
	1 Cor. 15:58
	Therefore, my beloved brethren, be ye **stedfast**, unmovable, always abounding in the work of the Lord, forasmuch as ye know that your labour is not in vain in the Lord. [KJV]
	Therefore, my beloved brethren, be **steadfast**, immovable, always abounding in the work of the Lord, knowing that your toil is not in vain in the Lord. [NASB]
	Therefore, my dear brothers, **stand firm**. Let nothing move you. Always give yourselves fully to the work of the Lord, because you know that your labor in the Lord is not in vain. [NIV]
	Therefore, my beloved brethren, be **steadfast**, immovable, always abounding in the work of the Lord, knowing that your labor is not in vain in the Lord. [NKJV]
	So, my dear brothers and sisters, be **strong** and steady, always enthusiastic about the Lord's work, for you know that nothing you do for the Lord is ever useless. [NLT]
	ὥστε, ἀδελφοί μου ἀγαπητοί, **ἑδραῖοι γίνεσθε**, ἀμετακίνητοι, περισσεύοντες ἐν τῷ ἔργῳ τοῦ Κυρίου πάντοτε, εἰδότες ὅτι ὁ κόπος ὑμῶν οὐκ ἔστι κενὸς ἐν Κυρίῳ. [GNS]
	Ὥστε, ἀδελφοί μου ἀγαπητοί, **ἑδραῖοι γίνεσθε**, ἀμετακίνητοι, περισσεύοντες ἐν τῷ ἔργῳ τοῦ κυρίου πάντοτε, εἰδότες ὅτι ὁ κόπος ὑμῶν οὐκ ἔστιν κενὸς ἐν κυρίῳ. [GNT]
		To stand firm; to be firm, fixed, determined, purposed, faithful.
		
		Practical Application
		The believer is to stand firm and fixed in his belief and labor for the Lord, determined to live for the Lord and to carry out his purpose for the Lord. The believer is to be steadfast and unmovable. Why? Because he has such a glorious hope: the hope of being resurrected and given an incorruptible and immortal body. The hope of this glorious fact should stir the believer to stand firm, letting nothing move him in serving the Lord Jesus Christ.

#3732 **Stand Firm**	στήκετε = *stëkete*
	Pronunciation: [stay'-keh-teh]
	Parsing (part of speech): verb
	    Mood—imperative
	    Tense—present
		To stand firm; to stand fast; to persist; to persevere; to stay true.

ENGLISH WORD	GREEK WORD AND VERSE	THE WORD MEANS...
Stand fast–KJV **Stand firm–NASB** **Stand firm–NIV** Stand fast–NKJV Stay true–NLT **POSB REFERENCE** (Philip.4:1) Note 1	Voice—active Person—2nd person Number—plural Stem or root—from στήκω Concordance References: ⇒ Strong's #4739 stëkö ⇒ NIV #5112 stëkö ⇒ NASB #4739 stëkö **Philip. 4:1** Therefore, my brethren dearly beloved and longed for, my joy and crown, so **stand fast** in the Lord, my dearly beloved. [KJV] Therefore, my beloved brethren whom I long to see, my joy and crown, so **stand firm** in the Lord, my beloved. [NASB] Therefore, my brothers, you whom I love and long for, my joy and crown, that is how you should **stand firm** in the Lord, dear friends! [NIV] Therefore, my beloved and longed-for brethren, my joy and crown, so **stand fast** in the Lord, beloved. [NKJV] Dear brothers and sisters, I love you and long to see you, for you are my joy and the reward for my work. So please **stay true** to the Lord, my dear friends. [NLT] Ὥστε, ἀδελφοί μου ἀγαπητοὶ καὶ ἐπιπόθητοι, χαρὰ καὶ στέφανός μου, οὕτω **στήκετε** ἐν Κυρίῳ, ἀγαπητοί. [GNS] Ὥστε, ἀδελφοί μου ἀγαπητοὶ καὶ ἐπιπόθητοι, χαρὰ καὶ στέφανός μου, οὕτως **στήκετε** ἐν κυρίῳ, ἀγαπητοί. [GNT]	**Practical Application** It is the picture of a soldier standing firm against the onslaught of an enemy. He refuses to give ground no matter the pressure and strength of attack. He does not flinch; he is not unstable, and he is never defeated. The Christian believer is to stand firm... • no matter how great the trial. • no matter the pressure of the temptation. • no matter the influence, offer, and allurement made by others. But how does a believer stand firm? When the temptation to surrender is so appealing and the trial is so terrible, where can the believer find the strength to stand firm? There are two places. 1. There is the believer's source of strength: the Lord Himself. 2. There is the encouragement: a minister or brother who loves and cares about his fellow-believer's standing firm.

**#3733
Stand Firm**
 	
Stablish–KJV
Strengthen–NASB
Stand firm–NIV
Establish–NKJV
Take courage–NLT
 	
**POSB
REFERENCE**
(James 5:7-9; esp. v.8)
Note 2, point 1
	στηρίξατε τὰς καρδίας = stërixate tas kardias
	Pronunciation: [stay-rid'-zah-teh tas kar-dee'-ahs]
	Parsing *stërixate* (part of speech): verb
	    Mood—imperative
	    Tense—aorist
	    Voice—active
	    Person—2nd person
	    Number—plural
	    Stem or root— from στηρίζω
	Parsing *kardias* (part of speech): noun
	    Case—accusative
	    Gender—feminine
	    Number—plural
	    Stem or root—from καρδία, ας
	Concordance References:
	⇒ Strong's #2588+3588+4741 kardia ho stërizo
	⇒ NIV #2840+3836+5114 kardia ho stërizo [stand firm]
	⇒ NASB #2588+3588+4741 kardia ho stërizo
	
	James 5:8
	Be ye also patient; **stablish** your hearts: for the coming of the Lord draweth nigh. [KJV]
	You too be patient; **strengthen** your hearts, for the coming of the Lord is at hand. [NASB]
	You too, be patient and **stand firm**, because the Lord's coming is near. [NIV]
	You also be patient. **Establish** your hearts, for the coming of the Lord is at hand. [NKJV]
	You, too, must be patient. And **take courage**, for the coming of the Lord is near. [NLT]
	μακροθυμήσατε καὶ ὑμεῖς, **στηρίξατε τὰς καρδίας** ὑμῶν, ὅτι ἡ παρουσία τοῦ Κυρίου ἤγγικε. [GNS]
	μακροθυμήσατε καὶ ὑμεῖς, **στηρίξατε τὰς καρδίας** ὑμῶν, ὅτι ἡ παρουσία τοῦ κυρίου ἤγγικεν. [GNT]
		To stand firm; to stablish; to strengthen; to take courage; to stand firm in one's mind, his inner self, his heart.
		
		Practical Application
		Believers must "stand firm" (*stërixate*) their hearts. The word means to set upon; to fix upon; to make fast (W.E. Vine. *Expository Dictionary of New Testament Words*, p.41). We must set our hearts upon the Lord's coming, for His coming is near. The idea is that it is drawing ever so close and can happen at any moment. We must focus and set our hearts upon His return—be looking for it every day just as the farmer looks for his great day of harvest. Looking for the great day of redemption—for the Lord's glorious return—will stir us to combat temptation and trial step by step. It will stir us to patiently endure no matter the situation, and by patiently enduring we shall gain the victory over all—no matter how bad the situation may be.

**#3734
Stand Firm,
Makes–
Stand Firm**
	βεβαιῶν = bebaiön
	Pronunciation: [beb-ah-yi'-own]
	Parsing (part of speech): verb
	    Mood—participle
	    Tense—present
		To establish; to confirm; to sustain; to keep strong; to strengthen, to make firm, steadfast, and constant.

ENGLISH WORD	GREEK WORD AND VERSE	THE WORD MEANS...
Stablisheth–KJV Establishes–NASB **Makes...stand firm–NIV** Establishes–NKJV **Stand firm–NLT** **POSB REFERENCE** (2 Cor.1:21-22; esp. v.21) Note 5	Voice—active Case—nominative Gender—masculine Number—singular Stem or root—from βεβαιόω Concordance References: ⇒ Strong's #950 bebaioö ⇒ NIV #1011 bebaioö ⇒ NASB #950 bebaioö **2 Cor. 1:21** Now he which **stablisheth** us with you in Christ, and hath anointed us, is God; [KJV] Now He who **establishes** us with you in Christ and anointed us is God, [NASB] Now it is God who **makes** both us and you **stand firm** in Christ. He anointed us, [NIV] Now He who **establishes** us with you in Christ and has anointed us *is* God, [NKJV] It is God who gives us, along with you, the ability to **stand firm** for Christ. He has commissioned us, [NLT] ὁ δὲ **βεβαιῶν** ἡμᾶς σὺν ὑμῖν εἰς Χριστὸν, καὶ χρίσας ἡμᾶς, Θεός, [GNS] ὁ δὲ **βεβαιῶν** ἡμᾶς σὺν ὑμῖν εἰς Χριστὸν καὶ χρίσας ἡμᾶς θεός, [GNT]	**Practical Application** The word "us" refers primarily to Paul. He is comparing himself with the Corinthians, and he is also including those who oppose him. In no uncertain terms, Paul says that the same God who has worked in the Corinthians has also worked in him.
#3735 **Stand In It** Grounded–KJV Established–NASB Established–NIV Grounded–NKJV **Stand in it–NLT** **POSB REFERENCE** (Col.1:23) Note 4, point 1	*τεθεμελιωμένοι* = *tethemeliömenoi* Pronunciation: [teh-them-el-ee-o'-mehn-oy] Parsing (part of speech): verb Mood—participle Tense—perfect Voice—passive Case—nominative Gender—masculine Person—2nd person Number—plural Stem or root—from θεμελιόω Concordance References: ⇒ Strong's #2311 themelioö ⇒ NIV #2530 themelioö ⇒ NASB #2311 themelioö **Col. 1:23** If ye continue in the faith **grounded** and settled, and be not moved away from the hope of the gospel, which ye have heard, and which was preached to every creature which is under heaven; whereof I Paul am made a minister; [KJV] If indeed you continue in the faith firmly **established** and steadfast, and not moved away from the hope of the gospel that you have heard, which was proclaimed in all creation under heaven, and of which I, Paul, was made a minister. [NASB] If you continue in your faith, **established** and firm, not moved from the hope held out in the gospel. This is the gospel that you heard and that has been proclaimed to every creature under heaven, and of which I, Paul, have become a servant. [NIV] If indeed you continue in the faith, **grounded** and steadfast, and are not moved away from the hope of the gospel which you heard, which was preached to every creature under heaven, of which I, Paul, became a minister. [NKJV] But you must continue to believe this truth and **stand in it** firmly. Don't drift away from the assurance you received when you heard the Good News. The Good News has been preached all over the world, and I, Paul, have been appointed by God to proclaim it. [NLT] εἴγε ἐπιμένετε τῇ πίστει **τεθεμελιωμένοι** καὶ ἑδραῖοι, καὶ μὴ μετακινούμενοι ἀπὸ τῆς ἐλπίδος τοῦ εὐαγγελίου οὗ ἠκούσατε, τοῦ κηρυχθέντος ἐν πάσῃ τῇ κτίσει τῇ ὑπὸ τὸν οὐρανόν, οὗ ἐγενόμην ἐγὼ Παῦλος	To be established; to be grounded; to be rooted; to make strong; to be fixed. It means to be grounded in Christ like the firm, solid foundation of a building. **Practical Application** This is the word that pictures the foundation of a building, the solid foundation that gives the greatest stability possible to a building. The believer must be so grounded in Christ that he can withstand the severest storms of life.

ENGLISH WORD	GREEK WORD AND VERSE	THE WORD MEANS...
	διάκονος. [GNS] εἴ γε ἐπιμένετε τῇ πίστει **τεθεμελιωμένοι** καὶ ἑδραῖοι καὶ μὴ μετακινούμενοι ἀπὸ τῆς ἐλπίδος τοῦ εὐαγγελίου οὗ ἠκούσατε, τοῦ κηρυχθέντος ἐν πάσῃ κτίσει τῇ ὑπὸ τὸν οὐρανόν, οὗ ἐγενόμην ἐγὼ Παῦλος διάκονος. [GNT]	
#3736 **Stand On The Side Of** Cleave–KJV Cling–NASB Cling–NIV Cling–NKJV **Stand on the side of–NLT** **POSB REFERENCE** (Rom.12:9-10; esp. v.9) Note 1, point 2	κολλώμενοι = kollōmenoi Pronunciation: [kol-lo'-mehn-oy] Parsing (part of speech): verb 　　Mood—participle (imperative sense) 　　Tense—present 　　Voice—passive 　　Case—nominative 　　Gender—masculine 　　Person—2nd person 　　Number—plural 　　Stem or root—from κολλάομαι Concordance References: 　⇒ Strong's #2853 kollaō 　⇒ NIV #3140 kollaō 　⇒ NASB #2853 kollaō **Romans 12:9** 　　Let love be without dissimulation. Abhor that which is evil; **cleave** to that which is good. [KJV] 　　Let love be without hypocrisy. Abhor what is evil; **cling** to what is good. [NASB] 　　Love must be sincere. Hate what is evil; **cling** to what is good. [NIV] 　　Let love be without hypocrisy. Abhor what is evil. **Cling** to what is good. [NKJV] 　　Don't just pretend that you love others. Really love them. Hate what is wrong. **Stand on the side of** the good. [NLT] 　　Ἡ ἀγάπη ἀνυπόκριτος. ἀποστυγοῦντες τὸ πονηρόν, **κολλώμενοι** τῷ ἀγαθῷ. [GNS] 　　Ἡ ἀγάπη ἀνυπόκριτος. ἀποστυγοῦντες τὸ Πονηρόν, **κολλώμενοι** τῷ ἀγαθῷ, [GNT]	To cling; to cleave; to stand on the side of; to join or fasten together, to attach or glue together. **Practical Application** 　　The believer is to love by standing on the side of the good. The believer is to desire only the very best—all the good possible—for people. He is to cleave to the good and to work for everyone to know and experience the good. The believer shows that he truly loves people by holding fast and working for the good.
#3737 **Stand Up– Stand Forth– Stand, Come And** **Stand forth–KJV** Rise and come–NASB **Stand up–NIV** Step forward–NKJV **Come and stand– NLT** **POSB REFERENCE** (Mk.3:3) Note 2	Ἔγειρε = Egeire Pronunciation: [eg-i'-reh] Parsing (part of speech): verb 　　Mood—imperative 　　Tense—present 　　Voice—active 　　Person—2nd person 　　Number—singular 　　Stem or root—from ἐγείρω Concordance References: 　⇒ Strong's #1453 egeirō 　⇒ NIV #1586 egeirō 　⇒ NASB #1453 egeirō **Mark 3:3** 　　And he saith unto the man which had the withered hand, **Stand forth**. [KJV] 　　And He said to the man with the withered hand, "**Rise and come** forward!" [NASB] 　　Jesus said to the man with the shriveled hand, "**Stand up** in front of everyone." [NIV] 　　And He said to the man who had the withered hand, "**Step forward**." [NKJV] 　　Jesus said to the man, "**Come and stand** in front of everyone." [NLT] 　　καὶ λέγει τῷ ἀνθρώπῳ τῷ ἐξηραμμένην ἔχοντι, τὴν χεῖρα Ἔγειρε εἰς τὸ μέσον. [GNS] 　　καὶ λέγει τῷ ἀνθρώπῳ τῷ τὴν ξηρὰν χεῖρα ἔχοντι, Ἔγειρε εἰς τὸ μέσον. [GNT]	To stand up; to rise and come; to get up. **Practical Application** 　　The words "stand up" (*egeirai eis to meson*) actually say, "Rise up, stand up in the midst." Jesus was calling for the man's will—his willingness to do exactly what the Messiah was saying. The man had to want help enough to be willing to stand before the audience and before the scornful religionists. By such a stand he would be confessing his faith in Jesus and in His power to save and heal.
#3738 **Stands Firm**	ὑπομείνας = upomeinas Pronunciation: [hoop-om-en'-ahs] Parsing (part of speech): verb 　　Mood—participle	To stand firm; to endure; to bear up under suffering, to stand firm, to be courageous in suffering, to persevere and endure patiently—but actively, not passively.

ENGLISH WORD	GREEK WORD AND VERSE	THE WORD MEANS...
Endure–KJV Endures–NASB **Stands firm–NIV** Endures–NKJV Endure–NLT **POSB REFERENCE** (Mk.13:13) Note 9, point 1 **See also POSB REF:** (Mt.24:13) Note 9	Tense—aorist Voice—active Case—nominative Gender—masculine Number—singular Stem or root—from ὑπομένω Concordance References: ⇒ Strong's #5278 hupomenō ⇒ NIV #5702 hupomenō ⇒ NASB #5278 hupomenō **Mark 13:13** And ye shall be hated of all men for my name's sake: but he that shall **endure** unto the end, the same shall be saved. [KJV] "And you will be hated by all on account of My name, but the one who **endures** to the end, he shall be saved. [NASB] All men will hate you because of me, but he who **stands firm** to the end will be saved. [NIV] And you will be hated by all for My name's sake. But he who **endures** to the end shall be saved. [KJV] And everyone will hate you because of your allegiance to me. But those who **endure** to the end will be saved. [NLT] καὶ ἔσεσθε μισούμενοι ὑπὸ πάντων διὰ τὸ ὄνομά μου. ὁ δὲ **ὑπομείνας** εἰς τέλος, οὗτος σωθήσεται. [GNS] καὶ ἔσεσθε μισούμενοι ὑπὸ πάντων διὰ τὸ ὄνομά μου. ὁ δὲ **ὑπομείνας** εἰς τέλος οὗτος σωθήσεται. [GNT]	**Practical Application** It is standing, actively bearing intense suffering. The believer is now called upon and will be called upon to stand firm through all forms of persecution and abuse, even if it leads to inhuman torture and death.
#3739 Stared At Looked on–KJV Fixing his gaze upon–NASB **Stared at–NIV** Observed–NKJV **Stared at–NLT** **POSB REFERENCE** (Acts 10:1-8; esp. v.4) Note 1, point 3c	ἀτενίσας = atenisas Pronunciation: [ah-ten-i'-sahs] Parsing (part of speech): verb Mood—participle Tense—aorist Voice—active Case—nominative Gender—masculine Number—singular Stem or root—from ἀτενίζω Concordance References: ⇒ Strong's #816 atenizō ⇒ NIV #867 atenizō ⇒ NASB #816 atenizō **Acts 10:4** And when he **looked on** him, he was afraid, and said, What is it, Lord? And he said unto him, Thy prayers and thine alms are come up for a memorial before God. [KJV] And **fixing his gaze upon** him and being much alarmed, he said, "What is it, Lord?" And he said to him, "Your prayers and alms have ascended as a memorial before God. [NASB] Cornelius **stared at** him in fear. "What is it, Lord?" he asked. The angel answered, "Your prayers and gifts to the poor have come up as a memorial offering before God. [NIV] And when he **observed** him, he was afraid, and said, "What is it, lord?" So he said to him, "Your prayers and your alms have come up for a memorial before God. [NKJV] Cornelius **stared at** him in terror. "What is it, sir?" he asked the angel. And the angel replied, "Your prayers and gifts to the poor have not gone unnoticed by God! [NLT] ὁ δὲ **ἀτενίσας** αὐτῷ καὶ ἔμφοβος γενόμενος εἶπε, Τί ἐστι, Κύριε; εἶπε δὲ αὐτῷ, Αἱ προσευχαί σου καὶ αἱ τε ἐλεημοσύναι σου ἀνέβησαν εἰς μνημόσυνον ἐνώπιον τοῦ Θεοῦ. [GNS] ὁ δὲ **ἀτενίσας** αὐτῷ καὶ ἔμφοβος γενόμενος εἶπεν, Τί ἐστιν, κύριε; εἶπεν δὲ αὐτῷ, Αἱ προσευχαί σου καὶ αἱ ἐλεημοσύναι σου ἀνέβησαν εἰς μνημόσυνον ἔμπροσθεν τοῦ Θεοῦ. [GNT]	To stare at; to look on; to fix one's gaze upon; to look straight at. **Practical Application** Cornelius "stared at," that is, fastening his eyes, gazing, focusing; he was startled, frightened.

ENGLISH WORD	GREEK WORD AND VERSE	THE WORD MEANS...

#3740
Stared At Him Intently
 	
Were fastened on Him–KJV
Were fixed upon Him–NASB
Were fastened on Him–NIV
Were fixed on Him–NKJV
Stared at him intently–NLT
 	
POSB REFERENCE
(Lk.4:20-21; esp. v.20)
Note 3
	ἦσαν ἀτενίζοντες αὐτῷ = ësan atenizontes autö
	Pronunciation: [ay-san at-en-id'-zon-tes au-tow]
	Parsing *atenizontes* (part of speech): verb
	    Mood—participle
	    Tense—present
	    Voice—active
	    Case—nominative
	    Gender—masculine
	    Number—plural
	    Stem or root—from ἀτενίζω
	Concordance References:
	  ⇒ Strong's #1488 eimi + 816 atenizo + 846 autos
	  ⇒ NIV #1639 eimi [were] + 867 atenizö [fastened] + 899 autos [Him]
	  ⇒ NASB #1488 eimi + 816 atenizo + 846 autos
	
	Luke 4:20
	And he closed the book, and he gave it again to the minister, and sat down. And the eyes of all them that were in the synagogue **were fastened on him**. [KJV]
	And He closed the book, and gave it back to the attendant, and sat down; and the eyes of all in the synagogue **were fixed upon Him**. [NASB]
	Then he rolled up the scroll, gave it back to the attendant and sat down. The eyes of everyone in the synagogue **were fastened on him**, [NIV]
	Then He closed the book, and gave it back to the attendant and sat down. And the eyes of all who were in the synagogue **were fixed on Him**. [NKJV]
	He rolled up the scroll, handed it back to the attendant, and sat down. Everyone in the synagogue **stared at him intently**. [NLT]
	καὶ πτύξας τὸ βιβλίον, ἀποδοὺς τῷ ὑπηρέτῃ, ἐκάθισε· καὶ πάντων ἐν τῇ συναγωγῇ οἱ ὀφθαλμοὶ **ἦσαν ἀτενίζοντες αὐτῷ**· [GNS]
	καὶ πτύξας τὸ βιβλίον ἀποδοὺς τῷ ὑπηρέτῃ ἐκάθισεν· καὶ πάντων οἱ ὀφθαλμοὶ ἐν τῇ συναγωγῇ **ἦσαν ἀτενίζοντες αὐτῷ**. [GNT]
		Fixed, gazing, spellbound; to stare at intently.
		
		Practical Application
		Note the context of this Scripture: Jesus closed the book, handed it to the minister, and sat down. Sitting was the posture for preaching in the synagogue. All eyes "stared at him intently" (*ësan atenizontes autö*), a descriptive phrase meaning fixed, gazing, spellbound. They stared at Him in rapt attention; their eyes were locked upon Him eagerly waiting to see what He had to say.

#3741
Start
 	
Author–KJV
Author–NASB
Author–NIV
Author–NKJV
Start–NLT
 	
POSB REFERENCE
(Heb.12:2)
Note 3, point 1
	τὸν ἀρχηγὸν = ton archëgon
	Pronunciation: [ton ar-khay-gon']
	Parsing (part of speech): noun
	    Case—accusative
	    Gender—masculine
	    Number—singular
	    Stem or root—from ἀρχηγός, οῦ
	Concordance References:
	  ⇒ Strong's #3588 ho + 747 archëgos
	  ⇒ NIV #3836 ho + 795 archëgos [author]
	  ⇒ NASB #3588 ho + 747 archëgos
	
	Hebrews 12:2
	Looking unto Jesus the **author** and finisher of our faith; who for the joy that was set before him endured the cross, despising the shame, and is set down at the right hand of the throne of God. [KJV]
	Fixing our eyes on Jesus, the **author** and perfecter of faith, who for the joy set before Him endured the cross, despising the shame, and has sat down at the right hand of the throne of God. [NASB]
	Let us fix our eyes on Jesus, the **author** and perfecter of our faith, who for the joy set before him endured the cross, scorning its shame, and sat down at the right hand of the throne of God. [NIV]
	Looking unto Jesus, the **author** and finisher of our faith, who for the joy that was set before Him endured the cross, despising the shame, and has sat down at the right hand of the throne of God. [NKJV]
	We do this by keeping our eyes on Jesus, on whom our faith depends from **start** to finish. He was willing to die a shameful death on the cross because of the joy he knew would be his afterward. Now he is seated in the place of
		Author, leader, pioneer, pathfinder, founder, originator, a perfect leader. It means the one who blazes forth and cuts through something so that others may follow.
		
		Practical Application
		Jesus Christ participated in the race Himself; He actually ran the race of faith. In fact, He is the very Starter and Finisher of faith. The "start" (*ton archëgon*) means that He authored, began, originated, created, and gave birth to the Christian race.

ENGLISH WORD	GREEK WORD AND VERSE	THE WORD MEANS...
	er who walks disorderly and not according to the tradition which he received from us. [NKJV] And now, dear brothers and sisters, we give you this command with the authority of our Lord Jesus Christ: **Stay away** from any Christian who lives in idleness and doesn't follow the tradition of hard work we gave you. [NLT] Παραγγέλλομεν δὲ ὑμῖν, ἀδελφοί, ἐν ὀνόματι τοῦ Κυρίου ἡμῶν Ἰησοῦ Χριστοῦ, **στέλλεσθαι** ὑμᾶς ἀπὸ παντὸς ἀδελφοῦ ἀτάκτως περιπατοῦντος, καὶ μὴ κατὰ τὴν παράδοσιν ἣν παρέλαβε παρ' ἡμῶν· [GNS] Παραγγέλλομεν δὲ ὑμῖν, ἀδελφοί, ἐν ὀνόματι τοῦ κυρίου [ἡμῶν] Ἰησοῦ Χριστοῦ **στέλλεσθαι** ὑμᾶς ἀπὸ παντὸς ἀδελφοῦ ἀτάκτως περιπατοῦντος καὶ μὴ κατὰ τὴν παράδοσιν ἣν παρελάβοσαν παρ' ἡμῶν. [GNT]	and in an act of sacrificial commitment they gave away *all they had*. The result was catastrophic. They were now having to sponge off the other believers in order to survive. Their action had been most unwise—unwise because believers are to *live life* as it should be lived so long as they are upon earth. Believers are to set the example as to how life is to be lived, and work is certainly one of the duties of men. Therefore, all people believers are to set an example in work. They are to be the very best workmen possible. Quitting work and not working is disorderly behavior; it is totally unacceptable for a true believer. It is so unacceptable that believers are commanded to withdraw from nonworkers. ⇒ What does the Lord mean by "stay away" (*stellesthai*)? The word means to stay away from the idle worker; to have no fellowship with him. His behavior is not to be indulged or condoned. We are not to put our stamp of approval upon him, nor are we to run the risk of becoming identified with him. ⇒ Who are the idle? They are the idle, the slothful, the lazy. They are the persons who refuse to work or who shirk their work or are slack in their work.

#3746
Stay Away From The Love Of Money
 	
Without covetousness–KJV
Free from the love of money–NASB
Free from the love of money–NIV
Without covetousness–NKJV
Stay away from the love of money–NLT
 	
POSB REFERENCE
(Heb.13:5-6; esp. v.5)
Note 5, point 1
	Ἀφιλάργυρος = *Aphilarguros*
	Pronunciation: [af-il-ar'-goo-ros]
	Parsing (part of speech): adjective
	    Case—nominative
	    Gender—masculine
	    Number—singular
	    Stem or root—from ἀφιλάργυρος, ον
	Concordance References:
	⇒ Strong's #866 aphilarguros
	⇒ NIV #921 aphilarguros
	⇒ NASB #866 aphilarguros
	
	Hebrews 13:5
	Let your conversation be **without covetousness**; and be content with such things as ye have: for he hath said, I will never leave thee, nor forsake thee. [KJV]
	
	Let your character be **free from the love of money**, being content with what you have; for He Himself has said, "I will never desert you, nor will I ever forsake you," [NASB]
	
	Keep your lives **free from the love of money** and be content with what you have, because God has said, "Never will I leave you; never will I forsake you." [NIV]
	
	Let your conduct be **without covetousness**; be content with such things as you have. For He Himself has said, *"I will never leave you nor forsake you."* [NKJV]
	
	Stay away from the love of money; be satisfied with what you have. For God has said, "I will never fail you. I will never forsake you." [NLT]
	
	ἀφιλάργυρος ὁ τρόπος, ἀρκούμενοι τοῖς παροῦσιν· αὐτὸς γὰρ εἴρηκεν, Οὐ μή σε ἀνῶ, οὐδ' οὐ μήσε ἐγκαταλίπω. [GNS]
	
	Ἀφιλάργυρος ὁ τρόπος, ἀρκούμενοι τοῖς παροῦσιν. αὐτὸς γὰρ εἴρηκεν, Οὐ μή σε ἀνῶ οὐδ' οὐ μή σε ἐγκαταλίπω, [GNT]
		Covetousness; a love of money; avarice; greed. It means a lover of money or possessions. A person can love money, property, estates, houses, cars—anything on earth.
		
		Practical Application
		Note what it is that brings contentment:
		⇒ living life being free from the love of money.
		⇒ being satisfied with what one has.
		⇒ knowing God personally: experiencing His constant companionship and care, knowing that He never leaves or forsakes us.

#3747
Stay True
 	
Stand fast–KJV
Stand firm–NASB
	στήκετε = *stēkete*
	Pronunciation: [stay'-keh-teh]
	Parsing (part of speech): verb
	    Mood—imperative
	    Tense—present
	    Voice—active
		To stand firm; to stand fast; to persist; to persevere; to stay true.
		
		Practical Application
		It is the picture of a soldier standing fast

ENGLISH WORD	GREEK WORD AND VERSE	THE WORD MEANS...
Stand firm–NIV Stand fast–NKJV **Stay true–NLT** **POSB** **REFERENCE** (Philip.4:1) Note 1	Person—2nd person Number—plural Stem or root—from στήκω Concordance References: ⇒ Strong's #4739 stëkö ⇒ NIV #5112 stëkö ⇒ NASB #4739 stëköt **Philip. 4:1** Therefore, my brethren dearly beloved and longed for, my joy and crown, so **stand fast** in the Lord, my dearly beloved. [KJV] Therefore, my beloved brethren whom I long to see, my joy and crown, so **stand firm** in the Lord, my beloved. [NASB] Therefore, my brothers, you whom I love and long for, my joy and crown, that is how you should **stand firm** in the Lord, dear friends! [NIV] Therefore, my beloved and longed-for brethren, my joy and crown, so **stand fast** in the Lord, beloved. [NKJV] Dear brothers and sisters, I love you and long to see you, for you are my joy and the reward for my work. So please **stay true** to the Lord, my dear friends. [NLT] Ὥστε, ἀδελφοί μου ἀγαπητοὶ καὶ ἐπιπόθητοι, χαρὰ καὶ στέφανός μου, οὕτω **στήκετε** ἐν Κυρίῳ, ἀγαπητοί. [GNS] Ὥστε, ἀδελφοί μου ἀγαπητοὶ καὶ ἐπιπόθητοι, χαρὰ καὶ στέφανός μου, οὕτως **στήκετε** ἐν κυρίῳ, ἀγαπητοί. [GNT]	against the onslaught of an enemy. He refuses to give ground no matter the pressure and strength of attack. He does not flinch; he is not unstable, and he is never defeated. The Christian believer is to stay true... • no matter how great the trial. • no matter the pressure of the temptation. • no matter the influence, offer, and allurement made by others. But how does a believer stay true? When the temptation to surrender is so appealing and the trial is so terrible, where can the believer find the strength to stay true? There are two places. 1. There is the believer's source of strength: the Lord Himself. 2. There is the encouragement: a minister or brother who loves and cares about his fellow-believer's staying true.
#3748 **Stay True** Continue–KJV Persevere in–NASB Persevere in–NIV Continue–NKJV **Stay true–NLT** **POSB** **REFERENCE** (1 Tim.4:16) Note 12	ἐπίμενε = epimene Pronunciation: [ep-ee-men'-eh] Parsing (part of speech): verb Mood—imperative Tense—present Voice—active Person—2nd person Number—singular Stem or root—from ἐπιμένω Concordance References: ⇒ Strong's #1961 epimenö ⇒ NIV #2152 epimenö ⇒ NASB #1961 epimenö **1 Tim. 4:16** Take heed unto thyself, and unto the doctrine; **continue** in them: for in doing this thou shalt both save thyself, and them that hear thee. [KJV] Pay close attention to yourself and to your teaching; **persevere in** these things; for as you do this you will insure salvation both for yourself and for those who hear you. [NASB] Watch your life and doctrine closely. **Persevere in** them, because if you do, you will save both yourself and your hearers. [NIV] Take heed to yourself and to the doctrine. **Continue** in them, for in doing this you will save both yourself and those who hear you. [NKJV] Keep a close watch on yourself and on your teaching. **Stay true** to what is right, and God will save you and those who hear you. [NLT] ἔπεχε σεαυτῷ καὶ τῇ διδασκαλίᾳ. **ἐπίμενε** αὐτοῖς· τοῦτο γὰρ ποιῶν καὶ σεαυτὸν σώσεις καὶ τοὺς ἀκούοντάς σου. [GNS] ἔπεχε σεαυτῷ καὶ τῇ διδασκαλίᾳ, **ἐπίμενε** αὐτοῖς· τοῦτο γὰρ ποιῶν καὶ σεαυτὸν σώσεις καὶ τοὺς ἀκούοντάς σου. [GNT]	To continue; to persevere in; to stay true; to persist in; to remain; to keep on. The word "stay true" (epimene) means to "stay by them," "stick to them," "see them through" (A.T. Robertson. *Word Pictures in the New Testament*, Vol.4, p.582). **Practical Application** Note what he does. He continues in the instructions of the Word of God. Why? Because by continuing in them, he saves both himself and those who hear him.
#3749 **Stayed**	κατεῖχον = kateichon Pronunciation: [kat-ay'-chon] Parsing (part of speech): verb Mood—indicative	Tried to prevent; hinder; stop; hold back; restrain; to physically try to keep someone from leaving.

ENGLISH WORD	GREEK WORD AND VERSE	THE WORD MEANS...
POSB REFERENCE (Jn.1:38-39; esp. v.38) Note 2, point 2	Concordance References: ⇒ Strong's #4226 pou + 3306 meno ⇒ NIV #4544 pou [where] + 3531 menō [staying] ⇒ NASB #4226 pou + 3306 meno **John 1:38** Then Jesus turned, and saw them following, and saith unto them, What seek ye? They said unto him, Rabbi, (which is to say, being interpreted, Master,) **where dwellest** thou? [KJV] And Jesus turned, and beheld them following, and said to them, "What do you seek?" And they said to Him, "Rabbi (which translated means Teacher), **where** are You **staying**?" [NASB] Turning around, Jesus saw them following and asked, "What do you want?" They said, "Rabbi" (which means Teacher), "**where** are you **staying**?" [NIV] Then Jesus turned, and seeing them following, said to them, "What do you seek?" They said to Him, "Rabbi" (which is to say, when translated, Teacher), "**where** are You **staying**?" [NKJV] Jesus looked around and saw them following. "What do you want?" he asked them. They replied, "Rabbi" (which means Teacher), "**where** are you **staying**?" [NLT] Στραφεὶς δὲ ὁ Ἰησοῦς, καὶ θεασάμενος αὐτοὺς ἀκολουθοῦντας, λέγει αὐτοῖς, Τί ζητεῖτε; οἱ δὲ εἶπον αὐτῷ, Ῥαββί -- ὃ λέγεται ἑρμηνευόμενον, Διδάσκαλε -- , **ποῦ μένεις**; [GNS] στραφεὶς δὲ ὁ Ἰησοῦς καὶ θεασάμενος αὐτοὺς ἀκολουθοῦντας λέγει αὐτοῖς, Τί ζητεῖτε; οἱ δὲ εἶπον αὐτῷ, Ῥαββί (ὃ λέγεται μεθερμηνευόμενον Διδάσκαλε), **ποῦ μένεις** [GNT]	road. They were asking to join Him in the quiet of His home, to open and pour out their hearts to Him and for Him to become their teacher. They wanted Him to meet the crying need of their heart and to do such in the quiet confines of His dwelling.

#3753
Steadfast
 	
Settled–KJV
Steadfast–NASB
Firm–NIV
Steadfast–NKJV
Firmly–NLT
 	
POSB REFERENCE (Col.1:23) Note 4, point 1
	ἑδραῖοι = *hedraioi*
	Pronunciation: [ed-rah'-ee-oy]
	Parsing (part of speech): adjective
	   Case—nominative
	   Gender—masculine
	   Number—plural
	   Stem or root—from ἑδραῖος, α, ον
	Concordance References:
	⇒ Strong's #1476 hedraios
	⇒ NIV #1612 hedraios
	⇒ NASB #1476 hedraios
	
	Col. 1:23
	If ye continue in the faith grounded and **settled**, and be not moved away from the hope of the gospel, which ye have heard, and which was preached to every creature which is under heaven; whereof I Paul am made a minister; [KJV]
	If indeed you continue in the faith firmly established and **steadfast**, and not moved away from the hope of the gospel that you have heard, which was proclaimed in all creation under heaven, and of which I, Paul, was made a minister. [NASB]
	If you continue in your faith, established and **firm**, not moved from the hope held out in the gospel. This is the gospel that you heard and that has been proclaimed to every creature under heaven, and of which I, Paul, have become a servant. [NIV]
	If indeed you continue in the faith, grounded and **steadfast**, and are not moved away from the hope of the gospel which you heard, which was preached to every creature under heaven, of which I, Paul, became a minister. [NKJV]
	But you must continue to believe this truth and stand in it **firmly**. Don't drift away from the assurance you received when you heard the Good News. The Good News has been preached all over the world, and I, Paul,
		To be firm; to be settled; to be steadfast; to stand firm.
		
		Practical Application
		The believer must stand firm and continue on. He must be steadfast if he wishes to be presented perfect before God.

ENGLISH WORD	GREEK WORD AND VERSE	THE WORD MEANS...
	have been appointed by God to proclaim it. [NLT] εἴγε ἐπιμένετε τῇ πίστει τεθεμελιωμένοι καὶ **ἑδραῖοι**, καὶ μὴ μετακινούμενοι ἀπὸ τῆς ἐλπίδος τοῦ εὐαγγελίου οὗ ἠκούσατε, τοῦ κηρυχθέντος ἐν πάσῃ τῇ κτίσει τῇ ὑπὸ τὸν οὐρανόν, οὗ ἐγενόμην ἐγὼ Παῦλος διάκονος. [GNS] εἴ γε ἐπιμένετε τῇ πίστει τεθεμελιωμένοι καὶ **ἑδραῖοι** καὶ μὴ μετακινούμενοι ἀπὸ τῆς ἐλπίδος τοῦ εὐαγγελίου οὗ ἠκούσατε, τοῦ κηρυχθέντος ἐν πάσῃ κτίσει τῇ ὑπὸ τὸν οὐρανόν, οὗ ἐγενόμην ἐγὼ Παῦλος διάκονος. [GNT]	

#3754
Steadfast
 	
Settle–KJV
Establish–NASB
Steadfast–NIV
Settle–NKJV
Place you on a firm foundation–NLT
 	
POSB REFERENCE
(1 Pt.5:10)
Note 2, point 4
	θεμελιώσει = *themeliösei*
	Pronunciation: [them-el-ee-o'-seh-ee]
	Parsing (part of speech): verb
	    Mood—indicative
	    Tense—future
	    Voice—active
	    Person—3rd person
	    Number—singular
	    Stem or root—from θεμελιόω
	Concordance References:
	⇒ Strong's #2311 themelioö
	⇒ NIV #2530 themelioö
	⇒ NASB #2311 themelioö
	
	1 Peter 5:10
	But the God of all grace, who hath called us unto his eternal glory by Christ Jesus, after that ye have suffered a while, make you perfect, stablish, strengthen, **settle** you. [KJV]
	And after you have suffered for a little while, the God of all grace, who called you to His eternal glory in Christ, will Himself perfect, confirm, strengthen and **establish** you. [NASB]
	And the God of all grace, who called you to his eternal glory in Christ, after you have suffered a little while, will himself restore you and make you strong, firm and **steadfast**. [NIV]
	But may the God of all grace, who called us to His eternal glory by Christ Jesus, after you have suffered a while, perfect, establish, strengthen, and **settle** *you.* [NKJV]
	In his kindness God called you to his eternal glory by means of Jesus Christ. After you have suffered a little while, he will restore, support, and strengthen you, and he will **place you on a firm foundation**. [NLT]
	ὁ δὲ Θεὸς πάσης χάριτος, ὁ καλέσας ὑμᾶς εἰς τὴν αἰώνιον αὐτοῦ δόξαν ἐν Χριστῷ Ἰησοῦ, ὀλίγον παθόντας αὐτὸς καταρτίσει ὑμᾶς, στηρίξει, σθενώσαι, **θεμελιώσαι**. [GNS]
	Ὁ δὲ θεὸς πάσης χάριτος, ὁ καλέσας ὑμᾶς εἰς τὴν αἰώνιον αὐτοῦ δόξαν ἐν Χριστῷ [Ἰησοῦ], ὀλίγον παθόντας αὐτὸς καταρτίσει, στηρίξει, σθενώσει, **θεμελιώσει**. [GNT]
		To be steadfast; to settle; to establish; to place on a firm foundation; to secure as in a foundation; to ground with security.
		
		Practical Application
		God Himself will make us strong, firm and steadfast. God is able to make us secure through all the sufferings of life, no matter what they are. He is able to settle and secure our nerves, thoughts, and fears—all the uneasy and unnerving emotions that disturb us. God can settle us if we will only do one thing: resist the devil and draw near to Him.

#3755
Steadfastness– Stedfastness
 	
Stedfastness–KJV
Stability–NASB
Firm–NIV
Steadfastness–NKJV
Strong–NLT
 	
POSB REFERENCE
(Col.2:5)
Note 4
	στερέωμα = *stereöma*
	Pronunciation: [ster-eh'-o-mah]
	Parsing (part of speech): noun
	    Case—accusative
	    Gender—neuter
	    Number—singular
	    Stem or root—from στερέωμα, τος
	Concordance References:
	⇒ Strong's #4733 stereöma
	⇒ NIV #5106 stereöma
	⇒ NASB #4733 stereöma
	
	Col. 2:5
	For though I be absent in the flesh, yet am I with you in the spirit, joying and beholding your order, and the **stedfastness** of your faith in Christ. [KJV]
	For even though I am absent in body, nevertheless I am with you in spirit, rejoicing to see your good discipline
		To be firm, steadfast, stable, strong. It means to stand fast and persevere; to be immovable, steady, and unyielding; to never crack, give in, or back up.
		
		Practical Application
		A mature people maintain discipline—order and steadfastness.
		⇒ The word "orderly" (*taxin*) means to maintain military discipline, array, and arrangement; to hold a solid front (The Amplified New Testament); to hold the military line unbroken and intact (A.T. Robertson, *Word Pictures in the New Testament*, Vol.4, p.489).
		⇒ The word "steadfastness" (*stereöma*) is also a military word. A.T. Robertson says

ENGLISH WORD	GREEK WORD AND VERSE	THE WORD MEANS...

and the **stability** of your faith in Christ. [NASB]

   For though I am absent from you in body, I am present with you in spirit and delight to see how orderly you are and how **firm** your faith in Christ is. [NIV]

   For though I am absent in the flesh, yet I am with you in spirit, rejoicing to see your *good* order and the **steadfastness** of your faith in Christ. [NKJV]

   For though I am far away from you, my heart is with you. And I am very happy because you are living as you should and because of your **strong** faith in Christ. [NLT]

   εἰ γὰρ καὶ τῇ σαρκὶ ἄπειμι, ἀλλὰ τῷ πνεύματι σὺν ὑμῖν εἰμι, χαίρων καὶ βλέπων ὑμῶν τὴν τάξιν, καὶ τὸ **στερέωμα** τῆς εἰς Χριστὸν πίστεως ὑμῶν. [GNS]

   εἰ γὰρ καὶ τῇ σαρκὶ ἄπειμι, ἀλλὰ τῷ πνεύματι σὺν ὑμῖν εἰμι, χαίρων καὶ βλέπων ὑμῶν τὴν τάξιν καὶ τὸ **στερέωμα** τῆς εἰς Χριστὸν πίστεως ὑμῶν. [GNT]

that it is "the solid part of the line which can and does stand the attack" of the seduction.

   Note that the believers of the Colossian church were being attacked by false teaching even as Paul was writing to them. But they were responding like a victorious army. They were maintaining their discipline and holding their order and standing fast. Note also the importance of the minister's encouragement: Paul says that he was with them *in spirit*, joying and watching them gain the victory over the false teachers.

#3756
Steadfast–
Stedfast

Stedfast–KJV
Steadfast–NASB
Stand firm–NIV
Steadfast–NKJV
Strong–NLT

POSB
REFERENCE
(1 Cor.15:58)
Note 6, point 2

ἑδραῖοι γίνεσθε = *hedraioi ginesthe*
Pronunciation: [hed-rah'-ee-yoy gin-es-theh]
Parsing *hedraioi* (part of speech): adjective
   Case—nominative
   Gender—masculine
   Number—plural
   Stem or root—from ἑδραῖος, α, ον
Concordance References:
  ⇒ Strong's #1096+1476 ginomai hedraios
  ⇒ NIV #1181+1612 ginomai hedraios [stand firm]
  ⇒ NASB #1096+1476 ginomai hedraios

1 Cor. 15:58

   Therefore, my beloved brethren, be ye **stedfast**, unmovable, always abounding in the work of the Lord, forasmuch as ye know that your labour is not in vain in the Lord. [KJV]

   Therefore, my beloved brethren, be **steadfast**, immovable, always abounding in the work of the Lord, knowing that your toil is not in vain in the Lord. [NASB]

   Therefore, my dear brothers, **stand firm**. Let nothing move you. Always give yourselves fully to the work of the Lord, because you know that your labor in the Lord is not in vain. [NIV]

   Therefore, my beloved brethren, be **steadfast**, immovable, always abounding in the work of the Lord, knowing that your labor is not in vain in the Lord. [NKJV]

   So, my dear brothers and sisters, be **strong** and steady, always enthusiastic about the Lord's work, for you know that nothing you do for the Lord is ever useless. [NLT]

   ὥστε, ἀδελφοί μου ἀγαπητοί, **ἑδραῖοι γίνεσθε**, ἀμετακίνητοι, περισσεύοντες ἐν τῷ ἔργῳ τοῦ Κυρίου πάντοτε, εἰδότες ὅτι ὁ κόπος ὑμῶν οὐκ ἔστι κενὸς ἐν Κυρίῳ. [GNS]

   Ὥστε, ἀδελφοί μου ἀγαπητοί, **ἑδραῖοι γίνεσθε**, ἀμετακίνητοι, περισσεύοντες ἐν τῷ ἔργῳ τοῦ κυρίου πάντοτε, εἰδότες ὅτι ὁ κόπος ὑμῶν οὐκ ἔστιν κενὸς ἐν κυρίῳ. [GNT]

To stand firm; to be firm, fixed, determined, purposed, faithful.

Practical Application

   The believer is to stand fast and fixed in his belief and labor for the Lord, determined to live for the Lord and to carry out his purpose for the Lord. The believer is to be steadfast and unmovable. Why? Because he has such a glorious hope: the hope of being resurrected and given an incorruptible and immortal body. The hope of this glorious fact should stir the believer to be steadfast and unmovable in serving the Lord Jesus Christ.

#3757
Steadfastness

Patience–KJV
Steadfastness–NASB
Endurance–NIV
Patience–NKJV
Endurance–NLT

POSB
REFERENCE
(Col.1:11)
Note 3, point 1

ὑπομονὴν = *hupomonën*
Pronunciation: [hoop-om-on-ayn']
Parsing (part of speech): noun
   Case—accusative
   Gender—feminine
   Number—singular
   Stem or root—from ὑπομονή, ῆς
Concordance References:
  ⇒ Strong's #5281 hupomone
  ⇒ NIV #5705 hupomone
  ⇒ NASB #5281 hupomone

Col. 1:11

   Strengthened with all might, according to his glorious power, unto all **patience** and longsuffering with joyfulness; [KJV]

Endurance, patience, steadfastness, fortitude, constancy, perseverance.

Practical Application

   The word (*hupomonën*) is not passive; it is active. It is not the spirit that sits back and puts up with the trials of life, taking whatever may come. Rather, it is the spirit that stands up and faces the trials of life, that actively goes about conquering and overcoming them. When trials confront a person who is truly justified, he is stirred to arise and face the trials head on. He immediately sets out to conquer and overcome them. He knows that God is allowing the trials in

ENGLISH WORD	GREEK WORD AND VERSE	THE WORD MEANS...
See also POSB REF: (2 Tim. 3:10) Note 1, point 7 (2 Thes.1:4-5; esp. v.4) Note 6 (1 Tim.6:11) Note 2, point 5 (Heb.12:11) Note 2, point 2	Strengthened with all power, according to His glorious might, for the attaining of all **steadfastness** and patience; joyously [NASB] Being strengthened with all power according to his glorious might so that you may have great **endurance** and patience, and joyfully [NIV] Strengthened with all might, according to His glorious power, for all **patience** and longsuffering with joy; [NKJV] We also pray that you will be strengthened with his glorious power so that you will have all the patience and **endurance** you need. May you be filled with joy, [NLT] ἐν πάσῃ δυνάμει δυναμούμενοι κατὰ τὸ κράτος τῆς δόξης αὐτοῦ, εἰς πᾶσαν **ὑπομονὴν** καὶ μακροθυμίαν, μετὰ χαρᾶς· [GNS] ἐν πάσῃ δυνάμει δυναμούμενοι κατὰ τὸ κράτος τῆς δόξης αὐτοῦ εἰς πᾶσαν **ὑπομονὴν** καὶ μακροθυμίαν. μετὰ χαρᾶς [GNT]	order to teach him more and more patience (endurance). The godly person follows the example of those who are actively patient, who endure by walking through the trials of life, conquering all for Christ.

#3758
Steady
 	
Unmovable–KJV
Immovable–NASB
Nothing move–NIV
Immovable–NKJV
Steady–NLT
 	
POSB REFERENCE
(1 Cor.15:58)
Note 6, point 2
	ἀμετακίνητοι = *ametakinētoi*
	Pronunciation: [am-et-ak-in'-ay-toy]
	Parsing (part of speech): adjective
	    Case—nominative
	    Gender—masculine
	    Number—plural
	    Stem or root—from ἀμετακίνητος, ον
	Concordance References:
	    ⇒ Strong's #277 ametakinētos
	    ⇒ NIV #293 ametakinētos
	    ⇒ NASB #277 ametakinētos
	
	1 Cor. 15:58
	Therefore, my beloved brethren, be ye stedfast, **unmovable**, always abounding in the work of the Lord, forasmuch as ye know that your labour is not in vain in the Lord. [KJV]
	Therefore, my beloved brethren, be steadfast, **immovable**, always abounding in the work of the Lord, knowing that your toil is not in vain in the Lord. [NASB]
	Therefore, my dear brothers, stand firm. Let **nothing move** you. Always give yourselves fully to the work of the Lord, because you know that your labor in the Lord is not in vain. [NIV]
	Therefore, my beloved brethren, be steadfast, **immovable**, always abounding in the work of the Lord, knowing that your labor is not in vain in the Lord. [NKJV]
	So, my dear brothers and sisters, be strong and **steady**, always enthusiastic about the Lord's work, for you know that nothing you do for the Lord is ever useless. [NLT]
	Ὥστε, ἀδελφοί μου ἀγαπητοί, ἑδραῖοι γίνεσθε, **ἀμετακίνητοι**, περισσεύοντες ἐν τῷ ἔργῳ τοῦ Κυρίου πάντοτε, εἰδότες ὅτι ὁ κόπος ὑμῶν οὐκ ἔστι κενὸς ἐν Κυρίῳ. [GNS]
	Ὥστε, ἀδελφοί μου ἀγαπητοί, ἑδραῖοι γίνεσθε, **ἀμετακίνητοι**,, περισσεύοντες ἐν τῷ ἔργῳ τοῦ κυρίου πάντοτε, εἰδότες ὅτι ὁ κόπος ὑμῶν οὐκ ἔστιν κενὸς ἐν κυρίῳ. [GNT]
		To be unyielding, unshaken, undisturbed. It means to be immovable and steady.
		
		Practical Application
		The believer is not to be fickle in his service for the Lord. He is to stand as solid as a rock in his beliefs and in his service for the Lord.

#3759
Steal–Stealing
 	
Steal–KJV
Steal–NASB
Steal–NIV
Steal–NKJV
Stealing–NLT
 	
POSB REFERENCE
(Rom.13:9)
Note 4
	κλέψεις = *klepseis*
	Pronunciation: [klep'-sees]
	Parsing (part of speech): verb
	    Mood—indicative or imperative
	    Tense—future or aorist
	    Voice—active
	    Person—2nd person
	    Number—singular
	    Stem or root—from κλέπτω
	Concordance References:
	    ⇒ Strong's #2813 kleptö
	    ⇒ NIV #3096 kleptö
	    ⇒ NASB #2813 kleptö
		To cheat, to take wrongfully from another person, either legally or illegally.
		
		Practical Application
		"Thou shalt not steal" (Exodus 20:15; Deut. 5:19). Note that the laws of men are not the determining rule governing whether a person is stealing or not. This is what is so often misunderstood about stealing.
		    ⇒ Men can sometimes use the law to steal.
		    ⇒ Men can take from others without ever breaking a law.
		    ⇒ Men can secure too much of something,

ENGLISH WORD	GREEK WORD AND VERSE	THE WORD MEANS...
	Romans 13:9 For this, Thou shalt not commit adultery, Thou shalt not kill, Thou shalt not **steal**, Thou shalt not bear false witness, Thou shalt not covet; and if there be any other commandment, it is briefly comprehended in this saying, namely, Thou shalt love thy neighbour as thyself. [KJV] For this, "You shall not commit adultery, You shall not murder, You shall not **steal**, You shall not covet," and if there is any other commandment, it is summed up in this saying, "You shall love your neighbor as yourself." [NASB] The commandments, "Do not commit adultery," "Do not murder," "Do not **steal**," "Do not covet," and whatever other commandment there may be, are summed up in this one rule: "Love your neighbor as yourself." [NIV] For the commandments, "You shall not commit adultery," "You shall not murder," "You shall not **steal**," "You shall not bear false witness," "You shall not covet," and if there is any other commandment, are all summed up in this saying, namely, "You shall love your neighbor as yourself." [NKJV] For the commandments against adultery and murder and **stealing** and coveting—and any other commandment—are all summed up in this one commandment: "Love your neighbor as yourself." [NLT] τὸ γὰρ, Οὐ μοιχεύσεις, οὐ φονεύσεις, οὐ **κλέψεις**, οὐ ψευδομαρτυρήσεις, οὐκ ἐπιθυμήσεις, καὶ εἴ τις ἑτέρα ἐντολή, ἐν τούτῳ τῷ λόγῳ ἀνακεφαλαιοῦται, ἐν τῷ Ἀγαπήσεις τὸν πλησίον σου ὡς σεαυτόν. [GNS] τὸ γὰρ Οὐ μοιχεύσεις, Οὐ φονεύσεις, Οὐ **κλέψεις**, Οὐκ ἐπιθυμήσεις, καὶ εἴ τις ἑτέρα ἐντολή, ἐν τῷ λόγῳ τούτῳ ἀνακεφαλαιοῦται [ἐν τῷ] Ἀγαπήσεις τὸν πλησίον σου ὡς σεαυτόν. [GNT]	well beyond what they need—something that rightfully belongs to others. Very simply stated, the Bible teaches that stealing is the taking of anything that rightfully belongs to others.

#3760
Steal From Pagan Temples
 	
Commit sacrilege–KJV
Rob temples–NASB
Rob temples–NIV
Rob temples–NKJV
Steal from pagan temples–NLT
 	
POSB REFERENCE
(Rom.2:21-24; esp. v.22)
Note 2, point 4
	ἱεροσυλεῖς = *hierosuleis*
	Pronunciation: [hee-er-os-ool-ice]
	Parsing (part of speech): verb
	    Mood—indicative
	    Tense—present
	    Voice—active
	    Person—2nd person
	    Number—singular
	    Stem or root—from ἱεροσυλέω
	Concordance References:
	  ⇒ Strong's #2416 hierosuleö
	  ⇒ NIV #2644 hierosuleö
	  ⇒ NASB #2416 hierosuleö
	
	Romans 2:22
	Thou that sayest a man should not commit adultery, dost thou commit adultery? thou that abhorrest idols, dost thou **commit sacrilege**? [KJV]
	You who say that one should not commit adultery, do you commit adultery? You who abhor idols, do you **rob temples**? [NASB]
	You who say that people should not commit adultery, do you commit adultery? You who abhor idols, do you **rob temples**? [NIV]
	You who say, "Do not commit adultery," do you commit adultery? You who abhor idols, do you **rob temples**? [NKJV]
	You say it is wrong to commit adultery, but do you do it? You condemn idolatry, but do you **steal from pagan temples**? [NLT]
	ὁ λέγων μὴ μοιχεύειν μοιχεύεις; ὁ βδελυσσόμενος τὰ εἴδωλα, **ἱεροσυλεῖς**; [GNS]
	ὁ λέγων μὴ μοιχεύειν μοιχεύεις; ὁ βδελυσσόμενος τὰ εἴδωλα **ἱεροσυλεῖς** [GNT]
		Commit sacrilege; rob temples; to violate one's commitment to God and to rob from God.
		
		Practical Application
		"You condemn idolatry, but do you steal from pagan temples?" The phrase "steal from pagan temples" (*hierosuleis*) means to consider something more important than God, something so important that it requires...
		  • the commitment that you owe God.
		  • the tithes and offerings that you owe God.
		
		You say that you worship God and abhor idols, yet you take what belongs to God–your commitment, your time, your energy, your tithes–and you give it to something else. You make something else more important than God; you make it an idol. This is one of the major sins of the religionists.

#3761 **Stealing– Steals–Stole**	κλέπτων = *kleptön* Pronunciation: [klep'-ton] Parsing (part of speech): verb Mood—participle	To steal; to cheat; to take wrongfully from another person, either legally or illegally.

ENGLISH WORD	GREEK WORD AND VERSE	THE WORD MEANS...
Stole–KJV **Steals–NASB** **Stealing–NIV** **Steal–NKJV** Thief–NLT **POSB REFERENCE** (Eph.4:28) Note 3	Tense—present Voice—active Case—nominative Gender—masculine Number—singular Stem or root— from κλέπτω Concordance References: ⇒ Strong's #2813 kleptö ⇒ NIV #3096 kleptö ⇒ NASB #2813 kleptö **Ephes. 4:28** Let him that **stole** steal no more: but rather let him labour, working with his hands the thing which is good, that he may have to give to him that needeth. [KJV] Let him who **steals** steal no longer; but rather let him labor, performing with his own hands what is good, in order that he may have something to share with him who has need. [NASB] He who has been **stealing** must steal no longer, but must work, doing something useful with his own hands, that he may have something to share with those in need. [NIV] Let him who stole **steal** no longer, but rather let him labor, working with *his* hands what is good, that he may have something to give him who has need. [NKJV] If you are a **thief**, stop stealing. Begin using your hands for honest work, and then give generously to others in need. [NLT] ὁ **ὀκλέπτων** μηκέτι κλεπτέτω· μᾶλλον δὲ κοπιάτω, ἐργαζόμενος τὸ ἀγαθόν ταῖς χερσὶν, ἵνα ἔχῃ μεταδιδόναι τῷ χρείαν ἔχοντι. [GNS] ὁ **κλέπτων** μηκέτι κλεπτέτω, μᾶλλον δὲ κοπιάτω ἐργαζόμενος ταῖς [ἰδίαις] χερσὶν τὸ ἀγαθόν, ἵνα ἔχῃ μεταδιδόναι τῷ χρείαν ἔχοντι. [GNT]	**Practical Application** Note that the laws of men are not the determining rule governing whether a person is stealing or not. This is what is so often misunderstood about stealing. ⇒ Men can sometimes use the law to steal. ⇒ Men can take from others without ever breaking a law. ⇒ Men can secure too much of something, well beyond what they need; and when they hoard, they are taking something that by nature belongs to others. Very simply stated, the Bible teaches that stealing is the taking of anything that *rightfully or by nature* belongs to others. There are at least three forms of stealing. 1. A person steals by taking something which is *actually possessed or personally owned* by another person. If a person owns it and we take it, then we are guilty of stealing. It may be something as simple as a pencil from the office or an answer to a test from a fellow student, or it may be something as complex as embezzlement of funds through bookkeeping procedures. If we take it, we have broken God's commandment and stand guilty as thieves. 2. A person steals by hoarding and banking more than he needs. *Keeping back* is stealing. It is... • keeping what is not needed for one's own needs. • keeping back what is desperately needed by others. • taking away what nature and the earth have provided to meet the needs of the human population. • hoarding the knowledge and gifts and blessings God gave to be used for the welfare of a desperate world filled with so many who are less privileged and gifted. We may call it by whatever name we wish, but to God it is stealing. God has put within the earth enough resources to meet the needs of His people, and He has given men both the *ability and command to subdue and have dominion over the earth.* 3. A person steals by living extravagantly, beyond what he needs. There are some who give to meet the crying needs of the world, yet they do not live sacrificially. They *keep plenty* for themselves, indulging their flesh... • in clothing • in food • in jewelry • in possessions • in housing • in transportation • in recreation • in property (See POSB note 3, Eph.4:28 for more discussion).

#3762
Step Forward
	Ἔγειρε = *Egeire*
	Pronunciation: [eg-i'-reh]
	Parsing (part of speech): verb
	    Mood—imperative
	    Tense—present
		To stand up; to rise and come; to get up.
		
		Practical Application
		The words "step forward" (*egeirai eis to meson*) actually say, "Rise up, stand up in the

ENGLISH WORD	GREEK WORD AND VERSE	THE WORD MEANS...
Stand forth–KJV Rise and come–NASB Stand up–NIV **Step forward–NKJV** Come and stand–NLT **POSB REFERENCE** (Mk.3:3) Note 2	Voice—active Person—2nd person Number—singular Stem or root—from ἐγείρω Concordance References: ⇒ Strong's #1453 egeirö ⇒ NIV #1586 egeirö ⇒ NASB #1453 egeirö **Mark 3:3** And he saith unto the man which had the withered hand, **Stand forth**. [KJV] And He said to the man with the withered hand, "**Rise and come** forward!" [NASB] Jesus said to the man with the shriveled hand, "**Stand up** in front of everyone." [NIV] And He said to the man who had the withered hand, "**Step forward**." [NKJV] Jesus said to the man, "**Come and stand** in front of everyone." [NLT] καὶ λέγει τῷ ἀνθρώπῳ τῷ ἐξηραμμένην ἔχοντι, τὴν χεῖρα Ἔγειρε εἰς τὸ μέσον. [GNS] καὶ λέγει τῷ ἀνθρώπῳ τῷ τὴν ξηρὰν χεῖρα ἔχοντι, Ἔγειρε εἰς τὸ μέσον. [GNT]	midst." Jesus was calling for the man's will—his willingness to do exactly what the Messiah was saying. The man had to want help enough to be willing to stand before the audience and before the scornful religionists. By such a stand he would be confessing his faith in Jesus and in His power to save and heal.
#3763 ## Stephen, At The Killing Of At that time–KJV On that day–NASB On that day–NIV At that time–NKJV **At the killing of Stephen–NLT** **POSB REFERENCE** (Acts 8:1) Note 1, point 2	ἐν ἐκείνῃ τῇ ἡμέρᾳ = en ekeinē tē hēmera Pronunciation: [en eh-keh-ee-nay tay hay-mer'-ah] Parsing hēmera (part of speech): noun Case—dative Gender—feminine Number—singular Stem or root—from ἡμέρα, ας Concordance References: ⇒ Strong's #1722 en + 1565 ekeinos + 3588 ho + 2250 hēmera ⇒ NIV #1877 en [On] + 1697 ekeinos [that] + 3836 ho + 2465 hēmera [day] ⇒ NASB #1722 en + 1565 ekeinos + 3588 ho + 2250 hēmera **Acts 8:1** And Saul was consenting unto his death. And **at that time** there was a great persecution against the church which was at Jerusalem; and they were all scattered abroad throughout the regions of Judaea and Samaria, except the apostles. [KJV] And Saul was in hearty agreement with putting him to death. And **on that day** a great persecution arose against the church in Jerusalem; and they were all scattered throughout the regions of Judea and Samaria, except the apostles. [NASB] And Saul was there, giving approval to his death. **On that day** a great persecution broke out against the church at Jerusalem, and all except the apostles were scattered throughout Judea and Samaria. [NIV] Now Saul was consenting to his death. **At that time** a great persecution arose against the church which was at Jerusalem; and they were all scattered throughout the regions of Judea and Samaria, except the apostles. [NKJV] Saul was one of the official witnesses **at the killing of Stephen**. A great wave of persecution began that day, sweeping over the church in Jerusalem, and all the believers except the apostles fled into Judea and Samaria. [NLT] Σαῦλος δὲ ἦν συνευδοκῶν τῇ ἀναιρέσει αὐτοῦ. Ἐγένετο δὲ ἐν ἐκείνῃ τῇ ἡμέρᾳ διωγμὸς μέγας ἐπὶ τὴν ἐκκλησίαν τὴν ἐν Ἱεροσολύμοις· πάντες τε διεσπάρησαν κατὰ τὰς χώρας τῆς Ἰουδαίας καὶ Σαμαρείας, πλὴν τῶν ἀποστόλων. [GNS] Σαῦλος δὲ ἦν συνευδοκῶν τῇ ἀναιρέσει αὐτοῦ. Ἐγένετο δὲ ἐν ἐκείνῃ τῇ ἡμέρᾳ διωγμὸς μέγας ἐπὶ τὴν ἐκκλησίαν τὴν ἐν Ἱεροσολύμοις, πάντες δὲ διεσπάρησαν κατὰ τὰς χώρας τῆς Ἰουδαίας καὶ Σαμαρείας πλὴν τῶν ἀποστόλων. [GNT]	On that day; at that time. **Practical Application** The words "at the killing of Stephen" mean on that very same day. Saul wished to act and to act quickly in wiping out the church. The believers were frightened and on the run. He had to strike immediately to catch them before they could escape.

ENGLISH WORD	GREEK WORD AND VERSE	THE WORD MEANS...

#3764
Sternly Warned
 	
Straitly charged–KJV
Sternly warned–NASB
Strong warning–NIV
Strictly warned–NKJV
Told him sternly–NLT
 	
POSB REFERENCE
(Mk.1:43)
Note 3, point 2
	ἐμβριμησάμενος = embrimesamenos
	Pronunciation: [em-brim-eh'-sah-mehn-os]
	Parsing (part of speech): verb
	    Mood—participle
	    Tense—aorist
	    Voice—middle deponent
	    Case—nominative
	    Gender—masculine
	    Number—singular
	    Stem or root—from ἐμβριμάομαι
	Concordance References:
	  ⇒ Strong's #1690 embrimaomai
	  ⇒ NIV #1839 embrimaomai
	  ⇒ NASB #1690 embrimaomai
	
	Mark 1:43
	And he **straitly charged** him, and forthwith sent him away; [KJV]
	And He **sternly warned** him and immediately sent him away, [NASB]
	Jesus sent him away at once with a **strong warning**: [NIV]
	And He **strictly warned** him and sent him away at once, [NKJV]
	Then Jesus sent him on his way and **told him sternly**, [NLT]
	καὶ ἐμβριμησάμενος αὐτῷ, εὐθέως ἐξέβαλεν αὐτόν, [GNS]
	καὶ ἐμβριμησάμενος αὐτῷ εὐθὺς ἐξέβαλεν αὐτόν [GNT]
		To sternly, strongly, powerfully, abruptly, bluntly warn.
		
		Practical Application
		It is a threatening phrase. It is a strong, severe warning to the man. It is the same kind of charge Jesus gave to the man who had been bedridden for thirty-eight years:
		
		See, you are well again. Stop sinning or something worse may happen to you. (John 5:14).

#3765
Sternness
 	
Severity–KJV
Severity–NASB
Sternness–NIV
Severity–NKJV
Severe–NLT
 	
POSB REFERENCE
(Rom.11:22)
Note 4, point 1
	ἀποτομίαν = apotomian
	Pronunciation: [ap-ot-om-ee'-ahn]
	Parsing (part of speech): noun
	    Case—accusative
	    Gender—feminine
	    Number—singular
	    Stem or root—from ἀποτομία,, ας
	Concordance References:
	  ⇒ Strong's #663 apotomia
	  ⇒ NIV #704 apotomia
	  ⇒ NASB #663 apotomia
	
	Romans 11:22
	Behold therefore the goodness and **severity** of God: on them which fell, severity; but toward thee, goodness, if thou continue in his goodness: otherwise thou also shalt be cut off. [KJV]
	Behold then the kindness and **severity** of God; to those who fell, severity, but to you, God's kindness, if you continue in His kindness; otherwise you also will be cut off. [NASB]
	Consider therefore the kindness and **sternness** of God: sternness to those who fell, but kindness to you, provided that you continue in his kindness. Otherwise, you also will be cut off. [NIV]
	Therefore consider the goodness and **severity** of God: on those who fell, severity; but toward you, goodness, if you continue in *His* goodness. Otherwise you also will be cut off. [NKJV]
	Notice how God is both kind and **severe**. He is severe to those who disobeyed, but kind to you as you continue to trust in his kindness. But if you stop trusting, you also will be cut off. [NLT]
	ἴδε οὖν χρηστότητα καὶ ἀποτομίαν Θεοῦ· ἐπὶ μὲν τοὺς πεσόντας, ἀποτομίαν· ἐπὶ δὲ σέ, χρηστότητα, ἐὰν ἐπιμένῃς τῇ χρηστότητι· ἐπεὶ καὶ σὺ ἐκκοπήσῃ. [GNS]
	ἴδε οὖν χρηστότητα καὶ ἀποτομίαν θεοῦ· ἐπὶ μὲν τοὺς πεσόντας ἀποτομία, ἐπὶ δὲ σὲ χρηστότης θεοῦ, ἐὰν ἐπιμένῃς τῇ χρηστότητι, ἐπεὶ καὶ σὺ ἐκκοπήσῃ [GNT]
		Severity, sternness, harshness, hardness, grievousness, strictness.
		
		Practical Application
		The Gentile believer must take a sharp look at the goodness and severity of God.
		The sternness of God is seen in the spiritual fall of Israel. The Jews had committed the very sins the Gentiles are being warned about in this passage. The Jews...
		  ⇒ had developed an attitude of arrogance and boasting toward other people, refusing to carry the Word of God to them.
		  ⇒ had felt highminded and complacent, feeling safe and secure, thinking themselves to be more acceptable to God than other people.
		
		In addition to these gross sins, the Jews had rejected God's prophets down through the centuries until they eventually killed God's very own Son. In one brief word, their sin was unbelief. The vast majority of the Jews never did believe God, not to the point that they loved God supremely. As a result, the judgment and severity of God fell upon them (see POSB *Deeper Study* #2, Judgment—Romans 11:7-10 for more discussion).

ENGLISH WORD	GREEK WORD AND VERSE	THE WORD MEANS...
	the Holy Spirit! [NIV] "*You* **stiffnecked** and uncircumcised in heart and ears! You always resist the Holy Spirit; as your fathers *did*, so *do* you. [NKJV] "You **stubborn** people! You are heathen at heart and deaf to the truth. Must you forever resist the Holy Spirit? But your ancestors did, and so do you! [NLT] Σκληροτράχηλοι καὶ ἀπερίτμητοι τῇ καρδίᾳ καὶ τοῖς ὠσίν, ὑμεῖς ἀεὶ τῷ Πνεύματι τῷ Ἁγίῳ ἀντιπίπτετε· ὡς οἱ πατέρες ὑμῶν, καὶ ὑμεῖς. [GNS] Σκληροτράχηλοι καὶ ἀπερίτμητοι καρδίαις καὶ τοῖς ὠσίν, ὑμεῖς ἀεὶ τῷ πνεύματι τῷ ἁγίῳ ἀντιπίπτετε ὡς οἱ πατέρες ὑμῶν καὶ ὑμεῖς. [GNT]	

#3771
Stir Up
 	
Stir up–KJV
Kindle afresh–NASB
Fan into flame–NIV
Stir up–NKJV
Fan into flames–NLT
 	
**POSB
REFERENCE**
(2 Tim.1:6)
Note 1
	ἀναζωπυρεῖν = *anazōpurein*
	Pronunciation: [an-ad-zo-poor-eh'-een]
	Parsing (part of speech): verb
	    Mood—infinitive
	    Tense—present
	    Voice—active
	    Stem or root—from ἀναζωπυρέω
	Concordance References:
	⇒ Strong's #329 anazōpureō
	⇒ NIV #351 anazōpureō
	⇒ NASB #329 anazōpureō
	
	2 Tim. 1:6
	Wherefore I put thee in remembrance that thou **stir up** the gift of God, which is in thee by the putting on of my hands. [KJV]
	And for this reason I remind you to **kindle afresh** the gift of God which is in you through the laying on of my hands. [NASB]
	For this reason I remind you to **fan into flame** the gift of God, which is in you through the laying on of my hands. [NIV]
	Therefore I remind you to **stir up** the gift of God which is in you through the laying on of my hands. [NKJV]
	This is why I remind you to **fan into flames** the spiritual gift God gave you when I laid my hands on you. [NLT]
	δι' ἣν αἰτίαν ἀναμιμνήσκω σε **ἀναζωπυρεῖν** τὸ χάρισμα τοῦ Θεοῦ, ὅ ἐστιν ἐν σοὶ διὰ τῆς ἐπιθέσεως τῶν χειρῶν μου. [GNS]
	δι' ἣν αἰτίαν ἀναμιμνήσκω σε **ἀναζωπυρεῖν** τὸ χάρισμα τοῦ θεοῦ, ὅ ἐστιν ἐν σοὶ διὰ τῆς ἐπιθέσεως τῶν χειρῶν μου. [GNT]
		To fan into flame; to stir up; to kindle afresh; to stir into flame. The word "stir up" (*anazōpurein*) can mean to keep blazing and to keep the flame of the fire burning. But it can also mean to rekindle and to restir the flame, indicating that the flame was about to go out.
		
		Practical Application
		Which is meant here? No doubt Timothy faced what we sometimes face: times when he needed to be restirred and rekindled. But there is no indication that Timothy's flame was about to go out.
		Keep this is mind: Paul was facing death; he was about to be executed. He clearly states this fact (2 Tim. 4:6-8). Therefore, Paul sensed the need to give Timothy charge after charge. One of the very first things Timothy needed to do was to keep his spiritual gifts blazing and burning to the hottest point possible. The idea is present tense, which means it is progressive and continuous action. The believer is to *keep on* stirring up his gift, never letting its flame lose any of its intensity. He is to use his gift to minister and minister, never slacking up nor losing his zeal. God has gifted the believer to minister, gifted him in a very, very special way; therefore, he must minister. He must do exactly what God has gifted him to do.

#3772
Stirred
 	
Moved–KJV
Stirred–NASB
Stirred–NIV
Moved–NKJV
Stirred–NLT
 	
**POSB
REFERENCE**
(Mt.21:10-11; esp.
v.10)
Note 5
	ἐσείσθη = *eseisthē*
	Pronunciation: [eh-sees'-thay]
	Parsing (part of speech): verb
	    Mood—indicative
	    Tense—aorist
	    Voice—passive
	    Person—3rd person
	    Number—singular
	    Stem or root—from σείω
	Concordance References:
	⇒ Strong's #4579 seiō
	⇒ NIV #4940 seiō
	⇒ NASB #4579 seiō
	
	Matthew 21:10
	And when he was come into Jerusalem, all the city was **moved**, saying, Who is this? [KJV]
	And when He had entered Jerusalem, all the city was **stirred**, saying, "Who is this?" [NASB]
	When Jesus entered Jerusalem, the whole city was **stirred** and asked, "Who is this?" [NIV]
	And when He had come into Jerusalem, all the city was **moved**, saying, "Who is this?" [NKJV]
	The entire city of Jerusalem was **stirred** as he
		To stir up; to be shaken to the core, to the foundations. This word implies that nothing is spared—everything that can be shaken will be shaken.
		
		Practical Application
		When Jesus Christ makes His presence known, every fabric of society is affected. Note what happened when He entered Jerusalem:
		⇒ The Romans sensed that a popular uprising might be in the making.
		⇒ The Herodians, who were the Jewish ruling party, feared they would be overthrown and lose their power.
		⇒ The Pharisees were stirred to new depths of envy and malice.
		⇒ The common people were convinced that their day of liberation had finally arrived in Jesus of Nazareth.

ENGLISH WORD	GREEK WORD AND VERSE	THE WORD MEANS...

entered. "Who is this?" they asked. [NLT]

καὶ εἰσελθόντος αὐτοῦ εἰς Ἱεροσόλυμα **ἐσείσθη** πᾶσα ἡ πόλις λέγουσα, Τίς ἐστιν οὗτος; [GNS]

καὶ εἰσελθόντος αὐτοῦ εἰς Ἱεροσόλυμα **ἐσείσθη** πᾶσα ἡ πόλις λέγουσα, Τίς ἐστιν οὗτος; [GNT]

#3773

Stirred

Stirred–KJV
Provoked–NASB
Greatly distressed–
NIV
Provoked–NKJV
Deeply troubled–NLT

**POSB
REFERENCE**
(Acts 17:16)
Note 1

παρωξύνετο = paröxuneto
Pronunciation: [par-ox-oo'-neh-tow]
Parsing (part of speech): verb
    Mood—indicative
    Tense—imperfect
    Voice—passive
    Person—3rd person
    Number—singular
    Stem or root—from *παροξύνομαι*
Concordance References:
⇒ Strong's #3947 paroxunö
⇒ NIV #4236 paroxunö
⇒ NASB #3947 paroxunö

Acts 17:16

Now while Paul waited for them at Athens, his spirit was **stirred** in him, when he saw the city wholly given to idolatry. [KJV]

Now while Paul was waiting for them at Athens, his spirit was being **provoked** within him as he was beholding the city full of idols. [NASB]

While Paul was waiting for them in Athens, he was **greatly distressed** to see that the city was full of idols. [NIV]

Now while Paul waited for them at Athens, his spirit was **provoked** within him when he saw that the city was given over to idols. [NKJV]

While Paul was waiting for them in Athens, he was **deeply troubled** by all the idols he saw everywhere in the city. [NLT]

Ἐν δὲ ταῖς Ἀθήναις ἐκδεχομένου αὐτοὺς τοῦ Παύλου, **παρωξύνετο** τὸ πνεῦμα αὐτοῦ ἐν αὐτῷ, θεωροῦντι κατείδωλον οὖσαν τὴν πόλιν. [GNS]

Ἐν δὲ ταῖς Ἀθήναις ἐκδεχομένου αὐτοὺς τοῦ Παύλου **παρωξύνετο** τὸ πνεῦμα αὐτοῦ ἐν αὐτῷ θεωροῦντος κατείδωλον οὖσαν τὴν πόλιν. [GNT]

To be greatly distressed; to be stirred; to be provoked; to be deeply troubled; to be aroused; to be agitated; to be irritated; to be greatly upset.

Practical Application

Paul in Athens, the great intellectual and cultural center of the world. Paul was alone, and no doubt he did as anyone would do—he toured the city. But note: he was not swept off his feet by the majestic buildings and splendor of the architecture. Contrariwise, what gripped him was the idolatry. The city was "wholly given to idolatry." The Greek says "full of idols." Ancient writers estimate that the city had thousands and thousands of idols, one or more for every person in the city. The idols sat everywhere, lining the streets and buildings, within and without every home. Seeing such a sight "stirred" (*paröxuneto*) the spirit of Paul. Paul was aroused...

- over the abuse of God's glory.
- over the spiritual blindness of man's mind and reason.
- against the devil's enslavement of lives.
- with compassion for the souls of men.

Note what happened: Paul could wait no longer. He had been waiting for Silas and Timothy, but he could not swallow the scene of idolatry anymore. He began to *reason* and *discuss* the gospel with men everywhere.

#3774

Stirred Up

Stirred up–KJV
Stirring up–NASB
Agitating–NIV
Stirred up–NKJV
Stirred up–NLT

**POSB
REFERENCE**
(Acts 17:13-15; esp.
v.13)
Note 7

σαλεύοντες = saleuontes
Pronunciation: [sal-yoo'-on-tehs]
Parsing (part of speech): verb
    Mood—participle
    Tense—present
    Voice—active
    Case—nominative
    Gender—masculine
    Number—plural
    Stem or root—from *σαλεύω*
Concordance References:
⇒ Strong's #4531 saleuö
⇒ NIV #4888 saleuö
⇒ NASB #4531 saleuö

Acts 17:13

But when the Jews of Thessalonica had knowledge that the word of God was preached of Paul at Berea, they came thither also, and **stirred up** the people. [KJV]

But when the Jews of Thessalonica found out that the word of God had been proclaimed by Paul in Berea also, they came there likewise, agitating and **stirring up** the crowds. [NASB]

When the Jews in Thessalonica learned that Paul was preaching the word of God at Berea, they went there too, **agitating** the crowds and stirring them up. [NIV]

But when the Jews from Thessalonica learned that the word of God was preached by Paul at Berea, they came there also and **stirred up** the crowds. [NKJV]

But when some Jews in Thessalonica learned that Paul

To agitate; to stir up; to shake; to sway; to be unsettled.

Practical Application

The idea is a volcanic stirring or shaking of the people. The stirring was of earthquake proportions. (Cp. the Galatian Jews who also pursued Paul to keep him from preaching, Acts 14:19.)

ENGLISH WORD	GREEK WORD AND VERSE	THE WORD MEANS...
	was preaching the word of God in Berea, they went there and **stirred up** trouble. [NLT] ὡς δὲ ἔγνωσαν οἱ ἀπὸ τῆς Θεσσαλονίκης Ἰουδαῖοι ὅτι καὶ ἐν τῇ Βεροίᾳ κατηγγέλη ὑπὸ τοῦ Παύλου ὁ λόγος τοῦ Θεοῦ, ἦλθον κἀκεῖ **σαλεύοντες** τοὺς ὄχλους. [GNS] Ὡς δὲ ἔγνωσαν οἱ ἀπὸ τῆς Θεσσαλονίκης Ἰουδαῖοι ὅτι καὶ ἐν τῇ Βεροίᾳ κατηγγέλη ὑπὸ τοῦ Παύλου ὁ λόγος τοῦ θεοῦ, ἦλθον κἀκεῖ **σαλεύοντες** καὶ ταράσσοντες τοὺς ὄχλους. [GNT]	

#3775
Stirred Up
 	
Stirred up–KJV
Stirred up–NASB
Stirred up–NIV
Stirred up–NKJV
Roused–NLT
 	
**POSB
REFERENCE**
(Acts 6:11-14; esp.
v.12)
Note 3, point 1
	συνεκίνησάν = sunekinēsan
	Pronunciation: [soon-eh-kin-eh'-san]
	Parsing (part of speech): verb
	   Mood—indicative
	   Tense—aorist
	   Voice—active
	   Person—3rd person
	   Number—plural
	   Stem or root—from συγκινέω
	Concordance References:
	  ⇒ Strong's #4787 sugkineo
	  ⇒ NIV #5167 sugkineö
	  ⇒ NASB #4787 sugkineo
	
	Acts 6:12
	And they **stirred up** the people, and the elders, and the scribes, and came upon him, and caught him, and brought him to the council, [KJV]
	And they **stirred up** the people, the elders and the scribes, and they came upon him and dragged him away, and brought him before the Council. [NASB]
	So they **stirred up** the people and the elders and the teachers of the law. They seized Stephen and brought him before the Sanhedrin. [NIV]
	And they **stirred up** the people, the elders, and the scribes; and they came upon *him,* seized him, and brought *him* to the council. [NKJV]
	Naturally, this **roused** the crowds, the elders, and the teachers of religious law. So they arrested Stephen and brought him before the high council. [NLT]
	συνεκίνησάν τε τὸν λαὸν καὶ τοὺς πρεσβυτέρους καὶ τοὺς γραμματεῖς, καὶ ἐπιστάντες συνήρπασαν αὐτὸν, καὶ ἤγαγον εἰς τὸ συνέδριον, [GNS]
	συνεκίνησάν τε τὸν λαὸν καὶ τοὺς πρεσβυτέρους καὶ τοὺς γραμματεῖς, καὶ ἐπιστάντες συνήρπασαν αὐτὸν καὶ ἤγαγον εἰς τὸ συνέδριον, [GNT]
		To stir up, arouse.
		
		Practical Application
		It means to shake as a volcano; to move and rock together as with a violent shaking. This was the first time the people themselves were aroused against the disciples.

#3776
Stomach
 	
Belly–KJV
Appetite–NASB
Stomach–NIV
Belly–NKJV
Appetite–NLT
 	
**POSB
REFERENCE**
(Philip.3:18-19; esp.
v.19)
Note 2, point 2
	κοιλία = koilia
	Pronunciation: [koy-lee'-ah]
	Parsing (part of speech): noun
	   Case—nominative
	   Gender—feminine
	   Number—singular
	   Stem or root—from κοιλία, ας
	Concordance References:
	  ⇒ Strong's #2836 koilia
	  ⇒ NIV #3120 koilia
	  ⇒ NASB #2836 koilia
	
	Philip. 3:19
	Whose end is destruction, whose God is their **belly**, and whose glory is in their shame, who mind earthly things.) [KJV]
	Whose end is destruction, whose god is their **appetite**, and whose glory is in their shame, who set their minds on earthly things. [NASB]
	Their destiny is destruction, their god is their **stomach**, and their glory is in their shame. Their mind is on earthly things. [NIV]
	Whose end *is* destruction, whose god *is their* **belly**, and *whose* glory *is* in their shame—who set their mind on earthly things. [NKJV]
	Their future is eternal destruction. Their god is their
		Stomach, belly, appetite.
		
		Practical Application
		Their god is their stomach (*koilia*), that is, their appetite, their sensuality, their desire for the physical pleasures of this world. Physical and material gratification is their god. They center their lives around...
		• possessions and property
		• houses and furnishings
		• food and appetite
		• comfort and plenty
		• position and success
		• pleasure and sex
		• acceptance and social standing
		• money and wealth
		• honor and fame
		Just take a moment to think about any of the above, how some persons center and focus their lives upon such things. Some persons spend more time in front of a mirror or eating or thinking about acceptance or success or possessions or some business deal than they do in prayer.

ENGLISH WORD	GREEK WORD AND VERSE	THE WORD MEANS...
	appetite, they brag about shameful things, and all they think about is this life here on earth. [NLT] ὧν τὸ τέλος ἀπώλεια, ὧν ὁ θεὸς ἡ **κοιλία**, καὶ ἡ δόξα ἐν τῇ αἰσχύνῃ αὐτῶν, οἱ τὰ ἐπίγεια φρονοῦντες. [GNS] ὧν τὸ τέλος ἀπώλεια, ὧν ὁ θεὸς ἡ **κοιλία** καὶ ἡ δόξα ἐν τῇ αἰσχύνῃ αὐτῶν, οἱ τὰ ἐπίγεια φρονοῦντες. [GNT]	

#3777
Stop
 	
Forbid–KJV
Hinder–NASB
Hinder–NIV
Forbid–NKJV
Stop–NLT
 	
**POSB
REFERENCE**
(Mk.10:14)
Deeper Study #3
	κωλύετε = *köluete*
	Pronunciation: [ko-loo'-eh-teh]
	Parsing (part of speech): verb
	    Mood—imperative
	    Tense—present
	    Voice—active
	    Person—2nd person
	    Number—plural
	    Stem or root—from κωλύω
	Concordance References:
	  ⇒ Strong's #2967 köluö
	  ⇒ NIV #3266 köluö
	  ⇒ NASB #2967 köluö
	
	Mark 10:14
	
	But when Jesus saw it, he was much displeased, and said unto them, Suffer the little children to come unto me, and **forbid** them not: for of such is the kingdom of God. [KJV]
	
	But when Jesus saw this, He was indignant and said to them, "Permit the children to come to Me; do not **hinder** them; for the kingdom of God belongs to such as these. [NASB]
	
	When Jesus saw this, he was indignant. He said to them, "Let the little children come to me, and do not **hinder** them, for the kingdom of God belongs to such as these. [NIV]
	
	But when Jesus saw it, He was greatly displeased and said to them, "Let the little children come to Me, and do not **forbid** them; for of such is the kingdom of God. [NKJV]
	
	But when Jesus saw what was happening, he was very displeased with his disciples. He said to them, "Let the children come to me. Don't **stop** them! For the Kingdom of God belongs to such as these. [NLT]
	
	ἰδὼν δὲ ὁ Ἰησοῦς ἠγανάκτησε, καὶ εἶπεν αὐτοῖς, ῎Αφετε τὰ παιδία ἔρχεσθαι πρός με, καὶ μὴ **κωλύετε** αὐτά. τῶν γὰρ τοιούτων ἐστὶν ἡ βασιλεία τοῦ Θεοῦ. [GNS]
	
	ἰδὼν δὲ ὁ Ἰησοῦς ἠγανάκτησεν καὶ εἶπεν αὐτοῖς, ῎Αφετε τὰ παιδία ἔρχεσθαι πρός με, μὴ **κωλύετε** αὐτά, τῶν γὰρ τοιούτων ἐστὶν ἡ βασιλεία τοῦ θεοῦ. [GNT]
		To hinder, forbid, stop, prevent, obstruct, block, impede, encumber, restrain, withhold, hamper.
		
		Practical Application
		The tense is a present imperative, a continuous command: stop hindering, stop preventing the children from coming to Me. In this case, His own disciples were hindering the children, continuously preventing their coming to Jesus.

#3778
Stop
 	
Charge–KJV
Instruct–NASB
Command–NIV
Charge–NKJV
Stop–NLT
 	
**POSB
REFERENCE**
(1 Tim.1:3)
Note 1
	παραγγείλης = *paraggeilës*
	Pronunciation: [par-ang-geh-i-lays]
	Parsing (part of speech): verb
	    Mood—subjunctive
	    Tense—aorist
	    Voice—active
	    Person—2nd person
	    Number—singular
	    Stem or root—from παραγγέλλω
	Concordance References:
	  ⇒ Strong's #3853 paraggellö
	  ⇒ NIV #4133 paraggellö
	  ⇒ NASB #3853 paraggellöt
	
	1 Tim. 1:3
	
	As I besought thee to abide still at Ephesus, when I went into Macedonia, that thou mightest **charge** some that they teach no other doctrine, [KJV]
	
	As I urged you upon my departure for Macedonia, remain on at Ephesus, in order that you may **instruct** certain men not to teach strange doctrines, [NASB]
	
	As I urged you when I went into Macedonia, stay there in Ephesus so that you may **command** certain men not to
		To command; to charge; to instruct; to give strict orders to stop.
		
		Practical Application
		Timothy was in Ephesus and Paul was in Macedonia, a great distance apart. Ephesus was in Asia and Macedonia was in Europe, north of Greece. Note that Paul had to urge Timothy to stay at Ephesus. The church was in trouble because false teaching had seeped in, and the church needed Timothy. Apparently, Timothy felt incapable and wanted to join Paul until Paul could return to Ephesus and handle the situation himself. However, false teaching is so serious a matter that it has to be handled immediately when it raises its ugly head. Therefore, Timothy had to remain in Ephesus so that he could *command* the church to stop the false teaching. The word "stop" (*paraggeilës*) is a strong word. It is a military word that means to pass commands down through the ranks. Timothy was to *give*

ENGLISH WORD	GREEK WORD AND VERSE	THE WORD MEANS...
	teach false doctrines any longer [NIV] As I urged you when I went into Macedonia—remain in Ephesus that you may **charge** some that they teach no other doctrine, [NKJV] When I left for Macedonia, I urged you to stay there in Ephesus and **stop** those who are teaching wrong doctrine. [NLT] Καθὼς παρεκάλεσά σε προσμεῖναι ἐν Ἐφέσῳ, πορευόμενος εἰς Μακεδονίαν, ἵνα **παραγγείλῃς** τισὶ μὴ ἑτεροδιδασκαλεῖν, [GNS] Καθὼς παρεκάλεσά σε προσμεῖναι ἐν Ἐφέσῳ πορευόμενος εἰς Μακεδονίαν, ἵνα **παραγγείλῃς** τισὶν μὴ ἑτεροδιδασκαλεῖν [GNT]	*orders and charge* the false teachers to stop teaching false doctrine, and if this did not work, he was to order and charge the church to handle the false teachers.

#3779
Stop Clinging To Me
 	
Touch me not–KJV
Stop clinging to me– NASB
Do not hold on to me– NIV
Do not cling to Me– NKJV
Don't cling to me– NLT
 	
POSB REFERENCE
(Jn.20:17-18; esp. v.17)
Note 4
	Μή μου ἅπτου = *mē mou haptou*
	Pronunciation: [may moo hap-too]
	Parsing *haptou* (part of speech): verb
	    Mood—imperative
	    Tense—present
	    Voice—middle
	    Person—2nd person
	    Number—singular
	    Stem or root—from **ἅπτω**
	Concordance References:
	⇒ Strong's #3361 me + 1473 ego + 680 hapto
	⇒ NIV #3590 me [not] + 1609 ego [me] + 721 hapto [hold on to]
	⇒ NASB #3361 me + 1473 ego + 680 hapto
	
	John 20:17
	Jesus saith unto her, **Touch me not**; for I am not yet ascended to my Father: but go to my brethren, and say unto them, I ascend unto my Father, and your Father; and to my God, and your God. [KJV]
	
	Jesus said to her, "**Stop clinging to Me**, for I have not yet ascended to the Father; but go to My brethren, and say to them, 'I ascend to My Father and your Father, and My God and your God.' [NASB]
	
	Jesus said, "**Do not hold on to me**, for I have not yet returned to the Father. Go instead to my brothers and tell them, 'I am returning to my Father and your Father, to my God and your God.' [NIV]
	
	Jesus said to her, "**Do not cling to Me**, for I have not yet ascended to My Father; but go to My brethren and say to them, 'I am ascending to My Father and your Father, and *to* My God and your God.' [NKJV]
	
	"**Don't cling to me**," Jesus said, "for I haven't yet ascended to the Father. But go find my brothers and tell them that I am ascending to my Father and your Father, my God and your God." [NLT]
	
	λέγει αὐτῇ ὁ Ἰησοῦς, **Μή μου ἅπτου**, οὔπω γὰρ ἀναβέβηκα πρὸς τὸν πατέρα μου· πορεύου δὲ πρὸς τοὺς ἀδελφούς μου, καὶ εἰπὲ αὐτοῖς, Ἀναβαίνω πρὸς τὸν πατέρα μου καὶ πατέρα ὑμῶν, καὶ Θεόν μου καὶ Θεὸν ὑμῶν. [GNS]
	
	λέγει αὐτῇ Ἰησοῦς, **Μή μου ἅπτου**, οὔπω γὰρ ἀναβέβηκα πρὸς τὸν πατέρα· πορεύου δὲ πρὸς τοὺς ἀδελφούς μου καὶ εἰπὲ αὐτοῖς, Ἀναβαίνω πρὸς τὸν πατέρα μου καὶ πατέρα ὑμῶν καὶ θεόν μου καὶ θεὸν ὑμῶν. [GNT]
		To not hold on to; to stop clinging; to resist touching; not to physically reach out and touch the body of Christ.
		
		Practical Application
		The words are present action, stop clinging to Me—do not hold on to Me. Mary's great love seemingly had one flaw. She wanted to revel in her love for the Lord and in the fellowship that that love brought her. She was reaching out to clutch and to cling to His body (physically), but in doing so, she was missing the point: His cross and resurrection had created a totally new relationship. He was no longer just her Rabboni, her Master. He was her Lord and God (cp. John 20:28). He was soon to ascend back to the Father, so she must not waste time clutching and clinging. She must run to tell her great discovery. The Master was now her Lord and God, for He had created a new spiritual relationship with people.

#3780
Stopped
 	
Stopped–KJV
Silenced–NASB
Silenced–NIV
Stopped–NKJV
Silenced–NLT
	ἐπιστομίζειν = *epistomizein*
	Pronunciation: [ep-ees-to-miz'-eh-een]
	Parsing (part of speech): verb
	    Mood—infinitive
	    Tense—present
	    Voice—active
	    Stem or root—from **ἐπιστομίζω**
	Concordance References:
	⇒ Strong's #1993 epistomizō
	⇒ NIV #2187 epistomizō
	⇒ NASB #1993 epistomizō
		Silenced, stopped. It means to muzzle or bridle, but it should be by reason and argument, not by physical force.
		
		Practical Application
		The false teachers had mouths that needed to be silenced. Their false teaching needed to be stopped, but not by physical force. False teachers must always be stopped. Their teaching is misleading and erroneous; therefore, their teaching must be restrained, stopped dead in its tracks. Their tongues must be silenced. False

ENGLISH WORD	GREEK WORD AND VERSE	THE WORD MEANS...
POSB REFERENCE (Tit.1:10-12; esp. v.11) Note 1, point 5	**Titus 1:11** Whose mouths must be **stopped**, who subvert whole houses, teaching things which they ought not, for filthy lucre's sake. [KJV] Who must be **silenced** because they are upsetting whole families, teaching things they should not teach, for the sake of sordid gain. [NASB] They must be **silenced**, because they are ruining whole households by teaching things they ought not to teach—and that for the sake of dishonest gain. [NIV] Whose mouths must be **stopped**, who subvert whole households, teaching things which they ought not, for the sake of dishonest gain. [NKJV] They must be **silenced**. By their wrong teaching, they have already turned whole families away from the truth. Such teachers only want your money. [NLT] οὓς δεῖ **ἐπιστομίζειν**· οἵτινες ὅλους οἴκους ἀνατρέπουσι, διδάσκοντες ἃ μὴ δεῖ, αἰσχροῦ κέρδους χάριν. [GNS] οὓς δεῖ **ἐπιστομίζειν**, οἵτινες ὅλους οἴκους ἀνατρέπουσιν διδάσκοντες ἃ μὴ δεῖ αἰσχροῦ κέρδους χάριν. [GNT]	teachers must not be allowed to sow the seeds of their error.

#3781
Stories
 	
Parables–KJV
Parables–NASB
Parables–NIV
Parables–NKJV
Stories–NLT
 	
POSB REFERENCE
(Mk.4:2)
Deeper Study #1
	παραβολαῖς = *parabolais*
	Pronunciation: [par-ab-ol-ah-ees]
	Parsing (part of speech): noun
	    Case—dative
	    Gender—feminine
	    Number—plural
	    Stem or root—from παραβολή, ῆς
	Concordance References:
	  ⇒ Strong's #3850 parabolë
	  ⇒ NIV #4130 parabolë
	  ⇒ NASB #3850 parabolë
	
	Mark 4:2
	And he taught them many things by **parables**, and said unto them in his doctrine, [KJV]
	And He was teaching them many things in **parables**, and was saying to them in His teaching, [NASB]
	He taught them many things by **parables**, and in his teaching said: [NIV]
	Then He taught them many things by **parables**, and said to them in His teaching: [NKJV]
	He began to teach the people by telling many **stories** such as this one: [NLT]
	καὶ ἐδίδασκεν αὐτοὺς ἐν **παραβολαῖς** πολλά, καὶ ἔλεγεν αὐτοῖς ἐν τῇ διδαχῇ αὐτοῦ, [GNS]
	καὶ ἐδίδασκεν αὐτοὺς ἐν **παραβολαῖς** πολλά καὶ ἔλεγεν αὐτοῖς ἐν τῇ διδαχῇ αὐτοῦ, [GNT]
		A parable, a story, a symbol, a figure, a proverb, placing a thing by the side of something else for the purpose of comparing.
		
		Practical Application
		The word *comparison* best describes a story or parable.
		1. A story or parable is a comparison: it is an earthly event pointing out a heavenly truth. It is a comparison between the earth and heaven.
		2. A story or parable is a comparison: the earthly story has to be delved into to discover the heavenly truth. The spiritual point is found only by active thought and effort, by actively comparing the physical world with the spiritual world. In fact, the more a man thinks and meditates upon a story or parable, the more he usually sees of the truth.
		Jesus is the *Master User* of the story or parable. No man ever used the story or parable so effectively. Why did He use the story or parable so much? (See POSB note—Luke 8:9-10; POSB notes—Matthew 13:10-17 for a full outline on why Jesus spoke in parables. for the reasons and for more discussion.)
		1. Jesus wanted the *open hearts*, the persons who were really seeking God, to learn all they could about the *mysteries* of the Kingdom of God. Parables required much thought in order to grasp their meaning. A person who really sought after God would seek, strive, think, and ask until he could find the meaning to the parable. And then he would chew upon the meaning, drawing all the meaning he could out of the parable so that he could learn everything possible about God.
		2. Jesus wanted the truth concealed from closed minds. Closed minds are hardened and unwilling to consider the *mysteries* of the Kingdom of God. Sitting there in the audience, they heard and understood the words and the pictures which the words painted. But there was only a little interest in searching into the hidden meaning (mysteries) of the parable. The time and effort required were

ENGLISH WORD	GREEK WORD AND VERSE	THE WORD MEANS...
		not worth it. The closed minded and carnal were just not that interested. Jesus and His message were interesting, for He was a very capable preacher, full of charisma and practical help for living. However, as far as committing one's life totally to His cause and commandments, as far as denying self completely and sacrificing all one is and has, it was not worth it, not to the carnal. Therefore, the carnal were not willing to take the time or effort required to search out the meaning of the parable. Jesus actually said that He wanted the meaning hidden from the closed-minded. Note something else as well. The closed minded, hard-hearted, and carnal often *react* to the truth when the truth points a finger at them and their wrong.

#3782
Storing Up
 	
Treasurest up–KJV
Storing up–NASB
Storing up–NIV
Treasuring up–NKJV
Storing up–NLT
 	
**POSB
REFERENCE**
(Rom.2:2-5; esp. v.5)
Note 2, point 4
	θησαυρίζεις = *thesaurizeis*
	Pronunciation: [thay-sow-rid'-zice]
	Parsing (part of speech): verb
	    Mood—indicative
	    Tense—present
	    Voice—active
	    Person—2nd person
	    Number—singular
	    Stem or root—from θησαυρίζω
	Concordance References:
	  ⇒ Strong's #2343 thësaurizo
	  ⇒ NIV #2564 thësaurizo
	  ⇒ NASB #2343 thësaurizo
	
	Romans 2:5
	But after thy hardness and impenitent heart **treasurest up** unto thyself wrath against the day of wrath and revelation of the righteous judgment of God; [KJV]
	But because of your stubbornness and unrepentant heart you are **storing up** wrath for yourself in the day of wrath and revelation of the righteous judgment of God, [NASB]
	But because of your stubbornness and your unrepentant heart, you are **storing up** wrath against yourself for the day of God's wrath, when his righteous judgment will be revealed. [NIV]
	But in accordance with your hardness and your impenitent heart you are **treasuring up** for yourself wrath in the day of wrath and revelation of the righteous judgment of God, [NKJV]
	But no, you won't listen. So you are **storing up** terrible punishment for yourself because of your stubbornness in refusing to turn from your sin. For there is going to come a day of judgment when God, the just judge of all the world, [NLT]
	κατὰ δὲ τὴν σκληρότητά σου καὶ ἀμετανόητον καρδίαν θησαυρίζεις σεαυτῷ ὀργὴν ἐν ἡμέρᾳ ὀργῆς καὶ ἀποκαλύψεως δικαιοκρισίας τοῦ Θεοῦ, [GNS]
	κατὰ δὲ τὴν σκληρότητά σου καὶ ἀμετανόητον καρδίαν θησαυρίζεις σεαυτῷ ὀργὴν ἐν ἡμέρᾳ ὀργῆς καὶ ἀποκαλύψεως δικαιοκρισίας τοῦ θεοῦ [GNT]
		Store up, save, put aside, heap up, lay up.
		
		Practical Application
		The man who hardens his heart and refuses to repent stores up more and more wrath against himself in the day of judgment.

#3783
Straining Their Eyes, Were
 	
While they looked
  steadfastly–KJV
Were gazing intently–
  NASB
Were looking intently
  up–NIV
	ἀτενίζοντες ἦσαν = *atenizontes ësan*
	Pronunciation: [at-en-id'-zon-tes hay-san]
	Parsing *atenizontes* (part of speech): verb
	    Mood—participle
	    Tense—present
	    Voice—active
	    Case—nominative
	    Gender—masculine
	    Number—plural
	    Stem or root—from ἀτενίζω
		To look intently; to look steadfastly; to gaze intently; to fix one's eyes on; to stare; to look directly at.
		
		Practical Application
		The Lord ascended somewhat slowly in a dramatic, spectacular fashion. Why depart in this way? For the sake of the disciples. There are several significant reasons why they needed such a dramatic departure. (See POSB note,

ENGLISH WORD	GREEK WORD AND VERSE	THE WORD MEANS...
While they looked steadfastly–NKJV **Were straining their eyes–NLT** **POSB REFERENCE** (Acts 1:9-10; esp. v.10) Note 4	Concordance References: ⇒ Strong's #816 atenizö + 1488 eimi ⇒ NIV #867 atenizö + 1639 eimi ⇒ NASB #816 atenizö + 1488 eimi **Acts 1:10** And **while they looked stedfastly** toward heaven as he went up, behold, two men stood by them in white apparel; [KJV] And as they **were gazing intently** into the sky while He was departing, behold, two men in white clothing stood beside them; [NASB] They **were looking intently up** into the sky as he was going, when suddenly two men dressed in white stood beside them. [NIV] And **while they looked steadfastly** toward heaven as He went up, behold, two men stood by them in white apparel, [NKJV] As they **were straining their eyes** to see him, two white-robed men suddenly stood there among them. [NLT] καὶ ὡς **ἀτενίζοντες ἦσαν** εἰς τὸν οὐρανὸν πορευομένου αὐτοῦ, καὶ ἰδοὺ ἄνδρες δύο παρειστήκεισαν αὐτοῖς ἐν ἐσθῆτι λευκῇ, [GNS] καὶ ὡς **ἀτενίζοντες ἦσαν** εἰς τὸν οὐρανὸν πορευομένου αὐτοῦ, καὶ ἰδοὺ ἄνδρες δύο παρειστήκεισαν αὐτοῖς ἐν ἐσθήσεσι λευκαῖς, [GNT]	Jesus Christ, Exaltation—Acts 2:33-36 for more discussion.) 1. Christ needed to dramatize and enforce His final departure. 2. Christ needed to dramatize and enforce His claim upon the disciples. 3. Christ needed to dramatize and enforce His return to earth, that it would take place exactly as He said. (See POSB note—Acts 1:10-11 for discussion.) 4. Christ needed to dramatize and enforce that the disciples were not to be standing around "straining their eyes." They were to get to the business at hand. They were to return to the upper room and... • "wait" and pray for the presence and power of the Holy Spirit. • move out witnessing to a world lost and reeling in desperate need. (See POSB note—Acts 1:9-10 for a detailed discussion of this topic.)

#3784
Straitened
 	
Straitened–KJV
Restrained–NASB
Withholding–NIV
Restricted–NKJV
Withheld–NLT
 	
POSB REFERENCE
(2 Cor.6:11-13; esp. v.12)
Note 1
	στενοχωρεῖσθε = *stenochöreisthe*
	Pronunciation: [sten-okh-o-reh'-ees-the]
	Parsing (part of speech): verb
	  Mood—indicative
	  Tense—present
	  Voice—passive
	  Person—2nd person
	  Number—plural
	  Stem or root—from στενοχωρέομαι
	Concordance References:
	⇒ Strong's #4729 stenochöreö
	⇒ NIV #5102 stenochöreö
	⇒ NASB #4729 stenochöreö
	
	2 Cor. 6:12
	Ye are not **straitened** in us, but ye are **straitened** in your own bowels. [KJV]
	You are not **restrained** by us, but you are **restrained** in your own affections. [NASB]
	We are not **withholding** our affection from you, but you are **withholding** yours from us. [NIV]
	You are not **restricted** by us, but you are restricted by your *own* affections. [NKJV]
	If there is a problem between us, it is not because of a lack of love on our part, but because you have **withheld** your love from us. [NLT]
	οὐ **στενοχωρεῖσθε** ἐν ἡμῖν, **στενοχωρεῖσθε** δὲ ἐν τοῖς σπλάγχνοις ὑμῶν. [GNS]
	οὐ **στενοχωρεῖσθε** ἐν ἡμῖν, **στενοχωρεῖσθε** δὲ ἐν τοῖς σπλάγχνοις ὑμῶν· [GNT]
		To withhold; to be restrained; to be restricted; to lack room; to be held in check; to be pressed or distressed; to be in anguish or straits.
		
		Practical Application
		Paul says there was no lack of room in his heart for the church; no restriction against the Corinthians. He held nothing against them. His heart was wide open to receive them.

#3785
Straitly Charged
 	
Straitly charged–KJV
Sternly warned–NASB
Strong warning–NIV
Strictly warned–NKJV
Told him sternly–NLT
	ἐμβριμησάμενος = *embrimesamenos*
	Pronunciation: [em-brim-eh'-sah-mehn-os]
	Parsing (part of speech): verb
	  Mood—participle
	  Tense—aorist
	  Voice—middle deponent
	  Case—nominative
	  Gender—masculine
	  Number—singular
	  Stem or root—from ἐμβριμάομαι
	Concordance References:
	⇒ Strong's #1690 embrimaomai
	⇒ NIV #1839 embrimaomai
	⇒ NASB #1690 embrimaomai
		To sternly, strongly, powerfully, abruptly, bluntly warn.
		
		Practical Application
		It is a threatening phrase. It is a strong, severe warning to the man. It is the same kind of charge Jesus gave to the man who had been bedridden for thirty-eight years:
		
		Afterward Jesus findeth him in the temple, and said unto him, Behold, thou art made whole: sin no more, lest a worse thing come unto thee. (John 5:14) [KJV]

ENGLISH WORD	GREEK WORD AND VERSE	THE WORD MEANS...
POSB REFERENCE (Mk.1:43) Note 3, point 2	**Mark 1:43** And he **straitly charged** him, and forthwith sent him away; [KJV] And He **sternly warned** him and immediately sent him away, [NASB] Jesus sent him away at once with a **strong warning**: [NIV] And He **strictly warned** him and sent him away at once, [NKJV] Then Jesus sent him on his way and **told him sternly**, [NLT] καὶ **ἐμβριμησάμενος** αὐτῷ, εὐθέως ἐξέβαλεν αὐτόν, [GNS] καὶ **ἐμβριμησάμενος** αὐτῷ εὐθὺς ἐξέβαλεν αὐτόν [GNT]	
#3786 **Stranger** Stranger–KJV Foreigner–NASB Foreigner–NIV Foreigner–NKJV Foreigner–NLT **POSB REFERENCE** (Lk.17:15-19; esp. v.18) Note 3, point 4	**ἀλλογενὴς** = allogenës Pronunciation: [al-log-en-ace'] Parsing (part of speech): pronominal adjective 　　Case—nominative 　　Gender—masculine 　　Number—singular 　　Stem or root—from ἀλλογενής, οὓς Concordance References: ⇒ Strong's #241 allogenës ⇒ NIV #254 allogenës ⇒ NASB #241 allogenëst **Luke 17:18** There are not found that returned to give glory to God, save this **stranger**. [KJV] "Was no one found who turned back to give glory to God, except this **foreigner**?" [NASB] Was no one found to return and give praise to God except this **foreigner**?" [NIV] Were there not any found who returned to give glory to God except this **foreigner**?" [NKJV] Does only this **foreigner** return to give glory to God?" [NLT] οὐχ εὑρέθησαν ὑποστρέψαντες δοῦναι δόξαν τῷ Θεῷ, εἰ μὴ ὁ **ἀλλογενής** οὗτος; [GNS] οὐχ εὑρέθησαν ὑποστρέψαντες δοῦναι δόξαν τῷ θεῷ εἰ μὴ ὁ **ἀλλογενής** οὗτος; [GNT]	A person who was a foreigner or stranger, a person from another nation. **Practical Application** The most rejected was the most thankful. In the context of this Scripture, it means that he was a "stranger from the covenants of promise, having no hope, and without God in the world." (Ephes. 2:12).
#3787 **Strangers** Strangers–KJV Strangers–NASB Foreigners–NIV Strangers–NKJV Strangers–NLT **POSB REFERENCE** (Eph.2:19) Note 1, point 1	**ξένοι** = xenoi Pronunciation: [xen'-oy] Parsing (part of speech): adjective 　　Case—nominative 　　Gender—masculine 　　Number—plural 　　Stem or root—from ξένος, η, ον Concordance References: ⇒ Strong's #3581 xenos ⇒ NIV #3828 xenos ⇒ NASB #3581 xenos **Ephes. 2:19** Now therefore ye are no more **strangers** and foreigners, but fellowcitizens with the saints, and of the household of God; [KJV] So then you are no longer **strangers** and aliens, but you are fellow citizens with the saints, and are of God's household, [NASB] j Consequently, you are no longer **foreigners** and aliens, but fellow citizens with God's people and members of God's household, [NIV] Now, therefore, you are no longer **strangers** and foreigners, but fellow citizens with the saints and members of the household of God, [NKJV] So now you Gentiles are no longer **strangers** and foreigners. You are citizens along with all of God's holy people. You are members of God's family. [NLT] ἄρα οὖν οὐκέτι ἐστὲ **ξένοι** καὶ πάροικοι, ἀλλὰ	Foreigners, strangers, an outsider, an unknown person, a person who does not belong. **Practical Application** There was a time when we... • were outside God and His kingdom. • were unknown to God and His kingdom. • did not belong to God and His kingdom. • were sojourners, living outside God and outside His kingdom. • were alien to God and to His kingdom. • were migrants, not belonging to God nor to His kingdom. • were exiles ton God and to His kingdom. There was a time when we were as stranger's and foreigner's to God, when we were not citizens of God's kingdom. We had no relationship and no fellowship with God and no home and no rights to citizenship in His kingdom. But note the glorious news: we are no longer strangers and foreigners to God. Jesus Christ has brought us to God (see POSB outline—Ephes. 2:13-18 and POSB notes—Ephes. 2:13-18). We are now *fellowcitizens* with all of God's people. We now have a home and all the rights of citizenship in God's kingdom.

ENGLISH WORD	GREEK WORD AND VERSE	THE WORD MEANS...
	συμπολῖται τῶν ἁγίων καὶ οἰκεῖοι τοῦ Θεοῦ, [GNS] ἄρα οὖν οὐκέτι ἐστὲ **ξένοι** καὶ πάροικοι ἀλλὰ ἐστὲ συμπολῖται τῶν ἁγίων καὶ οἰκεῖοι τοῦ θεοῦ, [GNT]	

#3788
Strangers
 	
Strangers–KJV
Aliens–NASB
Strangers–NIV
Pilgrims–NKJV
Foreigners–NLT
 	
POSB
REFERENCE
(1 Pt.1:1)
Note 1
 	
See also POSB REF:
(1 Pt.2:11)
Note 1, point 2
	παρεπιδήμοις = *parepidēmois*
	Pronunciation: [par-ep-id'-ay-moys]
	Parsing (part of speech): pronominal adjective
	    Case—dative
	    Gender—masculine
	    Number—plural
	    Stem or root—from παρεπίδημος, ου
	Concordance References:
	  ⇒ Strong's #3927 parepidēmos
	  ⇒ NIV #4215 parepidēmos
	  ⇒ NASB #3927 parepidēmos
	
	1 Peter 1:1
	Peter, an apostle of Jesus Christ, to the **strangers** scattered throughout Pontus, Galatia, Cappadocia, Asia, and Bithynia, [KJV]
	Peter, an apostle of Jesus Christ, to those who reside as **aliens**, scattered throughout Pontus, Galatia, Cappadocia, Asia, and Bithynia, who are chosen [NASB]
	Peter, an apostle of Jesus Christ, To God's elect, **strangers** in the world, scattered throughout Pontus, Galatia, Cappadocia, Asia and Bithynia, [NIV]
	Peter, an apostle of Jesus Christ, To the **pilgrims** of the Dispersion in Pontus, Galatia, Cappadocia, Asia, and Bithynia, [NKJV]
	This letter is from Peter, an apostle of Jesus Christ.I am writing to God's chosen people who are living as **foreigners** in the lands of Pontus, Galatia, Cappadocia, the province of Asia, and Bithynia. [NLT]
	Πέτρος, ἀπόστολος Ἰησοῦ Χριστοῦ, ἐκλεκτοῖς **παρεπιδήμοις** διασπορᾶς Πόντου, Γαλατίας, Καππαδοκίας, Ἀσίας, καὶ Βιθυνίας, [GNS]
	Πέτρος ἀπόστολος Ἰησοῦ Χριστοῦ ἐκλεκτοῖς **παρεπιδήμοις** διασπορᾶς Πόντου, Γαλατίας, Καππαδοκίας, Ἀσίας καὶ Βιθυνίας, [GNT]
		Strangers, aliens, pilgrims, foreigners. The word means pilgrim, sojourner, refugee, visitor, or exile.
		
		Practical Application
		The chosen are believers, believers who are only strangers scattered over the earth. This is the descriptive picture being painted in 1 Peter 1:1. Believers are only strangers (*parepidēmois*) on earth. The idea is that of a person visiting a place for a while, but he is not a permanent resident. Believers are citizens of heaven; their home is in heaven *with God*, not on earth with the rulers of this world. The rulers and people of this earth may persecute believers, but believers are here on earth only temporarily—only as strangers, pilgrims, sojourners, and exiles.

#3789
Strangers
 	
Sojourning–KJV
Stay–NASB
Strangers–NIV
Stay–NKJV
Foreigners–NLT
 	
POSB
REFERENCE
(1 Pt.1:17)
Note 3
	παροικίας = *paroikias*
	Pronunciation: [par-oy-kee'-ahs]
	Parsing (part of speech): noun
	    Case—genitive
	    Gender—feminine
	    Number—singular
	    Stem or root—from παροικία, ας
	Concordance References:
	  ⇒ Strong's #3940 paroikia
	  ⇒ NIV #4229 paroikia
	  ⇒ NASB #3940 paroikia
	
	1 Peter 1:17
	And if ye call on the Father, who without respect of persons judgeth according to every man's work, pass the time of your **sojourning** here in fear: [KJV]
	And if you address as Father the One who impartially judges according to each man's work, conduct yourselves in fear during the time of your **stay** upon earth; [NASB]
	Since you call on a Father who judges each man's work impartially, live your lives as **strangers** here in reverent fear. [NIV]
	And if you call on the Father, who without partiality judges according to each one's work, conduct yourselves throughout the time of your **stay** *here* in fear; [NKJV]
	And remember that the heavenly Father to whom you pray has no favorites when he judges. He will judge or reward you according to what you do. So you must live in reverent fear of him during your time as **foreigners** here on earth. [NLT]
	καὶ εἰ πατέρα ἐπικαλεῖσθε τὸν ἀπροσωπολήπτως κρίνοντα κατὰ τὸ ἑκάστου ἔργον, ἐν φόβῳ τὸν τῆς **παροικίας** ὑμῶν χρόνον ἀναστράφητε· [GNS]
		Strangers, foreigners, sojourning, staying. The word "strangers" (*paroikias*) means to dwell alongside; to be passing by.
		
		Practical Application
		It is the picture of a pilgrim or stranger who is in a foreign country and is only dwelling there or passing by for a brief time. This is the believer here on earth. He is not a permanent resident on earth. He is only passing through the earth to a better world. This means a most wonderful thing: when a person is a stranger or pilgrim in a foreign land, his mind and heart are home. He lives in a consciousness of home. So it is with the believer: his thoughts are upon home. He lives and walks in the consciousness of being in heaven with God. This is his attitude and his thoughts as he walks through his pilgrimage upon earth. He travels through life with his mind and heart upon heaven, his permanent home.

ENGLISH WORD	GREEK WORD AND VERSE	THE WORD MEANS...
	Καὶ εἰ πατέρα ἐπικαλεῖσθε τὸν ἀπροσωπολήμπτως κρίνοντα κατὰ τὸ ἑκάστου ἔργον, ἐν φόβῳ τὸν τῆς **παροικίας** ὑμῶν χρόνον ἀναστράφητε, [GNT]	

#3790
 	
Strategies And Tricks
 	
Wiles–KJV
Schemes–NASB
Schemes–NIV
Wiles–NKJV
Strategies and tricks– NLT
 	
POSB REFERENCE
(Eph.6:11)
Note 2
	μεθοδείας = *methodeias*
	Pronunciation: [meth-od-i'-ahs]
	Parsing (part of speech): noun
	   Case—accusative
	   Gender—feminine
	   Number—plural
	   Stem or root—from μεθοδεία, ας
	Concordance References:
	  ⇒ Strong's #3180 methodeia
	  ⇒ NIV #3497 methodeia
	  ⇒ NASB #3180 methodeiat
	
	<div align="center">**Ephes. 6:11**</div>Put on the whole armour of God, that ye may be able to stand against the **wiles** of the devil. [KJV]
	Put on the full armor of God, that you may be able to stand firm against the **schemes** of the devil. [NASB]
	Put on the full armor of God so that you can take your stand against the devil's **schemes**. [NIV]
	Put on the whole armor of God, that you may be able to stand against the **wiles** of the devil. [NKJV]
	Put on all of God's armor so that you will be able to stand firm against all **strategies and tricks** of the Devil. [NLT]
	ἐνδύσασθε τὴν πανοπλίαν τοῦ Θεοῦ, πρὸς τὸ δύνασθαι ὑμᾶς στῆναι πρὸς τὰς **μεθοδείας** τοῦ διαβόλου· [GNS]
	ἐνδύσασθε τὴν πανοπλίαν τοῦ θεοῦ πρὸς τὸ δύνασθαι ὑμᾶς στῆναι πρὸς τὰς **μεθοδείας** τοῦ διαβόλου· [GNT]
		Schemes, wiles, strategies and tricks; trickery. It means the deceits, craftiness, trickery, methods, and strategies which the devil uses to wage war against the believer.
		
		Practical Application
		The enemy is the devil and his strategies. He will do everything he can to deceive and capture the believer.

#3791
 	
Strength
 	
Strength–KJV
Strength–NASB
Strength–NIV
Strength–NKJV
Strength–NLT
 	
POSB REFERENCE
(Mk.12:30)
Note 2, point 2
	ἰσχύος = *ischuos*
	Pronunciation: [is-khoo-os']
	Parsing (part of speech): noun
	   Case—genitive
	   Gender—feminine
	   Number—singular
	   Stem or root—from ἰσχύς, ύος
	Concordance References:
	  ⇒ Strong's #2479 ischus
	  ⇒ NIV #2709 ischus
	  ⇒ NASB #2479 ischus
	
	<div align="center">**Mark 12:30**</div>And thou shalt love the Lord thy God with all thy heart, and with all thy soul, and with all thy mind, and with all thy **strength**: this is the first commandment. [KJV]
	And you shall love the Lord your God with all your heart, and with all your soul, and with all your mind, and with all your **STRENGTH**.' [NASB]
	Love the Lord your God with all your heart and with all your soul and with all your mind and with all your **strength**.' [NIV]
	And you shall love the Lord your God with all your heart, with all your soul, with all your mind, and with all your **strength**.' This is the first commandment. [NKJV]
	And you must love the Lord your God with all your heart, all your soul, all your mind, and all your **strength**.' [NLT]
	καὶ ἀγαπήσεις Κύριον τὸν Θεόν σου ἐξ ὅλης τῆς καρδίας σου, καὶ ἐξ ὅλης τῆς ψυχῆς σου, καὶ ἐξ ὅλης τῆς διανοίας σου, καὶ ἐξ ὅλης τῆς **ἰσχύος** σου. αὕτη πρώτη ἐντολή. [GNS]
	καὶ ἀγαπήσεις κύριον τὸν θεόν σου ἐξ ὅλης τῆς καρδίας σου καὶ ἐξ ὅλης τῆς ψυχῆς σου καὶ ἐξ ὅλης τῆς διανοίας σου καὶ ἐξ ὅλης τῆς **ἰσχύος** σου. [GNT]
		To love God with every amount of physical strength, force, vigor, or energy that a person can exert.
		
		Practical Application
		In this Scripture, Jesus is quoting from the familiar Old Testament command. What are the obvious lessons from this timeless passage?
		  ⇒ We are to love God completely and entirely, just as God has chosen to love us.
		  ⇒ There can be no suitable substitute for total devotion to love God with a person's entire being. We are to love Him...
		  • with all our mind
		  • with all our heart
		  • with all our soul
		  • with all our strength

#3792 **Strength**	κράτει = *kratei* Pronunciation: [krat'-eh-ee] Parsing (part of speech): noun Case—dative	Power, strength, might. The Lord's "power" (*kratei*) means His sovereign unlimited power and dominion over all.

ENGLISH WORD	GREEK WORD AND VERSE	THE WORD MEANS...
Power–KJV **Strength–NASB** Power–NIV Power–NKJV Power–NLT **POSB REFERENCE** (Eph.6:10-11; esp. v.10) Note 1, point 1	Gender—neuter Number—singular Stem or root—from κράτος, ους Concordance References: ⇒ Strong's #2904 kratos ⇒ NIV #3197 kratos ⇒ NASB #2904 kratos **Ephes. 6:10** Finally, my brethren, be strong in the Lord, and in the **power** of his might. [KJV] Finally, be strong in the Lord, and in the **strength** of His might. [NASB] Finally, be strong in the Lord and in his mighty **power**. [NIV] Finally, my brethren, be strong in the Lord and in the **power** of His might. [NKJV] A final word: Be strong with the Lord's mighty **power**. [NLT] Τὸ λοιπὸν, ἀδελφοί μου, ἐνδυναμοῦσθε ἐν Κυρίῳ, καὶ ἐν τῷ **κράτει** τῆς ἰσχύος αὐτοῦ. [GNS] Τοῦ λοιποῦ, ἐνδυναμοῦσθε ἐν κυρίῳ καὶ ἐν τῷ **κράτει** τῆς ἰσχύος αὐτοῦ. [GNT]	**Practical Application** The believer must be strong *in the Lord* and in the strength of His might. Note the stress upon power and strength. Three different words are used: ⇒ be *strong* ⇒ in the Lord's *strength* ⇒ in the Lord's *might* Each of these words is used to stress the utter necessity of the believer being strong and possessing power. ⇒ The word "strong" (*endunamoo*) means power, might, strength. The believer must possess power, might, and strength as he walks through the course of this life. ⇒ The Lord's "strength" (*kratei*) means His sovereign unlimited power and dominion over all. ⇒ The Lord's "might" (*ischuos*) means strength, force, ability. It means His ability to use His strength and force wisely, that is, in perfection. The believer is to be strong in the sovereign unlimited power of the Lord—in the power of His might—in His ability to use His power exactly as it should be used. (See POSB outline—Ephes. 1:19-23 and POSB notes—Ephes. 1:19-23 for more discussion on the power of God.) But note the critical point: the believer's strength is not human, fleshly strength; it is not the strength of anything within this world. The believer's strength is found *in the Lord*—in a living, dynamic relationship with Him. The Lord is the source of the believer's strength. There is no other source that can give man the strength to overcome this world with all its trials and temptations and death.
#3793 **Strength** Stablish–KJV Strengthen–NASB Strengthen–NIV Establish–NKJV **Strength–NLT** **POSB REFERENCE** (2 Thes.2:16-17; esp. v.17) Note 5, point 5 **See also POSB REF:** (2 Thes.3:3-5; esp. v.3) Note 2, point 1	στηρίξαι = *stērixai* Pronunciation: [stay-rix'-ah-ee] Parsing (part of speech): verb Mood—optative Tense—aorist Voice—active Person—3rd person Number—singular Stem or root—from στηρίζω Concordance References: ⇒ Strong's #4741 stērizō ⇒ NIV #5114 stērizō ⇒ NASB #4741 stērizō **2 Thes. 2:17** Comfort your hearts, and **stablish** you in every good word and work. [KJV] Comfort and **strengthen** your hearts in every good work and word. [NASB] Encourage your hearts and **strengthen** you in every good deed and word. [NIV] Comfort your hearts and **establish** you in every good word and work. [NKJV] Comfort your hearts and give you **strength** in every good thing you do and say. [NLT] παρακαλέσαι ὑμῶν τὰς καρδίας, καὶ **στηρίξαι** ὑμᾶς ἐν παντὶ λόγῳ καὶ ἔργῳ ἀγαθῷ. [GNS] παρακαλέσαι ὑμῶν τὰς καρδίας καὶ **στηρίξαι** ἐν παντὶ ἔργῳ καὶ λόγῳ ἀγαθῷ. [GNT]	To strengthen, secure, establish, make stable, set fast, and make firm. **Practical Application** The person who is saved is strengthened in every good word and work. The one thing men long for is to be secure, strong, and firmly established in life. God is able to fulfill this longing. God is able to establish and strengthen man and to give him a strong life.

ENGLISH WORD	GREEK WORD AND VERSE	THE WORD MEANS...

#3794
**Strength,
Increasing
In–
Strength,
Increased All
The More In**
 	
Increased the more in strength–KJV
Increasing in strength–NASB
More and more powerful–NIV
Increased all the more in strength–NKJV
More and more powerful–NLT
 	
**POSB
REFERENCE**
(Acts 9:22)
Note 5, point 1
	μᾶλλον ἐνεδυναμοῦτο = *mallon enedunamouto*
	Pronunciation: [mal'-lon en-doo-nam-oo'-tow]
	Parsing *mallon* (part of speech): adjective adverb
	    Type—comparative
	    Stem or root—from μᾶλλον
	Parsing *enedunamouto* (part of speech): verb
	    Mood—indicative
	    Tense—imperfect
	    Voice—passive
	    Person—3rd person
	    Number—singular
	    Stem or root—from ἐνδυναμόω
	Concordance References:
	⇒ Strong's #3123 mallon + 1743 endunamoö
	⇒ NIV #3437 mallon [more and] + 1904 endunamoö [powerful]
	⇒ NASB #3123 mallon + 1743 endunamoö
	
	Acts 9:22
	But Saul **increased the more in strength**, and confounded the Jews which dwelt at Damascus, proving that this is very Christ. [KJV]
	But Saul kept **increasing in strength** and confounding the Jews who lived at Damascus by proving that this Jesus is the Christ. [NASB]
	Yet Saul grew **more and more powerful** and baffled the Jews living in Damascus by proving that Jesus is the Christ. [NIV]
	But Saul **increased all the more in strength**, and confounded the Jews who dwelt in Damascus, proving that this *Jesus* is the Christ. [NKJV]
	Saul's preaching became **more and more powerful**, and the Jews in Damascus couldn't refute his proofs that Jesus was indeed the Messiah. [NLT]
	Σαῦλος δὲ **μᾶλλον ἐνεδυναμοῦτο**, καὶ συνέχυνε τοὺς Ἰουδαίους τοὺς κατοικοῦντας ἐν Δαμασκῷ, συμβιβάζων ὅτι οὗτός ἐστιν ὁ Χριστός. [GNS]
	Σαῦλος δὲ **μᾶλλον ἐνεδυναμοῦτο** καὶ συνέχυννεν [τοὺς] Ἰουδαίους τοὺς κατοικοῦντας ἐν Δαμασκῷ συμβιβάζων ὅτι οὗτός ἐστιν ὁ Χριστός. [GNT]
		More and more powerful; increasing in strength; to become strong within; to gain inner strength; to increase spiritually.
		
		Practical Application
		The more Saul (or Paul) grew in the Lord, the more he was able to "confound" (confuse) those who opposed and rebelled against the gospel. He was able to "prove" (affirm and confirm) it with more and more power as he grew and grew.

#3795
Strengthen
 	
Strengthen–KJV
Strengthen–NASB
Firm–NIV
Strengthen–NKJV
Strengthen–NLT
 	
**POSB
REFERENCE**
(1 Pt.5:10)
Note 2, point 3
	σθενώσει = *sthenösei*
	Pronunciation: [sthen-o'-seh-ee]
	Parsing (part of speech): verb
	    Mood—indicative
	    Tense—future
	    Voice—active
	    Person—3rd person
	    Number—singular
	    Stem or root—from σθενόω
	Concordance References:
	⇒ Strong's #4599 sthenoö
	⇒ NIV #4964 sthenoö
	⇒ NASB #4599 sthenoö
	
	1 Peter 5:10
	But the God of all grace, who hath called us unto his eternal glory by Christ Jesus, after that ye have suffered a while, make you perfect, stablish, **strengthen**, settle you. [KJV]
	And after you have suffered for a little while, the God of all grace, who called you to His eternal glory in Christ, will Himself perfect, confirm, **strengthen** and establish you. [NASB]
	And the God of all grace, who called you to his eternal glory in Christ, after you have suffered a little while, will himself restore you and make you strong, **firm** and steadfast. [NIV]
	But may the God of all grace, who called us to His eternal glory by Christ Jesus, after you have suffered a while, perfect, establish, **strengthen**, and settle *you*. [NKJV]
	In his kindness God called you to his eternal glory by means of Jesus Christ. After you have suffered a little while, he will restore, support, and **strengthen** you, and he will place you on a firm foundation. [NLT]
		Firm, strength, solid, established; to give energy, power, vigor and might.
		
		Practical Application
		God Himself will "strengthen" (*sthenösei*) us. This is the only time this word is used in the New Testament. Most translators say that it means strength. It would, therefore, mean to be filled with all strength, with all the strength necessary to overcome all the trials and temptations and sufferings of life. Again, remember that it is only God Himself who can give us such enormous strength. And He will if we will only draw near Him.

ENGLISH WORD	GREEK WORD AND VERSE	THE WORD MEANS...
	ὁ δὲ Θεὸς πάσης χάριτος, ὁ καλέσας ὑμᾶς εἰς τὴν αἰώνιον αὐτοῦ δόξαν ἐν Χριστῷ Ἰησοῦ, ὀλίγον παθόντας αὐτὸς καταρτίσει ὑμᾶς, στηρίξει, **σθενώσαι**, θεμελιώσαι. [GNS] Ὁ δὲ Θεὸς πάσης χάριτος, ὁ καλέσας ὑμᾶς εἰς τὴν αἰώνιον αὐτοῦ δόξαν ἐν Χριστῷ [Ἰησοῦ], ὀλίγον παθόντας αὐτὸς καταρτίσει, στηρίξει, **σθενώσει** θεμελιώσει. [GNT]	

#3796
Strengthen
 	
Stablish–KJV
Strengthen–NASB
Strengthen–NIV
Establish–NKJV
Strength–NLT
 	
**POSB
REFERENCE**
(2 Thes.2:16-17; esp.
v.17)
Note 5, point 5
 	
See also POSB REF:
(2 Thes.3:3-5; esp.
v.3)
Note 2, point 1
	στηρίξαι = *stērixai*
	Pronunciation: [stay-rix'-ah-ee]
	Parsing (part of speech): verb
	    Mood—optative
	    Tense—aorist
	    Voice—active
	    Person—3rd person
	    Number—singular
	    Stem or root—from στηρίζω
	Concordance References:
	⇒ Strong's #4741 stērizō
	⇒ NIV #5114 stērizō
	⇒ NASB #4741 stērizō
	
	2 Thes. 2:17
	Comfort your hearts, and **stablish** you in every good word and work. [KJV]
	Comfort and **strengthen** your hearts in every good work and word. [NASB]
	Encourage your hearts and **strengthen** you in every good deed and word. [NIV]
	Comfort your hearts and **establish** you in every good word and work. [NKJV]
	Comfort your hearts and give you **strength** in every good thing you do and say. [NLT]
	παρακαλέσαι ὑμῶν τὰς καρδίας, καὶ **στηρίξαι** ὑμᾶς ἐν παντὶ λόγῳ καὶ ἔργῳ ἀγαθῷ. [GNS]
	παρακαλέσαι ὑμῶν τὰς καρδίας καὶ **στηρίξαι** ἐν παντὶ ἔργῳ καὶ λόγῳ ἀγαθῷ. [GNT]
		To strengthen, secure, establish, make stable, set fast, and make firm.
		
		### Practical Application
		The person who is saved is strengthened in every good word and work. The one thing men long for is to be secure, strong, and firmly established in life. God is able to fulfill this longing. God is able to establish and strengthen man and to give him a strong life.

#3797
Strengthen
 	
Stablish–KJV
Strengthen–NASB
Stand firm–NIV
Establish–NKJV
Take courage–NLT
 	
**POSB
REFERENCE**
(James 5:7-9; esp. v.8)
Note 2, point 1
	στηρίξατε τὰς καρδίας = *stērixate tas kardias*
	Pronunciation: [stay-rid'-zah-teh tas kar-dee'-ahs]
	Parsing *stērixate* (part of speech): verb
	    Mood—imperative
	    Tense—aorist
	    Voice—active
	    Person—2nd person
	    Number—plural
	    Stem or root— from στηρίζω
	Parsing *kardias* (part of speech): noun
	    Case—accusative
	    Gender—feminine
	    Number—plural
	    Stem or root—from καρδία, ας
	Concordance References:
	⇒ Strong's #2588+3588+4741 kardia ho stērizō
	⇒ NIV #2840+3836+5114 kardia ho stērizō [stand firm]
	⇒ NASB #2588+3588+4741 kardia ho stērizō
	
	James 5:8
	Be ye also patient; **stablish** your hearts: for the coming of the Lord draweth nigh. [KJV]
	You too be patient; **strengthen** your hearts, for the coming of the Lord is at hand. [NASB]
	You too, be patient and **stand firm**, because the Lord's coming is near. [NIV]
	You also be patient. **Establish** your hearts, for the coming of the Lord is at hand. [NKJV]
	You, too, must be patient. And **take courage**, for the coming of the Lord is near. [NLT]
	μακροθυμήσατε καὶ ὑμεῖς, **στηρίξατε τὰς καρδίας** ὑμῶν, ὅτι ἡ παρουσία τοῦ Κυρίου ἤγγικε. [GNS]
	μακροθυμήσατε καὶ ὑμεῖς, **στηρίξατε τὰς καρδίας** ὑμῶν, ὅτι ἡ παρουσία τοῦ κυρίου ἤγγικεν. [GNT]
		To stand firm; to stablish; to strengthen; to take courage; to stand firm in one's mind, his inner self, his heart.
		
		### Practical Application
		Believers must "strengthen" (*stērixate*) their hearts. The word means to set upon; to fix upon; to make fast (W.E. Vine. *Expository Dictionary of New Testament Words*, p.41). We must set our hearts upon the Lord's coming, for His coming is near. The idea is that it is drawing ever so close and can happen at any moment. We must focus and set our hearts upon His return—be looking for it every day just as the farmer looks for his great day of harvest. Looking for the great day of redemption—for the Lord's glorious return—will stir us to combat temptation and trial step by step. It will stir us to patiently endure no matter the situation, and by patiently enduring we shall gain the victory over all—no matter how bad the situation may be.

ENGLISH WORD	GREEK WORD AND VERSE	THE WORD MEANS...
	am afraid that I will find **quarreling**, jealousy, outbursts of anger, selfishness, backstabbing, gossip, conceit, and disorderly behavior. [NLT] φοβοῦμαι γὰρ μή πως ἐλθὼν οὐχ οἵους θέλω εὕρω ὑμᾶς, κἀγὼ εὑρεθῶ ὑμῖν οἷον οὐ θέλετε· μή πως **ἔρις**, ζῆλοι, θυμοί, ἐριθεῖαι, καταλαλιαί, ψιθυρισμοί, φυσιώσεις, ἀκαταστασίαι· [GNS] φοβοῦμαι γὰρ μή πως ἐλθὼν οὐχ οἵους θέλω εὕρω ὑμᾶς κἀγὼ εὑρεθῶ ὑμῖν οἷον οὐ θέλετε· μή πως **ἔρις**, ζῆλος, θυμοί, ἐριθεῖαι, καταλαλιαί, ψιθυρισμοί, fusiῶσεις, ἀκαταστασίαι· [GNT]	

#3806
Strife
 	
Debate–KJV
Strife–NASB
Strife–NIV
Strife–NKJV
Fighting–NLT
 	
POSB
REFERENCE
(Rom.1:29)
Deeper Study #8
	ἔριδος = *eridos*
	Pronunciation: [er'-i-dos]
	Parsing (part of speech): noun
	   Case—genitive
	   Gender—feminine
	   Number—singular
	   Stem or root—from ἔρις, ιδος
	Concordance References:
	  ⇒ Strong's #2054 eris
	  ⇒ NIV #2251 eris
	  ⇒ NASB #2054 eris
	
	Romans 1:29
	Being filled with all unrighteousness, fornication, wickedness, covetousness, maliciousness; full of envy, murder, **debate**, deceit, malignity; whisperers, [KJV]
	
	being filled with all unrighteousness, wickedness, greed, evil; full of envy, murder, **strife**, deceit, malice; they are gossips, [NASB]
	
	They have become filled with every kind of wickedness, evil, greed and depravity. They are full of envy, murder, **strife**, deceit and malice. They are gossips, [NIV]
	
	Being filled with all unrighteousness, sexual immorality, wickedness, covetousness, maliciousness; full of envy, murder, **strife**, deceit, evil-mindedness; *they are* whisperers, [NKJV]
	
	Their lives became full of every kind of wickedness, sin, greed, hate, envy, murder, **fighting**, deception, malicious behavior, and gossip. [NLT]
	
	πεπληρωμένους πάσῃ ἀδικίᾳ πορνείᾳ, πονηρίᾳ πλεονεξίᾳ κακίᾳ· μεστοὺς φθόνου, φόνου, **ἔριδος**, δόλου, κακοηθείας· [GNS]
	
	πεπληρωμένους πάσῃ ἀδικίᾳ πονηρίᾳ πλεονεξίᾳ κακίᾳ, μεστοὺς φθόνου φόνου **ἔριδος** δόλου κακοηθείας, ψιθυριστάς [GNT]
		Selfish rivalry; arguments. The word strife (*eridos*) means debate, discord, contention, fighting, struggling, quarreling, dissension, wrangling.
		
		### Practical Application
		It means that a man fights against another person in order to get something: position, promotion, property, honor, recognition. He fights in a dishonest and evil way.

#3807
Strife
 	
Strife–KJV
Strife–NASB
Dissension–NIV
Strife–NKJV
Fighting–NLT
 	
POSB
REFERENCE
(Rom.13:13)
Note 4, point 5
	ἔριδι = *eridi*
	Pronunciation: [er'-i-di]
	Parsing (part of speech): noun
	   Case—dative
	   Gender—feminine
	   Number—singular
	   Stem or root—from ἔρις, ιδος
	Concordance References:
	  ⇒ Strong's #2054 eris
	  ⇒ NIV #2251 eris
	  ⇒ NASB #2054 eris
	
	Romans 13:13
	Let us walk honestly, as in the day; not in rioting and drunkenness, not in chambering and wantonness, not in **strife** and envying. [KJV]
	
	Let us behave properly as in the day, not in carousing and drunkenness, not in sexual promiscuity and sensuality, not in **strife** and jealousy. [NASB]
	
	Let us behave decently, as in the daytime, not in orgies and drunkenness, not in sexual immorality and debauchery, not in **dissension** and jealousy. [NIV]
	
	Let us walk properly, as in the day, not in revelry and drunkenness, not in lewdness and lust, not in **strife** and
		Dissension, strife, fighting, selfish rivalry, contention, quarreling, arguing, striving.
		
		### Practical Application
		It is the restless craving deep within a person that wants recognition, honor, position, and authority. It is a spirit that is in constant competition with others, that will push one forward...
		• by putting others down.
		• by bypassing others.
		• by ignoring others.
		• by holding others back.
		• by blaming others.
		• by neglecting others.

ENGLISH WORD	GREEK WORD AND VERSE	THE WORD MEANS...
	envy. [NKJV] We should be decent and true in everything we do, so that everyone can approve of our behavior. Don't participate in wild parties and getting drunk, or in adultery and immoral living, or in **fighting** and jealousy. [NLT] ὡς ἐν ἡμέρᾳ, εὐσχημόνως περιπατήσωμεν, μὴ κώμοις καὶ μέθαις, μὴ κοίταις καὶ ἀσελγείαις, μὴ **ἔριδι** καὶ ζήλῳ. [GNS] ὡς ἐν ἡμέρᾳ εὐσχημόνως περιπατήσωμεν, μὴ κώμοις καὶ μέθαις, μὴ κοίταις καὶ ἀσελγείαις, μὴ **ἔριδι** καὶ ζήλῳ, [GNT]	

#3808
Strife
 	
Variance–KJV
Strife–NASB
Discord–NIV
Contentions–NKJV
Quarrelling–NLT
 	
**POSB
REFERENCE**
(Gal.5:19-21; esp.
v.20)
Note 2
	ἔρις = eris
	Pronunciation: [er'-is]
	Parsing (part of speech): noun
	  Case—nominative
	  Gender—feminine
	  Number—singular
	  Stem or root—from **ἔρις**, ιδος
	Concordance References:
	  ⇒ Strong's #2054 eris
	  ⇒ NIV #2251 eris
	  ⇒ NASB #2054 eris
	
	Galatians 5:20
	Idolatry, witchcraft, hatred, **variance**, emulations, wrath, strife, seditions, heresies, [KJV]
	Idolatry, sorcery, enmities, **strife**, jealousy, outbursts of anger, disputes, dissensions, factions, [NASB]
	Idolatry and witchcraft; hatred, **discord**, jealousy, fits of rage, selfish ambition, dissensions, factions [NIV]
	Idolatry, sorcery, hatred, **contentions**, jealousies, outbursts of wrath, selfish ambitions, dissensions, heresies, [NKJV]
	Idolatry, participation in demonic activities, hostility, **quarreling**, jealousy, outbursts of anger, selfish ambition, divisions, the feeling that everyone is wrong except those in your own little group, [NLT]
	εἰδωλολατρία, φαρμακεία, ἔχθραι, **ἔρεις**, ζῆλοι, θυμοί, ἐριθεῖαι, διχοστασίαι, αἱρέσεις, [GNS]
	εἰδωλολατρία, φαρμακεία, ἔχθραι, **ἔρις**, ζῆλος, θυμοί, ἐριθεῖαι, διχοστασίαι, αἱρέσεις, [GNT]
		Discord, variance, strife, quarreling, contention, fighting, struggling, dissension, wrangling, selfish rivalry.
		
		Practical Application
		It means that a person fights against another person in order to get something: position, promotion, property, honor, recognition. He deceives, doing whatever has to be done to get what he is after.

#3809
Strifes
 	
Strifes–KJV
Disputes–NASB
Factions–NIV
Selfish ambitions–
NKJV
Selfishness–NLT
 	
**POSB
REFERENCE**
(2 Cor.12:19-21; esp.
v.20)
Note 3, point 2
 	
See also POSB REF:
(Gal.5:19-21; esp.
v.20)
Note 2
(Jas.3:14-16)
Note 2, point 1b
	ἐριθεῖαι = eritheiai
	Pronunciation: [er-ith-i'-ah-ee]
	Parsing (part of speech): noun
	  Case—nominative
	  Gender—feminine
	  Number—plural
	  Stem or root—from **ἐριθεία**, ας
	Concordance References:
	  ⇒ Strong's #2052 eritheia
	  ⇒ NIV #2249 eritheia
	  ⇒ NASB #2052 eritheia
	
	2 Cor. 12:20
	For I fear, lest, when I come, I shall not find you such as I would, and that I shall be found unto you such as ye would not: lest there be debates, envyings, wraths, **strifes**, backbitings, whisperings, swellings, tumults: [KJV]
	For I am afraid that perhaps when I come I may find you to be not what I wish and may be found by you to be not what you wish; that perhaps there may be strife, jealousy, angry tempers, **disputes**, slanders, gossip, arrogance, disturbances; [NASB]
	For I am afraid that when I come I may not find you as I want you to be, and you may not find me as you want me to be. I fear that there may be quarreling, jealousy, outbursts of anger, **factions**, slander, gossip, arrogance and disorder. [NIV]
	For I fear lest, when I come, I shall not find you such
		Factions, envying, disputes, selfishness; selfish ambitions; an envious spirit or clique that stands as a rival to others; a factious spirit caused by selfishness or self-seeking.
		
		Practical Application
		Paul was stricken with fear, fear lest the church fail to be what it should be and reject him and his ministry. Paul feared that the church would fail to deal with the carnal critics and continue putting up with their evil attacks against him. He lists eight evils—including "strifes" (*eritheiai*) that were and still are characteristic of divisive critics in the church.

ENGLISH WORD	GREEK WORD AND VERSE	THE WORD MEANS...

	as I wish, and *that* I shall be found by you such as you do not wish; lest *there be* contentions, jealousies, outbursts of wrath, **selfish ambitions**, backbitings, whisperings, conceits, tumults; [NKJV]
	
	    For I am afraid that when I come to visit you I won't like what I find, and then you won't like my response. I am afraid that I will find quarreling, jealousy, outbursts of anger, **selfishness**, backstabbing, gossip, conceit, and disorderly behavior. [NLT]
	
	    φοβοῦμαι γὰρ μή πως ἐλθὼν οὐχ οἵους θέλω εὕρω ὑμᾶς, κἀγὼ εὑρεθῶ ὑμῖν οἷον οὐ θέλετε· μή πως ἔρις, ζῆλοι, θυμοί, **ἐριθείαι**, καταλαλιαί, ψιθυρισμοί, φυσιώσεις, ἀκαταστασίαι· [GNS]
	
	    φοβοῦμαι γὰρ μή πως ἐλθὼν οὐχ οἵους θέλω εὕρω ὑμᾶς κἀγὼ εὑρεθῶ ὑμῖν οἷον οὐ θέλετε· μή πως ἔρις, ζῆλος, θυμοί, **ἐριθείαι** καταλαλιαί, ψιθυρισμοί, φυσιώσεις, ἀκαταστασίαι· [GNT]	

#3810
Strip Off
 	
Lay aside–KJV
Lay aside–NASB
Throw off–NIV
Lay aside–NKJV
Strip off–NLT
 	
**POSB
REFERENCE**
(Heb.12:1)
Note 2, point 1
	ἀποθέμενοι = *apothemenoi*
	Pronunciation: [ap-oth-eh'-mehn-oy]
	Parsing (part of speech): verb
	    Mood—participle
	    Tense—aorist
	    Voice—middle
	    Case—nominative
	    Gender—masculine
	    Person—1st person
	    Number—plural
	    Stem or root—from ἀποτίθημι
	Concordance References:
	    ⇒ Strong's #659 apotithēmi
	    ⇒ NIV #700 apotithēmi
	    ⇒ NASB #659 apotithēmi
	
	Hebrews 12:1
	    Wherefore seeing we also are compassed about with so great a cloud of witnesses, let us **lay aside** every weight, and the sin which doth so easily beset us, and let us run with patience the race that is set before us, [KJV]
	
	    Therefore, since we have so great a cloud of witnesses surrounding us, let us also **lay aside** every encumbrance, and the sin which so easily entangles us, and let us run with endurance the race that is set before us, [NASB]
	
	    Therefore, since we are surrounded by such a great cloud of witnesses, let us **throw off** everything that hinders and the sin that so easily entangles, and let us run with perseverance the race marked out for us. [NIV]
	
	    Therefore we also, since we are surrounded by so great a cloud of witnesses, let us **lay aside** every weight, and the sin which so easily ensnares us, and let us run with endurance the race that is set before us, [NKJV]
	
	    Therefore, since we are surrounded by such a huge crowd of witnesses to the life of faith, let us **strip off** every weight that slows us down, especially the sin that so easily hinders our progress. And let us run with endurance the race that God has set before us. [NLT]
	
	    Τοιγαροῦν καὶ ἡμεῖς τοσοῦτον ἔχοντες περικείμενον ἡμῖν νέφος μαρτύρων, ὄγκον **ἀποθέμενοι** πάντα καὶ τὴν εὐπερίστατον ἁμαρτίαν, δι' ὑπομονῆς τρέχωμεν τὸν προκείμενον ἡμῖν ἀγῶνα, [GNS]
	
	    Τοιγαροῦν καὶ ἡμεῖς τοσοῦτον ἔχοντες περικείμενον ἡμῖν νέφος μαρτύρων, ὄγκον **ἀποθέμενοι** πάντα καὶ τὴν εὐπερίστατον ἁμαρτίαν, δι' ὑπομονῆς τρέχωμεν τὸν προκείμενον ἡμῖν ἀγῶνα [GNT]
		To throw off; to lay aside; to strip off; to get rid of; to put off; to remove as in taking off clothes.
		
		### Practical Application
		    We must strip off every weight and strip off the sin that so easily traps us. Anything that does not build us up and make us stronger is excess weight that slows us down. The Christian runner must do exactly what the Olympic runner does: strain to remove all excess weight. He must do nothing—absolutely nothing—that hinders or hampers him from running at full speed. He must strip off all unnecessary weight.

#3811
Stripes
 	
Stripes–KJV
Beatings–NASB
	πληγαῖς = *plēgais*
	Pronunciation: [play-gah-ees]
	Parsing (part of speech): noun
	    Case—dative
	    Gender—feminine
	    Number—plural
		Scourgings, beatings, floggings, lashings, whippings; to wound.
		
		### Practical Application
		This was a savage, excruciating punishment.

ENGLISH WORD	GREEK WORD AND VERSE	THE WORD MEANS...
Beatings–NIV **Stripes–NKJV** Beaten–NLT **POSB REFERENCE** (2 Cor. 6:4-5; esp. v.5) Note 3	Stem or root—from πληγή, ῆς Concordance References: ⇒ Strong's #4127 plëgë ⇒ NIV #4435 plëgë ⇒ NASB #4127 plëgë **2 Cor. 6:5** In **stripes**, in imprisonments, in tumults, in labours, in watchings, in fastings; [KJV] In **beatings**, in imprisonments, in tumults, in labors, in sleeplessness, in hunger, [NASB] In **beatings**, imprisonments and riots; in hard work, sleepless nights and hunger; [NIV] In **stripes**, in imprisonments, in tumults, in labors, in sleeplessness, in fastings; [NKJV] We have been **beaten**, been put in jail, faced angry mobs, worked to exhaustion, endured sleepless nights, and gone without food. [NLT] ἐν **πληγαῖς**, ἐν φυλακαῖς, ἐν ἀκαταστασίαις, ἐν κόποις, ἐν ἀγρυπνίαις, ἐν νηστείαις, [GNS] ἐν **πληγαῖς** ἐν φυλακαῖς, ἐν ἀκαταστασίαις, ἐν κόποις, ἐν ἀγρυπνίαις, ἐν νηστείαις, [GNT]	The whip (*plëgais*) was made of leather straps with two small balls attached to the end of each strap. The balls were made of rough lead or sharp bones or spikes, so that they would cut deeply into the flesh. Paul's hands were tied to a post above his head as he was scourged. It was the custom for the prisoner to be lashed until he was judged near death by the presiding centurion (Jewish trials allowed only forty lashes.) The criminal's back was, of course, nothing more than an unrecognizable mass of torn flesh. Paul was scourged at least eight times—just imagine! Eight times—five times by the Jews and three times by the Gentiles (2 Cor. 11:24-25). Tragically, believers all over the world are sometimes whipped and abused because of their testimony for the Lord Jesus. In such times, only one thing can give the believer a consistent life and testimony: steadfast endurance.
#3812 **Strive** **Strive–KJV** **Strive–NASB** Make every effort–NIV **Strive–NKJV** Work hard–NLT **POSB REFERENCE** (Lk.13:24) Note 2, point 2	Ἀγωνίζεσθε = *Agōnizesthe* Pronunciation: [ag-o-nid'-zehs-theh] Parsing (part of speech): verb 　Mood—imperative 　Tense—present 　Voice—middle or passive deponent 　Person—2nd person 　Number—plural 　Stem or root—from ἀγωνίζομαι Concordance References: ⇒ Strong's #75 agonizomai ⇒ NIV #76 agōnizomai ⇒ NASB #75 agonizomai **Luke 13:24** **Strive** to enter in at the strait gate: for many, I say unto you, will seek to enter in, and shall not be able. [KJV] "**Strive** to enter by the narrow door; for many, I tell you, will seek to enter and will not be able. [NASB] "**Make every effort** to enter through the narrow door, because many, I tell you, will try to enter and will not be able to. [NIV] "**Strive** to enter through the narrow gate, for many, I say to you, will seek to enter and will not be able. [NKJV] "The door to heaven is narrow. **Work hard** to get in, because many will try to enter, [NLT] Ἀγωνίζεσθε εἰσελθεῖν διὰ τῆς στενῆς πύλης· ὅτι πολλοί, λέγω ὑμῖν, ζητήσουσιν εἰσελθεῖν, καὶ οὐκ ἰσχύσουσιν. [GNS] Ἀγωνίζεσθε εἰσελθεῖν διὰ τῆς στενῆς θύρας, ὅτι πολλοί, λέγω ὑμῖν, ζητήσουσιν εἰσελθεῖν καὶ οὐκ ἰσχύσουσιν. [GNT]	To make every effort; to agonize, strive, struggle, contend, work hard, exert to the fullest, labor fervently. **Practical Application** A person has to "strive" to be saved. Wholehearted dedication and effort are required. But note a critical point: the idea is not that a person works for his salvation, but that he diligently seeks God. He casts himself totally upon the belief that God is, that God actually exists (cp. Hebrews 11:6). It is the spirit, the attitude, the heart that sets itself upon God refusing to be diverted or to be committed to anything else. It is the total commitment of one's life to God for salvation.
#3813 **Strive** Exercise–KJV Best–NASB **Strive–NIV** **Strive–NKJV** Try–NLT **POSB REFERENCE** (Acts 24:14-16; esp. v.16) Note 3, point 4a	ἀσκω = *askö* Pronunciation: [as-ko'] Parsing (part of speech): verb 　Mood—indicative 　Tense—present 　Voice—active 　Person—1st person 　Number—singular 　Stem or root—from ἀσκέω Concordance References: ⇒ Strong's #778 askeö ⇒ NIV #828 askeö ⇒ NASB #778 askeö **Acts 24:16** And herein do I **exercise** myself, to have always a	To strive; to exercise; to try; to endeavor; to give one's best. **Practical Application** Paul exercised himself—actively trained, disciplined, practiced, labored, strove, struggled, even to the point of pain—to keep a pure conscience.

ENGLISH WORD	GREEK WORD AND VERSE	THE WORD MEANS...
	conscience void of offence toward God, and toward men. [KJV] "In view of this, I also do my **best** to maintain always a blameless conscience both before God and before men. [NASB] So I **strive** always to keep my conscience clear before God and man. [NIV] This *being* so, I myself always **strive** to have a conscience without offense toward God and men. [NKJV] Because of this, I always **try** to maintain a clear conscience before God and everyone else. [NLT] ἐν τούτῳ δὲ αὐτὸς **ἀσκῶ**, ἀπρόσκοπον συνείδησιν ἔχειν πρὸς τὸν Θεὸν καὶ τοὺς ἀνθρώπους διὰ παντός. [GNS] ἐν τούτῳ καὶ αὐτὸς **ἀσκῶ** ἀπρόσκοπον συνείδησιν ἔχειν πρὸς τὸν θεὸν καὶ τοὺς ἀνθρώπους διὰ παντός. [GNT]	

#3814
Striveth
 	
Striveth–KJV
Competes in the
  games–NASB
Competes in the
  games–NIV
Competes–NKJV
Athletes practice–NLT
 	
POSB
REFERENCE
(1 Cor.9:25)
Note 2
	ἀγωνιζόμενος = *agōnizomenos*
	Pronunciation: [ag-o-nid'-zom-eh-nos]
	Parsing (part of speech): verb
	   Mood—participle
	   Tense—present
	   Voice—middle or passive deponent
	   Case—nominative
	   Gender—masculine
	   Number—singular
	   Stem or root—from **ἀγωνίζομαι**
	Concordance References:
	⇒ Strong's #75 agōnizomai
	⇒ NIV #76 agōnizomai
	⇒ NASB #75 agōnizomai
	
	1 Cor. 9:25
	And every man that **striveth** for the mastery is temperate in all things. Now they do it to obtain a corruptible crown; but we an incorruptible. [KJV]
	
	And everyone who **competes in the games** exercises self-control in all things. They then do it to receive a perishable wreath, but we an imperishable. [NASB]
	
	Everyone who **competes in the games** goes into strict training. They do it to get a crown that will not last; but we do it to get a crown that will last forever. [NIV]
	
	And everyone who **competes** for the prize is temperate in all things. Now they do it to obtain a perishable crown, but we for an imperishable crown. [NKJV]
	
	All **athletes practice** strict self-control. They do it to win a prize that will fade away, but we do it for an eternal prize. [NLT]
	
	πᾶς δὲ ὁ **ἀγωνιζόμενος** πάντα ἐγκρατεύεται, ἐκεῖνοι μὲν οὖν ἵνα φθαρτὸν στέφανον λάβωσιν, ἡμεῖς δὲ ἄφθαρτον. [GNS]
	
	πᾶς δὲ ὁ **ἀγωνιζόμενος** πάντα ἐγκρατεύεται, ἐκεῖνοι μὲν οὖν ἵνα φθαρτὸν στέφανον λάβωσιν, ἡμεῖς δὲ ἄφθαρτον. [GNT]
		To compete in games; to compete as a highly disciplined athlete; to struggle in competition; to struggle; to make every effort.
		
		Practical Application
		Every runner and boxer is highly disciplined in body, mind, thought, spirit, exercise, workouts, and contests. He is disciplined...
		• in body: what he eats and how much he eats.
		• in mind and thought: his concentration on the goal and how to best gear his body, spirit, and mind to that end.
		• in spirit: keeping his spirit strong and motivated for the strain necessary to work out day by day and to reach his goal.
		The minister or believer is to do no less. He must be just as disciplined as the athlete. He disciplines himself to the point of pain. And note: the discipline "goes into strict training." It covers his body, mind, and spirit, the place where God's presence actually dwells. Therefore, he does not allow anything to touch or enter his body, not anything, that is corrupt, impure, polluted, or that will cause a more rapid deterioration of the temple.

#3815
Striving
  Together
 	
Striving together–
KJV
Striving together–
NASB
Contending as–NIV
Striving together–
NKJV
Fighting together–NLT
	συναθλοῦντες = *sunathlountes*
	Pronunciation: [soon-ath-loon'-tehs]
	Parsing (part of speech): verb
	   Mood—participle
	   Tense—present
	   Voice—active
	   Case—nominative
	   Gender—masculine
	   Person—2nd person
	   Number—plural
	   Stem or root—from **συναθλέω**
	Concordance References:
	⇒ Strong's #4866 sunathleō
	⇒ NIV #5254 sunathleō
	⇒ NASB #4866 sunathleō
		Contending as; striving together; struggling, fighting together; working together.
		
		Practical Application
		The word "striving together" (*sunathlountes*) is the word taken from an athletic contest. It is the picture of a team's working and struggling together against strong opposition (compare a football team). The church—every member of it—is to strive for the faith of the gospel: strive, work, struggle, push, exert all the energy possible; everyone's cooperating together, not a single person's letting up or turning aside or walking off the field. The opposition is difficult; therefore, the faith of the gospel needs for every member to work and struggle together.

ENGLISH WORD	GREEK WORD AND VERSE	THE WORD MEANS...
POSB REFERENCE (Philip.1:27) Note 3, point 2	**Philip. 1:27** Only let your conversation be as it becometh the gospel of Christ: that whether I come and see you, or else be absent, I may hear of your affairs, that ye stand fast in one spirit, with one mind **striving together** for the faith of the gospel; [KJV] Only conduct yourselves in a manner worthy of the gospel of Christ; so that whether I come and see you or remain absent, I may hear of you that you are standing firm in one spirit, with one mind **striving together** for the faith of the gospel; [NASB] Whatever happens, conduct yourselves in a manner worthy of the gospel of Christ. Then, whether I come and see you or only hear about you in my absence, I will know that you stand firm in one spirit, **contending as** one man for the faith of the gospel [NIV] Only let your conduct be worthy of the gospel of Christ, so that whether I come and see you or am absent, I may hear of your affairs, that you stand fast in one spirit, with one mind **striving together** for the faith of the gospel, [NKJV] But whatever happens to me, you must live in a manner worthy of the Good News about Christ, as citizens of heaven. Then, whether I come and see you again or only hear about you, I will know that you are standing side by side, **fighting together** for the Good News. [NLT] μόνον ἀξίως τοῦ εὐαγγελίου τοῦ Χριστοῦ πολιτεύεσθε, ἵνα εἴτε ἐλθὼν καὶ ἰδὼν ὑμᾶς, εἴτε ἀπὼν, ἀκούσω τὰ περὶ ὑμῶν, ὅτι στήκετε ἐν ἑνὶ πνεύματι, μιᾷ ψυχῇ **συναθλοῦντες** τῇ πίστει τοῦ εὐαγγελίου, [GNS] Μόνον ἀξίως τοῦ εὐαγγελίου τοῦ Χριστοῦ πολιτεύεσθε, ἵνα εἴτε ἐλθὼν καὶ ἰδὼν ὑμᾶς εἴτε ἀπὼν ἀκούω τὰ περὶ ὑμῶν, ὅτι στήκετε ἐν ἑνὶ πνεύματι, μιᾷ ψυχῇ **συναθλοῦντες** τῇ πίστει τοῦ εὐαγγελίου [GNT]	
#3816 Strong Waxed strong–KJV **Strong–NASB** **Strong–NIV** **Strong–NKJV** **Strong–NLT** **POSB REFERENCE** (Lk.2:40) Note 3, point 1	ἐκραταιοῦτο = *ekrataiouto* Pronunciation: [eh-krat-ah-ee'-oo-to] Parsing (part of speech): verb Mood—indicative Tense—imperfect Voice—passive Person—3rd person Number—singular Stem or root—from κραταιόομαι Concordance References: ⇒ Strong's #2901 krataioö ⇒ NIV #3194 krataioö ⇒ NASB #2901 krataioö **Luke 2:40** And the child grew, and **waxed strong** in spirit, filled with wisdom: and the grace of God was upon him. [KJV] And the Child continued to grow and become **strong**, increasing in wisdom; and the grace of God was upon Him. [NASB] And the child grew and became **strong**; he was filled with wisdom, and the grace of God was upon him. [NIV] And the Child grew and became **strong** in spirit, filled with wisdom; and the grace of God was upon Him. [NKJV] There the child grew up healthy and **strong**. He was filled with wisdom beyond his years, and God placed his special favor upon him. [NLT] Τὸ δὲ παιδίον ηὔξανε καὶ **ἐκραταιοῦτο** πνεύματι, πληρούμενον σοφίας· καὶ χάρις Θεοῦ ἦν ἐπ' αὐτό. [GNS] Τὸ δὲ παιδίον ηὔξανεν καὶ **ἐκραταιοῦτο** πληρούμενον σοφίᾳ, καὶ χάρις θεοῦ ἦν ἐπ' αὐτό. [GNT]	To be strong; to increase in strength. **Practical Application** The idea is that Jesus grew as a normal child. But note: No other child had ever been or ever will be perfect in growth at the various stages of childhood, but the Christ-child was. He grew as well as a child can grow: filled perfectly with all the qualities that fill a child.
#3817 Strong	ἑδραῖοι γίνεσθε = *hedraioi ginesthe* Pronunciation: [hed-rah'-ee-yoy gen-es-theh] Parsing *hedraioi* (part of speech): adjective Case—nominative Gender—masculine	To stand firm; to be firm, fixed, determined, purposed, faithful.

ENGLISH WORD	GREEK WORD AND VERSE	THE WORD MEANS...
Study–KJV Make it...ambition– NASB Make it...ambition– NIV Aspire–NKJV Ambition–NLT **POSB REFERENCE** (1 Thes.4:11) Note 2	Tense—present Voice—middle or passive deponent Stem or root—from φιλοτιμέομαι Concordance References: ⇒ Strong's #5389 philotimeomai ⇒ NIV #5818 philotimeomai ⇒ NASB #5389 philotimeomai **1 Thes. 4:11** And that ye **study** to be quiet, and to do your own business, and to work with your own hands, as we commanded you; [KJV] And to **make it** your **ambition** to lead a quiet life and attend to your own business and work with your hands, just as we commanded you; [NASB] **Make it** your **ambition** to lead a quiet life, to mind your own business and to work with your hands, just as we told you, [NIV] That you also **aspire** to lead a quiet life, to mind your own business, and to work with your own hands, as we commanded you, [NKJV] This should be your **ambition**: to live a quiet life, minding your own business and working with your hands, just as we commanded you before. [NLT] καὶ **φιλοτιμεῖσθαι** ἡσυχάζειν καὶ πράσσειν τὰ ἴδια, καὶ ἐργάζεσθαι ταῖς ἰδίαις χερσὶν ὑμῶν, καθὼς ὑμῖν παρηγγείλαμεν· [GNS] καὶ **φιλοτιμεῖσθαι** ἡσυχάζειν καὶ πράσσειν τὰ ἴδια καὶ ἐργάζεσθαι ταῖς [ἰδίαις] χερσὶν ὑμῶν, καθὼς ὑμῖν παρηγγείλαμεν, [GNT]	**Practical Application** The very meaning of the word *study* shows the supreme importance of quietness. We must seek to be quiet and learn to be quiet.
#3830 **Stumble** Offended–KJV Fall away–NASB Fall away–NIV **Stumble–NKJV** Desert–NLT **POSB REFERENCE** (Mt.26:31) *Deeper Study #1* **See also POSB REF:** (Mk.14:27) Note 1, point 1	*σκανδαλισθήσεσθε* = skandalisthēsesthe Pronunciation: [skan-dal-is'-thay-sehs-theh] Parsing (part of speech): verb Mood—indicative Tense—future Voice—passive Person—2nd person Number—plural Stem or root—from σκανδαλίζω Concordance References: ⇒ Strong's #4624 skandalizō ⇒ NIV #4997 skandalizō ⇒ NASB #4624 skandalizō **Matthew 26:31** Then saith Jesus unto them, All ye shall be **offended** because of me this night: for it is written, I will smite the shepherd, and the sheep of the flock shall be scattered abroad. [KJV] Then Jesus said to them, "You will all **fall away** because of Me this night, for it is written, 'I WILL STRIKE DOWN THE SHEPHERD, AND THE SHEEP OF THE FLOCK SHALL BE SCATTERED.' [NASB] Then Jesus told them, "This very night you will all **fall away** on account of me, for it is written:" 'I will strike the shepherd, and the sheep of the flock will be scattered.' [NIV] Then Jesus said to them, "All of you will be made to **stumble** because of Me this night, for it is written: 'I will strike the Shepherd, And the sheep of the flock will be scattered.' [NKJV] "Tonight all of you will **desert** me," Jesus told them. "For the Scriptures say, 'God will strike the Shepherd, and the sheep of the flock will be scattered.' [NLT] Τότε λέγει αὐτοῖς ὁ Ἰησοῦς, Πάντες ὑμεῖς **σκανδαλισθήσεσθε** ἐν ἐμοὶ ἐν τῇ νυκτὶ ταύτῃ, γέγραπται γάρ, Πατάξω τὸν ποιμένα, καὶ διασκορπισθήσεται τὰ πρόβατα τῆς ποίμνης· [GNS] Τότε λέγει αὐτοῖς ὁ Ἰησοῦς, Πάντες ὑμεῖς **σκανδαλισθήσεσθε** ἐν ἐμοὶ ἐν τῇ νυκτὶ ταύτῃ, γέγραπται γάρ, Πατάξω τὸν ποιμένα, καὶ διασκορπισθήσονται τὰ πρόβατα τῆς ποίμνης. [GNT]	To stumble; to cause to stumble; to be led into sin; to be offended; to fall (because of Christ). (See POSB *Deeper Study #1*—Matthew 26:31). **Practical Application** When facing Christ, men stumble over three things. (For a thorough discussion see POSB *Deeper Study #9*—Matthew 21:44 and POSB *Deeper Study #10*—Matthew 21:44 cp. POSB note—Luke 20:17-18.) 1. Men stumble over who Christ is (John 6:54-58, 60, 66). 2. Men stumble over the cross of Christ (1 Cor. 1:21-23, esp. 1 Cor. 1:23). 3. Men stumble over the cross God calls them to bear (see POSB note—Luke 9:23 and POSB *Deeper Study #1*—Luke 9:23).

ENGLISH WORD	GREEK WORD AND VERSE	THE WORD MEANS...

#3831
Stumble–
Stumbling
 	
Offended–KJV
Stumbling–NASB
Go astray–NIV
Stumble–NKJV
Fall away–NLT
 	
POSB
REFERENCE
(Jn.16:1)
Note 1
	σκανδαλισθῆτε = *skandalisthēte*
	Pronunciation: [skan-dal-is'-thay-teh]
	Parsing (part of speech): verb
	    Mood—subjunctive
	    Tense—aorist
	    Voice—passive
	    Person—2nd person
	    Number—plural
	    Stem or root—from σκανδαλίζω
	Concordance References:
	  ⇒ Strong's #4624 skandalizō
	  ⇒ NIV #4997 skandalizō
	  ⇒ NASB #4624 skandalizō
	
	John 16:1
	These things have I spoken unto you, that ye should not be **offended**. [KJV]
	"These things I have spoken to you, that you may be kept from **stumbling**. [NASB]
	"All this I have told you so that you will not **go astray**. [NIV]
	"These things I have spoken to you, that you should not be made to **stumble**. [NKJV]
	"I have told you these things so that you won't **fall away**. [NLT]
	Ταῦτα λελάληκα ὑμῖν, ἵνα μὴ **σκανδαλισθῆτε**· [GNS]
	Ταῦτα λελάληκα ὑμῖν ἵνα μὴ **σκανδαλισθῆτε**. [GNT]
		To go astray; to fall away; to cause to stumble or sin; to be offended; to stumble and to trip.
		
		Practical Application
		Jesus warned the believer that religionists would persecute His followers. Jesus warned the believer because He wants to prevent the believer from slipping away. The believer can stumble and fall over persecution. Persecution can...
		• cause a believer to question his beliefs.
		• cause a believer to weaken and return to the way of false religion.
		• silence a believer and his witness.
		• cause a believer to deny Jesus.

#3832
Stumble In
 	
Offend–KJV
Stumble in–NASB
Stumble in–NIV
Stumble in–NKJV
Make...mistakes–NLT
 	
POSB
REFERENCE
(Jas.3:2)
Note 2
	πταίομεν = *ptaiomen*
	Pronunciation: [ptah'-ee-o-mehn]
	Parsing (part of speech): verb
	    Mood—indicative
	    Tense—present
	    Voice—active
	    Person—1st person
	    Number—plural
	    Stem or root—from πταίω
	Concordance References:
	  ⇒ Strong's #4417 ptaiō
	  ⇒ NIV #4760 ptaiō
	  ⇒ NASB #4417 ptaiō
	
	James 3:2
	For in many things we offend all. If any man **offend** not in word, the same is a perfect man, and able also to bridle the whole body. [KJV]
	For we all **stumble in** many ways. If anyone does not stumble in what he says, he is a perfect man, able to bridle the whole body as well. [NASB]
	We all **stumble in** many ways. If anyone is never at fault in what he says, he is a perfect man, able to keep his whole body in check. [NIV]
	For we all stumble in many things. If anyone does not **stumble in** word, he *is* a perfect man, able also to bridle the whole body. [NKJV]
	We all **make** many **mistakes**, but those who control their tongues can also control themselves in every other way. [NLT]
	πολλὰ γὰρ **πταίομεν** ἅπαντες. εἴ τις ἐν λόγῳ οὐ πταίει, οὗτος τέλειος ἀνήρ, δυνατὸς χαλιναγωγῆσαι καὶ ὅλον τὸ σῶμα. [GNS]
	πολλὰ γὰρ **πταίομεν** ἅπαντες. εἴ τις ἐν λόγῳ οὐ πταίει, οὗτος τέλειος ἀνήρ δυνατὸς χαλιναγωγῆσαι καὶ ὅλον τὸ σῶμα. [GNT]
		To stumble in; to offend; to make mistakes; to go wrong, astray.
		
		Practical Application
		The tongue stumbles and sins often, stumbles in word after word. Note: "we all stumble in" (fall, sin). This includes teachers as well as other believers. No believer—no matter how great a teacher he is or who he is—is free from stumbling and falling. In fact, note what the verse says: "In many things" we all stumble. We do not just occasionally fall and sin; we are always coming up short before God. And this includes all teachers or preachers as well as all other believers. What is the proof of this? When some believers live such pure and righteous lives and walk so faithfully among us, how can Scripture say that they are always offending and stumbling? Look at the tongue; the tongue shows us.

#3833
Stumbling
Block
	προσκοπήν = *proskopēn*
	Pronunciation: [pros-kop-ayn']
	Parsing (part of speech): noun
	    Case—accusative
	    Gender—feminine
	    Number—singular
	    Stem or root—from προσκοπή, ῆς
		Stumbling block; to give cause for offense; to stumble; to strike against; to hinder someone from finding the Lord.
		
		Practical Application
		Paul wanted his life and ministry to be so

ENGLISH WORD	GREEK WORD AND VERSE	THE WORD MEANS...
Offence–KJV Offense–NASB **Stumbling block– NIV** Offense–NKJV Hindered from finding the Lord–NLT **POSB REFERENCE** (2 Cor.6:3) Note 1	Concordance References: ⇒ Strong's #4349 proskopë ⇒ NIV #4683 proskopë ⇒ NASB #4349 proskopë **2 Cor. 6:3** Giving no **offence** in any thing, that the ministry be not blamed: [KJV] Giving no cause for **offense** in anything, in order that the ministry be not discredited, [NASB] We put no **stumbling block** in anyone's path, so that our ministry will not be discredited. [NIV] We give no **offense** in anything, that our ministry may not be blamed. [NKJV] We try to live in such a way that no one will be **hindered from finding the Lord** by the way we act, and so no one can find fault with our ministry. [NLT] μηδεμίαν ἐν μηδενὶ διδόντες **προσκοπήν**, ἵνα μὴ μωμηθῇ ἡ διακονία· [GNS] μηδεμίαν ἐν μηδενὶ διδόντες **προσκοπήν**, ἵνα μὴ μωμηθῇ ἡ διακονία, [GNT]	consistent that he would never give any reason for anyone to reject or to turn sour on the Lord Jesus Christ. Paul was careful; he guarded his behavior and conduct lest he cause a person to stumble and fall and reject the gospel of Christ. Note the reason: he did not want to be a poor reflection upon the ministry. Paul knew the nature of man, that people looked for excuses to reject Christ and to avoid His church. He knew that some people were always searching for juicy gossip to use against the followers of Christ and especially against the ministers of the gospel. He also knew that God had called him to the ministry of His Son, the Lord Jesus Christ, and that no higher call could be issued. Therefore, Paul sought to bring only honor to the ministry and to the name of the Lord Jesus Christ.

#3834
**Stumbling
Block–
Stumbling-
block**
 	
Stumblingblock–KJV
**Stumbling block–
NASB**
**Stumbling block–
NIV**
**Stumbling block–
NKJV**
Cause...to stumble–
NLT
 	
**POSB
REFERENCE**
(1 Cor.8:9-11; esp. v.9)
Note 3
 	
See also POSB REF:
(Rom.14:13-15; esp.
v.13)
Note 6
	πρόσκομμα = proskomma
	Pronunciation: [pros'-kom-mah]
	Parsing (part of speech): noun
	  Case—nominative
	  Gender—neuter
	  Number—singular
	  Stem or root—from πρόσκομμα, τος
	Concordance References:
	⇒ Strong's #4348 proskomma
	⇒ NIV #4682 proskomma
	⇒ NASB #4348 proskomma
	
	1 Cor. 8:9
	But take heed lest by any means this liberty of yours become a **stumblingblock** to them that are weak. [KJV]
	But take care lest this liberty of yours somehow become a **stumbling block** to the weak. [NASB]
	Be careful, however, that the exercise of your freedom does not become a **stumbling block** to the weak. [NIV]
	But beware lest somehow this liberty of yours become a **stumbling block** to those who are weak. [NKJV]
	But you must be careful with this freedom of yours. Do not **cause** a brother or sister with a weaker conscience **to stumble.** [NLT]
	βλέπετε δὲ μήπως ἡ ἐξουσία ὑμῶν αὕτη **πρόσκομμα** γένηται τοῖς ἀσθενέσιν. [GNS]
	βλέπετε δὲ μή πως ἡ ἐξουσία ὑμῶν αὕτη **πρόσκομμα** γένηται τοῖς ἀσθενέσιν. [GNT]
		A stone, an obstacle, an occasion, an offense or something that causes a person to stumble and fall into sin.
		
		Practical Application
		A believer's liberty can cause a weak believer to fall into sin. In the case of the Corinthians, some believers were participating in the social functions where meat had been offered to idols. Some were even attending the functions in the idol's temple (1 Cor. 8:10). Apparently, this was causing some of the weaker believers to do the same. But they were not able to handle the situation.

#3835
Subjection
 	
Subjection–KJV
Submissive–NASB
Submissive–NIV
Submissive–NKJV
Accept the authority–
NLT
 	
**POSB
REFERENCE**
(1 Pt.3:1)
Note 1
 	
See also POSB REF:
(Col.3:18)
Note 1, point 1
(1 Pt.5:5)
Note 1
	ὑποτασσόμεναι = hupotassomenai
	Pronunciation: [hoop-ot-as'-so-mehn-ah-ee]
	Parsing (part of speech): verb
	  Mood—participle (imperative sense)
	  Tense—present
	  Voice—passive
	  Case—nominative
	  Gender—feminine
	  Person—2nd person
	  Number—plural
	  Stem or root—from ὑποτάσσω
	Concordance References:
	⇒ Strong's #5293 hupotassomenai
	⇒ NIV #5718 hupotassomenai
	⇒ NASB #5293 hupotassomenai
	
	1 Peter 3:1
	Likewise, ye wives, be in **subjection** to your own husbands; that, if any obey not the word, they also may without the word be won by the conversation of the wives; [KJV]
	In the same way, you wives, be **submissive** to your own husbands so that even if any of them are disobedient
		To be submissive; to accept the authority; to submit to; to be under the authority of.
		
		Practical Application
		The wife's duty is to subject herself to her own husband even if he does not obey God's Word. Scripture is clear and pointed about this. The word "subjection" (hupotassomenai) means just what it says—to be in subjection; to submit oneself. The Greek scholar Marvin Vincent says that it is used of the *submission of servants* (*Word Studies in the New Testament*, Vol.1, p.65). (Cp. 1 Peter 2:18.) The word means that a Christian wife is to place herself under the authority and control of her husband; that she is to subject and submit herself to her own husband's authority, control, and leadership. There is no question but that this is what the word means.
		⇒ W.E. Vine says that "subjection" is prima-

ENGLISH WORD	GREEK WORD AND VERSE	THE WORD MEANS...

to the word, they may be won without a word by the behavior of their wives, [NASB]

Wives, in the same way be **submissive** to your husbands so that, if any of them do not believe the word, they may be won over without words by the behavior of their wives, [NIV]

Wives, likewise, be **submissive** to your own husbands, that even if some do not obey the word, they, without a word, may be won by the conduct of their wives, [NKJV]

In the same way, you wives must **accept the authority** of your husbands, even those who refuse to accept the Good News. Your godly lives will speak to them better than any words. They will be won over [NLT]

Ὁμοίως, αἱ γυναῖκες **ὑποτασσόμεναι** τοῖς ἰδίοις ἀνδράσιν, ἵνα καὶ εἴ τινες ἀπειθοῦσι τῷ λόγῳ, διὰ τῆς τῶν γυναικῶν ἀναστροφῆς ἄνευ λόγου κερδηθήσωνται [GNS]

Ὁμοίως [αἱ] γυναῖκες, **ὑποτασσόμεναι** τοῖς ἰδίοις ἀνδράσιν, ἵνα καὶ εἴ τινες ἀπειθοῦσι τῷ λόγῳ, διὰ τῆς τῶν γυναικῶν ἀναστροφῆς ἄνευ λόγου κερδηθήσονται, [GNT]

rily a military term meaning to *rank under* (*Expository Dictionary of New Testament Words*).

⇒ A.T. Robertson says that the word has a military air and that the word is the same kind of obedience that a citizen is to give to the government. (See his comments on Col. 3:18, *Word Pictures in the New Testament*, Vol.6.)

(See **Submissive** for more discussion).

#3836
Submissive

Subjection–KJV
Submissive–NASB
Submissive–NIV
Submissive–NKJV
Accept the authority–
NLT

**POSB
REFERENCE**
(1 Pt.3:1)
Note 1

See also POSB REF:
(Col.3:18)
Note 1, point 1
(1 Pt.5:5)
Note 1

ὑποτασσόμεναι = *hupotassomenai*
Pronunciation: [hoop-ot-as'-so-mehn-ah-ee]
Parsing (part of speech): verb
Mood—participle (imperative sense)
Tense—present
Voice—passive
Case—nominative
Gender—feminine
Person—2nd person
Number—plural
Stem or root—from ὑποτάσσω
Concordance References:
⇒ Strong's #5293 hupotassomenai
⇒ NIV #5718 hupotassomenai
⇒ NASB #5293 hupotassomenai

1 Peter 3:1

Likewise, ye wives, be in **subjection** to your own husbands; that, if any obey not the word, they also may without the word be won by the conversation of the wives; [KJV]

In the same way, you wives, be **submissive** to your own husbands so that even if any of them are disobedient to the word, they may be won without a word by the behavior of their wives, [NASB]

Wives, in the same way be **submissive** to your husbands so that, if any of them do not believe the word, they may be won over without words by the behavior of their wives, [NIV]

Wives, likewise, be **submissive** to your own husbands, that even if some do not obey the word, they, without a word, may be won by the conduct of their wives, [NKJV]

In the same way, you wives must **accept the authority** of your husbands, even those who refuse to accept the Good News. Your godly lives will speak to them better than any words. They will be won over [NLT]

Ὁμοίως, αἱ γυναῖκες **ὑποτασσόμεναι** τοῖς ἰδίοις ἀνδράσιν, ἵνα καὶ εἴ τινες ἀπειθοῦσι τῷ λόγῳ, διὰ τῆς τῶν γυναικῶν ἀναστροφῆς ἄνευ λόγου κερδηθήσωνται [GNS]

Ὁμοίως [αἱ] γυναῖκες, **ὑποτασσόμεναι** τοῖς ἰδίοις ἀνδράσιν, ἵνα καὶ εἴ τινες ἀπειθοῦσι τῷ λόγῳ, διὰ τῆς τῶν γυναικῶν ἀναστροφῆς ἄνευ λόγου κερδηθήσονται, [GNT]

To be submissive; to accept the authority; to submit to; to be under the authority of.

Practical Application

The wife's duty is to subject herself to her own husband even if he does not obey God's Word. Scripture is clear and pointed about this. The word "submissive" (*hupotassomenai*) means just what it says—to be in subjection; to submit oneself. The Greek scholar Marvin Vincent says that it is used of the *submission of servants* (*Word Studies In The New Testament*, Vol.1, p.65). (Cp. 1 Peter 2:18.) The word means that a Christian wife is to place herself under the authority and control of her husband; that she is to subject and submit herself to her own husband's authority, control, and leadership. There is no question but that this is what the word means.

⇒ W.E. Vine says that "submissive" is primarily a military term meaning to *rank under* (*Expository Dictionary of New Testament Words*).

⇒ A.T. Robertson says that the word has a military air and that the word is the same kind of obedience that a citizen is to give to the government. (See his comments on Col. 3:18, *Word Pictures in the New Testament*, Vol.6.)

In modern society this is strong; in fact, it is too strong for many. Many reject the idea of woman's submission as archaic, outdated, and old-fashioned. Some even react in anger and hostility against the Word of God and those who preach the duty of wives.

Are they right? Has Scripture gone too far in declaring that wives should accept the authority of their husbands? Has God made a mistake within the order of the family? To the Christian, the answer is "no." The problem is not in what God has said, but in our *understanding of what He has said* or in our rebellion against what He wills. Any wife who reacts to God's command is reacting either because she does not understand

ENGLISH WORD	GREEK WORD AND VERSE	THE WORD MEANS...
	tation, he is able to **help** us when we are being tempted. [NLT] ἐν ᾧ γὰρ πέπονθεν αὐτὸς πειρασθείς, δύναται τοῖς πειραζομένοις **βοηθῆσαι.** [GNS] ἐν ᾧ γὰρ πέπονθεν αὐτὸς πειρασθείς, δύναται τοῖς πειραζομένοις **βοηθῆσαι.** [GNT]	• having his life threatened as a baby (Matthew 2:13f). • being the cause of unimaginable sorrow (Matthew 2:16f). • having to be moved and shifted about as a baby (Matthew 2:13f). • being reared in a despicable place, Nazareth (Luke 2:39). • having His father die during His youth (see POSB note, pt. 3—Matthew 13:53-58). • having to support His mother and brothers and sisters (see POSB note, pt. 3—Matthew 13:53-58). • having no home, not even a place to lay His head (Matthew 8:20; Luke 9:58). • being hated and opposed by religionists (Mark 14:1-2). • being charged with insanity (Mark 3:21). • being charged with demon possession (Mark 3:22). • being opposed by His own family (Mark 3:31-32). • being rejected, hated, and opposed by listeners (Matthew 13:53-58; Luke 4:28-29). • being betrayed by a close friend (Mark 14:10-11, 18). • being left alone, rejected, and forsaken by all of His friends (Mark 14:50). • being tried before the high court of the land on the charge of treason (John 18:33). • being executed by crucifixion, the worst possible death (John 19:16f). And Jesus Christ suffered so much more, but the point to note is this: in each of these experiences His suffering reached the depth of humiliation. Christ stooped to the lowest point of human experience in every condition in order to become the *Perfect Sympathizer* (Savior). This is the reason He can now identify with and feel for any person's circumstances. No person ever comes close to the depth of suffering and humiliation He bore. Jesus Christ can succor—help, feel for, care for, and look after—every person no matter their condition, trial, or temptation.

#3843
## Succourer 	
 	
Succourer–KJV
Helper–NASB
Great help–NIV
Helper–NKJV
Helped–NLT
 	
POSB
REFERENCE
(Rom.16:1-2; esp. v.2)
Note 1, point 4b
	προστάτις = *prostatis*
	Pronunciation: [pros-tat'-is]
	Parsing (part of speech): noun
	  Case—nominative
	  Gender—feminine
	  Number—singular
	  Stem or root—from προστάτις, ιδος
	Concordance References:
	  ⇒ Strong's #4368 prostatis
	  ⇒ NIV #4706 prostatis
	  ⇒ NASB #4368 prostatis
	
	### Romans 16:2
	That ye receive her in the Lord, as becometh saints, and that ye assist her in whatsoever business she hath need of you: for she hath been a **succourer** of many, and of myself also. [KJV]
	That you receive her in the Lord in a manner worthy of the saints, and that you help her in whatever matter she may have need of you; for she herself has also been a **helper** of many, and of myself as well. [NASB]
	I ask you to receive her in the Lord in a way worthy of the saints and to give her any help she may need from you,
		Great help; succorer; helper; helped; aided.
		
		### Practical Application
		Phoebe had been a "succorer" (*prostatis*) to many, including Paul himself. The word means that she protected, helped, looked after, and provided for people. Phoebe was a woman who ministered to the needs of many. Apparently she helped and looked after the welfare of any who had need.

ENGLISH WORD	GREEK WORD AND VERSE	THE WORD MEANS...
	for she has been a **great help** to many people, including me. [NIV] That you may receive her in the Lord in a manner worthy of the saints, and assist her in whatever business she has need of you; for indeed she has been a **helper** of many and of myself also. [NKJV] Receive her in the Lord, as one who is worthy of high honor. Help her in every way you can, for she has **helped** many in their needs, including me. [NLT] ἵνα αὐτὴν προσδέξησθε ἐν Κυρίῳ ἀξίως τῶν ἁγίων, καὶ παραστῆτε αὐτῇ ἐν ᾧ ἂν ὑμῶν χρῄζῃ πράγματι· καὶ γὰρ αὐτὴ **προστάτις** πολλῶν ἐγενήθη, καὶ αὐτοῦ ἐμοῦ. [GNS] ἵνα αὐτὴν προσδέξησθε ἐν κυρίῳ ἀξίως τῶν ἁγίων καὶ παραστῆτε αὐτῇ ἐν ᾧ ἂν ὑμῶν χρῄζῃ πράγματι· καὶ γὰρ αὐτὴ **προστάτις** πολλῶν ἐγενήθη καὶ ἐμοῦ αὐτοῦ. [GNT]	

#3844
 	
Suddenly Took Away
 	
Caught away–KJV
Snatched...away–NASB
Suddenly took... away–NIV
Caught...away–NKJV
Caught...away–NLT
 	
POSB REFERENCE
(Acts 8:39-40; esp. v.39)
Note 7, point 1
	ἥρπασεν = *hërpasen*
	Pronunciation: [heyr-pah'-sehn]
	Parsing (part of speech): verb
	    Mood—indicative
	    Tense—aorist
	    Voice—active
	    Person—3rd person
	    Number—singular
	    Stem or root—from ἁρπάζω
	Concordance References:
	⇒ Strong's #726 harpazö
	⇒ NIV #773 harpazö
	⇒ NASB #726 harpazö
	
	Acts 8:39
	And when they were come up out of the water, the Spirit of the Lord **caught away** Philip, that the eunuch saw him no more: and he went on his way rejoicing. [KJV]
	
	And when they came up out of the water, the Spirit of the Lord **snatched** Philip **away**; and the eunuch saw him no more, but went on his way rejoicing. [NASB]
	
	When they came up out of the water, the Spirit of the Lord **suddenly took** Philip **away**, and the eunuch did not see him again, but went on his way rejoicing. [NIV]
	
	Now when they came up out of the water, the Spirit of the Lord **caught** Philip **away**, so that the eunuch saw him no more; and he went on his way rejoicing. [NKJV]
	
	When they came up out of the water, the Spirit of the Lord **caught** Philip **away**. The eunuch never saw him again but went on his way rejoicing. [NLT]
	
	ὅτε δὲ ἀνέβησαν ἐκ τοῦ ὕδατος, Πνεῦμα Κυρίου **ἥρπασε** τὸν Φίλιππον· καὶ οὐκ εἶδεν αὐτὸν οὐκέτι ὁ εὐνοῦχος, ἐπορεύετο γὰρ τὴν ὁδὸν αὐτοῦ χαίρων. [GNS]
	
	ὅτε δὲ ἀνέβησαν ἐκ τοῦ ὕδατος, πνεῦμα κυρίου **ἥρπασεν** τὸν Φίλιππον καὶ οὐκ εἶδεν αὐτὸν οὐκέτι ὁ εὐνοῦχος, ἐπορεύετο γὰρ τὴν ὁδὸν αὐτοῦ χαίρων. [GNT]
		To be suddenly taken away; to be caught away; to be snatched away; to be taken by force.
		
		Practical Application
		The word for "suddenly took away" (*hërpasen*) is strong. It means to be snatched away quickly, immediately, miraculously. It is the same word used for the rapture of the church. It means to catch up into heaven during the rapture.

#3845
 	
Suffer
 	
Suffer–KJV
Suffer–NASB
Suffer–NIV
Suffer–NKJV
Suffer–NLT
 	
POSB REFERENCE
(Acts 26:22-23; esp. v.23)
Note 2, point 2
	παθητός = *pathëtos*
	Pronunciation: [path-ay-tos']
	Parsing (part of speech): adjective
	    Case—nominative
	    Gender—masculine
	    Number—singular
	    Stem or root—from παθητός, ή, όν
	Concordance References:
	⇒ Strong's #3805 pathëtos
	⇒ NIV #4078 pathëtos
	⇒ NASB #3805 pathëtos
	
	Acts 26:23
	That Christ should **suffer**, and that he should be the first that should rise from the dead, and should shew light unto the people, and to the Gentiles. [KJV]
	
	That the Christ was to **suffer**, and that by reason of
		To suffer, endure, tolerate, bear, stand.
		
		Practical Application
		The words "that Christ would suffer" are spoken from the Jewish point of view. Paul was declaring that Christ, the Messiah, must suffer; He was destined to suffer. The Messiah was a man who was not only capable of suffering, but He had to suffer. His death was ordained; it was a *must* in the mind of God and prophesied in the Scripture. There was no other way for God to save man other than by the death of His Son, the Messiah. (See POSB outline—Acts 2:22-24 and notes, Jesus Christ, Death—Acts 2:22-24; POSB *Deeper Study* #2—Acts 2:23 for more discussion.)

ENGLISH WORD	GREEK WORD AND VERSE	THE WORD MEANS...
	His resurrection from the dead He should be the first to proclaim light both to the Jewish people and to the Gentiles." [NASB] That the Christ would **suffer** and, as the first to rise from the dead, would proclaim light to his own people and to the Gentiles." [NIV] That the Christ would **suffer**, that He would be the first to rise from the dead, and would proclaim light to the *Jewish* people and to the Gentiles." [NKJV] That the Messiah would **suffer** and be the first to rise from the dead as a light to Jews and Gentiles alike." [NLT] εἰ **παθητὸς** ὁ Χριστός, εἰ πρῶτος ἐξ ἀναστάσεως νεκρῶν φῶς μέλλει καταγγέλλειν τῷ τε λαῷ καὶ τοῖς ἔθνεσι. [GNS] εἰ **παθητὸς** ὁ Χριστός, εἰ πρῶτος ἐξ ἀναστάσεως νεκρῶν φῶς μέλλει καταγγέλλειν τῷ τε λαῷ καὶ τοῖς ἔθνεσιν. [GNT]	

#3846
Suffer Grief
 	
Heaviness–KJV
Distressed–NASB
Suffer grief–NIV
Grieved–NKJV
Endure–NLT
 	
POSB REFERENCE
(1 Pt.1:6)
    Note 1, point 2
	λυπηθέντες = lupēthentes
	Pronunciation: [loo-pay'-then-tehs]
	Parsing (part of speech): verb
	    Mood—participle
	    Tense—aorist
	    Voice—passive
	    Case—nominative
	    Gender—masculine
	    Person—2nd person
	    Number—plural
	    Stem or root—from λυπέω
	Concordance References:
	⟹ Strong's #3076 lupeö
	⟹ NIV #3382 lupeö
	⟹ NASB #3076 lupeö
	
	1 Peter 1:6
	Wherein ye greatly rejoice, though now for a season, if need be, ye are in **heaviness** through manifold temptations: [KJV]
	
	In this you greatly rejoice, even though now for a little while, if necessary, you have been **distressed** by various trials, [NASB]
	
	In this you greatly rejoice, though now for a little while you may have had to **suffer grief** in all kinds of trials. [NIV]
	
	In this you greatly rejoice, though now for a little while, if need be, you have been **grieved** by various trials, [NKJV]
	
	So be truly glad! There is wonderful joy ahead, even though it is necessary for you to **endure** many trials for a while. [NLT]
	
	ἐν ᾧ ἀγαλλιᾶσθε ὀλίγον ἄρτι, εἰ δέον ἐστί, **λυπηθέντες** ἐν ποικίλοις πειρασμοῖς, [GNS]
	
	ἐν ᾧ ἀγαλλιᾶσθε, ὀλίγον ἄρτι εἰ δέον [ἐστὶν] **λυπηθέντες** ἐν ποικίλοις πειρασμοῖς, [GNT]
		To suffer grief, heaviness; to be distressed, sorrowful; to be hurt; to be made sorry; to be sad; to be grieving; to suffer sorrow, stress, pressure, and mental anguish.
		
		Practical Application
		Trials and temptations cause a heaviness within us. We all know what it is to feel heavy and weighed down with grief; to suffer stress and pressure; to be in mental anguish, wondering, questioning, and suffering under the weight of trial or temptation.

#3847
Suffereth Long–
Suffers Long
 	
Suffereth long–KJV
Patient–NASB
Patient–NIV
Suffers long–NKJV
Patient–NLT
 	
POSB REFERENCE
(1 Cor.13:4-7; esp. v.4)
    Note 2
	μακροθυμεῖ = makrothumei
	Pronunciation: [mak-roth-oo-meh'-ee]
	Parsing (part of speech): verb
	    Mood—indicative
	    Tense—present
	    Voice—active
	    Person—3rd person
	    Number—singular
	    Stem or root—from μακροθυμέω
	Concordance References:
	⟹ Strong's #3114 makrothumeö
	⟹ NIV #3428 makrothumeö
	⟹ NASB #3114 makrothumeö
	
	1 Cor. 13:4
	Charity **suffereth long**, and is kind; charity envieth not; charity vaunteth not itself, is not puffed up, [KJV]
		Patient, untiring, persevering; to suffer long; is patient with people.
		
		Practical Application
		The word always refers to being patient with people, not with circumstances (William Barclay. *The Letters to the Corinthians*, p.133).
		Love is patient; it is patient a long, long time..
		• no matter the evil and injury done by a person.
		• no matter the neglect or ignoring by a loved one.
		
		Love is patient a long, long time without resentment, anger, or seeking revenge. Love

ENGLISH WORD	GREEK WORD AND VERSE	THE WORD MEANS...
	Love is **patient**, love is kind, and is not jealous; love does not brag and is not arrogant, [NASB] Love is **patient**, love is kind. It does not envy, it does not boast, it is not proud. [NIV] Love **suffers long** *and* is kind; love does not envy; love does not parade itself, is not puffed up; [NKJV] Love is **patient** and kind. Love is not jealous or boastful or proud [NLT] ἡ ἀγάπη **μακροθυμεῖ**, χρηστεύεται· ἡ ἀγάπη, οὐ ζηλοῖ· ἡ ἀγάπη οὐ περπερεύεται, οὐ φυσιοῦται, [GNS] Ἡ ἀγάπη **μακροθυμεῖ** χρηστεύεται ἡ ἀγάπη, οὐ ζηλοῖ, [ἡ ἀγάπη] οὐ περπερεύεται, οὐ φυσιοῦται, [GNT]	controls itself in order to win the person and to help him live, work, and serve as he should.

#3848
Suffering
 	
Tribulation–KJV
Tribulation–NASB
Suffering–NIV
Tribulation–NKJV
Trials–NLT
 	
POSB
REFERENCE
(Rom.5:3-5; esp. v.3)
Note 5
	θλῖψις = *thlipsis*
	Pronunciation: [thlip'-sis]
	Parsing (part of speech): noun
	  Case—nominative
	  Gender—feminine
	  Number—singular
	  Stem or root—from θλίψις, εως
	Concordance References:
	⇒ Strong's #2347 thlipsis
	⇒ NIV #2568 thlipsis
	⇒ NASB #2347 thlipsis
	
	Romans 5:3
	And not only so, but we glory in tribulations also: knowing that **tribulation** worketh patience; [KJV]
	
	And not only this, but we also exult in our tribulations, knowing that **tribulation** brings about perseverance; [NASB]
	
	Not only so, but we also rejoice in our sufferings, because we know that **suffering** produces perseverance; [NIV]
	
	And not only *that,* but we also glory in tribulations, knowing that **tribulation** produces perseverance; [NKJV]
	
	We can rejoice, too, when we run into problems and **trials**, for we know that they are good for us—they help us learn to endure. [NLT]
	
	οὐ μόνον δέ, ἀλλὰ καὶ καυχώμεθα ἐν ταῖς θλίψεσιν, εἰδότες ὅτι ἡ **θλῖψις** ὑπομονὴν κατεργάζεται, [GNS]
	
	οὐ μόνον δέ, ἀλλὰ καὶ καυχώμεθα ἐν ταῖς θλίψεσιν, εἰδότες ὅτι ἡ **θλῖψις** ὑπομονὴν κατεργάζεται, [GNT]
		Trouble, distress, hard circumstances, trials, suffering. The word "suffering" (*thlipsis*) means pressure, oppression, affliction, and distress. It means to be pressed together ever so tightly. It means all kinds of pressure ranging from the day-to-day pressures to the pressure of confronting the most serious afflictions, even that of death itself.
		
		Practical Application
		When a man is truly justified, he is no longer defeated by trials and sufferings. Trials and sufferings no longer discourage and swamp him, no longer cast him down into the dungeon of despair and hopelessness. The very opposite is true. Trials and sufferings become purposeful and meaningful. The truly justified man knows...
		
		• that his life and welfare are completely under God's care and watchful eye.
		• therefore, whatever events come into his life—whether good or bad—they are allowed by God for a reason. The justified man knows that God will take the trials and sufferings of this world and work them out for good, even if God has to twist and move every event surrounding the believer.

#3849
Suffering
 	
Passion–KJV
Suffering–NASB
Suffering–NIV
Suffering–NKJV
Crucifixion–NLT
 	
POSB
REFERENCE
(Acts 1:3)
Note 3
	παθεῖν = *pathein*
	Pronunciation: [path'-een]
	Parsing (part of speech): verb
	  Mood—infinitive
	  Tense—aorist
	  Voice—active
	  Case—accusative
	  Stem or root—from πάσχω
	Concordance References:
	⇒ Strong's #3958 paschō
	⇒ NIV #4248 paschō
	⇒ NASB ##3958 paschō
	
	Acts 1:3
	To whom also he shewed himself alive after his **passion** by many infallible proofs, being seen of them forty days, and speaking of the things pertaining to the kingdom of God: [KJV]
	
	To these He also presented Himself alive, after His **suffering**, by many convincing proofs, appearing to them over a period of forty days, and speaking of the things concerning the kingdom of God. [NASB]
	
	After his **suffering**, he showed himself to these men and gave many convincing proofs that he was alive. He appeared to them over a period of forty days and spoke about the kingdom of God. [NIV]
	
	To whom He also presented Himself alive after His
		Suffering, passion, crucifixion.
		
		Practical Application
		The word "suffering" (*pathein*) means suffering; it refers to the sufferings or death of Christ. His death and resurrection assured the salvation of man.

ENGLISH WORD	GREEK WORD AND VERSE	THE WORD MEANS...

	suffering by many infallible proofs, being seen by them during forty days and speaking of the things pertaining to the kingdom of God. [NKJV]	
	During the forty days after his **crucifixion**, he appeared to the apostles from time to time and proved to them in many ways that he was actually alive. On these occasions he talked to them about the Kingdom of God. [NLT]	
	οἷς καὶ παρέστησεν ἑαυτὸν ζῶντα μετὰ τὸ **παθεῖν** αὐτὸν ἐν πολλοῖς τεκμηρίοις, δι' ἡμερῶν τεσσεράκοντα ὀπτανόμενος αὐτοῖς, καὶ λέγων τὰ περὶ τῆς βασιλείας τοῦ Θεοῦ. [GNS]	
	οἷς καὶ παρέστησεν ἑαυτὸν ζῶντα μετὰ τὸ **παθεῖν** αὐτὸν ἐν πολλοῖς τεκμηρίοις, δι' ἡμερῶν τεσσεράκοντα ὀπτανόμενος αὐτοῖς καὶ λέγων τὰ περὶ τῆς βασιλείας τοῦ θεοῦ· [GNT]	

#3850
Suffering
 	
Tribulation–KJV
Tribulation–NASB
Afflictions–NIV
Tribulation–NKJV
Suffering–NLT
 	
POSB
REFERENCE
(Rev.2:9)
Note 3, point 1
	θλῖψιν = thlipsin
	Pronunciation: [thlip'-sin]
	Parsing (part of speech): noun
	   Case—accusative
	   Gender—feminine
	   Number—singular
	   Stem or root—from θλῖψις, εως
	Concordance References:
	⇒ Strong's #2347 thlipsis
	⇒ NIV #2568 thlipsis
	⇒ NASB #2347 thlipsis
	
	Rev. 2:9
	I know thy works, and **tribulation**, and poverty, (but thou art rich) and I know the blasphemy of them which say they are Jews, and are not, but are the synagogue of Satan. [KJV]
	'I know your **tribulation** and your poverty (but you are rich), and the blasphemy by those who say they are Jews and are not, but are a synagogue of Satan. [NASB]
	I know your **afflictions** and your poverty—yet you are rich! I know the slander of those who say they are Jews and are not, but are a synagogue of Satan. [NIV]
	I know your works, **tribulation**, and poverty (but you are rich); and I know the blasphemy of those who say they are Jews and are not, but are a synagogue of Satan. [NKJV]
	"I know about your **suffering** and your poverty—but you are rich! I know the slander of those opposing you. They say they are Jews, but they really aren't because theirs is a synagogue of Satan. [NLT]
	Οἶδά σου τὰ ἔργα καὶ τὴν **θλῖψιν** καὶ τὴν πτωχείαν, -- πλούσιος δὲ εἶ -- , καὶ τὴν βλασφημίαν τῶν λεγόντων Ἰουδαίους εἶναι ἑαυτούς, καὶ οὐκ εἰσίν, ἀλλὰ συναγωγὴ τοῦ Σατανᾶ. [GNS]
	Οἶδά σου τὴν **θλῖψιν** καὶ τὴν πτωχείαν, ἀλλὰ πλούσιος εἶ, καὶ τὴν βλασφημίαν ἐκ τῶν λεγόντων Ἰουδαίους εἶναι ἑαυτούς, καὶ οὐκ εἰσὶν ἀλλὰ συναγωγὴ τοῦ Σατανᾶ. [GNT]
		Afflictions, trials, tribulation, persecution, suffering, trouble. It means the pressure of crushing affliction. It means troubles, hard circumstances, distress, pressure, strain, tension that comes both from within and without.
		
		Practical Application
		This word indicates that the trials and persecution were most severe. But the believers were holding up under the attacks and refusing to deny Christ. They were faithful to Christ despite all the ridicule, mockery, abuse, cursing, loss of property, possible imprisonment and martyrdom.

#3851
Sufficient
 	
Sufficient–KJV
Sufficient–NASB
Sufficient–NIV
Sufficient–NKJV
All you need–NLT
 	
POSB
REFERENCE
(2 Cor.12:7-10; esp.
v.9)
Note 3
	Ἀρκεῖ = Arkei
	Pronunciation: [ar-keh'-ee]
	Parsing (part of speech): verb
	   Mood—indicative
	   Tense—present
	   Voice—active
	   Person—3rd person
	   Number—singular
	   Stem or root—from ἀρκέω
	Concordance References:
	⇒ Strong's #714 arkeö
	⇒ NIV #758 arkeö
	⇒ NASB #714 arkeö
		Sufficient, all you need; to be enough; the power or strength to withstand any danger.
		
		Practical Application
		The presence, love, favor, and blessings of God are sufficient to help the believer walk through any suffering. God's grace within the believer can carry the believer through anything. In Paul's case, it was physical suffering. In our case it may be either physical or spiritual attacks; but no matter: God's grace is sufficient to see us through whatever the thorn is.

ENGLISH WORD	GREEK WORD AND VERSE	THE WORD MEANS...
	2 Cor. 12:9 And he said unto me, My grace is **sufficient** for thee: for my strength is made perfect in weakness. Most gladly therefore will I rather glory in my infirmities, that the power of Christ may rest upon me. [KJV] And He has said to me, "My grace is **sufficient** for you, for power is perfected in weakness." Most gladly, therefore, I will rather boast about my weaknesses, that the power of Christ may dwell in me. [NASB] But he said to me, "My grace is **sufficient** for you, for my power is made perfect in weakness." Therefore I will boast all the more gladly about my weaknesses, so that Christ's power may rest on me. [NIV] And He said to me, "My grace is **sufficient** for you, for My strength is made perfect in weakness." Therefore most gladly I will rather boast in my infirmities, that the power of Christ may rest upon me. [NKJV] Each time he said, "My gracious favor is **all you need**. My power works best in your weakness." So now I am glad to boast about my weaknesses, so that the power of Christ may work through me. [NLT] καὶ εἴρηκέ μοι· Ἀρκεῖ σοι ἡ χάρις μου· ἡ γὰρ δύναμις μου ἐν ἀσθενείᾳ τελειοῦται. ἥδιστα οὖν μᾶλλον καυχήσομαι ἐν ταῖς ἀσθενείαις μου, ἵνα ἐπισκηνώσῃ ἐπ' ἐμὲ ἡ δύναμις τοῦ Χριστοῦ. [GNS] καὶ εἴρηκέν μοι· Ἀρκεῖ σοι ἡ χάρις μου, ἡ γὰρ δύναμις ἐν ἀσθενείᾳ τελεῖται. ἥδιστα οὖν μᾶλλον καυχήσομαι ἐν ταῖς ἀσθενείαις μου, ἵνα ἐπισκηνώσῃ ἐπ' ἐμὲ ἡ δύναμις τοῦ Χριστοῦ. [GNT]	

#3852
Summing Up Of All Things
 	
Gather together in one all things–KJV
Summing up of all things–NASB
Bring...together under one head–NIV
Gather together in one all things–NKJV
Bring everything together–NLT
 	
POSB REFERENCE
(Eph.1:9-10; esp. v.10)
Note 6, point 3
	ἀνακεφαλαιώσασθαι = anakephalaiösasthai
	Pronunciation: [an-ak-ef-al-ah'ee-o-sahs-tha-ee]
	Parsing (part of speech): verb
	   Mood—infinitive
	   Tense—aorist
	   Voice—middle dep
	   Stem or root—from ἀνακεφαλαιόω
	Concordance References:
	⇒ Strong's #346 anakephalaioö
	⇒ NIV #368 anakephalaioö
	⇒ NASB #346 anakephalaioö
	Ephes. 1:10
	That in the dispensation of the fulness of times he might **gather together in one all things** in Christ, both which are in heaven, and which are on earth; even in him: [KJV]
	With a view to an administration suitable to the fulness of the times, that is, the **summing up of all things** in Christ, things in the heavens and things upon the earth. In Him [NASB]
	To be put into effect when the times will have reached their fulfillment—to **bring** all things in heaven and on earth **together under one head**, even Christ. [NIV]
	That in the dispensation of the fullness of the times He might **gather together in one all things** in Christ, both which are in heaven and which are on earth—in Him. [NKJV]
	And this is his plan: At the right time he will **bring everything together** under the authority of Christ—everything in heaven and on earth. [NLT]
	εἰς οἰκονομίαν τοῦ πληρώματος τῶν καιρῶν, **ἀνακεφαλαιώσασθαι** τὰ πάντα ἐν τῷ Χριστῷ, τά τε ἐν τοῖς οὐρανοῖς καὶ τὰ ἐπὶ τῆς γῆς· ἐν αὐτῷ, [GNS]
	εἰς οἰκονομίαν τοῦ πληρώματος τῶν καιρῶν, **ἀνακεφαλαιώσασθαι** τὰ πάντα ἐν τῷ Χριστῷ, τὰ ἐπὶ τοῖς οὐρανοῖς καὶ τὰ ἐπὶ τῆς γῆς ἐν αὐτῷ. [GNT]
		To bring together under one head; to gather together in one all things; to sum up all things; to bring everything together; to unite.
		
		Practical Application
		There is to be a consummation, a climax of history—a *fulness of the times*, a new order—in which all things will be unified and harmonized and brought to a peaceful state under the authority of Jesus Christ. History is in the hands of God.
		God is handling, planning, arranging, and administering all things toward a climactic consummation for Christ and His followers. In that climactic day all disharmony and division and evil will be subjected and harmonized (*anakephalaiösasthai*) under Christ. A new and perfect and eternal creation will be established for the Lord and His followers throughout the universe.

#3853
Sumptuously
	λαμπρῶς = lamprös
	Pronunciation: [lamp-rows]
	Parsing (part of speech): adjective
	   Type—adverb
	   Stem or root—from λαμπρῶς
		To live in luxury; to live in splendor. The word means that the rich man was flamboyant, displaying his wealth in materialistic ways.

ENGLISH WORD	GREEK WORD AND VERSE	THE WORD MEANS...

#3864
Swellings
 	
Swellings–KJV
Arrogance–NASB
Arrogance–NIV
Conceits–NKJV
Conceit–NLT
 	
**POSB
REFERENCE**
(2 Cor.12:19-21; esp.
v.20)
Note 3, point 2
	φυσιώσεις = *phusiöseis*
	Pronunciation: [foo-see'-o-seh-ees]
	Parsing (part of speech): noun
	   Case—nominative
	   Gender—feminine
	   Number—plural
	   Stem or root—from φυσίωσις, εως
	Concordance References:
	⇒ Strong's #5450 phusiösis
	⇒ NIV #5883 phusiösis
	⇒ NASB #5450 phusiösis
	
	2 Cor. 12:20
	For I fear, lest, when I come, I shall not find you such as I would, and that I shall be found unto you such as ye would not: lest there be debates, envyings, wraths, strifes, backbitings, whisperings, **swellings**, tumults: [KJV]
	For I am afraid that perhaps when I come I may find you to be not what I wish and may be found by you to be not what you wish; that perhaps there may be strife, jealousy, angry tempers, disputes, slanders, gossip, **arrogance**, disturbances; [NASB]
	For I am afraid that when I come I may not find you as I want you to be, and you may not find me as you want me to be. I fear that there may be quarreling, jealousy, outbursts of anger, factions, slander, gossip, **arrogance** and disorder. [NIV]
	For I fear lest, when I come, I shall not find you such as I wish, and that I shall be found by you such as you do not wish; lest there be contentions, jealousies, outbursts of wrath, selfish ambitions, backbitings, whisperings, **conceits**, tumults; [NKJV]
	For I am afraid that when I come to visit you I won't like what I find, and then you won't like my response. I am afraid that I will find quarreling, jealousy, outbursts of anger, selfishness, backstabbing, gossip, **conceit**, and disorderly behavior. [NLT]
	φοβοῦμαι γὰρ μή πως ἐλθὼν οὐχ οἵους θέλω εὕρω ὑμᾶς, κἀγὼ εὑρεθῶ ὑμῖν οἷον οὐ θέλετε· μή πως ἔρις, ζῆλοι, θυμοί, ἐριθείαι, καταλαλιαί, ψιθυρισμοί, **φυσιώσεις**, ἀκαταστασίαι· [GNS]
	φοβοῦμαι γὰρ μή πως ἐλθὼν οὐχ οἵους θέλω εὕρω ὑμᾶς κἀγὼ εὑρεθῶ ὑμῖν οἷον οὐ θέλετε· μή πως ἔρις, ζῆλος, θυμοί, ἐριθείαι, καταλαλιαί, ψιθυρισμοί, **φυσιώσεις**, ἀκαταστασίαι· [GNT]
		Conceit, pride, swellings, puffed up, arrogance, haughtiness, insolence, putting oneself above others, looking down upon others, scorn, contempt.
		
		Practical Application
		The arrogant, the conceited, the proud person feels that he is better than others. Note that this is a feeling within the heart. The proud person may appear quiet and humble, but within his heart, he secretly feels better than others. God resists the proud.

#3865
Swept
 	
Drew–KJV
Swept–NASB
Swept–NIV
Drew–NKJV
Dragged–NLT
 	
**POSB
REFERENCE**
(Rev.12:3-4; esp.v.4)
Note 2, point 2
	σύρει = *surei*
	Pronunciation: [soo'-reh-ee]
	Parsing (part of speech): verb
	   Mood—indicative
	   Tense—present
	   Voice—active
	   Person—3rd person
	   Number—singular
	   Stem or root—from σύρω
	Concordance References:
	⇒ Strong's #4951 surö
	⇒ NIV #5359 surö
	⇒ NASB #4951 surö
	
	Rev. 12:4
	And his tail **drew** the third part of the stars of heaven, and did cast them to the earth: and the dragon stood before the woman which was ready to be delivered, for to devour her child as soon as it was born. [KJV]
	And his tail **swept** away a third of the stars of heaven, and threw them to the earth. And the dragon stood before the woman who was about to give birth, so that when she gave birth he might devour her child. [NASB]
	His tail **swept** a third of the stars out of the sky and flung them to the earth. The dragon stood in front of the woman who was about to give birth, so that he might devour her child the moment it was born. [NIV]
		Swept, drew, dragged; to sweep; to drag down.
		
		Practical Application
		There is the origin of the dragon or devil. This statement is telling where Satan came from. This is clearly seen in the Greek tense of the statement. His tail "swept" (*surei*, present tense) a third part of heaven. That is, Satan draws, pulls, and drags a third of the stars, that is, angels of heaven.

ENGLISH WORD	GREEK WORD AND VERSE	THE WORD MEANS...
	His tail **drew** a third of the stars of heaven and threw them to the earth. And the dragon stood before the woman who was ready to give birth, to devour her Child as soon as it was born. [NKJV]	
	His tail **dragged** down one-third of the stars, which he threw to the earth. He stood before the woman as she was about to give birth to her child, ready to devour the baby as soon as it was born. [NLT]	
	καὶ ἡ οὐρὰ αὐτοῦ **σύρει** τὸ τρίτον τῶν ἀστέρων τοῦ οὐρανοῦ, καὶ ἔβαλεν αὐτοὺς εἰς τὴν γῆν· καὶ ὁ δράκων ἔστηκεν ἐνώπιον τῆς γυναικὸς τῆς μελλούσης τεκεῖν, ἵνα, ὅταν τέκῃ τὸ τέκνον αὐτῆς. καταφάγῃ. [GNS]	
	καὶ ἡ οὐρὰ αὐτοῦ **σύρει** τὸ τρίτον τῶν ἀστέρων τοῦ οὐρανοῦ καὶ ἔβαλεν αὐτοὺς εἰς τὴν γῆν. καὶ ὁ δράκων ἔστηκεν ἐνώπιον τῆς γυναικὸς τῆς μελλούσης τεκεῖν, ἵνα ὅταν τέκῃ τὸ τέκνον αὐτῆς καταφάγῃ. [GNT]	
#3866 **Swindlers** Extortioners–KJV **Swindlers–NASB** **Swindlers–NIV** Extortioners–NKJV **Swindlers–NLT** **POSB** **REFERENCE** (1 Cor.6:10) Note 3, point 5 **See also POSB REF:** (1 Cor.5:10) Note 4, point 3	**ἅρπαγες** = *harpages* Pronunciation: [har'-pah-gehs] Parsing (part of speech): pronominal adjective 　Case—nominative 　Gender—masculine 　Number—plural 　Stem or root—from ἅρπαξ, αγος Concordance References: ⇒ Strong's #727 harpax ⇒ NIV #774 harpax ⇒ NASB #727 harpax **1 Cor. 6:10** Nor thieves, nor covetous, nor drunkards, nor revilers, nor **extortioners**, shall inherit the kingdom of God. [KJV] Nor thieves, nor the covetous, nor drunkards, nor revilers, nor **swindlers**, shall inherit the kingdom of God. [NASB] Nor thieves nor the greedy nor drunkards nor slanderers nor **swindlers** will inherit the kingdom of God. [NIV] Nor thieves, nor covetous, nor drunkards, nor revilers, nor **extortioners** will inherit the kingdom of God. [NKJV] Thieves, greedy people, drunkards, abusers, and **swindlers**—none of these will have a share in the Kingdom of God. [NLT] οὔτε κλέπται, οὔτε πλεονέκται, οὐ μέθυσοι, οὐ λοίδοροι, οὐχ **ἅρπαγες**, βασιλείαν Θεοῦ οὐ κληρονομήσουσι. [GNS] οὔτε κλέπται, οὔτε πλεονέκται, οὐ μέθυσοι, οὐ λοίδοροι, οὐχ **ἅρπαγες** βασιλείαν θεοῦ κληρονομήσουσιν. [GNT]	Swindlers, extortioners, robbers, savage like a wolf. **Practical Application** Swindlers (*harpages*) are persons who take money and things from others either by scheme or force. They take advantage of the poor, the ignorant, the innocent, the unsuspecting, and sometimes even family and friends. They use whoever and whatever they can to get what they want. They grasp to get more and more.
#3867 **Symbolizes** Figure–KJV Corresponding–NASB **Symbolizes–NIV** Antitype–NKJV Picture–NLT **POSB** **REFERENCE** (1 Pt.3:21) Note 1, point 3	**ἀντίτυπον** = *antitupon* Pronunciation: [an-teet'-oo-pon] Parsing (part of speech): adjective adverb OR adjective 　Case—nominative 　Gender—neuter 　Number—singular 　Stem or root—from ἀντίτυπος, ον Concordance References: ⇒ Strong's #499 antitupos ⇒ NIV #531 antitupos ⇒ NASB #499 antitupos **1 Peter 3:21** The like **figure** whereunto even baptism doth also now save us (not the putting away of the filth of the flesh, but the answer of a good conscience toward God,) by the resurrection of Jesus Christ: [KJV] And **corresponding** to that, baptism now saves you—not the removal of dirt from the flesh, but an appeal to God for a good conscience—through the resurrection of Jesus Christ, [NASB]	Symbolize, figure, copy, antitype. **Practical Application** Jesus Christ saves the believer through baptism: not the baptism by water, but the baptism of a good conscience wrought by the power of the resurrection of Jesus Christ (1 Peter 3:21). The water which saved Noah and his family is a type of the cleansing that saves us. The water... • bore up the ark and saved them through the judgment of God. • delivered them from the ridicule and mockery of evil men. • delivered them from the corruption of the world and led them to a new life. • put to death the old world and gave them the hope of a new world. • put to death their old life and gave them a new beginning.

ENGLISH WORD	GREEK WORD AND VERSE	THE WORD MEANS...
	And this water **symbolizes** baptism that now saves you also—not the removal of dirt from the body but the pledge of a good conscience toward God. It saves you by the resurrection of Jesus Christ, [NIV] There is also an **antitype** which now saves us—baptism (not the removal of the filth of the flesh, but the answer of a good conscience toward God), through the resurrection of Jesus Christ, [NKJV] And this is a **picture** of baptism, which now saves you by the power of Jesus Christ's resurrection. Baptism is not a removal of dirt from your body; it is an appeal to God from a clean conscience. [NLT] ᾧ καὶ ἡμᾶς **ἀντίτυπον** νῦν σῴζει βάπτισμα, οὐ σαρκὸς ἀπόθεσις ῥύπου, ἀλλὰ συνειδήσεως ἀγαθῆς ἐπερώτημα εἰς Θεόν, δι' ἀναστάσεως Ἰησοῦ Χριστοῦ, [GNS] ὃ καὶ ὑμᾶς **ἀντίτυπον** νῦν σῴζει βάπτισμα, οὐ σαρκὸς ἀπόθεσις ῥύπου ἀλλὰ συνειδήσεως ἀγαθῆς ἐπερώτημα εἰς θεόν, δι' ἀναστάσεως Ἰησοῦ Χριστοῦ, [GNT]	• saved the race of man and created a new people of God. • delivered them from the old world right into the new world. What is Peter saying? Note the word "symbolizes" (*antitupon*). The figure or picture of baptism is just like the water that saved Noah and his family. ⇒ The *flooding waters* of Noah's day picture the judgment of God upon sin. The flooding waters picture how man was saved from a corruptible world and carried into a new world. ⇒ The *baptismal water* pictures the judgment of God upon Christ, a judgment of death that was due sinners. It pictures how man is saved from a corruptible life and world and carried into a new life and world by the resurrection of Christ.
#3868 **Sympathetic–** **Sympathy** Compassion–KJV **Sympathetic–NASB** **Sympathetic–NIV** Compassion–NKJV **Sympathy–NLT** **POSB** **REFERENCE** (1 Pt.3:8) Note 2	συμπαθεῖς = *sumpatheis* Pronunciation: [soom-path-ice'] Parsing (part of speech): adjective 　　Case—nominative 　　Gender—masculine 　　Number—plural 　　Stem or root—from συμπαθής, ές Concordance References: ⇒　Strong's #4835 sumpathēs ⇒　NIV #5218 sumpathēs ⇒　NASB #4835 sumpathēs **1 Peter 3:8** Finally, be ye all of one mind, having **compassion** one of another, love as brethren, be pitiful, be courteous: [KJV] To sum up, let all be harmonious, **sympathetic**, brotherly, kindhearted, and humble in spirit; [NASB] Finally, all of you, live in harmony with one another; be **sympathetic**, love as brothers, be compassionate and humble. [NIV] Finally, all *of you be* of one mind, having **compassion** for one another; love as brothers, *be* tenderhearted, *be* courteous; [NKJV] Finally, all of you should be of one mind, full of **sympathy** toward each other, loving one another with tender hearts and humble minds. [NLT] Τὸ δὲ τέλος, πάντες ὁμόφρονες, **συμπαθεῖς**, φιλάδελφοι, εὔσπλαγχνοι, φιλόφρονες· [GNS] Τὸ δὲ τέλος πάντες ὁμόφρονες, **συμπαθεῖς**, φιλάδελφοι, εὔσπλαγχνοι, ταπεινόφρονες, [GNT]	Compassion, sympathy; to actually feel with others. **Practical Application** It means to feel for others so much that... • one suffers with those who suffer. • one weeps with those who weep. • one rejoices when others are honored. • one understands the pressure that a leader is under when he has to lead. • one hurts with those who are criticized and attacked. • one grieves with the sorrows of others. Unity cannot exist unless believers feel compassion and sympathy for one another. Believers cannot be selfish and aloof; they cannot be seeking attention and seeking to get their own way if they are to be unified. Unity demands sympathy; unity demands that believers feel for one another—that they feel deeply, so deeply that they actually experience what other believers experience: pain, hurt, abuse, suffering, joy, and rejoicing.
#3869 **Sympathize** **With** Touched–KJV **Sympathize with–** **NASB** **Sympathize with–** **NIV** **Sympathize with–** **NKJV** Understands–NLT	συμπαθῆσαι = *sumpathēsai* Pronunciation: [soom-path-ay'-sah-ee] Parsing (part of speech): verb 　　Mood—infinitive 　　Tense—aorist 　　Voice—active 　　Stem or root—from συμπαθέω Concordance References: ⇒　Strong's #4834 sumpatheō ⇒　NIV #5217 sumpatheō ⇒　NASB #4834 sumpatheō **Hebrews 4:15** For we have not an high priest which cannot be **touched** with the feeling of our infirmities; but was in all points tempted like as we are, yet without sin. [KJV] For we do not have a high priest who cannot **sympathize with** our weaknesses, but One who has been tempt-	To sympathize with; to be touched with another persons hurt; to understand. The word "touched" (*sumpathēsai*) means to sympathize, feel, and suffer with. It means to sympathize and feel with a person to the point that the hurt and pain are actually felt within one's own heart. **Practical Application** We have a High Priest who feels with us. The idea is that Jesus Christ actually suffers when we suffer. He knows and suffers right along with us when we... • become sick • suffer trials • face temptations • fall into sin • have an accident

ENGLISH WORD	GREEK WORD AND VERSE	THE WORD MEANS...

**POSB
REFERENCE**
(Heb.4:15-16; esp.
v.15
Note 2, point 1

ed in all things as we are, yet without sin. [NASB]

For we do not have a high priest who is unable to **sympathize with** our weaknesses, but we have one who has been tempted in every way, just as we are—yet was without sin. [NIV]

For we do not have a High Priest who cannot **sympathize with** our weaknesses, but was in all *points* tempted as *we are, yet* without sin. [NKJV]

This High Priest of ours **understands** our weaknesses, for he faced all of the same temptations we do, yet he did not sin. [NLT]

οὐ γὰρ ἔχομεν ἀρχιερέα μὴ δυνάμενον **συμπαθῆσαι** ταῖς ἀσθενείαις ἡμῶν, πεπειρασμένον δὲ κατὰ πάντα καθ᾽ ὁμοιότητα, χωρὶς ἁμαρτίας. [GNS]

οὐ γὰρ ἔχομεν ἀρχιερέα μὴ δυνάμενον **συμπαθῆσαι** ταῖς ἀσθενείαις ἡμῶν, πεπειρασμένον δὲ κατὰ πάντα καθ᾽ ὁμοιότητα χωρὶς ἁμαρτίας. [GNT]

- feel lonely
- sense emptiness
- lack purpose
- lose a loved one
- lack money
- are hungry
- lack clothes
- suffer persecution
- face death

Name the trial or pain, temptation, or suffering—name the infirmity or weakness—name any and all human experiences—Jesus Christ actually sympathizes and feels with us. He actually suffers and hurts right along with us. We could ask for no greater Savior; we could crave no greater Intercessor; we could long for no greater High Priest to stand before God *for us*. Jesus Christ is our *great High Priest*. He is our representative before God. He is the One who carries on the glorious ministry and intercession for us, and He "sympathizes with our weaknesses"—with all of our human weaknesses and frailties.

**#3870
Synagogue**

Synagogue–KJV
Synagogue–NASB
Synagogue–NIV
Synagogue–NKJV
Synagogue–NLT

**POSB
REFERENCE**
(Mk.1:21)
Deeper Study #1

συναγωγὴν = *synagogen*
Pronunciation: [soon-ag-o-gayn']
Parsing (part of speech): noun
    Case—accusative
    Gender—feminine
    Number—singular
    Stem or root—from συναγωγή, ῆς
Concordance References:
  ⟹ Strong's #4864 sunagoge
  ⟹ NIV #5252 sunágögë
  ⟹ NASB #4864 sunagoge

Mark 1:21
And they went into Capernaum; and straightway on the sabbath day he entered into the **synagogue**, and taught. [KJV]

And they went into Capernaum; and immediately on the Sabbath He entered the **synagogue** and began to teach. [NASB]

They went to Capernaum, and when the Sabbath came, Jesus went into the **synagogue** and began to teach. [NIV]

Then they went into Capernaum, and immediately on the Sabbath He entered the **synagogue** and taught. [NKJV]

Jesus and his companions went to the town of Capernaum, and every Sabbath day he went into the **synagogue** and taught the people. [NLT]

Καὶ εἰσπορεύονται εἰς Καφερναούμ· καὶ εὐθέως τοῖς σάββασιν εἰσελθὼν εἰς τὴν **συναγωγὴν**, ἐδίδασκε. [GNS]

Καὶ εἰσπορεύονται εἰς Καφαρναούμ· καὶ εὐθὺς τοῖς σάββασιν εἰσελθὼν εἰς τὴν **συναγωγὴν** ἐδίδασκεν. [GNT]

A gathering, a community of people. It can also mean the building in which the gathering took place.

Practical Application
Synagogues were often held in homes. In fact, if ten Jews lived in a community, they were bound by law to conduct a synagogue meeting someplace. If there were enough Jewish citizens in a place and the local laws allowed, they constructed a synagogue building. There is no sure mention of synagogues in the Old Testament, but they are mentioned over fifty times in the New Testament.

Synagogues began to rise either during or right after the Jews returned from the Babylonian captivity. The leaders became convinced that the nation could never survive unless its people really knew and practiced the law of God. Therefore, it was established that wherever ten or more Jews lived, they were to meet together on a regular basis in a synagogue meeting. They were to study and practice the law of God. The growth of synagogues was staggering. The number can be imagined by keeping in mind how the Jews had been deported and dispersed all over the world, and by remembering that wherever ten Jews lived, they were to form a synagogue meeting (cp. Luke 4:16f; Acts 9:2).

The head of the synagogue was the Ruler of the Synagogue. He was the administrator, handling the business affairs and overseeing the services. He arranged for speakers and readers and the men who were to pray (cp. Mark 5:22; Luke 13:14; Acts 18:8). There was also the chazzan or sexton or minister. He was in charge of the sacred scrolls or Scripture, the teaching of the law in actual class sessions, and the care and maintenance of the synagogue building (cp. Luke 4:20).

The service of the synagogue meeting was very simple. There was prayer, the reading of the Scripture (scroll), and an exposition of the

ENGLISH WORD	GREEK WORD AND VERSE	THE WORD MEANS...
	παθημάτων τῇ ἐν τῷ κόσμῳ ὑμῶν ἀδελφότητι ἐπιτελεῖσθαι. [GNS] ᾧ **ἀντίστητε** στερεοὶ τῇ πίστει εἰδότες τὰ αὐτὰ τῶν παθημάτων τῇ ἐν [τῷ] κόσμῳ ὑμῶν ἀδελφότητι ἐπιτελεῖσθαι. [GNT]	• "Do your own thing." • "You're a fool if you don't get all you can." • "Live, drink, and be merry." A person's desires and lusts may want more and more of the possessions and pleasures of this world. The temptation will always be there to turn away from Christ and His righteousness, to turn away from one's faith and to return to the world and its ways. Our duty is to take a firm stand against the devil, trusting God for the necessary strength to conquer the temptation.

#3873
Take Care
 	
Ministered–KJV
Minister–NASB
Take care–NIV
Ministered–NKJV
Help–NLT
 	
**POSB
REFERENCE**
(Philip.2:25)
Note 1, point 5
	λειτουργὸν = *leitourgon*
	Pronunciation: [li-toorg-on']
	Parsing (part of speech): noun
	    Case—accusative
	    Gender—masculine
	    Number—singular
	    Stem or root—from **λειτουργός**, οῦ
	Concordance References:
	⇒ Strong's #3011 leitourgos
	⇒ NIV #3313 leitourgos
	⇒ NASB #3011 leitourgos
	
	Philip. 2:25
	Yet I supposed it necessary to send to you Epaphroditus, my brother, and companion in labour, and fellow soldier, but your messenger, and he that **ministered** to my wants. [KJV]
	But I thought it necessary to send to you Epaphroditus, my brother and fellow worker and fellow soldier, who is also your messenger and **minister** to my need; [NASB]
	But I think it is necessary to send back to you Epaphroditus, my brother, fellow worker and fellow soldier, who is also your messenger, whom you sent to **take care** of my needs. [NIV]
	Yet I considered it necessary to send to you Epaphroditus, my brother, fellow worker, and fellow soldier, but your messenger and the one who **ministered** to my need; [NKJV]
	Meanwhile, I thought I should send Epaphroditus back to you. He is a true brother, a faithful worker, and a courageous soldier. And he was your messenger to **help** me in my need. [NLT]
	ἀναγκαῖον δὲ ἡγησάμην Ἐπαφρόδιτον τὸν ἀδελφὸν καὶ συνεργὸν καὶ συστρατιώτην μου, ὑμῶν δὲ ἀπόστολον, καὶ **λειτουργὸν** τῆς χρείας μου, πέμψαι πρὸς ὑμᾶς· [GNS]
	Ἀναγκαῖον δὲ ἡγησάμην Ἐπαφρόδιτον τὸν ἀδελφὸν καὶ συνεργὸν καὶ συστρατιώτην μου, ὑμῶν δὲ ἀπόστολον, καὶ **λειτουργὸν** τῆς χρείας μου, πέμψαι πρὸς ὑμᾶς, [GNT]
		To take care; to minister; to help; to be a servant.
		
		Practical Application
		Epaphroditus was a very special minister (*leitourgon*). William Barclay points out that this word would have great meaning to the Greek minds of the Philippian church. The word (*leitourgon*) was a great word and was used only of great men. The title was bestowed only upon great benefactors, men who loved their city, culture, arts, or sports so much that they gave huge sums of money to support these functions. The person was looked upon as a great servant or minister given over to his cause. (*The Letters to the Phillipians, Colossians, and Thessalonians,* p.61.) Paul is here bestowing the great title of minister (*leitourgon*) upon Epaphroditus. Epaphroditus was an extraordinary minister of God who ministered to Paul's needs. He was not a quitter! He was not a coward!

#3874
Take Care
 	
Take heed–KJV
Take care–NASB
See to it–NIV
Beware–NKJV
Be careful then–NLT
 	
**POSB
REFERENCE**
(Heb.3:12)
Note 2
	Βλέπετε = *Blepete*
	Pronunciation: [blep'-eh-teh]
	Parsing (part of speech): verb
	    Mood—imperative
	    Tense—present
	    Voice—active
	    Person—2nd person
	    Number—plural
	    Stem or root—from **βλέπω**
	Concordance References:
	⇒ Strong's #991 blepö
	⇒ NIV #1063 blepö
	⇒ NASB #991 blepö
	
	Hebrews 3:12
	Take heed, brethren, lest there be in any of you an evil heart of unbelief, in departing from the living God. [KJV]
	Take care, brethren, lest there should be in any one
		Be alert and stay alert; be on the lookout and do it constantly; watch and keep on watching.
		
		Practical Application
		There is great danger that believers might depart from the living God. They might do just what Israel did. Therefore, take care (*Blepete*). Keep a watchful eye on your trust and obedience to God. Watch for an evil heart of unbelief. What is an evil heart of unbelief? It is a heart that...
		• stands off from God
		• stands aloof from God
		• renounces God
		• rebels against God
		• does not believe in God
		• does not trust God and His promises
		• does not follow God as He demands

ENGLISH WORD	GREEK WORD AND VERSE	THE WORD MEANS...
	of you an evil, unbelieving heart, in falling away from the living God. [NASB] **See to it**, brothers, that none of you has a sinful, unbelieving heart that turns away from the living God. [NIV] **Beware**, brethren, lest there be in any of you an evil heart of unbelief in departing from the living God; [NKJV] **Be careful then**, dear brothers and sisters. Make sure that your own hearts are not evil and unbelieving, turning you away from the living God. [NLT] βλέπετε, ἀδελφοί, μή ποτε ἔσται ἔν τινι ὑμῶν καρδία πονηρὰ ἀπιστίας, ἐν τῷ ἀποστῆναι ἀπὸ Θεοῦ ζῶντος· [GNS] Βλέπετε, ἀδελφοί, μήποτε ἔσται ἔν τινι ὑμῶν καρδία πονηρὰ ἀπιστίας ἐν τῷ ἀποστῆναι ἀπὸ θεοῦ ζῶντος, [GNT]	

#3875
Take Care Of
 	
Feed–KJV
Shepherd–NASB
Take care of–NIV
Tend–NKJV
Take care of–NLT
 	
POSB REFERENCE
(Jn.21:15-17; esp. v.16)
Note 3, point 3
	Ποίμαινε = poimaine
	Pronunciation: [poy-mah'ee-neh]
	Parsing (part of speech): verb
	  Mood—imperative
	  Tense—present
	  Voice—active
	  Person—2nd person
	  Number—singular
	  Stem or root—from ποιμαίνω
	Concordance References:
	  ⇒ Strong's #4165 poimaino
	  ⇒ NIV #4477 poimaino
	  ⇒ NASB #4165 poimaino
	
	John 21:16
	He saith to him again the second time, Simon, *son of* Jonas, lovest thou me? He saith unto him, Yea, Lord; thou knowest that I love thee. He saith unto him, **Feed** my sheep. [KJV]
	
	He said to him again a second time, "Simon, *son of* John, do you love Me?" He said to Him, "Yes, Lord; You know that I love You." He said to him, "**Shepherd** My sheep." [NASB]
	
	Again Jesus said, "Simon son of John, do you truly love me?" He answered, "Yes, Lord, you know that I love you."Jesus said, "**Take care of** my sheep." [NIV]
	
	He said to him again a second time, "Simon, son of Jonah, do you love Me?" He said to Him, "Yes, Lord; You know that I love You." He said to him, "**Tend** My sheep." [NKJV]
	
	Jesus repeated the question: "Simon son of John, do you love me?" "Yes, Lord," Peter said, "you know I love you." "Then **take care of** my sheep," Jesus said. [NLT]
	
	λέγει αὐτῷ πάλιν δεύτερον, Σίμων Ἰωνᾶ ἀγαπᾷς με; Λέγει αὐτῷ, Ναί, Κύριε· σὺ οἶδας ὅτι φιλῶ σε. λέγει αὐτῷ, Ποίμαινε τὰ πρόβατά μου. [GNS]
	
	λέγει αὐτῷ πάλιν δεύτερον, Σίμων Ἰωάννου, ἀγαπᾷς με; λέγει αὐτῷ, Ναί, κύριε, σὺ οἶδας ὅτι φιλῶ σε. λέγει αὐτῷ, Ποίμαινε τὰ πρόβατά μου. [GNT]
		To take care of; to feed; to shepherd; to rule; to tend.
		
		Practical Application
		What is the responsibility of the Shepherd to the sheep? The Shepherd leads and shepherds the sheep. He loves them as His own; therefore, He must lead them to the green pastures and still waters. He must see that they are nourished and protected and given the very best care possible. (See POSB note—Mark 6:34 for more discussion, what happens to sheep without a Shepherd.)
		1. He feeds the sheep even if He has to gather them in His arms to carry them to the pasture (Isaiah 40:11).
		2. He guides the sheep to the pasture and away from the rough places and precipices (Psalm 23:1-4).
		3. He seeks and saves the sheep who get lost (Matthew 18:11-12; Ezekiel 34:16).
		4. He protects the sheep. He even sacrifices His life for the sheep (John 10:11; Hebrews 13:20).
		5. He restores the sheep who go astray and return (1 Peter 2:25).
		6. He rewards the sheep for obedience and faithfulness (1 Peter 5:4).
		7. He will keep the sheep separate from the goats (Matthew 25:32-33).

#3876
Take Control
 	
Put on–KJV
Put on–NASB
Clothe with–NIV
Put on–NKJV
Take control–NLT
 	
POSB REFERENCE
(Rom.13:14)
Deeper Study #2
	ἐνδύσασθε = endusasthe
	Pronunciation: [en-doo'-sahs-theh]
	Parsing (part of speech): verb
	  Mood—imperative
	  Tense—aorist
	  Voice—middle
	  Person—2nd person
	  Number—plural
	  Stem or root—from ἐνδύω
	Concordance References:
	  ⇒ Strong's #1746 enduö
	  ⇒ NIV #1907 enduö
	  ⇒ NASB #1746 enduö
	
	Romans 13:14
	But **put** ye **on** the Lord Jesus Christ, and make not
		To clothe with; to put on; to wear; to dress; to take control.
		
		Practical Application
		Scripture lists seven things that the believer is to put on or with which he is to clothe himself.
		1. The believer is to take control and be endued or clothed (*endusesthe*) with the Holy Spirit (Luke 24:49).
		2. The believer is to take control and be clothed with the Lord Jesus Christ (Romans 13:14; Galatians 3:27).
		3. The believer is to take control and be clothed with immortality (1 Cor. 15:53-54; 2 Cor. 5:3).

ENGLISH WORD	GREEK WORD AND VERSE	THE WORD MEANS...
See also POSB REF: (Col.3:12-14; esp. v.12) Note 1	provision for the flesh, to *fulfil* the lusts *thereof*. [KJV] But **put on** the Lord Jesus Christ, and make no provision for the flesh in regard to *its* lusts. [NASB] Rather, **clothe** yourselves **with** the Lord Jesus Christ, and do not think about how to gratify the desires of the sinful nature. [NIV] But **put on** the Lord Jesus Christ, and make no provision for the flesh, to *fulfill its* lusts. [NKJV] But let the Lord Jesus Christ **take control** of you, and don't think of ways to indulge your evil desires. [NLT] ἀλλ᾽ **ἐνδύσασθε** τὸν Κύριον Ἰησοῦν Χριστόν, καὶ τῆς σαρκὸς πρόνοιαν μὴ ποιεῖσθε, εἰς ἐπιθυμίας. [GNS] ἀλλὰ **ἐνδύσασθε** τὸν κύριον Ἰησοῦν Χριστόν καὶ τῆς σαρκὸς πρόνοιαν μὴ ποιεῖσθε εἰς ἐπιθυμίας. [GNT]	4. The believer is to put on and be clothed with the new man (Ephes. 4:24; Col. 3:10). 5. The believer is to take control and be clothed with the nature of God (Col. 3:12). 6. The believer is to take control and be clothed with the armour of light and of God (Romans 13:14; Ephes. 6:11f). 7. The believer is to take control and be clothed with love (Col. 3:14).
#3877 **Take Courage** Good cheer–KJV **Take courage–NASB** **Take courage–NIV** Good cheer–NKJV Be encouraged–NLT **POSB REFERENCE** (Acts 23:11) Note 5	Θάρσει = *Tharsei* Pronunciation: [thar-seh'-ee] Parsing (part of speech): verb 　　Mood—imperfect 　　Tense—present 　　Voice—active 　　Person—2nd person 　　Number—singular 　　Stem or root—from θαρσέω Concordance References: 　⇒　Strong's #2293 tharseö 　⇒　NIV #2510 tharseö 　⇒　NASB #2293 tharseö **Acts 23:11** And the night following the Lord stood by him, and said, Be of **good cheer**, Paul: for as thou hast testified of me in Jerusalem, so must thou bear witness also at Rome. [KJV] But on the night *immediately* following, the Lord stood at his side and said, "**Take courage**; for as you have solemnly witnessed to My cause at Jerusalem, so you must witness at Rome also." [NASB] The following night the Lord stood near Paul and said, "**Take courage**! As you have testified about me in Jerusalem, so you must also testify in Rome." [NIV] But the following night the Lord stood by him and said, "Be of **good cheer**, Paul; for as you have testified for Me in Jerusalem, so you must also bear witness at Rome." [NKJV] That night the Lord appeared to Paul and said, "**Be encouraged**, Paul. Just as you have told the people about me here in Jerusalem, you must preach the Good News in Rome." [NLT] Τῇ δὲ ἐπιούσῃ νυκτὶ ἐπιστὰς αὐτῷ ὁ Κύριος εἶπε, **Θάρσει** Παῦλε· ὡς γὰρ διεμαρτύρω τὰ περὶ ἐμοῦ εἰς Ἱερουσαλήμ, οὕτω σε δεῖ καὶ εἰς Ῥώμην μαρτυρῆσαι. [GNS] Τῇ δὲ ἐπιούσῃ νυκτὶ ἐπιστὰς αὐτῷ ὁ κύριος εἶπεν, **Θάρσει** ὡς γὰρ διεμαρτύρω τὰ περὶ ἐμοῦ εἰς Ἱερουσαλήμ, οὕτω σε δεῖ καὶ εἰς Ῥώμην μαρτυρῆσαι. [GNT]	To take courage; to be of good cheer; to be encouraged; to cheer up; to take heart. **Practical Application** The Lord wishes His servants to always take courage (*Tharsei*), no matter the trial. The life of His servant is under the care and leadership of the Lord.
#3878 **Take Courage** Stablish–KJV Strengthen–NASB Stand firm–NIV Establish–NKJV **Take courage–NLT** **POSB REFERENCE** (James 5:7-9; esp. v.8) Note 2, point 1	στηρίξατε τὰς καρδίας = *stērixate tas kardias* Pronunciation: [stay-rid'-zah-teh tas kar-dee'-ahs] Parsing *stērixate* (part of speech): verb 　　Mood—imperative 　　Tense—aorist 　　Voice—active 　　Person—2nd person 　　Number—plural 　　Stem or root— from στηρίζω Parsing *kardias* (part of speech): noun 　　Case—accusative 　　Gender—feminine 　　Number—plural 　　Stem or root—from καρδία, ας Concordance References:	To stand firm; to stablish; to strengthen; to take courage; to stand firm in one's mind, his inner self, his heart. **Practical Application** Believers must "take courage" (*stērixate*) in their hearts. The word means to set upon; to fix upon; to make fast (W.E. Vine. *Expository Dictionary of New Testament Words*, p.41). We must set our hearts upon the Lord's coming, for His coming is near. The idea is that it is drawing ever so close and can happen at any moment. We must focus and set our hearts upon His return—be looking for it every day just as the farmer

ENGLISH WORD	GREEK WORD AND VERSE	THE WORD MEANS...
	⇒ Strong's #2588+3588+4741 kardia ho stērizō ⇒ NIV #2840+3836+5114 kardia ho stērizō [stand firm] ⇒ NASB #2588+3588+4741 kardia ho stērizō **James 5:8** Be ye also patient; **stablish** your hearts: for the coming of the Lord draweth nigh. [KJV] You too be patient; **strengthen** your hearts, for the coming of the Lord is at hand. [NASB] You too, be patient and **stand firm**, because the Lord's coming is near. [NIV] You also be patient. **Establish** your hearts, for the coing of the Lord is at hand. [NKJV] You, too, must be patient. And **take courage**, for the coming of the Lord is near. [NLT] μακροθυμήσατε καὶ ὑμεῖς, **στηρίξατε τὰς καρδίας** ὑμῶν, ὅτι ἡ παρουσία τοῦ Κυρίου ἤγγικε. [GNS] μακροθυμήσατε καὶ ὑμεῖς, **στηρίξατε τὰς καρδίας** ὑμῶν, ὅτι ἡ παρουσία τοῦ κυρίου ἤγγικεν. [GNT]	looks for his great day of harvest. Looking for the great day of redemption—for the Lord's glorious return—will stir us to combat temptation and trial step by step. It will stir us to patiently endure no matter the situation, and by patiently enduring we shall gain the victory over all—no matter how bad the situation may be.

#3879
Take Delight
 	
Preferring–KJV
Give preference–NASB
Above–NIV
Giving preference–NKJV
Take delight–NLT
 	
POSB REFERENCE
(Rom.12:9-10; esp. v.10)
Note 1, point 4
	προηγούμενοι = proëgoumenoi
	Pronunciation: [pro-ay-goo'-mehn-oy]
	Parsing (part of speech): verb
	    Mood—participle (imperative sense)
	    Tense—present
	    Voice—middle or passive deponent
	    Case—nominative
	    Gender—masculine
	    Person—2nd person
	    Number—plural
	    Stem or root—from προηγέομαι
	Concordance References:
	⇒ Strong's #4285 proëgeomai
	⇒ NIV #4605 proëgeomai
	⇒ NASB #4285 proëgeomai
	
	Romans 12:10
	Be kindly affectioned one to another with brotherly love; in honour **preferring** one another; [KJV]
	Be devoted to one another in brotherly love; **give preference** to one another in honor; [NASB]
	Be devoted to one another in brotherly love. Honor one another **above** yourselves. [NIV]
	Be kindly affectionate to one another with brotherly love, in honor **giving preference** to one another; [NKJV]
	Love each other with genuine affection, and **take delight** in honoring each other. [NLT]
	τῇ φιλαδελφίᾳ εἰς ἀλλήλους φιλόστοργοι· τῇ τιμῇ ἀλλήλους **προηγούμενοι**· [GNS]
	τῇ φιλαδελφίᾳ εἰς ἀλλήλους φιλόστοργοι, τῇ τιμῇ ἀλλήλους **προηγούμενοι**, [GNT]
		Above; preferring; to give preference; to take delight. It means to go before; to lead; to set an example.
		
		Practical Application
		The charge is clear: the believer is to take the lead in esteeming and expressing respect for others. Imagine a church full of believers with each taking the lead in esteeming and honoring the other. What a picture of true love and care, of real warmth and tenderness, of great strength and manliness.

#3880
Take Heed
 	
Take heed–KJV
Watch out–NASB
Careful, Be–NIV
Take heed–NKJV
Warned–NLT
 	
POSB REFERENCE
(Mk.8:15)
Deeper Study #1
	Ὁρᾶτε = Horate
	Pronunciation: [hor-ah'-teh]
	Parsing (part of speech): verb
	    Mood—imperative
	    Tense—present
	    Voice—active
	    Person—2nd person
	    Number—plural
	    Stem or root—from ὁράω
	Concordance References:
	⇒ Strong's #3708 horaö
	⇒ NIV #3972 horaö
	⇒ NASB #3708 horaö
	
	Mark 8:15
	And he charged them, saying, **Take heed**, beware of the leaven of the Pharisees, and *of* the leaven of Herod. [KJV]
	And He was giving orders to them, saying, "**Watch**
		To see, behold, discern, and acquaint oneself by closely observing and experiencing. It means to take heed; to watch out; to be warned; to be careful; to make sure.
		
		Practical Application
		Two things are needed for a person to "take heed": active thought and a discerning mind. The thing to be heeded must be actively observed, thought through, and discerned.
		In the present passage, the charge is a *present imperative*. The disciple is to "take heed" of yeast (leaven) beginning right now, and he is to continue being careful, always observing and discerning.

ENGLISH WORD	GREEK WORD AND VERSE	THE WORD MEANS...
	out! Beware of the leaven of the Pharisees and the leaven of Herod." [NASB] "**Be careful**," Jesus warned them. "Watch out for the yeast of the Pharisees and that of Herod." [NIV] Then He charged them, saying, "**Take heed**, beware of the leaven of the Pharisees and the leaven of Herod." [NKJV] As they were crossing the lake, Jesus **warned** them, "Beware of the yeast of the Pharisees and of Herod." [NLT] καὶ διεστέλλετο αὐτοῖς, λέγων, Ὁρᾶτε, βλέπετε ἀπὸ τῆς ζύμης τῶν Φαρισαίων, καὶ τῆς ζύμης Ἡρώδου. [GNS] καὶ διεστέλλετο αὐτοῖς λέγων, Ὁρᾶτε, βλέπετε ἀπὸ τῆς ζύμης τῶν Φαρισαίων καὶ τῆς ζύμης Ἡρώδου. [GNT]	
#3881 **Take Heed** **Take heed–KJV** On guard–NASB Careful–NIV **Take heed–NKJV** Watch out–NLT **POSB REFERENCE** (Lk.21:34-35; esp. v.34) Note 1	Προσέχετε = *prosechete* Pronunciation: [pros-ekh'-eh-teh] Parsing (part of speech): verb 　Mood—imperative 　Tense—present 　Voice—active 　Person—2nd person 　Number—plural 　Stem or root—from προσέχω Concordance References: ⇒ Strong's #4337 prosechö ⇒ NIV #4668 prosechö ⇒ NASB #4337 prosechö ### Luke 21:34 And **take heed** to yourselves, lest at any time your hearts be overcharged with surfeiting, and drunkenness, and cares of this life, and so that day come upon you unawares. [KJV] "Be **on guard**, that your hearts may not be weighted down with dissipation and drunkenness and the worries of life, and that day come on you suddenly like a trap; [NASB] "Be **careful**, or your hearts will be weighed down with dissipation, drunkenness and the anxieties of life, and that day will close on you unexpectedly like a trap. [NIV] "But **take heed** to yourselves, lest your hearts be weighed down with carousing, drunkenness, and cares of this life, and that Day come on you unexpectedly. [NKJV] "**Watch out**! Don't let me find you living in careless ease and drunkenness, and filled with the worries of this life. Don't let that day catch you unaware, [NLT] Προσέχετε δὲ ἑαυτοῖς, μήποτε βαρυνθῶσιν ὑμῶν αἱ καρδίαι ἐν κραιπάλῃ καὶ μέθῃ καὶ μερίμναις βιωτικαῖς, καὶ αἰφνίδιος ἐφ' ὑμᾶς ἐπιστῇ ἡ ἡμέρα ἐκείνη· [GNS] Προσέχετε δὲ ἑαυτοῖς μήποτε βαρηθῶσιν ὑμῶν αἱ καρδίαι ἐν κραιπάλῃ καὶ μέθῃ καὶ μερίμναις βιωτικαῖς καὶ ἐπιστῇ ἐφ' ὑμᾶς αἰφνίδιος ἡ ἡμέρα ἐκείνη [GNT]	To give attention; to focus one's mind; to watch out; to guard; to beware; to take care; to be on guard; to pay close attention to; to carefully consider. ### Practical Application The end time and the day of the Lord's return demands taking care. Note this important fact: the believer is to take heed; that is, to guard his life. How? By not engaging in worldliness. His heart is not to be weighed down (*barethosin*): heavy, weighed down, burdened, overloaded, filled up, indulged.
#3882 **Take Heed** **Take heed–KJV** Be on guard–NASB Keep watch over–NIV **Take heed–NKJV** Beware–NLT **POSB REFERENCE** (Acts 20:28) Note 1, point 1	προσέχετε = *prosechete* Pronunciation: [pros-ech'-eh-teh] Parsing (part of speech): verb 　Mood—imperfect 　Tense—present 　Voice— active 　Person—2nd person 　Number—plural 　Stem or root—from προσέχω Concordance References: ⇒ Strong's #4337 prosechö ⇒ NIV #4668 prosechö ⇒ NASB #4337 prosechö	To keep watch over; to take heed; to be on guard; to beware; to be careful, oh so careful. It means to give attention, concentrate upon, focus upon, attend to, watch after, and guard one's life. ### Practical Application There are specific areas the believer must take heed. 1. He must take heed against false teaching (Luke 12:1). 2. He must take heed against an unforgiving spirit (Luke 17:3-4). 3. He must take heed against self-indulgence,

ENGLISH WORD	GREEK WORD AND VERSE	THE WORD MEANS...
	Acts 20:28	drunkenness, and the possessions of this life (Luke 21:34).
	Take heed therefore unto yourselves, and to all the flock, over the which the Holy Ghost hath made you overseers, to feed the church of God, which he hath purchased with his own blood. [KJV]	4. He must take heed against the fables, myths, speculations, ideas, and false doctrines of men, and depending upon one's genealogy or heritage for salvation (1 Tim. 1:4).
	"**Be on guard** for yourselves and for all the flock, among which the Holy Spirit has made you overseers, to shepherd the church of God which He purchased with His own blood. [NASB]	5. He must watch and give himself to reading, exhortation and doctrine (1 Tim. 4:13).
	Keep watch over yourselves and all the flock of which the Holy Spirit has made you overseers. Be shepherds of the church of God, which he bought with his own blood. [NIV]	6. He must especially give himself to the doctrine (*te didaskalia*), the teaching of Scripture (1 Tim. 4:16).
	Therefore **take heed** to yourselves and to all the flock, among which the Holy Spirit has made you overseers, to shepherd the church of God which He purchased with His own blood. [NKJV]	
	"And now **beware**! Be sure that you feed and shepherd God's flock—his church, purchased with his blood—over whom the Holy Spirit has appointed you as elders. [NLT]	
	προσέχετε οὖν ἑαυτοῖς καὶ παντὶ τῷ ποιμνίῳ, ἐν ᾧ ὑμᾶς τὸ Πνεῦμα τὸ Ἅγιον ἔθετο ἐπισκόπους, ποιμαίνειν τὴν ἐκκλησίαν τοῦ Θεοῦ, ἣν περιεποιήσατο διὰ τοῦ ἰδίου αἵματος. [GNS]	
	προσέχετε ἑαυτοῖς καὶ παντὶ τῷ ποιμνίῳ, ἐν ᾧ ὑμᾶς τὸ πνεῦμα τὸ ἅγιον ἔθετο ἐπισκόπους ποιμαίνειν τὴν ἐκκλησίαν τοῦ θεοῦ, ἣν περιεποιήσατο διὰ τοῦ αἵματος τοῦ ἰδίου. [GNT]	
#3883 **Take Heed** **Take heed–KJV** Pay close attention–NASB Watch...closely–NIV **Take heed–NKJV** Keep a close watch–NLT **POSB REFERENCE** (1 Tim.4:16) Note 12	ἔπεχε = *epeche* Pronunciation: [ep-ekh'-eh] Parsing (part of speech): verb 　　Mood—imperative 　　Tense—present 　　Voice—active 　　Person—2nd person 　　Number—singular 　　Stem or root—from ἐπέχω Concordance References: ⇒ Strong's #1907 epechö ⇒ NIV #2091 epechö ⇒ NASB #1907 epechö **1 Tim. 4:16** **Take heed** unto thyself, and unto the doctrine; continue in them: for in doing this thou shalt both save thyself, and them that hear thee. [KJV] **Pay close attention** to yourself and to your teaching; persevere in these things; for as you do this you will insure salvation both for yourself and for those who hear you. [NASB] **Watch** your life and doctrine **closely**. Persevere in them, because if you do, you will save both yourself and your hearers. [NIV] **Take heed** to yourself and to the doctrine. Continue in them, for in doing this you will save both yourself and those who hear you. [NKJV] **Keep a close watch** on yourself and on your teaching. Stay true to what is right, and God will save you and those who hear you. [NLT] ἔπεχε σεαυτῷ καὶ τῇ διδασκαλίᾳ. ἐπίμενε αὐτοῖς· τοῦτο γὰρ ποιῶν καὶ σεαυτὸν σώσεις καὶ τοὺς ἀκούοντάς σου. [GNS] ἔπεχε σεαυτῷ καὶ τῇ διδασκαλίᾳ, ἐπίμενε αὐτοῖς· τοῦτο γὰρ ποιῶν καὶ σεαυτὸν σώσεις καὶ τοὺς ἀκούοντάς σου. [GNT]	To watch closely; to take heed; to pay close attention; to keep a close watch; to keep a strict eye upon or to keep on paying attention to oneself and to one's teaching. **Practical Application** The good minister guards himself and his teaching. ⇒ He guards his body, keeps it both morally and physically fit. He flees the temptations that assault and seduce him, and he controls his thoughts and keeps them pure from the lusts of the world and flesh. He neither eats too much nor succumbs to immoral thoughts or acts. He neither gives in to greed nor seeks the possessions or wealth of the world. ⇒ He guards his spirit and keeps it spiritually fit. He worships God every day and lives in God's Word and prayer all day long, and he shares the glorious gospel of Christ, witnessing to and exhorting people as he walks throughout the day. ⇒ He guards his study and teaching, avoiding the profane doctrines, teachings, notions, philosophies, ideas, and fables of men.

ENGLISH WORD	GREEK WORD AND VERSE	THE WORD MEANS...
#3884 **Take Heed** **Take heed–KJV** Take care–NASB See to it–NIV Beware–NKJV Be careful then–NLT **POSB** **REFERENCE** (Heb.3:12) Note 2	Βλέπετε = *Blepete* Pronunciation: [blep'-eh-teh] Parsing (part of speech): verb Mood—imperative Tense—present Voice—active Person—2nd person Number—plural Stem or root—from βλέπω Concordance References: ⇒ Strong's #991 blepö ⇒ NIV #1063 blepö ⇒ NASB #991 blepö **Hebrews 3:12** **Take heed**, brethren, lest there be in any of you an evil heart of unbelief, in departing from the living God. [KJV] **Take care**, brethren, lest there should be in any one of you an evil, unbelieving heart, in falling away from the living God. [NASB] **See to it**, brothers, that none of you has a sinful, unbelieving heart that turns away from the living God. [NIV] **Beware**, brethren, lest there be in any of you an evil heart of unbelief in departing from the living God; [NKJV] **Be careful then**, dear brothers and sisters. Make sure that your own hearts are not evil and unbelieving, turning you away from the living God. [NLT] βλέπετε, ἀδελφοί, μή ποτε ἔσται ἔν τινι ὑμῶν καρδία πονηρὰ ἀπιστίας, ἐν τῷ ἀποστῆναι ἀπὸ Θεοῦ ζῶντος· [GNS] Βλέπετε, ἀδελφοί, μήποτε ἔσται ἔν τινι ὑμῶν καρδία πονηρὰ ἀπιστίας ἐν τῷ ἀποστῆναι ἀπὸ θεοῦ ζῶντος, [GNT]	Be alert and stay alert; be on the lookout and do it constantly; watch and keep on watching. **Practical Application** There is great danger that believers might depart from the living God. They might do just what Israel did. Therefore, be careful—take heed (*Blepete*). Keep a watchful eye on your trust and obedience to God. Watch for an evil heart of unbelief. What is an evil heart of unbelief? It is a heart that... • stands off from God • stands aloof from God • renounces God • rebels against God • does not believe in God • does not trust God and His promises • does not follow God as He demands
#3885 **Take Money By Force** Violence–KJV **Take money...by** **force–NASB** Extort money–NIV Intimidate–NKJV Extort money–NLT **POSB** **REFERENCE** (Lk.3:10-14; esp. v.14) Note 5, point 3a	διασείσητε = *diaseisëte* Pronunciation: [dee-as-i'-say-teh] Parsing (part of speech): verb Mood—subjunctive OR imperative Tense—aorist Voice—active Person—2nd person Number—plural Stem or root—from διασείω Concordance References: ⇒ Strong's #1286 diaseiö ⇒ NIV #1398 diaseiö ⇒ NASB #1286 diaseiö **Luke 3:14** And the soldiers likewise demanded of him, saying, And what shall we do? And he said unto them, Do **violence** to no man, neither accuse any falsely; and be content with your wages. [KJV] And some soldiers were questioning him, saying, "And what about us, what shall we do?" And he said to them, "Do not **take money** from anyone **by force**, or accuse anyone falsely, and be content with your wages." [NASB] Then some soldiers asked him, "And what should we do?" He replied, "Don't **extort money** and don't accuse people falsely—be content with your pay." [NIV] Likewise the soldiers asked him, saying, "And what shall we do?" So he said to them, "Do not **intimidate** anyone or accuse falsely, and be content with your wages." [NKJV] "What should we do?" asked some soldiers. John replied, "Don't **extort money**, and don't accuse people of things you know they didn't do. And be content with your pay." [NLT] ἐπηρώτων δὲ αὐτὸν καὶ στρατευόμενοι, λέγοντες, Καὶ	To extort money; to take money by force; to shake violently, agitate, terrify. **Practical Application** The thought is that some took money by terrifying people. Roman soldiers were, of course, posted to protect the interests of Rome. It was common for soldiers to allow illegal things to go on for a bribe.

ENGLISH WORD	GREEK WORD AND VERSE	THE WORD MEANS...
	ἡμεῖς τί ποιήσομεν; καὶ εἶπε πρὸς αὐτοῖς, Μηδένα **διασείσητε** μηδὲ συκοφαντήσητε· καὶ ἀρκεῖσθε τοῖς ὀψωνίοις ὑμῶν. [GNS] ἐπηρώτων δὲ αὐτὸν καὶ στρατευόμενοι λέγοντες, Τί ποιήσωμεν καὶ ἡμεῖς; καὶ εἶπεν αὐτοῖς, Μηδένα **διασείσητε** μηδὲ συκοφαντήσητε καὶ ἀρκεῖσθε τοῖς ὀψωνίοις ὑμῶν. [GNT]	
#3886 **Take No Thought** **Take no thought–KJV** Anxious–NASB Worry about–NIV Worry about–NKJV Worry about–NLT **POSB REFERENCE** (Lk.12:22-34; esp. v.22) Outline Introduction **See also POSB REF:** (Mt.6:25) Note 1	**μεριμνᾶτε** = *merimnate* Pronunciation: [mer-im-nah'-teh] Parsing (part of speech): verb 　Mood—imperfect 　Tense—present 　Voice—active 　Person—2nd person 　Number—plural 　Stem or root—from **μεριμνάω** Concordance References: ⇒　Strong's #3309 merimnaö ⇒　NIV #3534 merimnaö ⇒　NASB #3309 merimnaö **Luke 12:22** And he said unto his disciples, Therefore I say unto you, **Take no thought** for your life, what ye shall eat; neither for the body, what ye shall put on. [KJV] And He said to His disciples, "For this reason I say to you, do not be **anxious** for *your* life, *as to* what you shall eat; nor for your body, *as to* what you shall put on. [NASB] Then Jesus said to his disciples: "Therefore I tell you, do not **worry about** your life, what you will eat; or about your body, what you will wear. [NIV] Then He said to His disciples, "Therefore I say to you, do not **worry about** your life, what you will eat; nor about the body, what you will put on. [NKJV] Then turning to his disciples, Jesus said, "So I tell you, don't **worry about** everyday life—whether you have enough food to eat or clothes to wear. [NLT] Εἶπε δὲ πρὸς τοὺς μαθητάς αὐτοῦ, Διὰ τοῦτο ὑμῖν λέγω, μὴ **μεριμνᾶτε** τῇ ψυχῇ ὑμῶν, τί φάγητε· μηδὲ τῷ σώματι, τί ἐνδύσησθε. [GNS] Εἶπεν δὲ πρὸς τοὺς μαθητάς [αὐτοῦ], Διὰ τοῦτο λέγω ὑμῖν· μὴ **μεριμνᾶτε** τῇ ψυχῇ τί φάγητε, μηδὲ τῷ σώματι τί ἐνδύσησθε. [GNT]	Do not worry; do not be anxious; do not be overly concerned and caring (cp. Phil. 4:6). **Practical Application** "Take no thought" for your life. Being worried and overly concerned, is a constant problem among men. It is not to be so among God's people. (See POSB outline—Matthew 6:25-34 and POSB notes—Matthew 6:25-34 for more discussion and application.)
#3887 **Take Note** Behold–KJV **Take note–NASB** Consider–NIV Look on–NKJV Hear–NLT **POSB REFERENCE** (Acts 4:29-30; esp. v.29) Note 4, point 1b	**ἔπιδε ἐπί** = *epide epi* Pronunciation: [ep-i'-deh ep-ee] 　Parsing *epide* (part of speech): verb 　Mood—imperative 　Tense—aorist 　Voice—active 　Person—2nd person 　Number—singular 　Stem or root—from **ἐπεῖδον** Parsing *epi* (part of speech): preposition 　Case—accusative 　Stem or root—from **ἐπι** Concordance References: ⇒　Strong's #1896 + 1909 epeidon epi ⇒　NIV #2078 + 2093 epeidon epi ⇒　NASB #1896 + 1909 epeidon epi **Acts 4:29** And now, Lord, **behold** their threatenings: and grant unto thy servants, that with all boldness they may speak thy word, , [KJV] "And now, Lord, **take note** of their threats, and grant that Thy bond-servants may speak Thy word with all confidence, [NASB] Now, Lord, **consider** their threats and enable your servants to speak your word with great boldness. [NIV]	To consider; to behold; to take note; to hear; to look upon. **Practical Application** The church was asking God to concentrate and focus upon the persecution; to deal with it and to overrule the enemy; to give whatever was necessary to endure through it all.

ENGLISH WORD	GREEK WORD AND VERSE	THE WORD MEANS...
	Now, Lord, **look on** their threats, and grant to Your servants that with all boldness they may speak Your word, [NKJV] And now, O Lord, **hear** their threats, and give your servants great boldness in their preaching. [NLT] καὶ τὰ νῦν, Κύριε, **ἔπιδε ἐπὶ** τὰς ἀπειλὰς αὐτῶν, καὶ δὸς τοῖς δούλοις σου μετὰ παρρησίας πάσης λαλεῖν τὸν λόγον σου, [GNS] καὶ τὰ νῦν, κύριε, **ἔπιδε ἐπὶ** τὰς ἀπειλὰς αὐτῶν καὶ δὸς τοῖς δούλοις σου μετὰ παρρησίας πάσης λαλεῖν τὸν λόγον σου, [GNT]	

#3888
Take Out
 	
Sever–KJV
Take out–NASB
Separate–NIV
Separate–NKJV
Separate–NLT
 	
POSB REFERENCE
(Mt.13:49)
Deeper Study #3
	ἀφοριοῦσιν = *aphoriousin*
	Pronunciation: [af-or-i-oo'-sin]
	Parsing (part of speech): verb
	    Mood—indicative
	    Tense—future
	    Voice—active
	    Person—3rd person
	    Number—plural
	    Stem or root—from ἀφορίζω
	Concordance References:
	⇒ Strong's #873 aphorizö
	⇒ NIV #928 aphorizö
	⇒ NASB #873 aphorizö
	
	Matthew 13:49
	So shall it be at the end of the world: the angels shall come forth, and **sever** the wicked from among the just, [KJV]
	
	"So it will be at the end of the age; the angels shall come forth, and **take out** the wicked from among the righteous, [NASB]
	
	This is how it will be at the end of the age. The angels will come and **separate** the wicked from the righteous [NIV]
	
	So it will be at the end of the age. The angels will come forth, and **separate** the wicked from among the just, [NKJV]
	
	That is the way it will be at the end of the world. The angels will come and **separate** the wicked people from the godly, [NLT]
	
	οὕτως ἔσται ἐν τῇ συντελείᾳ τοῦ αἰῶνος· ἐξελεύσονται οἱ ἄγγελοι, καὶ **ἀφοριοῦσι** τοὺς πονηροὺς ἐκ μέσου τῶν δικαίων, [GNS]
	
	οὕτως ἔσται ἐν τῇ συντελείᾳ τοῦ αἰῶνος· ἐξελεύσονται οἱ ἄγγελοι καὶ **ἀφοριοῦσιν** τοὺς πονηροὺς ἐκ μέσου τῶν δικαίων [GNT]
		To separate; to sever; to take out; to exclude; to set off by bounds; to set apart.
		
		Practical Application
		In this Scripture, the wicked are to be taken completely away. They are taken and cast completely out of the presence of the good.

#3889
Take Pride
 	
Puffed up–KJV
Become
  arrogant–NASB
Take pride–NIV
Puffed up–NKJV
Brag–NLT
 	
POSB REFERENCE
(1 Cor.4:6)
Note 1, point 2
	φυσιοῦσθε = *phusiousthe*
	Pronunciation: [foo-see-o'-oos-the]
	Parsing (part of speech): verb
	    Mood—indicative
	    Tense—present
	    Voice—passive
	    Person—2nd person
	    Number—plural
	    Stem or root—from φυσιόω
	Concordance References:
	⇒ Strong's #5448 phusioö
	⇒ NIV #5881 phusioö
	⇒ NASB #5448 phusioö
	
	1 Cor. 4:6
	And these things, brethren, I have in a figure transferred to myself and *to* Apollos for your sakes; that ye might learn in us not to think *of men* above that which is written, that no one of you be **puffed up** for one against another. [KJV]
	
	Now these things, brethren, I have figuratively applied to myself and Apollos for your sakes, that in us you might learn not to exceed what is written, in order that no one of you might **become arrogant** in behalf of one against
		To take pride; to become arrogant; to brag; to be conceited; to be inflated; to be puffed up.
		
		Practical Application
		It is a picture of puffed up air bags. The point is the judging of ministers and the feelings that one can judge ministers is nothing but hot air in *puffed up* or inflated balloons. It is meaningless. It means absolutely nothing to God. (Cp. 1 Cor. 4:18-19; 1 Cor. 5:2; 1 Cor. 8:1; 1 Cor. 13:4.)

ENGLISH WORD	GREEK WORD AND VERSE	THE WORD MEANS...

the other. [NASB]

Now, brothers, I have applied these things to myself and Apollos for your benefit, so that you may learn from us the meaning of the saying, "Do not go beyond what is written." Then you will not **take pride** in one man over against another. [NIV]

Now these things, brethren, I have figuratively transferred to myself and Apollos for your sakes, that you may learn in us not to think beyond what is written, that none of you may be **puffed up** on behalf of one against the other. [NKJV]

Dear brothers and sisters, I have used Apollos and myself to illustrate what I've been saying. If you pay attention to the Scriptures, you won't **brag** about one of your leaders at the expense of another. [NLT]

Ταῦτα δέ, ἀδελφοί, μετεσχημάτισα εἰς ἐμαυτὸν καὶ Ἀπολλῶν δι' ὑμᾶς, ἵνα ἐν ἡμῖν μάθητε τὸ μὴ ὑπὲρ ὃ γέγραπται φρονεῖν, ἵνα μὴ εἷς ὑπὲρ τοῦ ἑνὸς **φυσιοῦσθε** κατὰ τοῦ ἑτέρου. [GNS]

Ταῦτα δέ, ἀδελφοί, μετεσχημάτισα εἰς ἐμαυτὸν καὶ Ἀπολλῶν δι' ὑμᾶς, ἵνα ἐν ἡμῖν μάθητε τὸ Μὴ ὑπὲρ ἃ γέγραπται, ἵνα μὴ εἷς ὑπὲρ τοῦ ἑνὸς **φυσιοῦσθε** κατὰ τοῦ ἑτέρου. [GNT]

#3890

Taken Up

Received up–KJV
Ascension–NASB
Taken up–NIV
Received up–NKJV
Return–NLT

**POSB
REFERENCE**
(Lk.9:51)
Deeper Study #1

ἀναλήμψεως = analēmpseōs
Pronunciation: [an-al'-aimp-se-os]
Parsing (part of speech): noun
    Case—genitive
    Gender—feminine
    Number—singular
    Stem or root—from *ἀνάλημψις, εως*
Concordance References:
  ⇒ Strong's #354 analepsis
  ⇒ NIV #378 analēmpsis
  ⇒ NASB #354 analēmpsis

Luke 9:51

And it came to pass, when the time was come that he should be **received up**, he stedfastly set his face to go to Jerusalem, [KJV]

And it came about, when the days were approaching for His **ascension**, that He resolutely set His face to go to Jerusalem; [NASB]

As the time approached for him to be **taken up** to heaven, Jesus resolutely set out for Jerusalem. [NIV]

Now it came to pass, when the time had come for Him to be **received up**, that He steadfastly set His face to go to Jerusalem, [NKJV]

As the time drew near for his **return** to heaven, Jesus resolutely set out for Jerusalem. [NLT]

Ἐγένετο δὲ ἐν τῷ συμπληροῦσθαι τὰς ἡμέρας τῆς *ἀναλήμψεως* αὐτοῦ, καὶ αὐτὸς τὸ πρόσωπον αὐτοῦ ἐστήριξε τοῦ πορεύεσθαι εἰς Ἰερουσαλήμ, [GNS]

Ἐγένετο δὲ ἐν τῷ συμπληροῦσθαι τὰς ἡμέρας τῆς *ἀναλήμψεως* αὐτοῦ καὶ αὐτὸς τὸ πρόσωπον ἐστήρισεν τοῦ πορεύεσθαι εἰς Ἰερουσαλήμ. [GNT]

Taken up, ascensed, received up, returned.

Practical Application

This word refers to the ascension of Christ (cp. *analambano*, Acts 1:2, 11, 22; 1 Tim. 3:16). Salvation was to be secured by the ascension of Christ. How? The Ascended Lord means at least four things.

1. It means the *Risen Lord*. The ascension means that Christ arose from the dead. If He had remained in the grave, He would still be there in the form of dust. He could not have ascended. If He were to be "received up," He had to be raised up—quickened—made alive—taken up. No one can be taken up without first being raised up. Therefore, to speak of the ascension is to mean that Christ is risen. Death is conquered; man can now be saved from death.

2. It means the *Advocate* or *Representative* Lord. On earth, Christ lived a perfect life; He was without sin (2 Cor. 5:21; Hebrews 4:15; 1 Peter 1:19; 1 Peter 2:22; John 8:46). He was "obedient unto death, even the death of the cross. Wherefore God also hath highly exalted Him" (Phil. 2:8-9). He is "sitting on the right hand of God (Col. 3:1). He is "Jesus Christ the righteous"; therefore, He is our "advocate with the Father" (1 John 2:1). He is able to represent us before God because He has lived upon earth and secured a perfect righteousness. He is the Ideal Man (see note—Matthew 5:17-18), our advocate, the One who is qualified to plead our case before God and see to it that we are saved.

3. It means the *Priestly* or *Intercessory Lord*. Every man suffers while on earth: suffers pain, trial, need, want, temptation, loss, illness and, eventually, death. We are incapable of even knowing how to pray as we ought in order to secure the help we need. But Christ knows and understands because He has been to earth and suffered just as we suffer. Therefore, He knows how to intercede for us and how to deliver us.

ENGLISH WORD	GREEK WORD AND VERSE	THE WORD MEANS...
	Afterward Jesus and his disciples left Jerusalem, but they **stayed** in Judea for a while and baptized there. [NLT] Μετὰ ταῦτα ἦλθεν ὁ Ἰησοῦς καὶ οἱ μαθηταὶ αὐτοῦ εἰς τὴν Ἰουδαίαν γῆν· καὶ ἐκεῖ **διέτριβε** μετ' αὐτῶν καὶ ἐβάπτιζεν. [GNS] Μετὰ ταῦτα ἦλθεν ὁ Ἰησοῦς καὶ οἱ μαθηταὶ αὐτοῦ εἰς τὴν Ἰουδαίαν γῆν καὶ ἐκεῖ **διέτριβεν** μετ' αὐτῶν καὶ ἐβάπτιζεν. [GNT]	
#3895 **Taste Death** Taste...death–KJV Taste...death–NASB Taste death–NIV Taste...death–NKJV Die–NLT **POSB REFERENCE** (Jn.8:51; esp. v.52) *Deeper Study #1,* point 3	γεύσηται θανάτου = *geusëtai thanatou* Pronunciation: [ghyoo'-say-tah-ee thahn'-at-oo] Parsing *geusëtai* (part of speech): verb 　　Mood—subjunctive 　　Tense—aorist 　　Voice—middle deponent 　　Person—3rd person 　　Number—singular 　　Stem or root—from γεύομαι Parsing *thanatou* (part of speech): noun 　　Case—genitive 　　Gender—masculine 　　Number—singular 　　Stem or root—from θάνατος, ου Concordance References: ⇒　Strong's #1089 geuomai + 2288 thanatos ⇒　NIV #1174 geuomai [taste] + 2505 thanatos [death] ⇒　NASB #1089 geuomai + 2288 thanatos **John 8:52** Then said the Jews unto him, Now we know that thou hast a devil. Abraham is dead, and the prophets; and thou sayest, If a man keep my saying, he shall never **taste** of **death**. [KJV] The Jews said to Him, "Now we know that You have a demon. Abraham died, and the prophets *also*; and You say, 'If anyone keeps My word, he shall never **taste** of **death**.' [NASB] At this the Jews exclaimed, "Now we know that you are demon-possessed! Abraham died and so did the prophets, yet you say that if anyone keeps your word, he will never **taste death**. [NIV] Then said the Jews unto him, Now we know that thou hast a devil. Abraham is dead, and the prophets; and thou sayest, If a man keep my saying, he shall never **taste** of **death**. [NKJV] The people said, "Now we know you are possessed by a demon. Even Abraham and the prophets died, but you say that those who obey your teaching will never **die**! [NLT] εἶπον οὖν αὐτῷ οἱ Ἰουδαῖοι, Νῦν ἐγνώκαμεν ὅτι δαιμόνιον ἔχεις· Ἀβραὰμ ἀπέθανε καὶ οἱ προφῆται, καὶ σὺ λέγεις, Ἐάν τις τὸν λόγον μου τηρήσῃ, οὐ μὴ **γεύσεται θανάτου** εἰς τὸν αἰῶνα. [GNS] εἶπον [οὖν] αὐτῷ οἱ Ἰουδαῖοι, Νῦν ἐγνώκαμεν ὅτι δαιμόνιον ἔχεις· Ἀβραὰμ ἀπέθανεν καὶ οἱ προφῆται, καὶ σὺ λέγεις, Ἐάν τις τὸν λόγον μου τηρήσῃ, οὐ μὴ **γεύσηται θανάτου** εἰς τὸν αἰῶνα. [GNT]	To taste, experience death; to die; to eat of death. **Practical Application** The meaning is that a genuine follower of Christ will... ● never experience death nor see death. ● never know death nor partake of death. ● never face the condemnation of death. ● never experience the terror, the hurt, the pain, and the suffering of death. ● never experience the anguish of being separated from God and from the glory, beauty, perfection, and life of heaven. In a flash, quicker than lightning or the blinking of an eye, the follower of Christ passes from this world into the next. He never ceases to experience life and never loses consciousness. One moment he is in this world; the next moment he is in the presence of God Himself. 　Note the reason why the believer shall never "taste death": it is because Jesus came "by the grace of God [to] taste death for every man" (Hebrews 2:9).
#3896 **Tasted** Tasted–KJV Tasted–NASB Tasted–NIV Tasted–NKJV Experienced–NLT **POSB REFERENCE** (Heb.6:4-5, esp. v.4) Note 1	γευσαμένους = *geusamenous* Pronunciation: [ghyoo'-ahm-eh-noos] Parsing (part of speech): verb 　　Mood—participle 　　Tense—aorist 　　Voice—middle deponent 　　Case—accusative 　　Gender—masculine 　　Number—plural 　　Stem or root—from γεύομαι Concordance References: ⇒　Strong's #1089 geuomai ⇒　NIV #1174 geuomai ⇒　NASB #1089 geuomai	To taste; to experience; to eat. It means to partake of; to take in; to come to know. The Greek scholar Marvin Vincent says that it means to "have consciously partaken of" (*Word Studies in the New Testament*, Vol. 4, p.445). **Practical Application** The Greek Scripture definitely uses the aorist tense which means that the person had a *once-for-all* experience, an experience that was once-for-all completed, fulfilled, and finished. How could this apply to anyone else other than a

ENGLISH WORD	GREEK WORD AND VERSE	THE WORD MEANS...
	Hebrews 6:4 For *it is* impossible for those who were once enlightened, and have **tasted** of the heavenly gift, and were made partakers of the Holy Ghost, [KJV] For in the case of those who have once been enlightened and have **tasted** of the heavenly gift and have been made partakers of the Holy Spirit, [NASB] It is impossible for those who have once been enlightened, who have **tasted** the heavenly gift, who have shared in the Holy Spirit, [NIV] For *it is* impossible for those who were once enlightened, and have **tasted** of the heavenly gift, and were made partakers of the Holy Ghost, [NKJV] For it is impossible to restore to repentance those who were once enlightened—those who have **experienced** the good things of heaven and shared in the Holy Spirit, [NLT] ἀδύνατον γὰρ τοὺς ἅπαξ φωτισθέντας, **γευσαμένους** τε τῆς δωρεᾶς τῆς ἐπουρανίου, καὶ μετόχους γενηθέντας Πνεύματος Ἁγίου, [GNS] Ἀδύνατον γὰρ τοὺς ἅπαξ φωτισθέντας, **γευσαμένους** τε τῆς δωρεᾶς τῆς ἐπουρανίου καὶ μετόχους γενηθέντας πνεύματος ἁγίου [GNT]	believer? Note how each of these read in the aorist tense: the person... • *was once-for-all* enlightened. • *had once-for-all* tasted of the heavenly gift. • *was once-for-all* made a partaker of the Holy Spirit. • *had once-for-all* tasted of the good Word of God. • *had once-for-all tasted* of the power of the world to come. The very same word is used of Christ when it said that He "tasted death" for us (Hebrews 2:9). And one thing is sure: Christ tasted, that is, *consciously experienced*, death for us. Therefore, this passage must mean that this person *fully tasted and fully experienced* salvation. As stated, it seems that we have to twist Scripture to make it say any less than a conscious and full experience. Note the glorious experiences and privileges these persons received in Christ.

#3897
Taught Many
 	
Taught many–KJV
Made many disciples–NASB
Won a large number of disciples–NIV
Taught many–NKJV
Making many disciples–NLT
 	
POSB REFERENCE
(Acts 14:21)
Note 1, point 2
	μαθητεύσαντες ἱκανοὺς = *mathēteusantes hikanous*
	Pronunciation: [math-ayt-yoo'-san-tehs hik-an-oos']
	Parsing *mathēteusantes* (part of speech): verb
	  Mood—participle
	  Tense—aorist
	  Voice—active
	  Case—nominative
	  Gender—masculine
	  Number—plural
	  Stem or root—from μαθητεύω
	Parsing *hikanous* (part of speech): pronominal adjective
	  Case—accusative
	  Gender—masculine
	  Number—plural
	  Stem or root—from ἱκανός, ή, όν
	Concordance References:
	⇒ Strong's #3100 mathēteuō + 2425 hikanos
	⇒ NIV #3411 mathēteuō [won disciples]+ 2653 hikanos [large number]
	⇒ NASB #3100 mathēteuō + 2425 hikanos
	
	Acts 14:21
	And when they had preached the gospel to that city, and had **taught many**, they returned again to Lystra, and *to* Iconium, and Antioch, [KJV]
	And after they had preached the gospel to that city and had **made many disciples**, they returned to Lystra and to Iconium and to Antioch, [NASB]
	They preached the good news in that city and **won a large number of disciples**. Then they returned to Lystra, Iconium and Antioch, [NIV]
	And when they had preached the gospel to that city, and had **taught many**, they returned again to Lystra, and *to* Iconium, and Antioch, [NKJV]
	After preaching the Good News in Derbe and **making many disciples**, Paul and Barnabas returned again to Lystra, Iconium, and Antioch of Pisidia, [NLT]
	εὐαγγελισάμενοί τε τὴν πόλιν ἐκείνην καὶ **μαθητεύσαντες ἱκανοὺς**, ὑπέστρεψαν εἰς τὴν Λύστραν καὶ Ἰκόνιον καὶ Ἀντιόχειαν, [GNS]
	Εὐαγγελισάμενοί τε τὴν πόλιν ἐκείνην καὶ **μαθητεύσαντες ἱκανοὺς** ὑπέστρεψαν εἰς τὴν Λύστραν καὶ εἰς Ἰκόνιον καὶ εἰς Ἀντιόχειαν [GNT]
		Won a large number of disciples; taught many; made many disciples.
		
		Practical Application
		The ministry of the preachers (Paul and Barnabas) was to make disciples. They not only preached, but they had made disciples out of the believers (see POSB note, Discipleship—Acts 13:5-6 for discussion).

ENGLISH WORD	GREEK WORD AND VERSE	THE WORD MEANS...

#3898
Teach
 	
Teach–KJV
Make disciples–NASB
Make disciples–NIV
Make disciples–NKJV
Make disciples–NLT
 	
POSB
REFERENCE
(Mt.28:19-20; esp.
v.19)
Note 3, point 1
	μαθητεύσατε = *mathëteusate*
	Pronunciation: [math-ayt-yoo'-sa-tay]
	Parsing (part of speech): verb
	   Mood—imperative
	   Tense—aorist
	   Voice—active
	   Person—2nd person
	   Number—plural
	   Stem or root—from μαθητεύω
	Concordance References:
	  ⇒ Strong's #3100 mathëteuö
	  ⇒ NIV #3411 mathëteuö
	  ⇒ NASB #3100 mathëteuö
	
	Matthew 28:19
	Go ye therefore, and **teach** all nations, baptizing them in the name of the Father, and of the Son, and of the Holy Ghost: [KJV]
	"Go therefore and **make disciples** of all the nations, baptizing them in the name of the Father and the Son and the Holy Spirit, [NASB]
	Therefore go and **make disciples** of all nations, baptizing them in the name of the Father and of the Son and of the Holy Spirit, [NIV]
	Go therefore and **make disciples** of all nations, baptizing them in the name of the Father and of the Son and of the Holy Spirit, [NKJV]
	Therefore, go and **make disciples** of all the nations, baptizing them in the name of the Father and the Son and the Holy Spirit. [NLT]
	πορευθέντες οὖν **μαθητεύσατε** πάντα τὰ ἔθνη, βαπτίζοντες αὐτοὺς εἰς τὸ ὄνομα τοῦ Πατρὸς καὶ τοῦ Υἱοῦ καὶ τοῦ Ἁγίου Πνεύματος· [GNS]
	πορευθέντες οὖν **μαθητεύσατε** πάντα τὰ ἔθνη, βαπτίζοντες αὐτοὺς εἰς τὸ ὄνομα τοῦ πατρὸς καὶ τοῦ υἱοῦ καὶ τοῦ ἁγίου πνεύματος, [GNT]
		To make disciples; to teach; to attach ourselves to those persons who will follow our Lord until they can, in turn, make disciples.
		
		Practical Application
		Our Lord was not only telling us "to go and evangelize," He was telling us *how* to go and *how* to evangelize. He was not only giving His ultimate *objective* and overriding purpose, He was giving *the method* to use in evangelizing the world.
		Think about the word "teach" (*mathëteusate*). What does our Lord mean by "make disciples"? Does it not mean that we are to do what He did: make disciples and do things with them as He did. Is He not telling us to do exactly as He did?
		What *did* He do? Christ "came to seek and save that which was lost" (Luke 19:10). He sought the lost, those who were willing to commit their lives to Him. And when He found such a person, He saved that person. When Christ found a person who was willing to commit his life, Christ attached Himself to that person. Christ began to mold and make that person into His image. The word *attach* is the key word. It is probably the word that best describes discipleship. Christ made disciples of men by attaching Himself to them; and through that personal attachment, they were able to observe His life and conversation; and in seeing and hearing, they began to absorb and assimilate His very character and behavior. They began to follow Him and to serve Him more closely. In simple terms this is what our Lord did. This is the way He made disciples. This was His mission and His method, His obsession: to attach Himself to willing believers.

#3899
Teach
 	
Learning–KJV
Instruction–NASB
Teach–NIV
Learning–NKJV
Teach–NLT
 	
POSB
REFERENCE
(Rom. 15:4)
Note 2, point 1
	διδασκαλίαν = *didaskalian*
	Pronunciation: [did-ahs-kal-ee'-ahn]
	Parsing (part of speech): noun
	   Case—accusative
	   Gender—feminine
	   Number—singular
	   Stem or root—from διδασκαλία, ας
	Concordance References:
	  ⇒ Strong's #1319 didaskalia
	  ⇒ NIV #1436 didaskalia
	  ⇒ NASB #1319 didaskalia
	
	Romans 15:4
	For whatsoever things were written aforetime were written for our **learning**, that we through patience and comfort of the scriptures might have hope. [KJV]
	For whatever was written in earlier times was written for our **instruction**, that through perseverance and the encouragement of the Scriptures we might have hope. [NASB]
	For everything that was written in the past was written to **teach** us, so that through endurance and the encouragement of the Scriptures we might have hope. [NIV]
	For whatsoever things were written aforetime were written for our **learning**, that we through patience and comfort of the scriptures might have hope. [NKJV]
	Such things were written in the Scriptures long ago to **teach** us. They give us hope and encouragement as we wait patiently for God's promises. [NLT]
	ὅσα γὰρ προεγράφη, εἰς τὴν ἡμετέραν **διδασκαλίαν** προεγράφη, ἵνα διὰ τῆς ὑπομονῆς καὶ τῆς
		What is taught; teaching; doctrine; act of teaching; instruction.
		
		Practical Application
		In a strong church, everyone studies the Scripture. This is a great verse on the purpose of the Holy Scriptures. In very simple terms, it tells us why God gave us the Bible.
		The Scriptures were written for our...
		• learning,
		• instruction,
		• direction,
		• guidance.

ENGLISH WORD	GREEK WORD AND VERSE	THE WORD MEANS...
	παρακλήσεως τῶν γραφῶν τὴν ἐλπίδα ἔχωμεν. [GNS] ὅσα γὰρ προεγράφη, εἰς τὴν ἡμετέραν **διδασκαλίαν** ἐγράφη, ἵνα διὰ τῆς ὑπομονῆς καὶ διὰ τῆς παρακλήσεως τῶν γραφῶν τὴν ἐλπίδα ἔχωμεν. [GNT]	

#3900
Teach–
Teaching–
Taught
 	
Taught–KJV
Teaching–NASB
Teaching–NIV
Taught–NKJV
Teach–NLT
 	
POSB
REFERENCE
(Mk.9:31)
Note 2, point 1
 	
See also POSB REF:
(Mt.28:19-20; esp.
v.20)
Note 3, point 3
(Rom. 12:6-8, esp. v.7)
Note 2, point 3
	ἐδίδασκεν = *edidaske*
	Pronunciation: [eh-did-as'-keh]
	Parsing (part of speech): verb
	   Mood—indicative
	   Tense—imperfect
	   Voice—active
	   Person—3rd person
	   Number—singular
	   Stem or root—from **διδάσκω**
	Concordance References:
	  ⇒ Strong's #1321 didaskō
	  ⇒ NIV #1438 didaskō
	  ⇒ NASB #1321 didaskō
	
	Mark 9:31
	For he **taught** his disciples, and said unto them, The Son of man is delivered into the hands of men, and they shall kill him; and after that he is killed, he shall rise the third day. [KJV]
	For He was **teaching** His disciples and telling them, "The Son of Man is to be delivered into the hands of men, and they will kill Him; and when He has been killed, He will rise three days later." [NASB]
	Because he was **teaching** his disciples. He said to them, "The Son of Man is going to be betrayed into the hands of men. They will kill him, and after three days he will rise." [NIV]
	For He **taught** His disciples and said to them, "The Son of Man is being betrayed into the hands of men, and they will kill Him. And after He is killed, He will rise the third day." [NKJV]
	In order to spend more time with his disciples and **teach** them. He said to them, "The Son of Man is going to be betrayed. He will be killed, but three days later he will rise from the dead." [NLT]
	ἐδίδασκε γὰρ τοὺς μαθητὰς αὐτοῦ, καὶ ἔλεγεν αὐτοῖς, ὅτι Ὁ υἱὸς τοῦ ἀνθρώπου παραδίδοται εἰς χεῖρας ἀνθρώπων, καὶ ἀποκτενοῦσιν αὐτόν· καὶ ἀποκτανθείς, τῇ τρίτῃ ἡμέραι ἀναστήσεται. [GNS]
	ἐδίδασκεν γὰρ τοὺς μαθητὰς αὐτοῦ καὶ ἔλεγεν αὐτοῖς ὅτι Ὁ υἱὸς τοῦ ἀνθρώπου παραδίδοται εἰς χεῖρας ἀνθρώπων, καὶ ἀποκτενοῦσιν αὐτόν, καὶ ἀποκτανθεὶς μετὰ τρεῖς ἡμέρας ἀναστήσεται. [GNT]
		To continue to teach, to instruct, to educate, to train, to guide, to direct.
		
		Practical Application
		The Greek tense is imperfect; that is, He continued to teach them, kept right on teaching them. It was a continuous process, pulling one to the side, then another, then two, then four or five, then the whole group. He taught and taught, drilling the fact of His death and resurrection into them.

#3901
Teach Others
  What Is Good
 	
Teachers of good
  things–KJV
Teaching what is
  good–NASB
Teach what is
  good–NIV
Teachers of good
  things–NKJV
Teach others what is
  good–NLT
 	
POSB
REFERENCE
(Tit.2:3)
Note 3
	καλοδιδασκάλους = *kalodidaskalous*
	Pronunciation: [kal-od-id-as'-kal-oos]
	Parsing (part of speech): adjective
	   Case—accusative
	   Gender—feminine
	   Number—plural
	   Stem or root—from **καλοδιδάσκαλος**, ον
	Concordance References:
	  ⇒ Strong's #2567 kalodidaskalos
	  ⇒ NIV #2815 kalodidaskalos
	  ⇒ NASB #2567 kalodidaskalos
	
	Titus 2:3
	The aged women likewise, that *they be* in behaviour as becometh holiness, not false accusers, not given to much wine, **teachers of good things**; [KJV]
	Older women likewise are to be reverent in their behavior, not malicious gossips, nor enslaved to much wine, **teaching what is good**, [NASB]
	Likewise, teach the older women to be reverent in the way they live, not to be slanderers or addicted to much wine, but to **teach what is good**. [NIV]
	The older women likewise, that they be reverent in behavior, not slanderers, not given to much wine, **teach-**
		To teach what is good; to be teachers of good things. This refers to ministry in the home (Donald Guthrie. *The Pastoral Epistles.* "Tyndale New Testament Commentaries," p.193).
		
		Practical Application
		Elderly women are to *teach others what is good* (*kalodidaskalous*). Elderly women are to live such godly lives that they teach by their very example and testimony within the home. Note: they are to teach the young women how to live for Christ in a sinful and corruptible world.

ENGLISH WORD	GREEK WORD AND VERSE	THE WORD MEANS...

	ers of good things— [NKJV]
	    Similarly, teach the older women to live in a way that is appropriate for someone serving the Lord. They must not go around speaking evil of others and must not be heavy drinkers. Instead, they should **teach others what is good**. [NLT]
	    Πρεσβύτιδας ὡσαύτως ἐν καταστήματι ἱεροπρεπεῖς, μὴ διαβόλους, μὴ οἴνῳ πολλῷ δεδουλωμένας, **καλοδιδασκάλους**, [GNS]
	    πρεσβύτιδας ὡσαύτως ἐν καταστήματι ἱεροπρεπεῖς, μὴ διαβόλους μηδὲ οἴνῳ πολλῷ δεδουλωμένας, **καλοδιδασκάλους**, [GNT]	

#3902
**Teach
  Otherwise–
Teaches
  Otherwise**
 	
**Teach otherwise–
KJV**
Advocates a different doctrine–NASB
Teaches false doctrines–NIV
**Teaches otherwise–
NKJV**
Deny these things–NLT
 	
**POSB
REFERENCE**
(1 Tim.6:3)
  Note 1
	ἑτεροδιδασκαλεῖ = *heterodidaskalei*
	Pronunciation: [het-er-od-id-as-kal-eh'-ee]
	Parsing (part of speech): verb
	    Mood—indicative
	    Tense—present
	    Voice—active
	    Person—3rd person
	    Number—singular
	    Stem or root—from ἑτεροδιδασκαλέω
	Concordance References:
	⇒ Strong's #2085 heterodidaskaleö
	⇒ NIV #2281 heterodidaskaleö
	⇒ NASB #2085 heterodidaskaleö
	
	1 Tim. 6:3
	    If any man **teach otherwise**, and consent not to wholesome words, *even* the words of our Lord Jesus Christ, and to the doctrine which is according to godliness; [KJV]
	    If anyone **advocates a different doctrine**, and does not agree with sound words, those of our Lord Jesus Christ, and with the doctrine conforming to godliness, [NASB]
	    If anyone **teaches false doctrines** and does not agree to the sound instruction of our Lord Jesus Christ and to godly teaching, [NIV]
	    If anyone **teaches otherwise** and does not consent to wholesome words, *even* the words of our Lord Jesus Christ, and to the doctrine which accords with godliness, [NKJV]
	    Some false teachers may **deny these things**, but these are the sound, wholesome teachings of the Lord Jesus Christ, and they are the foundation for a godly life. [NLT]
	    Εἴ τις **ἑτεροδιδασκαλεῖ**, καὶ μὴ προσέρχεται ὑγιαίνουσι λόγοις, τοῖς τοῦ Κυρίου ἡμῶν Ἰησοῦ Χριστοῦ, καὶ τῇ κατ' εὐσέβειαν διδασκαλίᾳ, [GNS]
	    εἴ τις **ἑτεροδιδασκαλεῖ** καὶ μὴ προσέρχεται ὑγιαίνουσιν λόγοις τοῖς τοῦ κυρίου ἡμῶν Ἰησοῦ Χριστοῦ καὶ τῇ κατ' εὐσέβειαν διδασκαλίᾳ, [GNT]
		Teaches false doctrines; to advocate a different doctrine.
		
		Practical Application
		    The false teacher teaches a different doctrine. He does not teach the words of the Lord Jesus Christ. This is a terrible indictment. Imagine being in the pulpit of a Christian church and claiming to be a teacher of the Lord Jesus Christ, yet not teaching His words. How many of us are guilty of this indictment? How many of us are guilty of teaching a different doctrine?

#3903
**Teach,
  Teaching
  What Is Good**
 	
Teachers of good things–KJV
Teaching what is good–NASB
Teach what is good–NIV
Teachers of good things–NKJV
Teach others what is good–NLT
	καλοδιδασκάλους = *kalodidaskalous*
	Pronunciation: [kal-od-id-as'-kal-oos]
	Parsing (part of speech): adjective
	    Case—accusative
	    Gender—feminine
	    Number—plural
	    Stem or root—from καλοδιδάσκαλος, ον
	Concordance References:
	⇒ Strong's #2567 kalodidaskalos
	⇒ NIV #2815 kalodidaskalos
	⇒ NASB #2567 kalodidaskalos
	
	Titus 2:3
	    The aged women likewise, that *they be* in behaviour as becometh holiness, not false accusers, not given to much wine, **teachers of good things**; [KJV]
	    Older women likewise are to be reverent in their behavior, not malicious gossips, nor enslaved to much wine, **teaching what is good**, [NASB]
	    Likewise, teach the older women to be reverent in the
		To teach what is good; to be teachers of good things. This refers to ministry in the home (Donald Guthrie. *The Pastoral Epistles.* "Tyndale New Testament Commentaries," p.193).
		
		Practical Application
		    Elderly women are to *teach what is good* (*kalodidaskalous*). Elderly women are to live such godly lives that they teach by their very example and testimony within the home. Note: they are to teach the young women how to live for Christ in a sinful and corruptible world.

ENGLISH WORD	GREEK WORD AND VERSE	THE WORD MEANS...
POSB **REFERENCE** (Tit.2:3) Note 3	way they live, not to be slanderers or addicted to much wine, but to **teach what is good**. [NIV] The older women likewise, that they be reverent in behavior, not slanderers, not given to much wine, **teachers of good things—** [NKJV] Similarly, teach the older women to live in a way that is appropriate for someone serving the Lord. They must not go around speaking evil of others and must not be heavy drinkers. Instead, they should **teach others what is good**. [NLT] Πρεσβύτιδας ὡσαύτως ἐν καταστήματι ἱεροπρεπεῖς, μὴ διαβόλους, μὴ οἴνῳ πολλῷ δεδουλωμένας, **καλοδιδασκάλους**, [GNS] πρεσβύτιδας ὡσαύτως ἐν καταστήματι ἱεροπρεπεῖς, μὴ διαβόλους μηδὲ οἴνῳ πολλῷ δεδουλωμένας, **καλοδιδασκάλους** [GNT]	

#3904
Teacher
 	
Lord–KJV
Rabboni–NASB
Rabbi–NIV
Rabboni–NKJV
Teacher–NLT
 	
POSB
REFERENCE
(Mk.10:51-52; esp. v.51)
Note 6, point 4
	Ῥαββουνί = *Rabboni*
	Pronunciation: [hrab-bon-ee']
	Parsing (part of speech): noun
	  Case vocative
	  Gender—masculine
	  Number—singular
	  Stem or root—from ῥαββουνί
	Concordance References:
	  ⇒ Strong's #4462 rhabboni or *rhabbouni*
	  ⇒ NIV #4808 hrabbouni
	  ⇒ NASB #4462 hrabbouni
	
	Mark 10:51
	And Jesus answered and said unto him, What wilt thou that I should do unto thee? The blind man said unto him, **Lord**, that I might receive my sight. [KJV]
	
	And answering him, Jesus said, "What do you want Me to do for you?" And the blind man said to Him, "**Rabboni**, *I want* to regain my sight!" [NASB]
	
	"What do you want me to do for you?" Jesus asked him. The blind man said, "**Rabbi**, I want to see." [NIV]
	
	So Jesus answered and said to him, "What do you want Me to do for you?" The blind man said to Him, "**Rabboni**, that I may receive my sight."
	
	"What do you want me to do for you?" Jesus asked. "**Teacher**," the blind man said, "I want to see!" [NLT]
	
	καὶ ἀποκριθεὶς λέγει αὐτῷ ὁ Ἰησοῦς, Τί θέλεις ποιήσω σοι; Ὁ δὲ τυφλὸς εἶπεν αὐτῷ, **Ῥαββουνι**, ἵνα ἀναβλέψω. [GNS]
	
	καὶ ἀποκριθεὶς αὐτῷ ὁ Ἰησοῦς εἶπεν, Τί σοι θέλεις ποιήσω; ὁ δὲ τυφλὸς εἶπεν αὐτῷ, **Ῥαββουνι**, ἵνα ἀναβλέψω. [GNT]
		Rabbi, Lord, Rabboni, Teacher, Master.
		
		Practical Application
		It is a title of reverent respect. Note the possessive "my." The heart of Bartimaeus reached out to Jesus, desiring to belong to Him.

#3905
Teacher
 	
Master–KJV
Teacher–NASB
Teacher–NIV
Teacher–NKJV
Teacher–NLT
 	
POSB
REFERENCE
(Jn.11:28)
Deeper Study #1
	Ὁ διδάσκαλος = *ho didaskalos*
	Pronunciation: [ho did-as'-kal-os]
	Parsing *didaskalos* (part of speech): noun
	  Case—nominative
	  Gender—masculine
	  Number—singular
	  Stem or root—from διδάσκαλος, ου
	Concordance References:
	  ⇒ Strong's #1320 didaskalos
	  ⇒ NIV #1437 didaskalos
	  ⇒ NASB #1320 didaskalos
	
	John 11:28
	And when she had so said, she went her way, and called Mary her sister secretly, saying, **The Master** is come, and calleth for thee. [KJV]
	
	And when she had said this, she went away, and called Mary her sister, saying secretly, "**The Teacher** is here, and is calling for you." [NASB]
	
	And after she had said this, she went back and called her sister Mary aside. "**The Teacher** is here," she said, "and is asking for you." [NIV]
		The Teacher, Master, Rabbi.
		
		Practical Application
		The definite article "the" (*ho*) is important. Jesus is not just another teacher like all other teachers. He is *the* Teacher, the teaching Master. This means at least two things.
		1. Jesus is the Supreme Teacher, the very best teacher who has ever lived. He is known for being the greatest of teachers. No one compares or even comes close to comparing with Him. He stands alone as *the Teacher*.
		2. Jesus is the Master, the Lord, the Teacher of all men. In calling Jesus *the* Teacher, there is the idea of His Lordship and deity. Note that He claims deity Himself: "Ye call me 'Teacher' and 'Lord' and rightly so, for that is what I am" (John 13:13). His being *the Teacher* is tied closely with His being *the Lord*. In fact, logic alone would tell us that

ENGLISH WORD	GREEK WORD AND VERSE	THE WORD MEANS...

#3910
Teachers Of Good Things
 	
Teachers of good things–KJV
Teaching what is good–NASB
Teach what is good–NIV
Teachers of good things–NKJV
Teach others what is good–NLT
 	
POSB REFERENCE
(Tit.2:3)
Note 3
	καλοδιδασκάλους = kalodidaskalous
	Pronunciation: [kal-od-id-as'-kal-oos]
	Parsing (part of speech): adjective
	  Case—accusative
	  Gender—feminine
	  Number—plural
	  Stem or root—from καλοδιδάσκαλος, ον
	Concordance References:
	⇒ Strong's #2567 kalodidaskalos
	⇒ NIV #2815 kalodidaskalos
	⇒ NASB #2567 kalodidaskalos
	
	Titus 2:3
	The aged women likewise, that *they be* in behaviour as becometh holiness, not false accusers, not given to much wine, **teachers of good things**; [KJV]
	Older women likewise are to be reverent in their behavior, not malicious gossips, nor enslaved to much wine, **teaching what is good**, [NASB]
	Likewise, teach the older women to be reverent in the way they live, not to be slanderers or addicted to much wine, but to **teach what is good**. [NIV]
	The older women likewise, that they be reverent in behavior, not slanderers, not given to much wine, **teachers of good things**— [NKJV]
	Similarly, teach the older women to live in a way that is appropriate for someone serving the Lord. They must not go around speaking evil of others and must not be heavy drinkers. Instead, they should **teach others what is good**. [NLT]
	Πρεσβύτιδας ὡσαύτως ἐν καταστήματι ἱεροπρεπεῖς, μὴ διαβόλους, μὴ οἴνῳ πολλῷ δεδουλωμένας, **καλοδιδασκάλους**, [GNS]
	πρεσβύτιδας ὡσαύτως ἐν καταστήματι ἱεροπρεπεῖς, μὴ διαβόλους μηδὲ οἴνῳ πολλῷ δεδουλωμένας, **καλοδιδασκάλους**, [GNT]
		To teach what is good; to be teachers of good things. This refers to ministry in the home (Donald Guthrie. *The Pastoral Epistles.* "Tyndale New Testament Commentaries," p.193).
		
		Practical Application
		Elderly women are to be *teachers of good things* (kalodidaskalous). Elderly women are to live such godly lives that they teach by their very example and testimony within the home. Note: they are to teach the young women how to live for Christ in a sinful and corruptible world.

#3911
Teachers Of The Law– Teachers Of Religious Law
 	
Scribes–KJV
Scribes–NASB
Teachers of the law–NIV
Scribes–NKJV
Teachers of religious law–NLT
 	
POSB REFERENCE
(Mk.12:28)
Deeper Study #1
	γραμματέων = grammateön
	Pronunciation: [gram-mat-eh-own']
	Parsing (part of speech): noun
	  Case—genitive
	  Gender—masculine
	  Number—plural
	  Stem or root—from γραμματεύς, έως
	Concordance References:
	⇒ Strong's #1122 grammateus
	⇒ NIV #1208 grammateus
	⇒ NASB #1122 grammateus
	
	Mark 12:28
	And one of the **scribes** came, and having heard them reasoning together, and perceiving that he had answered them well, asked him, Which is the first commandment of all? [KJV]
	And one of the **scribes** came and heard them arguing, and recognizing that He had answered them well, asked Him, "What commandment is the foremost of all?" [NASB]
	One of the **teachers of the law** came and heard them debating. Noticing that Jesus had given them a good answer, he asked him, "Of all the commandments, which is the most important?" [NIV]
	Then one of the **scribes** came, and having heard them reasoning together, perceiving that He had answered them well, asked Him, "Which is the first commandment of all?" [NKJV]
	One of the **teachers of religious law** was standing there listening to the discussion. He realized that Jesus had answered well, so he asked, "Of all the commandments, which is the most important?" [NLT]
	Καὶ προσελθὼν εἷς τῶν **γραμματέων**, ἀκούσας αὐτῶν συζητούντων, εἰδὼς ὅτι καλῶς αὐτοῖς ἀπεκρίθη,
		Teachers of the law, teachers of religious law, scribes, scholars.
		
		Practical Application
		This word (grammateön) describes a profession of laymen who studied, taught, interpreted, and dealt with the practical questions of Jewish law. They were a specialization within the profession commonly called Scribes (cp. Matthew 22:35). They functioned both in the court and synagogues (cp. Luke 7:30; Luke 10:25; Luke 11:45, 46, 52; Luke 14:3; Titus 3:13). They were apparently a specialization dealing more with the study and interpretation of the law.

ENGLISH WORD	GREEK WORD AND VERSE	THE WORD MEANS...
	ἐπηρώτησεν αὐτόν, Ποία ἐστὶ πρώτη πάντων ἐντολή; [GNS] Καὶ προσελθὼν εἷς τῶν **γραμματέων** ἀκούσας αὐτῶν συζητούντων, ἰδὼν ὅτι καλῶς ἀπεκρίθη αὐτοῖς ἐπηρώτησεν αὐτόν, Ποία ἐστὶν ἐντολὴ πρώτη πάντων; [GNT]	
#3912 **Teaches False Doctrines** Teach otherwise–KJV Advocates a different doctrine–NASB **Teaches false doctrines–NIV** Teaches otherwise–NKJV Deny these things–NLT **POSB REFERENCE** (1 Tim.6:3) Note 1	ἑτεροδιδασκαλεῖ = *heterodidaskalei* Pronunciation: [het-er-od-id-as-kal-eh'-ee] Parsing (part of speech): verb 　Mood—indicative 　Tense—present 　Voice—active 　Person—3rd person 　Number—singular 　Stem or root—from ἑτεροδιδασκαλέω Concordance References: 　⇒ Strong's #2085 heterodidaskaleō 　⇒ NIV #2281 heterodidaskaleō 　⇒ NASB #2085 heterodidaskaleō **1 Tim. 6:3** If any man **teach otherwise**, and consent not to wholesome words, *even* the words of our Lord Jesus Christ, and to the doctrine which is according to godliness; [KJV] If anyone **advocates a different doctrine**, and does not agree with sound words, those of our Lord Jesus Christ, and with the doctrine conforming to godliness, [NASB] If anyone **teaches false doctrines** and does not agree to the sound instruction of our Lord Jesus Christ and to godly teaching, [NIV] If anyone **teaches otherwise** and does not consent to wholesome words, *even* the words of our Lord Jesus Christ, and to the doctrine which accords with godliness, [NKJV] Some false teachers may **deny these things**, but these are the sound, wholesome teachings of the Lord Jesus Christ, and they are the foundation for a godly life. [NLT] Εἴ τις **ἑτεροδιδασκαλεῖ**, καὶ μὴ προσέρχεται ὑγιαίνουσι λόγοις, τοῖς τοῦ Κυρίου ἡμῶν Ἰησοῦ Χριστοῦ, καὶ τῇ κατ' εὐσέβειαν διδασκαλίᾳ, [GNS] εἴ τις **ἑτεροδιδασκαλεῖ** καὶ μὴ προσέρχεται ὑγιαίνουσιν λόγοις τοῖς τοῦ κυρίου ἡμῶν Ἰησοῦ Χριστοῦ καὶ τῇ κατ' εὐσέβειαν διδασκαλίᾳ, [GNT]	Teaches false doctrines; to advocate a different doctrine. **Practical Application** The false teacher teaches a different doctrine. He does not teach the words of the Lord Jesus Christ. This is a terrible indictment. Imagine being in the pulpit of a Christian church and claiming to be a teacher of the Lord Jesus Christ, yet not teaching His words. How many of us are guilty of this indictment? How many of us are guilty of teaching a different doctrine?
#3913 **Teaching** Doctrine–KJV **Teaching–NASB** **Teaching–NIV** Doctrine–NKJV **Teaching–NLT** **POSB REFERENCE** (Acts 2:42) *Deeper Study* #2	διδαχῇ = *didachë* Pronunciation: [did-akh-ay'] Parsing (part of speech): noun 　Case—dative 　Gender—feminine 　Number—singular 　Stem or root—from διδαχή, ῆς Concordance References: 　⇒ Strong's #1322 didachë 　⇒ NIV #1439 didachë 　⇒ NASB #1322 didachë **Acts 2:42** And they continued stedfastly in the apostles' **doctrine** and fellowship, and in breaking of bread, and in prayers. [KJV] And they were continually devoting themselves to the apostles' **teaching** and to fellowship, to the breaking of bread and to prayer. [NASB] They devoted themselves to the apostles' **teaching** and to the fellowship, to the breaking of bread and to prayer. [NIV] And they continued steadfastly in the apostles' **doctrine** and fellowship, in the breaking of bread, and in prayers. [NKJV]	Teaching, doctrine, instruction, principle, training. **Practical Application** It is the teaching, the instruction of the apostles. This would include both what Christ taught and His death, resurrection, ascension, or exaltation. It would be the same teaching and instructions... 　• that are shared in the New Testament. 　• that the disciples wrote to various churches and bodies of believers. The teaching would be no different. There is only one message, only one Word that saves and grounds people in the Lord—the Word of God Himself, the message of the New Testament. On the day of Pentecost, the persons who were saved needed to be grounded in the faith. And the only message that could ground them was the message found in the New Testament. It was that message, that doctrine they were taught.

ENGLISH WORD	GREEK WORD AND VERSE	THE WORD MEANS...
	They joined with the other believers and devoted themselves to the apostles' **teaching** and fellowship, sharing in the Lord's Supper and in prayer. [NLT] ἦσαν δὲ προσκαρτεροῦντες τῇ **διδαχῇ** τῶν ἀποστόλων καὶ τῇ κοινωνίᾳ, καὶ τῇ κλάσει τοῦ ἄρτου καὶ ταῖς προσευχαῖς. [GNS] ἦσαν δὲ προσκαρτεροῦντες τῇ **διδαχῇ** τῶν ἀποστόλων καὶ τῇ κοινωνίᾳ, τῇ κλάσει τοῦ ἄρτου καὶ ταῖς προσευχαῖς. [GNT]	

#3914
Teaching
 	
Tradition–KJV
Tradition–NASB
Teaching–NIV
Tradition–NKJV
Tradition of hard work–NLT
 	
POSB REFERENCE
(2 Thes.3:6-11; esp. v.6)
Note 1
	παράδοσιν = *paradosin*
	Pronunciation: [par-ad'-os-in]
	Parsing (part of speech): noun
	    Case—accusative
	    Gender—feminine
	    Number—singular
	    Stem or root—from **παράδοσις**, εως
	Concordance References:
	⇒ Strong's #3862 paradosis
	⇒ NIV #4142 paradosis
	⇒ NASB #3862 paradosis
	
	2 Thes. 3:6
	Now we command you, brethren, in the name of our Lord Jesus Christ, that ye withdraw yourselves from every brother that walketh disorderly, and not after the **tradition** which he received of us. [KJV]
	
	Now we command you, brethren, in the name of our Lord Jesus Christ, that you keep aloof from every brother who leads an unruly life and not according to the **tradition** which you received from us. [NASB]
	
	In the name of the Lord Jesus Christ, we command you, brothers, to keep away from every brother who is idle and does not live according to the **teaching** you received from us. [NIV]
	
	But we command you, brethren, in the name of our Lord Jesus Christ, that you withdraw from every brother who walks disorderly and not according to the **tradition** which he received from us. [NKJV]
	
	And now, dear brothers and sisters, we give you this command with the authority of our Lord Jesus Christ: Stay away from any Christian who lives in idleness and doesn't follow the **tradition of hard work** we gave you. [NLT]
	
	Παραγγέλλομεν δὲ ὑμῖν, ἀδελφοί, ἐν ὀνόματι τοῦ Κυρίου ἡμῶν Ἰησοῦ Χριστοῦ, στέλλεσθαι ὑμᾶς ἀπὸ παντὸς ἀδελφοῦ ἀτάκτως περιπατοῦντος, καὶ μὴ κατὰ τὴν **παράδοσιν** ἣν παρέλαβε παρ' ἡμῶν. [GNS]
	
	Παραγγέλλομεν δὲ ὑμῖν, ἀδελφοί, ἐν ὀνόματι τοῦ κυρίου [ἡμῶν] Ἰησοῦ Χριστοῦ στέλλεσθαι ὑμᾶς ἀπὸ παντὸς ἀδελφοῦ ἀτάκτως περιπατοῦντος καὶ μὴ κατὰ τὴν **παράδοσιν** ἣν παρελάβοσαν παρ' ἡμῶν. [GNT]
		Teaching, tradition, tradition of hard work. It means all the Word of God, whether taught orally or written.
		
		Practical Application
		The idle worker disobeys the instructions of God (2 Thes. 3:6). Paul says that he had taught the believers the commandments of God that deal with work; therefore, they are without excuse. They know better than to sit around idle. If they continue to be idle, slothful, and lazy, the other believers are to withdraw from them. They are deliberately disobeying the instructions of God.

#3915
Teachings
 	
Ordinances–KJV
Traditions–NASB
Teachings–NIV
Traditions–NKJV
Christian teaching–NLT
 	
POSB REFERENCE
(1 Cor.11:2)
Note 1
 	
See also POSB REF:
(2 Thes.2:15)
Note 4
	παραδόσεις = *paradoseis*
	Pronunciation: [par-ad'-os-ees]
	Parsing (part of speech): noun
	    Case—accusative
	    Gender—feminine
	    Number—plural
	    Stem or root—from **παράδοσις**, εως
	Concordance References:
	⇒ Strong's #3862 paradosis
	⇒ NIV #4142 paradosis
	⇒ NASB #3862 paradosis
	
	1 Cor. 11:2
	Now I praise you, brethren, that ye remember me in all things, and keep the **ordinances**, as I delivered *them* to you. [KJV]
	
	Now I praise you because you remember me in everything, and hold firmly to the **traditions**, just as I delivered them to you. [NASB]
	
	I praise you for remembering me in everything and for
		Teachings, traditions or instructions that are passed down by word of mouth from generation to generation.
		
		Practical Application
		This is important to see, for this passage is dealing...
		• with traditions.
		• with unwritten laws of behavior.
		• with customs.
		• with local practice.
		• with preferences of a particular people or body.
		• with long-established patterns of a people or group.
		
		Leon Morris quotes J.B. Lightfoot: "The prominent idea of *paradoseis* [tradition]...is that

ENGLISH WORD	GREEK WORD AND VERSE	THE WORD MEANS...
	holding to the **teachings**, just as I passed them on to you. [NIV] Now I praise you, brethren, that you remember me in all things and keep the **traditions** just as I delivered *them* to you. [NKJV] I am so glad, dear friends, that you always keep me in your thoughts and you are following the **Christian teaching** I passed on to you. [NLT] Ἐπαινῶ δὲ ὑμᾶς, ἀδελφοί, ὅτι πάντα μου μέμνησθε καὶ καθὼς παρέδωκα ὑμῖν τὰς **παραδόσεις** κατέχετε. [GNS] Ἐπαινῶ δὲ ὑμᾶς ὅτι πάντα μου μέμνησθε καὶ, καθὼς παρέδωκα ὑμῖν, τὰς **παραδόσεις** κατέχετε. [GNT]	of an authority external to the teacher himself." Leon Morris himself says: *This is another way of putting the truth...that the gospel is not of human origin, and the preacher is not at liberty to substitute his own thoughts for that which he has received (The Epistles of Paul to the Thessalonians.* "Tyndale New Testament Commentaries," p.138).

#3916
Team Up
 	
Unequally yoked together–KJV
Bound together–NASB
Yoked together–NIV
Unequally yoked together–NKJV
Team up–NLT
 	
POSB REFERENCE
(2 Cor.6:14-16; esp. v.14)
Note 2
	ἑτεροζυγοῦντες = *heterozugountes*
	Pronunciation: [het-er-od-zoog-oon-tehs]
	Parsing (part of speech): verb
	    Mood—participle
	    Tense—present
	    Voice—active
	    Case—nominative
	    Gender—masculine
	    Person—2nd person
	    Number—plural
	    Stem or root—from ἑτεροζυγέω
	Concordance References:
	⇒ Strong's #2086 heterozugeö
	⇒ NIV #2282 heterozugeö
	⇒ NASB #2086 heterozugeö
	
	2 Cor. 6:14
	Be ye not **unequally yoked together** with unbelievers: for what fellowship hath righteousness with unrighteousness? and what communion hath light with darkness? [KJV]
	
	Do not be **bound together** with unbelievers; for what partnership have righteousness and lawlessness, or what fellowship has light with darkness? [NASB]
	
	Do not be **yoked together** with unbelievers. For what do righteousness and wickedness have in common? Or what fellowship can light have with darkness? [NIV]
	
	Do not be **unequally yoked together** with unbelievers. For what fellowship has righteousness with lawlessness? And what communion has light with darkness? [NKJV]
	
	Don't **team up** with those who are unbelievers. How can goodness be a partner with wickedness? How can light live with darkness? [NLT]
	
	Μὴ γίνεσθε **ἑτεροζυγοῦντες** ἀπίστοις· τίς γὰρ μετοχὴ δικαιοσύνῃ καὶ ἀνομίᾳ; τίς δὲ κοινωνία φωτὶ πρὸς σκότος; [GNS]
	
	Μὴ γίνεσθε **ἑτεροζυγοῦντες** ἀπίστοις· τίς γὰρ μετοχὴ δικαιοσύνῃ καὶ ἀνομίᾳ, ἢ τίς κοινωνία φωτὶ πρὸς σκότος; [GNT]
		To be yoked together; to be bound together; to team up; to be unequally yoked; to be mismated.
		
		### Practical Application
		It refers back to the Old Testament where God forbade the plowing of an ox with an ass (Deut. 22:10) or the union of different kinds of animals (Leviticus 19:19). The point is...
		• that the union of a genuine believer with an unbeliever would be as different as the union between two kinds of animals.
		• that the plowing through life of a believer with an unbeliever would be as difficult as the plowing of a field with an ox and an ass yoked together.
		
		Genuine believers are radically different from unbelievers.

#3917
Teammate
 	
Yokefellow–KJV
Comrade–NASB
Yokefellow–NIV
Companion–NKJV
Teammate–NLT
 	
POSB REFERENCE
(Philip.4:2-3; esp. v.3)
Note 2, point 2
	σύζυγε = *suzuge*
	Pronunciation: [sood'-zoo-geh]
	Parsing (part of speech): pronominal adjective
	    Case—vocative
	    Gender—masculine
	    Number—singular
	    Stem or root—from σύζυγος, ου
	Concordance References:
	⇒ Strong's #4805 suzugos
	⇒ NIV #5187 suzugos
	⇒ NASB #4805 suzugos
	
	Philip. 4:3
	And I intreat thee also, true **yokefellow**, help those women which laboured with me in the gospel, with Clement also, and with other my fellowlabourers, whose names are in the book of life. [KJV]
	
	Indeed, true **comrade**, I ask you also to help these
		Yokefellow, fellow worker, comrade, teammate.
		
		### Practical Application
		The need is for a true friend, a yokefellow, to step in to help any who are quarreling. The word "teammate" (*suzuge*) is thought by some to be a proper name given to some Christians when they were baptized. It was a common practice for believers to be given new names at their baptism in order to symbolize their spiritual birth. Just who this yokefellow was is not known, but he must have been a man deeply respected by the people of the church. His name refers to the *yoke* or *collar* that was fitted around the neck of oxen for plowing. The collar attached the plow and

ENGLISH WORD	GREEK WORD AND VERSE	THE WORD MEANS...
	women who have shared my struggle in the cause of the gospel, together with Clement also, and the rest of my fellow workers, whose names are in the book of life. [NASB] Yes, and I ask you, loyal **yokefellow**, help these women who have contended at my side in the cause of the gospel, along with Clement and the rest of my fellow workers, whose names are in the book of life. [NIV] And I urge you also, true **companion**, help these women who labored with me in the gospel, with Clement also, and the rest of my fellow workers, whose names are in the Book of Life. [NKJV] And I ask you, my true **teammate**, to help these women, for they worked hard with me in telling others the Good News. And they worked with Clement and the rest of my co-workers, whose names are written in the Book of Life. [NLT] καὶ ἐρωτῶ καὶ σέ, **σύζυγε** γνήσιε, συλλαμβάνου αὐταῖς, αἵτινες ἐν τῷ εὐαγγελίῳ συνήθλησάν μοι, μετὰ καὶ Κλήμεντος, καὶ τῶν λοιπῶν συνεργῶν μου, ὧν τὰ ὀνόματα ἐν βίβλῳ ζωῆς. [GNS] ναὶ ἐρωτῶ καὶ σέ, γνήσιε **σύζυγε**, συλλαμβάνου αὐταῖς, αἵτινες ἐν τῷ εὐαγγελίῳ συνήθλησάν μοι μετὰ καὶ Κλήμεντος καὶ τῶν λοιπῶν συνεργῶν μου, ὧν τὰ ὀνόματα ἐν βίβλῳ ζωῆς. [GNT]	held the two oxen together so that they would pull together and more quickly get the work done. Therefore, "teammate" means a person who pulls and works cooperatively with others. The very fact that Paul would ask him to help the two quarreling ladies shows that he was highly esteemed. Paul felt that he cared and that the two quarrelers would listen to him—that he could solve the dispute and bring about reconciliation. Most churches have one or more yokefellows, persons... • who love and care deeply for others. • who are always helping and ministering to others. • whom God has gifted and appointed to be ministerial helpers to the flock. • who are highly respected and esteemed by most in the congregation. The yokefellow is the person who should step in when quarrels and divisiveness begin to arouse their poisonous heads. The yokefellow is the person especially gifted by God to bring reconciliation and peace to the church.
#3918 **Tell** Charge–KJV Instruct–NASB Command–NIV Command–NKJV **Tell–NLT** **POSB REFERENCE** (1 Tim.6:17-19; esp. v.17) Note 1	*παράγγελλε = paraggelle* Pronunciation: [par-ang-gel'-leh] Parsing (part of speech): verb 　Mood—imperative 　Tense—present 　Voice—active 　Person—2ⁿᵈ person 　Number—singular 　Stem or root—from παραγγέλλω Concordance References: ⇒　Strong's #3853 paraggellö ⇒　NIV #4133 paraggellö ⇒　NASB #3853 paraggellö **1 Tim. 6:17** **Charge** them that are rich in this world, that they be not highminded, nor trust in uncertain riches, but in the living God, who giveth us richly all things to enjoy; [KJV] **Instruct** those who are rich in this present world not to be conceited or to fix their hope on the uncertainty of riches, but on God, who richly supplies us with all things to enjoy. [NASB] **Command** those who are rich in this present world not to be arrogant nor to put their hope in wealth, which is so uncertain, but to put their hope in God, who richly provides us with everything for our enjoyment. [NIV] **Command** those who are rich in this present age not to be haughty, nor to trust in uncertain riches but in the living God, who gives us richly all things to enjoy. [NKJV] **Tell** those who are rich in this world not to be proud and not to trust in their money, which will soon be gone. But their trust should be in the living God, who richly gives us all we need for our enjoyment. [NLT] Τοῖς πλουσίοις ἐν τῷ νῦν αἰῶνι **παράγγελλε** μὴ ὑψηλοφρονεῖν, μηδὲ ἠλπικέναι ἐπὶ πλούτου ἀδηλότητι, ἀλλ' ἐν Θεῷ τῷ ζῶντι, τῷ παρέχοντι ἡμῖν πλουσίως πάντα εἰς ἀπόλαυσιν· [GNS] Τοῖς πλουσίοις ἐν τῷ νῦν αἰῶνι **παράγγελλε** μὴ ὑψηλοφρονεῖν μηδὲ ἠλπικέναι ἐπὶ πλούτου ἀδηλότητι ἀλλ' ἐπὶ θεῷ τῷ παρέχοντι ἡμῖν πάντα πλουσίως εἰς ἀπόλαυσιν, [GNT]	To command; to charge; to instruct; to tell; to order; to rule. The word is a strong word. It has the force of a military command, yet it has the tenderness of an appeal to it. **Practical Application** It means to beg and beseech a person—strongly so—to the point that the person is commanded to act. In this charge, God is appealing and begging the rich person, but He is doing it so strongly that it is a command. The rich person is approached in love and tenderness and an appeal is made to him, but he is expected to do exactly what God says.

ENGLISH WORD	GREEK WORD AND VERSE	THE WORD MEANS...

#3919
Tell People
 	
Witnesses–KJV
Witnesses–NASB
Witnesses–NIV
Witnesses–NKJV
Tell people–NLT
 	
POSB REFERENCE
(Acts 1:8)
Note 3, point 2c
	μάρτυρες = *martures*
	Pronunciation: [mar'-toor-ehs]
	Parsing (part of speech): noun
	  Case—nominative
	  Gender—masculine
	  Number—plural
	  Stem or root—from μάρτυς, μάρτυρος
	Concordance References:
	⇒ Strong's #3144 martus
	⇒ NIV #3459 martus
	⇒ NASB #3144 martus
	
	Acts 1:8
	But ye shall receive power, after that the Holy Ghost is come upon you: and ye shall be **witnesses** unto me both in Jerusalem, and in all Judaea, and in Samaria, and unto the uttermost part of the earth. [KJV]
	But you shall receive power when the Holy Spirit has come upon you; and you shall be My **witnesses** both in Jerusalem, and in all Judea and Samaria, and even to the remotest part of the earth." [NASB]
	But you will receive power when the Holy Spirit comes on you; and you will be my **witnesses** in Jerusalem, and in all Judea and Samaria, and to the ends of the earth." [NIV]
	But you shall receive power when the Holy Spirit has come upon you; and you shall be **witnesses** to Me in Jerusalem, and in all Judea and Samaria, and to the end of the earth." [NKJV]
	But when the Holy Spirit has come upon you, you will receive power and will **tell people** about me everywhere—in Jerusalem, throughout Judea, in Samaria, and to the ends of the earth." [NLT]
	ἀλλὰ λήψεσθε δύναμιν ἐπελθόντος τοῦ Ἁγίου Πνεύματος ἐφ' ὑμᾶς· καὶ ἔσεσθέ μοι **μάρτυρες** ἔν τε Ἰερουσαλὴμ, καὶ ἐν πάσῃ τῇ Ἰουδαίᾳ καὶ Σαμαρείᾳ καὶ ἕως ἐσχάτου τῆς γῆς. [GNS]
	ἀλλὰ λήμψεσθε δύναμιν ἐπελθόντος τοῦ ἁγίου πνεύματος ἐφ' ὑμᾶς καὶ ἔσεσθέ μου **μάρτυρες** ἔν τε Ἰερουσαλὴμ καὶ [ἐν] πάσῃ τῇ Ἰουδαίᾳ καὶ Σαμαρείᾳ καὶ ἕως ἐσχάτου τῆς γῆς. [GNT]
		Witnesses; to tell people; martyr.
		
		Practical Application
		This is the same word as martyr. The believer is to be so committed to reaching men that he is ready to die as a martyr if need be. (See POSB *Deeper Study* #1—Acts 1:8 for verses on witnessing.)
		The term "tell people" (*martures*) is not a command. Rather, it is a natural result of the Holy Spirit within a person. So is power. The Lord says very simply that a Spirit-filled person has power and becomes a witness for Him throughout the world. This is important, for it makes power and witnessing trademarks of Christian believers. A genuine believer possesses both the Spirit and power in his life and becomes by nature a witness for the Lord.

#3920
Telling Them The Good News About
 	
Preaching–KJV
Preaching–NASB
Telling them the good news about–NIV
Preaching–NKJV
Preaching–NLT
 	
POSB REFERENCE
(Acts 11:19-30; esp. v.20)
Deeper Study #2, point 2
	εὐαγγελιζόμενοι = *euaggelizomenoi*
	Pronunciation: [yoo-ang-ghel-id'-zo-men-o-ee]
	Parsing (part of speech): verb
	  Mood—participle
	  Tense—present
	  Voice—middle
	  Case—nominative
	  Gender—masculine
	  Number—plural
	  Stem or root—from εὐαγγελίζω
	Concordance References:
	⇒ Strong's #2097 euaggelizo
	⇒ NIV #2294 euaggelizo
	⇒ NASB #2097 euaggelizo
	
	Acts 11:20
	And some of them were men of Cyprus and Cyrene, which, when they were come to Antioch, spake unto the Grecians, **preaching** the Lord Jesus. [KJV]
	But there were some of them, men of Cyprus and Cyrene, who came to Antioch and *began* speaking to the Greeks also, **preaching** the Lord Jesus. [NASB]
	Some of them, however, men from Cyprus and Cyrene, went to Antioch and began to speak to Greeks also, **telling them the good news about** the Lord Jesus. [NIV]
	But some of them were men from Cyprus and Cyrene, who, when they had come to Antioch, spoke to the Hellenists, **preaching** the Lord Jesus. [NKJV]
	However, some of the believers who went to Antioch
		Telling them the good news about preaching. This word means to declare and proclaim the gospel; to preach the glad tidings of Jesus Christ; to proclaim the Word, the truth about Jesus Christ.
		
		Practical Application
		It means that the believers who went to Antioch actually entered the city preaching and telling them the good news about the Lord Jesus. The picture is...
		• that of their entering the city to bring the Lord Jesus to its residents. The believers were set on reaching the city for God, and their method was telling them the good news about the Lord Jesus.
		• that of facing a person or persons, of standing before people and telling them the good news about Christ.

ENGLISH WORD	GREEK WORD AND VERSE	THE WORD MEANS...
	from Cyprus and Cyrene began **preaching** to Gentiles about the Lord Jesus. [NLT] ἦσαν δέ τινες ἐξ αὐτῶν ἄνδρες Κύπριοι καὶ Κυρηναῖοι, οἵτινες ἐλθόντες εἰς ᾿Αντιόχειαν, ἐλάλουν πρὸς τοὺς ῾Ελληνιστάς, **εὐαγγελιζόμενοι** τὸν Κύριον ᾿Ιησοῦν. [GNS] ἦσαν δέ τινες ἐξ αὐτῶν ἄνδρες Κύπριοι καὶ Κυρηναῖοι, οἵτινες ἐλθόντες εἰς ᾿Αντιόχειαν ἐλάλουν πρὸς τοὺς ῾Ελληνιστάς **εὐαγγελιζόμενοι** τὸν κύριον ᾿Ιησοῦν. [GNT]	

#3921
 	
Temperance
 	
Temperance–KJV
Self-control–NASB
Self-control–NIV
Self-control–NKJV
Self-control–NLT
 	
POSB REFERENCE
(Gal.5:22-23; esp. v.23)
Note 1
 	
See also POSB REF:
(2 Pt.1:5-7; esp. v.6)
Note 1, point 3
	ἐγκράτεια = egkrateia
	Pronunciation: [eng-krat'-i-ah]
	Parsing (part of speech): noun
	    Case—nominative
	    Gender—feminine
	    Number—singular
	    Stem or root—from ἐγκράτεια, ας
	Concordance References:
	  ⇒ Strong's #1466 egkrateia
	  ⇒ NIV #1602 egkrateia
	  ⇒ NASB #1466 egkrateia
	
	Galatians 5:23
	Meekness, **temperance**: against such there is no law. [KJV]
	Gentleness, **self-control**; against such things there is no law. [NASB]
	Gentleness and **self-control**. Against such things there is no law. [NIV]
	Gentleness, **self-control**. Against such there is no law. [NKJV]
	Gentleness, and **self-control**. Here there is no conflict with the law. [NLT]
	πραΰτης, **ἐγκράτεια**· κατὰ τῶν τοιούτων οὐκ ἔστι νόμος. [GNS]
	πραΰτης **ἐγκράτεια**· κατὰ τῶν τοιούτων οὐκ ἔστιν νόμος. [GNT]
		Self-control, temperance; to master and control the body or the sinful nature with all of its desires and lusts.
		
		Practical Application
		It means the master of desire, appetite and passion, especially sensual urges and cravings. It means to be strong and controlled and restrained. It means to stand against the cravings of sinful man, the lust of his eyes, and the boasting of what he has and does (1 John 2:15-16).

#3922
 	
Temperate
 	
Vigilant–KJV
Temperate–NASB
Temperate–NIV
Temperate–NKJV
Exhibit self-control–NLT
 	
POSB REFERENCE
(1 Tim.3:2-3; esp. v.2)
Note 2
	νηφάλιον = nëphalion
	Pronunciation: [nay-fal'-ee-on]
	Parsing (part of speech): adjective
	    Case—accusative
	    Gender—masculine
	    Number—singular
	    Stem or root—from νηφάλιος, α, ον
	Concordance References:
	  ⇒ Strong's #3524 nëphalios
	  ⇒ NIV #3767 nëphalios
	  ⇒ NASB #3524 nëphalios
	
	1 Tim. 3:2
	A bishop then must be blameless, the husband of one wife, **vigilant**, sober, of good behaviour, given to hospitality, apt to teach; [KJV]
	An overseer, then, must be above reproach, the husband of one wife, **temperate**, prudent, respectable, hospitable, able to teach, [NASB]
	Now the overseer must be above reproach, the husband of but one wife, **temperate**, self-controlled, respectable, hospitable, able to teach, [NIV]
	A bishop then must be blameless, the husband of one wife, **temperate**, sober-minded, of good behavior, hospitable, able to teach; [NKJV]
	For an elder must be a man whose life cannot be spoken against. He must be faithful to his wife. He must **exhibit self-control**, live wisely, and have a good reputation. He must enjoy having guests in his home and must be able to teach. [NLT]
	δεῖ οὖν τὸν ἐπίσκοπον ἀνεπίλημπτον εἶναι, μιᾶς γυναικὸς ἄνδρα, **νηφάλιον**, σώφρονα, κόσμιον, φιλόξενον, διδακτικόν· [GNS]
	δεῖ οὖν τὸν ἐπίσκοπον ἀνεπίλημπτον εἶναι, μιᾶς γυναικὸς ἄνδρα, **νηφάλιον** σώφρονα κόσμιον φιλόξενον διδακτικόν, [GNT]
		Temperate, vigilant sober; to exhibit self control.
		
		Practical Application
		The minister or overseer must be temperate (nëphalion). He must be self-controlled and watchful. He must be vigilant, watch over, and control his own life and the lives of his dear people.

ENGLISH WORD	GREEK WORD AND VERSE	THE WORD MEANS...

#3923
Temperate
 	
Sober–KJV
Temperate–NASB
Temperate–NIV
Sober–NKJV
Exercise self-control–NLT
 	
**POSB
REFERENCE**
(Tit.2:2)
Note 2, point 1
	νηφαλίους = *nēphalious*
	Pronunciation: [nay-fal'-ee'-oos]
	Parsing (part of speech): adjective
	  Case—accusative
	  Gender—masculine
	  Number—plural
	  Stem or root—from *νηφάλιος, α, ον*
	Concordance References:
	  ⇒ Strong's #3524 nēphalios
	  ⇒ NIV #3767 nēphalios
	  ⇒ NASB #3524 nēphalios
	
	Titus 2:2
	That the aged men be **sober**, grave, temperate, sound in faith, in charity, in patience. [KJV]
	Older men are to be **temperate**, dignified, sensible, sound in faith, in love, in perseverance. [NASB]
	Teach the older men to be **temperate**, worthy of respect, self-controlled, and sound in faith, in love and in endurance. [NIV]
	That the older men be **sober**, reverent, temperate, sound in faith, in love, in patience; [NKJV]
	Teach the older men to **exercise self-control**, to be worthy of respect, and to live wisely. They must have strong faith and be filled with love and patience. [NLT]
	πρεσβύτας **νηφαλίους** εἶναι, σεμνούς, σώφρονας, ὑγιαίνοντας τῇ πίστει, τῇ ἀγάπῃ, τῇ ὑπομονῇ· [GNS]
	πρεσβύτας **νηφαλίους** εἶναι, σεμνούς, σώφρονας, ὑγιαίνοντας τῇ πίστει, τῇ ἀγάπῃ, τῇ ὑπομονῇ· [GNT]
		To be temperate; to be sober; to exercise self-control; to be moderate.
		
		Practical Application
		It is the opposite of over indulgence in anything such as eating, drinking, recreation, or whatever.

#3924
Temperate
 	
Temperate–KJV
Sensible–NASB
Self-controlled–NIV
Temperate–NKJV
Live wisely–NLT
 	
**POSB
REFERENCE**
(Tit.2:2)
Note 2, point 3
	σώφρονας = *sōphronas*
	Pronunciation: [so'-fron-ahs]
	Parsing (part of speech): adjective
	  Case—accusative
	  Gender—masculine
	  Number—plural
	  Stem or root—from *σώφρων, ον*
	Concordance References:
	  ⇒ Strong's #4998 sōphrōn
	  ⇒ NIV #5409 sōphrōn
	  ⇒ NASB #4998 sōphrōn
	
	Titus 2:2
	That the aged men be sober, grave, **temperate**, sound in faith, in charity, in patience. [KJV]
	Older men are to be temperate, dignified, **sensible**, sound in faith, in love, in perseverance. [NASB]
	Teach the older men to be temperate, worthy of respect, **self-controlled**, and sound in faith, in love and in endurance. [NIV]
	That the older men be sober, reverent, **temperate**, sound in faith, in love, in patience; [NKJV]
	Teach the older men to exercise self-control, to be worthy of respect, and to **live wisely**. They must have strong faith and be filled with love and patience. [NLT]
	πρεσβύτας νηφαλίους εἶναι, σεμνούς, **σώφρονας**, ὑγιαίνοντας τῇ πίστει, τῇ ἀγάπῃ, τῇ ὑπομονῇ· [GNS]
	πρεσβύτας νηφαλίους εἶναι, σεμνούς, **σώφρονας**, ὑγιαίνοντας τῇ πίστει, τῇ ἀγάπῃ, τῇ ὑπομονῇ· [GNT]
		To be self-controlled; temperate, prudent; to live wisely; to be sensible; to have a mind that is sound; sensible, controlled, disciplined, chaste, sober—a mind that has complete control over all sensual desires.
		
		Practical Application
		Elderly men are to be "temperate" (*sōphronas*). Elderly men are to have minds that are sound, sensible, and chaste—minds that have complete control over all sensual desires. Neither age nor retirement gives the elderly a right to live a life of license, neither in drink, eating, sex, recreation, travel, play nor in any other area of life. The elderly who really know the Lord are not to waste time and fritter their life away. Far too many people—children, men, women—are destitute, poor, hurting, and dying from hunger, poor housing, loneliness, emptiness, and sin.

#3925
Tempered
 	
Tempered–KJV
Composed–NASB
Combined–NIV
Composed–NKJV
Put together–NLT
	συνεκέρασεν = *sunekerasen*
	Pronunciation: [soon-eh-ker'-ahn-sehn]
	Parsing (part of speech): verb
	  Mood—indicative
	  Tense—aorist
	  Voice—active
	  Person—3rd person
	  Number—singular
	  Stem or root—from *συγκεράννυμι*
	Concordance References:
	  ⇒ Strong's #4786 sugkerannumi
	  ⇒ NIV #5166 sugkerannumi
	  ⇒ NASB #4786 sugkerannumi
		To mix; to combine; to unite; to put together; to arrange and blend together.
		
		Practical Application
		God has arranged the church as it is: the gifted and less gifted mix, combine, and blend together. And He has done it in such a manner that more honor really belongs to those who are not as gifted. The prayer warrior is much more essential than the soloist who is out before the people. The lay witness for Christ is more necessary than the preacher who stands in the pul-

ENGLISH WORD	GREEK WORD AND VERSE	THE WORD MEANS...
		Vol. 6, p.11). The idea is that of many trials and temptations, of all sorts and of all kinds of temptations and trials. But we must always remember: no matter what the trial or temptation, it is for our good and for our benefit. It is to help us. It is to prove us—to make us stronger and much more pure and righteous—to make us much more dynamic witnesses for Christ. God allows trials and temptations to make us more and more like Jesus.

#3933
Tempted
 	
Tempted–KJV
Tempted–NASB
Tempted–NIV
Tempted–NKJV
Tempted–NLT
 	
**POSB
REFERENCE**
(Lk.4:1-2; esp. v.2)
Deeper Study #1
 	
See also POSB REF:
(Heb.3:7-11, esp. v.9)
Note 1
	πειραζόμενος = *peirazomenos*
	Pronunciation: [pi-rad'-zo-mehn-os]
	Parsing (part of speech): verb
	  Mood—participle
	  Tense—present
	  Voice—passive
	  Case—nominative
	  Gender—masculine
	  Number—singular
	  Stem or root—from πειράζω
	Concordance References:
	⇒ Strong's #3985 peirazö
	⇒ NIV #4279 peirazö
	⇒ NASB #3985 peirazö
	
	Luke 4:2
	Being forty days **tempted** of the devil. And in those days he did eat nothing: and when they were ended, he afterward hungered. [KJV]
	For forty days, being **tempted** by the devil. And He ate nothing during those days; and when they had ended, He became hungry. [NASB]
	Where for forty days he was **tempted** by the devil. He ate nothing during those days, and at the end of them he was hungry. [NIV]
	Being **tempted** for forty days by the devil. And in those days He ate nothing, and afterward, when they had ended, He was hungry. [NASB]
	Where the Devil **tempted** him for forty days. He ate nothing all that time and was very hungry. [NLT]
	ἡμέρας τεσσεράκοντα **πειραζόμενος** ὑπὸ τοῦ διαβόλου. καὶ οὐκ ἔφαγεν οὐδὲν ἐν ταῖς ἡμέραις ἐκείναις· καὶ συντελεσθεισῶν αὐτῶν, ὕστερον ἐπείνασε. [GNS]
	ἡμέρας τεσσεράκοντα **πειραζόμενος** ὑπὸ τοῦ διαβόλου. καὶ οὐκ ἔφαγεν οὐδὲν ἐν ταῖς ἡμέραις ἐκείναις καὶ συντελεσθεισῶν αὐτῶν ἐπείνασεν. [GNT]
		To tempt; to test; to try; to prove.
		
		Practical Application
		The word temptation is used here in both a good and a bad sense. In the good sense, it means to test, to try, to prove. It does not mean to seduce into sin. Its purpose is not to defeat or to destroy. The idea is not that one is tempted, seduced, enticed, and pulled into sin by the Holy Spirit (cp. James 1:13); but one is tested, proved, strengthened, reinforced, and purified through the trials of temptation.

#3934
Tend
 	
Feed–KJV
Tend–NASB
Feed–NIV
Feed–NKJV
Feed–NLT
 	
**POSB
REFERENCE**
(Jn.21:15; cp.
Jn.21:15, 17)
Note 3, point 3
	Βόσκε = *Boske*
	Pronunciation: [bos'-keh]
	Parsing (part of speech): verb
	  Mood—imperative
	  Tense—present
	  Voice—active
	  Person—2nd person
	  Number—singular
	  Stem or root—from βόσκω
	Concordance References:
	⇒ Strong's #1006 bosko
	⇒ NIV #1081 bosko
	⇒ NASB #1006 bosko
	
	John 21:15
	So when they had dined, Jesus saith to Simon Peter, Simon, *son* of Jonas, lovest thou me more than these? He saith unto him, Yea, Lord; thou knowest that I love thee. He saith unto him, **Feed** my lambs. [KJV]
	So when they had finished breakfast, Jesus said to Simon Peter, "Simon, *son* of John, do you love Me more than these?" He said to Him, "Yes, Lord; You know that I love You." He said to him, "**Tend** My lambs." [NASB]
	When they had finished eating, Jesus said to Simon Peter, "Simon son of John, do you truly love me more
		To feed; to tend; to nourish; to support; to sustain; to provide for.
		
		Practical Application
		Note that the word used for feeding or "tending" (*Boske*) is the word used for both the lambs (John 21:15) and the sheep (John 21:17). Both the lambs and sheep are to be fed on the same Word and fed in the same way. The ministry to the flock or church is twofold.
		1. The first ministry is to feed (*Boske*, John 21:15, 17).
		  ⇒ To give food, teaching both the milk and meat of the Word. (1 Peter 2:2-3; Hebrews 5:12-14).
		  ⇒ To guide into the study of the Word—showing oneself approved to God. (2 Tim. 2:15).
		2. The second ministry is to shepherd (*poimaine*, John 21:16). Shepherding involves all the works of the ministry.

ENGLISH WORD	GREEK WORD AND VERSE	THE WORD MEANS...
	than these?" "Yes, Lord," he said, "you know that I love you."Jesus said, "**Feed** my lambs." [NIV] So when they had eaten breakfast, Jesus said to Simon Peter, "Simon, *son* of Jonah, do you love Me more than these?" He said to Him, "Yes, Lord; You know that I love You." He said to him, "**Feed** My lambs." [NKJV] After breakfast Jesus said to Simon Peter, "Simon son of John, do you love me more than these?" "Yes, Lord," Peter replied, "you know I love you." "Then **feed** my lambs," Jesus told him. [NLT] Ὅτε οὖν ἠρίστησαν, λέγει τῷ Σίμωνι Πέτρῳ ὁ Ἰησοῦς, Σίμων Ἰωνᾶ, ἀγαπᾷς με πλέον τούτων; λέγει αὐτῷ, Ναί Κύριε· σὺ οἶδας ὅτι φιλῶ σε. λέγει αὐτῷ, **Βόσκε** τὰ ἀρνία μου. [GNS] Ὅτε οὖν ἠρίστησαν λέγει τῷ Σίμωνι Πέτρῳ ὁ Ἰησοῦς, Σίμων Ἰωάννου, ἀγαπᾷς με πλέον τούτων; λέγει αὐτῷ, Ναί, κύριε, σὺ οἶδας ὅτι φιλῶ σε. λέγει αὐτῷ, **Βόσκε** τὰ ἀρνία μου. [GNT] **NOTE ALSO THIS SCRIPTURE...** **John 21:17** He saith unto him the third time, Simon, *son* of Jonas, lovest thou me? Peter was grieved because he said unto him the third time, Lovest thou me? And he said unto him, Lord, thou knowest all things; thou knowest that I love thee. Jesus saith unto him, **Feed** my sheep. [KJV] He said to him the third time, "Simon, *son* of John, do you love Me?" Peter was grieved because He said to him the third time, "Do you love Me?" And he said to Him, "Lord, You know all things; You know that I love You." Jesus said to him, "**Tend** My sheep. [NASB] The third time he said to him, "Simon son of John, do you love me?"Peter was hurt because Jesus asked him the third time, "Do you love me?" He said, "Lord, you know all things; you know that I love you."Jesus said, "**Feed** my sheep. [NIV] He said to him the third time, "Simon, *son* of Jonah, do you love Me?" Peter was grieved because He said to him the third time, "Do you love Me?" And he said to Him, "Lord, You know all things; You know that I love You." Jesus said to him, "**Feed** My sheep. [NKJV] Once more he asked him, "Simon son of John, do you love me?"Peter was grieved that Jesus asked the question a third time. He said, "Lord, you know everything. You know I love you."Jesus said, "Then **feed** my sheep. [NLT] λέγει αὐτῷ τὸ τρίτον, Σίμων Ἰωνᾶ, φιλεῖς με; ἐλυπήθη ὁ Πέτρος, ὅτι εἶπεν αὐτῷ τὸ τρίτον, φιλεῖς με; καὶ εἶπεν αὐτῷ, Κύριε, σὺ πάντα οἶδας· σὺ γινώσκεις ὅτι φιλῶ σε. λέγει αὐτῷ ὁ Ἰησοῦς, **Βόσκε** τὰ πρόβατά μου. [GNS] λέγει αὐτῷ τὸ τρίτον, Σίμων Ἰωάννου, φιλεῖς με; ἐλυπήθη ὁ Πέτρος ὅτι εἶπεν αὐτῷ τὸ τρίτον, Φιλεῖς με; καὶ λέγει αὐτῷ, Κύριε, πάντα σὺ οἶδας, σὺ γινώσκεις ὅτι φιλῶ σε. λέγει αὐτῷ [ὁ Ἰησοῦς], **Βόσκε** τὰ πρόβατά μου. [GNT]	

#3935
Tend
 	
Feed–KJV
Shepherd–NASB
Take care of–NIV
Tend–NKJV
Take care of–NLT
 	
POSB REFERENCE
(Jn.21:15-17; esp. Jn.21:16)
	Ποίμαινε = *poimaine*
	Pronunciation: [poy-mah'ee-neh]
	Parsing (part of speech): verb
	    Mood—imperative
	    Tense—present
	    Voice—active
	    Person—2nd person
	    Number—singular
	    Stem or root—from ποιμαίνω
	Concordance References:
	  → Strong's #4165 poimaino
	  ⇒ NIV #4477 poimaino
	  ⇒ NASB #4165 poimaino
		To take care of; to feed; to shepherd; to rule.
		
		Practical Application
		What is the responsibility of the Shepherd to the sheep? The Shepherd leads and shepherds the sheep. He loves them as His own; therefore, He must lead them to the green pastures and still waters. He must see that they are nourished and protected and given the very best care possible. (See POSB note—Mark 6:34 for more discussion, what happens to sheep without a Shepherd.)
		1. He feeds the sheep even if He has to gather

ENGLISH WORD	GREEK WORD AND VERSE	THE WORD MEANS...
Note 3, point 3	**John 21:16** He saith to him again the second time, Simon, *son of* Jonas, lovest thou me? He saith unto him, Yea, Lord; thou knowest that I love thee. He saith unto him, **Feed** my sheep. [KJV] He said to him again a second time, "Simon, *son of* John, do you love Me?" He said to Him, "Yes, Lord; You know that I love You." He said to him, **Shepherd** My sheep." [NASB] Again Jesus said, "Simon son of John, do you truly love me?" He answered, "Yes, Lord, you know that I love you." Jesus said, "**Take care of** my sheep." [NIV] He said to him again a second time, "Simon, son of Jonah, do you love Me?" He said to Him, "Yes, Lord; You know that I love You." He said to him, "**Tend** My sheep." [NKJV] Jesus repeated the question: "Simon son of John, do you love me?" "Yes, Lord," Peter said, "you know I love you." "Then **take care of** my sheep," Jesus said. [NLT] λέγει αὐτῷ πάλιν δεύτερον, Σίμων Ἰωνᾶ ἀγαπᾷς με· Λέγει αὐτῷ, Ναί, Κύριε· σὺ οἶδας ὅτι φιλῶ σε. λέγει αὐτῷ, **Ποίμαινε** τὰ πρόβατά μου. [GNS] λέγει αὐτῷ πάλιν δεύτερον, Σίμων Ἰωάννου, ἀγαπᾷς με; λέγει αὐτῷ, Ναί, κύριε, σὺ οἶδας ὅτι φιλῶ σε. λέγει αὐτῷ, **Ποίμαινε** τὰ πρόβατά μου. [GNT]	them in His arms to carry them to the pasture (Isaiah 40:11). 2. He guides the sheep to the pasture and away from the rough places and precipices (Psalm 23:1-4). 3. He seeks and saves the sheep who get lost (Matthew 18:11-12; Ezekiel 34:16). 4. He protects the sheep. He even sacrifices His life for the sheep (John 10:11; Hebrews 13:20). 5. He restores the sheep who go astray and return (1 Peter 2:25). 6. He rewards the sheep for obedience and faithfulness (1 Peter 5:4). 7. He will keep the sheep separate from the goats (Matthew 25:32-33).

#3936
 	
Tender Hearts–Tender-hearted
 	
Pitiful–KJV
Kindhearted–NASB
Compassionate–NIV
Tenderhearted–NKJV
Tender hearts–NLT
 	
POSB REFERENCE
(1 Pt.3:8)
Note 4
	εὔσπλαγχνοι = *eusplagchnoi*
	Pronunciation: [yoo'-splangkh-noy]
	Parsing (part of speech): adjective
	    Case—nominative
	    Gender—masculine
	    Number—plural
	    Stem or root—from εὔσπλαγχνος, ον
	Concordance References:
	⇒ Strong's #2155 eusplagchnos
	⇒ NIV #2359 eusplagchnos
	⇒ NASB #2155 eusplagchnos
	
	1 Peter 3:8
	Finally, *be ye* all of one mind, having compassion one of another, love as brethren, *be* **pitiful**, *be* courteous: [KJV]
	
	To sum up, let all be harmonious, sympathetic, brotherly, **kindhearted**, and humble in spirit; [NASB]
	
	Finally, all of you, live in harmony with one another; be sympathetic, love as brothers, be **compassionate** and humble. [NIV]
	
	Finally, all *of you* be of one mind, having compassion for one another; love as brothers, *be* **tenderhearted**, *be* courteous; [NKJV]
	
	Finally, all of you should be of one mind, full of sympathy toward each other, loving one another with **tender hearts** and humble minds. [NLT]
	
	Τὸ δὲ τέλος, πάντες ὁμόφρονες, συμπαθεῖς, φιλάδελφοι, **εὔσπλαγχνοι**, φιλόφρονες· [GNS]
	
	Τὸ δὲ τέλος πάντες ὁμόφρονες, συμπαθεῖς, φιλάδελφοι, **εὔσπλαγχνοι**, ταπεινόφρονες, [GNT]
		To be compassionate; to pity; to be kindhearted; to have a tender heart. It means to be tenderhearted; to be sensitive and affectionate toward the needs of others; to be moved with tender feelings over the pain and sufferings of others.
		
		Practical Application
		We live in a world that desperately needs pity, a world of extreme suffering. So many suffer and continue to suffer without ever having their needs met. The means and resources to meet their needs exist, but so many within the world have become hardened to the sufferings of others. They bank, hoard, and build up asset after asset instead of sacrificing and reaching out to meet the needs of the world. But this is not to be true of the believer. Believers are to have pity upon the sufferings of others. Believers are to feel pity to the point that they are moved to act, sacrificing and reaching out to meet the needs of the suffering.
		
		Again, note how compassion leaves no room for selfishness. Compassion demands that a person deny himself and help others in their desperate needs and sufferings. Note also how pity draws people together. Helping and ministering to one another binds and knits people together. Having compassion—feeling for one another and sacrificing and reaching out to help one another—unites people together. A great bond is created between the believer and those to whom he ministers.

#3937
 	
Tender-hearted–Tender Hearted
 	
Tenderhearted–KJV
Tender-hearted–NASB
Compassionate–NIV
	εὔσπλαγχνοι = *eusplagchnoi*
	Pronunciation: [yoo'-splangkh-noy]
	Parsing (part of speech): adjective
	    Case—nominative
	    Gender—masculine
	    Number—plural
	    Stem or root—from εὔσπλαγχνος, ον
	Concordance References:
	⇒ Strong's #2155 eusplagchnos
	⇒ NIV #2359 eusplagchnos
	⇒ NASB #2155 eusplagchnos
		Compassionate, tenderhearted, kind. It means to show compassion, mercy, understanding, love, tenderness, and warmth.
		
		Practical Application
		It means to *be aware* of a person's hurts and sufferings, problems and difficulties, emotions and mental state, physical and spiritual condition. It means to be tenderhearted toward them.

ENGLISH WORD	GREEK WORD AND VERSE	THE WORD MEANS...
Tenderhearted–NKJV Tenderhearted–NLT **POSB REFERENCE** (Eph.4:32) Note 7, point 2	**Ephes. 4:32** And be ye kind one to another, **tenderhearted**, forgiving one another, even as God for Christ's sake hath forgiven you. [KJV] And be kind to one another, **tender-hearted**, forgiving each other, just as God in Christ also has forgiven you. [NASB] Be kind and **compassionate** to one another, forgiving each other, just as in Christ God forgave you. [NIV] And be kind to one another, **tenderhearted**, forgiving one another, just as God in Christ forgave you. [NKJV] Instead, be kind to each other, **tenderhearted**, forgiving one another, just as God through Christ has forgiven you. [NLT] γίνεσθε δὲ εἰς ἀλλήλους χρηστοί, **εὔσπλαγχνοι**, χαριζόμενοι ἑαυτοῖς, καθὼς καὶ ὁ Θεὸς ἐν Χριστῷ ἐχαρίσατο ὑμῖν. [GNS] γίνεσθε [δὲ] εἰς ἀλλήλους χρηστοί, **εὔσπλαγχνοι**, χαριζόμενοι ἑαυτοῖς, καθὼς καὶ ὁ θεὸς ἐν Χριστῷ ἐχαρίσατο ὑμῖν. [GNT]	

**#3938
Terrible Anger**
 	
Wrath–KJV
Wrath–NASB
Wrath–NIV
Wrath–NKJV
Terrible anger–NLT
 	
**POSB
REFERENCE**
(Col.3:5-7; esp. v.6)
Note 1, point 2
	ὀργὴ = *orgë*
	Pronunciation: [or-gay']
	Parsing (part of speech): noun
	    Case—nominative
	    Gender—feminine
	    Number—singular
	    Stem or root—from ὀργή, ῆς
	Concordance References:
	  ⇒ Strong's #3709 orgë
	  ⇒ NIV #3973 orgë
	  ⇒ NASB #3709 orgë
	
	Col. 3:6
	For which things' sake the **wrath** of God cometh on the children of disobedience: [KJV]
	For it is on account of these things that the **wrath** of God will come, [NASB]
	Because of these, the **wrath** of God is coming. [NIV]
	Because of these things the **wrath** of God is coming upon the sons of disobedience, [NKJV]
	God's **terrible anger** will come upon those who do such things. [NLT]
	δι' ἃ ἔρχεται ἡ **ὀργὴ** τοῦ Θεοῦ ἐπὶ τοὺς υἱοὺς τῆς ἀπειθείας; [GNS]
	δι' ἃ ἔρχεται ἡ **ὀργὴ** τοῦ θεοῦ [ἐπὶ τοὺς υἱοὺς τῆς ἀπειθείας]. [GNT]
		Wrath, terrible anger, retribution.
		
		Practical Application
		The words "terrible anger" (*orgë*) mean anger, but it is not the outburst of anger that quickly blazes up, not the anger that arises solely from emotion. Rather, it is a decisive and a deliberate anger. It is an anger that comes from a thoughtful decision, an anger that comes from the mind because someone has done something evil and hurtful. It is an anger that judges and condemns sin and evil, violence and slaughter, immorality and injustice. It is an anger that hates sin and evil and that metes out a just revenge and equal punishment.

**#3939
Terrible Worship Of Idols**
 	
Abominable idolatries–KJV
Abominable idolatries–NASB
Detestable idolatry–NIV
Abominable idolatries–NKJV
Terrible worship of idols–NLT
 	
**POSB
REFERENCE**
(1 Pt.4:3)
Note 3, point 6
	ἀθεμίτοις εἰδωλολατρίαις = *athemitois eidölolatriais*
	Pronunciation: [ath-em'-ee-toys i-do-lol-at-ri'-ah-ees]
	Parsing *athemitois* (part of speech): adjective
	    Case—dative
	    Gender—feminine
	    Number—plural
	    Stem or root—from ἀθέμιτος, ον
	Parsing *eidölolatriais* (part of speech): noun
	    Case—dative
	    Gender—feminine
	    Number—plural
	    Stem or root—from εἰδωλολατρία, ας
	Concordance References:
	  ⇒ Strong's #111 athemitos + 1495 eidölolatria
	  ⇒ NIV #116 athemitos [detestable] + 1630 eidölolatria [idolatry]
	  ⇒ NASB #111 athemitos + 1495 eidölolatria
	
	1 Peter 4:3
	For the time past of *our* life may suffice us to have wrought the will of the Gentiles, when we walked in lasciviousness, lusts, excess of wine, revellings, banquetings, and **abominable idolatries**: [KJV]
		Detestable, disgusting idolatry; abominable idolatries; the terrible worship of idols.
		
		Practical Application
		It is the worship of idols, whether mental or made by man's hands; the worship of some idea of what God is like, of an image of God within a person's mind; the giving of one's primary devotion (time and energy) to something other than God. (See POSB note, Idolatry—1 Cor. 6:9 for detailed discussion.)

ENGLISH WORD	GREEK WORD AND VERSE	THE WORD MEANS...
	For the time already past is sufficient *for you* to have carried out the desire of the Gentiles, having pursued a course of sensuality, lusts, drunkenness, carousals, drinking parties and **abominable idolatries**. [NASB] For you have spent enough time in the past doing what pagans choose to do—living in debauchery, lust, drunkenness, orgies, carousing and **detestable idolatry**. [NIV] For we *have spent* enough of our past lifetime in doing the will of the Gentiles—when we walked in lewdness, lusts, drunkenness, revelries, drinking parties, and **abominable idolatries**. [NKJV] You have had enough in the past of the evil things that godless people enjoy—their immorality and lust, their feasting and drunkenness and wild parties, and their **terrible worship of idols**. [NLT] ἀρκετὸς γὰρ ἡμῖν ὁ παρεληλυθὼς χρόνος τὸ βίου τὸ θέλημα τῶν ἐθνῶν κατεργάσασθαι, πεπορευμένους ἐν ἀσελγείαις, ἐπιθυμίαις, οἰνοφλυγίαις, κώμοις, πότοις, καὶ **ἀθεμίτοις εἰδωλολατρείαις**· [GNS] ἀρκετὸς γὰρ ὁ παρεληλυθὼς χρόνος τὸ βούλημα τῶν ἐθνῶν κατειργάσθαι πεπορευμένους ἐν ἀσελγείαις, ἐπιθυμίαις, οἰνοφλυγίαις, κώμοις, πότοις καὶ **ἀθεμίτοις εἰδωλολατρίαις**. [GNT]	

#3940
Terrified
 	
Terrified–KJV
Terrified–NASB
Frightened–NIV
Terrified–NKJV
Panic–NLT
 	
POSB REFERENCE
(Lk.21:9-10; esp. v.9)
Note 3, point 2
	πτοηθῆτε = *ptoëthëte*
	Pronunciation: [pto-eh'-thay-teh]
	Parsing (part of speech): verb
	   Mood—subjunctive OR imperative
	   Tense—aorist
	   Voice—passive
	   Person—2nd person
	   Number—plural
	   Stem or root—from πτοέομαι
	Concordance References:
	⇒ Strong's #4422 ptoeö
	⇒ NIV #4765 ptoeö
	⇒ NASB #4422 ptoeö
	
	Luke 21:9
	But when ye shall hear of wars and commotions, be not **terrified**: for these things must first come to pass; but the end *is* not by and by. [KJV]
	
	"And when you hear of wars and disturbances, do not be **terrified**; for these things must take place first, but the end *does* not *follow* immediately." [NASB]
	
	When you hear of wars and revolutions, do not be **frightened**. These things must happen first, but the end will not come right away." [NIV]
	
	But when you hear of wars and commotions, do not be **terrified**; for these things must come to pass first, but the end *will not come* immediately." [NKJV]
	
	And when you hear of wars and insurrections, don't **panic**. Yes, these things must come, but the end won't follow immediately." [NLT]
	
	ὅταν δὲ ἀκούσητε πολέμους καὶ ἀκαταστασίας, μὴ **πτοηθῆτε**· δεῖ γὰρ ταῦτα γενέσθαι πρῶτον, ἀλλ' οὐκ εὐθέως τὸ τέλος. [GNS]
	
	ὅταν δὲ ἀκούσητε πολέμους καὶ ἀκαταστασίας, μὴ **πτοηθῆτε**· δεῖ γὰρ ταῦτα γενέσθαι πρῶτον, ἀλλ' οὐκ εὐθέως τὸ τέλος. [GNT]
		To be terrified; to be frightened; to panic; to be scared; to be startled.
		
		Practical Application
		Believers are not to be "terrified" (*ptoëthëte*). They are not to let their hearts "be troubled" (John 14:1). World violence can trouble people; but the believer's heart and life are to be centered upon God, trusting His presence, care, and security—eternally.

#3941
Test
 	
Tempt–KJV
Try–NASB
Test–NIV
Tempt–NKJV
Test–NLT
	ἐκπειράζωμεν = *ekpeirazömen*
	Pronunciation: [ek-pi-rad'-zo-mehn]
	Parsing (part of speech): verb
	   Mood—subjunctive
	   Tense—present
	   Voice—active
	   Person—1st person
	   Number—plural
	   Stem or root—from ἐκπειράζω
	Concordance References:
	⇒ Strong's #1598 ekpeirazö
		To try the Lord's patience; to see how far a person can go; to test the patience of Christ.
		
		Practical Application
		The believers of Israel...
		• often felt that God and His leader Moses *demanded and expected too much*.
		• often longed for the things of the flesh which they had formerly known in Egypt (the world).

ENGLISH WORD	GREEK WORD AND VERSE	THE WORD MEANS...
POSB REFERENCE (1 Cor.10:6-10; esp. v.9) Note 2, point 4	⇒ NIV #1733 ekpeirazö ⇒ NASB #1598 ekpeirazö **1 Cor. 10:9** Neither let us **tempt** Christ, as some of them also tempted, and were destroyed of serpents. [KJV] Nor let us **try** the Lord, as some of them did, and were destroyed by the serpents. [NASB] We should not **test** the Lord, as some of them did—and were killed by snakes. [NIV] Nor let us **tempt** Christ, as some of them also tempted, and were destroyed by serpents; [NKJV] Nor should we put Christ to the **test**, as some of them did and then died from snakebites. [NLT] μηδὲ ἐκπειράζωμεν τὸν Χριστόν, καθώς τινες αὐτῶν ἐπείρασαν, καὶ ὑπὸ τῶν ὄφεων ἀπώλοντο. [GNS] μηδὲ ἐκπειράζωμεν τὸν Χριστόν, καθώς τινες αὐτῶν ἐπείρασαν καὶ ὑπὸ τῶν ὄφεων ἀπώλλυντο. [GNT]	They became discontent with the things God provided and longed to return to Egypt (the world). Therefore, many of them perished in the wilderness and were not allowed to enter the promised land.

#3942
Test And Approve
 	
Prove–KJV
Prove–NASB
Test and approve–NIV
Prove–NKJV
Will know–NLT
 	
POSB REFERENCE
(Rom. 12:2)
Note 4, point 2
	δοκιμάζειν = *dokimazein*
	Pronunciation: [dok-im-ahd'-zeen]
	Parsing (part of speech): verb
	  Mood—infinitive
	  Tense—present
	  Voice—active
	  Case—accusative
	  Stem or root—from δοκιμάζω
	Concordance References:
	⇒ Strong's #1381 dokimazö
	⇒ NIV #1507 dokimazö
	⇒ NASB #1381 dokimazö
	
	Romans 12:2
	And be not conformed to this world: but be ye transformed by the renewing of your mind, that ye may **prove** what is that good, and acceptable, and perfect, will of God. [KJV]
	And do not be conformed to this world, but be transformed by the renewing of your mind, that you may **prove** what the will of God is, that which is good and acceptable and perfect. [NASB]
	Do not conform any longer to the pattern of this world, but be transformed by the renewing of your mind. Then you will be able to **test and approve** what God's will is—his good, pleasing and perfect will. [NIV]
	And do not be conformed to this world, but be transformed by the renewing of your mind, that you may **prove** what *is* that good and acceptable and perfect will of God. [NKJV]
	Don't copy the behavior and customs of this world, but let God transform you into a new person by changing the way you think. Then you will know what God wants you to do, and you **will know** how good and pleasing and perfect his will really is. [NLT]
	καὶ μὴ συσχηματίζεσθε τῷ αἰῶνι τούτῳ, ἀλλὰ μεταμορφοῦσθε τῇ ἀνακαινώσει τοῦ νοός ὑμῶν, εἰς τὸ δοκιμάζειν ὑμᾶς τί τὸ θέλημα τοῦ Θεοῦ, τὸ ἀγαθὸν καὶ εὐάρεστον καὶ τέλειον. [GNS]
	καὶ μὴ συσχηματίζεσθε τῷ αἰῶνι τούτῳ, ἀλλὰ μεταμορφοῦσθε τῇ ἀνακαινώσει τοῦ νοός εἰς τὸ δοκιμάζειν ὑμᾶς τί τὸ θέλημα τοῦ Θεοῦ, τὸ ἀγαθὸν καὶ εὐάρεστον καὶ τέλειον. [GNT]
		Test, examine; interpret, discern, discover; approve; prove, demonstrate.
		
		Practical Application
		The reason why the believer is to be transformed is extremely significant. The believer must test and approve (*dokimazein*) the will of God. The words "test and approve" mean both to find and to follow God's will. This is certainly understandable. If a person's mind is not renewed and focused upon God...
		• how can the person ever find or discover and know the will of God?
		• how can the person ever follow or obey and do the will of God?
		
		The only conceivable way a person can ever find and follow God's will is to keep his mind focused upon God and upon the things of God.

#3943
Testament
 	
Testament–KJV
Covenant–NASB
Covenant–NIV
Covenant–NKJV
Covenant–NLT
	διαθήκης = *diathëkës*
	Pronunciation: [dee-ath-ay'-kays]
	Parsing (part of speech): noun
	  Case—genitive
	  Gender—feminine
	  Number—singular
	  Stem or root—from διαθήκη, ης
	Concordance References:
	⇒ Strong's #1242 diathëkë
		Covenant, testament, will. It means an agreement made between two parties; a contract drawn up between two or more people; a special relationship set up and established between persons.
		
		Practical Application
		In the Old Testament period of history, God had set up an old covenant between Himself and

ENGLISH WORD	GREEK WORD AND VERSE	THE WORD MEANS...

#3947
Testimony
 	
Testimony–KJV
Testimony–NASB
Testimony–NIV
Testimony–NKJV
Message–NLT
 	
POSB
REFERENCE
(1 Cor.2:1)
Note 1, point 3
	μυστήριον = *mustērion*
	Pronunciation: [mus-tay'-ree-on]
	Parsing (part of speech): noun
	  Case—accusative
	  Gender—neuter
	  Number—singular
	  Stem or root—from μυστήριον, ου
	Concordance References:
	  ⇒ Strong's #3142 mustērion
	  ⇒ NIV #3457 mustērion
	  ⇒ NASB #3142 mustērion
	
	1 Cor. 2:1
	  And I, brethren, when I came to you, came not with excellency of speech or of wisdom, declaring unto you the **testimony** of God. [KJV]
	  And when I came to you, brethren, I did not come with superiority of speech or of wisdom, proclaiming to you the **testimony** of God. [NASB]
	  When I came to you, brothers, I did not come with eloquence or superior wisdom as I proclaimed to you the **testimony** about God. [NIV]
	  And I, brethren, when I came to you, did not come with excellence of speech or of wisdom declaring to you the **testimony** of God. [NKJV]
	  Dear brothers and sisters, when I first came to you I didn't use lofty words and brilliant ideas to tell you God's **message**. [NLT]
	  Κἀγὼ ἐλθὼν πρὸς ὑμᾶς, ἀδελφοί, ἦλθον οὐ καθ' ὑπεροχὴν λόγου η σοφίας καταγγέλλων ὑμῖν τὸ **μυστήριον** τοῦ Θεοῦ. [GNS]
	  Κἀγὼ ἐλθὼν πρὸς ὑμᾶς, ἀδελφοί, ἦλθον οὐ καθ' ὑπεροχὴν λόγου η σοφίας καταγγέλλων ὑμῖν τὸ **μυστήριον** τοῦ θεοῦ. [GNT]
		The testimony, the witness, the message or revelation of God.
		
		Practical Application
		  The glorious testimony or revelation of God is Jesus Christ and Him crucified (1 Cor. 2:2). Preaching is not delivering eloquent speeches nor sound advice on...
		  • self-development
		  • self-image
		  • positive thinking
		  • philosophy
		  • religion and its rituals
		  • education
		  • science
		  • new and novel ideas
		  • history
		
		  All of these have their place, and what truth lies within each needs to be taught; but they are not the subjects that are to be preached by God's ministers to a lost world that is reeling under the weight of lonely, empty, starving, and suffering masses of people. The genuine preacher of God is to preach the testimony (marturion, mystery, revelation) of God.

#3948
Testing
 	
Proved–KJV
Testing–NASB
Tried–NIV
Tried–NKJV
Tried my patience–NLT
 	
POSB
REFERENCE
(Heb.3:7-11; esp. v.9)
Note 1
	δοκιμασία = *dokimasia*
	Pronunciation: [dok-im-ahs-see-ah]
	Parsing (part of speech): noun
	  Case—dative
	  Gender—feminine
	  Number—singular
	  Stem or root—from δοκιμασία, ας
	Concordance References:
	  ⇒ Strong's #1381 dokimazo
	  ⇒ NIV #1508 dokimasia
	  ⇒ NASB #1381b dokimasia
	
	Hebrews 3:9
	  When your fathers tempted me, **proved** me, and saw my works forty years. [KJV]
	  WHERE YOUR FATHERS TRIED *Me* BY **TESTING** *Me*, AND SAW MY WORKS FOR FORTY YEARS. [NASB]
	  Where your fathers tested and **tried** me and for forty years saw what I did. [NIV]
	  Where your fathers tested Me, **tried** Me, And saw My works forty years. [NKJV]
	  There your ancestors **tried my patience**, even though they saw my miracles for forty years. [NLT]
	  οὗ ἐπείρασαν με οἱ πατέρες ὑμῶν, **ἐδοκίμασάν** με, καὶ εἶδον τὰ ἔργα μου τεσσεράκοντα ἔτη· [GNS]
	  οὗ ἐπείρασαν οἱ πατέρες ὑμῶν ἐν **δοκιμασίᾳ** καὶ εἶδον τὰ ἔργα μου [GNT]
		Trying, proving, testing; to try God's patience; to test Him.
		
		Practical Application
		  They were testing (*dokimasia*) God. This means they put Him to the test to see if He met their approval. If God would prove faithful, then He would be worthy of their obedience and loyalty. They wanted Him to prove Himself first, then they would follow Him.
		  Note the unbelief and hardness of heart in all this. There is no belief or trust. They wanted God to prove Himself by giving the provision without any trial or suffering. They were unwilling to prove themselves, unwilling to show that they really believed and trusted God. They wanted God to prove Himself, that He was worthy of their trust and loyalty. What audacity! What an affront! What unbelief and hardness of heart—total disobedience!

#3949
Thanksgiving–
Thanksgivings
 	
Giving of thanks–KJV
Thanksgivings–NASB
Thanksgiving–NIV
	εὐχαριστίας = *eucharistias*
	Pronunciation: [yoo-khar-is-tee'-ahs]
	Parsing (part of speech): noun
	  Case–accusative
	  Gender–accusative
	  Number–feminine
	  Number–plural
	  Stem or root–from εὐχαριστία, ας
	Concordance References:
	  ⇒ Strong's #2169 eucharistia
		Thanksgiving, thankfulness, gratitude, giving of thanks; to give thanks.
		
		Practical Application
		  This means that we thank God for hearing and answering–thank Him for what He has done and is going to do for all men. We are to give thanks in all things. How can we thank God for terrible trials such as accidents and death and

ENGLISH WORD	GREEK WORD AND VERSE	THE WORD MEANS...
Giving of thanks– NKJV Give thanks–NLT **POSB REFERENCE** (1 Tim.2:1) Note 1 **See also POSB REF:** (Philip.4:6-7; esp. v.6) Note 1, point 2	⇒ NIV #2374 eucharistia ⇒ NASB #2169 eucharistia **1 Tim. 2:1** I exhort therefore, that, first of all, supplications, prayers, intercessions, *and* **giving of thanks**, be made for all men; [KJV] First of all, then, I urge that entreaties *and* prayers, petitions *and* **thanksgivings**, be made on behalf of all men, [NASB] I urge, then, first of all, that requests, prayers, intercession and **thanksgiving** be made for everyone–[NIV] Therefore I exhort first of all that supplications, prayers, intercessions, *and* **giving of thanks** be made for all men, [NKJV] I urge you, first of all, to pray for all people. As you make your requests, plead for God's mercy upon them, and **give thanks**. [NLT] Παρακαλῶ οὖν πρῶτον πάντων ποιεῖσθαι δεήσεις, προσευχάς, ἐντεύξεις, **εὐχαριστίας**, ὑπὲρ πάντων ἀνθρώπων· [GNS] Παρακαλῶ οὖν πρῶτον πάντων ποιεῖσθαι δεήσεις προσευχάς ἐντεύξεις **εὐχαριστίας** ὑπὲρ πάντων ἀνθρώπων, [GNT]	sin? We can not; this is not what Scripture means. What God means is to thank Him for His presence and power as we walk through such trials. In Christ Jesus there is victory and triumph over all, no matter how terrible. Therefore, *in* everything (not *for* everything)–as we walk through all–thank God for the victory He has given us through Christ.

#3950
That
 	
So be that–KJV
In order that–NASB
In order that–NIV
That–NKJV
We are to–NLT
 	
POSB REFERENCE
(Rom.8:16-17; esp. v.17)
Note 9, point 4
 	
See also POSB REF:
(Rom.8:18)
Note 1
	ἵνα = *hina*
	Pronunciation: [hin'-ah]
	Parsing (part of speech): conjunction
	    Kind of—subordinating
	    Stem or root—from **ἵνα**
	Concordance References:
	⇒ Strong's #2443 hina
	⇒ NIV #2671 hina
	⇒ NASB #2443 hina
	
	Romans 8:17
	And if children, then heirs; heirs of God, and joint-heirs with Christ; if **so be that** we suffer with him, that we may be also glorified together. [KJV]
	And if children, heirs also, heirs of God and fellow heirs with Christ, if indeed we suffer with Him **in order that** we may also be glorified with Him. [NASB]
	Now if we are children, then we are heirs—heirs of God and co-heirs with Christ, if indeed we share in his sufferings **in order that** we may also share in his glory. [NIV]
	And if children, then heirs—heirs of God and joint heirs with Christ, if indeed we suffer with Him, **that** we may also be glorified together. [NKJV]
	And since we are his children, we will share his treasures—for everything God gives to his Son, Christ, is ours, too. But if **we are to** share his glory, we must also share his suffering. [NLT]
	εἰ δὲ τέκνα, καὶ κληρονόμοι· κληρονόμοι μὲν Θεοῦ, συγκληρονόμοι δὲ Χριστοῦ· εἴπερ συμπάσχομεν, **ἵνα** καὶ συνδοξασθῶμεν. [GNS]
	εἰ δὲ τέκνα, καὶ κληρονόμοι· κληρονόμοι μὲν θεοῦ, συγκληρονόμοι δὲ Χριστοῦ, εἴπερ συμπάσχομεν **ἵνα** καὶ συνδοξασθῶμεν. [GNT]
		In order that; so that.
		
		Practical Application
		Note that the believer is to suffer with Christ in order "that" (*hina*—Greek) he may be glorified with Christ (Romans 8:17). Suffering prepares the believer to participate in the glory of Christ. It is the necessary condition for exaltation. Suffering and struggling are a refining process through which the believer must pass (1 Peter 1:6-7). It refines the believer by forcing him to expand his trust in God more and more.

#3951
That Can Never Perish
 	
Incorruptible–KJV
Imperishable–NASB
That can never perish–NIV
Incorruptible–NKJV
Pure–NLT
	ἄφθαρτον = *aphtharton*
	Pronunciation: [af'-thar-ton]
	Parsing (part of speech): adjective
	    Case—accusative
	    Gender—feminine
	    Number—singular
	    Stem or root—from **ἄφθαρτος**, ον
	Concordance References:
	⇒ Strong's #862 aphthartos
	⇒ NIV #915 aphthartos
	⇒ NASB #862 aphthartos
		Incorruptible, immortal, imperishable, pure, that can never perish; it cannot perish; it does not age, deteriorate, or die; it does not have the seed of corruption within it.
		
		Practical Application
		Matthew Henry points out that everything on earth changes from better to worse, but not our inheritance. It is perfect and incorruptible. It never changes, and it will never cease to be the most perfect inheritance and gift imaginable (*Matthew Henry's Commentary*, Vol.6, p.1005).

ENGLISH WORD	GREEK WORD AND VERSE	THE WORD MEANS...
POSB REFERENCE (1 Pt.1:4) Note 2, point 1	**1 Peter 1:4** To an inheritance **incorruptible**, and undefiled, and that fadeth not away, reserved in heaven for you, [KJV] To *obtain* an inheritance *which is* **imperishable** and undefiled and will not fade away, reserved in heaven for you, [NASB] And into an inheritance **that can never perish**, spoil or fade—kept in heaven for you, [NIV] To an inheritance **incorruptible** and undefiled and that does not fade away, reserved in heaven for you, [NKJV] For God has reserved a priceless inheritance for his children. It is kept in heaven for you, **pure** and undefiled, beyond the reach of change and decay. [NLT] εἰς κληρονομίαν **ἄφθαρτον** καὶ ἀμίαντον καὶ ἀμάραντον, τετηρημένην ἐν οὐρανοῖς εἰς ὑμᾶς [GNS] εἰς κληρονομίαν **ἄφθαρτον** καὶ ἀμίαντον καὶ ἀμάραντον, τετηρημένην ἐν οὐρανοῖς εἰς ὑμᾶς [GNT]	
#3952 **Theft–Thefts** Thefts–KJV Thefts–NASB Theft–NIV Thefts–NKJV Theft–NLT **POSB REFERENCE** (Mk.7:21) *Deeper Study #7*	κλοπαί = *klopai* Pronunciation: [klop-ah-ee'] Parsing (part of speech): noun Case—nominative Gender—feminine Number—plural Stem or root—from κλοπή, ῆς Concordance References: ⇒ Strong's #2829 klopë ⇒ NIV #3113 klopë ⇒ NASB #2829 klopë **Mark 7:21-22** For from within, out of the heart of men, proceed evil thoughts, adulteries, fornications, murders, **Thefts**, covetousness, wickedness, deceit, lasciviousness, an evil eye, blasphemy, pride, foolishness: [KJV] (Note: κλοπαί = *klopai* v.22 in KJV and NKJV only) "For from within, out of the heart of men, proceed the evil thoughts, fornications, **thefts**, murders, adulteries, deeds of coveting *and* wickedness, *as well as* deceit, sensuality, envy, slander, pride *and* foolishness. [NASB] For from within, out of men's hearts, come evil thoughts, sexual immorality, **theft**, murder, adultery, greed, malice, deceit, lewdness, envy, slander, arrogance and folly. [NIV] For from within, out of the heart of men, proceed evil thoughts, adulteries, fornications, murders, **thefts**, covetousness, wickedness, deceit, lewdness, an evil eye, blasphemy, pride, foolishness. [NKJV] (Note: κλοπαί = *klopai* v.22 in KJV and NKJV only) For from within, out of a person's heart, come evil thoughts, sexual immorality, **theft**, murder, adultery, greed, wickedness, deceit, eagerness for lustful pleasure, envy, slander, pride, and foolishness. [NLT] ἔσωθεν γὰρ ἐκ τῆς καρδίας τῶν ἀνθρώπων οἱ διαλογισμοὶ οἱ κακοὶ ἐκπορεύονται, μοιχεῖαι, πορνεῖαι, φόνοι, **κλοπαί**, πλεονεξίαι, πονηρίαι, δόλος, ἀσέλγεια, ὀφθαλμὸς πονηρός, βλασφημία, ὑπερηφανία, ἀφροσύνη· [GNS] ἔσωθεν γὰρ ἐκ τῆς καρδίας τῶν ἀνθρώπων οἱ διαλογισμοὶ οἱ κακοὶ ἐκπορεύονται, πορνεῖαι, **κλοπαί**, φόνοι, μοιχεῖαι, πλεονεξίαι, πονηρίαι, δόλος, ἀσέλγεια, ὀφθαλμὸς πονηρός, βλασφημία, ὑπερηφανία, ἀφροσύνη· [GNT]	Theft; to cheat and steal; to take wrongfully from another person, either legally or illegally. **Practical Application** Note exactly what Jesus was saying: "It is not things that defile a person. It is the heart that defiles a person." A person's heart is corrupt; therefore, he corrupts himself. A person is not made unclean by things; he is unclean because of his polluted heart. It is he himself who takes things and does unclean things with them (see POSB *Deeper Studies #3-15*—Mark 7:21-22 for discussion).

ENGLISH WORD	GREEK WORD AND VERSE	THE WORD MEANS...

#3953
Thefts
 	
Thefts–KJV
Thefts–NASB
Thefts–NIV
Thefts–NKJV
Thefts–NLT
 	
POSB REFERENCE
(Rev.9:20-21; esp.v.21)
Note 4, point 2e
	κλεμμάτων = *klemmatön*
	Pronunciation: [klem'-mah-ton]
	Parsing (part of speech): noun
	    Case—genitive
	    Gender—neuter
	    Number—plural
	    Stem or root—from κλέμμα, τος
	Concordance References:
	  ⇒ Strong's #2809 klemma
	  ⇒ NIV #3092 klemma
	  ⇒ NASB #2809 klemma
	
	Rev. 9:21
	Neither repented they of their murders, nor of their sorceries, nor of their fornication, nor of their **thefts**. [KJV]
	And they did not repent of their murders nor of their sorceries nor of their immorality nor of their **thefts**. [NASB]
	Nor did they repent of their murders, their magic arts, their sexual immorality or their **thefts**. [NIV]
	And they did not repent of their murders or their sorceries or their sexual immorality or their **thefts**. [NKJV]
	And they did not repent of their murders or their witchcraft or their immorality or their **thefts**. [NLT]
	καὶ οὐ μετενόησαν ἐκ τῶν φόνων αὐτῶν, οὔτε ἐκ τῶν φαρμακειῶν αὐτῶν, οὔτε ἐκ τῆς πορνείας αὐτῶν, οὔτε ἐκ τῶν **κλεμμάτων** αὐτῶν. [GNS]
	καὶ οὐ μετενόησαν ἐκ τῶν φόνων αὐτῶν οὔτε ἐκ τῶν φαρμάκων αὐτῶν οὔτε ἐκ τῆς πορνείας αὐτῶν οὔτε ἐκ τῶν **κλεμμάτων** αὐτῶν. [GNT]
		Thefts, robberies; to cheat and steal; to take wrongfully from another person, either legally or illegally.
		
		Practical Application
		
		There will be several gross sins for which the ungodly need to repent. And remember: there will be an enormous increase and intensification of the evils in the end time.
		1. There will be an increase in the worship of evil spirits and the worship of idols.
		2. There will be an increase in the sin of murder.
		3. There will be an increase in the sin of sorcery (*pharmakon*).
		4. There will be an increase in immorality (*porneias*).
		5. There will be an increase in thefts (*klemmatön*).

#3954
There
 	
Behold–KJV
Behold–NASB
Where–NIV
Behold–NKJV
There–NLT
 	
POSB REFERENCE
(Acts 16:1-3; esp. v.1)
Note 1, point 1
	καὶ ἰδού = *kai idou*
	Pronunciation: [kah-ee id-oo']
	Parsing *idou* (part of speech): particle sentence
	    Stem or root—from ἰδού
	Concordance References:
	  ⇒ Strong's #2400 + 2532 idou kai
	  ⇒ NIV #2627 + 2779 idou kai
	  ⇒ NASB #2400 + 2532 idou kai
	
	Acts 16:1
	Then came he to Derbe and Lystra: and, **behold**, a certain disciple was there, named Timotheus, the son of a certain woman, which was a Jewess, and believed; but his father *was* a Greek: [KJV]
	And he came also to Derbe and to Lystra. And **behold**, a certain disciple was there, named Timothy, the son of a Jewish woman who was a believer, but his father was a Greek, [NASB]
	He came to Derbe and then to Lystra, **where** a disciple named Timothy lived, whose mother was a Jewess and a believer, but whose father was a Greek. [NIV]
	Then he came to Derbe and Lystra. And **behold**, a certain disciple was there, named Timothy, *the* son of a certain Jewish woman who believed, but his father *was* Greek. [NKJV]
	Paul and Silas went first to Derbe and then on to Lystra. **There** they met Timothy, a young disciple whose mother was a Jewish believer, but whose father was a Greek. [NLT]
	Κατήντησε δὲ εἰς Δέρβην καὶ Λύστραν· **καὶ ἰδού**, μαθητής τις ἦν ἐκεῖ, ὀνόματι Τιμόθεος, υἱὸς γυναικὸς τινος Ἰουδαίας πιστῆς, πατρὸς δὲ Ἕλληνος. [GNS]
	Κατήντησεν δὲ [καὶ] εἰς Δέρβην καὶ εἰς Λύστραν. **καὶ ἰδού** μαθητής τις ἦν ἐκεῖ ὀνόματι Τιμόθεος, υἱὸς γυναικὸς Ἰουδαίας πιστῆς, πατρὸς δὲ Ἕλληνος, [GNT]
		To behold; to look and listen.
		
		Practical Application
		The word "there" (*kai idou*) has the idea of looking and gazing at a wonderful discovery, at an unexpected surprise.

ENGLISH WORD	GREEK WORD AND VERSE	THE WORD MEANS...
#3955 **These** Who–KJV **These–NASB** They–NIV **These–NKJV** They–NLT **POSB REFERENCE** (2 Thes.1:9) Note 1	οἵτινες = *hoitines* Pronunciation: [hoy'-ti-nehs] Parsing (part of speech): pronominal adjective 　　Type—relative 　　Case—nominative 　　Gender—masculine 　　Number—plural 　　Stem or root—from ὅστις, ἥτις, ὅ τι Concordance References: ⇒　Strong's #3748 hostis ⇒　NIV #4015 hostis ⇒　NASB #3748 hostis **2 Thes. 1:9** **Who** shall be punished with everlasting destruction from the presence of the Lord, and from the glory of his power; [KJV] And **these** will pay the penalty of eternal destruction, away from the presence of the Lord and from the glory of His power, [NASB] **They** will be punished with everlasting destruction and shut out from the presence of the Lord and from the majesty of his power [NIV] **These** shall be punished with everlasting destruction from the presence of the Lord and from the glory of His power, [NKJV] **They** will be punished with everlasting destruction, forever separated from the Lord and from his glorious power [NLT] οἵτινες δίκην τίσουσιν, ὄλεθρον αἰώνιον ἀπὸ προσώπου τοῦ Κυρίου καὶ ἀπὸ τῆς δόξης τῆς ἰσχύος αὐτοῦ, [GNS] οἵτινες δίκην τίσουσιν ὄλεθρον αἰώνιον ἀπὸ προσώπου τοῦ κυρίου καὶ ἀπὸ τῆς δόξης τῆς ἰσχύος αὐτοῦ, [GNT]	They, who, these, whoever, anyone. **Practical Application** The word "these" (*hoitines*) is used in a qualitative sense; that is, it means *"persons who are such as"* deserve this punishment; "persons who are of *such a kind as to*" deserve this punishment. The Greek word clearly shows that these persons deserve the punishment of the coming judgment. (This is pointed out by A.T. Robertson, *Word Pictures in the New Testament*, Vol.4, p.44; and Leon Morris, *The Epistles of Paul to the Thessalonians*. "Tyndale New Testament Commentaries," p.119.)
#3956 **They** Who–KJV These–NASB **They–NIV** These–NKJV **They–NLT** **POSB REFERENCE** (2 Thes.1:9) Note 1	οἵτινες = *hoitines* Pronunciation: [hoy'-ti-nehs] Parsing (part of speech): pronominal adjective 　　Type—relative 　　Case—nominative 　　Gender—masculine 　　Number—plural 　　Stem or root—from ὅστις, ἥτις, ὅ τι Concordance References: ⇒　Strong's #3748 hostis ⇒　NIV #4015 hostis ⇒　NASB #3748 hostis **2 Thes. 1:9** **Who** shall be punished with everlasting destruction from the presence of the Lord, and from the glory of his power; [KJV] And **these** will pay the penalty of eternal destruction, away from the presence of the Lord and from the glory of His power, [NASB] **They** will be punished with everlasting destruction and shut out from the presence of the Lord and from the majesty of his power [NIV] **These** shall be punished with everlasting destruction from the presence of the Lord and from the glory of His power, [NKJV] **They** will be punished with everlasting destruction, forever separated from the Lord and from his glorious power [NLT] οἵτινες δίκην τίσουσιν, ὄλεθρον αἰώνιον ἀπὸ προσώπου τοῦ Κυρίου καὶ ἀπὸ τῆς δόξης τῆς ἰσχύος αὐτοῦ, [GNS] οἵτινες δίκην τίσουσιν ὄλεθρον αἰώνιον ἀπὸ προσώπου τοῦ κυρίου καὶ ἀπὸ τῆς δόξης τῆς ἰσχύος αὐτοῦ, [GNT]	They, who, these, whoever, anyone. **Practical Application** The word "they" (*hoitines*) is used in a qualitative sense; that is, it means *"persons who are such as"* deserve this punishment; "persons who are of *such a kind as to*" deserve this punishment. The Greek word clearly shows that these persons deserve the punishment of the coming judgment. (This is pointed out by A.T. Robertson, *Word Pictures in the New Testament*, Vol.4, p.44; and Leon Morris, *The Epistles of Paul to the Thessalonians*. "Tyndale New Testament Commentaries," p.119.)

ENGLISH WORD·	GREEK WORD AND VERSE	THE WORD MEANS...

#3957
Thief
 	
Stole–KJV
Steals–NASB
Stealing–NIV
Stole–NKJV
Thief–NLT
 	
**POSB
REFERENCE**
(Eph.4:28)
Note 3
	κλέπτων = kleptön
	Pronunciation: [klep'-ton]
	Parsing (part of speech): verb
	  Mood—participle
	  Tense—present
	  Voice—active
	  Case—nominative
	  Gender—masculine
	  Number—singular
	  Stem or root— from κλέπτω
	Concordance References:
	  ⇒ Strong's #2813 kleptö
	  ⇒ NIV #3096 kleptö
	  ⇒ NASB #2813 kleptö
	
	Ephes. 4:28
	  Let him that **stole** steal no more: but rather let him labour, working with *his* hands the thing which is good, that he may have to give to him that needeth. [KJV]
	  Let him who **steals** steal no longer; but rather let him labor, performing with his own hands what is good, in order that he may have *something* to share with him who has need. [NASB]
	  He who has been **stealing** must steal no longer, but must work, doing something useful with his own hands, that he may have something to share with those in need. [NIV]
	  Let him who **stole** steal no longer, but rather let him labor, working with *his* hands what is good, that he may have something to give him who has need. [NKJV]
	  If you are a **thief**, stop stealing. Begin using your hands for honest work, and then give generously to others in need. [NLT]
	  ὁ **οκλέπτων** μηκέτι κλεπτέτω· μᾶλλον δὲ κοπιάτω, ἐργαζόμενος τὸ ἀγαθόν ταῖς χερσὶν, ἵνα ἔχῃ μεταδιδόναι τῷ χρείαν ἔχοντι. [GNS]
	  ὁ **κλέπτων** μηκέτι κλεπτέτω, μᾶλλον δὲ κοπιάτω ἐργαζόμενος ταῖς [ἰδίαις] χερσὶν τὸ ἀγαθόν, ἵνα ἔχῃ μεταδιδόναι τῷ χρείαν ἔχοντι. [GNT]
		To steal; to cheat; to take wrongfully from another person, either legally or illegally.
		
		Practical Application
		  Note that the laws of men are not the determining rule governing whether a person is stealing or not. This is what is so often misunderstood about stealing.
		  ⇒ Men can sometimes use the law to steal.
		  ⇒ Men can take from others without ever breaking a law.
		  ⇒ Men can secure too much of something, well beyond what they need; and when they hoard, they are taking something that by nature belongs to others.
		  Very simply stated, the Bible teaches that stealing is the taking of anything that *rightfully or by nature* belongs to others. There are at least three forms of stealing.
		1. A person steals by taking something which is *actually possessed or personally owned* by another person. If a person owns it and we take it, then we are guilty of stealing. It may be something as simple as a pencil from the office or an answer to a test from a fellow student, or it may be something as complex as embezzlement of funds through bookkeeping procedures. If we take it, we have broken God's commandment and stand guilty as thieves.
		2. A person steals by hoarding and banking more than he needs. *Keeping back* is stealing. It is...
		  • keeping what is not needed for one's own needs.
		  • keeping back what is desperately needed by others.
		  • taking away what nature and the earth have provided to meet the needs of the human population.
		  • hoarding the knowledge and gifts and blessings God gave to be used for the welfare of a desperate world filled with so many who are less privileged and gifted.
		    We may call it by whatever name we wish, but to God it is stealing. God has put within the earth enough resources to meet the needs of His people, and He has given men both the *ability and command to subdue and have dominion over the earth.*
		3. A person steals by living extravagantly, beyond what he needs. There are some who give to meet the crying needs of the world, yet they do not live sacrificially. They *keep plenty* for themselves, indulging their flesh...
		  • in clothing
		  • in food
		  • in jewelry
		  • in possessions
		  • in housing
		  • in transportation
		  • in recreation
		  • in property
		
		(See POSB note 3, Eph.4:28 for more discussion).

ENGLISH WORD	GREEK WORD AND VERSE	THE WORD MEANS...

#3958
Thieves
 	
Thieves–KJV
Thieves–NASB
Thieves–NIV
Thieves–NKJV
Thieves–NLT
 	
**POSB
REFERENCE**
(1 Cor.6:10)
Note 3
 	
See also POSB REF:
(Jn.10:1)
Note 2, point 2
	κλέπται = *kleptai*
	Pronunciation: [klep'-tah-ee]
	Parsing (part of speech): noun
	  Case—nominative
	  Gender—masculine
	  Number—plural
	  Stem or root—from κλέπτης, ου
	Concordance References:
	  ⇒ Strong's #2812 kleptēs
	  ⇒ NIV #3095 kleptēs
	  ⇒ NASB #2812 kleptēs
	
	1 Cor. 6:10
	Nor **thieves**, nor covetous, nor drunkards, nor revilers, nor extortioners, shall inherit the kingdom of God. [KJV]
	Nor **thieves**, nor *the* covetous, nor drunkards, nor revilers, nor swindlers, shall inherit the kingdom of God. [NASB]
	Nor **thieves** nor the greedy nor drunkards nor slanderers nor swindlers will inherit the kingdom of God. [NIV]
	Nor **thieves**, nor covetous, nor drunkards, nor revilers, nor extortioners will inherit the kingdom of God. [NKJV]
	Thieves, greedy people, drunkards, abusers, and swindlers—none of these will have a share in the Kingdom of God. [NLT]
	οὔτε **κλέπται**, οὔτε πλεονέκται, οὐ μέθυσοι, οὐ λοίδοροι, οὐχ ἅρπαγες, βασιλείαν Θεοῦ οὐ κληρονομήσουσι. [GNS]
	οὔτε **κλέπται** οὔτε πλεονέκται, οὐ μέθυσοι, οὐ λοίδοροι, οὐχ ἅρπαγες βασιλείαν θεοῦ κληρονομήσουσιν. [GNT]
		Thieves.
		
		Practical Application
		The word used here for thieves (*kleptai*) does not mean just the *professional thief* who lives by stealing. It means the petty, sneak thief: the shoplifter, the person who steals things here and there.

#3959
Things
 	
Things–KJV
Things–NASB
Things–NIV
Things–NKJV
Things–NLT
 	
**POSB
REFERENCE**
(Acts 5:32)
Note 3
	ῥημάτων = *hrēmaton*
	Pronunciation: [hray'-mah-toan]
	Parsing (part of speech): noun
	  Case—genitive
	  Gender—neuter
	  Number—plural
	  Stem or root—from ῥῆμα, τος
	Concordance References:
	  ⇒ Strong's #4487 hrēma
	  ⇒ NIV #4839 hrēma
	  ⇒ NASB #4487 hrēma
	
	Acts 5:32
	And we are his witnesses of these **things**; and *so is* also the Holy Ghost, whom God hath given to them that obey him. [KJV]
	"And we are witnesses of these **things**; and *so is* the Holy Spirit, whom God has given to those who obey Him." [NASB]
	We are witnesses of these **things**, and so is the Holy Spirit, whom God has given to those who obey him." [NIV]
	And we are His witnesses to these **things**, and *so also is* the Holy Spirit whom God has given to those who obey Him." [NKJV]
	We are witnesses of these **things** and so is the Holy Spirit, who is given by God to those who obey him." [NLT]
	καὶ ἡμεῖς ἐσμεν μάρτυρες τῶν **ῥημάτων** τούτων, καὶ τὸ Πνεῦμα δὲ τὸ Ἅγιον ὃ ἔδωκεν ὁ Θεὸς τοῖς πειθαρχοῦσιν αὐτῷ. [GNS]
	καὶ ἡμεῖς ἐσμεν μάρτυρες τῶν **ῥημάτων** τούτων καὶ τὸ πνεῦμα τὸ ἅγιον ὃ ἔδωκεν ὁ θεὸς τοῖς πειθαρχοῦσιν αὐτῷ. [GNT]
		Things or sayings, words, charges, messages.
		
		Practical Application
		What things, what sayings? These things: The believer is a witness that Jesus Christ is the Prince and Savior, the only Person who accepts repentance and can forgive sins. (See POSB note—Acts 1:8 and POSB *Deeper Study* #1—Acts 1:8 for more discussion and verses.)

ENGLISH WORD	GREEK WORD AND VERSE	THE WORD MEANS...

#3960
Things The World Considers Foolish
 	
Foolish things–KJV
Foolish things–NASB
Foolish things–NIV
Foolish things–NKJV
Things the world considers foolish–NLT
 	
POSB REFERENCE
(1 Cor.1:27-28; esp. v.27)
Note 2, point 1
	μωρὰ = möra
	Pronunciation: [mo-rah']
	Parsing (part of speech): pronominal adjective
	    Case—accusative
	    Gender—neuter
	    Number—plural
	    Stem or root—from μωρός, ά, όν
	Concordance References:
	  ⇒ Strong's #3474 möros
	  ⇒ NIV #3704 möros [foolish things]
	  ⇒ NASB #3474 möros
	
	1 Cor. 1:27
	But God hath chosen the **foolish things** of the world to confound the wise; and God hath chosen the weak things of the world to confound the things which are mighty; [KJV]
	But God has chosen the **foolish things** of the world to shame the wise, and God has chosen the weak things of the world to shame the things which are strong, [NASB]
	But God chose the **foolish things** of the world to shame the wise; God chose the weak things of the world to shame the strong. [NIV]
	But God has chosen the **foolish things** of the world to put to shame the wise, and God has chosen the weak things of the world to put to shame the things which are mighty; [NKJV]
	Instead, God deliberately chose **things the world considers foolish** in order to shame those who think they are wise. And he chose those who are powerless to shame those who are powerful. [NLT]
	ἀλλὰ τὰ **μωρὰ** τοῦ κόσμου ἐξελέξατο ὁ Θεός, ἵνα τοὺς σοφούς, καταισχύνῃ· καὶ τὰ ἀσθενῆ τοῦ κόσμου ἐξελέξατο ὁ Θεός, ἵνα καταισχύνῃ τὰ ἰσχυρά· [GNS]
	ἀλλὰ τὰ **μωρὰ** τοῦ κόσμου ἐξελέξατο ὁ θεός, ἵνα καταισχύνῃ τοὺς σοφούς, καὶ τὰ ἀσθενῆ τοῦ κόσμου ἐξελέξατο ὁ θεός, ἵνα καταισχύνῃ τὰ ἰσχυρά, [GNT]
		Foolish things, foolishness; things the world considers foolish.
		
		Practical Application
		God chooses the "things the world considers foolish." Note the term *"things"* is used instead of "people."
		Many of the wise in the world look upon those who have little or nothing as things. They look upon them as nothing more than tools for the rich and powerful to use as they wish. God chooses the ignorant, the unlearned, and the disadvantaged over the wise of the world.

#3961
Think About
 	
Consider–KJV
Consider–NASB
Fix...thoughts on–NIV
Consider–NKJV
Think about–NLT
 	
POSB REFERENCE
(Heb.3:1)
Note 1
	κατανοήσατε = katanoësate
	Pronunciation: [kat-an-o-ay-sah'-teh]
	Parsing (part of speech): verb
	    Mood—imperative
	    Tense—aorist
	    Voice—active
	    Person—2nd person
	    Number—plural
	    Stem or root—from κατανοέω
	Concordance References:
	  ⇒ Strong's #2657 katanoeö
	  ⇒ NIV #2917 katanoeö
	  ⇒ NASB #2657 katanoeö
	
	Hebrews 3:1
	Wherefore, holy brethren, partakers of the heavenly calling, **consider** the Apostle and High Priest of our profession, Christ Jesus; [KJV]
	Therefore, holy brethren, partakers of a heavenly calling, **consider** Jesus, the Apostle and High Priest of our confession. [NASB]
	Therefore, holy brothers, who share in the heavenly calling, **fix** your **thoughts on** Jesus, the apostle and high priest whom we confess. [NIV]
	Therefore, holy brethren, partakers of the heavenly calling, **consider** the Apostle and High Priest of our confession, Christ Jesus, [NKJV]
	And so, dear brothers and sisters who belong to God and are bound for heaven, **think about** this Jesus whom we declare to be God's Messenger and High Priest. [NLT]
	Ὅθεν, ἀδελφοὶ ἅγιοι, κλήσεως ἐπουρανίου μέτοχοι, **κατανοήσατε** τὸν ἀπόστολον καὶ ἀρχιερέα τῆς ὁμολογίας ἡμῶν Χριστὸν Ἰησοῦν, [GNS]
	Ὅθεν, ἀδελφοὶ ἅγιοι, κλήσεως ἐπουρανίου μέτοχοι, **κατανοήσατε** τὸν ἀπόστολον καὶ ἀρχιερέα τῆς ὁμολογίας ἡμῶν Ἰησοῦν, [GNT]
		To fix thoughts on; to consider; to think about; to observe; to look upon; to see; to fix one's thoughts and mind, attention and eyes upon Jesus Christ.
		
		Practical Application
		It means to concentrate; to seek to grasp; to focus and to be attentive in order to learn about Jesus Christ. Note: this exhortation is written to believers.

ENGLISH WORD	GREEK WORD AND VERSE	THE WORD MEANS...

#3962
Think About
 	
Consider–KJV
Consider–NASB
Consider–NIV
Consider–NKJV
Think about–NLT
 	
POSB
REFERENCE
(Heb.12:3)
Note 4
	ἀναλογίσασθε = *analogisasthe*
	Pronunciation: [an-al-og-i'-sahs-theh]
	Parsing (part of speech): verb
	    Mood—imperative
	    Tense—aorist
	    Voice—middle deponent
	    Person—2nd person
	    Number—plural
	    Stem or root—from ἀναλογίζομαι
	Concordance References:
	  ⇒ Strong's #357 analogizomai
	  ⇒ NIV #382 analogizomai
	  ⇒ NASB #357 analogizomai
	
	Hebrews 12:3
	    For **consider** him that endured such contradiction of sinners against himself, lest ye be wearied and faint in your minds. [KJV]
	    For **consider** Him who has endured such hostility by sinners against Himself, so that you may not grow weary and lose heart. [NASB]
	    Consider him who endured such opposition from sinful men, so that you will not grow weary and lose heart. [NIV]
	    For **consider** Him who endured such hostility from sinners against Himself, lest you become weary and discouraged in your souls. [NKJV]
	    Think about all he endured when sinful people did such terrible things to him, so that you don't become weary and give up. [NLT]
	    ἀναλογίσασθε γὰρ τὸν τοιαύτην ὑπομεμενηκότα ὑπὸ τῶν ἁμαρτωλῶν εἰς αὐτὸν ἀντιλογίαν, ἵνα μὴ κάμητε, ταῖς ψυχαῖς ὑμῶν ἐκλυόμενοι. [GNS]
	    ἀναλογίσασθε γὰρ τὸν τοιαύτην ὑπομεμενηκότα ὑπὸ τῶν ἁμαρτωλῶν εἰς ἑαυτὸν ἀντιλογίαν, ἵνα μὴ κάμητε ταῖς ψυχαῖς ὑμῶν ἐκλυόμενοι. [GNT]
		To consider; to think about. It means to compare, reckon, count up, weigh.
		
		Practical Application
		    Believers are to focus upon Jesus Christ and His sufferings and compare and weigh them against their sufferings. Christ endured so much more than we have to endure. Let any orphan, widow, criminal, prostitute, slave, or sufferer—any person whatsoever—compare himself with all this, and remember Jesus bore *all this*:
		⇒ being born to an unwed mother (Matthew 1:18-19).
		⇒ being born in a stable, the worst of conditions (Luke 2:7).
		⇒ being born to poor parents (Luke 2:24).
		⇒ having his life threatened as a baby (Matthew 2:13f).
		⇒ being the cause of unimaginable sorrow (Matthew 2:16f).
		⇒ having to be moved and shifted as a baby (Matthew 2:13f).
		⇒ being reared in a despicable place, Nazareth (Luke 2:39).
		⇒ having His father die during His youth (see POSB note, pt. 3—Matthew 13:53-58).
		⇒ having to support His mother and brothers and sisters (see POSB note, pt. 3—Matthew 13:53-58).
		⇒ having no home, not even a place to lay His head (Matthew 8:20; Luke 9:58).
		⇒ being hated and opposed by religionists (Mark 14:1-2).
		⇒ being charged with insanity (Mark 3:21).
		⇒ being charged with demon possession (Mark 3:22).
		⇒ being opposed by His own family (Mark 3:31-32).
		⇒ being rejected, hated, and opposed by audiences to whom He spoke (Matthew 13:53-58; Luke 4:28-29).
		⇒ being betrayed by a close friend (Mark 14:10-11, 18).
		⇒ being left alone, rejected, and forsaken by all His friends (Mark 14:50).
		⇒ being tried before the high court of the land on the charge of treason (John 18:33).
		⇒ being executed by crucifixion, the worst possible death (John 19:16f).

#3963
Think About–
Think On
 	
Think on–KJV
Let your mind dwell on–NASB
Think about–NIV
Meditate on–NKJV
Think about–NLT
 	
POSB
REFERENCE
(Philip.4:8-9; esp. v.8)
Note 2
	λογίζεσθε = *logizesthe*
	Pronunciation: [log-id'-zehs-theh]
	Parsing (part of speech): verb
	    Mood—imperative
	    Tense—present
	    Voice—middle or passive deponent
	    Person—2nd person
	    Number—plural
	    Stem or root—from λογίζομαι
	Concordance References:
	  ⇒ Strong's #3049 logizomai
	  ⇒ NIV #3357 logizomai
	  ⇒ NASB #3049 logizomai
	
	Philip. 4:8
	    Finally, brethren, whatsoever things are true, whatso-
		To think about; to think on; to let one's mind dwell on; to calculate; to evaluate; to consider, reflect, reason, and ponder.
		
		Practical Application
		    The idea is that of focusing our thoughts until they shape our behavior. The truth is:
		⇒ what we think is what we become.
		⇒ where we have kept our minds is where we are.
		⇒ our thoughts shape our behavior.
		⇒ what we do is what we think.
		William Barclay says,
		"...it is a law of life that, if a man thinks of something often enough and long enough, he

ENGLISH WORD	GREEK WORD AND VERSE	THE WORD MEANS...

ever things *are* honest, whatsoever things *are* just, whatsoever things *are* pure, whatsoever things *are* lovely, whatsoever things *are* of good report; if *there be* any virtue, and if *there be* any praise, **think on** these things. [KJV]

Finally, brethren, whatever is true, whatever is honorable, whatever is right, whatever is pure, whatever is lovely, whatever is of good repute, if there is any excellence and if anything worthy of praise, **let your mind dwell on** these things. [NASB]

Finally, brothers, whatever is true, whatever is noble, whatever is right, whatever is pure, whatever is lovely, whatever is admirable—if anything is excellent or praiseworthy—**think about** such things. [NIV]

Finally, brethren, whatever things are true, whatever things *are* noble, whatever things *are* just, whatever things *are* pure, whatever things *are* lovely, whatever things *are* of good report, if *there is* any virtue and if *there is* anything praiseworthy—**meditate on** these things. [NKJV]

And now, dear brothers and sisters, let me say one more thing as I close this letter. Fix your thoughts on what is true and honorable and right. Think about things that are pure and lovely and admirable. **Think about** things that are excellent and worthy of praise. [NLT]

Τὸ λοιπόν, ἀδελφοί, ὅσα ἐστὶν ἀληθῆ, ὅσα σεμνά, ὅσα δίκαια, ὅσα ἁγνά, ὅσα προσφιλῆ, ὅσα εὔφημα, εἴ τις ἀρετὴ καὶ εἴ τις ἔπαινος, ταῦτα **λογίζεσθε**· [GNS]

Τὸ λοιπόν, ἀδελφοί, ὅσα ἐστὶν ἀληθῆ, ὅσα σεμνά, ὅσα δίκαια, ὅσα ἁγνά, ὅσα προσφιλῆ, ὅσα εὔφημα, εἴ τις ἀρετὴ καὶ εἴ τις ἔπαινος, ταῦτα **λογίζεσθε**· [GNT]

will come to the stage when he cannot stop thinking about it. His thoughts will be quite literally in a groove out of which he cannot jerk them" (The Letters to the Philippians, Colossians, and Thessalonians, p.97).

A person who centers his thoughts upon the world and its things will live for the world and its things: money, wealth, lands, property, houses, possessions, position, power, recognition, honor, social standing, fame, and a host of other worldly pursuits. Very simply stated, a person who centers his thoughts...

- upon the flesh and its lusts will live to satisfy the flesh through such things as pride, self, greed, pleasure, and sex.
- upon the eyes and their lust will live to satisfy the eyes and their lust through such things as the immoral, pornographic filth flaunted in magazines, films, books, and television; the exposing of the human body; dressing to attract attention; looking a second time.
- upon the pride of life will live to satisfy such things as the desire for recognition, honor, position, and authority.

A mind set upon the world and the flesh is what leads to anxiety and worry, emptiness and restlessness (Phil. 4:6-7). A worldly mind never knows peace—not true peace, not the peace of God. God will never allow a worldly mind to have peace, for it is the restlessness of the human soul that He uses to reach men for salvation.

The point is this: when a person accepts Jesus Christ, his mind is renewed by the Spirit of God.

#3964
Think Of Ways

Consider–KJV
Consider–NASB
Consider–NIV
Consider–NKJV
Think of ways–NLT

**POSB
REFERENCE**
(Heb.10:24)
Note 3

κατανοῶμεν = *katanoömen*
Pronunciation: [kat-an-o-ow'-mehn]
Parsing (part of speech): verb
 Mood—subjunctive
 Tense—present
 Voice—active
 Person—1st person
 Number—plural
 Stem or root—from **κατανοέω**
Concordance References:
 ⇒ Strong's #2657 katanoeö
 ⇒ NIV #2917 katanoeö
 ⇒ NASB #2657 katanoeö

Hebrews 10:24

And let us **consider** one another to provoke unto love and to good works: [KJV]

And let us **consider** how to stimulate one another to love and good deeds, [NASB]

And let us **consider** how we may spur one another on toward love and good deeds. [NIV]

And let us **consider** one another in order to stir up love and good works, [NKJV]

Think of ways to encourage one another to outbursts of love and good deeds. [NLT]

καὶ **κατανοῶμεν** ἀλλήλους εἰς παροξυσμὸν ἀγάπης καὶ καλῶν ἔργων, [GNS]

καὶ **κατανοῶμεν** ἀλλήλους εἰς παροξυσμὸν ἀγάπης καὶ καλῶν ἔργων, [GNT]

To consider; to think of ways; to notice; to observe; to look upon; to be aware of. It means to give attention to; to fix our attention upon; to give continuous care; to watch over.

Practical Application
What an exhortation to believers!
⇒ Give attention to one another.
⇒ Fix your attention upon one another.
⇒ Give continuous care to one another.
⇒ Watch over one another.

How different the church would be—how much stronger we would be in Christ and in life—if we heeded this exhortation! And note what it is that we are to give attention to: to make sure that we are stirred up and living for Christ—that we are loving one another and doing good works. This simply means...

- that we are considerate of one another.
- that we show concern for one another.
- that we meet one another's needs.
- that we strengthen one another's weaknesses.
- that we help one another through every trial and temptation.

It means that we love—love in act and not in word—that we...

- feed the poor
- visit the sick and shut-ins
- look after the orphans and the children of broken homes and single parents

ENGLISH WORD	GREEK WORD AND VERSE	THE WORD MEANS...
		• become a friend to the lonely • give direction to the empty and those without purpose. Note the exhortation again: we give attention to one another. Why? To make sure none of us are slacking up—to stir one another to love and to do good works. This is the duty of the new, living faith Jesus Christ has wrought for us. It is not a dead faith. It is a faith that stirs us to action—that stirs us to live, truly live, live in love and good works—for the sake of a needful and sick world.

#3965
Thinketh No Evil–
Thinks No Evil
 	
Thinketh no evil–KJV
Does not take into account a wrong suffered–NASB
Record of wrongs–NIV
Thinks no evil–NKJV
No record of when it has been wronged–NLT
 	
POSB REFERENCE
(1 Cor.13:4-7; esp. v.5)
Note 2, point 9
	οὐ λογίζεται τὸ κακόν = *oo logizetai to kakon*
	Pronunciation: [log-id'-eh-tah-ee to kak-on']
	Parsing *logizetai* (part of speech): verb
	   Mood—indicative
	   Tense—present
	   Voice—middle or passive deponent
	   Person—3rd person
	   Number—singular
	   Stem or root—from λογίζομαι
	Parsing *kakon* (part of speech): pronominal adjective
	   Case—accusative
	   Gender—neuter
	   Number—singular
	   Stem or root—from κακός, ή, όν
	Concordance References:
	   Strong's #3049 logizomai + 2556 kakos
	   NIV #3357 logizomai [record of] + 2805 kakos [wrongs]
	   NASB #3049 logizomai + 2556 kakos
	
	1 Cor. 13:5
	   Doth not behave itself unseemly, seeketh not her own, is not easily provoked, **thinketh no evil**; [KJV]
	   Does not act unbecomingly; it does not seek its own, is not provoked, **does not take into account a wrong suffered,** [NASB]
	   It is not rude, it is not self-seeking, it is not easily angered, it keeps no **record of wrongs**. [NIV]
	   Does not behave rudely, does not seek its own, is not provoked, **thinks no evil**; [NKJV]
	   Or rude. Love does not demand its own way. Love is not irritable, and it keeps **no record of when it has been wronged**. [NLT]
	   οὐκ ἀσχημονεῖ, οὐ ζητεῖ τὰ ἑαυτῆς, οὐ παροξύνεται, οὐ λογίζεται τὸ κακόν, [GNS]
	   οὐκ ἀσχημονεῖ, οὐ ζητεῖ τὰ ἑαυτῆς, οὐ παροξύνεται, οὐ λογίζεται τὸ κακόν, [GNT]
		To count, to reckon; to claim a record of wrongs; not to think evil; to keep an account of wrongs suffered.
		
		Practical Application
		   Love does not consider the wrong suffered; is not resentful; does not hold the evil done to oneself. Love suffers the evil done to it and forgets it.

#3966
Thinking
 	
Imaginations–KJV
Speculations–NASB
Thinking–NIV
Thoughts–NKJV
Ideas–NLT
 	
POSB REFERENCE
(Rom.1:21)
Note 4, point 1
	διαλογισμοῖς = *dialogismois*
	Pronunciation: [dee-al-og-is-mo-ees']
	Parsing (part of speech): noun
	   Case—dative
	   Gender—masculine
	   Number—plural
	   Stem or root—from διαλογισμός, οῦ
	Concordance References:
	   ⇒ Strong's #1261 dialogismos
	   ⇒ NIV #1369 dialogismos
	   ⇒ NASB #1261 dialogismos
	
	Romans 1:21
	   Because that, when they knew God, they glorified *him* not as God, neither were thankful; but became vain in their **imaginations**, and their foolish heart was darkened. [KJV]
	   For even though they knew God, they did not honor Him as God, or give thanks; but they became futile in their **speculations**, and their foolish heart was darkened. [NASB]
	   For although they knew God, they neither glorified him as God nor gave thanks to him, but their **thinking**
		Thoughts, opinions, motives, reasonings; doubts, questions; arguments, disputes, deliberations, conclusions, speculations.
		
		Practical Application
		   When men push God out of their minds, their minds are void and empty of God. God is not in their thoughts. (Cp. Psalm 10:4.) Their minds are ready to be *filled* with some other *god* or *supremacy*.

ENGLISH WORD	GREEK WORD AND VERSE	THE WORD MEANS...
	became futile and their foolish hearts were darkened. [NIV] Because, although they knew God, they did not glorify *Him* as God, nor were thankful, but became futile in their **thoughts**, and their foolish hearts were darkened. [NKJV] Yes, they knew God, but they wouldn't worship him as God or even give him thanks. And they began to think up foolish **ideas** of what God was like. The result was that their minds became dark and confused. [NLT] διότι γνόντες τὸν Θεὸν οὐχ ὡς Θεὸν ἐδόξασαν ἢ ηὐχαρίστησαν, ἀλλ᾽ ἐματαιώθησαν ἐν τοῖς **διαλογισμοῖς** αὐτῶν, καὶ ἐσκοτίσθη ἡ ἀσύνετος αὐτῶν καρδία. [GNS] διότι γνόντες τὸν θεὸν οὐχ ὡς θεὸν ἐδόξασαν ἢ ηὐχαρίστησαν, ἀλλ᾽ ἐματαιώθησαν ἐν τοῖς **διαλογισμοῖς** αὐτῶν καὶ ἐσκοτίσθη ἡ ἀσύνετος αὐτῶν καρδία. [GNT]	

#3967
Thinking
 	
Mind–KJV
Mind–NASB
Thinking–NIV
Mind–NKJV
Not translated–NLT
 	
POSB REFERENCE
(Eph.4:17-19; esp. v.17)
Note 1, point 1
	νοὸς = noos
	Pronunciation: [noose]
	Parsing (part of speech): noun
	    Case—genitive
	    Gender—masculine
	    Number—singular
	    Stem or root—from νοῦς, νοός, νοΐ, νοῦν
	Concordance References:
	  ⇒ Strong's #3563 nous
	  ⇒ NIV #3808 nous
	  ⇒ NASB #3563 nous
	
	Ephes. 4:17
	This I say therefore, and testify in the Lord, that ye henceforth walk not as other Gentiles walk, in the vanity of their **mind**, [KJV]
	
	This I say therefore, and affirm together with the Lord, that you walk no longer just as the Gentiles also walk, in the futility of their **mind**, [NASB]
	
	So I tell you this, and insist on it in the Lord, that you must no longer live as the Gentiles do, in the futility of their **thinking**. [NIV]
	
	This I say, therefore, and testify in the Lord, that you should no longer walk as the rest of the Gentiles walk, in the futility of their **mind**, [NKJV]
	
	With the Lord's authority let me say this: Live no longer as the ungodly do, for they are hopelessly confused. [NLT]—NOT TRANSLATED
	
	Τοῦτο οὖν λέγω καὶ μαρτύρομαι ἐν Κυρίῳ, μηκέτι ὑμᾶς περιπατεῖν καθὼς καὶ τὰ λοιπὰ ἔθνη περιπατεῖ, ἐν ματαιότητι τοῦ **νοὸς** αὐτῶν, [GNS]
	
	Τοῦτο οὖν λέγω καὶ μαρτύρομαι ἐν κυρίῳ, μηκέτι ὑμᾶς περιπατεῖν, καθὼς καὶ τὰ ἔθνη περιπατεῖ ἐν ματαιότητι τοῦ **νοὸς** αὐτῶν, [GNT]
		Thinking, mind, discernment, purpose, thought. The thinking (*noos*) includes the ability to will and to do the truth as well as know the truth; it includes morality as well as reasoning and understanding.
		
		Practical Application
		When men push God out of their minds, their minds are void and empty of God and of His truth and morality. *God is not in their thoughts.* Their minds are ready to be filled with some other god or supremacy, that is, with the things of the world:
		
		⇒ worldly pleasures
		⇒ worldly possessions
		⇒ worldly power
		⇒ worldly position
		⇒ worldly religions
		⇒ worldly ideas
		⇒ worldly honor
		⇒ worldly gods

#3968
Thinks
 	
Judged–KJV
Examined–NASB
Judged–NIV
Judged–NKJV
Thinks–NLT
 	
POSB REFERENCE
(1 Cor.4:3)
Note 2
	ἀνακρίνω = anakrinō
	Pronunciation: [an-ak-ree'-no]
	Parsing (part of speech): verb
	    Mood—subjunctive
	    Tense—aorist
	    Voice—passive
	    Person—1st person
	    Number—singular
	    Stem or root—from ἀνακρίνω
	Concordance References:
	  ⇒ Strong's #350 anakrinō
	  ⇒ NIV #373 anakrinō
	  ⇒ NASB #350 anakrinō
	
	1 Cor. 4:3
	But with me it is a very small thing that I should be **judged** of you, or of man's judgment: yea, I judge not mine own self. [KJV]
	
	But to me it is a very small thing that I should be **examined** by you, or by any human court; in fact, I do not even examine myself. [NASB]
		To judge; to examine; to evaluate; to discern; to closely study; to scrutinize; to investigate; to question; and to cross-examine.
		
		Practical Application
		Note this: Paul does not even judge himself. Paul knew precisely what every honest and thinking prson knows.
		
		⇒ No minister can honestly judge his own ministry: its true success; his motives for every single thing he has done; how much fruit he has really borne in people's lives and how much should have been borne.
		
		⇒ A person who begins to judge his own works either begins to think too highly of himself or too lowly. To varying degrees, he becomes prideful or discouraged.

ENGLISH WORD	GREEK WORD AND VERSE	THE WORD MEANS...
	I care very little if I am **judged** by you or by any human court; indeed, I do not even judge myself. [NIV] But with me it is a very small thing that I should be **judged** by you or by a human court. In fact, I do not even judge myself. [NKJV] What about me? Have I been faithful? Well, it matters very little what you or anyone else **thinks**. I don't even trust my own judgment on this point. [NLT] ἐμοὶ δὲ εἰς ἐλάχιστόν ἐστιν ἵνα ὑφ' ὑμῶν ἀνακριθῶ, ἢ ὑπὸ ἀνθρωπίνης ἡμέρας· ἀλλ' οὐδὲ ἐμαυτὸν **ἀνακρίνω**. [GNS] ἐμοὶ δὲ εἰς ἐλάχιστόν ἐστιν, ἵνα ὑφ' ὑμῶν ἀνακριθῶ ἢ ὑπὸ ἀνθρωπίνης ἡμέρας· ἀλλ' οὐδὲ ἐμαυτὸν **ἀνακρίνω**. [GNT]	

#3969
Thirst–Thirsty
 	
Thirst–KJV
Thirst–NASB
Thirst–NIV
Thirst–NKJV
Thirsty–NLT
 	
POSB
REFERENCE
(Mt.5:6)
Note 5
	διψῶντες = *dipsóntes*
	Pronunciation: [dip-son'-tehs]
	Parsing (part of speech): verb
	   Mood—participle
	   Tense—present
	   Voice—active
	   Case—nominative
	   Gender—masculine
	   Number—plural
	   Stem or root—from διψάω
	Concordance References:
	  ⇒ Strong's #1372 dipsaö
	  ⇒ NIV #1498 dipsaö
	  ⇒ NASB #1372 dipsaö
	
	Matthew 5:6
	Blessed *are* they which do hunger and **thirst** after righteousness: for they shall be filled. [KJV]
	
	"Blessed are those who hunger and **thirst** for righteousness, for they shall be satisfied. [NASB]
	
	Blessed are those who hunger and **thirst** for righteousness, for they will be filled. [NIV]
	
	Blessed are those who hunger and **thirst** for righteousness, For they shall be filled. [NKJV]
	
	God blesses those who are hungry and **thirsty** for justice, for they will receive it in full. [NLT]
	
	Μακάριοι οἱ πεινῶντες καὶ **διψῶντες** τὴν δικαιοσύνην· ὅτι αὐτοὶ χορτασθήσονται. [GNS]
	
	μακάριοι οἱ πεινῶντες καὶ **διψῶντες** τὴν δικαιοσύνην, ὅτι αὐτοὶ χορτασθήσονται. [GNT]
		Thirst, thirsty; a parched, dying thirst.
		
		Practical Application
		In this Scripture it means to have a thirsty spirit. It is a parched and dying thirst. It is a starving spirit and a parched soul that craves after righteousness. But there is something more: righteousness means all righteousness. The true believer is starved and parched for all righteousness. This is shown by the Greek, for the verbs hunger (*peinao*) and thirst (*dipsöntes*) are usually in what is called the Greek genitive case. This simply means that a person sometimes feels a little hunger and a little thirst; therefore, he hungers and thirsts for a bit of something, for example, an apple or a glass of juice. But in the beatitude, hunger and thirst are in the accusative case. It means that a person must have a hunger and a thirst for the whole thing—for all righteousness, not for little tidbits. It means that the promise of a filled life is conditional. A person must starve and thirst for all righteousness if he wishes to be filled with the fullness of life.

#3970
This Fellow
 	
This fellow–KJV
This man–NASB
This fellow–NIV
This fellow–NKJV
This man–NLT
 	
POSB
REFERENCE
(Mt.26:60-61; esp. v.61)
Note 4, point 2
	Οὗτος = *houtos*
	Pronunciation: [who-tos]
	Parsing (part of speech): pronominal adjective
	   Type—demonstrative
	   Case—nominative
	   Gender—masculine
	   Number—singular
	   Stem or root—from οὗτος, αὕτη, τοῦτο
	Concordance References:
	  ⇒ Strong's #3778 houtos
	  ⇒ NIV #4047 houtos
	  ⇒ NASB #3778 houtos
	
	Matthew 26:61
	And said, **This** *fellow* said, I am able to destroy the temple of God, and to build it in three days. [KJV]
	
	And said, "**This man** stated, 'I am able to destroy the temple of God and to rebuild it in three days.' "[NASB]
	
	And declared, "**This fellow** said, 'I am able to destroy the temple of God and rebuild it in three days.' "[NIV]
	
	And said, "**This fellow** said, 'I am able to destroy the temple of God and to build it in three days.' " [NKJV]
	
	Who declared, "**This man** said, 'I am able to destroy the Temple of God and rebuild it in three days.'" [NLT]
	
	ὕστερον δὲ προσελθόντες δύο ψευδομάρτυρες εἶπον,
		This fellow; this man; a disrespectful, contemptuous address.
		
		Practical Application
		There was a total disregard for what Jesus Christ represented: God, come in the flesh. Open rebellion against God will cause people to do and say anything. When people are bent on doing something, they often go ahead and do it—regardless of the method.
		1. When a person is bent on rejecting Christ, he rationalizes and justifies himself and rejects Christ.
		2. When a person is bent on doing something wrong, he rationalizes and justifies himself and does it.

ENGLISH WORD	GREEK WORD AND VERSE	THE WORD MEANS...
	Οὗτος ἔφη, Δύναμαι καταλῦσαι τὸν ναὸν τοῦ Θεοῦ καὶ διὰ τριῶν ἡμερῶν οἰκοδομῆσαι αὐτόν. [GNS] εἶπαν, Οὗτος ἔφη, Δύναμαι καταλῦσαι τὸν ναὸν τοῦ θεοῦ καὶ διὰ τριῶν ἡμερῶν οἰκοδομῆσαι. [GNT]	

#3971
This Is His Plan
 	
Dispensation–KJV
Administration–NASB
Put into effect–NIV
Dispensation–NKJV
This is his plan–NLT
 	
POSB
REFERENCE
(Eph.1:9-10; esp. v.10)
Note 6, point 3
	οἰκονομίαν = oikonomian
	Pronunciation: [oy-kon-om-ee'-ahn]
	Parsing (part of speech): noun
	    Case—accusative
	    Gender—feminine
	    Number—singular
	    Stem or root—from οἰκονομία, ας
	Concordance References:
	  ⇒ Strong's #3622 oikonomia
	  ⇒ NIV #3873 oikonomia
	  ⇒ NASB #3622 oikonomia
	
	Ephes. 1:10
	That in the **dispensation** of the fulness of times he might gather together in one all things in Christ, both which are in heaven, and which are on earth; *even* in him: [KJV]
	With a view to an **administration** suitable to the fulness of the times, *that is*, the summing up of all things in Christ, things in the heavens and things upon the earth. In Him [NASB]
	To be **put into effect** when the times will have reached their fulfillment—to bring all things in heaven and on earth together under one head, even Christ. [NIV]
	That in the **dispensation** of the fullness of the times He might gather together in one all things in Christ, both which are in heaven and which are on earth—in Him. [NKJV]
	And **this is his plan**: At the right time he will bring everything together under the authority of Christ—everything in heaven and on earth. [NLT]
	εἰς οἰκονομίαν τοῦ πληρώματος τῶν καιρῶν, ἀνακεφαλαιώσασθαι τὰ πάντα ἐν τῷ Χριστῷ, τά τε ἐν τοῖς οὐρανοῖς καὶ τὰ ἐπὶ τῆς γῆς· ἐν αὐτῷ, [GNS]
	εἰς οἰκονομίαν τοῦ πληρώματος τῶν καιρῶν, ἀνακεφαλαιώσασθαι τὰ πάντα ἐν τῷ Χριστῷ, τὰ ἐπὶ τοῖς οὐρανοῖς καὶ τὰ ἐπὶ τῆς γῆς ἐν αὐτω. [GNT]
		To put into effect; administration; to have a plan. The word Paul uses literally means, "household arrangement."
		
		Practical Application
		The idea is that the universe is a house under the management of God. God is handling, planning, arranging, and administering all things toward a climactic consummation for Christ and His followers. In that climactic day all disharmony and division and evil will be subjected and harmonized (*anakephalaioo*) under Christ. A new and perfect and eternal creation will be established for the Lord and His followers throughout the universe.

#3972
This Is My Son, Whom I Have Chosen–
This Is My Son, My Chosen One–
This Is My Beloved Son
 	
This is my beloved Son–KJV
This is My Son, *My* Chosen One–NASB
This is my Son, whom I have chosen–NIV
This is My beloved Son–NKJV
This is my Son, my Chosen One–NLT
 	
POSB
REFERENCE
(Lk.9:35)
Note 7
	Οὗτός ἐστιν ὁ υἱός μου ὁ ἐκλελεγμένος = Houtos estin ho huios mou ho eklelegmenos
	Pronunciation: [oo-tos es-tin ha we-os moo ha ek-leh-leg-mehn-os]
	Parsing *Houtos* (part of speech): pronominal adjective
	    Type—demonstrative
	    Case—nominative
	    Gender—masculine
	    Number—singular
	    Stem or root—from οὗτος, αὕτη, τοῦτο
	Parsing *estin* (part of speech): verb
	    Mood—indicative
	    Tense—present
	    Voice—active
	    Person—3rd person
	    Number—singular
	    Stem or root—from εἰμί
	Parsing *huios* (part of speech): noun
	    Case—nominative
	    Gender—masculine
	    Number—singular
	    Stem or root—from υἱός, οῦ
	Parsing *mou* (part of speech): noun
	    Type—pronoun
	    Case—genitive
	    Person—1st person
	    Number—singular
	    Stem or root—from ἐγώ
	Parsing *eklelegmenos* (part of speech): verb
	    Mood—participle
	    Tense—perfect
		This is My Son, My beloved Son, My special Son whom I have chosen.
		
		Practical Application
		God was both telling and warning the disciples to listen to Christ...
		• He was God's Son, the beloved and chosen One.
		• He spoke the truth, even when He predicted His death and resurrection.

ENGLISH WORD	GREEK WORD AND VERSE	THE WORD MEANS...
	Voice—passive Case—nominative Gender—masculine Number—singular Stem or root—from ἐκλέγομαι Concordance References: ⇒ Strong's #3778 houtos + 1488+eimi + 1473 ego +5207 huios + 3588 ho + 1586 eklegomai ⇒ NIV #4047 houtos [this] + 1639 eimi [is] + 1609 egö [my] + 5626 huios [Son] + 3836 ho [whom] + 1721 eklegomai [chosen] ⇒ NASB #3778 houtos + 1488+eimi + 1473 ego +5207 huios + 3588 ho + 1586 eklegomai **Luke 9:35** And there came a voice out of the cloud, saying, **This is my beloved Son**: hear him. [KJV] And a voice came out of the cloud, saying, "**This is My Son,** *My* **Chosen One**; listen to Him!" [NASB] A voice came from the cloud, saying, "**This is my Son, whom I have chosen**; listen to him." [NIV] And a voice came out of the cloud, saying, "**This is My beloved Son**. Hear Him!" [NKJV] Then a voice from the cloud said, "**This is my Son, my Chosen One**. Listen to him." [NLT] καὶ φωνὴ ἐγένετο ἐκ τῆς νεφέλης, λέγουσα, **Οὗτός** ἐστιν ὁ υἱός μου ὁ **ἀγαπητὸς**, αὐτοῦ ἀκούετε. [GNS] καὶ φωνὴ ἐγένετο ἐκ τῆς νεφέλης λέγουσα, **Οὗτός** ἐστιν ὁ υἱός μου ὁ **ἐκλελεγμένος**, αὐτοῦ ἀκούετε. [GNT]	
#3973 **This Man** This fellow–KJV **This man–NASB** This fellow–NIV This fellow–NKJV **This man–NLT** **POSB REFERENCE** (Mt.26:60-61; esp. v.61) Note 4, point 2	**Οὗτος** = houtos Pronunciation: [who-tos] Parsing (part of speech): pronominal adjective Type—demonstrative Case—nominative Gender—masculine Number—singular Stem or root—from **οὗτος**, αὕτη, τοῦτο Concordance References: ⇒ Strong's #3778 houtos ⇒ NIV #4047 houtos ⇒ NASB #3778 houtos **Matthew 26:61** And said, **This** *fellow* said, I am able to destroy the temple of God, and to build it in three days. [KJV] And said, "**This man** stated, 'I am able to destroy the temple of God and to rebuild it in three days.'" [NASB] And declared, "**This fellow** said, 'I am able to destroy the temple of God and rebuild it in three days.' [NIV] And said, "**This fellow** said, 'I am able to destroy the temple of God and to build it in three days.' [NKJV] Who declared, "**This man** said, 'I am able to destroy the Temple of God and rebuild it in three days.' "[NLT] ὕστερον δὲ προσελθόντες δύο ψευδομάρτυρες εἶπον, **Οὗτος** ἔφη, Δύναμαι καταλῦσαι τὸν ναὸν τοῦ Θεοῦ καὶ διὰ τριῶν ἡμερῶν οἰκοδομῆσαι αὐτόν. [GNS] εἶπαν, **Οὗτος** ἔφη, Δύναμαι καταλῦσαι τὸν ναὸν τοῦ θεοῦ καὶ διὰ τριῶν ἡμερῶν οἰκοδομῆσαι. [GNT]	This fellow; this man; a disrespectful, contemptuous address. **Practical Application** There was a total disregard for what Jesus Christ represented: God, come in the flesh. Open rebellion against God will cause people to do and say anything. When people are bent on doing something, they often go ahead and do it—regardless of the method. 1. When a person is bent on rejecting Christ, he rationalizes and justifies himself and rejects Christ. 2. When a person is bent on doing something wrong, he rationalizes and justifies himself and does it.
#3974 **Thorn** **Thorn–KJV** **Thorn–NASB** **Thorn–NIV** **Thorn–NKJV** **Thorn–NLT**	**σκόλοψ** = skolops Pronunciation: [skol'-ops] Parsing (part of speech): noun Case—nominative Gender—masculine Number—singular Stem or root—from **σκόλοψ**, οπος Concordance References: ⇒ Strong's #4647 skolops ⇒ NIV #5022 skolops ⇒ NASB #4647 skolops	Thorn, splinter, briar, sharp point, prickle, quill. **Practical Application** Paul needed a "thorn" to keep him ever mindful that he was no better than other men. He was totally dependent upon God despite the indescribable spiritual experiences. What was his "thorn in my flesh?" There are many guesses as to what the

ENGLISH WORD	GREEK WORD AND VERSE	THE WORD MEANS...
POSB REFERENCE (2 Cor.12:7-10; esp. v.7) Note 3	**2 Cor. 12:7** And lest I should be exalted above measure through the abundance of the revelations, there was given to me a **thorn** in the flesh, the messenger of Satan to buffet me, lest I should be exalted above measure. [KJV] And because of the surpassing greatness of the revelations, for this reason, to keep me from exalting myself, there was given me a **thorn** in the flesh, a messenger of Satan to buffet me—to keep me from exalting myself! [NASB] To keep me from becoming conceited because of these surpassingly great revelations, there was given me a **thorn** in my flesh, a messenger of Satan, to torment me. [NIV] And lest I should be exalted above measure by the abundance of the revelations, a **thorn** in the flesh was given to me, a messenger of Satan to buffet me, lest I be exalted above measure. [NKJV] Even though I have received wonderful revelations from God. But to keep me from getting puffed up, I was given a **thorn** in my flesh, a messenger from Satan to torment me and keep me from getting proud. [NLT] καὶ τῇ ὑπερβολῇ τῶν ἀποκαλύψεων ἵνα μὴ ὑπεραίρωμαι, ἐδόθη μοι **σκόλοψ** τῇ σαρκί, ἄγγελος Σατᾶν, ἵνα με κολαφίζῃ, ἵνα μὴ ὑπεραίρωμαι. [GNS] καὶ τῇ ὑπερβολῇ τῶν ἀποκαλύψεων. διὸ ἵνα μὴ ὑπεραίρωμαι, ἐδόθη μοι **σκόλοψ** τῇ σαρκί, ἄγγελος Σατανᾶ, ἵνα με κολαφίζῃ, ἵνα μὴ ὑπεραίρωμαι [GNT]	"thorn" was: ⇒ some spiritual suffering such as constant attacks by Satan or opposition by men, or occasional evangelistic failure in order to keep Paul humble and on his face before God seeking supernatural strength. ⇒ some physical suffering such as a recurring fever (for example, malaria), or epilepsy, or poor eyesight. Just what the thorn was is not known. The best guess seems to be some physical ailment, for suffering is what this passage is all about (cp. 2 Cor. 11:16-12:10). The words flesh, strength, weakness, and infirmities are used; and, although these same words could be used to describe spiritual sufferings, the context does not weigh toward spiritual suffering (cp. also 2 Cor. 10:10). The clearest description of the thorn is probably eye trouble (cp. 2 Cor. 10:10; Galatians 4:13-15; Galatians 6:11). Paul had been stricken blind for three days at his conversion, and he had been badly beaten and stoned several times (2 Cor. 11:24-27). A serious injury to his eyes, or for that matter to any other part of his body, could have occurred at any of these tragedies.
#3975 Thoroughly Perfect–KJV Adequate–NASB **Thoroughly–NIV** Complete–NKJV Preparing us in every way–NLT **POSB REFERENCE** (2 Tim. 3:17) Note 5	ἄρτιος = *artios* Pronunciation: [ar'-tee-os] Parsing (part of speech): adjective Case—nominative Gender—masculine Number—singular Stem or root—from ἄρτιος, α, ον Concordance References: ⇒ Strong's #739 artios ⇒ NIV #787 artios ⇒ NASB #739 artios **2 Tim. 3:17** That the man of God may be **perfect**, throughly furnished unto all good works. [KJV] That the man of God may be **adequate**, equipped for every good work. [NASB] So that the man of God may be **thoroughly** equipped for every good work. [NIV] That the man of God may be **complete**, thoroughly equipped for every good work. [NKJV] It is God's way of **preparing us in every way**, fully equipped for every good thing God wants us to do. [NLT] ἵνα ἄρτιος ᾖ ὁ τοῦ Θεοῦ ἄνθρωπος, πρὸς πᾶν ἔργον ἀγαθὸν ἐξηρτισμένος. [GNS] ἵνα ἄρτιος ᾖ ὁ τοῦ θεοῦ ἄνθρωπος, πρὸς πᾶν ἔργον ἀγαθὸν ἐξηρτισμένος. [GNT]	To be thorough; to be perfect; to be adequate; to be prepared in every way. It means complete, matured, filled. **Practical Application** Scripture perfects a man and equips him for every good work. "Thoroughly" (*artios*) means complete, matured, perfect, filled. No person is complete or mature apart from Scripture. Man was made for God and he is to live by the Word of God. If he tries to live without God and His Word, man fails in life. He lives an incomplete, immature, and misfitted life. This is particularly true of the *man of God*, the person who claims to be a minister or teacher of God's Word.
#3976 Those Who Can Get Others To Work Together Governments–KJV Administrations– NASB Those with gifts of administration– NIV	κυβερνήσεις = *kubernēseis* Pronunciation: [koo-ber'-nay-sees] Parsing (part of speech): noun Case—accusative Gender—feminine Number—plural Stem or root—from κυβέρνησις, εως Concordance References: ⇒ Strong's #2941 kubernēsis ⇒ NIV #3236 kubernēsis ⇒ NASB #2941 kubernēsis **1 Cor. 12:28** And God hath set some in the church, first apostles, secondarily prophets, thirdly teachers, after that miracles,	Those with gifts of administration; those who can get others to work together; a God-given ability to lead. **Practical Application** The Greek word is descriptive (*kuberneseis*). It refers to the pilot of a ship, the person who steers the ship through the dangerous channels of the oceans. The church, of course, needs such persons who can give it direction as it moves along on its journey to reach the destination God has appointed for it.

ENGLISH WORD	GREEK WORD AND VERSE	THE WORD MEANS...

Administrations–
NKJV
Those who can get others to work together–NLT
 	
POSB REFERENCE
(1 Cor.12:27-30; esp. v.28)
Note 5, point 1g
	then gifts of healings, helps, **governments**, diversities of tongues. [KJV]
	    And God has appointed in the church, first apostles, second prophets, third teachers, then miracles, then gifts of healings, helps, **administrations**, *various* kinds of tongues. [NASB]
	    And in the church God has appointed first of all apostles, second prophets, third teachers, then workers of miracles, also those having gifts of healing, those able to help others, **those with gifts of administration**, and those speaking in different kinds of tongues. [NIV]
	    And God has appointed these in the church: first apostles, second prophets, third teachers, after that miracles, then gifts of healings, helps, **administrations**, varieties of tongues. [NKJV]
	    Here is a list of some of the members that God has placed in the body of Christ: first are apostles, second are prophets, third are teachers, then those who do miracles, those who have the gift of healing, those who can help others, **those who can get others to work together**, those who speak in unknown languages. [NLT]
	    καὶ οὓς μὲν ἔθετο ὁ Θεὸς ἐν τῇ ἐκκλησίᾳ πρῶτον ἀποστόλους, δεύτερον προφήτας, τρίτον διδασκάλους, ἔπειτα δυνάμεις, εἶτα χαρίσματα ἰαμάτων, ἀντιλήψεις, **κυβερνήσεις**, γένη γλωσσῶν. [GNS]
	    καὶ οὓς μὲν ἔθετο ὁ θεὸς ἐν τῇ ἐκκλησίᾳ πρῶτον ἀποστόλους, δεύτερον προφήτας, τρίτον διδασκάλους, ἔπειτα δυνάμεις, ἔπειτα χαρίσματα ἰαμάτων, ἀντιλήμψεις, **κυβερνήσεις**, γένη γλωσσῶν. [GNT]	

#3977
 	
Those Who Work For Peace
 	
Peacemakers–KJV
Peacemakers–NASB
Peacemakers–NIV
Peacemakers–NKJV
Those who work for peace–NLT
 	
POSB REFERENCE
(Mt.5:9)
Note 8
	εἰρηνοποιοί = *eirenopoios*
	Pronunciation: [i-ray-nop-oy-os]
	Parsing (part of speech): pronominal adjective
	    Case—nominative
	    Gender—masculine
	    Number—plural
	    Stem or root—from εἰρηνοποιός, ου
	Concordance References:
	  ⇒ Strong's #1518 eirenopoios
	  ⇒ NIV #1648 eirenopoios
	  ⇒ NASB #1518 eirenopoios
	
	Matthew 5:9
	Blessed *are* the **peacemakers**: for they shall be called the children of God. [KJV]
	    "Blessed are the **peacemakers**, for they shall be called sons of God. [NASB]
	    Blessed are the **peacemakers**, for they will be called sons of God. [NIV]
	    Blessed are the **peacemakers**, [NKJV]
	For they shall be called sons of God. Matthew 5:9
	    God blesses **those who work for peace**, for they will be called the children of God. [NLT]
	    Μακάριοι οἱ **εἰρηνοποιοί**· ὅτι αὐτοὶ υἱοὶ Θεοῦ κληθήσονται. [GNS]
	    μακάριοι οἱ **εἰρηνοποιοί**, ὅτι αὐτοὶ υἱοὶ θεοῦ κληθήσονται. [GNT]
		Peacemakers; to make peace; those who work for peace.
		
		Practical Application
		    A peacemaker brings people together; but even more important than this, he makes peace between people and God. A peacemaker...
		• solves disputes and erases divisions.
		• reconciles differences and eliminates strife.
		• silences tongues and builds right relationships.
		Who is the peacemaker?
		1. The person who strives to make peace with God (Romans 5:1; Ephes. 2:14-17). He conquers the inner struggle, settles the inner tension, handles the inner pressure. He takes the struggle within his heart between good and evil, and strives for the good and conquers the bad.
		2. The person who strives at every opportunity to make peace *within* others. He seeks and leads others to make their peace with God—to conquer their inner struggle, to settle their inner tension, to handle their inner pressure.
		3. The person who strives at every opportunity to make peace *between* others. He works to solve disputes and erase divisions, to reconcile differences and eliminate strife, to silence tongues and build relationships.

#3978
 	
Those With Gifts Of Administration
 	
Governments–KJV
Administrations–NASB
	κυβερνήσεις = *kubernëseis*
	Pronunciation: [koo-ber'-nay-sees]
	Parsing (part of speech): noun
	    Case—accusative
	    Gender—feminine
	    Number—plural
	    Stem or root—from κυβέρνησις, εως
	Concordance References:
	  ⇒ Strong's #2941 kubernësis
	  ⇒ NIV #3236 kubernësis
	  ⇒ NASB #2941 kubernësis
		Those with gifts of administration; those who can get others to work together; a God-given ability to lead.
		
		Practical Application
		    The Greek word is descriptive (*kuberneseis*). It refers to the pilot of a ship, the person who steers the ship through the dangerous channels of the oceans. The church, of course, needs such persons who can give it direction as it moves

ENGLISH WORD	GREEK WORD AND VERSE	THE WORD MEANS...
Those with gifts of administration–NIV Administrations–NKJV Those who can get others to work together–NLT **POSB REFERENCE** (1 Cor.12:27-30; esp. v.28) Note 5, point 1g	**1 Cor. 12:28** And God hath set some in the church, first apostles, secondarily prophets, thirdly teachers, after that miracles, then gifts of healings, helps, **governments**, diversities of tongues. [KJV] And God has appointed in the church, first apostles, second prophets, third teachers, then miracles, then gifts of healings, helps, **administrations**, *various* kinds of tongues. [NASB] And in the church God has appointed first of all apostles, second prophets, third teachers, then workers of miracles, also those having gifts of healing, those able to help others, **those with gifts of administration**, and those speaking in different kinds of tongues. [NIV] And God has appointed these in the church: first apostles, second prophets, third teachers, after that miracles, then gifts of healings, helps, **administrations**, varieties of tongues. [NKJV] Here is a list of some of the members that God has placed in the body of Christ: first are apostles, second are prophets, third are teachers, then those who do miracles, those who have the gift of healing, those who can help others, **those who can get others to work together**, those who speak in unknown languages. [NLT] καὶ οὓς μὲν ἔθετο ὁ Θεὸς ἐν τῇ ἐκκλησίᾳ πρῶτον ἀποστόλους, δεύτερον προφήτας, τρίτον διδασκάλους, ἔπειτα δυνάμεις, εἶτα χαρίσματα ἰαμάτων, ἀντιλήψεις, **κυβερνήσεις**, γένη γλωσσων. [GNS] καὶ οὓς μὲν ἔθετο ὁ θεὸς ἐν τῇ ἐκκλησίᾳ πρῶτον ἀποστόλους, δεύτερον προφήτας, τρίτον διδασκάλους, ἔπειτα δυνάμεις, ἔπειτα χαρίσματα ἰαμάτων, ἀντιλήμψεις, **κυβερνήσεις**, γένη γλωσσων. [GNT]	along on its journey to reach the destination God has appointed for it.

#3979
Though He Dies–
Though He Were Dead–
Though He May Die
Though They Die
 	
Though he were dead–KJV
Even if he dies–NASB
Though he dies–NIV
Though he may die–NKJV
Though they die–NLT
 	
POSB REFERENCE
(Jn.11:25-27; esp. v.25)
Note 4, point 2a
	καν ἀποθάνῃ = *kan apothanë*
	Pronunciation: [kahn ha-po-thah-nay]
	Parsing *kan* (part of speech): adjective
	    Type—adverb
	AND
	Parsing *kan* (part of speech): conjunction
	    Type—subordinating
	    Stem or root—from *κἄν*
	Parsing *apothanë* (part of speech): verb
	    Mood—subjunctive
	    Tense—aorist
	    Voice—active
	    Person—3rd person
	    Number—singular
	    Stem or root—from *ἀποθνήσκω*
	Concordance References:
	⇒ Strong's #2579 kan + 599 apothnesko
	⇒ NIV #2829 kan [even though] + 633 apothnesko [dies]
	⇒ NASB #2579 kan + 599 apothnesko
	
	John 11:25
	Jesus said unto her, I am the resurrection, and the life: he that believeth in me, **though he were dead**, yet shall he live: [KJV]
	Jesus said to her, "I am the resurrection and the life; he who believes in Me shall live **even if he dies**, [NASB]
	Jesus said to her, "I am the resurrection and the life. He who believes in me will live, even **though he dies**; [NIV]
	Jesus said to her, "I am the resurrection and the life. He who believes in Me, **though he may die**, he shall live. [NKJV]
	Jesus told her, "I am the resurrection and the life. Those who believe in me, even **though they die** like everyone else, will live again. [NLT]
	εἶπεν αὐτῇ ὁ Ἰησοῦς, Ἐγώ εἰμι ἡ ἀνάστασις καὶ ἡ ζωή. ὁ πιστεύων εἰς ἐμὲ **καν ἀποθάνῃ**, ζήσεται· [GNS]
	εἶπεν αὐτῇ ὁ Ἰησοῦς, Ἐγώ εἰμι ἡ ἀνάστασις καὶ ἡ ζωή· ὁ πιστεύων εἰς ἐμὲ **καν ἀποθάνῃ** ζήσεται, [GNT]
		Though He dies; though He were dead; even if He dies.
		
		Practical Application
		Note Jesus' great promise:
		"He who believes in me, will live, even though he dies (*kan apothanë*)" [NIV]. He lives in the other world: in heaven, in the spiritual dimension of being, in the very presence of God Himself. The believer who has passed from this world is not some place...
		• in a semi-conscious state.
		• in a deep sleep, locked up in a compartment someplace.
		• in space moving about and floating around on a fluffy cloud.
		The believer is fully alive: he lives in heaven, in the other world, in the very presence of God Himself. Another world exists just as this world exists. It is not a world that lies out in the future; it is a world that exists now—a spiritual world, a spiritual dimension—a world that the Bible calls heaven. It is the spiritual world and dimension where God and Christ and angels and all those who have gone on before now live.
		The point is this: when a person who has *believed in Jesus* Christ dies, he goes to live in heaven, in the spiritual world where God and Christ and the heavenly hosts live. *Hallelujah!* Only the word "hallelujah" can express the hope and joy that fills the soul of the true believer.

ENGLISH WORD	GREEK WORD AND VERSE	THE WORD MEANS...
tude–NKJV **Thousands–NLT** **POSB** **REFERENCE** (Lk.12:1) Note 1	an **innumerable multitude** of people, insomuch that they trode one upon another, he began to say unto his disciples first of all, Beware ye of the leaven of the Pharisees, which is hypocrisy. [KJV] Under these circumstances, after so **many thousands** of the multitude had gathered together that they were stepping on one another, He began saying to His disciples first *of all,* "Beware of the leaven of the Pharisees, which is hypocrisy. [NASB] Meanwhile, when a crowd of **many thousands** had gathered, so that they were trampling on one another, Jesus began to speak first to his disciples, saying: "Be on your guard against the yeast of the Pharisees, which is hypocrisy. [NIV] In the meantime, when an **innumerable multitude** of people had gathered together, so that they trampled one another, He began to say to His disciples first *of all,* "Beware of the leaven of the Pharisees, which is hypocrisy. [NKJV] Meanwhile, the crowds grew until **thousands** were milling about and crushing each other. Jesus turned first to his disciples and warned them, "Beware of the yeast of the Pharisees—beware of their hypocrisy. [NLT] Ἐν οἷς ἐπισυναχθεισῶν τῶν **μυριάδων** τοῦ ὄχλου, ὥστε καταπατεῖν ἀλλήλους, ἤρξατο λέγειν πρὸς τοὺς μαθητὰς αὐτοῦ πρῶτον, Προσέχετε ἑαυτοῖς ἀπὸ τῆς ζύμης τῶν Φαρισαίων, ἥτις ἐστὶν ὑπόκρισις. [GNS] Ἐν οἷς ἐπισυναχθεισῶν τῶν **μυριάδων** τοῦ ὄχλου, ὥστε καταπατεῖν ἀλλήλους, ἤρξατο λέγειν πρὸς τοὺς μαθητὰς αὐτοῦ πρῶτον, Προσέχετε ἑαυτοῖς ἀπὸ τῆς ζύμης, ἥτις ἐστὶν ὑπόκρισις, τῶν Φαρισαίων. [GNT]	

#3988
Threw
 	
Cast–KJV
Threw–NASB
Flung–NIV
Threw–NKJV
Threw–NLT
 	
POSB
REFERENCE
(Rev.12:3-4; esp.v.4)
Note 2
	ἔβαλεν = ebalen
	Pronunciation: [eh-bal'-lehn]
	Parsing (part of speech): verb
	   Mood—indicative
	   Tense—aorist
	   Voice—active
	   Person—3rd person
	   Number—singular
	   Stem or root—from βάλλω
	Concordance References:
	  ⇒ Strong's #906 ballö
	  ⇒ NIV #965 ballö
	  ⇒ NASB #906 ballö
	
	Rev. 12:4
	And his tail drew the third part of the stars of heaven, and did **cast** them to the earth: and the dragon stood before the woman which was ready to be delivered, for to devour her child as soon as it was born. [KJV]
	
	And his tail swept away a third of the stars of heaven, and **threw** them to the earth. And the dragon stood before the woman who was about to give birth, so that when she gave birth he might devour her child. [NASB]
	
	His tail swept a third of the stars out of the sky and **flung** them to the earth. The dragon stood in front of the woman who was about to give birth, so that he might devour her child the moment it was born. [NIV]
	
	His tail drew a third of the stars of heaven and **threw** them to the earth. And the dragon stood before the woman who was ready to give birth, to devour her Child as soon as it was born. [NKJV]
	
	His tail dragged down one-third of the stars, which he **threw** to the earth. He stood before the woman as she was about to give birth to her child, ready to devour the baby as soon as it was born. [NLT]
	
	καὶ ἡ οὐρὰ αὐτοῦ σύρει τὸ τρίτον τῶν ἀστέρων τοῦ οὐρανοῦ, καὶ **ἔβαλεν** αὐτοὺς εἰς τὴν γῆν· καὶ ὁ δράκων ἕστηκεν ἐνώπιον τῆς γυναικὸς τῆς μελλούσης τεκεῖν, ἵνα, ὅταν τέκῃ τὸ τέκνον αὐτῆς, καταφάγῃ. [GNS]
		Flung, cast, threw; to throw down; to banish; to swing.
		
		Practical Application
		He "threw" (*ebalen*) them down or cast them down. This is aorist tense which means a once-for-all act; that is, it tells us what Satan did long ago.
		
		The point is this: today, in the present moment, Satan has authority over one third of the stars or angels of heaven. How? Because in the past, he cast them down with himself.

ENGLISH WORD	GREEK WORD AND VERSE	THE WORD MEANS...
	καὶ ἡ οὐρὰ αὐτοῦ σύρει τὸ τρίτον τῶν ἀστέρων τοῦ οὐρανοῦ καὶ **ἔβαλεν** αὐτοὺς εἰς τὴν γῆν. καὶ ὁ δράκων ἕστηκεν ἐνώπιον τῆς γυναικὸς τῆς μελλούσης τεκεῖν, ἵνα ὅταν τέκῃ τὸ τέκνον αὐτῆς καταφάγῃ. [GNT]	

#3989
 	
Through Christ Jesus
 	
In Christ Jesus–KJV
In Christ Jesus–NASB
By Christ Jesus–NIV
In Christ Jesus–NKJV
Through Christ Jesus–NLT
 	
POSB REFERENCE
(Rom.3:24)
Note 3, point 2
	ἐν Χριστῷ Ἰησοῦ· = en Christō Iēsou
	Pronunciation: [en khris-tow' ee-ay-soo']
	Parsing en (part of speech): preposition
	  Case—dative
	  Stem or root—from **ἐν**
	Concordance References:
	⇒ Strong's #1722 en + 5547 Christos + 2424 Iēsous
	⇒ NIV #1877 en [by] + 5986 Christos [Christ] + 2652 Iēsous [Jesus]
	⇒ NASB #1722 en + 5547 Christos + 2424 Iēsous
	
	Romans 3:24
	Being justified freely by his grace through the redemption that is **in Christ Jesus**: [KJV]
	Being justified as a gift by His grace through the redemption which is **in Christ Jesus**; [NASB]
	And are justified freely by his grace through the redemption that came **by Christ Jesus**. [NIV]
	Being justified freely by His grace through the redemption that is **in Christ Jesus**, [NKJV]
	Yet now God in his gracious kindness declares us not guilty. He has done this **through Christ Jesus**, who has freed us by taking away our sins. [NLT]
	δικαιούμενοι δωρεὰν τῇ αὐτοῦ χάριτι διὰ τῆς ἀπολυτρώσεως τῆς **ἐν Χριστῷ Ἰησοῦ·** [GNS]
	δικαιούμενοι δωρεὰν τῇ αὐτοῦ χάριτι διὰ τῆς ἀπολυτρώσεως τῆς **ἐν Χριστῷ Ἰησοῦ·** [GNT]
		By Christ Jesus, *in* Christ Jesus, *through* Christ Jesus.
		
		Practical Application
		Redemption is "through Christ Jesus," wrought through His death and sufferings. Of this there can be no doubt; the fact is critical to a person's destiny. Redemption is not brought about...
		• by the life of Christ.
		• by the power of Christ.
		• by the example of Christ.
		Scripture is abundantly clear about this. His cross and His sacrifice in death are what brought about redemption. Redemption is because of the shed blood of Jesus Christ, God's very own Son. Through Christ and Christ alone, redemption is...
		• accomplished
		• a reality
		• wrought
		• a truth
		• a fact
		• fulfilled

#3990
 	
Through The Prophetic Writings
 	
By the scriptures of the prophets–KJV
By the Scriptures of the prophets–NASB
Through the prophetic writings–NIV
By the prophetic Scriptures–NKJV
As the prophets foretold–NLT
 	
POSB REFERENCE
(Rom.16:25-26, esp. v.26)
Note 3, point 2
	διὰ γραφῶν προφητικῶν = dia graphōn prophētikōn
	Pronunciation: [di-ah graf-own' prof-ay-tik-own']
	Parsing dia (part of speech): preposition
	  Case—genitive
	  Stem or root—from **διὰ**
	Parsing graphōn (part of speech): noun
	  Case—genitive
	  Gender—feminine
	  Number—plural
	  Stem or root—from **γραφή**, ῆς
	Parsing prophētikōn (part of speech): adjective
	  Case—genitive
	  Gender—feminine
	  Number—plural
	  Stem or root—from **προφητικός**, ή, όν
	Concordance References:
	⇒ Strong's #1223 dia + 1124 graphē + 4397 prophētikos
	⇒ NIV #1328 dia [through] + 1210 graphē [writings] + 4738 prophētikos [prophetic]
	⇒ NASB #1223 dia + 1124 graphē + 4397 prophētikos
	
	Romans 16:26
	But now is made manifest, and **by the scriptures of the prophets**, according to the commandment of the everlasting God, made known to all nations for the obedience of faith: [KJV]
	But now is manifested, and **by the Scriptures of the prophets**, according to the commandment of the eternal God, has been made known to all the nations, *leading* to obedience of faith; [NASB]
	But now revealed and made known **through the prophetic writings** by the command of the eternal God, so that all nations might believe and obey him—[NIV]
	But now has been made manifest, and **by the prophetic Scriptures** has been made known to all nations, according to the commandment of the everlasting
		Through the prophetic writings, by the Scriptures of the prophets, as the prophets foretold.
		
		Practical Application
		God wants the world to know the gospel; therefore, He has commanded that it be revealed and proclaimed to the world. But note the crucial point: it is revealed through the prophetic writings (*dia graphōn prophētikōn*). This is extremely important, for it tells us exactly where we are to find out about God and His message to the world. We do not discover God by natural reasoning: God reveals Himself to us.
		There are two questions that desperately need to be studied by everyone.
		1. Since God has revealed how men are to become acceptable to Him, why do men continue to create their own ideas about how to reach God? Why do men continue to think they will be acceptable to God if they can just do enough good to pacify God? Why do most men continue to think that God will never reject them, that they are not evil enough to be unacceptable to God?
		2. Since God has revealed the gospel in the prophetic Scriptures, why do men not rush to the Scriptures to find the truth? Why do men not search the Scriptures daily to find out what God has revealed? (cp. Acts 17:11).

ENGLISH WORD	GREEK WORD AND VERSE	THE WORD MEANS...
Time–NIV Day–NKJV Day...now–NLT **POSB REFERENCE** (Acts 20:18-19; esp. v.18) Note 2, point 1	Number—singular Stem or root— from χρόνος, ου Concordance References: ⇒ Strong's #5550 chronos ⇒ NIV #5989 chronos ⇒ NASB #5550 chronos ### Acts 20:18 And when they were come to him, he said unto them, Ye know, from the first day that I came into Asia, after what manner I have been with you at all **seasons**, [KJV] And when they had come to him, he said to them, "You yourselves know, from the first day that I set foot in Asia, how I was with you the whole **time**, [NASB] When they arrived, he said to them: "You know how I lived the whole **time** I was with you, from the first day I came into the province of Asia. [NIV] And when they had come to him, he said to them: "You know, from the first **day** that I came to Asia, in what manner I always lived among you, [NKJV] When they arrived he declared, "You know that from the **day** I set foot in the province of Asia until **now** [NLT] ὡς δὲ παρεγένοντο πρὸς αὐτὸν, εἶπεν αὐτοῖς, Ὑμεῖς ἐπίστασθε, ἀπὸ πρώτης ἡμέρας ἀφ' ἧς ἐπέβην εἰς τὴν Ἀσίαν, πῶς μεθ' ὑμῶν τὸν πάντα **χρόνον** ἐγενόμην, [GNS] ὡς δὲ παρεγένοντο πρὸς αὐτὸν εἶπεν αὐτοῖς, Ὑμεῖς ἐπίστασθε, ἀπὸ πρώτης ἡμέρας ἀφ' ἧς ἐπέβην εἰς τὴν Ἀσίαν πῶς μεθ' ὑμῶν τὸν πάντα **χρόνον** ἐγενόμην, [GNT]	first day" (*chronon*) through all kinds of situations and circumstances.
#3995 **Time, At That** At that time–KJV On that day–NASB On that day–NIV At that time–NKJV At the killing of Stephen–NLT **POSB REFERENCE** (Acts 8:1) Note 1, point 2	ἐν ἐκείνῃ τῇ ἡμέρᾳ = en ekeinē tē hēmera Pronunciation: [en eh-keh-ee-nay tay hay-mer'-ah] Parsing *hēmera* (part of speech): noun Case—dative Gender—feminine Number—singular Stem or root—from ἡμέρα, ας Concordance References: ⇒ Strong's #1722 en + 1565 ekeinos + 3588 ho + 2250 hēmera ⇒ NIV #1877 en [On] + 1697 ekeinos [that] + 3836 ho + 2465 hēmera [day] ⇒ NASB #1722 en + 1565 ekeinos + 3588 ho + 2250 hēmera ### Acts 8:1 And Saul was consenting unto his death. And **at that time** there was a great persecution against the church which was at Jerusalem; and they were all scattered abroad throughout the regions of Judaea and Samaria, except the apostles. [KJV] And Saul was in hearty agreement with putting him to death. And **on that day** a great persecution arose against the church in Jerusalem; and they were all scattered throughout the regions of Judea and Samaria, except the apostles. [NASB] And Saul was there, giving approval to his death. **On that day** a great persecution broke out against the church at Jerusalem, and all except the apostles were scattered throughout Judea and Samaria. [NIV] Now Saul was consenting to his death. **At that time** a great persecution arose against the church which was at Jerusalem; and they were all scattered throughout the regions of Judea and Samaria, except the apostles. [NKJV] Saul was one of the official witnesses **at the killing of Stephen**. A great wave of persecution began that day, sweeping over the church in Jerusalem, and all the believers except the apostles fled into Judea and Samaria. [NLT]	On that day; at that time. #### Practical Application The words "at that time" mean on that very same day. Saul wished to act and to act quickly in wiping out the church. The believers were frightened and on the run. He had to strike immediately to catch them before they could escape.

ENGLISH WORD	GREEK WORD AND VERSE	THE WORD MEANS...
	Σαῦλος δὲ ἦν συνευδοκῶν τῇ ἀναιρέσει αὐτοῦ. Ἐγένετο δὲ **ἐν ἐκείνῃ τῇ ἡμέρᾳ** διωγμὸς μέγας ἐπὶ τὴν ἐκκλησίαν τὴν ἐν Ἱεροσολύμοις· πάντες τε διεσπάρησαν κατὰ τὰς χώρας τῆς Ἰουδαίας καὶ Σαμαρείας, πλὴν τῶν ἀποστόλων. [GNS] Σαῦλος δὲ ἦν συνευδοκῶν τῇ ἀναιρέσει αὐτοῦ. Ἐγένετο δὲ **ἐν ἐκείνῃ τῇ ἡμέρᾳ** διωγμὸς μέγας ἐπὶ τὴν ἐκκλησίαν τὴν ἐν Ἱεροσολύμοις, πάντες δὲ διεσπάρησαν κατὰ τὰς χώρας τῆς Ἰουδαίας καὶ Σαμαρείας πλὴν τῶν ἀποστόλων. [GNT]	

#3996
Time, The
 	
The time–KJV
The time–NASB
The present time–NIV
The time–NKJV
Time–NLT
 	
POSB
REFERENCE
(Romans 13:11)
Note 1
	τὸν καιρόν = *ton kairon*
	Pronunciation: [ton kahee-ron']
	Parsing (part of speech): noun
	    Case—accusative
	    Gender—masculine
	    Number—singular
	    Stem or root—from **καιρός**, οῦ
	Concordance References:
	  ⇒ Strong's #3588 ho + 2540 kairos
	  ⇒ NIV #3836 ho [the] + 2789 kairos [present time]
	  ⇒ NASB #3588 ho + 2540 kairos
	
	### Romans 13:11
	And that, knowing **the time**, that now it is high time to awake out of sleep: for now is our salvation nearer than when we believed. [KJV]
	And this do, knowing **the time**, that it is already the hour for you to awaken from sleep; for now salvation is nearer to us than when we believed. [NASB]
	And do this, understanding **the present time**. The hour has come for you to wake up from your slumber, because our salvation is nearer now than when we first believed. [NIV]
	And *do* this, knowing **the time**, that now *it is* high time to awake out of sleep; for now our salvation *is* nearer than when we *first* believed. [NKJV]
	Another reason for right living is that you know how late it is; **time** is running out. Wake up, for the coming of our salvation is nearer now than when we first believed. [NLT]
	Καὶ τοῦτο, εἰδότες **τὸν καιρόν**, ὅτι ὥρα ὑμᾶς ἤδη ἐξ ὕπνου ἐγερθῆναι· νῦν γὰρ ἐγγύτερον ἡμῶν ἡ σωτηρία η ὅτε ἐπιστεύσαμεν. [GNS]
	Καὶ τοῦτο εἰδότες **τὸν καιρόν**, ὅτι ὥρα ἤδη ὑμᾶς ἐξ ὕπνου ἐγερθῆναι, νῦν γὰρ ἐγγύτερον ἡμῶν ἡ σωτηρία η ὅτε ἐπιστεύσαμεν. [GNT]
		The last time; opportunity. Time (viewed as an occasion rather than an extent), appointed or proper time, season, age. It means the critical period; the strategic or special period of time.
		
		#### Practical Application
		The believer is to know the time. The word "knowing" (*eridotes*) means to make sure that you know; do not dare miss knowing.
		What strategic or critical period of time is meant? What is the period of human history that we must not overlook?
		⇒ The day of "our salvation," the day which is nearer than when we first believed.
		⇒ The day which is at hand, the day when we will meet the Lord Jesus Christ face to face.

#3997
Timid
 	
Base–KJV
Meek–NASB
Timid–NIV
Lowly–NKJV
Timid–NLT
 	
POSB
REFERENCE
(2 Cor.10:1-2; esp. v.1)
Note 1
	ταπεινός = *tapeinos*
	Pronunciation: [tap-i-nos']
	Parsing (part of speech): adjective
	    Case—nominative
	    Gender—masculine
	    Number—singular
	    Stem or root—from **ταπεινός**, ή, όν
	Concordance References:
	  ⇒ Strong's #5011 tapeinos
	  ⇒ NIV #5424 tapeinos
	  ⇒ NASB #5011 tapeinos
	
	### 2 Cor. 10:1
	Now I Paul myself beseech you by the meekness and gentleness of Christ, who in presence *am* **base** among you, but being absent am bold toward you: [KJV]
	Now I, Paul, myself urge you by the meekness and gentleness of Christ— I who am **meek** when face to face with you, but bold toward you when absent! [NASB]
	By the meekness and gentleness of Christ, I appeal to you—I, Paul, who am "**timid**" when face to face with you, but "bold" when away! [NIV]
	Now I, Paul, myself am pleading with you by the
		Timid, meek, base, humble, lowly, gentle.
		
		#### Practical Application
		Some were saying that Paul was a coward. This is what is meant by the word "timid" (*tapeinos*). They were saying that Paul was bold in his instructions; that is, he rebuked the church when he was writing to them, but he was a coward when it came to speaking face to face with them.

ENGLISH WORD	GREEK WORD AND VERSE	THE WORD MEANS...
	meekness and gentleness of Christ—who in presence *am* **lowly** among you, but being absent am bold toward you. [NKJV] Now I, Paul, plead with you. I plead with the gentleness and kindness that Christ himself would use, even though some of you say I am bold in my letters but **timid** in person. [NLT] Αὐτὸς δὲ ἐγὼ Παῦλος παρακαλῶ ὑμᾶς διὰ τῆς πραότητος καὶ ἐπιεικείας τοῦ Χριστοῦ, ὃς κατὰ πρόσωπον μὲν **ταπεινὸς** ἐν ὑμῖν, ἀπὼν δὲ θαρρῶ εἰς ὑμᾶς· [GNS] Αὐτὸς δὲ ἐγὼ Παῦλος παρακαλῶ ὑμᾶς διὰ τῆς πραΰτητος καὶ ἐπιεικείας τοῦ Χριστοῦ, ὃς κατὰ πρόσωπον μὲν **ταπεινὸς** ἐν ὑμῖν, ἀπὼν δὲ θαρρῶ εἰς ὑμᾶς· [GNT]	

#3998
To Become Like
 	
Conformed to the image–KJV
Conformed to the image–NASB
Conformed to the likeness–NIV
Conformed to the image–NKJV
To become like–NLT
 	
POSB REFERENCE
(Rom.8:29)
Note 2, point 2
(Rom.8:29)
Note 2, point 2a
(Rom.8:29)
Note 2, point 2b
	συμμόρφους τῆς εἰκόνος = *summorphous tēs eikonos*
	Pronunciation: [soom-mor-foos' tace i-kone'-os]
	Parsing *summorphous* (part of speech): adjective
	    Case—accusative
	    Gender—masculine
	    Number—plural
	    Stem or root—from σύμμορφος, ον
	Parsing *eikonos* (part of speech): noun
	    Case—genitive
	    Gender—feminine
	    Number—singular
	    Stem or root—from εἰκών, όνος
	Concordance References:
	⇒ Strong's #4832 summorphos + 3588 ho + 1504 eikōn
	⇒ NIV #5215 summorphos [conformed] + 3836 ho [the] + 1635 eikōn [likeness]
	⇒ NASB #4832 summorphos + 3588 ho + 1504 eikōn
	
	Romans 8:29
	For whom he did foreknow, he also did predestinate to be **conformed to the image** of his Son, that he might be the firstborn among many brethren. [KJV]
	
	For whom He foreknew, He also predestined to become **conformed to the image** of His Son, that He might be the first-born among many brethren; [NASB]
	
	For those God foreknew he also predestined to be **conformed to the likeness** of his Son, that he might be the firstborn among many brothers. [NIV]
	
	For whom He foreknew, He also predestined *to be* **conformed to the image** of His Son, that He might be the firstborn among many brethren. [NKJV]
	
	For God knew his people in advance, and he chose them **to become like** his Son, so that his Son would be the firstborn, with many brothers and sisters. [NLT]
	
	ὅτι οὓς προέγνω, καὶ προώρισε **συμμόρφους τῆς εἰκόνος** τοῦ υἱοῦ αὐτοῦ, εἰς τὸ εἶναι αὐτὸν πρωτότοκον ἐν πολλοῖς ἀδελφοῖς· [GNS]
	
	ὅτι οὓς προέγνω, καὶ προώρισεν **συμμόρφους τῆς εἰκόνος** τοῦ υἱοῦ αὐτοῦ, εἰς τὸ εἶναι αὐτὸν πρωτότοκον ἐν πολλοῖς ἀδελφοῖς· [GNT]
		Conformed to the likeness, conformed to the image; to become like.
		
		### Practical Application
		"To become like" (*summorphous*) means the very same form or image as Christ. Within our nature—our being, our person—we will be made just like Christ. As He is perfect and eternal—without disease and pain, sin and death—so we will be perfected just like Him. We will be transformed into His very likeness. "Image" or "likeness" (*eikonos*) means a derived or a given likeness. The image or likeness of Christ is not something which believers merit or for which they work; it is not an image that comes from their own nature or character. No man can earn or produce the perfection and eternal life possessed by Christ. The image of Christ, His perfection and life, is a gift of God. To be conformed to the image of God's Son means...
		• to participate in the divine nature (2 Peter 1:4).
		• to be adopted as a son of God (Ephes. 1:5).
		• to be holy and without blame before Him (Ephes. 1:4; Ephes. 4:24).
		• to bear the image of the heavenly: which is an incorruptible, immortal body (1 Cor. 15:49-54; cp. 1 Cor. 15:42-44).
		• to have one's body fashioned (conformed) just like His glorious body (Phil. 3:21).
		• to be changed (transformed) into the same image of the Lord (2 Cor. 3:18).
		• to be recreated just like Him (1 John 3:2-3).

#3999
To It
 	
Into it–KJV
Into it–NASB
Into it–NIV
Into it–NKJV
To it–NLT
	εἰς αὐτήν = *eis autēn*
	Pronunciation: [ice ow-tayn']
	Parsing *eis* (part of speech): preposition
	    Case—accusative
	    Stem or root—from εἰς
	Parsing *autēn* (part of speech): noun
	    Type—pronoun
	    Case—accusative
	    Gender—feminine
	    Person—3rd person
	    Number—singular
	    Stem or root—from αὐτός, ή, ό
		Into it, to it.
		
		### Practical Application
		Believers will bring their glory and honor *to the heavenly city* and give all their glory and honor to the Lord who bestowed it upon them. Believers owe everything they are to God and Christ; therefore, they are going to acknowledge and praise God and Christ for giving them so great a salvation. Note that believers will bring their glory and honor *to the city*.
		⇒ This speaks as though believers will be

ENGLISH WORD	GREEK WORD AND VERSE	THE WORD MEANS...
POSB REFERENCE (Rev.21:24-27; esp. v.24) Note 1, point 5	Concordance References: ⇒ Strong's #1519 eis + 846 autos ⇒ NIV #1650 eis [into] + 899 autos [it] ⇒ NASB #1519 eis + 846 autos **Rev. 21:24** And the nations of them which are saved shall walk in the light of it: and the kings of the earth do bring their glory and honour **into it**. [KJV] And the nations shall walk by its light, and the kings of the earth shall bring their glory **into it**. [NASB] The nations will walk by its light, and the kings of the earth will bring their splendor **into it**. [NIV] And the nations of those who are saved shall walk in its light, and the kings of the earth bring their glory and honor **into it**. [NKJV] The nations of the earth will walk in its light, and the rulers of the world will come and bring their glory **to it**. [NLT] καὶ τὰ ἔθνη τῶν σωζομένων ἐν τῷ φωτὶ αὐτῆς περιπατήσουσι· καὶ οἱ βασιλεῖς τῆς γῆς φέρουσι τὴν δόξαν καὶ τὴν τιμῶν αὐτῶν **εἰς αὐτήν**· [GNS] καὶ περιπατήσουσιν τὰ ἔθνη διὰ τοῦ φωτὸς αὐτῆς, καὶ οἱ βασιλεῖς τῆς γῆς φέρουσιν τὴν δόξαν αὐτῶν **εἰς αὐτήν**, [GNT]	serving as kings of nations *outside the city*. ⇒ This speaks as though there will be special occasions when believers will gather *in the heavenly city*, gather to bring the glory and honor of their nations to God and Christ. Read it carefully (the Greek says *eis autën*), for this seems to be the picture being painted. One thing is sure: no matter what we may describe or picture, it is going to be far beyond anything we could ever describe or ask or even think. God's Word emphatically declares this. Believers will bring the glory and honor of their nations to (*eis autën*) the city. This shows that believers are the kings being spoken about, that believers will be coming from various rules or nations to bring the glory of their nations to God. Again the picture seems to be periodic celebrations of great worship. There will certainly be times when all believers come together from all corners of heaven (the spiritual world or universe) in a great celebration of worship. We would think that the Marriage Supper of the Lamb will not be the only time we will all be brought together to worship our dear Lord. Note again: Scripture says that as kings we enter "into" the city. It is as though we are coming from the far reaches of the spiritual world to bring the honor of our nations to God and Christ. But we must also repeat: whatever the case—wherever we are coming from—our minds could never imagine the glory and majesty of what will really happen.

#4000
To See
 	
To see–KJV
Look at–NASB
Look at–NIV
To see–NKJV
To see–NLT
 	
POSB REFERENCE (Mt.28:1) Note 2, point 2a
	θεωρῆσαι = *theōrēsai*
	Pronunciation: [theh-o-ray'-sah-ee]
	Parsing (part of speech): verb
	    Mood—infinitive
	    Tense—aorist
	    Voice—active
	    Stem or root—from θεωρέω
	Concordance References:
	⇒ Strong's #2334 theōreō
	⇒ NIV #2555 theōreō
	⇒ NASB #2334 theōreō
	
	Matthew 28:1
	In the end of the sabbath, as it began to dawn toward the first *day* of the week, came Mary Magdalene and the other Mary **to see** the sepulchre. [KJV]
	Now after the Sabbath, as it began to dawn toward the first *day* of the week, Mary Magdalene and the other Mary came to **look at** the grave. [NASB]
	After the Sabbath, at dawn on the first day of the week, Mary Magdalene and the other Mary went to **look at** the tomb. [NIV]
	Now after the Sabbath, as the first *day* of the week began to dawn, Mary Magdalene and the other Mary came **to see** the tomb. [NKJV]
	Early on Sunday morning, as the new day was dawning, Mary Magdalene and the other Mary went out **to see** the tomb. [NLT]
	Ὀψὲ δὲ σαββάτων, τῇ ἐπιφωσκούσῃ εἰς μίαν σαββάτων, ἦλθε Μαρία ἡ Μαγδαληνὴ καὶ ἡ ἄλλη Μαρία **θεωρῆσαι** τὸν τάφον. [GNS]
	Ὀψὲ δὲ σαββάτων, τῇ ἐπιφωσκούσῃ εἰς μίαν σαββάτων ἦλθεν Μαριὰμ ἡ Μαγδαληνὴ καὶ ἡ ἄλλη Μαρία **θεωρῆσαι** τὸν τάφον. [GNT]
		To look at; to see; to contemplate; to gaze; to observe in order to grasp; to perceive.
		
		Practical Application
		We can learn from the example of the two women who came to the empty tomb: They came to be close to their Lord, the One who meant so much to them, to mourn over Him, to think through all that had happened. This is an important point, for it perhaps explains why the women were more prepared to believe the miracle of the resurrection.

ENGLISH WORD	GREEK WORD AND VERSE	THE WORD MEANS...
	ered they are liars. [NLT] Οἶδα τὰ ἔργα σου, καὶ τὸν **κόπον** σου, καὶ τὴν ὑπομονήν σου, καὶ ὅτι οὐ δύνῃ βαστάσαι κακούς, καὶ ἐπειράσω τοὺς φάσκοντας εἶναι ἀποστόλους καὶ οὐκ εἰσί, καὶ εὗρες αὐτοὺς ψευδεῖς, [GNS] Οἶδα τὰ ἔργα σου καὶ τὸν **κόπον** καὶ τὴν ὑπομονήν σου καὶ ὅτι οὐ δύνῃ βαστάσαι κακούς, καὶ ἐπείρασας τοὺς λέγοντας ἑαυτοὺς ἀποστόλους καὶ οὐκ εἰσίν καὶ εὗρες αὐτοὺς ψευδεῖς, [GNT]	

#4005
Told
 	
Preached–KJV
Proclaiming–NASB
Proclaimed–NIV
Preached–NKJV
Told–NLT
 	
POSB
REFERENCE
(Acts 8:5)
Note 1
	ἐκήρυσσεν = ekērussen
	Pronunciation: [eh-kay-roos'-sen]
	Parsing (part of speech): verb
	  Mood—indicative
	  Tense—imperfect
	  Voice—active
	  Person—3rd person
	  Number—singular
	  Stem or root—from κηρύσσω
	Concordance References:
	⇒ Strong's #2784 kērussö
	⇒ NIV #3062 kērussö
	⇒ NASB #2784 kērussö
	
	Acts 8:5
	Then Philip went down to the city of Samaria, and **preached** Christ unto them. [KJV]
	And Philip went down to the city of Samaria and began **proclaiming** Christ to them. [NASB]
	Philip went down to a city in Samaria and **proclaimed** the Christ there. [NIV]
	Then Philip went down to the city of Samaria and **preached** Christ to them. [NKJV]
	Philip, for example, went to the city of Samaria and **told** the people there about the Messiah. [NLT]
	Φίλιππος δὲ κατελθὼν εἰς πόλιν τῆς Σαμαρείας, **ἐκήρυσσεν** αὐτοῖς τὸν Χριστόν. [GNS]
	Φίλιππος δὲ κατελθὼν εἰς [τὴν] πόλιν τῆς Σαμαρείας **ἐκήρυσσεν** αὐτοῖς τὸν Χριστόν. [GNT]
		To proclaim, make known, tell, preach.
		
		Practical Application
		This is important to note:
		⇒ The first great evangelistic thrust outside Jerusalem was carried out by a *layman*.
		⇒ The first time the term *evangelist* is used, it is used with a layman (Acts 21:8).
		
		Philip told (*ekērussen*) the people and preached Christ. Later on, he is said to preach (*euaggelizomeno*), to announce the good news, "concerning the kingdom of God" (Acts 8:12) [NIV]. These two great words are used in the New Testament for proclaiming the gospel. Philip, the layman, was a true servant of the Lord, a lay believer who preached Christ. He was a layman who dedicated his time and energy to proclaiming the things concerning the kingdom of God.

#4006
Told
 	
Charged–KJV
Gave [them] orders–NASB
Commanded–NIV
Commanded–NKJV
Told–NLT
 	
POSB
REFERENCE
(Mk.7:36)
Note 5
	διεστείλατο = diesteilato
	Pronunciation: [dee-es-teel'-ah-tow]
	Parsing (part of speech): verb
	  Mood—indicative
	  Tense—aorist
	  Voice—middle
	  Person—3rd person
	  Number—singular
	  Stem or root—from διαστέλλω
	Concordance References:
	⇒ Strong's #1291 diastellomai
	⇒ NIV #1403 diastellö
	⇒ NASB #1291 diastellö
	
	Mark 7:36
	And he **charged** them that they should tell no man: but the more he charged them, so much the more a great deal they published it; [KJV]
	And He **gave them orders** not to tell anyone; but the more He ordered them, the more widely they continued to proclaim it. [NASB]
	Jesus **commanded** them not to tell anyone. But the more he did so, the more they kept talking about it. [NIV]
	Then He **commanded** them that they should tell no one; but the more He commanded them, the more widely they proclaimed it. [NKJV]
	Jesus **told** the crowd not to tell anyone, but the more he told them not to, the more they spread the news, [NLT]
	καὶ **διεστείλατο** αὐτοῖς ἵνα μηδενὶ εἴπωσιν· ὅσον δὲ αὐτὸς αὐτοῖς διεστέλλετο μᾶλλον περισσότερον ἐκήρυσσον· [GNS]
	καὶ **διεστείλατο** αὐτοῖς ἵνα μηδενὶ λέγωσιν· ὅσον δὲ αὐτοῖς διεστέλλετο, αὐτοὶ μᾶλλον περισσότερον ἐκήρυσσον. [GNT]
		To charge; to give a command; to give orders; to tell someone what to do or what not to do; to warn.
		
		Practical Application
		The word for "told" (*diesteilato*) is strong. The order was clearly given. There is a lesson on humility in the command. Jesus was not after the applause or praise of people. The miracles were not done for that reason. All that He was and all that He had done was to help peoplemen by pointing them to God. People were lost, and He had come to seek and save the lost, not to win their applause (cp. Luke 19:10).

ENGLISH WORD	GREEK WORD AND VERSE	THE WORD MEANS...

#4007
Told Him Sternly
 	
Straitly charged–KJV
Sternly warned–NASB
Strong warning–NIV
Strictly warned–NKJV
Told him sternly–NLT
 	
POSB REFERENCE
(Mk.1:43)
Note 3, point 2
	ἐμβριμησάμενος = embrimesamenos
	Pronunciation: [em-brim-eh'-sah-mehn-os]
	Parsing (part of speech): verb
	    Mood—participle
	    Tense—aorist
	    Voice—middle deponent
	    Case—nominative
	    Gender—masculine
	    Number—singular
	    Stem or root—from ἐμβριμάομαι
	Concordance References:
	⇒ Strong's #1690 embrimaomai
	⇒ NIV #1839 embrimaomai
	⇒ NASB #1690 embrimaomai
	
	Mark 1:43
	And he **straitly charged** him, and forthwith sent him away; [KJV]
	And He **sternly warned** him and immediately sent him away, [NASB]
	Jesus sent him away at once with a **strong warning**: [NIV]
	And He **strictly warned** him and sent him away at once, [NKJV]
	Then Jesus sent him on his way and **told him sternly**, [NLT]
	καὶ **ἐμβριμησάμενος** αὐτῷ, εὐθέως ἐξέβαλεν αὐτόν, [GNS]
	καὶ **ἐμβριμησάμενος** αὐτῷ εὐθὺς ἐξέβαλεν αὐτόν [GNT]
		To sternly, strongly, powerfully, abruptly, bluntly warn.
		
		Practical Application
		It is a threatening phrase. It is a strong severe warning to the man. It is the same kind of charge Jesus gave to the man who had been bed-ridden for thirty-eight years:
		
		Now you are well; so stop sinning, or something even worse may happen to you (John 5:14). [NLT]

#4008
Tolerance–Tolerant
 	
Forbearance–KJV
Forbearance–NASB
Tolerance–NIV
Forbearance–NKJV
Tolerant–NLT
 	
POSB REFERENCE
(Romans 2:2-5; esp. v.4)
Note 2, point 2
	ἀνοχῆς = anochës
	Pronunciation: [an-okh-ays']
	Parsing (part of speech): noun
	    Case—genitive
	    Gender—feminine
	    Number—singular
	    Stem or root—from ἀνοχή, ῆς
	Concordance References:
	⇒ Strong's #463 anochë
	⇒ NIV #496 anochë
	⇒ NASB #463 anochë
	
	Romans 2:4
	Or despisest thou the riches of his goodness and **forbearance** and longsuffering; not knowing that the goodness of God leadeth thee to repentance? [KJV]
	Or do you think lightly of the riches of His kindness and **forbearance** and patience, not knowing that the kindness of God leads you to repentance? [NASB]
	Or do you show contempt for the riches of his kindness, **tolerance** and patience, not realizing that God's kindness leads you toward repentance? [NIV]
	Or do you despise the riches of His goodness, **forbearance**, and longsuffering, not knowing that the goodness of God leads you to repentance? [NKJV]
	Don't you realize how kind, **tolerant**, and patient God is with you? Or don't you care? Can't you see how kind he has been in giving you time to turn from your sin? [NLT]
	η τοῦ πλούτου τῆς χρηστότητος αὐτοῦ καὶ τῆς **ἀνοχῆς** καὶ τῆς μακροθυμίας καταφρονεῖς, ἀγνοῶν ὅτι τὸ χρηστὸν τοῦ Θεοῦ εἰς μετάνοιάν σε ἄγει; [GNS]
	η τοῦ πλούτου τῆς χρηστότητος αὐτοῦ καὶ τῆς **ἀνοχῆς** καὶ τῆς μακροθυμίας καταφρονεῖς, ἀγνοῶν ὅτι τὸ χρηστὸν τοῦ Θεοῦ εἰς μετάνοιάν σε ἄγει; [GNT]
		Forbearance, tolerance...
		• of God's tolerance (*anochës*): His refraining, holding back, abstaining and controlling His justice.
		• of God's long-suffering: His suffering a long time, being patient and slow in judging sin.
		
		Practical Application
		God, of course, is all this and much more. What the moralist fails to see is that God's goodness...
		• is not a blank check for sin.
		• does not give license to sin.
		• does not condone sin.
		• does not indulge sin.
		• does not overlook sin.

#4009
Took
 	
Took–KJV
Took–NASB
	παρέλαβεν = parelaben
	Pronunciation: [par-ee-la-ben']
	Parsing (part of speech): verb
	    Mood—indicative
	    Tense—aorist
	    Voice—active
		Took; to take along; that Christ took His disciples "aside."
		
		Practical Application
		Jesus took the disciples aside to get all alone.

ENGLISH WORD	GREEK WORD AND VERSE	THE WORD MEANS...
Took–NIV **Took–NKJV** **Took–NLT** **POSB REFERENCE** (Mt.20:17) Note 1	Person—3rd person Number—singular Stem or root—from παραλαμβάνω Concordance References: ⇒ Strong's #3880 paralambanō ⇒ NIV #4161 paralambanō ⇒ NASB #3880 paralambanō **Matthew 20:17** And Jesus going up to Jerusalem **took** the twelve disciples apart in the way, and said unto them, [KJV] And as Jesus was about to go up to Jerusalem, He **took** the twelve *disciples* aside by themselves, and on the way He said to them, [NASB] Now as Jesus was going up to Jerusalem, he **took** the twelve disciples aside and said to them, [NIV] Now Jesus, going up to Jerusalem, **took** the twelve disciples aside on the road and said to them, [NKJV] As Jesus was on the way to Jerusalem, he **took** the twelve disciples aside privately and told them what was going to happen to him. [NLT] Καὶ ἀναβαίνων ὁ Ἰησοῦς εἰς Ἱεροσόλυμα, **παρέλαβε** τοὺς δώδεκα μαθητὰς κατ' ἰδίαν, καὶ ἐν τῇ ὁδῷ, καὶ εἶπεν αὐτοῖς, [GNS] ὁμοία ἐστιν κόκκῳ σινάπεως, ὃν λαβὼν ἄνθρωπος ἔβαλεν εἰς κῆπον ἑαυτοῦ, καὶ ηὔξησεν καὶ ἐγένετο εἰς δένδρον, καὶ τὰ πετεινὰ τοῦ οὐρανοῦ κατεσκήνωσεν ἐν τοῖς κλάδοις αὐτοῦ. [GNT]	There is great meaning in these words. 1. There is tenderness and warmth and intimacy. He needed and wanted them close to Him, right by His side. He needed to feel and know their presence, in particular that they were with Him as He *went up to Jerusalem* to face death. They also needed His presence, to have Him right beside them and to feel what He felt. Such memories would help them as they faced the trials that lay ahead. 2. There was tremendous pressure and tension (also see POSB note—Matthew 20:19). The very air surrounding them was tight. There seemed to be a heavy weight hanging over the Lord's head. He seemed to be consumed in deep thought—the kind of thought that quickens a person's pace, tightens the muscles of the body, and strains the expressions of the face. The pressure and tension cannot be overstated. Mark expressed it well: "They were in the way going up to Jerusalem; and Jesus went before [walked ahead of] them. And they were amazed [bewildered, perplexed]; and as they followed, they were afraid [seized with alarm]" (Mark 10:32).

#4010
Took
 	
Took–KJV
Took–NASB
Took–NIV
Took–NKJV
Not Translated–NLT
 	
**POSB
REFERENCE**
(Lk.13:19)
Note 2, point 1
	λαβὼν = *labōn*
	Pronunciation: [la-bone']
	Parsing (part of speech): verb
	  Mood—participle
	  Tense—aorist
	  Voice—active
	  Case—nominative
	  Gender—masculine
	  Number—singular
	  Stem or root—from λαμβάνω
	Concordance References:
	⇒ Strong's #2983 lambanō
	⇒ NIV #3284 lambanō
	⇒ NASB #2983 lambanō
	
	Luke 13:19
	It is like a grain of mustard seed, which a man **took**, and cast into his garden; and it grew, and waxed a great tree; and the fowls of the air lodged in the branches of it. [KJV]
	"It is like a mustard seed, which a man **took** and threw into his own garden; and it grew and became a tree; and THE BIRDS OF THE AIR NESTED IN ITS BRANCHES." [NASB]
	It is like a mustard seed, which a man **took** and planted in his garden. It grew and became a tree, and the birds of the air perched in its branches." [NIV]
	It is like a mustard seed, which a man **took** and put in his garden; and it grew and became a large tree, and the birds of the air nested in its branches." [NKJV]
	It is like a tiny mustard seed planted in a garden; it grows and becomes a tree, and the birds come and find shelter among its branches." [NLT]—NOT TRANSLATED
	ὁμοία ἐστι κόκκῳ σινάπεως, ὃν **λαβὼν** ἄνθρωπος ἔβαλεν εἰς κῆπον ἑαυτοῦ· καὶ ηὔξησε, καὶ ἐγένετο εἰς δένδρον μέγα, καὶ τὰ πετεινὰ τοῦ οὐρανοῦ κατεσκήνωσεν ἐν τοῖς κλάδοις αὐτοῦ. [GNS]
	ὁμοία ἐστὶν κόκκῳ σινάπεως, ὃν **λαβὼν** ἄνθρωπος ἔβαλεν εἰς κῆπον ἑαυτου, καὶ ηὔξησεν καὶ ἐγένετο εἰς δένδρον, καὶ τὰ πετεινὰ τοῦ οὐρανοῦ κατεσκήνωσεν ἐν τοῖς κλάδοις αὐτοῦ. [GNT]
		To deliberately take; to take with purpose and thought; to seize.
		
		Practical Application
		The seed was not planted by chance; it did not just happen. With purpose and thought God planted and nourished the seed (kingdom).

ENGLISH WORD	GREEK WORD AND VERSE	THE WORD MEANS...

#4011
Took–
Took Aside
 	
Took–KJV
Took aside–NASB
Took aside–NIV
Took aside–NKJV
Took aside–NLT
 	
POSB
REFERENCE
(Mk.8:32-33; esp.
v.32)
Note 2, point 1a
 	
See also POSB REF:
(Mt.16:21-23; esp.
v.22),
Note 1, point 2
	προσλαβόμενος = *proslabomenos*
	Pronunciation: [pros-lam-bo'-mehn-os]
	Parsing (part of speech): verb
	    Mood—participle
	    Tense—aorist
	    Voice—middle
	    Case—nominative
	    Gender—masculine
	    Number—singular
	    Stem or root—from προσλαμβάνομαι
	Concordance References:
	⇒ Strong's #4355 proslambanö
	⇒ NIV #4689 proslambanö
	⇒ NASB #4355 proslambanö
	
	Mark 8:32
	And he spake that saying openly. And Peter **took** him, and began to rebuke him. [KJV]
	And He was stating the matter plainly. And Peter **took** Him **aside** and began to rebuke Him. [NASB]
	He spoke plainly about this, and Peter **took** him **aside** and began to rebuke him. [NIV]
	He spoke this word openly. And Peter **took** Him **aside** and began to rebuke Him. [NASB]
	As he talked about this openly with his disciples, Peter **took** him **aside** and told him he shouldn't say things like that. [NLT]
	καὶ παρρησίᾳ τὸν λόγον ἐλάλει. καὶ **προσλαβόμενος** αὐτὸν ὁ Πέτρος, ἤρξατο ἐπιτιμᾶν αὐτῷ. [GNS]
	καὶ παρρησίᾳ τὸν λόγον ἐλάλει. καὶ **προσλαβόμενος** ὁ Πέτρος αὐτὸν ἤρξατο ἐπιτιμᾶν αὐτῷ. [GNT]
		To take hold of; to take; to be caught hold of.
		
		Practical Application
		Peter took hold and grabbed Jesus. Peter bodily took Jesus aside for a conference. Peter was urging Jesus to follow his own human schemes instead of God's way. And by such, he was tempting Jesus with the very same compromises that Satan used to tempt Jesus, the compromises of power, fame, and sensations (Matthew 4:1-11). Peter was zealous for God, but He was mistaken and ignorant in his zeal. He did not understand that God was planning to save the world through the death of His Son (see POSB note, pt.3—Mark 8:31).
		Peter's behavior is the way of the world. It is the natural, carnal mind. Mankind just rebels and recoils against the idea of a Suffering Savior who dies for the sins of the world, a Suffering Savior who demands the same sacrifice and denial of His followers. Such an idea is unacceptable and repulsive.

#4012
Took–Took Up
 	
Took–KJV
Took–NASB
Took up–NIV
Took–NKJV
Took–NLT
 	
POSB
REFERENCE
(Mt.8:17)
Note 3
 	
See also POSB REF:
(Lk.13:19)
Note 2, point 1
	ἔλαβεν = *elaben*
	Pronunciation: [eh-la-ben]
	Parsing (part of speech): verb
	    Mood—indicative
	    Tense—aorist
	    Voice—active
	    Person—3rd person
	    Number—singular
	    Stem or root—from λαμβάνω
	Concordance References:
	⇒ Strong's #2983 lambanö
	⇒ NIV #3284 lambanö
	⇒ NASB #2983 lambanö
	
	Matthew 8:17
	That it might be fulfilled which was spoken by Esaias the prophet, saying, Himself **took** our infirmities, and bare *our* sicknesses. [KJV]
	In order that what was spoken through Isaiah the prophet might be fulfilled, saying, "HE HIMSELF **TOOK** OUR INFIRMITIES, AND CARRIED AWAY OUR DISEASES." [NASB]
	This was to fulfill what was spoken through the prophet Isaiah: "He **took up** our infirmities and carried our diseases." [NIV]
	That it might be fulfilled which was spoken by Isaiah the prophet, saying: "He Himself **took** our infirmities And bore our sicknesses." [NKJV]
	This fulfilled the word of the Lord through Isaiah, who said, "He **took** our sicknesses and removed our diseases." [NLT]
	ὅπως πληρωθῇ τὸ ῥηθὲν διὰ Ἡσαΐου τοῦ προφήτου, λέγοντος, Αὐτὸς τὰς ἀσθενείας ἡμῶν **ἔλαβε**, καὶ τὰς νόσους ἐβάστασεν. [GNS]
	ὅπως πληρωθῇ τὸ ῥηθὲν διὰ Ἡσαΐου τοῦ προφήτου λέγοντος, Αὐτὸς τὰς ἀσθενείας ἡμῶν **ἔλαβεν** καὶ τὰς νόσους ἐβάστασεν. [GNT]
		To take or take up; to receive; to pick up.
		
		Practical Application
		Christ did not heal our sicknesses as any other minister, but He "Himself took up [*elaben*] our infirmities, and carried [*ebastasen*] our sicknesses." This means at least two things.
		1. He carried our infirmities and sicknesses to the ultimate degree when He died on the cross for us. It was there that He bore them (see POSB *Deeper Study* #2—Mt.8:17 for discussion). (Cp. Jn.1:29.)
		2. He carried each fresh illness in a way that will never be understood.
		a. Each need that stood before Him was a reminder that He had to bear the sin of the world. And He knew what this meant and all that it was to include. Seeing the needs of men standing before Him reminded Him of the suffering He was to bear.
		b. Each need that He met was a foretaste of the cross. The thought of what He had to bear was upon His mind day by day and hour by hour as He went about ministering. This was bound to weigh ever so heavily upon Him.

ENGLISH WORD	GREEK WORD AND VERSE	THE WORD MEANS...

#4013
Took Counsel
 	
Took counsel–KJV
Intending-NASB
Wanted–NIV
Plotted–NKJV
Decided–NLT
 	
POSB
REFERENCE
(Acts 5:32-40; esp.
v.33)
Note 4, point 1
	ἐβούλοντο = eboulonto
	Pronunciation: [eh-bool-on-tow]
	Parsing (part of speech): verb
	    Mood—indicative
	    Tense—imperfect
	    Voice—middle or passive deponent
	    Person—3rd person
	    Number—plural
	    Stem or root—from βούλομαι
	Concordance References:
	  ⇒ Strong's #1014 boulomai
	  ⇒ NIV #1089 boulomai
	  ⇒ NASB #1014 boulomai
	
	Acts 5:33
	When they heard *that,* they were cut *to the heart,* and **took counsel** to slay them. [KJV]
	But when they heard this, they were cut to the quick and were **intending** to slay them. [NASB]
	When they heard this, they were furious and **wanted** to put them to death. [NIV]
	When they heard *this,* they were furious and **plotted** to kill them. [NKJV]
	At this, the high council was furious and **decided** to kill them. [NLT]
	Οἱ δὲ ἀκούσαντες διεπρίοντο, καὶ **ἐβούλοντο** ἀνελεῖν αὐτούς. [GNS]
	Οἱ δὲ ἀκούσαντες διεπρίοντο καὶ **ἐβούλοντο** ἀνελεῖν αὐτούς. [GNT]
		To want; to take counsel; to intend; to decide; to wish; to plan.
		
		Practical Application
		They were minded, were intending; were set on killing the disciples.

#4014
Took Issue
 	
Contended–KJV
Took issue–NASB
Criticized–NIV
Contended–NKJV
Criticized–NLT
 	
POSB
REFERENCE
(Acts 11:1-3; esp. v.2)
Note 1, point 2
	διεκρίνοντο = diekrinonto
	Pronunciation: [dee-eh-kree-non-tow]
	Parsing (part of speech): verb
	    Mood—indicative
	    Tense—imperfect
	    Voice—middle
	    Person—3rd person
	    Number—plural
	    Stem or root—from διακρίνω
	Concordance References:
	  ⇒ Strong's #1252 diakrinō
	  ⇒ NIV #1359 diakrinō
	  ⇒ NASB #1252 diakrinō
	
	Acts 11:2
	And when Peter was come up to Jerusalem, they that were of the circumcision **contended** with him, [KJV]
	And when Peter came up to Jerusalem, those who were circumcised **took issue** with him, [NASB]
	So when Peter went up to Jerusalem, the circumcised believers **criticized** him [NIV]
	And when Peter came up to Jerusalem, those of the circumcision **contended** with him, [NKJV]
	But when Peter arrived back in Jerusalem, some of the Jewish believers **criticized** him. [NLT]
	καὶ ὅτε δὲ ἀνέβη Πέτρος εἰς Ἰερουσαλήμ, **διεκρίνοντο** πρὸς αὐτὸν οἱ ἐκ περιτομῆς, [GNS]
	ὅτε δὲ ἀνέβη Πέτρος εἰς Ἰερουσαλήμ, **διεκρίνοντο** πρὸς αὐτὸν οἱ ἐκ περιτομῆς [GNT]
		To criticize; to contend; to debate; to dispute; to take issue with. The words "took issue" (*diekrinonto*) means to stand against, to take an opposite position, to take sides against, to oppose, to create a cleavage, a division. It is creating strife, struggle, and discord.
		
		Practical Application
		They (the circumcision, the religionists) readily and willingly opposed Peter, and the idea is that it was repeated: it went on and on; the issue was prolonged.
		Again keep in mind the issue: Peter had carried the Word of God to the Gentiles. He had allowed the non-Jews to receive the Word of God without circumcising them (Acts 11:1). He had broken the law of Moses by "going to the uncircumcised [non-Jews] and eating" with them (Acts 11:3).

#4015
Took Part
 	
Took part–KJV
Partook–NASB
Shared in–NIV
Shared in–NKJV
Became–NLT
	μετέσχεν = meteschen
	Pronunciation: [met-es-khehn]
	Parsing (part of speech): verb
	    Mood—indicative
	    Tense—aorist
	    Voice—active
	    Person—3rd person
	    Number—singular
	    Stem or root—from μετέχω
	Concordance References:
	  ⇒ Strong's #3348 metechō
	  ⇒ NIV #3576 metechō
	  ⇒ NASB #3348 metechō
		To share in; to take part of; to partake of; to become; to hold with.
		
		Practical Application
		Christ took part of or became (*meteschen*) human nature. The idea is that Christ became human nature and held human nature with man. He added human nature to His divine nature. His human nature was an addition to His divine nature. As God the Son, Jesus Christ had absolutely no part of flesh and blood; but as the Son of Man, He took hold of man's nature. The

ENGLISH WORD	GREEK WORD AND VERSE	THE WORD MEANS...
POSB REFERENCE (Heb.2:14-16; esp. v.14) Note 1. point 1	**Hebrews 2:14** Forasmuch then as the children are partakers of flesh and blood, he also himself likewise **took part** of the same; that through death he might destroy him that had the power of death, that is, the devil; [KJV] Since then the children share in flesh and blood, He Himself likewise also **partook** of the same, that through death He might render powerless him who had the power of death, that is, the devil; [NASB] Since the children have flesh and blood, he too **shared in** their humanity so that by his death he might destroy him who holds the power of death—that is, the devil—[NIV] Inasmuch then as the children have partaken of flesh and blood, He Himself likewise **shared in** the same, that through death He might destroy him who had the power of death, that is, the devil, [NKJV] Because God's children are human beings—made of flesh and blood—Jesus also **became** flesh and blood by being born in human form. For only as a human being could he die, and only by dying could he break the power of the Devil, who had the power of death. [NLT] ἐπεὶ οὖν τὰ παιδία κεκοινώνηκε σαρκός καὶ αἵματος, καὶ αὐτὸς παραπλησίως **μετέσχε** τῶν αὐτῶν, ἵνα διὰ τοῦ θανάτου καταργήσῃ τὸν τὸ κράτος ἔχοντα τοῦ θανάτου, τοῦτ ἔστι τὸν διάβολον, [GNS] ἐπεὶ οὖν τὰ παιδία κεκοινώνηκεν αἵματος καὶ σαρκός, καὶ αὐτὸς παραπλησίως **μετέσχεν** τῶν αὐτῶν, ἵνα διὰ τοῦ θανάτου καταργήσῃ τὸν τὸ κράτος ἔχοντα τοῦ θανάτου, τοῦτ' ἔστιν τὸν διάβολον, [GNT]	point is this: Jesus Christ became man, and as Man He became flesh and blood, willingly and voluntarily. Jesus Christ loves us so much that He would pay the ultimate price to deliver us. He would humble Himself to such a degree that He would leave heaven above in order to come to earth and live as a Man. (See POSB notes—Hebrews 2:17-18 for more discussion.) (Kenneth Wuest points this out in an excellent discussion and Marvin Vincent quotes the Biblical scholar B.F. Westcott as making the same point.)
#4016 **Took Place** Most surely believed–KJV Accomplished–NASB Fulfilled–NIV Fulfilled–NKJV **Took place–NLT** **POSB REFERENCE** (Lk.1:1) Note 1, point 2 **See also POSB REF:** (Lk.21:24) Note 5, point 1	**πεπληροφορημένων** = peplērophorēmenōn Pronunciation: [pe-play-rof-or-ee-men-own] Parsing (part of speech): verb 　　Mood—participle 　　Tense—perfect 　　Voice—passive 　　Case—genitive 　　Gender—neuter 　　Number—plural 　　Stem or root—from πληροφορέω Concordance References: ⇒　Strong's #4135 plērophoreō ⇒　NIV #4442 plērophoreō ⇒　NASB #4135 plērophoreō **Luke 1:1** Forasmuch as many have taken in hand to set forth in order a declaration of those things which are **most sure-ly believed** among us, [KJV] Inasmuch as many have undertaken to compile an account of the things **accomplished** among us, [NASB] Many have undertaken to draw up an account of the things that have been **fulfilled** among us, [NIV] Inasmuch as many have taken in hand to set in order a narrative of those things which have been **fulfilled** among us, [NKJV] Most honorable Theophilus: Many people have written accounts about the events that **took place** among us. [NLT] Ἐπειδήπερ πολλοὶ ἐπεχείρησαν ἀνατάξασθαι διήγησιν περὶ τῶν **πεπληροφορημένων** ἐν ἡμῖν πραγμάτων, [GNS] Ἐπειδήπερ πολλοὶ ἐπεχείρησαν ἀνατάξασθαι διήγησιν περὶ τῶν **πεπληροφορημένων** ἐν ἡμῖν πραγμάτων, [GNT]	To fill; to fill up; to make full; to come to an end; to bring to completion; to finish. It means things that were fulfilled, that were accomplished, that were actually performed, or that had run their full course (cp. 2 Tim. 4:5). **Practical Application** Luke is saying that the *things of Christ* were not only believed, but they were also accomplished or fulfilled among the believers of that day. The *things* (events, matters) of Christ actually took place; they were purposeful; they were destined to be accomplished and fulfilled. The point is this: the things of Christ are a record of historical events, things that actually happened and that actually fulfilled the purpose of God. Therefore, the things are "most surely believed among us [believers]." What are the *things* accomplished and believed? Both the things of the New Testament and of the Old Testament. The whole Bible is a record of "those things."

ENGLISH WORD	GREEK WORD AND VERSE	THE WORD MEANS...
	ἀναβέβηκα πρὸς τὸν πατέρα μου· πορεύου δὲ πρὸς τοὺς ἀδελφούς μου, καὶ εἰπὲ αὐτοῖς, Ἀναβαίνω πρὸς τὸν πατέρα μου καὶ πατέρα ὑμῶν, καὶ Θεόν μου καὶ Θεὸν ὑμῶν. [GNS] λέγει αὐτῇ Ἰησοῦς, **Μή μου ἅπτου**, οὔπω γὰρ ἀναβέβηκα πρὸς τὸν πατέρα· πορεύου δὲ πρὸς τοὺς ἀδελφούς μου καὶ εἰπὲ αὐτοῖς, Ἀναβαίνω πρὸς τὸν πατέρα μου καὶ πατέρα ὑμῶν καὶ θεόν μου καὶ θεὸν ὑμῶν. [GNT]	

#4021
Touched
 	
Handled–KJV
Handled–NASB
Touched–NIV
Handled–NKJV
Touched–NLT
 	
**POSB
REFERENCE**
(1 Jn.1:1)
Note 2, point 4
	ἐψηλάφησαν = epsëlaphësan
	Pronunciation: [epsay-laf-ay'-sahn]
	Parsing (part of speech): erb
	    Mood—indicative
	    Tense—aorist
	    Voice—actiye
	    Person—3rd person
	    Number—plural
	    Stem or root—from ψηλαφάω
	Concordance References:
	  ⇒ Strong's #5584 psëlaphaö
	  ⇒ NIV #6027 psëlaphaö
	  ⇒ NASB #5584 psëlaphaö
	
	1 John 1:1
	That which was from the beginning, which we have heard, which we have seen with our eyes, which we have looked upon, and our hands have **handled**, of the Word of life; [KJV]
	
	What was from the beginning, what we have heard, what we have seen with our eyes, what we beheld and our hands **handled**, concerning the Word of Life— [NASB]
	
	That which was from the beginning, which we have heard, which we have seen with our eyes, which we have looked at and our hands have **touched**—this we proclaim concerning the Word of life. [NIV]
	
	That which was from the beginning, which we have heard, which we have seen with our eyes, which we have looked upon, and our hands have **handled**, concerning the Word of life [NKJV]
	
	The one who existed from the beginning is the one we have heard and seen. We saw him with our own eyes and **touched** him with our own hands. He is Jesus Christ, the Word of life. [NLT]
	
	Ὃ ἦν ἀπ᾽ ἀρχῆς, ὃ ἀκηκόαμεν, ὃ ἑωράκαμεν τοῖς ὀφθαλμοῖς ἡμῶν, ὃ ἐθεασάμεθα, καὶ αἱ χεῖρες ἡμῶν **ἐψηλάφησαν**, περὶ τοῦ λόγου τῆς ζωῆς [GNS]
	
	Ὃ ἦν ἀπ᾽ ἀρχῆς, ὃ ἀκηκόαμεν, ὃ ἑωράκαμεν τοῖς ὀφθαλμοῖς ἡμῶν, ὃ ἐθεασάμεθα καὶ αἱ χεῖρες ἡμῶν **ἐψηλάφησαν** περὶ τοῦ λόγου τῆς ζωῆς [GNT]
		In a general sense to touch; to handle; to feel.
		
		Practical Application
		The word "touched" (epsëlaphësan) means more than just touching. It means to grope and grasp after in order to understand; to handle in order to examine closely (John RW Stott. *The Epistles of John.* "Tyndale New Testament Commentary," p.60). A.T. Robertson, the Greek scholar, says that it is a graphic word, the very same word that Jesus used to prove that He was not a spirit after His resurrection (*Word Pictures in the New Testament*, Vol.6, p.205).

#4022
Touched
 	
Touched–KJV
Sympathize with–NASB
Sympathize with–NIV
Sympathize with–NKJV
Understands–NLT
 	
**POSB
REFERENCE**
(Heb.4:15-16; esp.
v.15
Note 2, point 1
	συμπαθῆσαι = sumpathësai
	Pronunciation: [soom-path-ay'-sah-ee]
	Parsing (part of speech): verb
	    Mood—infinitive
	    Tense—aorist
	    Voice—active
	    Stem or root—from συμπαθέω
	Concordance References:
	  ⇒ Strong's #4834 sumpatheö
	  ⇒ NIV #5217 sumpatheö
	  ⇒ NASB #4834 sumpatheö
	
	Hebrews 4:15
	For we have not an high priest which cannot be **touched** with the feeling of our infirmities; but was in all points tempted like as *we are, yet* without sin. [KJV]
	
	For we do not have a high priest who cannot **sympathize with** our weaknesses, but One who has been tempted in all things as *we are, yet* without sin. [NASB]
	
	For we do not have a high priest who is unable to **sympathize with** our weaknesses, but we have one who has been tempted in every way, just as we are—yet was
		To sympathize with; to be touched with another persons hurt; to understand. The word "touched" (sumpathësai) means to sympathize, feel, and suffer with. It means to sympathize and feel with a person to the point that the hurt and pain are actually felt within one's own heart.
		
		Practical Application
		We have a High Priest who feels with us. The idea is that Jesus Christ actually suffers when we suffer. He knows and suffers right along with us when we...
		• become sick
		• suffer trials
		• face temptations
		• fall into sin
		• have an accident
		• feel lonely
		• sense emptiness
		• lack purpose

ENGLISH WORD	GREEK WORD AND VERSE	THE WORD MEANS...

without sin. [NIV]

For we do not have a High Priest who cannot **sympathize with** our weaknesses, but was in all *points* tempted as *we are, yet* without sin. [NKJV]

This High Priest of ours **understands** our weaknesses, for he faced all of the same temptations we do, yet he did not sin. [NLT]

οὐ γὰρ ἔχομεν ἀρχιερέα μὴ δυνάμενον **συμπαθῆσαι** ταῖς ἀσθενείαις ἡμῶν, πεπειρασμένον δὲ κατὰ πάντα καθ' ὁμοιότητα, χωρὶς ἁμαρτίας. [GNS]

οὐ γὰρ ἔχομεν ἀρχιερέα μὴ δυνάμενον **συμπαθῆσαι** ταῖς ἀσθενείαις ἡμῶν, πεπειρασμένον δὲ κατὰ πάντα καθ' ὁμοιότητα χωρὶς ἁμαρτίας. [GNT]

- lose a loved one
- are stricken with suffering
- lack money
- are hungry
- lack clothes
- suffer persecution
- face death

Name the trial or pain, temptation, or suffering—name the infirmity or weakness—name any and all human experiences—Jesus Christ actually sympathizes and feels with us. He actually suffers and hurts right along with us. We could ask for no greater Savior; we could crave no greater Intercessor; we could long for no greater High Priest to stand before God *for us*. Jesus Christ is our *great High Priest*. He is our representative before God. He is the One who carries on the glorious ministry and intercession for us, and He "is touched with the feelings of our infirmities"—with all of our human weaknesses and frailties.

#4023

Tough

Austere–KJV
Exacting–NASB
Hard–NIV
Austere–NKJV
Tough–NLT

**POSB
REFERENCE**
(Lk.19:15-23; esp.
v.22)
Note 5, point 6b

αὐστηρός = *austēros*
Pronunciation: [ow-stay-ros']
Parsing (part of speech): adjective
    Case—nominative
    Gender—masculine
    Number—singular
    Stem or root—from αὐστηρός, ά, όν
Concordance References:
  ⇒ Strong's #840 austēros
  ⇒ NIV #893 austēros
  ⇒ NASB #840 austēros

Luke 19:22

And he saith unto him, Out of thine own mouth will I judge thee, *thou* wicked servant. Thou knewest that I was an **austere** man, taking up that I laid not down, and reaping that I did not sow: [KJV]

"He said to him, 'By your own words I will judge you, you worthless slave. Did you know that I am an **exacting** man, taking up what I did not lay down, and reaping what I did not sow? [NASB]

"His master replied, 'I will judge you by your own words, you wicked servant! You knew, did you, that I am a **hard** man, taking out what I did not put in, and reaping what I did not sow? [NIV]

And he said to him, 'Out of your own mouth I will judge you, *you* wicked servant. You knew that I was an **austere** man, collecting what I did not deposit and reaping what I did not sow. [NKJV]

" 'You wicked servant!' the king roared. 'Hard, am I? If you knew so much about me and how **tough** I am, [NLT]

λέγει δὲ αὐτῷ, Ἐκ τοῦ στόματός σου κρίνω σε, πονηρὲ δοῦλε. ᾔδεις ὅτι ἐγὼ ἄνθρωπος **αὐστηρός** εἰμι, αἴρων ὃ οὐκ ἔθηκα, καὶ θερίζων ὃ οὐκ ἔσπειρα [GNS]

λέγει αὐτῷ, Ἐκ τοῦ στόματός σου κρίνω σε, πονηρὲ δοῦλε. ᾔδεις ὅτι ἐγὼ ἄνθρωπος **αὐστηρός** εἰμι, αἴρων ὃ οὐκ ἔθηκα καὶ θερίζων ὃ οὐκ ἔσπειρα; [GNT]

Sharp, hard, exacting, tough, austere, stringent.

Practical Application

In this Scripture, the unfaithful servant accused the Lord of being too tough. He felt that the Lord was too demanding and strict; and if he committed himself to the Lord's affairs, he would lose out on too much of the pleasures and comforts of life. But note: this was merely an excuse for his failure. He had chosen to live a life of selfishness and comfort and worldliness in the kingdom of the Lord without paying the price of helping to build it. He had been complacent and idle, doing very little. He had to cover up his failure or else face judgment, but his excuse was unacceptable. Perfect justice was executed. The very excuse, as well as the life, of the unfaithful servant determined his judgment.

#4024

Tradition

Tradition–KJV
Tradition–NASB
Teaching–NIV
Tradition–NKJV
Tradition of hard
  work–NLT

παράδοσιν = *paradosin*
Pronunciation: [par-ad'-os-in]
Parsing (part of speech): noun
    Case—accusative
    Gender—feminine
    Number—singular
    Stem or root—from παράδοσις, εως
Concordance References:
  ⇒ Strong's #3862 paradosis
  ⇒ NIV #4142 paradosis
  ⇒ NASB #3862 paradosis

Teaching, tradition, tradition of hard work. It means all the Word of God, whether taught orally or written.

Practical Application

The idle worker disobeys the instructions of God (2 Thes. 3:6). Paul says that he had taught the believers the commandments of God that deal with work; therefore, they are without excuse. They know better than to sit around idle.

ENGLISH WORD	GREEK WORD AND VERSE	THE WORD MEANS...

#4028
Training
 	
Admonition–KJV
Instruction–NASB
Instruction–NIV
Training–NKJV
Instruction–NLT
 	
POSB
REFERENCE
(Eph.6:4)
Note 2, point 2
	νουθεσία = nouthesia
	Pronunciation: [noo-thes-ee'-ah]
	Parsing (part of speech): noun
	  Case—dative
	  Gender—feminine
	  Number—singular
	  Stem or root—from νουθεσία, ας
	Concordance References:
	  ⇒ Strong's #3559 nouthesia
	  ⇒ NIV #3804 nouthesia
	  ⇒ NASB #3559 nouthesia
	
	Ephes. 6:4
	And, ye fathers, provoke not your children to wrath: but bring them up in the nurture and **admonition** of the Lord. [KJV]
	And, fathers, do not provoke your children to anger; but bring them up in the discipline and **instruction** of the Lord. [NASB]
	Fathers, do not exasperate your children; instead, bring them up in the training and **instruction** of the Lord. [NIV]
	And you, fathers, do not provoke your children to wrath, but bring them up in the **training** and admonition of the Lord. [NKJV]
	And now a word to you fathers. Don't make your children angry by the way you treat them. Rather, bring them up with the discipline and **instruction** approved by the Lord. [NLT]
	καὶ οἱ πατέρες, μὴ παροργίζετε τὰ τέκνα ὑμῶν, ἀλλ᾽ ἐκτρέφετε αὐτὰ ἐν παιδείᾳ καὶ **νουθεσίᾳ** Κυρίου. [GNS]
	Καὶ οἱ πατέρες, μὴ παροργίζετε τὰ τέκνα ὑμῶν ἀλλὰ ἐκτρέφετε αὐτὰ ἐν παιδείᾳ καὶ **νουθεσίᾳ** κυρίου. [GNT]
		Instruction, admonition, warning. It means counsel, exhortation, correction; to give strict orders.
		
		Practical Application
		Note that the parent is not to rear the child after his own ideas and notions of what is best for the child, but after the nurture and instruction *of the Lord*. The Lord's Word is to be the guide for Christian parents in rearing their child. The benefits in bringing up a child in the Lord are innumerable. Just a few are as follows:
		1. A child who is brought to Christ grows up learning love: that he is loved by God and by all who trust God. He grows no matter how evil some may act, knowing that he is to love even those who do wrong.
		2. A child who is brought to Christ grows up learning power and triumph: that God will help His followers through all; that there is a supernatural power available to help, a power to help when mother and dad and loved ones have done all they can.
		3. A child who is brought to Christ grows up learning hope and faith: that no matter what happens, no matter how great a trial, we can still trust God and hope in Him. He has provided a very special strength to carry us through the trials of this life (no matter how painful); that He has provided a very special place called heaven where He will carry us and our loved ones when we face death.
		4. A child who is brought to Christ grows up learning the truth of life and endurance (service): that God has given us the privilege of life and of living in a beautiful earth and universe; that the evil and bad which exists in the world is caused by evil and bad people; that despite such evil, we are to serve in appreciation for life and the beautiful earth upon which God has placed us. We are to work and work diligently, making the greatest contribution we can.
		5. A child who is brought to Christ grows up learning trust and endurance: that life is full of temptations and pitfalls which can easily rob us of joy and destroy our lives and the fulfillment of our purposes; that the way to escape the temptations and pitfalls is to follow Christ and endure in our work and purpose.
		6. A child who is brought to Christ grows up learning peace: that there is an inner peace despite the turbulent waters of this world; that peace is knowing and trusting Christ.

#4029
Training
 	
Exercise–KJV
Discipline–NASB
Training–NIV
Exercise–NKJV
Exercise–NLT
	γυμνασία = gumnasia
	Pronunciation: [goom-nas-ee'-ah]
	Parsing (part of speech): noun
	  Case—nominative
	  Gender—feminine
	  Number—singular
	  Stem or root—from γυμνασία, ας
	Concordance References:
	  ⇒ Strong's #1129 gumnasia
	  ⇒ NIV #1215 gumnasia
	  ⇒ NASB #1129 gumnasia
		Training, exercise, discipline.
		
		Practical Application
		The minister is to train (*gumnasia*) himself in godliness as much as an Olympic athlete exercises his body. How much energy, effort, time, and dedication does an Olympic athlete put into his training? His sport is his life—unequivocally so. So it is with the minister: godliness is to be his life. All of his energy, effort, time, and dedication are to be given over to godliness. The

ENGLISH WORD	GREEK WORD AND VERSE	THE WORD MEANS...
POSB REFERENCE (1 Tim.4:8) Note 4, point 1	**1 Tim. 4:8** For bodily **exercise** profiteth little: but godliness is profitable unto all things, having promise of the life that now is, and of that which is to come. [KJV] For bodily **discipline** is only of little profit, but godliness is profitable for all things, since it holds promise for the present life and *also* for the *life* to come. [NASB] For physical **training** is of some value, but godliness has value for all things, holding promise for both the present life and the life to come. [NIV] For bodily **exercise** profits a little, but godliness is profitable for all things, having promise of the life that now is and of that which is to come. [NKJV] Physical **exercise** has some value, but spiritual exercise is much more important, for it promises a reward in both this life and the next. [NLT] ἡ γὰρ σωματικὴ **γυμνασία** πρὸς ὀλίγον ἐστὶν ὠφέλιμος· ἡ δὲ εὐσέβεια πρὸς πάντα ὠφέλιμός ἐστιν, ἐπαγγελίαν ἔχουσα ζωῆς τῆς νῦν καὶ τῆς μελλούσης. [GNS] ἡ γὰρ σωματικὴ **γυμνασία** πρὸς ὀλίγον ἐστὶν ὠφέλιμος, ἡ δὲ εὐσέβεια πρὸς πάντα ὠφέλιμός ἐστιν ἐπαγγελίαν ἔχουσα ζωῆς τῆς νῦν καὶ τῆς μελλούσης. [GNT]	minister is to know *no training* but the training of godliness.
#4030 **Traitors** **Traitors**–KJV Treacherous–NASB Treacherous–NIV **Traitors**–NKJV Betray–NLT **POSB REFERENCE** (2 Tim. 3:2-4; esp. v.4) Note 2, point 15	προδόται = *prodotai* Pronunciation: [prod-ot'-ah-ee] Parsing (part of speech): noun Case—nominative Gender—masculine Number—plural Stem or root—from προδότης, ου Concordance References: ⇒ Strong's #4273 prodotēs ⇒ NIV #4595 prodotēs ⇒ NASB #4273 prodotēs **2 Tim. 3:4** **Traitors**, heady, highminded, lovers of pleasures more than lovers of God; [KJV] **Treacherous**, reckless, conceited, lovers of pleasure rather than lovers of God; [NASB] **Treacherous**, rash, conceited, lovers of pleasure rather than lovers of God—[NIV] **Traitors**, headstrong, haughty, lovers of pleasure rather than lovers of God, [NKJV] They will **betray** their friends, be reckless, be puffed up with pride, and love pleasure rather than God. [NLT] **προδόται**, προπετεῖς, τετυφωμένοι, φιλήδονοι μᾶλλον ἢ φιλόθεοι, [GNS] **προδόται** προπετεῖς τετυφωμένοι, φιλήδονοι μᾶλλον ἢ φιλόθεοι, [GNT]	Treacherous, traitor, to betray. **Practical Application** People will be traitors (*prodotai*): betraying a trust refers to a person who... • betrays his country • betrays his team • betrays his friends • betrays his family It refers to a person who betrays any trust or any commitment. The most tragic betrayal of all is the person who betrays Christ and the church—who turns his back upon Christ and returns to the world and its crowd. The last days will see an increase in traitors.
#4031 **Transfigured** **Transfigured**–KJV **Transfigured**–NASB **Transfigured**–NIV **Transfigured**–NKJV Appearance changed–NLT **POSB REFERENCE** (Mt.17:2) Note 2 **See also POSB REF:** (Mk.9:2-3; esp. v.2) *Deeper Study #2*	μετεμορφώθη = *metemorphōthē* Pronunciation: [met-am-or-fo'-thay] Parsing (part of speech): verb Mood—indicative Tense—aorist Voice—passive Person—3rd person Number—singular Stem or root—from μεταμορφόομαι Concordance References: ⇒ Strong's #3339 metamorphoö ⇒ NIV #3565 metamorphoö ⇒ NASB #3339 metamorphoö **Matthew 17:2** And was **transfigured** before them: and his face did shine as the sun, and his raiment was white as the light. [KJV] And He was **transfigured** before them; and His face shone like the sun, and His garments became as white as light. [NASB]	A change into another form; a transformation; a change of countenance; a complete change. **Practical Application** Luke said, "His face did shine as the sun" (Luke 9:29). Note how the gospel writers described what happened. *And was transfigured before them: and his face did shine as the sun, and his raiment was white as the light. (Matthew 17:2) [KJV]* *And His garments became radiant and exceedingly white, as no launderer on earth can whiten them. (Mark 9:3) [NASB]* *As he was praying, the appearance of his face changed, and his clothes became as bright as a flash of lightning. (Luke 9:29) [NIV]*

ENGLISH WORD	GREEK WORD AND VERSE	THE WORD MEANS...
	There he was **transfigured** before them. His face shone like the sun, and his clothes became as white as the light. [NIV] And He was **transfigured** before them. His face shone like the sun, and His clothes became as white as the light. [NKJV] As the men watched, Jesus' **appearance changed** so that his face shone like the sun, and his clothing became dazzling white. [NLT] καὶ **μετεμορφώθη** ἔμπροσθεν αὐτῶν, καὶ ἔλαμψε τὸ πρόσωπον αὐτοῦ ὡς ὁ ἥλιος, τὰ δὲ ἱμάτια αὐτοῦ ἐγένετο λευκὰ ὡς τὸ φῶς. [GNS] καὶ **μετεμορφώθη** ἔμπροσθεν αὐτῶν, καὶ ἔλαμψεν τὸ πρόσωπον αὐτοῦ ὡς ὁ ἥλιος, τὰ δὲ ἱμάτια αὐτοῦ ἐγένετο λευκὰ ὡς τὸ φῶς. [GNT]	
#4032 **Transform–Transformed** **Transformed–KJV** **Transformed–NASB** **Transformed–NIV** **Transformed–NKJV** **Transform–NLT** **POSB** **REFERENCE** (Rom.12:2) Note 4	**μεταμορφοῦσθε** = *metamorphousthe* Pronunciation: [met-am-or-foos'-theh] Parsing (part of speech): verb 　　Mood—imperative 　　Tense—present 　　Voice—passive 　　Person—2nd person → 2nd person 　　Number—plural 　　Stem or root—from **μεταμορφόομαι** Concordance References: 　⇒　Strong's #3339 metamorphoö 　⇒　NIV #3565 metamorphoö 　⇒　NASB #3339 metamorphoö **Romans 12:2** And be not conformed to this world: but be ye **transformed** by the renewing of your mind, that ye may prove what is that good, and acceptable, and perfect, will of God. [KJV] And do not be conformed to this world, but be **transformed** by the renewing of your mind, that you may prove what the will of God is, that which is good and acceptable and perfect. [NASB] Do not conform any longer to the pattern of this world, but be **transformed** by the renewing of your mind. Then you will be able to test and approve what God's will is—his good, pleasing and perfect will. [NIV] And do not be conformed to this world, but be **transformed** by the renewing of your mind, that you may prove what *is* that good and acceptable and perfect will of God. [NKJV] Don't copy the behavior and customs of this world, but let God **transform** you into a new person by changing the way you think. Then you will know what God wants you to do, and you will know how good and pleasing and perfect his will really is. [NLT] καὶ μὴ συσχηματίζεσθε τῷ αἰῶνι τούτῳ, ἀλλὰ **μεταμορφοῦσθε** τῇ ἀνακαινώσει τοῦ νοός ὑμῶν, εἰς τὸ δοκιμάζειν ὑμᾶς τί τὸ θέλημα τοῦ Θεοῦ, τὸ ἀγαθὸν καὶ εὐάρεστον καὶ τέλειον. [GNS] καὶ μὴ συσχηματίζεσθε τῷ αἰῶνι τούτῳ, ἀλλὰ **μεταμορφοῦσθε** τῇ ἀνακαινώσει τοῦ νοός εἰς τὸ δοκιμάζειν ὑμᾶς τί τὸ θέλημα τοῦ θεοῦ, τὸ ἀγαθὸν καὶ εὐάρεστον καὶ τέλειον. [GNT]	Transformed, changed, converted, metamorphosed. **Practical Application** 　The believer is to be transformed (*metamorphousthe*). The Greek root of the word is morphe. Morphe means the real being of a man. It is the very nature and essence, the inseparable part, the unchanging shape of a man. The man in evening clothes looks different than he does in work clothes, but he is still the same man inwardly. The elderly man is the same man inwardly that he was as a young man. 　What the Bible is saying is clearly evident: the believer must undergo a radical change within his inner being in order to escape the world and its doom. The believer must be transformed and changed inwardly. His real self—his very nature, essence, personality, inner being, his inner man—must be changed.
#4033 **Transformed** **Transformed–KJV** Disguise–NASB Masquerade–NIV **Transform–NKJV** Pretending–NLT	**μετασχηματίζονται** = *metaschëmatizontai* Pronunciation: [met-askh-ay-mat-id'-zon-tah-ee] Parsing (part of speech): verb 　　Mood—indicative 　　Tense—present 　　Voice—middle 　　Person—3rd person → 3rd person 　　Number—plural 　　Stem or root—from **μετασχηματίζω** Concordance References: 　⇒　Strong's #3345 metaschëmatizö	To masquerade; to disguise; to pretend; to transform; to fashion; to change one's outward appearance. **Practical Application** 　They pose as "gentlemen of the cloth," but they are nothing but cloth (A.T. Robertson. *Word Pictures in the New Testament*, Vol. 4, p.259). They are false ministers.

ENGLISH WORD	GREEK WORD AND VERSE	THE WORD MEANS...
POSB REFERENCE (2 Cor.11:13-15; esp. v.15) Note 6	⇒ NIV #3571 metaschēmatizō ⇒ NASB #3345 metaschēmatizō **2 Cor. 11:15** Therefore it is no great thing if his ministers also be **transformed** as the ministers of righteousness; whose end shall be according to their works. [KJV] Therefore it is not surprising if his servants also **disguise** themselves as servants of righteousness; whose end shall be according to their deeds. [NASB] It is not surprising, then, if his servants **masquerade** as servants of righteousness. Their end will be what their actions deserve. [NIV] Therefore *it is* no great thing if his ministers also **transform** themselves into ministers of righteousness, whose end will be according to their works. [NKJV] So it is no wonder his servants can also do it by **pretending** to be godly ministers. In the end they will get every bit of punishment their wicked deeds deserve. [NLT] οὐ μέγα οὖν εἰ καὶ οἱ διάκονοι αὐτοῦ **μετασχηματίζονται** ὡς διάκονοι δικαιοσύνης, ὧν τὸ τέλος ἔσται κατὰ τὰ ἔργα αὐτῶν. [GNS] οὐ μέγα οὖν εἰ καὶ οἱ διάκονοι αὐτοῦ **μετασχηματίζονται** ὡς διάκονοι δικαιοσύνης· ὧν τὸ τέλος ἔσται κατὰ τὰ ἔργα αὐτῶν. [GNT]	
#4034 **Transgres-sion** Transgression–KJV Transgression–NASB Violation–NIV Transgression–NKJV Violation of the law–NLT **POSB REFERENCE** (Heb.2:2) Note 2	παράβασις = *parabasis* Pronunciation: [par-ab'-as-is] Parsing (part of speech): noun 　　Case—nominative 　　Gender—feminine 　　Number—singular 　　Stem or root—from παράβασις, εως Concordance References: ⇒ Strong's #3847 parabasis ⇒ NIV #4126 parabasis ⇒ NASB #3847 parabasis **Hebrews 2:2** For if the word spoken by angels was stedfast, and every **transgression** and disobedience received a just recompence of reward; [KJV] For if the word spoken through angels proved unalterable, and every **transgression** and disobedience received a just recompense, [NASB] For if the message spoken by angels was binding, and every **violation** and disobedience received its just punishment, [NIV] For if the word spoken through angels proved steadfast, and every **transgression** and disobedience received a just reward, [NKJV] The message God delivered through angels has always proved true, and the people were punished for every **violation of the law** and every act of disobedience. [NLT] εἰ γὰρ ὁ δι' ἀγγέλων λαληθεὶς λόγος ἐγένετο βέβαιος, καὶ πᾶσα **παράβασις** καὶ παρακοὴ ἔλαβεν ἔνδικον μισθαποδοσίαν, [GNS] εἰ γὰρ ὁ δι' ἀγγέλων λαληθεὶς λόγος ἐγένετο βέβαιος καὶ πᾶσα **παράβασις** καὶ παρακοὴ ἔλαβεν ἔνδικον μισθαποδοσίαν, [GNT]	Violation, transgression, disobedience; to step aside; to step over the line. ### Practical Application It means to go against what the law says and to do what it forbids. To violate the law of God is sin and the violator is to be punished. The point is this: judgment under the law was very strict. Every transgression and disobedience had its appropriate punishment. If a person broke a law, he was judged, condemned, and bore the punishment laid out by the law.
#4035 **Transgressions** Trespasses–KJV Trespasses–NASB **Transgressions–NIV** Trespasses–NKJV Not translated–NLT	παραπτώμασιν = *paraptōmasin* Pronunciation: [par-ap'-to-mah-sin] Parsing (part of speech): noun 　　Case—dative 　　Gender—neuter 　　Number—plural 　　Stem or root—from παράπτωμα, τος Concordance References: ⇒ Strong's #3900 paraptōma ⇒ NIV #4183 paraptōma ⇒ NASB #3900 paraptōma	Transgressions, trespasses, sin, wrongdoing. It means to fall, slip, blunder, deviate, turn aside, or wander away. ### Practical Application It is a person who... • falls from the right way. • slips from doing what he should. • blunders and fails. • deviates off the right road.

ENGLISH WORD	GREEK WORD AND VERSE	THE WORD MEANS...

#4040
Treacherous
 	
Traitors–KJV
Treacherous–NASB
Treacherous–NIV
Traitors–NKJV
Betray–NLT
 	
POSB
REFERENCE
(2 Tim. 3:2-4; esp. v.4)
Note 2, point 15
	προδόται = *prodotai*
	Pronunciation: [prod-ot'-ah-ee]
	Parsing (part of speech): noun
	    Case—nominative
	    Gender—masculine
	    Number—plural
	    Stem or root—from προδότης, ου
	Concordance References:
	⇒ Strong's #4273 prodotēs
	⇒ NIV #4595 prodotēs
	⇒ NASB #4273 prodotēs
	
	2 Tim. 3:4
	Traitors, heady, highminded, lovers of pleasures more than lovers of God; [KJV]
	Treacherous, reckless, conceited, lovers of pleasure rather than lovers of God; [NASB]
	Treacherous, rash, conceited, lovers of pleasure rather than lovers of God—[NIV]
	Traitors, headstrong, haughty, lovers of pleasure rather than lovers of God, [NKJV]
	They will **betray** their friends, be reckless, be puffed up with pride, and love pleasure rather than God. [NLT]
	προδόται, προπετεῖς, τετυφωμένοι, φιλήδονοι μᾶλλον η φιλόθεοι, [GNS]
	προδόται προπετεῖς τετυφωμένοι, φιλήδονοι μᾶλλον η φιλόθεοι, [GNT]
		Treacherous, traitor, to betray.
		
		Practical Application
		People will be treacherous (*prodotai*): betraying a trust refers to a person who...
		• betrays his country
		• betrays his team
		• betrays his friends
		• betrays his family
		
		It refers to a person who betrays any trust or any commitment. The most tragic betrayal of all is the person who betrays Christ and the church—who turns his back upon Christ and returns to the world and its crowd. The last days will see an increase in traitors.

#4041
Treasurest–
Treasuring Up
 	
Treasurest up–KJV
Storing up–NASB
Storing up–NIV
Treasuring up–NKJV
Storing up–NLT
 	
POSB
REFERENCE
(Romans 2:2-5; esp. v.5)
Note 2, point 4
	θησαυρίζεις = *thēsaurizeis*
	Pronunciation: [thay-sow-rid'-zice]
	Parsing (part of speech): verb
	    Mood—indicative
	    Tense—present
	    Voice—active
	    Person—2nd person
	    Number—singular
	    Stem or root—from θησαυρίζω
	Concordance References:
	⇒ Strong's #2343 thēsaurizō
	⇒ NIV #2564 thēsaurizō
	⇒ NASB #2343 thēsaurizō
	
	Romans 2:5
	But after thy hardness and impenitent heart **treasurest up** unto thyself wrath against the day of wrath and revelation of the righteous judgment of God; [KJV]
	But because of your stubbornness and unrepentant heart you are **storing up** wrath for yourself in the day of wrath and revelation of the righteous judgment of God, [NASB]
	But because of your stubbornness and your unrepentant heart, you are **storing up** wrath against yourself for the day of God's wrath, when his righteous judgment will be revealed. [NIV]
	But in accordance with your hardness and your impenitent heart you are **treasuring up** for yourself wrath in the day of wrath and revelation of the righteous judgment of God [NKJV]
	But no, you won't listen. So you are **storing up** terrible punishment for yourself because of your stubbornness in refusing to turn from your sin. For there is going to come a day of judgment when God, the just judge of all the world, [NLT]
	κατὰ δὲ τὴν σκληρότητά σου καὶ ἀμετανόητον καρδίαν θησαυρίζεις σεαυτῷ ὀργὴν ἐν ἡμέρᾳ ὀργῆς καὶ ἀποκαλύψεως δικαιοκρισίας τοῦ Θεοῦ, [GNS]
	κατὰ δὲ τὴν σκληρότητά σου καὶ ἀμετανόητον καρδίαν θησαυρίζεις σεαυτῷ ὀργὴν ἐν ἡμέρᾳ ὀργῆς καὶ ἀποκαλύψεως δικαιοκρισίας τοῦ θεοῦ [GNT]
		Store up, save, put aside, heap up, lay up.
		
		Practical Application
		The man who hardens his heart and refuses to repent stores up more and more wrath against himself in the day of judgment.

#4042 **Treasury**	γαζοφυλάκιον = *gazophulakion* Pronunciation: [gad-zof-oo-lak'-ee-on] Parsing (part of speech): noun Case—accusative	The temple treasury; a collection box; an offering box; the place where the offerings were put.

ENGLISH WORD	GREEK WORD AND VERSE	THE WORD MEANS...
Treasury–KJV **Treasury–NASB** Temple treasury–NIV **Treasury–NKJV** Collection box–NLT **POSB REFERENCE** (Lk.21:1) *Deeper Study #1*	Gender—neuter Number—singular Stem or root—from γαζοφυλάκιον, ου Concordance References: ⇒ Strong's #1049 gazophulakion ⇒ NIV #1126 gazophulakion ⇒ NASB #1049 gazophulakion **Luke 21:1** And he looked up, and saw the rich men casting their gifts into the **treasury**. [KJV] And He looked up and saw the rich putting their gifts into the **treasury**. [NASB] As he looked up, Jesus saw the rich putting their gifts into the **temple treasury**. [NIV] And He looked up and saw the rich putting their gifts into the **treasury**, [NKJV] While Jesus was in the Temple, he watched the rich people putting their gifts into the **collection box**. [NLT] Ἀναβλέψας δὲ εἶδε τοὺς βάλλοντας τὰ δῶρα αὐτῶν εἰς τὸ **γαζοφυλάκιον** αὐτῶν πλουσίους· [GNS] Ἀναβλέψας δὲ εἶδεν τοὺς βάλλοντας εἰς τὸ **γαζοφυλάκιον** τὰ δῶρα αὐτῶν πλουσίους. [GNT]	**Practical Application** The treasury box was in the court of the women. A section of the court had thirteen trumpet shaped collection boxes. Each box had written on it the purpose for which the offerings were to be used. People simply dropped their offerings into the box of the ministry they wished to support.
#4043 Treat Provoke–KJV Provoke–NASB Exasperate–NIV Provoke–NKJV Treat–NLT **POSB REFERENCE** (Eph.6:4) Note 2	παροργίζετε = *parorgizete* Pronunciation: [par-org-id'-zeh-teh] Parsing (part of speech): verb Mood—imperative Tense—present Voice—active Person—2nd person Number—plural Stem or root—from παροργίζω Concordance References: ⇒ Strong's #3949 parorgizō ⇒ NIV #4239 parorgizō ⇒ NASB #3949 parorgizō **Ephes. 6:4** And, ye fathers, **provoke** not your children to wrath: but bring them up in the nurture and admonition of the Lord. [KJV] And, fathers, do not **provoke** your children to anger; but bring them up in the discipline and instruction of the Lord. [NASB] Fathers, do not **exasperate** your children; instead, bring them up in the training and instruction of the Lord. [NIV] And you, fathers, do not **provoke** your children to wrath, but bring them up in the training and admonition of the Lord. [NKJV] And now a word to you fathers. Don't make your children angry by the way you **treat** them. Rather, bring them up with the discipline and instruction approved by the Lord. [NLT] καὶ οἱ πατέρες, μὴ **παροργίζετε** τὰ τέκνα ὑμῶν, ἀλλ ἐκτρέφετε αὐτὰ ἐν παιδείᾳ καὶ νουθεσίᾳ Κυρίου. [GNS] Καὶ οἱ πατέρες, μὴ **παροργίζετε** τὰ τέκνα ὑμῶν ἀλλὰ ἐκτρέφετε αὐτὰ ἐν παιδείᾳ καὶ νουθεσίᾳ κυρίου. [GNT]	To exasperate; to provoke; to treat wrongly; to anger. The word "treat" (*parorgizete*) means to arouse to wrath or anger, to provoke to the point of utter exasperation and resentment. **Practical Application** Parents are not to make their children angry by treating them wrongly. Parents are bound to upset and irritate their children sometimes; we all upset and irritate people sometimes. Discipline, correction, and reproof are seldom enjoyable experiences. Their very nature is that of disturbance and irritation. This is not what this instruction means. Four things will provoke a child. 1. Failing to accept the fact that things do change. Time and generations do change. This does not mean that a child should participate in nor be allowed to do everything that his generation does. But it does mean that parents need to be alert to the changes between generations and allow the child to be a part of his own generation instead of trying to conform the child to the parent's childhood generation. The parent's childhood generation does not exist nor will it ever exist again. 2. Overcontrolling a child will also provoke a child to wrath. Overcontrol ranges all the way from stern restriction and discipline to child abuse. Disciplining and restricting a child too much will either stifle the growth of a child or stir him to react and rebel, causing the child to flee from the parent. What is too much discipline? How much should a child be restricted? Should he be allowed to do everything he wants? No! There is a limit, and the limit must be placed upon the child and discipline must be exercised when the limit is crossed. 3. Undercontrolling a child can provoke a child. It should be noted that this is the most prevalent problem in an industrialized society. There is a tendency for those with plenty or with wealth to pamper, indulge, and give a child everything imaginable—well beyond what a child needs and what is really best for him.

ENGLISH WORD	GREEK WORD AND VERSE	THE WORD MEANS...

#4048
Trials
 	
Tribulation–KJV
Tribulation–NASB
Suffering–NIV
Tribulation–NKJV
Trials–NLT
 	
**POSB
REFERENCE**
(Romans 5:3-5; esp.
v.3)
Note 5
 	
See also POSB REF:
(Rom.2:9)
Deeper Study #8
	θλῖψις = *thlipsis*
	Pronunciation: [thlip'-sis]
	Parsing (part of speech): noun
	    Case—nominative
	    Gender—feminine
	    Number—singular
	    Stem or root—from θλῖψις, εως
	Concordance References:
	⇒ Strong's #2347 thlipsis
	⇒ NIV #2568 thlipsis
	⇒ NASB #2347 thlipsis
	
	Romans 5:3
	And not only *so*, but we glory in tribulations also: knowing that **tribulation** worketh patience; [KJV]
	And not only this, but we also exult in our tribulations, knowing that **tribulation** brings about perseverance; [NASB]
	Not only so, but we also rejoice in our sufferings, because we know that **suffering** produces perseverance; [NIV]
	And not only *that*, but we also glory in tribulations, knowing that **tribulation** produces perseverance; [NKJV]
	We can rejoice, too, when we run into problems and **trials**, for we know that they are good for us—they help us learn to endure. [NLT]
	οὐ μόνον δέ, ἀλλὰ καὶ καυχώμεθα ἐν ταῖς θλίψεσιν, εἰδότες ὅτι ἡ **θλῖψις** ὑπομονὴν κατεργάζεται, [GNS]
	οὐ μόνον δέ, ἀλλὰ καὶ καυχώμεθα ἐν ταῖς θλίψεσιν, εἰδότες ὅτι ἡ **θλῖψις** ὑπομονὴν κατεργάζεται, [GNT]
		Trouble, distress, hard circumstances, trials, suffering. The word "trials" or "tribulations" (*thlipsis*) means pressure, oppression, affliction, and distress. It means to be pressed together ever so tightly. It means all kinds of pressure ranging from the day-to-day pressures to the pressure of confronting the most serious afflictions, even that of death itself.
		
		Practical Application
		When a man is truly justified, he is no longer defeated by trials and sufferings. Trials and sufferings no longer discourage and swamp him, no longer cast him down into the dungeon of despair and hopelessness. The very opposite is true. Trials and sufferings become purposeful and meaningful. The truly justified man knows...
		• that his life and welfare are completely under God's care and watchful eye.
		• therefore, whatever events come into his life—whether good or bad—they are allowed by God for a reason. The justified man knows that God will take the trials and sufferings of this world and work them out for good, even if God has to twist and move every event surrounding the believer.

#4049
Trials
 	
Temptations–KJV
Temptation–NASB
Trials–NIV
Temptations–NKJV
Trials–NLT
 	
**POSB
REFERENCE**
(2 Pt.2:3-9; esp. v.9)
Note 5, point 4
	πειρασμοῦ = *peirasmou*
	Pronunciation: [pi-ras-moo']
	Parsing (part of speech): noun
	    Case—genitive
	    Gender—masculine
	    Number—singular
	    Stem or root—from πειρασμός, οῦ
	Concordance References:
	⇒ Strong's #3986 peirasmos
	⇒ NIV #4280 peirasmos
	⇒ NASB #3986 peirasmos
	
	2 Peter 2:9
	The Lord knoweth how to deliver the godly out of **temptations**, and to reserve the unjust unto the day of judgment to be punished: [KJV]
	Then the Lord knows how to rescue the godly from **temptation**, and to keep the unrighteous under punishment for the day of judgment, [NASB]
	If this is so, then the Lord knows how to rescue godly men from **trials** and to hold the unrighteous for the day of judgment, while continuing their punishment. [NIV]
	Then the Lord knows how to deliver the godly out of **temptations** and to reserve the unjust under punishment for the day of judgment, [NKJV]
	So you see, the Lord knows how to rescue godly people from their **trials**, even while punishing the wicked right up until the day of judgment. [NLT]
	οἶδε Κύριος εὐσεβεῖς ἐκ **πειρασμῶν** ῥύεσθαι, ἀδίκους δὲ εἰς ἡμέραν κρίσεως κολαζομένους τηρεῖν· [GNS]
	οἶδεν κύριος εὐσεβεῖς ἐκ **πειρασμοῦ** ῥύεσθαι, ἀδίκους δὲ εἰς ἡμέραν κρίσεως κολαζομένους τηρεῖν, [GNT]
		Trials, temptations, testings, enticements.
		
		Practical Application
		God knows how to deliver the godly and reserve the unjust until the day of judgment to be punished. This verse completes the sentence begun in 2 Peter 2:4. Note what it is that God delivers the godly from: temptations and trials (*peirasmou*); all the temptations and trials of life. There is no excuse for a false teacher preaching or teaching false doctrine—no excuse for him to fear other preachers or teachers or other men within his church nor to shy away from the truth—for God knows how to meet the needs of the man. God knows how to deliver the man from every obstacle and through every difficulty, no matter how great a trial or temptation. No matter who opposes the teacher, God knows how to deliver him. He delivered Noah and Lot both through the most trying opposition and ungodliness. But note this: God also knows how to keep the ungodly until the day of judgment and doom. All false teachers will be judged and doomed to punishment.

#4050
Trials
 	
Temptations–KJV
Trials–NASB
Trials–NIV
	πειρασμοῖς = *peirasmois*
	Pronunciation: [pi-ras-moys']
	Parsing (part of speech): noun
	    Case—dative
	    Gender—masculine
	    Number—plural
	    Stem or root—from πειρασμός, οῦ
	Concordance References:
		Trials, temptations, troubles, testings.
		
		Practical Application
		The fact is certain—we will have many trials and temptations. The Greek word used for temptations or trials throughout James is *peirasmois*. It means to tempt; to try; to test; to prove.

ENGLISH WORD	GREEK WORD AND VERSE	THE WORD MEANS...
Trials–NKJV Trouble–NLT **POSB REFERENCE** (Jas.1:2) Note 1	⇒ Strong's #3986 peirasmos ⇒ NIV #4280 peirasmos ⇒ NASB #3986 peirasmos **James 1:2** My brethren, count it all joy when ye fall into divers **temptations**; [KJV] Consider it all joy, my brethren, when you encounter various **trials**, [NASB] Consider it pure joy, my brothers, whenever you face **trials** of many kinds, [NIV] My brethren, count it all joy when you fall into various **trials**, [NKJV] Dear brothers and sisters, whenever **trouble** comes your way, let it be an opportunity for joy. [NLT] Πᾶσαν χαρὰν ἡγήσασθε, ἀδελφοί μου, ὅταν **πειρασμοῖς** περιπέσητε ποικίλοις, [GNS] Πᾶσαν χαρὰν ἡγήσασθε, ἀδελφοί μου, ὅταν **πειρασμοῖς** περιπέσητε ποικίλοις, [GNT]	Throughout the Bible the word peirasmos and its various forms are used to refer to both the temptations and trials of life. But note that the word means far more than just to tempt; it means... • to test • to try • to prove That is, the temptations and trials of life are to prove us: they are for a beneficial purpose; they are permitted by God for a good purpose (W.E. Vine. *Expository Dictionary of New Testament Words*, p.116). What is that purpose? To make us stronger and more pure. ⇒ When we conquer temptation, we become much more pure persons—more holy, righteous, and just. ⇒ When we triumphantly go through the trials of life, we become much stronger persons—more steadfast, enduring, and persevering ⇒ When we stand up against trials and temptations, we become dynamic witnesses to all those who see us: we demonstrate the living presence and power of Christ—that He actually does live in our hearts and lives and is going to give us eternal life. As said, God allows temptations and trials for a good and beneficial purpose: to prove us—to make us much stronger and much more pure and righteous. God wants us to face the temptations and trials of life and to conquer them and, by conquering them, to become much more like Christ and to make Christ more fully known to the world. Note one other thing that James says: he says that we will *fall into all kinds* of temptations and trials. The Greek scholar A.T. Robertson says, "It is the picture of being surrounded (peri) by trials" (*Word Pictures in the New Testament*, Vol. 6, p.11). The idea is that of many trials and temptations, of all sorts and of all kinds of temptations and trials. But we must always remember: no matter what the trial or temptation, it is for our good and for our benefit. It is to help us. It is to prove us—to make us stronger and much more pure and righteous—to make us much more dynamic witnesses for Christ. God allows trials and temptations to make us more and more like Jesus.
#4051 **Tribulation** **Tribulation–KJV** **Tribulation–NASB** Suffering–NIV **Tribulation–NKJV** Trials–NLT **POSB REFERENCE** (Rom.5:3-5; esp. v.3) Note 5 **See also POSB REF:** (Rom.2:9) *Deeper Study #8*	θλῖψις = *thlipsis* Pronunciation: [thlip'-sis] Parsing (part of speech): noun 　Case—nominative 　Gender—feminine 　Number—singular 　Stem or root—from θλῖψις, εως Concordance References: ⇒ Strong's #2347 thlipsis ⇒ NIV #2568 thlipsis ⇒ NASB #2347 thlipsis **Romans 5:3** And not only *so,* but we glory in tribulations also: knowing that **tribulation** worketh patience; [KJV] And not only this, but we also exult in our tribulations, knowing that **tribulation** brings about perseverance; [NASB] Not only so, but we also rejoice in our sufferings,	Trouble, distress, hard circumstances, trials, suffering. The word "trials" or "tribulations" (*thlipsis*) means pressure, oppression, affliction, and distress. It means to be pressed together ever so tightly. It means all kinds of pressure ranging from the day-to-day pressures to the pressure of confronting the most serious afflictions, even that of death itself. **Practical Application** When a man is truly justified, he is no longer defeated by trials and sufferings. Tribulations and sufferings no longer discourage and swamp him, no longer cast him down into the dungeon of despair and hopelessness. The very opposite is true. Tribulations and sufferings become purposeful and meaningful. The truly justified man knows...

ENGLISH WORD	GREEK WORD AND VERSE	THE WORD MEANS...
	because we know that **suffering** produces perseverance; [NIV] And not only *that*, but we also glory in tribulations, knowing that **tribulation** produces perseverance; [NKJV] We can rejoice, too, when we run into problems and **trials**, for we know that they are good for us—they help us learn to endure. [NLT] οὐ μόνον δέ, ἀλλὰ καὶ καυχώμεθα ἐν ταῖς θλίψεσιν, εἰδότες ὅτι ἡ **θλίψις** ὑπομονὴν κατεργάζεται, [GNS] οὐ μόνον δέ, ἀλλὰ καὶ καυχώμεθα ἐν ταῖς θλίψεσιν, εἰδότες ὅτι ἡ **θλίψις** ὑπομονὴν κατεργάζεται, [GNT]	• that his life and welfare are completely under God's care and watchful eye. • therefore, whatever events come into his life—whether good or bad—they are allowed by God for a reason. The justified man knows that God will take the trials and sufferings of this world and work them out for good, even if God has to twist and move every event surrounding the believer.

#4052
Tribulation
 	
Tribulation–KJV
Affliction–NASB
Troubles–NIV
Tribulation–NKJV
Troubles–NLT
 	
**POSB
REFERENCE**
(2 Cor.1:4)
Note 2
 	
See also POSB REF:
(1 Thes.3:7-10; esp. v.7)
Note 4, point 1
	θλίψει = *thlipsei*
	Pronunciation: [thlip'-see]
	Parsing (part of speech): noun
	  Case—dative
	  Gender—feminine
	  Number—singular
	  Stem or root—from θλίψις, εως
	Concordance References:
	⇒ Strong's #2347 thlipsis
	⇒ NIV #2568 thlipsis
	⇒ NASB #2347 thlipsis
	
	2 Cor. 1:4
	Who comforteth us in all our **tribulation**, that we may be able to comfort them which are in any trouble, by the comfort wherewith we ourselves are comforted of God. [KJV]
	
	Who comforts us in all our **affliction** so that we may be able to comfort those who are in any affliction with the comfort with which we ourselves are comforted by God. [NASB]
	
	Who comforts us in all our **troubles**, so that we can comfort those in any trouble with the comfort we ourselves have received from God. [NIV]
	
	Who comforts us in all our **tribulation**, that we may be able to comfort those who are in any trouble, with the comfort with which we ourselves are comforted by God. [NKJV]
	
	He comforts us in all our **troubles** so that we can comfort others. When others are troubled, we will be able to give them the same comfort God has given us. [NLT]
	
	ὁ παρακαλῶν ἡμᾶς ἐπὶ πάσῃ τῇ θλίψει ἡμῶν, εἰς τὸ δύνασθαι ἡμᾶς παρακαλεῖν τοὺς ἐν πάσῃ **θλίψει**, διὰ τῆς παρακλήσεως ἧς παρακαλούμεθα αὐτοὶ ὑπὸ τοῦ Θεοῦ· [GNS]
	
	ὁ παρακαλῶν ἡμᾶς ἐπὶ πάσῃ τῇ θλίψει ἡμῶν, εἰς τὸ δύνασθαι ἡμᾶς παρακαλεῖν τοὺς ἐν πάσῃ **θλίψει** διὰ τῆς παρακλήσεως ἧς παρακαλούμεθα αὐτοὶ ὑπὸ τοῦ Θεοῦ· [GNT]
		To have trouble, tribulation, affliction, distress; to suffer from hard circumstances; to be weighed down exceedingly; to be pressed and crushed. It means persecution, affliction, crushing troubles, hard circumstances, terrible suffering.
		
		Practical Application
		It is the picture of a beast of burden being crushed beneath a load that is just too heavy. It is the picture of a person's having a heavy weight placed on his breast and being pressed and crushed to the point that he feels he is going to die. Note the word is used four times in 2 Cor. 1:3-7.

#4053
Tribulation
 	
Tribulation–KJV
Tribulation–NASB
Afflictions–NIV
Tribulation–NKJV
Suffering–NLT
 	
**POSB
REFERENCE**
(Rev.2:9)
Note 3, point 1
	θλίψιν = *thlipsin*
	Pronunciation: [thlip'-sin]
	Parsing (part of speech): noun
	  Case—accusative
	  Gender—feminine
	  Number—singular
	  Stem or root—from θλίψις, εως
	Concordance References:
	⇒ Strong's #2347 thlipsis
	⇒ NIV #2568 thlipsis
	⇒ NASB #2347 thlipsis
	
	Rev. 2:9
	I know thy works, and **tribulation**, and poverty, (but thou art rich) and *I know* the blasphemy of them which say they are Jews, and are not, but *are* the synagogue of Satan. [KJV]
	
	'I know your **tribulation** and your poverty (but you are rich), and the blasphemy by those who say they are Jews and are not, but are a synagogue of Satan. [NASB]
		Afflictions, trials, tribulations, persecutions, sufferings, troubles. It means the pressure of crushing affliction. It means troubles, hard circumstances, distresses, pressures, strains, tensions that come both from within and without.
		
		Practical Application
		This word indicates that the trials and persecution were most severe. But the believers were holding up under the attacks and refusing to deny Christ. They were faithful to Christ despite all the ridicule, mockery, abuse, cursing, loss of property, possible imprisonment and martyrdom.

ENGLISH WORD	GREEK WORD AND VERSE	THE WORD MEANS...
	I know your **afflictions** and your poverty—yet you are rich! I know the slander of those who say they are Jews and are not, but are a synagogue of Satan. [NIV] I know your works, **tribulation**, and poverty (but you are rich); and *I know* the blasphemy of those who say they are Jews and are not, but *are* a synagogue of Satan. [NKJV] "I know about your **suffering** and your poverty—but you are rich! I know the slander of those opposing you. They say they are Jews, but they really aren't because theirs is a synagogue of Satan. [NLT] Οἶδά σου τὰ ἔργα καὶ τὴν **θλῖψιν** καὶ τὴν πτωχείαν, -- πλούσιος δὲ εἶ -- , καὶ τὴν βλασφημίαν τῶν λεγόντων Ἰουδαίους εἶναι ἑαυτούς, καὶ οὐκ εἰσίν, ἀλλὰ συναγωγὴ τοῦ Σατανᾶ. [GNS] Οἶδά σου τὴν **θλῖψιν** καὶ τὴν πτωχείαν, ἀλλὰ πλούσιος εἶ, καὶ τὴν βλασφημίαν ἐκ τῶν λεγόντων Ἰουδαίους εἶναι ἑαυτούς, καὶ οὐκ εἰσὶν ἀλλὰ συναγωγὴ τοῦ Σατανᾶ. [GNT]	

#4054
Tribulations
 	
Afflictions–KJV
Afflictions–NASB
Troubles–NIV
Tribulations–NKJV
Troubles–NLT
 	
POSB REFERENCE
(2 Cor.6:4-5; esp. v.4)
Note 3
 	
See also POSB REF:
(2 Thes.1:4-5; esp. v.4)
Note 6
	θλίψεσιν = *thlipsesin*
	Pronunciation: [thlips'-seh-sin]
	Parsing (part of speech): noun
	   Case—dative
	   Gender—feminine
	   Number—plural
	   Stem or root—from θλῖψις, εως
	Concordance References:
	  ⇒ Strong's #2347 thlipsis
	  ⇒ NIV #2568 thlipsis
	  ⇒ NASB #2347 thlipsis
	
	2 Cor. 6:4
	But in all *things* approving ourselves as the ministers of God, in much patience, in **afflictions**, in necessities, in distresses, [KJV]
	
	But in everything commending ourselves as servants of God, in much endurance, in **afflictions**, in hardships, in distresses, [NASB]
	
	Rather, as servants of God we commend ourselves in every way: in great endurance; in **troubles**, hardships and distresses; [NIV]
	
	But in all *things* we commend ourselves as ministers of God: in much patience, in **tribulations**, in needs, in distresses, [NKJV]
	
	In everything we do we try to show that we are true ministers of God. We patiently endure **troubles** and hardships and calamities of every kind. [NLT]
	
	ἀλλ' ἐν παντὶ συνίσταντες ἑαυτοὺς ὡς Θεοῦ διάκονοι, ἐν ὑπομονῇ πολλῇ, ἐν **θλίψεσιν**, ἐν ἀνάγκαις, ἐν στενοχωρίαις, [GNS]
	
	ἀλλ' ἐν παντὶ συνίσταντες ἑαυτοὺς ὡς θεοῦ διάκονοι, ἐν ὑπομονῇ πολλῇ, ἐν **θλίψεσιν**, ἐν ἀνάγκαις, ἐν στενοχωρίαις, [GNT]
		To have trouble, tribulation, affliction, distress; to suffer from hard circumstances; to be weighed down exceedingly; to be pressed and crushed. It means persecution, affliction, crushing trouble, hard circumstance, terrible suffering.
		
		Practical Application
		Things often press in upon a man, weigh upon and burden down his heart. Sometimes the pressure is so heavy and tight that a man feels as though he is going to explode or be crushed. The pressure may come from some lustful temptation or from some strong trial, but no matter, he is to steadfastly endure all pressing troubles.

#4055
Trick
 	
Craftiness–KJV
Craftiness–NASB
Deception–NIV
Craftiness–NKJV
Trick–NLT
 	
POSB REFERENCE
(2 Cor.4:2)
Note 2
	πανουργία = *panourgia*
	Pronunciation: [pan-oorg-ee'-ah]
	Parsing (part of speech): noun
	   Case—dative
	   Gender—feminine
	   Number—singular
	   Stem or root—from πανουργία, ας
	Concordance References:
	  ⇒ Strong's #3834 panourgia
	  ⇒ NIV #4111 panourgia
	  ⇒ NASB #3834 panourgia
	
	2 Cor. 4:2
	But have renounced the hidden things of dishonesty, not walking in **craftiness**, nor handling the word of God deceitfully; but by manifestation of the truth commending ourselves to every man's conscience in the sight of God. [KJV]
		Deception, craftiness, trickery, cunning, cleverness, shrewdness, evil design. It means a man who will do anything and use any means to get what he wants.
		
		Practical Application
		Note the minister is not to "walk" this way; he is not to walk using and misusing people, circumstances, events, and things for his own end. The minister of God is to walk as Jesus walked.

ENGLISH WORD	GREEK WORD AND VERSE	THE WORD MEANS...

#4059
Tried–Trying
 	
Assayed–KJV
Trying–NASB
Tried–NIV
Tried–NKJV
Tried–NLT
 	
POSB REFERENCE
(Acts 9:26-28; esp. v.26)
Note 2, point 1
	ἐπείραζεν = *epeirazen*
	Pronunciation: [eh-peh-i'-rahd-zen]
	Parsing (part of speech): verb
	  Mood—indicative
	  Tense—imperfect
	  Voice—active
	  Person—3rd person
	  Number—singular
	  Stem or root—from *πειράζω*
	Concordance References:
	⇒ Strong's #3987 peirao
	⇒ NIV #4279 peirazō
	⇒ NASB #3985 peirazō
	
	Acts 9:26
	And when Saul was come to Jerusalem, he **assayed** to join himself to the disciples: but they were all afraid of him, and believed not that he was a disciple. [KJV]
	And when he had come to Jerusalem, he was **trying** to associate with the disciples; and they were all afraid of him, not believing that he was a disciple. [NASB]
	When he came to Jerusalem, he **tried** to join the disciples, but they were all afraid of him, not believing that he really was a disciple. [NIV]
	And when Saul had come to Jerusalem, he **tried** to join the disciples; but they were all afraid of him, and did not believe that he was a disciple. [NKJV]
	When Saul arrived in Jerusalem, he **tried** to meet with the believers, but they were all afraid of him. They thought he was only pretending to be a believer! [NLT]
	Παραγενόμενος δὲ ὁ Σαῦλος εἰς Ἰερουσαλήμ, **ἐπείρᾶτο** κολλᾶσθαι τοῖς μαθηταῖς· καὶ πάντες ἐφοβοῦντο αὐτόν, μὴ πιστεύοντες ὅτι ἐστὶ μαθητής. [GNS]
	Παραγενόμενος δὲ εἰς Ἰερουσαλὴμ **ἐπείραζεν** κολλᾶσθαι τοῖς μαθηταῖς, καὶ πάντες ἐφοβοῦντο αὐτόν μὴ πιστεύοντες ὅτι ἐστὶν μαθητής. [GNT]
		To try; to try repeatedly; to put to the test; to attempt.
		
		Practical Application
		Paul was faithful in seeking fellowship with believers, but they rejected him. Paul fled to Jerusalem. Note these facts.
		1. Paul tried and tried to join the disciples at Jerusalem.
		2. Paul's past as the arch-persecutor of believers haunted him; the believers would not accept him. They did not believe his testimony. They were suspicious, thinking he was an imposter trying to work his way into the circle of believers...
		  • to spy upon them.
		  • to identify all the disciples so he could arrest them.
		3. Paul was befriended by Barnabas. Somehow Barnabas began to sense Paul may be telling the truth. Apparently, he sat down with Paul and had Paul relate his experiences with Christ. Barnabas became thoroughly convinced that Paul was truthful and took Paul to the apostles. (By apostles is meant Peter and James, the half-brother of Jesus who was to become, if he were not already, the pastor of the church at Jerusalem [Galatians 1:18-19]. The other apostles were probably out of town on some mission.) Note that Barnabas, after introducing Paul to Peter and James, shared three things about Paul:
		⇒ that Paul's conversion was real—that he had actually seen the Lord on the road to Damascus.
		⇒ that the Lord had actually spoken to Paul.
		⇒ that Paul had been preaching boldly in Damascus.
		4. Paul was finally accepted. Peter was convinced and invited Paul to stay with him. Paul did, and he stayed fifteen glorious days, fellowshipping with the man whom the Lord Himself had chosen to be the first leader of His dear people (cp. Galatians 1:18. Note: Paul said his primary purpose for coming to Jerusalem was to see Peter.) This was important for it meant he had not gone for the purpose of ministering, but to learn about Jesus from the leader of the apostolic band. Note also that while there, Paul was not sitting around revelling in the fellowship of Peter and James. He still ministered, still bore witness of the saving grace of God. He went out to preach Jesus.
		  Note the great struggle Paul went through just to be able to worship and fellowship with other believers. There was no thought whatsoever about forsaking the assembly of believers, no thoughts about worshipping alone out in nature or wherever. He fought to fellowship with other believers, fought until they accepted him.

#4060
Tried My Patience
	δοκιμασία = *dokimasia*
	Pronunciation: [dok-im-ahs-see-ah]
	Parsing (part of speech): noun
	  Case—dative
	  Gender—feminine
	  Number—singular
		Trying, proving, testing; to try God's patience; to test Him.
		
		Practical Application
		They tried (*dokimasia*) God's patience. This

ENGLISH WORD	GREEK WORD AND VERSE	THE WORD MEANS...
Proved–KJV Testing–NASB Tried–NIV Tried–NKJV **Tried my patience–** **NLT** **POSB** **REFERENCE** (Heb.3:7-11; esp. v.9) Note 1	Stem or root—from **δοκιμασία**, ας Concordance References: ⇒ Strong's #1381 dokimazo ⇒ NIV #1508 dokimasia ⇒ NASB #1381b dokimasia **Hebrews 3:9** When your fathers tempted me, **proved** me, and saw my works forty years. [KJV] WHERE YOUR FATHERS TRIED *Me* BY TESTING *Me*, AND SAW MY WORKS FOR FORTY YEARS. [NASB] Where your fathers tested and **tried** me and for forty years saw what I did. [NIV] Where your fathers tested Me, **tried** Me, And saw My works forty years. [NKJV] There your ancestors **tried my patience**, even though they saw my miracles for forty years. [NLT] οὖ ἐπείρασαν με οἱ πατέρες ὑμῶν, **ἐδοκίμασάν** με, καὶ εἶδον τὰ ἔργα μου τεσσεράκοντα ἔτη· [GNS] οὖ ἐπείρασαν οἱ πατέρες ὑμῶν ἐν **δοκιμασίᾳ** καὶ εἶδον τὰ ἔργα μου [GNT]	means they tested Him, put Him to the test to see if He met their approval. If God would prove faithful, then He would be worthy of their obedience and loyalty. They wanted Him to prove Himself first, then they would follow Him. Note the unbelief and hardness of heart in all this. There is no belief or trust. They wanted God to prove Himself by giving the provision without any trial or suffering. They were unwilling to prove themselves, unwilling to show that they really believed and trusted God. They wanted God to prove Himself, that He was worthy of their trust and loyalty. What audacity! What an affront! What unbelief and hardness of heart—total disobedience!

#4061
Trouble
 	
Temptations–KJV
Trials–NASB
Trials–NIV
Trials–NKJV
Trouble–NLT
 	
POSB
REFERENCE
(Jas.1:2)
Note 1
	πειρασμοῖς = peirasmois
	Pronunciation: [pi-ras-moys']
	Parsing (part of speech): noun
	   Case—dative
	   Gender—masculine
	   Number—plural
	   Stem or root—from **πειρασμός**, οῦ
	Concordance References:
	⇒ Strong's #3986 peirasmos
	⇒ NIV #4280 peirasmos
	⇒ NASB #3986 peirasmos
	
	James 1:2
	My brethren, count it all joy when ye fall into divers **temptations**; [KJV]
	Consider it all joy, my brethren, when you encounter various **trials**, [NASB]
	Consider it pure joy, my brothers, whenever you face **trials** of many kinds, [NIV]
	My brethren, count it all joy when you fall into various **trials**, [NKJV]
	Dear brothers and sisters, whenever **trouble** comes your way, let it be an opportunity for joy. [NLT]
	Πᾶσαν χαρὰν ἡγήσασθε, ἀδελφοί μου, ὅταν **πειρασμοῖς** περιπέσητε ποικίλοις, [GNS]
	Πᾶσαν χαρὰν ἡγήσασθε, ἀδελφοί μου, ὅταν **πειρασμοῖς** περιπέσητε ποικίλοις, [GNT]
		Trials, temptations, troubles, testings.
		
		Practical Application
		The fact is certain—we will have many trials and temptations. The Greek word used for temptations or trials throughout James is *peirasmois*. It means to tempt; to try; to test; to prove. Throughout the Bible the word *peirasmos* and its various forms are used to refer to both the temptations and trials of life. But note that the word means far more than just to tempt; it means...
		• to test
		• to try
		• to prove
		That is, the temptations and trials of life are to prove us: they are for a beneficial purpose; they are permitted by God for a good purpose (W.E. Vine. *Expository Dictionary of New Testament Words*, p.116). What is that purpose? To make us stronger and more pure.
		⇒ When we conquer temptation, we become much more pure persons—more holy, righteous, and just.
		⇒ When we triumphantly go through the trials of life, we become much stronger persons—more stedfast, enduring, and persevering
		⇒ When we stand up against trials and temptations, we become dynamic witnesses to all those who see us: we demonstrate the living presence and power of Christ—that He actually does live in our hearts and lives and is going to give us eternal life.
		As said, God allows temptations and trials for a good and beneficial purpose: to prove us—to make us much stronger and much more pure and righteous. God wants us to face the temptations and trials of life and to conquer them and, by conquering them, to become much more like Christ and to make Christ more fully known to the world.
		Note one other thing that James says: he says that we'll *fall into all kinds* of temptations and trials. The Greek scholar A.T. Robertson says, "It is the picture of being surrounded (peri) by trials" (*Word Pictures in the New Testament*, Vol. 6, p.11). The idea is that of many trials and temp-

ENGLISH WORD	GREEK WORD AND VERSE	THE WORD MEANS...
#4066 **Troubled** Troubled–KJV Disturbed–NASB Disturbed–NIV Troubled–NKJV Troubled–NLT **POSB** **REFERENCE** (Acts 15:24) Note 2, point 1	ἐτάραξαν = etaraxan Pronunciation: [eh-tar-axs'-sahn] Parsing (part of speech): verb 　Mood—indicative 　Tense—aorist 　Voice—active 　Person—3rd person 　Number—plural 　Stem or root—from ταράσσω Concordance References: ⇒ Strong's #5015 tarassö ⇒ NIV #5429 tarassö ⇒ NASB #5015 tarassö **Acts 15:24** Forasmuch as we have heard, that certain which went out from us have **troubled** you with words, subverting your souls, saying, *Ye must* be circumcised, and keep the law: to whom we gave no *such* commandment: [KJV] "Since we have heard that some of our number to whom we gave no instruction have **disturbed** you with their words, unsettling your souls, [NASB] We have heard that some went out from us without our authorization and **disturbed** you, troubling your minds by what they said. [NIV] Since we have heard that some who went out from us have **troubled** you with words, unsettling your souls, saying, "You must be circumcised and keep the law"—to whom we gave no *such* commandment— [NKJV] "We understand that some men from here have **troubled** you and upset you with their teaching, but they had no such instructions from us. [NLT] Ἐπειδὴ ἠκούσαμεν ὅτι τινὲς ἐξ ἡμῶν ἐξελθόντες **ἐτάραξαν** ὑμᾶς λόγοις, ἀνασκευάζοντες τὰς ψυχὰς ὑμῶν, λέγοντες περιτέμνεσθαι καὶ τηρεῖν τὸν νόμον, οἷς οὐ διεστειλάμεθα· [GNS] Ἐπειδὴ ἠκούσαμεν ὅτι τινὲς ἐξ ἡμῶν [ἐξελθόντες] **ἐτάραξαν** ὑμᾶς λόγοις ἀνασκευάζοντες τὰς ψυχὰς ὑμῶν οἷς οὐ διεστειλάμεθα, [GNT]	Disturbed; troubled; terrified; startled; upset; frightened; stirred up; thrown into turmoil. **Practical Application** The picture is that of words heaped upon words, false words that "trouble," disturb, agitate, and shake violently.
#4067 **Troubled** Grieved–KJV Annoyed–NASB Troubled–NIV Annoyed–NKJV Exasperated–NLT **POSB** **REFERENCE** (Acts 16:18) Note 2, point 2	διαπονηθείς = diaponëtheis Pronunciation: [dee-ap-on-ay'-theh-ees] Parsing (part of speech): verb 　Mood—participle 　Tense—aorist 　Voice—passive deponent 　Case—nominative 　Gender—masculine 　Number—singular 　Stem or root—from διαπονέομαι Concordance References: ⇒ Strong's #1278 diaponeomai ⇒ NIV #1387 diaponeomai ⇒ NASB #1278 diaponeomai **Acts 16:18** And this did she many days. But Paul, being **grieved**, turned and said to the spirit, I command thee in the name of Jesus Christ to come out of her. And he came out the same hour. [KJV] And she continued doing this for many days. But Paul was greatly **annoyed**, and turned and said to the spirit, "I command you in the name of Jesus Christ to come out of her!" And it came out at that very moment. [NASB] She kept this up for many days. Finally Paul became so **troubled** that he turned around and said to the spirit, "In the name of Jesus Christ I command you to come out of her!" At that moment the spirit left her. [NIV] And this she did for many days. But Paul, greatly **annoyed**, turned and said to the spirit, "I command you in the name of Jesus Christ to come out of her." And he came out that very hour. [NKJV]	Troubled, grieved, annoyed, exasperated. The word means pained, deeply troubled, worked up, annoyed, and angry (a righteous anger). **Practical Application** Paul was troubled and hurting... • over the girl's being enslaved by sin. • over the girl's being so used by greedy and lustful men. • over the false witness to the Lord's name. • over the mockery and ridicule of his ministry as the servant of Christ.

ENGLISH WORD	GREEK WORD AND VERSE	THE WORD MEANS...
	This went on day after day until Paul got so **exasperated** that he turned and spoke to the demon within her. "I command you in the name of Jesus Christ to come out of her," he said. And instantly it left her. [NLT] τοῦτο δὲ ἐποίει ἐπὶ πολλὰς ἡμέρας. **διαπονηθεὶς** δὲ ὁ Παῦλος, καὶ ἐπιστρέψας, τῷ πνεύματι εἶπε, Παραγγέλλω σοι ἐν τῷ ὀνόματι Ἰησοῦ Χριστοῦ, ἐξελθεῖν ἀπ᾽ αὐτῆς. Καὶ ἐξῆλθεν αὐτῇ τῇ ὥρᾳ. [GNS] τοῦτο δὲ ἐποίει ἐπὶ πολλὰς ἡμέρας. **διαπονηθεὶς** δὲ Παῦλος καὶ ἐπιστρέψας τῷ πνεύματι εἶπεν, Παραγγέλλω σοι ἐν ὀνόματι Ἰησοῦ Χριστοῦ ἐξελθεῖν ἀπ᾽ αὐτῆς· καὶ ἐξῆλθεν αὐτῇ τῇ ὥρᾳ. [GNT]	

#4068
Troubled, Not
 	
Not troubled–KJV
Not frightened–NASB
Not alarmed–NIV
Not troubled–NKJV
Don't panic–NLT
 	
POSB
REFERENCE
(Mt.24:6-7; esp. v.6)
Note 3, point 2
 	
See also POSB REF:
(Mk.13:7-8; esp. v.7)
Note 3, point 2
	μὴ θροεῖσθε = *më throeisthe*
	Pronunciation: [meh-thro-eis'-the]
	Parsing *throeisthe* (part of speech): verb
	    Mood—imperfect
	    Tense—present
	    Voice—passive
	    Person—2nd person
	    Number—plural
	    Stem or root—from **θροέομαι**
	Concordance References:
	  ⇒ Strong's #3361 më + 2360 throeö
	  ⇒ NIV # 3590 më + 2583 throeö
	  ⇒ NASB #3361 më + 2360 throeö
	
	Matthew 24:6
	And ye shall hear of wars and rumours of wars: see that ye be **not troubled**: for all *these things* must come to pass, but the end is not yet. [KJV]
	"And you will be hearing of wars and rumors of wars; see that you are **not frightened**, for *those things* must take place, but *that* is not yet the end. [NASB]
	You will hear of wars and rumors of wars, but see to it that you are **not alarmed**. Such things must happen, but the end is still to come. [NIV]
	And you will hear of wars and rumors of wars. See that you are **not troubled**; for all *these things* must come to pass, but the end is not yet. [NKJV]
	And wars will break out near and far, but **don't panic**. Yes, these things must come, but the end won't follow immediately. [NLT]
	μελλήσετε δὲ ἀκούειν πολέμους καὶ ἀκοὰς πολέμων· ὁρᾶτε, **μὴ θροεῖσθε**· δεῖ γὰρ γενέσθαι· ἀλλ᾽ οὔπω ἐστὶ τὸ τέλος. [GNS]
	μελλήσετε δὲ ἀκούειν πολέμους καὶ ἀκοὰς πολέμων· ὁρᾶτε **μὴ θροεῖσθε**· δεῖ γὰρ γενέσθαι, ἀλλ᾽ οὔπω ἐστὶν τὸ τέλος. [GNT]
		Not to be disturbed, startled, frightened, alarmed, panicked, troubled, or confused.
		
		Practical Application
		World violence can disturb and frighten. It can lead us into confusion and commotion; to cry out within our inner being. But Christ says this is not to be the case with His disciples. Our hearts are to be fixed upon God, trusting His presence, care, and security (Matthew 10:28; Luke 12:4).
		Three things can happen to the believer in looking at worldwide trouble.
		1. The believer can become overly affected by the news of world affairs and turmoil. Such news can become so interesting and captivating that it can dominate the believer's life. He begins to live and thrive on the news.
		2. The believer can become overly apprehensive about the personal safety of himself and his family. He can begin to fear so much that he forgets that his security is in God, not in this world. Fear over world affairs tends to emphasize the importance of the earth over the importance of God; it tends to emphasize the worldly over the spiritual. The world, of course, is important; but what needs to be stressed is the spiritual. And it is the believer's responsibility to stress the spiritual, the security and peace of heart that is found in Christ.
		3. The believer can become so alarmed over world affairs that he neglects his spiritual duties. The believer is naturally concerned over the world, as all men should be. But he is not to allow world affairs to interfere with his witnessing for Christ. He is to be at peace and to be secure with God, and he is to demonstrate the peace and security of God, going about his daily duties as much as possible within a turbulent world. The point is, the believer is to be witnessing for Christ no matter the turbulence of the world.

#4069
Troubles
 	
Tribulation–KJV
Affliction–NASB
Troubles–NIV
Tribulation–NKJV
Troubles–NLT
 	
POSB
REFERENCE
(2 Cor.1:4)
Note 2
	θλίψει = *thlipsei*
	Pronunciation: [thlip'-see]
	Parsing (part of speech): noun
	    Case—dative
	    Gender—feminine
	    Number—singular
	    Stem or root—from **θλῖψις**, εως
	Concordance References:
	  ⇒ Strong's #2347 thlipsis
	  ⇒ NIV #2568 thlipsis
	  ⇒ NASB #2347 thlipsis
		To have trouble, tribulation, affliction, distress; to suffer from hard circumstances; to be weighed down exceedingly; to be pressed and crushed. It means persecution, affliction, crushing troubles, hard circumstances, terrible suffering.
		
		Practical Application
		It is the picture of a beast of burden being crushed beneath a load that is just too heavy. It is the picture of a person's having a heavy weight placed on his breast and being pressed and

ENGLISH WORD	GREEK WORD AND VERSE	THE WORD MEANS...
See also POSB REF: (1 Thes.3:7-10; esp. v.7) Note 4, point 1	**2 Cor. 1:4** Who comforteth us in all our **tribulation**, that we may be able to comfort them which are in any trouble, by the comfort wherewith we ourselves are comforted of God. [KJV] Who comforts us in all our **affliction** so that we may be able to comfort those who are in any affliction with the comfort with which we ourselves are comforted by God. [NASB] Who comforts us in all our **troubles**, so that we can comfort those in any trouble with the comfort we ourselves have received from God. [NIV] Who comforts us in all our **tribulation**, that we may be able to comfort those who are in any trouble, with the comfort with which we ourselves are comforted by God. [NKJV] He comforts us in all our **troubles** so that we can comfort others. When others are troubled, we will be able to give them the same comfort God has given us. [NLT] ὁ παρακαλῶν ἡμᾶς ἐπὶ πάσῃ τῇ θλίψει ἡμῶν, εἰς τὸ δύνασθαι ἡμᾶς παρακαλεῖν τοὺς ἐν πάσῃ **θλίψει**, διὰ τῆς παρακλήσεως ἧς παρακαλούμεθα αὐτοὶ ὑπὸ τοῦ Θεοῦ· [GNS] ὁ παρακαλῶν ἡμᾶς ἐπὶ πάσῃ τῇ θλίψει ἡμῶν, εἰς τὸ δύνασθαι ἡμᾶς παρακαλεῖν τοὺς ἐν πάσῃ **θλίψει** διὰ τῆς παρακλήσεως ἧς παρακαλούμεθα αὐτοὶ ὑπὸ τοῦ θεοῦ· [GNT]	crushed to the point that he feels he is going to die. Note the word is used four times in 2 Cor. 1:3-7.

#4070
Troubles
 	
Afflictions–KJV
Afflictions–NASB
Troubles–NIV
Tribulations–NKJV
Troubles–NLT
 	
POSB
REFERENCE
(2 Cor.6:4-5; esp. v.4)
Note 3
 	
See also POSB REF:
(2 Thes.1:4-5; esp.
v.4)
Note 6
	θλίψεσιν = *thlipsesin*
	Pronunciation: [thlips'-seh-sin]
	Parsing (part of speech): noun
	  Case—dative
	  Gender—feminine
	  Number—plural
	  Stem or root—from θλίψις, εως
	Concordance References:
	  ⇒ Strong's #2347 thlipsis
	  ⇒ NIV #2568 thlipsis
	  ⇒ NASB #2347 thlipsis
	
	2 Cor. 6:4
	But in all *things* approving ourselves as the ministers of God, in much patience, in **afflictions**, in necessities, in distresses, [KJV]
	But in everything commending ourselves as servants of God, in much endurance, in **afflictions**, in hardships, in distresses, [NASB]
	Rather, as servants of God we commend ourselves in every way: in great endurance; in **troubles**, hardships and distresses; [NIV]
	But in all *things* we commend ourselves as ministers of God: in much patience, in **tribulations**, in needs, in distresses, [NKJV]
	In everything we do we try to show that we are true ministers of God. We patiently endure **troubles** and hardships and calamities of every kind. [NLT]
	ἀλλ' ἐν παντὶ συνίσταντες ἑαυτοὺς ὡς Θεοῦ διάκονοι, ἐν ὑπομονῇ πολλῇ, ἐν **θλίψεσιν**, ἐν ἀνάγκαις, ἐν στενοχωρίαις, [GNS]
	ἀλλ' ἐν παντὶ συνίσταντες ἑαυτοὺς ὡς θεοῦ διάκονοι, ἐν ὑπομονῇ πολλῇ, ἐν **θλίψεσιν**, ἐν ἀνάγκαις, ἐν στενοχωρίαις, [GNT]
		To have trouble, tribulation, affliction, distress; to suffer from hard circumstances; to be weighed down exceedingly; to be pressed and crushed. It means persecution, affliction, crushing trouble, hard circumstance, terrible suffering.
		
		Practical Application
		Things often press in upon a man, weigh upon and burden down his heart. Sometimes the pressure is so heavy and tight that a man feels as though he is going to explode or be crushed. The pressure may come from some lustful temptation or from some strong trial, but no matter, he is to steadfastly endure all pressing troubles.

#4071
Troubling
 	
Subverting–KJV
Unsettling–NASB
Troubling–NIV
Unsettling–NKJV
Upset–NLT
	ἀνασκευάζοντες = *anaskeuazontes*
	Pronunciation: [an-ask-yoo-ad'-zon-tehs]
	Parsing (part of speech): verb
	  Mood—participle
	  Tense—present
	  Voice—active
	  Case—nominative
	  Gender—masculine
	  Number—plural
	  Stem or root—from ἀνασκευάζω
		Troubling, subverting, unsettling, upsetting, disturbing. The word means to devastate; to plunder; to dismantle; to ravage; to wreck; to cause havoc.
		
		Practical Application
		Ritual and law are not necessary to salvation. No matter what anyone teaches, no matter who they are or how influential they are, salvation is...

ENGLISH WORD	GREEK WORD AND VERSE	THE WORD MEANS...
POSB REFERENCE (Acts 15:24) Note 2, point 2	Concordance References: ⇒ Strong's #384 anaskeuazō ⇒ NIV #412 anaskeuazō ⇒ NASB #384 anaskeuazō ### Acts 15:24 Forasmuch as we have heard, that certain which went out from us have troubled you with words, **subverting** your souls, saying, *Ye must* be circumcised, and keep the law: to whom we gave no *such* commandment: [KJV] "Since we have heard that some of our number to whom we gave no instruction have disturbed you with *their* words, **unsettling** your souls, [NASB] We have heard that some went out from us without our authorization and disturbed you, **troubling** your minds by what they said. [NIV] Since we have heard that some who went out from us have troubled you with words, **unsettling** your souls, saying, "You must be circumcised and keep the law"—to whom we gave no such commandment— [NKJV] "We understand that some men from here have troubled you and **upset** you with their teaching, but they had no such instructions from us. [NLT] Ἐπειδὴ ἠκούσαμεν ὅτι τινὲς ἐξ ἡμῶν ἐξελθόντες ἐτάραξαν ὑμᾶς λόγοις, **ἀνασκευάζοντες** τὰς ψυχὰς ὑμῶν, λέγοντες περιτέμνεσθαι καὶ τηρεῖν τον νόμον, οἷς οὐ διεστειλάμεθα· [GNS] Ἐπειδὴ ἠκούσαμεν ὅτι τινὲς ἐξ ἡμῶν [ἐξελθόντες] ἐτάραξαν ὑμᾶς λόγοις **ἀνασκευάζοντες** τὰς ψυχὰς ὑμῶν οἷς οὐ διεστειλάμεθα, [GNT]	• "through the grace of our Lord Jesus Christ" and through His grace alone. Ritual and law are not necessary (Acts 15:11). • "by the miraculous signs and wonders God had done" and by His works alone (Acts 15:12). • by turning to God and turning to Him alone (Acts 15:19). The persons who taught otherwise, the false teachers, were strongly rebuked. 1. They troubled believers with their words. The picture is that of words heaped upon words, false words that "disturb" (*etaraxan*), agitate, disturb, and shake violently. But note: the false teachers proclaimed mere words, empty words, and believers must always remember this. Salvation is by grace alone, and nothing is to be added to it. God and God alone saves. A man either accepts God's salvation or rejects it. It is that simple. Man can do nothing to earn salvation. 2. They were "troubling" (*anaskeuazontes*) the believers' souls. 3. They were never commissioned by the church.

#4072
 Trucebreakers
 	
 Trucebreakers–KJV
 Irreconcilable–NASB
 Unforgiving–NIV
 Unforgiving–NKJV
 Unforgiving–NLT
 	
 POSB REFERENCE (2 Tim. 3:2-4; esp. v.3) Note 2, point 10
	ἄσπονδοι = aspondoi
	 Pronunciation: [as'-pon-doy]
	 Parsing (part of speech): adjective
	     Case—nominative
	     Gender—masculine
	     Number—plural
	     Stem or root—from ἄσπονδος, ον
	 Concordance References:
	 ⇒ Strong's #786 aspondos
	 ⇒ NIV #836 aspondos
	 ⇒ NASB #786 aspondos
	
	 ### 2 Tim. 3:3
	 Without natural affection, **trucebreakers**, false accusers, incontinent, fierce, despisers of those that are good, [KJV]
	 Unloving, **irreconcilable**, malicious gossips, without self-control, brutal, haters of good, [NASB]
	 Without love, **unforgiving**, slanderous, without self-control, brutal, not lovers of the good, [NIV]
	 Unloving, **unforgiving**, slanderers, without self-control, brutal, despisers of good, [NKJV]
	 They will be unloving and **unforgiving**; they will slander others and have no self-control; they will be cruel and have no interest in what is good. [NLT]
	 ἄστοργοι, **ἄσπονδοι**, διάβολοι, ἀκρατεῖς, ἀνήμεροι, ἀφιλάγαθοι, [GNS]
	 ἄστοργοι **ἄσπονδοι** διάβολοι ἀκρατεῖς ἀνήμεροι ἀφιλάγαθοι [GNT]
		Unforgiving, trucebreakers, irreconcilable, merciless, breakers of promises and agreements, untrustworthy, faithless, treacherous, and untruthful.
		
		 ### Practical Application
		 A trucebreaker is a man or some organization or body of people who tragically do not keep their word or promise. They are simply untrustworthy and undependable. What happens when a person's word can no longer be accepted?
		 ⇒ What happens in a home when the husband or wife breaks the truce of marriage?
		 ⇒ What happens between parent and child when one of them breaks his promise time and again?
		 ⇒ What happens when an employer breaks his promise to his workers?
		 ⇒ What happens when a worker breaks his truce and slacks up in his work?
		 ⇒ What happens when a nation breaks its agreement with another nation?
		
		 The last days will see what we are seeing in our society today: a barrage of broken truces, covenants, and promises.

#4073
 True
 	
 Indeed–KJV
 True–NASB
 Real–NIV
 Indeed–NKJV
 True–NLT
	ἀληθής = alēthēs
	 Pronunciation: [al-ay-thace']
	 Parsing (part of speech): adjective
	     Case—nominative
	     Gender—feminine
	     Number—singular
	     Stem or root—from ἀληθής, ές
	 Concordance References:
	 ⇒ Strong's #227 alēthēs
	 ⇒ NIV #239 alēthēs
	 ⇒ NASB #227 alēthēs
		True as opposed to false; real, honest, indeed, valid, genuine.
		
		 ### Practical Application
		 The words true, truth, and real are taken from two Greek words very much alike. But each has a different shade of meaning. (See POSB *Deeper Study* #1—John 8:32; POSB *Deeper Study* #2—John 14:6.)
		 1. "*Alēthēs*" means true, the opposite of false.
		 2. "*Alethinos*" means the true, the genuine, the real. It is the *opposite* of the unreal, the ficti-

ENGLISH WORD	GREEK WORD AND VERSE	THE WORD MEANS...

Commit–NKJV
Trust–NLT
 	
**POSB
REFERENCE**
(Jn.2:24)
Deeper Study #2
	Number—singular
	Stem or root—from πιστεύω
	Concordance References:
	⇒ Strong's #4100 pisteuo
	⇒ NIV #4409 pisteuō
	⇒ NASB #4100 pisteuo
	
	John 2:24
	But Jesus did not **commit** himself unto them, because he knew all men, [KJV]
	But Jesus, on His part, was not **entrusting** Himself to them, for He knew all men, [NASB]
	But Jesus would not **entrust** himself to them, for he knew all men. [NIV]
	But Jesus did not **commit** Himself to them, because He knew all *men*, [NKJV]
	But Jesus didn't **trust** them, because he knew what people were really like. [NLT]
	αὐτὸς δὲ ὁ Ἰησοῦς οὐκ **ἐπίστευεν** ἑαυτὸν αὐτοῖς, διὰ τὸ αὐτὸν γινώσκειν πάντας, [GNS]
	αὐτὸς δὲ Ἰησοῦς οὐκ **ἐπίστευεν** αὐτὸν αὐτοῖς διὰ τὸ αὐτὸν γινώσκειν πάντας [GNT]
		as "believe" (cp. John 2:23). This gives an excellent picture of saving faith, of what genuine faith is—of the kind of faith that really saves a person. Note the circumstances behind this Scripture.
		    Jesus did not trust nor believe in the people; He did not commit Himself into their lives or hands. The verb is continuous action: Jesus kept on refusing to trust men, kept on refusing to commit Himself into their lives. Two reasons are given for this continuing attitude of Jesus.
		1. Jesus knew all men. The idea is that He knew every single man personally. Not a person escaped His knowledge.
		2. Jesus knew what was in man. No one needed to tell Him about man. He knew man's nature: his depravity, evil, deception, and fickleness. He knew the men He could trust and could not trust. He knew every man who professed to believe, yet would...
		• betray Him.
		• deny his faith under pressure.
		• forsake Him, turning back to the world.
		• slip and fall back into sin.
		• be weak and easily influenced, tossed to and fro.
		• prove untrustworthy.
		• lack zeal and genuine commitment.
		• lack courage to stand.
		    Jesus knew all this about every man. Nothing was hid from Him. Therefore, He was not able to trust Himself and His blessings to some men despite the fact that they professed to believe.

#4078
Trust
 	
Dispensation–KJV
Stewardship–NASB
Trust–NIV
Stewardship–NKJV
Sacred trust–NLT
 	
**POSB
REFERENCE**
(1 Cor.9:16-17; esp. v.17)
Note 2
	οἰκονομίαν = oikonomian
	Pronunciation: [oy-kon-om-ee'-ahn]
	Parsing (part of speech): noun
	    Case—accusative
	    Gender—feminine
	    Number—singular
	    Stem or root—from οἰκονομία, ας
	Concordance References:
	⇒ Strong's #3622 oikonomia
	⇒ NIV #3873 oikonomia
	⇒ NASB #3622 oikonomia
	
	1 Cor. 9:17
	For if I do this thing willingly, I have a reward: but if against my will, a **dispensation** *of the gospel* is committed unto me. [KJV]
	For if I do this voluntarily, I have a reward; but if against my will, I have a **stewardship** entrusted to me. [NASB]
	If I preach voluntarily, I have a reward; if not voluntarily, I am simply discharging the **trust** committed to me. [NIV]
	For if I do this willingly, I have a reward; but if against my will, I have been entrusted with a **stewardship**. [NKJV]
	If I were doing this of my own free will, then I would deserve payment. But God has chosen me and given me this **sacred trust**, and I have no choice. [NLT]
	εἰ γὰρ ἑκὼν τοῦτο πράσσω, μισθὸν ἔχω· εἰ δὲ ἄκων, **οἰκονομίαν** πεπίστευμαι. [GNS]
	εἰ γὰρ ἑκὼν τοῦτο πράσσω, μισθὸν ἔχω· εἰ δὲ ἄκων, **οἰκονομίαν** πεπίστευμαι· [GNT]
		A stewardship; a sacred trust; a commission; a responsibility.
		
		Practical Application
		    The steward was the manager of a large household or estate. The minister of God is the manager of God's household and estate (church).
		    Once God had called Paul to preach, the stewardship and trust of preaching was his. Whether he followed through and preached did not matter; he was still responsible for preaching. There was no release from the call and duty. He would stand accountable for preaching the gospel, or he would stand accountable for not preaching the gospel.
		    The call to preach the gospel is an awesome responsibility. God places the stewardship of the gospel into the hands of the person He calls. Just think about it: whatever these persons do with the gospel is all that will be done with the gospel—nothing more, nothing less. God has placed His gospel—the stewardship of it—into the hands of the persons He calls. Only what they do with the gospel will be done. What an awesome responsibility!

#4079 **Trust**	πιστεύοντες = pisteuontes Pronunciation: [pist-yoo'-on-tehs] Parsing (part of speech): verb Mood—participle	To believe; to trust; to have faith in God and Christ; to have the utmost confidence in.

ENGLISH WORD	GREEK WORD AND VERSE	THE WORD MEANS...
Believing–KJV Believe–NASB Believe–NIV Believing–NKJV **Trust–NLT** **POSB REFERENCE** (1 Pt.1:8-9; esp. v.8) Note 3, point 2	Tense—present Voice—active Case—nominative Gender—masculine Person—2nd person Number—plural Stem or root—from πιστεύω Concordance References: ⇒ Strong's #4100 pisteuō ⇒ NIV #4409 pisteuō ⇒ NASB #4100 pisteuō **1 Peter 1:8** Whom having not seen, ye love; in whom, though now ye see *him* not, yet **believing**, ye rejoice with joy unspeakable and full of glory: [KJV] And though you have not seen Him, you love Him, and though you do not see Him now, but **believe** in Him, you greatly rejoice with joy inexpressible and full of glory, [NASB] Though you have not seen him, you love him; and even though you do not see him now, you **believe** in him and are filled with an inexpressible and glorious joy, [NIV] Whom having not seen you love. Though now you do not see *Him,* yet **believing**, you rejoice with joy inexpressible and full of glory, [NKJV] You love him even though you have never seen him. Though you do not see him, you **trust** him; and even now you are happy with a glorious, inexpressible joy. [NLT] ὃν οὐκ εἰδότες ἀγαπᾶτε, εἰς ὃν ἄρτι μὴ ὁρῶντες **πιστεύοντες** δὲ, ἀγαλλιᾶσθε χαρᾷ ἀνεκλαλήτῳ καὶ δεδοξασμένῃ, [GNS] ὃν οὐκ ἰδόντες ἀγαπᾶτε, εἰς ὃν ἄρτι μὴ ὁρῶντες **πιστεύοντες** δὲ ἀγαλλιᾶσθε χαρᾷ ἀνεκλαλήτῳ καὶ δεδοξασμένῃ [GNT]	**Practical Application** Trials and temptations are to be conquered by our belief in Jesus Christ. Note the verse: we do not see Jesus, but we do trust Him. The word "trust" (*pisteuontes*) is in the present continuous tense. That is, it is continuous action, continuous belief—a belief that continues on and on. It is believing and never ceasing to believe and trust Jesus Christ. The point is clear: if we are continuing to believe in Jesus Christ, then we are following Christ. We are doing what He says... • rejecting and turning away from all temptations. • standing firm and relying upon His presence and power to conquer and to carry us through all trials.
#4080 **Trust** Commit–KJV Entrust–NASB Commit–NIV Commit–NKJV **Trust–NLT** **POSB REFERENCE** (1 Pt.4:19) Note 7	*παρατιθέσθωσαν* = *paratithesthōsan* Pronunciation: [par-at-ith'-ehs-tho'-sahn] Parsing (part of speech): verb Mood—imperative Tense—present Voice—middle Person—3rd person Number—plural Stem or root—from παρατίθημι Concordance References: ⇒ Strong's #3908 paratithēmi ⇒ NIV #4192 paratithēmi ⇒ NASB #3908 paratithēmi **1 Peter 4:19** Wherefore let them that suffer according to the will of God **commit** the keeping of their souls to him in well doing, as unto a faithful Creator. [KJV] Therefore, let those also who suffer according to the will of God **entrust** their souls to a faithful Creator in doing what is right. [NASB] So then, those who suffer according to God's will should **commit** themselves to their faithful Creator and continue to do good. [NIV] Therefore let those who suffer according to the will of God **commit** their souls to Him in doing good, as to a faithful reator. [NKJV] So if you are suffering according to God's will, keep on doing what is right, and **trust** yourself to the God who made you, for he will never fail you. [NLT] ὥστε καὶ οἱ πάσχοντες κατὰ τὸ θέλημα τοῦ Θεοῦ, ὡς πιστῷ κτίστῃ **παρατιθέσθωσαν** τὰς ψυχὰς ἑαυτῶν ἐν ἀγαθοποιΐᾳ. [GNS] ὥστε καὶ οἱ πάσχοντες κατὰ τὸ θέλημα τοῦ θεοῦ πιστῷ κτίστῃ **παρατιθέσθωσαν** τὰς ψυχὰς αὐτῶν ἐν ἀγαθοποιΐᾳ. [GNT]	To commit; to entrust; to trust; to deposit; to entrust into the hands of a trusted banker or friend. **Practical Application** God can be trusted; He will not fail the believer. He will either deliver the believer through the suffering or else take him home to be with Christ forever. God will save the believer's soul. The believer can trust God, trust Him far more than any friend on earth, for God never fails. God is a faithful Creator. He has created us to be with Him eternally, and His plan will not be defeated. If we trust our souls to Him, no matter what men may do to us, God will save us. He will fulfill His plan and purpose in our lives.

ENGLISH WORD	GREEK WORD AND VERSE	THE WORD MEANS...

#4081
Trusted
 	
Trusted–KJV
Trusted–NASB
Confident–NIV
Trusted–NKJV
Self-confidence–NLT
 	
**POSB
REFERENCE**
(Lk.18:9)
Note 1, point 1
	πεποιθότας = pepoithotas
	Pronunciation: [peh-poy'-tho-tahs]
	Parsing (part of speech): verb
	  Mood—participle
	  Tense—perfect
	  Voice—active
	  Case—accusative
	  Gender—masculine
	  Number—plural
	  Stem or root—from πείθω
	Concordance References:
	⇒ Strong's #3982 peithö
	⇒ NIV #4275 peithö
	⇒ NASB #3982 peithö
	
	Luke 18:9
	And he spake this parable unto certain which **trusted** in themselves that they were righteous, and despised others: [KJV]
	And He also told this parable to certain ones who **trusted** in themselves that they were righteous, and viewed others with contempt: [NASB]
	To some who were **confident** of their own righteousness and looked down on everybody else, Jesus told this parable: [NIV]
	Also He spoke this parable to some who **trusted** in themselves that they were righteous, and despised others: [NKJV]
	Then Jesus told this story to some who had great **self-confidence** and scorned everyone else: [NLT]
	Εἶπε δὲ καὶ πρός τινας τοὺς **πεποιθότας** ἐφ' ἑαυτοῖς ὅτι εἰσὶ δίκαιοι, καὶ ἐξουθενοῦντας τοὺς λοιπούς, τὴν παραβολὴν ταύτην· [GNS]
	Εἶπεν δὲ καὶ πρός τινας τοὺς **πεποιθότας** ἐφ' ἑαυτοῖς ὅτι εἰσὶν δίκαιοι καὶ ἐξουθενοῦντας τοὺς λοιποὺς τὴν παραβολὴν ταύτην· [GNT]
		To be confident; to trust in one's own self; to have self-confidence; to rely upon oneself.
		
		Practical Application
		It means those who trust in themselves; that is, those who feel they are completely self-sufficient and have no need for anyone else. They feel all they need dwells within their own bodies and minds. There is a feeling that neither God nor anyone else is really needed—not too often, if ever—as one ploughs through life.

#4082
Trusted
 	
Trusted–KJV
Hoping–NASB
Hoped–NIV
Hoping–NKJV
Thought–NLT
 	
**POSB
REFERENCE**
(Lk.24:15-27; esp.
v.21)
Note 2, point 2a
	ἠλπίζομεν = ëlpizomen
	Pronunciation: [ayl-pid'-zo-men]
	Parsing (part of speech): verb
	  Mood—indicative
	  Tense—imperfect
	  Voice—active
	  Person—1st person
	  Number—plural
	  Stem or root—from ἐλπίζω
	Concordance References:
	⇒ Strong's #1679 elpizö
	⇒ NIV #1827 elpizö
	⇒ NASB #1679 elpizö
	
	Luke 24:21
	But we **trusted** that it had been he which should have redeemed Israel: and beside all this, to day is the third day since these things were done. [KJV]
	"But we were **hoping** that it was He who was going to redeem Israel. Indeed, besides all this, it is the third day since these things happened. [NASB]
	But we had **hoped** that he was the one who was going to redeem Israel. And what is more, it is the third day since all this took place. [NIV]
	But we were **hoping** that it was He who was going to redeem Israel. Indeed, besides all this, today is the third day since these things happened. [NKJV]
	We had **thought** he was the Messiah who had come to rescue Israel. That all happened three days ago. [NLT]
	ἡμεῖς δὲ **ἠλπίζομεν** ὅτι αὐτός ἐστιν ὁ μέλλων λυτροῦσθαι τὸν Ἰσραήλ. ἀλλά γε οὐ-ν σὺν πᾶσι τούτοις τρίτην ταύτην ἡμέραν ἄγει σήμερον, ἀφ' οὗ ταῦτα ἐγένετο. [GNS]
	ἡμεῖς δὲ **ἠλπίζομεν** ὅτι αὐτός ἐστιν ὁ μέλλων λυτροῦσθαι τὸν Ἰσραήλ· ἀλλά γε καὶ σὺν πᾶσιν τούτοις τρίτην ταύτην ἡμέραν ἄγει ἀφ' οὗ ταῦτα ἐγένετο. [GNT]
		To hope, trust, desire, expect.
		
		Practical Application
		When Scripture speaks of the believer's hope, it does not mean what the world means by hope. The hope of the world is a desire, a want. The world hopes—wants, desires—that something will happen. But this is not the hope of the believer. The hope of the believer is a surety: it is perfect assurance, confidence, and knowledge. How can hope be so absolute and assured? By being an inward possession. The believer's hope is based upon the presence of God's Spirit who dwells within the believer. In fact, the believer possesses the hope of glory only by the Spirit of God who dwells within him. (See POSB *Deeper Study* #1, Hope—Romans 8:24-25 for more detailed discussion.)

ENGLISH WORD	GREEK WORD AND VERSE	THE WORD MEANS...

#4083
Trustworthy
 	
Faithful–KJV
Faithful–NASB
Reliable–NIV
Faithful–NKJV
Trustworthy–NLT
 	
**POSB
REFERENCE**
(2 Tim. 2:2)
Note 2, point 2
	πιστοῖς = *pistois*
	Pronunciation: [pis-toys']
	Parsing (part of speech): adjective
	   Case—dative
	   Gender—masculine
	   Number—plural
	   Stem or root— from πιστός, ή, όν
	Concordance References:
	  ⇒ Strong's #4103 pistos
	  ⇒ NIV #4412 pistos
	  ⇒ NASB #4103 pistos
	
	2 Tim. 2:2
	And the things that thou hast heard of me among many witnesses, the same commit thou to **faithful** men, who shall be able to teach others also. [KJV]
	
	And the things which you have heard from me in the presence of many witnesses, these entrust to **faithful** men, who will be able to teach others also. [NASB]
	
	And the things you have heard me say in the presence of many witnesses entrust to **reliable** men who will also be qualified to teach others. [NIV]
	
	And the things that you have heard from me among many witnesses, commit these to **faithful** men who will be able to teach others also. [NKJV]
	
	You have heard me teach many things that have been confirmed by many reliable witnesses. Teach these great truths to **trustworthy** people who are able to pass them on to others. [NLT]
	
	καὶ ἃ ἤκουσας παρ' ἐμοῦ διὰ πολλῶν μαρτύρων, ταῦτα παράθου **πιστοῖς** ἀνθρώποις, οἵτινες ἱκανοὶ ἔσονται καὶ ἑτέρους διδάξαι. [GNS]
	
	καὶ ἃ ἤκουσας παρ' ἐμοῦ διὰ πολλῶν μαρτύρων, ταῦτα παράθου **πιστοῖς** ἀνθρώποις, οἵτινες ἱκανοὶ ἔσονται καὶ ἑτέρους διδάξαι. [GNT]
		Reliable, faithful, trustworthy, unfailing.
		
		Practical Application
		By trustworthy (*pistois*) is meant a person...
		• who *believes* in Christ and in the Word of God.
		• who is loyal, reliable, dependable, and faithful.
		
		Naturally, a person who does not believe in God or in God's Word cannot be said to be trustworthy to God. He is unfaithful and disloyal. God cannot trust or rely on him.
		The point is this: a strong teacher will not commit the truth to an unfaithful person. The strong teacher will look for trustworthy people and teach the truth to them.

#4084
Truth
 	
Truth–KJV
Truth–NASB
Truth–NIV
Truth–NKJV
Truth–NLT
 	
**POSB
REFERENCE**
(1 Cor.5:8)
Note 3
 	
See also POSB REF:
(Eph.5:9)
Deeper Study #2
	ἀληθείας = *alëtheias*
	Pronunciation: [al-ay'-thi-ahs]
	Parsing (part of speech): noun
	   Case—genitive
	   Gender—feminine
	   Number—singular
	   Stem or root—from ἀλήθεια, ας
	Concordance References:
	  ⇒ Strong's #225 alëtheia
	  ⇒ NIV #237 alëtheia
	  ⇒ NASB #225 alëtheia
	
	1 Cor. 5:8
	Therefore let us keep the feast, not with old leaven, neither with the leaven of malice and wickedness; but with the unleavened *bread* of sincerity and **truth**. [KJV]
	
	Let us therefore celebrate the feast, not with old leaven, nor with the leaven of malice and wickedness, but with the unleavened bread of sincerity and **truth**. [NASB]
	
	Therefore let us keep the Festival, not with the old yeast, the yeast of malice and wickedness, but with bread without yeast, the bread of sincerity and **truth**. [NIV]
	
	Therefore let us keep the feast, not with old leaven, nor with the leaven of malice and wickedness, but with the unleavened *bread* of sincerity and **truth**. [NKJV]
	
	So let us celebrate the festival, not by eating the old bread of wickedness and evil, but by eating the new bread of purity and **truth**. [NLT]
	
	ὥστε ἑορτάζωμεν, μὴ ἐν ζύμῃ παλαιᾷ, μηδὲ ἐν ζύμῃ κακίας καὶ πονηρίας, ἀλλ' ἐν ἀζύμοις εἰλικρινείας καὶ **ἀληθείας**. [GNS]
	
	ὥστε ἑορτάζωμεν μὴ ἐν ζύμῃ παλαιᾷ μηδὲ ἐν ζύμῃ κακίας καὶ πονηρίας ἀλλ' ἐν ἀζύμοις εἰλικρινείας καὶ **ἀληθείας**. [GNT]
		Truth, truthfulness. It means unadulterated, conformed to the nature of whatever is true.
		
		Practical Application
		God is truth; therefore, it means to be like God. It means to live and do the truth; therefore, the church must do precisely what is right.

ENGLISH WORD	GREEK WORD AND VERSE	THE WORD MEANS...

#4085
Truth
 	
Truth–KJV
Rightly–NASB
Truth–NIV
Truth–NKJV
Justice–NLT
 	
**POSB
REFERENCE**
(Romans 2:2-5; esp.
v.2)
Note 2
	ἀλήθειαν = alētheian
	Pronunciation: [al-ay'-thi-ahn]
	Parsing (part of speech): noun
	  Case—accusative
	  Gender—feminine
	  Number—singular
	  Stem or root—from ἀλήθεια, ας
	Concordance References:
	⇒ Strong's #225 alētheia
	⇒ NIV #237 alētheia
	⇒ NASB #2596 kata + 225 alētheia
	
	Romans 2:2
	But we are sure that the judgment of God is according to **truth** against them which commit such things. [KJV]
	And we know that the judgment of God **rightly** falls upon those who practice such things. [NASB]
	Now we know that God's judgment against those who do such things is based on **truth**. [NIV]
	But we know that the judgment of God is according to **truth** against those who practice such things. [NKJV]
	And we know that God, in his **justice**, will punish anyone who does such things. [NLT]
	οἴδαμεν δὲ ὅτι τὸ κρίμα τοῦ Θεοῦ ἐστι κατὰ ἀλήθειαν ἐπὶ τοὺς τὰ τοιαῦτα πράσσοντας. [GNS]
	οἴδαμεν δὲ ὅτι τὸ κρίμα τοῦ θεοῦ ἐστιν κατὰ ἀλήθειαν ἐπὶ τοὺς τὰ τοιαῦτα πράσσοντας. [GNT]
		Often truly, to be sure; with right motives (Php 1.18).
		
		Practical Application
		The judgment of God—of the only living and true God—is according to truth. God's judgment will be executed in perfect justice. The word "truth" (*alētheian*) means true as opposed to false. It means what really is; what actually exists; what exactly takes place. God's judgment is perfectly just, exactly what it should be, nothing more and nothing less. His judgment is based upon...
		• what really happens.
		• what the facts are.
		• what actually takes place.
		• what a person really is within his heart and what the person actually did.

#4086
Try
 	
Tempt–KJV
Try–NASB
Test–NIV
Tempt–NKJV
Test–NLT
 	
**POSB
REFERENCE**
(1 Cor.10:6-10; esp.
v.9)
Note 2, point 4
	ἐκπειράζωμεν = ekpeirazōmen
	Pronunciation: [ek-pi-rad'-zo-mehn]
	Parsing (part of speech): verb
	  Mood—subjunctive
	  Tense—present
	  Voice—active
	  Person—1st person
	  Number—plural
	  Stem or root—from ἐκπειράζω
	Concordance References:
	⇒ Strong's #1598 ekpeirazō
	⇒ NIV #1733 ekpeirazō
	⇒ NASB #1598 ekpeirazō
	
	1 Cor. 10:9
	Neither let us **tempt** Christ, as some of them also tempted, and were destroyed of serpents. [KJV]
	Nor let us **try** the Lord, as some of them did, and were destroyed by the serpents. [NASB]
	We should not **test** the Lord, as some of them did—and were killed by snakes. [NIV]
	Nor let us **tempt** Christ, as some of them also tempted, and were destroyed by serpents; [NKJV]
	Nor should we put Christ to the **test**, as some of them did and then died from snakebites. [NLT]
	μηδὲ ἐκπειράζωμεν τὸν Χριστόν, καθώς τινες αὐτῶν ἐπείρασαν, καὶ ὑπὸ τῶν ὄφεων ἀπώλοντο. [GNS]
	μηδὲ ἐκπειράζωμεν τὸν Χριστόν, καθώς τινες αὐτῶν ἐπείρασαν καὶ ὑπὸ τῶν ὄφεων ἀπώλλυντο. [GNT]
		To try the Lord's patience; to see how far a person can go; to test the patience of Christ.
		
		Practical Application
		The believers of Israel...
		• often felt that God and His leader Moses *demanded and expected too much*.
		• often longed for the things of the flesh which they had formerly known in Egypt (the world).
		
		They became discontent with the things God provided and longed to return to Egypt (the world). Therefore, many of them perished in the wilderness and were not allowed to enter the promised land.

#4087
Try
 	
Exercise–KJV
Best–NASB
Strive–NIV
Strive–NKJV
Try–NLT
 	
**POSB
REFERENCE**
(Acts 24:14-16; esp.
v.16)
Note 3, point 4a
	ἀσκῶ = askō
	Pronunciation: [as-ko']
	Parsing (part of speech): verb
	  Mood—indicative
	  Tense—present
	  Voice—active
	  Person—1st person
	  Number—singular
	  Stem or root—from ἀσκέω
	Concordance References:
	⇒ Strong's #778 askeō
	⇒ NIV #828 askeō
	⇒ NASB #778 askeō
		To strive; to exercise; to try; to endeavor; to give one's best.
		
		Practical Application
		Paul tried—actively trained, disciplined, practiced, labored, strove, struggled, even to the point of pain—to keep a clear conscience.

ENGLISH WORD	GREEK WORD AND VERSE	THE WORD MEANS...
	Acts 24:16 And herein do I **exercise** myself, to have always a conscience void of offence toward God, and *toward* men. [KJV] "In view of this, I also do my **best** to maintain always a blameless conscience *both* before God and before men. [NASB] So I **strive** always to keep my conscience clear before God and man. [NIV] This *being* so, I myself always **strive** to have a conscience without offense toward God and men. [NKJV] Because of this, I always **try** to maintain a clear conscience before God and everyone else. [NLT] ἐν τούτῳ δὲ αὐτὸς **ἀσκῶ**, ἀπρόσκοπον συνείδησιν ἔχειν πρὸς τὸν Θεὸν καὶ τοὺς ἀνθρώπους διὰ παντός. [GNS] ἐν τούτῳ καὶ αὐτὸς **ἀσκῶ** ἀπρόσκοπον συνείδησιν ἔχειν πρὸς τὸν θεὸν καὶ τοὺς ἀνθρώπους διὰ παντός. [GNT]	

#4088
Tumults
 	
Tumults–KJV
Tumults–NASB
Riots–NIV
Tumults–NKJV
Faced angry mobs–NLT
 	
**POSB
REFERENCE**
(2 Cor.6:4-5; esp. v.5)
Note 3
	ἀκαταστασίαις = akatastasiais
	Pronunciation: [ak-at-as-tah-see'-ah-ees]
	Parsing (part of speech): noun
	    Case—dative
	    Gender—feminine
	    Number—plural
	    Stem or root—from **ἀκαταστασία**, ας
	Concordance References:
	⇒ Strong's #181 akatastasia
	⇒ NIV #189 akatastasia
	⇒ NASB #181 akatastasia
	
	2 Cor. 6:5
	In stripes, in imprisonments, in **tumults**, in labours, in watchings, in fastings; [KJV]
	In beatings, in imprisonments, in **tumults**, in labors, in sleeplessness, in hunger, [NASB]
	In beatings, imprisonments and **riots**; in hard work, sleepless nights and hunger; [NIV]
	In stripes, in imprisonments, in **tumults**, in labors, in sleeplessness, in fastings; [NKJV]
	We have been beaten, been put in jail, **faced angry mobs**, worked to exhaustion, endured sleepless nights, and gone without food. [NLT]
	ἐν πληγαῖς, ἐν φυλακαῖς, ἐν **ἀκαταστασίαις**, ἐν κόποις, ἐν ἀγρυπνίαις, ἐν νηστείαις, [GNS]
	ἐν πληγαῖς, ἐν φυλακαῖς, ἐν **ἀκαταστασίαις**, ἐν κόποις, ἐν ἀγρυπνίαις, ἐν νηστείαις, [GNT]
		Riots, tumults, disorder, revolutions, insurrection; to face angry mob uprisings and attacks.
		
		Practical Application
		Paul often faced angered mobs: at Antioch of Pisidia (Acts 13:50); Lystra (Acts 14:19); Philippi (Acts 16:19); Ephesus (Acts 19:29); and at Jerusalem (Acts 21:30). Mob uprisings present one of the most difficult and frightening situations imaginable for a believer, for a mob cannot be controlled by reason. The believer is unable to be heard, so speech is useless. Believers often face the abuse and ridicule of crowds because of the righteous lives they live and because they refuse to join in the worldly pleasures and indulgences of life. At such times the believer must be consistent in his testimony—no matter the temptation to go along with the crowd. The true believer, layman and minister alike, must steadfastly endure.

#4089
Tumults
 	
Tumults–KJV
Disturbances–NASB
Disorder–NIV
Tumults–NKJV
Disorderly behavior–NLT
 	
**POSB
REFERENCE**
(2 Cor.12:19-21; esp. v.20)
Note 3, point 2
	ἀκαταστασίαι = akatastasiai
	Pronunciation: [ak-at-as-tah-see'-ah-ee]
	Parsing (part of speech): noun
	    Case—nominative
	    Gender—feminine
	    Number—plural
	    Stem or root—from **ἀκαταστασία**, ας
	Concordance References:
	⇒ Strong's #181 akatastasia
	⇒ NIV #189 akatastasia
	⇒ NASB #181 akatastasia
	
	2 Cor. 12:20
	For I fear, lest, when I come, I shall not find you such as I would, and that I shall be found unto you such as ye would not: lest there be debates, envyings, wraths, strifes, backbitings, whisperings, swellings, **tumults**: [KJV]
	For I am afraid that perhaps when I come I may find you to be not what I wish and may be found by you to be not what you wish; that perhaps there may be strife, jealousy, angry tempers, disputes, slanders, gossip, arrogance, **disturbances**; [NASB]
	For I am afraid that when I come I may not find you as I want you to be, and you may not find me as you want me
		Disorder, tumults, disturbances, disorderly behavior, insurrection, anarchy, confusion.
		
		Practical Application
		Paul was stricken with fear, fear lest the church fail to be what it should be and reject him and his ministry. Paul feared that the church would fail to deal with the carnal critics and continue putting up with their evil attacks against him. He lists eight evils, including "tumults" (*akatastasiai*), that were and still are characteristic of divisive critics in the church.

ENGLISH WORD	GREEK WORD AND VERSE	THE WORD MEANS...
	to be. I fear that there may be quarreling, jealousy, outbursts of anger, factions, slander, gossip, arrogance and **disorder**. [NIV] For I fear lest, when I come, I shall not find you such as I wish, and *that* I shall be found by you such as you do not wish; lest *there be* contentions, jealousies, outbursts of wrath, selfish ambitions, backbitings, whisperings, conceits, **tumults**; [NKJV] For I am afraid that when I come to visit you I won't like what I find, and then you won't like my response. I am afraid that I will find quarreling, jealousy, outbursts of anger, selfishness, backstabbing, gossip, conceit, and **disorderly behavior**. [NLT] φοβοῦμαι γὰρ μή πως ἐλθὼν οὐχ οἵους θέλω εὕρω ὑμᾶς, κἀγὼ εὑρεθῶ ὑμῖν οἷον οὐ θέλετε· μή πως ἔρις, ζῆλοι, θυμοί, ἐριθεῖαι, καταλαλιαί, ψιθυρισμοί, φυσιώσεις, **ἀκαταστασίαι**· [GNS] φοβοῦμαι γὰρ μή πως ἐλθὼν οὐχ οἵους θέλω εὕρω ὑμᾶς κἀγὼ εὑρεθῶ ὑμῖν οἷον οὐ θέλετε· μή πως ἔρις, ζῆλος, θυμοί, ἐριθεῖαι, καταλαλιαί, ψιθυρισμοί, φυσιώσεις, **ἀκαταστασίαι**· [GNT]	

#4090
Turn
 	
Converted–KJV
Converted–NASB
Change–NIV
Converted–NKJV
Turn–NLT
 	
POSB REFERENCE
(Mt.18:3)
Note 2
	στραφῆτε = *straphëte*
	Pronunciation: [stref'-ee-teh]
	Parsing (part of speech): verb
	    Mood—subjunctive
	    Tense—aorist
	    Voice—passive
	    Person—2nd person
	    Number—plural
	    Stem or root—from στρέφω
	Concordance References:
	  ⇒ Strong's #4762 strephö
	  ⇒ NIV #5138 strephö
	  ⇒ NASB #4762 strephö
	
	Matthew 18:3
	And said, Verily I say unto you, Except ye be **converted**, and become as little children, ye shall not enter into the kingdom of heaven. [KJV]
	
	And said, "Truly I say to you, unless you are **converted** and become like children, you shall not enter the kingdom of heaven. [NASB]
	
	And he said: "I tell you the truth, unless you **change** and become like little children, you will never enter the kingdom of heaven. [NIV]
	
	And said, "Assuredly, I say to you, unless you are **converted** and become as little children, you will by no means enter the kingdom of heaven. [NKJV]
	
	Then he said, "I assure you, unless you **turn** from your sins and become as little children, you will never get into the Kingdom of Heaven. [NLT]
	
	καὶ εἶπεν, Ἀμὴν λέγω ὑμῖν, ἐὰν μὴ **στραφῆτε** καὶ γένησθε ὡς τὰ παιδία, οὐ μὴ εἰσέλθητε εἰς τὴν βασιλείαν τῶν οὐρανῶν. [GNS]
	
	καὶ εἶπεν, Ἀμὴν λέγω ὑμῖν, ἐὰν μὴ **στραφῆτε** καὶ γένησθε ὡς τὰ παιδία, οὐ μὴ εἰσέλθητε εἰς τὴν βασιλείαν τῶν οὐρανῶν. [GNT]
		To change; to turn around; to be converted; to turn from one thing to something else.
		
		Practical Application
		How is a person changed or turned? By turning and becoming as a little child. What does it mean "to become as a little children"? When Christ *called* the child to Him, the child demonstrated exactly what Christ meant.
		1. The child *trusted Christ*. The child responded to the call of Christ. He sensed the openness, warmth, tenderness, care, and love of Christ; so he felt free to respond and to trust Christ's call.
		2. The child *surrendered* himself to Christ. He was willing to give up what he was doing to go to Christ, willing to surrender whatever it was that was occupying his thoughts and behavior.
		3. The child was *obedient* to Christ. He obeyed, doing exactly what Christ requested, and it was probably difficult to do so. There were at least thirteen adult men standing or sitting there, and the child was being asked to walk into the midst of these men. Note that he obeyed despite the difficulty and obeyed simply because Christ asked him.
		4. The child was *humble* before Christ. All the above traits show humility. However, there is something often overlooked and abused by the adult world. Little children do not push themselves forward. They are not interested in prominence, fame, power, wealth, or position. They do not want to be placed in the midst of a group of adults, for they prefer to be in the background, away from staring, gawking eyes. Such embarrasses them and makes them feel self-conscious. Therefore, they prefer to be left in their obscure world. They are by nature humble, knowing little if anything of the competitive world that surrounds them; that is, they know little of it until they are brought into it by adults.

#4091 **Turn Away**	παραπεσόντας = *parapesontas* Pronunciation: [par-ap-ehs-on'-tahs] Parsing (part of speech): verb Mood—participle	To fall away; to turn away; to commit apostasy. This means to turn aside; to deviate.

ENGLISH WORD	GREEK WORD AND VERSE	THE WORD MEANS...
Fall away–KJV Fallen away–NASB Fall away–NIV Fall away–NKJV **Turn away–NLT** **POSB REFERENCE** (Heb.6:6) Note 2	Tense—aorist Voice—active Case—accusative Gender—masculine Number—plural Stem or root—from παραπίπτω Concordance References: ⇒ Strong's #3895 parapiptö ⇒ NIV #4178 parapiptö ⇒ NASB #3895 parapiptö **Hebrews 6:6** If they shall **fall away**, to renew them again unto repentance; seeing they crucify to themselves the Son of God afresh, and put *him* to an open shame. [KJV] And *then* have **fallen away**, it is impossible to renew them again to repentance, since they again crucify to themselves the Son of God, and put Him to open shame. [NASB] If they **fall away**, to be brought back to repentance, because to their loss they are crucifying the Son of God all over again and subjecting him to public disgrace. [NIV] If they **fall away**, to renew them again to repentance, since they crucify again for themselves the Son of God, and put *Him* to an open shame. [NKJV] And who then **turn away** from God. It is impossible to bring such people to repentance again because they are nailing the Son of God to the cross again by rejecting him, holding him up to public shame. [NLT] καὶ **παραπεσόντας**, πάλιν ἀνακαινίζειν εἰς μετάνοιαν, ἀνασταυροῦντας ἑαυτοῖς τὸν υἱὸν τοῦ Θεοῦ καὶ παραδειγματίζοντας· [GNS] καὶ **παραπεσόντας**, πάλιν ἀνακαινίζειν εἰς μετάνοιαν, ἀνασταυροῦντας ἑαυτοῖς τὸν υἱὸν τοῦ θεοῦ καὶ παραδειγματίζοντας. [GNT]	**Practical Application** It means... • to turn aside from Christ. • to turn away from Christ. • to deviate from Christ.
#4092 **Turn Away From, To** To forsake–KJV To forsake–NASB **To turn away from– NIV** To forsake–NKJV To turn their backs on–NLT **POSB REFERENCE** (Acts 21:20-26; esp. v.21) Note 3, point 2	*ἀποστασίαν ἀπὸ* = *apostasian apo* Pronunciation: [ap-os-tahs-ee'-ahn apo'] Parsing *apostasian* (part of speech): noun Case—accusative Gender—feminine Number—singular Stem or root—from ἀποστασία, ας Parsing *apo* (part of speech): preposition Case—genitive Stem or root—from ἀπό Concordance References: ⇒ Strong's #575 + 646 apo apostasia ⇒ NIV #608 + 686 apo apostasia ⇒ NASB #575 + 646 apo apostasia **Acts 21:21** And they are informed of thee, that thou teachest all the Jews which are among the Gentiles **to forsake** Moses, saying that they ought not to circumcise *their* children, neither to walk after the customs. [KJV] And they have been told about you, that you are teaching all the Jews who are among the Gentiles **to forsake** Moses, telling them not to circumcise their children nor to walk according to the customs. [NASB] They have been informed that you teach all the Jews who live among the Gentiles **to turn away from** Moses, telling them not to circumcise their children or live according to our customs. [NIV] But they have been informed about you that you teach all the Jews who are among the Gentiles **to forsake** Moses, saying that they ought not to circumcise *their* children nor to walk according to the customs. [NKJV] Our Jewish Christians here at Jerusalem have been told that you are teaching all the Jews living in the Gentile world **to turn their backs on** the laws of Moses. They say that you teach people not to circumcise their children	To turn away from; to forsake; to turn one's back on. It means apostasy and rebellion. **Practical Application** The word "to turn away from" (*apostasian*) is the word for apostasy. This is the most serious accusation possible to a Jew, apostasy from Moses and the law of circumcision. Of course, Paul never said this. He said that... • a person could be circumcised and keep the customs of the law if he wished. • a person, however, did not have to be circumcised or keep the law *to be saved*. The law is not what saves a person. Christ alone saves. (See POSB note, Salvation vs. Ritual—Acts 15:1-3; POSB outline—Acts 15:6-22 and POSB notes—Acts 15:6-22 for more discussion.)

ENGLISH WORD	GREEK WORD AND VERSE	THE WORD MEANS...
	or follow other Jewish customs. [NLT] κατηχήθησαν δὲ περὶ σοῦ, ὅτι **ἀποστασίαν** διδάσκεις **ἀπὸ** Μωσέως τοὺς κατὰ τὰ ἔθνη πάντας Ἰουδαίους, λέγων μὴ περιτέμνειν αὐτοὺς τὰ τέκνα, μηδὲ τοῖς ἔθεσι περιπατεῖν. [GNS] κατηχήθησαν δὲ περὶ σοῦ ὅτι **ἀποστασίαν** διδάσκεις **ἀπὸ** Μωϋσέως τοὺς κατὰ τὰ ἔθνη πάντας Ἰουδαίους λέγων μὴ περιτέμνειν αὐτοὺς τὰ τέκνα μηδὲ τοῖς ἔθεσιν περιπατεῖν. [GNT]	
#4093 **Turn From** Mortify–KJV Putting to death–NASB Put to death–NIV Put to death–NKJV **Turn from–NLT** **POSB REFERENCE** (Romans 8:12-13, esp. v.13) Note 6, point 2c	**θανατοῦτε** = *thanatoute* Pronunciation: [than-at-oo'-teh] Parsing (part of speech): verb 　　Mood—indicative 　　Tense—present 　　Voice—active 　　Person—2nd person 　　Number—plural 　　Stem or root—from **θανατόω** Concordance References: ⇒　Strong's #2289 thanatoö ⇒　NIV #2506 thanatoö ⇒　NASB #2289 thanatoö **Romans 8:13** For if ye live after the flesh, ye shall die: but if ye through the Spirit do **mortify** the deeds of the body, ye shall live. [KJV] For if you are living according to the flesh, you must die; but if by the Spirit you are **putting to death** the deeds of the body, you will live. [NASB] For if you live according to the sinful nature, you will die; but if by the Spirit you **put to death** the misdeeds of the body, you will live, [NIV] For if you live according to the flesh you will die; but if by the Spirit you **put to death** the deeds of the body, you will live. [NKJV] For if you keep on following it, you will perish. But if through the power of the Holy Spirit you **turn from** it and its evil deeds, you will live. [NLT] εἰ γὰρ κατὰ σάρκα ζῆτε, μέλλετε ἀποθνῄσκειν· εἰ δὲ πνεύματι τὰς πράξεις τοῦ σώματος **θανατοῦτε**, ζήσεσθε. [GNS] εἰ γὰρ κατὰ σάρκα ζῆτε, μέλλετε ἀποθνῄσκειν· εἰ δὲ πνεύματι τὰς πράξεις τοῦ σώματος **θανατοῦτε**, ζήσεσθε. [GNT]	To put to death; to mortify; to turn from. The idea is that of denying, subjecting, subduing, deadening, destroying the strength of. **Practical Application** The power to turn from the evil deeds of the body comes "through the power of the Holy Spirit." However, note this: we deny the evil deeds, and then the Spirit gives the strength to deaden and to subdue their strength. We are involved just as the Spirit is involved. He cannot destroy the strength of sin unless we exercise our will and work to destroy it ourselves, and we cannot will and work at it apart from Him. Both the Spirit and ourselves have to be involved, each doing his part if we wish the evil deeds of the body to be put to death. To repeat the point above: we exercise our will to deny the evil deeds, and then the Spirit immediately steps in to deaden the pull and strength of the evil deed. If we do not want the evil deeds of our body destroyed, if we want to continue living in the sins of the flesh, if we want nothing to do with the Spirit—then the Spirit can do nothing for us. God loves us too much to force us; He will not override our choices. But if we honestly will to follow the Spirit and honestly desire to destroy the evil deeds of our body, the Spirit will step in and give the power to do so. He will break the power of sin: He will deaden and subdue the strength of it.
#4094 **Turn From Your Sins** Repent–KJV Repent–NASB Repent–NIV Repent–NKJV **Turn from your sins–NLT** **POSB REFERENCE** (Mt.3:2-6; esp. v.2) Note 1	**Μετανοεῖτε** = *Metanoeite* Pronunciation: [met-an-o-ee'-teh] Parsing (part of speech): verb 　　Mood—imperative 　　Tense—present 　　Voice—active 　　Person—2nd person 　　Number—plural 　　Stem or root—from **μετανοέω** Concordance References: ⇒　Strong's #3340 metanoeö ⇒　NIV #3566 metanoeö ⇒　NASB #3340 metanoeö **Matthew 3:2** And saying, **Repent** ye: for the kingdom of heaven is at hand. [KJV] "**Repent**, for the kingdom of heaven is at hand." [NASB] And saying, "**Repent**, for the kingdom of heaven is near." [NIV] And saying, "**Repent**, for the kingdom of heaven is at hand!" [NASB] "**Turn from your sins** and turn to God, because the Kingdom of Heaven is near." [NLT] καὶ λέγων, **Μετανοεῖτε**, ἤγγικε γὰρ ἡ βασιλεία τῶν	To repent; to turn from your sins; to change; to turn; to change one's mind; to turn one's life around. **Practical Application** In this Scripture, "turning from your sins" (repentance) is a turning away from sin and turning toward God. It is a change of mind, a forsaking of sin. It is putting sin out of one's thoughts and behavior. It is resolving never to think or do a thing again. (Cp. Mt.3:2; Lk.13:2-3; Acts 2:38; Acts 3:19; Acts 8:22; Acts 26:20.) The change is turning away from lying, stealing, cheating, immorality, cursing, drunkenness, and the other so-called glaring sins of the flesh. But the change is also turning away from the silent sins of the spirit such as self-centeredness, selfishness, envy, bitterness, pride, covetousness, anger, evil thoughts, hopelessness, laziness, jealousy, lust. 1. Turning from your sins involves two turns. There is a negative turn away from sin and a positive turn toward God. It is a turning to God

ENGLISH WORD	GREEK WORD AND VERSE	THE WORD MEANS...
	οὐρανῶν. [GNS] [καὶ] λέγων, Μετανοεῖτε· ἤγγικεν γὰρ ἡ βασιλεία τῶν οὐρανῶν. [GNT]	away from sin, whether sins of thought or action. (See POSB note, Repentance—Lk.3:3. Cp. 1 Thes. 1:9; Acts 14:15.) 2. Turning from your sins is more than sorrow. Sorrow may or may not be involved in repentance. A person may repent simply because he wills and acts to change; or a person may repent because he senses an agonizing sorrow within. But the sense or feeling of sorrow is not repentance. Repentance is both the change of mind and the actual turning of one's life away from sin and toward God. (See POSB *Deeper Study* #1—2 Cor. 7:10.)

#4095
Turn Their Backs On, To
 	
To forsake–KJV
To forsake–NASB
To turn away from–NIV
To forsake–NKJV
To turn their backs on–NLT
 	
POSB REFERENCE
(Acts 21:20-26; esp. v.21)
Note 3, point 2
	ἀποστασίαν ἀπὸ = *apostasian apo*
	Pronunciation: [ap-os-tahs-ee'-ahn apo']
	Parsing *apostasian* (part of speech): noun
	  Case—accusative
	  Gender—feminine
	  Number—singular
	  Stem or root—from ἀποστασία, ας
	Parsing *apo* (part of speech): preposition
	  Case—genitive
	  Stem or root—from ἀπό
	Concordance References:
	⇒ Strong's #575 + 646 apo apostasia
	⇒ NIV #608 + 686 apo apostasia
	⇒ NASB #575 + 646 apo apostasia
	
	Acts 21:21
	And they are informed of thee, that thou teachest all the Jews which are among the Gentiles **to forsake** Moses, saying that they ought not to circumcise *their* children, neither to walk after the customs. [KJV]
	And they have been told about you, that you are teaching all the Jews who are among the Gentiles **to forsake** Moses, telling them not to circumcise their children nor to walk according to the customs. [NASB]
	They have been informed that you teach all the Jews who live among the Gentiles **to turn away from** Moses, telling them not to circumcise their children or live according to our customs. [NIV]
	But they have been informed about you that you teach all the Jews who are among the Gentiles **to forsake** Moses, saying that they ought not to circumcise *their* children nor to walk according to the customs. [NKJV]
	Our Jewish Christians here at Jerusalem have been told that you are teaching all the Jews living in the Gentile world **to turn their backs on** the laws of Moses. They say that you teach people not to circumcise their children or follow other Jewish customs. [NLT]
	κατηχήθησαν δὲ περὶ σοῦ, ὅτι **ἀποστασίαν** διδάσκεις ἀπὸ Μωσέως τοὺς κατὰ τὰ ἔθνη πάντας Ἰουδαίους, λέγων μὴ περιτέμνειν αὐτοὺς τὰ τέκνα, μηδὲ τοῖς ἔθεσι περιπατεῖν. [GNS]
	κατηχήθησαν δὲ περὶ σοῦ ὅτι **ἀποστασίαν** διδάσκεις ἀπὸ Μωϋσέως τοὺς κατὰ τὰ ἔθνη πάντας Ἰουδαίους λέγων μὴ περιτέμνειν αὐτοὺς τὰ τέκνα μηδὲ τοῖς ἔθεσιν περιπατεῖν. [GNT]
		To turn away from; to forsake; to turn one's back on. It means apostasy and rebellion.
		
		Practical Application
		The word "to turn their backs on" (*apostasian*) is the word for apostasy. This is the most serious accusation possible to a Jew, apostasy from Moses and the law of circumcision. Of course, Paul never said this. He said that...
		• a person could be circumcised and keep the customs of the law if he wished.
		• a person, however, did not have to be circumcised or keep the law *to be saved*. The law is not what saves a person. Christ alone saves. (See POSB note, Salvation vs. Ritual—Acts 15:1-3; POSB outline—Acts 15:6-22 and POSB notes—Acts 15:6-22 for more discussion.)

#4096
Turn To
 	
Converted–KJV
Return–NASB
Turn to–NIV
Converted–NKJV
Turn to–NLT
	ἐπιστρέψατε = *epistrepsate*
	Pronunciation: [ep-ee-stref'-ah-teh]
	Parsing (part of speech): verb
	  Mood—imperative
	  Tense—aorist
	  Voice—active
	  Person—2nd person
	  Number—plural
	  Stem or root—from ἐπιστρέφω
	Concordance References:
	⇒ Strong's #1994 epistrephō
	⇒ NIV #2188 epistrephō
	⇒ NASB #1994 epistrephō
		Turn to; convert, return; to turn back; to turn around.
		
		Practical Application
		The word "turn to" (*epistrepsate*) means to turn again. Men must repent and turn again to God. (See POSB note—Acts 17:29-30 and POSB *Deeper Study* #1, Repentance—Acts 17:29-30.)

ENGLISH WORD	GREEK WORD AND VERSE	THE WORD MEANS...
POSB REFERENCE (Acts 3:19) Note 7	**Acts 3:19** Repent ye therefore, and be **converted**, that your sins may be blotted out, when the times of refreshing shall come from the presence of the Lord; [KJV] "Repent therefore and **return**, that your sins may be wiped away, in order that times of refreshing may come from the presence of the Lord; [NASB] Repent, then, and **turn to** God, so that your sins may be wiped out, that times of refreshing may come from the Lord, [NIV] Repent therefore and be **converted**, that your sins may be blotted out, so that times of refreshing may come from the presence of the Lord, [NKJV] Now turn from your sins and **turn to** God, so you can be cleansed of your sins. [NLT] μετανοήσατε οὖν καὶ **ἐπιστρέψατε**, εἰς τὸ ἐξαλειφθῆναι ὑμῶν τὰς ἁμαρτίας, [GNS] μετανοήσατε οὖν καὶ **ἐπιστρέψατε** εἰς τὸ ἐξαλειφθῆναι ὑμῶν τὰς ἁμαρτίας, [GNT]	
#4097 **Turned Again– Turned Back** Converted–KJV **Turned again–NASB** **Turned back–NIV** Returned–NKJV Repented and turned–NLT **POSB REFERENCE** (Lk.22:32) Note 2, point 2 **See also POSB REF:** (Acts 3:19) Note 7	**ἐπιστρέψας** = *epistrepsas* Pronunciation: [ep-ee-stref'-ahs] Parsing (part of speech): verb Mood—participle Tense—aorist Voice—active Case—nominative Gender—masculine Person—2nd person Number—singular Stem or root—from ἐπιστρέφω Concordance References: ⇒ Strong's #1994 epistrephö ⇒ NIV #2188 epistrephö ⇒ NASB #1994 epistrephö **Luke 22:32** But I have prayed for thee, that thy faith fail not: and when thou art **converted**, strengthen thy brethren." [KJV] But I have prayed for you, that your faith may not fail; and you, when once you have **turned again**, strengthen your brothers." [NASB] But I have prayed for you, Simon, that your faith may not fail. And when you have **turned back**, strengthen your brothers." [NIV] But I have prayed for you, that your faith should not fail; and when you have **returned** to *Me,* strengthen your brethren." [NKJV] But I have pleaded in prayer for you, Simon, that your faith should not fail. So when you have **repented and turned** to me again, strengthen and build up your brothers." [NLT] ἐγὼ δὲ ἐδεήθην περὶ σοῦ, ἵνα μὴ ἐκλείπῃ ἡ πίστις σου· καὶ σύ ποτε **ἐπιστρέψας**, στήριξον τοὺς ἀδελφούς σου. [GNS] ἐγὼ δὲ ἐδεήθην περὶ σοῦ ἵνα μὴ ἐκλίπῃ ἡ πίστις σου· καὶ σύ ποτε **ἐπιστρέψας** στήρισον τοὺς ἀδελφούς σου. [GNT]	To turn around; to convert; to turn back to; to repent and turn; to turn again. **Practical Application** It is a turning away from sin and turning toward God. It is a change of mind, a forsaking of sin. It is putting sin out of one's thoughts and behavior. It is resolving never to think or do a thing again.
#4098 **Turned Away From the Truth** Subverted–KJV Perverted–NASB Warped–NIV Warped–NKJV	**ἐξέστραπται** = *exestraptai* Pronunciation: [ek-ehs'-trap-tah-ee] Parsing (part of speech): verb Mood—indicative Tense—perfect Voice—passive Person—3rd person Number—singular Stem or root—from ἐκστρέφομαι Concordance References: ⇒ Strong's #1612 ekstrephö	Perverted, corrupted, warped, turned away from the truth. It means the heretic is "turned away from the truth" (*exestraptai*): which means he is twisted or turned out and away from the truth of Christ and His Word. **Practical Application** Note that the heretic sins. The idea is that he sins greatly. Therefore, he condemns himself. He

ENGLISH WORD	GREEK WORD AND VERSE	THE WORD MEANS...
Turned away from the truth–NLT **POSB REFERENCE** (Tit.3:10-11; esp. v.11) Note 3	⇒ NIV #1750 ekstrephö ⇒ NASB #1612 ekstrephö **Titus 3:11** Knowing that he that is such is **subverted**, and sinneth, being condemned of himself. [KJV] Knowing that such a man is **perverted** and is sinning, being self-condemned. [NASB] You may be sure that such a man is **warped** and sinful; he is self-condemned. [NIV] Knowing that such a person is **warped** and sinning, being self-condemned. [NKJV] For people like that have **turned away from the truth**. They are sinning, and they condemn themselves. [NLT] εἰδὼς ὅτι **ἐξέστραπται** ὁ τοιοῦτος, καὶ ἁμαρτάνει, ων αὐτοκατάκριτος. [GNS] εἰδὼς ὅτι **ἐξέστραπται** ὁ τοιοῦτος καὶ ἁμαρτάνει ων αὐτοκατάκριτος. [GNT]	himself has chosen the path of unbelief, and he will be condemned for his unbelief.
#4099 **Turned Away, All Have– Turned Aside** All gone out of the way–KJV **All have turned aside–NASB** **All have turned away–NIV** **All turned aside–NKJV** **All have turned away from God–NLT** **POSB REFERENCE** (Romans 3:10-12; esp. v.12) Note 2, point 4	πάντες ἐξέκλιναν = *pantes exeklinan* Pronunciation: [pahn-tehs ek-ehk-lee'-nahn] Parsing *exeklinan* (part of speech): verb 　Mood—indicative 　Tense—aorist 　Voice—active 　Person—3ʳᵈ person 　Number—plural 　Stem or root—from ἐκκλίνω Concordance References: ⇒ Strong's #3956 pas + 1578 ekklinö ⇒ NIV #4246 pas [all] + 1712 ekklinö [turned away] ⇒ NASB #3956 pas + 1578 ekklinö **Romans 3:12** They are **all gone out of the way**, they are together become unprofitable; there is none that doeth good, no, not one. [KJV] ALL HAVE TURNED ASIDE, TOGETHER THEY HAVE BECOME USELESS; THERE IS NONE WHO DOES GOOD, THERE IS NOT EVEN ONE." [NASB] **All have turned away**, they have together become worthless; there is no one who does good, not even one." [NIV] They have **all turned aside**; They have together become unprofitable; There is none who does good, no, not one." [NKJV] **All have turned away from God**; all have gone wrong. No one does good, not even one." [NLT] πάντες ἐξέκλιναν, ἅμα ἠχρειώθησαν· οὐκ ἔστι ὁ ποιῶν χρηστότητα, οὐκ ἔστιν ἕως ἑνός. [GNS] πάντες ἐξέκλιναν ἅμα ἠχρεώθησαν· οὐκ ἔστιν ὁ ποιῶν χρηστότητα, [οὐκ ἔστιν] ἕως ἑνός. [GNT]	To turn away; to turn aside; to go out of the way. **Practical Application** The Greek means that men lean out, turn away, and turn aside... • from God. • from the way that leads to God. • to another way. Men are crooked; they are not straight with God. They do not follow God nor pursue the right way to God. They take another path, another road, another way.
#4100 **Turned Down** Diminishing–KJV Failure–NASB Loss–NIV Failure–NKJV **Turned down–NLT** **POSB REFERENCE** (Romans 11:11-12, esp. v.12) Note 1, point 3	ἥττημα = *hëttëma* Pronunciation: [hayt'-tay-mah] Parsing (part of speech): noun 　Case—nominative 　Gender—neuter 　Number—singular 　Stem or root—from ἥττημα, τος Concordance References: ⇒ Strong's #2275 hëttëma ⇒ NIV #2488 hëttëma ⇒ NASB #2275 hëttëma **Romans 11:12** Now if the fall of them *be* the riches of the world, and the **diminishing** of them the riches of the Gentiles; how much more their fulness? [KJV] Now if their transgression be riches for the world and their **failure** be riches for the Gentiles, how much more	Defeat; failure; diminishing loss; turning down, downfall. **Practical Application** God assures the glorious restoration of Israel and a rich period for the whole earth. Note the sharp contrast... • between "full" and "riches." • between "turned down" and "riches." The phrase "turned down" (*hëttëma*) means diminishthing, defeat, injury. It means that Israel became impoverished spiritually. Israel was spiritually injured and defeated; the Jewish people lost the blessings of salvation. Now... • if the spiritual fall of Israel led to the riches of salvation being carried to the world...

ENGLISH WORD	GREEK WORD AND VERSE	THE WORD MEANS...
	will their fulfillment be! [NASB] But if their transgression means riches for the world, and their **loss** means riches for the Gentiles, how much greater riches will their fullness bring! [NIV] Now if their fall *is* riches for the world, and their **failure** riches for the Gentiles, how much more their fullness! [NKJV] Now if the Gentiles were enriched because the Jews **turned down** God's offer of salvation, think how much greater a blessing the world will share when the Jews finally accept it. [NLT] εἰ δὲ τὸ παράπτωμα αὐτῶν πλοῦτος κόσμου, καὶ τὸ ἥττημα αὐτῶν πλοῦτος ἐθνῶν, πόσῳ μᾶλλον τὸ πλήρωμα αὐτῶν; [GNS] εἰ δὲ τὸ παράπτωμα αὐτῶν πλοῦτος κόσμου καὶ τὸ ἥττημα αὐτῶν πλοῦτος ἐθνῶν, πόσῳ μᾶλλον τὸ πλήρωμα αὐτῶν. [GNT]	• if the spiritual loss of Israel led to the riches of salvation being carried to the Gentiles... ...how much more shall will the fullness (the restoration of Israel) bring the blessings of God to earth?

#4101
Turning Away
 	
Removed–KJV
Deserting–NASB
Deserting–NIV
Turning away–NKJV
Turning away–NLT
 	
**POSB
REFERENCE**
(Gal.1:6-7; esp. v.6)
Note 2, point 1
	μετατίθεσθε ἀπὸ = *metatithesthe apo*
	Pronunciation: [met-at-ith'-ehs-the ah-po]
	Parsing *metatithesthe* (part of speech): verb
	    Mood—indicative
	    Tense—present
	    Voice—middle or passive
	    Person—2nd person
	    Number—plural
	    Stem or root—from μετατίθημι
	Parsing *apo* (part of speech): preposition
	    Case—genitive
	    Stem or root—from ἀπό
	Concordance References:
	⇒ Strong's #575+3346 apo metatithēmi
	⇒ NIV #608+3572 apo metatithēmi [deserting]
	⇒ NASB #575+3346 apo metatithēmi
	
	Galatians 1:6
	I marvel that ye are so soon **removed** from him that called you into the grace of Christ unto another gospel: [KJV]
	
	I am amazed that you are so quickly **deserting** Him who called you by the grace of Christ, for a different gospel; [NASB]
	
	I am astonished that you are so quickly **deserting** the one who called you by the grace of Christ and are turning to a different gospel—[NIV]
	
	I marvel that you are **turning away** so soon from Him who called you in the grace of Christ, to a different gospel, [NKJV]
	
	I am shocked that you are **turning away** so soon from God, who in his love and mercy called you to share the eternal life he gives through Christ. You are already following a different way [NLT]
	
	Θαυμάζω ὅτι οὕτω ταχέως **μετατίθεσθε ἀπὸ** τοῦ καλέσαντος ὑμᾶς ἐν χάριτι Χριστοῦ εἰς ἕτερον εὐαγγέλιον· [GNS]
	
	Θαυμάζω ὅτι οὕτως ταχέως **μετατίθεσθε ἀπὸ** τοῦ καλέσαντος ὑμᾶς ἐν χάριτι [Χριστοῦ] εἰς ἕτερον εὐαγγέλιον, [GNT]
		To desert; to remove; to turn away; to change places; to transfer elsewhere.
		
		Practical Application
		The believers were deserting God, removing themselves away from God. The tense of the verb (*metatithesthe*) is present tense which means the Galatians were in the process of turning; they had not yet fully turned. There was still hope for them to repent and return to God.

#4102
Tutor
 	
Schoolmaster–KJV
Tutor–NASB
Put in charge to lead–NIV
Tutor–NKJV
Guardian and teacher–NLT
	παιδαγωγός = *paidagōgos*
	Pronunciation: [pahee-dag-o-gos']
	Parsing (part of speech): noun
	    Case—nominative
	    Gender—masculine
	    Number—singular
	    Stem or root—from παιδαγωγός, οῦ
	Concordance References:
	⇒ Strong's #3807 paidagōgos
	⇒ NIV #4080 paidagōgos
	⇒ NASB #3807 paidagōgos
	
	Galatians 3:24
	Wherefore the law was our **schoolmaster** to bring us
		Put in charge to lead, tutor, teacher, instructor, guide.
		
		Practical Application
		The law was man's tutor to lead him to see his need for Christ. The *paidagōgos* was usually a trusted slave who was in charge of a child's moral welfare, but he had one particular duty to which Paul was referring. Every day the guardian took the child to school to deliver him to the teacher. And then at the end of the day, he returned for the child and brought him safely back home. This was what the law was to do.

ENGLISH WORD	GREEK WORD AND VERSE	THE WORD MEANS...

**POSB
REFERENCE**
(Gal.3:23-25; esp.
v.24)
Note 1
 	
See also POSB REF:
(1 Cor.4:15)
Note 2
	unto Christ, that we might be justified by faith. [KJV]
	    Therefore the Law has become our **tutor** to lead us to Christ, that we may be justified by faith. [NASB]
	    So the law was **put in charge to lead** us to Christ that we might be **justified** by faith. [NIV]
	    Therefore the law was our **tutor** *to bring us* to Christ, that we might be justified by faith. [NKJV]
	    Let me put it another way. The law was our **guardian and teacher** to lead us until Christ came. So now, through faith in Christ, we are made right with God. [NLT]
	    ὥστε ὁ νόμος **παιδαγωγὸς** ἡμῶν γέγονεν εἰς Χριστόν, ἵνα ἐκ πίστεως δικαιωθῶμεν· [GNS]
	    ὥστε ὁ νόμος **παιδαγωγὸς** ἡμῶν γέγονεν εἰς Χριστόν, ἵνα ἐκ πίστεως δικαιωθῶμεν· [GNT]
		The law is to lead man to Christ, the true Teacher. The law does this by showing man that he is utterly unable to secure righteousness by himself. He must look to Christ, the real Teacher, for righteousness and acceptance by God, that is, for justification by faith. And once Christ (faith in Him) has come, there is no need for the law nor for any other tutor, for Jesus Christ brings us face to face with God.

**#4103
Tutors**
 	
Instructers–KJV
Tutors–NASB
Guardians–NIV
Instructors–NKJV
To teach–NLT
 	
**POSB
REFERENCE**
(1 Cor.4:15)
Note 2
	παιδαγωγοὺς = *paidagōgous*
	Pronunciation: [pahee-dag-o-goos']
	Parsing (part of speech): noun
	    Case—accusative
	    Gender—masculine
	    Number—plural
	    Stem or root—from παιδαγωγός, οῦ
	Concordance References:
	  ⇒ Strong's #3807 paidagōgos
	  ⇒ NIV #4080 paidagōgos
	  ⇒ NASB #3807 paidagōgos
	
	1 Cor. 4:15
	    For though ye have ten thousand **instructers** in Christ, yet *have ye* not many fathers: for in Christ Jesus I have begotten you through the gospel. [KJV]
	    For if you were to have countless **tutors** in Christ, yet *you would* not *have* many fathers; for in Christ Jesus I became your father through the gospel. [NASB]
	    Even though you have ten thousand **guardians** in Christ, you do not have many fathers, for in Christ Jesus I became your father through the gospel. [NIV]
	    For though you might have ten thousand **instructors** in Christ, yet you *do* not *have* many fathers; for in Christ Jesus I have begotten you through the gospel. [NKJV]
	    For even if you had ten thousand others **to teach** you about Christ, you have only one spiritual father. For I became your father in Christ Jesus when I preached the Good News to you. [NLT]
	    ἐὰν γὰρ μυρίους **παιδαγωγοὺς** ἔχητε ἐν Χριστῷ, ἀλλ' οὐ πολλοὺς πατέρας· ἐν γὰρ Χριστῷ Ἰησοῦ διὰ τοῦ εὐαγγελίου ἐγὼ ὑμᾶς ἐγέννησα. [GNS]
	    ἐὰν γὰρ μυρίους **παιδαγωγοὺς** ἔχητε ἐν Χριστῷ ἀλλ' οὐ πολλοὺς πατέρας· ἐν γὰρ Χριστῷ Ἰησοῦ διὰ τοῦ εὐαγγελίου ἐγὼ ὑμᾶς ἐγέννησα. [GNT]
		Guardian, instructor, tutor.
		
		Practical Application
		    The "tutor" (*paidagogous*) of Paul's day was a trusted slave who was placed in complete charge of a child's welfare and growth. He was even in charge of escorting the child to school to see that no harm came to him. He was responsible for the growth and development of the child until he was grown. Paul says that the Corinthian church had an unlimited number of capable instructors and teachers, but he alone was their spiritual father. He was the one who brought them to Christ Jesus for life and gave birth to the church. He was the one whom God had been using and was still using to oversee the growth of the church. Paul was stressing that he, as the minister of the church, bore more concern, tenderness, and care for the church than others.

**#4104
Twist And
Change**
 	
Pervert–KJV
Distort–NASB
Pervert–NIV
Pervert–NKJV
**Twist and change–
NLT**
 	
**POSB
REFERENCE**
(Gal.1:6-7; esp. v.7)
Note 2
	μεταστρέψαι = *metastrepsai*
	Pronunciation: [met-as-tref'-sah-ee]
	Parsing (part of speech): verb
	    Mood—infinitive
	    Tense—aorist
	    Voice—active
	    Stem or root—from μεταστρέφω
	Concordance References:
	  ⇒ Strong's #3344 metastrephō
	  ⇒ NIV #3570 metastrephō
	  ⇒ NASB #3344 metastrephō
	
	Galatians 1:7
	    Which is not another; but there be some that trouble you, and would **pervert** the gospel of Christ. [KJV]
	    Which is really not another; only there are some who are disturbing you, and want to **distort** the gospel of Christ. [NASB]
	    Which is really no gospel at all. Evidently some people are throwing you into confusion and are trying to **pervert** the gospel of Christ. [NIV]
		To distort; to turn about; to change completely; to alter.
		
		Practical Application
		    The false teachers were taking the gospel of God's love as demonstrated in His Son, Jesus Christ, and changing it. The false teachers claimed to be Christians, followers of Christ. They even believed with Paul...
		  • that God did love the world and sent His Son into the world.
		  • that Jesus Christ was the Son of God who did actually come to earth.
		  • that Jesus Christ did die and arise from the dead.
		However, the false teachers were adding to and taking away from the gospel, twisting its meaning and making it say something entirely different from the Holy Scripture.

ENGLISH WORD	GREEK WORD AND VERSE	THE WORD MEANS...
	Which is not another; but there are some who trouble you and want to **pervert** the gospel of Christ. [NKJV] That pretends to be the Good News but is not the Good News at all. You are being fooled by those who **twist and change** the truth concerning Christ. [NLT] ὃ οὐκ ἔστιν ἄλλο, εἰ μή τινές εἰσιν οἱ ταράσσοντες ὑμᾶς καὶ θέλοντες **μεταστρέψαι** τὸ εὐαγγέλιον τοῦ Χριστοῦ. [GNS] ὃ οὐκ ἔστιν ἄλλο, εἰ μή τινές εἰσιν οἱ ταράσσοντες ὑμᾶς καὶ θέλοντες **μεταστρέψαι** τὸ εὐαγγέλιον τοῦ Χριστοῦ. [GNT]	

ENGLISH WORD	GREEK WORD AND VERSE	THE WORD MEANS...
#4105 **Unashamed** Ashamed–KJV Shame–NASB **Unashamed–NIV** Ashamed–NKJV Shame–NLT **POSB REFERENCE** (1 Jn.2:28) Note 2	μὴ αἰσχυνθῶμεν = mē aischunthōmen Pronunciation: [may ahee-skhoo'-tho-mehn] Parsing (part of speech): verb 　Mood—subjunctive 　Tense—aorist 　Voice—passive deponent 　Person—1st person 　Number—plural 　Stem or root—from αἰσχύνομαι Concordance References: ⇒ Strong's #153+3361 aischunomai mē ⇒ NIV #159+3590 aischunomai mē [unashamed] ⇒ NASB #153+3361 aischunomai mē **1 John 2:28** And now, little children, abide in him; that, when he shall appear, we may have confidence, and not be **ashamed** before him at his coming. [KJV] And now, little children, abide in Him, so that when He appears, we may have confidence and not shrink away from Him in **shame** at His coming. [NASB] And now, dear children, continue in him, so that when he appears we may be confident and **unashamed** before him at his coming. [NIV] And now, little children, abide in Him, that when He appears, we may have confidence and not be **ashamed** before Him at His coming. [NKJV] And now, dear children, continue to live in fellowship with Christ so that when he returns, you will be full of courage and not shrink back from him in **shame**. [NLT] καὶ νῦν, τεκνία, μένετε ἐν αὐτῷ· ἵνα ὅταν φανερωθῇ ἔχωμεν παρρησίαν, καὶ μὴ **αἰσχυνθῶμεν** ἀπ' αὐτοῦ, ἐν τῇ παρουσίᾳ αὐτοῦ. [GNS] Καὶ νῦν, τεκνία, μένετε ἐν αὐτῷ, ἵνα ἐὰν φανερωθῇ σχῶμεν παρρησίαν καὶ μὴ **αἰσχυνθῶμεν** ἀπ' αὐτοῦ ἐν τῇ παρουσίᾳ αὐτοῦ. [GNT]	Unashamed, ashamed, shame. It means not to shrink back; to sense guilt and disgrace; to feel embarrassment. **Practical Application** If we do not continue in Christ, we will be ashamed when Jesus Christ returns to earth. Note a fact that is so often ignored by believers, a fact that is seldom if ever thought about. There will be shame, disgrace, and embarrassment when Christ returns. Some believers will shrink back from Christ. The picture of nothing but joy and rejoicing when Christ returns is not a true picture. There is going to be judgment: the judgment of every man's works no matter what the works are, and there will be the judgment of sinners no matter who they are, all unbelievers. There will be joy and rejoicing for some believers, for those who have been abiding in Christ. But there will be shame, guilt, disgrace, and embarrassment—a shrinking back—for those who have been walking unfaithfully.
#4106 **Unbelief** **Unbelief–KJV** Disobedience–NASB Disobedience–NIV Disobedience–NKJV Disobedience–NLT **POSB REFERENCE** (Rom.11:32) Note 5	ἀπείθειαν = apeitheian Pronunciation: [ap-i'-thi-ahn] Parsing (part of speech): noun 　Case—accusative 　Gender—feminine 　Number—singular 　Stem or root—from ἀπείθεια, ας Concordance References: ⇒ Strong's #543 apeitheia ⇒ NIV #577 apeitheia ⇒ NASB #543 apeitheia **Romans 11:32** For God hath concluded them all in **unbelief**, that he might have mercy upon all. [KJV] For God has shut up all in **disobedience** that He might show mercy to all. [NASB] For God has bound all men over to **disobedience** so that he may have mercy on them all. [NIV] For God has committed them all to **disobedience**, that He might have mercy on all. [NKJV] For God has imprisoned all people in their own **disobedience** so he could have mercy on everyone. [NLT] συνέκλεισε γὰρ ὁ Θεὸς τοὺς πάντας εἰς **ἀπείθειαν** ἵνα τοὺς πάντας ἐλεήσῃ. [GNS] συνέκλεισεν γὰρ ὁ θεὸς τοὺς πάντας εἰς **ἀπείθειαν** ἵνα τοὺς πάντας ἐλεήσῃ. [GNT]	Unbelief, disobedience, insubordination, defiance, disregard. **Practical Application** God has taken men, both Jews and Gentiles, and shut them up to *unbelief* (*apeitheian*) or disobedience. This is the judicial judgment of God (see POSB *Deeper Study* #2—Romans 11:7-10; POSB note—Romans 1:24; POSB *Deeper Study* #1—John 12:39-41). It is the picture of God's using sin and events for good. God takes sin and works it out for the good of the world. Man has chosen sin, choosing to go his own way in life, so God allows man to do his own thing. God locks man up in his own world of selfishness, allowing man to roam around in his world of sin. Why? So that man's true nature of sinfulness will be clearly seen, and thereby cause the honest and thinking man to seek God. God wishes to and will have mercy upon all, both Jew and Gentile; but before men can come to God, they must confess two things: ⇒ that they are sinful and dying creatures in desperate need of God. ⇒ that God exists and that He will have mercy upon the person who diligently seeks Him.
#4107 **Unbeliever** Infidel–KJV **Unbeliever–NASB**	ἀπίστου = apistou Pronunciation: [ap'-is-too] Parsing (part of speech): pronominal adjective 　Case—genitive 　Gender—masculine 　Number—singular	Unbeliever, an infidel, an unbelieving person, an unfaithful person. **Practical Application** It means a person who has chosen to disbelieve in Christ and has deliberately rejected Him.

ENGLISH WORD	GREEK WORD AND VERSE	THE WORD MEANS...
Unbeliever–NIV **Unbeliever–NKJV** **Unbeliever–NLT** **POSB** **REFERENCE** (2 Cor.6:14-16; esp. v.15) Note 2	Stem or root—from **ἄπιστος**, ον Concordance References: ⇒ Strong's #571 apistos ⇒ NIV #603 apistos ⇒ NASB #571 apistos **2 Cor. 6:15** And what concord hath Christ with Belial? or what part hath he that believeth with an **infidel**? [KJV] Or what harmony has Christ with Belial, or what has a believer in common with an **unbeliever**? [NASB] What harmony is there between Christ and Belial? What does a believer have in common with an **unbeliever**? [NIV] And what accord has Christ with Belial? Or what part has a believer with an **unbeliever**? [NKJV] What harmony can there be between Christ and the Devil? How can a believer be a partner with an **unbeliever**? [NLT] τίς δὲ συμφώνησις Χριστῷ πρὸς Βελίαλ; ἢ τίς μερὶς πιστῷ μετὰ **ἀπίστου**; [GNS] τίς δὲ συμφώνησις Χριστοῦ πρὸς Βελιάρ, ἢ τίς μερὶς πιστῷ μετὰ **ἀπίστου**; [GNT]	

#4108
Unbelieving
 	
Faithless–KJV
Unbelieving–NASB
Unbelieving–NIV
Faithless–NKJV
Faithless–NLT
 	
POSB
REFERENCE
(Lk.9:41)
Deeper Study #2
	ἄπιστος = apistos
	Pronunciation: [ap'-is-tos]
	Parsing (part of speech): adjective
	  Case—vocative
	  Gender—feminine
	  Number—singular
	  Stem or root—from **ἄπιστος**, ον
	Concordance References:
	⇒ Strong's #571 apistos
	⇒ NIV #603 apistos
	⇒ NASB #571 apistos
	
	Luke 9:41
	And Jesus answering said, O **faithless** and perverse generation, how long shall I be with you, and suffer you? Bring thy son hither. [KJV]
	And Jesus answered and said, "O **unbelieving** and perverted generation, how long shall I be with you, and put up with you? Bring your son here." [NASB]
	"O **unbelieving** and perverse generation," Jesus replied, "how long shall I stay with you and put up with you? Bring your son here." [NIV]
	Then Jesus answered and said, "O **faithless** and perverse generation, how long shall I be with you and bear with you? Bring your son here." [NKJV]
	"You stubborn, **faithless** people," Jesus said, "how long must I be with you and put up with you? Bring him here." [NLT]
	ἀποκριθεὶς δὲ ὁ Ἰησοῦς εἶπεν, Ὦ γενεὰ **ἄπιστος** καὶ διεστραμμένη, ἕως πότε ἔσομαι πρὸς ὑμᾶς, καὶ ἀνέξομαι ὑμῶν; προσάγαγε ὧδε τὸν υἱόν σου. [GNS]
	ἀποκριθεὶς δὲ ὁ Ἰησοῦς εἶπεν, Ὦ γενεὰ **ἄπιστος** καὶ διεστραμμένη, ἕως πότε ἔσομαι πρὸς ὑμᾶς καὶ ἀνέξομαι ὑμῶν; προσάγαγε ὧδε τὸν υἱόν σου. [GNT]
		Faithless; unbelieving; disbelieving; being without faith; being out of faith; not keeping faith (cp. Titus 1:15).
		
		Practical Application
		What is unbelief?
		1. Unbelief is doubting Christ Himself, the object of one's faith. It is questioning the power of Christ. Is He really strong enough to do what is needed: to save, deliver, heal, and help; and to remove evil empires, entrenched wickedness, destructive greed, and the threat of wars?
		2. Unbelief is doubting the power of the Lord within oneself. It is questioning if one is close enough to Christ for Him to hear and answer or to grant enough power to meet the need.
		3. Unbelief is doubting one's own faith. It is questioning the strength of one's own dependence and confidence in Christ.
		4. Unbelief is doubting if the thing needed is God's will. It is questioning if one should be seeking such a thing or if God is willing to do what is needed.

#4109
Unbelieving
 	
Unbelieving–KJV
Disbelieved–NASB
Refused to believe–NIV
Unbelieving–NKJV
Spurned God's message–NLT
	ἀπειθήσαντες = apeithēsantes
	Pronunciation: [ap-i-thoon'-tace]
	Parsing (part of speech): verb
	  Mood—participle
	  Tense—aorist
	  Voice—active
	  Case—nominative
	  Gender—masculine
	  Number—plural
	  Stem or root—from **ἀπειθέω**
	Concordance References:
	⇒ Strong's #544 apeitheō
	⇒ NIV #578 apeitheō
	⇒ NASB #544 apeitheō
		Refused to believe; unbelieving; disbelieved; to spurn God's message; to be disobedient; to be an unbeliever.
		
		Practical Application
		The idea is they were unwilling to believe or be persuaded. They deliberately withheld belief, disobeying God.

ENGLISH WORD	GREEK WORD AND VERSE	THE WORD MEANS...
POSB REFERENCE (Acts 14:2) Note 4, point 1	**Acts 14:2** But the **unbelieving** Jews stirred up the Gentiles, and made their minds evil affected against the brethren. [KJV] But the Jews who **disbelieved** stirred up the minds of the Gentiles, and embittered them against the brethren. [NASB] But the Jews who **refused to believe** stirred up the Gentiles and poisoned their minds against the brothers. [NIV] But the **unbelieving** Jews stirred up the Gentiles and poisoned their minds against the brethren. [NKJV] But the Jews who **spurned God's message** stirred up distrust among the Gentiles against Paul and Barnabas, saying all sorts of evil things about them. [NLT] οἱ δὲ **ἀπειθοῦντες** Ἰουδαῖοι ἐπήγειραν καὶ ἐκάκωσαν τὰς ψυχὰς τῶν ἐθνῶν κατὰ τῶν ἀδελφῶν. [GNS] οἱ δὲ **ἀπειθήσαντες** Ἰουδαῖοι ἐπήγειραν καὶ ἐκάκωσαν τὰς ψυχὰς τῶν ἐθνῶν κατὰ τῶν ἀδελφῶν. [GNT]	
#4110 **Unbelieving, Be Not– Unbelieving, Do Not Be** Be not faithless–KJV **Be not unbelieving– NASB** Stop doubting–NIV **Do not be unbelieving–NKJV** Don't be faithless any longer–NLT **POSB REFERENCE** (Jn.20:26-28; esp. v.27) Note 3, point 1b	μὴ γίνου ἄπιστος = *mē ginou apistos* Pronunciation: [may ghen-oo ha-pis-tos] Parsing *ginou* (part of speech): verb Mood—imperative Tense—present Voice—middle or passive deponent Person—2nd person Number—singular Stem or root—from γίνομαι Parsing *apistos* (part of speech): adjective Case—nominative Gender—masculine Number—singular Stem or root—from ἄπιστος, ον Concordance References: ⇒ Strong's #3361 mē + 571+1096 apistos ginomai ⇒ NIV #3590 mē [Stop] + 603+1181 apistos ginomai [doubting] ⇒ NASB #3361 mē + 571+1096 apistos ginomai **John 20:27** Then saith he to Thomas, reach hither thy finger, and behold my hands; and reach hither thy hand, and thrust *it* into my side: and **be not faithless**, but believing. [KJV] Then He said to Thomas, "Reach here your finger, and see My hands; and reach here your hand, and put it into My side; and **be not unbelieving**, but believing." [NASB] Then he said to Thomas, "Put your finger here; see my hands. Reach out your hand and put it into my side. **Stop doubting** and believe." [NIV] Then He said to Thomas, "Reach your finger here, and look at My hands; and reach your hand *here*, and put *it* into My side. **Do not be unbelieving**, but believing." [NKJV] Then he said to Thomas, "Put your finger here and see my hands. Put your hand into the wound in my side. **Don't be faithless any longer**. Believe!" [NLT] εἶτα λέγει τῷ Θωμᾷ, Φέρε τὸν δάκτυλόν σου ὧδε, καὶ ἴδε τὰς χεῖράς μου. καὶ φέρε τὴν χεῖρά σου καὶ βάλε εἰς τὴν πλευράν μου· καὶ **μὴ γίνου ἄπιστος** ἀλλὰ πιστός. [GNS] εἶτα λέγει τῷ Θωμᾷ, Φέρε τὸν δάκτυλόν σου ὧδε καὶ ἴδε τὰς χεῖράς μου, καὶ φέρε τὴν χεῖρά σου καὶ βάλε εἰς τὴν πλευράν μου, καὶ **μὴ γίνου ἄπιστος** ἀλλὰ πιστός. [GNT]	To stop doubting; to stop being faithless; to stop becoming an unbeliever. **Practical Application** In this Scripture, Jesus warned and called for belief. Thomas had been walking down a dangerous road. The disciples had witnessed to him time and again, but he had refused time and again to accept their testimony. Note the Lord's strong charge: ⇒ "Be not unbelieving" (*mē ginou apistos*): stop becoming an unbeliever. You are running the risk of *becoming faithless* and unbelieving, beyond the point of believing. You have carried your unbelief too far. It is now time to stop the foolishness. The others have been witnessing and witnessing the truth to you. Stop the stiff-necked, obstinate unbelief. You are in danger.
#4111 **Unblameable** **Unblameable–KJV** Blameless–NASB	ἀμώμους = *amōmous* Pronunciation: [am'-o-moos] Parsing (part of speech): adjective Case—accusative Gender—masculine Number—plural	Without blemish; without spot; without fault; without any defect whatsoever. **Practical Application** We must also be "unblameable" (*amōmous*). We must be without spot, faultless, without any

ENGLISH WORD	GREEK WORD AND VERSE	THE WORD MEANS...
Without blemish–NIV Blameless–NKJV Blameless–NLT **POSB REFERENCE** (Col.1:22) Note 3, point 2	Stem or root—from ἄμωμος, ον Concordance References: ⇒ Strong's #299 amōmos ⇒ NIV #320 amōmos ⇒ NASB #299 amōmos ### Col. 1:22 In the body of his flesh through death, to present you holy and **unblameable** and unreproveable in his sight: [KJV] Yet He has now reconciled you in His fleshly body through death, in order to present you before Him holy and **blameless** and beyond reproach—[NASB] But now he has reconciled you by Christ's physical body through death to present you holy in his sight, **without blemish** and free from accusation—[NIV] In the body of His flesh through death, to present you holy, and **blameless**, and above reproach in His sight [NKJV] Yet now he has brought you back as his friends. He has done this through his death on the cross in his own human body. As a result, he has brought you into the very presence of God, and you are holy and **blameless** as you stand before him without a single fault. [NLT] νυνὶ δὲ ἀποκατήλλαξεν ἐν τῷ σώματι τῆς σαρκὸς αὐτοῦ διὰ τοῦ θανάτου, παραστῆσαι ὑμᾶς ἁγίους καὶ **ἀμώμους** καὶ ἀνεγκλήτους κατενώπιον αὐτοῦ·[GNS] νυνὶ δὲ ἀποκατήλλαξεν ἐν τῷ σώματι τῆς σαρκὸς αὐτοῦ διὰ τοῦ θανάτου παραστῆσαι ὑμᾶς ἁγίους καὶ **ἀμώμους** καὶ ἀνεγκλήτους κατενώπιον αὐτοῦ, [GNT]	defect whatsoever.
#4112 ## Unblamable– ## Unblameable Unblameable–KJV Unblamable–NASB Blameless–NIV Blameless–NKJV Blameless–NLT **POSB REFERENCE** (1 Thes.3:13) Note 3	ἀμέμπτους = *amemptous* Pronunciation: [am'-ehmp-toos] Parsing (part of speech): adjective Case—accusative Gender—feminine Number—plural Stem or root—from ἄμεμπτος, ον Concordance References: ⇒ Strong's #273 amemptos ⇒ NIV #289 amemptos ⇒ NASB #273 amemptos ### 1 Thes. 3:13 To the end he may stablish your hearts **unblameable** in holiness before God, even our Father, at the coming of our Lord Jesus Christ with all his saints. [KJV] So that He may establish your hearts **unblamable** in holiness before our God and Father at the coming of our Lord Jesus with all His saints. [NASB] May he strengthen your hearts so that you will be **blameless** and holy in the presence of our God and Father when our Lord Jesus comes with all his holy ones. [NIV] So that He may establish your hearts **blameless** in holiness before our God and Father at the coming of our Lord Jesus Christ with all His saints. [NKJV] As a result, Christ will make your hearts strong, **blameless**, and holy when you stand before God our Father on that day when our Lord Jesus comes with all those who belong to him. [NLT] εἰς τὸ στηρίξαι ὑμῶν τὰς καρδίας **ἀμέμπτους** ἐν ἁγιωσύνη, ἔμπροσθεν τοῦ Θεοῦ καὶ πατρὸς ἡμῶν, ἐν τῇ παρουσίᾳ τοῦ Κυρίου ἡμῶν Ἰησοῦ Χριστοῦ μετὰ πάντων τῶν ἁγίων αὐτοῦ. [GNS] εἰς τὸ στηρίξαι ὑμῶν τὰς καρδίας **ἀμέμπτους** ἐν ἁγιωσύνη ἔμπροσθεν τοῦ θεοῦ καὶ πατρὸς ἡμῶν ἐν τῇ παρουσίᾳ τοῦ κυρίου ἡμῶν Ἰησοῦ μετὰ πάντων τῶν ἁγίων αὐτοῦ, [ἀμήν]. [GNT]	Blameless, unblameable, faultless. ### Practical Application The word "unblameable" (*amemptous*) means to be free from fault and blame; to be free from all charges (*Vine*). It is the Lord Jesus Christ who can make our hearts *unblameable in holiness* before God. He alone can free us from the faults and charges of sin; He alone can present us blameless and holy before God. Just think about it: Who else has such power? Do you know such a person? The thinking and honest person has to answer no. And to be honest, if Christ does not have the righteousness and power to present us unblameable before God, then we are hopelessly doomed. Why? Because He is the only Person who has ever risen from the dead, the only Person never to die again and to live eternally with God. If He is not our Savior, then we will die and never arise, never live with God. Man's only hope is Christ, the hope that He has the righteousness and power to set us blameless before God.

ENGLISH WORD	GREEK WORD AND VERSE	THE WORD MEANS...

#4113
Unchanging Plan
 	
Predestinated–KJV
Predestined–NASB
Predestined–NIV
Predestined–NKJV
Unchanging plan–NLT
 	
POSB REFERENCE
(Eph.1:5-6; esp. v.5)
Note 3
	προορίσας = *proorisas*
	Pronunciation: [pro-or-is-ahs]
	Parsing (part of speech): verb
	  Mood—participle
	  Tense—aorist
	  Voice—active
	  Case—nominative
	  Gender—masculine
	  Number—singular
	  Stem or root—from προορίζω
	Concordance References:
	  ⇒ Strong's #4309 proorizō
	  ⇒ NIV #4633 proorizō
	  ⇒ NASB #4309 proorizō
	
	Ephes. 1:5
	Having **predestinated** us unto the adoption of children by Jesus Christ to himself, according to the good pleasure of his will, [KJV]
	
	He **predestined** us to adoption as sons through Jesus Christ to Himself, according to the kind intention of His will, [NASB]
	
	He **predestined** us to be adopted as his sons through Jesus Christ, in accordance with his pleasure and will— [NIV]
	
	Having **predestined** us to adoption as sons by Jesus Christ to Himself, according to the good pleasure of His will, [NKJV]
	
	His **unchanging plan** has always been to adopt us into his own family by bringing us to himself through Jesus Christ. And this gave him great pleasure. [NLT]
	
	προορίσας ἡμᾶς εἰς υἱοθεσίαν διὰ Ἰησοῦ Χριστοῦ εἰς αὐτόν, κατὰ τὴν εὐδοκίαν τοῦ θελήματος αὐτοῦ, [GNS]
	
	προορίσας ἡμᾶς εἰς υἱοθεσίαν διὰ Ἰησοῦ Χριστοῦ εἰς αὐτόν, κατὰ τὴν εὐδοκίαν τοῦ θελήματος αὐτοῦ, [GNT]
		To destine or appoint before, to foreordain, to predetermine. The basic Greek word (*proorizō*) means to *mark off or to set off* the boundaries of something.
		
		### Practical Application
		God has adopted us as children. How unbelievable—what a glorious privilege to be adopted as a child of God! And note:
		⇒ It was predestinated, that is, foreordained (*proorisas*).
		⇒ It was the pleasure of God to adopt us—the good pleasure of His will. And it was His purpose to adopt us, and His purpose and pleasure and His will were all good.
		This is most striking when we consider how sinful and depraved we are and how much we have cursed, rebelled, and rejected God. The fact that God wills and finds pleasure in adopting us and that He counts it as good is too much to believe. Yet, it is exactly what He says. Now note: The word "foreordained" does not mean that God chooses some persons for salvation and everyone else for eternal punishment. Scripture teaches the exact opposite.
		The idea is a glorious picture of what God is doing for the believer. The boundary is marked and set off for the believer: the boundary of being adopted as a child of God. The believer will be adopted, made just like Christ and conformed to His very likeness and image. Nothing can stop God's purpose for the believer. It is predestinated, set and marked off. The believer may struggle and suffer through the sin and shame of this world; he may even stumble and fall or become discouraged and downhearted. But if he is a genuine child of God, he will not be defeated, not totally. He will soon arise from his fall and begin to follow Christ again. He is predestinated to be a brother of Christ, to worship and serve Christ throughout all eternity. And Christ will not be disappointed. God loves His Son too much to allow Him to be disappointed by losing a single brother. Jesus Christ will have His joy fulfilled; He will see every brother of His adopted and conformed perfectly to His image. He will receive the worship and service of every person chosen to be His. The believer's eternal destiny, that of being an adopted brother to the Lord Jesus Christ, is determined. The believer can rest assured of this glorious truth. God has predestinated him to be delivered from the suffering and struggling of this sinful world. (See POSB note, Predestination—John 6:37; POSB note—John 6:39; POSB note—John 6:44-46 for God's part and man's part in salvation. See POSB *Deeper Study #3*—Acts 2:23; POSB note—Romans 8:28-39; POSB note—POSB *Deeper Study #2*, Romans 9:11-13; and POSB note—Romans 9:14-33 for more discussion.)

#4114
Uncircumcised Hearts, In Heart
 	
Uncircumcised in heart–KJV
	ἀπερίτμητοι καρδίαις = *aperitmētoi kardiais*
	Pronunciation: [ap-er-eet'-may-to-ee kar-dee'-ah-ees]
	Parsing *aperitmētoi* (part of speech): pronominal adjective
	  Case—vocative
	  Gender—masculine
	  Number—plural
	  Stem or root—from ἀπερίτμητος, ον
		Uncircumcised hearts; to be a heathen at heart; to have a stubborn heart.
		
		### Practical Application
		Who are the "uncircumcised hearts" (*aperitmētoi kardiais*)? They are the pagan, lost, idolaters, false worshippers, ungodly of the world.

ENGLISH WORD	GREEK WORD AND VERSE	THE WORD MEANS...

Unclean spirit–KJV
Unclean spirit–NASB
Evil spirit–NIV
Unclean spirit–NKJV
Evil spirit–NLT
 	
POSB
REFERENCE
(Mk.1:23-24; esp.
v.23)
Note 1
	Parsing *akatharto* (part of speech): adjective
	    Case—dative
	    Gender—neuter
	    Number—singular
	    Stem or root—from ἀκάθαρτος, ον
	Concordance References:
	  ⇒ Strong's #169 akathartos + #4151 pneuma
	  ⇒ NIV #1877 en (by) + 176 akathartos [evil]
	      +4460 pneuma [spirit]
	  ⇒ NASB #169 akathartos + #4151 pneuma
	
	### Mark 1:23
	And there was in their synagogue a man **with an unclean spirit**; and he cried out, [KJV]
	And just then there was in their synagogue a man **with an unclean spirit**; and he cried out, [NASB]
	Just then a man in their synagogue who was possessed by an **evil spirit** cried out, [NIV]
	Now there was a man in their synagogue **with an unclean spirit**. And he cried out, [NKJV]
	A man possessed by an **evil spirit** was in the synagogue, [NLT]
	καὶ ἦν ἐν τῇ συναγωγῇ αὐτῶν ἄνθρωπος **ἐν πνεύματι ἀκαθάρτῳ**, καὶ ἀνέκραξε, [GNS]
	καὶ εὐθὺς ἦν ἐν τῇ συναγωγῇ αὐτῶν ἄνθρωπος **ἐν πνεύματι ἀκαθάρτῳ** καὶ ἀνέκραξεν [GNT]
		### Practical Application
		The man was in the grasp, in the possession of the unclean spirit. He was in the grip, captivated by the unclean spirit. He was under the spell, the will of the unclean spirit. To better understand the meaning, think of all the evil in the world, all the evil that occurs every hour and every day. Then note John's words, "The whole world is under the control of the evil one" (1 Jn.5:19).

#4119
Uncleanness
 	
Uncleanness–KJV
Impurity–NASB
Sexual impurity–NIV
Uncleanness–NKJV
Shameful things–NLT
 	
POSB
REFERENCE
(Romans 1:24-25; esp.
v.24)
Note 2
	ἀκαθαρσίαν = *akatharsian*
	Pronunciation: [ak-ath-ar-see'-ahn]
	Parsing (part of speech): noun
	    Case—accusative
	    Gender—feminine
	    Number—singular
	    Stem or root—from ἀκαθαρσία, ας
	Concordance References:
	  ⇒ Strong's #167 akatharsia
	  ⇒ NIV #174 akatharsia
	  ⇒ NASB #167 akatharsia
	
	### Romans 1:24
	Wherefore God also gave them up to **uncleanness** through the lusts of their own hearts, to dishonour their own bodies between themselves: [KJV]
	Therefore God gave them over in the lusts of their hearts to **impurity**, that their bodies might be dishonored among them. [NASB]
	Therefore God gave them over in the sinful desires of their hearts to **sexual impurity** for the degrading of their bodies with one another. [NIV]
	Therefore God also gave them up to **uncleanness**, in the lusts of their hearts, to dishonor their bodies among themselves, [NKJV]
	So God let them go ahead and do whatever **shameful things** their hearts desired. As a result, they did vile and degrading things with each other's bodies. [NLT]
	Διὸ καὶ παρέδωκεν αὐτοὺς ὁ Θεὸς ἐν ταῖς ἐπιθυμίαις τῶν καρδιῶν αὐτῶν εἰς **ἀκαθαρσίαν** τοῦ ἀτιμάζεσθαι τὰ σώματα αὐτῶν ἐν αὐτοῖς· [GNS]
	Διὸ παρέδωκεν αὐτοὺς ὁ Θεὸς ἐν ταῖς ἐπιθυμίαις τῶν καρδιῶν αὐτῶν εἰς **ἀκαθαρσίαν** τοῦ ἀτιμάζεσθαι τὰ σώματα αὐτῶν ἐν αὐτοῖς· [GNT]
		Impurity, immorality; impure motive; rottenness, filthiness, defilement, dirt, pollution, contamination, infection.
		
		### Practical Application
		God—the only living and true God—shows wrath by giving men up to uncleanness. The word "uncleanness" (*akatharsian*) means impurity, filthiness, immorality, defilement, dirt, pollution, contamination, infection. When men turn from God—abandon God to live unclean and immoral lives—God leaves men. He abandons them to their choice. God lets men wallow around in their filthiness. Men are judged and condemned to uncleanness.

#4120
Uncleanness
 	
Uncleanness–KJV
Impurity–NASB
Impurity–NIV
Uncleanness–NKJV
Impure thoughts–NLT
	ἀκαθαρσία = *akatharsia*
	Pronunciation: [ak-ath-ar-see'-ah]
	Parsing (part of speech): noun
	    Case—nominative
	    Gender—feminine
	    Number—singular
	    Stem or root—from ἀκαθαρσία, ας
	Concordance References:
	  ⇒ Strong's #167 akatharsia
	  ⇒ NIV #174 akatharsia
	  ⇒ NASB #167 akatharsia
		Impurity, uncleanness, impure thoughts, filth, rottenness, moral impurity; doing things that dirty, pollute, and soil life. It means to be dirty and filthy; to be infested with every kind of unclean, immoral, dirty, and polluted behavior. It is the most immoral behavior imaginable. It is *unbridled lust* turned loose.
		
		### Practical Application
		When men turn from God—abandon God to

ENGLISH WORD	GREEK WORD AND VERSE	THE WORD MEANS...
POSB REFERENCE (Gal.5:19-21; esp. v.19) Note 2	**Galatians 5:19**	live unclean and immoral lives—God leaves men. He abandons them to their choice. God lets men wallow around in their filthiness. Men are judged and condemned to impurity (cp. Ro.1:18-32).

Galatians 5:19

Now the works of the flesh are manifest, which are *these*; Adultery, fornication, **uncleanness**, lasciviousness, [KJV]

Now the deeds of the flesh are evident, which are: immorality, **impurity**, sensuality, [NASB]

The acts of the sinful nature are obvious: sexual immorality, **impurity** and debauchery; [NIV]

Now the works of the flesh are evident, which are: adultery, fornication, **uncleanness**, lewdness, [NKJV]

When you follow the desires of your sinful nature, your lives will produce these evil results: sexual immorality, **impure thoughts**, eagerness for lustful pleasure, [NLT]

φανερὰ δέ ἐστι τὰ ἔργα τῆς σαρκός, ἅτινά ἐστι μοιχεία, πορνεία, **ἀκαθαρσία**, ἀσέλγεια, [GNS]

φανερὰ δέ ἐστιν τὰ ἔργα τῆς σαρκός, ἅτινά ἐστιν πορνεία, **ἀκαθαρσία**, ἀσέλγεια, [GNT]

live unclean and immoral lives—God leaves men. He abandons them to their choice. God lets men wallow around in their filthiness. Men are judged and condemned to impurity (cp. Ro.1:18-32).

See also POSB REF:
(2 Cor.12:19-21; esp. v.21)
Note 3, point 2
(Eph.4:17-19; esp. v.19)
Note 1, point 6
(Col.3:5-7; esp. v.5)
Note 1, point 1

#4121
Uncontentious

Not a brawler–KJV
Uncontentious– NASB
Not quarrelsome–NIV
Not quarrelsome– NKJV
Peace loving–NLT

POSB REFERENCE
(1 Tim.3-2-3; esp. v.3)
Note 2, point 12

ἄμαχον = *amachon*
Pronunciation: [am'-akh-on]
Parsing (part of speech): adjective
 Case—accusative
 Gender—masculine
 Number—singular
 Stem or root—from ἄμαχος, ον
Concordance References:
 ⇒ Strong's #269 amachos
 ⇒ NIV #285 amachos
 ⇒ NASB #269 amachos

1 Tim. 3:3

Not given to wine, no striker, not greedy of filthy lucre; but patient, **not a brawler**, not covetous; [KJV]

Not addicted to wine or pugnacious, but gentle, **uncontentious**, free from the love of money. [NASB]

Not given to drunkenness, not violent but gentle, **not quarrelsome**, not a lover of money. [NIV]

Not given to wine, not violent, not greedy for money, but gentle, **not quarrelsome**, not covetous; [NKJV]

He must not be a heavy drinker or be violent. He must be gentle, **peace loving**, and not one who loves money. [NLT]

μὴ πάροινον, μὴ πλήκτην, μὴ αἰσχροκερδῆ, ἀλλ' ἐπιεικῆ, **ἄμαχον**, ἀφιλάργυρον· [GNS]

μὴ πάροινον μὴ πλήκτην, ἀλλὰ ἐπιεικῆ **ἄμαχον** ἀφιλάργυρον, [GNT]

Not quarrelsome; not a brawler; not contentious or a fighter; to be peace loving, peaceable, peaceful.

Practical Application

The minister or overseer must not be contentious (*amachon*): He must be a man of peace, a mild-mannered person, always under control. Again, this refers to the tongue as well as to the hands. He must be a man who is deeply touched when there is unrest, controversy, or disturbance in the church or among believers. He must be a person who is so touched that he will work and seek for peace.

#4122
Uncontentious

Brawlers–KJV
Uncontentious– NASB
Peaceable–NIV
Peaceable–NKJV
Quarreling–NLT

POSB REFERENCE
(Tit.3:2)
Note 4

ἀμάχους = *amachous*
Pronunciation: [am'-akh-oos]
Parsing (part of speech): adjective
 Case—accusative
 Gender—masculine
 Number—plural
 Stem or root—from ἄμαχος, ον
Concordance References:
 ⇒ Strong's #269 amachos
 ⇒ NIV #285 amachos
 ⇒ NASB #269 amachos

Titus 3:2

To speak evil of no man, to be no **brawlers**, *but* gentle, shewing all meekness unto all men. [KJV]

To malign no one, to be **uncontentious**, gentle, showing every consideration for all men. [NASB]

To slander no one, to be **peaceable** and considerate, and to show true humility toward all men. [NIV]

To speak evil of no one, to be **peaceable**, gentle, showing all humility to all men. [NKJV]

They must not speak evil of anyone, and they must avoid **quarreling**. Instead, they should be gentle and show true humility to everyone. [NLT]

μηδένα βλασφημεῖν, **ἀμάχους** εἶναι, ἐπιεικεῖς, πᾶσαν ἐνδεικνυμένους πρᾳότητα πρὸς πάντας ἀνθρώπους. [GNS]

μηδένα βλασφημεῖν, **ἀμάχους** εἶναι, ἐπιεικεῖς, πᾶσαν ἐνδεικνυμένους πραΰτητα πρὸς πάντας ἀνθρώπους. [GNT]

To be peaceable; uncontentious; not to be quarreling or brawling.

Practical Application

The Christian is not to be a fighting, contentious person; not to be a person who is always walking around looking for an argument or fight; not to be a person who walks around with a chip on his shoulder looking for some controversy or argument; not to be so opinionated and stubborn that everyone else is always wrong; not to be a person who is always criticizing or talking about others, stirring up trouble and disturbing feelings and causing division. The Christian citizen is to be the very opposite: meek and peaceful. This, of course, does not mean that the Christian citizen does not speak up for what is right; he does. And he is strong in his stand, refusing to give in to the license and indulgence of evil. But he seeks peace where it is possible, and he seeks to lead others to be peaceable.

ENGLISH WORD	GREEK WORD AND VERSE	THE WORD MEANS...

#4123
Uncontrollable
 	
Unruly–KJV
Restless–NASB
Restless–NIV
Unruly–NKJV
Uncontrollable–NLT
 	
POSB
REFERENCE
(Jas 3:7-12; esp. v.8)
Note 5, point 3
	ἀκατάστατον = *akatastaton*
	Pronunciation: [ak-at-as'-tah-ton]
	Parsing (part of speech): adjective
	    Case—nominative
	    Gender—neuter
	    Number—singular
	    Stem or root—from *ἀκατάστατος, ον*
	Concordance References:
	⇒ Strong's #183 akataschetos
	⇒ NIV #190 akatastatos
	⇒ NASB #182 akatastatos
	
	James 3:8
	But the tongue can no man tame; *it is* an **unruly** evil, full of deadly poison. [KJV]
	But no one can tame the tongue; *it is* a **restless** evil *and* full of deadly poison. [NASB]
	But no man can tame the tongue. It is a **restless** evil, full of deadly poison. [NIV]
	But no man can tame the tongue. *It is* an **unruly** evil, full of deadly poison. [NKJV]
	But no one can tame the tongue. It is an **uncontrollable** evil, full of deadly poison. [NLT]
	τὴν δὲ γλῶσσαν οὐδεὶς δύναται ἀνθρώπων δαμάσαι· **ἀκατάσχετον** κακόν, μεστὴ ἰοῦ θανατηφόρου. [GNS]
	τὴν δὲ γλῶσσαν οὐδεὶς δαμάσαι δύναται ἀνθρώπων, **ἀκατάστατον** κακόν, μεστὴ ἰοῦ θανατηφόρου. [GNT]
		Restless, unruly, uncontrollable, nervous, jittery, unsettled.
		
		Practical Application
		The tongue is "uncontrollable" (*akatastaton*), that is, restless, uneasy, unstable, always roaming about. And it is full of deadly poison. It can bless God in one breath and curse men in the next, men who are made in the image of God. Note how inconsistent the tongue is: it blesses God and curses men. Imagine! The very same tongue that blesses is the same tongue that curses. How many sit in church on Sunday or at meals blessing God and then turn around on Monday and curse or use foul and off-colored language? It is the same tongue that does both. How restless it is! It is just difficult to hold the tongue still, and when it speaks, it is just as liable to speak some curse word as it is to speak some blessing.

#4124
Uncorruptible
 	
Uncorruptible–KJV
Incorruptible–NASB
Immortal–NIV
Incorruptible–NKJV
Ever-living–NLT
 	
POSB
REFERENCE
(Romans 1:22-23; esp. v.23)
Note 5, point 2a
	ἀφθάρτου = *aphthartou*
	Pronunciation: [af'-thar-too]
	Parsing (part of speech): adjective
	    Case—genitive
	    Gender—masculine
	    Number—singular
	    Stem or root—from *ἄφθαρτος, ον*
	Concordance References:
	⇒ Strong's #862 aphthartos
	⇒ NIV #915 aphthartos
	⇒ NASB #862a aphthartos
	
	Romans 1:23
	And changed the glory of the **uncorruptible** God into an image made like to corruptible man, and to birds, and fourfooted beasts, and creeping things. [KJV]
	And exchanged the glory of the **incorruptible** God for an image in the form of corruptible man and of birds and four-footed animals and crawling creatures. [NASB]
	And exchanged the glory of the **immortal** God for images made to look like mortal man and birds and animals and reptiles. [NIV]
	And changed the glory of the **incorruptible** God into an image made like corruptible man—and birds and four-footed animals and creeping things. [NKJV]
	And instead of worshiping the glorious, **ever-living** God, they worshiped idols made to look like mere people, or birds and animals and snakes. [NLT]
	καὶ ἤλλαξαν τὴν δόξαν τοῦ **ἀφθάρτου** Θεοῦ ἐν ὁμοιώματι εἰκόνος φθαρτοῦ ἀνθρώπου καὶ πετεινῶν καὶ τετραπόδων καὶ ἑρπετῶν. [GNS]
	καὶ ἤλλαξαν τὴν δόξαν τοῦ **ἀφθάρτου** θεοῦ ἐν ὁμοιώματι εἰκόνος φθαρτοῦ ἀνθρώπου καὶ πετεινῶν καὶ τετραπόδων καὶ ἑρπετῶν. [GNT]
		Imperishable; incorruptible; lasting forever; deathless; ageless; eternal, ever living. God is said to be "uncorruptible" (*aphthartou*) which means non-decaying, imperishable, unchanging, and unaging.
		
		Practical Application
		Uncorruptible means that God is not subject to passing away; He is eternal. God always has been and always will be: God will always exist.

#4125
Undefiled
 	
Undefiled–KJV
Undefiled–NASB
Spoil–NIV
Undefiled–NKJV
Undefiled–NLT
	ἀμίαντον = *amianton*
	Pronunciation: [am-ee'-an-ton]
	Parsing (part of speech): adjective
	    Case—accusative
	    Gender—feminine
	    Number—singular
	    Stem or root—from *ἀμίαντος, ον*
	Concordance References:
	⇒ Strong's #283 amiantos
	⇒ NIV #299 amiantos
	⇒ NASB #283 amiantos
		Not spoiled, undefiled, unstained, pure.
		
		Practical Application
		The word means that it (the believer's inheritance) cannot be polluted or defiled, dirtied or infected. It means that our inheritance will be without any flaw or defect; it will be perfectly free from sickness, disease, infections, accident, pollution, dirt—from any defilement whatsoev-

ENGLISH WORD	GREEK WORD AND VERSE	THE WORD MEANS...
POSB REFERENCE (1 Pt.1:4) Note 2, point 2	**1 Peter 1:4** To an inheritance incorruptible, and **undefiled**, and that fadeth not away, reserved in heaven for you, [KJV] To *obtain* an inheritance *which is* imperishable and **undefiled** and will not fade away, reserved in heaven for you, [NASB] And into an inheritance that can never perish, **spoil** or fade—kept in heaven for you, [NIV] To an inheritance incorruptible and **undefiled** and that does not fade away, reserved in heaven for you, [NKJV] For God has reserved a priceless inheritance for his children. It is kept in heaven for you, pure and **undefiled**, beyond the reach of change and decay. [NLT] εἰς κληρονομίαν ἄφθαρτον καὶ ἀμίαντον καὶ **ἀμάραντον**, τετηρημένην ἐν οὐρανοῖς εἰς ὑμᾶς [GNS] εἰς κληρονομίαν ἄφθαρτον καὶ ἀμίαντον καὶ **ἀμάραντον**, τετηρημένην ἐν οὐρανοῖς εἰς ὑμᾶς [GNT]	er. There will never be any tears over what happens to oneself or over the damage or loss of some possession.

#4126
Undefiled
 	
Undefiled–KJV
Undefiled–NASB
Pure–NIV
Undefiled–NKJV
Unstained by sin–NLT
 	
POSB REFERENCE
(Heb.7:26)
Note 2
	ἀμίαντος = *amiantos*
	Pronunciation: [am-ee'-an-tos]
	Parsing (part of speech): adjective
	    Case—nominative
	    Gender—masculine
	    Number—singular
	    Stem or root—from ἀμίαντος, ον
	Concordance References:
	⇒ Strong's #283 amiantos
	⇒ NIV #299 amiantos
	⇒ NASB #283 amiantos
	
	Hebrews 7:26
	For such an high priest became us, *who is* holy, harmless, **undefiled**, separate from sinners, and made higher than the heavens; [KJV]
	For it was fitting that we should have such a high priest, holy, innocent, **undefiled**, separated from sinners and exalted above the heavens; [NASB]
	Such a high priest meets our need—one who is holy, blameless, **pure**, set apart from sinners, exalted above the heavens. [NIV]
	For such a High Priest was fitting for us, *who is* holy, harmless, **undefiled**, separate from sinners, and has become higher than the heavens; [NKJV]
	He is the kind of high priest we need because he is holy and blameless, **unstained by sin**. He has now been set apart from sinners, and he has been given the highest place of honor in heaven. [NLT]
	Τοιοῦτος γὰρ ἡμῖν ἔπρεπεν ἀρχιερεύς, ὅσιος, ἄκακος, **ἀμίαντος**, κεχωρισμένος ἀπὸ τῶν ἁμαρτωλῶν, καὶ ὑψηλότερος τῶν οὐρανῶν γενόμενος· [GNS]
	Τοιοῦτος γὰρ ἡμῖν καὶ ἔπρεπεν ἀρχιερεύς, ὅσιος ἄκακος **ἀμίαντος**, κεχωρισμένος ἀπὸ τῶν ἁμαρτωλῶν καὶ ὑψηλότερος τῶν οὐρανῶν γενόμενος, [GNT]
		Pure, undefiled, unstained by sin.
		
		Practical Application
		Jesus Christ is "undefiled" (*amiantos*): unstained by sin; absolutely free from all moral impurity, uncleanness, and defilement. Jesus Christ was completely free from anything that would keep Him from approaching God. He is absolutely *undefiled*.

#4127
Undefiled
 	
Undefiled–KJV
Undefiled–NASB
Pure–NIV
Undefiled–NKJV
Faithful–NLT
 	
POSB REFERENCE
(Heb.13:4)
Note 4
	ἀμίαντος = *amiantos*
	Pronunciation: [am-ee'-ahn-tos]
	Parsing (part of speech): adjective
	    Case—nominative
	    Gender—feminine
	    Number—singular
	    Stem or root—from ἀμίαντος, ον
	Concordance References:
	⇒ Strong's #283 amiantos
	⇒ NIV #299 amiantos
	⇒ NASB #283 amiantos
	
	Hebrews 13:4
	Marriage *is* honourable in all, and the bed **undefiled**: but whoremongers and adulterers God will judge. [KJV]
	Let marriage *be held* in honor among all, and let the
		Pure, undefiled, faithful, faultless, unstained, devoted, reliable, constant, unswerving, allegiant, unwavering, scrupulous.
		
		Practical Application
		The word "undefiled" (*amiantos*) means that the bed is unstained by sin, absolutely free from all moral impurity, uncleanness, and defilement. This is saying at least three things.
		⇒ First, husband and wife are free and encouraged to be close in bed. Closeness and intimacy are a gift from God; it is even a type of the church (cp. Ephes. 5:22f).

ENGLISH WORD	GREEK WORD AND VERSE	THE WORD MEANS...
	marriage bed *be* **undefiled**; for fornicators and adulterers God will judge. [NASB] Marriage should be honored by all, and the marriage bed kept **pure**, for God will judge the adulterer and all the sexually immoral. [NIV] Marriage *is* honorable among all, and the bed **undefiled**; but fornicators and adulterers God will judge. [NKJV] Give honor to marriage, and remain **faithful** to one another in marriage. God will surely judge people who are immoral and those who commit adultery. [NLT] τίμιος ὁ γάμος ἐν πᾶσι, καὶ ἡ κοίτη **ἀμίαντος**· πόρνους δὲ καὶ μοιχοὺς κρινεῖ ὁ Θεός. [GNS] Τίμιος ὁ γάμος ἐν πᾶσιν καὶ ἡ κοίτη **ἀμίαντος**, πόρνους γὰρ καὶ μοιχοὺς κρινεῖ ὁ θεός. [GNT]	⇒ Second, the closeness in bed between husband and wife will prevent unfaithfulness. ⇒ Third, the bed is to be kept undefiled. Only husband and wife are to be close in bed, and only with each other. There is absolutely no place for anyone else in the bed. The importance of the bed in marriage cannot be overemphasized. God's Word says that it is so important that husband and wife are not to separate for any period of time except for fasting and prayer, and even then separation is not to occur unless it is by mutual consent.
#4128 **Under Compulsion** Laid upon–KJV **Under compulsion– NASB** Compelled–NIV Laid upon–NKJV Compelled–NLT **POSB REFERENCE** (1 Cor.9:16) Note 1	ἀνάγκη ἐπίκειται = *anagkē epikeitai* Pronunciation: [an-ang-kay' ep-ik'-eh-ee-tah-ee] Parsing *anagkē* (part of speech): noun 　Case—nominative 　Gender—feminine 　Number—singular 　Stem or root—from ἀνάγκη, ης Parsing *epikeitai* (part of speech): verb 　Mood—indicative 　Tense—present 　Voice—middle or passive deponent 　Person—3rd person 　Number—singular 　Stem or root—from ἐπίκειμαι Concordance References: 　⇒ Strong's #318+1945 anagkē epikeimai 　⇒ NIV #340+2130 anagkē epikeimai [compelled] 　⇒ NASB #318+1945 anagkē epikeimai **1 Cor. 9:16** For though I preach the gospel, I have nothing to glory of: for necessity is **laid upon** me; yea, woe is unto me, if I preach not the gospel! [KJV] For if I preach the gospel, I have nothing to boast of, for I am **under compulsion**; for woe is me if I do not preach the gospel. [NASB] Yet when I preach the gospel, I cannot boast, for I am **compelled** to preach. Woe to me if I do not preach the gospel! [NIV] For if I preach the gospel, I have nothing to boast of, for necessity is **laid upon** me; yes, woe is me if I do not preach the gospel! [NKJV] For preaching the Good News is not something I can boast about. I am **compelled** by God to do it. How terrible for me if I didn't do it! [NLT] ἐὰν γὰρ εὐαγγελίζωμαι, οὐκ ἔστι μοι καύχημα· ἀνάγκη γάρ μοι ἐπίκειται· οὐαὶ δέ μοί ἐστιν, ἐὰν μὴ εὐαγγελίζωμαι. [GNS] ἐὰν γὰρ εὐαγγελίζωμαι, οὐκ ἔστιν μοι καύχημα· ἀνάγκη γάρ μοι ἐπίκειται· οὐαὶ γάρ μοί ἐστιν ἐὰν μὴ εὐαγγελίσωμαι. [GNT]	To be pressed, compelled, constrained, required; to be duty bound, gripped with a sense of duty; to preach the gospel. It means to be urged, under force, under compulsion, imposed upon. **Practical Application** God had called Paul to preach the gospel; therefore, it was his charge, his work, his business, his call in life. He could not do otherwise: he was compelled to preach. His preaching was not a matter of choice; he had not chosen to be a preacher. His preaching was a matter of duty. If he did not preach, he would be disobeying God and would be missing the very purpose for his life upon earth.
#4129 **Under Sin** **Under sin–KJV** **Under sin–NASB** **Under sin–NIV** **Under sin–NKJV** Under the power of sin–NLT **POSB REFERENCE** (Romans 3:9) Note 1	ὑφ' ἁμαρτίαν = *huph'hamartian* Pronunciation: [hoof' ham-ar-tee'-ahn] Parsing *huph'* (part of speech): preposition 　Case—accusative 　Stem or root—from ὑπό Parsing *hamartian* (part of speech): noun 　Case—accusative 　Gender—feminine 　Number—singular 　Stem or root—from ἁμαρτία, ας Concordance References: 　⇒ Strong's #5259 hupo + 266 hamartia 　⇒ NIV #5679 hupo [under] + 281 hamartia [sin] 　⇒ NASB #5259 hupo + 266 hamartia	To be subject to the power of or under the authority of; by means of; at the hands of; under the authority of. **Practical Application** All men are under sin. A man outside of Jesus Christ is under the power of sin, and he is helpless to escape from it (cp. Galatians 3:10, 25; Galatians 4:2, 21; Galatians 5:18; 1 Tim. 6:1).

ENGLISH WORD	GREEK WORD AND VERSE	THE WORD MEANS...
	Romans 3:9 What then? are we better *than they?* No, in no wise: for we have before proved both Jews and Gentiles, that they are all **under sin**; [KJV] What then? Are we better than they? Not at all; for we have already charged that both Jews and Greeks are all **under sin**; [NASB] What shall we conclude then? Are we any better? Not at all! We have already made the charge that Jews and Gentiles alike are all **under sin**. [NIV] What then? Are we better *than they?* Not at all. For we have previously charged both Jews and Greeks that they are all **under sin**. [NKJV] Well then, are we Jews better than others? No, not at all, for we have already shown that all people, whether Jews or Gentiles, are **under the power of sin**. [NLT] Τί οὖν; προεχόμεθα; οὐ πάντως· προῃτιασάμεθα γὰρ Ἰουδαίους τε καὶ Ἕλληνας πάντας **ὑφ' ἁμαρτίαν** εἶναι, [GNS] Τί οὖν; προεχόμεθα; οὐ πάντως· προῃτιασάμεθα γὰρ Ἰουδαίους τε καὶ Ἕλληνας πάντας **ὑφ' ἁμαρτίαν** εἶναι, [GNT]	
#4130 **Under Sin** **Under sin–KJV** **Under sin–NASB** Of sin–NIV **Under sin–NKJV** Of sin–NLT **POSB** **REFERENCE** (Gal.3:22) Note 5	**ὑπὸ ἁμαρτίαν** = *hupo hamartian* Pronunciation: [hoop-o' ham-ar-tee'-ahn] Parsing *hupo* (part of speech): preposition 　　Case—accusative 　　Stem or root—from ὑπό Parsing *hamartian* (part of speech): noun 　　Case—accusative 　　Gender—feminine 　　Number—singular 　　Stem or root—from ἁμαρτία, ας Concordance References: ⇒　Strong's #5259 hupo + 266 hamartia ⇒　NIV #5679 hupo [of] + 281 hamartia [sin] ⇒　NASB #5259 hupo + 266 hamartia **Galatians 3:22** But the scripture hath concluded all **under sin**, that the promise by faith of Jesus Christ might be given to them that believe. [KJV] But the Scripture has shut up all men **under sin**, that the promise by faith in Jesus Christ might be given to those who believe. [NASB] But the Scripture declares that the whole world is a prisoner **of sin**, so that what was promised, being given through faith in Jesus Christ, might be given to those who believe. [NIV] But the Scripture has confined all **under sin**, that the promise by faith in Jesus Christ might be given to those who believe. [NKJV] But the Scriptures have declared that we are all prisoners **of sin**, so the only way to receive God's promise is to believe in Jesus Christ. [NLT] ἀλλὰ συνέκλεισεν ἡ γραφὴ τὰ πάντα **ὑπὸ ἁμαρτίαν**, ἵνα ἡ ἐπαγγελία ἐκ πίστεως Ἰησοῦ Χριστοῦ δοθῇ τοῖς πιστεύουσι. [GNS] ἀλλὰ συνέκλεισεν ἡ γραφὴ τὰ πάντα **ὑπὸ ἁμαρτίαν**, ἵνα ἡ ἐπαγγελία ἐκ πίστεως Ἰησοῦ Χριστοῦ δοθῇ τοῖς πιστεύουσιν. [GNT]	Of sin, under sin; to be shut up as a prisoner in the hopeless depths or solitary confinement of a dungeon. **Practical Application** How do we know that the law does not justify or make a person acceptable to God? Because the law imprisons all men under sin.
#4131 **Under The** **Power Of Sin** Under sin–KJV Under sin–NASB Under sin–NIV Under sin–NKJV **Under the power of** **sin–NLT**	**ὑφ' ἁμαρτίαν** = *huph'hamartian* Pronunciation: [hoof' ham-ar-tee'-ahn] Parsing *huph'* (part of speech): preposition 　　Case—accusative 　　Stem or root—from ὑπό Parsing *hamartian* (part of speech): noun 　　Case—accusative 　　Gender—feminine 　　Number—singular 　　Stem or root—from ἁμαρτία, ας Concordance References:	To be subject to the power of or under the authority of; by means of; at the hands of; under the authority of. **Practical Application** All men are under the power of sin. A man outside of Jesus Christ is under the power of sin, and he is helpless to escape from it (cp. Galatians 3:10, 25; Galatians 4:2, 21; Galatians 5:18; 1 Tim. 6:1).

ENGLISH WORD	GREEK WORD AND VERSE	THE WORD MEANS...
POSB REFERENCE (Romans 3:9) Note 1	⇒ Strong's #5259 hupo + 266 hamartia ⇒ NIV #5679 hupo [under] + 281 hamartia [sin] ⇒ NASB #5259 hupo + 266 hamartia **Romans 3:9** What then? are we better *than they?* No, in no wise: for we have before proved both Jews and Gentiles, that they are all **under sin**; [KJV] What then? Are we better than they? Not at all; for we have already charged that both Jews and Greeks are all **under sin**; [NASB] What shall we conclude then? Are we any better? Not at all! We have already made the charge that Jews and Gentiles alike are all **under sin**. [NIV] What then? Are we better *than they?* Not at all. For we have previously charged both Jews and Greeks that they are all **under sin**. [NKJV] Well then, are we Jews better than others? No, not at all, for we have already shown that all people, whether Jews or Gentiles, are **under the power of sin**. [NLT] Τί οὖν; προεχόμεθα; οὐ πάντως· προῃτιασάμεθα γὰρ Ἰουδαίους τε καὶ Ἕλληνας πάντας **ὑφ' ἁμαρτίαν** εἶναι, [GNS] Τί οὖν; προεχόμεθα; οὐ πάντως· προῃτιασάμεθα γὰρ Ἰουδαίους τε καὶ Ἕλληνας πάντας **ὑφ' ἁμαρτίαν** εἶναι, [GNT]	
#4132 **Understand** Allow–KJV **Understand–NASB** **Understand–NIV** **Understand–NKJV** **Understand–NLT** **POSB REFERENCE** (Rom. 7:14-17; esp. v.15) Note 2, point 1a	γινώσκω = *ginöskö* Pronunciation: [ghin-oce'-ko] Parsing (part of speech): verb 　　Mood—indicative 　　Tense—present 　　Voice—active 　　Person—1st person 　　Number—singular 　　Stem or root—from γινώσκω Concordance References: ⇒ Strong's #1097 ginöskö ⇒ NIV #1182 ginöskö ⇒ NASB #1097 ginöskö **Romans 7:15** For that which I do I **allow** not: for what I would, that do I not; but what I hate, that do I. [KJV] For that which I am doing, I do not **understand**; for I am not practicing what I *would* like to *do,* but I am doing the very thing I hate. [NASB] I do not **understand** what I do. For what I want to do I do not do, but what I hate I do. [NIV] For what I am doing, I do not **understand**. For what I will to do, that I do not practice; but what I hate, that I do. [NKJV] I don't **understand** myself at all, for I really want to do what is right, but I don't do it. Instead, I do the very thing I hate. [NLT] ὃ γὰρ κατεργάζομαι, οὐ **γινώσκω**· οὐ γὰρ ὃ θέλω, τοῦτο πράσσω· ἀλλ' ὃ μισῶ, τοῦτο ποιῶ. [GNS] ὃ γὰρ κατεργάζομαι οὐ **γινώσκω**· οὐ γὰρ ὃ θέλω τοῦτο πράσσω, ἀλλ' ὃ μισῶ τοῦτο ποιῶ. [GNT]	To know; to have knowledge of; to find out; to learn; to understand; to perceive; to discern; to have knowledge; to acknowledge, to recognize; to be very certain; to remember. **Practical Application** Paul says that a carnal life is a helpless, unceasing struggle. A carnal man finds himself doing things, and he cannot understand why he is doing them. He fights and struggles against them, but before he knows it, he has sinned and come short. The sin was upon him before he even recognized and saw it. If he had known that the behavior was sin, he would have never done it, but he did not recognize it as coming short of God's glory and God's will for his life.
#4133 **Understand** **Understand–KJV** **Understand–NASB** **Understand–NIV** **Understand–NKJV** **Understand–NLT** **POSB REFERENCE** (Heb. 11:3) Note 3	νοοῦμεν = *nooumen* Pronunciation: [no-oo-meh] Parsing (part of speech): verb 　　Mood—indicative 　　Tense—present 　　Voice—active 　　Person—1st person 　　Number—plural 　　Stem or root—from νοέω Concordance References: ⇒ Strong's #3539 noeö ⇒ NIV #3783 noeö ⇒ NASB #3539 noeö	To understand; to discern. It means to perceive with the mind, to understand, to know a true fact. **Practical Application** Some say the belief that God made the world is only an assumption, that it is the beginning point in building Christian's beliefs and theology. There is both truth and error in this charge. The error is found in the word assumption. The truth is this: the Christian begins with a fact that is true: *God did create the world.* The Christian

ENGLISH WORD	GREEK WORD AND VERSE	THE WORD MEANS...

Hebrews 11:3

Through faith we **understand** that the worlds were framed by the word of God, so that things which are seen were not made of things which do appear. [KJV]

By faith we **understand** that the worlds were prepared by the word of God, so that what is seen was not made out of things which are visible. [NASB]

By faith we **understand** that the universe was formed at God's command, so that what is seen was not made out of what was visible. [NIV]

By faith we **understand** that the worlds were framed by the word of God, so that the things which are seen were not made of things which are visible. [NKJV]

By faith we **understand** that the entire universe was formed at God's command, that what we now see did not come from anything that can be seen. [NLT]

πίστει **νοοῦμεν** κατηρτίσθαι τοὺς αἰῶνας ῥήματι Θεοῦ, εἰς τὸ μὴ ἐκ φαινομένων τὸ βλεπόμενον γεγονέναι. [GNS]

Πίστει **νοοῦμεν** κατηρτίσθαι τοὺς αἰῶνας ῥήματι θεοῦ, εἰς τὸ μὴ ἐκ φαινομένων τὸ βλεπόμενον γεγονέναι. [GNT]

believer's starting point is more than an assumption—it is an understanding, a true fact, the very basic fact that God did create the world. This understanding is based upon four things:

⇒ The world itself: looking at and observing the world, and studying and thinking about its origin, purpose, and end.

⇒ The Bible, the Word of God, the written revelation of God.

⇒ The Lord Jesus Christ, the living revelation of God.

⇒ The witness of the Holy Spirit who is given to every believer. He bears witness that Jesus Christ and the Word of God are true. This is critical, for it is *a fact*, as any true Christian believer can testify. When a person believes in the Lord Jesus Christ, God puts His Spirit into the heart and life of the believer. The Holy Spirit seals, guarantees, bears witness that Jesus Christ is the Son of God and that the promises and teachings of God's Word are true.

The point is this: the Christian believer has four strong sources that show the origin, purpose, and end of all things; and all four are undeniable.

#4134

Understanding, Perfect

Perfect understanding–KJV

Investigated–NASB

Investigated–NIV

Perfect understanding–NKJV

Investigated–NLT

POSB REFERENCE

(Lk.1:3)

Note 3, point 1

παρηκολουθηκότι = *parëkolouthëkoti*
Pronunciation: [par-ak-ol-oo-thay'-ko-tee]
Parsing (part of speech): verb
  Mood—participle
  Tense—perfect
  Voice—active
  Case—dative
  Gender—masculine
  Person—1st person
  Number—singular
  Stem or root—from **παρακολουθέω**
Concordance References:
  ⇒ Strong's #3877 parakoloutheō
  ⇒ NIV #4158 parakoloutheō
  ⇒ NASB #3877 parakoloutheō

Luke 1:3

It seemed good to me also, having had **perfect understanding** of all things from the very first, to write unto thee in order, most excellent Theophilus, [KJV]

It seemed fitting for me as well, having **investigated** everything carefully from the beginning, to write *it* out for you in consecutive order, most excellent Theophilus; [NASB]

Therefore, since I myself have carefully **investigated** everything from the beginning, it seemed good also to me to write an orderly account for you, most excellent Theophilus, [NIV]

It seemed good to me also, having had **perfect understanding** of all things from the very first, to write to you an orderly account, most excellent Theophilus, [NKJV]

Having carefully **investigated** all of these accounts from the beginning, I have decided to write a careful summary for you, [NLT]

ἔδοξε κἀμοὶ **παρηκολουθηκότι** ἄνωθεν πᾶσιν ἀκριβῶς, καθεξῆς σοι γράψαι, κράτιστε Θεόφιλε, [GNS]

ἔδοξε κἀμοὶ **παρηκολουθηκότι** ἄνωθεν πᾶσιν ἀκριβῶς καθεξῆς σοι γράψαι, κράτιστε Θεόφιλε, [GNT]

To study; to follow up; to search out diligently; to investigate; to give careful attention; to trace accurately; to become acquainted with; to scrutinize.

Practical Application

Luke says that having been acquainted with and having investigated all things, he was determined to record the facts himself.

#4135

Understanding, Without

ἀσυνέτους = *asunetous*
Pronunciation: [as-oon'-ay-toos]
Parsing (part of speech): adjective
  Case—accusative

Without understanding, dull; senseless, foolish, without conscience.

ENGLISH WORD	GREEK WORD AND VERSE	THE WORD MEANS...
	Καὶ τοῦτο, εἰδότες τὸν καιρόν, ὅτι ὥρα ὑμᾶς ἤδη ἐξ ὕπνου ἐγερθῆναι· νῦν γὰρ ἐγγύτερον ἡμῶν ἡ σωτηρία η ὅτε ἐπιστεύσαμεν. [GNS] Καὶ τοῦτο εἰδότες τὸν καιρόν, ὅτι ὥρα ἤδη ὑμᾶς ἐξ ὕπνου ἐγερθῆναι, νῦν γὰρ ἐγγύτερον ἡμῶν ἡ σωτηρία η ὅτε ἐπιστεύσαμεν. [GNT]	

#4140
Understanding
 	
Prudence–KJV
Insight–NASB
Understanding–NIV
Prudence–NKJV
Understanding–NLT
 	
POSB
REFERENCE
(Eph.1:8)
Note 5, point 2
	φρονήσει = phronēsei
	Pronunciation: [fron´-ay-see]
	Parsing (part of speech): noun
	    Case—dative
	    Gender—feminine
	    Number—singular
	    Stem or root—from φρόνησις, εως
	Concordance References:
	  ⇒ Strong's #5428 phronēsis
	  ⇒ NIV #5860 phronēsis
	  ⇒ NASB #5428 phronēsis
	
	Ephes. 1:8
	Wherein he hath abounded toward us in all wisdom and **prudence**; [KJV]
	    Which He lavished upon us. In all wisdom and **insight** [NASB]
	    That he lavished on us with all wisdom and **understanding**. [NIV]
	    Which He made to abound toward us in all wisdom and **prudence**, [NKJV]
	    He has showered his kindness on us, along with all wisdom and **understanding**. [NLT]
	ἧς ἐπερίσσευσεν εἰς ἡμᾶς ἐν πάσῃ σοφίᾳ καὶ φρονήσει, [GNS]
	ἧς ἐπερίσσευσεν εἰς ἡμᾶς, ἐν πάσῃ σοφίᾳ καὶ φρονήσει, [GNT]
		Understanding, insight, wisdom, prudence, comprehension, discernment, intelligence, discretion, judgment.
		
		Practical Application
		    The word "understanding" (phronēsei) means seeing how to use and do the truth. It is seeing the direction to take. It is understanding, insight, the ability to solve day-to-day problems. It is a down-to-earth practical understanding of things.

#4141
Understanding
 	
Revelation–KJV
Revelation–NASB
Revelation–NIV
Revelation–NKJV
Understanding–NLT
 	
POSB
REFERENCE
(Eph.1:17-18; esp. v.17)
Note 2, point 2
	ἀποκαλύψεως = apokalupseōs
	Pronunciation: [ap-ok-al´-oop-seh-os]
	Parsing (part of speech): noun
	    Case—genitive
	    Gender—feminine
	    Number—singular
	    Stem or root—from ἀποκάλυψις, εως
	Concordance References:
	  ⇒ Strong's #602 apokalupsis
	  ⇒ NIV #637 apokalupsis
	  ⇒ NASB #602 apokalupsis
	
	Ephes. 1:17
	That the God of our Lord Jesus Christ, the Father of glory, may give unto you the spirit of wisdom and **revelation** in the knowledge of him: [KJV]
	    That the God of our Lord Jesus Christ, the Father of glory, may give to you a spirit of wisdom and of **revelation** in the knowledge of Him. [NASB]
	    I keep asking that the God of our Lord Jesus Christ, the glorious Father, may give you the Spirit of wisdom and **revelation**, so that you may know him better. [NIV]
	    That the God of our Lord Jesus Christ, the Father of glory, may give to you the spirit of wisdom and **revelation** in the knowledge of Him, [NKJV]
	    Asking God, the glorious Father of our Lord Jesus Christ, to give you spiritual wisdom and **understanding**, so that you might grow in your knowledge of God. [NLT]
	ἵνα ὁ Θεὸς τοῦ Κυρίου ἡμῶν Ἰησοῦ Χριστοῦ, ὁ πατὴρ τῆς δόξης, δῴη ὑμῖν πνεῦμα σοφίας καὶ ἀποκαλύψεως, ἐν ἐπιγνώσει αὐτοῦ· [GNS]
	ἵνα ὁ θεὸς τοῦ κυρίου ἡμῶν Ἰησοῦ Χριστοῦ, ὁ πατὴρ τῆς δόξης, δῴη ὑμῖν πνεῦμα σοφίας καὶ ἀποκαλύψεως ἐν ἐπιγνώσει αὐτοῦ, [GNT]
		Revelation, understanding. It means to manifest; to reveal; to unveil; to uncover; to open.
		
		Practical Application
		    It is the work of the Holy Spirit to reveal the knowledge of God to Christians. In fact, it is the work of the Holy Spirit to reveal the meaning of all truth to the Christian (John 14:26; John 16:12-15). This is clearly seen in 1 Cor. 1:9-16 where the wisdom of the world is contrasted with the wisdom of God. A spiritual Christian sees (through the Spirit revealing to him) the meaning behind world events as well as day to day experiences. He understands who and what is behind the events of history and human experience. Therefore, he gains a growing knowledge of God day by day.

ENGLISH WORD	GREEK WORD AND VERSE	THE WORD MEANS...

#4142

Understanding

Judgment–KJV
Discernment–NASB
Insight–NIV
Discernment–NKJV
Understanding–NLT

**POSB
REFERENCE**
(Philip.1:9-10; esp.
v.9)
Note 7

αἰσθήσει = aisthēsei
Pronunciation: [ah'ee-sthay-seh-ee]
Parsing (part of speech): noun
    Case—dative
    Gender—feminine
    Number—singular
    Stem or root—from *αἴσθησις, εως*
Concordance References:
  ⇒ Strong's #144 aisthēsis
  ⇒ NIV #151 aisthēsis
  ⇒ NASB #144 aisthēsis

Philip. 1:9

And this I pray, that your love may abound yet more and more in knowledge and in all **judgment**; [KJV]

And this I pray, that your love may abound still more and more in real knowledge and all **discernment**, [NASB]

And this is my prayer: that your love may abound more and more in knowledge and depth of **insight**, [NIV]

And this I pray, that your love may abound still more and more in knowledge and all **discernment**, [NKJV]

I pray that your love for each other will overflow more and more, and that you will keep on growing in your knowledge and **understanding**. [NLT]

καὶ τοῦτο προσεύχομαι, ἵνα ἡ ἀγάπη ὑμῶν ἔτι μᾶλλον καὶ μᾶλλον περισσεύῃ ἐν ἐπιγνώσει καὶ πάσῃ **αἰσθήσει**, [GNS]

καὶ τοῦτο προσεύχομαι, ἵνα ἡ ἀγάπη ὑμῶν ἔτι μᾶλλον καὶ μᾶλλον περισσεύῃ ἐν ἐπιγνώσει καὶ πάσῃ **αἰσθήσει** [GNT]

Insight, judgment, discernment, understanding, intelligence.

Practical Application

Love in the Bible never focuses upon *good feelings*. Feelings may and usually do come to the person who truly loves another person, but feelings are never the focus—not with true love. What then is the focus?

⇒ The focus of love is knowledge. If we truly love someone, we want to know that person. In fact, we want to know all we can about the person.

⇒ The force of love is understanding (*aisthēsei*). If we truly love someone, we not only want to know a person but we want to learn all we can about the person. We want to gather all the intelligence and facts possible and discern them so that we can please the person.

#4143

Understanding

Understanding–KJV
**Understanding–
NASB**
Understanding–NIV
**Understanding–
NKJV**
Wisdom–NLT

**POSB
REFERENCE**
(Col.1:9)
Note 1

συνέσει = sunesei
Pronunciation: [soon'-es-eh-ee]
Parsing (part of speech): noun
    Case—dative
    Gender—feminine
    Number—singular
    Stem or root—from *σύνεσις, εως*
Concordance References:
  ⇒ Strong's #4907 sunesis
  ⇒ NIV #5304 sunesis
  ⇒ NASB #4907 sunesis

Col. 1:9

For this cause we also, since the day we heard *it*, do not cease to pray for you, and to desire that ye might be filled with the knowledge of his will in all wisdom and spiritual **understanding**; [KJV]

For this reason also, since the day we heard *of it*, we have not ceased to pray for you and to ask that you may be filled with the knowledge of His will in all spiritual wisdom and **understanding**, [NASB]

For this reason, since the day we heard about you, we have not stopped praying for you and asking God to fill you with the knowledge of his will through all spiritual wisdom and **understanding**. [NIV]

For this reason we also, since the day we heard it, do not cease to pray for you, and to ask that you may be filled with the knowledge of His will in all wisdom and spiritual **understanding**; [NKJV]

So we have continued praying for you ever since we first heard about you. We ask God to give you a complete understanding of what he wants to do in your lives, and we ask him to make you wise with spiritual **wisdom**. [NLT]

Διὰ τοῦτο καὶ ἡμεῖς, ἀφ' ἧς ἡμέρας ἠκούσαμεν, οὐ παυόμεθα ὑπὲρ ὑμῶν προσευχόμενοι, καὶ αἰτούμενοι ἵνα πληρωθῆτε τὴν ἐπίγνωσιν τοῦ θελήματος αὐτοῦ ἐν πάσῃ σοφίᾳ καὶ **συνέσει** πνευματικῇ, [GNS]

Διὰ τοῦτο καὶ ἡμεῖς, ἀφ' ἧς ἡμέρας ἠκούσαμεν, οὐ παυόμεθα ὑπὲρ ὑμῶν προσευχόμενοι, καὶ αἰτούμενοι ἵνα πληρωθῆτε τὴν ἐπίγνωσιν τοῦ θελήματος αὐτοῦ ἐν πάσῃ σοφίᾳ καὶ **συνέσει** πνευματικῇ, [GNT]

Understanding, wisdom, insight, intelligence. Understanding" (*sunesei*) means that a person has the ability to apply the basic principles to everyday life, to the circumstances and decisions of life.

Practical Application

The believer needs both wisdom and understanding: he must learn all the basic principles of life, and he must learn how to apply them to everyday life. But how? How can he secure wisdom and understanding?

⇒ By studying God's Word.

⇒ By prayer—praying to be filled with the knowledge of God's will.

Think about the shallow lives that so many people live. Think about how little most people know about God's will. Compare this tragic fact with the kind of life God wills man to live. Is it any wonder...

- that so many have been deceived by false teaching?
- that so much of our ministry is superficial and formal?

ENGLISH WORD	GREEK WORD AND VERSE	THE WORD MEANS...
Unmerciful–KJV Unmerciful–NASB Ruthless–NIV Unmerciful–NKJV **Unforgiving–NLT** **POSB REFERENCE** (Romans 1:31) *Deeper Study #23*	Gender—masculine Number—plural Stem or root—from ἀνελέημων, ον Concordance References: ⇒ Strong's #415 aneleëmön ⇒ NIV #446 aneleëmön ⇒ NASB #415 aneleëmön **Romans 1:31** Without understanding, covenantbreakers, without natural affection, implacable, **unmerciful**: [KJV] Without understanding, untrustworthy, unloving, **unmerciful**; [NASB] They are senseless, faithless, heartless, **ruthless**. [NIV] Undiscerning, untrustworthy, unloving, unforgiving, **unmerciful**; [NKJV] They refuse to understand, break their promises, and are heartless and **unforgiving**. [NLT] ἀσυνέτους, ἀσυνθέτους, ἀστόργους, ἀσπόνδους, **ἀνελεήμονας**· [GNS] ἀσυνέτους ἀσυνθέτους ἀστόργους **ἀνελεήμονας**· [GNT]	**Practical Application** It is a person... • craving to have and to possess others regardless of their welfare. • craving to use others as one wills regardless of hurt and shame. • craving to satisfy one's own pleasure even if it means the hurt or death of others. It is an absence of consideration or feelings for others. What matters is one's own pleasure and rights, not the pleasure and rights of others.
#4149 Unforgiving Implacable–KJV Not translated–NASB Not translated–NIV **Unforgiving–NKJV** **Unforgiving–NLT** **POSB REFERENCE** (Romans 1:31) *Deeper Study #22*	ἀσπόνδους = *aspondous* Pronunciation: [as'-pon-doos] Parsing (part of speech): adjective Case—accusative Gender—masculine Number—plural Stem or root—from ἀνελέημων, ον Concordance References: ⇒ Strong's #786 aspondos ⇒ NIV #—NOT TRANSLATED ⇒ NASB #—NOT TRANSLATED **Romans 1:31** Without understanding, covenantbreakers, without natural affection, **implacable**, unmerciful: [KJV] Without understanding, untrustworthy, unloving, unmerciful; [NASB]—NOT TRANSLATED They are senseless, faithless, heartless, ruthless. [NIV]—NOT TRANSLATED Undiscerning, untrustworthy, unloving, **unforgiving**, unmerciful; [NKJV] They refuse to understand, break their promises, and are heartless and **unforgiving**. [NLT] ἀσυνέτους, ἀσυνθέτους, ἀστόργους, **ἀσπόνδους**, ἀνελεήμονας· [GNS] ἀσυνέτους ἀσυνθέτους ἀστόργους ἀνελεήμονας· [GNT]	Incapable of giving in, of being appeased or purified; to be unforgiving. **Practical Application** This word describes a person who is unwilling to make peace or come to an agreement.
#4150 Unforgiving Trucebreakers–KJV Irreconcilable–NASB **Unforgiving–NIV** **Unforgiving–NKJV** **Unforgiving–NLT** **POSB REFERENCE** (2 Tim. 3:2-4; esp. v.3) Note 2, point 10	ἄσπονδοι = *aspondoi* Pronunciation: [as'-pon-doy] Parsing (part of speech): adjective Case—nominative Gender—masculine Number—plural Stem or root—from ἄσπονδος, ον Concordance References: ⇒ Strong's #786 aspondos ⇒ NIV #836 aspondos ⇒ NASB #786 aspondos **2 Tim. 3:3** Without natural affection, **trucebreakers**, false accusers, incontinent, fierce, despisers of those that are good, [KJV] Unloving, **irreconcilable**, malicious gossips, without self-control, brutal, haters of good, [NASB] Without love, **unforgiving**, slanderous, without self-control, brutal, not lovers of the good, [NIV] Unloving, **unforgiving**, slanderers, without self-control, brutal, despisers of good, [NKJV]	Unforgiving, trucebreakers, irreconcilable, merciless, breakers of promises and agreements, untrustworthy, faithless, treacherous, and untruthful. **Practical Application** An unforgiving person is a man or some organization or body of people who tragically do not keep their word or promise. They are simply untrustworthy and undependable. What happens when a person's word can no longer be accepted? ⇒ What happens in a home when the husband or wife breaks the truce of marriage? ⇒ What happens between parent and child when one of them breaks his promise time and again? ⇒ What happens when an employer breaks his promise to his workers? ⇒ What happens when a worker breaks his truce and slacks up in his work?

ENGLISH WORD	GREEK WORD AND VERSE	THE WORD MEANS...
	They will be unloving and **unforgiving**; they will slander others and have no self-control; they will be cruel and have no interest in what is good. [NLT] ἄστοργοι, **ἄσπονδοι**, διάβολοι, ἀκρατεῖς, ἀνήμεροι, ἀφιλάγαθοι, [GNS] ἄστοργοι **ἄσπονδοι** διάβολοι ἀκρατεῖς ἀνήμεροι ἀφιλάγαθοι [GNT]	⇒ What happens when a nation breaks its agreement with another nation? The last days will see what we are seeing in our society today: a barrage of broken truces, covenants, and promises.

#4151
Ungodliness
 	
Ungodliness–KJV
Ungodliness–NASB
Godlessness–NIV
Ungodliness–NKJV
Sinful–NLT
 	
**POSB
REFERENCE**
(Rom. 1:18)
Note 1, point 3a
	ἀσέβειαν = *asebeian*
	Pronunciation: [as-eb'-i-ahn]
	Parsing (part of speech): noun
	  Case—accusative
	  Gender—feminine
	  Number—singular
	  Stem or root—from ἀσέβεια, ας
	Concordance References:
	  ⇒ Strong's #763 asebeia
	  ⇒ NIV #813 asebeia
	  ⇒ NASB #763 asebeia
	
	Romans 1:18
	For the wrath of God is revealed from heaven against all **ungodliness** and unrighteousness of men, who hold the truth in unrighteousness; [KJV]
	For the wrath of God is revealed from heaven against all **ungodliness** and unrighteousness of men, who suppress the truth in unrighteousness, [NASB]
	The wrath of God is being revealed from heaven against all the **godlessness** and wickedness of men who suppress the truth by their wickedness, [NIV]
	For the wrath of God is revealed from heaven against all **ungodliness** and unrighteousness of men, who suppress the truth in unrighteousness, [NKJV]
	But God shows his anger from heaven against all **sinful**, wicked people who push the truth away from themselves. [NLT]
	Ἀποκαλύπτεται γὰρ ὀργὴ Θεοῦ ἀπ' οὐρανοῦ ἐπὶ πᾶσαν **ἀσέβειαν** καὶ ἀδικίαν ἀνθρώπων τῶν τὴν ἀλήθειαν ἐν ἀδικίᾳ κατεχόντων, [GNS]
	Ἀποκαλύπτεται γὰρ ὀργὴ θεοῦ ἀπ' οὐρανοῦ ἐπὶ πᾶσαν **ἀσέβειαν** καὶ ἀδικίαν ἀνθρώπων τῶν τὴν ἀλήθειαν ἐν ἀδικίᾳ κατεχόντων, [GNT]
		Godlessness, ungodliness; sinful, wicked behavior that is contrary to God's nature.
		
		Practical Application
		The ungodly (*asebeian*) fail to love and obey God. They are those who do not live as God lives. They are not like God, not holy and righteous and pure. They do not work at developing a godly nature, do not honor God by word or deed, do not worship and obey God as the only living and true God, do not reverence Him by doing what He says. On the contrary, the ungodly are those who do what they want when they want, who may give lip service to God, but who ignore Him in their day-to-day lives.

#4152
Ungodliness
 	
Ungodliness–KJV
Ungodliness–NASB
Ungodliness–NIV
Ungodliness–NKJV
Godless living–NLT
 	
**POSB
REFERENCE**
(Tit.2:12)
Note 2, point 1
	ἀσέβειαν = *asebeian*
	Pronunciation: [as-eb'-i-ahn]
	Parsing (part of speech): noun
	  Case—accusative
	  Gender—feminine
	  Number—singular
	  Stem or root—from ἀσέβεια, ας
	Concordance References:
	  ⇒ Strong's #763 asebeia
	  ⇒ NIV #813 asebeia
	  ⇒ NASB #763 asebeia
	
	Titus 2:12
	Teaching us that, denying **ungodliness** and worldly lusts, we should live soberly, righteously, and godly, in this present world; [KJV]
	Instructing us to deny **ungodliness** and worldly desires and to live sensibly, righteously and godly in the present age, [NASB]
	It teaches us to say "No" to **ungodliness** and worldly passions, and to live self-controlled, upright and godly lives in this present age, [NIV]
	Teaching us that, denying **ungodliness** and worldly lusts, we should live soberly, righteously, and godly in the present age, [NKJV]
	And we are instructed to turn from **godless living** and sinful pleasures. We should live in this evil world with self-control, right conduct, and devotion to God, [NLT]
	παιδεύουσα ἡμᾶς ἵνα, ἀρνησάμενοι τὴν **ἀσέβειαν** καὶ
		Ungodliness, godless living, wickedness; anything that is not like God, not holy, righteous or pure; anything that does not honor God by word or deed, that does not show reverence and worship toward God; anything that does not obey God, that violates God's commandments and goes against His will.
		
		Practical Application
		God's grace—demonstrated in the Lord Jesus Christ—teaches us to deny ungodliness and worldly lusts, that is, to reject, renounce, give up, and have nothing to do with ungodliness and worldly lusts. God's grace teaches us "to say 'no' to ungodliness and worldly lusts" (Beck, *The New Testament in the Language of Today*).

ENGLISH WORD	GREEK WORD AND VERSE	THE WORD MEANS...
	τὰς κοσμικὰς ἐπιθυμίας σωφρόνως καὶ δικαίως καὶ εὐσεβῶς ζήσωμεν ἐν τῷ νῦν αἰῶνι, [GNS] παιδεύουσα ἡμᾶς, ἵνα ἀρνησάμενοι τὴν **ἀσέβειαν** καὶ τὰς κοσμικὰς ἐπιθυμίας σωφρόνως καὶ δικαίως καὶ εὐσεβῶς ζήσωμεν ἐν τῷ νῦν αἰῶνι, [GNT]	
#4153 **Ungodly** Ungodly–KJV Ungodly–NASB Ungodly–NIV Ungodly–NKJV Sinners–NLT **POSB REFERENCE** (Rom.5:6-7; esp. v.6) Note 1, point 2	**ἀσεβῶν** = asebön Pronunciation: [as-eb-own'] Parsing (part of speech): pronominal adjective Case—genitive Gender—masculine Number—plural Stem or root—from ἀσεβής, ές Concordance References: ⇒ Strong's #765 asebës ⇒ NIV #815 asebës ⇒ NASB #765 asebës **Romans 5:6** For when we were yet without strength, in due time Christ died for the **ungodly**. [KJV] For while we were still helpless, at the right time Christ died for the **ungodly**. [NASB] You see, at just the right time, when we were still powerless, Christ died for the **ungodly**. [NIV] For when we were still without strength, in due time Christ died for the **ungodly**. [NKJV] When we were utterly helpless, Christ came at just the right time and died for us **sinners**. [NLT] ἔτι γὰρ Χριστὸς ὄντων ἡμῶν ἀσθενῶν, ἔτι κατὰ καιρὸν ὑπὲρ **ἀσεβῶν** ἀπέθανε. [GNS] ἔτι γὰρ Χριστὸς ὄντων ἡμῶν ἀσθενῶν ἔτι κατὰ καιρὸν ὑπὲρ **ἀσεβῶν** ἀπέθανεν. [GNT]	Godless, impious, ungodly, irreverent, wicked. **Practical Application** We were ungodly (asebön): not like God, different from God, profane, having a different lifestyle than God. God is godly, that is, perfect; man is ungodly; that is, he is not like God; he is imperfect.
#4154 **Ungrateful** Unthankful–KJV Ungrateful–NASB Ungrateful–NIV Unthankful–NKJV Ungrateful–NLT **POSB REFERENCE** (2 Tim. 3:2-4; esp. v.2) Note 2, point 7	**ἀχάριστοι** = acharistoi Pronunciation: [ach-ar'-is-toy] Parsing (part of speech): adjective Case—nominative Gender—masculine Number—plural Stem or root—from ἀχάριστος, ον Concordance References: ⇒ Strong's #884 acharistos ⇒ NIV #940 acharistos ⇒ NASB #884 acharistos **2 Tim. 3:2** For men shall be lovers of their own selves, covetous, boasters, proud, blasphemers, disobedient to parents, **unthankful**, unholy, [KJV] For men will be lovers of self, lovers of money, boastful, arrogant, revilers, disobedient to parents, **ungrateful**, unholy, [NASB] People will be lovers of themselves, lovers of money, boastful, proud, abusive, disobedient to their parents, **ungrateful**, unholy, [NIV] For men will be lovers of themselves, lovers of money, boasters, proud, blasphemers, disobedient to parents, **unthankful**, unholy, [NKJV] For people will love only themselves and their money. They will be boastful and proud, scoffing at God, disobedient to their parents, and **ungrateful**. They will consider nothing sacred. [NLT] ἔσονται γὰρ οἱ ἄνθρωποι φίλαυτοι, φιλάργυροι, ἀλαζόνες, ὑπερήφανοι, βλάσφημοι, γονεῦσιν ἀπειθεῖς, **ἀχάριστοι**, ἀνόσιοι, [GNS] ἔσονται γὰρ οἱ ἄνθρωποι φίλαυτοι φιλάργυροι ἀλαζόνες ὑπερήφανοι βλάσφημοι, γονεῦσιν ἀπειθεῖς, **ἀχάριστοι** ἀνόσιοι [GNT]	Ungrateful, unthankful. **Practical Application** People will be "ungrateful" (acharistoi): no sense of gratitude or appreciation for what one has and receives; no giving of thanks to God or man. Many persons feel that the world and society or business and government owe them the good things of life. They have little if any sense of debt to others. This is the reason many waste time on the job, do mediocre work, and feel little obligation to the world and society. They fail to see how privileged they are to be alive and to live in such a beautiful world and to have a job and friends and neighbors. They fail to see how good God has been to them, and how caring and responsible some people are. Therefore, they reach out to get more and more without sensing any need to express thanks and appreciation. They take and take and forget all about the thanksgiving—the debt and contribution—they owe to God and men.
#4155 **Unholy**	**ἀνόσιοι** = anosioi Pronunciation: [an-os'-ee-oy] Parsing (part of speech): adjective Case—nominative	Profane, indecent, shameless, given over to the most base passions, being blind to modesty, decency, purity, and righteousness.

ENGLISH WORD	GREEK WORD AND VERSE	THE WORD MEANS...
Unholy–KJV **Unholy–NASB** **Unholy–NIV** **Unholy–NKJV** Consider nothing sacred–NLT **POSB REFERENCE** (2 Tim. 3:2-4; esp. v.2) Note 2, point 8	Gender—masculine Number—plural Stem or root—from ἀνόσιος, ον Concordance References: ⇒ Strong's #462 anosios ⇒ NIV #495 anosios ⇒ NASB #462 anosios **2 Tim. 3:2** For men shall be lovers of their own selves, covetous, boasters, proud, blasphemers, disobedient to parents, unthankful, **unholy**, [KJV] For men will be lovers of self, lovers of money, boastful, arrogant, revilers, disobedient to parents, ungrateful, **unholy**, [NASB] People will be lovers of themselves, lovers of money, boastful, proud, abusive, disobedient to their parents, ungrateful, **unholy**, [NIV] For men will be lovers of themselves, lovers of money, boasters, proud, blasphemers, disobedient to parents, unthankful, **unholy**, [NKJV] For people will love only themselves and their money. They will be boastful and proud, scoffing at God, disobedient to their parents, and ungrateful. They will **consider nothing sacred**. [NLT] ἔσονται γὰρ οἱ ἄνθρωποι φίλαυτοι, φιλάργυροι, ἀλαζόνες, ὑπερήφανοι, βλάσφημοι, γονεῦσιν ἀπειθεῖς, ἀχάριστοι, **ἀνόσιοι**, [GNS] ἔσονται γὰρ οἱ ἄνθρωποι φίλαυτοι φιλάργυροι ἀλαζόνες ὑπερήφανοι βλάσφημοι, γονεῦσιν ἀπειθεῖς, ἀχάριστοι **ἀνόσιοι** [GNT]	**Practical Application** People will "be unholy" (*anosioi*). The unholy person... • is mastered by passion. • seeks constant gratification of the flesh. • senses little shame. • is blind to decency. • seeks his pleasure in the abnormal. (Just think of the abnormal sex that is flaunted today.)

#4156
Unholy And Unclean
 	
Common or unclean–KJV
Unholy and unclean–NASB
Impure or unclean–NIV
Common or unclean–NKJV
Forbidden by our Jewish laws–NLT
 	
POSB REFERENCE
(Acts 10:11-16; esp. v.14)
Deeper Study #3
	κοινὸν καὶ ἀκάθαρτον = *koinon kai akatharton*
	Pronunciation: [koy-non' kah-ee ak-ath'-ar-ton]
	Parsing *koinon* (part of speech): adjective
	  Type— pronoun
	  Case—accusative
	  Gender—neuter
	  Number—singular
	  Stem or root—from κοινός, ή, όν
	Parsing *akatharton* (part of speech): adjective
	  Type— pronoun
	  Case—accusative
	  Gender—neuter
	  Number—singular
	  Stem or root—from ἀκάθαρτος, ον
	Concordance References:
	⇒ Strong's #2839 koinos + 2532 kai + 169 akathartos
	⇒ NIV #3123 koinos [impure] + 2779 kai [or] + 176 akathartos [unclean]
	⇒ NASB #2839 koinos + 2532 kai + 169 akathartos
	
	Acts 10:14
	But Peter said, Not so, Lord; for I have never eaten any thing that is **common or unclean**. [KJV]
	But Peter said, "By no means, Lord, for I have never eaten anything **unholy and unclean**." [NASB]
	"Surely not, Lord!" Peter replied. "I have never eaten anything **impure or unclean**." [NIV]
	But Peter said, "Not so, Lord! For I have never eaten anything **common or unclean**." [NKJV]
	"Never, Lord," Peter declared. "I have never in all my life eaten anything **forbidden by our Jewish laws**." [NLT]
	ὁ δὲ Πέτρος εἶπε, Μηδαμῶς Κύριε· ὅτι οὐδέποτε ἔφαγον πᾶν **κοινὸν** ἢ **ἀκάθαρτον**. [GNS]
	ὁ δὲ Πέτρος εἶπεν, Μηδαμῶς, κύριε, ὅτι οὐδέποτε ἔφαγον πᾶν **κοινὸν καὶ ἀκάθαρτον**. [GNT]
		Impure or unclean; common or unclean; unholy and unclean.
		
		Practical Application
		The words "unholy and unclean" (*koinon kai akatharton*) refer to being religiously or ceremonially unclean. The unclean animals were unhallowed, profaned. The Jews felt that eating them would not please God.

ENGLISH WORD	GREEK WORD AND VERSE	THE WORD MEANS...

and His saving grace together. When a couple shares God together day by day, God works supernaturally within their spirits, *melting* their beings and *moulding* them into what He calls *one flesh*. They actually become as *one person*. This is what is meant by "God has joined together" (Mt.19:6). The Greek word for "joined together" (*sunzeugen*) actually means to *yoke together*. It is God yoking, God joining, God binding the couple together into such a spiritual union that causes them to become one person.

#4160

Universe

Worlds–KJV
World–NASB
Universe–NIV
Worlds–NKJV
Universe and everything in it–NLT

**POSB
REFERENCE**
(Heb.1:2)
Note 3

αἰῶνας = *aiōnas*
Pronunciation: [ahee-ohn-ahs]
Parsing (part of speech): noun
  Case—accusative
  Gender—masculine
  Number—plural
  Stem or root—from αἰών, ῶνος
Concordance References:
  ⇒ Strong's #165 aiön
  ⇒ NIV #172 aiön
  ⇒ NASB #165 aiön

Hebrews 1:2

Hath in these last days spoken unto us by *his* Son, whom he hath appointed heir of all things, by whom also he made the **worlds**; [KJV]

In these last days has spoken to us in *His* Son, whom He appointed heir of all things, through whom also He made the **world**. [NASB]

But in these last days he has spoken to us by his Son, whom he appointed heir of all things, and through whom he made the **universe**. [NIV]

Has in these last days spoken to us by *His* Son, whom He has appointed heir of all things, through whom also He made the **worlds**; [NKJV]

But now in these final days, he has spoken to us through his Son. God promised everything to the Son as an inheritance, and through the Son he made the **universe and everything in it**. [NLT]

ἐπ' ἐσχάτων τῶν ἡμερῶν τούτων ἐλάλησεν ἡμῖν ἐν υἱῷ, ὃν ἔθηκε κληρονόμον πάντων, δι' οὗ καὶ τοὺς **αἰῶνας** ἐποίησεν, [GNS]

ἐπ' ἐσχάτου τῶν ἡμερῶν τούτων ἐλάλησεν ἡμῖν ἐν υἱῷ, ὃν ἔθηκεν κληρονόμον πάντων, δι' οὗ καὶ ἐποίησεν τοὺς **αἰῶνας**· [GNT]

Universe, worlds, the universe and everything in it.

Practical Application

Jesus Christ is the Creator and Maker of the worlds—all of the worlds. This is the third reason why Jesus Christ is superior to the prophets. The word "universe" (*aiōnas*) can also be translated as *ages*. Jesus Christ is the creator of both the universe and the ages that roll in one upon another, creator of both the worlds and time as it moves forward from event to event, and generation to generation. The Amplified New Testament states it well:

He [Christ] created the worlds and the reaches of space and the ages of time [that is], He made, produced, built, operated and arranged them in order (Hebrews 1:2).

Colossians states it even better:

For by him were all things created, that are in heaven, and that are in earth, visible and invisible, whether they be thrones, or dominions, or principalities, or powers: all things were created by him, and for him (Col. 1:16).

The point is this: the creation of Christ includes all the worlds, all the universes, of all the dimensions of being, wherever they are and however many there may be. This is exactly what is meant by the word universe. It is also what is meant when Colossians says that Christ created all things "in heaven and on earth, visible and invisible, whether thrones or powers, or rulers, or authorities."
  ⇒ If there are other *visible planets and living beings* in outer space, Christ created them.
  ⇒ If there are *invisible worlds and beings* in other dimensions, Christ created them.
  It does not matter what kind of world or creatures they may be—thrones, dominions, principalities, or powers—Christ created them all. There is nothing in existence that He has not created.

#4161

Universe And Everything In It

Worlds–KJV
World–NASB
Universe–NIV
Worlds–NKJV

αἰῶνας = *aiōnas*
Pronunciation: [ahee-ohn-ahs]
Parsing (part of speech): noun
  Case—accusative
  Gender—masculine
  Number—plural
  Stem or root—from αἰών, ῶνος
Concordance References:
  ⇒ Strong's #165 aiön
  ⇒ NIV #172 aiön
  ⇒ NASB #165 aiön

Universe, worlds, the universe and everything in it.

Practical Application

Jesus Christ is the Creator and Maker of the worlds—all of the worlds. This is the third reason why Jesus Christ is superior to the prophets. The phrase "universe and everything in it" (*aiōnas*) can also be translated as ages. Jesus Christ is the creator of both the universe and the ages

ENGLISH WORD	GREEK WORD AND VERSE	THE WORD MEANS...
Universe and everything in it–NLT POSB REFERENCE (Heb.1:2) Note 3	**Hebrews 1:2** Hath in these last days spoken unto us by *his* Son, whom he hath appointed heir of all things, by whom also he made the **worlds**; [KJV] In these last days has spoken to us in *His* Son, whom He appointed heir of all things, through whom also He made the **world**. [NASB] But in these last days he has spoken to us by his Son, whom he appointed heir of all things, and through whom he made the **universe**. [NIV] Has in these last days spoken to us by *His* Son, whom He has appointed heir of all things, through whom also He made the **worlds**; [NKJV] But now in these final days, he has spoken to us through his Son. God promised everything to the Son as an inheritance, and through the Son he made the **universe and everything in it**. [NLT] ἐπ' ἐσχάτων τῶν ἡμερῶν τούτων ἐλάλησεν ἡμῖν ἐν υἱῷ, ὃν ἔθηκε κληρονόμον πάντων, δι' οὗ καὶ τοὺς **αἰῶνας** ἐποίησεν, [GNS] ἐπ' ἐσχάτου τῶν ἡμερῶν τούτων ἐλάλησεν ἡμῖν ἐν υἱῷ, ὃν ἔθηκεν κληρονόμον πάντων, δι' οὗ καὶ ἐποίησεν τοὺς **αἰῶνας**· [GNT]	that roll in one upon another, creator of both the worlds and time as it moves forward from event to event, and generation to generation. The Amplified New Testament states it well: (See **Universe** for more discussion).

#4162
Unknown God
 	
Unknown GOD–KJV
Unknown GOD–NASB
Unknown GOD–NIV
Unknown GOD–NKJV
Unknown God–NLT
 	
POSB REFERENCE
(Acts 17:23)
Note 3
	Ἀγνώστῳ θεῷ = *Agnōstō theō*
	Pronunciation: [ag'-nos-tow theh'-o]
	Parsing *Agnōstō* (part of speech): adjective
	    Case—dative
	    Gender—masculine
	    Number—singular
	    Stem or root—from ἄγνωστος, ον
	Concordance References:
	⇒ Strong's #57 agnōstos + 2316 theos
	⇒ NIV #58 agnōstos [Unknown] + 2536 theos [God]
	⇒ NASB #57 agnōstos + 2316 theos
	
	Acts 17:23
	For as I passed by, and beheld your devotions, I found an altar with this inscription, TO THE **UNKNOWN GOD**. Whom therefore ye ignorantly worship, him declare I unto you. [KJV]
	"For while I was passing through and examining the objects of your worship, I also found an altar with this inscription, 'TO AN **UNKNOWN GOD**.' What therefore you worship in ignorance, this I proclaim to you. [NASB]
	For as I walked around and looked carefully at your objects of worship, I even found an altar with this inscription: TO AN **UNKNOWN GOD**. Now what you worship as something unknown I am going to proclaim to you. [NIV]
	For as I was passing through and considering the objects of your worship, I even found an altar with this inscription: TO THE **UNKNOWN GOD**. Therefore, the One whom you worship without knowing, Him I proclaim to you: [NKJV]
	For as I was walking along I saw your many altars. And one of them had this inscription on it—'To an **Unknown God**.' You have been worshiping him without knowing who he is, and now I wish to tell you about him. [NLT]
	διερχόμενος γὰρ καὶ ἀναθεωρῶν τὰ σεβάσματα ὑμῶν, εὗρον καὶ βωμὸν ἐν ᾧ ἐπεγέγραπτο, Ἀγνώστῳ Θεῷ. ὃν οὖν ἀγνοοῦντες εὐσεβεῖτε, τοῦτον ἐγὼ καταγγέλλω ὑμῖν. [GNS]
	διερχόμενος γὰρ καὶ ἀναθεωρῶν τὰ σεβάσματα ὑμῶν εὗρον καὶ βωμὸν ἐν ᾧ ἐπεγέγραπτο, Ἀγνώστῳ θεῷ. ὃ οὖν ἀγνοοῦντες εὐσεβεῖτε, τοῦτο ἐγὼ καταγγέλλω ὑμῖν. [GNT]
		Unfamiliar, hidden, undiscovered, unknown God.
		
		Practical Application
		God is not hid, not unknown. As Paul had walked throughout the great city of Athens, he had read many of the inscriptions written on the monuments and idols. One in particular had caught his attention: the altar "TO AN UNKNOWN GOD" (*Agnōstō theō*). Note several facts.
		1. The word "devotions" (*ta sebasmata*) means the objects of worship such as idols, altars, images.
		2. The people acknowledged there was an unknown god, and they worshipped him. But they did not know him.
		   None of the gods satisfied the people. Their lives and their religions were still empty and missing something. The restlessness and hunger and fear were still in their hearts and minds, especially in lonely moments. None of the religions or gods created by man's imagination satisfied and met their needs. All they could do was worship *an unknown god*; they knew nothing about him, yet they worshipped him.
		   Note what Paul did: he declared that he knew the unknown God. He personally knew Him and it was He whom Paul declared.

#4163 **Unloving**	ἀστόργους = *astorgous* Pronunciation: [as'-tor-goos] Parsing (part of speech): adjective Case—accusative	Heartless; unloving; lacking normal human affection; inhuman; without natural affection; abnormal affection and love; without human

ENGLISH WORD	GREEK WORD AND VERSE	THE WORD MEANS...
Without natural affection–KJV **Unloving–NASB** Heartless–NIV **Unloving–NKJV** Heartless–NLT **POSB REFERENCE** (Romans 1:31) *Deeper Study #21*	Gender—masculine Number—plural Stem or root—from ἄστοργος, ον Concordance References: ⇒ Strong's #794 astorgos ⇒ NIV #845 astorgos ⇒ NASB #794 astorgos **Romans 1:31** Without understanding, covenantbreakers, **without natural affection**, implacable, unmerciful: [KJV] Without understanding, untrustworthy, **unloving**, unmerciful; [NASB] They are senseless, faithless, **heartless**, ruthless. [NIV] Undiscerning, untrustworthy, **unloving**, unforgiving, unmerciful; [NKJV] They refuse to understand, break their promises, and are **heartless** and unforgiving. [NLT] ἀσυνέτους, ἀσυνθέτους, **ἀστόργους**, ἀσπόνδους, ἀνελεήμονας· [GNS] ἀσυνέτους ἀσυνθέτους **ἀστόργους** ἀνελεήμονας·[GNT]	emotion or love; a lack of feeling for others; abuse of normal affection and love. **Practical Application** Others become little more than pawns for a man's own use and benefit, pleasure and purposes, excitement and stimulation. Abnormal affection, sex and perversion prevail.
#4164 **Unloving** Without natural affection–KJV **Unloving–NASB** Without love–NIV **Unloving–NKJV** **Unloving–NLT** **POSB REFERENCE** (2 Tim. 3:2-4; esp. v.3) Note 2, point 9	**ἄστοργοι** = astorgoi Pronunciation: [as'-tor-goy] Parsing (part of speech): adjective Case—nominative Gender—masculine Number—plural Stem or root—from **ἄστοργος**, ον Concordance References: ⇒ Strong's #794 astorgos ⇒ NIV #845 astorgos ⇒ NASB #794 astorgos **2 Tim. 3:3** **Without natural affection**, trucebreakers, false accusers, incontinent, fierce, despisers of those that are good, [KJV] **Unloving**, irreconcilable, malicious gossips, without self-control, brutal, haters of good, [NASB] **Without love**, unforgiving, slanderous, without self-control, brutal, not lovers of the good, [NIV] **Unloving**, unforgiving, slanderers, without self-control, brutal, despisers of good, [NKJV] They will be **unloving** and unforgiving; they will slander others and have no self-control; they will be cruel and have no interest in what is good. [NLT] **ἄστοργοι**, ἄσπονδοι, διάβολοι, ἀκρατεῖς, ἀνήμεροι, ἀφιλάγαθοι, [GNS] **ἄστοργοι** ἄσπονδοι διάβολοι ἀκρατεῖς ἀνήμεροι ἀφιλάγαθοι [GNT]	Unloving, without love, without natural affection, abnormal affection and love; heartless, without human emotion or love; a lack of feeling for others; abuse of normal affection and love. It means others become little more than pawns for a man's own use and benefit, pleasure and purposes, excitement and stimulation. **Practical Application** Man has been created to be affectionate—to have affection for others. It is normal and natural for a person to have affection for his family, friends, neighbors, coworkers, and to a certain extent for the stranger and fellow-citizens of the world. But in the end time, people will be so set on satisfying their flesh and pleasure that they will forget family, friends, and everything else. They will be so set on doing their own thing and so self-centered that they will have little affection for anyone or anything else.
#4165 **Unmerciful** Unmerciful–KJV **Unmerciful–NASB** Ruthless–NIV **Unmerciful–NKJV** Unforgiving–NLT **POSB REFERENCE** (Romans 1:31) *Deeper Study #23*	**ἀνελεήμονας** = aneleëmonas Pronunciation: [an-eleh-ay'-mone-ahs] Parsing (part of speech): adjective Case—accusative Gender—masculine Number—plural Stem or root—from **ἀνελεήμων**, ον Concordance References: ⇒ Strong's #415 aneleëmön ⇒ NIV #446 aneleëmön ⇒ NASB #415 aneleëmön **Romans 1:31** Without understanding, covenantbreakers, without natural affection, implacable, **unmerciful**: [KJV] Without understanding, untrustworthy, unloving, **unmerciful**; [NASB] They are senseless, faithless, heartless, **ruthless**. [NIV]	Unmerciful, cruel, savage, pitiless, hardhearted, harsh, uncompassionate. without pity; unwilling to show mercy. **Practical Application** It is a person... • craving to have and to possess others regardless of their welfare. • craving to use others as one wills regardless of hurt and shame. • craving to satisfy one's own pleasure even if it means the hurt or death of others. It is an absence of consideration or feelings for others. What matters is one's own pleasure and rights, not the pleasure and rights of others.

ENGLISH WORD	GREEK WORD AND VERSE	THE WORD MEANS...
	Undiscerning, untrustworthy, unloving, unforgiving, **unmerciful**; [NKJV] They refuse to understand, break their promises, and are heartless and **unforgiving**. [NLT] ἀσυνέτους, ἀσυνθέτους, ἀστόργους, ἀσπόνδους, **ἀνελεήμονας·** [GNS] ἀσυνέτους ἀσυνθέτους ἀστόργους **ἀνελεήμονας·** [GNT]	

#4166
Unmovable
 	
Unmovable–KJV
Immovable–NASB
Nothing move–NIV
Immovable–NKJV
Steady–NLT
 	
POSB
REFERENCE
(1 Cor.15:58)
Note 6, point 2
	ἀμετακίνητοι = ametakinētoi
	Pronunciation: [am-et-ak-in'-ay-toy]
	Parsing (part of speech): adjective
	  Case—nominative
	  Gender—masculine
	  Number—plural
	  Stem or root—from ἀμετακίνητος, ον
	Concordance References:
	⇒ Strong's #277 ametakinētos
	⇒ NIV #293 ametakinētos
	⇒ NASB #277 ametakinētos
	
	1 Cor. 15:58
	Therefore, my beloved brethren, be ye stedfast, **unmovable**, always abounding in the work of the Lord, forasmuch as ye know that your labour is not in vain in the Lord. [KJV]
	
	Therefore, my beloved brethren, be steadfast, **immovable**, always abounding in the work of the Lord, knowing that your toil is not *in* vain in the Lord. [NASB]
	
	Therefore, my dear brothers, stand firm. Let **nothing move** you. Always give yourselves fully to the work of the Lord, because you know that your labor in the Lord is not in vain. [NIV]
	
	Therefore, my beloved brethren, be steadfast, **immovable,** always abounding in the work of the Lord, knowing that your labor is not in vain in the Lord. [NKJV]
	
	So, my dear brothers and sisters, be strong and **steady**, always enthusiastic about the Lord's work, for you know that nothing you do for the Lord is ever useless. [NLT]
	
	ὥστε, ἀδελφοί μου ἀγαπητοί, ἑδραῖοι γίνεσθε, **ἀμετακίνητοι**, περισσεύοντες ἐν τῷ ἔργῳ τοῦ Κυρίου πάντοτε, εἰδότες ὅτι ὁ κόπος ὑμῶν οὐκ ἔστι κενὸς ἐν Κυρίῳ. [GNS]
	
	Ὥστε, ἀδελφοί μου ἀγαπητοί, ἑδραῖοι γίνεσθε, **ἀμετακίνητοι**, περισσεύοντες ἐν τῷ ἔργῳ τοῦ κυρίου πάντοτε, εἰδότες ὅτι ὁ κόπος ὑμῶν οὐκ ἔστιν κενὸς ἐν κυρίῳ. [GNT]
		To be unyielding, unshaken, undisturbed. It means to be immovable and steady.
		
		Practical Application
		The believer is not to be fickle in his service for the Lord. He is to stand as solid as a rock in his beliefs and in his service for the Lord.

#4167
Unnoticed, Have Not Gone
 	
For...memorial–KJV
As...memorial–NASB
Memorial offering–NIV
For...memorial–NKJV
Have not gone unnoticed–NLT
 	
POSB
REFERENCE
(Acts 10:1-6; esp. v.4)
Deeper Study #1
	εἰς μνημόσυνον = eis mnēmosunon
	Pronunciation: [ice mnay-mos'-oo-non]
	Parsing mnēmosunon (part of speech): noun
	  · Case—accusative
	  Gender—neuter
	  Number—singular
	  Stem or root—from μνημόσυνον, ου
	Concordance References:
	⇒ Strong's #1519 eis + 3422 mnēmosunon
	⇒ NIV #1650 eis [as] + 3649 mnēmosunon [memorial offering]
	⇒ NASB #1519 eis + 3422 mnēmosunon
	
	Acts 10:4
	And when he looked on him, he was afraid, and said, What is it, Lord? And he said unto him, Thy prayers and thine alms are come up **for a memorial** before God. [KJV]
	
	And fixing his gaze upon him and being much alarmed, he said, "What is it, Lord?" And he said to him, "Your prayers and alms have ascended **as a memorial** before God. [NASB]
	
	Cornelius stared at him in fear. "What is it, Lord?" he
		A memorial offering; a memorial.
		
		Practical Application
		The word means that the sincerity of Cornelius' heart caught God's eye. Cornelius was seeking God, desiring to please God, to know God and to do God's will. Therefore, God could not miss him. He had to make sure that Cornelius heard the message of salvation.

ENGLISH WORD	GREEK WORD AND VERSE	THE WORD MEANS...
	asked.The angel answered, "Your prayers and gifts to the poor have come up **as a memorial offering** before God. [NIV] And when he observed him, he was afraid, and said, "What is it, lord?" So he said to him, "Your prayers and your alms have come up **for a memorial** before God. [NKJV] Cornelius stared at him in terror. "What is it, sir?" he asked the angel.And the angel replied, "Your prayers and gifts to the poor **have not gone unnoticed** by God! [NLT] ὁ δὲ ἀτενίσας αὐτῷ καὶ ἔμφοβος γενόμενος εἶπε, Τί ἐστι, Κύριε; εἶπε δὲ αὐτῷ, Αἱ προσευχαί σου καὶ αἱ τε ἐλεημοσύναι σου ἀνέβησαν **εἰς μνημόσυνον** ἐνώπιον τοῦ Θεοῦ. [GNS] ὁ δὲ ἀτενίσας αὐτῷ καὶ ἔμφοβος γενόμενος εἶπεν, Τί ἐστιν, κύριε; εἶπεν δὲ αὐτῷ, Αἱ προσευχαί σου καὶ αἱ ἐλεημοσύναι σου ἀνέβησαν **εἰς μνημόσυνον** ἔμπροσθεν τοῦ θεοῦ. [GNT]	

#4168
Unquenchable Fire
 	
Everlasting fire–KJV
Eternal fire–NASB
Eternal fire–NIV
Everlasting fire–NKJV
Unquenchable fire–NLT
 	
POSB REFERENCE
(Mt.18:8)
Deeper Study #1
 	
See also POSB REF:
(Mt.25:41)
Deeper Study #3
	πῦρ τὸ αἰώνιον = *pur to aiönion*
	Pronunciation: [poor tow ahee-o'-nee-on]
	Parsing *pur* (part of speech): noun
	  Case—accusative
	  Gender—neuter
	  Number—singular
	  Stem or root—from πῦρ, ός
	Parsing *aiönion* (part of speech): adjective
	  Case—accusative
	  Gender—neuter
	  Number—singular
	  Stem or root—from αἰώνιος, ον
	Concordance References:
	⇒ Strong's #4442 pur + 166 aiönios
	⇒ NIV #4786 pur [fire] + 173 aiönios [eternal]
	⇒ NASB #4442 pur + 166 aiönios
	
	Matthew 18:8
	Wherefore if thy hand or thy foot offend thee, cut them off, and cast them from thee: it is better for thee to enter into life halt or maimed, rather than having two hands or two feet to be cast into **everlasting fire**. [KJV]
	
	"And if your hand or your foot causes you to stumble, cut it off and throw it from you; it is better for you to enter life crippled or lame, than having two hands or two feet, to be cast into the **eternal fire**. [NASB]
	
	If your hand or your foot causes you to sin cut it off and throw it away. It is better for you to enter life maimed or crippled than to have two hands or two feet and be thrown into **eternal fire**. [NIV]
	
	If your hand or foot causes you to sin, cut it off and cast it from you. It is better for you to enter into life lame or maimed, rather than having two hands or two feet, to be cast into the **everlasting fire**. [NKJV]
	
	So if your hand or foot causes you to sin, cut it off and throw it away. It is better to enter heaven crippled or lame than to be thrown into the **unquenchable fire** with both of your hands and feet. [NLT]
	
	εἰ δὲ ἡ χείρ σου ἢ ὁ πούς σου σκανδαλίζει σε, ἔκκοψον αὐτὰ καὶ βάλε ἀπὸ σοῦ· καλόν σοί ἐστιν εἰσελθεῖν εἰς τὴν ζωὴν χωλόν η κυλλὸν, η δύο χεῖρας η δύο πόδας ἔχοντα βληθῆναι εἰς τὸ **πῦρ τὸ αἰώνιον**. [GNS]
	
	Εἰ δὲ ἡ χείρ σου η ὁ πούς σου σκανδαλίζει σε, ἔκκοψον αὐτὸν καὶ βάλε ἀπὸ σοῦ· καλόν σοί ἐστιν εἰσελθεῖν εἰς τὴν ζωὴν κυλλὸν η χωλόν η δύο χεῖρας η δύο πόδας ἔχοντα βληθῆναι εἰς τὸ **πῦρ τὸ αἰώνιον**. [GNT]
		Eternal fire, everlasting fire, unquenchable fire, a fire without end.
		
		Practical Application
		This is the first time the words *unquenchable fire* (*pur to aiönion*) are used. The words point to an awful fate, a terrible and horrible eternity. Everlasting means for the duration, on and on without end. The fact that the unforgiven sinner is to suffer so great a punishment should cause all sinners to cease from being stumbling blocks. It should stir them to become stepping stones to God (see POSB *Deeper Study #2*—Matthew 5:22; POSB *Deeper Study #3*—Luke 16:23; POSB *Deeper Study #4*—Luke 16:24).

#4169
Unreproveable
 	
Unreproveable–KJV
Beyond reproach–NASB
	ἀνεγκλήτους = *anegklëtous*
	Pronunciation: [an-eng'-klay-toos]
	Parsing (part of speech): adjective
	  Case—accusative
	  Gender—masculine
	  Number—plural
		To be free from accusation; to be beyond reproach; to have nothing against them; to be without a single fault, unreproveable, blameless, unchargeable.

ENGLISH WORD	GREEK WORD AND VERSE	THE WORD MEANS...
Free from accusa-tion–NIV Above reproach–NKJV Without a single fault–NLT **POSB REFERENCE** (Col.1:22) Note 3, point 3	Stem or root—from ἀνέγκλητος, ον Concordance References: ⇒ Strong's #410 anegklētos ⇒ NIV #441 anegklētos ⇒ NASB #410 anegklētos **Col. 1:22** In the body of his flesh through death, to present you holy and unblameable and **unreproveable** in his sight: [KJV] Yet He has now reconciled you in His fleshly body through death, in order to present you before Him holy and blameless and **beyond reproach**— [NASB] But now he has reconciled you by Christ's physical body through death to present you holy in his sight, without blemish and **free from accusation**— [NIV] In the body of His flesh through death, to present you holy, and blameless, and **above reproach** in His sight— [NKJV] Yet now he has brought you back as his friends. He has done this through his death on the cross in his own human body. As a result, he has brought you into the very presence of God, and you are holy and blameless as you stand before him **without a single fault**. [NLT] νυνὶ δὲ ἀποκατήλλαξεν ἐν τῷ σώματι τῆς σαρκὸς αὐτοῦ διὰ τοῦ θανάτου, παραστῆσαι ὑμᾶς ἁγίους καὶ ἀμώμους καὶ **ἀνεγκλήτους** κατενώπιον αὐτοῦ·[GNS] νυνὶ δὲ ἀποκατήλλαξεν ἐν τῷ σώματι τῆς σαρκὸς αὐτοῦ διὰ τοῦ θανάτου παραστῆσαι ὑμᾶς ἁγίους καὶ ἀμώμους καὶ **ἀνεγκλήτους** κατενώπιον αὐτοῦ, [GNT]	**Practical Application** Imagine standing before God holy, unre-proveable, unblameable, and beyond reproach. Imagine how pleased God would be! How He would joy and rejoice in us—that we had hon-ored Christ, His only Son, by trusting Him so much! As we are presented to God, what would He say? What would His first words be to us? We would be speechless, no doubt. But what a day of coronation, of glory, of greatness—stand-ing face to face with our Father, the God of all glory, the Sovereign Majesty of the whole uni-verse. This is God's one great purpose in reconcilia-tion: to present us perfect before Him.
#4170 **Unrighteous-ness** Unrighteousness–KJV Unrighteousness–NASB Wickedness–NIV Unrighteousness–NKJV Wicked–NLT **POSB REFERENCE** (Romans 1:18) Note 1, point 3a See also POSB REF: (Rom.1:29) *Deeper Study #1*	ἀδικίαν = adikian Pronunciation: [ad-ee-kee'-ahn] Parsing (part of speech): noun 　　Case—accusative 　　Gender—feminine 　　Number—singular 　　Stem or root—from ἀδικία, ας Concordance References: ⇒ Strong's #93 adikia ⇒ NIV #94 adikia ⇒ NASB #93 adikia **Romans 1:18** For the wrath of God is revealed from heaven against all ungodliness and **unrighteousness** of men, who hold the truth in unrighteousness; [KJV] For the wrath of God is revealed from heaven against all ungodliness and **unrighteousness** of men, who sup-press the truth in unrighteousness, [NASB] The wrath of God is being revealed from heaven against all the godlessness and **wickedness** of men who suppress the truth by their wickedness, [NIV] For the wrath of God is revealed from heaven against all ungodliness and **unrighteousness** of men, who sup-press the truth in unrighteousness, [NKJV] But God shows his anger from heaven against all sin-ful, **wicked** people who push the truth away from them-selves. [NLT] Ἀποκαλύπτεται γὰρ ὀργὴ Θεοῦ ἀπ' οὐρανοῦ ἐπὶ πᾶσαν ἀσέβειαν καὶ **ἀδικίαν** ἀνθρώπων τῶν τὴν ἀλήθειαν ἐν ἀδικίᾳ κατεχόντων, [GNS] Ἀποκαλύπτεται γὰρ ὀργὴ θεοῦ ἀπ' οὐρανοῦ ἐπὶ πᾶσαν ἀσέβειαν καὶ **ἀδικίαν** ἀνθρώπων τῶν τὴν ἀλήθειαν ἐν ἀδικίᾳ κατεχόντων, [GNT]	Wrongdoing, evil, sin, injustice **Practical Application** The unrighteous (*adikian*) fail to love others. They are those who do not live with men as they should. They act against men: cheating, stealing, lying, abusing, enslaving, destroying and taking advantage of them.
#4171 **Unrighteous-ness** Iniquity–KJV Unrighteousness–NASB	ἀδικία = adikia Pronunciation: [ad-ee-kee'-ah] Parsing (part of speech): noun 　　Case—dative 　　Gender—feminine 　　Number—singular 　　Stem or root—from ἀδικία, ας	Evil, iniquity, wickedness, sin, unrighteous-ness, wrongdoing, harmful injustice. **Practical Application** Love does not take pleasure in the unright-eousness and sin of others; it does not feed upon

ENGLISH WORD	GREEK WORD AND VERSE	THE WORD MEANS...
Evil–NIV Iniquity–NKJV Injustice–NLT **POSB REFERENCE** (1 Cor.13:4-7; esp. v.6) Note 2, point 10 **See also POSB REF:** (Rom.2:8) *Deeper Study #5*	Concordance References: ⇒ Strong's #93 adikia ⇒ NIV #94 adikia ⇒ NASB #93 adikia **1 Cor. 13:6** Rejoiceth not in **iniquity**, but rejoiceth in the truth; [KJV] Does not rejoice in **unrighteousness**, but rejoices with the truth; [NASB] Love does not delight in **evil** but rejoices with the truth. [NIV] Does not rejoice in **iniquity**, but rejoices in the truth; [NKJV] It is never glad about **injustice** but rejoices whenever the truth wins out. [NLT] οὐ χαίρει ἐπὶ τῇ **ἀδικίᾳ**, συγχαίρει δὲ τῇ ἀληθείᾳ· [GNS] οὐ χαίρει ἐπὶ τῇ **ἀδικίᾳ**, συγχαίρει δὲ τῇ ἀληθείᾳ· [GNT]	sin and wrong, nor does it pass along the stories of sin and wrong. Man's nature is too often fed the tragedy of evil, whether personal sin or natural disaster. (Cp. the daily news reports and the subjects of conversation between so many people).
#4172 **Unruly** Unruly–KJV Restless–NASB Restless–NIV Unruly–NKJV Uncontrollable–NLT **POSB REFERENCE** (Jas. 3:7-12; esp. v.8) Note 5, point 3	ἀκατάστατον = akatastaton Pronunciation: [ak-at-as'-tah-ton] Parsing (part of speech): adjective 　Case—nominative 　Gender—neuter 　Number—singular 　Stem or root—from ἀκατάστατος, ον Concordance References: ⇒ Strong's #183 akataschetos ⇒ NIV #190 akatastatos ⇒ NASB #182 akatastatos **James 3:8** But the tongue can no man tame; *it is* an **unruly** evil, full of deadly poison. [KJV] But no one can tame the tongue; *it is* a **restless** evil *and* full of deadly poison. [NASB] But no man can tame the tongue. It is a **restless** evil, full of deadly poison. [NIV] But no man can tame the tongue. It is an **unruly** evil, full of deadly poison. [NKJV] But no one can tame the tongue. It is an **uncontrollable** evil, full of deadly poison. [NLT] τὴν δὲ γλῶσσαν οὐδεὶς δύναται ἀνθρώπων δαμάσαι· **ἀκατάσχετον** κακόν, μεστὴ ἰοῦ θανατηφόρου. [GNS] τὴν δὲ γλῶσσαν οὐδεὶς δαμάσαι δύναται ἀνθρώπων, **ἀκατάστατον** κακόν, μεστὴ ἰοῦ θανατηφόρου. [GNT]	Restless, unruly, uncontrollable, nervous, jittery, unsettled. **Practical Application** The tongue is "unruly" (*akatastaton*), that is, restless, uneasy, unstable, always roaming about. And it is full of deadly poison. It can bless God in one breath and curse men in the next, men who are made in the image of God. Note how inconsistent the tongue is: it blesses God and curses men. Imagine! The very same tongue that blesses is the same tongue that curses. How many sit in church on Sunday or at meals blessing God and then turn around on Monday and curse or use foul and off-colored language? It is the same tongue that does both. How restless it is! It is just difficult to hold the tongue still, and when it speaks, it is just as liable to speak some curse word as it is to speak some blessing.
#4173 **Unruly** Unruly–KJV Rebellious–NASB Rebellious–NIV Insubordinate–NKJV Rebel–NLT **POSB REFERENCE** (Tit.1:10-12; esp. v.10) Note 1, point 1	ἀνυπότακτοι = anupotaktoi Pronunciation: [an-oo-pot'-ak-toy] Parsing (part of speech): pronominal adjective 　Case—nominative 　Gender—masculine 　Number—plural 　Stem or root—from ἀνυπότακτος, ον Concordance References: ⇒ Strong's #506 anupotaktos ⇒ NIV #538 anupotaktos ⇒ NASB #506 anupotaktos **Titus 1:10** For there are many **unruly** and vain talkers and deceivers, specially they of the circumcision: [KJV] For there are many **rebellious** men, empty talkers and deceivers, especially those of the circumcision, [NASB] For there are many **rebellious** people, mere talkers and deceivers, especially those of the circumcision group. [NIV] For there are many **insubordinate**, both idle talkers and deceivers, especially those of the circumcision, [NKJV] For there are many who **rebel** against right teaching;	Rebellious, unruly; insubordinate; to rebel. **Practical Application** They were "unruly" (*anupotaktoi*): undisciplined, rebellious, disloyal, insubordinate against God and the truth. They refused to submit to God and to the truth of the gospel and of God's Word.

ENGLISH WORD	GREEK WORD AND VERSE	THE WORD MEANS...
	they engage in useless talk and deceive people. This is especially true of those who insist on circumcision for salvation. [NLT] Εἰσὶ γὰρ πολλοὶ καὶ **ἀνυπότακτοι**, ματαιολόγοι καὶ φρεναπάται, μάλιστα οἱ ἐκ τῆς περιτομῆς, [GNS] Εἰσὶν γὰρ πολλοὶ [καὶ] **ἀνυπότακτοι**, ματαιολόγοι καὶ φρεναπάται, μάλιστα οἱ ἐκ τῆς περιτομῆς, [GNT]	

#4174
Unsettling
 	
Subverting–KJV
Unsettling–NASB
Troubling–NIV
Unsettling–NKJV
Upset–NLT
 	
POSB REFERENCE
(Acts 15:24)
Note 2, point 2
	ἀνασκευάζοντες = anaskeuazontes
	Pronunciation: [an-ask-yoo-ad'-zon-tehs]
	Parsing (part of speech): verb
	    Mood—participle
	    Tense—present
	    Voice—active
	    Case—nominative
	    Gender—masculine
	    Number—plural
	    Stem or root—from **ἀνασκευάζω**
	Concordance References:
	  ⇒ Strong's #384 anaskeuazō
	  ⇒ NIV #412 anaskeuazō
	  ⇒ NASB #384 anaskeuazō
	
	Acts 15:24
	Forasmuch as we have heard, that certain which went out from us have troubled you with words, **subverting** your souls, saying, *Ye must* be circumcised, and keep the law: to whom we gave no *such* commandment: [KJV]
	
	"Since we have heard that some of our number to whom we gave no instruction have disturbed you with *their* words, **unsettling** your souls, [NASB]
	
	We have heard that some went out from us without our authorization and disturbed you, **troubling** your minds by what they said. [NIV]
	
	Since we have heard that some who went out from us have troubled you with words, **unsettling** your souls, saying, "You must be circumcised and keep the law"—to whom we gave no such commandment— [NKJV]
	
	"We understand that some men from here have troubled you and **upset** you with their teaching, but they had no such instructions from us. [NLT]
	
	Ἐπειδὴ ἠκούσαμεν ὅτι τινὲς ἐξ ἡμῶν ἐξελθόντες ἐτάραξαν ὑμᾶς λόγοις, **ἀνασκευάζοντες** τὰς ψυχὰς ὑμῶν, λέγοντες περιτέμνεσθαι καὶ τηρεῖν τον νόμον, οἷς οὐ διεστειλάμεθα· [GNS]
	
	Ἐπειδὴ ἠκούσαμεν ὅτι τινὲς ἐξ ἡμῶν [ἐξελθόντες] ἐτάραξαν ὑμᾶς λόγοις **ἀνασκευάζοντες** τὰς ψυχὰς ὑμῶν οἷς οὐ διεστειλάμεθα, [GNT]
		Troubling, subverting, unsettling, upsetting, disturbing. The word means to devastate; to plunder; to dismantle; to ravage; to wreck; to cause havoc.
		
		Practical Application
		Ritual and law are not necessary to salvation. No matter what anyone teaches, no matter who they are or how influential they are, salvation is...
		
		• "through the grace of the Lord Jesus Christ" and through His grace alone. Ritual and law are not necessary (Acts 15:11).
		• "by the signs and wonders of God" and by His works alone (Acts 15:12).
		• by turning to God and turning to Him alone (Acts 15:19).
		
		The persons who taught otherwise, the false teachers, were strongly rebuked.
		1. They troubled believers with their words. The picture is that of words heaped upon words, false words that "disturb" (*etaraxan*), agitate, disturb, and shake violently. But note: the false teachers proclaimed mere words, empty words, and believers must always remember this. Salvation is by grace alone and nothing is to be added to it. God and God alone saves. A man either accepts God's salvation or rejects it. It is that simple. Man can do nothing to earn salvation.
		2. They "unsettled" (*anaskeuazontes*) the believers' souls.
		3. They were never commissioned by the church.

#4175
Unskillful–Unskilled
 	
Unskillful–KJV
Not accustomed to–NASB
Not acquainted with–NIV
Unskilled–NKJV
Doesn't know much–NLT
 	
POSB REFERENCE
(Heb.5:13)
Note 3
	ἄπειρος = apeiros
	Pronunciation: [ap'-i-ros]
	Parsing (part of speech): adjective
	    Case—nominative
	    Gender—masculine
	    Number—singular
	    Stem or root—from **ἄπειρος**, ον
	Concordance References:
	  ⇒ Strong's #552 apeiros
	  ⇒ NIV #586 apeiros
	  ⇒ NASB #552 apeiros
	
	Hebrews 5:13
	For every one that useth milk *is* **unskillful** in the word of righteousness: for he is a babe. [KJV]
	
	For everyone who partakes *only* of milk is **not accustomed to** the word of righteousness, for he is a babe. [NASB]
	
	Anyone who lives on milk, being still an infant, is **not acquainted with** the teaching about righteousness. [NIV]
	
	For everyone who partakes *only* of milk *is* **unskilled** in the word of righteousness, for he is a babe. [NKJV]
	
	And a person who is living on milk isn't very far along
		Not acquainted with; unskillful; not accustomed to; does not know much; inexperienced in.
		
		Practical Application
		A person becomes immature because of being unskilled in the Word. The Hebrew believers remained unskillful in the Word of righteousness. They professed Christ and His righteousness, but they had never grasped or experienced Him—not fully—not in a mature sense. Note the verse: although this person is a church member, "he is a babe."

ENGLISH WORD	GREEK WORD AND VERSE	THE WORD MEANS...
	in the Christian life and **doesn't know much** about doing what is right. [NLT] πᾶς γὰρ ὁ μετέχων γάλακτος **ἄπειρος** λόγου δικαιοσύνης· νήπιος γάρ ἐστι. [GNS] πᾶς γὰρ ὁ μετέχων γάλακτος **ἄπειρος** λόγου δικαιοσύνης, νήπιος γάρ ἐστιν· [GNT]	

#4176
Unspiritual
 	
Carnal–KJV
Flesh–NASB
Unspiritual–NIV
Carnal–NKJV
With me–NLT
 	
**POSB
REFERENCE**
(Rom.7:14-17; esp.
v.14)
Note 2
	σάρκινός = sarkinos
	Pronunciation: [sahr-kee-nos']
	Parsing (part of speech): adjective
	    Case—nominative
	    Gender—masculine
	    Number—singular
	    Stem or root—from σάρκινος, η, ον
	Concordance References:
	⇒ Strong's #4559 sarkikos
	⇒ NIV #4921 sarkikos
	⇒ NASB #4560 sarkikos
	
	Romans 7:14
	For we know that the law is spiritual: but I am **carnal**, sold under sin. [KJV]
	For we know that the Law is spiritual; but I am of **flesh**, sold into bondage to sin. [NASB]
	We know that the law is spiritual; but I am **unspiritual**, sold as a slave to sin. [NIV]
	x For we know that the law is spiritual, but I am **carnal**, sold under sin. [NKJV]
	The law is good, then. The trouble is not with the law but **with me**, because I am sold into slavery, with sin as my master. [NLT]
	οἴδαμεν γὰρ ὅτι ὁ νόμος πνευματικός ἐστιν· ἐγὼ δὲ **σάρκικός** εἰμι, πεπραμένος ὑπὸ τὴν ἁμαρτίαν. [GNS]
	οἴδαμεν γὰρ ὅτι ὁ νόμος πνευματικός ἐστιν, ἐγὼ δὲ **σάρκινός** εἰμι πεπραμένος ὑπὸ τὴν ἁμαρτίαν. [GNT]
		Unspiritual, carnal, fleshly, human, worldly; by sinful nature; to belong to this world; to be made of flesh; to consist of flesh; to have a body of flesh and blood. It means the flesh with which a man is born, the fleshly nature one inherits from his parents when he is born.
		
		Practical Application
		The word unspiritual also means to be given up to the sinful nature, that is, to live a fleshly, sensual life; to be given over to animal appetites; to be controlled by one's sinful nature. (See POSB *Deeper Study* #1, Carnal—1 Cor. 3:1-4 for more discussion.)

#4177
Unstained By Sin
 	
Undefiled–KJV
Undefiled–NASB
Pure–NIV
Undefiled–NKJV
**Unstained by sin–
NLT**
 	
**POSB
REFERENCE**
(Heb.7:26)
Note 2
	ἀμίαντος = amiantos
	Pronunciation: [am-ee'-an-tos]
	Parsing (part of speech): adjective
	    Case—nominative
	    Gender—masculine
	    Number—singular
	    Stem or root—from ἀμίαντος, ον
	Concordance References:
	⇒ Strong's #283 amiantos
	⇒ NIV #299 amiantos
	⇒ NASB #283 amiantos
	
	Hebrews 7:26
	For such an high priest became us, *who is* holy, harmless, **undefiled**, separate from sinners, and made higher than the heavens; [KJV]
	For it was fitting that we should have such a high priest, holy, innocent, **undefiled**, separated from sinners and exalted above the heavens; [NASB]
	Such a high priest meets our need—one who is holy, blameless, **pure**, set apart from sinners, exalted above the heavens. [NIV]
	For such a High Priest was fitting for us, *who is* holy, harmless, **undefiled**, separate from sinners, and has become higher than the heavens; [NKJV]
	He is the kind of high priest we need because he is holy and blameless, **unstained by sin**. He has now been set apart from sinners, and he has been given the highest place of honor in heaven. [NLT]
	Τοιοῦτος γὰρ ἡμῖν ἔπρεπεν ἀρχιερεύς, ὅσιος, ἄκακος, **ἀμίαντος**, κεχωρισμένος ἀπὸ τῶν ἁμαρτωλῶν, καὶ ὑψηλότερος τῶν οὐρανῶν γενόμενος· [GNS]
	Τοιοῦτος γὰρ ἡμῖν καὶ ἔπρεπεν ἀρχιερεύς, ὅσιος ἄκακος **ἀμίαντος**, κεχωρισμένος ἀπὸ τῶν ἁμαρτωλῶν καὶ ὑψηλότερος τῶν οὐρανῶν γενόμενος, [GNT]
		Pure, undefiled, unstained by sin.
		
		Practical Application
		Jesus Christ is "unstained by sin" (*amiantos*): undefiled; absolutely free from all moral impurity, uncleanness, and defilement. Jesus Christ was completely free from anything that would keep Him from approaching God. He is absolutely *unstained by sin*.

ENGLISH WORD	GREEK WORD AND VERSE	THE WORD MEANS...

#4178
Unthankful
 	
Unthankful–KJV
Ungrateful–NASB
Ungrateful–NIV
Unthankful–NKJV
Ungrateful–NLT
 	
**POSB
REFERENCE**
(2 Tim. 3:2-4; esp. v.2)
Note 2, point 7
	ἀχάριστοι = acharistoi
	Pronunciation: [ach-ar'-is-toy]
	Parsing (part of speech): adjective
	    Case—nominative
	    Gender—masculine
	    Number—plural
	    Stem or root—from ἀχάριστος, ον
	Concordance References:
	⇒ Strong's #884 acharistos
	⇒ NIV #940 acharistos
	⇒ NASB #884 acharistos
	
	2 Tim. 3:2
	For men shall be lovers of their own selves, covetous, boasters, proud, blasphemers, disobedient to parents, **unthankful**, unholy, [KJV]
	For men will be lovers of self, lovers of money, boastful, arrogant, revilers, disobedient to parents, **ungrateful**, unholy, [NASB]
	People will be lovers of themselves, lovers of money, boastful, proud, abusive, disobedient to their parents, **ungrateful**, unholy, [NIV]
	For men will be lovers of themselves, lovers of money, boasters, proud, blasphemers, disobedient to parents, **unthankful**, unholy, [NKJV]
	For people will love only themselves and their money. They will be boastful and proud, scoffing at God, disobedient to their parents, and **ungrateful**. They will consider nothing sacred. [NLT]
	ἔσονται γὰρ οἱ ἄνθρωποι φίλαυτοι, φιλάργυροι, ἀλαζόνες, ὑπερήφανοι, βλάσφημοι, γονεῦσιν ἀπειθεῖς, **ἀχάριστοι**, ἀνόσιοι, [GNS]
	ἔσονται γὰρ οἱ ἄνθρωποι φίλαυτοι φιλάργυροι ἀλαζόνες ὑπερήφανοι βλάσφημοι, γονεῦσιν ἀπειθεῖς, **ἀχάριστοι** ἀνόσιοι [GNT]
		Ungrateful, unthankful.
		
		Practical Application
		People will be "unthankful" (acharistoi): no sense of gratitude or appreciation for what one has and receives; no giving of thanks to God or man. Many persons feel that the world and society or business and government owe them the good things of life. They have little if any sense of debt to others. This is the reason many waste time on the job, do mediocre work, and feel little obligation to the world and society. They fail to see how privileged they are to be alive and to live in such a beautiful world and to have a job and friends and neighbors. They fail to see how good God has been to them, and how caring and responsible some people are. Therefore, they reach out to get more and more without sensing any need to express thanks and appreciation. They take and take and forget all about the thanksgiving—the debt and contribution—they owe to God and men.

#4179
Untoward
 	
Untoward–KJV
Perverse–NASB
Corrupt–NIV
Perverse–NKJV
Astray–NLT
 	
**POSB
REFERENCE**
(Acts 2:40)
Note 5, point 2
	σκολιᾶς = skolias
	Pronunciation: [skol-ee-ahs']
	Parsing (part of speech): adjective
	    Case—genitive
	    Gender—feminine
	    Number—singular
	    Stem or root—from σκολιός, ά, όν
	Concordance References:
	⇒ Strong's #4646 skolios
	⇒ NIV #5021 skolios
	⇒ NASB #4646 skolios
	
	Acts 2:40
	And with many other words did he testify and exhort, saying, Save yourselves from this **untoward** generation. [KJV]
	And with many other words he solemnly testified and kept on exhorting them, saying, "Be saved from this **perverse** generation!" [NASB]
	With many other words he warned them; and he pleaded with them, "Save yourselves from this **corrupt** generation." [NIV]
	And with many other words he testified and exhorted them, saying, "Be saved from this **perverse** generation." [NKJV]
	Then Peter continued preaching for a long time, strongly urging all his listeners, "Save yourselves from this generation that has gone **astray**!" [NLT]
	ἑτέροις τε λόγοις πλείοσι διεμαρτύρετο καὶ παρεκάλει, λέγων, Σώθητε ἀπὸ τῆς γενεᾶς τῆς **σκολιᾶς** ταύτης. [GNS]
	ἑτέροις τε λόγοις πλείοσιν διεμαρτύρατο καὶ παρεκάλει αὐτοὺς λέγων, Σώθητε ἀπὸ τῆς γενεᾶς τῆς **σκολιᾶς** ταύτης. [GNT]
		To be corrupt; to be harsh; to be perverse; to go astray; to be crooked or bent out of shape.
		
		Practical Application
		People are far from being straight and far from being in the shape intended by God. They are crooked and bent, unrighteous and ungodly, sinful and corrupt.

ENGLISH WORD	GREEK WORD AND VERSE	THE WORD MEANS...

#4180
Untrustworthy
 	
Covenantbreakers–KJV
Untrustworthy–NASB
Faithless–NIV
Untrustworthy–NKJV
Break their promises–NLT
 	
POSB REFERENCE
(Romans 1:31)
Deeper Study #20
	ἀσυνθέτους = *asunthetous*
	Pronunciation: [as-oon'-thet-oos]
	Parsing (part of speech): adjective
	    Case—accusative
	    Gender—masculine
	    Number—plural
	    Stem or root—from ἀσύνθετος, ον
	Concordance References:
	  ⇒ Strong's #802 asunthetos
	  ⇒ NIV #853 asunthetos
	  ⇒ NASB #802 asunthetos
	
	Romans 1:31
	Without understanding, **covenantbreakers**, without natural affection, implacable, unmerciful: [KJV]
	Without understanding, **untrustworthy**, unloving, unmerciful; [NASB]
	They are senseless, **faithless**, heartless, ruthless. [NIV]
	Undiscerning, **untrustworthy**, unloving, unforgiving, unmerciful; [NKJV]
	They refuse to understand, **break their promises**, and are heartless and unforgiving. [NLT]
	ἀσυνέτους, **ἀσυνθέτους**, ἀστόργους, ἀσπόνδους, ἀνελεήμονας· [GNS]
	ἀσυνέτους **ἀσυνθέτους** ἀστόργους ἀνελεήμονας· [GNT]
		Faithless; covenant breakers; untrustworthy; disloyal; one who breaks his promises; disloyal breakers of promises or agreements; untruthful.
		
		Practical Application
		It is a person who tragically does not keep his word or promise. He is simply untrustworthy, not dependable.

#4181
Unusual Miracles
 	
Special miracles–KJV
Extraordinary miracles–NASB
Extraordinary miracles–NIV
Unusual miracles–NKJV
Unusual miracles–NLT
 	
POSB REFERENCE
(Acts 19:10-20; esp. v.11)
Note 3, point 2
	Δυνάμεις τε οὐ τὰς τυχούσας = *Dunameis te ou tas tuchousas*
	Pronunciation: [doo'-nam-eh-is the oo tahs too-choo'-sahs]
	Parsing *Dunameis* (part of speech): noun
	    Case—accusative
	    Gender—feminine
	    Number—plural
	    Stem or root—from δύναμις, εως
	Parsing *tuchousas* (part of speech): verb
	    Mood—participle
	    Tense—aorist
	    Voice—active
	    Case—accusative
	    Gender—feminine
	    Number—plural
	    Stem or root—from τυγχάνω
	Concordance References:
	  ⇒ Strong's #1411 dunamis + 5037 te + 3588 + 3756 + 5177 ho ou tugchanō
	  ⇒ NIV #1539 dunamis [miracles] + 5445 te + 3836 + 4024 + 5593 ho ou tugchanō [extraordinary]
	  ⇒ NASB #1411 dunamis + 5037 te + 3588 + 3756 + 5177 ho ou tugchanō
	
	Acts 19:11
	And God wrought **special miracles** by the hands of Paul: [KJV]
	And God was performing **extraordinary miracles** by the hands of Paul, [NASB]
	God did **extraordinary miracles** through Paul, [NIV]
	Now God worked **unusual miracles** by the ands of Paul, [NKJV]
	God gave Paul the power to do **unusual miracles**, [NLT]
	δυνάμεις τε οὐ τὰς τυχούσας ἐποίει ὁ Θεὸς διὰ τῶν χειρῶν Παύλου, [GNS]
	Δυνάμεις τε οὐ τὰς τυχούσας ὁ θεὸς ἐποίει διὰ τῶν χειρῶν Παύλου, [GNT]
		Extraordinary miracles; special miracles; unusual miracles; supernatural miracles.
		
		Practical Application
		The phrase actually means two things:
		⇒ They were miracles, powers that were not regular happenings; powers that were not the day-to-day experiences of men.
		⇒ They were miracles that were unusual; that were usually not seen; that were uncommon; that were usually not performed. Even the disciples had not witnessed such miracles, not on a regular basis.

#4182 **Unwavering**	ἀδιάκριτος = *adiakritos* Pronunciation: [ad-ee-ak-'ree-tos] Parsing (part of speech): adjective Case—nominative	Impartial, without partiality, unwavering, no partiality, no favoritism.

ENGLISH WORD	GREEK WORD AND VERSE	THE WORD MEANS...
Without partiality–KJV **Unwavering–NASB** Impartial–NIV Without partiality–NKJV No partiality–NLT **POSB REFERENCE** (Jas. 3:17-18; esp. v.17) Note 3, point 2g	Gender—feminine Number—singular Stem or root—from ἀδιάκριτος, ον Concordance References: ⇒ Strong's #87 adiakritos ⇒ NIV #88 adiakritos ⇒ NASB #87 adiakritos **James 3:17** But the wisdom that is from above is first pure, then peaceable, gentle, *and* easy to be intreated, full of mercy and good fruits, **without partiality**, and without hypocrisy. [KJV] But the wisdom from above is first pure, then peaceable, gentle, reasonable, full of mercy and good fruits, **unwavering**, without hypocrisy. [NASB] But the wisdom that comes from heaven is first of all pure; then peace-loving, considerate, submissive, full of mercy and good fruit, **impartial** and sincere. [NIV] But the wisdom that is from above is first pure, then peaceable, gentle, willing to yield, full of mercy and good fruits, **without partiality** and without hypocrisy. [NKJV] But the wisdom that comes from heaven is first of all pure. It is also peace loving, gentle at all times, and willing to yield to others. It is full of mercy and good deeds. It shows **no partiality** and is always sincere. [NLT] ἡ δὲ ἄνωθεν σοφία πρῶτον μὲν ἁγνή ἐστιν, ἔπειτα εἰρηνική, ἐπιεικής, εὐπειθής, μεστὴ ἐλέους καὶ καρπῶν ἀγαθῶν, **ἀδιάκριτος** καὶ ἀνυπόκριτος. [GNS] ἡ δὲ ἄνωθεν σοφία πρῶτον μὲν ἁγνή ἐστιν, ἔπειτα εἰρηνική, ἐπιεικής, εὐπειθής, μεστὴ ἐλέους καὶ καρπῶν ἀγαθῶν, **ἀδιάκριτος**, ἀνυπόκριτος. [GNT]	**Practical Application** True wisdom is unwavering (*adiakritos*). This word in the Greek actually means two things. 1. The wise teacher is impartial; he shows no partiality or favoritism to anyone. 2. The wise teacher is undivided in his convictions and judgments. He knows the truth, exactly what God's Word says, and he will not entertain false ideas or teachings. He is totally committed and undivided in following and teaching God's Word.
#4183 ## Unwholesome Corrupt–KJV **Unwholesome–NASB** **Unwholesome–NIV** Corrupt–NKJV Foul or abusive–NLT **POSB REFERENCE** (Eph.4:29) Note 4	σαπρός = *sapros* Pronunciation: [sap-ros'] Parsing (part of speech): adjective Case—nominative Gender—masculine Number—singular Stem or root—from σαπρός, ά, όν Concordance References: ⇒ Strong's #4550 sapros ⇒ NIV #4911 sapros ⇒ NASB #4550 saprost **Ephes. 4:29** Let no **corrupt** communication proceed out of your mouth, but that which is good to the use of edifying, that it may minister grace unto the hearers. [KJV] Let no **unwholesome** word proceed from your mouth, but only such *a word* as is good for edification according to the need *of the moment,* that it may give grace to those who hear. [NASB] Do not let any **unwholesome** talk come out of your mouths, but only what is helpful for building others up according to their needs, that it may benefit those who listen. [NIV] Let no **corrupt** word proceed out of your mouth, but what is good for necessary edification, that it may impart grace to the hearers. [NKJV] Don't use **foul or abusive** language. Let everything you say be good and helpful, so that your words will be an encouragement to those who hear them. [NLT] πᾶς λόγος **σαπρὸς** ἐκ τοῦ στόματος ὑμῶν μὴ ἐκπορευέσθω, ἀλλ εἴ τις ἀγαθὸς πρὸς οἰκοδομὴν τῆς χρείας, ἵνα δῷ χάριν τοῖς ἀκούουσι. [GNS] πᾶς λόγος **σαπρὸς** ἐκ τοῦ στόματος ὑμῶν μὴ ἐκπορευέσθω, ἀλλὰ εἴ τις ἀγαθὸς πρὸς οἰκοδομὴν τῆς χρείας, ἵνα δῷ χάριν τοῖς ἀκούουσιν. [GNT]	Rotten, foul, corrupt, abusive, putrid, bad, unwholesome, polluting. **Practical Application** The believer is to strip away filthy and foul talk. The word "unwholesome" (*sapros*) means rotten, foul, putrid and polluting. Unwholesome talk, of course, would include cursing and unholy talk and even the worthless conversation that is so often carried on by people. The Amplified New Testament has a good description. *Let no foul or polluting language, nor evil word, nor unwholesome or worthless talk [ever] come out of your mouth (Ephes. 4:29).*

ENGLISH WORD	GREEK WORD AND VERSE	THE WORD MEANS...
#4184 **Upright** Just–KJV Just–NASB **Upright–NIV** Just–NKJV Fair–NLT **POSB** **REFERENCE** (Tit.1:7-8; esp. v.8) Note 3, point 2d	δίκαιον = *dikaion* Pronunciation: [dik'-ah-ee-on] Parsing (part of speech): adjective 　　Case—accusative 　　Gender—masculine 　　Number—singular 　　Stem or root—from δίκαιος, α, ον Concordance References: 　⇒　Strong's #1342 dikaios 　⇒　NIV #1465 dikaios 　⇒　NASB #1342 dikaios **Titus 1:8** But a lover of hospitality, a lover of good men, sober, **just**, holy, temperate; [KJV] But hospitable, loving what is good, sensible, **just**, devout, self-controlled, [NASB] Rather he must be hospitable, one who loves what is good, who is self-controlled, **upright**, holy and disciplined. [NIV] But hospitable, a lover of what is good, sober-minded, **just**, holy, self-controlled, [NKJV] He must enjoy having guests in his home and must love all that is good. He must live wisely and be **fair**. He must live a devout and disciplined life. [NLT] ἀλλὰ φιλόξενον, φιλάγαθον, σώφρονα, **δίκαιον**, ὅσιον, ἐγκρατῆ, [GNS] ἀλλὰ φιλόξενον φιλάγαθον σώφρονα **δίκαιον** ὅσιον ἐγκρατῆ, [GNT]	Upright, just, fair, honest, innocent, proper, above board in his behavior and dealings with both God and man. **Practical Application** There is no deception, lying, cheating, stealing, meanness, misbehavior, or irresponsibility whatsoever in the minister's dealings—not with men nor with God.
#4185 **Upright** Righteously–KJV Righteously–NASB **Upright–NIV** Righteously–NKJV Right conduct–NLT **POSB** **REFERENCE** (Tit.2:12) Note 2, point 2b	δικαίως = *dikaiōs* Pronunciation: [dik-ah'-yoce] Parsing (part of speech): adjective 　　Type—adverb 　　Stem or root—from δικαίως Concordance References: 　⇒　Strong's #1346 dikaiōs 　⇒　NIV #1469 dikaiōs 　⇒　NASB #1346 dikaiōs **Titus 2:12** Teaching us that, denying ungodliness and worldly lusts, we should live soberly, **righteously**, and godly, in this present world; [KJV] Instructing us to deny ungodliness and worldly desires and to live sensibly, **righteously** and godly in the present age, [NASB] It teaches us to say "No" to ungodliness and worldly passions, and to live self-controlled, **upright** and godly lives in this present age, [NIV] Teaching us that, denying ungodliness and worldly lusts, we should live soberly, **righteously**, and godly in the present age, [NKJV] And we are instructed to turn from godless living and sinful pleasures. We should live in this evil world with self-control, **right conduct**, and devotion to God, [NLT] παιδεύουσα ἡμᾶς ἵνα, ἀρνησάμενοι τὴν ἀσέβειαν καὶ τὰς κοσμικὰς ἐπιθυμίας σωφρόνως καὶ **δικαίως** καὶ εὐσεβῶς ζήσωμεν ἐν τῷ νῦν αἰῶνι, [GNS] παιδεύουσα ἡμᾶς, ἵνα ἀρνησάμενοι τὴν ἀσέβειαν καὶ τὰς κοσμικὰς ἐπιθυμίας σωφρόνως καὶ **δικαίως** καὶ εὐσεβῶς ζήσωμεν ἐν τῷ νῦν αἰῶνι, [GNT]	Righteously, doing right, treating others like one should, doing good to them, giving them their due share, right conduct. **Practical Application** What an indictment! How selfish we are in our hoarding and banking while a world dies from starvation, disease, war, evil, and sin. Every person is due his share. We are to live righteously, giving and seeing to it that every man is treated right, that every man receives his due share. If they are well-off physically and materially, we are to treat them righteously, just like we would want to be treated. If they are needy, poor, destitute, hungry, diseased, lonely, bedridden, and sinful, we are to do right toward them and meet their needs. They are to receive their due share of this earth just as we are.
#4186 **Upset** Troubled–KJV Bothered–NASB **Upset–NIV** Troubled–NKJV **Upset–NLT**	θορυβάζη = *thorubazē* Pronunciation: [tho-ru-bad'-zay] Parsing (part of speech): verb 　　Mood—indicative 　　Tense—present 　　Voice—passive 　　Person—2nd person 　　Number—singular 　　Stem or root—from θορυβάζω	To be upset; to be bothered; to be troubled; to be disturbed, agitated, in turmoil, stirred up, ruffled. **Practical Application** In this Scripture, Martha sought to please Jesus with her service and ministering, but two things were wrong. 　⇒　She was looking after "many things," too

ENGLISH WORD	GREEK WORD AND VERSE	THE WORD MEANS...
POSB REFERENCE (Lk.10:41-42; esp. v.41) Note 4, point 2	Concordance References: ⇒ Strong's #5182 thorubazö ⇒ NIV #2571 thorubazö ⇒ NASB #2350a thorubazö **Luke 10:41** And Jesus answered and said unto her, Martha, Martha, thou art careful and **troubled** about many things: [KJV] But the Lord answered and said to her, "Martha, Martha, you are worried and **bothered** about so many things; [NASB] "Martha, Martha," the Lord answered, "you are worried and **upset** about many things, [NIV] And Jesus answered and said to her, "Martha, Martha, you are worried and **troubled** about many things. [NKJV] But the Lord said to her, "My dear Martha, you are so **upset** over all these details! [NLT] ἀποκριθεὶς δὲ εἶπεν αὐτῇ ὁ Ἰησοῦς, Μάρθα Μάρθα, μεριμνᾷς καὶ **τυρβάζῃ** περὶ πολλά· [GNS] ἀποκριθεὶς δὲ εἶπεν αὐτῇ ὁ κύριος, Μάρθα Μάρθα, μεριμνᾷς καὶ **θορυβάζῃ** περὶ πολλά, [GNT]	many. She was trying to do too much for so many. ⇒ She had become worried and upset.

#4187
Upset
 	
Careful–KJV
Worried–NASB
Worried–NIV
Worried–NKJV
Upset–NLT
 	
POSB REFERENCE (Lk.10:41-42; esp. v.41) Note 4, point 2
	μεριμνᾷς = *merimnas*
	Pronunciation: [mer-im-nahs']
	Parsing (part of speech): verb
	   Mood—indicative
	   Tense—present
	   Voice—active
	   Person—2nd person
	   Number—singular
	   Stem or root—from μεριμνάω
	Concordance References:
	⇒ Strong's #3309 merimnaö
	⇒ NIV #3534 merimnaö
	⇒ NASB #3309 merimnaö
	
	Luke 10:41
	And Jesus answered and said unto her, Martha, Martha, thou art **careful** and troubled about many things: [KJV]
	But the Lord answered and said to her, "Martha, Martha, you are **worried** and bothered about so many things; [NASB]
	"Martha, Martha," the Lord answered, "you are **worried** and upset about many things, [NIV]
	And Jesus answered and said to her, "Martha, Martha, you are **worried** and troubled about many things. [NKJV]
	But the Lord said to her, "My dear Martha, you are so **upset** over all these details! [NLT]
	ἀποκριθεὶς δὲ εἶπεν αὐτῇ ὁ Ἰησοῦς, Μάρθα Μάρθα, **μεριμνᾷς** καὶ τυρβάζῃ περὶ πολλά· [GNS]
	ἀποκριθεὶς δὲ εἶπεν αὐτῇ ὁ κύριος, Μάρθα Μάρθα, **μεριμνᾷς** καὶ θορυβάζῃ περὶ πολλά, [GNT]
		To worry; to be anxious; to be cautious; to be mindful; to be upset; to be overly concerned and caring (cp. Phil. 4:6).
		
		Practical Application
		It has the idea of being inwardly torn and divided in two, of being distracted from what one's mind and heart and life should be focused upon.

#4188
Upset
 	
Subverting–KJV
Unsettling–NASB
Troubling–NIV
Unsettling–NKJV
Upset–NLT
 	
POSB REFERENCE (Acts 15:24) Note 2, point 2
	ἀνασκευάζοντες = *anaskeuazontes*
	Pronunciation: [an-ask-yoo-ad'-zon-tehs]
	Parsing (part of speech): verb
	   Mood—participle
	   Tense—present
	   Voice—active
	   Case—nominative
	   Gender—masculine
	   Number—plural
	   Stem or root—from ἀνασκευάζω
	Concordance References:
	⇒ Strong's #384 anaskeuazö
	⇒ NIV #412 anaskeuazö
	⇒ NASB #384 anaskeuazö
	
	Acts 15:24
	Forasmuch as we have heard, that certain which went
		Troubling, subverting, unsettling, upsetting, disturbing. The word means to devastate; to plunder; to dismantle; to ravage; to wreck; to cause havoc.
		
		Practical Application
		Ritual and law are not necessary to salvation. No matter what anyone teaches, no matter who they are or how influential they are, salvation is...
		• "through the grace of the Lord Jesus Christ" and by Him alone. Ritual and law are not necessary (Acts 15:11).
		• by the "many miracles and wonders of God" and by Him alone (Acts 15:12).
		• by turning to God and turning to Him alone (Acts 15:19).

ENGLISH WORD	GREEK WORD AND VERSE	THE WORD MEANS...
	out from us have troubled you with words, **subverting** your souls, saying, *Ye must* be circumcised, and keep the law: to whom we gave no *such* commandment: [KJV] "Since we have heard that some of our number to whom we gave no instruction have disturbed you with *their* words, **unsettling** your souls, [NASB] We have heard that some went out from us without our authorization and disturbed you, **troubling** your minds by what they said. [NIV] Since we have heard that some who went out from us have troubled you with words, **unsettling** your souls, saying, "You must be circumcised and keep the law"—to whom we gave no such commandment— [NKJV] "We understand that some men from here have troubled you and **upset** you with their teaching, but they had no such instructions from us. [NLT] Ἐπειδὴ ἠκούσαμεν ὅτι τινὲς ἐξ ἡμῶν ἐξελθόντες ἐτάραξαν ὑμᾶς λόγοις, **ἀνασκευάζοντες** τὰς ψυχὰς ὑμῶν, λέγοντες περιτέμνεσθαι καὶ τηρεῖν τὸν νόμον, οἷς οὐ διεστειλάμεθα· [GNS] Ἐπειδὴ ἠκούσαμεν ὅτι τινὲς ἐξ ἡμῶν [ἐξελθόντες] ἐτάραξαν ὑμᾶς λόγοις **ἀνασκευάζοντες** τὰς ψυχὰς ὑμῶν οἷς οὐ διεστειλάμεθα, [GNT]	The persons who taught otherwise, the false teachers, were strongly rebuked. 1. They troubled believers with their words. The picture is that of words heaped upon words, false words that "trouble" (*etaraxan*), agitate, disturb, and shake violently. But note: the false teachers proclaimed mere words, empty words, and the believers must always remember this. Salvation is by grace alone and nothing is to be added to it. God and God alone saves. A man either accepts God's salvation or rejects it. It is that simple. Man can do nothing to earn salvation. 2. They "upset" (*anaskeuazontes*) the believers' souls. 3. They were never commissioned by the church.

#4189
Upset People's Faith
 	
Offences–KJV
Hindrances–NASB
Obstacles–NIV
Offenses–NKJV
Upset people's faith–NLT
 	
POSB REFERENCE
(Rom.16:17-18; esp. v.17)
Note 1, point 1
	σκάνδαλα = *skandala*
	Pronunciation: [skan'-dal-ah]
	Parsing (part of speech): noun
	  Case—accusative
	  Gender—neuter
	  Number—plural
	  Stem or root—from σκάνδαλον, ου
	Concordance References:
	  ⇒ Strong's #4625 skandalon
	  ⇒ NIV #4998 skandalon
	  ⇒ NASB #4625 skandalon
	
	Romans 16:17
	Now I beseech you, brethren, mark them which cause divisions and **offences** contrary to the doctrine which ye have learned; and avoid them. [KJV]
	
	Now I urge you, brethren, keep your eye on those who cause dissensions and **hindrances** contrary to the teaching which you learned, and turn away from them. [NASB]
	
	I urge you, brothers, to watch out for those who cause divisions and put **obstacles** in your way that are contrary to the teaching you have learned. Keep away from them. [NIV]
	
	Now I urge you, brethren, note those who cause divisions and **offenses**, contrary to the doctrine which you learned, and avoid them. [NKJV]
	
	And now I make one more appeal, my dear brothers and sisters. Watch out for people who cause divisions and **upset people's faith** by teaching things that are contrary to what you have been taught. Stay away from them. [NLT]
	
	Παρακαλῶ δὲ ὑμᾶς, ἀδελφοί, σκοπεῖν τοὺς τὰς διχοστασίας καὶ τὰ **σκάνδαλα**, παρὰ τὴν διδαχὴν ἣν ὑμεῖς ἐμάθετε, ποιοῦντας· καὶ ἐκκλίνατε ἀπ' αὐτῶν. [GNS]
	
	Παρακαλῶ δὲ ὑμᾶς, ἀδελφοί, σκοπεῖν τοὺς τὰς διχοστασίας καὶ τὰ **σκάνδαλα** παρὰ τὴν διδαχὴν ἣν ὑμεῖς ἐμάθετε ποιοῦντας, καὶ ἐκκλίνετε ἀπ' αὐτῶν· [GNT]
		That which causes sin or gives occasion for sin; that which causes stumbling or trouble, obstacle. The words "upset people's faith" (*skandala*) mean laying a stumbling block in someone's way or causing someone to fall.
		
		### Practical Application
		The most effective way for Satan to get a foothold into a strong church is to quietly and insidiously move a divisive person into some teaching or leadership position where he can influence immature believers. Paul knew this, so he left the warning until the end of his letter. It is a warning that must be heeded by a strong church if it is to keep its witness for the Lord.

#4190
Urge
 	
Pray–KJV
Beg–NASB
Implore–NIV
Implore–NKJV
Urge–NLT
	δεόμεθα = *deometha*
	Pronunciation: [deh'-om-eh-tha]
	Parsing (part of speech): verb
	  Mood—indicative
	  Tense—present
	  Voice—middle or passive deponent
	  Person—1st person
	  Number—plural
	  Stem or root—from δέομαι
		To implore; to pray; to beg; to urge; to intreat; to cry; to ask; and to plead with.
		
		### Practical Application
		Note that it is "for Christ's sake" that we are to plead with men. Christ has paid the ultimate price to make reconciliation available to men: He has taken the sins of men upon Himself and

ENGLISH WORD	GREEK WORD AND VERSE	THE WORD MEANS...
POSB REFERENCE (2 Cor.5:20) Note 3	Concordance References: ⇒ Strong's #1189 deomai ⇒ NIV #1289 deomai ⇒ NASB #1189a deomai ### 2 Cor. 5:20 Now then we are ambassadors for Christ, as though God did beseech *you* by us: we **pray** *you* in Christ's stead, be ye reconciled to God. [KJV] Therefore, we are ambassadors for Christ, as though God were entreating through us; we **beg** you on behalf of Christ, be reconciled to God. [NASB] We are therefore Christ's ambassadors, as though God were making his appeal through us. We **implore** you on Christ's behalf: Be reconciled to God. [NIV] Now then, we are ambassadors for Christ, as though God were pleading through us: we **implore** *you* on Christ's behalf, be reconciled to God. [NKJV] We are Christ's ambassadors, and God is using us to speak to you. We **urge** you, as though Christ himself were here pleading with you, "Be reconciled to God!" [NLT] ὑπὲρ Χριστοῦ οὖν πρεσβεύομεν, ὡς τοῦ Θεοῦ παρακαλοῦντος δι' ἡμῶν· **δεόμεθα** ὑπὲρ Χριστοῦ, καταλλάγητε τῷ Θεῷ. [GNS] ὑπὲρ Χριστοῦ οὖν πρεσβεύομεν ὡς τοῦ θεοῦ παρακαλοῦντος δι' ἡμῶν· **δεόμεθα** ὑπὲρ Χριστοῦ, καταλλάγητε τῷ θεῷ. [GNT]	borne the condemnation for them. Because He has done so much, every man owes his life to Christ—every man owes it to Christ to be reconciled to God. For Christ's sake, a man should give himself to God.
#4191 ## Urge Beseech–KJV **Urge–NASB** **Urge–NIV** Beseech–NKJV **Plead with–NLT** **POSB REFERENCE** (Rom.12:1) Note 1	*Παρακαλῶ* = *Parakalō* Pronunciation: [par-ak-al-o] Parsing (part of speech): verb Mood—indicative Tense—present Voice—active Person—1st person Number—singular Stem or root—from παρακαλέω Concordance References: ⇒ Strong's #3870 parakaleō ⇒ NIV #4151 parakaleō ⇒ NASB #3870 parakaleō ### Romans 12:1 I **beseech** you therefore, brethren, by the mercies of God, that ye present your bodies a living sacrifice, holy, acceptable unto God, *which is* your reasonable service. [KJV] I **urge** you therefore, brethren, by the mercies of God, to present your bodies a living and holy sacrifice, acceptable to God, *which is* your spiritual service of worship. [NASB] Therefore, I **urge** you, brothers, in view of God's mercy, to offer your bodies as living sacrifices, holy and pleasing to God—this is your spiritual act of worship. [NIV] I **beseech** you therefore, brethren, by the mercies of God, that you present your bodies a living sacrifice, holy, acceptable to God, *which is* your reasonable service. [NKJV] And so, dear brothers and sisters, I **plead with** you to give your bodies to God. Let them be a living and holy sacrifice—the kind he will accept. When you think of what he has done for you, is this too much to ask? [NLT] **Παρακαλῶ** οὖν ὑμᾶς, ἀδελφοί, διὰ τῶν οἰκτιρμῶν τοῦ Θεοῦ, παραστῆσαι τὰ σώματα ὑμῶν θυσίαν ζῶσαν, ἁγίαν εὐάρεστον τῷ Θεῷ, τὴν λογικὴν λατρείαν ὑμῶν. [GNS] **Παρακαλῶ** οὖν ὑμᾶς, ἀδελφοί, διὰ τῶν οἰκτιρμῶν τοῦ θεοῦ παραστῆσαι τὰ σώματα ὑμῶν θυσίαν ζῶσαν ἁγίαν εὐάρεστον τῷ θεῷ, τὴν λογικὴν λατρείαν ὑμῶν· [GNT]	To urge; to beseech; to plead with; to beg; to request; to ask. ### Practical Application Note a significant point: what is about to be said is not being said to the world, that is, to the lost. It is being directed to brothers in Christ: "I *urge* you, brothers." Devotion to God is strongly urged.

ENGLISH WORD	GREEK WORD AND VERSE	THE WORD MEANS...
	εἰ δὲ Χριστὸς οὐκ ἐγήγερται, **κενὸν** ἄρα τὸ κήρυγμα ἡμῶν, κενὴ δὲ καὶ ἡ πίστις ὑμῶν, [GNS] εἰ δὲ Χριστὸς οὐκ ἐγήγερται, **κενὸν** ἄρα [καὶ] τὸ κήρυγμα ἡμῶν, κενὴ καὶ ἡ πίστις ὑμῶν· [GNT]	ies and make them perfect by changing their corruptible nature into an incorruptible nature. Therefore, to deny the resurrection of Christ or of believers is to deny what we preach. Our preaching of the resurrected Lord and of our living forever is empty and meaningless. We may as well be doing something else; there is no need to preach a false hope. 2. The message we preach is that Jesus Christ is the Son of God who died for our sins and rose again conquering death for us. The fact that God raised Him from the dead is the glorious proof that He is the Son of God, the proof that God accepted His sacrifice for our sins (Romans 1:4). If Christ did not arise, then it means that God left Him in the grave, that He is no more than what other men are, a man doomed to die and remain in the grave forever with all other men. But if God did raise Christ up from the grave, then it means that death is conquered and that He will raise us up to live forever with Him. The point is this: if there is no resurrection—no resurrection of Christ and no resurrection of us—then the consequence is terrible. Jesus Christ is not the Son of God. What we are preaching is useless and meaningless. We may as well keep quiet.

#4196
Useless
 	
Vain–KJV
Worthless–NASB
Futile–NIV
Futile–NKJV
Useless–NLT
 	
**POSB
REFERENCE**
(1 Cor.15:16-19; esp. v.17)
Note 3, point 2
	ματαία = *matzaia*
	Pronunciation: [mat'-ah-ee-ah]
	Parsing (part of speech): adjective
	    Case—nominative
	    Gender—feminine
	    Number—singular
	    Stem or root—from **μάταιος**, α, ον
	Concordance References:
	    ⇒ Strong's #3152 mataios
	    ⇒ NIV #3469 mataios
	    ⇒ NASB #3152 mataios
	
	1 Cor. 15:17
	And if Christ be not raised, your faith is **vain**; ye are yet in your sins. [KJV]
	And if Christ has not been raised, your faith is **worthless**; you are still in your sins. [NASB]
	And if Christ has not been raised, your faith is **futile**; you are still in your sins. [NIV]
	And if Christ is not risen, your faith *is* **futile**; you are still in your sins! [NKJV]
	And if Christ has not been raised, then your faith is **useless**, and you are still under condemnation for your sins. [NLT]
	εἰ δὲ Χριστὸς οὐκ ἐγήγερται, **ματαία** ἡ πίστις ὑμῶν· ἔτι ἐστὲ ἐν ταῖς ἁμαρτίαις ὑμῶν. [GNS]
	εἰ δὲ Χριστὸς οὐκ ἐγήγερται, **ματαία** ἡ πίστις ὑμῶν, ἔτι ἐστὲ ἐν ταῖς ἁμαρτίαις ὑμῶν, [GNT]
		Fruitless or futile; that is, we are still in our sins; worthless; useless.
		
		### Practical Application
		To deny the resurrection (either of Christ or of us) means that our faith is useless (*matzaia*). If Jesus Christ has not risen from the dead, then He is still dead, still in the grave; therefore, there is no redemption, no forgiveness of sins.

#4197
Useless
 	
Barren–KJV
Useless–NASB
Ineffective–NIV
Unfruitful–NKJV
Productive–NLT
	ἀργοὺς = *argous*
	Pronunciation: [ar-goos']
	Parsing (part of speech): adjective
	    Case—accusative
	    Gender—masculine
	    Number—plural
	    Stem or root—from **ἀργός**, ή, όν
	Concordance References:
	    ⇒ Strong's #692 argos
	    ⇒ NIV #734 argos
	    ⇒ NASB #692 argos
		To be ineffective; to be barren; to be lazy; to be careless; to be doing nothing. It means to be idle and slothful, empty and useless.
		
		### Practical Application
		It is the very opposite of being fruitful and productive in life. Therefore if we possess *these qualities*, if we really work at our salvation, we will not live an ineffective, dry life. We will not be unfruitful nor live a life that is empty and useless, idle and slothful. On the contrary, we will

ENGLISH WORD	GREEK WORD AND VERSE	THE WORD MEANS...
POSB REFERENCE (2 Pt.1:8-11; esp. v.8) Note 2, point 1	**2 Peter 1:8** For if these things be in you, and abound, they make *you that ye shall* neither *be* **barren** nor unfruitful in the knowledge of our Lord Jesus Christ. [KJV] For if these *qualities* are yours and are increasing, they render you neither **useless** nor unfruitful in the true knowledge of our Lord Jesus Christ. [NASB] For if you possess these qualities in increasing measure, they will keep you from being **ineffective** and unproductive in your knowledge of our Lord Jesus Christ. [NIV] For if these things are yours and abound, *you will be* neither barren nor **unfruitful** in the knowledge of our Lord Jesus Christ. [NKJV] The more you grow like this, the more you will become **productive** and useful in your knowledge of our Lord Jesus Christ. [NLT] ταῦτα γὰρ ὑμῖν ὑπάρχοντα, καὶ πλεονάζοντα, οὐκ **ἀργοὺς** οὐδὲ ἀκάρπους καθίστησιν εἰς τὴν τοῦ Κυρίου ἡμῶν Ἰησοῦ Χριστοῦ ἐπίγνωσιν· [GNS] ταῦτα γὰρ ὑμῖν ὑπάρχοντα καὶ πλεονάζοντα οὐκ **ἀργοὺς** οὐδὲ ἀκάρπους καθίστησιν εἰς τὴν τοῦ κυρίου ἡμῶν Ἰησοῦ Χριστοῦ ἐπίγνωσιν· [GNT]	live a life that flows with nourishment and that bears the ripest of fruit: love, joy, and peace (cp. Galatians 5:22-23). But note the source of such a life: the source is our Lord Jesus Christ. We must know Him and grow in the knowledge of Him. The knowledge of Him must be our aim and purpose in life. Only as we know Him can we overcome the barrenness and unfruitfulness of life. He and He alone can give us real life. Therefore, we must possess *these qualities*—really work at our salvation—really seek fellowship and communion with Christ moment by moment and day by day—in order not to be barren or unfruitful in the knowledge of Him. We must learn to pray all day long and to take *set times* for prayer every day, set times for concentrated prayer. We must learn to *keep our minds* on Christ.
#4198 **Useless Talk** Vain talkers–KJV Empty talkers–NASB Mere talkers–NIV Idle talkers–NKJV **Useless talk–NLT** **POSB REFERENCE** (Tit.1:10-12; esp. v.10) Note 1, point 2	**ματαιολόγοι** = *mataiologoi* Pronunciation: [mat-ah-yol-og'-oy] Parsing (part of speech): pronominal adjective Case—nominative Gender—masculine Number—plural Stem or root—from **ματαιολόγος**, ου Concordance References: ⇒ Strong's #3151 mataiologos ⇒ NIV #3468 mataiologos ⇒ NASB #3151 mataiologos **Titus 1:10** For there are many unruly and **vain talkers** and deceivers, specially they of the circumcision: [KJV] For there are many rebellious men, **empty talkers** and deceivers, especially those of the circumcision, [NASB] For there are many rebellious people, **mere talkers** and deceivers, especially those of the circumcision group. [NIV] For there are many insubordinate, both **idle talkers** and deceivers, especially those of the circumcision, [NKJV] For there are many who rebel against right teaching; they engage in **useless talk** and deceive people. This is especially true of those who insist on circumcision for salvation. [NLT] Εἰσὶ γὰρ πολλοὶ καὶ ἀνυπότακτοι, **ματαιολόγοι** καὶ φρεναπάται, μάλιστα οἱ ἐκ τῆς περιτομῆς, [GNS] Εἰσὶν γὰρ πολλοὶ [καὶ] ἀνυπότακτοι, **ματαιολόγοι** καὶ φρεναπάται, μάλιστα οἱ ἐκ τῆς περιτομῆς, [GNT]	Mere talkers, vain talkers, empty talkers, useless talk. **Practical Application** They were saying and teaching things that amounted to nothing and were worthless. Their teaching helped no one—not permanently and not eternally. Their teaching was not able to overcome sin and death—not able to bring true forgiveness of sin and eternal life to a person.
#4199 **Utterly Destroyed From** Destroyed–KJV **Utterly destroyed from–NASB** Completely cut off from–NIV **Utterly destroyed from–NKJV** Cut off from–NLT	**ἐξολεθρευθήσεται ἐκ** = *exolethreuthēsetai ek* Pronunciation: [ex-ol-eth-ryoo'-thay-seh-tah-ee ek] Parsing *exolethreuthēsetai* (part of speech): verb Mood—indicative or imperative Tense—future or aorist Voice—passive Person—3rd person Number—singular Stem or root—from **ἐξολεθρεύω** Concordance References: ⇒ Strong's #1537 + 1842 ek exolethreuō ⇒ NIV #1666 + 2017 ek exolethreuō ⇒ NASB #1537 + 1842 ek exolethreuō **Acts 3:23** And it shall come to pass, that every soul, which will	To be completely cut off from; to be utterly destroyed or slayed; to lose one's well-being; to be wasted and ruined and given a worthless existence. **Practical Application** It does not mean that a person will cease to exist. It means a person will be destroyed and devastated and condemned to a worthless existence. He will suffer waste and loss and ruin forever and ever.

ENGLISH WORD	GREEK WORD AND VERSE	THE WORD MEANS...
POSB REFERENCE (Acts 3:23) *Deeper Study #4*	not hear that prophet, shall be **destroyed** from among the people. [KJV] 'And it shall be that every soul that does not heed that prophet shall be **utterly destroyed from** among the people.' [NASB] Anyone who does not listen to him will be **completely cut off from** among his people.' [NIV] *And it shall be that every soul who will not hear that Prophet shall be **utterly destroyed from** among the people.'* [NKJV] Then Moses said, 'Anyone who will not listen to that Prophet will be **cut off from** God's people and utterly destroyed.' [NLT] ἔσται δὲ, πᾶσα ψυχὴ ἥτις ἐὰν μὴ ἀκούσῃ τοῦ προφήτου ἐκείνου, **ἐξολεθρευθήσεται ἐκ** τοῦ λαοῦ. [GNS] ἔσται δὲ πᾶσα ψυχὴ ἥτις ἐὰν μὴ ἀκούσῃ τοῦ προφήτου ἐκείνου **ἐξολεθρευθήσεται ἐκ** τοῦ λαοῦ. [GNT]	

#4200
Uttermost
 	
Uttermost–KJV
Forever–NASB
Completely–NIV
Uttermost–NKJV
Once and forever–NLT
 	
POSB REFERENCE (Heb.7:25) Note 1, point 3
	εἰς τὸ παντελές = *eis to panteles*
	Pronunciation: [ice to pan-tel-ehs]
	Parsing *panteles* (part of speech): pronominal adjective
	    Case—accusative
	    Gender—neuter
	    Number—singular
	    Stem or root—from παντελής, ές
	Concordance References:
	⇒ Strong's #1519+3588+3838 eis ho pantelēs
	⇒ NIV #1650+3836+4117 eis ho pantelēs [completely]
	⇒ NASB #1519+3588+3838 eis ho pantelēs
	
	Hebrews 7:25
	Wherefore he is able also to save them to the **uttermost** that come unto God by him, seeing he ever liveth to make intercession for them. [KJV]
	Hence, also, He is able to save **forever** those who draw near to God through Him, since He always lives to make intercession for them. [NASB]
	Therefore he is able to save **completely** those who come to God through him, because he always lives to intercede for them. [NIV]
	Therefore He is also able to save to the **uttermost** those who come to God through Him, since He always lives to make intercession for them. [NKJV]
	Therefore he is able, **once and forever**, to save everyone who comes to God through him. He lives forever to plead with God on their behalf. [NLT]
	ὅθεν καὶ σῴζειν **εἰς τὸ παντελὲς** δύναται τοὺς προσερχομένους δι' αὐτοῦ τῷ Θεῷ, πάντοτε ζῶν εἰς τὸ ἐντυγχάνειν ὑπὲρ αὐτῶν. [GNS]
	ὅθεν καὶ σῴζειν **εἰς τὸ παντελὲς** δύναται τοὺς προσερχομένους δι' αὐτοῦ τῷ Θεῷ, πάντοτε ζῶν εἰς τὸ ἐντυγχάνειν ὑπὲρ αὐτῶν. [GNT]
		Completely; to the uttermost; forever, once and forever.
		
		Practical Application
		Jesus Christ is able to save all persons to the uttermost. What does it mean to be saved completely, to the uttermost (*panteles*)? It means to be saved "completely, perfectly, finally and for all time and eternity" (Amplified New Testament). It means that Jesus Christ presents us to God as perfect. He presents us in His righteousness as perfected forever. Therefore in Christ—because He makes intercession for us and because He stands before God as the perfect and eternal sacrifice for our sins—we become acceptable to God. But it means much more. In outline form, when Jesus Christ saves us to the uttermost, it means...
		• that He saves us from sin, death and condemnation (John 5:24; Romans 8:34).
		• that He saves us to live with God eternally (John 3:16; Romans 8:39).
		• that He saves us to be the citizens of the new heaven and earth (2 Peter 3:10-13; Rev. 21:1f).
		• that He saves us to rule and reign over the universe right along with Him throughout all of eternity (Luke 12:42-44; Luke 22:28-29; 1 Cor. 6:2-3).

ENGLISH WORD	GREEK WORD AND VERSE	THE WORD MEANS...

#4201
Vain
 	
Vain–KJV
Vain–NASB
Useless–NIV
Empty–NKJV
Useless–NLT
 	
**POSB
REFERENCE**
(1 Cor.15:13-15; esp.
v.14)
Note 2, point 2
	κενòν = *kenon*
	Pronunciation: [ken-on']
	Parsing (part of speech): adjective
	    Case—nominative
	    Gender—neuter
	    Number—singular
	    Stem or root—from κενός, ή, όν
	Concordance References:
	  ⇒ Strong's #2756 kenos
	  ⇒ NIV #3031 kenos
	  ⇒ NASB #2756 kenos
	
	1 Cor. 15:14
	And if Christ be not risen, then is our preaching **vain**, and your faith is also vain. [KJV]
	And if Christ has not been raised, then our preaching is **vain**, your faith also is vain. [NASB]
	And if Christ has not been raised, our preaching is **useless** and so is your faith. [NIV]
	And if Christ is not risen, then our preaching *is* **empty** and your faith *is* also empty. [NKJV]
	And if Christ was not raised, then all our preaching is **useless**, and your trust in God is useless. [NLT]
	εἰ δὲ Χριστὸς οὐκ ἐγήγερται, **κενòν** ἄρα τὸ κήρυγμα ἡμῶν, κενὴ δὲ καὶ ἡ πίστις ὑμῶν, [GNS]
	εἰ δὲ Χριστὸς οὐκ ἐγήγερται, **κενòν** ἄρα [καὶ] τὸ κήρυγμα ἡμῶν, κενὴ καὶ ἡ πίστις ὑμῶν· [GNT]
		Useless, vain, empty, senseless, groundless, foolish, void of all truth and meaning.
		
		Practical Application
		How does denying the resurrection of the body make our preaching meaningless? There are two ways.
		1. The message we preach is the gospel (*good news*) of the resurrected Lord who has been raised to give us the glorious privilege:
		  ⇒ of living forever in the presence of God.
		  ⇒ of having a personal face-to-face relationship with God.
		  ⇒ of being made perfect and serving God face to face in a new heavens and earth.
		    There is no way *disembodied spirits* can serve God. What is a disembodied spirit anyway? It takes a *body*, a whole and real person, to serve God. If we are not to be whole and real persons, then we cannot be alive and serving God. The only way we can live with God eternally is for God to resurrect our bodies and make them perfect by changing their corruptible nature into an incorruptible nature.
		    Therefore, to deny the resurrection of Christ or of believers is to deny what we preach. Our preaching of the resurrected Lord and of our living forever is empty and meaningless. We may as well be doing something else; there is no need to preach a false hope.
		2. The message we preach is that Jesus Christ is the Son of God who died for our sins and rose again conquering death for us. The fact that God raised Him from the dead is the glorious proof that He is the Son of God, the proof that God accepted His sacrifice for our sins (Romans 1:4). If Christ did not arise, then it means that God left Him in the grave, that He is no more than what other men are, a man doomed to die and remain in the grave forever with all other men. But if God did raise Christ up from the grave, then it means that death is conquered and that He will raise us up to live forever with Him.
		    The point is this: if there is no resurrection—no resurrection of Christ and no resurrection of us—then the consequence is terrible. Jesus Christ is not the Son of God. What we are preaching is empty and meaningless. We may as well keep quiet.

#4202
Vain
 	
Vain–KJV
Worthless–NASB
Futile–NIV
Futile–NKJV
Useless–NLT
 	
**POSB
REFERENCE**
(1 Cor.15:16-19; esp.
v.17)
Note 3, point 2
	ματαία = *mataia*
	Pronunciation: [mat'-ah-ee-ah]
	Parsing (part of speech): adjective
	    Case—nominative
	    Gender—feminine
	    Number—singular
	    Stem or root—from μάταιος, α, ον
	Concordance References:
	  ⇒ Strong's #3152 mataios
	  ⇒ NIV #3469 mataios
	  ⇒ NASB #3152 mataios
	
	1 Cor. 15:17
	And if Christ be not raised, your faith is **vain**; ye are yet in your sins. [KJV]
	And if Christ has not been raised, your faith is **worthless**; you are still in your sins. [NASB]
		Fruitless or futile; that is, we are still in our sins; worthless; useless.
		
		Practical Application
		To deny the resurrection (either of Christ or of us) means that our faith is vain (*mataia*). If Jesus Christ has not risen from the dead, then He is still dead, still in the grave; therefore, there is no redemption, no forgiveness of sins.

ENGLISH WORD	GREEK WORD AND VERSE	THE WORD MEANS...
	And if Christ has not been raised, your faith is **futile**; you are still in your sins. [NIV] And if Christ is not risen, your faith *is* **futile**; you are still in your sins! [NKJV] And if Christ has not been raised, then your faith is **useless**, and you are still under condemnation for your sins. [NLT] εἰ δὲ Χριστὸς οὐκ ἐγήγερται, **ματαία** ἡ πίστις ὑμῶν· ἔτι ἐστὲ ἐν ταῖς ἁμαρτίαις ὑμῶν. [GNS] εἰ δὲ Χριστὸς οὐκ ἐγήγερται, **ματαία** ἡ πίστις ὑμῶν, ἔτι ἐστὲ ἐν ταῖς ἁμαρτίαις ὑμῶν, [GNT]	

#4203
Vain
 	
Vain–KJV
Futile–NASB
Futile–NIV
Futile–NKJV
Foolish–NLT
 	
POSB
REFERENCE
(Romans 1:21)
Note 4, point 1
	ἐματαιώθησαν = *emataiōthēsan*
	Pronunciation: [eh-mat-ah-i'-o-thay-sahn]
	Parsing (part of speech): verb
	    Mood—indicative
	    Tense—aorist
	    Voice—passive
	    Person—3rd person
	    Number—plural
	    Stem or root—from ματαιόομαι
	Concordance References:
	  ⇒ Strong's #3154 mataioö
	  ⇒ NIV #3471 mataioö
	  ⇒ NASB #3154 mataioö
	
	Romans 1:21
	Because that, when they knew God, they glorified him not as God, neither were thankful; but became **vain** in their imaginations, and their foolish heart was darkened. [KJV]
	
	For even though they knew God, they did not honor Him as God, or give thanks; but they became **futile** in their speculations, and their foolish heart was darkened. [NASB]
	
	For although they knew God, they neither glorified him as God nor gave thanks to him, but their thinking became **futile** and their foolish hearts were darkened. [NIV]
	
	Because, although they knew God, they did not glorify *Him* as God, nor were thankful, but became **futile** in their thoughts, and their foolish hearts were darkened. [NKJV]
	
	Yes, they knew God, but they wouldn't worship him as God or even give him thanks. And they began to think up **foolish** ideas of what God was like. The result was that their minds became dark and confused. [NLT]
	
	διότι γνόντες τὸν Θεὸν οὐχ ὡς Θεὸν ἐδόξασαν η ηὐχαρίστησαν, ἀλλ' **ἐματαιώθησαν** ἐν τοῖς διαλογισμοῖς αὐτῶν, καὶ ἐσκοτίσθη ἡ ἀσύνετος αὐτῶν καρδία. [GNS]
	
	διότι γνόντες τὸν Θεὸν οὐχ ὡς Θεὸν ἐδόξασαν η ηὐχαρίστησαν, ἀλλ' **ἐματαιώθησαν** ἐν τοῖς διαλογισμοῖς αὐτῶν καὶ ἐσκοτίσθη ἡ ἀσύνετος αὐτῶν καρδία. [GNT]
		To be given to worthless or futile speculation. The word vain means empty, futile, unsuccessful, senseless, worthless.
		
		Practical Application
		The mind of man has been affected by sin. It desperately needs to be renewed. The mind is far from perfect. It is *basically worldly*, that is...
		• selfish
		• self-centered
		• self-seeking
		• centered on this world
		• centered on the flesh
		• centered on this life
		
		Scripture is clear about the corruption of man's mind. The human mind has been tragically corrupted by man's selfishness and sin.

#4204
Vain Babblings
 	
Vain babblings–KJV
Empty chatter–NASB
Chatter–NIV
Idle babblings–NKJV
Foolish discussions–
  NLT
 	
POSB
REFERENCE
(1 Tim.6:20)
Note 2, point 2a
	κενοφωνίας = *kenophönias*
	Pronunciation: [ken-of-o-nee'-ahs]
	Parsing (part of speech): noun
	    Case—accusative
	    Gender—feminine
	    Number—plural
	    Stem or root—from κενοφωνία, ας
	Concordance References:
	  ⇒ Strong's #2757 kenophönia
	  ⇒ NIV #3032 kenophönia
	  ⇒ NASB #2757 kenophönia
	
	1 Tim. 6:20
	O Timothy, keep that which is committed to thy trust, avoiding profane and **vain babblings**, and oppositions of science falsely so called: [KJV]
	
	O Timothy, guard what has been entrusted to you,
		Chatter; vain babblings; idle babblings; empty chatter; foolish discussions; foolish talk.
		
		Practical Application
		The charge is to take all *empty talk* and turn away from it. Have absolutely nothing to do with common, irreverent, godless, and *empty voices*—no matter who is sounding forth the words. This would, of course, include...
		⇒ false claims to truth
		⇒ worldly philosophy
		⇒ cursing
		⇒ criticism
		⇒ suggestive talk
		⇒ all forms of false teaching
		⇒ novel ideas of religion

ENGLISH WORD	GREEK WORD AND VERSE	THE WORD MEANS...

	avoiding worldly and **empty chatter** and the opposing arguments of what is falsely called "knowledge"— [NASB]
	
	    Timothy, guard what has been entrusted to your care. Turn away from godless **chatter** and the opposing ideas of what is falsely called knowledge, [NIV]
	
	    O Timothy! Guard what was committed to your trust, avoiding the profane and **idle babblings** and contradictions of what is falsely called knowledge— [NKJV]
	
	    Timothy, guard what God has entrusted to you. Avoid godless, **foolish discussions** with those who oppose you with their so-called knowledge. [NLT]
	
	    Ὦ Τιμόθεε, τὴν παρακαταθήκην φύλαξον, ἐκτρεπόμενος τὰς βεβήλους **κενοφωνίας** καὶ ἀντιθέσεις τῆς ψευδωνύμου γνώσεως· [GNS]
	
	    Ὦ Τιμόθεε, τὴν παραθήκην φύλαξον ἐκτρεπόμενος τὰς βεβήλους **κενοφωνίας** καὶ ἀντιθέσεις τῆς ψευδωνύμου γνώσεως, [GNT]
		⇒ gossip
		⇒ off-colored jokes

#4205
## Vain Repetitions 	
 	
Vain repetitions–KJV
Meaningless repetitions–NASB
Babbling–NIV
Vain repetitions–NKJV
Babble–NLT
 	
POSB REFERENCE
(Mt.6:7)
Deeper Study #1
	βατταλογήσητε = *battologesete*
	Pronunciation: [bat-tol-og-ehs'-tay]
	Parsing (part of speech): verb
	    Mood—subjunctive or imperative
	    Tense—aorist
	    Voice—active
	    Person—2nd person
	    Number—plural
	    Stem or root—from βατταλογέω
	Concordance References:
	  ⇒ Strong's #945 battalogeö
	  ⇒ NIV #1006 battalogeö
	  ⇒ NASB #945 battalogeö
	
	### Matthew 6:7
	But when ye pray, use not **vain repetitions**, as the heathen do: for they think that they shall be heard for their much speaking. [KJV]
	
	    "And when you are praying, do not use **meaningless repetition**, as the Gentiles do, for they suppose that they will be heard for their many words. [NASB]
	
	    And when you pray, do not keep on **babbling** like pagans, for they think they will be heard because of their many words. [NIV]
	
	    And when you pray, do not use **vain repetitions** as the heathen do. For they think that they will be heard for their many words. [NKJV]
	
	    "When you pray, don't **babble** on and on as people of other religions do. They think their prayers are answered only by repeating their words again and again. [NLT]
	
	    Προσευχόμενοι δὲ μὴ **βατταλογήσητε**, ὥσπερ οἱ ἐθνικοί· δοκοῦσι γὰρ ὅτι ἐν τῇ πολυλογίᾳ αὐτῶν εἰσακουσθήσονται. [GNS]
	
	    Προσευχόμενοι δὲ μὴ **βατταλογήσητε** ὥσπερ οἱ ἐθνικοί, δοκοῦσιν γὰρ ὅτι ἐν τῇ πολυλογίᾳ αὐτῶν εἰσακουσθήσονται. [GNT]
		To babble much; to use many phrases; to speak idle or vain words; to speak meaningless words.
		
		### Practical Application
		The phrase "vain repetitions" (*battologesete*) means at least two things.
		1. It means saying the same words over and over again without putting one's heart and thought into what is being said.
		2. It means using certain religious words or phrases (sometimes over and over again) and thinking God hears because one is using such religious talk.

#4206
## Vain Talkers 	
 	
Vain talkers–KJV
Empty talkers–NASB
Mere talkers–NIV
Idle talkers–NKJV
Useless talk–NLT
 	
POSB REFERENCE
(Tit.1:10-12; esp. v.10)
Note 1, point 2
	ματαιολόγοι = *mataiologoi*
	Pronunciation: [mat-ah-yol-og'-oy]
	Parsing (part of speech): pronominal adjective
	    Case—nominative
	    Gender—masculine
	    Number—plural
	    Stem or root—from ματαιολόγος, ου
	Concordance References:
	  ⇒ Strong's #3151 mataiologos
	  ⇒ NIV #3468 mataiologos
	  ⇒ NASB #3151 mataiologos
	
	### Titus 1:10
	For there are many unruly and **vain talkers** and deceivers, specially they of the circumcision: [KJV]
	
	    For there are many rebellious men, **empty talkers** and deceivers, especially those of the circumcision,
		Mere talkers, vain talkers, empty talkers, useless talk.
		
		### Practical Application
		They were saying and teaching things that amounted to nothing and were worthless. Their teaching helped no one—not permanently and not eternally. Their teaching was not able to overcome sin and death—not able to bring true forgiveness of sin and eternal life to a person.

ENGLISH WORD	GREEK WORD AND VERSE	THE WORD MEANS...
	[NASB] For there are many rebellious people, **mere talkers** and deceivers, especially those of the circumcision group. [NIV] For there are many insubordinate, both **idle talkers** and deceivers, especially those of the circumcision, [NKJV] For there are many who rebel against right teaching; they engage in **useless talk** and deceive people. This is especially true of those who insist on circumcision for salvation. [NLT] Εἰσὶ γὰρ πολλοὶ καὶ ἀνυπότακτοι, **ματαιολόγοι** καὶ φρεναπάται, μάλιστα οἱ ἐκ τῆς περιτομῆς, [GNS] Εἰσὶν γὰρ πολλοὶ [καὶ] ἀνυπότακτοι, **ματαιολόγοι** καὶ φρεναπάται, μάλιστα οἱ ἐκ τῆς περιτομῆς, [GNT]	

#4207
Valid
 	
True–KJV
True–NASB
Valid–NIV
True–NKJV
Valid–NLT
 	
POSB REFERENCE
(Jn.8:14)
Note 2
 	
See also POSB REF:
(Philip.4:8-9; esp. v.8)
Note 2
	ἀληθής = alëthës
	Pronunciation: [al-ay-thace']
	Parsing (part of speech): adjective
	    Case—nominative
	    Gender—feminine
	    Number—singular
	    Stem or root—from ἀληθής, ές
	Concordance References:
	  ⇒ Strong's #227 alëthës
	  ⇒ NIV #239 alëthës
	  ⇒ NASB #227 alëthës
	
	John 8:14
	Jesus answered and said unto them, Though I bear record of myself, yet my record is **true**: for I know whence I came, and whither I go; but ye cannot tell whence I come, and whither I go. [KJV]
	Jesus answered and said to them, "Even if I bear witness of Myself, My witness is **true**; for I know where I came from, and where I am going; but you do not know where I come from, or where I am going. [NASB]
	Jesus answered, "Even if I testify on my own behalf, my testimony is **valid**, for I know where I came from and where I am going. But you have no idea where I come from or where I am going. [NIV]
	Jesus answered and said to them, "Even if I bear witness of Myself, My witness is **true**, for I know where I came from and where I am going; but you do not know where I come from and where I am going. [NKJV]
	Jesus told them, "These claims are **valid** even though I make them about myself. For I know where I came from and where I am going, but you don't know this about me. [NLT]
	ἀπεκρίθη Ἰησοῦς καὶ εἶπεν αὐτοῖς, Κἂν ἐγὼ μαρτυρῶ περὶ ἐμαυτοῦ, **ἀληθής** ἐστιν ἡ μαρτυρία μου· ὅτι οἶδα πόθεν ἦλθον, καὶ ποῦ ὑπάγω. ὑμεῖς δὲ οὐκ οἴδατε πόθεν ἔρχομαι, καὶ ποῦ ὑπάγω. [GNS]
	ἀπεκρίθη Ἰησοῦς καὶ εἶπεν αὐτοῖς, Κἂν ἐγὼ μαρτυρῶ περὶ ἐμαυτοῦ, **ἀληθής** ἐστιν ἡ μαρτυρία μου, ὅτι οἶδα πόθεν ἦλθον καὶ ποῦ ὑπάγω· ὑμεῖς δὲ οὐκ οἴδατε πόθεν ἔρχομαι η ποῦ ὑπάγω. [GNT]
		To be valid; to be true; to be accurate; to be factual, bona fide, genuine, real.
		
		Practical Application
		Jesus knew His origin and destiny. He declared, "I am the Light of the world," and He declared that His witness was enough. He said, "My testimony is valid" (alëthës).
		⇒ It is not false.
		⇒ It is not a lie.
		⇒ It is not a deceptive claim.
		⇒ It is not the claim of an egomaniac setting Himself up as a *god*.
		⇒ It is not the claim of a man who is out to shatter men's dreams.
		⇒ It is not the claim of a man who is set on destroying men.
		
		The witness of Jesus Christ was valid, and His witness was sufficient evidence for a very strong reason. Jesus knew His origin and destiny, where He had come from and where He was going. He was "*out of*" heaven, "*out of*" the spiritual dimension of being, and He was to return to heaven.

#4208
Valued Highly
 	
Dear–KJV
Highly regarded–NASB
Valued highly–NIV
Dear–NKJV
Highly valued–NLT
 	
POSB REFERENCE
(Lk.7:2)
Note 2
	ἦν ἔντιμος = ën entimos
	Pronunciation: [ayn en'-tee-mos]
	Parsing *ën* (part of speech):verb
	    Mood—indicative
	    Tense—imperfect
	    Voice—active
	    Person—3rd person
	    Number—singular
	    Stem or root—from εἰμί
	Parsing *entimos* (part of speech): adjective
	    Case—nominative
	    Gender—masculine
	    Number—singular
	    Stem or root—from ἔντιμος, ον
	Concordance References:
	  ⇒ Strong's #1488 eimi + 1784 entimos
	  ⇒ NIV #1639 eimi + 1952 entimos
	  ⇒ NASB #1488 eimi + 1784 entimos
		Valued highly, to be highly regarded; to be held dear, esteemed, honored, distinguished, precious, prized.
		
		Practical Application
		In the society of that day, a slave was nothing, only a tool or a thing to be used as the owner wished. He had no rights whatsoever, not even the right to live. An owner could mistreat or kill a slave without having to give an account. But this soldier loved his slave. This reveals a deep concern and care for people. It would have been much less bother to dispose of the slave or to ignore him and just let him die, but not this soldier. He cared. Note how he personally looked after the slave, a person who meant nothing to the rest of society.

ENGLISH WORD	GREEK WORD AND VERSE	THE WORD MEANS...
	Luke 7:2 And a certain centurion's servant, who was **dear** unto him, was sick, and ready to die. [KJV] And a certain centurion's slave, who was **highly regarded** by him, was sick and about to die. [NASB] There a centurion's servant, whom his master **valued highly**, was sick and about to die. [NIV] And a certain centurion's servant, who was **dear** to him, was sick and ready to die. [NKJV] Now the **highly valued** slave of a Roman officer was sick and near death. [NLT] Ἑκατοντάρχου δέ τινος δοῦλος κακῶς ἔχων ἤμελλε τελευτᾶν, ὃς ἦν αὐτῷ ἔντιμος. [GNS] Ἑκατοντάρχου δέ τινος δοῦλος κακῶς ἔχων ἤμελλεν τελευτᾶν, ὃς ἦν αὐτῷ ἔντιμος. [GNT]	

#4209
Vanity
 	
Vanity–KJV
Futility–NASB
Frustration–NIV
Futility–NKJV
Curse–NLT
 	
**POSB
REFERENCE**
(Romans 8:19-22, esp.
v.20)
Note 2, point 1
	ματαιότητι = mataiotēti
	Pronunciation: [mat-ah-yot'-ay-tee]
	Parsing (part of speech): noun
	    Case—dative
	    Gender—feminine
	    Number—singular
	    Stem or root—from ματαιότης, ητος
	Concordance References:
	⇒ Strong's #3153 mataiotēs
	⇒ NIV #3470 mataiotēs
	⇒ NASB #3153 mataiotēs
	
	Romans 8:20
	For the creature was made subject to **vanity**, not willingly, but by reason of him who hath subjected the same in hope, [KJV]
	For the creation was subjected to **futility**, not of its own will, but because of Him who subjected it, in hope [NASB]
	For the creation was subjected to **frustration**, not by its own choice, but by the will of the one who subjected it, in hope [NIV]
	For the creation was subjected to **futility**, not willingly, but because of Him who subjected *it* in hope; [NKJV]
	Against its will, everything on earth was subjected to God's **curse**. [NLT]
	τῇ γὰρ **ματαιότητι** ἡ κτίσις ὑπετάγη, οὐχ ἑκοῦσα ἀλλὰ διὰ τὸν ὑποτάξαντα, ἐφ' ἑλπίδι· [GNS]
	τῇ γὰρ **ματαιότητι** ἡ κτίσις ὑπετάγη, οὐχ ἑκοῦσα ἀλλὰ διὰ τὸν ὑποτάξαντα, ἐφ' ἑλπίδι [GNT]
		Worthlessness, futility; emptiness, frustration; cursed.
		
		Practical Application
		Creation is subject to corruption. This is clearly seen by men; and what men see is constantly confirmed by such authorities as the botanist, zoologist, geologist, and astronomer of the world. All of creation, whether mineral, plant, or animal, suffers just as men do. All creation suffers hurt, damage, loss, deterioration, erosion, death, and decay—all creation struggles for life. It is full of "vanity" (*mataiotēti*), that is, condemned to futility and frustration, unable to realize its purpose, subject to corruption.

#4210
Vanity
 	
Vanity–KJV
Futility–NASB
Futility–NIV
Futility–NKJV
Hopelessly con-
  fused–NLT
 	
**POSB
REFERENCE**
(Eph.4:17-19; esp.
v.17)
Note 1, point 1
	ματαιότητι = mataiotēti
	Pronunciation: [mat-ah-yot'-ay-tee]
	Parsing (part of speech): noun
	    Case—dative
	    Gender—feminine
	    Number—singular
	    Stem or root—from ματαιότης, ητος
	Concordance References:
	⇒ Strong's #3153 mataiotēs
	⇒ NIV #3470 mataiotēs
	⇒ NASB #3153 mataiotēs
	
	Ephes. 4:17
	This I say therefore, and testify in the Lord, that ye henceforth walk not as other Gentiles walk, in the **vanity** of their mind, [KJV]
	This I say therefore, and affirm together with the Lord, that you walk no longer just as the Gentiles also walk, in the **futility** of their mind, [NASB]
	So I tell you this, and insist on it in the Lord, that you must no longer live as the Gentiles do, in the **futility** of their thinking. [NIV]
	This I say, therefore, and testify in the Lord, that you should no longer walk as the rest of the Gentiles walk, in the **futility** of their mind, [NKJV]
	With the Lord's authority let me say this: Live no
		Futility, vanity; emptiness, frustration; to be hopelessly confused; to be empty, futile, senseless, aimless, unsuccessful, worthless.
		
		Practical Application
		When men push God out of their minds, their minds are void and empty of God, of His truth and morality. *God is not in their thoughts.* Their minds are ready to be filled with some other god or supremacy, that is, with the things of the world:
		⇒ worldly pleasures
		⇒ worldly possessions
		⇒ worldly power
		⇒ worldly position
		⇒ worldly religions
		⇒ worldly ideas
		⇒ worldly honor
		⇒ worldly gods

ENGLISH WORD	GREEK WORD AND VERSE	THE WORD MEANS...
Vengeance–NLT **POSB REFERENCE** (Lk.21:22) *Deeper Study #1*	Concordance References: ⇒ Strong's #1557 ekdikēsis ⇒ NIV #1689 ekdikēsis ⇒ NASB #1557 ekdikēsis **Luke 21:22** For these be the days of **vengeance**, that all things which are written may be fulfilled. [KJV] Because these are days of **vengeance**, in order that all things which are written may be fulfilled. [NASB] For this is the time of **punishment** in fulfillment of all that has been written. [NIV] For these are the days of **vengeance**, that all things which are written may be fulfilled. [NKJV] For those will be days of God's **vengeance**, and the prophetic words of the Scriptures will be fulfilled. [NLT] ὅτι ἡμέραι **ἐκδικήσεως** αὐταί εἰσι, τοῦ πληρωθῆναι πάντα τὰ γεγραμμένα. [GNS] ὅτι ἡμέραι **ἐκδικήσεως** αὐταί εἰσιν τοῦ πλησθῆναι πάντα τὰ γεγραμμένα. [GNT]	self-gratification or selfish reaction in the word at all. It is judgment that executes perfect justice. It is judgment that makes things right, exactly as they should be.

#4215
Very Heavy
 	
Very heavy–KJV
Distressed–NASB
Troubled–NIV
Deeply distressed–NKJV
Deep distress–NLT
 	
POSB REFERENCE
(Mt.26:37)
Deeper Study #3
 	
See also POSB REF:
(Mk.14:33-34; esp. v.33)
Note 2
	ἀδημονεῖν = adēmonein
	Pronunciation: [ad-ay-mon-een]
	Parsing (part of speech): verb
	  Mood—infinitive
	  Tense—present
	  Voice—active
	  Stem or root—from ἀδημονέω
	Concordance References:
	⇒ Strong's #85 adēmoneō
	⇒ NIV #86 adēmoneō
	⇒ NASB #85 adēmoneō
	
	Matthew 26:37
	And he took with him Peter and the two sons of Zebedee, and began to be sorrowful and **very heavy**. [KJV]
	And He took with Him Peter and the two sons of Zebedee, and began to be grieved and **distressed**. [NASB]
	He took Peter and the two sons of Zebedee along with him, and he began to be sorrowful and **troubled**. [NIV]
	And He took with Him Peter and the two sons of Zebedee, and He began to be sorrowful and **deeply distressed**. [NKJV]
	He took Peter and Zebedee's two sons, James and John, and he began to be filled with anguish and **deep distress**. [NLT]
	καὶ παραλαβὼν τὸν Πέτρον καὶ τοὺς δύο υἱοὺς Ζεβεδαίου, ἤρξατο λυπεῖσθαι καὶ **ἀδημονεῖν**. [GNS]
	καὶ παραλαβὼν τὸν Πέτρον καὶ τοὺς δύο υἱοὺς Ζεβεδαίου ἤρξατο λυπεῖσθαι καὶ **ἀδημονεῖν**. [GNT]
		To be troubled, dismayed, disturbed. It means to be *gripped* with intense heaviness of soul.
		
		Practical Application
		Troubled, very heavy, or *distressed* pictures the trouble and dismay that is caused by an *unexpected calamity*. It is consternation, a heaviness that drives a man to be alone, for he is unfit for company. He desperately needs quiet, and he needs a few companions who understand and can help bear the trouble.

#4216
Vessel
 	
Vessel–KJV
Vessel–NASB
Body–NIV
Vessel–NKJV
Body–NLT
 	
POSB REFERENCE
(1 Thes.4:3-5; esp. v.4)
Note 2, point 2
	σκεῦος = skeuos
	Pronunciation: [skyoo'-os]
	Parsing (part of speech): noun
	  Case—accusative
	  Gender—neuter
	  Number—singular
	  Stem or root—
	Concordance References:
	⇒ Strong's #4632 skeuos
	⇒ NIV #5007 skeuos
	⇒ NASB #4632 skeuos
	
	1 Thes. 4:4
	That every one of you should know how to possess his **vessel** in sanctification and honour; [KJV]
	That each of you know how to possess his own **vessel** in sanctification and honor, [NASB]
	That each of you should learn to control his own **body** in a way that is holy and honorable, [NIV]
	That each of you should know how to possess his own **vessel** in sanctification and honor, [NKJV]
		Body, vessel.
		
		Practical Application
		Sanctification means that a person knows how to control his body and his spouse. Leon Morris points out that the word body or "vessel" (*skeuos*) can refer either to a person's own body or to a person's spouse (*The Epistles of Paul to the Thessalonians,* "Tyndale New Testament Commentaries," p.75). Both hold great meaning for the Christian believer. A believer is to know how to control his own body and how to control his spouse. A person can neglect, ignore, and abuse his body and a person can neglect, ignore, and abuse his or her spouse. In discussing a person's spouse it is important to note 1 Cor. 7:4-5. Neglecting, ignoring, or abusing one's spouse can bring about temptation and can contribute significantly to the spouse becoming unfaithful and impure.

ENGLISH WORD	GREEK WORD AND VERSE	THE WORD MEANS...
	Then each of you will control your **body** and live in holiness and honor—[NLT] εἰδέναι ἕκαστον ὑμῶν τὸ ἑαυτοῦ **σκεῦος** κτᾶσθαι ἐν ἁγιασμῷ καὶ τιμῇ [GNS] εἰδέναι ἕκαστον ὑμῶν τὸ ἑαυτοῦ **σκεῦος** κτᾶσθαι ἐν ἁγιασμῷ καὶ τιμῇ, [GNT]	Note that the believer is to *learn how to control*, to possess his or her body and spouse in a way that is holy and honorable. There is no excuse for ignorance in this matter nor for disobedience. The believer is to learn that it is his duty to keep his body and spouse pure, learn this... • beyond a shadow of a doubt • without equivocation • without question The point is strong: it is unthinkable that a believer would engage in sexual immorality, that he would bring dishonor to his Lord and to his spouse, family, and himself. The believing husband and wife are to know that they must keep themselves and each other in sanctification and honor. They must not give themselves to dishonorable and immoral neighbors nor to harlots.

#4217
Vex
 	
Vex–KJV
Mistreat–NASB
Persecute–NIV
Harass–NKJV
Persecute–NLT
 	
POSB REFERENCE
(Acts 12:1-4, esp. v.1)
Note 1, point 1
	κακῶσαί = *kakōsai*
	Pronunciation: [kak-o'-sah-ee]
	Parsing (part of speech): verb
	    Mood—infinitive
	    Tense—aorist
	    Voice—active
	    Stem or root—from *κακόω*
	Concordance References:
	⇒ Strong's #2559 kakoö
	⇒ NIV #2808 kakoö
	⇒ NASB #2559 kakoö
	
	Acts 12:1
	Now about that time Herod the king stretched forth his hands to **vex** certain of the church. [KJV]
	Now about that time Herod the king laid hands on some who belonged to the church, in order to **mistreat** them. [NASB]
	It was about this time that King Herod arrested some who belonged to the church, intending to **persecute** them. [NIV]
	Now about that time Herod the king stretched out his hand to **harass** some from the church. [NKJV]
	About that time King Herod Agrippa began to **persecute** some believers in the church. [NLT]
	Κατ' ἐκεῖνον δὲ τὸν καιρὸν ἐπέβαλεν Ἡρῴδης ὁ βασιλεὺς τὰς χεῖρας **κακῶσαί** τινας τῶν ἀπὸ τῆς ἐκκλησίας. [GNS]
	Κατ' ἐκεῖνον δὲ τὸν καιρὸν ἐπέβαλεν Ἡρῴδης ὁ βασιλεὺς τὰς χεῖρας **κακῶσαί** τινας τῶν ἀπὸ τῆς ἐκκλησίας. [GNT]
		To persecute; to mistreat; to vex; to harass; to oppress, torment, do evil against, harm; to be cruel.
		
		Practical Application
		Certain leaders in the church were arrested and imprisoned and apparently tortured. A person can just imagine believers' being man-handled and molested as the persecuted of every generation so often are with their homes and property being destroyed and confiscated or stolen.

#4218
Viewed Others With Contempt
 	
Despised–KJV
Viewed others with contempt–NASB
Looked down on–NIV
Despised–NKJV
Scorned–NLT
 	
POSB REFERENCE
(Lk.18:9)
Note 1, point 3
	ἐξουθενοῦντας = *exouthenountas*
	Pronunciation: [ex-oo-then-oon'-tas]
	Parsing (part of speech): verb
	    Mood—participle
	    Tense—present
	    Voice—active
	    Case—accusative
	    Gender—masculine
	    Number—plural
	    Stem or root—from *ἐξουθενέω*
	Concordance References:
	⇒ Strong's #1848 exoutheneö
	⇒ NIV #2024 exoutheneö
	⇒ NASB #1848 exoutheneö
	
	Luke 18:9
	And he spake this parable unto certain which trusted in themselves that they were righteous, and **despised** others: [KJV]
	And He also told this parable to certain ones who trust-
		To despise; to view others with contempt; to look down on; to scorn; to set at naught; to count as nothing, as unimportant and insignificant.
		
		Practical Application
		Such persons feel and act as though they are above and better, more important and significant, than others. They shy away from, ignore and neglect, pass by and downgrade, criticize and talk about...
		• the poor
		• the unfortunate
		• the poorly dressed
		• the homeless
		• the downcast
		• the derelict
		• the undernourished

ENGLISH WORD	GREEK WORD AND VERSE	THE WORD MEANS...
	public debate. Using the Scriptures, he explained to them, "The Messiah you are looking for is Jesus." [NLT] εὐτόνως γὰρ τοῖς Ἰουδαίοις διακατηλέγχετο δημοσίᾳ ἐπιδεικνὺς διὰ τῶν γραφῶν εἶναι τὸν Χριστὸν, Ἰησοῦν. [GNS] εὐτόνως γὰρ τοῖς Ἰουδαίοις διακατηλέγχετο δημοσίᾳ ἐπιδεικνὺς διὰ τῶν γραφῶν εἶναι τὸν Χριστὸν Ἰησοῦν. [GNT]	

#4223
Vile Affections, Passions
 	
Vile affections–KJV
Degrading passions–NASB
Shameful lusts–NIV
Vile passions–NKJV
Shameful desires–NLT
 	
POSB REFERENCE
(Romans 1:26-27; esp. v.26)
Note 3, point 1
	πάθη ἀτιμίας = pathë atimias
	Pronunciation: [path'-ay at-ee-mee'-ahs]
	Parsing pathë (part of speech): noun
	  Case—accusative
	  Gender—neuter
	  Number—plural
	  Stem or root—from πάθος, ους
	Parsing atimias (part of speech): noun
	  Case—genitive
	  Gender—feminine
	  Number—singular
	  Stem or root—from ἀτιμία, ας
	Concordance References:
	  ⇒ Strong's #3806 pathos + 819 atimia
	  ⇒ NIV #4079 pathos [lusts] + 871 atimia [shameful]
	  ⇒ NASB #3806 pathos + 819 atimia
	
	Romans 1:26
	For this cause God gave them up unto **vile affections**: for even their women did change the natural use into that which is against nature: [KJV]
	For this reason God gave them over to **degrading passions**; for their women exchanged the natural function for that which is unnatural, [NASB]
	Because of this, God gave them over to **shameful lusts**. Even their women exchanged natural relations for unnatural ones. [NIV]
	For this reason God gave them up to **vile passions**. For even their women exchanged the natural use for what is against nature. [NKJV]
	That is why God abandoned them to their **shameful desires**. Even the women turned against the natural way to have sex and instead indulged in sex with each other. [NLT]
	Διὰ τοῦτο παρέδωκεν αὐτοὺς ὁ Θεὸς εἰς **πάθη ἀτιμίας**· αἵ τε γὰρ θήλειαι αὐτῶν μετήλλαξαν τὴν φυσικὴν χρῆσιν εἰς τὴν παρὰ φύσιν· [GNS]
	διὰ τοῦτο παρέδωκεν αὐτοὺς ὁ θεὸς εἰς **πάθη ἀτιμίας**, αἵ τε γὰρ θήλειαι αὐτῶν μετήλλαξαν τὴν φυσικὴν χρῆσιν εἰς τὴν παρὰ φύσιν, [GNT]
		Shameful lusts, vile affections, degrading passions, shameful desires. It means to be dishonored, disgraced, shamed, and degraded. It means passions that cannot be controlled or governed, that run loose and wild, no matter how much a person tries to control them.
		
		Practical Application
		The reason God gives men up to vile affections (pathë atimias) is because of their unnatural passion. Men lust and lust, craving the illegitimate and unlawful. They burn in their lust one for another. And note what Scripture is talking about: unnatural affection, that is, homosexuality.
		  ⇒ Women burn and lust and exchange the "natural use into that which is against nature." [KJV] And note, it is against nature.
		  ⇒ Men burn in their "lust one toward another; men with men doing that which is shameful." (Rom.1:27) [KJV]

#4224
Villainy
 	
All subtilty–KJV
All deceit–NASB
All...deceit–NIV
All deceit–NKJV
Villainy–NLT
 	
POSB REFERENCE
(Acts 13:8-11; esp. v.10)
Note 4, point 3
	παντὸς δόλου = pantos dolou
	Pronunciation: [pahn-tos dol'-oo]
	Parsing pantos (part of speech): adjective
	  Case—genative
	  Gender—masculine
	  Number—singular
	  Stem or root—from πᾶς
	Parsing dolou [deceit] (part of speech): noun
	  Case—genative
	  Gender—masculine
	  Number—singular
	  Stem or root—from δόλος
	Concordance References:
	  ⇒ Strong's #3956 pas + 1388 dolos
	  ⇒ NIV #4246 pas + 1515 dolos
	  ⇒ NASB #3956 pas + 1388 dolos
	
	Acts 13:10
	And said, O full of **all subtilty** and all mischief, thou child of the devil, thou enemy of all righteousness, wilt thou not cease to pervert the right ways of the Lord? [KJV]
	And said, "You who are full of **all deceit** and fraud, you son of the devil, you enemy of all righteousness, will
		All deceit, subtilty, villainy, treachery.
		
		Practical Application
		It means to be full of all craftiness, guile, trickery, deceit, treachery, seeking to bait and catch, to enslave in error and untruth.

ENGLISH WORD	GREEK WORD AND VERSE	THE WORD MEANS...
	you not cease to make crooked the straight ways of the Lord? [NASB] "You are a child of the devil and an enemy of everything that is right! You are full of **all** kinds of **deceit** and trickery. Will you never stop perverting the right ways of the Lord? [NIV] And said, "O full of **all deceit** and all fraud, you son of the devil, you enemy of all righteousness, will you not cease perverting the straight ways of the Lord? [NKJV] "You son of the Devil, full of every sort of trickery and **villainy**, enemy of all that is good, will you never stop perverting the true ways of the Lord? [NLT] εἶπεν, Ὦ πλήρης **παντὸς δόλου** καὶ πάσης ῥᾳδιουργίας, υἱὲ διαβόλου, ἐχθρὲ πάσης δικαιοσύνης, οὐ παύσῃ διαστρέφων τὰς ὁδοὺς Κυρίου τὰς εὐθείας; [GNS] εἶπεν, Ὦ πλήρης **παντὸς δόλου** καὶ πάσης ῥᾳδιουργίας, υἱὲ διαβόλου, ἐχθρὲ πάσης δικαιοσύνης, οὐ παύσῃ διαστρέφων τὰς ὁδοὺς [τοῦ] κυρίου τὰς εὐθείας; [GNT]	

#4225
Violation
 	
Transgression–KJV
Transgression–NASB
Violation–NIV
Transgression–NKJV
Violation of the law–NLT
 	
POSB REFERENCE
(Hcb.2:2)
Note 2
	παράβασις = *parabasis*
	Pronunciation: [par-ab'-as-is]
	Parsing (part of speech): noun
	  Case—nominative
	  Gender—feminine
	  Number—singular
	  Stem or root—from παράβασις, εως
	Concordance References:
	  ⇒ Strong's #3847 parabasis
	  ⇒ NIV #4126 parabasis
	  ⇒ NASB #3847 parabasis
	
	Hebrews 2:2
	For if the word spoken by angels was stedfast, and every **transgression** and disobedience received a just recompence of reward; [KJV]
	For if the word spoken through angels proved unalterable, and every **transgression** and disobedience received a just recompense, [NASB]
	For if the message spoken by angels was binding, and every **violation** and disobedience received its just punishment, [NIV]
	For if the word spoken through angels proved steadfast, and every **transgression** and disobedience received a just reward, [NKJV]
	The message God delivered through angels has always proved true, and the people were punished for every **violation of the law** and every act of disobedience. [NLT]
	εἰ γὰρ ὁ δι' ἀγγέλων λαληθεὶς λόγος ἐγένετο βέβαιος, καὶ πᾶσα **παράβασις** καὶ παρακοὴ ἔλαβεν ἔνδικον μισθαποδοσίαν, [GNS]
	εἰ γὰρ ὁ δι' ἀγγέλων λαληθεὶς λόγος ἐγένετο βέβαιος καὶ πᾶσα **παράβασις** καὶ παρακοὴ ἔλαβεν ἔνδικον μισθαποδοσίαν, [GNT]
		Violation, transgression, disobedience; to step aside; to step over the line.
		
		Practical Application
		It means to go against what the law says and to do what it forbids. To violate the law of God is sin and the violator is to be punished.
		The point is this: judgment under the law was very strict. Every transgression and disobedience had its appropriate punishment. If a person broke a law, he was judged, condemned, and bore the punishment laid out by the law.

#4226
Violation Of The Law
 	
Transgression–KJV
Transgression–NASB
Violation–NIV
Transgression–NKJV
Violation of the law–NLT
 	
POSB REFERENCE
(Heb.2:2)
Note 2
	παράβασις = *parabasis*
	Pronunciation: [par-ab'-as-is]
	Parsing (part of speech): noun
	  Case—nominative
	  Gender—feminine
	  Number—singular
	  Stem or root—from παράβασις, εως
	Concordance References:
	  ⇒ Strong's #3847 parabasis
	  ⇒ NIV #4126 parabasis
	  ⇒ NASB #3847 parabasis
	
	Hebrews 2:2
	For if the word spoken by angels was stedfast, and every **transgression** and disobedience received a just recompence of reward; [KJV]
	For if the word spoken through angels proved unalterable, and every **transgression** and disobedience
		Violation, transgression, disobedience; to step aside, to step over the line.
		
		Practical Application
		It means to go against what the law says and to do what it forbids. To violate the law of God is sin and the violator is to be punished.
		The point is this: judgment under the law was very strict. Every transgression and disobedience had its appropriate punishment. If a person broke a law, he was judged, condemned, and bore the punishment laid out by the law.

ENGLISH WORD	GREEK WORD AND VERSE	THE WORD MEANS...

	received a just recompense, [NASB]
	    For if the message spoken by angels was binding, and every **violation** and disobedience received its just punishment, [NIV]
	    For if the word spoken through angels proved steadfast, and every **transgression** and disobedience received a just reward, [NKJV]
	    The message God delivered through angels has always proved true, and the people were punished for every **violation of the law** and every act of disobedience. [NLT]
	    εἰ γὰρ ὁ δι' ἀγγέλων λαληθεὶς λόγος ἐγένετο βέβαιος, καὶ πᾶσα **παράβασις** καὶ παρακοὴ ἔλαβεν ἔνδικον μισθαποδοσίαν, [GNS]
	    εἰ γὰρ ὁ δι' ἀγγέλων λαληθεὶς λόγος ἐγένετο βέβαιος, καὶ πᾶσα **παράβασις** καὶ παρακοὴ ἔλαβεν ἔνδικον μισθαποδοσίαν, [GNT]	

#4227
Violence
 	
Violence–KJV
Take money...by force–NASB
Extort money–NIV
Intimidate–NKJV
Extort money–NLT
 	
POSB REFERENCE
(Lk.3:10-14; esp. v.14)
Note 5, point 3a
	διασείσητε = *diaseisēte*
	Pronunciation: [dee-as-i'-say-teh]
	Parsing (part of speech): verb
	    Mood—subjunctive OR imperative
	    Tense—aorist
	    Voice—active
	    Person—2nd person
	    Number—plural
	    Stem or root—from *διασείω*
	Concordance References:
	  ⇒ Strong's #1286 diaseiö
	  ⇒ NIV #1398 diaseiö
	  ⇒ NASB #1286 diaseiö
	
	Luke 3:14
	    And the soldiers likewise demanded of him, saying, And what shall we do? And he said unto them, Do **violence** to no man, neither accuse any falsely; and be content with your wages. [KJV]
	    And some soldiers were questioning him, saying, "And what about us, what shall we do?" And he said to them, "Do not **take money** from anyone **by force**, or accuse anyone falsely, and be content with your wages." [NASB]
	    Then some soldiers asked him, "And what should we do?" He replied, "Don't **extort money** and don't accuse people falsely--be content with your pay." [NIV]
	    Likewise the soldiers asked him, saying, "And what shall we do?" So he said to them, "Do not **intimidate** anyone or accuse falsely, and be content with your wages." [NKJV]
	    "What should we do?" asked some soldiers. John replied, "Don't **extort money**, and don't accuse people of things you know they didn't do. And be content with your pay." [NLT]
	    ἐπηρώτων δὲ αὐτὸν καὶ στρατευόμενοι, λέγοντες, Καὶ ἡμεῖς τί ποιήσομεν; καὶ εἶπε πρὸς αὐτοῖς, Μηδένα **διασείσητε** μηδὲ συκοφαντήσητε· καὶ ἀρκεῖσθε τοῖς ὀψωνίοις ὑμῶν. [GNS]
	    ἐπηρώτων δὲ αὐτὸν καὶ στρατευόμενοι λέγοντες, Τί ποιήσωμεν καὶ ἡμεῖς; καὶ εἶπεν αὐτοῖς, Μηδένα **διασείσητε** μηδὲ συκοφαντήσητε καὶ ἀρκεῖσθε τοῖς ὀψωνίοις ὑμῶν. [GNT]
		To extort money; to take money by force; to shake violently, agitate, terrify.
		
		Practical Application
		    The thought is that some persons extorted money by terrifying people. Roman soldiers were, of course, posted to protect the interests of Rome. It was common for soldiers to allow illegal things to go on for a bribe.

#4228
Violent
 	
Despiteful–KJV
Insolent–NASB
Insolent–NIV
Violent–NKJV
Insolent–NLT
	ὑβριστάς = *hubristas*
	Pronunciation: [hoo-bris-tahs']
	Parsing (part of speech): noun
	    Case—accusative
	    Gender—masculine
	    Number—plural
	    Stem or root—from *ὑβριστής*, οῦ
	Concordance References:
	  ⇒ Strong's #5197 hubristēs
	  ⇒ NIV #5616 hubristēs
	  ⇒ NASB #5197 hubristēs
		Insolent, despiteful, insulting, and defying; a violent man.
		
		Practical Application
		    It is a spirit of spite, of attack and assault, verbally or physically. It is despising and attacking, inflicting injury either by word or act. It is a man who...
		• lives his own life as he wishes, ignoring both God and men.
		• lives as though his rights and affairs are the

ENGLISH WORD	GREEK WORD AND VERSE	THE WORD MEANS...
POSB **REFERENCE** (Romans 1:30) *Deeper Study #14*	**Romans 1:30** Backbiters, haters of God, **despiteful**, proud, boasters, inventors of evil things, disobedient to parents, [KJV] Slanderers, haters of God, **insolent**, arrogant, boastful, inventors of evil, disobedient to parents, [NASB] Slanderers, God-haters, **insolent**, arrogant and boastful; they invent ways of doing evil; they disobey their parents; [NIV] Backbiters, haters of God, **violent**, proud, boasters, inventors of evil things, disobedient to parents, [NKJV] They are backstabbers, haters of God, **insolent**, proud, and boastful. They are forever inventing new ways of sinning and are disobedient to their parents. [NLT] ψιθυριστάς, καταλάλους, θεοστυγεῖς, **ὑβριστάς**, ὑπερηφάνους, ἀλαζόνας, ἐφευρετὰς κακῶν, γονεῦσιν ἀπειθεῖς, [GNS] καταλάλους θεοστυγεῖς **ὑβριστάς** ὑπερηφάνους ἀλαζόνας, ἐφευρετὰς κακῶν, γονεῦσιν ἀπειθεῖς, [GNT]	only rights and affairs which matter. • stands toe to toe with both God and men, acting as though he needs neither. • acts so independent in life that he dares God or men to get in his way. • does what he wants when he wants, even if it hurts or destroys others. The sin of despite, of being violent and insulting, is the spirit that hurts and harms others in order to do what one wants.
#4229 **Violent Aggressor** Injurious–KJV **Violent aggressor–NASB** Violent man–NIV Insolent man–NKJV Harming–NLT **POSB REFERENCE** (1 Tim.1:12-14; esp. v.13) Note 1, point 3	ὑβριστήν = *hubristēn* Pronunciation: [hoo-bris-tayn'] Parsing (part of speech): noun 　Case—accusative 　Gender—masculine 　Number—singular 　Stem or root—from ὑβριστής, οῦ Concordance References: ⇒ Strong's #5197 hubristēs ⇒ NIV #5616 hubristēs ⇒ NASB #5197 hubristēs **1 Tim. 1:13** Who was before a blasphemer, and a persecutor, and **injurious**: but I obtained mercy, because I did it ignorantly in unbelief. [KJV] Even though I was formerly a blasphemer and a persecutor and a **violent aggressor**. And yet I was shown mercy, because I acted ignorantly in unbelief; [NASB] Even though I was once a blasphemer and a persecutor and a **violent man**, I was shown mercy because I acted in ignorance and unbelief. [NIV] Although I was formerly a blasphemer, a persecutor, and an **insolent man**; but I obtained mercy because I did *it* ignorantly in unbelief. [NKJV] Even though I used to scoff at the name of Christ. I hunted down his people, **harming** them in every way I could. But God had mercy on me because I did it in ignorance and unbelief. [NLT] τὸν πρότερον ὄντα βλάσφημον καὶ διώκτην καὶ **ὑβριστήν**· ἀλλ' ἠλεήθην, ὅτι ἀγνοῶν ἐποίησα ἐν ἀπιστίᾳ [GNS] τὸ πρότερον ὄντα βλάσφημον καὶ διώκτην καὶ **ὑβριστήν**, ἀλλὰ ἠλεήθην, ὅτι ἀγνοῶν ἐποίησα ἐν ἀπιστίᾳ· [GNT]	A violent man; a violent aggressor; injurious, harmful; an insulting person; insolent; to treat and use others despitefully; to enjoy being brutal and violent; to be in a fiery rage and to inflict it upon others. **Practical Application** William Barclay says that the word "indicates a kind of arrogant sadism; it describes the man who is out to inflict pain and injury for the sheer joy of inflicting it....that is what Paul was once like in regard to the Christian Church. Not content with words of insult, he went to the limit of legal persecution. Not content with legal persecution, he went to the limit of sadistic brutality in his attempt to stamp out the Christian faith" (*The Letters to Timothy, Titus, and Philemon*, p.52). However despite all this evil, God had mercy upon Paul. Paul had not known that Christ was really the true Messiah. He thought that he knew God and that his religion was the true religion. He felt that any religion that stood against his religion was to be stamped out. Therefore, when Paul attacked Christ and His followers, he did it ignorantly in unbelief. He just did not believe that Jesus Christ could possibly be the Messiah. The point is this: God had mercy upon Paul. He took pity upon Paul despite his terrible sins (see POSB *Deeper Study #2*, Mercy—1 Tim. 1:2).
#4230 **Violent Man** Injurious–KJV Violent aggressor–NASB **Violent man–NIV** Insolent man–NKJV Harming–NLT **POSB REFERENCE** (1 Tim.1:12-14; esp. v.13) Note 1, point 3	ὑβριστήν = *hubristēn* Pronunciation: [hoo-bris-tayn'] Parsing (part of speech): noun 　Case—accusative 　Gender—masculine 　Number—singular 　Stem or root—from ὑβριστής, οῦ Concordance References: ⇒ Strong's #5197 hubristēs ⇒ NIV #5616 hubristēs ⇒ NASB #5197 hubristēs **1 Tim. 1:13** Who was before a blasphemer, and a persecutor, and **injurious**: but I obtained mercy, because I did it ignorantly in unbelief. [KJV] Even though I was formerly a blasphemer and a perse-	A violent man; a violent aggressor; injurious, harmful; an insulting person; insolent; to treat and use others despitefully; to enjoy being brutal and violent; to be in a fiery rage and to inflict it upon others. **Practical Application** William Barclay says that the word "indicates a kind of arrogant sadism; it describes the man who is out to inflict pain and injury for the sheer joy of inflicting it....that is what Paul was once like in regard to the Christian Church. Not content with words of insult, he went to the limit of legal persecution. Not content with legal persecution, he went to the limit of sadistic brutality in his attempt to stamp out the Christian faith"

ENGLISH WORD	GREEK WORD AND VERSE	THE WORD MEANS...
Excellent–NIV **Virtue–NKJV** Excellent–NLT **POSB REFERENCE** (Philip.4:8-9; esp. v.8) Note 2, point 1g	Stem or root—from ἀρετή, ῆς Concordance References: ⇒ Strong's #703 aretē ⇒ NIV #746 aretē ⇒ NASB #703 aretē **Philip. 4:8** Finally, brethren, whatsoever things are true, whatsoever things are honest, whatsoever things are just, whatsoever things are pure, whatsoever things are lovely, whatsoever things are of good report; if there be any **virtue**, and if there be any praise, think on these things. [KJV] Finally, brethren, whatever is true, whatever is honorable, whatever is right, whatever is pure, whatever is lovely, whatever is of good repute, if there is any **excellence** and if anything worthy of praise, let your mind dwell on these things. [NASB] Finally, brothers, whatever is true, whatever is noble, whatever is right, whatever is pure, whatever is lovely, whatever is admirable—if anything is **excellent** or praiseworthy—think about such things. [NIV] Finally, brethren, whatever things are true, whatever things *are* noble, whatever things *are* just, whatever things *are* pure, whatever things *are* lovely, whatever things *are* of good report, if *there is* any **virtue** and if *there is* anything praiseworthy—meditate on these things. [NKJV] And now, dear brothers and sisters, let me say one more thing as I close this letter. Fix your thoughts on what is true and honorable and right. Think about things that are pure and lovely and admirable. Think about things that are **excellent** and worthy of praise. [NLT] Τὸ λοιπόν, ἀδελφοί, ὅσα ἐστὶν ἀληθῆ, ὅσα σεμνά, ὅσα δίκαια, ὅσα ἁγνά, ὅσα προσφιλῆ, ὅσα εὔφημα, εἴ τις **ἀρετὴ** καὶ εἴ τις ἔπαινος, ταῦτα λογίζεσθε· [GNS] Τὸ λοιπόν, ἀδελφοί, ὅσα ἐστὶν ἀληθῆ, ὅσα σεμνά, ὅσα δίκαια, ὅσα ἁγνά, ὅσα προσφιλῆ, ὅσα εὔφημα, εἴ τις **ἀρετὴ** καὶ εἴ τις ἔπαινος, ταῦτα λογίζεσθε· [GNT]	⇒ what we think is what we become. ⇒ where we have kept our minds is where we are. ⇒ our thoughts shape our behavior. ⇒ what we do is what we think. William Barclay says, "...*it is a law of life that, if a man thinks of something often enough and long enough, he will come to the stage when he cannot stop thinking about it. His thoughts will be quite literally in a groove out of which he cannot jerk them*" (*The Letters to the Philippians, Colossians, and Thessalonians*, p.97). A person who centers his thoughts upon the world and its things will live for the world and its things: money, wealth, lands, property, houses, possessions, position, power, recognition, honor, social standing, fame, and a host of other worldly pursuits.

**#4234
Virtue**
 	
Virtue–KJV
Moral excellence–
NASB
Goodness–NIV
Virtue–NKJV
Moral excellence–NLT
 	
**POSB
REFERENCE**
(2 Pt.1:5-7; esp. v.5)
Note 1, point 1
	ἀρετήν = *aretēn*
	Pronunciation: [ar-et-ayn']
	Parsing (part of speech): noun
	    Case—accusative
	    Gender—feminine
	    Number—singular
	    Stem or root—from ἀρετή, ῆς
	Concordance References:
	⇒ Strong's #703 aretē
	⇒ NIV #746 aretē
	⇒ NASB #703 aretē
	2 Peter 1:5
	And beside this, giving all diligence, add to your faith **virtue**; and to virtue knowledge; [KJV]
	Now for this very reason also, applying all diligence, in your faith supply **moral excellence**, and in your moral excellence, knowledge; [NASB]
	For this very reason, make every effort to add to your faith **goodness**; and to goodness, knowledge; [NIV]
	But also for this very reason, giving all diligence, add to your faith **virtue**, to virtue knowledge, [NKJV]
	So make every effort to apply the benefits of these promises to your life. Then your faith will produce a life of **moral excellence**. A life of moral excellence leads to knowing God better. [NLT]
	καὶ αὐτὸ τοῦτο δὲ σπουδὴν πᾶσαν παρεισενέγκαντες, ἐπιχορηγήσατε ἐν τῇ πίστει ὑμῶν τὴν **ἀρετήν**, ἐν δὲ τῇ ἀρετῇ τὴν γνῶσιν, [GNS]
	καὶ αὐτὸ τοῦτο δὲ σπουδὴν πᾶσαν παρεισενέγκαντες ἐπιχορηγήσατε ἐν τῇ πίστει ὑμῶν τὴν **ἀρετήν**, ἐν δὲ τῇ ἀρετῇ τὴν γνῶσιν, [GNT]
		Goodness, virtue; moral excellence and goodness of character; moral strength and moral courage.
		
		Practical Application
		It means manliness; being an excellent person in life, a real man or a real woman in life; living life just like one should, in the most excellent way. It means always choosing the excellent way.

ENGLISH WORD	GREEK WORD AND VERSE	THE WORD MEANS...

#4235
Visible
 	
Observation–KJV
Observed–NASB
Careful observation–
NIV
Observation–NKJV
Visible–NLT
 	
**POSB
REFERENCE**
(Lk.17:20-21; esp.
v.20)
Note 1, point 1
	παρατηρήσεως = paratērēseōs
	Pronunciation: [par-at-ay'-ray-seh-os]
	Parsing (part of speech): noun
	  Case—genitive
	  Gender—feminine
	  Number—singular
	  Stem or root—from παρατήρησις, εως
	Concordance References:
	  ⇒ Strong's #3907 paratērēsis
	  ⇒ NIV #4191 paratērēsis
	  ⇒ NASB #3907 paratērēsis
	
	Luke 17:20
	And when he was demanded of the Pharisees, when the kingdom of God should come, he answered them and said, The kingdom of God cometh not with **observation**: [KJV]
	Now having been questioned by the Pharisees as to when the kingdom of God was coming, He answered them and said, "The kingdom of God is not coming with signs to be **observed**; [NASB]
	Once, having been asked by the Pharisees when the kingdom of God would come, Jesus replied, "The kingdom of God does not come with your **careful observation**, [NIV]
	Now when He was asked by the Pharisees when the kingdom of God would come, He answered them and said, "The kingdom of God does not come with **observation**; [NKJV]
	One day the Pharisees asked Jesus, "When will the Kingdom of God come?" Jesus replied, "The Kingdom of God isn't ushered in with **visible** signs. [NLT]
	Ἐπερωτηθεὶς δὲ ὑπὸ τῶν Φαρισαίων, πότε ἔρχεται ἡ βασιλεία τοῦ Θεοῦ, ἀπεκρίθη αὐτοῖς καὶ εἶπεν, Οὐκ ἔρχεται ἡ βασιλεία τοῦ Θεοῦ μετὰ **παρατηρήσεως**· [GNS]
	Ἐπερωτηθεὶς δὲ ὑπὸ τῶν Φαρισαίων πότε ἔρχεται ἡ βασιλεία τοῦ θεοῦ ἀπεκρίθη αὐτοῖς καὶ εἶπεν, Οὐκ ἔρχεται ἡ βασιλεία τοῦ θεοῦ μετὰ **παρατηρήσεως**, [GNT]
		To watch closely; to give close observation to (as in astronomical observations); to make careful observation.
		
		Practical Application
		The kingdom cannot be seen with the naked eye. This means at least two things.
		1. The Kingdom of God does not come with an outward, dramatic, thunderous show. It does not come in such a way that men say, "Lo here! or, lo there!" It comes with a silent, pervasive influence. It is coming, and its coming will permeate the whole world, but its coming is to be silent, not showy (cp. the yeast or leaven which silently permeates the whole lump, see POSB note—Matthew 13:33).
		2. The Kingdom of God cannot be seen with the naked eye. The Lord's kingdom is not of this world, not of the physical and material dimension of being. It is not the kind of kingdom men see when they observe the nations of the world.

#4236
Visions
 	
Visions–KJV
Visions–NASB
Visions–NIV
Visions–NKJV
Visions–NLT
 	
**POSB
REFERENCE**
(Acts 2:17-21; esp.
v.17)
Note 2, point 1c
	ὁράσεις = horaseis
	Pronunciation: [hor'-as-is]
	Parsing (part of speech): noun
	  Case—accusative
	  Gender—feminine
	  Number—plural
	  Stem or root—from ὅρασις, εως
	Concordance References:
	  ⇒ Strong's #3706 horasis
	  ⇒ NIV #3970 horasis
	  ⇒ NASB #3706 horasis
	
	Acts 2:17
	And it shall come to pass in the last days, saith God, I will pour out of my Spirit upon all flesh: and your sons and your daughters shall prophesy, and your young men shall see **visions**, and your old men shall dream dreams: [KJV]
	'And it shall be in the last days,' God says, 'That I will pour forth of My Spirit upon all MANKIND; And your sons and your daughters shall prophesy, And your young men shall see **visions**, And your old men shall dream dreams; [NASB]
	"'In the last days, God says, I will pour out my Spirit on all people. Your sons and daughters will prophesy, your young men will see **visions**, your old men will dream dreams. [NIV]
	'And it shall come to pass in the last days, says God, That I will pour out of My Spirit on all flesh; Your sons and your daughters shall prophesy, Your young men shall see **visions**, Your old men shall dream dreams. [NKJV]
	'In the last days, God said, I will pour out my Spirit
		Visions; an appearance, an ecstatic revelation.
		
		Practical Application
		In Scripture the Greek word is used for both what a man can envision (see, imagine, think, cause to appear) within his own mind and what is given him by God through a special revelation (Rev. 9:17).
		Note the purpose of visions:
		  ⇒ To convert and call men to the ministry (Acts 26:19, cp. Acts 26:1-18).
		  ⇒ To encourage believers. (Acts 18:9-11; 2 Cor. 12:1-7).
		  ⇒ To guide and direct believers (Acts 9:10-16; Acts 10:17, cp. Acts 9:1-48; Acts 16:8-11).
		  ⇒ To reveal spiritual things to believers (Rev. 1:10).
		  ⇒ To reveal the truth of Christ (Luke 24:23).
		  ⇒ To show men that they are living in the last days (Acts 2:17-21).

ENGLISH WORD	GREEK WORD AND VERSE	THE WORD MEANS...
	upon all people. Your sons and daughters will prophesy, your young men will see **visions**, and your old men will dream dreams. [NLT] Καὶ ἔσται ἐν ταῖς ἐσχάταις ἡμέραις, -- λέγει ὁ Θεός -- ἐκχεῶ ἀπὸ τοῦ πνεύματός μου ἐπὶ πᾶσαν σάρκα· καὶ προφητεύσουσιν οἱ υἱοὶ ὑμῶν καὶ αἱ θυγατέρες ὑμῶν, καὶ οἱ νεανίσκοι ὑμῶν **ὁράσεις** ὄψονται, καὶ οἱ πρεσβύτεροι ὑμῶν ἐνυπνία ἐνυπνιασθήσονται [GNS] Καὶ ἔσται ἐν ταῖς ἐσχάταις ἡμέραις, λέγει ὁ θεός, ἐκχεῶ ἀπὸ τοῦ πνεύματός μου ἐπὶ πᾶσαν σάρκα, καὶ προφητεύσουσιν οἱ υἱοὶ ὑμῶν καὶ αἱ θυγατέρες ὑμῶν καὶ οἱ νεανίσκοι ὑμῶν **ὁράσεις** ὄψονται καὶ οἱ πρεσβύτεροι ὑμῶν ἐνυπνίοις ἐνυπνιασθήσονται [GNT]	

#4237
Visit–Visited
 	
Visit–KJV
Concerned–NASB
Showed...concern–
NIV
Visited–NKJV
Visited–NLT
 	
POSB
REFERENCE
(Acts 15:13-21; esp.
v.14)
Note 4, point 1
	ἐπεσκέψατο = *epeskepsato*
	Pronunciation: [ep-eh-skep'-sah-tow]
	Parsing (part of speech): verb
	    Mood—indicative
	    Tense—aorist
	    Voice—middle deponent
	    Person—3rd person
	    Number—singular
	    Stem or root—from **ἐπισκέπτομαι**
	Concordance References:
	  ⇒ Strong's #1980 episkeptomai
	  ⇒ NIV #2170 episkeptomai
	  ⇒ NASB #1980a episkeptomai
	
	Acts 15:14
	Simeon hath declared how God at the first did **visit** the Gentiles, to take out of them a people for his name. [KJV]
	"Simeon has related how God first **concerned** Himself about taking from among the Gentiles a people for His name. [NASB]
	Simon has described to us how God at first **showed** his **concern** by taking from the Gentiles a people for himself. [NIV]
	Simon has declared how God at the first **visited** the Gentiles to take out of them a people for His name. [NKJV]
	Peter has told you about the time God first **visited** the Gentiles to take from them a people for himself. [NLT]
	Συμεὼν ἐξηγήσατο καθὼς πρῶτον ὁ Θεὸς **ἐπεσκέψατο** λαβεῖν ἐξ ἐθνῶν λαὸν ἐπὶ τῷ ὀνόματι αὐτοῦ. [GNS]
	Συμεὼν ἐξηγήσατο καθὼς πρῶτον ὁ θεὸς **ἐπεσκέψατο** λαβεῖν ἐξ ἐθνῶν λαὸν τῷ ὀνόματι αὐτοῦ. [GNT]
		To show concern; to visit; to care for; to look after.
		
		Practical Application
		James supported Peter's great declaration. The way James worded his support is significant.
		⇒ "God...did visit (*epeskepsato*) for the Gentiles."
		⇒ "to take *from among the Gentiles* a people": to choose; to appoint; to remove them from the Gentile nations and select a chosen people. The word "people" (*laon*) is the same word used of the Jewish people (cp. Acts 10:2). The point is that God was calling out *a new people*—a new body, a new nation, a new race—to be His chosen people, just as He had done with Abraham and the Jews. (See POSB *Deeper Study* #8, pt.6—Matthew 21:43; POSB note—Ephes. 2:11-18; POSB note—Ephes. 2:14-15; POSB note—Ephes. 2:19-22; and POSB note—Ephes. 4:17-19 for more discussion.)
		⇒ "For His name": two verses clearly show what God means by choosing a people "for His name."
		
		"You are My witnesses," says the Lord, "And My servant whom I have chosen, That you may know and believe Me, And understand that I am He. Before Me there was no God formed, Nor shall there be after Me" (Isaiah 43:10) [NKJV].
		"For as the sash clings to the waist of a man, so I have caused the whole house of Israel and the whole house of Judah to cling to Me,' says the Lord, 'that they may become My people, for renown, for praise, and for glory; but they would not hear'" (Jeremiah 13:11) [NKJV].

#4238
Voice Against
 	
Voice against–KJV
Cast...vote against–
NASB
Cast...vote against–
NIV
Cast...vote against–
NKJV
Cast...vote against–
NLT
	κατήνεγκα ψῆφον = *katënegka psëphon*
	Pronunciation: [kat-ay-nehg'-kah psay'-fon]
	Parsing *katënegka* (part of speech): verb
	    Mood—indicative
	    Tense—aorist
	    Voice—active
	    Person—1st person
	    Number—singular
	    Stem or root—from **καταφέρω**
	Parsing *psëphon* (part of speech): noun
	    Case—accusative
	    Gender—feminine
	    Number—singular
	    Stem or root—from **ψῆφος**
		To cast a vote against; to vote against.
		
		Practical Application
		The word actually means a little stone or pebble used by the Sanhedrin that was thrown into an urn indicating how a person was voting. A black pebble meant condemnation. The point to note is this: Paul was saying that he was a member of the Sanhedrin, actually casting a vote against the Christian believers.

ENGLISH WORD	GREEK WORD AND VERSE	THE WORD MEANS...
POSB REFERENCE (Acts 26:9-11; esp. v.10) Note 4	Concordance References: ⇒ Strong's #2702 katapherö + 5586 psëphos ⇒ NIV #2965 katapherö [cast against] + 6029 psëphos [vote] ⇒ NASB #2702 katapherö + 5586 psëphos ### Acts 26:10 Which thing I also did in Jerusalem: and many of the saints did I shut up in prison, having received authority from the chief priests; and when they were put to death, I gave my **voice against** them. [KJV] "And this is just what I did in Jerusalem; not only did I lock up many of the saints in prisons, having received authority from the chief priests, but also when they were being put to death I **cast** my **vote against** them. [NASB] And that is just what I did in Jerusalem. On the authority of the chief priests I put many of the saints in prison, and when they were put to death, I **cast** my **vote against** them. [NIV] This I also did in Jerusalem, and many of the saints I shut up in prison, having received authority from the chief priests; and when they were put to death, I **cast** my **vote against** them. [NKJV] Authorized by the leading priests, I caused many of the believers in Jerusalem to be sent to prison. And I **cast** my **vote against** them when they were condemned to death. [NLT] ὃ καὶ ἐποίησα ἐν Ἱεροσολύμοις, καὶ πολλούς τῶν ἁγίων ἐγὼ φυλακαῖς κατέκλεισα, τὴν παρὰ τῶν ἀρχιερέων ἐξουσίαν λαβών, ἀναιρουμένων τε αὐτῶν **κατήνεγκα ψῆφον**. [GNS] ὃ καὶ ἐποίησα ἐν Ἱεροσολύμοις, καὶ πολλούς τε τῶν ἁγίων ἐγὼ ἐν φυλακαῖς κατέκλεισα τὴν παρὰ τῶν ἀρχιερέων ἐξουσίαν λαβὼν ἀναιρουμένων τε αὐτῶν **κατήνεγκα ψῆφον**. [GNT]	

#4239
## Void Of Offence 	
 	
Void of offence–KJV
Blameless–NASB
Clear–NIV
Without offense–NKJV
Clear–NLT
 	
POSB REFERENCE
(Acts 24:14-16; esp. v.16) Note 3, point 4b
	ἀπρόσκοπον = *aproskopon*
	Pronunciation: [ap-ros'-kop-on]
	Parsing (part of speech): adjective
	    Case—accusative
	    Gender—feminine
	    Number—singular
	    Stem or root—from ἀπρόσκοπος
	Concordance References:
	⇒ Strong's #677 aproskopos
	⇒ NIV #718 aproskopos
	⇒ NASB #677 aproskopos
	
	### Acts 24:16
	And herein do I exercise myself, to have always a conscience **void of offence** toward God, and toward men. [KJV]
	"In view of this, I also do my best to maintain always a **blameless** conscience both before God and before men. [NASB]
	So I strive always to keep my conscience **clear** before God and man. [NIV]
	This being so, I myself always strive to have a conscience **without offense** toward God and men. [NKJV]
	Because of this, I always try to maintain a **clear** conscience before God and everyone else. [NLT]
	ἐν τούτῳ δὲ αὐτὸς ἀσκῶ, **ἀπρόσκοπον** συνείδησιν ἔχειν πρὸς τὸν Θεὸν καὶ τοὺς ἀνθρώπους διὰ παντός. [GNS]
	ἐν τούτῳ καὶ αὐτὸς ἀσκῶ **ἀπρόσκοπον** συνείδησιν ἔχειν πρὸς τὸν θεὸν καὶ τοὺς ἀνθρώπους διὰ παντός. [GNT]
		To be clear; to be blameless; to be clear in conscience.
		
		### Practical Application
		It means to keep from stumbling, to keep from causing others to stumble, to keep from hurting oneself and from hurting others.

#4240 ## Vulnerable Women	γυναικάρια = *gunaikaria* Pronunciation: [goo-nahee-kar'-ee-ah] Parsing (part of speech): noun Case—accusative	Weak-willed women, silly women, vulnerable women, morally weak women. The Greek word means *little women, little* in the sense of being spiritually dead, weak, immature, and unstable.

ENGLISH WORD	GREEK WORD AND VERSE	THE WORD MEANS...
Silly women–KJV Weak women–NASB Weak-willed women–NIV Gullible women–NKJV **Vulnerable women–NLT** **POSB REFERENCE** (2 Tim. 3:6-9; esp. v.6) Note 4, point 1	Gender—neuter Number—plural Stem or root—from γυναικάριον, ου Concordance References: ⇒ Strong's #1133 gunaikarion ⇒ NIV #1220 gunaikarion ⇒ NASB #1133 gunaikarion ### 2 Tim. 3:6 For of this sort are they which creep into houses, and lead captive **silly women** laden with sins, led away with divers lusts, [KJV] For among them are those who enter into households and captivate **weak women** weighed down with sins, led on by various impulses, [NASB] They are the kind who worm their way into homes and gain control over **weak-willed women**, who are loaded down with sins and are swayed by all kinds of evil desires, [NIV] For of this sort are those who creep into households and make captives of **gullible women** loaded down with sins, led away by various lusts, [NKJV] They are the kind who work their way into people's homes and win the confidence of **vulnerable women** who are burdened with the guilt of sin and controlled by many desires. [NLT] ἐκ τούτων γάρ εἰσιν οἱ ἐνδύνοντες εἰς τὰς οἰκίας, καὶ αἰχμαλωτεύοντες τὰ **γυναικάρια** σεσωρευμένα ἁμαρτίαις, ἀγόμενα ἐπιθυμίαις ποικίλαις, [GNS] ἐκ τούτων γάρ εἰσιν οἱ ἐνδύνοντες εἰς τὰς οἰκίας καὶ αἰχμαλωτίζοντες **γυναικάρια** σεσωρευμένα ἁμαρτίαις, ἀγόμενα ἐπιθυμίαις ποικίλαις, [GNT]	However, it should always be remembered that men are just as gullible as women, just as spiritually dead, weak, immature, and unstable. ### Practical Application The present passage zeros in on women because of the local situation in Ephesus; some of the women in the Ephesian church were following the corrupt ministers. But the warning is applicable to us all: both men and women must guard against corrupt ministers. Note what the corrupt minister does. He seeks after people... • who are laden or burdened down with sins and guilt. • who are easily swayed and led away by all kinds of desires and lusts. • who are seeking after truth—who are listening and learning all they can from anybody who claims to have the truth. This is the person the false minister goes after and eventually captivates. When a person begins to seek the truth because he senses a need in his life, senses that he has been living only for his own selfish desires and lusts—that person is wide open for a corrupt minister to step in and lead him astray. Unfortunately, this is exactly what happens ever too often. And note the great tragedy: the person never comes to the knowledge of the truth. Why? Because he never seek the truth in Christ. He only seek a "form of godliness,"—acting as if they are religious—not true godliness. True godliness is found in Christ alone and nowhere else.
#4241 ## Vultures, The The eagles–KJV **The vultures–NASB** **The vultures–NIV** The eagles–NKJV **Vultures–NLT** **POSB REFERENCE** (Lk.17:37) Note 8	οἱ ἀετοὶ = hoi aetoi Pronunciation: [hoi ah-et-o-ee] Parsing aetoi (part of speech): noun Case—nominative Gender—masculine Number—plural Stem or root—from ἀετός, οῦ Concordance References: ⇒ Strong's #3588 ho + 105 aetos ⇒ NIV #3836 ho [the] + 108 aetos [vultures] ⇒ NASB #3588 ho + 105 aetos ### Luke 17:37 And they answered and said unto him, Where, Lord? And he said unto them, Wheresoever the body is, thither will **the eagles** be gathered together. [KJV] And answering they said to Him, "Where, Lord?" And He said to them, "Where the body is, there also will **the vultures** be gathered." [NASB] "Where, Lord?" they asked. He replied, "Where there is a dead body, there **the vultures** will gather." [NIV] And they answered and said to Him, "Where, Lord?" So He said to them, "Wherever the body is, there **the eagles** will be gathered together." [NKJV] "Lord, where will this happen?" the disciples asked. Jesus replied, "Just as the gathering of **vultures** shows there is a carcass nearby, so these signs indicate that the end is near." [NLT] καὶ ἀποκριθέντες λέγουσιν αὐτῷ, Ποῦ, Κύριε; ὁ δὲ εἶπεν αὐτοῖς, Ὅπου τὸ σῶμα, ἐκεῖ συναχθήσονται **οἱ ἀετοί.** [GNS] καὶ ἀποκριθέντες λέγουσιν αὐτῷ, Ποῦ, κύριε; ὁ δὲ εἶπεν αὐτοῖς, Ὅπου τὸ σῶμα, ἐκεῖ καὶ **οἱ ἀετοὶ** ἐπισυναχθήσονται. [GNT]	Eagle or vulture. ### Practical Application It probably should be translated vulture here, for they are the ones who gather universally as scavengers over dead bodies. Vultures gather where the dead are and feast upon them. Since death is universal, vultures are found everywhere.

ENGLISH WORD	GREEK WORD AND VERSE	THE WORD MEANS...

#4242
Wailed For
 	
Lamented–KJV
Lamenting–NASB
Wailed for–NIV
Lamented–NKJV
Grief-stricken–NLT
 	
**POSB
REFERENCE**
(Lk.23:27)
Note 2
	ἐθρήνουν = ethrēnoun
	Pronunciation: [eh-thray-noon]
	Parsing (part of speech): verb
	    Mood—indicative
	    Tense—imperfect
	    Voice—active
	    Person—3rd person
	    Number—plural
	    Stem or root—from θρηνέω
	Concordance References:
	⇒ Strong's #2354 thrēneö
	⇒ NIV #2577 thrēneö
	⇒ NASB #2354 thrēneö
	
	Luke 23:27
	And there followed him a great company of people, and of women, which also bewailed and **lamented** him. [KJV]
	And there were following Him a great multitude of the people, and of women who were mourning and **lamenting** Him. [NASB]
	A large number of people followed him, including women who mourned and **wailed for** him. [NIV]
	And a great multitude of the people followed Him, and women who also mourned and **lamented** Him. [NKJV]
	Great crowds trailed along behind, including many **grief-stricken** women. [NLT]
	Ἠκολούθει δὲ αὐτῷ πολὺ πλῆθος τοῦ λαοῦ, καὶ γυναικῶν αἳ καὶ ἐκόπτοντο καὶ **ἐθρήνουν** αὐτόν. [GNS]
	Ἠκολούθει δὲ αὐτῷ πολὺ πλῆθος τοῦ λαοῦ καὶ γυναικῶν αἳ ἐκόπτοντο καὶ **ἐθρήνουν** αὐτόν. [GNT]
		To be grief-stricken; to lament; to wail; to cry out loud; to mourn; to groan; to weep for; to sing out a dirge.
		
		Practical Application
		In this Scripture, the women were crying out, unable to hold back the pain cutting their hearts. Some of the people, of course, had been followers of Jesus for a long time and were feeling the depth of their Lord's sufferings. Other onlookers, as in any crowd witnessing severe suffering, felt only a natural tenderness and lament over one suffering so much.

#4243
Wait On
 	
Serve–KJV
Serve–NASB
Wait on–NIV
Serve–NKJV
Administering–NLT
 	
**POSB
REFERENCE**
(Acts 6:2)
Deeper Study #1
	διακονεῖν = diakonein
	Pronunciation: [dee-ak-on-een']
	Parsing (part of speech): verb
	    Mood—infinitive
	    Tense—present
	    Voice—active
	    Stem or root—from διακονέω
	Concordance References:
	⇒ Strong's #1247 diakoneö
	⇒ NIV #1354 diakoneö
	⇒ NASB #1247 diakoneö
	
	Acts 6:2
	Then the twelve called the multitude of the disciples *unto them,* and said, It is not reason that we should leave the word of God, and **serve** tables. [KJV]
	And the twelve summoned the congregation of the disciples and said, "It is not desirable for us to neglect the word of God in order to **serve** tables. [NASB]
	So the Twelve gathered all the disciples together and said, "It would not be right for us to neglect the ministry of the word of God in order to **wait on** tables. [NIV]
	Then the twelve summoned the multitude of the disciples and said, "It is not desirable that we should leave the word of God and **serve** tables. [NKJV]
	So the Twelve called a meeting of all the believers."We apostles should spend our time preaching and teaching the word of God, not **administering** a food program," they said. [NLT]
	προσκαλεσάμενοι δὲ οἱ δώδεκα τὸ πλῆθος τῶν μαθητῶν, εἶπον, Οὐκ ἀρεστόν ἐστιν ἡμᾶς, καταλείψαντας τὸν λόγον τοῦ Θεοῦ, **διακονεῖν** τραπέζαις. [GNS]
	προσκαλεσάμενοι δὲ οἱ δώδεκα τὸ πλῆθος τῶν μαθητῶν εἶπαν, Οὐκ ἀρεστόν ἐστιν ἡμᾶς καταλείψαντας τὸν λόγον τοῦ θεοῦ **διακονεῖν** τραπέζαις. [GNT]
		To wait on; to serve; to administer; to minister; to care for; to see after; to provide for.
		
		Practical Application
		The phrase "wait on" *diakonein* is used of ministers throughout the New Testament, both preachers of the Word and deacons who serve as ministers in meeting the day-to-day needs of the flock (cp. Acts 6:4; Acts 12:25; Acts 21:19; Romans 11:13). The deacons were being chosen to minister as much as the apostles, but in a different area of concentration.
		This does not mean the apostles never met day-to-day needs of the flock nor that the deacons never shared the Word. Both apostles and deacons served in both areas, but each concentrated upon his primary call and mission. (See POSB *Deeper Study* #1, Deacon—1 Tim. 3:8-13 for more discussion.)

#4244
Waiting Eagerly For
	ἀποκαραδοκία = apokaradokia
	Pronunciation: [ap-ok-ar-ad-ok-ee'-ah]
	Parsing (part of speech): noun
	    Case—nominative
	    Gender—feminine
		Eager longing, deep desire, eager expectation; earnest expectation of; waiting eagerly for.

ENGLISH WORD	GREEK WORD AND VERSE	THE WORD MEANS...
Earnest expectation of–KJV Anxious longing of–NASB Eager expectation for–NIV Eagerly waits for–NKJV **Waiting eagerly for–NLT** **POSB REFERENCE** (Romans 8:19-22; esp. v.19) Note 2	Number—singular Stem or root—from ἀποκαραδοκία, ας Concordance References: ⇒ Strong's #603 apokaradokia ⇒ NIV #638 apokaradokia ⇒ NASB #603 apokaradokia **Romans 8:19** For the **earnest expectation of** the creature waiteth for the manifestation of the sons of God. [KJV] For the **anxious longing of** the creation waits eagerly for the revealing of the sons of God. [NASB] The creation waits in **eager expectation for** the sons of God to be revealed. [NIV] For the earnest expectation of the creation **eagerly waits for** the revealing of the sons of God. [NKJV] For all creation is **waiting eagerly for** that future day when God will reveal who his children really are. [NLT] ἡ γὰρ **ἀποκαραδοκία** τῆς κτίσεως τὴν ἀποκάλυψιν τῶν υἱῶν τοῦ Θεοῦ ἀπεκδέχεται· [GNS] ἡ γὰρ **ἀποκαραδοκία** τῆς κτίσεως τὴν ἀποκάλυψιν τῶν υἱῶν τοῦ θεοῦ ἀπεκδέχεται. [GNT]	**Practical Application** The creation suffers and struggles for deliverance from corruption. The word "creation" refers to everything under man: animal, plant, and mineral. All creation is pictured as living and waiting expectantly for the day when the sons of God will be glorified. The words "waiting eagerly for" (*apokaradokia*) mean to watch with the neck outstretched and the head erect. It is a persistent, unswerving expectation, an expectation that does not give up but keeps looking until the event happens.
#4245 **Wake Up** Awake–KJV Awaken–NASB **Wake up–NIV** Awake–NKJV **Wake up–NLT** **POSB REFERENCE** (Rom.13:11-12; esp. v.11) Note 2	ἐγερθῆναι = egerthēnai Pronunciation: [eg-er'-thay-nah-ee] Parsing (part of speech): verb Mood—infinitive Tense—aorist Voice—passive Stem or root—from ἐγείρω Concordance References: ⇒ Strong's #1453 egeirō ⇒ NIV #1586 egeirō ⇒ NASB #1453 egeirō **Romans 13:11** And that, knowing the time, that now it is high time to **awake** out of sleep: for now is our salvation nearer than when we believed. [KJV] And this do, knowing the time, that it is already the hour for you to **awaken** from sleep; for now salvation is nearer to us than when we believed. [NASB] And do this, understanding the present time. The hour has come for you to **wake up** from your slumber, because our salvation is nearer now than when we first believed. [NIV] And do this, knowing the time, that now it is high time to **awake** out of sleep; for now our salvation is nearer than when we first believed. [NKJV] Another reason for right living is that you know how late it is; time is running out. **Wake up**, for the coming of our salvation is nearer now than when we first believed. [NLT] Καὶ τοῦτο, εἰδότες τὸν καιρόν, ὅτι ὥρα ὑμᾶς ἤδη ἐξ ὕπνου **ἐγερθῆναι**· νῦν γὰρ ἐγγύτερον ἡμῶν ἡ σωτηρία ἢ ὅτε ἐπιστεύσαμεν. [GNS] Καὶ τοῦτο εἰδότες τὸν καιρόν, ὅτι ὥρα ἤδη ὑμᾶς ἐξ ὕπνου **ἐγερθῆναι**, νῦν γὰρ ἐγγύτερον ἡμῶν ἡ σωτηρία ἢ ὅτε ἐπιστεύσαμεν. [GNT]	To wake up; to awake; to get up; to raise up. **Practical Application** Too many believers are slumbering and paying no attention to what is going on in the world; too many are not watching; too many are not observing the signs of the time. Too many are complacent and slothful, lazily passing through life with little commitment to serving Christ. Too few are meeting the needs of the suffering and dying masses of the world. It is time to "wake up" (*egerthenai*) out of sleep: time to wake up, to be aroused and stirred. It is time to get up and move and act—now—before it is too late.
#4246 **Walk** **Walk–KJV** **Walk–NASB** Live–NIV **Walk–NKJV** Live–NLT	περιπατήσωμεν = peripatēsōmen Pronunciation: [per-ee-pat-ay'-so-mehn] Parsing (part of speech): verb Mood—subjunctive Tense—aorist Voice—active Person—1st person Number—plural Stem or root—from περιπατέω Concordance References: ⇒ Strong's #4043 peripateō ⇒ NIV #4344 peripateō ⇒ NASB #4043 peripateō	To walk; to go or move about; to live; to conduct oneself. **Practical Application** God's purpose for raising us up with Christ is dynamic and meaningful. It involves walking in a whole new life. The word "walk" (*peripateo*) means to walk about, to walk step by step, to control and order our behavior, to constantly and habitually walk in "newness of life." Think about it for a moment. When Christ

ENGLISH WORD	GREEK WORD AND VERSE	THE WORD MEANS...
POSB REFERENCE (Romans 6:3-5, esp. v.4) Note 2, point 2b	**Romans 6:4** Therefore we are buried with him by baptism into death: that like as Christ was raised up from the dead by the glory of the Father, even so we also should **walk** in newness of life. [KJV] Therefore we have been buried with Him through baptism into death, in order that as Christ was raised from the dead through the glory of the Father, so we too might **walk** in newness of life. [NASB] We were therefore buried with him through baptism into death in order that, just as Christ was raised from the dead through the glory of the Father, we too may **live** a new life. [NIV] Therefore we were buried with Him through baptism into death, that just as Christ was raised from the dead by the glory of the Father, even so we also should **walk** in newness of life. [NKJV] For we died and were buried with Christ by baptism. And just as Christ was raised from the dead by the glorious power of the Father, now we also may **live** new lives. [NLT] συνετάφημεν οὖν αὐτῷ διὰ τοῦ βαπτίσματος εἰς τὸν θάνατον· ἵνα ὥσπερ ἠγέρθη Χριστὸς ἐκ νεκρῶν διὰ τῆς δόξης τοῦ πατρός, οὕτως καὶ ἡμεῖς ἐν καινότητι ζωῆς **περιπατήσωμεν**. [GNS] συνετάφημεν οὖν αὐτῷ διὰ τοῦ βαπτίσματος εἰς τὸν θάνατον, ἵνα ὥσπερ ἠγέρθη Χριστὸς ἐκ νεκρῶν διὰ τῆς δόξης τοῦ πατρός, οὕτως καὶ ἡμεῖς ἐν καινότητι ζωῆς **περιπατήσωμεν**. [GNT]	died, he laid aside His old life and left it behind Him. Therefore, when He arose, He took on a totally new life, a changed life, a resurrected life. It is His new life, His changed and resurrected life, that is given to us. In the Bible the word "new" often carries the idea of purity, righteousness, holiness, godliness. The believer... • receives a "new birth" (1 Peter 1:23; 1 Peter 2:2). • receives a "new heart" (Ezekiel 11:19; Ezekiel 18:31). • becomes a "new creature" (2 Cor. 5:17; Galatians 6:15). • becomes a "new man" (Ephes. 4:24; Col. 3:10). God's very purpose for placing us in the resurrected life of Jesus Christ is that we might walk in Christ, walk soberly, righteously and godly in this present world. The true believer puts off the old man of sin and puts on the new man of righteousness and godliness. He lives a pure, clean, and holy life.

#4247 **Walk**
 	
Walk–KJV **Walk–NASB** **Walk–NIV** **Walk–NKJV** Live–NLT
 	
POSB REFERENCE (1 Jn.2:6) Note 4
	περιπατεῖν = *peripatein*
	Pronunciation: [per-ee-pat-een]
	Parsing (part of speech): verb
	   Mood—infinitive
	   Tense—present
	   Voice—active
	   Stem or root—from περιπατέω
	Concordance References:
	  ⇒ Strong's #4043 peripateō
	  ⇒ NIV #4344 peripateō
	  ⇒ NASB #4043 peripateō
	
	1 John 2:6
	He that saith he abideth in him ought himself also so to **walk**, even as he walked. [KJV]
	The one who says he abides in Him ought himself to **walk** in the same manner as He walked. [NASB]
	Whoever claims to live in him must **walk** as Jesus did. [NIV]
	He who says he abides in Him ought himself also to **walk** just as He walked. [NKJV]
	Those who say they **live** in God should live their lives as Christ did. [NLT]
	ὁ λέγων ἐν αὐτῷ μένειν ὀφείλει, καθὼς ἐκεῖνος περιεπάτησε, καὶ αὐτὸς οὕτω **περιπατεῖν**. [GNS]
	ὁ λέγων ἐν αὐτῷ μένειν ὀφείλει καθὼς ἐκεῖνος περιεπάτησεν καὶ αὐτὸς [οὕτως] **περιπατεῖν**. [GNT]
		To walk; to live; to act; to behave. The word "walk" (*peripatein*) is continuous action. It means to keep on walking; to continuously walk.
		
		Practical Application
		If a person says that he abides in Christ, he must be a responsible person. He ought to walk as Jesus Christ walked. In fact, the word *ought* means debt, constraint, obligation. The person who professes Jesus Christ, who claims that he knows God, is obligated to walk as Jesus Christ walked. He is in debt to walk as Christ walked. How did Christ walk upon earth? He walked...
		• believing and trusting God.
		• worshipping and praying to God.
		• fellowshipping and communing with God.
		• giving and sacrificing all He was and had to God.
		• seeking and following after God.
		• teaching and telling others about God.
		• loving and caring for others just as God said to do.
		• obeying and keeping all of God's commandments.
		This is the responsible man, the man who lives what he professes. If he professes to know God, he walks even as the Lord Jesus Christ walked upon earth. He believes and trusts God; he worships and prays to God, and he does all the other things that Christ did. He walks in the footsteps of Christ, doing exactly what Christ did. This is the person who knows God.

#4248 **Walked Along With– Walking Beside**	**συνεπορεύετο** = *suneporeueto*
	Pronunciation: [soon-eh-por-yoo'-eh-to]
	Parsing (part of speech): verb
	   Mood—indicative
	   Tense—imperfect
		To go together; to travel with; to walk beside; to go with.
		
		Practical Application
		The idea is that they were so absorbed in their

ENGLISH WORD	GREEK WORD AND VERSE	THE WORD MEANS...
Went with them—KJV Traveling with—NASB **Walked along with–NIV** Went with them–NKJV **Walking beside–NLT** **POSB REFERENCE** (Lk.24:15-27; esp. v.15) Note 2	Voice—middle or passive deponent Person—3rd person Number—singular Stem or root—from συμπορεύομαι Concordance References: ⇒ Strong's #4848 sumporeuomai ⇒ NIV #5233 sumporeuomai ⇒ NASB #4848 sumporeuomai ### Luke 24:15 And it came to pass, that, while they communed together and reasoned, Jesus himself drew near, and **went with them**. [KJV] And it came about that while they were conversing and discussing, Jesus Himself approached, and began **traveling with** them. [NASB] As they talked and discussed these things with each other, Jesus himself came up and **walked along with** them; [NIV] So it was, while they conversed and reasoned, that Jesus Himself drew near and **went with them**. [NKJV] Suddenly, Jesus himself came along and joined them and began **walking beside** them. [NLT] καὶ ἐγένετο ἐν τῷ ὁμιλεῖν αὐτοὺς καὶ συζητεῖν, καὶ αὐτὸς ὁ Ἰησοῦς ἐγγίσας **συνεπορεύετο** αὐτοῖς· [GNS] καὶ ἐγένετο ἐν τῷ ὁμιλεῖν αὐτοὺς καὶ συζητεῖν καὶ αὐτὸς Ἰησοῦς ἐγγίσας **συνεπορεύετο** αὐτοῖς, [GNT]	despair and talk that Jesus was already walking along with them when they noticed Him. But note: they did not know Him. His resurrected body differed enough that He was not recognized as Jesus without close observation (see POSB *Deeper Study* #1—John 21:1).

#4249
 	
Wander Beyond
 	
Whosoever transgresseth—KJV
Anyone who goes too far–NASB
Anyone who runs ahead–NIV
Whoever transgresses–NKJV
Wander beyond–NLT
 	
POSB REFERENCE
(2 Jn.1:9)
Note 3
	πᾶς ὁ προάγων = pas ho proagōn
	Pronunciation: [pro-ag'-on]
	Parsing *proagōn* (part of speech): verb
	    Mood—participle
	    Tense—present
	    Voice—active
	    Case—nominative
	    Gender—masculine
	    Number—singular
	    Stem or root—from προάγω
	Concordance References:
	⇒ Strong's #3956 pas + 3588 ho + 3845 parabaino
	⇒ NIV #4246 pas [Anyone] + 3836 ho [who] +
	⇒ 4575 proagō [runs ahead]
	   NASB #3956 pas + 3588 ho + 4254 proagō
	
	### 2 John 1:9
	Whosoever transgresseth, and abideth not in the doctrine of Christ, hath not God. He that abideth in the doctrine of Christ, he hath both the Father and the Son. [KJV]
	Anyone who goes too far and does not abide in the teaching of Christ, does not have God; the one who abides in the teaching, he has both the Father and the Son. [NASB]
	Anyone who runs ahead and does not continue in the teaching of Christ does not have God; whoever continues in the teaching has both the Father and the Son. [NIV]
	Whoever transgresses and does not abide in the doctrine of Christ does not have God. He who abides in the doctrine of Christ has both the Father and the Son. [NKJV]
	For if you **wander beyond** the teaching of Christ, you will not have fellowship with God. But if you continue in the teaching of Christ, you will have fellowship with both the Father and the Son. [NLT]
	πᾶς ὁ παραβαίνω καὶ μὴ μένων ἐν τῇ διδαχῇ τοῦ Χριστοῦ, Θεὸν οὐκ ἔχει· ὁ μένων ἐν τῇ διδαχῇ τοῦ Χριστοῦ, οὗτος καὶ τὸν πατέρα καὶ τὸν υἱὸν ἔχει. [GNS]
	πᾶς ὁ προάγων καὶ μὴ μένων ἐν τῇ διδαχῇ τοῦ Χριστοῦ θεὸν οὐκ ἔχει· ὁ μένων ἐν τῇ διδαχῇ, οὗτος καὶ τὸν πατέρα καὶ τὸν υἱὸν ἔχει. [GNT]
		To transgress against God by going too far, by trying to move out ahead of Christ; to wander beyond.
		
		### Practical Application
		The person who wanders beyond the teachings of Christ does not have or possess God. There are many teachers, ministers and laymen alike, who would like to be progressive and creative, to come up with a novel idea, to make some advancement in thought. They want people to recognize and approve them; therefore, they try to impress people. In so doing, they go beyond Christ and what He taught. They twist or branch off from the teachings of Christ. John warns against this: if a person does not stay in the teachings of Christ, then he does not have God. He is not saved; he is not truly born of God. The only person who is born of God is the person who stays in the teachings of Christ. This does not mean that believers are not to be creative and thoughtful. It means that we must not move out beyond Christ and what He taught.

ENGLISH WORD	GREEK WORD AND VERSE	THE WORD MEANS...

#4250
Wanted
 	
Took counsel–KJV
Intending–NASB
Wanted–NIV
Plotted–NKJV
Decided–NLT
 	
**POSB
REFERENCE**
(Acts 5:32-40; esp.
v.33)
Note 4, point 1
	ἐβούλοντο = *eboulonto*
	Pronunciation: [eh-bool-on-tow]
	Parsing (part of speech): verb
	   Mood—indicative
	   Tense—imperfect
	   Voice—middle or passive deponent
	   Person—3rd person
	   Number—plural
	   Stem or root—from βούλομαι
	Concordance References:
	⇒ Strong's #1014 boulomai
	⇒ NIV #1089 boulomai
	⇒ NASB #1014 boulomai
	
	Acts 5:33
	When they heard that, they were cut to the heart, and **took counsel** to slay them. [KJV]
	But when they heard this, they were cut to the quick and were **intending** to slay them. [NASB]
	When they heard this, they were furious and **wanted** to put them to death. [NIV]
	When they heard this, they were furious and **plotted** to kill them. [NKJV]
	At this, the high council was furious and **decided** to kill them. [NLT]
	Οἱ δὲ ἀκούσαντες διεπρίοντο, καὶ **ἐβούλοντο** ἀνελεῖν αὐτούς. [GNS]
	Οἱ δὲ ἀκούσαντες διεπρίοντο καὶ **ἐβούλοντο** ἀνελεῖν αὐτούς. [GNT]
		To want; to take counsel; to intend; to decide; to wish; to plan.
		
		Practical Application
		They were minded, were intending; were set on killing the disciples.

#4251
Wantonness
 	
Wantonness–KJV
Sensuality–NASB
Debauchery–NIV
Lust–NKJV
Immoral living–NLT
 	
**POSB
REFERENCE**
(Rom.13:13)
Note 4, point 4
	ἀσελγείαις = *aselgeiais*
	Pronunciation: [as-elg'-i-ah-is]
	Parsing (part of speech): noun
	   Case—dative
	   Gender—feminine
	   Number—plural
	   Stem or root—from ἀσέλγεια, ας
	Concordance References:
	⇒ Strong's #766 aselgeia
	⇒ NIV #816 aselgeia
	⇒ NASB #766 aselgeia
	
	Romans 13:13
	Let us walk honestly, as in the day; not in rioting and drunkenness, not in chambering and **wantonness**, not in strife and envying. [KJV]
	Let us behave properly as in the day, not in carousing and drunkenness, not in sexual promiscuity and **sensuality**, not in strife and jealousy. [NASB]
	Let us behave decently, as in the daytime, not in orgies and drunkenness, not in sexual immorality and **debauchery**, not in dissension and jealousy. [NIV]
	Let us walk properly, as in the day, not in revelry and drunkenness, not in lewdness and **lust**, not in strife and envy. [NKJV]
	We should be decent and true in everything we do, so that everyone can approve of our behavior. Don't participate in wild parties and getting drunk, or in adultery and **immoral living**, or in fighting and jealousy. [NLT]
	ὡς ἐν ἡμέρᾳ, εὐσχημόνως περιπατήσωμεν, μὴ κώμοις καὶ μέθαις, μὴ κοίταις καὶ **ἀσελγείαις**, μὴ ἔριδι καὶ ζήλῳ. [GNS]
	ὡς ἐν ἡμέρᾳ εὐσχημόνως περιπατήσωμεν, μὴ κώμοις καὶ μέθαις, μὴ κοίταις καὶ **ἀσελγείαις**, μὴ ἔριδι καὶ ζήλῳ, [GNT]
		Debauchery; sensuality; lust; running wild; licentiousness; wantonness; homosexuality; lasciviousness; living a wild, partying, and immoral life.
		
		Practical Application
		It is excess lust, unbridled lust that consumes one's thoughts and behavior through...
		• looks and dress
		• films and pictures
		• dances and parties
		• suggestions and gestures
		• books and pamphlets
		• songs and music
		• talk and jokes
		• touch and behavior
		• sensuality, indecency, vice

#4252
Wants
 	
Will–KJV
Wishes–NASB
Would–NIV
	θέλει = *thelē*
	Pronunciation: [thel'-ee]
	Parsing (part of speech): verb
	   Mood—indicative
	   Tense—present
	   Voice—active
	   Person—3rd person
		To desire, wish, design, purpose, resolve, determine.
		
		Practical Application
		It is a deliberate willingness, a deliberate choice, a determined resolve to follow Christ.

ENGLISH WORD	GREEK WORD AND VERSE	THE WORD MEANS...
Desires–NKJV Wants–NLT **POSB REFERENCE** (Mt.16:24) Note 2, point 1	Number—singular Stem or root—from θέλω Concordance References: ⇒ Strong's #2309 thelö ⇒ NIV #2527 thelö ⇒ NASB #2309 thelö **Matthew 16:24** Then said Jesus unto his disciples, If any man **will** come after me, let him deny himself, and take up his cross, and follow me. [KJV] Then Jesus said to His disciples, "If anyone **wishes** to come after Me, let him deny himself, and take up his cross, and follow Me. [NASB] Then Jesus said to his disciples, "If anyone **would** come after me, he must deny himself and take up his cross and follow me. [NIV] Then Jesus said to His disciples, "If anyone **desires** to come after Me, let him deny himself, and take up his cross, and follow Me. [NKJV] Then Jesus said to the disciples, "If any of you **wants** to be my follower, you must put aside your selfish ambition, shoulder your cross, and follow me. [NLT] τότε ὁ Ἰησοῦς εἶπε τοῖς μαθηταῖς αὐτοῦ, Εἴ τις θέλει ὀπίσω μου ἐλθεῖν, ἀπαρνησάσθω ἑαυτὸν, καὶ ἀράτω τὸν σταυρὸν αὐτοῦ καὶ ἀκολουθείτω μοι. [GNS] Τότε ὁ Ἰησοῦς εἶπεν τοῖς μαθηταῖς αὐτοῦ, Εἴ τις θέλει ὀπίσω μου ἐλθεῖν, ἀπαρνησάσθω ἑαυτὸν καὶ ἀράτω τὸν σταυρὸν αὐτοῦ καὶ ἀκολουθείτω μοι. [GNT]	If a person really wills and deliberately chooses to follow Christ, then he has to do the three things mentioned. Note: the choice is voluntary; it is made by the person.

#4253
Warn
 	
Exhort–KJV
Encourage–NASB
Encourage–NIV
Exhort–NKJV
Warn–NLT
 	
**POSB
REFERENCE**
(Heb.3:13-19; esp.
v.13)
Note 3
	παρακαλεῖτε = parakaleite
	Pronunciation: [par-ak-al-eh'-ee-teh]
	Parsing (part of speech): verb
	  Mood—imperative
	  Tense—present
	  Voice—active
	  Person—2nd person
	  Number—plural
	Stem or root—from *παρακαλέω*
	Concordance References:
	⇒ Strong's #3870 parakaleö
	⇒ NIV #4151 parakaleö
	⇒ NASB #3870 parakaleö
	
	Hebrews 3:13
	But **exhort** one another daily, while it is called To day; lest any of you be hardened through the deceitfulness of sin. [KJV]
	But **encourage** one another day after day, as long as it is still called "Today," lest any one of you be hardened by the deceitfulness of sin. [NASB]
	But **encourage** one another daily, as long as it is called Today, so that none of you may be hardened by sin's deceitfulness. [NIV]
	But **exhort** one another daily, while it is called "Today," lest any of you be hardened through the deceitfulness of sin. [NKJV]
	You must **warn** each other every day, as long as it is called "today," so that none of you will be deceived by sin and hardened against God. [NLT]
	ἀλλὰ **παρακαλεῖτε** ἑαυτοὺς καθ' ἑκάστην ἡμέραν, ἄχρις οὗ τὸ Σήμερον καλεῖται, ἵνα μὴ σκληρυνθῇ τις ἐξ ὑμῶν ἀπάτῃ τῆς ἁμαρτίας· [GNS]
	ἀλλὰ **παρακαλεῖτε** ἑαυτοὺς καθ' ἑκάστην ἡμέραν, ἄχρις οὗ τὸ Σήμερον καλεῖται, ἵνα μὴ σκληρυνθῇ τις ἐξ ὑμῶν ἀπάτῃ τῆς ἁμαρτίας [GNT]
		To encourage; to exhort; to warn; to plead with; to console. The word "warn" (*parakaleite*) means to "beg, entreat, beseech, exhort" (Kenneth Wuest. *Hebrews*, Vol. 2, p.79).
		
		Practical Application
		It is from the same word that the Comforter or Paraclete (the Holy Spirit) is taken. This means that the word "warn" also includes comfort, the kind of comfort that will "strengthen and encourage the believer each single day so that when a crises arises he may be able to stand fast" (Thomas Hewitt. *The Epistle to the Hebrews.* "Tyndale New Testament Commentaries." Grand Rapids, MI: Eerdmans, 1960, p.83). Believers are to constantly exhort one another to guard themselves against unbelief and sin.

#4254
**Warn–
Warning**
	νουθετῶν = noutheton
	Pronunciation: [noo-thet-own']
	Parsing (part of speech): verb
	  Mood—participle
	  Tense—present
	  Voice—active
		To warn; to admonish; to watch and care; to instruct; to teach.
		
		Practical Application
		The word means both to give advice and to

ENGLISH WORD	GREEK WORD AND VERSE	THE WORD MEANS...
Warn–KJV Admonish–NASB **Warning–NIV** **Warn–NKJV** Watch and care–NLT **POSB REFERENCE** (Acts 20:28-31; esp. v.31) Note 2, point 4a **See also POSB REF:** (Rom.15:14) Note 1, point 2c	Case—nominative Gender—masculine Person—1st person Number—singular Stem or root—from νουθετέω Concordance References: ⇒ Strong's #3560 noutheteö ⇒ NIV #3805 noutheteö ⇒ NASB #3560 noutheteö ### Acts 20:31 Therefore watch, and remember, that by the space of three years I ceased not to **warn** every one night and day with tears. [KJV] "Therefore be on the alert, remembering that night and day for a period of three years I did not cease to **admonish** each one with tears. [NASB] So be on your guard! Remember that for three years I never stopped **warning** each of you night and day with tears. [NIV] Therefore watch, and remember that for three years I did not cease to **warn** everyone night and day with tears. [NKJV] Watch out! Remember the three years I was with you—my constant **watch and care** over you night and day, and my many tears for you. [NLT] διὸ γρηγορεῖτε, μνημονεύοντες ὅτι τριετίαν νύκτα καὶ ἡμέραν οὐκ ἐπαυσάμην μετὰ δακρύων **νουθετῶν** ἕνα ἕκαστον. [GNS] διὸ γρηγορεῖτε μνημονεύοντες ὅτι τριετίαν νύκτα καὶ ἡμέραν οὐκ ἐπαυσάμην μετὰ δακρύων **νουθετῶν** ἕνα ἕκαστον. [GNT]	warn. It is a picture of urgency; of a desperate need to share the truth. The message is so important that the messenger is overcome with tears—both night and day.
#4255 Warned Spake on–KJV **Warned–NASB** **Warned–NIV** Spoke–NKJV Not translated–NLT **POSB REFERENCE** (Heb.12:25) Note 1	χρηματίζοντα = chrēmatizonta Pronunciation: [khray-mat-id'-zon-tah] Parsing (part of speech): verb Mood—participle Tense—present Voice—active Case—accusative Gender—masculine Number—singular Stem or root—from χρηματίζω Concordance References: ⇒ Strong's #5537 chrēmatizo ⇒ NIV #5976 chrēmatizo ⇒ NASB #5537 chrēmatizo ### Hebrews 12:25 See that ye refuse not him that speaketh. For if they escaped not who refused him that **spake on** earth, much more shall not we escape, if we turn away from him that speaketh from heaven: [KJV] See to it that you do not refuse Him who is speaking. For if those did not escape when they refused him who **warned** them on earth, much less shall we escape who turn away from Him who warns from heaven. [NASB] See to it that you do not refuse him who speaks. If they did not escape when they refused him who **warned** them on earth, how much less will we, if we turn away from him who warns us from heaven? [NIV] See that you do not refuse Him who speaks. For if they did not escape who refused Him who **spoke** on earth, much more shall we not escape if we turn away from Him who speaks from heaven, [NKJV] See to it that you obey God, the one who is speaking to you. For if the people of Israel did not escape when they refused to listen to Moses, the earthly messenger, how terrible our danger if we reject the One who speaks to us from heaven! [NLT]—NOT TRANSLATED βλέπετε μὴ παραιτήσησθε τὸν λαλοῦντα. εἰ γὰρ ἐκεῖνοι οὐκ ἔφυγον, τὸν ἐπὶ τῆς γῆς παραιτησάμενοι	To warn; to speak; to disclose; to reveal. It means transmitter or mouthpiece (William Barclay. *The Letter to the Hebrews*, p.215). ### Practical Application There shall be no escape whatsoever for the close-minded. Moses is the person who spoke on earth and gave the law of God to man, but Jesus Christ is the One who spoke and brought the Word of God down *out of* heaven.

ENGLISH WORD	GREEK WORD AND VERSE	THE WORD MEANS...
	χρηματίζοντα, πολλῷ μᾶλλον ἡμεῖς οἱ τὸν ἀπ' οὐρανῶν ἀποστρεφόμενοι [GNS] Βλέπετε μὴ παραιτήσησθε τὸν λαλοῦντα· εἰ γὰρ ἐκεῖνοι οὐκ ἐξέφυγον ἐπὶ γῆς παραιτησάμενοι τὸν χρηματίζοντα, πολὺ μᾶλλον ἡμεῖς οἱ τὸν ἀπ' οὐρανῶν ἀποστρεφόμενοι, [GNT]	

#4256
 Warned
 	
 Take heed–KJV
 Watch out–NASB
 Careful, Be–NIV
 Take heed–NKJV
 Warned–NLT
 	
 POSB
 REFERENCE
 (Mk.8:15)
 Deeper Study #1
	Ὁρᾶτε = *Horate*
	 Pronunciation: [hor-ah'-teh]
	 Parsing (part of speech): verb
	     Mood—imperative
	     Tense—present
	     Voice—active
	     Person—2nd person
	     Number—plural
	     Stem or root—from ὁράω
	 Concordance References:
	   ⇒ Strong's #3708 horaö
	   ⇒ NIV #3972 horaö
	   ⇒ NASB #3708 horaö
	
	 Mark 8:15
	 And he charged them, saying, **Take heed**, beware of the leaven of the Pharisees, and of the leaven of Herod. [KJV]
	
	 And He was giving orders to them, saying, "**Watch out**! Beware of the leaven of the Pharisees and the leaven of Herod." [NASB]
	
	 "**Be careful**," Jesus warned them. "Watch out for the yeast of the Pharisees and that of Herod." [NIV]
	
	 Then He charged them, saying, "**Take heed**, beware of the leaven of the Pharisees and the leaven of Herod." [NKJV]
	
	 As they were crossing the lake, Jesus **warned** them, "Beware of the yeast of the Pharisees and of Herod." [NLT]
	
	 καὶ διεστέλλετο αὐτοῖς, λέγων, Ὁρᾶτε, βλέπετε ἀπὸ τῆς ζύμης τῶν Φαρισαίων, καὶ τῆς ζύμης Ἡρώδου. [GNS]
	
	 καὶ διεστέλλετο αὐτοῖς λέγων, Ὁρᾶτε, βλέπετε ἀπὸ τῆς ζύμης τῶν Φαρισαίων καὶ τῆς ζύμης Ἡρῴδου. [GNT]
		To see, behold, discern, and acquaint oneself by closely observing and experiencing. It means to take heed; to watch out; to be warned; to be careful; to make sure.
		
		 Practical Application
		 Two things are needed for a person to be "warned": active thought and a discerning mind. The thing to be heeded must be actively observed, thought through, and discerned.
		
		 In the present passage, the charge is a *present imperative*. Beginning right now, the disciple is "warned" of yeast (leaven) and he is to continue being careful, always observing and discerning.

#4257
 Warped
 	
 Subverted–KJV
 Perverted–NASB
 Warped–NIV
 Warped–NKJV
 Turned away from the truth–NLT
 	
 POSB
 REFERENCE
 (Tit.3:10-11; esp. v.11)
 Note 3
	ἐξέστραπται = *exestraptai*
	 Pronunciation: [ek-ehs'-trap-tah-ee]
	 Parsing (part of speech): verb
	     Mood—indicative
	     Tense—perfect
	     Voice—passive
	     Person—3rd person
	     Number—singular
	     Stem or root—
	 Concordance References:
	   ⇒ Strong's #1612 ekstrephö
	   ⇒ NIV #1750 ekstrephö
	   ⇒ NASB #1612 ekstrephö
	
	 Titus 3:11
	 Knowing that he that is such is **subverted**, and sinneth, being condemned of himself. [KJV]
	
	 Knowing that such a man is **perverted** and is sinning, being self-condemned. [NASB]
	
	 You may be sure that such a man is **warped** and sinful; he is self-condemned. [NIV]
	
	 Knowing that such a person is **warped** and sinning, being self-condemned. [NKJV]
	
	 For people like that have **turned away from the truth**. They are sinning, and they condemn themselves. [NLT]
	
	 εἰδὼς ὅτι ἐξέστραπται ὁ τοιοῦτος, καὶ ἁμαρτάνει, ων αὐτοκατάκριτος. [GNS]
	
	 εἰδὼς ὅτι ἐξέστραπται ὁ τοιοῦτος καὶ ἁμαρτάνει ων αὐτοκατάκριτος. [GNT]
		Perverted, corrupted, warped, turned away from the truth. It means the heretic is "warped" (*exestraptai*): which means he is twisted or turned out and away from the truth of Christ and His Word.
		
		 Practical Application
		 Note that the heretic sins. The idea is that he sins greatly. Therefore, he condemns himself. He himself has chosen the path of unbelief, and he will be condemned for his unbelief.

ENGLISH WORD	GREEK WORD AND VERSE	THE WORD MEANS...

#4258
Was
 	
Was–KJV
Was–NASB
Was–NIV
Was–NKJV
Was–NLT
 	
POSB REFERENCE
(Jn.1:1-2; esp. v.1)
Note 1, point 1b
	ἦν = *ën*
	Pronunciation: [heyn]
	Parsing (part of speech): verb
	    Mood—indicative
	    Tense—imperfect
	    Voice—active
	    Person—3rd person
	    Number—singular
	    Stem or root—from εἰμί
	Concordance References:
	⇒ Strong's #1488 eimi
	⇒ NIV #1639 eimi
	⇒ NASB #1488 eimi
	
	John 1:1
	In the beginning **was** the Word, and the Word was with God, and the Word was God. [KJV]
	In the beginning **was** the Word, and the Word was with God, and the Word was God. [NASB]
	In the beginning **was** the Word, and the Word was with God, and the Word was God. [NIV]
	In the beginning **was** the Word, and the Word was with God, and the Word was God. [NKJV]
	In the beginning the Word **already existed**. He was with God, and he was God. [NLT]
	Ἐν ἀρχῇ ἦν ὁ λόγος, καὶ ὁ λόγος ἦν πρὸς τὸν Θεόν, καὶ Θεὸς ἦν ὁ λόγος. [GNS]
	Ἐν ἀρχῇ ἦν ὁ λόγος, καὶ ὁ λόγος ἦν πρὸς τὸν θεόν, καὶ θεὸς ἦν ὁ λόγος. [GNT]
		To be or I am; to exist.
		
		Practical Application
		The word "was" (*ën*) is the Greek imperfect tense of *eimi* which is the word so often used for deity. It means *to be* or *I am*. *To be* means continuous existence, without beginning or origin. (See POSB *Deeper Study #1*—John 6:20.)

#4259
Was
 	
Was made–KJV
Was born–NASB
Was–NIV
Was born–NKJV
Came–NLT
 	
POSB REFERENCE
(Romans 1:1-4; esp. v.3)
Note 3, point 2a
	γενομένου = *genomenou*
	Pronunciation: [ghin'-om-hen-oo]
	Parsing (part of speech): verb
	    Mood—participle
	    Tense—aorist
	    Voice—middle deponent
	    Case—genitive
	    Gender—masculine
	    Number—singular
	    Stem or root—from γίνομαι
	Concordance References:
	⇒ Strong's #1096 ginomai
	⇒ NIV #1181 ginomai
	⇒ NASB #1096 ginomai
	
	Romans 1:3
	Concerning his Son Jesus Christ our Lord, which **was made** of the seed of David according to the flesh; [KJV]
	Concerning His Son, who **was born** of a descendant of David according to the flesh, [NASB]
	Regarding his Son, who as to his human nature **was** a descendant of David, [NIV]
	Concerning His Son Jesus Christ our Lord, who **was born** of the seed of David according to the flesh, [NKJV]
	It is the Good News about his Son, Jesus, who **came** as a man, born into King David's royal family line. [NLT]
	περὶ τοῦ υἱοῦ αὐτοῦ τοῦ **γενομένου** ἐκ σπέρματος Δαβὶδ κατὰ σάρκα, [GNS]
	περὶ τοῦ υἱοῦ αὐτοῦ τοῦ **γενομένου** ἐκ σπέρματος Δαυὶδ κατὰ σάρκα, [GNT]
		Was; was made; was born; came; became; happened; came into being.
		
		Practical Application
		The point is this: God sent His Son into the world in human flesh. God's Son became a man—flesh and blood—just like all other men. He had a human nature, and because He had a human nature...
		
		• He suffered all the trials of life which we suffer.
		• He is able to help us through all the trials of life.

#4260
Was
 	
Being–KJV
Existed–NASB
Being–NIV
Being–NKJV
Was–NLT
	ὑπάρχων = *huparchön*
	Pronunciation: [hoop-ar'-khown]
	Parsing (part of speech): verb
	    Mood—participle
	    Tense—present
	    Voice—active
	    Case—nominative
	    Gender—masculine
	    Number—singular
	    Stem or root—from ὑπάρχω
	Concordance References:
	⇒ Strong's #5225 huparchö
		Being, existed, was. The word "was" (*huparchön*) means existence, what a person is within and without.
		
		Practical Application
		It is the very essence of a person, what a person is; that part of a person that cannot be changed. It is who a person is and all that he is.
		This is a most glorious truth because it means that *Jesus Christ is God*; He is the very *being of God*.

ENGLISH WORD	GREEK WORD AND VERSE	THE WORD MEANS...
POSB REFERENCE (Philip.2:6) Note 2, point 1	⇒ NIV #5639 huparchö ⇒ NASB #5225 huparchö **Philip. 2:6** Who, **being** in the form of God, thought it not robbery to be equal with God: [KJV] Who, although He **existed** in the form of God, did not regard equality with God a thing to be grasped, [NASB] Who, **being** in very nature God, did not consider equality with God something to be grasped, [NIV] Who, **being** in the form of God, did not consider it robbery to be equal with God, [NKJV] Though he **was** God, he did not demand and cling to his rights as God. [NLT] ὃς ἐν μορφῇ Θεοῦ **ὑπάρχων**, οὐχ ἁρπαγμὸν ἡγήσατο τὸ εἶναι ἴσα Θεῷ, [GNS] ὃς ἐν μορφῇ θεοῦ **ὑπάρχων** οὐχ ἁρπαγμὸν ἡγήσατο τὸ εἶναι ἴσα θεῷ, [GNT]	

#4261
Was Before Me
 	
Was before me–KJV
Existed before me–NASB
Was before me–NIV
Was before me–NKJV
Existed long before I did–NLT
 	
POSB REFERENCE (Jn.1:15) Note 3
	ὅτι πρῶτός μου = hoti prötos mou
	Pronunciation: [ho-tee pro-tos moo]
	Parsing *hoti* (part of speech): conjunction
	    Type—subordinating
	    Stem or root—from ὅτι
	Parsing *prötos* (part of speech): adjective
	    Type—ordinal
	    Case—nominative
	    Gender—masculine
	    Number—singular
	    Stem or root—from πρῶτος, η, ον
	Parsing *mou* (part of speech): noun
	    Type—pronoun
	    Case—genitive
	    Person—1st person
	    Number—singular
	    Stem or root—from ἐγώ
	Concordance References:
	⇒ Strong's #3754 hoti +4413 prötos + 1473 ego
	⇒ NIV #4022 hoti [was] + 4755 prötos [before] + 1609 egö [me]
	⇒ NASB #3754 hoti +4413 prötos + 1473 ego
	
	John 1:15
	John bare witness of him, and cried, saying, This was he of whom I spake, He that cometh after me is preferred before me: for he **was before me**. [KJV]
	John bore witness of Him, and cried out, saying, "This was He of whom I said, 'He who comes after me has a higher rank than I, for He **existed before me**.'" [NASB]
	John testifies concerning him. He cries out, saying, "This was he of whom I said, 'He who comes after me has surpassed me because he **was before me**.'" [NIV]
	John bore witness of Him and cried out, saying, "This was He of whom I said, 'He who comes after me is preferred before me, for He **was before me**.'" [NKJV]
	John pointed him out to the people. He shouted to the crowds, "This is the one I was talking about when I said, 'Someone is coming who is far greater than I am, for he **existed long before I did**.'" [NLT]
	Ἰωάννης μαρτυρεῖ περὶ αὐτοῦ καὶ κέκραγε λέγων, Οὗτος ἦν ὃν εἶπον, Ὁ ὀπίσω μου ἐρχόμενος ἔμπροσθέν μου γέγονεν· **ὅτι πρῶτός μου** ἦν. [GNS]
	Ἰωάννης μαρτυρεῖ περὶ αὐτοῦ καὶ κέκραγεν λέγων, Οὗτος ἦν ὃν εἶπον, Ὁ ὀπίσω μου ἐρχόμενος ἔμπροσθέν μου γέγονεν, **ὅτι πρῶτός μου** ἦν. [GNT]
		Was before me; existed before me; existed long before I did; literally *first to me* or *first of me*.
		
		Practical Application
		It refers both to time and importance. Jesus Christ was first in time, existing before John. He existed "in the beginning"—throughout all eternity. John proclaimed, "He was before me": He always existed; He was the First; He was the very cause for John's existence. John also declared that Jesus was first in importance. He was first in superiority, Being, Person. His very name is the First and the Last, the Alpha and the Omega, the Beginning and the End.

#4262
Was Born
 	
Was made–KJV
Was born–NASB
Was–NIV
	γενομένου = genomenou
	Pronunciation: [ghin'-om-hen-oo]
	Parsing (part of speech): verb
	    Mood—participle
	    Tense—aorist
	    Voice—middle deponent
	    Case—genitive
		Was; was made; was born; came; became; happened; came into being.
		
		Practical Application
		The point is this: God sent His Son into the world in human flesh. God's Son became a

ENGLISH WORD	GREEK WORD AND VERSE	THE WORD MEANS...
Was born–NKJV Came–NLT **POSB REFERENCE** (Romans 1:1-4; esp. v.3) Note 3, point 2a	Gender—masculine Number—singular Stem or root—from γίνομαι Concordance References: ⇒ Strong's #1096 ginomai ⇒ NIV #1181 ginomai ⇒ NASB #1096 ginomai **Romans 1:3** Concerning his Son Jesus Christ our Lord, which **was made** of the seed of David according to the flesh; [KJV] Concerning His Son, who **was born** of a descendant of David according to the flesh, [NASB] Regarding his Son, who as to his human nature **was** a descendant of David, [NIV] Concerning His Son Jesus Christ our Lord, who **was born** of the seed of David according to the flesh, [NKJV] It is the Good News about his Son, Jesus, who **came** as a man, born into King David's royal family line. [NLT] περὶ τοῦ υἱοῦ αὐτοῦ τοῦ **γενομένου** ἐκ σπέρματος Δαβὶδ κατὰ σάρκα, [GNS] περὶ τοῦ υἱοῦ αὐτοῦ τοῦ **γενομένου** ἐκ σπέρματος Δαυίδ κατὰ σάρκα, [GNT]	man—flesh and blood—just like all other men. He had a human nature, and because He had a human nature... • He suffered all the trials of life which we suffer. • He is able to help us through all the trials of life.
#4263 Was Dead Was dead–KJV Was dead–NASB Who died–NIV Was dead–NKJV Who died–NLT **POSB REFERENCE** (Rev.2:8) Note 2, point 2	ὃς ἐγένετο νεκρός = hos egeneto nekros Pronunciation: [hos eh-ghin'-eh-to nek-ros'] Parsing *egeneto* (part of speech): verb 　Mood—indicative 　Tense—aorist 　Voice—middle deponent 　Person—3rd person 　Number—singular 　Stem or root—from γίνομαι Parsing *nekros* (part of speech): adjective 　Case—nominative 　Gender—masculine 　Number—singular 　Stem or root—from νεκρός, ά, όν Concordance References: ⇒ Strong's #3739 hos + 1096+3498 ginomai nekros ⇒ NIV #4005 hos [who] + 1181+3738 ginomai nekros [died] ⇒ NASB #3739 hos + 1096+3498 ginomai nekros **Rev. 2:8** And unto the angel of the church in Smyrna write; These things saith the first and the last, which **was dead**, and is alive; [KJV] "And to the angel of the church in Smyrna write:The first and the last, who **was dead**, and has come to life, says this: [NASB] "To the angel of the church in Smyrna write: These are the words of him who is the First and the Last, **who died** and came to life again. [NIV] "And to the angel of the church in Smyrna write,'These things says the First and the Last, who **was dead**, and came to life: [NKJV] "Write this letter to the angel of the church in Smyrna. This is the message from the one who is the First and the Last, **who died** and is alive: [NLT] Καὶ τῷ ἀγγέλῳ τῆς ἐκκλησίας Σμυρναίων γράψον, Τάδε λέγει ὁ πρῶτος καὶ ὁ ἔσχατος, **ὃς ἐγένετο νεκρὸς** καὶ ἔζησεν· [GNS] Καὶ τῷ ἀγγέλῳ τῆς ἐν Σμύρνῃ ἐκκλησίας γράψον· Τάδε λέγει ὁ πρῶτος καὶ ὁ ἔσχατος, **ὃς ἐγένετο νεκρὸς** καὶ ἔζησεν· [GNT]	Was dead; who died. **Practical Application** Christ says that He is the One who *was dead and is alive again*. The word "was" (*genomenos*) really means *became*. Christ *became* dead. His death was only a passing phase, an episode He had to go through. He experienced death, but death was only a passing thing for Him. He triumphed over it. *Alive* is aorist tense in the Greek, a once-for-all act. Once it is done, it is done—completed, finished. Jesus *came to life again*. He arose. Therefore, the message to the church at Smyrna is that no matter what they experience, it is a passing episode. Even if they experience death, it has been conquered. Christ has personally been there and triumphed over both pain and death. Therefore, the believer will live forever even if he is martyred.
#4264 Was Made Was made–KJV Was born–NASB	γενομένου = genomenou Pronunciation: [ghin'-om-hen-oo] Parsing (part of speech): verb 　Mood—participle 　Tense—aorist	Was; was made; was born; came; to become; to happen; came into being. **Practical Application** The point is this: God sent His Son into the

ENGLISH WORD	GREEK WORD AND VERSE	THE WORD MEANS...
Was–NIV Was born–NKJV Came–NLT **POSB REFERENCE** (Romans 1:1-4; esp. v.3) Note 3, point. 2a	Voice—middle deponent Case—genitive Gender—masculine Number—singular Stem or root—from γίνομαι Concordance References: ⇒ Strong's #1096 ginomai ⇒ NIV #1181 ginomai ⇒ NASB #1096 ginomait **Romans 1:3** Concerning his Son Jesus Christ our Lord, which **was made** of the seed of David according to the flesh; [KJV] Concerning His Son, who **was born** of a descendant of David according to the flesh, [NASB] Regarding his Son, who as to his human nature **was** a descendant of David, [NIV] Concerning His Son Jesus Christ our Lord, who **was born** of the seed of David according to the flesh, [NKJV] It is the Good News about his Son, Jesus, who **came** as a man, born into King David's royal family line. [NLT] περὶ τοῦ υἱοῦ αὐτοῦ τοῦ **γενομένου** ἐκ σπέρματος Δαβὶδ κατὰ σάρκα, [GNS] περὶ τοῦ υἱοῦ αὐτοῦ τοῦ **γενομένου** ἐκ σπέρματος Δαυὶδ κατὰ σάρκα, [GNT]	world in human flesh. God's Son became a man—flesh and blood—just like all other men. He had a human nature, and because He had a human nature... • He suffered all the trials of life which we suffer. • He is able to help us through all the trials of life.
#4265 **Washed** Washed–KJV Washed–NASB Washed–NIV Washed–NKJV Washed–NLT **POSB REFERENCE** (1 Cor.6:11) Note 4, point 3	ἀπελούσασθε = *apelousasthe* Pronunciation: [ap-el-oo'-sahs-theh] Parsing (part of speech): verb Mood—indicative Tense—aorist Voice—middle Person—2nd person Number—plural Stem or root—from ἀπολούομαι Concordance References: ⇒ Strong's #628 apolouö ⇒ NIV #666 apolouö ⇒ NASB #628 apolouö **1 Cor. 6:11** And such were some of you: but ye are **washed**, but ye are sanctified, but ye are justified in the name of the Lord Jesus, and by the Spirit of our God. [KJV] And such were some of you; but you were **washed**, but you were sanctified, but you were justified in the name of the Lord Jesus Christ, and in the Spirit of our God. [NASB] And that is what some of you were. But you were **washed**, you were sanctified, you were justified in the name of the Lord Jesus Christ and by the Spirit of our God. [NIV] And such were some of you. But you were **washed**, but you were sanctified, but you were justified in the name of the Lord Jesus and by the Spirit of our God. [NKJV] There was a time when some of you were just like that, but now your sins have been **washed** away, and you have been set apart for God. You have been made right with God because of what the Lord Jesus Christ and the Spirit of our God have done for you. [NLT] καὶ ταῦτά τινες ἦτε· ἀλλὰ **ἀπελούσασθε**, ἀλλὰ ἡγιάσθητε, ἀλλὰ ἐδικαιώθητε ἐν τῷ ὀνόματι τοῦ Κυρίου Ἰησοῦ, καὶ ἐν τῷ Πνεύματι τοῦ Θεοῦ ἡμῶν. [GNS] καὶ ταῦτά τινες ἦτε· ἀλλὰ **ἀπελούσασθε**, ἀλλὰ ἡγιάσθητε, ἀλλὰ ἐδικαιώθητε ἐν τῷ ὀνόματι τοῦ κυρίου Ἰησοῦ Χριστοῦ καὶ ἐν τῷ πνεύματι τοῦ θεοῦ ἡμῶν. [GNT]	To wash off; to wash away (sin). **Practical Application** It means that a person comes to Jesus Christ to have his sins washed away, and when he comes, Jesus actually washes his sins away. The word is in the Greek aorist tense which is the past tense a once-for-all act; that is, it is referring to their conversion experience. When the believer is washed from sin, he is supposed to be washed and cleansed. Sin and its defilement are supposed to be washed away forever. By the power of Christ, the believer is supposed to stay away from the dirt and the filth of the world.
#4266 **Washed**	λύσαντι = *lusanti* Pronunciation: [loo'-sahn-tee] Parsing (part of speech): verb Mood—participle	To be freed, washed, loosed, set free, and released from sin.

ENGLISH WORD	GREEK WORD AND VERSE	THE WORD MEANS...
Washed–KJV Released–NASB Freed–NIV **Washed–NKJV** Freed–NLT **POSB** **REFERENCE** (Rev.1:5-6; esp.v.5) Note 2, point 4	Tense—aorist Voice—active Case—dative Gender—masculine Number—singular Stem or root—from λύω Concordance References: ⇒ Strong's #3089 luō ⇒ NIV #3395 luō ⇒ NASB #3089 luō **Rev. 1:5** And from Jesus Christ, who is the faithful witness, and the first begotten of the dead, and the prince of the kings of the earth. Unto him that loved us, and **washed** us from our sins in his own blood, [KJV] And from Jesus Christ, the faithful witness, the first-born of the dead, and the ruler of the kings of the earth. To Him who loves us, and **released** us from our sins by His blood, [NASB] And from Jesus Christ, who is the faithful witness, the firstborn from the dead, and the ruler of the kings of the earth. To him who loves us and has **freed** us from our sins by his blood, [NIV] And from Jesus Christ, the faithful witness, the first-born from the dead, and the ruler over the kings of the earth. To Him who loved us and **washed** us from our sins in His own blood, [NKJV] And from Jesus Christ, who is the faithful witness to these things, the first to rise from the dead, and the commander of all the rulers of the world. All praise to him who loves us and has **freed** us from our sins by shedding his blood for us. [NLT] καὶ ἀπὸ Ἰησοῦ Χριστοῦ, ὁ μάρτυς ὁ πιστός, ὁ πρωτότοκος τῶν νεκρῶν καὶ ὁ ἄρχων τῶν βασιλέων τῆς γῆς. τῷ ἀγαπήσαντι ἡμᾶς, καὶ **λούσαντι** ἡμᾶς ἀπὸ τῶν ἁμαρτιῶν ἡμῶν ἐν τῷ αἵματι αὐτοῦ· [GNS] καὶ ἀπὸ Ἰησοῦ Χριστοῦ, ὁ μάρτυς ὁ πιστός, ὁ πρωτότοκος τῶν νεκρῶν καὶ ὁ ἄρχων τῶν βασιλέων τῆς γῆς. Τῷ ἀγαπῶντι ἡμᾶς καὶ **λύσαντι** ἡμᾶς ἐκ τῶν ἁμαρτιῶν ἡμῶν ἐν τῷ αἵματι αὐτοῦ, [GNT]	**Practical Application** Jesus Christ has redeemed us. He *"loves us and has washed us from our sins in His own blood"* (Rev. 1:5). The word *love* is in the present tense in the Greek. This means that Jesus Christ *always loves* us. He loves us today just as He has loved us in the past. How did the blood of Jesus Christ set us free from sin? Jesus Christ took our sins and died for them. He had lived a sinless and perfect life as a Man upon earth. Therefore, He was able to present Himself as the Ideal and Perfect Man before God. He was able to die as the Ideal and Perfect Sacrifice. He was able to take our sins—the guilt and the judgment of our sins—upon Himself to bear the punishment for them. He was the Ideal and Perfect Man; therefore, God is able to accept His death as the Ideal and Perfect Sacrifice for sin. The point is this: Jesus Christ died for our sins. He actually took our sins off of us, removed them, and died for them. Therefore, we are free and loosed from sin. Sin has been removed from us. We stand before God free of sin and acceptable to Him. But remember how: by the shed blood of Jesus Christ upon the cross. It is the shed blood of Christ upon the cross—His dying for our sins—that washes us from sin.
#4267 **Washed Away** Washing–KJV Washing–NASB Washing–NIV Washing–NKJV **Washed away–NLT** **POSB** **REFERENCE** (Tit.3:5) Note 2, point 1	λουτροῦ = *loutrou* Pronunciation: [loo-troo'] Parsing (part of speech): noun Case—genitive Gender—neuter Number—singular Stem or root—from λουτρόν, οῦ Concordance References: ⇒ Strong's #3067 loutron ⇒ NIV #3373 loutron ⇒ NASB #3067 loutron **Titus 3:5** Not by works of righteousness which we have done, but according to his mercy he saved us, by the **washing** of regeneration, and renewing of the Holy Ghost; [KJV] He saved us, not on the basis of deeds which we have done in righteousness, but according to His mercy, by the **washing** of regeneration and renewing by the Holy Spirit, [NASB] He saved us, not because of righteous things we had done, but because of his mercy. He saved us through the **washing** of rebirth and renewal by the Holy Spirit, [NIV] Not by works of righteousness which we have done, but according to His mercy He saved us, through the **washing** of regeneration and renewing of the Holy Spirit, [NKJV] He saved us, not because of the good things we did, but because of his mercy. He **washed away** our sins and gave us a new life through the Holy Spirit. [NLT]	Washing, washed away, cleansing with water. **Practical Application** Note that the new birth is so radical a change in a person's life that it is described as a "washing away" (*loutrou*) which means a bath, a complete immersion. Salvation is so dramatic it is just like the washing away of the old life and the receiving of a new life. All that concerns a person's old life is washed away, all the... • sin and evil • corruption and injustice • selfishness and greed • guilt and doubt • dirt and immorality • pollution and worldliness • failure and shortcoming The Spirit of God cleanses a person—immerses the person in the cleansing blood of Jesus Christ.

ENGLISH WORD	GREEK WORD AND VERSE	THE WORD MEANS...
	οὐκ ἐξ ἔργων τῶν ἐν δικαιοσύνῃ ὧν ἐποιήσαμεν ἡμεῖς, ἀλλὰ κατὰ τὸν αὐτοῦ ἔλεον ἔσωσεν ἡμᾶς, διὰ **λουτροῦ** παλιγγενεσίας καὶ ἀνακαινώσεως Πνεύματος Ἁγίου, [GNS] οὐκ ἐξ ἔργων τῶν ἐν δικαιοσύνῃ ἃ ἐποιήσαμεν ἡμεῖς ἀλλὰ κατὰ τὸ αὐτοῦ ἔλεος ἔσωσεν ἡμᾶς διὰ **λουτροῦ** παλιγγενεσίας καὶ ἀνακαινώσεως πνεύματος ἁγίου, [GNT]	
#4268 **Washing** Washing–KJV Washing–NASB Washing–NIV Washing–NKJV Washed away–NLT **POSB** **REFERENCE** (Tit.3:5) Note 2, point 1	**λουτροῦ** = *loutrou* Pronunciation: [loo-troo'] Parsing (part of speech): noun 　Case—genitive 　Gender—neuter 　Number—singular 　Stem or root—from λουτρόν, οῦ Concordance References: ⇒ Strong's #3067 loutron ⇒ NIV #3373 loutron ⇒ NASB #3067 loutron **Titus 3:5** Not by works of righteousness which we have done, but according to his mercy he saved us, by the **washing** of regeneration, and renewing of the Holy Ghost; [KJV] He saved us, not on the basis of deeds which we have done in righteousness, but according to His mercy, by the **washing** of regeneration and renewing by the Holy Spirit, [NASB] He saved us, not because of righteous things we had done, but because of his mercy. He saved us through the **washing** of rebirth and renewal by the Holy Spirit, [NIV] Not by works of righteousness which we have done, but according to His mercy He saved us, through the **washing** of regeneration and renewing of the Holy Spirit, [NKJV] He saved us, not because of the good things we did, but because of his mercy. He **washed away** our sins and gave us a new life through the Holy Spirit. [NLT] οὐκ ἐξ ἔργων τῶν ἐν δικαιοσύνῃ ὧν ἐποιήσαμεν ἡμεῖς, ἀλλὰ κατὰ τὸν αὐτοῦ ἔλεον ἔσωσεν ἡμᾶς, διὰ **λουτροῦ** παλιγγενεσίας καὶ ἀνακαινώσεως Πνεύματος Ἁγίου, [GNS] οὐκ ἐξ ἔργων τῶν ἐν δικαιοσύνῃ ἃ ἐποιήσαμεν ἡμεῖς ἀλλὰ κατὰ τὸ αὐτοῦ ἔλεος ἔσωσεν ἡμᾶς διὰ **λουτροῦ** παλιγγενεσίας καὶ ἀνακαινώσεως πνεύματος ἁγίου, [GNT]	Washing, washed away, cleansing with water. **Practical Application** Note that the new birth is so radical a change in a person's life that it is described as a "washing" (*loutrou*) which means a bath, a complete immersion. Salvation is so dramatic it is just like the washing away of the old life and the receiving of a new life. All that concerns a person's old life is washed away, all the... ● sin and evil ● corruption and injustice ● selfishness and greed ● guilt and doubt ● dirt and immorality ● pollution and worldliness ● failure and shortcoming The Spirit of God cleanses a person—immerses the person in the cleansing blood of Jesus Christ.
#4269 **Wasted** Wasted–KJV Destroy–NASB Destroy–NIV Destroy–NKJV Get rid of–NLT **POSB** **REFERENCE** (Gal.1:13-16; esp. v.13) Note 3, point 1a	**ἐπόρθουν** = *eporthoun* Pronunciation: [eh-por-thoon'] Parsing (part of speech): verb 　Mood—indicative 　Tense—imperfect 　Voice—active 　Person—1st person 　Number—singular 　Stem or root—from πορθέω Concordance References: ⇒ Strong's #4199 portheö ⇒ NIV #4514 portheö ⇒ NASB #4199 portheö **Galatians 1:13** For ye have heard of my conversation in time past in the Jews' religion, how that beyond measure I persecuted the church of God, and **wasted** it: [KJV] For you have heard of my former manner of life in Judaism, how I used to persecute the church of God beyond measure, and tried to **destroy** it; [NASB] For you have heard of my previous way of life in Judaism, how intensely I persecuted the church of God and tried to **destroy** it. [NIV] For you have heard of my former conduct in Judaism,	To destroy; to get rid of; to make havoc; to utterly rack or lay waste; to devastate, destroy, ruin, or wipe out. **Practical Application** The point is that Paul had been bent on violence; he had sought to utterly stamp out the church; to wipe believers off the face of the earth. (See POSB note, Church, Persecution of—Acts 8:3 for more discussion.)

ENGLISH WORD	GREEK WORD AND VERSE	THE WORD MEANS...
	how I persecuted the church of God beyond measure and *tried to* **destroy** it. [NKJV] You know what I was like when I followed the Jewish religion—how I violently persecuted the Christians. I did my best to **get rid of** them. [NLT] ἠκούσατε γὰρ τὴν ἐμὴν ἀναστροφήν ποτε ἐν τῷ Ἰουδαϊσμῷ, ὅτι καθ᾽ ὑπερβολὴν ἐδίωκον τὴν ἐκκλησίαν τοῦ Θεοῦ, καὶ **ἐπόρθουν** αὐτήν· [GNS] Ἠκούσατε γὰρ τὴν ἐμὴν ἀναστροφήν ποτε ἐν τῷ Ἰουδαϊσμῷ, ὅτι καθ᾽ ὑπερβολὴν ἐδίωκον τὴν ἐκκλησίαν τοῦ θεοῦ καὶ **ἐπόρθουν** αὐτήν, [GNT]	

#4270
Watch
 	
Watch–KJV
Be on the alert–NASB
Keep watch–NIV
Watch–NKJV
Be prepared–NLT
 	
**POSB
REFERENCE**
(Mt.24:42)
Note 1
 	
See also POSB REF:
(Mk.13:37)
Deeper Study #1
(1 Pt.5:8)
Note 1, point 2
	γρηγορεῖτε = grēgoreite
	Pronunciation: [gray-gor-ee'-teh]
	Parsing (part of speech):verb
	   Mood—imperative
	   Tense—present
	   Voice—active
	   Person—2nd person
	   Number—plural
	   Stem or root—from γρηγορέω
	Concordance References:
	⇒ Strong's #1127 gregoreuo
	⇒ NIV #1213 grēgoreō
	⇒ NASB #1127 gregoreuo
	
	Matthew 24:42
	Watch therefore: for ye know not what hour your Lord doth come. [KJV]
	"Therefore **be on the alert**, for you do not know which day your Lord is coming. [NASB]
	"Therefore **keep watch**, because you do not know on what day your Lord will come. [NIV]
	Watch therefore, for you do not know what hour your Lord is coming. [NKJV]
	So **be prepared**, because you don't know what day your Lord is coming. [NLT]
	γρηγορεῖτε οὖν, ὅτι οὐκ οἴδατε ποίᾳ ὥρᾳ ὁ Κύριος ὑμῶν ἔρχεται. [GNS]
	γρηγορεῖτε οὖν, ὅτι οὐκ οἴδατε ποίᾳ ὥρᾳ ὁ Κύριος ὑμῶν ἔρχεται. [GNT]
		To watch; to stay alert; to be ready; to pay strict attention; to keep awake; to be watchful and sleepless; to be vigilant; to be prepared.
		
		Practical Application
		It also includes the idea of being motivated, of keeping one's attention (mind) upon a thing. Being on the alert also has the idea of being alert at the right time. It is at night that a person really needs to stay awake to watch for the thief (cp. 1 Thes. 5:4-9).

#4271
Watch
 	
Watch–KJV
On...alert–NASB
On...guard–NIV
Watch–NKJV
On guard–NLT
 	
**POSB
REFERENCE**
(1 Cor.16:13-14; esp. v.13)
Note 4
	Γρηγορεῖτε = Grēgoreite
	Pronunciation: [gray-gor-ee'-teh]
	Parsing (part of speech): verb
	   Mood—imperative
	   Tense—present
	   Voice—active
	   Person—2nd person
	   Number—plural
	   Stem or root—from γρηγορέω
	Concordance References:
	⇒ Strong's #1127 grēgoreō
	⇒ NIV #1213 grēgoreō
	⇒ NASB #1127 gregoreō
	
	1 Cor. 16:13
	Watch ye, stand fast in the faith, quit you like men, be strong. [KJV]
	Be **on** the **alert**, stand firm in the faith, act like men, be strong. [NASB]
	Be **on** your **guard**; stand firm in the faith; be men of courage; be strong. [NIV]
	Watch, stand fast in the faith, be brave, be strong. [NKJV]
	Be **on guard**. Stand true to what you believe. Be courageous. Be strong. [NLT]
	Γρηγορεῖτε, στήκετε ἐν τῇ πίστει, ἀνδρίζεσθε, κραταιοῦσθε. [GNS]
	Γρηγορεῖτε, στήκετε ἐν τῇ πίστει, ἀνδρίζεσθε, κραταιοῦσθε. [GNT]
		To be on guard; to be on alert; to watch; to be awake, alert, alive, and constantly on guard; never to be sleepy-eyed or sluggish; never to let one's guard down.
		
		Practical Application
		There are five charges in this exhortation, and all five are in the present tense; that is, this is the way believers are to live. These things are to be continually done.
		1. "Watch" (*Grēgoreite*): to be awake, alert, and constantly on guard; never to be sleepy-eyed or sluggish; never to let one's guard down.
		2. "Stand fast in the faith": do not listen or give heed to false teachers and false doctrine; do not question the word and truth of Christ. Stand against those who mishandle and abuse the Word of God.
		3. "Quit you like men" or "be brave" means either to be courageous as real men or to quit living like immature men. It means to live as courageous men of God.
		4. "Be strong": to grow in strength; to be men of real strength; to stand against the world and its enticements.
		5. Do everything in love (v.17): The believer is to live "in" love and to do everything "in" love. Remember the love chapter, 1 Cor. 13. The greatest answer to the division

ENGLISH WORD	GREEK WORD AND VERSE	THE WORD MEANS...
		and other problems within the church is love. Love must prevail in the hearts and behavior of believers and their church.

#4272
Watch
 	
Considering–KJV
Looking–NASB
Watch–NIV
Considering–NKJV
Be careful–NLT
 	
**POSB
REFERENCE**
(Gal.6:1)
Note 3
	σκοπῶν = *skopōn*
	Pronunciation: [skop-own]
	Parsing (part of speech): verb
	    Mood—participle (imperative sense)
	    Tense—present
	    Voice—active
	    Case—nominative
	    Gender—masculine
	    Person—2nd person
	    Number—singular
	    Stem or root—from σκοπέω
	Concordance References:
	  ⇒ Strong's #4648 skopeö
	  ⇒ NIV #5023 skopeö
	  ⇒ NASB #4648 skopeö
	
	Galatians 6:1
	Brethren, if a man be overtaken in a fault, ye which are spiritual, restore such an one in the spirit of meekness; **considering** thyself, lest thou also be tempted. [KJV]
	Brethren, even if a man is caught in any trespass, you who are spiritual, restore such a one in a spirit of gentleness; each one **looking** to yourself, lest you too be tempted. [NASB]
	Brothers, if someone is caught in a sin, you who are spiritual should restore him gently. But **watch** yourself, or you also may be tempted. [NIV]
	Brethren, if a man is overtaken in any trespass, you who are spiritual restore such a one in a spirit of gentleness, **considering** yourself lest you also be tempted. [NKJV]
	Dear brothers and sisters, if another Christian is overcome by some sin, you who are godly should gently and humbly help that person back onto the right path. And **be careful** not to fall into the same temptation yourself. [NLT]
	Ἀδελφοί, ἐὰν καὶ προληφθῇ ἄνθρωπος ἔν τινι παραπτώματι, ὑμεῖς οἱ πνευματικοὶ καταρτίζετε τὸν τοιοῦτον ἐν πνεύματι πραότητος, **σκοπῶν** σεαυτόν, μὴ καὶ σὺ πειρασθῇς. [GNS]
	Ἀδελφοί, ἐὰν καὶ προλημφθῇ ἄνθρωπος ἔν τινι παραπτώματι, ὑμεῖς οἱ πνευματικοὶ καταρτίζετε τὸν τοιοῦτον ἐν πνεύματι πραΰτητος, **σκοπῶν** σεαυτόν μὴ καὶ σὺ πειρασθῇς. [GNT]
		To watch; to carefully consider; to look to oneself; to keep one's attention on; to fix eyes on; to take note of; to think about oneself and to give attention to oneself. It means to keep an attentive eye on oneself.
		
		Practical Application
		If we really watch and consider the matter, then we will reach out in love and gentleness to help our fallen brothers. We have to help them, for we are all ever so subject to being caught in a sin.

#4273
**Watch–
Watchful**
 	
Watch–KJV
Sober–NASB
Keep [your] head–NIV
Watchful–NKJV
Keep [a] clear mind–
NLT
 	
**POSB
REFERENCE**
(2 Tim. 4:5)
Note 4, point 1
	νῆφε = *nēphe*
	Pronunciation: [nay'-feh]
	Parsing (part of speech): verb
	    Mood—imperative
	    Tense—present
	    Voice—active
	    Person—2nd person
	    Number—singular
	    Stem or root—from νήφω
	Concordance References:
	  ⇒ Strong's #3525 nēphö
	  ⇒ NIV #3768 nēphö
	  ⇒ NASB #3525 nēphö
	
	2 Tim. 4:5
	But **watch** thou in all things, endure afflictions, do the work of an evangelist, make full proof of thy ministry. [KJV]
	But you, be **sober** in all things, endure hardship, do the work of an evangelist, fulfill your ministry. [NASB]
	But you, **keep** your **head** in all situations, endure hardship, do the work of an evangelist, discharge all the duties of your ministry. [NIV]
	But you be **watchful** in all things, endure afflictions,
		To keep your head; to watch; to keep a clear mind. It means to be sober, calm, and alert; to keep a cool, calm, and collected mind; to maintain a controlled and disciplined life and spirit.
		
		Practical Application
		The minister must watch in all things. And note: the minister is to be this way in all things: in body, mind, and spirit—in thought, word and behavior. The minister is to always watch—always be alert, calm, controlled, and disciplined—no matter the activity or behavior.

ENGLISH WORD	GREEK WORD AND VERSE	THE WORD MEANS...
	do the work of an evangelist, fulfill your ministry. [NKJV] But you should **keep** a **clear mind** in every situation. Don't be afraid of suffering for the Lord. Work at bringing others to Christ. Complete the ministry God has given you. [NLT] σὺ δὲ **νῆφε** ἐν πᾶσι, κακοπάθησον, ἔργον ποίησον εὐαγγελιστοῦ, τὴν διακονίαν σου πληροφόρησον. [GNS] σὺ δὲ **νῆφε** ἐν πᾶσιν, κακοπάθησον, ἔργον ποίησον εὐαγγελιστοῦ, τὴν διακονίαν σου πληροφόρησον. [GNT]	
#4274 **Watch–** **Watchful** **Watch–KJV** Sober spirit–NASB Self-controlled–NIV **Watchful–NKJV** Disciplined–NLT **POSB** **REFERENCE** (1 Pt.4:7) Note 2 **See also POSB REF:** (1 Pt.1:13) Note 1, point 2	νήψατε = *nëpsate* Pronunciation: [nay'-psah-teh] Parsing (part of speech): verb 　Mood—imperative 　Tense—aorist 　Voice—active 　Person—2nd person 　Number—plural 　Stem or root—from νήφω Concordance References: 　⇒ Strong's #3525 nëphö 　⇒ NIV #3768 nëphö 　⇒ NASB #3525 nëphö **1 Peter 4:7** But the end of all things is at hand: be ye therefore sober, and **watch** unto prayer. [KJV] 　The end of all things is at hand; therefore, be of sound judgment and **sober spirit** for the purpose of prayer. [NASB] 　The end of all things is near. Therefore be clear minded and **self-controlled** so that you can pray. [NIV] 　But the end of all things is at hand; therefore be serious and **watchful** in your prayers. [NKJV] 　The end of the world is coming soon. Therefore, be earnest and **disciplined** in your prayers. [NLT] 　Πάντων δὲ τὸ τέλος ἤγγικε· σωφρονήσατε οὖν καὶ **νήψατε** εἰς τὰς προσευχάς· [GNS] 　Πάντων δὲ τὸ τέλος ἤγγικεν. σωφρονήσατε οὖν καὶ **νήψατε** εἰς προσευχάς· [GNT]	To be self-controlled; to watch; to have a sober spirit; to be disciplined; to stay sober and alert and awake at all times. **Practical Application** This says two things. 1. The believer is to keep his mind sober, always watching. He is not to drink intoxicating beverages or take drugs or do anything else that dulls and numbs his mind. He is to keep his mind sober and alert at all times. He is not to be escaping reality; he is to be grasping reality. He is to be praying always for all things, and he cannot be praying if his mind is dull and numb because of drink and drugs. 2. The believer is to keep his mind alert, keep it from being sleepy-eyed and lazy and wandering about. The mind is always thinking; it is always upon something; it is never without thought. Therefore, the believer is to keep his mind alert and active. He is to control his thoughts even to the point of captivating every thought. Every moment that his thoughts are not engaged with the necessary activities of life, he is to focus his thoughts upon prayer. Even while carrying on the activities of life, he needs to flicker his thoughts to prayer here and there. He needs to acknowledge God in all His ways. This is what it means to watch and pray. The believer is to stay sober and watch for every opportunity to pray.
#4275 **Watch–** **Watch,** **Constant–** **Watch, On The** **Watch–KJV** On the alert–NASB **On the watch–NIV** **Watch–NKJV** **Constant watch–NLT** **POSB** **REFERENCE** (Lk.21:36) Note 2	ἀγρυπνεῖτε = *agrupneite* Pronunciation: [ag-roop-neeh'-te] Parsing (part of speech): verb 　Mood—imperative 　Tense—present 　Voice—active 　Person—2nd person 　Number—plural 　Stem or root—from ἀγρυπνέω Concordance References: 　⇒ Strong's #69 agrupneö 　⇒ NIV #70 agrupneö 　⇒ NASB #69 agrupneö **Luke 21:36** **Watch** ye therefore, and pray always, that ye may be accounted worthy to escape all these things that shall come to pass, and to stand before the Son of man. [KJV] 　"But keep **on the alert** at all times, praying in order that you may have strength to escape all these things that are about to take place, and to stand before the Son of Man." [NASB] 　Be always **on the watch**, and pray that you may be able to escape all that is about to happen, and that you may be able to stand before the Son of Man." [NIV] 　**Watch** therefore, and pray always that you may be counted worthy to escape all these things that will come	To be sleepless, awake, on guard; to be on a constant watch. **Practical Application** 　It means a spirit of being wakeful; of being restless; of guarding. In this Scripture, to watch is to pray. What does it mean to watch and pray? Praying always means the believer is to live in a spirit of prayer... 　• praying all day, as he walks throughout the day. 　• praying on all occasions and about everything. 　• Praying at appointed times, times set aside for nothing but prayer and devotions or quiet times.

ENGLISH WORD	GREEK WORD AND VERSE	THE WORD MEANS...
	to pass, and to stand before the Son of Man." [NKJV] Keep a **constant watch**. And pray that, if possible, you may escape these horrors and stand before the Son of Man." [NLT] Ἀγρυπνεῖτε οὖν ἐν παντὶ καιρῷ δεόμενοι ἵνα καταξιωθῆτε ἐκφυγεῖν ταῦτα πάντα τὰ μέλλοντα γίνεσθαι, καὶ σταθῆναι ἔμπροσθεν τοῦ υἱοῦ τοῦ ἀνθρώπου. [GNS] ἀγρυπνεῖτε δὲ ἐν παντὶ καιρῷ δεόμενοι ἵνα κατισχύσητε ἐκφυγεῖν ταῦτα πάντα τὰ μέλλοντα γίνεσθαι καὶ σταθῆναι ἔμπροσθεν τοῦ υἱοῦ τοῦ ἀνθρώπου. [GNT]	

#4276
Watch And Care
 	
Warn–KJV
Admonish–NASB
Warning–NIV
Warn–NKJV
Watch and care–NLT
 	
POSB REFERENCE
(Acts 20:28-31; esp. v.31)
Note 2, point 4a
 	
See also POSB REF:
(Rom.15:14)
Note 1, point 2c
	νουθετῶν = *noutheton*
	Pronunciation: [noo-thet-own']
	Parsing (part of speech): verb
	  Mood—participle
	  Tense—present
	  Voice—active
	  Case—nominative
	  Gender—masculine
	  Person—1st person
	  Number—singular
	  Stem or root—from νουθετέω
	Concordance References:
	⇒ Strong's #3560 noutheteö
	⇒ NIV #3805 noutheteö
	⇒ NASB #3560 noutheteö
	
	Acts 20:31
	Therefore watch, and remember, that by the space of three years I ceased not to **warn** every one night and day with tears. [KJV]
	"Therefore be on the alert, remembering that night and day for a period of three years I did not cease to **admonish** each one with tears. [NASB]
	So be on your guard! Remember that for three years I never stopped **warning** each of you night and day with tears. [NIV]
	Therefore watch, and remember that for three years I did not cease to **warn** everyone night and day with tears. [NKJV]
	Watch out! Remember the three years I was with you—my constant **watch and care** over you night and day, and my many tears for you. [NLT]
	διὸ γρηγορεῖτε, μνημονεύοντες ὅτι τριετίαν νύκτα καὶ ἡμέραν οὐκ ἐπαυσάμην μετὰ δακρύων **νουθετῶν** ἕνα ἕκαστον. [GNS]
	διὸ γρηγορεῖτε μνημονεύοντες ὅτι τριετίαν νύκτα καὶ ἡμέραν οὐκ ἐπαυσάμην μετὰ δακρύων **νουθετῶν** ἕνα ἕκαστον. [GNT]
		To warn; to admonish; to watch and care; to instruct; to teach.
		
		Practical Application
		The word means both to give advice and to warn. It is a picture of urgency; of a desperate need to share the truth. The message is so important that the messenger is overcome with tears—both night and day.

#4277
Watch Closely
 	
Take heed–KJV
Pay close attention–NASB
Watch closely–NIV
Take heed–NKJV
Keep a close watch–NLT
 	
POSB REFERENCE
(1 Tim.4:16)
Note 12
	ἔπεχε = *epeche*
	Pronunciation: [ep-ekh'-eh]
	Parsing (part of speech): verb
	  Mood—imperative
	  Tense—present
	  Voice—active
	  Person—2nd person
	  Number—singular
	  Stem or root—from ἐπέχω
	Concordance References:
	⇒ Strong's #1907 epechö
	⇒ NIV #2091 epechö
	⇒ NASB #1907 epechö
	
	1 Tim. 4:16
	Take heed unto thyself, and unto the doctrine; continue in them: for in doing this thou shalt both save thyself, and them that hear thee. [KJV]
	Pay close attention to yourself and to your teaching; persevere in these things; for as you do this you will insure salvation both for yourself and for those who hear you. [NASB]
		To watch closely; to take heed; to pay close attention; to keep a close watch; to keep a strict eye upon or to keep on paying attention to oneself and to one's teaching.
		
		Practical Application
		The good minister guards himself and his teaching.
		⇒ He guards his body, keeps it both morally and physically fit. He flees the temptations that assault and seduce him, and he controls his thoughts and keeps them pure from the lusts of the world and flesh. He neither eats too much nor succumbs to immoral thoughts or acts. He neither gives in to greed nor seeks the possessions or wealth of the world.
		⇒ He guards his spirit and keeps it spiritually fit. He worships God every day and lives in God's Word and prayer all day long, and he shares the glorious gospel of Christ, witness-

ENGLISH WORD	GREEK WORD AND VERSE	THE WORD MEANS...
	Watch your life and doctrine **closely**. Persevere in them, because if you do, you will save both yourself and your hearers. [NIV] **Take heed** to yourself and to the doctrine. Continue in them, for in doing this you will save both yourself and those who hear you. [NKJV] **Keep a close watch** on yourself and on your teaching. Stay true to what is right, and God will save you and those who hear you. [NLT] ἔπεχε σεαυτῷ καὶ τῇ διδασκαλίᾳ. ἐπίμενε αὐτοῖς· τοῦτο γὰρ ποιῶν καὶ σεαυτὸν σώσεις καὶ τοὺς ἀκούοντάς σου. [GNS] ἔπεχε σεαυτῷ καὶ τῇ διδασκαλίᾳ, ἐπίμενε αὐτοῖς· τοῦτο γὰρ ποιῶν καὶ σεαυτὸν σώσεις καὶ τοὺς ἀκούοντάς σου. [GNT]	ing to and exhorting people as he walks throughout the day. ⇒ He guards his study and teaching, avoiding the profane doctrines, teachings, notions, philosophies, ideas, and fables of men.
#4278 **Watch Out** Beware–KJV Beware–NASB **Watch out–NIV** Beware–NKJV Beware–NLT **POSB REFERENCE** (Mt.7:15) Note 1	Προσέχετε = *Prosechete* Pronunciation: [pros-ekh'-eh-teh] Parsing (part of speech): verb 　Mood—imperative 　Tense—present 　Voice—active 　Person—2nd person 　Number—plural 　Stem or root—from προσέχω Concordance References: ⇒ Strong's #4337 prosechō ⇒ NIV #4668 prosechō ⇒ NASB #4337 prosechō **Matthew 7:15** **Beware** of false prophets, which come to you in sheep's clothing, but inwardly they are ravening wolves. [KJV] "**Beware** of the false prophets, who come to you in sheep's clothing, but inwardly are ravenous wolves. [NASB] "**Watch out** for false prophets. They come to you in sheep's clothing, but inwardly they are ferocious wolves. [NIV] "**Beware** of false prophets, who come to you in sheep's clothing, but inwardly they are ravenous wolves. [NKJV] "**Beware** of false prophets who come disguised as harmless sheep, but are really wolves that will tear you apart. [NLT] Προσέχετε δὲ ἀπὸ τῶν ψευδοπροφητῶν, οἵτινες ἔρχονται πρὸς ὑμᾶς ἐν ἐνδύμασι προβάτων, ἔσωθεν δέ εἰσι λύκοι ἅρπαγες. [GNS] Προσέχετε ἀπὸ τῶν ψευδοπροφητῶν, οἵτινες ἔρχονται πρὸς ὑμᾶς ἐν ἐνδύμασιν προβάτων, ἔσωθεν δέ εἰσιν λύκοι ἅρπαγες. [GNT]	To beware, take heed, guard, watch, keep yourself. It means to pay close attention to; to be careful. **Practical Application** The word is emphatic; the warning is clear and strong. The believer has been warned; therefore, he must now beware, guard and stand against the error of false teachers. If he does not stay alert and guard against the teaching of false teachers, he will be led away by their error. The believer will fall and no longer be steadfast. He will lose the exciting hope of the Lord's return and no longer look forward to the glorious union with Christ nor to eternal life with God the Father.
#4279 **Watch Out** Take heed–KJV On guard–NASB Careful–NIV Take heed–NKJV **Watch out–NLT** **POSB REFERENCE** (Lk.21:34-35; esp. v.34) Note 1	Προσέχετε = *prosechete* Pronunciation: [pros-ekh'-eh-teh] Parsing (part of speech): verb 　Mood—imperative 　Tense—present 　Voice—active 　Person—2nd person 　Number—plural 　Stem or root—from προσέχω Concordance References: ⇒ Strong's #4337 prosechō ⇒ NIV #4668 prosechō ⇒ NASB #4337 prosechō **Luke 21:34** And **take heed** to yourselves, lest at any time your hearts be overcharged with surfeiting, and drunkenness, and cares of this life, and so that day come upon you unawares. [KJV] "Be **on guard**, that your hearts may not be weighted	To give attention; to focus one's mind; to watch out; to guard; to beware; to take care; to be on guard; to pay close attention to; to carefully consider. **Practical Application** The end time and the day of the Lord's return demands taking care. Note this important fact: the believer is to watch out; that is, to guard his life. How? By not engaging in worldliness. His heart is not to be weighed down (*barethosin*): heavy, weighed down, burdened, overloaded, filled up, indulged.

ENGLISH WORD	GREEK WORD AND VERSE	THE WORD MEANS...
	down with dissipation and drunkenness and the worries of life, and that day come on you suddenly like a trap; [NASB] "Be **careful**, or your hearts will be weighed down with dissipation, drunkenness and the anxieties of life, and that day will close on you unexpectedly like a trap. [NIV] "But **take heed** to yourselves, lest your hearts be weighed down with carousing, drunkenness, and cares of this life, and that Day come on you unexpectedly. [NKJV] "**Watch out**! Don't let me find you living in careless ease and drunkenness, and filled with the worries of this life. Don't let that day catch you unaware, [NLT] Προσέχετε δὲ ἑαυτοῖς, μήποτε βαρυνθῶσιν ὑμῶν αἱ καρδίαι ἐν κραιπάλη καὶ μέθη καὶ μερίμναις βιωτικαῖς, καὶ αἰφνίδιος ἐφ' ὑμᾶς ἐπιστῇ ἡ ἡμέρα ἐκείνη· [GNS] Προσέχετε δὲ ἑαυτοῖς μήποτε βαρηθῶσιν ὑμῶν αἱ καρδίαι ἐν κραιπάλη καὶ μέθη καὶ μερίμναις βιωτικαῖς καὶ ἐπιστῇ ἐφ' ὑμᾶς αἰφνίδιος ἡ ἡμέρα ἐκείνη [GNT]	

#4280
Watch Out
 	
Vigilant–KJV
Be on the alert–NASB
Alert–NIV
Vigilant–NKJV
Watch out–NLT
 	
POSB REFERENCE
(1 Pt.5:8)
Note 1, point 2
	γρηγορήσατε = grēgorēsate
	Pronunciation: [gray-gor-ay'-sah-teh]
	Parsing (part of speech): verb
	    Mood—imperative
	    Tense—aorist
	    Voice—active
	    Person—2nd person
	    Number—plural
	    Stem or root—from γρηγορέω
	Concordance References:
	⇒ Strong's #1127 grēgoreō
	⇒ NIV #1213 grēgoreō
	⇒ NASB #1127 grēgoreō
	
	1 Peter 5:8
	Be sober, be **vigilant**; because your adversary the devil, as a roaring lion, walketh about, seeking whom he may devour: [KJV]
	
	Be of sober *spirit*, **be on the alert**. Your adversary, the devil, prowls about like a roaring lion, seeking someone to devour. [NASB]
	
	Be self-controlled and **alert**. Your enemy the devil prowls around like a roaring lion looking for someone to devour. [NIV]
	
	Be sober, be **vigilant**; because your adversary the devil walks about like a roaring lion, seeking whom he may devour. [NKJV]
	
	Be careful! **Watch out** for attacks from the Devil, your great enemy. He prowls around like a roaring lion, looking for some victim to devour. [NLT]
	
	νήψατε, **γρηγορήσατε**, ὅτι ὁ ἀντίδικος ὑμῶν διάβολος, ὡς λέων ὠρυόμενος περιπατεῖ ζητῶν τινα καταπίη· [GNS]
	
	Νήψατε, **γρηγορήσατε**. ὁ ἀντίδικος ὑμῶν διάβολος ὡς λέων ὠρυόμενος περιπατεῖ ζητῶν [τινα] καταπιεῖν· [GNT]
		To be alert; to be vigilant; to watch out. The word means to be watchful and awake.
		
		Practical Application
		It has the idea of being constantly aroused and on the lookout; to always be aroused, awake, and watching for the devil and his attacks. If a person's mind and body are dull, flabby, and weak from drink, drugs, overeating, slothfulness, or in anything else—that person cannot be watching and waiting; he cannot be constantly aroused to look for the devil's temptations and attacks.
		
		The believer must be sober and serious about the devil; he must be alert and vigilant in looking for the devil's temptations and attacks. It is the only conceivable way the believer can conquer and overcome in this life; it is the only way he can keep his life and testimony from being destroyed by the devil.

#4281
Watch Out
 	
Beware–KJV
Beware–NASB
Watch out–NIV
Beware–NKJV
Beware–NLT
 	
POSB REFERENCE
(Mk.8:15)
Deeper Study #2
	βλέπετε = blepete
	Pronunciation: [blep'-eh-teh]
	Parsing (part of speech): verb
	    Mood—imperative
	    Tense—present
	    Voice—active
	    Person—2nd person
	    Number—plural
	    Stem or root—from βλέπω
	Concordance References:
	⇒ Strong's #991 blepō
	⇒ NIV #1063 blepō
	⇒ NASB #991 blepō
		To watch out; to beware; to see, perceive, grasp, and understand in order to watch out for something; to turn the mind upon an object and consider and keep a watchful eye upon it; to guard and protect against something.
		
		Practical Application
		Again, the charge is a *present imperative*. The person is to begin immediately to beware and to continue his watch, always looking out for the danger.

ENGLISH WORD	GREEK WORD AND VERSE	THE WORD MEANS...
	Mark 8:15 And he charged them, saying, Take heed, **beware** of the leaven of the Pharisees, and of the leaven of Herod. [KJV] And He was giving orders to them, saying, "Watch out! **Beware** of the leaven of the Pharisees and the leaven of Herod." [NASB] "Be careful," Jesus warned them. "**Watch out** for the yeast of the Pharisees and that of Herod." [NIV] Then He charged them, saying, "Take heed, **beware** of the leaven of the Pharisees and the leaven of Herod." [NKJV] As they were crossing the lake, Jesus warned them, "**Beware** of the yeast of the Pharisees and of Herod." [NLT] καὶ διεστέλλετο αὐτοῖς, λέγων, Ὁρᾶτε, **βλέπετε** ἀπὸ τῆς ζύμης τῶν Φαρισαίων, καὶ τῆς ζύμης Ἡρώδου. [GNS] καὶ διεστέλλετο αὐτοῖς λέγων, Ὁρᾶτε, **βλέπετε** ἀπὸ τῆς ζύμης τῶν Φαρισαίων καὶ τῆς ζύμης Ἡρῴδου. [GNT]	
#4282 **Watch Out** Take heed–KJV **Watch out–NASB** Careful, Be–NIV Take heed–NKJV Warned–NLT **POSB REFERENCE** (Mk.8:15) *Deeper Study #1*	Ὁρᾶτε = *Horate* Pronunciation: [hor-ah'-teh] Parsing (part of speech): verb 　　Mood—imperative 　　Tense—present 　　Voice—active 　　Person—2nd person 　　Number—plural 　　Stem or root—from ὁράω Concordance References: 　⇒　Strong's #3708 horaō 　⇒　NIV #3972 horaō 　⇒　NASB #3708 horaō **Mark 8:15** And he charged them, saying, **Take heed**, beware of the leaven of the Pharisees, and of the leaven of Herod. [KJV] And He was giving orders to them, saying, "**Watch out**! Beware of the leaven of the Pharisees and the leaven of Herod." [NASB] "**Be careful**," Jesus warned them. "Watch out for the yeast of the Pharisees and that of Herod." [NIV] Then He charged them, saying, "**Take heed**, beware of the leaven of the Pharisees and the leaven of Herod." [NKJV] As they were crossing the lake, Jesus **warned** them, "Beware of the yeast of the Pharisees and of Herod." [NLT] καὶ διεστέλλετο αὐτοῖς, λέγων, Ὁρᾶτε, βλέπετε ἀπὸ τῆς ζύμης τῶν Φαρισαίων, καὶ τῆς ζύμης Ἡρώδου. [GNS] καὶ διεστέλλετο αὐτοῖς λέγων, Ὁρᾶτε, βλέπετε ἀπὸ τῆς ζύμης τῶν Φαρισαίων καὶ τῆς ζύμης Ἡρῴδου. [GNT]	To see, behold, discern, and acquaint oneself by closely observing and experiencing. It means to take heed; to watch out; to be warned; to be careful; to make sure. **Practical Application** Two things are needed for a person to "watch out": active thought and a discerning mind. The thing to be heeded must be actively observed, thought through, and discerned. In the present passage, the charge is a *present imperative*. Beginning right now, the disciple is to "watch out" for yeast (leaven) and he is to continue being careful, always observing and discerning.
#4283 **Watch Out For** Mark–KJV Keep your eye on– 　NASB **Watch out for–NIV** Note–NKJV **Watch out for–NLT** **POSB REFERENCE** (Rom.16:17-18; esp. v.17) Note 1, point 1c	σκοπεῖν = *skopein* Pronunciation: [skop-een'] Parsing (part of speech): verb 　　Mood—infinitive 　　Tense—present 　　Voice—active 　　Stem or root—from σκοπέω Concordance References: 　⇒　Strong's #4648 skopeō 　⇒　NIV #5023 skopeō 　⇒　NASB #4648 skopeō **Romans 16:17** Now I beseech you, brethren, **mark** them which cause divisions and offences contrary to the doctrine which ye have learned; and avoid them. [KJV]	To mark; to note; to keep one's eye on; to look at; to observe; to focus upon; to contemplate; to scrutinize; to pay attention to; to watch out (for); to be careful. **Practical Application** "Watch out for" the divisive person. The phrase "watch out for" (*skopeite*) means to keep one's eye on, to look at, to observe, to focus upon, to contemplate, to scrutinize. Note: it is the divisive person himself who is to be avoided and turned away from, not just his sin. We are not to have anything to do with a divisive person... 　• for we give the appearance of approving of

ENGLISH WORD	GREEK WORD AND VERSE	THE WORD MEANS...
	Now I urge you, brethren, **keep your eye on** those who cause dissensions and hindrances contrary to the teaching which you learned, and turn away from them. [NASB] I urge you, brothers, to **watch out for** those who cause divisions and put obstacles in your way that are contrary to the teaching you have learned. Keep away from them. [NIV] Now I urge you, brethren, **note** those who cause divisions and offenses, contrary to the doctrine which you learned, and avoid them. [NKJV] And now I make one more appeal, my dear brothers and sisters. **Watch out for** people who cause divisions and upset people's faith by teaching things that are contrary to what you have been taught. Stay away from them. [NLT] Παρακαλῶ δὲ ὑμᾶς, ἀδελφοί, **σκοπεῖν** τοὺς τὰς διχοστασίας καὶ τὰ σκάνδαλα, παρὰ τὴν διδαχὴν ἣν ὑμεῖς ἐμάθετε, ποιοῦντας· καὶ ἐκκλίνατε ἀπ' αὐτῶν. [GNS] Παρακαλῶ δὲ ὑμᾶς, ἀδελφοί, **σκοπεῖν** τοὺς τὰς διχοστασίας καὶ τὰ σκάνδαλα παρὰ τὴν διδαχὴν ἣν ὑμεῖς ἐμάθετε ποιοῦντας, καὶ ἐκκλίνετε ἀπ' αὐτῶν· [GNT]	what he is doing. • for we run the risk of being influenced by and stumbling over what he says and does.

#4284
Watched
 	
Beheld–KJV
Observing–NASB
Watched–NIV
Saw–NKJV
Watched–NLT
 	
**POSB
REFERENCE**
(Mk.12:41-42; esp.
v.41)
Note 1
	ἐθεώρει = etheōrei
	Pronunciation: [eh-theh-o-reh'-ee]
	Parsing (part of speech): verb
	    Mood—indicative
	    Tense—imperfect
	    Voice—active
	    Person—3rd person
	    Number—singular
	    Stem or root—from θεωρέω
	Concordance References:
	  ⇒ Strong's #2334 theōreō
	  ⇒ NIV #2555 theōreō
	  ⇒ NASB #2334 theōreō
	
	Mark 12:41
	And Jesus sat over against the treasury, and **beheld** how the people cast money into the treasury: and many that were rich cast in much. [KJV]
	
	And He sat down opposite the treasury, and began **observing** how the multitude were putting money into the treasury; and many rich people were putting in large sums. [NASB]
	
	Jesus sat down opposite the place where the offerings were put and **watched** the crowd putting their money into the temple treasury. Many rich people threw in large amounts. [NIV]
	
	Now Jesus sat opposite the treasury and **saw** how the people put money into the treasury. And many who were rich put in much. [NKJV]
	
	Jesus went over to the collection box in the Temple and sat and **watched** as the crowds dropped in their money. Many rich people put in large amounts. [NLT]
	
	Καὶ καθίσας ὁ Ἰησοῦς κατέναντι τοῦ γαζοφυλακίου, **ἐθεώρει** πῶς ὁ ὄχλος βάλλει χαλκὸν εἰς τὸ γαζοφυλάκιον· καὶ πολλοὶ πλούσιοι ἔβαλλον πολλά. [GNS]
	
	Καὶ καθίσας κατέναντι τοῦ γαζοφυλακίου **ἐθεώρει** πῶς ὁ ὄχλος βάλλει χαλκὸν εἰς τὸ γαζοφυλάκιον. καὶ πολλοὶ πλούσιοι ἔβαλλον πολλά· [GNT]
		To observe, watch, behold, look at, notice; to see; to carefully observe; to look on; to gaze upon; to perceive.
		
		Practical Application
		Christ was deliberately watching, discerning the motives of the people as they made their offerings. Christ knows the motives—the sacrifices made or the "tips" offered—behind every gift given to Him.
		
		There is a great difference between giving what one can spare and giving sacrificially, actually giving up something in order to give. Sacrificial giving costs something. Sacrificial giving is giving when it hurts, when a person has nothing left, nothing to spare. The difference needs to be stressed, for God expects sacrificial giving. If the world is ever to be reached for Christ and its desperate needs met, then every believer must give sacrificially.

#4285
Watched–
Watched...
  Closely–
Watching...
  Closely–
	παρετηροῦντο = paretērounto
	Pronunciation: [par-at-ay-roon'-to]
	Parsing (part of speech): verb
	    Mood—indicative
	    Tense—imperfect
	    Voice—middle
	    Person—3rd person
	    Number—singular
	    Stem or root—from παρατηρέω
	Concordance References:
		To watch carefully; to observe with a sinister purpose: to look for something wrong, to search for the incorrect, to watch for error. It means to look with critical and cynical eyes.
		
		Practical Application
		The religionists "watched" Jesus. The meaning is that they watched closely just as an animal

ENGLISH WORD	GREEK WORD AND VERSE	THE WORD MEANS...
Watched–KJV **Watching closely–** **NASB** **Watched...closely–** **NIV** **Watched...closely–** **NKJV** **Watched closely–** **NLT** **POSB** **REFERENCE** (Lk.6:6-11; esp. v.7) Note 3, point 2 **See also POSB REF:** (Lk.14:1) Note 1	⇒ Strong's #3906 paratēreō ⇒ NIV #4190 paratēreō ⇒ NASB #3906 paratēreō **Luke 6:7** And the scribes and Pharisees **watched** him, whether he would heal on the sabbath day; that they might find an accusation against him. [KJV] And the scribes and the Pharisees were **watching** Him **closely**, to see if He healed on the Sabbath, in order that they might find reason to accuse Him. [NASB] The Pharisees and the teachers of the law were looking for a reason to accuse Jesus, so they **watched** him **close-ly** to see if he would heal on the Sabbath. [NIV] So the scribes and Pharisees **watched** Him **closely**, whether He would heal on the Sabbath, that they might find an accusation against Him. [NKJV] The teachers of religious law and the Pharisees **watched closely** to see whether Jesus would heal the man on the Sabbath, because they were eager to find some legal charge to bring against him. [NLT] παρετήρουν δὲ αὐτὸν οἱ γραμματεῖς καὶ οἱ Φαρισαῖοι, εἰ ἐν τῷ σαββάτῳ θεραπεύει· ἵνα εὕρωσι κατηγορεῖν αὐτοῦ. [GNS] παρετηροῦντο δὲ αὐτὸν οἱ γραμματεῖς καὶ οἱ Φαρισαῖοι εἰ ἐν τῷ σαββάτῳ θεραπεύει, ἵνα εὕρωσιν κατηγορεῖν αὐτοῦ. [GNT]	does its prey. Note their purpose was to accuse Him.
#4286 **Watched–** **Watching** Beheld–KJV Looking on–NASB Before...eyes–NIV Watched–NKJV **Watching–NLT** **POSB** **REFERENCE** (Acts 1:9) Note 4	βλεπόντων = blepontōn Pronunciation: [blep'-own-tone] Parsing (part of speech): verb Mood—participle Tense—present Voice—active Case—genitive Gender—masculine Number—plural Stem or root—from βλέπω Concordance References: ⇒ Strong's #991 blepō ⇒ NIV #1063 blepō ⇒ NASB #991 blepō **Acts 1:9** And when he had spoken these things, while they **beheld**, he was taken up; and a cloud received him out of their sight. [KJV] And after He had said these things, He was lifted up while they were **looking on**, and a cloud received Him out of their sight. [NASB] After he said this, he was taken up **before** their very **eyes**, and a cloud hid him from their sight. [NIV] Now when He had spoken these things, while they **watched**, He was taken up, and a cloud received Him out of their sight. [NKJV] It was not long after he said this that he was taken up into the sky while they were **watching**, and he disap-peared into a cloud. [NLT] καὶ ταῦτα εἰπών, βλεπόντων αὐτῶν ἐπήρθη, καὶ νεφέλη ὑπέλαβεν αὐτὸν ἀπὸ τῶν ὀφθαλμῶν αὐτῶν. [GNS] καὶ ταῦτα εἰπὼν βλεπόντων αὐτῶν ἐπήρθη, καὶ νεφέλη ὑπέλαβεν αὐτὸν ἀπὸ τῶν ὀφθαλμῶν αὐτῶν. [GNT]	To see; to behold; to look upon; to watch. **Practical Application** Jesus Christ began to slowly arise from the earth, ascending ever upward toward the sky above. The disciples were shocked and spell-bound, gazing at the spectacular sight. They were watching one of the most dramatic and phenomenal events ever experienced: ⇒ the Ascension of the Lord Jesus Christ. ⇒ the return of God's Son into heaven, into the spiritual world and dimension of being.
#4287 **Watchful** Watch–KJV Keeping alert–NASB **Watchful–NIV** Being vigilant–NKJV Alert–NLT	γρηγοροῦντες = grēgorountes Pronunciation: [gray-gor-yoon'-tehs] Parsing (part of speech): verb Mood—participle (imperative sense) Tense—present Voice—active Case—nominative Gender—masculine Person—2nd person Number—plural	To be watchful; to keep alert; to be alive; to stay awake, be sleepless, be active, concentrate. **Practical Application** It means to fight against distractions, drowsi-ness, sluggishness, wandering thoughts, and use-less daydreaming. It means to discipline our minds and control our thoughts in prayer. Being very honest, this is a problem that afflicts every

ENGLISH WORD	GREEK WORD AND VERSE	THE WORD MEANS...
POSB REFERENCE (Col.4:2-4; esp. v.2) Note 1, point 2	Stem or root—from γρηγορέω Concordance References: ⇒ Strong's #1127 grĕgoreŏ ⇒ NIV #1213 grĕgoreŏ ⇒ NASB #1127 grĕgoreŏ **Col. 4:2** Continue in prayer, and **watch** in the same with thanksgiving; [KJV] Devote yourselves to prayer, **keeping alert** in it with an attitude of thanksgiving; [NASB] Devote yourselves to prayer, being **watchful** and thankful. [NIV] Continue earnestly in prayer, **being vigilant** in it with thanksgiving; [NKJV] Devote yourselves to prayer with an **alert** mind and a thankful heart. [NLT] Τῇ προσευχῇ προσκαρτερεῖτε, **γρηγοροῦντες** ἐν αὐτῇ ἐν εὐχαριστίᾳ· [GNS] Τῇ προσευχῇ προσκαρτερεῖτε, **γρηγοροῦντες** ἐν αὐτῇ ἐν εὐχαριστίᾳ, [GNT]	believer sometime. Overwork, tiredness, pressure, strain—an innumerable list of things can make it very difficult to concentrate in prayer. This is the very reason Paul stresses the need to watch in prayer. But note: vigilance in prayer is the duty of the believer. Again, it is not something that God does for us. We are responsible for watching and concentrating. We are the ones who are to discipline our minds and control our thoughts. For this reason, we must never give up in prayer. We must... • always struggle against drowsiness and wandering thoughts. • learn to concentrate—to discipline our minds and control our thoughts. • teach ourselves to be watchful in prayer.

#4288
Watching
 	
Beheld–KJV
Watching–NASB
Saw–NIV
Saw–NKJV
Saw–NLT
 	
POSB REFERENCE (Lk.10:18) Note 2
	Ἐθεώρουν = etheŏroun
	Pronunciation: [eh-theh-o-reh'-o]
	Parsing (part of speech): verb
	   Mood—indicative
	   Tense—imperfect
	   Voice—active
	   Person—1st person
	   Number—singular
	   Stem or root—from θεωρέω
	Concordance References:
	⇒ Strong's #2334 theŏreŏ
	⇒ NIV #2555 theŏreŏ
	⇒ NASB #2334 theŏreŏ
	
	Luke 10:18
	And he said unto them, I **beheld** Satan as lightning fall from heaven. [KJV]
	And He said to them, "I was **watching** Satan fall from heaven like lightning. [NASB]
	He replied, "I **saw** Satan fall like lightning from heaven. [NIV]
	And He said to them, "I **saw** Satan fall like lightning from heaven. [NKJV]
	"Yes," he told them, "I **saw** Satan falling from heaven as a flash of lightning! [NLT]
	εἶπε δὲ αὐτοῖς, Ἐθεώρουν τὸν Σατανᾶν ὡς ἀστραπὴν ἐκ τοῦ οὐρανοῦ πεσόντα. [GNS]
	εἶπεν δὲ αὐτοῖς, Ἐθεώρουν τὸν Σατανᾶν ὡς ἀστραπὴν ἐκ τοῦ οὐρανοῦ πεσόντα. [GNT]
		To see; to carefully observe; to behold; to watch; to look on; to gaze upon; to perceive; to notice.
		
		Practical Application
		The word means that Jesus thought upon, gave full attention to, contemplated, envisioned Satan's falling from his summit of power as the god and prince of this world (see POSB *Deeper Study* #1, Satan—Rev. 12:9).

#4289
Watchings
 	
Watchings–KJV
Sleeplessness–NASB
Sleepless nights–NIV
Sleeplessness–NKJV
Sleepless nights–NLT
 	
POSB REFERENCE (2 Cor.6:5) Note 4
	ἀγρυπνίαις = agrupniais
	Pronunciation: [ag-roop-nee'-ah-ees]
	Parsing (part of speech): noun
	   Case—dative
	   Gender—feminine
	   Number—plural
	   Stem or root—from ἀγρυπνία, ας
	Concordance References:
	⇒ Strong's #70 agrupnia
	⇒ NIV #71 agrupnia
	⇒ NASB #70 agrupnia
	
	2 Cor. 6:5
	In stripes, in imprisonments, in tumults, in labours, in **watchings**, in fastings; [KJV]
	In beatings, in imprisonments, in tumults, in labors, in **sleeplessness**, in hunger, [NASB]
	In beatings, imprisonments and riots; in hard work, **sleepless nights** and hunger; [NIV]
	In stripes, in imprisonments, in tumults, in labors, in **sleeplessness**, in fastings; [NKJV]
		Sleepless nights, sleeplessness; to go without sleep.
		
		Practical Application
		The record of Paul's life indicates that he arose early and rested only as he needed. He spent nights in prayer, and sometimes found the weight of the churches on his mind so much that he could sleep little if any. The point to see is Paul's great concern for people and their needs: concern so great that it would keep him awake at nights praying and figuring out how to better reach and help people for Christ. Paul was steadfast in the ministry, even enduring sleepless nights for the cause of Christ.

ENGLISH WORD	GREEK WORD AND VERSE	THE WORD MEANS...
	We have been beaten, been put in jail, faced angry mobs, worked to exhaustion, endured **sleepless nights**, and gone without food. [NLT] ἐν πληγαῖς, ἐν φυλακαῖς, ἐν ἀκαταστασίαις, ἐν κόποις, ἐν **ἀγρυπνίαις**, ἐν νηστείαις, [GNS] ἐν πληγαῖς, ἐν φυλακαῖς, ἐν ἀκαταστασίαις, ἐν κόποις, ἐν **ἀγρυπνίαις**, ἐν νηστείαις, [GNT]	

#4290
Waver–
Wavered
 	
Staggered–KJV
Waver–NASB
Waver–NIV
Waver–NKJV
Wavered–NLT
 	
POSB
REFERENCE
(Romans 4:18-22; esp. v.20)
Note 2, point 1b
	διεκρίθη = diekrithë
	Pronunciation: [dee-ek-ree'-thay]
	Parsing (part of speech): verb
	  Mood—indicative
	  Tense—aorist
	  Voice—passive
	  Person—3rd person
	  Number—singular
	  Stem or root—from διακρίνω
	Concordance References:
	⇒ Strong's #1252 diakrinö
	⇒ NIV #1359 diakrinö
	⇒ NASB #1252 diakrinö
	
	Romans 4:20
	He **staggered** not at the promise of God through unbelief; but was strong in faith, giving glory to God; [KJV]
	Yet, with respect to the promise of God, he did not **waver** in unbelief, but grew strong in faith, giving glory to God, [NASB]
	Yet he did not **waver** through unbelief regarding the promise of God, but was strengthened in his faith and gave glory to God, [NIV]
	He did not **waver** at the promise of God through unbelief, but was strengthened in faith, giving glory to God, [NKJV]
	Abraham never **wavered** in believing God's promise. In fact, his faith grew stronger, and in this he brought glory to God. [NLT]
	εἰς δὲ τὴν ἐπαγγελίαν τοῦ Θεοῦ οὐ **διεκρίθη** τῇ ἀπιστίᾳ, ἀλλ' ἐνεδυναμώθη τῇ πίστει, δοὺς δόξαν τῷ Θεῷ, [GNS]
	εἰς δὲ τὴν ἐπαγγελίαν τοῦ θεοῦ οὐ **διεκρίθη** τῇ ἀπιστίᾳ ἀλλ' ἐνεδυναμώθη τῇ πίστει, δοὺς δόξαν τῷ θεῷ [GNT]
		To waver; to stagger; to fluctuate; to take issue; to doubt.
		
		Practical Application
		Abraham was strong in faith—not staggering at the promise of God. Instead he walked about glorifying and praising God for His glorious promise. The word "waver" (diakrino) means he did not stagger, did not vacillate, did not question God's ability to fulfill His promise.

#4291
Waxed Strong
 	
Waxed strong–KJV
Strong–NASB
Strong–NIV
Strong–NKJV
Strong–NLT
 	
POSB
REFERENCE
(Lk.2:40)
Note 3, point 1
	ἐκραταιοῦτο = ekrataiouto
	Pronunciation: [eh-krat-ah-ee'-oo-to]
	Parsing (part of speech): verb
	  Mood—indicative
	  Tense—imperfect
	  Voice—passive
	  Person—3rd person
	  Number—singular
	  Stem or root—from κραταιόομαι
	Concordance References:
	⇒ Strong's #2901 krataioö
	⇒ NIV #3194 krataioö
	⇒ NASB #2901 krataioö
	
	Luke 2:40
	And the child grew, and **waxed strong** in spirit, filled with wisdom: and the grace of God was upon him. [KJV]
	And the Child continued to grow and become **strong**, increasing in wisdom; and the grace of God was upon Him. [NASB]
	And the child grew and became **strong**; he was filled with wisdom, and the grace of God was upon him. [NIV]
	And the Child grew and became **strong** in spirit, filled with wisdom; and the grace of God was upon Him. [NKJV]
	There the child grew up healthy and **strong**. He was filled with wisdom beyond his years, and God placed his special favor upon him. [NLT]
		To be strong; to increase in strength.
		
		Practical Application
		The idea is that Jesus grew as a normal child. But note: No other child had ever been or ever will be perfect in growth at the various stages of childhood, but the Christ-child was. He grew as well as a child can grow: filled perfectly with all the qualities that fill a child.

ENGLISH WORD	GREEK WORD AND VERSE	THE WORD MEANS...
	No, much rather, those members of the body which seem to be **weaker** are necessary. [NKJV]	
	In fact, some of the parts that seem **weakest and least important** are really the most necessary. [NLT]	
	ἀλλὰ πολλῷ μᾶλλον τὰ δοκοῦντα μέλη τοῦ σώματος **ἀσθενέστερα** ὑπάρχειν, ἀναγκαῖά ἐστι· [GNS]	
	ἀλλὰ πολλῷ μᾶλλον τὰ δοκοῦντα μέλη τοῦ σώματος **ἀσθενέστερα** ὑπάρχειν ἀναγκαῖά ἐστιν, [GNT]	
#4296 **Weakest And Least Important** Feeble–KJV Weaker–NASB Weaker–NIV Weaker–NKJV **Weakest and least important–NLT** **POSB REFERENCE** (1 Cor.12:21-23; esp. v.22) Note 3	**ἀσθενέστερα** = asthenestera Pronunciation: [as-then-ehs'-teh-rah] Parsing (part of speech): adjective 　Type—comparative 　Case—nominative 　Gender—neuter 　Number—plural 　Stem or root—from **ἀσθενής**, ές Concordance References: 　⇒ Strong's #772 asthenēs 　⇒ NIV #822 asthenēs 　⇒ NASB #772 asthenēs **1 Cor. 12:22** Nay, much more those members of the body, which seem to be more **feeble**, are necessary: [KJV] On the contrary, it is much truer that the members of the body which seem to be **weaker** are necessary; [NASB] On the contrary, those parts of the body that seem to be **weaker** are indispensable, [NIV] No, much rather, those members of the body which seem to be **weaker** are necessary. [NKJV] In fact, some of the parts that seem **weakest and least important** are really the most necessary. [NLT] ἀλλὰ πολλῷ μᾶλλον τὰ δοκοῦντα μέλη τοῦ σώματος **ἀσθενέστερα** ὑπάρχειν, ἀναγκαῖά ἐστι· [GNS] ἀλλὰ πολλῷ μᾶλλον τὰ δοκοῦντα μέλη τοῦ σώματος **ἀσθενέστερα** ὑπάρχειν ἀναγκαῖά ἐστιν, [GNT]	Feeble, sick, sickly, weak, delicate, fragile, helpless. **Practical Application** In appearance the lesser parts of the body may seem unimportant, but they are not; they are essential. In fact, they are actually more necessary. The average layman who serves as a personal worker, although he is never seen by the crowds, is much more essential to decisions for Christ than the evangelist who is in the center of the scene. The dear saint who has become a *prayer warrior* is much more essential to the strength of the church than the most eloquent preacher who ever fills the pulpit.
#4297 **Wear** Adorn–KJV Adorn–NASB Dress–NIV Adorn–NKJV **Wear–NLT** **POSB REFERENCE** (1 Tim.2:9-10; esp. v.9) Note 1	**κοσμεῖν** = kosmein Pronunciation: [kos-meh'-in] Parsing (part of speech): verb 　Mood—infinitive 　Tense—present 　Voice—active 　Stem or root—from **κοσμέω** Concordance References: 　⇒ Strong's #2885 kosmeō 　⇒ NIV #3175 kosmeō 　⇒ NASB #2885 kosmeō **1 Tim. 2:9** In like manner also, that women **adorn** themselves in modest apparel, with shamefacedness and sobriety; not with broided hair, or gold, or pearls, or costly array; [KJV] Likewise, I want women to **adorn** themselves with proper clothing, modestly and discreetly, not with braided hair and gold or pearls or costly garments; [NASB] I also want women to **dress** modestly, with decency and propriety, not with braided hair or gold or pearls or expensive clothes, [NIV] In like manner also, that the women **adorn** themselves in modest apparel, with propriety and moderation, not with braided hair or gold or pearls or costly clothing, [NKJV] And I want women to be modest in their appearance. They should **wear** decent and appropriate clothing and not draw attention to themselves by the way they fix their hair or by wearing gold or pearls or expensive clothes. [NLT] ὡσαύτως καὶ τὰς γυναῖκας ἐν καταστολῇ κοσμίῳ, μετὰ αἰδοῦς καὶ σωφροσύνης, **κοσμεῖν** ἑαυτάς, μὴ ἐν πλέγμασιν, ἢ χρυσῷ, ἢ μαργαρίταις, ἢ ἱματισμῷ πολυτελεῖ, [GNS]	To dress; to adorn; to wear. **Practical Application** The word "adorn" (*kosmein*) is really a better translation of what Scripture means. The word means the dress, ornaments, and arrangement of clothing upon the body. But the word *wear* also refers to behavior and demeanor, that is, the way a woman carries herself, walks, moves, and behaves in public. Remember: this passage is being written to genuine Christian women—women who truly believe in the Lord and wish to honor the Lord and to have a strong testimony for Him. The Christian woman wants to guard her clothing in order to dress modestly; she wants to watch the way she dresses, walks, moves, and behaves in public. She wants to bring honor to the Lord and to build a strong testimony—a testimony that she loves the Lord and has committed her life... • to help people, not to seduce them. • to serve people, not to destroy them. • to point people to Jesus, not to attract them to herself. • to teach people righteous behavior, not fleshly and worldly behavior.

ENGLISH WORD	GREEK WORD AND VERSE	THE WORD MEANS...
	ὡσαύτως [καὶ] γυναῖκας ἐν καταστολῇ κοσμίῳ μετὰ αἰδοῦς καὶ σωφροσύνης **κοσμεῖν** ἑαυτάς, μὴ ἐν πλέγμασιν καὶ χρυσίῳ η μαργαρίταις η ἱματισμῷ πολυτελεῖ, [GNT]	

#4298
Wear Me Out
 	
Weary me–KJV
Wear me out–NASB
Wear me out–NIV
Weary me–NKJV
Wearing me out–NLT
 	
POSB REFERENCE
(Lk.18:2-5; esp. v.5)
Note 2, point 4
	ὑπωπιάζῃ με = *hupöpiazë me*
	Pronunciation: [hoop-o-pee-ad'-zay meh]
	Parsing *hupöpiazë* (part of speech): verb
	    Mood—subjunctive
	    Tense—present
	    Voice—active
	    Person—3rd person
	    Number—singular
	    Stem or root—from ὑπωπιάζω
	Concordance References:
	  ⇒ Strong's #1473 më + 5299 hupöpiazö
	  ⇒ NIV #3590 më [me] + 5724 hupöpiazö [wear out]
	  ⇒ NASB #1473 më + 5299 hupöpiazö
	
	Luke 18:5
	    Yet because this widow troubleth me, I will avenge her, lest by her continual coming she **weary me**. [KJV]
	    Yet because this widow bothers me, I will give her legal protection, lest by continually coming she **wear me out**.' [NASB]
	    Yet because this widow keeps bothering me, I will see that she gets justice, so that she won't eventually **wear me out** with her coming!' [NIV]
	    Yet because this widow troubles me I will avenge her, lest by her continual coming she **weary me**.' [NKJV]
	    'But this woman is driving me crazy. I'm going to see that she gets justice, because she is **wearing me out** with her constant requests!' [NLT]
	    διά γε τὸ παρέχειν μοι κόπον τὴν χήραν ταύτην, ἐκδικήσω αὐτήν, ἵνα μὴ εἰς τέλος ἐρχομένη **ὑπωπιάζῃ με**. [GNS]
	    διά γε τὸ παρέχειν μοι κόπον τὴν χήραν ταύτην ἐκδικήσω αὐτήν, ἵνα μὴ εἰς τέλος ἐρχομένη **ὑπωπιάζῃ με** [GNT]
		To annoy, weary, wear out.
		
		Practical Application
		    The literal meaning is, unless she "give me a black eye." She was persistent—refusing to let the judge go!
		    The point is this: the judge gave in. "For some time he refused," but the poor widow kept on coming and coming, pleading and pleading. She would not let the judge rest. Now note the stress. The judge...
		• did not fear God,
		• did not regard man's opinions,
		...yet he gave in to the widow and avenged her of her adversary.
		    Why? Because of "her coming." He could not get rid of her. She would not accept silence nor take no for an answer. She kept coming and coming.

#4299
Wearing Me Out
 	
Weary me–KJV
Wear me out–NASB
Wear me out–NIV
Weary me–NKJV
Wearing me out–NLT
 	
POSB REFERENCE
(Lk.18:2-5; esp. v.5)
Note 2, point 4
	ὑπωπιάζῃ με = *hupöpiazë me*
	Pronunciation: [hoop-o-pee-ad'-zay meh]
	Parsing *hupöpiazë* (part of speech): verb
	    Mood—subjunctive
	    Tense—present
	    Voice—active
	    Person—3rd person
	    Number—singular
	    Stem or root—from ὑπωπιάζω
	Concordance References:
	  ⇒ Strong's #1473 më + 5299 hupöpiazö
	  ⇒ NIV #3590 më [me] + 5724 hupöpiazö [wear out]
	  ⇒ NASB #1473 më + 5299 hupöpiazö
	
	Luke 18:5
	    Yet because this widow troubleth me, I will avenge her, lest by her continual coming she **weary me**. [KJV]
	    Yet because this widow bothers me, I will give her legal protection, lest by continually coming she **wear me out**.' [NASB]
	    Yet because this widow keeps bothering me, I will see that she gets justice, so that she won't eventually **wear me out** with her coming!' [NIV]
	    Yet because this widow troubles me I will avenge her, lest by her continual coming she **weary me**.' [NKJV]
	    'But this woman is driving me crazy. I'm going to see that she gets justice, because she is **wearing me out** with her constant requests!' [NLT]
	    διά γε τὸ παρέχειν μοι κόπον τὴν χήραν ταύτην, ἐκδικήσω αὐτήν, ἵνα μὴ εἰς τέλος ἐρχομένη **ὑπωπιάζῃ με**. [GNS]
	    διά γε τὸ παρέχειν μοι κόπον τὴν χήραν ταύτην ἐκδικήσω αὐτήν, ἵνα μὴ εἰς τέλος ἐρχομένη **ὑπωπιάζῃ με** [GNT]
		To annoy, weary, wear out.
		
		Practical Application
		    The literal meaning is, unless she "give me a black eye." She was persistent—refusing to let the judge go!
		    The point is this: the judge gave in. "The judge ignored her for awhile," but the poor widow kept on coming and coming, pleading and pleading. She would not let the judge rest. Now note the stress. The judge...
		• did not fear God,
		• did not regard man's opinions,
		...yet he gave in to the widow and avenged her of her adversary.
		    Why? Because of "her constant requests." He could not get rid of her. She would not accept silence nor take no for an answer. She kept coming and coming.

ENGLISH WORD	GREEK WORD AND VERSE	THE WORD MEANS...

#4300
Weary

Fainted–KJV
Distressed–NASB
Harassed–NIV
Weary–NKJV
Problems were so
  great–NLT

**POSB
REFERENCE**
(Mt.9:36)
Deeper Study #3

ἐσκυλμένοι = eskulmenoi
Pronunciation: [es-kool-me'-noi]
Parsing (part of speech): verb
    Mood—participle
    Tense—perfect
    Voice—passive
    Case—nominative
    Gender—masculine
    Number—plural
    Stem or root—from σκύλλω
Concordance References:
⇒ Strong's #4660 skullö
⇒ NIV #5035 skullö
⇒ NASB #4660 skullö

Matthew 9:36

But when he saw the multitudes, he was moved with compassion on them, because they **fainted**, and were scattered abroad, as sheep having no shepherd. [KJV]

And seeing the multitudes, He felt compassion for them, because they were **distressed** and downcast like sheep without a shepherd. [NASB]

When he saw the crowds, he had compassion on them, because they were **harassed** and helpless, like sheep without a shepherd. [NIV]

But when He saw the multitudes, He was moved with compassion for them, because they were **weary** and scattered, like sheep having no shepherd. [NKJV]

He felt great pity for the crowds that came, because their **problems were so great** and they didn't know where to go for help. They were like sheep without a shepherd. [NLT]

Ἰδὼν δὲ τοὺς ὄχλους, ἐσπλαγχνίσθη περὶ αὐτῶν, ὅτι ἦσαν **ἐκλελυμένοι** καὶ ἐρριμμένοι ὡσεὶ πρόβατα μὴ ἔχοντα ποιμένα. [GNS]

Ἰδὼν δὲ τοὺς ὄχλους ἐσπλαγχνίσθη περὶ αὐτῶν, ὅτι ἦσαν **ἐσκυλμένοι** καὶ ἐρριμμένοι ὡσεὶ πρόβατα μὴ ἔχοντα ποιμένα. [GNT]

To be harassed; to faint; to grow weary; to be troubled; to lose heart; to lack courage; to worry; to bother; to be annoyed; to be distressed, faint-hearted, bewildered. It means to be completely overwhelmed with problems.

Practical Application

The word is used when a person has struggled and struggled against sin or stood against the barrage of insult after insult until he can stand no more. It means that a person has undergone trial after trial until he is ready to collapse (Heb.12:3).

#4301
Weary Me

Weary me–KJV
Wear me out–NASB
Wear me out–NIV
Weary me–NKJV
Wearing me out–NLT

**POSB
REFERENCE**
(Lk.18:2-5; esp. v.5)
Note 2, point 4

ὑπωπιάζῃ με = hupöpiazë me
Pronunciation: [hoop-o-pee-ad'-zay meh]
Parsing hupöpiazë (part of speech): verb
    Mood—subjunctive
    Tense—present
    Voice—active
    Person—3rd person
    Number—singular
    Stem or root—from ὑπωπιάζω
Concordance References:
⇒ Strong's #1473 më + 5299 hupöpiazö
⇒ NIV #3590 më [me] + 5724 hupöpiazö [wear out]
⇒ NASB #1473 më + 5299 hupöpiazö

Luke 18:5

Yet because this widow troubleth me, I will avenge her, lest by her continual coming she **weary me**. [KJV]

Yet because this widow bothers me, I will give her legal protection, lest by continually coming she **wear me out**.' [NASB]

Yet because this widow keeps bothering me, I will see that she gets justice, so that she won't eventually **wear me out** with her coming!'" [NIV]

Yet because this widow troubles me I will avenge her, lest by her continual coming she **weary me**.' [NKJV]

'But this woman is driving me crazy. I'm going to see that she gets justice, because she is **wearing me out** with her constant requests!' [NLT]

διά γε τὸ παρέχειν μοι κόπον τὴν χήραν ταύτην, ἐκδικήσω αὐτήν, ἵνα μὴ εἰς τέλος ἐρχομένη **ὑπωπιάζῃ με**. [GNS]

διά γε τὸ παρέχειν μοι κόπον τὴν χήραν ταύτην ἐκδικήσω αὐτήν, ἵνα μὴ εἰς τέλος ἐρχομένη **ὑπωπιάζῃ με** [GNT]

To annoy, weary, wear out.

Practical Application

The literal meaning is, unless she "give me a black eye." She was persistent—refusing to let the judge go!

The point is this: the judge gave in. "He would not for a while," but the poor widow kept on coming and coming, pleading and pleading. She would not let the judge rest. Now note the stress. The judge...

• did not fear God,
• did not regard man's opinions,

...yet he gave in to the widow and avenged her of her adversary.

Why? Because of "her coming." He could not get rid of her. She would not accept silence nor take no for an answer. She kept coming and coming.

ENGLISH WORD	GREEK WORD AND VERSE	THE WORD MEANS...

#4302

Weep And Groan

Weep and howl–KJV
Weep and howl–NASB
Weep and wail–NIV
Weep and howl–NKJV
Weep and groan–NLT

POSB REFERENCE
(Jas 5:1)
Note 1

κλαύσατε ὀλολύζοντες = klausate ololuzontes
Pronunciation: [klah'-sah-teh ol-ol-ood'-zon-tehs]
Parsing *klausate* (part of speech): verb
    Mood—imperative
    Tense—aorist
    Voice—active
    Person—2nd person
    Number—plural
    Stem or root—from κλαίω
Parsing *ololuzontes* (part of speech): verb
    Mood—participle (imperative sense)
    Tense—present
    Voice—active
    Case—nominative
    Gender—masculine
    Person—2nd person
    Number—plural
    Stem or root—from ὀλολύζω
Concordance References:
⇒ Strong's #2799 klaiō + 3649 ololuzō
⇒ NIV #3081 klaiō [weep] + 3909 ololuzō [wail]
⇒ NASB #2799 klaiō + 3649 ololuzō

James 5:1
Go to now, ye rich men, **weep and howl** for your miseries that shall come upon you. [KJV]
Come now, you rich, **weep and howl** for your miseries which are coming upon you. [NASB]
Now listen, you rich people, **weep and wail** because of the misery that is coming upon you. [NIV]
Come now, you rich, **weep and howl** for your miseries that are coming upon you! [NKJV]
Look here, you rich people, **weep and groan** with anguish because of all the terrible troubles ahead of you. [NLT]
Ἄγε νῦν οἱ πλούσιοι, **κλαύσατε ὀλολύζοντες** ἐπὶ ταῖς ταλαιπωρίαις ὑμῶν ταῖς ἐπερχομέναις. [GNS]
Ἄγε νῦν οἱ πλούσιοι, **κλαύσατε ὀλολύζοντες** ἐπὶ ταῖς ταλαιπωρίαις ὑμῶν ταῖς ἐπερχομέναις. [GNT]

Weep and howl, weep and wail, weep and groan.

Practical Application
This is a strong summons to rich people.

"Look here, you rich people, weep and groan with anguish because of all the terrible troubles ahead of you." (James 5:1) [NLT]

"Weep and groan" (*klausate ololuzontes*) means to burst into weeping and to howl with grief if you are hoarding money (A.T. Robertson. *Word Pictures in the New Testament*, Vol. 6, p.57). Why? Because *troubles* (plural) are coming upon you—such troubles that are so terrible that you need to begin weeping and groaning now. There will be...

- troubles of afflictions
- troubles of emptiness
- troubles of loneliness
- troubles of purposelessness
- troubles of mind
- troubles of insecurity
- troubles of passion
- troubles in this world
- troubles in eternity
- troubles in judgment
- troubles in hell

Riches that are hoarded will fail a person; they will not satisfy and they will doom a person. They will bring all kinds of troubles upon a person. Therefore, weigh the summons of God.

#4303

Weep And Howl

Weep and howl–KJV
Weep and howl–NASB
Weep and wail–NIV
Weep and howl–NKJV
Weep and groan–NLT

POSB REFERENCE
(Jas. 5:1)
Note 1

κλαύσατε ὀλολύζοντες = klausate ololuzontes
Pronunciation: [klah'-sah-teh ol-ol-ood'-zon-tehs]
Parsing *klausate* (part of speech): verb
    Mood—imperative
    Tense—aorist
    Voice—active
    Person—2nd person
    Number—plural
    Stem or root—from κλαίω
Parsing *ololuzontes* (part of speech): verb
    Mood—participle (imperative sense)
    Tense—present
    Voice—active
    Case—nominative
    Gender—masculine
    Person—2nd person
    Number—plural
    Stem or root—from ὀλολύζω
Concordance References:
⇒ Strong's #2799 klaiō + 3649 ololuzō
⇒ NIV #3081 klaiō [weep] + 3909 ololuzō [wail]
⇒ NASB #2799 klaiō + 3649 ololuzō

James 5:1
Go to now, ye rich men, **weep and howl** for your miseries that shall come upon you. [KJV]
Come now, you rich, **weep and howl** for your miseries which are coming upon you. [NASB]
Now listen, you rich people, **weep and wail** because of the misery that is coming upon you. [NIV]
Come now, you rich, **weep and howl** for your miseries that are coming upon you! [NKJV]
Look here, you rich people, **weep and groan** with

Weep and howl, weep and wail, weep and groan.

Practical Application
This is a strong summons to rich people.

"You rich men, weep and howl for your miseries that shall come upon you" (James 5:1). [KJV]

"Weep and howl" (*klausate ololuzontes*) means to burst into weeping and to howl with grief if you are hoarding money (A.T. Robertson. *Word Pictures in the New Testament*, Vol. 6, p.57). Why? Because *miseries* (plural) are coming upon you—such miseries that are so terrible that you need to begin weeping and howling now. There will be...

- miseries of afflictions
- miseries of emptiness
- miseries of loneliness
- miseries of purposelessness
- miseries of mind
- miseries of insecurity
- miseries of passion
- miseries in this world
- miseries in eternity
- miseries in judgment
- miseries in hell

ENGLISH WORD	GREEK WORD AND VERSE	THE WORD MEANS...
	anguish because of all the terrible troubles ahead of you. [NLT] Ἄγε νῦν οἱ πλούσιοι, **κλαύσατε ὀλολύζοντες** ἐπὶ ταῖς ταλαιπωρίαις ὑμῶν ταῖς ἐπερχομέναις. [GNS] Ἄγε νῦν οἱ πλούσιοι, **κλαύσατε ὀλολύζοντες** ἐπὶ ταῖς ταλαιπωρίαις ὑμῶν ταῖς ἐπερχομέναις. [GNT]	Riches that are hoarded will fail a person; they will not satisfy and they will doom a person. They will bring all kinds of miseries upon a person. Therefore, weigh the summons of God.

#4304
Weep And Wail
 	
Weep and howl–KJV
Weep and howl–
  NASB
Weep and wail–NIV
Weep and howl–
  NKJV
Weep and groan–NLT
 	
**POSB
REFERENCE**
(Jas. 5:1)
  Note 1
	κλαύσατε ὀλολύζοντες = klausate ololuzontes
	Pronunciation: [klah'-sah-teh ol-ol-ood'-zon-tehs]
	Parsing *klausate* (part of speech): verb
	    Mood—imperative
	    Tense—aorist
	    Voice—active
	    Person—2nd person
	    Number—plural
	    Stem or root—from κλαίω
	Parsing *ololuzontes* (part of speech): verb
	    Mood—participle (imperative sense)
	    Tense—present
	    Voice—active
	    Case—nominative
	    Gender—masculine
	    Person—2nd person
	    Number—plural
	    Stem or root—from ὀλολύζω
	Concordance References:
	⇒ Strong's #2799 klaiö + 3649 ololuzö
	⇒ NIV #3081 klaiö [weep] + 3909 ololuzö [wail]
	⇒ NASB #2799 klaiö + 3649 ololuzö
	
	James 5:1
	Go to now, ye rich men, **weep and howl** for your miseries that shall come upon you. [KJV]
	Come now, you rich, **weep and howl** for your miseries which are coming upon you. [NASB]
	Now listen, you rich people, **weep and wail** because of the misery that is coming upon you. [NIV]
	Come now, you rich, **weep and howl** for your miseries that are coming upon you! [NKJV]
	Look here, you rich people, **weep and groan** with anguish because of all the terrible troubles ahead of you. [NLT]
	
	Ἄγε νῦν οἱ πλούσιοι, **κλαύσατε ὀλολύζοντες** ἐπὶ ταῖς ταλαιπωρίαις ὑμῶν ταῖς ἐπερχομέναις. [GNS]
	Ἄγε νῦν οἱ πλούσιοι, **κλαύσατε ὀλολύζοντες** ἐπὶ ταῖς ταλαιπωρίαις ὑμῶν ταῖς ἐπερχομέναις. [GNT]
		Weep and howl, weep and wail, weep and groan.
		
		Practical Application
		This is a strong summons to rich people.
		
		"Now listen, you rich people, weep and wail because of the misery that is coming upon you. " (James 5:1). [NIV]
		
		"Weep and wail" (*klausate ololuzontes*) means to burst into weeping and to howl with grief if you are hoarding money (A.T. Robertson. *Word Pictures in the New Testament*, Vol. 6, p.57). Why? Because *miseries* (plural) are coming upon you—such miseries that are so terrible that you need to begin weeping and wailing now. There shall be...
		• miseries of afflictions
		• miseries of emptiness
		• miseries of loneliness
		• miseries of purposelessness
		• miseries of mind
		• miseries of insecurity
		• miseries of passion
		• miseries in this world
		• miseries in eternity
		• miseries in judgment
		• miseries in hell
		
		Riches that are hoarded will fail a person; they will not satisfy and they will doom a person. They will bring all kinds of miseries upon a person. Therefore, weigh the summons of God.

#4305
Weeping
 	
Weeping–KJV
Weeping–NASB
Weeping–NIV
Weeping–NKJV
Weeping–NLT
 	
**POSB
REFERENCE**
(Lk.13:28)
Deeper Study #1
	ὁ **κλαυθμός** = ho klauthmos
	Pronunciation: [ha klowth-mos']
	Parsing *klauthmos* (part of speech): noun
	    Case—nominative
	    Gender—masculine
	    Number—singular
	    Stem or root—from κλαυθμός, οῦ
	Concordance References:
	⇒ Strong's #2805 klauthmos + 3588 ho
	⇒ NIV #3088 klauthmos + 3836 ho
	⇒ NASB #2805 klauthmos + 3588 ho
	
	Luke 13:28
	There shall be **weeping** and gnashing of teeth, when ye shall see Abraham, and Isaac, and Jacob, and all the prophets, in the kingdom of God, and you yourselves thrust out. [KJV]
	"There will be **weeping** and gnashing of teeth there when you see Abraham and Isaac and Jacob and all the prophets in the kingdom of God, but yourselves being cast out. [NASB]
	"There will be **weeping** there, and gnashing of teeth, when you see Abraham, Isaac and Jacob and all the prophets in the kingdom of God, but you yourselves thrown out. [NIV]
	There will be **weeping** and gnashing of teeth, when
		Loud grief, mourning, groaning, bitter crying, wailing, floods and floods of tears.
		
		Practical Application
		Note the reason: they will actually see their fathers, godly men from whose roots they came, enter God's kingdom; but they themselves will be thrust out. Note: the lost are able to see believers in heaven, in God's kingdom (see POSB note, pt.2—Luke 16:23-31).

ENGLISH WORD	GREEK WORD AND VERSE	THE WORD MEANS...
	you see Abraham and Isaac and Jacob and all the prophets in the kingdom of God, and yourselves thrust out. [NKJV] "And there will be great **weeping** and gnashing of teeth, for you will see Abraham, Isaac, Jacob, and all the prophets within the Kingdom of God, but you will be thrown out. [NLT] ἐκεῖ ἔσται **ὁ κλαυθμὸς** καὶ ὁ βρυγμὸς τῶν ὀδόντων, ὅταν ὄψησθε Ἀβραὰμ καὶ Ἰσαὰκ καὶ Ἰακὼβ καὶ πάντας τοὺς προφήτας ἐν τῇ βασιλείᾳ τοῦ Θεοῦ, ὑμᾶς δὲ ἐκβαλλομένους ἔξω. [GNS] ἐκεῖ ἔσται **ὁ κλαυθμὸς** καὶ ὁ βρυγμὸς τῶν ὀδόντων, ὅταν ὄψεσθε Ἀβραὰμ καὶ Ἰσαὰκ καὶ Ἰακὼβ καὶ πάντας τοὺς προφήτας ἐν τῇ βασιλείᾳ τοῦ θεοῦ, ὑμᾶς δὲ ἐκβαλλομένους ἔξω. [GNT]	

#4306
 Weighed Down–Weighted Down
 	
 Overcharged–KJV
 Weighted down–NASB
 Weighed down–NIV
 Weighed down–NKJV
 Filled with–NLT
 	
 POSB REFERENCE
 (Lk.21:34-35, esp. v.34)
 Note 1
	βαρηθῶσιν = *barēthōsin*
	 Pronunciation: [ba-ray'-tho-sin]
	 Parsing (part of speech): verb
	    Mood—subjunctive
	    Tense—aorist
	    Voice—passive
	    Person—3rd person
	    Number—plural
	    Stem or root—from βαρέω
	 Concordance References:
	 ⇒ Strong's #925 baruno or #916 bareō
	 ⇒ NIV #976 bareō
	 ⇒ NASB #916 bareō
	
	 Luke 21:34
	 And take heed to yourselves, lest at any time your hearts be **overcharged** with surfeiting, and drunkenness, and cares of this life, and so that day come upon you unawares. [KJV]
	
	 "Be on guard, that your hearts may not be **weighted down** with dissipation and drunkenness and the worries of life, and that day come on you suddenly like a trap; [NASB]
	
	 "Be careful, or your hearts will be **weighed down** with dissipation, drunkenness and the anxieties of life, and that day will close on you unexpectedly like a trap. [NIV]
	
	 "But take heed to yourselves, lest your hearts be **weighed down** with carousing, drunkenness, and cares of this life, and that Day come on you unexpectedly. [NKJV]
	
	 "Watch out! Don't let me find you living in careless ease and drunkenness, and **filled with** the worries of this life. Don't let that day catch you unaware, [NLT]
	
	 Προσέχετε δὲ ἑαυτοῖς, μήποτε **βαρυνθῶσιν** ὑμῶν αἱ καρδίαι ἐν κραιπάλῃ καὶ μέθῃ καὶ μερίμναις βιωτικαῖς, καὶ αἰφνίδιος ἐφ' ὑμᾶς ἐπιστῇ ἡ ἡμέρα ἐκείνη· [GNS]
	
	 Προσέχετε δὲ ἑαυτοῖς μήποτε **βαρηθῶσιν** ὑμῶν αἱ καρδίαι ἐν κραιπάλῃ καὶ μέθῃ καὶ μερίμναις βιωτικαῖς καὶ ἐπιστῇ ἐφ' ὑμᾶς αἰφνίδιος ἡ ἡμέρα ἐκείνη [GNT]
		Heavy, weighed down, burdened, overloaded, filled up, indulged.
		
		 Practical Application
		 The believer's heart is not to be weighed down with the worldliness described in this verse. Three worldly acts in particular are mentioned.
		 1. Dissipation (*kraipale*). The word means to be light-hearted, silly, frivolous, giddy. Medically, it referred to drunken nausea or headaches. It is the kind of light-heartedness, silliness, frivolity, and giddiness that comes from partying and drinking.
		 2. Drunkenness (*methei*). The word comes from the word meaning wine (*methu*). It means to be drunk with wine (or any other strong drink or drug), to be intoxicated.
		 3. Anxieties of this life. This means to indulge one's cravings for more and more of the things of this world. Man too often gives his attention and focuses his mind upon more and more of this world. He desires far more than what he needs, more...
		 • food and delicacies
		 • clothes and the latest styles
		 • houses and furnishings
		 • property and holdings
		 • cars and other vehicles
		 • free time and recreation
		 • money and wealth
		 • recognition and esteem

#4307
 Welcomed
 	
 Embraced–KJV
 Welcomed–NASB
 Welcomed–NIV
 Embraced–NKJV
 Welcomed–NLT
 	
 POSB REFERENCE
 (Heb.11:13-15; esp. v.13)
 Note 1, point 2
	ἀσπασάμενοι = *aspasamenoi*
	 Pronunciation: [as-pas'-ah-mehn-oy]
	 Parsing (part of speech): verb
	    Mood—participle
	    Tense—aorist
	    Voice—middle deponent
	    Case—nominative
	    Gender—masculine
	    Number—plural
	    Stem or root—from ἀσπάζομαι
	 Concordance References:
	 ⇒ Strong's #782 aspazomai
	 ⇒ NIV #832 aspazomai
	 ⇒ NASB #782 aspazomai
		To welcome; to embrace; to receive with warmth and respect.
		
		 Practical Application
		 Their faith was a *growing faith*.
		 ⇒ They saw the promise of God and were thankful to God for the privilege of seeing it.
		 ⇒ They were assured of the promises of God. They believed that the promises were true, that there was a promised land and that God was going to give it to them. They believed in God and that what God promised He was going to fulfill.
		 ⇒ They welcomed (*aspasamenoi*) the promises. They were ever so thankful and appreciative

ENGLISH WORD	GREEK WORD AND VERSE	THE WORD MEANS...
	Hebrews 11:13 These all died in faith, not having received the promises, but having seen them afar off, and were persuaded of them, and **embraced** them, and confessed that they were strangers and pilgrims on the earth. [KJV] All these died in faith, without receiving the promises, but having seen them and having **welcomed** them from a distance, and having confessed that they were strangers and exiles on the earth. [NASB] All these people were still living by faith when they died. They did not receive the things promised; they only saw them and **welcomed** them from a distance. And they admitted that they were aliens and strangers on earth. [NIV] These all died in faith, not having received the promises, but having seen them afar off were assured of them, **embraced** them and confessed that they were strangers and pilgrims on the earth. [NKJV] All these faithful ones died without receiving what God had promised them, but they saw it all from a distance and **welcomed** the promises of God. They agreed that they were no more than foreigners and nomads here on earth. [NLT] Κατὰ πίστιν ἀπέθανον οὗτοι πάντες, μὴ λαβόντες τὰς ἐπαγγελίας, ἀλλὰ πόρρωθεν αὐτὰς ἰδόντες, καὶ πεισθέντες, καὶ **ἀσπασάμενοι**, καὶ ὁμολογήσαντες ὅτι ξένοι καὶ παρεπίδημοί εἰσιν ἐπὶ τῆς γῆς. [GNS] Κατὰ πίστιν ἀπέθανον οὗτοι πάντες, μὴ λαβόντες τὰς ἐπαγγελίας ἀλλὰ πόρρωθεν αὐτὰς ἰδόντες καὶ **ἀσπασάμενοι** καὶ ὁμολογήσαντες ὅτι ξένοι καὶ παρεπίδημοί εἰσιν ἐπὶ τῆς γῆς. [GNT]	to God for such a glorious hope as the promised land. They rejoiced and loved the promise, setting their eyes upon it and not looking away.

#4308
Welcomed
 	
Received–KJV
Received–NASB
Welcomed–NIV
Received–NKJV
Welcomed–NLT
 	
POSB
REFERENCE
(Acts 15:4-5; esp. v.4)
Note 2, point 1
	παρεδέχθησαν = *paredechthēsan*
	Pronunciation: [par-eh-d-ech'-thay-sahn]
	Parsing (part of speech): verb
	    Mood—indicative
	    Tense—aorist
	    Voice—passive
	    Person—3rd person
	    Number—plural
	    Stem or root—from παραδέχομαι
	Concordance References:
	⇒ Strong's #588 apodechomai
	⇒ NIV #4138 paradechomai
	⇒ NASB #3858 paradechomai
	
	Acts 15:4
	And when they were come to Jerusalem, they were **received** of the church, and of the apostles and elders, and they declared all things that God had done with them. [KJV]
	And when they arrived at Jerusalem, they were **received** by the church and the apostles and the elders, and they reported all that God had done with them. [NASB]
	When they came to Jerusalem, they were **welcomed** by the church and the apostles and elders, to whom they reported everything God had done through them. [NIV]
	And when they had come to Jerusalem, they were **received** by the church and the apostles and the elders; and they reported all things that God had done with them. [NKJV]
	When they arrived in Jerusalem, Paul and Barnabas were **welcomed** by the whole church, including the apostles and elders. They reported on what God had been doing through their ministry. [NLT]
	παραγενόμενοι δὲ εἰς Ἰερουσαλὴμ, **ἀπεδέχθησαν** ὑπὸ τῆς ἐκκλησίας καὶ τῶν ἀποστόλων καὶ τῶν πρεσβυτέρων, ἀνήγγειλάν τε ὅσα ὁ Θεὸς ἐποίησε μετ' αὐτῶν. [GNS]
	παραγενόμενοι δὲ εἰς Ἰερουσαλὴμ **παρεδέχθησαν** ἀπὸ τῆς ἐκκλησίας καὶ τῶν ἀποστόλων καὶ τῶν πρεσβυτέρων, ἀνήγγειλάν τε ὅσα ὁ Θεὸς ἐποίησε μετ' αὐτῶν. [GNT]
		To welcome; to receive; to recognize; to accept.
		
		Practical Application
		The word "welcomed" (*paredechthēsan*) has the idea of a formal meeting of the church.

ENGLISH WORD	GREEK WORD AND VERSE	THE WORD MEANS...
#4309 **Welcomes** Receive–KJV Receives–NASB **Welcomes–NIV** Receives–NKJV **Welcomes–NLT** **POSB** **REFERENCE** (Mt.18:5) Note 1	δέξηται = *dexëtai* Pronunciation: [dekh'-ee-tie] Parsing (part of speech): verb 　Mood—subjunctive 　Tense—aorist 　Voice—middle deponent 　Person—3rd person 　Number—singular 　Stem or root— Concordance References: 　⇒ Strong's #1209 dechomai 　⇒ NIV #1312 dechomai 　⇒ NASB #1209 dechomai **Matthew 18:5** And whoso shall **receive** one such little child in my name receiveth me. [KJV] "And whoever **receives** one such child in My name receives Me; [NASB] "And whoever **welcomes** a little child like this in my name welcomes me. [NIV] Whoever **receives** one little child like this in My name receives Me. [NKJV] And anyone who **welcomes** a little child like this on my behalf is welcoming me. [NLT] καὶ ὃς ἐὰν **δέξηται** παιδίον τοιοῦτο ἕν ἐπὶ τῷ ὀνόματί μου, ἐμὲ δέχεται· [GNS] καὶ ὃς ἐὰν **δέξηται** ἓν παιδίον τοιοῦτο ἐπὶ τῷ ὀνόματί μου, ἐμὲ δέχεται. [GNT]	To receive; to accept unconditionally; to welcome. To make a deliberate choice to welcome a child in every way possible. **Practical Application** In this Scripture... ⇒ It means to welcome the child as a person: with tenderness, warmth, care, affection and love—no matter how low or unimportant or poor. Christ is contrasting the child with the greatest person, the person over whom the disciples had just been arguing (see POSB notes—Matthew 18:1-4; POSB note—Matthew 8:1-2). ⇒ It means to welcome the child when he is in need physically or materially: to feed, cloth, shelter, visit, and help him (Matthew 25:35f; James 1:27). ⇒ It means to welcome the child spiritually: to help him grow, build him up, encourage, and motivate him to follow Christ and to share his faith.
#4310 **Well** Whole–KJV **Well–NASB** Healed–NIV **Well–NKJV** All right–NLT **POSB** **REFERENCE** (Lk.8:49-56; esp. v.50) Note 4, point 2 **See also POSB REF:** (Acts 4:9-10; esp. v.9) *Deeper Study #4*	σωθήσεται = *sōthësetai* Pronunciation: [so-they'-se-tah-ee] Parsing (part of speech): verb 　Mood—indicative 　Tense—future 　Voice—passive 　Person—3rd person 　Number—singular 　Stem or root—from σώζω Concordance References: 　⇒ Strong's #4982 sozo 　⇒ NIV #5392 sözö 　⇒ NASB #4982 sozo **Luke 8:50** But when Jesus heard *it,* he answered him, saying, Fear not: believe only, and she shall be made **whole**. [KJV] But when Jesus heard *this,* He answered him, "Do not be afraid *any longer;* only believe, and she shall be made **well**." [NASB] Hearing this, Jesus said to Jairus, "Don't be afraid; just believe, and she will be **healed**." [NIV] But when Jesus heard *it,* He answered him, saying, "Do not be afraid; only believe, and she will be made **well**." [NKJV] But when Jesus heard what had happened, he said to Jairus, "Don't be afraid. Just trust me, and she will be **all right**." [NLT] ὁ δὲ Ἰησοῦς ἀκούσας ἀπεκρίθη αὐτῷ, λέγων, Μὴ φοβοῦ. μόνον πίστευε, καὶ **σωθήσεται**. [GNS] ὁ δὲ Ἰησοῦς ἀκούσας ἀπεκρίθη αὐτῷ, Μὴ φοβοῦ, μόνον πίστευσον, καὶ **σωθήσεται**. [GNT]	Restored, made alive, saved; to make well; to preserve; to make all right. **Practical Application** Imagine the strong faith required to believe simply because of Jesus' Word, because of what He said. Jesus demonstrated His great love and amazing power. He raised Jairus' daughter. He showed that He cared for the man and the family who approached Him in belief and trust.
#4311 **Well Repsected** Honest report–KJV Good reputation– 　NASB Known–NIV	μαρτυρουμένους = *marturoumenous* Pronunciation: [mar-too-roo'-men-oos] Parsing (part of speech): verb 　Mood—participle 　Tense—present 　Voice—passive 　Case—accusative 　Gender—masculine 　Number—plural	To be known; to have a good reputation; well respected; well attested; well reported of; bearing a good witness. **Practical Application** The deacon's character was to be proven beyond reproach. They were to be men of integrity, faithful and trustworthy; moral and upright, men trusted by all.

ENGLISH WORD	GREEK WORD AND VERSE	THE WORD MEANS...
Good reputation–NKJV **Well repsected–NLT** **POSB REFERENCE** (Acts 6:3) Note 3, point 1	Stem or root—from μαρτυρέω Concordance References: ⇒ Strong's #3140 martureö ⇒ NIV #3455 martureö ⇒ NASB #3140 martureö **Acts 6:3** Wherefore, brethren, look ye out among you seven men of **honest report**, full of the Holy Ghost and wisdom, whom we may appoint over this business. [KJV] "But select from among you, brethren, seven men of **good reputation**, full of the Spirit and of wisdom, whom we may put in charge of this task. [NASB] Brothers, choose seven men from among you who are **known** to be full of the Spirit and wisdom. We will turn this responsibility over to them [NIV] Therefore, brethren, seek out from among you seven men of **good reputation**, full of the Holy Spirit and wisdom, whom we may appoint over this business; [NKJV] "Now look around among yourselves, brothers, and select seven men who are **well respected** and are full of the Holy Spirit and wisdom. We will put them in charge of this business. [NLT] ἐπισκέψασθε οὖν, ἀδελφοί, ἄνδρας ἐξ ὑμῶν **μαρτυρουμένους** ἑπτά, πλήρεις Πνεύματος Ἁγίου καὶ σοφίας, οὓς καταστήσομεν ἐπὶ τῆς χρείας ταύτης. [GNS] ἐπισκέψασθε δέ, ἀδελφοί, ἄνδρας ἐξ ὑμῶν **μαρτυρουμένους** ἑπτά, πλήρεις πνεύματος καὶ σοφίας, οὓς καταστήσομεν ἐπὶ τῆς χρείας ταύτης, [GNT]	

#4312
 	
Well, Had Faith To Be Made
 	
Had faith to be healed–KJV
Had faith to be made well–NASB
Had faith to be healed–NIV
Had faith to be healed–NKJV
Had faith to be healed–NLT
 	
POSB REFERENCE
(Acts 14:8-13; esp. v.9)
Note 2, point 1d
	ἔχει πίστιν τοῦ σωθῆναι = echei pistin tou sōthë-nai
	Pronunciation: [ech-eh-ee pis'-tin too sow-they'-nah-ee]
	Parsing *pistin* (part of speech): noun
	    Case—accusative
	    Gender—feminine
	    Number—singular
	    Stem or root—from πίστις, εως
	Parsing *sōthēnai* (part of speech): verb
	    Mood—infinitive
	    Tense—aorist
	    Voice—passive
	    Case—genitive
	    Stem or root—from σῴζω
	Concordance References:
	⇒ Strong's #2192 echö + 4102 pistis + 3588 ho + 4982 sözö
	⇒ NIV #2400 echö [had] + 4411 pistis [faith] + 3836 ho [Not in English] + 5392 sözö [healed]
	⇒ NASB #2192 echö + 4102 pistis +3588 ho + 4982 sözö
	
	Acts 14:9
	The same heard Paul speak: who stedfastly beholding him, and perceiving that he **had faith to be healed**, [KJV]
	This man was listening to Paul as he spoke, who, when he had fixed his gaze upon him, and had seen that he **had faith to be made well**, [NASB]
	He listened to Paul as he was speaking. Paul looked directly at him, saw that he **had faith to be healed** [NIV]
	This man heard Paul speaking. Paul, observing him intently and seeing that he **had faith to be healed**, [NKJV]
	He was listening as Paul preached, and Paul noticed him and realized he **had faith to be healed**. [NLT]
	οὗτος ἤκουε τοῦ Παύλου λαλοῦντος. ὃς ἀτενίσας αὐτῷ, καὶ ἰδὼν ὅτι **πίστιν ἔχει τοῦ σωθῆναι**, [GNS]
	οὗτος ἤκουσεν τοῦ Παύλου λαλοῦντος· ὃς ἀτενίσας αὐτῷ καὶ ἰδὼν ὅτι **ἔχει πίστιν τοῦ σωθῆναι**, [GNT]
		Had faith to be healed, made well, saved, made better. It means both to be cured and to be saved.
		
		Practical Application
		Paul, of course, was preaching the gospel, and the man's heart was stirred to believe and trust Jesus to save him. Paul noticed this; he saw a faith rise up in the man, a faith strong enough to heal him as well as save his soul. All the man needed was to be pointed toward such power in the name of Jesus.

ENGLISH WORD	GREEK WORD AND VERSE	THE WORD MEANS...
#4313 **Went Forth– Went Out** **Went forth–KJV** **Went forth–NASB** Left–NIV **Went out–NKJV** Crossed–NLT **POSB REFERENCE** (Jn.18:1-3; esp. v.1) Note 1	ἐξῆλθεν = exēlthen Pronunciation: [ex-ayl'-thehn] Parsing (part of speech): verb 　Mood—indicative 　Tense—aorist 　Voice—active 　Person—3rd person 　Number—singular 　Stem or root—from ἐξέρχομαι Concordance References: 　⇒　Strong's #1831 exerchomai 　⇒　NIV #2002 exerchomai 　⇒　NASB #1831 exerchomai **John 18:1** 　When Jesus had spoken these words, he **went forth** with his disciples over the brook Cedron, where was a garden, into the which he entered, and his disciples. [KJV] 　When Jesus had spoken these words, He **went forth** with His disciples over the ravine of the Kidron, where there was a garden, into which He Himself entered, and His disciples. [NASB] 　When he had finished praying, Jesus **left** with his disciples and crossed the Kidron Valley. On the other side there was an olive grove, and he and his disciples went into it. [NIV] 　When Jesus had spoken these words, He **went out** with His disciples over the Brook Kidron, where there was a garden, which He and His disciples entered. [NKJV] 　After saying these things, Jesus **crossed** the Kidron Valley with his disciples and entered a grove of olive trees. [NLT] 　Ταῦτα εἰπὼν ὁ Ἰησοῦς **ἐξῆλθε** σὺν τοῖς μαθηταῖς αὐτοῦ πέραν τοῦ χειμάρρου τοῦ Κεδρὼν, ὅπου ἦν κῆπος, εἰς ὃν εἰσῆλθεν αὐτὸς καὶ οἱ μαθηταὶ αὐτοῦ. [GNS] 　Ταῦτα εἰπὼν Ἰησοῦς **ἐξῆλθεν** σὺν τοῖς μαθηταῖς αὐτοῦ πέραν τοῦ χειμάρρου τοῦ Κεδρὼν ὅπου ἦν κῆπος, εἰς ὃν εἰσῆλθεν αὐτὸς καὶ οἱ μαθηταὶ αὐτοῦ. [GNT]	To leave; to go forth; to cross over; to go; to set out. **Practical Application** 　The idea being conveyed is purpose. Jesus was going forth deliberately, for a specific purpose, knowing exactly what He was doing. 　Jesus "went forth" to prepare Himself spiritually. He was facing *the hour* to which God had called Him, the hour of His death (See POSB note, Hour—John 2:3-5; POSB *Deeper Study* #1—John 12:23-24). He knew that God's will was for Him to die for the sins of the world. He knew the awful separation from God that sin causes; therefore, He knew that He was to be cut off from God's presence, that God would have to forsake and turn His back upon Him because of sin. He was feeling the awful pressure of God's coming judgment upon sin which was to be exercised upon Him. In the flesh, He wanted to flee; He wanted another way to be chosen to save man (Matthew 26:39, 42, 44). Yet He... 　• was *committed* to God. 　• was totally *devoted* to His Father. 　• *must* do God's will. 　But to do God's will, He had to have God's help. He had to pray and seek God's face. In some special way He desperately needed God to meet His need. It was for this reason that He headed for the garden. He was seeking to be alone with His Father, to have His Father strengthen Him for the terrible ordeal and judgment of the cross.
#4314 **Went With Them** **Went with them– KJV** Traveling with–NASB Walked along with– NIV **Went with them– NKJV** Walking beside–NLT **POSB REFERENCE** (Lk.24:15-27; esp. v.15) Note 2	συνεπορεύετο = suneporeueto Pronunciation: [soon-eh-por-yoo'-eh-to] Parsing (part of speech): verb 　Mood—indicative 　Tense—imperfect 　Voice—middle or passive deponent 　Person—3rd person 　Number—singular 　Stem or root—from συμπορεύομαι Concordance References: 　⇒　Strong's #4848 sumporeuomai 　⇒　NIV #5233 sumporeuomai 　⇒　NASB #4848 sumporeuomai **Luke 24:15** 　And it came to pass, that, while they communed together and reasoned, Jesus himself drew near, and **went with them**. [KJV] 　And it came about that while they were conversing and discussing, Jesus Himself approached, and began **traveling with** them. [NASB] 　As they talked and discussed these things with each other, Jesus himself came up and **walked along with** them; [NIV] 　So it was, while they conversed and reasoned, that Jesus Himself drew near and **went with them**. [NKJV] 　Suddenly, Jesus himself came along and joined them and began **walking beside** them. [NLT] 　καὶ ἐγένετο ἐν τῷ ὁμιλεῖν αὐτοὺς καὶ συζητεῖν, καὶ αὐτὸς ὁ Ἰησοῦς ἐγγίσας **συνεπορεύετο** αὐτοῖς· [GNS] 　καὶ ἐγένετο ἐν τῷ ὁμιλεῖν αὐτοὺς καὶ συζητεῖν καὶ αὐτὸς Ἰησοῦς ἐγγίσας **συνεπορεύετο** αὐτοῖς, [GNT]	To go together; to travel with; to walk beside; to go with. **Practical Application** 　The idea is that they were so absorbed in their despair and talk that Jesus was already walking along with them when they noticed Him. But note: they did not know Him. His resurrected body differed enough that He was not recognized as Jesus without close observation (see POSB *Deeper Study* #1—John 21:1).

ENGLISH WORD	GREEK WORD AND VERSE	THE WORD MEANS...

#4315
Wept
 	
Wept–KJV
Wept–NASB
Wept–NIV
Wept–NKJV
Cry–NLT
 	
POSB
REFERENCE
(Lk.19:41-42; esp.
v.41)
Note 1, point 1a
	ἔκλαυσεν = eklausen
	Pronunciation: [eh-klahs'-sen]
	Parsing (part of speech): verb
	    Mood—indicative
	    Tense—aorist
	    Voice—active
	    Person—3rd person
	    Number—singular
	    Stem or root—from κλαίω
	Concordance References:
	  ⇒ Strong's #2799 klaiö
	  ⇒ NIV #3081 klaiö
	  ⇒ NASB #2799 klaiö
	
	Luke 19:41
	And when he was come near, he beheld the city, and **wept** over it, [KJV]
	And when He approached, He saw the city and **wept** over it, [NASB]
	As he approached Jerusalem and saw the city, he **wept** over it [NIV]
	Now as He drew near, He saw the city and **wept** over it, [NKJV]
	But as they came closer to Jerusalem and Jesus saw the city ahead, he began to **cry**. [NLT]
	Καὶ ὡς ἤγγισεν, ἰδὼν τὴν πόλιν, **ἔκλαυσεν** ἐπ' αὐτῇ, [GNS]
	Καὶ ὡς ἤγγισεν ἰδὼν τὴν πόλιν **ἔκλαυσεν** ἐπ' αὐτήν [GNT]
		To burst into tears; to weep out loud; to sob; to wail; to mourn.
		
		Practical Application
		Jesus was literally heartbroken over Jerusalem. Jesus was weeping while the city was engaged in the excitement of feasting and fellowshipping in a jovial, party-like spirit. The whole atmosphere was like that of a present-day convention. The scene can be imagined. But while the people were in such a partying mood, Jesus was off on the hillside weeping over the city and its people.

#4316
Were Fastened
On Him
 	
Were fastened on
Him–KJV
Were fixed upon
Him–NASB
Were fastened on
Him–NIV
Were fixed on Him–
NKJV
Stared at him intently–NLT
 	
POSB
REFERENCE
(Lk.4:20-21; esp. v.20)
Note 3
	ἦσαν ἀτενίζοντες αὐτῷ = ēsan atenizontes autö
	Pronunciation: [ay-san at-en-id'-zon-tes au-tow]
	Parsing atenizontes (part of speech): verb
	    Mood—participle
	    Tense—present
	    Voice—active
	    Case—nominative
	    Gender—masculine
	    Number—plural
	    Stem or root—from ἀτενίζω
	Concordance References:
	  ⇒ Strong's #1488 eimi + 816 atenizö + 846 autos
	  ⇒ NIV #1639 eimi [were] + 867 atenizö [fastened] + 899 autos [Him]
	  ⇒ NASB #1488 eimi + 816 atenizö + 846 autos
	
	Luke 4:20
	And he closed the book, and he gave it again to the minister, and sat down. And the eyes of all them that were in the synagogue **were fastened on him**. [KJV]
	And He closed the book, and gave it back to the attendant, and sat down; and the eyes of all in the synagogue **were fixed upon Him**. [NASB]
	Then he rolled up the scroll, gave it back to the attendant and sat down. The eyes of everyone in the synagogue **were fastened on him**, [NIV]
	Then He closed the book, and gave it back to the attendant and sat down. And the eyes of all who were in the synagogue **were fixed on Him**. [NKJV]
	He rolled up the scroll, handed it back to the attendant, and sat down. Everyone in the synagogue **stared at him intently**. [NLT]
	καὶ πτύξας τὸ βιβλίον, ἀποδοὺς τῷ ὑπηρέτῃ, ἐκάθισε· καὶ πάντων ἐν τῇ συναγωγῇ οἱ ὀφθαλμοὶ **ἦσαν ἀτενίζοντες αὐτῷ·** [GNS]
	καὶ πτύξας τὸ βιβλίον ἀποδοὺς τῷ ὑπηρέτῃ ἐκάθισεν· καὶ πάντων οἱ ὀφθαλμοὶ ἐν τῇ συναγωγῇ **ἦσαν ἀτενίζοντες αὐτῷ**. [GNT]
		Fixed, gazing, spellbound; to stare at intently.
		
		Practical Application
		Note the context of this Scripture: Jesus closed the book, handed it to the minister, and sat down. Sitting was the posture for preaching in the synagogue. All eyes "were fastened on Him" (ēsan atenizontes autö), a descriptive phrase meaning fixed, gazing, spellbound. They stared at Him in rapt attention; their eyes were locked upon Him eagerly waiting to see what He had to say.

#4317 **Were Fixed** **Upon Him–**	ἦσαν ἀτενίζοντες αὐτῷ = ēsan atenizontes autö Pronunciation: [ay-san at-en-id'-zon-tes au-tow] Parsing atenizontes (part of speech): verb Mood—participle	Fixed, gazing, spellbound; to stare at intently. **Practical Application** Note the context of this Scripture: Jesus

ENGLISH WORD	GREEK WORD AND VERSE	THE WORD MEANS...
Were Fixed On Him Were fastened on Him–KJV **Were fixed upon Him–NASB** Were fastened on Him–NIV **Were fixed on Him–NKJV** Stared at him intently–NLT **POSB REFERENCE** (Lk.4:20-21; esp. v.20) Note 3	Tense—present Voice—active Case—nominative Gender—masculine Number—plural Stem or root—from ἀτενίζω Concordance References: ⇒ Strong's #1488 eimi + 816 atenizo + 846 autos ⇒ NIV #1639 eimi [were] + 867 atenizō [fastened] + 899 autos [Him] ⇒ NASB #1488 eimi + 816 atenizō + 846 autos **Luke 4:20** And he closed the book, and he gave it again to the minister, and sat down. And the eyes of all them that were in the synagogue **were fastened on him**. [KJV] And He closed the book, and gave it back to the attendant, and sat down; and the eyes of all in the synagogue **were fixed upon Him**. [NASB] Then he rolled up the scroll, gave it back to the attendant and sat down. The eyes of everyone in the synagogue **were fastened on him**, [NIV] Then He closed the book, and gave it back to the attendant and sat down. And the eyes of all who were in the synagogue **were fixed on Him**. [NKJV] He rolled up the scroll, handed it back to the attendant, and sat down. Everyone in the synagogue **stared at him intently**. [NLT] καὶ πτύξας τὸ βιβλίον, ἀποδοὺς τῷ ὑπηρέτῃ, ἐκάθισε· καὶ πάντων ἐν τῇ συναγωγῇ οἱ ὀφθαλμοὶ **ἦσαν** ἀτενίζοντες αὐτῷ· [GNS] καὶ πτύξας τὸ βιβλίον ἀποδοὺς τῷ ὑπηρέτῃ ἐκάθισεν· καὶ πάντων οἱ ὀφθαλμοὶ ἐν τῇ συναγωγῇ **ἦσαν** ἀτενίζοντες αὐτῷ. [GNT]	closed the book, handed it to the minister, and sat down. Sitting was the posture for preaching in the synagogue. All eyes "were fixed upon Him" (*ēsan atenizontes autō*), a descriptive phrase meaning fixed, gazing, spellbound. They stared at Him in rapt attention; their eyes were locked upon Him eagerly waiting to see what He had to say.
#4318 **Were Made** **Were made–KJV** Came into being–NASB **Were made–NIV** **Were made–NKJV** Created–NLT **POSB REFERENCE** (Jn.1:3) Note 2, point 2	ἐγένετο = egeneto Pronunciation: [eh-ghin'-eh-tow] Parsing (part of speech): verb Mood—indicative Tense—aorist Voice—middle dep Person—3rd person Number—singular Stem or root—from γίνομαι Concordance References: ⇒ Strong's #1096 ginomai ⇒ NIV #1181 ginomai ⇒ NASB #1096 ginomai **John 1:3** All things **were made** by him; and without him was not any thing made that was made. [KJV] All things **came into being** by Him, and apart from Him nothing came into being that has come into being. [NASB] Through him all things **were made**; without him nothing was made that has been made. [NIV] All things **were made** through Him, and without Him nothing was made that was made. [NKJV] He **created** everything there is. Nothing exists that he didn't make. [NLT] πάντα δι' αὐτοῦ **ἐγένετο**, καὶ χωρὶς αὐτοῦ **ἐγένετο** οὐδὲ ἕν, ὃ γέγονεν. [GNS] πάντα δι' αὐτοῦ **ἐγένετο**, καὶ χωρὶς αὐτοῦ **ἐγένετο** οὐδὲ ἕν. ὃ γέγονεν [GNT]	Were made, came into being or became, created; to take place; to happen. **Practical Application** Note what this is saying. Nothing was existing—no substance, no matter whatsoever. Matter is not eternal. God did not take something outside of Himself, something less than perfect (evil) to create the world. Christ, the Word, took nothing but His will and power; and He spoke the Word and created every single thing out of nothing (*ex nihilo*).
#4319 **Were Together** **Were together–KJV** **Were together–NASB** **Were together–NIV**	ἦσαν ἐπὶ τὸ αὐτὸ = ēsan epi to auto Pronunciation: [ay-san eh-pee to aw-to] Parsing *ēsan* (part of speech): verb Mood—indicative Tense—imperfect Voice—active Person—3rd person	Were together; met together. **Practical Application** This means they were together in the same place because they were of the same call, mind, and purpose. It does not mean just being in the same location and place. They would not have

ENGLISH WORD	GREEK WORD AND VERSE	THE WORD MEANS...
Were together– **NKJV** Met together–NLT **POSB REFERENCE** (Acts 2:44-45; esp. v.44) Note 4, point 2	Number—plural Stem or root—from εἰμί Parsing *epi* (part of speech): preposition Case—accusative Stem or root—from ἐπί Parsing *auto* (part of speech): pronominal adjective Case—accusative Gender—neuter Number—singular Stem or root—αὐτός, ή, ό Concordance References: ⇒ Strong's #1488 eimi + 846 + 1909 + 3588 autos epi ho ⇒ NIV #1639 eimi [were] + 899+ 2093+ 3836 ⇒ autos epi ho [together] NASB #1488 eimi + 846 + 1909 + 3588 autos epi ho **Acts 2:44** And all that believed **were together**, and had all things common; [KJV] And all those who had believed **were together**, and had all things in common; [NASB] All the believers **were together** and had everything in common. [NIV] And all those who had believed **were together**, and had all things in common; [NASB] Now all who believed **were together**, and had all things in common, [NKJV] And all the believers **met together** constantly and shared everything they had. [NLT] πάντες δὲ οἱ πιστεύοντες **ἦσαν ἐπὶ τὸ αὐτὸ** καὶ εἶχον ἅπαντα κοινά, [GNS] πάντες δὲ οἱ πιστεύοντες **ἦσαν ἐπὶ τὸ αὐτὸ** καὶ εἶχον ἅπαντα κοινά [GNT]	been together unless they had been of the same spirit and purpose. This is critical to God's call.
#4320 **What [Is] Right** Honest–KJV **What [is] right–** **NASB** **What [is] right–NIV** What [is] honorable– NKJV Right–NLT **POSB REFERENCE** (2 Cor.13:7-10; esp. v.7) Note 2	τὸ καλὸν = *to kalon* Pronunciation: [to kal-on'] Parsing *kalon* (part of speech): pronominal adjective Case—accusative Gender—neuter Number—singular Stem or root—from καλός, ή, όν Concordance References: ⇒ Strong's #3588 ho + 2566 kalos ⇒ NIV #3836 ho [what] + 2819 kalos [right] ⇒ NASB #3588 ho + 2566 kalos **2 Cor. 13:7** Now I pray to God that ye do no evil; not that we should appear approved, but that ye should do that which is **honest**, though we be as reprobates. [KJV] Now we pray to God that you do no wrong; not that we ourselves may appear approved, but that you may do **what** is **right**, even though we should appear unapproved. [NASB] Now we pray to God that you will not do anything wrong. Not that people will see that we have stood the test but that you will do **what** is **right** even though we may seem to have failed. [NIV] Now I pray to God that you do no evil, not that we should appear approved, but that you should do **what** is **honorable**, though we may seem disqualified. [NKJV] We pray to God that you will not do anything wrong. We pray this, not to show that our ministry to you has been successful, but because we want you to do **right** even if we ourselves seem to have failed. [NLT] εὐχόμαι δὲ πρὸς τὸν Θεὸν, μὴ ποιῆσαι ὑμᾶς κακὸν μηδέν, οὐχ ἵνα ἡμεῖς δόκιμοι φανῶμεν, ἀλλ' ἵνα ὑμεῖς **τὸ καλὸν** ποιῆτε, ἡμεῖς δὲ ὡς ἀδόκιμοι ὦμεν. [GNS] εὐχόμεθα δὲ πρὸς τὸν θεὸν μὴ ποιῆσαι ὑμᾶς κακὸν μηδέν, οὐχ ἵνα ἡμεῖς δόκιμοι φανῶμεν, ἀλλ' ἵνα ὑμεῖς **τὸ καλὸν** ποιῆτε, ἡμεῖς δὲ ὡς ἀδόκιμοι ὦμεν. [GNT]	Right, noble, honest, proper, good, pleasing. **Practical Application** Paul was under attack, and suffered the tension and pressure of the attack, but that was not the reason he wanted his critics to repent. His purpose was not selfish or self-centered: he wanted his critics to repent for the sake of righteousness, that the good and right thing might be done. He wanted this despite the fact that they treated him as a reprobate. They might not love him, but he loved them and wanted only the best for them. He did not want to discipline them; he wanted them to repent before he arrived.

ENGLISH WORD	GREEK WORD AND VERSE	THE WORD MEANS...
#4321 **What [Is] Honorable** Honest–KJV What right–NASB What right–NIV **What honorable–NKJV** Right–NLT **POSB REFERENCE** (2 Cor.13:7-10; esp. v.7) Note 2	τὸ καλὸν = *to kalon* Pronunciation: [to kal-on'] Parsing *kalon* (part of speech): pronominal adjective 　Case—accusative 　Gender—neuter 　Number—singular 　Stem or root—from καλός, ή, όν Concordance References: ⇒ Strong's #3588 ho + 2566 kalos ⇒ NIV #3836 ho [what] + 2819 kalos [right] ⇒ NASB #3588 ho + 2566 kalos **2 Cor. 13:7** 　Now I pray to God that ye do no evil; not that we should appear approved, but that ye should do that which is **honest**, though we be as reprobates. [KJV] 　Now we pray to God that you do no wrong; not that we ourselves may appear approved, but that you may do **what** is **right**, even though we should appear unapproved. [NASB] 　Now we pray to God that you will not do anything wrong. Not that people will see that we have stood the test but that you will do **what** is **right** even though we may seem to have failed. [NIV] 　Now I pray to God that you do no evil, not that we should appear approved, but that you should do **what** is **honorable**, though we may seem disqualified. [NKJV] 　We pray to God that you will not do anything wrong. We pray this, not to show that our ministry to you has been successful, but because we want you to do **right** even if we ourselves seem to have failed. [NLT] 　εὐχόμαι δὲ πρὸς τὸν Θεὸν, μὴ ποιῆσαι ὑμᾶς κακὸν μηδέν, οὐχ ἵνα ἡμεῖς δόκιμοι φανῶμεν, ἀλλ' ἵνα ὑμεῖς **τὸ καλὸν** ποιῆτε, ἡμεῖς δὲ ὡς ἀδόκιμοι ὦμεν. [GNS] 　εὐχόμεθα δὲ πρὸς τὸν θεὸν μὴ ποιῆσαι ὑμᾶς κακὸν μηδέν, οὐχ ἵνα ἡμεῖς δόκιμοι φανῶμεν, ἀλλ' ἵνα ὑμεῖς **τὸ καλὸν** ποιῆτε, ἡμεῖς δὲ ὡς ἀδόκιμοι ὦμεν. [GNT]	Right, noble, honest, proper, good, pleasing. **Practical Application** 　Paul was under attack and suffered the tension and pressure of the attack, but that was not the reason he wanted his critics to repent. His purpose was not selfish or self-centered: he wanted his critics to repent for the sake of righteousness, that the good and right thing might be done. He wanted this despite the fact that they treated him as a reprobate. They might not love him, but he loved them and wanted only the best for them. He did not want to discipline them; he wanted them to repent before he arrived.
#4322 **What Magician Has Cast An Evil Spell** Bewitched–KJV Bewitched–NASB Bewitched–NIV Bewitched–NKJV **What magician has cast an evil spell–NLT** **POSB REFERENCE** (Gal.3:1) Note 1	ἐβάσκανεν = *ebaskanen* Pronunciation: [eh-bas-kah'-nen] Parsing (part of speech): verb 　Mood—indicative 　Tense—aorist 　Voice—active 　Person—3rd person 　Number—singular 　Stem or root—from βασκαίνω Concordance References: ⇒ Strong's #940 baskainō ⇒ NIV #1001 baskainō ⇒ NASB #940 baskainō **Galatians 3:1** 　O foolish Galatians, who hath **bewitched** you, that ye should not obey the truth, before whose eyes Jesus Christ hath been evidently set forth, crucified among you? [KJV] 　You foolish Galatians, who has **bewitched** you, before whose eyes Jesus Christ was publicly portrayed as crucified? [NASB] 　You foolish Galatians! Who has **bewitched** you? Before your very eyes Jesus Christ was clearly portrayed as crucified. [NIV] 　O foolish Galatians! Who has **bewitched** you that you should not obey the truth, before whose eyes Jesus Christ was clearly portrayed among you as crucified? [NKJV] 　Oh, foolish Galatians! **What magician has cast an evil spell** on you? For you used to see the meaning of Jesus Christ's death as clearly as though I had shown you a signboard with a picture of Christ dying on the cross. [NLT] 　Ὦ ἀνόητοι Γαλάται, τίς ὑμᾶς **ἐβάσκανε** τῇ ἀληθείᾳ	To be bewitched; to be placed under an evil spell; to cast a spell upon; to mislead, deceive. **Practical Application** 　The false teachers were charismatic, very capable, fluent, and persuasive speakers. They had dynamic personalities. Their teaching sounded reasonable and logical: ⇒ A man must keep the ritual of religion. ⇒ A man must do good works to be good. ⇒ A man must keep the law in order to be acceptable to God. 　It all sounded reasonable and logical, especially to a person who was not thinking and comparing the teaching to the gospel of Christ. The error was *casting an evil spell*, deceiving the believers.

ENGLISH WORD	GREEK WORD AND VERSE	THE WORD MEANS...

μὴ πείθεσθαι, οἷς κατ' ὀφθαλμοὺς Ἰησοῦς Χριστὸς προεγράφη ἐν ὑμῖν ἐσταυρωμένος; [GNS]

Ὦ ἀνόητοι Γαλάται, τίς ὑμᾶς **ἐβάσκανεν**, οἷς κατ' ὀφθαλμοὺς Ἰησοῦς Χριστὸς προεγράφη ἐσταυρωμένος; [GNT]

#4323

What You Need

Supplication–KJV
Supplication–NASB
Petition–NIV
Supplication–NKJV
What you need–NLT

**POSB
REFERENCE**
(Philip.4:6-7; esp. v.6)
Note 1, point 2

δεήσει = *deësei*
Pronunciation: [deh'-ay-seh-ee]
Parsing (part of speech): noun
  Case—dative
  Gender—feminine
  Number—singular
  Stem or root—from δέησις, εως
Concordance References:
  ⇒ Strong's #1162 deësis
  ⇒ NIV #1255 deësis
  ⇒ NASB #1162 deësis

Philip. 4:6

Be careful for nothing; but in every thing by prayer and **supplication** with thanksgiving let your requests be made known unto God. [KJV]

Be anxious for nothing, but in everything by prayer and **supplication** with thanksgiving let your requests be made known to God. [NASB]

Do not be anxious about anything, but in everything, by prayer and **petition**, with thanksgiving, present your requests to God. [NIV]

Be anxious for nothing, but in everything by prayer and **supplication**, with thanksgiving, let your requests be made known to God; [NKJV]

Don't worry about anything; instead, pray about everything. Tell God **what you need**, and thank him for all he has done. [NLT]

μηδὲν μεριμνᾶτε, ἀλλ' ἐν παντὶ τῇ προσευχῇ καὶ τῇ **δεήσει** μετὰ εὐχαριστίας τὰ αἰτήματα ὑμῶν γνωριζέσθω πρὸς τὸν Θεόν, [GNS]

μηδὲν μεριμνᾶτε, ἀλλ' ἐν παντὶ τῇ προσευχῇ καὶ τῇ **δεήσει** μετὰ εὐχαριστίας τὰ αἰτήματα ὑμῶν γνωριζέσθω πρὸς τὸν θεόν. [GNT]

Petition, supplication, prayer, what you need.

Practical Application

The words "what you need" (*deësei*) refer to the prayers that focus upon special needs. We feel a deep, intense need, therefore, we go before God and *petition*, that is, pour out our soul to God. Need—great need—confronts us, and the only possible help and deliverance is God. Therefore, we come and lay our need before Him as a child: crying, pleading and begging for His help, comfort, deliverance, and peace.

#4324

Whatever You Choose To Obey

Servants–KJV
Slaves–NASB
Slaves–NIV
Slaves–NKJV
Whatever you choose to obey–NLT

**POSB
REFERENCE**
(Rom.6:16)
Note 2

δούλους = *doulous*
Pronunciation: [doo'-loos]
Parsing (part of speech): noun
  Case—accusative
  Gender—masculine
  Number—plural
  Stem or root—from δοῦλος, η, ον
Concordance References:
  ⇒ Strong's #1401 doulos
  ⇒ NIV #1528 doulos1
  ⇒ NASB #1401 doulos

Romans 6:16

Know ye not, that to whom ye yield yourselves **servants** to obey, his servants ye are to whom ye obey; whether of sin unto death, or of obedience unto righteousness? [KJV]

Do you not know that when you present yourselves to someone as **slaves** for obedience, you are slaves of the one whom you obey, either of sin resulting in death, or of obedience resulting in righteousness? [NASB]

Don't you know that when you offer yourselves to someone to obey him as **slaves**, you are slaves to the one whom you obey—whether you are slaves to sin, which leads to death, or to obedience, which leads to righteousness? [NIV]

Do you not know that to whom you present yourselves **slaves** to obey, you are that one's slaves whom you obey, whether of sin leading to death, or of obedience leading to righteousness? [NKJV]

Don't you realize that **whatever you choose to obey** becomes your master? You can choose sin, which

---

Slaves, servants; whatever you choose to obey.

Practical Application

A person is either the slave of sin or of God, and there is a very simple test to tell which master a person serves.
⇒ Do you yield to sin, that is, serve sin?
⇒ Do you yield to God, that is, serve God?
If you yield to sin, you will die. If you yield to God and obey Him, you will be counted righteous and live.

Now note a crucial point. Either sin is your master or God is your Master. You either yield to sin or you yield to God. This does not mean that you become sinless and perfect, but that...
• you do not plan to sin.
• you hate sin and fight against it.
• you struggle to please God by not sinning.
• you diligently seek to make God the Master of your life by obeying Him.
• you study God's Word so that you will know His commandments and can obey Him.
• you immediately seek God's forgiveness when you do sin and you repent—you turn away from the sin (1 John 1:9; 1 John 2:1-2).
• you walk in open confession before God, talking to Him all day long, ever gaining an

ENGLISH WORD	GREEK WORD AND VERSE	THE WORD MEANS...
	leads to death, or you can choose to obey God and receive his approval. [NLT] οὐκ οἴδατε ὅτι ᾧ παριστάνετε ἑαυτοὺς **δούλους** εἰς ὑπακοήν, δοῦλοί ἐστε ᾧ ὑπακούετε, ἤτοι ἁμαρτίας εἰς θάνατον, ἢ ὑπακοῆς εἰς δικαιοσύνην; [GNS] οὐκ οἴδατε ὅτι ᾧ παριστάνετε ἑαυτοὺς **δούλους** εἰς ὑπακοήν, δοῦλοί ἐστε ᾧ ὑπακούετε, ἤτοι ἁμαρτίας εἰς θάνατον ἢ ὑπακοῆς εἰς δικαιοσύνην; [GNT]	unbroken fellowship with Him as the Master of your life. Again, note the results, for whom we serve determines our destiny. If we yield to sin, we will die; but if we yield to God, we will be counted righteous and live eternally.

#4325
Where
 	
Behold–KJV
Behold–NASB
Where–NIV
Behold–NKJV
There–NLT
 	
**POSB
REFERENCE**
(Acts 16:1-3; esp. v.1)
Note 1, point 1
	καὶ ἰδοὺ = *kai idou*
	Pronunciation: [kah-ee id-oo']
	Parsing *idou* (part of speech): particle sentence
	    Stem or root—from ἰδού
	Concordance References:
	  ⇒ Strong's #2400 + 2532 idou kai
	  ⇒ NIV #2627 + 2779 idou kai
	  ⇒ NASB #2400 + 2532 idou kai
	
	Acts 16:1
	Then came he to Derbe and Lystra: and, **behold**, a certain disciple was there, named Timotheus, the son of a certain woman, which was a Jewess, and believed; but his father was a Greek: [KJV]
	
	And he came also to Derbe and to Lystra. And **behold**, a certain disciple was there, named Timothy, the son of a Jewish woman who was a believer, but his father was a Greek, [NASB]
	
	He came to Derbe and then to Lystra, **where** a disciple named Timothy lived, whose mother was a Jewess and a believer, but whose father was a Greek. [NIV]
	
	Then he came to Derbe and Lystra. And **behold**, a certain disciple was there, named Timothy, the son of a certain Jewish woman who believed, but his father was Greek. [NKJV]
	
	Paul and Silas went first to Derbe and then on to Lystra. **There** they met Timothy, a young disciple whose mother was a Jewish believer, but whose father was a Greek. [NLT]
	
	Κατήντησε δὲ εἰς Δέρβην καὶ Λύστραν· **καὶ ἰδοὺ**, μαθητής τις ἦν ἐκεῖ, ὀνόματι Τιμόθεος, υἱὸς γυναικὸς τινος Ἰουδαίας πιστῆς, πατρὸς δὲ Ἕλληνος. [GNS]
	
	Κατήντησεν δὲ [καὶ] εἰς Δέρβην καὶ εἰς Λύστραν· **καὶ ἰδοὺ** μαθητής τις ἦν ἐκεῖ ὀνόματι Τιμόθεος, υἱὸς γυναικὸς Ἰουδαίας πιστῆς, πατρὸς δὲ Ἕλληνος, [GNT]
		To behold, to look and listen.
		
		Practical Application
		The word "where" (*kai idou*) has the idea of looking and gazing at a wonderful discovery, at an unexpected surprise.

#4326
Whisperers
 	
Whisperers–KJV
Gossips–NASB
Gossips–NIV
Whisperers–NKJV
Gossip–NLT
 	
**POSB
REFERENCE**
(Romans 1:29)
Deeper Study #11
	ψιθυριστάς = *psithuristas*
	Pronunciation: [psith-u-ris-tahs']
	Parsing (part of speech): noun
	    Case—accusative
	    Gender—masculine
	    Number—plural
	    Stem or root—from ψιθυριστής, οῦ
	Concordance References:
	  ⇒ Strong's #5588 psithuristës
	  ⇒ NIV #6031 psithuristës
	  ⇒ NASB #5588 psithuristës
	
	Romans 1:29
	Being filled with all unrighteousness, fornication, wickedness, covetousness, maliciousness; full of envy, murder, debate, deceit, malignity; **whisperers**, [KJV]
	
	Being filled with all unrighteousness, wickedness, greed, evil; full of envy, murder, strife, deceit, malice; they are **gossips**, [NASB]
	
	They have become filled with every kind of wickedness, evil, greed and depravity. They are full of envy, murder, strife, deceit and malice. They are **gossips**, [NIV]
	
	Being filled with all unrighteousness, sexual immorality, wickedness, covetousness, maliciousness; full of envy, murder, strife, deceit, evil-mindedness; they are **whisperers**, [NKJV]
	
	Their lives became full of every kind of wickedness, sin, greed, hate, envy, murder, fighting, deception, mali-
		Gossips, whisperers, slanderers, backbiters, murderers, tale bearers.
		
		Practical Application
		It is a person...
		• who gossips behind another person's back, chewing and tearing him up.
		• who passes on tales about others, whether true or not.
		• who destroys the reputation of others.

ENGLISH WORD	GREEK WORD AND VERSE	THE WORD MEANS...

cious behavior, and **gossip**. [NLT]

πεπληρωμένους πάσῃ ἀδικίᾳ πορνείᾳ, πονηρίᾳ πλεονεξίᾳ κακίᾳ· μεστοὺς φθόνου, φόνου, ἔριδος, δόλου, **κακοηθείας**· [GNS]

πεπληρωμένους πάσῃ ἀδικίᾳ πονηρίᾳ πλεονεξίᾳ κακίᾳ, μεστοὺς φθόνου φόνου ἔριδος δόλου κακοηθείας, **ψιθυριστάς** [GNT]

#4327
Whisperings

Whisperings–KJV
Gossip–NASB
Gossip–NIV
Whisperings–NKJV
Gossip–NLT

**POSB
REFERENCE**
(2 Cor.12:19-21; esp.
v.20)
Note 3, point 2

ψιθυρισμοί = *psithurismoi*
Pronunciation: [psith-oo-ris-moy']
Parsing (part of speech): noun
    Case—nominative
    Gender—masculine
    Number—plural
    Stem or root—from ψιθυρισμός, οῦ
Concordance References:
  ⇒ Strong's #5587 psithurismos
  ⇒ NIV #6030 psithurismos
  ⇒ NASB #5587 psithurismos

2 Cor. 12:20
For I fear, lest, when I come, I shall not find you such as I would, and that I shall be found unto you such as ye would not: lest there be debates, envyings, wraths, strifes, backbitings, **whisperings**, swellings, tumults: [KJV]

For I am afraid that perhaps when I come I may find you to be not what I wish and may be found by you to be not what you wish; that perhaps there may be strife, jealousy, angry tempers, disputes, slanders, **gossip**, arrogance, disturbances; [NASB]

For I am afraid that when I come I may not find you as I want you to be, and you may not find me as you want me to be. I fear that there may be quarreling, jealousy, outbursts of anger, factions, slander, **gossip**, arrogance and disorder. [NIV]

For I fear lest, when I come, I shall not find you such as I wish, and that I shall be found by you such as you do not wish; lest there be contentions, jealousies, outbursts of wrath, selfish ambitions, backbitings, **whisperings**, conceits, tumults; [NKJV]

For I am afraid that when I come to visit you I won't like what I find, and then you won't like my response. I am afraid that I will find quarreling, jealousy, outbursts of anger, selfishness, backstabbing, **gossip**, conceit, and disorderly behavior. [NLT]

φοβοῦμαι γὰρ μή πως ἐλθὼν οὐχ οἵους θέλω εὕρω ὑμᾶς, κἀγὼ εὑρεθῶ ὑμῖν οἷον οὐ θέλετε· μή πως ἔρις, ζῆλοι, θυμοί, ἐριθεῖαι, καταλαλιαί, **ψιθυρισμοί**, φυσιώσεις, ἀκαταστασίαι· [GNS]

φοβοῦμαι γὰρ μή πως ἐλθὼν οὐχ οἵους θέλω εὕρω ὑμᾶς κἀγὼ εὑρεθῶ ὑμῖν οἷον οὐ θέλετε· μή πως ἔρις, ζῆλος, θυμοί, ἐριθεῖαι, καταλαλιαί, **ψιθυρισμοί**, φυσιώσεις, ἀκαταστασίαι· [GNT]

Gossip, whisperings, behind-the-back talk, spicy rumor.

Practical Application
Paul was stricken with fear, fear lest the church fail to be what it should be and reject him and his ministry. Paul feared that the church would fail to deal with the carnal critics and continue putting up with their evil attacks against him. He lists eight evils, including whisperings (*psithurismoi*), that are characteristic of divisive critics in the church.

#4328
Who

Who–KJV
These–NASB
They–NIV
These–NKJV
They–NLT

**POSB
REFERENCE**
(2 Thes.1:9)
Note 1

οἵτινες = *hoitines*
Pronunciation: [hoy'-ti-nehs]
Parsing (part of speech): pronominal adjective
    Type—relative
    Case—nominative
    Gender—masculine
    Number—plural
    Stem or root—from ὅστις, ἥτις, ὅ τι
Concordance References:
  ⇒ Strong's #3748 hostis
  ⇒ NIV #4015 hostis
  ⇒ NASB #3748 hostis

2 Thes. 1:9
Who shall be punished with everlasting destruction from the presence of the Lord, and from the glory of his power; [KJV]

And **these** will pay the penalty of eternal destruction, away from the presence of the Lord and from the glory of

They, who, these, whoever, anyone.

Practical Application
The word "who" (*hoitines*) is used in a qualitative sense; that is, it means *"persons who are such as"* deserve this punishment; "persons who are of *such a kind as to*" deserve this punishment. The Greek word clearly shows that these persons deserve the punishment of the coming judgment. (This is pointed out by A.T. Robertson, *Word Pictures in the New Testament*, Vol.4, p.44; and Leon Morris, *The Epistles of Paul to the Thessalonians*. "Tyndale New Testament Commentaries," p.119.)

ENGLISH WORD	GREEK WORD AND VERSE	THE WORD MEANS...

	His power, [NASB]
	    They will be punished with everlasting destruction and shut out from the presence of the Lord and from the majesty of his power [NIV]
	    These shall be punished with everlasting destruction from the presence of the Lord and from the glory of His power, [NKJV]
	    They will be punished with everlasting destruction, forever separated from the Lord and from his glorious power [NLT]
	    οἵτινες δίκην τίσουσιν, ὄλεθρον αἰώνιον ἀπὸ προσώπου τοῦ Κυρίου καὶ ἀπὸ τῆς δόξης τῆς ἰσχύος αὐτοῦ, [GNS]
	    οἵτινες δίκην τίσουσιν ὄλεθρον αἰώνιον ἀπὸ προσώπου τοῦ κυρίου καὶ ἀπὸ τῆς δόξης τῆς ἰσχύος αὐτοῦ, [GNT]	

#4329
Who Died
 	
Was dead–KJV
Was dead–NASB
Who died–NIV
Was dead–NKJV
Who died–NLT
 	
**POSB
REFERENCE**
(Rev.2:8)
Note 2, point 2
	ὃς ἐγένετο νεκρὸς = *hos egeneto nekros*
	Pronunciation: [hos eh-ghin'-eh-to nek-ros']
	Parsing *egeneto* (part of speech): verb
	    Mood—indicative
	    Tense—aorist
	    Voice—middle deponent
	    Person—3rd person
	    Number—singular
	    Stem or root—from γίνομαι
	Parsing *nekros* (part of speech): adjective
	    Case—nominative
	    Gender—masculine
	    Number—singular
	    Stem or root—from νεκρός, ά, όν
	Concordance References:
	  ⇒ Strong's #3739 hos + 1096+3498 ginomai nekros
	  ⇒ NIV #4005 hos [who] + 1181+3738 ginomai nekros [died]
	  ⇒ NASB #3739 hos + 1096+3498 ginomai nekros
	
	Rev. 2:8
	    And unto the angel of the church in Smyrna write; These things saith the first and the last, which **was dead**, and is alive; [KJV]
	    "And to the angel of the church in Smyrna write:The first and the last, who **was dead**, and has come to life, says this: [NASB]
	    "To the angel of the church in Smyrna write: These are the words of him who is the First and the Last, **who died** and came to life again. [NIV]
	    "And to the angel of the church in Smyrna write,' These things says the First and the Last, who **was dead**, and came to life: [NKJV]
	    "Write this letter to the angel of the church in Smyrna. This is the message from the one who is the First and the Last, **who died** and is alive: [NLT]
	    Καὶ τῷ ἀγγέλῳ τῆς ἐκκλησίας Σμυρναίων γράψον, Τάδε λέγει ὁ πρῶτος καὶ ὁ ἔσχατος, ὃς ἐγένετο νεκρὸς καὶ ἔζησεν· [GNS]
	    Καὶ τῷ ἀγγέλῳ τῆς ἐν Σμύρνῃ ἐκκλησίας γράψον· Τάδε λέγει ὁ πρῶτος καὶ ὁ ἔσχατος, ὃς ἐγένετο νεκρὸς καὶ ἔζησεν· [GNT]
		Was dead, who died.
		
		Practical Application
		    Christ says that He is the One who *died and came to life again*. Christ *became* dead. His death was only a passing phase, an episode He had to go through. He experienced death, but death was only a passing thing for Him. He triumphed over it. *Alive* is aorist tense in the Greek, a once-for-all act. Once it is done, it is done—completed, finished. Jesus *came to life again*. He arose. Therefore, the message to the church at Smyrna is that no matter what they experience, it is a passing episode. Even if they experience death, it has been conquered. Christ has personally been there and triumphed over both pain and death. Therefore, the believer shall live forever even if he is martyred.

#4330
**Who Does Not Obey–
Who Don't Obey**
 	
Believeth not–KJV
**Who does not obey–
NASB**
Whoever rejects–NIV
	ὁ ἀπειθῶ = *ho apeithön*
	Pronunciation: [ho ap-i-thown']
	Parsing *apeithön* (part of speech): verb
	    Mood—participle
	    Tense—present
	    Voice—active
	    Case—nominative
	    Gender—masculine
	    Number—singular
	    Stem or root—from ἀπειθέω
	Concordance References:
	  ⇒ Strong's #3588 ho + 544 apeitheö
		To reject; to believe not; to obey not; to disobey; to be an unbeliever.
		
		Practical Application
		    If a person does not obey, he does not really believe. Conversely, if a person really believes, he obeys. (See POSB note—John 2:24 and POSB *Deeper Study* #2—John 2:24; POSB *Deeper Study* #1—Hebrews 5:9.) The man who believes *on* the Son has everlasting life (see POSB *Deeper Study* #2—John 1:4; POSB

ENGLISH WORD	GREEK WORD AND VERSE	THE WORD MEANS...

Does not believe–NKJV
Who don't obey–
NLT
 	
POSB
REFERENCE
(Jn.3:36)
Deeper Study #4
	⇒ NIV #3836 ho [whoever] + 578 apeitheō
	  [rejects]
	⇒ NASB #3588 ho + 544 apeitheō
	
	John 3:36
	He that believeth on the Son hath everlasting life: and he that **believeth not** the Son shall not see life; but the wrath of God abideth on him. [KJV]
	"He who believes in the Son has eternal life; but he **who does not obey** the Son shall not see life, but the wrath of God abides on him." [NASB]
	Whoever believes in the Son has eternal life, but **whoever rejects** the Son will not see life, for God's wrath remains on him." [NIV]
	He who believes in the Son has everlasting life; and he who **does not believe** the Son shall not see life, but the wrath of God abides on him." [NKJV]
	And all who believe in God's Son have eternal life. Those **who don't obey** the Son will never experience eternal life, but the wrath of God remains upon them." [NLT]
	ὁ πιστεύων εἰς τὸν υἱὸν ἔχει ζωὴν αἰώνιον· ὁ δὲ **ἀπειθῶν** τῷ υἱῷ, οὐκ ὄψεται ζωήν, ἀλλ' ἡ ὀργὴ τοῦ Θεοῦ μένει ἐπ' αὐτόν. [GNS]
	ὁ πιστεύων εἰς τὸν υἱὸν ἔχει ζωὴν αἰώνιον· ὁ δὲ **ἀπειθῶν** τῷ υἱῷ οὐκ ὄψεται ζωήν, ἀλλ' ἡ ὀργὴ τοῦ θεοῦ μένει ἐπ' αὐτόν. [GNT]
		Deeper Study #1—John 10:10; POSB *Deeper Study* #1—John 17:2-3). God will receive and honor anyone who receives and honors His Son whom He loves so much. It does not matter who the person is or what the person has done. If the person believes on God's only Son, God gives everlasting life to him.
		  The person who does not obey the Son faces two things.
		1. He will not see life. He perishes (see POSB *Deeper Study* #2, Perish—John 3:16).
		2. The wrath of God abides on him (see POSB *Deeper Study* #5—John 3:36).

#4331
Who Have The
Spirit
 	
Spiritual–KJV
Spiritual–NASB
Spiritual–NIV
Spiritual–NKJV
Who have the
Spirit–NLT
 	
POSB
REFERENCE
(1 Cor.2:15-16; esp.
v.15)
Note 2
	πνευματικός = *pneumatikos*
	Pronunciation: [pnyoo-mat-ik-os']
	Parsing (part of speech): pronominal adjective
	  Case—nominative
	  Gender—masculine
	  Number—singular
	  Stem or root—from πνευματικός, ή, όν
	Concordance References:
	⇒ Strong's #4152 pneumatikos
	⇒ NIV #4461 pneumatikos
	⇒ NASB #4152 pneumatikos
	
	1 Cor. 2:15
	But he that is **spiritual** judgeth all things, yet he himself is judged of no man. [KJV]
	But he who is **spiritual** appraises all things, yet he himself is appraised by no man. [NASB]
	The **spiritual** man makes judgments about all things, but he himself is not subject to any man's judgment: [NIV]
	But he who is **spiritual** judges all things, yet he himself is rightly judged by no one. [NKJV]
	We **who have the Spirit** understand these things, but others can't understand us at all. [NLT]
	ὁ δὲ **πνευματικὸς** ἀνακρίνει μὲν πάντα, αὐτὸς δὲ ὑπ' οὐδενὸς ἀνακρίνεται. [GNS]
	ὁ δὲ **πνευματικὸς** ἀνακρίνει [τὰ] πάντα, αὐτὸς δὲ ὑπ' οὐδενὸς ἀνακρίνεται. [GNT]
		Spiritual; the person who has the Spirit; that the spiritual man is a person in whom the Holy Spirit dwells.
		
		Practical Application
		  A man has the Spirit because the Holy Spirit dwells in him. He is not spiritual because he...
		• has received some superior, human gift.
		• has received some unusual ability.
		• has become more intelligent than before.
		• has become greater than he was before.
		• has become better than he was before.
		
		A man becomes spiritual because he has received the Spirit of God and is living under the influence of the Spirit of God.

#4332
Whoever
Rejects
 	
Believeth not–KJV
Who does not obey–
NASB
Whoever rejects–NIV
Does not believe–
NKJV
Who don't obey–NLT
	ὁ ἀπειθῶν = *ho apeithōn*
	Pronunciation: [ho hap-i-thown']
	Parsing *apeithōn* (part of speech): verb
	  Mood—participle
	  Tense—present
	  Voice—active
	  Case—nominative
	  Gender—masculine
	  Number—singular
	  Stem or root—from ἀπειθέω
	Concordance References:
	⇒ Strong's #3588 ho + 544 apeitheō
	⇒ NIV #3836 ho [whoever] + 578 apeitheō
	  [rejects]
	⇒ NASB #3588 ho + 544 apeitheō
		To reject; to believe not; to obey not; to disobey; to be an unbeliever.
		
		Practical Application
		  If a person does not obey, he does not really believe. Conversely, if a person really believes, he obeys. (See POSB note—John 2:24 and POSB *Deeper Study* #2—John 2:24; POSB *Deeper Study* #1—Hebrews 5:9.) The man who believes *on* the Son has everlasting life (see POSB *Deeper Study* #2—John 1:4; POSB *Deeper Study* #1—John 10:10; POSB *Deeper Study* #1—John 17:2-3). God will receive and honor anyone who receives and honors His Son

ENGLISH WORD	GREEK WORD AND VERSE	THE WORD MEANS...
POSB REFERENCE (Jn.3:36) *Deeper Study #4*	**John 3:36** He that believeth on the Son hath everlasting life: and he that **believeth not** the Son shall not see life; but the wrath of God abideth on him. [KJV] "He who believes in the Son has eternal life; but he **who does not obey** the Son shall not see life, but the wrath of God abides on him." [NASB] Whoever believes in the Son has eternal life, but **whoever rejects** the Son will not see life, for God's wrath remains on him." [NIV] He who believes in the Son has everlasting life; and he who **does not believe** the Son shall not see life, but the wrath of God abides on him." [NKJV] And all who believe in God's Son have eternal life. Those **who don't obey** the Son will never experience eternal life, but the wrath of God remains upon them." [NLT] ὁ πιστεύων εἰς τὸν υἱὸν ἔχει ζωὴν αἰώνιον· **ὁ δὲ ἀπειθῶν** τῷ υἱῷ, οὐκ ὄψεται ζωήν, ἀλλ᾽ ἡ ὀργὴ τοῦ Θεοῦ μένει ἐπ᾽ αὐτόν. [GNS] ὁ πιστεύων εἰς τὸν υἱὸν ἔχει ζωὴν αἰώνιον· **ὁ δὲ ἀπειθῶν** τῷ υἱῷ οὐκ ὄψεται ζωήν, ἀλλ᾽ ἡ ὀργὴ τοῦ Θεοῦ μένει ἐπ᾽ αὐτόν. [GNT]	whom He loves so much. It does not matter who the person is or what the person has done. If the person believes on God's only Son, God gives everlasting life to him. The person who rejects the Son faces two things. 1. He will not see life. He perishes (see POSB *Deeper Study #2*, Perish—John 3:16). 2. The wrath of God remains on him (see POSB *Deeper Study #5*—John 3:36).
#4333 Whole **Whole–KJV** Well–NASB Healed–NIV Well–NKJV All right–NLT **POSB REFERENCE** (Lk.8:49-56; esp. v.50) Note 4, point 2 **See also POSB REF:** (Acts 4:9-10; esp. v.9) *Deeper Study #4*	σωθήσεται = *sōthēsetai* Pronunciation: [so-they'-se-tah-ee] Parsing (part of speech): verb Mood—indicative Tense—future Voice—passive Person—3rd person Number—singular Stem or root—from σῴζω Concordance References: ⇒ Strong's #4982 sōzō ⇒ NIV #5392 sōzō ⇒ NASB #4982 sōzō **Luke 8:50** But when Jesus heard *it*, he answered him, saying, Fear not: believe only, and she shall be made **whole**. [KJV] But when Jesus heard *this*, He answered him, "Do not be afraid *any longer*; only believe, and she shall be made **well**." [NASB] Hearing this, Jesus said to Jairus, "Don't be afraid; just believe, and she will be **healed**." [NIV] But when Jesus heard *it*, He answered him, saying, "Do not be afraid; only believe, and she will be made **well**." [NKJV] But when Jesus heard what had happened, he said to Jairus, "Don't be afraid. Just trust me, and she will be **all right**." [NLT] ὁ δὲ Ἰησοῦς ἀκούσας ἀπεκρίθη αὐτῷ, λέγων, Μὴ φοβοῦ. μόνον πίστευε, καὶ **σωθήσεται**. [GNS] ὁ δὲ Ἰησοῦς ἀκούσας ἀπεκρίθη αὐτῷ, Μὴ φοβοῦ, μόνον πίστευσον, καὶ **σωθήσεται**. [GNT]	Restored, made alive, saved; to make well; to preserve; to make all right. **Practical Application** Imagine the strong faith required to believe simply because of Jesus' Word, because of what He said. Jesus demonstrated His great love and amazing power. He raised Jairus' daughter. He showed that He cared for the man and the family who approached Him in belief and trust.
#4334 Whole, Maketh **Maketh...whole–KJV** Heals–NASB Healed–NLT Heals–NKJV Heals–NIV **POSB REFERENCE** (Acts 9:34) Note 4, point 3	ἰᾶται = *iatai* Pronunciation: [ee-ah'-tah-ee] Parsing (part of speech): verb Mood—indicative Tense—present Voice—middle or passive deponent Person—3rd person Number—singular Stem or root—from ἰάομαι Concordance References: ⇒ Strong's #2390 iaomai ⇒ NIV #2615 iaomai ⇒ NASB #2390 iaomai	Heals; to make whole; to cure; to restore; to free. **Practical Application** It means to be healed immediately, here and now. It was not a drawn out thing. The man was to be healed right then. The word has the idea of being made completely whole, within as well as without, spiritually as well as physically. The man, if not already saved, was made whole spiritually as well as physically. (See POSB note—Matthew 14:36 for more discussion.)

ENGLISH WORD	GREEK WORD AND VERSE	THE WORD MEANS...
	Acts 9:34 And Peter said unto him, Aeneas, Jesus Christ **maketh** thee **whole**: arise, and make thy bed. And he arose immediately. [KJV] And Peter said to him, "Aeneas, Jesus Christ **heals** you; arise, and make your bed." And immediately he arose. [NASB] "Aeneas," Peter said to him, "Jesus Christ **heals** you. Get up and take care of your mat." Immediately Aeneas got up. [NIV] And Peter said to him, "Aeneas, Jesus the Christ **heals** you. Arise and make your bed." Then he arose immediately. [NKJV] Peter said to him, "Aeneas, Jesus Christ heals you! Get up and make your bed!" And he was **healed** instantly. [NLT] καὶ εἶπεν αὐτῷ ὁ Πέτρος, Αἰνέα, **ἰᾶταί** σε Ἰησοῦς ὁ Χριστός· ἀνάστηθι καὶ στρῶσον σεαυτῷ. Καὶ εὐθέως ἀνέστη. [GNS] καὶ εἶπεν αὐτῷ ὁ Πέτρος, Αἰνέα, **ἰᾶταί** σε Ἰησοῦς Χριστός· ἀνάστηθι καὶ στρῶσον σεαυτῷ. καὶ εὐθέως ἀνέστη. [GNT]	

#4335
Wholesome Thinking
 	
Pure minds–KJV
Sincere mind–NASB
Wholesome thinking–NIV
Pure minds–NKJV
Wholesome thinking–NLT
 	
POSB REFERENCE
(2 Pt.3:1-2; esp. v.1)
Note 1
	εἰλικρινῆ διάνοιαν = eilikrinë dianoian
	Pronunciation: [i-lik-ree-nay' dee-an'-oy-ahn]
	Parsing eilikrinë (part of speech): adjective
	  Case—accusative
	  Gender—feminine
	  Number—singular
	  Stem or root—from εἰλικρινής, ές
	Parsing dianoian (part of speech): noun
	  Case—accusative
	  Gender—feminine
	  Number—singular
	  Stem or root—from διάνοια, ας
	Concordance References:
	⇒ Strong's #1506 eilikrinës + 1271 dianoia
	⇒ NIV #1637 eilikrinës [wholesome] + 1379 dianoia [thinking]
	⇒ NASB #1506 eilikrinës + 1271 dianoia
	
	2 Peter 3:1
	This second epistle, beloved, I now write unto you; in both which I stir up your **pure minds** by way of remembrance: [KJV]
	This is now, beloved, the second letter I am writing to you in which I am stirring up your **sincere mind** by way of reminder, [NASB]
	Dear friends, this is now my second letter to you. I have written both of them as reminders to stimulate you to **wholesome thinking**. [NIV]
	Beloved, I now write to you this second epistle (in both of which I stir up your **pure minds** by way of reminder), [NKJV]
	This is my second letter to you, dear friends, and in both of them I have tried to stimulate your **wholesome thinking** and refresh your memory. [NLT]
	Ταύτην ἤδη, ἀγαπητοί, δευτέραν ὑμῖν γράφω ἐπιστολήν, ἐν αἷς διεγείρω ὑμῶν ἐν ὑπομνήσει τὴν **εἰλικρινῆ διάνοιαν**, [GNS]
	Ταύτην ἤδη, ἀγαπητοί, δευτέραν ὑμῖν γράφω ἐπιστολήν, ἐν αἷς διεγείρω ὑμῶν ἐν ὑπομνήσει τὴν **εἰλικρινῆ διάνοιαν** [GNT]
		Wholesome thinking, pure minds, sincere mind, thoughts, attitudes. It means to have a clear, pure, unmixed, uncontaminated, focused, and concentrating mind.
		
		Practical Application
		It is the picture of thoughts being sifted just like wheat is sifted in order to be separated from the chaff. Thoughts are to be sifted in order to separate the true and pure from the untrue and impure. There is always so much false teaching about the end time that the mind must be pure in order to sift the true teaching from the false. The picture of a pure mind is this: the mind must be exposed to the light of the sun and be found flawless. The mind must be pure and clear from wandering and impure thoughts if it is to study the Word of God to learn its great teachings. The mind must be pure and clear if it is to grasp the great truth of the return of Jesus Christ to earth.

#4336
Whoremonger
 	
Whoremonger–KJV
Immoral–NASB
Immoral–NIV
Fornicator–NKJV
Immoral–NLT
	πόρνος = pornos
	Pronunciation: [por'-nos]
	Parsing (part of speech): noun
	  Case—nominative
	  Gender—masculine
	  Number—singular
	  Stem or root—from πόρνος, ου
	Concordance References:
	⇒ Strong's #4205 pornos
	⇒ NIV #4521 pornos
	⇒ NASB #4205 pornos
		To be sexually immoral; to be a whoremonger. It is illicit sexual intercourse, fornication, prostitution, immoral behavior.
		
		Practical Application
		Uncleanness has no part with God, no part whatsoever. The profession of a person does not matter: if he practices these things, he will not share in the kingdom of Christ and of God. And, note, *the doom* pronounced is not future, it is

ENGLISH WORD	GREEK WORD AND VERSE	THE WORD MEANS...
POSB REFERENCE (Eph.5:5-6; esp. v.5) Note 5, point 1	**Ephes. 5:5** For this ye know, that no **whoremonger**, nor unclean person, nor covetous man, who is an idolater, hath any inheritance in the kingdom of Christ and of God. [KJV] For this you know with certainty, that no **immoral** or impure person or covetous man, who is an idolater, has an inheritance in the kingdom of Christ and God. [NASB] For of this you can be sure: No **immoral**, impure or greedy person—such a man is an idolater—has any inheritance in the kingdom of Christ and of God. [NIV] For this you know, that no **fornicator**, unclean person, nor covetous man, who is an idolater, has any inheritance in the kingdom of Christ and God. [NKJV] You can be sure that no **immoral**, impure, or greedy person will inherit the Kingdom of Christ and of God. For a greedy person is really an idolater who worships the things of this world. [NLT] τοῦτο γὰρ ἔστε γινώσκοντες, ὅτι πᾶς **πόρνος**, ἢ ἀκάθαρτος, ἢ πλεονέκτης, ὅς ἐστιν εἰδωλολάτρης, οὐκ ἔχει κληρονομίαν ἐν τῇ βασιλείᾳ τοῦ Χριστοῦ καὶ Θεοῦ. [GNS] τοῦτο γὰρ ἴστε γινώσκοντες, ὅτι πᾶς **πόρνος** ἢ ἀκάθαρτος ἢ πλεονέκτης, ὅ ἐστιν εἰδωλολάτρης, οὐκ ἔχει κληρονομίαν ἐν τῇ βασιλείᾳ τοῦ Χριστοῦ καὶ θεοῦ. [GNT]	present. It does not say, "he shall not have," but rather, "he does not have an inheritance with God." He may have houses, lands, and all kinds of possessions; but he does not have one scrap of the kingdom. He has lost all that is really worth having.
#4337 **Whoever Transgresses– Whosoever Transgresseth** **Whosoever transgresseth–KJV** Anyone who goes too far–NASB Anyone who runs ahead–NIV **Whoever transgresses–NKJV** Wander beyond–NLT **POSB REFERENCE** (2 Jn.1:9) Note 3	πᾶς ὁ προάγων = pas ho proagön Pronunciation: [pas ho pro-ag'-on] Parsing proagön (part of speech): verb Mood—participle Tense—present Voice—active Case—nominative Gender—masculine Number—singular Stem or root—from προάγω Concordance References: ⇒ Strong's #3956 pas + 3588 ho + 3845 parabaino ⇒ NIV #4246 pas [Anyone] + 3836 ho [who] + 4575 proagö [runs ahead] ⇒ NASB #3956 pas + 3588 ho + 4254 proagö **2 John 1:9** **Whosoever transgresseth**, and abideth not in the doctrine of Christ, hath not God. He that abideth in the doctrine of Christ, he hath both the Father and the Son. [KJV] **Anyone who goes too far** and does not abide in the teaching of Christ, does not have God; the one who abides in the teaching, he has both the Father and the Son. [NASB] **Anyone who runs ahead** and does not continue in the teaching of Christ does not have God; whoever continues in the teaching has both the Father and the Son. [NIV] **Whoever transgresses** and does not abide in the doctrine of Christ does not have God. He who abides in the doctrine of Christ has both the Father and the Son. [NKJV] For if you **wander beyond** the teaching of Christ, you will not have fellowship with God. But if you continue in the teaching of Christ, you will have fellowship with both the Father and the Son. [NLT] πᾶς ὁ **παραβαίνω** καὶ μὴ μένων ἐν τῇ διδαχῇ τοῦ Χριστοῦ, Θεὸν οὐκ ἔχει· ὁ μένων ἐν τῇ διδαχῇ τοῦ Χριστοῦ, οὗτος καὶ τὸν πατέρα καὶ τὸν υἱὸν ἔχει. [GNS] πᾶς ὁ **προάγων** καὶ μὴ μένων ἐν τῇ διδαχῇ τοῦ Χριστοῦ θεὸν οὐκ ἔχει· ὁ μένων ἐν τῇ διδαχῇ, οὗτος καὶ τὸν πατέρα καὶ τὸν υἱὸν ἔχει. [GNT]	To transgress against God by going too far, by trying to move out ahead of Christ; to wander beyond. **Practical Application** The person who does not abide in the doctrines of Christ does not have or possess God. There are many teachers, ministers and laymen alike, who would like to be progressive and creative, to come up with a novel idea, to make some advancement in thought. They want people to recognize and approve them; therefore, they try to impress people. In so doing, they go beyond Christ and what He taught. They twist or branch off from the teachings of Christ. John warns against this: if a person does not abide in the doctrines of Christ, then he does not have God. He is not saved; he is not truly born of God. The only person who is born of God is the person who abides in the doctrines of Christ. This does not mean that believers are not to be creative and thoughtful. It means that we must not move out beyond Christ and what He taught.

ENGLISH WORD	GREEK WORD AND VERSE	THE WORD MEANS...

#4338
Wicked–
Wickedness
 	
Unrighteousness–KJV
Unrighteousness–NASB
Wickedness–NIV
Unrighteousness–NKJV
Wicked–NLT
 	
POSB
REFERENCE
(Romans 1:18)
Note 1, point 3a
 	
See also POSB REF:
(Rom.1:29)
Deeper Study #1
	ἀδικίαν = *adikian*
	Pronunciation: [ad-ee-kee'-ahn]
	Parsing (part of speech): noun
	  Case—accusative
	  Gender—feminine
	  Number—singular
	  Stem or root—from ἀδικία, ας
	Concordance References:
	  ⇒ Strong's #93 adikia
	  ⇒ NIV #94 adikia
	  ⇒ NASB #93 adikia
	
	Romans 1:18
	For the wrath of God is revealed from heaven against all ungodliness and **unrighteousness** of men, who hold the truth in unrighteousness; [KJV]
	For the wrath of God is revealed from heaven against all ungodliness and **unrighteousness** of men, who suppress the truth in unrighteousness, [NASB]
	The wrath of God is being revealed from heaven against all the godlessness and **wickedness** of men who suppress the truth by their wickedness, [NIV]
	For the wrath of God is revealed from heaven against all ungodliness and **unrighteousness** of men, who suppress the truth in unrighteousness, [NKJV]
	But God shows his anger from heaven against all sinful, **wicked** people who push the truth away from themselves. [NLT]
	'Αποκαλύπτεται γὰρ ὀργὴ Θεοῦ ἀπ' οὐρανοῦ ἐπὶ πᾶσαν ἀσέβειαν καὶ **ἀδικίαν** ἀνθρώπων τῶν τὴν ἀλήθειαν ἐν ἀδικίᾳ κατεχόντων, [GNS]
	'Αποκαλύπτεται γὰρ ὀργὴ θεοῦ ἀπ' οὐρανοῦ ἐπὶ πᾶσαν ἀσέβειαν καὶ **ἀδικίαν** ἀνθρώπων τῶν τὴν ἀλήθειαν ἐν ἀδικίᾳ κατεχόντων, [GNT]
		Wrongdoing, evil, sin; injustice.
		
		Practical Application
		The wicked (*adikia*) fail to love others. They are those who do not live with men as they should. They act against men: cheating, stealing, lying, abusing, enslaving, destroying and taking advantage of them.

#4339
Wicked Spirits
In The
Heavenly
Realms
 	
Spiritual wickedness in high places–KJV
Spiritual forces of wickedness in the heavenly places–NASB
Spiritual forces of evil in the heavenly realms–NIV
Spiritual hosts of wickedness in the heavenly places–NKJV
Wicked spirits in the heavenly realms–NLT
 	
POSB
REFERENCE
(Eph.6:12)
Note 3, point 5
	πνευματικὰ τῆς πονηρίας ἐπουρανίοις = *pneumatika ponërias epouraniois*
	Pronunciation: [pnyoo-mat-ik-ah' tace pon-ay-ree'-ahs ep-oo-ran'-ee-os]
	Parsing *pneumatika* (part of speech): pronominal adjective
	  Case—accusative
	  Gender—neuter
	  Number—plural
	  Stem or root—from πνευματικός, ή, όν
	Parsing *ponërias* (part of speech): noun
	  Case—genitive
	  Gender—feminine
	  Number—singular
	  Stem or root—from πονηρία, ας
	Parsing *epouraniois* (part of speech): pronominal adjective
	  Case—dative
	  Gender—neuter
	  Number—plural
	  Stem or root—from ἐπουράνιος, ον
	Concordance References:
	  ⇒ Strong's #4152 pneumatikos + 4189 ponëria + 1722 en + 3588 ho + 2032 epouranios
	  ⇒ NIV #4461 pneumatikos [spiritual] +4504 ponëria [evil] + 1877 en [in] + 3836 ho [the] + 2230 epouranios [heavenly realms]
	  NASB #4152 pneumatikos + 4189 ponëria + 1722 en + 3588 ho + 2032 epouranios
	
	Ephes. 6:12
	For we wrestle not against flesh and blood, but against principalities, against powers, against the rulers of the darkness of this world, against **spiritual wickedness in high places**. [KJV]
	For our struggle is not against flesh and blood, but against the rulers, against the powers, against the world
		Spiritual wickedness in high places, spiritual forces of evil in the heavenly realms, spiritual forces of wickedness in the heavenly places, wicked spirits in the heavenly realms.
		
		Practical Application
		Wicked spirits in the heavenly realms (*pneumatika tes ponerias*): Satan and all his demonic forces.

ENGLISH WORD	GREEK WORD AND VERSE	THE WORD MEANS...

forces of this darkness, against the **spiritual forces of wickedness in the heavenly places**. [NASB]

For our struggle is not against flesh and blood, but against the rulers, against the authorities, against the powers of this dark world and against the **spiritual forces of evil in the heavenly realms**. [NIV]

For we do not wrestle against flesh and blood, but against principalities, against powers, against the rulers of the darkness of this age, against **spiritual *hosts* of wickedness in the heavenly *places***. [NKJV]

For we are not fighting against people made of flesh and blood, but against the evil rulers and authorities of the unseen world, against those mighty powers of darkness who rule this world, and against **wicked spirits in the heavenly realms**. [NLT]

ὅτι οὐκ ἔστιν ἡμῖν ἡ πάλη πρὸς αἷμα καὶ σάρκα, ἀλλὰ πρὸς τὰς ἀρχάς, πρὸς τὰς ἐξουσίας, πρὸς τοὺς κοσμοκράτορας τοῦ σκότους τοῦ αἰῶνος τούτου, πρὸς τὰ **πνευματικὰ τῆς πονηρίας** ἐν τοῖς **ἐπουρανίοις**. [GNS]

ὅτι οὐκ ἔστιν ἡμῖν ἡ πάλη πρὸς αἷμα καὶ σάρκα, ἀλλὰ πρὸς τὰς ἀρχάς, πρὸς τὰς ἐξουσίας, πρὸς τοὺς κοσμοκράτορας τοῦ σκότους τούτου, πρὸς τὰ **πνευματικὰ τῆς πονηρίας** ἐν τοῖς **ἐπουρανίοις**. [GNT]

#4340
Wickedness

Wickedness–KJV
Wickedness–NASB
Malice–NIV
Wickedness–NKJV
Wickedness–NLT

POSB REFERENCE
(Mk.7:22)
Deeper Study #9

See also POSB REF:
(Lk.11:39-41; esp. v.39)
Note 2, point 1

πονηρίαι = *poneriai*
Pronunciation: [pon-ay-ree'-ah-ee]
Parsing (part of speech): noun
  Case—nominative
  Gender—feminine
  Number—plural
  Stem or root—from πονηρία, ας
Concordance References:
⇒ Strong's #4189 ponëria
⇒ NIV #4504 ponëria
⇒ NASB #4189 ponëria

Mark 7:22
Thefts, covetousness, **wickedness**, deceit, lasciviousness, an evil eye, blasphemy, pride, foolishness: [KJV]

Deeds of coveting and **wickedness**, as well as deceit, sensuality, envy, slander, pride and foolishness. [NASB]

Greed, **malice**, deceit, lewdness, envy, slander, arrogance and folly. [NIV]

Thefts, covetousness, **wickedness**, deceit, lewdness, an evil eye, blasphemy, pride, foolishness. [NKJV]

Adultery, greed, **wickedness**, deceit, eagerness for lustful pleasure, envy, slander, pride, and foolishness. [NLT]

πλεονεξίαι, **πονηρίαι**, δόλος, ἀσέλγεια, ὀφθαλμὸς πονηρός, βλασφημία, ὑπερηφανία, ἀφροσύνη· [GNS]

μοιχεῖαι, πλεονεξίαι, **πονηρίαι**, δόλος, ἀσέλγεια, ὀφθαλμὸς πονηρός, βλασφημία, ὑπερηφανία, ἀφροσύνη· [GNT]

To be depraved; to be malicious; to be wicked; to be actively evil; to do mischief; to trouble others and cause harm; to be malicious; to be dangerous and destructive.

Practical Application
It is malice, hatred, and ill will. It is an active wickedness, a desire within the heart to do harm and to corrupt people. It is actually pursuing others in order to seduce them or to harm them.

#4341
Wickedness

Iniquity–KJV
Lawlessness–NASB
Wickedness–NIV
Lawlessness–NKJV
Sin will be rampant–NLT

POSB REFERENCE
(Mt.24:12)
Deeper Study #6

ἀνομίαν = *anomian*
Pronunciation: [an-om-ee'-ahn]
Parsing (part of speech): noun
  Case—accusative
  Gender—feminine
  Number—singular
  Stem or root—from ἀνομία, ας
Concordance References:
⇒ Strong's #458 anomia
⇒ NIV #490 anomia
⇒ NASB #458 anomia

Matthew 24:12
And because **iniquity** shall abound, the love of many shall wax cold. [KJV]

"And because **lawlessness** is increased, most people's love will grow cold. [NASB]

Because of the increase of **wickedness**, the love of

Lawlessness, wickedness, iniquity, unrighteousness; sin that is rampant; a gross transgression of the law; unauthorized acts or conduct; evil-doing.

Practical Application
Unbelievers do not obey God. They live and do as they wish, not as God says. They reject God and what God says and go about doing their own thing. They rebel against God and His commandments, living lawless and unrighteous lives. What is lawlessness? It is taking license...
• with the law and righteousness
• with morality and discipline

It is neglect of or opposition to the law of God; it is substituting the will of self in the place

ENGLISH WORD	GREEK WORD AND VERSE	THE WORD MEANS...
See also POSB REF: (Mt.7:23) Note 3, point 2 (2 Cor.6:14-16; esp. v.14) Note 2	most will grow cold. [NIV] And because **lawlessness** will abound, the love of many will grow cold. [NKJV] **Sin will be rampant** everywhere, and the love of many will grow cold. [NLT] καὶ διὰ τὸ πληθυνθῆναι τὴν **ἀνομίαν** ψυγήσεται ἡ ἀγάπη τῶν πολλῶν· [GNS] καὶ διὰ τὸ πληθυνθῆναι τὴν **ἀνομίαν** ψυγήσεται ἡ ἀγάπη τῶν πολλῶν. [GNT]	of God's will (1 John 3:4). It is looking to self or to the world instead of looking to God. It is following the course of self and the desires of self instead of following the course of God. (See POSB *Deeper Study* #1—Matthew 7:23 for discussion).

#4342
Wickedness
 	
Malice–KJV
Malice–NASB
Malice–NIV
Malice–NKJV
Wickedness–NLT
 	
**POSB
REFERENCE**
(1 Cor.5:8)
Note 3
 	
See also POSB REF:
(Eph.4:7-10; esp. v.10)
Note 1
(Col.3:8-11; esp. v.8)
Note 2, point 1c
(1 Pt.2:1)
Note 1, point 1
	κακίας = *kakias*
	Pronunciation: [kak-ee'-ahs]
	Parsing (part of speech): noun
	    Case—genitive
	    Gender—feminine
	    Number—singular
	    Stem or root—from κακία, ας
	Concordance References:
	  ⇒ Strong's #2549 kakia
	  ⇒ NIV #2798 kakia
	  ⇒ NASB #2549 kakia
	
	1 Cor. 5:8
	Therefore let us keep the feast, not with old leaven, neither with the leaven of **malice** and wickedness; but with the unleavened bread of sincerity and truth. [KJV]
	Let us therefore celebrate the feast, not with old leaven, nor with the leaven of **malice** and wickedness, but with the unleavened bread of sincerity and truth. [NASB]
	Therefore let us keep the Festival, not with the old yeast, the yeast of **malice** and wickedness, but with bread without yeast, the bread of sincerity and truth. [NIV]
	Therefore let us keep the feast, not with old leaven, nor with the leaven of **malice** and wickedness, but with the unleavened bread of sincerity and truth. [NKJV]
	So let us celebrate the festival, not by eating the old bread of **wickedness** and evil, but by eating the new bread of purity and truth. [NLT]
	ὥστε ἑορτάζωμεν, μὴ ἐν ζύμῃ παλαιᾷ, μηδὲ ἐν ζύμῃ **κακίας** καὶ πονηρίας, ἀλλ' ἐν ἀζύμοις εἰλικρινείας καὶ ἀληθείας. [GNS]
	ὥστε ἑορτάζωμεν μὴ ἐν ζύμῃ παλαιᾷ μηδὲ ἐν ζύμῃ **κακίας** καὶ πονηρίας ἀλλ' ἐν ἀζύμοις εἰλικρινείας καὶ ἀληθείας. [GNT]
		Malice, wickedness, hateful feelings.
		
		Practical Application
		The word "wickedness" (*kakias*) indicates that some in the church were apparently opposing the shameful man's presence in the church (1 Cor.5:6). But those who supported the man stood their ground, and malice set in between the two groups. The word means two things.
		1. In a general sense, it means wickedness, all kinds and forms of evil. It is a word that strikes at all the vices of men.
		2. In a narrow sense, it means malice, deep-seated feelings against a person; hatred that lasts on and on; intense and long-lasting bitterness against a person. It means ill will, actually wishing that something bad would happen to a person. It means to be vicious, to be spiteful, and to hold a grudge. It means that a person has turned his heart over to evil:
		⇒ He no longer has any good feelings toward the other person—none whatsoever.
		⇒ He could care less if something bad happened to the person.
		
		The charge is strong: believers are to strip off malice—all of their evil and wickedness and all of their ill feelings against others. Believers are to be pure and clean, and they are to live pure and clean lives before their brothers and sisters in the Lord.

#4343
Wickedness
 	
Wickedness–KJV
Wickedness–NASB
Wickedness–NIV
Wickedness–NKJV
Evil–NLT
 	
**POSB
REFERENCE**
(1 Cor.5:8)
Note 3
	πονηρίας = *ponërias*
	Pronunciation: [pon-ay-ree'-ahs]
	Parsing (part of speech): noun
	    Case—genitive
	    Gender—feminine
	    Number—singular
	    Stem or root—from πονηρία, ας
	Concordance References:
	  ⇒ Strong's #4189 ponëria
	  ⇒ NIV #4504 ponëria
	  ⇒ NASB #4189 ponëria
	
	1 Cor. 5:8
	Therefore let us keep the feast, not with old leaven, neither with the leaven of malice and **wickedness**; but with the unleavened bread of sincerity and truth. [KJV]
	Let us therefore celebrate the feast, not with old leaven, nor with the leaven of malice and **wickedness**, but with the unleavened bread of sincerity and truth. [NASB]
	Therefore let us keep the Festival, not with the old yeast, the yeast of malice and **wickedness**, but with bread without yeast, the bread of sincerity and truth. [NIV]
	Therefore let us keep the feast, not with old leaven, nor with the leaven of malice and **wickedness**, but with the unleavened bread of sincerity and truth. [NKJV]
	So let us celebrate the festival, not by eating the old bread of wickedness and **evil**, but by eating the new bread
		Wickedness, evil.
		
		Practical Application
		The word "wickedness" (*ponerias*) means more than just sin and coming short. It means taking pleasure in evil. The church must purge itself of its pride in prestigious men who are living in shameful sin. Such wickedness must be purged out.

ENGLISH WORD	GREEK WORD AND VERSE	THE WORD MEANS...
	of purity and truth. [NLT] ὥστε ἑορτάζωμεν, μὴ ἐν ζύμῃ παλαιᾷ, μηδὲ ἐν ζύμῃ κακίας καὶ **πονηρίας**, ἀλλ' ἐν ἀζύμοις εἰλικρινείας καὶ ἀληθείας. [GNS] ὥστε ἑορτάζωμεν μὴ ἐν ζύμῃ παλαιᾷ μηδὲ ἐν ζύμῃ κακίας καὶ **πονηρίας** ἀλλ' ἐν ἀζύμοις εἰλι κρινείας καὶ ἀληθείας. [GNT]	

#4344
Wickedness
 	
Wickedness–KJV
Evil–NASB
Evil–NIV
Wickedness–NKJV
Sin–NLT
 	
POSB REFERENCE
(Romans 1:29)
Deeper Study #3
	πονηρία = ponēria
	Pronunciation: [pon-ay-ree'-ah]
	Parsing (part of speech): noun
	   Case—dative
	   Gender—feminine
	   Number—singular
	   Stem or root—from πονηρία, ας
	Concordance References:
	  ⇒ Strong's #4189 ponēria
	  ⇒ NIV #4504 ponēria
	  ⇒ NASB #4189 ponēria
	
	Romans 1:29
	Being filled with all unrighteousness, fornication, **wickedness**, covetousness, maliciousness; full of envy, murder, debate, deceit, malignity; whisperers, [KJV]
	Being filled with all unrighteousness, wickedness, greed, **evil**; full of envy, murder, strife, deceit, malice; they are gossips, [NASB]
	They have become filled with every kind of wickedness, **evil**, greed and depravity. They are full of envy, murder, strife, deceit and malice. They are gossips, [NIV]
	Being filled with all unrighteousness, sexual immorality, **wickedness**, covetousness, maliciousness; full of envy, murder, strife, deceit, evil-mindedness; they are whisperers, [NKJV]
	Their lives became full of every kind of wickedness, **sin**, greed, hate, envy, murder, fighting, deception, malicious behavior, and gossip. [NLT]
	
	πεπληρωμένους πάσῃ ἀδικίᾳ **πορνείᾳ**, πονηρίᾳ πλεονεξίᾳ κακίᾳ· μεστοὺς φθόνου, φόνου, ἔριδος, δόλου, κακοηθείας· [GNS]
	
	πεπληρωμένους πάσῃ ἀδικίᾳ **πονηρίᾳ** πλεονεξίᾳ κακίᾳ, μεστοὺς φθόνου φόνου ἔριδος δόλου κακοηθείας, ψιθυριστάς [GNT]
		To be depraved; to be actively evil; to do mischief; to trouble others and cause harm; to be malicious; to be dangerous and destructive. It is malice, wickedness, sin, hatred, evil intention and ill will.
		
		### Practical Application
		It is an active wickedness, a desire within the heart to do harm and to corrupt people. It is a person who actually pursues others to seduce or to injure them.

#4345
Wild Parties
 	
Revelings–KJV
Carousing–NASB
Orgies–NIV
Revelries–NKJV
Wild parties–NLT
 	
POSB REFERENCE
(Gal.5:19-21; esp. v.21)
Note 2
 	
See also POSB REF:
(Rom.13:13)
Note 4, point 1
	κῶμοι = kōmoi
	Pronunciation: [ko'-moy]
	Parsing (part of speech): noun
	   Case—nominative
	   Gender—masculine
	   Number—plural
	   Stem or root—from κῶμος, ου
	Concordance References:
	  ⇒ Strong's #2970 kōmos
	  ⇒ NIV #3269 kōmos
	  ⇒ NASB #2970 kōmos
	
	Galatians 5:21
	Envyings, murders, drunkenness, **revellings**, and such like: of the which I tell you before, as I have also told you in time past, that they which do such things shall not inherit the kingdom of God. [KJV]
	Envying, drunkenness, **carousing**, and things like these, of which I forewarn you just as I have forewarned you that those who practice such things shall not inherit the kingdom of God. [NASB]
	And envy; drunkenness, **orgies**, and the like. I warn you, as I did before, that those who live like this will not inherit the kingdom of God. [NIV]
	Envy, murders, drunkenness, **revelries**, and the like; of which I tell you beforehand, just as I also told you in time past, that those who practice such things will not inherit the kingdom of God. [NKJV]
	Envy, drunkenness, **wild parties**, and other kinds of
		Orgies, rioting, carousing, wild parties. It means revelling, carousing, partying, feasting, intemperance, debauchery, unrestrained revelry and indulgence, giving license to basic urges.
		
		### Practical Application
		This word graphically describes a life of uncontrolled license, indulgence, and pleasure; taking part in wild parties or in drinking parties; lying around indulging in feeding the lusts of the flesh; orgies.

ENGLISH WORD	GREEK WORD AND VERSE	THE WORD MEANS...
	sin. Let me tell you again, as I have before, that anyone living that sort of life will not inherit the Kingdom of God. [NLT] φθόνοι, φόνοι, μέθαι, **κῶμοι**, καὶ τὰ ὅμοια τούτοις· ἃ προλέγω ὑμῖν, καθὼς καὶ προεῖπον, ὅτι οἱ τὰ τοιαῦτα πράσσοντες βασιλείαν Θεοῦ οὐ κληρονομήσουσιν. [GNS] φθόνοι, μέθαι, **κῶμοι** καὶ τὰ ὅμοια τούτοις, ἃ προλέγω ὑμῖν καθὼς προεῖπον ὅτι οἱ τὰ τοιαῦτα πράσσοντες βασιλείαν θεοῦ οὐ κληρονομήσουσιν. [GNT]	

#4346
Wild Parties
 	
Banquetings–KJV
Drinking parties–
  NASB
Carousing–NIV
Drinking parties–
  NKJV
Wild parties–NLT
 	
**POSB
REFERENCE**
(1 Pt.4:3)
  Note 3, point 5
	πότοις = *potois*
	Pronunciation: [pot'-oys]
	Parsing (part of speech): noun
	  Case—dative
	  Gender—masculine
	  Number—plural
	  Stem or root—from **πότος**, ου
	Concordance References:
	  ⇒ Strong's #4224 potos
	  ⇒ NIV #4542 potos
	  ⇒ NASB #4224 potos
	
	1 Peter 4:3
	For the time past of our life may suffice us to have wrought the will of the Gentiles, when we walked in lasciviousness, lusts, excess of wine, revellings, **banquetings**, and abominable idolatries: [KJV]
	
	For the time already past is sufficient for you to have carried out the desire of the Gentiles, having pursued a course of sensuality, lusts, drunkenness, carousals, **drinking parties** and abominable idolatries. [NASB]
	
	For you have spent enough time in the past doing what pagans choose to do—living in debauchery, lust, drunkenness, orgies, **carousing** and detestable idolatry. [NIV]
	
	For we have spent enough of our past lifetime in doing the will of the Gentiles—when we walked in lewdness, lusts, drunkenness, revelries, **drinking parties**, and abominable idolatries. [NKJV]
	
	You have had enough in the past of the evil things that godless people enjoy—their immorality and lust, their feasting and drunkenness and **wild parties**, and their terrible worship of idols. [NLT]
	
	ἀρκετὸς γὰρ ἡμῖν ὁ παρεληλυθὼς χρόνος τὸ βίου τὸ θέλημα τῶν ἐθνῶν κατεργάσασθαι, πεπορευμένους ἐν ἀσελγείαις, ἐπιθυμίαις, οἰνοφλυγίαις, κώμοις, **πότοις**, καὶ ἀθεμίτοις εἰδωλολατρείαις·[GNS]
	
	ἀρκετὸς γὰρ ὁ παρεληλυθὼς χρόνος τὸ βούλημα τῶν ἐθνῶν κατειργάσθαι πεπορευμένους ἐν ἀσελγείαις, ἐπιθυμίαις, οἰνοφλυγίαις, κώμοις, **πότοις** καὶ ἀθεμίτοις εἰδωλολατρίαις. [GNT]
		Carousing, banquetings, drunkenness; drinking parties; wild parties; partying and getting drunk; a drunken orgy.
		
		Practical Application
		The believer's life is divided into two parts: *his old life and his new life*. Note the force of this verse: in his *old life*, he sinned enough. He has already followed the desires and lusts of the ungodly (Gentiles) enough. He has already worked the will of the ungodly. He has walked after them, walked just as they walk, and enough is enough. The believer is no longer to fulfill the desires of the flesh.

#4347
Wiles
 	
Wiles–KJV
Schemes–NASB
Schemes–NIV
Wiles–NKJV
Strategies and
  tricks–NLT
 	
**POSB
REFERENCE**
(Eph.6:11)
  Note 2
	μεθοδείας = *methodeias*
	Pronunciation: [meth-od-i'-ahs]
	Parsing (part of speech): noun
	  Case—accusative
	  Gender—feminine
	  Number—plural
	  Stem or root—from **μεθοδεία**, ας
	Concordance References:
	  ⇒ Strong's #3180 methodeia
	  ⇒ NIV #3497 methodeia
	  ⇒ NASB #3180 methodeia
	
	Ephes. 6:11
	Put on the whole armour of God, that ye may be able to stand against the **wiles** of the devil. [KJV]
	
	Put on the full armor of God, that you may be able to stand firm against the **schemes** of the devil. [NASB]
	
	Put on the full armor of God so that you can take your stand against the devil's **schemes**. [NIV]
	
	Put on the whole armor of God, that you may be able to stand against the **wiles** of the devil. [NKJV]
		Schemes, wiles, strategies and tricks; trickery. It means the deceits, craftiness, trickery, methods, and strategies which the devil uses to wage war against the believer.
		
		Practical Application
		The enemy is the devil and his strategies. He will do everything he can to deceive and capture the believer.

ENGLISH WORD	GREEK WORD AND VERSE	THE WORD MEANS...
	Put on all of God's armor so that you will be able to stand firm against all **strategies and tricks** of the Devil. [NLT] ἐνδύσασθε τὴν πανοπλίαν τοῦ Θεοῦ, πρὸς τὸ δύνασθαι ὑμᾶς στῆναι πρὸς τὰς **μεθοδείας** τοῦ διαβόλου [GNS] ἐνδύσασθε τὴν πανοπλίαν τοῦ θεοῦ πρὸς τὸ δύνασθαι ὑμᾶς στῆναι πρὸς τὰς **μεθοδείας** τοῦ διαβόλου [GNT]	

#4348
Will
 	
Will–KJV
Wishes–NASB
Would–NIV
Desires–NKJV
Wants–NLT
 	
POSB REFERENCE
(Mt.16:24)
Note 2, point 1
	θέλει = thelë
	Pronunciation: [thel'-ee]
	Parsing (part of speech): verb
	    Mood—indicative
	    Tense—present
	    Voice—active
	    Person—3rd person
	    Number—singular
	    Stem or root—from θέλω
	Concordance References:
	  ⇒ Strong's #2309 thelö
	  ⇒ NIV #2527 thelö
	  ⇒ NASB #2309 thelö
	
	Matthew 16:24
	Then said Jesus unto his disciples, If any man **will** come after me, let him deny himself, and take up his cross, and follow me. [KJV]
	Then Jesus said to His disciples, "If anyone **wishes** to come after Me, let him deny himself, and take up his cross, and follow Me. [NASB]
	Then Jesus said to his disciples, "If anyone **would** come after me, he must deny himself and take up his cross and follow me. [NIV]
	Then Jesus said to His disciples, "If anyone **desires** to come after Me, let him deny himself, and take up his cross, and follow Me. [NKJV]
	Then Jesus said to the disciples, "If any of you **wants** to be my follower, you must put aside your selfish ambition, shoulder your cross, and follow me. [NLT]
	τότε ὁ Ἰησοῦς εἶπε τοῖς μαθηταῖς αὐτοῦ, Εἴ τις **θέλει** ὀπίσω μου ἐλθεῖν, ἀπαρνησάσθω ἑαυτὸν, καὶ ἀράτω τὸν σταυρὸν αὐτοῦ καὶ ἀκολουθείτω μοι. [GNS]
	Τότε ὁ Ἰησοῦς εἶπεν τοῖς μαθηταῖς αὐτοῦ, Εἴ τις **θέλει** ὀπίσω μου ἐλθεῖν, ἀπαρνησάσθω ἑαυτὸν καὶ ἀράτω τὸν σταυρὸν αὐτοῦ καὶ ἀκολουθείτω μοι. [GNT]
		To desire, wish, design, purpose, resolve, determine.
		
		Practical Application
		It is a deliberate willingness, a deliberate choice, a determined resolve to follow Christ.
		If a person really wills and deliberately chooses to follow Christ, then he has to do the three things mentioned. Note: the choice is voluntary; it is made by the person.

#4349
Will Come True
 	
Have an end–KJV
Fulfillment–NASB
Reaching [its] fulfillment–NIV
Have an end–NKJV
Will come true–NLT
 	
POSB REFERENCE
(Lk.22:33-37; esp. v.37)
Note 3, point 4c
	τέλος ἔχει = telos echei
	Pronunciation: [tel'-os ex-eh-ee]
	Parsing telos (part of speech): noun
	    Case—accusative
	    Gender—neuter
	    Number—singular
	    Stem or root—from τέλος, ους
	Parsing echei (part of speech): verb
	    Mood—indicative
	    Tense—present
	    Voice—active
	    Person—3rd person
	    Number—singular
	    Stem or root—from ἔχω
	Concordance References:
	  ⇒ Strong's #2192 echö + 5056 telos
	  ⇒ NIV #2400 echö [reaching] + 5465 telos [fulfillment]
	  ⇒ NASB #2192 echö + 5056 telos
	
	Luke 22:37
	For I say unto you, that this that is written must yet be accomplished in me, And he was reckoned among the transgressors: for the things concerning me **have an end**. [KJV]
	"For I tell you, that this which is written must be fulfilled in Me, 'And He was numbered with transgressors'; for that which refers to Me has its **fulfillment**." [NASB]
		Reaching an end, an accomplishment, fulfillment, completion.
		
		Practical Application
		It means that The Suffering Servant of God would fulfill Isaiah 53 and man's salvation would be finally settled, finished. He was to proclaim upon the cross, "It is finished," and then bow His head and give up His Spirit (Jn.19:30).

ENGLISH WORD	GREEK WORD AND VERSE	THE WORD MEANS...
	It is written: 'And he was numbered with the transgressors'; and I tell you that this must be fulfilled in me. Yes, what is written about me is **reaching its fulfillment**." [NIV] For I say to you that this which is written must still be accomplished in Me: 'And He was numbered with the transgressors.' For the things concerning Me **have an end**." [NKJV] For the time has come for this prophecy about me to be fulfilled: 'He was counted among those who were rebels.' Yes, everything written about me by the prophets **will come true**." [NLT] λέγω γὰρ ὑμῖν ὅτι ἔτι τοῦτο τὸ γεγραμμένον δεῖ τελεσθῆναι ἐν ἐμοί, τὸ Καὶ μετὰ ἀνόμων ἐλογίσθη· καὶ γὰρ τὰ περὶ ἐμοῦ **τέλος ἔχει**. [GNS] λέγω γὰρ ὑμῖν ὅτι τοῦτο τὸ γεγραμμένον δεῖ τελεσθῆναι ἐν ἐμοί, τὸ Καὶ μετὰ ἀνόμων ἐλογίσθη· καὶ γὰρ τὸ περὶ ἐμοῦ **τέλος ἔχει**. [GNT]	

#4350
Will Know
 	
Prove–KJV
Prove–NASB
Test and approve–NIV
Prove–NKJV
Will know–NLT
 	
**POSB
REFERENCE**
(Rom. 12:2)
Note 4, point 2
	δοκιμάζειν = *dokimazein*
	Pronunciation: [dok-im-ahd'-zeen]
	Parsing (part of speech): verb
	    Mood—infinitive
	    Tense—present
	    Voice—active
	    Case—accusative
	    Stem or root—from δοκιμάζω
	Concordance References:
	  ⇒ Strong's #1381 dokimazō
	  ⇒ NIV #1507 dokimazō
	  ⇒ NASB #1381 dokimazō
	
	Romans 12:2
	And be not conformed to this world: but be ye transformed by the renewing of your mind, that ye may **prove** what is that good, and acceptable, and perfect, will of God. [KJV]
	
	And do not be conformed to this world, but be transformed by the renewing of your mind, that you may **prove** what the will of God is, that which is good and acceptable and perfect. [NASB]
	
	Do not conform any longer to the pattern of this world, but be transformed by the renewing of your mind. Then you will be able to **test and approve** what God's will is—his good, pleasing and perfect will. [NIV]
	
	And do not be conformed to this world, but be transformed by the renewing of your mind, that you may **prove** what is that good and acceptable and perfect will of God. [NKJV]
	
	Don't copy the behavior and customs of this world, but let God transform you into a new person by changing the way you think. Then you will know what God wants you to do, and you **will know** how good and pleasing and perfect his will really is. [NLT]
	
	καὶ μὴ συσχηματίζεσθε τῷ αἰῶνι τούτῳ, ἀλλὰ μεταμορφοῦσθε τῇ ἀνακαινώσει τοῦ νοός ὑμῶν, εἰς τὸ **δοκιμάζειν** ὑμᾶς τί τὸ θέλημα τοῦ Θεοῦ, τὸ ἀγαθὸν καὶ εὐάρεστον καὶ τέλειον. [GNS]
	
	καὶ μὴ συσχηματίζεσθε τῷ αἰῶνι τούτῳ, ἀλλὰ μεταμορφοῦσθε τῇ ἀνακαινώσει τοῦ νοός εἰς τὸ **δοκιμάζειν** ὑμᾶς τί τὸ θέλημα τοῦ θεοῦ, τὸ ἀγαθὸν καὶ εὐάρεστον καὶ τέλειον. [GNT]
		To test; to examine; to interpret; to discern; to discover; to approve; to prove; to demonstrate.
		
		Practical Application
		The reason why the believer is to be transformed is extremely significant. The believer will know (*dokimazein*) the will of God. The phrase "will know" means both to find and to follow God's will. This is certainly understandable. If a person's mind is not renewed and focused upon God...
		
		• how can the person ever find or discover and know the will of God?
		• how can the person ever follow or obey and do the will of God?
		
		The only conceivable way a person can ever find and follow God's will is to keep his mind focused upon God and upon the things of God.

#4351
Will Of Man
 	
Will of man–KJV
Will of man–NASB
Husband's will–NIV
Will of man–NKJV
Human...plan–NLT
	ἐκ θελήματος ἀνδρὸς = *ek thelēmatos andros*
	Pronunciation: [ek thel'-ay-mah-tos an'-dros]
	Parsing *thelēmatos* (part of speech): noun
	    Case—genitive
	    Gender—neuter
	    Number—singular
	    Stem or root—from θέλημα, τος
	Parsing *andros* (part of speech): noun
	    Case—genitive
	    Gender—masculine
		A man's will; a man's plan.
		
		Practical Application
		The idea is that even man (the husband, the stronger member, the one who is usually the leader) cannot bring about the spiritual birth of others. No man, no matter who he is—husband or world leader—can make a person a child of God.

ENGLISH WORD	GREEK WORD AND VERSE	THE WORD MEANS...
POSB REFERENCE (Jn.1:12-13; esp. v13) Note 3, point 3a	Number—singular Stem or root—from ἀνήρ, ἀνδρός Concordance References: ⇒ Strong's #1537 ek + 2307 thelëma + 435 aner ⇒ NIV #1666 ek + 2525 thelëma [will] + 467 anër [husband's] ⇒ NASB #1537 ek + 2307 thelëma + 435 anër **John 1:13** Which were born, not of blood, nor of the will of the flesh, nor of the **will of man**, but of God. [KJV] Who were born not of blood, nor of the will of the flesh, nor of the **will of man**, but of God. [NASB] Children born not of natural descent, nor of human decision or a **husband's will**, but born of God. [NIV] Who were born, not of blood, nor of the **will of man**, but of God. [NKJV] They are reborn! This is not a physical birth resulting from **human** passion or **plan**—this rebirth comes from God. [NLT] οἳ οὐκ ἐξ αἱμάτων, οὐδὲ ἐκ θελήματος σαρκός, οὐδὲ **ἐκ θελήματος ἀνδρός**, ἀλλ' ἐκ Θεοῦ ἐγεννήθησαν. [GNS] οἳ οὐκ ἐξ αἱμάτων οὐδὲ ἐκ θελήματος σαρκὸς οὐδὲ **ἐκ θελήματος ἀνδρὸς** ἀλλ' ἐκ θεοῦ ἐγεννήθησαν. [GNT]	

#4352
Will Of The Flesh
 	
Will of the flesh–KJV
Will of the flesh–NASB
Human decision–NIV
Will of the flesh–NKJV
Human passion–NLT
 	
POSB REFERENCE (Jn.1:12-13; esp. v.13) Note 3, point 3a
	ἐκ θελήματος σαρκὸς = *ek thelëmatos sarkos*
	Pronunciation: [ek thel'-ay-mah-tos sar-kos]
	Parsing *thelëmatos* (part of speech): noun
	  Case—genitive
	  Gender—neuter
	  Number—singular
	  Stem or root—from θέλημα, τος
	Parsing *sarkos* (part of speech): noun
	  Case—genitive
	  Gender—feminine
	  Number—singular
	  Stem or root—from σάρξ, σαρκός
	Concordance References:
	⇒ Strong's #1537 ek + 2307 thelëma + 4561 sarx
	⇒ NIV #1666 ek + 2525 thelëma [will] + 4922 sarx [human]
	⇒ NASB #1537 ek + 2307 thelëma + 4561 sarx
	
	John 1:13
	Which were born, not of blood, nor of the **will of the flesh**, nor of the will of man, but of God. [KJV]
	Who were born not of blood, nor of the **will of the flesh**, nor of the will of man, but of God. [NASB]
	Children born not of natural descent, nor **of human decision** or a husband's will, but born of God. [NIV]
	Who were born, not of blood, nor of the **will of the flesh**, nor of the will of man, but of God. [NKJV]
	They are reborn! This is not a physical birth resulting from **human passion** or plan—this rebirth comes from God. [NLT]
	οἳ οὐκ ἐξ αἱμάτων, οὐδὲ **ἐκ θελήματος σαρκός**, οὐδὲ ἐκ θελήματος ἀνδρός, ἀλλ' ἐκ Θεοῦ ἐγεννήθησαν. [GNS]
	οἳ οὐκ ἐξ αἱμάτων οὐδὲ **ἐκ θελήματος σαρκὸς** οὐδὲ ἐκ θελήματος ἀνδρὸς ἀλλ' ἐκ θεοῦ ἐγεννήθησαν. [GNT]
		Sexual desire, the will of the flesh, human passion, human decision.
		
		Practical Application
		The idea is that a person is not spiritually born again by willing to become a child of God just like a person wills to have an earthly child. These words picture a person who seeks pleasure, who is driven to please himself, but finds it impossible to achieve.

#4353
Will Ruin Your Life
 	
Excess–KJV
Dissipation–NASB
Debauchery–NIV
Dissipation–NKJV
Will ruin your life–NLT
	ἀσωτία = *asötia*
	Pronunciation: [as-o-tee'-ah]
	Parsing (part of speech): noun
	  Case—nominative
	  Gender—feminine
	  Number—singular
	  Stem or root—from ἀσωτία, ας
	Concordance References:
	⇒ Strong's #810 asötia
	⇒ NIV #861 asötia
	⇒ NASB #810 asötia
		Debauchery, excess behavior, wild, dissipation, reckless living, a ruined life. The word means...
		• the dissipation and wasting away of the body.
		• uncontrolled behavior.
		• rioting, debauchery, wild and outrageous behavior and conduct.

ENGLISH WORD	GREEK WORD AND VERSE	THE WORD MEANS...
POSB REFERENCE (Eph.5:18) Note 4	**Ephes. 5:18** And be not drunk with wine, wherein is **excess**; but be filled with the Spirit; [KJV] And do not get drunk with wine, for that is **dissipation**, but be filled with the Spirit, [NASB] Do not get drunk on wine, which leads to **debauchery**. Instead, be filled with the Spirit. [NIV] And do not be drunk with wine, in which is **dissipation**; but be filled with the Spirit, [NKJV] Don't be drunk with wine, because that **will ruin your life**. Instead, let the Holy Spirit fill and control you. [NLT] καὶ μὴ μεθύσκεσθε οἴνῳ, ἐν ᾧ ἐστιν **ἀσωτία**, ἀλλὰ πληροῦσθε ἐν Πνεύματι, [GNS] καὶ μὴ μεθύσκεσθε οἴνῳ, ἐν ᾧ ἐστιν **ἀσωτία**, ἀλλὰ πληροῦσθε ἐν πνεύματι, [GNT]	**Practical Application** Drunkenness is a work of the flesh that often leads to other sins of the flesh: partying, loose behavior, immodest clothing, exposure of the body, sexual thoughts, immorality, wicked or evil and unjust behavior or violence and physical abuse, notions of grandeur, strength or power. The Bible says several things about drunkenness. 1. Drunkenness excludes a person from the kingdom of God. 2. Drunkenness leads to other forms of misbehavior and sin. 3. Drunkenness makes it impossible to grasp the fleeting opportunities of time.

#4354
 Willing To Yield– Willing To Yield To Others
 	
 Easy to be intreated–KJV
 Reasonable–NASB
 Sumissive–NIV
 Willing to yield– NKJV
 Willing to yield to others–NLT
 	
 POSB REFERENCE (Jas. 3:17-18; esp. v.17) Note 3, point 2d
	εὐπειθής = *eupeithës*
	 Pronunciation: [yoo-pi-thace']
	 Parsing (part of speech): adjective
	     Case—nominative
	     Gender—feminine
	     Number—singular
	     Stem or root—from εὐπειθής, ές
	 Concordance References:
	 ⇒ Strong's #2138 eupeithës
	 ⇒ NIV #2340 eupeithës
	 ⇒ NASB #2138 eupeithës
	
	 James 3:17
	 But the wisdom that is from above is first pure, then peaceable, gentle, and **easy to be intreated**, full of mercy and good fruits, without partiality, and without hypocrisy. [KJV]
	 But the wisdom from above is first pure, then peaceable, gentle, **reasonable**, full of mercy and good fruits, unwavering, without hypocrisy. [NASB]
	 But the wisdom that comes from heaven is first of all pure; then peace-loving, considerate, **submissive**, full of mercy and good fruit, impartial and sincere. [NIV]
	 But the wisdom that is from above is first pure, then peaceable, gentle, **willing to yield**, full of mercy and good fruits, without partiality and without hypocrisy. [NKJV]
	 But the wisdom that comes from heaven is first of all pure. It is also peace loving, gentle at all times, and **willing to yield to others**. It is full of mercy and good deeds. It shows no partiality and is always sincere. [NLT]
	 ἡ δὲ ἄνωθεν σοφία πρῶτον μὲν ἀγνή ἐστιν, ἔπειτα εἰρηνική, ἐπιεικής, **εὐπειθής**, μεστὴ ἐλέους καὶ καρπῶν ἀγαθῶν, ἀδιάκριτος καὶ ἀνυπόκριτος. [GNS]
	 ἡ δὲ ἄνωθεν σοφία πρῶτον μὲν ἀγνή ἐστιν, ἔπειτα εἰρηνική, ἐπιεικής, **εὐπειθής**, μεστὴ ἐλέους καὶ καρπῶν ἀγαθῶν, ἀδιάκριτος, ἀνυπόκριτος. [GNT]
		To be submissive; to be reasonable; to be willing to yield to others, easy to be entreated, open to reason. The word means reasonable; being willing to listen to reason and to appeal; being willing to change when one is wrong.
		
		 Practical Application
		 True wisdom is not stubborn or hard. The wise teacher listens to the voice and reasoning of God and of his fellow believers; and when he is wrong, he changes his behavior.

#4355
 Winked
 	
 Winked–KJV
 Overlooked–NASB
 Overlooked–NIV
 Overlooked–NKJV
 Overlooked–NLT
 	
 POSB REFERENCE (Acts 17:29-30; esp. v.30) Note 7, point 2
	ὑπεριδών = *huperidön*
	 Pronunciation: [hoop-er-i'-doawn]
	 Parsing (part of speech): verb
	     Mood—participle
	     Tense—aorist
	     Voice—active
	     Case—nominative
	     Gender—masculine
	     Number—singular
	     Stem or root—from ὑπεροράω
	 Concordance References:
	 ⇒ Strong's #5237 huperoraö
	 ⇒ NIV #5666 huperoraö
	 ⇒ NASB #5237 huperoraö
	
	 Acts 17:30
	 And the times of this ignorance God **winked** at; but now commandeth all men every where to repent: [KJV]
		To overlook; to wink; to disregard.
		
		 Practical Application
		 Before now God overlooked or winked at man's ignorance—not in the sense of closing His eyes or of condoning man's idolatry, but He overlooked man's ignorance until He could prepare man for the coming of His Son. Now God's Son has come, and God demands that all men repent (see POSB *Deeper Study #1*—Acts 17:29-30).

ENGLISH WORD	GREEK WORD AND VERSE	THE WORD MEANS...
	"Therefore having **overlooked** the times of ignorance, God is now declaring to men that all everywhere should repent, [NASB] In the past God **overlooked** such ignorance, but now he commands all people everywhere to repent. [NIV] Truly, these times of ignorance God **overlooked**, but now commands all men everywhere to repent, [NKJV] God **overlooked** people's former ignorance about these things, but now he commands everyone everywhere to turn away from idols and turn to him. [NLT] τοὺς μὲν οὖν χρόνους τῆς ἀγνοίας **ὑπεριδὼν** ὁ Θεὸς, τὰ νῦν παραγγέλλει τοῖς ἀνθρώποις πᾶσι πανταχοῦ μετανοεῖν· [GNS] τοὺς μὲν οὖν χρόνους τῆς ἀγνοίας **ὑπεριδὼν** ὁ θεὸς, τὰ νῦν παραγγέλλει τοῖς ἀνθρώποις πάντας πανταχοῦ μετανοεῖν, [GNT]	

#4356
Winnowing Fork, Fan
 	
Fan–KJV
Winnowing fork–NASB
Winnowing fork–NIV
Winnowing fan–NKJV
Winnowing fork–NLT
 	
POSB REFERENCE
(Lk.3:15-17; esp.v.17)
Note 6, point 3a
	πτύον = *ptuon*
	Pronunciation: [ptoo'-on]
	Parsing (part of speech): noun
	    Case—nominative
	    Gender—neuter
	    Number—singular
	    Stem or root—from πτύον, ου
	Concordance References:
	⇒ Strong's #4425 ptuon
	⇒ NIV #4768 ptuon
	⇒ NASB #4425 ptuon
	
	Luke 3:17
	Whose **fan** is in his hand, and he will throughly purge his floor, and will gather the wheat into his garner; but the chaff he will burn with fire unquenchable. [KJV]
	
	"And His **winnowing fork** is in His hand to thoroughly clear His threshing floor, and to gather the wheat into His barn; but He will burn up the chaff with unquenchable fire." [NASB]
	
	His **winnowing fork** is in his hand to clear his threshing floor and to gather the wheat into his barn, but he will burn up the chaff with unquenchable fire." [NIV]
	
	His **winnowing fan** is in His hand, and He will thoroughly clean out His threshing floor, and gather the wheat into His barn; but the chaff He will burn with unquenchable fire." [NKJV]
	
	He is ready to separate the chaff from the grain with his **winnowing fork**. Then he will clean up the threshing area, storing the grain in his barn but burning the chaff with never-ending fire." [NLT]
	
	οὗτο **πτύον** ἐν τῇ χειρὶ αὐτοῦ, διακαθαριεῖ τὴν ἅλωνα αὐτοῦ, καὶ συνάξει τὸν σῖτον εἰς τὴν ἀποθήκην αὐτοῦ, τὸ δὲ ἄχυρον κατακαύσει πυρὶ ἀσβέστῳ. [GNS]
	
	οὗ τὸ **πτύον** ἐν τῇ χειρὶ αὐτοῦ διακαθᾶραι τὴν ἅλωνα αὐτοῦ καὶ συναγαγεῖν τὸν σῖτον εἰς τὴν ἀποθήκην αὐτοῦ, τὸ δὲ ἄχυρον κατακαύσει πυρὶ ἀσβέστῳ. [GNT]
		A winnowing fork, fan, or shovel that was used to throw grain up in the air to separate the wheat from the chaff.
		
		Practical Application
		In this Scripture, the winnowing fork is the Messiah's power to pick up both the wheat and the chaff.

#4357
Wiped Away
 	
Blotted out–KJV
Wiped away–NASB
Wiped out–NIV
Blotted out–NKJV
Cleansed–NLT
 	
POSB REFERENCE
(Acts 3:19)
Note 7, point 1
	ἐξαλειφθῆναι = *exaleiphthēnai*
	Pronunciation: [ex-al-eef'-thay-nah-ee]
	Parsing (part of speech): verb
	    Mood—infinitive
	    Tense—aorist
	    Voice—passive
	    Case—accusative
	    Stem or root—from ἐξαλείφω
	Concordance References:
	⇒ Strong's #1813 exaleiphō
	⇒ NIV #1981 exaleiphō
	⇒ NASB #1813 exaleiphō
	
	Acts 3:19
	Repent ye therefore, and be converted, that your sins may be **blotted out**, when the times of refreshing shall come from the presence of the Lord; [KJV]
	
	"Repent therefore and return, that your sins may be
		Wiped out; wiped away; blotted out; cleansed; destroyed; removed; canceled.
		
		Practical Application
		It means erased, smeared out, rubbed off, wiped out, obliterated—just like handwriting is erased and wiped off a wall.

ENGLISH WORD	GREEK WORD AND VERSE	THE WORD MEANS...
	wiped away, in order that times of refreshing may come from the presence of the Lord; [NASB] Repent, then, and turn to God, so that your sins may be **wiped out**, that times of refreshing may come from the Lord, [NIV] Repent therefore and be converted, that your sins may be **blotted out**, so that times of refreshing may come from the presence of the Lord, [NKJV] Now turn from your sins and turn to God, so you can be **cleansed** of your sins. [NLT] μετανοήσατε οὖν καὶ ἐπιστρέψατε, εἰς τὸ ἐξαλειφθῆναι ὑμῶν τὰς ἁμαρτίας, [GNS] μετανοήσατε οὖν καὶ ἐπιστρέψατε εἰς τὸ ἐξαλειφθῆναι ὑμῶν τὰς ἁμαρτίας, [GNT]	

#4358
Wiped Out
 	
Blotted out–KJV
Wiped away–NASB
Wiped out–NIV
Blotted out–NKJV
Cleansed–NLT
 	
POSB
REFERENCE
(Acts 3:19)
Note 7, point 1
	ἐξαλειφθῆναι = exaleiphthēnai
	Pronunciation: [ex-al-eef'-thay-nah-ee]
	Parsing (part of speech): verb
	    Mood—infinitive
	    Tense—aorist
	    Voice—passive
	    Case—accusative
	    Stem or root—from ἐξαλείφω
	Concordance References:
	  ⇒ Strong's #1813 exaleiphō
	  ⇒ NIV #1981 exaleiphō
	  ⇒ NASB #1813 exaleiphō
	
	Acts 3:19
	Repent ye therefore, and be converted, that your sins may be **blotted out**, when the times of refreshing shall come from the presence of the Lord; [KJV]
	
	"Repent therefore and return, that your sins may be **wiped away**, in order that times of refreshing may come from the presence of the Lord; [NASB]
	
	Repent, then, and turn to God, so that your sins may be **wiped out**, that times of refreshing may come from the Lord, [NIV]
	
	Repent therefore and be converted, that your sins may be **blotted out**, so that times of refreshing may come from the presence of the Lord, [NKJV]
	
	Now turn from your sins and turn to God, so you can be **cleansed** of your sins. [NLT]
	
	μετανοήσατε οὖν καὶ ἐπιστρέψατε, εἰς τὸ ἐξαλειφθῆναι ὑμῶν τὰς ἁμαρτίας, [GNS]
	
	μετανοήσατε οὖν καὶ ἐπιστρέψατε εἰς τὸ ἐξαλειφθῆναι ὑμῶν τὰς ἁμαρτίας, [GNT]
		Wiped out; wiped away; blotted out; cleansed; destroyed; removed; canceled.
		
		Practical Application
		It means erased, smeared out, rubbed off, wiped out, obliterated—just like handwriting is erased and wiped off a wall.

#4359
Wisdom
 	
Wisdom–KJV
Wisdom–NASB
Wisdom–NIV
Wisdom–NKJV
Wisdom–NLT
 	
POSB
REFERENCE
(Eph.1:17-18; esp. v.17)
Note 2, point 1
 	
See also POSB REF:
(Eph.1:8)
Note 5
(Col.1:9)
Note 1
	σοφίας = sophias
	Pronunciation: [sof-ee'-ahs]
	Parsing (part of speech): noun
	    Case—genitive
	    Gender—feminine
	    Number—singular
	    Stem or root—from σοφία, ας
	Concordance References:
	  ⇒ Strong's #4678 sophia
	  ⇒ NIV #5053 sophia
	  ⇒ NASB #4678 sophia
	
	Ephes. 1:17
	That the God of our Lord Jesus Christ, the Father of glory, may give unto you the spirit of **wisdom** and revelation in the knowledge of him: [KJV]
	
	That the God of our Lord Jesus Christ, the Father of glory, may give to you a spirit of **wisdom** and of revelation in the knowledge of Him. [NASB]
	
	I keep asking that the God of our Lord Jesus Christ, the glorious Father, may give you the Spirit of **wisdom** and revelation, so that you may know him better. [NIV]
	
	That the God of our Lord Jesus Christ, the Father of glory, may give to you the spirit of **wisdom** and revelation in the knowledge of Him, [NKJV]
		Wisdom, insight, intelligence, knowledge.
		
		Practical Application
		To grow in the knowledge of God a believer must have the *spirit of wisdom* (*sophia*).
		
		What the believer needs from God is a *spirit...*
		• a spirit that reaches out and grasps after wisdom.
		• a spirit that hungers and thirsts after wisdom.
		• a spirit that seeks and seeks after wisdom.
		
		Wisdom can best be understood by the single words *what* and *how*. Wisdom means knowing what something is, what is behind something, and what can be done. It is knowing how to use or relate to something. Therefore, spiritual wisdom means...
		• knowing who God is and how to relate to Him.
		• knowing the truth and how to use it.
		• knowing what to do and how to do it.
		• knowing how to live more and more fruit-

ENGLISH WORD	GREEK WORD AND VERSE	THE WORD MEANS...
	Asking God, the glorious Father of our Lord Jesus Christ, to give you spiritual **wisdom** and understanding, so that you might grow in your knowledge of God. [NLT] ἵνα ὁ Θεὸς τοῦ Κυρίου ἡμῶν Ἰησοῦ Χριστοῦ, ὁ πατὴρ τῆς δόξης, δώῃ ὑμῖν πνεῦμα **σοφίας** καὶ ἀποκαλύψεως, ἐν ἐπιγνώσει αὐτοῦ· [GNS] ἵνα ὁ θεὸς τοῦ κυρίου ἡμῶν Ἰησοῦ Χριστοῦ, ὁ πατὴρ τῆς δόξης, δώῃ ὑμῖν πνεῦμα **σοφίας** καὶ ἀποκαλύψεως ἐν ἐπιγνώσει αὐτοῦ, [GNT]	ful lives—for the glory of God and for the welfare of men. Wisdom differs from knowledge. Knowledge is the grasping of facts, but grasping facts is not enough. Much more is needed: a person must know how to use the facts. That is where wisdom comes in. Wisdom knows how to use the facts. The point is this: it is not enough to know the facts about God; a person must know God personally. He must know how to experience the facts about God. He must use the facts to develop a personal relationship with God—a growing relationship—a relationship that is intimate, that grows deeper and deeper. This is the meaning of the word "knowledge" (*epignosei*): a personal and intimate relationship with God; a personal experience with God. It is not an intellectual knowledge of God, but an experiential knowledge of God.

#4360
Wisdom
 	
Understanding–KJV
Understanding–NASB
Understanding–NIV
Understanding–NKJV
Wisdom–NLT
 	
POSB
REFERENCE
(Col.1:9)
Note 1
	συνέσει = *sunesei*
	Pronunciation: [soon'-es-eh-ee]
	Parsing (part of speech): noun
	   Case—dative
	   Gender—feminine
	   Number—singular
	   Stem or root—from σύνεσις, εως
	Concordance References:
	  ⇒ Strong's #4907 sunesis
	  ⇒ NIV #5304 sunesis
	  ⇒ NASB #4907 sunesis
	
	### Col. 1:9
	For this cause we also, since the day we heard it, do not cease to pray for you, and to desire that ye might be filled with the knowledge of his will in all wisdom and spiritual **understanding**; [KJV]
	For this reason also, since the day we heard of it, we have not ceased to pray for you and to ask that you may be filled with the knowledge of His will in all spiritual wisdom and **understanding**, [NASB]
	For this reason, since the day we heard about you, we have not stopped praying for you and asking God to fill you with the knowledge of his will through all spiritual wisdom and **understanding**. [NIV]
	For this reason we also, since the day we heard it, do not cease to pray for you, and to ask that you may be filled with the knowledge of His will in all wisdom and spiritual **understanding**; [NKJV]
	So we have continued praying for you ever since we first heard about you. We ask God to give you a complete understanding of what he wants to do in your lives, and we ask him to make you wise with spiritual **wisdom**. [NLT]
	
	Διὰ τοῦτο καὶ ἡμεῖς, ἀφ' ἧς ἡμέρας ἠκούσαμεν, οὐ παυόμεθα ὑπὲρ ὑμῶν προσευχόμενοι, καὶ αἰτούμενοι ἵνα πληρωθῆτε τὴν ἐπίγνωσιν τοῦ θελήματος αὐτοῦ ἐν πάσῃ σοφίᾳ καὶ **συνέσει** πνευματικῇ, [GNS]
	
	Διὰ τοῦτο καὶ ἡμεῖς, ἀφ' ἧς ἡμέρας ἠκούσαμεν, οὐ παυόμεθα ὑπὲρ ὑμῶν προσευχόμενοι καὶ αἰτούμενοι, ἵνα πληρωθῆτε τὴν ἐπίγνωσιν τοῦ θελήματος αὐτοῦ ἐν πάσῃ σοφίᾳ καὶ **συνέσει** πνευματικῇ, [GNT]
		Understanding, wisdom, insight, intelligence. "Wisdom" (*sunesei*) means that a person has the ability to apply the basic principles to everyday life, to the circumstances and decisions of life.
		
		### Practical Application
		The believer needs both wisdom and understanding: he must learn all the basic principles of life, and he must learn how to apply them to everyday life. But how? How can he secure wisdom and understanding?
		  ⇒ By studying God's Word.
		  ⇒ By prayer—praying to be filled with the knowledge of God's will.
		
		Think about the shallow lives that so many people live. Think about how little most people know about God's will. Compare this tragic fact with the kind of life God wills man to live. Is it any wonder...
		  • that so many have been deceived by false teaching?
		  • that so much of our ministry is superficial and formal?

#4361
Wisdom, Filled With–
Wisdom,
Increasing In
	πληρούμενον σοφίᾳ = *plēroumenon sophias*
	Pronunciation: [play-roo'-men-on sof-ee'-ahs]
	Parsing *plēroumenon* (part of speech): verb
	   Mood—participle
	   Tense—present
	   Voice—passive
	   Case—nominative
	   Gender—neuter
	   Number—singular
		Understanding, insight, common sense, prudence, discretion, tact, diplomacy.
		
		### Practical Application
		The word "wisdom" (*sophia*) means seeing and knowing the truth. It is seeing and knowing what to do. It grasps the great truths of life. It sees the answers to the problems of life and

ENGLISH WORD	GREEK WORD AND VERSE	THE WORD MEANS...

Filled with wisdom–KJV
 	
Increasing in wisdom–NASB
 	
Filled with wisdom–NIV
 	
Filled with wisdom–NKJV
 	
Filled with wisdom–NLT
 	
POSB REFERENCE
(Lk.2:40)
Note 3, point 1
 	
See also POSB REF:
(Col.2:3)
Deeper Study #1
	Stem or root—from πληρόω
	Parsing *sophias* (part of speech): noun
	   Case—dative
	   Gender—feminine
	   Number—singular
	   Stem or root—from σοφία, ας
	Concordance References:
	⇒ Strong's #4137 plëroö + 4678 sophia
	⇒ NIV #4444 plëroö [filled *with*] + 5053 sophia [wisdom]
	⇒ NASB #4137 plëroö + 4678 sophia
	
	### Luke 2:40
	And the child grew, and waxed strong in spirit, **filled with wisdom**: and the grace of God was upon him. [KJV]
	
	And the Child continued to grow and become strong, **increasing in wisdom**; and the grace of God was upon Him. [NASB]
	
	And the child grew and became strong; he was **filled with wisdom**, and the grace of God was upon him. [NIV]
	
	And the Child grew and became strong in spirit, **filled with wisdom**; and the grace of God was upon Him. [NKJV]
	
	There the child grew up healthy and strong. He was **filled with wisdom** beyond his years, and God placed his special favor upon him. [NLT]
	
	Τὸ δὲ παιδίον ηὔξανε καὶ ἐκραταιοῦτο πνεύματι, **πληρούμενον σοφίας**· καὶ χάρις Θεοῦ ἦν ἐπ' αὐτό. [GNS]
	
	Τὸ δὲ παιδίον ηὔξανεν καὶ ἐκραταιοῦτο **πληρούμενον σοφίᾳ**, καὶ χάρις θεοῦ ἦν ἐπ' αὐτό. [GNT]
		death, God and man, time and eternity, good and evil—the deep things of God and of the universe.
		
		This wisdom is found only in Jesus Christ and is promised only to those who search after Him with all their hearts (1 Cor. 1:30; 1 Cor. 2:10-16; Ephes. 1:8; Phil. 2:5f; James 1:5).

#4362
Wise
 	
Wise–KJV
Wise–NASB
Wise–NIV
Wise–NKJV
Wise–NLT
 	
POSB REFERENCE
(Jas. 3:13)
Note 1
	σοφός = *sophos*
	Pronunciation: [sof-os']
	Parsing (part of speech): adjective
	   Case—nominative
	   Gender—masculine
	   Number—singular
	   Stem or root—from σοφός, ή, όν
	Concordance References:
	⇒ Strong's #4680 sophos
	⇒ NIV #5055 sophos
	⇒ NASB #4680 sophos
	
	### James 3:13
	Who is a **wise** man and endued with knowledge among you? let him shew out of a good conversation his works with meekness of wisdom. [KJV]
	
	Who among you is **wise** and understanding? Let him show by his good behavior his deeds in the gentleness of wisdom. [NASB]
	
	Who is **wise** and understanding among you? Let him show it by his good life, by deeds done in the humility that comes from wisdom. [NIV]
	
	Who is **wise** and understanding among you? Let him show by good conduct that his works are done in the meekness of wisdom. [NKJV]
	
	If you are **wise** and understand God's ways, live a life of steady goodness so that only good deeds will pour forth. And if you don't brag about the good you do, then you will be truly wise! [NLT]
	
	Τίς **σοφὸς** καὶ ἐπιστήμων ἐν ὑμῖν; δειξάτω ἐκ τῆς καλῆς ἀναστροφῆς τὰ ἔργα αὐτοῦ ἐν πραΰτητι σοφίας. [GNS]
	
	Τίς **σοφὸς** καὶ evpisτήμων ἐν ὑμῖν; δειξάτω ἐκ τῆς καλῆς ἀναστροφῆς τὰ ἔργα αὐτοῦ ἐν πραΰτητι σοφίας. [GNT]
		Wise, experienced, clever, learned; skilled
		
		### Practical Application
		There is the wise and understanding man. Note the question, "Who is a wise man and endued with knowledge among you?" The term "wise man" (*sophos*) refers to the teacher; *knowledge* refers to the expert, the skilled, the scientific, or knowledgeable person (A.T. Robertson. *Word Pictures in the New Testament*, Vol. 6, p.45). By teacher, of course, is meant anyone among us who teaches the Word of God including ministers and teachers. Within our church, who are the wise teachers and leaders? Who among us is knowledgeable or understanding? Let us ask another question. What teacher among us wants to be unwise and ignorant? Are there any? Of course not. The point being stressed is this: "Do you want to be a wise teacher? Do you want to be a teacher of knowledge? Then here is how. You must do some things."
		
		But note this: some of the teachers to whom James was writing did not understand the meaning of true wisdom and knowledge. Some of them were acting most unwisely and about as empty headed as a person can act, yet they thought they were wise and knowledgeable. Too often the same unwise behavior has characterized ministers and teachers down through the ages, even today. This is the very reason for this passage: to stir ministers and teachers to think about how wise and knowledgeable they really are.

ENGLISH WORD	GREEK WORD AND VERSE	THE WORD MEANS...

#4363
Wishes
 	
Will–KJV
Wishes–NASB
Would–NIV
Desires–NKJV
Wants–NLT
 	
**POSB
REFERENCE**
(Mt.16:24)
Note 2, point 1
	θέλει = thelë
	Pronunciation: [thel'-ee]
	Parsing (part of speech): verb
	    Mood—indicative
	    Tense—present
	    Voice—active
	    Person—3rd person
	    Number—singular
	    Stem or root—from θέλω
	Concordance References:
	  ⇒ Strong's #2309 thelö
	  ⇒ NIV #2527 thelö
	  ⇒ NASB #2309 thelö
	
	Matthew 16:24
	Then said Jesus unto his disciples, If any man **will** come after me, let him deny himself, and take up his cross, and follow me. [KJV]
	Then Jesus said to His disciples, "If anyone **wishes** to come after Me, let him deny himself, and take up his cross, and follow Me. [NASB]
	Then Jesus said to his disciples, "If anyone **would** come after me, he must deny himself and take up his cross and follow me. [NIV]
	Then Jesus said to His disciples, "If anyone **desires** to come after Me, let him deny himself, and take up his cross, and follow Me. [NKJV]
	Then Jesus said to the disciples, "If any of you **wants** to be my follower, you must put aside your selfish ambition, shoulder your cross, and follow me. [NLT]
	τότε ὁ Ἰησοῦς εἶπε τοῖς μαθηταῖς αὐτοῦ, Εἴ τις **θέλει** ὀπίσω μου ἐλθεῖν, ἀπαρνησάσθω ἑαυτὸν, καὶ ἀράτω τὸν σταυρὸν αὐτοῦ καὶ ἀκολουθείτω μοι. [GNS]
	Τότε ὁ Ἰησοῦς εἶπεν τοῖς μαθηταῖς αὐτοῦ, Εἴ τις **θέλει** ὀπίσω μου ἐλθεῖν, ἀπαρνησάσθω ἑαυτὸν καὶ ἀράτω τὸν σταυρὸν αὐτοῦ καὶ ἀκολουθείτω μοι. [GNT]
		To desire, wish, design, purpose, resolve, determine.
		
		Practical Application
		It is a deliberate willingness, a deliberate choice, a determined resolve to follow Christ.
		If a person really wills and deliberately chooses to follow Christ, then he has to do the three things mentioned. Note: the choice is voluntary; it is made by the person.

#4364
Witchcraft
 	
Witchcraft–KJV
Sorcery–NASB
Witchcraft–NIV
Sorcery–NKJV
Participation in
   demonic activi-
   ties–NLT
 	
**POSB
REFERENCE**
(Gal.5:19-21; esp.
v.20)
Note 2
	φαρμακεία = pharmakeia
	Pronunciation: [far-mak-i'-ah]
	Parsing (part of speech): noun
	    Case—nominative
	    Gender—feminine
	    Number—singular
	    Stem or root—from φαρμακεία, ας
	Concordance References:
	  ⇒ Strong's #5331 pharmakeia
	  ⇒ NIV #5758 pharmakeia
	  ⇒ NASB #5331 pharmakeia
	
	Galatians 5:20
	Idolatry, **witchcraft**, hatred, variance, emulations, wrath, strife, seditions, heresies, [KJV]
	Idolatry, **sorcery**, enmities, strife, jealousy, outbursts of anger, disputes, dissensions, factions, [NASB]
	Idolatry and **witchcraft**; hatred, discord, jealousy, fits of rage, selfish ambition, dissensions, factions [NIV]
	Idolatry, **sorcery**, hatred, contentions, jealousies, outbursts of wrath, selfish ambitions, dissensions, heresies, [NKJV]
	Idolatry, **participation in demonic activities**, hostility, quarreling, jealousy, outbursts of anger, selfish ambition, divisions, the feeling that everyone is wrong except those in your own little group, [NLT]
	εἰδωλολατρία, **φαρμακεία**, ἔχθραι, ἔρεις, ζῆλοι, θυμοί, ἐριθεῖαι, διχοστασίαι, αἱρέσεις, [GNS]
	εἰδωλολατρία, **φαρμακεία**, ἔχθραι, ἔρις, ζῆλος, θυμοί, ἐριθεῖαι, διχοστασίαι, αἱρέσεις, [GNT]
		Witchcraft, sorcery, participation in demonic activities; the use of drugs or of evil spirits to gain control over the lives of others or over one's own life.
		
		Practical Application
		It would include all forms of seeking the control of one's fate through astrology, palm reading, seances, fortune telling, crystals, and other forms of witchcraft.

#4365
Witchcraft
	φαρμάκων = pharmakön
	Pronunciation: [far-mak-own']
	Parsing (part of speech): noun
	    Case—genitive
	    Gender—neuter
		Magic arts, sorceries, witchcraft.
		
		Practical Application
		Note that the Greek word (pharmakön) is

ENGLISH WORD	GREEK WORD AND VERSE	THE WORD MEANS...
Sorceries–KJV Sorceries–NASB Magic arts–NIV Sorceries–NKJV **Witchcraft–NLT** **POSB REFERENCE** (Rev.9:20-21; esp.v.21) Note 4, point 2c	Number—plural Stem or root—from **φάρμακον**, ου Concordance References: ⇒ Strong's #5331 pharmakon ⇒ NIV #5760 pharmakon ⇒ NASB #5331 pharmakon **Rev. 9:21** Neither repented they of their murders, nor of their **sorceries**, nor of their fornication, nor of their thefts. [KJV] And they did not repent of their murders nor of their **sorceries** nor of their immorality nor of their thefts. [NASB] Nor did they repent of their murders, their **magic arts**, their sexual immorality or their thefts. [NIV] And they did not repent of their murders or their **sorceries** or their sexual immorality or their thefts. [NKJV] And they did not repent of their murders or their **witchcraft** or their immorality or their thefts. [NLT] καὶ οὐ μετενόησαν ἐκ τῶν φόνων αὐτῶν, οὔτε ἐκ τῶν **φαρμακειῶν** αὐτῶν, οὔτε ἐκ τῆς πορνείας αὐτῶν, οὔτε ἐκ τῶν κλεμμάτων αὐτῶν. [GNS] καὶ οὐ μετενόησαν ἐκ τῶν φόνων αὐτῶν οὔτε ἐκ τῶν **φαρμάκων** αὐτῶν οὔτε ἐκ τῆς πορνείας αὐτῶν οὔτε ἐκ τῶν κλεμμάτων αὐτῶν. [GNT]	close to the spelling of the English word *pharmacy*, that is, a place that handles drugs. Sorcery includes all kinds of witchcraft, the use of drugs or of evil spirits to gain control over the lives of others or over one's own life. In the present context, it would include all forms of sorcery including astrology, palm reading, seances, fortune telling, crystals, and other forms of witchcraft.

#4366
With
 	
With–KJV
With–NASB
In presence–NIV
With–NKJV
With–NLT
 	
**POSB
REFERENCE**
(Jn.8:38)
Note 4, point 1
	παρά = *para*
	Pronunciation: [pa-rah]
	Parsing (part of speech): preposition
	    Case—dative
	    Stem or root— from **παρά**
	Concordance References:
	⇒ Strong's #3844 para
	⇒ NIV #4123 para
	⇒ NASB #3844 para
	
	John 8:38
	I speak that which I have seen **with** my Father: and ye do that which ye have seen with your father. [KJV]
	"I speak the things which I have seen **with** My Father; therefore you also do the things which you heard from your father." [NASB]
	I am telling you what I have seen **in** the Father's **presence**, and you do what you have heard from your father." [NIV]
	I speak what I have seen **with** My Father, and you do what you have seen with your father." [NKJV]
	I am telling you what I saw when I was **with** my Father. But you are following the advice of your father." [NLT]
	ἐγὼ ὃ ἑώρακα **παρὰ** τῷ πατρὶ μου, λαλῶ· καὶ ὑμεῖς οὖν ὃ ἑωράκατε παρὰ τῷ πατρὶ ὑμῶν ποιεῖτε. [GNS]
	ἃ ἐγὼ ἑώρακα **παρὰ** τῷ πατρὶ λαλῶ· καὶ ὑμεῖς οὖν ἃ ἠκούσατε παρὰ τοῦ πατρὸς ποιεῖτε. [GNT]
		In the presence of; by the side of; with, in the company of; among; in association.
		
		Practical Application
		What Christ saw came from the very side of the Father. Christ was from the very presence of God, so what He spoke was God's Word. His message was the Word of God Himself. What was His message?
		⇒ A person must "believe Him" (John 8:31).
		⇒ A person must "hold on to His teaching [His Word]" (John 8:31).
		⇒ A person is "a slave to sin" (John 8:34).
		⇒ A person can be freed and adopted as a child of God's by the eternal Son (John 8:35-36).

#4367
With
 	
With–KJV
With–NASB
With–NIV
With–NKJV
With–NLT
 	
**POSB
REFERENCE**
(Jn.1:1-2; esp. v.1)
Note 1, point 2
	πρός = *pros*
	Pronunciation: [pros]
	Parsing (part of speech): preposition
	    Case—accusative
	    Stem or root—from **πρός**
	Concordance References:
	⇒ Strong's #4314 pros
	⇒ NIV #4639 pros
	⇒ NASB #4314 pros
	
	John 1:1
	In the beginning was the Word, and the Word was **with** God, and the Word was God. [KJV]
	In the beginning was the Word, and the Word was **with** God, and the Word was God. [NASB]
	In the beginning was the Word, and the Word was **with** God, and the Word was God. [NIV]
		The idea of both being with and acting toward. Jesus Christ (the Word) was both with God and acting with God.
		
		Practical Application
		He was "with God": by God's side, acting, living, and moving in the closest of relationships. Christ had the ideal and perfect relationship with God the Father. Their life together—their relationship, communion, fellowship, and connection—was a perfect eternal bond. This is exactly what is said: "The same was in the beginning with God" (John 1:2).

ENGLISH WORD	GREEK WORD AND VERSE	THE WORD MEANS...
	In the beginning was the Word, and the Word was **with** God, and the Word was God. [NKJV] In the beginning the Word already existed. He was **with** God, and he was God. [NLT] Ἐν ἀρχῇ ἦν ὁ λόγος, καὶ ὁ λόγος ἦν **πρὸς** τὸν Θεόν, καὶ Θεὸς ἦν ὁ λόγος. [GNS] Ἐν ἀρχῇ ἦν ὁ λόγος, καὶ ὁ λόγος ἦν **πρὸς** τὸν θεόν, καὶ θεὸς ἦν ὁ λόγος. [GNT]	

#4368
With All Your Heart
 	
From the heart–KJV
From the heart–NASB
From your heart–NIV
From the heart–NKJV
With all your heart–NLT
 	
POSB REFERENCE
(Eph.6:5-8; esp. v.6)
Note 1, point 4
 	
See also POSB REF:
(Col.3:22-25; esp. v.23)
Note 1, point 4
	ἐκ ψυχῆς = ek psuchēs
	Pronunciation: [ek psoo-khays']
	Parsing ek (part of speech): preposition
	  Case—genitive
	  Stem or root—from ἐκ
	Parsing psuchēs (part of speech): noun
	  Case—genitive
	  Gender—feminine
	  Number—singular
	  Stem or root—from ψυχή, ῆς
	Concordance References:
	⇒ Strong's #1537 ek + 5590 psuchē
	⇒ NIV #1666 ek [from] + 6034 psuchē [heart]
	⇒ NASB #1537 ek + 5590 psuchē
	
	Ephes. 6:6
	Not with eyeservice, as menpleasers; but as the servants of Christ, doing the will of God **from the heart**; [KJV]
	Not by way of eyeservice, as men-pleasers, but as slaves of Christ, doing the will of God **from the heart**. [NASB]
	Obey them not only to win their favor when their eye is on you, but like slaves of Christ, doing the will of God **from your heart**. [NIV]
	Not with eyeservice, as men-pleasers, but as bondservants of Christ, doing the will of God **from the heart**, [NKJV]
	Work hard, but not just to please your masters when they are watching. As slaves of Christ, do the will of God **with all your heart**. [NLT]
	μὴ κατ' ὀφθαλμοδουλείαν ὡς ἀνθρωπάρεσκοι, ἀλλ' ὡς δοῦλοι τοῦ Χριστοῦ, ποιοῦντες τὸ θέλημα τοῦ Θεοῦ **ἐκ ψυχῆς**, [GNS]
	μὴ κατ' ὀφθαλμοδουλίαν ὡς ἀνθρωπάρεσκοι ἀλλ' ὡς δοῦλοι Χριστοῦ ποιοῦντες τὸ θέλημα τοῦ θεοῦ **ἐκ ψυχῆς**, [GNT]
		From your heart; from the heart; with all your heart; out of the soul; with interest and energy.
		
		Practical Application
		The Christian workman is to work as the slave of Christ doing the will of God *with all his heart*. It is the opposite of routiness and listlessness, of having no energy or heart for the work. The Christian workman must always remember this: even if the boss is not looking, Christ sees what kind of work he is doing. Therefore, he must work as though he is working for Christ. In fact, the very drive of his heart and life must be to work for Christ. He must work...
		• to serve Christ
		• to do the will of God
		• to do both *from the heart*

#4369
With Grace
 	
With grace–KJV
With grace–NASB
Full of grace–NIV
With grace–NKJV
Gracious–NLT
 	
POSB REFERENCE
(Col.4:6)
Note 3
	ἐν χάριτι = en chariti
	Pronunciation: [en khar'-ih-tee]
	Parsing en (part of speech): preposition
	  Case—dative
	  Stem or root—from ἐν
	Parsing chariti (part of speech): noun
	  Case—dative
	  Gender—feminine
	  Number—singular
	  Stem or root—from χάρις, ιτος
	Concordance References:
	⇒ Strong's #1722 en + 5485 charis
	⇒ NIV #1877 en [full of] + 5921 charis [grace]
	⇒ NASB #1722 en + 5485 charis
	
	Col. 4:6
	Let your speech be alway **with grace**, seasoned with salt, that ye may know how ye ought to answer every man. [KJV]
	Let your speech always be **with grace**, seasoned, as it were, with salt, so that you may know how you should respond to each person. [NASB]
	Let your conversation be always full **of grace**, seasoned with salt, so that you may know how to answer everyone. [NIV]
	Let your speech always be **with grace**, seasoned with
		To be full of grace; to be with grace; to be gracious; to be kind; to be courteous.
		
		Practical Application
		As a believer, you must speak always with grace, answering and sharing what it is that makes your life different. What an expectation God has of us: to be living a life so different and righteous that men ask us what it is that makes us different. How many live a life that is that different? That godly and righteous? Note exactly what is said.
		When we are walking among unbelievers, we are to guard our speech and conversation. We are...
		• to make sure that we speak with grace (*en chariti*), that is, with kindness, courtesy, and graciousness.
		• to season our conversation with salt; that is, we are to flavor and turn the conversation to tasteful and enjoyable subjects and away from corruptible and tasteless subjects.
		What happens when this is done is striking: unbelievers will begin to notice our lives and

ENGLISH WORD	GREEK WORD AND VERSE	THE WORD MEANS...
	salt, that you may know how you ought to answer each one. [NKJV] Let your conversation be **gracious** and effective so that you will have the right answer for everyone. [NLT] ὁ λόγος ὑμῶν πάντοτε ἐν χάριτι, ἅλατι ἠρτυμένος, εἰδέναι πῶς δεῖ ὑμᾶς ἑνὶ ἑκάστῳ ἀποκρίνεσθαι. [GNS] ὁ λόγος ὑμῶν πάντοτε ἐν χάριτι, ἅλατι ἠρτυμένος, εἰδέναι πῶς δεῖ ὑμᾶς ἑνὶ ἑκάστῳ ἀποκρίνεσθαι. [GNT]	conversation—that we are different in a good and wholesome way. And some will ask us what it is that gives us such peace and security and assurance in life. Then it is that we have a unique opportunity to witness. Then it is that we can reach out and bring in those who are so tragically without Christ, lost and doomed in despair and hopelessness forever.

#4370
With Me
 	
Carnal–KJV
Flesh–NASB
Unspiritual–NIV
Carnal–NKJV
With me–NLT
 	
POSB
REFERENCE
(Rom.7:14-17; esp. v.14)
Note 2
	σάρκινός = sarkinos
	Pronunciation: [sahr-kee-nos']
	Parsing (part of speech): adjective
	    Case—nominative
	    Gender—masculine
	    Number—singular
	    Stem or root—from σάρκινος, η, ον
	Concordance References:
	  ⇒ Strong's #4559 sarkikos
	  ⇒ NIV #4921 sarkinos
	  ⇒ NASB #4560 sarkinos
	
	Romans 7:14
	For we know that the law is spiritual: but I am **carnal**, sold under sin. [KJV]
	
	For we know that the Law is spiritual; but I am of **flesh**, sold into bondage to sin. [NASB]
	
	We know that the law is spiritual; but I am **unspiritual**, sold as a slave to sin. [NIV]
	
	For we know that the law is spiritual, but I am **carnal**, sold under sin. [NKJV]
	
	The law is good, then. The trouble is not with the law but **with me**, because I am sold into slavery, with sin as my master. [NLT]
	
	οἴδαμεν γὰρ ὅτι ὁ νόμος πνευματικός ἐστιν· ἐγὼ δὲ **σάρκικός** εἰμι, πεπραμένος ὑπὸ τὴν ἁμαρτίαν. [GNS]
	
	οἴδαμεν γὰρ ὅτι ὁ νόμος πνευματικός ἐστιν, ἐγὼ δὲ **σάρκινός** εἰμι πεπραμένος ὑπὸ τὴν ἁμαρτίαν. [GNT]
		Unspiritual, carnal, fleshly, human, worldy; by sinful nature; to belong to this world; to be made of flesh; to consist of flesh; to have a body of flesh and blood. It means the flesh with which a man is born, the fleshly nature one inherits from his parents when he is born.
		
		Practical Application
		The word carnal also means to be given up to the flesh, that is, to live a fleshly, sensual life; to be given over to animal appetites; to be controlled by one's sinful nature. (See POSB *Deeper Study* #1, Carnal—1 Cor. 3:1-4 for more discussion.)

#4371
Withdraw
 	
Withdraw–KJV
Keep aloof–NASB
Keep away–NIV
Withdraw–NKJV
Stay away–NLT
 	
POSB
REFERENCE
(2 Thes.3:6-11; esp. v.6)
Note 1
	στέλλεσθαι = stellesthai
	Pronunciation: [stel'-les-tha-ee]
	Parsing (part of speech): verb
	    Mood—infinitive
	    Tense—present
	    Voice—middle
	    Stem or root—from στέλλομαι
	Concordance References:
	  ⇒ Strong's #4724 stellō
	  ⇒ NIV #5097 stellō
	  ⇒ NASB #4724 stellō
	
	2 Thes. 3:6
	Now we command you, brethren, in the name of our Lord Jesus Christ, that ye **withdraw** yourselves from every brother that walketh disorderly, and not after the tradition which he received of us. [KJV]
	
	Now we command you, brethren, in the name of our Lord Jesus Christ, that you **keep aloof** from every brother who leads an unruly life and not according to the tradition which you received from us. [NASB]
	
	In the name of the Lord Jesus Christ, we command you, brothers, to **keep away** from every brother who is idle and does not live according to the teaching you received from us. [NIV]
	
	But we command you, brethren, in the name of our Lord Jesus Christ, that you **withdraw** from every brother who walks disorderly and not according to the tradition which he received from us. [NKJV]
	
	And now, dear brothers and sisters, we give you this command with the authority of our Lord Jesus Christ: **Stay away** from any Christian who lives in idleness and doesn't follow the tradition of hard work we gave you. [NLT]
		To keep away; to withdraw; to avoid; to keep aloof; to stay away; to shun.
		
		Practical Application
		We are to withdraw from every brother who walks disorderly, that is, who does not work. Note: this is a very strong command. It has the force of a military command: it is given "in the name of our Lord Jesus Christ," the supreme commander. There is to be no discussion about the matter. What is being said is to be obeyed.
		
		"Withdraw...from every brother that walks disorderly" (2 Thes. 3:6). Who are the disorderly? Those who do not work. A strange thing had happened in the Thessalonian church. Some of the believers had become excited over the return of the Lord and the promise of being with Him forever in the new heavens and earth. They became so excited that they began to sacrifice all they could to meet the needs of people. But some went too far. They ignored the Lord's words that only God knew when He would be returning, and they began to project dates and declare that His return was about to take place. Therefore, some quit their jobs in order to have more time to minister, and in an act of sacrificial commitment they gave away *all they had*. The result was catastrophic. They were now having to sponge off the other believers in order to survive. Their action had been most unwise—unwise because believers are to *live life* as it

ENGLISH WORD	GREEK WORD AND VERSE	THE WORD MEANS...
	Παραγγέλλομεν δὲ ὑμῖν, ἀδελφοί, ἐν ὀνόματι τοῦ Κυρίου ἡμῶν Ἰησοῦ Χριστοῦ, **στέλλεσθαι** ὑμᾶς ἀπὸ παντὸς ἀδελφοῦ ἀτάκτως περιπατοῦντος, καὶ μὴ κατὰ τὴν παράδοσιν ἣν παρέλαβε παρ' ἡμῶν· [GNS] Παραγγέλλομεν δὲ ὑμῖν, ἀδελφοί, ἐν ὀνόματι τοῦ κυρίου [ἡμῶν] Ἰησοῦ Χριστοῦ **στέλλεσθαι** ὑμᾶς ἀπὸ παντὸς ἀδελφοῦ ἀτάκτως περιπατοῦντος καὶ μὴ κατὰ τὴν παράδοσιν ἣν παρελάβοσαν παρ' ἡμῶν. [GNT]	should be lived so long as they are upon earth. Believers are to set the example as to how life is to be lived, and work is certainly one of the duties of men. Therefore, all people believers are to set an example in work. They are to be the very best workmen possible. Quitting work and not working is disorderly behavior; it is totally unacceptable for a true believer. It is so unacceptable that believers are commanded to withdraw from non-workers. ⇒ What does the Lord mean by "withdraw" (*stellesthai*)? The word means to stay away from the idle worker; to have no fellowship with him. His behavior is not to be indulged or condoned. We are not to put our stamp of approval upon him, nor are we to run the risk of becoming identified with him. ⇒ Who are the disorderly? They are the idle, the slothful, the lazy. They are the persons who refuse to work or who shirk their work or who are slack in their work.
#4372 **Withers–** **Withered** **Withered–KJV** Dries up–NASB **Withers–NIV** **Withered–NKJV** **Withers–NLT** **POSB** **REFERENCE** (Jn.15:4-6; esp. v.6) Note 4, point 4b	ἐξηράνθη = *exëranthë* Pronunciation: [ex-ay-rah'n-thay] Parsing (part of speech): verb 　　Mood—indicative 　　Tense—aorist 　　Voice—passive 　　Person—3rd person 　　Number—singular 　　Stem or root—from ξηραίνω Concordance References: ⇒ Strong's #3583 xërainö ⇒ NIV #3830 xërainö ⇒ NASB #3583 xërainö **John 15:6** If a man abide not in me, he is cast forth as a branch, and is **withered**; and men gather them, and cast them into the fire, and they are burned. [KJV] "If anyone does not abide in Me, he is thrown away as a branch, and **dries up**; and they gather them, and cast them into the fire, and they are burned. [NASB] If anyone does not remain in me, he is like a branch that is thrown away and **withers**; such branches are picked up, thrown into the fire and burned. [NIV] If anyone does not abide in Me, he is cast out as a branch and is **withered**; and they gather them and throw them into the fire, and they are burned. [NKJV] Anyone who parts from me is thrown away like a useless branch and **withers**. Such branches are gathered into a pile to be burned. [NLT] ἐὰν μή τις μείνῃ ἐν ἐμοί, ἐβλήθη ἔξω ὡς τὸ κλῆμα, καὶ **ἐξηράνθη**, καὶ συνάγουσιν αὐτὰ, καὶ εἰς πῦρ βάλλουσι, καὶ καίεται. [GNS] ἐὰν μή τις μένῃ ἐν ἐμοί, ἐβλήθη ἔξω ὡς τὸ κλῆμα καὶ **ἐξηράνθη** καὶ συνάγουσιν αὐτὰ καὶ εἰς τὸ πῦρ βάλλουσιν καὶ καίεται. [GNT]	To be dried up, wrinkled, peeled; to become sapless and bare; to lose energy and strength. **Practical Application** The unattached branch experiences everything withering away—its... • gifts and abilities • life and body • family and friends • fate and destiny • hopes and dreams • confidence and assurance • purpose and meaning
#4373 **Withered Hand** **Withered hand–KJV** **Withered hand–** **NASB** Shriveled hand–NIV **Withered hand–** **NKJV** Deformed hand–NLT	ἐξηραμμένην ἔχων τὴν χεῖρα = *exerammenen echon ten cheira* Pronunciation: [ex-ay-rahm'mehn-ayn ekh'-own tayn khir-ah] Parsing *exerammenen* (part of speech): verb 　　Mood—participle 　　Tense—perfect 　　Voice—passive 　　Case—accusative 　　Gender—feminine 　　Number—singular 　　Stem or root—from ξηραίνω	To have an injured or sick hand. This phrase describes a hand that was withered, shriveled, dried up, wilted, wasted, dropped, scorched. **Practical Application** His hand had been injured or become diseased. He was not born with a withered hand. His plight, of course, was desperate; for he was unable to work for a livelihood with a withered hand. Tradition says he was a stone mason who beseeched Jesus to heal him so that he might not

ENGLISH WORD	GREEK WORD AND VERSE	THE WORD MEANS...

POSB REFERENCE (Mk.3:1-2; esp. v.1) Note 1, point 1	Parsing *econ* (part of speech): verb
	  Mood—participle
	  Tense—present
	  Voice—active
	  Case—nominative
	  Gender—masculine
	  Number—singular
	  Stem or root—from ἔχω
	Parsing *ten* (part of speech): determiner [definite article]
	  Case—accusative
	  Gender—feminine
	  Number—singular
	  Stem or root—from ὁ, ἡ, τό
	Parsing *cheira* (part of speech): noun
	  Case—accusative
	  Gender—feminine
	  Number—singular
	  Stem or root—from χείρ, χειρός
	Concordance References:
	  ⇒ Strong's #3583 xĕrainō + #5495 cheir
	  ⇒ NIV #2400 echō [with] + 3830 xĕrainō [shriveled] + 5931 cheir [hand]
	  ⇒ NASB #3583 xĕrainō + #5495 cheir
	
	Mark 3:1
	And he entered again into the synagogue; and there was a man there which had a **withered hand**. [KJV]
	And He entered again into a synagogue; and a man was there with a **withered hand**. [NASB]
	Another time he went into the synagogue, and a man with a **shriveled hand** was there. [NIV]
	And He entered the synagogue again, and a man was there who had a **withered hand**. [NKJV]
	Jesus went into the synagogue again and noticed a man with a **deformed hand**. [NLT]
	Καὶ εἰσῆλθε πάλιν εἰς τὴν συναγωγήν, καὶ ἦν ἐκεῖ ἄνθρωπος **ἐξηραμμένην ἔχων τὴν χεῖρα**. [GNS]
	Καὶ εἰσῆλθεν πάλιν εἰς τὴν συναγωγήν. καὶ ἦν ἐκεῖ ἄνθρωπος **ἐξηραμμένην ἔχων τὴν χεῖρα**. [GNT]
		have to beg in shame (see POSB notes—Matthew 12:9-13).

#4374
Withheld
 	
Straitened–KJV
Restrained–NASB
Withholding–NIV
Restricted–NKJV
Withheld–NLT
 	
POSB REFERENCE (2 Cor.6:11-13; esp. v.12) Note 1
	στενοχωρεῖσθε = *stenochōreisthe*
	Pronunciation: [sten-okh-o-reh'-ees-the]
	Parsing (part of speech): verb
	  Mood—indicative
	  Tense—present
	  Voice—passive
	  Person—2nd person
	  Number—plural
	  Stem or root—from στενοχωρέομαι
	Concordance References:
	  ⇒ Strong's #4729 stenochōreō
	  ⇒ NIV #5102 stenochōreō
	  ⇒ NASB #4729 stenochōreō
	
	2 Cor. 6:12
	Ye are not **straitened** in us, but ye are **straitened** in your own bowels. [KJV]
	You are not **restrained** by us, but you are **restrained** in your own affections. [NASB]
	We are not **withholding** our affection from you, but you are **withholding** yours from us. [NIV]
	You are not **restricted** by us, but you are **restricted** by your own affections. [NKJV]
	If there is a problem between us, it is not because of a lack of love on our part, but because you have **withheld** your love from us. [NLT]
	οὐ στενοχωρεῖσθε ἐν ἡμῖν, **στενοχωρεῖσθε** δὲ ἐν τοῖς σπλάγχνοις ὑμῶν. [GNS]
	οὐ **στενοχωρεῖσθε** ἐν ἡμῖν, **στενοχωρεῖσθε** δὲ ἐν τοῖς σπλάγχνοις ὑμῶν· [GNT]
		To withhold; to be restrained; to be restricted; to lack room; be held in check; to be pressed or distressed; to be in anguish or straits.
		
		Practical Application
		Paul says there was no lack of room in his heart for the church; no restriction against the Corinthians. He held nothing against them. His heart was wide open to receive them.

#4375 **Withholding**	στενοχωρεῖσθε = *stenochōreisthe* Pronunciation: [sten-okh-o-reh'-ees-the] Parsing (part of speech): verb Mood—indicative	To withhold; to be restrained; to be restricted; to lack room; to be held in check; to be pressed or distressed; to be in anguish or straits.

ENGLISH WORD	GREEK WORD AND VERSE	THE WORD MEANS...
Straitened–KJV Restrained–NASB **Withholding–NIV** Restricted–NKJV Withheld–NLT **POSB REFERENCE** (2 Cor.6:11-13; esp. v.12) Note 1	Tense—present Voice—passive Person—2nd person Number—plural Stem or root—from στενοχωρέομαι Concordance References: ⇒ Strong's #4729 stenochöreö ⇒ NIV #5102 stenochöreö ⇒ NASB #4729 stenochöreö **2 Cor. 6:12** Ye are not **straitened** in us, but ye are **straitened** in your own bowels. [KJV] You are not **restrained** by us, but you are **restrained** in your own affections. [NASB] We are not **withholding** our affection from you, but you are **withholding** yours from us. [NIV] You are not **restricted** by us, but you are restricted by your own affections. [NKJV] If there is a problem between us, it is not because of a lack of love on our part, but because you have **withheld** your love from us. [NLT] οὐ στενοχωρεῖσθε ἐν ἡμῖν, **στενοχωρεῖσθε** δὲ ἐν τοῖς σπλάγχνοις ὑμῶν. [GNS] οὐ **στενοχωρεῖσθε** ἐν ἡμῖν, **στενοχωρεῖσθε** δὲ ἐν τοῖς σπλάγχνοις ὑμῶν· [GNT]	**Practical Application** Paul says there was no lack of room in his heart for the church; no restriction against the Corinthians. He held nothing against them. His heart was wide open to receive them.

#4376
Within You
 	
Within you–KJV
In your midst–NASB
Within you–NIV
Within you–NKJV
Among you–NLT
 	
**POSB
REFERENCE**
(Lk.17:20-21; esp.
v.21)
Note 1, point 2
	ἐντὸς ὑμῶν = entos humön
	Pronunciation: [en-tos' hu-mown]
	Parsing entos (part of speech): preposition
	    Case—genitive
	    Stem or root—from ἐντός
	Parsing humön (part of speech): noun pronoun
	    Case—genitive
	    Person—2nd person
	    Number—plural
	    Stem or root—from σύ
	Concordance References:
	⇒ Strong's #1787 entos + 5216 humon
	⇒ NIV #1955 entos [within] + 5148 su [you]
	⇒ NASB #1787 entos + 5216 humon
	
	Luke 17:21
	Neither shall they say, Lo here! or, lo there! for, behold, the kingdom of God is **within you**. [KJV]
	Nor will they say, 'Look, here *it is!*' or, 'There *it is!*' For behold, the kingdom of God is **in your midst.**" [NASB]
	Nor will people say, 'Here it is,' or 'There it is,' because the kingdom of God is **within you**." [NIV]
	Nor will they say, 'See here!' or 'See there!' For indeed, the kingdom of God is **within you**." [NKJV]
	You won't be able to say, 'Here it is!' or 'It's over there!' For the Kingdom of God is **among you**." [NLT]
	οὐδὲ ἐροῦσιν, Ἰδοὺ ὧδε, ἤ, Ἰδοὺ ἐκεῖ. ἰδοὺ γὰρ, ἡ βασιλεία τοῦ Θεοῦ **ἐντὸς ὑμῶν** ἐστιν. [GNS]
	οὐδὲ ἐροῦσιν, Ἰδοὺ ὧδε ἤ, Ἐκεῖ, ἰδοὺ γὰρ ἡ βασιλεία τοῦ θεοῦ **ἐντὸς ὑμῶν** ἐστιν. [GNT]
		Within you, among you, inside of you, or in your midst.
		
		Practical Application
		Some say this should be translated "among you." If so, then Christ is saying that He is the embodiment of the Kingdom of God. He is setting up the Kingdom of God among them, right there and then. God is already beginning to rule and reign in the lives He is touching.
		Others say the words mean "within you." If so, then the kingdom is to be looked for within the hearts and lives of people. The Kingdom of God is spiritual; it is the changing of hearts, the rule and reign of God within men's lives. It is the power of God to take a sinful, immoral, and unjust man and change him into a servant of God.

#4377
**Without A
Single Fault**
 	
Unreproveable–KJV
Beyond reproach–
NASB
Free from accusation–
NIV
Above reproach–
NKJV
**Without a single
fault–NLT**
	ἀνεγκλήτους = anegklëtous
	Pronunciation: [an-eng'-klay-toos]
	Parsing (part of speech): adjective
	    Case—accusative
	    Gender—masculine
	    Number—plural
	    Stem or root—from ἀνέγκλητος, ον
	Concordance References:
	⇒ Strong's #410 anegklëtos
	⇒ NIV #441 anegklëtos
	⇒ NASB #410 anegklëtos
	
	Col. 1:22
	In the body of his flesh through death, to present you
		To be free from accusation; to be beyond reproach; to have nothing against them; to be without a single fault, unreproveable, blameless, unchargeable.
		
		Practical Application
		Imagine standing before God holy, unblameable, and beyond reproach. Imagine how pleased God would be! How He would joy and rejoice in us—that we had honored Christ, His only Son, by trusting Him so much! As we are presented to God, what would He say? What would His first words be to us? We would be speechless, no

ENGLISH WORD	GREEK WORD AND VERSE	THE WORD MEANS...
POSB REFERENCE (Col.1:22) Note 3, point 3	holy and unblameable and **unreproveable** in his sight: [KJV] Yet He has now reconciled you in His fleshly body through death, in order to present you before Him holy and blameless and **beyond reproach**—[NASB] But now he has reconciled you by Christ's physical body through death to present you holy in his sight, without blemish and **free from accusation**—[NIV] In the body of His flesh through death, to present you holy, and blameless, and **above reproach** in His sight—[NKJV] Yet now he has brought you back as his friends. He has done this through his death on the cross in his own human body. As a result, he has brought you into the very presence of God, and you are holy and blameless as you stand before him **without a single fault**. [NLT] νυνὶ δὲ ἀποκατήλλαξεν ἐν τῷ σώματι τῆς σαρκὸς αὐτοῦ διὰ τοῦ θανάτου, παραστῆσαι ὑμᾶς ἁγίους καὶ ἀμώμους καὶ **ἀνεγκλήτους** κατενώπιον αὐτοῦ·[GNS] νυνὶ δὲ ἀποκατήλλαξεν ἐν τῷ σώματι τῆς σαρκὸς αὐτοῦ διὰ τοῦ θανάτου παραστῆσαι ὑμᾶς ἁγίους καὶ ἀμώμους καὶ **ἀνεγκλήτους** κατενώπιον αὐτοῦ, [GNT]	doubt. But what a day of coronation, of glory, of greatness—standing face to face with our Father, the God of all glory, the Sovereign Majesty of the whole universe. This is God's one great purpose in reconciliation: to present us perfect before Him.

#4378
 	
Without Blemish
 	
Unblameable–KJV
Blameless–NASB
Without blemish–NIV
Blameless–NKJV
Blameless–NLT
 	
POSB REFERENCE (Col.1:22) Note 3, point 2
	ἀμώμους = amōmous
	Pronunciation: [am'-o moos]
	Parsing (part of speech): adjective
	    Case—accusative
	    Gender—masculine
	    Number—plural
	    Stem or root—from ἄμωμος, ον
	Concordance References:
	  ⇒ Strong's #299 amōmos
	  ⇒ NIV #320 amōmos
	  ⇒ NASB #299 amōmos
	
	Col. 1:22
	In the body of his flesh through death, to present you holy and **unblameable** and unreproveable in his sight: [KJV]
	
	Yet He has now reconciled you in His fleshly body through death, in order to present you before Him holy and **blameless** and beyond reproach—[NASB]
	
	But now he has reconciled you by Christ's physical body through death to present you holy in his sight, **without blemish** and free from accusation—[NIV]
	
	In the body of His flesh through death, to present you holy, and **blameless**, and above reproach in His sight–[NKJV]
	
	Yet now he has brought you back as his friends. He has done this through his death on the cross in his own human body. As a result, he has brought you into the very presence of God, and you are holy and **blameless** as you stand before him without a single fault. [NLT]
	
	νυνὶ δὲ ἀποκατήλλαξεν ἐν τῷ σώματι τῆς σαρκὸς αὐτοῦ διὰ τοῦ θανάτου, παραστῆσαι ὑμᾶς ἁγίους καὶ ἀμώμους καὶ ἀνεγκλήτους κατενώπιον αὐτοῦ· [GNS]
	
	νυνὶ δὲ ἀποκατήλλαξεν ἐν τῷ σώματι τῆς σαρκὸς αὐτοῦ διὰ τοῦ θανάτου παραστῆσαι ὑμᾶς ἁγίους καὶ ἀμώμους καὶ ἀνεγκλήτους κατενώπιον αὐτοῦ, [GNT]
		Without blemish; without spot; without fault; without any defect whatsoever.
		
		Practical Application
		We must also be "without blemish" (*amōmous*): We must be without spot, faultless, without any defect whatsoever.

#4379
 	
Without Ceasing
 	
Without ceasing–KJV
Fervently–NASB
Earnestly–NIV
Constant–NKJV
Earnestly–NLT
	ἐκτενῶς = ektenōs
	Pronunciation: [ek-ten-os']
	Parsing (part of speech): adjective adverb
	    Stem or root—from ἐκτενῶς
	Concordance References:
	  ⇒ Strong's #1618 ektenes
	  ⇒ NIV #1757 ektenōs
	  ⇒ NASB #1619 ektenōs
	
	Acts 12:5
	Peter therefore was kept in prison: but prayer was made **without ceasing** of the church unto God for him. [KJV]
		Earnestly, deeply, ceaselessly, fervently, constantly.
		
		Practical Application
		The idea is intense prayer, prayer that captivates and focuses a person's concentration. The root meaning of the word is "to stretch out." The picture is that the church was stretched out, prostrate before God, earnestly and fervently crying out for God's sovereign deliverance of Peter. The church could do nothing and they knew it. Peter's only hope was God.

ENGLISH WORD	GREEK WORD AND VERSE	THE WORD MEANS...
POSB REFERENCE (Acts 12:5-17; esp. v.5) Note 2, point 1c)	So Peter was kept in the prison, but prayer for him was being made **fervently** by the church to God. [NASB] So Peter was kept in prison, but the church was **earnestly** praying to God for him. [NIV] Peter was therefore kept in prison, but **constant** prayer was offered to God for him by the church. [NKJV] But while Peter was in prison, the church prayed very **earnestly** for him. [NLT] ὁ μὲν οὖν Πέτρος ἐτηρεῖτο ἐν τῇ φυλακῇ· προσευχὴ δὲ ἦν **ἐκτενῶς** γινομένη ὑπὸ τῆς ἐκκλησίας πρὸς τὸν Θεὸν ὑπὲρ αὐτοῦ. [GNS] ὁ μὲν οὖν Πέτρος ἐτηρεῖτο ἐν τῇ φυλακῇ· προσευχὴ δὲ ἦν **ἐκτενῶς** γινομένη ὑπὸ τῆς ἐκκλησίας πρὸς τὸν θεὸν περὶ αὐτοῦ. [GNT]	

#4380
Without Fault
 	
Without rebuke–KJV
Above reproach–NASB
Without fault–NIV
Without fault–NKJV
Innocent lives–NLT
 	
POSB REFERENCE (Philip.2:15) Note 4, point 3
	ἄμωμα = *amōma*
	Pronunciation: [am-o'-mah]
	Parsing (part of speech): adjective
	    Case—nominative
	    Gender—neuter
	    Number—plural
	    Stem or root—from ἄμωμος, ον
	Concordance References:
	⇒ Strong's #298 amōmetos
	⇒ NIV #320 amōmos
	⇒ NASB #299b amōmos
	
	Philip. 2:15
	That ye may be blameless and harmless, the sons of God, **without rebuke**, in the midst of a crooked and perverse nation, among whom ye shine as lights in the world; [KJV]
	
	That you may prove yourselves to be blameless and innocent, children of God **above reproach** in the midst of a crooked and perverse generation, among whom you appear as lights in the world, [NASB]
	
	So that you may become blameless and pure, children of God **without fault** in a crooked and depraved generation, in which you shine like stars in the universe [NIV]
	
	That you may become blameless and harmless, children of God **without fault** in the midst of a crooked and perverse generation, among whom you shine as lights in the world, [NKJV]
	
	So that no one can speak a word of blame against you. You are to live clean, **innocent lives** as children of God in a dark world full of crooked and perverse people. Let your lives shine brightly before them. [NLT]
	
	ἵνα γένησθε ἄμεμπτοι καὶ ἀκέραιοι, τέκνα Θεοῦ **ἀμώμητα** ἐν μέσῳ γενεᾶς σκολιᾶς καὶ διεστραμμένης, ἐν οἷς φαίνεσθε ὡς φωστῆρες ἐν κόσμῳ, [GNS]
	
	ἵνα γένησθε ἄμεμπτοι καὶ ἀκέραιοι, τέκνα θεοῦ **ἄμωμα** μέσον γενεᾶς σκολιᾶς καὶ διεστραμμένης, ἐν οἷς φαίνεσθε ὡς φωστῆρες ἐν κόσμῳ, [GNT]
		To be without fault; to be without rebuke; to be above reproach; to live an innocent life; to be without blemish, spot, or defect.
		
		Practical Application
		This is a word that is taken from the Old Testament sacrifices made to God. The idea is that the believer is to live upon earth under the eyes and scrutiny of God. He is to walk without any blemish, spot, or defect.
		
		However, note a fact: the believer lives in a crooked and perverse generation. The world is wicked and evil, twisted and perverted; therefore, the believer has a difficult path to walk. But walk he must, for he is to be the light of the world. He is to shine as a light in the world. He is to reflect the purity, holiness and witness of God Himself.

#4381
Without Fault
 	
Faultless–KJV
Blameless–NASB
Without fault–NIV
Faultless–NKJV
Innocent of sin–NLT
 	
POSB REFERENCE (Jude 1:24-25; esp. v.24) Note 4, point 2
	ἀμώμους = *amōmous*
	Pronunciation: [am'-o-moos]
	Parsing (part of speech): adjective
	    Case—accusative
	    Gender—masculine
	    Number—plural
	    Stem or root—from ἄμωμος, ον
	Concordance References:
	⇒ Strong's #299 amōmos
	⇒ NIV #320 amōmos
	⇒ NASB #299 amōmos
	
	Jude 1:24
	Now unto him that is able to keep you from falling, and to present you **faultless** before the presence of his glory with exceeding joy, [KJV]
	
	Now to Him who is able to keep you from stumbling, and to make you stand in the presence of His glory
		To be without fault, blameless; to be innocent of sin; to be faultless, without blemish; to be spotless and pure, without any defilement whatsoever.
		
		Practical Application
		God is *able to present us without fault* when we come face to face with Him. God is able to accept us in Jesus Christ, the spotless Lamb of God. If we will continue to approach God in Christ—in the name of Christ and His death—then God will accept us and count our faith as righteousness. He will accept us in the righteousness of His Son, the Lord Jesus Christ. God is able to do this, and He will do it if we will draw near Him *in Christ*.

ENGLISH WORD	GREEK WORD AND VERSE	THE WORD MEANS...
	blameless with great joy, [NASB] To him who is able to keep you from falling and to present you before his glorious presence **without fault** and with great joy—[NIV] Now to Him who is able to keep you from stumbling, And to present you **faultless** before the presence of His glory with exceeding joy, [NKJV] And now, all glory to God, who is able to keep you from stumbling, and who will bring you into his glorious presence **innocent of sin** and with great joy. [NLT] Τῷ δὲ δυναμένῳ φυλάξαι ὑμᾶς ἀπταίστους, καὶ στῆσαι κατενώπιον τῆς δόξης αὐτοῦ **ἀμώμους** ἐν ἀγαλλιάσει, [GNS] Τῷ δὲ δυναμένῳ φυλάξαι ὑμᾶς ἀπταίστους καὶ στῆσαι κατενώπιον τῆς δόξης αὐτοῦ **ἀμώμους** ἐν ἀγαλλιάσει, [GNT]	
#4382 **Without Law–Without The Law** Without law–KJV Without the Law–NASB Apart from the law–NIV Without law–NKJV Never had God's written law–NLT **POSB REFERENCE** (Romans 2:11-15; esp. v.12) Note 4, point 1a	**ἀνόμως** = anomōs Pronunciation: [an-om'-oce] Parsing (part of speech): adjective adverb 　　Stem or root—from **ἀνόμως** Concordance References: ⇒　Strong's #460 anomōs ⇒　NIV #492 anomōs ⇒　NASB #460 anomōs **Romans 2:12** For as many as have sinned **without law** shall also perish without law: and as many as have sinned in the law shall be judged by the law; [KJV] For all who have sinned **without the Law** will also perish without the Law; and all who have sinned under the Law will be judged by the Law; [NASB] All who sin **apart from the law** will also perish apart from the law, and all who sin under the law will be judged by the law. [NIV] For as many as have sinned **without law** will also perish without law, and as many as have sinned in the law will be judged by the law [NKJV] God will punish the Gentiles when they sin, even though they **never had God's written law**. And he will punish the Jews when they sin, for they do have the law. [NLT] ὅσοι γὰρ **ἀνόμως** ἥμαρτον, ἀνόμως καὶ ἀπολοῦνται· καὶ ὅσοι ἐν νόμῳ ἥμαρτον, διὰ νόμου κριθήσονται· [GNS] ὅσοι γὰρ **ἀνόμως** ἥμαρτον, ἀνόμως καὶ ἀπολοῦνται, καὶ ὅσοι ἐν νόμῳ ἥμαρτον, διὰ νόμου κριθήσονται [GNT]	Apart from the law; to be without the law; to never have God's written law. **Practical Application** The man who sins "without the law" (*anomos*) will also perish apart from the law. The word for "law" is a general word. It refers to the law of God in both the Scriptures and nature. Therefore, the man who does not have the law of Scripture does have the law of nature to guide him. If he sins against the law of nature, he will still be judged and perish. He had the opportunity to know through nature itself.
#4383 **Without Love** Without natural affection–KJV Unloving–NASB Without love–NIV Unloving–NKJV Unloving–NLT **POSB REFERENCE** (2 Tim. 3:2-4; esp. v.3) Note 2, point 9	**ἄστοργοι** = astorgoi Pronunciation: [as'-tor-goy] Parsing (part of speech): adjective 　　Case—nominative 　　Gender—masculine 　　Number—plural 　　Stem or root—from **ἄστοργος**, ον Concordance References: ⇒　Strong's #794 astorgos ⇒　NIV #845 astorgos ⇒　NASB #794 astorgos **2 Tim. 3:3** **Without natural affection**, trucebreakers, false accusers, incontinent, fierce, despisers of those that are good, [KJV] **Unloving**, irreconcilable, malicious gossips, without self-control, brutal, haters of good, [NASB] **Without love**, unforgiving, slanderous, without self-control, brutal, not lovers of the good, [NIV] **Unloving**, unforgiving, slanderers, without self-control, brutal, despisers of good, [NKJV] They will be **unloving** and unforgiving; they will	Unloving, without love, without natural affection, abnormal affection and love; heartless, without human emotion or love; a lack of feeling for others; abuse of normal affection and love. It means others become little more than pawns for a man's own use and benefit, pleasure and purposes, excitement and stimulation. **Practical Application** Man has been created to be affectionate—to have affection for others. It is normal and natural for a person to have affection for his family, friends, neighbors, co-workers, and to a certain extent for the stranger and fellow citizens of the world. But in the end time, people will be so set on satisfying their flesh and pleasure that they will forget family, friends, and everything else. They will be so set on doing their own thing and so self-centered that they will have little affection for anyone or anything else.

ENGLISH WORD	GREEK WORD AND VERSE	THE WORD MEANS...
	slander others and have no self-control; they will be cruel and have no interest in what is good. [NLT] ἄστοργοι, ἄσπονδοι, διάβολοι, ἀκρατεῖς, ἀνήμεροι, ἀφιλάγαθοι, [GNS] ἄστοργοι ἄσπονδοι διάβολοι ἀκρατεῖς ἀνήμεροι ἀφιλάγαθοι [GNT]	
#4384 **Without Misgivings** Nothing doubting–KJV **Without misgivings–NASB** No hesitation–NIV Doubting nothing–NKJV Not to worry about–NLT **POSB REFERENCE** (Acts 11:4-15; esp. v.12) Note 2, point 3	μηδὲν διακρίναντα = mēden diakrinanta Pronunciation: [may-dehn' dee-ak-ree'-nahn-tah] Parsing diakrinanta (part of speech): verb 　Mood—participle 　Tense—aorist 　Voice—active 　Case—accusative 　Gender—masculine 　Person—1st person 　Number—singular 　Stem or root—from διακρίνω Concordance References: ⇒　Strong's #3367 mēdeis + 1252 diakrinō ⇒　NIV #3594 mēdeis [no] + 1359 diakrinō [hesitation] ⇒　NASB #3367 mēdeis + 1252 diakrinō **Acts 11:12** And the spirit bade me go with them, **nothing doubting**. Moreover these six brethren accompanied me, and we entered into the man's house: [KJV] "And the Spirit told me to go with them **without misgivings**. And these six brethren also went with me, and we entered the man's house. [NASB] The Spirit told me to have **no hesitation** about going with them. These six brothers also went with me, and we entered the man's house. [NIV] Then the Spirit told me to go with them, **doubting nothing**. Moreover these six brethren accompanied me, and we entered the man's house. [NKJV] The Holy Spirit told me to go with them and **not to worry about** their being Gentiles. These six brothers here accompanied me, and we soon arrived at the home of the man who had sent for us. [NLT] εἶπε δέ μοι τὸ Πνεῦμά συνελθεῖν αὐτοῖς, **μηδὲν διακρινόμενον**. ἦλθον δὲ σὺν ἐμοὶ καὶ οἱ ἓξ ἀδελφοὶ οὗτοι, καὶ εἰσήλθομεν εἰς τὸν οἶκον τοῦ ἀνδρός· [GNS] εἶπεν δὲ τὸ πνεῦμά μοι συνελθεῖν αὐτοῖς **μηδὲν διακρίναντα**. ἦλθον δὲ σὺν ἐμοὶ καὶ οἱ ἓξ ἀδελφοὶ οὗτοι καὶ εἰσήλθομεν εἰς τὸν οἶκον τοῦ ἀνδρός. [GNT]	Not to hesitate; not to have misgivings; not to worry about; not to doubt. **Practical Application** 　God tells Peter in no uncertain terms, "Go with them [the Gentiles] making no distinctions." 　The same command is given to all believers of all generations. Believers are not to make distinctions, not to discriminate in proclaiming the gospel. What an indictment against so many! How many *withdraw* from the poor? How many do not reach out to people of other races and social classes?
#4385 **Without Natural Affection** **Without natural affection–KJV** Unloving–NASB Heartless–NIV Unloving–NKJV Heartless–NLT **POSB REFERENCE** (Romans 1:31) *Deeper Study #21*	ἀστόργους = astorgous Pronunciation: [as'-tor-goos] Parsing (part of speech): adjective 　Case—accusative 　Gender—masculine 　Number—plural 　Stem or root—from ἄστοργος, ον Concordance References: ⇒　Strong's #794 astorgos ⇒　NIV #845 astorgos ⇒　NASB #794 astorgos **Romans 1:31** Without understanding, covenantbreakers, **without natural affection**, implacable, unmerciful: [KJV] Without understanding, untrustworthy, **unloving**, unmerciful; [NASB] They are senseless, faithless, **heartless**, ruthless. [NIV] Undiscerning, untrustworthy, **unloving**, unforgiving, unmerciful; [NKJV] They refuse to understand, break their promises, and are **heartless** and unforgiving. [NLT] ἀσυνέτους, ἀσυνθέτους, **ἀστόργους**, ἀσπόνδους, ἀνελεήμονας·[GNS] ἀσυνέτους ἀσυνθέτους **ἀστόργους** ἀνελεήμονας [GNT]	Heartless; unloving; lacking normal human affection; inhuman; without natural affection; abnormal affection and love; without human emotion or love; a lack of feeling for others; abuse of normal affection and love. **Practical Application** 　Others become little more than pawns for a man's own use and benefit, pleasure and purposes, excitement and stimulation. Abnormal affection, sex and perversion prevail.

ENGLISH WORD	GREEK WORD AND VERSE	THE WORD MEANS...
#4386 **Without Natural Affection** **Without natural affection–KJV** Unloving–NASB Without love–NIV Unloving–NKJV Unloving–NLT **POSB REFERENCE** (2 Tim. 3:2-4; esp. v.3) Note 2, point 9	ἄστοργοι = *astorgoi* Pronunciation: [as'-tor-goy] Parsing (part of speech): adjective Case—nominative Gender—masculine Number—plural Stem or root—from ἄστοργος, ον Concordance References: ⇒ Strong's #794 astorgos ⇒ NIV #845 astorgos ⇒ NASB #794 astorgos **2 Tim. 3:3** **Without natural affection**, trucebreakers, false accusers, incontinent, fierce, despisers of those that are good, [KJV] **Unloving**, irreconcilable, malicious gossips, without self-control, brutal, haters of good, [NASB] **Without love**, unforgiving, slanderous, without self-control, brutal, not lovers of the good, [NIV] **Unloving**, unforgiving, slanderers, without self-control, brutal, despisers of good, [NKJV] They will be **unloving** and unforgiving; they will slander others and have no self-control; they will be cruel and have no interest in what is good. [NLT] ἄστοργοι, ἄσπονδοι, διάβολοι, ἀκρατεῖς, ἀνήμεροι, ἀφιλάγαθοι, [GNS] ἄστοργοι ἄσπονδοι διάβολοι ἀκρατεῖς ἀνήμεροι ἀφιλάγαθοι [GNT]	Unloving, without love, without natural affection, abnormal affection and love; heartless, without human emotion or love; a lack of feeling for others; abuse of normal affection and love. It means others become little more than pawns for a man's own use and benefit, pleasure and purposes, excitement and stimulation. **Practical Application** Man has been created to be affectionate—to have affection for others. It is normal and natural for a person to have affection for his family, friends, neighbors, coworkers, and to a certain extent for the stranger and fellow-citizens of the world. But in the end time, people will be so set on satisfying their flesh and pleasure that they will forget family, friends, and everything else. They will be so set on doing their own thing and so self-centered that they will have little affection for anyone or anything else.
#4387 **Without Offense** Void of offence–KJV Blameless–NASB Clear–NIV **Without offense–NKJV** Clear–NLT **POSB REFERENCE** (Acts 24:14-16; esp. v.16) Note 3, point 4b	ἀπρόσκοπον = *aproskopon* Pronunciation: [ap-ros'-kop-on] Parsing (part of speech): adjective Case—accusative Gender—feminine Number—singular Stem or root—from ἀπρόσκοπος Concordance References: ⇒ Strong's #677 aproskopos ⇒ NIV #718 aproskopos ⇒ NASB #677 aproskopos **Acts 24:16** And herein do I exercise myself, to have always a conscience **void of offence** toward God, and toward men. [KJV] "In view of this, I also do my best to maintain always a **blameless** conscience both before God and before men. [NASB] So I strive always to keep my conscience **clear** before God and man. [NIV] This being so, I myself always strive to have a conscience **without offense** toward God and men. [NKJV] Because of this, I always try to maintain a **clear** conscience before God and everyone else. [NLT] ἐν τούτῳ δὲ αὐτὸς ἀσκῶ, **ἀπρόσκοπον** συνείδησιν ἔχειν πρὸς τὸν Θεὸν καὶ τοὺς ἀνθρώπους διὰ παντός. [GNS] ἐν τούτῳ καὶ αὐτὸς ἀσκῶ **ἀπρόσκοπον** συνείδησιν ἔχειν πρὸς τὸν θεὸν καὶ τοὺς ἀνθρώπους διὰ παντός. [GNT]	To be clear; to be blameless; to be clear in conscience. **Practical Application** It means to keep from stumbling, to keep from causing others to stumble, to keep from hurting oneself and from hurting others.
#4388 **Without Partiality** **Without partiality–KJV** Unwavering–NASB Impartial–NIV **Without partiality–NKJV**	ἀδιάκριτος = *adiakritos* Pronunciation: [ad-ee-ak-'ree-tos] Parsing (part of speech): adjective Case—nominative Gender—feminine Number—singular Stem or root—from ἀδιάκριτος, ον Concordance References: ⇒ Strong's #87 adiakritos ⇒ NIV #88 adiakritos ⇒ NASB #87 adiakritos	Impartial, without partiality, unwavering, no partiality, no favoritism. **Practical Application** True wisdom is without partiality (*adiakritos*). This word in the Greek actually means two things. 1. The wise teacher is impartial; he shows no partiality or favoritism to anyone. 2. The wise teacher is undivided in his convic-

ENGLISH WORD	GREEK WORD AND VERSE	THE WORD MEANS...
No partiality–NLT **POSB REFERENCE** (Jas 3:17-18; esp. v.17) Note 3, point 2g	**James 3:17** But the wisdom that is from above is first pure, then peaceable, gentle, and easy to be intreated, full of mercy and good fruits, **without partiality**, and without hypocrisy. [KJV] But the wisdom from above is first pure, then peaceable, gentle, reasonable, full of mercy and good fruits, **unwavering**, without hypocrisy. [NASB] But the wisdom that comes from heaven is first of all pure; then peace-loving, considerate, submissive, full of mercy and good fruit, **impartial** and sincere. [NIV] But the wisdom that is from above is first pure, then peaceable, gentle, willing to yield, full of mercy and good fruits, **without partiality** and without hypocrisy. [NKJV] But the wisdom that comes from heaven is first of all pure. It is also peace loving, gentle at all times, and willing to yield to others. It is full of mercy and good deeds. It shows **no partiality** and is always sincere. [NLT] ἡ δὲ ἄνωθεν σοφία πρῶτον μὲν ἁγνή ἐστιν, ἔπειτα εἰρηνική, ἐπιεικής, εὐπειθής, μεστὴ ἐλέους καὶ καρπῶν ἀγαθῶν, **ἀδιάκριτος** καὶ ἀνυπόκριτος. [GNS] ἡ δὲ ἄνωθεν σοφία πρῶτον μὲν ἁγνή ἐστιν, ἔπειτα εἰρηνική, ἐπιεικής, εὐπειθής, μεστὴ ἐλέους καὶ καρπῶν ἀγαθῶν, **ἀδιάκριτος**, ἀνυπόκριτος. [GNT]	tions and judgments. He knows the truth, exactly what God's Word says, and he will not entertain false ideas or teachings. He is totally committed and undivided in following and teaching God's Word.

#4389
Without Rebuke
 	
Without rebuke–KJV
Above
  reproach–NASB
Without fault–NIV
Without fault–NKJV
Innocent lives–NLT
 	
**POSB
REFERENCE**
(Philip.2:15)
Note 4, point 3
	ἄμωμα = *amöma*
	Pronunciation: [am-o'-mah]
	Parsing (part of speech): adjective
	    Case—nominative
	    Gender—neuter
	    Number—plural
	    Stem or root—from **ἄμωμος**, ον
	Concordance References:
	  ⇒ Strong's #298 amömetos
	  ⇒ NIV #320 amömos
	  ⇒ NASB #299b amömos
	
	Philip. 2:15
	That ye may be blameless and harmless, the sons of God, **without rebuke**, in the midst of a crooked and perverse nation, among whom ye shine as lights in the world; [KJV]
	That you may prove yourselves to be blameless and innocent, children of God **above reproach** in the midst of a crooked and perverse generation, among whom you appear as lights in the world, [NASB]
	So that you may become blameless and pure, children of God **without fault** in a crooked and depraved generation, in which you shine like stars in the universe [NIV]
	That you may become blameless and harmless, children of God **without fault** in the midst of a crooked and perverse generation, among whom you shine as lights in the world, [NKJV]
	So that no one can speak a word of blame against you. You are to live clean, **innocent lives** as children of God in a dark world full of crooked and perverse people. Let your lives shine brightly before them. [NLT]
	ἵνα γένησθε ἄμεμπτοι καὶ ἀκέραιοι, τέκνα Θεοῦ **ἀμώμητα** ἐν μέσῳ γενεᾶς σκολιᾶς καὶ διεστραμμένης, ἐν οἷς φαίνεσθε ὡς φωστῆρες ἐν κόσμῳ, [GNS]
	ἵνα γένησθε ἄμεμπτοι καὶ ἀκέραιοι, τέκνα θεοῦ **ἄμωμα** μέσον γενεᾶς σκολιᾶς καὶ διεστραμμένης, ἐν οἷς φαίνεσθε ὡς φωστῆρες ἐν κόσμῳ, [GNT]
		To be without fault; to be without rebuke; to be above reproach; to live an innocent life; to be without blemish, spot, or defect.
		
		Practical Application
		This is a word that is taken from the Old Testament sacrifices made to God. The idea is that the believer is to live upon earth under the eyes and scrutiny of God. He is to walk without any blemish, spot, or defect.
		However, note a fact: the believer lives in a crooked and perverse generation. The world is wicked and evil, twisted and perverted; therefore, the believer has a difficult path to walk. But walk he must, for he is to be the light of the world. He is to shine as a light in the world. He is to reflect the purity, holiness and witness of God Himself.

#4390
**Without Self
Control**
	ἀκρατεῖς = *akrateis*
	Pronunciation: [ak-rat'-eh-ees]
	Parsing (part of speech): adjective
	    Case—nominative
	    Gender—masculine
	    Number—plural
	    Stem or root—from **ἀκρατής**, ές
		Without self control, incontinent, undisciplined and uncontrolled; having no power to discipline.
		
		Practical Application
		It is being given over...

ENGLISH WORD	GREEK WORD AND VERSE	THE WORD MEANS...
Incontinent–KJV **Without self control–NASB** **Without self control–NIV** **Without self-control–NKJV** No self control–NLT **POSB REFERENCE** (2 Tim. 3:2-4; esp. v.3) Note 2, point 12	Concordance References: ⇒ Strong's #193 akratēs ⇒ NIV #203 akratēs ⇒ NASB #193 akratēs **2 Tim. 3:3** Without natural affection, trucebreakers, false accusers, **incontinent**, fierce, despisers of those that are good, [KJV] Unloving, irreconcilable, malicious gossips, **without self-control**, brutal, haters of good, [NASB] Without love, unforgiving, slanderous, **without self-control**, brutal, not lovers of the good, [NIV] Unloving, unforgiving, slanderers, **without self-control**, brutal, despisers of good, [NKJV] They will be unloving and unforgiving; they will slander others and have **no self-control**; they will be cruel and have no interest in what is good. [NLT] ἄστοργοι, ἄσπονδοι, διάβολοι, **ἀκρατεῖς**, ἀνήμεροι, ἀφιλάγαθοι, [GNS] ἄστοργοι ἄσπονδοι διάβολοι **ἀκρατεῖς** ἀνήμεροι ἀφιλάγαθοι [GNT]	• to pleasure and indulgence • to passion and sexual craving • to lust and lewdness It is a person who cannot control his passion for recreation, food, sex, pornography, sensuality, drink, drugs, smoking, whatever. It is a passion that grips and enslaves a person until it becomes an unbreakable habit and bondage.
#4391 **Without Strength** Without strength–**KJV** Helpless–NASB Powerless–NIV Without strength–**NKJV** Helpless–NLT **POSB REFERENCE** (Romans 5:6-7, esp. v.6) Note 1, point 1	ἀσθενῶ = asthenōn Pronunciation: [as-then-own'] Parsing (part of speech): adjective Case—genitive Gender—masculine Number—plural Stem or root—from ἀσθενής, ές Concordance References: ⇒ Strong's #772 asthenes ⇒ NIV #820 astheneō ⇒ NASB #772 asthenes **Romans 5:6** For when we were yet **without strength**, in due time Christ died for the ungodly. [KJV] For while we were still **helpless**, at the right time Christ died for the ungodly. [NASB] You see, at just the right time, when we were still **powerless**, Christ died for the ungodly. [NIV] For when we were still **without strength**, in due time Christ died for the ungodly. [NKJV] When we were utterly **helpless**, Christ came at just the right time and died for us sinners. [NLT] ἔτι γὰρ Χριστὸς ὄντων ἡμῶν **ἀσθενῶν**, ἔτι κατὰ καιρὸν ὑπὲρ ἀσεβῶν ἀπέθανε. [GNS] ἔτι γὰρ Χριστὸς ὄντων ἡμῶν **ἀσθενῶν** ἔτι κατὰ καιρὸν ὑπὲρ ἀσεβῶν ἀπέθανεν. [GNT]	Sick, weak, delicate, helpless, worthless, useless, hopeless, destitute. **Practical Application** We were ungodly and without strength, yet Christ died for us. God's great love is seen in this unbelievable act. We were "without strength" (asthenōn), powerless. We were spiritually worthless and useless and unable to help ourselves.
#4392 **Witness** Martyr–KJV **Witness–NASB** **Witness–NIV** Martyr–NKJV **Witness–NLT** **POSB REFERENCE** (Rev.2:13) Note 3, point 3	μάρτυς = martus Pronunciation: [mar'-tus] Parsing (part of speech): noun Case—nominative Gender—masculine Number—singular Stem or root—from μάρτυς, μάρτυρος Concordance References: ⇒ Strong's #3144 martus ⇒ NIV #3459 martus ⇒ NASB #3144 martus **Rev. 2:13** I know thy works, and where thou dwellest, even where Satan's seat is: and thou holdest fast my name, and hast not denied my faith, even in those days wherein Antipas was my faithful **martyr**, who was slain among you, where Satan dwelleth. [KJV] 'I know where you dwell, where Satan's throne is; and you hold fast My name, and did not deny My faith, even in the days of Antipas, My **witness**, My faithful one, who was killed among you, where Satan dwells. [NASB]	Witness, martyr, victim. **Practical Application** The church was standing fast in persecution. At least one believer had been martyred, Antipas. Nothing is known about this dear believer other than what is recorded here. Tradition says that he was placed inside a brazen bull and slowly roasted to death (A.T. Robertson. *Word Pictures in the New Testament*, Vol.6, p.305). Note: the word "witness" (martus) is the regular Greek word for witness. A.T. Robertson says that Antipas was a witness just as Jesus said we should be (Acts 1:8). Christ gave this dear man His own title: "my faithful one" (cp. Rev. 1:5; Rev. 3:14). He was faithful unto death. This is a sharp rebuke to us today. Just think: the word *witness* and *martyr* mean the same thing. The early believers knew exactly what it

ENGLISH WORD	GREEK WORD AND VERSE	THE WORD MEANS...
	I know where you live—where Satan has his throne. Yet you remain true to my name. You did not renounce your faith in me, even in the days of Antipas, my faithful **witness**, who was put to death in your city—where Satan lives. [NIV] I know your works, and where you dwell, where Satan's throne is. And you hold fast to My name, and did not deny My faith even in the days in which Antipas was My faithful **martyr**, who was killed among you, where Satan dwells. [NKJV] "I know that you live in the city where that great throne of Satan is located, and yet you have remained loyal to me. And you refused to deny me even when Antipas, my faithful **witness**, was martyred among you by Satan's followers. [NLT] Οἶδα τὰ ἔργα σου, καὶ ποῦ κατοικεῖς, ὅπου ὁ θρόνος τοῦ Σατανᾶ· καὶ κρατεῖς τὸ ὄνομά μου, καὶ οὐκ ἠρνήσω τὴν πίστιν, μου, καὶ ἐν ταῖς ἡμέραις ἐν αἷς Ἀντιπᾶς ὁ **μάρτυς** μου, ὁ πιστός, ὃς ἀπεκτάνθη παρ' ὑμῖν, ὅπου κατοικεῖ ὁ Σατανᾶ· [GNS] Οἶδα ποῦ κατοικεῖς, ὅπου ὁ θρόνος τοῦ Σατανᾶ, καὶ κρατεῖς τὸ ὄνομά μου καὶ οὐκ ἠρνήσω τὴν πίστιν μου καὶ ἐν ταῖς ἡμέραις Ἀντιπᾶς ὁ **μάρτυς** μου ὁ πιστός μου, ὃς ἀπεκτάνθη παρ' ὑμῖν, ὅπου ὁ Σατανᾶς κατοικεῖ. [GNT]	meant to become a follower of Christ: it meant the commitment of all they were and had. It meant the possibility of death.

#4393
Witnesses
 	
Witnesses–KJV
Witnesses–NASB
Witnesses–NIV
Witnesses–NKJV
Tell people–NLT
 	
POSB
REFERENCE
(Acts 1:8)
Note 3, point 2c
	μάρτυρες = *martures*
	Pronunciation: [mar'-toor-ehs]
	Parsing (part of speech): noun
	    Case—nominative
	    Gender—masculine
	    Number—plural
	    Stem or root—from μάρτυς, μάρτυρος
	Concordance References:
	  ⇒ Strong's #3144 martus
	  ⇒ NIV #3459 martus
	  ⇒ NASB #3144 martus
	
	Acts 1:8
	But ye shall receive power, after that the Holy Ghost is come upon you: and ye shall be **witnesses** unto me both in Jerusalem, and in all Judaea, and in Samaria, and unto the uttermost part of the earth. [KJV]
	
	But you shall receive power when the Holy Spirit has come upon you; and you shall be My **witnesses** both in Jerusalem, and in all Judea and Samaria, and even to the remotest part of the earth." [NASB]
	
	But you will receive power when the Holy Spirit comes on you; and you will be my **witnesses** in Jerusalem, and in all Judea and Samaria, and to the ends of the earth." [NIV]
	
	But you shall receive power when the Holy Spirit has come upon you; and you shall be **witnesses** to Me in Jerusalem, and in all Judea and Samaria, and to the end of the earth." [NKJV]
	
	But when the Holy Spirit has come upon you, you will receive power and will **tell people** about me everywhere—in Jerusalem, throughout Judea, in Samaria, and to the ends of the earth." [NLT]
	
	ἀλλὰ λήψεσθε δύναμιν ἐπελθόντος τοῦ Ἁγίου Πνεύματος ἐφ' ὑμᾶς· καὶ ἔσεσθέ μοι **μάρτυρες** ἔν τε Ἰερουσαλὴμ, καὶ ἐν πάσῃ τῇ Ἰουδαίᾳ καὶ Σαμαρείᾳ καὶ ἕως ἐσχάτου τῆς γῆς. [GNS]
	
	ἀλλὰ λήμψεσθε δύναμιν ἐπελθόντος τοῦ ἁγίου πνεύματος ἐφ' ὑμᾶς καὶ ἔσεσθέ μου **μάρτυρες** ἔν τε Ἰερουσαλὴμ καὶ [ἐν] πάσῃ τῇ Ἰουδαίᾳ καὶ Σαμαρείᾳ καὶ ἕως ἐσχάτου τῆς γῆς. [GNT]
		Witnesses; to tell people; martyr.
		
		Practical Application
		This is the same word as martyr. The believer is to be so committed to reaching men that he is ready to die as a martyr if need be. (See POSB *Deeper Study* #1—Acts 1:8 for verses on witnessing.)
		
		The word "witnesses" (*martures*) is not a command. Rather, it is a natural result of the Holy Spirit within a person. So is power. The Lord says very simply that a Spirit-filled person has power and becomes a witness for Him throughout the world. This is important, for it makes power and witnessing trademarks of Christian believers. A genuine believer possesses both the Spirit and power in his life and becomes by nature a witness for the Lord.

#4394
Woe
	Οὐαί = *Ouai*
	Pronunciation: [oo-ah'ee]
	Parsing (part of speech): particle
	    Type—sentence
	    Stem or root—from οὐαί
		Both wrath and sorrow, anger and pity. There is no single English word to express what it means. It is a grieving denunciation; a sorrowful wrath; a pitying anger. It is a godly threat.

ENGLISH WORD	GREEK WORD AND VERSE	THE WORD MEANS...

Woe–KJV
Woe–NASB
Woe–NIV
Woe–NKJV
How terrible it will be–NLT

POSB REFERENCE
(Mt.23:13)
Deeper Study #1

Concordance References:
⇒ Strong's #3759 ouai
⇒ NIV #4026 ouai
⇒ NASB #3759 ouai

Matthew 23:13
But **woe** unto you, scribes and Pharisees, hypocrites! for ye shut up the kingdom of heaven against men: for ye neither go in yourselves, neither suffer ye them that are entering to go in. [KJV]

"But **woe** to you, scribes and Pharisees, hypocrites, because you shut off the kingdom of heaven from men; for you do not enter in yourselves, nor do you allow those who are entering to go in. [NASB]

"**Woe** to you, teachers of the law and Pharisees, you hypocrites! You shut the kingdom of heaven in men's faces. You yourselves do not enter, nor will you let those enter who are trying to. [NIV]

But **woe** to you, scribes and Pharisees, hypocrites! For you shut up the kingdom of heaven against men; for you neither go in yourselves, nor do you allow those who are entering to go in. [NKJV]

"**How terrible it will be** for you teachers of religious law and you Pharisees. Hypocrites! For you won't let others enter the Kingdom of Heaven, and you won't go in yourselves. [NLT]

Οὐαὶ δὲ ὑμῖν, γραμματεῖς καὶ Φαρισαῖοι ὑποκριταί, ὅτι κλείετε τὴν βασιλείαν τῶν οὐρανῶν ἔμπροσθεν τῶν ἀνθρώπων· ὑμεῖς γὰρ οὐκ εἰσέρχεσθε, οὐδὲ τοὺς εἰσερχομένους ἀφίετε εἰσελθεῖν. [GNS]

Οὐαὶ δὲ ὑμῖν, γραμματεῖς καὶ Φαρισαῖοι ὑποκριταί, ὅτι κλείετε τὴν βασιλείαν τῶν οὐρανῶν ἔμπροσθεν τῶν ἀνθρώπων· ὑμεῖς γὰρ οὐκ εἰσέρχεσθε οὐδὲ τοὺς εἰσερχομένους ἀφίετε εἰσελθεῖν. [GNT]

Practical Application
Note just a few examples from Scripture:
Woe to you, Korazin! Woe to you, Bethsaida! If the miracles that were performed in you had been performed in Tyre and Sidon, they would have repented long ago in sackcloth and ashes. (Matthew 11:21)

Woe to the world because of the things that cause people to sin! Such things must come, but woe to the man through whom they come! (Matthew 18:7)

Woe to you, teachers of the law and Pharisees, you hypocrites! You shut the kingdom of heaven in men's faces. You yourselves do not enter, nor will you let those enter who are trying to. (Matthew 23:13)

Woe to you, teachers of the law and Pharisees, you hypocrites! You give a tenth of your spices—mint, dill and cummin. But you have neglected the more important matters of the law—justice, mercy and faithfulness. You should have practiced the latter, without neglecting the former. (Matthew 23:23)

Woe to you, teachers of the law and Pharisees, you hypocrites! You clean the outside of the cup and dish, but inside they are full of greed and self-indulgence. (Matthew 23:25)

Woe to you, teachers of the law and Pharisees, you hypocrites! You are like whitewashed tombs, which look beautiful on the outside but on the inside are full of dead men's bones and everything unclean. (Matthew 23:27)

Woe to you, teachers of the law and Pharisees, you hypocrites! You build tombs for the prophets and decorate the graves of the righteous. (Matthew 23:29)

The Son of Man will go just as it is written about him. But woe to that man who betrays the Son of Man! It would be better for him if he had not been born." (Matthew 26:24)

#4395
Won A Large Number Of Disciples

Taught many–KJV
Made many disciples–NASB
Won a large number of disciples–NIV
Made many disciples–NKJV
Making many disciples–NLT

POSB REFERENCE
(Acts 14:21)
Note 1, point 2

μαθητεύσαντες ἱκανούς = *mathēteusantes hikanous*
Pronunciation: [math-ayt-yoo'-san-tehs hik-an-oos']
Parsing *mathēteusantes* (part of speech): verb
    Mood—participle
    Tense—aorist
    Voice—active
    Case—nominative
    Gender—masculine
    Number—plural
    Stem or root—from μαθητεύω
Parsing *hikanous* (part of speech): pronominal adjective
    Case—accusative
    Gender—masculine
    Number—plural
    Stem or root—from ἱκανός, ή, όν
Concordance References:
⇒ Strong's #3100 mathēteuö + 2425 hikanos
⇒ NIV #3411 mathēteuö [won disciples]+ 2653 hikanos [large number]
⇒ NASB #3100 mathēteuö + 2425 hikanos

Acts 14:21
And when they had preached the gospel to that city,

Won a large number of disciples; taught many; made many disciples.

Practical Application
The ministry of the preachers (Paul and Barnabas) was to make disciples. They not only preached, but they had made disciples out of the believers (see POSB note, Discipleship—Acts 13:5-6 for discussion).

ENGLISH WORD	GREEK WORD AND VERSE	THE WORD MEANS...
	and had **taught many**, they returned again to Lystra, and to Iconium, and Antioch, [KJV] And after they had preached the gospel to that city and had **made many disciples**, they returned to Lystra and to Iconium and to Antioch, [NASB] They preached the good news in that city and **won a large number of disciples**. Then they returned to Lystra, Iconium and Antioch, [NIV] And when they had preached the gospel to that city and **made many disciples**, they returned to Lystra, Iconium, and Antioch, [NKJV] After preaching the Good News in Derbe and **making many disciples**, Paul and Barnabas returned again to Lystra, Iconium, and Antioch of Pisidia, [NLT] εὐαγγελισάμενοί τε τὴν πόλιν ἐκείνην καὶ **μαθητεύσαντες ἱκανούς**, ὑπέστρεψαν εἰς τὴν Λύστραν καὶ Ἰκόνιον καὶ Ἀντιόχειαν, [GNS] Εὐαγγελισάμενοί τε τὴν πόλιν ἐκείνην καὶ **μαθητεύσαντες ἱκανούς** ὑπέστρεψαν εἰς τὴν Λύστραν καὶ εἰς Ἰκόνιον καὶ εἰς Ἀντιόχειαν [GNT]	

#4396
## Wonder 	
 	
Fear–KJV
Fear–NASB
Awe–NIV
Fear–NKJV
Wonder–NLT
 	
POSB REFERENCE
(Lk.1:64-66; esp. v.65)
Note 3, point 2
 	
See also POSB REF:
(Acts 2:43)
Note 3
(Acts 9:31)
Deeper Study #1
	φόβος = *phobos*
	Pronunciation: [fob'-os]
	Parsing (part of speech): noun
	  Case—nominative
	  Gender—masculine
	  Number—singular
	  Stem or root—from φόβος, ου
	Concordance References:
	  ⇒ Strong's #5401 phobos
	  ⇒ NIV #5832 phobos
	  ⇒ NASB #5401 phobos
	
	### Luke 1:65
	And **fear** came on all that dwelt round about them: and all these sayings were noised abroad throughout all the hill country of Judaea. [KJV]
	
	And **fear** came on all those living around them; and all these matters were being talked about in all the hill country of Judea. [NASB]
	
	The neighbors were all filled with **awe**, and throughout the hill country of Judea people were talking about all these things. [NIV]
	
	Then **fear** came on all who dwelt around them; and all these sayings were discussed throughout all the hill country of Judea. [NKJV]
	
	Wonder fell upon the whole neighborhood, and the news of what had happened spread throughout the Judean hills. [NLT]
	
	καὶ ἐγένετο ἐπὶ πάντας **φόβος** τοὺς περιοικοῦντας αὐτούς· καὶ ἐν ὅλῃ τῇ ὀρεινῇ τῆς Ἰουδαίας διελαλεῖτο πάντα τὰ ῥήματα ταῦτα, [GNS]
	
	καὶ ἐγένετο ἐπὶ πάντας **φόβος** τοὺς περιοικοῦντας αὐτούς, καὶ ἐν ὅλῃ τῇ ὀρεινῇ τῆς Ἰουδαίας διελαλεῖτο πάντα τὰ ῥήματα ταῦτα, [GNT]
		Awe, fear, wonder.
		
		### Practical Application
		It does not mean to fear God's presence, to shrink and withdraw from Him. To the contrary, it means that a person reverences and stands in awe of Him, wanting to approach and know Him because He is the majestic and sovereign Being of the universe. It means that a person does not fear...
		• to trust and believe Him.
		• to approach and worship Him.
		• to do His will.
		• to serve Him.
		Fear does not mean terror or fright. It means...
		• a godly fear, a fear of God, of His displeasure and judgment.
		• a holy sense of God's presence.
		• a consciousness that God is working.
		• a reverence for God and for what is happening.
		• a sense of awe and wonder.

#4397
## Wonder 	
 	
Wonder–KJV
Sign–NASB
Wondrous sign–NIV
Sign–NKJV
Event of great significance–NLT
 	
POSB REFERENCE
(Rev.12:1-2; esp.v.1)
Note 1
	σημεῖον = *sēmeion*
	Pronunciation: [say-mi'-on]
	Parsing (part of speech): noun
	  Case—nominative
	  Gender—neuter
	  Number—singular
	  Stem or root—from σημεῖον, ου
	Concordance References:
	  ⇒ Strong's #4592 sēmeion
	  ⇒ NIV #4956 sēmeion
	  ⇒ NASB #4592 sēmeion
	
	### Rev. 12:1
	And there appeared a great **wonder** in heaven; a woman clothed with the sun, and the moon under her feet, and upon her head a crown of twelve stars: [KJV]
	
	And a great **sign** appeared in heaven: a woman
		A wondrous sign; a wonder; a sign; an event of great significance; a miraculous sign.
		
		### Practical Application
		Note how the woman bursts upon the scene. She is said to be a "great wonder" (*sēmeion*) or a great sign in heaven. Note also that she is in heaven. This means that she is the heavenly representative of some earthly people.

ENGLISH WORD	GREEK WORD AND VERSE	THE WORD MEANS...
	clothed with the sun, and the moon under her feet, and on her head a crown of twelve stars; [NASB] A great and **wondrous sign** appeared in heaven: a woman clothed with the sun, with the moon under her feet and a crown of twelve stars on her head. [NIV] Now a great **sign** appeared in heaven: a woman clothed with the sun, with the moon under her feet, and on her head a garland of twelve stars. [NKJV] Then I witnessed in heaven an **event of great significance**. I saw a woman clothed with the sun, with the moon beneath her feet, and a crown of twelve stars on her head. [NLT] Καὶ **σημεῖον** μέγα ὤφθη ἐν τῷ οὐρανῷ, γυνὴ περιβεβλημένη τὸν ἥλιον, καὶ ἡ σελήνη ὑποκάτω τῶν ποδῶν αὐτῆς, καὶ ἐπὶ τῆς κεφαλῆς αὐτῆς στέφανος ἀστέρων δώδεκα· [GNS] Καὶ **σημεῖον** μέγα ὤφθη ἐν τῷ οὐρανῷ, γυνὴ περιβεβλημένη τὸν ἥλιον, καὶ ἡ σελήνη ὑποκάτω τῶν ποδῶν αὐτῆς καὶ ἐπὶ τῆς κεφαλῆς αὐτῆς στέφανος ἀστέρων δώδεκα, [GNT]	
#4398 **Wondered** Doubted–KJV Perplexed–NASB Puzzled–NIV **Wondered–NKJV** Perplexed–NLT **POSB REFERENCE** (Acts 5:21-25; esp. v.24) Note 4, point 3	διηπόρουν = diëporoun Pronunciation: [dee-ap-or-oon] Parsing (part of speech): verb Mood—indicative Tense—imperfect Voice—active Person—3rd person Number—plural Stem or root—from διαπορέω Concordance References: ⇒ Strong's #1280 diaporeö ⇒ NIV #1389 diaporeö ⇒ NASB #1280 diaporeö **Acts 5:24** Now when the high priest and the captain of the temple and the chief priests heard these things, they **doubted** of them whereunto this would grow. [KJV] Now when the captain of the temple guard and the chief priests heard these words, they were greatly **perplexed** about them as to what would come of this. [NASB] On hearing this report, the captain of the temple guard and the chief priests were **puzzled**, wondering what would come of this. [NIV] Now when the high priest, the captain of the temple, and the chief priests heard these things, they **wondered** what the outcome would be. [NKJV] When the captain of the Temple guard and the leading priests heard this, they were **perplexed**, wondering where it would all end. [NLT] ὡς δὲ ἤκουσαν τοὺς λόγους τούτους ὅ τε ἱερεὺς καὶ ὁστρατηγὸς τοῦ ἱεροῦ καὶ οἱ ἀρχιερεῖς, **διηπόρουν** περὶ αὐτῶν, τί ἂν γένοιτο τοῦτο. [GNS] ὡς δὲ ἤκουσαν τοὺς λόγους τούτους ὅ τε στρατηγὸς τοῦ ἱεροῦ καὶ οἱ ἀρχιερεῖς, **διηπόρουν** περὶ αὐτῶν τί ἂν γένοιτο τοῦτο. [GNT]	To be puzzled; to be perplexed; to be completely baffled; to be at a loss; to wonder about. **Practical Application** They could not understand how the disciples could be delivered "out of their hand." They were apprehensive about the growth of the *new movement*. In the present situation, the authorities probably thought some of the guards had either willfully released the prisoners or else been careless while on duty.
#4399 **Wondered–Wondering** **Wondered–KJV** **Wondering–NASB** Amazed–NIV Marveled–NKJV Amazed–NLT	ἐθαύμαζον = ethaumazon Pronunciation: [eh-thou-mad'-zon] Parsing (part of speech): verb Mood—indicative Tense—imperfect Voice—active Person—3rd person Number—plural Stem or root—from θαυμάζω Concordance References: ⇒ Strong's #2296 thaumazö ⇒ NIV #2513 thaumazö ⇒ NASB #2296 thaumazö	To wonder; to be amazed; to marvel. **Practical Application** The people of Jesus' home town began to marvel and to be amazed at the gracious words flowing from His mouth. They were taking pride in one of the sons of their neighbors, a son who was so capable.

ENGLISH WORD	GREEK WORD AND VERSE	THE WORD MEANS...
POSB REFERENCE (Lk.4:22-23; esp. v.22) Note 4, point 1	**Luke 4:22** And all bare him witness, and **wondered** at the gracious words which proceeded out of his mouth. And they said, Is not this Joseph's son? [KJV] And all were speaking well of Him, and **wondering** at the gracious words which were falling from His lips; and they were saying, "Is this not Joseph's son?" [NASB] All spoke well of him and were **amazed** at the gracious words that came from his lips. "Isn't this Joseph's son?" they asked. [NIV] So all bore witness to Him, and **marveled** at the gracious words which proceeded out of His mouth. And they said, "Is this not Joseph's son?" [NKJV] All who were there spoke well of him and were **amazed** by the gracious words that fell from his lips. "How can this be?" they asked. "Isn't this Joseph's son?" [NLT] καὶ πάντες ἐμαρτύρουν αὐτῷ, καὶ **ἐθαύμαζον** ἐπὶ τοῖς λόγοις τῆς χάριτος, τοῖς ἐκπορευομένοις ἐκ τοῦ στόματος αὐτοῦ, καὶ ἔλεγον, Οὐχ οὗτος ἐστιν οἱ υἱός Ἰωσήφ; [GNS] Καὶ πάντες ἐμαρτύρουν αὐτῷ καὶ **ἐθαύμαζον** ἐπὶ τοῖς λόγοις τῆς χάριτος τοῖς ἐκπορευομένοις ἐκ τοῦ στόματος αὐτοῦ καὶ ἔλεγον, Οὐχὶ υἱός ἐστιν Ἰωσήφ οὗτος; [GNT]	
#4400 Wonderful Blessed–KJV Blessed–NASB Blessed–NIV Blessed–NKJV **Wonderful–NLT** **POSB REFERENCE** (Tit.2:13) Note 3	μακαρίαν = *makarian* Pronunciation: [mak-ar'-ee-ahn] Parsing (part of speech): adjective Case—accusative Gender—feminine Number—singular Stem or root—from μακάριος, α, ον Concordance References: ⇒ Strong's #3107 makarios ⇒ NIV #3421 makarios ⇒ NASB #3107 makarios **Titus 2:13** Looking for that **blessed** hope, and the glorious appearing of the great God and our Saviour Jesus Christ; [KJV] Looking for the **blessed** hope and the appearing of the glory of our great God and Savior, Christ Jesus; [NASB] While we wait for the **blessed** hope—the glorious appearing of our great God and Savior, Jesus Christ, [NIV] Looking for the **blessed** hope and glorious appearing of our great God and Savior Jesus Christ, [NKJV] While we look forward to that **wonderful** event when the glory of our great God and Savior, Jesus Christ, will be revealed. [NLT] προσδεχόμενοι τὴν **μακαρίαν** ἐλπίδα καὶ ἐπιφάνειαν τῆς δόξης τοῦ μεγάλου Θεοῦ καὶ σωτῆρος ἡμῶν Ἰησοῦ Χριστοῦ, [GNS] προσδεχόμενοι τὴν **μακαρίαν** ἐλπίδα καὶ ἐπιφάνειαν τῆς δόξης τοῦ μεγάλου θεοῦ καὶ σωτῆρος ἡμῶν Ἰησοῦ Χριστοῦ, [GNT]	Blessed, wonderful. It means to be filled with happiness, prosperity, richness, benefits, the highest good—all the great and glorious benefits imaginable. **Practical Application** The wonderful hope of the Lord's return is to be filled with all that one can imagine and more... • all the *happiness* imaginable and more. • all the *prosperity* imaginable and more. • all the *richness* imaginable and more. • all the *benefits* imaginable and more. If one can imagine the highest good and all the richness of life possible, the appearing of the glory of the Lord Jesus Christ will be this and more—much more.
#4401 Wonderful Miracles Wonderful things–KJV Wonderful things– NASB Wonderful things–NIV Wonderful things– NKJV **Wonderful miracles– NLT**	τὰ θαυμάσια = *ta thaumasia* Pronunciation: [ta thow-mas'-ee-ah] Parsing *thaumasia* (part of speech): pronominal adjective Case—accusative Gender—neuter Number—plural Stem or root—from θαυμάσιος, α, ον Concordance References: ⇒ Strong's #3588 ho + 2297 thaumasios ⇒ NIV #3836 ho + 2514 thaumasios [wonderful things] ⇒ NASB #3588 ho + 2297 thaumasios **Matthew 21:15** And when the chief priests and scribes saw the won-	Wonders, wonderful things, wonderful works, wonderful miracles. **Practical Application** It refers to all the things Christ was doing in the temple. This is the only time the word is used in the New Testament. What a beautiful description of what the church is to be: a place where wonderful things are to be done for God.

ENGLISH WORD	GREEK WORD AND VERSE	THE WORD MEANS...
POSB REFERENCE (Mt.21:15) Note 4	derful things that he did, and the children crying in the temple, and saying, Hosanna to the Son of David; they were sore displeased, [KJV] But when the chief priests and the scribes saw the **wonderful things** that He had done, and the children who were crying out in the temple and saying, "Hosanna to the Son of David," they became indignant, [NASB] But when the chief priests and the teachers of the law saw the **wonderful things** he did and the children shouting in the temple area, "Hosanna to the Son of David," they were indignant. [NIV] But when the chief priests and scribes saw the **wonderful things** that He did, and the children crying out in the temple and saying, "Hosanna to the Son of David!" they were indignant [NKJV] The leading priests and the teachers of religious law saw these **wonderful miracles** and heard even the little children in the Temple shouting, "Praise God for the Son of David." But they were indignant [NLT] ἰδόντες δὲ οἱ ἀρχιερεῖς καὶ οἱ γραμματεῖς **τὰ θαυμάσια** ἃ ἐποίησε, καὶ τοὺς παῖδας τοὺς κράζοντας ἐν τῷ ἱερῷ καὶ λέγοντας, Ὡσαννὰ τῷ υἱῷ Δαβίδ, ἠγανάκτησαν [GNS] ἰδόντες δὲ οἱ ἀρχιερεῖς καὶ οἱ γραμματεῖς **τὰ θαυμάσια** ἃ ἐποίησεν καὶ τοὺς παῖδας τοὺς κράζοντας ἐν τῷ ἱερῷ καὶ λέγοντας, Ὡσαννὰ τῷ υἱῷ Δαυίδ, ἠγανάκτησαν [GNT]	

#4402 **Wonderful Things**
 	
Wonderful things– KJV
Wonderful things– NASB
Wonderful things– NIV
Wonderful things– NKJV
Wonderful miracles– NLT
 	
POSB REFERENCE (Mt.21:15) Note 4
	τὰ θαυμάσια = *ta thaumasia*
	Pronunciation: [ta thow-mas'-ee-ah]
	Parsing *thaumasia* (part of speech): pronominal adjective
	    Case—accusative
	    Gender—neuter
	    Number—plural
	    Stem or root—from **θαυμάσιος**, α, ον
	Concordance References:
	⇒ Strong's #3588 ho + 2297 thaumasios
	⇒ NIV #3836 ho + 2514 thaumasios [wonderful things]
	⇒ NASB #3588 ho + 2297 thaumasios
	
	Matthew 21:15
	And when the chief priests and scribes saw the **wonderful things** that he did, and the children crying in the temple, and saying, Hosanna to the Son of David; they were sore displeased, [KJV]
	
	But when the chief priests and the scribes saw the **wonderful things** that He had done, and the children who were crying out in the temple and saying, "Hosanna to the Son of David," they became indignant, [NASB]
	
	But when the chief priests and the teachers of the law saw the **wonderful things** he did and the children shouting in the temple area, "Hosanna to the Son of David," they were indignant. [NIV]
	
	But when the chief priests and scribes saw the **wonderful things** that He did, and the children crying out in the temple and saying, "Hosanna to the Son of David!" they were indignant [NKJV]
	
	The leading priests and the teachers of religious law saw these **wonderful miracles** and heard even the little children in the Temple shouting, "Praise God for the Son of David." But they were indignant [NLT]
	
	ἰδόντες δὲ οἱ ἀρχιερεῖς καὶ οἱ γραμματεῖς **τὰ θαυμάσια** ἃ ἐποίησε, καὶ τοὺς παῖδας τοὺς κράζοντας ἐν τῷ ἱερῷ καὶ λέγοντας, Ὡσαννὰ τῷ υἱῷ Δαβίδ, ἠγανάκτησαν [GNS]
	
	ἰδόντες δὲ οἱ ἀρχιερεῖς καὶ οἱ γραμματεῖς **τὰ θαυμάσια** ἃ ἐποίησεν καὶ τοὺς παῖδας τοὺς κράζοντας ἐν τῷ ἱερῷ καὶ λέγοντας, Ὡσαννὰ τῷ υἱῷ Δαυίδ, ἠγανάκτησαν [GNT]
		Wonders, wonderful things, wonderful works, wonderful miracles.
		
		Practical Application
		It refers to all the things Christ was doing in the temple. This is the only time the word is used in the New Testament. What a beautiful description of what the church is to be: a place where wonderful things are to be done for God.

ENGLISH WORD	GREEK WORD AND VERSE	THE WORD MEANS...

#4403
Wonders
 	
Wonders–KJV
Wonders–NASB
Wonders–NIV
Wonders–NKJV
Wonders–NLT
 	
POSB
REFERENCE
(Acts 2:19-20; esp.
v.19)
Deeper Study #1,
point 1a
 	
See also POSB REF:
(2 Cor.12:11-12; esp.
v.12)
Note 1
	τέρατα = *terata*
	Pronunciation: [ter'-ah-tah]
	Parsing (part of speech): noun
	    Case—accusative
	    Gender—neuter
	    Number—plural
	    Stem or root—from τέρας, ατος
	Concordance References:
	⇒ Strong's #5059 teras
	⇒ NIV #5469 teras
	⇒ NASB #5059 teras
	
	### Acts 2:19
	And I will shew **wonders** in heaven above, and signs in the earth beneath; blood, and fire, and vapour of smoke: [KJV]
	'And I will grant **wonders** in the sky above, And signs on the earth beneath, Blood, and fire, and vapor of smoke. [NASB]
	I will show **wonders** in the heaven above and signs on the earth below, blood and fire and billows of smoke. [NIV]
	I will show **wonders** in heaven above and signs in the earth beneath: blood and fire and vapor of smoke. [NKJV]
	And I will cause **wonders** in the heavens above and signs on the earth below—blood and fire and clouds of smoke. [NLT]
	καὶ δώσω τέρατα ἐν τῷ οὐρανῷ ἄνω, καὶ σημεῖα ἐπὶ τῆς γῆς κάτω, αἷμα καὶ πῦρ καὶ ἀτμίδα καπνοῦ· [GNS]
	καὶ δώσω τέρατα ἐν τῷ οὐρανῷ ἄνω καὶ σημεῖα ἐπὶ τῆς γῆς κάτω, αἷμα καὶ πῦρ καὶ ἀτμίδα καπνοῦ· [GNT]
		Wonders; an omen; signs of awe, astonishment; the effect of miracles upon the observers.
		
		### Practical Application
		It means marvels, signs, happenings, portents in heaven above, that is, in outer space; happenings and marvels that point to something unusual about to happen.

#4404
Wondrous Sign
 	
Wonder–KJV
Sign–NASB
Wondrous sign–NIV
Sign–NKJV
Event of great significance–NLT
 	
POSB
REFERENCE
(Rev.12:1-2; esp.v.1)
Note 1
	σημεῖον = *sëmeion*
	Pronunciation: [say-mi'-on]
	Parsing (part of speech): noun
	    Case—nominative
	    Gender—neuter
	    Number—singular
	    Stem or root—from σημεῖον, ου
	Concordance References:
	⇒ Strong's #4592 sëmeion
	⇒ NIV #4956 sëmeion
	⇒ NASB #4592 sëmeion
	
	### Rev. 12:1
	And there appeared a great **wonder** in heaven; a woman clothed with the sun, and the moon under her feet, and upon her head a crown of twelve stars: [KJV]
	And a great **sign** appeared in heaven: a woman clothed with the sun, and the moon under her feet, and on her head a crown of twelve stars; [NASB]
	A great and **wondrous sign** appeared in heaven: a woman clothed with the sun, with the moon under her feet and a crown of twelve stars on her head. [NIV]
	Now a great **sign** appeared in heaven: a woman clothed with the sun, with the moon under her feet, and on her head a garland of twelve stars. [NKJV]
	Then I witnessed in heaven an **event of great significance**. I saw a woman clothed with the sun, with the moon beneath her feet, and a crown of twelve stars on her head. [NLT]
	Καὶ σημεῖον μέγα ὤφθη ἐν τῷ οὐρανῷ, γυνὴ περιβεβλημένη τὸν ἥλιον, καὶ ἡ σελήνη ὑποκάτω τῶν ποδῶν αὐτῆς, καὶ ἐπὶ τῆς κεφαλῆς αὐτῆς στέφανος ἀστέρων δώδεκα· [GNS]
	Καὶ σημεῖον μέγα ὤφθη ἐν τῷ οὐρανῷ, γυνὴ περιβεβλημένη τὸν ἥλιον, καὶ ἡ σελήνη ὑποκάτω τῶν ποδῶν αὐτῆς καὶ ἐπὶ τῆς κεφαλῆς αὐτῆς στέφανος ἀστέρων δώδεκα, [GNT]
		A wondrous sign; a wonder; a sign; an event of great significance; a miraculous sign.
		
		### Practical Application
		Note how the woman bursts upon the scene. She is said to be a great "wondrous sign" (*sëmeion*) or a great sign in heaven. Note also that she is in heaven. This means that she is the heavenly representative of some earthly people.

#4405 **Word**	λόγος = *logos* Pronunciation: [log'-os] Parsing (part of speech): noun Case—nominative	The Word. The *Word* (*logos*) is Jesus Christ. ### Practical Application John faced a serious problem in writing to the

ENGLISH WORD	GREEK WORD AND VERSE	THE WORD MEANS...
Word–KJV Word–NASB Word–NIV Word–NKJV Word–NLT **POSB** **REFERENCE** (Jn.1:1-5; esp. v.1) *Deeper Study #1*	Gender—masculine Number—singular Stem or root—from **λόγος**, ου Concordance References: ⇒ Strong's #3056 logos ⇒ NIV #3364 logos ⇒ NASB #3056 logos **John 1:1** In the beginning was the **Word**, and the Word was with God, and the **Word** was God. [KJV] In the beginning was the **Word**, and the **Word** was with God, and the **Word** was God. [NASB] In the beginning was the **Word**, and the **Word** was with God, and the **Word** was God. [NIV] In the beginning was the **Word**, and the Word was with God, and the Word was God. [NKJV] In the beginning the **Word** already existed. He was with God, and he was God. [NLT] Ἐν ἀρχῇ ἦν ὁ **λόγος**, καὶ ὁ **λόγος** ἦν πρὸς τὸν Θεόν, καὶ Θεὸς ἦν ὁ **λόγος**. [GNS] Ἐν ἀρχῇ ἦν ὁ **λόγος**, καὶ ὁ **λόγος** ἦν πρὸς τὸν θεόν, καὶ θεὸς ἦν ὁ **λόγος**. [GNT]	Gentiles, that is, the non-Jewish world. Most Gentiles had never heard of the Messiah or Savior who was expected by the Jews. The idea was foreign to them. However, the Messiah was the very center of Christianity. How was John going to present Christ so that a Gentile could understand? The answer lay in the idea of the *Word*, for the *Word* was understood by both Gentile and Jew. 1. The Jews saw a word as something more than a mere sound. A word was something active and existing. It was power—it possessed the power to express something, to do something. This is seen in the many Old Testament references where *The Word of God* was seen as the creative power of God, the power that made the world and gave light and life to every man (Genesis 1:3, 6, 11; Psalm 33:6; Psalm 107:20; Psalm 147:15; Isaiah 55:11). 2. The Gentiles or Greeks saw the *Word* more philosophically. a. When they looked at the world of nature, they saw that things were not chaotic, but orderly. Everything had its place and moved or grew in an orderly fashion, including the stars above and the vegetation below. Therefore, the Greeks said that behind the world was a mind, a reason, a power that made and kept things in their proper place. This creative and sustaining mind, this supreme reason, this unlimited power was said to be the *Word*. b. The *Word* was also seen as the power that enabled men to think and reason. It was the power that brought light and understanding to man's mind, enabling him to express his jumbled thoughts in an orderly fashion. c. More importantly, the *Word* was the power by which men came into contact with God and expressed their feelings to God. 3. John grabbed hold of this common idea of the Jews and Gentiles. He proclaimed that Jesus Christ was the *Word*. John saw that a word is the expression of an idea, a thought, an image in the mind of a person. He saw that a word describes what is in the mind of a person. Thus, he proclaimed that in the life of Jesus Christ, God was speaking to the world, speaking and demonstrating just what He wanted to say to man. John said three things. a. God has given us much more than mere words in the Holy Scriptures. God has given us Jesus Christ, *The Word*. As *The Word*, Jesus Christ was the picture, the expression, the pattern, the very image of what God wished to say to man. The very image within God's mind of the *Ideal Man* was demonstrated in the life of Jesus Christ. Jesus Christ was the perfect expression of all that God wishes man to be. Jesus Christ was God's utterance, God's speech, *God's Word* to man. Jesus Christ was *the Word* of God who came down to earth in human flesh to bring man into a face-to-face relationship with God (cp. John 1:1-2). Jesus was *the Word of God who came to earth to live out the written Word of God.*

ENGLISH WORD	GREEK WORD AND VERSE	THE WORD MEANS...
		b. Jesus Christ is the Mind, the Reason, the Power that both made and keeps things in their proper order. He is the creative and sustaining Mind, the Supreme Reason, the unlimited Power (cp. John 1:3). c. Jesus Christ is the Light, the Illumination, the Power that penetrates the darkness of the world. He, the Life and Light of the world, is what makes sense of the world and enables men to understand the world (cp. John 1:4-5).

#4406
Word
 	
Word–KJV
Word–NASB
Spiritual–NIV
Word–NKJV
Spiritual–NLT
 	
POSB
REFERENCE
(1 Pt.2:2-3; esp. v.2)
Note 2
	λογικὸν = *logikon*
	Pronunciation: [log-ik-on']
	Parsing (part of speech): adjective
	  Case—accusative
	  Gender—neuter
	  Number—singular
	  Stem or root—from λογικός, ή, όν
	Concordance References:
	⇒ Strong's #3050 logikos
	⇒ NIV #3358 logikos
	⇒ NASB #3050 logikos
	
	1 Peter 2:2
	As newborn babes, desire the sincere milk of the **word**, that ye may grow thereby: [KJV]
	Like newborn babes, long for the pure milk of the **word**, that by it you may grow in respect to salvation, [NASB]
	Like newborn babies, crave pure **spiritual** milk, so that by it you may grow up in your salvation, [NIV]
	As newborn babes, desire the pure milk of the **word**, that you may grow thereby, [NKJV]
	You must crave pure **spiritual** milk so that you can grow into the fullness of your salvation. Cry out for this nourishment as a baby cries for milk, [NLT]
	ὡς ἀρτιγέννητα βρέφη, τὸ **λογικὸν** ἄδολον γάλα ἐπιποθήσατε, ἵνα ἐν αὐτῷ αὐξηθῆτε, [GNS]
	ὡς ἀρτιγέννητα βρέφη τὸ **λογικὸν** ἄδολον γάλα ἐπιποθήσατε, ἵνα ἐν αὐτῷ αὐξηθῆτε εἰς σωτηρίαν, [GNT]
		Spiritual, word, rational.
		
		Practical Application
		The Greek word that is translated "the word" (*logikon*) is translated by some commentators as *spiritual* or *reasonable*. That is, the verse is made to read "desire pure spiritual milk" or "desire the reasonable and intelligent milk." However, the correct translation seems to be "desire the sincere milk of the Word." This has clearly been the emphasis of Peter throughout this whole passage. His subject and thrust has been the Word of God (cp. 1 Peter 1:23-25). William Barclay states it as well as it can be stated:
		
		"Logos is the Greek for word, and logikos means belonging to the word. This is the sense in which the Authorized Version takes the word, and we think that it is entirely correct. Peter has just been talking about the word of God which lives and abides for ever (1 Peter 1:23-25). It is the word of God which is in his mind; and we think that what Peter means here is that the Christian must desire with his whole heart the nourishment which comes from the word of God, for by that nourishment he can thrive and grow up until he reaches salvation itself. In face of all the evil of the heathen world the Christian must strengthen his soul and his life with the pure food of the word of God" (The Letters of James and Peter. "The Daily Study Bible," p.227).

#4407
Word Of Blame
 	
Blameless–KJV
Blameless–NASB
Blameless–NIV
Blameless–NKJV
Word of blame–NLT
 	
POSB
REFERENCE
(Philip.2:15)
Note 4
	ἄμεμπτοι = *amemptoi*
	Pronunciation: [am'-emp-toy]
	Parsing (part of speech): adjective
	  Case—nominative
	  Gender—masculine
	  Number—plural
	  Stem or root—from ἄμεμπτος, ον
	Concordance References:
	⇒ Strong's #273 amemptos
	⇒ NIV #289 amemptos
	⇒ NASB #273 amemptos
	
	Philip. 2:15
	That ye may be **blameless** and harmless, the sons of God, without rebuke, in the midst of a crooked and perverse nation, among whom ye shine as lights in the world; [KJV]
	That you may prove yourselves to be **blameless** and innocent, children of God above reproach in the midst of a crooked and perverse generation, among whom you appear as lights in the world, [NASB]
	So that you may become **blameless** and pure, children of God without fault in a crooked and depraved gen-
		To be blameless, faultless, free from fault and censure; to be above reproach and rebuke; to have nothing wrong with.
		
		Practical Application
		The believer is to live a blameless, faultless and pure life, both in the church and in the world. No person should be able to point to the believer to accuse him with anything. The believer is to be clean, unpolluted, spotless, holy, righteous, and pure before man and God.

ENGLISH WORD	GREEK WORD AND VERSE	THE WORD MEANS...
	eration, in which you shine like stars in the universe [NIV] That you may become **blameless** and harmless, children of God without fault in the midst of a crooked and perverse generation, among whom you shine as lights in the world, [NKJV] So that no one can speak a **word of blame** against you. You are to live clean, innocent lives as children of God in a dark world full of crooked and perverse people. Let your lives shine brightly before them. [NLT] ἵνα γένησθε **ἄμεμπτοι** καὶ ἀκέραιοι, τέκνα Θεοῦ ἀμώμητα ἐν μέσῳ γενεᾶς σκολιᾶς καὶ διεστραμμένης, ἐν οἷς φαίνεσθε ὡς φωστῆρες ἐν κόσμῳ, [GNS] ἵνα γένησθε **ἄμεμπτοι** καὶ ἀκέραιοι, τέκνα θεοῦ ἄμωμα μέσον γενεᾶς σκολιᾶς καὶ διεστραμμένης, ἐν οἷς φαίνεσθε ὡς φωστῆρες ἐν κόσμῳ, [GNT]	

#4408
Word Of Knowledge
 	
Word of knowl-edge–KJV
Word of knowl-edge–NASB
Message of knowl-edge–NIV
Word of knowl-edge–NKJV
Gift of special knowl-edge–NLT
 	
POSB REFERENCE
(1 Cor.12:8-10; esp. v.8)
Note 3, point 2
	λόγος γνώσεως = *logos gnōseōs*
	Pronunciation: [gno'-seh-os]
	Parsing *gnōseōs* (part of speech): noun
	  Case—genitive
	  Gender—feminine
	  Number—singular
	  Stem or root—from γνῶσις, εως
	Concordance References:
	⇒ Strong's #3056 logos + 1108 gnōsis
	⇒ NIV #3364 logos [message of] + 1194 gnōsis [knowledge]
	⇒ NASB #3056 logos + 1108 gnōsis
	
	1 Cor. 12:8
	For to one is given by the Spirit the word of wisdom; to another the **word of knowledge** by the same Spirit; [KJV]
	
	For to one is given the word of wisdom through the Spirit, and to another the **word of knowledge** according to the same Spirit; [NASB]
	
	To one there is given through the Spirit the message of wisdom, to another the **message of knowledge** by means of the same Spirit, [NIV]
	
	For to one is given the word of wisdom through the Spirit, to another the **word of knowledge** through the same Spirit, [NKJV]
	
	To one person the Spirit gives the ability to give wise advice; to another he gives the **gift of special knowl-edge**. [NLT]
	
	ᾧ μὲν γὰρ διὰ τοῦ Πνεύματος δίδοται λόγος σοφίας, ἄλλῳ δὲ **λόγος γνώσεως**, κατὰ τὸ αὐτὸ Πνεῦμα· [GNS]
	
	ᾧ μὲν γὰρ διὰ τοῦ πνεύματος δίδοται λόγος σοφίας, ἄλλῳ δὲ **λόγος γνώσεως** κατὰ τὸ αὐτὸ πνεῦμα, [GNT]
		Message, word of knowledge; a gift of practical knowledge.
		
		Practical Application
		This is practical knowledge. It is knowing what to do in the day-to-day situations that arise. It is knowing how to apply the wisdom that one has to daily living. It is being able to make practical application of truth to life. It does no good to know truth unless a person knows how to use the truth.
		
		The word *of knowledge* is the gift to share with others how they should live; the ability to apply truth to their lives in day-to-day living; the ability to make practical application of truth to life.

#4409
Word Of Prophecy
 	
Word of prophecy–KJV
Prophetic word–NASB
Word of the prophets–NIV
Prophetic word–NKJV
Message proclaimed by the prophets–NLT
 	
POSB REFERENCE
(2 Pt.1:19-21; esp. v.19)
Deeper Study #2
	προφητικὸν λόγον = *prophētikon logon*
	Pronunciation: [prof-ay-tik-on' log'-on]
	Parsing *prophētikon* (part of speech): adjective
	  Case—accusative
	  Gender—masculine
	  Number—singular
	  Stem or root—from προφητικός, ή, όν
	Parsing *logon* (part of speech): noun
	  Case—accusative
	  Gender—masculine
	  Number—singular
	  Stem or root—from λόγος, ου
	Concordance References:
	⇒ Strong's #4397 prophētikos + 3056 logos
	⇒ NIV #4738 prophētikos [of prophets] + 3364 [word]
	⇒ NASB #4397 prophētikos + 3056 logos
	
	2 Peter 1:19
	We have also a more sure **word of prophecy**; whereunto ye do well that ye take heed, as unto a light that shineth in a dark place, until the day dawn, and the day
		The word of the prophets; the word of prophecy; the prophetic word; the message proclaimed by the prophets.
		
		Practical Application
		"The word of prophecy" (*prophētikon logon*) is better translated *prophetic word*, referring to the whole prophetic message centered in Jesus Christ. The *prophetic word* did not begin or originate in the mind of man, but in the mind of God. However, God used men as instruments and authors to communicate His message to the world. Over a period of some 1500 years, He chose kings, soldiers, peasants, farmers, scholars, priests, statesmen—approximately thirty-five authors from different nations, professions, and social strata. The original manuscripts were written in three different languages—Hebrew, Aramaic, and Greek.
		1. The word "Bible" comes from the Greek

ENGLISH WORD	GREEK WORD AND VERSE	THE WORD MEANS...
	star arise in your hearts: [KJV] And so we have the **prophetic word** made more sure, to which you do well to pay attention as to a lamp shining in a dark place, until the day dawns and the morning star arises in your hearts. [NASB] And we have the **word of the prophets** made more certain, and you will do well to pay attention to it, as to a light shining in a dark place, until the day dawns and the morning star rises in your hearts. [NIV] And so we have the **prophetic word** confirmed, which you do well to heed as a light that shines in a dark place, until the day dawns and the morning star rises in your hearts; [NKJV] Because of that, we have even greater confidence in the **message proclaimed by the prophets**. Pay close attention to what they wrote, for their words are like a light shining in a dark place—until the day Christ appears and his brilliant light shines in your hearts. [NLT] καὶ ἔχομεν βεβαιότερον τὸν **προφητικὸν λόγον**, ᾧ καλῶς ποιεῖτε προσέχοντες ὡς λύχνῳ φαίνοντι ἐν αὐχμηρῷ τόπῳ, ἕως οὗ ἡμέρα διαυγάσῃ, καὶ φωσφόρος ἀνατείλῃ ἐν ταῖς καρδίαις ὑμῶν· [GNS] καὶ ἔχομεν βεβαιότερον τὸν **προφητικὸν λόγον**, ᾧ καλῶς ποιεῖτε προσέχοντες ὡς λύχνῳ φαίνοντι ἐν αὐχμηρῷ τόπῳ, ἕως οὗ ἡμέρα διαυγάσῃ καὶ φωσφόρος ἀνατείλῃ ἐν ταῖς καρδίαις ὑμῶν, [GNT]	word *biblos*, meaning *a book*. The Bible is also called "the Scriptures" (1 Cor. 15:3-4) and "the Word of God" (Hebrews 4:12). The Bible is divided into two parts: ⇒ The first part, the *Old* Testament, was written before Christ. ⇒ The second part, the *New* Testament, was written after Christ came. The word *testament* means a *covenant or an agreement*. Therefore, the Bible is God's covenant, an agreement He has made with man. The Old Testament is His covenant with man before Christ came, and the New Testament is His covenant with man after Christ came. 2. The Old Testament has thirty-nine books which were designated as "the Law, the Prophets, and the Holy Writings or Psalms" (Luke 24:25-27). The books are sometimes divided as follows: ⇒ Five Law Books: Genesis, Exodus, Leviticus, Numbers and Deuteronomy. These five are known as the Pentateuch. ⇒ Twelve History Books: Joshua, Judges, Ruth, I and II Samuel, I and II Kings, I and II Chronicles, Ezra, Nehemiah, and Esther. ⇒ Five Poetic Books: Job, Psalms, Proverbs, Ecclesiastes, and the Song of Solomon. ⇒ Five Long or Major Prophetic Books: Isaiah, Jeremiah, Lamentations, Ezekiel, and Daniel. ⇒ Twelve Short or Minor Prophetic Books: Hosea, Joel, Amos, Obadiah, Jonah, Micah, Nahum, Habakkuk, Zephaniah, Haggai, Zechariah, and Malachi. 3. The New Testament has twenty-seven books which are sometimes divided as follows: ⇒ Four Gospels which cover the life of Christ: Matthew, Mark, Luke, and John. ⇒ One History Book which deals with the early believers and early church: Acts. ⇒ Fourteen Pauline Letters or Epistles written to specific churches or individual Christians: Romans, I and II Corinthians, Galatians, Ephesians, Philippians, Colossians, I and II Thessalonians, I and II Timothy, Titus, Philemon, and perhaps Hebrews. ⇒ Seven General Letters or Epistles written by other men to specific groups, each bearing the author's name: James, 1 Peter, 2 Peter, 1 John, 2 John, 3 John, and Jude. ⇒ One Prophetic Book: Revelation. 4. The Bible has one central theme: Jesus Christ. He is the key to understanding what God reveals. He is the focal point of human history. In Him God reveals His purpose and program for the ages (Hebrews 1:1-2). 5. The unity of the Bible is a miracle of God. Think of the facts: thirty-five different authors from so many diverse backgrounds wrote over a 1500-year period. Think of the number and diversity of subjects, yet look at the harmony of purpose and theme. There is only one explanation. God has spoken and has preserved an authoritative record of His

ENGLISH WORD	GREEK WORD AND VERSE	THE WORD MEANS...
		message: "Holy men of God spoke as they were moved by the Holy Ghost" (1 Peter 1:21). 6. The Bible claims to be the record of Jesus Christ (John 5:39), and it claims to be the written Word of God (2 Peter 1:21). As such it is inseparably linked with the living Word of God, Jesus Christ (Hebrews 4:12; 1 Peter 1:23). Jesus Christ is the *living Word of God* and the Bible is the *written Word of God*. The written Word testifies to the living Word even as the living Word [Christ Himself] testified to the written Word.

#4410
## Word Of The Prophets 	
 	
Word of prophecy–KJV
Prophetic word–NASB
Word of the prophets–NIV
Prophetic word–NKJV
Message proclaimed by the prophets–NLT
 	
POSB REFERENCE
(2 Pt.1:19-21; esp. v.19)
Deeper Study #2
	προφητικὸν λόγον = *prophëtikon logon*
	Pronunciation: [prof-ay-tik-on' log'-on]
	Parsing *prophëtikon* (part of speech): adjective
	    Case—accusative
	    Gender—masculine
	    Number—singular
	    Stem or root—from προφητικός, ή, όν
	Parsing *logon* (part of speech): noun
	    Case—accusative
	    Gender—masculine
	    Number—singular
	    Stem or root—from λόγος, ου
	Concordance References:
	⇒ Strong's #4397 prophëtikos + 3056 logos
	⇒ NIV #4738 prophëtikos [of prophets] + 3364 [word]
	⇒ NASB #4397 prophëtikos + 3056 logos
	
	2 Peter 1:19
	We have also a more sure **word of prophecy**; whereunto ye do well that ye take heed, as unto a light that shineth in a dark place, until the day dawn, and the day star arise in your hearts: [KJV]
	And so we have the **prophetic word** made more sure, to which you do well to pay attention as to a lamp shining in a dark place, until the day dawns and the morning star arises in your hearts. [NASB]
	And we have the **word of the prophets** made more certain, and you will do well to pay attention to it, as to a light shining in a dark place, until the day dawns and the morning star rises in your hearts. [NIV]
	And so we have the **prophetic word** confirmed, which you do well to heed as a light that shines in a dark place, until the day dawns and the morning star rises in your hearts; [NKJV]
	Because of that, we have even greater confidence in the **message proclaimed by the prophets**. Pay close attention to what they wrote, for their words are like a light shining in a dark place—until the day Christ appears and his brilliant light shines in your hearts. [NLT]
	καὶ ἔχομεν βεβαιότερον τὸν **προφητικὸν λόγον**, ᾧ καλῶς ποιεῖτε προσέχοντες ὡς λύχνῳ φαίνοντι ἐν αὐχμηρῷ τόπῳ, ἕως οὗ ἡμέρα διαυγάσῃ, καὶ φωσφόρος ἀνατείλῃ ἐν ταῖς καρδίαις ὑμῶν· [GNS]
	καὶ ἔχομεν βεβαιότερον τὸν **προφητικὸν λόγον**, ᾧ καλῶς ποιεῖτε προσέχοντες ὡς λύχνῳ φαίνοντι ἐν αὐχμηρῷ τόπῳ, ἕως οὗ ἡμέρα διαυγάσῃ καὶ φωσφόρος ἀνατείλῃ ἐν ταῖς καρδίαις ὑμῶν, [GNT]
		The word of the prophets; the word of prophecy; the prophetic word; the message proclaimed by the prophets.
		
		### Practical Application
		"The word of the prophets" (*prophëtikon logon*) is better translated *prophetic word*, referring to the whole prophetic message centered in Jesus Christ. The *prophetic word* did not begin or originate in the mind of man, but in the mind of God. However, God used men as instruments and authors to communicate His message to the world. Over a period of some 1500 years, He chose kings, soldiers, peasants, farmers, scholars, priests, statesmen—approximately thirty-five authors from different nations, professions, and social strata. The original manuscripts were written in three different languages—Hebrew, Aramaic, and Greek. (See **Word Of Prophecy** for more discussion).

#4411
## Word Of Wisdom 	
 	
Word of wisdom–KJV
Word of wisdom–NASB
	σοφίας λόγος = *sophias logos*
	Pronunciation: [sof-ee'-ahs log'-os]
	Parsing *sophias* (part of speech): noun
	    Case—genitive
	    Gender—feminine
	    Number—singular
	    Stem or root—from σοφία, ας
	Concordance References:
	⇒ Strong's #3056 logos + 4678 sophia
		Message or word of wisdom; the ability to give wise advice; insight, intelligence, knowledge, the wisdom of God.
		
		### Practical Application
		The wisdom of God is the truth which God has now revealed to man; it is the whole system of truth revealed by God—the truth about God and man and the world. Therefore, the message

ENGLISH WORD	GREEK WORD AND VERSE	THE WORD MEANS...
Message of wisdom–NIV **Word of wisdom–NKJV** Ability to give wise advice–NLT **POSB REFERENCE** (1 Cor.12:8-10; esp. v.8) Note 3, point 1	⇒ NIV #3364 logos [message of] + 5053 sophia [wisdom] ⇒ NASB #3056 logos + 4678 sophia **1 Cor. 12:8** For to one is given by the Spirit the **word of wisdom**; to another the word of knowledge by the same Spirit; [KJV] For to one is given the **word of wisdom** through the Spirit, and to another the word of knowledge according to the same Spirit; [NASB] To one there is given through the Spirit the **message of wisdom**, to another the message of knowledge by means of the same Spirit, [NIV] For to one is given the **word of wisdom** through the Spirit, to another the word of knowledge through the same Spirit, [NKJV] To one person the Spirit gives the **ability to give wise advice**; to another he gives the gift of special knowledge. [NLT] ᾧ μὲν γὰρ διὰ τοῦ Πνεύματος δίδοται λόγος **σοφίας**, ἄλλῳ δὲ **λόγος** γνώσεως, κατὰ τὸ αὐτὸ Πνεῦμα· [GNS] ᾧ μὲν γὰρ διὰ τοῦ πνεύματος δίδοται λόγος **σοφίας**, ἄλλῳ δὲ **λόγος** γνώσεως κατὰ τὸ αὐτὸ πνεῦμα, [GNT]	of wisdom is the gift to share the wisdom and truth of God with men—to share the truth in simple and understandable language.

#4412
Word, The
 	
Preaching, the–KJV
Word, the–NASB
Message, the–NIV
Message, the–NKJV
Message, the–NLT
 	
POSB REFERENCE
(1 Cor.1:18)
Note 3
	Ὁ λόγος = *Ho logos*
	Pronunciation: [ho log'-os]
	Parsing *logos* (part of speech): noun
	    Case—nominative
	    Gender—masculine
	    Number—singular
	    Stem or root—from λόγος, ου
	Concordance References:
	⇒ Strong's #3588 ho + 3056 logos
	⇒ NIV #3836 ho [the] + 3364 logos [message]
	⇒ NASB #3588 ho + 3056 logos
	
	1 Cor. 1:18
	For **the preaching** of the cross is to them that perish foolishness; but unto us which are saved it is the power of God. [KJV]
	For **the word** of the cross is to those who are perishing foolishness, but to us who are being saved it is the power of God. [NASB]
	For **the message** of the cross is foolishness to those who are perishing, but to us who are being saved it is the power of God. [NIV]
	For **the message** of the cross is foolishness to those who are perishing, but to us who are being saved it is the power of God. [NKJV]
	I know very well how foolish **the message** of the cross sounds to those who are on the road to destruction. But we who are being saved recognize this message as the very power of God. [NLT]
	Ὁ λόγος γὰρ ὁ τοῦ σταυροῦ τοῖς μὲν ἀπολλυμένοις μωρία ἐστί, τοῖς δὲ σωζομένοις ἡμῖν δύναμις Θεοῦ ἐστι. [GNS]
	Ὁ λόγος γὰρ ὁ τοῦ σταυροῦ τοῖς μὲν ἀπολλυμένοις μωρία ἐστίν, τοῖς δὲ σωζομένοις ἡμῖν δύναμις θεοῦ ἐστιν. [GNT]
		The message; the preaching; the word; the account; the teaching.
		
		Practical Application
		It literally means "the word" (see POSB *Deeper Study* #1, The Word—John 1:1-5). A sharp contrast is being drawn between the "wisdom of words" (1 Cor. 1:17) and "the Word of the cross." The world's wisdom includes many words, that is, many ways to find the truth and meaning to life. But the Word of the cross is the only way to the truth and meaning of life.

#4413
Work
 	
Business–KJV
Diligence–NASB
Zeal–NIV
Diligence–NKJV
Work–NLT
	σπουδῇ = *spoudē*
	Pronunciation: [spoo-day']
	Parsing (part of speech): noun
	    Case—dative
	    Gender—feminine
	    Number—singular
	    Stem or root—from σπουδή, ῆς
	Concordance References:
	⇒ Strong's #4710 spoudē
	⇒ NIV #5082 spoudē
	⇒ NASB #4710 spoudē
		Zeal, diligence, work, earnestness, effort.
		
		Practical Application
		The exhortation is clear: the believer must...
		• not be lazy or slow moving in zeal.
		• not be sluggish or lethargic in diligence.
		• not be hesitating or delaying in earnestness.
		
		The believer just cannot approach life in a lackadaisical, easygoing, slow moving fashion.

ENGLISH WORD	GREEK WORD AND VERSE	THE WORD MEANS...
POSB **REFERENCE** (Rom.12:11) Note 2, point	**Romans 12:11** Not slothful in **business**; fervent in spirit; serving the Lord; [KJV] Not lagging behind in **diligence**, fervent in spirit, serving the Lord; [NASB] Never be lacking in **zeal**, but keep your spiritual fervor, serving the Lord. [NIV] Not lagging in **diligence**, fervent in spirit, serving the Lord; [NKJV] Never be lazy in your **work**, but serve the Lord enthusiastically. [NLT] τῇ **σπουδῇ** μὴ ὀκνηροί· τῷ πνεύματι ζέοντες· τῷ Κυρίῳ δουλεύοντες· [GNS] τῇ **σπουδῇ** μὴ ὀκνηροί, τῷ πνεύματι ζέοντες, τῷ κυρίῳ δουλεύοντες, [GNT]	The world is reeling in pain, with millions starving and suffering due to man's selfishness and sin, hoarding, disease, war, death—and the list could go on and on. The believer must not give in to sluggishness and complacency. He must serve the Lord with all diligence and zeal and earnestness. He must be enthusiastic in his service.

#4414
Work
 	
Labour–KJV
Labor–NASB
Labor–NIV
Labor–NKJV
Work–NLT
 	
POSB
REFERENCE
(Col.1:29)
Note 5, point 1
	κοπιῶ = *kopiö*
	Pronunciation: [kop-ee-o']
	Parsing (part of speech): verb
	  Mood—indicative
	  Tense—present
	  Voice—active
	  Person—1st person
	  Number—singular
	  Stem or root —from κοπιάω
	Concordance References:
	⇒ Strong's #2872 kopiaö
	⇒ NIV #3159 kopiaö
	⇒ NASB #2872 kopiaö
	
	Col. 1:29
	Whereunto I also **labour**, striving according to his working, which worketh in me mightily. [KJV]
	And for this purpose also I **labor**, striving according to His power, which mightily works within me. [NASB]
	To this end I **labor**, struggling with all his energy, which so powerfully works in me. [NIV]
	To this *end* I also **labor**, striving according to His working which works in me mightily. [NKJV]
	I **work** very hard at this, as I depend on Christ's mighty power that works within me. [NLT]
	εἰς ὃ καὶ **κοπιῶ**, ἀγωνιζόμενος κατὰ τὴν ἐνέργειαν αὐτοῦ, τὴν ἐνεργουμένην ἐν ἐμοὶ ἐν δυνάμει. [GNS]
	εἰς ὃ καὶ **κοπιῶ** ἀγωνιζόμενος κατὰ τὴν ἐνέργειαν αὐτοῦ τὴν ἐνεργουμένην ἐν ἐμοὶ ἐν δυνάμει. [GNT]
		To labor; to work; to work hard; to toil and to struggle in labor and work to the point of exhaustion, fatigue, and pain.
		
		Practical Application
		It is the picture of an athlete struggling, agonizing, and pushing himself well beyond his capacity in order to achieve his objective. This is the call of God to the minister: to labor and work just as diligently as Paul and as the most dedicated athlete.

#4415
Work Hard
 	
Strive–KJV
Strive–NASB
Make every effort–
NIV
Strive–NKJV
Work hard–NLT
 	
POSB
REFERENCE
(Lk.13:24)
Note 2, point 2
	Ἀγωνίζεσθε = *Agönizesthe*
	Pronunciation: [ag-o-nid'-zehs-theh]
	Parsing (part of speech): verb
	  Mood—imperative
	  Tense—present
	  Voice—middle or passive deponent
	  Person—2nd person
	  Number—plural
	  Stem or root—from ἀγωνίζομαι
	Concordance References:
	⇒ Strong's #75 agönizomai
	⇒ NIV #76 agönizomai
	⇒ NASB #75 agönizomai
	
	Luke 13:24
	Strive to enter in at the strait gate: for many, I say unto you, will seek to enter in, and shall not be able. [KJV]
	"**Strive** to enter by the narrow door; for many, I tell you, will seek to enter and will not be able. [NASB]
	"**Make every effort** to enter through the narrow door, because many, I tell you, will try to enter and will not be able to. [NIV]
	"**Strive** to enter through the narrow gate, for many, I say to you, will seek to enter and will not be able. [NKJV]
	"The door to heaven is narrow. **Work hard** to get in, because many will try to enter, [NLT]
		To make every effort; to agonize, strive, struggle, contend, work hard, exert to the fullest, labor fervently.
		
		Practical Application
		A person has to "work hard" to be saved. Wholehearted dedication and effort are required. But note a critical point: the idea is not that a person works for his salvation, but that he diligently seeks God. He casts himself totally upon the belief that God is, that God actually exists (cp. Hebrews 11:6). It is the spirit, the attitude, the heart that sets itself upon God refusing to be diverted or to be committed to anything else. It is the total commitment of one's life to God for salvation.

ENGLISH WORD	GREEK WORD AND VERSE	THE WORD MEANS...

Ἀγωνίζεσθε εἰσελθεῖν διὰ τῆς στενῆς πύλης· ὅτι πολλοί, λέγω ὑμῖν, ζητήσουσιν εἰσελθεῖν, καὶ οὐκ ἰσχύσουσιν. [GNS]

Ἀγωνίζεσθε εἰσελθεῖν διὰ τῆς στενῆς θύρας, ὅτι πολλοί, λέγω ὑμῖν, ζητήσουσιν εἰσελθεῖν καὶ οὐκ ἰσχύσουσιν. [GNT]

#4416
Work Hard

Labour–KJV
Labor–NASB
Labor–NIV
Labor–NKJV
Work hard–NLT

**POSB
REFERENCE**
(1 Tim.4:10)
Note 6

κοπιῶμεν = kopiōmen
Pronunciation: [kop-ee-o'-mehn]
Parsing (part of speech): verb
　　Mood—indicative
　　Tense—present
　　Voice—active
　　Person—1st person
　　Number—plural
　　Stem or root—from κοπιάω
Concordance References:
⇒ Strong's #2872 kopiaō
⇒ NIV #3159 kopiaō
⇒ NASB #2872 kopiaō

1 Tim. 4:10

For therefore we both **labour** and suffer reproach, because we trust in the living God, who is the Saviour of all men, specially of those that believe. [KJV]

For it is for this we **labor** and strive, because we have fixed our hope on the living God, who is the Savior of all men, especially of believers. [NASB]

(And for this we **labor** and strive), that we have put our hope in the living God, who is the Savior of all men, and especially of those who believe. [NIV]

For to this end we both **labor** and suffer reproach, because we trust in the living God, who is the Savior of all men, especially of those who believe. [NKJV]

We **work hard** and suffer much in order that people will believe the truth, for our hope is in the living God, who is the Savior of all people, and particularly of those who believe. [NLT]

εἰς τοῦτο γὰρ **ΚΟΠΙΩΜΕΝ** καὶ ὀνειδιζόμεθα, ὅτι ἠλπίκαμεν ἐπὶ Θεῷ ζῶντι, ὅς ἐστι σωτὴρ πάντων ἀνθρώπων, μάλιστα πιστῶν. [GNS]

εἰς τοῦτο γὰρ **ΚΟΠΙΩΜΕΝ** καὶ ἀγωνιζόμεθα, ὅτι ἠλπίκαμεν ἐπὶ θεῷ ζῶντι, ὅς ἐστιν σωτὴρ πάντων ἀνθρώπων μάλιστα πιστῶν. [GNT]

To labor; to work; to work hard. It means arduous labor, strenuous work.

Practical Application
The good minister labors and labors, works and works to the point of fatigue and exhaustion; to the point that he can go no further. He exerts every ounce of energy and effort in his body for the sake of God and Christ. And note: he is even willing to suffer reproach for Christ. He continues to minister even when men ridicule, revile, mock, curse, and persecute him. Why?

⇒ Because God is the living God. The minister's work and message are based upon the truth; what he is doing is truth. It is all for the living God.

⇒ Because Jesus Christ is the Savior of all men. All men can be saved, actually delivered from the grip of sin, death, and condemnation.

Therefore the good minister must labor, no matter the reproach. He must share the glorious news: man can now be reconciled to God and live forever.

#4417
Work Hard

Ensue–KJV
Pursue–NASB
Pursue–NIV
Pursue–NKJV
Work hard–NLT

**POSB
REFERENCE**
(1 Pt.3:11)
Note 3

διωξάτω = diōxatō
Pronunciation: [dee-o'-kaht-o']
Parsing (part of speech): verb
　　Mood—imperative
　　Tense—aorist
　　Voice—active
　　Person—3rd person
　　Number—singular
　　Stem or root—from διώκω
Concordance References:
⇒ Strong's #1377 diōkō
⇒ NIV #1503 diōkō
⇒ NASB #1377 diōkō

1 Peter 3:11

Let him eschew evil, and do good; let him seek peace, and **ensue** it. [KJV]

"And let him turn away from evil and do good; Let him seek peace and **pursue** it. [NASB]

He must turn from evil and do good; he must seek peace and **pursue** it. [NIV]

Let him turn away from evil and do good; Let him seek peace and **pursue** it. [NKJV]

Turn away from evil and do good. **Work hard** at living in peace with others. [NLT]

ἐκκλινάτω ἀπὸ κακοῦ, καὶ ποιησάτω ἀγαθόν· ζητησάτω εἰρήνην, καὶ **διωξάτω** αὐτήν. [GNS]

ἐκκλινάτω δὲ ἀπὸ κακοῦ καὶ ποιησάτω ἀγαθόν, ζητησάτω εἰρήνην καὶ **διωξάτω** αὐτήν· [GNT]

To pursue; to ensue; to work hard; to strive for; to seek after. The phrase "work hard" (diōxatō) means to run after, chase after, press after, and to pursue. It has the idea of swiftness and endurance—of hotly pursuing and staying after peace.

Practical Application
Believers are not only to desire peace, but they are to actively work hard and go after it. We live in a world that is full of corruptible and evil people who could care less about peace and holiness just so they get what they are after. However, the believer must not give up, for peace is the very reason he is on earth.

The believer is to follow after peace (eirenen) with all men. The fact that he has to follow after peace means that peace is not always possible.

⇒ Some persons within the church are troublemakers: grumblers, complainers, gossipers, criticizers; some are self-centered leaders full of pride; some people within the church are just selfish and self-centered and care more about pushing themselves forward and getting their own way than they do about peace. Self is put before

ENGLISH WORD	GREEK WORD AND VERSE	THE WORD MEANS...
		Christ and the church and its mission. ⇒ Some persons within the world are troublemakers and they cause great trouble for the believer. They oppose the believer: ridicule, mock, poke fun at, curse, abuse, persecute, ignore, and isolate him. ⇒ Sonme persons within the world are troublemakers for the world at large: dissenters, dividers, fighters, egotists, power-builders, and warmongers. Some people have no interest in peace whatever unless they can have their own way. The point is this: the believer is to follow after peace with *all men*—no matter who they are. The very purpose for the believer being on earth is to bring peace between men and God and between men and all other men. Therefore, the believer is to do all he can to live at peace with everyone and to lead others to live in peace.

#4418
Work In–
Worketh In–
Working In–
Works In
 	
Worketh in–KJV
Work in–NASB
Works in–NIV
Works in–NKJV
Working in–NLT
 	
POSB
REFERENCE
(Philip.2:13)
Note 2
	ἐνεργῶν ἐν = energön en
	Pronunciation: [en-erg-eh'-own en]
	Parsing (part of speech): verb
	  Mood—infinitive
	  Tense—present
	  Voice—active
	  Case—accusative
	  Stem or root—from ἐνεργέω
	Concordance References:
	⇒ Strong's #1722+1754 en energeö
	⇒ NIV #1877+1919 en energeö [works in]
	⇒ NASB #1722+1754 en energeö
	
	Philip. 2:13
	For it is God which **worketh in** you both to will and to do of his good pleasure. [KJV]
	For it is God who is at **work in** you, both to will and to work for His good pleasure. [NASB]
	For it is God who **works in** you to will and to act according to his good purpose. [NIV]
	For it is God who **works in** you both to will and to do for His good pleasure. [NKJV]
	For God is **working in** you, giving you the desire to obey him and the power to do what pleases him. [NLT]
	ὁ Θεὸς γάρ ἐστιν ὁ **ἐνεργῶν ἐν** ὑμῖν καὶ τὸ θέλειν καὶ τὸ ἐνεργεῖν ὑπὲρ τῆς εὐδοκίας. [GNS]
	θεὸς γάρ ἐστιν ὁ **ἐνεργῶν ἐν** ὑμῖν καὶ τὸ θέλειν καὶ τὸ ἐνεργεῖν ὑπὲρ τῆς εὐδοκίας. [GNT]
		To work in; to energize.
		
		Practical Application
		God arouses, stirs, and energizes the heart of the believer to do God's will. This is a most wonderful truth. Just think about it: we all experience movements and stirrings within our heart toward God. These stirrings are of God. God is working within us—energizing us—giving us both *the will and power* to do what pleases Him.
		As stated, this is a most wonderful truth. Our duty is to grab hold of the stirrings—not to let them pass. We are to grab hold of them and do exactly what the *stirrings* are arousing and energizing us to do.
		This is a most wonderful truth. It means that God does not leave us alone to work out our salvation and deliverance. He works within us: moves, stirs, energizes, and arouses us to get up and get to it. And whatever the energy points toward is what we need to do. God uses the energy and stirring to direct and guide us. The point to see is that God is forever working within us—never leaving us alone—working and stirring us to complete our salvation.

#4419
Work Out
 	
Work out–KJV
Work out–NASB
Work out–NIV
Work out–NKJV
Put into action–NLT
 	
POSB
REFERENCE
(Philip.2:12)
Note 1
	κατεργάζεσθε = katergazesthe
	Pronunciation: [kat-er-gad'-zehs-theh]
	Parsing (part of speech): verb
	  Mood—imperative
	  Tense—present
	  Voice—middle or passive deponent
	  Person—2nd person
	  Number—plural
	  Stem or root—from κατεργάζομαι
	Concordance References:
	⇒ Strong's #2716 katergazomai
	⇒ NIV #2981 katergazomai
	⇒ NASB #2716 katergazomai
	
	Philip. 2:12
	Wherefore, my beloved, as ye have always obeyed, not as in my presence only, but now much more in my absence, **work out** your own salvation with fear and trembling. [KJV]
	So then, my beloved, just as you have always obeyed, not as in my presence only, but now much more in my absence, **work out** your salvation with fear and trembling; [NASB]
		To work out; to put into action; to produce; to carry out. It means to work on to the finish, to completion, to perfection.
		
		Practical Application
		It always means to complete the effort and the work begun; to accomplish it perfectly; to bring it to completion. The point is: do not go halfway in salvation. Do not take bits and pieces when there is a whole parcel. Do not be satisfied with a little when you can have much. Go on, grow until salvation is completed in you. It is your own salvation. No friend, no pastor can work it out for you. You alone must do it.
		The point is clearly stated: once God has saved a person, that person is to get busy obeying God. He is to take hold of the new life and salvation God has given him, and he is to work on it until it is completed and finished, that is, until God takes him home and perfects him.

ENGLISH WORD	GREEK WORD AND VERSE	THE WORD MEANS...
	Therefore, my dear friends, as you have always obeyed—not only in my presence, but now much more in my absence—continue to **work out** your salvation with fear and trembling, [NIV] Therefore, my beloved, as you have always obeyed, not as in my presence only, but now much more in my absence, **work out** your own salvation with fear and trembling; [NKJV] Dearest friends, you were always so careful to follow my instructions when I was with you. And now that I am away you must be even more careful to **put into action** God's saving work in your lives, obeying God with deep reverence and fear. [NLT] Ὥστε, ἀγαπητοί μου, καθὼς πάντοτε ὑπηκούσατε, μὴ ὡς ἐν τῇ παρουσίᾳ μου μόνον, ἀλλὰ νῦν πολλῷ μᾶλλον ἐν τῇ ἀπουσίᾳ μου, μετὰ φόβου καὶ τρόμου τὴν ἑαυτῶν σωτηρίαν **κατεργάζεσθε**· [GNS] Ὥστε, ἀγαπητοί μου, καθὼς πάντοτε ὑπηκούσατε, μὴ ὡς ἐν τῇ παρουσίᾳ μου μόνον ἀλλὰ νῦν πολλῷ μᾶλλον ἐν τῇ ἀπουσίᾳ μου, μετὰ φόβου καὶ τρόμου τὴν ἑαυτῶν σωτηρίαν **κατεργάζεσθε**· [GNT]	

#4420
Work Through
 	
Rest upon–KJV
Dwell in–NASB
Rest on–NIV
Rest upon–NKJV
Work through–NLT
 	
POSB REFERENCE
(2 Cor.12:7-10; esp. v.9)
Note 3, point 3b
	ἐπισκηνώσῃ ἐπ' = episkēnōsē ep'
	Pronunciation: [ep-ee-skay-no'-say hep]
	Parsing *episkēnōsē* (part of speech): verb
	    Mood—subjunctive
	    Tense—aorist
	    Voice—active
	    Person—3rd person
	    Number—singular
	    Stem or root—from *ἐπισκηνόω*
	Concordance References:
	⇒ Strong's #1909+1981 epi episkēnoö
	⇒ NIV #2093+2172 epi episkēnoö [rest on]
	⇒ NASB #1909+1981 epi episkēnoö
	
	2 Cor. 12:9
	And he said unto me, My grace is sufficient for thee: for my strength is made perfect in weakness. Most gladly therefore will I rather glory in my infirmities, that the power of Christ may **rest upon** me. [KJV]
	
	And He has said to me, "My grace is sufficient for you, for power is perfected in weakness." Most gladly, therefore, I will rather boast about my weaknesses, that the power of Christ may **dwell in** me. [NASB]
	
	But he said to me, "My grace is sufficient for you, for my power is made perfect in weakness." Therefore I will boast all the more gladly about my weaknesses, so that Christ's power may **rest on** me. [NIV]
	
	And He said to me, "My grace is sufficient for you, for My strength is made perfect in weakness." Therefore most gladly I will rather boast in my infirmities, that the power of Christ may **rest upon** me. [NKJV]
	
	Each time he said, "My gracious favor is all you need. My power works best in your weakness." So now I am glad to boast about my weaknesses, so that the power of Christ may **work through** me. [NLT]
	
	καὶ εἴρηκέ μοι, Ἀρκεῖ σοι ἡ χάρις μου· ἡ γὰρ δύναμις μου ἐν ἀσθενείᾳ τελειοῦται. ἥδιστα οὖν μᾶλλον καυχήσομαι ἐν ταῖς ἀσθενείαις μου, ἵνα **ἐπισκηνώσῃ** ἐπ' ἐμὲ ἡ δύναμις τοῦ Χριστοῦ. [GNS]
	
	καὶ εἴρηκέν μοι· Ἀρκεῖ σοι ἡ χάρις μου· ἡ γὰρ δύναμις μου ἐν ἀσθενείᾳ τελεῖται. ἥδιστα οὖν μᾶλλον καυχήσομαι ἐν ταῖς ἀσθενείαις μου, ἵνα **ἐπισκηνώσῃ** ἐπ' ἐμὲ ἡ δύναμις τοῦ Χριστοῦ. [GNT]
		To rest on; to rest upon; to dwell in; to live in; to work through; to fix a tent upon.
		
		### Practical Application
		The idea is that the power of Christ rests upon the suffering believer just as the Shekinah glory dwelt in the holy place of the tabernacle. What a glorious thought! The strength of Christ fixes itself upon and dwells within the believer—filling him with the Shekinah glory of God—when he suffers.

#4421
Work Together
 	
Work together–KJV
Work together–NASB
	συνεργεῖ = sunergei
	Pronunciation: [soon-erg-ehee']
	Parsing (part of speech): verb
	    Mood—indicative
	    Tense—present
	    Voice—active
	    Person—3rd person
		To work with; to work together with; to cooperate with; to help.
		
		### Practical Application
		The words "work together" (*sunergei*) mean to create and eliminate, place and replace, con-

ENGLISH WORD	GREEK WORD AND VERSE	THE WORD MEANS...
Works–NIV **Work together–NKJV** **Work together–NLT** **POSB REFERENCE** (Rom.8:28) Note 1, point 2	Number—singular Stem or root—from συνεργέω Concordance References: ⇒ Strong's #4903 sunergeō ⇒ NIV #5300 sunergeō ⇒ NASB #4903 sunergeō **Romans 8:28** And we know that all things **work together** for good to them that love God, to them who are the called according to his purpose. [KJV] And we know that God causes all things to **work together** for good to those who love God, to those who are called according to His purpose. [NASB] And we know that in all things God **works** for the good of those who love him, who have been called according to his purpose. [NIV] And we know that all things **work together** for good to those who love God, to those who are the called according to His purpose. [NKJV] And we know that God causes everything to **work together** for the good of those who love God and are called according to his purpose for them. [NLT] οἴδαμεν δὲ ὅτι τοῖς ἀγαπῶσι τὸν Θεὸν πάντα **συνεργεῖ** εἰς ἀγαθόν, τοῖς κατὰ πρόθεσιν κλητοῖς οὖσιν. [GNS] οἴδαμεν δὲ ὅτι τοῖς ἀγαπῶσιν τὸν θεὸν πάντα **συνεργεῖ** εἰς ἀγαθόν, τοῖς κατὰ πρόθεσιν κλητοῖς οὖσιν. [GNT]	nect and group, interrelate and intermingle, shape and forge, press and stretch, move and operate, control and guide, arrange and influence. The words "work together" are also present action which means that all things are continually working together for good. God is in control of the believer's life. Daily, moment by moment, God is arranging and rearranging all things for the believer's good.
#4422 **Work Toward Complete** Perfecting–KJV Perfecting–NASB Perfecting–NIV Perfecting–NKJV **Work toward complete–NLT** **POSB REFERENCE** (2 Cor.7:1) Note 4	ἐπιτελοῦντες = *epitelountes* Pronunciation: [ep-ee-tel-oon-tace] Parsing (part of speech): verb Mood—participle Tense—present Voice—active Case—nominative Gender—masculine Person—1st person Number—plural Stem or root—from ἐπιτελέω Concordance References: ⇒ Strong's #2005 epiteleō ⇒ NIV #2200 epiteleō ⇒ NASB #2005 epiteleō **2 Cor. 7:1** Having therefore these promises, dearly beloved, let us cleanse ourselves from all filthiness of the flesh and spirit, **perfecting** holiness in the fear of God. [KJV] Therefore, having these promises, beloved, let us cleanse ourselves from all defilement of flesh and spirit, **perfecting** holiness in the fear of God. [NASB] Since we have these promises, dear friends, let us purify ourselves from everything that contaminates body and spirit, **perfecting** holiness out of reverence for God. [NIV] Therefore, having these promises, beloved, let us cleanse ourselves from all filthiness of the flesh and spirit, **perfecting** holiness in the fear of God. [NKJV] Because we have these promises, dear friends, let us cleanse ourselves from everything that can defile our body or spirit. And let us **work toward complete** purity because we fear God. [NLT] ταύτας οὖν ἔχοντες τὰς ἐπαγγελίας, ἀγαπητοί, καθαρίσωμεν ἑαυτοὺς ἀπὸ παντὸς μολυσμοῦ σαρκὸς καὶ πνεύματος, **ἐπιτελοῦντες** ἁγιωσύνην ἐν φόβῳ Θεοῦ. [GNS] ταύτας οὖν ἔχοντες τὰς ἐπαγγελίας, ἀγαπητοί, καθαρίσωμεν ἑαυτοὺς ἀπὸ παντὸς μολυσμοῦ σαρκὸς καὶ πνεύματος, **ἐπιτελοῦντες** ἁγιωσύνην ἐν φόβῳ θεοῦ. [GNT]	Perfecting, completing, accomplishing, finishing. **Practical Application** God expects us to perfect holiness in the fear of God. Note that this is continuous action. The word translated "work toward complete" (*epitelountes*) is an aggressive word demanding aggressive action. It means not only to practice but to finish and complete. The believer is, of course, to *practice holiness*. That is, he is to practice doing the things that will make him holy. But he is to do *much more*: he is to pursue holiness aggressively, seeking to perfect and complete holiness in his life. Of course, the believer can never become perfectly holy: he cannot become God. But he is to set his mind and heart upon becoming holy.

ENGLISH WORD	GREEK WORD AND VERSE	THE WORD MEANS...

#4423
 	
Work, To This Very Day–Worketh Hitherto–Working, Has Been–Working Until Now–Working, Never Stops
 	
Worketh hitherto–KJV
 	
Working until now–NASB
 	
At his work to this very day–NIV
 	
Has been working–NKJV
 	
Never stops working–NLT
 	
POSB REFERENCE
(Jn.5:17-18; esp. v.17)
Note 1
	ἕως ἄρτι ἐργάζεται = heös arti ergazetai
	Pronunciation: [eh'-oce ar'-tee er-gad'-zeh-tah-ee]
	Parsing *ergazetai* (part of speech): verb
	   Mood—indicative
	   Tense—present
	   Voice—middle or passive deponent
	   Person—3rd person
	   Number—singular
	   Stem or root—from ἐργάζομαι
	Concordance References:
	⇒ Strong's #2193 heös + 737 arti + 2038 erga-zomai
	⇒ NIV #2401 heös [to] + 785 arti [this very day] + 2237 ergazomai [at work]
	⇒ NASB # heös + 737 arti + 2038 ergazomai
	
	John 5:17
	But Jesus answered them, My Father **worketh hitherto**, and I work. [KJV]
	But He answered them, "My Father is **working until now**, and I Myself am working." [NASB]
	Jesus said to them, "My Father is always **at his work to this very day**, and I, too, am working." [NIV]
	But Jesus answered them, "My Father **has been working** until now, and I have been working." [NKJV]
	But Jesus replied, "My Father **never stops working**, so why should I?" [NLT]
	ὁ δὲ Ἰησοῦς ἀπεκρίνατο αὐτοῖς, Ὁ πατήρ μου **ἕως ἄρτι ἐργάζεται**, κἀγὼ ἐργάζομαι. [GNS]
	ὁ δὲ [Ἰησοῦς] ἀπεκρίνατο αὐτοῖς, Ὁ πατήρ μου **ἕως ἄρτι ἐργάζεται**, κἀγὼ ἐργάζομαι. [GNT]
		Working until now, has been working, never stops working.
		
		Practical Application
		God never ceases to work, even on the Sabbath (Sunday). It is true that when God created the world, Scripture says He rested on the Sabbath day; but this means He rested from His creative work, not from His other work. His work of love and mercy, helping and caring (compassion), looking after and overseeing (sovereignty) continued.

#4424
 	
Worked
 	
Laboured–KJV
Labored–NASB
Worked–NIV
Labored–NKJV
Worked–NLT
 	
POSB REFERENCE
(1 Cor.15:8-10; esp. v.10)
Note 5, point 3
	ἐκοπίασα = ekopiasa
	Pronunciation: [eh-kop-ee'-ah-sah]
	Parsing (part of speech): verb
	   Mood—indicative
	   Tense—aorist
	   Voice—active
	   Person—1st person
	   Number—singular
	   Stem or root—from κοπιάω
	Concordance References:
	⇒ Strong's #2872 kopiaö
	⇒ NIV #3159 kopiaö
	⇒ NASB #2872 kopiaö
	
	1 Cor. 15:10
	But by the grace of God I am what I am: and his grace which was bestowed upon me was not in vain; but I **laboured** more abundantly than they all: yet not I, but the grace of God which was with me. [KJV]
	But by the grace of God I am what I am, and His grace toward me did not prove vain; but I **labored** even more than all of them, yet not I, but the grace of God with me. [NASB]
	But by the grace of God I am what I am, and his grace to me was not without effect. No, I **worked** harder than all of them—yet not I, but the grace of God that was with me. [NIV]
	But by the grace of God I am what I am, and His grace toward me was not in vain; but I **labored** more abundantly than they all, yet not I, but the grace of God which was with me. [NKJV]
	But whatever I am now, it is all because God poured out his special favor on me—and not without results. For I have **worked** harder than all the other apostles, yet it was not I but God who was working through me by his grace. [NLT]
	χάριτι δὲ Θεοῦ εἰμι ὅ εἰμι, καὶ ἡ χάρις αὐτοῦ ἡ εἰς ἐμὲ οὐ κενὴ ἐγενήθη, ἀλλὰ περισσότερον αὐτῶν πάντων **ἐκοπίασα**, οὐκ ἐγὼ δὲ ἀλλ ἡ χάρις τοῦ Θεοῦ ἡ σὺν ἐμοί. [GNS]
		To labor to the point of being weary and exhausted; to become tired because of hard work.
		
		Practical Application
		Because God had done so much for him, Paul worked ever so diligently for God. Note his statement: he worked more than all the others that served Christ. Why? Because he owed it to Christ: he had sinned so terribly against the Lord. Note that he even gives the credit for his work to the grace of God.

ENGLISH WORD	GREEK WORD AND VERSE	THE WORD MEANS...
	χάριτι δὲ θεοῦ εἰμι ὅ εἰμι, καὶ ἡ χάρις αὐτοῦ ἡ εἰς ἐμὲ οὐ κενὴ ἐγενήθη, ἀλλὰ περισσότερον αὐτῶν πάντων **ἐκοπίασα**, οὐκ ἐγὼ δὲ ἀλλὰ ἡ χάρις τοῦ θεοῦ [ἡ] σὺν ἐμοί. [GNT]	

#4425
 	
 Worked To Exhaustion
 	
 Labours–KJV
 Labors–NASB
 Hard work–NIV
 Labors–NKJV
 Worked to exhaustion–NLT
 	
 POSB REFERENCE
 (2 Cor.6:5)
 Note 4
	κόποις = *kopois*
	 Pronunciation: [kop'-oys]
	 Parsing (part of speech): noun
	     Case—dative
	     Gender—masculine
	     Number—plural
	     Stem or root—from κόπος, ου
	 Concordance References:
	   ⇒ Strong's #2873 kopos
	   ⇒ NIV #3160 kopos
	   ⇒ NASB #2873 kopos
	
	 2 Cor. 6:5
	 In stripes, in imprisonments, in tumults, in **labours**, in watchings, in fastings; [KJV]
	 In beatings, in imprisonments, in tumults, in **labors**, in sleeplessness, in hunger, [NASB]
	 In beatings, imprisonments and riots; in **hard work**, sleepless nights and hunger; [NIV]
	 In stripes, in imprisonments, in tumults, in **labors**, in sleeplessness, in fastings; [NKJV]
	 We have been beaten, been put in jail, faced angry mobs, **worked to exhaustion**, endured sleepless nights, and gone without food. [NLT]
	 ἐν πληγαῖς, ἐν φυλακαῖς, ἐν ἀκαταστασίαις, ἐν **κόποις**, ἐν ἀγρυπνίαις, ἐν νηστείαις, [GNS]
	 ἐν πληγαῖς, ἐν φυλακαῖς, ἐν ἀκαταστασίαις, ἐν **κόποις**, ἐν ἀγρυπνίαις, ἐν νηστείαις, [GNT]
		Hard work, labors, toil, laborous work to the point of exhaustion.
		
		 Practical Application
		 As we study the life of Paul, one striking characteristic about Paul's ministry becomes clear: he never stopped preaching, teaching, or ministering—not until he just had to have rest. He was not lazy, lethargic, slothful, or complacent. He got up in the mornings and put his hand to the plow: working, praying, studying, ministering, and witnessing—just as God had called him.

#4426
 	
 Workers At Home
 	
 Chaste, keepers at home–KJV
 Workers at home–NASB
 Busy at home–NIV
 Chaste, homemakers–NKJV
 Pure...take care of their homes–NLT
 	
 POSB REFERENCE
 (Tit.2:4-5; esp. v.5)
 Note 4, point 6
	οἰκουργούς = *oikourgous*
	 Pronunciation: [oy-koor-goos']
	 Parsing (part of speech): pronominal adjective OR adjective
	     Case—accusative
	     Gender—feminine
	     Number—plural
	     Stem or root—from οἰκουργός, όν
	 Concordance References:
	   ⇒ Strong's #3626 oikourgos
	   ⇒ NIV #3877 oikourgos
	   ⇒ NASB #3626 oikourgos
	
	 Titus 2:5
	 To be discreet, **chaste**, **keepers at home**, good, obedient to their own husbands, that the word of God be not blasphemed. [KJV]
	 To be sensible, pure, **workers at home**, kind, being subject to their own husbands, that the word of God may not be dishonored. [NASB]
	 To be self-controlled and pure, to be **busy at home**, to be kind, and to be subject to their husbands, so that no one will malign the word of God. [NIV]
	 To be discreet, **chaste, homemakers**, good, obedient to their own husbands, that the word of God may not be blasphemed. [NKJV]
	 To live wisely and be **pure**, to **take care of their homes**, to do good, and to be submissive to their husbands. Then they will not bring shame on the word of God. [NLT]
	 σώφρονας, ἀγνάς, **οἰκουργούς** ἀγαθάς, ὑποτασσομένας τοῖς ἰδίοις ἀνδράσιν, ἵνα μὴ ὁ λόγος τοῦ Θεοῦ βλασφημῆται [GNS]
	 σώφρονας ἀγνάς **οἰκουργούς** ἀγαθάς, ὑποτασσομένας τοῖς ἰδίοις ἀνδράσιν, ἵνα μὴ ὁ λόγος τοῦ θεοῦ βλασφημῆται. [GNT]
		To be busy at home; to be keepers at home; to be workers at home; to take care of business [at home]; to be homemakers, devoted to duties at home.
		
		 Practical Application
		 Young women are to be "workers at home." No better exposition of this command could be given than that written by Oliver Greene:
		
		 "This does not mean that the wife is never to go out of the home, never to take part in any outside interests; but she is not to neglect the duties of the home in order to participate in things outside the home. In other words, she is not to be better known outside the home than in the home, by her own husband and family. She is to be diligent at home—not lazy or slothful, not unconcerned about the home and the things pertaining thereto—but to give her best to the home, seeing that things are in order and that the home is kept as becomes a Christian....The duty of a Christian mother is first to her home, and these other interests must be secondary" (The Epistles of Paul the Apostle to Timothy and Titus, p.444f).

#4427 **Working**	**ἐνέργειαν** = *energeian* Pronunciation: [en-erg'-i-ahn] Parsing (part of speech): noun Case—accusative	Energy, working, power. The word "working" (*energeian*) means energy and efficiency, and is only used of superhuman power (Kenneth

ENGLISH WORD	GREEK WORD AND VERSE	THE WORD MEANS...
Working–KJV Power–NASB Energy–NIV **Working–NKJV** Power–NLT **POSB REFERENCE** (Col.1:29) Note 5, point 2	Gender—feminine Number—singular Stem or root—from ἐνέργεια, ας Concordance References: ⇒ Strong's #1753 energeia ⇒ NIV #1918 energeia ⇒ NASB #1753 energeia ### Col. 1:29 Whereunto I also labour, striving according to his **working**, which worketh in me mightily. [KJV] And for this purpose also I labor, striving according to His **power**, which mightily works within me. [NASB] To this end I labor, struggling with all his **energy**, which so powerfully works in me. [NIV] To this *end* I also labor, striving according to His **working** which works in me mightily. [NKJV] I work very hard at this, as I depend on Christ's mighty **power** that works within me. [NLT] εἰς ὃ καὶ κοπιῶ, ἀγωνιζόμενος κατὰ τὴν **ἐνέργειαν** αὐτοῦ, τὴν ἐνεργουμένην ἐν ἐμοὶ ἐν δυνάμει. [GNS] εἰς ὃ καὶ κοπιῶ ἀγωνιζόμενος κατὰ τὴν **ἐνέργειαν** αὐτοῦ τὴν ἐνεργουμένην ἐν ἐμοὶ ἐν δυνάμει. [GNT]	Wuest, *Ephesians and Colossians,* Vol.1, p.195). In this case, it is the power of Christ. #### Practical Application When the minister has gone as far as he can, Christ steps in and infuses energy and power into his body—an energy and power that works in him powerfully. The minister who has truly labored to the point of exhaustion and experienced the energy and power of Christ knows how glorious the experience is. It is just tragic that there are too few who so labor and even fewer who consistently labor to the point that Christ has to step in with His energy and power. We seem to forget too easily: ⇒ as long as we have physical strength and energy left to labor, the energy and power of Christ are not needed. The only way we can experience the physical energy and power of Christ is to use up all of our own strength. When we are completely empty, then Christ has to step in or else leave us and abandon us and disregard the promise of His Word. And this He will never do. Therefore, when we have no more strength to walk and labor, it is then that He infuses us with His own supernatural energy and power.
#4428 ## Working Operation–KJV **Working–NASB** Power–NIV **Working–NKJV** Power–NLT **POSB REFERENCE** (Col.2:11-12; esp. v.12) Note 2, point 3	*ἐνεργείας = energeias* Pronunciation: [en-erg'-i-ahs] Parsing (part of speech): noun Case—genitive Gender—feminine Number—singular Stem or root—from ἐνέργεια, ας Concordance References: ⇒ Strong's #1753 energeia ⇒ NIV #1918 energeia ⇒ NASB #1753 energeia ### Col. 2:12 Buried with him in baptism, wherein also ye are risen with him through the faith of the **operation** of God, who hath raised him from the dead. [KJV] Having been buried with Him in baptism, in which you were also raised up with Him through faith in the **working** of God, who raised Him from the dead. [NASB] Having been buried with him in baptism and raised with him through your faith in the **power** of God, who raised him from the dead. [NIV] Buried with Him in baptism, in which you also were raised with Him through faith in the **working** of God, who raised Him from the dead. [NKJV] For you were buried with Christ when you were baptized. And with him you were raised to a new life because you trusted the mighty **power** of God, who raised Christ from the dead. [NLT] συνταφέντες αὐτῷ ἐν τῷ βαπτίσματι, ἐν ᾧ καὶ συνηγέρθητε διὰ τῆς πίστεως τῆς **ἐνεργείας** τοῦ Θεοῦ, τοῦ ἐγείραντος αὐτὸν ἐκ τῶν νεκρῶν. [GNS] συνταφέντες αὐτῷ ἐν τῷ βαπτισμῷ, ἐν ᾧ καὶ συνηγέρθητε διὰ τῆς πίστεως τῆς **ἐνεργείας** τοῦ θεοῦ τοῦ ἐγείραντος αὐτὸν ἐκ νεκρῶν· [GNT]	Operation, working, power, energy. #### Practical Application Real religion is an operation of God and an operation of God alone. God has to perform the operation or work upon a person if the person is to be acceptable to God. No person can operate upon any other person and make him acceptable to God. God alone has the ability and power to make a person acceptable to Him.
#4429 ## Workmanship **Workmanship–KJV** **Workmanship–NASB** **Workmanship–NIV**	*ποίημα = poiēma* Pronunciation: [poy'-ee-mah] Parsing (part of speech): noun Case—nominative Gender—neuter Number—singular Stem or root—from ποίημα, τος	Workmanship, masterpiece; that which is created or made. #### Practical Application 1. We are God's workmanship, created in Christ Jesus. The believer experiences two creations, both a natural birth and a spiritual

ENGLISH WORD	GREEK WORD AND VERSE	THE WORD MEANS...
Workmanship– **NKJV** Masterpiece–NLT **POSB** **REFERENCE** (Eph.2:10) Note 2	Concordance References: ⇒ Strong's #4161 poiëma ⇒ NIV #4473 poiëma ⇒ NASB #4161 poiëma **Ephes. 2:10** For we are his **workmanship**, created in Christ Jesus unto good works, which God hath before ordained that we should walk in them. [KJV] For we are His **workmanship**, created in Christ Jesus for good works, which God prepared beforehand, that we should walk in them. [NASB] For we are God's **workmanship**, created in Christ Jesus to do good works, which God prepared in advance for us to do. [NIV] For we are His **workmanship**, created in Christ Jesus for good works, which God prepared beforehand that we should walk in them. [NKJV] For we are God's **masterpiece**. He has created us anew in Christ Jesus, so that we can do the good things he planned for us long ago. [NLT] αὐτοῦ γάρ ἐσμεν **ποίημα**, κτισθέντες ἐν Χριστῷ Ἰησοῦ ἐπὶ ἔργοις ἀγαθοῖς, οἷς προητοίμασεν ὁ Θεὸς, ἵνα ἐν αὐτοῖς περιπατήσωμεν. [GNS] αὐτοῦ γάρ ἐσμεν **ποίημα**, κτισθέντες ἐν Χριστῷ Ἰησοῦ ἐπὶ ἔργοις ἀγαθοῖς οἷς προητοίμασεν ὁ θεὸς, ἵνα ἐν αὐτοῖς περιπατήσωμεν. [GNT]	birth. The spiritual birth is the point of this verse. When a man believes in Jesus Christ, God *creates him in Christ*. What does this mean? ⇒ It means that God *quickens the spirit* of the believer, making his spirit alive. Whereas the believer's spirit was dead to God, God creates it anew and makes it alive to God. ⇒ It means that God causes the believer to be *born again spiritually*. ⇒ It means that God actually places His *divine nature* into the heart of the believer. ⇒ It means that God actually makes a *new creature* of the believer. ⇒ It means that God actually creates a *new man* out of the believer. ⇒ It means that God *renews the believer* by the Holy Spirit. 2. We are created to do good works. God saves man *for good works* not by good works. F.F. Bruce points out that the believer is God's "workmanship" (*poiema*), God's work of art (*The Epistle to the Ephesians*, p.52). God fashions man and creates a masterpiece. God's workmanship is always a work of art. The believer does not create the beauty, the art that shows in the canvas of his life. The believer just shows that he is God's workmanship, by the life he lives and displays. Works are an evidence of salvation. Those who walk in trespasses and sins (Ephes. 2:1-2) show that they are not God's workmanship no matter what profession they make. God's people give ample evidence of the *power of a new life* which operates in them. Note that God has *ordained* us to walk in good works. Doing good works is not an option for the believer; it is the very nature of the believer. If a man has been created in Christ—if God has truly worked in him—the man does good works. His very nature dictates it. He cannot do otherwise. He is not perfect, and he fails; but he keeps coming back to God and falling upon his knees, believing and asking forgiveness, and getting back up and going forth once again to do all the good he can. As stated, it is his nature. He is a new creature created to do good works. Therefore, he does them. Just like a tree, he bears the fruit of his nature.

#4430
Works
 	
Work together–KJV
Work together–NASB
Works–NIV
Work together–NKJV
Work together–NLT
 	
POSB
REFERENCE
(Rom.8:28)
Note 1, point 2
	συνεργει = *sunergei*
	Pronunciation: [soon-erg-ehee']
	Parsing (part of speech): verb
	  Mood—indicative
	  Tense—present
	  Voice—active
	  Person—3rd person
	  Number—singular
	  Stem or root—from συνεργγέω
	Concordance References:
	⇒ Strong's #4903 sunergeō
	⇒ NIV #5300 sunergeō
	⇒ NASB #4903 sunergeō
	
	Romans 8:28
	And we know that all things **work together** for good to them that love God, to them who are the called accord-
		To work with; to work together with; to cooperate with; to help.
		
		Practical Application
		The word "works" (*sunergei*) means to create and eliminate, place and replace, connect and group, interrelate and intermingle, shape and forge, press and stretch, move and operate, control and guide, arrange and influence. The word "works" is also present action which means that all things are continually working together for good. God is in control of the believer's life. Daily, moment by moment, God is arranging and rearranging all things for the believer's good.

ENGLISH WORD	GREEK WORD AND VERSE	THE WORD MEANS...
	ing to his purpose. [KJV] And we know that God causes all things to **work together** for good to those who love God, to those who are called according to His purpose. [NASB] And we know that in all things God **works** for the good of those who love him, who have been called according to his purpose. [NIV] And we know that all things **work together** for good to those who love God, to those who are the called according to His purpose. [NKJV] And we know that God causes everything to **work together** for the good of those who love God and are called according to his purpose for them. [NLT] οἴδαμεν δὲ ὅτι τοῖς ἀγαπῶσι τὸν Θεὸν πάντα **συνεργεῖ** εἰς ἀγαθόν, τοῖς κατὰ πρόθεσιν κλητοῖς οὖσιν. [GNS] οἴδαμεν δὲ ὅτι τοῖς ἀγαπῶσιν τὸν θεὸν πάντα **συνεργεῖ** εἰς ἀγαθόν, τοῖς κατὰ πρόθεσιν κλητοῖς οὖσιν. [GNT]	
#4431 **Works Hard** Perfect–KJV Fully trained–NASB Fully trained–NIV Perfectly trained–NKJV **Works hard–NLT** **POSB REFERENCE** (Lk.6:40) Note 2, point 1	*κατηρτισμένος = katērtismenos* Pronunciation: [kat-tayr-tis'-me-nos] Parsing (part of speech): verb 　　Mood—participle 　　Tense—perfect 　　Voice—passive 　　Case—nominative 　　Gender—masculine 　　Number—singular 　　Stem or root—from **καταρτίζω** Concordance References: ⇒　Strong's #2675 katartizō ⇒　NIV #2936 katartizō ⇒　NASB #2675 katartizō **Luke 6:40** The disciple is not above his master: but every one that is **perfect** shall be as his master. [KJV] "A pupil is not above his teacher; but everyone, after he has been **fully trained**, will be like his teacher. [NASB] A student is not above his teacher, but everyone who is **fully trained** will be like his teacher. [NIV] A disciple is not above his teacher, but everyone who is **perfectly trained** will be like his teacher. [NKJV] A student is not greater than the teacher. But the student who **works hard** will become like the teacher. [NLT] οὐκ ἔστι μαθητὴς ὑπὲρ τὸν διδάσκαλον αὐτοῦ· **κατηρτισμένος** δὲ πᾶς ἔσται ὡς ὁ διδάσκαλος αὐτοῦ. [GNS] οὐκ ἔστιν μαθητὴς ὑπὲρ τὸν διδάσκαλον· **κατηρτισμένος** δὲ πᾶς ἔσται ὡς ὁ διδάσκαλος αὐτοῦ. [GNT]	To be fully trained; to work hard. It means to complete, render fit, mend. It is a common word often used for mending, repairing, or restoring broken things such as nets (Matthew 4:21) or men (Galatians 6:1). **Practical Application** The point is forceful: "the student is not greater than the teacher" (see POSB note, pt.1—Matthew 10:24-25). The disciple is not better than his Lord; therefore, he cannot expect to be treated better, nor can he expect to receive more in this world than his Lord. The disciple cannot expect to be better by having more honor, praise, recognition, or esteem. He cannot expect to have more comfort, rest, or pleasure. The Lord suffered, humbled, and denied Himself for the sake of the world and its needs. The disciple, as a follower of the Lord, does the same; he denies himself in order to reach the world for his Lord (see POSB note—Luke 9:23 and POSB *Deeper Study* #1—Luke 9:23).
#4432 **World** **World–KJV** Age–NASB Age–NIV Age–NKJV **World–NLT** **POSB REFERENCE** (1 Cor.2:6) Note 2, point 2	*αἰῶνος = aiōnos* Pronunciation: [ahee-ohn'-os] Parsing (part of speech): noun 　　Case—genitive 　　Gender—masculine 　　Number—singular 　　Stem or root—from **αἰών**, ῶνος Concordance References: ⇒　Strong's #165 aiōn ⇒　NIV #172 aiōn ⇒　NASB #165 aiōn **1 Cor. 2:6** Howbeit we speak wisdom among them that are perfect: yet not the wisdom of this **world**, nor of the princes of this **world**, that come to nought: [KJV] Yet we do speak wisdom among those who are mature; a wisdom, however, not of this **age**, nor of the rulers of	This age, this world that is passing on as fast as the flower of the field which is here today and gone tomorrow. **Practical Application** The wisdom of this age and of its leaders is here today and gone tomorrow. Man's ideas about God and truth fade and pass away almost as quickly as man himself does.

ENGLISH WORD	GREEK WORD AND VERSE	THE WORD MEANS...
	this **age**, who are passing away; [NASB] We do, however, speak a message of wisdom among the mature, but not the wisdom of this **age** or of the rulers of this **age**, who are coming to nothing. [NIV] However, we speak wisdom among those who are mature, yet not the wisdom of this **age**, nor of the rulers of this age, who are coming to nothing. [NKJV] Yet when I am among mature Christians, I do speak with words of wisdom, but not the kind of wisdom that belongs to this **world**, and not the kind that appeals to the rulers of this **world**, who are being brought to nothing. [NLT] Σοφίαν δὲ λαλοῦμεν ἐν τοῖς τελείοις· σοφίαν δὲ οὐ τοῦ **αἰῶνος** τούτου, οὐδὲ τῶν ἀρχόντων τοῦ **αἰῶνος** τούτου, τῶν καταργουμένων· [GNS] Σοφίαν δὲ λαλοῦμεν ἐν τοῖς τελείοις, σοφίαν δὲ οὐ τοῦ **αἰῶνος** τούτου οὐδὲ τῶν ἀρχόντων τοῦ **αἰῶνος** τούτου τῶν κταργουμένων· [GNT]	
#4433 **World** World–KJV World–NASB World–NIV World–NKJV World–NLT **POSB** **REFERENCE** (Rom.12:2) Note 3, point 2	**αἰῶνι** = aiöni Pronunciation: [ahee-ohn'-ee] Parsing (part of speech): noun 　　Case—dative 　　Gender—masculine 　　Number—singular 　　Stem or root—from **αἰών**, ῶνος Concordance References: 　⇒　Strong's #165 aiön 　⇒　NIV #172 aiön 　⇒　NASB #165 aiön **Romans 12:2** And be not conformed to this **world**: but be ye transformed by the renewing of your mind, that ye may prove what is that good, and acceptable, and perfect, will of God. [KJV] And do not be conformed to this **world**, but be transformed by the renewing of your mind, that you may prove what the will of God is, that which is good and acceptable and perfect. [NASB] Do not conform any longer to the pattern of this **world**, but be transformed by the renewing of your mind. Then you will be able to test and approve what God's will is—his good, pleasing and perfect will. [NIV] And do not be conformed to this **world**, but be transformed by the renewing of your mind, that you may prove what is that good and acceptable and perfect will of God. [NKJV] Don't copy the behavior and customs of this **world**, but let God transform you into a new person by changing the way you think. Then you will know what God wants you to do, and you will know how good and pleasing and perfect his will really is. [NLT] καὶ μὴ συσχηματίζεσθε τῷ **αἰῶνι** τούτῳ, ἀλλὰ μεταμορφοῦσθε τῇ ἀνακαινώσει τοῦ νοός ὑμῶν, εἰς τὸ δοκιμάζειν ὑμᾶς τί τὸ θέλημα τοῦ Θεοῦ, τὸ ἀγαθὸν καὶ εὐάρεστον καὶ τέλειον. [GNS] καὶ μὴ συσχηματίζεσθε τῷ **αἰῶνι** τούτῳ, ἀλλὰ μεταμορφοῦσθε τῇ ἀνακαινώσει τοῦ νοός εἰς τὸ δοκιμάζειν ὑμᾶς τί τὸ θέλημα τοῦ θεοῦ, τὸ ἀγαθὸν καὶ εὐάρεστον καὶ τέλειον. [GNT]	Age; world. ### Practical Application The word "world" (aion) in the simplest of terms means the world itself and everything in it, for it is all corruptible. The world, including the heavens and earth and all therein, is aging, deteriorating and dying; and it will pass away. The world is not perfect: not in being, order, morality, or justice.
#4434 **World** World–KJV World–NKJV World–NIV World–NASB World–NLT	**κόσμον** = kosmon Pronunciation: [kos'-mown] Parsing (part of speech): noun 　　Case—accusative 　　Gender—masculine 　　Number—singular 　　Stem or root—from **κόσμος**, ου Concordance References: 　⇒　Strong's #2889 kosmos 　⇒　NIV #3180 kosmos 　⇒　NASB #2889 kosmos	World; world order. ### Practical Application God made the world and all things therein (kosmon, the whole universe). The point is striking. There is only One God, One who... ● is supreme ● is absolute ● is all powerful ● is all encompassing

ENGLISH WORD	GREEK WORD AND VERSE	THE WORD MEANS...
POSB REFERENCE (Acts 17:24-25; esp. v.24) Note 4, point 1	**Acts 17:24** God that made the **world** and all things therein, seeing that he is Lord of heaven and earth, dwelleth not in temples made with hands; [KJV] "The God who made the **world** and all things in it, since He is Lord of heaven and earth, does not dwell in temples made with hands; [NASB] "The God who made the **world** and everything in it is the Lord of heaven and earth and does not live in temples built by hands. [NIV] God, who made the **world** and everything in it, since He is Lord of heaven and earth, does not dwell in temples made with hands. [NKJV] "He is the God who made the **world** and everything in it. Since he is Lord of heaven and earth, he doesn't live in man-made temples, [NLT] ὁ Θεὸς ὁ ποιήσας τὸν **κόσμον** καὶ πάντα τὰ ἐν αὐτῷ, οὗτος, οὐρανοῦ καὶ γῆς κύριος ὑπάρχων, οὐκ ἐν χειροποιήτοις ναοῖς κατοικεῖ, [GNS] ὁ θεὸς ὁ ποιήσας τὸν **κόσμον** καὶ πάντα τὰ ἐν αὐτῷ, οὗτος οὐρανοῦ καὶ γῆς ὑπάρχων, κύριος οὐκ ἐν χειροποιήτοις ναοῖς κατοικεῖ [GNT]	• has created the world (*kosmon*, universe) • has created everything in the world • has created man himself (who is part of the universe)
#4435 World Forces Rulers...of...world– KJV **World forces–NASB** Powers of...world– NIV Rulers of...age–NKJV Mighty powers...who rule this world–NLT **POSB REFERENCE** (Eph.6:12) Note 3, point 5	**κοσμοκράτορας** = *kosmokratoras* Pronunciation: [kos-mok-rat'-ore-ahs] Parsing (part of speech): noun Case—accusative Gender—masculine Number—plural Stem or root—from **κοσμοκράτωρ**, ορος Concordance References: ⇒ Strong's #2888 kosmokratōr ⇒ NIV #3179 kosmokratōr ⇒ NASB #2888 kosmokratōr **Ephes. 6:12** For we wrestle not against flesh and blood, but against principalities, against powers, against the **rulers** of the darkness **of** this **world**, against spiritual wickedness in high places. [KJV] For our struggle is not against flesh and blood, but against the rulers, against the powers, against the **world forces** of this darkness, against the spiritual forces of wickedness in the heavenly places. [NASB] For our struggle is not against flesh and blood, but against the rulers, against the authorities, against the **powers of** this dark **world** and against the spiritual forces of evil in the heavenly realms. [NIV] For we do not wrestle against flesh and blood, but against principalities, against powers, against the **rulers of** the darkness of this **age**, against spiritual hosts of wickedness in the heavenly places. [NKJV] For we are not fighting against people made of flesh and blood, but against the evil rulers and authorities of the unseen world, against those **mighty powers** of darkness **who rule this world**, and against wicked spirits in the heavenly realms. [NLT] ὅτι οὐκ ἔστιν ἡμῖν ἡ πάλη πρὸς αἷμα καὶ σάρκα, ἀλλὰ πρὸς τὰς ἀρχάς, πρὸς τὰς ἐξουσίας, πρὸς τοὺς **κοσμοκράτορας** τοῦ σκότους τοῦ αἰῶνος τούτου, πρὸς τὰ πνευματικὰ τῆς πονηρίας ἐν τοῖς ἐπουρανίοις. [GNS] ὅτι οὐκ ἔστιν ἡμῖν ἡ πάλη πρὸς αἷμα καὶ σάρκα, ἀλλὰ πρὸς τὰς ἀρχάς, πρὸς τὰς ἐξουσίας, πρὸς τοὺς **κοσμοκράτορας** τοῦ σκότους τούτου, πρὸς τὰ πνευματικὰ τῆς πονηρίας ἐν τοῖς ἐπουρανίοις. [GNT]	Powers of the world, rulers of the world, world forces, the mighty powers who rule this world. **Practical Application** Who is this? It refers to Satan and his demons. The forces of evil are the rulers of darkness, the rulers who blind the minds of men lest they believe the glorious gospel of eternal salvation. F.F. Bruce words it well: Satan and his demonic forces *"rank among the highest angel-princes in the hierarchy of the heavenly places, yet all of them owe their existence to Christ, through whom they were created [Col. 1:16], and who is accordingly the head of all principality and power' [Col. 2:10]. But some at least of the principalities and powers have embarked upon rebellion against God and not only seek to force men to pay them the worship that is due to Him, but launched an assault upon the crucified Christ at a time when they thought they had Him at their mercy. But He, far from suffering their assault without resistance, grappled with them and overcame them, stripping them of their armor and driving them before Him in His triumphal procession [Col. 2:15]. Thus the hostile powers of evil which Christians must encounter are already vanquished powers, but it is only through faith-union with the victorious Christ that Christians can make His triumph theirs"* (The Epistle to the Ephesians, p.127f).
#4436 Worldly Carnal–KJV Men of flesh–NASB **Worldly–NIV**	**σάρκινος** = *sarkinois* Pronunciation: [sar-kee'-noys] Parsing (part of speech): pronominal adjective Case—dative Gender—masculine Number—plural Stem or root—from **σάρκινος**, η, ον	Worldly, carnal, fleshly, controlled by your own sinful desires, unspiritual, belonging to this world;. **Practical Application** The ending "inois" [*sarkinois*] means "to be

ENGLISH WORD	GREEK WORD AND VERSE	THE WORD MEANS...
Carnal–NKJV Belonged to this world–NLT **POSB REFERENCE** (1 Cor.3:1-4; esp. v.1) *Deeper Study #1*	Concordance References: ⇒ Strong's #4560 sarkinos ⇒ NIV #4921 sarkinos ⇒ NASB #4560 sarkinos **1 Cor. 3:1** And I, brethren, could not speak unto you as unto spiritual, but as unto **carnal**, even as unto babes in Christ. [KJV] And I, brethren, could not speak to you as to spiritual men, but as to **men of flesh**, as to babes in Christ. [NASB] Brothers, I could not address you as spiritual but as **worldly**—mere infants in Christ. [NIV] And I, brethren, could not speak to you as to spiritual people but as to **carnal**, as to babes in Christ. [NKJV] Dear brothers and sisters, when I was with you I couldn't talk to you as I would to mature Christians. I had to talk as though you **belonged to this world** or as though you were infants in the Christian life. [NLT] Καὶ ἐγώ, ἀδελφοί, οὐκ ἠδυνήθην λαλῆσαι ὑμῖν ὡς πνευματικοῖς, ἀλλ᾽ ὡς **σαρκίνοις**, ὡς νηπίοις ἐν Χριστῷ. [GNS] Κἀγώ, ἀδελφοί, οὐκ ἠδυνήθην λαλῆσαι ὑμῖν ὡς πνευματικοῖς ἀλλ᾽ ὡς **σαρκίνοις**, ὡς νηπίοις ἐν Χριστῷ. [GNT]	made of." Paul is saying that the Corinthians were human beings, made of flesh. Their problem was that they were living as though they were nothing but flesh. They were still living at the human level of life. They had never gotten beyond the affairs and material things of this life. They acted as though this world was all there was.

#4437
Worldly
 	
Carnal–KJV
Fleshly–NASB
Worldly–NIV
Carnal–NKJV
Controlled by your own sinful desires–NLT
 	
POSB REFERENCE
(1 Cor.3:1-4; esp. v.3)
Deeper Study #1
	σαρκικοί = *sarkikoi*
	Pronunciation: [sar-kee-koy']
	Parsing (part of speech): adjective
	  Case—nominative
	  Gender—masculine
	  Number—plural
	  Stem or root—from σαρκικός, ή, όν
	Concordance References:
	⇒ Strong's #4559 sarkikos
	⇒ NIV #4920 sarkikos
	⇒ NASB #4559 sarkikos
	
	1 Cor. 3:3
	For ye are yet **carnal**: for whereas there is among you envying, and strife, and divisions, are ye not carnal, and walk as men? [KJV]
	For you are still **fleshly**. For since there is jealousy and strife among you, are you not fleshly, and are you not walking like mere men? [NASB]
	You are still **worldly**. For since there is jealousy and quarreling among you, are you not worldly? Are you not acting like mere men? [NIV]
	For you are still carnal. For where there are envy, strife, and divisions among you, are you not **carnal** and behaving like mere men? [NKJV]
	For you are still **controlled by your own sinful desires**. You are jealous of one another and quarrel with each other. Doesn't that prove you are controlled by your own desires? You are acting like people who don't belong to the Lord. [NLT]
	ἔτι γὰρ **σαρκικοί** ἐστε· ὅπου γὰρ ἐν ὑμῖν ζῆλος καὶ ἔρις καὶ διχοστασίαι, οὐχὶ σαρκικοί ἐστε, καὶ κατὰ ἄνθρωπον περιπατεῖτε; [GNS]
	ἔτι γὰρ **σαρκικοί** ἐστε. ὅπου γὰρ ἐν ὑμῖν ζῆλος καὶ ἔρις, οὐχὶ σαρκικοί ἐστε καὶ κατὰ ἄνθρωπον περιπατεῖτε; [GNT]
		Worldly, carnal, fleshly, controlled by your own sinful desires.
		
		Practical Application
		The ending "*ikoi*" means to be "characterized by." Paul is saying that the Corinthians were not only "made of flesh" but characterized and "dominated by the flesh." They were allowing the flesh and its passions to captivate and control their behavior. They were living on the level of the flesh, dominated by it.

#4438
Worldly
 	
Profane–KJV
Worldly–NASB
Godless–NIV
Profane–NKJV
Godless–NLT
	βεβήλους = *bebēlous*
	Pronunciation: [beb'-ay-loos]
	Parsing (part of speech): adjective
	  Case—accusative
	  Gender—feminine
	  Number—plural
	  Stem or root—from βέβηλος, ον
	Concordance References:
	⇒ Strong's #952 bebēlos
		Godless, profane, worldly, irreligious. It means common, irreverent, and godless talk. It means to be unhallowed and sensual; to be neglectful of spiritual things and a lover of the world and its things.
		
		Practical Application
		The minister is to turn away from false teach-

ENGLISH WORD	GREEK WORD AND VERSE	THE WORD MEANS...
POSB REFERENCE (1 Tim.6:20-21; esp. v.20) Note 2, point 2 **See also POSB REF:** (2 Tim. 2:16-18, esp. v.16) Note 3 (Heb.12:15-17; esp. v.16) Note 2, point 4	⇒ NIV #1013 bebëlos ⇒ NASB #952 bebëlos **1 Tim. 6:20** O Timothy, keep that which is committed to thy trust, avoiding **profane** and vain babblings, and oppositions of science falsely so called: [KJV] O Timothy, guard what has been entrusted to you, avoiding **worldly** and empty chatter and the opposing arguments of what is falsely called "knowledge"— [NASB] Timothy, guard what has been entrusted to your care. Turn away from **godless** chatter and the opposing ideas of what is falsely called knowledge, [NIV] O Timothy! Guard what was committed to your trust, avoiding the **profane** and idle babblings and contradictions of what is falsely called knowledge– [NKJV] Timothy, guard what God has entrusted to you. Avoid **godless**, foolish discussions with those who oppose you with their so-called knowledge. [NLT] Ὦ Τιμόθεε, τὴν παρακαταθήκην φύλαξον, ἐκτρεπόμενος τὰς **βεβήλους** κενοφωνίας καὶ ἀντιθέσεις τῆς ψευδωνύμου γνώσεως· [GNS] Ὦ Τιμόθεε, τὴν παραθήκην φύλαξον ἐκτρεπόμενος τὰς **βεβήλους** κενοφωνίας καὶ ἀντιθέσεις τῆς ψευδωνύμου γνώσεως, [GNT]	ing. The description of false teaching is graphic. 1. False teaching is described as worldly and empty chatter. 2. False teaching is described as "arguments of what is falsely called knowledge." The charge is strong, very strong: turn away from men and their teachings when they stand against Christ and the teachings of God's Word; have nothing to do with the false science or false knowledge of men. The men and their false teachings may concern philosophy, psychology, education, sociology, religion—any area of science or knowledge—but turn away from them if they are false. How do you tell if they are false? By the Word of God, the revelation and record of Christ and of the truth of God. If the science or knowledge stands in opposition to the Word of God, turn away from it. The charge is direct and forceful: avoid, shun, keep away from godless and empty talk. What are some examples of talk that is godless and empty? There is such talk as... • false teaching • worldly philosophy • cursing • theological theories • criticism • gossip • off-colored conversations • indecent insinuations • immoral suggestions • suggestive enticements

#4439
Worldly
 	
Worldly–KJV
Worldly–NASB
Worldly–NIV
Worldly–NKJV
Sinful–NLT
 	
POSB REFERENCE (Tit.2:12) Note 2, point 1b
	κοσμικὰς = *kosmikas*
	Pronunciation: [kos-mee-kahs']
	Parsing (part of speech): adjective
	  Case—accusative
	  Gender—feminine
	  Number—plural
	  Stem or root—from **κοσμικός**, ή, όν
	Concordance References:
	⇒ Strong's #2886 kosmikos
	⇒ NIV #3176 kosmikos
	⇒ NASB #2886 kosmikos
	
	Titus 2:12
	Teaching us that, denying ungodliness and **worldly** lusts, we should live soberly, righteously, and godly, in this present world; [KJV]
	Instructing us to deny ungodliness and **worldly** desires and to live sensibly, righteously and godly in the present age, [NASB]
	It teaches us to say "No" to ungodliness and **worldly** passions, and to live self-controlled, upright and godly lives in this present age, [NIV]
	Teaching us that, denying ungodliness and **worldly** lusts, we should live soberly, righteously, and godly, in the present age, [NKJV]
	And we are instructed to turn from godless living and **sinful** pleasures. We should live in this evil world with self-control, right conduct, and devotion to God, [NLT]
	παιδεύουσα ἡμᾶς, ἵνα, ἀρνησάμενοι τὴν ἀσέβειαν καὶ τὰς **κοσμικὰς** ἐπιθυμίας σωφρόνως καὶ δικαίως καὶ εὐσεβῶς ζήσωμεν ἐν τῷ νῦν αἰῶνι, [GNS]
	παιδεύουσα ἡμᾶς, ἵνα ἀρνησάμενοι τὴν ἀσέβειαν καὶ τὰς **κοσμικὰς** ἐπιθυμίας σωφρόνως καὶ δικαίως καὶ εὐσεβῶς ζήσωμεν ἐν τῷ νῦν αἰῶνι, [GNT]
		Worldly, sinful; all the desires of this world that are not fit for heaven and could not be presented to God; all the desires that push us away from God.
		
		Practical Application
		It means all the desires and lusts of the world that stir us...
		• to look when we should not look.
		• to do when we should not do.
		• to get more when we should give more.
		• to be selfish and vicious when we should be sacrificial and kind.
		• to be sensual and immoral when we should be disciplined and pure.
		• to seek the recognition of men when we should seek the recognition of God.

ENGLISH WORD	GREEK WORD AND VERSE	THE WORD MEANS...

#4440
World-Worlds
 	
Worlds–KJV
World–NASB
Universe–NIV
Worlds–NKJV
Universe and every-
thing in it–NLT
 	
**POSB
REFERENCE**
(Heb.1:2)
Note 3
	αἰῶνας = aiönas
	Pronunciation: [ahee-ohn-ahs]
	Parsing (part of speech): noun
	  Case—accusative
	  Gender—masculine
	  Number—plural
	  Stem or root—from αἰών, ῶνος
	Concordance References:
	⇒ Strong's #165 aiön
	⇒ NIV #172 aiön
	⇒ NASB #165 aiön
	
	Hebrews 1:2
	Hath in these last days spoken unto us by his Son, whom he hath appointed heir of all things, by whom also he made the **worlds**; [KJV]
	In these last days has spoken to us in His Son, whom He appointed heir of all things, through whom also He made the **world**. [NASB]
	But in these last days he has spoken to us by his Son, whom he appointed heir of all things, and through whom he made the **universe**. [NIV]
	Has in these last days spoken to us by His Son, whom He has appointed heir of all things, through whom also He made the **worlds**; [NKJV]
	But now in these final days, he has spoken to us through his Son. God promised everything to the Son as an inheritance, and through the Son he made the **universe and everything in it**. [NLT]
	ἐπ' ἐσχάτων τῶν ἡμερῶν τούτων ἐλάλησεν ἡμῖν ἐν υἱῷ, ὃν ἔθηκε κληρονόμον πάντων, δι' οὗ καὶ τοὺς **αἰῶνας** ἐποίησεν, [GNS]
	ἐπ' ἐσχάτου τῶν ἡμερῶν τούτων ἐλάλησεν ἡμῖν ἐν υἱῷ, ὃν ἔθηκεν κληρονόμον πάντων, δι' οὗ καὶ ἐποίησεν τοὺς **αἰῶνας**· [GNT]
		Universe, worlds, the universe and every-thing in it.
		
		Practical Application
		Jesus Christ is the Creator and Maker of the worlds—all of the worlds. This is the third reason why Jesus Christ is superior to the prophets. The word "worlds" (*aiönas*) can also be translated as ages. Jesus Christ is the creator of both the universe and the ages that roll in one upon another, creator of both the worlds and time as it moves forward from event to event, and generation to generation. The *Amplified New Testament* states it well:
		
		He [Christ] created the worlds and the reaches of space and the ages of time [that is], He made, produced, built, operated and arranged them in order (Hebrews 1:2).
		
		Colossians states it even better:
		For by him were all things created, that are in heaven, and that are in earth, visible and invisible, whether they be thrones, or dominions, or principalities, or powers: all things were created by him, and for him (Col. 1:16).
		
		The point is this: the creation of Christ includes all the worlds (plural) of all the dimensions of being, wherever they are and however many there may be. This is exactly what is meant by the plural "worlds." It is also what is meant when Colossians says that Christ created all things "that are in heaven, and in earth, visible and invisible, whether they be thrones, or dimensions, or principalities, or powers."
		⇒ If there are other *visible planets and living beings* in outer space, Christ created them.
		⇒ If there are *invisible worlds and beings* in other dimensions, Christ created them.
		  It does not matter what kind of world or creatures they may be—thrones, dominions, principalities, or powers—Christ created them all. There is nothing in existence that He has not created.

#4441
Worried
 	
Careful–KJV
Worried–NASB
Worried–NIV
Worried–NKJV
Upset–NLT
 	
**POSB
REFERENCE**
(Lk.10:41-42; esp.
v.41)
Note 4, point 2
	μεριμνᾷς = merimnas
	Pronunciation: [mer-im-nahs']
	Parsing (part of speech): verb
	  Mood—indicative
	  Tense—present
	  Voice—active
	  Person—2nd person
	  Number—singular
	  Stem or root—from μεριμνάω
	Concordance References:
	⇒ Strong's #3309 merimnaö
	⇒ NIV #3534 merimnaö
	⇒ NASB #3309 merimnaö
	
	Luke 10:41
	And Jesus answered and said unto her, Martha, Martha, thou art **careful** and troubled about many things: [KJV]
	But the Lord answered and said to her, "Martha, Martha, you are **worried** and bothered about so many things; [NASB]
	"Martha, Martha," the Lord answered, "you are **wor-**
		To worry; to be anxious; to be cautious; to be mindful; to be upset; to be overly concerned and caring (cp. Phil. 4:6).
		
		Practical Application
		It has the idea of being inwardly torn and divided in two, of being distracted from what one's mind and heart and life should be focused upon.

ENGLISH WORD	GREEK WORD AND VERSE	THE WORD MEANS...
	ried and upset about many things, [NIV] And Jesus answered and said to her, "Martha, Martha, you are **worried** and troubled about many things. [NKJV] But the Lord said to her, "My dear Martha, you are so **upset** over all these details! [NLT] ἀποκριθεὶς δὲ εἶπεν αὐτῇ ὁ Ἰησοῦς, Μάρθα Μάρθα, **μεριμνᾷς** καὶ τυρβάζῃ περὶ πολλά· [GNS] ἀποκριθεὶς δὲ εἶπεν αὐτῇ ὁ κύριος, Μάρθα Μάρθα, **μεριμνᾷς** καὶ θορυβάζῃ περὶ πολλά, [GNT]	

#4442
 	
Worries And Cares
 	
Care–KJV
Anxiety–NASB
Anxiety–NIV
Care–NKJV
Worries and cares– NLT
 	
POSB REFERENCE
(1 Pt.5:6-7; esp. v.7)
Note 3, point 3
	μέριμναν = *merimnan*
	Pronunciation: [mer'-im-nahn]
	Parsing (part of speech): noun
	    Case—accusative
	    Gender—feminine
	    Number—singular
	    Stem or root—from μέριμνα, ης
	Concordance References:
	  ⇒ Strong's #3308 merimna
	  ⇒ NIV #3533 merimna
	  ⇒ NASB #3308 merimna
	
	1 Peter 5:7
	Casting all your **care** upon him; for he careth for you. [KJV]
	Casting all your **anxiety** upon Him, because He cares for you. [NASB]
	Cast all your **anxiety** on him because he cares for you. [NIV]
	Casting all your **care** upon Him, for He cares for you. [NKJV]
	Give all your **worries and cares** to God, for he cares about what happens to you. [NLT]
	πᾶσαν τὴν **μέριμναν** ὑμῶν ἐπιρρίψαντες ἐπ' αὐτόν, ὅτι αὐτῷ μέλει περὶ ὑμῶν. [GNS]
	πᾶσαν τὴν **μέριμναν** ὑμῶν ἐπιρίψαντες ἐπ' αὐτόν, ὅτι αὐτῷ μέλει περὶ ὑμῶν. [GNT]
		Anxiety, care, worries, concern, distress, pressure.
		
		Practical Application
		God cares for us; He cares about all our worries and cares. Remember: the believers of Peter's day were suffering terrible persecution. They had been forced to flee for their lives, leaving everything behind: homes, jobs, and possessions. They had only what they could carry by hand, and they fled to whatever places they felt were safe. They were, so to speak, an underground people. They had to live, work, and worship in secret and to find housing and food wherever they could. They never knew when they would be discovered and forced to flee again.
		The point is this: imagine the anxiety, the pressure, tension, and stress being experienced by the believers. Yet there was great help: God was available to help them. Note that the exhortation is not only clearly stated; it is a command: "give all your worries and cares" (*merimna*) upon Him, because He cares for you." God's mighty hand will...
		• save and deliver you
		• look after and care for you
		• strengthen and secure you
		• provide and protect you
		• give you assurance and confidence

#4443
 	
Worry About
 	
Take no thought–KJV
Anxious–NASB
Worry about–NIV
Worry about–NKJV
Worry about–NLT
 	
POSB REFERENCE
(Lk.12:22-34; esp. v.22)
Outline
Introduction
 	
See also POSB REF:
(Mt.6:25)
Note 1
	μεριμνᾶτε = *merimnate*
	Pronunciation: [mer-im-nah'-teh]
	Parsing (part of speech): verb
	    Mood—imperfect
	    Tense—present
	    Voice—active
	    Person—2nd person
	    Number—plural
	    Stem or root—from μεριμνάω
	Concordance References:
	  ⇒ Strong's #3309 merimnaō
	  ⇒ NIV #3534 merimnaō
	  ⇒ NASB #3309 merimnaō
	
	Luke 12:22
	And he said unto his disciples, Therefore I say unto you, **Take no thought** for your life, what ye shall eat; neither for the body, what ye shall put on. [KJV]
	And He said to His disciples, "For this reason I say to you, do not be **anxious** for *your* life, *as to* what you shall eat; nor for your body, *as to* what you shall put on. [NASB]
	Then Jesus said to his disciples: "Therefore I tell you, do not **worry about** your life, what you will eat; or about your body, what you will wear. [NIV]
	Then He said to His disciples, "Therefore I say to you, do not **worry about** your life, what you will eat; nor about the body, what you will put on. [NKJV]
	Then turning to his disciples, Jesus said, "So I tell you, don't **worry about** everyday life—whether you have
		Do not worry; do not be anxious; do not be overly concerned and caring (cp. Phil. 4:6).
		
		Practical Application
		"Do not worry about" your life. Being anxious and overly concerned, is a constant problem among men. It is not to be so among God's people. (See POSB outline—Matthew 6:25-34 and POSB notes—Matthew 6:25-34 for more discussion and application.)

ENGLISH WORD	GREEK WORD AND VERSE	THE WORD MEANS...
	enough food to eat or clothes to wear. [NLT] Εἶπε δὲ πρὸς τοὺς μαθητάς αὐτοῦ, Διὰ τοῦτο ὑμῖν λέγω, μὴ **μεριμνᾶτε** τῇ ψυχῇ ὑμῶν, τί φάγητε· μηδὲ τῷ σώματι, τί ἐνδύσησθε. [GNS] Εἶπεν δὲ πρὸς τοὺς μαθητάς [αὐτοῦ], Διὰ τοῦτο λέγω ὑμῖν· μὴ **μεριμνᾶτε** τῇ ψυχῇ τί φάγητε, μηδὲ τῷ σώματι τί ἐνδύσησθε. [GNT]	

#4444
Worry About
 	
Careful for–KJV
Anxious for–NASB
Anxious about–NIV
Anxious for–NKJV
Worry about–NLT
 	
POSB REFERENCE
(Philip.4:6-7; esp. v.6)
Note 1
	μεριμνᾶτε = merimnate
	Pronunciation: [mer-im-nah'-teh]
	Parsing (part of speech): verb
	    Mood—imperative
	    Tense—present
	    Voice—active
	    Person—2nd person
	    Number—plural
	    Stem or root—from **μεριμνάω**
	Concordance References:
	    ⇒ Strong's #3309 merimnaō
	    ⇒ NIV #3534 merimnaō
	    ⇒ NASB #3309 merimnaō
	
	Philip. 4:6
	Be **careful for** nothing; but in every thing by prayer and supplication with thanksgiving let your requests be made known unto God. [KJV]
	
	Be **anxious for** nothing, but in everything by prayer and supplication with thanksgiving let your requests be made known to God. [NASB]
	
	Do not be **anxious about** anything, but in everything, by prayer and petition, with thanksgiving, present your requests to God. [NIV]
	
	Be **anxious for** nothing, but in everything by prayer and supplication, with thanksgiving, let your requests be made known to God; [NKJV]
	
	Don't **worry about** anything; instead, pray about everything. Tell God what you need, and thank him for all he has done. [NLT]
	
	πᾶσαν τὴν **μέριμναν** ὑμῶν ἐπιρρίψαντες ἐπ' αὐτόν, ὅτι αὐτῷ μέλει περὶ ὑμῶν. [GNS]
	
	μηδὲν **μεριμνᾶτε**, ἀλλ' ἐν παντὶ τῇ προσευχῇ καὶ τῇ δεήσει μετὰ εὐχαριστίας τὰ αἰτήματα ὑμῶν γνωριζέσθω πρὸς τὸν θεόν. [GNT]
		To be anxious about; to be anxious for; to be careful for; to worry about; to be concerned about.
		
		Practical Application
		The idea is that the believer is not to worry or fret about a single thing. The word "anything" (*meden*) means not even one thing. Humanly speaking, the Philippians had every reason to worry and be anxious.
		    ⇒ They were suffering severe persecution (Phil. 1:18-19).
		    ⇒ They were facing a disturbance in the church, some disunity and quarreling (Phil. 1:27, 42).
		    ⇒ They had some carnal members within their fellowship, some members who were prideful, super-spiritual, and self-centered (Phil. 2:3-4; Phil. 3:12).
		    ⇒ They were facing some false teachers who had joined their fellowship, and the teachers were fierce in attacking the cross of Christ (Phil. 3:2-3, 18-19).
		    ⇒ Some of the believers were having to struggle for the necessities of life: food, clothing, and shelter (Phil. 4:19).
		
		There was little else that could confront these dear believers. They were facing about every trial and temptation imaginable, the kind of trouble that arouses anxiety and worry. Humanly, a person is going to fret, worry and suffer anxiety...
		    • when he is either about to lose or lacks food, clothing, or shelter.
		    • when he is persecuted, ridiculed, abused, or threatened.
		    • when he is surrounded by quarrels, disturbance, carnality, or false teaching.
		
		In the midst of such circumstances, the only way a person can keep from worrying is to receive an injection of supernatural power.
		    This is the very point of Scripture. There is an answer to worry and anxiety, a supernatural answer: the peace of God. God will *enable* the believer to conquer worry and anxiety. God will overcome the trials of life for the believer, no matter how terrible and pressuring they may be. God will infuse the believer with peace—with the very peace of God Himself—a peace so great and so wonderful that it carries the believer right through the trial. Of course, this does not mean the believer is not to be concerned about the problems of life. He is, but there is a difference between concern and anxiety or worry. Concern drives us to arise and tackle the problems of life with an indomitable courage and diligence. Concern drives us to tackle and conquer all that we can handle. Anxiety and worry cause all kinds of problems.

ENGLISH WORD	GREEK WORD AND VERSE	THE WORD MEANS...

#4445
Worrying
 	
Cumbered–KJV
Distracted–NASB
Distracted–NIV
Distracted–NKJV
Worrying–NLT
 	
POSB
REFERENCE
(Lk.10:40)
Note 3
	περιεσπᾶτο = periespato
	Pronunciation: [per-ee-spah'-tow]
	Parsing (part of speech): verb
	  Mood—indicative
	  Tense—imperfect
	  Voice—passive
	  Person—3rd person
	  Number—singular
	  Stem or root—from περισπάομαι
	Concordance References:
	⇒ Strong's #4049 perispaō
	⇒ NIV #4352 perispaō
	⇒ NASB #4049 perispaō
	
	Luke 10:40
	But Martha was **cumbered** about much serving, and came to him, and said, Lord, dost thou not care that my sister hath left me to serve alone? bid her therefore that she help me. [KJV]
	But Martha was **distracted** with all her preparations; and she came up to Him, and said, "Lord, do You not care that my sister has left me to do all the serving alone? Then tell her to help me." [NASB]
	But Martha was **distracted** by all the preparations that had to be made. She came to him and asked, "Lord, don't you care that my sister has left me to do the work by myself? Tell her to help me!" [NIV]
	But Martha was **distracted** with much serving, and she approached Him and said, "Lord, do You not care that my sister has left me to serve alone? Therefore tell her to help me." [NKJV]
	But Martha was **worrying** over the big dinner she was preparing. She came to Jesus and said, "Lord, doesn't it seem unfair to you that my sister just sits here while I do all the work? Tell her to come and help me." [NLT]
	ἡ δὲ Μάρθα **περιεσπᾶτο** περὶ πολλὴν διακονίαν· ἐπιστᾶσα δὲ εἶπε, Κύριε, οὐ μέλει σοι ὅτι ἡ ἀδελφή μου μόνην με κατέλιπε διακονεῖν; εἰπὲ οὖν αὐτῇ ἵνα μοι συναντιλάβηται. [GNS]
	ἡ δὲ Μάρθα **περιεσπᾶτο** περὶ πολλὴν διακονίαν· ἐπιστᾶσα δὲ εἶπεν, Κύριε, οὐ μέλει σοι ὅτι ἡ ἀδελφή μου μόνην με κατέλιπεν διακονεῖν; εἰπὲ οὖν αὐτῇ ἵνα μοι συναντιλάβηται. [GNT]
		To be distracted; to worry; to draw around; to twist; to be drawn here and there.
		
		Practical Application
		The idea is that Martha was drawn around and twisted with anxiety and worry. She was distracted, running here and there, being drawn by the cares of this and that person.

#4446
Worship Of Idols
 	
Idolatry–KJV
Idolatry–NASB
Idolatry–NIV
Idolatry–NKJV
Worship of idols–NLT
 	
POSB
REFERENCE
(1 Cor.10:14)
Note 1
 	
See also POSB REF:
(Gal.5:19-21; esp. v.20)
Note 2
	εἰδωλολατρίας = eidōlolatrias
	Pronunciation: [i-do-lol-at-ri'-ahs]
	Parsing (part of speech): noun
	  Case—genitive
	  Gender—feminine
	  Number—singular
	  Stem or root—from εἰδωλολατρία, ας
	Concordance References:
	⇒ Strong's #1495 eidōlolatria
	⇒ NIV #1630 eidōlolatria
	⇒ NASB #1495 eidōlolatria
	
	1 Cor. 10:14
	Wherefore, my dearly beloved, flee from **idolatry**. [KJV]
	Therefore, my beloved, flee from **idolatry**. [NASB]
	Therefore, my dear friends, flee from **idolatry**. [NIV]
	Therefore, my beloved, flee from **idolatry**. [NKJV]
	So, my dear friends, flee from the **worship of idols**. [NLT]
	Διόπερ, ἀγαπητοί μου, φεύγετε ἀπὸ τῆς **εἰδωλολατρίας**. [GNS]
	Διόπερ, ἀγαπητοί μου, φεύγετε ἀπὸ τῆς **εἰδωλολατρίας**. [GNT]
		Both the worship of false gods and the failure to have a right relationship with God. Any person who does not worship God is worshipping some idol, and almost everything upon earth can become an idol and consume the heart and passion of man.
		
		Practical Application
		In practical terms, an idol is anything that consumes a person's mind, heart, soul, and body. An idol is that to which a person gives himself.
		⇒ Some people give themselves and are consumed by some purpose or possession on earth.
		⇒ Other people give themselves and pray to their own idea of god; that is, to the *god* which they imagine in their own mind. (This is actually the worship of most people in industrialized societies.) They have a concept of god and worship that concept. They choose their own concept of god instead of the living and true God revealed by Jesus Christ.
		⇒ Still other people give themselves and pray to some idol, picture, or image which they have made or purchased. (The idol may either rep-

ENGLISH WORD	GREEK WORD AND VERSE	THE WORD MEANS...
		resent some god or be considered the god himself.) From this, one can readily see that most men are idolaters, for most people are consumed by something other than God Himself. They reject the only living and true God, Jehovah Himself who has revealed Himself in Jesus Christ and the Holy Scriptures. (See POSB note—1 Cor. 8:1-13 as background for this passage).
#4447 **Worshiped–** **Worshipped–** **Worshiping** **Worshipped–KJV** Bowed down–NASB Knelt–NIV **Worshiped–NKJV** **Worshiping–NLT** **POSB** **REFERENCE** (Mt.8:2) Note 2, point 2	προσεκύνει = prosekunei Pronunciation: [pros-koo-neh'-ee] Parsing (part of speech): verb Mood—indicative Tense—imperfect Voice—active Person—3rd person Number—singular Stem or root—from προσκυνέω Concordance References: ⇒ Strong's #4352 proskuneö ⇒ NIV #4686 proskuneö ⇒ NASB #4352 proskuneö **Matthew 8:2** And, behold, there came a leper and **worshipped** him, saying, Lord, if thou wilt, thou canst make me clean. [KJV] And behold, a leper came to Him, and **bowed down** to Him, saying, "Lord, if You are willing, You can make me clean." [NASB] A man with leprosy came and **knelt** before him and said, "Lord, if you are willing, you can make me clean." [NIV] And behold, a leper came and **worshiped** Him, saying, "Lord, if You are willing, You can make me clean." [NKJV] Suddenly, a man with leprosy approached Jesus. He knelt before him, **worshiping**. "Lord," the man said, "if you want to, you can make me well again." [NLT] καὶ ἰδού, λεπρὸς ἐλθὼν **προσεκύνει** αὐτῷ λέγων, Κύριε, ἐὰν θέλῃς δύνασαί με καθαρίσαι. [GNS] καὶ ἰδοὺ λεπρὸς προσελθὼν **προσεκύνει** αὐτῷ λέγων, Κύριε, ἐὰν θέλῃς δύνασαί με καθαρίσαι. [GNT]	To worship; to bow down; to reverence; to pay homage. **Practical Application** In this Scripture, it is a bowing down, a genuine worship that is directed to the Lord. The leper demonstrated two significant things by rushing up and worshipping Jesus. ⇒ His desire and willingness to break away from the world and its restrictions. ⇒ His acknowledgment that Jesus was worthy of worship.
#4448 **Worth** Dear–KJV Dear–NASB **Worth–NIV** Dear–NKJV **Worth–NLT** **POSB** **REFERENCE** (Acts 20:24) Note 6, point 1	τιμίαν = timian Pronunciation: [tim'-ee-ahn] Parsing (part of speech): adjective Case—accusative Gender—feminine Number—singular Stem or root—from τίμιος, α, ον Concordance References: ⇒ Strong's #5093 timios ⇒ NIV #5508 timios ⇒ NASB #5093 timios **Acts 20:24** But none of these things move me, neither count I my life **dear** unto myself, so that I might finish my course with joy, and the ministry, which I have received of the Lord Jesus, to testify the gospel of the grace of God. [KJV] "But I do not consider my life of any account as **dear** to myself, in order that I may finish my course, and the ministry which I received from the Lord Jesus, to testify solemnly of the gospel of the grace of God. [NASB] However, I consider my life **worth** nothing to me, if only I may finish the race and complete the task the Lord Jesus has given me—the task of testifying to the gospel of God's grace. [NIV] But none of these things move me; nor do I count my	Precious, dear, costly, of great value, priceless, honored. It means precious and valuable, of extreme worth. **Practical Application** Paul's life was not for himself, not for his own use. His life was the precious and valuable possesion of the Lord.

ENGLISH WORD	GREEK WORD AND VERSE	THE WORD MEANS...

life **dear** to myself, so that I may finish my race with joy, and the ministry which I received from the Lord Jesus, to testify to the gospel of the grace of God. [NKJV]

But my life is **worth** nothing unless I use it for doing the work assigned me by the Lord Jesus—the work of telling others the Good News about God's wonderful kindness and love. [NLT]

ἀλλ' οὐδενὸς λόγου ποιοῦμαι, οὐδὲ ἔχω τὴν ψυχήν μου **τιμίαν** ἐμαυτῷ, ὡς τελειῶσαι τὸν δρόμον μου μετὰ χαρᾶς, καὶ τὴν διακονίαν ἣν ἔλαβον παρὰ τοῦ Κυρίου Ἰησοῦ, διαμαρτύρασθαι τὸ εὐαγγέλιον τῆς χάριτος τοῦ Θεοῦ. [GNS]

ἀλλ' οὐδενὸς λόγου ποιοῦμαι τὴν ψυχὴν **τιμίαν** ἐμαυτῷ ὡς τελειῶσαι τὸν δρόμον μου καὶ τὴν διακονίαν ἣν ἔλαβον παρὰ τοῦ κυρίου Ἰησοῦ, διαμαρτύρασθαι τὸ εὐαγγέλιον τῆς χάριτος τοῦ θεοῦ. [GNT]

#4449

Worthless

Vain–KJV
Worthless–NASB
Futile–NIV
Futile–NKJV
Useless–NLT

POSB REFERENCE
(1 Cor.15:16-19; esp. v.17)
Note 3, point 2

ματαία = *mataia*
Pronunciation: [mat'-ah-ee-ah]
Parsing (part of speech): adjective
    Case—nominative
    Gender—feminine
    Number—singular
    Stem or root—from μάταιος, α, ον
Concordance References:
  ⇒ Strong's #3152 mataios
  ⇒ NIV #3469 mataios
  ⇒ NASB #3152 mataios

1 Cor. 15:17

And if Christ be not raised, your faith is **vain**; ye are yet in your sins. [KJV]

And if Christ has not been raised, your faith is **worthless**; you are still in your sins. [NASB]

And if Christ has not been raised, your faith is **futile**; you are still in your sins. [NIV]

And if Christ is not risen, your faith *is* **futile**; you are still in your sins! [NKJV]

And if Christ has not been raised, then your faith is **useless**, and you are still under condemnation for your sins. [NLT]

εἰ δὲ Χριστὸς οὐκ ἐγήγερται, **ματαία** ἡ πίστις ὑμῶν· ἔτι ἐστὲ ἐν ταῖς ἁμαρτίαις ὑμῶν. [GNS]

εἰ δὲ Χριστὸς οὐκ ἐγήγερται, **ματαία** ἡ πίστις ὑμῶν, ἔτι ἐστὲ ἐν ταῖς ἁμαρτίαις ὑμῶν, [GNT]

Fruitless or futile; that is, we are still in our sins; worthless; useless.

Practical Application

To deny the resurrection (either of Christ or of us) means that our faith is worthless (*mataia*). If Jesus Christ has not risen from the dead, then He is still dead, still in the grave; therefore, there is no redemption, no forgiveness of sins.

#4450

Worthy

Worthy–KJV
Worthy–NASB
Worthy–NIV
Worthy–NKJV
Always honor–NLT

POSB REFERENCE
(Col.1:10)
Note 2

ἀξίως = *axiōs*
Pronunciation: [ax-ee'-oce]
Parsing (part of speech): adjective
    Type—adverb
    Stem or root—from ἀξίως
Concordance References:
  ⇒ Strong's #516 axiōs
  ⇒ NIV #547 axiōs
  ⇒ NASB #516 axiōs

Col. 1:10

That ye might walk **worthy** of the Lord unto all pleasing, being fruitful in every good work, and increasing in the knowledge of God; [KJV]

So that you may walk in a manner **worthy** of the Lord, to please Him in all respects, bearing fruit in every good work and increasing in the knowledge of God; [NASB]

And we pray this in order that you may live a life **worthy** of the Lord and may please him in every way: bearing fruit in every good work, growing in the knowledge of God, [NIV]

That you may walk **worthy** of the Lord, fully pleasing Him, being fruitful in every good work and increasing in the knowledge of God; [NKJV]

Then the way you live will **always honor** and please

Worthy; in a manner worthy of; to always honor.

Practical Application

Knowing the will of God is of no value until we have committed our lives to do it. The word "worthy" (*axios*) means to have the weight of something else or to weigh as much as something else (Kenneth Wuest, *Ephesians and Colossians,* Vol.1, p.176).

This means an amazing thing: our walk is to weigh as much as the walk of Christ. Our conduct is to conform to the will of God as much as the conduct of Christ. We are to live a life just as worthy as the life of Christ. The will of God is to control our behavior as much as it did the behavior of Christ.

ENGLISH WORD	GREEK WORD AND VERSE	THE WORD MEANS...
	the Lord, and you will continually do good, kind things for others. All the while, you will learn to know God better and better. [NLT] περιπατῆσαι ὑμᾶς **ἀξίως** τοῦ Κυρίου εἰς πᾶσαν ἀρεσκείαν, ἐν παντὶ ἔργῳ ἀγαθῷ καρποφοροῦντες καὶ αὐξανόμενοι εἰς τὴν ἐπιγνώσιν τοῦ Θεοῦ· [GNS] περιπατῆσαι **ἀξίως** τοῦ κυρίου εἰς πᾶσαν ἀρεσκείαν, ἐν παντὶ ἔργῳ ἀγαθῷ καρποφοροῦντες καὶ αὐξανόμενοι τῇ ἐπιγνώσει τοῦ θεοῦ, [GNT]	

#4451
Worthy Of Praise
 	
Praise–KJV
Worthy of praise–NASB
Praiseworthy–NIV
Praiseworthy–NKJV
Worthy of praise–NLT
 	
POSB REFERENCE
(Philip.4:8-9; esp. v.8)
Note 2, point 1g
	ἔπαινος = epainos
	Pronunciation: [ep'-ahee-nos]
	Parsing (part of speech): noun
	  Case—nominative
	  Gender—masculine
	  Number—singular
	  Stem or root—from **ἔπαινος**, ου
	Concordance References:
	  ⇒ Strong's #1868 epainos
	  ⇒ NIV #2047 epainos
	  ⇒ NASB #1868 epainos
	
	Philip. 4:8
	Finally, brethren, whatsoever things are true, whatsoever things are honest, whatsoever things are just, whatsoever things are pure, whatsoever things are lovely, whatsoever things are of good report; if there be any virtue, and if there be any **praise**, think on these things. [KJV]
	Finally, brethren, whatever is true, whatever is honorable, whatever is right, whatever is pure, whatever is lovely, whatever is of good repute, if there is any excellence and if anything **worthy of praise**, let your mind dwell on these things. [NASB]
	Finally, brothers, whatever is true, whatever is noble, whatever is right, whatever is pure, whatever is lovely, whatever is admirable—if anything is excellent or **praiseworthy**—think about such things. [NIV]
	Finally, brethren, whatever things are true, whatever things *are* noble, whatever things *are* just, whatever things *are* pure, whatever things *are* lovely, whatever things *are* of good report, if *there is* any virtue and if *there is* anything **praiseworthy**—meditate on these things. [NKJV]
	And now, dear brothers and sisters, let me say one more thing as I close this letter. Fix your thoughts on what is true and honorable and right. Think about things that are pure and lovely and admirable. Think about things that are excellent and **worthy of praise**. [NLT]
	
	Τὸ λοιπόν, ἀδελφοί, ὅσα ἐστὶν ἀληθῆ, ὅσα σεμνά, ὅσα δίκαια, ὅσα ἁγνά, ὅσα προσφιλῆ, ὅσα εὔφημα, εἴ τις ἀρετὴ καὶ εἴ τις **ἔπαινος**, ταῦτα λογίζεσθε· [GNS]
	Τὸ λοιπόν, ἀδελφοί, ὅσα ἐστὶν ἀληθῆ, ὅσα σεμνά, ὅσα δίκαια, ὅσα ἁγνά, ὅσα προσφιλῆ, ὅσα εὔφημα, εἴ τις ἀρετὴ καὶ εἴ τις **ἔπαινος**, ταῦτα λογίζεσθε· [GNT]
		Praiseworthy, commendation, applause, acclaim, approval, endorsement, worthy of praise.
		
		Practical Application
		The truth is:
		⇒ what we think is what we become.
		⇒ where we have kept our minds is where we are.
		⇒ our thoughts shape our behavior.
		⇒ what we do is what we think.
		
		William Barclay says, *"...it is a law of life that, if a man thinks of something often enough and long enough, he will come to the stage when he cannot stop thinking about it. His thoughts will be quite literally in a groove out of which he cannot jerk them"* (*The Letters to the Philippians, Colossians, and Thessalonians*, p.97).
		
		Thus the charge: "If there is any *excellence and worthy praise*—think about such things." Positive thinking is the answer to peace for the Christian believer.

#4452
Worthy Of Respect
 	
Grave–KJV
Dignity–NASB
Worthy of respect–NIV
Reverent–NKJV
Respected–NLT
 	
POSB REFERENCE
(1 Tim.3:8)
Note 1, point 1
	σεμνούς = semnous
	Pronunciation: [sem-noos']
	Parsing (part of speech): adjective
	  Case—accusative
	  Gender—masculine
	  Number—plural
	  Stem or root—from **σεμνός**, ή, όν
	Concordance References:
	  ⇒ Strong's #4586 semnos
	  ⇒ NIV #4948 semnos
	  ⇒ NASB #4586 semnos
	
	1 Tim. 3:8
	Likewise must the deacons be **grave**, not double-tongued, not given to much wine, not greedy of filthy lucre; [KJV]
	Deacons likewise must be men of **dignity**, not dou-
		Worthy of respect, grave, dignity, highly respected, serious, honorable, worthy, revered, noble.
		
		Practical Application
		It is being serious-minded, the very opposite...
		• of being flippant.
		• of dishonoring oneself.
		• of being shallow by being over talkative.
		• of having little respect because one is not grave or serious enough.
		• of having a surface religion only.
		
		However, this does not mean that the deacon

ENGLISH WORD	GREEK WORD AND VERSE	THE WORD MEANS...

See also POSB REF:
(1 Tim.3:8)
  Note 1, point 1
(Tit.2:2)
  Note 2
	ble-tongued, or addicted to much wine or fond of sordid gain, [NASB]
	
	  Deacons, likewise, are to be men **worthy of respect**, sincere, not indulging in much wine, and not pursuing dishonest gain. [NIV]
	
	  Likewise deacons must be **reverent**, not double-tongued, not given to much wine, not greedy for money, [NKJV]
	
	  In the same way, deacons must be people who are **respected** and have integrity. They must not be heavy drinkers and must not be greedy for money. [NLT]
	
	  διακόνους ὡσαύτως **σεμνούς**, μὴ διλόγους, μὴ οἴνῳ πολλῷ προσέχοντας, μὴ αἰσχροκερδεῖς, [GNS]
	
	  Διακόνους ὡσαύτως **σεμνούς**, μὴ διλόγους, μὴ οἴνῳ πολλῷ προσέχοντας, μὴ αἰσχροκερδεῖς, [GNT]
		is to walk around with a long face, never smiling, joking, or having fun. It simply means that he is to be serious-minded and committed to Christ and to the mission of the church: the mission of reaching the lost and meeting the desperate needs of the world.

#4453
Worthy, Be
 	
Becometh–KJV
In a manner worthy–NASB
In a manner worthy–NIV
Be worthy–NKJV
In a manner worthy–NLT
 	
POSB REFERENCE
(Philip.1:27)
Note 2
	ἀξίως = axiōs
	Pronunciation: [ax-ee'-oce]
	Parsing (part of speech): adjective adverb
	  Stem or root—from ἀξίως
	Concordance References:
	  ⇒ Strong's #516 axiōs
	  ⇒ NIV #547 axiōs
	  ⇒ NASB #516 axiōs
	
	Philip. 1:27
	  Only let your conversation be as it **becometh** the gospel of Christ: that whether I come and see you, or else be absent, I may hear of your affairs, that ye stand fast in one spirit, with one mind striving together for the faith of the gospel; [KJV]
	  Only conduct yourselves **in a manner worthy** of the gospel of Christ; so that whether I come and see you or remain absent, I may hear of you that you are standing firm in one spirit, with one mind striving together for the faith of the gospel; [NASB]
	  Whatever happens, conduct yourselves **in a manner worthy** of the gospel of Christ. Then, whether I come and see you or only hear about you in my absence, I will know that you stand firm in one spirit, contending as one man for the faith of the gospel [NIV]
	  Only let your conduct **be worthy** of the gospel of Christ, so that whether I come and see you or am absent, I may hear of your affairs, that you stand fast in one spirit, with one mind striving together for the faith of the gospel, [NKJV]
	  But whatever happens to me, you must live **in a manner worthy** of the Good News about Christ, as citizens of heaven. Then, whether I come and see you again or only hear about you, I will know that you are standing side by side, fighting together for the Good News. [NLT]
	  μόνον **ἀξίως** τοῦ εὐαγγελίου τοῦ Χριστοῦ πολιτεύεσθε, ἵνα εἴτε ἐλθὼν καὶ ἰδὼν ὑμᾶς, εἴτε ἀπών, ἀκούσω τὰ περὶ ὑμῶν, ὅτι στήκετε ἐν ἑνὶ πνεύματι, μιᾷ ψυχῇ συναθλοῦντες τῇ πίστει τοῦ εὐαγγελίου, [GNS]
	  Μόνον **ἀξίως** τοῦ εὐαγγελίου τοῦ Χριστοῦ πολιτεύεσθε, ἵνα εἴτε ἐλθὼν καὶ ἰδὼν ὑμᾶς εἴτε ἀπὼν ἀκούω τὰ περὶ ὑμῶν, ὅτι στήκετε ἐν ἑνὶ πνεύματι, μιᾷ ψυχῇ συναθλοῦντες τῇ πίστει τοῦ εὐαγγελίου [GNT]
		To fit; to be suitable; to correspond; to be worthy.
		
		Practical Application
		The believer's behavior is to...
		• fit the gospel he professes.
		• correspond to the gospel he professes.
		• be suitable to the gospel he professes.
		• be worthy of the gospel he professes.
		
		No church and no believer within the church is to bring dishonor to the gospel. If a person professes the gospel, he is to live worthy of the gospel. His conduct and behavior is to fit and correspond to the gospel he professes.

#4454
Worthy, In A Manner
 	
Becometh–KJV
In a manner worthy–NASB
In a manner worthy–NIV
Be worthy –NKJV
In a manner worthy–NLT
	ἀξίως = axiōs
	Pronunciation: [ax-ee'-oce]
	Parsing (part of speech): adjective adverb
	  Stem or root—from ἀξίως
	Concordance References:
	  ⇒ Strong's #516 axiōs
	  ⇒ NIV #547 axiōs
	  ⇒ NASB #516 axiōs
	
	Philip. 1:27
	  Only let your conversation be as it **becometh** the gospel of Christ: that whether I come and see you, or else be absent, I may hear of your affairs, that ye stand fast in
		In a manner worthy; to fit, correspond, be suitable; to be worthy.
		
		Practical Application
		The believer's behavior is to...
		• fit the gospel he professes.
		• correspond to the gospel he professes.
		• be suitable to the gospel he professes.
		• be worthy of the gospel he professes.
		
		No church and no believer within the church is to bring dishonor to the gospel. If a person

ENGLISH WORD	GREEK WORD AND VERSE	THE WORD MEANS...
POSB REFERENCE (Philip.1:27) Note 2	one spirit, with one mind striving together for the faith of the gospel; [KJV] Only conduct yourselves **in a manner worthy** of the gospel of Christ; so that whether I come and see you or remain absent, I may hear of you that you are standing firm in one spirit, with one mind striving together for the faith of the gospel; [NASB] Whatever happens, conduct yourselves **in a manner worthy** of the gospel of Christ. Then, whether I come and see you or only hear about you in my absence, I will know that you stand firm in one spirit, contending as one man for the faith of the gospel [NIV] Only let your conduct **be worthy** of the gospel of Christ, so that whether I come and see you or am absent, I may hear of your affairs, that you stand fast in one spirit, with one mind striving together for the faith of the gospel, [NKJV] But whatever happens to me, you must live **in a manner worthy** of the Good News about Christ, as citizens of heaven. Then, whether I come and see you again or only hear about you, I will know that you are standing side by side, fighting together for the Good News. [NLT] μόνον **ἀξίως** τοῦ εὐαγγελίου τοῦ Χριστοῦ πολιτεύεσθε, ἵνα εἴτε ἐλθὼν καὶ ἰδὼν ὑμᾶς, εἴτε ἀπών, ἀκούσω τὰ περὶ ὑμῶν, ὅτι στήκετε ἐν ἑνὶ πνεύματι, μιᾷ ψυχῇ συναθλοῦντες τῇ πίστει τοῦ εὐαγγελίου, [GNS] Μόνον **ἀξίως** τοῦ εὐαγγελίου τοῦ Χριστοῦ πολιτεύεσθε, ἵνα εἴτε ἐλθὼν καὶ ἰδὼν ὑμᾶς εἴτε ἀπὼν ἀκούω τὰ περὶ ὑμῶν, ὅτι στήκετε ἐν ἑνὶ πνεύματι, μιᾷ ψυχῇ συναθλοῦντες τῇ πίστει τοῦ εὐαγγελίου [GNT]	professes the gospel, he is to live worthy of the gospel. His conduct and behavior is to fit and correspond to the gospel he professes.

#4455
Would
 	
Will–KJV
Wishes–NASB
Would–NIV
Desires–NKJV
Wants–NLT
 	
POSB REFERENCE (Mt.16:24) Note 2, point 1
	θέλει = thelë
	Pronunciation: [thel'-ee]
	Parsing (part of speech): verb
	   Mood—indicative
	   Tense—present
	   Voice—active
	   Person—3rd person
	   Number—singular
	   Stem or root—from θέλω
	Concordance References:
	  ⇒ Strong's #2309 thelo
	  ⇒ NIV #2527 thelö
	  ⇒ NASB #2309 thelo
	
	Matthew 16:24
	Then said Jesus unto his disciples, If any man **will** come after me, let him deny himself, and take up his cross, and follow me. [KJV]
	
	Then Jesus said to His disciples, "If anyone **wishes** to come after Me, let him deny himself, and take up his cross, and follow Me. [NASB]
	
	Then Jesus said to his disciples, "If anyone **would** come after me, he must deny himself and take up his cross and follow me. [NIV]
	
	Then Jesus said to His disciples, "If anyone **desires** to come after Me, let him deny himself, and take up his cross, and follow Me. [NKJV]
	
	Then Jesus said to the disciples, "If any of you **wants** to be my follower, you must put aside your selfish ambition, shoulder your cross, and follow me. [NLT]
	
	τότε ὁ Ἰησοῦς εἶπε τοῖς μαθηταῖς αὐτοῦ, Εἴ τις **θέλει** ὀπίσω μου ἐλθεῖν, ἀπαρνησάσθω ἑαυτὸν, καὶ ἀράτω τὸν σταυρὸν αὐτοῦ καὶ ἀκολουθείτω μοι. [GNS]
	
	Τότε ὁ Ἰησοῦς εἶπεν τοῖς μαθηταῖς αὐτοῦ, Εἴ τις **θέλει** ὀπίσω μου ἐλθεῖν, ἀπαρνησάσθω ἑαυτὸν καὶ ἀράτω τὸν σταυρὸν αὐτοῦ καὶ ἀκολουθείτω μοι. [GNT]
		To desire, wish, design, purpose, resolve, determine.
		
		Practical Application
		It is a deliberate willingness, a deliberate choice, a determined resolve to follow Christ.
		
		If a person really wills and deliberately chooses to follow Christ, then he has to do the three things mentioned. Note: the choice is voluntary; it is made by the person.

#4456
Wrapped Together
	ἐντετυλιγμένον = entetuligmenon
	Pronunciation: [en-teh-too-lig-meh'n-on]
	Parsing (part of speech): verb
	   Mood—participle
	   Tense—perfect
		Folded up, wrapped together, rolled up.
		
		Practical Application
		The Greek word "wrapped together" (ente-

ENGLISH WORD	GREEK WORD AND VERSE	THE WORD MEANS...
Wrapped together– KJV Rolled up–NASB Folded up–NIV Folded together– NKJV Folded up–NLT **POSB REFERENCE** (Jn.20:7-10; esp. v.7) Note 3, point 1	Voice—passive Case—accusative Gender—neuter Number—singular Stem or root—from ἐντυλίσσω Concordance References: ⇒ Strong's #1794 entulisso ⇒ NIV #1962 entulisso ⇒ NASB #1794 entulisso **John 20:7** And the napkin, that was about his head, not lying with the linen clothes, but **wrapped together** in a place by itself. [KJV] And the face-cloth, which had been on His head, not lying with the linen wrappings, but **rolled up** in a place by itself. [NASB] As well as the burial cloth that had been around Jesus' head. The cloth was **folded up** by itself, separate from the linen. [NIV] And the handkerchief that had been around His head, not lying with the linen cloths, but **folded together** in a place by itself. [NKJV] while the cloth that had covered Jesus' head was **folded up** and lying to the side. [NLT] καὶ τὸ σουδάριον, ὃ ἦν ἐπὶ τῆς κεφαλῆς αὐτοῦ, οὐ μετὰ τῶν ὀθονίων κείμενον, ἀλλὰ χωρὶς **ἐντετυλιγμένον** εἰς ἕνα τόπον. [GNS] καὶ τὸ σουδάριον, ὃ ἦν ἐπὶ τῆς κεφαλῆς αὐτοῦ, οὐ μετὰ τῶν ὀθονίων κείμενον ἀλλὰ χωρὶς **ἐντετυλιγμένον** εἰς ἕνα τόπον. [GNT]	*tuligmenon*) is the verb which is used for actually winding the linens around a body for burial. The Greek word is saying that the linens were "still in their fold," wrapped just like they would be wrapped around a body—as if the body had just evaporated. They were not disheveled or disarranged. This says at least four things. 1. It would be impossible to extract a body from its wrappings and leave them in such good order. 2. The wrappings would have been taken with the body if the body had been removed. 3. The wrappings would have been disheveled and disarranged and scattered if thieves had ransacked the tomb. 4. The wrappings (under any circumstances that might be conceived in removing the body) could never be placed in the exact spot on the rock slab where the body lay. Yet, this is just how they were lying according to the Greek text. It was this that led John to an immediate belief.
#4457 Wrath Wrath–KJV Wrath–NASB Wrath–NIV Wrath–NKJV Wrath–NLT **POSB REFERENCE** (Jn.3:36) *Deeper Study #5*	ὀργή = *orgë* Pronunciation: [or-gay'] Parsing (part of speech): noun Case—nominative Gender—feminine Number—singular Stem or root—from ὀργή, ῆς Concordance References: ⇒ Strong's #3709 orgë ⇒ NIV #3973 orgë ⇒ NASB #3709 orgë **John 3:36** He that believeth on the Son hath everlasting life: and he that believeth not the Son shall not see life; but the **wrath** of God abideth on him. [KJV] "He who believes in the Son has eternal life; but he who does not obey the Son shall not see life, but the **wrath** of God abides on him." [NASB] Whoever believes in the Son has eternal life, but whoever rejects the Son will not see life, for God's **wrath** remains on him." [NIV] He who believes in the Son has everlasting life; and he who does not believe the Son shall not see life, but the **wrath** of God abides on him." [NKJV] And all who believe in God's Son have eternal life. Those who don't obey the Son will never experience eternal life, but the **wrath** of God remains upon them." [NLT] ὁ πιστεύων εἰς τὸν υἱὸν ἔχει ζωὴν αἰώνιον· ὁ δὲ ἀπειθῶν τῷ υἱῷ, οὐκ ὄψεται ζωήν, ἀλλ' ἡ **ὀργὴ** τοῦ Θεοῦ μένει ἐπ' αὐτόν. [GNS] ὁ πιστεύων εἰς τὸν υἱὸν ἔχει ζωὴν αἰώνιον· ὁ δὲ ἀπειθῶν τῷ υἱῷ οὐκ ὄψεται ζωήν, ἀλλ' ἡ **ὀργὴ** τοῦ Θεοῦ μένει ἐπ' αὐτόν. [GNT]	Anger, temper, wrath, indignation. It is not an uncontrolled, unthinking, violent reaction. It is deep, permanent, settled, thoughtful, controlled anger and temper. **Practical Application** The wrath or anger of God is aroused for four reasons. 1. People do not believe on the Son of God. They allow their hearts to become hardened and impenitent (Romans 2:5). They spurn and wound God's love—rejecting, abusing, cursing and denying His Son, the dearest thing to His heart (John 3:36; 2 Thes. 1:7-9. See POSB note—John 3:18-20; POSB note—John 3:35-36.) 2. People reject God's mercy, which is ever attempting to reach out to save them (Romans 2:3-6). 3. People transgress God's law (Romans 1:18f; Col. 3:6). 4. People sin and come short of God's will, violating His holiness (Ephes. 5:6). God's wrath is real and active. God is holy, righteous, and pure as well as loving, gracious, and merciful. He executes justice as well as love. He shows wrath and anger as well as compassion. His wrath is both present and future. 1. God's wrath is present and active in this life. His wrath abides upon men now. His wrath is manifested against all ungodliness and unrighteousness of men (Romans 1:18). God punishes sin in this life by giving people up... • to uncleanness. • to vile affections. • to reprobate minds. 2. God's wrath is future, and it is to be actively

ENGLISH WORD	GREEK WORD AND VERSE	THE WORD MEANS...
		executed in the next life (see POSB *Deeper Study* #2—Matthew 5:22; POSB *Deeper Study* #4—Luke 16:24; POSB *Deeper Study* #1—Hebrews 9:27). God will punish sin by giving men up... • to eternal fire (Matthew 25:41; Matthew 25:46). • to hell (Matthew 5:22). • to outer darkness (Matthew 8:12). • to weeping and gnashing of teeth (Matthew 8:12). • to the Lake of Fire (Rev. 20:15). 3. God's wrath will be especially revealed or manifested and active in the last days (cp. Rev. 6:16; Rev. 11:8; Rev. 14:10; Rev. 16:19; Rev. 19:15). There is another Greek word which also means wrath (*thumos*), and it is also used of God's wrath. *Thumos* is anger that arises more quickly, blazes forth, and just as quickly cools down. It is an anger that is more turbulent, more sudden, but the agitation lasts for only a short period of time. This simply means that God does not dodge His responsibility to execute justice and to punish injustice and sin (cp. Romans 1:22).

#4458
Wrath
 	
Indignation–KJV
Wrath–NASB
Wrath–NIV
Indignation–NKJV
Wrath–NLT
 	
POSB REFERENCE
(Romans 2:8)
Deeper Study #6
	ὀργὴ = *orgē*
	Pronunciation: [or-gay']
	Parsing (part of speech): noun
	    Case—nominative
	    Gender—feminine
	    Number—singular
	    Stem or root—from ὀργή, ῆς
	Concordance References:
	  ⇒ Strong's #3709 orgē
	  ⇒ NIV #3973 orgē
	  ⇒ NASB #3709 orgē
	
	Romans 2:8
	But unto them that are contentious, and do not obey the truth, but obey unrighteousness, **indignation** and wrath, [KJV]
	But to those who are selfishly ambitious and do not obey the truth, but obey unrighteousness, **wrath** and indignation. [NASB]
	But for those who are self-seeking and who reject the truth and follow evil, there will be **wrath** and anger. [NIV]
	But to those who are self-seeking and do not obey the truth, but obey unrighteousness—**indignation** and wrath, [NKJV]
	But he will pour out his anger and **wrath** on those who live for themselves, who refuse to obey the truth and practice evil deeds. [NLT]
	τοῖς δὲ ἐξ ἐριθείας, καὶ ἀπειθοῦσι μὲν τῇ ἀληθείᾳ πειθομένοις δὲ τῇ ἀδικίᾳ, θυμός καὶ **ὀργὴ**, [GNS]
	τοῖς δὲ ἐξ ἐριθείας καὶ ἀπειθοῦσι τῇ ἀληθείᾳ πειθομένοις δὲ τῇ ἀδικίᾳ **ὀργὴ** καὶ θυμός. [GNT]
		Wrath, anger; retribution, punishment; revenge. Wrath (*orgē*) means God's anger against sin. (See POSB *Deeper Study* #1, God's Wrath—Romans 1:18 for discussion).
		
		Practical Application
		    It is anger, not an agitated outburst of violence. It is not the anger that quickly blazes up and just as quickly fades away, not the anger that arises solely from emotion. Rather, it is decisive anger. It is an anger that has arisen from a thoughtful decision, an anger that arises from the mind much more than from the emotions. When used of God, it is always an anger that is *righteous and just and good*. It is an anger that stands against the sin and evil, violence and slaughter, immorality and injustices of men. It is an anger that abhors and hates sin and evil and that dishes out a just revenge and equal justice. However, it is an anger that is *deeply felt*; in fact, it must be felt, for evil and corruption must be opposed and erased from the face of the earth if there is to be a "new heavens and a new earth." And God has promised a new heavens and a new earth where righteousness and perfection dwell forever.

#4459
Wrath
 	
Wrath–KJV
Indignation–NASB
Anger–NIV
Wrath–NKJV
Anger–NLT
	θυμός = *thumos*
	Pronunciation: [thoo-mos']
	Parsing (part of speech): noun
	    Case—nominative
	    Gender—masculine
	    Number—singular
	    Stem or root—from θυμός, ου
	Concordance References:
	  ⇒ Strong's #2372 thumos
	  ⇒ NIV #2596 thumos
	  ⇒ NASB #2372 thumos
		Anger, wrath, fury, indignation, rage. It means God's wrath against sin.
		
		Practical Application
		    Thumos is an anger that is felt more deeply than the *orge* anger of God; therefore, it arises more quickly. *Thumos* anger is the anger that arises out of deep hurt; therefore, it bursts forth with terrifying judgment. (See POSB *Deeper Study* #1, God's Wrath—Romans 1:18 for verses.)

ENGLISH WORD	GREEK WORD AND VERSE	THE WORD MEANS...
POSB REFERENCE (Romans 2:8) *Deeper Study #7*	**Romans 2:8** But unto them that are contentious, and do not obey the truth, but obey unrighteousness, indignation and **wrath**, [KJV] But to those who are selfishly ambitious and do not obey the truth, but obey unrighteousness, wrath and **indignation**. [NASB] But for those who are self-seeking and who reject the truth and follow evil, there will be wrath and **anger**. [NIV] But to those who are self-seeking and do not obey the truth, but obey unrighteousness—indignation and **wrath**, [NKJV] But he will pour out his **anger** and wrath on those who live for themselves, who refuse to obey the truth and practice evil deeds. [NLT] τοῖς δὲ ἐξ ἐριθείας, καὶ ἀπειθοῦσι μὲν τῇ ἀληθείᾳ πειθομένοις δὲ τῇ ἀδικίᾳ, **θυμός** καὶ ὀργή, [GNS] τοῖς δὲ ἐξ ἐριθείας καὶ ἀπειθοῦσι τῇ ἀληθείᾳ πειθομένοις δὲ τῇ ἀδικίᾳ ὀργὴ καὶ **θυμός**. [GNT]	
#4460 **Wrath** **Wrath–KJV** Outbursts of anger– NASB Fits of rage–NIV Outbursts of wrath– NKJV Outbursts of anger– NLT **POSB REFERENCE** (Gal.5:19-21; esp. v.20) Note 2	**θυμοί** = *thumoi* Pronunciation: [thoo-moy'] Parsing (part of speech): noun Case—nominative Gender—masculine Number—plural Stem or root—from θυμός, ου Concordance References: ⇒ Strong's #2372 thumos ⇒ NIV #2596 thumos ⇒ NASB #2372 thumos **Galatians 5:20** Idolatry, witchcraft, hatred, variance, emulations, **wrath**, strife, seditions, heresies, [KJV] Idolatry, sorcery, enmities, strife, jealousy, **outbursts of anger**, disputes, dissensions, factions, [NASB] Idolatry and witchcraft; hatred, discord, jealousy, **fits of rage**, selfish ambition, dissensions, factions [NIV] Idolatry, sorcery, hatred, contentions, jealousies, **outbursts of wrath**, selfish ambitions, dissensions, heresies, [NKJV] Idolatry, participation in demonic activities, hostility, quarreling, jealousy, **outbursts of anger**, selfish ambition, divisions, the feeling that everyone is wrong except those in your own little group, [NLT] εἰδωλολατρία, φαρμακεία, ἔχθραι, ἔρεις, ζῆλοι, **θυμοί**, ἐριθείαι, διχοστασίαι, αἱρέσεις, [GNS] εἰδωλολατρία, φαρμακεία, ἔχθραι, ἔρις, ζῆλος, **θυμοί**, ἐριθείαι, διχοστασίαι, αἱρέσεις, [GNT]	Fits of rage; outbursts of anger; wrath; an intense feeling of indignation. **Practical Application** It is a violent, explosive temper; quick-tempered explosive reactions that arise from stirred and boiling emotions. But it is anger which fades away just as quickly as it arose. It is not anger that lasts.
#4461 **Wrath** **Wrath–KJV** **Wrath–NASB** Rage–NIV **Wrath–NKJV** Rage–NLT **POSB REFERENCE** (Eph.4:31) Note 6, point 2 **See also POSB REF:** (Col.3:8-11; esp. v.8) Note 2, point 1b	**θυμός** = *thumos* Pronunciation: [thoo-mos'] Parsing (part of speech): noun Case—nominative Gender—masculine Number—singular Stem or root—from θυμός, ου Concordance References: ⇒ Strong's #2372 thumos ⇒ NIV #2596 thumos ⇒ NASB #2372 thumos **Ephes. 4:31** Let all bitterness, and **wrath**, and anger, and clamour, and evil speaking, be put away from you, with all malice: [KJV] Let all bitterness and **wrath** and anger and clamor and slander be put away from you, along with all malice. [NASB] Get rid of all bitterness, **rage** and anger, brawling and slander, along with every form of malice. [NIV]	Rage, wrath, intense anger. **Practical Application** This kind of wrath (*thumos*) is bursts of anger. It is indignation, a violent, explosive temper. It is being quick-tempered, having explosive reactions that arise from stirred and boiling emotions. But it is anger which fades away just as quickly as it arose. It is not anger that lasts.

ENGLISH WORD	GREEK WORD AND VERSE	THE WORD MEANS...
	Let all bitterness, **wrath**, anger, clamor, and evil speaking be put away from you, with all malice. [NKJV] Get rid of all bitterness, **rage**, anger, harsh words, and slander, as well as all types of malicious behavior. [NLT] πᾶσα πικρία καὶ **θυμὸς** καὶ ὀργὴ καὶ κραυγὴ καὶ βλασφημία ἀρθήτω ἀφ' ὑμῶν, σὺν πάσῃ κακίᾳ· [GNS] πᾶσα πικρία καὶ **θυμὸς** καὶ ὀργὴ καὶ κραυγὴ καὶ βλασφημία ἀρθήτω ἀφ' ὑμῶν σὺν πάσῃ κακίᾳ. [GNT]	
#4462 **Wrath** Wrath–KJV Wrath–NASB Wrath–NIV Wrath–NKJV Terrible anger–NLT **POSB REFERENCE** (Col.3:5-7; esp. v.6) Note 1, point 2	**ὀργὴ** = orgë Pronunciation: [or-gay'] Parsing (part of speech): noun 　　Case—nominative 　　Gender—feminine 　　Number—singular 　　Stem or root—from ὀργή, ῆς Concordance References: ⇒　Strong's #3709 orgë ⇒　NIV #3973 orgë ⇒　NASB #3709 orgë **Col. 3:6** For which things' sake the **wrath** of God cometh on the children of disobedience: [KJV] For it is on account of these things that the **wrath** of God will come, [NASB] Because of these, the **wrath** of God is coming. [NIV] Because of these things the **wrath** of God is coming upon the sons of disobedience, [NKJV] God's **terrible anger** will come upon those who do such things. [NLT] δι' ἃ ἔρχεται ἡ **ὀργὴ** τοῦ Θεοῦ ἐπὶ τοὺς υἱοὺς τῆς ἀπειθείας; [GNS] δι' ἃ ἔρχεται ἡ **ὀργὴ** τοῦ θεοῦ [ἐπὶ τοὺς υἱοὺς τῆς ἀπειθείας]. [GNT]	Wrath, terrible anger, retribution. **Practical Application** 　The word "wrath" (orgë) means anger, but it is not the outburst of anger that quickly blazes up, not the anger that arises solely from emotion. Rather, it is a decisive and a deliberate anger. It is an anger that comes from a thoughtful decision, an anger that comes from the mind because someone has done something evil and hurtful. It is an anger that judges and condemns sin and evil, violence and slaughter, immorality and injustice. It is an anger that hates sin and evil and that metes out a just revenge and equal punishment.
#4463 **Wraths** Wraths–KJV Angry tempers–NASB Outbursts of anger–NIV Outbursts of wrath–NKJV Outbursts of anger–NLT **POSB REFERENCE** (2 Cor.12:19-21; esp. v.20) Note 3, point 2	**θυμοί** = thumoi Pronunciation: [thoo-moy'] Parsing (part of speech): noun 　　Case—nominative 　　Gender—masculine 　　Number—plural 　　Stem or root—from θυμός, ου Concordance References: ⇒　Strong's #2372 thumos ⇒　NIV #2596 thumos ⇒　NASB #2372 thumos **2 Cor. 12:20** For I fear, lest, when I come, I shall not find you such as I would, and that I shall be found unto you such as ye would not: lest there be debates, envyings, **wraths**, strifes, backbitings, whisperings, swellings, tumults: [KJV] For I am afraid that perhaps when I come I may find you to be not what I wish and may be found by you to be not what you wish; that perhaps there may be strife, jealousy, **angry tempers**, disputes, slanders, gossip, arrogance, disturbances; [NASB] For I am afraid that when I come I may not find you as I want you to be, and you may not find me as you want me to be. I fear that there may be quarreling, jealousy, **outbursts of anger**, factions, slander, gossip, arrogance and disorder. [NIV] For I fear lest, when I come, I shall not find you such as I wish, and that I shall be found by you such as you do not wish; lest there be contentions, jealousies, **outbursts of wrath**, selfish ambitions, backbitings, whisperings, conceits, tumults; [NKJV] For I am afraid that when I come to visit you I won't like what I find, and then you won't like my response. I am afraid that I will find quarreling, jealousy, **outbursts of anger**, selfishness, backstabbing, gossip, conceit, and	Outbursts of anger; angry tempers; fiery anger; intense fits of anger. **Practical Application** 　Paul was stricken with fear, fear lest the church fail to be what it should be and reject him and his ministry. Paul feared that the church would fail to deal with the carnal critics and continue putting up with their evil attacks against him. He lists eight evils, including wraths (thumoi) that were and still are characteristic of divisive critics in the church.

ENGLISH WORD	GREEK WORD AND VERSE	THE WORD MEANS...
	disorderly behavior. [NLT] φοβοῦμαι γὰρ μή πως ἐλθὼν οὐχ οἴους θέλω εὕρω ὑμᾶς, κἀγὼ εὑρεθῶ ὑμῖν οἷον οὐ θέλετε· μή πως ἔρις, ζῆλοι, **θυμοί**, ἐριθείαι, καταλαλιαί, ψιθυρισμοί, φυσιώσεις, ἀκαταστασίαι [GNS] φοβοῦμαι γὰρ μή πως ἐλθὼν οὐχ οἴους θέλω εὕρω ὑμᾶς κἀγὼ εὑρεθῶ ὑμῖν οἷον οὐ θέλετε· μή πως ἔρις, ζῆλος, **θυμοί**, ἐριθείαι, καταλαλιαί, ψιθυρισμοί, φυσιώσεις, ἀκαταστασίαι· [GNT]	
#4464 **Wrestle** **Wrestle–KJV** Struggle–NASB Struggle–NIV **Wrestle–NKJV** Fighting against–NLT **POSB** **REFERENCE** (Eph.6:12) Note 3	*πάλη* = *palë* Pronunciation: [pal'-ay] Parsing (part of speech): noun 　　Case—nominative 　　Gender—feminine 　　Number—singular 　　Stem or root—from *πάλη*, ης Concordance References: ⇒ Strong's #3823 palë ⇒ NIV #4097 palë ⇒ NASB #3823 palë **Ephes. 6:12** For we **wrestle** not against flesh and blood, but against principalities, against powers, against the rulers of the darkness of this world, against spiritual wickedness in high places. [KJV] For our **struggle** is not against flesh and blood, but against the rulers, against the powers, against the world forces of this darkness, against the spiritual forces of wickedness in the heavenly places. [NASB] For our **struggle** is not against flesh and blood, but against the rulers, against the authorities, against the powers of this dark world and against the spiritual forces of evil in the heavenly realms. [NIV] For we do not **wrestle** against flesh and blood, but against principalities, against powers, against the rulers of the darkness of this age, against spiritual hosts of wickedness in the heavenly places. [NKJV] For we are not **fighting against** people made of flesh and blood, but against the evil rulers and authorities of the unseen world, against those mighty powers of darkness who rule this world, and against wicked spirits in the heavenly realms. [NLT] ὅτι οὐκ ἔστιν ἡμῖν ἡ **πάλη** πρὸς αἷμα καὶ σάρκα, ἀλλὰ πρὸς τὰς ἀρχάς, πρὸς τὰς ἐξουσίας, πρὸς τοὺς κοσμοκράτορας τοῦ σκότους τοῦ αἰῶνος τούτου, πρὸς τὰ πνευματικὰ τῆς πονηρίας ἐν τοῖς ἐπουρανίοις. [GNS] ὅτι οὐκ ἔστιν ἡμῖν ἡ **πάλη** πρὸς αἷμα καὶ σάρκα, ἀλλὰ πρὸς τὰς ἀρχάς, πρὸς τὰς ἐξουσίας, πρὸς τοὺς κοσμοκράτορας τοῦ σκότους τούτου, πρὸς τὰ πνευματικὰ τῆς πονηρίας ἐν τοῖς ἐπουρανίοις. [GNT]	To struggle; to wrestle; to fight against, grapple, scuffle, tussle. **Practical Application** The warfare is not human or physical, but spiritual. Kenneth Wuest has a descriptive picture of the believer's great spiritual struggle: *"In the word 'wrestle' [pale], Paul uses a Greek athletic term. Thayer defines as follows: 'a contest between two in which each endeavors to throw the other, and which is decided when the victor is able to press and hold down his prostate antagonist, namely, hold him down with his hand upon his neck.' When we consider that the loser in a Greek wrestling contest had his eyes gouged out with resulting blindness for the rest of his days, we can form some conception of the Ephesian Greek's reaction to Paul's illustration. The Christian's wrestling against the powers of darkness is no less desperate and fateful"* (Ephesians and Colossians, Vol.1, p.141). The point to see is that the believer's struggle is not against flesh and blood. His foes are not human or physical: they are spiritual—spiritual forces that possess unbelievable power. Note exactly what is said: the believer fights... • against principalities • against power • against the rulers of darkness • against spiritual wickedness
#4465 **Wretched** **Wretched–KJV** **Wretched–NASB** **Wretched–NIV** **Wretched–NKJV** **Wretched–NLT** **POSB** **REFERENCE** (Rev.3:16-17; esp. v.17) Note 4, point 2	*ὁ ταλαίπωρος* = *ho talaipõros* Pronunciation: [ho tal-ah'ee-po-ros] Parsing (part of speech): pronominal adjective 　　Case—nominative 　　Gender—masculine 　　Number—singular 　　Stem or root—from *ταλαίπωρος*, ον Concordance References: ⇒ Strong's #3588 ho + 5005 talaipõros ⇒ NIV #3836 ho + 5417 talaipõros [wretched] ⇒ NASB #3588 ho + 5005 talaipõros **Rev. 3:17** Because thou sayest, I am rich, and increased with goods, and have need of nothing; and knowest not that thou art **wretched**, and miserable, and poor, and blind, and naked: [KJV] 'Because you say, "I am rich, and have become wealthy, and have need of nothing," and you do not know	Miserable, wretched, distressed, dejected, depressed, unhappy. **Practical Application** The lukewarm are rejected because of their true condition: they are wretched, miserable, poor, blind, and naked. What does this mean? All of these refer to the spiritual life of the church and its believers. a. The church was spiritually "wretched" (*hotalaiporos*). The word actually says *the wretched one* in the Greek. The church had its full staff and all the programs—so much so that it felt it needed nothing. But the church was really *the wretched one*. The word means to be afflicted spiritually; to be spiritually contemptible; to be spiritually inferior. In God's eyes they were spiritually

ENGLISH WORD	GREEK WORD AND VERSE	THE WORD MEANS...
	that you are **wretched** and miserable and poor and blind and naked, [NASB] You say, 'I am rich; I have acquired wealth and do not need a thing.' But you do not realize that you are **wretched**, pitiful, poor, blind and naked. [NIV] Because you say, 'I am rich, have become wealthy, and have need of nothing'—and do not know that you are **wretched**, miserable, poor, blind, and naked— [NKJV] You say, 'I am rich. I have everything I want. I don't need a thing!' And you don't realize that you are **wretched** and miserable and poor and blind and naked. [NLT] ὅτι λέγεις, ὅτι Πλούσιός εἰμι, καὶ πεπλούτηκα καὶ οὐδενὸς χρείαν ἔχω, καὶ οὐκ οἶδας ὅτι σὺ εἶ ὁ **ταλαίπωρος** καὶ ἐλεεινὸς καὶ πτωχὸς καὶ τυφλὸς καὶ γυμνός· [GNS] ὅτι λέγεις ὅτι Πλούσιός εἰμι καὶ πεπλούτηκα καὶ οὐδὲν χρείαν ἔχω, καὶ οὐκ οἶδας ὅτι σὺ εἶ ὁ **ταλαίπωρος** καὶ ἐλεεινὸς καὶ πτωχὸς καὶ τυφλὸς καὶ γυμνός, [GNT]	lacking, very much so—so much so that they were afflicted, contemptible, and inferior.

#4466
Written Code
 	
Handwriting–KJV
Certificate of debt–NASB
Written code–NIV
Handwriting–NKJV
Record–NLT
 	
POSB REFERENCE
(Col.2:14)
Note 2, point 1
	χειρόγραφον = *cheirographon*
	Pronunciation: [khi-rog'-raf-on]
	Parsing (part of speech): noun
	    Case —accusative
	    Gender—neuter
	    Number—singular
	    Stem or root—from χειρόγραφον, ου
	Concordance References:
	  ⇒ Strong's #5498 cheirographon
	  ⇒ NIV #5934 cheirographon
	  ⇒ NASB #5498 cheirographon
	
	Col. 2:14
	Blotting out the **handwriting** of ordinances that was against us, which was contrary to us, and took it out of the way, nailing it to his cross; [KJV]
	
	Having canceled out the **certificate of debt** consisting of decrees against us and which was hostile to us; and He has taken it out of the way, having nailed it to the cross. [NASB]
	
	Having canceled the **written code**, with its regulations, that was against us and that stood opposed to us; he took it away, nailing it to the cross. [NIV]
	
	Having wiped out the **handwriting** of requirements that was against us, which was contrary to us. And He has taken it out of the way, having nailed it to the cross. [NKJV]
	
	He canceled the **record** that contained the charges against us. He took it and destroyed it by nailing it to Christ's cross. [NLT]
	
	ἐξαλείψας τὸ καθ' ἡμῶν **χειρόγραφον** τοῖς δόγμασιν, ὃ ἦν ὑπεναντίον ἡμῖν· καὶ αὐτὸ ἦρκεν ἐκ τοῦ μέσου, προσηλώσας αὐτὸ τῷ σταυρῷ· [GNS]
	
	ἐξαλείψας τὸ καθ' ἡμῶν **χειρόγραφον** τοῖς δόγμασιν ὃ ἦν ὑπεναντίον ἡμῖν, καὶ αὐτὸ ἦρκεν ἐκ τοῦ μέσου προσηλώσας αὐτὸ τῷ σταυρῷ· [GNT]
		Written code, handwriting, certificate of debt, record of one's debts. It actually means a legal note or debt, what Barclay calls *a charge list* or a list of charges against man (*The Letters to the Philippians, Colossians, and Thessalonians*, p.170).
		
		Practical Application
		Man's concept of the law is twofold.
		1. Some men see the law as a list of rules that God has led great religious men to write down in either the Bible or other religious books.
		2. Other men see the laws of God as unwritten laws that are rooted in the nature of man and the world. Man just instinctively senses what is right and wrong, and he is to live as his instinct tells him (cp. Romans 2:14-15).
		
		Man just senses the written code of laws against him—laws that condemn him when he goes contrary to what they say or what he senses. The point is this: man senses the list of charges against him. And he should sense the wrong he has done, for it is his violation of God's law that condemns him to eternal death. Only as he senses and acknowledges his transgressions will he ever turn to God to save him.

#4467
Wrought
 	
Wrought–KJV
Wrought–NASB
Done–NIV
Done–NKJV
Doing–NLT
 	
POSB REFERENCE
(Jn.3:21)
Note 4, point 3
	ἐστιν εἰργασμένα = *estin eirgasmena*
	Pronunciation: [eh-stin eerg-ahs-mehn-ah]
	Parsing *estin* (part of speech): verb
	    Mood—indicative
	    Tense—present
	    Voice—active
	    Person—3rd person
	    Number—singular
	    Stem or root—from εἰμί
	Parsing *eirgasmena* (part of speech): verb
	    Mood—participle
	    Tense—perfect
	    Voice—passive
	    Case—nominative
	    Gender—neuter
		To work, produce, perform, originate, and to fashion from something.
		
		Practical Application
		The idea is that the person comes to Christ (the Light) so that his works will be wrought, originated, and worked in and of God. The person who comes to Christ lives close to God. He walks and talks and listens to God (His Word) and he does what God says (cp. 2 Cor. 1:12).

ENGLISH WORD	GREEK WORD AND VERSE	THE WORD MEANS...
	Number—plural Stem or root—from ἐργάζομαι Concordance References: ⇒ Strong's #1488+2038 eimi ergazomai ⇒ NIV #1639+2237 eimi ergazomai ⇒ NASB #1488+2038 eimi ergazomai ### John 3:21 But he that doeth truth cometh to the light, that his deeds may be made manifest, that they are **wrought** in God. [KJV] "But he who practices the truth comes to the light, that his deeds may be manifested as having been **wrought** in God." [NASB] But whoever lives by the truth comes into the light, so that it may be seen plainly that what he has done has been **done** through God." [NIV] But he who does the truth comes to the light, that his deeds may be clearly seen, that they have been **done** in God." [NKJV] But those who do what is right come to the light gladly, so everyone can see that they are **doing** what God wants." [NLT] ὁ δὲ ποιῶν τὴν ἀλήθειαν, ἔρχεται πρὸς τὸ φῶς, ἵνα φανερωθῇ αὐτοῦ τὰ ἔργα, ὅτι ἐν Θεῷ **ἐστιν εἰργασμένα**. [GNS] ὁ δὲ ποιῶν τὴν ἀλήθειαν ἔρχεται πρὸς τὸ φῶς, ἵνα φανερωθῇ αὐτοῦ τὰ ἔργα ὅτι ἐν θεῷ **ἐστιν εἰργασμένα**. [GNT]	

ENGLISH WORD	GREEK WORD AND VERSE	THE WORD MEANS...

#4468
Yield
 	
Yield–KJV
Presenting–NASB
Offer–NIV
Present–NKJV
Let–NLT
 	
POSB
REFERENCE
(Rom.6:13)
Deeper Study #2
	παριστάνετε = *paristanete*
	Pronunciation: [par-is'-tahn-eh-teh]
	Parsing (part of speech): verb
	  Mood—imperative
	  Tense—present
	  Voice—active
	  Person—2nd person
	  Number—plural
	  Stem or root—from παρίστημι and παριστάνω
	Concordance References:
	⇒ Strong's #3936 paristēmi
	⇒ NIV #4225 paristēmi
	⇒ NASB #3936 paristēmi
	
	Romans 6:13
	Neither **yield** ye your members as instruments of unrighteousness unto sin: but yield yourselves unto God, as those that are alive from the dead, and your members as instruments of righteousness unto God. [KJV]
	And do not go on **presenting** the members of your body to sin as instruments of unrighteousness; but present yourselves to God as those alive from the dead, and your members as instruments of righteousness to God. [NASB]
	Do not **offer** the parts of your body to sin, as instruments of wickedness, but rather offer yourselves to God, as those who have been brought from death to life; and offer the parts of your body to him as instruments of righteousness. [NIV]
	And do not **present** your members as instruments of unrighteousness to sin, but present yourselves to God as being alive from the dead, and your members as instruments of righteousness to God. [NKJV]
	Do not **let** any part of your body become a tool of wickedness, to be used for sinning. Instead, give yourselves completely to God since you have been given new life. And use your whole body as a tool to do what is right for the glory of God. [NLT]
	μηδὲ **παριστάνετε** τὰ μέλη ὑμῶν ὅπλα ἀδικίας τῇ ἁμαρτίᾳ· ἀλλὰ παραστήσατε ἑαυτοὺς τῷ Θεῷ ὡς ἐκ νεκρῶν ζῶντας, καὶ τὰ μέλη ὑμῶν ὅπλα δικαιοσύνης τῷ Θεῷ. [GNS]
	μηδὲ **παριστάνετε** τὰ μέλη ὑμῶν ὅπλα ἀδικίας τῇ ἁμαρτίᾳ, ἀλλὰ παραστήσατε ἑαυτοὺς τῷ θεῷ ὡσεὶ ἐκ νεκρῶν ζῶντας καὶ τὰ μέλη ὑμῶν ὅπλα δικαιοσύνης τῷ θεῷ. [GNT]
		To present; to bring into one's presence; to show; to yield; to dedicate; to provide; to send; to prove. It means to offer; to put at the disposal of; to give; to grant; to turn over to.
		
		Practical Application
		The believer must not yield the members of his body sin. The believer is not to yield the members of his body to be instruments or tools of unrighteousness. If he takes a member of his body and uses it as an instrument or tool of unrighteousness, he sins. The members of a person's body refer to all the parts of the body: the eyes, ears, mouth, tongue, hands, feet, mind, or any of the covered and dressed parts. No believer is to offer or give any part of his body over to unrighteousness. To do so is to sin. The tense is present action, so the believer is to be constantly on guard against allowing any member of his body to be yielded to sin. Note: the word "yield" has the idea of struggling. It is a struggle to fight against sin and to control and protect the members of our bodies.

#4469
Yielded Up,
His Spirit,
The Ghost
 	
Yielded up the
  ghost–KJV
Yielded up His
  Spirit–NASB
Gave up his
  spirit–NIV
Yielded up His spirit–NKJV
Gave up his
  spirit–NLT
 	
POSB
REFERENCE
(Mt.27:50)
Note 3, point 2
	ἀφῆκεν τὸ πνεῦμα = *aphēken to pneuma*
	Pronunciation: [af-ee'-ken to pnyoo'-mah]
	Parsing *aphēken* (part of speech): verb
	  Mood—indicative
	  Tense—aorist
	  Voice—active
	  Person—3rd person
	  Number—singular
	  Stem or root—from ἀφίημι
	Parsing *pneuma* (part of speech): noun
	  Case—accusative
	  Gender—neuter
	  Number—singular
	  Stem or root—from πνεῦμα, τος
	Concordance References:
	⇒ Strong's #863 aphiemi + 4151 pneuma
	⇒ NIV #918 aphiēmi [gave up] + 3836 ho [his] +
	  4460 pneuma [spirit]
	  NASB #863 aphiemi + 4151 pneuma
	
	Matthew 27:50
	Jesus, when he had cried again with a loud voice, **yielded up the ghost.** [KJV]
	And Jesus cried out again with a loud voice, and **yielded up His spirit.** [NASB]
	And when Jesus had cried out again in a loud voice, he
		Christ willingly yielded and gave up His spirit.
		
		Practical Application
		It must always be remembered that Jesus willingly died. He willingly came to this moment of yielding and giving up His spirit to death.
		His death was the supreme act of obedience. It was voluntary; He willingly died. No man took His life; He sacrificed it Himself. The power to take it was His and His alone.
		Note the critical point: this "commandment" to die was of God (cp. John 10:17-18). This gives a higher meaning to the death of Jesus than just meeting man's need. It means that Jesus did not die just because of sin, but because He wished to glorify and honor God. He wished above all else to show His love and adoration for God.
		This is an aspect of Jesus' death that is often overlooked—an aspect that rises far above the mere meeting of our need. For in giving Himself as an "offering to God," Christ was looking

ENGLISH WORD	GREEK WORD AND VERSE	THE WORD MEANS...
	gave up his spirit. [NIV] And Jesus cried out again with a loud voice, and **yielded up His spirit**. [NKJV] Then Jesus shouted out again, and he **gave up his spirit**. [NLT] ὁ δὲ Ἰησοῦς πάλιν κράξας φωνῇ μεγάλῃ **ἀφῆκε** τὸ πνεῦμα. [GNS] ὁ δὲ Ἰησοῦς πάλιν κράξας φωνῇ μεγάλῃ **ἀφῆκεν** τὸ πνεῦμα. [GNT]	beyond our need to the majestic responsibility of glorifying God. This means that His first purpose was the glory of God. He was concerned primarily with doing the will of God, with obeying God. God had been terribly dishonored by the first man, Adam, and by all those who followed after him. Jesus Christ wished to honor God by showing that at least one man thought more of God's glory than of anything else. Jesus wished to show that God's will meant more than any personal desire or ambition which He might have.

#4470
Yoke
 	
Yoke–KJV
Yoke–NASB
Yoke–NIV
Yoke–NKJV
Not translated–NLT
 	
POSB
REFERENCE
(1 Tim.6:1)
Note 1
	ζυγὸν = *zugon*
	Pronunciation: [dzoo-gon']
	Parsing (part of speech): noun
	  Case—accusative
	  Gender—masculine
	  Number—singular
	  Stem or root—from ζυγός, οῦ
	Concordance References:
	  ⇒ Strong's #2218 zugos
	  ⇒ NIV #2433 zugos
	  ⇒ NASB #2218 zugos
	
	1 Tim. 6:1
	Let as many servants as are under the **yoke** count their own masters worthy of all honour, that the name of God and his doctrine be not blasphemed. [KJV]
	
	Let all who are under the **yoke** as slaves regard their own masters as worthy of all honor so that the name of God and our doctrine may not be spoken against. [NASB]
	
	All who are under the **yoke** of slavery should consider their masters worthy of full respect, so that God's name and our teaching may not be slandered. [NIV]
	
	Let as many bondservants as are under the **yoke** count their own masters worthy of all honor, so that the name of God and His doctrine may not be blasphemed. [NKJV]
	
	Christians who are slaves should give their masters full respect so that the name of God and his teaching will not be shamed. [NLT]—NOT TRANSLATED
	
	Ὅσοι εἰσὶν ὑπὸ **ζυγὸν** δοῦλοι, τοὺς ἰδίους δεσπότας πάσης τιμῆς ἀξίους ἡγείσθωσαν, ἵνα μὴ τὸ ὄνομα τοῦ Θεοῦ καὶ ἡ διδασκαλία βλασφημῆται [GNS]
	
	Ὅσοι εἰσὶν ὑπὸ **ζυγὸν** δοῦλοι, τοὺς ἰδίους δεσπότας πάσης τιμῆς ἀξίους ἡγείσθωσαν, ἵνα μὴ τὸ ὄνομα τοῦ θεοῦ καὶ ἡ διδασκαλία βλασφημῆται. [GNT]
		Yoke; to be under bondage, enslaved, weighed down ever so heavily.
		
		Practical Application
		Paul does not hesitate to call slavery just what it is: a yoke that does not belong upon any man. Paul is expressing a heartfelt compassion for the slaves.

#4471
Yoked Together
 	
Unequally yoked together–KJV
Bound together–NASB
Yoked together–NIV
Unequally yoked together–NKJV
Team up–NLT
 	
POSB
REFERENCE
(2 Cor.6:14-16; esp. v.14)
Note 2
	ἑτεροζυγοῦντες = *heterozugountes*
	Pronunciation: [het-er-od-zoog-oon-tehs]
	Parsing (part of speech): verb
	  Mood—participle
	  Tense—present
	  Voice—active
	  Case—nominative
	  Gender—masculine
	  Person—2nd person
	  Number—plural
	  Stem or root—from ἑτεροζυγέω
	Concordance References:
	  ⇒ Strong's #2086 heterozugeō
	  ⇒ NIV #2282 heterozugeō
	  ⇒ NASB #2086 heterozugeō
	
	2 Cor. 6:14
	Be ye not **unequally yoked together** with unbelievers: for what fellowship hath righteousness with unrighteousness? and what communion hath light with darkness? [KJV]
	
	Do not be **bound together** with unbelievers; for what partnership have righteousness and lawlessness, or what fellowship has light with darkness? [NASB]
		To be yoked together; to be bound together; to team up; to be unequally yoked; to be mismated.
		
		Practical Application
		It refers back to the Old Testament where God forbade the plowing of an ox with an ass (Deut. 22:10) or the union of different kinds of animals (Leviticus 19:19). The point is...
		
		• that the union of a genuine believer with an unbeliever would be as different as the union between two kinds of animals.
		• that the plowing through life of a believer with an unbeliever would be as difficult as the plowing of a field with an ox and an ass yoked together.
		
		Genuine believers are radically different from unbelievers.

ENGLISH WORD	GREEK WORD AND VERSE	THE WORD MEANS...
	Do not be **yoked together** with unbelievers. For what do righteousness and wickedness have in common? Or what fellowship can light have with darkness? [NIV] Do not be **unequally yoked together** with unbelievers. For what fellowship has righteousness with lawlessness? And what communion has light with darkness? [NKJV] Don't **team up** with those who are unbelievers. How can goodness be a partner with wickedness? How can light live with darkness? [NLT] Μὴ γίνεσθε **ἑτεροζυγοῦντες** ἀπίστοις· τίς γὰρ μετοχὴ δικαιοσύνη καὶ ἀνομία; τίς δὲ κοινωνία φωτὶ πρὸς σκότος; [GNS] Μὴ γίνεσθε **ἑτεροζυγοῦντες** ἀπίστοις· τίς γὰρ μετοχὴ δικαιοσύνη καὶ ἀνομία, η τίς κοινωνία φωτὶ πρὸς σκότος; [GNT]	

#4472
Yokefellow
 	
Yokefellow–KJV
Comrade–NASB
Yokefellow–NIV
Companion–NKJV
Teammate–NLT
 	
POSB REFERENCE
(Philip.4:2-3; esp. v.3)
Note 2, point 2
	σύζυγε = *suzuge*
	Pronunciation: [sood'-zoo-geh]
	Parsing (part of speech): pronominal adjective
	    Case—vocative
	    Gender—masculine
	    Number—singular
	    Stem or root—from σύζυγος, ου
	Concordance References:
	⇒ Strong's #4805 suzugos
	⇒ NIV #5187 suzugos
	⇒ NASB #4805 suzugos
	
	Philip. 4:3
	And I intreat thee also, true **yokefellow**, help those women which laboured with me in the gospel, with Clement also, and with other my fellowlabourers, whose names are in the book of life. [KJV]
	
	Indeed, true **comrade**, I ask you also to help these women who have shared my struggle in the cause of the gospel, together with Clement also, and the rest of my fellow workers, whose names are in the book of life. [NASB]
	
	Yes, and I ask you, loyal **yokefellow**, help these women who have contended at my side in the cause of the gospel, along with Clement and the rest of my fellow workers, whose names are in the book of life. [NIV]
	
	And I urge you also, true **companion**, help these women who labored with me in the gospel, with Clement also, and the rest of my fellow workers, whose names are in the Book of Life. [NKJV]
	
	And I ask you, my true **teammate**, to help these women, for they worked hard with me in telling others the Good News. And they worked with Clement and the rest of my co-workers, whose names are written in the Book of Life. [NLT]
	
	καὶ ἐρωτῶ καὶ σέ, **σύζυγε** γνήσιε, συλλαμβάνου αὐταῖς, αἵτινες ἐν τῷ εὐαγγελίῳ συνήθλησάν μοι, μετὰ καὶ Κλήμεντος, καὶ τῶν λοιπῶν συνεργῶν μου, ὧν τὰ ὀνόματα ἐν βίβλῳ ζωῆς. [GNS]
	
	ναὶ ἐρωτῶ καὶ σέ, γνήσιε **σύζυγε**, συλλαμβάνου αὐταῖς, αἵτινες ἐν τῷ εὐαγγελίῳ συνήθλησάν μοι μετὰ καὶ Κλήμεντος καὶ τῶν λοιπῶν συνεργῶν μου, ὧν τὰ ὀνόματα ἐν βίβλῳ ζωῆς. [GNT]
		Yokefellow, fellow worker, comrade, teammate.
		
		Practical Application
		The need is for a true friend, a yokefellow, to step in to help any who are quarreling. The word "yokefellow" (*suzuge*) is thought by some to be a proper name given to some Christians when they were baptized. It was a common practice for believers to be given new names at their baptism in order to symbolize their spiritual birth. Just who this yokefellow was is not known, but he must have been a man deeply respected by the people of the church. His name refers to the *yoke* or *collar* that was fitted around the neck of oxen for plowing. The collar attached the plow and held the two oxen together so that they would pull together and more quickly get the work done. Therefore, "yokefellow" means a person who pulls and works cooperatively with others. The very fact that Paul would ask him to help the two quarreling ladies shows that he was highly esteemed. Paul felt that he cared and that the two quarrelers would listen to him—that he could solve the dispute and bring about reconciliation.
		
		Most churches have one or more yokefellows, persons...
		• who love and care deeply for others.
		• who are always helping and ministering to others.
		• whom God has gifted and appointed to be ministerial helpers to the flock.
		• who are highly respected and esteemed by most in the congregation.
		
		The yokefellow is the person who should step in when quarrels and divisiveness begin to arouse their poisonous heads. The yokefellow is the person especially gifted by God to bring reconciliation and peace to the church.

#4473
You Fool
 	
Raca–KJV
Raca–NASB
Raca–NIV
You fool–NKJV
You idiot–NLT
	Ῥακά = *hraka*
	Pronunciation: [hrak-ah']
	Parsing (part of speech): noun
	    Case—vocative
	    Gender—masculine
	    Number—singular
	    Stem or root—from ῥακά
	Concordance References:
	⇒ Strong's #4469 hraka
	⇒ NIV #4819 hraka
	⇒ NASB #4469 hraka
		Raca, you idiot; literally, an empty-headed fool.
		
		Practical Application
		To use this expression against another person during the New Testament period was considered to be a grave insult, a striking verbal assault.

ENGLISH WORD	GREEK WORD AND VERSE	THE WORD MEANS...
POSB **REFERENCE** (Mt.5:22) Note 3, point 2	**Matthew 5:22** But I say unto you, That whosoever is angry with his brother without a cause shall be in danger of the judgment: and whosoever shall say to his brother, **Raca**, shall be in danger of the council: but whosoever shall say, Thou fool, shall be in danger of hell fire. [KJV] "But I say to you that everyone who is angry with his brother shall be guilty before the court; and whoever shall say to his brother, '**Raca**,' shall be guilty before the supreme court; and whoever shall say, 'You fool,' shall be guilty enough to go into the fiery hell. [NASB] But I tell you that anyone who is angry with his brother will be subject to judgment. Again, anyone who says to his brother, '**Raca**,' is answerable to the Sanhedrin. But anyone who says, 'You fool!' will be in danger of the fire of hell. [NIV] But I say to you that whoever is angry with his brother without a cause shall be in danger of the judgment. And whoever says to his brother, 'Raca!' shall be in danger of the council. But whoever says, '**You fool**!' shall be in danger of hell fire. [NKJV] But I say, if you are angry with someone, you are subject to judgment! If you say to your friend, '**You idiot**,' you are in danger of being brought before the court. And if you curse someone, you are in danger of the fires of hell. [NLT] ἐγὼ δὲ λέγω ὑμῖν ὅτι πᾶς ὁ ὀργιζόμενος τῷ ἀδελφῷ αὐτοῦ εἰκῆ ἔνοχος ἔσται τῇ κρίσει· ὃς δ' ἂν εἴπῃ τῷ ἀδελφῷ αὐτοῦ, **ῥακά**, ἔνοχος ἔσται τῷ συνεδρίῳ· ὃς δ' ἂν εἴπῃ, Μωρέ, ἔνοχος ἔσται εἰς τὴν γέενναν τοῦ πυρός. [GNS] ἐγὼ δὲ λέγω ὑμῖν ὅτι πᾶς ὁ ὀργιζόμενος τῷ ἀδελφῷ αὐτοῦ ἔνοχος ἔσται τῇ κρίσει· ὃς δ' ἂν εἴπῃ τῷ ἀδελφῷ αὐτοῦ, **Ῥακά**, ἔνοχος ἔσται τῷ συνεδρίῳ· ὃς δ' ἂν εἴπῃ, Μωρέ, ἔνοχος ἔσται εἰς τὴν γέενναν τοῦ πυρός. [GNT]	

#4474
You Idiot
 	
Raca–KJV
Raca–NASB
Raca–NIV
You fool–NKJV
You idiot–NLT
 	
POSB
REFERENCE
(Mt.5:22)
Note 3, point 2
	Ῥακά = hraka
	Pronunciation: [hrak-ah']
	Parsing (part of speech): noun
	    Case—vocative
	    Gender—masculine
	    Number—singular
	    Stem or root—from **ῥακά**
	Concordance References:
	  ⇒ Strong's #4469 hraka
	  ⇒ NIV #4819 hraka
	  ⇒ NASB #4469 hraka
	
	Matthew 5:22
	But I say unto you, That whosoever is angry with his brother without a cause shall be in danger of the judgment: and whosoever shall say to his brother, **Raca**, shall be in danger of the council: but whosoever shall say, Thou fool, shall be in danger of hell fire. [KJV]
	
	"But I say to you that everyone who is angry with his brother shall be guilty before the court; and whoever shall say to his brother, '**Raca**,' shall be guilty before the supreme court; and whoever shall say, 'You fool,' shall be guilty enough to go into the fiery hell. [NASB]
	
	But I tell you that anyone who is angry with his brother will be subject to judgment. Again, anyone who says to his brother, '**Raca**,' is answerable to the Sanhedrin. But anyone who says, 'You fool!' will be in danger of the fire of hell. [NIV]
	
	But I say to you that whoever is angry with his brother without a cause shall be in danger of the judgment. And whoever says to his brother, 'Raca!' shall be in danger of the council. But whoever says, '**You fool**!' shall be in danger of hell fire. [NKJV]
	
	But I say, if you are angry with someone, you are subject to judgment! If you say to your friend, '**You idiot**,'
		Raca, you idiot; literally, an empty-headed fool.
		
		Practical Application
		To use this expression against another person during the New Testament period was considered to be a grave insult, a striking verbal assault.

ENGLISH WORD	GREEK WORD AND VERSE	THE WORD MEANS...
	you are in danger of being brought before the court. And if you curse someone, you are in danger of the fires of hell. [NLT] ἐγὼ δὲ λέγω ὑμῖν ὅτι πᾶς ὁ ὀργιζόμενος τῷ ἀδελφῷ αὐτοῦ εἰκῇ ἔνοχος ἔσται τῇ κρίσει· ὃς δ' ἂν εἴπῃ τῷ ἀδελφῷ αὐτοῦ, ʽρακά, ἔνοχος ἔσται τῷ συνεδρίῳ· ὃς δ' ἂν εἴπῃ, Μωρέ, ἔνοχος ἔσται εἰς τὴν γέενναν τοῦ πυρός. [GNS] ἐγὼ δὲ λέγω ὑμῖν ὅτι πᾶς ὁ ὀργιζόμενος τῷ ἀδελφῷ αὐτοῦ ἔνοχος ἔσται τῇ κρίσει· ὃς δ' ἂν εἴπῃ τῷ ἀδελφῷ αὐτοῦ, ʽΡακά, ἔνοχος ἔσται τῷ συνεδρίῳ· ὃς δ' ἂν εἴπῃ, Μωρέ, ἔνοχος ἔσται εἰς τὴν γέενναν τοῦ πυρός. [GNT]	

#4475
Your Own Plans
 	
Boastings–KJV
Arrogance–NASB
Brag–NIV
Arrogance–NKJV
Your own plans–NLT
 	
POSB REFERENCE
(Jas.4:16)
Note 4
	ἐν ταῖς ἀλαζονείαις = en tais alazoneiais
	Pronunciation: [en tace hal-ad-zon-i'-ah-is]
	Parsing *alazoneiais* (part of speech): noun
	    Case—dative
	    Gender—feminine
	    Number—plural
	    Stem or root—from ἀλαζονεία, ας
	Concordance References:
	  ⇒ Strong's #212+1722+3588 alazoneia en ho
	  ⇒ NIV #224+1877+3836 alazoneia en ho [brag]
	  ⇒ NASB #212+1722+3588 alazoneia en ho
	
	James 4:16
	But now ye rejoice in your **boastings**: all such rejoicing is evil. [KJV]
	
	But as it is, you boast in your **arrogance**; all such boasting is evil. [NASB]
	
	As it is, you boast and **brag**. All such boasting is evil. [NIV]
	
	But now you boast in your **arrogance**. All such boasting is evil. [NKJV]
	
	Otherwise you will be boasting about **your own plans**, and all such boasting is evil. [NLT]
	
	νῦν δὲ καυχᾶσθε **ἐν ταῖς ἀλαζονείαις** ὑμῶν· πᾶσα καύχησις τοιαύτη πονηρά ἐστιν. [GNS]
	
	νῦν δὲ καυχᾶσθε **ἐν ταῖς ἀλαζονείαις** ὑμῶν· πᾶσα καύχησις τοιαύτη πονηρά ἐστιν. [GNT]
		To brag; boasting, pride, and arrogance.
		
		Practical Application
		The phrase "your own plans" (*alazoniais*) means an empty boaster (A.T. Robertson. *Word Pictures in the New Testament*, Vol. 6, p.56). That is, it is a person who boasts about something he thinks he has, but he does not really have it. He lives in an unreal world. Any person who goes through life without God is just like this. He lives and plans, thinking that he controls his life and the future. His life is one big boast of self-sufficiency, and it is wrong, totally wrong. A thousand things can happen to change his plans—to injure him or to radically change his life and work, or to snatch his life right out of this world.
		
		Most people boast—laymen and ministers alike—boast of their work, what they have done, their ability and possessions. But note a fact seldom thought about: most boasting is not done by word of mouth. It is done by the way we live. We boast by flaunting our abilities and successes through our possessions and activities such as expensive houses, clothes and cars, exclusive clubs, friendships, and recreation.
		
		We have an urge, a tendency to boast and to be seen and recognized as better and more successful than others. And note what Scripture says: we rejoice in our boastings—that we are more successful in our work than some others. But such boastings—such pride and arrogance—are evil. Why? Because a man's ability and life are due to God and rest in the hands of God. And in addition to this: the future—tomorrow and even one hour from now—is in the hands of God. It may be a heart attack—it may be a thief—it may be an accident—it is all in the hands of God. What a person needs to do is trust God and commit all his ways into the hands of God, acknowledging Him in all things and at every turn of every day.

ENGLISH WORD	GREEK WORD AND VERSE	THE WORD MEANS...

#4476
Zeal
 	
Business–KJV
Diligence–NASB
Zeal–NIV
Diligence–NKJV
Work–NLT
 	
**POSB
REFERENCE**
(Rom.12:11)
Note 2, point 1
	σπουδή = *spoudë*
	Pronunciation: [spoo-day']
	Parsing (part of speech): noun
	    Case—dative
	    Gender—feminine
	    Number—singular
	    Stem or root—from σπουδή, ῆς
	Concordance References:
	⇒ Strong's #4710 spoudë
	⇒ NIV #5082 spoudë
	⇒ NASB #4710 spoudë
	
	Romans 12:11
	Not slothful in **business**; fervent in spirit; serving the Lord; [KJV]
	Not lagging behind in **diligence**, fervent in spirit, serving the Lord; [NASB]
	Never be lacking in **zeal**, but keep your spiritual fervor, serving the Lord. [NIV]
	Not lagging in **diligence**, fervent in spirit, serving the Lord; [NKJV]
	Never be lazy in your **work**, but serve the Lord enthusiastically. [NLT]
	τῇ **σπουδῇ** μὴ ὀκνηροί· τῷ πνεύματι ζέοντες· τῷ Κυρίῳ δουλεύοντες· [GNS]
	τῇ **σπουδῇ** μὴ ὀκνηροί, τῷ πνεύματι ζέοντες, τῷ κυρίῳ δουλεύοντες, [GNT]
		Zeal, diligence, work, earnestness, effort.
		
		Practical Application
		The exhortation is clear: the believer must...
		• not be lazy or slow moving in zeal.
		• not be sluggish or lethargic in diligence.
		• not be hesitating or delaying in earnestness.
		
		The believer just cannot approach life in a lackadaisical, easygoing, slow moving fashion. The world is reeling in pain, with millions starving and suffering due to man's selfishness and sin, hoarding, disease, war, death—and the list could go on and on. The believer must not give in to sluggishness and complacency. He must serve the Lord with all diligence and zeal and earnestness. He must be enthusiastic in his service.

#4477
Zealous
 	
Diligent–KJV
Diligent–NASB
Zealous–NIV
Diligent–NKJV
Earnest–NLT
 	
**POSB
REFERENCE**
(2 Cor.8:22)
Note 4
	σπουδαῖον = *spoudaion*
	Pronunciation: [spoo-dah'-ee-on]
	Parsing (part of speech): adjective
	    Case—accusative
	    Gender—masculine
	    Number—singular
	    Stem or root—from σπουδαῖος, α, ον
	Concordance References:
	⇒ Strong's #4705 spoudaios
	⇒ NIV #5080 spoudaios
	⇒ NASB #4705 spoudaios
	
	2 Cor. 8:22
	And we have sent with them our brother, whom we have oftentimes proved **diligent** in many things, but now much more diligent, upon the great confidence which *I have* in you. [KJV]
	And we have sent with them our brother, whom we have often tested and found **diligent** in many things, but now even more diligent, because of *his* great confidence in you. [NASB]
	In addition, we are sending with them our brother who has often proved to us in many ways that he is **zealous**, and now even more so because of his great confidence in you. [NIV]
	And we have sent with them our brother whom we have often proved **diligent** in many things, but now much more diligent, because of the great confidence which *we have* in you. [NKJV]
	And we are also sending with them another brother who has been thoroughly tested and has shown how **earnest** he is on many occasions. He is now even more enthusiastic because of his increased confidence in you. [NLT]
	συνεπέμψαμεν δὲ αὐτοῖς τὸν ἀδελφὸν ἡμῶν, ὃν ἐδοκιμάσαμεν ἐν πολλοῖς πολλάκις **σπουδαῖον**, ὄντα, νυνὶ δὲ πολὺ σπουδαιότερον πεποιθήσει πολλῇ τῇ εἰς ὑμᾶς. [GNS]
	συνεπέμψαμεν δὲ αὐτοῖς τὸν ἀδελφὸν ἡμῶν ὃν ἐδοκιμάσαμεν ἐν πολλοῖς πολλάκις **σπουδαῖον** ὄντα, νυνὶ δὲ πολὺ σπουδαιότερον πεποιθήσει πολλῇ τῇ εἰς ὑμᾶς. [GNT]
		Zealous, diligent, earnest, enthusiastic, eager, devoted.
		
		Practical Application
		Men who handle collections (ushers) are zealous in many things, but especially in collections. Who this unnamed brother was is not known. Three significant points are made about him, points that should speak to the heart of every church usher and person who handles collections.
		1. He was a brother, a true believer who was in fellowship with other believers and cooperated with the church in its mission endeavors.
		2. He had often been "zealous" (*spoudaion*) when other ministries had been assigned to him. He gave himself wholeheartedly to whatever task the church gave him.
		3. He observed and was alert to the testimony of churches. When Paul told him about the Corinthian church—about the great revival of the church—he became excited and was more willing than ever to serve Christ in the midst of the church.

ENGLISH WORD	GREEK WORD AND VERSE	THE WORD MEANS...

#4478
Zealous
 	
Followers–KJV
Zealous–NASB
Eager–NIV
Followers–NKJV
Eager–NLT
 	
**POSB
REFERENCE**
(1 Pt.3:13-14; esp.
v.13)
Note 1
	ζηλωταί = *zēlōtai*
	Pronunciation: [dzay-lo-tah-ee]
	Parsing (part of speech): noun
	    Case—nominative
	    Gender—masculine
	    Number—plural
	    Stem or root—from ζηλωτής, οῦ
	Concordance References:
	  ⇒ NIV #2421 zēlōtēs
	  ⇒ Strong's #2207 zēlōtēs
	  ⇒ NASB #2207 zēlōtēs
	
	1 Peter 3:13
	And who *is* he that will harm you, if ye be **followers** of that which is good? [KJV]
	And who is there to harm you if you prove **zealous** for what is good? [NASB]
	Who is going to harm you if you are **eager** to do good? [NIV]
	And who *is* he who will harm you if you become **followers** of what is good? [NKJV]
	Now, who will want to harm you if you are **eager** to do good? [NLT]
	Καὶ τίς ὁ κακώσων ὑμᾶς, ἐὰν τοῦ ἀγαθοῦ **μιμηταὶ** γέγενσθε; [GNS]
	Καὶ τίς ὁ κακώσων ὑμᾶς ἐὰν τοῦ ἀγαθοῦ **ζηλωταὶ** γένησθε; [GNT]
		To be eager; to be a follower, a strongly committed follower; to be zealous; to be a Zealot.
		
		Practical Application
		Note the verse: it actually says to become "prove zealous for what is good." The believer is to be so zealous for what is right that he is actually known as a zealot for good. Imagine being gripped with so much passion and zeal for good that one becomes known as a zealot! This is the challenge of this passage. Several attitudes toward doing good permeate society.
		⇒ Some persons have a *"care less" attitude* toward goodness. Doing what is right and good matters little. What is right and good is rebelled against, ignored, cursed, and rejected. The person has little conscience about right and wrong. His values are ever so weak. He could not care less if he does what is right and good.
		⇒ Some persons have a *selfish attitude* toward goodness. If doing what is right and good benefits them, then they do it. If it helps them, meets their need and enlarges their holdings, then they do what is right. But if it costs them, demands discipline and control, and takes away from their pleasure and holdings, then they reject the good, refusing to do what is right.
		⇒ Some persons have a *surface or sentimental attitude* to what is good and right. They readily profess to believe in what is good and right in an effort to be known as moral and upright. But behind the scenes, they go ahead and live like they want, doing their own thing.
		⇒ Some persons, of course, have a zealous attitude toward what is right and good. They have committed their lives to seeking and doing what they should. This is exactly what Scripture is saying: "Be a zealot—be a fanatic—be a passionate follower—after that which is good and right."

A SIMPLIFIED GREEK PRIMER FOR BEGINNERS

The purpose of this Greek primer is to simplify, as much as possible, the terms that make up New Testament Greek. Please note: attention has been given to simplification. The help this chart offers to serious Greek students is limited. No one should pin a major point of doctrine solely on the information provided in this chart.

Key: The words in **BOLD CAPS** type are major subjects. Note the flow of thought:
⇒ Part of Speech or Grammatical term
⇒ What the part of speech or term means
⇒ The importance or substance of the part of speech or term

Part Of Speech Or Grammatical Term	The Meaning Of...	The Importance Of...
MOOD	The speaker has a particular perspective in mind toward the action of the verb.	It indicates the expectation of the speaker in regard to the action being expressed.
Indicative	The speaker is making an assertion.	The speaker is clearly not implying a wish/desire or a command.
Subjunctive	The speaker is implying a wish, desire or a potential/hypothetical circumstance.	The speaker is clearly not making an assertion.
Infinitive	This mood of the verb is not directly tied to a person, number or gender. It functions as a verbal noun. However, it usually expresses the state of being or action for the subject of the clause in which it is found. The most common translation is "to, plus the verb." e.g. to look.	This construction most commonly indicates purpose or result, often being translated "in order that..." or "with the result that..." It can also be translated temporally, "while, when, or during."
Imperative	This verb form always indicates a command.	The speaker is making a command.
Participle	This form is a verbal noun. Usually it is translated using some form of "ing" on the end of the verb or the accompanying helping verb. e.g. seeing, looking, having looked etc.	This is perhaps one of the more exclusively characteristic features of the Greek language. These words reflect some action which is closely related to the action of the main verb in a sentence. e.g. "Having lost the coin, the woman was sad," or "While riding in the chariot, Philip was talking."
Participle (imperative sense)	This verb form can also take an imperative force.	This is seen in the idea: "Go and preach" which is literally "Having gone, preach." The participle here can take the same force as the main verb, preach which is an imperative
TENSE	This term refers to the time of the action occurring and the quality of the action. e.g. The action is currently going on or is completed.	The tense of Greek verbs is quite specific. However, care should be taken not to read too much theologically into the use of tenses in relation to various doctrines.
Present	The action is going on at the moment.	**Translation possibilities:** "I go, am going, do go."

SIMPLIFIED GREEK PRIMER

Part Of Speech Or Grammatical Term	The Meaning Of...	The Importance Of...
Imperfect	The action is occurring in past time, but this tense can indicate a past habitual/continual/customary action or origin.	**Translation possibilities:** "I was going, used to go, began to go."
Perfect	This action occurred in the past, but the effect of the action reaches to the present.	**Translation possibilities:** "I have gone" (Perhaps this is more clearly seen in the phrase "I have arrived.")
Pluperfect	The action was finished in past time.	**Translation possibilities:** "I had gone."
Aorist	The action took place in the past, as a simple once and for all past action which could have lasting results. Also, this tense is sometimes used in proverbs to indicate a general truth. When thus used, it can be translated as a present.	**Translation possibilities:** "I went, once and for all or simply I went. (Caution: Often too much is made of this tense distinction theologically.
Future	The action will take place in the future.	**Translation possibilities:** "I will go, or I shall go."
Future Perfect	The action will be finished in future time.	**Translation possibilities:** "I will have gone."
VOICE	Expresses the relationship of the verb to the speaker and the thing or person being acted upon.	Tells you who is doing what to whom.
Active	The subject is performing the action.	Tells you who is doing an action.
Passive	The subject is being acted upon.	Tells you that the subject is not doing anything, but he/she/it is receiving some sort of action.
Middle	This voice usually indicates a reflexive action, that is the subject is acting upon himself/herself.	Some verbs take particular meanings in this voice. e.g. "to persuade" in middle voice becomes "to obey" i.e. "to persuade oneself." Caution: One should be careful not to push this Greek grammatical aspect too far as well.
Deponent	This is really more of a grammatical convention than a verb voice. The verb may take a passive/middle form but be translated as an a active voice verb.	Certain verbs simply take this form. This fact should be noted but not overly considered.
PERSON	This indicates the person doing or receiving the action.	Personal pronouns in Greek do not need to be expressed since they are implied in the verb itself. When they do occur, it is usually for emphasis.

SIMPLIFIED GREEK PRIMER

Part Of Speech Or Grammatical Term	The Meaning Of...	The Importance Of...
First Person	Indicates the person speaking is doing the action.	**Translation possibilities:** "I or We."
Second Person	Indicates the person speaking is directing his/her remarks to someone else.	**Translation possibilities:** "You or You (plural)."
Third Person	Indicates the speaker is talking about someone else other than himself/herself or the person to whom he/she is talking.	**Translation possibilities:** "He, she or it, they."
NUMBER	The number of people, items, events etc. involved in a thought.	Tells you how many.
Singular	One person or event.	(See explanation for **NUMBER**)
Plural	More than one person or event.	(See explanation for **NUMBER**)
CASE	The endings which occur on a Greek noun or verbal noun which indicate how it is used in the sentence. This is called inflection.	Tells you how the words used in a sentence fit together
Nominative	Usually indicates the subject of a sentence.	**Translation possibilities:** "Man or if plural, men."
Genitive	Usually indicates possession. It can also be the object of certain prepositions.	**Translation possibilities:** "Of a man or men."
Dative	Usually indicates an indirect object or agency.	**Translation possibilities:** "To or for a man or men" or "by means of or with a man or men."
Accusative	Usually indicates the direct object or even the object of a preposition. (Note: Some prepositions take a different case, such as the dative or genitive.)	**Translation possibilities:** "Man or men."
Vocative	Usually indicates direct address.	**Translation possibilities:** "O man" or "O men" or simply "man or men."
GENDER	This can indicate male, female, or neuter. However since Greek is like some other languages in that all nouns have gender, this gender does not always correspond to the actual person place or thing named by the noun. e.g. the word "road" is feminine.	All Greek words must agree in person, number and gender. This fact can be helpful in determining which helping/modifying word is connected to which word it is helping/modifying.

SIMPLIFIED GREEK PRIMER

Part Of Speech Or Grammatical Term	The Meaning Of...	The Importance Of...
STEM OR ROOT	This is the base word to which the inflected noun or verb endings are added.	You need to know this in order to look up the word in a Greek dictionary or concordance. You can also make certain connections between the meanings of words sharing the same root. Caution: These word connections can sometimes be overdone. One should exercise care in making such connections.
PRONOUN	A word used in the place of a noun. In Greek, these words are usually used for emphasis since the verb already has the pronoun implied by its ending. However, objective pronouns are used quite frequently.	These are such words as: He, she, it, I, you, they, we, him her them.
NOUN	The name of a person, place, thing or idea.	These are the basic building blocks of any language.
VERB	A word that expresses action or state of being.	These words usually connect nouns in some way.
ADJECTIVE	A word that describes a noun by telling which one, how many or what kind. These words in Greek can sometimes take the place of a noun as in the "good" die young. (Substantive)	These words add clarity to a sentence and specificity.
ADVERB	A word that modifies verbs or other adverbs answering the questions how, when, and where.	These words continue to refine the details of a sentence.
PREPOSITION	A word that is connected to a noun or pronoun in a phrase by expressing some relationship between it and the rest of the sentence.	These can be used as adverbs. e.g. "After five years," "Inside the house," etc.
PARTICLE/CONJUNCTION	Usually these are words that express some kind of connection between the words in a sentence. The connection may be simple, resultant, purposeful, temporal, contingent etc.	**Translation possibilities:** "And, in order that, so that, with the result that, in as much as, when, while, as long as, if, then etc."

Sources:

Blass, F. and DeBrunner, A. *A Greek Grammar of the New Testament and Other Early Christian Literature*. Translated by Robert Funk. Chicago: University of Chicago Press, 1974.

Chase, Alston and Phillips, Henry. *A New Introduction to Greek*. Cambridge, Mass.: Harvard University Press, 1961.

Goodwin, William. *Greek Grammar*. London: Macmillan, 1971.

Machen, Gresham. *New Testament Greek for Beginners*. Toronto, Ontario: Macmillan, 1923.

Wallace, Daniel B. *Greek Grammar Beyond the Basics: An Exegetical Syntax of the New Testament*. Grand Rapids, Michigan: Zondervan, 1996.

GREEK INDEX for the Practical Word Study

(Including PWS & POSB References)

A

Ἀβαδδὼν = *Abaddön* **#1**
POSB Reference:
(Rev.9:11) Note 6, pt. 4

Αββα = *Abba* **#4**
POSB Reference:
(Mk.14:36) Note 3, pt. 3

ἀχάριστοι = *acharistoi* **#4154, #4178**
POSB Reference:
(2 Tim. 3:2-4; esp. v.2) Note 2, pt. 7

ἀδημονεῖν = *adëmonein* **#1117, #4062, #4215**
POSB Reference:
(Mt.26:37) *Deeper Study* #3

ἀδιάκριτος = *adiakritos* **#2093, #2668, #4182, #4388**
POSB Reference:
(Jas.3:17-18; esp. v.17) Note 3, pt. 2g

ἀδικία = *adikia* **#1341, #2150, #2152, #4171**
POSB Reference:
(1 Cor.13:4-7; esp. v.6) Note 2, pt. 10

ἀδικίαν = *adikian* **#4170, #4338**
POSB Reference:
(Rom.1:18) Note 1, pt. 3a

ἀδόκιμοί ἐστε = *adokimoi este* **#1101, #1418, #3254**
POSB Reference:
(2 Cor.13:1-6; esp. v.5) Note 1, pt. 3

ἀδόκιμον νοῦν = *adokimon noun* **#892, #962, #1353, #3253**
POSB Reference:
(Rom.1:28-31; esp. v.28) Note 4, pt. 1

ἀδόκιμος = *adokimos* **#523, #1100**
POSB Reference:
(1 Cor.9:27) Note 6, pt. 2

ἄδολον = *adolon,* **#3100, #3580**
POSB Reference:
(1 Pt.2:2-3; esp. v.2) Note 2, pt. 1b

Ἀδύνατον = *Adunaton,* **#2100**
POSB Reference:
(Heb.6:6; esp. v.4) Note 2 (commentary for v. 4 is in v. 6)

ἀγανακτοῦντες = *aganaktountes* **#2139, #2142**
POSB Reference:
(Mk.14:4-5; esp. v.4) Note 2

ἀγαπᾷς = *agapas* **#2444**
POSB Reference:
(Jn.21:15) Note 2

ἀγαπᾶτε = *agapate* **#2426**
POSB Reference:
(Mt.5:44) *Deeper Study* #1

ἀγαπᾶτε = *agapate* **#2429**
POSB Reference:
(Eph.5:25-33; esp. v.25) Note 2, pt. 1

ἀγάπη = *agapë* **#2428**
POSB Reference:
(Gal.5:22-23; esp. v.22) Note 1

ἀγάπην = *agapën* **#549, #2427**
POSB Reference:
(1 Cor.13:1-13; esp. v.1) *Deeper Study* #1

ἀγάπην ἠγάπησεν = *agapën ëgapësen* **#2432**
POSB Reference:
(Eph.2:4-5; esp. v.4) Note 1, pt. 1b

ἀγαθάς = *agathas* **#1745, #2253**
POSB Reference:
(Tit.2:4-5; esp. v.5) Note 4 , pt. 7

ἀγαθῇ = *agathë,* **#1738**
POSB Reference:
(Lk.8:11-15; esp. v.15) Note 4, pt. 4b

ἀγαθόν = *agathon* **#1742**
POSB Reference:
(Rom.8:28) Note 1, pt. 3

ἀγαθωσύνη = *agathösunë* **#1763**
POSB Reference:
(Gal.5:22-23; esp. v.22) Note 1

ἀγγαρεύσει = *aggareusei* **#675, #949, #1572**
POSB Reference:
(Mt.5:39-41, esp.v.41) Note 3, pt. 3

ἀγγέλων = *aggelön,* **#139**
POSB Reference:
(Heb.1:4-14; esp. v.4) *Deeper Study* #1

ἄγκυραν = *agkuran* **#136**
POSB Reference:
(Heb.6:18-20; esp. v.19) Note 6, pt. 2

Ἀγνώστῳ θεῷ = *Agnöstö theö* **#4162**
POSB Reference:
(Acts 17:23) Note 3

ἀγῶνα = *agöna* **#86, #717, #3826**
POSB Reference:
(Col.2:1) Note 1

Ἀγωνίζεσθε = *Agönizesthe* **#2503, #3812, #4415**
POSB Reference:
(Lk.13:24) Note 2, pt. 2

ἀγωνίζου = *agönizomai* **#1481**
POSB Reference:
(1 Tim.6:12) Note 3

ἀγωνιζόμενος = *agönizomenos* **#234, #679, #3814**
POSB Reference:
(1 Cor.9:25) Note 2

ἄγονται = *agontai* **#2318**
POSB Reference:
(Rom.8:14) Note 7

ἀγρυπνεῖτε = *agrupneite* **#102, #4275**
POSB Reference:
(Lk.21:36) Note 2

ἀγρυπνίαις = *agrupniais* **#3619, #3620, #4289**
POSB Reference:
(2 Cor.6:5) Note 4

αἰῶνα = *aiöna* **#815, #2347, #4292**
POSB Reference:
(Eph.2:1-2; esp. v.2) Note 2

αἰῶνας = *aiönas* **#4160, #4161, #4440**
POSB Reference:
(Heb.1:2) Note 3

αἰῶνι = *aiöni* **#4433**
POSB Reference:
(Rom.12:2) Note 3, pt. 2

αἰώνιος = *aiönios* **#1319**
POSB Reference:
(Jn.17:2-3; esp. v.3) *Deeper Study* #1

αἰῶνος = *aiönos* **#83, #4432**
POSB Reference:
(1 Cor.2:6) Note 2, pt. 2

αἰῶσιν = *aiösin* **#84**
POSB Reference:
(Eph.2:7) Note 4

αἴρει = *airei* **#868, #3892**
POSB Reference:
(Jn.15:2) Note 2, pt. 3

αἴρων = *airön* **#3891**
POSB Reference:
(Jn.1:29) Note 1, pt. 4a

αἰσχρολογίαν = *aischrologian* **#25,
#1047, #1496, #1497**
POSB Reference:
(Col.3:8-11; esp. v.8) Note 2, pt. 1e

αἰσχρότης = *aischrotës* **#1495, #2728,
#2729**
POSB Reference:
(Eph.5:4) Note 4, pt. 1

αἰσχύνης = *aischunës* **#1073, #3502**
POSB Reference:
(2 Cor.4:2) Note 2

αἰσθήσει = *aisthësei* **#1055, #2162,
#2216, #4142**
POSB Reference:
(Philip.1:9-10; esp. v.9) Note 7

αἰτήματα = *aitëmata* **#3261**
POSB Reference:
(Philip.4:6-7; esp. v.6) Note 1, pt. 2

ἄκακος = *akakos* **#391, #1869, #2156**
POSB Reference:
(Heb.7:26) Note 2, pt. 2

ἀκαταστασίαι = *akatastasiai* **#1082,
#1083, #1124, #4089**
POSB Reference:
(2 Cor.12:19-21; esp. v.20) Note 3, pt. 2

ἀκαταστασίαις = *akatastasiais* **#1412,
#3333, #4088**
POSB Reference:
(2 Cor.6:4-5; esp. v.5) Note 3

ἀκαταστασίας = *akatastasias* **#663,
#1123, #2178, #3313**
POSB Reference:
(Lk.21:9-10; esp. v.9) Note 3, pt. 1

ἀκατάστατον = *akatastaton* **#3283,
#4123, #4172**
POSB Reference:
(Jas.3:7-12; esp. v.8) Note 5, pt. 3

ἀκαθαρσία = *akatharsia* **#2105, #2107,
#4120**
POSB Reference:
(Gal.5:19-21; esp. v.19) Note 2

ἀκαθαρσίαν = *akatharsian* **#2106,
#3494, #3507, #4119**
POSB Reference:
(Rom.1:24-25; esp. v.24) Note 2

ἀκάθαρτος = *akathartos* **#2103, #4117**
POSB Reference:
(Eph.5:5-6; esp. v.5) Note 5, pt. 1

ἀκαθάρτου = *akathartou* **#1339, #4116**
POSB Reference:
(Lk.4:33-37; esp. v.33) Note 3, pt. 2

ἀκέραιοι = *akeraioi* **#592, #1870,
#2155, #3097**
POSB Reference:
(Philip.2:15) Note 4, pt. 2

ἀκεραίους = *akeraious* **#2154, #3564**
POSB Reference:
(Rom.16:19-20; esp. v.19) Note 2, pt. 2

Ἀκολούθει = *akolouthei* **#616, #1542**
POSB Reference:
(Jn.1:43) *Deeper Study* #1

ἀκολουθείτω = *akoloutheitö* **#1541**
POSB Reference:
(Mt.16:24) Note 2, pt. 4

ἀκούοντα = *akouonta* **#1069, #1909,
#2355**
POSB Reference:
(Lk.2:46-47; esp. v.46) Note 3, pt. 2a

ἀκούσαντες = *akousantes* **#1907**
POSB Reference:
(Mk.3:21) Note 2

ἀκρατεῖς = *akrateis* **#2130, #2670,
#4390**
POSB Reference:
(2 Tim. 3:2-4; esp. v.3) Note 2, pt. 12

ἀκριβῶς = *akribös* **#40, #1040**
POSB Reference:
(Acts 18:25) Note 5

ἀκριβῶς = *akribös* **#497, #589**
POSB Reference:
(Eph.5:15) Note 1

ἀκυροῦντες = *akurountes* **#439, #2186,
#2677 #2716, #2744**
POSB Reference:
(Mk.7:13) *Deeper Study* #2

ἀλαζόνας = *alazonas* **#413**
POSB Reference:
(Rom.1:30) *Deeper Study* #16

ἀλήθειαν = *alëtheian* **#2221, #3330,
#4085**
POSB Reference:
(Rom.2:2-5; esp. v.2) Note 2

ἀληθείας = *alëtheias* **#4084**
POSB Reference:
(1 Cor.5:8) Note 3

ἀληθής = *alëthës* **#2137, #3171,
#4073**
POSB Reference:
(Jn.6:55) Note 3, pt. 1

ἀληθής = *alëthës* **#4074, #4207**
POSB Reference:
(Jn.8:14) Note 2

ἀληθινός = *alëthinos* **#4075**
POSB Reference:
(Rev.3:7) Note 2, pt. 2

ἀλλαχόθεν = *allachothen* **#2798,
#3630**
POSB Reference:
(Jn.10:1) Note 2, pt. 2

ἀλλογενής = *allogenës* **#1573, #3786**
POSB Reference:
(Lk.17:15-19; esp. v.18) Note 3, pt. 4

ἄλλος = *allos* **#156, #3647**
POSB Reference:
(Jn.5:32) Note 2

ἄμαχον = *amachon* **#435, #2868,
#3138, #4121**
POSB Reference:
(1 Tim.3-2-3; esp. v.3) Note 2, pt. 12

ἀμάχους = *amachous* **#436, #2872,
#3135, #4122**
POSB Reference:
(Tit.3:2) Note 4

ἀμίαντον = *amaranton* **#378, #1417**
POSB Reference:
(1 Pt.1:4) Note 2, pt. 3

ἀμελήσαντες = *amelësantes* **#2075,
#2479, #2822**
POSB Reference:
(Mt.22:3-7; esp. v.5) Note 2, pt. 3

ἄμεμπτοι = *amemptoi* **#393, #4407**
POSB Reference:
(Philip.2:15) Note 4

ἀμέμπτους = *amemptous* **#389, #4112**
POSB Reference:
(1 Thes.3:13) Note 3

ἀμετακίνητοι = *ametakinëtoi* **#2092,
#2712, #3758, #4166**
POSB Reference:
(1 Cor.15:58) Note 6, pt. 2

ἀμάραντον = *amianton* **#3716, #4125**
POSB Reference:
(1 Pt.1:4) Note 2, pt. 2

ἀμίαντος = *amiantos* **#1430, #3102,
#4127**
POSB Reference:
(Heb.13:4) Note 4

GREEK INDEX

ἀμίαντος = *amiantos* **#3101, #4126, #4177**
POSB Reference:
(Heb.7:26) Note 2

ἄμωμα = *amöma* **#19, #2157, #4380, #4389**
POSB Reference:
(Philip.2:15) Note 4, pt. 3

ἀμώμητοι = *amömëtoi* **#395**
POSB Reference:
(2 Pt.3:14) Note 4, pt. 3

ἀμώμους = *amömous* **#385, #388, #1450**
POSB Reference:
(Eph.1:4) Note 2, pt. 2

ἀμώμους = *amömous* **#394, #4111, #4378**
POSB Reference:
(Col.1:22) Note 3, pt. 2

ἀμώμους = *amömous* **#396, #1451, #2158, #4381**
POSB Reference:
(Jude 1:24-25; esp. v.24) Note 4, pt. 2

ἀνάγκαις = *anagkais* **#1867, #2654, #2655**
POSB Reference:
(2 Cor.6:4-5; esp. v.4) Note 3

ἀνάγκη ἐπίκειται = *anagkë epikeitai* **#676, #2291, #4128**
POSB Reference:
(1 Cor.9:16) Note 1

ἀνακαινώσει = *anakainösei* **#541, #3249**
POSB Reference:
(Rom.12:2) Note 4, pt. 1

ἀνακαινώσεως = *anakainöseös* **#3246**
POSB Reference:
(Tit.3:5) Note 2, pt. 2

ἀνακεφαλαιώσασθαι = *anakephalaiösasthai* **#445, #447, #1638, #3852**
POSB Reference:
(Eph.1:9-10; esp. v.10) Note 6, pt. 3

ἀνακρίνεται = *anakrinetai* **#186, #1052, #2551**
POSB Reference:
(1 Cor.2:14) Note 1, pt. 3

ἀνακρίνω = *anakrinö* **#1364, #2212, #3968**
POSB Reference:
(1 Cor.4:3) Note 2

ἀναλήμψεως = *analëmpseös* **#207, #3190, #3291, #3890**
POSB Reference:
(Lk.9:51) *Deeper Study* #1

ἀναλογίσασθε = *analogisasthe* **#732, #3962**
POSB Reference:
(Heb.12:3) Note 4

ἀναλῦσαι = *analusai* **#957, #1709**
POSB Reference:
(Philip.1:22-23; esp. v.23) Note 3, pts. 1, 2

ἀναλύσεώς = *analuseös* **#891, #959**
POSB Reference:
(2 Tim. 4:6) Note 1, pt. 2

ἀνανεοῦσθαι = *ananeousthai* **#2480, #3247, #3709**
POSB Reference:
(Eph.4:23) *Deeper Study* #2

ἀναπαήσονται = *anapaësontai* **#3277**
POSB Reference:
(Rev.14:13) Note 2, pt. 1

ἀνάπαυσιν = *anapausin* **#3275**
POSB Reference:
(Mt.11:29) Note 2 *Deeper Study* #1

ἀνασκευάζοντες = *anaskeuazontes* **#3841, #4071, #4174, #4188**
POSB Reference:
(Acts 15:24) Note 2, pt. 2

ἀναστενάξας τῷ πνεύματι = *anastenazas tö pneumati* **#3556**
POSB Reference:
(Mk.8:12) *Deeper Study* #2

ἀναστρέφεσθαι = *anastrephesthai* **#323, #705**
POSB Reference:
(1 Tim.3:14-15; esp. v.15) Note 1

ἀνάθεμα = *anathema* **#41, #135, #856**
POSB Reference:
(1 Cor.16:19-24; esp. v.22) Note 6, pt. 2

ἀνάθεμα = *anathema* **#42, #858**
POSB Reference:
(Rom.9:1-3; esp. v.3) Note 1, pt. 3

ἀναζητῆσαι = *anazëteö* **#1499, #2390, #3412**
POSB Reference:
(Acts 11:25-26; esp. v.25) Note 3

ἀναζωπυρεῖν = *anazöpurein* **#1444, #2256, #3771**
POSB Reference:
(2. Tim.1:6) Note 1

ἀνεχόμενοι = *anechomenoi* **#290, #1569, #2500**
POSB Reference:
(Col.3:13) Note 7

ἀνεγκλήτους = *anegklëtous* **#20, #377, #1601, #4169, #4377**
POSB Reference:
(Col.1:22) Note 3, pt. 3

ἀνεγκλήτους = *anegklëtous* **#386, #1602**
POSB Reference:
(1 Cor.1:8) Note 3

ἀνῆκεν = *anëken* **#1518**
POSB Reference:
(Col.3:18) Note 1, pt. 2

ἀνελεήμονας = *aneleëmonas* **#3353, #4148, #4165**
POSB Reference:
(Rom.1:31) *Deeper Study* #23

ἀνήμεροι = *anëmeroi* **#458, #847, #1480**
POSB Reference:
(2 Tim. 3:2-4; esp. v.3) Note 2, pt. 13

ἀνεπίλημπτον = *anepilëmpton* **#18, #390, #2343**
POSB Reference:
(1 Tim.3:2-3; esp. v.2) Note 2, pt. 1

ἀνὴρ λόγιος = *anër logios* **#1245, #1246, #2315**
POSB Reference:
(Acts 18:24) Note 2

ἀνέστησαν = *anestësan* **#198, #2787, #3340, #3742**
POSB Reference:
(Acts 6:9-10; esp. v.9) Note 2, pt. 2

ἀνεθάλετε = *anethalete* **#81, #1536, #3248, #3312**
POSB Reference:
(Philip.4:10) Note 1

ἀνεθεμάτισαν = *anethematisan* **#857, #2719**
POSB Reference:
(Acts 23:12-15; esp. v.12) Note 1, pt. 1

ἀνοχῆς = *anochës* **#1568, #4008**
POSB Reference:
(Rom.2:2-5; esp. v.4) Note 2, pt. 2

ἀνόητοι = *anoëtoi* **#1558**
POSB Reference:
(Gal.3:1) Note 1

ἀνομίαν = anomian #2149, #2306, #3574, #4341
POSB Reference:
(Mt.24:12) Deeper Study #6

ἀνόμως = anomös #167, #2659, #4382
POSB Reference:
(Rom.2:11-15; esp. v.12) Note 4, pt. 1a

ἀνόσιοι = anosioi #734, #4155
POSB Reference:
(2 Tim. 3:2-4; esp. v.2) Note 2, pt. 8

ἄνωθεν = anöthen #319, #1511
POSB Reference:
(Lk.1:3) Note 3, pt. 2

ἄνωθεν = anöthen #80
POSB Reference:
(Jn.3:3) Note 2, pt. 1

ἄνωθεν = anöthen #1610
POSB Reference:
(Jn.3:31) Deeper Study #1

ἀνθρώπινος = anthröpinos #662, #2665
POSB Reference:
(1 Cor.10:11-13; esp. v.13) Note 3, pt. 3

ἀνθυπάτῳ = anthupatö #964, #1771, #3051
POSB Reference:
(Acts 13:7) Note 3

ἀντίδικος = antidikos #67, #1285
POSB Reference:
(1 Pt.5:8) Note 2

ἀντίλυτρον = antilutron #3092, #3161
POSB Reference:
(1 Tim.2:3-7; esp. v 6) Note 3, pt. 4

ἀντίστητε = antistëte #3265, #3872
POSB Reference:
(1 Pt.5:9) Note 3, pt. 1

ἀντιτάσσεται = antitassetai #2785, #3266, #3482
POSB Reference:
(1 Pt.5:5) Note 2, pt. 3a

ἀντιθέσεις = antitheseis #768, #2784, #2786, #2788
POSB Reference:
(1 Tim.6:20-21; esp. v.20) Note 2, pt. 2b

ἀντίτυπον = antitupon #160, #801, #1487, #2935, #3867
POSB Reference:
(1 Pt.3:21) Note 1, pt. 3a

ἀνυπόκριτος = anupokritos #1106, #2054, #3036, #3576
POSB Reference:
(Rom.12:9-10; esp. v.9) Note 1

ἀνυπότακτοι = anupotaktoi #2176, #3177, #4173
POSB Reference:
(Tit.1:10-12; esp. v.10 Note 1, pt. 1

ἀπαρνησάσθω = aparnësasthö #953, #3117
POSB Reference:
(Mt.16:24) Note 2, pt. 2

ἀπέχετε = apechete #1886, #3189
POSB Reference:
(Lk.6:24-26; esp. v.24) Note 2, pt. 1d

ἀπέδειξεν = apedeixen #1090, #1386, #3125, #3479
POSB Reference:
(1 Cor.4:9-10; esp. v.9) Note 4

ἄπειρος = apeiros #1142, #2679, #2680, #4175
POSB Reference:
(Heb.5:13) Note 3

ἀπείθειαν = apeitheian #1075, #4106
POSB Reference:
(Rom.11:32) Note 5

ἀπειθεῖς = apeitheis #1079
POSB Reference:
(Tit.3:3) Deeper Study #2

ἀπειθήσαντες = apeithësantes #1051, #3212, #3722, #4109
POSB Reference:
(Acts 14:2) Note 4, pt. 1

ἀπειθήσασιν = apeithësasin #346, #1078, #1081, #2723
POSB Reference:
(Heb.3:13-19; esp. v.18) Note 3, pt. 7

ἀπεκδεχόμεθα = apekdechometha #1201, #2385
POSB Reference:
(Philip.3:20-21; esp. v.20) Note 3, pt. 2

ἀπηλγηκότες = apëlgëkotes #1147, #1889, #2423, #2841
POSB Reference:
(Eph.4:17-19; esp. v.19) Note 1, pt. 4

ἀπηλλοτριωμένους = apëllotriömenous #103, #3632
POSB Reference:
(Col.1:21-22; esp. v.21) Note 2

ἀπελούσασθε = apelousasthe #4265
POSB Reference:
(1 Cor.6:11) Note 4, pt. 3

ἀπερίτμητοι καρδίαις = aperitmëtoi kardiais #1914, #4114
POSB Reference:
(Acts7:42-53; esp. v.51) Note 6, pt. 5

ἀπεσταλμένος = apestalmenos #3447
POSB Reference:
(Jn.1:6) Deeper Study #1

ἀφῆκεν τὸ πνεῦμα = aphëken to pneuma #1647, #4469
POSB Reference:
(Mt.27:50) Note 3, pt. 2

ἀφελότητι = aphelotëti #1653, #3566, #3577, #3586, #3596
POSB Reference:
(Acts 2:46-47; esp. v.46) Note 6, pt. 3

ἄφεσιν = aphesin #1587, #3242
POSB Reference:
(Mt.26:28) Deeper Study #4

ἄφεσιν = aphesin #1588
POSB Reference:
(Eph.1:7) Deeper Study #1

ἀφιλάγαθοι = aphilagathoi #991, #1883, #2667, #2688
POSB Reference:
(2 Tim. 3:2-4; esp. v.3) Note 1, pt. 14

Ἀφιλάργυρος = Aphilarguros #825, #1603, #3746
POSB Reference:
(Heb.13:5-6; esp. v.5) Note 5, point 1

ἀφοριοῦσιν = aphoriousin #3451, #3488, #3888
POSB Reference:
(Mt.13:49) Deeper Study #3

ἀφωρισμένος = aphörismenos #3450, #3452, #3477
POSB Reference:
(Rom.1:1-4; esp. v.1) Note 3

ἀφορῶντες = aphoröntes #1521, #2402, #2244
POSB Reference:
(Heb.12:2) Note 3

ἀφρόνων = aphronön #1557, #2073
POSB Reference:
(Rom.2:17-20; esp. v.20) Note 1, pt. 8

ἀφροσύνη = aphrosune #1553, #1563
POSB Reference:
(Mk.7:22) Deeper Study #15

ὀφθαλμὸς πονηρός = *aphthalmos poneros* **#1306, #1351**
POSB Reference:
(Mk.7:22) *Deeper Study* #12

ἀφθαρσίαν = *aphtharsian* **#2091**
POSB Reference:
(Rom.2:7) *Deeper Study* #3

ἄφθαρτον = *aphtharton* **#2095, #2132, #3099, #3951**
POSB Reference:
(1 Pt.1:4) Note 2, pt. 1

ἀφθάρτου = *aphthartou* **#1328, #2090, #2131, #4124**
POSB Reference:
(Rom.1:22-23; esp. v.23) Note 5, pt. 2a

ἄπιστος = *apistos* **#1432, #4108**
POSB Reference:
(Lk.9:41) *Deeper Study* #2

ἀπίστου = *apistou* **#2145, #4107**
POSB Reference:
(2 Cor.6:14-16; esp. v.15) Note 2

ἀποχωρεῖτε ἀπ' = *apochöreite ap'* **#250, #956**
POSB Reference:
(Mt.7:23) *Deeper Study* #1

ἀποδεδειγμένον = *apodedeigmenon* **#39, #189, #238, #1271**
POSB Reference:
(Acts 2:22-24; esp. v.22) Note 3, pt. 1

ἀποδείξει = *apodeixei* **#951, #2982**
POSB Reference:
(1 Cor.2:4) Note 4, pt. 3

ἀποκαλύψει = *apokalupsei* **#177, #3296**
POSB Reference:
(2 Thes.1:7-8; esp. v.7) Note 2, pt. 1

ἀποκαλύψεως = *apokalupseös* **#3297, #4141**
POSB Reference:
(Eph.1:17-18; esp. v.17) Note 2, pt. 2

Ἀποκάλυψις = *Apokalupsis* **#3298**
POSB Reference:
(Rev.1:1-3; esp. v.1) Introduction

ἀποκαραδοκία = *apokaradokia* **#164, #1199, #1202, #1215**
POSB Reference:
(Rom.8:19-22; esp. v.19) Note 2

ἀποκαραδοκίαν = *apokaradokian* **#1204, #1214**
POSB Reference:
(Philip.1:20) Note 1, pt. 1

ἀποκαταλλάξῃ = *apokatallaxë* **#3200**
POSB Reference:
(Eph.2:16-17; esp. v.16) Note 4

ἀποκαταστάσεως = *apokatastaseös* **#3282, #3287**
POSB Reference:
(Acts 3:21) *Deeper Study* #3

ἀποκρίσεσιν = *apokrisesin* **#159**
POSB Reference:
(Lk.2:46-47; esp. v.47) Note 3, pt. 2c

ἀπώλεια = *apöleia* **#1003, #1321**
POSB Reference:
(Philip.3:18-19; esp. v.19) Note 2, pt. 1

ἀπωλείας = *apöleias* **#870, #1005**
POSB Reference:
(2 Pt.2:1) Note 2, pt. 2

ἀπωλείας = *apöleias* **#1004, #1154, #2884**
POSB Reference:
(2 Thes.2:3; see v.4 for commentary) Note 1, pt. 2c

ἀπολέσαι = *apolesai* **#993**
POSB Reference:
(Mt.10:28) *Deeper Study* #1

ἀπολέσαι = *apolesai* **#994, #2250**
POSB Reference:
(Lk.19:47-48; esp. v.47) Note 3, pt. 1a

ἀπόληται = *apolëtai* **#2901**
POSB Reference:
(Jn.3:16) *Deeper Study* #2

ἀπολλύμενοι = *apollumenoi* **#1000, #2234**
POSB Reference:
(2 Cor.4:7-9; esp. v.9) Note 2, pt. 4

ἀπολλυμένοις = *apollumenois* **#2422, #2902**
POSB Reference:
(2 Cor.4:3-4; esp. v.3) Note 3

ἀπολλύων = *Apolluön* **#168**
POSB Reference:
(Rev.9:11) Note 6

ἀπολογίαν = *apologian* **#158, #932, #1400**
POSB Reference:
(1 Pt.3:15) Note 3

ἀπολωλὸς = *apolölos* **#2421**
POSB Reference:
(Lk.15:4) *Deeper Study* #1

ἀπολυτρώσεως = *apolutröseös* **#1605, #3209**
POSB Reference:
(Rom.3:24) *Deeper Study* #2

ἀπολύτρωσιν = *apolutrösin* **#3094, #3208**
POSB Reference:
(Eph.1:7) Note 4

ἀπορούμενοι = *aporoumenoi* **#2903**
POSB Reference:
(2 Cor.4:7-9; esp. v.8) Note 2

ἀπωσάμενοι = *apösamenoi* **#939, #3118, #3224**
POSB Reference:
(1 Tim.1:19-20; esp. v.19) Note 3

ἀπώσατο = *apösato* **#518, #3221**
POSB Reference:
(Rom.11:1) Note 1

ἀποστασίαν ἀπὸ = *apostasian apo* **#1596, #4092, #4095**
POSB Reference:
(Acts 21:20-26; esp. v.21) Note 3, pt. 2

ἀποστόλων = *apostolön* **#169**
POSB Reference:
(Mt.10:2) *Deeper Study* #5

ἀποστυγοῦντες = *apostugountes* **#5, #1878**
POSB Reference:
(Romans. 12:9-10, esp. v.9) Note 1, pt. 1

ἀποθανεῖν = *apothanein* **#1031**
POSB Reference:
(Heb.9:27) *Deeper Study* #1

ἀποθέμενοι = *apothemenoi* **#2308, #3810, #3991**
POSB Reference:
(Heb.12:1) Note 2, pt. 1

Ἀποθέμενοι = *Apothemenoi* **#2310, #3130, #3315**
POSB Reference:
(1 Pt.2:1) Note 1

ἀποτομίαν = *apotomian* **#3490, #3765**
POSB Reference:
(Rom.11:22) Note 4, pt. 1

ἀπρόσκοποι = *aproskopoi* **#392, #2747**
POSB Reference:
(Philip.1:9-10; esp. v.10) Note 7, pt. 3

ἀπρόσκοπον = *aproskopon* **#387, #595, #4239, #4387**
POSB Reference:
(Acts 24:14-16; esp. v.16) Note 3, pt. 4b

ἀρχάς = *archas* **#1355, #3042, #3350**
POSB Reference:
(Eph.6:12) Note 3, pt. 5

ἀρχή = *archë* **#317, #1513**
POSB Reference:
(Col.1:18) Note 2

ἀρχηγὸν = *archëgon* **#241, #487, #2891**
POSB Reference:
(Heb.2:9-13; esp. v.10) Note 3, pt. 2b

ἀρχηγὸν = *archëgon* **#3041**
POSB Reference:
(Acts 5:31) *Deeper Study #1*

ἀρχῆς = *archës* **#318, #1209, #1510**
POSB Reference:
(Lk.1:3, esp. v.2) Note 3, pt. 2

ἀρχιποίμενος = *archipoimenos* **#3521**
POSB Reference:
(1 Pt.5:4) Note 3, pt. 1

ἀρχιτέκτων = *architektön* **#1397, #2542**
POSB Reference:
(1 Cor.3:10) Note 1

ἀρετὰς = *aretas* **#1375, #1764, #2996**
POSB Reference:
(1 Pt.2:9) Note 2

ἀρετὴ = *aretë* **#1374, #1378, #4233**
POSB Reference:
(Philip.4:8-9; esp. v.8) Note 2, pt. 1g

ἀρετήν = *aretën* **#1765, #2619, #4234**
POSB Reference:
(2 Pt.1:5-7; esp. v.5) Note 1, pt. 1

ἀργὸν = *argon* **#502, #2065**
POSB Reference:
(Mt.12:36) *Deeper Study #1*

ἀργοὺς = *argous* **#269, #2143, #3052, #4197**
POSB Reference:
(2 Pt.1:8-11; esp. v.8) Note 2, pt. 1

Ἀρκεῖ = *Arkei* **#114, #3851**
POSB Reference:
(2 Cor.12:7-10; esp. v.9) Note 3

ἀρνία = *arnia* **#2293**
POSB Reference:
(Jn.21:16; esp. v.15) Note 3, pt. 2

ἀρνίον = *arnion* **#2292**
POSB Reference:
(Rev.5:6-7; esp. v.6) Note 2, pt. 2

ἀρραβὼν = *arrabön* **#960, #1212, #1827, #2962**
POSB Reference:
(Eph.1:13-14; esp. v.14) Note 8

ἀρραβῶνα = *arraböna* **#961, #1210, #1512, #1826, #2961**
POSB Reference:
(2 Cor.1:21-22; esp. v.22) Note 5

ἀρσενοκοῖται = *arsenokoitai* **#22, #1983, #1984, #3643**
POSB Reference:
(1 Cor.6:9) Note 2, pt. 4

ἄρτιος = *artios* **#48, #683, #2887, #3026, #3975**
POSB Reference:
(2 Tim. 3:17) Note 5

ἄρτους τῆς προθέσεως = *artous tace protheseös* **#723, #3539, #3683**
POSB Reference:
(Lk.6:4) *Deeper Study #2*

ἀσχημονεῖ = *aschëmonei* **#44, #324, #325, #3345**
POSB Reference:
(1 Cor.13:4-7; esp. v.5) Note 2, pt. 6

ἀσέβειαν = *asebeian* **#1725, #4152**
POSB Reference:
(Tit.2:12) Note 2, pt. 1

ἀσέβειαν = *asebeian* **#1726, #3588, #4151**
POSB Reference:
(Rom.1:18) Note 1, pt. 3a

ἀσεβῶν = *asebön* **#3599, #4153**
POSB Reference:
(Rom.5:6-7; esp. v.6) Note 1, pt. 2

ἀσέλγεια = *aselgeia* **#1206, #2298, #2329, #3444**
POSB Reference:
(Mk.7:22) *Deeper Study #11*

ἀσελγείαις = *aselgeiais* **#896, #2086, #2460, #3445, #4251**
POSB Reference:
(Rom.13:13) Note 4, pt. 4

ἀσελγείαις = *aselgeiais* **#898, #2088, #2331, #3446**
POSB Reference:
(1 Pt.4:3) Note 3, pt. 1

ἀσέλγειαν = *aselgeian* **#2085, #2299, #2332, #2335, #2336**
POSB Reference:
(Jude 1:4) Note 5

ἄσκω = *askö* **#362, #1382, #3813, #4087**
POSB Reference:
(Acts 24:14-16; esp. v.16) Note 3, pt. 4a

ἀσωτία = *asötia* **#897, #1108, #1380, #4353**
POSB Reference:
(Eph.5:18) Note 4

ἀσπασάμενοι = *aspasamenoi* **#1247, #4307**
POSB Reference:
(Heb.11:13-15; esp. v.13) Note 1, pt. 2

ἀσφαλῶς γινωσκέτω = *asphalös ginösketö* **#223, #533, #598**
POSB Reference:
(Acts 2:33-36; esp. v.36) Note 4, pt. 3

ἄσπονδοι = *aspondoi* **#2192, #4072, #4150**
POSB Reference:
(2 Tim. 3:2-4; esp. v.3) Note 2, pt. 10

ἀσπόνδους = *aspondous* **#2096, #4149**
POSB Reference:
(Rom.1:31) *Deeper Study #22*

ἀσθενέστερα = *asthenestera* **#1461, #4295, #4296**
POSB Reference:
(1 Cor.12:21-23; esp. v.22) Note 3

ἀσθενῶ = *asthenön* **#1936, #2987, #4391**
POSB Reference:
(Rom.5:6-7, esp. v.6) Note 1, pt. 1

ἄστοργοι = *astorgoi* **#4164, #4383, #4386**
POSB Reference:
(2 Tim. 3:2-4; esp. v.3) Note 2, pt. 9

ἀστόργους = *astorgous* **#1912, #4163, #4385**
POSB Reference:
(Rom.1:31) *Deeper Study #21*

ἀσύνετος = *asunetos* **#1556**
POSB Reference:
(Rom.1:21) Note 4, pt. 2

ἀσυνέτους = *asunetous* **#3439, #4135, #4137, #4146**
POSB Reference:
(Rom.1:31) *Deeper Study #19*

ἀσυνθέτους = *asunthetous* **#441, #819, #1433, #4180**
POSB Reference:
(Rom.1:31) *Deeper Study #20*

ἀτενίσας = atenisas **#1524, #2399, #2732, #3739**
POSB Reference:
(Acts 10:1-8; esp. v.4) Note 1, pt. 3c

ἀτενίζοντες ἦσαν = atenizontes ësan **#1649, #2400, #2407, #3783**
POSB Reference:
(Acts 1:9-10; esp. v.10) Note 4

ἀθεμίτοις εἰδωλολατρίαις = athemitois eidölolatriais **#2072, #3939**
POSB Reference:
(1 Pt.4:3) Note 3, pt. 6

ἀθετῶ = athetö **#1613, #2549, #2717, #3478**
POSB Reference:
(Gal.2:19-21; esp. v.21) Note 5

ἀτόμῳ = atomö **#1525, #2616**
POSB Reference:
(1 Cor.15:51-52; esp. v.52) Note 2, pt. 2

αὐλὸς = aulos **#1539, #2939**
POSB Reference:
(1 Cor.14:6-14 esp. v.7) Note 3

αὐστηρός = austeros **#240, #1361, #1857, #4023**
POSB Reference:
(Lk.19:15-23; esp. v.22) Note 5, pt. 6b

αὐταρκείας = autarkeias **#757**
POSB Reference:
(1 Tim.6:6-8; esp. v.6) Note 1

αὐτάρκης = autarkës **#751, #1851**
POSB Reference:
(Philip.4:11-14; esp. v.11) Note 2, pt. 1

αὐθάδη = authadë **#204, #2810, #3436**
POSB Reference:
(Tit.1:7-8; esp. v.7) Note 3, pt. 1a

αὐτομάτη = automate **#1943, #2196, #2818**
POSB Reference:
(Mk.4:28) Note 4

ἀξίως = axiös **#309, #4453, #4454**
POSB Reference:
(Philip.1:27) Note 2

ἀξίως = axiös **#122, #4450**
POSB Reference:
(Col.1:10) Note 2

B

βαλλάντιον = ballantion **#2618, #3112**
POSB Reference:
(Lk.10:4) Note 4, pt. 1

βαπτίσει = baptisei **#266**
POSB Reference:
(Mt.3:11) Deeper Study #2

βαρηθῶσιν = barëthösin **#1488, #2811, #4306**
POSB Reference:
(Lk.21:34-35, esp. v.34) Note 1

βασανιζόμενον = basanizomenon **#276, #459, #1482, #4019**
POSB Reference:
(Mt.14:24-27, esp.v.24) Note 2, pt. 1

βασιλευέτω = basileuetö **#773, #3220**
POSB Reference:
Rom.6:12 Note 2, pt. 1

βασιλικὸς = basilikos **#1769, #2675, #3344**
POSB Reference:
(Jn.4:46-47; esp. v.46) Note 1

βατταλογήσητε = battologesete **#255, #2550, #4205**
POSB Reference:
(Mt.6:7) Deeper Study #1

βδέλυγμα ἐρημώσεως = bdelugma erëmöseös **#13, #965, #3358**
POSB Reference:
(Mt.24:15) Deeper Study #1

βεβαιῶν = bebaiön **#1318, #3728, #3734**
POSB Reference:
(2 Cor.1:21-22; esp. v.21) Note 5

βεβαιώσει = bebaiösei **#714, #2240**
POSB Reference:
(1 Cor.1:8) Note 3

βεβήλους = bebëlous **#1724, #3053, #4438**
POSB Reference:
(1 Tim.6:20-21; esp. v.20) Note 2, pt. 2

Βηθανίαν = Bëthanian **#364**
POSB Reference:
(Mt.21:17-18; esp. v.17) Note 1

Βηθφαγὴ = Bëthphagë **#365**
POSB Reference:
(Mt.21:1) Deeper Study #2

βλασφημεῖ = blasphëmei **#398**
POSB Reference:
(Mt.9:3) Deeper Study #4

βλασφημία = blasphemia **#399, #3605**
POSB Reference:
(Mk.7:22) Deeper Study #13

βλασφημία = blasphëmia **#1356, #3606**
POSB Reference:
(Eph.4:31) Note 6, pt. 5

βλάσφημοι = blasphëmoi **#23, #397, #3310, #3390**
POSB Reference:
(2 Tim.3:2-4; esp. v.2) Note 2, pt. 5

Βλέπετε = Blepete **#281, #374, #3408, #3874, #3884**
POSB Reference:
(Heb.3:12) Note 2

βλέπετε = blepete **#371, #4281**
POSB Reference:
(Mk.8:15) Deeper Study #2

βλέπετε = blepete **#375, #1149, #3407**
POSB Reference:
(Col.2:8) Note 1

βλεπόντων = blepontön **#311, #329, #2408, #4286**
POSB Reference:
(Acts 1:9) Note 4

βοηθῆσαι = boëthësai **#94, #622, #1925, #3842**
POSB Reference:
(Heb 2:17-18, esp. v.18) Note 2, pt. 4

Βόσκε = Boske **#1462, #3934**
POSB Reference:
(Jn.21:16; cp. Jn.21:15, 17) Note 3, pt. 3

βουλῇ = boulë **#808, #2950, #3111**
POSB Reference:
(Acts 2:23) Deeper Study #3, pt. 2

βρυγμὸς = brugmos **#1708**
POSB Reference:
(Mt.8:12) Note 3, pt. 3

C

Χαίρετε. = Chairete **#1805, #1841, #3225**
POSB Reference:
(Mt.28:9) Deeper Study #2

χαρακτὴρ = charaktër **#1360, #1404, #3252**
POSB Reference:
(Heb.1:3) Note 5

χαρᾶς = charas **#1854, #2206**
POSB Reference:
(Rom. 15:13) Note 5, pt. 1

χαρᾶς = charas **#2207**
POSB Reference:
(Philip.1:4) Note 3

χάριν = *charin* **#1772, #1948**
POSB Reference:
(Rom.5:2) Note 3, pt. 1

χάρις = *charis* **#1715, #1775**
POSB Reference:
(1 Pt.1:2) Note 5, pt. 1

χάρις = *charis* **#1774**
POSB Reference:
(Eph.1:2) *Deeper Study* #1

χάρισμα = *charisma* **#406, #1671**
POSB Reference:
(Rom.1:10-13; esp. v.11) Note 4, pt. 1

χάρισμα = *charisma* **#1672**
POSB Reference:
(1 Pt.4:10-11; esp. v. 10) Note 5

χαρίσματα = *charismata* **#10, #1674**
POSB Reference:
(Rom.12:6-8; esp. v.6) Note 2

χάριτι = *chariti* **#1654, #1773**
POSB Reference:
(1 Cor.1:4) *Deeper Study* #1

χαριζόμενοι = *charizomenoi* **#1586**
POSB Reference:
(Col.3:13) Note 8

χειρόγραφον = *cheirographon* **#536, #1849, #3202, #4466**
POSB Reference:
(Col.2:14) Note 2, pt. 1

χειροτονήσαντες = *cheirotonēsantes* **#182, #2790**
POSB Reference:
(Acts 14:23) *Deeper Study* #3

χρηματίζοντα = *chrēmatizonta* **#3673, #3718, #4255**
POSB Reference:
(Heb.12:25) Note 1

χρηστοί = *chrēstoi* **#2251**
POSB Reference:
(Eph.4:32) Note 7, pt. 1

χρηστόν = *chrēston* **#1762, #2254**
POSB Reference:
(Rom.2:2-5; esp. v.4) Note 2, pt. 2

χρηστός = *chrēstos* **#1223, #1520**
POSB Reference:
(Mt.11:29-30, esp.v.30) Note 2, pt. 1

χρηστότης = *chrēstotēs* **#1662, #2258**
POSB Reference:
(Gal.5:22-23; esp. v.22) Note 1, pt. 5

χρηστότης = *chrēstotēs* **#2259**
POSB Reference:
(Tit..3:4-5; esp. v.4) Note 1, pt. 1

χρηστότητα = *chrēstotēta* **#1740**
POSB Reference:
(Rom.3:10-12; esp. v.12) Note 2, pt. 6

χρίσας = *chrisas* **#155, #652**
POSB Reference:
(2 Cor.1:21-22; esp. v.21) Note 5

Χριστοῦ = *Christou* **#581, #2580**
POSB Reference:
(Mk.1:1) *Deeper Study* #2

Χριστοῦ = *Christou* **#582**
POSB Reference:
(Jas.1:1) Note 1

χρόνον = *chronon* **#880, #3399, #3994**
POSB Reference:
(Acts 20:18-19; esp. v.18) Note 2, pt. 1

D

δεήσει = *deēsei* **#2932, #3856, #4323**
POSB Reference:
(Philip.4:6-7; esp. v.6) Note 1, pt. 2

δεήσεις = *deēseis* **#1299, #3262, #3857**
POSB Reference:
(1 Tim.2:1) Note 1, pt. 1

δεῖ = *dei* **#1839, #2637**
POSB Reference:
(Mt.16:21-23; esp. v.21) Note 1

δεῖν = *dein* **#2638, #2799, #3527**
POSB Reference:
(Lk.18:1) Note 1, pt. 2

δειξάτω = *deixatō* **#2361, #3534**
POSB Reference:
(Jas.3:13) Note 1

δελεαζόμενος = *deleazomenos* **#1294, #2459**
POSB Reference:
(Jas.1:14-16; esp. v.14) Note 2, pt. 1

δεόμενος = *deomenos* **#3001**
POSB Reference:
(Acts 10:1-8; esp. v.2) Note 1, pt. 2

δεόμεθα = *deometha* **#312, #2098, #2999, #4190**
POSB Reference:
(2 Cor.5:20) Note 3

δέους = *deous* **#253, #1731**
POSB Reference:
(Heb.12:28-29; esp. v.28) Note 3, pt. 2

δήσητε = *dēsēte* **#379, #3057**
POSB Reference:
(Mt.18:17-18; esp. v.18) Note 2, pt. 2

Δέσποτα = *Despota* **#2414, #3671**
POSB Reference:
(Acts 4:24) *Deeper Study* #1

δέξηται = *dexētai* **#3185, #4309**
POSB Reference:
(Mt.18:5) Note 1

διά γραφῶν προφητικῶν = *dia graphōn prophētikōn* **#206, #467, #468, #3990**
POSB Reference:
(Rom.16:25-26, esp. v.26) Note 3, pt. 2

διάβολοι = *diaboloi* **#3607**
POSB Reference:
(2 Tim. 3:2-4; esp. v.3) Note 2, pt. 11

διάβολος = *diabolos* **#1010**
POSB Reference:
(1 Pt.5:8) Note 2, pt. 2

διαβόλους = *diabolous* **#1441, #2524, #3613, #3679**
POSB Reference:
(Tit.2:3) Note 3, pt. 2

διαδήματα = *diadēmata* **#844, #1024**
POSB Reference:
(Rev.19:12) Note 2, pt. 2

διακατηλέγχετο = *diakatēlegcheto* **#197, #791, #3215**
POSB Reference:
(Acts 18:27-28; esp. v.28) Note 8, pt. 2b

διακονεῖν = *diakonein* **#49, #3468, #4243**
POSB Reference:
(Acts 6:2) *Deeper Study* #1

διακονίαν = *diakonian* **#2603, #3473, #3475**
POSB Reference:
(Rom.12:6-8; esp. v.7) Note 2, pt. 2

διάκονοι = *diakonoi* **#2601, #3463**
POSB Reference:
(1 Cor.3:5) Note 1

διακόνοις = *diakonois* **#95, #236, #3462**
POSB Reference:
(Mt.22:11-14; esp. v.13) Note 4, pt. 2

διάκονον = *diakonon* **#884, #3459**
POSB Reference:
(Rom.16:1-2; esp. v.1) Note 1, pt. 3

διακονῶν = *diakonön* **#3458, #3469**
POSB Reference:
(Lk.22:26-27 esp. v.26) Note 3, pt. 2

Διακόνους = *Diakonous* **#885**
POSB Reference:
(1 Tim.3:8-13 esp. v.8) *Deeper Study* #1

διακρίνων = *diakrinön* **#1054, #2006, #2211, #3199**
POSB Reference:
(1 Cor.11:27-30; esp. v.29) Note 4, pt. 2

διαλεγόμενος = *dialegomenos* **#193, #1099, #3176**
POSB Reference:
(Acts 19:2-9; esp. v.8) Note 2, pt. 2a

διαλογισμοὶ οἱ κακοὶ = *dialogismoi hoi kakoi* **#1359**
POSB Reference:
(Mk.7:21) *Deeper Study* #3

διαλογισμοῖς = *dialogismois* **#2063, 2197, #3689, #3966, #3984**
POSB Reference:
(Rom.1:21) Note 4, pt. 1

διαλογισμῶν = *dialogismön* **#192**
POSB Reference:
(Philip.2:14) Note 3

διαμαρτυρόμενος = *diamarturomenos* **#924, #2575, #3946**
POSB Reference:
(Acts 20:20-21; esp. v.21) Note 3, pt. 3

διαμεριζόμεναι = *diamerizomenai* **#609, #1122, #1127, #3453**
POSB Reference:
(Acts 2:2-4; esp. v.3) Note 4, pt. 2

διανοίας = *dianoia* **#2591**
POSB Reference:
(Mk.12:30) Note 2, pt. 2

διαφθοράν = *diaphthoran* **#806, #901, #1777, #3341**
POSB Reference:
(Acts 2:25-28; esp. v.27) Note 1, pt. 2c
(Acts 2:27) *Deeper Study* #1, pt. 2

διαπονηθεὶς = *diaponëtheis* **#154, #1371, #1816, #4067**
POSB Reference:
(Acts 16:18) Note 2, pt. 2

διασείσητε = *diaseisëte* **#1406, #2184, #3885, #4227**
POSB Reference:
(Lk.3:10-14; esp. v.14) Note 5, pt. 3a

διασπαρέντες = *diasparentes* **#1527, #3383**
POSB Reference:
(Acts 8:4) Note 4, pt. 1

διασπορᾷ = *diaspora* **#1088, #3385, #3386**
POSB Reference:
(Jas.1:1) Note 2, pt. 2

διαθήκην = *diathëkën* **#818**
POSB Reference:
(Gal.3:15) Note 1

διαθήκης = *diathëkës* **#817, #3943**
POSB Reference:
(2 Cor.3:6) Note 1

διχοστασίαι = *dichostasiai* **#1098, #1105, #1130, #3402**
POSB Reference:
(Gal.5:19-21; esp. v.20) Note 2

διχοστασίας = *dichostasias* **#1104, #1129**
POSB Reference:
(Rom.16:17-18; esp. v.17) Note 1, pt. 1

διδαχῇ = *didachë* **#1141, #3913**
POSB Reference:
(Acts 2:42) *Deeper Study* #2

Διδάσκαλε = *Didaskale* **#2541, #3907**
POSB Reference:
(Mt.8:19) *Deeper Study* #2

διδασκαλίαν = *didaskalian* **#2172, #2316, #3899**
POSB Reference:
(Rom.15:4) Note 2, pt. 1

διδάσκαλοι = *didaskaloi* **#2544, #3909**
POSB Reference:
(Jas.3:1-12; esp v.1) Note 1

διδασκάλους = *didaskalous* **#3908**
POSB Reference:
(Eph.4:11) Note 3, pt. 5

διδάσκων = *didaskön* **#3906**
POSB Reference:
(Rom.12:6-8; esp. v.7) Note 2, pt. 3

διεκρίνοντο = *diekrinonto* **#749, #839, #4014**
POSB Reference:
(Acts 11:1-3; esp. v.2) Note 1, pt. 2

διεκρίθη = *diekrithë* **#3729, #4290**
POSB Reference:
(Rom.4:18-22; esp. v.20) Note 2, pt. 1b

διελέγετο = *dielegeto* **#894, #1096, #3175**
POSB Reference:
(Acts 17:17) Note 2

διελογίζεσθε = *dielogizesthe* **#194, #1068, #1095**
POSB Reference:
(Mk.9:33) Note 1

διελογίζοντο = *dielogizonto* **#1067, #3174, #3893**
POSB Reference:
(Mk.11:29-32; esp. v.31) Note 3, pt. 2

διεφέρετο = *diephereto* **#3084, #3720**
POSB Reference:
(Acts 13:46-52; esp. v.49) Note 2, pt. 2d

διηπόρουν = *diëporoun* **#1155, #2905**
POSB Reference:
(Acts 2:12-13; esp. v.12) Note 6, pt. 1

διηπόρουν = *diëporoun* **#1156, #2904, #3131, #4398**
POSB Reference:
(Acts 5:21-25; esp. v.24) Note 4, pt. 3

διεπρίοντο = *dieprionto* **#865, #866, #1629**
POSB Reference:
(Acts 5:32-40; esp. v.33) Note 4, pt. 1

διεπρίοντο ταῖς καρδίαις = *dieprionto tais kardiais* **#864, #867, #1630, #2146**
(Acts 7:54) Note 1, pt. 2

διεσώθησαν = *diesöthësan* **#853, #1898, #2487, #2489**
POSB Reference:
(Mt.14:36) Note 6

διεστείλατο = *diesteilato* **#547, #647, #1642, #4006**
POSB Reference:
(Mk.7:36) Note 5

διεστραμμένη = *diestrammenë* **#2927, #2929, #3827**
POSB Reference:
(Lk.9:41) *Deeper Study* #3

διέτριβεν = *dietriben* **#3239, #3694, #3695, #3750**
POSB Reference:
(Jn.3:22-26; esp. v.22) Note 1, pt. 1

διϊκνούμενος = *diiknoumenos* **#869, #2878, #2937**
POSB Reference:
(Heb.4:11-13; esp. v.22) Note 5, pt. 2

ἔβαλεν = *ebalen* **#516, #1538, #3988**
POSB Reference:
(Rev.12:3-4; esp.v.4) Note 2

ἐβάσκανεν = *ebaskanen* **#376, #4322**
POSB Reference:
(Gal.3:1) Note 1

ἐβάστασεν = *ebastasen* **#267, #421, #514, #3243**
POSB Reference:
(Mt.8:17) Note 3

ἐβλήθη ἔξω = *eblëthë exö* **#520, #3992**
POSB Reference:
(Jn.15:4-6; esp. v.6) Note 4, pt. 4a

ἐβούλοντο = *eboulonto* **#917, #2180, #2963, #4013**
POSB Reference:
(Acts 5:32-40; esp. v.33) Note 4, pt. 1

ἔβρυχον = *ebruchon* **#1707, #3525**
POSB Reference:
(Acts 7:54) Note 1, pt. 3

ἐχάρησαν = *echarësan* **#1695, #1788, #3228**
POSB Reference:
(Acts 15:30-35; esp. v.31) Note 5, pt. 1

ἐχάρητε = *echarëte* **#1693, #1853, #3226**
POSB Reference:
(Jn.14:28-29; esp. v.28) Note 2

ἔχει πίστιν τοῦ σωθῆναι = *echei pistin tou söthënai* **#1901, #4312**
POSB Reference:
(Acts 14:8-13; esp. v.9) Note 2, pt. 1d

ἠχρεώθησαν = *ëchreöthësan* **#305, #306, #308, #1736**
POSB Reference:
(Rom.3:10-12; esp. v.12) Note 2, pt. 5

ἔχθραι = *echthrai* **#1290, #1884, #2019**
POSB Reference:
(Gal.5:19-21; esp. v.20) Note 2

ἐχθροί = *echthroi* **#1283**
POSB Reference:
(Rom.11:28-29, esp. v. 28) Note 3, pt. 1

ἐχθροὺς = *echthrous* **#1284, #2018**
POSB Reference:
(Col.1:21-22; esp. v.21) Note 2, pt. 2

ἤδη κέκριται = *ëdë kekritai* **#702, #2214, #2215**
POSB Reference:
(Jn.3:18) Note 2

ἐδίδασκεν = *edidaske* **#3900**
POSB Reference:
(Mk.9:31) Note 2, pt. 1

ἔδωκεν = *edoken* **#1645, #2757**
POSB Reference:
(Mk.14:23-24; esp. v.23) Note 2, pt. 3

ἔδωκεν = *edöken* **#1641**
POSB Reference:
(Jn.3:16) Note 2, pt. 2

ἐδολιοῦσαν = *edoliousan* **#1493, #2233, #2991, #4193**
POSB Reference:
(Rom.3:13-14; esp. v.13) Note 3, pt. 2

ἐδόξαζον τὸν θεὸν = *edoxazon ton theon* **#1700, #2995**
POSB Reference:
(Lk.7:16-17; esp. v.16) Note 4, pt. 1

ἠγαλλιάσατο = *ëgalliasato* **#1410, #1696, #3229, #3529**
POSB Reference:
(Acts 2:25-28; esp. v.26) Note 1, pt. 1b

ἠγανάκτησεν = *ëganaktësen* **#1092, #2138**
POSB Reference:
(Mk.10:14) *Deeper Study #2*

Ἔγειρε = *Egeire* **#3334, #3737, #3762**
POSB Reference:
(Mk.3:3) Note 2

ἐγένετο = *egeneto* **#479, #831, #4318**
POSB Reference:
(Jn.1:3) Note 2, pt. 2

ἐγένετο ἐπ' ἔκστασις = *egeneto ep' ekstasis* **#1467**
POSB Reference:
Acts 10:9-22; esp. v.10) Note 2, pt. 3

ἐγερθῆναι = *egerthënai* **#248, #4245**
POSB Reference:
(Rom.13:11-12; esp. v.11) Note 2

ἤγετο ἐν τῷ πνεύματι = *ëgeto en tö pneumati* **#3700**
POSB Reference:
(Lk.4:1-2; esp. v.1) Note 1, pt. 1b

ἐγκαταλειπόμενοι = *egkataleipomenoi* **#3, #1597**
POSB Reference:
(2 Cor.4:7-9; esp. v.9) Note 2, pt. 3

ἐγκαταλείψεις = *egkataleipseis* **#2, #2317**
POSB Reference:
(Acts 2:25-28; esp. v.27) Note 1, pt. 2a

ἐγκομβώσασθε = *egkombösasthe* **#282, #606, #608, #3470**
POSB Reference:
(1 Pt.5:5) Note 2, pt. 2

ἐγκράτεια = *egkrateia* **#3422, #3921**
POSB Reference:
(Gal.5:22-23; esp. v.23) Note 1

Ἐγώ εἰμι = *ego eimi* **#2057**
POSB Reference:
(Mk.14:62) Note 5, pt. 1

Ἐγώ εἰμι = *Egö eimi* **#2058, #2195**
POSB Reference:
(Jn.6:20) *Deeper Study #1*

Ἐγόγγυζον = *Egogguzon* **#680, #1824, #2634**
POSB Reference:
(Jn.6:41-43; esp. v.41) Note 1

ἠγοράσθητε = *ëgorasthëte* **#424**
POSB Reference:
(1 Cor.6:20) *Deeper Study #2*

εἰδέναι = *eidenai* **#187, #1995, #2267, #3198, #3270**
POSB Reference:
(1 Thes.5:12-13; esp.v.12) Note 1, pt. 1

εἰδωλολάτραι = *eidölolatrai* **#2069, #2070**
POSB Reference:
(1 Cor.6:9) Note 2, pt. 2

εἰδωλολατρίας = *eidölolatrias* **#2071, #4446**
POSB Reference:
(1 Cor.10:14) Note 1

εἰδότες = *eidotes* **#2269, #4139**
POSB Reference:
(Rom.13:11) Note 1

εἰκὼν = *eikön* **#2076**
POSB Reference:
(Col.1:15) Note 1

εἰλικρινῆ διάνοιαν = *eilikrinë dianoian* **#3105, #3582, #4335**
POSB Reference:
(2 Pt.3:1-2; esp. v.1) Note 1

εἰλικρινείᾳ τοῦ θεοῦ = *eilikrineia too theou* **#1733, #3575, #3587**
POSB Reference:
(2 Cor.1:12) Note 1

εἰλικρινείας = *eilikrineias* **#3585**
POSB Reference:
(2 Cor.2:16-17; esp. v.17) Note 4

εἰλικρινεῖς = *eilikrineis #3096, #3578*
POSB Reference:
(Philip.1:9-10; esp. v.9) Note 7, pt. 2

εἶπεν μεγάλῃ φωνῇ = *eipen megalë phönë #475, #2425*
POSB Reference:
(Acts 14:8-13; esp. v.10) Note 2, pt. 1e

εἰρήνη = *eirënë #2866*
POSB Reference:
(Gal.1:3) Note 3

εἰρήνην = *eirënë #2864*
POSB Reference:
(Lk.19:42) *Deeper Study #1*

εἰρήνην = *eirënën #2865, #3276*
POSB Reference:
(Acts 9:31) Note 1

Εἰρήνην = *Eirënën #2867*
POSB Reference:
(Heb.12:14) Note 1, pt. 1

εἰρηνεύετε = *eirëneuete #2365*
POSB Reference:
(2 Cor.13:11-13; esp. v.11) Note 3

εἰρηνική = *eirënikë #2870, #2871*
POSB Reference:
(Jas.3:17-18; esp. v.17) Note 3, pt. 2b

εἰρηνοποιοί = *eirenopoios #2873, #3977*
POSB Reference:
(Mt.5:9) Note 8

εἰς αὐτήν = *eis autën #2185, #3999*
POSB Reference:
(Rev.21:24-27; esp. v.24) Note 1, pt. 5

εἰς μνημόσυνον = *eis mnëmosunon #2560, #2561, #4167*
POSB Reference:
(Acts 10:1-6; esp. v.4) *Deeper Study #1*

εἰς τὰ ἴδια = *eis ta idia #1958*
POSB Reference:
(Jn.1:10-11; esp. v.11) Note 2, pt. 2

εἰς τὸ ἐμὸν ὄνομα = *eis to emon onoma #298, #2121*
POSB Reference:
(Mt.18:19-20; esp . v.20) *Deeper Study #3*

εἰς τὸ παντελές = *eis to panteles #686, #1584, #2771, #4200*
POSB Reference:
(Heb.7:25) Note 1, pt. 3

ἐκ = *ek #1609, #2804*
POSB Reference:
(Jn.6:33) Note 3, pt. 1a

ἐκ ψυχῆς = *ek psuchës #1612, #4368*
POSB Reference:
(Eph.6:5-8; esp. v.6) Note 1, pt. 4

ἐκ θελήματος ἀνδρὸς = *ek thelëmatos andros #2032, #2051, #4351*
POSB Reference:
(Jn.1:12-13; esp. v.13) Note 3, pt. 3a

ἐκ θελήματος σαρκὸς = *ek thelëmatos sarkos #2029, #2031, #4352*
POSB Reference:
(Jn.1:12-13; esp. v.13) Note 3, pt. 3a

ἐκάθευδον = *ekatheudön #214, #3618*
POSB Reference:
(Mt.25:5) *Deeper Study #4*

ἐκάθισεν = *ekathisen #3280, #3281, #3373, #3486*
POSB Reference:
(Acts 2:2-4; esp. v.3) Note 4, pt. 2b

ἐκβάλλει = *ekballei #677, #1175, #1177, #2094, #3449*
POSB Reference:
(Mk.1:12) Note 2

ἐκβληθήσεται ἔξω = *ekblëthësetai exö #521, #1174*
POSB Reference:
(Jn.12:31) *Deeper Study #3*, pt. 3

ἐκχεῶ = *ekcheö #2969*
POSB Reference:
(Acts 2:17-21; esp. v.17) Note 2, pt. 1

ἐκδικήσεως = *ekdikëseös #3089, #4214*
POSB Reference:
(Lk.21:22) *Deeper Study #1*

ἐκένωσεν = *ekenösen #1249, #2481, #3258*
POSB Reference:
(Philip.2:7) Note 3, pt.1

ἐκήρυσσεν = *ekërussen #3006, #3047, #4005*
POSB Reference:
(Acts 8:5) Note 1

ἐκκλησία = *ekklësia #218, #587, #721*
POSB Reference:
(Acts 7:38) *Deeper Study #4*

ἐκκλησίαν = *ekklësian #586*
POSB Reference:
(Mt.16:18) *Deeper Study #1*

ἐκκλίνετε = *ekklinete #246, #249*
POSB Reference:
(Rom.16:17-18; esp. v.17) Note 1, pt. 1b

ἐκκοπήσῃ = *ekkopësë #861*
POSB Reference:
(Rom.11:22) Note 4, pt. 2

ἔκλαυσεν = *eklausen #849, #4315*
POSB Reference:
(Lk.19:41-42; esp. v.41) Note 1, pt. 1a

ἐκλεκτῇ = *eklektë #573, #1240*
POSB Reference:
(2 Jn.1:1) Note 1

ἐκλεκτῶν = *eklektön #571, #1238*
POSB Reference:
(Lk.18:7) *Deeper Study #1*

ἐκλεκτῶν = *eklektön #574, #1239*
POSB Reference:
(Tit.1:1) Note 2

ἐκλεκτοὺς = *eklektous #577, #1237*
POSB Reference:
(Mt.24:31) Note 6

ἐκληρώθημεν = *eklëröthëmen #572, #2148*
POSB Reference:
(Eph.1:11-13; esp. v.11) Note 7, pt. 2

ἐκλύου = *ekluou #1065, #1420, #2416*
POSB Reference:
(Heb.12:5-7, esp. v.5) Note 1, pt. 2

ἐκνήψατε = *eknëpsate #247, #304, #619*
POSB Reference:
(1 Cor.15:34) Note 4

ἠκολούθει = *ëkolouthei #1549*
POSB Reference:
(Jn.6:1-6; esp. v.2) Note 1

ἠκολούθησαν = *ëkolouthësan #1547*
POSB Reference:
(Jn.1:35-37; esp. v.37) Note 1, pt. 3

ἐκοπίασα = *ekopiasa #2282, #4424*
POSB Reference:
(1 Cor.15:8- 10; esp. v.10) Note 5, pt. 3

ἐκόπτοντο = *ekoptonto #369, #1811, #2629*
POSB Reference:
(Lk.23:27) Note 2

ἤκουεν = *ëkouen #1906, #2353*
POSB Reference:
(Acts 16:14) Note 4

ἐκπειράζωμεν = *ekpeirazömen #3929, #3941, #4086*
POSB Reference:
(1 Cor.10:6-10; esp. v.9) Note 2, pt. 4

ἐκραταιοῦτο = ekrataiouto #3816, #4291
POSB Reference:
(Lk.2:40) Note 3, pt. 1

ἔκραξεν = ekraxen #474, #837, #3528
POSB Reference:
(Jn.7:37-39; esp. v.37) Note 2

ἔκραξεν = ekraxen #474, #838
POSB Reference:
(Jn.7:25-31; esp. v.28) Note 2

ἔκρινά = ekrina #2059, #2060, #2062
POSB Reference:
(1 Cor.2:2) Note 2

ἐκτενῇ = ektenë #927, #1472
POSB Reference:
(1 Pt.4:8) Note 3

ἐκτενῶς = ektenös #744, #1217, #1474, #4379
POSB Reference:
(Acts 12:5-17; esp. v.5) Note 2, pt. 1c

ἐκτενῶς = ektenös #929, #1475, #2181
POSB Reference:
(1 Pt.1:22-25; esp. v.22) Note 1

ἐκθαμβεῖσθαι = ekthambeisthai #1119, #1492, #3657
POSB Reference:
(Mk.14:33-34; esp. v.33) Note 2

ἐκτίσθη = ektisthë #832
POSB Reference:
(Col.1:16) Note 1, pt. 3

ἐκτρέφει = ektrephei #504, #1465, #2715
POSB Reference:
(Eph.5:25-33; esp. v.29) Note 2, pt. 2

ἐκζητῶν = ekzëtön #3415
POSB Reference:
(Rom.3:10-12; esp. v.11) Note, pt. 3

ἐκζητοῦσιν = ekzëtousin #1041, #1218, #3413, #3584
POSB Reference:
(Heb.11:6) Note 5, pt. 2b

ἔλαβεν = elaben #4012
POSB Reference:
(Mt.8:17) Note 3

ἔλαβεν φόβος = elaben phobos #1456, #1490
POSB Reference:
(Lk.7:16-17; esp. v.16) Note 4

ἐλάλουν = elaloun #3672, #3675, #3717
POSB Reference:
(Acts 11:19-30; esp. v.20) Deeper Study #2, pt. 1

ἐλέει = eleei #2569
POSB Reference:
(Eph.2:4-5; esp. v.4) Note 1, pt. 1a

ἐλεεινός = eleeinos #2607, #2941
POSB Reference:
(Rev.3:16-17; esp. v.17) Note 4, pt. 2b

ἐλεήμονες = eleëmones #2567
POSB Reference:
(Mt.5:7) Note 6

ἐλεημοσυνῶν ἐποίει = eleëmosunön epoiei #119, #548, #1934
POSB Reference:
(Acts 9:36-39; esp. v.36) Note 2, pt. 1c

ἐλέγχειν = elegchein #783, #788, #3214. #3535
POSB Reference:
(Tit.1:9) Note 4, pt. 2

ἐλέγχετε = elegchete #1402, #3255
POSB Reference:
(Eph.5:11-12; esp. v.11) Note 4, pt. 2

ἐλέγξει = elegxei #784, #786, #3257
POSB Reference:
(Jn.16:8-11; esp. v.8) Note 2

ἔλεγξον = elegxon #787, #797, #3256
POSB Reference:
(2 Tim. 4:2) Note 2, pt. 3

ἐλεῶν = eleön #3545, #3547, #3548
POSB Reference:
(Rom.12:6-8; esp. v.8) Note 2, pt. 7

ἐλογίσθη = elogisthë #38, #834, #923, #2108, #3196
POSB Reference:
(Rom.4:22) Deeper Study #1

Ἐλογίσθη = elogisthë #37, #833, #922, #3195
POSB Reference:
(Rom. 4:9) Note 2

ἐλπίδα = elpida #712, #2008
POSB Reference:
(Rom.5:3-5; esp. v.4) Note 5, pt. 3

ἐλπίδι = elpidi #1205, #2009
POSB Reference:
(Rom.8:24-25, esp. v.24) Deeper Study #1

ἠλπίζομεν = ëlpizomen #2010, #3980, #4082
POSB Reference:
(Lk.24:15-27; esp. v.21) Note 2, pt. 2a

ἐλυμαίνετο = elumaineto #998, #1008, #1890, #3164
POSB Reference:
(Acts 8:3) Note 3

ἐλυτρώθητε = elutröthëte #2820, #3207
POSB Reference:
(1 Pt.1:18-20; esp. v.18) Note 4

Ἐμάχοντο = Emachonto #191, #3132, #3822
POSB Reference:
(Jn.6:52-53; esp. v.52) Note 1

ἐματαιώθησαν = emataiöthësan #1555, #1632, #4203
POSB Reference:
(Rom.1:21) Note 4, pt. 1

ἐμβλέψας = emblepsas #330, #2396, 2406
POSB Reference:
(Jn.1:42) Note 6, pt. 1

ἐμβριμησάμενος = embrimesamenos #3764, #3785, #3803, #3821, #4007
POSB Reference:
(Mk.1:43) Note 3, pt. 2

Ἐμμανουήλ = Emmanouël #1248, #2080
POSB Reference:
(Mt.1:23) Deeper Study #9

ἐμοίχευσεν = emoicheusen #64
POSB Reference:
(Mt.5:28) Note 2

ἐμφανῇ γενέσθαι = emphanë genesthai #171, #307, #3418, #3544
POSB Reference:
(Acts 10:40-41; esp. v.40) Note 6, pt. 1

ἐμφανίσω = emphanisö #1063, #2529, #3295, #3530, #3532
POSB Reference:
(Jn.14:21) Deeper Study #3

ἔμφυτον = emphuton #1288, #2097, #2951
POSB Reference:
(Jas.1:19-21; esp. v.21) Note 1, pt. 5

ἔμφυτον = emphuton #1289, #2015
POSB Reference:
(1 Tim.3:2-3; esp. v.2) Note 2, pt. 6

ἦν = *ën* **#4258**
POSB Reference:
(Jn.1:1-2; esp. v.1) Note 1, pt. 1b

Ἐν ἀρχῇ = *En archë* **#2124**
POSB Reference:
(Jn.1:1-2; esp. v.1) Note 1, pt. 1a

ἐν αὐτῷ = *en autö* **#465, #583**
POSB Reference:
(Col.1:16) Note 1, pt. 1

ἐν χάριτι = *en chariti* **#1776, #4369**
POSB Reference:
(Col.4:6) Note 3

ἐν Χριστῷ Ἰησοῦ· = *en Christö Iësou* **#464, #2111, #3989**
POSB Reference:
(Rom.3:24) Note 3, pt. 2

ἐν ἐκείνῃ τῇ ἡμέρᾳ = *en ekeinë të hëmera* **#881, #3763, #3995**
POSB Reference:
(Acts 8:1) Note 1, pt. 2

ἦν ἔντιμος = *ën entimos* **#889, #1949, #1950, #4208**
POSB Reference:
(Lk.7:2) Note 2

ἐν ἁπλότητι = *en haplotëti* **#2334, #1655, #3568**
POSB Reference:
(Rom.12:6-8; esp. v.8) Note 2, pt. 5

ἐν ἱλαρότητι = *en hilarotëti* **#560, #1697**
POSB Reference:
(Rom.12:6-8; esp. v.8) Note 2, pt. 7

ἐν κυρίῳ = *en kuriö* **#299, #2126**
POSB Reference:
(Eph.6:1-3; esp. v.1) Note 1, pt. 1

ἐν λύπῃ = *en lupë* **#2117, #2823, #3658**
POSB Reference:
(2 Cor.2:1) Note 2

ἐν μυστηρίῳ = *en mustëriö* **#2642, #3400**
POSB Reference:
(1 Cor.2:7) *Deeper Study* #1

ἐν οἰκονόμοις = *en oikonomois* **#1684, #3119, #3766**
POSB Reference:
(1 Cor.4:1-2; esp. v.2) Note 1, pt. 2

ἐν παντὶ = *en panti* **#2116, #2766**
POSB Reference:
(2 Cor.4:7-9; esp. v.8) Note 2, pt. 1

ἐν πνεύματι ἀκαθάρτῳ = *en pneumati akatharto* **#1357, #4118**
POSB Reference:
(Mk.1:23-24; esp. v.23) Note 1

ἐν σπουδῇ = *en spoudë* **#1037, #3455**
POSB Reference:
(Rom.12:6-8; esp. v.8) Note 2, pt. 6

ἐν ταῖς ἀλαζονείαις = *en tais alazoneiais* **#201, #414, #432, #4475**
POSB Reference:
(Jas.4:16) Note 4

Ἦν θυμομαχῶν = *Ën thumomachön* **#144, #145, #1093, #3136**
POSB Reference:
(Acts 12:18- 23; esp. v.20) Note 3, pt. 1

ἐν τῷ καθεξῆς = *en tö kathexës* **#78, #79**
POSB Reference:
(Lk.8:1) Note 1

ἐν τοῖς ὑψίστοις = *en tois hupsistos* **#2118, #2125**
POSB Reference:
(Mk.11:10) *Deeper Study* #8

ἐναντίους = *enantious* **#82, #770, #1896**
POSB Reference:
(Acts 27:4-12; esp. v.4) Note 2, pt. 1a

ἐνδεής = *endeës* **#2288, #2656, #2972**
POSB Reference:
(Acts 4:34-37; esp. v.34) Note 3, pt. 1

ἐνδυναμώσαντί = *endunamösanti* **#1254, #1686, #3800**
POSB Reference:
(1 Tim.1:12-14; esp. v.12) Note 1, pt. 1

ἐνδυναμοῦσθε = *endunamousthe* **#3818**
POSB Reference:
(Eph.6:10-11; esp. v.10) Note 1, pt. 1

ἐνδύσασθε = *endusasthe* **#605, #3124, #3876**
POSB Reference:
(Rom.13:14) *Deeper Study* #2

ἐνδύσησθε = *endusësthe* **#607, #624, #1272**
POSB Reference:
(Lk.24:44-49; esp. v.49) Note 2, pt. 4c

ἐνεβριμῶντο = *eneboimonto* **#840, #2635, #3182, #3391, #3392**
POSB Reference:
(Mk.14:4-5; esp. v.5) Note 2

ἐνεβριμήσατο = *enebrimësato* **#930, #1818, #2631**
POSB Reference:
(Jn.11:33-36; esp. v.33) Note 5, pt. 1

ἐνέκοψεν = *enekopsen* **#860, #1953, #2183**
POSB Reference:
(Gal.5:7) Note 1, pt. 1

ἐνέργειαν = *energeian* **#1286, #2977, #4427**
POSB Reference:
(Col.1:29) Note 5, pt. 2

ἐνέργειαν πλάνης = *energeian planës* **#946, #1783, #2985, #3820**
POSB Reference:
(2 Thes.2:11) Note 3

ἐνεργείας = *energeias* **#2783, #2978, #4428**
POSB Reference:
(Col.2:11-12; esp. v.12) Note 2, pt. 3

ἐνηργεῖτο ἐν = *enërgeito en* **#233, #1025**
POSB Reference:
(Rom.7:5) Note 1, pt. 1

ἐνεργὴς = *energës* **#45, #2979, #2983**
POSB Reference:
(Heb.4:11-13; esp. v.12) Note 5, pt. 2a

ἐνεργῶν ἐν = *energön en* **#4418**
POSB Reference:
(Philip.2:13) Note 2

ἐνοικείτω ἐν = *enoikeitö en* **#1187, #2363**
POSB Reference:
(Col.3:16) Note 2, pt. 1

ἐντετυλιγμένον = *entetuligmenon* **#1540, #3338, #4456**
POSB Reference:
(Jn.20:7-10; esp. v.7) Note 3, pt. 1

ἐντεύξεις = *enteuxeis* **#2182, #2933, #2953**
POSB Reference:
(1 Tim.2:1) Note 1, pt. 3

ἐνθυμήσεως = *enthumëseös* **#968, #1009, #1011, #3981**
POSB Reference:
(Acts 17:29-30; esp. v.29) Note 7, pt. 1

ἐντὸς ὑμῶν = *entos humön* **#134, #2128, #4376**
POSB Reference:
(Lk.17:20-21; esp. v.21) Note 1, pt. 2

ἐνύσταξαν = *enustaxan* **#1178, #2309, #3625**
POSB Reference:
(Mt.25:5) *Deeper Study* #3

ἔπαινος = *epainos* **#2993, #4451**
POSB Reference:
(Philip.4:8-9; esp. v.8) Note 2, pt. 1g

ἐπακολουθήσητε = *epakolouthësëte* **#1546**
POSB Reference:
(1 Pt.2:21) Note 1

ἐπαρρησιασάμεθα = *eparrësiasametha* **#416, #814, #874**
POSB Reference:
(1 Thes.2:2) Note 2

ἔπεχε = *epeche* **#2229, #2862, #3883, #4277**
POSB Reference:
(1 Tim.4:16) Note 12

ἐπείραζεν = *epeirazen* **#216, #4059**
POSB Reference:
(Acts 9:26-28; esp. v.26) Note 2, pt. 1

ἔπειθέν = *epeithen* **#789, #2919, #2920**
POSB Reference:
(Acts 18:4) Note 4, pt. 2

ἠπείθουν = *ëpeithoun* **#341, #345, #1077, #3213, #3222**
POSB Reference:
(Acts 19:2-9; esp. v.9) Note 2, pt. 2d

ἐπενθήσατε = *epenthësate* **#1491, #2628**
POSB Reference:
(1 Cor.5:2) Note 2

ἐπέπεσεν ἐπὶ = *epepesen epi* **#482, #1468**
POSB Reference:
(Acts 10:44-45; esp. v.44) Note 1, pt. 3

ἐπερωτῶντα = *eperötönta* **#213, #1070**
POSB Reference:
(Lk.2:46-47; esp. v.46) Note 3, pt. 2b

ἐπεσκέψατο = *epeskepsato* **#694, #695, #3543, #4237**
POSB Reference:
(Acts 15:13-21; esp. v.14) Note 4, pt. 1

ἐφευρετὰς κακῶν = *epheuretas kakön* **#2187, #2188**
POSB Reference:
(Rom.1:30) *Deeper Study* #17

ἐφιμώθη = *ephimöthë* **#2669, #3690**
POSB Reference:
(Mt.22:11-14; esp. v.12) Note 4, pt. 1c

ἐφώνει = *ephönei* **#472, #836**
POSB Reference:
(Lk.8:5-8; esp. v.8) Note 2, pt. 4

ἐφρουρούμεθα = *ephrouroumetha* **#1920, #2248, #2249**
POSB Reference:
(Gal.3:23-25; esp. v.23) Note 1

ἐφρύαξαν = *ephruaxan* **#3153**
POSB Reference:
(Acts 4:25-28; esp. v.25) Note 3, pt. 1a

ἐπιβαλὼν = *epibalon* **#450, #3982, #3983**
POSB Reference:
(Mk.14:72) Note 5

ἐπιβλέψαι ἐπὶ = *epiblepsai epi* **#2388, #2392, #2395**
POSB Reference:
(Lk.9:37-40; esp. v.38) Note 1, pt. 1

ἐπιχορηγήσατε = *epichorëgësate* **#46, #180**
POSB Reference:
(2 Pt.1:5-7; esp. v.5) Note 1

ἔπιδε ἐπὶ = *epide epi* **#332, #729, #1905, #2393, #3887**
POSB Reference:
(Acts 4:29-30; esp. v.29) Note 4, pt. 1b

ἐπιδεικνύμεναι = *epideiknumenai* **#3546**
POSB Reference:
(Acts 9:36-39; esp. v.39) Note 2, pt. 5

ἐπιεικῆ = *epieikë* **#1657, #2852**
POSB Reference:
(1 Tim.3:3; esp. v.3) Note 2, pt. 11

ἐπιεικής = *epieikës* **#735, #1659, #1661**
POSB Reference:
(Jas.3:17-18; esp. v.17) Note 3, pt. 2c

ἐπιγνώσει = *epignösei* **#621, #2273**
POSB Reference:
(2 Pt.1:2) Note 3, pt. 3

ἐπίγνωσιν = *epignösin* **#2275**
POSB Reference:
(Heb.10:26-27; esp. v.26) Note 1

ἐπικεῖσθαι = *epikeisthai* **#842, #3035**
POSB Reference:
(Lk.5:1) Note 2

ἐπιλαμβάνεται = *epilambanetai* **#93, #1892, #1937**
POSB Reference:
(Heb.2:14-16; esp. v.16) Note 1, pt. 5

ἐπίμενε = *epimene* **#762, #2911, #3748**
POSB Reference:
(1 Tim.4:16) Note 12

ἤπιον = *ëpion* **#1658, #2252**
POSB Reference:
(2 Tim. 2:24-26 esp. v.24) Note 4

ἐπιφανείᾳ = *epiphaneia* **#172, #443, #3713**
POSB Reference:
(2 Thes.2:8) Note 4, pt. 2

ἐπιφάνειαν = *epiphaneian* **#176**
POSB Reference:
(2 Tim.4:1) Note 1, pt. 2

ἐπιπλήξῃς = *epiplëxës* **#3179, #3181, #3516**
POSB Reference:
(1 Tim.5:1-3; esp. v.1) Introduction

ἐπιποθήσατε = *epipothësate* **#829, #971, #2379**
POSB Reference:
(1 Pt.2:2-3; esp. v.2) Note 2

ἐπισκηνώσῃ ἐπ' = *episkënösë ep'* **#1189, #3279, #4420**
POSB Reference:
(2 Cor.12:7-10; esp. v.9) Note 3, pt. 3b

ἐπισκοπὴν = *episkopën* **#382, #2760, #2943, #2967**
POSB Reference:
(Acts 1:16-20; esp. v.20) Note 2, pt. 6a

ἐπισκόποις = *episkopois* **#383, #1235, #2816**
POSB Reference:
(Philip.1:1) Note 4, pt. 1

ἐπίσκοπον = *episkopon* **#381, #1830, #2814**
POSB Reference:
(1 Pt.2:25) Note 3, pt. 2

ἐπισκοποῦντες = *episkopountes* **#2386, #2403, #2404, #3409**
POSB Reference:
(Heb.12:15-17; esp. v.15) Note 2

ἐπισκόπους = *episkopous* **#1234, #2815**
POSB Reference:
(Acts 20:28-31; esp. v.28) Note 2, pt. 2

ἐπιστάντες = *epistantes* **#485**
POSB Reference:
(Acts 6:11-14; esp. v.12) Note 3, pt. 2

ἐπιστάτα = epistata **#2539**
POSB Reference:
(Lk.17:12-14; esp. v.13) Note 2, pt. 3a

ἐπιστηρίζοντες = epistērizontes **#716, #3801**
POSB Reference:
(Acts 14:21-27; esp. v.22) Note 2, pt. 1

ἐπίστηθι = epistēthi **#2166, #2916, #3024, #3169**
POSB Reference:
(2 Tim. 4:2) Note 2, pt. 2a

ἐπίστευεν = episteuen **#653, #1302, #4077**
POSB Reference:
(Jn.2:24) Deeper Study #2

ἐπίστευσαν = episteusan **#344, #790**
POSB Reference:
(Jn.2:23) Note 1, pt. 1

ἐπιστομίζειν = epistomizein **#3561, #3780**
POSB Reference:
(Tit.1:10-12; esp. v.11) Note 1, pt. 5

ἠπίστουν = ēpistoun **#343**
POSB Reference:
(Lk.24:9-11; esp. v.11) Note 6

ἐπιστρέψας = epistrepsas **#781, #3251, #3294, #4097**
POSB Reference:
(Lk.22:32) Note 2, pt. 2

ἐπιστρέψατε = epistrepsate **#782, #3292, #4096**
POSB Reference:
(Acts 3:19) Note 7

ἐπιταγὴν = epitagēn **#642, #646**
POSB Reference:
(1 Tim.1:1) Note 1, pt. 1

ἐπιτελοῦντες = epitelountes **#2897, #4422**
POSB Reference:
(2 Cor.7:1) Note 4

ἐπιθανατίους = epithanatious **#185, #703**
POSB Reference:
(1 Cor.4:9-10; esp. v.9) Note 4, pt. 1

ἐπιθυμεῖ κατὰ = epithumei kata **#981, #2452, #2465, #3483**
POSB Reference:
(Gal.5:16-18; esp. v.17) Note 1

ἐπιθυμήσεις = epithumēseis **#820**
POSB Reference:
(Rom.13:9) Note 6

ἐπιθυμίαις = epithumiais **#2463**
POSB Reference:
(1 Pt.4:3) Note 3

ἐπιθυμίαις = epithumiais **#975, #2467, #3590**
POSB Reference:
(Rom.1:24-25; esp. v.24) Note 2, pt. 1

ἐπιθυμίαν κακήν = epithumian kakēn **#1346, #1350, #3505**
POSB Reference:
(Col.3:5-7; esp. v.5) Note 1, pt. 1d

ἐπιθυμίας = epithumias **#977, #1347, #2462,**
POSB Reference:
(Jas.1:14-16; esp. v.14) Note 2

ἐπιθυμίας = epithumias **#978, #2469**
POSB Reference:
(2 Tim. 4:3-4; esp. v.3) Note 3, pt. 2

ἐπιθυμίας = epithumias **#980, #2471, #2840**
POSB Reference:
(Tit.3:3) Note 2

ἐπιθυμίας = epithumias **#972, #2466, #1358**
POSB Reference:
(Jn.8:44) Deeper Study #1

ἐπιθυμίας = epithumias **#1348, #2468**
POSB Reference:
(2 Tim. 2:22) Note 1

ἐπιτιμᾶν = epitiman **#798, #3180**
POSB Reference:
(Mt.16:21-23; esp. v.22) Note 1, pt. 2

ἐπλήσθησαν ἀνοίας = eplēsthēsan anoias **#1628, #2491, #3155**
POSB Reference:
(Lk.6:6-11; esp. v.11) Note 3, pt. 5

ἐποίησεν = epoiesen **#181, #2789, #3420**
POSB Reference:
(Mk.3:14) Deeper Study #1

ἐπορεύθη μετὰ σπουδῆς = eporeuthē meta spoudēs **#1875, #2049**
POSB Reference:
(Lk.1:39-42; esp. v.39) Note 1

ἐπόρθουν = eporthoun **#995, #1668, #4269**
POSB Reference:
(Gal.1:13-16; esp. v.13) Note 3, pt. 1a

ἐψηλάφησαν = epsēlaphēsan **#1846, #4021**
POSB Reference:
(1 Jn.1:1) Note 2, pt. 4

ἐράπισαν = erapisan **#3614, #3627, #3823**
POSB Reference:
(Mt.26:67-68; esp. v.67) Note 8, pt. 1

ἐραυνᾶτε = eraunate **#1042, #3398**
POSB Reference:
(Jn.5:39) Note 6, pt. 1

ἔρχεται = erchetai **#617, 639**
POSB Reference:
(Jn.4:25) Note 1, pt. 1

ἔρημος. = erēmos **#983**
POSB Reference:
(Mt.23:38) Deeper Study #2

ἔργα = erga **#925, #1152**
POSB Reference:
(Rom.2:6-10; esp. v.6) Note 3

ἔργων ἀγαθῶν = ergōn agathōn **#926, #1144, #1145, #1761**
POSB Reference:
(Acts 9:36-39; esp. v.36) Note 2, pt. 1b

ἔριδες = erides **#195, #753, #3137**
POSB Reference:
(1 Cor.1:11) Note 2

ἔριδι = eridi **#1103, #1484, #3807**
POSB Reference:
(Rom.13:13) Note 4, pt. 5

ἔριδος = eridos **#893, #1483, #3806**
POSB Reference:
(Rom.1:29) Deeper Study #8

ἔρις = eris **#754, #895, #3133, #3805**
POSB Reference:
(2 Cor.12:19-21; esp. v.20) Note 3

ἔρις = eris **#755, #1064, #3134, #3808, #4211**
POSB Reference:
(Gal.5:19-21; esp. v.20) Note 2

ἐριθεῖαι = eritheiai **#1097, #1414, #3433, #3435, #3809**
POSB Reference:
(2 Cor.12:19-21; esp. v.20) Note 3, pt. 2

ἐριθείας = eritheias **#756, #2362, #3432, #3434**
POSB Reference:
(Rom.2:8) Deeper Study #4

ἠρώτα = erota **#313, #358, #2247**
POSB Reference:
(Mk.7:26-28; esp. v.26) Note 3

ἠρώτα = *ëröta* **#315, #360, #2099, #3260**
POSB Reference:
(Jn.4:46-47; esp. v.47) Note 1, pt. 4

ἐρωτῶμεν = *erötömen* **#356, #210, #3259, #4192**
POSB Reference:
(1 Thes.4:1-2) Note 1, pt. 1

ἐρριμμένοι = *errimmenoi* **#1026, #1159, #1935, #3384**
POSB Reference:
(Mt.9:36) *Deeper Study* #4

ἐρρύσατο = *errusato* **#944, #3264**
POSB Reference:
(Col.1:13) Note 2, pt. 2

ἦσαν ἐπὶ τὸ αὐτὸ = *ësan epi to auto* **#2581, #4319**
POSB Reference:
(Acts 2:44-45; esp. v.44) Note 4, pt. 2

ἦσαν ἀτενίζοντες αὐτῷ = *ësan atenizontes autö* **#3740, #4316, #4317**
POSB Reference:
(Lk.4:20-21; esp. v.20) Note 3

ἦσαν νηστεύοντες. = *esan nesteuontes* **#1447**
POSB Reference:
(Mk.2:18) Note 1

ἦσαν προσκαρτεροῦντες = *ësan proskarterountes* **#759, #764, #1018**
POSB Reference:
(Acts 2:42) *Deeper Study* #1

ἦσαν προσκαρτεροῦντες = *ësan proskarterountes* **#758, #765, #2204, #2582**
POSB Reference:
(Acts 1:12-15; esp. v.14) Note 1, pt. 4

ἐσχάτη ὥρα = *eschatë höra* **#2300, #2301**
POSB Reference:
(1 Jn.2:18) Note 1, pt. 1

ἔσῃ ζωγρῶν = *esë zögrön* **#524, #1517**
POSB Reference:
(Lk.5:10) Note 7, pt. 2

ἐσείσθη = *eseisthë* **#2630, #3772**
POSB Reference:
(Mt.21:10-11; esp. v.10) Note 5

ἐσκληρύνοντο = *esklërunonto* **#1865, #2736, #3223**
POSB Reference:
(Acts 19:2-9; esp. v.9) Note 2, pt. 2d

ἐσκοτίσθη = *eskotisthë* **#875, #877**
POSB Reference:
(Rom.1:21) Note 4, pt. 2

ἐσκυλμένοι = *eskulmenoi* **#1114, #1423, #1856, #3043, #4300**
POSB Reference:
(Mt.9:36) *Deeper Study* #3

ἐσπλαγχνίσθη = *esplagchnisthë* **#668, #2942**
POSB Reference:
(Mt.9:36) *Deeper Study* #2

ἐσπλαγχνίσθη = *esplagchnisthë* **#669, #1911**
POSB Reference:
(Lk.7:13) *Deeper Study* #1

ἔσται συλαγωγῶν = *estai sulagögön* **#228, #488, #555, #3715**
POSB Reference:
(Col.2:8) Note 1

ἐστὲ πεπληρωμένοι = *este peplërömenoi* **#1685**
POSB Reference:
(Col.2:9-10; esp. v.10) Note 2, pt. 2

ἐστέναξεν = *estenaxen* **#3555**
POSB Reference:
(Mk.7:34-35; esp. v.34) Note 4, pt. 2

ἐστιν εἰργασμένα = *estin eirgasmena* **#1151, #4467**
POSB Reference:
(Jn.3:21) Note 4, pt. 3

ἔστιν προσωπολήμπτης = *estin prosöpolëmptës* **#3273, #3536, #3538**
POSB Reference:
(Acts 10:34-35; esp. v.34) Note 1

ἐτάραξαν = *etaraxan* **#1125, #4066**
POSB Reference:
(Acts 15:24) Note 2, pt. 1

ἔταξαν = *etaxan* **#47, #1015, #3693**
POSB Reference:
(1 Cor.16:15-18; esp. v.15) Note 5

ἐτελειώθη = *eteleiöthë* **#2478, #2484, #2894**
POSB Reference:
(Jas.2:21-24; esp. v.22) Note 5

ἐθαμβήθησαν = *ethambethesan* **#129**
POSB Reference:
(Mk.1:27-28; esp. v.27) Note 3, pt. 1

ἐθαύμαζον = *ethaumazon* **#126, #2536, #4399**
POSB Reference:
(Lk.4:22-23; esp. v.22) Note 4, pt. 1

ἐθαύμαζον = *ethaumazon* **#227, #2537, #3863**
POSB Reference:
(Jn.4:27) Note 3

ἐθεασάμεθα = *etheasametha* **#331, #2397, #3382**
POSB Reference:
(1 Jn.1:1) Note 2, pt. 3

ἐθεασάμεθα = *etheasametha* **#328, #3417**
POSB Reference:
(Jn.1:14) Note 1

ἐθεώρει = *etheörei* **#326, #2733, #3379, #4284**
POSB Reference:
(Mk.12:41-42; esp. v.41) Note 1

Ἐθεώρουν = *etheöroun* **#327, #3380, #4288**
POSB Reference:
(Lk.10:18) Note 2

ἔθνος ἅγιον = *ethnos hagion* **#1979**
POSB Reference:
(1 Pt.2:9) Note 1, pt. 3

ἐθρήνουν = *ethrënoun* **#1810, #2295, #4242**
POSB Reference:
(Lk.23:27) Note 2

ἐτυμπανίσθησαν = *etumpanisthësan* **#4018**
POSB Reference:
(Heb.11:35-38; esp. v.35) Note 1

ἔτυπτον = *etupton* **#292, #3626, #3823**
POSB Reference:
(Mt.27:26-38; esp. v.30) Note 2, pt. 7

εὖ πράξετε = *eu praxete* **#1140**
POSB Reference:
(Acts 15:28-29; esp. v.29) Note 4, pt. 2

εὐαγγέλιον = *euaggelion* **#1755, #1766**
POSB Reference:
(Mt.4:23) Note 2

Εὐαγγελισάμενοί = *Euaggelisamenoi* **#3007, #3009**
POSB Reference:
(Acts 14:21) Note 1, pt. 1

εὐαγγελίσασθαι = euaggelisasthai
#3003, #3004
POSB Reference:
(Lk.4:17-19; esp. v.18) Note 2, pt. 3

εὐαγγελιστάς = euaggelistas **#1325**
POSB Reference:
(Eph.4:11) Note 3, pt. 3

εὐαγγελιζόμενοι = euaggelizomenoi
#3014, #3920
POSB Reference:
(Acts 11:19-30; esp. v.20) *Deeper Study*
#2, pt. 2

εὐαγγελιζόμενοι τὸν λόγον = euaggelizomenoi ton logon **#3008, #3015**
(Acts 8:4) Note 4, pt. 2

εὐαγγελιζόμενος = euaggelizomenos
#115, #449, #3050, #3549
POSB Reference:
(Lk.8:1) *Deeper Study* #2

εὐάρεστοι εἶναι = euarestoi einai **#30,**
#2956
POSB Reference:
(2 Cor.5:9-10; esp. v.9) Note 4

εὐάρεστον = euareston **#27, #2957**
POSB Reference:
(Rom.12:1) Note 4, pt. 2

εὐχαριστίας = eucharistias **#1680,**
#1691, #3949
POSB Reference:
(1 Tim.2:1) Note 1

εὐδοκία = eudokia **#970, #2381**
POSB Reference:
(Rom.10:1-3; esp. v.1) Note 1

εὐεργέται = euergetai **#352, #1606**
POSB Reference:
(Lk.22:25) Note 2, pt. 2

εὐλαβείας = eulabeias **#1978, #3304**
POSB Reference:
(Heb.12:28-29; esp. v.28) Note 3, pt. 2

εὐλαβεῖς = eulabeis **#1022, #1720,**
#1728
POSB Reference:
(Acts 2:5-11; esp. v.5) Note 5, pt. 1

εὐλαβής = eulabës **#1021**
POSB Reference:
(Lk.2:25-27; esp. v.25) Note 1, pt. 1

εὐλαβηθείς = eulabëtheis **#1455,**
#1730, #1977, #2724, #3305
POSB Reference:
(Heb.11:7) Note 1, pt. 1

εὐλογεῖτε = eulogeite **#401**
POSB Reference:
(Rom.12:14) Note 1

εὐλογητοῦ = eulogëtou **#402**
POSB Reference:
(Mk.14:61) Note 5

εὐπειθής = eupeithës **#1224, #3173,**
#3837, #4354
POSB Reference:
(Jas.3:17-18; esp. v.17) Note 3, pt. 2d

εὐπερίστατον = euperistaton **#1220,**
#1221, #1291, #3624
POSB Reference:
(Heb.12:1) Note 2, pt. 1b

εὔφημα = euphëma **#53, #1757, #1760**
POSB Reference:
(Philip.4:8-9; esp. v.8) Note 2, pt. 1f

ηὐφράνθη = ëuphranthë **#1694, #2208,**
#3227
POSB Reference:
(Acts 2:25-28; esp. v.26) Note 1, pt. 1b

εὐσχημόνων = euschëmön **#2007,**
#3058
POSB Reference:
(Acts 17:12) Note 6

εὐσχημόνως = euschëmonös **#914,**
#915, #1993, #3061
POSB Reference:
(Rom.13:13) Note 4

εὐσέβειαν = eusebeian **#1727, #1732**
POSB Reference:
(1 Tim.6:11) Note 2, pt. 2

εὐσεβῶς = eusebös **#1019, #1729**
POSB Reference:
(Tit.2:12) Note 2, pt. 2c

εὔσπλαγχνοι = eusplagchnoi **#673,**
#3937
POSB Reference:
(Eph.4:32) Note 7, pt. 2

εὔσπλαγχνοι = eusplagchnoi **#674,**
#2255, #2940, #3936
POSB Reference:
(1 Pt.3:8) Note 4

εὐτόνως = eutonös **#2584, #2984,**
#4222
POSB Reference:
(Acts 18:27-28; esp. v.28) Note 8, pt. 2a

εὐτραπελία = eutrapelia **#610, #611,**
#2201
POSB Reference:
(Eph.5:4) Note 4, pt. 3

ηὔξανεν καὶ ἐπληθύνετο = ëuxanen kai
eplëthuneto **#1807, #1820, #2134,**
#3721
POSB Reference:
(Acts 12:24-25; esp. v.24) Note 4, pt. 1

ἐξ αὐτοῦ = ex autou **#297, #466,**
#1716, #2743
POSB Reference:
(1 Cor.1:30-31; esp. v.30) Note 4

ἐξαλειφθῆναι = exaleiphthënai **#409,**
#594, #4357, #4358
POSB Reference:
(Acts 3:19) Note 7, pt. 1

ἐξαπορούμενοι = exaporoumenoi **#985,**
#1681, #2114
POSB Reference:
(2 Cor.4:7-9; esp. v.8) Note 2, pt. 2

ἐξαστράπτων = exastraptön **#883,**
#1526, #1698, #1699
POSB Reference:
(Lk.9:29) Note 3, pt. 2

ἐξήγειρά = exëgeira **#183, #3158**
POSB Reference:
(Rom.9:15-18; esp. v.17) Note 2, pt. 2a

ἐξεκρέματο = exekremato **#237, #1850,**
#2045
POSB Reference:
(Lk.19:47-48; esp. v.48) Note 3, pt. 2

ἐξέληται = exelëtai **#940, #3263**
POSB Reference:
(Gal.1:4-5; esp. v.4) Note 4, pt. 2

ἐξελέξατο = exelexato **#567**
POSB Reference:
(1 Cor.1:27-28) Note 2

ἐξῆλθεν = exëlthen **#841, #2319,**
#4313
POSB Reference:
(Jn.18:1-3; esp. v.1) Note 1

ἐξεπλήσσοντο = exeplëssonto **#125,**
#251
POSB Reference:
(Lk.9:42-43; esp. v.43) Note 3, pt. 2

ἐξηραμμένην ἔχων τὴν χεῖρα = exer-
ammenen echon ten cheira **#935,**
#1845, #3551, #4373
POSB Reference:
(Mk.3:1-2; esp. v.1) Note 1, pt. 1

ἐξηράνθη = exëranthë **#1170, #4372**
POSB Reference:
(Jn.15:4-6; esp. v.6) Note 4, pt. 4b

ξέστημεν = exestëmen #357, #830, #2805
POSB Reference:
(2 Cor.5:13) Note 3

ἐξέστραπται = exestraptai #2930, #3840, #4098, #4257
POSB Reference:
(Tit.3:10-11; esp. v.11) Note 3

ἐξῃτήσατο = exëtësato #211, #947, #974
POSB Reference:
(Lk.22:31) Note 1, pt. 2

ἐξεθαμβήθησαν = exethambëthësan #128, #254, #1794, #2817
POSB Reference:
(Mk.9:15) Deeper Study #1

ἐξίσταντο = existanto #127, #225
POSB Reference:
(Acts 9:21) Note 4

ἐξίσταντο = existanto #130
POSB Reference:
(Acts 2:12-13; esp. v.12) Note 6

ἐξίσταντο δὲ = existanto de #124, #226
POSB Reference:
(Lk.2:46-47; esp. v.47) Note 3, pt. 2c

ἔξοδον = exodon #903, #958, #1195
POSB Reference:
(Lk.9:30-31; esp. v.31) Note 4, pt. 2

ἐξολεθρευθήσεται ἐκ = exo- lethreuthësetai ek #687, #862, #1001, #4199
POSB Reference:
(Acts 3:23) Deeper Study #4

ἐξουσίαν = exousia #244, #2973
POSB Reference:
(Mt.10:1) Deeper Study #2

ἐξουσίαν = exousian #2974, #3319
POSB Reference:
(1 Cor.9:4-11; esp. v.4-6) Note 2

ἐξουσίας = exousias #243, #2988
POSB Reference:
(Eph.6:12) Note 3, pt. 5

ἐξουθενείτω = exoutheneitö #986, #2389, #3216
POSB Reference:
(Rom.14:3-4, esp. v.3) Note 2

ἐξουθενήσας = exouthenësas #748, #2714, #3316
POSB Reference:
(Lk.23:8-11; esp. v.11) Note 3, pt. 4

ἐξουθενοῦντας = exouthenountas #989, #2398, #3393, #4218
POSB Reference:
(Lk.18:9) Note 1, pt. 3

G

Γαβριὴλ = Gabriël #1635
POSB Reference:
(Lk.1:19) Deeper Study #1

γαζοφυλάκιον = gazophulakion #614, #3928, #4042
POSB Reference:
(Lk.21:1) Deeper Study #1

γέενναν = geennan #1921
POSB Reference:
(Mt.5:22) Deeper Study #2

γεγέννηκά = gegennëka #301, #320
POSB Reference:
(Heb.1:4-6; esp. v.5) Note 1, pt. 1

γελάσετε = gelasete #2304
POSB Reference:
(Lk.6:20-23; esp. v.21) Note 1, pt. 3c

γενέσεως = geneseös #1650, #1651, #3203
POSB Reference:
(Mt.1:1) Note 1

γένησθε = genësthe #277, #300
POSB Reference:
(Jn.12:34-36; esp. v.36) Note 5, pt. 2

γεννηθὲν = gennëthen #693
POSB Reference:
(Mt.1:20-21; esp. v.20) Note 3

γενομένης φωνῆς = genomenës phönës #1908, #2676, #3668
POSB Reference:
(Acts 2:5-11; esp. v.6) Note 5, pt. 2

γενόμενον ἐκ γυναικός = genomenon ek gunaikos #422, #2482
POSB Reference:
(Gal.4:4-7; esp. v.4) Note 2

γενόμενος = genTomenos #174, #641, #2474
POSB Reference:
(Philip.2:7) Note 3, pt. 2

γενόμενος ἐν ἀγωνίᾳ = genomenos en agönia #88, #146
POSB Reference:
(Lk.22:43-44; esp. v.44) Note 4, pt. 2

γενομένου = genomenou #477, #4259, #4262, #4264
POSB Reference:
(Rom.1:1-4; esp. v.3) Note 3, pt.. 2a

γένος ἐκλεκτόν = genos eklekton #576, #578, #579
POSB Reference:
(1 Pt.2:9) Note 1, pt. 1

Γεθσημανί = Gethsëmani #1669
POSB Reference:
(Mt.26:36) Deeper Study #1

γευσαμένους = geusamenous #1396, #3896
POSB Reference:
(Heb.6:4-5, esp. v.4) Note 1

γεύσηται θανάτου = geusëtai thanatou #1029, #3895
POSB Reference:
(Jn.8:51; esp. v.52) Deeper Study #1, pt. 3

γίνεσθε = ginesthe #278, #1544
POSB Reference:
(Eph.5:1) Note 1

γινώσκω = ginöskö #4132
POSB Reference:
(Rom.7:14-17; esp. v.15) Note 2, pt. 1a

γνησίως = gnësiös #1666, #2650, #3583
POSB Reference:
(Philip.2:20) Note 1

Γνωρίζω = Gnörizö #537, #2266, #2509, #3645
POSB Reference:
(Gal.1:11-12; esp. v.11) Note 2

Γνωρίζω = Gnörizö #919, #2508, #3241
POSB Reference:
(1 Cor.15:1-2; esp. v.1) Note 1

γνώσει = gnösei #2276, #4138
POSB Reference:
(2 Cor.6:6-7; esp. v.6) Note 5

γνῶσιν = gnösin #2272, #2274
POSB Reference:
(2 Pt.1:5-7; esp. v.5) Note 1

γογγυσμῶν = goggusmön #681, #1825, #2636
POSB Reference:
(Philip.2:14) Note 3

Γολγοθᾶν = Golgothan #1734
POSB Reference:
(Mk.15:22) Note 4

γονεῦσιν ἀπειθεῖς = goneusin apeitheis #1080
POSB Reference:
(2 Tim. 3:2-4; esp. v.2) Note 2, pt. 6

ραμματέων = *grammateön* **#3395, #3911**
POSB Reference:
(Mk.12:28) *Deeper Study* #1

γρηγορεῖτε = *grëgoreite* **#101, #2237, #3025, #4270**
POSB Reference:
(Mt.24:42) Note 1

Γρηγορεῖτε = *Grëgoreite* **#2764, #2769, #4271**
POSB Reference:
(1 Cor.16:13-14; esp. v.13) Note 4

γρηγορήσατε = *grëgorësate* **#99, #288, #4221, #4280**
POSB Reference:
(1 Pt.5:8) Note 1, pt. 2

γρηγοροῦντες = *grëgorountes* **#100, #2243, #4219, #4287**
POSB Reference:
(Col.4:2-4; esp. v.2) Note 1, pt. 2

γυμνασία = *gumnasia* **#1059, #1383, #4029**
POSB Reference:
(1 Tim.4:8) Note 4, pt. 1

γυμνός = *gumnos* **#2645**
POSB Reference:
(Rev.3:16-17; esp. v.17) Note 4, pt. 2e

γυναικάρια = *gunaikaria* **#1836, #3563, #4240, #4294**
POSB Reference:
(2 Tim. 3:6-9; esp. v.6) Note 4, pt. 1

H

ᾅδη = *hadë* **#1839, #1922, #2944**
POSB Reference:
(Lk.16:23) *Deeper Study* #3

ᾅδην = *hadën* **#886, #1778, #1840, #1923**
POSB Reference:
(Acts 2:25-28; esp. v.27) Note 1, pt. 2b

ἁγιασμῶ = *hagiasmö* **#1973, #3368, 3372**
POSB Reference:
(1 Pt.1:2) Note 2

ἁγιασμόν = *hagiasmon* **#1969, #3369**
POSB Reference:
(Rom.6:19-20, esp. v.19)

ἁγίασον = *hagiason* **#3104, #3371**
POSB Reference:
(Jn.17:17) *Deeper Study* #4

ἁγιασθήτω = *hagiasthëtö* **#1843, #2004**
POSB Reference:
(Mt.6:9) *Deeper Study* #4

ἅγιοι = *hagioi* **#350, #1975**
POSB Reference:
(Heb.3:1) Note 1, pt. 1

ἅγιοι = *hagioi* **#1974**
POSB Reference:
(1 Pt.1:15-16; esp. v.15) Note 3

ἁγίοις = *hagiois* **#1713, #3362**
POSB Reference:
(Eph.1:1-2; esp. v.1) Note 2

ἁγίοις = *hagiois* **#1714, #1972, #3363**
POSB Reference:
(Col.1:2) Note 3, pt. 1

ἁγίοις = *hagiois* **#1971, #3360**
POSB Reference:
(1 Cor.1:2) *Deeper Study* #2

ἁγίους = *hagious* **#585, #3361**
POSB Reference:
(2 Cor.9:1-2; esp. v.1) Note 1

ἁγνα = *hagna* **#3098**
POSB Reference:
(Philip.4:8-9; esp. v.8) Note 2, pt. 1d

ἁγνήν = *hagnën* **#551, #3103, #3110**
POSB Reference:
(1 Pt.3:2) Note 2)

ἁγνότητι = *hagnotëti* **#3107, #3109**
POSB Reference:
(2 Cor.6:6-7; esp. v.6) Note 5

αἱρέσεις = *haireseis* **#1466, #1415, #1939**
POSB Reference:
(Gal.5:19-21; esp. v.20) Note 2

αἱρέσεις = *haireseis* **#1940**
POSB Reference:
(2 Pt.2:1) Note 2, pt. 1

αἱρετικὸν = *hairetikon* **#1131, #1132, #1416, #1941**
POSB Reference:
(Tit.3:10-11; esp. v.10) Note 3

ἁμαρτία = *hamartia* **#3572**
POSB Reference:
(1 Jn.3:4) *Deeper Study* #1

ἁμαρτίαις = *hamartiais* **#3602**
POSB Reference:
(Eph.2:1-2; esp. v.1) Note 2

ἁμαρτίαν = *hamartian* **#3570**
POSB Reference:
(Jn.1:29) Note 1, pt. 4b

ἅπαξ = *hapax* **#2770**
POSB Reference:
(Heb.9:27-28; esp. v.27) Note 3, pt. 1

ἁπλότητος = *haplotëtos* **#2333, #1652**
POSB Reference:
(2 Cor.8:1-5; esp. v.2) Note 1, pt. 1

ἁπλότητος = *haplotëtos* **#3565, #3567, #3581**
POSB Reference:
(2 Cor.11:3) Note 2

ἅρπαγες = *harpages* **#1408, #3867**
POSB Reference:
(1 Cor.6:10) Note 3, pt. 5

ἁρπαγῆς = *harpagës* **#1799, #3165, #3337**
POSB Reference:
(Lk.11:39-41; esp. v.39) Note 2, pt. 1

ἅρπαξιν = *harpaxin* **#1407**
POSB Reference:
(1 Cor.5:9-10; esp. v.9) Note 4, pt. 3

ἡ ἔπαυλις αὐτοῦ = *hë epaulis autou* **#1193, #1837, #1981, #1982, #2946**
POSB Reference:
(Acts 1:16-20; esp. v.20) Note 2, pt. 6a

ἡ σωτηρία = *hë sötëria* **#3364**
POSB Reference:
(Jn.4:22) Note 3, pt. 1

ἡδοναῖς = *hëdonais* **#2960**
POSB Reference:
(Tit.3:3) Note 2

ἡδονῶν = *hëdonön* **#979, #982, #2470, #2958**
POSB Reference:
(Jas.4:1) Note 1

ἑδραῖοι = *hedraioi* **#1507, #3487, #3753**
POSB Reference:
(Col.1:23) Note 4, pt. 1

ἑδραῖοι γίνεσθε = *hedraioi ginesthe* **#3731, #3756, #3817**
POSB Reference:
(1 Cor.15:58) Note 6, pt. 2

εἵλκυσαν = *heilkusan* **#1161, #1168**
POSB Reference:
(Acts 16:19-24; esp. v.19) Note 3, pt. 1

εἷς ὑπὲρ πάντων ἀπέθανεν = *heis huper pantön apethanen* **#115, #1336**
POSB Reference:
(2 Cor.5:14-16; esp. v.14) Note 4, pt. 1

Ἑκατὸν βάτους = *hekaton batous*
#1233, #2043, #2044, #3986
POSB Reference:
(Lk.16:6-7; esp. v.6) *Deeper Study* #1

ἡλικίαν = *hëlikian* **#2340, #2342,
#3743**
POSB Reference:
(Lk.12:22-28; esp. v.25) Note 1, pt. 3

ἑλκύσῃ = *helkusë* **#1166**
POSB Reference:
(Jn.6:44-46; esp. v.44) Note 2, pt. 1

ἥμαρτον = *hëmarton* **#3597**
POSB Reference:
(Rom.3:22-23; esp. v.23) Note 2, pt. 2a

ἡμέραι ἱκαναι = *hëmerai hikanai* **#77,
#2531, #3646, #1479, #3489**
POSB Reference:
(Acts 9:23) *Deeper Study* #1

ἡμέρας τινάς = *hëmeras tinas* **#3646,
#1479, #3489**
POSB Reference:
(Acts 9:23) *Deeper Study* #1

ἡμέρας τινάς = *hëmeras tinas* **#534,
#1479, #3489**
POSB Reference:
(Acts 9:19) Note 2

ἑορτάζωμεν = *heortazömen* **#1458,
#1459, #1477, #1478**
POSB Reference:
(1 Cor.5:8) Note 3, pt. 5

ἕως ἄρτι ἐργάζεται = *heös arti
ergazetai* **#4423**
POSB Reference:
(Jn.5:17-18; esp. v.17) Note 1

ἥρπασεν = *hërpasen* **#526, #3629,
#3844**
POSB Reference:
(Acts 8:39-40; esp. v.39) Note 7, pt. 1

ἡσυχία = *hësuchia* **#3147, #3148,
#3560**
POSB Reference:
(1 Tim.2:11-14; esp. v.11) Note 2

ἑτεροδιδασκαλεῖ = *heterodidaskalei*
#69, #955, #3902, #3912
POSB Reference:
(1 Tim.6:3) Note 1

ἕτερον = *heteron* **#157, #1032**
POSB Reference:
(Gal.1:6-7; esp. v.6) Note 2

ἑτεροζυγοῦντες = *heterozugountes*
#428, #3916, #4147, #4471
POSB Reference:
(2 Cor.6:14-16; esp. v.14) Note 2

ἑτοίμους = *hetoimous* **#3170**
POSB Reference:
(Tit.3:1) Note 2

ἥττημα = *hëttëma* **#2419, #1043,
#1419, #4100**
POSB Reference:
(Rom.11:11-12, esp. v.12) Note 1, pt. 3

ἱερόν = *hieron* **#3927**
POSB Reference:
(Mt.21:12-16; esp. v.12) *Deeper Study*
#1

ἱεροπρεπεῖς = *hieroprepeis* **#188,
#1968, #3307**
POSB Reference:
(Tit.2:3) Note 3, pt. 1

ἱεροσυλεῖς = *hierosuleis* **#656, #3336,
#3760**
POSB Reference:
(Rom.2:21-24; esp. v.22) Note 2, pt. 4

ἱλαρὸν = *hilaron* **#559**
POSB Reference:
(2 Cor.9:7) Note 4

ἱλάσκεσθαι = *hilaskesthai* **#2501,
#2511, #2512, #2756**
POSB Reference:
(Heb.2:17-18; esp. v.17) Note 2, pt. 3

ἱλασμός = *hilasmos* **#235, #3066,
#3356**
POSB Reference:
(1 Jn.2:1-2; esp. v.2) Note 3, pt. 2

ἱλαστήριον = *hilastërion* **#3065,
#3091, #3357**
POSB Reference:
(Rom.3:25) Note 4

ἱλάσθητί = *hilasthëti* **#2568, #2572**
POSB Reference:
(Lk.18:13) Note 4, pt. 3b

ἵνα = *hina* **#2122, #3631, #3950,
#4293**
POSB Reference:
(Rom.8:16-17; esp. v.17) Note 9, pt. 4

ὁ ἀπειθῶ = *ho apeithön* **#342, #347,
#4330, #4332**
POSB Reference:
(Jn.3:36) *Deeper Study* #4

ὁ ἄρτος = *ho artos* **#438**
POSB Reference:
(Jn.6:33) Note 3, pt. 1d

ὁ ἄρτος ὁ ζῶν = *ho artos ho zön*
#2377
POSB Reference:
(Jn.6:47-51; esp. v.51) Note 3, pt. 3a

Ὁ διδάσκαλος = *ho didaskalos* **#2540,
#3905**
POSB Reference:
(Jn.11:28) *Deeper Study* #1

ὁ κλαυθμὸς = *ho klauthmos* **#4305**
POSB Reference:
(Lk.13:28) *Deeper Study* #1

Ὁ λόγος = *Ho logos* **#2579, #3016,
#4412**
POSB Reference:
(1 Cor.1:18) Note 3

ὁ ταλαίπωρος = *ho talaipöros* **#4465**
POSB Reference:
(Rev.3:16-17; esp. v.17) Note 4, pt. 2

Ὁ θεὸς τῆς δόξης = *Ho theos tës
doxës* **#1702, #1719**
POSB Reference:
(Acts 7:2) *Deeper Study* #1

οἱ ἀετοὶ = *hoi aetoi* **#1208, #4241**
POSB Reference:
(Lk.17:37) Note 8

οἱ ἡμέτεροι = *hoi hëmeteroi* **#2802,
#2803**
POSB Reference:
(Tit.3:14) Note 6

οἵτινες = *hoitines* **#3955, #3956,
#4328**
POSB Reference:
(2 Thes.1:9) Note 1

ὁλοκληρίαν = *holoklërian* **#1902,
#1904, #3669**
POSB Reference:
(Acts 3:16) *Deeper Study* #2

ὁλόκληροι = *holoklëroi* **#684, #1297**
POSB Reference:
(Jas.1:4) Note 3, pt. 2

ὁμοιοπαθεῖς = *homoiopatheis* **#2028,
#2030, #2345, #3367, #3366**
POSB Reference:
(Acts 14:14-18; esp. v.15) Note 3, pt. 1

ὁμόφρονες = homophrones **#2364,**
#1871, #2778
POSB Reference:
(1 Pt.3:8) Note 1

ὁμοθυμαδὸν = homothumadon **#2773,**
#2776, #4002
POSB Reference:
(Acts 1:14) *Deeper Study* #1

ὅπως ἐξαγγείλητε = hopōs exaggeilëte
#920, #3046, #3533, #3537
POSB Reference:
(1 Pt.2:9) Note 2

ὁράσεις = horaseis **#4236**
POSB Reference:
(Acts 2:17-21; esp. v.17) Note 2, pt. 1c

Ὁρᾶτε = Horate **#500, #3880, #4256,**
#4282
POSB Reference:
(Mk.8:15) *Deeper Study* #1

ὡρισμένη = hörismenë **#3476, #1007,**
#3017, #3021
POSB Reference:
(Acts 2:23) *Deeper Study* #3, pt. 2

ὡς δεισιδαιμονεστέρους = hös
deisidaimonesterous **#3235, #3855**
POSB Reference:
(Acts 17:22) Note 2

ὃς ἐγένετο νεκρὸς = hos egeneto
nekros **#4263, #4329**
POSB Reference:
(Rev.2:8) Note 2, pt. 2

Ὡσαννά = Hosanna **#2014, #2994**
POSB Reference:
(Mk.11:9) *Deeper Study* #5

ὡσεὶ λῆρος = hösei lëros **#2067,**
#2678
POSB Reference:
(Lk.24:9-11; esp. v.11) Note 6

ὅσιος = hosios **#1976**
POSB Reference:
(Heb.7:26) Note 2, pt. 1

ὅσους ἂν προσκαλέσηται = hosous an
proskalesëtai **#471**
POSB Reference:
(Acts 2:39) *Deeper Study* #3

ὅτι πρῶτός μου = hoti prötos mou
#1393, #4261
POSB Reference:
(Jn.1:15) Note 3

Οὗτος = houtos **#3970, #3973**
POSB Reference:
(Mt.26:60-61; esp. v.61) Note 4, pt. 2

Οὗτός ἐστιν ὁ υἱός μου ὁ
ἐκλελεγμένος = Houtos estin ho
huios mou ho eklelegmenos **#3972**
POSB Reference:
(Lk.9:35) Note 7

ῥᾳδιουργίας = hradiourgias **#1599,**
#2606, #4056
POSB Reference:
(Acts 13:8-11; esp. v.10) Note 4, pt. 3

Ῥακά = hraka **#3151, #4473, #4474**
POSB Reference:
(Mt.5:22) Note 3, pt. 2

ῥημάτων = hrëmatön **#3959**
POSB Reference:
(Acts 5:32) Note 3

ῥητῶς = hrëtös **#597, #1401, #1405**
POSB Reference:
(1 Tim.4:1) Note 1

ῥυπαρίαν = hruparian **#1494, #2620**
POSB Reference:
(Jas.1:19-21; esp. v.21) Note 1, pt. 3

ὑβριστάς = hubristas **#992, #2163,**
#4228
POSB Reference:
(Rom.1:30) *Deeper Study* #14

ὑβριστήν = hubristën **#1868, #2151,**
#2164, #4229, #4230
POSB Reference:
(1 Tim.1:12-14; esp. v.13) Note 1, pt. 3

ὑβρισθήσεται = hubristhësetai **#2177,**
#2611, #3712, #4044
POSB Reference:
(Lk.18:32-33; esp. v.32) Note 2, pt. 1b

ὑγιαινόντων = hugiainontön **#3318,**
#3664
POSB Reference:
(2 Tim. 1:13) Note 1

υἱοί = huioi **#564, #3651**
POSB Reference:
(Jn.12:34-36; esp. v.36) Note 5, pt. 2

υἱοθεσίαν = huiothesian **#56, #57,**
#1620
POSB Reference:
(Gal.4:5-6; esp. v.5) *Deeper Study* #2

ὕλην = hulën **#1583, #2545**
POSB Reference:
(Jas.3:5-6; esp. v.5) Note 4

ὑπακούετε = hupakouete **#2722**
POSB Reference:
(Eph.6:1-3; esp. v.1) Note 1

ὑπάρχων = huparchön **#336, #1392,**
#4260
POSB Reference:
(Philip.2:6) Note 2, pt. 1

ὑπέλαβεν = hupelaben **#1049, #1944,**
#3187
POSB Reference:
(Acts 1:10-11; esp. v.9) Note 5, pt. 1

ὑπὲρ = huper **#1565**
POSB Reference:
(Jn.10:11) *Deeper Study* #2

ὑπὲρ ὑμῶν = huper humön **#1567**
POSB Reference:
(1 Cor.11:23-26; esp. v.24) Note 3, pt.
1b

ὑπεραυξάνει = huperauxanei **#1373,**
#1537, #1796, #1822
POSB Reference:
(2 Thes.1:3) Note 4

ὑπερβάλλον = huperballon **#1372,**
#2129, #2136, #3862
POSB Reference:
(Eph.1:19) Note 1

ὑπερηφανία = huperephania **#199,**
#3039
POSB Reference:
(Mk.7:22) *Deeper Study* #14

ὑπερηφάνους = huperëphanous **#203,**
#3072
POSB Reference:
(Rom.1:30) *Deeper Study* #15

ὑπηρέτας = hupëretas **#2602, #3464**
POSB Reference:
(1 Cor.4:1-2; esp. v.1) Note 1

ὑπηρέτην = hupëretën **#1929, #220,**
#2599
POSB Reference:
(Acts 13:5-6; esp. v.5) Note 2, pt. 2

ὑπεριδὼν = huperidön **#2813, #4355**
POSB Reference:
(Acts 17:29-30; esp. v.30) Note 7, pt. 2

ὑπεροχὴν λόγου ἢ σοφίας = huper-
ochën logou ë sophias **#2378,**
#1244, #1376, #1377, #3854
POSB Reference:
(1 Cor.2:1) Note 1, pt. 1

ὑφ' ἁμαρτίαν = huph'hamartian
#4129, #4131
POSB Reference:
(Rom.3:9) Note 1

ὑπὸ ἁμαρτίαν = *hupo hamartian* **#2745, #4130**
POSB Reference:
(Gal.3:22) Note 5

ὑποδείγματι = *hupodeigmati* **#795, #1368**
POSB Reference:
(Heb.8:4-5, esp. v.5) Note 5

ὑπογραμμὸν = *hupogrammon* **#1367**
POSB Reference:
(1 Pt.2:21) Note 1

ὑποκρίσεις = *hupokriseis* **#2053**
POSB Reference:
(1 Pt.2:1) Note 1, pt. 3

ὑποκριταί = *hupokritai* **#2056**
POSB Reference:
(Mt.23:13) *Deeper Study* #2

ὑποκριταὶ = *hupokritai* **#2055**
POSB Reference:
(Mt.6:2) Note 2, pt. 2

ὑπομένει = *hupomenei* **#1282, #2913**
POSB Reference:
(1 Cor.13:4-7; esp. v.7) Note 2, pt. 15

ὑπομένοντες = *hupomenontes* **#2851, #2914**
POSB Reference:
(Rom.12:12) Note 3, pt. 2

ὑπομονῇ = *hupomonë* **#1277, #2843**
POSB Reference:
(2 Cor.6:4) Note 2

ὑπομονήν = *hupomonën* **#1276, #2849, #2910**
POSB Reference:
(Jas.1:2-4; esp. v.3) Note 2, pt. 1

ὑπομονήν = *hupomonën* **#2848**
POSB Reference:
(2 Pt.1:5-7; esp. v.6) Note 1, pt. 4

ὑπομονὴν = *hupomonën* **#1273, #2845, #3757**
POSB Reference:
(Col.1:11) Note 3, pt. 1

ὑπομονὴν = *hupomonën* **#2855, #2908, #2915**
POSB Reference:
(Rom.2:6-10; esp. v.7) Note 3, pt. 1b

ὑπομονῆς = *hupomonës* **#1274, #2846, #2856, #2912**
POSB Reference:
(Heb.10:32-39; esp. v.36) Note 4

ὑπομονῆς = *hupomonës* **#1275, #2847, #2909**
POSB Reference:
(Heb.12:1) Note 2, pt. 2

ὑπωπιάζῃ με = *hupöpiazë me* **#4298, #4299, #4301**
POSB Reference:
(Lk.18:2-5; esp. v.5) Note 2, pt. 4

ὑποστάσεως = *hupostaseös* **#335, #1712, #2653, #2917**
POSB Reference:
(Heb.1:3) Note 5

ὑπόστασις = *hupostasis* **#711, #222, #3839, #3860**
POSB Reference:
(Heb.11:1) Note 1

ὑποστρέφειν εἰς διαφθοράν = *hupostrephein eis diaphthoran* **#807, #902, #1030**
POSB Reference:
(Acts 13:32-37; esp. v.34) *Deeper Study* #4

ὑποτάγητε = *hupotagëte* **#2033, #3838**
POSB Reference:
(Jas.4:7) Note 4

ὑποτασσόμεναι = *hupotassomenai* **#28, #3835, #3836**
POSB Reference:
(1 Pt.3:1) Note 1

ὑποτιθέμενος = *hupotithemenos* **#1399, #2169, #2964, #3121**
POSB Reference:
(1 Tim.4:6) Note 1

ὑστέροις καιροῖς = *husterois kairois* **#2302, #2303**
POSB Reference:
(1 Tim.4:1) Note 1

I

ἰᾶται = *iatai* **#1903, #4334**
POSB Reference:
(Acts 9:34) Note 4, pt. 3

ἰδόντες = *idontes* **#3381**
POSB Reference:
(Jn.20:20) *Deeper Study* #2

Ἰησοῦν· = *Iësoun* **#2202**
POSB Reference:
(Mt.1:21) *Deeper Study* #5

ἰσάγγελοι = *isaggeloi* **#140**
POSB Reference:
(Lk.20:36) Note 5, pt. 1

ἰσχύος = *ischuos* **#2583**
POSB Reference:
(Eph.6:10-11; esp. v.10) Note 1, pt. 1

ἰσχύος = *ischuos* **#3791**
POSB Reference:
(Mk.12:30) Note 2, pt. 2

ἰσότιμον = *isotimon* **#205, #2346, #3365, #3367**
POSB Reference:
(2 Pt.1:1) Note 2

K

καὶ = *kai* **#137**
POSB Reference:
(Jn.3:5) *Deeper Study* #2

καὶ ἰδοὺ = *kai idou* **#333, #3954, #4325**
POSB Reference:
(Acts 16:1-3; esp. v.1) Note 1, pt. 1

καίεται = *kaietai* **#461**
POSB Reference:
(Jn.15:4-6; esp. v.6) Note 4, pt. 4d

καινὸν ἄνθρωπον = *kainon anthröpon* **#2661, #2662, #2663**
POSB Reference:
(Eph.4:24) *Deeper Study* #3

καιρός = *kairos* **#184, #3993**
POSB Reference:
(Mt.26:17-19; esp. v.18) Note 1, pt. 2

κακία = *kakia* **#936, #1342, #1879, #2525**
POSB Reference:
(Rom.1:29) *Deeper Study* #5

κακία = *kakia* **#1345, #2522**
POSB Reference:
(Tit.3:3) *Deeper Study* #4

κακίας = *kakias* **#2520, #4342**
POSB Reference:
(1 Cor.5:8) Note 3

κακοηθείας = *kakoëtheias* **#1352, #2521, #2523, #2526**
POSB Reference:
(Rom.1:29) *Deeper Study* #10

κακοπάθησον = *kakopathëson* **#1146, #1280, #1281**
POSB Reference:
(2 Tim. 4:5) Note 4, pt. 2

κακῶσαί = *kakösai* **#1855, #2610, #2906, #4217**
POSB Reference:
(Acts 12:1-4; esp. v.1) Note 1, pt. 1

καλῇ = *kalë* **#1986, #2672**
POSB Reference:
(Lk.8:11-15; esp. v.15) Note 4, pt. 4a

καλήν = *kalën* **#280, #1379, #1744, #1990, #1999**
POSB Reference:
(1 Pt.2:12) Note 3

καλοδιδασκάλους = *kalodidaskalous* **#3901, #3903, #3910**
POSB Reference:
(Tit.2:3) Note 3

καλὸν = *kalon* **#1739**
POSB Reference:
(1 Cor.7:1) Note 1

καλοῦ = *kalou* **#1500, #1743, #2001, #2674**
POSB Reference:
(1 Tim.3:1) Note 1

καν ἀποθάνη = *kan apothanë* **#1326, #3979**
POSB Reference:
(Jn.11:25-27; esp. v.25) Note 4, pt. 2a

φκαπηλεύοντες = *kapëleuontes* **#2876, #802, #2026, #2877**
POSB Reference:
(2 Cor.2:16-17; esp. v.17) Note 4

καρδίαν = *kardian* **#1910**
POSB Reference:
(Mk.7:20; esp. v.19) *Deeper Study* #1

καρπῶν ἀγαθῶν = *karpön agathön* **#1750, #1754**
POSB Reference:
(Jas.3:17-18; esp. v.17) Note 3, pt. 2f

κατὰ καιρὸν = *kata kairon* **#1183, #3322**
POSB Reference:
(Rom. (5:6-7; esp. v.6) Note 1, pt. 3

καταβαλλόμενοι = *kataballomenoi* **#519, #2265, #3824**
POSB Reference:
(2 Cor.4:7-9; esp. v.9) Note 2, pt. 4

καταβάς = *katabas* **#478**
POSB Reference:
(Jn.6:47-51; esp. v.51) Note 3, pt. 3b

καταβραβευέτω = *katabrabeuetö* **#322, #556, #699, #936, #1102**
POSB Reference:
(Col.2:18-19; esp. v.18) Note 2

καταγγέλλετε = *kataggellete* **#153, #3045, #3531**
POSB Reference:
(1 Cor.11:23-26; esp. v.26) Note 3, pt. 3

καταισχύνη = *kataischunë* **#721, #3500**
POSB Reference:
(1 Cor.1:27-28; esp. v.27) Note 2, pt. 1

καταισχύνει = *kataischunei* **#208, #1050**
POSB Reference:
(Rom.5:3-5; esp. v.5) Note 5, pt. 4

καταλαλεῖτε = *katalaleite* **#3608, #3676, #3677**
POSB Reference:
(Jas.4:11) Note 1, pt. 1

καταλαλιαι = *katalaliai* **#258, #260, #3609**
POSB Reference:
(2 Cor.12:19-21; esp. v.20) Note 3, pt. 2

καταλάλους = *katalalous* **#257, #259, #3612**
POSB Reference:
(Rom.1:30) *Deeper Study* #12

κατανοήσατε = *katanoësate* **#730, #1522, #3961**
POSB Reference:
(Heb.3:1) Note 1

κατανοῶμεν = *katanoömen* **#731, #3964**
POSB Reference:
(Heb.10:24) Note 3

καταπέτασμα = *katapetasma* **#859, #4213**
POSB Reference:
(Mk.15:38) Note 15, pt. 1

καταφρονηταί = *kataphronëtai* **#990, #2613, #3389**
POSB Reference:
(Acts 13:23-41; esp. v.41) Note 3, pt. 7

καταφυγόντες = *kataphugontes* **#1528, #1529**
POSB Reference:
(Heb.6:18-20; esp. v.18) Note 6, pt. 1

κατάραν = *kataran* **#855**
POSB Reference:
(Gal.3:10-12; esp. v.10) Note 3

καταργήσῃ = *katargësë* **#440, #996, #3245**
POSB Reference:
(Heb.2:14-16; esp. v.14) Note 1, pt. 3

καταρτίσει = *katartisei* **#2888, #3286**
POSB Reference:
(1 Pt.5:10) Note 2, pt. 1

κατάρτισιν = *katartisin* **#2477, #2899, #3284**
POSB Reference:
(2 Cor.13:7-10; esp. v.9) Note 2

καταρτισμὸν = *katartismon* **#1311, #2898, #3023**
POSB Reference:
(Eph.4:12-16; esp. v.12) Note 4, pt. 1

καταρτίζεσθε = *katartizesthe* **#96, #285, #289, #303, #540**
POSB Reference:
(2 Cor.13:11-13; esp. v.11) Note 3

καταρτίζετε = *katartizete* **#1926, #3285**
POSB Reference:
(Gal.6:1-5; esp. v.1) Introduction

κατασκηνώσει = *kataskënösei* **#7, #2357, #3278**
POSB Reference:
(Acts 2:25-28; esp. v.26) Note 1, pt. 1c

καταξιωθῆναι = *kataxiöthënai* **#737, #811, #2516**
POSB Reference:
(2 Thes.1:4-5; esp. v.5) Note 3

κατέχετε = *katechete* **#1508, #1966, #1967, #2235**
POSB Reference:
(1 Cor.15:1-2; esp. v.2) Note 1, pt. 3

κατεχόντων = *katechontön* **#1965, #3116, #3859**
POSB Reference:
(Rom.1:18) Note 1, pt. 3b

κατεῖχον = *kateichon* **#314, #2223, #3749**
POSB Reference:
(Lk.4:43-44; esp. v.42) Note 8

κατηλλάγημεν = *katëllagëmen* **#3201, #3288**
POSB Reference:
(Rom.5:10) *Deeper Study* #1

κατήνεγκα ψῆφον = *katënegka psëphon* **#522, #4238**
POSB Reference:
(Acts 26:9-11; esp. v.10) Note 4

κατενόησεν = *katenoësen* **#733, #747, #1413, #2263**
POSB Reference:
(Rom.4:18-22; esp. v.19) Note 2, pt. 1a

κατενύγησαν = *katenugësan* **#785,
#863, #2936, #3038**
POSB Reference:
(Acts 2:37) Note 1

κατεργάζεσθε = *katergazesthe* **#3122,
#4419**
POSB Reference:
(Philip.2:12) Note 1

κατηργήθημεν = *katërgëthëmen* **#943,
#3231**
POSB Reference:
(Rom.7:6) Note 4

κατηρτισμένος = *katërtismenos* **#1626,
#2886, #4431**
POSB Reference:
(Lk.6:40) Note 2, pt. 1

κατευθύναι = *kateuthunai* **#444, #1044**
POSB Reference:
(2 Thes.3:3-5; esp. v.5) Note 2, pt. 3

καθαίρει = *kathairei* **#3083, #3108**
POSB Reference:
(Jn.15:2-4; esp. v.2) Note 3, pt. 3

καθαρίσθητι = *katharisthëti* **#593,
#1899**
POSB Reference:
(Mt.8:3) Note 3

καθαροὶ = *katharoi* **#3095**
POSB Reference:
(Mt.5:8) Note 7

καθεξῆς = *kathexës* **#499, #724, #2793**
POSB Reference:
(Lk.1:3) Note 3, pt. 3

κατοικεῖ = *katoikei* **#2372, #1186**
POSB Reference:
(Col.2:9-10; esp. v.9) Note 2, pt. 1

κατοικῆσαι = *katoikësai* **#1185, #2621**
POSB Reference:
(Eph.3:17) Note 3

καυχᾶσαι = *kauchasai* **#410, #433**
POSB Reference:
(Rom.2:17-20; esp. v.17) Note 1, pt. 2

καύχημα = *kauchëma* **#412, #1706**
POSB Reference:
(1 Cor.5:6) Note 1

κεκοινώνηκεν = *kekoinönëken* **#1887,
#2831, #3509**
POSB Reference:
(Hcb.2:14-16; esp. v.14) Note 1, pt. 1

κεκρυμμένον = *kekrummenon* **#1945**
POSB Reference:
(Lk.18:34) Note 3

κενὸν = *kenon* **#1250, #4195, #4201**
POSB Reference:
(1 Cor.15:13-15; esp. v.14) Note 2, pt. 2

κενοφωνίας = *kenophönias* **#554,
#1251, #1560, #2066, #4204**
POSB Reference:
(1 Tim.6:20) Note 2, pt. 2a

κηρύσσειν = *kërussein* **#3002**
POSB Reference:
(Mk.3:14) *Deeper Study* #2

κηρύσσων = *kërussön* **#150, #3013,
#3049**
POSB Reference:
(Lk.8:1) *Deeper Study* #1

κηρύσσων = *kërussön* **#152, #3011,
#3048**
POSB Reference:
(Mt.9:35) *Deeper Study* #1

κῆρυξ = *kërux* **#1938, #3010**
POSB Reference:
(1 Tim.2:3-7; esp. v.7) Note 3, pt. 5

κιθάρα = *kithara* **#1873**
POSB Reference:
(1 Cor.13:6-14; esp. v.7) Note 3

κλαύσατε ὀλολύζοντες = *klausate
ololuzontes* **#4302, #4303, #4304**
POSB Reference:
(Jas.5:1) Note 1

κλεμμάτων = *klemmatön* **#3953**
POSB Reference:
(Rev.9:20-21; esp.v.21) Note 4, pt. 2e

κλέψεις = *klepseis* **#3759**
POSB Reference:
(Rom.13:9) Note 4

κλέπται = *kleptai* **#3958**
POSB Reference:
(1 Cor.6:10) Note 3

κλέπτων = *kleptön* **#3761, #3957**
POSB Reference:
(Eph.4:28) Note 3

κλήρων = *klërön* **#116, #219, #1305,
#1942**
POSB Reference:
(1 Pt.5:2-3; esp. v.3) Note 2, pt. 3

κληρονομίαν = *klëronomian* **#2147**
POSB Reference:
(Acts 20:32) Note 3, pt. 2

κλητοῖς = *klëtois* **#473**
POSB Reference:
(Jude 1:1-2; esp. v.1) Note 2, pt. 3

κλοπαί = *klopai* **#3952**
POSB Reference:
(Mk.7:21) *Deeper Study* #7

κοιλία = *koilia* **#349, #178, #3776**
POSB Reference:
(Philip.3:18-19; esp. v.19) Note 2, pt. 2

κοιλίᾳ = *koilia* **#179, #348, #2918**
POSB Reference:
(Rom.16:17-18; esp. v.18) Note 1, pt. 2

κοινοῖ = *koinoi* **#934, #4115**
POSB Reference:
(Mt.15:10-11, esp.v.11) Note 3

κοινὸν καὶ ἀκάθαρτον = *koinon kai
akatharton* **#661, #1571, #2104,
#4156**
POSB Reference:
(Acts 10:11-16; esp. v.14) *Deeper Study*
#3

κοινωνία = *koinönia* **#664, #1470,
#2370**
POSB Reference:
(2 Cor.6:14-16; esp. v.14) Note 2, pt. 2

κοινωνοῦντες = *kuinönountes* **#771,
#1121, #1927, #3511**
POSB Reference:
(Rom.12:13) Note 4, pt. 1

κοίταις = *koitais* **#65, #538, #2330,
#3492, #3496**
POSB Reference:
(Rom.13:13) Note 4, pt. 3

κολληθήσεται = *kollëthësetai* **#601,
#2203, #4158**
POSB Reference:
(Mt.19:5) *Deeper Study* #2

κολλώμενοι = *kollömenoi* **#600, #603,
#3736**
POSB Reference:
(Rom.12:9-10; esp. v.9) Note 1, pt. 2

κωλύετε = *köluete* **#1570, #1952,
#3777**
POSB Reference:
(Mk.10:14) *Deeper Study* #3

κῶμοι = *kömoi* **#511, #2795, #3299,
#3301, #4345**
POSB Reference:
(Gal.5:19-21; esp. v.21) Note 2

κώμοις = kōmois **#510, #1460, #2796, #3300, #3302**
POSB Reference:
(1 Pt.4:3) Note 3, pt. 4

κοπιῶ = kopiō **#2280, #4414**
POSB Reference:
(Col.1:29) Note 5, pt. 1

κοπιῶμεν = kopiōmen **#2278, #4416**
POSB Reference:
(1 Tim.4:10) Note 6

κοπιῶντα = kopiōnta **#2283, #1864**
POSB Reference:
(2 Tim. 2:6) Note 5

κόποις = kopois **#2284, #1862, #4425**
POSB Reference:
(2 Cor.6:5) Note 4

κόπον = kopon **#1863, #2281, #2287, #4004**
POSB Reference:
(Rev.2:2-3; esp. v.2) Note 3, pt. 1

κόπος = kopos **#2279, #2713, 4003**
POSB Reference:
(1 Cor.15:58) Note 6, pt. 3

κοσμεῖν = kosmein **#58, #1167, #4297**
POSB Reference:
(1 Tim.2:9-10; esp. v.9) Note 1

κοσμικὰς = kosmikas **#3589, #4439**
POSB Reference:
(Tit.2:12) Note 2, pt. 1b

κόσμιον = kosmion **#1747, #1759, #3271**
POSB Reference:
(1 Tim.3:2-3; esp. v.2) Note 2, pt. 5

κοσμοκράτορας = kosmokratoras **#2587, #2989, #3351, #4435**
POSB Reference:
(Eph.6:12) Note 3, pt. 5

κόσμον = kosmon **#4434**
POSB Reference:
(Acts 17:24-25; esp. v.24) Note 4, pt. 1

κόσμος = kosmos **#59, #294**
POSB Reference:
(1 Pt.3:3) Note 4

κραιπάλῃ = kraipalē **#503, #513, #1107, #3861**
POSB Reference:
(Lk.21:34-35; esp. v.34) Note 1, pt. 1

κράτει = kratei **#2976, #3792**
POSB Reference:
(Eph.6:10-11; esp. v.10) Note 1, pt. 1

κράτιστε = kratiste **#2624**
POSB Reference:
(Lk.1:3) Note 3, pt. 4a

κραυγὴ = kraugē **#437, #591, #1874**
POSB Reference:
(Eph.4:31) Note 6, pt. 4

κρίμα = krima **#700, #871, #2217, #3090**
POSB Reference:
(Rom.13:1-2; esp. v.2) Note 2, pt. 2

κριθῆτε = krinete **#2209**
POSB Reference:
(Mt.7:1) Note 1

κρινέτω = krinetō **#698**
POSB Reference:
(Rom.14:3-4; esp. v.3) Note 2

κριθῶσιν = krithōsin **#701, #872, #2213**
POSB Reference:
(2 Thes.2:12) Note 4

κριτικὸς = kritikos **#1053, #1403, #2210**
POSB Reference:
(Heb.4:11-13; esp. v.12) Note 5, pt. 2e

κυβερνήσεις = kubernēseis **#52, #1770, #3976, #3978**
POSB Reference:
(1 Cor.12:27-30; esp. v.28) Note 5, pt. 1g

κύνας = kunas **#1143**
POSB Reference:
(Philip.3:2) Note 3, pt. 1

Κύριε = Kurie **#2412, #3604**
POSB Reference:
(Jn.6:34-35; esp. v.34) Note 4, pt. 1

Κύριος = Kurios **#2413**
POSB Reference:
(1 Cor.12:3) Note 4

κύριος = kurios **#2415**
POSB Reference:
(Philip.2:11) *Deeper Study* #1

L

λαβὼν = labōn **#4010**
POSB Reference:
(Lk.13:19) Note 2, pt. 1

λαχοῦσιν = lachousin **#2737, #3186, #3508**
POSB Reference:
(2 Pt.1:1) Note 2, pt. 2

λαλοῦντα = lalounta **#3681**
POSB Reference:
(Heb.12:25) Note 1

λαλοῦντες διεστραμμένα = lalountes diestrammena **#1111, #3680**
POSB Reference:
(Acts 20:29-30; esp. v.30) *Deeper Study* #2, pt. 3

λαμπρῶς = lamprōs **#2472, #3714, #3853**
POSB Reference:
(Lk.16:19-21; esp. v.19) *Deeper Study* #1 pt. 1

λαὸν = laon **#2879**
POSB Reference:
(Acts 15:13-21; esp. v.14) Note 4, pt. 1

λαὸς εἰς περιποίησιν = laos eis peripoiēsin **#1959, #1963, #2875, #2880, #2881**
POSB Reference:
(1 Pt.2:9) Note 1

λατρείαν = latreian **#43, #3472, #3474**
POSB Reference:
(Rom.12:1) Note 2, pt. 2b

λατρεύω = latreuō **#3467**
POSB Reference:
(Ro.1:9) *Deeper Study* #1

λειτουργὸν = leitourgon **#1924, #2598, #2600, #3873**
POSB Reference:
(Philip.2:25) Note 1, pt. 5

λειτουργὸν = leitourgon **#2598, #3685**
POSB Reference:
(Rom.15:16) Note 3

λεπρὸς = lepros **#2323, #2324**
POSB Reference:
(Mk.1:40) Note 1

λίθος μυλικὸς = lithos mulikos **#2297, #2588**
POSB Reference:
(Lk.17:2) Deeper Study #1

λόγος = logos **#4405**
POSB Reference:
(Jn.1:1-5; esp. v.1) *Deeper Study* #1

λογικὴν = logikēn **#3172, #3704**
POSB Reference:
(Rom.12:1) Note 2, pt. 2b

λογικὸν = logikon **#3705, #4406**
POSB Reference:
(1 Pt.2:2-3; esp. v.2) Note 2

λογισμοὺς = *logismous* **#196, #1334, #2077, #3688**
POSB Reference:
(2 Cor.10:3-5; esp. v.5) Note 2

λογίζεσθε = *logizesthe* **#728, #810, #3194**
POSB Reference:
(Rom.6:11) *Deeper Study* #1

λογίζεσθε = *logizesthe* **#2328, #2553, #3963**
POSB Reference:
(Philip.4:8-9; esp. v.8) Note 2

λογίζεται = *logizetai* **#835, #921, #2109, #3197**
POSB Reference:
(Rom.4:6-8; esp. v.6) Note 3, pt. 1

λογιζόμενος = *logizomenos* **#812, #2110**
POSB Reference:
(2 Cor.5:18-19; esp. v.19) Note 2, pt. 2

λόγος γνώσεως = *logos gnöseös* **#1673, #2576, #4408**
POSB Reference:
(1 Cor.12:8-10; esp. v.8) Note 3, pt. 2

λοίδοροι = *loidoroi* **#21, #3311, #3611**
POSB Reference:
(1 Cor.6:10) Note 3, pt. 4

λοίδορος = *loidoros* **#24, #3156, #3309, #3610**
POSB Reference:
(1 Cor.5:11) Note 5

λουτροῦ = *loutrou* **#4267, #4268**
POSB Reference:
(Tit.3:5) Note 2, pt. 1

λύπη = *lupë* **#1916, #3659**
POSB Reference:
(Rom.9:1-3; esp. v.2) Note 1, pt. 2

λυπεῖσθαι = *lupeisthai* **#147, #1814, #3661**
POSB Reference:
(Mt.26:37) *Deeper Study* #3

λυπεῖτε = *lupeite* **#446, #1812**
POSB Reference:
(Eph.4:30) Note 5

λυπηθέντες = *lupëthentes* **#1116, #1278, #1817, #1917, #3846**
POSB Reference:
(1 Pt.1:6) Note 1, pt. 2

λύσαντι = *lusanti* **#1604, #3232, #4266**
POSB Reference:
(Rev.1:5-6; esp.v.5) Note 2, pt. 4

λύσητε = *lusëte* **#117, #2409**
POSB Reference:
(Mt.18:17-18; esp. v.18) Note 2, pt. 2

λύτρον ἀντὶ πολλῶν = *lutron anti pollon* **#3162**
POSB Reference:
(Mt.20:28) *Deeper Study* #5

λυτρώσηται = *lutrösëtai* **#1600, #3206**
POSB Reference:
(Tit.2:14) Note 4, pt. 1

M

μακαρίαν = *makarian* **#404, #4400**
POSB Reference:
(Tit.2:13) Note 3

μακάριοι = *makarioi* **#403, #1737, #3684**
POSB Reference:
(Lk.12:35-40; esp. v.37) Note 1, pt. 3

Μακάριος = *Makarios* **#405**
POSB Reference:
(Jas.1:12) Note 3, pt. 1

μακροθυμεῖ = *makrothumei* **#2383, #2853**
POSB Reference:
(2 Pt.3:9) Note 2

μακροθυμεῖ = *makrothumei* **#2850, #3847**
POSB Reference:
(1 Cor.13:4-7; esp. v.4) Note 2

Μακροθυμήσατε = *Makrothumësate* **#2854**
POSB Reference:
(Jas.5:7) Note 1

μακροθυμία = *makrothumia* **#2382, #2844**
POSB Reference:
(Gal.5:22-23; esp. v.22) Note 1

μαλακοὶ = *malakoi* **#1232, #1985, #2518**
POSB Reference:
(1 Cor.6:9) Note 2, pt. 4

μᾶλλον ἐνεδυναμοῦτο = *mallon enedunamouto* **#2986, #3794**
POSB Reference:
(Acts 9:22) Note 5, pt. 1

ἀμωνᾷ = *mamöna* **#2527, #2617**
POSB Reference:
(Mt.6:24) Note 3

Μαρανα θα = *Marana tha* **#623, #2533**
POSB Reference:
(1 Cor.16:19-24; esp. v.22) Note 6, pt. 2

μάρτυρες = *martures* **#3919, #4393**
POSB Reference:
(Acts 1:8) Note 3, pt. 2c

μαρτυρουμένους = *marturoumenous* **#1758, #1991, #2277, #4311**
POSB Reference:
(Acts 6:3) Note 3, pt. 1

μάρτυς = *martus* **#2535, #4392**
POSB Reference:
(Rev.2:13) Note 3, pt. 3

ματαία = *mataia* **#1631, #4202, #4449**
POSB Reference:
(1 Cor.15:16-19; esp. v.17) Note 3, pt. 2

ματαιολόγοι = *mataiologoi* **#1252, #2068, #2573, #4198, #4206**
POSB Reference:
(Tit.1:10-12; esp. v.10) Note 1, pt. 2

ματαιότητι = *mataiotëti* **#854, #1614, #1633, #4209**
POSB Reference:
(Rom.8:19-22, esp. v.20) Note 2, pt. 1

ματαιότητι = *mataiotëti* **#1634, #2011, #4210**
POSB Reference:
(Eph.4:17-19; esp. v.17) Note 1, pt. 1

μαθητεύσαντες ἱκανοὺς = *mathëteusantes hikanous* **#1056, #1057, #3897, #4395**
POSB Reference:
(Acts 14:21) Note 1, pt. 2

μαθητεύσατε = *mathëteusate* **#2502, #3898**
POSB Reference:
(Mt.28:19-20; esp. v.19) Note 3, pt. 1

ματαία = *matzaia* **#1631, #4196**
POSB Reference:
(1 Cor.15:16-19; esp. v.17) Note 3, pt. 2

μὴ αἰσχυνθῶμεν = *më aischunthömen* **#209, #3501, #4105**
POSB Reference:
(1 Jn.2:28) Note 2

μὴ ἀπολέσω = më apolesö **#2418**
POSB Reference:
(Jn.6:39) Note 4, pt. 2

μὴ ἀπόλλυε = më apollue **#997, #999, #1150, #3347, #4395**
POSB Reference:
(Rom.14:13-15; esp. v.15) Note 6, pt. 2

μὴ διαβόλους = më diabolous **#2690, #2691, #2703, #2705**
POSB Reference:
(1 Tim.3:11-12; esp. v.11) Note 3, pt. 1b

μὴ διλόγους = më dilogous **#2179, #2683, #3579**
POSB Reference:
(1 Tim.3:8) Note 1, pt. 2

μὴ ἐγκακεῖν = më egkakein **#2417, #1422, #1682**
POSB Reference:
(Lk.18:1) Note 1, pt. 4

μὴ γένοιτο = më genoito **#535, #1718, #2548, #2682, #2741**
POSB Reference:
(Rom.3:5-8; esp. v.4) Note 3, pt. 1

μὴ γίνου ἄπιστος = më ginou apistos **#1158, #1434, #1435, #4110**
POSB Reference:
(Jn.20:26-28; esp. v.27) Note 3, pt. 1b

Μή μου ἅπτου = më mou haptou **#1135, #1136, #3779, #4020**
POSB Reference:
(Jn.20:17-18; esp. v.17) Note 4

μὴ νεόφυτον = më neophuton **#2694, #2695, #2696, #2699**
POSB Reference:
(1 Tim.3:6) Note 4

Μὴ ὀκνήσῃς = Më oknësës **#231, #620, #938, #2706**
POSB Reference:
(Acts 9:36-39; esp. v.38) Note 2, pt. 3c

μὴ ὀλιγώρει = më oligörei **#987, #988, #1148, #2689, #2700**
POSB Reference:
(Heb.12:5-7; esp. v.5) Note 1

Μὴ φοβοῦ = më phobou **#76, #1457**
POSB Reference:
(Lk.8:49-56; esp. v.50) Note 4, pt. 2

μὴ πλανᾶσθε = më planasthe **#913, #1554, #2609**
POSB Reference:
(1 Cor.15:33) Note 3

μὴ πλήκτην = më plëktën **#2671, #2697, #2708**
POSB Reference:
(1 Tim.3:2-3; esp. v.3) Note 2, pt. 9

μὴ θροεῖσθε = më throeisthe **#98, #1608, #2826, #4068**
POSB Reference:
(Mt.24:6-7; esp. v.6) Note 3, pt. 2

μηδὲ αἰσχροκερδῶς = mëde aischrokerdös **#1072, #1498, #1803, #1823, #3656**
POSB Reference:
(1 Pt.5:2-3; esp. v.2) Note 2, pt. 2

μηδὲν = mëden **#166**
POSB Reference:
(Philip.4:6-7; esp. v.6) Note 1

μηδὲν διακρίναντα = mëden diakrinanta **#16, #1157, #2666, #2707, #2711, #4384**
POSB Reference:
(Acts 11:4-15; esp. v.12) Note 2, pt. 3

μεγαλειότητι = megaleiotëti **#1089, #1797, #2498, #2586**
POSB Reference:
(Lk.9:42-43; esp. v.43) Note 3, pt. 2

μεγαλειότητος = megaleiotëtos **#2497, #2499**
POSB Reference:
(2 Pt.1:16-18; esp. v.16) Note 2

Μεγαλύνει = Megalunei **#1363, #1701, #2493, #2992**
POSB Reference:
(Lk.1:46) Note 1, pt. 2

μεγαλυνόντων τὸν θεόν = megalunontön ton theon **#1362, #2494, #2997**
POSB Reference:
(Acts 10:46) Note 2

μέγεθος = megethos **#1782**
POSB Reference:
(Eph.1:19) Note 1

μείνατε = meinate **#6, #3236**
POSB Reference:
(Jn.15:4) Deeper Study #2

μείνητε = meinëte **#8, #760**
POSB Reference:
(Jn.8:31) Note 1, pt. 2

μείνητε = meinëte **#1964, #2236**
POSB Reference:
(Jn.8:31) Note 1, pt. 2

μεμαρτύρηκεν = memarturëken **#268, #3005, #3945**
POSB Reference:
(Jn.5:33-35; esp. v.33) Note 3, pt. 1

μεμονωμένη = memonömenë **#984, #2320, #2321, #4076**
POSB Reference:
(1 Tim.5:4-8; esp. v.5) Note 2, pt. 2

μένε = mene **#763, #3238**
POSB Reference:
(2 Tim. 3:14) Note 1

μένει = menei **#9, #3237, #1192**
POSB Reference:
(Jn.6:56) Note 4

μέριμναν = merimnan **#161, #489, #4442**
POSB Reference:
(1 Pt.5:6-7; esp. v.7) Note 3, pt. 3

μεριμνᾷς = merimnas **#493, #4187, #4441**
POSB Reference:
(Lk.10:41-42; esp. v.41) Note 4, pt. 2

μεριμνᾶτε = merimnate **#162, #3886 #4443**
POSB Reference:
(Lk.12:22-34; esp. v.22) Outline
Introduction

μεριμνᾶτε = merimnate **#163, #498, #4444**
POSB Reference:
(Philip.4:6-7; esp. v.6) Note 1

μερὶς = meris **#2113, #2830**
POSB Reference:
(2 Cor.6:14-16; esp. v.15) Note 2, pt. 4

μεσίτης = mesitës **#2552, #2780**
POSB Reference:
(Heb.8:6) Note 1

μετὰ πάσης προθυμίας = meta pasës prothumias **#1200, #1207, #3167**
POSB Reference:
(Acts 17:11) Note 5

μετὰ πάσης ταπεινοφροσύνης = meta pasës tapeinophrosunës **#2036, #2040, #2041, #2042**
POSB Reference:
(Acts 20:18-19; esp. v.19) Note 2, pt. 3

μεταδιδοὺς = metadidous **#772, #1687, #3510**
POSB Reference:
(Rom.12:6-8; esp. v.8) Note 2, pt. 5

μεταμορφοῦσθε = metamorphousthe **#4032**
POSB Reference:
(Rom.12:2) Note 4

Μετανοεῖτε = Metanoeite **#3250, #4094**
POSB Reference:
(Mt.3:2-6; esp. v.2) Note 1

μετασχηματίζονται = metaschëmati-zontai **#1071, #2538, #3037, #4033**
POSB Reference:
(2 Cor.11:13-15; esp. v.15) Note 6

μεταστρέψαι = metastrepsai **#1110, #2928, #4104**
POSB Reference:
(Gal.1:6-7; esp. v.7) Note 2

μετατίθεσθε ἀπὸ = metatithesthe apo **#967, #4101**
POSB Reference:
(Gal.1:6-7, esp. v.6) Note 2, pt. 1

μετεμορφώθη = metemorphöthë **#173, #4031**
POSB Reference:
(Mt.17:2) Note 2

μετέσχεν = meteschen **#295, #2837, #3512, #4015**
POSB Reference:
(Heb.2:14-16; esp. v.14) Note 1. pt. 1

μέθαις = methais **#1670**
POSB Reference:
(Rom.13:13) Note 4, pt. 2

μέθη = methë **#1180**
POSB Reference:
(Lk.21:34-35; esp. v.34) Note 1, pt. 2

μεθοδείας = methodeias **#3387, #3790, #4347**
POSB Reference:
(Eph.6:11) Note 2

μέθυσοι = methusoi **#1179**
POSB Reference:
(1 Cor.6:10) Note 3, pt. 3

μετοχή = metochë **#1469, #2112, #2836**
POSB Reference:
(2 Cor.6:14-16; esp. v.14) Note 2, pt. 1c

μετόχους γενηθέντας = metochous genëthentas **#2832, #3513**
POSB Reference:
(Heb.6:4-5; esp. v.4) Note 1, pt. 3

μιμηταί = mimëtai **#1366, #1551, #2079**
POSB Reference:
(Eph.5:1) Note 1

μιμηταί γίνεσθε. = mimëtai ginesthe **#1365, #1550, #2078**
POSB Reference:
(1 Cor.4:16) Note 3

μνᾶς = mnas **#2590, #2968**
POSB Reference:
(Lk.19:13)
  Deeper Study #1

Μνημονεύετε = Mnëmoneuete **#3240**
POSB Reference:
(Heb.13:7) Note 6

μοιχεία = moicheia **#63**
POSB Reference:
(Gal.5:19-21; esp. v.19) Note 2

μοιχεῖαι = moicheiai **#66**
POSB Reference:
(Mk.7:21) *Deeper Study* #4

μοιχοί = moichoi **#61**
POSB Reference:
(1 Cor.6:9) Note 2, pt. 3

μοναι = monai **#1194, #2530, #3339**
POSB Reference:
(Jn.14:2) Note 2, pt. 3

μωρὰ = möra **#1562, #3960**
POSB Reference:
(1 Cor.1:27-28; esp. v.27) Note 2, pt. 1

μωρὰς = möras **#1559**
POSB Reference:
(Tit.3:9) Note 2, pt. 1

μωρία = möria **#1564, #3670**
POSB Reference:
(1 Cor.2:14) Note 1, pt. 2

μωρολογία = mörologia **#1561, #3562**
POSB Reference:
(Eph.5:4) Note 4, pt. 21

μορφῇ = morphë **#1590, #2652**
POSB Reference:
(Philip.2:6) Note 2, pt. 2

μυκτηρίζεται = muktërizetai **#2074, #2612**
POSB Reference:
(Gal.6:7-9; esp. v.7) Note 2, pt. 1

μύλος ὀνικὸς = mulos onikos **#2589**
POSB Reference:
(Mt.18:6) Note 2, pt. 1

μυριάδων = muriadön **#2159, #3987**
POSB Reference:
(Lk.12:1) Note 1

μύρου = murou **#2762, #2763, #2900**
POSB Reference:
(Jn.12:3) Note 2, pt. 2

μυστήριον = mustërion **#2574, #3947**
POSB Reference:
(1 Cor.2:1) Note 1, pt. 3

μυστηρίου = mustëriou **#2643, #3401**
POSB Reference:
(Rom.16:25-26; esp. v.25) Note 3, pt. 1

μύθοις = muthois **#1411, #2644**
POSB Reference:
(1 Tim.1:4) Note 2, pt. 1

N

ναός = naos **#3926**
POSB Reference:
(1 Cor.3:16) Note 6

νεκροὺς = nekrous **#887**
POSB Reference:
(Eph.2:1) Note 1

νηφάλιον = nëphalion **#1385, #3922, #4220**
POSB Reference:
(1 Tim.3:2-3; esp. v.2) Note 2

νηφαλίους = nëphalious **#1384, #3636, #3923**
POSB Reference:
(Tit.2:2) Note 2, pt. 1

νῆφε = nëphe **#2228, #2232, #3634, #4273**
POSB Reference:
(2 Tim. 4:5) Note 4, pt. 1

νηπίων = nëpiön **#256, #565, #2081, #2144**
POSB Reference:
(Rom.2:17-20; esp. v.20) Note 1, pt. 9

Νήψατε = Nëpsate **#495, #3427, #3637**
POSB Reference:
(1 Pt.5:8) Note 1

νήψατε = nëpsate **#1061, #3426, #3640, #4274**
POSB Reference:
(1 Pt.4:7) Note 2

νηστείαις = nësteiais **#1448, #1735, #2046**
POSB Reference:
(2 Cor.6:5) Note 4

νομικὸς = nomikos **#1398, #2307**
POSB Reference:
(Mt.22:35) *Deeper Study* #1

νόμον = nomon **#2305**
POSB Reference:
(Mt.5:17-18; esp. v.17) Note 1, *Deeper Study* #2

νοός = nuos **#2592, #3967**
POSB Reference:
(Eph.4:17-19; esp. v.17) Note 1, pt. 1

νοοῦμεν = *nooumen #4133*
POSB Reference:
(Heb.11:3) Note 3

νωθροί = *nöthroi #1184, #1859,*
#3623
POSB Reference:
(Heb.5:11) Note 1

νουθεσία = *nouthesia #55, #2173*
POSB Reference:
(Eph.6:4) Note 2, pt. 2

νουθετῶν = *nouthetön #54, #4254,*
#4276
POSB Reference:
(Acts 20:28-31; esp. v.31) Note 2, pt. 4a

Ο

Ὁ κύριος = *o kurios #2410*
POSB Reference:
(Mt.21:2-5; esp. v.3) Note 2, pt. 1a

ὁλόκληροι = *holoklëroi #1623*
POSB Reference:
(Jas.1:4) Note 3, pt. 2

ὠδῖνας = *ödinas #87, #2012, #2824*
POSB Reference:
(Acts 2:24) *Deeper Study* #4, pt. 2

ὠδίνων = *ödinön #380, #2013, #3662*
POSB Reference:
(Mt.24:8) *Deeper Study* #5

ὀδύνη = *odunë #149, #1809, #3660*
POSB Reference:
(Rom.9:1-3; esp. v.2), Note 1, pt. 2

ὄγκον πάντα = *ogkon panta #1333,*
#1335, #1337
POSB Reference:
(Heb.12:1) Note 2, pt. 1a

οἰκεῖ = *oikei #1188, #2374*
POSB Reference:
(Rom.8:9) Note 4, pt. 1

οἴκῳ = *oikö #2022*
POSB Reference:
(1 Tim.3:15) Note 2, pt. 1

οἰκοδομεῖτε = *oikodomeite #460,*
#1231
POSB Reference:
(1 Thes.5:11) Note 4

οἰκοδομὴν = *oikodomën #1229,*
#1932, #3802
POSB Reference:
(1 Cor.14:3) *Deeper Study* #1, pt. 1

οἰκοδομουμένη = *oikodomoumenë*
#337, #1230, #1808, #3799
POSB Reference:
(Acts 9:31) Note 2

οἰκονομίαν = *oikonomian #50, #1085,*
#3123, #3971
POSB Reference:
(Eph.1:9-10; esp. v.10) Note 6, pt. 3

οἰκονομίαν = *oikonomian #51, #1086,*
#3686, #3768
POSB Reference:
(Eph.3:2) Note 1, pt. 2

οἰκονομίαν = *oikonomian #651,*
#3274
POSB Reference:
(Col.1:25) Note 2

οἰκονομίαν = *oikonomian #1084,*
#3355, #3767, #4078
POSB Reference:
(1 Cor.9:16-17; esp. v.17) Note 2

οἰκουργούς = *oikourgous #463, #552,*
#3106, #4426
POSB Reference:
(Tit.2:4-5; esp. v.5) Note 4, pt. 6

οἰκτιρμῶν = *oiktirmön #670, #2565,*
#2571
POSB Reference:
(2 Cor.1:3) Note 1

οἰκτιρμοῦ = *oiktirmou #671, #2566,*
#2570
POSB Reference:
(Col.3:12) Note 2

οἰνοφλυγίαις = *oinophlugiais #1181,*
#1381
POSB Reference:
(1 Pt.4:3) Note 3, pt. 3

οἰκονομίαν = *oikonomian #1087,*
#3769
POSB Reference:
(Col.1:25) Note 2

ὀκνηροί = *oknëroi #2289, #2290,*
#2311, #3622
POSB Reference:
(Rom.12:11) Note 2, pt. 1

ὄλεθρον αἰώνιον = *olethron aiönion*
#1322, #1331
POSB Reference:
(2 Thes.1:9) Note 4, pt. 3

ων = *ön #334, #2194*
POSB Reference:
(Heb.1:3) Note 4

οὐ λογίζεται τὸ κακόν =*oo logizetai to*
kakon #36, #3204, #3205, #3965
POSB Reference:
(1 Cor.13:4-7; esp. v.5) Note 2, pt. 9

ὀφειλήματα = *opheilëmata #900,*
#3600
POSB Reference:
(Mt.6:12) *Deeper Study* #8

ὀφειλέτης = *opheiletës #899, #1791,*
#2727
POSB Reference:
(Rom.1:14-15; esp. v.14) Note 5, pt. 1

ὀφείλομεν = *opheilomen #426, #2800*
POSB Reference:
(2 Thes.1:3) Note 4

ὠφέλιμος = *öphelimos #3056, #4194*
POSB Reference:
(2 Tim. 3:16) Note 4

ὄψεσθε = *opsesthe #3405*
POSB Reference:
(Jn.1:39-40; esp. v.39) Note 3, pt. 2

ὀργὴ = *orgë #2140, #4458*
POSB Reference:
(Rom.2:8) *Deeper Study* #6

ὀργὴ = *orgë #3938, #4462*
POSB Reference:
(Col.3:5-7; esp. v.6) Note 1, pt. 2

ὀργὴ = *orgë #4457*
POSB Reference:
(Jn.3:36) *Deeper Study* #5

ὀργίλον = *orgilon #3140, #3653*
POSB Reference:
(Tit.1:7-8; esp. v.7) Note 3, pt. 1b

ὀργίζεσθε = *orgizesthe #142*
POSB Reference:
(Eph.4:26-27; esp. v.26) Note 2

ὀρφανούς = *orphanous #638, #2797*
POSB Reference:
(Jn.14:18-20; esp. v.18) Note 4, pt. 1

ὀρθοτομοῦντα = *orthotomounta #799,*
#800, #1847, #3331
POSB Reference:
(2 Tim. 2:15) Note 2

οὐ δέχεται = *ou dechetai #29, #486,*
#2698, #3191
POSB Reference:
(1 Cor.2:14) Note 1, pt. 1

οὐ γὰρ δύνῃ = *ou gar dunë #296,*
#1074, #2380
POSB Reference:
(Lk.16:1-7; esp. v.2) Note 1, pt. 2a

οὐ μισεῖ = *ou misei* **#1880, #2640, #2684**
POSB Reference:
(Lk.14:26) Note 2

οὐ φρονεῖς = *ou phroneis* **#2685, #2692, #2702, #3378, #3410**
POSB Reference:
(Mk.8:32-33; esp. v.33) Note 2, pt. 3

Οὐαὶ = *Ouai* **#2025, 4394**
POSB Reference:
(Mt.23:13) *Deeper Study #1*

οὐχὶ ἔδει = *ouchi edei* **#599, #2686, #2693, #2801**
POSB Reference:
(Lk.24:15-27; esp. v.26) Note 2, pt. 3b

οὐδὲ ἕν = *oude hen* **#2681, #2710**
POSB Reference:
(Jn.1:3) Note 2, pt. 4b

Οὐδὲν κατάκριμα = *Ouden katakrima* **#2664**
POSB Reference:
(Rom.8:1) Note 1, pt. 1

οὐκ ἐδέξαντο = *ouk edexanto* **#3184, #3210**
POSB Reference:
(2 Thes.2:10) Note 2

οὐκ ἐγκακοῦμεν = *ouk egkakoumen* **#1421, #2657, #2687**
POSB Reference:
(2 Cor.4:1) Note 1

οὐκ ἐφείσατο = *ouk epheisato* **#2704, #3674**
POSB Reference:
(Rom.8:31-33; esp. v.32) Note 4, pt. 1

οὐκέτι ἦλθον = *ouketi ëlthon* **#480, #481, #1027, #2701**
POSB Reference:
(2 Cor.1:23-2:4; esp. v.23) Note 1, 2

οὐρανοῖς = *ouranois* **#1915**
POSB Reference:
(Mt.6:9) *Deeper Study #3*

οὔσῃ ἡγιασμένοις = *ousë hëgiasmenois* **#1970, #3370**
POSB Reference:
(1 Cor.1:2) *Deeper Study #1*

P

παγίς = *pagis* **#3628, #4037**
POSB Reference:
(Lk.21:35) *Deeper Study #1*

παιδαγωγὸς = *paidagögos* **#1831, #3120, #3388, #4102**
POSB Reference:
(Gal.3:23-25; esp. v.24) Note 1

παιδαγωγοὺς = *paidagögous* **#1832, #2171, #4001, #4103**
POSB Reference:
(1 Cor.4:15) Note 2

παιδείᾳ = *paideia* **#1058, #2718, 4027**
POSB Reference:
(Eph.6:4) Note 2, pt. 2

παιδεύει = *paideuei* **#553, #1062**
POSB Reference:
(Heb.12:5-13; esp. v.6)

πάλη = *palë* **#1485, #3825, #4464**
POSB Reference:
(Eph.6:12) Note 3

παλιγγενεσίας = *paliggenesias* **#2660, #3178, #3219**
POSB Reference:
(Tit.3:5) Note 2, pt. 1

πανουργίᾳ = *panourgia* **#828, #916, #4055**
POSB Reference:
(2 Cor.4:2) Note 2

πάντα = *panta* **#106**
POSB Reference:
(Lk.9:1) Note 1, pt. 4a

πάντα = *panta* **#113, #1338**
POSB Reference:
(Jn.1:3) Note 2, pt. 1

πάντες ἐξέκλιναν = *pantes exeklinan* **#108, #4099**
POSB Reference:
(Rom.3:10-12; esp. v.12) Note 2, pt. 4

παντοκράτωρ = *pantokratör* **#118**
POSB Reference:
(Rev.1:8) Note 4, pt. 3

παντὸς δόλου = *pantos dolou* **#107, #112, #4224**
POSB Reference:
(Acts 13:8-11; esp. v.10) Note 4, pt. 3

πάντοτε δὸς = *pantote dos* **#1683**
POSB Reference:
(Jn.6:34-35; esp. v.34) Note 4, pt. 1

παρὰ = *para* **#2123, #4366**
POSB Reference:
(Jn.8:38) Note 4, pt. 1

παρὰ θεοῦ = *para theou* **#1611**
POSB Reference:
(Jn.1:6) Note 1, pt. 2b

παράβασις = *parabasis* **#4034, #4225, #4226**
POSB Reference:
(Heb.2:2) Note 2

παραβολαῖς = *parabolais* **#2827, #3781**
POSB Reference:
(Mk.4:2) *Deeper Study #1*

παραβολευσάμενος = *paraboleusamenos* **#3213, #3335**
POSB Reference:
(Philip.2:28-30; esp. v.30) Note 4

παράδεισον = *paradeison* **#2829**
POSB Reference:
(2 Cor.12:4) *Deeper Study #2*

παραδόσεις = *paradoseis* **#584, #2794, #3915, #4026**
POSB Reference:
(1 Cor.11:2) Note 1

παράδοσιν = *paradosin* **#3914, #4024, #4025**
POSB Reference:
(2 Thes.3:6-11; esp. v.6) Note 1

παραδοθήσεται = *paradothesetai* **#367, #941, #1844**
POSB Reference:
(Mk.10:33) Note 4

παραδοθήσεται = *paradothësetai* **#368, #942**
POSB Reference:
(Mt.20:18) Note 2, pt. 1

παραγγείλῃς = *paraggeilës* **#544, #643, #2168, #3778**
POSB Reference:
(1 Tim.1:3) Note 1

παραγγελίαν = *paraggelian* **#545, #644, #2174**
POSB Reference:
(1 Tim.1:18) Note 1

παράγγελλε = *paraggelle* **#546, #645, #2170, #3918**
POSB Reference:
(1 Tim.6:17-19; esp. v.17) Note 1

παραγγέλλων = *paraggellön* **#918, #1046, #2175, #2563**
POSB Reference:
(1 Cor.11:17) Note 1

αραιτήσησθε = *paraitësësthe* **#3211**
POSB Reference:
(Heb.12:25-29; esp. v.25) Introduction

παρακαλεî = *parakalei* **#359, #1298, #2955**
POSB Reference:
(Mk.5:22-24; esp. v.23) Note 2 pt. 3

παρακαλεîσθε = *parakaleisthe* **#633, #636, #1260, #2351**
POSB Reference:
(2 Cor.13:11-13; esp. v.11) Note 3

παρακαλεîτε = *parakaleite* **#1258, #1389, #4253**
POSB Reference:
(Heb.3:13-19; esp. v.13) Note 3

παρακαλέσαι = *parakalesai* **#630, #1256**
POSB Reference:
(2 Thes.2:16-17; esp. v.17) Note 5, pt. 4

παρακάλεσον = *parakaleson* **#1257, #1388**
POSB Reference:
(2 Tim. 4:2) Note 2, pt. 5

Παρακαλῶ = *Parakalö* **#354, #170, #1387, #2952**
POSB Reference:
(1 Cor.1:10) Note 1

Παρακαλῶ = *Parakalö* **#355, #2954, #4191**
POSB Reference:
(Rom.12:1) Note 1

παρακλήσει = *paraklësei* **#628, #1263**
POSB Reference:
(Acts 9:31) Note 3, pt. 2

παρακλήσει = *paraklësei* **#740, #1261, #1267**
POSB Reference:
(Acts 15:30-35; esp. v.31) Note 5, pt. 1

παρακλήσει = *paraklësei* **#1255, #1390**
POSB Reference:
(Rom.12:6-8, esp. v.8) Note 2

παρακλήσεως = *paraklëseös* **#632**
POSB Reference:
(2 Cor.1:3) Note 1

παράκλησιν = *paraklësin* **#627, #739, #1852**
POSB Reference:
(Lk.6:24-26; esp. v.24) Note 2, pt. 1d

παράκλησιν αἰωνίαν = *paraklësin aiönian* **#1320, #1323, #1329, #1330**
POSB Reference:
(2 Thes. 2:16-17, esp. v.16) Note 5, pt. 2

παράκλησις = *paraklësis* **#742, #1262**
POSB Reference:
(Philip.2:1) Note 1

παρακληθῶσιν = *paraklëthösin* **#634, #1264**
POSB Reference:
(Col.2:2-3; esp. v.2) Note 2

παράκλητον = *paraklëton* **#68, #638, #3648, #3682**
POSB Reference:
(1 Jn.2:1-2; esp. v.1) Note 3, pt. 1

παράκλητον = *paraklëton* **#637, #809, #1930**
POSB Reference:
(Jn.14:16) *Deeper Study* #1

παρακοή = *parakoë* **#1076**
POSB Reference:
(Heb.2:2) Note 2

παραλογίζηται = *paralogizëtai* **#321, #909, #945**
POSB Reference:
(Col.2:4) Note 3

παραμυθίαν = *paramuthian* **#631, #741**
POSB Reference:
(1 Cor.14:3) *Deeper Study* #1, pt. 3

παραμύθιον = *paramuthion* **#629, #743**
POSB Reference:
(Philip.2:1) Note 2

παραπεσόντας = *parapesontas* **#1438, #4091**
POSB Reference:
(Heb.6:6) Note 2

παραφέρεσθε = *parapheresthe* **#239, #515**
POSB Reference:
(Heb.13:9-11; esp. v.9) Note 1

παραπτώμασιν = *paraptömasin*, **#4035, #4047**
POSB Reference:
(Eph.2:1-2; esp. v.1) Note 2

παραπτώματα = *paraptömata* **#3569, #3573, #4036, #4045**
POSB Reference:
(Mt.6:14) Note 1

παραπτωμάτων = *paraptömatön* **#3601, #4046**
POSB Reference:
(Eph.1:7) *Deeper Study* #1

παραρυῶμεν = *pararuömen* **#1171, #3621**
POSB Reference:
(Heb.2:1) Note 1

παρατηρήσεως = *paratërëseös* **#2730, #4235**
POSB Reference:
(Lk.17:20-21; esp. v.20) Note 1, pt. 1

παραθήκην = *parathëkën* **#659, #1304**
POSB Reference:
(2 Tim. 1:11-12 esp. v.12) Note 5, pt. 2b

παρατίθεμαι = *paratithemai* **#649, #654, #1300**
POSB Reference:
(Acts 20:32) Note 3

παρατιθέσθωσαν = *paratithesthösan* **#655, #1301, #4080**
POSB Reference:
(1 Pt.4:19) Note 7

παρεδέχθησαν = *paredechthësan* **#3188, #4308**
POSB Reference:
(Acts 15:4-5; esp. v.4) Note 2, pt. 1

παρεδίδου = *paredidou* **#658, #1303, #2322**
POSB Reference:
(1 Pt.2:21-24; esp. v.23) Note 2, pt. 3c

παρεκάλει = *parekalei* **#1259, #1391**
POSB Reference:
(Acts 11:19-30; esp. v.23) *Deeper Study* #2, pt. 3

παρεκάλουν = *parekaloun* **#212, #316, #361, #2191**
POSB Reference:
(Acts 13:42-45; esp. v.42) Note 1, pt. 1

παρηκολουθηκότι = *parëkolouthëkoti* **#2190, #2892, #4134**
POSB Reference:
(Lk.1:3) Note 3, pt. 1

παρηκολούθησάς = *parëkolouthësas* **#1548, #1625, #2268, #2270**
POSB Reference:
(2 Tim. 3:10) Note 1

παρέλαβεν = *parelaben* **#4009**
POSB Reference:
(Mt.20:17) Note 1

παρεπιδήμοις = *parepidëmois* **#105, #1576, #2938, #3788**
POSB Reference:
(1 Pt.2:11) Note 1, pt. 2

παρέστησεν = parestēsen **#175, #3031, #3540, #3542**
POSB Reference:
(Acts 1:3) Note 3, pt. 1

παρετηροῦντο = paretērounto **#4285**
POSB Reference:
(Lk.6:6-11; esp. v.7) Note 3, pt. 2

παριστάνετε = paristanete **#2325, #2755, #3027, #4468**
POSB Reference:
(Rom.6:13) *Deeper Study #2*

παροικίας = paroikias **#1577, #3644, #3744, #3789**
POSB Reference:
(1 Pt.1:17) Note 3

πάροικοι = paroikoi **#104, #1575**
POSB Reference:
(Eph.2:19) Note 1

παροργίζετε = parorgizete **#1370, #3078, #4043**
POSB Reference:
Eph.6:4) Note 2

παρουσίας = parousias **#640**
POSB Reference:
(2 Thes.2:8) Note 4, pt. 2

παροξύνεται = paroxunetai **#1219, #1222, #2193, #3079**
POSB Reference:
1 Cor.13:4-7; esp. v.5) Note 2, pt. 8

παρωξύνετο = parŏxuneto **#931, #1795, #3080, #3773**
POSB Reference:
(Acts 17:16) Note 1

παροξυσμός = paroxusmos **#752, #1048, #3514**
POSB Reference:
(Acts 15:39) Note 2, pt. 1

παρρησία = parresia **#2782, #2948**
POSB Reference:
(Mk.8:32-33; esp. v.32) Note 2

παρρησίαν = parrēsian **#417, #707**
POSB Reference:
(Heb.10:19-20; esp. v.19) Note 1

παρθένος = parthenos **#4231**
POSB Reference:
(Mt.1:23) *Deeper Study #8*

πᾶς ὁ προάγων = pas ho proagōn
#165, #4249, #4337
POSB Reference:
(2 Jn.1:9) Note 3

πᾶσα ἐξουσία = pasa exousia **#245, #2981**
POSB Reference:
(Mt.28:18) Note 2

πάσῃ μακροθυμίᾳ = pasë makrothumia **#110, #1789, #2857**
POSB Reference:
(2 Tim. 4:2) Note 2, pt. 5a

Πάτερ = Patër **#1449**
POSB Reference:
(Lk.22:41-42; esp. v.42) Note 3, pt. 2

πάθη ἀτιμίας = pathë atimias **#937, #3504, #3506, #4223**
POSB Reference:
(Rom.1:26-27; esp. v.26) Note 3, pt. 1

παθεῖν = pathein **#845, #2838, #3849**
POSB Reference:
(Acts 1:3) Note 3

παθητός = pathëtos **#3845**
POSB Reference:
(Acts 26:22-23; esp. v.23) Note 2, pt. 2

πάθος = pathos **#2160, #2461, #2839**
POSB Reference:
(Col.3:5-7; esp. v.5) Note 1, pt. 1c

πῆχυν = pëchun **#850, #2020, #2614**
POSB Reference:
(Mt.6:27) Note 4

πῆχυν = pëchun **#851, #2021, #2615**
POSB Reference:
(Lk.12:22-28; esp. v.25) Note 1, pt. 3

πειρασμοῖς = peirasmois **#3932, #4050, #4061**
POSB Reference:
(Jas.1:2) Note 1

πειρασμόν = peirasmon **#3930**
POSB Reference:
(Mt.6:13) *Deeper Study #9*

πειρασμοῦ = peirasmou **#3931, #4049**
POSB Reference:
(2 Pt.2:3-9; esp. v.9) Note 5, pt. 4

πειραζόμενος = peirazomenos **#3933**
POSB Reference:
(Lk.4:1-2; esp. v.2) *Deeper Study #1*

πεισμονή = peismonë **#2922**
POSB Reference:
(Gal.5:8) Note 2

πειθοῖ[ς] = peithois **#1295, #2923**
POSB Reference:
(1 Cor.2:4) Note 4, pt. 2

πείθων = peithön **#2921, #2925**
POSB Reference:
(Acts 19:2-9; esp. v.8) Note 2, pt. 2b

πέμπω = pempö **#3438**
POSB Reference:
(Jn.20:21) Note 3 pt. 3

πενιχρὰν = penichran **#2966**
POSB Reference:
(Lk.21:2) Note 2

πενθοῦντες = penthountes **#2627**
POSB Reference:
(Mt.5:4) Note 3

πεπληρωμένοι πάσης γνώσεως = peplërömenoi pasës gnöseös **#685, #1489, #2271**
POSB Reference:
(Rom.15:14) Note 1, pt. 2b

πεπληροφορημένων = peplërophorë-menön **#34, #1615, #2625, #4016**
POSB Reference:
(Lk.1:1) Note 1, pt. 2

πεπλήρωται = peplërötai **#618**
POSB Reference:
(Jn.7:6-9; esp. v.8) Note 3, pt. 3

πέποιθάς = pepoithas **#713, #792**
POSB Reference:
(Rom.2:17-20; esp. v.19) Note 1, pt. 6

πεποιθότας = pepoithotas **#709, #3421, #4081**
POSB Reference:
(Lk.18:9) Note 1, pt. 1

πεπτωκότα = peptökota **#1439**
POSB Reference:
(Rev.9:1) Note 2

πήραν = përan **#261, #2261, #3396, #4038**
POSB Reference:
(Lk.10:4) Note 4, pt. 1

περὶ ἁμαρτιῶν = peri hamartiön **#1566**
POSB Reference:
(1 Pt.3:18) Note 1, pt. 1

περιεποιήσατο = periepoiësato **#425, #3093**
POSB Reference:
(Acts 20:28-31; esp. v.28) Note 2, pt. 1b

περιεσπᾶτο = periespato **#852, #1112, #4445**
POSB Reference:
Lk.10:40) Note 3

περιούσιον = *periousion* **#1960,**
#1961, #1962, #2874
POSB Reference:
(Tit.2:14) Note 4, pt. 2

περιπατεῖν = *peripatein* **#2359, #4247**
POSB Reference:
(1 Jn.2:6) Note 4

περιπατῆσαι = *peripatësai* **#2360**
POSB Reference:
(Col.1:10) Note 2

περιπατήσωμεν = *peripatësömen*
#2356, #4246
POSB Reference:
(Rom.6:3-5, esp. v.4) Note 2, pt. 2b

περισσεύσαι = *perisseusai* **#15, #2812**
POSB Reference:
(1 Th.3:12) Note 2

περπερεύεται = *perpereuetai* **#411,**
#431, #2828, #4212
POSB Reference:
(1 Cor.13:4-7; esp. v.4) Note 2, pt. 4

Πέτρον = *Petron* **#2931**
POSB Reference:
(Mk.3:16) *Deeper Study* #4

φάγῃ = *phagë* **#1225**
POSB Reference:
(Jn.6:47-51; esp. v.50) Note 3, pt. 2b

φαρμακεία = *pharmakeia* **#2833,**
#3655, #4364
POSB Reference:
(Gal.5:19-21; esp. v.20) Note 2

φαρμάκων = *pharmakön* **#2492,**
#3654, #4365
POSB Reference:
(Rev.9:20-21; esp.v.21) Note 4, pt. 2c

φιλαδελφία = *philadelphia* **#2454,**
#2435, #2440, #454
POSB Reference:
(Heb.13:1) Note 1, pt. 1

φιλαδελφίαν = *philadelphian* **#2436,**
#2437, #2439
POSB Reference:
(1 Pt.1:22-25; esp. v.22)

φιλαδελφίαν = *philadelphian* **#2438**
POSB Reference:
(2 Pt.1:5-7; esp. v.7) Note 1, pt. 6

φιλαδελφίας = *philadelphias* **#453,**
#452
POSB Reference:
(1 Thes.4:9-10; esp. v.9) Note 1

φιλάδελφοι = *philadelphoi* **#451,**
#2434, #2455
POSB Reference:
(1 Pt.3:8) Note 3

φιλάγαθον = *philagathon* **#2447,**
#2433, #2446, #2453
POSB Reference:
(Tit.1:7-8; esp. v.8) Note 3, pt. 2b

φιλάνδρους = *philandrous* **#2442**
POSB Reference:
(Tit.2:4-5; esp. v.4) Note 4, pt. 2

φιλανθρωπία = *philanthröpia* **#2431**
POSB Reference:
(Tit.3:4-5; esp. v.4) Note 1, pt. 2

φιλάργυροι = *philarguroi* **#823,**
#2443, #2448
POSB Reference:
(2 Tim. 3:2-4; esp. v.2) Note 2, pt. 2

φίλαυτοι = *philautoi* **#2441, #2449,**
#2450, #2451
POSB Reference:
(2 Tim. 3:2-4; esp. v.2) Note 2, pt. 1

φιλῶ = *philö* **#2430**
POSB Reference:
(Rev.3:18-20; esp. v.19) Note 5, pt. 2

φιλονεικία = *philoneikia* **#190, #1094,**
#3804
POSB Reference:
(Lk.22:24) Note 1, pt. 1

φιλόστοργοι = *philostorgoi* **#1016,**
#1667, #2257
POSB Reference:
(Rom.12:9-10; esp. v.10) Note 1, pt. 3

φιλοτιμεῖσθαι = *philotimeisthai* **#133,**
#215, 3829
POSB Reference:
(1 Thes.4:11) Note 2

φιλοτιμούμεθα = *philotimoumetha* **#97,**
#132, #2285, #2507
POSB Reference:
(2 Cor.5:9-10; esp. v.9) Note 4

φιλόξενον = *philoxenon* **#1289,**
#2015, #2016
POSB Reference:
(1 Tim.3:2-3; esp. v.2) Note 2, pt. 6

φοβεῖσθε = *phobeisthe* **#75, #1452**
POSB Reference:
(Mt.10:29) *Deeper Study* #2 [Note: the
word afraid is used in Mt.10:26, 28, 31]

φόβῳ = *phobö* **#1454, #3308**
POSB Reference:
(1 Pt.1:17) Note 2

φόβος = *phobos* **#252, #1453, #4396**
POSB Reference:
(Lk.1:64-66; esp. v.65) Note 3, pt. 2

φόνοι = *phonoi* **#2633**
POSB Reference:
(Gal.5:19-21; esp. v.21) Note 2

φόνου = *phonou* **#2632**
POSB Reference:
(Rom.1:29) *Deeper Study* #7

φωτός = *phötos* **#2344**
POSB Reference:
(Jn.12:36) *Deeper Study* #5

φραγελλώσας = *phragellösas* **#1535,**
#3394
POSB Reference:
(Mt.27:26-38; esp. v.26) Note 2, pt. 1

φρεναπάται = *phrenapatai* **#911**
POSB Reference:
(Tit.1:10-12; esp. v.10) Note 1, pt. 3

φρονεῖτε = *phroneite* **#70, #2595,**
#3985
POSB Reference:
Col.3:1-4; esp. v.2) Note 2

φρονήσει = *phronësei* **#2161, #3082,**
#4140
POSB Reference:
(Eph.1:8) Note 5, pt. 2

φροντίζωσιν = *phrontizösin* **#496**
POSB Reference:
(Tit.3:8) Note 1

φρουρήσει = *phrourësei* **#1828, #2226**
POSB Reference:
(Philip.4:6-7; esp. v.7) Note 1, pt. 3b

φρουρουμένους = *phrouroumenous*
#2245, #3069, #3523
POSB Reference:
(1 Pt.1:5) Note 3, pt. 1

φθερεῖ = *phtheirei* **#933, #1002,**
#3348
POSB Reference:
(1 Cor.3:17) Note 7

φθόνῳ = *phthonö* **#1307**
POSB Reference:
(Tit.3:3) *Deeper Study* #5

φυλακαῖς = *phulakais* **#310, #2101**
POSB Reference:
(2 Cor.6:4-5; esp. v.5) Note 3

φυλάσσεσθε = *phulassesthe* **#372,**
#2767
POSB Reference:
(Rom.12:15-19; esp. v.15) Note 2, pt. 1

φυλάξει = *phulaxei #1829, #2227, #3068*
POSB Reference:
(2 Thes.3:3-5; esp. v.3) Note 2, pt. 1

φύσει = *phusei #2167, #2651*
POSB Reference:
(Rom.2:11-15; esp. v.14) Note 4, pt. 3a

φυσιώσεις = *phusiöseis #200, #690, #3864*
POSB Reference:
(2 Cor.12:19-21; esp. v.20) Note 3, pt. 2

φυσιοῦσθε = *phusiousthe #302, #430, #3085, #3889*
POSB Reference:
(1 Cor.4:6) Note 1, pt. 2

φυσιοῦται = *phusioutai #202, #3071, #3086*
POSB Reference:
(1 Cor.13:4-7; esp. v.4) Note 2, pt. 5

πικρία = *pikria #384*
POSB Reference:
(Eph.4:31) Note 1, pt. 1

πίνοντες = *pinontes #1172, #2834*
POSB Reference:
(Mt.24:38) *Deeper Study #4*

πιστεύετε = *pisteuete #339, #3129*
POSB Reference:
(Jn.12:34-36; esp. v.36) Note 5, pt. 2

πιστεύοντες = *pisteuontes #340, #4079*
POSB Reference:
(1 Pt.1:8-9; esp. v.8) Note 3, pt. 2

πιστεῦσαι δεῖ = *pisteusai dei #2639*
POSB Reference:
(Heb.11:6) Note 5, pt. 2a

πίστιν = *pistin #1425*
POSB Reference:
(Mk.2:5) Note 3, pt. 1

πίστις = *pistis #1426, #1431*
POSB Reference:
(Gal.5:22-23; esp. v.22) Note 1

πιστοῖς = *pistois #1428*
POSB Reference:
(Eph.1:1-2; esp. v.1) Note 2, pt. 1b

πιστοῖς = *pistois #1429, #3233, #4083*
POSB Reference:
(2 Tim. 2:2) Note 2, pt. 2

πιθανολογία = *pithanologia #1296, #1501, #2924*
POSB Reference:
(Col.2:4) Note 3

πλανώμενοι = *planömenoi #912, #2608*
POSB Reference:
(Tit.3:3) *Deeper Study #3*
See also POSB REF: (Gal.6:7-9; esp. v.7) Note 2

πλανώντων = *planöntön #2312, #910, #3403*
POSB Reference:
(1 Jn.2:26) Note 3

πληγαῖς = *plëgais #293, #3811*
POSB Reference:
(2 Cor. 6:4-5; esp. v.5) Note 3

πλεῖστος = *pleistos #1781, #2296*
POSB Reference:
(Mk.4:1-2; esp. v.1) Note 1

πλεονέκταις = *pleonektais #822, #1802, #824*
POSB Reference:
(1 Cor.5:9-10; esp. v.9) Note 4, pt. 2

πλεονέκτης = *pleonektës #824, #1804*
POSB Reference:
(Eph.5:5-6; esp. v.5) Note 5, pt. 1

πλεονεξία = *pleonexia #1800, #2464*
POSB Reference:
(Eph.4:17-19; esp. v.19) Note 1, pt. 7

πλεονεξίαι = *pleonexiai #821, #826, #1798*
POSB Reference:
(Mk.7:22) *Deeper Study #8*

πλεονεξίας = *pleonexias #827, #1801*
POSB Reference:
(Lk.12:15) *Deeper Study #1*

πλήρωμα = *plëröma #1617, #1622, #1793*
POSB Reference:
(Rom.11:11-12) Note 1, pt. 3

πληρώματος = *plërömatos #1621, #3314*
POSB Reference:
(Jn.1:16-17; esp. v.16) Note 4

πληρωθῶσιν = *plëröthösin #625, #1616*
POSB Reference:
(Lk.21:24) Note 5, pt. 1

πληρούμενον σοφίᾳ = *plëroumenon sophias #4361*
POSB Reference:
(Lk.2:40) Note 3, pt. 1

πληθυνθῆναι = *plëthunthënai #14, #2133, #3160*
POSB Reference:
(Mt.24:12) *Deeper Study #7*

πνεῦμα πύθωνα = *pneuma puthöna #950, #3697, #3699*
POSB Reference:
Acts 16:16-17; esp. v.16) Note 1, pt. 1

πνεύματι = *pneumati #442, #3696*
POSB Reference:
(2 Thes.2:8) Note 4, pt. 1

πνευματικὰ τῆς πονηρίας ἐπουρανίοις = *pneumatika ponërias epouraniois #3707, #3708, #3710, #4339*
POSB Reference:
(Eph.6:12) Note 3, pt. 5

πνευματικόν σῶμα = *pneumatikon söma #3706*
POSB Reference:
(1 Cor.15:42-44; esp. v.44) Note 3, pt. 4

πνευματικός = *pneumatikos #1741, #3703*
POSB Reference:
(Rom.7:14) Note 1, pt. 1

πνευματικός = *pneumatikos #3702, #4331*
POSB Reference:
(1 Cor.2:15-16; esp. v.15) Note 2

ποίημα = *poiëma #2543, #4429*
POSB Reference:
(Eph.2:10) Note 2

Ποίμαινε = *poimaine #1463, #3519, #3875, #3935*
POSB Reference:
(Jn.21:16; cp. Jn.21:15, 17) Note 3, pt. 3

ποιμάνατε = *poimanate #491, #1464, #3520, #3522*
POSB Reference:
(1 Pt.5:2-3) Note 2

ποιμένας = *poimenas #2842*
POSB Reference:
(Eph.4:11) Note 3, pt. 4

ποιῶν τὴν ἁμαρτίαν = *poiön tën hamartian #3603*
POSB Reference:
(Jn.8:34-36; esp. v.34) Note 2

πολιτεύεσθε = *politeuesthe #704, #776, #2358*
POSB Reference:
(Philip.1:27) Note 1

πολίτευμα = *politeuma #590, #777*
POSB Reference:
(Philip.3:20-21; esp. v.20) Note 1, pt. 1

Πολυμερῶς = *Polumerös* **#230, #232,
#2119, #2532**
POSB Reference:
(Heb.1:1-2; esp. v.1) Note 1, pt. 1

πολυτρόπως = *polutropös* **#2116,
#2120, #2127**
POSB Reference:
(Heb.1:1-2; esp. v.1) Note 1, pt. 1

πονηρία = *ponëria* **#1343, #3571,
#4344**
POSB Reference:
(Rom.1:29) *Deeper Study* #3

πονηρίαι = *poneriai* **#2519, #4340**
POSB Reference:
(Mk.7:22) *Deeper Study* #9

πονηρίας = *ponërias* **#1340, #4343**
POSB Reference:
(1 Cor.5:8) Note 3

πονηροῦ = *ponërou* **#1344**
POSB Reference:
(2 Thes.3:3-5, esp. v.3) Note 2, pt. 1

πορνεία = *porneia* **#1591, #2087,
#3493**
POSB Reference:
(Gal.5:19-21; esp. v.19) Note 2

πορνεία = *porneiai* **#1593, #3491**
POSB Reference:
(Rom.1:29) *Deeper Study* #2

πορνείας = *porneias* **#62, #1592,
#2089**
POSB Reference:
(Rev.18:2-7; esp. v.3) Note 2

πόρνοις = *pornois* **#1595, #2883,
#2086, #3498**
POSB Reference:
(1 Cor.5:9-10; esp. v.9) Note 4

πόρνος = *pornos* **#1594, #2083,
#3497**
POSB Reference:
(Heb.12:15-17; esp. v.16) Note 2, pt. 3

πόρνος = *pornos* **#2082, #4336**
POSB Reference:
(Eph.5:5-6; esp. v.5) Note 5, pt. 1

πώρωσιν = *pörösin* **#408, #1866,
#3552**
POSB Reference:
(Eph.4:17-19; esp. v.18) Note 1, pt. 3

πορφυρόπωλις = *porphuropölis* **#888,
#2564, #3437**
POSB Reference:
(Acts 16:14) Note 2

πόσαι μυριάδες = *posai muriades*
#2023, #2024
POSB Reference:
(Acts 21:20-26; esp. v.20) Note 3, pt. 1

πότοις = *potois* **#264, #512, 1173,
#4346**
POSB Reference:
(1 Pt.4:3) Note 3, pt. 5

ποῦ μένεις = *pou meneis* **#1191,
#3752**
POSB Reference:
(Jn.1:38-39; esp. v.38) Note 2, pt. 2

πραεῖς = *praeis* **#1660, #2554**
POSB Reference:
(Mt.5:5) Note 4

Πραγματεύσασθε = *Pragmateusasthe*
#1134, #2189, #2740, #3127
POSB Reference:
(Lk.19:13) Note 3, pt. 2 *Deeper Study* #2

πράσσης = *prassës* **#2225, #2721,
#2731, #2990**
POSB Reference:
(Rom.2:25-27; esp. v.25) Note 3

πραϋπαθίαν = *praupathian* **#1665,
#2557**
POSB Reference:
(1 Tim.6:11) Note 2, pt. 6

πραΰτης = *prautës* **#1663, #2556**
POSB Reference:
(Gal.5:22-23; esp. v.23) Note 1, pt. 8

πραΰτητα = *prautëta* **#736, #2039**
POSB Reference:
(Tit.3:2) Note 6

πραΰτητι = *prautëti* **#434, #1664,
#2038, #2558**
POSB Reference:
(Jas.3:13) Note 1, pt. 2

πρᾶξιν = *praxin* **#1627, #2759**
POSB Reference:
(Rom.12:3-5, esp.v.4) Note 1, pt. 2

πρεσβεύομεν = *presbeuomen* **#131**
POSB Reference:
(2 Cor.5:20) Note 3, pt. 1

πρεσβυτέρους = *presbuterous* **#1236**
POSB Reference:
(Tit.1:5-9; esp. v.5) *Deeper Study* #1

πρόβατά = *probata* **#3517**
POSB Reference:
(Jn.21:16) Note 3, pt. 2

προδόται = *prodotai* **#366, #4030,
#4040**
POSB Reference:
(2 Tim. 3:2-4; esp. v.4) Note 2, pt. 15

προέγνω = *proegnö* **#1578, #1579,
#2264**
POSB Reference:
(Rom.8:29) Note 2, pt. 3

προεγνωσμένου πρὸ = *proegnösmenou
pro* **#568, #575, #575, #1581,
#1582**
POSB Reference:
(1 Pt.1:18-20; esp. v.20) Note 4, pt. 3b

προηγούμενοι = *proëgoumenoi* **#17,
#1679, #1692, #3022, #3879**
POSB Reference:
(Rom.12:9-10; esp. v.10) Note 1, pt. 4

προέκοπτεν = *proekopten* **#2135,
#1806**
POSB Reference:
(Lk.2:52) *Deeper Study* #1

προεστῶτες = *proestötes* **#1045,
#1138, #3349**
POSB Reference:
(1 Tim.5:17-18;esp. v.17) Note 1

προέθετο = *proetheto* **#1091, #3030,
#3480, #3448**
POSB Reference:
(Rom.3:25) Note 4, pt. 1a

πρόγνωσιν = *prognösin* **#570, #1580**
POSB Reference:
(1 Pt.1:2) *Deeper Study* #1

προϊστάμενος = *proistamenos* **#2313,
#2314, #3352**
POSB Reference:
(Rom.12:6-8, esp. v.8) Note 2, pt. 6

προΐστασθαι = *proistasthai* **#1013,
#1133, #1287, #2496**
POSB Reference:
(Tit.3:8) Note 1

προκεχειροτονημένοις = *prokecheiro-
tonëmenois* **#580**
POSB Reference:
(Acts 10:40-41; esp. v.41) Note 6, pt. 2

προνοούμενοι = *pronooumenoi* **#494,
#1139, #3077, #3217, #3267**
POSB Reference:
Rom.12:17) Note 4, pt. 2

πειρασμοῖς = *peirasmois* **#3932,
#4050, #4061**
POSB Reference:
(Jas.1:2) Note 1

προσεῖχον = *proseichon* **#1643, #1690, #1919, #2354**
POSB Reference:
(Acts 8:6) Note 2, pt. 2

ψιθυριστάς = *psithuristas* **#1768, #4326**
POSB Reference:
(Rom.1:29) *Deeper Study* #11

προορίσας = *proorisas* **#3020, #4113**
POSB Reference:
(Eph.1:5-6; esp. v.5) Note 3

προώρισεν = *proörisen* **#569, #3018, #3019**
POSB Reference:
(Rom.8:29) Note 2, pt. 3

προπετεῖς = *propeteis* **#1895, #1897, #3163, #3192**
POSB Reference:
(2 Tim. 3:2-4; esp. v.4) Note 2, pt. 16

προφήτας = *prophëtas* **#3064**
POSB Reference:
(Eph.4:11) Note 3, pt. 2

προφητεύων = *prophëteuön* **#3062**
POSB Reference:
(1 Cor.14:3) *Deeper Study* #1

προφητικὸν λόγον = *prophëtikon logon* **#2578, #3063, #3063, #4409, #4410**
POSB Reference:
(2 Pt.1:19-21; esp. v.19) *Deeper Study* #2

πρός = *pros* **#4367**
POSB Reference:
(Jn.1:1-2; esp. v.1) Note 1, pt. 2

προσαγωγὴν = *prosagögën* **#31, #457, #2738**
POSB Reference:
(Rom.5:2) Note 3, pt. 2

προσαγωγὴν = *prosagögën* **#32, #2547**
POSB Reference:
(Eph.2:18) Note 5

προσδοκῶντας = *prosdoköntas* **#2391, #2405**
POSB Reference:
(2 Pt.3:12) Note 2, pt. 1

προσέχειν = *prosechein* **#1216, #1918, #2350, #2861**
POSB Reference:
(Heb.2:1) Note 1

προσέχετε = *prosechete* **#287, #373, #2238 #3882**
POSB Reference:
(Acts 20:28) Note 1, pt. 1

Προσέχετε = *Prosechete* **#370, #4278**
POSB Reference:
(Mt.7:15) Note 1

Προσέχετε = *prosechete* **#492, #2768, #3881, #4279**
POSB Reference:
(Lk.21:34-35; esp. v.34) Note 1

προσεῖχον = *proseichon* **#2354, #1643, #2821**
POSB Reference:
(Acts 8:6) Note 2, pt. 2

προσεκύνει = *prosekunei* **#429, #2262, #4447**
POSB Reference:
(Mt.8:2) Note 2, pt. 2

προσήλυτον = *prosëluton* **#3067, #4447**
POSB Reference:
(Mt.23:15) *Deeper Study* #4

προσέφερον = *prosepheron* **#448, #455**
POSB Reference:
(Mk.10:13) *Deeper Study* #1

προσέρχεται = *proserchetai* **#91, #726, #954**
POSB Reference:
(1 Tim.6:3) Note 1, pt. 1 & 2

προσέταξεν = *prosetaxen* **#648, #1646, #2791**
POSB Reference:
(Acts 10:48) Note 4

προσεύξασθαι = *proseuchasthai* **#2998**
POSB Reference:
(Mk.6:46) Note 2

προσευχῇ = *proseuchë* **#3000**
POSB Reference:
(Philip.4:6-7; esp. v.6) Note 1, pt. 2

προσκαρτερεῖτε = *proskartereite* **#761, #1012**
POSB Reference:
(Col.4:2-4; esp. v.2) Note 1, pt. 1

προσκαρτερήσομεν = *proskarterësomen* **#1014, #1675, #1678, #3692**
POSB Reference:
(Acts 6:4) Note 4, pt. 2

προσκαρτεροῦντες = *proskarterountes* **#121, #766, #767, #1017, #1427**
POSB Reference:
(Rom.12:12) Note 3, pt. 3

προσκολληθήσεται πρός = *proskollëthësetai pros* **#602, #2205, #4159**
POSB Reference:
(Eph.5:31) *Deeper Study* #1

πρόσκομμα = *proskomma* **#527, #3834**
POSB Reference:
(1 Cor.8:9-11; esp. v.9) Note 3

προσκοπήν = *proskopën* **#1954, #2746, #3833**
POSB Reference:
(2 Cor.6:3) Note 1

προσλαβόμενος = *proslabomenos* **#4011**
POSB Reference:
(Mk.8:32-33; esp. v.32) Note 2, pt. 1a

προσλαμβάνεσθε = *proslambanesthe* **#26, #3183**
POSB Reference:
(Rom.14:1-2; esp. v.1) Note 1

προσφιλῆ = *prosphilë* **#2445**
POSB Reference:
(Philip.4:8-9; esp. v.8) Note 2, pt. 1e

προστάτις = *prostatis* **#1787, #1928, #3843**
POSB Reference:
(Rom.16:1-2; esp. v.2) Note 1, pt. 4b

πρόθυμον = *prothumon* **#1196, #3168**
POSB Reference:
(Rom.1:14-15; esp. v.15) Note 5, pt. 2

πρῶτος = *prötos* **#562, #1509**
POSB Reference:
(Mt.20:23-28; esp. v.27) Note 3, pt. 3

πρωτότοκον = *prötotokon* **#1515, #1516, #2005**
POSB Reference:
(Heb.1:4-6; esp. v.6) Note 1, pt. 3

Πρωΐ = *proi* **#2622**
POSB Reference:
(Mt.21:18) *Deeper Study* #1

ψεύδεσθε = *pseudesthe* **#2337**
POSB Reference:
(Col.3:8-11; esp. v.9) Note 2, pt. 1f

ψεῦδος = *pseudos* **#2473, #1442**
POSB Reference:
(Eph.4:25) Note 1

ψιθυρισμοί = *psithurismoi* **#1767, #4327**
POSB Reference:
(2 Cor.12:19-21; esp. v.20) Note 3, pt. 2

ψιθυριστάς = psithuristas **#1768, #4326**
POSB Reference:
(Rom.1:29) *Deeper Study* #11

ψυχῇ = psuchë **#3663**
POSB Reference:
(Mt.22:37) *Deeper Study* #5

ψυχὴν = psuchën **#2339**
POSB Reference:
(Lk.9:24) Note 2

ψυχικόν σῶμα = psuchikon söma **#2647, #2648**
POSB Reference:
(1 Cor.15:42-44; esp. v.44) Note 3, pt. 4

ψυχικός = psuchikos **#2528, #2649, #2882**
POSB Reference:
(1 Cor.2:14) Note 1

πταίομεν = ptaiomen **#2510, #2751, #3832**
POSB Reference:
(Jas.3:2) Note 2

πτωχὴ = ptöchë **#2965**
POSB Reference:
(Lk.21:3) Note 3

πτοηθῆτε = ptoëthëte **#1607, #2825, #3940, #3940**
POSB Reference:
(Lk.21:9-10; esp. v.9) Note 3, pt. 2

πτύον = ptuon **#1443, #4356**
POSB Reference:
(Lk.3:15-17; esp.v.17) Note 6, pt. 3a

πῦρ τὸ αἰώνιον = pur to aiönion **#1324, #1332, #4168**
POSB Reference:
(Mt.18:8) *Deeper Study* #1

πυρὶ ἀσβέστῳ = puri asbesto **#1504**
POSB Reference:
(Lk.3:17) *Deeper Study* #2

R

Ῥαββουνι = Rabboni **#2411, #3149, #3150, #3904**
POSB Reference:
(Mk.10:51-52; esp. v.51) Note 6, pt. 4

S

σάββασιν = sabbasin **#3354**
POSB Reference:
(Mt.12:1) *Deeper Study* #1

σαλεύοντες = saleuontes **#85, #3774**
POSB Reference:
(Acts 17:13-15; esp.v.13) Note 7

σαπρός = sapros **#804, #1598, #4183**
POSB Reference:
(Eph.4:29) Note 4

σαρκι = sarki **#3593, #4183, #1532**
POSB Reference:
(Rom.7:18-20; esp. v.18) Note 3

εσαρκικοί = sarkikoi **#507, #1533, #774, #4437**
POSB Reference:
(1 Cor.3:1-4; esp. v.3) *Deeper Study* #1

σαρκικῶν ἐπιθυμιῶν = sarkikön epithumiön **#1349, #1534, #3592**
POSB Reference:
(1 Pt.2:11) Note 2

σαρκίνοις = sarkinois **#351, #506, #2562, #4436**
POSB Reference:
(1 Cor.3:1-4; esp. v.1) *Deeper Study* #1

σάρκινός = sarkinos **#508, #1531, #4176, #4370**
POSB Reference:
(Rom.7:14-17; esp. v.14) Note 2

σάρξ = sarx **#1530, #2027**
POSB Reference:
(Jn.1:14) Note 1

Σατανᾶς = Satanas **#3374**
POSB Reference:
(Rev.12:9) Note 1 *Deeper Study* #1

σχῆμα = schëma **#109, #1445, #1589, #3028**
POSB Reference:
(1 Cor.7:29-31; esp. v.31) Note 3

σχίσματα = schismata **#1128**
POSB Reference:
(1 Cor.1:10) Note 1

σχιζομένους = schizamenous **#2781, #2835**
POSB Reference:
(Mk.1:10) Note 3

σχῶμεν παρρησίαν = schömen parrësian **#708, #1619**
POSB Reference:
(1 Jn.2:28) Note 2, pt. 2

σεβομένοις = sebomenois **#1023, #1656, #1721, #1722**
POSB Reference:
(Acts 17:17) Note 3

σημεῖα = sëmeia **#2605, #3558**
POSB Reference:
(Jn.2:23) Note 1, pt. 2

σημείοις = sëmeiois **#3559**
POSB Reference:
(2 Cor.12:11-12; esp. v.12) Note 1

σημεῖον = sëmeion **#1327, #3557, #4397, #4404**
POSB Reference:
(Rev.12:1-2; esp.v.1) Note 1

σεμνά = semna **#1989, #2000, #2673**
POSB Reference:
(Philip.4:8-9; esp. v.8) Note 2, pt. 1b

σεμνότητος = semnotëtos **#1034, #1780, #3268, #3303**
POSB Reference:
(1 Tim.3:4-5; esp. v.4) Note 3

σεμνούς = semnous **#1035, #1779, #3272, #3306, #4452**
POSB Reference:
(1 Tim.3:8) Note 1, pt. 1

σέσηπεν = sesëpen **#805, #3342**
POSB Reference:
(Jas.5:2-3) Note 2

σέσωκέν = sesöken **#2488, #2490**
POSB Reference:
(Lk.17:15-19; esp. v.19) Note 3, pt. 5

σιαγόνα = siagona **#557**
POSB Reference:
(Lk.6:27-31; esp. v.29) Note 1, pt. 1e

σινιάσαι = siniasai **#3554**
POSB Reference:
(Lk.22:31) Note 1, pt. 3

Σιώπα πεφίμωσο = siopa pephimoso **#2052, #2869, #3145, #3146**
POSB Reference:
(Mk.4:38-39; esp. v.39) Note 3

σκάνδαλα = skandala **#1955, #2735, #2748, #4189**
POSB Reference:
(Rom.16:17-18; esp. v.17) Note 1, pt. 1

σκανδαλίσῃ = skandalisë **#530, #531, #532, #2750**
POSB Reference:
(Mk.9:42) Note 1

σκανδαλίσωμεν = skandalisömen **#2752**
POSB Reference:
(Mt.17:27) Note 4

σκανδαλισθήσεσθε = *skandalisthëses-the* **#966, #3829, #1436, #2753**
POSB Reference:
(Mt.26:31) *Deeper Study* #1

σκανδαλισθῆτε = *skandalisthëte* **#1437, #1710, #2754, #3831**
POSB Reference:
(Jn.16:1) Note 1

σκανδαλίζει = *skandalizei* **#528, #529, #2517, #2749**
POSB Reference:
(Mt.5:29) Note 4

σκάνδαλον = *skandalon* **#2734, #2739**
POSB Reference:
(Rom.14:13-15; esp. v.13) Note 6

σκηνάς = *skënas* **#3518, #3550, #3871**
POSB Reference:
(Mt.17:4) Note 4, pt. 1

σκεῦος = *skeuos* **#415, #4216**
POSB Reference:
(1 Thes.4:3-5; esp. v.4) Note 2, pt. 2

Σκιὰν = *Skian* **#3499**
POSB Reference:
(Heb.10:1-4, esp. v.1) Note 1, pt. 1

Σκληρός = *sklëros* **#1033, #1858**
POSB Reference:
(Jn.6:59-60; esp. v.60) Note 1

Σκληροτράχηλοι = *Sklërotrachëloi* **#3770, #3828**
POSB Reference:
(Acts 7:42-53; esp. v.51) Note 6, pt. 5

σκωληκόβρωτος = *skölëkobrötos* **#746, #1226**
POSB Reference:
(Acts 12:18-23; esp. v.23) Note 3, pt. 2

σκολιᾶς = *skolias* **#229, #803, #2926, #4179**
POSB Reference:
(Acts 2:40) Note 5, pt. 2

σκόλοψ = *skolops* **#3974**
POSB Reference:
(2 Cor.12:7-10; esp. v.7) Note 3

σκοπεῖν = *skopein* **#2241, #2534, #2709, #4283**
POSB Reference:
(Rom.16:17-18; esp. v.17) Note 1, pt. 1c

σκοπῶν = *skopön* **#2401, #501, #738, #4272**
POSB Reference:
(Gal.6:1) Note 3

σκοπούντων = *skopountön* **#2384, #1523**
POSB Reference:
(2 Cor.4:17-18; esp. v.18) Note 8, pt. 2

σκότει = *skotei* **#876**
POSB Reference:
(Rom.2:17-20; esp. v.19) Note 1, pt. 7

σκοτία = *skotia* **#879**
POSB Reference:
(1 Jn.1:5) *Deeper Study* #1

σκότος = *skotos* **#878**
POSB Reference:
(2 Cor.6:14) *Deeper Study* #1

σκυθρωποί = *skuthröpoi* **#1160, #3359**
POSB Reference:
(Lk.24:15-27; esp. v.17) Note 2, pt. 1

σοφίας = *sophias* **#4359**
POSB Reference:
(Eph.1:17-18; esp. v.17) Note 2, pt. 1

σοφίας λόγος = *sophias logos* **#11, #2577, #4411**
POSB Reference:
(1 Cor.12:8-10; esp. v.8) Note 3, pt. 1

σοφός = *sophos* **#4362**
POSB Reference:
(Jas.3:13) Note 1

σώφρονα = *söphrona* **#2366, #3081, #3424, #3633**
POSB Reference:
(1 Tim.3:2; esp. v.2) Note 2, pt. 4

σώφρονας = *söphronas* **#2367, #3425, #3440, #3924**
POSB Reference:
(Tit.2:2) Note 2, pt. 3

σώφρονας = *söphronas* **#2368, #1066, #3428, #3441**
POSB Reference:
(Tit.2:4-5; esp. v.5) Note 4, pt. 4

σωφρονεῖν = *söphronein* **#2369, #3429, #3442, #3639**
POSB Reference:
(Tit.2:6) Note 5

σωφρονεῖν = *söphronein* **#1992, #3638, #3641, #3665**
POSB Reference:
(Rom.12:3-5; esp. v.3) Note 1, pt. 1

σωφρονήσατε = *söphronësate* **#596, #1213, #3454, #3635, #3666**
POSB Reference:
(1 Pt.4:7) Note 1

σωφρονισμοῦ = *söphronismou* **#1060, #3430, #3667**
POSB Reference:
(2 Tim. 1:7) Note 2, pt. 3

σωφρόνως = *söphronös* **#3423, #3443, #3642**
POSB Reference:
(Tit.2:12) Note 2, pt. 2

σώσει = *sösei* **#3375**
POSB Reference:
(Mt.1:20-21; esp. v.21) *Deeper Study* #6

σωτὴρ = *sötër* **#3377**
POSB Reference:
(Jn.4:42) *Deeper Study* #1

σωθήσεται = *söthësetai* **#111, #1900, #4310, #4333**
POSB Reference:
(Lk.8:49-56; esp. v.50) Note 4, pt. 2

σουδαρίῳ = *soudariö* **#604, #1894, #2646**
POSB Reference:
(Jn.11:44) *Deeper Study* #2

σωζομένους = *sözomenous* **#3376**
POSB Reference:
(Acts 2:46-47; esp. v.47) Note 6, pt. 5

σπαράξαν = *sparaxan* **#793, #794, #3526, #4017**
POSB Reference:
(Mk.1:25-26; esp. v.26) Note 2, pt. 2

σπεῖραν = *speiran* **#262, #275, #613, #1006**
POSB Reference:
(Jn.18:3) *Deeper Study* #1

σπεῖραν = *speiran* **#263, #274, #612, #666, #1636**
POSB Reference:
(Mt.27:26-38; esp. v.27) Note 2, pt. 2

σπένδομαι = *spendomai* **#2758, #2970, #2971**
POSB Reference:
(2 Tim. 4:6) Note 1, pt. 1

σπεύδοντας = *speudontas* **#1876, #1877, #2050, #3691**
POSB Reference:
(2 Pt.3:12) Note 2, pt. 2

σφραγισάμενος =*sphragisamenos* **#2064, #3397, #3481**
POSB Reference:
(2 Cor.1:21-22; esp. v.22) Note 5

σπιλάδες = *spilades* **#400, #873, #1946, #3719**
POSB Reference:
(Jude 1:12) Note 14

σπουδαῖον = *spoudaion* **#1038, #1211, #4477**
POSB Reference:
(2 Cor.8:22) Note 4

σπουδάσατε = *spoudasate* **#283, #2505**
POSB Reference:
(2 Pt.3:14) Note 4

σπουδάσωμεν = *spoudasömen* **#1039, #1137, #2286, #2506**
POSB Reference:
(Heb.4:11-13; esp. v.11) Note 5, pt. 1

σπουδάζοντες = *spoudazontes* **#123, #338, #1270, #2504**
POSB Reference:
(Eph.4:3) Note 2

σπουδῇ = *spoudë* **#462, #1036, #4413, #4476**
POSB Reference:
(Rom.12:11) Note 2, pt. 1

σπυρίδας πλήρεις:= *spuridas plëreis* **#273**
POSB Reference:
(Mt.15:37) *Deeper Study* #1

Σταύρωσον = *stauröson* **#846**
POSB Reference:
(Mk.15:12-14, esp. v.13) Note 5, pt. 2

στέγει = *stegei* **#291, #2658, #3070**
POSB Reference:
(1 Cor.13:4-7; esp. v.7) Note 2, pt. 12

στήκετε = *stëkete* **#3730, #3732, #3747**
POSB Reference:
(Philip.4:1) Note 1

στέλλεσθαι = *stellesthai* **#2230, #2231, #3745, #4371**
POSB Reference:
(2 Thes.3:6-11; esp. v.6) Note 1

στενοχωρεῖσθε = *stenochöreisthe* **#3289, #3290, #3784, #4374, #4375**
POSB Reference:
(2 Cor.6:11-13; esp. v.12) Note 1

στενοχωρία = *stenochöria* **#148, #470, #1113**
POSB Reference:
(Rom.2:9) *Deeper Study* #9

στενοχωρίαις = *stenochöriais* **#469, #1120**
POSB Reference:
(2 Cor.6:4-5; esp. v.4) Note 3

στενοχωρούμενοι = *stenochöroumenoi* **#848, #1115**
POSB Reference:
(2 Cor.4:7-9; esp. v.8) Note 2, pt. 1

στέφανος = *stephanos* **#843**
POSB Reference:
(Rev.6:1-2; esp. v.2) Note 1, pt. 2

στερέωμα = *stereöma* **#1505, #3723, #3755, #3819**
POSB Reference:
(Col.2:5) Note 4

στηριχθῆναι = *stërichthënai* **#1316, #1821, #2513**
POSB Reference:
(Rom.1:10-13; esp. v.11) Note 4, pt. 1

στηρίξαι = *stërixai* **#1312, #2514, #3724**
POSB Reference:
(Rom.16:25-27, esp. v.25)

στηρίξαι = *stërixai* **#3725, #3793, #3796**
POSB Reference:
(2 Thes.2:16-17; esp. v.17) Note 5, pt. 5

στηρίξατε τὰς καρδίας = *stërixate tas kardias* **#1314, #3727, #3733, #3797, #3878**
POSB Reference:
(James 5:7-9; esp. v.8) Note 2, pt. 1

στηρίξει = *stërixei* **#715, #1315, #2515, #3726, #3858**
POSB Reference:
(1 Pt.5:10) Note 2, pt. 2

σθενώσει = *sthenösei* **#1506, #3795**
POSB Reference:
(1 Pt.5:10) Note 2, pt. 3

στίλβοντα λίαν = *stilbonta lian* **#882, #3152, #3524**
POSB Reference:
(Mk.9:2-3; esp. v.3) *Deeper Study* #2 pt. 1

στοιχεῖα τῆς ἀρχῆς = *stoicheia tës archës* **#272, #1242, #1243, #1514**
POSB Reference:
(Heb.5:12) Note 2

στοιχείων = *stoicheiön* **#271, #1241, #1354, #3346**
POSB Reference:
(Col.2:20) Note 1

στραφῆτε = *straphëte* **#539, #780, #4090**
POSB Reference:
(Mt.18:3) Note 2

στρατιᾶς = *stratias* **#2017**
POSB Reference:
(Lk.2:13-14; esp. v.13) Note 4

στυγητοί = *stugëtoi* **#1881**
POSB Reference:
(Tit.3:3) *Deeper Study* #6

σὺ δὲ = *su de* **#138**
POSB Reference:
(Rom.11:17) Note 1, pt. 2

συγγενη = *suggenë* **#3230, #813, #2260**
POSB Reference:
(Rom.16:11) Note 11

Συγκαλεσάμενος = *sugkalesamenos* **#476**
POSB Reference:
(Lk.9:1) Note 1

συγκατάθεσις = *sugkatathesis* **#92, #4157**
POSB Reference:
(2 Cor.6:14-16; esp. v.16) Note 2

συλλυπούμενος = *sullupoumenos* **#1118, #1126, #1815**
POSB Reference:
(Mk.3:5) *Deeper Study* #1

συμβιβάζοντες = *sumbibazontes* **#224, #696**
POSB Reference:
(Acts 16:10) Note 3

συμμόρφους τῆς εἰκόνος = *summorphous tës eikonos* **#719, #3998**
POSB Reference:
(Rom.8:29) Note 2, pt. 2

συμπαρακληθῆναι = *sumparaklëthënai* **#635, #1265, #1266, #2641**
POSB Reference:
(Rom.1:10-13; esp. v.12) Note 4, pt. 2

συμπαθεῖς = *sumpatheis* **#672, #3868**
POSB Reference:
(1 Pt.3:8) Note 2

συμπαθῆσαι = *sumpathësai* **#3869, #4022, #4144**
POSB Reference:
(Heb.4:15-16; esp. v.15) Note 2, pt. 1

σύμφημι = *sumphëmi* **#90, #725**
POSB Reference:
(Rom.7:14-17; esp. v.16) Note 2, pt. 2

συμφέρει = sumpherei #353, #1394, #1753, #1931, #3055
POSB Reference:
(1 Cor.6:12) Note 1, pt. 1

συμφέρον = sumpheron #660, #1933, #3054
POSB Reference:
(1 Cor.12:7) Note 2

συμφωνήσωσιν = sumphönësösin #89
POSB Reference:
(Mt.18:19-20; esp. v.19) *Deeper Study* #3

συνάγουσιν = sunagousin #1637, #2934
POSB Reference:
(Jn.15:4-6; esp. v.6) Note 4, pt. 4c

συναγωγὴν = synagogen #3870
POSB Reference:
(Mk.1:21) *Deeper Study* #1

συναίρειν = sunairein #3485, #3044, #3193
POSB Reference:
(Mt.18:23-27; esp. v.24) Note 2, pt. 1

συναναμίγνυσθαι = sunanamignusthai #221, #667
POSB Reference:
(1 Cor.5:9-10; esp. v.9) Note 4

συναθλοῦντες = sunathlountes #750, #1486, #3815
POSB Reference:
(Philip.1:27) Note 3, pt. 2

συνέχει = sunechei #678, #745, #775
POSB Reference:
(2 Cor.5:14-16; esp. v.14) Note 4

συνήγειρεν = sunëgeiren #3157, #3159
POSB Reference:
(Eph.2:6) Note 3

συνεκέρασεν = sunekerasen #615, #688, #3128, #3925
POSB Reference:
(1 Cor.12:24-26; esp. v.24) Note 4

συνεκίνησάν = sunekinësan #3343, #3775, #456, #525, #1163, #3419
POSB Reference:
(Acts 6:11-14; esp. v.12) Note 3, pt. 1

συνέκλεισεν = sunekleisen #427, #657, #697, #2102, #3553
POSB Reference:
(Rom.11:32) Note 5

συνεπορεύετο = suneporeueto #4039, #4248, #4314
POSB Reference:
(Lk.24:15-27; esp. v.15) Note 2

συνέρχονται = sunerchontai #217, #484, #1639
POSB Reference:
(Mk.14:53) Note 1

συνεργεῖ = sunergei #4421, #4430
POSB Reference:
(Rom.8:28) Note 1, pt. 2

συνήρπασαν = sunërpasan #456, #525, #1163, #3419
POSB Reference:
(Acts 6:11-14; esp. v.12) Note 3, pt. 3

συνέσει = sunesei #4143, #4360
POSB Reference:
(Col.1:9) Note 1

συνευδοκῶν = suneudokön #727, #1689, #1913, #2761
POSB Reference:
(Acts 8:1) Note 1, pt. 1

συνεζωοποίησεν = sunezöopoiësen #1648, #2476
POSB Reference:
(Eph.2:4-5; esp. v.5) Note 1, pt. 2b

συνεζωοποίησεν = sunezöopoiësen #3142, #2475, #3143
POSB Reference:
(Col.2:13) Note 1, pt. 2b

συνίετε = suniete #4136
POSB Reference:
(Eph.5:17) Note 3

συνίων = suniön #4145
POSB Reference:
(Rom.3:10-12; esp. v.11) Note 2, pt. 2

συνίστησιν = sunistësin #650, #952, #3541
POSB Reference:
(Rom.5:8-9; esp. v.8) Note 2

συνοικοῦντες = sunoikountes #2371, #1190, #1676
POSB Reference:
(1 Pt.3:7) Note 1

σύρει = surei #1162, #1169, #3865
POSB Reference:
(Rev.12:3-4; esp.v.4) Note 2, pt. 2

σύρων = surön #1164, #1842
POSB Reference:
(Acts 8:3) Note 3, pt. 2

συσχηματίζεσθε = suschëmatizesthe #718, #796
POSB Reference:
(Rom.12:2) Note 3, pt. 1

Συστρεφομένων = Sustrephomenön #12, #483, #1640, #3293, #3751
POSB Reference:
(Mt.17:22) Note 1, pt. 1

σύζυγε = suzuge #665, #689, #3917, #4472
POSB Reference:
(Philip.4:2-3; esp. v.3) Note 2, pt. 2

T

τὰ παθήματα τῶν ἁμαρτιῶν = ta pathëmata tön hamartiön #2626, #3591, #3595
POSB Reference:
(Rom.7:5) Note 3, pt. 1b

τὰ σεβάσματα = ta sebasmata #120, #1020, #2726
POSB Reference:
(Acts 17:23) Note 3, pt. 1

τὰ θαυμάσια = ta thaumasia #4401, #4402
POSB Reference:
(Mt.21:15) Note 4

ταλαιπωρήσατε = talaipörësate #279, #286, #928, #1813, #2294
POSB Reference:
(Jas.4:9) Note 3

ταπεινόφρονες = tapeinophrones #816, #2034
POSB Reference:
(1 Pt.3:8) Note 5

ταπεινοφροσύνῃ = tapeinophrosunë #2037, #2457
POSB Reference:
(Philip.2:3) *Deeper Study* #1

ταπεινὸς = tapeinos #270, #2458, #2555, #3997
POSB Reference:
(2 Cor.10:1-2; esp. v.1) Note 1

ταπεινῶν = tapeinön #2035
POSB Reference:
(Lk.14:11) *Deeper Study* #1

τὰς πρωτοκλισίας = tas prötoklisias #363, #563, #1893, #2947
POSB Reference:
(Lk.14:7) Note 1

τάξιν = *taxin #1752, #1756, #2376, #2792*
POSB Reference:
(Col.2:5) Note 4

τεκμηρίοις = *tekmēriois #3060*
POSB Reference:
(Acts 1:3) Note 3, pt. 2a

τέκνα θεοῦ = *tekna theou #566, #3652*
POSB Reference:
(Jn.1:12-13; esp. v.12) Note 3, pt. 2

Τέκνον = *teknon #3649*
POSB Reference:
(Mk.2:5) Note 3, pt. 2b

τέλειοι = *teleioi #1624, #2546, #2889*
POSB Reference:
(Jas.1:4) Note 3

τέλειός = *teleios #2885*
POSB Reference:
(Mt.5:48) Note 4

τελειωτὴν = *teleiōtēn #1502, #2896*
POSB Reference:
(Heb.12:2) Note 3

τελειοῦμαι = *teleioumai #33, #2593, #3166*
POSB Reference:
(Lk.13:31-33; esp. v.32) Note 2, pt. 1

τελεῖτε = *teleite #2860*
POSB Reference:
(Rom. 13:6-7) Note 4, pt. 3

τέλος = *telos #35, #1269*
POSB Reference:
(Rom.10:4) Note 2

τέλος = *telos #1268*
POSB Reference:
(1 Cor.15:24-28; esp. v.24) Note 2

τέλος ἔχει = *telos echei #1618, #1888, #4349*
POSB Reference:
(Lk.22:33-37; esp. v.37) Note 3, pt. 4c

τὴν ὀφειλὴν = *tēn opheilēn #1182, #1956, #1957, #3495*
POSB Reference:
(1 Cor.7:3) Note 3

τέρατα = *terata #4403*
POSB Reference:
(Acts 2:19-20; esp. v.19) *Deeper Study* #1, pt. 1a

τηρῇ = *tērē #2242, #2725*
POSB Reference:
(1 Jn.2:5) Note 3

τηρήσετε = *tērēsete #2224, #2720*
POSB Reference:
(Jn.14:15) Note 1, pt. 1

τῆς ἐκκλησίας = *tēs ekklēsias #588*
POSB Reference:
(Rom.16:1-2; esp. v.1) Note 1

τετάρακται = *tetaraktai #4064*
POSB Reference:
(Jn.12:27-30; esp. v.27) Note 3, pt. 1

τετελειωμένοι = *teteleiōmenoi #682, #2890*
POSB Reference:
(Jn.17:23) *Deeper Study* #2

τετελειωμένον = *teteleiōmenon #722, #2483, #2895*
POSB Reference:
(Heb.7:28) Note 4

Τετέλεσται = *Tetelestai #1503*
POSB Reference:
(Jn.19:30) Note 7, pt. 1

τετηρημένοις = *tetērēmenois #490, #2246, #3032*
POSB Reference:
(Jude 1:1-2; esp. v.1) Note 2, pt. 2

τεθεμελιωμένοι = *tethemeliōmenoi #1317, #1819, #3735*
POSB Reference:
(Col.1:23) Note 4, pt. 1

τετυφωμένοι = *tetuphōmenoi #692, #1885, #1951, #3087*
POSB Reference:
(2 Tim. 3:2-4; esp. v.4) Note 2, pt. 17

τετύφωται = *tetuphōtai #691, #3073*
POSB Reference:
(1 Tim.6:4) Note 2

θάλπει = *thalpei #505, #561, #2456*
POSB Reference:
(Eph.5:25-33; esp. v.29) Note 2, pt. 2a

θανατοῦτε = *thanatoute #2623, #3126, #4093*
POSB Reference:
(Rom.8:12-13, esp. v.13) Note 6, pt. 2c

Θαρροῦντες = *Tharrountes #710, #1749*
POSB Reference:
(2 Cor.5:5-8; esp. v.6) Note 3

Θάρσει = *Tharsei #284, #1748, #3877*
POSB Reference:
(Acts 23:11) Note 5

Θάρσει = *tharsei #558, #626*
POSB Reference:
(Lk.8:43-48; esp. v.48) Note 3, pt. 5b

θεάσασθαι = *theasasthai #2394, #2559, #3404*
POSB Reference:
(Mt.22:11-14; esp. v.11) Note 4, pt. 1

θέλει = *thelē #976, #4252, #4348, #4363, #4455*
POSB Reference:
(Mt.16:24) Note 2, pt. 1

θεμελιώσει = *themeliōsei #1313, #2945, #3484, #3754*
POSB Reference:
(1 Pt.5:10) Note 2, pt. 4

θεόπνευστος = *theopneustos #1717, #2165*
POSB Reference:
(2 Tim. 3:16) Note 3, pt. 2

θεωρῆσαι = *theōrēsai #2387, #4000*
POSB Reference:
(Mt.28:1) Note 2, pt. 2a

θεωρήσῃ θάνατον = *theōrēsē thanaton #1028, #3406*
POSB Reference:
(Jn.8:51) *Deeper Study* #1, pt. 3

θεὸς = *theos #1711*
POSB Reference:
(Jn.1:1-2; esp. v.1) Note 1, pt. 3

θεοστυγεῖς = *theostugeis #1723, #1882*
POSB Reference:
(Rom.1:30) *Deeper Study* #13

θησαυρίζεις = *thēsaurizeis #3782, #4041*
POSB Reference:
(Rom.2:2-5; esp. v.5) Note 2, pt. 4

Θέσθε ὑμεῖς εἰς τὰ ὦτα ὑμῶν = *Thesthe humeis eis ta ōta humōn #2352, #2326, #2327, #2349*
POSB Reference:
(Lk.9:44-45; esp. v.44) Note 4, pt. 1

θλιβόμενοι = *thlibomenoi #71, #1861, #3034, #4065*
POSB Reference:
(2 Cor.4:7-9; esp. v.8) Note 2

θλίψει = thlipsei **#72, #4052, #4069**
POSB Reference:
(2 Cor.1:4) Note 2

θλίψεσιν = thlipsesin **#74, #4054, #4070**
POSB Reference:
(2 Cor.6:4-5; esp. v.4) Note 3

θλῖψιν = thlipsin **#73, #3850, #4053**
POSB Reference:
(Rev.2:9) Note 3, pt. 1

θλῖψις = thlipsis **#3848, #4048, #4051**
POSB Reference:
(Rom.5:3-5; esp. v.3) Note 5

θορυβάζη = thorubazë **#423, #4063, #4186**
POSB Reference:
(Lk.10:41-42; esp. v.41) Note 4, pt. 2

θρησκεία = thrëskeia **#3234**
POSB Reference:
(Jas. 1:26) Note 3

θρόμβοι = thromboi **#1176, #1784**
POSB Reference:
(Lk.22:43-44; esp. v.44) Note 4, pt. 3

θυμοί = thumoi **#143, #2806, #2808, #4463**
POSB Reference:
(2 Cor.12:19-21; esp. v.20) Note 3, pt. 2

θυμοί = thumoi **#1519, #2807, #2809, #4460**
POSB Reference:
(Gal.5:19-21; esp. v.20) Note 2

θυμός = thumos **#141, #2141, #4459**
POSB Reference:
(Rom.2:8) Deeper Study #7

θυμός = thumos **#3154, #4461**
POSB Reference:
(Eph.4:31) Note 6, pt. 2

τίμα = tima **#1996**
POSB Reference:
(Eph.6:1-3; esp. v.2) Note 1, pt. 2

τιμήν = timën **#1998, #3269**
POSB Reference:
(1 Pt.3:7) Note 3

τιμῆς = timës **#1994, #2819**
POSB Reference:
(1 Tim.5:17)

τιμίαν = timian **#890, #4448**
POSB Reference:
(Acts 20:24) Note 6, pt. 1

Τίμιος = Timios **#1997, #2002**
POSB Reference:
(Heb.13:4) Note 4, pt. 1

τὸ αὐτὸ φρονεῖτε = to auto phroneite **#2348, #1872, #2775, #2777**
POSB Reference:
(2 Cor.13:11-13; esp. v.11) Note 3, pt. 3

τὸ εἶναι ἴσα = to einai isa **#1310, #3332**
POSB Reference:
(Philip.2:6) Note 2, pt. 3

τῷ ἐκτρώματι = tö ektrömati **#2061, #2772, #2774, #2779**
POSB Reference:
(1 Cor.15:8-10; esp. v.8) Note 5

τὸ καλὸν = to kalon **#1988, #2003, #3320, #3323, #4320, #4321**
POSB Reference:
(2 Cor.13:7-10; esp. v.7) Note 2

τὸ φρόνημα τῆς σαρκὸς = to phronëma tës sarkos **#509, #2594, #2596, #3594**
POSB Reference:
(Rom.8:5-8; esp. v.6) Note 3, pt. 1

τὸ φρόνημα τοῦ πνεύματος = to phronëma tou pneumatos **#1980, #2593, #2597, #3711**
POSB Reference:
(Romans 8:5-8, esp. v.6) Note 3, pt. 2

τὸ πνεῦμα Ἰησου = to pneuma Iësou **#3698, #3701**
POSB Reference:
(Acts 16:7) Deeper Study #1

τομώτερος = tomöteros **#3515**
POSB Reference:
(Heb.4:11-13; esp. v.12) Note 5, pt. 2c

τὸν ἀρχηγὸν = ton archëgon **#242, #3741**
POSB Reference:
(Heb.12:2) Note 3, pt. 1

τὸν καιρόν = ton kairon **#3029, #3996**
POSB Reference:
(Rom.13:11) Note 1

τὸν παῖδα = ton paida **#3460, #3650**
POSB Reference:
(Acts 3:12-13; esp. v.13) Note 2, pt. 2c

τοῦ ἀποσπᾶν = tou apospan **#1165**
POSB Reference:
(Acts 20:29-30; esp. v.30) Deeper Study #2, pt. 4

τοῦ θεοῦ = tou theou **#2742**
POSB Reference:
(Jn.1:29) Note 1, pt. 3

τοὐναντίον = tounantion **#769, #2765**
POSB Reference:
(Gal.2:7-10; esp. v.7) Note 5

τρώγων = trögön **#1228**
POSB Reference:
(Jn.6:54) Note 2, pt. 1

τρώγοντες = trögontes **#265, #1227**
POSB Reference:
(Mt.24:38) Deeper Study #3

τρόπος = tropos **#542, #706, #778, #2373**
POSB Reference:
(Heb.13:5-6; esp. v.5) Note 5

τῷ ἁμαρτωλῷ = tö hamartölö **#3598**
POSB Reference:
(Lk.18:13) Note 4, pt. 3a

τυφλὸς = tuphlos **#407**
POSB Reference:
(Rev.3:16-17; esp. v.17) Note 4

τύπον = tupon **#1369, #2859**
POSB Reference:
(Tit.2:7-8; esp. v.7) Note 6, pt. 1

τύπον = tupon **#1446, #2858, #2949**
POSB Reference:
(Acts 7:42-53; esp. v.44) Note 6, pt. 3a

U

ὑπομείνας = upomeinas **#1279, #3738**
POSB Reference:
(Mk.13:13) Note 9, pt. 1

X

ξένοι = xenoi **#1574, #3787**
POSB Reference:
(Eph.2:19) Note 1, pt. 1

Z

ζηλοῖ = zëloi **#1308, #2198**
POSB Reference:
(1 Cor.13:4-7; esp. v.4) Note 2, pt. 3

ζῆλος = zëlos **#1253, #2200**
POSB Reference:
(Gal.5:19-21; esp. v.20) Note 2, pt. 9

ζῆλος = zëlos **#1309, #2199**
POSB Reference:
(2 Cor.12:19-21; esp. v.20) Note 3, pt. 2

ζηλωταί = *zēlōtai* **#1197, #1552, #4478**
POSB Reference:
(1 Pt.3:13-14; esp. v.13) Note 1

ζηλοῦτε = *zēloute* **#969, #973, #1203**
POSB Reference:
(1 Cor.14:1) Note 1, pt. 2

ζημιωθείς = *zēmiōtheis* **#517, #1585, #2420**
POSB Reference:
(Lk.9:25) *Deeper Study #2*

ζέων τῷ πνεύματι = *zeōn tō pneumati* **#1473, #1785, #1786**
POSB Reference:
(Acts 18:25) Note 4

ζέοντες = *zeontes* **#1293, #1471, #1476**
POSB Reference:
(Rom.12:11) Note 2, pt. 2

ζητεῖ τὰ ἑαυτῆς = *zētei ta heautēs* **#949, #3414**
POSB Reference:
(1 Cor.13:4-7; esp. v.5) Note 2, pt. 7

ζητεῖ τὰ ἑαυτῆς = *zētei ta heautēs* **#948, 3416, #3431**
POSB Reference:
(1 Cor.13:4-7; esp. v.5) Note 2, pt. 7

ζητεῖτε = *zēteite* **#3040, #3411**
POSB Reference:
(Mt.6:33) Note 7

ζωὴν = *zōēn* **#2341**
POSB Reference:
(Jn.10:10) *Deeper Study #1*

Ζῶν = *Zōn* **#2375, #3139**
POSB Reference:
(Heb.4:11-13; esp. v.12) Note 5, pt. 2a

ζῳογονοῦντος = *zōogonountos* **#1688, #3144**
POSB Reference:
(1 Tim.6:13-16; esp. v.13) Note 4, pt. 1

ζῳοποιήσει = *zōopoiēsei* **#1677, #3141**
POSB Reference:
(Rom.8:10-11; esp. v.11) Note 5, pt. 2a

ζυγὸν = *zugon* **#4470**
POSB Reference:
(1 Tim.6:1) Note 1

BIBLIOGRAPHY

Every child of God is precious to the Lord and deeply loved. And every child as a servant of the Lord touches the lives of those who come in contact with him or his ministry. The writing ministry of the following servants have touched this work, and we are grateful that God brought their writings our way. We hereby acknowledge their ministry to us, being fully aware that there are so many others down through the years whose writings have touched our lives and who deserve mention, but the weaknesses of our minds have caused them to fade from memory. May our wonderful Lord continue to bless the ministry of these dear servants, and the ministry of us all as we diligently labor to reach the world for Christ and to meet the desperate needs of those who suffer so much.

THE GREEK SOURCES

1. Analytical Greek New Testament AGNT2 (GNM) Greek NT Grammatical Analysis Database, Version 2 Copyright © 1994 Timothy and Barbara Friberg. All rights reserved. Source: Bushell, Michael S. *BibleWorks For Windows, Version 3.5.* 1996.

2. Bauer, Walter. *A Greek-English Lexicon of the New Testament and Other Early Christian Literature*. Second Edition. Revised and augmented by F. Wilbur Gingrich and Frederick W. Danker. Chicago: University of Chicago Press, 1979.

3. Blass, F. and DeBrunner, A. *A Greek Grammar of the New Testament and Other Early Christian Literature*. Translated by Robert Funk. Chicago: University of Chicago Press, 1974.

4. Chase, Alston and Phillips, Henry. *A New Introduction to Greek*. Cambridge, Mass.: Harvard University Press, 1961.

5. Dana, H.E. Th.D. & Mantey, Julius R. Mantey, Th.D., D.D. *A Manual Grammar of the Greek New Testament*. Toronto, Ontario (Printed in the USA): Copyright The Macmillian Company, 1927, Tommie P. Dana & Julius R. Mantey, 1955, 50th printing.

6. *Expositor's Greek Testament*, Edited by W. Robertson Nicoll. Grand Rapids, MI: Eerdmans Publishing Co., 1970

7. Goodrick, Edward W. & Kohlenberger, John R. III. *The NIV Exhaustive Concordance*. Grand Rapids, MI: Zondervan Publishing House, 1990.

8. Goodwin, William. *Greek Grammar*. London: Macmillan, 1971.

9. Jay, Eric G. *New Testament Greek: An Introductory Grammar*. London: SPCK Holy Trinity Church, The Camelot Press Ltd., Southhampton, Tenth impression, 1981.

10. Machen, Gresham. *New Testament Greek for Beginners*. Toronto, Ontario: Macmillan, 1923.

11. Moulton, Harold K. *The Analytical Greek Lexicon Revised, 1978 Edition*. Grand Rapids, MI: The Zondervan Corporation, 1982.

12. *New American Standard Greek and Hebrew Dictionary*. Copyright © 1960, 1962, 1963, 1968, 1971, 1973, 1975, 1977, 1988, 1995. The Lockman Foundation. All rights reserved. Database copyright © NavPress Software.

13. Robertson, A.T. *Word Pictures in the New Testament*. Nashville, TN: Broadman Press, 1930.

14. *Strong's Exhaustive Concordance of the Bible* [Greek & Hebrew Dictionary]. Database copyright © 1990-1993 NavPress Software.

15. Thayer, Joseph Henry. *Greek-English Lexicon of the New Testament*. New York: American Book Co, No date listed.

16. *The Complete WordStudy Bible & Reference CD*. Chattanooga, TN: AMG Publishers, 1997.

17. *The Greek New Testament*. Aland, Black, Martini, Metzger, & Wikgren, Editors. New York, NY: American Bible Society, 1975.

18. *The Hebrew-Greek Key Study Bible, NIV Version*. Zodhiates, Spiros, Th.D., Editor. Chattanooga, TN: AMG International, Inc., 1996.

19. *The New International Dictionary of New Testament Theology* (Three Volumes). Brown, Colin, Editor. Grand Rapids, MI: Regency Reference Library from Zondervan Publishing House, 1978.

20. *The NIV Complete Bible Library* (software). Grand Rapids, MI: The Zondervan Corporation, 1997.

21. *The Zondervan Parallel New Testament in Greek and English*. Grand Rapids, MI: Zondervan Corporation, 1980.

22. *Theological Dictionary of the New Testament* (10 Volumes). Gerhard Friedrich, Editor. Grand Rapids, MI: Eerdmans Publishing Co., 1971.

BIBLIOGRAPHY for the Practical Word Study

23. Vincent, Marvin R. *Word Studies in the New Testament.* Grand Rapids, MI: Eerdmans Publishing Co., 1969.

24. Vine, W.E. *Expository Dictionary of New Testament Words.* Old Tappan, NJ: Fleming H. Revell Co. No date listed.

25. Wallace, Daniel B. *Greek Grammar Beyond the Basics: An Exegetical Syntax of the New Testament.* Grand Rapids, Michigan: Zondervan, 1996.

26. *WordSearch Greek + Hebrew Library ,5.0* (software),. Austin, TX: NavPress Software (iExalt), 1997-1998.

27. Wuest, Kenneth S. *Word Studies in the Greek New Testament.* Grand Rapids, MI: Eerdmans Publishing Co., 1966.

THE BIBLE TRANSLATIONS

28. *The Holy Bible, King James Version.* KJV database (but not KJV text) copyright © 1987, 1990 by WORDworks Software Architects. Source: NavPress Software.

29. *The Holy Bible, New International Version NIV.* Copyright © 1973, 1978, 1984 by International Bible Society. Used by permission of Zondervan Publishing House. All rights reserved. (American Edition Copyright.) Source: NavPress Software.

30. *The Holy Bible, New Living Translation,* Copyright © 1996 by Tyndale Charitable Trust. All rights reserved. Database © 1997, NavPress Software.

31. *The New American Standard Bibe. NASB,* Copyright © 1960, 1962, 1963, 1968, 1971, 1973, 1975, 1977, 1988, 1995. The Lockman Foundation. All rights reserved - International copyright secured. Source: NavPress Software.

32. *The New King James Version NKJV (NKJV),* Copyright © 1982, Thomas Nelson, Inc. All rights reserved. NKJV database copyright © 1990 by WORDworks Software Architects. Source: NavPress Software.

THE GREEK TEXTS

33. The F. H. A. Scrivener 1881 - Theodore Beza 1598 Textus Receptus Greek New Testament (GNS),ASCII edition Copyright © 1992 by Dr. Kirk D. DiVietro, Grace Baptist Church. All rights reserved. Source: *BibleWorks For Windows, Version 3.5.* 1996.

34. The Greek New Testament (GNT UBS4 - NA27), edited by Barbara Aland, Kurt Aland, Johannes Karavidopoulos, Carlo M. Martini, and Bruce M. Metzger, in cooperation with the Institute for New Testament Textual Research, Munster/Westphalia, Fourth Revised Edition (with exactly the same text as the Nestle - Aland 27th Edition of the Greek New Testament), Copyright © 1966, 1968, 1975 by the United Bible Societies (UBS) and 1993, 1994 by Deutsche Bibelgesellschaft (German Bible Society), Stuttgart. Used by permission. Used by arrangement through United Bible Societies and Drs. Timothy and Barbara Friberg (AGNT/ANLEX). The computer form for the UBS Second Edition (© 1968) was prepared by the TLG Project. The computer form for the UBS Third Edition (© 1975) was derived from the MRT (machine readable text) created by Timothy and Barara Friberg at the University of Minnesota, Academic Computing Services and Systems. Source: *BibleWorks For Windows, Version 3.5.* 1996.

THE GREEK FONT

35. Bushell, Michael S. *BWGrkl BibleWorks For Windows, Version 3.5.* 1996. BWGRKL [Greek] Postscript® Type 1 and TrueType™ fonts Copyright © 1994-1997 Michael S. Bushell. All rights reserved.

THE REFERENCE WORKS

36. *Cruden's Complete Concordance of the Old & New Testament.* Philadelphia, PA: The John C. Winston Co., 1930.

37. *Josephus' Complete Works.* Grand Rapids, MI: Kregel Publications, 1981.

38. Lockyer, Herbert. Series of Books, including his Books on *All the Men, Women, Miracles, and Parables of the Bible.* Grand Rapids, MI: Zondervan Publishing House, 1958-1967.

39. *Nave's Topical Bible.* Nashville, TN: The Southwestern Co., No date listed.

40. *The Amplified New Testament.* (Scripture Quotations are from the Amplified New Testament, Copyright 1954, 1958, 1987 by the Lockman Foundation. Used by permission.)

41. *The Four Translation New Testament (Including King James, New American Standard, Williams - New Testament In the Language of the People, Beck - New Testament In the Language of Today.)* Minneapolis, MN: World Wide Publications.

BIBLIOGRAPHY for the Practical Word Study

42. *The New Compact Bible Dictionary*, Edited by T. Alton Bryant. Grand Rapids, MI: Zondervan Publishing House, 1967.

43. *The New Thompson Chain Reference Bible*. Indianapolis, IN: B.B. Kirkbride Bible Co., 1964,

44. *The Zondervan Pictorial Encyclopedia Of The Bible*, Edited by Merrill C. Tenney. Grand Rapds, MI: Zondervan Publishing House, 1982.

THE COMMENTARIES

45. Barclay, William. *Daily Study Bible Series*. Philadelphia, PA: Westminster Press, Began in 1953.

46. Bruce, F. F. *History of the Bible in English, Third Edition*. New York: Oxford University Press, 1978.

47. Bruce, F.F. *Epistle to the Hebrews*. Grand Rapids, MI: Eerdmans Publishing Co., 1964.

48. Bruce, F.F. *The Epistle to the Ephesians*. Westwood, NJ: Fleming H. Revell Co., 1968.

49. Bruce, F.F. *The Epistles of John*. Old Tappan, NJ: Fleming H. Revell Co., 1970.

50. Criswell, W.A. *Expository Sermons on Revelation*. Grand Rapids, MI: Zondervan Publishing House, 1962-66.

51. Greene, Oliver. *The Epistles of John*. Greenville, SC: The Gospel Hour, Inc., 1966.

52. Greene, Oliver. *The Epistles of Paul the Apostle to the Hebrews*. Greenville, SC: The Gospel Hour, Inc., 1965.

53. Greene, Oliver. *The Revelation Verse by Verse Study*. Greenville, SC: The Gospel Hour, Inc., 1963.

54. Greene, Oliver. *The Epistles of Paul the Apostle to Timothy & Titus*. Greenville, SC: The Gospel Hour, Inc., 1964.

55. Henry, Matthew. *Commentary on the Whole Bible*. Old Tappan, NJ: Fleming H. Revell Co.

56. Hodge, Charles. *Exposition on Romans & on Corinthians*. Grand Rapids, MI: Eerdmans Publishing Co., 1972-1973.

57. Ladd, George Eldon. *A Commentary On the Revelation of John*. Grand Rapids, MI: Eerdmans Publishing Co., 1972-1973.

58. Leupold, H.C. *Exposition of Daniel*. Grand Rapids, MI: Baker Book House, 1969.

59. Morris, Leon. *The Gospel According to John*. Grand Rapids, MI: Eerdmans Publishing Co., 1971.

60. Newell, William R. *Hebrews, Verse by Verse*. Chicago, IL: Moody Press, 1947.

61. Sailhamer, John H. *How We Got The Bible*. Grand Rapids, MI: Zondervan Publishing House, 1998.

62. Strauss, Lehman. *Devotional Studies in Philippians*. Neptune, NJ: Loizeaux Brothers, 1959.

63. Strauss, Lehman. *The Book of the Revelation*. Neptune, NJ: Loizeaux Brothers, 1964.

64. Strauss, Lehman. *Devotional Studies in Galatians & Ephesians*. Neptune, NJ: Loizeaux Brothers, 1957.

65. Strauss, Lehman. *James, Your Brother*. Neptune, NJ: Loizeaux Brothers, 1956.

66. *The New Testament & Wycliffe Bible Commentary*, Edited by Charles F. Pfeiffer & Everett F. Harrison. New York: The Iverson Associates, 1971. Produced for Moody Monthly. Chicago Moody Press, 1962.

67. *The Preacher's Outline and Sermon Bible®*. Chattanooga, TN: Leadership Ministries Worldwide, 1991.

68. *The Pulpit Commentary*, Edited by H.D.M. Spence & Joseph S. Exell. Grand Rapids, MI: Eerdmans Publishing Co., 1950.

69. Thomas, W.H. Griffith. *Hebrews, A Devotional Commentary*. Grand Rapids, MI: Eerdmans Publishing Co., 1970.

70. Thomas, W.H. Griffith. *Outline Studies in the Acts of the Apostles*. Grand Rapids, MI: Eerdmans Publishing Co., 1956.

71. Thomas, W.H. Griffith. *St. Paul's Epistle to the Romans*. Grand Rapids, MI: Eerdmans Publishing Co., 1946.

72. Thomas, W.H. Griffith. *Studies in Colossians & Philemon*. Grand Rapids, MI: Baker Book House, 1973.

73. *Tyndale New Testament Commentaries*. Grand Rapids, MI: Eerdmans Publishing Co., Began in 1958.

74. Walker, Thomas. *Acts of the Apostles*. Chicago, IL: Moody Press, 1965.

75. Walvoord, John. *The Thessalonian Epistles*. Grand Rapids, MI: Zondervan Publishing House, 1973.

BIBLIOGRAPHY for the Practical Word Study
OTHER SOURCES

76. Bruce, F.F. *History of the English Bible*. New York, NY: Oxford University Press, 1978, Third Edition.

77. Holy Bible, *New Living Translation*. Wheaton, IL: Tyndale House Publishers, Inc., 1996.

78. The Lockman Foundation web site http://www.gospelcom.net/lockman.

79. *The New Open Bible, Study Edition, The New King James Version*. Nashville, TN: Thomas Nelson Publishers, 1990.

80. *The NIV Study Bible*. Grand Rapids, MI: The Zondervan Corporation, 1985.

81. Tyndale House Publishers web site http://www.newlivingtranslation.com/about.html.

OUTLINE BIBLE RESOURCES

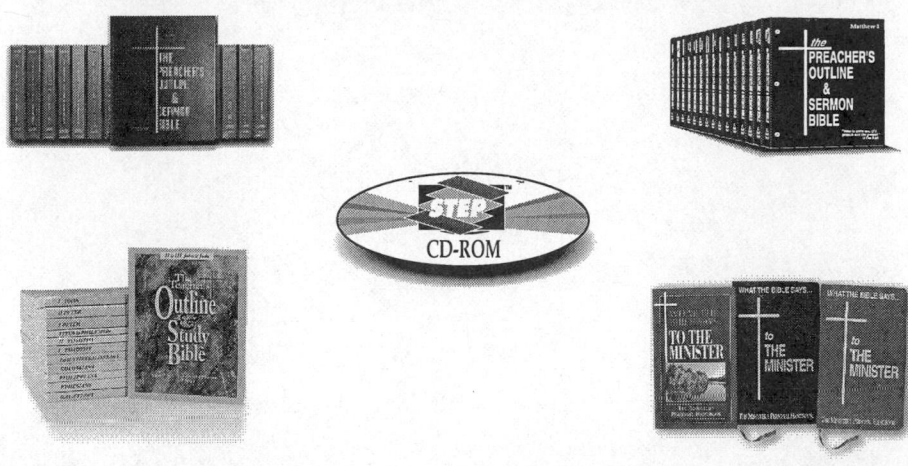

This material, like similar works, has come from imperfect man and is thus susceptible to human error. We are nevertheless grateful to God for both calling us and empowering us through His Holy Spirit to undertake this task. Because of His goodness and grace The Preacher's Outline & Sermon Bible® - New Testament is complete in 14 volumes, and the Old Testament volumes release periodically. **The Minister's Handbook** is available and *OUTLINE* Bible materials are releasing electonically on **POSB-CD** and our **Web site**.

God has given the strength and stamina to bring us this far. Our confidence is that, as we keep our eyes on Him and grounded in the undeniable truths of the Word, we will continue working through the Old Testament volumes and the second series known as **The Teacher's Outline & Study Bible.** The future includes helpful *Outline Bible* books and **Handbook** materials for God's dear servants.

To everyone everywhere who preaches and teaches the Word, we offer this material firstly to Him in whose name we labor and serve, and for whose glory it has been produced.

Our daily prayer is that each volume will lead thousands, millions, yes even billions, into a better understanding of the Holy Scriptures and a fuller knowledge of Jesus Christ the incarnate Word, of whom the Scriptures so faithfully testify.

> As you have purchased this volume, you will be pleased to know that a small portion of the price you have paid has gone to underwrite and provide similar volumes in other languages (Russian, Korean, Spanish and others yet to come) — To a preacher, pastor, lay leader, or Bible student somewhere around the world, who will present God's message with clarity, authority, and understanding beyond their own. *Amen.*

For information and prices, kindly contact your *OUTLINE* Bible bookseller or:

LEADERSHIP MINISTRIES WORLDWIDE

P.O. Box 21310, 515 Airport Road, Suite 107
Chattanooga, TN 37424-0310
(423) 855-2181 FAX (423) 855-8616
E-Mail - outlinebible@compuserve.com
www.outlinebible.org — *FREE* download materials

9/98